Hotel Guide 2012

AA Lifestyle Guides

45th edition September 2011.
First published by the Automobile Association as the Hotel and Restaurant Guide, 1967

Assessments of AA inspected establishments are based on the experience of the Hotel and Restaurant Inspectors on the occasion(s) of their visit(s) and therefore descriptions given in this guide necessarily contain an element of subjective opinion which may not reflect or dictate a reader's own opinion on another occasion. See 'AA Star Classification' in the preliminary section for a clear explanation of how, based on our Inspectors' inspection experiences, establishments are graded. If the meal or meals experienced by an Inspector or Inspectors during an inspection fall between award levels the restaurant concerned may be awarded the lower of any award levels considered applicable.

AA Media Limited strives to ensure accuracy of the information in this guide at the time of printing. Due to the constantly evolving nature of the subject matter the information is subject to change. AA Media Limited will gratefully receive any advice from our readers of any necessary updated information.

Please contact:
Advertising Sales Department: advertisingsales@theAA.com
Editorial Department: lifestyleguides@theAA.com
AA Hotel Scheme Enquiries: 01256 844455

Web site addresses are included in some entries and specified by the respective establishment. Such web sites are not under the control of AA Media Limited and as such AA Media Limited has no control over them and will not accept any responsibility or liability in respect of any and all matters whatsoever relating to such web sites including access, content, material and functionality. By including the addresses of third party Web Sites the AA does not intend to solicit business or offer any security to any person in any country, directly or indirectly.

Every effort has been made to trace copyright holders, and we apologise in advance for any unintentional omisions or errors. We would be pleased to apply any corrections in a following edition of this publication.

Front Cover: (t) Ballygarry House Hotel & Spa; (bl) St Brides Spa Hotel; (br) Gilpin Hotel & Lake House
Back Cover: (l) Black Swan Hotel; (c) BrookLodge Hotel & Wells Spa; (r) Loch Ness Lodge

Typeset/Repro: Servis Filmsetting Ltd, Manchester
Printed and bound by Graficas Estella, Spain

This directory is compiled by AA Lifestyle Guides; managed in the Librios Information Management System and generated by the AA establishment database system.

Published by AA Publishing, a trading name of AA Media Limited, whose registered office is Fanum House, Basing View, Basingstoke, Hampshire RG21 4EA.
Registered number 06112600
A CIP catalogue record for this book is available from the British Library
ISBN: 978-0-7495-7071-2
A04610

Maps prepared by the Mapping Services Department of AA Publishing.

Information on National Parks in England provided by the Countryside Agency (Natural England).

Information on National Parks in Scotland provided by Scottish Natural Heritage.

Information on National Parks in Wales provided by The Countryside Council for Wales.

Contents

How to Use the Guide

1 LOCATION

Town listed alphabetically within country (the county name appears under the town name)

2 MAP REFERENCE

Map page number followed by a 2-figure National Grid reference (see also page 7)

3 HOTEL NAME

Where the name appears in *italic* type the information that follows has not been confirmed by the establishment for 2012

4 GRADING

Hotels are listed in star rating and merit score order within each location (for full explanation of ratings and awards see page 24)

★ Star rating

% Merit score

❁ Rosette award

5 TYPE OF HOTEL

(see opposite)

6 HOTEL LOGO

If a symbol appears here it represents a hotel group or consortium (See pages 29-37)

7 PICTURE

Optional photograph supplied by establishment

8 ADDRESS AND CONTACT DETAILS

9 DIRECTIONS

Brief details of how to find the hotel

10 DESCRIPTION

Written by the AA inspector at the time of the last visit

11 ROOMS

Number of rooms and prices (see page 6)

12 FACILITIES

Additional facilities including those for children and for leisure activities

13 CONFERENCE

Conference facilities as available (see page 6)

14 NOTES

Additional information (see pages 6-7)

1
3
4
5
7
2
6
TAVISTOCK
Devon
Map 3 SX47
Horn of Plenty
LOGO
★★★ 85% ❁❁ HOTEL
☎ 01822 832528 01822 834390
Gulworthy PL19 8JD
e-mail: enquiries@thehornofplenty.co.uk
web: www.thehornofplenty.co.uk
dir: From Tavistock take A390 W for 3m. Right at Gulworthy Cross. In 400yds turn left, hotel in 400yds on right
With stunning views over the Tamar Valley, The Horn of Plenty maintains a good reputation as an excellent country-house hotel. Bedrooms are well equipped and have many thoughtful extras, with garden rooms offering impressive levels of both quality and comfort. Award-winning cuisine is prepared with skill and there is a passion to use the best ingredients the area has to offer.
Rooms 10 (6 annexe) (3 fmly) (4 GF) S £85-£215; D £95-£225 (incl. bkfst)* Facilities FTV Xmas New Year Wi-fi Conf Class 22 Board 14 Thtr 22 Del from £120 to £150* Parking 25 Notes LB Civ Wed 80
8
9
10
11
13
12
14

KEY TO SYMBOLS AND ABBREVIATIONS

★	Black stars
★	Red stars – indicate AA Inspectors' Choice
◎	AA Rosettes – indicate an AA award for food *For full explanation of AA ratings and awards see page 24*
%	Inspector's Merit score (see page 6)
A	Associate Hotels (see this page)
O	Hotel due to open during the currency of the guide
U	Star rating not confirmed (see this page)
Fmly	Number of family rooms available
GF	Ground floors rooms available
Smoking	Number of bedrooms allocated for smokers
pri facs	Bedroom with separate private facilities (Restaurant with Rooms only)
S	Single room
D	Double room
*	2011 prices
fr	From
incl. bkfst	Breakfast included in the price
FTV	Freeview
STV	Satellite television
Wi-fi	Wireless network connection
Air con	Air conditioning
	Heated indoor swimming pool
	Outdoor swimming pool
	Heated outdoor swimming pool
♫	Entertainment
Child facilities	Children's facilities (see page 6)
Xmas/New Year	Special programme for Christmas/New Year
	Tennis court
	Croquet lawn
	Golf course
CONF	Conference facilities
Thtr	Number of theatre style seats
Class	Number of classroom style seats
Board	Number of boardroom style seats
	No dogs allowed (guide dogs for the blind and assist dogs should be allowed)
No children	Children cannot be accommodated
RS	Restricted opening time
Civ Wed	Establishment licensed for civil weddings (+ maximum number of guests at ceremony)
LB	Special leisure breaks available
Spa	Hotel has its own spa

TYPES OF HOTEL

The majority of establishments in this guide come under the category of Hotel; other categories are listed below.

TOWN HOUSE HOTEL A small, individual city or town centre property, which provides a high degree of personal service and privacy

COUNTRY HOUSE HOTEL These are quietly located in a rural area

SMALL HOTEL Has fewer than 20 bedrooms and is owner-managed

METRO HOTEL A hotel in an urban location that does not offer an evening meal

BUDGET HOTEL These are usually purpose built modern properties offering inexpensive accommodation. Often located near motorways and in town or city centres

RESTAURANT WITH ROOMS This category of accommodation is now assessed under the AA's Guest Accommodation scheme, therefore, although they continue to have an entry in this guide, we do not include their star rating. Most Restaurants with Rooms have been awarded AA Rosettes for their food and the rooms will meet the required AA standard. For more detailed information about any Restaurant with Rooms please consult The AA Bed and Breakfast Guide or see **theAA.com**

A These are establishments that have not been inspected by the AA but which have been inspected by the national tourist boards in Britain and Northern Ireland. An establishment marked as "Associate" has paid to belong to the AA Associate Hotel Scheme and therefore receives a limited entry in the guide. Descriptions of these hotels can be found on the AA website.*

U A small number of hotels in the guide have this symbol because their star classification was not confirmed at the time of going to press. This may be due to a change of ownership or because the hotel has only recently joined the AA rating scheme.

O These hotels were not open at the time of going to press, but will open in late 2011, or in 2012.

* Check the AA website **theAA.com** for current information and ratings

How to Use the Guide *continued*

Merit Score (%)

AA inspectors supplement their reports with an additional quality assessment of everything the hotel provides, including hospitality, based on their findings as a 'mystery guest'. This wider ranging quality assessment results in an overall Merit Score which is shown as a percentage beside the hotel name. When making your selection of hotel accommodation this enables you to see at a glance that a three star hotel with a Merit Score of 79% offers a higher standard overall than one in the same star classification but with a Merit Score of 69%. To gain AA recognition, a hotel must achieve a minimum score of 50%.

AA Awards

Every year the AA presents a range of awards to the finest AA-inspected and rated hotels from England, Scotland, Wales and the Republic of Ireland. The Hotel of the Year is our ultimate accolade and is awarded to those hotels that are recognised as outstanding examples in their field. Often innovative, the winning hotels always set high standards in hotel keeping. The winners for all the 2011-2012 awards are listed on pages 9-15.

Rooms

Each entry shows the total number of en suite rooms available (this total will include any annexe rooms). The total number may be followed by a breakdown of the type of rooms available, i.e. the number of annexe rooms; number of family rooms (fmly); number of ground-floor rooms (GF); number of rooms available for smokers.

Bedrooms in an annexe or extension are only noted if they are at least equivalent in quality to those in the main building, but facilities and prices may differ. In some hotels all bedrooms are in an annexe or extension.

If the hotel has highspeed or broadband internet access in the bedrooms, this may be chargeable.

Prices

Prices are per room per night and are provided by the hoteliers in good faith. These prices are indications and not firm quotations. * indicates 2011 prices. Perhaps due to the economic climate at the time we were collecting the data for this guide, fewer hotels were willing to tell us their room prices for 2012. Many hotels have introduced special rates so it is worth looking at their websites for the latest information.

Payment

As most hotels now accept credit or debit cards we only indicate if an establishment does not accept any cards for payment. Credit cards may be subject to a surcharge – check when booking if this is how you intend to pay.

Children

Child facilities may include baby intercom, baby sitting service, playroom, playground, laundry, drying/ironing facilities, cots, high chairs or special meals. In some hotels children can sleep in parents' rooms at no extra cost – check when booking.

If 'No children' is indicated a minimum age may be also given e.g. No children 4yrs indicates that no children under 4 years of age would be accepted.

Some hotels, although accepting children, may not have any special facilities for them.

Leisure breaks (LB)

Some hotels offer special leisure breaks, and these prices may differ from those quoted in this guide and the availability may vary through the year.

Parking

We indicate the number of parking spaces available for guests. This may include covered parking. Please note that some hotels make a charge to use their car park.

Civil Weddings (Civ Wed)

Indicates that the establishment holds a civil wedding licence, and we indicate the number of guests that can be accommodated at the ceremony.

Conference Facilities

We include three types of meeting layouts – Theatre, Classroom and Boardroom style and include the maximum number of delegates for each. The price shown is the maximum 24-hour rate per delegate. Please note that as arrangements vary between a hotel and a business client, VAT may or may not be included in the price quoted in the guide. We also show if Wi-fi connectivity is available, but please check with the hotel that this is suitable for your requirements.

Dogs

Although many hotels allow dogs, they may be excluded from some areas of the hotel and some breeds, particularly those requiring an exceptional licence, may not be acceptable at all. Under the Disability Discrimination Act 1995 access should be allowed for guide dogs and assistance dogs. Please check the hotel's policy when making your booking.

Entertainment (♫)

This indicates that live entertainment should be available at least once a week all year. Some hotels provide live entertainment only in summer or on special occasions.

Hotel logos

If an establishment belongs to a hotel group

or consortium their logo is included in their entry (pages 29-37).

Map references

Each town is given a map reference – the map page number and a two-figure map reference based on the National Grid. For example: **Map 05 SU 48**:
05 refers to the page number of the map section at back of the guide
SU is the National Grid lettered square (representing 100,000sq metres) in which the location will be found
4 is the figure reading across the top or bottom of the map page
8 is the figure reading down at each side of the map page

Restricted service

Some hotels have restricted service (RS) during quieter months, usually during the winter, and at this time some of the listed facilities will not be available. If your booking is out-of-season, check with the hotel and enquire specifically.

Smoking regulations

If a bedroom has been allocated for smokers, the hotel is obliged to clearly indicate that this is the case. If either the freedom to smoke, or to be in a non-smoking environment is important to you, please check with the hotel when you book.

Spa

For the purposes of this guide the word **Spa** in an entry indicates that the hotel has its own spa which is either managed by themselves or outsourced to an external management company. Facilities will vary but will include a minimum of two treatment rooms. Any specific details are also given, and these are as provided to us by the establishment (i.e. steam room, beauty therapy etc).

Hotels of the Year

ENGLAND

GILPIN HOTEL & LAKE HOUSE

WINDERMERE, CUMBRIA Page 514

★★★★ ◎◎◎

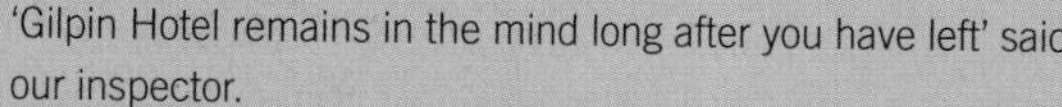

'Gilpin Hotel remains in the mind long after you have left' said our inspector.

Set in delightful gardens with woodland leading to the fells, this smart hotel is just the place to escape from the hustle and bustle of modern life. Right from the time of arrival the Cunliffe family and their team make a special effort to get to know you, and vise versa - there's even a directory of the staff in each room. The hospitality is attentive but not at all intrusive.

An award-winning designer has created a modern and superbly stylish interior, from day rooms with deeply comfortable sofas, welcoming fires, magazines, newspapers and books to spacious, individually designed bedrooms and suites. Guests can choose from Classic and Master bedrooms with sitting areas, stunning Junior Suites with patios leading directly onto the gardens, or the Garden Suites, each with a completely private, outdoor cedar wood hot tub.

There are four dining rooms, each distinctly different in feel and design. The award-winning menu, based on the finest, mainly locally-sourced ingredients, is split into 'signature dishes' and 'classic dishes'. The 200-strong wine list offers an excellent range representing no less than 13 countries.

That's not all - The Lake House, a short drive from the hotel, is the ultimate retreat. Here, there is a spa with a pool and a long list of rejuvenating treatments.

The Cunliffe family are passionate about what they do, and it shows.

LONDON

THE SAVOY

LONDON SW1 Page 319

★★★★★ ◎◎

This iconic hotel has undergone a much publicised and costly restoration. Given its heritage, and fondness of both the industry and its guests alike, the sense of expectation has probably been higher than any other hotel re-opening.

The refurbishment has delivered impressive results but the key elements of the English Edwardian architecture and Art Deco design have remained and the attention to detail is clear to see. Underpinning the changes is a commitment to energy efficiency through the implementation of 'green' technology. As an inspiration there's the Elements Package - guests can take advantage of a personal butler to assist and advise on the hotel's green initiatives, complimentary use of a bike (and helmet), organic meals, one-day travel card for London's public transport plus a donation by the hotel on behalf of the guest to a London waterway charity.

Public areas ooze sophistication and character, be it the Savoy Grill (the favourite of many an illustrious diner and now under Gordon Ramsay's watchful eye), The River Room overlooking the Thames, the American Bar or the new Beaufort Bar, the place to enjoy champagne, cocktails and a nightly cabaret.

The bedrooms and suites, with views of either the Thames or the city, are appointed with the finest furnishings and latest technologys. Among the myriad of facilities is a fitness gallery on the third floor with a pool, a gym and a variety of relaxing treatments and therapies.

The Savoy is clearly back – stronger and better.

Hotels of the Year *continued*

SCOTLAND

BLYTHSWOOD SQUARE

GLASGOW Page 575

★★★★★ 88%

This new 'boutique' hotel overlooking a delightful green space in Glasgow, Blythswood Square is a restoration of a grand 1823 building that was once the headquarters of the Royal Scottish Automobile Club and one of eight official starting points for the 1955 Monte Carlo Rally. Now a Grade B listed building, it is located within the Glasgow City Central Conservation Area.

Remaining true to its original design, the interior has been painstakingly refurbished to create real wow factor. Intricate cornices, marble fireplaces, wood panelling and Harris tweed furnishings all combine to create a sense of luxury in keeping with the hotel's Scottish heritage. Nowhere is this more evident than the popular 35-metre Salon Lounge where cocktails, champagne, afternoon tea and light meals are served. The former RSAC's grand ballroom, now the main restaurant, is the venue for enjoying award-winning cuisine. The modern British menu serves up bold contemporary dishes alongside comforting classics.

Hues of purple, grey and beige together with black and white images set the style in the sumptuous bedrooms and suites. All have touches of luxury, but for the ultimate stay there's the Penthouse; on its own floor, accessed by a private lift, this stunning suite has a dining area, bar, rooftop terrace and breathtaking views. The hotel's spa features a fantastic Thermal Suite with a whole array of luxurious treatments, two relaxation pools, a lounge and café.

WALES

ST BRIDES SPA HOTEL

SAUNDERSFOOT, PEMBROKESHIRE Page 650

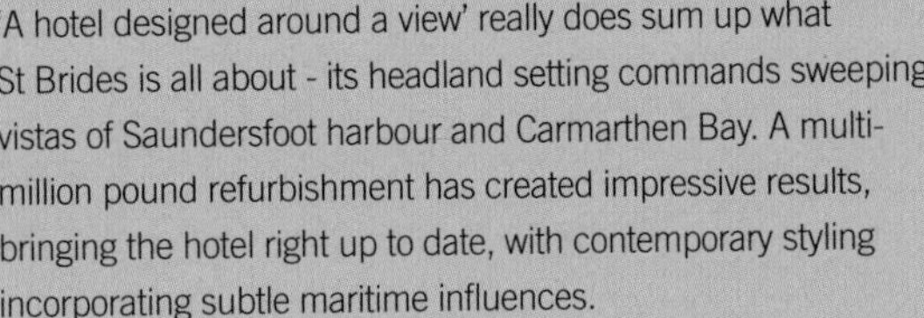

★★★★ 82%

'A hotel designed around a view' really does sum up what St Brides is all about - its headland setting commands sweeping vistas of Saundersfoot harbour and Carmarthen Bay. A multi-million pound refurbishment has created impressive results, bringing the hotel right up to date, with contemporary styling incorporating subtle maritime influences.

Family owned and run with great dedication, it is evident that guest care is given much focus and attention by all the staff.

The sleek public spaces make the most of the property's setting and it is not hard to find a spot to sit and relax, perhaps with your feet up, and watch the changing scene on the beach and out to sea. Alongside paintings inspired by Wales, mainly by Welsh artists, are little touches such as shells and driftwood that serve as reminders of the hotel's coastal location. The Cliff Restaurant, with its open terrace in the summer, is the place to sample simply cooked dishes based on the best Pembrokeshire produce.

The elegant bedrooms (named good, better and best) come in different shapes and sizes, and the majority have sea views and balconies. Six two-bedrooms apartments, situated adjacent to the main building, are the most luxurious choices. Each has a kitchenette, dining area, and either a balcony or terrace.

The marine spa perched on the cliff top offers treatments using seaweed, mud and clay; the thermal suite includes an infinity salt water pool, steam room and sensation shower.

REPUBLIC OF IRELAND

GREGANS CASTLE

BALLYVAUGHN, CO CLARE **Page 665**

With ownership seamlessly changing to Simon Haden and Frederieke (Freddie) McMurray from Simon's parents, this delightful country house hotel continues to impress. It is a real luxury hideaway set amidst the unique landscape of The Burren.

Freddie has overseen a refurbishment and the house style is a mix of antique furniture, modern art and open log or turf fires. It's not difficult to relax in the cosy bar over a casual lunch or afternoon tea or in the elegant Drawing Room, perhaps enjoying an after-dinner coffee while watching the sun setting over Galway Bay.

Any adverse impact on the environment is taken seriously here, so they source food from local producers and promote activities such as walking, birdwatching and cycling. As founder members of the Burren Ecotourism Network, they endorse responsible travel in order to help protect the environment.

The bedrooms and suites are individually designed in calming colours. Some have their own garden areas, and all have either bay, mountain or garden views. Top of the range are the Premier suites each with a sitting room and a BOSE sound system, and some with a four-poster bed.

The food will be the highlight of a visit here. Chef Michael Viljanen's passion for cooking is evident in the modern European dishes showcased on well thought out and imaginative menus. After such delights, guests might like to stretch their legs in the 13-acre grounds where they might chance upon ducks, cats, two donkeys and a pony, not to mention red squirrels.

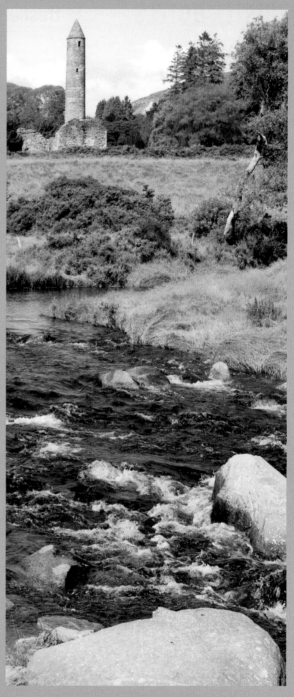

Hotel Group of the Year

THISTLE HOTELS

thistle

The Thistle Hotel Group has been on long journey of evolution and progression and now shows a dedicated focus on customer care and a commitment to ongoing investment in the refurbishment of their properties. Their portfolio of hotels has undergone major re-branding which now demonstrates consistently high levels of hospitality, service, cuisine and housekeeping.

Thistle takes a pro-active approach to its wider role in the hospitality industry and under the banner of corporate social responsibility they are gaining 'green' tourism awards.

With 9 hotels in London, 12 in England from Poole on the south coast to Newcastle upon Tyne in the north east, 6 in Scotland, and one in Wales they provide a diverse choice of popular destinations.

The Grand

ENGLAND

BRISTOL The Grand, Bristol
CHELTENHAM Thistle Cheltenham Hotel
EAST MIDLANDS AIRPORT Thistle East Midlands Airport
EXETER The Rougemont Hotel, Exeter
HAYDOCK Thistle Haydock
LIVERPOOL Atlantic Tower, Liverpool
LONDON EC1 Thistle City Barbican
LONDON NW1 Thistle Euston
LONDON SW1 Thistle Westminster
LONDON W1 Thistle Marble Arch
LONDON W1 Thistle Piccadilly
LONDON W2 Thistle Hyde Park
LONDON W2 Thistle Kensington Gardens
LONDON WC1 The Kingsley by Thistle
LONDON WC2 The Royal Trafalgar, London
MANCHESTER The Portland by Thistle, Manchester
MIDDLESBROUGH Thistle Hotel Middlesbrough
NEWCASTLE UPON TYNE County Hotel, Newcastle
POOLE Thistle Poole
ST ALBANS Thistle St Albans
WEST DRAYTON Thistle London Heathrow

SCOTLAND

ABERDEEN Thistle Aberdeen Altens
ABERDEEN Thistle Aberdeen Airport
ABERDEEN The Calendonian, Aberdeen
EDINBURGH The King James, Edinburgh
GLASGOW Thistle Glasgow
INVERNESS Thistle Inverness

WALES

CARDIFF The Parc Hotel, Cardiff

Small Hotel Group of the Year

WARNER LEISURE HOTELS

Warner Leisure Hotels

This group has created its own niche market – venues exclusively for adults (over 21 years old). Their properties are carefully chosen and range from grand estates to modern buildings. The majority of the hotels are certainly grand places, from Grade I listed mansions to Grade II listed stately homes. After significant investment in 2010 and 2011 these hotels have become even more memorable places to stay. Short breaks at any of the Warner Leisure Hotels are extremely popular – by choosing perhaps a spa break, pamper weekend or valentine's break you can make the most of what they have to offer.

Cricket St Thomas Hotel

ENGLAND

BEMBRIDGE Bembridge Coast Hotel
CHARD Cricket St Thomas Hotel
HARROGATE Nidd Hall Hotel
HAYLING ISLAND Sinah Warren Hotel
HOLME LACEY Holme Lacy House Hotel
HUNGERFORD Littlecote House Hotel
NANTWICH Alvaston Hall Hotel
OLLERTON Thoresby Hall Hotel & Spa

WALES

BODELWYDDAN Bodelwyddan Castle Hotel

Thoresby Hall Hotel & Spa

Littlecote House Hotel

Eco Hotel of the Year Sponsored by

As the guide went to press the judging process for these awards was still ongoing, and the winners will be announced at the AA Hospitality Awards ceremony at the end of September 2011. The winners will be shown on the AA website theAA.com after that date.

Last year's winners from The Scarlet Hotel, Cornwall

AA Eco Hotel of the Year 2011-12

Shortlist of finalists

The County Hotel, Chelmsford, Essex

The Crown Spa Hotel, Scarborough, North Yorkshire

The Lancaster, London W2

The Crown Spa Hotel

AA Eco Hotel Group of the Year 2011-12

Shortlist of finalists

Accor Hotels

Park Plaza Hotels

Q Hotels

Red Carnation Hotels

Rubens at the Palace (Red Carnation Hotels)

The Lancaster

Behind THE scenes

The family-run Goring hotel – just a stone's throw from Buckingham Palace – is at the top of its game with five red stars, and even hosted Kate Middleton on the night before her marriage to HRH Prince William. Fiona Griffiths went behind the scenes for a day to find out just what makes this top hotel tick...

ONE HUNDRED YEARS ONE FAMILY
(The Goring's motto)

Jeremy Goring, the fourth generation of his family to run The Goring hotel in London's Belgravia, is looking a little anxious.

It's Thursday 24th March 2011 – a little over four weeks to go until the wedding of the century, that of HRH Prince William and Kate Middleton – and up on the top floor of the hotel, the new 'Royal Suite' is far from ready.

Four bedrooms are being knocked through to form a huge, two-bedroom, two-bathroom suite, complete with a pair of lounges, its own bar and a large balcony overlooking the garden.

At this stage, Jeremy is refusing to confirm rumours in the press that Kate will be spending her last night as a single woman at The Goring, saying that the Royal Suite is so-named because of its regal theme that includes a painting of Queen Victoria and the same silks as on the walls of Buckingham Palace.

But a few weeks later all the suspicions are confirmed as the royal wedding route is announced, and on 28th April Kate arrived at the hotel, following in the footsteps of her husband-to-be's great grandmother, the late Queen Elizabeth, the Queen Mother, a Goring regular.

As I imagine Kate relaxing in the luxury of her suite on the night before the big day, I can't help but wonder whether she'll try the 'eggs Drumkilbo' – a recreation ▷

Right: The Royal Suite

Above: The Dining Room

Right: Jeremy Goring

Far right: Morning briefing

of one of the Queen Mother's favourite dishes (a mixture of chopped egg, lobster, tomato and herbs, bound in mayonnaise and topped with a chicken jelly), and a staple on the Goring menu.

A Royal Suite in the making

Anyway, back to my visit, and while Jeremy is clearly nervous about the forthcoming stay of his VIP guest (The Goring has different categories of VIP guest, and of course Kate will be at the very top), he's also very excited. He's an extremely 'hands-on' hotelier – visibly brimming over with energy and enthusiasm for his role as host – and so, as with all refurbishment projects at The Goring (and there have been many), he's been working closely with a top designer, in this case Russell Sage, on the plans for the Royal Suite.

"There's a famous painting I saw in the Tate of Queen Victoria, and we're going to have a replica of it on the wall in the shower," he says, grabbing his laptop eagerly to show me a picture of the artwork in question, along with a painting of a scene from the BBC's *Blackadder* comedy series, which they plan to hang in the toilet.

"We're calling the toilet 'the throne room' because it has a proper throne toilet. On the walls there'll be beautiful dark red silk, the same as the Throne

> “We have what we call ‘profile notes’ – an individual record for every guest.”

Room at Buckingham Palace, which we’ve been given special permission to use.”

Jeremy is thrilled that he’ll soon be in a far better position to compete with the capital’s larger five-star hotels by offering this superior two-bedroom suite, as well as having a fantastic story to tell about its first guest. Now, even actor Will Smith, who has made enquiries about a suite of rooms before, will be able look forward to The Goring’s hospitality.

“I can imagine it will be popular with Hollywood stars because they can hold press interviews up there, they can bring their entourage or their family with them, and they can entertain in there too,” comments Jeremy.

Every guest is special

At many thousands of pounds a night, it’s fair to say the Royal Suite is beyond the means of most of us, but The Goring has many customers who are happy with more modest accommodation – and most of these are regulars who tend to have their favourite rooms.

In fact, repeat guests make up 50 per cent of The Goring’s business, and as front office manager Clive Bullock tells me, it can be a tough job meeting all the requests for specific rooms.

“At The Goring no two rooms are quite the same size, design or layout. We take special requests at the time of reservation, and it’s a great challenge for me because I make the allocations; it can take a fair amount of time to work it all out,” says Clive. Other guest requirements are also noted at the time of booking and added to the hotel’s database.

“We have what we call ‘profile notes’ – an individual record for every guest – which tells us about allergies, what people love and what they dislike,” explains Clive. “For instance, we have a guest arriving on Saturday who likes Evian water which we don’t normally stock in the hotel, but when we know they’re coming we make sure we have it in.”

Clearly, it’s that kind of attention to detail and individual service that keeps guests coming back time and again, which is something that’s brought home to me even more at the morning briefing – the ▷

daily get together at 8.45am of all the hotel's department heads.

At the briefing, Clive, who has worked at The Goring for 12 years, takes centre stage, reading out the arrivals list for the day to the assembled throng of managers – including the night manager, executive chef, head of housekeeping, head of IT, head of maintenance, and Jeremy Goring himself.

Amongst the 25 new arrivals today, there's Mr Price who's on his 11th stay, Mr Thompson who's on his 34th, Mr Ellis who's on his 135th, Mrs Woods who's celebrating her 70th birthday and Mr Simpson, who, Clive adds, is "on crutches, so no bed spread, and two foot stools in the bathroom".

There's a brief mention of places still being available for staff on the 'name recognition course', and then everyone goes off to begin – or in many cases continue – their daily duties.

For the maintenance team there's the sink drainage to check in room 58, plus a whole host of other things that general manager Graham Copeman has noted on his early morning walk around the hotel – the smallest things amiss don't escape his eagle eye.

Seamless housekeeping

For executive housekeeper Teresa Doyle – affectionately known as 'matron' – there are 69 rooms to be cleaned in eight hours by a team of just six maids. As well as checking their work is up to "Mr Jeremy's very strict standards", Teresa mucks in herself, especially when a guest arrives before their room is ready – which happens quite often because of The Goring's flexible approach to check-in and check-out times.

"If reception rang me now and said 'we need room 43', I would go into that room

"Jeremy and myself have been all over the country to find good artisan suppliers and producers."

with a maid and clean it with her. If we've got three housekeepers on one room it'll be done in 15 minutes, because we don't like to keep guests waiting," says Teresa. "If a guest does arrive before their room is ready and there's another room empty, we'll offer them that one in the meantime so they can go in and have a shower."

The heat of the kitchen

While Teresa and her team are dispersed around the hotel cleaning rooms, down in the basement, executive chef Derek Quelch is holding his daily kitchen briefing.

Today, Thursday, there are 55 diners booked in for lunch (a full house), with the same number expected in the evening, plus there's a private dinner in one of the function rooms for which two trays of canapés need to be ready for 7pm.

As well as the main restaurant with its menu full of British classics (including the aforementioned eggs Drumkilbo as a starter), Derek is also responsible for the food served in the bar, the lounge (where afternoon teas are big business) and room service.

Without many functions taking place in the hotel, today is quiet by his standards. However, standing in the kitchen during lunch service, to me it feels anything but.

No sooner has the first guest been seated upstairs in the restaurant than the little printer which sits at the end of the pass – the area Derek refers to as "the nerve station" – springs into life. Every couple of minutes it whirs gently as the orders come flooding in, which prompts Derek to call out to his team, "one whitebait, one lamb, one sea bass, one lobster omelette for the bar – gluten free". ▷

Each time he listens out for someone to claim the order so he knows it's being taken care of. Each chef is working on different elements of a dish – one is roasting the Peterhead cod, while another is cooking the Shetland mussel stew to accompany it; another chef is roasting the fillet of Dorset plaice while a young chef is cooking spinach to go with it. Derek is tasting and plating up dishes on the pass. He takes a little of the spinach to check that it tastes as it should, but it's over salty and the chef has to start again.

While it's getting hotter and hotter in the heart of the kitchen, in the cold section another printer is constantly churning out orders for sandwiches for the bar and lounge, and a young chef is feeling the heat as he single-handedly makes them up at impressive speed.

The waiting staff come in a steady stream to load up their trays to take upstairs to the restaurant, lounge and bar, and eventually everyone has been served and the pressure is off again – until dinnertime at least.

Although breakfast, lunch and dinner are the busiest times for Derek and his team, food is available 24 hours at The Goring – you can even order eggs Drumkilbo at 4am in the bar if you wish – the kitchen never shuts down.

Derek's day is a long one, starting at around 7.30am and finishing anywhere between 7-10pm, but he does get some perks, including fairly regular trips away with Jeremy to find new suppliers.

"Jeremy and myself have been all over the country to find good artisan suppliers and producers – from cheese, to meat and fish". In addition to the quality produce from the markets at Covent Garden or Billingsgate, Derek thinks it important to seek out excellent ingredients from British producers to feature on his British inspired menus.

"We do pay a bit more for our produce now but we've absorbed the cost because that's what we need to do to give our customers the best. It shows that we care and that we're trying to give them something different."

Little things that matter

Back at the front desk, Clive is dealing with an unhappy customer. A little girl of about seven is leaving to go back to America today, and she wants to take home the sheep cuddly toy from the bedroom. Clive knows just how to diffuse the issue.

"We stock them in the hotel shop, so this afternoon I'm sending one up to the room as a little present," he says, with the knowing look of a man who's encountered this sort of problem before.

I'm sure the little girl and her parents will be thrilled, and perhaps they'll write a 'thank you' letter when they get home, just as many other guests do.

"So many people do write to us saying things like, 'I want to come back to our home-from-home in London'," says Clive. "One of the nicest comments I had was from a lady who wrote to say, 'It's just like being at home, but with staff'."

Having spent some time at The Goring, I can quite see where she's coming from.

It's a luxurious but entirely unstuffy hotel, with charming staff who give the impression they really would do anything to make you happy.

I wouldn't be surprised if the name 'HRH Duchess of Cambridge' appeared on a list at a future morning briefing – with cosseting like this she'll surely make another visit.

Right: Clive Bullock, Front Office Manager

Below: Splendid Silk Room

“One of the nicest comments I had was from a lady who wrote to say, ‘It’s just like being at home, but with staff’.”

AA Star Classifications & Rosette Awards

AA Assessment

In collaboration with VisitBritain, VisitScotland and VisitWales, the AA developed Common Quality Standards for inspecting and rating accommodation. These standards and rating categories are now applied throughout the British Isles.

Any hotel applying for AA recognition receives an unannounced visit from an AA inspector to check standards. The hotels with full entries in this guide have all paid an annual fee for AA inspection, recognition and rating.

AA inspectors pay as a guest for their inspection visit, they do not accept free hospitality of any kind. Although AA inspectors do not stay overnight at Budget Hotels they do carry out regular visits to verify standards and procedures.

A guide to some of the general expectations for each star classification is as follows:

★ One Star

Polite, courteous staff providing a relatively informal yet competent style of service, available during the day and evening to receive guests

- At least one designated eating area open to residents for breakfast
- If dinner is offered it should be on at least five days a week, with last orders no earlier than 6.30pm
- Television in bedroom
- Majority of rooms en suite, bath or shower room available at all times

★★ Two Star

As for one star, plus

- At least one restaurant or dining room open to residents for breakfast (and for dinner at least five days a week)
- Last orders for dinner no earlier than 7pm
- En suite or private bath or shower and WC

★★★ Three Star

- Management and staff smartly and professionally presented and usually uniformed
- A dedicated receptionist on duty at peak times
- At least one restaurant or dining room open to residents and non-residents for breakfast and dinner whenever the hotel is open
- Last orders for dinner no earlier than 8pm
- Remote-control television, direct-dial telephone
- En suite bath or shower and WC.

★★★★ Four Star

- A formal, professional staffing structure with smartly presented, uniformed staff anticipating and responding to your needs or requests. Usually spacious, well-appointed public areas
- Reception staffed 24 hours by well-trained staff
- Express checkout facilities where appropriate
- Porterage available on request
- Night porter available
- At least one restaurant open to residents and non-residents for breakfast and dinner seven days per week, and lunch to be available in a designated eating area
- Last orders for dinner no earlier than 9pm
- En suite bath with fixed overhead shower and WC

AA Rosette Awards

Out of the many thousands of restaurants in the UK, the AA identifies over 2,000 as the best. The following is an outline of what to expect from restaurants with AA Rosette Awards.

◎ Excellent local restaurants serving food prepared with care, understanding and skill, using good quality ingredients.

◎◎ The best local restaurants, which aim for and achieve higher standards, better consistency and where a greater precision is apparent in the cooking. There will be obvious attention to the selection of quality ingredients.

◎◎◎ Outstanding restaurants that demand recognition well beyond their local area.

◎◎◎◎ Amongst the very best restaurants in the British Isles, where the cooking demands national recognition.

◎◎◎◎◎ The finest restaurants in the British Isles, where the cooking stands comparison with the best in the world.

★★★★★ Five Star

- Luxurious accommodation and public areas with a range of extra facilities. First time guests shown to their bedroom
- Multilingual service
- Guest accounts well explained and presented
- Porterage offered
- Guests greeted at hotel entrance, full concierge service provided
- At least one restaurant open to residents and non-residents for all meals seven days per week
- Last orders for dinner no earlier than 10pm
- High-quality menu and wine list
- Evening service to turn down the beds. Remote-control television, direct-dial telephone at bedside and desk, a range of luxury toiletries, bath sheets and robes. En suite bathroom incorporating fixed overhead shower and WC

★ Inspectors' Choice
Each year we select the best hotels in each rating. These hotels stand out as the very best in the British Isles, regardless of style. Red Star hotels appear in highlighted panels throughout the guide. Inspectors' Choice Restaurant with Rooms are establishments that have been awarded the highest accommodation rating under the AA Bed & Breakfast scheme.

Additional information

Hints on booking your stay

It's always worth booking as early as possible, particularly for the peak holiday period from the beginning of June to the end of September. Bear in mind that Easter and other public holidays may be busy too and in some parts of Scotland, the ski season is a peak holiday period.

Some hotels will ask for a deposit or full payment in advance, especially for one-night bookings. And some hotels charge half-board (bed, breakfast and dinner) whether you require the meals or not, while others may only accept full-board bookings. Not all hotels will accept advance bookings for bed and breakfast, overnight or short stays. Some will not take reservations from mid week.

Once a booking is confirmed, let the hotel know at once if you are unable to keep your reservation. If the hotel cannot re-let your room you may be liable to pay about two-thirds of the room price (a deposit will count towards this payment).

In Britain a legally binding contract is made when you accept an offer of accommodation, either in writing or by telephone, and illness is not accepted as a release from this contract. You are advised to take out insurance against possible cancellation, for example AA Single Trip Insurance (telephone 0845 092 1677).

Booking online

Locating and booking somewhere to stay can be a time-consuming process, but you can search quickly and easily online for a place that best suits your needs. Simply visit theAA.com to search for full details of over 6,000 quality rated hotels and B&Bs in Great Britain and Ireland. Check availability and click on the 'Book it' button.

Prices

The AA encourages the use of the Hotel Industry Voluntary Code of Booking Practice, which aims to ensure that guests know how much they will have to pay and what services and facilities are included, before entering a financially binding agreement. If the price has not previously been confirmed in writing, guests should be given a card stipulating the total obligatory charge when they register at reception.

Facilities for disabled guests

The Equality Act 2010 provides legal rights for disabled people including access to goods, services and facilities, and means that service providers may have to consider making adjustments to their premises. For more information about the Act see: www.equalities.gov.uk. or www.direct.gov.uk/en/DisabledPeople/RightsAndObligations/DisabilityRights/DG_4001068

The establishments in this guide should be aware of their obligations under the Act. We recommend that you always telephone in advance to ensure that the establishment you have chosen has appropriate facilities.

Please note: AA inspectors are not accredited to make inspections under the National Accessibility Scheme. We indicate in entries if an establishment has ground floor rooms; and if a hotel tells us that they have disabled facilities this is included in the description.

Useful Websites

www.holidaycare.org.uk
www.dptac.gov.uk/door-to-door

Licensing Laws

Licensing laws differ in England, Wales, Scotland, the Republic of Ireland, the Isle of Man, the Isles of Scilly and the Channel Islands. Public houses are generally open from mid morning to early afternoon, and from about 6 or 7pm until 11pm, although closing times may be earlier or later and some pubs are open all afternoon. Unless otherwise stated, establishments listed are licensed to serve alcohol. Hotel residents can obtain alcoholic drinks at all times, if the licensee is prepared to serve them. Non-residents eating at the hotel restaurant can have drinks with meals. Children under 14 may be excluded from bars where no food is served. Those under 18 may not purchase or consume alcoholic drinks.

Club licence means that drinks are served to club members only, 48 hours must lapse between joining and ordering.

The Fire Precautions Act does not apply to the Channel Islands, Republic of Ireland, or the Isle of Man, which have their own rules. As far as we are aware, all hotels listed in Great Britain have applied for and not been refused a fire certificate.

For information on Ireland see page 658.

Bank and Public Holidays 2012

New Year's Day	1st January
New Year's Holiday	4th January (Scotland)
Good Friday	6th April
Easter Monday	9th April
Early May Bank Holiday	7th May
Spring Bank Holiday	4th June
Diamond Jubilee Holiday	5th June
August Holiday	2nd August (Scotland)
Summer Bank Holiday	27th August
St Andrew's Day (Scotland)	30th November
Christmas Day	25th December
Boxing Day	26th December

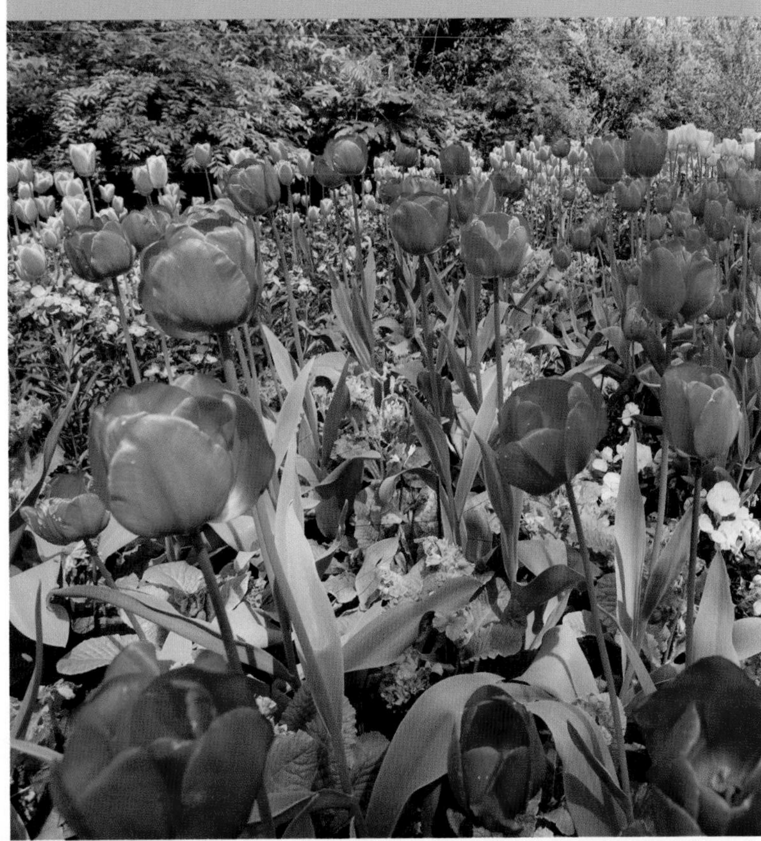

Hotel Groups Information

AKKERON	**Akkeron** A collection of three and four star hotels located throughout England and Scotland.	*0845 906 9966* *www.akkeron-hotels.com*
APEX HOTELS	**Apex Hotels** A group of contemporary four star hotels. One in Dundee, four in Edinburgh and two in London. Spa and gym facilities are available at a number of the hotels.	*0845 365 0000* *www.apexhotels.co.uk*
Barceló	**Barceló** An international group of predominantly four star hotels in the UK in 2 brands – Barceló Hotels and Barceló Premium Hotels.	*0870 168 8833* *www.barcelo-hotels.co.uk*
"bespoke" HOTELS	**Bespoke** A growing group of personally managed three and four star hotels in leisure locations.	*0870 423 3550* *www.bespokehotels.com*
Best Western	**Best Western** Britain's largest consortia group has over 280 independently owned and managed hotels, modern and traditional, in the two, three and four star range. Many have leisure facilities and rosette awards.	*08457 76 76 76* *www.bestwestern.co.uk*
Best Western PREMIER	**Best Western Premier** These hotels are selected for their beautiful settings, range of facilities and enhanced levels of service. There are currently 7 Best Western Great Britain hotels that have achieved Premier status. These join over 45 Best Western Premier accredited hotels across Europe and Asia.	*08457 76 76 76* *www.bestwestern.co.uk*
Bewleys Hotels.com	**Bewley's Hotels** Part of the Moran Hotel Group. A privately owned group of high quality, contemporary three star hotels in key locations in the UK and Ireland.	*0845 234 5959* *www.bewleyshotels.com*
Brend Hotels	**Brend** A privately owned group of 11 three and four star hotels in Devon and Cornwall.	*01271 344 496* *www.brendhotels.co.uk*
Campanile HOTEL RESTAURANT	**Campanile** An American owned and French managed company, Campanile has 20 properties in the UK offering modern accommodation in budget hotels.	*020 8326 1500* *www.envergure.fr*
CARLTON HOTEL GROUP	**Carlton Hotels** An international hotel brand based in Ireland renowned for leisure, family and relaxing spa breaks, with hotels in major cities and scenic destinations throughout Ireland.	*+353 1 866 7555* *www.carlton.ie*
CHOICE HOTELS EUROPE	**Choice** Choice has four different brands in the UK: Clarion and Quality Hotels are three and four star hotels, Comfort Inns are two and three star hotels, and Sleep Inns are budget hotels.	*0800 44 44 44* *www.choicehotelseurope.com*
CLASSIC BRITISH HOTELS	**Classic British Hotels** A consortium of four star and high-quality three star independent hotels marketed under the Classic British Hotels hallmark. Many have spas, health clubs and award-winning fine dining.	*0845 070 7090* *www.classicbritishhotels.com*
CLASSIC LODGES	**Classic Lodges** A small group of three and four star hotels mainly situated in the Cotswolds.	*0845 603 8892* *www.classiclodges.co.uk*
MILLENNIUM HOTELS AND RESORTS MILLENNIUM • COPTHORNE	**Copthorne** Part of the Millennium and Copthorne group, with 11 four star hotels in primary provincial locations as well as London.	*0800 41 47 41* *www.millenniumhotels.com*
Cotswold Inns & Hotels	**Cotswold Inns & Hotels** Charming three and four star small hotels located in the Cotswolds.	*www.* *cotswold-inns-hotels.co.uk*

Hotel Groups Information *continued*

Logo	Description	Contact
CROWNE PLAZA HOTELS & RESORTS	**Crowne Plaza** Four star hotels predominantly found in key city centre locations.	*0871 423 4876* *www.crowneplaza.co.uk*
DAYS INN	**Days Inn** Good quality modern budget hotels with good coverage across the UK.	*0800 028 0400* *www.daysinn.com*
DE VERE Hotels & Resorts	**De Vere Hotels & Resorts** A growing group of four and five star hotels with good coverage across the UK.	*0845 375 2808* *www.devere.co.uk*
EXCLUSIVE HOTELS	**Exclusive** A small privately owned group of luxury five and four red star hotels, all located in the south of England.	*01276 471 774* *www.exclusivehotels.co.uk*
Express by Holiday Inn	**Express by Holiday Inn** A major international hotel brand with over 100 hotels across the UK and over 60 across Continental Europe.	*0871 423 4876* *www.hiexpress.co.uk*
FBD Hotels	**FBD Hotels** An Irish owned and operated group offering quality hotels in convenient locations throughout Ireland.	*353 (0)1 428 2400* *www.fdbhotels.com*
focus hotels	**Focus Hotels** A group of three star hotels in both city and country locations across England. All offer Wi-fi and a number have spa facilities.	*0844 225 1625* *www.focushotels.co.uk*
fh	**Forestdale Hotels** A privately owned group of 19 three star hotels located across the UK.	*0808 144 9494* *www.forestdale.com*
FOUR PILLARS HOTELS	**Four Pillars Hotels** A group of three and four star hotels in the Oxfordshire area.	*0800 374 692* *www.four-pillars.co.uk*
GUOMAN HOTELS	**Guoman Hotels** A collection of large hotels in London, all four star, with the exception of The Royal Horseguards which has five stars.	*www.gouman.com*
HandPICKED HOTELS	**Handpicked Hotels** A group of 14 predominantly four star, high quality country house hotels, with a real emphasis on quality food. Some provide stylish spa facilities.	*0845 458 0901* *www.handpicked.co.uk*
Holiday Inn	**Holiday Inn** A major international group with many hotels across the UK.	*0871 423 4876* *www.holiday-inn.co.uk*
Hotel du Vin & Bistro	**Hotel du Vin** A small expanding group of high quality four star hotels, that places a strong emphasis on its destination restaurant concept and appealing menus.	*0845 365 4438* *www.hotelduvin.com*
ibis HOTEL	**Ibis** A growing chain of modern budget hotels with properties across the UK.	*0871 663 0628* *www.ibishotel.com*
THE INDEPENDENTS HOTEL ASSOCIATION	**Independents** A consortium of independently owned, mainly two, three and four star hotels, across Britain.	*0800 885 544* *www.theindependents.co.uk*
IRELAND'S BLUE BOOK	**Ireland's Blue Book** A collection of country houses, historic hotels, castles and restaurants throughout Ireland.	*00 353 1 676 9914* *www.irelands-blue-book.ie*

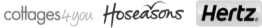

Hotel Groups Information *continued*

Logo	Description	Contact
IRISH COUNTRY HOTELS	**Irish Country Hotels** A collection of over 30 family run hotels, located all across Ireland.	*00 353 1 295 8900 (local)* *0818 281 281* *www.irishcountryhotels.com*
LAKE DISTRICT HOTELS	**Lake District Hotels** A small collection of hotels situated in some of the most beautiful parts of the Lake District countryside and in Lakeland towns.	*0800 840 1240* *www.lakedistricthotels.net*
LEGACY HOTELS	**Legacy Hotels** A small group of three star hotels growing its coverage across the UK.	*0844 411 9023* *www.legacy-hotels.co.uk*
Leisureplex	**Leisureplex** A group of 17 two star hotels located in many popular seaside resorts.	*08451 305 666 (Head Office)* *www.alfatravel.co.uk*
MACDONALD HOTELS & RESORTS	**Macdonald** A large group of predominantly four star hotels, both traditional and modern in style and located across the UK. Many hotels enjoy rural settings and state-of-the-art spa facilities	*0844 879 9000* *www.macdonaldhotels.co.uk*
Malmaison	**Malmaison** A growing brand of modern, three star city centre hotels that provide deeply comfortable bedrooms, exciting restaurants and carefully selected wine lists.	*0845 365 4247* *www.malmaison.com*
MANOR HOUSE HOTELS	**Manor House** Located throughout Ireland, this group offers a selection of independent, high quality country and manor house hotels.	*00 353 1 295 8900 (local)* *0818 281 281* *www.manorhousehotels.com*
Marriott HOTELS & RESORTS	**Marriott** This international brand has four and five star hotels in primary locations. Most are modern and have leisure facilities with a focus on activities such as golf.	*00800 1927 1927* *www.marriott.co.uk*
MAYBOURNE HOTEL GROUP	**Maybourne Hotels** A hotel group representing the prestigious London five star hotels - The Berkeley, Claridge's and The Connaught.	*020 7107 8830 (Head Office)* *www.maybourne.com*
MenziesHotels	**Menzies Hotels** A group of predominantly four star hotels in key locations across the UK.	*0845 850 3030* *www.menzies-hotels.co.uk*
Mercure	**Mercure Hotels** A fast growing group with the original hotels in London and Bristol joined by a further 24 throughout the country.	*0871 663 0627* *www.mercure.com*
MILLENNIUM HOTELS AND RESORTS	**Millennium** Part of the Millennium and Copthorne group with 6 high-quality four star hotels, mainly in central London.	*0800 41 47 41* *www.millenniumhotels.com*
minthotel	**Mint Hotels** A small group of four star contemporary hotels located in prime city centre locations.	*www.minthotel.com*
MORAN HOTELS	**Moran Hotels** A privately owned group with 4 four star Moran Hotels, and 6 three star Bewley's Hotels. All have strategic locations in the UK and Ireland.	*00 353 1 459 3650* *www.moranhotels.com*
NEW FOREST HOTELS	**New Forest Hotels** A collection of properties situated in the New Forest National Park, each with its own distinct character. All have an AA Rosette award for culinary excellence.	*0800 44 44 41* *www.newforesthotels.co.uk*

Hotel Groups Information *continued*

Logo	Description	Contact
NOVOTEL HOTELS	**Novotel** Part of French group Accor, Novotel provides mainly modern three star hotels and a new generation of four star hotels in key locations throughout the UK.	*0871 663 0626* *www.novotel.com*
OldEnglish	**Old English Inns** A large collection of former coaching inns that are mainly graded at two and three stars.	*0800 917 3085* *& 0845 608 6040* *www.oldenglishinns.co.uk*
OXFORD HOTELS & INNS	**Oxford Hotels and Inns** A large group of 45 hotels with good coverage across the UK, and particularly in Scotland. Each hotel has its own individual style and character.	*0871 376 9900* *www.oxfordhotelsandinns.com*
Park Plaza Hotels & Resorts	**Park Plaza Hotels** A European based group increasing its presence in the UK with quality four star hotels in primary locations.	*0800 169 6128* *www.parkplaza.com*
Peel Hotels plc	**Peel Hotels** A group of mainly three star hotels located across the UK.	*0845 601 7335* *www.peelhotels.co.uk*
Premier Inn	**Premier Inns** The largest and fastest growing budget hotel group with over 590 hotels offering quality, modern accommodation in key locations throughout the UK and Ireland. Each hotel is located adjacent to a family restaurant and bar.	*0871 527 8000* *www.premierinn.com*
	Pride of Britain A consortium of privately owned high quality British hotels, often in the country house style, many of which have been awarded red stars and AA Rosettes.	*0800 089 3929* *www.prideofbritainhotels.com*
PRIMA HOTEL GROUP	**Prima Hotels** A small hotel group which currently has 6 four star hotels. Five hotels are in England and one is in Scotland.	*www.primahotels.co.uk*
PH principal hayley	**Principal Hayley** A small group of four star hotels currently represented by 12 hotels situated in prime city centre locations.	*0870 242 7474* *www.principal-hotels.com*
QHotels	**QHotels** An expanding hotel group currently with 21 individually styled four star hotels across the UK.	*0845 074 0060* *www.qhotels.co.uk*
Radisson BLU Hotels & Resorts	**Radisson Blu** A recognised international brand increasing its hotels in the UK and Ireland, and offering high-quality four star hotels in key locations. (Formerly known as Radisson SAS).	*0800 374 411* *www.radisson.com*
RAMADA	**Ramada** A large hotel group with many properties throughout the UK in three brands - Ramada Plaza, Ramada and Ramada Hotel & Resort.	*0845 2070 100* *www.ramadajarvis.co.uk*
The Red Carnation Hotel Collection	**Red Carnation** A unique collection of prestigious four and five star central London hotels, providing luxurious surroundings and attentive service.	*0845 634 2665* *www.redcarnationhotels.com*
Relais & Chateaux	**Relais et Chateaux** An international consortium of rural, privately owned hotels, mainly in the country house style.	*00800 2000 0002* *www.relaischateaux.com*

Hotel Groups Information *continued*

Logo	Hotel group	Contact
RENAISSANCE. HOTELS & RESORTS	**Renaissance** One of the Marriott brands, Renaissance is a collection of individual hotels offering comfortable guest rooms, quality cuisine and good levels of service.	*00800 1927 1927* *www.marriott.co.uk*
RICHARDSON	**Richardson Hotels** A group of 6 three and four star hotels located in Cornwall and Devon, plus one hotel in Lancashire.	*www.richardsonhotels.co.uk*
THE ROCCO FORTE COLLECTION	**Rocco Forte Hotels** A small group of luxury hotels spread across Europe. Owned by Sir Rocco Forte, three hotels in the UK, all situated in major city locations.	*0870 458 4040* *www.roccofortecollection.com*
	Scotland's Hotels of Distinction A consortium of independent Scottish hotels in the three and four star range.	*01333 360 888* *www.hotels-of-distinction.com*
Sheraton	**Sheraton** Represented in the UK by a small number of four and five star hotels in London and Scotland.	*0800 35 35 35* *www.starwoodhotels.com*
shire hotels & spas	**Shire** A small group of mostly four star hotels many of which feature spa facilities and well-equipped bedrooms ideal for both the business and leisure guest.	*01254 267 444 (Head Office)* *www.shirehotels.com*
slh.com	**Small Luxury Hotels of the World** Part of an international consortium of mainly privately owned hotels, often in the country house style.	*00800 5254 8000* *www.slh.com*
THE CIRCLE	**The Circle** A consortium of independently owned, mainly two and three star hotels, across Britain.	*0845 345 1965* *www.circle-hotels.co.uk*
thistle	**Thistle** A large group of approximately 30 hotels across the UK with a significant number in London.	*0870 414 1516* *www.thistlehotels.com*
VENTURE HOTELS	**Venture Hotels** Small group of business and leisure hotels located in the north of England.	*www.venturehotels.co.uk*
von Essen hotels A PRIVATE COLLECTION	**Von Essen** A privately owned collection of country house hotels, all individual in style and offered in 3 main catagories: classic, luxury family and country.	*01761 240 121* *www.vonessenhotels.co.uk*
Warner Leisure Hotels	**Warner Leisure Hotels** Exclusively for adults, a collection of four star country hotels.	*0800 138 2633* *www.warnerleisurehotels.co.uk*
WELCOMEBREAK	**Welcome Break** Good quality, modern, budget accommodation at motorway services.	*01908 299 705* *www.welcomebreak.co.uk*

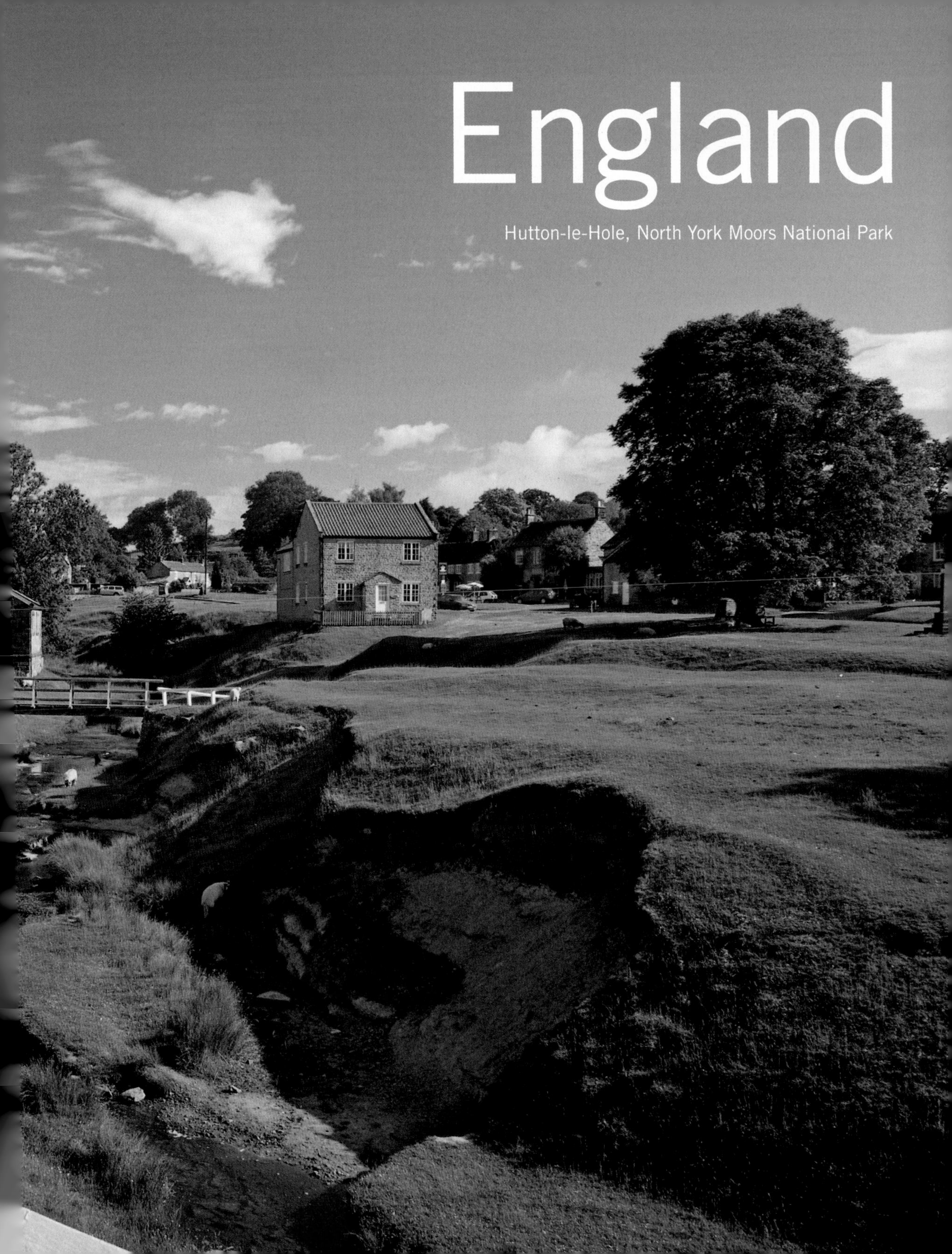

England

Hutton-le-Hole, North York Moors National Park

A

ABBERLEY Map 10 SO76
Worcestershire

The Elms Hotel

von Essen hotels A PRIVATE COLLECTION www.vonessenhotels.com

★★★ 88% HOTEL

☎ 01299 896666 01299 896804
Stockton Rd WR6 6AT
e-mail: info@theelmshotel.co.uk
web: www.theelmshotel.co.uk
dir: On A443, 2m beyond Great Witley

This imposing Queen Anne mansion, set in delightful grounds, dates back to 1710 and offers a sophisticated yet relaxed atmosphere throughout. The spacious public rooms and generously proportioned bedrooms offer elegance and charm. The hotel is particularly well geared for families, with a host of child-friendly facilities including a crèche, a play area and wonderful high teas. Imaginative cooking is served in the elegant restaurant.

Rooms 23 (6 annexe) (1 fmly) (3 GF) **D** £185-£515 (incl. bkfst) **Facilities** Spa FTV Gym Xmas New Year Wi-fi Child facilities **Conf** Class 30 Board 22 Thtr 50 Del from £165 to £195* **Parking** 100 **Notes** LB Civ Wed 70

ABINGDON Map 5 SU49
Oxfordshire

Abingdon Four Pillars Hotel

★★★ 75% HOTEL

☎ 0800 374 692 & 01235 553456
01235 554117
Marcham Rd OX14 1TZ
e-mail: abingdon@four-pillars.co.uk
web: www.four-pillars.co.uk/abingdon
dir: A34 at junct with A415, in Abingdon, turn right at rdbt, hotel on right

On the outskirts of Abingdon, this busy commercial hotel is well located for access to major roads. The bedrooms are comfortable and well equipped with extras such as safes and trouser presses. All day refreshments are offered in the stylish lounge and conservatory.

Rooms 66 (5 fmly) (32 GF) **S** £50-£120; **D** £60-£130* **Facilities** FTV Xmas New Year Wi-fi **Conf** Class 80 Board 40 Thtr 140 Del from £99 to £172* **Parking** 85 **Notes** LB Civ Wed 120

Upper Reaches

★★★ 73% HOTEL

☎ 01235 522536 & 462143 01235 555682
Thames St OX14 3JA
e-mail: reservations@upperreaches-abingdon.co.uk
web: www.upperreaches-abingdon.co.uk
dir: From A415 in Abingdon follow Dorchester signs, turn left just before bridge over Thames

Built from Abingdon Abbey's old corn mill, the hotel enjoys an attractive location. It offers well-appointed rooms, individually styled and with a wide range of amenities. The aptly named Millrace Restaurant is situated in the ancient mill house which still features a working wheel, and the river can be seen flowing beneath.

Rooms 31 (5 GF) **Facilities** FTV Fishing Xmas New Year **Parking** 60 **Notes**

Crown & Thistle

★★ 68% HOTEL

☎ 01235 522556 01235 553281
18 Bridge St OX14 3HS
e-mail: reception@crownandthistle.com
dir: Follow A415 to Dorchester town centre

A cosy hotel situated at the edge of a historical market town and a stone's throw from the Thames. There is a variety of bar and lounge areas and a maze of bright, airy corridors linking individually-styled bedrooms. The spacious reception leads to an outdoor courtyard for alfresco drinks and snacks. The Gallery Restaurant provides a pleasant atmosphere with satisfying cuisine served by friendly, efficient staff. Alternatively Stocks Bar offers pub dishes and a wide-screen TV for big sporting events.

Rooms 19 (3 fmly) **Facilities** Pool table Xmas **Conf** Class 8 Board 12 Thtr 12 **Parking** 35 **Notes**

Premier Inn Abingdon

BUDGET HOTEL

☎ 0871 527 8014 0871 527 8015
Marcham Rd OX14 1AD
dir: On A415. Approx 0.5m from A34 at Abingdon South junct (Marcham Interchange)

High quality, budget accommodation ideal for both families and business travellers. Spacious, en suite bedrooms feature tea and coffee making facilities, and Freeview TV in most hotels. Internet access and Wi-fi are available for a small fee. The adjacent family restaurant features a wide and varied menu. See also the Hotel Groups pages.

Rooms 27 **D** £60-£67*

ACCRINGTON Map 18 SD72
Lancashire

Mercure Dunkenhalgh Hotel & Spa

★★★★ 74% HOTEL

☎ 01254 398021 01254 872230
Blackburn Rd, Clayton-le-Moors BB5 5JP
e-mail: H6617@accor.com
web: www.mercure.com
dir: M65 junct 7, left at rdbt, left at lights, hotel 100yds on left

Set in delightfully tended grounds yet only a stone's throw from the M65, this fine mansion has conference and banqueting facilities that attract the wedding and corporate markets. The state-of-the-art thermal suite allows guests to relax and take life easy. Bedrooms come in a variety of styles, sizes and standards; some are located away from the main hotel building.

Rooms 175 (119 annexe) (36 fmly) (43 GF) **Facilities** Spa STV Gym Thermal suite Aerobics studio Xmas New Year Wi-fi **Conf** Class 200 Board 100 Thtr 400 **Services** Lift **Parking** 400 **Notes** Civ Wed 300

Sparth House Hotel

★★★ 76% SMALL HOTEL

☎ 01254 872263 🖹 01254 872263
Whalley Rd, Clayton Le Moors BB5 5RP
e-mail: mail.sparth@btinternet.com
web: www.sparthhousehotel.co.uk
dir: A6185 to Clitheroe along Dunkenhalgh Way, right at lights onto A678, left at next lights, A680 to Whalley. Hotel on left after 2 sets of lights

This 18th-century listed building sits in three acres of well-tended gardens. Bedrooms come in a choice of styles, from the cosy modern rooms ideal for business guests, to the spacious classical rooms - including one with furnishings from one of the great cruise liners. Public rooms feature a panelled restaurant and plush lounge bar.

Rooms 16 (3 fmly) **Facilities** FTV **Conf** Class 50 Board 40 Thtr 160 **Parking** 50 **Notes** ® Civ Wed

ALCESTER Warwickshire **Map 10 SP05**

Kings Court

★★★ 73% HOTEL

☎ 01789 763111 🖹 01789 400242
Kings Coughton B49 5QQ
e-mail: info@kingscourthotel.co.uk
web: www.kingscourthotel.co.uk
dir: 1m N on A435

This privately owned hotel dates back to Tudor times and the bedrooms in the original house have oak beams. Most guests are accommodated in the well-appointed modern wings. The bar and restaurant offer good cooking on interesting menus. The hotel is licensed to hold civil ceremonies and the pretty garden is ideal for summer weddings.

Rooms 62 (58 annexe) (3 fmly) (32 GF) **S** £58-£68; **D** £58-£90 (incl. bkfst)* **Facilities** STV Gym Wi-fi **Conf** Class 60 Board 40 Thtr 100 Del from £89 to £120* **Parking** 200 **Notes** Civ Wed 100

ALDEBURGH Suffolk **Map 13 TM45**

Brudenell Hotel

★★★★ 85% ®® HOTEL

☎ 01728 452071 🖹 01728 454082
The Parade IP15 5BU
e-mail: info@brudenellhotel.co.uk
web: www.brudenellhotel.co.uk
dir: A12, A1094. In town, turn right into High St. Hotel on seafront adjoining Fort Green car park

Situated at the far end of the town centre just a step away from the beach, this hotel has a contemporary appearance, enhanced by subtle lighting and quality soft furnishings. Many of the bedrooms have superb sea views; they include deluxe rooms with king-sized beds and superior rooms suitable for families. The informal restaurant showcases skilfully prepared dishes that use fresh, seasonal produce especially local fish, seafood and game.

Rooms 44 (17 fmly) **S** £80-£117; **D** £147-£314 (incl. bkfst) **Facilities** Xmas New Year Wi-fi **Conf** Class 20 Board 20 Thtr 20 **Services** Lift **Parking** 18 **Notes** LB

Wentworth

★★★ 88% ®® HOTEL

☎ 01728 452312 🖹 01728 454343
Wentworth Rd IP15 5BD
e-mail: stay@wentworth-aldeburgh.co.uk
web: www.wentworth-aldeburgh.com
dir: Off A12 onto A1094, 6m to Aldeburgh, with church on left, left at bottom of hill

A delightful privately owned hotel overlooking the beach. The attractive, well-maintained public rooms include three stylish lounges as well as a cocktail bar and elegant restaurant. Bedrooms are smartly decorated with co-ordinated fabrics and have many thoughtful touches; some rooms have superb sea views. Several very spacious Mediterranean-style rooms are located across the road.

Rooms 35 (7 annexe) (2 fmly) (5 GF) **S** £83-£129; **D** £141-£290 (incl. bkfst & dinner)* **Facilities** FTV Xmas New Year Wi-fi **Conf** Class 12 Board 12 Thtr 15 **Parking** 30 **Notes** LB

The White Lion Hotel

★★★ 86% ® HOTEL

☎ 01728 452720 🖹 01728 452986
Market Cross Place IP15 5BJ
e-mail: info@whitelion.co.uk
web: www.whitelion.co.uk
dir: A12 onto A1094, follow signs to Aldeburgh at junct on left. Hotel on right

A popular 15th-century hotel situated at the quiet end of town overlooking the sea. Bedrooms are pleasantly decorated and thoughtfully equipped, many rooms have lovely sea views. Public areas include two lounges and an elegant restaurant, where locally-caught fish and seafood are served. There is also a modern brasserie.

Rooms 38 (1 fmly) **Facilities** STV Xmas New Year Wi-fi **Conf** Class 50 Board 50 Thtr 120 **Parking** 15 **Notes** Civ Wed 100

A

ALDERLEY EDGE Cheshire **Map 16 SJ87**

Alderley Edge Hotel

★★★ 86% ®®® HOTEL

☎ 01625 583033 📠 01625 586343
Macclesfield Rd SK9 7BJ
e-mail: sales@alderleyedgehotel.com
web: www.alderleyedgehotel.com
dir: Off A34 in Alderley Edge onto B5087 towards Macclesfield. Hotel 200yds on right

This well-furnished hotel, with its charming grounds, was originally a country house built for one of the region's 'cotton kings'. The bedrooms and suites are attractively furnished, offering excellent quality and comfort. The welcoming bar and adjacent lounge lead into the split-level conservatory restaurant where imaginative, memorable food and friendly, attentive service form highlights of any visit.

Rooms 50 (4 fmly) (6 GF) **S** £89.50-£260; **D** £130-£400* **Facilities** STV ♫ Wi-fi **Conf** Class 40 Board 30 Thtr 120 Del from £130 to £165* **Services** Lift **Parking** 90 **Notes** LB ⊗ Closed 1 Jan RS 25 & 26 Dec Civ Wed 114

Premier Inn Alderley Edge

BUDGET HOTEL

☎ 0871 527 8016 📠 0871 527 8017
Congleton Rd SK9 7AA
dir: From N: M56 junct 6, A538 towards Wilmslow, onto A34 towards Birmingham. From S: M6 junct 17, A534 towards Congleton, onto A34 towards Manchester. Hotel adjacent to De Trafford Arms

High quality, budget accommodation ideal for both families and business travellers. Spacious, en suite bedrooms feature tea and coffee making facilities, and Freeview TV in most hotels. Internet access and Wi-fi are available for a small fee. The adjacent family restaurant features a wide and varied menu. See also the Hotel Groups pages.

Rooms 37 **D** £52-£57*

ALDERMINSTER Warwickshire **Map 10 SP24**

INSPECTORS' CHOICE

Ettington Park Hotel

HandPICKED HOTELS

★★★★ ®® HOTEL

☎ 01789 450123 & 0845 072 7454
📠 01789 450472
CV37 8BU
e-mail: ettingtonpark@handpicked.co.uk
web: www.handpicked.co.uk
dir: Off A3400, 5m S of Stratford, just outside Alderminster

Set in 40-acre grounds in the picturesque Stour Valley, Ettington Park offers the best of both worlds - the peace of the countryside and easy access to main roads and motorway networks. Bedrooms are spacious and individually decorated; views include the delightful grounds and gardens, or the historic chapel. Luxurious day rooms extend to the period drawing room, the oak-panelled dining room with inlays of family crests, a range of contemporary meeting rooms and indoor leisure centre.

Rooms 48 (20 annexe) (5 fmly) (10 GF) **Facilities** STV Clay pigeon shooting Archery Sauna Steam room Xmas New Year Wi-fi **Conf** Class 48 Board 48 Thtr 90 Del from £165 to £210* **Services** Lift **Parking** 100 **Notes** ⊗ Civ Wed 96

ALDERSHOT Hampshire **Map 5 SU85**

Potters International

★★★ 68% HOTEL

☎ 01252 344000 📠 01252 311611
1 Fleet Rd GU11 2ET
e-mail: reservations@pottersinthotel.com
dir: Access via A325 & A321 towards Fleet

This modern hotel is located within easy reach of Aldershot. Extensive air-conditioned public areas include ample lounge areas, a pub and a more formal restaurant; there are also conference rooms and a very good leisure club. Bedrooms, mostly spacious, are well equipped and have been attractively decorated and furnished.

Rooms 103 (9 fmly) (9 GF) **S** £82-£102; **D** £103-£124 (incl. bkfst)* **Facilities** STV Gym Wi-fi **Conf** Class 250 Board 100 Thtr 400 **Services** Lift **Parking** 120 **Notes** ⊗

Premier Inn Aldershot

BUDGET HOTEL

☎ 0871 527 8018 📠 0871 527 8019
7 Wellington Av GU11 1SQ
dir: M3 junct 4, A331. A325 through Farnborough. Pass Barons BMW then Queens Rdbt. Adjacent to Willems Park Brewers Fayre

High quality, budget accommodation ideal for both families and business travellers. Spacious, en suite bedrooms feature tea and coffee making facilities, and Freeview TV in most hotels. Internet access and Wi-fi are available for a small fee. The adjacent family restaurant features a wide and varied menu. See also the Hotel Groups pages.

Rooms 60 **D** £52-£71*

ALDWARK North Yorkshire **Map 19 SE46**

Aldwark Manor Golf & Spa Hotel

★★★★ 74% HOTEL

☎ 01347 838146 📠 01347 833950
YO61 1UF
e-mail: aldwarkmanor@qhotels.co.uk
web: www.qhotels.co.uk
dir: A1/A59 towards Green Hammerton, then B6265 Little Ouseburn. Follow signs for Aldwark Bridge/ Manor. A19 through Linton-on-Ouse

Mature parkland forms the impressive backdrop for this rambling 19th-century mansion, with the River Ure flowing gently through the hotel's own 18-hole golf course. Bedrooms vary - the main-house rooms are traditional and those in the extension are modern in design. Impressive conference and banqueting facilities and a stylish, very well equipped leisure club are available.

Rooms 54 (6 fmly) **Facilities** Spa FTV ⓢ ⛳ 18 Putt green Gym Health & beauty Xmas New Year Wi-fi **Conf** Class 100 Board 80 Thtr 240 **Services** Lift **Parking** 150 **Notes** ⊗ Civ Wed 140

ALFRISTON East Sussex **Map 6 TQ50**

Deans Place

★★★ 86% ❀❀ HOTEL

☎ 01323 870248 📠 01323 870918
Seaford Rd BN26 5TW
e-mail: mail@deansplacehotel.co.uk
web: www.deansplacehotel.co.uk
dir: Off A27 between Eastbourne & Brighton, signed Alfriston & Drusillas Zoo Park. Continue south through village towards Seaford

Situated on the southern fringe of the village, this friendly hotel is set in attractive gardens. Bedrooms vary in size and are well appointed with good facilities. A wide range of food is offered including an extensive bar menu and a fine dining option in Harcourt's Restaurant.

Rooms 36 (4 fmly) (8 GF) **S** £80-£95; **D** £120-£185 (incl. bkfst)* **Facilities** STV FTV ⛳ Putt green 🎣 Boules Xmas New Year Wi-fi **Conf** Class 100 Board 60 Thtr 200 Del from £150 to £200* **Parking** 100 **Notes** LB Civ Wed 150

The Star Alfriston

★★★ 77% ❀ HOTEL

☎ 01323 870495 📠 01323 870922
BN26 5TA
e-mail: bookings@thestaralfriston.co.uk
dir: 2m off A27, at Drusillas rdbt follow Alfriston signs. Hotel on right in centre of High St

Built in the 13th century and reputedly one of the country's oldest inns, this charming establishment is ideally situated for walking the South Downs or exploring the Sussex coast. Bedrooms, including two feature rooms and a mini suite, are traditionally decorated but with comfortable, modern facilities. Public areas include cosy lounges with open log fires, a bar and a popular restaurant serving a wide choice of dishes using mainly local produce. Guests can also enjoy luxury spa treatments by appointment.

Rooms 37 (1 fmly) (11 GF) **S** £70-£90; **D** £110-£135 (incl. bkfst) **Facilities** Xmas New Year Wi-fi **Conf** Class 60 Board 46 Thtr 85 Del from £120 to £145* **Parking** 35 **Notes** LB Closed 3-31 Jan Civ Wed 120

ALMONDSBURY Gloucestershire **Map 4 ST68**

Aztec Hotel & Spa

shire hotels & spas

★★★★ 80% ❀ HOTEL

☎ 01454 201090 📠 01454 201593
Aztec West Business Park, Almondsbury BS32 4TS
e-mail: aztec@shirehotels.com
web: www.aztechotelbristol.com

(For full entry see Bristol)

ALNWICK Northumberland **Map 21 NU11**

See also **Embleton**

White Swan Hotel

CLASSIC LODGES

★★★ 79% HOTEL

☎ 01665 602109 📠 01665 510400
Bondgate Within NE66 1TD
e-mail: info.whiteswan@classiclodges.co.uk
web: www.classiclodges.co.uk
dir: From A1 follow town centre signs. Hotel in town centre near Bondgate Tower

Situated in the heart of the historic town, this charming 300-year-old coaching inn still retains many authentic period features. The Olympic Suite dining room, with its original oak panelling, mirrors and stained glass windows salvaged from *RMS Olympic* (sister ship of the ill fated *Titanic*) blends well with the modern Hardy's bistro. All the bedrooms are stylishly appointed and well equipped.

Rooms 56 (5 fmly) (11 GF) **Facilities** Xmas New Year Wi-fi **Conf** Class 50 Board 40 Thtr 150 **Parking** 25 **Notes** ⊗ Civ Wed 150

ALSTON Cumbria **Map 18 NY74**

Alston House

RESTAURANT WITH ROOMS

☎ 01434 382200 📠 01434 382493
Townfoot CA9 3RN
e-mail: alstonhouse@fsmail.net
web: www.alstonhouse.co.uk
dir: On A686 opposite Spar garage

Located at the foot of the town, this family-owned restaurant with rooms provides well-equipped, stylish and comfortable accommodation. The kitchen serves both modern and traditional dishes with flair and creativity. Alston House runs a café during the day serving light meals and afternoon teas.

Rooms 7 (3 fmly)

ALTRINCHAM Greater Manchester **Map 15 SJ78**

Mercure Altrincham Bowden Hotel

★★★ 73% HOTEL

☎ 0161 928 7121 & 941 1866 📠 0161 927 7560
Langham Rd, Bowdon WA14 2HT
e-mail: enquiries@hotels-altrincham.com
dir: A556 towards Manchester, into Park Rd at lights, hotel 1m on right

Situated within easy access of Manchester and the Airport, this hotel offers comfortable and well equipped bedrooms. Public areas include the Café Bar and The Restaurant, both serving a good choice of dishes. A well-equipped leisure centre has an indoor heated pool, spa, sauna and comprehensive air-condition gym. There is free Wi-fi throughout.

Rooms 87 (8 fmly) (13 GF) **S** £40-£99; **D** £45-£125* **Facilities** FTV ⓢ supervised Gym Sauna Steam room Xmas New Year Wi-fi **Conf** Board 40 Thtr 140 Del from £89 to £159 **Parking** 125 **Notes** LB Civ Wed 125

A

ALTRINCHAM *continued*

Premier Inn Manchester Altrincham

BUDGET HOTEL

☎ 0871 527 8738 🖷 0871 527 8739
Manchester Rd WA14 4PH
dir: From N: M60 junct 7, A56 towards Altrincham. From S: M6 junct 19, A556 then A56 towards Sale

High quality, budget accommodation ideal for both families and business travellers. Spacious, en suite bedrooms feature tea and coffee making facilities, and Freeview TV in most hotels. Internet access and Wi-fi are available for a small fee. The adjacent family restaurant features a wide and varied menu. See also the Hotel Groups pages.

Rooms 46 **D** £52-£58*

ALVELEY Shropshire — **Map 10 SO78**

Mill Hotel & Restaurant

★★★★ 78% HOTEL

☎ 01746 780437 🖷 01746 780850
WV15 6HL
e-mail: info@themill-hotel.co.uk
web: www.themill-hotel.co.uk
dir: Midway between Kidderminster & Bridgnorth, exit A442 signed Enville & Turley Green

Built around a 17th-century water mill, with the original water wheel still on display, this extended and renovated hotel is set in eight acres of landscaped grounds. Bedrooms are pleasant, well equipped and include some superior rooms which have sitting areas. There are also some rooms with four-poster beds. The restaurant provides carefully prepared dishes and there are extensive wedding and function facilities.

Rooms 41 (5 fmly) **Facilities** STV Gym Xmas New Year Wi-fi **Conf** Class 180 Board 80 Thtr 250 **Services** Lift **Parking** 212 **Notes** ⊗ Civ Wed 140

ALVESTON Gloucestershire — **Map 4 ST68**

Alveston House Hotel

★★★ 81% ◎ HOTEL

☎ 01454 415050 🖷 01454 415425
Davids Ln, Alveston BS35 2LA
e-mail: info@alvestonhousehotel.co.uk
web: www.alvestonhousehotel.co.uk
dir: M5 junct 14 from N or junct 16 from S, on A38

In a quiet area with easy access to the city and a short drive from both the M4 and M5, this smartly presented hotel provides an impressive combination of good service, friendly hospitality and a relaxed atmosphere. The comfortable bedrooms are well equipped for both business and leisure guests. The restaurant offers carefully prepared fresh food, and the pleasant bar and conservatory area is perfect for enjoying a pre-dinner drink.

Rooms 30 (1 fmly) (6 GF) **S** £80-£95; **D** £110-£120 (incl. bkfst)* **Facilities** FTV Beauty treatments Xmas New Year Wi-fi **Conf** Class 48 Board 50 Thtr 85 Del from £140 to £160* **Parking** 75 **Notes** LB Civ Wed 75

AMBERLEY West Sussex — **Map 6 TQ01**

INSPECTORS' CHOICE

Amberley Castle Hotel

von Essen hotels

★★★★ ◎◎◎ COUNTRY HOUSE HOTEL

☎ 01798 831992 🖷 01798 831998
BN18 9LT
e-mail: info@amberleycastle.co.uk
web: www.amberleycastle.co.uk
dir: On B2139, off A29 between Bury & Storrington

This delightful castle idyllically set in the Sussex countryside boasts 900 years of history. The battlements, complete with a mighty portcullis (one of the few in Europe that still works) enclose the hotel. Beyond these walls are acres of stunning parkland that feature formal gardens, Koi ponds and Mistletoe Lodge, a thatched tree house accessed by a rope bridge. Here, from May to September, it is possible to dine on a special seasonal menu for two. In a more formal setting guests can enjoy award-winning cuisine in the magnificent Queen's Room - pre-booking is essential. Named after Sussex castles each of the sumptuously furnished bedrooms and suites is unique in design; some have four-poster beds. All have whirlpool baths and have lots of little luxuries such as fruit, biscuits and chocolates.

Rooms 19 (5 annexe) (6 GF) **Facilities** ♨ Putt green ⛳ Xmas New Year **Conf** Class 18 Board 28 Thtr 40 **Parking** 40 **Notes** ⊗ No children 12yrs Civ Wed 110

AMBLESIDE Cumbria — **Map 18 NY30**

See also **Elterwater**

Waterhead Hotel

★★★★ 77% ◎ TOWN HOUSE HOTEL

☎ 015394 32566 🖷 015394 31255
Lake Rd LA22 0ER
e-mail: waterhead@englishlakes.co.uk
web: www.englishlakes.co.uk
dir: A591 to Ambleside. Hotel opposite Waterhead Pier

With an enviable location opposite the bay, this well-established hotel offers contemporary and comfortable accommodation with CD/DVD players, plasma-screen TVs and internet access. There is a bar with a garden terrace overlooking the lake and a stylish restaurant serving classical cuisine with a modern twist. Staff are very attentive and friendly. Guests can enjoy full use of the Low Wood Hotel leisure facilities nearby.

Rooms 41 (3 fmly) (7 GF) **S** £86-£143; **D** £113-£226 (incl. bkfst)* **Facilities** FTV Free use of leisure facilities at sister hotel (1m) Xmas New Year Wi-fi **Conf** Class 30 Board 26 Thtr 40 Del from £99 to £165* **Parking** 43 **Notes** LB

Rothay Manor

★★★ 83% ❁ HOTEL

☎ 015394 33605 📠 015394 33607
Rothay Bridge LA22 0EH
e-mail: hotel@rothaymanor.co.uk
web: www.rothaymanor.co.uk/aa
dir: In Ambleside follow signs for Coniston (A593). Hotel 0.25m SW of Ambleside opposite rugby pitch

A long-established hotel, this attractive listed building built in Regency style, is a short walk from both the town centre and Lake Windermere. Spacious bedrooms, including suites, family rooms and rooms with balconies, are comfortably equipped and furnished to a very high standard. Public areas include a choice of lounges, a spacious restaurant and conference facilities.

Rooms 19 (2 annexe) (7 fmly) (3 GF) **S** £95-£165; **D** £160-£240 (incl. bkfst)* **Facilities** STV Nearby leisure centre free to guests Free fishing permits Xmas New Year Wi-fi **Conf** Board 18 Thtr 22 Del from £180 to £200* **Parking** 45 **Notes** LB ⊗ Closed 3-20 Jan

See advert on this page

Best Western Ambleside Salutation Hotel

Best Western

★★★ 80% HOTEL

☎ 015394 32244 📠 015394 34157
Lake Rd LA22 9BX
e-mail: ambleside@hotelslakedistrict.com
web: www.hotelslakedistrict.com
dir: A591 to Ambleside, onto one-way system, Wansfell Rd into Compston Rd. Right at lights into village

A former coaching inn, this hotel lies in the centre of the town. Bedrooms are tastefully appointed and thoughtfully equipped; many boast balconies and fine views. Inviting public areas include an attractive restaurant and a choice of comfortable lounges for relaxing, and for the more energetic there is a swimming pool and small gym.

Rooms 51 (12 annexe) (4 fmly) **S** £56.50-£70.50; **D** £113-£141 (incl. bkfst)* **Facilities** Spa Ⓢ Gym Sauna Steam room Xmas New Year Wi-fi **Conf** Class 36 Board 26 Thtr 80 Del from £122 to £134.50 **Services** Lift **Parking** 51 **Notes** LB

Regent

★★★ 79% HOTEL

☎ 015394 32254 📠 015394 31474
Waterhead Bay LA22 0ES
e-mail: info@regentlakes.co.uk
dir: 1m S on A591

This attractive holiday hotel, situated close to Waterhead Bay, offers a warm welcome. Bedrooms come in a variety of styles, including three suites and five bedrooms in the garden wing. There is a modern swimming pool and the restaurant offers a fine dining experience in a contemporary setting.

Rooms 30 (7 fmly) **S** £75-£115; **D** £95-£155 (incl. bkfst)* **Facilities** FTV Ⓢ ♫ New Year Wi-fi **Parking** 39 **Notes** LB Closed 19-27 Dec

Skelwith Bridge

★★★ 75% HOTEL

☎ 015394 32115 📠 015394 34254
Skelwith Bridge LA22 9NJ
e-mail: info@skelwithbridgehotel.co.uk
web: www.skelwithbridgehotel.co.uk
dir: 2.5m W on A593 at junct with B5343 to Langdale

This 17th-century inn is now a well-appointed tourist hotel located at the heart of the Lake District National Park and renowned for its friendly and attentive service. Bedrooms include two rooms with four-poster beds. Spacious public areas include a choice of lounges and bars, and an attractive restaurant overlooking the gardens to the bridge from which the hotel takes its name.

Rooms 28 (6 annexe) (2 fmly) (1 GF) **S** £48-£66; **D** £108-£132 (incl. bkfst)* **Facilities** Xmas New Year Wi-fi **Parking** 60 **Notes** LB

A

AMBLESIDE *continued*

Queens

★★ 69% HOTEL

☎ 015394 32206 📠 015394 32721
Market Place LA22 9BU
e-mail: enquiries@queenshotelambleside.com
web: www.queenshotelambleside.com
dir: A591 to Ambleside, follow town centre signs on one-way system. Take right lane at lights, hotel on right

Situated in the heart of the village, this traditional Lakeland stone-clad hotel offers good tourist facilities. Bedrooms are equipped with both practical and thoughtful extras, and corridors and stairways feature a fine collection of monarchy memorabilia. Public areas include an open-plan bar and lounge area, an intimate restaurant and a themed Cellar Bar with flat-screen TVs for sporting events.

Rooms 26 (4 fmly) **S** £33-£48; **D** £66-£96 (incl. bkfst)* **Facilities** STV Xmas New Year Wi-fi **Parking** 6 **Notes** LB ⊗

The Log House

RESTAURANT WITH ROOMS

☎ 015394 31077
Lake Rd LA22 0DN
e-mail: info@loghouse.co.uk
web: www.loghouse.co.uk
dir: From Windermere into Ambleside on A591. On left after Hayes Garden Centre

This charming and historic Norwegian building is located midway between the town centre and the shore of Lake Windermere, just five minutes' walk to each. Guests can enjoy delicious meals in the attractive restaurant, which also has a bar area. There are three comfortable bedrooms, each equipped with thoughtful accessories such as DVD/VCR players and hairdryers. Wi-fi is also available.

Rooms 3

AMESBURY Wiltshire **Map 5 SU14**

Holiday Inn Salisbury - Stonehenge

★★★★ 76% HOTEL

☎ 0845 241 3535 📠 0845 241 3535
Midsummer Place, Solstice Park SP4 7SQ
e-mail: reservations@hisalisbury-stonehenge.co.uk
web: www.hisalisbury-stonehenge.co.uk
dir: Exit A303, follow signs into Solstice Park. Hotel adjacent to service area

This hotel of striking modern design is located on the A303 very close to Stonehenge. All bedrooms have been appointed to the highest standards with unique headboards, air conditioning and broadband connection included in the generous amenities. Fluffy towels and powerful showers are provided in the modern bathrooms. The Solstice Bar and Grill is open from 7am-11pm offering a range of snacks and meals.

Rooms 103 (24 fmly) (8 GF) **Facilities** FTV Xmas New Year Wi-fi **Conf** Class 20 Board 20 Thtr 25
Del from £120 to £160* **Services** Lift Air con **Parking** 168 **Notes** ⊗

ANDOVER Hampshire **Map 5 SU34**

Esseborne Manor

★★★ 80% HOTEL

☎ 01264 736444 📠 01264 736725
Hurstbourne Tarrant SP11 0ER
e-mail: info@esseborne-manor.co.uk
web: www.esseborne-manor.co.uk
dir: Halfway between Andover & Newbury on A343, 1m N of Hurstbourne Tarrant

Set in two acres of well-tended gardens, this attractive manor house is surrounded by the open countryside of the North Wessex Downs. Bedrooms are delightfully individual and are split between the main house, an adjoining courtyard and separate garden cottage. There's a wonderfully relaxed atmosphere throughout, and public rooms combine elegance with comfort.

Rooms 19 (8 annexe) (2 fmly) (6 GF) **S** £80-£110; **D** £100-£180 (incl. bkfst)* **Facilities** STV FTV Xmas New Year Wi-fi **Conf** Class 40 Board 30 Thtr 60 **Parking** 50 **Notes** LB Civ Wed 100

Quality Hotel Andover

★★★ 62% HOTEL

☎ 01264 369111 📠 01264 369000
Micheldever Rd SP11 6LA
e-mail: andover@quality-hotels.co.uk
dir: At A303 & A3093 junct. At 1st rdbt 1st exit, at 2nd rdbt 1st exit. Left immediately before Total petrol station, left again

Located on the outskirts of the town, this hotel is popular with business guests. Bedrooms provide useful accessories; public areas consist of a cosy lounge, a hotel bar and a traditional style restaurant serving a range of meals. There is also a large conference suite available and a pleasant garden with patio seating.

Rooms 49 (36 annexe) (13 GF) **Facilities** Wi-fi **Conf** Class 60 Board 60 Thtr 180 **Parking** 100 **Notes** Civ Wed 85

Premier Inn Andover

BUDGET HOTEL

☎ 0871 527 8020 📠 0871 527 8021
West Portway Industrial Estate, Joule Rd SP10 3UX
dir: From A303 follow A342/A343 signs. Hotel at rdbt junct of A342 & A343 adjacent to Portway Inn Brewers Fayre

High quality, budget accommodation ideal for both families and business travellers. Spacious, en suite bedrooms feature tea and coffee making facilities, and Freeview TV in most hotels. Internet access and Wi-fi are available for a small fee. The adjacent family restaurant features a wide and varied menu. See also the Hotel Groups pages.

Rooms 50 **D** £65*

A

ANSTY Map 11 SP48
Warwickshire

Macdonald Ansty Hall

★★★★ 76% HOTEL

☎ 0844 879 9031 024 7660 2155
Main Rd CV7 9HZ
e-mail: ansty@macdonald-hotels.co.uk
web: www.macdonald-hotels.co.uk/anstyhall
dir: M6 junct 2 onto B4065 signed Ansty. Hotel 1.5m on left

Dating back to 1678, this Grade II listed Georgian house is set in eight acres of attractive grounds and woodland. The hotel enjoys a central yet tranquil location. Spacious bedrooms feature a traditional decorative style and a range of extras. Rooms are divided between the main house and the newer annexe.

Rooms 62 (39 annexe) (4 fmly) (22 GF) **S** £75-£219; **D** £75-£252* **Facilities** FTV Xmas New Year Wi-fi **Conf** Class 60 Board 60 Thtr 150 Del from £145 to £195* **Services** Lift **Parking** 100 **Notes** Civ Wed 100

APPLEBY-IN-WESTMORLAND Map 18 NY62
Cumbria

Appleby Manor Country House Hotel

★★★★ 76% COUNTRY HOUSE HOTEL

☎ 017683 51571 017683 52888
Roman Rd CA16 6JB
e-mail: reception@applebymanor.co.uk
web: www.applebymanor.co.uk
dir: M6 junct 40, A66 towards Brough. Take Appleby turn, immediately right. 0.5m to hotel

This imposing country mansion is set in extensive grounds amid stunning Cumbrian scenery. The Dunbobbin family and their experienced staff ensure a warm welcome and attentive service. The thoughtfully equipped bedrooms vary in style and include the impressive Heelis Suite; some rooms also have patio areas. The bar offers a wide range of malt whiskies and the restaurant serves carefully prepared meals.

Rooms 30 (7 annexe) (9 fmly) (10 GF) **D** £150-£280 (incl. bkfst)* **Facilities** FTV Putt green Steam room Spa bath Sauna Table tennis Pool table New Year Wi-fi **Conf** Class 25 Board 28 Thtr 38 Del from £140 to £180* **Parking** 51 **Notes** LB Closed 24-26 Dec RS 6-13 Jun Civ Wed 60

ARLINGHAM Map 4 SO71
Gloucestershire

The Old Passage Inn

RESTAURANT WITH ROOMS

☎ 01452 740547 01452 741871
Passage Rd GL2 7JR
e-mail: oldpassage@ukonline.co.uk
dir: A38 onto B4071 through Arlingham. Through village to river

Delightfully located on the very edge of the River Severn, this relaxing restaurant with rooms combines high quality food with an air of tranquillity. Bedrooms and bathrooms are decorated in a modern style and include a range of welcome extras such as air conditioning and a well-stocked mini-bar. The menu offers a wide range of seafood and shellfish dishes including crab, oysters and lobsters from Cornwall (kept alive in seawater tanks). An outdoor terrace is available in warmer months.

Rooms 3

ARUNDEL Map 6 TQ00
West Sussex

White Swan Hotel

★★★ 78% HOTEL

☎ 01903 882677 01903 884154
16 Chichester Rd BN18 0AD
e-mail: thewhiteswan.arundel@pebblehotels.com
dir: From Chichester take A27 towards Arundel. Hotel on left approx 1m W of Arundel

This hotel offers very comfortable and stylish guest accommodation. There is a character bar, lounge and restaurant, and an informal service is provided by the friendly team. Substantial snacks and meals can be ordered throughout the day and evening. Complimentary Wi-fi is available in the public areas.

Rooms 20 (20 fmly) (6 GF) **Facilities** FTV Wi-fi **Conf** Class 50 Board 40 Thtr 130 **Parking** 110 **Notes** Civ Wed 80

Norfolk Arms

★★★ 74% HOTEL

☎ 01903 882101 01903 884275
High St BN18 9AB
e-mail: norfolk.arms@forestdale.com
web: www.norfolkarmshotel.com
dir: On High St in centre

Built by the 10th Duke of Norfolk, this Georgian coaching inn enjoys a superb setting beneath the battlements of Arundel Castle. Bedrooms vary in sizes and character - all are comfortable and well equipped. Public areas include two bars serving real ales, comfortable lounges with roaring log fires, a traditional restaurant and a range of meeting and function rooms.

Rooms 33 (13 annexe) (4 fmly) (8 GF) **Facilities** FTV Xmas New Year Wi-fi **Conf** Class 36 Board 40 Thtr 100 **Parking** 34 **Notes** LB Civ Wed 60

Comfort Inn

★★ 65% HOTEL

☎ 01903 840840 01903 849849
Crossbush BN17 7QQ
e-mail: reservations@comfortinnarundel.co.uk
dir: A27/A284, 1st right into services

This modern, purpose-built hotel provides a good base for exploring the nearby historic town. Good access to local road networks and a range of meeting rooms, all air-conditioned, also make this an ideal venue for business guests. Bedrooms are spacious, smartly decorated and well equipped.

Rooms 53 (4 fmly) (25 GF) (12 smoking) **Facilities** STV FTV Xmas New Year Wi-fi **Conf** Class 30 Board 30 Thtr 30 **Parking** 53

Premier Inn Arundel

BUDGET HOTEL

☎ 0871 527 8022 0871 527 8023
Crossbush Ln BN18 9PQ
dir: At junct of A27 &A284, 1m E of Arundel

High quality, budget accommodation ideal for both families and business travellers. Spacious, en suite bedrooms feature tea and coffee making facilities, and Freeview TV in most hotels. Internet access and Wi-fi are available for a small fee. The adjacent family restaurant features a wide and varied menu. See also the Hotel Groups pages.

Rooms 30 **D** £67*

A

ARUNDEL *continued*

The Townhouse

RESTAURANT WITH ROOMS

☎ 01903 883847
65 High St BN18 9AJ
e-mail: enquiries@thetownhouse.co.uk
web: www.thetownhouse.co.uk
dir: A27 to Arundel, into High Street, establishment on left at top of hill

This is an elegant, Grade II-listed Regency building overlooking Arundel Castle, just a short walk from the shops and centre of the town. Bedrooms and public areas retain the building's unspoilt character. The ceiling in the dining room is particularly spectacular and originated in Florence in the 16th century. The owners can be justifiably proud of the enterprise they undertook just a few years ago.

Rooms 4

ASCOT
Berkshire — **Map 6 SU96**

Coworth Park

★★★★★ 86% HOTEL

☎ 01344 876600 📠 01344 876660
London Rd SL5 7SE
e-mail: info@coworthpark.com
dir: M25 junct 13 S onto A30 to Sunningdale. Hotel on left 2 min past Wentworth Golf Club

Set in 240 acres of stunning parkland, Coworth Park is part of the luxury Dorchester Collection, sister to The Dorchester in London. The hotel offers luxurious guest rooms and suites, polo grounds, stables and a spa. Children are well cared for too, with a 'Kids Concierge' who can arrange a wide variety of activities for them. The hotel maintains a strong 'green' policy, as does the kitchen team where local quality suppliers are a priority. A skilful mix of flavours and textures is provided in the fine dining restaurant (3 AA Rosettes) on the local 'Shire menu' and a tasting menu under the guidance of John Campbell. Casual dining is available in the popular Barn restaurant (1 AA Rosette), in a converted stable block.

Rooms 70 (30 fmly) (21 GF) **S** £252-£535; **D** £252-£535 (incl. bkfst) **Facilities** Spa STV FTV Fishing Gym Polo Club & tuition Table tennis Xmas New Year Wi-fi **Conf** Class 54 Board 40 Thtr 100 Del from £295 to £495 **Services** Lift Air con **Notes** LB Civ Wed 250

Macdonald Berystede Hotel & Spa

★★★★ 78% HOTEL

☎ 0844 879 9104 📠 01344 872301
Bagshot Rd, Sunninghill SL5 9JH
e-mail: general.berystede@macdonald-hotels.co.uk
web: www.macdonald-hotels.co.uk/berystede
dir: A30, B3020 (Windmill Pub). 1.25m to hotel on left just before junct with A330

This impressive Victorian mansion, close to Ascot Racecourse, offers executive bedrooms that are spacious, comfortable and particularly well equipped. Public rooms include a cosy bar and an elegant restaurant in which creative dishes are served. An impressive self-contained conference centre and spa facility appeal to both conference and leisure guests.

Rooms 126 (61 fmly) (33 GF) **S** £90-£245; **D** £100-£255* **Facilities** Spa STV Gym Leisure complex (thermal & beauty treatments) Outdoor garden spa Xmas New Year Wi-fi **Conf** Class 220 Board 150 Thtr 330 Del from £165 to £300* **Services** Lift **Parking** 200 **Notes** LB Civ Wed 300

Brockenhurst Hotel

★★ 60% HOTEL

☎ 01344 621912 📠 01344 873252
Brockenhurst Rd SL5 9HA
e-mail: info@brockenhurst.com
dir: On A330 (near Ascot race course), pass course on left, right at mini rdbt, 0.5m, hotel on right

Sitting in well kept grounds and gardens, this hotel is in a convenient location in a leafy suburb in south Ascot, a short distance from the railway station. Bedrooms are comfortable and each is individually designed to reflect the hotel's unique character. Dinner is served in the contemporary dining room and offers a good range of home cooked dishes. Parking is available at this property.

Rooms 10 (3 fmly) **S** £60-£180; **D** £70-£200 (incl. bkfst)* **Facilities** Wi-fi **Parking** 30 **Notes**

Premier Inn Ascot

BUDGET HOTEL

☎ 0871 527 8024 📠 0871 527 8025
London Rd SL5 8DR
dir: M3 junct 3, A322 signed Bracknell & Ascot, follow Ascot signs. At next rdbt 1st exit to Bracknell. Hotel on right after lights. Or M4 junct 6 follow Ascot/A322 signs. Racecourse on left, at rdbt follow Bracknell/A329 signs. Hotel on right after lights

High quality, budget accommodation ideal for both families and business travellers. Spacious, en suite bedrooms feature tea and coffee making facilities, and Freeview TV in most hotels. Internet access and Wi-fi are available for a small fee. The adjacent family restaurant features a wide and varied menu. See also the Hotel Groups pages.

Rooms 28 **D** £60-£75*

ASHBOURNE
Derbyshire — **Map 10 SK14**

See also **Thorpe**

Callow Hall

★★★ 82% HOTEL

☎ 01335 300900 📠 01335 300512
Mappleton Rd DE6 2AA
e-mail: info@callowhall.co.uk
dir: A515 through Ashbourne towards Buxton, left at Bowling Green pub, then 1st right

This delightful, creeper-clad, early Victorian house, set on a 44-acre estate, enjoys views over Bentley Brook and the Dove Valley. The atmosphere is relaxed and welcoming, and some of the spacious bedrooms in the main house have comfortable sitting areas. Public rooms feature high ceilings, ornate plasterwork and antique furniture. There is a good range of dishes offered on both the carte and the fixed-price, daily-changing menus.

Rooms 16 (2 fmly) (2 GF) **Facilities** STV Xmas New Year Wi-fi **Conf** Class 25 Board 28 Thtr 30 Del from £80 to £160* **Parking** 21 **Notes** LB Civ Wed 40

ASHBY-DE-LA-ZOUCH
Leicestershire
Map 11 SK31

The Royal Hotel

★★★ 64% HOTEL

☎ 01530 412833 📠 01530 564548
Station Rd LE65 2GP
e-mail: reservations@royalhotelashby.com
web: www.royalhotelashby.com
dir: A42 junct 13/A511 towards Ashby-de-la-Zouch. A511 along Nottingham Rd to Station Rd, & Main Rd into town. Left at rdbt, left & left again

This Grade II listed Regency building retains much of its original character. The bedrooms, although varying in size are comfortable and well equipped; one room has a four-poster bed. The Castle Room Restaurant overlooks the lovely landscaped gardens. The staff are friendly and efficient.

Rooms 34 (4 fmly) **S** £45-£75; **D** £65-£110 (incl. bkfst)* **Facilities** STV Wi-fi **Conf** Class 26 Board 26 Thtr 70 Del from £120 to £140* **Parking** 200 **Notes** LB ⊗ Civ Wed 65

Premier Inn Ashby-de-la-Zouch

BUDGET HOTEL

☎ 0871 527 8026 📠 0871 527 8027
Flagstaff Island LE65 1DS
dir: M1 junct 23a, follow A42 (M42), Tamworth & Birmingham signs. Hotel at rdbt at A42 junct 13. (NB for Sat Nav use LE65 1JP)

High quality, budget accommodation ideal for both families and business travellers. Spacious, en suite bedrooms feature tea and coffee making facilities, and Freeview TV in most hotels. Internet access and Wi-fi are available for a small fee. The adjacent family restaurant features a wide and varied menu. See also the Hotel Groups pages.

Rooms 40 **D** £49-£60*

ASHFORD
Kent
Map 7 TR04

INSPECTORS' CHOICE

Eastwell Manor

★★★★  HOTEL

☎ 01233 213000 📠 01233 635530
Eastwell Park, Boughton Lees TN25 4HR
e-mail: enquiries@eastwellmanor.co.uk
dir: M20 junct 9, follow Faversham A251 signs. On A251 hotel on left on entering Boughton Lees

Set in 62 acres of landscaped grounds, this lovely hotel dates back to the Norman Conquest and boasts a number of interesting features, including carved wood-panelled rooms and huge baronial stone fireplaces. Accommodation is divided between the manor house and the courtyard mews cottages. The luxury Pavilion Spa in the grounds has an all-day brasserie, and award-winning fine dining is offered in the main restaurant.

Rooms 62 (39 annexe) (2 fmly) (15 GF) **S** £110-£190; **D** £140-£445 (incl. bkfst)* **Facilities** Spa STV 🏊 ⛳ 9 Putt green Gym Boules Xmas New Year Wi-fi **Conf** Class 70 Board 60 Thtr 180 Del from £140 to £240* **Services** Lift **Parking** 200 **Notes** LB Civ Wed 450

Ashford International Hotel

★★★★ 80% HOTEL

☎ 01233 219988 📠 01233 647743
Simone Weil Av TN24 8UX
e-mail: ashford@qhotels.co.uk
web: www.qhotels.co.uk
dir: M20 junct 9, exit for Ashford/Canterbury. Left at 1st rdbt, hotel 200mtrs on left

Situated just off the M20 and with easy links to the Eurotunnel, Eurostar and ferry terminals, this hotel has been stunningly appointed. The slick, stylishly presented bedrooms are equipped with the latest amenities. Public areas include the spacious Horizons Wine Bar and Restaurant serving a competitively priced menu, and Quench Sports Bar for relaxing drinks. The Reflections leisure club boasts a pool, fully-equipped gym, spa facilities and treatment rooms.

Rooms 179 (29 fmly) (57 GF) **S** £75-£250; **D** £85-£260 (incl. bkfst)* **Facilities** Spa 🏊 Gym Aroma steam room Rock sauna Feature shower Ice fountain Xmas New Year Wi-fi **Conf** Class 180 Board 26 Thtr 400 Del from £119 to £159* **Services** Lift Air con **Parking** 400 **Notes** LB Civ Wed 400

Holiday Inn Ashford-Central

★★★ 79% HOTEL

☎ 0870 400 9001 📠 01233 643176
Canterbury Rd TN24 8QQ
e-mail: reservations-ashford@ihg.com
web: www.holidayinn.co.uk
dir: A28, at 2nd lights turn left. Hotel approx 90mtrs on right

Ideally situated within easy reach of Eurostar and Eurotunnel terminals and a short drive to historic Canterbury, this popular hotel offers stylish facilities for both business and leisure travellers. Comfortable, well-equipped bedrooms vary in size and include spacious family rooms with modern sofa beds. Public areas include a casual restaurant, lounges, bar and attractive garden area.

Rooms 103 (40 fmly) (50 GF) (12 smoking) **Facilities** STV Xmas Wi-fi **Conf** Class 64 Board 40 Thtr 120 **Parking** 120 **Notes** ⊗ Civ Wed 130

A

ASHFORD *continued*

Holiday Inn Ashford-North A20

★★★ 75% HOTEL

☎ 01233 713333 📠 01233 712082
Maidstone Rd, Hothfield TN26 1AR
e-mail: reception.ashford@hiashford.com
web: www.holidayinn.co.uk
dir: M20 junct 9, at rdbt take 3rd exit signed Ashford/Canterbury. At next rdbt 4th exit signed Lenham. Straight on at next rdbt. Hotel approx 3.5m on left just after Esso petrol station

This hotel is ideally situated to meet the needs of business and leisure travellers. It enjoys a rural outlook whilst occupying a convenient location for travel via the Eurostar terminal at Ashford, the channel port of Dover and the M20. There's a small bar, gym and restaurant with a 'local pub' in the grounds. Ample free parking is available.

Rooms 92 (5 fmly) (20 GF) (7 smoking) **Facilities** STV Gym Xmas New Year Wi-fi **Conf** Class 28 Board 32 Thtr 125 Del from £115 to £135* **Services** Lift Air con **Parking** 140 **Notes** ® Civ Wed 60

Premier Inn Ashford Central

BUDGET HOTEL

☎ 0871 527 8030 📠 0871 527 8031
Hall Av, Orbital Park, Sevington TN24 0GN
dir: M20 junct 10 S'bound: 4th exit at rdbt. N'bound: 1st exit onto A2070 signed Brenzett. Hotel on right at next rdbt

High quality, budget accommodation ideal for both families and business travellers. Spacious, en suite bedrooms feature tea and coffee making facilities, and Freeview TV in most hotels. Internet access and Wi-fi are available for a small fee. The adjacent family restaurant features a wide and varied menu. See also the Hotel Groups pages.

Rooms 60 **D** £57*

Premier Inn Ashford (Eureka Leisure Park)

BUDGET HOTEL

☎ 0871 527 8028 📠 0871 527 8029
Eureka Leisure Park TN25 4BN
dir: M20 junct 9, take 1st exit on left

Rooms 74 **D** £59*

Premier Inn Ashford North

BUDGET HOTEL

☎ 0871 527 8032 📠 0871 527 8033
Maidstone Road (A20), Hothfield Common TN26 1AP
dir: M20 junct 9, A20 follow Lenham signs. Hotel between Ashford & Charing

Rooms 60 **D** £56*

The Wife of Bath

®® RESTAURANT WITH ROOMS

☎ 01233 812232 📠 01233 813630
4 Upper Bridge St, Wye TN25 5AF
e-mail: relax@thewifeofbath.com
dir: 4m NE of Ashford. M20 junct 9, A28 for Canterbury, 3m right to Wye

The Wife of Bath is set in the medieval village of Wye which is close to Dover, Canterbury and Ashford. Bedrooms are tastefully decorated and provide guests with comfortable accommodation; each is equipped with LCD TVs and DVD players (a range of DVDs is available). The stylish restaurant, with a small separate bar area, is open for lunch and dinner daily; a cooked or continental breakfast is served here in the morning. Free Wi-fi is available throughout.

Rooms 5 (2 annexe)

ASHFORD IN THE WATER — Map 16 SK16
Derbyshire

Riverside House

★★★ 88% ®® HOTEL

☎ 01629 814275 📠 01629 812873
Fennel St DE45 1QF
e-mail: riversidehouse@enta.net
dir: Off A6 (Bakewell/Buxton road) 2m from Bakewell, hotel at end of main street

This delightful and welcoming hotel, with outstanding service, is establishing a good reputation for its high quality accommodation and fine dining. In parts dating back to 1630, it enjoys a peaceful location by the River Wye. Individually styled bedrooms are thoughtfully equipped, and the smart public rooms include a bright conservatory, an oak-panelled lounge with inglenook fireplace, a drawing room and two dining rooms.

Rooms 14 (4 GF) **S** £120-£155; **D** £145-£195 (incl. bkfst) **Facilities** STV Xmas New Year **Conf** Class 15 Board 15 Thtr 15 **Parking** 40 **Notes** LB ® No children 16yrs Civ Wed 32

ASHINGTON — Map 21 NZ28
Northumberland

Premier Inn Ashington

BUDGET HOTEL

☎ 0871 527 8034 📠 0871 527 8035
Queen Elizabeth Country Park, Woodhorn NE63 9AT
dir: From A1 follow signs to Morpeth then Woodhorn Colliery Museum/Ashington. Through Ashington. Hotel in Queen Elizabeth II Country Park

High quality, budget accommodation ideal for both families and business travellers. Spacious, en suite bedrooms feature tea and coffee making facilities, and Freeview TV in most hotels. Internet access and Wi-fi are available for a small fee. The adjacent family restaurant features a wide and varied menu. See also the Hotel Groups pages.

Rooms 20 **D** £53-£59*

ASHWATER — Map 3 SX39
Devon

INSPECTORS' CHOICE

Blagdon Manor

®® RESTAURANT WITH ROOMS

☎ 01409 211224 📠 01409 211634
EX21 5DF
e-mail: stay@blagdon.com
web: www.blagdon.com
dir: A388 towards Launceston/Holsworthy. Approx 2m N of Chapman's Well take 2nd right for Ashwater. Next right beside Blagdon Lodge, 0.25m to manor

Located on the borders of Devon and Cornwall within easy reach of the coast, and set in its own beautifully kept natural gardens, this small and friendly restaurant with rooms offers a charming home-from-home atmosphere. The tranquillity of the secluded setting, the character and charm of the house and its unhurried pace ensure calm and relaxation. High levels of service, personal touches and thoughtful extras are all part of a stay here. Steve Morey cooks with passion and his commitment to using only the finest local ingredients speaks volumes.

Rooms 7

ASKRIGG North Yorkshire **Map 18 SD99**

White Rose

★★ 72% SMALL HOTEL

☎ 01969 650515 📠 01969 650176
Main St DL8 3HG
e-mail: stay@thewhiterosehotelaskrigg.co.uk
dir: M6 or A1 onto A684. Follow signs to Askrigg, hotel in village centre

This family-run hotel dates from the 19th century, and is situated in the heart of Askrigg which was the fictional town of Darrowby in the BBC's *All Creatures Great and Small* series. The friendliness of the staff is noteworthy. The accommodation is tastefully decorated and comfortably furnished, and home cooked food is served in the conservatory overlooking the beer garden.

Rooms 12 **S** £47.50; **D** £75-£85 (incl. bkfst)* **Facilities** New Year **Parking** 20 **Notes** Closed 24-25 Dec

ASPLEY GUISE Bedfordshire **Map 11 SP93**

Best Western Moore Place

★★★ 77% HOTEL

☎ 01908 282000 📠 01908 281888
The Square MK17 8DW
e-mail: manager@mooreplace.com
dir: M1 junct 13, take A507 signed Aspley Guise & Woburn Sands. Hotel on left in village square

This impressive Georgian house, set in delightful gardens in the village centre, is very conveniently located for the M1. Bedrooms do vary in size, but consideration has been given to guest comfort, with many thoughtful extras provided. There is a wide range of meeting rooms and private dining options.

Rooms 62 (27 annexe) (16 GF) **S** £65-£109; **D** £79-£145* **Facilities** FTV Wi-fi **Conf** Class 24 Board 20 Thtr 40 Del from £109 to £169* **Parking** 70 **Notes** LB Civ Wed 65

ATHERSTONE Warwickshire **Map 10 SP39**

Chapel House Restaurant With Rooms

🏵 RESTAURANT WITH ROOMS

☎ 01827 718949 📠 01827 717702
Friar's Gate CV9 1EY
e-mail: info@chapelhouse.eu
web: www.chapelhouse.eu
dir: A5 to town centre, right onto Church St. Right onto Sheepy Rd & left onto Friar's Gate

Sitting next to the church this 18th-century town house offers excellent hospitality and service while the cooking, using much local produce, is very notable. Bedrooms are well equipped and lounges are extensive; there is also a delightful walled garden for guests to use.

Rooms 11

AUSTWICK North Yorkshire **Map 18 SD76**

The Traddock

🏵🏵 RESTAURANT WITH ROOMS

☎ 015242 51224 📠 015242 51796
LA2 8BY
e-mail: info@austwicktraddock.co.uk
dir: From Skipton take A65 towards Kendal, 3m after Settle turn right signed Austwick, cross hump back bridge, 100yds on left

Situated within the Yorkshire Dales National Park and a peaceful village environment, this fine Georgian country house with well-tended gardens offers a haven of calm and good hospitality. There are two comfortable lounges with real fires and fine furnishings, as well as a cosy bar and an elegant dining room serving fine dinners. Bedrooms are individually styled with many homely touches.

Rooms 12 (2 fmly)

AXMINSTER Devon **Map 4 SY29**

See also **Colyford**

Fairwater Head Hotel

★★★ 75% 🏵 HOTEL

☎ 01297 678349 📠 01297 678459
Hawkchurch EX13 5TX
e-mail: stay@fairwaterheadhotel.co.uk
web: www.fairwaterheadhotel.co.uk
dir: Off B3165 (Crewkerne to Lyme Regis road). Hotel signed to Hawkchurch

This elegant Edwardian country house provides a perfect location for anyone looking for a peaceful break. Surrounded by extensive gardens and rolling countryside, the setting guarantees relaxation. Bedrooms are located both within the main house and the garden wing; all provide good levels of comfort. Public areas have much appeal and include lounge areas, a bar and an elegant restaurant. Food is a highlight with excellent local produce prepared with care and skill.

Rooms 16 (4 annexe) (8 GF) **S** £70-£125; **D** £85-£180 (incl. bkfst)* **Facilities** FTV Library Xmas New Year Wi-fi **Conf** Class 25 Board 20 Thtr 35 Del from £152 to £185* **Parking** 30 **Notes** LB Closed 1-30 Jan Civ Wed 50

AYCLIFFE Co Durham **Map 19 NZ22**

The County Restaurant with Rooms

RESTAURANT WITH ROOMS

☎ 01325 312273 📠 01325 317131
12 The Green DL5 6LX
e-mail: info@thecountyaycliffevillage.com
dir: A1(M) junct 59, A167 towards Newton Aycliffe. At Aycliffe turn onto village green

Located overlooking the pretty village green yet convenient for the A1, the focus here is on fresh, home-cooked meals, real ales and friendly service. There is a relaxed atmosphere in the bar area, and the restaurant where attractive artwork is displayed. The bedrooms in the smart townhouse next door are all furnished to a high standard.

Rooms 7

A

AYLESBURY
Buckinghamshire
Map 11 SP81

INSPECTORS' CHOICE

Hartwell House Hotel, Restaurant & Spa

★★★★ ◎◎◎ HOTEL

☎ 01296 747444 🖹 01296 747450
Oxford Rd HP17 8NR
e-mail: info@hartwell-house.com
web: www.hartwell-house.com
dir: From S: M40 junct 7, A329 to Thame, then A418 towards Aylesbury. After 6m, through Stone, hotel on left. From N: M40 junct 9 for Bicester. A41 to Aylesbury, A418 to Oxford for 2m. Hotel on right

This beautiful, historic house is set in 90 acres of unspoilt parkland. The grand public rooms are truly magnificent, and feature many fine works of art. The service standards are very high; guests will find that the staff offer attentive and traditional hospitality without stuffiness. There is an elegant, award-winning restaurant where carefully prepared dishes use the best local produce. Bedrooms are spacious, elegant and very comfortable. Most are in the main house, but some, including suites, are in the nearby, renovated coach house, which also houses an excellent spa.

Rooms 46 (16 annexe) (3 fmly) (10 GF) **S** £175; **D** £205-£290 (incl. bkfst)* **Facilities** Spa STV supervised Gym Sauna treatment rooms Steam rooms Xmas New Year Wi-fi
Conf Class 40 Board 40 Thtr 100 Del from £225 to £265* **Services** Lift **Parking** 91 **Notes** LB No children 4yrs RS Xmas/New Year Civ Wed 120

Holiday Inn Aylesbury

★★★ 78% HOTEL

☎ 01296 734000 🖹 01296 392211
Aston Clinton Rd HP22 5AA
e-mail: aylesbury@ihg.com
web: www.holidayinn.co.uk
dir: M25 junct 20, follow A41. Hotel on left on entering Aylesbury

Situated to the south of town, this hotel is conveniently located for local businesses and the town centre. Public areas are extensive including the well-equipped health club and a superb range of meeting rooms. Bedrooms are comfortable and are equipped with a host of extras.

Rooms 139 (45 fmly) (69 GF) (8 smoking)
Facilities Spa STV supervised Gym Steam room Sauna Dance studio Gym New Year Wi-fi
Conf Class 50 Board 50 Thtr 120 **Services** Air con
Parking 160 **Notes** Civ Wed 120

Premier Inn Aylesbury

BUDGET HOTEL

☎ 0871 527 8036 🖹 0871 527 8037
Buckingham Rd HP19 9QL
dir: From Aylesbury on A413 towards Buckingham. Hotel in 1m on left adjacent to lights

High quality, budget accommodation ideal for both families and business travellers. Spacious, en suite bedrooms feature tea and coffee making facilities, and Freeview TV in most hotels. Internet access and Wi-fi are available for a small fee. The adjacent family restaurant features a wide and varied menu. See also the Hotel Groups pages.

Rooms 64 **D** £56-£62*

AYLESFORD
Kent
Map 6 TQ75

Hamlets Hotel & Restaurant

★★★ 62% HOTEL

☎ 01732 846858 🖹 01732 846786
802 London Rd ME20 6HJ
e-mail: reservations@hamletshotel.com
dir: M20 junct 4, A228, A20. Hotel on left adjacent to B&Q

This Georgian house was rebuilt in 1846 and retains much of traditional charm. It is conveniently located within easy reach of London as well as Gatwick and Heathrow airports, the south coast and the Channel Tunnel. The accommodation is comfortable and the public areas include a well-stocked, pub-style bar.

Rooms 52 (4 fmly) (9 GF) **S** £46-£66; **D** £63-£83 (incl. bkfst) **Facilities** FTV New Year Wi-fi **Conf** Class 35 Board 35 Thtr 90 Del from £105 to £155* **Parking** 45 **Notes** LB ⊗ Civ Wed 80

AYNHO
Northamptonshire
Map 11 SP53

Cartwright Hotel

★★★ 79% HOTEL

☎ 01869 811885 🖹 01869 812809
1-5 Croughton Rd OX17 3BE
e-mail: cartwright@oxfordshire-hotels.co.uk
dir: M40 junct 10, A43, B4100 to Aynho

This former coaching inn is located between Banbury and Oxford, making it ideally located for visiting the many tourist attractions the area has to offer including the race track at Silverstone and Blenheim Palace. The hotel features individually designed bedrooms which range from double to executive, and premiere standards with flat-screen digital TVs and complimentary Wi-fi. Secure parking is available.

Rooms 21 (12 annexe) (2 fmly) (12 GF) **S** £79-£119; **D** £79-£119 (incl. bkfst)* **Facilities** STV FTV Xmas New Year Wi-fi **Conf** Class 40 Board 20 Thtr 60 Del from £120 to £150* **Parking** 15 **Notes** LB ⊗

BABBACOMBE

See Torquay

B

BAGSHOT Map 6 SU96
Surrey

INSPECTORS' CHOICE

Pennyhill Park Hotel & The Spa

★★★★★ @@@@@
COUNTRY HOUSE HOTEL

☎ 01276 471774 📠 01276 473217
London Rd GU19 5EU
e-mail: enquiries@pennyhillpark.co.uk
web: www.exclusivehotels.co.uk
dir: M3 junct 3, follow signs to Camberley. On A30 between Bagshot & Camberley

This delightful country-house hotel, set in 120-acre grounds, provides every modern comfort. The stylish bedrooms are individually designed and have impressive bathrooms. Leisure facilities include a jogging trail, a golf course and a state-of-the-art spa with a thermal sequencing experience, ozone treated swimming and hydrotherapy pools along with a comprehensive range of therapies and treatments. The Latymer restaurant, overseen by chef Michael Wignall, has become a true dining destination in its own right. The cooking is outstanding and great care is made to source first-rate ingredients, much from local suppliers. There is an eight-seater chef's table for enjoying the tasting menu while watching the action in the kitchen. In addition there are other eating options, and lounges and bars to relax in.

Rooms 123 (97 annexe) (6 fmly) (26 GF) **S** £315-£1375; **D** £315-£1375* **Facilities** Spa STV 🏊 🎾 ⛳ 9 🏌 Fishing 🏋 Gym Archery Clay shooting Plunge pool Turkish steam room Rugby/football pitch 🎵 Xmas New Year Wi-fi **Conf** Class 80 Board 60 Thtr 160 Del from £375* **Services** Lift **Parking** 500 **Notes** LB Civ Wed 140

Premier Inn Bagshot

BUDGET HOTEL

☎ 0871 527 8040 📠 0871 527 8041
1 London Rd GU19 5HR
dir: On A30 (London Rd) just before junct with A322 (Bracknell Rd). Adjacent to Cricketers Beefeater

High quality, budget accommodation ideal for both families and business travellers. Spacious, en suite bedrooms feature tea and coffee making facilities, and Freeview TV in most hotels. Internet access and Wi-fi are available for a small fee. The adjacent family restaurant features a wide and varied menu. See also the Hotel Groups pages.

Rooms 39 **D** £57-£75*

BAINBRIDGE Map 18 SD99
North Yorkshire

Yorebridge House

@@ RESTAURANT WITH ROOMS

☎ 01969 652060 📠 01969 650258
DL8 3EE
e-mail: enquiries@yorebridgehouse.co.uk

Yorebridge House is situated by the river on the edge of Bainbridge, in the heart of the North Yorkshire Dales. Formerly a schoolmaster's house and school in the Victorian era, this building now offers luxury boutique-style accommodation. Each bedroom is individually designed with high quality furnishings and thoughtful extras. All rooms have stunning views of the Dales and some have their own terrace with hot tubs. There is a comfortable lounge bar where guests can relax before enjoying dinner in the attractive and elegant dining room.

Rooms 11 (4 annexe) (11 fmly)

BAKEWELL Map 16 SK26
Derbyshire

Monsal Head Hotel

★★ 83% @ HOTEL

☎ 01629 640250 📠 01629 640815
Monsal Head DE45 1NL
e-mail: enquiries@monsalhead.com
web: www.monsalhead.com
dir: A6 from Bakewell to Buxton. In 2m turn into Ashford-in-the-Water, take B6465 for 1m. Hotel on left through public car park entrance

Situated three miles from Bakewell and overlooking the picturesque Monsal Dale in the Peak District National Park, this hotel is full of charm and character. The bedrooms have beautiful views, and public areas include the Ashford Room, a quiet residents' lounge, and Longstone Restaurant. The converted stables bar adjacent to the hotel has an excellent choice of cask ales and lagers.

Rooms 7 (1 fmly) **S** £65-£70; **D** £90-£100 (incl. bkfst)* **Facilities** Xmas New Year **Conf** Class 30 Board 20 Thtr 50 Del from £120* **Parking** 20 **Notes** LB RS 25 Dec

BALDOCK Map 12 TL23
Hertfordshire

Days Inn Stevenage North - A1

BUDGET HOTEL

☎ 01462 730598 📠 01462 835037
Baldock Extra Motorways, A1(M) Junction 10, Radwell SG7 5TR
e-mail: stevenage.hotel@welcomebreak.co.uk
dir: A1(M) junct 10 Baldock Extra Services

This modern, purpose built accommodation offers smartly appointed, well-equipped bedrooms, with good power showers. There is a choice of adjacent food outlets where guests may enjoy breakfast, snacks and meals. See also the Hotel Groups pages.

Rooms 62 (7 fmly) (30 GF) (13 smoking) **S** £39.95-£59.95; **D** £49.95-£69.95

BALSALL COMMON Map 10 SP27
West Midlands

Nailcote Hall

CLASSIC BRITISH HOTELS

★★★★ 75% @ HOTEL

☎ 024 7646 6174 📠 024 7647 0720
Nailcote Ln, Berkswell CV7 7DE
e-mail: info@nailcotehall.co.uk
web: www.nailcotehall.co.uk
dir: On B4101

This 17th-century house, set in 15 acres of grounds, boasts a 9-hole championship golf course and Roman bath-style swimming pool amongst its many facilities. Rooms are spacious and elegantly furnished. The eating options are the fine dining restaurant where smart casual dress is required, or The Piano Bar where more informal meals are served.

Rooms 40 (19 annexe) (2 fmly) (15 GF) **S** £100-£145; **D** £120-£165 (incl. bkfst)* **Facilities** STV 🏊 supervised ⛳ 9 🏌 Putt green 🏋 Gym 🎵 Xmas New Year Wi-fi **Conf** Class 80 Board 44 Thtr 140 Del from £135 to £165* **Services** Lift **Parking** 200 **Notes** LB ⊗ Civ Wed 120

BALSALL COMMON ***continued***

Haigs Hotel

★★★ 73% HOTEL

☎ 01676 533004 🖷 01676 535132
Kenilworth Rd CV7 7EL
e-mail: info@haigshotel.co.uk
dir: A45 towards Coventry, at Stonebridge Island turn right, 4m S of M42 junct 6

Conveniently located just five miles from Birmingham Airport and twelve miles from Stratford-upon-Avon. This small family-run hotel offers its guests a comfortable stay. Enjoyable meals on a monthly changing menu can be taken in McKee's Restaurant.

Rooms 23 (2 fmly) (5 GF) **Facilities** Xmas New Year Wi-fi **Conf** Board 20 Thtr 25 Del from £95.50* **Parking** 23 **Notes** Civ Wed 60

Premier Inn Balsall Common (Near NEC)

BUDGET HOTEL

☎ 0871 527 8042 🖷 0871 527 8043
Kenilworth Rd CV7 7EX
dir: M42 junct 6, A45 towards Coventry for 0.5m. A452 signed Leamington/Kenilworth. In 3m hotel on right

High quality, budget accommodation ideal for both families and business travellers. Spacious, en suite bedrooms feature tea and coffee making facilities, and Freeview TV in most hotels. Internet access and Wi-fi are available for a small fee. The adjacent family restaurant features a wide and varied menu. See also the Hotel Groups pages.

Rooms 42 **D** £54-£60*

BAMBURGH Map 21 NU13
Northumberland

Waren House

★★★ 82% COUNTRY HOUSE HOTEL

☎ 01668 214581 🖷 01668 214484
Waren Mill NE70 7EE
e-mail: enquiries@warenhousehotel.co.uk
web: www.warenhousehotel.co.uk
dir: 2m E of A1 turn onto B1342 to Waren Mill, at T-junct turn right, hotel 100yds on right

This delightful Georgian mansion is set in six acres of woodland and offers a welcoming atmosphere and views of the coast. The individually themed bedrooms and suites include many with large bathrooms. Good, home-cooked food is served in the elegant dining room. A comfortable lounge and library are also available.

Rooms 15 (4 annexe) (3 GF) **S** £95-£130; **D** £130-£185 (incl. bkfst) **Facilities** FTV Xmas New Year Wi-fi **Conf** Class 16 Board 16 **Parking** 20 **Notes** No children 14yrs

The Lord Crewe

★★ 81% HOTEL

☎ 01668 214243 & 214613 🖷 01668 214273
Front St NE69 7BL
e-mail: enquiries@lordcrewe.co.uk
dir: Just below castle

Located in the heart of the village in the shadow of impressive Bamburgh Castle, this hotel has been developed from an old inn. Public areas combine modern and traditional very well and include a choice of lounges, a cosy bar and a smart modern Italian restaurant. Bedrooms vary in size, but all are well equipped and offer modern amenities.

Rooms 17 **S** £65-£75; **D** £105-£145 (incl. bkfst)* **Facilities** FTV Wi-fi **Parking** 20 **Notes** ⊗ No children 5yrs Closed Dec & Jan

BANBURY Map 11 SP44
Oxfordshire

Best Western Wroxton House

★★★ 81% HOTEL

☎ 01295 730777 🖷 01295 730800
Wroxton St Mary OX15 6QB
e-mail: reservations@wroxtonhousehotel.com
dir: M40 junct 11, A422 signed Banbury & Wroxton. Approx 3m, hotel on right on entering Wroxton

Dating in parts from 1649, this partially thatched hotel is set just off the main road and has undergone considerable refurbishment in last few years. Bedrooms, either created from cottages or situated in a contemporary wing, are comfortable and well equipped with Wi-fi and LCD TVs. The public areas are open plan and the low-beamed Restaurant 1649 has a peaceful atmosphere for dining.

Rooms 32 (3 annexe) (5 fmly) (8 GF) **S** £80-£120; **D** £95-£135 (incl. bkfst) **Facilities** FTV Xmas New Year Wi-fi **Conf** Class 40 Board 40 Thtr 80 Del from £140 to £150 **Parking** 60 **Notes** LB ⊗ Civ Wed 80

Mercure Whately Hall

★★★ 74% HOTEL

☎ 01295 253261
Banbury Cross OX16 0AN
e-mail: h6633@accor.com
web: www.mercure.com
dir: M40 junct 11, straight over 2 rdbts, left at 3rd, 0.25m to Banbury Cross, hotel on right

Dating back to 1677, this historic inn boasts many original features such as stone passages, priests' holes and a fine wooden staircase. Spacious public areas include the oak-panelled restaurant, which overlooks the attractive well-tended gardens, a choice of lounges and a traditional bar. Smartly appointed bedrooms vary in size and style but all are thoughtfully equipped.

Rooms 69 (6 fmly) (2 GF) **Facilities** FTV Xmas New Year Wi-fi **Conf** Class 40 Board 40 Thtr 120 **Services** Lift **Parking** 52 **Notes** ⊗ Civ Wed 150

Holiday Inn Express Banbury M40 Jct 11

BUDGET HOTEL

☎ 01295 234567 📠 01295 234568
Ermont Way, Stroud Park OX16 4TJ
e-mail: reception@exhibanbury.co.uk
web: www.hiexpress.co.uk
dir: M40 junct 11, A422 towards Banbury. 1st left, next left by Frankie & Benny's. Hotel on left. (NB postcode not always recognised by Sat Nav)

A modern hotel ideal for families and business travellers. Fresh and uncomplicated, the spacious rooms include Sky TV, power shower and tea and coffee-making facilities. Continental buffet breakfast is included in the room rate; other meals may be taken at the nearby family pub or restaurant. See also the Hotel Groups pages.

Rooms 120 (71 fmly) (14 GF) **S** £49-£140; (incl. bkfst) **Conf** Class 30 Board 30 Thtr 70 Del from £112.45 to £134.45

Premier Inn Banbury

BUDGET HOTEL

☎ 0871 527 8044 📠 0871 527 8045
Warwick Rd, Warmington OX17 1JJ
dir: From N: M40 junct 12, B4451, B4100 towards Warmington. From S: M40 junct 11, A423, A422, B4100. Hotel adjacent to Wobbly Wheel Brewers Fayre

High quality, budget accommodation ideal for both families and business travellers. Spacious, en suite bedrooms feature tea and coffee making facilities, and Freeview TV in most hotels. Internet access and Wi-fi are available for a small fee. The adjacent family restaurant features a wide and varied menu. See also the Hotel Groups pages.

Rooms 39 **D** £55-£60*

BARFORD
Warwickshire — **Map 10 SP26**

The Glebe at Barford

★★★ 71% HOTEL

☎ 01926 624218 📠 01926 624625
Church St CV35 8BS
e-mail: sales@glebehotel.co.uk
dir: M40 junct 15/A429 (Stow). At mini island turn left, hotel 500mtrs on right

The giant Lebanese cedar tree in front of this hotel was ancient even in 1820, when the original rectory was built. Public rooms within the house include a lounge bar and the aptly named Cedars Conservatory Restaurant which offers interesting cuisine. Individually appointed bedrooms are tastefully decorated in soft pastel fabrics, with coronet, tented ceiling or four-poster style beds.

Rooms 39 (3 fmly) (4 GF) **S** £75-£105; **D** £80-£140 (incl. bkfst)* **Facilities** STV ⓢ Gym Beauty salon Xmas New Year Wi-fi **Conf** Class 40 Board 40 Thtr 120 **Services** Lift **Parking** 60 **Notes** LB Civ Wed 120

BARKING
Greater London

See LONDON SECTION plan 1 H4

Ibis London East Barking

BUDGET HOTEL

☎ 020 8477 4100 📠 020 8477 4101
Highbridge Rd IG11 7BA
e-mail: H2042@accor.com
web: www.ibishotel.com
dir: Exit Barking from A406 or A13

Modern, budget hotel offering comfortable accommodation in bright and practical bedrooms. Breakfast is self-service and dinner is available in the restaurant. See also the Hotel Groups pages.

Rooms 86 (26 GF) (9 smoking)

Premier Inn Barking

BUDGET HOTEL

☎ 0871 527 8048 📠 0871 527 8049
Highbridge Rd IG11 7BA
dir: A13 onto A406 signed Barking/Ilford. At Barking, exit at Tesco/A406 slip road. Hotel on left

High quality, budget accommodation ideal for both families and business travellers. Spacious, en suite bedrooms feature tea and coffee making facilities, and Freeview TV in most hotels. Internet access and Wi-fi are available for a small fee. The adjacent family restaurant features a wide and varied menu. See also the Hotel Groups pages.

Rooms 88 **D** £60-£74*

BARLBOROUGH
Derbyshire — **Map 16 SK47**

Ibis Sheffield North

BUDGET HOTEL

☎ 01246 813222 📠 01246 813444
Tallys End, Chesterfield Rd S43 4TX
e-mail: H3157@accor.com
web: www.ibishotel.com
dir: M1 junct 30. Towards A619, right at rdbt towards Chesterfield. Hotel immediately left

Modern, budget hotel offering comfortable accommodation in bright and practical bedrooms. Breakfast is self-service and dinner is available in the restaurant. See also the Hotel Groups pages.

Rooms 86 (22 fmly) **D** £45-£53* **Conf** Board 18 Thtr 35

BARNARD CASTLE
Co Durham — **Map 19 NZ01**

The Morritt

★★★★ 77% HOTEL

☎ 01833 627232 📠 01833 627392
Greta Bridge DL12 9SE
e-mail: relax@themorritt.co.uk
web: www.themorritt.co.uk
dir: Exit A1(A1(M)) at Scotch Corner onto A66 W'bound towards Penrith. Greta Bridge 9m on left

Set off the main road at Greta Bridge, this 17th-century former coaching house provides comfortable public rooms full of character. The bar, with its interesting Dickensian mural, is very much focused on food, but in addition a fine dining is offered in the oak-panelled restaurant. Bedrooms come in individual styles and of varying sizes. The attentive service is noteworthy.

Rooms 27 (6 annexe) (3 fmly) (4 GF) **S** £85-£155; **D** £95-£200 (incl. bkfst) **Facilities** FTV Xmas New Year Wi-fi **Conf** Class 60 Board 50 Thtr 200 Del from £125 **Parking** 40 **Notes** LB Civ Wed 200

B

BARNBY MOOR Nottinghamshire **Map 16 SK68**

Ye Olde Bell Hotel & Restaurant

★★★★ 74% HOTEL

☎ 01777 705121 🖹 01777 860424
DN22 8QS
e-mail: enquiries@yeoldebell-hotel.co.uk
web: www.yeoldebell-hotel.co.uk
dir: A1(M) south near junct 24, exit Barnby Moor or A1(M) north exit A620 Retford. Hotel on A638 between Retford & Bawtry

A 17th-century coaching inn situated in the rural village of Barnby Moor near Retford. Public rooms have a wealth of original character such as traditional log fires, ornate plaster work and wood panelling. The tastefully appointed bedrooms have superb co-ordinated soft furnishings and many thoughtful touches.

Rooms 49 (5 fmly) **Facilities** FTV Xmas New Year Wi-fi **Conf** Class 100 Board 50 Thtr 250 Del from £99 to £145* **Parking** 200 **Notes** LB ® Civ Wed 250

BARNET Greater London **Map 6 TQ29**

Savoro Restaurant with Rooms

® RESTAURANT WITH ROOMS

☎ 020 8449 9888 🖹 020 8449 7444
206 High St EN5 5SZ
e-mail: savoro@savoro.co.uk
web: www.savoro.co.uk
dir: M25 junct 23, A1000. In crescent behind Hadley Green Jaguar Garage

Set back from the main high street, the traditional frontage of this establishment belies the stylishly modern bedrooms and well designed bathrooms within. The award-winning restaurant is an additional bonus.

Rooms 11 (3 GF)

BARNHAM BROOM Norfolk **Map 13 TG00**

Barnham Broom Hotel, Golf & Restaurant

★★★★ 74% ®® HOTEL

☎ 01603 759393 🖹 01603 758224
NR9 4DD
e-mail: amortimer@barnham-broom.co.uk
web: www.barnham-broom.co.uk
dir: A11/A47 towards Swaffham, follow brown tourist signs

Situated in a peaceful rural location just a short drive from Norwich, this hotel offers contemporary style bedrooms that are tastefully furnished and thoughtfully equipped. The Sports Bar serves a range of snacks and meals throughout the day, or guests can choose from the carte menu in Flints Restaurant. There also are extensive leisure, conference and banqueting facilities.

Rooms 46 (11 fmly) (22 GF) **S** £70-£125; **D** £90-£150 (incl. bkfst) **Facilities** Spa STV supervised 36 Putt green Gym Squash Sauna Steam room Personal trainers Xmas New Year Wi-fi **Conf** Class 100 Board 80 Thtr 250 Del from £110 to £140 **Parking** 150 **Notes** LB ® Civ Wed 200

BARNSLEY South Yorkshire **Map 16 SE30**

Tankersley Manor

QHOTELS

★★★★ 77% HOTEL

☎ 01226 744700 🖹 01226 745405
Church Ln S75 3DQ
e-mail: tankersleymanor@qhotels.co.uk
web: www.qhotels.co.uk

(For full entry see Tankersley)

Best Western Ardsley House Hotel

★★★ 79% HOTEL

☎ 01226 309955 🖹 01226 205374
Doncaster Rd, Ardsley S71 5EH
e-mail: ardsley.house@forestdale.com
web: www.ardsleyhousehotel.co.uk
dir: On A635, 0.75m from Stairfoot rdbt

This late 18th-century building has retained many of its original Georgian features. Bedrooms are both comfortable and well equipped. The excellent leisure facilities including a gym, pool and beauty salon. The Allendale Restaurant, with views of the nearby woodlands, offers an extensive menu.

Rooms 75 (12 fmly) (14 GF) **Facilities** Spa supervised Gym Xmas New Year Wi-fi **Conf** Class 250 Board 40 Thtr 350 **Parking** 200 **Notes** Civ Wed 250

Premier Inn Barnsley Central M1 Jct 37

BUDGET HOTEL

☎ 0871 527 9204 🖹 0871 527 9205
Gateway Plaza, Sackville St S70 2RD
dir: M1 junct 37, A628 (Dodworth Rd) signed Barnsley. In approx 1m 2nd exit at rdbt into Shambles St, car park entrance on left

High quality, budget accommodation ideal for both families and business travellers. Spacious, en suite bedrooms feature tea and coffee making facilities, and Freeview TV in most hotels. Internet access and Wi-fi are available for a small fee. The adjacent family restaurant features a wide and varied menu. See also the Hotel Groups pages.

Rooms 110 **D** £53-£63*

BARNSTAPLE Devon **Map 3 SS53**

The Imperial

★★★★ 77% HOTEL

☎ 01271 345861 🖹 01271 324448
Taw Vale Pde EX32 8NB
e-mail: reservations@brend-imperial.co.uk
web: www.brend-imperial.co.uk
dir: M5 junct 27/A361 to Barnstaple. Follow town centre signs, passing Tesco. Straight on at next 2 rdbts. Hotel on right

This smart and attractive hotel is pleasantly located at the centre of Barnstaple and overlooks the river. The staff are friendly and offer attentive service. The comfortable bedrooms are of various sizes; some have balconies and many overlook the river. Afternoon tea is available in the lounge, and the appetising cuisine is freshly prepared.

Rooms 63 (9 fmly) (4 GF) **S** £87-£185; **D** £97-£185* **Facilities** FTV Leisure facilities at sister hotel Xmas New Year Wi-fi **Conf** Class 40 Board 30 Thtr 60 **Services** Lift **Parking** 80 **Notes** LB ®

See advert on opposite page

B

Barnstaple Hotel

★★★ 80% HOTEL

☎ 01271 376221 📠 01271 324101
Braunton Rd EX31 1LE
e-mail: reservations@barnstaplehotel.co.uk
web: www.barnstaplehotel.co.uk
dir: Outskirts of Barnstaple on A361

This well-established hotel enjoys a convenient location on the edge of town. Bedrooms are spacious and well equipped, many with access to a balcony overlooking the outdoor pool and garden. A wide choice is offered from various menus based on local produce, served in the Brasserie Restaurant. There is an extensive range of leisure and conference facilities.

Rooms 60 (2 fmly) (17 GF) **S** £65-£100; **D** £69-£110* **Facilities** FTV Gym Barnstable health & leisure club part of hotel Xmas New Year Wi-fi **Conf** Class 100 Board 50 Thtr 250 Del from £70 to £99.50* **Parking** 250 **Notes** LB Civ Wed 150

Royal & Fortescue

★★★ 78% HOTEL

☎ 01271 342289 📠 01271 340102
Boutport St EX31 1HG
e-mail: reservations@royalfortescue.co.uk
web: www.royalfortescue.co.uk
dir: A361 along Barbican Rd signed town centre, right into Queen St, left into Boutport St, hotel on left

Formerly a coaching inn, this friendly and convivial hotel is conveniently located in the centre of town. Bedrooms vary in size and all are decorated and furnished to a consistently high standard. In addition to the formal restaurant, guests can take snacks in the popular coffee shop or dine more informally in The Bank, a bistro and café bar.

Rooms 49 (4 fmly) (4 GF) **S** £60-£100; **D** £100-£140* **Facilities** FTV Leisure facilities available at sister hotel ♫ Xmas New Year Wi-fi **Conf** Class 25 Board 25 Thtr 25 **Services** Lift **Parking** 40 **Notes** LB

Park Hotel

★★★ 77% HOTEL

☎ 01271 372166 📠 01271 323157
Taw Vale EX32 9AE
e-mail: reservations@parkhotel.co.uk
web: www.parkhotel.co.uk
dir: Opposite Rock Park, 0.5m from town centre

Enjoying views across the park and within easy walking distance of the town centre, this modern hotel offers a choice of bedrooms in both the main building and the Garden Court, just across the car park. Public rooms are open-plan in style and the friendly staff offer attentive service in a relaxed atmosphere.

Rooms 40 (17 annexe) (3 fmly) (2 GF) **S** £57-£72; **D** £62-£82* **Facilities** FTV Leisure facilities available at sister hotel Xmas New Year Wi-fi **Conf** Class 50 Board 30 Thtr 80 **Parking** 80 **Notes** LB Civ Wed 100

B

BARNSTAPLE *continued*

Premier Inn Barnstaple

BUDGET HOTEL

☎ 0871 527 8052 🖷 0871 527 8053
Whiddon Dr, off Eastern Av EX32 8RY
dir: Off A361 (North Devon Link Rd) towards Barnstaple. Right at Portmore rdbt

High quality, budget accommodation ideal for both families and business travellers. Spacious, en suite bedrooms feature tea and coffee making facilities, and Freeview TV in most hotels. Internet access and Wi-fi are available for a small fee. The adjacent family restaurant features a wide and varied menu. See also the Hotel Groups pages.

Rooms 40 **D** £69*

BARROW-IN-FURNESS Cumbria **Map 18 SD26**

Clarence House Country Hotel & Restaurant

★★★★ 72% ®® HOTEL

☎ 01229 462508 🖷 01229 467177
Skelgate LA15 8BQ
e-mail: clarencehsehotel@aol.com
web: www.clarencehouse-hotel.co.uk
dir: A590 through Ulverston & Lindal, 2nd exit at rdbt & 1st exit at next. Follow signs to Dalton, hotel at top of hill on right

This hotel is located in ornamental grounds with unrestricted countryside views. Bedrooms are individually themed with those in the main hotel being particularly stylish and comfortable. The public rooms are spacious and also furnished to a high standard. The popular conservatory restaurant and contemporary brasserie offer well-prepared dishes from extensive menus. There is a delightful barn conversion that is ideal for weddings.

Rooms 19 (12 annexe) (1 fmly) (5 GF) **Facilities** FTV ♫ New Year Wi-fi **Conf** Class 40 Board 15 Thtr 100 **Parking** 40 **Notes** Closed 25-26 Dec Civ Wed 100

Abbey House Hotel

★★★ 77% HOTEL

☎ 01229 838282 🖷 01229 820403
Abbey Rd LA13 0PA
e-mail: enquiries@abbeyhousehotel.com
dir: A590, follow signs for Furness general hospital/ Furness Abbey. Hotel approx 100yds on left

Set in its own gardens, this smart hotel provides stylish public areas, as well as extensive function and conference facilities. The well-equipped bedrooms vary in style - the more traditional rooms are in the main house and a more contemporary style of accommodation can be found in the extension. Service is friendly and helpful.

Rooms 57 (6 fmly) (2 GF) **Facilities** Xmas Wi-fi **Conf** Class 120 Board 80 Thtr 280 **Services** Lift **Parking** 100 **Notes** Civ Wed 120

Clarke's Hotel

★★★ 71% HOTEL

☎ 01229 820303 🖷 01229 430954
Rampside LA13 0PX
e-mail: bookings@clarkeshotel.co.uk
dir: A590 to Ulverston then A5087, take coast road for 8m, turn left at rdbt into Rampside

This smart, well-maintained hotel enjoys a peaceful location on the south Cumbrian coast, overlooking Morecambe Bay. The tastefully appointed bedrooms come in a variety of sizes and are thoughtfully equipped particularly for the business guest. Inviting public areas include an open-plan bar and brasserie offering freshly prepared food throughout the day.

Rooms 14 (1 fmly) **Facilities** FTV **Parking** 50

BARTON Lancashire **Map 18 SD53**

Barton Grange Hotel

★★★★ 77% HOTEL

☎ 01772 862551 🖷 01772 861267
Garstang Rd PR3 5AA
e-mail: stay@bartongrangehotel.com
web: www.bartongrangehotel.co.uk
dir: M6 junct 32, follow Garstang (A6) signs for 2.5m. Hotel on right

Situated close to the M6, this modern, stylish hotel benefits from extensive public areas that include leisure facilities with a swimming pool, sauna and gym. Comfortable, well-appointed bedrooms include executive rooms and family rooms, as well as attractive accommodation in an adjacent cottage. The unique Walled Garden Bistro offers all-day eating.

Rooms 51 (8 annexe) (4 fmly) (4 GF) **S** £50-£92; **D** £60-£117* **Facilities** STV ⓢ Gym Sauna Xmas New Year Wi-fi **Conf** Class 100 Board 80 Thtr 300 Del from £95 to £145* **Services** Lift **Parking** 250 **Notes** LB ⊗ Civ Wed 300

BARTON-ON-SEA Hampshire Map 5 SZ29

Pebble Beach

RESTAURANT WITH ROOMS

☎ 01425 627777 📠 01425 610689
Marine Dr BH25 7DZ
e-mail: mail@pebblebeach.uk.com
dir: A35 from Southampton onto A337 to New Milton, left onto Barton Court Ave to clifftop

Situated on the cliff top the restaurant at this establishment boasts stunning views towards The Needles. Bedrooms and bathrooms, situated above the restaurant, are well equipped and provide a range of accessories to enhance guest comfort. A freshly cooked breakfast is served in the main restaurant.

Rooms 4

BARTON-UPON-HUMBER Lincolnshire Map 17 TA02

Best Western Reeds Country Hotel

★★★ 77% HOTEL

☎ 01652 632313 📠 01652 636361
Westfield Lakes, Far Ings Rd DN18 5RG
e-mail: info@reedshotel.co.uk
dir: At A15 rdbt take 2nd exit (Humber Bridge) & exit at Barton-upon-Humber, left at rdbt. In 200yds right at hotel sign, down hill & hotel at junct

This hotel is situated in a quiet wildlife sanctuary just upstream from the Humber Bridge. A very attractive lakeside restaurant commands tranquil views, and there is a health spa offering various alternative therapies. Bedrooms are comfortable and well equipped, and service is both friendly and helpful.

Rooms 26 (5 fmly) **Facilities** Spa STV FTV Xmas New Year Wi-fi **Conf** Class 200 Board 70 Thtr 300 **Services** Lift **Parking** 100 **Notes** LB ⊗ Civ Wed 300

BASILDON Essex Map 6 TQ78

Holiday Inn Basildon

★★★ 79% HOTEL

☎ 0870 400 9003 & 01268 824000
📠 01268 530119
Waterfront Walk, Festival Leisure Park SS14 3DG
e-mail: reservations-basildon@ihg.com
web: www.holidayinn.co.uk
dir: From A127 take A176/Basildon Billericay exit. Follow brown signs to Festival Leisure Park

This modern hotel sits alongside the river in a convenient location in the heart of town. It enjoys delightful views and is ideally placed for leisurely walks beside the river or for easy access to the town. The contemporary bedrooms are comfortable and particularly well equipped, with safes, Wi-fi and flat-screen TVs. There are a host of other facilities including a range of meeting rooms and leisure facilities, as well as a car park.

Rooms 148 (10 fmly) (8 GF) (16 smoking) **S** £49-£130; **D** £49-£130* **Facilities** STV Use of nearby leisure club New Year Wi-fi **Conf** Class 80 Board 80 Thtr 300 Del from £95 to £170* **Services** Lift Air con **Parking** 152 **Notes** LB Civ Wed 300

Chichester

★★★ 77% HOTEL

☎ 01268 560555 📠 01268 560580
Old London Rd, Wickford SS11 8UE
e-mail: reception@chichester-hotel.com
web: www.chichester-hotel.com
dir: Off A129

Set in landscaped gardens and surrounded by farmland, this friendly hotel has been owned and run by the same family for over 25 years. Spacious bedrooms are located around an attractive courtyard, and each is pleasantly decorated and thoughtfully equipped. Public rooms include a cosy lounge bar and a smart restaurant.

Rooms 35 (32 annexe) (12 fmly) (17 GF) **S** £41-£69; **D** £41-£69* **Facilities** FTV Wi-fi **Parking** 150 **Notes** LB ⊗

Campanile Basildon

Campanile HOTEL RESTAURANT

BUDGET HOTEL

☎ 01268 530810 📠 01268 286710
Pipps Hill, Southend Arterial Rd SS14 3AE
e-mail: basildon@campanile.com
dir: M25 junct 29 Basildon exit, back under A127, then left at rdbt

This modern building offers accommodation in smart, well-equipped bedrooms, all with en suite bathrooms. Refreshments may be taken at the informal bistro. See also the Hotel Groups pages.

Rooms 97 (97 annexe) (8 fmly) (44 GF) **Conf** Class 18 Board 24 Thtr 35

Premier Inn Basildon (East Mayne)

BUDGET HOTEL

☎ 0871 527 8054 📠 0871 527 8055
Felmores, East Mayne SS13 1BW
dir: M25 junct 29 , A127 towards Southend, take A132 S signed Basildon & Wickford at Neverdon exit. Hotel on left

High quality, budget accommodation ideal for both families and business travellers. Spacious, en suite bedrooms feature tea and coffee making facilities, and Freeview TV in most hotels. Internet access and Wi-fi are available for a small fee. The adjacent family restaurant features a wide and varied menu. See also the Hotel Groups pages.

Rooms 32 **D** £53-£62*

Premier Inn Basildon (Festival Park)

BUDGET HOTEL

☎ 0871 527 8056 📠 0871 527 8057
Festival Leisure Park, Pipps Hill Road South, Off Cranes Farm Rd SS14 3WB
dir: M25 junct 9, A217 towards Basildon. Take A17. Hotel just off A1235 adjacent to David Lloyd Leisure Club

Rooms 64 **D** £57-£67*

B

BASILDON *continued*

Premier Inn Basildon South

BUDGET HOTEL

☎ 0871 527 8060 📠 0871 527 8061
High Rd, Fobbing, Stanford-Le-Hope SS17 9NR
dir: M2 junct 30/31, A13 towards Southend. 10m to Five Bells Rdbt junct with A176. Right into Fobbing High Rd. Hotel on left

Rooms 61 **D** £55-£65*

BASINGSTOKE Hampshire **Map 5 SU65**

See also **Odiham**

INSPECTORS' CHOICE

Tylney Hall Hotel

★★★★ ®® HOTEL

☎ 01256 764881 📠 01256 768141
RG27 9AZ
e-mail: sales@tylneyhall.com
web: www.tylneyhall.com
(For full entry see Rotherwick)

Oakley Hall Hotel

★★★★ 83% ® COUNTRY HOUSE HOTEL

☎ 01256 783350 📠 01256 783351
Rectory Rd RG23 7EL
e-mail: enquiries@oakleyhall-park.com
web: www.oakleyhall-park.com
dir: M3 junct 7, follow Basingstoke signs. In 500yds before lights turn left onto A30 towards Oakley, immediately right onto unclass road towards Oakley. In 3m left at T-junct into Rectory Rd. Left onto B3400. Hotel signed 1st on left

An impressive drive leads to this country house which benefits from delightful country views across north Hampshire. Built in 1795, it was once owned by the Bramston family who were friends of Jane Austen. An ideal wedding venue, Oakley Hall also has an excellent range of conference facilities, and is a great place to spend a relaxing leisure break. The bedrooms are spacious; many are located in the impressively restored courtyard and are particularly well equipped; there is also the delightful Garden Cottage. Service is delivered by a friendly team, and cuisine is contemporary and satisfying.

Rooms 18 (18 annexe) (8 fmly) (18 GF) **S** £119-£295; **D** £155-£295 (incl. bkfst)* **Facilities** FTV Clay pigeon shooting Xmas New Year Wi-fi **Conf** Class 82 Board 50 Thtr 300 Del from £169 to £245* **Services** Air con **Parking** 100 **Notes** ⊗ Civ Wed 100

The Hampshire Court Hotel

QHOTELS

★★★★ 79% HOTEL

☎ 01256 319700 📠 01256 319730
Centre Dr, Chineham RG24 8FY
e-mail: hampshirecourt@qhotels.co.uk
web: www.qhotels.co.uk
dir: Off A33 (Reading road) behind Chineham Shopping Centre via Great Binfields Rd

This hotel boasts a range of smart, comfortable and stylish bedrooms, and leisure facilities that are unrivalled locally. Facilities include indoor and outdoor tennis courts, two swimming pools, a gym and a number of treatment rooms.

Rooms 90 (6 fmly) **Facilities** Spa STV Gym Steam room Beauty salon Sauna Exercise studios Xmas New Year Wi-fi **Conf** Class 130 Board 60 Thtr 220 **Services** Lift **Parking** 220 **Notes** Civ Wed 220

Barceló Basingstoke Country Hotel

Barceló

★★★★ 75% HOTEL

☎ 01256 764161 📠 01256 768341
Scures Hill, Nately Scures, Hook RG27 9JS
e-mail: basingstokecountry.mande@barcelo-hotels.co.uk
web: www.barcelo-hotels.co.uk
dir: M3 junct 5, A287 towards Newnham. Left at lights. Hotel 200mtrs on right

This popular hotel is close to Basingstoke and its country location ensures a peaceful stay. Bedrooms are available in a number of styles - all have air conditioning, Wi-fi, in-room safes and hairdryers. Guests have a choice of dining in the formal restaurant, or for lighter meals and snacks there is a relaxed café and a smart bar. Extensive wedding, conference and leisure facilities complete the picture.

Rooms 100 (26 GF) **Facilities** Spa STV supervised Gym Sauna Solarium Steam room Dance studio Beauty treatments New Year Wi-fi **Conf** Class 85 Board 80 Thtr 240 **Services** Lift Air con **Parking** 200 **Notes** RS 24 Dec-2 Jan Civ Wed 90

Audleys Wood

HandPICKED HOTELS

★★★★ 74% HOTEL

☎ 01256 817555 📠 01256 817500
Alton Rd RG25 2JT
e-mail: audleyswood@handpicked.co.uk
web: www.handpickedhotels.co.uk/audleyswood
dir: M3 junct 6. From Basingstoke take A339 towards Alton, hotel on right

A long sweeping drive leads to what was once a Victorian hunting lodge. This traditional country-house hotel offers bedrooms with flat-screen TVs and MP3 player connections. Smart and traditional public areas have log fires, and good food is served in the contemporary conservatory with a small minstrels' gallery.

Rooms 72 (23 fmly) (34 GF) **S** £71-£147; **D** £81-£157 (incl. bkfst)* **Facilities** STV FTV Xmas New Year Wi-fi **Conf** Class 80 Board 60 Thtr 200 Del from £155 to £190* **Parking** 60 **Notes** LB ⊗ Civ Wed 100

Apollo Hotel

★★★★ 72% ® HOTEL

☎ 01256 796700 📠 01256 796701
Aldermaston Roundabout RG24 9NU
e-mail: admin@apollohotels.com
web: www.apollohotels.com
dir: M3 junct 6. Follow ring road N, exit A340 (Aldermaston). Hotel on rdbt, 5th exit into Popley Way for access

This modern hotel provides well-equipped accommodation and spacious public areas, appealing to both the leisure and business guest. Facilities include a smartly appointed leisure club, a business centre, along with a good choice of formal and informal eating in two restaurants; Vespers is the fine dining option.

Rooms 125 (32 GF) **S** £120-£200; **D** £120-£200* **Facilities** Spa FTV supervised Gym Sauna Steam room Wi-fi **Conf** Class 196 Board 30 Thtr 255 Del from £135 to £170* **Services** Lift Air con **Parking** 200 **Notes** LB ⊗ Civ Wed 100

Holiday Inn Basingstoke

★★★ 79% HOTEL

☎ 0871 942 9004 📠 01256 840081
Grove Rd RG21 3EE
e-mail: reservations-basingstoke@ihg.com
web: www.hibasingstokehotel.co.uk
dir: On A339 (Alton road) S of Basingstoke

Located conveniently on the southern approach to Basingstoke and close to the M3, this modern, comfortable hotel offers well-equipped, air-conditioned bedrooms. There is a busy Conference Academy on site. The staff are friendly throughout the hotel. Free parking is available.

Rooms 86 (1 fmly) (43 GF) **Facilities** STV FTV Complimentary passes available at nearby leisure centre Xmas New Year Wi-fi **Conf** Class 70 Board 70 Thtr 140 Del from £120 to £190 **Services** Air con **Parking** 150 **Notes** LB ⊗ Civ Wed 140

Premier Inn Basingstoke Central

BUDGET HOTEL

☎ 0871 527 8062 📠 0871 527 8063
Basingstoke Leisure Park, Worting Rd RG22 6PG
dir: M3 junct 6, A339 towards Newbury. A340 follow brown Leisure Park signs. At next rdbt right onto B3400 (Churchill Way West). Right on next rdbt into Leisure Park. Hotel adjacent to Spruce Goose Beefeater

High quality, budget accommodation ideal for both families and business travellers. Spacious, en suite bedrooms feature tea and coffee making facilities, and Freeview TV in most hotels. Internet access and Wi-fi are available for a small fee. The adjacent family restaurant features a wide and varied menu. See also the Hotel Groups pages.

Rooms 71 **D** £58-£68*

BASLOW
Derbyshire
Map 16 SK27

INSPECTORS' CHOICE

Fischer's Baslow Hall

★★★ ⊛⊛⊛ HOTEL

☎ 01246 583259 📠 01246 583818
Calver Rd DE45 1RR
e-mail: reservations@fischers-baslowhall.co.uk
web: www.fischers-baslowhall.co.uk
dir: On A623 between Baslow & Calver

Located at the end of a chestnut tree-lined drive on the edge of the Chatsworth Estate, in marvellous gardens, this beautiful Derbyshire manor house offers sumptuous accommodation and facilities. Staff provide very friendly and personally attentive service. There are two styles of bedroom available - traditional, individually-themed rooms in the main house and spacious, more contemporary-styled rooms with Italian marble bathrooms in the Garden House. The cuisine is excellent and will prove the highlight of any stay.

Rooms 11 (5 annexe) (4 GF) **S** £115-£145; **D** £155-£225 (incl. bkfst)* **Facilities** Wi-fi **Conf** Board 16 Thtr 20 Del from £205 to £225* **Parking** 40 **Notes** LB ⊗ No children 12 yrs Closed 25-26 Dec RS 31 Dec & 1 Jan Civ Wed 38

Cavendish

★★★ 86% ⊛⊛ HOTEL

☎ 01246 582311 📠 01246 582312
DE45 1SP
e-mail: info@cavendish-hotel.net
web: www.cavendish-hotel.net
dir: M1 junct 29/A617 W to Chesterfield & A619 to Baslow. Hotel in village centre, off main road

This stylish property, dating back to the 18th century, is delightfully situated on the outskirts of the Chatsworth Estate. Elegantly appointed bedrooms offer a host of thoughtful amenities, while comfortable public areas are furnished with period pieces and paintings. Guests have a choice of dining in either the informal conservatory Garden Room or the elegant Gallery Restaurant.

Rooms 24 (3 fmly) (2 GF) **S** £133-£177; **D** £169-£219* **Facilities** FTV Putt green Fishing Xmas New Year Wi-fi **Conf** Class 8 Board 18 Thtr 25 **Parking** 50 **Notes** LB ⊗ RS 25 Dec evening

B

BASSENTHWAITE
Cumbria
Map 18 NY23

INSPECTORS' CHOICE

Armathwaite Hall Country House & Spa

★★★★ ® COUNTRY HOUSE HOTEL

☎ 017687 76551 📠 017687 76220
CA12 4RE
e-mail: reservations@armathwaite-hall.com
web: www.armathwaite-hall.com
dir: M6 junct 40/A66 to Keswick rdbt then A591 signed Carlisle. 8m to Castle Inn junct, turn left. Hotel 300yds

Enjoying fine views over Bassenthwaite Lake, this impressive mansion, dating from the 17th century, is situated amid 400 acres of deer park. Comfortably furnished bedrooms and refurbished bathrooms are complemented by a choice of public rooms that have many original features. The new spa is an outstanding addition to the leisure facilities; it offers an infinity pool, thermal suite, sauna, state-of-the-art gym, treatments, exercise classes and a hot tub overlooking the landscaped gardens.

Rooms 42 (4 fmly) (8 GF) **S** £135-£170; **D** £270-£380 (incl. bkfst) **Facilities** Spa STV supervised Fishing Gym Archery Clay shooting Quad & mountain bikes Falconry Xmas New Year Wi-fi **Conf** Class 50 Board 60 Thtr 200 **Services** Lift **Parking** 100 **Notes** Civ Wed 150

Best Western Castle Inn Hotel

★★★★ 76% HOTEL

☎ 017687 76401 📠 017687 76604
CA12 4RG
e-mail: reservations@castleinncumbria.co.uk
web: www.castleinncumbria.co.uk
dir: A591 to Carlisle, pass Bassenthwaite village on right. Hotel on left of T-junct

Overlooking some of England's highest fells and Bassenthwaite Lake, this fine hotel is ideally situated for exploring Bassenthwaite, Keswick and the Lake District. The accommodation, extensive leisure facilities and friendly service are certainly strong points here. Ritson's Restaurant and Laker's Lounge offer a range of dishes using locally sourced meats from the fells, sustainable fish and seasonal ingredients.

Rooms 42 (4 fmly) (9 GF) **S** £90-£190; **D** £100-£200 (incl. bkfst)* **Facilities** FTV supervised Putt green Gym Sauna Steam room Xmas New Year Wi-fi **Conf** Class 108 Board 60 Thtr 200 Del from £120 to £150* **Parking** 120 **Notes** LB Civ Wed 180

The Pheasant

★★★ 86% ® HOTEL

☎ 017687 76234 📠 017687 76002
CA13 9YE
e-mail: info@the-pheasant.co.uk
web: www.the-pheasant.co.uk
dir: Midway between Keswick & Cockermouth, signed from A66

Enjoying a rural setting, within well-tended gardens, on the western side of Bassenthwaite Lake, this friendly 500-year-old inn is steeped in tradition. The attractive oak-panelled bar has seen few changes over the years and features log fires and a great selection of malt whiskies. The individually decorated bedrooms are stylish and thoughtfully equipped.

Rooms 15 (2 annexe) (2 GF) **S** £90-£110; **D** £140-£200 (incl. bkfst)* **Facilities** New Year Wi-fi **Parking** 40 **Notes** LB No children 12yrs Closed 25 Dec

Ravenstone

★★ 82% HOTEL

☎ 017687 76240 📠 017687 76733
CA12 4QG
e-mail: andrew@ravenstone-hotel.co.uk
dir: From M6 junct 40 follow A66 W for 17m. At rdbt turn right onto A591, 4m on right

A Victorian country house where a friendly welcome is guaranteed. It has been tastefully extended over the years yet retains many original features. Stylish bedrooms have fine views across to the Lakeland Fells. Day rooms include a spacious lounge, traditional bar and games room. The dining room has pleasant views and local produce featured on the dinner menus.

Rooms 19 (1 fmly) **S** £70-£80; **D** £140-£200 (incl. bkfst & dinner)* **Facilities** FTV Xmas New Year Wi-fi **Parking** 30 **Notes** LB

BATH
Somerset
Map 4 ST76

See also **Colerne & Hinton Charterhouse**

Macdonald Bath Spa

★★★★★ 86% ®® HOTEL

☎ 0844 879 9106 & 01225 444424
📠 01225 444006
Sydney Rd BA2 6JF
e-mail: sales.bathspa@macdonald-hotels.co.uk
web: www.macdonaldhotels.co.uk/bathspa
dir: A4, left onto A36 at 1st lights. Right at lights after pedestrian crossing left into Sydney Place. Hotel 200yds on right

A delightful Georgian mansion set amidst seven acres of pretty landscaped grounds, just a short walk from the many and varied delights of the city centre. A timeless elegance pervades the gracious public areas and bedrooms. Facilities include a popular leisure club, a choice of dining options and a number of meeting rooms.

Rooms 129 (3 fmly) (17 GF) **Facilities** Spa STV FTV supervised Gym Beauty treatment Thermal suite Outdoor hydro pool Whirlpool Xmas New Year Wi-fi **Conf** Class 100 Board 50 Thtr 130 **Services** Lift Air con **Parking** 160 **Notes** Civ Wed 130

The Royal Crescent

★★★★★ 85% ®® HOTEL

☎ 01225 823333 📠 01225 339401
16 Royal Crescent BA1 2LS
e-mail: info@royalcrescent.co.uk
web: www.vonessenhotels.co.uk
dir: From A4, right at lights. 2nd left into Bennett St. Continue into The Circus, 2nd exit into Brock St

John Wood's masterpiece of fine Georgian architecture provides the setting for this elegant hotel in the centre of the world famous Royal Crescent. Spacious, air-conditioned bedrooms are individually designed and furnished with antiques. Delightful central grounds lead to a second house, which is home to further rooms, the award-winning Dower House restaurant and the Bath House which offers therapies and treatments.

Rooms 45 (8 fmly) (7 GF) **S** £179-£325; **D** £199-£345 (incl. bkfst)* **Facilities** Spa STV FTV Gym 1920s river launch Xmas New Year Wi-fi **Conf** Class 25 Board 24 Thtr 50 Del from £250 to £305* **Services** Lift Air con **Parking** 27 **Notes** LB Civ Wed 50

The Bath Priory Hotel, Restaurant & Spa

★★★★★ 81% HOTEL

☎ 01225 331922 01225 448276
Weston Rd BA1 2XT
e-mail: mail@thebathpriory.co.uk
web: www.thebathpriory.co.uk
dir: Adjacent to Victoria Park

Set in delightful walled gardens, this attractive Georgian house provides peace and tranquillity, within easy reach of the city. An extensive display of paintings and fine art adorn the sumptuously furnished day rooms, whilst bedrooms are equally stylishly and boast beautifully appointed en suites. The stylish, award-winning restaurant is overseen by Michael Caines and offers memorable, classic dishes. The Garden Spa has extensive facilities including a pool, sauna, steam pod, treatment rooms and a fitness centre.

Rooms 31 (4 annexe) (6 fmly) (1 GF) **D** £270-£625 (incl. bkfst)* **Facilities** Spa STV Gym Xmas New Year Wi-fi **Conf** Class 25 Board 25 Thtr 32 Del from £210 to £280* **Parking** 40 **Notes** LB Civ Wed 70

Barceló Combe Grove Manor

★★★★ 74% COUNTRY HOUSE HOTEL

☎ 01225 834644 01225 834961
Brassknocker Hill, Monkton Combe BA2 7HS
e-mail: combegrovemanor@barcelo-hotels.co.uk
web: www.barcelo-hotels.co.uk
dir: Exit A36 at Limpley Stoke onto Brassknocker Hill. Hotel 0.5m up hill on left

Set in over 80 acres of gardens, this Georgian mansion commands stunning views over Limpley Stoke Valley. Most bedrooms are in the Garden Lodge, a short walk from the main house. The superb range of indoor and outdoor leisure facilities includes a beauty clinic with holistic therapies, golf, tennis and two pools. The Eden Brasserie is in the cellar (please note that the narrow steps may prove a problem for less able guests).

Rooms 42 (33 annexe) (5 fmly) (8 GF) **Facilities** Spa STV supervised 5 Putt green Gym Squash Driving range Xmas New Year Wi-fi **Conf** Class 60 Board 30 Thtr 90 **Parking** 150 **Notes** Civ Wed 50

INSPECTORS' CHOICE

Queensberry

★★★ HOTEL

☎ 01225 447928 01225 446065
Russel St BA1 2QF
e-mail: reservations@thequeensberry.co.uk
web: www.thequeensberry.co.uk
dir: 100mtrs from the Assembly Rooms

This charming family-run hotel, situated in a quiet residential street near the city centre, consists of four delightful townhouses. The spacious bedrooms offer deep armchairs, marble bathrooms and a range of modern comforts. Sumptuously furnished sitting rooms add to The Queensberry's appeal and allow access to the very attractive and peaceful walled gardens. The Olive Tree is a stylish restaurant that combines Georgian opulence with contemporary simplicity. Innovative menus are based on best quality ingredients and very competent cooking. Valet parking proves a useful service.

Rooms 29 (2 fmly) (2 GF) **S** £130-£190; **D** £130-£460* **Facilities** FTV Wi-fi **Conf** Class 12 Board 25 Thtr 35 Del from £225 to £295* **Services** Lift **Parking** 9 **Notes**

B

BATH *continued*

Best Western The Cliffe

★★★ 83% HOTEL

☎ 01225 723226 01225 723871
Cliffe Dr, Crowe Hill, Limpley Stoke BA2 7FY
e-mail: cliffe@bestwestern.co.uk
dir: A36 S from Bath onto B3108 at lights left towards Bradford-on-Avon, 0.5m. Right before bridge through village, 2nd hotel on right

With stunning countryside views, this attractive country house is just a short drive from the City of Bath. Bedrooms vary in size and style but are well equipped; several are particularly spacious and a number of rooms are on the ground floor. The restaurant overlooks the well-tended garden and offers a tempting selection of carefully prepared dishes. Wi-fi is available throughout.

Rooms 11 (3 annexe) (2 fmly) (4 GF) **Facilities** FTV Xmas New Year Wi-fi **Conf** Class 12 Board 8 Thtr 20 **Parking** 20

Dukes

★★★ 82% SMALL HOTEL

☎ 01225 787960 01225 787961
Great Pulteney St BA2 4DN
e-mail: info@dukesbath.co.uk
web: www.dukesbath.co.uk
dir: A46 to Bath, at rdbt right on A4. 4th set of lights turn left (A36), then right into Great Pulteney St. Hotel on left

A fine elegant, Grade I listed Georgian building, just a few minutes' walk from Pulteney Bridge. The well-equipped bedrooms, which differ in size and style, provide plenty of comfort and have flat-screen TVs; suites and ground-floor rooms are available. Staff are particularly friendly and attentive and contribute to the engaging and welcoming atmosphere. There is a courtyard terrace, leading from the lounge/bar, where guests can enjoy an aperitif or lunch during the summer months. The Cavendish Restaurant offers a very creative and interesting menu in a relaxed, light and airy environment.

Rooms 17 (5 fmly) (2 GF) **S** £99-£132; **D** £139-£251.40 (incl. bkfst) **Facilities** FTV Xmas New Year Wi-fi **Conf** Board 20 Thtr 35 Del from £182 to £202

Bailbrook House Hotel

★★★ 79% HOTEL

☎ 01225 855100 01225 855200
Eveleigh Av, London Road West BA1 7JD
e-mail: bailbrook@hilwoodresorts.com
web: www.bailbrookhouse.co.uk
dir: M4 junct 18/A46, at bottom of long hill take slip road to city centre. At rdbt take 1st exit, London Rd. Hotel 200mtrs on left

Located in its own grounds, just a short drive or bus ride from the city centre, this establishment is made up of a historic main house with annexe buildings where the bedrooms, restaurant and bar are situated. It is suited to both business and leisure guests; extensive conference facilities are available. There is a first-floor bar, and a ground-floor restaurant where freshly made dishes may be enjoyed.

Rooms 78 (78 annexe) (2 fmly) (26 GF) **Facilities** FTV Gym Sauna Wi-fi **Conf** Class 72 Board 40 Thtr 160 **Parking** 120 **Notes** Closed 24-30 Dec Civ Wed 120

Haringtons

★★★ 78% METRO HOTEL

☎ 01225 461728 & 445883 01225 444804
8-10 Queen St BA1 1HE
e-mail: post@haringtonshotel.co.uk
web: www.haringtonshotel.co.uk
dir: A4 to George St, into Milsom St. 1st right into Quiet St, 1st left into Queen St

Dating back to the 18th century, this hotel is situated in the heart of the city and provides all the expected modern facilities and comforts. Although a full dinner in a restaurant is not offered, the comfortably furnished lounge is light and airy and open throughout the day for light snacks and refreshments. A warm welcome is assured from the proprietors and staff, making this a delightful place to stay.

Rooms 13 (3 fmly) **Facilities** STV FTV Wi-fi **Conf** Class 10 Board 12 Thtr 18 **Parking** 11 **Notes** LB

Mercure Francis

★★★ 77% HOTEL

☎ 01225 424105 & 338970 01225 319715
Queen Square BA1 2HH
e-mail: h6636@accor.com
web: www.mercure.com
dir: M4 junct 18/A46 to Bath junct. 3rd exit onto A4, right into George St, left into Gay St into Queen Sq. Hotel on left

Overlooking Queen Square in the centre of the city, this elegant Georgian hotel is situated within walking distance of Bath's many attractions. Public rooms provide a variety of options where guests can eat, drink and relax - from the informal café-bar to the traditional lounge and more formal restaurant. Bedrooms have air conditioning.

Rooms 95 (17 fmly) (5 smoking) **Facilities** Xmas New Year Wi-fi **Conf** Class 40 Board 30 Thtr 80 **Services** Lift **Parking** 40 **Notes** Civ Wed 100

Pratt's Hotel

★★★ 72% HOTEL

☎ 01225 460441 01225 448807
South Pde BA2 4AB
e-mail: pratts@forestdale.com
web: www.prattshotel.co.uk
dir: A46 into city centre. Left at 1st lights (Curfew Pub), right at next lights. 2nd exit at next rdbt, right at lights, left at next lights, 1st left into South Pde

Built in 1743 this popular Georgian hotel still has many original features and is centrally placed for exploring Bath. The bedrooms, each with their own individual character and style, offer great comfort. The lounge has original open fireplaces and offers a relaxing venue for afternoon tea.

Rooms 46 (2 fmly) **Facilities** FTV Xmas New Year Wi-fi **Conf** Class 12 Board 20 Thtr 50 **Services** Lift **Notes** LB

B

Old Malt House

THE INDEPENDENTS HOTEL ASSOCIATION

★★ 75% HOTEL

☎ 01761 470106 01761 472726
Radford, Timsbury BA2 0QF
e-mail: hotel@oldmalthouse.co.uk
dir: A367 towards Radstock for 1m, pass Park & Ride, right onto B3115 towards Tunley & Timsbury. At sharp bend straight ahead, hotel 2nd left in 50mtrs

Dating back to 1835, this building was originally the malt house for the Radford Brewery. Just six miles from Bath, this small and welcoming family-run hotel is an ideal base for exploring the many places of interest in the area. Bedrooms are individual in style and have lovely countryside views. In addition to the convivial bar/lounge, the patio is a popular venue for drinks before enjoying good, honest home-cooking in the restaurant.

Rooms 11 (1 fmly) (2 GF) **Facilities** FTV Wi-fi **Parking** 20 **Notes** ® Closed Xmas & New Year

Wentworth House Hotel

★★ 69% HOTEL

☎ 01225 339193 01225 310460
106 Bloomfield Rd BA2 2AP
e-mail: stay@wentworthhouse.co.uk
web: www.wentworthhouse.co.uk
dir: A36 towards Bristol at railway arches, hotel on right

This hotel is located on the outskirts of Bath yet is within walking distance of the city centre. Bedrooms vary in size and style; ground-floor rooms have their own conservatory seating area, some have four-posters and one has superb city views. The dinner menu features authentic home-cooked Indian dishes. There is a garden, which has a pool to enjoy in fine weather.

Rooms 19 (2 fmly) (6 GF) **Facilities** STV FTV Xmas Wi-fi **Conf** Class 40 Board 35 **Parking** 19 **Notes** LB ® No children 7yrs

Carfax Hotel

★★ TOWN HOUSE HOTEL

☎ 01225 462089 01225 443257
13-15 Great Pulteney St BA2 4BS
e-mail: reservations@carfaxhotel.co.uk
dir: A36 onto Great Pulteney St

Rooms 30 (5 fmly) (4 GF) **S** £85-£105; **D** £120-£180 (incl. bkfst)* **Facilities** FTV Wi-fi **Conf** Class 18 Board 12 Thtr 30 Del from £106 to £165* **Services** Lift **Parking** 13 **Notes** LB ®

The Halcyon Hotel

U

☎ 01225 444100 01225 331200
2-3 South Pde BA2 4AA
e-mail: info@thehalcyon.com
web: www.thehalcyon.com

Currently the rating for this establishment is not confirmed. This may be due to a change of ownership or because it has only recently joined the AA rating scheme. For further details please see the AA website: theAA.com

Rooms 21 (3 GF) **S** £85-£125; **D** £99-£155* **Facilities** STV Wi-fi **Notes** LB ®

Holiday Inn Express Bath

Holiday Inn Express

BUDGET HOTEL

☎ 01225 303000 01225 303030
Lower Bristol Rd, Brougham Hayes BA2 3QU
e-mail: info@expressbath.co.uk
web: www.hiexpress.co.uk/bath
dir: From A4, right into Bathwick St, over rdbt onto Pulteney Rd. Into Claverton St, straight over at next rdbt (Lower Bristol Rd). Hotel opposite Sainsburys

A modern hotel ideal for families and business travellers. Fresh and uncomplicated, the spacious rooms include Sky TV, power shower and tea and coffee-making facilities. Continental buffet breakfast is included in the room rate; other meals may be taken at the nearby family pub or restaurant. See also the Hotel Groups pages.

Rooms 126 (33 fmly) (31 GF) **D** £75-£169* **Conf** Class 10 Board 20 Thtr 20

Milsoms Bath

RESTAURANT WITH ROOMS

☎ 01225 750128 01225 750121
24 Milsom St BA1 1DG
e-mail: bath@milsomshotel.co.uk

Located at the end of the main street in busy, central Bath, this stylish restaurant with rooms offers a range of comfortable, well equipped rooms. The ground-floor Loch Fyne Restaurant serves an excellent selection of dishes at both lunch and dinner with an emphasis on freshest quality fish and shellfish. A good selection of hot and cold items is also available in the same restaurant at breakfast.

Rooms 9

BATTLE
East Sussex — **Map 7 TQ71**

Powder Mills

★★★ 80% HOTEL

☎ 01424 775511 01424 774540
Powdermill Ln TN33 0SP
e-mail: powdc@aol.com
web: www.powdermillshotel.com
dir: M25 junct 5, A21 towards Hastings. At St Johns Cross take A2100 to Battle. Pass Abbey on right, 1st right into Powdermills Ln. 1m, hotel on right

A delightful 18th-century country-house hotel set amidst 150 acres of landscaped grounds with lakes and woodland. The individually decorated bedrooms are tastefully furnished and thoughtfully equipped; some rooms have sun terraces with lovely views over the lake. Public rooms include a cosy lounge bar, music room, drawing room, library, restaurant and conservatory.

Rooms 40 (10 annexe) (5 GF) **S** £95-£115; **D** £140-£350 (incl. bkfst)* **Facilities** STV FTV Fishing Jogging trails Woodland walks Clay pigeon shooting Xmas New Year Wi-fi **Conf** Class 50 Board 16 Thtr 250 Del from £135 to £165* **Parking** 101 **Notes** LB Civ Wed 100

B

BATTLE *continued*

Brickwall Hotel

★★★ 78% HOTEL

☎ 01424 870253 & 870339 📠 01424 870785
The Green, Sedlescombe TN33 0QA
e-mail: info@brickwallhotel.com
web: www.brickwallhotel.com
dir: Off A21 on B2244 at top of Sedlescombe Green

This is a well-maintained Tudor house, which is situated in the heart of this pretty village and overlooks the green. The spacious public rooms feature a lovely wood-panelled restaurant with a wealth of oak beams, a choice of lounges and a smart bar. Bedrooms are pleasantly decorated and some have garden views.

Rooms 25 (2 fmly) (17 GF) **S** £60-£75; **D** £85-£125 (incl. bkfst)* **Facilities** STV Xmas New Year Wi-fi **Conf** Class 40 Board 30 Thtr 30 **Parking** 40 **Notes** LB ®

BEAMINSTER
Dorset — Map 4 ST40

BridgeHouse

★★★ 81% ®® HOTEL

☎ 01308 862200 📠 01308 863700
3 Prout Bridge DT8 3AY
e-mail: enquiries@bridge-house.co.uk
web: www.bridge-house.co.uk
dir: Off A3066, 100yds from town square

Dating back to the 13th century, this property offers friendly and attentive service. The stylish bedrooms feature finest Italian cotton linens, flat-screen TVs and Wi-fi. There are five types of room to choose from including four-poster and coach house rooms. Smartly presented public areas include the Georgian dining room, cosy bar and adjacent lounge, and a breakfast room together with the Beaminster Brasserie with its alfresco eating area under a canopy overlooking the attractive walled garden.

Rooms 13 (4 annexe) (2 fmly) (4 GF) **S** £86-£120; **D** £126-£215 (incl. bkfst)* **Facilities** FTV Xmas New Year Wi-fi Child facilities **Conf** Class 14 Board 10 Thtr 24 **Parking** 20 **Notes** LB Civ Wed 100

BEAMISH
Co Durham — Map 19 NZ25

Beamish Park Hotel

★★★ 82% ®® HOTEL

☎ 01207 230666 📠 01207 281260
Beamish Burn Rd, Marley Hill NE16 5EG
e-mail: reception@beamish-park-hotel.co.uk
web: www.beamish-park-hotel.co.uk
dir: A1 junct 63 onto A693 Stanley. Exit rdbt onto A6076, hotel 2m on right

The Metro Centre, Beamish Museum and south Tyneside are all within striking distance of this modern hotel, set in open countryside alongside its own golf course and floodlit range. Bedrooms are tastefully decorated and well equipped; some have their own patios. The conservatory bistro offers an interesting menu using fine ingredients.

Rooms 42 (4 fmly) (27 GF) **S** £95-£150; **D** £105-£175* **Facilities** FTV 9 Putt green New Year Wi-fi **Conf** Class 50 Board 50 Thtr 100 Del from £145 to £182* **Parking** 100 **Notes** LB Closed 24 Dec-1 Jan Civ Wed 100

BEAULIEU
Hampshire — Map 5 SU30

Montagu Arms

★★★★ 82% ®®® HOTEL

☎ 01590 612324 & 624467 📠 01590 612188
Palace Ln SO42 7ZL
e-mail: reservations@montaguarmshotel.co.uk
web: www.montaguarmshotel.co.uk
dir: M27 junct 2, turn left at rdbt, follow signs for Beaulieu. Continue to Dibden Purlieu, then right at rdbt. Hotel on left

Situated at the heart of this charming village and surrounded by glorious New Forest scenery, this lovely hotel dates back to 1742 and still retains the character of a traditional country house. The individually designed bedrooms include some with four-posters. Public rooms include a choice of two dining options, the informal Monty's brasserie serving home-cooked classics, and the stylish, award-winning Terrace Restaurant. Much produce comes from the kitchen garden project which saw a derelict piece of land to the rear transformed to produce organic fruit, vegetables and herbs plus free-range eggs from the hens. In warmer weather there is a sheltered alfresco eating area overlooking the pretty terraced garden. Complimentary use of leisure and spa facilities is available to guests at a sister hotel six miles away.

Rooms 22 (3 fmly) **Facilities** FTV Complimentary use of spa in Brockenhurst Xmas New Year Wi-fi **Conf** Class 16 Board 26 Thtr 50 **Parking** 86 **Notes** ® Civ Wed 100

The Master Builders at Bucklers Hard

★★★ 79% ® HOTEL

☎ 01590 616253 📠 01590 616297
Buckler's Hard SO42 7XB
e-mail: enquiries@themasterbuilders.co.uk
web: www.themasterbuilders.co.uk
dir: M27 junct 2, follow Beaulieu signs. At T-junct left onto B3056, 1st left to Buckler's Hard. Hotel 2m on left before village

A tranquil historic riverside setting creates the backdrop for this delightful property. The main house bedrooms are full of historical features and of individual design, and in addition there are some bedrooms in the newer wing. Public areas include a popular bar and guest lounge, whilst grounds are an ideal location for alfresco dining in the summer months. Award-winning cuisine is served in the stylish dining room.

Rooms 25 (17 annexe) (4 fmly) (8 GF) **S** fr £95; **D** fr £105 (incl. bkfst)* **Facilities** FTV Xmas New Year Wi-fi **Conf** Class 30 Board 20 Thtr 40 **Parking** 40

Beaulieu Hotel

NEW FOREST HOTELS

★★★ 78% ® HOTEL

☎ 023 8029 3344 📠 023 8029 2729
Beaulieu Rd SO42 7YQ
e-mail: beaulieu@newforesthotels.co.uk
web: www.newforesthotels.co.uk
dir: M27 junct 1/A337 towards Lyndhurst. Left at lights, through Lyndhurst, right onto B3056, hotel in 3m

Located in the heart of the beautiful New Forest and close to Beaulieu Road railway station, this popular, small hotel provides an ideal base for exploring this remarkable area. Once a coaching inn, the hotel now particularly welcomes families; children will delight in seeing the ponies on the doorstep! Bedrooms, all with free Wi-fi and flat-screen TVs with Freeview, range from cosy Keeper rooms to Crown rooms which also have four-posters and iPod docking stations. The relaxing Exbury Restaurant has doors that lead out onto the patio area and the landscaped gardens, and alfresco eating is possible in the summer. Facilities include an indoor swimming pool and an adjoining pub.

Beaulieu Hotel

Rooms 28 (7 annexe) (5 fmly) (4 GF) **D** £120-£190 (incl. bkfst)* **Facilities** FTV Steam room Xmas New Year Wi-fi **Conf** Class 100 Board 100 Thtr 250 Del from £95 to £110* **Services** Lift **Parking** 60 **Notes** LB Civ Wed 205

BECCLES Map 13 TM48
Suffolk

Waveney House

★★★ 83% HOTEL

☎ 01502 712270 01502 470370
Puddingmoor NR34 9PL
e-mail: enquiries@waveneyhousehotel.co.uk
web: www.waveneyhousehotel.co.uk
dir: From A146 onto Common Lane North, left into Pound Rd, left into Ravensmere, right onto Smallgate, right onto Old Market, continue to Puddingmoor

An exceptionally well presented, privately owned hotel is situated by the River Waveney on the edge of a busy little market town. The stylish public rooms include a smart lounge bar and a contemporary-style restaurant with views over the river. The spacious bedrooms are attractively decorated with co-ordinated fabrics and have many thoughtful touches.

Rooms 12 (3 fmly) **Facilities** FTV Xmas New Year Wi-fi **Conf** Class 100 Board 50 Thtr 160 **Parking** 45 **Notes** ® Civ Wed 80

BEDFORD Map 12 TL04
Bedfordshire

The Bedford Swan

★★★★ 73% @@ HOTEL

☎ 01234 346565 01234 212009
The Embankment MK40 1RW
e-mail: info@bedfordswanhotel.co.uk

This historic hotel successfully combines original features with modern comforts. The bedrooms ooze style and quality and do not forget the needs of the modern traveller. The award-winning River Room Restaurant offers a varied choice of freshly prepared dishes. The hotel also offers meeting and function rooms, spa facilities and secure parking.

Rooms 113 (10 fmly) (12 smoking) **S** £89-£199; **D** £99-£209 **Facilities** STV Spa treatments Xmas New Year Wi-fi **Conf** Class 40 Board 60 Thtr 250 **Services** Lift Air con **Parking** 80 **Notes** Civ Wed 250

The Barns Hotel

★★★★ 73% HOTEL

☎ 0844 855 9101 01234 273102
Cardington Rd MK44 3SA
e-mail: foh@barnshotelbedford.co.uk
web: www.barnshotelbedford.co.uk
dir: From M1 junct 13, A421, approx 10m to A603 Sandy/Bedford exit, hotel on right at 2nd rdbt

A tranquil location on the outskirts of Bedford, friendly staff and well-equipped bedrooms all combine to make this a good choice. Cosy day rooms and two informal bars add to the hotel's appeal, while large windows in the restaurant make the most of the view over the river. The original barn houses the conference and function suite.

Rooms 49 (18 GF) **S** £79-£159; **D** £89-£169 (incl. bkfst)* **Facilities** Free use of local leisure centre (1m) New Year Wi-fi **Conf** Class 40 Board 40 Thtr 120 Del from £130 to £155* **Parking** 90 **Notes** LB ® Civ Wed 90

Park Inn Bedford

park inn by Radisson

★★★ 70% HOTEL

☎ 01234 799988 & 799900 01234 799902
2 St Marys St MK40 1DZ
e-mail: info.bedford@rezidorparkinn.com
dir: B531, left A5141/Cauldwell St, right St Mary's St then left into Duck Mill Lane

This modern hotel sits alongside the river in a convenient location in the heart of town and enjoys delightful views. The comfortable bedrooms are contemporary in style and particularly well equipped, with safes, Wi-fi and flat-screen TVs. The hotel also offers a host of other facilities including a leisure facilities and a range of meeting rooms.

Rooms 120 (1 fmly) (16 GF) **Facilities** FTV Gym Steam room Treatment room Cardio vascular equipment Wi-fi **Conf** Class 200 Board 160 Thtr 450 Del from £110 to £160* **Services** Lift Air con **Parking** 90 **Notes** ® Civ Wed 100

Woodland Manor Hotel

★★★ 68% HOTEL

☎ 01234 363281 01234 272390
Green Ln, Clapham MK41 6EP
e-mail: reception@woodlandmanorhotel.co.uk
dir: A6 towards Kettering. On entering village 1st right into Green Ln. Hotel 200mtrs on right

Sitting in acres of wooded grounds and gardens, this secluded Grade II listed, Victorian manor house offers a warm welcome. The hotel has spacious bedrooms, ample parking plus meeting rooms that are suitable for a variety of occasions. Traditional public areas include a cosy bar and a smart restaurant, where traditional English dishes, with a hint of French flair, are served.

Rooms 34 (6 fmly) (3 GF) **S** £55-£90; **D** £65-£150 (incl. bkfst)* **Facilities** Wi-fi **Conf** Class 25 Board 22 Thtr 80 **Parking** 60 **Notes** LB ® Civ Wed 80

Holiday Inn Express Bedford

BUDGET HOTEL

☎ 01234 224100 01234 224166
Elstow Interchange A6/A421, Bedford Bypass Junction, Wilstead Rd MK42 9BF
e-mail: info@expressbedford.co.uk
web: www.expressbedford.co.uk
dir: 2m S of Bedford town centre at Elstow interchange at junct of A421/A6

A modern hotel ideal for families and business travellers. Fresh and uncomplicated, the spacious rooms include Sky TV, power shower and tea and coffee-making facilities. Continental buffet breakfast is included in the room rate; other meals may be taken at the nearby family pub or restaurant. See also the Hotel Groups pages.

Rooms 80 (44 fmly) (18 GF) **S** £50-£120; (incl. bkfst) **Conf** Class 18 Board 20 Thtr 35 Del from £75 to £145

B

BEDFORD *continued*

Premier Inn Bedford (Priory Marina)

BUDGET HOTEL

☎ 0871 527 8066 📠 0871 527 8067
Priory Country Park, Barkers Ln MK41 9DJ
dir: M1 junct 13, A421, A6, A428 signed Cambridge. Cross River Ouse, right at next rdbt into Barkers Lane. Follow Priory Country Park signs. Hotel adjacent to Priory Marina Beefeater

High quality, budget accommodation ideal for both families and business travellers. Spacious, en suite bedrooms feature tea and coffee making facilities, and Freeview TV in most hotels. Internet access and Wi-fi are available for a small fee. The adjacent family restaurant features a wide and varied menu. See also the Hotel Groups pages.

Rooms 57 **D** £49-£60*

BELFORD Map 21 NU13
Northumberland

Purdy Lodge

★★ 76% HOTEL

☎ 01668 213000 📠 01668 213111
Adderstone Services NE70 7JU
e-mail: stay@purdylodge.co.uk
web: www.purdylodge.co.uk
dir: A1 onto B1341 then immediately left

Situated off the A1, this family-owned lodge provides modern bedrooms that look out over the fields towards Bamburgh Castle. Food is readily available in the attractive restaurant, Café One, and the lounge bar. This is a great stop-off hotel where a friendly welcome is guaranteed.

Rooms 20 (4 fmly) (10 GF) **Facilities** FTV New Year Wi-fi **Parking** 60 **Notes** Closed 25 Dec

BELPER Map 11 SK34
Derbyshire

Makeney Hall Hotel

★★★★ 73% HOTEL

☎ 0845 609 9966 📠 01332 842777
Makeney, Milford DE56 0RS
e-mail: reservations@akkeron-hotels.com
web: www.akkeron-hotels.com
dir: Off A6 at Milford, signed Makeney. Hotel 0.25m on left

This restored Victorian mansion stands in six acres of landscaped gardens and grounds above the River Derwent. Bedrooms vary in style and are generally very spacious. They are divided between the main house and the ground floor courtyard. Comfortable public rooms include a lounge, bar and spacious restaurant with views of the gardens.

Rooms 46 (18 annexe) (4 fmly) **Facilities** STV FTV Xmas New Year Wi-fi **Conf** Class 60 Board 50 Thtr 180 **Services** Lift **Parking** 150 **Notes** Civ Wed 180

BELTON Map 11 SK42
Leicestershire

The Queen's Head

@@ RESTAURANT WITH ROOMS

☎ 01530 222359 📠 01530 224680
2 Long St LE12 9TP
e-mail: enquiries@thequeenshead.org
web: www.thequeenshead.org
dir: From Loughborough left onto B5324, 3m to Belton

This well furnished establishment is found in the village centre and has public rooms with a modern feel. The individually designed bedrooms feature crisp white linen, fluffy duvets and pillows, 19-inch LCD TVs with Freeview and DVD players. The restaurant has earned a well deserved reputation for its award-winning cuisine; the menus are based on the freshest, locally sourced produce quality.

Rooms 6 (2 fmly)

BELTON Map 11 SK93
Lincolnshire

De Vere Belton Woods

DE VERE Hotels & Resorts

★★★★ 71% HOTEL

☎ 01476 593200 📠 01476 574547
NG32 2LN
e-mail: belton.woods@devere-hotels.com
web: www.devere.co.uk
dir: A1 to Gonerby Moor Services. B1174 towards Great Gonerby. At top of hill turn left towards Manthorpe/Belton. At T-junct turn left onto A607. Hotel 0.25m on left

Beautifully located amidst 475 acres of picturesque countryside, this is a destination venue for lovers of sport, especially golf, as well as a relaxing executive retreat for seminars. Comfortable and well-equipped accommodation complements the elegant and spacious public areas, which provide a good choice of drinking and dining options.

Rooms 136 (136 fmly) (68 GF) **Facilities** Spa supervised 45 Putt green Fishing Gym Squash Outdoor activity centre (quad biking, laser shooting etc) Xmas New Year Wi-fi **Conf** Class 180 Board 80 Thtr 245 **Services** Lift **Parking** 350 **Notes** Civ Wed 80

BEMBRIDGE Map 5 SZ68
Isle of Wight

Bembridge Coast Hotel

Warner Leisure Hotels

★★★ 75% HOTEL

☎ 01983 873931
Fishermans Walk PO35 5TH

This hotel occupies a delightful, peaceful location on the east coast of the Isle of Wight in 23-acre grounds. The accommodation is comfortable, and there are a number of rooms with sea views for which a small supplementary charge applies. A full activities itinerary ensures that guests can make the most of what the hotel, and this beautiful island, have to offer. The helpful reservations team can also arrange ferry bookings from the UK mainland. Please note that this is an adults-only (over 21 years old) hotel. Warner Leisure Hotels – AA Small Hotel Group of the Year 2011-12.

Rooms 244 **Notes** No children

BERWICK-UPON-TWEED Map 21 NT95
Northumberland

Marshall Meadows Country House

★★★ 74% COUNTRY HOUSE HOTEL

☎ 01289 331133 🖹 01289 331438
TD15 1UT
e-mail: gm.marshallmeadows@classiclodges.co.uk
web: www.classiclodges.co.uk
dir: Signed directly off A1, 300yds from Scottish border

This stylish Georgian mansion is set in wooded grounds flanked by farmland and has convenient access from the A1. A popular venue for weddings and conferences, it offers comfortable and well-equipped bedrooms. Public rooms include a cosy bar, a relaxing lounge and a two-tier restaurant which serves imaginative dishes.

Rooms 19 (1 fmly) **Facilities** Xmas New Year **Conf** Class 120 Board 40 Thtr 200 **Parking** 87 **Notes** Civ Wed 200

Queens Head

★★★ 73% SMALL HOTEL

☎ 01289 307852 🖹 01289 307858
Sandgate TD15 1EP
e-mail: info@queensheadberwick.co.uk
dir: A1 towards centre & town hall, along High St. Right at bottom to Hide Hill. Hotel adjacent to cinema

This small hotel is situated in the town centre, close to the old walls of this former garrison town. Bedrooms provide many thoughtful extras as standard. Dining remains a strong aspect with a carte menu that offers an impressive choice of tasty, freshly prepared dishes served in the comfortable lounge or dining room.

Rooms 6 (1 fmly) **S** £57.50-£65; **D** £80-£90 (incl. bkfst)* **Facilities** STV FTV Wi-fi **Notes** ⊗

BEVERLEY Map 17 TA03
East Riding of Yorkshire

Tickton Grange

★★★ 82% ◎◎ HOTEL

☎ 01964 543666 🖹 01964 542556
Tickton HU17 9SH
e-mail: info@ticktongrange.co.uk
dir: 3m NE on A1035

A charming Georgian country house situated in four acres of private grounds and attractive gardens. Bedrooms are individually designed and decorated to a high specification. Pre-dinner drinks may be enjoyed in the comfortable library lounge, prior to enjoying fine, modern British cooking in the restaurant. The hotel has excellent facilities for both weddings and business conferences.

Rooms 20 (3 annexe) (2 fmly) (4 GF) **S** £95; **D** £128 (incl. bkfst)* **Facilities** STV FTV Gym Wi-fi **Conf** Class 100 Board 80 Thtr 200 Del from £118.95 to £131.50* **Parking** 90 **Notes** LB ⊗ RS 25-29 Dec Civ Wed 200

Best Western Lairgate Hotel

★★★ 72% HOTEL

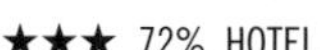

☎ 01482 882141 🖹 01482 861067
30/32 Lairgate HU17 8EP
e-mail: mail@thelairgateinbeverley.co.uk
dir: A63 towards town centre. Hotel 220yds on left, follow one-way system

Located just off the market square, this pleasing Georgian hotel has been appointed to offer stylish accommodation. Bedrooms are elegant and well equipped, and public rooms include a comfortable lounge, a lounge bar, and restaurant with a popular sun terrace.

Rooms 30 (1 fmly) (8 GF) **Facilities** FTV New Year Wi-fi **Conf** Class 20 Board 20 Thtr 20 **Parking** 18 **Notes** ⊗ Closed 26 Dec & 1 Jan RS 25 Dec Civ Wed 70

BEXHILL Map 6 TQ70
East Sussex

Cooden Beach Hotel

★★★ 80% HOTEL

☎ 01424 842281 🖹 01424 846142
Cooden Beach TN39 4TT
e-mail: rooms@thecoodenbeachhotel.co.uk
web: www.thecoodenbeachhotel.co.uk
dir: A259 towards Cooden. Signed at rdbt in Little Common Village. Hotel at end of road

This privately owned hotel is situated in private gardens which have direct access to the beach. With a train station within walking distance the location is perfectly suited for both business and leisure guests. Bedrooms are comfortably appointed, and public areas include a spacious restaurant, lounge, bar and leisure centre with swimming pool.

Rooms 41 (8 annexe) (10 fmly) (4 GF) **Facilities** FTV Gym Sauna Steam room Spa bath ♫ Xmas New Year Wi-fi **Conf** Class 40 Board 40 Thtr 150 **Parking** 60 **Notes** Civ Wed 160

B

BEXLEY Map 6 TQ47
Greater London

Bexleyheath Marriott Hotel

Marriott HOTELS & RESORTS

★★★★ 76% HOTEL

☎ 020 8298 1000 🖷 020 8298 1234
1 Broadway DA6 7JZ
e-mail: bexleyheath@marriotthotels.co.uk
web: www.bexleyheathmarriott.co.uk
dir: M25 junct 2/A2 towards London. Exit at Black Prince junct onto A220, signed Bexleyheath. Left at 2nd lights into hotel

Well positioned for access to major road networks, this large, modern hotel offers spacious, air-conditioned bedrooms with a comprehensive range of extra facilities. Planters Bar is a popular venue for pre-dinner drinks and offers guests a choice of lighter dining, whilst a more formal restaurant is also available. The hotel boasts a well-equipped leisure centre and undercover parking.

Rooms 142 (16 fmly) (26 GF) **Facilities** Spa STV FTV supervised Gym Steam room Xmas New Year Wi-fi **Conf** Class 120 Board 34 Thtr 250 Del from £135* **Services** Lift Air con **Parking** 77 **Notes** Civ Wed 60

Holiday Inn London - Bexley

★★★ 80% HOTEL

Holiday Inn

☎ 0871 942 9006 & 01322 625513
🖷 01322 625584
Black Prince Interchange, Southwold Rd DA5 1ND
e-mail: bexley@ihg.com
web: www.holidayinn.co.uk
dir: M25 junct 2, A2 towards London. Exit at Black Prince Interchange (signed Bexley, Bexleyheath, A220, A223). Hotel on left

This hotel is within easy access of London and the Kent countryside; only 10 minutes from the famous Bluewater Shopping Centre and 15 minutes from Brands Hatch motor racing circuit. All bedrooms are air conditioned; suites are available. The hotel has a range of meeting rooms.

Rooms 107 (11 fmly) (33 GF) (16 smoking) **S** £45-£195; **D** £45-£195* **Facilities** STV FTV Xmas New Year Wi-fi **Conf** Class 42 Board 50 Thtr 120 Del from £99 to £175* **Services** Lift Air con **Parking** 200 **Notes** LB Civ Wed 80

BIBURY Map 5 SP10
Gloucestershire

Bibury Court

★★★ 85% ◎◎ COUNTRY HOUSE HOTEL

☎ 01285 740337 & 741171 🖷 01285 740660
GL7 5NT
e-mail: info@biburycourt.com
web: www.biburycourt.com
dir: On B4425, 6m N of Cirencester (A4179). 8m S of Burford (A40), entrance by River Coln

Dating back to Tudor times, this elegant manor is the perfect antidote to the hustle and bustle of the modern world. Public areas have abundant charm and character. Bedrooms are spacious and offer traditional quality with modern comforts. A choice of interesting dishes is available in the conservatory at lunchtime, whereas dinner is served in the more formal restaurant. Staff are friendly and helpful.

Rooms 18 (3 fmly) (1 GF) **S** £150-£410; **D** £150-£425 (incl. bkfst)* **Facilities** FTV Fishing Xmas New Year Wi-fi **Conf** Class 50 Board 30 Thtr 50 **Parking** 40 **Notes** LB Civ Wed 80

Swan

Cotswold Inns & Hotels

★★★ 83% ◎ HOTEL

☎ 01285 740695 🖷 01285 740473
GL7 5NW
e-mail: info@swanhotel.co.uk
web: www.cotswold-inns-hotels.co.uk/swan
dir: 9m S of Burford A40 onto B4425. 6m N of Cirencester A4179 onto B4425

This hotel, built in the 17th century as a coaching inn, is set in peaceful and picturesque surroundings. It provides well-equipped and smartly presented accommodation, including four luxury cottage suites set just outside the main hotel. The elegant public areas are comfortable and have feature fireplaces. There is a choice of dining options to suit all tastes.

Swan

Rooms 22 (4 annexe) (1 fmly) **S** £140-£200; **D** £160-£200 (incl. bkfst)* **Facilities** Fishing Xmas New Year Wi-fi **Conf** Class 50 Board 32 Thtr 80 Del from £155* **Services** Lift **Parking** 22 **Notes** LB Civ Wed 110

BICESTER Map 11 SP52
Oxfordshire

Bignell Park Hotel & Oaks Restaurant

THE INDEPENDENTS HOTEL ASSOCIATION

★★★ 75% ◎ HOTEL

☎ 01869 326550 🖷 01869 322729
Chesterton OX26 1UE
e-mail: enq@bignellparkhotel.co.uk
dir: M40 junct 9/A41 to Bicester, over 1st & 2nd rdbts, left at mini-rdbt, follow signs to Witney A4095. Hotel 0.5m

This pleasant property is situated in the peaceful village of Chesterton, just a short drive from Bicester Village Retail Outlet, the M40 and Oxford. Public rooms feature a superb oak-beamed restaurant, a smart bar and a comfortable lounge with plush sofas. Bedrooms are smartly decorated, well maintained and equipped with modern facilities.

Rooms 23 (4 fmly) (9 GF) **Facilities** FTV Xmas New Year Wi-fi **Conf** Class 16 Board 60 Thtr 100 **Parking** 40 **Notes** LB Civ Wed 60

BIDEFORD Map 3 SS42
Devon

Yeoldon Country House

★★★ 74% SMALL HOTEL

☎ 01237 474400 📠 01237 476618
Durrant Ln, Northam EX39 2RL
e-mail: yeoldonhouse@aol.com
web: www.yeoldonhousehotel.co.uk
dir: A39 from Barnstaple over River Torridge Bridge. At rdbt right onto A386 towards Northam, 3rd right into Durrant Lane

In a tranquil location with superb views over attractive grounds and the River Torridge, this is a charming Victorian house. The well-equipped bedrooms are individually decorated and some have balconies with breathtaking views. The public rooms are full of character with many interesting features and artefacts. The daily-changing dinner menu offers imaginative dishes.

Rooms 10 **S** £80-£90; **D** £120-£140 (incl. bkfst) **Facilities** FTV Wi-fi **Parking** 20 **Notes** LB Closed 24-27 Dec Civ Wed 50

Royal

★★★ 74% HOTEL

☎ 01237 472005 📠 01237 478957
Barnstaple St EX39 4AE
e-mail: reservations@royalbideford.co.uk
web: www.royalbideford.co.uk
dir: At eastern end of Bideford Bridge

A quiet and relaxing hotel, the Royal is set near the river within a five-minute walk of the busy town centre and the quay. The bright, well maintained public areas retain much of the charm and style of its 16th-century origins, particularly in the wood-panelled Kingsley Suite. Bedrooms are well equipped and comfortable. The meals at dinner and the lounge snacks are appetising.

Rooms 32 (2 fmly) (2 GF) **S** £59-£120; **D** £75-£120* **Facilities** FTV Xmas New Year Wi-fi **Conf** Class 100 Board 100 Thtr 100 **Services** Lift **Parking** 70 **Notes** LB ⊗ Civ Wed 130

Durrant House

★★★ 🅰 HOTEL

☎ 01237 472361 📠 01237 421709
Heywood Rd, Northam EX39 3QB
e-mail: info@durranthousehotel.com
dir: A39 to Bideford, over New Torridge Bridge, right at rdbt, hotel 500yds on right

Rooms 125 (25 fmly) (14 GF) **S** £45-£85; **D** £70-£185 (incl. bkfst) **Facilities** FTV Gym Sauna Xmas New Year Wi-fi **Conf** Class 100 Board 80 Thtr 350 **Services** Lift **Parking** 200 **Notes** LB Civ Wed 100

BIGBURY-ON-SEA Map 3 SX64
Devon

Henley

★★ 83% SMALL HOTEL

☎ 01548 810240 📠 01548 810240
TQ7 4AR
e-mail: thehenleyhotel@btconnect.com
dir: Through Bigbury, past Golf Centre into Bigbury-on-Sea. Hotel on left

Built in Edwardian times and complete with its own private cliff path to a sandy beach, this small hotel boasts stunning views from an elevated position. Family run, it is a perfect choice for guests wishing to escape the hurried pace of life to a peaceful retreat. Personal service, friendly hospitality and food cooked with care that uses local, fresh produce combine to make this an uncomplicated yet special place to stay.

Rooms 6 **S** £80; **D** £120-£144 (incl. bkfst)* **Facilities** FTV Wi-fi **Parking** 9 **Notes** No children 12yrs Closed Nov-Mar

BILDESTON Map 13 TL94
Suffolk

INSPECTORS' CHOICE

Bildeston Crown

★★★ @@@ HOTEL

☎ 01449 740510 📠 01449 741843
104 High St IP7 7EB
e-mail: hayley@thebildestoncrown.co.uk
web: www.thebildestoncrown.co.uk
dir: A12 junct 31, turn right onto B1070 & follow signs to Hadleigh. At T-junct turn left onto A1141, then immediately right onto B1115. Hotel 0.5m

A charming inn situated in a peaceful village close to the historic town of Lavenham. Public areas feature beams, exposed brickwork and oak floors, with contemporary style decor; they include a choice of bars, a lounge and a restaurant. The tastefully decorated bedrooms have lovely co-ordinated fabrics and modern facilities that include Yamaha music systems and LCD TVs. Food here is the real focus and draw; guests can expect fresh, high-quality local produce and accomplished technical skills in both modern and classic dishes.

Bildeston Crown

Rooms 13 **Facilities** STV FTV Xmas New Year Wi-fi **Conf** Class 25 Board 16 Thtr 40 Del from £150 to £190* **Services** Lift **Parking** 30 **Notes** Civ Wed 50

BILLINGHAM Map 19 NZ42
Co Durham

Wynyard Hall Hotel

★★★★ 82% @ HOTEL

☎ 01740 644811 📠 01740 644769
Wynyard Village TS22 5NF
e-mail: enq@wynyardhall.co.uk
web: www.wynyardhall.co.uk
dir: A19, A1027 towards Stockton. At rdbt take B1274 (Junction Rd). At next rdbt take A177 (Durham Rd). Right onto Wynyard Rd signed Wolviston. Left into estate

Drive though the gates, over the lion bridge and Wynyard Hall will immediately impress with its grandeur and elegance. The opulent public areas are as much a feature of the property as are the grounds and gardens. The individually designed bedrooms and suites are stunning with a combination of modern and period style furniture. The elegant, award-winning Duke of Wellington restaurant is also impressive. The Essential Time Treatment Suite offers many relaxing therapies and beauty treatments. As a wedding venue the hall provides the option for a civil ceremony, or a religious service in the chapel, followed by a memorable reception.

Rooms 17 (1 annexe) (1 fmly) **S** £90-£120; **D** £180 (incl. bkfst) **Facilities** Spa FTV ⛳ Clay pigeon shooting Xmas New Year Wi-fi **Conf** Class 240 Board 50 Thtr 300 Del from £175 to £205 **Services** Lift **Parking** 200 **Notes** LB ⊗ Civ Wed 150

BINGLEY Map 19 SE13
West Yorkshire

Five Rise Locks Hotel & Restaurant

★★★ 75% @ SMALL HOTEL

☎ 01274 565296 📠 01274 568828
Beck Ln BD16 4DD
e-mail: info@five-rise-locks.co.uk
dir: Main St into Park Rd, 0.5m, left into Beck Lane

A warm welcome and comfortable accommodation await guests at this impressive Victorian building. Bedrooms are of a good size and feature homely extras. The restaurant offers imaginative dishes and the bright breakfast room overlooks open countryside.

Rooms 9 (2 GF) **S** £60-£67; **D** £89-£110 (incl. bkfst)* **Facilities** FTV Wi-fi **Conf** Class 16 Board 18 Thtr 25 Del from £95 to £125* **Parking** 20 **Notes** LB

BIRCHANGER GREEN MOTORWAY SERVICE AREA (M11) Map 6 TL52
Essex

Days Inn Bishop's Stortford - M11

BUDGET HOTEL

☎ 01279 656477 📠 01279 656590
CM23 5QZ
e-mail: birchanger.hotel@welcomebreak.co.uk
web: www.welcomebreak.co.uk
dir: M11 junct 8

This modern building offers accommodation in smart, spacious and well-equipped bedrooms, suitable for families and business travellers, and all with en suite bathrooms. Continental breakfast is available and other refreshments may be taken at the nearby family restaurant. See also the Hotel Groups pages.

Rooms 60 (57 fmly) (10 smoking) **S** £49.95-£69.95; **D** £59.95-£79.95

BIRKENHEAD Map 15 SJ38
Merseyside

The RiverHill Hotel

★★★ 80% HOTEL

☎ 0151 653 3773 📠 0151 653 7162
Talbot Rd, Prenton CH43 2HJ
e-mail: reception@theriverhill.co.uk
dir: M53 junct 3, A552. Left onto B5151 at lights, hotel 0.5m on right

Pretty lawns and gardens provide the setting for this friendly, privately owned hotel, which is conveniently situated about a mile from the M53. Attractively furnished, well-equipped bedrooms include ground floor, family, and four-poster rooms. Business meetings and weddings can be catered for. A wide choice of dishes, on both carte and set menus, is available in the restaurant which overlooks the garden.

Rooms 15 (1 fmly) **Facilities** STV FTV Free use of local leisure facilities Wi-fi **Conf** Class 30 Board 52 Thtr 50 **Parking** 32 **Notes** ⊗ Civ Wed 40

Premier Inn Wirral (Greasby)

BUDGET HOTEL

☎ 0871 527 9176 📠 0871 527 9177
Greasby Rd, Greasby CH49 2PP
dir: 9m from Liverpool city centre. 2m from M53 junct 2. Just off B5139

High quality, budget accommodation ideal for both families and business travellers. Spacious, en suite bedrooms feature tea and coffee making facilities, and Freeview TV in most hotels. Internet access and Wi-fi are available for a small fee. The adjacent family restaurant features a wide and varied menu. See also the Hotel Groups pages.

Rooms 30 **D** £54-£57*

BIRMINGHAM Map 10 SP08
West Midlands

See also **Bromsgrove, Lea Marston, Oldbury & Sutton Coldfield**

Birmingham Marriott Hotel

Marriott HOTELS & RESORTS

★★★★ 78% HOTEL

☎ 0121 452 1144 📠 0121 456 3442
12 Hagley Rd, Five Ways B16 8SJ
e-mail: pascal.demarchi@marriotthotels.com
web: www.birminghammarriott.co.uk
dir: Leebank Middleway to Five Ways rdbt, 1st left then right. Follow signs for hotel

Situated in the suburb of Edgbaston, this Edwardian hotel is a prominent landmark on the outskirts of the city centre. Air-conditioned bedrooms are decorated in a comfortable, modern style and provide a comprehensive range of extra facilities. Public rooms include the contemporary, brasserie-style West 12 Bar and Restaurant.

Rooms 104 **Facilities** Spa STV Gym Steam room Wi-fi **Conf** Board 35 Thtr 80 **Services** Lift Air con **Parking** 50 **Notes** ⊗ Civ Wed 60

Hotel du Vin Birmingham

★★★★ 76% ◎

TOWN HOUSE HOTEL

☎ 0121 200 0600 📠 0121 236 0889
25 Church St B3 2NR
e-mail: info@birmingham.hotelduvin.com
web: www.hotelduvin.com
dir: M6 junct 6/A38(M) to city centre, over flyover. Keep left & exit at St Chads Circus signed Jewellery Quarter. At lights & rdbt take 1st exit, follow signs for Colmore Row, opposite cathedral. Right into Church St, across Barwick St. Hotel on right

The former Birmingham Eye Hospital has become a chic and sophisticated hotel. The stylish, high-ceilinged rooms, all with a wine theme, are luxuriously appointed and feature stunning bathrooms, sumptuous duvets and Egyptian cotton sheets. The Bistro offers relaxed dining and a top-notch wine list, while other attractions include a champagne bar, a wine boutique and a health club.

Rooms 66 **Facilities** Spa STV Gym Treatment rooms Steam room Sauna Xmas New Year Wi-fi **Conf** Class 40 Board 40 Thtr 84 **Services** Lift Air con **Notes** LB Civ Wed 84

B

BIRMINGHAM ***continued***

Mint Hotel Birmingham

★★★★ 76% ® HOTEL

☎ 0845 838 1255 & 0121 643 1003
🖹 0121 643 1005
1 Brunswick Square, Brindley Place B1 2HW
e-mail: birmingham.reservations@minthotel.com
web: www.minthotel.com
dir: M6 junct 6/A38M follow signs for A456. Right into Sheepcote St, hotel straight ahead

This large modern hotel is conveniently situated close to the heart of the city in the popular Brindley Place. Modern and contemporary in style, air-conditioned bedrooms are comfortable and well laid out, and feature iMacs, TV with Sky channels and free high speed Wi-fi. Public areas include a range of meeting rooms, the City Café and the restaurant which offers modern cuisine.

Rooms 238 (17 smoking) **S** £69-£225; **D** £69-£225* **Facilities** STV FTV Gym Xmas New Year Wi-fi **Conf** Class 50 Board 50 Thtr 120 Del from £130 to £185* **Services** Lift Air con **Parking** 24 **Notes** LB ⊗ Civ Wed 100

Macdonald Burlington

★★★★ 76% HOTEL

☎ 0844 879 9019 & 0121 643 9191
🖹 0121 628 5005
Burlington Arcade, 126 New St B2 4JQ
e-mail: events.burlington@macdonald-hotels.co.uk
web: www.macdonaldhotels.co.uk/burlington
dir: M6 junct 6, follow signs for city centre, then take A38

The Burlington's original Victorian grandeur - the marble and iron staircases and the high ceilings - blend seamlessly with modern facilities. Bedrooms are equipped to a good standard and public areas include a stylish bar and coffee lounge. The Berlioz Restaurant specialises in innovative dishes using fresh produce.

Rooms 115 (6 fmly) **S** £72-£234; **D** £142-£304* **Facilities** STV New Year Wi-fi **Conf** Class 175 Board 60 Thtr 400 Del from £139 to £195* **Services** Lift **Notes** LB Closed 24-26 Dec Civ Wed 400

Radisson Blu Hotel Birmingham

★★★★ 74% HOTEL

☎ 0121 654 6000 🖹 0121 654 6001
12 Holloway Circus, Queensway B1 1BT
e-mail: info.birmingham@radissonblu.com
dir: A3844, through A38 underpass, left, merge into Suffolk St Queensway. Hotel on corner of Holloway Circus Queensway

This modern glass structure of 39 floors sits in the heart of the city dominating the area with its concept design. The interior continues the modern look and feel. Public areas have wooden floors, leather seating and a stylish Italian restaurant. The bedrooms are individually designed with bold colours and designer pieces of furniture that create the wow factor. The small gym, sauna suite and spa areas add to the hotel's impressive facilities.

Rooms 211 (16 smoking) **Facilities** Spa STV FTV Gym Wi-fi **Conf** Class 48 Board 40 Thtr 130 **Services** Lift Air con **Notes** ⊗ Civ Wed 130

Novotel Birmingham Centre

★★★★ 71% HOTEL

☎ 0121 643 2000 🖹 0121 643 9786
70 Broad St B1 2HT
e-mail: h1077@accor.com
web: www.novotel.com
dir: A38/A456, hotel on right beyond International Convention Centre

This large, modern, purpose-built hotel benefits from an excellent city centre location, with the bonus of secure parking. Bedrooms are spacious, modern and well equipped especially for business users; four rooms have facilities for less able guests. Public areas include the Garden Brasserie, function rooms and a fitness room.

Rooms 148 (148 fmly) (11 smoking) **Facilities** Gym Fitness room Cardio-vascular equipment Sauna Steam room Wi-fi **Conf** Class 120 Board 90 Thtr 300 **Services** Lift Air con **Parking** 53 **Notes** LB

Copthorne Hotel Birmingham

★★★★ 69% HOTEL

☎ 0121 200 2727 🖹 0121 200 1197
Paradise Circus B3 3HJ
e-mail: reservations.birmingham@millenniumhotels.co.uk
web: www.millenniumhotels.co.uk
dir: M6 junct 6, city centre A38(M). After Queensway Tunnel, left, follow International Convention Centre signs. At Paradise Circus island take right lane

This hotel is one of the few establishments in the city that benefits from its own car park. Bedrooms are spacious and come in a choice of styles, all with excellent facilities. Guests can eat in the Bugis Street Brasserie that offers traditional Chinese, Singaporean and Malay cuisine.

Rooms 211 **Facilities** FTV Gym Xmas New Year Wi-fi **Conf** Class 120 Board 30 Thtr 200 Del from £99 to £199* **Services** Lift **Parking** 78 **Notes** LB ⊗ Civ Wed 150

Malmaison Birmingham

★★★ 83% ® HOTEL

☎ 0121 246 5000 🖹 0121 246 5002
1 Wharfside St, The Mailbox B1 1RD
e-mail: birmingham@malmaison.com
web: www.malmaison.com
dir: M6 junct 6, A38 towards Birmingham. Hotel within The Mailbox, signed from A38

The 'Mailbox' development, of which this stylish and contemporary hotel is a part, incorporates the very best in fashionable shopping, an array of restaurants and ample parking. Air-conditioned bedrooms are stylishly decorated and feature comprehensive facilities. Public rooms include a contemporary bar and brasserie which prove a hit with guests and locals alike. There's also Gymtonic, and Petit Spa that offers rejuvenating treatments.

Rooms 189 **Facilities** Gym Wi-fi **Conf** Class 40 Board 24 Thtr 50 **Services** Lift Air con

B

Best Western Westley

★★★ 82% HOTEL

☎ 0121 706 4312 📠 0121 706 2824
80-90 Westley Rd, Acocks Green B27 7UJ
e-mail: reservations@westley-hotel.co.uk
dir: A41 signed Birmingham on Solihull by-pass, continue to Acocks Green. At rdbt, 2nd exit B4146 Westley Rd. Hotel 200yds on left

Situated in the city suburbs and conveniently located for the N.E.C. and the airport, this friendly hotel provides well-equipped, smartly presented bedrooms. In addition to the main restaurant, there is also a lively bar and brasserie together with a large function room.

Rooms 37 (11 annexe) (1 fmly) (3 GF) **Facilities** STV ♫ New Year Wi-fi **Conf** Class 80 Board 50 Thtr 200 **Parking** 150 **Notes** ⊗ Civ Wed 200

Thistle Birmingham City

thistle

★★★ 80% HOTEL

☎ 0871 376 9005 📠 0871 376 9105
St Chads, Queensway B4 6HY
e-mail: birminghamcity@thistle.co.uk
web: www.thistle.com/birminghamcity
dir: From M6 junct 6 onto Aston Expressway towards city centre, after 1m exit A38 signed Jewellery Quarter. Hotel on left

This hotel benefits from a central location and is convenient for both the motorway network and nearby extensive parking facilities. Bedrooms range in size and style with most bedrooms providing air conditioning, along with a host of thoughtful guest extras. A modern comfortable lounge bar links to a terrace area. Thistle Hotels – AA Hotel Group of the Year 2011-12.

Rooms 133 (3 fmly) **Facilities** STV Xmas New Year Wi-fi **Conf** Class 90 Board 35 Thtr 180 **Services** Lift **Notes** ⊗ Civ Wed 170

Holiday Inn Birmingham City

Holiday Inn

★★★ 79% HOTEL

☎ 0871 942 9008 📠 0121 631 2528
Smallbrook Queensway B5 4EW
e-mail: reservations-birminghamcity@ihg.com
web: www.holidayinn.co.uk
dir: M6 junct 6, A38(M) to city centre, keep left after flyover & two underpasses. 2nd left into Suffolk Place. 1st right into St Jude's Passage

This is a large hotel in the city centre with extensive meeting rooms and a business centre. The lounge bar with a roof terrace is a popular meeting place. The Albany Restaurant offers lunch and dinner; room service is also available.

Rooms 241 (8 fmly) **D** £99-£139* **Facilities** STV FTV Xmas New Year Wi-fi **Conf** Class 300 Board 150 Thtr 630 Del from £119 to £189* **Services** Lift Air con **Parking** 10 **Notes** LB Civ Wed 630

Menzies Strathallan

MenziesHotels

★★★ 75% HOTEL

☎ 0121 455 9777 📠 0121 454 9432
225 Hagley Rd, Edgbaston B16 9RY
e-mail: strathallan@menzieshotels.co.uk
web: www.menzies-hotels.co.uk
dir: From A38 follow signs for ICC into Broad St, towards Five Ways island, take underpass to Hagley Rd. Hotel 1m

Located just a few minutes from the city's central attractions and with the benefit of excellent parking, this hotel provides a range of comfortable and well-equipped bedrooms. A modern lounge bar and contemporary restaurant offer a good range of dining options.

Rooms 135 **Facilities** Xmas New Year Wi-fi **Conf** Class 90 Board 50 Thtr 170 **Services** Lift **Parking** 120 **Notes** ⊗ Civ Wed 40

Edgbaston Palace

★★★ 72% HOTEL

☎ 0121 452 1577 📠 0121 455 7933
198-200 Hagley Rd, Edgbaston B16 9PQ
e-mail: enquiries@edgbastonpalacehotel.com
dir: M5 junct 3 N, A456 for 4.3m. Hotel on right

Dating back to the 19th century, this Grade II listed Victorian property has bedrooms that are modern, well appointed and offer good comfort levels. The hospitality is warm, personal and refreshing. Supervised children under 18 are welcome.

Rooms 48 (21 annexe) (3 fmly) (16 GF) **Facilities** FTV Wi-fi **Conf** Class 70 Board 60 Thtr 200 **Parking** 70 **Notes** ⊗

Holiday Inn Birmingham M6 Jct 7

Holiday Inn

★★★ 72% HOTEL

☎ 0871 942 9009 & 0121 357 7303
📠 0121 357 7503
Chapel Ln, Great Barr B43 7BG
e-mail: birminghamgreatbarr@ihg.com
web: www.holidayinn.co.uk
dir: M6 junct 7, A34 signed Walsall. Hotel 200yds on right across carriageway in Chapel Ln

Situated in pleasant surroundings, this modern hotel offers well-equipped and comfortable bedrooms. Public areas include the popular Traders restaurant and a comfortable lounge where a menu is available to guests all day. There is also 24-hour room service; a courtyard patio and a garden.

Rooms 190 (45 fmly) (67 GF) (12 smoking) **S** £59-£119; **D** £69-£129 (incl. bkfst)* **Facilities** STV FTV supervised Gym Xmas New Year Wi-fi **Conf** Class 75 Board 50 Thtr 160 **Services** Air con **Parking** 250 **Notes** LB Civ Wed 160

Ramada Encore Birmingham City Centre

★★★ 71% HOTEL

☎ 0121 622 8800 📠 0121 622 8810
Ernerst Street/Holloway Head B1 1NS
e-mail: reservations@encorebirmingham.co.uk
dir: M6 junct 6/A38, merge onto A5127, follow A38 onto A41 exit onto Suffolk Queensway, at rdbt take 4th exit onto Holloway Head

Located in the heart of the city, this hotel offers stylish and comfortable accommodation. 'The Hub' is a smart, modern, open plan bar and restaurant with a choice of seating areas and offers a full dining menu all day. Secure on site parking is a plus.

Rooms 131 (11 fmly) **D** £49-£149 **Facilities** STV Xmas New Year Wi-fi **Conf** Class 10 Board 20 Thtr 30 Del from £89 to £119* **Services** Lift **Parking** 24 **Notes** ⊗

B

BIRMINGHAM *continued*

Great Barr Hotel & Conference Centre

★★★ 67% HOTEL

☎ 0121 357 1141 📠 0121 357 7557
Pear Tree Dr, Newton Rd, Great Barr B43 6HS
e-mail: sales@thegreatbarrhotel.com
web: www.thegreatbarrhotel.com
dir: M6 junct 7, at Scott Arms x-rds right towards West Bromwich (A4010) Newton Rd. Hotel 1m on right

This busy hotel, situated in a leafy residential area, is particularly popular with business clients. It has excellent, state-of-the-art training and seminar facilities. There is a traditional oak-panelled bar and formal restaurant. The bedrooms are appointed to a good standard and have the expected amenities.

Rooms 92 (6 fmly) **Facilities** STV Xmas Wi-fi **Conf** Class 90 Board 60 Thtr 200 **Parking** 200 **Notes** ⊗ RS Bank Hols - restaurant may close Civ Wed 200

Park Inn Birmingham Walsall, M6 Jct 9

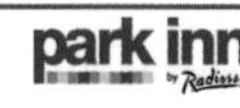

★★★ 66% HOTEL

☎ 01922 639100 📠 01922 709764
Bescot Crescent WS1 4SE
e-mail: reservations.walsall@rezidorparkinn.com
dir: M6 junct 9 (signed Wednesbury), A461 (signed Walsall). At lights right onto A4148 (signed Ring Road/Birmingham/ A34). At lights right into Bescot Cres (signed Bescot Stadium) pass stadium, hotel on left. (NB use WS1 4SA for Sat Nav)

This hotel is set just off the motorway and within easy reach of all the attractions around Birmingham, including the NEC. The bedrooms are bright and modern; all have air conditioning and spacious work desks. There are family rooms, twin rooms and double rooms. The spacious Hub Bar & Restaurant is where a hot buffet breakfast is served. A meeting room and a fitness suite are also available.

Rooms 121

Comfort Inn Birmingham

★★ 62% METRO HOTEL

☎ 0121 643 1134 📠 0121 643 3209
Station St B5 4DY
e-mail: enquiries@thecomfortinnbirmingham.co.uk
dir: M6 junct 6, A38(M) towards city centre. Take Queensway Ring Road, Holloway Head to Smallbridge Queensway. Left into Hill St, 2nd right into Station St

Conveniently located next to New Street station, this hotel offers practical and comfortable accommodation. Public areas include a breakfast room and a public bar with large-screen TV.

Rooms 40 (3 fmly) (10 smoking) **Facilities** Wi-fi **Conf** Class 25 Board 25 Thtr 45 **Services** Lift **Notes** ⊗

Crowne Plaza Birmingham City Centre

U

☎ 0121 224 5000
Central Square, Holliday St B1 1HH
e-mail: enquiries@cpbhamcity.com
web: www.crowneplaza.com
dir: A38, follow city centre signs. After 2nd tunnel (Suffolk Queensway) into left slip road, follow signs for New St Station & The Mailbox. Hotel adjacent to The Mailbox

Currently the rating for this establishment is not confirmed. This may be due to a change of ownership or because it has only recently joined the AA rating scheme. For further details please see the AA website: theAA.com

Rooms 312 (115 fmly) **S** £70-£225; **D** £70-£225 **Facilities** STV FTV Gym Wi-fi **Conf** Class 150 Board 40 Thtr 300 Del from £120 to £250 **Services** Lift Air con **Notes** LB Civ Wed 200

Campanile Birmingham

Campanile HOTEL RESTAURANT

BUDGET HOTEL

☎ 0121 359 3330 📠 0121 359 1223
Chester St, Aston B6 4BE
e-mail: birmingham@campanile.com
dir: Next to rdbt at junct of A4540/A38

This modern building offers accommodation in smart, well-equipped bedrooms, all with en suite bathrooms. Refreshments may be taken at the informal bistro. See also the Hotel Groups pages.

Rooms 110 (5 fmly) **Conf** Class 100 Board 100 Thtr 250

Express by Holiday Inn Birmingham

BUDGET HOTEL

☎ 0121 747 6633 📠 0121 747 6644
1200 Chester Rd, Castle Bromwich B35 7AF
e-mail: castlebromwich@holidayinnexpress.co.uk
web: www.hiexpress.com/birminghamex
dir: M6 junct 5/6/A38 for Tyburn, right into Chester Rd, follow Park signs

A modern hotel ideal for families and business travellers. Fresh and uncomplicated, the spacious rooms include Sky TV, power shower and tea and coffee-making facilities. Continental buffet breakfast is included in the room rate; other meals may be taken at the nearby family pub or restaurant. See also the Hotel Groups pages.

Rooms 110 (21 fmly) (12 GF) **Conf** Class 16 Board 16 Thtr 20

Holiday Inn Express Birmingham City Centre

BUDGET HOTEL

☎ 0845 1126151 📠 0121 200 1910
65 Lionel St B3 1JE
e-mail: enquiries@hiexpressbirminghamcitycentre.co.uk
web: www.hiexpress.com/exb'minghamc
dir: A38 to City Centre until Paradise Circus, take 4th exit on Queensway, 1st left into Lionel St, hotel on right

A modern hotel ideal for families and business travellers. Fresh and uncomplicated, the spacious rooms include Sky TV, power shower and tea and coffee-making facilities. Continental buffet breakfast is included in the room rate; other meals may be taken at the nearby family pub or restaurant. See also the Hotel Groups pages.

Rooms 120 (80 fmly) **S** £55-£150; **D** £55-£150 (incl. bkfst)* **Conf** Class 16 Board 16 Thtr 30

Holiday Inn Express Birmingham-South A45

BUDGET HOTEL

☎ 0121 289 3333 📠 0121 289 3334
1270 Coventry Rd, Yardley B25 8BS
e-mail: reservations@hiex-birmingham.co.uk

Rooms 83

Ibis Birmingham Bordesley Circus

BUDGET HOTEL

☎ 0121 506 2600 📠 0121 506 2610
1 Bordesley Park Rd, Bordesley B10 0PD
e-mail: H2178@accor.com
web: www.ibishotel.com

Modern, budget hotel offering comfortable accommodation in bright and practical bedrooms. Breakfast is self-service and dinner is available in the restaurant. See also the Hotel Groups pages.

Rooms 87 (16 GF)

Ibis Birmingham City Centre

BUDGET HOTEL

☎ 0121 622 6010 📠 0121 622 6020
Arcadian Centre, Ladywell Walk B5 4ST
e-mail: h1459@accor-hotels.com
web: www.ibishotel.com
dir: From motorways follow city centre signs. Then follow Bullring or Indoor Market signs. Hotel adjacent to market

Rooms 159 (5 fmly) **Conf** Class 60 Board 50 Thtr 120

Ibis Birmingham Holloway Circus

BUDGET HOTEL

☎ 0121 622 4925 📠 0121 622 4195
55 Irving St B1 1DH
e-mail: H2092@accor.com
web: www.ibishotel.com
dir: From M6 take A38/City Centre, left after 2nd tunnel. Right at rdbt, 4th left (Sutton St) into Irving St. Hotel on left

Rooms 51 (2 fmly) (26 GF) **S** £52-£125; **D** £52-£125*

Premier Inn Birmingham Broad Street (Brindley Place)

BUDGET HOTEL

☎ 0871 527 8076 📠 0871 527 8077
80 Broad St B15 1AU
dir: M6 junct 6, A38 (Aston Expressway). Follow City Centre, ICC & NIA signs into Broad St. Right into Sheepcote St. 2nd left at rdbt into Essington St. Hotel on left. (NB for Sat Nav use B16 8AL)

High quality, budget accommodation ideal for both families and business travellers. Spacious, en suite bedrooms feature tea and coffee making facilities, and Freeview TV in most hotels. Internet access and Wi-fi are available for a small fee. The adjacent family restaurant features a wide and varied menu. See also the Hotel Groups pages.

Rooms 62 **D** £63-£69*

Premier Inn Birmingham Broad Street Canal Side

BUDGET HOTEL

☎ 0871 527 8078 📠 0871 527 8079
20 Bridge St B1 2JH
dir: M6 junct 6, A3(M) towards city centre. Follow signs for city centre/ICC/A456 (Broad St). Left at Hyatt Hotel, hotel on right at bottom of Bridge St

Rooms 83 **D** £62-£69*

Premier Inn Birmingham Central East

BUDGET HOTEL

☎ 0871 527 8080 📠 0871 527 8081
Richard St, Aston, Waterlinks B7 4AA
dir: M6 junct 6, signed city centre. A38(M) signed A4540 (ring road). At rdbt 1st exit 50mtrs left into Richard St, hotel on left (barrier access to car park)

Rooms 61 **D** £58-£65*

Premier Inn Birmingham Central (Hagley Road)

BUDGET HOTEL

☎ 0871 527 8082 📠 0871 527 8083
Hagley Rd B16 9NY
dir: M6 junct 6, A38 (Aston Express Way). Follow city centre, ICC & NIA signs, into Broad St. From M5 junct 3, A456 for approx 3m, hotel on left

Rooms 62 **D** £62-£68*

Premier Inn Birmingham City Centre (Waterloo Street)

BUDGET HOTEL

☎ 0871 527 8074 📠 0871 527 8075
3-6 Waterloo St B2 5PG
dir: M6 junct 6, A38 (Corporation St). Follow West Bromwich/A41 signs. Merge into St Chad's Queensway. 2nd exit for Great Charles St Queensway, becomes Livery St. Left into Waterloo St

Rooms 109 **D** £63-£71*

Premier Inn Birmingham (Great Barr/M6 Jct 7)

BUDGET HOTEL

☎ 0871 527 8072 📠 0871 527 8073
Birmingham Rd, Great Barr B43 7AG
dir: M6 junct 7, A34 towards Walsall. Hotel on left behind Beacon Harvester

Rooms 32 **D** £50-£59*

Premier Inn Birmingham South (Hall Green)

BUDGET HOTEL

☎ 0871 527 8092 📠 0871 527 8093
Stratford Rd, Hall Green B28 9ES
dir: M42 junct 4, A34 towards Shirley signed Birmingham. Straight on at 6 rdbts. At 7th rdbt 4th exit. Hotel on left

Rooms 51 **D** £52-£60*

BIRMINGHAM AIRPORT
West Midlands — **Map 10 SP08**

Novotel Birmingham Airport

★★★★ 71% HOTEL

☎ 0121 782 7000 & 782 4111 📠 0121 782 0445
B26 3QL
e-mail: H1158@accor.com
web: www.novotel.com
dir: M42 junct 6/A45 to Birmingham, signed to airport. Hotel opposite main terminal

This large, purpose-built hotel is located opposite the main passenger terminal. Bedrooms are spacious, modern in style and well equipped, including Playstations to keep the children busy. Several rooms have facilities for less able guests. The Garden Brasserie is open from noon until midnight; the bar is open 24 hours and a full room service is available.

Rooms 195 (24 fmly) **Facilities** STV Gym Fitness room Wi-fi **Conf** Class 10 Board 20 Thtr 35 **Services** Lift Air con

B

BIRMINGHAM AIRPORT *continued*

Ibis Birmingham Airport

BUDGET HOTEL

☎ 0121 780 5800 📠 0121 780 5810
Ambassador Rd, Bickenhill, Solihull B26 3AW
e-mail: H6359@accor.com
dir: M42 junct 6, A45 follow signs to Birmingham Airport

Modern, budget hotel offering comfortable accommodation in bright and practical bedrooms. Breakfast is self-service and dinner is available in the restaurant. See also the Hotel Groups pages.

Rooms 162 (2 fmly)

BIRMINGHAM (NATIONAL EXHIBITION CENTRE) Map 10 SP18
West Midlands

Nailcote Hall

★★★★ 75% ® HOTEL

☎ 024 7646 6174 📠 024 7647 0720
Nailcote Ln, Berkswell CV7 7DE
e-mail: info@nailcotehall.co.uk
web: www.nailcotehall.co.uk

(For full entry see Balsall Common)

Best Western Premier Moor Hall Hotel & Spa

★★★★ 75% HOTEL

☎ 0121 308 3751 📠 0121 308 8974
Moor Hall Dr, Four Oaks B75 6LN
e-mail: mail@moorhallhotel.co.uk
web: www.moorhallhotel.co.uk

(For full entry see Sutton Coldfield)

Crowne Plaza Birmingham NEC

★★★★ 74% HOTEL

☎ 0871 942 9160 📠 0121 781 4321
National Exhibition Centre, Pendigo Way B40 1PS
e-mail: necroomsales@ihg.com
web: www.crowneplaza.co.uk
dir: M42 junct 6, follow signs for NEC, take 2nd exit on left, South Way for hotel entrance 50mtrs on right

On the doorstep of the NEC and overlooking Pendigo Lake, this hotel has contemporary design and offers well-equipped bedrooms with air conditioning. Rooms have ample working space and high-speed internet access (for an additional charge). Eating options include the modern Pendigo Restaurant overlooking the lake, the bar and 24-hour room service.

Rooms 242 (12 fmly) (15 smoking) **Facilities** STV Gym Sauna Wi-fi **Conf** Class 140 Board 56 Thtr 200 **Services** Lift Air con **Parking** 348 **Notes** ⊗

Arden Hotel & Leisure Club

★★★ 73% HOTEL

☎ 01675 443221 📠 01675 445604
Coventry Rd, Bickenhill B92 0EH
e-mail: enquiries@ardenhotel.co.uk
dir: M42 junct 6/A45 towards Birmingham. Hotel 0.25m on right, just off Birmingham International railway island

This smart hotel neighbouring the NEC offers modern rooms and well-equipped leisure facilities. After dinner in the formal restaurant, the place to relax is the spacious lounge area. A buffet breakfast is served in the bright and airy Meeting Place.

Rooms 216 (6 fmly) (6 GF) (12 smoking) **Facilities** Spa STV 🏊 supervised Gym Sports therapy Beautician ♫ Xmas New Year Wi-fi **Conf** Class 40 Board 60 Thtr 200 **Services** Lift **Parking** 300 **Notes** Closed 25-28 Dec Civ Wed 100

Haigs Hotel

★★★ 73% HOTEL

☎ 01676 533004 📠 01676 535132
Kenilworth Rd CV7 7EL
e-mail: info@haigshotel.co.uk

(For full entry see Balsall Common)

Heath Lodge Hotel

★★ 70% HOTEL

☎ 0121 779 2218 & 07860 887212
📠 0121 770 5648
117 Coleshill Rd, Marston Green B37 7HT
e-mail: enquiries@heathlodgehotel.co.uk
dir: 1m N of NEC or Birmingham International Airport & station. M6 junct 4, A446 signed North/Coleshill, 400yds, at rdbt left onto Coleshill Heath Rd. 0.5m, straight on at rdbt to Marston Green. Hotel at 2nd junct on right

This privately owned and personally run hotel is ideally located for visitors to the NEC and Birmingham Airport. Hospitality and service standards are high and while some bedrooms are compact, all are well equipped and comfortable. Public areas include a bar and a lounge, and a dining room that overlooks the pretty garden.

Rooms 23 (1 fmly) (6 GF) **Facilities** FTV Xmas Wi-fi **Conf** Class 30 Board 20 Thtr 35 **Parking** 23 **Notes** LB No children 2yrs

Holiday Inn Express Birmingham NEC

BUDGET HOTEL

☎ 0121 782 3222 📠 0121 780 4323
Bickenhill Parkway, Bickenhill B40 1QA
e-mail: birmingham@morethanhotels.com
web: www.hiexpressbirminghamnec.co.uk
dir: Follow signs for NEC from M42 junct 6

A modern hotel ideal for families and business travellers. Fresh and uncomplicated, the spacious rooms include Sky TV, power shower and tea and coffee-making facilities. Continental buffet breakfast is included in the room rate; other meals may be taken at the nearby family pub or restaurant. See also the Hotel Groups pages.

Rooms 179 (91 fmly) (23 GF) (3 smoking) **Conf** Class 32 Board 32 Thtr 80

Premier Inn Birmingham NEC/Airport

BUDGET HOTEL

☎ 0871 527 8086 📠 0871 527 8087
Off Bickenhill Parkway, National Exhibition Centre B40 1QA
dir: M42 junct 6 signed NEC. Turn right towards North Way. Follow Premier Inn signs. Hotel on left at 5th rdbt

High quality, budget accommodation ideal for both families and business travellers. Spacious, en suite bedrooms feature tea and coffee making facilities, and Freeview TV in most hotels. Internet access and Wi-fi are available for a small fee. The adjacent family restaurant features a wide and varied menu. See also the Hotel Groups pages.

Rooms 199 **D** £65-£75*

BILSBORROW Map 18 SD53
Lancashire

Premier Inn Preston North

BUDGET HOTEL

☎ 0871 527 8912 📠 0871 527 8913
Garstang Rd PR3 0RN
dir: 4m from M6 junct 32 on A6 towards Garstang. 7m from Preston

High quality, budget accommodation ideal for both families and business travellers. Spacious, en suite bedrooms feature tea and coffee making facilities, and Freeview TV in most hotels. Internet access and Wi-fi are available for a small fee. The adjacent family restaurant features a wide and varied menu. See also the Hotel Groups pages.

Rooms 40 **D** £55*

BISHOP AUCKLAND Map 19 NZ22
Co Durham

Premier Inn Bishop Auckland

BUDGET HOTEL

☎ 0871 527 8096 📠 0871 527 8097
West Auckland Rd DL14 9AP
dir: From S: A1 junct 58, left onto A68 signed Corbridge/Bishop Auckland. At 1st rdbt 2nd exit onto A6072 signed Shildon. Straight on at 4 rdbts, follow Shildon/Bishop Auckland signs. Hotel approx 1m on left

High quality, budget accommodation ideal for both families and business travellers. Spacious, en suite bedrooms feature tea and coffee making facilities, and Freeview TV in most hotels. Internet access and Wi-fi are available for a small fee. The adjacent family restaurant features a wide and varied menu. See also the Hotel Groups pages.

Rooms 49 **D** £53-£58*

BISHOP'S STORTFORD Map 6 TL42
Hertfordshire

Down Hall Country House

★★★★ 75% ◎◎ HOTEL

☎ 01279 731441 📠 01279 730416
Hatfield Heath CM22 7AS
e-mail: reservations@downhall.co.uk
web: www.downhall.co.uk
dir: A1060, at Hatfield Heath keep left. Turn right into lane opposite Hunters Meet restaurant, left at end, follow sign

Imposing country-house hotel set amidst 100 acres of mature grounds in a peaceful location just a short drive from Stansted Airport. Bedrooms are generally quite spacious; each one is pleasantly decorated, tastefully furnished and equipped with modern facilities. Public rooms include a choice of restaurants, a cocktail bar, two lounges and leisure facilities.

Rooms 99 (20 GF) **Facilities** FTV Giant chess Whirlpool Sauna Snooker room Gym equipment Xmas New Year Wi-fi **Conf** Class 140 Board 68 Thtr 200 Del from £149 to £209* **Services** Lift **Parking** 150 **Notes** Civ Wed 150

Days Hotel London Stansted - M11

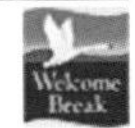

BUDGET HOTEL

☎ 01279 213900 📠 01279 213901
M11 Motorway, Junction 8, Old Dunmow Rd CM23 5QZ
dir: Adjacent to M11 junct 8

This modern building offers accommodation in smart, spacious and well-equipped bedrooms, suitable for families and business travellers, and all with en suite bathrooms. There is an attractive lounge area and a dining room where breakfast is served and other refreshments may be taken. See also the Hotel Groups pages.

Rooms 77 (16 fmly) (16 GF) (8 smoking) **S** £49.95-£69.95; **D** £59.95-£79.95

BISHOPSTEIGNTON Map 3 SX97
Devon

Cockhaven Manor Hotel

THE INDEPENDENTS HOTEL ASSOCIATION

★★ 71% HOTEL

☎ 01626 775252 📠 01626 775572
Cockhaven Rd TQ14 9RF
e-mail: cockhaven@btconnect.com
web: www.cockhavenmanor.com
dir: M5/A380 towards Torquay, then A381 towards Teignmouth. Left at Metro Motors. Hotel 500yds on left

A friendly, family-run inn that dates back to the 16th century. Bedrooms are well equipped and many enjoy views across the beautiful Teign estuary. A choice of dining options is offered, and traditional and interesting dishes, along with locally caught fish, prove popular.

Rooms 12 (2 fmly) **S** £50-£65; **D** £75-£90 (incl. bkfst)* **Facilities** FTV Petanque Wi-fi **Conf** Class 50 Board 30 Thtr 50 Del from £75 to £90* **Parking** 50 **Notes** LB Closed 25-26 Dec

BLACKBURN Map 18 SD62
Lancashire

See also **Langho**

Mercure Blackburn Foxfields Country Hotel

★★★ 76% HOTEL

☎ 01254 822556 📠 01254 824613
Whalley Rd, Billington BB7 9HY
e-mail: enquiries@hotels-blackburn.com
dir: Just off A59

This modern hotel is easily accessible from major road networks. Bedrooms are comfortable and spacious, and include some suites and others with separate dressing areas. Facilities include a good-sized swimming pool, a small gym and conference suites. The traditional restaurant serves an interesting range of cuisine.

Rooms 44 (16 annexe) (27 fmly) (13 GF) (8 smoking) **S** £55-£125; **D** £65-£135 **Facilities** STV FTV Gym Sauna Steam room Xmas New Year Wi-fi **Conf** Class 60 Board 60 Thtr 140 Del from £110 to £145 **Parking** 194 **Notes** LB Civ Wed 200

Millstone at Mellor

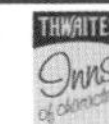

★★ 85% ◎◎ HOTEL

☎ 01254 813333 📠 01254 812628
Church Ln, Mellor BB2 7JR
e-mail: relax@millstonehotel.co.uk
web: www.millstonehotel.co.uk
dir: 3m NW off A59

Once a coaching inn, the Millstone is situated in a village just outside the town. The hotel provides a very high standard of accommodation, professional and friendly service and good food. Bedrooms, some in an adjacent house, are comfortable and generally spacious, and all are very well equipped. A room for less able guests is also available.

Rooms 23 (6 annexe) (5 fmly) (8 GF) **S** £90-£150; **D** £100-£200 (incl. bkfst)* **Facilities** STV New Year Wi-fi **Parking** 40 **Notes** LB Civ Wed 60

B

BLACKBURN *continued*

Premier Inn Blackburn North West

BUDGET HOTEL

☎ 0871 527 8098 🖷 0871 527 8099
Myerscough Rd, Balderstone BB2 7LE
dir: M6 junct 31, A59 towards Clitheroe. Hotel opposite British Aerospace, adjacent to Boddington Arms

High quality, budget accommodation ideal for both families and business travellers. Spacious, en suite bedrooms feature tea and coffee making facilities, and Freeview TV in most hotels. Internet access and Wi-fi are available for a small fee. The adjacent family restaurant features a wide and varied menu. See also the Hotel Groups pages.

Rooms 20 **D** £50-£56*

Premier Inn Blackburn South

BUDGET HOTEL

☎ 0871 527 8100 🖷 0871 527 8101
Off Eccleshill Rd, Riversway Dr, Lower Darwen BB3 0SN
dir: At M65 junct 4

Rooms 43 **D** £50-£56*

BLACKPOOL Lancashire **Map 18 SD33**

Barceló Blackpool Imperial Hotel

★★★★ 73% HOTEL

☎ 01253 623971 🖷 01253 751784
North Promenade FY1 2HB
e-mail: imperialblackpool@barcelo-hotels.co.uk
web: www.barcelo-hotels.co.uk
dir: M55 junct 2, take A583 North Shore, follow signs to North Promenade. Hotel on seafront, north of tower

Enjoying a prime seafront location, this grand Victorian hotel offers smartly appointed, well-equipped bedrooms and spacious, elegant public areas. Facilities include a smart leisure club, a comfortable lounge, the No.10 bar and an attractive split-level restaurant that overlooks the seafront. Conferences and functions are extremely well catered for.

Rooms 180 (16 fmly) **Facilities** Spa STV 🏊 supervised Gym Xmas New Year Wi-fi **Conf** Class 280 Board 70 Thtr 600 **Services** Lift **Parking** 150 **Notes** Civ Wed 200

Big Blue Hotel

★★★★ 72% HOTEL

☎ 0871 222 4000 & 01253 400045
🖷 01253 400046
Ocean Boulevard FY4 1ND
e-mail: reservations@bigbluehotel.com
dir: M6 junct 32 onto M55. Follow tourist signs for Pleasure Beach. Hotel on Pleasure Beach near rail station

This stylish hotel is ideally located adjacent to the Pleasure Beach, boasting excellent family facilities. A large proportion of family suites offer separate children's rooms furnished with bunk beds, each with their own individual TV screens. Spacious executive rooms boast seating areas with flat-screen TVs and DVD players. Public areas include a smart bar and brasserie, a range of meeting facilities and a residents' gym.

Rooms 157 (84 fmly) (37 GF) (4 smoking) **S** £71-£129; **D** £81-£139 (incl. bkfst)* **Facilities** FTV Gym New Year Wi-fi **Conf** Class 25 Board 30 Thtr 55 Del from £105 to £179* **Services** Lift Air con **Parking** 80 **Notes** LB ⊗ Closed 20-28 Dec Civ Wed 40

Best Western Carlton Hotel

★★★ 78% ◎ HOTEL

☎ 01253 628966 🖷 01253 752587
282-286 North Promenade FY1 2EZ
e-mail: mail@carltonhotelblackpool.co.uk
web: www.bw-carltonhotel.co.uk
dir: M6 junct 32/M55 follow signs for North Shore. Between Blackpool Tower & Gynn Sq

Enjoying a prime seafront location, this hotel offers bedrooms that are attractively furnished in modern style. Public areas include a choice of bar lounge and seafront lounges. The fine dining Jali Indian Restaurant is a contrast to the traditional dining room; extensive function facilities are available and a warm welcome is assured.

Rooms 58 (9 fmly) **S** £50-£75; **D** £60-£115 (incl. bkfst) **Facilities** STV FTV Xmas New Year Wi-fi **Conf** Class 40 Board 40 Thtr 90 Del from £85 to £135 **Services** Lift **Parking** 43 **Notes** LB ⊗ Civ Wed 80

Carousel

★★★ 77% HOTEL

☎ 01253 402642 🖷 01253 341100
663-671 New South Prom FY4 1RN
e-mail: carousel.reservations@sleepwellhotels.com
web: www.sleepwellhotels.com
dir: From M55 follow signs to airport, pass airport to lights. Turn right, hotel 100yds on right

This friendly seafront hotel, close to the Pleasure Beach, offers smart, contemporary accommodation. Bedrooms are comfortably appointed and have a modern, stylish feel to them. An airy restaurant and a spacious bar/lounge both overlook the Promenade. The hotel has good conference/meeting facilities and its own car park.

Rooms 92 (22 fmly) **S** £50-£90; **D** £60-£140 (incl. bkfst) **Facilities** FTV ♫ Xmas New Year Wi-fi **Conf** Class 30 Board 40 Thtr 100 Del from £125 to £175 **Services** Lift **Parking** 46 **Notes** LB ⊗ Civ Wed 150

Claremont

★★ 75% HOTEL

☎ 0845 458 4222 🖷 01253 754222
270 North Promenade FY1 1SA
e-mail: reservations@choice-hotels.co.uk
dir: M55 junct 3 follow sign for promenade. Hotel beyond North Pier

Conveniently situated this is a popular family holiday hotel. The bedrooms are bright and attractively decorated. The extensive public areas include a spacious air-conditioned restaurant which offers a good choice of dishes. There is a well equipped, supervised children's play room, and entertainment is provided during the season.

Rooms 143 (50 fmly) **Facilities** 🏊 ♫ Xmas New Year Wi-fi **Conf** Class 300 Board 75 Thtr 530 **Services** Lift **Parking** 40 **Notes** LB ⊗

The Viking Hotel

★★ 75% HOTEL

☎ 0845 458 4222 🖷 01253 754222
479 South Promenade FY4 1AY
e-mail: reservations@choice-hotels.co.uk
dir: M55 junct 3, follow Pleasure Beach signs

Located close to the centre of the South Promenade, this establishment offers well equipped accommodation and a warm welcome. Meals are served in the attractive sea view restaurant and entertainment is available in the renowned 'Talk of the Coast' night club. Leisure facilities at sister hotels are also available free of charge.

Rooms 101 (10 GF) (25 smoking) **Facilities** Cabaret club ♫ Xmas New Year **Services** Lift **Parking** 50 **Notes** LB ⊗ No children 18yrs

The Cliffs Hotel

★★ 74% HOTEL

☎ 0845 458 4222 & 01253 595559
🖷 01253 754222
Queens Promenade FY2 9SG
e-mail: reservations@choice-hotels.co.uk
dir: M55 junct 3, follow Promenade signs. Hotel just after rdbt

This large, privately owned and extremely popular hotel is within easy reach of the town centre. The bedrooms, including spacious family rooms, vary in size. Public areas offer an all-day coffee shop, a smart restaurant and a family room where children are entertained.

Rooms 163 (53 fmly) **Facilities** ⓢ supervised Gym Beauty treatments ♫ Xmas New Year Wi-fi **Conf** Class 210 Board 50 Thtr 475 **Services** Lift **Parking** 30 **Notes** LB ⊗

Hotel Sheraton

★★ 72% HOTEL

☎ 01253 352723 🖷 01253 595499
54-62 Queens Promenade FY2 9RP
e-mail: email@hotelsheraton.co.uk
web: www.hotelsheraton.co.uk
dir: 1m N from Blackpool Tower towards Fleetwood

This family-owned and run hotel is situated at the quieter, northern end of the promenade. Public areas include a choice of spacious lounges with sea views, a large function suite where popular dancing and cabaret evenings are held, and a heated indoor swimming pool. The smartly appointed bedrooms come in a range of sizes and styles.

Rooms 104 (45 fmly) (15 smoking) **Facilities** ⓢ Table tennis Darts ♫ Xmas New Year **Conf** Class 100 Board 150 Thtr 200 **Services** Lift **Parking** 20 **Notes** ⊗

Headlands

★★ 68% HOTEL

☎ 01253 341179 🖷 01253 342657
611-613 South Promenade FY4 1NJ
e-mail: headlandshotel@aol.com
dir: From end of M55 follow South Promenade signs

This friendly, family owned hotel stands on the South Promenade, close to the Pleasure Beach and many of the town's major attractions. Bedrooms are traditionally furnished and many enjoy sea views. There is a choice of lounges and live entertainment is provided regularly. Home cooked food is served in the panelled dining room.

Rooms 41 (10 fmly) **S** £25-£51.95; **D** £50-£103.90 (incl. bkfst)* **Facilities** Darts Games room Pool Snooker ♫ Xmas New Year **Services** Lift **Parking** 46 **Notes** LB Closed 2-15 Jan

Lyndene

★★ 🅰 HOTEL

☎ 01253 346779 🖷 01253 346466
303/315 Promenade FY1 6AN
e-mail: enquiries@lyndenehotel.com

Rooms 140 (60 fmly) (12 GF) (140 smoking) **Facilities** FTV ♫ Xmas New Year Wi-fi **Services** Lift **Parking** 70 **Notes** ⊗ No children 5yrs

Premier Inn Blackpool Airport

BUDGET HOTEL

☎ 0871 527 8106 🖷 0871 527 8107
Squire Gate Ln FY4 2QS
dir: M55 junct 4, A5230, left at 1st rdbt towards airport. Hotel just before Squires Gate rail station

High quality, budget accommodation ideal for both families and business travellers. Spacious, en suite bedrooms feature tea and coffee making facilities, and Freeview TV in most hotels. Internet access and Wi-fi are available for a small fee. The adjacent family restaurant features a wide and varied menu. See also the Hotel Groups pages.

Rooms 39 **D** £65*

Premier Inn Blackpool (Bispham)

BUDGET HOTEL

☎ 0871 527 8102 🖷 0871 527 8103
Devonshire Rd, Bispham FY2 0AR
dir: M55 junct 4, A583. At 5th lights turn right (Whitegate Drive). Approx 4.5m onto A587 (Devonshire Rd)

Rooms 40 **D** £65*

Premier Inn Blackpool Central

BUDGET HOTEL

☎ 0871 527 8108 🖷 0871 527 8109
Yeadon Way, South Shore FY1 6BF
dir: M55 junct 4 to Blackpool, straight on at last island onto Yeaden Way. Follow signs for Central Car Park/Coach Area. Left at Total garage

Rooms 82 **D** £65*

Premier Inn Blackpool East (M55 Jct 4)

BUDGET HOTEL

☎ 0871 527 8110 🖷 0871 527 8111
Whitehills Park, Preston New Rd FY4 5NZ
dir: Just off M55 junct 4. 1st left off rdbt. Hotel on right

Rooms 81 **D** £65*

BLAKENEY
Norfolk **Map 13 TG04**

INSPECTORS' CHOICE

Morston Hall

★★★ ◎◎◎ HOTEL

☎ 01263 741041 🖷 01263 740419
Morston, Holt NR25 7AA
e-mail: reception@morstonhall.com
web: www.morstonhall.com
dir: 1m W of Blakeney on A149 (King's Lynn to Cromer road)

This delightful 17th-century country-house hotel enjoys a tranquil setting amid well-tended gardens. The comfortable public rooms offer a choice of attractive lounges and a sunny conservatory, while the elegant dining room is the perfect setting to enjoy Galton Blackiston's award-winning cuisine. The spacious bedrooms are individually decorated and stylishly furnished with modern opulence.

Rooms 13 (6 annexe) (7 GF) **S** £200-£270; **D** £310-£360 (incl. bkfst & dinner)* **Facilities** STV FTV ⛳ New Year Wi-fi **Parking** 40 **Notes** Closed 1 Jan-last Fri in Jan & 2 days Xmas

B

BLAKENEY *continued*

The Blakeney

★★★ 85% HOTEL

☎ 01263 740797 01263 740795
The Quay NR25 7NE
e-mail: reception@blakeneyhotel.co.uk
web: www.blakeneyhotel.co.uk
dir: From A148 between Fakenham & Holt, take B1156 to Langham & Blakeney

A traditional, privately owned hotel situated on the quayside with superb views across the estuary and the salt marshes to Blakeney Point. Public rooms feature an elegant restaurant, ground-floor lounge, a bar and a first-floor sun lounge overlooking the harbour. Bedrooms are smartly decorated and equipped with modern facilities; some enjoy the lovely sea views.

Rooms 63 (16 annexe) (20 fmly) (17 GF) **S** £89-£145; **D** £178-£314 (incl. bkfst & dinner)* **Facilities** FTV Gym Billiards Snooker Table tennis Sauna Steam room Spa bath Xmas New Year Wi-fi **Conf** Class 100 Board 100 Thtr 150 **Services** Lift **Parking** 60

Blakeney Manor Hotel

★★ 76% HOTEL

☎ 01263 740376 01263 741116
The Quay NR25 7ND
e-mail: reception@blakeneymanor.co.uk
web: www.blakeneymanor.co.uk
dir: Exit A149 at Blakeney towards Blakeney Quay. Hotel at end of quay between Mariner's Hill & Friary Hills

An attractive Norfolk flint building overlooking Blakeney Marshes close to the town centre and quayside. The bedrooms are located in flint-faced barns in a courtyard adjacent to the main building. The spacious public rooms include a choice of lounges, a conservatory, a popular bar and a large restaurant offering an interesting choice of dishes.

Rooms 35 (28 annexe) (26 GF) **Facilities** Xmas New Year Wi-fi **Parking** 40 **Notes** No children 14yrs

BLEADON Somerset **Map 4 ST35**

Premier Inn Weston-Super-Mare

BUDGET HOTEL

☎ 0871 527 9154 0871 527 9155
Bridgwater Rd, Lympsham BS24 0BP
dir: M5 junct 22, A38 (Bristol Rd) signed Weston-Super-Mare. At 1st rdbt take 1st exit into Bridgewater Rd (A370). Approx 2m to hotel

High quality, budget accommodation ideal for both families and business travellers. Spacious, en suite bedrooms feature tea and coffee making facilities, and Freeview TV in most hotels. Internet access and Wi-fi are available for a small fee. The adjacent family restaurant features a wide and varied menu. See also the Hotel Groups pages.

Rooms 24 **D** £69*

BLETCHINGDON Oxfordshire **Map 11 SP51**

The Oxfordshire Inn

★★★ 64% HOTEL

☎ 01869 351444 01869 351555
Heathfield Village OX5 3DX
e-mail: staff@oxfordshireinn.co.uk
web: www.oxfordshireinn.co.uk
dir: M40 junct 9, A34 towards Oxford, then A4027 towards Bletchingdon. Hotel signed 0.7m on right

A converted farmhouse with additional outbuildings that is located close to major motorway networks. Accommodation is set around an open courtyard, and includes suites that have four-poster beds. There is a spacious bar and restaurant.

Rooms 28 (4 fmly) (15 GF) **Facilities** Putt green Golf driving range Xmas New Year Wi-fi **Conf** Class 80 Board 30 Thtr 140 **Parking** 50 **Notes** LB

BLYTH Nottinghamshire **Map 16 SK68**

Best Western Charnwood Hotel

★★★ 82% HOTEL

☎ 01909 591610 01909 591429
Sheffield Rd S81 8HF
e-mail: reception@thecharnwood.com
web: www.thecharnwood.com
dir: A614 into Blyth, right past church onto A634 (Sheffield road). Hotel 0.5m on right past humpback bridge

In peaceful rural setting surrounded by attractive gardens with lovely views, this hotel offers a range of carefully prepared meals and snacks in either the formal restaurant, or the comfortable lounge bar. Bedrooms are comfortably furnished and attractively decorated. Service is friendly and attentive.

Rooms 45 (14 GF) **Facilities** STV FTV New Year Wi-fi **Conf** Class 60 Board 45 Thtr 140 Del from £105 to £135* **Services** Lift **Parking** 165 **Notes** Civ Wed 110

BODMIN Cornwall **Map 2 SX06**

Trehellas House Hotel & Restaurant

★★★ 74% SMALL HOTEL

☎ 01208 72700 01208 73336
Washaway PL30 3AD
e-mail: enquiries@trehellashouse.co.uk
web: www.trehellashouse.co.uk
dir: A389 from Bodmin towards Wadebridge. Hotel on right 0.5m beyond road to Camelford

This 18th-century former posting inn retains many original features and provides comfortable accommodation. Bedrooms are located in both the main house and adjacent coach house - all provide the same high standards. An interesting choice of cuisine, with an emphasis on locally-sourced ingredients, is offered in the impressive slate-floored restaurant.

Rooms 12 (7 annexe) (2 fmly) (5 GF) **S** £50-£70; **D** £50-£170 (incl. bkfst)* **Facilities** FTV Xmas New Year Wi-fi **Conf** Board 20 Thtr 20 Del from £95 to £150 **Parking** 32 **Notes** LB

Westberry

★★ 81% HOTEL

☎ 01208 72772 🖷 01208 72212
Rhind St PL31 2EL
e-mail: westberry@btconnect.com
web: www.westberryhotel.net
dir: On ring road off A30 & A38. St Petroc's Church on right, at mini rdbt turn right. Hotel on right

This popular hotel is conveniently located for both Bodmin town centre and the A30. The bedrooms are attractive and well equipped. A spacious bar lounge and a billiard room are also provided. The restaurant serves a variety of dishes, ranging from bar snacks to a more extensive carte menu.

Rooms 20 (8 annexe) (2 fmly) (6 GF) **Facilities** STV Full sized snooker table Wi-fi **Conf** Class 80 Board 80 Thtr 100 **Parking** 30 **Notes** LB

Premier Inn Bodmin

BUDGET HOTEL

☎ 0871 527 8112 🖷 0871 527 8113
Launceston Rd PL31 2AR
dir: From A30 S'bound exit onto A389, hotel 0.5m on right. N'bound exit onto A38, follow A389 signs. Left at T-junct

High quality, budget accommodation ideal for both families and business travellers. Spacious, en suite bedrooms feature tea and coffee making facilities, and Freeview TV in most hotels. Internet access and Wi-fi are available for a small fee. The adjacent family restaurant features a wide and varied menu. See also the Hotel Groups pages.

Rooms 44 **D** £70*

BOGNOR REGIS West Sussex **Map 6 SZ99**

The Russell Hotel

★★★ 77% HOTEL

☎ 01243 871300 🖷 01243 871301
King's Pde PO21 2QP
e-mail: russell.hotel@actionforblindpeople.org.uk
dir: A27 follow signs for town centre, hotel on seafront

Situated in a pleasant location close to the seafront, the Russell Hotel offers large and well-appointed bedrooms; some are fully accessible and many have sea views. This hotel also caters for visually impaired people, their families, friends and their guide dogs, as well as offering a warm welcome to business and leisure guests. There are of course special facilities for the guide dogs. Leisure facilities are also available.

Rooms 40 (5 fmly) **S** £39.90-£99; **D** £49.90-£110 (incl. bkfst) **Facilities** FTV supervised Gym Xmas New Year **Conf** Class 40 Board 20 Thtr 50 Del from £49.90 to £99 **Services** Lift **Parking** 6 **Notes** LB

Best Western Beachcroft Hotel

★★★ 71% HOTEL

☎ 01243 827142 🖷 01243 863500
Clyde Rd, Felpham Village PO22 7AH
e-mail: reservations@beachcroft-hotel.co.uk
web: www.beachcroft-hotel.co.uk
dir: From A259 between Chichester & Littlehampton at Felpham, follow village signs, hotel signed

This popular hotel overlooks a secluded part of the seafront. Bedrooms are bright and spacious, and facilities include a heated indoor swimming pool and free Wi-fi in the bedrooms. Diners may choose from varied, traditional restaurant menus or from those served in the more informal cosy bar.

Rooms 35 (4 fmly) (6 GF) **S** £49-£74; **D** £69-£94 (incl. bkfst)* **Facilities** STV Xmas New Year Wi-fi **Conf** Class 60 Board 40 Thtr 100 **Parking** 30 **Notes** LB

The Inglenook

★★★ 67% SMALL HOTEL

☎ 01243 262495 & 265411 🖷 01243 262668
255 Pagham Rd, Nyetimber PO21 3QB
e-mail: reception@the-inglenook.com
dir: A27 to Vinnetrow Road left at Walnut Tree, 2.5m on right

This 16th-century inn retains much of its original character, including exposed beams throughout. Bedrooms are individually decorated and vary in size. There is a cosy lounge, a well-kept garden and a bar that offers a popular evening menu and convivial atmosphere. The restaurant, overlooking the garden, also serves enjoyable cuisine.

Rooms 18 (1 fmly) (2 GF) **S** £55-£75; **D** £95-£200 (incl. bkfst)* **Facilities** FTV Xmas New Year Wi-fi **Conf** Class 50 Board 50 Thtr 100 Del from £95 to £125* **Parking** 35 **Notes** LB Civ Wed 80

The Royal Norfolk Hotel

★★ 74% HOTEL

☎ 01243 826222 🖷 01243 826325
The Esplanade PO21 2LH
e-mail: royalnorfolk@alfatrvale.co.uk
web: www.leisureplex.co.uk
dir: From A259 follow Longford Rd through lights to Canada Grove to T-junct. Right, take 2nd exit at rdbt. Hotel on right

Located on the seafront, but set back behind well tended lawns and gardens, is this fine looking Regency hotel. The bedrooms are traditionally furnished and provide guests with modern comforts. There are sea views from the bar, the restaurant and the lounges.

Rooms 60 (7 GF) **S** £39-£55; **D** £62-£94 (incl. bkfst) **Facilities** FTV Xmas New Year Wi-fi **Services** Lift **Parking** 25 **Notes** LB Closed 2 Jan-14 Feb

Premier Inn Bognor Regis

BUDGET HOTEL

☎ 0871 527 8114 🖷 0871 527 8115
Shripney Rd PO22 9PA
dir: From A27 & A29 rdbt junct follow Bognor Regis signs. Approx 4m, hotel on left

High quality, budget accommodation ideal for both families and business travellers. Spacious, en suite bedrooms feature tea and coffee making facilities, and Freeview TV in most hotels. Internet access and Wi-fi are available for a small fee. The adjacent family restaurant features a wide and varied menu. See also the Hotel Groups pages.

Rooms 24 **D** £67*

BOLTON Map 15 SD70
Greater Manchester

B

Holiday Inn Bolton Centre

★★★★ 70% HOTEL

☎ 0871 9429 050 & 01204 879988
Fax 01204 879983
1 Higher Bridge St BL1 2EW
e-mail: reservations.hibolton@qmh-hotels.com
web: www.holidayinn.co.uk
dir: M61 junct 3/A666, left at lights (Gordons Ford). Left at next lights, onto Higher Bridge St, hotel on right

Located close to the town centre this modern hotel offers well-equipped accommodation. There is an attractive lounge bar, and dinner and breakfast are available in Hardies Restaurant. Club Motivation provides an indoor pool, small gym and a sauna.

Rooms 132 (2 fmly) (8 smoking) **Facilities** STV Gym Sauna Sunbed Xmas New Year Wi-fi **Conf** Class 125 Board 80 Thtr 340 **Services** Lift Air con **Parking** 100 **Notes** Civ Wed 150

Egerton House

★★★ 81% HOTEL

☎ 01204 307171 Fax 01204 593030
Blackburn Rd, Egerton BL7 9SB
e-mail: reservation@egertonhouse-hotel.co.uk
web: www.egertonhouse-hotel.co.uk
dir: M61, A666 (Bolton road), pass ASDA on right. Hotel 2m on just passed war memorial on right

Peace and relaxation come as standard at this popular, privately owned hotel, that sits in acres of well-tended woodland gardens. Public rooms are stylishly appointed and have an inviting, relaxing atmosphere. Many of the individually styled, attractive guest bedrooms enjoy delightful garden views. Conferences and meetings are well catered for.

Rooms 29 (7 fmly) **S** £73-£76; **D** £83-£96 (incl. bkfst) **Facilities** FTV Xmas New Year Wi-fi **Conf** Class 90 Board 60 Thtr 150 Del from £130 to £145* **Parking** 135 **Notes** LB Civ Wed 140

Mercure Last Drop Village Hotel & Spa

★★★ 77% HOTEL

☎ 01204 591131 Fax 01204 304122
Hospital Rd, Bromley Cross BL7 9PZ
e-mail: h6634@accor.com
web: www.mercure.com
dir: 3m N of Bolton off B5472

A collection of 18th-century farmhouses set on cobbled streets with various shops and a local pub. Extensive self-contained conference rooms, a modern health and beauty spa and breathtaking views of the West Pennine Moors make this a popular choice with both corporate and leisure guests. The bedrooms are well equipped and spacious.

Rooms 128 (10 annexe) (29 fmly) (20 GF) **Facilities** Spa FTV Gym Craft shops Thermal suite Rock sauna Steam bath Bio sauna Xmas New Year Wi-fi **Conf** Class 300 Board 95 Thtr 700 **Services** Lift **Parking** 400 **Notes** LB Civ Wed 500

Premier Inn Bolton (Reebok Stadium)

BUDGET HOTEL

☎ 0871 527 8116 Fax 0871 527 8117
Arena Approach 3, Horwich BL6 6LB
dir: M61 junct 6, right at rdbt, left at 2nd rdbt

High quality, budget accommodation ideal for both families and business travellers. Spacious, en suite bedrooms feature tea and coffee making facilities, and Freeview TV in most hotels. Internet access and Wi-fi are available for a small fee. The adjacent family restaurant features a wide and varied menu. See also the Hotel Groups pages.

Rooms 74 **D** £51-£60*

Premier Inn Bolton West

BUDGET HOTEL

☎ 0871 527 8118 Fax 0871 527 8119
991 Chorley New Rd, Horwich BL6 4BA
dir: M61 junct 6, follow dual carriageway signed Bolton/Horwich (Reebok Stadium on left). Hotel at 2nd rdbt

Rooms 60 **D** £51-£60*

BOLTON ABBEY Map 19 SE05
North Yorkshire

INSPECTORS' CHOICE

The Devonshire Arms Country House Hotel & Spa

★★★★ HOTEL

☎ 01756 710441 & 718111 Fax 01756 710564
BD23 6AJ
e-mail: res@thedevonshirehotels.co.uk
web: www.thedevonshirearms.co.uk
dir: On B6160, 250yds N of junct with A59

With stunning views of the Wharfedale countryside this beautiful hotel, owned by the Duke and Duchess of Devonshire, dates back to the 17th century. Bedrooms are elegantly furnished; those in the old part of the house are particularly spacious and have four-posters and fine antiques. The sitting rooms are delightfully cosy with log fires, and the dedicated staff deliver service with a blend of friendliness and professionalism. The Burlington Restaurant offers award-winning, highly accomplished cuisine together with an impressive wine list, while the Brasserie provides a lighter alternative.

Rooms 40 (1 fmly) (17 GF) **S** fr £206; **D** £248-£457 (incl. bkfst)* **Facilities** Spa STV supervised Fishing Gym Classic cars Falconry Laser pigeon shooting Fly fishing Cricket Xmas New Year Wi-fi **Conf** Class 80 Board 30 Thtr 90 Del from £135 to £195* **Parking** 150 **Notes** LB Civ Wed 90

BOREHAMWOOD
Hertfordshire Map 6 TQ19

Holiday Inn London - Elstree

★★★★ 73% HOTEL

☎ 0871 942 9071 & 020 8214 9988
020 8207 6817
Barnet Bypass WD6 5PU
e-mail: hielstree@qmh-hotels.com
web: www.holidayinn.co.uk
dir: M25 junct 23, A1 S towards London. In 2m, B5135 towards Borehamwood. Hotel at 1st rdbt

Ideally located for motorway links and easy travel into the city, this hotel boasts excellent conference and event facilities, secure parking and leisure and beauty treatment options. A range of bedroom sizes is available; all are well equipped and have air conditioning. Dining is available in either the restaurant, which offers both carvery and carte choices, or in the bar serving a range of dishes.

Rooms 135 (5 fmly) (25 GF) (9 smoking) **D** £79-£155 (incl. bkfst)* **Facilities** STV Gym Steam room Beauty salon Wi-fi **Conf** Class 150 Board 60 Thtr 400 Del from £135 to £165 **Services** Lift Air con **Parking** 350 **Notes** LB Civ Wed 250

Ibis London Elstree Borehamwood

BUDGET HOTEL

☎ 020 8736 2600 020 8736 2610
Elstree Way WD6 1JY
e-mail: H6186@accor.com
dir: M25 junct 23 then A1 exit at Borehamwood, follow A5135 Elstree Way

Modern, budget hotel offering comfortable accommodation in bright and practical bedrooms. Breakfast is self-service and dinner is available in the restaurant. See also the Hotel Groups pages.

Rooms 122 (16 fmly) (16 GF)

Premier Inn London Elstree/Borehamwood

BUDGET HOTEL

☎ 0871 527 8654 0871 527 8655
Warwick Rd WD6 1US
dir: Exit A1 signed Borehamwood onto A5135 (Elstree Way). Pass BP Garage, left into Warwick Rd

High quality, budget accommodation ideal for both families and business travellers. Spacious, en suite bedrooms feature tea and coffee making facilities, and Freeview TV in most hotels. Internet access and Wi-fi are available for a small fee. The adjacent family restaurant features a wide and varied menu. See also the Hotel Groups pages.

Rooms 120 **D** £49-£65*

BOROUGHBRIDGE
North Yorkshire Map 19 SE36

Best Western Crown

★★★ 77% HOTEL

☎ 01423 322328 01423 324512
Horsefair YO51 9LB
e-mail: sales@crownboroughbridge.co.uk
web: www.crownboroughbridge.co.uk
dir: A1(M) junct 48 towards Boroughbridge. Hotel 1m

Situated in the centre of town but convenient for the A1(M), The Crown provides a full leisure complex, conference rooms and a secure car park. Bedrooms are well appointed. A wide range of well-prepared dishes can be enjoyed in both the restaurant and bar.

Rooms 37 (3 fmly) (2 GF) **S** £70.50-£95.50; **D** £99-£142 (incl. bkfst)* **Facilities** STV FTV supervised Gym Xmas New Year Wi-fi **Conf** Class 80 Board 80 Thtr 150 Del from £128 to £136.95 **Services** Lift **Parking** 60 **Notes** LB Civ Wed 120

BORROWDALE
Cumbria Map 18 NY21

See also **Keswick & Rosthwaite**

B

Lodore Falls Hotel

LAKE DISTRICT HOTELS

★★★★ 77% HOTEL

☎ 017687 77285 & 0800 840 1246
017687 77343
CA12 5UX
e-mail: lodorefalls@lakedistricthotels.net
web: www.lakedistricthotels.net/lodorefalls
dir: M6 junct 40 take A66 to Keswick, then B5289 to Borrowdale. Hotel on left

This impressive hotel has an enviable location overlooking Derwentwater. The bedrooms, many with lake or fell views, are comfortably equipped; family rooms and suites are also available. The dining room, bar and lounge areas are appointed to a very high standard. One of the treatments in the hotel's Elemis Spa actually makes use of the Lodore Waterfall!

Rooms 69 (11 fmly) **S** £90-£156; **D** £181-£450 (incl. bkfst) **Facilities** Spa STV FTV Fishing Gym Squash Sauna Xmas New Year Wi-fi **Conf** Class 90 Board 45 Thtr 200 Del from £145 to £175 **Services** Lift **Parking** 93 **Notes** LB Civ Wed 130

See advert on page 242

Borrowdale Gates Country House Hotel

★★★ 80% COUNTRY HOUSE HOTEL

☎ 017687 77204 017687 77195
CA12 5UQ
e-mail: hotel@borrowdale-gates.com
dir: From A66 follow B5289 for approx 4m. Turn right over bridge, hotel 0.25m beyond village

This friendly hotel is peacefully located in the Borrowdale Valley, close to the village but in its own three acres of wooded grounds. Public rooms include comfortable lounges and a restaurant with lovely views. Bedrooms vary in size and style.

Rooms 27 (10 GF) **Facilities** FTV Xmas New Year Wi-fi **Services** Lift **Parking** 29 **Notes** Closed 3 Jan-4 Feb

B

BORROWDALE *continued*

Borrowdale Hotel

★★★ 78% HOTEL

☎ 017687 77224 📠 017687 77338
CA12 5UY
e-mail: borrowdale@lakedistricthotels.net
dir: 3m from Keswick, on B5289 at S end of Lake Derwentwater

Situated in the beautiful Borrowdale Valley overlooking Derwentwater, this traditionally styled hotel guarantees a friendly welcome. Extensive public areas include a choice of lounges, traditional dining room, lounge bar and popular conservatory which serves more informal meals. Bedrooms vary in style and size, including two that are suitable for less able guests.

Rooms 36 (2 fmly) (2 GF) **S** £101-£121; **D** £202-£242 (incl. bkfst & dinner)* **Facilities** STV FTV Leisure facilities available at nearby sister hotel Xmas New Year Wi-fi **Conf** Class 30 Board 24 Thtr 80 **Parking** 30 **Notes** LB

See advert on page 242

Leathes Head

LAKE DISTRICT HOTELS

U

☎ 017687 77247 & 77650 📠 017687 77363
CA12 5UY
e-mail: reservations@leatheshead.co.uk
web: www.leatheshead.co.uk
dir: 3.5m from Keswick on B5289 (Borrowdale road). Hotel on left 0.25m before Grange Bridge

Currently the rating for this establishment is not confirmed. This may be due to a change of ownership or because it has only recently joined the AA rating scheme For further details please see the AA website: theAA.com

Rooms 12 (2 fmly) (3 GF) **Facilities** FTV Wi-fi **Parking** 16 **Notes** LB ® No children 15yrs Closed late Nov-mid Feb

BOSCASTLE
Cornwall — Map 2 SX09

The Wellington Hotel

U

☎ 01840 250202
The Harbour PL35 0AQ
e-mail: info@boscastle-wellington.com
web: www.boscastle-wellington.com
dir: A30/A395 at Davidstowe follow Boscastle signs. B3266 to village. Right into Old Rd

Currently the rating for this establishment is not confirmed. This may be due to a change of ownership or because it has only recently joined the AA rating scheme. For further details please see the AA website: theAA.com

Rooms 14 **S** £35-£50; **D** £60-£145* **Conf** Class 6 Board 24 Thtr 40

BOSHAM
West Sussex — Map 5 SU80

The Millstream Hotel & Restaurant

★★★ 85% ®® HOTEL

☎ 01243 573234 📠 01243 573459
Bosham Ln PO18 8HL
e-mail: info@millstream-hotel.co.uk
web: www.millstream-hotel.co.uk
dir: 4m W of Chichester on A259, left at Bosham rdbt. After 0.5m right at T-junct signed to church & quay. Hotel 0.5m on right

Lying in the idyllic village of Bosham, this attractive hotel provides comfortable, well-equipped and tastefully decorated bedrooms. Many guests regularly return here for the relaxed atmosphere created by the notably efficient and friendly staff. Public rooms include a cocktail bar that opens onto the garden, and a pleasant restaurant where varied and freshly prepared cuisine can be enjoyed.

Rooms 35 (2 annexe) (2 fmly) (9 GF) **Facilities** FTV Painting & Bridge breaks ♫ Xmas New Year Wi-fi **Conf** Class 20 Board 20 Thtr 45 **Parking** 44 **Notes** LB ® Civ Wed 97

BOSTON
Lincolnshire — Map 12 TF34

Supreme Inns Boston

★★★ 74% HOTEL

☎ 01205 822804 📠 01205 822888
Donnington Rd, Bicker Bar Roundabout PE20 3AN
e-mail: enquiries@supremeinns.co.uk
web: www.supremeinns.co.uk
dir: At A52 & A17 rdbt junct

Situated south west of Boston and surrounded by the Lincolnshire Fens, this modern, purpose-built hotel offers well equipped bedrooms that have flat-screen TVs and internet access. Food is available in the restaurant or all day in the relaxing bar area. Wedding, private dinner and conference facilities are all available.

Rooms 55 (27 GF) **S** £49-£60; **D** £49-£80* **Facilities** FTV Xmas New Year Wi-fi **Conf** Board 35 Thtr 60 Del from £65 to £80* **Parking** 65 **Notes** LB ® Civ Wed 60

Boston West Hotel

★★★ 73% HOTEL

☎ 01205 292969 & 290670 📠 01205 290725
Hubberts Bridge PE20 3QX
e-mail: info@bostonwesthotel.co.uk
dir: A1121 signed Boston, hotel on left after speed camera

A modern, purpose-built hotel situated in a rural location on the outskirts of town. The smartly appointed bedrooms are spacious and thoughtfully equipped; some rooms have balconies with stunning countryside views. Public rooms include a restaurant and a large open-plan lounge bar which overlooks the golf course.

Rooms 24 (5 fmly) (12 GF) **S** £49-£60; **D** £49-£60 **Facilities** FTV ⛳ 18 Putt green Driving range New Year Wi-fi **Conf** Class 60 Board 40 Thtr 80 Del from £75 to £85* **Services** Lift **Parking** 24 **Notes** ® Civ Wed 110

Poacher's Country Hotel

U

☎ 01205 290310 📠 01205 290254
Swineshead Rd, Kirton Holme PE20 1SQ
e-mail: enquiries@poachershotel.co.uk
dir: Just off A52, a short distance from A52/A17 rdbt

Currently the rating for this establishment is not confirmed. This may be due to a change of ownership or because it has only recently joined the AA rating scheme. For further details please see the AA website: theAA.com

Rooms 14 (1 fmly) (8 GF) **S** £50; **D** £50* **Facilities** FTV Xmas New Year Wi-fi **Conf** Class 150 Board 50 Thtr 175 **Parking** 55 **Notes** LB ⊗ Civ Wed 200

Premier Inn Boston

BUDGET HOTEL

☎ 0871 527 8120 📠 0871 527 8121
Wainfleet Rd PE21 9RW
dir: A52, 300yds E of junct with A16 (Boston to Grimsby road)

High quality, budget accommodation ideal for both families and business travellers. Spacious, en suite bedrooms feature tea and coffee making facilities, and Freeview TV in most hotels. Internet access and Wi-fi are available for a small fee. The adjacent family restaurant features a wide and varied menu. See also the Hotel Groups pages.

Rooms 54 **D** £57-£60*

BOTLEY Map 5 SU51
Hampshire

Macdonald Botley Park, Golf & Country Club

★★★★ 76% ◎ COUNTRY HOUSE HOTEL

☎ 01489 780 888 & 0870 194 2132
📠 01489 789 242
Winchester Rd, Boorley Green SO32 2UA
e-mail: botleypark@macdonald-hotels.co.uk
web: www.macdonald-hotels.co.uk/botleypark
dir: M27 junct 7, A334 towards Botley. At 1st rdbt left, past M&S store, over at next 5 mini rdbts. At 6th mini rdbt turn right. In 0.5m hotel on left

This modern and spacious hotel sits peacefully in the midst of its own 176-acre parkland golf course. Bedrooms are comfortably appointed with a good range of extras and an extensive range of leisure facilities is on offer. Attractive public areas include a relaxing restaurant and the more informal Swing and Divot Bar.

Rooms 130 (30 fmly) (44 GF) **S** £89-£180; **D** £89-£245 (incl. bkfst)* **Facilities** **Spa** STV 🏊 ⛳ 18 Putt green Gym Squash Dance studio Xmas New Year Wi-fi **Conf** Class 180 Board 100 Thtr 450 Del from £135 to £225 **Services** Air con **Parking** 250 **Notes** LB ⊗ Civ Wed 400

BOURNEMOUTH Map 5 SZ19
Dorset

See also **Christchurch**

Bournemouth Highcliff Marriott Hotel

Marriott HOTELS & RESORTS

★★★★ 80% ◎◎ HOTEL

☎ 01202 557702 📠 01202 293155
St Michaels Rd, West Cliff BH2 5DU
e-mail: mhrs.bohbm.ays@marriotthotels.co.uk
web: www.bournemouthhighcliffmarriott.co.uk
dir: A338 through Bournemouth. Follow BIC signs to West Cliff Rd. 2nd right into St Michaels Rd. Hotel at end of road on left

Originally built as a row of coastguard cottages, this establishment has expanded over the years into a very elegant and charming hotel. Impeccably maintained throughout, many of the bedrooms have sea views. An excellent range of leisure, business and conference facilities are offered, as well as private dining and banqueting rooms. The hotel also has direct access to the Bournemouth International Centre.

Rooms 160 (19 annexe) (22 fmly) (4 GF) (8 smoking) **S** £140-£330; **D** £140-£330 **Facilities** STV FTV 🏊 🏊 Putt green 🎾 Gym Beautician 🎵 Xmas New Year Wi-fi **Conf** Class 180 Board 90 Thtr 350 Del from £145 to £195* **Services** Lift Air con **Parking** 92 **Notes** LB ⊗ Civ Wed 250

Menzies East Cliff Court

MenziesHotels

★★★★ 79% HOTEL

☎ 01202 554545 📠 01202 557456
East Overcliff Dr BH1 3AN
e-mail: eastcliff@menzieshotels.co.uk
web: www.menzieshotels.co.uk
dir: Telephone or check the website for directions

Enjoying panoramic views across the bay, this popular hotel offers bedrooms that are modern and contemporary in style; they are appointed to a very high standard, and may have the benefit of balconies and sea views. Stylish public areas include a range of inviting lounges, a spacious restaurant and a selection of conference rooms.

Rooms 67 (4 fmly) (2 GF) (5 smoking) **Facilities** 🏊 Full leisure facilities at adjacent Menzies Carlton Xmas New Year Wi-fi **Conf** Class 80 Board 50 Thtr 200 **Services** Lift **Parking** 45 **Notes** Civ Wed 250

The Green House

★★★★ 77% TOWN HOUSE HOTEL

☎ 01202 498900 📠 01202 551559
4 Grove Rd BH1 3AX
e-mail: reception@thegreenhousehotel.com

This latest addition to the Bournemouth hotel scene has a clear commitment to the environment which goes beyond just energy efficient lighting; everything has been designed and built to be sympathetic to the environment. The beautifully appointed bedrooms and bathrooms demonstrate the 'green' principle from the locally-made 100% wool carpets and solid wood furniture to the wallpapers and paint that have been used. The ingredients used for the menus are locally sourced and organic.

Rooms 32 (3 fmly) (6 GF) **D** £140-£240 (incl. bkfst)* **Facilities** FTV Xmas New Year Wi-fi **Conf** Class 40 Board 40 Thtr 100 Del from £160 to £290* **Services** Lift **Parking** 32 **Notes** ⊗ Civ Wed 100

B

BOURNEMOUTH ***continued***

Menzies Carlton

MenziesHotels

★★★★ 74% HOTEL

☎ 01202 552011 📠 01202 299573
East Overcliff BH1 3DN
e-mail: carlton@menzieshotels.co.uk
web: www.menzieshotels.co.uk
dir: From M3/M27, approach Bournemouth on A338 (leads onto Wessex Way), follow signs to the East Cliff, hotel on seafront

Enjoying a prime location on the East Cliff, and with views of the Isle of Wight and Dorset coastline, the Carlton has attractive gardens and pool area. Most of the spacious bedrooms enjoy sea views. Leisure facilities include an indoor and outdoor pool as well as a gym. Guests can enjoy an interesting range of carefully prepared dishes in Frederick's restaurant. The conference and banqueting facilities are varied.

Rooms 76 (17 fmly) (8 GF) (9 smoking) **Facilities** STV FTV Gym Hair & beauty salon Xmas New Year Wi-fi **Conf** Class 120 Board 50 Thtr 250 **Services** Lift **Parking** 87 **Notes** Civ Wed 200

De Vere Royal Bath

DE VERE Hotels & Resorts

★★★★ 73% HOTEL

☎ 01202 555555 📠 01202 554158
Bath Rd BH1 2EW
e-mail: royalbath@devere-hotels.com
web: www.devere.co.uk
dir: A338, follow signs for pier & beaches. Hotel on seafront before BIC

Overlooking the bay, this well-established seafront hotel is surrounded by beautifully kept gardens. Public rooms, which include lounges, a choice of restaurants and indoor leisure facilities, are of a scale and style befitting the Victorian era in which the hotel was built. Parking space is limited but valet parking, at a charge, is provided.

Rooms 140 (31 fmly) (23 GF) **Facilities** Spa STV supervised Gym Beauty salon Hairdressing Xmas New Year Wi-fi **Conf** Class 220 Board 100 Thtr 400 **Services** Lift **Parking** 70 **Notes** LB Civ Wed 400

Norfolk Royale

★★★★ 72% HOTEL

☎ 01202 551521 📠 01202 299729
Richmond Hill BH2 6EN
e-mail: gm@norfolkroyale-hotel-bournemouth.com
web: www.norfolk-royale.co.uk
dir: A338 into Bournemouth take Richmond Hill exit to A347 Wimborne, turn left at top into Richmond Hill. Hotel on right

Easily recognisable by its wrought iron balconies, this Edwardian hotel is conveniently located for the centre of the town. Most of the bedrooms are contained in a modern wing at the side of the building, overlooking the pretty landscaped gardens. There is a car park at rear of the hotel.

Rooms 95 (7 fmly) (9 GF) (4 smoking) **S** £79-£150; **D** £114-£185 (incl. bkfst)* **Facilities** Spa STV Membership of nearby health club Xmas New Year Wi-fi Child facilities **Conf** Class 50 Board 40 Thtr 150 Del from £135 to £155* **Services** Lift **Parking** 95 **Notes** LB Civ Wed 150

Hallmark Bournemouth

★★★★ 71% HOTEL

☎ 01202 751000 📠 01202 757585
Durley Chine Rd, West Cliff BH2 5JS
e-mail: bournemouth.sales@hallmarkhotels.co.uk
dir: A338 follow signs to West Cliff & BIC, hotel on right

This refurbished property is conveniently located and offers a friendly atmosphere and attentive service. The comfortable bedrooms are tastefully appointed and are suitable for both business and leisure guests. The restaurant and bar serve a good choice of dishes, and the well-appointed leisure area is popular with both residents and locals alike. There is also a good range of conference facilities and meeting rooms.

Rooms 78 (12 annexe) **Facilities** Spa FTV Gym Sauna Steam room Aromatherapy Ice zone Xmas New Year Wi-fi **Conf** Class 80 Board 40 Thtr 250 Del from £99 to £190* **Services** Lift **Parking** 80 **Notes** Civ Wed 200

Best Western Connaught Hotel

★★★ 85% HOTEL

☎ 01202 298020 📠 01202 298028
West Hill Rd, West Cliff BH2 5PH
e-mail: reception@theconnaught.co.uk
web: www.theconnaught.co.uk
dir: Follow Town Centre West & BIC signs

Conveniently located on the West Cliff, close to the BIC, beaches and town centre, this privately-owned hotel offers well equipped, neatly decorated rooms, some with balconies. The hotel boasts a very well equipped leisure complex with a large pool and gym. Breakfast and dinner offer imaginative dishes made with quality local ingredients.

Rooms 83 (27 annexe) (10 fmly) **S** £45-£75; **D** £60-£130 (incl. bkfst)* **Facilities** Spa FTV supervised Gym Sauna Steam room Xmas New Year Wi-fi **Conf** Class 60 Board 35 Thtr 180 Del from £98 to £150* **Services** Lift **Parking** 66 **Notes** Civ Wed 200

See advert on opposite page

Hermitage Hotel

★★★ 85% ⊛ HOTEL

☎ 01202 557363 🖷 01202 559173
Exeter Rd BH2 5AH
e-mail: info@hermitage-hotel.co.uk
web: www.hermitage-hotel.co.uk
dir: A338 Ringwood, follow signs for BIC & pier. Hotel directly opposite

Occupying an impressive location overlooking the seafront, at the heart of the town centre, the Hermitage offers friendly and attentive service. The majority of the smart bedrooms are comfortably appointed and all are very well equipped; many rooms have sea views. The wood-panelled lounge provides an elegant and tranquil area, as does the restaurant where well-prepared and interesting dishes are served.

Rooms 74 (11 annexe) (9 fmly) (7 GF) **S** £50.50-£77; **D** £101-£154 (incl. bkfst)* **Facilities** FTV Xmas New Year Wi-fi **Conf** Class 60 Board 60 Thtr 180 Del from £78 to £160* **Services** Lift **Parking** 58 **Notes** ⊗

See advert on page 92

Cumberland

★★★ 85% HOTEL

☎ 01202 290722 & 298350 🖷 01202 311394
East Overcliff Dr BH1 3AF
e-mail: info@cumberlandbournemouth.co.uk
dir: A35 towards East Cliff & beaches, right onto Holdenhurst Rd, straight over 2 rdbts, left at junct to East Overcliff Drive, hotel on seafront

A purpose built, art deco hotel where many of the bedrooms are appointed in keeping with the hotel's original character. Front-facing bedrooms have balconies with superb sea views. The comfortable public areas are spacious and striking in their design. The Mirabelle Restaurant and the Red Door Brasserie offer cuisine prepared from local produce.

Rooms 102 (20 fmly) **S** £25-£85; **D** £50-£170 (incl. bkfst)* **Facilities** FTV ⓢ Gym Squash Sauna Xmas New Year Wi-fi **Conf** Class 180 Board 40 Thtr 250 Del from £50 to £95* **Services** Lift **Parking** 50 **Notes** LB Civ Wed 100

See advert on page 95

Langtry Manor - Lovenest of a King

★★★ 82% ⊛ HOTEL

☎ 0844 3725 432 🖷 01202 290115
Derby Rd, East Cliff BH1 3QB
e-mail: lillie@langtrymanor.com
web: www.langtrymanor.co.uk
dir: A31/A338, 1st rdbt by rail station turn left. Over next rdbt, 1st left into Knyveton Rd. Hotel opposite

Retaining a stately air, this property was originally built in 1877 by Edward VII for his mistress Lillie Langtry. The individually furnished and decorated bedrooms include several with four-poster beds. Enjoyable cuisine is served in the magnificent dining hall, that displays several large Tudor tapestries. There is an Edwardian banquet on Saturday evenings.

Rooms 20 (8 annexe) (2 fmly) (3 GF) **Facilities** FTV Free use of health club (200yds) ♫ Xmas New Year Wi-fi **Conf** Class 60 Board 40 Thtr 100 Del from £110 to £150 **Parking** 30 **Notes** LB Civ Wed 100

B

BOURNEMOUTH *continued*

Hotel Miramar

★★★ 82% HOTEL

☎ 01202 556581 📠 01202 291242
East Overcliff Dr, East Cliff BH1 3AL
e-mail: sales@miramar-bournemouth.com
web: www.miramar-bournemouth.com
dir: Wessex Way rdbt turn into St Pauls Rd, right at next rdbt. 3rd exit at next rdbt, 2nd exit at next rdbt into Grove Rd. Hotel car park on right

Conveniently located on the East Cliff, this Edwardian hotel enjoys glorious sea views. The Miramar was a favoured destination of famed author JRR Tolkien, who often stayed here. The bedrooms are comfortable and well equipped, and there are spacious public areas and a choice of lounges. The friendly staff and the relaxing environment are noteworthy here.

Hotel Miramar

Rooms 43 (6 fmly) **S** £39.95-£74.95; **D** £79.90-£197.40 (incl. bkfst)* **Facilities** FTV ♫ Xmas New Year Wi-fi **Conf** Class 50 Board 50 Thtr 200 Del from £90 to £120* **Services** Lift **Parking** 80 **Notes** LB Civ Wed 110

Chine Hotel

★★★ 81% ❀ HOTEL

☎ 01202 396234 & 0845 337 1550
📠 01202 391737
Boscombe Spa Rd BH5 1AX
e-mail: reservations@fjbhotels.co.uk
web: www.fjbhotels.co.uk
dir: Follow BIC signs, A338/Wessex Way to St Pauls rdbt. 1st exit, to next rdbt, 2nd exit signed Eastcliff, Boscombe, Southbourne. Next rdbt, 1st exit into Christchurch Rd. After 2nd lights, right into Boscombe Spa Rd

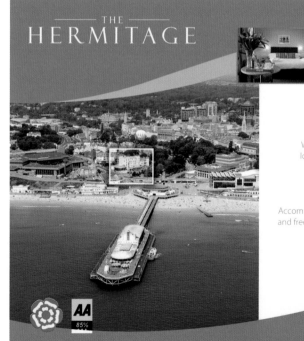

Benefiting from superb views this popular hotel is set in delightful gardens with private access to the seafront and beach. The excellent range of facilities includes an indoor and outdoor pool, a small leisure centre and a selection of meeting rooms. The spacious bedrooms, some with balconies, are well appointed and thoughtfully equipped.

Rooms 88 (23 annexe) (16 fmly) (8 GF) **Facilities** STV supervised supervised Putt green Gym Games room Children's indoor play area Xmas New Year Wi-fi Child facilities **Conf** Class 70 Board 40 Thtr 140 **Services** Lift **Parking** 55 **Notes** Civ Wed 120

Best Western Hotel Royale

★★★ 80% HOTEL

☎ 01202 554794 01202 299615
16 Gervis Rd BH1 3EQ
e-mail: reservations@thehotelroyale.com
web: www.thehotelroyale.com
dir: M27 junct 1, A31 onto A338 to Bournemouth, follow signs for East Cliff & seafront. Over 2 rdbts into Gervis Rd. Hotel on right

Located on the East Cliff, just a short walk from the seafront and local shops and amenities, this is a privately owned hotel. Public areas are contemporary in style, and facilities include a small health club and spacious function rooms. Bedrooms are comfortable and well furnished.

Rooms 64 (8 annexe) (22 fmly) (8 GF) **S** £45-£75; **D** £55-£130 (incl. bkfst) **Facilities** STV FTV Gym Xmas New Year Wi-fi **Conf** Class 60 Board 40 Thtr 100 Del from £80 to £130 **Services** Lift **Parking** 80 **Notes** LB

Elstead

★★★ 80% HOTEL

☎ 01202 293071 01202 293827
Knyveton Rd BH1 3QP
e-mail: info@the-elstead.co.uk
web: www.the-elstead.co.uk
dir: A338 Wessex Way to St Pauls rdbt, left & left again

Ideal as a base for both business and leisure travellers, this popular hotel is conveniently located for the town centre, seafront and BIC. An impressive range of facilities is offered, including meeting rooms, an indoor leisure centre and comfortable lounges.

Rooms 50 (15 fmly) **Facilities** supervised Gym Steam room Pool & snooker tables Xmas New Year Wi-fi **Conf** Class 60 Board 40 Thtr 80 **Services** Lift **Parking** 40 **Notes** Civ Wed 60

Royal Exeter

★★★ 79% HOTEL

☎ 01202 438000 01202 789664
Exeter Rd BH2 5AG
e-mail: enquiries@royalexeterhotel.com
web: www.royalexeterhotel.com
dir: Opposite Bournemouth International Centre

Ideally located opposite the Bournemouth International Centre, and convenient for the beach and town centre, this busy hotel caters for both business and leisure guests. Public areas are smart and there's a modern open-plan lounge bar and restaurant together with an exciting adjoining bar complex.

Rooms 54 (13 fmly) (12 smoking) **Facilities** FTV Gym Wi-fi **Conf** Class 40 Board 40 Thtr 100 **Services** Lift **Parking** 50 **Notes** LB

See advert on this page

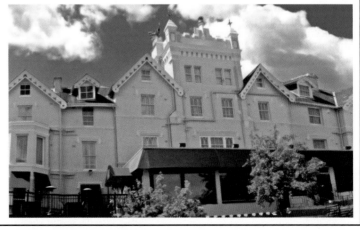

B

BOURNEMOUTH *continued*

Queens

★★★ 78% HOTEL

☎ 01202 554415 01202 294810
Meyrick Rd, East Cliff BH1 3DL
e-mail: reception@queenshotelbournemouth.com
web: www.queenshotelbournemouth.com
dir: M3/M27 onto A338 leading onto Wessex Way. Follow signs to East Cliff

This attractive hotel enjoys a good location near the seafront and is popular for conferences and functions. Public areas include a bar, lounge and a large restaurant. Leisure facilities include indoor pool and small gym. Bedrooms vary in size and style, many have sea views.

Rooms 109 (44 fmly) **S** £49.50-£99; **D** £90-£180 (incl. bkfst)* **Facilities** Spa Gym Beauty salon Snooker & pool tables Xmas New Year Wi-fi **Conf** Class 200 Board 100 Thtr 380 Del from £99.50 to £137.50 **Services** Lift **Parking** 60 **Notes** LB Civ Wed 120

Trouville Hotel

★★★ 78% HOTEL

☎ 01202 552262 01202 293324
Priory Rd BH2 5DH
e-mail: reception@trouvillehotel.com
dir: Follow Town Centre West signs. Exit at rdbt signed BIC/West Cliff/Beaches. 2nd exit at next rdbt, left at next rdbt. Hotel on left near end of Priory Rd

Located near Bournemouth International Centre, the seafront and the shops, this hotel has the advantage of indoor leisure facilities and a large car park. Bedrooms are generally a good size with comfortable furnishings; there are plenty of family rooms here. The air-conditioned restaurant offers a daily changing menu.

Rooms 95 (19 annexe) (17 fmly) (2 GF) **S** £43.95-£70.95; **D** £87.90-£141.90 (incl. bkfst) **Facilities** FTV Gym Sauna Xmas New Year Wi-fi **Conf** Class 75 Board 40 Thtr 200 Del from £77.50 to £97.50 **Services** Lift **Parking** 70 **Notes** LB Civ Wed 100

Carrington House

★★★ 77% HOTEL

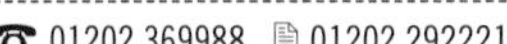

☎ 01202 369988 01202 292221
31 Knyveton Rd BH1 3QQ
e-mail: carrington.house@forestdale.com
web: www.carringtonhousehotel.co.uk
dir: A338 at St Paul's rdbt, 200mtrs & left into Knyveton Rd. Hotel 400mtrs on right

This hotel occupies a prominent position on a tree-lined avenue and a short walk from the seafront. The bedrooms are comfortable, well equipped and include many purpose-built family rooms. There are two dining options, Mortimers restaurant, and the Kings bar which serves light meals and snacks. Guests can relax in the comfortable lounge areas whilst the leisure complex offers a whole host of activities.

Rooms 145 (42 fmly) (2 GF) **Facilities** FTV Children's play area Xmas New Year Wi-fi **Conf** Class 250 Board 110 Thtr 500 **Services** Lift **Parking** 85 **Notes** LB Civ Wed 60

The Riviera

★★★ 77% HOTEL

☎ 01202 763653 01202 768422
Burnaby Rd, Alum Chine BH4 8JF
e-mail: info@rivierabournemouth.co.uk
web: www.rivierabournemouth.co.uk
dir: A338, follow signs to Alum Chine

The Riviera offers a range of comfortable, well-furnished bedrooms and bathrooms. Welcoming staff provide efficient service delivered in a friendly manner. In addition to a spacious lounge with regular entertainment, there is an indoor and an outdoor pool, and all just a short walk from the beach.

Rooms 73 (4 annexe) (25 fmly) (11 GF) **S** £37-£78; **D** £74-£156 (incl. bkfst)* **Facilities** FTV Games room Sauna Spa bath Treatments available Xmas New Year Wi-fi **Conf** Class 120 Board 50 Thtr 180 Del from £65 to £125* **Services** Lift **Parking** 45 **Notes** LB Civ Wed 160

Wessex

★★★ 77% HOTEL

☎ 01202 551911 01202 297354
West Cliff Rd BH2 5EU
e-mail: wessex@forestdale.com
web: www.thewessexhotel.co.uk
dir: Follow M27/A35 or A338 from Dorchester & A347 N. Hotel on West Cliff side of town

Centrally located and handy for the beach, the Wessex is a popular, relaxing hotel. Bedrooms are well equipped and comfortable with a range of modern amenities. The Lulworth Restaurant provides a range of appetizing dishes. The excellent leisure facilities boast both indoor and outdoor pools, sauna, ample function rooms and an open-plan bar and lounge.

Rooms 109 (32 fmly) (17 GF) **Facilities** FTV Gym Table tennis Sauna Steam room Xmas New Year Wi-fi **Conf** Class 150 Board 100 Thtr 400 **Services** Lift **Parking** 160 **Notes** LB Civ Wed 200

Cliffeside

★★★ 76% HOTEL

☎ 01202 555724 & 298350 01202 314534
East Overcliff Dr BH1 3AQ
e-mail: info@cliffesidebournemouth.co.uk
dir: Off A35/A338 to East Cliff & beaches, right into Holdenhurst Rd, over next 2 rdbts, at junct left into East Overcliff Drive, hotel on left

Benefiting from an elevated position on the seafront and just a short walk to town, it's no wonder that this friendly hotel has many returning guests. Bedrooms and public areas are attractively appointed, many with sea views. The Atlantic Restaurant offers guests a fixed-price menu.

Rooms 62 (5 fmly) (2 GF) **S** £22-£75; **D** £44-£150 (incl. bkfst)* **Facilities** Gym Squash Sauna Xmas New Year Wi-fi **Conf** Class 70 Board 40 Thtr 120 Del from £45 to £85* **Services** Lift **Parking** 32 **Notes** LB Civ Wed 120

See advert on opposite page

Hotel Piccadilly

★★★ 75% HOTEL

☎ 01202 298024 01202 298235
25 Bath Rd BH1 2NN
e-mail: enquiries@hotelpiccadilly.co.uk
dir: From A338 take 1st exit rdbt, signed East Cliff. 3rd exit at next rdbt signed Lansdowne, 3rd exit at next rdbt into Bath Rd

This hotel offers a friendly welcome to guests, many of whom return on a regular basis, particularly for the superb ballroom dancing facilities and small break packages which are a feature here. Bedrooms are smartly decorated, well maintained and comfortable. Dining in the attractive restaurant is always popular and dishes are freshly prepared and appetising.

Rooms 45 (2 fmly) (5 GF) **Facilities** FTV Xmas New Year Wi-fi **Services** Lift **Parking** 35 **Notes**

Suncliff

★★★ 75% HOTEL

☎ 01202 291711 & 298350 🖷 01202 293788
29 East Overcliff Dr BH1 3AG
e-mail: info@suncliffbournemouth.co.uk
dir: A338/A35 towards East Cliff & beaches, right into Holdenhurst Rd, straight over 2 rdbts, left at junct into East Overcliff Drive, hotel on seafront

Enjoying splendid views from the East Cliff and catering mainly for leisure guests, this friendly hotel offers a range of facilities and services. Bedrooms are well equipped and comfortable, and many have sea views. Public areas include a large conservatory, an attractive bar and pleasant lounges.

Rooms 97 (29 fmly) (14 GF) **S** £22-£75; **D** £44-£150 (incl. bkfst)* **Facilities** Gym Squash Xmas New Year Wi-fi **Conf** Class 70 Board 60 Thtr 100 Del from £45 to £85* **Services** Lift **Parking** 62 **Notes** LB Civ Wed 80

Hinton Firs

★★★ 74% HOTEL

☎ 01202 555409 🖷 01202 299607
Manor Rd, East Cliff BH1 3ET
e-mail: info@hintonfirshotel.co.uk
web: www.hintonfirshotel.co.uk
dir: A338 turn W at St Paul's rdbt, straight on at next 2 rdbts, fork left to side of church. Hotel at next corner

This family owned and friendly hotel is conveniently located on East Cliff, just a short stroll from the sea. The smart, well-appointed bedrooms are light and airy; there are family rooms and also one bedroom, with a wet room, that is suitable for less able guests. The leisure facilities include indoor and outdoor pools, a sauna, beauty treatments and supervised children's activities in the school holidays. There is also a spacious lounge, a restaurant and bar.

Hinton Firs

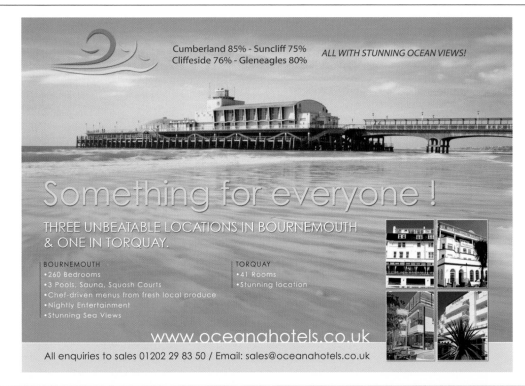

Rooms 52 (6 annexe) (12 fmly) (6 GF) **Facilities** STV Games room Xmas New Year Wi-fi **Conf** Class 40 Board 30 Thtr 50 **Services** Lift **Parking** 40 **Notes** LB

B

BOURNEMOUTH *continued*

Mayfair Hotel

★★★ 74% HOTEL

☎ 01202 551983 Fax 01202 551002
27 Bath Rd BH1 2NW
e-mail: info@themayfair.com
web: www.themayfair.com
dir: Exit A338 at St Pauls Rd (Asda rdbt), right into Holdenhurst Rd, 3rd exit from Lansdowne rdbt

Occupying a central location in the heart of Bournemouth and within walking distance of both the town centre and the seafront, this hotel offers guests comfortable, modern accommodation. There is a spacious restaurant and bar area, plus a pleasant outdoor patio and function room.

Rooms 40 (6 fmly) (1 GF) **Facilities** Ballroom dancing programme on request Xmas New Year **Conf** Class 40 Board 30 Thtr 60 Del from £80 to £105 **Services** Lift **Parking** 30 **Notes** LB ⊗ Civ Wed 80

Hotel Collingwood

★★★ 70% HOTEL

☎ 01202 557575 Fax 01202 293219
11 Priory Rd, West Cliff BH2 5DF
e-mail: info@hotel-collingwood.co.uk
web: www.hotel-collingwood.co.uk
dir: A338 left at West Cliff sign, over 1st rdbt, left at 2nd rdbt. Hotel 500yds on left

This privately owned and managed hotel is situated close to the BIC. Bedrooms are airy, with the emphasis on comfort. An excellent range of leisure facilities is available and the public areas are spacious and welcoming. Pinks Restaurant offers carefully prepared cuisine and a fixed-price, five-course dinner.

Rooms 53 (16 fmly) (6 GF) **S** £39-£65; **D** £78-£130 (incl. bkfst) **Facilities** FTV ⓢ Gym Steam room Sauna Games room Snooker room ♫ Xmas New Year Wi-fi **Conf** Class 60 Board 20 Thtr 100 Del from £105 to £150 **Services** Lift **Parking** 55

Belvedere Hotel

★★★ 67% HOTEL

☎ 01202 297556 & 293336 Fax 01202 294699
Bath Rd BH1 2EU
e-mail: enquiries@belvedere-hotel.co.uk
web: www.belvedere-hotel.co.uk
dir: From A338 with railway station and Asda on left. At rdbt 1st left then 3rd exit at next 2 rdbts. Hotel on Bath Hill after 4th rdbt

Close to the town centre and the seafront, this friendly, family-run hotel includes a choice of bars, a small indoor leisure club with beauty treatments and an attractive restaurant. There is a range of meeting rooms, which provide an ideal location for conferences or functions.

Rooms 100 (20 fmly) **S** £36-£59; **D** £58-£100 (incl. bkfst)* **Facilities** FTV ⓢ Gym Sauna Treatment room ♫ Xmas New Year Wi-fi **Conf** Class 60 Board 50 Thtr 120 Del from £59 to £127.50* **Services** Lift **Parking** 90 **Notes** LB ⊗

Durley Dean Hotel

★★★ 67% HOTEL

☎ 01202 557711 Fax 01202 292815
West Cliff Rd BH2 5HE
e-mail: reservations@durleydean.co.uk
dir: In Bournemouth follow signs for Westcliff. Onto Durley Chine Rd South to next rdbt, hotel off 2nd exit on left

Situated close to the seafront on the West Cliff, this modern hotel has bedrooms which vary in size and style. There is a restaurant, a comfortable bar and several meeting rooms. Parking is also a bonus.

Rooms 117 (36 fmly) (6 GF) **Facilities** FTV ⓢ Gym ♫ Xmas New Year Wi-fi **Conf** Class 40 Board 40 Thtr 150 **Services** Lift **Parking** 30 **Notes** ⊗ Civ Wed 200

Burley Court

★★★ 61% HOTEL

☎ 01202 552824 & 556704 Fax 01202 298514
Bath Rd BH1 2NP
e-mail: info@burleycourthotel.co.uk
dir: Exit A338 at St Paul's rdbt, take 3rd exit at next rdbt into Holdenhurst Rd. 3rd exit at next rdbt into Bath Rd, over crossing, 1st left

Located on Bournemouth's West Cliff, this well-established hotel is well located and convenient for the town and beaches. Bedrooms are pleasantly furnished and decorated in bright colours. A daily-changing menu is served in the spacious dining room.

Rooms 38 (8 fmly) (4 GF) **Facilities** ⤨ Xmas **Conf** Class 15 Board 15 Thtr 30 **Services** Lift **Parking** 35 **Notes** Closed 30 Dec-14 Jan RS 15-31 Jan

The Whitehall

★★ 78% HOTEL

☎ 01202 554682 Fax 01202 292637
Exeter Park Rd BH2 5AX
e-mail: reservations@thewhitehallhotel.co.uk
web: www.thewhitehallhotel.co.uk
dir: Follow BIC signs then turn into Exeter Park Rd off Exeter Rd

This friendly hotel enjoys an elevated position overlooking the park and is also close to the town centre and seafront. The spacious public areas include a choice of lounges, a cosy bar and a well-presented restaurant. The well-equipped and inviting bedrooms are spread over three floors.

Rooms 46 (5 fmly) (3 GF) **Facilities** ♫ Xmas **Conf** Class 40 Board 32 Thtr 70 **Services** Lift **Parking** 25

Tower House

★★ 76% HOTEL

☎ 01202 290742 Fax 01202 553305
West Cliff Gardens BH2 5HP
e-mail: towerhouse.hotel@btconnect.com

A popular family owned and run hotel on the West Cliff. The owners and their staff are friendly and helpful. The bedrooms are comfortable and well maintained and the hotel provides good off-road parking.

Rooms 32 (12 fmly) (3 GF) **Facilities** FTV Xmas New Year Wi-fi **Services** Lift **Parking** 30

Durley Grange

★★ 74% HOTEL

☎ 01202 554473 📠 01202 293774
6 Durley Rd, West Cliff BH2 5JL
e-mail: reservations@durleygrange.com
dir: A338/Bournemouth West rdbt. Over next rdbt, 1st left into Sommerville Rd & right into Durley Rd

Located in a quiet area, with parking, the town and beaches are all in walking distance of this welcoming, friendly hotel. Bedrooms are brightly decorated, comfortable and well equipped. There is an indoor pool and sauna for all-year round use. Enjoyable meals are served in the smart dining room.

Rooms 52 (8 fmly) (4 GF) **S** £46-£66; **D** £92-£132 (incl. bkfst & dinner)* **Facilities** Sauna ♫ Xmas New Year Wi-fi **Services** Lift **Parking** 35 **Notes** LB

Devon Towers

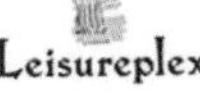

★★ 71% HOTEL

☎ 01202 553863 📠 01202 315265
58-62 St Michael's Rd, West Cliff BH2 5ED
e-mail: devontowers.bournemouth@alfatravel.co.uk
dir: A338 into Bournemouth, follow signs for BIC. Left into St. Michaels Rd at top of hill. Hotel 100mtrs on left

Located in a quiet road within walking distance of the West Cliff and shops, this hotel appeals to the budget leisure market. The four-course menus offer plenty of choice and entertainment is featured most evenings. The bar and lobby area provide plenty of space for relaxing.

Rooms 62 (6 GF) **S** £37-£52; **D** £58-£88 (incl. bkfst) **Facilities** FTV ♫ Xmas **Services** Lift **Parking** 6 **Notes** LB Closed Jan-mid Feb (ex Xmas) RS Nov, mid-end Feb & Mar

Ullswater

★★ 71% HOTEL

☎ 01202 555181 📠 01202 317896
West Cliff Gardens BH2 5HW
e-mail: enquiries@ullswater-hotel.co.uk
web: www.ullswater-hotel.co.uk
dir: In Bournemouth follow signs to West Cliff. Hotel just off Westcliff Rd

A welcoming family run hotel conveniently located for the city and the seafront. This popular establishment attracts a loyal following. The well-equipped bedrooms vary in size, and the charming lounge bar and dining room are very smart. Cuisine is hearty and homemade offering a good choice from the daily-changing menu.

Rooms 42 (8 fmly) (2 GF) **S** £43-£56; **D** £86-£110 (incl. bkfst)* **Facilities** FTV Snooker room Table tennis ♫ Xmas New Year Wi-fi **Conf** Class 30 Board 24 Thtr 40 **Services** Lift **Parking** 12 **Notes** LB

Arlington Hotel

★★ 69% HOTEL

☎ 01202 552879 & 553012 📠 01202 298317
Exeter Park Rd BH2 5BD
e-mail: enquiries@arlingtonbournemouth.co.uk
dir: Follow BIC signs through Priory Rd, onto rdbt and exit at Royal Exeter Hotel sign

Well-equipped bedrooms and comfortable accommodation along with friendly hospitality are offered at this privately owned and run hotel. Conveniently located, midway between the square and the pier and ideally situated for the BIC, the Arlington has direct access to the Winter Gardens, which are overlooked from the hotel's lounge and terrace bar.

Rooms 28 (1 annexe) (6 fmly) **Facilities** Xmas **Services** Lift **Parking** 21 **Notes** LB No children 2yrs Closed 4-15 Jan

Bourne Hall Hotel

★★ 63% HOTEL

☎ 01202 299715 📠 01202 552669
14 Priory Rd, West Cliff BH2 5DN
e-mail: info@bournehall.co.uk
web: www.bournehall.co.uk
dir: M27/A31 from Ringwood into Bournemouth on A338, Wessex Way. Follow signs to BIC, onto West Cliff. Hotel on right

This friendly, comfortable hotel is conveniently located close to the Bournemouth International Centre and the seafront. Bedrooms are well equipped, some located on the ground floor and some with sea views. In addition to the spacious lounge, there are two bars and a meeting room. A daily-changing menu is offered in the dining room.

Rooms 48 (9 fmly) (5 GF) **S** £29-£55; **D** £58-£110 (incl. bkfst)* **Facilities** STV Free leisure facilities for guests at Marriott Highcliff Hotel ♫ Xmas New Year Wi-fi **Conf** Class 60 Board 40 Thtr 130 Del from £150 to £950 **Services** Lift **Parking** 35

Premier Inn Bournemouth Central

BUDGET HOTEL

☎ 0871 527 8124 📠 0871 527 8125
Westover Rd BH1 2BZ
dir: M27 junct 1, A31. Left at Ashley Heath junct. A338 towards Bournemouth. At rdbt 1st exit. At next rdbt 3rd exit (Holdenhurst Rd). At next rdbt 3rd exit (Bath Rd). At next rdbt 3rd exit onto Bath Hill. At next rdbt into Westover Rd, right into Hinton Rd, hotel on right

High quality, budget accommodation ideal for both families and business travellers. Spacious, en suite bedrooms feature tea and coffee making facilities, and Freeview TV in most hotels. Internet access and Wi-fi are available for a small fee. The adjacent family restaurant features a wide and varied menu. See also the Hotel Groups pages.

Rooms 120 **D** £70-£80*

Premier Inn Bournemouth East

BUDGET HOTEL

☎ 0871 527 8126 📠 0871 527 8127
47 Christchurch Rd, Boscombe BH1 3PA
dir: M27 junct 1, A31, 9m, left at Ashley Heath junct, take A338 signed Bournemouth. At 1st rdbt take 1st exit into Saint Paul's Rd. At 2nd rdbt 1st exit onto Christchurch Rd. Hotel on right

Rooms 20 **D** £65-£70*

B

BOURNEMOUTH *continued*

Premier Inn Bournemouth Westcliffe

BUDGET HOTEL

☎ 0871 527 8128 📠 0871 527 8129
Poole Rd BH2 5QU
dir: M27 junct 1, A31. At Ashley Heath junction, left. Take A338 signed Bournemouth. At Bournemouth West rdbt 1st exit signed Ring Road, West Cliff. At next rdbt (St Michael's) 3rd exit (signed Westbourne) into Poole Rd. Hotel on right

Rooms 101 **D** £60-£70*

BOURTON-ON-THE-WATER Map 10 SP12
Gloucestershire

The Dial House Hotel

★★★ 79% @@ SMALL HOTEL

☎ 01451 822244 📠 01451 810126
The Chestnuts, High St GL54 2AN
e-mail: info@dialhousehotel.com
dir: Off A429, 0.5m to village centre

Located in the main street of this popular Cotswold town, The Dial House offers high quality and comfort throughout. Bedrooms and bathrooms, in a wide variety of shapes and sizes, are luxuriously decorated and furnished. The building itself dates from 1698 and has intimate public areas full of character and quality. Dinner, in the delightful award-winning restaurant, utilises the finest produce and should not be missed.

Rooms 15 (4 annexe) (7 GF) **Facilities** Xmas New Year Wi-fi **Conf** Class 12 Board 12 Thtr 12 **Parking** 20 **Notes** No children 12yrs

Chester House

★★★ 72% SMALL HOTEL

☎ 01451 820286 📠 01451 820471
Victoria St GL54 2BU
e-mail: info@chesterhousehotel.com
dir: On A429 between Northleach & Stow-on-the-Wold

This hotel occupies a secluded but central location in this delightful Cotswold village. Bedrooms, some at ground floor level, are situated in the main house and adjoining coach house. The public areas are stylish, light and airy. Breakfast is taken in the main building whereas dinner is served in the attractive restaurant just a few yards away.

Rooms 22 (10 annexe) (3 fmly) (8 GF) **S** £80-£125; **D** £90-£125 (incl. bkfst)* **Facilities** FTV Beauty therapist New Year Wi-fi **Parking** 18 **Notes** Closed 7 Jan-1 Feb

BOWNESS ON WINDERMERE

See Windermere

BOXWORTH Map 12 TL36
Cambridgeshire

Days Inn Cambridge - A1

BUDGET HOTEL

☎ 01954 267176 📠 01954 267864
Cambridge Extra Services, Junction A14/M11 CB3 8WU
e-mail: cambridge.hotel@welcomebreak.co.uk
dir: A14/M11 Cambridge Extra Services

This modern, purpose built accommodation offers smartly appointed, well-equipped bedrooms, with good power showers. There is a choice of adjacent food outlets where guests may enjoy breakfast, snacks and meals. See also the Hotel Groups pages.

Rooms 82 (14 fmly) (40 GF) (19 smoking) **S** £49.95-£69.95; **D** £59.95-£79.95

BRACKNELL Map 5 SU86
Berkshire

Coppid Beech

★★★★ 75% @ HOTEL

☎ 01344 303333 📠 01344 301200
John Nike Way RG12 8TF
e-mail: sales@coppidbeech.com
web: www.coppidbeech.com
dir: M4 junct 10 take Wokingham/Bracknell onto A329. In 2m take B3408 to Binfield at rdbt. Hotel 200yds on right

This chalet designed hotel offers extensive facilities and includes a ski-slope, ice rink, nightclub, health club and Bier Keller. Bedrooms range from suites to standard rooms - all are impressively equipped. A choice of dining is offered; there's a full bistro menu available in the Keller, and for more formal dining, Rowan's restaurant provides award-winning cuisine.

Rooms 205 (6 fmly) (16 GF) **S** £80-£165; **D** £110-£205 (incl. bkfst) **Facilities** Spa STV Gym Ice rink Dry ski slope Snow boarding Freestyle park New Year Wi-fi **Conf** Class 161 Board 24 Thtr 350 Del from £155 to £195 **Services** Lift Air con **Parking** 350 **Notes** LB Civ Wed 200

Stirrups Country House

★★★ 80% HOTEL

☎ 01344 882284 📠 01344 882300
Maidens Green RG42 6LD
e-mail: reception@stirrupshotel.co.uk
web: www.stirrupshotel.co.uk
dir: 3m N on B3022 towards Windsor

Situated in a peaceful location between Maidenhead, Bracknell and Windsor, this hotel has high standards of comfort particularly in the bedrooms; some rooms have a small sitting room area. There is a popular bar, a restaurant, function rooms and delightful grounds.

Rooms 30 (4 fmly) (2 GF) **D** £82.50-£102.50* **Facilities** STV New Year Wi-fi **Conf** Class 50 Board 40 Thtr 100 Del from £170* **Services** Lift **Parking** 100 **Notes** LB Civ Wed 100

Premier Inn Bracknell Central

BUDGET HOTEL

☎ 0871 527 8132 📠 0871 527 8133
Wokingham Rd RG42 1NA
dir: M4 junct 10, A329(M) (Bracknell) to lights. 1st left, 3rd exit rdbt by Morrisons to town centre. Left at rdbt, left at next rdbt. Hotel on left

High quality, budget accommodation ideal for both families and business travellers. Spacious, en suite bedrooms feature tea and coffee making facilities, and Freeview TV in most hotels. Internet access and Wi-fi are available for a small fee. The adjacent family restaurant features a wide and varied menu. See also the Hotel Groups pages.

Rooms 60 **D** £60-£77*

Premier Inn Bracknell (Twin Bridges)

BUDGET HOTEL

☎ 0871 527 8130 📠 0871 527 8131
Downshire Way RG12 7AA
dir: M4 junct 10, A329(M) towards Bracknell. Straight on at mini rdbt. At Twin Bridges rdbt take 2nd exit. Hotel on right adjacent to Downshire Arms Beefeater

Rooms 28 **D** £60-£70*

BRADFORD Map 19 SE13
West Yorkshire

See also **Gomersal & Shipley**

Cedar Court

★★★★ 71% HOTEL

☎ 01274 406606 & 0845 409 0426
🖷 01274 406600
Mayo Av, Off Rooley Ln BD5 8HZ
e-mail: sales@cedarcourtbradford.co.uk
dir: M62 junct 26/M606. To end of motorway, take 1st left

This purpose built, modern hotel is conveniently located just off the motorway and close to the city centre and the airport. The hotel boasts extensive function and conference facilities, a well-equipped leisure club and an elegant restaurant. Bedrooms are comfortably appointed for both business and leisure guests.

Rooms 131 (7 fmly) (23 GF) (4 smoking) **S** £70-£135; **D** £80-£135 (incl. bkfst) **Facilities** STV FTV Gym Steam room New Year Wi-fi **Conf** Class 300 Board 100 Thtr 800 Del from £99 to £145 **Services** Lift **Parking** 350 **Notes** LB Civ Wed 550

Midland Hotel

★★★ 80% HOTEL

☎ 01274 735735 🖷 01274 720003
Forster Square BD1 4HU
e-mail: info@midland-hotel-bradford.com
web: www.midland-hotel-bradford.com
dir: M62 junct 26/M606, left opp ASDA, left at rdbt onto A650. Through 2 rdbts & 2 lights. Follow A6181/ Haworth signs. Up hill, next left into Manor Row. Hotel 400mtrs

Ideally situated in the heart of the city, this grand Victorian hotel provides modern, very well equipped accommodation and comfortable, spacious day rooms. Ample parking is available in what was once the city's railway station, and a Victorian walkway linking the hotel to the old platform can still be used today.

Rooms 90 (5 fmly) (10 smoking) **S** £65-£110; **D** £75-£165 (incl. bkfst) **Facilities** STV FTV Xmas New Year Wi-fi **Conf** Class 150 Board 100 Thtr 450 Del from £115 to £165* **Services** Lift **Parking** 60 **Notes** LB Civ Wed 450

Best Western Guide Post Hotel

★★★ 75% HOTEL

☎ 0845 409 1362 & 01274 607866
🖷 01274 671085
Common Rd, Low Moor BD12 0ST
e-mail: sue.barnes@guideposthotel.net
web: www.guideposthotel.net
dir: From M606 rdbt take 2nd exit. At next rdbt take 1st exit (Cleckheaton Rd). 0.5m, turn right at bollard into Common Rd

Situated south of the city, this hotel offers attractively styled, modern, comfortable bedrooms. The restaurant offers an extensive range of food using fresh, local produce; lighter snack meals are served in the bar. There is also a choice of well-equipped meeting and function rooms. There is disabled access to the hotel, restaurant and one function room.

Rooms 42 (10 fmly) (13 GF) (8 smoking) **Facilities** STV FTV Complimentary use of nearby swimming & gym facilities Wi-fi **Conf** Class 80 Board 60 Thtr 120 Del from £114.50 to £131.50* **Parking** 100 **Notes** Civ Wed 120

Campanile Bradford

Campanile HOTEL RESTAURANT

★★★ 73% HOTEL

☎ 01274 683683 🖷 0844 800 5769
6 Roydsdale Way, Euroway Estate BD4 6SA
e-mail: bradford@campanile.com
web: www.campanile.com
dir: M62 junct 26 onto M606. Exit Euroway Estate East onto Merrydale Rd, right onto Roydsdale Way

This modern building offers accommodation in smart, well-equipped bedrooms, all with en suite bathrooms. Refreshments may be taken at the informal bistro.

Rooms 130 (37 fmly) (22 GF) (8 smoking) **S** £63; **D** £69* **Facilities** STV FTV Wi-fi **Conf** Class 100 Board 100 Thtr 300 Del from £99 to £125.40* **Services** Lift **Parking** 200 **Notes** Civ Wed 170

Express by Holiday Inn Bradford City Centre

BUDGET HOTEL

☎ 01274 302100 🖷 01274 302132
Vicra Ln, Leisure Exchange BD1 5LD
e-mail: bradford@morethanhotels.com
web: www.hiexpress.com/exbradfordcc
dir: M62 junct 26/M606 last exit at rdbt onto A6177 take 2nd left on to A650 & follow signs for The Leisure Exchange

A modern hotel ideal for families and business travellers. Fresh and uncomplicated, the spacious rooms include Sky TV, power shower and tea and coffee-making facilities. Continental buffet breakfast is included in the room rate; other meals may be taken at the nearby family pub or restaurant. See also the Hotel Groups pages.

Rooms 120 (96 fmly) **Conf** Class 30 Board 30 Thtr 40

BRADFORD-ON-AVON Map 4 ST86
Wiltshire

Woolley Grange

★★★ 82% ◎◎ HOTEL

☎ 01225 864705 🖷 01225 864059
Woolley Green BA15 1TX
e-mail: info@woolleygrangehotel.co.uk
web: www.woolleygrangehotel.co.uk
dir: A4 onto B3109. Bradford Leigh, left at x-roads, hotel 0.5m on right at Woolley Green

This splendid Cotswold manor house is set in beautiful countryside. Children are made especially welcome; there is a trained nanny on duty in the nursery. Bedrooms and public areas are charmingly furnished and decorated in true country-house style, with many thoughtful touches and luxurious extras. The hotel offers a varied and well-balanced menu selection, including ingredients from the hotel's own garden.

Rooms 26 (14 annexe) (20 fmly) (3 GF) **D** £120-£490 (incl. bkfst)* **Facilities** Spa FTV Beauty treatments Football Table tennis Trampoline Boules Cricket Steam room Xmas New Year Wi-fi Child facilities **Conf** Class 12 Board 22 Thtr 35 Del from £150 to £160* **Parking** 40 **Notes** Civ Wed 50

B

BRADFORD-UPON-AVON *continued*

Widbrook Grange

★★★ 77% ® COUNTRY HOUSE HOTEL

☎ 01225 864750 & 863173 📠 01225 862890
Trowbridge Rd, Widbrook BA15 1UH
e-mail: stay@widbrookgrange.com
dir: 1m SE from Bradford on A363, hotel diagonally opposite Bradford Marina & Arabian Stud

This former farmhouse, built as a model farm in the 18th century, has been carefully renovated to provide modern comforts, suitable for both business and leisure guests. Some bedrooms are in the main house, but most are in adjacent converted buildings, and these rooms have their own courtyard entrance and many are located on the ground floor. The lounges offer a good level of comfort. The friendly staff provide a personal and relaxed service.

Rooms 20 (15 annexe) (6 fmly) (13 GF) **S** £95-£125; **D** £135-£145 (incl. bkfst)* **Facilities** FTV ⓢ Gym Children's weekend play room Beauty treatments New Year Wi-fi Child facilities **Conf** Class 35 Board 25 Thtr 50 Del from £115 to £155* **Parking** 50 **Notes** LB ⊗ Closed 24-30 Dec Civ Wed 50

The Old Manor Hotel

★★ 72% HOTEL

☎ 01225 777393 📠 01225 765443
Trowle Common BA14 9BL
e-mail: romanticbeds@oldmanorhotel.com
dir: On A363 between Bradford-on-Avon & Trowbridge

This hotel stands in its own grounds and has been developed from farm buildings that retain much character and charm, and is filled with antiques. Bedrooms are mostly located in annexes and are individually styled; some having four-poster beds. The lounge and restaurant are open-plan and the atmosphere is relaxed.

Rooms 19 (15 annexe) (4 fmly) (15 GF) **Facilities** Wi-fi **Conf** Class 40 Board 30 Thtr 70 **Parking** 60

BRAINTREE Essex **Map 7 TL72**

White Hart Hotel

OldEnglish

★★★ 68% HOTEL

☎ 01376 321401 📠 01376 552628
Bocking End CM7 9AB
e-mail: whitehart.braintree@greeneking.co.uk
web: www.oldenglish.co.uk
dir: Off A120 towards town centre. Hotel at junct B1256 & Bocking Causeway

This 18th-century former coaching inn is conveniently located in the heart of the bustling town centre. The smartly appointed public rooms include a large lounge bar, a restaurant and meeting rooms. The pleasantly decorated bedrooms have co-ordinated fabrics and many thoughtful touches.

Rooms 31 (8 fmly) **S** fr £50; **D** £60-£70 (incl. bkfst)* **Facilities** Xmas New Year Wi-fi **Conf** Class 16 Board 24 Thtr 40 Del from £99* **Parking** 52 **Notes** ⊗ Civ Wed 35

Premier Inn Braintree (A120)

BUDGET HOTEL

☎ 0871 527 8138 📠 0871 527 8139
Cressing Rd, Galley's Corner CM77 8GG
dir: On A120 (Stansted to Braintree link road). Adjacent to Mulberry Tree Brewers Fayre

High quality, budget accommodation ideal for both families and business travellers. Spacious, en suite bedrooms feature tea and coffee making facilities, and Freeview TV in most hotels. Internet access and Wi-fi are available for a small fee. The adjacent family restaurant features a wide and varied menu. See also the Hotel Groups pages.

Rooms 60 **D** £55-£64*

Premier Inn Braintree (Freeport Village)

BUDGET HOTEL

☎ 0871 527 8140 📠 0871 527 8141
Fowlers Farm, Cressing Rd CM77 8DH
dir: M11 junct 8, follow signs to A120 Colchester & Freeport Shopping Village. At Galley's Corner rdbt, 4th exit, left into Wyevale Garden Centre. Hotel adjacent

Rooms 47 **D** £55-£64*

BRAITHWAITE Cumbria **Map 18 NY22**

The Cottage in the Wood

®® RESTAURANT WITH ROOMS

☎ 017687 78409
Whinlatter Pass CA12 5TW
e-mail: relax@thecottageinthewood.co.uk
dir: M6 junct 40, A66 W. After Keswick exit for Braithwaite via Whinlatter Pass (B5292), establishment at top of pass

This charming property sits on wooded hills with striking views of Skiddaw, and it is in a conveniently placed for Keswick. The professional owners provide excellent hospitality in a relaxed manner. The award-winning food, freshly prepared and locally sourced, is served in the bright and welcoming conservatory restaurant that has stunning views. The comfortable bedrooms are well appointed and have many useful extras.

Rooms 9

BRAMPTON Cumbria **Map 21 NY56**

INSPECTORS' CHOICE

Farlam Hall

★★★ HOTEL

☎ 016977 46234 016977 46683
CA8 2NG
e-mail: farlam@relaischateaux.com
web: www.farlamhall.co.uk
dir: On A689 (Brampton to Alston). Hotel 2m on left, (NB not in Farlam village)

This delightful country house has a history dating back to 1428, although the building today is very much the result of alterations carried out in the mid-19th century. The hotel is run by a friendly family team and their enthusiastic staff and is set in beautifully landscaped Victorian gardens complete with an ornamental lake and stream. Lovingly restored over many years, it provides the highest standards of comfort and hospitality. Gracious public rooms invite relaxation, whilst every thought has gone into the beautiful bedrooms, many of which are simply stunning. Nearby are Hadrian's Wall and the Northern Pennines Area of Outstanding Natural Beauty which provide endless opportunities for walking and sightseeing.

Rooms 12 (1 annexe) (2 GF) **S** £160-£190; **D** £300-£360 (incl. bkfst & dinner)* **Facilities** FTV New Year Wi-fi **Conf** Class 24 Board 12 Thtr 24 Del from £185 to £215* **Parking** 25 **Notes** LB No children 5yrs Closed 24-30 Dec & 4-13 Jan Civ Wed 45

BRANCASTER STAITHE Norfolk **Map 13 TF74**

White Horse

★★★ 79% HOTEL

☎ 01485 210262 01485 210930
PE31 8BY
e-mail: reception@whitehorsebrancaster.co.uk
web: www.whitehorsebrancaster.co.uk
dir: On A149 (coast road) midway between Hunstanton & Wells-next-the-Sea

A charming hotel situated on the north Norfolk coast with contemporary bedrooms in two wings, some featuring an interesting cobbled fascia. Each room is attractively decorated and thoughtfully equipped. There is a large bar and a lounge area leading through to the conservatory restaurant, with stunning tidal marshland views across to Scolt Head Island.

Rooms 15 (8 annexe) (4 fmly) (8 GF) **S** £77-£125; **D** £94-£190 (incl. bkfst)* **Facilities** Xmas New Year Wi-fi **Parking** 60 **Notes** LB

BRANDESBURTON East Riding of Yorkshire **Map 17 TA14**

Burton Lodge

★★ 71% HOTEL

☎ 01964 542847 01964 544771
YO25 8RU
e-mail: enquiries@burton-lodge.co.uk
dir: 7m from Beverley off A165, at Hainsworth Park Golf Club

A tennis court, sports play area and extensive lawns are features of this friendly hotel, which is situated in two acres of grounds adjoining a golf course. The modern bedrooms look out either onto the golf course or the countryside; there is a comfortable lounge with a small bar and a spacious restaurant that offers tasty home cooking.

Rooms 9 (2 annexe) (3 fmly) (2 GF) **Facilities** 18 Putt green Pitch and putt **Conf** Class 20 **Parking** 15 **Notes** Closed 25-26 Dec

BRANDON Suffolk **Map 13 TL78**

Brandon House

U

☎ 01842 810171 01842 814859
High St IP27 0AX
e-mail: book@brandonhouse.co.uk

Currently the rating for this establishment is not confirmed. This may be due to a change of ownership or because it has only recently joined the AA rating scheme. For further details please see the AA website: theAA.com

Rooms 16 **S** £55-£75; **D** £65-£95 (incl. bkfst)*

BRANDON Warwickshire **Map 11 SP47**

Mercure Brandon Hall Hotel & Spa

★★★ 77% HOTEL

☎ 024 7654 6000 024 7654 4909
Main St CV8 3FW
e-mail: h6625@accor.com
web: www.mercure.com
dir: A45 towards Coventry S. After Peugeot-Citroen garage on left, at island take 5th exit to M1 South/ London (back onto A45). After 200yds, immediately after Texaco garage, left into Brandon Ln, hotel after 2.5m

An impressive tree lined avenue leads to this 17th-century property which sits in 17 acres of grounds. The hotel provides a peaceful and friendly sanctuary away from the hustle and bustle. The bedrooms provide comfortable facilities and a good range of extras for guest comfort. There is a Spa Naturel with health, beauty and fitness facilities in a separate building with ample parking.

Rooms 120 (30 annexe) (50 GF) (8 smoking) **Facilities** Spa STV Gym New Year Wi-fi **Conf** Thtr 250 **Services** Lift **Parking** 200 **Notes** Civ Wed 150

B

BRANDS HATCH
Kent — Map 6 TQ56

Brandshatch Place Hotel & Spa
HandPICKED HOTELS

★★★★ 79% ®® HOTEL

☎ 01474 875000 🖹 01474 879652
Brands Hatch Rd, Fawkham DA3 8NQ
e-mail: brandshatchplace@handpicked.co.uk
web: www.handpicked.co.uk
dir: M25 junct 3/A20 West Kingsdown. Left at paddock entrance/Fawkham Green sign. 3rd left signed Fawkham Rd. Hotel 500mtrs on right

This charming 18th-century Georgian country house close to the famous racing circuit offers stylish and elegant rooms. Bedrooms are appointed to a very high standard, offering impressive facilities and excellent levels of comfort and quality. The hotel also features a comprehensive leisure club with substantial crèche facilities.

Rooms 38 (12 annexe) (1 fmly) (6 GF) **S** £89-£194; **D** £99-£204 (incl. bkfst)* **Facilities** Spa FTV Gym Squash Aerobic dance studio Sauna Steam room Xmas New Year Wi-fi **Conf** Class 60 Board 50 Thtr 160 **Services** Lift **Parking** 100 **Notes** LB Civ Wed 110

Thistle Brands Hatch
thistle

★★★★ 76% HOTEL

☎ 0871 376 9008 🖹 0871 376 9108
DA3 8PE
e-mail: brandshatch@thistle.co.uk
web: www.thistle.com/brandshatch
dir: Follow Brands Hatch signs, hotel on left of racing circuit entrance

Ideally situated overlooking Brands Hatch race track and close to the major road networks (M20/M25). The open-plan public areas include a choice of bars, large lounge and a restaurant. Bedrooms are stylishly appointed and well equipped for both leisure and business guests. Extensive meeting rooms and Otium leisure facilities are also available. Thistle Hotels – AA Hotel Group of the Year 2011-12.

Rooms 121 (5 fmly) (60 GF) (6 smoking) **Facilities** Spa Gym New Year Wi-fi **Conf** Class 120 Board 60 Thtr 270 Del from £130 to £165 **Parking** 200 **Notes** Civ Wed 100

BRANKSOME

See Poole

BRANSCOMBE
Devon — Map 4 SY18

Bulstone

★★ 68% HOTEL

☎ 01297 680446 🖹 01297 680000
High Bulstone EX12 3BL
e-mail: bulstone@aol.com
web: www.childfriendlyhotels.com
dir: A3052, Exeter to Lyme Regis, Branscombe Cross, follow brown hotel sign

Situated in a peaceful location close to the beautiful east Devon coast, this family-friendly hotel is ideally placed for a relaxing break with plenty of attractions within easy reach. All bedrooms comprise a main bedroom and separate children's room, each being practically furnished and equipped. Additional facilities include a playroom, a snug lounge, and the dining room where enjoyable home-cooked meals are offered. There is no charge for children under ten, and children's tea is at 5pm.

Rooms 7 (7 fmly) (4 GF) **S** £65-£110; **D** £90-£110 (incl. bkfst)* **Facilities** FTV Children's playroom Xmas New Year Wi-fi **Conf** Class 25 Board 25 **Services** Air con **Parking** 25 **Notes** LB

BREADSALL
Derbyshire — Map 11 SK33

Breadsall Priory, A Marriott Hotel & Country Club
Marriott HOTELS & RESORTS

★★★★ 75% ® COUNTRY HOUSE HOTEL

☎ 01332 832235 🖹 01332 833509
Moor Rd DE7 6DL
web: www.marriottbreadsallpriory.co.uk
dir: A52 to Derby, at Pentagon rdbt 3rd exit towards A61/Chesterfield. At 3rd rdbt take 3rd exit & 1st left into village, left at church into Moor Rd. Hotel 1.5m on left

This extended mansion house is set in 400 acres of parkland and well-tended gardens. The smart bedrooms are mostly contained in the modern wing. There is a vibrant café-bar, a more formal restaurant and a large room-service menu. The extensive leisure facilities include two golf courses and a swimming pool. Dinner in the Priory Restaurant is a highlight.

Rooms 112 (100 annexe) (40 fmly) **Facilities** Spa STV 36 Putt green Gym Health, beauty & hair salon Dance studio Leisure club Xmas New Year Wi-fi **Conf** Class 50 Board 36 Thtr 120 Del from £135 to £165* **Services** Lift **Parking** 300 **Notes** Civ Wed 100

BRENTFORD
Greater London

See LONDON plan 1 C3

Premier Inn London Kew

BUDGET HOTEL

☎ 0871 527 8670 🖹 0871 527 8671
52 High St TW8 0BB
dir: At junct of A4 (M4), A205 & A406, Chiswick rdbt, take A205 towards Kew & Brentford. 200yds right fork onto A315 (High St), for 0.5m. Hotel on left

High quality, budget accommodation ideal for both families and business travellers. Spacious, en suite bedrooms feature tea and coffee making facilities, and Freeview TV in most hotels. Internet access and Wi-fi are available for a small fee. The adjacent family restaurant features a wide and varied menu. See also the Hotel Groups pages.

Rooms 141 **D** £69-£83*

BRENT KNOLL
Somerset — Map 4 ST35

Woodlands Country House Hotel

★★★ 74% ® SMALL HOTEL

☎ 01278 760232 🖹 01278 769090
Hill Ln TA9 4DF
e-mail: info@woodlands-hotel.co.uk
web: www.woodlands-hotel.co.uk
dir: A38 take 1st left into village, then 5th right & 1st left, follow brown tourist signs

Located at the foot of Brent Knoll in four-acre grounds, this is an ideal base for both business and leisure travellers as it is within easy reach of the M5. The atmosphere is relaxed and welcoming with attentive service at all times. Bedrooms are all individually styled and reflect much charm. The elegant dining room has lovely views across the countryside and offers a well balanced menu featuring excellent local produce.

Rooms 9 (1 fmly) (1 GF) **Facilities** Xmas New Year **Conf** Class 20 Board 30 Thtr 30 **Parking** 16 **Notes** RS Sun Civ Wed 65

Brent Knoll Lodge & Fox & Goose Inn

★★ 78% HOTEL

☎ 01278 760008 🖹 01278 769236
Bristol Rd TA9 4HH
e-mail: reception@brentknolllodge.com
web: www.brentknolllodge.com
dir: On A38 approx 500mtrs N of M5 junct 22

The lodge is conveniently located just a few minutes drive from the M5 and is next door to the Fox & Goose Inn which offers a wide range of beverages and freshly prepared dishes. The American-style diner provides something that is distinctly different. Bedrooms, some at ground-floor level, are well equipped and spacious.

Rooms 14 (3 fmly) (7 GF) **S** £60-£80; **D** £65-£95* **Facilities** FTV Children's outdoor play area Xmas Wi-fi **Conf** Class 32 Board 20 Thtr 32 Del from £100 to £120* **Services** Lift Air con **Parking** 60 **Notes** LB

BRENTWOOD Map 6 TQ59
Essex

Marygreen Manor

CLASSIC BRITISH HOTELS

★★★★ 75% ◎◎ HOTEL

☎ 01277 225252 🖹 01277 262809
London Rd CM14 4NR
e-mail: info@marygreenmanor.co.uk
web: www.marygreenmanor.co.uk
dir: M25 junct 28, onto A1023 over 2 sets of lights, hotel on right

A 16th-century house which was built by Robert Wright, who named the house 'Manor of Mary Green' after his young bride. Public rooms exude character and have a wealth of original features that include exposed beams, carved panelling and the impressive Tudors Restaurant. Bedrooms are tastefully decorated and thoughtfully equipped.

Rooms 44 (40 annexe) (35 GF) (9 smoking) **Facilities** STV Wi-fi **Conf** Class 20 Board 25 Thtr 50 Del from £185 to £220 **Parking** 100 **Notes** LB ⊗ Civ Wed 60

De Rougemont Manor

★★★★ 74% HOTEL

☎ 01277 226418 & 220483 🖹 01277 239020
Great Warley St CM13 3JP
e-mail: info@derougemontmanor.co.uk
web: www.derougemontmanor.co.uk
dir: M25 junct 29, A127 to Southend then B186 towards Great Warley

Expect a warm welcome at this family owned and managed hotel, situated on the outskirts of Brentwood just off the M25. The stylish bedrooms are divided between the main hotel and a bedroom wing; each one is tastefully appointed and well equipped. Public rooms include a smart lounge bar, restaurant and a choice of seating areas.

Rooms 79 (10 annexe) (6 fmly) (16 GF) (10 smoking) **S** £79-£99; **D** £99-£129 (incl. bkfst)* **Facilities** FTV Gym 3-acre nature reserve Xmas New Year Wi-fi **Conf** Class 120 Board 16 Thtr 200 Del from £150 to £180* **Services** Lift Air con **Parking** 133 **Notes** ⊗ Civ Wed 90

Holiday Inn Brentwood

Holiday Inn

★★★ 80% HOTEL

☎ 0871 942 9012 🖹 01277 264264
Brook St CM14 5NF
e-mail: reservations-brentwoodm25@ihg.com
web: www.holidayinn.co.uk
dir: Exit M25 junct 28 (or A12 at M25 interchange). Follow signs to Brentwood/A1023. Hotel 200yds

Ideally located just off the M25, this hotel is only 40 minutes from central London and 25 minutes from Stansted Airport, making it the perfect choice for business and leisure travellers alike. The public areas are smartly appointed; the health and fitness club has an indoor swimming pool.

Rooms 149 (28 fmly) (43 GF) (8 smoking) **Facilities** STV Gym New Year Wi-fi **Conf** Class 60 Board 50 Thtr 140 Del from £115 to £180 **Services** Lift Air con **Parking** 276 **Notes** ⊗ Civ Wed

Premier Inn Brentwood

BUDGET HOTEL

☎ 0871 527 8142 🖹 0871 527 8143
Brentwood House, 169 Kings Rd CM14 4EF
dir: From S: M25 junct 28 take A1023 (or from N: at Brook Street rdbt 2nd exit onto A1023). Right at lights into Kings Rd, at rdbt 2nd exit into Kings Rd

High quality, budget accommodation ideal for both families and business travellers. Spacious, en suite bedrooms feature tea and coffee making facilities, and Freeview TV in most hotels. Internet access and Wi-fi are available for a small fee. The adjacent family restaurant features a wide and varied menu. See also the Hotel Groups pages.

Rooms 122 **D** £58-£66*

BRIDGNORTH Map 10 SO79
Shropshire

Old Vicarage Hotel

★★★ 83% ◎◎◎ SMALL HOTEL

☎ 01746 716497 🖹 01746 716552
Worfield WV15 5JZ
e-mail: admin@oldvicarageworfield.co.uk
web: www.oldvicarageworfield.com
dir: Off A454, approx 3.5m NE of Bridgnorth, 5m S of Telford's southern business area. Follow brown signs

This delightful property is set in acres of wooded farmland in a quiet and peaceful area of Shropshire. Service is friendly and helpful, and customer care is one the many strengths of this charming small hotel. The well-equipped bedrooms are individually appointed, and thoughtfully and luxuriously furnished. The lounge and conservatory are the perfect places to enjoy a pre-dinner drink or the complimentary afternoon tea. The restaurant is a joy, serving award-winning modern British cuisine in elegant surroundings.

Rooms 14 (4 annexe) (1 fmly) (2 GF) **S** £70-£110; **D** £80-£150 (incl. bkfst) **Facilities** FTV New Year Wi-fi **Conf** Class 40 Board 30 Thtr 60 **Parking** 30 **Notes** LB Civ Wed 60

B

BRIDGWATER
Somerset

Map 4 ST23

See also **Holford**

Walnut Tree Hotel

★★★ 77% ® HOTEL

☎ 01278 662255 🖷 01278 663946
North Petherton TA6 6QA
e-mail: reservations@walnuttreehotel.com
web: www.walnuttreehotel.com
dir: M5 junct 24. Follow North Petherton signs. 1.3m. Hotel in village centre

Popular with both business and leisure guests, this 18th-century former coaching inn is conveniently located within easy reach of the M5. The spacious and smartly decorated bedrooms are well furnished to ensure a comfortable and relaxing stay. An extensive selection of dishes is offered in either the restaurant, or the more informal setting of the bistro.

Rooms 30 (3 fmly) (3 GF) **S** £79-£99; **D** £99-£129 (incl. bkfst)* **Facilities** FTV Xmas New Year Wi-fi **Conf** Class 60 Board 50 Thtr 100 Del from £100 to £150* **Parking** 70 **Notes** LB ® Civ Wed 100

Apple Tree Hotel

★★★ 68% HOTEL

☎ 01278 733238 🖷 01278 732693
Keenthorne TA5 1HZ
e-mail: reservations@appletreehotel.com
web: www.appletreehotel.com

(For full entry see Nether Stowey)

Premier Inn Bridgwater

BUDGET HOTEL

☎ 0871 527 8148 🖷 0871 527 8149
Express Park, Bristol Rd TA6 4RR
dir: M5 junct 23, A38 to Bridgwater. Hotel on right in 2m

High quality, budget accommodation ideal for both families and business travellers. Spacious, en suite bedrooms feature tea and coffee making facilities, and Freeview TV in most hotels. Internet access and Wi-fi are available for a small fee. The adjacent family restaurant features a wide and varied menu. See also the Hotel Groups pages.

Rooms 40 **D** £59*

BRIDLINGTON
East Riding of Yorkshire

Map 17 TA16

Expanse

★★★ 75% HOTEL

☎ 01262 675347 🖷 01262 604928
North Marine Dr YO15 2LS
e-mail: reservations@expanse.co.uk
web: www.expanse.co.uk
dir: Follow North Beach signs, pass under railway arch for North Marine Drive. Hotel at bottom of hill

This traditional seaside hotel overlooks the bay and has been in the same family's ownership for many years. Service is relaxed and friendly and the modern bedrooms are well equipped. Comfortable public areas include a conference suite, a choice of bars and an inviting lounge.

Rooms 47 (5 fmly) **S** £29.95-£79; **D** £89.90-£140 (incl. bkfst)* **Facilities** FTV ♫ Xmas New Year Wi-fi **Conf** Class 50 Board 50 Thtr 180 **Services** Lift **Parking** 23 **Notes** LB ® Civ Wed 140

BRIDPORT
Dorset

Map 4 SY49

Haddon House

★★★ 67% HOTEL

☎ 01308 423626 & 425323 🖷 01308 427348
West Bay DT6 4EL
e-mail: info@haddonhousehotel.co.uk
dir: At Crown Inn rdbt take B3157 West Bay Rd, hotel 0.5m on right at mini-rdbt

This attractive, creeper-clad hotel offers good standards of accommodation and is situated a few minutes' walk from the seafront and the quay. A friendly and relaxed style of service is provided. An extensive range of dishes, from lighter bar snacks to main meals, is on offer in the Tudor-style restaurant.

Rooms 12 (2 fmly) (1 GF) **Facilities** FTV New Year Wi-fi **Conf** Class 20 Board 26 Thtr 60 **Parking** 44 **Notes** LB ®

Bridge House

THE INDEPENDENTS HOTEL ASSOCIATION

★★ 76% HOTEL

☎ 01308 423371 🖷 01308 459573
115 East St DT6 3LB
e-mail: info@bridgehousebridport.co.uk
dir: Follow signs to town centre from A35 rdbt, hotel 200mtrs on right

A short stroll from the town centre, this 18th-century Grade II listed property offers well-equipped bedrooms that vary in size. In addition to the main lounge, there is a small bar-lounge and a separate breakfast room. An interesting range of home-cooked meals is provided in the wine bar and brasserie.

Rooms 10 (3 fmly) **S** £69-£105; **D** £98-£148 (incl. bkfst)* **Facilities** FTV New Year Wi-fi **Conf** Class 20 Board 15 Thtr 36 **Parking** 13 **Notes** LB

BRIGHOUSE
West Yorkshire Map 16 SE12

Holiday Inn Leeds-Brighouse

★★★ 81% HOTEL

☎ 0871 942 9013 🖹 01484 400068
Clifton Village HD6 4HW
e-mail: brighouse@ihg.com
web: www.holidayinn.co.uk
dir: M62 junct 25, A644 signed Brighouse. Remain in right lane, 1st right, hotel at next left

A modern hotel built from traditional Yorkshire stone, and easily accessible from the M62. The bedrooms are spacious and include executive rooms. Other facilities include a leisure club, meeting rooms and ample parking.

Rooms 94 (14 fmly) (43 GF) **Facilities** STV supervised Gym Xmas New Year Wi-fi **Conf** Class 120 Board 50 Thtr 200 **Services** Air con **Parking** 197 **Notes** Civ Wed 200

Premier Inn Huddersfield North

BUDGET HOTEL

☎ 0871 527 8530 🖹 0871 527 8531
Wakefield Rd HD6 4HA
dir: M62 junct 25, A644 signed Huddersfield, Dewsbury & Wakefield. Hotel 500mtrs up hill on right

High quality, budget accommodation ideal for both families and business travellers. Spacious, en suite bedrooms feature tea and coffee making facilities, and Freeview TV in most hotels. Internet access and Wi-fi are available for a small fee. The adjacent family restaurant features a wide and varied menu. See also the Hotel Groups pages.

Rooms 71 **D** £51-£58*

BRIGHTON & HOVE
East Sussex Map 6 TQ30

See also **Steyning**

Thistle Brighton

thistle

★★★★ 78% HOTEL

☎ 01273 206700 🖹 0870 333 9229
King's Rd BN1 2GS
e-mail: brighton@thistle.co.uk
web: www.thistlehotels.com/brighton
dir: A23 to seafront. At rdbt turn right, hotel 200yds on right

Situated overlooking the sea and within easy reach of the town's many attractions this hotel is built around an atrium and offers air-conditioned rooms including luxury suites. The restaurant provides stunning sea views, and a comfortable, spacious lounge and bar offer a full range of drinks, light refreshments and meals. The Otium Health & Fitness Club has a pool, sauna and gym facilities plus health and beauty treatments. Thistle Hotels – AA Hotel Group of the Year 2011-12.

Rooms 210 (29 fmly) **Facilities** STV FTV supervised Sauna Solarium Beauty treatment rooms Xmas New Year Wi-fi **Conf** Class 180 Board 120 Thtr 300 **Services** Lift Air con **Parking** 68 **Notes** Civ Wed 300

Hotel du Vin Brighton

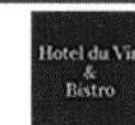

★★★★ 77%
TOWN HOUSE HOTEL

☎ 01273 718588 🖹 01273 718599
2-6 Ship St BN1 1AD
e-mail: info@brighton.hotelduvin.com
web: www.hotelduvin.com
dir: From A23 follow seafront/city centre signs. Right at seafront, right into Middle St. Follow to end bear right into Ship St. Hotel on right

This tastefully converted mock-Tudor building occupies a convenient location in a quiet side street close to the seafront. The individually designed bedrooms have a wine theme, and all are comprehensively equipped. Public areas offer a spacious split-level bar, an atmospheric and locally popular restaurant, plus useful private dining and meeting facilities.

Rooms 49 (2 fmly) (4 GF) **Facilities** STV Xmas New Year Wi-fi **Conf** Class 50 Board 60 Thtr 80 **Services** Air con **Notes** Civ Wed 120

Barceló Brighton Old Ship Hotel

★★★★ 74% HOTEL

☎ 01273 329001 🖹 01273 820718
King's Rd BN1 1NR
e-mail: oldship@barcelo-hotels.co.uk
web: www.barcelo-hotels.co.uk
dir: A23 to seafront, right at rdbt along Kings Rd. Hotel 200yds on right

This historic hotel enjoys a stunning seafront location and offers guests elegant surroundings to relax in. Bedrooms are well designed, with modern facilities ensuring comfort. Many original features have been retained, including the Paganini Ballroom. Facilities include a sleek bar, alfresco dining and a variety of conference rooms.

Rooms 152 **Facilities** STV Xmas New Year Wi-fi **Conf** Class 100 Board 35 Thtr 250 **Services** Lift **Parking** 40 **Notes** Civ Wed 150

Holiday Inn Brighton - Seafront

★★★★ 71% HOTEL

☎ 01273 828250 🖹 01273 775877
137 Kings Rd BN1 2JF
e-mail: reservations@hibrighton.com
web: www.holidayinn.co.uk
dir: M25 junct 7 to M23 southbound, A23 to town centre, follow signs to seafront, hotel on A259 opposite West Pier

Overlooking the seafront and within walking distance to the town centre, restaurants and pier, this spacious hotel offers modern amenities for leisure and business guests. The bedrooms are spacious and well equipped, and the executive rooms have additional facilities. Public areas include spacious lounges, sports bar and a modern restaurant with an outdoor terrace. A range of meeting rooms is also available.

Rooms 131 (23 fmly) **S** £99-£200; **D** £99-£200 **Facilities** STV Xmas New Year Wi-fi **Conf** Class 200 Board 50 Thtr 450 **Services** Lift Air con **Parking** 64 **Notes** LB Civ Wed 400

B

BRIGHTON & HOVE *continued*

Lansdowne Place Hotel & Spa

★★★★ 70% HOTEL

☎ 01273 736266 📠 01273 729802
Lansdowne Place BN3 1HQ
e-mail: info.brighton@rezidorparkinn.com
web: www.brighton.parkinn.co.uk
dir: A23 to seafront. Right at Brighton Pier, along seafront, right at Lansdowne Place

Following a £2 million refurbishment this establishment, now known as a 'boutique' hotel, proves a very stylish choice. The bright and spacious bedrooms, many with sea views, include plasma screen TVs and walk-in showers; suites are also available. The hotel offers a full range of beauty treatments and therapies in its state-of-the-art spa, and for the energetic there is a well-equipped gym. Weddings and meetings are also catered for.

Rooms 84 **Facilities** Spa Gym Wi-fi **Conf** Class 217 Board 206 Thtr 340 **Services** Lift **Parking** 14 **Notes** ® Civ Wed 200

Best Western Princes Marine

★★★ 75% HOTEL

☎ 01273 207660 📠 01273 325913
153 Kingsway BN3 4GR
e-mail: princesmarine@bestwestern.co.uk
dir: Right at Brighton Pier, follow seafront for 2m. Hotel 200yds from King Alfred leisure centre

This friendly hotel enjoys a seafront location and offers spacious, comfortable bedrooms equipped with a good range of facilities including free Wi-fi. There is a stylish restaurant, modern bar and selection of roof-top meeting rooms with sea views. Limited parking is available at the rear.

Rooms 48 (4 fmly) **Facilities** Xmas **Conf** Class 40 Board 40 Thtr 80 **Services** Lift **Parking** 30

Best Western Brighton Hotel

★★★ 74% METRO HOTEL

☎ 01273 820555 📠 01273 821555
143/145 King's Rd BN1 2PQ
e-mail: info@thebrightonhotel.com
web: www.thebrightonhotel.co.uk
dir: M23 onto A23 to pier. Right at rdbt, hotel just past West Pier

This friendly hotel is well placed in a prime seafront location close to the historic West Pier. The contemporary bedrooms are spaciously appointed and well equipped. The lounge, bar and restaurant are sunny, bright and comfortable with great sea views. Dinner is not available in the restaurant but a 24-hour room service menu is in place, and restaurants are within easy walking distance. Parking facilities, though limited, are a real bonus in this area of town.

Rooms 55 (6 fmly) **S** £34-£110; **D** £35-£250* **Facilities** FTV Xmas New Year Wi-fi **Conf** Class 30 Board 40 Thtr 70 Del from £110 to £185* **Services** Lift **Parking** 10 **Notes** ® Civ Wed 140

Imperial Hotel

★★★ 74% HOTEL

☎ 01273 777320 📠 01273 777310
First Av BN3 2GU
e-mail: info@imperial-hove.com
web: www.imperial-hove.com
dir: M23 to Brighton seafront, right at rdbt to Hove. 1.5m to First Ave, turn right

Located within minutes of the seafront, this Regency property is constantly being improved and upgraded. A good range of conference suites complement the comfortable public rooms, which include a lounge, a smart bar area and an attractive restaurant. Bedrooms are generally of comfortable proportions, well appointed and with a good range of facilities.

Rooms 76 (2 fmly) **Facilities** FTV Xmas New Year Wi-fi **Conf** Class 30 Board 34 Thtr 110 Del from £95 to £150 **Services** Lift **Notes** ®

The Kings Hotel

★★★ 70% METRO HOTEL

☎ 01273 820854
139-141 Kings Rd BN1 2NA
dir: Follow signs to seafront. At Brighton Pier rdbt take 3rd exit & drive west (seafront on left). Hotel adjacent to West Pier

Located on the seafront adjacent to West Pier, this Grade II listed, Regency building has been restored to offer contemporary accommodation. Although the hotel does not provide a full dinner service, light snacks are available throughout the day and evening in the public areas and also in the guests' bedrooms. There is limited parking space which is a bonus in Brighton.

Rooms 90 (3 fmly) (6 GF) **Conf** Class 25 Board 30 Thtr 70 **Notes** ®

Queens Hotel

★★★ 68% HOTEL

☎ 01273 321222 & 0800 970 7570
01273 203059
1-3 King's Rd BN1 1NS
e-mail: info@queenshotelbrighton.com
dir: A23 to Brighton town centre, follow signs for seafront. At Brighton Pier right onto seafront, hotel 500mtrs

This hotel has a fantastic location with views of the beach and pier. The modern bedrooms and bathrooms are spacious, and many benefit from uninterrupted sea views. All bedrooms have LCD TVs and free Wi-fi. There is a spacious bar and restaurant area plus fully equipped spa, gym and swimming pool.

Rooms 94 (24 fmly) (10 smoking) **S** £59-£160; **D** £69-£200 (incl. bkfst)* **Facilities** Spa FTV supervised Gym Beauty salon Wi-fi **Conf** Class 50 Board 50 Thtr 150 Del from £120 to £195* **Services** Lift **Notes** LB Civ Wed 120

The Courtlands Hotel & Conference Centre

★★★ 64% HOTEL

☎ 01273 731055 01273 328295
15-27 The Drive BN3 3JE
e-mail: info@courtlandshotel.com
dir: At junct of A23 & A27. Take 1st exit to Hove, 2nd exit at rdbt, right at 1st junct. Left at shops. Straight on at junct. Hotel on left

This hotel is located on a tree-lined avenue within walking distance of the seafront and has its own small car park. The bedrooms come in a variety of styles and include executive rooms and suites. Guests have the use of a comfortable lounge, a light and spacious restaurant. Service is both friendly and attentive.

Rooms 67 (7 annexe) (8 fmly) **S** £44-£85; **D** £65-£125 **Facilities** STV FTV Xmas New Year Wi-fi **Conf** Class 100 Board 80 Thtr 100 Del from £95 to £130 **Services** Lift **Parking** 30 **Notes** LB

Preston Park Hotel

★★ 67% HOTEL

☎ 01273 507853 01273 540039
216 Preston Rd BN1 6UU
e-mail: manager@prestonparkhotel.co.uk
dir: On A23 towards town centre. 5 mins from Preston Park train station

This hotel enjoys a convenient roadside location on the outskirts of Brighton. Bedrooms are modern in style and well provisioned for both the leisure and business guest. Freshly prepared meals are offered in the spacious Sussex Bar (open 24 hours to residents) and in the more intimate and relaxing restaurant. Guests can enjoy a drink on the patio in summer.

Rooms 33 (4 fmly) **Facilities** Gym Xmas New Year **Conf** Class 80 Board 80 Thtr 200 Del from £110 to £160 **Parking** 60 **Notes** Civ Wed 150

De Vere Grand, Brighton

DE VERE Hotels & Resorts

U

☎ 01273 224300 01273 224321
King's Rd BN1 2FW
e-mail: reservations@grandbrighton.co.uk
web: www.devere.co.uk
dir: On A259, seafront road between piers, adjacent to Brighton Centre

Currently the rating for this establishment is not confirmed. This may be due to a change of ownership or because it has only recently joined the AA rating scheme. For further details please see the AA website: theAA.com

Rooms 200 (60 fmly) **S** fr £105; **D** fr £115 (incl. bkfst)* **Facilities** STV Gym In room therapies Xmas New Year Wi-fi **Conf** Class 420 Board 50 Thtr 700 Del from £150 to £245* **Services** Lift **Parking** 50 **Notes** Civ Wed 800

Drakes

U

☎ 01273 696934 01273 684805
43-44 Marine Pde BN2 1PE
e-mail: info@drakesofbrighton.com
dir: From A23 at Brighton Pier rdbt. Left into Marine Pde towards marina. Hotel on left before lights (ornate water feature at front)

Currently the rating for this establishment is not confirmed. This may be due to a change of ownership or because it has only recently joined the AA rating scheme. For further details please see the AA website: theAA.com

Rooms 20 (2 GF) **Facilities** STV Wi-fi **Conf** Class 18 Board 12 Thtr 18 **Services** Air con **Parking** 13 **Notes** LB Civ Wed 45

Premier Inn Brighton City Centre

BUDGET HOTEL

☎ 0871 527 8150 0871 527 8151
144 North St BN1 1RE
dir: From A23 follow signs for city centre. Right at lights near Royal Pavilion, take road ahead on left (runs adjacent to Pavilion) into Church St, 1st left into New Rd leading North St

High quality, budget accommodation ideal for both families and business travellers. Spacious, en suite bedrooms feature tea and coffee making facilities, and Freeview TV in most hotels. Internet access and Wi-fi are available for a small fee. The adjacent family restaurant features a wide and varied menu. See also the Hotel Groups pages.

Rooms 160 **D** £69-£72*

B

BRISTOL
Bristol — Map 4 ST57

Doubletree by Hilton Cadbury House

★★★★ 80% HOTEL

☎ 01934 834343 01934 834390
Frost Hill, Congresbury BS49 5AD
e-mail: info@cadburyhouse.com
web: www.cadburyhouse.com
dir: On B3133, approx 0.25m from A370 at Congresbury

Externally this hotel presents an interesting blend of old and new, but inside there's contemporary, stylish accommodation with a wide range of facilities, suitable for both business and leisure guests. The bar has a vibrant atmosphere while the restaurant is relaxed and the service friendly. Just a stroll away from the main building is the leisure club and spa featuring a good sized pool, treatment rooms and an air-conditioned gym with state-of-the-art equipment.

Rooms 72 (4 fmly) **Facilities** Spa FTV Gym Xmas New Year Wi-fi **Conf** Class 150 Board 60 Thtr 250 **Services** Lift Air con **Parking** 350 **Notes** Civ Wed 130

B

BRISTOL ***continued***

Aztec Hotel & Spa

★★★★ 80% HOTEL

☎ 01454 201090 01454 201593
Aztec West Business Park, Almondsbury BS32 4TS
e-mail: aztec@shirehotels.com
web: www.aztechotelbristol.com
dir: Access via M5 junct 16 & M4

Situated close to Cribbs Causeway shopping centre and major motorway links, this stylish hotel offers comfortable, very well-equipped bedrooms. Built in a Nordic style, public rooms boast log fires and vaulted ceilings. Leisure facilities include a popular gym and good size pool. The Quarterjacks restaurant offers relaxed informal dining with a focus on simply prepared, quality regional foods.

Rooms 128 (8 fmly) (29 GF) **S** £100-£200; **D** £110-£210* **Facilities** Spa STV Gym Steam room Sauna Children's splash pool Activity studio New Year Wi-fi **Conf** Class 120 Board 36 Thtr 200 Del from £135 to £185* **Services** Lift **Parking** 240 **Notes** LB Civ Wed 120

Bristol Marriott Royal Hotel

★★★★ 79% HOTEL

☎ 0117 925 5100 0117 925 1515
College Green BS1 5TA
e-mail: bristol.royal@marriotthotels.co.uk
web: www.bristolmarriottroyal.co.uk
dir: Adjacent to cathedral

A truly stunning hotel located in the centre of the city, next to the cathedral. Public areas are particularly impressive with luxurious lounges and a leisure club. Dining options include the informal Terrace and the really spectacular, restaurant adjacent to the champagne bar. The spacious bedrooms have the benefit of air conditioning, comfortable armchairs and marble bathrooms.

Rooms 242 (6 smoking) **S** £80-£120; **D** £110-£350* **Facilities** Gym Hair & beauty salon Xmas New Year Wi-fi **Conf** Class 80 Board 84 Thtr 300 Del from £140 to £195* **Services** Lift Air con **Parking** 200 **Notes** LB Civ Wed 200

Mint Hotel Bristol

★★★★ 78% HOTEL

☎ 0117 925 1001 0117 907 4116
Temple Way BS1 6BF
e-mail: bristol.reservations@minthotel.com
web: www.minthotel.com
dir: M4 junct 19 onto M32. Continue to end, turn left, follow Temple Meads Station signs. Through underpass, hotel on right

This hotel enjoys a good central location on Temple Way, and offers contemporary bedrooms that feature iMacs, complimentary high-speed Wi-fi, power showers, and 24-hour room service; many rooms have views of the park. The popular City Café offers a high standard of modern cooking along with friendly and attentive service. Several meeting rooms and parking (though limited) are further bonuses.

Rooms 167 (3 GF) **Facilities** STV FTV Gym Wi-fi **Conf** Class 26 Board 28 Thtr 50 **Services** Lift Air con **Parking** 45 **Notes** LB Civ Wed 50

Mercure Bristol Holland House Hotel & Spa

★★★★ 77% HOTEL

☎ 0117 968 9900 0117 968 9866
Redcliffe Hill BS1 6SQ
e-mail: h6698@accor.com
web: www.mercure.com
dir: M4 junct 19 towards city centre, follow signs A4 then A370, take A38 Redcliffe Hill. Hotel opposite St Mary Redcliffe Church

This modern hotel, just a ten-minute walk from Bristol Temple Meads, has striking, contemporary style throughout, and offers some impressive facilities including a spa, a fitness suite and meeting rooms. The hotel has a green-bicycle service for guests. Bedrooms are stylishly designed with large plasma screen TVs, comfortable beds and free internet access. Dining is offered in the Phoenix Restaurant and bar.

Rooms 275 (44 GF) **S** £75-£145; **D** £85-£175 (incl. bkfst) **Facilities** Spa FTV Gym Free bike rental & laptop use Wi-fi **Conf** Class 150 Board 80 Thtr 240 Del from £125 to £215 **Services** Lift Air con **Parking** 140 **Notes** LB Civ Wed 220

Bristol Marriott City Centre

★★★★ 76% HOTEL

☎ 0117 929 4281 0117 927 6377
Lower Castle St BS1 3AD
web: www.bristolmarriottcitycentre.co.uk
dir: M32 follow signs to Broadmead, take slip road to large rdbt, take 3rd exit. Hotel on right

Situated at the foot of the picturesque Castle Park, this mainly business-orientated hotel is well placed for the city centre. Executive and deluxe bedrooms have high speed internet access. In addition to a coffee bar and lounge menu, the Mediterrano Restaurant offers an interesting selection of well-prepared dishes.

Rooms 300 (135 fmly) **Facilities** STV FTV Gym Steam room Sauna Spa pool New Year Wi-fi **Conf** Class 280 Board 40 Thtr 600 **Services** Lift Air con **Notes** Civ Wed 700

Radisson Blu Hotel Bristol

★★★★ 76% HOTEL

☎ 01179 349500 01179 175518
Broad Quay BS1 4BY
dir: Telephone for directions (NB use BS1 4AQ for Sat Nav)

This city centre hotel has a great location and impressive facilities. There are a range of meeting rooms, a spa and a ground-floor bar which specialises in cocktails and opens out to Bristol's main shopping and business area. The bedrooms are spacious and very well equipped, so too are the stylish bathrooms. The Italian themed Filini Restaurant enjoys views across the city.

Rooms 176

The Grand, Bristol

thistle

★★★★ 75% HOTEL

☎ 0871 376 9042 📠 0871 376 9142
Broad St BS1 2EL
e-mail: thegrand@thistle.co.uk
web: www.thistle.com/thegrand
dir: In city centre pass The Galleries. 3rd right into Broad St

This large hotel is situated in the heart of the city, and benefits from its own secure parking. Bedrooms are well equipped and comfortably appointed, and include a number of Premium Executive rooms. The public areas include leisure and therapy treatment rooms and there is an impressive range of conference and banqueting facilities. Thistle Hotels – AA Hotel Group of the Year 2011-12.

Rooms 182 (10 fmly) **Facilities** Spa STV supervised Gym Steam room Sauna Solarium Xmas New Year Wi-fi **Conf** Class 250 Board 40 Thtr 600 **Services** Lift Air con **Parking** 150 **Notes** Civ Wed 500

Hotel du Vin Bristol

Hotel du Vin & Bistro

★★★★ 74% TOWN HOUSE HOTEL

☎ 0117 925 5577 📠 0117 925 1199
The Sugar House, Narrow Lewins Mead BS1 2NU
e-mail: info.bristol@hotelduvin.com
web: www.hotelduvin.com
dir: From A4 follow city centre signs. After 400yds pass Rupert St NCP on right. Hotel on opposite carriageway

This hotel is part of one of Britain's most innovative hotel groups that offer high standards of hospitality and accommodation. Housed in a Grade II listed, converted 18th-century sugar refinery, it provides great facilities with a modern, minimalist design. The bedrooms are exceptionally well designed and the bistro offers an excellent menu and wine list.

Rooms 40 (10 fmly) **S** £125-£375; **D** £125-£375* **Facilities** STV FTV Xmas New Year Wi-fi **Conf** Class 36 Board 34 Thtr 72 Del from £175 to £225* **Services** Lift **Parking** 12 **Notes** LB Civ Wed 65

Holiday Inn Bristol Filton

Holiday Inn

★★★★ 74% HOTEL

☎ 0871 942 9014 📠 0117 956 0933
Filton Rd, Hambrook BS16 1QX
e-mail: bristol@ihg.com
web: www.hibristolfiltonhotel.co.uk
dir: M4 junct 19/M32 junct 1/A4174 towards Filton & Bristol. Hotel 800yds on left

With easy access of both the M4 and M5 this is, understandably, a popular hotel in particular with business guests. Public areas are spacious and relaxing with a wide choice of comfortable seating options. There are two restaurants - Sampans with a selection of dishes from the Far East, and the more traditional Junction Restaurant. Bedrooms vary in size, but all are well furnished and well equipped. A large car park, leisure facilities and range of conference rooms are all available.

Rooms 211 (40 fmly) (18 GF) (12 smoking) **D** £59-£149* **Facilities** STV FTV supervised Fishing Gym Treatment room Xmas New Year Wi-fi **Conf** Class 180 Board 75 Thtr 250 Del from £69 to £190* **Services** Lift Air con **Parking** 250 **Notes** LB Civ Wed 250

Mercure Brigstow Bristol

★★★★ 74% HOTEL

☎ 0117 929 1030 📠 0117 929 2030
5-7 Welsh Back BS1 4SP
e-mail: H6548@accor.com
web: www.mercure.com
dir: From the centre follow Baldwin St then right into Queen Charlotte St

In a prime position on the river this handsome purpose-built hotel is designed and finished with care. The shopping centre and theatres are within easy walking distance. The stylish bedrooms are extremely well equipped, including plasma TV screens in the bathrooms. There is an integrated state-of-the-art conference and meeting centre, and a smart restaurant and bar overlooking the harbour. Guests have complimentary use of a squash and health club, plus free internet access.

Rooms 116 **Facilities** STV Gym Free access to nearby gym & squash courts New Year Wi-fi **Conf** Class 40 Board 30 Thtr 85 **Services** Lift Air con **Notes** LB Civ Wed 80

Grange

RAMADA JARVIS

★★★★ 73% COUNTRY HOUSE HOTEL

☎ 0844 8159063 📠 01454 777447
Northwoods, Winterbourne BS36 1RP
e-mail: sales.grange@ramadajarvis.co.uk
web: www.ramadajarvis.co.uk
dir: A38 towards Filton/Bristol. At rdbt 1st exit into Bradley Stoke Way, at lights 1st left into Woodlands Ln, at 2nd rdbt left into Tench Ln. In 1m left at T-junct, hotel 200yds on left

Built in the 19th century and surrounded by 18 acres of attractive grounds, this is a pleasant hotel situated only a short drive from the city centre. The bedrooms are spacious and well equipped; there is a leisure centre with a pool plus a range of meeting facilities. The conservatory bar has a terrace which makes a delightful place to enjoy a drink under the shade of a 200-year-old cedar tree. The hotel is popular as a wedding venue.

Rooms 68 (20 fmly) (22 GF) **S** £79-£150; **D** £79-£150* **Facilities** Spa STV FTV supervised Gym Sauna Xmas New Year Wi-fi **Conf** Class 120 Board 134 Thtr 150 Del from £120 to £155* **Parking** 150 **Notes** LB Civ Wed 150

Ramada Bristol City

RAMADA JARVIS

★★★★ 72% HOTEL

☎ 0844 815 9100 📠 0117 926 1853
Redcliffe Way BS1 6NJ
e-mail: sales.bristol@ramadajarvis.co.uk
web: www.ramadajarvis.co.uk
dir: 1m from M32. 400yds from Temple Meads BR station, before church

This large modern hotel is situated in the heart of the city centre and offers spacious public areas and ample parking. Bedrooms are well equipped for both business and leisure guests. Dining options include a relaxed bar and a unique kiln restaurant where a good selection of freshly prepared dishes is available.

Rooms 201 (4 fmly) (18 smoking) **S** £69-£150; **D** £69-£150 **Facilities** FTV supervised Gym Sauna Steam room New Year Wi-fi **Conf** Class 120 Board 75 Thtr 300 Del from £99 to £175 **Services** Lift Air con **Parking** 150 **Notes** LB Civ Wed 250

BRISTOL *continued*

Novotel Bristol Centre

★★★★ 70% HOTEL

☎ 0117 976 9988 📠 0117 925 5040
Victoria St BS1 6HY
e-mail: H5622@accor.com
web: www.novotel.com
dir: At end of M32 follow signs for Temple Meads station to rdbt. Final exit, hotel immediately on right

This city centre hotel provides smart, contemporary style accommodation. Most of the bedrooms demonstrate the Novotel 'Novation' style with unique swivel desk, internet access, air-conditioning and a host of extras. The hotel is convenient for the mainline railway station and also has its own car park.

Rooms 131 (20 fmly) **S** £69-£149; **D** £69-£149* **Facilities** STV Gym Wi-fi **Conf** Class 70 Board 35 Thtr 210 Del from £125 to £145* **Services** Lift **Parking** 120 **Notes** LB Civ Wed 100

The Berkeley Square

★★★ 78% ⊛⊛ HOTEL

☎ 0117 925 4000 📠 0117 925 2970
15 Berkeley Square, Clifton BS8 1HB
e-mail: berkeley@cliftonhotels.com
web: www.cliftonhotels.com/chg.html
dir: M32 follow Clifton signs. 1st left at lights by Nills Memorial Tower (University) into Berkeley Sq

Set in a pleasant square close to the university, art gallery and Clifton Village, this smart, elegant Georgian hotel has modern, stylishly decorated bedrooms that feature many welcome extras. There is a cosy lounge and stylish restaurant on the ground floor and a smart, contemporary bar in the basement. A small garden is also available at the rear of the hotel.

Rooms 43 (4 GF) **Facilities** Use of local gym & swimming pool **Services** Lift **Parking** 20

Best Western Henbury Lodge Hotel

★★★ 77% ⊛ HOTEL

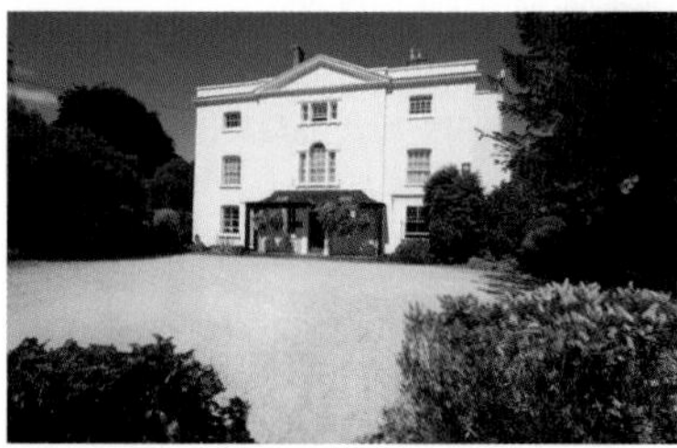

☎ 0117 950 2615 📠 0117 950 9532
Station Rd, Henbury BS10 7QQ
e-mail: info@henburyhotel.com
web: www.henburyhotel.com
dir: M5 junct 17/A4018 towards city centre, 3rd rdbt right into Crow Ln. At end turn right, hotel 200mtrs on right

This quietly located hotel is popular with both business and leisure guests. Bedrooms, in a wide range of shapes and sizes, are divided between the main house and a converted stable block; all are comfortable furnished and equipped. The small and friendly team offer a very personal welcome and many guests here are regulars. Dinner and breakfast are taken in the stylish restaurant where high quality local produce is used.

Rooms 20 (9 annexe) (4 fmly) (6 GF) **S** £85-£105; **D** £95-£125 (incl. bkfst)* **Facilities** FTV Wi-fi **Conf** Class 15 Board 20 Thtr 20 Del from £149 to £169* **Parking** 20 **Notes** LB ⊗ Closed 22 Dec-9 Jan

The Avon Gorge

★★★ 74% ⊛ HOTEL

☎ 0117 973 8955 📠 0117 923 8125
Sion Hill, Clifton BS8 4LD
e-mail: rooms@theavongorge.com
dir: From S: M5 junct 19, A369 to Clifton Toll, over suspension bridge, 1st right into Sion Hill. From N: M5 junct 18A, A4 to Bristol, under suspension bridge, follow signs to bridge, exit Sion Hill

After a number of changes this delightful terrace property, overlooking the Clifton Suspension Bridge, offers bedrooms of varying shapes and sizes with either views across the river or of Clifton Village. For eating there is the contemporary Bridge Café restaurant where a range of carefully prepared, tempting dishes is available. There is a limited amount of free parking space at the rear of the hotel or on-street (no restrictions) in the vicinity.

Rooms 75 (8 fmly) **S** £69-£99; **D** £79-£125 (incl. bkfst)* **Facilities** STV Xmas New Year Wi-fi **Conf** Class 40 Board 30 Thtr 100 Del from £115 to £150* **Services** Lift **Parking** 25 **Notes** LB Civ Wed 100

Arnos Manor Hotel

★★★ 74% HOTEL

☎ 0117 971 1461 📠 0117 971 5507
470 Bath Rd, Arno's Vale BS4 3HQ
e-mail: arnos.manor@forestdale.com
web: www.arnosmanorhotel.co.uk
dir: From end of M32 follow signs for Bath. On A4 in 2m, hotel on right, adjacent to ITV West TV studio

Once the home of a wealthy merchant, this historic 18th-century building is now a comfortable hotel and offers spacious, well-appointed bedrooms with plenty of workspace. The lounge was once the chapel and has many original features, while meals are taken in the atmospheric, conservatory-style restaurant.

Rooms 73 (5 fmly) (7 GF) **Facilities** FTV Xmas New Year Wi-fi **Conf** Class 50 Board 30 Thtr 150 **Services** Lift **Parking** 200 **Notes** LB Civ Wed 100

Rodney Hotel

★★★ 68% ⊛ HOTEL

☎ 0117 973 5422 📠 0117 946 7092
4 Rodney Place, Clifton BS8 4HY
e-mail: rodney@cliftonhotels.com
dir: Off Clifton Down Rd

With easy access from the M5, this attractive, listed building in Clifton is conveniently close to the city centre. The individually decorated bedrooms provide a useful range of extra facilities for the business traveller; the public areas include a smart bar and small restaurant offering enjoyable and carefully prepared dishes. A pleasant rear garden provides additional seating in the summer months.

Rooms 31 (1 fmly) (2 GF) **S** £67-£94; **D** £77-£112* **Facilities** FTV Wi-fi **Conf** Class 20 Board 20 Thtr 30 Del from £114 to £130* **Parking** 10 **Notes** LB Closed 22 Dec-3 Jan RS Sun

Best Western Victoria Square

★★ 79% HOTEL

☎ 0117 973 9058 Fax 0117 970 6929
Victoria Square, Clifton BS8 4EW
e-mail: info@victoriasquarehotel.co.uk
dir: M5 junct 19, follow Clifton signs. Over suspension/toll bridge, right into Clifton Down Rd. Left into Merchants Rd then into Victoria Square

This welcoming hotel offers high quality, individual bedrooms and bathrooms of varying of shapes and sizes. Ideally located, the hotel is just one mile from the city centre and a two-minute stroll from the heart of Clifton Village. The atmosphere is relaxed, and guests have a choice of dining options - from lighter meals in the bar to a range of imaginative dishes in the main restaurant.

Rooms 41 (20 annexe) (3 fmly) (3 GF) **Facilities** FTV Wi-fi **Conf** Class 15 Board 20 Thtr 25 Del from £135 to £145* **Parking** 25

Clifton

★★ 75% HOTEL

☎ 0117 973 6882 Fax 0117 974 1082
St Pauls Rd, Clifton BS8 1LX
e-mail: clifton@cliftonhotels.com
web: www.cliftonhotels.com/clifton
dir: M32 follow Bristol/Clifton signs, along Park St. Left at lights into St Pauls Rd

This popular hotel offers very well equipped bedrooms and relaxed, friendly service. There is a welcoming lounge by the reception, and in summer months drinks and meals can be enjoyed on the terrace. Racks Bar and Restaurant offers an interesting selection of modern dishes in informal surroundings. There is street parking, but for a small charge, secure garage parking is available.

Rooms 59 (2 fmly) (12 GF) (8 smoking) **S** £41-£75; **D** £50-£91* **Facilities** STV FTV Wi-fi **Services** Lift **Parking** 12

Express by Holiday Inn Bristol - North

BUDGET HOTEL

☎ 0117 317 2700 Fax 0117 317 2727
New Rd, Bristol Parkway Business Park BS34 8SJ
e-mail: managerbristolnorth@expressholidayinn.co.uk
web: www.hiexpress.com/bristolnorth
dir: M4 junct 19 or M32 junct 1. Follow Bristol Parkway Station signs, right at main rdbt, hotel on left. For access, left at next 2 rdbts onto New Rd, hotel entrance 100yds past Bristol & West building

A modern hotel ideal for families and business travellers. Fresh and uncomplicated, the spacious rooms include Sky TV, power shower and tea and coffee-making facilities. Continental buffet breakfast is included in the room rate; other meals may be taken at the nearby family pub or restaurant. See also the Hotel Groups pages.

Rooms 133 (106 fmly) **Conf** Class 20 Board 24 Thtr 30

Holiday Inn Express Bristol City Centre

BUDGET HOTEL

☎ 0117 930 4800 Fax 0117 930 4900
South End, Temple Gate House BS1 6PL
e-mail: bristol@morethanhotels.com
web: www.hiexpressbristol.co.uk
dir: M4 junct 19/M32 into Bristol. Keep left, follow Temple Meads train station signs. Hotel opposite station

A modern hotel ideal for families and business travellers. Fresh and uncomplicated, the spacious rooms include Sky TV, power shower and tea and coffee-making facilities. Continental buffet breakfast is included in the room rate; other meals may be taken at the nearby family pub or restaurant. See also the Hotel Groups pages.

Rooms 96 (10 fmly) **S** £49-£139; **D** £49-£139 (incl. bkfst)*

Ibis Bristol Centre (AKA Harbourside)

BUDGET HOTEL

☎ 0117 9897200 Fax 0117 9897210
Explore Ln BS1 5TY
e-mail: H5547-GM@accor.com
dir: Off A4 in harbourside district

Modern, budget hotel offering comfortable accommodation in bright and practical bedrooms. Breakfast is self-service and dinner is available in the restaurant. See also the Hotel Groups pages.

Rooms 182 (2 fmly) **S** £57-£120; **D** £57-£120*

Ibis Bristol Temple Meads

BUDGET HOTEL

☎ 0117 954 3600 Fax 0117 954 3610
Avon St BS2 0PS
e-mail: H6593@accor.com
dir: M4 junct 19, M32, follow Temple Meads train station signs. Left after underpass

Rooms 141 (7 fmly)

Premier Inn Bristol Airport (Sidcot)

BUDGET HOTEL

☎ 0871 527 8154 Fax 0871 527 8155
Bridgwater Rd, Winscombe BS25 1NN
dir: Between M5 junct 21 & 22 (9m from Bristol Airport), onto A371 towards Banwell, Winscombe to A38. Right at lights, Hotel 300yds on left

High quality, budget accommodation ideal for both families and business travellers. Spacious, en suite bedrooms feature tea and coffee making facilities, and Freeview TV in most hotels. Internet access and Wi-fi are available for a small fee. The adjacent family restaurant features a wide and varied menu. See also the Hotel Groups pages.

Rooms 31 **D** £69*

Premier Inn Bristol (Alveston)

BUDGET HOTEL

☎ 0871 527 8152 Fax 0871 527 8153
Thornbury Rd, Alveston BS35 3LL
dir: Just off M5. From N: exit at junct 14 onto A38 towards Bristol. From S: exit at junct 16 onto A38 towards Gloucester

Rooms 75 **D** £56-£69*

B

BRISTOL *continued*

Premier Inn Bristol City Centre (Haymarket)

BUDGET HOTEL

☎ 0871 527 8156 🖷 0871 527 8157
The Haymarket BS1 3LR
dir: M4 junct 19, M32 towards city centre. Through 2 sets of lights, at 3rd lights turn right, to rdbt, take 2nd exit. Hotel on left

Rooms 224 **D** £58-£68*

Premier Inn Bristol City Centre King St

BUDGET HOTEL

☎ 0871 527 8158 🖷 0871 527 8159
Llandoger Trow, King St BS1 4ER
dir: A38 into city centre. Left onto B4053 Baldwin St. Right into Queen Charlotte St, follow one-way system, bear right at river. Hotel on right

Rooms 60 **D** £60-£68*

Premier Inn Bristol Cribbs Causeway

BUDGET HOTEL

☎ 0871 527 8160 🖷 0871 527 8161
Cribbs Causeway, Catbrain Ln BS10 7TQ
dir: M5 junct 17, A4018. 1st left at rdbt into Lysander Rd. Right into Catbrain Hill, leads to Catbrain Lane

Rooms 106 **D** £60-£72*

Premier Inn Bristol East (Emersons Green)

BUDGET HOTEL

☎ 0871 527 8162 🖷 0871 527 8163
200/202 Westerleigh Rd, Emersons Green BS16 7AN
dir: M4 junct 19 onto M32 junct 1, left onto A4174 (Avon Ring Rd). Hotel at 3rd rdbt

Rooms 67 **D** £56-£67*

Premier Inn Bristol Filton

BUDGET HOTEL

☎ 0871 527 8164 🖷 0871 527 8165
Shield Retail Park, Gloucester Road North, Filton BS34 7BR
dir: M5 junct 16, A38 signed Filton/Patchway. Pass airport & Royal Mail on right. Left at 2nd rdbt, 1st left into retail park

Rooms 62 **D** £56-£72*

Premier Inn Bristol South

BUDGET HOTEL

☎ 0871 527 8166 🖷 0871 527 8167
Hengrove Leisure Park, Hengrove Way BS14 0HR
dir: From city centre take A37 to Wells & Shepton Mallet. Right onto A4174. Hotel at 3rd lights

Rooms 56 **D** £57-£66*

BRIXHAM Devon — Map 3 SX95

Quayside

★★★ 75% 🏵 HOTEL

☎ 01803 855751 🖷 01803 882733
41-49 King St TQ5 9TJ
e-mail: reservations@quaysidehotel.co.uk
web: www.quaysidehotel.co.uk
dir: A380, at 2nd rdbt at Kinkerswell towards Brixham on A3022

With views over the harbour and bay, this hotel was formerly six cottages, and the public rooms retain a certain cosiness and intimacy, and include the lounge, residents' bar and Ernie Lister's public bar. Freshly landed fish features on the menus, alongside a number of creative and skilfully prepared dishes, served in the well-appointed restaurant. Good food is also available in the public bar. The owners and their team of local staff provide friendly and attentive service.

Rooms 29 (2 fmly) **Facilities** FTV ♫ Xmas New Year Wi-fi **Conf** Class 18 Board 18 Thtr 25 **Parking** 30

Berry Head Hotel

THE INDEPENDENTS HOTEL ASSOCIATION

★★★ 72% HOTEL

☎ 01803 853225 🖷 01803 882084
Berry Head Rd TQ5 9AJ
e-mail: stay@berryheadhotel.com
dir: From marina, 1m, hotel on left

From its stunning cliff-top location, this imposing property that dates back to 1809, has spectacular views across Torbay. Public areas include two comfortable lounges, an outdoor terrace, a swimming pool, together with a bar serving a range of popular dishes. Many of the bedrooms have the benefit of the splendid sea views.

Rooms 32 (7 fmly) **S** £55-£70; **D** £110-£164 (incl. bkfst)* **Facilities** FTV Petanque Sailing Deep sea fishing Yacht charter ♫ Xmas New Year Wi-fi **Conf** Class 250 Board 40 Thtr 300 Del from £80 to £130* **Services** Lift **Parking** 200 **Notes** LB Civ Wed 200

BROADSTAIRS

See **Kingsgate**

BROADWAY Worcestershire — Map 10 SP03

See also **Buckland**

Barceló The Lygon Arms

★★★★ 80% 🏵🏵 HOTEL

☎ 01386 852255 🖷 01386 854470
High St WR12 7DU
e-mail: thelygonarms@barcelo-hotels.co.uk
web: www.barcelo-hotels.co.uk
dir: From Evesham take A44 signed Oxford, 5m. Follow Broadway signs. Hotel on left

A hotel with a wealth of historic charm and character, the Lygon Arms dates back to the 16th century. There is a choice of restaurants, a stylish cosy bar, an array of lounges and a smart spa and leisure club. Bedrooms vary in size and style, but all are thoughtfully equipped and include a number of stylish contemporary rooms as well as a cottage in the grounds.

Rooms 78 (16 fmly) (17 GF) **S** £119-£250; **D** £119-£750* **Facilities** Spa STV FTV supervised Gym Beauty treatments Billiard table ♫ Xmas New Year Wi-fi **Conf** Class 42 Board 30 Thtr 100 Del from £140 to £195* **Parking** 200 **Notes** LB Civ Wed 100

Dormy House

★★★★ 77% HOTEL

01386 852711 01386 858636
Willersey Hill WR12 7LF
e-mail: reservations@dormyhouse.co.uk.
web: www.dormyhouse.co.uk
dir: 2m E of Broadway off A44, at top of Fish Hill, turn for Saintbury/Picnic area. In 0.5m left, hotel on left

A converted 17th-century farmhouse set in extensive grounds and with stunning views over Broadway. Some rooms are in an annexe at ground-floor level, some have a contemporary style. The best traditions are retained - customer care, real fires, comfortable sofas and afternoon teas. Dinner features an interesting choice of dishes created by a skilled kitchen brigade.

Rooms 45 (20 annexe) (8 fmly) (21 GF) **S** £115-£145; **D** £165-£245 (incl. bkfst & dinner)* **Facilities** STV FTV Putt green Gym Nature & jogging trail Sauna Steam room Xmas New Year Wi-fi **Conf** Class 100 Board 25 Thtr 170 Del from £180 to £198* **Parking** 90 **Notes** Civ Wed 170

Broadway

★★★ 78% HOTEL

01386 852401 01386 853879
The Green, High St WR12 7AA
e-mail: info@broadwayhotel.info
web: www.cotswold-inns-hotels.co.uk/broadway
dir: Follow signs to Evesham, then Broadway

A half-timbered Cotswold stone property, built in the 15th century as a retreat for the Abbots of Pershore. The hotel combines modern, attractive decor with original charm and character. Bedrooms are tastefully furnished and well equipped while public rooms include a relaxing lounge, cosy bar and charming restaurant; alfresco all-day dining in summer months proves popular.

Rooms 19 (1 fmly) (3 GF) **S** £115-£155; **D** £155-£175 (incl. bkfst)* **Facilities** Xmas New Year Wi-fi **Conf** Board 12 Thtr 20 Del from £130* **Parking** 20 **Notes** LB Civ Wed 50

Russell's

RESTAURANT WITH ROOMS

01386 853555 01386 853555
20 High St WR12 7DT
e-mail: info@russellsofbroadway.co.uk
dir: Opposite village green

Situated in the centre of a picturesque Cotswold village this restaurant with rooms makes a great base for exploring local attractions. The superbly appointed bedrooms, each with its own character, have air conditioning and a wide range of extras for guests. The cuisine is a real draw here with freshly-prepared, local produce skilfully utilised.

Rooms 7 (3 annexe) (4 fmly)

BROCKENHURST Map 5 SU30
Hampshire

INSPECTORS' CHOICE

Rhinefield House

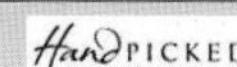

★★★★ HOTEL

01590 622922 & 0845 072 7516
01590 622800
Rhinefield Rd SO42 7QB
e-mail: rhinefieldhouse@handpicked.co.uk
web: www.handpicked.co.uk
dir: A35 towards Christchurch. 3m from Lyndhurst turn left to Rhinefield, 1.5m to hotel

This stunning 19th-century, mock-Elizabethan mansion is set in 40 acres of beautifully landscaped gardens and forest. Bedrooms are spacious and great consideration is given to guest comfort. The elegant and award-winning Armada Restaurant is richly furnished, and features a fireplace carving (nine years in the making) that is worth taking time to admire. If the weather permits, the delightful terrace is just the place for enjoying alfresco eating.

Rooms 50 (10 fmly) (18 GF) **S** £99-£405; **D** £109-£415 (incl. bkfst)* **Facilities** Spa STV Gym Hydro-therapy pool Plunge pool Steam room Sauna Treatment rooms Xmas New Year Wi-fi **Conf** Class 72 Board 56 Thtr 160 Del from £155 to £220 **Services** Lift **Parking** 100 **Notes** LB Civ Wed 110

B

BROCKENHURST *continued*

Careys Manor

★★★★ 84% ◎◎ HOTEL

☎ 01590 624467 🖷 01590 622799
SO42 7RH
e-mail: stay@careysmanor.com
web: www.careysmanor.com
dir: M27 junct 3, M271, A35 to Lyndhurst. A337 towards Brockenhurst. Hotel on left after Beaulieu sign

This smart property offers a host of facilities that include an Oriental-style spa and leisure suite with an excellent range of unusual treatments, and three very contrasting restaurants that offer a choice of Thai, French or modern British cuisine. Many of the spacious and well appointed bedrooms have balconies overlooking the gardens. Extensive function and conference facilities are also available.

Rooms 79 (61 annexe) (31 GF) **Facilities** Spa FTV Gym Steam room Beauty therapists Treatment rooms Hydrotherapy pool Xmas New Year Wi-fi **Conf** Class 70 Board 40 Thtr 120 **Services** Lift **Parking** 180 **Notes** No children 16yrs Civ Wed 100

Balmer Lawn

★★★★ 74% ◎ HOTEL

☎ 01590 623116 🖷 01590 623864
Lyndhurst Rd SO42 7ZB
e-mail: info@balmerlawnhotel.com
dir: Just off A337 from Brockenhurst towards Lymington

Situated in the heart of the New Forest, this peacefully located hotel provides comfortable public rooms and a wide range of bedrooms. A selection of carefully prepared and enjoyable dishes is offered in the spacious restaurant. The extensive function and leisure facilities make this popular with both families and conference delegates.

Rooms 54 (10 fmly) **Facilities** FTV Gym Squash Indoor leisure suite Treatment room Sauna Xmas New Year Wi-fi **Conf** Class 76 Board 48 Thtr 150 **Services** Lift **Parking** 100 **Notes** Civ Wed 120

INSPECTORS' CHOICE

The Pig

★★★ ◎◎ COUNTRY HOUSE HOTEL

☎ 01590 622354
Beaulieu Rd SO42 7QL
dir: Telephone for detailed directions

Rebranded as The Pig and having opened its doors in the Summer of 2011, this country house has undergone a complete change. Now the focus is very much on the food with the chef, gardener and forager working as a team to create menus of seasonal, locally sourced produce; all ingredients are found within a 15-mile radius. The result of such a policy is that menus change daily, and sometimes even more frequently! The stylish dining room is an authentically reproduced Victorian greenhouse, and alfresco eating is possible as there is a wood-fired oven in the courtyard. The bedrooms have eclectic furnishings, good beds and views of either the forest or the garden; two suites with private courtyards are available.

Rooms 26

New Park Manor

von Essen hotels
A PRIVATE COLLECTION
www.vonessenhotels.com

★★★ 80% ◎◎
COUNTRY HOUSE HOTEL

☎ 01590 623467 🖷 01590 622268
Lyndhurst Rd SO42 7QH
e-mail: info@newparkmanorhotel.co.uk
web: www.newparkmanorhotel.co.uk
dir: M27 junct 1, A337 to Lyndhurst & Brockenhurst. Hotel 1.5m on right

Once the favoured hunting lodge of King Charles II, this well presented hotel enjoys a peaceful setting in the New Forest and comes complete with an equestrian centre. The bedrooms are divided between the old house and a purpose-built wing. Food in the restaurant is based on seasonally available produce, including game and venison. An impressive spa offers a range of treatments.

Rooms 26

Forest Park

★★★ 71% HOTEL

☎ 01590 622844 🖷 01590 623948
Rhinefield Rd SO42 7ZG
e-mail: forest.park@forestdale.com
web: www.forestparkhotel.co.uk
dir: A337 to Brockenhurst into Meerut Rd, through Waters Green. Right at T-junct into Rhinefield Rd

Situated in the heart of the New Forest, this former vicarage and war field hospital is now a hotel which offers a warm and friendly welcome to all its guests. The hotel has a heated pool, riding stables, a log cabin sauna and tennis courts. The bedrooms and public areas are comfortable and stylish.

Rooms 38 (2 fmly) (7 GF) **Facilities** FTV Horse riding stables Sauna Xmas New Year Wi-fi **Conf** Class 20 Board 30 Thtr 50 **Parking** 80 **Notes** LB Civ Wed 50

INSPECTORS' CHOICE

Cloud Hotel

★★ SMALL HOTEL

☎ 01590 622165 & 622354 🖷 01590 622818
Meerut Rd SO42 7TD
e-mail: enquiries@cloudhotel.co.uk
web: www.cloudhotel.co.uk
dir: M27 junct 1 signed New Forest, A337 through Lyndhurst to Brockenhurst. On entering Brockenhurst 1st right. Hotel 300mtrs

This charming hotel enjoys a peaceful location on the edge of the village. The bedrooms are bright and comfortable with pine furnishings and smart en suite facilities. Public rooms include a selection of cosy lounges, a delightful rear garden with outdoor seating and a restaurant specialising in home-cooked, wholesome English food.

Rooms 18 (1 fmly) (2 GF) **Facilities** FTV Xmas Wi-fi **Conf** Class 12 Board 12 Thtr 40 **Parking** 20 **Notes** LB No children 12yrs Closed 27 Dec-12 Jan

Watersplash

★★ 63% HOTEL

☎ 01590 622344
The Rise SO42 7ZP
e-mail: bookings@watersplash.co.uk
web: www.watersplash.co.uk
dir: M3 junct 13/M27 junct 1/A337 S through Lyndhurst & Brockenhurst. The Rise on left, hotel on left

This popular, welcoming hotel that dates from Victorian times has been in the same family for over 40 years. Bedrooms have co-ordinated decor and good facilities. The restaurant overlooks the neatly tended garden and there is also a comfortably furnished lounge, separate bar and an outdoor pool.

Rooms 23 (6 fmly) (3 GF) **Facilities** ⥼ Xmas New Year **Conf** Class 20 Board 20 Thtr 80 **Parking** 29

BROMBOROUGH
Merseyside — **Map 15 SJ38**

Premier Inn Wirral (Bromborough)

BUDGET HOTEL

☎ 0871 527 9172 🖷 0871 527 9173
High St, Bromborough Cross CH62 7EZ
dir: On A41 (New Chester Rd), 2m from M53 junct 5

High quality, budget accommodation ideal for both families and business travellers. Spacious, en suite bedrooms feature tea and coffee making facilities, and Freeview TV in most hotels. Internet access and Wi-fi are available for a small fee. The adjacent family restaurant features a wide and varied menu. See also the Hotel Groups pages.

Rooms 32 **D** £53-£57*

BROMLEY
Greater London

See LONDON SECTION plan 1 H1

Best Western Bromley Court

★★★ 77% HOTEL

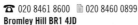

☎ 020 8461 8600 🖷 020 8460 0899
Bromley Hill BR1 4JD
e-mail: enquiries@bromleycourthotel.co.uk
web: www.bw-bromleycourthotel.co.uk
dir: N of town centre, off A21. Private drive opposite Volkswagen garage on Bromley Hill

Set amid three acres of grounds, this smart hotel enjoys a peaceful location, in a residential area on the outskirts of town. Well maintained bedrooms are smartly appointed and thoughtfully equipped. The contemporary-style restaurant offers a good choice of meals in comfortable surroundings. Extensive facilities include a leisure club and a good range of meeting rooms.

Rooms 114 (4 fmly) **Facilities** STV FTV Gym Steam room Spa pool Wi-fi **Conf** Class 80 Board 45 Thtr 150 Del from £135 to £155* **Services** Lift Air con **Parking** 100 **Notes** ⊗ Civ Wed 65

BROMSGROVE
Worcestershire — **Map 10 SO97**

Holiday Inn Birmingham - Bromsgrove

★★★★ 71% HOTEL

☎ 01527 576600 & 0871 942 9142
🖷 01527 878981
Kidderminster Rd B61 9AB
e-mail: info@hi-birminghambromsgrove.co.uk
dir: From S: M5 junct 5, A38 to Bromsgrove 2m. At rdbt left, B4091,1.5m. Left at 2nd rdbt A448. Hotel 0.5m on left. From N: M5 junct 4, A38/Bromsgrove for 2m. Through lights, straight on at rdbt. Filter right at lights. Right at 2nd rdbt onto A448. Hotel 0.5m on left

Public areas in this striking building are comfortable and spacious. A selection of meeting rooms is available, along with function suites, a courtyard garden and plenty of natural light. Bedrooms come in a variety of styles - some are more compact than others but all offer an excellent working environment for the business guest. Leisure facilities include a steam room, sauna, pool and gym. There is an extensive car park.

Rooms 110 (11 fmly) (31 GF) **S** £48-£120; **D** £48-£120* **Facilities** Spa STV ⛆ Gym Sauna Steam room Spa bath Xmas Wi-fi **Conf** Class 120 Board 50 Thtr 220 Del from £99 to £149* **Services** Lift Air con **Parking** 220 **Notes** LB ⊗ Civ Wed 180

Premier Inn Bromsgrove Central

BUDGET HOTEL

☎ 0871 527 8168 🖷 0871 527 8169
Birmingham Rd B61 0BA
dir: M42 junct 1 (S'bound access only) or M5 junct 4 S'bound or M5 junct 5 N'bound onto A38 towards Bromsgrove. Hotel adjacent to Guild Brewers Fayre. (NB for Sat Nav use B60 1GJ)

High quality, budget accommodation ideal for both families and business travellers. Spacious, en suite bedrooms feature tea and coffee making facilities, and Freeview TV in most hotels. Internet access and Wi-fi are available for a small fee. The adjacent family restaurant features a wide and varied menu. See also the Hotel Groups pages.

Rooms 78 **D** £49-£58*

Premier Inn Bromsgrove South (Worcester Road)

BUDGET HOTEL

☎ 0871 527 8170 🖷 0871 527 8171
Worcester Rd, Upton Warren B61 7ET
dir: M5 junct 5, A38 towards Bromsgrove, 1.2m. Or M42 junct 1, A38 S (cross over A448)

Rooms 27 **D** £49-£58*

BROOK (NEAR CADNAM)
Hampshire — **Map 5 SU21**

Bell Inn

★★★ 83% ®® HOTEL

☎ 023 8081 2214 🖷 023 8081 3958
SO43 7HE
e-mail: bell@bramshaw.co.uk
web: www.bellinnbramshaw.co.uk
dir: M27 junct 1 onto B3079, hotel 1.5m on right

The inn is part of the Bramshaw Golf Club and has tailored its style to suit this market, but it is also an ideal base for visiting the New Forest. Bedrooms are comfortable and attractively furnished, and the

continued

BROOK (NEAR CADNAM) *continued*

B

public areas, particularly the welcoming bar, have a cosy and friendly atmosphere.

Rooms 27 (2 annexe) (1 fmly) (8 GF) **Facilities** FTV ⛳ 54 Putt green Xmas New Year Wi-fi **Conf** Class 20 Board 30 Thtr 50 **Parking** 150 **Notes** LB ⊗

BROXTON Map 15 SJ45
Cheshire

De Vere Carden Park

DE VERE Hotels & Resorts

★★★★ 81% ◎ HOTEL

☎ 01829 731000 📠 01829 731599
Carden Park CH3 9DQ
e-mail: reservations.carden@devere-hotels.com
web: www.cardenpark.co.uk
dir: M56 junct 15/M53 Chester. Take A41 signed Whitchurch. 8m. At Broxton rdbt right onto A534 (signed Wrexham). Hotel 1.5m on left

This impressive Cheshire estate dates back to the 17th century and consists of 1000 acres of mature parkland. The hotel offers a choice of dining options along with superb leisure facilities that include golf courses, a fully equipped gym, a swimming pool and popular spa. Spacious, thoughtfully equipped bedrooms have excellent business and in-room entertainment facilities.

Rooms 196 (83 annexe) (24 fmly) (68 GF) **Facilities** Spa STV supervised ⛳ 36 Putt green Gym Archery Quad bikes Off-roading Cycle & walking trails Laser clay shooting Xmas New Year Wi-fi **Conf** Class 240 Board 125 Thtr 400 **Services** Lift **Parking** 700 **Notes** Civ Wed 375

BRYHER Map 2 SV81
Cornwall (Isles of Scilly)

INSPECTORS' CHOICE

Hell Bay Hotel

★★★ ◎◎◎ HOTEL

☎ 01720 422947 📠 01720 423004
TR23 0PR
e-mail: contactus@hellbay.co.uk
web: www.hellbay.co.uk
dir: Access by helicopter or boat from Penzance, plane from Bristol, Exeter, Newquay, Southampton, Land's End

Located on the smallest of the inhabited islands of the Scilly Isles on the edge of the Atlantic, this hotel makes a really special destination. The owners have filled the hotel with original works of art by artists who have connections with the islands, and the interior is decorated in cool blues and greens creating an extremely restful environment. The contemporary bedrooms are equally stylish and many have garden access and stunning sea views. Eating here is a delight, and naturally, seafood features strongly on the award-winning, daily-changing menus.

Rooms 25 (25 annexe) (3 fmly) (15 GF) **S** £200-£600; **D** £320-£600 (incl. bkfst & dinner) **Facilities** STV FTV ⛳ 7 Gym Wi-fi **Conf** Class 36 Board 36 Thtr 36 Del from £200 to £600 **Notes** LB Closed Nov-Feb

BUCKHURST HILL Map 6 TQ49
Essex

Premier Inn Loughton/ Buckhurst Hill

BUDGET HOTEL

☎ 0871 527 8686 📠 0871 527 8687
High Rd IG9 5HT
dir: M25 junct 26 towards Loughton. A121 into Buckhurst Hill (approx 5m), hotel on left

High quality, budget accommodation ideal for both families and business travellers. Spacious, en suite bedrooms feature tea and coffee making facilities, and Freeview TV in most hotels. Internet access and Wi-fi are available for a small fee. The adjacent family restaurant features a wide and varied menu. See also the Hotel Groups pages.

Rooms 49 **D** £65-£75*

BUCKINGHAM Map 11 SP63
Buckinghamshire

Villiers

CLASSIC BRITISH HOTELS

★★★★ 72% ◎◎ HOTEL

☎ 01280 822444 📠 01280 822113
3 Castle St MK18 1BS
e-mail: villiers@oxfordshire-hotels.co.uk
web: www.oxfordshire-hotels.co.uk
dir: M1 junct 13 (N) or junct 15 (S) follow signs to Buckingham. Castle St by Old Town Hall

Guests can enjoy a town centre location with a high degree of comfort at this 400-year-old former coaching inn. Relaxing public areas feature flagstone floors, oak panelling and real fires whilst bedrooms are modern, spacious and equipped to a high level. Diners can unwind in the atmospheric bar before taking dinner in the award-winning restaurant.

Rooms 49 (4 fmly) (3 GF) **S** £90-£140; **D** £110-£180 (incl. bkfst)* **Facilities** STV FTV Xmas New Year Wi-fi **Conf** Class 120 Board 80 Thtr 250 Del from £140 to £160* **Services** Lift **Parking** 52 **Notes** ⊗ Civ Wed 180

Best Western Buckingham Hotel

★★★ 77% HOTEL

☎ 01280 822622 📠 01280 823074
Buckingham Ring Rd MK18 1RY
e-mail: info@thebuckinghamhotel.co.uk
dir: Follow A421 for Buckingham, take ring road S towards Brackley & Bicester. Hotel on left

A purpose-built hotel, which offers comfortable and spacious rooms with well designed working spaces for business travellers. There are also extensive conference facilities. The open-plan restaurant and bar offer a good range of dishes, and the well-equipped leisure suite is popular with guests.

Rooms 70 (6 fmly) (31 GF) **S** £68-£125; **D** £76-£135 (incl. bkfst)* **Facilities** STV FTV supervised Gym Sauna Steam room Xmas New Year Wi-fi **Conf** Class 60 Board 60 Thtr 200 Del from £75 to £125* **Parking** 200 **Notes** LB Civ Wed 120

BUCKLAND (NEAR BROADWAY) Map 10 SP03
Gloucestershire

INSPECTORS' CHOICE

Buckland Manor

★★★
COUNTRY HOUSE HOTEL

01386 852626 01386 853557
WR12 7LY
e-mail: info@bucklandmanor.co.uk
web: www.bucklandmanor.co.uk
dir: Off B4632 (Broadway to Winchcombe road)

A grand 13th-century manor house that is surrounded by well-kept and beautiful gardens that feature a stream and waterfall. Everything at this hotel is geared to encourage rest and relaxation. Spacious bedrooms and public areas are furnished with high quality pieces and decorated in keeping with the style of the manor; crackling log fires warm the wonderful lounges. The elegant dining room, with views over the rolling hills, is the perfect place to enjoy dishes that use high quality local produce.

Rooms 13 (2 fmly) (4 GF) **S** £290-£505; **D** £300-£515 (incl. bkfst) **Facilities** STV Putt green Xmas New Year **Parking** 30 **Notes** LB No children 12yrs Civ Wed 40

BUDE Map 2 SS20
Cornwall

Falcon

★★★ 79% HOTEL

01288 352005 01288 356359
Breakwater Rd EX23 8SD
e-mail: reception@falconhotel.com
web: www.falconhotel.com
dir: A39 to Bude, to Widemouth Bay. Hotel on right over canal bridge

Dating back to 1798, this long-established hotel boasts delightful walled gardens, ideal for afternoon teas. Bedrooms offer high standards of comfort and quality; there is also a four-poster room complete with spa bath. A choice of menus is offered in the elegant restaurant and the friendly bar. The hotel has an impressive function room.

Rooms 29 (7 fmly) **S** £57-£70; **D** £114-£140 (incl. bkfst)* **Facilities** STV FTV New Year Wi-fi **Conf** Class 50 Board 50 Thtr 200 **Services** Lift **Parking** 40 **Notes** LB RS 25 Dec Civ Wed 160

Hartland

★★★ 77% HOTEL

01288 355661 01288 355664
Hartland Ter EX23 8JY
e-mail: hartlandhotel@aol.com
dir: A39 to Bude, follow town centre signs. Left into Hartland Terrace opposite Boots the chemist. Hotel at seaward end of road

This long established hotel has an enduring and timeless elegance with a reassuring sense of tradition. Its location is a wonderful asset, overlooking Summerleaze Beach with panoramic views of the town and coast. The bedrooms are individually styled and a number have four-poster beds and sea views. The spacious public areas include the convivial bar, lounges and attractive dining room where a varied menu is on offer. A pool is available for lazing away the summer days.

Rooms 28 (2 fmly) **Facilities** Xmas **Services** Lift **Parking** 30 **Notes** Closed mid Nov-Etr (ex Xmas & New Year)

Camelot

★★★ 75% HOTEL

01288 352361 01288 355470
Downs View EX23 8RE
e-mail: stay@camelot-hotel.co.uk
web: www.camelot-hotel.co.uk
dir: Off A39 into town centre, hotel close to golf course

This friendly and welcoming Edwardian property offers a range of facilities including a smart and comfortable conservatory bar and lounge, a games room and Hawkers Restaurant, which offers skilfully produced dishes using much local produce. The bedrooms are light and airy, with high standards of housekeeping and maintenance.

Rooms 24 (2 fmly) (7 GF) **S** £49-£66.50; **D** £59-£133 (incl. bkfst) **Facilities** FTV Games room Wi-fi **Conf** Class 10 Board 10 Thtr 15 **Parking** 21 **Notes** LB

Hotel Penarvor

★★ 74% SMALL HOTEL

01288 352036 01288 355027
Crooklets Beach EX23 8NE
e-mail: stay@hotelpenarvor.co.uk
dir: A39 towards Bude for 1.5m. At 2nd rdbt turn right, pass shops. Top of hill, left signed Crooklets Beach

Adjacent to the golf course and overlooking Crooklets Beach, this family owned hotel has a relaxed and friendly atmosphere. Bedrooms vary in size but are all equipped to a similar standard. An interesting selection of dishes, using fresh local produce, is available in the restaurant; bar meals are also provided.

Rooms 16 (6 fmly) (3 GF) **S** £37-£43; **D** £74-£86 (incl. bkfst)* **Facilities** FTV Wi-fi **Parking** 20 **Notes** LB Closed 24-28 Dec

B

BURFORD Oxfordshire **Map 5 SP21**

The Lamb Inn

★★★ 83% ®® SMALL HOTEL

☎ 01993 823155 📠 01993 822228
Sheep St OX18 4LR
e-mail: info@lambinn-burford.co.uk
web: www.cotswold-inns-hotels.co.uk/lamb
dir: A40 into Burford, downhill, 1st left into Sheep St, hotel last on right

This enchanting old inn is just a short walk from the centre of this delightful Cotswold village. Inside an abundance of character and charm is found in the cosy lounge with log fire, and intimate bar with flagged floors. An elegant restaurant offers locally sourced produce in carefully prepared dishes. Bedrooms, some with original features, are comfortable and well appointed.

Rooms 17 (1 fmly) (4 GF) **S** £120-£155; **D** £155-£180 (incl. bkfst)* **Facilities** Xmas New Year Wi-fi **Notes** LB

The Bay Tree Hotel

★★★ 81% ® HOTEL

☎ 01993 822791 📠 01993 823008
Sheep St OX18 4LW
e-mail: info@baytreehotel.info
web: www.cotswold-inns-hotels.co.uk/bay-tree
dir: A40 or A361 to Burford. From High St turn into Sheep St, next to old market square. Hotel on right

The modern decorative style combines seamlessly with features from this delightful inn's long history. Bedrooms are tastefully furnished and some have four-poster and half-tester beds. Public areas consist of a character bar, a sophisticated airy restaurant, a selection of meeting rooms and an attractive walled garden.

Rooms 21 (13 annexe) (2 fmly) (3 GF) **S** £120-£130; **D** £170-£180 (incl. bkfst)* **Facilities** Xmas New Year Wi-fi **Conf** Class 12 Board 25 Thtr 40 Del from £155* **Parking** 50 **Notes** LB Civ Wed 60

Cotswold Gateway

★★★ 73% HOTEL

☎ 01993 822695 📠 01993 823600
Cheltenham Rd OX18 4HX
e-mail: cotswoldgateway@btconnect.com
dir: From A40 at rdbt in Burford take A361 (High St) towards town centre. Hotel on left

Ideally located for both business and leisure guests, this hotel prominently situated on the A40 and yet only a short walk from Burford. Bedrooms are comfortable and well appointed with many guest comforts. Dinner menus have an extensive choice of popular dishes and there is the option of eating in the character bar, the coffee shop or brasserie-style restaurant.

Rooms 20 (5 annexe) (2 fmly) (4 GF) **Facilities** FTV New Year Wi-fi **Parking** 30 **Notes** Closed 25-26 Dec

The Bull at Burford

®® RESTAURANT WITH ROOMS

☎ 01993 822220 📠 01993 824055
105 High St OX18 4RG
e-mail: info@bullatburford.co.uk
dir: In town centre

Situated in the heart of a pretty Cotswold town, The Bull has undergone major refurbishment. Originally built in 1475 as a rest house for the local priory, it now has stylish, attractively presented bedrooms that still reflect charm and character. Dinner should not be missed and the award-winning restaurant has an imaginative menu along with an excellent choice of wines. Lunch is served daily and afternoon tea is popular. There is a residents' lounge, and free Wi-fi is available.

Rooms 12 (1 fmly)

The Inn For All Seasons

RESTAURANT WITH ROOMS

☎ 01451 844324 📠 01451 844375
The Barringtons OX18 4TN
e-mail: sharp@innforallseasons.com
web: www.innforallseasons.com
dir: 3m W of Burford on A40 towards Cheltenham

This charming 16th-century coaching inn is close to the pretty village of Burford. The individually styled bedrooms are comfortable, and include a four-poster room, and a family room that sleeps four. The public areas include a cosy bar with oak beams and real fires. There is a good choice on the bar menu, and evening meals feature the best of local Cotswold produce. The inn is a dog-friendly establishment and two of the ground-floor bedrooms have direct access to the garden and an exercise area.

Rooms 10

BURGESS HILL West Sussex **Map 6 TQ31**

Premier Inn Burgess Hill

BUDGET HOTEL

☎ 0871 527 8172 📠 0871 627 8173
Charles Av RH15 9AG
dir: M25 junct 7, M23, A23. Left at Burgess Hill follow A2300 signs. At rdbt 2nd exit onto A2300. At next rdbt 4th exit onto A273, straight on at next 2 rdbts, at 3rd rdbt (Tesco) 1st left. Hotel 2nd left

High quality, budget accommodation ideal for both families and business travellers. Spacious, en suite bedrooms feature tea and coffee making facilities, and Freeview TV in most hotels. Internet access and Wi-fi are available for a small fee. The adjacent family restaurant features a wide and varied menu. See also the Hotel Groups pages.

Rooms 60 **D** £56-£64*

BURLEY
Hampshire   Map 5 SU20

Moorhill House

NEW FOREST HOTELS

★★★ 78% ®
COUNTRY HOUSE HOTEL

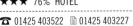

☎ 01425 403285 📠 01425 403715
BH24 4AH
e-mail: moorhill@newforesthotels.co.uk
web: www.newforesthotels.co.uk
dir: M27, A31, follow signs to Burley, through village, up hill, right opposite school & cricket grounds

Situated deep in the heart of the New Forest and formerly a grand gentleman's residence, this charming hotel offers a relaxed and friendly environment. Bedrooms, of varying sizes, are smartly decorated. A range of facilities is provided and guests can relax by walking around the extensive grounds. Both dinner and breakfast offer a choice of interesting and freshly prepared dishes.

Rooms 31 (13 fmly) (3 GF) **S** £60-£65; **D** £120-£170 (incl. bkfst)* **Facilities** FTV Putt green Badminton (Apr-Sep) Sauna Xmas New Year Wi-fi **Conf** Class 60 Board 65 Thtr 120 **Parking** 50 **Notes** LB Civ Wed 80

Burley Manor

★★★ 76% HOTEL

☎ 01425 403522 📠 01425 403227
Ringwood Rd BH24 4BS
e-mail: burley.manor@forestdale.com
web: www.theburleymanorhotel.co.uk
dir: Exit A31 at Burley sign, hotel 3m on left

Set in extensive grounds, this 18th-century mansion house enjoys a relaxed ambience and a peaceful setting. Half of the well-equipped, comfortable bedrooms, including several with four-posters, are located in the main house. The remainder, many with balconies, are in the adjacent converted stable block overlooking the outdoor pool. Cosy public rooms benefit from log fires in winter.

Rooms 38 (17 annexe) (2 fmly) (17 GF) **Facilities** FTV Horse riding stables Xmas New Year Wi-fi **Conf** Class 24 Board 40 Thtr 70 **Parking** 60 **Notes** LB Civ Wed 70

BURNHAM
Buckinghamshire   Map 6 SU98

Grovefield House Hotel

★★★★ 76% ®® HOTEL

☎ 01628 603131 📠 01628 668078
Taplow Common Rd SL1 8LP
e-mail: info.grovefield@classiclodges.co.uk
web: www.classiclodges.co.uk
dir: M4 junct 7, A4 towards Maidenhead. Next rdbt right under rail bridge. Straight over mini rdbt, garage on right. 1.5m, hotel on right

Set in its own spacious grounds, the Grovefield is conveniently located for Heathrow Airport as well as Slough and Maidenhead. Accommodation is spacious and well presented and most rooms have views over the attractive gardens. Public areas include a range of meeting rooms, comfortable bar/lounge area and Hamilton's restaurant.

Rooms 40 (5 fmly) (7 GF) **Facilities** Putt green Fishing Xmas New Year **Conf** Class 80 Board 80 Thtr 180 **Services** Lift **Parking** 155 **Notes** Civ Wed 200

Burnham Beeches Hotel

★★★★ 74% ® HOTEL

☎ 0844 736 8603 📠 01628 603994
Grove Rd SL1 8DP
e-mail: burnhambeeches@corushotels.com
web: www.corushotels.com/burnham
dir: M40 junct 2, A355 towards Slough, right at 2nd rdbt, 1st right to Grove Rd

Set in attractive mature grounds on the fringes of woodland, this extended Georgian manor house has spacious, comfortable and well-equipped bedrooms. Public rooms include a cosy lounge/bar offering all-day snacks and an elegant wood-panelled restaurant that serves interesting cuisine; there are also conference facilities, a fitness centre and pool.

Rooms 82 (22 fmly) (12 GF) **Facilities** FTV Gym Xmas New Year Wi-fi **Conf** Class 80 Board 60 Thtr 150 **Del** from £163.95 to £265* **Services** Lift **Parking** 200 **Notes** LB Civ Wed 120

B

BURNHAM MARKET Map 13 TF84
Norfolk

Hoste Arms

★★★ 87% ®® HOTEL

☎ 01328 738777 📠 01328 730103
The Green PE31 8HD
e-mail: reception@hostearms.co.uk
web: www.hostearms.co.uk
dir: Signed on B1155, 5m W of Wells-next-the-Sea

A stylish, privately-owned inn situated in the heart of a bustling village close to the north Norfolk coast. The extensive public rooms feature a range of dining areas that include a conservatory with plush furniture, a sunny patio and a traditional pub. The tastefully furnished and thoughtfully equipped bedrooms are generally very spacious and offer a high degree of comfort.

Rooms 34 (7 GF) **S** £122-£241; **D** £149-£241 (incl. bkfst)* **Facilities** Spa STV Beauty treatment rooms Xmas New Year Wi-fi **Conf** Class 40 Board 16 Thtr 25 **Services** Air con **Parking** 45 **Notes** LB

See advert on page 119

BURNLEY Map 18 SD83
Lancashire

Rosehill House

★★★ 79% HOTEL

☎ 01282 453931 📠 01282 455628
Rosehill Av BB11 2PW
e-mail: rhhotel@provider.co.uk
dir: 0.5m S of town centre, off A682

This fine Grade II listed building stands its own leafy grounds in a quiet area of town. The hotel features original and beautifully ornate ceilings and mosaic flooring. The boutique-style bedrooms are tastefully furnished and comfortably equipped; the two loft conversions and the former coach house offer spacious yet more traditional-style accommodation.

Rooms 34 (3 fmly) (4 GF) **S** £40-£55; **D** £50-£75 (incl. bkfst)* **Facilities** STV FTV Snooker room Wi-fi **Conf** Class 30 Board 30 Thtr 50 Del from £75 to £95 **Parking** 52 **Notes** ⊗ Civ Wed 90

Holiday Inn Express Burnley

BUDGET HOTEL

☎ 01282 855955 & 01282 855963
📠 0845 217 1374
55 Pendle Way BB12 0TJ
e-mail: cathy@starboardhotels.com
dir: M65 junct 10, 3rd exit at rdbt, Pendle Way, hotel on right

A modern hotel ideal for families and business travellers. Fresh and uncomplicated, the spacious rooms include Sky TV, power shower and tea and coffee-making facilities. Continental buffet breakfast is included in the room rate; other meals may be taken at the nearby family pub or restaurant. See also the Hotel Groups pages.

Rooms 102 (67 fmly) (4 GF) **S** £59.95-£79.95; **D** £59.95-£79.95 (incl. bkfst)* **Conf** Class 28 Board 28 Thtr 80 Del from £85 to £100*

Premier Inn Burnley

BUDGET HOTEL

☎ 0871 527 8174 📠 0871 527 8175
Queen Victoria Rd BB10 3EF
dir: M65 junct 12, 5th exit at rdbt, 1st exit at rdbt, keep in right lane at lights, 2nd exit at next rdbt, 3rd at next rdbt, under bridge, left before football ground

High quality, budget accommodation ideal for both families and business travellers. Spacious, en suite bedrooms feature tea and coffee making facilities, and Freeview TV in most hotels. Internet access and Wi-fi are available for a small fee. The adjacent family restaurant features a wide and varied menu. See also the Hotel Groups pages.

Rooms 43 **D** £51-£56*

BURNSALL Map 19 SE06
North Yorkshire

Red Lion Hotel & Manor House

★★ 75% HOTEL

☎ 01756 720204 📠 01756 720292
By the Bridge BD23 6BU
e-mail: redlion@daelnet.co.uk
web: www.redlion.co.uk
dir: On B6160 between Grassington & Bolton Abbey

This delightful 16th-century Dales' inn stands adjacent to a five-arch bridge over the scenic River Wharfe. Stylish, comfortable bedrooms are individually decorated, and well equipped. Public areas include a tasteful lounge traditional oak-panelled bar and impressive function rooms. The elegant restaurant makes good use of fresh local ingredients. Additional bed and breakfast based accommodation is now available in the Manor House.

Rooms 25 (15 annexe) (5 fmly) (4 GF) **Facilities** FTV Fishing Xmas New Year Wi-fi **Conf** Class 50 Board 25 Thtr 60 **Parking** 80 **Notes** Civ Wed 125

The Devonshire Fell

®® RESTAURANT WITH ROOMS

☎ 01756 729000 📠 01756 729009
BD23 6BT
e-mail: manager@devonshirefell.co.uk
web: www.devonshirefell.co.uk
dir: On B6160, 6m from Bolton Abbey rdbt, A59 junct

Located on the edge of the attractive village of Burnsall, this establishment offers comfortable, well-equipped accommodation in a relaxing atmosphere. There is an extensive menu featuring local produce, and meals can be taken either in the bar area or the more formal restaurant. A function room with views over the valley is also available.

Rooms 12 (2 fmly)

BURRINGTON (NEAR PORTSMOUTH ARMS STATION) Map 3 SS61
Devon

INSPECTORS' CHOICE

Northcote Manor

★★★ COUNTRY HOUSE HOTEL

☎ 01769 560501 01769 560770
EX37 9LZ
e-mail: rest@northcotemanor.co.uk
web: www.northcotemanor.co.uk
dir: Off A377 opposite Portsmouth Arms, into hotel drive. (NB do not enter Burrington village)

A warm and friendly welcome is assured at this beautiful country-house hotel, built in 1716 and surrounded by 20 acres of grounds and woodlands. Guests can enjoy wonderful views over the Taw River Valley whilst relaxing in the delightful environment created by the attentive staff. A meal in either the intimate, more formal Manor House Restaurant or the Walled Garden Restaurant will prove a highlight; each offers menus of the finest local produce used in well-prepared dishes. Bedrooms, including some suites, are individually styled, spacious and well appointed.

Rooms 11 **S** £110-£170; **D** £160-£260 (incl. bkfst)* **Facilities** FTV Xmas New Year Wi-fi **Conf** Class 50 Board 30 Thtr 80 **Parking** 30 **Notes** LB Civ Wed 100

BURTON UPON TRENT Map 10 SK22
Staffordshire

Three Queens

★★★ 78% HOTEL

☎ 01283 523800 & 0845 230 1332
01283 523823
One Bridge St DE14 1SY
e-mail: hotel@threequeenshotel.co.uk
web: www.threequeenshotel.co.uk
dir: On A511 in Burton upon Trent at junct of Bridge St & High St. Town side of Old River Bridge

Located in the centre of the town close to the river, this smartly presented hotel provides an appealing, high quality base from which to tour the area. Bedrooms come in a mix of styles that include spacious duplex suites and executive rooms located in the original Jacobean heart of the building. Smart day rooms include the medieval styled Grill Restaurant, a modern bar and a contemporary breakfast room. A warm welcome is assured from the professional staff.

Rooms 38 (7 smoking) **S** £55-£88; **D** £60-£95 (incl. bkfst)* **Facilities** STV FTV Xmas New Year Wi-fi **Conf** Class 40 Board 30 Thtr 60 Del from £95 to £120* **Services** Lift Air con **Parking** 40 **Notes** LB

Premier Inn Burton upon Trent East

BUDGET HOTEL

☎ 0871 527 8176 0871 527 8177
Ashby Road East DE15 0PU
dir: 2m E of Burton upon Trent on A50

High quality, budget accommodation ideal for both families and business travellers. Spacious, en suite bedrooms feature tea and coffee making facilities, and Freeview TV in most hotels. Internet access and Wi-fi are available for a small fee. The adjacent family restaurant features a wide and varied menu. See also the Hotel Groups pages.

Rooms 34 **D** £49-£60*

BURY Map 15 SD81
Greater Manchester

Red Hall Hotel

★★★ 80% HOTEL

☎ 01706 822476 01706 828086
Manchester Rd, Walmersley BL9 5NA
e-mail: info@red-hall.co.uk
dir: M66 junct 1, A56. Over motorway bridge, hotel approx 300mtrs on right

Originally a farmhouse this hotel, located in the picturesque village of Warmersley on the outskirts of Ramsbottom, is just off the M66 making it ideal for both business and leisure guests alike. Bedrooms are contemporary and well equipped. There is a restaurant and lounge bar, plus meeting and event facilities.

Rooms 37 (2 fmly) (18 GF) **Facilities** STV Xmas New Year Wi-fi **Conf** Class 60 Board 30 Thtr 140 **Services** Lift **Parking** 100 **Notes** Civ Wed

B

BURY *continued*

Premier Inn Bury

BUDGET HOTEL

☎ 0871 527 9294 🖷 0871 527 9295
5 Knowsley Place, Duke St BL9 0EJ
dir: M66 junct 2, A58 towards Bolton & Bury. At rdbt in Bury centre follow A58 (Angouleme Way). Left in Knowsley St, hotel on left

High quality, budget accommodation ideal for both families and business travellers. Spacious, en suite bedrooms feature tea and coffee making facilities, and Freeview TV in most hotels. Internet access and Wi-fi are available for a small fee. The adjacent family restaurant features a wide and varied menu. See also the Hotel Groups pages.

BURY ST EDMUNDS — Map 13 TL86
Suffolk

Angel Hotel

★★★★ 83% ◎◎ TOWN HOUSE HOTEL

☎ 01284 714000 🖷 01284 714001
Angel Hill IP33 1LT
e-mail: staying@theangel.co.uk
web: www.theangel.co.uk
dir: From A134, left at rdbt into Northgate St. Continue to lights, right into Mustow St, left into Angel Hill. Hotel on right

An impressive building situated just a short walk from the town centre. One of the Angel's more notable guests over the last 400 years was Charles Dickens who is reputed to have written part of the *Pickwick Papers* whilst in residence. The hotel offers a range of individually designed bedrooms that includes a selection of four-poster rooms and a suite.

Rooms 75 (5 fmly) (15 GF) **D** £125-£170 (incl. bkfst)* **Facilities** FTV Xmas Wi-fi **Conf** Board 16 Del from £150 to £250* **Services** Lift **Parking** 20

Ravenwood Hall

★★★ 88% ◎◎ COUNTRY HOUSE HOTEL

☎ 01359 270345 🖷 01359 270788
Rougham IP30 9JA
e-mail: enquiries@ravenwoodhall.co.uk
web: www.ravenwoodhall.co.uk
dir: 3m E off A14, junct 45. Hotel on left

Delightful 15th-century property set in seven acres of woodland and landscaped gardens. The building has many original features including carved timbers and inglenook fireplaces. The spacious bedrooms are attractively decorated, tastefully furnished with well-chosen pieces and equipped with many thoughtful touches. Public rooms include an elegant restaurant and a smart lounge bar with an open fire.

Rooms 14 (7 annexe) (5 GF) **S** £102-£136; **D** £125-£175 (incl. bkfst)* **Facilities** Shooting, fishing & horse riding can be arranged Xmas New Year Wi-fi Child facilities **Conf** Class 80 Board 40 Thtr 130 **Parking** 150 **Notes** LB Civ Wed 130

Best Western Priory

Best Western

★★★ 83% ◎◎ HOTEL

☎ 01284 766181 🖷 01284 767604
Mildenhall Rd IP32 6EH
e-mail: reservations@prioryhotel.co.uk
web: www.prioryhotel.co.uk
dir: From A14 take Bury St Edmunds W slip road. Follow signs to Brandon. At mini-rdbt turn right. Hotel 0.5m on left

An 18th-century Grade II listed building set in landscaped grounds on the outskirts of town. The attractively decorated, tastefully furnished and thoughtfully equipped bedrooms are split between the main house and garden wings, which have their own sun terraces. Public rooms feature a smart restaurant, a conservatory dining room and a lounge bar.

Rooms 36 (29 annexe) (1 fmly) (30 GF) **Facilities** FTV Xmas New Year Wi-fi **Conf** Class 35 Board 35 Thtr 75 **Parking** 60 **Notes** Civ Wed 75

Grange

★★★ 74% COUNTRY HOUSE HOTEL

☎ 01359 231260 🖷 01359 231387
Barton Rd, Thurston IP31 3PQ
e-mail: info@grangecountryhousehotel.com
web: www.grangecountryhousehotel.com
dir: A14 junct 45 towards Gt Barton, right at T-junct. At x-rds left into Barton Rd to Thurston. At rdbt, left after 0.5m, hotel on right

A Tudor-style country-house hotel situated on the outskirts of town. The individually decorated bedrooms have co-ordinated fabrics and many thoughtful touches; some rooms have nice views of the gardens. Public areas include a smart lounge bar, two private dining rooms, the Garden Restaurant and banqueting facilities.

Rooms 18 (5 annexe) (1 fmly) (3 GF) **S** £79.50; **D** £110 (incl. bkfst)* **Facilities** FTV Xmas New Year Wi-fi **Conf** Class 40 Board 30 Thtr 135 Del £129.50* **Parking** 100 **Notes** LB Civ Wed 150

Suffolk Hotel Golf & Leisure Club

OXFORD HOTELS & INNS

★★★ 74% HOTEL

☎ 01284 706777 🖷 01284 754767
Fornham St Genevieve IP28 6JQ
e-mail: reservations.suffolkgolf@ohiml.com
web: www.oxfordhotelsandinns.com
dir: A14 junct 42, B1106, through Fornham All Saints towards Thetford. Hotel 0.75m on right

Situated on the outskirts of this historic town just a few minutes from the A14. The modern, well equipped bedrooms are suitable for both business and leisure guests alike; some rooms have superb countryside views. Public rooms include a smart lounge bar and an intimate restaurant. The hotel has an 18-hole golf course, gym, heated indoor pool and spa facilities.

Rooms 40 (3 fmly) (15 GF) **Facilities** Spa FTV 18 Putt green Gym Xmas New Year Wi-fi **Conf** Class 60 Board 60 Thtr 100 **Services** Lift **Parking** 100 **Notes** Civ Wed 70

Ramada Bury St Edmunds

U

☎ 01284 760884 📠 01284 755476
A14 Bury East Exit, Symonds Rd IP32 7DZ
e-mail: reception@ramadaburystedmunds.co.uk
dir: Bury St Edmunds E exit off A14

Currently the rating for this establishment is not confirmed. This may be due to a change of ownership or because it has only recently joined the AA rating scheme. For further details please see the AA website: theAA.com

Rooms 71 **Conf** Class 20 Board 25 Thtr 50

BUXTON Map 16 SK07
Derbyshire

Barceló Buxton Palace Hotel

★★★★ 72% HOTEL

☎ 01298 22001 📠 01298 72131
Palace Rd SK17 6AG
e-mail: palace@barcelo-hotels.co.uk
web: www.barcelo-hotels.co.uk
dir: M6 junct 20, follow M56/M60 signs to Stockport then A6 to Buxton, hotel adjacent to railway station

This impressive Victorian hotel is located on the hill overlooking the town. Public areas are traditional and elegant in style, and include chandeliers and decorative ceilings. The bedrooms are spacious and equipped with modern facilities, and The Dovedale Restaurant provides modern British cuisine. Good leisure facilities are available.

Rooms 122 (18 fmly) **Facilities** Spa supervised Gym Beauty facilities Xmas New Year Wi-fi **Conf** Class 125 Board 80 Thtr 350 **Services** Lift **Parking** 180 **Notes** Civ Wed 100

Best Western Lee Wood

★★★ 81% HOTEL

☎ 01298 23002 📠 01298 23228
The Park SK17 6TQ
e-mail: reservations@leewoodhotel.co.uk
web: www.leewoodhotel.co.uk
dir: From town centre take A5004 NE, hotel 300mtrs beyond Devonshire Royal Hospital

This elegant Georgian hotel offers high standards of comfort and hospitality. The individually furnished bedrooms are generally spacious, with all of the expected modern conveniences. There is a choice of two comfortable lounges and a conservatory restaurant. The quality cooking, good service and fine hospitality are noteworthy.

Rooms 39 (5 annexe) (4 fmly) **S** £55-£95; **D** £75-£140 (incl. bkfst)* **Facilities** STV FTV New Year Wi-fi **Conf** Class 65 Board 40 Thtr 120 Del from £110 to £150* **Services** Lift **Parking** 50 **Notes** LB Civ Wed 120

Nat's Kitchen

RESTAURANT WITH ROOMS

☎ 01298 214642
9-11 Market St SK17 6JY
e-mail: natskitchen@btconnect.com
dir: On Market St, just off Buxton's market place

Set in one of the Peak Districts most well known destinations, Nat's Kitchen offers an intimate restaurant with a warm welcome. Accessed via a separate entrance, the accommodation is situated above the dining room and comes in a range of bedrooms with en suite facilities.

Rooms 5

CADNAM Map 5 SU31
Hampshire

Bartley Lodge Hotel

★★★ 80% HOTEL

☎ 023 8081 2248 📠 023 8081 2075
Lyndhurst Rd SO40 2NR
e-mail: bartley@newforesthotels.co.uk
web: www.newforesthotels.co.uk
dir: M27 junct 1 at 1st rdbt 1st exit, at 2nd rdbt 3rd exit onto A337. Hotel sign on left

This 18th-century former hunting lodge is very quietly situated, yet is just minutes from the M27. Bedrooms vary in size but all are well equipped. There is a selection of small lounge areas, a cosy bar and an indoor pool, together with a small fitness suite. The Crystal dining room offers a tempting choice of well prepared dishes.

Rooms 40 (15 fmly) (4 GF) **S** £60-£75; **D** £120-£160 (incl. bkfst)* **Facilities** FTV Sauna Xmas New Year Wi-fi **Conf** Class 60 Board 60 Thtr 120 Del from £95 to £110* **Parking** 60 **Notes** LB Civ Wed 80

See advert on this page

C

CALNE Map 4 ST97
Wiltshire

Bowood Hotel, Spa and Golf Resort

★★★★ 82% COUNTRY HOUSE HOTEL

01249 822228 01249 822218
Derry Hill SN11 9PQ
e-mail: resort@bowood.org
web: www.bowood-hotel.co.uk
dir: M4 junct 17, 2.5m W of Calne off A4

Located within the Bowood Estate this hotel is furnished to a luxury standard, very much with guest comfort in mind. Bedrooms and bathrooms are very well appointed, with contemporary artwork adorning the walls and quality linen on the deeply comfortable beds. The stylish Shelburne Restaurant, with views overlooking the beautiful 'Capability' Brown designed parkland, offers award-winning cuisine, and the Spa Bar offers more casual dining. The spa features an infinity pool and crystal steam room, and there is a championship golf course within the grounds.

Rooms 43 (2 fmly) (10 GF) **S** £150-£200; **D** £170-£220 (incl. bkfst)* **Facilities** Spa FTV 18 Putt green Gym Adventure playground Stately home & gardens New Year Wi-fi **Conf** Class 140 Board 85 Thtr 240 **Services** Lift Air con **Parking** 200 **Notes** LB Civ Wed 60

Lansdowne

★★★ 66% HOTEL

01249 812488 01249 815323
The Strand SN11 0EH
e-mail: reservations@lansdownestrand.co.uk
dir: From Chippenham take A4 signed Calne. Straight on at 2 rdbts, hotel in town centre

Situated in a picturesque market town, The Lansdowne was originally built in the 16th century as a coaching inn, and it still retains much of the charm and character of that era. Bedrooms are spacious and furnished in a traditional style. Guests can enjoy dinner in the pleasant bistro, in either of the bar areas, or choose from a varied room-service menu. An outdoor courtyard seating area is also available.

Rooms 26 (2 fmly) **Facilities** STV FTV Wi-fi **Conf** Class 60 Board 50 Thtr 60 **Parking** 15 **Notes** RS 25 Dec

CAMBERLEY Map 6 SU86
Surrey

See also **Yateley**

Macdonald Frimley Hall Hotel & Spa

★★★★ 76% HOTEL

0844 879 9110 01276 670362
Lime Av GU15 2BG
e-mail: sales.frimleyhall@macdonald-hotels.co.uk
web: www.macdonaldhotels.co.uk/frimleyhall
dir: M3 junct 3, A321 follow Bagshot signs. Through lights, left onto A30 signed Camberley & Basingstoke. To rdbt, 2nd exit onto A325, take 5th right

The epitome of classic English elegance, this ivy-clad Victorian manor house is set in two acres of immaculate grounds in the heart of Surrey. The bedrooms and public areas are smart and have a modern decorative theme. The hotel boasts an impressive health club and spa with treatment rooms, a fully equipped gym and heated indoor swimming pool.

Rooms 98 (15 fmly) **Facilities** Spa STV Gym Beauty treatment rooms Technogym Sauna Steam room Relaxation room Xmas New Year Wi-fi **Conf** Class 100 Board 60 Thtr 250 Del from £170 to £240 **Parking** 150 **Notes** Civ Wed 220

Lakeside International

★★★ 75% HOTEL

01252 838000 01252 837857
Wharf Rd, Frimley Green GU16 6JR
e-mail: info@lakesideinthotel.com
dir: Off A321 at mini-rdbt turn into Wharf Rd. Lakeside complex on right

This hotel, geared towards the business market, enjoys a lakeside location with noteworthy views. Bedrooms are modern, comfortable and with a range of facilities. Public areas are spacious and include a residents' lounge, bar and games room, a smart restaurant and an established health and leisure club.

Rooms 98 (1 fmly) (31 GF) **S** £55-£200; **D** £77-£230 (incl. bkfst)* **Facilities** Gym Squash Sauna Steam room Wi-fi **Conf** Class 100 Board 40 Thtr 120 **Services** Lift **Parking** 250 **Notes** Civ Wed 100

The Ely

★★★ 70% HOTEL

01252 860444 01252 878265
London Road (A30), Blackwater GU17 9LJ
e-mail: ely.yateley@newbridgeinns.co.uk
dir: M3 junct 4A, A327 towards Yateley. Right onto A30

This establishment benefits from being conveniently located close to Camberley and the M3. Bedrooms are particularly spacious and families are well catered for. A variety of enjoyable, substantial dishes is available throughout the day with the addition of a specials board in the evening. The range of options at breakfast is impressive. There is ample free parking on site and free Wi-fi throughout the hotel.

Rooms 35

Premier Inn Sandhurst

BUDGET HOTEL

0871 527 8958 0871 527 8959
221 Yorktown Rd, College Town, Sandurst GU47 0RT
dir: M3 junct 4, A331 to Camberley. At large rdbt take A321 towards Bracknell. At 3rd lights, hotel on left

High quality, budget accommodation ideal for both families and business travellers. Spacious, en suite bedrooms feature tea and coffee making facilities, and Freeview TV in most hotels. Internet access and Wi-fi are available for a small fee. The adjacent family restaurant features a wide and varied menu. See also the Hotel Groups pages.

Rooms 40 **D** £57-£75*

CAMBOURNE Map 12 TL35
Cambridgeshire

The Cambridge Belfry

QHOTELS

★★★★ 79% HOTEL

☎ 01954 714600 📠 01954 714610
Back St CB3 6BW
e-mail: cambridgebelfry@qhotels.co.uk
web: www.qhotels.co.uk
dir: M11 junct 13, A428 towards Bedford, follow signs to Cambourne. Exit at Cambourne, keep left. Left at rdbt, hotel on left

This exciting hotel, built beside the water, is located at the gateway to Cambourne Village and Business Park. Contemporary in style throughout, the hotel boasts state-of-the-art leisure facilities, including Reflections Spa offering a range of therapies and treatments, and extensive conference and banqueting rooms. There are two eating options - the Bridge Restaurant and the Brooks Brasserie. Original artwork is displayed throughout the hotel.

Rooms 120 (30 GF) **Facilities** Spa FTV Gym Beauty treatments Xmas New Year Wi-fi **Conf** Class 70 Board 70 Thtr 250 Del from £125 to £159* **Services** Lift **Parking** 200 **Notes** Civ Wed 160

CAMBRIDGE Map 12 TL45
Cambridgeshire

Hotel Felix

★★★★ 82% HOTEL

☎ 01223 277977 📠 01223 277973
Whitehouse Ln CB3 0LX
e-mail: help@hotelfelix.co.uk
web: www.hotelfelix.co.uk
dir: M11 junct 13. From A1 N, take A14 onto A1307. At 'City of Cambridge' sign left into Whitehouse Ln

A beautiful Victorian mansion set amidst three acres of landscaped gardens, this property was originally built in 1852 for a surgeon from the famous Addenbrookes Hospital. The contemporary-style bedrooms have carefully chosen furniture and many thoughtful touches, whilst public rooms feature an open-plan bar, the adjacent Graffiti restaurant and a small quiet lounge.

Rooms 52 (5 fmly) (26 GF) **S** £160-£215; **D** £198-£315 (incl. bkfst)* **Facilities** STV Xmas New Year Wi-fi **Conf** Class 36 Board 34 Thtr 60 **Services** Lift **Parking** 90 **Notes** LB Civ Wed 60

Menzies Cambridge Hotel & Golf Club

MenziesHotels

★★★★ 77% HOTEL

☎ 01954 249988 📠 01954 780010
Bar Hill CB23 8EU
e-mail: cambridge@menzieshotels.co.uk
web: www.menzieshotels.co.uk
dir: M11 N & S to A14 follow signs for Huntingdon. A14 turn off B1050 Bar Hill, hotel 1st exit on rdbt

Ideally situated amidst 200 acres of open countryside, just five miles from the university city of Cambridge. Public rooms include a brasserie restaurant and the popular Gallery Bar. The contemporary-style bedrooms are smartly decorated and equipped with a good range of useful facilities. The hotel also has a leisure club, swimming pool and golf course.

Rooms 136 (35 fmly) (68 GF) (12 smoking) **Facilities** STV 18 Putt green Gym Hair & beauty salon Steam room Sauna Xmas New Year Wi-fi **Conf** Class 90 Board 45 Thtr 200 **Services** Lift **Parking** 200 **Notes** Civ Wed 200

Hotel du Vin Cambridge

Hotel du Vin & Bistro

★★★★ 75% TOWN HOUSE HOTEL

☎ 01223 227330 📠 01223 227331
15-19 Trumpington St CB2 1QA
e-mail: info.cambridge@hotelduvin.com
web: www.hotelduvin.com
dir: M11 junct 11 Cambridge S, pass Trumpington Park & Ride on left. Hotel 2m on right after double rdbt

This beautiful building, which dates back in part to medieval times, has been transformed to enhance its many quirky architectural features. The bedrooms and suites, some with private terraces, have the company's trademark monsoon showers and Egyptian linen. The French-style bistro has an open-style kitchen and the bar is set in the unusual labyrinth of vaulted cellar rooms. There is also a library, specialist wine tasting room and private dining room.

Rooms 41 (3 annexe) (6 GF) **Facilities** STV Xmas New Year Wi-fi **Conf** Class 18 Board 18 Thtr 30 **Services** Lift Air con **Parking** 24

Crowne Plaza Cambridge

★★★★ 73% HOTEL

☎ 01223 556554 & 0871 942 9180
📠 01223 322374
20 Downing St CB2 3DT
e-mail: chris.darcy@ihg.com
web: www.crowneplaza.co.uk
dir: From M11 (either junct 11, 12 or 13). Follow signs to city centre then Grand Arcade car park. Hotel adjacent. Or from A14 take Cambridge exit, onto Huntingdon Rd, follow one-way system

Located in the heart of the city, this hotel enjoys an enviable position, with many of the universities and the town centre within easy walking distance. It is located adjacent to the Grand Arcade shopping centre: on site parking, although limited, is a plus. The hotel offers modern accommodation and large open-plan public areas; a fitness room and several conference rooms are also available.

Rooms 198 **S** £120-£275; **D** £140-£295* **Facilities** STV Gym Sauna New Year Wi-fi **Conf** Class 70 Board 50 Thtr 250 Del from £150 to £350* **Services** Lift Air con **Parking** 50 **Notes** LB Civ Wed 250

De Vere University Arms

DE VERE Hotels & Resorts

★★★★ 73% HOTEL

☎ 01223 273000 📠 01223 273037
Regent St CB2 1AD
e-mail: dua.sales@devere-hotels.com
web: www.devere.co.uk
dir: M11 junct 11, follow city centre signs for 3m. Right at 2nd mini rdbt, left at lights into Regent St. Hotel 600yds on right

Built in 1834, the University Arms has an enviable position in the very heart of the city, overlooking Parker's Piece. Public rooms include an elegant domed lounge, a smart restaurant, a bar and lounge overlooking the park. Conference and banqueting rooms are extensive, many with oak panelling. Given the hotel's central location parking for guests is a bonus.

Rooms 119 (2 fmly) **Facilities** STV Complimentary use of local fitness centre Xmas New Year Wi-fi **Conf** Class 150 Board 80 Thtr 300 **Services** Lift **Parking** 56 **Notes** Civ Wed 250

C

CAMBRIDGE *continued*

Arundel House Hotel

★★★ 82% HOTEL

☎ 01223 367701 Fax 01223 367721
Chesterton Rd CB4 3AN
e-mail: info@arundelhousehotels.co.uk
web: www.arundelhousehotels.co.uk
dir: City centre on A1303

Overlooking the River Cam and enjoying views over open parkland, this popular and smart hotel was originally a row of townhouses dating from Victorian times. Bedrooms are attractive and have a special character. The smart public areas feature a conservatory for informal snacks, a spacious bar and an elegant restaurant for more serious dining.

Rooms 103 (22 annexe) (7 fmly) (14 GF) **S** £75-£125; **D** £95-£150 (incl. bkfst)* **Facilities** FTV New Year Wi-fi **Conf** Class 24 Board 22 Thtr 50 Del from £145* **Parking** 70 **Notes** LB ⊗ Closed 25-26 Dec

Best Western Cambridge Quy Mill Hotel

★★★ 80% ⚘⚘ HOTEL

☎ 01223 293383 Fax 01223 293770
Church Rd, Stow Cum Quy CB25 9AF
e-mail: cambridgequy@bestwestern.co.uk
web: www.bw-cambridgequymill.co.uk
dir: Exit A14 at junct 35, E of Cambridge, onto B1102 for 50yds. Entrance opposite church

Set in open countryside, this 19th-century former watermill is conveniently situated for access to Cambridge. Bedroom styles differ, yet each room is smartly appointed and brightly decorated; superior, spacious courtyard rooms are noteworthy. Well-designed public areas include several spacious bar/lounges, with a choice of casual and formal eating areas; service is both friendly and helpful. There is a smart leisure club with state-of-the-art equipment.

Rooms 49 (26 annexe) (2 fmly) (26 GF) **Facilities** STV Gym Wi-fi **Conf** Class 30 Board 24 Thtr 80 **Parking** 90 **Notes** LB ⊗ Closed 24-30 Dec RS 31 Dec Civ Wed 80

Best Western The Gonville Hotel

★★★ 78% HOTEL

☎ 01223 366611 & 221111 Fax 01223 315470
Gonville Place CB1 1LY
e-mail: all@gonvillehotel.co.uk
web: www.bw-gonvillehotel.co.uk
dir: M11 junct 11, on A1309 follow city centre signs. At 2nd mini rdbt right into Lensfield Rd, over junct with lights. Hotel 25yds on right

A well established hotel situated on the inner ring road, a short walk across the green from the city centre. The air-conditioned public areas are cheerfully furnished, and include a lounge bar and brasserie; bedrooms are well appointed and appealing, offering a good range of facilities for both corporate and leisure guests.

Rooms 80 (2 fmly) (8 GF) **S** £78-£146; **D** £78-£156* **Facilities** FTV New Year Wi-fi **Conf** Class 100 Board 50 Thtr 200 **Services** Lift **Parking** 80 **Notes** LB RS 24-29 Dec Civ Wed 100

Holiday Inn Cambridge

★★★ 78% HOTEL

☎ 0871 942 9015 Fax 01223 233426
Lakeview, Bridge Rd, Impington CB24 9PH
e-mail: reservations-cambridge@ihg.com
web: www.holidayinn.co.uk
dir: 2.5m N, on N side of rdbt junct A14/B1049

A modern, purpose-built hotel conveniently situated just off the A14 junction, a short drive from the city centre. Public areas include a popular bar, the Junction Restaurant and a large open-plan lounge. Bedrooms come in a variety of styles and are suited to both business and leisure guests alike.

Rooms 161 (14 fmly) (75 GF) **Facilities** Spa STV supervised Gym Wi-fi **Conf** Class 40 Board 45 Thtr 120 **Services** Air con **Parking** 175 **Notes** ⊗ Civ Wed 100

Lensfield

★★★ 78% METRO HOTEL

☎ 01223 355017 Fax 01223 312022
53-57 Lensfield Rd CB2 1EN
e-mail: reservations@lensfieldhotel.co.uk
web: www.lensfieldhotel.co.uk
dir: M11 junct 11/12/13, follow signs to city centre, approach hotel via Silver St, Trumpington St, left into Lensfield Rd

Located close to all the city's attractions, this constantly improving hotel provides a range of attractive bedrooms, equipped with thoughtful extras. Comprehensive breakfasts are taken in an elegant dining room and a comfortable bar and cosy foyer lounge are also available.

Rooms 28 (3 fmly) (4 GF) **S** £69-£116; **D** £105-£128 (incl. bkfst)* **Facilities** STV Wi-fi **Parking** 5 **Notes** LB ⊗ Closed last 2 wks in Dec-4 Jan

Royal Cambridge

★★★ 75% HOTEL

☎ 01223 351631 Fax 01223 352972
Trumpington St CB2 1PY
e-mail: royal.cambridge@forestdale.com
web: www.theroyalcambridgehotel.co.uk
dir: M11 junct 11, signed city centre. At 1st mini rdbt left into Fen Causeway. Hotel 1st right

This elegant Georgian hotel is situated in the heart of Cambridge. The bedrooms are well equipped and provide great comfort. The stylish restaurant and bar are a popular choice with locals and guests alike. The complimentary parking proves a real benefit in this city centre location.

Rooms 57 (5 fmly) (3 GF) **Facilities** FTV Xmas New Year Wi-fi **Conf** Class 60 Board 40 Thtr 120 **Services** Lift **Parking** 80 **Notes** LB Civ Wed 100

Centennial Hotel

★★★ 70% HOTEL

☎ 01223 314652 📠 01223 315443
63-71 Hills Rd CB2 1PG
e-mail: reception@centennialhotel.co.uk
dir: M11 junct 11 take A1309 to Cambridge. Right onto Brooklands Ave to end. Left, hotel 100yds on right

This friendly hotel is convenient for the railway station and town centre. Well-presented public areas include a welcoming lounge, a relaxing bar and restaurant on the lower-ground level. Bedrooms are generally spacious, well maintained and thoughtfully equipped with a good range of facilities; several rooms are available on the ground floor.

Rooms 39 (1 fmly) (7 GF) **S** £70-£80; **D** £88-£96 (incl. bkfst)* **Facilities** FTV Wi-fi **Conf** Class 25 Board 25 Thtr 25 Del from £115 to £125* **Parking** 28 **Notes** ® Closed 23 Dec-1 Jan

Ashley Hotel

★★ 81% METRO HOTEL

☎ 01223 350059 & 367701 📠 01223 350900
74-76 Chesterton Rd CB4 1ER
e-mail: info@arundelhousehotels.co.uk
dir: On city centre ring road

Expect a warm welcome at this delightful Victorian property situated just a short walk from the River Cam. The smartly decorated bedrooms are generally quite spacious and equipped with a good range of useful extras. Breakfast is served at individual tables in the smart lower ground floor dining room.

Rooms 16 (5 fmly) (5 GF) **S** £65-£85; **D** £75-£95 (incl. bkfst)* **Facilities** FTV Wi-fi **Parking** 12 **Notes** ® Closed 24-26 Dec

Helen Hotel

★★ 80% METRO HOTEL

☎ 01223 246465 📠 01223 214406
167-169 Hills Rd CB2 2RJ
e-mail: enquiries@helenhotel.co.uk
dir: On A1307, 1.25m from city centre (south side). Cherry-Hinton Rd junct, opposite Homerton College

This extremely well maintained, privately owned hotel is situated close to the city centre and a range of popular eateries. Public areas include a smart lounge bar with plush sofas and a cosy breakfast room. Bedrooms are pleasantly decorated with co-ordinated fabrics and have many thoughtful touches.

Rooms 19 (2 fmly) (2 GF) **Facilities** STV Wi-fi **Parking** 12 **Notes** ® Closed Xmas & New Year

Holiday Inn Express Cambridge

BUDGET HOTEL

☎ 01223 866800 📠 01223 866857
15/17 Coldhams Park, Norman Way CB1 3LH
e-mail: info@expresscambridge.co.uk
web: www.expresscambridge.co.uk
dir: B1047 Fen Ditton. 1m to T-junct, right, at rdbt left onto Barnwell Rd, to rdbt. Left, to Toyota garage, right into Business Park

A modern hotel ideal for families and business travellers. Fresh and uncomplicated, the spacious rooms include Sky TV, power shower and tea and coffee-making facilities. Continental buffet breakfast is included in the room rate; and a choice of light meals are served in the smart restaurant. See also the Hotel Groups pages.

Rooms 100 (8 smoking) **Conf** Class 20 Board 24 Thtr 50

Holiday Inn Express Cambridge - Duxford

BUDGET HOTEL

☎ 01223 497070 📠 01223 497071
Duxford M11 Jct 10, 42 Station Rd, East Whittlesford Bridge CB22 4NL
e-mail: reception@hiexpresscambridgeduxford.co.uk
dir: Located 1m from Imperial War Museum Duxford

Rooms 73 (40 fmly) (6 GF) **Conf** Class 10 Board 16 Thtr 25

Premier Inn Cambridge (A14 Jct 32)

BUDGET HOTEL

☎ 0871 527 8186 📠 0871 527 8187
Ring Fort Rd CB4 2GW
dir: A14 junct 32, follow B1049/city centre signs. At 1st lights left onto Kings Hedges Rd, 2nd left into Ring Fort Rd

High quality, budget accommodation ideal for both families and business travellers. Spacious, en suite bedrooms feature tea and coffee making facilities, and Freeview TV in most hotels. Internet access and Wi-fi are available for a small fee. The adjacent family restaurant features a wide and varied menu. See also the Hotel Groups pages.

Rooms 154 **D** £70*

CANNOCK
Staffordshire — Map 10 SJ91

Premier Inn Cannock (Orbital)

BUDGET HOTEL

☎ 0871 527 8190 📠 0871 527 8191
Eastern Way WS11 8XR
dir: N'bound: M6 (Toll) junct 7, A5. At rdbt 1st exit (A5), 4th exit onto A460, 1st exit. S'bound: (no access from M6 Toll). M6 junct 11, A460 signed Cannock. At next 2 rdbts take 3rd exit. At next rdbt 1st exit onto service road. Hotel adjacent to Orbital Brewers Fayre

High quality, budget accommodation ideal for both families and business travellers. Spacious, en suite bedrooms feature tea and coffee making facilities, and Freeview TV in most hotels. Internet access and Wi-fi are available for a small fee. The adjacent family restaurant features a wide and varied menu. See also the Hotel Groups pages.

Rooms 21 **D** £70*

Premier Inn Cannock South

BUDGET HOTEL

☎ 0871 527 8192 📠 0871 527 8193
Watling St WS11 1SJ
dir: At junct of A5/A460, 2m from M6 juncts 11 & 12

Rooms 60 **D** £51-£58*

CANTERBURY Kent **Map 7 TR15**

Holiday Inn Express Canterbury

BUDGET HOTEL

☎ 01227 865000 🖷 01227 865100
A2 Dover Rd, Upper Harbledown CT2 9HX
e-mail: canterbury@exbhi.co.uk
web: www.hiexpresscanterbury.co.uk
dir: M2 junct 7, take A2 towards Dover. 4m. Hotel access via Texaco service area

A modern hotel ideal for families and business travellers. Fresh and uncomplicated, the spacious rooms include Sky TV, power shower and tea and coffee-making facilities. Continental buffet breakfast is included in the room rate; other meals may be taken at the nearby family pub or restaurant. See also the Hotel Groups pages.

Rooms 89 (38 GF) **S** £49-£125; **D** £59-£135 (incl. bkfst) **Conf** Class 20 Board 10 Thtr 36 Del from £79 to £99

CARBIS BAY

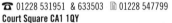

See St Ives (Cornwall)

CARLISLE Cumbria **Map 18 NY35**

Hallmark Hotel Carlisle

★★★★ 71% HOTEL

☎ 01228 531951 & 633503 🖷 01228 547799
Court Square CA1 1QY
e-mail: carlisle.reservations@hallmarkhotels.co.uk
dir: M6 junct 43, to city centre, then follow road to left & railway station

This refurbished hotel is at the heart of the town, opposite the railway station. Most of the bedrooms have benefited from an investment programme, and the smart ground-floor areas include a popular bar and restaurant. A number of meeting rooms are available and at the rear of the hotel is a small car park.

Rooms 70 (3 fmly) **Facilities** FTV Xmas New Year Wi-fi **Conf** Class 100 Board 30 Thtr 240 **Services** Lift **Parking** 26 **Notes** LB Civ Wed 200

Crown

★★★ 81% HOTEL

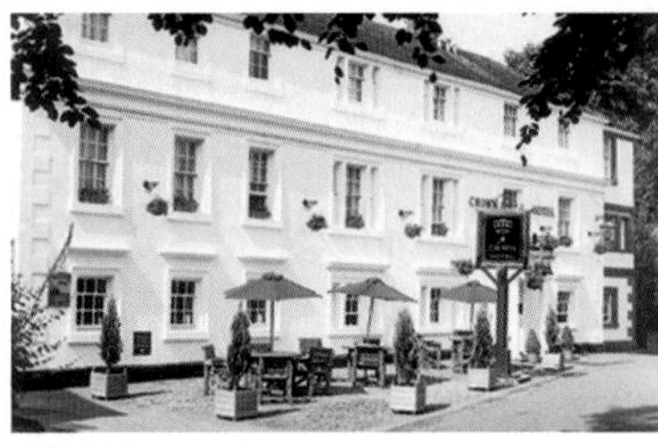

☎ 01228 561888 🖷 01228 561637
Station Rd, Wetheral CA4 8ES
e-mail: info@crownhotelwetheral.co.uk
web: www.crownhotelwetheral.co.uk
dir: M6 junct 42, B6263 to Wetheral, right at village shop, car park at rear of hotel

Set in the attractive village of Wetheral and with landscaped gardens to the rear, this hotel is well suited to both business and leisure guests. Rooms vary in size and style and include two apartments in an adjacent house ideal for long stays. A choice of dining options is available, with the popular Waltons Bar an informal alternative to the main restaurant.

Rooms 51 (2 annexe) (10 fmly) (3 GF) **S** £65-£80; **D** £110-£130 (incl. bkfst)* **Facilities** Spa STV supervised Gym Squash Children's splash pool Steam room Beauty room Sauna Xmas New Year Wi-fi **Conf** Class 90 Board 50 Thtr 175 Del from £110 to £135* **Parking** 80 **Notes** LB Civ Wed 120

Best Western Cumbria Park

★★★ 73% HOTEL

☎ 01228 522887 🖷 01228 514796
32 Scotland Rd, Stanwix CA3 9DG
e-mail: cumbriaparkhotel@wightcablenorth.net
web: www.bw-cumbriaparkhotel.co.uk
dir: M6 junct 44, A7 towards Carlisle. Hotel on left in 1.5m

Just minutes from the M6, this privately-owned hotel, with its a feature garden, is conveniently placed for the city centre. Well-equipped bedrooms come in a variety of sizes, and several have four-poster beds and whirlpool baths. Functions, conferences and weddings are all well catered for in a wide choice of rooms. Wi-fi is available throughout.

Rooms 47 (3 fmly) (7 GF) (2 smoking) **S** £55-£80; **D** £65-£120 (incl. bkfst)* **Facilities** STV FTV Wi-fi **Conf** Class 50 Board 35 Thtr 120 **Services** Lift **Parking** 51 **Notes** LB Closed 25-26 Dec Civ Wed 70

The Crown & Mitre

★★★ 70% HOTEL

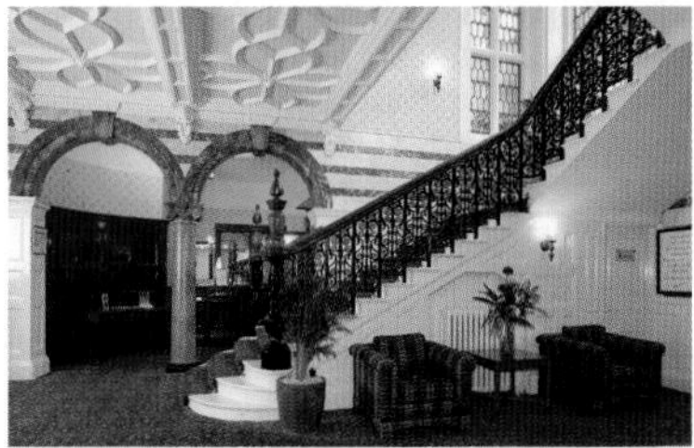

☎ 01228 525491 🖷 01228 514553
4 English St CA3 8HZ
e-mail: info@crownandmitre-hotel-carlisle.com
web: www.crownandmitre-hotel-carlisle.com
dir: A6 to city centre, pass station on left. Right into Blackfriars St. Rear entrance at end

Located in the heart of the city, this Edwardian hotel is close to the cathedral and a few minutes' walk from the castle. Bedrooms vary in size and style, from smart executive rooms to more functional standard rooms. Public rooms include a comfortable lounge area and the lovely bar with its feature stained-glass windows.

Rooms 95 (20 annexe) (4 fmly) (11 smoking) **Facilities** FTV Xmas New Year Wi-fi **Conf** Class 250 Board 50 Thtr 400 Del from £110 to £120* **Services** Lift **Parking** 42 **Notes** Civ Wed 100

Ibis Carlisle

BUDGET HOTEL

☎ 01228 518000 🖷 01228 518010
Portlands, Botchergate CA1 1RP
e-mail: H3443@accor-hotels.com
web: www.ibishotels.com
dir: M6 junct 42/43 follow signs for city centre. Hotel on Botchergate

Modern, budget hotel offering comfortable accommodation in bright and practical bedrooms. Breakfast is self-service and dinner is available in the restaurant See also the Hotel Groups pages.

Rooms 102 (17 fmly)

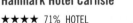

Premier Inn Carlisle Central

BUDGET HOTEL

☎ 0871 527 8210 📠 0871 527 8211
Warwick Rd CA1 2WF
dir: M6 junct 43, on A69

High quality, budget accommodation ideal for both families and business travellers. Spacious, en suite bedrooms feature tea and coffee making facilities, and Freeview TV in most hotels. Internet access and Wi-fi are available for a small fee. The adjacent family restaurant features a wide and varied menu. See also the Hotel Groups pages.

Rooms 44 **D** £60*

Premier Inn Carlisle Central North

BUDGET HOTEL

☎ 0871 527 8212 📠 0871 527 8213
Kingstown Rd CA3 0AT
dir: M6 junct 44, A7 towards Carlisle, hotel 1m on left

Rooms 49 **D** £60*

Premier Inn Carlisle (M6 Jct 42)

BUDGET HOTEL

☎ 0871 527 8206 📠 0871 527 8207
Carleton CA4 0AD
dir: Just off M6 junct 42, S of Carlisle

Rooms 61 **D** £60*

Premier Inn Carlisle (M6 Jct 44)

BUDGET HOTEL

☎ 0871 527 8208 📠 0871 527 8209
Parkhouse Rd CA3 0HR
dir: M6 junct 44, A7 signed Carlisle. Hotel on right at 1st set of lights

Rooms 127 **D** £60*

CARTMEL
Cumbria **Map 18 SD37**

Aynsome Manor Hotel

★★★ 78% ◎ COUNTRY HOUSE HOTEL

☎ 015395 36653 📠 015395 36016
LA11 6HH
e-mail: aynsomemanor@btconnect.com
dir: M6 junct 36, A590 signed Barrow-in-Furness towards Cartmel. Left at end of road, hotel before village

Dating back, in part, to the early 16th century, this manor house overlooks the fells and the nearby priory. Spacious bedrooms, including some courtyard rooms, are comfortably furnished. Dinner in the elegant restaurant features local produce whenever possible, and there is a choice of lounges to relax in.

Rooms 12 (2 annexe) (2 fmly) **S** £75-£105; **D** £140-£180 (incl. bkfst & dinner)* **Facilities** FTV New Year **Parking** 20 **Notes** LB Closed 2-31 Jan RS Sun

INSPECTORS' CHOICE

L'Enclume

◎◎◎◎◎ RESTAURANT WITH ROOMS

☎ 015395 36362
Cavendish St LA11 6PZ
e-mail: info@lenclume.co.uk
dir: From A590 turn left for Cartmel before Newby Bridge

A delightful 13th-century property in the heart of this lovely village offering 21st-century cooking that is more than worth travelling some distance for. Simon Rogan cooks imaginative and adventurous food in this stylish restaurant. Individually designed, modern, en suite rooms vary in size and style, and are either in the main property or dotted about the village only a few moments' walk from the restaurant.

Rooms 12 (5 annexe) (3 fmly)

CASTLE CARY
Somerset **Map 4 ST63**

The George Hotel

★★ 67% HOTEL

☎ 01963 350761 📠 01963 350035
Market Place BA7 7AH
e-mail: castlecarygeorge@aol.co.uk
dir: A303 onto A371. Signed Castle Cary, 2m on left

This 15th-century coaching inn provides well-equipped bedrooms that are generally spacious. Most bedrooms are at the back of the house, enjoying a quiet aspect, and some are on the ground floor; one is suitable for less able guests. Diners can choose to eat in the more formal dining room, or in one of the two cosy bars.

Rooms 17 (5 annexe) (1 fmly) (5 GF) **S** fr £65; **D** fr £85 (incl. bkfst) **Facilities** Xmas New Year Wi-fi **Conf** Class 40 Board 20 Thtr 50 **Parking** 7 **Notes** LB

CASTLE COMBE
Wiltshire **Map 4 ST87**

INSPECTORS' CHOICE

Manor House Hotel and Golf Club

★★★★ ◎◎◎ COUNTRY HOUSE HOTEL

☎ 01249 782206 📠 01249 782159
SN14 7HR
e-mail: enquiries@manorhouse.co.uk
web: www.exclusivehotels.co.uk
dir: M4 junct 17 follow Chippenham signs onto A420 Bristol, then right onto B4039. Through village, right after bridge

This delightful hotel is situated in a secluded valley adjacent to a picturesque village, where there have been no new buildings for 300 years. There are 365 acres of grounds to enjoy, complete with an Italian garden and an 18-hole golf course. Bedrooms, some in the main house and some in a row of stone cottages, have been superbly furnished, and public rooms include a number of cosy lounges with roaring fires. Service is a pleasing blend of professionalism and friendliness. The award-winning food utilises top quality local produce.

Rooms 48 (26 annexe) (8 fmly) (12 GF) **S** £245-£650; **D** £245-£650 (incl. bkfst)* **Facilities** STV ⛳ 18 Putt green Fishing Jogging track Hot air ballooning Xmas New Year Wi-fi **Conf** Class 70 Board 30 Thtr 100 Del from £ to £345* **Parking** 100 **Notes** LB Civ Wed 110

CASTLE DONINGTON

See East Midlands Airport

C

CASTLEFORD
West Yorkshire
Map 16 SE42

Premier Inn Castleford M62 Jct 31

BUDGET HOTEL

☎ 0871 527 8216 🖹 0871 527 8217
Pioneer Way WF10 5TG
dir: M62 junct 31, A655 towards Castleford, right at 1st lights, then left

High quality, budget accommodation ideal for both families and business travellers. Spacious, en suite bedrooms feature tea and coffee making facilities, and Freeview TV in most hotels. Internet access and Wi-fi are available for a small fee. The adjacent family restaurant features a wide and varied menu. See also the Hotel Groups pages.

Rooms 62 **D** £48-£55*

Premier Inn Castleford M62 Jct 32

BUDGET HOTEL

☎ 0871 527 8218 🖹 0871 527 8219
Colarado Way WF10 4TA
dir: M62 junct 32, follow signs for Xscape. Hotel adjacent to Xscape complex

Rooms 119 (GF) **D** £55-£62*

CAVENDISH
Suffolk
Map 13 TL84

The George

RESTAURANT WITH ROOMS

☎ 01787 280248
The Green CO10 8BA
e-mail: thegeorgecavendish@gmail.com
web: www.thecavendishgeorge.co.uk
dir: A1092 into Cavendish, The George next to village green

The George is situated in the heart of the pretty village of Cavendish and has four very stylish bedrooms. The front-facing rooms overlook the village; the comfortable, spacious bedrooms retain many of their original features. The award-winning restaurant is very well appointed and dinner should not be missed. Guests are guaranteed to receive a warm welcome, attentive friendly service and great food.

Rooms 4 (1 fmly)

CHADDESLEY CORBETT
Worcestershire
Map 10 SO87

INSPECTORS' CHOICE

Brockencote Hall Country House

★★★ HOTEL

☎ 01562 777876 🖹 01562 777872
DY10 4PY
e-mail: info@brockencotehall.com
web: www.brockencotehall.com
dir: 0.5m W, off A448, opposite St Cassians Church

Glorious countryside extends all around this magnificent mansion, and grazing sheep can be seen from the conservatory. Not surprisingly, relaxation comes high on the list of priorities here. Despite its very English location the hotel's owner actually hails from Alsace and the atmosphere is very much that of a provincial French château. The spacious, chandeliered dining room is a popular venue for accomplished classical French cuisine which has modern British influences.

Rooms 17 (2 fmly) (5 GF) **S** £96-£145; **D** £120-£190 (incl. bkfst)* **Facilities** FTV Fishing Reflexology Aromatherapy Massage Facials Xmas New Year Wi-fi **Conf** Class 20 Board 20 Thtr 30 Del from £175 to £190* **Services** Lift **Parking** 45 **Notes** LB Civ Wed 80

CHAGFORD
Devon
Map 3 SX78

INSPECTORS' CHOICE

Gidleigh Park

★★★★★ COUNTRY HOUSE HOTEL

☎ 01647 432367 🖹 01647 432574
TQ13 8HH
e-mail: gidleighpark@gidleigh.co.uk
web: www.gidleigh.com
dir: From Chagford, right at Lloyds Bank into Mill St. After 150yds fork right, follow lane 2m to end

Built in 1928 as a private residence for an Australian shipping magnate and set in 107 acres of lovingly tended grounds, this world-renowned hotel retains a timeless charm and a very endearing, homely atmosphere. The individually styled bedrooms are sumptuously furnished; some with separate seating areas, some with balconies and many enjoying panoramic views. There are spa suites, a loft suite, ideal for families, and the stunning thatched Pavilion in the grounds, which has two bedrooms, two bathrooms, a lounge and kitchen diner. The spacious public areas feature antique furniture, beautiful flower arrangements and magnificent artwork. The award-winning cuisine created by Michael Caines, together with the top quality wine list, will make a stay here a truly memorable experience.

Rooms 24 (4 fmly) (4 GF) **D** £310-£1155 (incl. bkfst)* **Facilities** STV FTV Putt green Fishing Bowls Xmas New Year Wi-fi **Conf** Board 22 **Parking** 45 **Notes** LB Civ Wed 28

Mill End Hotel

★★ 85% HOTEL

☎ 01647 432282 📠 01647 433106
Dartmoor National Park TQ13 8JN
e-mail: info@millendhotel.com
web: www.millendhotel.com
dir: From A30 at Whiddon Down take A382 to Moretonhampstead. In 3.5m, hump back bridge at Sandy Park, hotel on right

Originally an 18th-century working water mill, this engaging hotel sits alongside the River Teign and offers six miles of angling. Surrounded by picturesque Devon countryside, the atmosphere is akin to a family home where guests are encouraged to relax and enjoy the peace and informality. Bedrooms are available in a range of sizes and all are stylishly decorated and thoughtfully equipped. Dining is certainly a highlight of any stay here with the menus offering exciting dishes based on local produce.

Rooms 14 (3 GF) **Facilities** FTV Fishing Xmas New Year Wi-fi **Conf** Class 20 Board 30 Thtr 30 **Parking** 25 **Notes** LB

CHARD Somerset — Map 4 ST30

Cricket St Thomas Hotel

Warner Leisure Hotels

★★★★ 73% COUNTRY HOUSE HOTEL

☎ 01460 30111 📠 01460 30817
TA20 4DD
e-mail: cricket.sales@bourne-leisure.co.uk
dir: M5 junct 25/A358 to Chard, A30 to Crewkerne. Hotel 3m out of Chard

This Grade II listed house has an interesting history including the fact that Lord Nelson and Lady Hamilton were frequent visitors. The hotel is set in splendid parkland, with colourful gardens, lakes, and a unique woodland area. Various holiday packages are available, and there are extensive leisure facilities, as well as live entertainment and various dining venues, including Fenocchi's, with an Italian-themed menu. The bedrooms are spacious and well appointed. Please note that this is an adults-only (over 21 years old) hotel. Warner Leisure Hotels – AA Small Hotel Group of the Year 2011-12.

Rooms 239 (84 GF) **Facilities** Spa Putt green Gym Rifle shooting Archery Clay pigeon Short mat bowls Xmas New Year Wi-fi **Conf** Class 50 Board 25 Thtr 80 **Services** Lift **Parking** 351 **Notes** No children Civ Wed 60

Lordleaze

THE INDEPENDENTS HOTEL ASSOCIATION

★★★ 77% HOTEL

☎ 01460 61066 📠 01460 66468
Henderson Dr, Forton Rd TA20 2HW
e-mail: info@lordleazehotel.com
web: www.lordleazehotel.com
dir: A358 from Chard, left at St Mary's Church to Forton & Winsham on B3162. Follow signs to hotel

Conveniently and quietly located, this hotel is close to the Devon, Dorset and Somerset borders, and only minutes from Chard. All bedrooms are well equipped and comfortable. The friendly lounge bar has a wood-burning stove and serves tempting bar meals. The conservatory restaurant offers more formal dining.

Rooms 25 (2 fmly) (7 GF) **S** £75-£78; **D** £115-£120 (incl. bkfst)* **Facilities** FTV Xmas New Year Wi-fi **Conf** Class 60 Board 40 Thtr 180 Del from £125 to £137* **Parking** 55 **Notes** LB Civ Wed 100

C

CHARINGWORTH Gloucestershire — Map 10 SP13

Charingworth Manor

★★★★ 73% COUNTRY HOUSE HOTEL

☎ 01386 593555 📠 01386 593353
Charingworth Manor GL55 6NS
e-mail: gm.charingworthmanor@classiclodges.co.uk
web: www.classiclodges.co.uk/charingworthmanor

This 14th-century manor house retains many original features including flagstone floors, exposed beams and open fireplaces. The house has a beautiful setting in 50 acres of grounds and has been carefully extended to provide high quality accommodation and a delightful, small leisure spa. Spacious bedrooms are furnished with period pieces and modern amenities.

continued

CHARINGWORTH ***continued***

Rooms 26 (18 annexe) (2 fmly) (12 GF) **Facilities** Gym Sauna Steam room Solarium Xmas New Year **Conf** Class 30 Board 40 Thtr 80 **Parking** 50 **Notes** Civ Wed 60

See advert on page 131

CHARMOUTH Dorset **Map 4 SY39**

Fernhill Hotel

★★★ 80% HOTEL

☎ 01297 560492 01297 561159
Fernhill DT6 6BX
e-mail: mail@fernhill-hotel.co.uk
dir: A35 onto A3052 to Lyme Regis. Hotel 0.25m on left

A small, friendly hotel on top of the hill in well tended grounds. It boasts an outside pool and treatment rooms, together with comfortable rooms and pleasant public areas. Each bedroom is individually styled and many have views of the Char Valley and beyond. The menus are based on seasonal, locally sourced produce.

Rooms 10 (1 fmly) **Facilities** Fishing Holistic treatment centre Air/Massage baths Xmas New Year Wi-fi **Conf** Class 20 Board 24 Thtr 60 **Parking** 30 **Notes**

CHARNOCK RICHARD MOTORWAY SERVICE AREA (M6) Lancashire **Map 15 SD51**

Days Inn Charnock Richard - M6

BUDGET HOTEL

☎ 01257 791746 01257 793596
Welcome Break Service Area PR7 5LR
e-mail: charnockhotel@welcomebreak.co.uk
web: www.welcomebreak.co.uk
dir: Between junct 27 & 28 of M6 N'bound. 500yds from Camelot Theme Park via Mill Lane

This modern building offers accommodation in smart, spacious and well-equipped bedrooms, suitable for families and business travellers, and all with en suite bathrooms. Continental breakfast is available and other refreshments may be taken at the nearby family restaurant. See also the Hotel Groups pages.

Rooms 100 (68 fmly) (32 GF) (20 smoking) **S** £39.95-£59.95; **D** £49.95-£69.95 **Conf** Class 16 Board 24 Thtr 40

CHATHAM Kent **Map 7 TQ76**

Bridgewood Manor

★★★★ 74% HOTEL

☎ 01634 201333 01634 201330
Bridgewood Roundabout, Walderslade Woods ME5 9AX
e-mail: bridgewoodmanor@qhotels.co.uk
web: www.qhotels.co.uk
dir: Adjacent to Bridgewood rdbt on A229. Take 3rd exit signed Walderslade & Lordswood. Hotel 50mtrs on left

A modern, purpose-built hotel situated on the outskirts of Rochester. Bedrooms are pleasantly decorated, comfortably furnished and equipped with many thoughtful touches. The hotel has an excellent range of leisure and conference facilities. Guests can dine in the informal Terrace Bistro or experience fine dining in the more formal Squires restaurant, where the service is both attentive and friendly.

Rooms 100 (12 fmly) (26 GF) **S** £69-£149; **D** £89-£169 (incl. bkfst) **Facilities** Spa STV supervised Gym Beauty treatments Xmas New Year Wi-fi **Conf** Class 110 Board 80 Thtr 200 Del from £99 to £159* **Services** Lift **Parking** 170 **Notes** LB Civ Wed 130

Holiday Inn Rochester-Chatham

★★★ 77% HOTEL

☎ 0871 942 9069 & 07736 746229
01322 625584
Maidstone Rd ME5 9SF
e-mail: adrienne.reader@ihg.com
web: www.holidayinn.co.uk
dir: M2 junct 3 or M20 junct 6, then A229 for Chatham

A modern, well-equipped hotel close to Rochester, Canterbury and the historic Chatham Dockyards. Bedrooms, including family rooms, are comfortable and spacious; all have air conditioning and broadband access. Public facilities include a lounge, bar and modern restaurant. There is a gym, indoor pool, sauna, spa and an impressive self-contained conference centre.

Rooms 149 (29 fmly) (53 GF) (16 smoking) **Facilities** STV FTV supervised Gym Steam room Sauna Pilates & beauty evenings Wi-fi **Conf** Class 45 Board 45 Thtr 100 **Services** Lift Air con **Parking** 200 **Notes** Civ Wed 100

Ramada Encore Chatham

★★★ 68% HOTEL

☎ 01634 891677 01634 895152
Western Av, Chatham Historic Dockyard ME4 4NT
e-mail: operations@encorechatham.co.uk
dir: Follow signs for Chatham Historic Dockyard

Located in the historic dockyard and just minutes from the town centre, this hotel offers stylish, comfortable accommodation. The smart open-plan bar and restaurant are modern in design and provide a choice of seating areas; a full menu is on offer all day and in the evening. Free Wi-fi is available throughout the public areas, and there is a meeting room.

Rooms 90 (14 fmly) (8 smoking) **S** £49.95-£99.95; **D** £49.95-£99.95* **Facilities** STV FTV Wi-fi **Conf** Class 12 Board 12 Thtr 20 Del from £99 to £129* **Services** Lift Air con **Parking** 60 **Notes**

CHATHILL Northumberland **Map 21 NU12**

Doxford Hall Hotel & Spa

★★★★ 83% COUNTRY HOUSE HOTEL

☎ 01665 589700 & 589713 01665 589141
NE67 5DN
e-mail: info@doxfordhall.com
dir: 8m N of Alnwick just off A1, signed Christon Bank & Seahouses. B6347 then follow signs for Doxford

A beautiful country-house hotel set in a private estate, surrounded by countryside yet convenient for visiting nearby historic towns and attractions. Bedrooms are spacious and luxuriously furnished, each named after Northumbrian Castles. The dining room and lounges are very attractive. There is an impressive grand staircase, beautiful wood throughout the hotel and a spa also adds to the range of facilities.

Rooms 31 (1 fmly) (5 GF) **S** £100-£200; **D** £140-£280 (incl. bkfst)* **Facilities** Spa FTV supervised Gym Sauna Steam room Xmas New Year Wi-fi **Conf** Class 100 Board 22 Thtr 250 Del from £120 to £160* **Services** Lift **Parking** 100 **Notes** LB Civ Wed 250

CHEADLE Map 16 SJ88
Greater Manchester

Premier Inn Manchester (Cheadle)

BUDGET HOTEL

☎ 0871 527 8728 📠 0871 527 8729
Royal Crescent SK8 3FE
dir: Off A34, at Cheadle Royal rdbt behind TGI Friday's

High quality, budget accommodation ideal for both families and business travellers. Spacious, en suite bedrooms feature tea and coffee making facilities, and Freeview TV in most hotels. Internet access and Wi-fi are available for a small fee. The adjacent family restaurant features a wide and varied menu. See also the Hotel Groups pages.

Rooms 65 **D** £57-£59*

CHELMSFORD Map 6 TL70
Essex

County Hotel

★★★ 80% HOTEL

☎ 01245 455700 📠 01245 492762
29 Rainsford Rd CM1 2PZ
e-mail: kloftus@countyhotelgroup.co.uk
web: www.countyhotelgroup.co.uk
dir: From town centre, past rail & bus station. Hotel 300yds left beyond lights

This popular hotel is ideally situated within easy walking distance of the railway station, bus depot and town centre. Stylish bedrooms offer spacious comfort and plentiful extras including free Wi-fi. There is a smart restaurant, bar and lounge as well as sunny outdoor terraces for making the most of warm weather. The hotel also has a range of meeting rooms and banqueting facilities.

Rooms 50 (2 fmly) **S** £50-£90; **D** £65-£140* **Facilities** FTV Xmas New Year Wi-fi **Conf** Class 84 Board 64 Thtr 160 **Services** Lift **Parking** 80 **Notes** ⊗ Closed 27-30 Dec Civ Wed 80

Best Western Ivy Hill

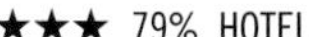

★★★ 79% HOTEL

☎ 01277 353040 & 355111 📠 01277 355038
Writtle Rd, Margaretting CM4 0EH
e-mail: sales@ivyhillhotel.co.uk
web: www.heritageleisure.co.uk
dir: Just off A12 junct 14. Hotel on left at top of slip road

A smartly appointed hotel conveniently situated just off the A12. The spacious bedrooms are tastefully decorated, have co-ordinated fabrics and all the expected facilities. Public rooms include a choice of lounges, a cosy bar, a smart conservatory and restaurant, as well as a range of conference and banqueting facilities.

Rooms 33 (5 fmly) (11 GF) **D** £90-£139 (incl. bkfst)* **Facilities** FTV Wi-fi **Conf** Class 80 Board 40 Thtr 180 Del from £150 to £161* **Parking** 60 **Notes** ⊗ Closed 23-30 Dec Civ Wed 100

Best Western Atlantic Hotel

★★★ 77% HOTEL

☎ 01245 268168 📠 01245 268169
New St CM1 1PP
e-mail: info@atlantichotel.co.uk
dir: From Chelmsford rail station, left into Victoria Rd, left at lights into New St, hotel on right

Ideally situated just a short walk from the railway station with its quick links to London, this modern, purpose-built hotel has contemporary-style bedrooms equipped with modern facilities. The open-plan public areas include Sapori Ristorante, an Italian restaurant, a lounge bar and a conservatory.

Rooms 59 (3 fmly) (27 GF) **Facilities** FTV Gym Complimentary use of facilities at Fitness First ♫ Wi-fi **Conf** Class 40 Board 10 Thtr 15 **Services** Air con **Parking** 60 **Notes** LB ⊗ Closed 23 Dec-3 Jan

Pontlands Park Country Hotel

★★★ 77% HOTEL

☎ 01245 476444 📠 01245 478393
West Hanningfield Rd, Great Baddow CM2 8HR
e-mail: sales@pontlandsparkhotel.co.uk
web: www.heritageleisure.co.uk
dir: A12/A130/A1114 to Chelmsford. 1st exit at rdbt, 1st slip road on left. Left towards Great Baddow, 1st left into West Hanningfield Rd. Hotel 400yds on left

A Victorian country-house hotel situated in a peaceful rural location amidst attractive landscaped grounds. The stylishly furnished bedrooms are generally quite spacious; each is individually decorated and equipped with modern facilities. The elegant public rooms include a tastefully furnished sitting room, a cosy lounge bar, smart conservatory restaurant and an intimate dining room.

Rooms 35 (10 fmly) (11 GF) **D** £75-£146 (incl. bkfst)* **Facilities** FTV Gym Beauty room Wi-fi **Conf** Class 40 Board 40 Thtr 100 Del from £152 to £164* **Parking** 100 **Notes** LB ⊗ Closed 24 Dec-3 Jan (ex 31 Dec) Civ Wed 100

Premier Inn Chelmsford (Boreham)

BUDGET HOTEL

☎ 0871 527 8220 📠 0871 527 8221
Main Rd, Boreham CM3 3HJ
dir: M25 junct 28, A12 to Colchester, B1137 to Boreham

High quality, budget accommodation ideal for both families and business travellers. Spacious, en suite bedrooms feature tea and coffee making facilities, and Freeview TV in most hotels. Internet access and Wi-fi are available for a small fee. The adjacent family restaurant features a wide and varied menu. See also the Hotel Groups pages.

Rooms 78 **D** £56-£64*

Premier Inn Chelmsford (Springfield)

BUDGET HOTEL

☎ 0871 527 8222 📠 0871 527 8223
Chelmsford Service Area, Colchester Rd, Springfield CM2 5PY
dir: At A12 junct 19, Chelmsford bypass, signed Chelmsford Service Area

Rooms 61 **D** £56-£64*

CHELTENHAM Map 10 SO92
Gloucestershire

Hotel du Vin Cheltenham

★★★★ 80% HOTEL

☎ 01242 588450 📠 01242 588455
Parabola Rd GL50 3AQ
e-mail: info@cheltenham.hotelduvin.com
web: www.hotelduvin.com
dir: M5 junct 11, follow signs for city centre. At rdbt opposite Morgan Estate Agents take 2nd left, 200mtrs to Parabola Rd

This hotel, in the Montpellier area of the town, has spacious public areas that are packed with stylish features. The pewter-topped bar has comfortable seating and the spacious restaurant has the Hotel du Vin trademark design; alfresco dining is possible on the extensive terrace area. Bedrooms are very comfortable, with Egyptian linen, deep baths and power showers. The spa is the ideal place to relax and unwind. Although parking is limited, it is a definite bonus. Service is friendly and attentive.

Rooms 49 (2 fmly) (5 GF) **Facilities** Spa STV Wi-fi **Conf** Class 24 Board 24 Thtr 30 **Services** Lift Air con **Parking** 26 **Notes** Civ Wed 60

C

CHELTENHAM *continued*

The Cheltenham Chase Hotel

★★★★ 80% HOTEL

☎ 01452 519988 📠 01452 519977
Shurdington Rd, Brockworth GL3 4PB
e-mail: cheltenhamreservations@qhotels.co.uk
web: www.qhotels.co.uk
dir: M5 junct 11a onto A417 Cirencester. 1st exit A46 to Stroud, hotel 500yds on left.

Conveniently positioned for Cheltenham, Gloucester, and the M5, this hotel is set in landscaped grounds with ample parking. Bedrooms are spacious with attractive colour schemes and excellent facilities; executive rooms and suites benefit from air conditioning. Public areas include an open-plan bar/lounge, Hardey's restaurant, extensive meeting and functions rooms and a well-equipped leisure club.

Rooms 122 (19 fmly) (44 GF) **S** £139-£159; **D** £159-£179 (incl. bkfst)* **Facilities** **Spa** STV FTV Gym Steam room Sauna Xmas New Year Wi-fi **Conf** Class 150 Board 70 Thtr 400 **Services** Lift Air con **Parking** 240 **Notes** Civ Wed 344

Mercure Queen's Hotel

★★★★ 77% HOTEL

☎ 0870 400 8107 📠 01242 224145
The Promenade GL50 1NN
e-mail: h6632@accor.com
web: www.mercure.com
dir: Follow town centre signs. Left at Montpellier Walk rdbt. Entrance 500mtrs right

With its spectacular position at the top of the main promenade, this landmark hotel is an ideal base from which to explore the charms of this Regency spa town and also the Cotswolds. Bedrooms are very comfortable and include two beautiful four-poster rooms. Smart public rooms include the popular Gold Cup bar and a choice of dining options.

Rooms 79 (5 smoking) **Facilities** STV Xmas New Year Wi-fi **Conf** Class 60 Board 40 Thtr 100 **Services** Lift Air con **Parking** 80 **Notes** Civ Wed 100

Barceló Cheltenham Park Hotel

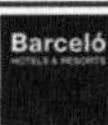

★★★★ 73% HOTEL

☎ 01242 222021 📠 01242 254880
Cirencester Rd, Charlton Kings GL53 8EA
e-mail: cheltenhampark@barcelo-hotels.co.uk
web: www.barcelo-hotels.co.uk
dir: On A435, 2m SE of Cheltenham near Lilley Brook Golf Course

Located south of Cheltenham, this attractive Georgian property is set in its own landscaped gardens, adjacent to Lilley Brook Golf Course. All bedrooms, whether premium or standard, are spacious and well equipped for both business and leisure guests. The hotel has an impressive health and leisure club with the latest gym equipment plus a pool, steam room and beauty salon; extensive meeting facilities are available. The Lakeside Restaurant serves carefully prepared cuisine.

Rooms 152 (119 annexe) **Facilities** STV supervised Gym Beauty treatment rooms Xmas New Year Wi-fi **Conf** Class 180 Board 110 Thtr 320 **Parking** 170 **Notes** Civ Wed 100

Thistle Cheltenham Hotel

thistle

★★★★ 73% HOTEL

☎ 0871 376 9013 📠 0871 376 9113
Gloucester Rd GL51 0TS
e-mail: cheltenham@thistle.co.uk
web: www.thistlehotels.com/cheltenham
dir: M5 junct 11/A40 signed Cheltenham, at 1st rdbt take 2nd exit. Hotel immediately on left

Conveniently located for easy access to the M5, this large hotel offers a good range of dining options in addition to extensive leisure facilities. Bedrooms and bathrooms are well equipped and provide good ease of use for both the business and leisure guest. Ample parking and a range of conference rooms are provided. Thistle Hotels – AA Hotel Group of the Year 2011-12.

Rooms 122 (9 fmly) (40 GF) **Facilities** FTV Gym Sauna Steam room Xmas New Year Wi-fi **Conf** Class 220 Board 45 Thtr 400 **Services** Lift Air con **Parking** 300 **Notes** Civ Wed 300

The Greenway Spa Hotel

★★★ 86% @@
COUNTRY HOUSE HOTEL

☎ 01242 862352 📠 01242 862780
Shurdington GL51 4UG
e-mail: info@thegreenway.co.uk
web: www.thegreenway.co.uk
dir: From Cheltenham centre 2.5m S on A46

This hotel, with a wealth of history, is peacefully located in a delightful setting close within easy reach of the many attractions of the Cotswolds and also the M5. The Manor House bedrooms are luxuriously appointed - traditional in style yet with plasma TVs and internet access. The tranquil Coach House rooms, in the converted stable block, have direct access to the beautiful grounds. The attractive dining room overlooks the sunken garden and is the venue for excellent food, proudly served by dedicated and attentive staff. The Elan Spa opened in April 2011.

Rooms 17 (6 annexe) (4 fmly) **Facilities** **Spa** FTV Clay pigeon shooting Horse riding Mountain biking Archery Xmas New Year Wi-fi **Conf** Class 18 Board 24 Thtr 42 Del from £165 to £195* **Parking** 50 **Notes** Civ Wed 45

George Hotel

★★★ 81% @@ HOTEL

☎ 01242 235751 📠 01242 224359
St Georges Rd GL50 3DZ
e-mail: hotel@stayatthegeorge.co.uk
web: www.stayatthegeorge.co.uk
dir: M5 junct 11 follow town centre signs. At 2nd lights left into Gloucester Rd, past rail station over mini-rdbt. At lights right into St Georges Rd. Hotel 0.75m on left

A genuinely friendly, privately-owned hotel occupying part of a Regency terrace, just two-minutes walk from the town centre. The contemporary interior is elegant and stylish, and the well-equipped, modern bedrooms offer a relaxing haven; individually designed junior suites and deluxe double rooms are available. Lunch or dinner can be enjoyed in a lively atmosphere of Monty's Brasserie, perhaps followed by an evening in the vibrant and sophisticated cocktail bar which hosts live entertainment on Friday and Saturday evenings.

Rooms 31 (1 GF) **D** £120-£185 (incl. bkfst)* **Facilities** STV Complimentary membership to local health club Live music at wknds Wi-fi **Conf** Class 18 Board 24 Thtr 30 **Parking** 30 **Notes** LB RS 24-26 Dec

Best Western Cheltenham Regency Hotel

★★★ 78% HOTEL

☎ 01452 713226 & 0845 194 9867
📠 01452 857590
Gloucester Rd, Staverton GL51 0ST
e-mail: info@cheltenhamregency.co.uk
dir: M5 junct 11 onto A40 to Cheltenham. Left at rdbt, hotel 1m on left

This hotel provides high standards of quality and comfort. The large bedrooms, including several suites, are very well equipped and ideal for both the business and leisure guest. A good selection of carefully prepared dishes is available from either the extensive lounge/bar menu or a more formal offering, utilising high quality produce, can be found in the main restaurant.

Rooms 47 (2 fmly) (16 GF) **Facilities** FTV New Year Wi-fi **Conf** Class 90 Board 80 Thtr 170 **Services** Lift Air con **Parking** 120 **Notes** LB Ⓧ Civ Wed 140

Charlton Kings

★★★ 74% SMALL HOTEL

☎ 01242 231061 📠 01242 241900
London Rd, Charlton Kings GL52 6UU
e-mail: enquiries@charltonkingshotel.co.uk
dir: From E (London or Oxford) on A40, hotel 1st building on left on entering Cheltenham. From M5 towards town centre follow Oxford/A40 signs. Through town, hotel last building on right on exiting Cheltenham

Personally run by the resident proprietors, the relatively small size of this hotel enables a good deal of individual guest care and attention. Bedrooms are very well decorated and furnished and include some welcome extras. Breakfast and dinner, served in the comfortable conservatory-style restaurant, offer a good selection of carefully prepared ingredients. There's a pleasant garden and rear car park.

Rooms 14 (3 GF) **Facilities** STV FTV Wi-fi **Parking** 15

Royal George

OldEnglish

★★★ 71% HOTEL

☎ 01452 862506 📠 01452 862277
Birdlip GL4 8JH
e-mail: royalgeorge.birdlip@greeneking.co.uk
web: www.oldenglish.co.uk
dir: M5 junct 11A take A417 towards Cirencester. At Air Balloon rdbt take 2nd exit then 1st right into Birdlip, hotel on right

This attractive 18th-century Cotswold building has been sympathetically converted and extended into a pleasant hotel. Bedrooms are spacious and comfortably furnished with modern facilities. The public areas have been designed around a traditional English pub with the bar leading on to a terrace overlooking extensive lawns.

Rooms 34 (4 fmly) (12 GF) **Facilities** ♫ Xmas **Conf** Class 60 Board 40 Thtr 90 **Notes** Ⓧ Civ Wed 80

Cotswold Grange

★★ 78% HOTEL

☎ 01242 515119 📠 01242 241537
Pittville Circus Rd GL52 2QH
e-mail: info@cotswoldgrange.co.uk
dir: From town centre, follow Prestbury signs. Right at 1st rdbt, next rdbt straight over, hotel 100yds on left

A delightful building located in a quieter, mainly residential area of Cheltenham, near Pittville Park and just a short walk to the town centre. The hotel offers a relaxed and welcoming atmosphere; there are many useful extras such as Wi-fi in the bedrooms. A range of carefully cooked and presented dishes is served in the comfortable restaurant.

Rooms 24 (2 fmly) **Facilities** Wi-fi **Conf** Class 24 Board 28 Thtr 50 **Parking** 20 **Notes** Closed 25 Dec-1 Jan

Premier Inn Cheltenham Central

BUDGET HOTEL

☎ 0871 527 8224 📠 0871 527 8225
374 Gloucester Rd GL51 7AY
dir: M5 junct 11, A40 (Cheltenham). Follow dual carriageway to end, straight on at 1st rdbt, right at 2nd rdbt

High quality, budget accommodation ideal for both families and business travellers. Spacious, en suite bedrooms feature tea and coffee making facilities, and Freeview TV in most hotels. Internet access and Wi-fi are available for a small fee. The adjacent family restaurant features a wide and varied menu. See also the Hotel Groups pages.

Rooms 43 **D** £55-£59*

Premier Inn Cheltenham West

BUDGET HOTEL

☎ 0871 527 8226 📠 0871 527 8227
Tewkesbury Rd, Uckington GL51 9SL
dir: M5 junct 10 (S'bound exit only), A4019, hotel in 2m. Or M5 junct 11, A40 towards Cheltenham. At Benhall Rdbt left onto A4103 (Princess Elizabeth Way) follow racecourse signs. At rdbt left onto A4019 signed Tewkesbury/M5 North. Hotel opposite Sainsbury's

Rooms 40 **D** £55-£59*

CHENIES Buckinghamshire — Map 6 TQ09

The Bedford Arms Hotel

★★★ 79% HOTEL

☎ 01923 283301 📠 01923 284825
WD3 6EQ
e-mail: contact@bedfordarms.co.uk
web: www.bedfordarms.co.uk
dir: M25 junct 18/A404 towards Amersham, hotel signed after 2m on right

This attractive, 19th-century country inn enjoys a peaceful rural setting. Comfortable bedrooms are decorated in traditional style and feature a range of thoughtful extras. Each room is named after a relation of the Duke of Bedford, whose family has an historic association with the property. There are two bars, a lounge and a cosy, wood-panelled restaurant.

Rooms 18 (8 annexe) (2 fmly) (8 GF) **S** £60-£110; **D** £95-£140 (incl. bkfst)* **Facilities** STV FTV Wi-fi **Conf** Class 16 Board 24 Thtr 50 Del from £130 to £170 **Parking** 60 **Notes** RS 27 Dec-4 Jan Civ Wed 55

CHESHUNT Hertfordshire — Map 6 TL30

Cheshunt Marriott

Marriott HOTELS & RESORTS

★★★★ 76% HOTEL

☎ 01992 451245 📠 01992 440120
Halfhide Ln, Turnford EN10 6NG
web: www.cheshuntmarriott.co.uk
dir: Exit A10 at Broxbourne, right & right again at rdbt, hotel on right at next rdbt

This popular suburban hotel has an attractive courtyard garden, overlooked by many of the guest bedrooms. All bedrooms are spacious and air conditioned. Public areas include a small, unsupervised leisure facility, along with the busy Washington Bar and Restaurant.

Rooms 143 (37 fmly) (39 GF) **Facilities** STV Gym Xmas New Year Wi-fi **Conf** Class 72 Board 56 Thtr 150 **Services** Lift Air con **Parking** 200 **Notes** Ⓧ Civ Wed 120

C

CHESSINGTON
Greater London Map 6 TQ16

Holiday Inn London-Chessington

★★★★ 71% HOTEL

☎ 01372 734600 01372 734698
Leatherhead Rd KT9 2NE
e-mail: enquiries@holidayinnchessington.co.uk
web: www.holidayinnchessington.co.uk
dir: Follow signs for Chessington World of Adventures. Hotel at North Car Park entrance

In a convenient location just off the M25 (junction 9), two miles from the A3 and just 12 miles from London, this hotel is, of course, ideal for those visiting Chessington World of Adventures and the zoo. The bedrooms are safari-themed and include family rooms with a separate sleeping area for children with their own TV. The Merula Bar and lounge is a great place to relax, and guests can eat in the Langata brasserie. The leisure facilities are extensive and there's ample parking.

Rooms 150 (56 fmly) (6 smoking) **Facilities** Spa STV FTV Gym Sauna Steam room Xmas New Year Wi-fi **Conf** Class 150 Board 70 Thtr 300 **Services** Lift Air con **Parking** 120 **Notes** Civ Wed 100

Premier Inn Chessington

BUDGET HOTEL

☎ 0871 527 8228 0871 527 8229
Leatherhead Rd KT9 2NE
dir: M25 junct 9, A243 towards Kingston-upon-Thames for approx 2m. Hotel adjacent to Chessington World of Adventures

High quality, budget accommodation ideal for both families and business travellers. Spacious, en suite bedrooms feature tea and coffee making facilities, and Freeview TV in most hotels. Internet access and Wi-fi are available for a small fee. The adjacent family restaurant features a wide and varied menu. See also the Hotel Groups pages.

Rooms 42 **D** £65-£75*

CHESTER
Cheshire Map 15 SJ46

See also **Puddington**

INSPECTORS' CHOICE

The Chester Grosvenor & Spa

★★★★★ @@@@ HOTEL

☎ 01244 324024 01244 313246
Eastgate CH1 1LT
e-mail: hotel@chestergrosvenor.com
dir: A56 follow signs for city centre hotels. On Eastgate St next to the Eastgate clock

Located within the Roman walls of the city, this Grade II listed, half-timbered building is the essence of Englishness. Furnished with fine fabrics and queen or king-size beds, the suites and bedrooms are of the highest standard, each designed with guest comfort as a priority. The eating options are the art deco La Brasserie, a bustling venue awarded 2 AA Rosettes, the Arkle Bar and Lounge for morning coffee, light lunches, afternoon tea and drinks plus the fine dining restaurant 'Simon Radley at The Chester Grosvenor' which offers creative cuisine with flair and style, and awarded 4 AA Rosettes. The hotel has a luxury spa and small fitness centre, and complimentary undercover parking is available to guests in an adjacent car park.

Rooms 80 (7 fmly) **D** £220-£1250* **Facilities** Spa STV Gym New Year Wi-fi **Conf** Class 120 Board 48 Thtr 250 Del from £265* **Services** Lift Air con **Notes** LB Closed 25-26 Dec RS Sun & Mon, 1-20 Jan Civ Wed 250

Rowton Hall Country House Hotel & Spa

★★★★ 81% @ HOTEL

☎ 01244 335262 01244 335464
Whitchurch Rd, Rowton CH3 6AD
e-mail: reception@rowtonhallhotelandspa.co.uk
web: www.rowtonhallhotel.co.uk
dir: M56 junct 12, A56 to Chester. At rdbt left onto A41 towards Whitchurch. Approx 1m, follow hotel signs

This delightful Georgian manor house, set in mature grounds, retains many original features such as a superb carved staircase and several eye-catching fireplaces. Bedrooms vary in size but all have been stylishly fitted and have impressive en suites. Public areas include a smart leisure centre, extensive function facilities and a striking restaurant that serves imaginative dishes.

Rooms 37 (4 fmly) (8 GF) **S** £95-£185; **D** £95-£185* **Facilities** Spa STV FTV Gym Sauna Steam room Xmas New Year Wi-fi **Conf** Class 48 Board 50 Thtr 170 Del from £135 to £205* **Parking** 200 **Notes** LB Civ Wed 170

Crowne Plaza Chester

★★★★ 79% HOTEL

☎ 0871 942 9162 & 01244 899988
01244 899911
Trinity St CH1 2BD
e-mail: cpchester@qmh-hotels.com
web: www.crowneplaza.co.uk
dir: M53 junct 12 to A56 onto St Martins Way, under foot bridge, left at lights, 1st right, hotel on right

Conveniently located in the heart of the city, this modern hotel offers spacious public areas that include the Silks restaurant, leisure club and a range of meeting rooms. Smart air-conditioned bedrooms are comfortably appointed and particularly well equipped. The hotel's own car park is a real bonus.

Rooms 160 (4 fmly) **Facilities** Spa STV FTV Gym Beauty salon Wi-fi **Conf** Class 250 Board 100 Thtr 600 Del from £130* **Services** Lift **Parking** 80 **Notes** Civ Wed 150

Best Western The Queen Hotel

★★★★ 76% HOTEL

☎ 01244 305000 📠 01244 318483
City Rd CH1 3AH
e-mail: queenhotel@feathers.uk.com
web: www.feathers.uk.com
dir: Follow signs for railway station, hotel opposite

This hotel is ideally located opposite the railway station and just a couple minutes' walk from the city. Public areas include a restaurant, small gym, waiting room bar, separate lounge and Roman-themed gardens. Bedrooms are generally spacious and reflect the hotel's Victorian heritage.

Rooms 218 (11 fmly) (12 GF) **S** £79-£169; **D** £89-£199 **Facilities** STV FTV Gym Treatment room Table tennis ♫ Xmas New Year Wi-fi **Conf** Class 150 Board 60 Thtr 400 Del from £125 to £165 **Services** Lift **Parking** 150 **Notes** LB ⊗ Civ Wed 400

Grosvenor Pulford Hotel & Spa

★★★★ 74% HOTEL

☎ 01244 570560 📠 01244 570809
Wrexham Rd, Pulford CH4 9DG
e-mail: reservations@grosvenorpulfordhotel.co.uk
web: www.grosvenorpulfordhotel.co.uk
dir: M53/A55 at junct signed A483 Chester/Wrexham & North Wales. Left onto B5445, hotel 2m on right

Set in rural surroundings, this modern, stylish hotel features a magnificent spa with a large Roman-style swimming pool. Among the bedrooms are several executive suites and others that have spiral staircases leading to the bedroom sections. A smart brasserie restaurant and bar provide a wide range of imaginative dishes in a relaxed atmosphere.

Rooms 73 (10 fmly) (21 GF) (6 smoking) **S** £99-£165; **D** £135-£180 (incl. bkfst)* **Facilities** Spa STV FTV Gym Steam room Sauna Xmas New Year Wi-fi **Conf** Class 100 Board 50 Thtr 200 Del from £117 to £150* **Services** Lift **Parking** 200 **Notes** Civ Wed 200

Ramada Chester

RAMADA JARVIS

★★★★ 72% HOTEL

☎ 01244 332121 & 0844 815 9001
📠 01244 335287
Whitchurch Rd, Christleton CH3 5QL
e-mail: sales.chester@ramadajarvis.co.uk
web: www.ramadajarvis.co.uk/chester
dir: A41 Whitchurch, hotel on right 200mtrs from A41, 1.3m from city centre

This smart, modern hotel is located just a short drive from the city centre; with extensive meeting and function facilities, a well-equipped leisure club and ample parking, it is a popular conference venue. Bedrooms vary in size and style but all are well equipped for both business and leisure guests. Food is served in the airy restaurant and also in the large open-plan bar lounge.

Rooms 126 (6 fmly) (58 GF) (10 smoking) **S** £59-£170; **D** £59-£205* **Facilities** STV Gym Xmas New Year Wi-fi **Conf** Class 80 Board 60 Thtr 230 Del from £99 to £195* **Services** Lift **Parking** 160 **Notes** LB ⊗ Civ Wed 180

Macdonald New Blossoms

★★★★ 71% HOTEL

☎ 01244 323186 & 0844 8799113
📠 01244 346433
St John St CH1 1HL
e-mail: events.blossoms@macdonald-hotels.co.uk
web: www.macdonaldhotels.co.uk/blossoms
dir: M53 junct 12 follow city centre signs for Eastgate, through pedestrian zone, hotel on left

Ideally located to explore the historic city of Chester this is a modern and contemporary hotel. Bedrooms range from executive to feature four-poster rooms, with many retaining the charm of the original Victorian building. A stylish brasserie restaurant and bar offer an informal dining experience.

Rooms 67 (1 fmly) **Facilities** Xmas New Year Wi-fi **Conf** Class 50 Board 40 Thtr 90 **Services** Lift **Notes** ⊗

Best Western Westminster

★★★ 80% HOTEL

☎ 01244 317341 📠 01244 325369
City Rd CH1 3AF
e-mail: westminsterhotel@feathers.uk.com
web: www.feathers.uk.com
dir: A56, 3m to city centre, left signed rail station. Hotel opposite station, on right

Situated close to the railway station and city centre, the Westminster is an old, established hotel. It has an attractive Tudor-style exterior, while bedrooms are brightly decorated with a modern theme. Family rooms are available. There is a choice of bars and lounges, and the dining room serves a good range of dishes.

Rooms 75 (8 fmly) (6 GF) **Facilities** STV FTV Free gym facilities at sister hotel Wi-fi **Conf** Class 60 Board 40 Thtr 150 **Services** Lift **Notes** LB ⊗ Civ Wed 100

Mill Hotel & Spa Destination

★★★ 78% HOTEL

☎ 01244 350035 📠 01244 345635
Milton St CH1 3NF
e-mail: reservations@millhotel.com
web: www.millhotel.com
dir: M53 junct 12, onto A56, left at 2nd rdbt (A5268), then 1st left , 2nd left

This hotel is a stylish conversion of an old corn mill and enjoys an idyllic canalside location next to the inner ring road and close to the city centre. The bedrooms offer varying styles, and public rooms are spacious and comfortable. There are several dining options and dinner is often served on a large boat that cruises Chester's canal system. A well-equipped leisure centre is also provided.

Rooms 128 (49 annexe) (57 fmly) **Facilities** Spa STV supervised Gym Aerobic studio Hairdresser Sauna Steam room Kenesis studio ♫ Xmas New Year Wi-fi **Conf** Class 27 Board 28 Thtr 40 **Services** Lift **Parking** 120 **Notes** LB ⊗

C

CHESTER ***continued***

Holiday Inn Chester South

★★★ 73% HOTEL

☎ 0871 942 9019 & 01244 688770
🖹 01244 674100
Wrexham Rd CH4 9DL
e-mail: reservations-chester@ihg.com
web: www.holidayinn.co.uk
dir: Near Wrexham junct on A483, off A55

Located close to the A55 and opposite the Park & Ride for the city centre, this hotel offers spacious and comfortable accommodation. Meals can be taken in the attractive bar or in the restaurant. There is also a well-equipped leisure club for residents, and extensive conference facilities are available.

Rooms 143 (21 fmly) (71 GF) **Facilities** STV FTV supervised Gym Xmas New Year Wi-fi **Conf** Class 70 Board 70 Thtr 80 Del from £110 to £150 **Services** Air con **Parking** 150 **Notes** Civ Wed 50

Brookside

★★ 75% HOTEL

☎ 01244 381943 & 390898 🖹 01244 651910
Brook Ln CH2 2AN
e-mail: info@brookside-hotel.co.uk
web: www.brookside-hotel.co.uk
dir: M53 junct 12, A56 towards Chester, then A41. 0.5m left signed Newton (Plas Newton Ln). 0.5m right into Brook Ln. Hotel 0.5m on right. Or from Chester inner ring road follow A5116/Ellesmere Port/Hospital signs (keep in right lane to take right fork). Immediately left. At mini-rdbt 2nd right

This hotel is conveniently located in a residential area just north of the city centre. The attractive public areas consist of a foyer lounge, a small bar and a split-level restaurant. The homely bedrooms are thoughtfully furnished and some feature four-poster beds.

Rooms 26 (9 fmly) (4 GF) **Facilities** Wi-fi **Conf** Class 20 Board 12 **Parking** 20 **Notes** Closed 20 Dec-3 Jan

Holiday Inn Express at Chester Racecourse

BUDGET HOTEL

☎ 0870 9904065 & 01244 327900
🖹 0870 9904066
The Racecourse, New Crane St CH1 2LY
e-mail: hotel@chester-races.com
web: www.hiexpress.com/exchesterrac
dir: M53, A483/Wrexham. Follow ring road follow signs for A548. Turn right onto New Crane St. Hotel 0.5m on left at racecourse

A modern hotel ideal for families and business travellers. Fresh and uncomplicated, the spacious rooms include Sky TV, power shower and tea and coffee-making facilities. Continental buffet breakfast is included in the room rate; other meals may be taken at the nearby family pub or restaurant. See also the Hotel Groups pages.

Rooms 97 (66 fmly) (4 GF) **S** fr £49; **D** fr £49 (incl. bkfst)* **Conf** Class 30 Board 25 Thtr 20

Premier Inn Chester Central (North)

BUDGET HOTEL

☎ 0871 527 8230 🖹 0871 527 8231
76 Liverpool Rd CH2 1AU
dir: M53 junct 12, A56. At 2nd rdbt right signed A41 to Chester Zoo. At 1st lights left into Heath Rd, leads into Mill Ln. Under small rail bridge. Hotel at end on right

High quality, budget accommodation ideal for both families and business travellers. Spacious, en suite bedrooms feature tea and coffee making facilities, and Freeview TV in most hotels. Internet access and Wi-fi are available for a small fee. The adjacent family restaurant features a wide and varied menu. See also the Hotel Groups pages.

Rooms 31 **D** £63*

Premier Inn Chester Central (South East)

BUDGET HOTEL

☎ 0871 527 8232 🖹 0871 527 8233
Caldy Valley Rd, Boughton CH3 5PR
dir: M53 junct 12, A56 to Chester. At 1st lights onto A41 (Whitchurch). At 2nd rdbt rd exit into Caldy Valley Rd (Huntington). Hotel on right

Rooms 94 **D** £56-£59*

Premier Inn Chester City Centre

BUDGET HOTEL

☎ 0871 527 8234 🖹 0871 527 8235
20-24 City Rd CH1 3AE
dir: M53 junct 12, follow A56/Chester City Centre signs. At rdbt 1st exit onto A5268 (St Oswalds Way) follow railway station signs. At Bar's Rdbt 1st. Hotel on right

Rooms 120 **D** £56-£59*

Oddfellows

RESTAURANT WITH ROOMS

☎ 01244 400001
20 Lower Bridge St CH1 1RS
e-mail: reception@oddfellows.biz

Surrounded by designer shops and only a few minutes' walk from the Chester Rows, old meets new at this stylish Georgian mansion. The upper ground floor comprises a walled garden with ornamental moat, Arabic tents, a roofed patio, a cocktail bar with an excellent wine selection, a bustling brasserie and an Alice in Wonderland tea room. Fine dining, featuring local produce, is skilfully prepared in a second-floor formal restaurant and a sumptuous 'members' lounge is also available to diners and resident guests. Bedrooms have the wow factor with super beds and every conceivable guest extra.

Rooms 4

Coach House Restaurant with Rooms

RESTAURANT WITH ROOMS

☎ 01244 251900 🖹 01244 351436
29 Northgate St CH1 2HQ
web: www.coachhousechester.co.uk

Ideally located in the centre of the city, this restaurant with rooms has been renovated to provide high standards of comfort and good facilities. Its sumptuous bedrooms have a wealth of thoughtful extras, and imaginative food is available in the bistro style restaurant or in the cosy bar area. A warm welcome is assured.

Rooms 9 (3 fmly)

CHESTERFIELD Map 16 SK37
Derbyshire

Casa Hotel

★★★★ 81% HOTEL

☎ 01246 245999 01246 245998
Lockoford Ln S41 7JB
e-mail: enquiries@casahotels.co.uk
dir: M1 junct 29 to A617 Chesterfield/A61 Sheffield, 1st exit at rdbt, hotel on left

A luxurious hotel with a contemporary Spanish theme throughout. The stylish bedrooms feature air conditioning, Hypnos beds and bathrooms with rain showers. Some also have jacuzzi baths and two have balconies with hot tubs. Cocina Restaurant offers appealing menus featuring ingredients from the hotel's own organic farm. The conference and events facilities are excellent and complimentary Wi-fi is offered.

Rooms 100 (6 fmly) **S** £90-£125; **D** £99-£140 (incl. bkfst)* **Facilities** FTV Gym Xmas New Year Wi-fi **Conf** Class 140 Board 50 Thtr 280 Del from £140* **Services** Lift Air con **Parking** 200 **Notes** LB Civ Wed 280

Ringwood Hall

THE INDEPENDENTS HOTEL ASSOCIATION

★★★ 85% HOTEL

☎ 01246 280077 01246 472241
Brimington S43 1DQ
e-mail: reception@ringwoodhallhotel.com
web: www.ringwoodhallhotel.com
dir: M1 junct 30, A619 to Chesterfield through Staveley. Hotel on left

This is a splendid Georgian manor house set in 29 acres of award-winning grounds, between the M1 and Chesterfield. Modern, comfortable bedrooms complement the traditional, spacious lounges. The health and fitness club has a pool, sauna, steam room and fitness suite.

Rooms 70 (6 annexe) (32 fmly) (25 GF) **S** £75-£98; **D** £85-£128 (incl. bkfst) **Facilities** FTV Gym Steam room Sauna Beauty therapy Aqua aerobics Xmas Wi-fi **Conf** Class 80 Board 60 Thtr 250 Del from £105 to £145* **Parking** 150 **Notes** LB Civ Wed 250

Sandpiper

THE INDEPENDENTS HOTEL ASSOCIATION

★★★ 67% HOTEL

☎ 01246 450550 01246 452805
Sheffield Rd, Sheepbridge S41 9EH
e-mail: sue@sandpiperhotel.co.uk
web: www.sandpiperhotel.co.uk
dir: M1 junct 29, A617 to Chesterfield then A61 to Sheffield. 1st exit take Dronfield/Unstone sign. Hotel 0.5m on left

Conveniently situated for both the A61 and M1 and providing a good touring base, being just three miles from Chesterfield, this modern hotel offers comfortable and well-furnished bedrooms. Public areas are situated in a separate building across the car park, and include a cosy bar and open plan restaurant, serving a range of interesting and popular dishes.

Rooms 46 (11 fmly) (16 GF) **Facilities** FTV New Year Wi-fi **Conf** Class 35 Board 35 Thtr 100 **Services** Lift **Parking** 120 **Notes** Civ Wed 90

Ibis Chesterfield

BUDGET HOTEL

☎ 01246 221333 01246 221444
Lordsmill St S41 7RW
e-mail: h3160@accor.com
web: www.ibishotel.com
dir: M1 junct 29/A617 to Chesterfield. 2nd exit at 1st rdbt. Hotel on right at 2nd rdbt

Modern, budget hotel offering comfortable accommodation in bright and practical bedrooms. Breakfast is self-service and dinner is available in the restaurant. See also the Hotel Groups pages.

Rooms 86 (21 fmly) (8 GF) **S** £48-£65; **D** £48-£65* **Conf** Board 12 Thtr 25

Premier Inn Chesterfield North

BUDGET HOTEL

☎ 0871 527 8238 0871 527 8239
Tapton Lock Hill, off Rotherway S41 7NJ
dir: Adjacent to Tesco, at A61 & A619 rdbt, 1m N of city centre

High quality, budget accommodation ideal for both families and business travellers. Spacious, en suite bedrooms feature tea and coffee making facilities, and Freeview TV in most hotels. Internet access and Wi-fi are available for a small fee. The adjacent family restaurant features a wide and varied menu. See also the Hotel Groups pages.

Rooms 60 **D** £49-£58*

Premier Inn Chesterfield West

BUDGET HOTEL

☎ 0871 527 8240 0871 527 8241
Baslow Rd, Eastmoor S42 7DA
dir: M1 junct 29, A617. At next rdbt 2nd exit. At next rdbt 1st exit into Markham Rd. At next rdbt 2nd exit into Wheatbridge Rd, left into Chatsworth Rd. 2.5m to hotel

Rooms 23 **D** £52-£58*

CHICHESTER Map 5 SU80
West Sussex

The Goodwood Hotel

★★★★ 79% HOTEL

☎ 01243 775537 01243 520120
PO18 0QB
e-mail: reservations@goodwood.com
web: www.goodwood.com

(For full entry see Goodwood)

The Millstream Hotel & Restaurant

★★★ 85% HOTEL

☎ 01243 573234 01243 573459
Bosham Ln PO18 8HL
e-mail: info@millstream-hotel.co.uk
web: www.millstream-hotel.co.uk

(For full entry see Bosham)

C

CHICHESTER *continued*

Crouchers Country Hotel & Restaurant

★★★ 81% @@ HOTEL

☎ 01243 784995 📠 01243 539797
Birdham Rd PO20 7EH
e-mail: crouchers@btconnect.com
dir: From A27 Chichester bypass onto A286 towards West Wittering, 2m, hotel on left between Chichester Marina & Dell Quay

This friendly, family-run hotel, situated in open countryside, is just a short drive from the harbour. The stylish and well-equipped bedrooms are situated in a separate barn, coach house and stable block, and include four-poster rooms and rooms with patios that overlook the fields. The modern oak-beamed restaurant, with country views, serves award-winning cuisine.

Rooms 26 (23 annexe) (2 fmly) (15 GF) **Facilities** STV FTV Xmas New Year Wi-fi **Conf** Class 80 Board 50 Thtr 80 Del from £120 to £155 **Parking** 80 **Notes** Civ Wed 70

The Ship Hotel

★★★ 73% HOTEL

☎ 01243 778000 📠 01243 788000
57 North St PO19 1NH
e-mail: enquiries@theshiphotel.net
dir: From A27, onto inner ring road to Northgate. At Northgate rdbt left into North St, hotel on left

This well-presented Grade II listed, Georgian property occupies a prime position at the top of North Street. The stylish bedrooms have flat-screen TVs, Egyptian cotton linen and high-speed Wi-fi access. The bar and restaurant are contemporary venues for enjoying meals and refreshments which are served all day. The hotel is just a few minutes' away is the famous Festival Theatre, and Goodwood, for motorsport and horse racing, is also close by.

Rooms 36 (2 fmly) **S** £82.50; **D** £110-£185 (incl. bkfst)* **Facilities** Xmas New Year Wi-fi **Conf** Class 50 Board 30 Thtr 50 Del from £130 to £220* **Services** Lift **Parking** 35 **Notes** LB

Premier Inn Chichester

BUDGET HOTEL

☎ 0871 527 8242 📠 0871 527 8243
Chichester Gate Leisure Park, Terminus Rd PO19 8EL
dir: A27 towards city centre. Follow Terminus Road Industrial Estate signs. Left at 1st lights, left at next lights into Chichester Gate Leisure Park. Hotel on right

High quality, budget accommodation ideal for both families and business travellers. Spacious, en suite bedrooms feature tea and coffee making facilities, and Freeview TV in most hotels. Internet access and Wi-fi are available for a small fee. The adjacent family restaurant features a wide and varied menu. See also the Hotel Groups pages.

Rooms 83 **D** £70*

CHILDER THORNTON Cheshire **Map 15 SJ37**

Brook Meadow

★★★ 74% HOTEL

☎ 0151 339 9350 📠 0151 347 4221
Health Ln CH66 7NS
e-mail: reservations.brookmeadow@ohiml.com
web: www.oxfordhotelsandinns.com
dir: M53 junct 5, A41, right onto A550, 2nd right into Heath Ln

This delightful country hotel, set in its own lovely gardens, is within easy reach of Liverpool, Chester, the M53 and M56. Bedrooms are tastefully decorated and well equipped; the bathrooms have spa baths. There is a comfortable lounge, and the dining room has a conservatory which overlooks the grounds. Two function suites are available.

Rooms 25 (7 fmly) (7 GF) **Facilities** FTV Xmas New Year Wi-fi **Conf** Class 60 Board 60 Thtr 180 **Services** Lift Air con **Parking** 80 **Notes** LB ⊗ Civ Wed 160

Premier Inn Wirral (Childer Thornton)

BUDGET HOTEL

☎ 0871 527 9174 📠 0871 527 9175
New Chester Rd CH66 1QW
dir: M53 junct 5, A41 towards Chester. Hotel on right (same entrance as Burleydam Garden Centre)

High quality, budget accommodation ideal for both families and business travellers. Spacious, en suite bedrooms feature tea and coffee making facilities, and Freeview TV in most hotels. Internet access and Wi-fi are available for a small fee. The adjacent family restaurant features a wide and varied menu. See also the Hotel Groups pages.

Rooms 31 **D** £53-£57*

CHIPPENHAM Wiltshire **Map 4 ST97**

Stanton Manor Hotel

★★★ 79% @ HOTEL

☎ 01666 837552 & 0870 890 02880
📠 01666 837022
SN14 6DQ
e-mail: reception@stantonmanor.co.uk
web: www.stantonmanor.co.uk

(For full entry see Stanton St Quintin)

Best Western Angel Hotel

★★★ 78% HOTEL

☎ 01249 652615 📠 01249 443210
Market Place SN15 3HD
e-mail: reception@angelhotelchippenham.co.uk
web: www.angelhotelchippenham.co.uk
dir: Follow tourist signs for Bowood House. Under railway arch, follow 'Borough Parade Parking' signs. Hotel adjacent to car park

Several impressive buildings combine to make a smart and comfortable hotel. The well-equipped bedrooms vary from those in the main house where character is the key, to the smart executive-style, courtyard rooms. The lounge and restaurant are bright and modern, and offer an imaginative carte and an all-day menu.

Rooms 50 (35 annexe) (3 fmly) (12 GF) **S** £64.85-£101.85; **D** £79.85-£111.85 **Facilities** STV FTV Gym Wi-fi **Conf** Class 50 Board 50 Thtr 100 **Parking** 50 **Notes** LB

Premier Inn Chippenham

BUDGET HOTEL

☎ 0871 527 8244 📠 0871 527 8245
Cepen Park, West Cepen Way SN14 6UZ
dir: M4 junct 17, A350 towards Chippenham. Hotel at 1st main rdbt

High quality, budget accommodation ideal for both families and business travellers. Spacious, en suite bedrooms feature tea and coffee making facilities, and Freeview TV in most hotels. Internet access and Wi-fi are available for a small fee. The adjacent family restaurant features a wide and varied menu. See also the Hotel Groups pages.

Rooms 79 **D** £63*

CHIPPING CAMPDEN Gloucestershire **Map 10 SP13**

Three Ways House

★★★ 82% HOTEL

☎ 01386 438429 📠 01386 438118
Mickleton GL55 6SB
e-mail: reception@puddingclub.com
web: www.threewayshousehotel.com
dir: In Mickleton centre, on B4632 (Stratford-upon-Avon to Broadway road)

Built in 1870, this charming hotel has welcomed guests for over 100 years and is home to the world famous Pudding Club, formed in 1985 to promote traditional English puddings. Individuality is a hallmark here, as reflected in a number of the bedrooms that have been designed around to a pudding theme. Public areas are stylish and include the air-conditioned restaurant, lounges and meeting rooms.

Rooms 48 (7 fmly) (14 GF) **S** £85-£90; **D** £145-£250 (incl. bkfst)* **Facilities** Xmas New Year Wi-fi **Conf** Class 40 Board 35 Thtr 100 **Services** Lift **Parking** 37 **Notes** LB Civ Wed 100

Noel Arms

★★★ 78% HOTEL

☎ 01386 840317 📠 01386 841136
High St GL55 6AT
e-mail: reception@noelarmshotel.com
web: www.noelarmshotel.com
dir: Off A44 onto B4081 to Chipping Campden, 1st right down hill into town. Hotel on right

This historic 14th-century hotel has a wealth of character and charm, and retains some of its original features. Bedrooms are very individual in style, but all have high levels of comfort and interesting interior design. Such distinctiveness is also evident throughout the public areas, which include the popular bar, conservatory lounge and attractive restaurant.

Rooms 28 (1 fmly) (8 GF) **Facilities** Use of spa at sister hotel (charged) Xmas New Year Wi-fi **Conf** Class 40 Board 40 Thtr 80 **Parking** 28 **Notes** LB Civ Wed 100

The Kings

RESTAURANT WITH ROOMS

☎ 01386 840256 & 841056 📠 01386 841598
The Square GL55 6AW
e-mail: info@kingscampden.co.uk
dir: In centre of town square

Located in the centre of this delightful Cotswold town, The Kings effortlessly blends a relaxed and friendly welcome with efficient service. Bedrooms and bathrooms come in a range of shapes and sizes but all are appointed to high levels of quality and comfort. Dining options, whether in the main restaurant or the comfortable bar area, include a tempting menu to suit all tastes, from light salads and pasta to meat and fish dishes.

Rooms 19 (5 annexe) (3 fmly)

CHIPPING NORTON Oxfordshire **Map 10 SP32**

Crowne Plaza Heythrop Park - Oxford

U

☎ 01608 673333 📠 01608 673799
Heythrop Park Resort, Enstone OX7 5UE
e-mail: info@heythroppark.co.uk
dir: From Woodstock take A44 towards Chipping Norton. Hotel off A44 on right. For detailed directions contact hotel

Currently the rating for this establishment is not confirmed. This may be due to a change of ownership or because it has only recently joined the AA rating scheme. For further details please see the AA website: theAA.com

Rooms 197 (56 fmly) (9 GF) **Facilities** Spa STV 18 Putt green Fishing Gym Xmas New Year Wi-fi **Conf** Class 280 Board 100 Thtr 450 **Services** Lift Air con **Parking** 350 **Notes** Civ Wed 350

CHORLEY Lancashire **Map 15 SD51**

Premier Inn Chorley North

BUDGET HOTEL

☎ 0871 527 8246 📠 0871 527 8247
Malthouse Farm, Moss Ln, Whittle-le-Woods PR6 8AB
e-mail: malthousefarm20@hotmail.com
dir: M61 junct 8 onto A674 (Wheelton), 400yds on left into Moss Ln

High quality, budget accommodation ideal for both families and business travellers. Spacious, en suite bedrooms feature tea and coffee making facilities, and Freeview TV in most hotels. Internet access and Wi-fi are available for a small fee. The adjacent family restaurant features a wide and varied menu. See also the Hotel Groups pages.

Rooms 81 **D** £50-£56*

Premier Inn Chorley South

BUDGET HOTEL

☎ 0871 527 8248 📠 0871 527 8249
Bolton Rd PR7 4AB
dir: From N: M61 junct 8, A6 to Chorley. From S: M6 junct 27 follow Standish signs. Left onto A5106 to Chorley, A6 towards Preston. Hotel 0.5m on right

Rooms 29 **D** £50-£56*

CHRISTCHURCH Dorset **Map 5 SZ19**

Christchurch Harbour Hotel

★★★★ 82% HOTEL

☎ 01202 483434 📠 01202 479004
95 Mudeford BH23 3NT
e-mail: christchurch@harbourhotels.co.uk
web: www.christchurch-harbour-hotel.co.uk
dir: On A35 to Christchurch onto A337 to Highcliffe. Right at rdbt, hotel 1.5m on left

Delightfully situated on the side of Mudeford Quay close to sandy beaches and conveniently located for Bournemouth Airport and the BIC, this hotel boasts an impressive spa and leisure facility. The bedrooms are particularly well appointed and stylishly finished; many have excellent views and some have balconies.

continued

CHRISTCHURCH *continued*

Guests can eat in the award-winning Harbour Restaurant, or the waterside Rhodes South.

Rooms 64 (7 fmly) (14 GF) **Facilities** Spa FTV Gym Steam room Sauna Exercise classes Hydrotherapy pool Xmas New Year Wi-fi **Conf** Class 20 Board 24 Thtr 70 **Services** Lift **Parking** 55 **Notes** LB Civ Wed 80

Captain's Club Hotel and Spa

★★★★ 81% HOTEL

☎ 01202 475111 01202 490111
Wick Ferry, Wick Ln BH23 1HU
e-mail: enquiries@captainsclubhotel.com
web: www.captainsclubhotel.com
dir: B3073 to Christchurch. On Fountain rdbt take 5th exit (Sopers Ln) 2nd left (St Margarets Ave) 1st right onto Wick Ln

Situated in the heart of the town on the banks of the River Stour at Christchurch Quay, and only ten minutes from Bournemouth. All bedrooms, including the suites and apartments have views overlooking the river. Guests can relax in the hydrotherapy pool, enjoy a spa treatment or enjoy the cuisine in Tides Restaurant.

Rooms 29 (12 fmly) **Facilities** Spa STV FTV Hydrotherapy pool Sauna Xmas New Year Wi-fi **Conf** Class 72 Board 64 Thtr 140 **Services** Lift Air con **Parking** 41 **Notes** Civ Wed 100

The Kings Hotel & Jacks Bar & Brasserie

★★★ 82% HOTEL

☎ 01202 588933 01202 588930
18 Castle St BH23 1DT
e-mail: kings@harbourhotels.co.uk
dir: Exit A35 into Christchurch High St, left at rdbt, hotel 20mtrs on left

This small hotel offers guests a luxury stay in the heart of Christchurch. Elegant and sumptuous bedrooms, with huge beds, are equipped with many modern extras such as iPod docking stations and Wi-fi. The luxury bathrooms have huge soft towels, bathrobes and an array of toiletries. The sleek modern restaurant serves dishes based mainly on produce sourced either in the nearby New Forest National Park, or a little further afield in the southwest of England. The cosy bar has an extensive list of tempting cocktails.

Rooms 19 (4 fmly) **S** £75-£115; **D** £115-£180 (incl. bkfst)* **Facilities** FTV Use of spa & pool at Christchurch Harbour Hotel Xmas New Year Wi-fi **Conf** Class 40 Board 40 Thtr 80 Del from £160 to £250* **Services** Lift **Parking** 7 **Notes** Civ Wed 100

Best Western Waterford Lodge

★★★ 78% HOTEL

☎ 01425 282100 & 282101 01425 278396
87 Bure Ln, Friars Cliff BH23 4DN
e-mail: waterfordlodgehotel@yahoo.co.uk
web: www.waterfordlodgehotel.co.uk
dir: A35 onto A337 towards Highcliffe. Turn right from rdbt signed Mudeford. Hotel 0.5m on left

Originally, the West Lodge to Highcliffe Castle and former home of the Dowager Duchess of Waterford, this hotel provides modern facilities whilst still retaining character, style and charm. The bedrooms vary - some are traditional in style, while others in the newer wing are more modern. It is ideally positioned for easy access to the medieval town of Christchurch and to Highcliffe Castle.

Rooms 18 (2 fmly) (3 GF) **S** £50-£120; **D** £80-£170 (incl. bkfst) **Facilities** FTV Xmas New Year Wi-fi **Conf** Class 60 Board 50 Thtr 90 Del from £75 to £170 **Parking** 38 **Notes** LB

Premier Inn Christchurch East

BUDGET HOTEL

☎ 0871 527 8250 0871 527 8251
Somerford Rd BH23 3QG
dir: In Christchurch from A35 & B3059 rdbt junct take B3059 (Somerford Rd)

High quality, budget accommodation ideal for both families and business travellers. Spacious, en suite bedrooms feature tea and coffee making facilities, and Freeview TV in most hotels. Internet access and Wi-fi are available for a small fee. The adjacent family restaurant features a wide and varied menu. See also the Hotel Groups pages.

Rooms 102 **D** £65*

Premier Inn Christchurch West

BUDGET HOTEL

☎ 0871 527 8252 0871 527 8253
Barrack Rd BH23 2BN
dir: From A338 take A3060 towards Christchurch. Left onto A35. Hotel on right

Rooms 41 **D** £65*

CHURCH STRETTON Map 15 SO49
Shropshire

Longmynd Hotel

★★★ 73% HOTEL

☎ 01694 722244 01694 722718
Cunnery Rd SY6 6AG
e-mail: info@longmynd.co.uk
web: www.longmynd.co.uk
dir: A49 into town centre on Sandford Ave, left at Lloyds TSB, over mini-rdbt, 1st right into Cunnery Rd, hotel at top of hill on left

Built in 1901 as a spa, this family-run hotel overlooks the town, and the views from many of the rooms and public areas are breathtaking. The attractive wooded grounds include a unique wood sculpture trail. Bedrooms, with smart modern bathrooms, are comfortable and well equipped; suites are available. Facilities include a choice of relaxing lounges. An ethical approach to climatic issues is observed, and a warm welcome is assured.

Rooms 50 (3 fmly) **S** £44-£59; **D** £88-£118 (incl. bkfst)* **Facilities** FTV Putt green Pitch and putt Sauna Xmas New Year Wi-fi **Conf** Class 50 Board 40 Thtr 100 Del from £115* **Services** Lift **Parking** 100 **Notes** LB Civ Wed 100

CHURT Map 5 SU83
Surrey

Best Western Frensham Pond Hotel

★★★ 79% HOTEL

☎ 01252 795161 01252 792631
Bacon Ln GU10 2QB
e-mail: info@frenshampondhotel.co.uk
web: www.frenshampondhotel.co.uk
dir: A3 onto A287. 4m left at 'Beware Horses' sign. Hotel 0.25m

This 15th-century house occupies a superb location on the edge of Frensham Pond. The bedrooms are mainly spacious, and the superior, garden annexe rooms have their own patio and air conditioning. The contemporary bar and lounge offers a range of snacks, and the leisure club has good facilities.

Rooms 51 (12 annexe) (14 fmly) (27 GF) **Facilities** STV FTV supervised Gym Squash Steam room Sauna Xmas New Year Wi-fi **Conf** Class 45 Board 40 Thtr 120 **Parking** 120 **Notes** LB Civ Wed 130

CIRENCESTER
Gloucestershire
Map 5 SP00

INSPECTORS' CHOICE

Barnsley House

★★★★ COUNTRY HOUSE HOTEL

01285 740000 01285 740925
Barnsley GL7 5EE
e-mail: info@barnsleyhouse.com
dir: 4m NE of Cirencester on B4425

This delightful Cotswold country house has been appointed to provide the highest levels of quality, comfort and relaxation. Bedrooms come in a range of shapes and sizes, from the large character rooms in the main house to the more contemporary-style stable rooms; all rooms are packed with guest extras and little luxuries. The delightful gardens include a fruit and vegetable area from where much produce is used in the delicious cuisine on offer at lunch and dinner. A spa and cinema are also available.

Rooms 18 (12 annexe) (10 GF) **S** £257-£527; **D** £275-£545 (incl. bkfst)* **Facilities** Spa STV FTV Cinema Bicycles Hydrotherapy pool Relaxation rooms Xmas New Year Wi-fi **Conf** Class 20 Board 18 Thtr 30 **Parking** 30 **Notes** LB Civ Wed 100

Best Western Stratton House

★★★ 77% HOTEL

01285 651761 01285 640024
Gloucester Rd GL7 2LE
e-mail: stratton.house@forestdale.com
web: www.strattonhousehotel.co.uk
dir: M4 junct 15, A419 to Cirencester. Hotel on left on A417 or M5 junct 11 to Cheltenham onto B4070 to A417. Hotel on right

This attractive 17th-century manor house is quietly situated about half a mile from the town centre. Bedrooms are well presented, and spacious, stylish premier rooms are available. The comfortable drawing rooms and restaurant have views over well-tended gardens - the perfect place to enjoy pre-dinner drinks on a summer evening.

Rooms 39 (9 GF) **Facilities** FTV Xmas New Year Wi-fi **Conf** Class 50 Board 30 Thtr 150 **Parking** 100 **Notes** LB Civ Wed 100

The Crown of Crucis

★★★ 73% HOTEL

01285 851806 01285 851735
Ampney Crucis GL7 5RS
e-mail: reception@thecrownofcrucis.co.uk
web: www.thecrownofcrucis.co.uk
dir: A417 to Fairford, hotel 2.5m on left

This delightful hotel consists of two buildings; one a 16th-century coaching inn, which houses the bar and restaurant, and a more modern bedroom block which surrounds a courtyard. Rooms are attractively appointed and offer modern facilities; the restaurant serves a range of imaginative dishes.

Rooms 25 (2 fmly) (13 GF) (4 smoking) **D** £80-£105 (incl. bkfst)* **Facilities** FTV Wi-fi **Conf** Class 50 Board 40 Thtr 100 Del from £115 to £135* **Parking** 82 **Notes** LB RS 25-26 Dec Civ Wed 90

Fleece Hotel

THE INDEPENDENTS HOTEL ASSOCIATION

★★★ 73% HOTEL

01285 658507 01285 651017
Market Place GL7 2NZ
e-mail: relax@fleecehotel.co.uk
web: www.fleecehotel.co.uk
dir: A417/A419 Burford road junct, follow signs for town centre. Right at lights into 'The Waterloo', car park 250yds on left

This town centre coaching inn, which dates back to the Tudor period, retains many original features such as flagstone-floors and oak beams. Well-equipped bedrooms vary in size and shape, but all offer good levels of comfort and have plenty of character. The bar lounge is a popular venue for morning coffee, and the stylish restaurant offers a range of dishes in an informal and convivial atmosphere.

Rooms 28 (3 fmly) (4 GF) **Facilities** Xmas New Year Wi-fi **Parking** 10

Corinium Hotel & Restaurant

★★★ SMALL HOTEL

01285 659711 01285 885807
12 Gloucester St GL7 2DG
e-mail: info@coriniumhotel.co.uk
web: www.coriniumhotel.co.uk
dir: From A417/A419/A429 towards Cirencester. A435 at rdbt. After 500mtrs turn left at lights, then 1st right, car park on left

Rooms 15 (2 fmly) (2 GF) **S** £55-£79; **D** £65-£115 (incl. bkfst)* **Facilities** FTV Wi-fi **Conf** Class 30 Board 34 Thtr 70 Del from £95 to £125* **Parking** 30 **Notes** LB

C

CLACTON-ON-SEA Map 7 TM11
Essex

Esplanade Hotel

★★ 65% HOTEL

☎ 01255 220450 📠 01255 221800
27-29 Marine Parade East CO15 1UU
e-mail: mjs@esplanadehoteluk.com
web: www.esplanadehoteluk.com
dir: From A133 to Clacton-on-Sea, follow seafront signs. At seafront turn right. Hotel on right in 50yds

Ideally situated on the seafront overlooking the pier and just a short walk from the town centre. Bedrooms vary in size and style: each one is pleasantly decorated and well equipped; some rooms have lovely sea views. Public rooms include a comfortable lounge bar and Coasters Restaurant.

Rooms 29 (2 fmly) (3 GF) **Facilities** Xmas New Year Wi-fi **Conf** Class 50 Board 50 Thtr 80 **Parking** 13 **Notes** LB ® Civ Wed 85

Premier Inn Clacton-on-Sea

BUDGET HOTEL

☎ 0871 527 8254 📠 0871 527 8255
Crown Green Roundabout, Colchester Rd, Trending CO16 9AA
dir: A12, A120 towards Harwich. In 4m take A133 to Clacton-on-Sea. Hotel off rdbt

High quality, budget accommodation ideal for both families and business travellers. Spacious, en suite bedrooms feature tea and coffee making facilities, and Freeview TV in most hotels. Internet access and Wi-fi are available for a small fee. The adjacent family restaurant features a wide and varied menu. See also the Hotel Groups pages.

Rooms 40 **D** £53-£60*

CLAVERDON Map 10 SP16
Warwickshire

Ardencote Manor Hotel, Country Club & Spa

★★★★ 77% ® HOTEL

☎ 01926 843111 📠 01926 842646
The Cumsey, Lye Green Rd, Claverdon CV35 8LT
e-mail: hotel@ardencote.com
web: www.ardencote.com
dir: Telephone for directions

Originally built as a gentleman's residence around 1860, this hotel is set in 83 acres of landscaped grounds. Public rooms include a choice of lounge areas, a cocktail bar and conservatory breakfast room. Main meals are served in the Lodge Restaurant, a separate building with a light contemporary style, which sits beside a small lake. An extensive range of leisure and conference facilities is provided and bedrooms are smartly decorated and tastefully furnished.

Rooms 110 (10 fmly) (30 GF) **S** £80-£110; **D** £90-£165 (incl. bkfst) **Facilities** Spa STV 9 Putt green Gym Squash Sauna Steam room Dance studio Xmas New Year Wi-fi **Conf** Class 70 Board 50 Thtr 175 Del from £130 to £180 **Services** Lift Air con **Parking** 350 **Notes** LB ® Civ Wed 150

CLEARWELL Map 4 SO50
Gloucestershire

Tudor Farmhouse Hotel & Restaurant

★★★ 79% ®® HOTEL

☎ 01594 833046 📠 01594 837093
High St GL16 8JS
e-mail: info@tudorfarmhousehotel.co.uk
web: www.tudorfarmhousehotel.co.uk
dir: A4136 onto B4228, through Coleford, right into Clearwell, hotel on right just before War Memorial Cross

Dating from the 13th century, this idyllic former farmhouse retains a host of original features including exposed stonework, oak beams, wall panelling and wonderful inglenook fireplaces. Bedrooms have great individuality and style and are located either in the main house or in converted buildings in the grounds. Creative menus offer quality cuisine, served in the intimate, candlelit restaurant.

Rooms 20 (15 annexe) (3 fmly) (8 GF) **S** £85-£140; **D** £100-£160 (incl. bkfst)* **Facilities** STV FTV New Year Wi-fi **Conf** Class 20 Board 12 Thtr 30 **Parking** 30 **Notes** LB Closed 24-27 Dec

Wyndham Arms

★★★ 68% ® HOTEL

☎ 01594 833666 📠 01594 836450
GL16 8JT
e-mail: nigel@thewyndhamhotel.co.uk
dir: Off B4228, in village centre on B4231

The history of this charming village inn can be traced back over 600 years. It has exposed stone walls, original beams and an impressive inglenook fireplace in the friendly bar. Most bedrooms are in a modern extension, whilst the other rooms, in the main house, are more traditional in style. A range of dishes is offered in the bar or restaurant.

Rooms 18 (12 annexe) (3 fmly) (6 GF) **S** £45-£55; **D** £75-£175 (incl. bkfst) **Facilities** FTV Xmas Wi-fi **Conf** Class 30 Board 22 Thtr 56 Del from £65 **Parking** 52 **Notes** LB Civ Wed 80

CLEATOR Cumbria **Map 18 NY01**

Ennerdale Country House

★★★ 74% HOTEL

☎ 01946 813907 📠 01946 815260
CA23 3DT
e-mail: reservations.ennerdale@ohiml.com
web: www.oxfordhotelsandinns.com
dir: M6 junct 40 to A66, A5086 for 12m, hotel on left

This fine Grade II listed building lies on the edge of the village and has landscaped gardens. Impressive bedrooms, including split-level suites and four-poster rooms, are richly furnished, smartly decorated and offer a range of facilities. Attractive public areas include a stylish restaurant and an American themed bar which offers a good range of bar meals.

Rooms 30 (2 fmly) (10 GF) **Facilities** STV Xmas New Year Wi-fi **Conf** Class 60 Board 60 Thtr 160 Del from £100 to £160* **Parking** 40 **Notes** Civ Wed 160

CLECKHEATON West Yorkshire **Map 19 SE12**

The Whitcliffe

★★★ 70% HOTEL

☎ 0845 833 5362 📠 01274 870376
Prospect Rd BD19 3HD
e-mail: info@thewhitcliffehotel.co.uk
web: www.thewhitcliffehotel.co.uk
dir: M62 junct 26, A638 to Dewsbury, over 1st lights, right into Mount St, to T-junct, right then 1st left

This popular and conveniently located commercial hotel offers comfortably equipped bedrooms. Spacious public areas provide a variety of amenities, including several meeting rooms, The Sportsman's bar and The Blue bar.

Rooms 41 (6 annexe) (3 fmly) (7 GF) **Facilities** FTV ♫ Wi-fi **Conf** Class 60 Board 40 Thtr 120 **Parking** 150 **Notes** ⊗ Civ Wed 80

Premier Inn Bradford South

BUDGET HOTEL

☎ 0871 527 8136 📠 0871 527 8137
Whitehall Rd, Dye House Dr BD19 6HG
dir: On A58 at intersection with M62 & M606

High quality, budget accommodation ideal for both families and business travellers. Spacious, en suite bedrooms feature tea and coffee making facilities, and Freeview TV in most hotels. Internet access and Wi-fi are available for a small fee. The adjacent family restaurant features a wide and varied menu. See also the Hotel Groups pages.

Rooms 40 **D** £52-£59*

CLEETHORPES Lincolnshire **Map 17 TA30**

Kingsway

★★★ 77% HOTEL

☎ 01472 601122 📠 0871 236 0671
Kingsway DN35 0AE
e-mail: reception@kingsway-hotel.com
web: www.kingsway-hotel.com
dir: Exit A180 at Grimsby, to Cleethorpes seafront. Hotel at Kingsway & Queen Parade junct (A1098)

This seafront hotel has been in the same family for four generations and continues to provide traditional comfort and friendly service. The lounges are comfortable and good food is served in the pleasant dining room. The bedrooms are bright and nicely furnished - most are comfortably proportioned.

Rooms 49 **S** £77-£90; **D** £94-£107 (incl. bkfst)* **Facilities** STV FTV Wi-fi **Conf** Board 18 Thtr 22 **Services** Lift **Parking** 50 **Notes** ⊗ No children 5yrs Closed 25-26 Dec

CLIMPING West Sussex **Map 6 SU90**

INSPECTORS' CHOICE

Bailiffscourt Hotel & Spa

★★★ ◎◎ HOTEL

☎ 01903 723511 📠 01903 723107
Climping St BN17 5RW
e-mail: bailiffscourt@hshotels.co.uk
web: www.hshotels.co.uk
dir: A259, follow Climping Beach signs. Hotel 0.5m on right

This delightful moated 'medieval manor' dating back only to the 1920s has the appearance of having been in existence for centuries. In fact it was built for Lord Moyne, a member of the Guinness family, who wanted to create an ancient manor house. It became a hotel just over 60 years ago and sits in 30 acres of delightful parkland that leads to the beach. Bedrooms vary from atmospheric feature rooms with log fires, oak beams and four-poster beds to spacious, stylish and contemporary rooms located in the grounds. The Tapestry Restaurant serves award-winning classic European cuisine, and in summer the Courtyard is the place for informal light lunches and afternoon tea. Superb facilities are to be found in the health spa.

Rooms 39 (30 annexe) (25 fmly) (16 GF) **S** £158-£398; **D** £210-£530 (incl. bkfst)* **Facilities** Spa STV FTV Gym Sauna Steam room Dance/fitness studio Yoga/Pilates/gym inductions Xmas New Year Wi-fi **Conf** Class 20 Board 26 Thtr 40 **Parking** 100 **Notes** LB Civ Wed 60

C

CLITHEROE
Lancashire Map 18 SD74

Eaves Hall Country Hotel

RICHARDSON

★★★ 77% HOTEL

☎ 01200 425271 📠 01200 425131
Eaves Hall Ln, West Bradford BB7 3JG
e-mail: reservations@eaveshall.co.uk
web: www.eaveshall.co.uk
dir: A59 onto Pimlico link West Bradford. At T-junct turn left, hotel 1st on right

A 19th century country-house set in 13 acres of landscaped gardens with its own crown bowling green, tennis courts and pitch & putt among other activities. Eaves Hall has a long history which can be traced to Tudor times, and during WW2 the Brooke Bond tea company established their headquarters here. Today the hotel is a good place to relax and 'get away from it all'. The bedrooms are spacious and well equipped. Jonathan's Restaurant, with lovely views over the grounds, is the elegant setting for meals, and the hotel is a popular venue for weddings.

Rooms 34 (7 fmly) **Facilities** ⛳ 9 🎾 Putt green Fishing Snooker table Pitch & putt Bowling green Xmas New Year Wi-fi **Conf** Class 90 Board 50 Thtr 100 **Services** Lift **Parking** 70 **Notes** Civ Wed 100

CLOVELLY
Devon Map 3 SS32

Red Lion Hotel

★★ 75% HOTEL

☎ 01237 431237 📠 01237 431044
The Quay EX39 5TF
e-mail: redlion@clovelly.co.uk
web: www.clovelly.co.uk
dir: Exit A39 at Clovelly Cross onto B3237. Pass visitor centre, 1st left by white rails to harbour

'Idyllic' is the only word to describe the harbour-side setting of this charming 18th-century inn, with the famous fishing village forming a spectacular backdrop. Bedrooms are stylish and enjoy delightful views. The inn's relaxed atmosphere is conducive to switching off from the pressures of modern life, even when the harbour comes alive with the activities of the local fishermen during the day.

Rooms 11 (2 fmly) (1 GF) **S** £61.75-£88.75; **D** £123.50-£141.50 (incl. bkfst)* **Facilities** FTV Tennis can be arranged Sea fishing Diving Xmas New Year Wi-fi **Parking** 11 **Notes** LB Civ Wed 70

New Inn

★★ 72% HOTEL

☎ 01237 431303 📠 01237 431636
High St EX39 5TQ
e-mail: newinn@clovelly.co.uk
dir: At Clovelly Cross, off A39 onto B3237. Follow down hill for 1.5m. Right at sign 'All vehicles for Clovelly'

Famed for its cobbled descent to the harbour, this fascinating fishing village is a traffic-free zone. Consequently, luggage is conveyed by sledge or donkey to this much-photographed hotel. Carefully renovated bedrooms and public areas are smartly presented with quality, locally-made furnishings. Meals may be taken in the elegant restaurant or the popular Upalong bar.

Rooms 8 (2 fmly) **Facilities** FTV Tennis can be arranged Sea fishing Diving Xmas New Year Wi-fi **Notes** LB Civ Wed 50

CLOWNE
Derbyshire Map 16 SK47

Hotel Van Dyk

★★★★ 79% ⚜ SMALL HOTEL

☎ 01246 810219 📠 01246 819566
Worksop Rd S43 4TD
e-mail: marcus@hotelvandyk.co.uk
dir: M1 junct 30, 2nd right towards Worksop, 2nd rdbt 1st exit, 3rd rdbt straight over. Through lights, hotel 100yds on right

A sympathetic renovation has resulted in a small vibrant boutique-style hotel where staff are always on hand to offer friendly and welcoming service. Accommodation is luxurious and equipped with many thoughtful extras. Bowdens Restaurant offers fine dining and makes the ideal setting for a memorable evening; alternatively there's Southgate Grill for those looking for a more casual eating option.

Rooms 15 (4 fmly) **Facilities** FTV ♫ Xmas New Year Wi-fi **Conf** Class 50 Board 60 Thtr 200 **Parking** 78 **Notes** ⊗ Civ Wed 250

COALVILLE
Leicestershire Map 11 SK41

Hermitage Park Hotel

★★★ 73% HOTEL

☎ 01530 814814 📠 01530 814202
Whitwick Rd LE67 3FA
e-mail: hotel@hermitageparkhotel.co.uk
dir: A511 to outskirts of Coalville. Follow brown tourist signs around bypass. Into Coalville at Morrisons supermarket. Hotel on left

There's a relaxed and friendly environment throughout this modern building which sits within easy access of major road networks. Bedrooms are contemporary and well equipped; ground-floor rooms are available. Open-plan public areas include a lounge bar and informal dining area.

Rooms 28 (5 fmly) (14 GF) **Facilities** STV ♫ Xmas New Year Wi-fi **Conf** Class 30 Board 30 Thtr 50 **Parking** 40 **Notes** ⊗ Civ Wed 100

COBHAM
Surrey Map 6 TQ16

Premier Inn Cobham

BUDGET HOTEL

☎ 0871 527 8256 📠 0871 527 8257
Portsmouth Rd, Fairmile KT11 1BW
dir: M25 junct 10, A3 towards London, A245 towards Cobham. In Cobham town centre left onto A307 (Portsmouth Rd). Hotel on left

High quality, budget accommodation ideal for both families and business travellers. Spacious, en suite bedrooms feature tea and coffee making facilities, and Freeview TV in most hotels. Internet access and Wi-fi are available for a small fee. The adjacent family restaurant features a wide and varied menu. See also the Hotel Groups pages.

Rooms 48 **D** £65-£79*

COCKERMOUTH
Cumbria Map 18 NY13

The Trout Hotel

★★★★ 77% HOTEL

☎ 01900 823591 📠 01900 827514
Crown St CA13 0EJ
e-mail: enquiries@trouthotel.co.uk
web: www.trouthotel.co.uk
dir: Adjacent to Wordsworth House

Dating back to 1670, this privately owned hotel has an enviable setting on the banks of the River Derwent. The well-equipped bedrooms, some contained in a wing overlooking the river, are comfortable and mostly spacious. The Terrace Bar & Bistro, serving food all day, has a sheltered patio area. There is also a cosy bar, a choice of lounge areas and an attractive, traditional-style dining room that offers a good choice of set-price dishes.

Rooms 49 (4 fmly) (15 GF) **S** £70-£100; **D** £110-£150 (incl. bkfst)* **Facilities** STV Fishing Xmas New Year Wi-fi **Conf** Class 20 Board 20 Thtr 25 Del from £179.95 to £209.95* **Parking** 40 **Notes** LB Civ Wed 60

Shepherds Hotel

★★★ 74% HOTEL

☎ 0845 459 9770 📠 01301 703327
Lakeland Sheep & Wool Centre, Egremont Rd CA13 0QX
e-mail: info@argyllholidays.com
web: www.shepherdshotel.co.uk
dir: At junct of A66 & A5086 S of Cockermouth, entrance off A5086, 200mtrs off rdbt

This hotel is modern in style and offers thoughtfully equipped accommodation. It is well situated for the northern lakes area and has good road links. The restaurant, open all day, serves a wide variety of meals and snacks; the Black Rock dishes are recommended. Free Wi-fi is available in the bedrooms.

Rooms 26 (4 fmly) (13 GF) **Facilities** FTV Pool table Small children's play area Wi-fi **Conf** Class 30 Board 30 Thtr 40 **Services** Lift **Parking** 100 **Notes** Closed 25-26 Dec & 4-18 Jan

COGGESHALL
Essex Map 7 TL82

White Hart Hotel

OldEnglish

★★★ 73% HOTEL

☎ 01376 561654 📠 01376 561789
Market End CO6 1NH
e-mail: 6529@greeneking.co.uk
web: www.oldenglish.co.uk
dir: From A12 through Kelvedon & onto B1024 to Coggeshall

A delightful inn situated in the centre of this bustling market town. Bedrooms vary in size and style; each one offers good quality and comfort with extras such as CD players, fruit and mineral water. The heavily beamed public areas include a popular bar serving a varied menu, a large restaurant offering European style cuisine and a cosy residents' lounge.

Rooms 18 (1 fmly) **Facilities** ♫ Xmas **Conf** Class 10 Board 22 Thtr 30 **Parking** 47

COLCHESTER
Essex Map 13 TL92

Five Lakes Hotel, Golf, Country Club & Spa

★★★★ 77% ◉ HOTEL

☎ 01621 868888 📠 01621 869696
Colchester Rd CM9 8HX
e-mail: enquiries@fivelakes.co.uk
web: www.fivelakes.co.uk

(For full entry see Tolleshunt Knights)

Best Western Marks Tey

Best Western

★★★★ 70% HOTEL

☎ 01206 210001 📠 01206 212167
London Rd, Marks Tey CO6 1DU
e-mail: info@marksteyhotel.co.uk
web: www.marksteyhotel.co.uk
dir: Off A12/A120 junct signed Marks Tey/Stansted. At rdbt follow Stanway signs. Follow over A12, at next rdbt take 1st exit. Hotel on left

A purpose-built hotel situated just off the A12 on the outskirts of Colchester. Public rooms include a brasserie restaurant, a choice of lounges, a bar and a conservatory. Bedrooms come in a variety of styles; each one is smartly furnished and equipped with modern facilities. The hotel also has conference and leisure facilities.

Rooms 110 (57 GF) **S** £59-£89; **D** £69-£99* **Facilities** FTV supervised Gym Steam room Beauty treatments Sauna Xmas New Year Wi-fi **Conf** Class 100 Board 60 Thtr 200 Del from £129 to £149* **Services** Lift **Parking** 200 **Notes** LB ⊗ Civ Wed 160

Stoke by Nayland Hotel, Golf & Spa

★★★ 82% ◉ HOTEL

☎ 01206 262836 📠 01206 265840
Keepers Ln, Leavenheath CO6 4PZ
e-mail: sales@stokebynayland.com
web: www.stokebynaylandclub.co.uk
dir: Off A134 at Leavenheath onto B1068, hotel 0.75m on right

This hotel is situated on the edge of Dedham Vale, an Area of Outstanding Natural Beauty, in 300 acres of undulating countryside with lakes and two golf courses. The spacious bedrooms are attractively decorated and equipped with modern facilities, including ISDN lines. Free Wi-fi is available throughout. Public rooms include the Spikes bar, a conservatory, a lounge, a smart restaurant, conference and banqueting suites. The superb Peake Spa and Fitness Centre offers extensive facilities including health and beauty treatments.

Rooms 80 (4 fmly) (26 GF) **Facilities** Spa STV FTV supervised ⛳ 36 Putt green Fishing Gym Squash Driving range Snooker tables ♫ New Year Wi-fi **Conf** Class 300 Board 60 Thtr 450 **Services** Lift **Parking** 335 **Notes** ⊗ Civ Wed 200

North Hill

★★★ 81% ◉ HOTEL

☎ 01206 574001 📠 01206 562941
51 North Hill CO1 1PY
e-mail: info@northhillhotel.com
dir: Follow signs for town centre. Up North Hill, hotel on right

This hotel is situated in the centre of this historic town. The contemporary open-plan public areas include a small lounge bar and the Green Room restaurant. The smartly appointed bedrooms are modern and well equipped with large flat-screen TVs and many thoughtful touches.

Rooms 17 (3 fmly) (1 GF) **S** £62.50; **D** £87.50-£117.50 (incl. bkfst)* **Facilities** FTV Xmas New Year Wi-fi **Notes** ⊗

C

COLCHESTER *continued*

Best Western The Rose & Crown

★★★ 80% HOTEL

☎ 01206 866677 📠 01206 866616
East St CO1 2TZ
e-mail: info@rose-and-crown.com
web: www.rose-and-crown.com
dir: From A12 follow Rollerworld signs, hotel by level crossing

This delightful 14th-century coaching inn is situated close to the shops and is full of charm and character. Public areas feature a wealth of exposed beams and timbered walls, and includes the contemporary East St Grill. Although the bedrooms vary in size, all are stylishly decorated and equipped with many thoughtful extras suitable for both business and leisure guests; luxury executive rooms are available.

Rooms 39 (3 fmly) (12 GF) **Facilities** Wi-fi **Conf** Class 50 Board 45 Thtr 100 **Services** Lift **Parking** 50 **Notes** LB ⊗ Civ Wed 80

Holiday Inn Colchester

★★★ 80% HOTEL

☎ 0871 942 9020 📠 01206 766577
Abbotts Ln, Eight Ash Green CO6 3QL
web: www.hicolchester.co.uk
dir: Exit A12 at junct with A1124, follow Halstead signs. 0.25m, hotel at rdbt on left

This hotel is situated three miles from Colchester and is ideally located just off the A12 in a quiet village setting. All bedrooms are air conditioned and have high-speed internet access. Trader's bar and grill offers a relaxed and informal environment; a range of conference rooms can cater for meetings and weddings.

Rooms 109 (25 fmly) (54 GF) **S** £59-£136; **D** £59-£136 (incl. bkfst)* **Facilities** Spa STV supervised Gym Health club Xmas New Year Wi-fi **Conf** Class 60 Board 50 Thtr 120 **Services** Air con **Parking** 130 **Notes** ⊗ Civ Wed 100

The George Hotel

★★★ 71% HOTEL

☎ 01206 578494 📠 01206 761732
116 High St CO1 1TD
e-mail: reservations.thegeorgehotel@ohiml.com
web: www.oxfordhotelsandinns.com
dir: In town centre, 200yds from Town Hall

Ideally situated in the centre of town, this 500-year-old establishment has much to offer. The medieval cellar has, preserved behind glass, evidence of the Roman road than once ran through this town. The individually decorated bedrooms are equipped with a range of amenities. There's a popular lounge in which to relax and enjoy good food and real ales. The Bubbles Wine Bar offers an alternative to the traditional lounge.

Rooms 47 (7 fmly) **Facilities** FTV Wi-fi **Conf** Class 40 Board 34 Thtr 70 **Parking** 50 **Notes** ⊗

Ramada Hotel

RAMADA JARVIS

U

☎ 01206 230900 📠 01206 231095
A12/A120 Ardveigh Junction CO7 7QY
e-mail: reception@ramadacolchester.co.uk
dir: From A12 Colchester north rdbt junct 29, continue straight on, hotel on left of slip road leading to A120

Currently the rating for this establishment is not confirmed. This may be due to a change of ownership or because it has only recently joined the AA rating scheme. For further details please see the AA website: theAA.com

Rooms 50 **Conf** Class 60 Board 50 Thtr 90

Holiday Inn Express Colchester

BUDGET HOTEL

☎ 01206 321510 📠 01206 321511
Birchwood Rd CO7 6HX

A modern hotel ideal for families and business travellers. Fresh and uncomplicated, the spacious rooms include Sky TV, power shower and tea and coffee-making facilities. Continental buffet breakfast is included in the room rate; other meals may be taken at the nearby family pub or restaurant. See also the Hotel Groups pages.

Rooms 101

Premier Inn Colchester (A12)

BUDGET HOTEL

☎ 0871 527 8260 📠 0871 527 8261
Ipswich Rd CO4 9WP
dir: From A12 exit at Colchester Nrth/A1232 junct off towards Colchester. Hotel on right, 200yds from rdbt. (NB for Sat Nav use CO4 9TD)

High quality, budget accommodation ideal for both families and business travellers. Spacious, en suite bedrooms feature tea and coffee making facilities, and Freeview TV in most hotels. Internet access and Wi-fi are available for a small fee. The adjacent family restaurant features a wide and varied menu. See also the Hotel Groups pages.

Rooms 60 **D** £55-£63*

Premier Inn Colchester Central

BUDGET HOTEL

☎ 0871 527 8258 📠 0871 527 8259
Cowdray Av CO1 1UT
dir: From Ipswich A12 junct 29. At rdbt onto A1232 (Ipswich road). At 2nd rdbt 2nd exit onto A133 (Cowdray Ave). Hotel approx 0.5m on right

Rooms 20 **D** £55-£64*

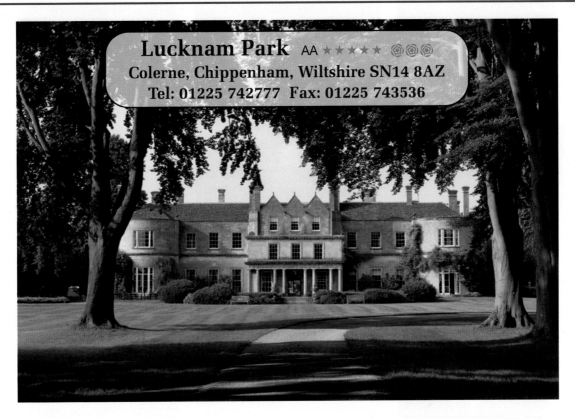

C

COLEFORD Gloucestershire Map 4 SO51

Bells Hotel & The Forest of Dean Golf Club

★★ 72% HOTEL

☎ 01594 832583 📠 01594 832584
Lords Hill GL16 8BE
e-mail: enquiries@bells-hotel.co.uk
dir: 0.25m from Coleford. Off B4228

Set in its own grounds, with an 18-hole golf course, this purpose-built establishment offers a range of facilities. Bedrooms vary in style and space, and a number are on the ground floor. There is a small gym, and a comfortable bar and lounge which is available until late. The hotel's club house, just yards away, has a bar with all-day meals and snacks, a restaurant, a games/TV room and conference and function rooms.

Rooms 53 (12 fmly) (36 GF) (5 smoking) **Facilities** FTV 18 Putt green Bowling green Short mat bowling room Xmas New Year Wi-fi **Conf** Class 250 Board 100 Thtr 350 **Parking** 100 **Notes** Civ Wed 150

COLERNE Wiltshire Map 4 ST87

INSPECTORS' CHOICE

Lucknam Park

★★★★★ COUNTRY HOUSE HOTEL

☎ 01225 742777 📠 01225 743536
SN14 8AZ
e-mail: reservations@lucknampark.co.uk
web: www.lucknampark.co.uk
dir: M4 junct 17, A350 towards Chippenham, then A420 towards Bristol for 3m. At Ford left to Colerne, 3m, right at x-rds, entrance on right

Guests on arrival at this Palladian mansion may well experience a sense of the theatrical as they drive along a magnificent mile-long avenue of beech and lime trees. Surrounded by 500 acres of parkland and beautiful gardens, this fine hotel offers a wealth of choices ranging from enjoying pampering treatments in the truly luxurious spa to trying the facilities at the equestrian centre. There are also tennis courts, walking trails, a 5-a-side football pitch, a croquet lawn and much more. The elegant bedrooms and suites are split between the main building and adjacent courtyard. Dining options range from the informal Brasserie, awarded 1 AA Rosette, to the formal, and very accomplished, main restaurant, The Park (awarded 3 Rosettes).

Rooms 42 (18 annexe) (16 GF) **S** £315-£1065; **D** £315-£1065* **Facilities** Spa STV FTV Gym Cross country course Mountain bikes Equestrian centre Five-a-side football Xmas New Year Wi-fi **Conf** Class 24 Board 24 Thtr 60 **Parking** 70 **Notes** LB Civ Wed 110

See advert on page 149

COLESHILL Warwickshire Map 10 SP28

Grimstock Country House

★★★ 71% COUNTRY HOUSE HOTEL

☎ 01675 462121 📠 01675 467646
Gilson Rd, Gilson B46 1LJ
e-mail: enquiries@grimstockhotel.co.uk
web: www.grimstockhotel.co.uk
dir: Off A446 at rdbt onto B4117 to Gilson, hotel 100yds on right

This privately owned hotel is convenient for Birmingham International Airport and the NEC, and benefits from a peaceful rural setting. Bedrooms are spacious and comfortable. Public rooms include two restaurants, a wood-panelled bar, good conference facilities and a gym featuring the latest cardiovascular equipment.

Rooms 44 (1 fmly) (13 GF) **S** £62-£95; **D** £70-£109 (incl. bkfst) **Facilities** STV Gym Xmas New Year Wi-fi **Conf** Class 60 Board 50 Thtr 100 Del from £110 to £140 **Parking** 100 **Notes** LB Civ Wed 100

COLN ST ALDWYNS Gloucestershire Map 5 SP10

INSPECTORS' CHOICE

New Inn at Coln

★★ HOTEL

☎ 01285 750651 📠 01285 750657
GL7 5AN
e-mail: info@thenewinnatcoln.co.uk
web: www.new-inn.co.uk
dir: 8m E of Cirencester, between Bibury & Fairford

This delightful village inn has origins dating back to the 16th century. The stylish, individually designed bedrooms retain original features yet include all the modern amenities such as flat-screen TVs and power showers. The rooms come in a variety of shapes and sizes and display bold, impressive colour schemes. Relaxed and welcoming hospitality mixes easily with efficient service from a dedicated team of staff. Dinner, utilising the best of local produce, is a real treat whether served in the relaxing dining room or, weather permitting, outside on the terrace.

Rooms 14 (6 annexe) (1 fmly) (1 GF) **S** £105-£150; **D** £115-£170 (incl. bkfst) **Facilities** FTV New Year Wi-fi **Conf** Board 10 **Parking** 24

COLYFORD
Devon — Map 4 SY29

Swallows Eaves

★★ 82% HOTEL

☎ 01297 553184 📠 01297 553574
Swan Hill Rd EX24 6QJ
e-mail: info@swallowseaves.co.uk
web: www.swallowseaves.co.uk
dir: On A3052 between Lyme Regis & Sidmouth, in village centre, opposite post office store

Close to the Devon and Dorset border, this intimate and welcoming hotel is ideally located for exploring this beautiful area. The relaxed atmosphere is matched with attentive service. Comfortable bedrooms come complete with Egyptian cotton bedding and large fluffy towels. Local produce features on the menu which is offered in the stylish Reeds restaurant.

Rooms 8 (1 GF) **S** £48-£60; **D** £70-£110 (incl. bkfst) **Facilities** FTV Wi-fi **Conf** Thtr 20 **Parking** 10 **Notes** LB ⊗ No children 14yrs

CONSETT
Co Durham — Map 19 NZ15

Best Western Derwent Manor

★★★ 75% HOTEL

☎ 01207 592000 📠 01207 502472
Allensford DH8 9BB
e-mail: reservations.derwentmanor@ohiml.com
web: www.oxfordhotelsandinns.com
dir: On A68

This hotel, built in the style of a manor house, is set in open grounds overlooking the River Derwent. Spacious bedrooms, including a number of suites, are comfortably equipped. A popular wedding venue, there are also extensive conference facilities and an impressive leisure suite. The Grouse & Claret bar serves a wide range of drinks and light meals, and Guinevere's restaurant offers the fine dining option.

Rooms 48 (29 fmly) (26 GF) **S** £55-£125; **D** £70-£150 (incl. bkfst)* **Facilities** STV FTV (indoor pool) supervised Gym Xmas New Year Wi-fi **Conf** Class 200 Board 60 Thtr 300 Del from £99 to £155* **Services** Lift **Parking** 100 **Notes** LB Civ Wed 300

COPTHORNE

See Gatwick Airport

CORBY
Northamptonshire — Map 11 SP88

Holiday Inn Corby-Kettering A43

★★★ 71% HOTEL

☎ 01536 401020 📠 01536 400767
Geddington Rd NN18 8ET
e-mail: paulnoble@hicorby.com
web: www.hicorby.com
dir: M1 junct 19, A14 towards Kettering. Exit at junct 7 towards Corby. Follow Stamford & Corby East, A43. At end of road left through Geddington. After Eurohub rdbt turn left at next lights

Situated just one hour from three major airports and close to major motorway networks this establishment proves a good destination for both the business and leisure traveller. The comfortable bedrooms are well equipped and include free Wi-fi. The facilities include a 15-metre pool, steam room, sauna and fully equipped gym.

Rooms 105 (9 GF) **Facilities** Spa STV FTV (indoor pool) Gym Sauna Steam room Xmas New Year Wi-fi **Conf** Class 70 Board 44 Thtr 250 **Services** Lift Air con **Parking** 250 **Notes** Civ Wed 200

Best Western Rockingham Forest Country Hotel

U

☎ 01536 401348 📠 01536 266383
Rockingham Rd NN17 1AE
e-mail: reception@bwrockinghamforest.com
dir: From A14 or A427 take A6003 to junct with A6116 & Rockingham Castle. In Corby, hotel on right

Currently the rating for this establishment is not confirmed. This may be due to a change of ownership or because it has only recently joined the AA rating scheme. For further details please see the AA website: theAA.com

Rooms 70

Premier Inn Corby

BUDGET HOTEL

☎ 0871 527 8264 📠 0871 527 8264
1 Little Colliers Field NN18 8TJ
dir: M1 junct 19, A14 E'bound. Exit at junct 7, left at rdbt onto A43. At next rdbt left onto A6003. Hotel at next rdbt (NB for Sat Nav use NN18 9EX)

High quality, budget accommodation ideal for both families and business travellers. Spacious, en suite bedrooms feature tea and coffee making facilities, and Freeview TV in most hotels. Internet access and Wi-fi are available for a small fee. The adjacent family restaurant features a wide and varied menu. See also the Hotel Groups pages.

Rooms 56 **D** £51-£60*

CORFE CASTLE
Dorset — Map 4 SY98

Mortons House Hotel

★★★ 86% ®® HOTEL

☎ 01929 480988 📠 01929 480820
49 East St BH20 5EE
e-mail: stay@mortonshouse.co.uk
web: www.mortonshouse.co.uk
dir: On A351 between Wareham & Swanage

Set in delightful gardens and grounds with excellent views of Corfe Castle, this impressive building dates back to Tudor times. The oak-panelled drawing room has a roaring log fire in cooler months and an interesting range of enjoyable cuisine is available in the well-appointed dining room. Bedrooms, many with views of the castle, are comfortable and well equipped.

Rooms 21 (7 annexe) (2 fmly) (7 GF) **S** £75-£100; **D** £135-£160 (incl. bkfst)* **Facilities** Xmas New Year Wi-fi **Conf** Class 45 Board 20 Thtr 45 Del from £130 to £155* **Parking** 40 **Notes** LB ⊗ Civ Wed 60

C

CORLEY MOTORWAY SERVICE AREA (M6) Map 10 SP38
Warwickshire

Days Inn Corley - NEC - M6

BUDGET HOTEL

☎ 01676 543800 & 540111 📠 01676 540128
Junction 3-4, M6 North, Corley CV7 8NR
e-mail: corley.hotel@welcomebreak.co.uk
dir: On M6 between juncts 3 & 4 N'bound

This modern building offers accommodation in smart, spacious and well-equipped bedrooms, suitable for families and business travellers, and all with en suite bathrooms. Continental breakfast is available and other refreshments may be taken at the nearby family restaurant. See also the Hotel Groups pages.

Rooms 50 (13 fmly) (24 GF) (8 smoking)
S £39.95-£59.95; **D** £49.95-£69.95

CORNHILL-ON-TWEED Map 21 NT83
Northumberland

Tillmouth Park Country House
★★★ 86% ® COUNTRY HOUSE HOTEL

☎ 01890 882255 📠 01890 882540
TD12 4UU
e-mail: reception@tillmouthpark.f9.co.uk
web: www.tillmouthpark.co.uk
dir: Exit A1(M) at East Ord rdbt at Berwick-upon-Tweed. Take A698 signed Cornhill & Coldstream. Hotel 9m on left

An imposing mansion set in landscaped grounds by the River Till. Gracious public rooms include a stunning galleried lounge with a drawing room adjacent. The quiet, elegant dining room overlooks the gardens, whilst lunches and early dinners are available in the bistro. Bedrooms retain much traditional character and include several magnificent master rooms.

Rooms 14 (2 annexe) (4 smoking) **S** £79-£205; **D** £158-£225 (incl. bkfst)* **Facilities** FTV Game shooting Fishing New Year Wi-fi **Conf** Class 20 Board 20 Thtr 50 Del from £160* **Parking** 50 **Notes** LB Closed 3 Jan-1 Apr Civ Wed 50

CORSE LAWN Map 10 SO83
Gloucestershire

INSPECTORS' CHOICE

Corse Lawn House
★★★ ®® HOTEL

☎ 01452 780771 📠 01452 780840
GL19 4LZ
e-mail: enquiries@corselawn.com
web: www.corselawn.com
dir: On B4211 5m SW of Tewkesbury

This gracious Grade II listed Queen Anne house, in 12-acre grounds, has been home to the Hine family for 33 years. Aided by an enthusiastic and committed team, the family continues to preside over all aspects of the hotel, creating a wonderfully relaxed environment. Bedrooms offer a reassuring mix of comfort and quality, and include four-poster rooms. In both The Restaurant and The Bistro the impressive cuisine is based on excellent produce, much of it locally sourced.

Rooms 19 (2 fmly) (5 GF) **S** £100; **D** £160 (incl. bkfst)* **Facilities** STV FTV Badminton Table tennis New Year Wi-fi **Conf** Class 30 Board 25 Thtr 50 Del from £150 **Parking** 62 **Notes** LB Closed 24-26 Dec Civ Wed 70

CORSHAM Map 4 ST87
Wiltshire

The Methuen Arms
®® RESTAURANT WITH ROOMS

☎ 01249 717060
2 High St SN13 0HB
e-mail: info@themethuenarms.com
web: www.themethuenarms.com
dir: M4 junct 17, A350 towards Chippenham, at rdbt take A4 towards Bath. 1m after lights, at next rdbt turn sharp left into Pickwick Rd, establishment 0.5m on left

This well established inn in the centre of the thriving town of Corsham has undergone a complete refurbished to provide high levels of quality and comfort. The bedrooms are modern and stylish with large comfortable beds and spacious, well-equipped bathrooms. Guests can enjoy a drink in the relaxing bar, a light snack in the day or evening, and should not miss the award-winning, high quality, carefully prepared dishes at dinner.

Rooms 12 (3 fmly)

COVENTRY Map 10 SP37
West Midlands

See also **Brandon, Meriden & Nuneaton**

Holiday Inn Coventry

★★★ 78% HOTEL

☎ 0871 942 9021 & 024 7658 7420
📠 024 7658 7404
Hinckley Rd CV2 2HP
e-mail: reservations-coventrym6@ihg.com
web: www.holidayinn.co.uk
dir: M6 junct 2. Hotel on A4600

Situated close to the city centre and major motorway networks, this hotel offers comfortable and modern accommodation. Facilities include the Spirit Leisure Suite, Traders Restaurant, spacious lounges where food is served all day and extensive conference services.

Rooms 158 (11 fmly) (64 GF) (16 smoking) **S** £69-£109; **D** £79-£119 (incl. bkfst)* **Facilities** STV supervised Gym Steam room Sauna Aqua aerobic classes New Year Wi-fi **Conf** Class 120 Board 105 Thtr 250 Del from £99 to £155* **Services** Lift Air con **Parking** 246 **Notes** LB Civ Wed 150

Novotel Coventry
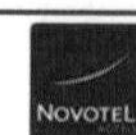
★★★ 75% HOTEL

☎ 024 7636 5000 📠 024 7636 2422
Wilsons Ln CV6 6HL
e-mail: h0506@accor-hotels.com
web: www.novotel.com
dir: M6 junct 3. Follow signs for B4113 towards Longford & Bedworth. 3rd exit on large rdbt

A modern hotel convenient for Birmingham, Coventry and the motorway network, offering spacious, well-equipped accommodation. The bright brasserie has extended dining hours, and alternatively there is an extensive room-service menu. Family rooms and a play area make this a child-friendly hotel, and there is also a selection of meeting rooms.

Rooms 98 (25 GF) **Facilities** STV Wi-fi **Conf** Class 100 Board 40 Thtr 200 **Services** Lift **Parking** 120 **Notes** Civ Wed 50

Quality Hotel

★★★ 64% HOTEL

☎ 024 7640 3835 📠 024 7640 3081
Birmingham Rd, Allesley CV5 9BA
e-mail: enquiries@qualityhotelcoventry.co.uk
dir: A45 onto A4114 towards Allesley. Follow brown signs for hotel

Conveniently situated on the A45 close to Birmingham Airport and the National Exhibition Centre. The bedrooms offer good comfort and space for both the business traveller or leisure guest. There is a sauna and steam room on site.

Rooms 80 (1 fmly) (21 GF) (27 smoking) **S** £45-£65; **D** £65-£95 **Facilities** STV FTV Sauna Steam room Xmas New Year Wi-fi **Conf** Class 40 Board 30 Thtr 120 Del from £70 to £99 **Parking** 150 **Notes** LB Civ Wed 75

Windmill Village Hotel, Golf & Leisure Club

U

☎ 02476 404040 📠 02476 404042
Birmingham Rd, Allesley CV5 9AL
e-mail: reservations@windmillvillagehotel.co.uk

Currently the rating for this establishment is not confirmed. This may be due to a change of ownership or because it has only recently joined the AA rating scheme. For further details please see the AA website: theAA.com

Rooms 105

Ibis Coventry Centre

BUDGET HOTEL

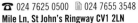

☎ 024 7625 0500 📠 024 7655 3548
Mile Ln, St John's Ringway CV1 2LN
e-mail: H2793@accor.com
web: www.ibishotel.com
dir: A45 to Coventry, then A4114 signed Jaguar Assembly Plant. At inner ring road towards ring road S. Off exit 5 for Mile Lane

Modern, budget hotel offering comfortable accommodation in bright and practical bedrooms. Breakfast is self-service and dinner is available in the restaurant. See also the Hotel Groups pages.

Rooms 89 (15 fmly) (25 GF) **D** £54-£65*

Ibis Coventry South

BUDGET HOTEL

☎ 024 7663 9922 📠 024 7630 6898
Abbey Rd, Whitley CV3 4BJ
e-mail: H2094@accor.com
web: www.ibishotel.com
dir: Signed from A46/A423 rdbt. Take A423 towards A45. Follow signs for Racquets Health Club & Jaguar Engineering Plant. 1st exit from Jaguar rdbt, hotel at end of lane by The Racquets

Rooms 51 (51 annexe) (25 GF) **S** £44-£74; **D** £44-£74* **Conf** Class 20 Board 16 Thtr 20 Del from £84 to £200*

Premier Inn Coventry (Binley/A46)

BUDGET HOTEL

☎ 0871 527 8268 📠 0871 527 8269
Rugby Rd, Binley Woods CV3 2TA
dir: M6 junct 2 follow Warwick, A46 & M40 signs. Follow 'All traffic' signs, under bridge onto A46. Left at 1st rdbt to Binley. Hotel on right at next rdbt

High quality, budget accommodation ideal for both families and business travellers. Spacious, en suite bedrooms feature tea and coffee making facilities, and Freeview TV in most hotels. Internet access and Wi-fi are available for a small fee. The adjacent family restaurant features a wide and varied menu. See also the Hotel Groups pages.

Rooms 76 **D** £47-£52*

Premier Inn Coventry City Centre

BUDGET HOTEL

☎ 0871 527 8272 📠 0871 527 8273
Belgrade Plaza, Bond St CV1 4AH
dir: A4053 (ring road) junct 9, follow Belgrade Plaza car park signs. Hotel in same complex

Rooms 119 **D** £50-£55*

Premier Inn Coventry East (Ansty)

BUDGET HOTEL

☎ 0871 527 8274 📠 0871 527 8275
Coombe Fields Rd, Ansty CV7 9JP
dir: M6 junct 2, B4065 towards Ansty. After village right onto B4029 signed Brinklow. Right into Coombe Fields Rd, hotel on right

Rooms 27 **D** £47-£57*

C

COVENTRY *continued*

Premier Inn Coventry (M6 Jct 2)

BUDGET HOTEL

☎ 0871 527 8266 📠 0871 527 8267
Gielgud Way, Cross Point Business Park CV2 2SZ
dir: M6 junct 2 towards Coventry onto A4600 (Hinckley road). At rdbt 1st exit into Parkway, left at next rdbt into Olivier Way. At next rdbt straight on into retail park towards cinema, hotel on right

Rooms 48 **D** £47-£57*

Premier Inn Coventry South (A45)

BUDGET HOTEL

☎ 0871 527 8270 📠 0871 527 8271
Kenpas Highway CV3 6PB
dir: M6 junct 2, A46. Follow A45 towards Birmingham

Rooms 37 **D** £47-£57*

COWES Isle of Wight — Map 5 SZ49

Best Western New Holmwood

★★★ 72% HOTEL

☎ 01983 292508 📠 01983 295020
Queens Rd, Egypt Point PO31 8BW
e-mail: reception@newholmwoodhotel.co.uk
dir: From A3020 at Northwood Garage lights, left & follow to rdbt. 1st left then sharp right into Baring Rd, 4th left into Egypt Hill. At bottom turn right, hotel on right

Just by the Esplanade, this hotel has an enviable outlook. Bedrooms are comfortable and very well equipped, and the light and airy, glass-fronted restaurant looks out to sea and serves a range of interesting meals. The sun terrace is delightful in the summer and there is a small pool area.

Rooms 26 (1 fmly) (9 GF) **Facilities** STV Xmas New Year Wi-fi **Conf** Class 60 Board 50 Thtr 120 **Parking** 20

See advert on page 153

CRAMLINGTON Northumberland — Map 21 NZ27

Premier Inn Newcastle Gosforth/Cramlington

BUDGET HOTEL

☎ 0871 527 8788 📠 0871 527 8789
Moor Farm Roundabout, Off Front St, Annitsford NE23 7QA
dir: At rdbt junct of A19 & A189, S of Cramlington

High quality, budget accommodation ideal for both families and business travellers. Spacious, en suite bedrooms feature tea and coffee making facilities, and Freeview TV in most hotels. Internet access and Wi-fi are available for a small fee. The adjacent family restaurant features a wide and varied menu. See also the Hotel Groups pages.

Rooms 40 **D** £53-£59*

CRANTOCK Cornwall — Map 2 SW76

Crantock Bay

★★★ 75% HOTEL

☎ 01637 830229 📠 01637 831111
West Pentire TR8 5SE
e-mail: stay@crantockbayhotel.co.uk
web: www.crantockbayhotel.co.uk
dir: At Newquay A3075 to Redruth. After 500yds right towards Crantock, follow signs to West Pentire

This family-run hotel has spectacular sea views and a tradition of friendly and attentive service. With direct access to the beach from its four acres of grounds, and its extensive leisure facilities, the hotel is a great place for families. There are separate lounges, a spacious bar and enjoyable cuisine is served in the dining room.

Rooms 31 (3 fmly) (9 GF) **Facilities** FTV Putt green Gym Children's games room Xmas New Year Wi-fi **Conf** Class 12 Board 12 Thtr 60 **Parking** 40 **Notes** LB Closed 2 wks Nov & Jan RS Dec & Feb

CRATHORNE North Yorkshire — Map 19 NZ40

INSPECTORS' CHOICE

Crathorne Hall

HandPICKED HOTELS

★★★★ @@ HOTEL

☎ 01642 700398 📠 01642 700814
TS15 0AR
e-mail: crathornehall@handpicked.co.uk
web: www.handpicked.co.uk
dir: Off A19, take slip road signed Teesside Airport & Kirklevington, then right signed Crathorne to hotel

This splendid Edwardian hall sits in its own landscaped grounds and enjoys fine views of the Leven Valley and rolling Cleveland Hills. Both the impressively equipped bedrooms and the delightful public areas offer sumptuous levels of comfort, with elegant antique furnishings that complement the hotel's architectural style. All bedrooms and suites offer oversize flat-screen TVs and free broadband among their many facilities. The elegant Leven Restaurant is a traditional setting for fine dining; there's also the Drawing Room for lighter food options. Weather permitting, alfresco eating is available on the terrace, and afternoon tea is always popular. Conference and banqueting facilities are available.

Rooms 37 (4 fmly) **S** £90-£137; **D** £115-£178 (incl. bkfst) **Facilities** STV FTV Jogging track Clay pigeon shooting Xmas Wi-fi **Conf** Class 75 Board 60 Thtr 120 Del from £140 to £161* **Services** Lift **Parking** 88 **Notes** LB Civ Wed 90

CRAWLEY

See Gatwick Airport

CREWE
Cheshire — Map 15 SJ75

Crewe Hall

★★★★ 77% HOTEL

☎ 01270 253333 01270 253322
Weston Rd CW1 6UZ
e-mail: crewehall@qhotels.co.uk
web: www.qhotels.co.uk
dir: M6 junct 16 follow A500 to Crewe. Last exit at rdbt onto A5020. 1st exit next rdbt to Crewe. Crewe Hall 150yds on right

Standing in 500 acres of mature grounds, this historic hall dates back to the 17th century. It retains an elaborate interior with Victorian-style architecture. Bedrooms are spacious, well equipped and comfortable with traditionally styled rooms in the main hall and modern suites in the west wing. Guests have a choice of formal dining in the elegant Ranulph restaurant (2 AA Rosettes) or the more relaxed atmosphere of the modern Brasserie (1 AA rosette). The health and beauty spa ensure that it is a popular choice with both corporate and leisure guests.

Rooms 117 (91 annexe) (5 fmly) (35 GF) **S** £75-£299; **D** £85-£309 (incl. bkfst)* **Facilities** Spa STV Gym Enclosed events field Wi-fi **Conf** Class 172 Board 96 Thtr 364 Del from £130 to £190* **Services** Lift **Parking** 500 **Notes** LB Civ Wed 180

Hunters Lodge

★★★ 78% HOTEL

☎ 01270 539100 01270 500553
Sydney Rd, Sydney CW1 5LU
e-mail: info@hunterslodge.co.uk
web: www.hunterslodge.co.uk
dir: M6 junct 16. 1m from Crewe station, off A534

Dating back to the 18th century, the hotel has been extended and modernised. Accommodation, mainly located in adjacent well-equipped bedroom wings, includes family and four-poster rooms. Imaginative dishes are served in the spacious restaurant, and the popular bar also offers a choice of tempting meals. Service throughout is friendly and efficient.

Rooms 57 (4 fmly) (31 GF) (2 smoking) **S** £52.50-£106; **D** £77-£160 (incl. bkfst)* **Facilities** STV FTV Gym Wi-fi **Conf** Class 100 Board 80 Thtr 160 Del from £125.30 to £146.15* **Parking** 240 **Notes** RS Sun Civ Wed 130

The Crewe Arms Hotel

★★★ 71% HOTEL

☎ 01270 213204 01270 588615
Nantwich Rd CW2 6DN
e-mail: reservations@crewearmshotel.com
web: www.crewearmshotel.com
dir: M6 junct 6 towards Crewe. At 1st rdbt take 3rd exit, at 2nd rdbt 1st exit. Hotel at end, opposite rail station

Close to Crewe station this popular, busy commercial hotel offers attractive, well-equipped accommodation. Meals are served in the comfortable Carriages lounge bar and the more formal Sophia's Restaurant. There is also a range of conference and meeting rooms.

Rooms 61 (3 fmly) (1 GF) (12 smoking) **Facilities** Wi-fi **Conf** Class 40 Board 40 Thtr 90 Del from £90 to £145 **Parking** 140 **Notes** Civ Wed 90

Premier Inn Crewe Central

BUDGET HOTEL

☎ 0871 527 8276 0871 527 8277
Weston Rd CW1 6FX
dir: M6 junct 16, A500, at rdbt 3rd exit onto A5020 (Old Park Rd). At next rdbt 2nd exit into Western Rd, at next rdbt 3rd exit, hotel on left

High quality, budget accommodation ideal for both families and business travellers. Spacious, en suite bedrooms feature tea and coffee making facilities, and Freeview TV in most hotels. Internet access and Wi-fi are available for a small fee. The adjacent family restaurant features a wide and varied menu. See also the Hotel Groups pages.

Rooms 20 **D** £53-£58*

Premier Inn Crewe West

BUDGET HOTEL

☎ 0871 527 8278 0871 527 8279
Coppenhall Ln, Woolstanwood CW2 8SD
dir: At junct of A530 & A532, 9m from M6 junct 16 N'bound

Rooms 42 **D** £53-£58*

CRICK
Northamptonshire — Map 11 SP57

Holiday Inn Rugby/ Northampton

★★★ 72% HOTEL

☎ 0871 942 9059 & 01788 824800
01788 823 8955
M1, Jct 18 NN6 7XR
e-mail: rugbyhi@ihg.com
web: www.holidayinn.co.uk
dir: 0.5m from M1 junct 18

Situated in pleasant surroundings, located just off the M1, this modern hotel offers well-equipped and comfortable bedrooms. Public areas include the popular Traders restaurant and a comfortable lounge where an all-day menu is available. The Spirit Health Club provides indoor swimming and a good fitness facility.

Rooms 90 (19 fmly) (42 GF) (12 smoking) **Facilities** STV Gym New Year Wi-fi **Conf** Class 90 Board 64 Thtr 170 **Services** Lift Air con **Parking** 250 **Notes** Civ Wed

Ibis Rugby

BUDGET HOTEL

☎ 01788 824331 01788 824332
Parklands NN6 7EX
e-mail: H3588@accor.com
web: www.ibishotel.com
dir: M1 junct 18, follow Daventry/Rugby A5 signs. At rdbt 3rd exit signed DIRFT East. Hotel on right

Modern, budget hotel offering comfortable accommodation in bright and practical bedrooms. Breakfast is self-service and dinner is available in the restaurant. See also the Hotel Groups pages.

Rooms 111 (47 fmly) (12 GF) **Conf** Class 25 Board 25 Thtr 30

C

CRICKLADE
Wiltshire
Map 5 SU09

Cricklade House

★★★ 78% HOTEL

☎ 01793 750751 📠 01793 751767
Common Hill SN6 6HA
e-mail: reception@crickladehotel.co.uk
dir: Off A419 onto B4040. Turn left at clock tower. Right at rdbt. Hotel 0.5m up hill on left

A haven of peace and tranquillity with spectacular views, this hotel is set in over 30 acres of beautiful countryside. Bedrooms vary in size and style; there are main building rooms and courtyard rooms - all offer high levels of comfort and quality. Public areas include an elegant lounge, dining room and a Victorian-style conservatory that runs the full length of the building. The extensive leisure facilities include a 9-hole golf course, an indoor pool and a gym.

Rooms 46 (21 annexe) (2 fmly) (5 GF) **S** £57.50-£75; **D** £57.50-£95* **Facilities** STV FTV 9 Gym Aromatherapy Beautician Xmas New Year Wi-fi **Conf** Class 60 Board 30 Thtr 80 **Parking** 100 **Notes** LB Civ Wed 120

See advert on opposite page

CROMER
Norfolk
Map 13 TG24

Sea Marge Hotel

★★★ 87% HOTEL

☎ 01263 579579 📠 01263 579524
16 High St, Overstrand NR27 0AB
e-mail: info@mackenziehotels.com
dir: A140 from Norwich then A149 to Cromer, B1159 to Overstrand. Hotel in village centre

An elegant Grade II listed Edwardian mansion perched on the clifftop amidst pretty landscaped gardens which lead down to the beach. Bedrooms are tastefully decorated and thoughtfully equipped; many have superb sea views. Public rooms offer a wide choice of areas in which to relax, including Frazer's restaurant and a smart lounge bar.

Rooms 25 (6 annexe) (6 fmly) (2 GF) **Facilities** Xmas New Year Wi-fi **Conf** Class 55 Board 30 Thtr 70 **Services** Lift **Parking** 50

The Cliftonville

★★★ 75% HOTEL

☎ 01263 512543 📠 01263 515700
Seafront NR27 9AS
e-mail: reservations@cliftonvillehotel.co.uk
web: www.cliftonvillehotel.co.uk
dir: From A149 (coast road), 500yds from town centre, N'bound on clifftop by sunken gardens

An imposing Edwardian hotel situated on the main coast road with stunning views of the sea. Public rooms feature a magnificent staircase, minstrels' gallery, coffee shop, lounge bar, a further residents' lounge, Boltons Bistro and an additional restaurant. The pleasantly decorated bedrooms are generally quite spacious and have lovely sea views.

Rooms 30 (5 fmly) **S** £62-£75; **D** £124-£150 (incl. bkfst)* **Facilities** Xmas New Year Wi-fi **Conf** Class 100 Board 60 Thtr 150 **Services** Lift **Parking** 21

Hotel de Paris

Leisureplex

★★ 72% HOTEL

☎ 01263 513141 📠 01263 515217
High St NR27 9HG
e-mail: deparis.cromer@alfatravel.co.uk
dir: Enter Cromer on A140 (Norwich road). Left at lights onto Mount St. At 2nd lights right into Prince of Wales Rd. 2nd right into New St leading into High St

An imposing, traditional-style resort hotel, situated in a prominent position overlooking the pier and beach. The bedrooms are pleasantly decorated and equipped with a good range of useful extras; many rooms have lovely sea views. The spacious public areas include a large lounge bar, restaurant, games room and a further lounge.

Rooms 63 (8 fmly) **S** £39-£55; **D** £31-£47 (incl. bkfst) **Facilities** FTV Games room Xmas New Year **Services** Lift **Parking** 14 **Notes** LB Closed Jan-Feb RS Mar, Nov & Dec

Williams Restaurant

RESTAURANT WITH ROOMS

☎ 01263 519619
2 Brook St NR27 9EY
e-mail: eat@williams-restaurant.co.uk

A lovely restored Victorian property situated just a stone's throw from the beach and pier. The bedroom is situated above the restaurant; it has been appointed with stylish fixtures and fittings, and provides high levels of quality and comfort. Breakfast and dinner are served at individual tables in the contemporary restaurant.

Rooms 1

CROOKLANDS
Cumbria
Map 18 SD58

Crooklands

★★★ 78% HOTEL

☎ 015395 67432 📠 015395 67525
LA7 7NW
e-mail: reception@crooklands.com
web: www.crooklands.com
dir: M6 junct 36 onto A65. Left at rdbt. Hotel 1.5m on right past garage

Although only a stone's throw from the M6, this hotel enjoys a peaceful rural location. Housed in a converted 200-year-old farmhouse, the restaurant retains many original features such as the beams and stone walls. Bedrooms are a mix of modern and traditional and vary in size. The hotel is a popular stop-over for both leisure and corporate guests travelling between England and Scotland.

Rooms 30 (3 fmly) (14 GF) **S** £70-£95; **D** £88-£130 (incl. bkfst) **Facilities** FTV New Year Wi-fi **Conf** Class 50 Board 40 Thtr 80 Del from £110 to £130 **Services** Lift **Parking** 80 **Notes** LB Closed 24-28 Dec

C

CROSTHWAITE Map 18 SD49
Cumbria

Damson Dene

★★★ 72% HOTEL

☎ 015395 68676 📠 015395 68227
LA8 8JE
e-mail: info@damsondene.co.uk
web: www.bestlakesbreaks.co.uk
dir: M6 junct 36, A590 signed Barrow-in-Furness, 5m right onto A5074. Hotel on right in 5m

A short drive from Lake Windermere, this hotel enjoys a tranquil and scenic setting. Bedrooms include a number with four-poster beds and jacuzzi baths. The spacious restaurant serves a daily-changing menu, with some of the produce coming from the hotel's own kitchen garden. Real fires warm the lounge in the cooler months, and leisure facilities are available.

Rooms 40 (3 annexe) (7 fmly) (9 GF) **S** £79-£99; **D** £118-£148 (incl. bkfst)* **Facilities** Spa Gym Beauty salon Xmas New Year Wi-fi **Conf** Class 60 Board 40 Thtr 140 Del from £105 to £145* **Parking** 45 **Notes** LB Civ Wed 120

CROYDON Map 6 TQ36
Greater London

Croydon Park Hotel

★★★★ 73% HOTEL

☎ 020 8680 9200 📠 020 8286 7676
7 Altyre Rd CR9 5AA
e-mail: info@croydonparkhotel.com
dir: 3 min walk to East Croydon Station

This hotel is located in the heart of the town centre, a 3-minute walk to East Croydon train station and with easy access to both Gatwick Airport and central London. Bedrooms vary in style, but all are comfortably appointed. The two dining options are Whistlers Bar with a menu available throughout the day, and Oscars Brasserie with a daily buffet and carte menu. Conference and leisure facilities are available.

Rooms 211 (36 fmly) (6 GF) (25 smoking) **Facilities** FTV supervised Gym Squash Sauna Solarium Xmas New Year Wi-fi **Conf** Class 100 Board 30 Thtr 220 Del from £119.50 to £145* **Services** Lift Air con **Parking** 91 **Notes** Civ Wed 220

Coulsdon Manor

★★★★ 70% HOTEL

☎ 020 8668 0414 📠 020 8668 3118
Coulsdon Court Rd, Coulsdon CR5 2LL
e-mail: reservations.coulsdon@ohiml.com
web: www.oxfordhotelsandinns.com
dir: M23/25 junct 7, A23 for 2.5m, B2030 for 1m, left onto Coulsdon Rd, then 0.5m to hotel

This delightful Victorian manor house is peacefully set amidst 140 acres of landscaped parkland, complete with its own professional 18-hole golf course. Bedrooms are spacious and comfortable, whilst public areas include a choice of lounges and an elegant restaurant serving carefully prepared, imaginative food.

Rooms 37 (4 fmly) **Facilities** STV FTV 18 Putt green Gym Squash Aerobic studio Steam room Sauna Xmas New Year Wi-fi **Conf** Class 90 Board 70 Thtr 180 **Services** Lift **Parking** 200 **Notes** Civ Wed 60

Selsdon Park Hotel & Golf Club

principal hayley

★★★★ 70% HOTEL

☎ 020 8657 8811 📠 020 8651 6171
Addington Rd, Sanderstead CR2 8YA
dir: 3m SE of Croydon, off A2022

Surrounded by 200 acres of mature parkland with it's own 18-hole golf course, this imposing Jacobean mansion is less than 20 minutes from central London. The hotel's impressive range of conference rooms along with the spectacular views of the North Downs countryside, make this a popular venue for both weddings and meetings. The leisure facilities are impressive.

Rooms 199 (19 fmly) (33 GF) **Facilities** Spa STV supervised supervised 18 Putt green Gym Squash Xmas Wi-fi **Conf** Class 250 Board 100 Thtr 350 Del from £139 to £199* **Services** Lift **Parking** 300 **Notes** Civ Wed 350

South Park Hotel

THE INDEPENDENTS HOTEL ASSOCIATION

★★★ 73% HOTEL

☎ 020 8688 5644 📠 020 8760 0861
3-5 South Park Hill Rd, South Croydon CR2 7DY
e-mail: reception@southparkhotel.co.uk
web: www.southparkhotel.co.uk
dir: Follow A235 to town centre. At Coombe Rd lights turn right (A212) towards Addington, 0.5m to rdbt take 3rd exit into South Park Hill Rd, hotel on left

This intimate hotel has easy access to rail and road networks and off-street parking is available. Attractively decorated bedrooms vary in size and offer a good range of in-room facilities. Public areas consist of a bar and lounge with large sofas and an informal dining area where meals are served.

Rooms 30 (2 fmly) (9 GF) **Facilities** FTV Wi-fi **Conf** Class 50 Board 30 Thtr 60 **Parking** 15 **Notes**

Holiday Inn Express London-Croydon

BUDGET HOTEL

☎ 0208 2531200 📠 0208 2531201
1 Priddys Yard, Off Frith Rd CR0 1TS
e-mail: admin@exhicroydon.com
web: www.hiexpress.com/london-croydon
dir: A235 into Lower Coombe St, at rdbt take 1st exit, at next rdbt 2nd exit onto dual carriageway, right to Centrale Shopping Centre, under car park, follow to right, 1st left

A modern hotel ideal for families and business travellers. Fresh and uncomplicated, the spacious rooms include Sky TV, power shower and tea and coffee-making facilities. Continental buffet breakfast is included in the room rate; other meals may be taken at the nearby family pub or restaurant. See also the Hotel Groups pages.

Rooms 156 (62 fmly) (16 smoking) **Conf** Class 30 Board 30 Thtr 60

Premier Inn Croydon South

BUDGET HOTEL

☎ 0871 527 8280 🖷 0871 527 8281
104 Coombe Rd CR0 5RB
dir: M25 junct 7, A23 to Purley, A235 to Croydon. Pass Tree House pub on left. Right at lights onto A212

High quality, budget accommodation ideal for both families and business travellers. Spacious, en suite bedrooms feature tea and coffee making facilities, and Freeview TV in most hotels. Internet access and Wi-fi are available for a small fee. The adjacent family restaurant features a wide and varied menu. See also the Hotel Groups pages.

Rooms 39 **D** £65-£76*

Premier Inn Croydon West

BUDGET HOTEL

☎ 0871 527 8282 🖷 0871 527 8283
The Colonnades Leisure Park, 619 Purley Way CR0 4RQ
dir: From N: M1, M25, A23 towards Croydon. From S: M25 junct 7, A23 towards Purley Way, 8m, hotel close to junct with Waddon Way

Rooms 84 **D** £65-£76*

CUCKFIELD Map 6 TQ32
West Sussex

INSPECTORS' CHOICE

Ockenden Manor

★★★  HOTEL

☎ 01444 416111 🖷 01444 415549
Ockenden Ln RH17 5LD
e-mail: reservations@ockenden-manor.com
web: www.hshotels.co.uk
dir: A23 towards Brighton. 4.5m left onto B2115 towards Haywards Heath. Cuckfield 3m. Ockenden Lane off High St. Hotel at end

This charming 16th-century property enjoys fine views of the South Downs. The individually designed bedrooms and suites offer high standards of accommodation, some with unique historic features. Public rooms, retaining much original character, include an elegant sitting room with all the elements for a relaxing afternoon in front of the fire. Imaginative, noteworthy cuisine is the highlight to any stay. The beautiful rooms and lovely garden make Ockenden a popular wedding venue. The hotel has a new spa, situated in a walled garden, that offers a pool, hot tub, spa bath, rain shower, floatation room, gym, sauna, steam room plus health and beauty treatments.

Rooms 28 (6 annexe) (4 fmly) (4 GF) **S** £113-£210; **D** £190-£395 (incl. bkfst)* **Facilities** Spa STV FTV Gym Xmas New Year Wi-fi **Conf** Class 20 Board 26 Thtr 50 Del from £215 to £250* **Parking** 98 **Notes** LB Civ Wed 150

CULLOMPTON Map 3 ST00
Devon

Padbrook Park

★★★ 77% HOTEL

☎ 01884 836100 🖷 01884 836101
EX15 1RU
e-mail: info@padbrookpark.co.uk
dir: 1m from M5 junct 28, follow brown signs

This purpose-built hotel is part of a golf and leisure complex located in the Culm Valley, just one mile from the M5. Set in 100 acres of parkland with an 18-hole golf course, Padbrook Park has a friendly, relaxed atmosphere and a contemporary feel. A variety of room types is available, including family, inter-connecting, superior and deluxe rooms.

Rooms 40 (4 fmly) (11 GF) **S** £45-£70; **D** £60-£110* **Facilities** STV FTV 18 Putt green Fishing Gym 3 rink bowling centre Crazy golf Xmas New Year Wi-fi **Conf** Class 150 Board 50 Thtr 200 Del from £85 to £120* **Services** Lift **Parking** 250 **Notes** LB Civ Wed 200

D

DARLINGTON Map 19 NZ21
Co Durham

Rockliffe Hall

★★★★★ 86% HOTEL

☎ 01325 729999 🖷 01325 720464
Rockliffe Park, Hurworth on Tees DL2 2DU
e-mail: enquiries@rockliffehall.com
dir: A1(M) junct 57, A66 (M), A66 towards Darlington, A167, through Hurworth-on-Tees. In Croft-on-Tees left into Hurworth Rd, follow signs

This impressive hotel enjoys a peaceful setting on a wonderfully restored 18th-century estate on the banks of the River Tees. Luxurious, spacious bedrooms, which are contemporary in style, are split between the original old hall, the new hall and Tiplady Lodge. Guests have a choice of eating options - the informal Waterhouse Bistro or the fine-dining experience in The Orangery which showcases the confident cooking of Kenny Atkinson. A state-of-the-art spa and championship golf course, with a first-class club house, complete the picture.

Rooms 61 (5 fmly) (17 GF) **S** £140-£425; **D** £165-£450 (incl. bkfst)* **Facilities** Spa STV FTV 18 Putt green Fishing Gym Xmas New Year Wi-fi **Conf** Class 190 Board 40 Thtr 250 Del from £175 to £195* **Services** Lift **Parking** 200 **Notes** LB Civ Wed 250

DARLINGTON ***continued***

Headlam Hall

★★★★ 75% HOTEL

☎ 01325 730238 01325 730790
Headlam, Gainford DL2 3HA
e-mail: admin@headlamhall.co.uk
web: www.headlamhall.co.uk
dir: 2m N of A67 between Piercebridge & Gainford

This impressive Jacobean hall lies in farmland north-east of Piercebridge and has its own 9-hole golf course. The main house retains many historical features, including flagstone floors and a pillared hall. Bedrooms are well proportioned and traditionally styled; a converted coach house contains the more modern rooms. There are extensive conference facilities, and the hotel is popular as a wedding venue. There is a stunning spa complex with a 14-metre pool, an outdoor hot spa, drench shower, sauna and steam room. There is also a gym with the latest cardio and resistance equipment, and five treatment rooms offering a range of therapies and beauty treatments.

Rooms 40 (22 annexe) (4 fmly) (10 GF) **S** £95-£130; **D** £120-£195 (incl. bkfst)* **Facilities** Spa STV FTV 9 Putt green Fishing Gym New Year Wi-fi **Conf** Class 40 Board 40 Thtr 120 Del from £140 to £150* **Services** Lift **Parking** 80 **Notes** LB Closed 24-26 Dec Civ Wed 150

The Blackwell Grange Hotel

★★★ 79% HOTEL

☎ 0870 609 6121 & 01325 509955
01325 380899
Blackwell Grange DL3 8QH
e-mail: blackwell.grange@forestdale.com
web: www.blackwellgrangehotel.com
dir: On A167, 1.5m from central ring road

This beautiful 17th-century mansion is peacefully situated in nine acres of its own grounds yet is convenient for the motorway network. The pick of the bedrooms are in a courtyard building or the impressive feature rooms in the original house. The Havelock Restaurant offers a range of traditional and continental menus.

Rooms 108 (11 annexe) (3 fmly) (36 GF) **Facilities** FTV Gym Beauty room Xmas New Year Wi-fi **Conf** Class 110 Board 50 Thtr 250 **Services** Lift **Parking** 250 **Notes** LB Civ Wed 200

Best Western Walworth Castle Hotel

★★★ 77% HOTEL

☎ 01325 485470 01325 462257
Walworth DL2 2LY
e-mail: enquiries@walworthcastle.co.uk
web: www.walworthcastle.co.uk
dir: A1(M) junct 58 follow signs to Corbridge. Left at The Dog pub. Hotel on left after 2m

This 12th-century castle is privately owned and has been tastefully converted. Accommodation is offered in a range of styles, including an impressive suite and more compact rooms in an adjoining wing. Dinner can be taken in the fine dining Hansards Restaurant or the more relaxed Farmer's Bar. This is a popular venue for conferences and weddings.

Rooms 32 (14 annexe) (4 fmly) (8 GF) **S** £70-£95; **D** £110-£290 (incl. bkfst)* **Facilities** Spa FTV Beauty rooms Hair salon Xmas New Year Wi-fi **Conf** Class 60 Board 40 Thtr 120 Del from £105 to £145* **Parking** 100 **Notes** LB Civ Wed 100

Hall Garth Hotel, Golf and Country Club

★★★ 75% HOTEL

☎ 0844 855 9110 01325 310083
Coatham Mundeville DL1 3LU
dir: A1(M) junct 59, A167 towards Darlington. After 600yds left at top of hill, hotel on right

Peacefully situated in grounds that feature a golf course, this hotel is just a few minutes from the motorway network. The well-equipped bedrooms come in various styles - it's worth asking for one of the trendy, modern rooms. Public rooms include relaxing lounges, a fine-dining restaurant and a separate pub. The extensive leisure and conference facilities are an important focus here.

Rooms 52 (12 annexe) (2 fmly) (1 GF) **Facilities** Spa STV FTV supervised 9 Putt green Gym Steam room Beauty Salon Xmas New Year Wi-fi **Conf** Class 160 Board 80 Thtr 250 **Parking** 150 **Notes** Civ Wed 170

Premier Inn Darlington

BUDGET HOTEL

☎ 0871 527 8286 0871 527 8287
Morton Park Way, Morton Park DL1 4PJ
dir: A1(M) junct 57, A66(M), A66 towards Teeside. At 3rd rdbt left onto B6280. Hotel on right. From N: A1(M) junct 57 onto A167, A1150, A66 towards Darlington, right onto B6280. Hotel on right

High quality, budget accommodation ideal for both families and business travellers. Spacious, en suite bedrooms feature tea and coffee making facilities, and Freeview TV in most hotels. Internet access and Wi-fi are available for a small fee. The adjacent family restaurant features a wide and varied menu. See also the Hotel Groups pages.

Rooms 58 **D** £54-£60*

Raby Hunt Inn and Restaurant with Rooms

RESTAURANT WITH ROOMS

☎ 01325 374237
Summerhouse DL2 3UD
e-mail: enquiries@rabyhuntrestaurant.co.uk
web: www.rabyhuntrestaurant.co.uk
dir: A1(M) junct 58 onto A68 N, onto B6275 then B6279

This Grade II listed building, situated in the quiet village of Summerhouse, is a family-owned restaurant with rooms providing well-equipped, stylish and comfortable accommodation. Both bedrooms are en suite and have many thoughtful extras. The comfortable and contemporary restaurant serves modern British and European dishes with flair and creativity.

Rooms 2

DARTFORD Map 6 TQ57
Kent

Rowhill Grange Hotel & Utopia Spa

★★★★ 81% HOTEL

☎ 01322 615136 📠 01322 615137
DA2 7QH
e-mail: admin@rowhillgrange.co.uk
web: www.rowhillgrange.co.uk
dir: M25 junct 3 take B2173 to Swanley, then B258 to Hextable

Set in nine acres of mature woodland, this hotel enjoys a tranquil setting, yet is accessible to road networks. Bedrooms are stylishly and individually decorated; many have four-poster or sleigh beds. The elegant lounge is popular for afternoon teas, and the leisure and conference facilities are impressive. There is a smart, conservatory restaurant and also a more informal brasserie.

Rooms 38 (8 annexe) (4 fmly) (3 GF) **Facilities** Spa STV FTV Gym Beauty treatment Hair salon Aerobic studio Japanese Therapy pool Xmas New Year Wi-fi **Conf** Class 64 Board 34 Thtr 160 **Services** Lift **Parking** 150 **Notes** Civ Wed 150

Campanile Dartford

Campanile HOTEL RESTAURANT

BUDGET HOTEL

☎ 01322 278925 📠 01322 278948
1 Clipper Boulevard West, Crossways Business Park DA2 6QN
e-mail: dartford@campanile.com
dir: Follow signs for Ferry Terminal from Dartford Bridge

This modern building offers accommodation in smart, well-equipped bedrooms, all with en suite bathrooms. Refreshments may be taken at the informal bistro. See also the Hotel Groups pages.

Rooms 125 (14 fmly) **Conf** Class 30 Board 30 Thtr 40

Express by Holiday Inn Dartford Bridge

BUDGET HOTEL

☎ 01322 290333 📠 01322 290444
Dartford Bridge, University Way DA1 5PA
e-mail: gm.dartford@expressholidayinn.co.uk
web: www.hiexpress.com/dartfordbridge
dir: A206 to Erith. Hotel off University Way via signed slip road

A modern hotel ideal for families and business travellers. Fresh and uncomplicated, the spacious rooms include Sky TV, power shower and tea and coffee-making facilities. Continental buffet breakfast is included in the room rate; other meals may be taken at the nearby family pub or restaurant. See also the Hotel Groups pages.

Rooms 126 (34 fmly) **Conf** Board 25 Thtr 35

DARTMOUTH Map 3 SX85
Devon

The Dart Marina

★★★★ 80% HOTEL

☎ 01803 832580 & 837120 📠 01803 835040
Sandquay Rd TQ6 9PH
e-mail: reservations@dartmarina.com
web: www.dartmarina.com
dir: A3122 from Totnes to Dartmouth. Follow road which becomes College Way, before Higher Ferry. Hotel sharp left in Sandquay Rd

Boasting a stunning riverside location with its own marina, this is a special place to stay. Bedrooms vary in style, and all have wonderful views; some have private balconies to sit and soak up the atmosphere. The stylish public areas take full advantage of the waterside setting with opportunities to dine alfresco. In addition to the Wildfire Bar & Bistro, the River Restaurant is the venue for accomplished cooking.

Rooms 49 (4 annexe) (4 fmly) (4 GF) **S** £95-£155; **D** £140-£200 (incl. bkfst)* **Facilities** Spa Gym Canoeing Sailing Xmas New Year Wi-fi **Services** Lift **Parking** 50 **Notes** LB Civ Wed 40

Royal Castle

★★★ 81% HOTEL

☎ 01803 833033 📠 01803 835445
11 The Quay TQ6 9PS
e-mail: enquiry@royalcastle.co.uk
web: www.royalcastle.co.uk
dir: In centre of town, overlooking Inner Harbour

At the edge of the harbour, this imposing 17th-century former coaching inn is filled with charm and character. Bedrooms are well equipped and comfortable; many have harbour views. A choice of quiet seating areas is offered in addition to both the traditional and contemporary bars. A variety of eating options is available, including the main restaurant which has lovely views.

Rooms 25 (3 fmly) **S** £95-£110; **D** £140-£210 (incl. bkfst)* **Facilities** FTV Xmas New Year Wi-fi **Conf** Class 30 Board 20 Thtr 50 **Parking** 15 **Notes** Civ Wed 80

Stoke Lodge

★★★ 73% HOTEL

☎ 01803 770523 📠 01803 770851
Stoke Fleming TQ6 0RA
e-mail: mail@stokelodge.co.uk
web: www.stokelodge.co.uk
dir: 2m S A379

This family-run hotel continues to attract returning guests and is set in three acres of gardens and grounds with lovely views across to the sea. A range of leisure facilities is offered including both indoor and outdoor pools, along with a choice of comfortable lounges. Bedrooms are pleasantly appointed. The restaurant offers a choice of menus and an impressive wine list.

Rooms 25 (5 fmly) (7 GF) **S** £71-£75.50; **D** £99-£129 (incl. bkfst)* **Facilities** FTV Putt green Table tennis Pool & Snooker tables Sauna Xmas New Year Wi-fi **Conf** Class 60 Board 30 Thtr 80 Del from £88 to £130* **Parking** 50 **Notes** LB

D

D

DAVENTRY Map 11 SP56
Northamptonshire

INSPECTORS' CHOICE

Fawsley Hall

★★★★ HOTEL

☎ 01327 892000 ⎙ 01327 892001
Fawsley NN11 3BA
e-mail: reservations@fawsleyhall.com
web: www.fawsleyhall.com
dir: A361 S of Daventry, between Badby & Charwelton, hotel signed (single track lane)

Dating back to the 15th century, this delightful hotel is peacefully located in beautiful gardens designed by 'Capability' Brown. Spacious, individually designed bedrooms and stylish public areas are beautifully furnished with antique and period pieces. Afternoon tea is served in the impressive Great Hall. The AA Rosette award for the cuisine in Equilibrium is temporarily suspended due to a change of chef. An award will be in place once our inspectors have assessed the food cooked by the new kitchen brigade.

Rooms 58 (14 annexe) (2 GF) **S** fr £185; **D** £185-£495 (incl. bkfst)* **Facilities** Spa STV Gym Health & beauty treatment rooms Fitness studio 29-seat cinema Xmas New Year Wi-fi **Conf** Class 64 Board 40 Thtr 120 **Parking** 140 **Notes** LB Civ Wed 120

Barceló Daventry Hotel

Barceló

★★★★ 71% HOTEL

☎ 01327 307000 ⎙ 01327 706313
Sedgemoor Way NN11 0SG
e-mail: daventry@barcelo-hotels.co.uk
web: www.barcelo-hotels.co.uk
dir: M1 junct 16/A45 to Daventry, at 1st rdbt turn right to Kilsby/M1(N). Hotel on right in 1m

This modern, striking hotel overlooking Drayton Water boasts spacious public areas that include a good range of banqueting, meeting and leisure facilities. It is a popular venue for conferences. Bedrooms are suitable for both business and leisure guests.

Rooms 155 (17 fmly) **Facilities** STV supervised Gym Steam room Health & beauty salon Xmas New Year Wi-fi **Conf** Class 200 Board 100 Thtr 600 **Services** Lift **Parking** 350 **Notes** Civ Wed 280

Premier Inn Daventry

BUDGET HOTEL

☎ 0871 527 8288 ⎙ 0871 527 8289
High St, Weedon NN7 4PX
dir: M1 junct 16, A45 towards Daventry. Through Upper Heyford & Flore. Hotel on left before Weedon & A5 junct

High quality, budget accommodation ideal for both families and business travellers. Spacious, en suite bedrooms feature tea and coffee making facilities, and Freeview TV in most hotels. Internet access and Wi-fi are available for a small fee. The adjacent family restaurant features a wide and varied menu. See also the Hotel Groups pages.

Rooms 47 **D** £51-£64*

DAWLISH Map 3 SX97
Devon

Langstone Cliff

THE INDEPENDENTS HOTEL ASSOCIATION

★★★ 78% HOTEL

☎ 01626 868000 ⎙ 01626 868006
Dawlish Warren EX7 0NA
e-mail: reception@langstone-hotel.co.uk
web: www.langstone-hotel.co.uk
dir: 1.5m NE off A379 (Exeter road) to Dawlish Warren

A family owned and run hotel, the Langstone Cliff offers a range of leisure, conference and function facilities. Bedrooms, many with sea views and balconies, are spacious, comfortable and well equipped. There are a number of attractive lounges and a well-stocked bar. Dinner is served, often carvery style, in the restaurant.

Rooms 66 (4 annexe) (52 fmly) (10 GF) **S** £81-£95; **D** £148-£212 (incl. bkfst)* **Facilities** STV FTV Gym Table tennis Golf practice area Hair & beauty salon Therapy room Ballroom Xmas New Year Wi-fi Child facilities **Conf** Class 200 Board 80 Thtr 400 **Services** Lift **Parking** 200 **Notes** LB Civ Wed 400

DEAL Map 7 TR35
Kent

Dunkerleys Hotel & Restaurant

★★★ 80% HOTEL

☎ 01304 375016 ⎙ 01304 380187
19 Beach St CT14 7AH
e-mail: info@dunkerleys.co.uk
web: www.dunkerleys.co.uk
dir: From M20 or M2 follow signs for A258 Deal. Hotel close to Pier

This hotel is centrally located and on the seafront. Bedrooms are furnished to a high standard with a good range of amenities. The restaurant and bar offer a comfortable and attractive environment in which to relax and to enjoy the cuisine that makes the best use of local ingredients. Service throughout is friendly and attentive.

Rooms 16 (2 fmly) **S** £80-£110; **D** £120-£150 (incl. bkfst) **Facilities** FTV Xmas New Year Wi-fi **Notes** LB RS Sun eve & Mon

DEDDINGTON Map 11 SP43
Oxfordshire

Deddington Arms

★★★ 77% HOTEL

☎ 01869 338364 ⎙ 01869 337010
Horsefair OX15 0SH
e-mail: deddarms@oxfordshire-hotels.co.uk
web: www.oxfordshire-hotels.co.uk
dir: From S: M40 junct 10/A43. 1st rdbt left to Aynho (B4100) & left to Deddington (B4031). From N: M40 junct 11 to hospital & Adderbury on A4260, then to Deddington

This charming and friendly old inn is conveniently located off the market square. The well-equipped bedrooms are comfortably appointed and situated either in the main building or a purpose-built courtyard wing. The bar is full of character, and the delightful restaurant enjoys a well-deserved reputation locally.

Rooms 27 (4 fmly) (10 GF) (2 smoking) **S** £69-£109; **D** £69-£109 (incl. bkfst)* **Facilities** STV Xmas New Year Wi-fi **Conf** Class 20 Board 25 Thtr 40 Del from £120 to £150* **Parking** 36 **Notes** LB

DEDHAM
Essex Map 13 TM03

INSPECTORS' CHOICE

Maison Talbooth

★★★ ◎◎ COUNTRY HOUSE HOTEL

☎ 01206 322367 📠 01206 322752
Stratford Rd CO7 6HN
e-mail: maison@milsomhotels.co.uk
dir: A12 towards Ipswich, 1st turn signed Dedham, follow to left bend, turn right. Hotel 1m on right

Warm hospitality and quality service are to be expected at this Victorian country-house hotel, which is situated in a peaceful rural location amidst pretty landscaped grounds overlooking the Stour River Valley. Public areas include a comfortable drawing room where guests may take afternoon tea or snacks. Residents are chauffeured to the popular Le Talbooth Restaurant just a mile away for dinner. The spacious bedrooms are individually decorated and tastefully furnished with lovely co-ordinated fabrics and many thoughtful touches.

Rooms 12 (1 fmly) (5 GF) **S** £165-£290; **D** £200-£405 (incl. bkfst)* **Facilities** Spa STV Xmas Wi-fi **Conf** Class 20 Board 16 Thtr 30 **Parking** 40 **Notes** LB Civ Wed 50

milsoms

★★★ 81% ◎ SMALL HOTEL

☎ 01206 322795 📠 01206 323689
Stratford Rd, Dedham CO7 6HW
e-mail: milsoms@milsomhotels.com
web: www.milsomhotels.com
dir: 6m N of Colchester off A12, follow Stratford St Mary/Dedham signs. Turn right over A12, hotel on left

Situated in the Dedham Vale, an Area of Outstanding Natural Beauty, this is the perfect base to explore the countryside on the Essex/Suffolk border. This establishment is styled along the lines of a contemporary 'gastro bar' combining good food served in an informal atmosphere, with stylish and well-appointed accommodation.

Rooms 15 (3 fmly) (4 GF) **S** £97-£133; **D** £117-£184* **Facilities** STV Use of spa at sister hotel nearby ♫ Xmas Wi-fi **Conf** Board 24 Del from £155* **Parking** 90 **Notes** LB

DELPH
Greater Manchester Map 16 SD90

The Saddleworth Hotel

★★★★ 83% ◎◎◎ COUNTRY HOUSE HOTEL

☎ 01457 871888 📠 01457 871889
Huddersfield Rd OL3 5LX
e-mail: enquiries@thesaddleworthhotel.co.uk
web: www.thesaddleworthhotel.co.uk
dir: M62 junct 21, A640 towards Huddersfield. At Junction Inn take A6052 towards Delph; at White Lion left onto unclassified road; in 0.5m left on A62 towards Huddersfield. Hotel 0.5m on right

Situated in nine acres of landscaped gardens and woodlands in the Castleshaw Valley, this lovingly restored 17th-century building, once a coaching station, has stunning views. The hotel offers comfort and opulence together with a team of staff who provide delightful customer care. Antique pieces have been acquired from far and wide, and no expense has been spared to provide guests with the latest up-to-date facilities. The restaurant, with black table linen and crystal glassware, offers an award-winning, fashionably understated, modern European menu.

Rooms 13 (5 annexe) (3 fmly) (1 GF) **Facilities** STV Xmas New Year Wi-fi **Conf** Class 40 Board 40 Thtr 70 **Parking** 142 **Notes** ⊗ Civ Wed 250

DERBY
Derbyshire Map 11 SK33

See also **Morley**

Hallmark Derby

★★★★ 79% HOTEL

☎ 01332 345894 📠 01332 293522
Midland Rd DE1 2SQ
e-mail: derby.reservations@hallmarkhotels.co.uk
web: www.hallmarkhotels.co.uk
dir: Directly opposite rail station

This early Victorian hotel situated opposite Derby Midland Station provides very comfortable accommodation. The executive rooms are ideal for business travellers as they are equipped with writing desks and high speed internet access. Public rooms include a comfortable lounge and a popular restaurant. Service is skilled, attentive and friendly. There is also a walled garden and private parking.

Rooms 100 **Facilities** ♫ Wi-fi **Conf** Class 50 Board 35 Thtr 150 **Services** Lift **Parking** 90 **Notes** ⊗ Closed 24-26 Dec & 1 Jan Civ Wed 150

Breadsall Priory, A Marriott Hotel & Country Club

Marriott HOTELS & RESORTS

★★★★ 75% ◎ COUNTRY HOUSE HOTEL

☎ 01332 832235 📠 01332 833509
Moor Rd DE7 6DL
web: www.marriottbreadsallpriory.co.uk

(For full entry see Breadsall)

Holiday Inn Derby Riverlights

★★★★ 73% HOTEL

☎ 01332 412644 & 412533 📠 01332 412645
Derby Riverlights, Mortledge DE1 2AY
e-mail: reservations@hiderby.co.uk
dir: M1 junct 25/A52 to Derby. Follow signs to City Centre/Westfield Shopping Centre. Hotel on Morledge on right by bus station

With a central location adjacent to the Westfield Shopping Centre, this new hotel is ideal for both business and leisure guests. The lobby area is a four storey atrium. The stylish bedrooms are well equipped, and there is air conditioning throughout. The contemporary restaurant, Stresa, offers Italian cooking in a relaxed environment; complimentary

continued

D

DERBY ***continued***

Wi-fi is available in the bar. Discounted rates for guests are offered at the Riverside car park.

Rooms 105 (11 smoking) **S** £59-£119; **D** £59-£119 **Facilities** FTV Gym Wi-fi **Conf** Class 60 Board 50 Thtr 130 Del from £95 to £145 **Services** Lift Air con **Notes** LB

Menzies Mickleover Court

MenziesHotels

★★★★ 73% HOTEL

☎ 01332 521234 📠 01332 521238
Etwall Rd, Mickleover DE3 0XX
e-mail: mickleovercourt@menzieshotels.co.uk
web: www.menzieshotels.co.uk
dir: A50 towards Derby, exit at junct 5. A516 towards Derby, take exit signed Mickleover

Located close to Derby, this modern hotel is well suited to both the conference and leisure markets. Bedrooms are spacious, air conditioned, well equipped and include some smart executive rooms and suites. The well presented leisure facilities are amongst the best in the region.

Rooms 99 (20 fmly) (5 smoking) **Facilities** STV Gym Beauty salon Steam room Xmas New Year Wi-fi **Conf** Class 80 Board 40 Thtr 225 **Services** Lift Air con **Parking** 270 **Notes** Civ Wed 150

Ramada Encore Derby

★★★ 73% HOTEL

☎ 0844 801 3680 📠 0844 8013681
Locomotive Way, Pride Park DE24 8PU
e-mail: admin@encorederby.co.uk
dir: M1 junct 22, A52 towards Derby. (Telephone for detailed directions)

This hotel offers stylish and comfortable accommodation. The Hub is a smart, modern, open-plan bar and restaurant with a choice of seating areas - it offers an extensive menu throughout the day. Secure on-site parking is available, and the hotel is within walking distance of Derby railway station.

Rooms 112 (16 fmly) **Facilities** STV Gym Sauna Wi-fi **Conf** Class 40 Board 20 Thtr 60 **Services** Lift Air con **Parking** 110 **Notes** ⊗

European Inn

★★★ 72% METRO HOTEL

☎ 01332 292000 📠 01332 293940
Midland Rd DE1 2SL
e-mail: enquiries@euro-derby.co.uk
web: www.euro-derby.co.uk
dir: City centre, 200yds from railway station

This is a contemporary hotel, offering quality accommodation plus a lounge bar, free Wi-fi and free parking. Situated just a 100 metres from the railway station and a not far from the city centre where there is an abundance of shops and restaurants.

Rooms 87 (18 fmly) **S** £60-£80; **D** £70-£95 (incl. bkfst)* **Facilities** FTV Wi-fi **Conf** Class 20 Board 30 Thtr 60 **Services** Lift **Parking** 90 **Notes** ⊗

Littleover Lodge

★★★ 69% HOTEL

☎ 01332 510161 📠 01332 514010
222 Rykneld Rd, Littleover DE23 4AN
e-mail: enquiries@littleoverlodge.co.uk
web: www.littleoverlodge.co.uk
dir: A38 towards Derby approx 1m on left slip lane signed Littleover/Mickleover/Findon, take 2nd exit off island marked Littleover 0.25m on right

Situated in a rural location this friendly hotel offers modern bedrooms with direct access from the car park. Two styles of dining are available - an informal carvery operation which is very popular locally, and a more formal restaurant which is open for lunch and dinner each day. Service is excellent with the long serving staff being particularly friendly.

Rooms 16 (3 fmly) (6 GF) **Facilities** STV ♫ Xmas New Year Wi-fi **Parking** 75 **Notes** LB Civ Wed 100

See advert on this page

Holiday Inn Express Derby Pride Park

BUDGET HOTEL

☎ 01332 388000 📠 01332 388038
Wheelwright Way, Pride Park DE24 8HX
e-mail: info@expressderby.co.uk
web: www.expressderby.co.uk
dir: A52 towards Derby, after 7m follow Pride Park signs. Over 1st 3 rdbts. Right at 4th, left at next. Take 1st left, hotel on right

A modern hotel ideal for families and business travellers. Fresh and uncomplicated, the spacious rooms include Sky TV, power shower and tea and coffee-making facilities. Continental buffet breakfast is included in the room rate; other meals may be taken at the nearby family pub or restaurant. See also the Hotel Groups pages.

Rooms 103 (64 fmly) (25 GF) **Conf** Class 28 Thtr 20

Premier Inn Derby East

BUDGET HOTEL

☎ 0871 527 8292 📠 0871 527 8293
The Wyvern, Stanier Way DE21 6BF
dir: M1 junct 25, A52 towards Derby. After 6.5m exit for Wyvern/Pride Park. 1st exit at rdbt (A52 Nottingham), straight on at next rdbt. Hotel on left

High quality, budget accommodation ideal for both families and business travellers. Spacious, en suite bedrooms feature tea and coffee making facilities, and Freeview TV in most hotels. Internet access and Wi-fi are available for a small fee. The adjacent family restaurant features a wide and varied menu. See also the Hotel Groups pages.

Rooms 83 **D** £53-£57*

Premier Inn Derby North West

BUDGET HOTEL

☎ 0871 527 8294 📠 0871 527 8295
95 Ashbourne Rd, Mackworth DE22 4LZ
dir: Exit M1 junct 25 onto A52 towards Derby. At Pentagon Island straight ahead towards city centre. Follow A52/Ashbourne signs into Mackworth

Rooms 22 **D** £53-£62*

Premier Inn Derby South

BUDGET HOTEL

☎ 0871 527 8296 📠 0871 527 8297
Foresters Leisure Park, Osmaston Park Rd DE23 8AG
dir: M1 junct 24, A6 towards Derby. Left onto A5111 (ring road), hotel in 2m

Rooms 27 **D** £53-£62*

Premier Inn Derby West

BUDGET HOTEL

☎ 0871 527 8298 📠 0871 527 8299
Manor Park Way, Uttoxeter New Rd DE22 3HN
dir: M1 junct 25, A38 W towards Burton upon Trent (approx 15m). Left at island (city hospital), right at lights, 3rd exit at city hospital island

Rooms 66 **D** £53-£62*

DERBY SERVICE AREA (A50) Map 11 SK42
Derbyshire

Days Inn Donington - A50

BUDGET HOTEL

☎ 01332 799666 📠 01332 794166
Welcome Break Services, A50 Westbound DE72 2WA
e-mail: derby.hotel@welcomebreak.co.uk
web: www.welcomebreak.co.uk
dir: M1 junct 24/24a, onto A50 towards Stoke/Derby. Hotel between juncts 1 & 2

This modern building offers accommodation in smart, spacious and well-equipped bedrooms, suitable for families and business travellers, and all with en suite bathrooms. Continental breakfast is available and other refreshments may be taken at the nearby family restaurant. See also the Hotel Groups pages.

Rooms 47 (39 fmly) (17 GF) (8 smoking) **S** £39.95-£59.95; **D** £49.95-£69.95 **Conf** Class 20 Board 40 Thtr 40

DEVIZES Map 4 SU06
Wiltshire

Bear Hotel

★★★ 80% HOTEL

☎ 01380 722444 📠 01380 722450
Market Place SN10 1HS
e-mail: info@thebearhotel.net
dir: In town centre, follow Market Place signs

Tracing its history back over three centuries, this friendly establishment occupies a prominent position in a bustling town. Staff and management are keen to please and offer friendly and hospitable service. The bedrooms are pleasantly appointed and have flat-screen TVs and broadband connection. The hotel has two restaurants - Lambtons Restaurant for fine dining, and the Lawrence Room Bistro open for lunch; in summer there is a courtyard for alfresco dining. The hotel is a popular venue for conferences and weddings.

Rooms 25 (5 fmly) **S** £87.50-£92.50; **D** £117.50-£145 (incl. bkfst)* **Facilities** ♫ Wi-fi **Conf** Class 55 Board 48 Thtr 110 **Services** Lift **Parking** 14 **Notes** LB ⊗ Closed 25-26 Dec Civ Wed 100

DEWSBURY Map 16 SE22
West Yorkshire

Heath Cottage Hotel & Restaurant

★★★ 72% HOTEL

☎ 01924 465399 📠 01924 459405
Wakefield Rd WF12 8ET
e-mail: info@heathcottage.co.uk
dir: M1 junct 40/A638 for 2.5m towards Dewsbury. Hotel before lights, opposite Earlsheaton Cemetery

Standing in an acre of grounds, Heath Cottage is just two and a half miles from the M1. The service is friendly and professional. All the bedrooms are modern and well appointed, and some are in a converted stable building. The lounge bar and restaurant are air conditioned. Extensive parking is available.

Rooms 28 (6 annexe) (3 fmly) (3 GF) **Facilities** Wi-fi **Conf** Class 56 Board 32 Thtr 100 **Parking** 60 **Notes** RS 23-27 Dec Civ Wed 100

D

DIDCOT
Oxfordshire Map 5 SU59

Premier Inn Oxford South (Didcot)

BUDGET HOTEL

☎ 0871 527 8868 🖷 0871 527 8869
Milton Heights, Milton OX14 4TX
dir: On A4130. Just off A34 at Milton interchange, between Oxford & Newbury

High quality, budget accommodation ideal for both families and business travellers. Spacious, en suite bedrooms feature tea and coffee making facilities, and Freeview TV in most hotels. Internet access and Wi-fi are available for a small fee. The adjacent family restaurant features a wide and varied menu. See also the Hotel Groups pages.

Rooms 83 **D** £55-£67*

DISLEY
Cheshire Map 16 SJ98

Best Western Moorside Grange Hotel & Spa

★★★ 73% HOTEL

☎ 01663 764151 🖷 01663 762794
Mudhurst Ln, Higher Disley SK12 2AP
e-mail: sales@moorsidegrangehotel.com
web: www.moorsidegrangehotel.com
dir: Exit A6 at Rams Head in Disley, onto Buxton Old Rd for 1m, right onto Mudhurst Ln, hotel on left

Situated on the edge of the Peak District National Park, and with spectacular views of the moors above Higher Disley, this large complex is in an area considered a walkers' paradise. The hotel has excellent conference and function facilities, a well-equipped leisure centre and two tennis courts in the extensive grounds. Suites, and bedrooms with four-poster beds, are available.

Rooms 98 (3 fmly) **Facilities** Spa supervised Putt green Gym Squash Xmas New Year Wi-fi **Conf** Class 140 Board 100 Thtr 280 Del from £99 to £129* **Services** Lift **Parking** 250 **Notes** Civ Wed 280

DOGMERSFIELD
Hampshire Map 5 SU75

INSPECTORS' CHOICE

Four Seasons Hotel Hampshire

★★★★★ HOTEL

☎ 01252 853000 🖷 01252 853010
Dogmersfield Park, Chalky Ln RG27 8TD
e-mail: reservations.ham@fourseasons.com
dir: M3 junct 5 onto A287 Farnham. After 1.5m left for Dogmersfield, hotel 0.6m on left

This Georgian manor house, set in 500 acres of rolling grounds and English Heritage listed gardens, offers the upmost in luxury and relaxation, just an hour from London. The spacious and stylish bedrooms are particularly well appointed and offer up-to-date technology. Fitness and spa facilities include nearly every conceivable indoor and outdoor activity, in addition to luxurious pampering. An elegant restaurant, a healthy eating spa café and a trendy bar are popular venues.

Rooms 133 (23 GF) **Facilities** Spa STV Fishing Gym Clay pigeon shooting Bikes Canal boat Falconry Horse riding Jogging trails Xmas New Year Wi-fi **Conf** Class 110 Board 60 Thtr 260 **Services** Lift Air con **Parking** 165 **Notes** Civ Wed 200

DONCASTER
South Yorkshire Map 16 SE50

Best Western Premier Mount Pleasant Hotel

★★★★ 76% HOTEL

☎ 01302 868696 & 868219 🖷 01302 865130
Great North Rd DN11 0HW
e-mail: reception@mountpleasant.co.uk
web: www.mountpleasant.co.uk

(For full entry see Rossington)

Holiday Inn Doncaster A1(M) Jct 36

★★★ 79% HOTEL

☎ 0871 9429061 & 01302 799988
🖷 01302 310197
High Rd, Warmsworth DN4 9UX
e-mail: hidoncaster@qmh-hotels.com
web: www.holidayinn.co.uk
dir: 200mtrs W of A1(M) junct 36

This hotel is situated in the grounds of the 17th-century Warmsworth Hall; the hall as been splendidly restored and is now the conference centre. All the bedrooms are very well appointed, and include rooms designed for disabled guests. The informal and relaxing restaurant provides a wide range of dishes.

Rooms 102 (6 fmly) (22 GF) **S** £68-£99; **D** £68-£119* **Facilities** STV supervised Gym Beautician Steam room Sauna New Year Wi-fi **Conf** Class 250 Board 100 Thtr 250 Del from £110 to £145* **Services** Lift Air con **Parking** 250 **Notes** LB Civ Wed 250

Ramada Encore Doncaster Airport

★★★ 73% HOTEL

☎ 01302 718520 🖷 01302 772045
Robin Hood Airport DN9 3RH
e-mail: rm@encoredoncaster.co.uk
dir: M180 junct 1, follow signs for airport

Conveniently situated only a few minutes' walk from the main terminal at Robin Hood Airport, this purpose-built hotel is an good base for both the business and the leisure traveller. The air-conditioned bedrooms are spacious and bright, with power shower rooms. Public areas include the Hub Bar and Lounge. Secure parking is available on site.

Rooms 102 (36 fmly) (3 GF) (9 smoking) **S** £46-£106; **D** £46-£106* **Facilities** STV FTV Wi-fi **Conf** Class 20 Board 20 Thtr 40 Del from £89 to £109* **Services** Lift Air con **Parking** 144 **Notes** LB

Danum

★★★ 68% HOTEL

☎ 01302 342261 🖷 01302 329034
High St DN1 1DN
e-mail: info@danumhotel.com
dir: M18 junct 3, A6182 to Doncaster. Over rdbt, right at next. Right at 'give way' sign, left at mini rdbt, hotel ahead

Situated in the centre of the town, this Edwardian hotel offers well equipped conference rooms together with comfortable bedrooms. A contemporary lounge area provides modern dining and especially negotiated rates at a local leisure centre are offered.

Rooms 64 (5 fmly) **Facilities** STV FTV Special rates at Cannons Health Club ♫ Xmas New Year Wi-fi **Conf** Class 160 Board 100 Thtr 350 **Services** Lift **Parking** 36 **Notes** RS 26-30 Dec Civ Wed 250

Grand St Leger

★★★ 68% HOTEL

☎ 01302 364111 🖷 01302 329865
Bennetthorpe DN2 6AX
e-mail: sales@grandstleger.com
web: www.grandstleger.com
dir: Follow Doncaster Racecourse signs. At racecourse rdbt hotel on corner

This friendly hotel is located next to the racecourse and is only ten minutes' walk from the town centre. There is a cheerful bar-lounge and a pleasant restaurant offering an extensive choice of dishes. The bedrooms are comfortable and thoughtfully equipped, including Wi-fi access.

Rooms 20 **Facilities** FTV Wi-fi **Conf** Class 50 Board 30 Thtr 80 **Parking** 28 **Notes** ⊗ RS 25 Dec Civ Wed 65

Park Inn Doncaster

★★★ 67% HOTEL

☎ 01302 760710 🖷 01302 762380
Decoy Bank S DN4 5PD
e-mail: info.doncaster@rezidorparkinn.com
dir: Telephone for directions

Situated in a thriving business park close to the city centre, this hotel has easy access to the A1 (north and south) and M18. A modern contemporary hotel that offers comfortable, spacious accommodation with individual climate control and complimentary Wi-fi access. An air-conditioned meeting room is available. The on-site parking is a real plus.

Rooms 85 **Facilities** Wi-fi

Campanile Doncaster

BUDGET HOTEL

☎ 01302 370770 🖷 01302 370813
Doncaster Leisure Park, Bawtry Rd DN4 7PD
e-mail: doncaster@campanile.com
dir: Follow signs to Doncaster Leisure Centre, left at rdbt before Dome complex

This modern building offers accommodation in smart, well-equipped bedrooms, all with en suite bathrooms. Refreshments may be taken at the informal bistro. See also the Hotel Groups pages.

Rooms 50 (25 GF) **Conf** Class 15 Board 15 Thtr 25

Holiday Inn Express Doncaster

BUDGET HOTEL

☎ 01302 314100 🖷 01302 314168
Catesby Business Park, Bullrush Grove DN4 8SJ
e-mail: doncaster@holidayinnexpress.org.uk
web: www.hiexpress.com/doncaster
dir: M18 junct 3/A6182, left at 1st rdbt onto Woodfield Way, straight over next rdbt, hotel on left

A modern hotel ideal for families and business travellers. Fresh and uncomplicated, the spacious rooms include Sky TV, power shower and tea and coffee-making facilities. Continental buffet breakfast is included in the room rate; other meals may be taken at the nearby family pub or restaurant. See also the Hotel Groups pages.

Rooms 94 (63 fmly) (16 GF) (14 smoking) **Conf** Class 16 Board 20 Thtr 40

Premier Inn Doncaster Central

BUDGET HOTEL

☎ 0871 527 8302 🖷 0871 527 8303
High Fishergate DN1 1QZ
dir: Off A630 (Church Way)

High quality, budget accommodation ideal for both families and business travellers. Spacious, en suite bedrooms feature tea and coffee making facilities, and Freeview TV in most hotels. Internet access and Wi-fi are available for a small fee. The adjacent family restaurant features a wide and varied menu. See also the Hotel Groups pages.

Rooms 140 **D** £55-£62*

Premier Inn Doncaster Central East

BUDGET HOTEL

☎ 0871 527 8304 🖷 0871 527 8305
Doncaster Leisure Park, Herten Way DN4 7NW
dir: M18 junct 3, signed Doncaster racecourse. Left into Whiterose Way (B&Q on left). Straight on at rdbt into Wilmington Dr, right at next rdbt into Lakeside Boulevard. At next rdbt 2nd exit. Straight on at next rdbt, hotel ahead

Rooms 47 **D** £52-£59*

Premier Inn Doncaster (Lakeside)

BUDGET HOTEL

☎ 0871 527 8300 🖷 0871 527 8301
Wilmington Dr, Doncaster Carr DN4 5PJ
dir: M18 junct 3, A6182. Hotel near junct with access road

Rooms 42 **D** £52-£59*

D

DORCHESTER
Dorset **Map 4 SY69**

Best Western King's Arms

★★★ 75% HOTEL

☎ 01305 265353 🖷 01305 260269
30 High East St DT1 1HF
e-mail: info@kingsarmsdorchester.com
web: www.kingsarmsdorchester.com
dir: In town centre

Previous guests at this 18th-century hotel, set in the very heart of Dorchester, have included Queen Victoria and John Lennon. Built in 1720, many Georgian features still remain, including beams in the cosy bar. Guests can dine in the bar, or in the restaurant which offers a traditional English menu. Bedrooms have suitable facilities, including a number with four-posters.

Rooms 37 (2 fmly) (3 GF) **Facilities** FTV Wi-fi **Conf** Class 40 Board 30 Thtr 80 **Services** Lift **Parking** 37 **Notes** ⊗ Civ Wed 80

The Wessex Royale

★★★ 73% HOTEL

☎ 01305 262660 🖷 01305 251941
High West St DT1 1UP
e-mail: info@wessexroyalehotel.co.uk
web: www.wessexroyaledorchester.com
dir: From A35 follow town centre signs. Straight on, hotel at top of hill on left

This centrally situated Georgian townhouse dates from 1756 and successfully combines historic charm with modern comforts. The restaurant is a relaxed location for enjoying innovative food, and the hotel offers the benefit of a smart conservatory, ideal for functions. Limited courtyard parking is available.

Rooms 27 (2 annexe) (2 fmly) (2 GF) **Facilities** STV FTV Wi-fi **Conf** Class 40 Board 40 Thtr 80 **Parking** 11 **Notes** ⊗ Closed 23-30 Dec

D

DORCHESTER (ON THAMES) Map 5 SU59
Oxfordshire

White Hart Hotel

★★★ 77% HOTEL

☎ 01865 340074 01865 341082
High St OX10 7HN
e-mail: whitehart@oxfordshire-hotels.co.uk
web: www.oxfordshire-hotels.co.uk
dir: M40 junct 6, take B4009 through Watlington & Benson to A4074. Follow signs to Dorchester. Hotel on right

Period charm and character are plentiful throughout this 17th-century coaching inn, which is situated in the heart of a picturesque village. The spacious bedrooms are individually decorated and thoughtfully equipped. Public rooms include a cosy bar, a choice of lounges and an atmospheric restaurant, complete with vaulted timber ceiling.

Rooms 26 (4 annexe) (2 fmly) (9 GF) **Facilities** Xmas Wi-fi **Conf** Class 20 Board 18 Thtr 30 **Parking** 36

George Hotel

★★ 71% HOTEL

☎ 01865 340404 01865 341620
25 High St OX10 7HH
e-mail: thegeorgehotel@fsmail.net
dir: M40 junct 6 onto B4009 through Watlington & Benson. Take A4074 at BP petrol station, follow Dorchester signs. Hotel on left

Located on the quaint High Street, The George is directly opposite the stunning abbey. Once a coaching inn, this historic property provides comfortable accommodation in the main house and also in a separate building which was once the stable. The food is freshly prepared and can be enjoyed in the formal beamed restaurant, in the more relaxed Potboys Bar with open fires, or in the garden in warmer months. Complimentary Wi-fi is available throughout.

Rooms 17 (8 annexe) (1 fmly) (6 GF) **Conf** Class 20 Board 24 Thtr 40 **Parking** 50 **Notes**

DORKING Map 6 TQ14
Surrey

Mercure Burford Bridge

Mercure

★★★★ 76% HOTEL

☎ 01306 884561 01306 880386
Burford Bridge, Box Hill RH5 6BX
e-mail: h6635@accor.com
web: www.mercure.com
dir: M25 junct 9/A245 towards Dorking. Hotel within 5m on A24

Steeped in history, this hotel was reputedly where Lord Nelson and Lady Hamilton met for the last time, and it is said that the landscape around the hotel has inspired many poets. The hotel has a contemporary feel throughout. The grounds, running down to the River Mole, are extensive, and there are good transport links to major centres, including London. The elegant Emlyn Restaurant offers a modern award-winning menu.

Rooms 57 (22 fmly) (3 GF) **Facilities** Xmas New Year Wi-fi **Conf** Class 80 Board 60 Thtr 120 **Parking** 130 **Notes** Civ Wed 200

Gatton Manor Hotel & Golf Club

★★★ 80% HOTEL

☎ 01306 627555 01306 627713
Standon Ln RH5 5PQ
e-mail: info@gattonmanor.co.uk
web: www.gattonmanor.co.uk

(For full entry see Ockley)

Mercure White Horse

★★★ 68% HOTEL

☎ 01306 881138 01306 887241
High St RH4 1BE
e-mail: h6637@accor.com
web: www.mercure.com
dir: M25 junct 9, A24 S towards Dorking. Hotel in town centre

The hotel was first established as an inn in 1750, although parts of the building date back as far as the 15th century. Its town centre location and Dickensian charm have long made this a popular destination for travellers. There's beamed ceilings, open fires and four-poster beds; more contemporary rooms can be found in the garden wing.

Rooms 78 (41 annexe) (2 fmly) (5 GF) **S** £60-£90; **D** £65-£140 (incl. bkfst)* **Facilities** FTV Discount for local leisure centre Xmas Wi-fi **Conf** Class 30 Board 30 Thtr 50 Del from £130 to £150* **Parking** 73 **Notes** LB

DORRIDGE Map 10 SP17
West Midlands

The Forest

RESTAURANT WITH ROOMS

☎ 01564 772120 01564 732680
25 Station Rd B93 8JA
e-mail: info@forest-hotel.com
web: www.forest-hotel.com
dir: In town centre near station

This very individual and stylish restaurant with rooms is well placed for routes to Birmingham, Stratford-upon-Avon and Warwick. The twelve individually designed bedrooms are very well equipped with modern facilities, and imaginative food is served in the bars and intimate restaurant. A warm welcome is assured.

Rooms 12

DOVER Map 7 TR34
Kent

Wallett's Court Country House Hotel & Spa

★★★★ 74% HOTEL

☎ 01304 852424 & 0800 035 1628
01304 853430
West Cliffe, St Margarets-at-Cliffe CT15 6EW
e-mail: wc@wallettscourt.com
web: www.wallettscourt.com
dir: From Dover take A258 towards Deal. 1st right to St Margarets-at-Cliffe & West Cliffe, 1m on right opposite West Cliffe church

A lovely Jacobean manor situated in a peaceful location on the outskirts of town. Bedrooms in the original house are traditionally furnished whereas the rooms in the courtyard buildings are more modern; all are equipped to a high standard. Public rooms include a smart bar, a lounge and a restaurant that utilises local organic produce. An impressive spa facility is housed in converted barn buildings in the grounds.

Rooms 16 (13 annexe) (2 fmly) (7 GF) **S** £110-£140; **D** £140-£250 (incl. bkfst)* **Facilities** Spa FTV Putt green Gym Treatment suite Aromatherapy massage Beauty therapy Golf pitching range New Year Wi-fi **Conf** Class 25 Board 16 Thtr 25 **Parking** 30 **Notes** LB Closed 24-26 Dec Civ Wed

Ramada Hotel Dover

★★★★ 74% HOTEL

☎ 01304 821230 🖷 01304 825576
Singledge Ln, Whitfield CT16 3EL
e-mail: reservations@ramadadover.co.uk
web: www.ramadadover.co.uk
dir: From M20 follow signs to A2 towards Canterbury. Turn right after Whitfield rdbt. From A2 towards Dover, turn left before Whitfield rdbt

A modern purpose-built hotel situated in a quiet location between Dover and Canterbury, close to the ferry port and seaside. The open-plan public areas are contemporary in style and include a lounge, a bar and The Olive Tree Restaurant. The stylish bedrooms are simply decorated with co-ordinated soft furnishings and many thoughtful extras.

Rooms 68 (68 GF) **S** fr £69; **D** fr £69* **Facilities** STV Gym Xmas New Year Wi-fi **Conf** Class 25 Board 20 Thtr 400 Del from £99* **Parking** 110 **Notes** ® Civ Wed

White Cliffs

★★★ 77% ® HOTEL

☎ 01304 852229 & 852400 🖷 0800 756 5574
High St, St Margaret's-at-Cliffe CT15 6AT
e-mail: mail@thewhitecliffs.com
dir: Opposite church in village centre

This fresh-looking traditional weather boarded inn has a contemporary feel although it still retains much traditional character. Comfortably appointed bedrooms, divided between the main house and The Mews, boast luxurious beds and well co-ordinated furnishings. Public areas are styled to create a relaxed beachside atmosphere. The Bay Restaurant is open for lunch and dinner all week.

Rooms 15 (9 annexe) (2 fmly) (4 GF) **Facilities** FTV Xmas New Year Wi-fi **Conf** Class 20 Board 14 Thtr 20 **Parking** 20 **Notes** LB

Best Western Dover Marina Hotel

★★★ 77% HOTEL

☎ 01304 203633 🖷 01304 216320
Dover Waterfront CT17 9BP
e-mail: reservations@dovermarinahotel.co.uk
web: www.dovermarinahotel.co.uk
dir: A20 follow Hoverport signs, left onto seafront, hotel in 800yds

An attractive terraced waterfront hotel overlooking the harbour that offers a wide range of facilities including meeting rooms, health club, hairdresser and beauty treatments. Some of the tastefully decorated bedrooms have balconies, some have broadband access and many of the rooms have superb sea views. Public rooms include a large, open-plan lounge bar and a smart bistro restaurant.

Rooms 81 (5 fmly) **Facilities** STV Gym Xmas New Year Wi-fi **Conf** Class 60 Board 50 Thtr 110 **Services** Lift **Notes** ®

Premier Inn Dover (A20)

BUDGET HOTEL

☎ 0871 527 8310 🖷 0871 527 8311
Folkestone Rd CT15 7AB
dir: A20 to Dover. Through tunnel, take 2nd exit onto B2011. 1st left at rdbt. In 1m hotel on left

High quality, budget accommodation ideal for both families and business travellers. Spacious, en suite bedrooms feature tea and coffee making facilities, and Freeview TV in most hotels. Internet access and Wi-fi are available for a small fee. The adjacent family restaurant features a wide and varied menu. See also the Hotel Groups pages.

Rooms 64 **D** £56*

Premier Inn Dover East

BUDGET HOTEL

☎ 0871 527 8308 🖷 0871 527 8309
Jubilee Way, Guston Wood CT15 5FD
dir: At rdbt junct of A2 & A258

Rooms 40 **D** £56*

Premier Inn Dover (Eastern Ferry Terminal)

BUDGET HOTEL

☎ 0871 527 8306 🖷 0871 527 8307
Marine Court, Marine Pde CT16 1LW
dir: In town centre adjacent to ferry terminal. M20 junct 13 onto A20 for 8.2m

Rooms 100 **D** £60*

The Marquis at Alkham

®® RESTAURANT WITH ROOMS

☎ 01304 873410 🖷 01304 873418
Alkham Valley Rd, Alkham CT15 7DF
e-mail: info@themarquisatalkham.co.uk
web: www.themarquisatalkham.co.uk
dir: From Dover take A256, at rdbt 1st exit onto London Rd, left onto Alkham Rd, Alkham Valley Rd. Establishment 1.5m after sharp bend

Located between Dover and Folkestone, this modern, contemporary restaurant with rooms offers luxury accommodation with modern features - flat-screen TVs, Wi-fi, power showers and bathrobes to name but a few. All the stylish bedrooms are individually designed and have fantastic views of the Kent Downs. The award-winning restaurant, open for lunch and dinner, serves modern British cuisine. Continental and a choice of cooked breakfasts are offered.

Rooms 5 (1 fmly)

DOWNHAM MARKET Norfolk Map 12 TF60

Castle Hotel

★★★ 73% HOTEL

☎ 01366 384311 🖷 01366 384311
High St PE38 9HF
e-mail: howards@castle-hotel.com
dir: M11 take A10 for Ely into Downham Market. Hotel opposite lights on corner of High St

This popular coaching inn is situated close to the centre of town and has been welcoming guests for over 300 years. Well maintained public areas include a cosy lounge bar and two smartly appointed restaurants. Inviting bedrooms, some with four-poster beds, are attractively decorated, thoughtfully equipped, and have bright, modern decor.

Rooms 12 (2 fmly) **S** £79-£85; **D** £99-£145 (incl. bkfst)* **Facilities** New Year Wi-fi **Conf** Class 30 Board 40 Thtr 60 Del from £109 to £129* **Parking** 26 **Notes** LB

D

DRIFFIELD (GREAT) East Riding of Yorkshire — Map 17 TA05

Best Western Bell Hotel

★★★ 78% HOTEL

☎ 01377 256661 01377 253228
46 Market Place YO25 6AN
e-mail: bell@bestwestern.co.uk
web: www.bw-bellhotel.co.uk
dir: From A164, right at lights. Car park 50yds on left behind black railings

This 250-year-old hotel incorporates the old corn exchange and the old town hall. It is furnished with antique and period pieces, and contains many items of local historical interest. The bedrooms vary in size, but all offer modern facilities and some have their own sitting rooms. The hotel has a relaxed and very friendly atmosphere. There is a spa and gym providing a very good range of facilities and treatments.

Rooms 16 (3 GF) **S** £81-£93; **D** £98-£112 (incl. bkfst)* **Facilities** Spa FTV Gym Squash Masseur Hairdressing Chiropody Snooker New Year Wi-fi **Conf** Class 100 Board 40 Thtr 150 **Services** Lift **Parking** 18 **Notes** LB No children 16yrs Closed 25 Dec & 1 Jan RS 24 & 26 Dec Civ Wed 120

DROITWICH Worcestershire — Map 10 SO86

Express by Holiday Inn Droitwich M5 Jct 5

BUDGET HOTEL

☎ 0870 442 5658 0870 442 5659
Worcester Rd, Wychbold WR9 7PA
e-mail: dgmdroitwich@expressholidayinn.co.uk
web: www.hiexpress.com/droitwichm5j
dir: M5 junct 5, at rdbt take A38 towards Bromsgrove. Hotel 300yds on left next to MacDonalds

A modern hotel ideal for families and business travellers. Fresh and uncomplicated, the spacious rooms include Sky TV, power shower and tea and coffee-making facilities. Continental buffet breakfast is included in the room rate; other meals may be taken at the nearby family pub or restaurant. See also the Hotel Groups pages.

Rooms 94 (44 fmly) **Conf** Class 18 Board 20 Thtr 40

DUDLEY West Midlands — Map 10 SO99

Copthorne Hotel Merry Hill - Dudley

MILLENNIUM HOTELS AND RESORTS
MILLENNIUM • COPTHORNE

★★★★ 73% HOTEL

☎ 01384 482882 01384 482773
The Waterfront, Level St, Brierley Hill DY5 1UR
e-mail: reservations.merryhill@millenniumhotels.co.uk
web: www.millenniumhotels.co.uk/copthornedudley
dir: Follow signs for Merry Hill Centre

This hotel enjoys a waterfront location and is close to the Merry Hill Shopping Mall. Polished marble floors, rich fabrics and striking interior design are all in evidence in the stylish public areas. Bedrooms are spacious and some have Connoisseur status, which includes the use of a private lounge. A modern leisure centre with pool occupies the lower level.

Rooms 138 (14 fmly) **Facilities** STV supervised Gym Aerobics Beauty/massage therapists Steam room Sauna Dance studio Xmas New Year Wi-fi **Conf** Class 240 Board 60 Thtr 570 Del from £115 to £150* **Services** Lift **Parking** 100 **Notes** Civ Wed 400

DUMBLETON Gloucestershire — Map 10 SP03

Dumbleton Hall Hotel

★★★ 78% COUNTRY HOUSE HOTEL

☎ 01386 881240 01386 882142
WR11 7TS
e-mail: dh@pofr.co.uk
dir: M5 junct 9/A46. 2nd exit at rdbt signed Evesham. Through Beckford for 1m, turn right signed Dumbleton. Hotel at S end of village

Standing on the site of a 16th-century building also known as Dumbleton Hall, the current mansion, surrounded by 19 acres of landscaped gardens and parkland, was built in the mid-18th century. Panoramic views of the Vale of Evesham can be seen from every window, and the spacious public rooms make this an ideal venue for weddings, conferences or just as a hideaway retreat. The individually designed bedrooms vary in size and layout; one room is adapted for less able guests.

Dumbleton Hall Hotel

Rooms 34 (9 fmly) **Facilities** Xmas New Year Wi-fi **Conf** Class 60 Board 60 Thtr 100 Del from £155 to £185* **Services** Lift **Parking** 60 **Notes** Civ Wed 100

DUNSTABLE Bedfordshire — Map 11 TL02

Premier Inn Dunstable/ Luton

BUDGET HOTEL

☎ 0871 527 8330 0871 527 8331
350 Luton Rd LU5 4LL
dir: M1 junct 11, follow Dunstable signs. At 1st rdbt turn right. Hotel on left on A505

High quality, budget accommodation ideal for both families and business travellers. Spacious, en suite bedrooms feature tea and coffee making facilities, and Freeview TV in most hotels. Internet access and Wi-fi are available for a small fee. The adjacent family restaurant features a wide and varied menu. See also the Hotel Groups pages.

Rooms 42 **D** £53-£66*

Premier Inn Dunstable South (A5)

BUDGET HOTEL

☎ 0871 527 8332 0871 527 8333
Watling St, Kensworth LU6 3QP
dir: M1 junct 9 towards Dunstable on A5, hotel on right after Packhorse pub

Rooms 40 **D** £50-£64*

DUNSTER Somerset Map 3 SS94

The Luttrell Arms Hotel

★★★ 73% HOTEL

☎ 01643 821555 📠 01643 821567
High St TA24 6SG
e-mail: info@luttrellarms.fsnet.co.uk
web: www.luttrellarms.co.uk/main.htm
dir: A39/A396 S towards Tiverton. Hotel on left opposite Yarn Market

Occupying an enviable position on the high street, this 15th-century hotel looks up towards the town's famous castle. Beautifully renovated and decorated, high levels of comfort can be found throughout. Some of the spacious bedrooms have four-poster beds. The warm and friendly staff provide attentive service in a relaxed atmosphere.

Rooms 28 (3 fmly) **Facilities** FTV Exmoor safaris Historic tours Walking tours New Year **Conf** Class 20 Board 20 Thtr 35 **Notes** LB

Yarn Market Hotel

★★★ HOTEL

☎ 01643 821425 📠 01643 821475
25-33 High St TA24 6SF
e-mail: hotel@yarnmarkethotel.co.uk
web: www.yarnmarkethotel.co.uk
dir: M5 junct 23, follow A39. Hotel in village centre

Rooms 20 (5 annexe) (3 fmly) **S** £60-£80; **D** £90-£160 (incl. bkfst)* **Facilities** FTV Xmas New Year Wi-fi **Conf** Class 30 Board 25 Thtr 60 **Parking** 4 **Notes** LB

DUNWICH Suffolk Map 13 TM47

The Ship Inn

★★ 80% SMALL HOTEL

☎ 01728 648219 & 07921 061060
Saint James St IP17 3DT
e-mail: info@shipatdunwich.co.uk
dir: From N: A12, exit at Blythburgh onto B1125, then left to village. Inn at end of road. From S: A12, turn right to Westleton. Follow signs for Dunwich

A delightful inn situated in the heart of this quiet village, surrounded by nature reserves and heathland, and just a short walk from the beach. Public rooms feature a smart lounge bar with an open fire and real ales on tap. The comfortable bedrooms are traditionally furnished; some rooms have lovely views across the sea or marshes.

Rooms 15 (4 annexe) (4 fmly) (4 GF) **D** £95-£125 (incl. bkfst)* **Facilities** FTV Xmas New Year **Parking** 15

DURHAM Co Durham Map 19 NZ24

Durham Marriott Hotel, Royal County

Marriott HOTELS & RESORTS

★★★★ 78% HOTEL

☎ 0191 386 6821 📠 0191 386 0704
Old Elvet DH1 3JN
e-mail: mhrs.xvudm.frontdesk@marriotthotels.com
web: www.durhammarriottroyalcounty.co.uk
dir: From A1(M) junct 62, then A690 to Durham, over 1st rdbt, left at 2nd rdbt left at lights, hotel on left

In a wonderful position on the banks of the River Wear, the hotel's central location makes it ideal for visiting the attractions of this historic city. The building was developed from a series of Jacobean town houses. The bedrooms are tastefully styled. Eating options include the County Restaurant, for formal dining, and the Cruz Restaurant.

Rooms 150 (8 annexe) (10 fmly) (15 GF) (4 smoking) **S** £99-£140; **D** £99-£140 (incl. bkfst)* **Facilities** STV FTV supervised Gym Turkish steam room Plunge pool Sanarium Tropical fun shower Wi-fi **Conf** Class 50 Board 50 Thtr 120 Del from £140 to £180* **Services** Lift **Parking** 76 **Notes** LB Civ Wed 120

Radisson Blu Durham

Radisson BLU HOTELS & RESORTS

★★★★ 77% HOTEL

☎ 0191 372 7200 📠 0191 372 7201
Framwellgate Waterside DH1 5TL
e-mail: info.durham@radissonsas.com

Situated on the River Wear this smart hotel is a short walk from the city centre and the castle. The stylish accommodation includes business class rooms and a range of suites; most rooms have views of the cathedral and the old part of the city. Filini Restaurant serves Italian cuisine. The PACE Health Club boasts an indoor pool, steam room, sauna, gym and five treatment rooms, and the impressive conference facilities include a business centre.

Rooms 207 (8 fmly) **Facilities** Spa STV Gym New Year Wi-fi **Conf** Class 200 Board 120 Thtr 450 **Services** Lift Air con **Parking** 130 **Notes** ⊗ Civ Wed 80

Ramside Hall

★★★★ 73% HOTEL

☎ 0191 386 5282 📠 0191 386 0399
Carrville DH1 1TD
e-mail: mail@ramsidehallhotel.co.uk
web: www.ramsidehallhotel.co.uk
dir: A1(M) junct 62, A690 to Sunderland. Straight on at lights. 200mtrs after rail bridge turn right

With its proximity to the motorway and delightful parkland setting, this establishment combines the best of both worlds - convenience and tranquillity. The hotel boasts 27 holes of golf, a choice of lounges, two eating options and two bars. Bedrooms are furnished and decorated to a very high standard and include two very impressive presidential suites.

Rooms 80 (10 fmly) (28 GF) **Facilities** STV ⛳ 27 Putt green Steam room Sauna Golf academy Driving range ♫ Xmas New Year Wi-fi **Conf** Class 160 Board 40 Thtr 500 Del from £135 to £160* **Services** Lift **Parking** 500 **Notes** Civ Wed 500

Best Western Whitworth Hall Hotel

★★★ 79% HOTEL

☎ 01388 811772 📠 01388 818669
Whitworth Hall Country Park DL16 7QX
e-mail: enquiries@whitworthhall.co.uk
web: www.whitworthhall.co.uk

(For full entry see Spennymoor)

Best Western Honest Lawyer Hotel

★★★ 78% HOTEL

☎ 0191 378 3780 📠 0191 378 3782
Croxdale Bridge, Croxdale DH1 3SP
e-mail: enquiries@honestlawyerhotel.com
dir: A1(M) junct 61, A688 towards Bishops Auckland. Right at rdbt (continue on A688), right at next rdbt onto A167 towards Durham. In 2.5m hotel on right

This hotel offers a mixture of smart motel-style bedrooms along with six junior suites in the main building that have four-poster beds. 40" LCD TVs, power showers and complimentary Wi-fi are provided as standard. Bailey's Bar & Restaurant, with its open kitchen, offers a seasonally changing menu and friendly service. There are good transportation links to Durham and the motorway.

Rooms 46 (40 annexe) (6 fmly) (40 GF) **S** £58-£78; **D** £63.50-£83.50* **Facilities** FTV ♫ Xmas New Year Wi-fi **Conf** Class 27 Board 24 Thtr 50 Del from £105 to £117.50* **Services** Air con **Parking** 150 **Notes** LB Civ Wed 40

D

DURHAM *continued*

Hallgarth Manor Country Hotel & Restaurant

★★★ 71% HOTEL

☎ 0191 372 1188 📠 0191 372 1249
Pittington DH6 1AB
e-mail: sales@hallgarthmanorhotel.com
dir: A1(M) junct 62/A690 signed Sunderland. In 0.5m turn right across dual carriageway, follow brown tourist signs to hotel

This traditional 16th-century country house is set in quiet and beautifully maintained grounds just a few miles from Durham. The public areas and the restaurant have been tastefully modernised yet retain many original features. The individually styled bedrooms are all situated on the top two floors of the building. A large function room is available.

Rooms 23 (2 fmly) **Facilities** Xmas New Year Wi-fi **Conf** Class 75 Board 60 Thtr 250 **Parking** 200 **Notes** ⊗ Civ Wed 200

Premier Inn Durham City Centre

BUDGET HOTEL

☎ 0871 527 8338 📠 0871 527 8339
Freemans Place, Walkergate DH1 1SQ
dir: A1(M) junct 62, A690 (Leazes Rd) towards city centre. In Durham follow Watergate signs, under bridge immediately left into Walkergate (one way). Back under A690, hotel on right

High quality, budget accommodation ideal for both families and business travellers. Spacious, en suite bedrooms feature tea and coffee making facilities, and Freeview TV in most hotels. Internet access and Wi-fi are available for a small fee. The adjacent family restaurant features a wide and varied menu. See also the Hotel Groups pages.

D £63*

Premier Inn Durham East

BUDGET HOTEL

☎ 0871 527 8340 📠 0871 527 8341
Broomside Park, Belmont Industrial Estate DH1 1GG
dir: A1(M) junct 62, A690 W towards Durham. In 1m left. Hotel on left

Rooms 40 **D** £54-£59*

Premier Inn Durham North

BUDGET HOTEL

☎ 0871 527 8342 📠 0871 527 8343
adj. Arnison Retail Centre, Pity Me DH1 5GB
dir: A1 junct 63, A167 to Durham. Straight on at 5 rbts, left at 6th rbt. Hotel on right after 200yds

Rooms 60 **D** £54-£59*

DUXFORD Cambridgeshire **Map 12 TL44**

Duxford Lodge

THE INDEPENDENTS HOTEL ASSOCIATION

★★★ 77% ❀ HOTEL

☎ 01223 836444 📠 01223 832271
Ickleton Rd CB22 4RT
e-mail: admin@duxfordlodgehotel.co.uk
web: www.duxfordlodgehotel.co.uk
dir: M11 junct 10, onto A505 to Duxford. 1st right at rdbt, hotel 0.75m on left

A warm welcome is assured at this attractive red-brick hotel in the hart of a delightful village. Public areas include a cosy relaxing bar, separate lounge, and an attractive restaurant, where an excellent and imaginative menu is offered. The bedrooms are well appointed, comfortable and smartly furnished.

Rooms 15 (4 annexe) (2 fmly) (4 GF) **S** £78.50-£88.50; **D** £108-£118.50 (incl. bkfst)* **Facilities** FTV Wi-fi **Conf** Class 20 Board 26 Thtr 45 **Parking** 34 **Notes** Closed 25 Dec-2 Jan Civ Wed 50

See advert on this page

EAST GRINSTEAD
West Sussex
Map 6 TQ33

Felbridge Hotel & Spa

★★★★ 86% @@ HOTEL

☎ 01342 337700 📠 01342 337715
London Rd RH19 2BH
e-mail: sales@felbridgehotel.co.uk
dir: From W: M23 junct 10, follow signs to A22. From N: M25 junct 6. Hotel on A22 at Felbridge

This luxurious hotel is within easy of the M25 and Gatwick as well as Eastbourne and the glorious south coast. All bedrooms are beautifully styled and offer a wealth of amenities. Diners can choose from the Bay Tree Brasserie, Anise Fine Dining Restaurant or contemporary QUBE Bar. Facilities include a selection of modern meeting rooms, the luxurious Chakra Spa and swimming pool.

Rooms 120 (16 fmly) (53 GF) (9 smoking) **S** £89-£160; **D** £89-£160* **Facilities** Spa STV FTV supervised Gym Sauna Steam room Hairdresser Xmas New Year Wi-fi **Conf** Class 120 Board 100 Thtr 500 Del from £135 to £185 **Services** Air con **Parking** 300 **Notes** LB Civ Wed 150

Premier Inn East Grinstead

BUDGET HOTEL

☎ 0871 527 8348 📠 0871 527 8349
London Rd, Felbridge RH19 2QR
dir: M25 junct 6. Hotel at junction of A22 & A264

High quality, budget accommodation ideal for both families and business travellers. Spacious, en suite bedrooms feature tea and coffee making facilities, and Freeview TV in most hotels. Internet access and Wi-fi are available for a small fee. The adjacent family restaurant features a wide and varied menu. See also the Hotel Groups pages.

Rooms 41 **D** £55-£67*

EAST MIDLANDS AIRPORT
Leicestershire
Map 11 SK42

Best Western Premier Yew Lodge Hotel & Spa

★★★★ 79% @@ HOTEL

☎ 01509 672518 📠 01509 674730
Packington Hill DE74 2DF
e-mail: info@yewlodgehotel.co.uk
web: www.yewlodgehotel.co.uk
dir: M1 junct 24. Follow signs to Loughborough & Kegworth on A6. On entering village, 1st right, after 400yds hotel on right

This smart, family-owned hotel is close to both the motorway and airport, yet is peacefully located. Modern, stylish bedrooms and public areas are thoughtfully appointed and smartly presented. The restaurant serves interesting dishes, while lounge service and extensive conference facilities are available. A very well equipped spa and leisure centre complete the picture.

Rooms 103 (22 fmly) **Facilities** Spa STV Gym Beauty therapy suite Steam room Sauna Power plate Xmas New Year Wi-fi **Conf** Class 150 Board 84 Thtr 330 **Services** Lift **Parking** 180 **Notes** Civ Wed 260

The Priest House

★★★★ 78% @@ HOTEL

☎ 01332 810649 & 815334 📠 01332 811141
Kings Mills DE74 2RR
e-mail: enquiries.priesthouse@handpicked.co.uk
web: www.handpickedhotels.co.uk
dir: M1 junct 24, onto A50, take 1st slip road signed Castle Donington. Right at lights, hotel in 2m

A historic hotel peacefully situated in a picturesque riverside setting. Public areas include a fine dining restaurant, a modern brasserie and conference rooms. Bedrooms are situated in both the main building and converted cottages, and the executive rooms feature state-of-the-art technology.

Rooms 42 (18 annexe) (5 fmly) (16 GF) **S** £72-£125; **D** £97-£250 (incl. bkfst)* **Facilities** STV FTV Fishing Xmas New Year Wi-fi **Conf** Class 40 Board 40 Thtr 120 Del from £130 to £180* **Parking** 200 **Notes** LB Civ Wed 100

Thistle East Midlands Airport

thistle

★★★★ 77% HOTEL

☎ 0871 376 9015 📠 0871 376 9115
DE74 2SH
e-mail: eastmidlandsairport@thistle.co.uk
web: www.thistle.com/eastmidlandsairport
dir: On A453, at entrance to East Midlands Airport

This large, well-presented hotel is conveniently located next to East Midlands Airport with easy access to the M1. Accommodation is generally spacious. Substantial public areas include the popular Lord Byron bar, a comprehensive range of meeting rooms and an Otium health and leisure club. Thistle Hotels – AA Hotel Group of the Year 2011-12.

Rooms 164 (11 fmly) (82 GF) (6 smoking) **Facilities** STV FTV supervised Gym Sauna Steam room Spa bath Xmas New Year Wi-fi **Conf** Class 150 Board 54 Thtr 250 **Services** Air con **Parking** 350 **Notes** LB Civ Wed 250

Express by Holiday Inn East Midlands Airport

BUDGET HOTEL

☎ 01509 678000 📠 01509 670954
Hunter Rd, Pegasus Business Park DE74 2TQ
e-mail: ema@expressholidayinn.co.uk
web: www.hiexpress.com/emidlandsapt
dir: Follow East Midlands Airport signs, right into Pegasus Business Park, hotel on left

A modern hotel ideal for families and business travellers. Fresh and uncomplicated, the spacious rooms include Sky TV, power shower and tea and coffee-making facilities. Continental buffet breakfast is included in the room rate; other meals may be taken at the nearby family pub or restaurant. See also the Hotel Groups pages.

Rooms 90 (55 fmly) **Conf** Class 26 Board 20 Thtr 40

Premier Inn East Midlands Airport

BUDGET HOTEL

☎ 0871 527 8350 📠 0871 527 8351
Pegasus Business Park, Herald Way DE74 2TQ
dir: From S: M1 junct 23a, A453 signed to airport. From N: M1 junct 24, A456 signed to airport.

High quality, budget accommodation ideal for both families and business travellers. Spacious, en suite bedrooms feature tea and coffee making facilities, and Freeview TV in most hotels. Internet access and Wi-fi are available for a small fee. The adjacent family restaurant features a wide and varied menu. See also the Hotel Groups pages.

Rooms 80 **D** £52-£62*

E

EASINGTON
North Yorkshire — Map 19 NZ71

The Grinkle Park Hotel

★★★★ 74%
COUNTRY HOUSE HOTEL

☎ 01287 640515 📠 01287 641278
TS13 4UB
e-mail: info.grinklepark@classiclodges.co.uk
web: www.classiclodges.co.uk
dir: Take A171 from Guisborough towards Whitby. Hotel signed on left

A baronial hall built in 1880 situated between the North Yorkshire Moors and the coast, and surrounded by 35 acres of parkland and gardens where peacocks roam. It retains many original features including fine wood panelling, and the bedrooms are individually designed. The comfortable lounge and bar have welcoming log fires. The Camelia Room is ideal for smaller weddings and private dining.

Rooms 20 (1 fmly) **Facilities** Xmas New Year Wi-fi **Conf** Class 80 Board 40 Thtr 120 **Parking** 150 **Notes** Civ Wed 150

EASINGWOLD
North Yorkshire — Map 19 SE56

George Hotel

★★ 76% SMALL HOTEL

☎ 01347 821698 📠 01347 823448
Market Place YO61 3AD
e-mail: info@the-george-hotel.co.uk
web: www.the-george-hotel.co.uk
dir: Off A19 midway between York & Thirsk, in Market Place

A friendly welcome awaits at this former coaching inn that faces the Georgian market square. Bedrooms are very comfortably furnished and well equipped, and the mews rooms have their own external access. An extensive range of well-produced food is available both in the bar and restaurant. There are two comfortable lounges and complimentary use of a local fitness centre.

Rooms 15 (2 fmly) (6 GF) **S** £75-£85; **D** £80-£110 (incl. bkfst)* **Facilities** FTV Complimentry use of local fitness centre New Year Wi-fi **Conf** Board 12 Del from £100 to £145* **Parking** 10 **Notes** LB

EASTBOURNE
East Sussex — Map 6 TV69

The Grand Hotel

★★★★★ 84% HOTEL

☎ 01323 412345 📠 01323 412233
King Edward's Pde BN21 4EQ
e-mail: reservations@grandeastbourne.com
web: www.grandeastbourne.com
dir: On seafront W of Eastbourne, 1m from railway station

This famous Victorian hotel offers high standards of service and hospitality, and is in close proximity to both the beach and the South Downs National Park. The extensive public rooms feature a magnificent Great Hall, with marble columns and high ceilings, where guests can relax and enjoy afternoon tea. The spacious bedrooms provide high levels of comfort; many with stunning sea views and a number with private balconies. Guests can choose to eat in the fine dining The Mirabelle or the Garden Restaurant and there are bars as well as superb spa and leisure facilities.

Rooms 152 (20 fmly) (4 GF) **S** £169-£425; **D** £199-£455 (incl. bkfst)* **Facilities** Spa STV supervised Putt green Gym Hairdressing Beauty therapy Xmas New Year Child facilities **Conf** Class 200 Board 40 Thtr 350 Del from £190* **Services** Lift **Parking** 80 **Notes** LB Civ Wed 300

Langham

★★★ 82% HOTEL

☎ 01323 731451 📠 01323 646623
Royal Pde BN22 7AH
web: www.langhamhotel.co.uk
dir: Follow seafront signs. Hotel 0.5m E of pier

This popular hotel is situated in a prominent position with superb views of the sea and pier. Bedrooms are pleasantly decorated and equipped with modern facilities. Superior rooms, some with four-poster beds are stylish and offer sea views. The spacious public rooms include the Grand Parade bar, a lounge and a fine dining conservatory restaurant.

Rooms 81 (2 fmly) **S** £30-£65; **D** £60-£120 (incl. bkfst)* **Facilities** Xmas New Year Wi-fi Child facilities **Conf** Class 40 Board 30 Thtr 80 Del from £90 to £115* **Services** Lift **Parking** 43 **Notes** LB Civ Wed 140

The Waterside Hotel

★★★ 81% HOTEL

☎ 01323 646566 📠 01323 416857
11-12 Royal Pde BN22 7AR

This stylish small hotel is conveniently located a stone's throw from the popular beach and pier, and a moment's walk from the town centre. Bedrooms, individually designed with original contemporary artwork, are smartly appointed and well equipped with many thoughtful extras; some have sea views. Public areas include a bar/lounge and restaurant areas providing comfortable seating in well designed surroundings.

Rooms 20

Hydro

★★★ 80% HOTEL

☎ 01323 720643 📠 01323 641167
Mount Rd BN20 7HZ
e-mail: sales@hydrohotel.com
dir: From pier/seafront, right along Grand Parade. At Grand Hotel follow Hydro Hotel sign. Up South Cliff 200yds

This well-managed and popular hotel enjoys an elevated position with views of attractive gardens and the sea beyond. The spacious bedrooms are attractive and well equipped. In addition to the comfortable lounges, guests also have access to fitness facilities and a hairdressing salon. Service is both professional and efficient throughout.

Rooms 84 (3 fmly) (3 GF) **Facilities** FTV Putt green Beauty room Hair salon 3/4 size snooker table Xmas New Year Wi-fi **Conf** Class 90 Board 40 Thtr 140 Del from £60 to £110* **Services** Lift **Parking** 40 **Notes** RS 24-28 & 30-31 Dec Civ Wed 120

Devonshire Park

★★★ 79% HOTEL

☎ 01323 728144 📠 01323 419734
27-29 Carlisle Rd BN21 4JR
e-mail: info@devonshire-park-hotel.co.uk
web: www.devonshire-park-hotel.co.uk
dir: Follow signs to seafront, exit at Wish Tower. Hotel opposite Congress Theatre

A handsome family-run hotel handily placed for the seafront and theatres. Attractively furnished rooms are spacious and comfortable; many boast king-sized beds and all are equipped with Wi-fi and satellite TV. Guests can relax in the well presented lounges, the cosy bar or, when the weather's fine, on the garden terrace.

Rooms 35 (8 GF) **S** £40-£75; **D** £80-£150 (incl. bkfst) **Facilities** STV Xmas New Year Wi-fi **Services** Lift **Parking** 25 **Notes** LB ⊗ No children 12yrs

Best Western Lansdowne

★★★ 78% HOTEL

☎ 01323 725174 & 745483 📠 01323 739721
King Edward's Pde BN21 4EE
e-mail: reception@lansdowne-hotel.co.uk
web: www.bw-lansdownehotel.co.uk
dir: At W end of seafront opposite Western Lawns

Enjoying an enviable position at the quieter end of the parade, this hotel overlooks the Western Lawns and Wish Tower, and is just a few minutes' walk from many of the town's attractions. Public rooms include a variety of lounges, a range of meeting rooms and games rooms. Bedrooms are attractively decorated and many offer sea views. The hotel has a wheelchair lift near the front entrance that operates between the pavement and one of the ground-floor public rooms.

Rooms 102 (10 fmly) (7 smoking) **S** £55-£82; **D** £99-£180 (incl. bkfst) **Facilities** STV FTV Table tennis Pool table 2 Snooker tables Xmas New Year Wi-fi **Conf** Class 40 Board 40 Thtr 80 Del from £95 to £135 **Services** Lift **Parking** 22 **Notes** LB Civ Wed 60

Chatsworth

★★★ 78% HOTEL

☎ 01323 411016 & 748700 📠 01323 643270
Grand Pde BN21 3YR
e-mail: chatsworth@lionhotelsltd.com
web: www.lionhotelsltd.com
dir: M23 then A27 to Polegate. A2270 into Eastbourne, follow seafront signs. Hotel near pier

Within minutes of the town centre and pier, this attractive Edwardian hotel is located on the seafront. The public areas consist of the Chatsworth Bar, a cosy lounge and the Devonshire Restaurant. Bedrooms, many with sea views, are traditional in style and have a range of facilities. Service is friendly and helpful throughout.

Rooms 45 (2 fmly) **S** £45-£60; **D** £80-£120 (incl. bkfst)* **Facilities** Spa STV FTV Gym Hairdresser Sauna Massage Beauty treatments ♫ Xmas New Year Wi-fi **Conf** Class 60 Board 40 Thtr 100 Del from £110 to £130* **Services** Lift **Notes** LB ⊗ Civ Wed 140

Albany Lions Hotel

★★★ 73% HOTEL

☎ 01323 722788 & 748700 📠 01323 419373
Grand Pde BN21 4DJ
e-mail: albany@lionhotelsltd.com
dir: From town centre follow Seafront/Pier signs

This hotel, close to the bandstand, has a seafront location that is within walking distance of the main town shopping. A carvery dinner is served in the restaurant, which has great sea views from most tables, and a relaxing drink or afternoon tea can be enjoyed in the sun lounge.

Rooms 61 (5 fmly) **S** £45-£60; **D** £80-£120 (incl. bkfst)* **Facilities** STV Hairdresser Massage ♫ Xmas New Year Wi-fi **Conf** Class 60 Board 40 Thtr 120 Del from £110 to £130* **Services** Lift **Notes** LB ⊗

New Wilmington

★★★ 73% HOTEL

☎ 01323 721219 📠 01323 746255
25-27 Compton St BN21 4DU
e-mail: info@new-wilmington-hotel.co.uk
web: www.new-wilmington-hotel.co.uk
dir: A22 to Eastbourne seafront. Right along promenade to Wish Tower. Right, then left at end of road, hotel 2nd on left

This friendly, family-run hotel is conveniently located close to the seafront, the Congress Theatre and Winter Gardens. Public rooms are well presented and include a cosy bar, a small comfortable lounge and a spacious restaurant. Bedrooms are comfortably appointed and tastefully decorated; family and superior bedrooms are available.

Rooms 40 (14 fmly) (3 GF) **S** £40-£52; **D** £55-£114* **Facilities** STV ♫ Xmas New Year Wi-fi **Conf** Class 20 Board 20 Thtr 40 **Services** Lift **Parking** 3 **Notes** LB Closed 3 Jan-mid Feb

Mansion Lions Hotel

★★★ 72% HOTEL

☎ 01323 727411 & 748700 📠 01323 720665
Grand Pde BN21 3YS
e-mail: mansion@lionhotelsltd.com
dir: From town centre follow Seafront/Pier signs. Hotel on seafront

Directly overlooking the beach, this Victorian hotel is only two minutes' walk from the magnificent pier, the shopping centre and bandstand. The well-equipped bedrooms are spacious, comfortably furnished and some have sea views. An enjoyable four-course evening meal and a filling breakfast are served in the stylish Hartington Restaurant. There is an attractive lounge, and a pretty garden can be found at the back of the hotel.

Rooms 108 (6 fmly) (4 GF) **S** £45-£60; **D** £80-£120 (incl. bkfst)* **Facilities** STV ♫ Xmas New Year Wi-fi **Conf** Class 80 Board 40 Thtr 150 Del from £110 to £130* **Services** Lift **Notes** LB ⊗ Closed 2-31 Jan Civ Wed 150

Claremont Lions

★★★ 70% HOTEL

☎ 01323 731417 📠 01323 720413
Grand Pde BN21 3YL
e-mail: claremont@lionhotelsltd.com
dir: A27 E to Eastbourne. Follow seafront signs, hotel opposite pier

Located directly opposite the beautiful Carpet Gardens, the seafront and pier this majestic hotel offers spacious bedrooms that are comfortably furnished; all have fridges and many have sea views. Public areas including the elegant dining room are attractively presented and comfortable. Ground floor rooms are well equipped for less able guests.

Rooms 67 (2 fmly) (4 GF) **S** £45-£60; **D** £80-£120 (incl. bkfst)* **Facilities** STV ♫ Xmas New Year Wi-fi **Conf** Class 50 Board 40 Thtr 100 Del from £110 to £130* **Services** Lift **Parking** 6 **Notes** LB ⊗ Closed 2 Jan-28 Feb

E

EASTBOURNE *continued*

Courtlands

★★★ 66% HOTEL

☎ 01323 723737 📠 01323 732902
3-5 Wilmington Gardens BN21 4JN
e-mail: bookings@courtlandseastbourne.com
dir: Exit Grand Parade at Carlisle Rd

Situated opposite the Congress Theatre, this hotel is just a short walk from both the seafront and Devonshire Park. Bedrooms are comfortably furnished and pleasantly decorated. Public areas are smartly appointed and include a cosy bar, a separate lounge and an attractive dining room.

Rooms 46 (4 fmly) (3 GF) **Facilities** STV FTV ♫ Xmas New Year **Conf** Class 60 Board 60 Thtr 60 **Services** Lift **Parking** 36 **Notes** Civ Wed 100

Congress

★★ 75% HOTEL

☎ 01323 732118 📠 01323 720016
31-41 Carlisle Rd BN21 4JS
e-mail: reservations@congresshotel.co.uk
web: www.congresshotel.co.uk
dir: From Eastbourne seafront W towards Beachy Head. Right at Wishtower into Wilmington Sq, cross Compton St, hotel on left

An attractive Victorian property ideally located close to the seafront, Wish Tower and Congress Theatre. The bedrooms are bright and spacious. Family rooms are available plus facilities for less able guests. Entertainment is provided in a large dining room that has a dance floor and bar.

Rooms 62 (6 fmly) (8 GF) **Facilities** FTV Games room ♫ Xmas New Year Wi-fi **Services** Lift **Parking** 12 **Notes** LB RS Jan-Feb

Queens Hotel

★★ 75% HOTEL

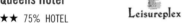

☎ 01323 722822 📠 01323 731056
Marine Pde BN21 3DY
e-mail: queens.eastbourne@alfatravel.co.uk
dir: Follow signs for seafront, hotel opposite pier

Popular with tour groups, this long-established hotel enjoys a central, prominent seafront location overlooking the pier. Spacious public areas include a choice of lounges, and regular entertainment is also provided. Bedrooms are suitably appointed and equipped.

Rooms 122 (5 fmly) **S** £39-£55; **D** £62-£94 (incl. bkfst) **Facilities** FTV Snooker ♫ Xmas New Year **Services** Lift **Parking** 50 **Notes** LB ⊗ Closed Jan (ex New Year) RS Nov, Feb-Mar

Alexandra Hotel

★★ 72% HOTEL

☎ 01323 720131 📠 01323 417769
King Edwards Pde BN21 4DR
e-mail: alexandrahotel@mistral.co.uk
web: http://alexandrahotel.eastbourne.biz/
dir: On seafront at junct of Carlisle Road & King Edward Parade

Located at the west end of the town, opposite the Wishing Tower, this hotel boasts panoramic views of the sea from many rooms. Bedrooms vary in size but are comfortable with good facilities for guests. A warm welcome is guaranteed at this long-standing, family run establishment.

Rooms 38 (2 fmly) (3 GF) **S** £33-£47; **D** £66-£110 (incl. bkfst)* **Facilities** ♫ Xmas New Year **Services** Lift **Notes** LB ⊗ Closed Jan & Feb RS Mar

Palm Court

★★ 71% HOTEL

☎ 01323 725811 📠 01323 430236
15 Burlington Place BN21 4AR
e-mail: thepalmcourt@btconnect.com
dir: From pier, W along seafront, Burlington Place 5th right

This family-run hotel is ideally situated close to the seafront and local theatres. The well appointed public areas include the lounge, spacious bar and stylish restaurant. Bedrooms vary in size but all offer plenty of handy accessories, comfortable furnishings and bright modern bathrooms. Good mobility facilities are provided.

Rooms 38 (5 GF) **S** £38-£45; **D** £76-£90 (incl. bkfst) **Facilities** Xmas New Year Wi-fi **Services** Lift **Notes** LB ⊗

Savoy Court

★★ 68% HOTEL

☎ 01323 723132 📠 01323 737902
11-15 Cavendish Place BN21 3EJ
e-mail: info@savoycourthotel.co.uk
web: www.savoycourthotel.co.uk
dir: M25 junct 6, A22 to Eastbourne. Hotel 50mtrs from pier

Located close to the pier and within easy walking distance of the beaches and open-air bandstand this hotel offers bedrooms that are pleasantly decorated and furnished. The public areas include a cosy lounge and spacious bar/lounge for relaxing at the end of the day.

Rooms 29 (3 fmly) (5 GF) **S** £35-£55; **D** £65-£95 (incl. bkfst) **Facilities** FTV Xmas New Year Wi-fi **Conf** Class 40 Board 30 Thtr 60 Del from £60 to £110 **Services** Lift **Notes** LB ⊗

Afton

★★ 64% HOTEL

☎ 01323 733162 📠 01323 645720
2-8 Cavendish Place BN21 3EJ
e-mail: info@aftonhotel.com
dir: From A22, A27 or A259, follow seafront signs. Hotel by pier

This friendly family run hotel is ideally located in the centre of town, opposite the pier and close to the shopping centre. Bedrooms vary in size but are all comfortable and well co-ordinated. The spacious restaurant serves traditional home cooking. A full programme of entertainment is provided.

Rooms 56 (4 fmly) (4 GF) **S** £30-£40; **D** £70-£80 (incl. bkfst)* **Facilities** ♫ Xmas New Year Wi-fi **Conf** Class 50 Board 50 Thtr 100 Del from £175 to £225* **Services** Lift

West Rocks

★★ 64% HOTEL

☎ 01323 725217 📠 01323 720421
Grand Pde BN21 4DL
e-mail: westrockshotel@btinternet.com
dir: West end of seafront

Ideally located near to the pier and bandstand, this hotel is only a short walk from the town centre. Bedrooms vary in size, with many offering stunning sea views. Guests have the choice of two comfortable lounges and a bar.

Rooms 47 (8 fmly) (6 GF) **Facilities** ♫ Xmas **Conf** Class 12 Board 12 Thtr 20 Del from £50 to £75 **Services** Lift **Notes** ⊗ Closed 3 Jan-20 Feb

Premier Inn Eastbourne

BUDGET HOTEL

☎ 0871 527 8352 📠 0871 527 8353
Willingdon Dr BN23 8AL
dir: From A22 or A27 at Polegate, take bypass signed Eastbourne (A22). Continue to Shinewater rdbt. Left towards Langney. Hotel 0.25m on left

High quality, budget accommodation ideal for both families and business travellers. Spacious, en suite bedrooms feature tea and coffee making facilities, and Freeview TV in most hotels. Internet access and Wi-fi are available for a small fee. The adjacent family restaurant features a wide and varied menu. See also the Hotel Groups pages.

Rooms 47 **D** £64*

Premier Inn Eastbourne (Polegate)

BUDGET HOTEL

☎ 0871 527 8354 📠 0871 527 8355
Hailsham Rd, Polegate BN26 6QL
dir: At rdbt junct of A22 & A27

Rooms 40 **D** £64*

EASTLEIGH Map 5 SU41
Hampshire

Holiday Inn Southampton-Eastleigh M3 Jct 13

★★★ 79% HOTEL

☎ 0871 942 9075 📠 023 8064 3945
Leigh Rd SO50 9PG
e-mail: reservations-eastleigh@ihg.com
web: www.holidayinn.co.uk
dir: M3 junct 13, right at lights, follow signs to Eastleigh, hotel on right

Located close to the M3 and convenient for Southampton Airport and the New Forest , this hotel is suitable for both the business and leisure traveller. All bedrooms have air conditioning and work desks as standard, but there are also executive rooms and suites with extra facilities. Junction Restaurant serves international dishes and there is a cocktail lounge. The popular leisure area includes a swimming pool, jacuzzi, aerobics studio, steam room, sauna and beauty treatments.

Rooms 129 (3 fmly) (27 GF) (12 smoking) **Facilities** Spa FTV supervised Gym Wi-fi **Conf** Class 60 Board 50 Thtr 120 **Services** Lift Air con **Parking** 175 **Notes** Civ Wed 100

Ellington Lodge Hotel

★★★ HOTEL

☎ 023 8065 1478 & 8061 3989 📠 023 8065 1479
The Concorde Club SO50 9HQ
e-mail: hotel@theconcordeclub.com
web: www.theconcordeclub.com
dir: M27 junct 5, at rdbt follow Chandlers Ford signs, hotel 500yds on right

Rooms 35 (18 GF) **Facilities** FTV Fishing Wi-fi **Conf** Class 50 Board 40 Thtr 200 **Services** Lift Air con **Parking** 250 **Notes** LB No children 18yrs Closed 24-26 Dec

Premier Inn Southampton (Eastleigh)

BUDGET HOTEL

☎ 0871 527 8994 📠 0871 527 8995
Leigh Rd SO50 9YX
dir: M3 junct 13, A335 towards Eastleigh. Hotel on right

High quality, budget accommodation ideal for both families and business travellers. Spacious, en suite bedrooms feature tea and coffee making facilities, and Freeview TV in most hotels. Internet access and Wi-fi are available for a small fee. The adjacent family restaurant features a wide and varied menu. See also the Hotel Groups pages.

Rooms 60 **D** £52-£65*

EDGWARE Map 6 TQ19
Greater London

Premier Inn London Edgware

BUDGET HOTEL

☎ 0871 527 8652 📠 0871 527 8653
435 Burnt Oak Broadway HA8 5AQ
dir: M1 junct 4, A41, A5 towards Edgware. 3m to hotel

High quality, budget accommodation ideal for both families and business travellers. Spacious, en suite bedrooms feature tea and coffee making facilities, and Freeview TV in most hotels. Internet access and Wi-fi are available for a small fee. The adjacent family restaurant features a wide and varied menu. See also the Hotel Groups pages.

Rooms 111 **D** £66-£78*

EGGESFORD Map 3 SS61
Devon

Fox & Hounds Country Hotel

★★★ 72% HOTEL

☎ 01769 580345 📠 01271 410200
EX18 7JZ
e-mail: relax@foxandhoundshotel.co.uk
web: www.foxandhoundshotel.co.uk
dir: M5 junct 27, A361 towards Tiverton. Take B3137 signed Witheridge. After Nomans Land follow signs for Eggesford Station. Hotel 50mtrs up hill from station

Situated midway between Exeter and Barnstaple, in the beautiful Taw Valley, this extensively developed hotel was originally a coaching inn dating back to the 1800s. Many of the comfortable, elegant bedrooms have lovely countryside views. Good cooking utilises excellent local produce and can be enjoyed in either restaurant or the convivial bar. For fishing enthusiasts, the hotel has direct access to the River Taw, and equipment and tuition can be provided if required.

Rooms 19 (6 fmly) (3 GF) **S** £62.50-£75; **D** £125-£145 (incl. bkfst)* **Facilities** FTV Fishing Health & beauty suite Xmas New Year Wi-fi **Conf** Class 60 Board 60 Thtr 100 **Parking** 100 **Notes** LB Civ Wed 130

E

EGHAM Map 6 TQ07
Surrey

Great Fosters

★★★★ 80% ◎◎◎ HOTEL

☎ 01784 433822 📠 01784 472455
Stroude Rd TW20 9UR
e-mail: enquiries@greatfosters.co.uk
web: www.greatfosters.co.uk
dir: From A30 (Bagshot to Staines), right at lights by Wheatsheaf pub into Christchurch Rd. Straight on at rdbt (pass 2 shop parades on right). Left at lights into Stroude Rd. Hotel 0.75m on right

This Grade I listed mansion dates back to the 16th century. The main house rooms are very much in keeping with the house's original style but are, of course, up-to-date with modern amenities. The stables and cloisters provide particularly stylish and luxurious accommodation. Public areas include a cosy bar and the award-winning Oak Room Restaurant, as well as a host of meeting and event facilities. Alfresco dining, overlooking the well manicured grounds, in the summer months is a must.

Rooms 44 (22 annexe) (1 fmly) (13 GF) **Facilities** STV ⚲ 🏌 🏇 Xmas New Year Wi-fi **Conf** Class 72 Board 50 Thtr 150 **Parking** 200 **Notes** ⊗ Civ Wed 180

the runnymede-on-thames

★★★★ 80% HOTEL

☎ 01784 220600 📠 01784 436340
Windsor Rd TW20 0AG
e-mail: info@therunnymede.co.uk
web: www.therunnymede.co.uk
dir: M25 junct 13, onto A308 towards Windsor

Enjoying a peaceful location beside the River Thames, this large modern hotel, with its excellent range of facilities, balances both leisure and corporate business well. The extensive function suites, together with spacious lounges and stylish, well laid out bedrooms are impressive. Superb spa facilities are available, and the good food and beverage venues offer wonderful river views.

Rooms 181 (19 fmly) **S** £127-£263; **D** £164-£302 (incl. bkfst)* **Facilities** Spa STV ⓢ supervised ⚲ supervised 🏌 🏇 Gym Dance studio Children's play area River boat hire Group treatment suite Xmas New Year Wi-fi Child facilities **Conf** Class 250 Board 76 Thtr 300 Del from £229 to £326* **Services** Lift Air con **Parking** 300 **Notes** LB ⊗ Civ Wed 140

See advert on this page

ELLESMERE PORT
Cheshire

Holiday Inn Ellesmere Port/ Chester

★★★ 75% HOTEL

☎ 0151 356 8111 📠 0151 356 8444
Waterways, Lower Mersey St CH65 2AL
e-mail: reservations@hiellesmereport.com
web: www.hiellesmereport.com
dir: At M53 junct 9

This smart, modern hotel enjoys a waterside location on the canal docks. The well equipped bedrooms are spacious and comfortable. Extensive meeting facilities, a well-equipped gym and swimming pool, and its proximity to local tourist attractions make it popular with business travellers and families alike. Meals are served in the restaurant overlooking the water.

Rooms 83

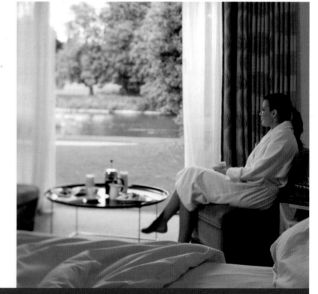

Mercure Chester North Woodhey House Hotel

★★★ 68% HOTEL

☎ 0151 339 5121 📠 0151 339 3214
Berwick Road West / Welsh Rd, Little Sutton CH66 4PS
e-mail: enquiries@woodheyhouse-hotel-chester.com
dir: A41 S, right at 2nd set of lights onto A550 towards Queensferry. Hotel 1m on left

Located in a quiet rural setting, yet in easy reach of the M53, the hotel provides and ideal stop off for both business and leisure guests. All bedrooms are well equipped. Day rooms are stylishly appointed and include a bar, restaurant and a very good range of meeting and conference facilities. Leisure facilities include an indoor pool, gym and steam room.

Rooms 75 (8 fmly) (23 GF) **Facilities** FTV Gym Sauna Steam room Xmas New Year Wi-fi **Conf** Class 120 Board 80 Thtr 250 Del from £90 to £140* **Services** Lift **Parking** 150 **Notes** Civ Wed 100

ELTERWATER — Cumbria — Map 18 NY30

Langdale Hotel & Spa

★★★★ 77% COUNTRY HOUSE HOTEL

☎ 015394 38014 📠 015394 37694
LA22 9JD
e-mail: info@langdale.co.uk
web: www.langdale.co.uk
dir: In Langdale Valley, W of Ambleside

Founded on the site of an abandoned 19th-century gunpowder works, this modern hotel is set in 35 acres of woodland and waterways. Comfortable bedrooms, many with spa baths, vary in size. Extensive public areas include a choice of stylish restaurants, conference and leisure facilities and an elegant bar with an interesting selection of snuff. There is also a traditional pub run by the hotel just along the main road.

Rooms 57 (52 annexe) (5 fmly) (25 GF) **Facilities** Spa STV FTV supervised Fishing Gym Steam room Cycle hire Solarium Aerobics studio Health & beauty salon Xmas New Year Wi-fi **Conf** Class 40 Board 35 Thtr 80 **Parking** 65 **Notes** Civ Wed 65

New Dungeon Ghyll

★★ 76% HOTEL

☎ 015394 37213 📠 015394 37666
Langdale LA22 9JX
e-mail: enquiries@dungeon-ghyll.com
web: www.dungeon-ghyll.com
dir: From Ambleside follow A593 towards Coniston for 3m, at Skelwith Bridge right onto B5343 towards 'The Langdales'

This friendly hotel enjoys a tranquil, idyllic position at the head of the valley, set among the impressive peaks of Langdale. Bedrooms vary in size and style; the rooms are brightly decorated and smartly furnished. Bar meals are served all day, and dinner can be enjoyed in the restaurant overlooking the landscaped gardens; there is also a cosy lounge/bar.

Rooms 20 (1 fmly) (3 GF) **S** £55-£75; **D** £110-£130 (incl. bkfst) **Facilities** FTV Xmas New Year Wi-fi **Conf** Class 30 Board 20 Thtr 20 **Parking** 30 **Notes** LB

ELTISLEY — Cambridgeshire — Map 12 TL25

The Eltisley

RESTAURANT WITH ROOMS

☎ 01480 880308
2 The Green PE19 6TG
e-mail: theeltisley@btconnect.com
dir: Close to A428

This popular restaurant with rooms is situated between St Neots and the historic City of Cambridge. The bedrooms are adjacent to the main building in a timber-framed block; each is pleasantly decorated and well equipped. The open-plan public rooms include a smart lounge bar, a restaurant and an alfresco dining area.

Rooms 7

ELY — Cambridgeshire — Map 12 TL58

Lamb Hotel

★★★ HOTEL

☎ 01353 663574 📠 01353 662023
2 Lynn Rd CB7 4EJ
e-mail: lamb.ely@oldenglishinns.co.uk
web: www.oldenglish.co.uk
dir: From A10 into Ely, hotel in town centre

Rooms 31 (6 fmly) **Facilities** Xmas **Conf** Class 40 Board 70 Thtr 100 **Parking** 20

The Anchor Inn

RESTAURANT WITH ROOMS

☎ 01353 778537 📠 01353 776180
Sutton Gault CB6 2BD
e-mail: anchorinn@popmail.bta.com
dir: 6m W of Ely. Sutton Gault signed off B1381 at S end of Sutton

Located beside the New Bedford River with stunning country views, this 17th-century inn has a wealth of original features enhanced by period furniture. The spacious bedrooms are tastefully appointed and equipped with many thoughtful touches. The friendly team of staff offer helpful and attentive service.

Rooms 4 (2 fmly)

EMBLETON — Northumberland — Map 21 NU22

Dunstanburgh Castle Hotel

★★ 82% HOTEL

☎ 01665 576111 📠 0870 706 0394
NE66 3UN
e-mail: stay@dunstanburghcastlehotel.co.uk
web: www.dunstanburghcastlehotel.co.uk
dir: From A1, take B1340 to Denwick past Rennington & Masons Arms. Take next right signed Embleton

The focal point of the village, this friendly, family-run hotel has a dining room and grill room that offer different menus, plus a cosy bar and two lounges. In addition to the main bedrooms, a barn conversion houses three stunning suites, each with a lounge and gallery bedroom above.

Rooms 32 (12 annexe) (6 fmly) **S** £45.50-£68.50; **D** £91-£137 (incl. bkfst)* **Facilities** Wi-fi **Parking** 33 **Notes** LB Closed Dec-Jan

E

E

EMSWORTH
Hampshire
Map 5 SU70

Brookfield

★★★ 80% HOTEL

☎ 01243 373363 📠 01243 376342
Havant Rd PO10 7LF
e-mail: bookings@brookfieldhotel.co.uk
dir: From A27 onto A259 towards Emsworth. Hotel 0.5m on left

This well-established family-run hotel has spacious public areas with popular conference and banqueting facilities. Bedrooms are in a modern style, and comfortably furnished. The popular Hermitage Restaurant offers a seasonally changing menu and an interesting wine list.

Rooms 39 (6 fmly) (16 GF) (2 smoking) **Facilities** STV FTV Free pass to local leisure club New Year Wi-fi **Conf** Class 50 Board 50 Thtr 100 Del from £130 to £150 **Parking** 80 **Notes** ® Closed 24-27 Dec Civ Wed 100

36 on the Quay

◎◎◎ RESTAURANT WITH ROOMS

☎ 01243 375592 & 372257
47 South St PO10 7EG

Occupying a prime position with far reaching views over the estuary, this 16th-century house is the scene for some accomplished and exciting cuisine. The elegant restaurant occupies centre stage with peaceful pastel shades, local art and crisp napery together with glimpses of the bustling harbour outside. The contemporary bedrooms offer style, comfort and thoughtful extras.

Rooms 5

ENFIELD
Greater London
Map 6 TQ39

Royal Chace

★★★★ 75% ◎ HOTEL

☎ 020 8884 8181 📠 020 8884 8150
The Ridgeway EN2 8AR
e-mail: reservations@royalchacehotel.co.uk
dir: M25 junct 24 take A1005 towards Enfield. Hotel 3m on right

This professionally run, privately owned hotel enjoys a peaceful location with open fields to the rear. Public rooms are smartly appointed; the first-floor Chace Brasserie is particularly appealing with its warm colour schemes and friendly service. Bedrooms are well presented and thoughtfully equipped.

Rooms 92 (5 fmly) (32 GF) **Facilities** FTV ⛳ Gym New Year Wi-fi **Conf** Class 100 Board 40 Thtr 250 **Parking** 200 **Notes** ® Closed 24-30 Dec RS Lunchtime/Sun eve Civ Wed 220

Comfort Hotel Enfield

BUDGET HOTEL

☎ 020 8366 3511 📠 020 8366 2432
52 Rowantree Rd EN2 8PW
e-mail: admin@comfortenfield.co.uk
web: www.comfortenfield.co.uk
dir: M25 junct 24 follow signs for A1005 towards Enfield. Hospital on left, across mini-rdbt, 3rd left onto Bycullah Rd, 2nd left into Rowantree Rd

This hotel is situated in a quiet residential area, close to the centre of Enfield. Comfortable accommodation is provided in the thoughtfully equipped bedrooms, which include ground floor and family rooms. Public areas include a cosy bar and lounge, conference and function rooms and the smart Etruscan Restaurant.

Rooms 34 (34 annexe) (3 fmly) **Conf** Class 25 Board 25 Thtr 65

Premier Inn Enfield

BUDGET HOTEL

☎ 0871 527 8374 📠 0871 527 8375
Innova Park, Corner of Solar Way EN3 7XY
dir: M25 junct 25, A10 towards London, left into Bullsmoor Lane & Mollison Ave. Over rdbt, right at lights into Innova Science Park

High quality, budget accommodation ideal for both families and business travellers. Spacious, en suite bedrooms feature tea and coffee making facilities, and Freeview TV in most hotels. Internet access and Wi-fi are available for a small fee. The adjacent family restaurant features a wide and varied menu.

Rooms 160 **D** £59-£65*

EPPING
Essex
Map 6 TL40

The Bell Hotel Epping

U

☎ 01992 573138 📠 01992 560402
High Rd, Bell Common CM16 4DG
e-mail: reservations@bellhotelepping.com
web: www.bellhotelepping.com
dir: M11 junct 7/B1393 to Epping. Hotel on right past town centre

Currently the rating for this establishment is not confirmed. This may be due to a change of ownership or because it has only recently joined the AA rating scheme. For further details please see the AA website: theAA.com

Rooms 79 (79 annexe) (5 fmly) (38 GF) (10 smoking) **S** £55-£105; **D** £65-£145 **Facilities** FTV Xmas New Year Wi-fi **Conf** Class 50 Board 50 Thtr 85 Del from £100 to £145 **Parking** 80 **Notes** ® Civ Wed 60

EPSOM
Surrey
Map 6 TQ26

Chalk Lane Hotel

★★★ 80% HOTEL

☎ 01372 721179 📠 01372 727878
Chalk Ln, Woodcote End KT18 7BB
e-mail: smcgregor@chalklanehotel.com
web: www.chalklanehotel.com
dir: M25 junct 9 onto A24 to Epsom. Right at lights by BP garage. Left into Avenue Rd, right into Worple Rd. Left at T-junct & hotel on right

This delightful, privately owned hotel enjoys a peaceful location just a ten minute walk from Epsom Racecourse. Stylish bedrooms are generally spacious and all are appointed to a high standard. Public areas are attractively furnished and include a choice of lounges, an excellent range of function and meeting facilities. A smartly appointed restaurant offers imaginative, accomplished cuisine.

Rooms 22 (1 fmly) **S** £85-£100; **D** £100-£200 (incl. bkfst)* **Facilities** FTV Wi-fi **Conf** Class 40 Board 30 Thtr 140 **Parking** 60 **Notes** Civ Wed 100

Holiday Inn Express London-Epsom Downs

BUDGET HOTEL

☎ 01372 755200 📠 01372 755201
Langley Vale Rd KT18 5LG
e-mail: epsom@holidayinnexpress.org.uk
dir: Just off M25 junct 9

A modern hotel ideal for families and business travellers. Fresh and uncomplicated, the spacious rooms include Sky TV, power shower and tea and coffee-making facilities. Continental buffet breakfast is included in the room rate; other meals may be taken at the nearby family pub or restaurant. See also the Hotel Groups pages.

Rooms 120 **Conf** Class 20 Board 12 Thtr 20

Premier Inn Epsom Central

BUDGET HOTEL

☎ 0871 527 8376 📠 0871 527 8377
2-4 St Margarets Dr, off Dorking Rd KT18 7LB
dir: M25 junct 9, A24 towards Epsom, hotel on left, just before town centre

High quality, budget accommodation ideal for both families and business travellers. Spacious, en suite bedrooms feature tea and coffee making facilities, and Freeview TV in most hotels. Internet access and Wi-fi are available for a small fee. The adjacent family restaurant features a wide and varied menu. See also the Hotel Groups pages.

Rooms 58 **D** £67-£79*

Premier Inn Epsom North

BUDGET HOTEL

☎ 0871 527 8380 📠 0871 527 8381
272 Kingston Rd, Ewell KT19 0SH
dir: M25 junct 8, A217 towards Sutton. A240 towards Ewell. At Beggars Hill rdbt 2nd exit into Kingston Rd

Rooms 29 **D** £65-£77*

ESCRICK North Yorkshire **Map 16 SE64**

Parsonage Country House Hotel

★★★ 78% ® COUNTRY HOUSE HOTEL

☎ 01904 728111 📠 01904 728151
York Rd YO19 6LF
e-mail: reservations@parsonagehotel.co.uk
web: www.parsonagehotel.co.uk
dir: A64 onto A19 Selby. Follow to Escrick. Hotel by St Helens Church

This 19th-century, former parsonage has been carefully restored and extended to provide delightful accommodation, set in well-tended gardens. Bedrooms are smartly appointed and well equipped both for business and leisure guests. Spacious public areas include an elegant restaurant, excellent meeting and conference facilities and a choice of attractive lounges.

Rooms 50 (13 annexe) (4 fmly) (9 GF) (8 smoking) **S** £69-£95; **D** £80-£140 (incl. bkfst) **Facilities** STV Putt green Xmas New Year Wi-fi **Conf** Class 80 Board 50 Thtr 180 **Services** Lift **Parking** 100 **Notes** LB ⊗ Civ Wed 150

EVERSHOT Dorset **Map 4 ST50**

INSPECTORS' CHOICE

Summer Lodge Country House Hotel, Restaurant & Spa

★★★★ ®®® COUNTRY HOUSE HOTEL

☎ 01935 482000 📠 01935 482040
DT2 0JR
e-mail: summer@relaischateaux.com
dir: 1m W of A37 halfway between Dorchester & Yeovil

This picturesque hotel is situated in the heart of Dorset and is the ideal retreat for getting 'away from it all', and it's worth arriving in time for the excellent afternoon tea. Bedrooms are appointed to a very high standard; each is individually designed with upholstered walls and come with a wealth of luxurious facilities. Expect plasma screen TVs, DVD players, radios, air conditioning and Wi-fi access, plus little touches such as homemade shortbread, fresh fruit and scented candles. The delightful public areas include a sumptuous lounge complete with an open fire, and the elegant restaurant where the cuisine continues to be the high point of any stay.

Rooms 24 (14 annexe) (6 fmly) (2 GF) (1 smoking) **S** £185-£535; **D** £210-£560 (incl. bkfst)* **Facilities** Spa STV FTV Gym Sauna Xmas New Year Wi-fi **Conf** Class 16 Board 16 Thtr 24 Del from £295* **Services** Air con **Parking** 41 **Notes** LB Civ Wed 30

George Albert Hotel

★★★ 77% HOTEL

☎ 01935 483430 📠 01935 483431
Wardon Hill DT2 9PW
e-mail: enquiries@gahotel.co.uk
dir: On A37 (between Yeovil & Dorchester). Adjacent to Southern Counties Shooting Ground

Situated mid-way between Dorchester and Yeovil, this hotel has much to offer for both business and leisure guests. The bedrooms offer impressive levels of comfort and many also having wonderful views across the Dorset countryside. Stylish public areas include extensive function rooms, a relaxing lounge, and a choice of dining options. Additional facilities include a karting track and clay pigeon shooting.

Rooms 39 (3 fmly) **S** £60-£79; **D** £75-£95 (incl. bkfst)* **Facilities** FTV Games room Xmas New Year Wi-fi **Conf** Class 60 Board 90 Thtr 250 **Services** Lift Air con **Parking** 200 **Notes** LB ⊗ Civ Wed 405

E

EVESHAM Worcestershire **Map 10 SP04**

Northwick Hotel

★★★ 82% ® HOTEL

☎ 01386 40322 📠 01386 41070
Waterside WR11 1BT
e-mail: enquiries@northwickhotel.co.uk
dir: Off A46 onto A44 over lights, right at next lights onto B4035. Past hospital, hotel on right

Located close to the centre of the town, this hotel benefits a good position overlooking the River Avon and adjacent park. The bedrooms are traditional in style and have broadband access; one room has been adapted for provide disabled access. Public areas offer a choice of drinking options, a restaurant and function and meeting rooms.

Rooms 29 (4 fmly) (1 GF) **Facilities** STV FTV New Year Wi-fi **Conf** Class 150 Board 80 Thtr 240 **Parking** 110 **Notes** ⊗ Closed 25-28 Dec Civ Wed 70

Dumbleton Hall Hotel

★★★ 78% COUNTRY HOUSE HOTEL

☎ 01386 881240 📠 01386 882142
WR11 7TS
e-mail: dh@pofr.co.uk

(For full entry see Dumbleton)

EVESHAM *continued*

The Evesham

★★★ 77% HOTEL

☎ 01386 765566 & 0800 716969 (Res)
📠 01386 765443
Coopers Ln, Off Waterside WR11 1DA
e-mail: reception@eveshamhotel.com
web: www.eveshamhotel.com
dir: M5 junct 9, A46 to Evesham. At rdbt on entering Evesham, take B4184 towards town, right at new bridge lights, 800yds, right into Coopers Ln

Dating from 1540 and set in extensive grounds, this delightful hotel has well-equipped accommodation that includes a selection of quirkily themed rooms - Alice in Wonderland, Egyptian, and Aquarium (which has a tropical fish tank in the bathroom). A reputation for food is well deserved, with a particularly strong choice for vegetarians. Children are welcome and toys are always available.

Rooms 40 (1 annexe) (3 fmly) (11 GF) **S** £77-£89; **D** £123-£126 (incl. bkfst)* **Facilities** FTV Putt green New Year Wi-fi Child facilities **Conf** Class 12 Board 12 Thtr 12 **Parking** 50 **Notes** LB Closed 25-26 Dec

Premier Inn Evesham

BUDGET HOTEL

☎ 0871 527 8384 📠 0871 527 8385
Evesham Country Park, A46 Trunk Rd, Twyford WR11 4TP
dir: At rdbt junct of A46(T) & A4184 at N end of Evesham bypass. Adjacent to Evesham Country Park

High quality, budget accommodation ideal for both families and business travellers. Spacious, en suite bedrooms feature tea and coffee making facilities, and Freeview TV in most hotels. Internet access and Wi-fi are available for a small fee. The adjacent family restaurant features a wide and varied menu. See also the Hotel Groups pages.

Rooms 40 **D** £53-£59*

EWEN Gloucestershire — **Map 4 SU09**

The Wild Duck

★★ 71% HOTEL

☎ 01285 770310 📠 01285 770492
Drakes Island GL7 6BY
e-mail: duckreservations@aol.com
dir: From Cirencester take A429 towards Malmesbury. At Kemble left to Ewen. Inn in village centre

This lovely 16th-century, family run inn sits in a delightful Cotswold location and offers a wealth of character and interest. Log fires crackle and there are heaps of nooks and crannies in the bar and restaurant where guests can enjoy the hearty cuisine and an extensive choice of beers and wines. There is a lovely courtyard for alfresco dining in the warmer weather. The individually designed bedrooms have a contemporary look, and each has a black lacquered four-poster; the Chinese Suite is in the oldest part of the building.

Rooms 12 (8 GF) **S** £50-£70; **D** £85-£165 (incl. bkfst) **Facilities** FTV Wi-fi **Parking** 50 **Notes** Closed 25 Dec evening

EXETER Devon — **Map 3 SX99**

Mercure Southgate Hotel

★★★★ 75% HOTEL

☎ 01392 412812 📠 01392 413549
Southernhay East EX1 1QF
e-mail: h6624@accor.com
web: www.mercure.com
dir: M5 junct 30, 3rd exit (Exeter), 2nd left towards city centre, 3rd exit at next rdbt, hotel 2m on right

Centrally located and with excellent parking, The Southgate offers a diverse range of leisure and business facilities. Public areas are pleasantly spacious with comfortable seating in the bar and lounge; there is also a pleasant terrace. The bedrooms, in differing sizes, are well equipped and have modern facilities.

Rooms 154 (6 fmly) (23 GF) (8 smoking) **Facilities** FTV supervised Gym Sauna Sun shower Spa pool New Year Wi-fi **Conf** Class 70 Board 50 Thtr 150 **Services** Lift **Parking** 101 **Notes** RS Sat/Sun Civ Wed 80

The Rougemont Hotel, Exeter thistle

★★★★ 72% HOTEL

☎ 0871 376 9018 📠 0871 376 9118
Queen St EX4 3SP
e-mail: exeter@thistle.co.uk
web: www.thistlehotels.com/exeter
dir: M5 junct 30 follow signs to services at 1st rdbt, then 1st left towards city centre. In city centre follow Museum/Central Station signs. Hotel opposite

Centrally located, this elegant hotel is well situated for those visiting the city for business or leisure. There is a charming, old-fashioned atmosphere here, with traditional hospitality to the fore. All bedrooms offer high levels of comfort and a number of suites are available. A choice of bars is provided - the convivial Drakes Bar and the smart and more formal cocktail bar. Thistle Hotels – AA Hotel Group of the Year 2011-12.

Rooms 98 (2 fmly) **Facilities** STV Wi-fi **Conf** Class 110 Board 70 Thtr 250 **Services** Lift **Parking** 24 **Notes** Civ Wed 200

Buckerell Lodge Hotel

★★★★ 71% HOTEL

☎ 0844 855 9112 📠 01392 424333
Topsham Rd EX2 4SQ
e-mail: reservations@akkeron-hotels.com
web: www.akkeron-hotels.com
dir: M5 junct 30 follow city centre signs, hotel 0.5m from Exeter

Although situated outside the city centre, this hotel is easily accessed by car or public transport. Bedrooms, all appointed in modern styles, are comfortable, fairly spacious and generally quiet. Public areas include a popular bar and restaurant and a variety of function rooms. The attractive and extensive gardens are a lovely feature and ideal for alfresco dining during warmer weather.

Rooms 54 (17 GF) **Facilities** FTV Wi-fi **Conf** Class 32 Board 35 Thtr 90 Del from £120 to £155* **Parking** 60 **Notes** Civ Wed 70

Devon Hotel

★★★ 76% HOTEL

☎ 01392 259268 📠 01392 413142
Exeter Bypass, Matford EX2 8XU
e-mail: reservations@devonhotel.co.uk
web: www.devonhotel.co.uk
dir: M5 junct 30 follow Marsh Barton Ind Est signs on A379. Hotel on Marsh Barton rdbt

Within easy access of the city centre, the M5 and the city's business parks, this smart Georgian hotel offers modern, comfortable accommodation. The Carriages Bar and Brasserie is popular with guests and locals alike, offering a wide range of dishes as well as a carvery at both lunch and dinner. Service is friendly and attentive, and extensive meeting and business facilities are available.

Rooms 40 (40 annexe) (2 fmly) (11 GF) **S** £59-£75; **D** £79-£85* **Facilities** FTV Xmas New Year Wi-fi **Conf** Class 80 Board 40 Thtr 150 **Parking** 250 **Notes** LB Civ Wed 100

Queens Court

★★★ 75% @@ HOTEL

☎ 01392 272709 🖹 01392 491390
6-8 Bystock Ter EX4 4HY
e-mail: enquiries@queenscourt-hotel.co.uk
web: www.queenscourt-hotel.co.uk
dir: Exit dual carriageway at junct 30 onto B5132 (Topsham Rd) towards city centre. Hotel 200yds from Central Station

Quietly located within walking distance of the city centre, this privately owned hotel is a listed, early Victorian property that provides friendly hospitality. The smart public areas and contemporary bedrooms are tastefully furnished, and the stylish and attractive Olive Tree restaurant offers an award-winning selection of dishes. Rooms are available for conferences, meetings, weddings and parties. Complimentary parking is available in a public car park directly opposite the hotel entrance.

Rooms 18 (1 fmly) **Facilities** FTV Wi-fi **Conf** Class 30 Board 30 Thtr 60 **Services** Lift **Notes** ⊗ Closed Xmas & New Year RS 25-30 Dec Civ Wed 60

St Olaves Hotel

★★★ 75% HOTEL

☎ 01392 217736 🖹 01392 413054
Mary Arches St EX4 3AZ
e-mail: info@olaves.co.uk
dir: In city centre, signed to Mary Arches Car Park. Hotel entrance opposite car park entrance

Only a short stroll from the cathedral and city centre, and set in an attractive walled garden, St Olaves seems to be a country house in an almost hidden location. Bedrooms are comfortably furnished and full of character. The Treasury Restaurant is the venue for enjoyable dishes with local produce very much in evidence.

Rooms 18 (3 annexe) (1 fmly) (1 GF) **S** £85-£99; **D** £105-£165 (incl. bkfst)* **Facilities** STV New Year Wi-fi **Conf** Class 80 Board 50 Thtr 120 Del from £127.50 to £155* **Parking** 15 **Notes** LB Civ Wed 120

Best Western Lord Haldon Country Hotel

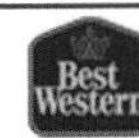

★★★ 74% HOTEL

☎ 01392 832483 🖹 01392 833765
Dunchideock EX6 7YF
e-mail: enquiries@lordhaldonhotel.co.uk
web: www.lordhaldonhotel.co.uk
dir: M5 junct 31, 1st exit off A30, follow signs through Ide to Dunchideock

Set amidst rural tranquillity, this attractive country house goes from strength to strength. Guests are assured of a warm welcome from the professional team of staff, and the well-equipped bedrooms are comfortable; many have stunning views. The daily-changing menu features skilfully cooked dishes with most of the produce sourced locally.

Rooms 23 (3 fmly) **S** £49-£160; **D** £60-£200 (incl. bkfst)* **Facilities** FTV Xmas New Year Wi-fi **Conf** Class 100 Board 40 Thtr 250 Del from £110 to £129.95* **Parking** 120 **Notes** LB Civ Wed 120

Barton Cross Hotel & Restaurant

★★★ 71% @ HOTEL

☎ 01392 841245 🖹 01392 841942
Huxham, Stoke Canon EX5 4EJ
e-mail: bartonxhuxham@aol.com
dir: 0.5m off A396 at Stoke Canon, 3m N of Exeter

17th-century charm combined with 21st-century luxury perfectly sums up the appeal of this lovely country hotel. The bedrooms are spacious, tastefully decorated and well maintained. Public areas include the cosy first-floor lounge and the lounge/bar with its warming log fire. The restaurant offers a seasonally changing menu of consistently enjoyable cuisine.

Rooms 9 (2 fmly) (2 GF) (2 smoking) **Facilities** STV FTV Xmas New Year Wi-fi **Conf** Class 20 Board 20 Thtr 20 **Parking** 35 **Notes** LB

See advert on this page

E

EXETER *continued*

Gipsy Hill Hotel

THE INDEPENDENTS HOTEL ASSOCIATION

★★★ 71% HOTEL

☎ 01392 465252 📠 01392 464302
Gipsy Hill Ln, Monkerton EX1 3RN
e-mail: stay@gipsyhillhotel.co.uk
web: www.gipsyhillhotel.co.uk
dir: M5 junct 29 towards Exeter. Right at 1st rdbt, right again at next rdbt. Hotel 0.5m on right

Located on the edge of the city, with easy access to the M5 and the airport, this popular hotel is set in attractive, well-tended gardens and boasts far-reaching country views. The hotel offers a range of conference and function rooms, comfortable bedrooms and modern facilities. An intimate bar and lounge are adjacent to the elegant restaurant.

Rooms 37 (17 annexe) (4 fmly) (12 GF) (1 smoking) **Facilities** STV FTV Xmas New Year Wi-fi **Conf** Class 80 Board 80 Thtr 300 **Parking** 60 **Notes** LB ⊗ Civ Wed 160

Red House

★★ 71% HOTEL

☎ 01392 256104 📠 01392 666145
2 Whipton Village Rd EX4 8AR
e-mail: info@redhousehotelexeter.co.uk
dir: M5 junct 30. Left before Middlemoor services, right at rdbt towards Pinhoe & University. 0.75m left to Whipton/University, hotel 1m on right

Located just a mile from the city centre, this family owned establishment has a warm and welcoming atmosphere; the convivial bar is a popular meeting place for visitors and locals alike. Bedrooms are soundly appointed and provide good levels of comfort. An extensive menu is offered either in the bar area or separate restaurant with a carvery at lunchtimes.

Rooms 12 (5 fmly) (4 GF) **Facilities** FTV **Conf** Board 24 Thtr 40 **Parking** 25 **Notes** ⊗

Great Western

★★ 64% HOTEL

☎ 01392 274039 📠 01392 425529
St David's Station Approach EX4 4NU
e-mail: bookings@greatwesternhotel.co.uk
dir: M5 junct 30, follow City Centre signs then St Davids Station signs. Hotel on A377 W of city

This long-established railway hotel has been providing rest and refreshment for weary travellers for many years. Its long tradition of hospitality is still very much in evidence in the convivial bar which is a popular venue with both visitors and locals alike. Bedrooms, in a variety of sizes, are soundly appointed. In addition to the bar menu, guests also have the option of eating in the attractive restaurant.

Rooms 35 (1 fmly) **S** £42-£49; **D** £62-£72 (incl. bkfst)* **Facilities** FTV Wi-fi **Conf** Class 12 Board 20 Thtr 35 Del from £42 to £100*

Express by Holiday Inn Exeter M5 Jct 29

BUDGET HOTEL

☎ 01392 261000 📠 01392 261061
Guardian Rd EX1 3PE
e-mail: managerexeter@expressholidayinn.co.uk
web: www.expressexeter.com
dir: M5 junct 29, follow signs for Exeter city centre. Hotel on 1st rdbt

A modern hotel ideal for families and business travellers. Fresh and uncomplicated, the spacious rooms include Sky TV, power shower and tea and coffee-making facilities. Continental buffet breakfast is included in the room rate; other meals may be taken at the nearby family pub or restaurant. See also the Hotel Groups pages.

Rooms 149 (94 fmly) (41 GF) (6 smoking) **Conf** Class 20 Board 20 Thtr 30

Premier Inn Exeter Central St Davids

BUDGET HOTEL

☎ 0871 527 9278 📠 0871 527 9279
Bonhay Rd EX4 4BG
dir: M5 junct 31, A30 towards Bodmin & Oakehampton. Exit onto A377 towards Exeter & Crediton. Hotel on left

High quality, budget accommodation ideal for both families and business travellers. Spacious, en suite bedrooms feature tea and coffee making facilities, and Freeview TV in most hotels. Internet access and Wi-fi are available for a small fee. The adjacent family restaurant features a wide and varied menu. See also the Hotel Groups pages.

Rooms 102 **D** £72-£76*

Premier Inn Exeter (Countess Wear)

BUDGET HOTEL

☎ 0871 527 8386 📠 0871 527 8387
398 Topsham Rd EX2 6HE
dir: 2m from M5 junct 30/A30 junct 29. Follow signs for Exeter & Dawlish (A379). On dual carriageway take 2nd slip road on left at Countess Wear rdbt. Hotel adjacent to Beefeater

Rooms 44 **D** £70-£72*

Chi Restaurant & Bar with Accommodation

RESTAURANT WITH ROOMS

☎ 01626 890213 📠 01626 891678
Fore St, Kenton EX6 8LD
e-mail: enquiries@chi-restaurant.co.uk
web: www.chi-restaurant.co.uk
dir: 5m S of Exeter. M5 junct 30, A379 towards Dawlish, in village centre

This former pub has been spectacularly transformed into a chic and contemporary bar, allied with a stylish Chinese restaurant. Dishes are beautifully presented with an emphasis on quality produce and authenticity, resulting in a memorable dining experience. Bedrooms are well equipped and all provide good levels of space and comfort, along with modern bathrooms.

Rooms 5 (2 fmly)

EXFORD Map 3 SS83
Somerset

Crown

★★★ 79% ® HOTEL

☎ 01643 831554 📠 01643 831665
TA24 7PP
e-mail: info@crownhotelexmoor.co.uk
web: www.crownhotelexmoor.co.uk
dir: M5 junct 25, follow Taunton signs. Take A358 from Taunton, then B3224 via Wheddon Cross to Exford

Guest comfort is certainly the hallmark here. Afternoon tea is served in the lounge beside a roaring fire, and tempting menus in the bar and restaurant are all part of the charm of this delightful old coaching inn that specialises in breaks for shooting and other country sports. Bedrooms retain a traditional style yet offer a range of modern comforts and facilities, many have views of this pretty moorland village.

Rooms 16 (3 fmly) **S** £69-£77; **D** £119-£155 (incl. bkfst)* **Facilities** Xmas New Year Wi-fi **Conf** Board 15 **Parking** 30 **Notes** LB

EXMOUTH Map 3 SY08
Devon

Royal Beacon

★★★ 79% HOTEL

☎ 01395 264886 📠 01395 268890
The Beacon EX8 2AF
e-mail: info@royalbeaconhotel.co.uk
web: www.royalbeaconhotel.co.uk
dir: From M5 take A376 & Marine Way. Follow seafront signs. On Imperial Rd turn left at T-junct then 1st right. Hotel 100yds on left

This elegant Georgian property sits in an elevated position overlooking the town and has fine views of the estuary towards the sea. Bedrooms are individually styled and many have sea views. Public areas include a well stocked bar, a cosy lounge, an impressive function suite, and a choice of restaurants where freshly prepared and enjoyable cuisine is offered.

Rooms 52 (17 annexe) (2 fmly) (8 GF) **Facilities** FTV Xmas New Year Wi-fi **Conf** Class 100 Board 60 Thtr 160 **Services** Lift **Parking** 28 **Notes** ® Civ Wed 160

Manor Hotel

★★ 72% HOTEL

☎ 01395 272549 📠 01395 225519
The Beacon EX8 2AG
e-mail: post@manorexmouth.co.uk
dir: M5 junct 30 take A376 to Exmouth. Hotel 300yds from seafront overlooking Manor Gardens

Conveniently located for easy access to the town centre and with views overlooking the sea, this friendly hotel offers traditional values of hospitality and service, drawing guests back year after year. The well-equipped bedrooms vary in style and size; many have far-reaching views. The fixed price menu offers a varied selection of dishes.

Rooms 39 (3 fmly) **S** £40-£48; **D** £70-£96 (incl. bkfst) **Facilities** FTV Xmas New Year Wi-fi **Conf** Class 60 Board 60 Thtr 100 **Services** Lift **Parking** 12 **Notes** LB ®

Cavendish Hotel

★★ 69% HOTEL

☎ 01395 272528 📠 01395 269361
11 Morton Crescent, The Esplanade EX8 1BE
e-mail: cavendish.exmouth@alfatravel.co.uk
dir: Follow seafront signs, hotel in centre of large crescent

Situated on the seafront, this terraced hotel attracts many groups from around the country. With fine views out to sea, the hotel is within walking distance of the town centre. The bedrooms are neatly presented; front-facing rooms are always popular. Entertainment is provided on most evenings during the summer.

Rooms 76 (3 fmly) (19 GF) **S** £39-£53; **D** £62-£90 (incl. bkfst) **Facilities** FTV Snooker ♫ Xmas New Year **Services** Lift **Parking** 25 **Notes** LB ® Closed Dec-Jan (ex Xmas) RS Nov & Mar

EYE Map 13 TM17
Suffolk

Cornwallis

★★★★ 73% ® HOTEL

☎ 01379 870326 & 08444 146524
📠 01379 870326
Rectory Rd, Brome IP23 8AJ
e-mail: reservations.cornwallis@ohiml.com
web: www.oxfordhotelsandinns.com

Peacefully situated just off the A140 at the end of a tree lined lane in 23 acres of wooded grounds, this charming Grade II listed property has a wealth of original character such as exposed beams, open fireplaces and wood carvings. Public rooms include a 15th-century Tudor bar, a lounge, a conservatory and a fine-dining restaurant. The individually designed bedrooms are tastefully appointed and have lovely views out over the gardens.

Rooms 16 (5 annexe) (1 fmly) (3 GF) **Facilities** Xmas New Year Wi-fi **Conf** Class 50 Board 30 Thtr 70 **Parking** 100 **Notes** ® Civ Wed 80

F

FALFIELD Gloucestershire Map 4 ST69

Best Western The Gables

★★★ 74% HOTEL

☎ 01454 260502 📠 01454 261821
Bristol Rd GL12 8DL
e-mail: mail@thegablesbristol.co.uk
web: www.thegablesbristol.co.uk
dir: M5 junct 14 N'bound. Left at end of sliproad. Right onto A38, hotel 300yds on right

Conveniently located, just a few minutes from the motorway this establishment is ideally suited to both business and leisure guests, with easy access to Cheltenham, Gloucester, Bristol and Bath. Bedrooms are spacious and well equipped. Relaxing public areas consist of a light and airy bar and restaurant where meals and all-day snacks are available; a more formal restaurant is open for dinner. There is also a range of meeting rooms.

Rooms 46 (4 fmly) (18 GF) **S** £60-£130; **D** £60-£130 (incl. bkfst)* **Facilities** FTV Wi-fi **Conf** Class 90 Board 50 Thtr 200 Del from £135 to £150* **Parking** 104 **Notes** LB ㊗ Civ Wed 150

FALMOUTH Cornwall Map 2 SW83

See also **Mawnan Smith**

Royal Duchy

★★★★ 79% ®® HOTEL

☎ 01326 313042 & 214001 📠 01326 319420
Cliff Rd TR11 4NX
e-mail: reservations@royalduchy.com
web: www.royalduchy.com
dir: On Cliff Rd, along Falmouth seafront

Looking out over the sea and towards Pendennis Castle, this hotel provides a friendly environment. The comfortable lounge and cocktail bar are well appointed, and leisure facilities and meeting rooms are also available. The award-winning restaurant serves carefully prepared dishes, and bedrooms vary in size and aspect, with many rooms having sea views.

Rooms 43 (6 fmly) (1 GF) **S** £80-£120; **D** £140-£290 (incl. bkfst)* **Facilities** FTV ③ Games room Beauty salon Sauna ♫ Xmas New Year Wi-fi Child facilities **Conf** Class 50 Board 50 Thtr 50 **Services** Lift **Parking** 50 **Notes** LB ㊗ Civ Wed 100

See advert on this page

St Michael's Hotel and Spa

★★★★ 75% HOTEL

☎ 01326 312707 📠 01326 211772
Gyllyngvase Beach, Seafront TR11 4NB
e-mail: info@stmichaelshotel.co.uk
dir: A39 into Falmouth, follow beach signs, at 2nd mini-rdbt into Pennance Rd. Take 2nd left & 2nd left again

Overlooking the bay this hotel is in an excellent position and commands lovely views. It is appointed in a fresh, contemporary style that reflects its location by the sea. The Flying Fish restaurant has a great atmosphere and a buzz. The light and bright bedrooms, some with balconies, are well equipped. There are excellent leisure facilities including a fitness and health club together with the spa offering many treatments; the attractive gardens also provide a place to relax and unwind.

Rooms 61 (8 annexe) (7 fmly) (12 GF) **S** £60-£125; **D** £120-£310 (incl. bkfst)* **Facilities** Spa FTV ③ Gym Sauna Steam room Aqua-aerobics Fitness classes Xmas New Year Wi-fi **Conf** Class 150 Board 50 Thtr 200 Del from £95 to £155* **Parking** 30 **Notes** LB ㊗ Civ Wed 80

The Greenbank Hotel

★★★★ 74% HOTEL

01326 312440 01326 211362
Harbourside TR11 2SR
e-mail: reception@greenbank-hotel.co.uk
web: www.greenbank-hotel.co.uk
dir: 500yds past Falmouth Marina on Penryn River

Located by the marina, and with its own private quay dating from the 17th century, this smart hotel has a strong maritime theme throughout. Set at the water's edge, the lounge, restaurant and many bedrooms all benefit from harbour views. The restaurant provides a choice of interesting and enjoyable dishes.

Rooms 60 (6 fmly) **S** £89-£119; **D** £145-£269 (incl. bkfst)* **Facilities** FTV Private beach & quay Xmas New Year Wi-fi **Conf** Class 90 Board 25 Thtr 90 Del from £145* **Services** Lift **Parking** 68 **Notes** Civ Wed 90

Best Western Penmere Manor

★★★ 80% HOTEL

01326 211411 01326 317588
Mongleath Rd TR11 4PN
e-mail: reservations@penmere.co.uk
web: www.penmere.co.uk
dir: Exit A39 at Hillhead rdbt, over double mini rdbt. After 0.75m left into Mongleath Rd

Set in five acres on the outskirts of town, this Georgian manor house was originally built for a ship's captain. Now a family owned hotel it provides friendly service and a good range of facilities. Bedrooms vary in size and a located in the manor house and the garden wing. Various menus are available in the bar and the smart restaurant. There is a health and beauty centre offering a wide range of treatments and the water in the indoor pool is UV filtered.

Rooms 37 (12 fmly) (13 GF) **S** £64-£74; **D** £64-£95 (incl. bkfst)* **Facilities** FTV Gym Sauna New Year Wi-fi **Conf** Class 20 Board 30 Thtr 60 Del from £144.50 to £173* **Parking** 50 **Notes** LB Closed 22-27 Dec Civ Wed 40

Best Western Falmouth Beach Hotel

★★★ 78% HOTEL

01326 310500 01326 319147
Gyllyngvase Beach, Seafront TR11 4NA
e-mail: info@falmouthbeachhotel.co.uk
web: www.bw-falmouthbeachhotel.co.uk
dir: A39 to Falmouth, follow seafront signs

Enjoying wonderful views, this popular hotel is situated opposite the beach and within easy walking distance of Falmouth's attractions and port. A friendly atmosphere is maintained and guests have a good choice of leisure, fitness, entertainment and dining options. Bedrooms, many with balconies and sea views, are well equipped and comfortable.

Rooms 120 (20 fmly) (4 GF) **Facilities** Spa FTV supervised Gym Sauna Steam room Hair & beauty salon Xmas New Year Wi-fi **Conf** Class 200 Board 250 Thtr 300 **Services** Lift **Parking** 88 **Notes** Civ Wed 220

Green Lawns

THE INDEPENDENTS HOTEL ASSOCIATION

★★★ 77% HOTEL

01326 312734 01326 211427
Western Ter TR11 4QJ
e-mail: info@greenlawnshotel.com
web: www.greenlawnshotel.com
dir: On A39

This attractive property enjoys a convenient location close to the town centre and within easy reach of the sea. Spacious public areas include inviting lounges, an elegant restaurant, conference and meeting facilities and a leisure centre. Bedrooms vary in size and style but all are well equipped and comfortable. The friendly service is particularly noteworthy.

Rooms 39 (8 fmly) (11 GF) **S** £60-£70; **D** £109-£189 (incl. bkfst)* **Facilities** FTV Gym Squash Sauna Steam room Spa bath New Year Wi-fi **Conf** Class 80 Board 80 Thtr 200 Del from £95 to £115* **Parking** 69 **Notes** LB Closed 24-30 Dec Civ Wed 100

Falmouth

★★★ 75% HOTEL

01326 312671 & 0800 019 3121
01326 319533
Castle Beach TR11 4NZ
e-mail: reservations@falmouthhotel.com
web: www.falmouthhotel.com
dir: A30 to Truro then A390 to Falmouth. Follow signs for beaches, hotel on seafront near Pendennis Castle

This spectacular beach-front Victorian property affords wonderful sea views from many of its comfortable bedrooms, some of which have their own balconies. Spacious public areas include a number of inviting lounges, a choice of dining options and an impressive range of leisure facilities.

Rooms 70 (16 fmly) **Facilities** Spa FTV Putt green Gym Beauty salon & Therapeutic rooms Xmas New Year Wi-fi **Conf** Class 150 Board 100 Thtr 250 **Services** Lift **Parking** 120 **Notes** Civ Wed 250

Penmorvah Manor

★★★ 72% HOTEL

01326 250277 01326 250509
Budock Water TR11 5ED
e-mail: reception@penmorvah.co.uk
web: www.penmorvah.co.uk
dir: A39 to Hillhead rdbt, take 2nd exit. Right at Falmouth Football Club, through Budock. Hotel opposite Penjerrick Gardens

Situated within two miles of central Falmouth, this extended Victorian manor house is a peaceful hideaway, set in six acres of private woodland and gardens. Penmorvah is well positioned for visiting the local gardens, and offers many garden-tour breaks. Dinner features locally sourced, quality ingredients such as Cornish cheeses, meat, fish and game.

Rooms 27 (1 fmly) (10 GF) **S** fr £55; **D** £105-£160 (incl. bkfst)* **Facilities** FTV Xmas Wi-fi **Conf** Class 100 Board 56 Thtr 250 Del from £100* **Parking** 100 **Notes** LB Closed 31 Dec-Jan Civ Wed 120

F

FALMOUTH *continued*

Rosslyn

★★ 69% HOTEL

☎ 01326 312699 & 315373 📠 01326 312699
110 Kimberley Park Rd TR11 2JJ
e-mail: mail@rosslynhotel.co.uk
web: www.rosslynhotel.co.uk
dir: On A39 towards Falmouth, to Hillend rdbt, turn right, straight on at next mini rdbt. At 2nd mini rdbt left into Trescobeas Rd. Hotel on left past hospital

A relaxed and friendly atmosphere is maintained at this family-run hotel. Situated on the northern edge of Falmouth, the Rosslyn is easily located and is suitable for both business and leisure guests. A comfortable lounge overlooks the well-tended garden, and enjoyable freshly prepared dinners are offered in the restaurant.

Rooms 25 (3 fmly) (6 GF) **Facilities** FTV Internet access in lounge New Year **Conf** Class 60 Board 20 **Parking** 22

Madeira Hotel

★★ 68% HOTEL

☎ 01326 313531 📠 01326 319143
Cliff Rd TR11 4NY
e-mail: madeira.falmouth@alfatravel.co.uk
dir: A39 (Truro to Falmouth), follow 'Hotel' tourist signs to seafront

This popular hotel offers splendid sea views and a pleasant, convenient location, which is close to the town. Extensive sun lounges are popular haunts in which to enjoy the views, while additional facilities include an oak panelled cocktail bar. Bedrooms, many with sea views, are available in a range of sizes.

Rooms 50 (8 fmly) (7 GF) **S** £39-£55; **D** £62-£94 (incl. bkfst) **Facilities** FTV ♫ Xmas New Year **Services** Lift **Parking** 11 **Notes** LB ⊗ Closed Dec-Feb (ex Xmas) RS Nov & Mar

Membly Hall

★★ 68% HOTEL

☎ 01326 312869 & 311115 📠 01326 211751
Sea Front, Cliff Rd TR11 4NT
e-mail: memblyhallhotel@tiscali.co.uk
dir: A39 to Falmouth. Follow seafront & beaches signs

Located conveniently on the seafront and enjoying splendid views, this family-run hotel offers friendly service. Bedrooms are pleasantly spacious and well equipped. Carefully prepared and enjoyable meals are served in the spacious dining room. Live entertainment is provided on some evenings and there is also a sauna and spa pool.

Rooms 35 (3 fmly) (6 GF) **Facilities** FTV Gym Indoor short bowls Table tennis Pool table Sauna Spa pool ♫ New Year Wi-fi **Conf** Class 130 Board 60 Thtr 150 **Services** Lift **Parking** 30 **Notes** LB ⊗ Closed Xmas week RS Dec-Jan

FAREHAM
Hampshire — Map 5 SU50

Solent Hotel & Spa

★★★★ 80% ❀ HOTEL

☎ 01489 880000 📠 01489 880007
Rookery Av, Whiteley PO15 7AJ
e-mail: solent@shirehotels.com
web: www.solenthotel.com
dir: M27 junct 9, hotel on Solent Business Park

Close to the M27 with easy access to Portsmouth, the New Forest and other attractions, this smart, purpose-built hotel enjoys a peaceful location. Bedrooms are spacious and very well appointed and there is a well-equipped spa with health and beauty facilities.

Rooms 111 (9 fmly) (39 GF) **S** £100-£200; **D** £110-£210* **Facilities** Spa STV Gym Steam room Sauna Children's splash pool Activity studio Xmas New Year Wi-fi **Conf** Class 100 Board 80 Thtr 200 Del from £135 to £185* **Services** Lift **Parking** 200 **Notes** LB ⊗ Civ Wed 160

Holiday Inn Fareham-Solent

★★★ 79% HOTEL

☎ 0871 942 9028 📠 01329 844666
Cartwright Dr, Titchfield PO15 5RJ
e-mail: fareham@ihg.com
web: www.holidayinn.co.uk
dir: M27 junct 9, follow signs for A27. Over Segensworth rdbt 1.5m, left at next rdbt

This hotel is well positioned and attracts both the business and leisure markets. Bedrooms are spacious and smart, and stylish public areas include a number of conference rooms. Beauty treatments are available in the leisure area which has a swimming pool, aerobics studio and gym.

Rooms 124 (4 fmly) (72 GF) (7 smoking) **Facilities** supervised Gym Sauna Treatment rooms Wi-fi **Conf** Class 64 Board 45 Thtr 140 **Services** Air con **Parking** 160 **Notes** ⊗ Civ Wed 100

Lysses House

★★★ 73% HOTEL

☎ 01329 822622 📠 01329 822762
51 High St PO16 7BQ
e-mail: lysses@lysses.co.uk
web: www.lysses.co.uk
dir: M27 junct 11 follow Fareham signs, stay in left lane to Delme rdbt. At rdbt 3rd exit into East St, follow into High St. Hotel at top on right

This attractive Georgian hotel is situated on the edge of the town in a quiet location and provides spacious and well-equipped accommodation. There are conference facilities, and a lounge bar serving a range of snacks together with the Richmond Restaurant that offers imaginative cuisine.

Rooms 21 (2 fmly) (7 GF) **Facilities** FTV Free entry to nearby Fitness First Wi-fi **Conf** Class 42 Board 28 Thtr 95 **Services** Lift **Parking** 30 **Notes** ⊗ Closed 25 Dec-1 Jan RS 24 Dec & BHs Civ Wed 100

Red Lion Hotel

OldEnglish

★★★ 67% HOTEL

☎ 01329 822640 📠 01329 823579
East St PO16 0BP
e-mail: redlion.fareham@oldenglishinns.co.uk

This hotel, which was formerly a coaching inn, is conveniently located within a few moments' walk of the market town of Fareham. An array of substantial hot and cold meals is served throughout the day in the bright informal restaurant and bar area. Bedrooms provide good comfort levels. The hotel has pretty gardens and benefits from barrier operated parking.

Rooms 46 **Conf** Class 60 Board 40 Thtr 100

Premier Inn Fareham

BUDGET HOTEL

☎ 0871 527 8396 📠 0871 527 8397
Southampton Rd, Park Gate SO31 6AF
dir: M27 junct 9, follow Fareham West, A27 signs. (NB for Sat Nav use SO31 6BZ)

High quality, budget accommodation ideal for both families and business travellers. Spacious, en suite bedrooms feature tea and coffee making facilities, and Freeview TV in most hotels. Internet access and Wi-fi are available for a small fee. The adjacent family restaurant features a wide and varied menu. See also the Hotel Groups pages.

Rooms 41 **D** £60-£64*

FARINGDON
Oxfordshire Map 5 SU29

Best Western Sudbury House Hotel & Conference Centre

★★★ 74% HOTEL

☎ 01367 241272 📠 01367 242346
London St SN7 8AA
e-mail: stay@sudburyhouse.co.uk
web: www.sudburyhouse.co.uk
dir: Off A420, signed Folly Hill

Situated on the edge of the Cotswolds and set in nine acres of pleasant grounds, this hotel offers spacious and well-equipped bedrooms that are attractively decorated in warm colours. Dining options include the comfortable restaurant for a good selection of carefully presented dishes, and also the bar for lighter options. A comprehensive room service menu is available.

Rooms 49 (2 fmly) (10 GF) (2 smoking) **S** £72-£140; **D** £92-£160 (incl. bkfst)* **Facilities** STV Gym Boules New Year Wi-fi **Conf** Class 40 Board 34 Thtr 100 Del from £99 to £160* **Services** Lift **Parking** 100 **Notes** LB Civ Wed 160

FARNBOROUGH
Hampshire Map 5 SU85

Aviator

★★★★ 80% HOTEL

☎ 01252 555890 📠 01252 555899
Farnborough Rd GU14 6EL
e-mail: enquiries@aviatorfarnborough.co.uk
web: www.aviatorfarnborough.co.uk
dir: A325 to Aldershot, continue for 3m, hotel on right

A striking property with a modern, sleek interior overlooking Farnborough airfield and located close to the main transport networks. This hotel is suitable for both the business and leisure travellers. The bedrooms have are well designed and provide complimentary Wi-fi. Both the Brasserie and the Deli source local ingredients for their menus.

Rooms 169 **D** £200-£330* **Facilities** STV Gym Exercise studio Xmas New Year Wi-fi **Conf** Class 30 Board 40 Thtr 110 Del from £250 to £280* **Services** Lift Air con **Parking** 169 **Notes** LB RS Sat Civ Wed 120

Holiday Inn Farnborough

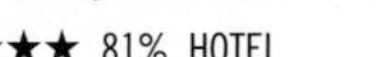

★★★ 81% HOTEL

☎ 0871 942 9029 & 01252 894300
📠 01252 523166
Lynchford Rd GU14 6AZ
e-mail: reservations-farnborough@ihg.com
web: www.holidayinn.co.uk
dir: M3 junct 4, follow A325 through Farnborough towards Aldershot. Hotel on left at The Queen's rdbt

This hotel occupies a perfect location for events in Aldershot and Farnborough with ample parking on site and easy access to the M3. Modern bedrooms provide good comfort levels, and internet access is provided throughout. Leisure facilities comprise a swimming pool, gym and beauty treatment rooms. Smart meeting rooms are also available.

Rooms 142 (31 fmly) (35 GF) (7 smoking) **Facilities** Spa STV supervised Gym Sauna Steam room Beauty room Xmas New Year Wi-fi **Conf** Class 80 Board 60 Thtr 180 Del from £99 to £210* **Services** Air con **Parking** 170 **Notes** Civ Wed 180

Premier Inn Farnborough

BUDGET HOTEL

☎ 0871 527 8398 📠 0871 527 8399
Ively Rd, Southwood GU14 0JP
dir: M3 junct 4a, A327 to Farnborough. Hotel on left at 5th rdbt (Monkey Puzzle Rdbt)

High quality, budget accommodation ideal for both families and business travellers. Spacious, en suite bedrooms feature tea and coffee making facilities, and Freeview TV in most hotels. Internet access and Wi-fi are available for a small fee. The adjacent family restaurant features a wide and varied menu. See also the Hotel Groups pages.

Rooms 62 **D** £52-£71*

FARNHAM
Surrey Map 5 SU84

Best Western Frensham Pond Hotel

★★★ 79% HOTEL

☎ 01252 795161 📠 01252 792631
Bacon Ln GU10 2QB
e-mail: info@frenshampondhotel.co.uk
web: www.frenshampondhotel.co.uk

(For full entry see Churt)

Mercure Bush Hotel

★★★ 77% HOTEL

☎ 01252 715237 📠 01252 719297
The Borough GU9 7NN
e-mail: H6621@accor.com
web: www.mercure.com
dir: M3 junct 4, A31, follow town centre signs. At East Street lights turn left, hotel on right

Dating back to the 17th century, this extended former coaching inn is attractively presented and has a courtyard and a lawned garden. The bedrooms are well appointed, with quality fabrics and good facilities. The public areas include the panelled Oak Lounge, a smart cocktail bar and a conference facility in an adjoining building.

Rooms 94 (3 fmly) (27 GF) **Facilities** FTV Xmas Wi-fi **Conf** Class 80 Board 30 Thtr 140 **Parking** 70 **Notes** Civ Wed 90

FELIXSTOWE
Suffolk Map 13 TM33

The Brook Hotel

★★★ 77% HOTEL

☎ 01394 278441 📠 01394 670422
Orwell Rd IP11 7PF
e-mail: welcome@brookhotel.com

A modern, well furnished hotel ideally situated in a residential area close to the town centre and the sea. Public areas include a lounge bar, a large open-plan restaurant with a bar area and a residents' lounge. Bedrooms are generally quite spacious; each one is pleasantly decorated and equipped with modern facilities.

Rooms 25 (5 fmly) (3 GF) **S** £60-£80; **D** £70-£120 (incl. bkfst) **Facilities** FTV Xmas New Year Wi-fi **Conf** Class 60 Board 60 Thtr 100 Del from £100 to £200 **Parking** 20 **Notes** LB Civ Wed 150

Marlborough

★★ 72% HOTEL

☎ 01394 285621 📠 01394 670724
Sea Front IP11 2BJ
e-mail: hsm@marlborough-hotel-felix.com
web: www.marlborough-hotel-felix.com
dir: From A14 follow 'Docks' signs. Over Dock rdbt, rail crossing & lights. Left at T-junct. Hotel 400mtrs on left

Situated on the seafront, overlooking the beach and just a short stroll from the pier and town centre. This traditional resort hotel offers a good range of facilities including the smart Rattan Restaurant, Flying Boat Bar and L'Aperitif lounge. The pleasantly

continued

F

FELIXSTOWE ***continued***

decorated bedrooms come in a variety of styles; some have lovely sea views.

Rooms 48 (1 fmly) **S** £49-£56; **D** £70-£95 (incl. bkfst)* **Facilities** STV Pool table Xmas New Year Wi-fi **Conf** Class 60 Board 40 Thtr 80 Del from £79 to £99* **Services** Lift **Parking** 16 **Notes** LB ®

FERNDOWN — Map 5 SU00
Dorset

Premier Inn Bournemouth/ Ferndown

BUDGET HOTEL

☎ 0871 527 8122 🖹 0871 527 8123
Ringwood Rd, Tricketts Cross BH22 9BB
dir: Off A348 just before Tricketts Cross rdbt

High quality, budget accommodation ideal for both families and business travellers. Spacious, en suite bedrooms feature tea and coffee making facilities, and Freeview TV in most hotels. Internet access and Wi-fi are available for a small fee. The adjacent family restaurant features a wide and varied menu. See also the Hotel Groups pages.

Rooms 32 **D** £68*

FLAMBOROUGH — Map 17 TA27
East Riding of Yorkshire

North Star

★★ 76% SMALL HOTEL

☎ 01262 850379 🖹 01262 850379
North Marine Dr YO15 1BL
web: www.thenorthstarhotel.co.uk
dir: B1229 or B1255 to Flamborough. Follow signs for North Landing along North Marine Dr. Hotel 100yds from sea

Standing close to the North Landing of Flamborough Head, this family-run hotel overlooks delightful countryside. It provides excellent accommodation and caring hospitality. A good range of fresh local food, especially fish, is available in both the bar and the dining room.

Rooms 7 **S** £55-£65; **D** £60-£100 (incl. bkfst)* **Parking** 60 **Notes** LB ® Closed Xmas RS Nov-Etr

FLEET MOTORWAY SERVICE AREA (M3) — Map 5 SU75
Hampshire

Days Inn Fleet - M3

BUDGET HOTEL

☎ 01252 815587 🖹 01252 815587
Fleet Services GU51 1AA
e-mail: fleet.hotel@welcomebreak.co.uk
web: www.welcomebreak.co.uk
dir: Between junct 4a & 5 southbound on M3

This modern building offers accommodation in smart, spacious and well-equipped bedrooms, suitable for families and business travellers, and all with en suite bathrooms. Continental breakfast is available and other refreshments may be taken at the nearby family restaurant. See also the Hotel Groups pages.

Rooms 58 (46 fmly) (5 smoking) **S** £39.95-£59.95; **D** £49.95-£69.95

FLITWICK — Map 11 TL03
Bedfordshire

Menzies Flitwick Manor

MenziesHotels

★★★★ 73% ® COUNTRY HOUSE HOTEL

☎ 01525 712242 🖹 01525 718753
Church Rd MK45 1AE
e-mail: flitwick@menzieshotels.co.uk
web: www.menzieshotels.co.uk
dir: M1 junct 12, follow signs for Flitwick, turn left into Church Rd, hotel on left

With its picturesque setting in acres of gardens and parkland, yet only minutes by car from the motorway, this lovely Georgian house combines the best of both worlds, being both accessible and peaceful. Bedrooms are individually decorated and furnished with period pieces; some are air conditioned. Cosy and intimate, the lounge and restaurant help give the hotel a home-from-home feel.

Rooms 18 (1 fmly) (5 GF) (1 smoking) **Facilities** STV Putt green Xmas New Year Wi-fi **Conf** Class 30 Board 22 Thtr 40 **Parking** 18 **Notes** Civ Wed 50

FOLKESTONE — Map 7 TR23
Kent

Best Western Clifton Hotel

★★★ 75% HOTEL

☎ 01303 851231 🖹 01303 223949
The Leas CT20 2EB
e-mail: reservations@thecliftonhotel.com
dir: M20 junct 13, 0.25m W of town centre on A259

This privately-owned Victorian-style hotel occupies a prime location, looking out across the English Channel. The bedrooms are comfortably appointed and most have views of the sea. Public areas include a traditionally furnished lounge, a popular bar serving a good range of beers and several well-appointed conference rooms.

Rooms 80 (5 fmly) **S** £65-£75; **D** £85-£110 (incl. bkfst)* **Facilities** FTV Games room Xmas New Year Wi-fi **Conf** Class 36 Board 32 Thtr 80 Del from £95 to £135* **Services** Lift **Notes** LB ®

The Southcliff

★★ 69% HOTEL

☎ 01303 850075 🖹 01303 850070
22-26 The Leas CT20 2DY
e-mail: sales@thesouthcliff.co.uk
web: www.thesouthcliff.co.uk
dir: M20 junct 13, follow signs for The Leas. Left at rdbt onto Sandgate Rd, right at Blockbusters, right at end of road, hotel on right

Located on the town's panoramic promenade with a bird's eye view of the sea, this historical Victorian hotel is perfectly located for cross channel connections and is only minutes from the town centre. The bedrooms are spacious and airy with some boasting balconies and sea views. Enjoy dinner in the spacious restaurant or relax in the contemporary bar. Parking is available by arrangement.

Rooms 68 (2 fmly) **S** £30-£45; **D** £39-£89 (incl. bkfst) **Facilities** STV ♫ Xmas New Year Wi-fi **Conf** Class 120 Board 50 Thtr 200 Del from £55 to £99 **Services** Lift **Parking** 24 **Notes** LB ®

Premier Inn Folkestone (Channel Tunnel)

BUDGET HOTEL

☎ 0871 527 8400 🖹 0871 527 8401
Cherry Garden Ln CT19 4AP
dir: M20 junct 13. Follow Folkestone, A20 signs. At lights turn right, hotel on right

High quality, budget accommodation ideal for both families and business travellers. Spacious, en suite bedrooms feature tea and coffee making facilities, and Freeview TV in most hotels. Internet access and Wi-fi are available for a small fee. The adjacent family restaurant features a wide and varied menu. See also the Hotel Groups pages.

Rooms 79 **D** £56*

FOREST ROW
East Sussex — Map 6 TQ43

INSPECTORS' CHOICE

Ashdown Park Hotel & Country Club

★★★★ @@ HOTEL

☎ 01342 824988 📠 01342 826206
Wych Cross RH18 5JR
e-mail: reservations@ashdownpark.com
web: www.ashdownpark.com
dir: A264 to East Grinstead, then A22 to Eastbourne. 2m S of Forest Row at Wych Cross lights. Left to Hartfield, hotel on right 0.75m

Situated in 186 acres of landscaped gardens and parkland, this impressive country house enjoys a peaceful countryside setting in the heart of the Ashdown Forest. Bedrooms are individually styled and decorated. Public rooms include a restored 18th-century chapel, ideal for exclusive meetings and wedding parties, plus three drawing rooms, a cocktail bar and the award-winning Anderida Restaurant. The extensive indoor and outdoor leisure facilities include the Country Club and Spa plus an 18-hole, par 3 golf course and driving range.

Rooms 106 (16 GF) **D** £199-£465 (incl. bkfst)* **Facilities** Spa FTV 18 Putt green Gym Beauty salon Aerobics studio Steam room Treatment rooms Mountain bike hire Xmas New Year Wi-fi **Conf** Class 70 Board 40 Thtr 160 **Parking** 200 **Notes** LB Civ Wed 150

FORMBY
Merseyside — Map 15 SD30

Formby Hall Golf Resort & Spa

★★★★ 75% HOTEL

☎ 01704 875699 📠 01704 832134
Southport Old Rd L37 0AB
e-mail: gm@formbyhallgolfresort.co.uk
web: www.formbyhallgolfresort.co.uk
dir: A565 to 2nd rdbt, follow brown signs

This hotel offers modern, boutique-style bedrooms with state-of-the-art facilities, some with excellent views over the championship golf course. The lavish spa offers peace and tranquillity along with a superbly equipped gym. Two golf courses and a driving range also add to the hotel's outstanding facilities. The Brasserie is an informal eating option and guests can enjoy a relaxing drink in the 19th Hole bar.

Rooms 62 (10 fmly) (29 GF) **Facilities** Spa STV FTV 18 Putt green Gym Kinesis studio Driving range Short ball area Xmas New Year Wi-fi **Conf** Class 60 Board 40 Thtr 300 **Services** Lift Air con **Parking** 457 **Notes** Civ Wed 100

FOWEY
Cornwall — Map 2 SX15

Fowey Hall

★★★★ 77% @@ HOTEL

☎ 01726 833866 📠 01726 834100
Hanson Dr PL23 1ET
e-mail: info@foweyhallhotel.co.uk
web: www.foweyhallhotel.co.uk
dir: In Fowey, over mini rdbt into town centre. Pass school on right, 400mtrs right into Hanson Drive

Built in 1899, this listed mansion looks out on to the English Channel. The imaginatively designed bedrooms offer charm, individuality and sumptuous comfort; the Garden Wing rooms adding a further dimension to staying here. The beautifully appointed public rooms include the wood-panelled dining room where accomplished cuisine is served. Enjoying glorious views, the well-kept grounds have a covered pool and sunbathing area.

Rooms 36 (8 annexe) (30 fmly) (6 GF) **S** £90-£230; **D** £170-£245 (incl. bkfst)* **Facilities** Spa STV FTV Table tennis Basketball Trampoline Pool table Xmas New Year Wi-fi **Conf** Class 20 Board 20 Thtr 30 Del from £165* **Parking** 30 **Notes** LB Civ Wed 120

The Fowey Hotel

★★★★ 73% @ HOTEL

☎ 01726 832551 📠 01726 832125
The Esplanade PL23 1HX
e-mail: reservations@thefoweyhotel.co.uk
web: www.thefoweyhotel.co.uk
dir: A30 to Okehampton, continue to Bodmin. Then B3269 to Fowey for 1m, on right bend left junct then right into Dagands Rd. Hotel 200mtrs on left

This attractive hotel stands proudly above the estuary, with marvellous views of the river from the public areas and the majority of the bedrooms. High standards are evident throughout, augmented by a relaxed and welcoming atmosphere. There is a spacious bar, elegant restaurant and smart drawing room. Imaginative dinners make good use of quality local ingredients.

Rooms 37 (2 fmly) **S** £118-£158; **D** £118-£158 (incl. bkfst) **Facilities** Xmas New Year Wi-fi **Conf** Class 60 Board 20 Thtr 100 **Services** Lift **Parking** 20 **Notes** Civ Wed 120

F

FOWEY ***continued***

INSPECTORS' CHOICE

Old Quay House

★★ ◎◎ HOTEL

☎ 01726 833302 📠 01726 833668
28 Fore St PL23 1AQ
e-mail: info@theoldquayhouse.com
dir: M5 junct 31 onto A30 to Bodmin. Then A389 through town, then B3269 to Fowey

Looking out across Fowey's busy waterways and situated at the end of steep and winding streets so typical of Cornwall, this boutique-style hotel offers something a little different. The bedrooms, including the Penthouse room, have much individuality and most have balconies for enjoying the ever changing harbour scene. Each room has goosedown duvets, Egyptian cotton bedding, luxury toiletries and power showers. The award-winning and accomplished cuisine features fish and shellfish strongly; and eating or just having a drinking on the harbourside terrace is a delight. Breakfasts are also noteworthy.

Rooms 11 **S** £150-£180; **D** £180-£320 (incl. bkfst)* **Facilities** STV Wi-fi **Notes** ⊗ No children 12yrs Civ Wed 100

FRADDON Cornwall **Map 2 SW95**

Premier Inn Newquay (A30/Fraddon)

BUDGET HOTEL

☎ 0871 527 8816 📠 0871 527 8817
Penhale Round TR9 6NA
dir: On A30, 2m S of Indian Queens

High quality, budget accommodation ideal for both families and business travellers. Spacious, en suite bedrooms feature tea and coffee making facilities, and Freeview TV in most hotels. Internet access and Wi-fi are available for a small fee. The adjacent family restaurant features a wide and varied menu. See also the Hotel Groups pages.

Rooms 40 **D** £70*

FRESHWATER Isle of Wight **Map 5 SZ38**

Albion Hotel

★★★ 67% HOTEL

☎ 01983 755755 📠 01983 755295
PO40 9RA
e-mail: info@albion-hotel.net

In an idyllic location on the island's southern heritage coast, the hotel is right on the seafront with stunning views of Freshwater Bay. The bedrooms and bathrooms are spacious and offer guests modern, comfortable accommodation; many rooms have balconies. Breakfast and dinner are served in the traditionally styled restaurant that also enjoys the lovely views.

Rooms 41 **Facilities** ⓢ **Conf** Class 30 Board 40 Thtr 60 **Notes** Closed Nov-Apr

FRITTON Norfolk **Map 13 TG40**

Fritton House

★★★ 86% ◎ SMALL HOTEL

☎ 01493 484008 📠 01493 488 621
Church Ln NR31 9HA
e-mail: fritton.house@adnams.co.uk
web: www.adnams.co.uk/stay-with-us/fritton-house
dir: On A143 between Beccles & Great Yarmouth, at Fritton Lake, hotel 1m on right

This charming 15th-century property is set amidst parkland on the banks of Fritton Lake on the Somerleyton Estate. The contemporary-style public rooms include a large open-plan lounge bar, a dining room, a further lounge and a terraced area for alfresco dining. The individually decorated bedrooms are tastefully appointed and thoughtfully equipped.

Rooms 9 (2 fmly) **D** £120-£160 (incl. bkfst) **Facilities** FTV Putt green Fishing Children's play area Horse riding Wi-fi **Conf** Class 75 Board 50 Thtr 100 **Parking** 50 **Notes** LB Civ Wed 100

Caldecott Hall Golf & Leisure

★★★ 79% HOTEL

☎ 01493 488488 📠 01493 488561
Caldecott Hall, Beccles Rd NR31 9EY
e-mail: hotel@caldecotthall.co.uk
web: www.caldecotthall.co.uk
dir: On A143 (Beccles to Great Yarmouth road), 4m from Great Yarmouth

Ideally situated in its own attractive, landscaped grounds that has a golf course, fishing lakes and the Redwings horse sanctuary. The individually decorated bedrooms are spacious, and equipped with many thoughtful touches. Public rooms include a smart sitting room, a lounge bar, restaurant, clubhouse and smart leisure complex.

Rooms 8 (3 fmly) **Facilities** FTV ⓢ supervised ⛳ 36 Putt green Gym Driving range Wi-fi **Conf** Class 80 Board 20 Thtr 100 **Parking** 100 **Notes** ⊗ Civ Wed 150

FROME Somerset **Map 4 ST74**

Premier Inn Frome

BUDGET HOTEL

☎ 9871 527 8404 📠 0871 527 8405
Commerce Park, Jenson Av BA11 2LD
dir: M4 junct 18, A46 follow Warminster & Frome signs. Hotel off A361 (Frome bypass) in Commerce Park

High quality, budget accommodation ideal for both families and business travellers. Spacious, en suite bedrooms feature tea and coffee making facilities, and Freeview TV in most hotels. Internet access and Wi-fi are available for a small fee. The adjacent family restaurant features a wide and varied menu. See also the Hotel Groups pages.

Rooms 40 **D** £65*

Archangel

◎ RESTAURANT WITH ROOMS

☎ 01373 456111 📠 01373 456110
1 King St BA11 1BH
e-mail: hello@archangelfrome.com

Located in the centre of Frome, this welcoming property has been completely refurbished to create a stylish, contemporary ambience in a building that is full of character. The bedrooms might be described as funky; they come in a varied range of shapes and sizes but plenty of welcome extras are included. There is a variety of lounges and bars, an outdoor patio with seating, and a comfortable restaurant where high quality ingredients are utilised at both dinner and breakfast.

Rooms 6

GAINSBOROUGH — Map 17 SK88
Lincolnshire

Hickman Hill Hotel

★★ 68% HOTEL

☎ 01427 613639 ⎙ 01427 677591
Cox's Hill DN21 1HH
e-mail: info@hickmanhill.co.uk
web: www.hickmanhill.co.uk
dir: Right off B1433 after rail bridge, hotel up hill 100mtrs on right

Dating back to 1795, and once a school, this establishment became a hotel over 25 years ago; it retains many original features. The stylish and spacious bedrooms are named after the school's head teachers. The two-acre gardens are ideal for relaxing in after the stressful day. The restaurant is in the old school hall and offers tasty home-made dishes that use many locally sourced ingredients.

Rooms 10 (1 fmly) (1 GF) **S** £80-£105; **D** £95-£150 (incl. bkfst)* **Facilities** FTV Wi-fi **Conf** Class 40 Board 30 Thtr 60 **Parking** 32 **Notes** ⊗

GARFORTH — Map 16 SE43
West Yorkshire

Holiday Inn Leeds Garforth

★★★ 83% HOTEL

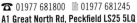

☎ 0113 286 6556 ⎙ 0113 286 8326
Wakefield Rd LS25 1LH
e-mail: reservations@hileedsgarforth.com
web: www.holidayinn.co.uk
dir: At junct of A63/A642. Hotel opposite rdbt

Located just outside Leeds, this hotel has excellent access to the M1 and M62 making it an ideal base for exploring the area. Well-equipped accommodation includes executive bedrooms. Public areas are attractively designed and include meeting rooms and leisure club. Aioli's Restaurant serves contemporary cuisine.

Rooms 144 (30 fmly) (35 GF) (15 smoking) **Facilities** FTV supervised Gym New Year Wi-fi **Conf** Class 120 Board 50 Thtr 350 **Services** Air con **Parking** 250 **Notes** Civ Wed 140

Best Western Milford Hotel

★★★ 81% HOTEL

☎ 01977 681800 ⎙ 01977 681245
A1 Great North Rd, Peckfield LS25 5LQ
e-mail: enquiries@mlh.co.uk
web: www.mlh.co.uk
dir: On A63, 1.5m W of A1(M) junct 42 & 4.5m E of M1 junct 46

This friendly, family owned and run hotel is conveniently situated, and provides very comfortable, modern accommodation. The air-conditioned bedrooms are particularly spacious and well equipped, and ten boutique-style superior rooms are available. Public areas include a relaxing lounge area, the contemporary Watermill Restaurant and lounge bar which has a working waterwheel.

Rooms 46 (13 GF) (6 smoking) **Facilities** FTV Xmas New Year Wi-fi **Conf** Class 35 Board 30 Thtr 60 **Services** Air con **Parking** 80 **Notes** LB

GARSTANG — Map 18 SD44
Lancashire

Best Western Garstang Country Hotel & Golf Centre

★★★ 77% HOTEL

☎ 01995 600100 ⎙ 01995 600950
Garstang Rd, Bowgreave PR3 1YE
e-mail: reception@ghgc.co.uk
web: www.garstanghotelandgolf.com
dir: M6 junct 32 take 1st right after Rogers Esso garage on A6 onto B6430. 1m, hotel on left

This smart, purpose-built hotel enjoys a peaceful location alongside its own 18-hole golf course. Comfortable and spacious bedrooms are well equipped for both business and leisure guests, whilst inviting public areas include a restaurant and a choice of bars - one serving food.

Rooms 32 (16 GF) **Facilities** STV FTV 18 Putt green Golf driving range Xmas New Year Wi-fi **Conf** Class 150 Board 80 Thtr 250 **Services** Lift **Parking** 172 **Notes** ⊗ Civ Wed 200

Pickerings Country House Hotel

★★★ 77% HOTEL

☎ 01995 600999 ⎙ 01995 602100
Garstang Rd, Catterall PR3 0HD
e-mail: info@pickerings-hotel.co.uk
dir: On B6430, S of Garstang in Catterall opposite Cock Robin lane junct

An 18th-century country house, in large immaculately kept gardens, that has been sympathetically renovated to provide good standards of comfort and extensive facilities. Some bedrooms are very spacious, and all are equipped with a range of practical and thoughtful extras. Public areas include a choice of lounges, and well-equipped function rooms are also available.

Rooms 12 (1 fmly) **Facilities** FTV Children's play area Xmas New Year Wi-fi **Conf** Class 90 Board 40 Thtr 150 **Parking** 51 **Notes** ⊗ Civ Wed 150

GATESHEAD — Map 21 NZ26
Tyne & Wear

See also **Beamish & Whickham**

G

Newcastle Marriott Hotel MetroCentre

Marriott HOTELS & RESORTS

★★★★ 77% HOTEL

☎ 0191 493 2233 ⎙ 0191 493 2030
MetroCentre NE11 9XF
e-mail: reservations.newcastle.england.metrocentre@marriotthotels.co.uk
web: www.newcastlemarriottmetrocentre.co.uk
dir: From N exit A1 at MetroCentre exit, take 'Other Routes'. From S exit A1 at MetroCentre exit, turn right

Set just off the A1 and on the doorstep of the popular Metro shopping centre, this stylish purpose-built hotel provides modern amenities including a leisure centre, conference facilities and an informal stylish restaurant offering a range of dining styles. All bedrooms are smartly laid out and thoughtfully equipped to suit both the business traveller and the leisure guest.

Rooms 150 (147 fmly) (5 smoking) **Facilities** Spa STV Gym Health & beauty clinic Dance studio Hairdresser Spinning studio Wi-fi **Conf** Class 172 Board 48 Thtr 400 **Services** Lift Air con **Parking** 300 **Notes** ⊗ Civ Wed 100

GATESHEAD *continued*

Eslington Villa Hotel

★★★ 79% HOTEL

☎ 0191 487 6017 & 420 0666 0191 420 0667
8 Station Rd, Low Fell NE9 6DR
e-mail: home@eslingtonvilla.co.uk
dir: From A1(M) exit for Team Valley Trading Estate. Right at 2nd rdbt along Eastern Av. Left at car show room, hotel 100yds on left

Set in a residential area, this smart hotel combines a bright, contemporary atmosphere with the period style of a fine Victorian villa. The overall ambience is relaxed and inviting. Chunky sofas grace the cocktail lounge, while tempting dishes can be enjoyed in either the classical dining room or modern conservatory overlooking the Team Valley.

Rooms 17 (2 fmly) (3 GF) **S** £74.50-£79.50; **D** £89.50-£94.50 (incl. bkfst)* **Facilities** FTV Wi-fi **Conf** Class 30 Board 25 Thtr 36 Del from £110 to £125* **Parking** 28 **Notes** LB Closed 25-26 Dec RS Sun/BHs

Express by Holiday Inn Newcastle Metro Centre

BUDGET HOTEL

☎ 01207 541100 01207 541136
Clasper Way, Riverside Way NE16 3BE
e-mail: newcastle@morethanhotels.com
web: www.hiexpress.com/gatesheaduk
dir: Follow signs for Metro Centre. Hotel on A1114 next to TGI Friday's & opposite Shell/Honda garage

A modern hotel ideal for families and business travellers. Fresh and uncomplicated, the spacious rooms include Sky TV, power shower and tea and coffee-making facilities. Continental buffet breakfast is included in the room rate; other meals may be taken at the nearby family pub or restaurant. See also the Hotel Groups pages.

Rooms 134 (69 fmly) **Conf** Class 20 Board 20 Thtr 30

Premier Inn Newcastle (Metro Centre)

BUDGET HOTEL

☎ 0871 527 8792 0871 527 8793
Derwent Haugh Rd, Swalwell NE16 3BL
dir: From A1 & A694 junct into Derwent Haugh Rd. 1m N of Metro Centre

High quality, budget accommodation ideal for both families and business travellers. Spacious, en suite bedrooms feature tea and coffee making facilities, and Freeview TV in most hotels. Internet access and Wi-fi are available for a small fee. The adjacent family restaurant features a wide and varied menu. See also the Hotel Groups pages.

Rooms 69 **D** £59-£60*

Premier Inn Newcastle South

BUDGET HOTEL

☎ 0871 527 8806 0871 527 8807
Lobley Hill Rd NE11 9NA
dir: A1 onto A692

Rooms 42 **D** £59-£60*

Premier Inn Newcastle (Team Valley)

BUDGET HOTEL

☎ 0871 527 8794 0871 527 8795
Maingate, Kingsway North, Team Valley NE11 0BE
dir: A1 onto B1426 signed Team Valley (S'bound) or Teams/Consett (N'bound). Take Gateshead exit at rdbt. At bottom of hill straight on at rdbt. Hotel opposite

Rooms 115 **D** £60-£66*

GATWICK AIRPORT (LONDON) Map 6 TQ24

West Sussex

See also **Dorking, East Grinstead & Reigate**

INSPECTORS' CHOICE

Langshott Manor

★★★★ COUNTRY HOUSE HOTEL

☎ 01293 786680 01293 783905
Langshott Ln RH6 9LN
e-mail: admin@langshottmanor.com
dir: From A23 take Ladbroke Rd, off Chequers rdbt to Langshott, after 0.75m hotel on right

On the outskirts of town this charming timber-framed Tudor manor house is set amidst beautifully landscaped grounds with an ancient moat. The stylish public areas feature a choice of inviting lounges with polished oak panelling, exposed beams and crackling log fires. Each bedroom, whether in the manor itself or in one of three mews buildings in the grounds, has been designed with flair and imagination. Expect sumptuous furnishings, Egyptians linens, flat-screen TVs and bathrooms with deep baths and powers showers. The Mulberry restaurant overlooks a picturesque pond and offers an imaginative menu.

Rooms 22 (15 annexe) (2 fmly) (8 GF) **S** £150-£440; **D** £180-£440 (incl. bkfst)* **Facilities** STV FTV Xmas New Year Wi-fi **Conf** Class 20 Board 22 Thtr 40 **Parking** 25 **Notes** LB Civ Wed 60

Sofitel London Gatwick

★★★★ 77% HOTEL

☎ 01293 567070 & 555000 01293 567739
North Terminal RH6 0PH
e-mail: h6204-re@accor.com
dir: M23 junct 9, follow to 2nd rdbt. Hotel straight ahead

One of the closest hotels to the airport, this modern, purpose-built hotel is located only minutes from the terminals. Bedrooms are contemporary and all are air conditioned. Guests have a choice of eating options including a French-style café, a brasserie and an oriental restaurant.

Rooms 518 (19 fmly) **S** £102-£191; **D** £102-£191 **Facilities** Gym Wi-fi **Conf** Class 150 Board 90 Thtr 300 Del from £135 to £165 **Services** Lift Air con **Parking** 200 **Notes** LB

Copthorne Hotel London Gatwick

★★★★ 72% HOTEL

☎ 01342 348800 & 348888 01342 348833
Copthorne Way RH10 3PG
e-mail: sales.gatwick@millenniumhotels.co.uk
web: www.millenniumhotels.co.uk
dir: On A264, 2m E of A264/B2036 rdbt

Situated in a tranquil position, the Copthorne is set in 100 acres of wooded, landscaped gardens containing jogging tracks, a putting green and a petanque pit. The sprawling building is built around a 16th-century farmhouse and has comfortable bedrooms; many are air conditioned. There are three dining options, ranging from the informal bar and carvery to the more formal Lion d'Or.

Rooms 227 (10 fmly) **Facilities** STV Gym Squash Aerobic studio Wi-fi **Conf** Class 60 Board 40 Thtr 135 **Parking** 300 **Notes** Civ Wed 100

Menzies Chequers

MenziesHotels

★★★★ 72% HOTEL

☎ 01293 766750 01293 820625
Brighton Rd RH6 8PH
e-mail: chequers@menzieshotels.co.uk
web: www.menzieshotels.co.uk
dir: M23 junct 9, A23 towards Redhill. At 'Longbridge' rdbt take 3rd exit signed Horley/A23. 1m to Sainsburys/Shell rdbt. Take 1st exit, hotel on right

A popular hotel located close to the town centre and also convenient for Gatwick Airport; original parts of the building date back to the 1750s. Bedrooms are comfortable and well equipped with good facilities. Dining areas include the contemporary restaurant and the traditional Chequers pub. Secure parking is available.

Rooms 104 (10 fmly) (46 GF) (6 smoking) **Facilities** Xmas New Year Wi-fi **Conf** Class 25 Board 32 Thtr 70 **Services** Lift **Parking** 140 **Notes**

Copthorne Hotel Effingham Gatwick

★★★★ 71% HOTEL

☎ 01342 714994 01342 716039
West Park Rd RH10 3EU
e-mail: sales.effingham@millenniumhotels.co.uk
web: www.millenniumhotels.co.uk
dir: M23 junct 10, A264 towards East Grinstead. Over rdbt, at 2nd rdbt left onto B2028. Effingham Park on right

A former stately home, set in 40 acres of grounds, this hotel is popular for conference and weekend functions. The main restaurant is an open-plan brasserie serving modern continental cuisine, and snacks are also available in the bar. Bedrooms are spacious and well equipped. Facilities include a golf course and a leisure club.

Rooms 122 (7 fmly) (20 GF) **Facilities** STV 9 Putt green Gym Aerobic & Dance studios Xmas New Year Wi-fi **Conf** Class 450 Board 250 Thtr 900 **Services** Lift **Parking** 500 **Notes** LB Civ Wed 600

Crowne Plaza London - Gatwick Airport

★★★★ 71% HOTEL

☎ 01293 608608 01293 515913
Langley Dr RH11 7SX
e-mail: info@cpgatwick.co.uk
web: www.cpgatwick.co.uk
dir: M23 junct 10, 3rd exit at rdbt & 3rd exit at next rdbt. At lights take 3rd exit at rdbt

Ideally located for Gatwick Airport, this contemporary hotel offers comfortable and well-furnished rooms suitable for both the leisure and business travellers. Elite Health and Fitness Centre is the leisure centre which houses a stunning indoor swimming pool. Cube Restaurant & Bar offers a relaxed dining experience and the Gallery Sports Bar, an informal alternative. The hotel also has extensive conference facilities.

Rooms 294 (15 fmly) **Facilities** STV FTV supervised Gym Saunas Steam room Bubble spa Xmas New Year Wi-fi **Conf** Class 110 Board 40 Thtr 230 **Services** Lift Air con **Parking** 200 **Notes** Civ Wed 150

Best Western Gatwick Moat House

★★★ 80% HOTEL

☎ 0870 443 1671 & 01293 899988
01293 899904
Longbridge Roundabout RH6 0AB
e-mail: gatwick@qmh-hotels.com
web: www.bestwestern.co.uk
dir: M23 junct 9, follow signs for North Terminal, take 4th exit at rdbt signed A23/Redhill. At 1st rdbt take 1st exit then 1st left

Ideally situated for either terminal, this hotel provides a shuttle service to the airport plus secure undercover parking. Modern conference facilities and a spacious break-out area are provided. The smart bedrooms have air conditioning and a contemporary feel; some family suites can sleep up to seven guests.

Rooms 125 (20 fmly) **Facilities** Xmas New Year Wi-fi **Conf** Class 20 Board 18 Thtr 40 **Services** Lift Air con **Parking** 138 **Notes**

Holiday Inn London - Gatwick Airport

★★★ 79% HOTEL

☎ 0871 942 9030 & 01293 787648
01293 771054
Povey Cross Rd RH6 0BA
web: www.holidayinn.co.uk
dir: M23 junct 9, follow Gatwick, then Reigate signs. Hotel on left after 3rd rdbt

Situated close to the airport, this modern hotel provides air conditioned, smart accommodation with facilities suiting both the business and leisure guest. There is a restaurant and bar, and a variety of conference rooms plus a supporting business centre. Park and Fly stays are popular.

Rooms 216 (13 fmly) (37 GF) (22 smoking) **Facilities** STV Wi-fi **Conf** Class 100 Board 70 Thtr 210 **Services** Lift Air con **Parking** 600

Gatwick Worth Hotel

★★★ 67% HOTEL

☎ 01293 884806 01293 882444
Crabbet Park, Turners Hill Rd, Worth RH10 4ST
e-mail: reception@gatwickworthhotel.co.uk
web: www.gatwickworthhotel.co.uk
dir: M23 junct 10, left to A264. At 1st rdbt take last exit. 1st left, 1st right at T-junct, hotel next right

This purpose-built hotel is ideally placed for access to Gatwick Airport. The bedrooms are spacious and suitably appointed with good facilities. Public areas consist of a light and airy bar area and a brasserie

continued

G

GATWICK AIRPORT (LONDON) *continued*

restaurant offering good value meals. Guests have use of the superb leisure club next door.

Rooms 118 (24 fmly) (56 GF) **Facilities** Wi-fi **Conf** Class 110 Board 100 Thtr 360 **Parking** 150 **Notes** ® Civ Wed 70

Express by Holiday Inn Gatwick - Crawley

BUDGET HOTEL

☎ 01293 529991 🖹 01293 525529
Haslett Av, The Squareabout RH10 1UA
e-mail: ebhi-crawley@btconnect.com
web: www.hiexpress.com/crawleyuk

A modern hotel ideal for families and business travellers. Fresh and uncomplicated, the spacious rooms include Sky TV, power shower and tea and coffee-making facilities. Continental buffet breakfast is included in the room rate; other meals may be taken at the nearby family pub or restaurant. See also the Hotel Groups pages.

Rooms 74 (55 fmly) **Conf** Class 12 Board 16 Thtr 35

Ibis London Gatwick Airport

BUDGET HOTEL

☎ 01293 590300 🖹 01293 590310
London Rd, County Oak RH10 9GY
e-mail: H1889@accor.com
web: www.ibishotel.com
dir: M23 junct 10, A2011 towards Crawley. Onto A23 left towards Crawley/Brighton. Hotel on left

Modern, budget hotel offering comfortable accommodation in bright and practical bedrooms. Breakfast is self-service and dinner is available in the restaurant. See also the Hotel Groups pages.

Rooms 141

Premier Inn Crawley East

BUDGET HOTEL

☎ 0871 527 8412 🖹 0871 527 8413
Crawley Av, Gossops Green RH10 8BA
dir: M23 junct 11, A23 towards Crawley & Gatwick Airport

High quality, budget accommodation ideal for both families and business travellers. Spacious, en suite bedrooms feature tea and coffee making facilities, and Freeview TV in most hotels. Internet access and Wi-fi are available for a small fee. The adjacent family restaurant features a wide and varied menu. See also the Hotel Groups pages.

Rooms 83 **D** £49-£64*

Premier Inn Crawley (Pound Hill)

BUDGET HOTEL

☎ 0871 527 8410 🖹 0871 527 8411
Balcombe Rd, Worth RH10 3NL
dir: M23 junct 10, B2036 S towards Crawley

Rooms 41 **D** £49-£64*

Premier Inn Crawley South (Goffs Park)

BUDGET HOTEL

☎ 0871 527 8414 🖹 0871 527 8415
45 Goffs Park Rd RH11 8AX
dir: M23 junct 11, A23 towards Crawley. At 2nd rdbt take 3rd exit for town centre, then 2nd right into Goffs Park Rd

Rooms 49 **D** £49-£64*

Premier Inn Gatwick Airport Central

BUDGET HOTEL

☎ 0871 527 8406 🖹 0871 527 8407
Longbridge Way, North Terminal RH6 0NX
dir: M23 junct 9/9A towards North Terminal, at rdbt take 3rd exit, hotel on right

Rooms 219 **D** £59-£69*

Premier Inn Gatwick Airport South

BUDGET HOTEL

☎ 0871 527 8408 🖹 0871 527 8409
London Rd, Lowfield Heath RH10 9ST
dir: M23 junct 9a towards North Terminal rdbt. Follow A23 & Crawley signs. Hotel in 2m

Rooms 102 **D** £54-£68*

Premier Inn Gatwick Manor Royal

BUDGET HOTEL

☎ 0871 527 9214 🖹 0871 527 9215
Crawley Business Quarter, Fleming Way RH10 9DF
dir: M23 junct 10, A2011 (Crawley Ave). At rdbt 4th exit onto A23 (London Rd), at rdbt right into Fleming Way. Hotel 300yds on left

Rooms 180 **D** £55-£69*

GILLINGHAM
Kent — Map 7 TQ76

Premier Inn Gillingham Business Park

BUDGET HOTEL

☎ 0871 527 8416 🖹 0871 527 8417
Will Adams Way ME8 6BY
dir: M2 junct 44, A278 to A2. Left at Tesco. Hotel at next rdbt

High quality, budget accommodation ideal for both families and business travellers. Spacious, en suite bedrooms feature tea and coffee making facilities, and Freeview TV in most hotels. Internet access and Wi-fi are available for a small fee. The adjacent family restaurant features a wide and varied menu. See also the Hotel Groups pages.

Rooms 46 **D** £57-£64*

Premier Inn Gillingham/Rainham

BUDGET HOTEL

☎ 0871 527 9268 🖹 0871 527 9269
High St, Rainham ME8 7JE
dir: M25 junct 2 (Canterbury/Dover/A2), A2 to M2 (Dover). Exit at junct 4 (Rainham/Medway Tunnel), straight on at 2 rdbts. At 3rd rdbt take 3rd exit (Rainham High St). Hotel on right at 3rd lights

Rooms 26 **D** £54-£59*

GIRTON
Cambridgeshire — Map 12 TL46

Premier Inn Cambridge North (Girton)

BUDGET HOTEL

☎ 0871 527 8188 🖹 0871 527 8189
Huntingdon Rd CB3 0DR
dir: A14 junct 31 follow signs towards Cambridge. Pass BP garage, next right. Hotel adjacent to Traveller's Rest Beefeater

High quality, budget accommodation ideal for both families and business travellers. Spacious, en suite bedrooms feature tea and coffee making facilities, and Freeview TV in most hotels. Internet access and Wi-fi are available for a small fee. The adjacent family restaurant features a wide and varied menu. See also the Hotel Groups pages.

Rooms 20 **D** £70*

GISBURN
Lancashire Map 18 SD84

Stirk House

★★★ 80% HOTEL

☎ 01200 445581 01200 445744
BB7 4LJ
e-mail: reservations@stirkhouse.co.uk
dir: W of village, on A59. Hotel 0.5m on left

This delightful historic hotel enjoys a peaceful location in its own grounds, amid rolling countryside. Extensive public areas include excellent conference and banqueting facilities, a leisure centre and an elegant restaurant. The stylish bedrooms and suites vary in size and style but all are comfortable and well equipped. Hospitality is warm and friendly, and service attentive.

Rooms 30 (10 annexe) (2 fmly) (12 GF) **S** £100-£180; **D** £130-£210 (incl. bkfst)* **Facilities** STV supervised Gym Aromatherapy Personal training Kick boxing Xmas New Year Wi-fi **Conf** Class 150 Board 45 Thtr 200 Del from £98.50 to £125 **Parking** 400 **Notes** LB Civ Wed 200

GLAZEBROOK
Cheshire Map 15 SJ69

The Rhinewood Country House Hotel

★★★ 78% HOTEL

☎ 0161 775 5555 0161 775 7965
Glazebrook Ln, Glazebrook WA3 5BB
e-mail: info@therhinewoodhotel.co.uk
dir: M6 junct 21, A57 towards Irlam. Left at Glazebrook sign, hotel 0.25m on left

This privately owned hotel stands in spacious landscaped gardens is a short drive from Manchester and Warrington. The attractively presented bedrooms are well equipped. There is a popular restaurant and the stylish bar is ideal for more informal dining. Facilities include conference and function rooms and the hotel is a popular wedding venue.

Rooms 32 (4 fmly) (16 GF) (8 smoking) **Facilities** STV Complimentary membership at nearby health spa Xmas Wi-fi **Conf** Class 70 Board 40 Thtr 100 **Parking** 120 **Notes** Civ Wed 100

GLENRIDDING
Cumbria Map 18 NY31

The Inn on the Lake

LAKE DISTRICT HOTELS

★★★ 83% HOTEL

☎ 017684 82444 017684 82303
Lake Ullswater CA11 0PE
e-mail: innonthelake@lakedistricthotels.net
web: www.lakedistricthotels.com
dir: M6 junct 40, A66 to Keswick. At rdbt take A592 to Ullswater Lake. Along lake to Glenridding. Hotel on left on entering village

In a picturesque lakeside setting, this restored Victorian hotel is a popular leisure destination as well as catering for weddings and conferences. Superb views can be enjoyed from the bedrooms and from the garden terrace where afternoon teas are served during warmer months. There is a popular pub in the grounds, and moorings for yachts are available to guests. Sailing tuition can be arranged.

Rooms 47 (6 fmly) (1 GF) **Facilities** 9 Putt green Fishing Gym Sailing 9 hole pitch & putt Bowls Xmas New Year Wi-fi **Conf** Class 24 Board 24 Thtr 60 **Services** Lift **Parking** 200 **Notes** Civ Wed 100

See advert on page 388

Best Western Glenridding Hotel

★★★ 77% HOTEL

☎ 017684 82228 & 82289 017684 82555
CA11 0PB
e-mail: glenridding@bestwestern.co.uk
dir: N'bound M6 junct 36, A591 Windermere then A592, for 14m. S'bound M6 junct 40, A592 for 13m

This friendly hotel benefits from a picturesque location in the village centre, and many rooms have fine views of the lake and fells. Public areas are extensive and include a choice of dining options including Ratchers Restaurant and a café. Leisure facilities are available along with a conference room and a garden function room.

Rooms 36 (7 fmly) (8 GF) **Facilities** STV Sauna Snooker Table tennis Xmas New Year Wi-fi **Conf** Class 30 Board 24 Thtr 30 **Services** Lift **Parking** 30 **Notes** Civ Wed 120

GLOSSOP
Derbyshire Map 16 SK09

Wind in the Willows Hotel

★★ 83% HOTEL

☎ 01457 868001 01457 853354
Derbyshire Level SK13 7PT
e-mail: info@windinthewillows.co.uk
dir: 1m E of Glossop on A57, turn right opposite Royal Oak, hotel 400yds on right

This impressive house sits in peaceful grounds with lovely views of the Peak District National Park. Individually furnished bedrooms are in keeping with the Victorian style of the house. Beautiful original oak panelling and crackling log fires add to the charm of the lounges and dining room. There is also a conference suite that is perfect for meetings, private dining or special occasions.

Rooms 12 **S** £88-£110; **D** £135-£165 (incl. bkfst)* **Facilities** FTV Fishing New Year Wi-fi **Conf** Class 12 Board 16 Thtr 40 Del from £139 to £159* **Parking** 16 **Notes** LB No children 10yrs

GLOUCESTER
Gloucestershire Map 10 SO81

Holiday Inn Gloucester-Cheltenham

★★★ 79% HOTEL

☎ 0871 942 9034 01452 371036
Crest Way, Barnwood GL4 3RX
e-mail: reservations-gloucester@ihg.com
web: www.holidayinn.co.uk
dir: A40 to Gloucester. At rdbt take 2nd exit signed A417/Cirencester. At next rdbt 2nd exit 1st left

This hotel is conveniently located close to the M5, and within easy driving distance of both Gloucester and Cheltenham. Bedrooms vary in size from the larger, well-equipped executive rooms to smaller style standard doubles. A good selection of dining options is available in either the lounge/bar, the relaxing restaurant or via room service. Guests can also enjoy the well-equipped leisure facilities.

Rooms 125 (19 fmly) (62 GF) (6 smoking) **S** £29-£134; **D** £29-£134* **Facilities** Spa STV FTV Gym Dance studio Wi-fi **Conf** Class 65 Board 50 Thtr 140 Del from £85 to £175* **Services** Air con **Parking** 180 **Notes** LB Civ Wed 120

G

GLOUCESTER *continued*

Hatherley Manor

★★★ 78% HOTEL

☎ 01452 730217 🖹 01452 731032
Down Hatherley Ln GL2 9QA
e-mail: reservations@hatherleymanor.com
web: www.hatherleymanor.com
dir: Off A38 into Down Hatherley Lane, signed. Hotel 600yds on left

Within easy striking distance of the M5, Gloucester, Cheltenham and the Cotswolds, this stylish 17th-century manor, set in attractive grounds, remains popular with both business and leisure guests. Bedrooms are well appointed and offer contemporary comforts. A particularly impressive range of meeting and function rooms is available.

Rooms 50 (5 fmly) (18 GF) **Facilities** FTV Xmas New Year Wi-fi **Conf** Class 90 Board 75 Thtr 400 **Parking** 250 **Notes** LB Civ Wed 300

Hatton Court

★★★ 75% HOTEL

☎ 01452 617412 🖹 01452 612945
Upton Hill, Upton St Leonards GL4 8DE
e-mail: res@hatton-court.co.uk
web: www.hatton-court.co.uk
dir: From Gloucester on B4073 (Painswick road). Hotel at top of hill on right

Built in the style of a 17th-century Cotswold manor house, and set in seven acres of well-kept gardens this hotel is popular with both business and leisure guests. It stands at the top of Upton Hill and commands truly spectacular views of the Severn Valley. Bedrooms are comfortable and tastefully furnished with many extra facilities. The elegant Carringtons Restaurant offers a varied choice of menus, and there is also a bar and foyer lounge.

Rooms 45 (28 annexe) **Facilities** Gym Xmas New Year Wi-fi **Conf** Class 30 Board 30 Thtr 60 **Parking** 80 **Notes** LB Civ Wed 80

Express by Holiday Inn Gloucester-South M5

BUDGET HOTEL

☎ 01452 726400 🖹 01452 722922
Waterwells Business Park, Quedgeley GL2 2AB
e-mail: gloucester@morethanhotels.com
web: www.hiexpress.com/exgloucesterso

A modern hotel ideal for families and business travellers. Fresh and uncomplicated, the spacious rooms include Sky TV, power shower and tea and coffee-making facilities. Continental buffet breakfast is included in the room rate; other meals may be taken at the nearby family pub or restaurant. See also the Hotel Groups pages.

Rooms 106 **S** £55-£250; **D** £55-£250 (incl. bkfst)* **Conf** Class 20 Board 20 Thtr 35 Del from £95 to £300*

Premier Inn Gloucester (Barnwood)

BUDGET HOTEL

☎ 0871 527 8456 🖹 0871 527 8457
Barnwood GL4 3HR
dir: M5 junct 11, A40 towards Gloucester. At 1st rdbt A417 towards Cirencester, at next rdbt 4th exit

High quality, budget accommodation ideal for both families and business travellers. Spacious, en suite bedrooms feature tea and coffee making facilities, and Freeview TV in most hotels. Internet access and Wi-fi are available for a small fee. The adjacent family restaurant features a wide and varied menu. See also the Hotel Groups pages.

Rooms 83 **D** £52-£60*

Premier Inn Gloucester Business Park

BUDGET HOTEL

☎ 0871 527 8462 🖹 0871 527 8463
Gloucester Business Park, Brockworth GL3 4AJ
dir: M5 junct 11a, A417 towards Cirencester. At Brockworth Rdbt follow Gloucester Business Park signs, onto dual carriageway (Valiant Way). At next rdbt left into Delta Way. Hotel adjacent to Tesco

Rooms 48 **D** £50-£60*

Premier Inn Gloucester (Little Witcombe)

BUDGET HOTEL

☎ 0871 527 8458 🖹 0871 527 8459
Witcombe GL3 4SS
dir: M5 junct 11a, A417signed Cirencester. At 1st exit turn right onto A46 towards Stroud & Witcombe. Left at next rdbt by Crosshands pub

Rooms 39 **D** £50-£60*

Premier Inn Gloucester (Longford)

BUDGET HOTEL

☎ 0871 527 8460 🖹 0871 527 8461
Tewkesbury Rd, Longford GL2 9BE
dir: M5 junct 11, A40 towards Gloucester & Ross-on-Wye. Hotel on A38 towards Gloucester

Rooms 60 **D** £50-£60*

Premier Inn Gloucester North

BUDGET HOTEL

☎ 0871 527 8464 🖹 0871 527 8465
Tewkesbury Rd, Twigworth GL2 9PG
dir: On A38, 1m N from junct with A40

Rooms 50 **D** £49-£58*

The Wharf House

RESTAURANT WITH ROOMS

☎ 01452 332900 & 332900 🖹 01452 332901
Over GL2 8DB
e-mail: thewharfhouse@yahoo.co.uk

The Wharf House was built to replace the old lock cottage and, as the name suggests, it is located at the very edge of the river; it has pleasant views and an outdoor terrace. The bedrooms and bathrooms have been decorated and appointed to high levels of quality and comfort, and there are plenty of guest extras. Seasonal, local produce can be enjoyed both at breakfast and dinner in the delightfully relaxing restaurant.

Rooms 7 (1 fmly)

GODALMING Surrey — **Map 6 SU94**

Premier Inn Godalming

BUDGET HOTEL

☎ 0871 527 8466 🖹 0871 527 8467
Guildford Rd GU7 3BX
dir: Exit A3 onto A3000 signed Godalming. 1m to rdbt, turn right into Guildford Rd towards Godalming. Hotel on left in 500yds

High quality, budget accommodation ideal for both families and business travellers. Spacious, en suite bedrooms feature tea and coffee making facilities, and Freeview TV in most hotels. Internet access and Wi-fi are available for a small fee. The adjacent family restaurant features a wide and varied menu. See also the Hotel Groups pages.

Rooms 17 **D** £57-£78*

GOLANT Map 2 SX15
Cornwall

Cormorant Hotel & Restaurant

★★★ 77% HOTEL

☎ 01726 833426 01726 833219
PL23 1LL
e-mail: relax@cormoranthotel.co.uk
web: www.cormoranthotel.co.uk
dir: A390 onto B3269 signed Fowey. In 3m left to Golant, through village to end of road, hotel on right

This hotel focuses on traditional hospitality, attentive service and good food. All the bedrooms enjoy the river view and guests can expect goose and down duvets, flat-screen digital TVs and free Wi-fi access. Breakfast and lunch may be taken on the terrace which overlooks the river.

Rooms 14 (4 GF) **S** £70-£200; **D** £80-£250 (incl. bkfst)* **Facilities** FTV Xmas New Year Wi-fi **Parking** 20 **Notes** LB No children 13yrs

GOMERSAL Map 19 SE22
West Yorkshire

Gomersal Park

CLASSIC BRITISH HOTELS

★★★ 79% HOTEL

☎ 01274 869386 01274 861042
Moor Ln BD19 4LJ
e-mail: enquiries@gomersalparkhotel.com
web: www.gomersalparkhotel.com
dir: A62 to Huddersfield. At junct with A65, by Greyhound Pub right, after 1m take 1st right after Oakwell Hall

Constructed around a 19th-century house, this stylish, modern hotel enjoys a peaceful location and pleasant grounds. Deep sofas ensure comfort in the open-plan lounge and imaginative meals are served in the popular Brasserie 101. The well-equipped bedrooms provide high quality and comfort. Extensive public areas include a well-equipped leisure complex and pool, and a wide variety of air-conditioned conference rooms.

Rooms 100 (3 fmly) (32 GF) **Facilities** FTV supervised Gym Wi-fi **Conf** Class 130 Board 60 Thtr 250 **Services** Lift **Parking** 150 **Notes** LB Civ Wed 200

GOODRINGTON

See Paignton

GOODWOOD Map 6 SU81
West Sussex

The Goodwood Hotel

★★★★ 79% HOTEL

☎ 01243 775537 01243 520120
PO18 0QB
e-mail: reservations@goodwood.com
web: www.goodwood.com
dir: Off A285, 3m NE of Chichester

Set at the centre of the 12,000-acre Goodwood Estate, this attractive hotel boasts extensive indoor and outdoor leisure facilities, along with a range of meeting rooms plus conference and banqueting facilities. Bedrooms are furnished to a consistently high standard, including a luxury suite located in the old coaching inn, and Executive rooms, each with a patio. Eating options are varied - the Richmond Arms sourcing produce extensively from the estate farm, The Richmond Arms Bar, and the Goodwood Bar and Grill. Overnight guests can also choose to dine in The Kennels, a private members' clubhouse.

Rooms 91 (48 GF) **S** £105-£300 (incl. bkfst) **Facilities** Spa STV FTV 18 Putt green Gym Golf driving range Sauna Steam room Fitness studio Xmas New Year Wi-fi **Conf** Class 60 Board 50 Thtr 150 Del from £162 to £216 **Parking** 350 **Notes** LB Civ Wed 120

GOOLE Map 17 SE72
East Riding of Yorkshire

Lowther Hotel

★★★ 80% HOTEL

☎ 01405 767999 01405 769321
Aire St DN14 5QW
dir: M62 junct 36, A614, follow town centre signs. At clock tower rdbt, right into Aire St

A beautifully restored Georgian Grade II* listed building that combines historic features with contemporary design. Set in a unique location, its overlooks the port yet is within easy reach of motorway links. The bedrooms are stylish, well equipped and have free Wi-fi. Public areas include the New Bridge Lounge and The Burlington Restaurant, and the impressive Mural Rooms are perfect for weddings, conferences and meetings.

Lowther Hotel

Rooms 14 (1 fmly) **S** £65-£99; **D** £85-£190 (incl. bkfst) **Facilities** FTV Xmas New Year Wi-fi **Conf** Class 90 Board 50 Thtr 90 Del from £125-£250 **Parking** 30 **Notes** LB Civ Wed 90

Premier Inn Goole

BUDGET HOTEL

☎ 0871 527 8468 0871 527 8469
Rawcliffe Rd, Airmyn DN14 8JS
dir: M62 junct 36, A614 signed Rawcliffe. Hotel immediately on left

High quality, budget accommodation ideal for both families and business travellers. Spacious, en suite bedrooms feature tea and coffee making facilities, and Freeview TV in most hotels. Internet access and Wi-fi are available for a small fee. The adjacent family restaurant features a wide and varied menu. See also the Hotel Groups pages.

Rooms 41 **D** £51-£59*

GORDANO SERVICE AREA (M5) Map 4 ST57
Somerset

Days Inn Bristol West - M5

BUDGET HOTEL

☎ 01275 373709 & 373624 01275 374104
BS20 7XG
e-mail: gordano.hotel@welcomebreak.co.uk
web: www.welcomebreak.co.uk
dir: M5 junct 19, follow signs for Gordano Services

This modern building offers accommodation in smart, spacious and well-equipped bedrooms, suitable for families and business travellers, and all with en suite bathrooms. Continental breakfast is available and other refreshments may be taken at the nearby family restaurant. See also the Hotel Groups pages.

Rooms 60 (52 fmly) (29 GF) (10 smoking) **S** £39.95-£59.95; **D** £49.95-£69.95 **Conf** Board 10

G

GORING Oxfordshire **Map 5 SU68**

The Miller of Mansfield

RESTAURANT WITH ROOMS

☎ 01491 872829 📠 01491 873100
High St RG8 9AW
e-mail: reservations@millerofmansfield.com
web: www.millerofmansfield.com
dir: M40 junct 7, S on A329 towards Benson, A4074 towards Reading, B4009 towards Goring. Or M4 junct 12, S on A4 towards Newbury. 3rd rdbt onto A340 to Pangbourne. A329 to Streatley, right at lights onto B4009 into Goring

G

The frontage of this former coaching inn hides sumptuous rooms with a distinctive and individual style, an award-winning restaurant that serves appealing dishes using locally sourced ingredients and a comfortable bar, which serves real ales, fine wines, afternoon tea and a bar menu for a quick bite to eat.

Rooms 13 (2 fmly)

GORLESTON ON SEA Norfolk **Map 13 TG50**

The Pier Hotel

★★★ 82% HOTEL

☎ 01493 662631 📠 01493 440263
Harbourmouth, South Pier NR31 6PL
e-mail: bookings@pierhotelgorleston.co.uk
dir: From A47 W of Great Yarmouth take A12 signed Lowestoft. At 3rd rdbt 1st left (Beccles Rd) signed Gorleston. At rdbt 2nd left (Church Rd). Next rdbt 1st left (Baker St). Right into Pier Plain, then Pier Walk to Pier Gdns

Ideally situated on the seafront this hotel offers smartly appointed bedrooms that are thoughtfully equipped and have a good range of useful extras; some rooms have superb sea views. The public areas include a large restaurant and a conservatory, which leads to a terrace and bar.

Rooms 19 (1 fmly) **S** £55-£65; **D** £80-£125 (incl. bkfst)* **Facilities** STV FTV ♫ New Year Wi-fi **Parking** 14 **Notes** ⊗

GRANGE-OVER-SANDS Cumbria **Map 18 SD47**

Netherwood

★★★ 80% HOTEL

☎ 015395 32552 📠 015395 34121
Lindale Rd LA11 6ET
e-mail: enquiries@netherwood-hotel.co.uk
web: www.netherwood-hotel.co.uk
dir: On B5277 before station

This imposing hotel stands in terraced grounds and enjoys fine views of Morecambe Bay. Though a popular conference and wedding venue, good levels of hospitality and service ensure all guests are well looked after. Bedrooms vary in size but all are well furnished and have smart modern bathrooms. Magnificent woodwork is a feature of the public areas.

Rooms 34 (5 fmly) **S** £70-£100; **D** £80-£180 (incl. bkfst) **Facilities** Spa FTV supervised Gym Beauty salon Steam room Spa bath Sunbed New Year Wi-fi **Conf** Class 150 Board 60 Thtr 150 Del from £120 to £160 **Services** Lift **Parking** 100 **Notes** LB Civ Wed 200

Cumbria Grand

★★★ 68% HOTEL

☎ 015395 32331 📠 015395 34534
LA11 6EN
e-mail: salescumbria@strathmorehotels.com
dir: M6 junct 36, A590 & follow Grange-over-Sands signs

Set within extensive grounds, this large hotel offers fine views over Morecambe Bay and caters well for a mixed market. Public areas are pure nostalgia, and include a grand dining room and fine ballroom. Bedrooms are comfortably equipped and some have views of the bay.

Rooms 122 (10 fmly) (25 GF) **Facilities** STV Putt green Snooker & pool table Table tennis Darts ♫ Xmas New Year **Services** Lift **Parking** 75

See advert on page 550

Graythwaite Manor

★★★ 68% HOTEL

☎ 015395 32001 & 33755 📠 015395 35549
Fernhill Rd LA11 7JE
e-mail: enquiries@graythwaitemanor.co.uk
dir: B5277 through Grange. Fernhill Rd opposite fire station, hotel 1st left

This well established hotel is set in beautiful gardens complete with sub-tropical plants, and affords delightful views out over Morecambe Bay. Public areas include an Orangery, a number of comfortable lounges and an elegant restaurant. The bedrooms, which vary in size, are traditional in style.

Rooms 24 (2 fmly) (4 GF) **Facilities** STV FTV Xmas New Year Wi-fi **Services** Lift **Parking** 34 **Notes** Civ Wed 100

Hampsfell House

★★ 81% HOTEL

☎ 015395 32567 📠 015395 35995
Hampsfell Rd LA11 6BG
e-mail: enquiries@hampsfellhouse.co.uk
web: www.hampsfellhouse.co.uk
dir: A590 at junct with B5277, signed to Grange-over-Sands. Left at rdbt into Main St, right at 2nd rdbt & right at x-rds. Hotel on left

Dating back to 1800, this owner managed hotel is peacefully set in two acres of private grounds yet is just a comfortable walk from the town centre. Bedrooms are smartly decorated and well maintained. There is a cosy bar where guests can relax and enjoy pre-dinner drinks. Comprehensive and imaginative dinners are taken in an attractive dining room.

Rooms 8 (1 fmly) **S** £35-£60; **D** £50-£90 (incl. bkfst)* **Facilities** FTV New Year Wi-fi **Parking** 20 **Notes** LB

INSPECTORS' CHOICE

Clare House

★ ◎ HOTEL

☎ 015395 33026 & 34253 📠 015395 34310
Park Rd LA11 7HQ
e-mail: info@clarehousehotel.co.uk
web: www.clarehousehotel.co.uk
dir: Off A590 onto B5277, through Lindale into Grange, keep left, hotel 0.5m on left past Crown Hill & St Paul's Church

A warm, genuine welcome awaits guests at this delightful hotel, proudly run by the Read family for over 40 years. Situated in its own secluded gardens, it provides a relaxed haven in which to enjoy the panoramic views across Morecambe Bay. The stylish bedrooms and public areas are comfortable and attractively furnished. Skilfully prepared dinners and hearty breakfasts are served in the elegant dining room.

Rooms 18 (4 GF) **S** £87-£92; **D** £174-£184 (incl. bkfst & dinner) **Facilities** FTV Putt green Wi-fi **Parking** 18 **Notes** LB ⊗ Closed 12 Nov-early Mar

GRANTHAM
Lincolnshire — Map 11 SK93

Ramada Grantham

RAMADA

★★★★ 72% HOTEL

☎ 01476 593000 📠 01476 592592
Swingbridge Rd NG31 7XT
e-mail: info@ramadagrantham.co.uk
web: www.ramadagrantham.co.uk
dir: Exit A1 at Grantham/Melton Mowbray junct onto A607. From N: 1st exit at mini rdbt, hotel on right. From S: at rdbt 2nd exit. Next left at T-junct. At mini rdbt 2nd exit. Hotel on right

A modern, purpose-built hotel ideally placed for touring the area. Bedrooms are spacious, smartly decorated and equipped with modern facilities. Public rooms include a large open-plan lounge/bar area with comfortable seating and an intimate restaurant as well as conference and banqueting facilities. The property also has smart leisure facilities.

Rooms 89 (44 GF) (2 smoking) **Facilities** STV Gym Steam room Sauna Xmas New Year Wi-fi **Conf** Class 90 Board 60 Thtr 200 **Parking** 102 **Notes** ⊗ Civ Wed 200

Premier Inn Grantham

BUDGET HOTEL

☎ 0871 527 8470 📠 0871 527 8471
A1/607 Junction, Harlaxton Rd NG31 7UA
dir: A1 onto A607. N'bound: hotel on right. S'bound: under A1, hotel on left

High quality, budget accommodation ideal for both families and business travellers. Spacious, en suite bedrooms feature tea and coffee making facilities, and Freeview TV in most hotels. Internet access and Wi-fi are available for a small fee. The adjacent family restaurant features a wide and varied menu. See also the Hotel Groups pages.

Rooms 59 **D** £50-£62*

GRASMERE
Cumbria — Map 18 NY30

Rothay Garden

★★★★ 80% ◎◎ HOTEL

☎ 015394 35334 📠 015394 35723
Broadgate LA22 9RJ
e-mail: stay@rothaygarden.com
web: www.rothaygarden.com
dir: Off A591, opposite Swan Hotel, into Grasmere, 300yds on left

On the edge of the village, and sitting in two acres of riverside gardens, Rothay Garden offers an impressive combination of stylish design and luxurious comfort. Bedrooms include five Loft Suites, each named after one of the fells they overlook; they feature original beams and designer bathrooms with plasma TVs. There is a chic lounge bar and an elegant candlelit conservatory restaurant. The friendly staff provide attentive service.

Rooms 30 (3 fmly) (8 GF) **Facilities** FTV Hydro spa pool Sauna Aromatherapy room Infra red loungers Reflexology Xmas New Year Wi-fi **Parking** 38 **Notes** No children 5yrs

See advert on page 202

G

G

GRASMERE *continued*

Wordsworth Hotel & Spa

★★★★ 79% HOTEL

015394 35592 015394 35765
LA22 9SW
e-mail: enquiry@thewordsworthhotel.co.uk
web: www.thewordsworthhotel.co.uk
dir: Off A591 centre of village adjacent to St Oswald's Church

Named after the famous poet, this charming hotel is set in two acres of landscaped gardens. Peaceful lounges, furnished with antiques, look out over well-kept lawns and the friendly staff provide professional service. Bedrooms are individually furnished and well equipped. There are comprehensive leisure facilities, and diners have a choice between the popular pub and the more formal Prelude Restaurant.

Rooms 36 (2 fmly) (2 GF) **S** £40-£175; **D** £120-£375 (incl. bkfst)* **Facilities** Spa FTV Gym Treatment room Mixed sauna Nail bar Xmas New Year Wi-fi **Conf** Class 50 Board 40 Thtr 100 Del from £150 to £250 **Services** Lift **Parking** 60 **Notes** LB Civ Wed 100

See advert on opposite page

Best Western Grasmere Red Lion

★★★ 80% HOTEL

015394 35456 015394 35579
Red Lion Square LA22 9SS
e-mail: reservations@grasmereredlionhotel.co.uk
dir: Off A591, signed Grasmere Village. Hotel in village centre

This modernised and extended 18th-century coaching inn, located in the heart of the village, offers spacious well-equipped rooms and a number of meeting and conference facilities. A range of pub meals complement the more formal Courtyard restaurant. The spacious and comfortable lounge area is ideal for relaxing, and for the more energetic guest there is a pool and gym.

Rooms 47 **Facilities** STV Gym Sauna Steam room Spa bath Xmas New Year Wi-fi **Conf** Class 24 Board 28 Thtr 60 **Services** Lift **Parking** 35 **Notes** LB

See advert on opposite page

Oak Bank Hotel

★★★ 79% HOTEL

015394 35217 015394 35685
Broadgate LA22 9TA
e-mail: info@lakedistricthotel.co.uk
web: www.lakedistricthotel.co.uk
dir: N'bound: M6 junct 36 onto A591 to Windermere, Ambleside, then Grasmere. S'bound: M6 junct 40 onto A66 to Keswick, A591 to Grasmere

Privately owned and personally run by the friendly proprietors, Oak Bank is a Victorian house in the charming village of Grasmere. Bedrooms are well-equipped and include one with a four-poster bed, as well as a suite with jacuzzi bath. In colder weather, welcoming log fires burn in the comfortable lounges. The restaurant has a conservatory extension overlooking the garden, and there is also a pleasant bar.

Rooms 14 (1 GF) **S** £82-£120; **D** £110-£193 (incl. bkfst & dinner) **Facilities** FTV Use of nearby leisure facilities New Year Wi-fi **Parking** 14 **Notes** LB Closed 2-26 Jan

Macdonald Swan

MACDONALD HOTELS & RESORTS

★★★ 79% HOTEL

0844 879 9120 015394 43432
LA22 9RF
e-mail: sales/oldengland@macdonald-hotels.co.uk
web: www.macdonaldhotels.co.uk
dir: M6 junct 36, A591 towards Kendal, A590 to Keswick through Ambleside. Hotel on right on entering village

Close to Dove Cottage and occupying a prominent position on the edge of the village, this 300-year-old

continued

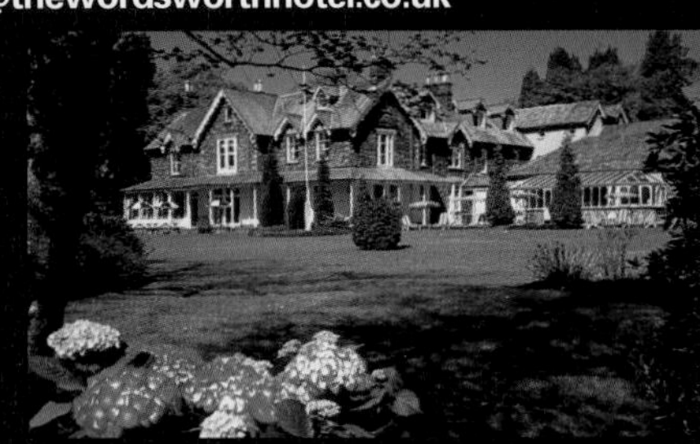

G

GRASMERE *continued*

inn is mentioned in Wordsworth's poem *The Waggoner*. Attractive public areas are spacious and comfortable, and bedrooms are equally stylish with some having CD players. A good range of bar meals is available, while the elegant restaurant offers more formal dining.

Rooms 38 (1 fmly) (28 GF) **Facilities** FTV Xmas New Year Wi-fi **Conf** Class 20 Board 30 Thtr 40 **Parking** 45 **Notes** Civ Wed 60

Gold Rill Country House

★★★ 78% HOTEL

☎ 015394 35486 📠 015394 35486
Red Bank Rd LA22 9PU
e-mail: reception@goldrill.co.uk
dir: A591 into village centre, turn into road opposite St Oswald's Church. Hotel 300yds on left

This popular hotel enjoys a fine location on the edge of the village with spectacular views of the lake and surrounding fells. Attractive bedrooms, some with balconies, are tastefully decorated and many have separate, comfortable seating areas. The hotel boasts a private pier, an outdoor heated pool and a putting green. Public areas include a well-appointed restaurant and choice of lounges.

Rooms 31 (6 annexe) (2 fmly) (11 GF) **Facilities** STV FTV ⛱ Putt green New Year Wi-fi **Parking** 35 **Notes** ⊗ Closed mid Dec-mid Jan (open New Year)

G

Grasmere

★★ 81% HOTEL

☎ 015394 35277
Broadgate LA22 9TA
e-mail: enquiries@grasmerehotel.co.uk
web: www.grasmerehotel.co.uk
dir: From Ambleside take A591 N, 2nd left into Grasmere. Over humpback bridge, past playing field. Hotel on left

Attentive and hospitable service contribute to the atmosphere at this family-run hotel, set in secluded gardens by the River Rothay. There are two inviting lounges (one with residents' bar) and an attractive dining room looking onto the garden. The thoughtfully prepared dinner menu makes good use of fresh ingredients. Quality antique furniture is featured in most bedrooms, along with welcome personal touches.

Rooms 14 (1 annexe) (2 GF) **S** £55-£63; **D** £90-£125 (incl. bkfst)* **Facilities** Full leisure facilities at nearby country club Fishing permit available Xmas New Year Wi-fi **Parking** 14 **Notes** LB No children 10yrs Closed 3 Jan-early Feb

See advert on page 203

GRASSINGTON North Yorkshire — Map 19 SE06

Grassington House

◎◎ RESTAURANT WITH ROOMS

☎ 01756 752406 📠 01756 752050
5 The Square BD23 5AQ
e-mail: bookings@grassingtonhousehotel.co.uk
web: www.grassingtonhousehotel.co.uk
dir: A59 into Grassington, in town square opposite post office

Located in the square of the popular village of Grassington this beautifully converted Georgian house is personally run by owners John and Sue. Delicious food, individually designed bedrooms and warm hospitality ensure an enjoyable stay. There is a stylishly appointed lounge bar looking out to the square and the restaurant is split between two rooms; here guests will find the emphasis is on fresh, local ingredients and attentive, yet friendly service.

Rooms 9 (2 fmly)

GRAVESEND Kent — Map 6 TQ67

Premier Inn Gravesend (A2/Singlewell)

Premier Inn

BUDGET HOTEL

☎ 0871 527 8472 📠 0871 527 8473
Hevercourt Rd, Singlewell DA12 5UQ
dir: At Gravesend East exit on A2

High quality, budget accommodation ideal for both families and business travellers. Spacious, en suite bedrooms feature tea and coffee making facilities, and Freeview TV in most hotels. Internet access and Wi-fi are available for a small fee. The adjacent family restaurant features a wide and varied menu. See also the Hotel Groups pages.

Rooms 31 **D** £57-£69*

Premier Inn Gravesend Central

BUDGET HOTEL

☎ 0871 527 8474 📠 0871 527 8475
Wrotham Rd DA11 7LF
dir: A2 onto A227 towards town centre, 1m to hotel

Rooms 36 **D** £57-£69*

GRAYS Essex — Map 6 TQ67

Park Inn Thurrock

park inn by Radisson

★★★ 70% HOTEL

☎ 01708 719988 📠 01708 719980
High Rd, North Stifford RM16 5UE
e-mail: info.thurrock@rezidorparkinn.com
dir: M25 junct 30/31, follow A13 towards Brentwood/Southend, A1012 (Grays), hotel is 1st exit on rdbt.

This hotel is conveniently located just 20 minutes from London, and is within close proximity of the Lakeside Shopping Centre and Dartford. It is a Georgian manor house set in landscaped gardens that offers comfortable bedrooms with satellite TV; Wi-fi is available. There is a range of modern meeting rooms, a sport-themed bar and a large Regency restaurant which is open for lunch and dinner daily; hot dishes and a continental buffet are on offer at breakfast. The hotel is a popular wedding venue.

Rooms 97 **Conf** Class 134 Board 185 Thtr 445

GREAT BIRCHAM Norfolk — Map 13 TF73

Kings Head

★★★ 86% HOTEL

☎ 01485 578265 📠 01485 578635
PE31 6RJ
e-mail: welcome@the-kings-head-bircham.co.uk
web: www.the-kings-head-bircham.co.uk
dir: From King's Lynn take A149 towards Fakenham. After Hillington, turn left onto B1153, to Great Bircham

This inn is situated in a peaceful village location close to the north Norfolk coastline. The spacious, individually decorated bedrooms are tastefully appointed with superb co-ordinated furnishings and many thoughtful touches. The contemporary, public rooms include a brasserie restaurant, a relaxing lounge, a smart bar and a private dining room.

Rooms 12 (2 fmly) **Facilities** Xmas Wi-fi **Conf** Class 16 Board 20 Thtr 30 **Parking** 25 **Notes** Civ Wed 130

GREAT CHESTERFORD
Essex
Map 12 TL54

The Crown House

★★★ 72% HOTEL

☎ 01799 530515 📠 01799 530683
CB10 1NY
e-mail: reservations@crownhousehotel.com
web: www.crownhousehotel.com
dir: From N: M11 at junct 9 (from S: junct 10) follow Saffron Walden signs, then Great Chesterford (B1383) signs

This Georgian coaching inn, situated in a peaceful village close to the M11, has been sympathetically restored and retains much original character. The bedrooms are well equipped and individually decorated; some rooms have delightful four-poster beds. Public rooms include an attractive lounge bar, an elegant oak-panelled restaurant and an airy conservatory.

Rooms 18 (10 annexe) (1 fmly) (5 GF)
S £69.50-£79.50; **D** £99.50-£145 (incl. bkfst)*
Facilities FTV New Year Wi-fi **Conf** Class 14 Board 12 Thtr 30 Del from £120 to £160* **Parking** 30 **Notes** LB Closed 27-30 Dec Civ Wed 50

GREAT MILTON
Oxfordshire
Map 5 SP60

INSPECTORS' CHOICE

Le Manoir Aux Quat' Saisons

★★★★★ ❀❀❀❀❀ HOTEL

☎ 01844 278881 📠 01844 278847
Church Rd OX44 7PD
e-mail: lemanoir@blanc.co.uk
web: www.manoir.com
dir: From A329 2nd right to Great Milton Manor, hotel 200yds on right

Even though Le Manoir is now very much part of the British scene, its iconic chef patron, Raymond Blanc, still fizzes with new ideas and projects. His first loves are his kitchen and his garden and the vital link between them. The fascinating grounds feature a Japanese tea garden and two acres of vegetables and herbs that supply the kitchen with an almost never ending supply of top notch produce. Even the car park has a stunning artichoke sculpture. The kitchen is the epicentre, with outstanding cooking highlighting freshness and seasonality. Bedrooms in this idyllic 'grand house on a small scale' are either in the main house or around an outside courtyard; all offer the highest levels of comfort and quality, have magnificent marble bathrooms and are equipped with a host of thoughtful extra touches. For something really special there is the 15th-century dovecot with a stunning upper-floor bedroom and a bathroom below. La Belle Epoque is the private dining room, ideal for weddings, celebrations and corporate events.

Rooms 32 (23 annexe) (13 GF) **S** £480-£1550; **D** £480-£1550 (incl. bkfst)* **Facilities** STV FTV Cookery school Water gardens Bikes Spa treatment Xmas New Year Wi-fi **Conf** Board 20 Thtr 24 **Parking** 60 **Notes** LB ⊗ Civ Wed 50

GREAT TOTHAM
Essex
Map 7 TL81

The Bull at Great Totham

❀❀ RESTAURANT WITH ROOMS

☎ 01621 893385 & 894020 📠 01621 894029
2 Maldon Rd CM9 8NH
e-mail: reservations@thebullatgreattotham.co.uk
web: www.thebullatgreattotham.co.uk
dir: Exit A12 at Witham junct to Great Totham

Located in the village of Great Totham, this stylish restaurant with rooms has been tastefully restored following a complete refurbishment. A 16th-century coaching inn, The Bull now offers comfortable en suite bedrooms with stylish decor and furnishings and satellite TVs with Freeview; Wi-fi is available throughout. Guests can enjoy dinner in the gastropub or in the AA 2-Rosette, fine dining restaurant, The Willow Room.

Rooms 4 en suite (2 GF)

G

GREAT YARMOUTH
Norfolk
Map 13 TG50

Imperial

THE INDEPENDENTS HOTEL ASSOCIATION

★★★★ 75% ❀ HOTEL

☎ 01493 842000 📠 01493 852229
North Dr NR30 1EQ
e-mail: reservations@imperialhotel.co.uk
web: www.imperialhotel.co.uk
dir: Follow signs to seafront, turn left. Hotel opposite tennis courts

This friendly, family-run hotel is situated at the quieter end of the seafront within easy walking distance of the town centre. Bedrooms are attractively decorated with co-ordinated soft furnishings and many thoughtful touches; most rooms have superb sea views. Public areas include the smart Savoie Lounge Bar and the Rambouillet Restaurant.

Rooms 39 (4 fmly) **S** £75-£100; **D** £85-£120 (incl. bkfst) **Facilities** FTV New Year Wi-fi **Conf** Class 40 Board 30 Thtr 140 Del from £120 to £160 **Services** Lift **Parking** 50 **Notes** LB Civ Wed 140

GREAT YARMOUTH *continued*

Comfort Hotel Great Yarmouth

★★★ 75% HOTEL

☎ 01493 855070 & 850044 📠 01493 853798
Albert Square NR30 3JH
e-mail: sales@comfortgreatyarmouth.co.uk
web: www.comfortgreatyarmouth.co.uk
dir: From seafront left at Wellington Pier into Kimberley Terr. Left into Albert Sq, hotel on left

A large hotel situated in the quieter end of town, just off the seafront and within easy walking distance of the town centre. The pleasantly decorated, well-equipped bedrooms are generally quite spacious and include Wi-fi. Public rooms include a comfortable lounge, a bar and smart brasserie-style restaurant.

Rooms 50 (6 fmly) (3 GF) **Facilities** FTV Xmas New Year Wi-fi **Conf** Class 50 Board 30 Thtr 120 **Parking** 15 **Notes** ⊗ Civ Wed 120

Furzedown

★★★ 75% HOTEL

☎ 01493 844138 📠 01493 844138
19-20 North Dr NR30 4EW
e-mail: paul@furzedownhotel.co.uk
web: www.furzedownhotel.co.uk
dir: At end of A47 or A12, towards seafront, left, hotel opposite Waterways

Expect a warm welcome at this family-run hotel situated at the northern end of the seafront overlooking the town's Venetian Waterways. Bedrooms are pleasantly decorated and thoughtfully equipped; many rooms have superb sea views. The stylish public areas include a comfortable lounge bar, a smartly appointed restaurant and a cosy TV room.

Rooms 20 (11 fmly) **Facilities** FTV New Year Wi-fi **Conf** Class 80 Board 40 Thtr 75 **Parking** 30

The Prom Hotel

★★★ 75% HOTEL

☎ 01493 842308 📠 01493 851297
77 Marine Pde NR30 2DH
e-mail: info@promhotel.co.uk

Ideally situated on the seafront close to the bright lights and attractions of Marine Parade. The open-plan public areas include a smart lounge bar with views of the sea, and a relaxed restaurant; guests also have the use of a further quieter lounge bar with plush seating. The modern contemporary bedrooms are smartly appointed and have many thoughtful touches; many rooms have lovely sea views.

Rooms 23 (1 fmly) **S** £65-£85; **D** £85-£110 (incl. bkfst)* **Facilities** STV FTV Xmas Wi-fi

Burlington Palm Hotel

★★★ 67% HOTEL

☎ 01493 844568 & 842095 📠 01493 331848
11 North Dr NR30 1EG
e-mail: enquiries@burlington-hotel.co.uk
web: www.burlington-hotel.co.uk
dir: A12 to seafront, left at Britannia Pier. Hotel near tennis courts

This privately owned hotel is situated at the quiet end of the resort, overlooking the sea. Bedrooms come in a variety of sizes and styles; they are pleasantly decorated and well equipped, and many have lovely sea views. The spacious public rooms include a range of seating areas, a choice of dining rooms, two bars and a heated indoor swimming pool.

Rooms 70 (9 fmly) (1 GF) **S** £65-£100; **D** £90-£150 (incl. bkfst) **Facilities** FTV Ⓢ Turkish steam room Xmas Wi-fi **Conf** Class 60 Board 30 Thtr 120 **Services** Lift **Parking** 70 **Notes** LB ⊗ Closed 28 Dec RS Dec-Feb

See advert on opposite page

Arden Court Hotel

★★ 80% HOTEL

☎ 01493 855310 📠 01493 843413
93-94 North Denes Rd NR30 4LW
e-mail: info@ardencourthotel.co.uk.
web: www.ardencourthotel.co.uk
dir: At seafront left along North Drive. At boating lake left along Beaconsfield Rd. At mini rdbt right into North Denes Rd

A friendly, family-run hotel situated in a residential area just a short walk from the seafront. The individually decorated bedrooms are smartly furnished and equipped with a good range of useful extras. Public rooms are attractively presented; they include a smart lounge bar and a restaurant serving an interesting choice of dishes.

Rooms 14 (5 fmly) (2 GF) **S** £47-£57; **D** £74-£84 (incl. bkfst)* **Facilities** Xmas Wi-fi **Parking** 10 **Notes** LB ⊗

New Beach Hotel

★★ 69% HOTEL

☎ 01493 332300 📠 01493 331880
67 Marine Pde NR30 2EJ
e-mail: newbeach.gtyarmouth@alfatravel.co.uk
dir: Follow signs to seafront. Hotel facing Britannia Pier

This Victorian building is centrally located on the seafront, overlooking Britannia Pier and the sandy beach. Bedrooms are pleasantly decorated and equipped with modern facilities; many have lovely sea views. Dinner is taken in the restaurant which doubles as the ballroom, and guests can also relax in the bar or sunny lounge.

Rooms 76 (3 fmly) **S** £36-£50; **D** £56-£84 (incl. bkfst) **Facilities** FTV ♫ Xmas New Year **Services** Lift **Notes** LB ⊗ Closed Dec-Feb (ex Xmas) RS Nov & Mar

Hadleigh Gables Hotel

★★ 61% HOTEL

☎ 01493 843078 📠 01493 843078
5-7 North Dr NR30 1ED
e-mail: hadleighgables@btconnect.com

Situated on the seafront overlooking the tennis courts, just a short walk from Wellesley Recreation Ground, the Bowling Green and Britannia Pier. The bedrooms are pleasantly decorated and equipped with modern facilities; some of the rooms have balconies with views of the sea. Public rooms include a large lounge bar and a smart dining room.

Rooms 62 (12 fmly) (8 GF) **Facilities** ♫ Xmas New Year Wi-fi **Services** Lift **Parking** 20 **Notes** ⊗

Andover House

RESTAURANT WITH ROOMS

☎ 01493 843490 📠 01493 852546
28-30 Camperdown NR30 3JB
e-mail: info@andoverhouse.co.uk
web: www.andoverhouse.co.uk
dir: Opposite Wellington Pier into Shadingfield Close, right into Kimberley Terrace, follow into Camperdown. Property on left

A lovely three-storey Victorian town house which was totally transformed by the current owners a few years ago. The property features a series of contemporary spaces that include a large open-plan lounge bar, a brasserie-style restaurant serving modern British cuisine, a cosy lounge and a smart sun terrace. Bedrooms are tastefully appointed with co-ordinated soft furnishings and have many thoughtful touches.

Rooms 20

GREAT YELDHAM Map 13 TL73
Essex

The White Hart

RESTAURANT WITH ROOMS

☎ 01787 237250 📠 01787 238044
Poole St CO9 4HJ
e-mail: mjwmason@yahoo.co.uk
dir: On A1017 in village

A large timber-framed character building houses the main restaurant and bar areas whilst the bedrooms are located in the converted coach house; all are smartly appointed and well equipped with many thoughtful extras. A comfortable lounge-bar area and beautifully landscaped gardens provide areas for relaxation. Locally sourced produce is used for the main house restaurant menus, which are popular with local residents and guests alike.

Rooms 11 (2 fmly)

GREENFORD
Greater London

See LONDON SECTION plan 1 B4

Premier Inn London Greenford

BUDGET HOTEL

☎ 0871 527 8658 📠 0871 527 8659
Western Av UB6 8TE
dir: From A40 (Western Avenue) E'bound, exit at Perivale. Right, left at 2nd lights. Hotel opposite Hoover Building

High quality, budget accommodation ideal for both families and business travellers. Spacious, en suite bedrooms feature tea and coffee making facilities, and Freeview TV in most hotels. Internet access and Wi-fi are available for a small fee. The adjacent family restaurant features a wide and varied menu. See also the Hotel Groups pages.

Rooms 39 **D** £66-£80*

GREETHAM Map 11 SK91
Rutland

Greetham Valley

★★★ 71% HOTEL

☎ 01780 460444 📠 01780 460623
Wood Ln LE15 7SN
e-mail: info@greethamvalley.co.uk
web: www.greethamvalley.co.uk
dir: A1/B668. Left towards Greetham, Cottesmore & Oakham. Left at x-rds after 0.5m, follow brown signs to golf club entrance

Spacious bedrooms with storage facilities designed for golfers, offer high levels of comfort and many have superb views over the two golf courses. Meals are taken in the clubhouse restaurants with a choice of informal or more formal styles. A beauty suite and extensive conference facilities are ideal for both large and small groups.

Rooms 35 (17 GF) **S** £54-£84; **D** £72-£92 (incl. bkfst)* **Facilities** Spa FTV ⛳ 45 Putt green Fishing Gym 4x4 off-road course Archery centre Bowls green Driving range New Year Wi-fi **Conf** Class 150 Board 80 Thtr 200 Del from £117* **Services** Lift **Parking** 300 **Notes** LB ⊗ Civ Wed 200

G

GRIMSBY Map 17 TA21
Lincolnshire

See also **Stallingborough**

Millfields

THE INDEPENDENTS HOTEL ASSOCIATION

★★★ HOTEL

☎ 01472 356068 📠 01472 250286
53 Bargate DN34 5AD
e-mail: info@millfieldshotel.co.uk
web: www.millfieldshotel.co.uk
dir: A180, right at KFC rdbt then left at next rdbt. Right at 2nd lights & right onto Bargate, hotel 0.5m on left after Wheatsheaf pub

Rooms 27 (4 annexe) (7 fmly) (13 GF) **S** fr £75; **D** fr £85 (incl. bkfst)* **Facilities** FTV Gym Squash Sauna Steam room Hairdresser Beauty salon Aromatherapist Wi-fi **Conf** Class 25 Board 25 Thtr 50 Del from £125* **Parking** 75 **Notes** LB Civ Wed 50

Premier Inn Grimsby

Premier Inn

BUDGET HOTEL

☎ 0871 527 8478 📠 0871 527 8479
Europa Park, Appian Way, off Gilbey Rd DN31 2UT
dir: M180 junct 5, A180 towards town centre. At 1st rdbt take 2nd exit. 1st left, left at mini rdbt into Appian Way

High quality, budget accommodation ideal for both families and business travellers. Spacious, en suite bedrooms feature tea and coffee making facilities, and Freeview TV in most hotels. Internet access and Wi-fi are available for a small fee. The adjacent family restaurant features a wide and varied menu. See also the Hotel Groups pages.

Rooms 40 **D** £52-£59*

GRIMSTON Map 11 SK62
Leicestershire

Best Western Leicester North

★★★ 73% HOTEL

☎ 01664 823212 📠 01664 823371
A46 Fosse Way, Station Rd, Upper Broughton LE14 3BH
e-mail: info@lnhotel.co.uk
dir: A46 towards Grantham. Hotel at junct for Upper Broughton & Willoughby

Very conveniently located right next to the Fosse Way (A46), this hotel offers well equipped and smart bedrooms. This makes an ideal base for visits to Nottingham, Leicester, Loughborough and Belvoir Castle. There is a small restaurant and bar area as well as very large conferencing facilities. Ample parking is a bonus.

Rooms 75 **Facilities** STV FTV Wi-fi **Conf** Class 100 Board 100 Thtr 300 **Parking** 200 **Notes** ⊗

GRIMSTON Map 12 TF72
Norfolk

INSPECTORS' CHOICE

Congham Hall Country House Hotel

★★★ ◎◎ COUNTRY HOUSE HOTEL

☎ 01485 600250 📠 01485 601191
Lynn Rd PE32 1AH
e-mail: info@conghamhallhotel.co.uk
web: www.conghamhallhotel.co.uk
dir: At A149/A148 junct, NE of King's Lynn, take A148 towards Fakenham for 100yds. Right to Grimston, hotel 2.5m on left

An elegant 18th-century Georgian manor set amid 30 acres of mature landscaped grounds and surrounded by parkland. The inviting public rooms provide a range of tastefully furnished areas in which to sit and relax. Imaginative cuisine is served in the Orangery Restaurant which has an intimate atmosphere and panoramic views of the gardens. The bedrooms, tastefully furnished with period pieces, have modern facilities and many thoughtful touches.

Rooms 14 (1 GF) **Facilities** Putt green Xmas New Year Wi-fi **Conf** Class 12 Board 28 Thtr 50 **Parking** 50 **Notes** ⊗ Civ Wed 100

GRINDLEFORD Map 16 SK27
Derbyshire

Maynard

★★★ 79% ◎◎ HOTEL

☎ 01433 630321 📠 01433 630445
Main Rd S32 2HE
e-mail: info@themaynard.co.uk
dir: From Sheffield take A625 to Castleton. Left into Grindleford on B6521. On left after Fox House Hotel

This building, dating back over 100 years, is situated in a beautiful and tranquil location yet is within easy reach of Sheffield and the M1. The bedrooms are contemporary in style and offer a wealth of accessories. The Peak District views from the restaurant and garden are stunning.

Rooms 10 (1 fmly) **Facilities** STV Wi-fi **Conf** Class 60 Board 40 Thtr 120 **Parking** 70 **Notes** LB Civ Wed 130

GUILDFORD
Surrey — Map 6 SU94

Holiday Inn Guildford

★★★ 80% HOTEL

☎ 0871 942 9036 📠 01483 457256
Egerton Rd GU2 7XZ
e-mail: reservations-guildford@ihg.com
web: www.higuildfordhotel.co.uk
dir: A3 to Guildford. Exit at sign for Research Park/Onslow Village. 3rd exit at 1st rdbt, 2nd exit at 2nd rdbt

This hotel is in a convenient location just off the A3 and within a 25 minute-drive of the M25. Public areas are stylish, and on-site facilities include a swimming pool and gym. The accommodation is spacious and comfortable and caters well for both the business and leisure markets. A number of well-equipped meeting rooms is available. There is ample free parking.

Rooms 168 (89 fmly) (66 GF) **S** £79-£215; **D** £89-£225 (incl. bkfst)* **Facilities** Spa STV FTV Gym Fitness studio Beauty treatments Wi-fi **Conf** Class 100 Board 60 Thtr 180 Del from £150 to £230* **Services** Air con **Parking** 230 **Notes** LB Civ Wed 180

Premier Inn Guildford Central

BUDGET HOTEL

☎ 0871 527 8482 📠 0871 527 8483
Parkway GU1 1UP
dir: M25 junct 10, follow Portsmouth (A3) signs. Exit for Guildford Centre/Leisure Complex (A322/A320/A25). Turn left, hotel on left

High quality, budget accommodation ideal for both families and business travellers. Spacious, en suite bedrooms feature tea and coffee making facilities, and Freeview TV in most hotels. Internet access and Wi-fi are available for a small fee. The adjacent family restaurant features a wide and varied menu. See also the Hotel Groups pages.

Rooms 87 **D** £57-£78*

Premier Inn Guildford (Worplesdon)

BUDGET HOTEL

☎ 0871 527 8480 📠 0871 527 8481
Perry Hill GU3 3RY
dir: A3 onto A322 towards Bagshot. In Wolpesdon hotel on right. Or from M3 junct 3, A322 S towards Guildford. In Worplesdon hotel on left

Rooms 19 **D** £57-£78*

GUISBOROUGH
North Yorkshire — Map 19 NZ61

Macdonald Gisborough Hall

★★★★ 80% HOTEL

☎ 0844 879 9149 📠 01287 610844
Whitby Ln TS14 6PT
e-mail: general.gisboroughhall@macdonald-hotels.co.uk
web: www.macdonald-hotels.co.uk
dir: A171, follow signs for Whitby to Waterfall rdbt then 3rd exit into Whitby Lane, hotel 500yds on right

Dating back to the mid-19th century, this elegant establishment provides a pleasing combination of original features and modern facilities. Bedrooms, including four-poster and family rooms, are richly furnished, and there is a choice of welcoming lounges with log fires. Imaginative food is served in Tockett's restaurant.

Rooms 71 (2 fmly) (12 GF) **Facilities** STV Beauty treatment rooms Xmas New Year Wi-fi **Conf** Class 150 Board 32 Thtr 400 **Services** Lift **Parking** 180 **Notes** Closed 2-6 Jan Civ Wed 250

Premier Inn Middlesborough South (Guisborough)

BUDGET HOTEL

☎ 0871 527 8772 📠 0871 527 8773
Middlesbrough Rd, Upsall TS14 6RW
dir: Off A171 towards Whitby

High quality, budget accommodation ideal for both families and business travellers. Spacious, en suite bedrooms feature tea and coffee making facilities, and Freeview TV in most hotels. Internet access and Wi-fi are available for a small fee. The adjacent family restaurant features a wide and varied menu. See also the Hotel Groups pages.

Rooms 20 **D** £54-£60*

HACKNESS
North Yorkshire — Map 17 SE99

Hackness Grange Country House

★★★ 62% HOTEL

☎ 01723 882345 & 374374 📠 01723 882391
North York National Park YO13 0JW
e-mail: admin@englishrosehotels.co.uk
dir: A64 to Scarborough, then A171 to Whitby & Scalby. Follow Hackness & Forge Valley National Park signs, through Hackness, hotel on left

Close to Scarborough, and situated in the North Yorkshire Moors National Park, Hackness Grange is surrounded by attractive gardens. The comfortable bedrooms have views of the open countryside; those in the cottages are ideally suited to families, and the courtyard rooms include facilities for the less able. The lounges and the restaurant are spacious and relaxing.

Rooms 33 (21 annexe) (5 fmly) (8 GF) **S** £55-£80; **D** £105-£175 (incl. bkfst) **Facilities** Putt green Xmas New Year **Conf** Board 14 Thtr 20 Del from £95 to £150 **Parking** 60 **Notes** LB

H

HADLEY WOOD
Greater London — Map 6 TQ29

West Lodge Park

★★★★ 80% HOTEL

☎ 020 8216 3900 & 8216 3903 📠 020 8216 3937
Cockfosters Rd EN4 0PY
e-mail: westlodgepark@bealeshotels.co.uk
web: www.bealeshotels.co.uk
dir: On A111, 1m S of M25 junct 24

A stylish country house set in stunning parkland and gardens, yet only 12 miles from central London and a few miles from the M25. Bedrooms are individually decorated in traditional style and offer excellent in-room facilities. Annexe rooms feature air-conditioning and have access to an outdoor patio area. Public rooms include the award-winning Cedar Restaurant, cosy bar area and separate lounge.

Rooms 59 (13 annexe) (1 fmly) (11 GF) **S** £95; **D** £145-£250* **Facilities** STV FTV Putt green Free use of nearby leisure club New Year Wi-fi **Conf** Class 30 Board 30 Thtr 64 Del from £205 to £225* **Services** Lift **Parking** 200 **Notes** LB Civ Wed 72

HADLOW
Kent — Map 6 TQ65

Hadlow Manor

★★★ 73% HOTEL

☎ 01732 851442 📠 01732 851875
Goose Green TN11 0JH
e-mail: hotel@hadlowmanor.co.uk
dir: On A26 (Maidstone to Tonbridge road). 1m E of Hadlow

This is a friendly, independently owned country-house hotel, ideally situated between Maidstone and Tonbridge. Traditionally styled bedrooms are spacious and attractively furnished with many amenities. Public areas include a sunny restaurant, bar and lounge. The gardens are delightful and there's a seated area ideal for relaxation in warmer weather. Meeting and banqueting facilities are available.

Rooms 29 (2 fmly) (8 GF) **S** £59-£85; **D** £59-£100* **Facilities** STV New Year Wi-fi **Conf** Class 90 Board 103 Thtr 200 **Parking** 120 **Notes** LB ⊗ Civ Wed 200

HADNALL
Shropshire — Map 15 SJ52

Saracens at Hadnall

◎◎ RESTAURANT WITH ROOMS

☎ 01939 210877 📠 01939 210877
Shrewsbury Rd SY4 4AG
e-mail: reception@saracensathadnall.co.uk
web: www.saracensathadnall.co.uk
dir: M54 onto A5, at junct of A5/A49 take A49 towards Whitchurch. Follow A49 to Hadnall, diagonally opposite church

This Georgian Grade II listed former farmhouse and village pub has been tastefully converted into a very smart restaurant with rooms, without any loss of original charm and character. The bedrooms are thoughtfully equipped and include a family room. Skilfully prepared meals are served in either the elegant dining room or the adjacent conservatory where there's a glass-topped well.

Rooms 5 (1 fmly)

HAGLEY
Worcestershire — Map 10 SO98

Premier Inn Hagley

BUDGET HOTEL

☎ 0871 527 8484 📠 0871 527 8485
Birmingham Rd DY9 9JS
dir: M5 junct 3, A456 towards Kidderminster (dual carriageway). Hotel visible on opposite side of road. At next rdbt double back follow A456 Birmingham signs. Hotel on left

High quality, budget accommodation ideal for both families and business travellers. Spacious, en suite bedrooms feature tea and coffee making facilities, and Freeview TV in most hotels. Internet access and Wi-fi are available for a small fee. The adjacent family restaurant features a wide and varied menu. See also the Hotel Groups pages.

Rooms 40 **D** £51-£60*

HAILSHAM
East Sussex — Map 6 TQ50

Boship Farm Hotel

★★★ 72% HOTEL

☎ 01323 844826 & 442600 📠 01323 843945
Lower Dicker BN27 4AT
e-mail: info@boshipfarmhotel.co.uk
dir: On A22. At A267 & 271 junct (Boship rdbt)

Dating back to 1652, a lovely old farmhouse forms the hub of this hotel, which is set in 17 acres of well-tended grounds. Guests have the use of an all-weather tennis court, an outdoor pool and a croquet lawn. Bedrooms are smartly appointed and well equipped; most have views across open fields and countryside.

Rooms 47 (3 fmly) (21 GF) **Facilities** Gym Badminton Sauna Steam room Xmas New Year **Conf** Class 40 Board 46 Thtr 175 **Parking** 110 **Notes** Civ Wed 140

The Olde Forge Hotel & Restaurant

★★ 79% HOTEL

☎ 01323 842893 📠 01323 842893
Magham Down BN27 1PN
e-mail: theoldeforgehotel@tesco.net
web: www.theoldeforgehotel.co.uk
dir: Off Boship Rdbt on A271 to Bexhill & Herstmonceux. Hotel 3m on left

In the heart of the countryside, this family-run hotel offers a friendly welcome and an informal atmosphere. The bedrooms are attractively decorated with thoughtful extras. The restaurant, with its timbered beams and log fires, was a forge in the 16th century; today it has a good local reputation for both its cuisine and service.

Rooms 7 **S** fr £48; **D** fr £85 (incl. bkfst)* **Facilities** Wi-fi **Parking** 11 **Notes** LB

HALIFAX
West Yorkshire — Map 19 SE02

Holdsworth House

★★★ 86% ◎◎ HOTEL

☎ 01422 240024 📠 01422 245174
Holdsworth HX2 9TG
e-mail: info@holdsworthhouse.co.uk
web: www.holdsworthhouse.co.uk
dir: From town centre take A629 (Keighley road). Right at garage up Shay Ln after 1.5m. Hotel on right after 1m

This delightful 17th-century Jacobean manor house, set in well tended gardens, offers individually decorated, thoughtfully equipped bedrooms. Public rooms, adorned with beautiful paintings and antique pieces, include a choice of inviting lounges and superb conference and function facilities. Dinner provides the highlight of any stay and is served in the elegant restaurant by friendly, attentive staff.

Rooms 40 (2 fmly) (15 GF) **S** £80-£100; **D** £100-£150 (incl. bkfst)* **Facilities** FTV New Year Wi-fi **Conf** Class 75 Board 50 Thtr 150 Del from £125 to £155* **Parking** 60 **Notes** Civ Wed 120

The White Swan Hotel

★★★ 74% HOTEL

☎ 01422 355541 📠 01422 357311
Princess St HX1 1TS
e-mail: info@whiteswanhalifax.com
dir: Adjacent to Town Hall

A well established hotel noted for its friendly staff. Located in the heart of the town it offers comfortable, well-equipped bedrooms plus conference and function facilities. The lounge area is ideal for relaxing, and for the more energetic guest there is a small fitness room.

Rooms 40 (2 fmly) **S** £59-£89; **D** £59-£101.50 (incl. bkfst)* **Facilities** STV Gym New Year Wi-fi **Conf** Class 35 Board 35 Thtr 80 **Services** Lift **Parking** 9

Premier Inn Halifax

BUDGET HOTEL

☎ 0871 527 8486 📠 0871 527 8487
Salterhebble Hill, Huddersfield Rd HX3 0QT
dir: Just off M62 junct 24 on A629 towards Halifax

High quality, budget accommodation ideal for both families and business travellers. Spacious, en suite bedrooms feature tea and coffee making facilities, and Freeview TV in most hotels. Internet access and Wi-fi are available for a small fee. The adjacent family restaurant features a wide and varied menu. See also the Hotel Groups pages.

Rooms 31 **D** £52-£58*

HALLAND
East Sussex — Map 6 TQ41

Halland Forge

★★ 67% HOTEL

☎ 01825 840456 📠 01825 840773
BN8 6PW
e-mail: info@hallandforgehotel.co.uk
dir: On A22 at junct with B2192, 4.5m S of Uckfield

Conveniently located, this hotel offers comfortable annexed accommodation with parking spaces directly outside the bedrooms. Public areas include a spacious lounge bar, attractive outdoor seating (weather permitting) and an informal restaurant serving generous portions at dinner. An attractively presented room is available for private dining, special occasions or for meetings by prior arrangement.

Rooms 20 (20 annexe) (2 fmly) (8 GF) **Conf** Class 20 Board 26 Thtr 45 **Parking** 70 **Notes** ⊗

HALSTEAD
Kent — Map 6 TQ46

7 Hotel Diner

★★★ 73% HOTEL

☎ 01959 535890
London Rd, Polhill TN14 7AA
e-mail: reservations@7hoteldiner.co.uk
dir: M25 junct 4, hotel in 2m towards Sevenoaks

This hotel, conveniently located off the M25 and just a short drive to Sevenoaks. The well-equipped bedrooms have been stylishly decorated to offer modern, comfortable accommodation; all have custom-made furniture, flat-screen TVs and free Wi-fi. There is an American-themed diner complete with authentic jukebox and leather booths, and all-day dining is available from 7am in the 7 Lounge. Secure parking is available.

Rooms 25 (2 fmly) (6 GF) **S** £45-£55; **D** £59-£92* **Facilities** STV FTV Xmas New Year Wi-fi Child facilities **Conf** Board 10 Del from £110* **Parking** 70 **Notes** ⊗

HAMPTON COURT
Greater London

See LONDON SECTION plan 1 C1

The Carlton Mitre

★★★★ 71% HOTEL

☎ 020 8979 9988 & 8783 3505 📠 020 8979 9777
Hampton Court Rd KT8 9BN
e-mail: gmmitre@carltonhotels.co.uk
dir: M3 junct 1 follow signs to Sunbury & Hampton Court Palace. At Hampton Court Palace rdbt right, hotel on right

This hotel, dating back in parts to 1655, enjoys an enviable setting on the banks of the River Thames opposite Hampton Court Palace. The riverside restaurant and Edge bar/brasserie command wonderful views as well as spacious terraces for alfresco dining. Bedrooms are spacious and elegant with excellent facilities. Parking is limited.

Rooms 36 (2 fmly) **D** £125-£265* **Facilities** STV FTV Xmas New Year Wi-fi **Conf** Class 60 Board 40 Thtr 120 **Services** Lift Air con **Parking** 13 **Notes** LB ⊗ Civ Wed 100

HANDFORTH

See Manchester Airport

HARLOW
Essex — Map 6 TL41

Park Inn by Radisson Harlow

park inn by Radisson

★★★ 64% HOTEL

☎ 01279 829988 📠 01279 829906
Southern Way CM18 7BA
e-mail: info.harlow@rezidorparkinn.com
web: www.parkinn.co.uk/hotel-harlow
dir: M11 junct 7/A414 towards Harlow, 1st exit at 1st rdbt then 1st left

This is provides a convenient and comfortable place to stay. Bedrooms are comfortably appointed with flat-screen TVs, Wi-fi and safes included. The RBG Restaurant dining concept offers a versatile format and service is attentive and unfussy. Conference facilities and convenient parking complete the picture.

Rooms 119 (2 fmly) (60 GF) **Facilities** FTV Gym Treatment room Dance studio & classes Xmas New Year Wi-fi **Conf** Class 110 Board 80 Thtr 200 **Services** Lift Air con **Parking** 100 **Notes** LB ⊗ Civ Wed 180

HARPENDEN
Hertfordshire — Map 6 TL11

Harpenden House Hotel

CLASSIC BRITISH HOTELS

★★★★ 72% HOTEL

☎ 01582 855 9113 📠 01582 760511
18 Southdown Rd AL5 1PE
e-mail: reservations@harpendenhouse.co.uk
web: www.harpendenhouse.co.uk
dir: M1 junct 10 left at rdbt. Next rdbt right onto A1081 to Harpenden. Over 2 mini rdbts, through town centre. Next rdbt left, hotel 200yds on left

This attractive Grade II listed Georgian building overlooks East Common. The hotel gardens are particularly attractive and the public areas are stylishly decorated, including the restaurant that has an impressive ceiling. Some of the bedrooms and a large suite are located in the original house but most of the accommodation is in the annexe.

Rooms 76 (59 annexe) (13 fmly) (2 GF) **Facilities** Complimentary use of local leisure centre Wi-fi **Conf** Class 60 Board 60 Thtr 150 **Parking** 80 **Notes** ⊗ RS wknds & BHs Civ Wed 120

H

HARROGATE
North Yorkshire
Map 19 SE35

See also **Knaresborough**

INSPECTORS' CHOICE

Rudding Park Hotel, Spa & Golf

★★★★ ⊛⊛ HOTEL

☎ 01423 871350 🖷 01423 872286
Rudding Park, Follifoot HG3 1JH
e-mail: reservations@ruddingpark.com
web: www.ruddingpark.co.uk
dir: From A61 at rdbt with A658 take York exit, follow signs to Rudding Park

In the heart of 200-year-old landscaped parkland, this modern hotel is elegant and stylish. Bedrooms, including two luxurious suites, are very smartly presented and thoughtfully equipped. Carefully prepared meals and Yorkshire tapas are served in the Clocktower, with its striking, contemporary decor. The stylish bar leads to the conservatory with a generous terrace for alfresco dining. The grandeur of the mansion house and the grounds make this a very popular venue for weddings. There is an adjoining 18-hole, par 72 golf course and an 18-bay floodlit, covered driving range; this hotel also provides extensive facilities for corporate activities.

Rooms 90 (31 GF) **S** fr £105; **D** fr £126 (incl. bkfst)* **Facilities** Spa STV FTV ⛳ 18 Putt green Gym Driving range Jogging trail Sauna Hammam ♫ Xmas New Year Wi-fi **Conf** Class 150 Board 40 Thtr 300 Del from £150 **Services** Lift **Parking** 250 **Notes** ® Civ Wed 300

Hotel du Vin Harrogate

Hotel du Vin & Bistro

★★★★ 81% ⊛⊛
TOWN HOUSE HOTEL

☎ 01423 856800 🖷 01423 856801
Prospect Place HG1 1LB
e-mail: info@harrogate.hotelduvin.com
web: www.hotelduvin.com
dir: A1(M) junct 47, A59 to Harrogate, follow town centre signs to Prince of Wales rdbt, 3rd exit, remain in right lane. Right at lights into Albert St, right into Prospect Place

This town house was created from eight Georgian-style properties and overlooks The Stray. The spacious, open-plan lobby has seating, a bar and the reception desk. Hidden downstairs is a cosy snug cellar. The French-influenced bistro offers high quality cooking and a great choice of wines. Bedrooms face front and back, and are smart and modern, with excellent 'deluge' showers.

Rooms 48 (4 GF) **S** £110-£170; **D** £110-£170 **Facilities** Spa STV FTV Xmas New Year Wi-fi **Conf** Class 20 Board 30 Thtr 60 Del from £180 to £195 **Services** Lift **Parking** 30 **Notes** LB Civ Wed 90

The Balmoral Hotel

★★★★ 77% ⊛⊛ HOTEL

☎ 01423 508208
16/18 Franklin Mount HG1 5EJ
e-mail: info@balmoralhotel.co.uk
web: www.balmoralhotel.co.uk
dir: A1 onto A59, then A661 to Harrogate. In town centre at 1st rdbt into Skipton Rd. 4th left into Kings Rd (Nat West bank on corner). Or from A61 follow signs to Harrogate. Into West Park St, Parliament St (Betty's Tea Rooms on left). Right into Kings Rd. Keep in left lane, 0.25m to hotel on right

Set in a peaceful residential area of Harrogate, the property has been tastefully converted into very stylish hotel. The individually designed bedrooms, including suites, are beautifully furnished with luxury touches such as handmade quilts and designer wallpaper. The dining room, with a wooden floor, highly polished tables and bench-style leather seating, offers award-winning cuisine and a great wine list. The staff are well informed and help to create a memorable stay.

The Balmoral Hotel

Rooms 23 (2 fmly) (2 GF) **S** £70-£105; **D** £110-£255 (incl. bkfst)* **Facilities** FTV Xmas New Year Wi-fi **Conf** Class 20 Board 16 Thtr 20 Del from £120 to £200* **Parking** 14

Holiday Inn Harrogate

Holiday Inn

★★★★ 76% HOTEL

☎ 0871 942 9261 🖷 01423 524435
Kings Rd HG1 1XX
e-mail: gm.hiharrogate@qmh-hotels.com
web: www.holidayinn.co.uk
dir: A1 to A59. Hotel adjoins International Conference Centre

Situated just a short walk from the town centre, this impressive hotel lies adjacent to the Harrogate International Conference Centre. Bedrooms are stylishly furnished. Extensive conference facilities and a business centre are provided. Public areas include the first-floor restaurant and ground floor lounge bar. Nearby private parking is a bonus.

Rooms 214 (7 fmly) **D** £69-£250* **Facilities** STV Gym Complimentary use of Harrogate Academy & Spa complex Wi-fi **Conf** Class 150 Board 100 Thtr 300 Del from £89 to £250* **Services** Lift **Parking** 180 **Notes** LB ®

Old Swan Hotel

★★★★ 76% HOTEL

☎ 01423 500055 📠 01423 501154
Swan Rd HG1 2SR
e-mail: info.theoldswan@classiclodges.co.uk
dir: From A1, A59 Ripon, left Empress rdbt, keep left, right at Prince of Wales rdbt. Straight across lights, left into Swan Rd

In the heart of Harrogate and within walking distance of the Harrogate International Centre and Valley Gardens, this hotel is famed as being Agatha Christie's hiding place during her disappearance in 1926. The bedrooms are stylishly furnished, and the public areas include the Library Restaurant, the Wedgwood Room and the lounge bar. Extensive conference and banqueting facilities are available.

Rooms 136 **Facilities** STV Xmas New Year Wi-fi **Conf** Class 130 Board 100 Thtr 450 **Services** Lift **Parking** 175 **Notes** Civ Wed 300

Studley Hotel

★★★★ 75% HOTEL

☎ 01423 560425 📠 01423 530967
Swan Rd HG1 2SE
e-mail: info@studleyhotel.co.uk
web: www.studleyhotel.co.uk
dir: Adjacent to Valley Gardens, opposite Mercer Gallery

This friendly, well-established hotel, close to the town centre and Valley Gardens, is well known for its Orchid Restaurant, which provides a dynamic and authentic approach to Pacific Rim and Asian cuisine. Bedrooms are modern and come in a variety of styles and sizes, while the stylish bar lounge provides an excellent place for relaxing. A PC is available for guests' use.

Rooms 30 (1 fmly) **S** £70-£140; **D** £80-£200 (incl. bkfst)* **Facilities** STV Free use of facilities at local Health Club Wi-fi **Conf** Class 15 Board 12 Thtr 15 **Services** Lift **Parking** 15 **Notes** Closed 23-30 Dec

Nidd Hall Hotel

Warner Leisure Hotels

★★★★ 75% COUNTRY HOUSE HOTEL

☎ 01423 771598 📠 01423 770931
Nidd HG3 3BN
dir: A59 through Knaresborough, follow signs for Ripley. Hotel on right

This fine hotel is set in 45 acres of Victorian and Edwardian gardens. The bedrooms are spacious and appointed to a high standard. Public areas are delightful and retain many original features. Leisure and spa facilities are available along with a variety of outdoor activities. Please note that this is an adults-only (over 21 years old) hotel. Warner Leisure Hotels – AA Small Hotel Group of the Year 2011-12.

Rooms 183 (47 GF) **Facilities** Spa FTV supervised Putt green Fishing Gym Xmas New Year **Conf** Class 40 Board 30 Thtr 60 **Services** Lift **Notes** No children

Barceló Harrogate Majestic Hotel

★★★★ 75% HOTEL

☎ 01423 700300 📠 01423 502283
Ripon Rd HG1 2HU
e-mail: majestic@barcelo-hotels.co.uk
web: www.barcelo-hotels.co.uk
dir: M1 onto A1(M) at Wetherby. Take A661 to Harrogate. Hotel in town centre adjacent to Royal Hall

Popular for conferences and functions, this grand Victorian hotel is set in 12 acres of landscaped grounds that is within walking distance of the town centre. It benefits from spacious public areas, and the comfortable bedrooms, including some spacious suites, come in a variety of sizes.

Rooms 174 (8 fmly) **Facilities** Spa STV supervised Gym Golf practice net Xmas New Year Wi-fi **Conf** Class 260 Board 70 Thtr 500 **Services** Lift **Parking** 250 **Notes** Civ Wed 200

The White Hart Hotel

★★★★ 74% HOTEL

☎ 01423 505681
2 Cold Bath Rd HG2 0NF
e-mail: reception@whitehart.net
web: www.whitehart.net
dir: A59 to Harrogate. A661 3rd exit on rdbt to Harrogate. Left at rdbt onto A6040 for 1m. Right onto A61. Bear left down Montpellier Hill

This hotel has an excellent location in Harrogate and has been welcoming guests for over 200 years. The bedrooms, including executive rooms with four-posters and views over the Montpellier Quarter, are attractively designed. The Tearooms serve from early morning until late afternoon, and the hotel has introduced a pub concept called the Fat Badger, with real ales, an extensive wine list and high quality food. Alfresco eating and drinking are possible in good weather. Secure parking is available and there is Wi-fi throughout.

The White Hart Hotel

Rooms 53 (1 fmly) **S** £60-£80; **D** £80-£100 (incl. bkfst) **Facilities** FTV Xmas New Year Wi-fi **Conf** Class 40 Board 30 Thtr 80 Del from £100 to £150 **Services** Lift **Parking** 80 **Notes** Civ Wed 80

The Kimberley Hotel

★★★★ 74% HOTEL

☎ 01423 505613 & 0800 783 7642
📠 01423 530276
11-19 Kings Rd HG1 5JY
e-mail: info@thekimberley.co.uk
dir: A661 Wetherby Road into town centre. Over 1st rdbt onto Skipton Rd. Kings Rd is 4th turn on left at Natwest Bank

This independently owned hotel is located close to the centre of the town and only a short walk from the Harrogate International Centre. Bedrooms, all now refurbished, are well equipped for both business and leisure guests and have a thoughtful range of extras including Wi-fi. There is a stylish lounge-bar and a contemporary bistro offering an extensive choice of dishes.

Rooms 93 (21 annexe) (3 fmly) (18 GF) **S** £49-£125; **D** £79-£250* **Facilities** STV FTV Xmas New Year Wi-fi **Conf** Class 12 Board 16 Thtr 30 Del from £99 to £279* **Services** Lift **Parking** 42 **Notes** LB

HARROGATE *continued*

Best Western Cedar Court Hotel

★★★★ 70% HOTEL

☎ 01423 858585 & 858595 (Res)
🖹 01423 504950
Queens Buildings, Park Pde HG1 5AH
e-mail: cedarcourt@bestwestern.co.uk
web: www.cedarcourthotels.co.uk
dir: From A1(M) follow signs to Harrogate on A661 past Sainsburys. At rdbt left onto A6040. Hotel right after church

This Grade II listed building was Harrogate's first hotel and enjoys a peaceful location in landscaped grounds, close to the town centre. It provides spacious, well-equipped accommodation. Public areas include a brasserie-style restaurant, a small gym and an open-plan lounge and bar. Functions and conferences are particularly well catered for.

Rooms 100 (8 fmly) (7 GF) **Facilities** FTV Gym Xmas New Year Wi-fi **Conf** Class 300 Board 240 Thtr 650 **Services** Lift **Parking** 150 **Notes** LB ⊗ Civ Wed 200

The Boar's Head

★★★ 83% ◎◎ HOTEL

☎ 01423 771888 🖹 01423 771509
Ripley Castle Estate HG3 3AY
e-mail: reservations@boarsheadripley.co.uk
dir: On A61 (Harrogate to Ripon road). Hotel in town centre

Part of the Ripley Castle estate, this delightful and popular hotel is renowned for its warm hospitality and as a dining destination. Bedrooms offer many comforts, and the luxurious day rooms feature works of art from the nearby castle. The banqueting suites in the castle are very impressive.

Rooms 25 (6 annexe) (2 fmly) **S** £105-£125; **D** £125-£150 (incl. bkfst)* **Facilities** Fishing Tennis Xmas New Year Wi-fi **Parking** 50 **Notes** LB

The Yorkshire Hotel

★★★ 75% HOTEL

☎ 0845 906 9966 🖹 01423 500082
Prospect Place HG1 1LA
e-mail: reservations@akkeron-hotels.com
web: www.akkeron-hotels.com
dir: A1 junct 24/A59 to town centre, right at Betty's Tea Rooms

Ideally situated in the heart of this beautiful spa town, The Yorkshire was transformed from a typical Victorian property to one that is fresh and contemporary, yet retains all the elegance of its original era. The stylish Hg1 Bar & Brasserie, very popular with both guests and local residents, serves meals and light bites throughout the day.

Rooms 80 (1 fmly) **S** £35-£120; **D** £59-£160 **Facilities** FTV Xmas New Year Wi-fi **Conf** Class 60 Board 45 Thtr 120 Del from £95 to £150 **Services** Lift **Parking** 33 **Notes** LB ⊗ Civ Wed 100

Cairn

★★★ A HOTEL

☎ 01423 504005 🖹 01423 500056
Ripon Rd HG1 2JD
e-mail: salescairn@strathmorehotels.com

Rooms 135 (7 fmly) **Facilities** Gym Xmas New Year Wi-fi **Conf** Class 170 Board 100 Thtr 500 **Services** Lift **Parking** 150 **Notes** Civ Wed

See advert on page 550

Premier Inn Harrogate

BUDGET HOTEL

☎ 0871 527 8490 🖹 0871 527 8491
Hornbeam Park Av HG2 8RA
dir: A1(M) junct 46, A661 to Harrogate. Left at The Woodlands lights. Left in 1.5m

High quality, budget accommodation ideal for both families and business travellers. Spacious, en suite bedrooms feature tea and coffee making facilities, and Freeview TV in most hotels. Internet access and Wi-fi are available for a small fee. The adjacent family restaurant features a wide and varied menu. See also the Hotel Groups pages.

Rooms 50 **D** £66*

HARROW
Greater London

See LONDON SECTION plan 1 B5

Best Western Cumberland Hotel

★★★ 72% METRO HOTEL

☎ 020 8863 4111 🖹 020 8861 5668
1 St Johns Rd HA1 2EF
e-mail: reservations@cumberlandhotel.co.uk
web: www.cumberlandhotel.co.uk
dir: On reaching Harrow using Station or Sheepcote Rd, turn into Gayton Rd, then Lyon Rd, becomes St Johns Rd

Situated within walking distance of the town centre, this hotel is ideally located for all local attractions and amenities. Bedrooms provide good levels of comfort and are practically equipped to meet the requirements of all travellers. The public areas comprise a well-stocked pub-style bar, which serves homemade food. Parking is located at the rear of the building.

Rooms 84 (53 annexe) (5 fmly) (15 GF) (23 smoking) **Facilities** FTV Gym Sauna Xmas New Year Wi-fi **Conf** Class 70 Board 62 Thtr 130 Del from £95 to £140* **Parking** 67 **Notes** ⊗ Civ Wed 150

HARROW WEALD
Greater London

See LONDON plan 1 B5

Grim's Dyke Hotel

★★★ 82% ◎◎ HOTEL

☎ 020 8385 3100 & 020 8954 4227
🖹 020 8954 4560
Old Redding HA3 6SH
e-mail: reservations@grimsdyke.com
web: www.grimsdyke.com
dir: A410 onto A409 north towards Bushey, at top of hill at lights turn left into Old Redding

Once home to Sir William Gilbert, this Grade II mansion contains many references to well-known Gilbert and Sullivan productions. The house is set in over 40 acres of beautiful parkland and gardens. Bedrooms in the main house are elegant and traditional, while those in the adjacent lodge are aimed more at the business guest.

Rooms 46 (37 annexe) (4 fmly) (17 GF) **S** £60-£125; **D** £70-£150 (incl. bkfst)* **Facilities** STV Gilbert &

Sullivan opera dinner Murder mystery & Sabrage evenings ♫ Xmas New Year Wi-fi **Conf** Class 49 Board 32 Thtr 90 **Parking** 97 **Notes** LB RS 24-31 Dec Civ Wed 90

HARTINGTON Map 16 SK16
Derbyshire

Biggin Hall Hotel

★★ A HOTEL

☎ 01298 84451
SK17 0DH
e-mail: enquiries@bigginhall.co.uk
web: www.bigginhall.co.uk
dir: 0.5m off A515 midway between Ashbourne & Buxton

Rooms 20 (12 annexe) (2 fmly) (4 GF) **S** £60-£116; **D** £80-£136 (incl. bkfst)* **Facilities** STV FTV Xmas New Year Wi-fi **Conf** Class 20 Board 20 Thtr 20 Del from £125 to £145* **Parking** 25 **Notes** LB No children 12yrs Civ Wed 60

HARTLEPOOL Map 19 NZ53
Co Durham

Best Western Grand

★★★ 77% HOTEL

☎ 01429 266345 📠 01429 265217
Swainson St TS24 8AA
e-mail: grandhotel@tavistockleisure.com
dir: A689 into town centre. Left onto Victoria Rd, hotel on right

This hotel retains many original features and the public areas include a grand ballroom, an open-plan lounge bar and the basement restaurant, Italia. The bedrooms are modern in design and have high spec fixtures and fittings. The staff provide attentive and friendly service.

Rooms 48 (1 fmly) **S** £57-£87; **D** £69-£97 (incl. bkfst)* **Facilities** STV FTV Affiliation with local gym ♫ New Year Wi-fi **Conf** Class 200 Board 60 Thtr 250 **Services** Lift **Parking** 50 **Notes** LB ⊗ Civ Wed 200

Premier Inn Hartlepool Marina

BUDGET HOTEL

☎ 0871 527 8492 📠 0871 527 8493
Maritime Av, Hartlepool Marina TS24 0XZ
dir: Approx 1m from A689/A179 junct. On marina

High quality, budget accommodation ideal for both families and business travellers. Spacious, en suite bedrooms feature tea and coffee making facilities, and Freeview TV in most hotels. Internet access and Wi-fi are available for a small fee. The adjacent family restaurant features a wide and varied menu. See also the Hotel Groups pages.

Rooms 60 **D** £54-£60*

HARTLEY WINTNEY Map 5 SU75
Hampshire

The Elvetham Hotel

★★★ 79% HOTEL

☎ 01252 844871 📠 01252 844161
RG27 8AR
e-mail: enq@theelvetham.co.uk
web: www.theelvetham.co.uk
dir: M3 junct 4A W, junct 5 E (or M4 junct 11, A33, B3011). Hotel signed from A323 between Hartley Wintney & Fleet

A spectacular 19th-century mansion set in 35 acres of grounds with an arboretum. All bedrooms are individually styled and many have views of the manicured gardens. A popular venue for weddings and conferences, the hotel lends itself to team building events and outdoor pursuits.

Rooms 72 (29 annexe) (10 fmly) (7 GF) **S** £80-£120; **D** £100-£140 (incl. bkfst)* **Facilities** STV Putt green Gym Badminton Boules Volleyball New Year Wi-fi **Conf** Class 80 Board 48 Thtr 110 Del from £180 to £235* **Parking** 200 **Notes** Closed 24-27 Civ Wed 200

HARTSHEAD MOOR MOTORWAY SERVICE AREA (M62) Map 19 SE12
West Yorkshire

Days Inn Bradford - M62

BUDGET HOTEL

☎ 01274 851706 📠 01274 855169
Hartshead Moor Service Area, Clifton HD6 4JX
e-mail: hartshead.hotel@welcomebreak.co.uk
web: www.welcomebreak.co.uk
dir: M62 between junct 25 & 26

This modern building offers accommodation in smart, spacious and well-equipped bedrooms, suitable for families and business travellers, and all with en suite bathrooms. Continental breakfast is available and other refreshments may be taken at the nearby family restaurant. See also the Hotel Groups pages.

Rooms 38 (33 fmly) (16 GF) **S** £39.95-£59.95; **D** £49.95-£69.95 **Conf** Board 10

HARWICH Map 13 TM23
Essex

The Pier at Harwich

★★★ 87% @@ HOTEL

☎ 01255 241212 📠 01255 551922
The Quay CO12 3HH
e-mail: pier@milsomhotels.com
web: www.milsomhotels.com
dir: From A12, take A120 to Quay. Hotel opposite lifeboat station

Situated on the quay, overlooking the ports of Harwich and Felixstowe. The bedrooms are tastefully decorated, thoughtfully equipped, and furnished in a contemporary style; many rooms have superb sea views. The public rooms include the informal Ha'Penny Bistro, the first-floor Harbourside Restaurant, a smart lounge bar and a plush residents' lounge.

Rooms 14 (7 annexe) (5 fmly) (1 GF) **S** £87-£142; **D** £112-£192 (incl. bkfst)* **Facilities** STV Day cruises on yachts Golf breaks arranged with nearby course Sea bass fishing Xmas Wi-fi **Conf** Board 16 Del from £155* **Parking** 10 **Notes** LB ⊗ Civ Wed 50

H

HARWICH *continued*

Tower Hotel

★★★ 75% HOTEL

☎ 01255 504952 📠 01255 504952
Dovercourt CO12 3PJ
e-mail: reception@tower-hotel-harwich.co.uk
web: www.tower-hotel-harwich.co.uk
dir: Follow main road into Harwich. Past BP garage on left

This hotel is an impressive late 17th-century Italian-style building. There is a wealth of ornamental ceiling cornices, beautiful architraves and an impressive balustrade. Bedrooms, many named after prominent people from Harwich's past, are spacious and furnished to a very high standard. Evening meals and breakfast are served in the decorative dining rooms, and Rigby's bar offers tempting meals and a wide range of refreshments.

Rooms 13 (2 fmly) (2 GF) **S** £50-£73; **D** £57-£85* **Facilities** Wi-fi **Conf** Class 30 Board 30 Thtr 30 **Parking** 30 **Notes** ⊗ Civ Wed 40

Cliff

★★ 67% HOTEL

☎ 01255 503345 & 507373 📠 01255 240358
Marine Pde, Dovercourt CO12 3RE
e-mail: reception@cliffhotelharwich.fsnet.co.uk
web: www.thecliffhotelharwich.co.uk
dir: A120 to Parkeston rdbt, take road to Dovercourt, on seafront after Dovercourt town centre

Conveniently situated on the seafront close to the railway station and ferry terminal. Public rooms are smartly appointed and include the Shade Bar, a comfortable lounge, a restaurant and the Marine Bar with views of Dovercourt Bay. The pleasantly decorated bedrooms have co-ordinated soft furnishings and modern facilities; many have sea views.

Rooms 26 (3 fmly) **S** £40-£50; **D** £50-£70* **Facilities** STV New Year Wi-fi **Conf** Class 150 Board 40 Thtr 200 Del from £80 to £120* **Parking** 50 **Notes** ⊗ RS Xmas & New Year

Premier Inn Harwich

BUDGET HOTEL

☎ 0871 527 8494 📠 0871 527 8495
Parkstone Rd, Dovercourt CO12 4NX
dir: A120 to Harwich, hotel opposite Morrisons. Right at rdbt. Hotel entrance through Lidl car park

High quality, budget accommodation ideal for both families and business travellers. Spacious, en suite bedrooms feature tea and coffee making facilities, and Freeview TV in most hotels. Internet access and Wi-fi are available for a small fee. The adjacent family restaurant features a wide and varied menu. See also the Hotel Groups pages.

Rooms 45 **D** £49-£60*

HASLEMERE Map 6 SU93
Surrey

Lythe Hill Hotel and Spa

★★★★ 74% ◎ HOTEL

☎ 01428 651251 📠 01428 644131
Petworth Rd GU27 3BQ
e-mail: lythe@lythehill.co.uk
web: www.lythehill.co.uk
dir: From High St onto B2131. Hotel 1.25m on right

This privately owned hotel sits in 30 acres of attractive parkland with lakes, complete with roaming geese. The hotel has been described as a hamlet of character buildings, each furnished in a style that complements the age of the property; the oldest one dating back to 1475. Cuisine in the adjacent 'Auberge de France' offers interesting, quality dishes, whilst breakfast is served in the hotel dining room. The bedrooms are split between a number of 15th-century buildings and vary in size. The stylish spa includes a 16-metre swimming pool.

Rooms 41 (8 fmly) (18 GF) **Facilities** Spa FTV Fishing Gym Boules Giant chess Xmas New Year Wi-fi **Conf** Class 40 Board 30 Thtr 128 **Parking** 200 **Notes** Civ Wed 128

HASTINGS & ST LEONARDS Map 7 TQ80
East Sussex

The Chatsworth Hotel

★★★ 73% ◎ HOTEL

☎ 01424 720188 📠 01424 445865
Carlisle Pde TN34 1JG
e-mail: info@chatsworthhotel.com
dir: A21 to town centre. At seafront turn right before next lights

Enjoying a central position on the seafront, close to the pier, this hotel is a short walk from the old town and within easy reach of the county's many attractions. Bedrooms are smartly decorated, equipped with a range of extras and many rooms enjoy splendid sea views. Guests can also enjoy an exciting Indian meal in the contemporary restaurant.

Rooms 52 (5 fmly) **Facilities** Xmas New Year Wi-fi **Conf** Class 20 Board 20 Thtr 40 **Services** Lift **Parking** 8 **Notes** ⊗

Best Western Royal Victoria

★★★ 73% HOTEL

☎ 01424 445544 📠 01424 721995
Marina, St Leonards-on-Sea TN38 0BD
e-mail: reception@royalvichotel.co.uk
web: www.royalvichotel.co.uk
dir: On A259 (seafront road) 1m W of Hastings pier

This imposing 18th-century property is situated in a prominent position overlooking the sea. A superb marble staircase leads up from the lobby to the main public areas on the first floor which has panoramic views of the sea. The spacious bedrooms are pleasantly decorated and well equipped, and include duplex and family suites.

Rooms 50 (15 fmly) **Facilities** Xmas **Conf** Class 40 Board 40 Thtr 100 **Services** Lift **Parking** 6 **Notes** Civ Wed 50

Premier Inn Hastings

BUDGET HOTEL

☎ 0871 527 8496 📠 0871 527 8497
1 John Macadam Way, St Leonards on Sea TN37 7DB
dir: A21 into Hastings. Hotel on right after junct with A2100 (Battle road)

High quality, budget accommodation ideal for both families and business travellers. Spacious, en suite bedrooms feature tea and coffee making facilities, and Freeview TV in most hotels. Internet access and Wi-fi are available for a small fee. The adjacent family restaurant features a wide and varied menu. See also the Hotel Groups pages.

Rooms 44 **D** £65*

HATFIELD Hertfordshire **Map 6 TL20**

Beales Hotel

★★★★ 78% ◎◎ HOTEL

☎ 01707 288500 🖹 01707 256282
Comet Way AL10 9NG
e-mail: hatfield@bealeshotels.co.uk
web: www.bealeshotels.co.uk
dir: On A1001 opposite Galleria Shopping Mall - follow signs for Galleria

This hotel is a stunning contemporary property. Within easy access of the M25, its striking exterior incorporates giant glass panels and cedar wood slats. Bedrooms have luxurious beds, flat-screen TVs and smart bathrooms. Public areas include a small bar and attractive restaurant, which opens throughout the day. The hotel is fully air-conditioned and free wired broadband is available in bedrooms, conference and banqueting rooms.

Rooms 53 (3 fmly) (21 GF) **Facilities** STV Use of nearby leisure club Xmas New Year Wi-fi **Conf** Class 124 Board 64 Thtr 300 **Services** Lift Air con **Parking** 126 **Notes** ⊗ RS 27-30 Dec Civ Wed 300

Mercure Hatfield Oak Hotel

★★★ 73% HOTEL

☎ 01707 275701 🖹 01707 266033
Roehyde Way AL10 9AF
e-mail: enquiries@hotels-hatfield.com
dir: M25 junct 23 between juncts 2 & 3 of A1(M). Roehyde Way runs parallel to A1(M)

The hotel enjoys an enviable location for both leisure and business guests, it is within easy reach of major roads and central London. In addition, the University of Hertfordshire is situated nearby. The accommodation has been appointed to a good standard, with flat-screen TVs and Wi-fi to name but a few facilities. The hotel also caters for conference and banqueting.

Rooms 76 (5 fmly) (36 GF) **Facilities** FTV Wi-fi **Conf** Class 50 Board 50 Thtr 100 Del from £100 to £140 **Parking** 85 **Notes** ⊗ Civ Wed 120

Premier Inn Hatfield

BUDGET HOTEL

☎ 0871 527 8498 🖹 0871 527 8499
Lemsford Rd AL10 0DZ
dir: From A1(M) junct 4, A1001 towards Hatfield. At rbt take 2nd exit, 1st right

High quality, budget accommodation ideal for both families and business travellers. Spacious, en suite bedrooms feature tea and coffee making facilities, and Freeview TV in most hotels. Internet access and Wi-fi are available for a small fee. The adjacent family restaurant features a wide and varied menu. See also the Hotel Groups pages.

Rooms 40 **D** £53-£65*

HATHERSAGE Derbyshire **Map 16 SK28**

George Hotel

★★★ 81% ◎◎ HOTEL

☎ 01433 650436 🖹 01433 650099
Main Rd S32 1BB
e-mail: info@george-hotel.net
web: www.george-hotel.net
dir: In village centre on A6187, SW of Sheffield

The George is a relaxing 500-year-old hostelry in the heart of this picturesque town. The beamed bar lounge has great character and traditional comfort, and the restaurant is light, modern and spacious with original artworks. Upstairs the decor is simpler with lots of light hues; the split-level and four-poster rooms are especially appealing. The quality cooking is a key feature of the hotel.

Rooms 22 (2 fmly) (3 GF) **S** £94-£107; **D** £132-£188 (incl. bkfst)* **Facilities** Xmas New Year Wi-fi **Conf** Class 20 Board 36 Thtr 80 Del from £148 to £168* **Parking** 40 **Notes** LB ⊗ Civ Wed 70

HAVANT Hampshire **Map 5 SU70**

Premier Inn Portsmouth (Havant)

BUDGET HOTEL

☎ 0871 527 8900 🖹 0871 527 8901
65 Bedhampton Hill, Bedhampton PO9 3JN
dir: At rdbt just off A3(M) junct 5 towards Bedhampton

High quality, budget accommodation ideal for both families and business travellers. Spacious, en suite bedrooms feature tea and coffee making facilities, and Freeview TV in most hotels. Internet access and Wi-fi are available for a small fee. The adjacent family restaurant features a wide and varied menu. See also the Hotel Groups pages.

Rooms 37 **D** £67*

HAVERHILL Suffolk **Map 12 TL64**

Days Inn Haverhill

DAYS INN

BUDGET HOTEL

☎ 01440 716950 🖹 01440 716951
Phoenix Road & Bumpstead Rd, Haverhill Business Park CB9 7AE
e-mail: reservations@daysinnhaverhill.co.uk
web: www.haverhilldaysinn.co.uk
dir: A1017 (Haverhill bypass). Hotel on 5th rdbt

This modern building offers accommodation in smart, spacious and well-equipped bedrooms, suitable for families and business travellers, and all with en suite bathrooms. Continental breakfast is available and other refreshments may be taken at the nearby family restaurant. See also the Hotel Groups pages.

Rooms 80 (8 fmly) (14 GF) **S** £49.50-£88.50; **D** £59.50-£98.50 (incl. bkfst)* **Conf** Class 28 Board 24 Thtr 60 Del from £117 to £130*

HAWES North Yorkshire Map 18 SD88

Simonstone Hall

★★ 82% HOTEL

☎ 01969 667255 📠 01969 667741
Simonstone DL8 3LY
e-mail: email@simonstonehall.demon.co.uk
web: www.simonstonehall.co.uk
dir: 1.5m N of Hawes on road signed Muker & Buttertubs

This former hunting lodge provides professional, friendly service and a relaxed atmosphere. There is an inviting drawing room, stylish fine dining restaurant, a bar and conservatory. The generally spacious bedrooms are elegantly designed to reflect the style of the house, and many offer spectacular views of the countryside.

Rooms 18 (10 fmly) (2 GF) **Facilities** Xmas Wi-fi **Conf** Class 20 Board 20 Thtr 50 **Parking** 40 **Notes** LB Civ Wed 72

HAWORTH West Yorkshire Map 19 SE03

Weavers Restaurant with Rooms

RESTAURANT WITH ROOMS

☎ 01535 643822 📠 01535 644832
13/17 West Ln BD22 8DU
e-mail: weaversltd@btconnect.com
dir: In village centre. Pass Brontë Weaving Shed on right, 100yds left to Parsonage car park

Centrally located on the cobbled main street, this family-owned restaurant with rooms provides well-equipped, stylish and comfortable accommodation. Each of the three en suite bedrooms has many thoughtful extras. The kitchen serves both modern and traditional dishes with flair and creativity.

Rooms 3

HAYDOCK Merseyside Map 15 SJ59

Thistle Haydock

thistle

★★★★ 76% HOTEL

☎ 0871 376 9044 📠 0871 376 9144
Penny Ln WA11 9SG
e-mail: haydock@thistle.co.uk
web: www.thistle.com/haydock
dir: M6 junct 23, follow Haydock Racecourse signs (A49) N towards Ashton-in-Makerfield, 1st left, after bridge 1st turn left

A smart, purpose-built hotel which offers an excellent standard of thoughtfully equipped accommodation. It is conveniently situated between Liverpool and Manchester, just off the M6. The wide range of leisure and meeting facilities prove popular with guests. Thistle Hotels – AA Hotel Group of the Year 2011-12.

Rooms 137 (10 fmly) (65 GF) **Facilities** STV FTV supervised Gym Children's play area Sauna Steam room Wi-fi **Conf** Class 140 Board 40 Thtr 300 Del from £90 to £160* **Parking** 210 **Notes** LB Civ Wed 220

Premier Inn Haydock

Premier Inn

BUDGET HOTEL

☎ 0871 527 8500 📠 0871 527 8501
Yew Tree Way, Golbourne WA3 3JD
dir: M6 junct 23, A580 towards Manchester. Approx 2m. Straight on at major rdbt. Hotel on left

High quality, budget accommodation ideal for both families and business travellers. Spacious, en suite bedrooms feature tea and coffee making facilities, and Freeview TV in most hotels. Internet access and Wi-fi are available for a small fee. The adjacent family restaurant features a wide and varied menu. See also the Hotel Groups pages.

Rooms 60 **D** £50-£56*

HAYLE Cornwall Map 2 SW53

Premier Inn Hayle

Premier Inn

BUDGET HOTEL

☎ 0871 527 8506 📠 0871 527 8507
Carwin Rise, Loggans TR27 4PN
dir: On A30 at Loggans Moor rdbt exit into Carwin Rise. Hotel on right

High quality, budget accommodation ideal for both families and business travellers. Spacious, en suite bedrooms feature tea and coffee making facilities, and Freeview TV in most hotels. Internet access and Wi-fi are available for a small fee. The adjacent family restaurant features a wide and varied menu. See also the Hotel Groups pages.

Rooms 56 **D** £70*

HAYLING ISLAND Hampshire Map 5 SU70

Langstone Hotel

★★★★ 73% HOTEL

☎ 023 9246 5011 📠 023 9246 6468
Northney Rd PO11 0NQ
e-mail: info@langstonehotel.co.uk
dir: From A27 take A3023 signed Havant/Hayling Island. Over bridge onto Hayling Island, sharp left after bridge

This hotel is located on the north shore of Hayling Island, yet is only minutes from the M27 and has easy access to Fareham, Havant and Chichester. All the smartly designed, air-conditioned bedrooms, including 45 superior rooms, have views over Langstone harbour. The Brasserie offers a good choice of dishes and overlooks the harbour. There's a gym, indoor pool, sauna, steam, beauty salon and a fitness club.

Rooms 148 (40 fmly) (60 GF) (5 smoking) **Facilities** Spa STV supervised Gym Xmas New Year Wi-fi **Conf** Class 80 Board 50 Thtr 180 Del from £115 to £175* **Services** Lift Air con **Parking** 150 **Notes** LB Civ Wed 150

Sinah Warren Hotel

Warner Leisure Hotels

★★★ 77% HOTEL

☎ 023 9246 6421 📠 023 9246 0068
Ferry Rd PO11 0BZ
e-mail: sinahwarren2@bourne-leisure.co.uk
dir: A27 at Havant junct take A3023 to Hayling Island, 2nd exit off rdbt towards Manor Rd, 3rd exit off rdbt into Ferry Rd. Hotel 1.5m on right

Located in a beautiful part of Hampshire, this hotel offers a great range of leisure facilities and numerous daily in-house and external activities catering for all. The accommodation is spacious, and some rooms have sea views. The packages range from a minimum two-night, half board stay. Please note that this is an adults-only (over 21 years old) hotel. Warner Leisure Hotels – AA Small Hotel Group of the Year 2011-12.

Rooms 246 (116 GF) **S** £194-£339; **D** £388-£678 (incl. bkfst & dinner)* **Facilities** Spa FTV supervised Gym Xmas New Year Wi-fi **Conf** Class 300 Board 250 Thtr 500 **Services** Lift **Parking** 260 **Notes** LB No children

H

HAYTOR VALE Map 3 SX77
Devon

Rock Inn

★★ 79% ® HOTEL

☎ 01364 661305 & 661465 📠 01364 661242
TQ13 9XP
e-mail: inn@rock-inn.co.uk
web: www.rock-inn.co.uk
dir: A38 onto A382 to Bovey Tracey, in 0.5m left onto B3387 to Haytor

Dating back to the 1750s, this former coaching inn is in a pretty hamlet on the edge of Dartmoor. Each named after a Grand National winner, the individually decorated bedrooms have some nice extra touches. Bars are full of character, with flagstone floors and old beams and offer a wide range of dishes, cooked with imagination.

Rooms 9 (2 fmly) **S** £75-£100; **D** £85-£135 (incl. bkfst)* **Facilities** FTV New Year Wi-fi **Parking** 20 **Notes** ⊗ Closed 25-26 Dec

HAYWARDS HEATH Map 6 TQ32
West Sussex

Best Western The Birch Hotel

★★★ 74% HOTEL

☎ 01444 451565 📠 01444 440109
Lewes Rd RH17 7SF
e-mail: info@birchhotel.co.uk
dir: On A272 opposite Princess Royal Hospital & behind Shell Garage

Originally the home of an eminent Harley Street surgeon, this attractive Victorian property has been extended to combine modern facilities with the charm of its original period. Public rooms include the conservatory-style Pavilion Restaurant, along with an open-plan lounge and brasserie-style bar serving a range of light meals.

Rooms 51 (3 fmly) (12 GF) **S** £80-£90; **D** £90-£116 (incl. bkfst) **Facilities** STV Wi-fi **Conf** Class 30 Board 26 Thtr 60 Del from £120 to £135 **Parking** 60 **Notes** LB Civ Wed 60

HEACHAM Map 12 TF63
Norfolk

Heacham Manor Hotel

★★★ 86% HOTEL

☎ 01485 536030 & 579800 📠 01485 533815
Hunstanton Rd PE31 7JX
e-mail: info@heacham-manor.co.uk
dir: On A149 between Heacham & Hunstanton. Near Hunstanton rdbt with water tower

This delightful 16th-century, Grade II listed house has been beautifully restored. The property is approached via a winding driveway through landscaped grounds to the front of the hotel. Public areas include a smart dining room, a sunny conservatory and a cosy bar which leads out onto a terrace. The bedrooms are very stylish and have modern facilities.

Heacham Manor Hotel

Rooms 45 (32 annexe) (10 fmly) (12 GF) **Facilities** FTV ⛳ 18 Swimming pools & leisure facilities available at sister resort Xmas New Year Wi-fi **Conf** Class 35 Board 20 Thtr 40 **Parking** 55 **Notes** ⊗

See advert on this page

HEATHROW AIRPORT (LONDON)
Greater London

See also Slough & Staines
See LONDON SECTION plan 1 A2/A3

Sheraton Skyline

★★★★ 82% HOTEL

☎ 020 8759 2535 & 8759 2535 📠 020 8750 9150
Bath Rd UB3 5BP
e-mail: res268-skyline@sheraton.com
dir: M4 junct 4 for Heathrow, follow Terminal 1,2 & 3 signs. Before airport entrance take slip road to left for 0.25m signed A4/Central London

Within easy reach of all terminals this hotel offers well appointed bedrooms featuring air conditioning. Bedrooms provide excellent levels of quality and comfort. The extensive, contemporary public areas are light and spacious, and include a wide range of eating and drinking options, function rooms, club lounge and a gym.

Rooms 350 (58 fmly) (27 smoking) **S** £275; **Facilities** STV FTV supervised Gym Fitness centre Xmas New Year Wi-fi **Conf** Class 325 Board 100 Thtr 500 **Services** Lift Air con **Parking** 327 **Notes** LB Civ Wed 360

London Heathrow Marriott

★★★★ 77% HOTEL

☎ 020 8990 1100 & 8990 1119 📠 020 8990 1110
Bath Rd UB3 5AN
e-mail: mhrs.lhrhr.ays@marriott.com
web: www.londonheathrowmarriott.co.uk
dir: M4 junct 4, follow signs for Heathrow Terminals 1, 2 & 3. Left at rdbt onto A4 towards central London. Hotel 0.5m on left

This smart, modern hotel, with its striking design, meets all the expectations of a successful airport hotel. The light and airy atrium offers several eating and drinking options, each with a different theme. Spacious bedrooms are appointed to a good standard with an excellent range of facilities, and there is a leisure club and business centre.

Rooms 393 (139 fmly) (30 smoking) **S** £178.80-£226.80; **D** £178.80-£226.80* **Facilities** STV supervised Gym Steam room Sauna Spa pool Xmas Wi-fi **Conf** Class 300 Board 65 Thtr 550 **Services** Lift Air con **Parking** 280 **Notes** LB Civ Wed 414

Crowne Plaza London - Heathrow

★★★★ 76% HOTEL

☎ 0871 942 9140 📠 01895 445122
Stockley Rd UB7 9NA
e-mail: lonha.reservations@ihg.com
web: www.crowneplaza.com/lon-heathrow
dir: M4 junct 4 follow signs to Uxbridge on A408, hotel 400yds on left

This smart hotel is conveniently located for access to Heathrow Airport and the motorway network. Excellent facilities include versatile conference and meeting rooms, a spa and leisure complex. Guests have the choice of two bars, both serving food plus two restaurants. Air-conditioned bedrooms are furnished and decorated to a high standard and feature a comprehensive range of extra facilities.

Rooms 465 (204 fmly) (37 GF) (20 smoking) **Facilities** STV supervised ⛳ 9 Putt green Gym Steam room Sauna Wi-fi **Conf** Class 120 Board 75 Thtr 200 **Services** Lift Air con **Parking** 800 **Notes**

Heathrow/Windsor Marriott

★★★★ 75% HOTEL

☎ 01753 544244 📠 01753 540240
Ditton Rd, Langley SL3 8PT
e-mail: mhrs.lhrsl.conferenceandevents@marriotthotels.com
web: www.heathrowwindsormarriott.co.uk
dir: M4 junct 5, follow 'Langley' signs, left at lights

Ideally located for access to Heathrow and the M4, this smart hotel offers a wide range of facilities. There is a well-appointed leisure centre, extensive conference facilities, a bar offering 24-hour snacks and light meals, and a restaurant with a wide ranging cuisine. Spacious bedrooms are well equipped for both leisure and business guests.

Rooms 382 (120 fmly) (96 GF) (20 smoking) **S** £72-£190.80; **D** £72-£190.80* **Facilities** STV FTV supervised Gym Sauna Steam room Wi-fi **Conf** Class 220 Board 42 Thtr 400 Del from £159 to £205* **Services** Lift Air con **Parking** 550 **Notes** LB Civ Wed 300

Renaissance London Heathrow Hotel

★★★★ 75% HOTEL

☎ 020 8897 6363 📠 020 8897 1113
Bath Rd TW6 2AQ
e-mail: rhi.lhrbr.guest.services@renaissancehotels.com
web: www.renaissancelondonheathrow.co.uk
dir: M4 junct 4 follow spur road towards airport, then 2nd left. At rdbt take 2nd exit signed 'Renaissance Hotel'. Hotel adjacent to Customs House

Located right on the perimeter of the airport, this hotel commands superb views over the runways. The smart bedrooms are fully soundproofed and equipped with air conditioning - each is well suited to meet the needs of today's business travellers. The hotel boasts extensive conference facilities, and is a very popular venue for air travellers and conference organisers.

Rooms 649 (59 GF) (30 smoking) **S** £90-£190; **D** £90-£190* **Facilities** STV Gym Steam room Fitness studio Massage treatment Personal trainer Solarium Xmas Wi-fi **Conf** Class 300 Board 80 Thtr 450 Del from £145 to £219* **Services** Lift Air con **Parking** 700 **Notes** Civ Wed 150

The Continental Hotel

★★★★ 74% HOTEL

☎ 020 8572 3131 📠 020 8572 3334
29-31 Lampton Rd TW3 1JA
e-mail: reservation@thecontinental-hotel.com
dir: A4, right onto A3006, left onto A3005 then left onto Lampton Rd

This hotel enjoys a prime location just a few minutes walk from Hounslow Central Line; central London can be reached in 40 minutes. The bedrooms are air conditioned, and complimentary broadband is available. The bedroom en suites are marble-clad wet rooms with power showers. The on-site Golds Gym has a 21-metre indoor pool, a state-of-the-art fitness centre and beauty treatment rooms.

Rooms 71 (8 fmly) **S** £89-£199; **D** £99-£199 **Facilities** Spa STV FTV Gym Xmas New Year Wi-fi **Services** Lift Air con **Parking** 40 **Notes** LB

Park Inn Heathrow

★★★★ 73% HOTEL

☎ 020 8759 6611 🖹 020 8759 7028
Bath Rd UB7 0DU
e-mail: info.heathrow@rezidorparkinn.com
dir: M4 junct 4, follow signs for T1, 2 & 3. Hotel on left, take exit on left up ramp

Ideally located for Heathrow Airports and central London. This hotel is spacious, purpose-built and offers a range of well-appointed bedrooms, conference rooms, a choice of bars and a fully-equipped health club. The restaurant offers varied dining ideal for a transient market, and there is plenty of parking available.

Rooms 895 (121 fmly) (95 GF) (95 smoking) **S** £70-£254; **D** £75-£259* **Facilities** STV supervised Gym Treatment room Xmas New Year Wi-fi **Conf** Class 360 Board 120 Thtr 700 Del from £174 to £254* **Services** Lift Air con **Parking** 475 **Notes** Civ Wed 500

Ramada London Heathrow

★★★★ 73% HOTEL

☎ 0844 815 9041 🖹 020 8897 7014
Bath Rd, Cranford TW5 9QE
e-mail: fo.lhr@ramadajarvis.co.uk
dir: M4 junct 3 follow signs to Heathrow Terminals 1, 2 & 3. Hotel on right of A4 Bath Rd

This well presented hotel is conveniently situated just three miles from Heathrow Airport. Bedrooms are located in a smart block and all are well appointed for both business and leisure guests; each has a flat-screen TV with multi-channel choice, climate control and good lighting. Arts Bar and Brasserie lead from a contemporary open-plan reception area. Chargeable car park on site.

Rooms 200 (18 fmly) (37 GF) **S** £109-£204; **D** £119-£204* **Facilities** FTV Wi-fi **Conf** Class 45 Board 40 Thtr 70 **Services** Lift Air con **Parking** 60 **Notes** LB ⊗ Civ Wed 65

Novotel London Heathrow

★★★★ 72% HOTEL

☎ 01895 431431 🖹 01895 431221
Cherry Ln UB7 9HB
e-mail: H1551-gm@accor.com
web: www.novotel.com
dir: M4 junct 4, follow Uxbridge signs on A408. Keep left, take 2nd exit off traffic island into Cherry Ln signed West Drayton. Hotel on left

Conveniently located for Heathrow Airport and the motorway network, this modern hotel provides comfortable accommodation. The large, airy indoor atrium creates a sense of space to the public areas, which include an all-day restaurant and bar, meeting rooms, fitness centre and swimming pool. Ample secure parking is available.

Rooms 178 (178 fmly) (10 GF) **S** £65-£139; **D** £65-£139* **Facilities** STV Gym Wi-fi **Conf** Class 100 Board 90 Thtr 250 Del from £159 to £199* **Services** Lift Air con **Parking** 100

Holiday Inn London Heathrow M4 Jct 4

★★★★ 71% HOTEL

☎ 0871 942 9095 🖹 020 8897 8659
Sipson Rd UB7 0JU
e-mail: reservations-heathrowm4@ihg.com
web: www.holidayinn.co.uk
dir: M4 junct 4, keep left, take 1st left into Holloway Lane, left at mini rdbt then left. For detailed instructions contact hotel

This landmark hotel can be seen from for miles when travelling on the M4 and is situated close to Heathrow Airport; it is an ideal base for the airport and for families visiting local attractions. The bedrooms are air conditioned and well equipped. There are two restaurants, a small gym and ample parking.

Rooms 617 (25 smoking) **S** £66-£336; **D** £76-£346* **Facilities** STV Xmas New Year Wi-fi **Conf** Class 60 Board 35 Thtr 130 Del from £125 to £330* **Services** Lift Air con **Parking** 450 **Notes** LB ⊗

Holiday Inn London - Heathrow

★★★★ 70% HOTEL

☎ 020 8990 0000 🖹 020 8564 7744
Bath Rd, Corner Sipson Way UB7 0DP
web: www.holidayinnheathrow.co.uk
dir: Exit airport via main tunnel, at end left towards A4/Other Routes, follow signs for A4. At main lights (hotel visable) turn right, 1st left into Sipson Way

A property close to the terminals and with a frequent bus service to the airport. Public areas include a large brasserie-style restaurant and bar plus shop, mini gym and parking. Bedrooms are spacious and air conditioned, with facilities to suit the business traveller; there are a number of executive rooms available.

Rooms 230 (15 fmly) (58 GF) (23 smoking) **Facilities** Gym New Year Wi-fi **Conf** Class 50 Board 50 Thtr 130 Del from £130 to £165* **Services** Lift Air con **Notes** ⊗ Civ Wed 80

Holiday Inn London Heathrow Ariel

★★★ 78% HOTEL

☎ 0871 942 9040 🖹 020 8564 9265
118 Bath Rd UB3 5AJ
e-mail: reservations-heathrow@ihg.com
web: www.holidayinn.co.uk
dir: M4 junct 4, take spur road to Heathrow Airport, 1st left onto A4 Bath Rd, through 3 sets of lights. Hotel on left

Located close to Heathrow Airport with good public transport links to all terminals, this well sited hotel is suitable for both the business and leisure traveller. Public areas benefit from a spacious lounge bar area, brasserie-style restaurant and extensive conference facilities. Ample secure parking is an additional plus.

Rooms 184 (18 smoking) **Facilities** STV Xmas Wi-fi **Conf** Class 35 Board 25 Thtr 50 **Services** Lift Air con **Parking** 100 **Notes** ⊗ Civ Wed 50

HEATHROW AIRPORT (LONDON) ***continued***

Thistle London Heathrow

thistle

★★★ 73% HOTEL

☎ 0871 376 9021 Fax 0871 376 9121
Bath Rd, Longford UB7 0EQ
e-mail: londonheathrow@thistle.co.uk
web: www.thistlehotels.com/londonheathrow
dir: M25 junct 14 signed Terminal 4 & Cargo Area. Right at 1st rdbt signed Heathrow. Left at lights onto A3044 signed Colnbrook & Longford

Located adjacent to the airport and with the benefit of secure parking and regular coach transfers, this long established hotel provides a range of well equipped bedrooms for both the business and leisure guest. Imaginative food is available in an attractive restaurant and comprehensive breakfasts are served in a separate first-floor dining room. Thistle Hotels – AA Hotel Group of the Year 2011-12.

Rooms 264 (3 fmly) (132 GF) **Facilities** STV FTV Use of nearby health club Xmas New Year Wi-fi **Conf** Class 300 Board 25 Thtr 700 **Services** Air con **Parking** 450 **Notes** ⊗ Civ Wed 540

Days Hotel Hounslow

DAYS INN

★★★ 72% HOTEL

☎ 020 8538 1230 Fax 020 8570 5053
8-10 Lampton Rd TW3 1JL
e-mail: gm@dhhounslow.com
dir: A4 (Bath Rd), then A3006 follow onto Lampton Rd (A3005)

A purpose built hotel situated in the centre of Hounslow and within walking distance of the tube station and with easy access to the motorway network. The accommodation is comfortable and offers a range of amenities that the modern traveller expects. The public areas are light and airy, and parking is available.

Rooms 96 (11 fmly) (4 GF) **S** £89-£99; **D** £99-£119* **Facilities** FTV ♫ Xmas New Year Wi-fi **Conf** Class 50 Board 60 Thtr 100 Del from £139 to £179* **Services** Lift Air con **Parking** 20 **Notes** LB ⊗ Civ Wed 120

Comfort Hotel Heathrow

Comfort INN

★★★ 71% HOTEL

☎ 020 8573 6162 Fax 020 8848 1057
Shepiston Ln UB3 1LP
e-mail: info@comfortheathrow.com
web: www.comfortheathrow.com
dir: M4 junct 4, follow directions to Hayes & Shepiston Lane, hotel approx 1m, next to fire station

This hotel is located a short drive from the airport, and guests may prefer its quieter position. There is a frequent bus service, which runs to and from the hotel throughout the day. Bedrooms are thoughtfully equipped and many benefit from air conditioning.

Rooms 184 (7 fmly) (50 GF) (6 smoking) **S** £42-£199; **D** £42-£199 **Facilities** STV FTV Gym Wi-fi **Conf** Class 72 Board 90 Thtr 150 Del from £89 to £159 **Services** Lift **Parking** 120 **Notes** LB ⊗ Civ Wed 90

Ibis London Heathrow Airport

ibis HOTEL

BUDGET HOTEL

☎ 020 8759 4888 Fax 020 8564 7894

112/114 Bath Rd UB3 5AL
e-mail: H0794@accor.com
web: www.ibishotel.com
dir: Follow Heathrow Terminals 1, 2 & 3 signs, then onto spur road, exit at sign for A4/Central London. Hotel 0.5m on left

Modern, budget hotel offering comfortable accommodation in bright and practical bedrooms. Breakfast is self-service and dinner is available in the restaurant. See also the Hotel Groups pages.

Rooms 351 (24 fmly) (39 GF) **Conf** Class 16 Board 16 Thtr 20

Premier Inn Hayes Heathrow

Premier Inn

BUDGET HOTEL

☎ 0871 527 8504 Fax 0871 527 8505
362 Uxbridge Rd UB4 0HF
dir: M4 junct 3, A312 N straight across next rdbt onto dual carriageway, at A4020 junct turn left, hotel 100yds on right

High quality, budget accommodation ideal for both families and business travellers. Spacious, en suite bedrooms feature tea and coffee making facilities, and Freeview TV in most hotels. Internet access and Wi-fi are available for a small fee. The adjacent family restaurant features a wide and varied menu. See also the Hotel Groups pages.

Rooms 62 **D** £54-£79*

Premier Inn Heathrow Airport (Bath Road)

BUDGET HOTEL

☎ 0871 527 8508 Fax 0871 527 8509
15 Bath Rd TW6 2AB
dir: M4 junct 4, follow signs for Heathrow Terminals 1, 2 & 3. Left onto Bath Rd signed A4/London. Hotel on right after 0.5m

Rooms 590 **D** £49-£65*

Premier Inn Heathrow Airport (M4 Jct 4)

BUDGET HOTEL

☎ 0871 527 8510 Fax 0871 527 8511
Shepiston Ln, Heathrow Airport UB3 1RW
dir: M4 junct 4 take 3rd exit off rdbt. Hotel on right

Rooms 134 **D** £47-£65*

HEBDEN BRIDGE — Map 19 SD92
West Yorkshire

Moyles

RESTAURANT WITH ROOMS

☎ 01422 845272 Fax 01422 847663
6-10 New Rd HX7 8AD
e-mail: enquire@moyles.com
dir: A646 to Hebden Bridge, opposite marina

Centrally located in the charming town of Hebden Bridge, this Victorian building as been modernised to offer a high standard of contemporary accommodation. Fresh, local produce features on the imaginative menus served in the bar and in the restaurant. There's a relaxing ambience throughout.

Rooms 12 (6 fmly)

HEDDON-ON-THE-WALL — Map 21 NZ16
Northumberland

Close House

★★★★ 74% HOTEL

☎ 01661 852255 Fax 01661 853322
NE15 0HT
e-mail: reservations@closehouse.co.uk
web: www.closehouse.co.uk
dir: A1 N, A69 W. Follow B6528 at junct turn left, hotel signed

Dating back to 1779, this is a magnificent country house set in 300 acres of woodland and parkland in the secluded and beautiful Tyne Valley. It is just 20 minutes from Newcastle city centre which has good national and international transport links. The hotel provides accommodation designed to make a stay relaxing and special. All the bedrooms are equipped with high-tech mod cons. There is a magnificent restaurant and bar, and 24-hour room service is also available. There is a golf course in the grounds.

Rooms 31 (12 annexe) (6 GF) **Facilities** STV 36 Putt green Driving range Xmas New Year Wi-fi **Conf** Class 30 Board 30 Thtr 140 **Services** Air con **Parking** 87 **Notes** Civ Wed 100

HELLIDON
Northamptonshire — Map 11 SP55

Hellidon Lakes Golf & Spa Hotel

QHOTELS

★★★★ 74% HOTEL

☎ 01327 262550 📠 01327 262559
NN11 6GG
e-mail: hellidonlakes@qhotels.co.uk
web: www.qhotels.co.uk
dir: Off A361 between Daventry & Banbury, signed

Some 220 acres of beautiful countryside, which include 27 holes of golf and 12 lakes, combine to form a rather spectacular backdrop to this impressive hotel. Bedroom styles vary, from ultra smart, modern rooms through to those in the original wing that offer superb views. There is an extensive range of facilities available from meeting rooms to a swimming pool, gym and ten-pin bowling. Golfers of all levels can try some of the world's most challenging courses on the indoor golf simulator.

Rooms 110 (5 fmly) **S** £65-£120; **D** £75-£130 (incl. bkfst)* **Facilities** Spa STV 27 Putt green Fishing Gym Beauty therapist Indoor smart golf 10-pin bowling Steam room Coarse fishing lake Xmas New Year Wi-fi **Conf** Class 150 Board 80 Thtr 300 Del from £135 to £175* **Services** Lift **Parking** 200 **Notes** LB Civ Wed 220

HELMSLEY
North Yorkshire — Map 19 SE68

INSPECTORS' CHOICE

Feversham Arms Hotel & Verbena Spa

★★★★ ◎◎◎ HOTEL

☎ 01439 770766 📠 01439 770346
1 High St YO62 5AG
e-mail: info@fevershamarmshotel.com
web: www.fevershamarmshotel.com
dir: A168 (signed Thirsk) from A1 then A170 or A64 (signed York) from A1 to York North, then B1363 to Helmsley. Hotel 125mtrs from Market Place

This long established hotel lies just round the corner from the main square, and under its caring ownership proves to be a refined operation, yet without airs and graces. There are several lounge areas and a high-ceilinged conservatory restaurant where good local ingredients are prepared with skill and minimal fuss. The bedrooms, including four poolside suites, have their own individual character and decor.

Rooms 33 (9 fmly) (8 GF) **S** £193-£473; **D** £240-£520 (incl. bkfst & dinner)* **Facilities** Spa STV FTV Sauna Saunarium Spa Xmas New Year Wi-fi **Conf** Class 20 Board 24 Thtr 35 Del from £ to £265* **Services** Lift **Parking** 50 **Notes** LB Civ Wed 50

Black Swan Hotel

★★★ 81% ◎◎ HOTEL

☎ 01439 770466 📠 01439 770174
Market Place YO62 5BJ
e-mail: enquiries@blackswan-helmsley.co.uk
web: www.blackswan-helmsley.co.uk
dir: A1 junct 49, A168, A170 east, hotel 14m from Thirsk

People have been visiting this establishment for over 200 years and it has become a landmark that dominates the market square. The hotel is renowned for its hospitality and friendliness; many of the staff are long-serving and dedicated. The bedrooms are stylish and include a junior suite and feature rooms. Dinner in the award-winning restaurant is the highlight of any stay. The hotel has a Tearoom and Patisserie that is open daily.

Rooms 45 (4 fmly) **S** £92-£157; **D** £132-£197 (incl. bkfst)* **Facilities** STV Xmas New Year Wi-fi **Conf** Class 30 Board 26 Thtr 50 Del from £145* **Parking** 50 **Notes** Civ Wed 130

HELSTON
Cornwall — Map 2 SW62

Premier Inn Helston

BUDGET HOTEL

☎ 0871 527 8512 📠 0871 527 8513
Clodgey Ln TR13 8FZ
dir: A39 from Truro towards Falmouth. Right onto A394 towards Helston, 8m. At rdbt 1st exit onto Helston bypass signed Penzance (A394)/Lizard. Hotel at next rdbt on left (NB for Sat Nav use TR13 0QD)

High quality, budget accommodation ideal for both families and business travellers. Spacious, en suite bedrooms feature tea and coffee making facilities, and Freeview TV in most hotels. Internet access and Wi-fi are available for a small fee. The adjacent family restaurant features a wide and varied menu. See also the Hotel Groups pages.

Rooms 50 **D** £70*

HEMEL HEMPSTEAD Map 6 TL00
Hertfordshire

Holiday Inn Hemel Hempstead

★★★ 77% HOTEL

☎ 0871 942 9041 📠 01442 211283
Breakspear Way HP2 4UA
e-mail: reservations-hemelhempsteadm1@ihg.com
web: www.holidayinn.co.uk/hemelhempstead
dir: M1 junct 8, over rdbt, 1st left after BP garage

A modern, purpose-built hotel that is convenient for the motorway networks. Bedrooms are spacious and well suited to the business traveller. Executive rooms and public areas are particularly well styled. Other facilities include a leisure club and a range of meeting rooms.

Rooms 144 (38 fmly) (42 GF) (12 smoking) **Facilities** Spa STV supervised Gym Beauty treaments & physiotherapy by appointment Wi-fi **Conf** Class 22 Board 30 Thtr 80 **Services** Lift Air con **Parking** 200 **Notes** LB Civ Wed 60

The Bobsleigh Hotel

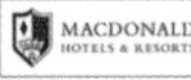

★★★ 75% HOTEL

☎ 0844 879 9033 📠 01442 832471
Hempstead Rd, Bovingdon HP3 0DS
e-mail: bobsleigh@macdonald-hotels.co.uk
web: www.macdonald-hotels.co.uk
dir: M1 junct 8, A414 signed Hemel Hempstead. At Plough Rdbt follow railway station signs. Pass rail station on left, straight on at rdbt, under 2 bridges. Left onto B4505 (Box Lane) signed Chesham. Hotel 1.5m on left

Located just outside the town, the hotel enjoys a pleasant rural setting, yet is within easy reach of local transport links and the motorway network. Bedrooms vary in size; all are modern in style. There is an open-plan lobby, a bar area and an attractive dining room with views over the garden.

Rooms 47 (15 annexe) (8 fmly) (29 GF) **S** £45-£120; **D** £45-£120* **Facilities** STV Xmas New Year Wi-fi **Conf** Class 50 Board 40 Thtr 150 Del from £80 to £140* **Parking** 60 **Notes** LB Civ Wed 100

Best Western The Watermill

★★★ 74% HOTEL

☎ 01442 349955 📠 01442 866130
London Rd, Bourne End HP1 2RJ
e-mail: info@hotelwatermill.co.uk
web: www.hotelwatermill.co.uk
dir: From M25 & M1 follow signs to Aylesbury on A41, A4251 to Bourne End. Hotel 0.25m on right

In the heart of the county this modern hotel has been built around an old flour mill on the banks of the River Bulbourne with water meadows adjacent. The thoughtfully equipped, contemporary bedrooms are located in three annexes situated around the complex. A good range of air-conditioned conference and meeting rooms complement the lounge bar and restaurant.

Rooms 71 (67 annexe) (9 fmly) (35 GF) (8 smoking) **Facilities** STV Fishing Xmas New Year Wi-fi **Conf** Class 150 Board 125 Thtr 200 **Parking** 100 **Notes** Civ Wed 180

Holiday Inn Express Hemel Hempstead

BUDGET HOTEL

☎ 01442 206600 📠 01442 206749
Stationers Place, Apsley Lock HP3 9RH
e-mail: info@expresshemel.co.uk
web: www.hiexpress.com/hemelhempstead
dir: M25 junct 20, Kings Langley, hotel on right after 3rd rdbt

A modern hotel ideal for families and business travellers. Fresh and uncomplicated, the spacious rooms include Sky TV, power shower and tea and coffee-making facilities. Continental buffet breakfast is included in the room rate; other meals may be taken at the nearby family pub or restaurant. See also the Hotel Groups pages.

Rooms 116 (82 fmly) (28 smoking) **Conf** Class 18 Board 18 Thtr 40

Premier Inn Hemel Hempstead Central

BUDGET HOTEL

☎ 0871 527 8514 📠 0871 527 8515
Moor End Rd HP1 1DL
dir: M1 junct 8, A414, follow town centre signs. Right at 1st mini rdbt, right at 2nd mini rdbt into Seldon Hill Rd, follow Riverside car park sings (footbridge to hotel from floor 3). (NB for Sat Nav use HP1 1BT)

High quality, budget accommodation ideal for both families and business travellers. Spacious, en suite bedrooms feature tea and coffee making facilities, and Freeview TV in most hotels. Internet access and Wi-fi are available for a small fee. The adjacent family restaurant features a wide and varied menu. See also the Hotel Groups pages.

Rooms 113 **D** £49-£64*

Premier Inn Hemel Hempstead West

BUDGET HOTEL

☎ 0871 527 8516 📠 0871 527 8517
A41 Service Area, Bourne End HP1 2SB
dir: M25 junct 20, A41 exit at services. Or from M1 junct 8, A414, A41, exit at services

Rooms 61 **D** £49-£60*

HENLEY-ON-THAMES Map 5 SU78
Oxfordshire

Hotel du Vin Henley-on-Thames

★★★★ 76% TOWN HOUSE HOTEL

☎ 01491 848400 📠 01491 848401
New St RG9 2BP
e-mail: info.henley@hotelduvin.com
web: www.hotelduvin.com
dir: M4 junct 8/9 signed High Wycombe, 2nd exit onto A404 in 2m. A4130 into Henley, over bridge, through lights, up Hart St, right onto Bell St, right onto New St, hotel on right

Situated just 50 yards from the water's edge, this hotel retains the character and much of the architecture of the former brewery. Food, and naturally wine, take on a strong focus here and guests will find an interesting mix of dishes to choose from; there are three private dining rooms where the fermentation room and old malt house once were; alfresco dining is popular when the weather permits. Bedrooms provide comfort, style and a good range of facilities including power showers. Parking is available and there is a drop-off point in the courtyard.

Rooms 43 (4 fmly) (4 GF) **S** £110-£435; **D** £110-£435* **Facilities** STV Use of local spa & gym Xmas New Year Wi-fi **Conf** Class 20 Board 36 Thtr 56 Del from £180 to £260* **Services** Air con **Parking** 36 **Notes** LB Civ Wed 60

Milsoms Henley-on-Thames

RESTAURANT WITH ROOMS

☎ 01491 845789 📠 01491 845781
20 Market Place RG9 2AH
e-mail: henley@milsomshotel.co.uk

The seven en suite bedrooms are located in a listed building above the Loch Fyne Restaurant in Henley's Market Place. Each bedroom is individually appointed and equipped to meet the needs of the modern traveller; particular care has been taken to incorporate original features into the contemporary design. The restaurant has a commitment to offer ethically sourced seafood.

Rooms 7

HEREFORD
Herefordshire — Map 10 SO54

See also **Leominster**

Holme Lacy House Hotel

Warner Leisure Hotels

★★★★ 74% COUNTRY HOUSE HOTEL

☎ 01432 870870 Fax 01432 870892
Holme Lacy HR2 6LP
web: www.holmelacyhouse.co.uk
dir: B4399 at Holme Lacy, take lane opposite college. Hotel 500mtrs on right

This is a grand Grade I listed mansion has a rich history. Just a short drive from Hereford and in a peaceful location, it is set in 20 acres of superb parkland in the heart of the Wye Valley. The well-appointed bedrooms are comfortable and vary in size and style. This hotel is exclusively for adults (over 21 years old) and there is much to do here, with a full, daily entertainment programme, an indoor pool, and health and beauty treatments. The three restaurants provide carefully selected menus of quality cuisine. Warner Leisure Hotels – AA Small Hotel Group of the Year 2011-12.

Rooms 180 (150 annexe) (53 GF) **S** £89-£105; **D** £178-£210 (incl. bkfst)* **Facilities Spa** FTV Putt green Fishing Gym Archery Rifle shooting Aquafit Salsa-cise classes Yoga Fencing Xmas New Year Wi-fi **Services** Lift **Parking** 200 **Notes** LB No children

Castle House

★★★ 86% TOWN HOUSE HOTEL

☎ 01432 356321 Fax 01432 365909
Castle St HR1 2NW
e-mail: info@castlehse.co.uk
web: www.castlehse.co.uk
dir: Follow signs to City Centre East. At junct of Commercial Rd & Union St follow hotel signs

Enjoying a prime city centre location and with a terraced garden leading to the castle moat, this delightful Grade II listed Georgian mansion is the epitome of elegance and sophistication. The character bedrooms are equipped with every luxury to ensure a memorable stay and are complemented perfectly by the well-proportioned and restful lounge and bar, together with the elegant topiary-themed restaurant where award-winning modern British cuisine is served.

Castle House

Rooms 15 (1 GF) **Facilities** FTV Free membership at local spa Xmas New Year Wi-fi **Services** Lift **Parking** 12 **Notes**

See advert on this page

HEREFORD *continued*

Three Counties Hotel

★★★ 75% HOTEL

H

☎ 01432 299955 🖷 01432 275114
Belmont Rd HR2 7BP
e-mail: enquiries@threecountieshotel.co.uk
web: www.threecountieshotel.co.uk
dir: On A465 (Abergavenny road)

Just a mile west of the city centre, this large, privately owned, modern complex has well-equipped, spacious bedrooms; many are located in separate single-storey buildings around the extensive car park. There is a spacious, comfortable lounge, a traditional bar and an attractive restaurant.

Rooms 60 (32 annexe) (4 fmly) (46 GF) **S** £67-£71.50; **D** £77-£92.50 (incl. bkfst)* **Facilities** STV FTV Wi-fi **Conf** Class 200 Board 120 Thtr 450 Del from £85 to £95* **Parking** 250 **Notes** LB Civ Wed 250

See advert on this page

Premier Inn Hereford

BUDGET HOTEL

☎ 0871 527 8518 🖷 0871 527 8519
Holmer Rd, Holmer HR4 9RS
dir: From N: M5 junct 7, A4103 to Worcester. M50 junct 4, A49 (Leominster road). Hotel 800yds on left

High quality, budget accommodation ideal for both families and business travellers. Spacious, en suite bedrooms feature tea and coffee making facilities, and Freeview TV in most hotels. Internet access and Wi-fi are available for a small fee. The adjacent family restaurant features a wide and varied menu. See also the Hotel Groups pages.

Rooms 81 **D** £53-£59*

HERNE BAY
Kent — Map 7 TR16

Premier Inn Canterbury North/Herne Bay

BUDGET HOTEL

☎ 0871 527 8520 🖷 0871 527 8521
Blacksole Farm, Margate Rd CT6 6LA
dir: From M2 junct 7 follow Canterbury signs, A299 signed Ramsgate/Margate. Exit at Broomfield & Beltinge. Hotel just off rdbt

High quality, budget accommodation ideal for both families and business travellers. Spacious, en suite bedrooms feature tea and coffee making facilities, and Freeview TV in most hotels. Internet access and Wi-fi are available for a small fee. The adjacent family restaurant features a wide and varied menu. See also the Hotel Groups pages.

Rooms 50 **D** £62-£65*

HERTFORD
Hertfordshire — Map 6 TL31

White Horse Hotel

★★★ 68% HOTEL

☎ 01992 586791 🖷 01992 550809
Hertingfordbury Rd, Hertingfordbury SG14 2LB
e-mail: bgray@aquariushotels.co.uk
dir: From A10 follow A414 signs. From Hertford under rail bridge, over rdbt, left at next rdbt, hotel 300yds on right

The Georgian façade of this former coaching inn belies a much older interior with oak beams dating back 400 years. Many of the spacious bedrooms overlook the picturesque gardens. Public rooms include a beamed bar with its open fireplace and a spacious conservatory restaurant.

Rooms 42 (4 fmly) **Facilities** FTV Xmas New Year Wi-fi **Conf** Class 30 Board 26 Thtr 60 **Services** Air con **Parking** 50 **Notes** ⊗ Civ Wed 75

HESWALL
Merseyside — Map 15 SJ28

Premier Inn Wirral (Heswall)

BUDGET HOTEL

☎ 0871 527 9178 🖷 0871 527 9179
Chester Rd, Gayton CH60 3SD
dir: M53 junct 4, A5137 signed Heswall. In 3m left at next rdbt, hotel on left

High quality, budget accommodation ideal for both families and business travellers. Spacious, en suite bedrooms feature tea and coffee making facilities, and Freeview TV in most hotels. Internet access and

Wi-fi are available for a small fee. The adjacent family restaurant features a wide and varied menu. See also the Hotel Groups pages.

Rooms 37 **D** £53-£57*

HETHERSETT Norfolk **Map 13 TG10**

Park Farm Hotel

★★★★ 76% ◎ HOTEL

☎ 01603 810264 📠 01603 812104
NR9 3DL
e-mail: enq@parkfarm-hotel.co.uk
web: www.parkfarm-hotel.co.uk
dir: 5m S of Norwich, off A11 on B1172

An elegant Georgian farmhouse set in landscaped grounds surrounded by open countryside. The property has been owned and run by the Gowing family since 1958. Bedrooms are pleasantly decorated and tastefully furnished; some rooms have patio doors with a sun terrace. Public rooms include a stylish conservatory, a lounge bar, a smart restaurant and superb leisure facilities.

Rooms 53 (16 annexe) (15 fmly) (26 GF) **S** £99-£150; **D** £120-£180 (incl. bkfst) **Facilities** Spa FTV supervised Gym Beauty salon Hairdressing Xmas New Year Wi-fi **Conf** Class 50 Board 50 Thtr 120 Del from £130 to £155 **Parking** 150 **Notes** LB Civ Wed 100

HETTON North Yorkshire **Map 18 SD95**

The Angel Inn

◎◎ RESTAURANT WITH ROOMS

☎ 01756 730263 📠 01756 730363
BD23 6LT
e-mail: info@angelhetton.co.uk
dir: B6265 from Skipton towards Grassington. At Rylstone turn left by pond, follow signs to Hetton

This roadside inn is steeped in history; parts of the building go back over 500 years. The restaurant and bar are in the main building which has ivy and green canopies at the front. The large and stylish bedrooms are across the road in a converted barn which has great views of the Dales, its own wine cave and private parking.

Rooms 9

HEXHAM Northumberland **Map 21 NY96**

Langley Castle

★★★★ 82% ◎◎ HOTEL

☎ 01434 688888 📠 01434 684019
Langley NE47 5LU
e-mail: manager@langleycastle.com
web: www.langleycastle.com
dir: From A69 S on A686 for 2m. Hotel on right

Langley is a magnificent 14th-century fortified castle, with its own chapel, set in ten acres of parkland. There is an award-winning restaurant, a comfortable drawing room and a cosy bar. Bedrooms are furnished with period pieces and most feature window seats. Restored buildings in the grounds have been converted into very stylish Castle View bedrooms.

Rooms 27 (18 annexe) (8 fmly) (9 GF) **Facilities** STV Xmas Wi-fi **Conf** Class 60 Board 40 Thtr 120 **Parking** 70 **Notes** LB Civ Wed 120

De Vere Slaley Hall

DE VERE Hotels & Resorts

★★★★ 80% ◎ HOTEL

☎ 01434 673350 📠 01434 673962
Slaley NE47 0BX
e-mail: slaley.hall@devere-hotels.com
web: www.devere.co.uk
dir: A1 from S to A68 link road follow signs for Slaley Hall

One thousand acres of Northumbrian forest and parkland, two championship golf courses and indoor leisure facilities can all be found here. Spacious bedrooms are fully air conditioned, equipped with a range of extras and the deluxe rooms offer excellent standards. Public rooms include a number of lounges and dining options of the fine-dining Dukes Grill, informal Claret Jug and impressive main restaurant overlooking the golf course.

Rooms 142 (18 fmly) (37 GF) **Facilities** Spa supervised ⛳ 36 Putt green Gym Quad bikes Archery Clay pigeon shooting 4x4 driving Xmas New Year Wi-fi **Conf** Class 220 Board 150 Thtr 300 **Services** Lift Air con **Parking** 500 **Notes** Civ Wed 250

Best Western Beaumont Hotel

★★★ 80% HOTEL

☎ 01434 602331 📠 01434 606184
Beaumont St NE46 3LT
e-mail: reservations@beaumonthotel.eclipse.co.uk
dir: A69 towards town centre

In a region steeped in history, this family-run hotel is located in the centre of Hexham, overlooking the park and 7th-century abbey. The hotel has two bars, a comfortable reception lounge and a first-floor restaurant. Bedrooms are a mix of traditional and contemporary; the South Wing rooms are spacious with a more contemporary feel and have 37" flat-screen TVs.

Rooms 34 (3 fmly) **S** £80-£120; **D** £120-£180 (incl. bkfst) **Facilities** FTV Wi-fi **Conf** Class 60 Board 40 Thtr 100 Del from £105 to £150 **Services** Lift **Parking** 16 **Notes** LB Closed 25-26 Dec Civ Wed 50

The County Hotel & Restaurant

★★ 71% SMALL HOTEL

☎ 01434 603601 📠 01434 603601
Priestpopple NE46 1PS
e-mail: reception@thecountyhexham.co.uk
dir: Off A69, follow signs for General Hospital. Hotel at top of hill

The resident owners of this establishment, located in the centre of this popular market town, provide their guests with a caring and personal service. Bedrooms are comfortably equipped. The County Restaurant offers an interesting selection of freshly prepared dishes that utilise local produce.

Rooms 8 (1 fmly) **S** £55-£70; **D** £80-£90 (incl. bkfst) **Facilities** Wi-fi **Notes**

HICKSTEAD West Sussex — Map 6 TQ22

Hickstead

★★★ 78%
COUNTRY HOUSE HOTEL

☎ 01444 248023 📠 01444 245280
Jobs Ln, Bolney RH17 5NZ
e-mail: info.hickstead@classiclodges.co.uk
web: www.classiclodges.co.uk
dir: M23 south, take A2300 exit (Burgess Hill), 1st left, next right, hotel 100yds on left

This hotel is located in seven acres of grounds not far from the main London to Brighton road. The smart bedrooms have satellite TV, free Wi-fi and power showers. Guests can choose to eat in the Oak Tree Bistro or in the Grange Bar. The indoor leisure centre is very popular. The hotel is close to a business park and within easy striking distance of the south coast.

Rooms 52 (5 fmly) (26 GF) **Facilities** STV Xmas New Year Wi-fi **Conf** Class 60 Board 55 Thtr 150 **Parking** 100 **Notes** LB ⊗ Civ Wed 80

HIGHAM Derbyshire — Map 16 SK35

Santo's Higham Farm Hotel

★★★ 79% ◎ HOTEL

☎ 01773 833812 📠 01773 520525
Main Rd DE55 6EH
e-mail: reception@santoshighamfarm.co.uk
web: www.santoshighamfarm.co.uk
dir: M1 junct 28, A38 towards Derby, then A61 towards Chesterfield. Onto B6013 towards Belper, hotel 300yds on right

With panoramic views across the rolling Amber Valley, this 15th-century crook barn and farmhouse has been expertly restored and extended. There's an Italian wing and an international wing of themed bedrooms and mini suites. Freshly prepared dishes, especially fish, are available in Guiseppe's restaurant. This hotel makes an ideal romantic hideaway.

Rooms 28 (2 fmly) (7 GF) **S** £80-£125; **D** £120-£150 (incl. bkfst)* **Facilities** Xmas New Year Wi-fi **Conf** Class 40 Board 34 Thtr 100 **Parking** 100 **Notes** LB ⊗ Civ Wed 100

HIGHCLIFFE Dorset — Map 5 SZ29

Premier Inn Christchurch/ Highcliffe

BUDGET HOTEL

☎ 0871 527 9276 📠 0871 527 9277
266 Lymington Rd BH23 5ET
dir: From A35 (Christchurch rdbt) onto A337 towards New Milton & Lymington. Approx 2m hotel on left

High quality, budget accommodation ideal for both families and business travellers. Spacious, en suite bedrooms feature tea and coffee making facilities, and Freeview TV in most hotels. Internet access and Wi-fi are available for a small fee. The adjacent family restaurant features a wide and varied menu. See also the Hotel Groups pages.

Rooms 62 **D** £54-£59*

HIGH WYCOMBE Buckinghamshire — Map 5 SU89

Holiday Inn High Wycombe

★★★ 75% HOTEL

☎ 0871 942 9042 📠 01494 439071
Handy Cross HP11 1TL
web: www.holidayinn.co.uk
dir: M40 junct 4, take A4010 towards Aylesbury

A modern, purpose-built hotel, convenient for the motorway networks. Bedrooms are spacious and well-equipped for the business traveller and feature a comprehensive range of extra facilities. Public rooms are particularly stylish, while the Academy offers a full range of meeting and conference services.

Rooms 112 (7 fmly) (10 smoking) **Facilities** FTV Wi-fi **Conf** Class 72 Board 50 Thtr 140 **Services** Air con **Parking** 200 **Notes** ⊗ Civ Wed 120

Fox Country Inn

★★★ 67% HOTEL

☎ 01491 639333 📠 01491 639444
Ibstone HP14 3XT
e-mail: info@foxcountryinn.co.uk
dir: M40 junct 5 follow signs to Ibstone, hotel 1.5m on left

This stylish modern hotel enjoys a peaceful rural location on the outskirts of High Wycombe. The modern bedrooms are all attractively presented and have a host of thoughtful little extras. Free Wi-fi is available throughout the hotel. The bar and restaurant have a contemporary open-plan style and food is served throughout the day in the bar and on the terrace.

Rooms 18 (2 fmly) (10 GF) **S** £77-£137; **D** £87-£167 (incl. bkfst)* **Facilities** FTV Xmas New Year Wi-fi **Conf** Class 40 Board 35 Thtr 45 **Parking** 45 **Notes** Civ Wed 100

Premier Inn High Wycombe

BUDGET HOTEL

☎ 0871 527 8522 📠 0871 527 8523
Thanstead Farm, London Rd, Loudwater HP10 9YL
dir: M40 junct 3, A40 towards High Wycombe

High quality, budget accommodation ideal for both families and business travellers. Spacious, en suite bedrooms feature tea and coffee making facilities, and Freeview TV in most hotels. Internet access and Wi-fi are available for a small fee. The adjacent family restaurant features a wide and varied menu. See also the Hotel Groups pages.

Rooms 108 **D** £57-£72*

HIMLEY Staffordshire — Map 10 SO89

Best Western Himley Hotel Dudley

U

☎ 01902 896716 📠 01902 896668
School Rd DY3 4LG
e-mail: reservations@bestwesternhimleyhotel
dir: Exit A449 at lights near Dudley Arms into School Rd, hotel 75yds on right

Currently the rating for this establishment is not confirmed. This may be due to a change of ownership or because it has only recently joined the AA rating scheme. For further details please see the AA website: theAA.com

Rooms 65 **Conf** Class 80 Board 50 Thtr 150

HINCKLEY Leicestershire — Map 11 SP49

Sketchley Grange

★★★★ 81% ◎◎ HOTEL

☎ 01455 251133 📠 01455 631384
Sketchley Ln, Burbage LE10 3HU
e-mail: info@sketchleygrange.co.uk
web: www.sketchleygrange.co.uk
dir: SE of town, off A5/M69 junct 1, take B4109 to Hinckley. Left at 2nd rdbt. 1st right onto Sketchley Lane

Close to motorway connections, this hotel is peacefully set in its own grounds, and enjoys open country views. Extensive leisure facilities include a stylish health and leisure spa. Modern meeting facilities, a choice of bars, and two dining options, together with comfortable bedrooms furnished with many extras, make this a special hotel.

Rooms 94 (9 fmly) (6 GF) **S** £65-£130; **D** £65-£130* **Facilities** Spa STV FTV Gym Steam room Sauna Xmas New Year Wi-fi **Conf** Class 150 Board 30 Thtr 300 Del from £110 to £145* **Services** Lift **Parking** 270 **Notes** LB Civ Wed 120

Barceló Hinckley Island Hotel

★★★★ 76% HOTEL

☎ 01455 631122 📠 01455 634536
Watling Street (A5) LE10 3JA
e-mail: hinckleyisland@barcelo-hotels.co.uk
web: www.barcelo-hotels.co.uk
dir: On A5, S of junct 1 on M69

A large, constantly improving hotel offering good facilities for both leisure and business guests. Bedrooms are well equipped, with the Club Floors providing high levels of comfort and workspace. A choice of dining styles is available in the Brasserie or Conservatory restaurants and the Triumph Bar is a must for motor cycle enthusiasts. The modern leisure club also offers a range of spa treatments.

Rooms 362 (14 GF) **Facilities** STV supervised Gym Steam room Wi-fi **Conf** Class 240 Board 40 Thtr 400 **Services** Lift Air con **Parking** 600 **Notes** Civ Wed 350

Premier Inn Hinckley

BUDGET HOTEL

☎ 0871 527 8524 📠 0871 527 8525
Coventry Rd LE10 0NB
dir: M69 junct 1, A5 towards Nuneaton. In 2.5m right at rdbt onto B4666 signed Hinckley Town Centre. Hotel on right (entrance via Total petrol station)

High quality, budget accommodation ideal for both families and business travellers. Spacious, en suite bedrooms feature tea and coffee making facilities, and Freeview TV in most hotels. Internet access and Wi-fi are available for a small fee. The adjacent family restaurant features a wide and varied menu. See also the Hotel Groups pages.

Rooms 53 **D** £45-£55*

HINTLESHAM Suffolk — Map 13 TM04

INSPECTORS' CHOICE

Hintlesham Hall Hotel

★★★★ HOTEL

☎ 01473 652334 📠 01473 652463
George St IP8 3NS
e-mail: reservations@hintleshamhall.com
web: www.hintleshamhall.com
dir: 4m W of Ipswich on A1071 to Hadleigh & Sudbury

Hospitality and service are key features at this imposing Grade I listed country-house hotel, situated in 175 acres of grounds and landscaped gardens. Originally a manor house dating from the Elizabethan era, the building was extended in the 17th and 18th centuries. It was a Red Cross hospital in World War II and has been a hotel for nearly forty years. Individually decorated bedrooms offer a high degree of comfort; each one is tastefully furnished and equipped with many thoughtful touches. The spacious public rooms include a series of comfortable lounges, and an elegant restaurant which serves fine classical cuisine based on top-notch ingredients. Wi-fi is available throughout.

Rooms 33 (10 GF) **S** £119-£149; **D** £129-£199 (incl. bkfst)* **Facilities** FTV 18 Putt green Gym Health & Beauty services Clay pigeon shooting Xmas New Year Wi-fi **Conf** Class 50 Board 32 Thtr 80 Del from £179 to £209* **Parking** 60 **Notes** LB RS Sat Civ Wed 110

HINTON CHARTERHOUSE Somerset — Map 4 ST75

INSPECTORS' CHOICE

Homewood Park

von Essen hotels A PRIVATE COLLECTION www.vonessenhotels.com

★★★ COUNTRY HOUSE HOTEL

☎ 01225 723731 📠 01225 723820
BA2 7TB
e-mail: info@homewoodpark.co.uk
web: www.homewoodpark.co.uk
dir: 6m SE of Bath on A36, turn left at 2nd sign for Freshford

Homewood Park, an unassuming yet stylish Georgian house set in delightful grounds, offers relaxed surroundings and maintains high standards of quality and comfort throughout. Bedrooms, all individually decorated, include thoughtful extras to ensure a comfortable stay. The spa includes a hydrotherapy pool, sauna, steam room, outdoor pool plus a range of luxury treatments. The hotel has a reputation for excellent cuisine, however the AA Rosette award is temporarily suspended as there has been a change of chef. A new award will be in place, once our inspectors have completed their assessments of meals cooked by the new kitchen team.

Rooms 21 (2 annexe) (3 fmly) (2 GF) **Facilities** Spa FTV Sauna Steam room Xmas New Year Wi-fi **Conf** Class 30 Board 25 Thtr 40 **Parking** 30 **Notes** Civ Wed 50

HITCHIN Hertfordshire Map 12 TL12

Redcoats Farmhouse Hotel

★★★ 71% ❀ SMALL HOTEL

☎ 01438 729500 🖷 01438 723322
Redcoats Green SG4 7JR
e-mail: sales@redcoats.co.uk
web: www.redcoats.co.uk
dir: A602 to Wymondley. Turn left to Redcoats Green. At top of hill straight over at junct

This delightful 15th-century property is situated in four acres of landscaped grounds only a short drive from the A1(M). Bedrooms in the main house and courtyard annexe are well appointed and spacious. Breakfast and dinner are served in the conservatory which overlooks the garden, and a series of intimate dining rooms is also available.

Rooms 13 (9 annexe) (1 fmly) (9 GF) **Facilities** FTV New Year Wi-fi **Conf** Board 15 Thtr 30 **Parking** 50 **Notes** Closed BH & Xmas-7 Jan Civ Wed 75

H

HOCKLEY HEATH West Midlands Map 10 SP17

Nuthurst Grange Country House & Restaurant

★★★ 86% ❀❀ HOTEL

☎ 01564 783972 🖷 01564 783919
Nuthurst Grange Ln B94 5NL
e-mail: info@nuthurst-grange.co.uk
web: www.nuthurst-grange.co.uk
dir: Off A3400, 0.5m south of Hockley Heath. Turn at sign into Nuthurst Grange Lane

A stunning avenue drive is the approach to this country-house hotel, set amid several acres of well-tended gardens and mature grounds with views over rolling countryside. The spacious bedrooms and bathrooms offer considerable luxury and comfort, and public areas include restful lounges, meeting rooms and a sunny restaurant. The kitchen brigade produces highly imaginative British and French cuisine, complemented by very attentive, professional restaurant service.

Rooms 19 (19 fmly) (2 GF) **Facilities** STV FTV Wi-fi **Conf** Class 50 Board 45 Thtr 100 **Parking** 80 **Notes** ® Civ Wed 100

HOLFORD Somerset Map 4 ST14

Combe House

★★★ 75% ❀ HOTEL

☎ 01278 741382 & 741213 🖷 01278 741322
TA5 1RZ
e-mail: enquiries@combehouse.co.uk
web: www.combehouse.co.uk
dir: From A39 W left in Holford then left at T-junct. Left at fork, 0.25m to Holford Combe

Located in a peaceful wooded valley with four acres of tranquil gardens to explore, the atmosphere here is relaxed and welcoming. The individually styled bedrooms have lots of comfort - all are designed for a cosseted and pampered stay. Public areas have equal charm with traditional features interwoven with contemporary style. Food comes highly recommended with a dedicated kitchen team producing accomplished, seasonal dishes.

Rooms 18 (1 annexe) (3 fmly) (2 GF) **Facilities** Sauna Small gym Beauty therapy treatments Xmas New Year Wi-fi **Conf** Class 30 Board 20 Thtr 30 **Parking** 36 **Notes** Civ Wed 130

HOLKHAM Norfolk Map 13 TF84

The Victoria at Holkham

★★ 83% ❀❀ SMALL HOTEL

☎ 01328 711008 🖷 01328 711009
Park Rd NR23 1RG
e-mail: victoria@holkham.co.uk
web: www.victoriaatholkham.co.uk
dir: A149, 2m W of Wells-next-the-Sea

A Grade II listed property, built from local flint, is ideally situated on the north Norfolk coast road and forms part of the Holkham Estate. Decor is very much influenced by the local landscape: the stylish bedrooms are individually decorated and tastefully furnished with pieces specially made for the hotel in India. The brasserie-style restaurant serves an interesting choice of dishes.

Rooms 10 (1 annexe) (2 fmly) (1 GF) **Facilities** Fishing Shooting on Holkham Estate, Bird watching reserve nearby Xmas **Conf** Class 40 Board 30 Thtr 12 **Parking** 30 **Notes** ® Civ Wed 70

HOLT Norfolk Map 13 TG03

The Lawns Wine Bar

❀ RESTAURANT WITH ROOMS

☎ 01263 713390
26 Station Rd NR25 6BS
e-mail: mail@lawnsatholt.co.uk
dir: A148 (Cromer road). 0.25m from Holt rdbt, turn left, 400yds along Station Rd

A superb Georgian house situated in the centre of this delightful north Norfolk market town. The open-plan public areas include a large wine bar with plush sofas, a conservatory and a smart restaurant. The spacious bedrooms are tastefully appointed with co-ordinated soft furnishings and have many thoughtful touches.

Rooms 8

HONITON
Devon Map 4 ST10

INSPECTORS' CHOICE

Combe House - Devon

★★★ @@ COUNTRY HOUSE HOTEL

☎ 01404 540400
Gittisham EX14 3AD
e-mail: stay@combehousedevon.com
web: www.combehousedevon.com
dir: Off A30 1m S of Honiton, follow Gittisham Heathpark signs. From M5 exit 29 for Honiton. Exit Pattesons Cross

Standing proudly in an elevated position, this Elizabethan mansion enjoys uninterrupted views over acres of its own woodland, meadow and pasture. Bedrooms are a blend of comfort and quality with relaxation being the ultimate objective; the Linen Room suite combines many original features with contemporary style. A range of atmospheric public rooms retain all the charm and history of the old house. Dining is equally impressive - a skilled kitchen brigade maximises the best of local and home-grown produce, augmented by excellent wines.

Rooms 16 (1 annexe) (1 fmly) **S** £169-£379; **D** £199-£399 (incl. bkfst)* **Facilities** Fishing Xmas New Year Wi-fi **Conf** Class 25 Board 26 Thtr 50 **Parking** 39 **Notes** LB Closed 3-18 Jan Civ Wed 150

Home Farm Hotel & Restaurant

★★ 75% SMALL HOTEL

☎ 01404 831278 Fax 01404 831411
Wilmington EX14 9JR
e-mail: info@thatchedhotel.co.uk
dir: 3m E of Honiton on A35

Set in well-tended gardens, this thatched former farmhouse is now a comfortable hotel. Many of the original features have been retained, including the cobbled courtyard. A range of interesting dishes is offered in the intimate restaurant, with bar meals available at lunchtime and most evenings. Bedrooms, some with private gardens, are individually styled, well equipped and comfortably furnished.

Rooms 12 (5 annexe) (2 fmly) (4 GF) **Facilities** FTV Wi-fi **Conf** Class 12 Board 15 Thtr 40 **Parking** 25 **Notes** ®

Monkton Court

@ RESTAURANT WITH ROOMS

☎ 01404 42309
Monkton EX14 9QH
e-mail: enquiries@monktoncourthotel.co.uk
dir: 2m E A30

Located on the A30 near Honiton and on the edge of the ancient Blackdown Hills, Monkton Court is a former vicarage steeped in history. There is a range of well-equipped and comfortably furnished bedrooms and bathrooms in addition to a relaxing lounge and spacious restaurant. Both dinner and breakfast utilise a range of local produce, and offer an enjoyable selection of dishes.

Rooms 7 (1 fmly)

HOOK
Hampshire Map 5 SU75

Raven Hotel

OldEnglish

★★★ 66% HOTEL

☎ 01256 762541 Fax 01256 768677
Station Rd RG27 9HS
e-mail: raven.hook@newbridgeinns.co.uk

This former coaching inn, conveniently located close to Hook railway station and a short distance from the M3, has been tastefully converted into a hotel. Bedrooms are comfortable and well appointed and have free Wi-fi. The popular restaurant offers an inviting menu of freshly prepared dishes, plus daily-changing specials. Function rooms are available as is parking.

Rooms 41 (2 fmly) (5 GF) **Facilities** FTV New Year Wi-fi **Conf** Class 60 Board 70 Thtr 100 **Parking** 60 **Notes** LB ® Civ Wed 120

HOPE
Derbyshire Map 16 SK18

Losehill House Hotel & Spa

★★★★ 76% @@ HOTEL

☎ 01433 621219 Fax 01433 622501
Lose Hill Ln, Edale Rd S33 6AF
e-mail: info@losehillhouse.co.uk
web: www.losehillhouse.co.uk
dir: A6187 into Hope. Take turn opposite church into Edale Rd. 1m, left & follow signs to hotel

Situated down a quiet leafy lane, this hotel occupies a secluded spot in the Peak District National Park. Bedrooms are comfortable and beautifully appointed. The outdoor hot tub, with stunning views over the valley, is a real indulgence; a heated swimming pool, sauna and spa treatments are also on offer. The views from the Orangery Restaurant are a real delight.

Rooms 24 (4 annexe) (4 fmly) (3 GF) **S** £120-£190; **D** £160-£250 (incl. bkfst)* **Facilities** Spa Sauna Cross trainer Xmas New Year Wi-fi **Conf** Class 20 Board 15 Thtr 30 Del from £145 to £225* **Services** Lift **Parking** 20 **Notes** LB ® Civ Wed 100

HOPE COVE
Devon Map 3 SX63

Lantern Lodge

★★ 78% HOTEL

☎ 01548 561280 Fax 01548 561736
TQ7 3HE
e-mail: lanternlodge@hopecove.wanadoo.co.uk
web: www.lantern-lodge.co.uk
dir: From Kingsbridge on A381 towards Salcombe turn right. 1st right after passing Hope Cove sign then 1st left along Grand View Rd

This attractive hotel, close to the South Devon coastal path, benefits from a friendly team of loyal staff. Bedrooms are well furnished and some have balconies. An imaginative range of home cooked meals is available. There is a choice of lounges and a pretty garden with putting green. The indoor pool has large doors opening directly on to the garden.

Rooms 14 (1 fmly) (1 GF) **D** £110-£180 (incl. bkfst & dinner) **Facilities** FTV Putt green Running machine Sauna Wi-fi **Parking** 15 **Notes** LB ® No children 12yrs Closed Dec-Feb

HORLEY

Hotels are listed under Gatwick Airport

H

HORNCASTLE Lincolnshire **Map 17 TF26**

Best Western Admiral Rodney Hotel

★★★ 71% HOTEL

☎ 01507 523131 🖷 01507 523104
North St LN9 5DX
e-mail: reception@admiralrodney.com
web: www.admiralrodney.com
dir: Off A153 (Louth to Horncastle)

Once a coaching inn and enjoying a prime location in the town centre, this smart hotel offers a high standard of accommodation. Bedrooms are well appointed and thoughtfully equipped for both business and leisure guests. Public areas include the Rodney Bar ideal for enjoying a drink, a range of meeting and conference rooms plus a conservatory-style restaurant and adjoining lounge.

Rooms 31 (3 fmly) (7 GF) **Facilities** Xmas New Year Wi-fi **Conf** Class 60 Board 50 Thtr 140 **Services** Lift **Parking** 60 **Notes** ⊗ Civ Wed 30

HORNS CROSS Devon **Map 3 SS32**

The Hoops Inn & Country Hotel

★★★ 72% ® HOTEL

☎ 01237 451222 🖷 01237 451247
The Hoops EX39 5DL
e-mail: sales@hoopsinn.co.uk
web: www.hoopsinn.co.uk
dir: M5 junct 27 follow Barnstaple signs. A39, by-passing Bideford, towards Bude. Hotel in dip just outside Horns Cross

The Hoops, with its whitewashed walls, thatched roof and real fires, has been welcoming guests for many centuries. Bedrooms have plenty of character and include a number that have four-poster or half-tester beds. Guests have the use of a quiet lounge and a pleasant seating area in the delightful rear garden. A fine selection of home-cooked meals can be enjoyed in the bar or restaurant.

Rooms 13 (9 annexe) (1 fmly) (1 GF) **S** £60-£65; (incl. bkfst) **Facilities** FTV Xmas New Year Wi-fi **Conf** Class 25 Board 20 Thtr 35 Del from £150 to £250 **Parking** 101 **Notes** LB

HORRINGER Suffolk **Map 13 TL86**

The Ickworth Hotel & Apartments

★★★★ 75% ®® COUNTRY HOUSE HOTEL

☎ 01284 735350 🖷 01284 736300
IP29 5QE
e-mail: info@ickworthhotel.co.uk
web: www.ickworthhotel.co.uk
dir: A14 exit for Bury St Edmunds, follow brown signs for Ickworth House, 4th exit at rdbt, cross staggered x-rds. Then onto T-junct, right into village, almost immediately right into Ickworth Estate

Gifted to the National Trust in 1956 this stunning property is in part a luxurious hotel that combines the glorious design and atmosphere of the past with a reputation for making children very welcome. The staff are friendly and easy going, there is a children's play area, crèche, horses and bikes to ride, and wonderful 'Capability' Brown gardens to roam in. Plus tennis, swimming, beauty treatments and an impressive dining room.

Rooms 39 (12 annexe) (35 fmly) (4 GF) **S** £229.50-£526.50; **D** £255-£585 (incl. bkfst & dinner)* **Facilities** Spa FTV Children's crèche Massage Manicures Adventure playground Vineyard Xmas New Year Wi-fi Child facilities **Conf** Class 30 Board 24 Thtr 45 **Services** Lift **Parking** 40 **Notes** LB Civ Wed 40

HORSHAM West Sussex **Map 6 TQ13**

Premier Inn Horsham

BUDGET HOTEL

☎ 0871 527 8526 🖷 0871 527 8527
57 North St RH12 1RB
dir: Opposite railway station, 5m from M23 junct 11

High quality, budget accommodation ideal for both families and business travellers. Spacious, en suite bedrooms feature tea and coffee making facilities, and Freeview TV in most hotels. Internet access and Wi-fi are available for a small fee. The adjacent family restaurant features a wide and varied menu. See also the Hotel Groups pages.

Rooms 40 **D** £56-£65*

HORSLEY Derbyshire **Map 11 SK34**

Horsley Lodge Hotel & Golf Club

★★★ 79% HOTEL

☎ 01332 780838 🖷 01332 781118
Smalley Mill Rd DE21 5BL
e-mail: reception@horsleylodge.co.uk
web: www.horsleylodge.co.uk
dir: A61 N, A38 signed 'Ripley'. Right at Coxbench. Follow to end, turn right, hotel 1m on left

This family-run hotel is full of character. Situated equidistant from Derby and Nottingham, it is ideal for exploring the Peak District. Bedrooms and bathrooms have been fully refurbished with stylish decor, beautiful fabrics and quality furnishings. Barn Cottage offers even greater luxury and is tucked away not far from the main building. The Brasserie overlooks the 18-hole golf course.

Rooms 11 (1 annexe) (2 fmly) **S** £80-£120; **D** £100-£150 (incl. bkfst) **Facilities** STV FTV 18 Putt green Fishing Golf driving range Xmas New Year Wi-fi **Conf** Class 70 Board 50 Thtr 100 **Parking** 100 **Notes** LB Civ Wed 100

HORWICH
Herefordshire Map 15 SD61

De Vere Whites

DE VERE venues

★★★★ 74% HOTEL

☎ 01204 667788 📠 01204 474663
De Havilland Way BL6 6SF
e-mail: whites@deverevenues.co.uk
web: www.deverevenues.co.uk
dir: M61 junct 6. 3rd right from slip road rdbt onto A6027 Mansell Way. Follow visitors car park A for hotel

Fully integrated within the Reebok Stadium, home of Bolton Wanderers FC, this modern hotel is a popular venue for business and conferences. Bedrooms are contemporary in style and equipped with a range of extras; many offer views of the pitch. There is an informal brasserie restaurant, the Pure bar/lounge area as well as the private dining restaurant. A fully equipped indoor leisure centre, the Premier Suite conference and exhibition centre are also available.

Rooms 125 (1 fmly) **S** £39-£129; **D** £39-£129 **Facilities** Spa STV supervised Gym Steam room Sauna Sun shower Xmas New Year Wi-fi **Conf** Class 1080 Board 72 Thtr 1500 Del from £99 **Services** Lift **Parking** 2750 **Notes** LB Civ Wed 1000

HOUGHTON-LE-SPRING
Tyne & Wear Map 19 NZ34

Chilton Country Pub & Hotel

★★ 76% HOTEL

☎ 0191 385 2694 📠 0191 385 6762
Black Boy Rd, Chilton Moor, Fencehouses DH4 6PY
e-mail: reception@chiltoncountrypub.co.uk
dir: A1(M) junct 62, onto A690 towards Sunderland. Left at Rainton Bridge & Fencehouses sign, right at rdbt, next rdbt straight over, next left. At next junct left, hotel on right

This country pub and hotel has been extended from the original farm cottages. Bedrooms are modern and comfortable and some rooms are particularly spacious. This hotel is popular for weddings and functions; there is also a well stocked bar, and a wide range of dishes is served in the Orangery and restaurant.

Rooms 25 (7 fmly) (11 GF) **S** £45-£48; **D** £55-£58 (incl. bkfst)* **Facilities** STV Xmas Wi-fi **Conf** Class 50 Board 30 Thtr 150 **Parking** 100 **Notes**

See advert on this page

HOVE

See Brighton & Hove

HOVINGHAM
North Yorkshire Map 19 SE67

Worsley Arms

★★★ 73% HOTEL

☎ 01653 628234 📠 01653 628130
High St YO62 4LA
e-mail: worsleyarms@aol.co.uk
dir: A64, signed York, towards Malton. At dual carriageway left to Hovingham. At Slingsby left, then 2m

Overlooking the village green, this hotel has relaxing and attractive lounges with welcoming open fires. Bedrooms are also comfortable and several are contained in cottages across the green. The restaurant provides interesting quality cooking, with less formal dining in the Cricketers' Bar and Bistro to the rear.

Rooms 20 (8 annexe) (2 fmly) (4 GF) **Facilities** FTV Shooting Xmas New Year Wi-fi **Conf** Class 40 Board 20 Thtr 40 Del from £120 to £160* **Parking** 25 **Notes** Civ Wed 100

H

H

HOWTOWN (NEAR POOLEY BRIDGE) Map 18 NY41
Cumbria

INSPECTORS' CHOICE

Sharrow Bay Country House

★★★ @@
COUNTRY HOUSE HOTEL

☎ 017684 86301 📠 017684 86349
Sharrow Bay CA10 2LZ
e-mail: info@sharrowbay.co.uk
web: www.vonessenhotels.co.uk
dir: M6 junct 40. From Pooley Bridge right fork by church towards Howtown. Right at x-rds right, follow lakeside road for 2m

Enjoying breathtaking views and an idyllic location on the shores of Lake Ullswater, Sharrow Bay is often described as the first country-house hotel. Individually styled bedrooms, all with a host of thoughtful extras, are situated either in the main house, in delightful buildings in the grounds or at Bank House - an Elizabethan farmhouse complete with lounges and breakfast room. Opulently furnished public areas include a choice of inviting lounges and two elegant dining rooms.

Rooms 24 (14 annexe) (5 GF) **S** £160; **D** £280-£780 (incl. bkfst & dinner)* **Facilities** FTV Xmas New Year Wi-fi **Conf** Class 15 Board 20 Thtr 30 Del from £250 to £300* **Parking** 35 **Notes** LB ⊗ No children 10yrs Civ Wed 30

HUCKNALL Map 16 SK54
Nottinghamshire

Premier Inn Nottingham North West (Hucknall)

BUDGET HOTEL

☎ 0871 527 8852 📠 0871 527 8853
Nottingham Rd NG15 7PY
dir: A611, A6002, straight on at 2 rdbts. Hotel 500yds on right

High quality, budget accommodation ideal for both families and business travellers. Spacious, en suite bedrooms feature tea and coffee making facilities, and Freeview TV in most hotels. Internet access and Wi-fi are available for a small fee. The adjacent family restaurant features a wide and varied menu. See also the Hotel Groups pages.

Rooms 35 **D** £54-£57*

HUDDERSFIELD Map 16 SE11
West Yorkshire

Cedar Court

★★★★ 71% HOTEL

☎ 01422 375431 📠 01422 314050
Ainley Top HD3 3RH
e-mail: sales@cedarcourthotels.co.uk
web: www.cedarcourthotels.co.uk
dir: 500yds from M62 junct 24

Sitting adjacent to the M62, this hotel is an ideal location for business travellers and for those touring the West Yorkshire area. Bedrooms are comfortably appointed; there is a busy lounge with snacks available all day, as well as a modern restaurant and a fully equipped leisure centre. In addition the hotel has extensive meeting and banqueting facilities.

Rooms 113 (6 fmly) (9 GF) **S** £50-£120; **D** £60-£130 (incl. bkfst) **Facilities** STV FTV supervised Gym Steam room Sauna Wi-fi **Conf** Class 150 Board 100 Thtr 500 Del from £90 to £155 **Services** Lift **Parking** 250 **Notes** Civ Wed 400

Pennine Manor Hotel

★★★ 77% HOTEL

☎ 01484 642368 📠 01484 642866
Nettleton Hill Rd, Scapegoat Hill HD7 4NH
e-mail: penninemanor@thedeckersgroup.com
dir: M62 junct 23, signed Rochdale (A640)/Outlane Village, left after Commercial pub, hotel signed

Set high in The Pennines, this attractive stone-built hotel enjoys magnificent panoramic views. The stylish, contemporary bedrooms are thoughtfully equipped. The popular bar with a log burning stove that creates a cosy atmosphere, offers a good selection of snacks and meals. The restaurant and meeting rooms enjoy fine views over the valley. Free Wi-fi is available.

Rooms 30 (4 fmly) (15 GF) **Facilities** STV Wi-fi **Conf** Class 56 Board 40 Thtr 132 **Parking** 115 **Notes** ⊗ Civ Wed 100

Bagden Hall

★★★ 74% HOTEL

☎ 01484 865330 📠 01484 861001
Wakefield Rd, Scissett HD8 9LE
e-mail: info@bagdenhallhotel.co.uk
web: www.bagdenhallhotel.co.uk
dir: On A636, between Scissett & Denby Dale

This elegant mansion house with wonderful views over the valley boasts its own 9-hole golf course. Comfortable bedrooms include classical feature rooms in the main house and contemporary rooms in a separate building. Guests can dine in the all-day Mediterranean bistro or the more formal elegant restaurant. The airy, stylish conference suite and beautiful grounds make this a popular wedding destination.

Rooms 36 (3 fmly) (15 GF) **Facilities** STV ⛳ 9 Putt green Wi-fi **Conf** Class 120 Board 50 Thtr 180 **Parking** 96 **Notes** ⊗ RS 25-26 Dec Civ Wed 150

Premier Inn Huddersfield Central

BUDGET HOTEL

☎ 0871 527 8528 📠 0871 527 9529
St Andrews Way HD1 3AQ
dir: Telephone for detailed directions

High quality, budget accommodation ideal for both families and business travellers. Spacious, en suite bedrooms feature tea and coffee making facilities, and Freeview TV in most hotels. Internet access and Wi-fi are available for a small fee. The adjacent family restaurant features a wide and varied menu. See also the Hotel Groups pages.

Rooms 52 **D** £45-£55*

Premier Inn Huddersfield West

BUDGET HOTEL

☎ 0871 527 8532 📠 0871 527 8533
New Hey Rd, Ainley Top HD2 2EA
dir: Just off M62 junct 24. From M62 take Brighouse exit from rdbt (A643). 1st left into Grimescar Rd, right into New Hey Rd

Rooms 42 **D** £51-£58*

HUNGERFORD Berkshire Map 5 SU36

Littlecote House Hotel

Warner Leisure Hotels

★★★★ 74% COUNTRY HOUSE HOTEL

☎ 01488 682509 01488 682341
RG17 0SU
e-mail: marie.jones@bourne-leisure.co.uk
dir: M4 junct 14, left onto A338, right onto A4, right onto B4192, left onto Littlecote Road, hotel 0.5m on right at top of hill

This hotel provides comfortable, spacious accommodation and is located in stunning grounds close to the Cotswolds and only a 10-minute drive from Hungerford. There are traditional-style bedrooms in the ornate Grade I listed Tudor building and more contemporary rooms in the main building. Facilities include a regular programme of entertainment, beauty treatments and a choice of dining locations in either Oliver's Bistro or Pophams Restaurant. Please note that this is an adults-only (over 21 years) hotel. Warner Leisure Hotels – AA Small Hotel Group of the Year 2011-12.

Rooms 201 (12 annexe) (55 GF) **S** £90-£120; **D** £180-£360 (incl. bkfst & dinner)* **Facilities** Spa FTV Putt green Gym Xmas New Year Wi-fi **Services** Lift **Parking** 520 **Notes** No children Civ Wed 120

The Bear Hotel

★★★ 80% HOTEL

☎ 01488 682512 01488 684357
41 Charnham St RG17 0EL
e-mail: info@thebearhotelhungerford.co.uk
web: www.thebearhotelhungerford.co.uk
dir: M4 junct 14, A338 to Hungerford for 3m, left at T-junct onto A4, hotel on left

Situated five miles south of the M4 this hotel dates back as far as early 13th century and was once owned by King Henry VIII. It now has a contemporary feel throughout. Bedrooms are split between the main house, the courtyard and Bear Island. The award-winning restaurant is open for lunch and dinner, and lighter snacks are available in the bar and lounge. Guests can enjoy the sun terrace in the summer and log fires in the winter.

Rooms 39 (26 annexe) (2 fmly) (24 GF) **S** £89-£119; **D** £99-£149 (incl. bkfst)* **Facilities** FTV Xmas New Year Wi-fi **Conf** Class 35 Board 34 Thtr 80 Del from £150 to £185 **Parking** 68 **Notes** LB Civ Wed 80

Three Swans Hotel

★★★ 70% HOTEL

☎ 01488 682721 01488 681708
117 High St RG17 0LZ
e-mail: info@threeswans.net
web: www.threeswans.net
dir: M4 junct 14 follow signs to Hungerford. Hotel half way along High St on left

Centrally located in the bustling market town of Hungerford this charming former inn, dating back some 700 years, has been renovated in a fresh and airy style. Visitors will still see the original arch under which the horse-drawn carriages once passed. There is a wood panelled bar, a spacious lounge and attractive rear garden to relax in. The informal restaurant is decorated with artwork by local artists. Bedrooms are well appointed and comfortable.

Rooms 25 (10 annexe) (1 fmly) (5 GF) (3 smoking) **Facilities** FTV Access to local private gym Xmas New Year Wi-fi **Conf** Class 40 Board 30 Thtr 55 **Parking** 30

HUNSTANTON Norfolk Map 12 TF64

Caley Hall

★★★ 83% HOTEL

☎ 01485 533486 01485 533348
Old Hunstanton Rd PE36 6HH
e-mail: mail@caleyhallhotel.co.uk
web: www.caleyhallhotel.co.uk
dir: 1m from Hunstanton, on A149

Situated within easy walking distance of the seafront. The tastefully decorated bedrooms are in a series of converted outbuildings; each is smartly furnished and thoughtfully equipped. Public rooms feature a large open-plan lounge/bar with plush leather seating, and a restaurant offering an interesting choice of dishes.

Rooms 39 (20 fmly) (30 GF) **S** £50-£200; **D** £80-£200 (incl. bkfst) **Facilities** STV Wi-fi Child facilities **Parking** 50 **Notes** LB Closed 18 Dec-20 Jan

Best Western Le Strange Arms

★★★ 82% HOTEL

☎ 01485 534411 01485 534724
Golf Course Rd, Old Hunstanton PE36 6JJ
e-mail: reception@lestrangearms.co.uk
dir: Off A149 1m N of Hunstanton. Left at sharp right bend by pitch & putt course

An impressive hotel with superb views from the wide lawns down to the sandy beach and across The Wash. Bedrooms in the main house have period furnishings whereas the rooms in the wing are more contemporary in style. Public rooms include a comfortable lounge bar and a conference and banqueting suite, plus a choice of dining options - Le Strange Restaurant and the Ancient Mariner.

Rooms 43 (7 annexe) (2 fmly) **Facilities** STV Xmas New Year Wi-fi **Conf** Class 150 Board 50 Thtr 180 **Services** Lift **Parking** 80 **Notes** Civ Wed 70

The Neptune Restaurant with Rooms

RESTAURANT WITH ROOMS

☎ 01485 532122
85 Old Hunstanton Rd, Old Hunstanton PE36 6HZ
e-mail: reservations@theneptune.co.uk
web: www.theneptune.co.uk
dir: On A149, past Hunstanton, 200mtrs on left after post office

This charming 18th-century coaching inn, now a restaurant with rooms, is ideally situated for touring the Norfolk coastline. The smartly appointed bedrooms are brightly finished with co-ordinated fabrics and handmade New England furniture. Public rooms feature white clapboard walls, polished dark wood floors, fresh flowers and Lloyd Loom furniture. The food is very much a draw here with the carefully prepared, award-winning cuisine utilising excellent local produce, from oysters and mussels from Thornham to quinces grown on a neighbouring farm.

Rooms 6

H

HUNTINGDON Cambridgeshire — Map 12 TL27

Huntingdon Marriott Hotel

★★★★ 77% HOTEL

☎ 01480 446000 01480 451111
Kingfisher Way, Hinchingbrooke Business Park PE29 6FL
e-mail: mhrs.cbghd.front.office@marriotthotels.com
web: www.huntingdonmarriott.co.uk
dir: On A14, 1m from Huntington centre close to Brampton racecourse

With its excellent road links, this modern, purpose-built hotel is a popular venue for conferences and business meetings, and is convenient for Huntingdon, Cambridge and racing at Newmarket. Bedrooms are spacious and offer every modern comfort, including air conditioning. The leisure facilities are also impressive.

Rooms 150 (5 fmly) (45 GF) **Facilities** supervised Gym Sauna Steam room Xmas New Year Wi-fi **Conf** Class 150 Board 100 Thtr 300 **Services** Lift Air con **Parking** 200 **Notes** Civ Wed 300

The Old Bridge Hotel

★★★ 86% HOTEL

☎ 01480 424300 01480 411017
1 High St PE29 3TQ
e-mail: oldbridge@huntsbridge.co.uk
web: www.huntsbridge.com
dir: From A14 or A1 follow Huntingdon signs. Hotel visible from inner ring road

An imposing 18th-century building situated close to shops and amenities. This charming hotel offers superb accommodation in stylish and individually decorated bedrooms that include many useful extras. Guests can choose from the same menu whether dining in the open-plan terrace, or the more formal restaurant with its bold colour scheme. There is also an excellent business centre.

Rooms 24 (2 fmly) (2 GF) **S** £99-£150; **D** £140-£220 (incl. bkfst)* **Facilities** STV FTV Fishing Private mooring for boats Xmas New Year Wi-fi **Conf** Class 50 Board 30 Thtr 60 **Services** Air con **Parking** 50 **Notes** LB Civ Wed 100

The George

★★★ 75% HOTEL

☎ 01480 432444 01480 453130
George St PE29 3AB
e-mail: george.huntingdon@oldenglishinns.co.uk
web: www.oldenglish.co.uk
dir: Exit A14 for Huntingdon racecourse. 3m to junct with ring road. Hotel opposite

This former coaching inn is ideally situated in the centre of town and was once the home of Oliver Cromwell's grandfather. The public rooms include a spacious lounge bar with plush seating and a smart brasserie offering an interesting choice of dishes. Bedrooms are pleasantly decorated and equipped with modern facilities.

Rooms 24 (3 fmly) **Facilities** Xmas Wi-fi **Conf** Class 60 Board 60 Thtr 80 **Parking** 55 **Notes** Civ Wed 120

Premier Inn Huntingdon (A1/A14)

BUDGET HOTEL

☎ 0871 527 8540 0871 527 8541
Great North Rd, Brampton PE28 4NQ
dir: At junct of A1 & A14. (NB from N do not use junct 14. Take exit for Huntingdon & Brampton). Access to hotel via Services

High quality, budget accommodation ideal for both families and business travellers. Spacious, en suite bedrooms feature tea and coffee making facilities, and Freeview TV in most hotels. Internet access and Wi-fi are available for a small fee. The adjacent family restaurant features a wide and varied menu. See also the Hotel Groups pages.

Rooms 80 **D** £49-£60*

HURLEY Berkshire — Map 5 SU88

Black Boys Inn

RESTAURANT WITH ROOMS

☎ 01628 824212
Henley Rd SL6 5NQ
e-mail: info@blackboysinn.co.uk
web: www.blackboysinn.co.uk
dir: 1m W of Hurley on A4130

Just a short drive from Henley, the traditional exterior of this friendly establishment is a contrast to the smart modernity within. Popular with locals, the restaurant is the stage for Simon Bonwick's imaginative cuisine, and has a buzzing atmosphere. The well-appointed bedrooms are situated in converted barns close by.

Rooms 8 (8 annexe)

HYDE Greater Manchester — Map 16 SJ99

Premier Inn Manchester (Hyde)

BUDGET HOTEL

☎ 0871 527 8712 0871 527 8713
Stockport Rd, Mottram SK14 3AU
dir: At end of M67 between A57 & A560

High quality, budget accommodation ideal for both families and business travellers. Spacious, en suite bedrooms feature tea and coffee making facilities, and Freeview TV in most hotels. Internet access and Wi-fi are available for a small fee. The adjacent family restaurant features a wide and varied menu. See also the Hotel Groups pages.

Rooms 83 **D** £52-£58*

HYTHE Kent — Map 7 TR13

Mercure Hythe Imperial

★★★★ 71% HOTEL

☎ 01303 267441 01303 264610
Princes Pde CT21 6AE
e-mail: h6862@accor.com
web: www.mercure.com
dir: M20, junct 11 onto A261. In Hythe follow Folkestone signs. Right into Twiss Rd to hotel

This imposing seafront hotel is enhanced by impressive grounds including a 13-hole golf course, tennis court and extensive gardens. Bedrooms are varied in style but all offer modern facilities, and many enjoy stunning sea views. The elegant restaurant, bar and lounges are traditional in style and retain many original features. The leisure club includes a gym, a squash court, an indoor pool, and the spa offers a range of luxury treatments.

Rooms 80 (6 fmly) (6 GF) **S** £60-£90; **D** £70-£135* **Facilities** Spa STV 13 Putt green Gym Squash Snooker & pool table Aerobic studio Table tennis Sauna Steam room Xmas New Year Wi-fi **Conf** Class 120 Board 80 Thtr 220 Del from £125 to £165* **Services** Lift **Parking** 207 **Notes** Civ Wed 120

Best Western Stade Court

★★★ 74% HOTEL

☎ 01303 268263 01303 261803
Stade St, West Pde CT21 6DT
e-mail: stadecourt@bestwestern.co.uk
dir: M20 junct 11 follow signs for Hythe town centre. Follow brown tourist sign for hotel

This hotel is situated right on the seafront with many bedrooms having the benefit of uninterrupted views of the English Channel. The comfortable bedrooms are tastefully decorated and provide free Wi-fi and in-room beverage-making facilities. Guests can enjoy traditional English or Indian cuisine in the sea facing restaurant.

Rooms 42 (5 fmly) **Facilities** FTV Fishing ♫ Xmas New Year Wi-fi **Conf** Class 20 Board 30 Thtr 40 **Services** Lift **Parking** 11 **Notes** Civ Wed 60

ILFORD
Greater London

See LONDON SECTION plan 1 H5

Express by Holiday Inn London Newbury Park

BUDGET HOTEL

☎ 020 8709 2200 🖷 020 8554 6232
713 Eastern Av IG2 7RH
web: www.hiexpress.com/londongantshil
dir: On A12 hotel on left between Gants Hill & Newbury Park station

A modern hotel ideal for families and business travellers. Fresh and uncomplicated, the spacious rooms include Sky TV, power shower and tea and coffee-making facilities. Continental buffet breakfast is included in the room rate; other meals may be taken at the nearby family pub or restaurant. See also the Hotel Groups pages.

Rooms 126 **S** £69-£199; **D** £69-£199 (incl. bkfst)* **Conf** Class 50 Board 50 Thtr 200 Del from £120 to £220*

Premier Inn Ilford

BUDGET HOTEL

☎ 0871 527 8542 🖷 0871 527 8543
Redbridge Lane East IG4 5BG
dir: At end of M11 follow London East, A12 & Chelmsford signs onto A12, hotel on left at bottom of slip road

High quality, budget accommodation ideal for both families and business travellers. Spacious, en suite bedrooms feature tea and coffee making facilities, and Freeview TV in most hotels. Internet access and Wi-fi are available for a small fee. The adjacent family restaurant features a wide and varied menu. See also the Hotel Groups pages.

Rooms 44 **D** £65-£75*

ILFRACOMBE
Devon
Map 3 SS54

Darnley

★★ 72% HOTEL

☎ 01271 863955
3 Belmont Rd EX34 8DR
e-mail: darnleyhotel@yahoo.co.uk
web: www.darnleyhotel.co.uk
dir: A361 to Barnstaple & Ilfracombe. Left at Church Hill, 1st left into Belmont Rd. 3rd entrance on left under walled arch

Standing in award-winning, mature gardens, with a wooded path to the High Street and the beach (about a five minute stroll away), this former Victorian gentleman's residence offers friendly, informal service. The individually furnished and decorated bedrooms vary in size. Dinners feature honest home cooking, with 'old fashioned puddings' always proving popular.

Rooms 10 (2 fmly) (2 GF) **S** £40-£45; **D** £59-£80 (incl. bkfst)* **Facilities** FTV Xmas New Year Wi-fi **Parking** 10 **Notes** No children 3yrs

Imperial Hotel

★★ 69% HOTEL

☎ 01271 862536 🖷 01271 862571
Wilder Rd EX34 9AL
e-mail: imperial.ilfracombe@alfatravel.co.uk
dir: Opposite Landmark Theatre

This popular hotel is just a short walk from the shops and harbour, overlooking gardens and the sea. Public areas include the spacious sun lounge, where guests can relax and enjoy the excellent views. Comfortable bedrooms are well equipped, with several having the added bonus of sea views.

Rooms 104 (6 fmly) **S** £36-£50; **D** £56-£84 (incl. bkfst) **Facilities** FTV ♫ Xmas New Year **Services** Lift **Parking** 10 **Notes** LB ⊗ Closed Dec-Feb (ex Xmas) RS Mar & Nov

ILKLEY
West Yorkshire
Map 19 SE14

Best Western Rombalds Hotel & Restaurant

★★★ 83% ® HOTEL

☎ 01943 603201 🖷 01943 816586
11 West View, Wells Rd LS29 9JG
e-mail: reception@rombalds.demon.co.uk
web: www.rombalds.co.uk
dir: A65 from Leeds. Left at 3rd main lights, follow Ilkley Moor signs. Right at HSBC Bank onto Wells Rd. Hotel 600yds on left

This elegantly furnished Georgian townhouse is located in a peaceful terrace between the town and the moors. Delightful day rooms include a choice of comfortable lounges and an attractive restaurant that provides a relaxed venue in which to sample the skilfully prepared, imaginative meals. The bedrooms are tastefully furnished, well equipped and include several spacious suites.

Rooms 15 (2 fmly) **Facilities** STV Xmas Wi-fi **Conf** Class 40 Board 25 Thtr 70 **Parking** 28 **Notes** Closed 28 Dec-2 Jan Civ Wed 70

The Craiglands Hotel

★★★ 70% HOTEL

☎ 01943 430001 & 886450 🖷 01943 430002
Cowpasture Rd LS29 8RQ
e-mail: reservations@craiglands.co.uk
web: www.craiglands.co.uk
dir: A65 into Ilkley. Left at T-junct. Past rail station, fork right into Cowpasture Rd. Hotel opposite school

This grand Victorian hotel is ideally situated close to the town centre. Spacious public areas and a good range of services are ideal for business or leisure. Extensive conference facilities are available along with an elegant restaurant and traditionally styled bar and lounge. Bedrooms, varying in size and style, are comfortably furnished and well equipped.

Rooms 62 (6 fmly) **S** £59-£111; **D** £69-£121 (incl. bkfst)* **Facilities** STV Xmas New Year Wi-fi **Conf** Class 200 Board 100 Thtr 500 Del from £104 to £124* **Services** Lift **Parking** 200 **Notes** LB ⊗ Civ Wed 500

ILSINGTON Devon Map 3 SX77

Ilsington Country House

CLASSIC BRITISH HOTELS

★★★ 86% COUNTRY HOUSE HOTEL

01364 661452 01364 661307
Ilsington Village TQ13 9RR
e-mail: hotel@ilsington.co.uk
web: www.ilsington.co.uk
dir: M5 onto A38 to Plymouth. Exit at Bovey Tracey. 3rd exit from rdbt to 'Ilsington', then 1st right. Hotel in 5m by Post Office

This friendly, family owned hotel, offers tranquillity and far-reaching views from its elevated position on the southern slopes of Dartmoor. The stylish suites and bedrooms, some on the ground floor, are individually furnished. The restaurant provides a stunning backdrop for the innovative, daily changing menus which feature local fish, meat and game. Additional facilities include an indoor pool and the Blue Tiger Inn, where a pint, a bite to eat and convivial banter can all be enjoyed.

Rooms 25 (4 fmly) (6 GF) **S** £85-£110; **D** £85-£215 (incl. bkfst)* **Facilities** FTV supervised Gym Steam room Sauna Beauty treatments Xmas New Year Wi-fi **Conf** Class 60 Board 40 Thtr 100 Del from £135 to £160* **Services** Lift **Parking** 100 **Notes** LB Civ Wed 120

INSTOW Devon Map 3 SS43

Commodore

★★★ 79% HOTEL

01271 860347 01271 861233
Marine Pde EX39 4JN
e-mail: admin@commodore-instow.co.uk
web: www.commodore-instow.co.uk
dir: M5 junct 27 follow N Devon link road to Bideford. Right before bridge, hotel in 3m

Maintaining its links with the local maritime and rural communities, The Commodore provides an interesting place to stay. Situated at the mouth of the Taw and Torridge estuaries and overlooking a sandy beach, it offers well-equipped bedrooms, many with balconies. There are five ground-floor suites. Eating options include the restaurant, the Quarterdeck bar, or the terrace in the warmer months.

Rooms 25 (1 fmly) (5 GF) **S** £79-£100; **D** £140-£220 (incl. bkfst & dinner)* **Facilities** FTV Xmas New Year Wi-fi **Parking** 200 **Notes** LB No children 3yrs

See advert on page 73

IPSWICH Suffolk Map 13 TM14

INSPECTORS' CHOICE

Hintlesham Hall Hotel

slh.com

★★★★ HOTEL

01473 652334 01473 652463
George St IP8 3NS
e-mail: reservations@hintleshamhall.com
web: www.hintleshamhall.com

(For full entry see Hintlesham)

INSPECTORS' CHOICE

Salthouse Harbour

★★★★ TOWN HOUSE HOTEL

01473 226789 01473 226927
No 1 Neptune Quay IP4 1AX
e-mail: staying@salthouseharbour.co.uk
dir: From A14 junct 56 follow signs for town centre, then Salthouse signs

Situated just a short walk from the town centre, this waterfront warehouse conversion is a clever mix of contemporary styles and original features. The hotel is stylish designed throughout with modern art, sculptures, interesting artefacts and striking colours. The spacious bedrooms provide luxurious comfort; some have feature bathrooms and some have balconies. Two air-conditioned penthouse suites, with stunning views, have extras such as state-of-the-art sound systems and telescopes. Award-winning food is served in the busy, ground-floor brasserie, and alfresco eating is possible in warmer weather.

Rooms 70 (6 fmly) **D** £125-£170 (incl. bkfst)* **Facilities** FTV Wi-fi **Services** Lift **Parking** 30

milsoms Kesgrave Hall

★★★★ 76% HOTEL

☎ 01473 333741 📠 01473 617614
Hall Rd, Kesgrave IP5 2PU
e-mail: reception@kesgravehall.com
web: www.milsomshotels.com
dir: A12 N of Ipswich, left at Ipswich/Woodbridge rdbt onto B1214. Right after 0.5m into Hall Rd. Hotel 200yds on left

A superb 18th-century, Grade II listed Georgian mansion set amidst 38 acres of mature grounds. Appointed in a contemporary style, the large open-plan public areas include a smart bar, a lounge with plush sofas, and a restaurant where guests can watch the chefs in action. Bedrooms are tastefully appointed and thoughtfully equipped.

Rooms 23 (8 annexe) (4 fmly) (8 GF) **S** £97-£184; **D** £122-£250* **Facilities** STV FTV Xmas Wi-fi **Conf** Class 200 Board 24 Thtr 300 **Parking** 100 **Notes** LB

Best Western Claydon Country House Hotel

★★★ 82% HOTEL

☎ 01473 830382 📠 01473 832476
16-18 Ipswich Rd, Claydon IP6 0AR
e-mail: reception@hotelsipswich.com
dir: From A14, NW of Ipswich. After 4m take Great Blakenham Rd (B1113) to Claydon, hotel on left

A delightful hotel situated just off the A14, within easy driving distance of the town centre. The pleasantly decorated bedrooms are thoughtfully equipped and one room has a lovely four-poster bed. An interesting choice of freshly prepared dishes is available in the smart restaurant, and guests have the use of a relaxing lounge bar.

Rooms 36 (5 fmly) (13 GF) **S** £59-£89; **D** £79-£99 **Facilities** STV Xmas New Year Wi-fi **Conf** Class 60 Board 55 Thtr 120 Del from £105 to £125 **Services** Air con **Parking** 85 **Notes** LB Civ Wed 100

Novotel Ipswich Centre

★★★ 82% HOTEL

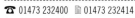

☎ 01473 232400 📠 01473 232414
Greyfriars Rd IP1 1UP
e-mail: h0995@accor.com
web: www.novotel.com
dir: From A14 towards Felixstowe. Left onto A137, 2m into town centre. Hotel on double rdbt by Stoke Bridge

A modern, red brick hotel perfectly placed in the centre of town close to shops, bars and restaurants. The open-plan public areas include a Mediterranean-style restaurant and a bar with a small games area. The bedrooms are smartly appointed and have many thoughtful touches; three rooms are suitable for less mobile guests.

Rooms 101 (8 fmly) **Facilities** STV Gym Xmas New Year Wi-fi **Conf** Class 75 Board 45 Thtr 180 **Services** Lift Air con **Parking** 53 **Notes** Civ Wed 75

Best Western The Gatehouse

★★★ 78% HOTEL

☎ 01473 741897 📠 01473 744236
799 Old Norwich Rd IP1 6LH
dir: A14 junct 53, A1156 signed Ipswich, left at lights into Norwich Rd, hotel on left

A Regency-style property set amidst three acres of landscaped grounds, on the outskirts of town in a quiet road just a short drive from the A14. The spacious bedrooms have co-ordinated soft furnishings and many thoughtful touches. Public rooms include a smart lounge bar, an intimate restaurant and a cosy drawing room with plush leather sofas.

Rooms 15 (4 annexe) (3 fmly) (6 GF) **S** £69-£89; **D** £79-£99 (incl. bkfst)* **Facilities** STV FTV Wi-fi **Parking** 25 **Notes** LB

Holiday Inn Ipswich

★★★ 77% HOTEL

☎ 0871 942 9045 📠 01473 680412
London Rd IP2 0UA
e-mail: reservations-ipswich@ichotelsgroup.com
web: www.holidayinn.co.uk
dir: From A14 & A12 junct take A1214 to West Ipswich. Over 1st rdbt. Hotel on left on A1071

A modern, purpose built hotel conveniently situated just off the A12/A14 junction to the west of the town centre. Public areas include a popular bar, the Junction Restaurant and a large open-plan lounge. Bedrooms come in a variety of styles and are suited to the needs of both the business and leisure guest alike.

Rooms 108 (40 fmly) (48 GF) (7 smoking) **Facilities** STV FTV supervised Gym Sauna Xmas New Year Wi-fi **Conf** Class 50 Board 40 Thtr 120 **Services** Lift Air con **Parking** 200 **Notes** Civ Wed 80

Ramada Encore Ipswich

★★★ 75% HOTEL

☎ 01473 694600 📠 01473 694610
Ranelagh Rd IP2 0AD
e-mail: reservations@encoreipswich.co.uk
dir: A14/A1214. Hotel 0.3m from Ipswich rail station

Modern ,purpose-built hotel situated close to the railway station and within easy walking distance of Ipswich Town FC. The contemporary, open-plan public areas feature a smart lounge bar which leads through to a bright and airy restaurant. The smart bedrooms are very well equipped and have interactive flat-screen TVs with internet access. The hotel also has a small gym.

Rooms 126 (9 fmly) (16 GF) **Facilities** Gym Wi-fi **Conf** Class 16 Board 20 Thtr 30 **Services** Lift Air con **Parking** 24 **Notes** LB

I

Premier Inn Ipswich (Chantry Park)

BUDGET HOTEL

☎ 0871 527 8548 📠 0871 527 8549
Old Hadleigh Rd IP8 3AR
dir: From A12/A14 junct take A1214 to Ipswich town centre. Left at lights by Holiday Inn, left onto A1071. At mini rdbt turn right. Hotel on right

High quality, budget accommodation ideal for both families and business travellers. Spacious, en suite bedrooms feature tea and coffee making facilities, and Freeview TV in most hotels. Internet access and Wi-fi are available for a small fee. The adjacent family restaurant features a wide and varied menu. See also the Hotel Groups pages.

Rooms 49 **D** £50-£60*

Premier Inn Ipswich North

BUDGET HOTEL

☎ 0871 527 8550 📠 0871 527 8551
Paper Mill Ln, Claydon IP6 0BE
e-mail: ipswich.mti@whitbread.com
dir: A14 junct 52. At rdbt exit onto Paper Mill Lane. Hotel 1st left

Rooms 59 **D** £53-£62*

IPSWICH *continued*

Premier Inn Ipswich South

BUDGET HOTEL

☎ 0871 527 8552 📠 0871 527 8553
Bourne Hill, Wherstead IP2 8ND
dir: From A14 follow Ipswich Central A137 signs, then Ipswich Central & Docks signs. At bottom of hill at rdbt 2nd exit. Hotel on right

Rooms 40 **D** £50-£62*

Premier Inn Ipswich South East

BUDGET HOTEL

☎ 0871 527 8554 📠 0871 527 8555
Augusta Close, Ransomes Euro Park IP3 9SS
dir: A14 junct 57, stay in right lane. At rdbt 2nd exit, then 1st left. Hotel adjacent to Swallow Restaurant

Rooms 20 **D** £53-£65*

I

IREBY Map 18 NY23
Cumbria

Overwater Hall

★★★ 86% ®® COUNTRY HOUSE HOTEL

☎ 017687 76566 📠 017687 76921
CA7 1HH
e-mail: welcome@overwaterhall.co.uk
dir: From A591 take turn to Ireby at Castle Inn. Hotel signed after 2m on right

This privately owned country house dates back to 1811 and is set in lovely gardens surrounded by woodland. The owners have lovingly restored this Georgian property over the years paying great attention to the authenticity of the original design; guests will receive warm hospitality and attentive service in a relaxed manner. The elegant and well appointed bedrooms include the more spacious Superior Rooms and the Garden Room; all bedrooms have Wi-fi. Creative dishes are served in the traditional-style dining room.

Rooms 11 (2 fmly) (1 GF) **S** £100-£175; **D** £200-£270 (incl. bkfst & dinner)* **Facilities** FTV Xmas New Year Wi-fi **Parking** 20 **Notes** LB Civ Wed 30

KEGWORTH

See East Midlands Airport

KEIGHLEY Map 19 SE04
West Yorkshire

Dalesgate

★★ 70% HOTEL

☎ 01535 664930 📠 01535 611253
406 Skipton Rd, Utley BD20 6HP
e-mail: stephen.e.atha@btinternet.com
dir: In town centre follow A629 over rdbt onto B6265. Right after 0.75m into St. John's Rd. 1st right into hotel car park

Originally the residence of a local chapel minister, this modern, well-established hotel provides well-equipped, comfortable bedrooms. It also boasts a cosy bar and pleasant restaurant, serving an imaginative range of dishes. A large car park is provided to the rear.

Rooms 20 (2 fmly) (3 GF) **Parking** 25 **Notes** RS 22 Dec-4 Jan

Premier Inn Bradford North (Bingley)

BUDGET HOTEL

☎ 0871 527 8134 📠 0871 527 8135
502 Bradford Rd, Sandbeds BD20 5NG
dir: M62 juncts 26 or 27, follow A650/Keighley & Skipton signs. From Bingley Bypass (A650 Cottingley) right at 1st rdbt signed Crossflatts & Micklethwaite. Hotel 50yds on left. (NB for Sat Nav use BD20 5NH)

High quality, budget accommodation ideal for both families and business travellers. Spacious, en suite bedrooms feature tea and coffee making facilities, and Freeview TV in most hotels. Internet access and Wi-fi are available for a small fee. The adjacent family restaurant features a wide and varied menu. See also the Hotel Groups pages.

Rooms 40 **D** £53-£58*

KENDAL Map 18 SD59
Cumbria

See also **Crooklands**

Best Western Castle Green Hotel in Kendal

★★★ 82% ®® HOTEL

☎ 01539 734000 📠 01539 735522
LA9 6RG
e-mail: reception@castlegreen.co.uk
web: www.castlegreen.co.uk
dir: M6 junct 37, A684 towards Kendal. Hotel on right in 5m

This smart, modern hotel enjoys a peaceful location and is conveniently situated for access to both the town centre and the M6. Stylish bedrooms are thoughtfully equipped for both the business and leisure guest. The Greenhouse Restaurant provides imaginative dishes and boasts a theatre kitchen; alternatively Alexander's pub serves food all day. The hotel has a fully equipped business centre and leisure club.

Rooms 99 (3 fmly) (25 GF) **S** £82-£113; **D** £102-£154 (incl. bkfst)* **Facilities** Spa FTV Gym Steam room Aerobics Yoga Beauty salon Xmas New Year Wi-fi **Conf** Class 120 Board 100 Thtr 300 Del from £130 to £150* **Services** Lift **Parking** 200 **Notes** LB Civ Wed 250

Riverside Hotel Kendal

★★★ 77% HOTEL

☎ 01539 734861 📠 01539 734863
Beezon Rd, Stramongate Bridge LA9 6EL
e-mail: info@riversidekendal.co.uk
web: www.bestlakesbreaks.co.uk
dir: M6 junct 36 Sedburgh, Kendal 7m, left at end of Ann St, 1st right onto Beezon Rd, hotel on left

Centrally located in this market town, and enjoying a peaceful riverside location, this 17th-century former tannery provides a suitable base for both business travellers and tourists. The comfortable bedrooms are well equipped, and open-plan day rooms include the attractive restaurant and bar. Conference facilities are available, and the state-of-the-art leisure club has a heated pool, sauna, steam room, solarium and gym.

Rooms 50 (18 fmly) (10 GF) **S** £79-£99; **D** £118-£158 (incl. bkfst)* **Facilities** STV supervised Gym Sauna Steam room Spa bath Xmas New Year Wi-fi **Conf** Class 200 Board 90 Thtr 200 Del from £105 to £125* **Services** Lift **Parking** 60 **Notes** LB Civ Wed 250

Stonecross Manor

★★★ 75% HOTEL

☎ 01539 733559 📠 01539 736386
Milnthorpe Rd LA9 5HP
e-mail: info@stonecrossmanor.co.uk
web: www.stonecrossmanor.co.uk
dir: M6 junct 36, A590, follow signs to Windermere, take exit for Kendal South. Hotel just past 30mph sign on left

Located on the edge of Kendal, this smart hotel offers a good combination of traditional style and modern facilities. Bedrooms are comfortable, well equipped and some feature four-poster beds. Guests can relax in the lounges or bar and enjoy an extensive choice of home cooked meals in the pleasant restaurant. Facilities also include a swimming pool.

Rooms 30 (4 fmly) **S** £87-£145; **D** £98-£156 (incl. bkfst)* **Facilities** FTV Xmas New Year Wi-fi **Conf** Class 80 Board 40 Thtr 140 **Services** Lift **Parking** 55 **Notes** LB Civ Wed 130

Premier Inn Kendal Central

BUDGET HOTEL

Premier Inn

☎ 0871 527 8562 📠 0871 527 8563
Maude St LA9 4QD
dir: M6 junct 36, A591 to Kendal. (NB ignore exit for Kendal South). At Plumbgarm Rdbt, take 3rd exit, 0.5m to Kendal. Hotel on right

High quality, budget accommodation ideal for both families and business travellers. Spacious, en suite bedrooms feature tea and coffee making facilities, and Freeview TV in most hotels. Internet access and Wi-fi are available for a small fee. The adjacent family restaurant features a wide and varied menu. See also the Hotel Groups pages.

Rooms 55 **D** £59*

KENILWORTH
Warwickshire — Map 10 SP27

Chesford Grange

QHOTELS

★★★★ 79% HOTEL

☎ 01926 859331 📠 01926 859272
Chesford Bridge CV8 2LD
e-mail: chesfordreservations@qhotels.co.uk
web: www.qhotels.co.uk
dir: 0.5m SE of junct A46/A452. At rdbt turn right signed Leamington Spa, follow signs to hotel

This much-extended hotel set in 17 acres of private grounds is well situated for Birmingham International Airport, the NEC and major routes. Bedrooms range from traditional style to contemporary rooms featuring state-of-the-art technology. Public areas include a leisure club and extensive conference and banqueting facilities.

Rooms 205 (20 fmly) (43 GF) **S** £95-£140; **D** £100-£150 (incl. bkfst)* **Facilities** Spa STV supervised Gym Steam room Solarium Xmas New Year Wi-fi **Conf** Class 350 Board 50 Thtr 710 Del from £130 to £179* **Services** Lift **Parking** 650 **Notes** LB Civ Wed 700

Best Western Peacock Hotel

★★★ 78% HOTEL

☎ 01926 851156 & 864500 📠 01926 864644
149 Warwick Rd CV8 1HY
e-mail: reservations@peacockhotel.com
dir: A46/A452 signed Kenilworth. Hotel 0.25m on right after St John's Church

Conveniently located for the town centre, the Peacock offers a peaceful retreat, and service is delivered in a very professional manner by friendly staff. The accommodation is attractive, and vibrant colour schemes run throughout the pleasant public rooms; there are two dining options: the Malabar Room offering modern European dining, and the Coconut Lagoon serving southern Indian dishes.

Rooms 29 (6 annexe) (5 fmly) (10 GF) **S** £55-£75; **D** £59-£125 (incl. bkfst)* **Facilities** FTV Xmas Wi-fi **Conf** Class 24 Board 28 Thtr 60 Del from £99 to £129* **Parking** 30 **Notes** LB ® Civ Wed 70

KENTON
Greater London

See LONDON SECTION plan 1 C5

Premier Inn London Harrow

BUDGET HOTEL

☎ 0871 527 8664 📠 0871 527 8665
Kenton Rd HA3 8AT
dir: M1 junct 5, follow Harrow & Kenton signs. Hotel between Harrow & Wembley on A4006 opposite Kenton railway station

High quality, budget accommodation ideal for both families and business travellers. Spacious, en suite bedrooms feature tea and coffee making facilities, and Freeview TV in most hotels. Internet access and Wi-fi are available for a small fee. The adjacent family restaurant features a wide and varied menu. See also the Hotel Groups pages.

Rooms 101 **D** £66-£76*

K

KESWICK
Cumbria — Map 18 NY22

Highfield

★★★ 79% @@ SMALL HOTEL

☎ 017687 72508 📠 017687 80837
The Heads CA12 5ER
e-mail: info@highfieldkeswick.co.uk
web: www.highfieldkeswick.co.uk
dir: M6 junct 40, A66, 2nd exit at rdbt. Left to T-junct, left again. Right at mini-rdbt. Take 4th right

This friendly hotel, close to the centre of town, offers stunning views of Skiddaw, Cats Bells and Derwentwater. Attractively furnished bedrooms, many of them spacious, are thoughtfully equipped. Public areas include a choice of comfortable lounges and an elegant restaurant, where imaginative, modern cuisine is served.

Rooms 18 (1 fmly) (2 GF) **S** £95; **D** £170-£220 (incl. bkfst & dinner)* **Facilities** STV Wi-fi **Parking** 20 **Notes** ® Closed Jan

Dale Head Hall Lakeside

★★★ 79% @ COUNTRY HOUSE HOTEL

☎ 017687 72478 📠 0871 900 7234
Lake Thirlmere CA12 4TN
e-mail: onthelakeside@daleheadhall.co.uk
web: www.daleheadhall.co.uk
dir: Between Keswick & Grasmere. Exit A591 onto private drive

Set in attractive, tranquil grounds on the shores of Lake Thirlmere, this historic lakeside residence dates from the 16th century. Comfortable and inviting

continued

THE LODORE FALLS HOTEL

BORROWDALE, KESWICK,
CUMBRIA CA12 5UX
Reservations: 0800 840 1246

Situated in the picturesque Borrowdale Valley, with 40 acres of lake frontage and landscaped gardens and with the famous Lodore waterfalls in the grounds, this 69 bedroom hotel offers not only a magnificent setting in the heart of the Lake District, but also the very best in hospitality. Extensive leisure facilities including indoor & outdoor swimming pools, tennis & squash, a beauty salon and a new outdoor hot tub.

LAKE DISTRICT HOTELS

www.lakedistricthotels.net

K

The Skiddaw Hotel is a well-known landmark in the picturesque town centre of Keswick, offering guests a warm welcome in comfortable and elegant surroundings. With 44 bedrooms, including family suites and 4 poster rooms. The restaurant features an extensive table d'hôte menu with emphasis on local produce, lounge bar and conservatory overlooking Keswick town centre are open all day for coffees, lunches, afternoon teas and evening meals.

LAKE DISTRICT HOTELS

THE SKIDDAW HOTEL

MAIN STREET, KESWICK,
CUMBRIA CA12 5BN
Resevations: 0800 840 1243

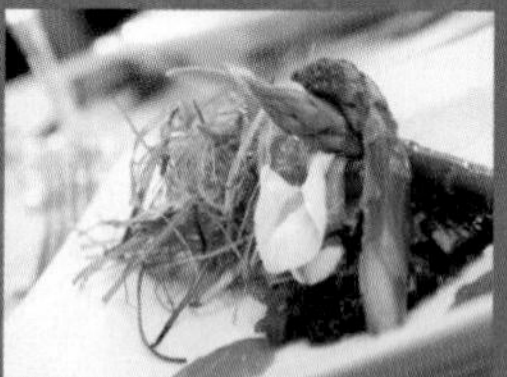

www.lakedistricthotels.net

A delightful hotel full of atmosphere and tradition with beautiful gardens and traditional conservatory. Nestled at the foot of Shepherds Crag in the beautiful valley of Borrowdale this hotel is the ideal base for a Lake District break. Most of the 36 bedrooms have recently been refurbished to a high standard, as have the ground floor lounges and restaurant. Famous for Sunday lunches and afternoon teas.

LAKE DISTRICT HOTELS

THE BORROWDALE HOTEL

BORROWDALE, KESWICK,
CUMBRIA CA12 5UY
Reservations: 0800 840 1244

www.lakedistricthotels.net

KESWICK ***continued***

public areas include a choice of lounges and a traditionally furnished restaurant featuring a daily-changing menu. Most bedrooms are spacious and have views of the lake or surrounding mountains.

Rooms 12 (1 fmly) (2 GF) **Facilities** STV Fishing Fishing permits Boating Xmas New Year Wi-fi **Conf** Class 20 Board 20 Thtr 20 Del from £110 to £150 **Parking** 34 **Notes** Closed 3-30 Jan Civ Wed 50

Skiddaw

★★★ 77% HOTEL

017687 72071 017687 74850
Main St CA12 5BN
e-mail: info@skiddawhotel.co.uk
web: www.skiddawhotel.co.uk
dir: A66 to Keswick, follow town centre signs. Hotel in market square

Occupying a central position overlooking the market square, this hotel provides smartly furnished bedrooms that include several family suites and a room with a four-poster bed. In addition to the restaurant, food is served all day in the bar and in the conservatory bar. There is also a quiet residents' lounge and two conference rooms.

Rooms 43 (7 fmly) (3 smoking) **Facilities** STV Use of leisure facilities at sister hotel (3m) Xmas New Year Wi-fi **Conf** Class 60 Board 40 Thtr 70 **Services** Lift **Parking** 35 **Notes** LB Civ Wed 90

See advert on opposite page

Keswick Country House

LAKE DISTRICT HOTELS

★★★ 72% HOTEL

0845 458 4333 01253 754222
Station Rd CA12 4NQ
e-mail: reservations@choice-hotels.co.uk
web: www.thekeswickhotel.co.uk
dir: M6 junct 40/A66, 1st slip road into Keswick, follow signs for leisure pool

This impressive Victorian hotel is set amid attractive gardens close to the town centre. Eight superior bedrooms are available in the Station Wing, which is accessed through a conservatory. The attractively appointed main house rooms are modern in style and offer a good range of amenities. Public areas include a well-stocked bar, a spacious and relaxing lounge, and a restaurant serving interesting dinners.

Rooms 74 (6 fmly) (4 GF) **Facilities** Putt green Leisure facilities close by Xmas New Year Wi-fi **Conf** Class 70 Board 60 Thtr 110 **Services** Lift **Parking** 70 **Notes** LB Civ Wed 100

Swinside Lodge Country House Hotel

★★ 85% COUNTRY HOUSE HOTEL

017687 72948 017687 73312
Grange Rd, Newlands CA12 5UE
e-mail: info@swinsidelodge-hotel.co.uk
web: www.swinsidelodge-hotel.co.uk
dir: A66, exit at Portinscale towards Grange for 2m (NB ignore Swinside & Newlands Valley signs). Hotel on right

Surrounded by fells, this beautifully maintained Georgian property is situated at the foot of Cat Bells and is only a five-minute stroll from the shores of Derwentwater. Guests are made to feel genuinely welcome with the friendly proprietors on hand to provide attentive service. The elegantly furnished lounges are an ideal place to relax before dinner. The four-course set dinner menu is creative, featuring high quality ingredients and beautifully presented dishes.

Rooms 7 (7 fmly) **S** £118-£174; **D** £176-£288 (incl. bkfst & dinner)* **Facilities** New Year Wi-fi **Parking** 12 **Notes** LB No children 12yrs Closed 20-26 Dec & Jan

KETTERING Northamptonshire **Map 11 SP87**

Rushton Hall Hotel and Spa

★★★★ 79% COUNTRY HOUSE HOTEL

01536 713001 01536 713010
NN14 1RR
e-mail: enquiries@rushtonhall.com
web: www.rushtonhall.com
dir: A14 junct 7. A43 to Corby then A6003 to Rushton, turn after bridge

An elegant country house hotel set amidst 30 acres of parkland and surrounded by open countryside. The stylish public rooms include a library, a superb open-plan lounge bar with a magnificent vaulted ceiling and plush sofas, and an oak-panelled dining hall. The tastefully appointed bedrooms have co-ordinated fabrics and many thoughtful touches.

Rooms 45 (5 fmly) (3 GF) **S** £150-£170; **D** £150-£170 (incl. bkfst)* **Facilities** Spa FTV Gym Billiard table Sauna Steam room Xmas New Year Wi-fi **Conf** Class 100 Board 40 Thtr 200 Del from £175 to £215* **Services** Lift **Parking** 140 **Notes** Civ Wed 160

See advert on page 244

Kettering Park Hotel & Spa

shire hotels & spas

★★★★ 79% HOTEL

01536 416666 01536 416171
Kettering Parkway NN15 6XT
e-mail: kpark@shirehotels.com
web: www.ketteringparkhotel.com
dir: Off A14 junct 9 (M1 to A1 link road), hotel in Kettering Venture Park

Expect a warm welcome at this stylish hotel situated just off the A14. The spacious, smartly decorated bedrooms are well equipped and meticulously maintained. Guests can choose from classical or contemporary dishes in the restaurant or lighter meals that are served in the bar. The extensive leisure facilities are impressive.

Rooms 119 (29 fmly) (35 GF) **S** £100-£200; **D** £110-£210* **Facilities** STV FTV Gym Steam room Sauna Treatment room Children's splash pool Activity studio New Year Wi-fi **Conf** Class 120 Board 40 Thtr 260 Del from £135 to £185* **Services** Lift Air con **Parking** 200 **Notes** LB Civ Wed 120

Holiday Inn Express Kettering

BUDGET HOTEL

01536 210210 01536 210211
Rockingham Rd NN14 1QF
e-mail: reception@exhikettering.co.uk
dir: A43 (N) to 1st rdbt. Stay in left lane, take 1st left. A6003, stay in left lane to lights. Filter back across dual carriageway. Hotel behind Harvester Restaurant

A modern hotel ideal for families and business travellers. Fresh and uncomplicated, the spacious rooms include Sky TV, power shower and tea and coffee-making facilities. Continental buffet breakfast is included in the room rate; other meals may be taken at the nearby family pub or restaurant. See also the Hotel Groups pages.

Rooms 120 (72 fmly) (13 GF) **S** £48-£103.50; **D** £48-£103.50 (incl. bkfst)* **Conf** Class 24 Board 18 Thtr 70

KETTERING *continued*

Premier Inn Kettering

BUDGET HOTEL

☎ 0871 527 8564 🖷 0871 527 8565
Rothwell Rd NN16 8XF
dir: Off A14 junct 7

High quality, budget accommodation ideal for both families and business travellers. Spacious, en suite bedrooms feature tea and coffee making facilities, and Freeview TV in most hotels. Internet access and Wi-fi are available for a small fee. The adjacent family restaurant features a wide and varied menu. See also the Hotel Groups pages.

Rooms 59 **D** £51-£60*

KIDDERMINSTER Worcestershire **Map 10 SO87**

Stone Manor

★★★★ 78% HOTEL

☎ 01562 777555 🖷 01562 777834
Stone DY10 4PJ
e-mail: enquiries@stonemanorhotel.co.uk
web: www.stonemanorhotel.co.uk
dir: 2.5m from Kidderminster on A448, on right

This converted, much extended former manor house stands in 25 acres of impressive grounds and gardens. The well-equipped accommodation includes rooms with four-poster beds and luxuriously appointed annexe bedrooms. Quality furnishing and decor styles throughout the public areas highlight the intrinsic charm of the interior; the hotel is a popular venue for wedding receptions.

Rooms 57 (5 annexe) (7 GF) **Facilities** STV Pool table Complimentary use of local leisure centre **Conf** Class 48 Board 60 Thtr 150 Del from £120 to £150* **Parking** 400 **Notes** Civ Wed 150

The Granary Hotel & Restaurant

★★★ 78% HOTEL

☎ 01562 777535 🖷 01562 777722
Heath Ln, Shenstone DY10 4BS
e-mail: info@granary-hotel.co.uk
web: www.granary-hotel.co.uk
dir: On A450 between Stourbridge & Worcester, 1m from Kidderminster

This modern hotel offers spacious, well-equipped accommodation with many rooms enjoying views towards Great Witley and the Amberley Hills. Public areas include a cocktail lounge, and an attractive modern restaurant serving dishes created from locally sourced produce, cooked with flair and imagination. There are also extensive conference facilities, and the hotel is popular as a wedding venue.

The Granary Hotel & Restaurant

Rooms 18 (1 fmly) (18 GF) **S** £60-£90; **D** £70-£140 (incl. bkfst)* **Facilities** FTV Wi-fi **Conf** Class 80 Board 70 Thtr 200 Del from £135 to £144* **Parking** 96 **Notes** LB Civ Wed 120

Gainsborough House Hotel

THE INDEPENDENTS HOTEL ASSOCIATION

★★★ 78% HOTEL

☎ 01562 820041 🖷 01562 66179
Bewdley Hill DY11 6BS
e-mail: reservations@gainsboroughhousehotel.com
web: www.gainsboroughhousehotel.com
dir: Follow A456 to Kidderminster (West Midlands Safari Park), pass hospital, hotel 500yds on left

This listed Georgian hotel provides a wide range of thoughtfully furnished bedrooms with smart modern bathrooms. The contemporary decor and furnishing throughout the public areas highlights the many retained period features. A large function suite and several meeting rooms are also available.

Rooms 42 (16 fmly) (12 GF) **S** £63-£93; **D** £69-£99 (incl. bkfst)* **Facilities** STV FTV Xmas New Year Wi-fi **Conf** Board 60 Thtr 250 Del from £85* **Services** Air con **Parking** 90 **Notes** LB Civ Wed 250

KINGHAM Oxfordshire Map 10 SP22

Mill House Hotel & Restaurant

★★★ 77% HOTEL

☎ 01608 658188 01608 658492
OX7 6UH
e-mail: stay@millhousehotel.co.uk
web: www.millhousehotel.co.uk
dir: Off A44 onto B4450. Hotel signed

This Cotswold-stone, former mill house is a stylish and peaceful hotel, set in well-kept grounds bordered by its own trout stream. The individually designed bedrooms are very comfortable and provide thoughtfully equipped facilities; most rooms have lovely views out over the extensive lawned gardens to the Cotswold Hills beyond. There is a peaceful lounge and bar, plus an atmospheric restaurant. The hotel is a popular venue for weddings.

Rooms 23 (2 annexe) (1 fmly) (7 GF) **D** £145-£190 (incl. bkfst & dinner) **Facilities** STV FTV Fishing Xmas New Year Wi-fi **Conf** Class 24 Board 24 Thtr 70 Del from £140-£190 (incl. bkfst & dinner) **Parking** 62 **Notes** LB Civ Wed 100

KINGSGATE Kent Map 7 TR37

The Fayreness

★★★ 79% HOTEL

☎ 01843 868641 & 861103 01843 608750
Marine Dr CT10 3LG
e-mail: info@fayreness.co.uk
web: www.fayreness.co.uk
dir: A28 onto B2051 which becomes B2052. Pass Holy Trinity Church on right & '19th Hole' public house. Next left, into Kingsgate Ave, hotel at end on left

Situated on the cliff top overlooking the English Channel, just a few steps from a sandy beach and adjacent to the North Foreland Golf Club. The spacious bedrooms are tastefully furnished with many thoughtful touches including free Wi-fi; some rooms have stunning sea views. Public rooms include a large open-plan lounge/bar, a function room, dining room and conservatory restaurant.

Rooms 29 (3 fmly) (5 GF) (4 smoking) **Facilities** STV New Year Wi-fi **Conf** Class 28 Board 36 Thtr 50 **Parking** 70 **Notes** Civ Wed 80

KING'S LANGLEY Hertfordshire Map 6 TL00

Premier Inn King's Langley

BUDGET HOTEL

☎ 0871 527 8568 0871 527 8569
Hempstead Rd WD4 8BR
dir: 1m from M25 junct 20 on A4251 after King's Langley

High quality, budget accommodation ideal for both families and business travellers. Spacious, en suite bedrooms feature tea and coffee making facilities, and Freeview TV in most hotels. Internet access and Wi-fi are available for a small fee. The adjacent family restaurant features a wide and varied menu. See also the Hotel Groups pages.

Rooms 60 **D** £53-£60*

KING'S LYNN Norfolk Map 12 TF62

INSPECTORS' CHOICE

Congham Hall Country House Hotel

★★★ COUNTRY HOUSE HOTEL

☎ 01485 600250 01485 601191
Lynn Rd PE32 1AH
e-mail: info@conghamhallhotel.co.uk
web: www.conghamhallhotel.co.uk
(For full entry see Grimston)

Bank House Hotel

★★★ 83% HOTEL

☎ 01553 660492
King's Staithe Square PE30 1RD
e-mail: info@thebankhouse.co.uk
dir: In King's Lynn Old Town follow quayside, through floodgates, hotel on right opposite Custom House

This Grade II listed, 18th-century town house is situated on the quay side in the heart of King's Lynn's historical quarter. Bedrooms are individually decorated and have high quality fabrics and furnishings along with a range of useful facilities. Public rooms include the Counting House coffee shop, a wine bar and brasserie restaurant, as well as a residents' lounge.

Rooms 11 (5 fmly) **S** £80-£110; **D** £100-£140 (incl. bkfst)* **Facilities** FTV Xmas New Year Wi-fi **Conf** Class 20 Board 15 Thtr 30 **Notes** LB

Best Western Knights Hill

★★★ 78% HOTEL

☎ 01553 675566 01553 675568
Knights Hill Village, South Wootton PE30 3HQ
e-mail: reception@knightshill.co.uk
dir: At junct A148 & A149

This hotel village complex is set on a 16th-century site on the outskirts of town. The smartly decorated, well-equipped bedrooms are situated in extensions of the original hunting lodge. Public areas have a wealth of historic charm including the Garden Restaurant and the Farmers Arms pub. The hotel also has conference and leisure facilities, including Imagine Spa.

Rooms 79 (12 annexe) (1 fmly) (38 GF) **S** £40-£100; **D** £50-£110* **Facilities** Spa STV Gym Xmas New Year Wi-fi **Conf** Class 150 Board 30 Thtr 200 Del from £100 to £135* **Parking** 350 **Notes** LB Civ Wed 90

Stuart House

★★★ 71% HOTEL

☎ 01553 772169 01553 774788
35 Goodwins Rd PE30 5QX
e-mail: reception@stuarthousehotel.co.uk
web: www.stuarthousehotel.co.uk
dir: At A47/A10/A149 rdbt follow signs to town centre. Under Southgate Arch, right into Guanock Terrace, right into Goodwins Rd

Small privately-owned hotel situated in a peaceful residential area just a short walk from the town centre. Bedrooms come in a variety of styles and sizes; all are pleasantly decorated and thoughtfully equipped. There is a choice of dining options with informal dining in the bar and a daily-changing menu in the elegant restaurant.

Rooms 18 (2 fmly) (3 GF) **S** £82; **D** £96-£160 (incl. bkfst) **Facilities** FTV Wi-fi **Conf** Class 30 Board 20 Thtr 50 **Parking** 30 **Notes** LB RS 25-26 Dec & 1 Jan Civ Wed 60

K

KING'S LYNN *continued*

Grange

★★ 71% HOTEL

☎ 01553 673777 & 671222 📠 01553 673777
Willow Park, South Wootton Ln PE30 3BP
e-mail: info@thegrangehotelkingslynn.co.uk
dir: A148 towards King's Lynn for 1.5m. At lights left into Wootton Rd, 400yds, right into South Wootton Ln. Hotel 1st on left

Expect a warm welcome at this Edwardian house which is situated in a quiet residential area in its own grounds. Public rooms include a smart lounge bar and a cosy restaurant. The spacious bedrooms are pleasantly decorated and equipped with many thoughtful touches; some are located in an adjacent wing.

Rooms 9 (4 annexe) (2 fmly) (4 GF) **Facilities** Xmas **Conf** Class 15 Board 12 Thtr 20 **Parking** 15

Ramada King's Lynn

U

☎ 01553 771707 📠 01553 768027
Beveridge Way, Hardwick Narrows PE30 4NB
e-mail: reception@ramadakingslynn.co.uk
dir: A47 Norwich Road, exit before flyover, 2nd exit off rdbt, follow signs to Hardwick Narrows Estate

Currently the rating for this establishment is not confirmed. This may be due to a change of ownership or because it has only recently joined the AA rating scheme. For further details please see the AA website: theAA.com

Rooms 50 **Conf** Class 20 Board 40 Thtr 80

Premier Inn King's Lynn

Premier Inn

BUDGET HOTEL

☎ 0871 527 8570 📠 0871 527 8571
Clenchwarton Rd, West Lynn PE34 3LJ
dir: At junct of A47 & A17

High quality, budget accommodation ideal for both families and business travellers. Spacious, en suite bedrooms feature tea and coffee making facilities, and Freeview TV in most hotels. Internet access and Wi-fi are available for a small fee. The adjacent family restaurant features a wide and varied menu. See also the Hotel Groups pages.

Rooms 61 **D** £65*

KINGSTON BAGPUIZE — Map 5 SU49
Oxfordshire

Fallowfields Country House Hotel & Restaurant

★★★ 73% HOTEL

☎ 01865 820416 📠 01865 821275
Faringdon Rd OX13 5BH
e-mail: stay@fallowfields.com
web: www.fallowfields.com
dir: A34 (Oxford Ring road), A420 towards Swindon. At junct with A415 left, 100yds, exit at mini rdbt. Hotel on left in 1m

Located in rural Oxfordshire just ten miles from Oxford city centre, this small family-run hotel offers the personal touch. The bedrooms are generous in size and some have delightful views over the croquet lawn. The grounds are home to several breeds of cattle, pigs and chickens along with the kitchen garden where much of the produce for the menus is sourced.

Rooms 10 (2 fmly) **S** £75-£125; **D** £125-£175 (incl. bkfst)* **Facilities** FTV Xmas New Year Wi-fi **Conf** Class 25 Board 20 Thtr 60 Del from £145 to £185* **Parking** 50 **Notes** Civ Wed 100

KINGSTON UPON HULL — Map 17 TA02
East Riding of Yorkshire

Portland

★★★★ 73% HOTEL

☎ 01482 326462 📠 01482 213460
Paragon St HU1 3JP
e-mail: info@portland-hotel.co.uk
web: www.portland-hull.com
dir: M62 junct 38 onto A63, to 1st main rdbt. Left at 2nd lights, over x-rds. Right at next junct onto Carr Ln, follow one-way system

A modern hotel situated adjacent to the City Hall that provides a good range of accommodation. Most of the public rooms are on the first floor and Wi-fi is available. The Bay Tree Café, at street level, is open during the day and evening. Staff are friendly and helpful, and will take care of parking cars for their guests.

Rooms 126 (4 fmly) **Facilities** STV FTV Complimentary use of nearby health & fitness centre Xmas New Year Wi-fi **Conf** Class 100 Board 50 Thtr 220 **Services** Lift **Notes** LB Civ Wed 100

The Townhouse

★★★★ 71% TOWN HOUSE HOTEL

☎ 01482 219878 📠 01482 226164
Albion St HU1 3TD
e-mail: stay@thetownhousehull.co.uk
web: www.thetownhousehull.co.uk
dir: M62 junct 38 to Hull. After Humber Bridge continue over flyover, follow Railway Station signs. Stay in right lane, right into Spencer St. 3rd left into Albion St, hotel on left

Built in 1846 for Queen Victoria's physician, this attractive Grade II listed building is situated in the heart of the city just a two-minute walk from the bus and rail station and St Stephen's Shopping Centre. Much care is taken to provide the highest levels of comfort in the bedrooms, which prove suitable for both business and leisure guests. The hotel has a spacious basement breakfast room, offering a wide selection including a full Yorkshire breakfast. There is a cosy club-style lounge, plus fully-equipped conference rooms.

Rooms 27 (5 fmly) (9 GF) **Facilities** FTV Wi-fi **Conf** Class 20 Board 20 Thtr 50 Del from £109 to £129* **Services** Lift Air con **Notes** ⊗ Civ Wed 40

Best Western Willerby Manor Hotel

★★★ 83% ◎ HOTEL

☎ 01482 652616 📠 01482 653901
Well Ln HU10 6ER
e-mail: willerbymanor@bestwestern.co.uk
web: www.willerbymanor.co.uk

(For full entry see Willerby)

Holiday Inn Hull Marina

★★★ 81% HOTEL

☎ 0871 942 9043 & 01482 386300
🖷 01482 386325
The Marina, Castle St HU1 2BX
e-mail: reservations-hull@ihg.com
web: www.holidayinn.co.uk
dir: M62 junct 38, A63 to Hull. Follow Marina & Ice Arena signs. Hotel on left adjacent to Ice Arena

Situated overlooking the marina just off the A63. The well-equipped accommodation includes executive rooms. Public areas are attractively designed and include meeting rooms and a leisure club. The Junction restaurant serves contemporary cuisine, and guests can eat alfresco on the patio if weather permits.

Rooms 100 (10 fmly) **S** £49-£119; **D** £59-£129* **Facilities** STV supervised Gym New Year Wi-fi **Conf** Class 70 Board 50 Thtr 120 Del from £99 to £135* **Services** Lift Air con **Parking** 151 **Notes** LB Civ Wed 120

Mercure Hull Royal Hotel

Mercure

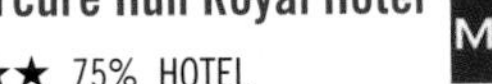

★★★ 75% HOTEL

☎ 01482 325087 🖷 01482 228833
170 Ferensway HU1 3UF
e-mail: reservations@hotels-hull.co.uk
dir: A63 to city centre. Follow signs to railway station, hotel adjacent

A 'railway hotel' in Victorian times, this impressive building, has been modernised in recent years. The stunning central lounge area is the focal point and there are extensive conference and banqueting facilities, with complimentary parking and Wi-fi access also provided. The contemporary bedrooms have bold colour schemes with good facilities including flat-screen TVs; many have air conditioning. There is a leisure club adjacent to the hotel.

Rooms 155 (29 fmly) (20 smoking) **Facilities** FTV Xmas New Year Wi-fi **Conf** Class 150 Board 70 Thtr 400 **Services** Lift **Parking** 84 **Notes** Civ Wed 400

Campanile Hull

Campanile HOTEL RESTAURANT

BUDGET HOTEL

☎ 01482 325530 🖷 01482 587538
Beverley Rd, Freetown Way (City Centre) HU2 9AN
e-mail: hull@campanile.com
dir: M62 junct 38, A63 to Hull, pass Humber Bridge on right. Over flyover, follow railway station signs onto A1079. Hotel at bottom of Ferensway

This modern building offers accommodation in smart, well-equipped bedrooms, all with en suite bathrooms. Refreshments may be taken at the informal bistro. See also the Hotel Groups pages.

Rooms 47 (47 annexe) (22 GF) **S** £46-£49; **D** £46-£49* **Conf** Class 15 Board 15 Thtr 25 Del from £80 to £90*

Ibis Hull

ibis HOTEL

BUDGET HOTEL

☎ 01482 387500 🖷 01482 385510
Osborne St HU1 2NL
e-mail: h3479-gm@accor-hotels.com
web: www.ibishotel.com
dir: M62/A63 straight across at rdbt, follow signs for Princes Quay onto Myton St. Hotel on corner of Osborne St & Ferensway

Modern, budget hotel offering comfortable accommodation in bright and practical bedrooms. Breakfast is self-service and dinner is available in the restaurant. See also the Hotel Groups pages.

Rooms 106 (19 GF)

Premier Inn Hull City Centre

BUDGET HOTEL

☎ 0871 527 8534 🖷 0871 527 8535
Tower St HU9 1TQ
dir: M62, A63 into Hull city centre. At rdbt left onto A1165 (Great Union St), left into Citadel Way. Hotel at end on right

High quality, budget accommodation ideal for both families and business travellers. Spacious, en suite bedrooms feature tea and coffee making facilities, and Freeview TV in most hotels. Internet access and Wi-fi are available for a small fee. The adjacent family restaurant features a wide and varied menu. See also the Hotel Groups pages.

Rooms 136 **D** £55-£62*

Premier Inn Hull North

BUDGET HOTEL

☎ 0871 527 8536 🖷 0871 527 8537
Ashcombe Rd, Kingswood Park HU7 3DD
dir: A63 to town centre, take A1079 N for approx 5m. Right at rdbt onto A1033. Hotel at 2nd rdbt in New Kingswood Park

Rooms 42 **D** £52-£60*

Premier Inn Hull West

BUDGET HOTEL

☎ 0871 527 8538 🖷 0871 527 8539
Ferriby Rd, Hessle HU13 0JA
dir: A63, A15 to Humber Bridge (Beverley & Hessle Viewpoint) Hotel at 1st rdbt

Rooms 61 **D** £52-£60*

KINGSWINFORD

West Midlands **Map 10 SO88**

Premier Inn Dudley (Kingswinford)

BUDGET HOTEL

☎ 0871 527 8314 🖷 0871 527 8315
Dudley Rd DY6 8WT
dir: A4123 to Dudley, A461 follow signs for Russell's Hall Hospital. On A4101 to Kingswinford, hotel opposite Pensnett Trading Estate

High quality, budget accommodation ideal for both families and business travellers. Spacious, en suite bedrooms feature tea and coffee making facilities, and Freeview TV in most hotels. Internet access and Wi-fi are available for a small fee. The adjacent family restaurant features a wide and varied menu. See also the Hotel Groups pages.

Rooms 45 **D** £50-£60*

K

KINGTON Herefordshire Map 9 SO25

Burton

★★★ 74% HOTEL

☎ 01544 230323 🖷 01544 239023
Mill St HR5 3BQ
e-mail: info@burtonhotel.co.uk
web: www.burtonhotel.co.uk
dir: At A44 & A411 rdbt junct follow Town Centre signs

Situated in the town centre, this friendly, privately-owned hotel offers spacious, pleasantly proportioned and well-equipped bedrooms. Smartly presented public areas include a lounge bar, leisure facilities including a swimming pool, and an attractive restaurant where carefully prepared cuisine can be enjoyed. There are function and meeting facilities available in a purpose-built, modern wing.

Rooms 16 (5 fmly) **S** £54-£79; **D** £94-£127 (incl. bkfst)* **Facilities** Spa FTV supervised Putt green Gym Steam room Therapy rooms Xmas New Year Wi-fi **Conf** Class 100 Board 20 Thtr 150 Del from £125 to £130 **Services** Lift **Parking** 50 **Notes** LB Civ Wed 120

KIRKBY FLEETHAM North Yorkshire Map 19 SE29

The Black Horse

RESTAURANT WITH ROOMS

☎ 01609 749010 & 749011 🖷 01423 507836
Lumley Ln DL7 0SH
e-mail: gm@blackhorsekirkbyfleetham.com
web: www.blackhorsekirkbyfleetham.com
dir: A1 onto A684 then Ham Hall Ln. On Lumley Ln, on left past Post Office

Set in a small village, the Black Horse provides everything needed for a getaway break including award-winning food. The spacious bedrooms, named after famous racehorses, are beautifully designed in New England/French style with pastel colours, co-ordinating fabrics and excellent beds; many of the superb bathrooms feature slipper or roll top baths. The inn has a large dining room and bar that attracts locals as well as visitors from further afield.

Rooms 7 (1 fmly)

KIRKBY LONSDALE Cumbria Map 18 SD67

The Whoop Hall

★★ 76% HOTEL

☎ 015242 71284 🖷 015242 72154
Burrow with Burrow LA6 2HP
e-mail: info@whoophall.co.uk
dir: On A65, 1m SE of Kirkby Lonsdale

This popular inn combines traditional charm with modern facilities, that include a very well-equipped leisure complex. Bedrooms, some with four-poster beds, and some housed in converted barns, are appointed to a smart, stylish standard. A fire warms the bar on chillier days, and an interesting choice of dishes is available in both the bar and galleried restaurant throughout the day and evening.

Rooms 24 (4 fmly) (2 GF) **Facilities** supervised Gym Beauty salon Pool table Xmas **Conf** Class 72 Board 56 Thtr 169 **Parking** 100 **Notes** Civ Wed 120

Hipping Hall

RESTAURANT WITH ROOMS

☎ 015242 71187 🖷 015242 72452
Cowan Bridge LA6 2JJ
e-mail: info@hippinghall.com
dir: M6 junct 36 take A65 through Kirkby Lonsdale towards Skipton. On right after Cowan Bridge

Close to the market town of Kirkby Lonsdale, Hipping Hall offers spacious, feature bedrooms, designed in soft shades with sumptuous textures and fabrics; the bathrooms use natural stone, slate and limestone to great effect. There are also three spacious cottage suites that create a real hideaway experience. The sitting room, with large, comfortable sofas has a traditional feel. The restaurant is a 15th-century hall with tapestries and a minstrels' gallery that is as impressive as it is intimate.

Rooms 9 (3 annexe)

Plato's

RESTAURANT WITH ROOMS

☎ 01524 274180
2 Mill Brow LA6 2AT
e-mail: sally@platoskirkby.co.uk
dir: M6 junct 36, A65 signed Kirkby Lonsdale, after 5m at rdbt take 1st exit onto one-way system

Tucked away in the heart of the popular market town Plato's is steeped in history. Sumptuous bedrooms have a wealth of thoughtful extras, and imaginative food is available in the elegant restaurant with its open-plan kitchen. The lounge bar is more rustic in style with fires to relax by. A warm welcome and professional service is assured. The Pop Shop offers Plato's cuisine to take away.

Rooms 8

KIRKHAM Lancashire Map 18 SD43

Premier Inn Blackpool Kirkham M55 Jct 3

BUDGET HOTEL

☎ 0871 527 8104 🖷 0871 527 8105
Fleetwood Rd, Greenhalgh PR4 3HE
dir: M6 junct 32, M55 towards Blackpool. Hotel just off junct 3 towards Kirkham

High quality, budget accommodation ideal for both families and business travellers. Spacious, en suite bedrooms feature tea and coffee making facilities, and Freeview TV in most hotels. Internet access and Wi-fi are available for a small fee. The adjacent family restaurant features a wide and varied menu. See also the Hotel Groups pages.

Rooms 28 **D** £65*

KNARESBOROUGH North Yorkshire Map 19 SE35

General Tarleton Inn

RESTAURANT WITH ROOMS

☎ 01423 340284 🖷 01423 340288
Boroughbridge Rd, Ferrensby HG5 0PZ
e-mail: gti@generaltarleton.co.uk
dir: A1(M) junct 48 at Boroughbridge, take A6055 to Knaresborough. 4m on right

Food is a real feature here with skilfully prepared meals served in the restaurant, traditional bar and modern conservatory. Accommodation is provided in brightly decorated and airy rooms, and the bathrooms are thoughtfully equipped. Enjoying a country location, yet close to the A1(M), the inn remains popular with both business and leisure guests.

Rooms 14

KNIPTON Leicestershire Map 11 SK83

The Manners Arms

RESTAURANT WITH ROOMS

☎ 01476 879222 🖷 01476 879228
Croxton Rd NG32 1RH
e-mail: info@mannersarms.com
web: www.mannersarms.com
dir: Off A607 into Knipton

Part of the Rutland Estate and built as a hunting lodge for the 6th Duke, the Manners Arms offers thoughtfully furnished bedrooms designed by the present Duchess. Public areas include the intimate themed Beater's Bar and attractive Red Coats Restaurant, popular for its imaginative menus.

Rooms 10 (1 fmly)

KNOWSLEY Map 15 SJ49
Merseyside

Suites Hotel Knowsley

THE INDEPENDENTS HOTEL ASSOCIATION

★★★★ 73% HOTEL

☎ 0151 549 2222 🖹 0151 549 1116
Ribblers Ln L34 9HA
e-mail: enquiries@suiteshotelgroup.com
web: www.suiteshotelgroup.com
dir: Off M57 junct 4. Telephone for detailed directions

Located a close to the M57, this hotel is just a 10-minute drive from Liverpool's city centre. It offers superior, well-equipped accommodation and there is a choice of lounges plus Handley's Restaurant. Guests have the use of the impressive leisure centre, and there are extensive conference facilities.

Rooms 101 (39 fmly) (20 GF) (6 smoking) **S** £89-£157; **D** £94-£240 (incl. bkfst)* **Facilities** STV supervised Gym Xmas New Year Wi-fi **Conf** Class 60 Board 50 Thtr 240 Del from £99 to £142* **Services** Lift Air con **Parking** 200 **Notes** LB Civ Wed 140

KNUTSFORD Map 15 SJ77
Cheshire

Cottons Hotel & Spa

shire hotels & spas

★★★★ 78% HOTEL

☎ 01565 650333 🖹 01565 755351
Manchester Rd WA16 0SU
e-mail: cottons@shirehotels.com
web: www.cottonshotel.com
dir: On A50, 1m from M6 junct 19

The superb leisure facilities and quiet location are great attractions at this hotel, which is just a short distance from Manchester Airport. Bedrooms are smartly appointed in various styles, and executive rooms have very good working areas. The hotel has spacious lounge areas and an excellent leisure centre.

Rooms 109 (14 fmly) (38 GF) **S** £100-£200; **D** £110-£210* **Facilities** Spa STV Gym Steam room Activity studio for exercise classes Sauna Children's splash pool Xmas New Year Wi-fi **Conf** Class 100 Board 36 Thtr 200 Del from £135 to £185* **Services** Lift Air con **Parking** 180 **Notes** LB Civ Wed 120

Mere Court Hotel & Conference Centre

★★★★ 77% HOTEL

☎ 01565 831000 🖹 01565 831001
Warrington Rd, Mere WA16 0RW
e-mail: sales@merecourt.co.uk
web: www.merecourt.co.uk
dir: A50, 1m W of junct with A556, on right

This is a smart and attractive hotel, set in extensive, well-tended gardens. The elegant and spacious bedrooms are individually styled and offer a host of thoughtful extras. Conference facilities are particularly impressive and there is a large, self contained, conservatory function suite. Dining is available in the fine dining Arboreum Restaurant.

Rooms 34 (24 fmly) (12 GF) **Facilities** STV Wi-fi **Conf** Class 75 Board 50 Thtr 200 **Services** Lift **Parking** 150 **Notes** Civ Wed 120

See advert on this page

K

KNUTSFORD *continued*

The Longview Hotel & Stuffed Olive Restaurant

★★ 81% HOTEL

☎ 01565 632119 📠 01565 652402
55 Manchester Rd WA16 0LX
e-mail: enquiries@longviewhotel.com
web: www.longviewhotel.com
dir: M6 junct 19 take A556 W towards Chester. Left at lights onto A5033, 1.5m to rdbt then left. Hotel 200yds on right

This friendly Victorian hotel offers high standards of hospitality and service. Attractive public areas include a cellar bar and foyer lounge area. The restaurant has a traditional feel and offers an imaginative selection of dishes. Bedrooms, some located in a superb renovation of nearby houses, are individually styled and offer a good range of thoughtful amenities, including broadband internet access.

Rooms 32 (19 annexe) (1 fmly) (5 GF) **S** £92; **D** £112 (incl. bkfst)* **Facilities** FTV Wi-fi **Conf** Class 20 Board 20 Del from £130 to £170* **Parking** 20 **Notes** LB RS 19 Dec-4 Jan

K

Premier Inn Knutsford (Bucklow Hill)

BUDGET HOTEL

☎ 0871 527 8572 📠 0871 527 8573
Bucklow Hill WA16 6RD
dir: M6 junct 19, A556 towards Manchester Airport & Stockport

High quality, budget accommodation ideal for both families and business travellers. Spacious, en suite bedrooms feature tea and coffee making facilities, and Freeview TV in most hotels. Internet access and Wi-fi are available for a small fee. The adjacent family restaurant features a wide and varied menu. See also the Hotel Groups pages.

Rooms 69 **D** £57*

Premier Inn Knutsford (Mere)

BUDGET HOTEL

☎ 0871 527 8574 📠 0871 527 8575
Warrington Rd, Hoo Green, Mere WA16 0PZ
dir: M6 junct 19, A556, follow Manchester signs. At 1st lights left onto A50 towards Warrington. Hotel 1m on right

Rooms 28 **D** £57*

LANCASTER
Lancashire — Map 18 SD46

Lancaster House

★★★★ 76% HOTEL

☎ 01524 844822 📠 01524 844766
Green Ln, Ellel LA1 4GJ
e-mail: lancaster@elhmail.co.uk
web: www.elh.co.uk/hotels/lancaster
dir: M6 junct 33 N towards Lancaster. Through Galgate, into Green Ln. Hotel before university on right

This modern hotel enjoys a rural setting south of the city and close to the university. The attractive open-plan reception and lounge boast a roaring log fire in colder months. Bedrooms are spacious, and include 19 rooms that are particularly well equipped for business guests. There are leisure facilities with a hot tub and a function suite.

Rooms 99 (29 fmly) (44 GF) **Facilities** Spa STV supervised Gym Beauty salon Xmas New Year Wi-fi **Conf** Class 60 Board 48 Thtr 250 **Parking** 120 **Notes** LB Civ Wed 140

Holiday Inn Lancaster

★★★ 79% HOTEL

☎ 01524 541325 & 0871 942 9047
📠 01524 841265
Waterside Park, Caton Rd LA1 3RA
e-mail: reservations-lancaster@ihg.com
web: www.holidayinn.co.uk
dir: M6 junct 34 towards Lancaster. Hotel 1st on right

Close to the M6 and Lancaster, this modern hotel caters well for business and leisure guests, including families. The ground floor is open plan, with an informal atmosphere in the lounge-bar and Traders restaurant. The Spirit Health Club features a 15-metre pool, sauna, steam room, beauty treatment rooms and a well-equipped gym.

Rooms 156 (72 fmly) (25 GF) (8 smoking) **Facilities** STV supervised Gym Fitness classes Xmas New Year Wi-fi **Conf** Class 60 Board 60 Thtr 120 **Services** Lift Air con **Parking** 200 **Notes** Civ Wed 110

Penny Street Bridge

★★★ 73% TOWN HOUSE HOTEL

☎ 01524 599900 📠 01524 599901
Penny St LA1 1XT
e-mail: relax@pennystreetbridge.co.uk
dir: In town centre

Ideally situated in the heart of the city, Penny Street Bridge has been transformed from a typical Victorian property to one that is fresh and contemporary, yet retains all the elegance of its original era. Bedrooms are modern and very well equipped. The stylish Bar & Brasserie are popular with both guests and local residents, serving meals and light bites throughout the day.

Rooms 28 (2 fmly) **S** £69-£95; **D** £75-£101 (incl. bkfst)* **Facilities** FTV Wi-fi **Services** Lift Air con **Parking** 4 **Notes** LB

The Royal Kings Arms

★★★ 70% HOTEL

☎ 01524 32451 📠 01524 841698
Market St LA1 1HP
e-mail: reservations.lancaster@ohiml.com
web: www.oxfordhotelsandinns.com
dir: M6 junct 33, A6 to city centre, 1st left, after Market Hotel. Hotel at lights before Lancaster Castle

A distinctive period building located in the town centre, close to the castle. Bedrooms are comfortable and suitable for both business and leisure guests. Public areas include a small lounge on the ground floor and The Castle Bar and Brasserie Restaurant on the first floor. The hotel also has a private car park.

Rooms 55 (14 fmly) **Facilities** FTV Xmas Wi-fi **Conf** Class 60 Board 40 Thtr 100 **Services** Lift **Parking** 26 **Notes** Civ Wed 100

Premier Inn Lancaster

BUDGET HOTEL

☎ 0871 527 8576 📠 0871 527 8577
Lancaster Business Park, Caton Rd LA1 3PE
dir: M6 junct 34, A683 towards Lancaster. Hotel 0.25m on left at entrance to Business Park

High quality, budget accommodation ideal for both families and business travellers. Spacious, en suite bedrooms feature tea and coffee making facilities, and Freeview TV in most hotels. Internet access and Wi-fi are available for a small fee. The adjacent family restaurant features a wide and varied menu. See also the Hotel Groups pages.

Rooms 85 **D** £57-£59*

LAND'S END — Map 2 SW32
Cornwall

The Land's End Hotel

★★★ 71% HOTEL

☎ 01736 871844 📠 01736 871599
TR19 7AA
e-mail: reservations@landsendhotel.co.uk
web: www.landsendhotel.co.uk
dir: From Penzance take A30, follow Land's End signs. After Sennen 1m to Land's End

This famous location provides a memorable setting for this well-established hotel. Bedrooms, many with stunning views of the Atlantic, are pleasantly decorated and comfortable. Refurbished public areas provide plenty of style and comfort with the relaxing lounge and convivial bar. The restaurant is equally impressive with accomplished cuisine complementing the amazing views out to sea.

Rooms 32 (2 fmly) **Facilities** Free entry to Land's End Visitor Centre Xmas New Year **Conf** Class 100 Board 50 Thtr 200 **Parking** 1000 **Notes** Civ Wed 110

LANGAR — Map 11 SK73
Nottinghamshire

Langar Hall

★★★ 81% ◎◎ HOTEL

☎ 01949 860559 📠 01949 861045
NG13 9HG
e-mail: info@langarhall.co.uk
web: www.langarhall.com
dir: Via Bingham from A52 or Cropwell Bishop from A46, both signed. Hotel behind church

This delightful hotel enjoys a picturesque rural location, yet is only a short drive from Nottingham. Individually styled bedrooms are furnished with fine period pieces and benefit from some thoughtful extras. There is a choice of lounges, warmed by real fires, and a snug little bar. Imaginative food is served in a dining room and the garden conservatory provides a lighter menu.

Rooms 12 (1 fmly) (1 GF) **Facilities** FTV Fishing Xmas New Year Wi-fi **Conf** Class 16 Board 12 Thtr 16 **Parking** 20 **Notes** Civ Wed 50

LANGHO — Map 18 SD73
Lancashire

INSPECTORS' CHOICE

Northcote

★★★★ ◎◎◎◎ SMALL HOTEL

☎ 01254 240555 📠 01254 246568
Northcote Rd BB6 8BE
e-mail: reception@northcote.com
web: www.northcote.com
dir: M6 junct 31, 9m to Northcote. Follow Clitheroe (A59) signs, Hotel on left before rdbt

This is a gastronomic haven where guests return to sample the delights of its famous kitchen. The outstanding cooking includes Lancashire's finest fare, and fruit and herbs from the hotel's own beautifully laid out organic gardens. Drinks can be enjoyed in the comfortable, elegantly furnished lounges and bar. Each of the luxury bedrooms has its own identity with sumptuous fabrics and soft furnishings, sophisticated lighting and ultra modern bathrooms; some have a garden patio.

Rooms 14 (2 fmly) (4 GF) **S** £179.50-£220.50; **D** £215.50-£267 (incl. bkfst)* **Facilities** STV FTV Wi-fi **Conf** Class 10 Board 22 Thtr 36 **Parking** 50 **Notes** LB ⊗ Closed 25 Dec Civ Wed 40

See advert on page 252

Best Western Mytton Fold Hotel and Golf Complex

★★★ 🅰 HOTEL

☎ 01254 240662 & 245392 📠 01254 248119
Whalley Rd BB6 8AB
e-mail: reception@myttonfold.co.uk
web: www.myttonfold.co.uk
dir: At large rdbt on A59, follow signs for Whalley, exit into Whalley Rd. Hotel on right

Rooms 43 (12 fmly) (10 GF) **Facilities** STV ⛳ 18 Putt green Wi-fi **Conf** Class 60 Board 40 Thtr 290 **Services** Lift **Parking** 300 **Notes** LB ⊗ Closed 24-26 Dec & 1 Jan Civ Wed 150

L

LASTINGHAM
North Yorkshire **Map 19 SE79**

Lastingham Grange

★★★ 81% HOTEL

☎ 01751 417345 & 417402 📠 01751 417358
YO62 6TH
e-mail: reservations@lastinghamgrange.com
dir: From A170 follow signs for Appleton-le-Moors, continue into Lastingham, pass church on left, right, then left up hill. Hotel on right

A warm welcome and sincere hospitality have been the hallmarks of this hotel for over 50 years. Antique furniture is plentiful, and the lounge and the dining room both look out onto the terrace and sunken rose garden below. There is a large play area for older children and the moorland views are breathtaking.

Rooms 12 (2 fmly) **S** £100-£135; **D** £150-£199 (incl. bkfst)* **Facilities** FTV Large adventure playground Wi-fi **Parking** 30 **Notes** LB Closed Dec-Feb

LAUNCESTON
Cornwall **Map 3 SX38**

See also **Lifton**

Eagle House

★★ 74% SMALL HOTEL

☎ 01566 772036 & 774488 📠 01566 772036
Castle St PL15 8BA
e-mail: eaglehousehotel@aol.com
dir: From Launceston on Holsworthy Rd follow brown hotel signs

Next to the castle, this elegant Georgian house dates back to 1767 and is within walking distance of all the local amienties. Many of the bedrooms have wonderful views over the Cornish countryside. A short carte is served each evening in the restaurant.

Rooms 14 (1 fmly) **S** £47-£49; **D** £72 (incl. bkfst)* **Facilities** Wi-fi **Conf** Class 170 Board 170 Thtr 170 **Parking** 80 **Notes** Civ Wed 170

LAVENHAM
Suffolk **Map 13 TL94**

The Swan

★★★★ 83% HOTEL

☎ 01787 247477 📠 01787 248286
High St CO10 9QA
e-mail: info@theswanatlavenham.co.uk
web: www.theswanatlavenham.co.uk
dir: From Bury St Edmunds take A134 (S), then A1141 to Lavenham

A delightful collection of listed buildings dating back to the 14th century, lovingly restored to retain their original charm. Public rooms include comfortable lounge areas, a charming rustic bar, an informal brasserie and a fine-dining restaurant. Bedrooms are tastefully furnished and equipped with many thoughtful touches. The friendly staff are helpful, attentive and offer professional service.

Rooms 45 (11 fmly) (13 GF) **S** £95-£155; **D** £180-£300 (incl. bkfst)* **Facilities** STV FTV Xmas New Year Wi-fi **Conf** Class 36 Board 30 Thtr 50 Del from £165 to £185* **Parking** 62 **Notes** Civ Wed 100

Lavenham Great House 'Restaurant With Rooms'

RESTAURANT WITH ROOMS

☎ 01787 247431 📠 01787 248007
Market Place CO10 9QZ
e-mail: info@greathouse.co.uk
web: www.greathouse.co.uk
dir: Off A1141 onto Market Ln, behind cross on Market Place

The 18th-century frontage on Market Place conceals a 15th-century timber-framed building that is a restaurant with rooms. The Great House remains a pocket of France offering high-quality rural cuisine served by French staff. The spacious bedrooms are individually decorated and thoughtfully equipped with many useful extras; some rooms have a separate lounge area.

Rooms 5 (1 fmly)

The Angel

RESTAURANT WITH ROOMS

☎ 01787 247388 📠 01787 248344
Market Place CO10 9QZ
e-mail: angel@maypolehotels.com
web: www.maypolehotels.com
dir: From A14 onto A143 signed Bury E & Sudbury. In 4m take A1141 to Lavenham. Establishment off High Street

A delightful 15th-century property overlooking the market place in the heart of this historic medieval town. The Angel is well known for its cuisine and offers an imaginative menu based on fresh ingredients. Public rooms include a residents' lounge and open-plan bar/dining area. Bedrooms are tastefully furnished, attractively decorated and thoughtfully equipped.

Rooms 8 (1 fmly)

LEA MARSTON
Warwickshire **Map 10 SP29**

Lea Marston Hotel

★★★★ 76% HOTEL

☎ 01675 470468 📠 01675 470871
Haunch Ln B76 0BY
e-mail: info@leamarstonhotel.co.uk
web: www.leamarstonhotel.co.uk
dir: M42 junct 9, A4097 to Kingsbury. Hotel signed 1.5m on right

Excellent access to the motorway network and a good range of sports facilities make this hotel a popular choice for conferences and leisure breaks. Bedrooms are mostly set around an attractive quadrangle and are generously equipped. Diners can choose between the popular Sportsman's Lounge Bar and the elegant Adderley Restaurant.

Rooms 88 (18 fmly) (49 GF) **S** £62-£142; **D** £72-£152 (incl. bkfst)* **Facilities** Spa FTV 9 Putt green Gym Golf driving range Golf simulator Xmas New Year Wi-fi **Conf** Class 50 Board 30 Thtr 140 Del from £130 to £170 **Services** Lift **Parking** 200 **Notes** LB Civ Wed 100

LEAMINGTON SPA (ROYAL) Map 10 SP36
Warwickshire

INSPECTORS' CHOICE

Mallory Court

★★★ ®®® HOTEL

L

☎ 01926 330214 🖷 01926 451714
Harbury Ln, Bishop's Tachbrook CV33 9QB
e-mail: reception@mallory.co.uk
web: www.mallory.co.uk
dir: M40 junct 13 N'bound left, left again towards Bishops Tachbrook, right into Harbury Ln after 0.5m. M40 junct 14 S'bound A452 to Leamington, at 2nd rdbt left into Harbury Ln

With its tranquil rural setting, this elegant Lutyens-style country house is an idyllic retreat. Set in ten acres of landscaped gardens with immaculate lawns and an orchard. Relaxation is easy in the two sumptuous lounges, drawing room or conservatory. Dining is a treat in either the elegant restaurant or the brasserie. Simon Haigh heads up a team of expert chefs producing dishes that continue to delight. Bedrooms in the main house are luxuriously decorated and most have wonderful views. Those in the Knights Suite are more contemporary and have their own access via a smart conference and banqueting facility.

Rooms 30 (11 annexe) (2 fmly) (4 GF) **S** fr £129; **D** £149-£475 (incl. bkfst)* **Facilities** FTV Use of nearby club facilities Xmas New Year Wi-fi **Conf** Class 160 Board 50 Thtr 200 Del from £165 to £355* **Services** Lift **Parking** 100 **Notes** LB ⊗ Civ Wed 160

Angel Hotel

★★★ 77% HOTEL

☎ 01926 881296 🖷 01926 313853
143 Regent St CV32 4NZ
e-mail: angelhotel143@hotmail.com
web: www.angelhotelleamington.co.uk
dir: In town centre at junct of Regent St & Holly Walk

This centrally located hotel is divided in two parts - the original inn and a more modern extension. Public rooms include a comfortable foyer lounge area, a smart restaurant and an informal bar. Bedrooms are individual in style, and, whether modern or traditional, all have the expected facilities.

Rooms 48 (3 fmly) (3 GF) **S** £59-£85; **D** £79-£105 (incl. bkfst)* **Facilities** STV FTV Xmas **Conf** Class 40 Board 40 Thtr 70 **Services** Lift **Parking** 38 **Notes** LB

Best Western Falstaff

★★★ 71% HOTEL

☎ 01926 312044 🖷 01926 450574
16-20 Warwick New Rd CV32 5JQ
e-mail: sales@falstaffhotel.com
web: www.falstaffhotel.com
dir: M40 junct 13 or 14, follow Leamington Spa signs. Over 4 rdbts, under bridge. Left into Princes Dr, right at mini-rdbt

Bedrooms at this hotel come in a variety of sizes and styles and are well equipped, with many thoughtful extras. Snacks can be taken in the relaxing lounge bar, and an interesting selection of English and continental dishes is offered in the restaurant; 24-hour room service is also available. Conference and banqueting facilities are extensive.

Rooms 63 (2 fmly) (16 GF) **Facilities** FTV Arrangement with local health club Xmas New Year Wi-fi **Conf** Class 30 Board 30 Thtr 70 **Parking** 50 **Notes** Civ Wed 60

LEATHERHEAD Map 6 TQ15
Surrey

Bookham Grange Hotel

★★ 67% HOTEL

☎ 01372 452742 & 459899 🖷 01372 450080
Little Bookham Common, Bookham KT23 3HS
e-mail: bookhamgrange@easynet.co.uk
web: www.bookham-grange.co.uk
dir: Off A246 at Bookham High St onto Church Rd, 1st right after Bookham railway station

This smart property enjoys a tranquil setting yet is only a short drive from Leatherhead, Guildford and Epsom, with good access to the M25 and London's major airports. Bedrooms are generally spacious and all are smartly appointed. Public areas include a lounge, bar and restaurant as well as conference and meeting facilities. Weddings are well catered for.

Rooms 27 (3 fmly) **Facilities** Xmas New Year Wi-fi **Conf** Class 30 Board 24 Thtr 80 **Parking** 60 **Notes** ⊗ Civ Wed 100

LEDBURY Map 10 SO73
Herefordshire

Verzon House

★★★ 86% ®® HOTEL

☎ 01531 670381 🖷 01531 670830
Hereford Rd, Trumpet HR8 2PZ
e-mail: info@verzonhouse.com
web: www.verzonhouse.com
dir: M5 junct 8/M50 junct 2, follow Hereford/A438 signs. Hotel on right

Dating back to 1790 this elegant establishment stands in extensive gardens with far-reaching views over the Malvern Hills. Bedrooms are very well appointed and spacious; one has a four-poster bed. Stylish public areas include the popular bar and brasserie restaurant where a range of well-executed dishes can be enjoyed.

Rooms 8 (1 fmly) **Facilities** FTV Wi-fi **Conf** Class 15 Board 24 Thtr 50 Del from £195 to £210 **Parking** 70 **Notes** ⊗ No children 8yrs Civ Wed 50

Feathers

★★★ 81% ® HOTEL

☎ 01531 635266 & 638950 🖷 01531 638955
High St HR8 1DS
e-mail: mary@feathers-ledbury.co.uk
web: www.feathers-ledbury.co.uk
dir: S from Worcester on A449, E from Hereford on A438, N from Gloucester on A417. Hotel in town centre

A wealth of authentic features can be found at this historic timber-framed hotel, set in the middle of town. The comfortably equipped bedrooms are tastefully decorated; in the grounds are Eve's Cottage, and Lanark House, a two-bedroom apartment that is ideal for families and self catering use. Well-prepared meals can be taken in Fuggles Brasserie with its adjoining bar, and breakfast is served in Quills Restaurant.

Rooms 22 (3 annexe) (2 fmly) **S** £92.50-£127.50; **D** £137.50-£234 (incl. bkfst) **Facilities** STV Gym Steam room New Year Wi-fi **Conf** Class 80 Board 40 Thtr 140 Del from £120 **Parking** 30 **Notes** LB Civ Wed 100

LEEDS
West Yorkshire
Map 19 SE23

See also **Gomersal, Shipley & Wakefield**

Thorpe Park Hotel & Spa

★★★★ 84% HOTEL

☎ 0113 264 1000 0113 264 1010
Century Way, Thorpe Park LS15 8ZB
e-mail: thorpepark@shirehotels.com
web: www.thorpeparkhotel.com
dir: M1 junct 46, follow signs off rdbt for Thorpe Park

Conveniently close to the M1, this hotel offers bedrooms that are modern in both style and facilities. The terrace and courtyard offer all-day casual dining and refreshments, and the restaurant features a Mediterranean-themed menu. There is also a state-of-the-art spa and leisure facility.

Rooms 111 (3 fmly) (25 GF) **S** £100-£200; **D** £110-£210* **Facilities** Spa STV Gym Activity studio Steam room Sauna New Year Wi-fi **Conf** Class 100 Board 50 Thtr 200 **Services** Lift Air con **Parking** 200 **Notes** LB Civ Wed 150

De Vere Oulton Hall

★★★★ 83% HOTEL

☎ 0113 282 1000 0113 282 8066
Rothwell Ln, Oulton LS26 8HN
e-mail: oulton.hall@devere-hotels.com
web: www.devere.co.uk
dir: 2m from M62 junct 30, follow Rothwell signs, then 'Oulton 1m' sign. 1st exit at next 2 rdbts. Hotel on left. Or 1m from M1 junct 44, follow Castleford & Pontefract signs on A639

Surrounded by the beautiful Yorkshire Dales, yet only 15 minutes from the city centre, this elegant 19th-century house offers the best of both worlds. Impressive features include stylish, opulent day rooms and delightful formal gardens, which have been restored to their original design. The hotel boasts a choice of dining options, extensive leisure facilities and golfers can book preferential tee times at the adjacent golf club.

Rooms 152 **Facilities** 27 Gym 9 treatment rooms Beauty therapy Aerobics Xmas New Year **Conf** Class 150 Board 40 Thtr 350 **Services** Lift Air con **Parking** 260 **Notes** Civ Wed 200

Mint Hotel Leeds

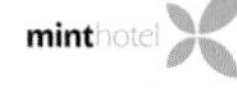

★★★★ 80% HOTEL

☎ 0113 241 1000
Granary Wharf, 2 Wharf Aproach LS1 4BR
e-mail: leeds.reservations@minthotel.com
dir: M1 junct 43 onto M621, follow Leeds (Centre)/ M621 signs. At junct 3 exit towards Holbeck. Merge onto A653 (Dewsbury road), into Neville St. 1st left at lights into Water Ln. 2nd right into Wharf Approach, over bridge, to hotel on right

This large, modern hotel is conveniently located next to both the canal and the railway station, and just a few minutes' walk from the city centre. Contemporary, air-conditioned bedrooms feature iMacs and complimentary high speed Wi-fi. Spacious public areas include meeting rooms and the popular City Café restaurant offering notable modern, British cuisine with alfresco eating possible in the warmer months. Guests can relax and take refreshments in the sky lounge on the 13th floor which offers stunning panoramic views.

Rooms 333 **S** £65-£165; **D** £65-£185* **Facilities** STV FTV Gym Wi-fi **Conf** Class 140 Board 30 Thtr 300 Del from £120 to £200* **Services** Lift Air con **Parking** 55 **Notes** LB Civ Wed 200

The Queens

★★★★ 80% HOTEL

☎ 0113 243 1323 0113 243 5315
City Square LS1 1PJ
e-mail: queensreservations@qhotels.co.uk
web: www.qhotels.co.uk
dir: M621, M1 & M62 follow signs for city centre & rail station, along Neville St towards City Square. Under rail bridge, at lights left into slip road in front of hotel

A legacy from the golden age of railways and located in the heart of the city, overlooking City Square. This grand Victorian hotel retains much of its original splendour. Public rooms include the spacious lounge bar, a range of conference and function rooms along with the grand Ballroom. Bedrooms vary in size but all are very well equipped, and there is a choice of suites available.

Rooms 215 (16 fmly) **Facilities** STV Xmas New Year Wi-fi **Conf** Class 255 Board 80 Thtr 600 **Services** Lift Air con **Parking** 80 **Notes** Civ Wed 600

Leeds Marriott Hotel

★★★★ 74% HOTEL

☎ 0113 236 6366 0113 236 6367
4 Trevelyan Square, Boar Ln LS1 6ET
e-mail: london.regional.reservations@marriott.com
web: www.leedsmarriott.co.uk
dir: M621/M1 junct 3. Follow signs for city centre on A653. Stay in right lane. Energis building on left, turn right, follow signs to hotel

With a charming courtyard setting in the heart of the city, this modern, elegant hotel provides the perfect base for shopping and sightseeing. Air-conditioned bedrooms are tastefully decorated and offer good workspace. Public areas include a leisure club, an informal bar, lobby lounge area and a choice of restaurants including Georgetown which offers Colonial Malaysian cuisine. Valet parking is available.

Rooms 244 (29 fmly) (10 smoking) **Facilities** STV supervised Gym Sauna Steam Room Wi-fi **Conf** Class 144 Board 80 Thtr 300 Del from £139* **Services** Lift Air con **Notes** Civ Wed 300

Radisson Blu Hotel Leeds

★★★★ 74% HOTEL

☎ 0113 236 6000 0113 236 6100
No 1 The Light, The Headrow LS1 8TL
e-mail: sales.leeds@radissonblu.com
web: www.radissonblu.co.uk
dir: Follow city centre 'loop' towards The Headrow/ Light Complex. Hotel access on Cockeridge St off The Headrow

Situated in the shopping complex known as 'The Light', the hotel occupies a converted building that was formerly the headquarters of the Leeds Permanent Building Society. Three styles of bedrooms are available but all have air conditioning and excellent business facilities. The lobby bar area serves substantial meals and is ideal for relaxation. Public parking is available, contact the hotel for details.

Rooms 147 (9 smoking) **S** £75-£125; **D** £85-£135* **Facilities** STV FTV Gym Access to Esporta Health Club Xmas New Year Wi-fi **Conf** Class 30 Board 28 Thtr 60 Del from £139 to £159* **Services** Lift Air con **Notes** LB Civ Wed

LEEDS *continued*

Crowne Plaza Hotel Leeds

★★★★ 73% HOTEL

☎ 0871 942 9170 📠 0113 244 0460
Wellington St LS1 4DL
e-mail: sales.cpleeds@ihg.com
web: www.crowneplaza.co.uk
dir: From M1 follow signs to city centre. Left at City Sq into Wellington St

With easy access to the motorway and city centre, this modern hotel is an ideal choice for the business traveller. Bedrooms are of a good size with excellent facilities including air conditioning. There's a good sized pool and large gym - both are well worth a visit.

Rooms 135 (38 fmly) **Facilities** Spa STV Gym Xmas New Year Wi-fi **Conf** Class 80 Board 60 Thtr 180 **Services** Lift Air con **Parking** 120 **Notes** Civ Wed 180

The Met

PH | principal hayley

★★★★ 73% HOTEL

☎ 0113 245 0841 📠 0113 242 5156
King St LS1 2HQ
e-mail: metropole.sales@principal-hotels.com
web: www.principal-hotels.com
dir: From M1, M62 & M621 follow city centre signs. A65 into Wellington St. At 1st traffic island right into King St, hotel on right

Said to be the best example of this type of building in the city, this splendid terracotta-fronted hotel is centrally located and convenient for the railway station. All bedrooms are appointed to suit the business traveller, with hi-speed internet access and a working area. The Restaurant and the Tempest Bar make convenient dining options. There are impressive conference and banqueting facilities. Some parking space is available.

Rooms 120 **S** £50-£149; **D** £69-£169* **Facilities** STV FTV Wi-fi **Conf** Class 100 Board 80 Thtr 250 Del from £100 to £179 **Services** Lift **Parking** 40 **Notes** LB ⊗ RS 24 Dec-1 Jan Civ Wed 200

Park Plaza Leeds

Park Plaza Hotels & Resorts

★★★★ 71% HOTEL

☎ 0113 380 4000 📠 0113 380 4100
Boar Ln LS1 5NS
e-mail: pplinfo@parkplazahotels.co.uk
web: www.parkplaza.com
dir: Follow signs for city centre

Chic, stylish, ultra modern, city-centre hotel located just opposite City Square. Chino Latino, located on the first floor, is a fusion Far East and modern Japanese restaurant with a Latino bar. Stylish, air-conditioned bedrooms are spacious and have a range of modern facilities, including high-speed internet connection.

Rooms 185 **Facilities** STV Gym Wi-fi **Conf** Class 70 Board 40 Thtr 160 **Services** Lift Air con **Notes** Civ Wed 120

Malmaison Leeds

★★★ 83% ⊛ HOTEL

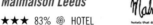

☎ 0113 398 1000 📠 0113 398 1002
1 Swinegate LS1 4AG
e-mail: leeds@malmaison.com
web: www.malmaison.com
dir: M621/M1 junct 3, follow city centre signs. At KPMG building, right into Sovereign Street. Hotel at end on right

Close to the waterfront, this stylish property offers striking bedrooms with CD players and air conditioning. The popular bar and brasserie feature vaulted ceilings, intimate lighting and offer a choice of a full three-course meal or a substantial snack. Service is both willing and friendly. A small fitness centre and impressive meeting rooms complete the package.

Rooms 100 (4 fmly) **Facilities** STV Gym Xmas New Year Wi-fi **Conf** Class 20 Board 24 Thtr 45 **Services** Lift Air con **Notes** LB Civ Wed 40

Best Western Milford Hotel

★★★ 81% HOTEL

☎ 01977 681800 📠 01977 681245
A1 Great North Rd, Peckfield LS25 5LQ
e-mail: enquiries@mlh.co.uk
web: www.mlh.co.uk

(For full entry see Garforth)

Novotel Leeds Centre

★★★ 80% HOTEL

☎ 0113 242 6446 📠 0113 242 6445
4 Whitehall, Whitehall Quay LS1 4HR
e-mail: H3270@accor.com
web: www.novotel.com
dir: M621 junct 3, follow signs to rail station. Into Aire St & left at lights

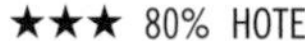

With a minimalist style, this contemporary hotel provides a quality, value-for-money experience close to the city centre. Spacious, climate-controlled bedrooms are provided, whilst public areas offer deep leather sofas and an eye-catching water feature in reception. Light snacks are provided in the airy bar, and the restaurant doubles as a bistro. Staff are committed to guest care and nothing is too much trouble.

Rooms 195 (50 fmly) **Facilities** Gym Playstation in rooms Play area Steam room Xmas **Conf** Class 50 Board 50 Thtr 100 **Services** Lift Air con **Parking** 140 **Notes** Civ Wed 70

The Cosmopolitan

★★★ 78% HOTEL

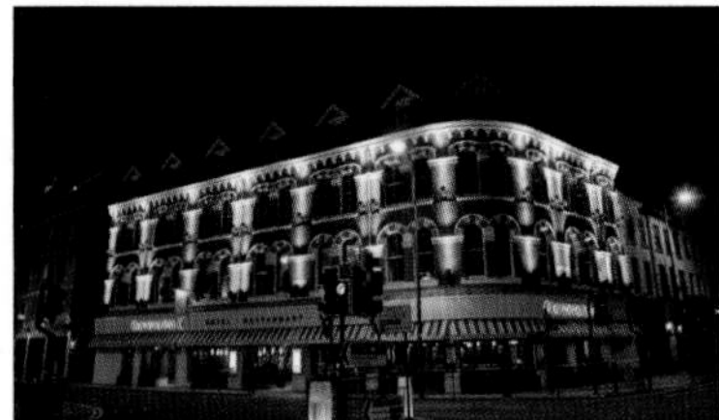

☎ 0113 243 6454 📠 0113 243 4241
2 Lower Briggate LS1 4AE
e-mail: info@cosmopolitan-hotel-leeds.com
web: www.cosmopolitan-hotel-leeds.com
dir: M621 junct 3. Keep in right lane. Follow until road splits into 4 lanes. Keep right, right at lights (ASDA House on left). Left at lights. Over bridge, turn left, hotel opposite. Parking in 150mtrs

This smartly presented, Victorian building is located on the south side of the city. The well-equipped bedrooms offer a choice of standard or executive grades. Staff are friendly and helpful ensuring a warm and welcoming atmosphere. Discounted overnight parking is provided in the adjacent 24-hour car park.

Rooms 89 (5 fmly) (14 smoking) **S** £89-£115; **D** £99-£130 (incl. bkfst)* **Facilities** STV FTV Xmas Wi-fi **Conf** Class 45 Board 40 Thtr 120 Del from £99 to £145* **Services** Lift

Bewleys Hotel Leeds

★★★ 75% HOTEL

☎ 0113 234 2340 📠 0113 234 2349
City Walk, Sweet St LS11 9AT
e-mail: leeds@bewleyshotels.com
web: www.bewleyshotels.com
dir: M621 junct 3, at 2nd lights left into Sweet St, right & right again

Located on the edge of the city centre, this hotel has the added advantage of secure underground parking. Bedrooms are spacious and comfortable with an extensive room service menu. Downstairs, the light and airy bar lounge leads into a brasserie where a wide selection of popular dishes is offered. High quality meeting rooms are also available.

Rooms 334 (99 fmly) **Facilities** Xmas New Year Wi-fi **Conf** Class 36 Board 18 Thtr 40 **Services** Lift **Parking** 160 **Notes** LB ⊗ Closed 24-29 Dec Civ Wed

Chevin Country Park Hotel & Spa

★★★ 74% HOTEL

☎ 01943 467818 📠 01943 850335
Yorkgate LS21 3NU
e-mail: chevin@crerarhotels.com

(For full entry see Otley)

The New Ellington

U

☎ 0844 815 9838 📠 0844 815 9836
23-25 York Place LS1 2EY
e-mail: info.thenewellington@bespokehotels.com

Currently the rating for this establishment is not confirmed. This may be due to a change of ownership or because it has only recently joined the AA rating scheme. For further details please see the AA website: theAA.com

Rooms 35

Holiday Inn Express Leeds City Centre

BUDGET HOTEL

☎ 0113 242 6200 📠 0113 242 6300
Cavendish St LS3 1LY
e-mail: reservations@expressleeds.co.uk
web: www.hiexpress.com/leedscityctr
dir: M621 junct 2, A643 to city centre. At large rdbt 3rd exit signed A58(M). 1st left onto A65. Right after pedestrian crossing & right again

A modern hotel ideal for families and business travellers. Fresh and uncomplicated, the spacious rooms include Sky TV, power shower and tea and coffee-making facilities. Continental buffet breakfast is included in the room rate; other meals may be taken at the nearby family pub or restaurant. See also the Hotel Groups pages.

Rooms 112 (44 fmly) **Conf** Class 15 Board 20 Thtr 35

Holiday Inn Express Leeds City Centre Armouries

BUDGET HOTEL

☎ 0113 380 4400 📠 0113 380 4455
Armouries Dr LS10 1LT
e-mail: leeds@holidayinnexpress.org.uk
web: www.hiexpress.com/leeds
dir: M1 junct 43, follow Royal Armouries brown tourist signs. M621 junct 4 follow Leeds City Centre signs to A61

Rooms 130 (72 fmly) (19 smoking) **Conf** Class 18 Board 20 Thtr 30

Holiday Inn Express Leeds - East

BUDGET HOTEL

☎ 0845 112 6039 📠 0845 393 4178
Aberford Rd, Oulton LS26 8EJ
e-mail: reservations@hiexpressleedseast.co.uk
web: www.hiexpressleedseast.co.uk
dir: M62 junct 29, E towards Pontefract. Exit at junct 30, A642 signed Rothwell. Lodge opposite at 1st rdbt

Rooms 77 **Conf** Thtr 40

Ibis Leeds Centre

BUDGET HOTEL

☎ 0113 220 4100 📠 0113 220 4110
Marlborough St LS1 4PB
e-mail: H3652@accor.com
web: www.ibishotel.com
dir: M1 junct 43 or M62 junct 2 take A643, follow city centre signs. Left on slip road opposite Yorkshire Post. Hotel opposite

Modern, budget hotel offering comfortable accommodation in bright and practical bedrooms. Breakfast is self-service and dinner is available in the restaurant See also the Hotel Groups pages.

Rooms 168 (14 fmly)

Premier Inn Leeds/ Bradford Airport

BUDGET HOTEL

☎ 0871 527 8578 📠 0871 527 8579
Victoria Av, Yeadon LS19 7AW
dir: On A658, near Leeds/Bradford Airport

High quality, budget accommodation ideal for both families and business travellers. Spacious, en suite bedrooms feature tea and coffee making facilities, and Freeview TV in most hotels. Internet access and Wi-fi are available for a small fee. The adjacent family restaurant features a wide and varied menu. See also the Hotel Groups pages.

Rooms 60 **D** £52-£60*

Premier Inn Leeds/Bradford (South)

BUDGET HOTEL

☎ 0871 527 8580 📠 0871 527 8581
Wakefield Rd, Drighlington BD11 1EA
dir: On Drighlington bypass, adjacent to M62 junct 27. Take A650, right to Drighlington, right, hotel on left

Rooms 42 **D** £52-£59*

Premier Inn Leeds City Centre

BUDGET HOTEL

☎ 0871 527 8582 📠 0871 527 8583
Citygate, Wellington St LS3 1LW
dir: At A65 & A58 junct

Rooms 140 **D** £60-£69*

Premier Inn Leeds City West

BUDGET HOTEL

☎ 0871 527 8584 📠 0871 527 8585
City West One Office Park, Gelderd Rd LS12 6LX
dir: M621 junct 1 take ring road towards Leeds. At 1st lights right into Gelderd Rd, right at rdbt

Rooms 126 **D** £52-£64*

Premier Inn Leeds East

BUDGET HOTEL

☎ 0871 527 8586 📠 0871 527 8587
Selby Rd, Whitkirk LS15 7AY
dir: M1 junct 46 towards Leeds. At 2nd rdbt follow Temple Newsam signs. Hotel 500mtrs on right

Rooms 87 **D** £52-£59*

L

LEEK Staffordshire

Map 16 SJ95

Three Horseshoes Inn & Country Hotel

★★★ 77% ◎◎ HOTEL

☎ 01538 300296 📠 01538 300320
Buxton Rd, Blackshaw Moor ST13 8TW
e-mail: enquires@threeshoesinn.co.uk
web: www.threeshoesinn.co.uk
dir: 2m N of Leek on A53

This traditional, family-owned hostelry provides stylish, individually designed, modern bedrooms, including several four-poster rooms. The smart brasserie, with an open kitchen and countryside views, offers modern English and Thai dishes, and there is also a pub and carvery; the award-winning

continued

LEEK *continued*

gardens and grounds are ideal for alfresco dining. The staff are attentive and friendly.

Rooms 26 (2 fmly) (10 GF) **S** £77.50-£113; **D** £85-£156 (incl. bkfst) **Facilities** FTV **Conf** Class 50 Board 25 Thtr 60 Del from £140 to £170 **Services** Lift **Parking** 80 **Notes** ⊗ Closed 24 Dec-1 Jan Civ Wed 120

LEEMING BAR
North Yorkshire — Map 19 SE28

Lodge at Leeming Bar

THE INDEPENDENTS HOTEL ASSOCIATION

★★ 71% HOTEL

☎ 01677 422122 📠 01677 424507
The Great North Rd DL8 1DT
e-mail: thelodgeatleemingbar@btinternet.com
dir: Off A1 at Bedale/Northallerton A684 junct. Follow signs for Leeming Bar/Services & Motel

Conveniently located just off the A1, this hotel offers bedrooms that vary in style, but all are well equipped for business and leisure guests; some feature flat-screen TVs and air conditioning. Meals are served in the bar and Old Market Square Restaurant. A meeting room is also available, and there is ample parking as well as a shop and café on site.

Rooms 39 **Notes** Closed 25-26 Dec

LEICESTER
Leicestershire — Map 11 SK50

See also **Rothley**

Leicester Marriott

Marriott HOTELS & RESORTS

★★★★ 79% HOTEL

☎ 0116 282 0100 📠 0116 282 0101
Smith Way, Grove Park, Enderby LE19 1SW
e-mail: mhrs.emalm.frontoffice@marriotthotels.com
web: www.leicestermarriott.co.uk
dir: M1 junct 21/A563 signed Leicester. At rdbt take 1st left onto A563. Into right lane, at 2nd slip road turn right. At rdbt take last exit, hotel straight ahead

This purpose-built hotel offers stylish bedrooms, some of which are executive rooms with access to the executive lounge. There is a popular brasserie, cocktail bar, atrium lounge, indoor heated pool, gym, sauna and steam room. 18 meeting rooms provide conference facilities for up to 500 delegates and parking is extensive.

Rooms 227 (91 fmly) **Facilities** STV ⓢ supervised Gym Wi-fi **Conf** Class 180 Board 52 Thtr 500 **Services** Lift Air con **Parking** 280 **Notes** ⊗ Civ Wed 300

Hotel Maiyango

★★★★ 73% ◎ SMALL HOTEL

☎ 0116 251 8898 📠 0116 242 1339
13-21 St Nicholas Place LE1 4LD
e-mail: reservations@maiyango.com
dir: B4114 (Narborough Rd) to city centre, right onto A47 (Hinkley Rd), keep right into St Nicholas Place

A boutique hotel offering a warm welcome and professional service. Access to the public areas is via a discreet foyer adjacent to a Middle Eastern themed restaurant (under the same ownership) where imaginative food is sure to be a memorable experience. Spacious bedrooms, decorated in minimalist style are enhanced by quality modern art, fine furnishings and superb bathrooms. Parking is available close by.

Rooms 14 **D** £91-£170 (incl. bkfst)* **Facilities** FTV ♫ Xmas New Year Wi-fi **Conf** Class 50 Board 30 Thtr 70 Del from £149* **Services** Lift Air con **Notes** ⊗

Belmont Hotel

★★★ 81% HOTEL

☎ 0116 254 4773 📠 0116 247 0804
De Montfort St LE1 7GR
e-mail: info@belmonthotel.co.uk
web: www.belmonthotel.co.uk
dir: From A6 take 1st right after rail station. Hotel 200yds on left

This well established hotel, under the same family ownership, has been welcoming guests for over 70 years. It is conveniently situated within easy walking distance of the railway station and city centre though it sits in a quiet leafy residential area. Extensive public rooms are smartly appointed and include the informal Bowie's Bistro, Jamie's Bar with its relaxed atmosphere, and the more formal Cherry Restaurant.

Rooms 75 (7 fmly) (9 GF) (2 smoking) **S** £55-£115; **D** £55-£135* **Facilities** FTV Gym Wi-fi **Conf** Class 75 Board 65 Thtr 175 Del from £120 to £160* **Services** Lift **Parking** 70 **Notes** LB Closed 25-26 Dec Civ Wed 150

Holiday Inn Leicester

★★★ 79% HOTEL

☎ 0871 942 9048 📠 0116 251 3169
St Nicholas Circle LE1 5LX
web: www.holidayinn.co.uk
dir: From S: M1 junct 21, A5460 towards city centre. In approx 3m follow Castle Gardens signs. Hotel at next rdbt. From N: M1 junct 22, A50 to city centre. Into Vaughan Way, follow signs for A47 (avoid underpass). Hotel at rdbt

This purpose-built city centre hotel offers impressive accommodation suitable for both business and leisure guests. The smartly appointed bar and restaurant are open throughout the day and there is a well-equipped leisure club. Overnight guests are offered free parking at the adjacent multi-storey car park.

Rooms 188 (12 smoking) **Facilities** ⓢ supervised Gym Wi-fi **Conf** Class 140 Board 90 Thtr 260 **Services** Lift Air con **Notes** Civ Wed 200

Regency

★★★ 71% HOTEL

☎ 0116 270 9634 📠 0116 270 1375
360 London Rd LE2 2PL
e-mail: info@the-regency-hotel.com
dir: On A6, 1.5m from city centre

This friendly hotel is located on the edge of town and provides smart accommodation, suitable for both business and leisure guests. Dining options include a cosy conservatory brasserie and a formal restaurant. A relaxing lounge bar is also available, along with good banqueting and conference facilities. Bedrooms come in a variety of styles and sizes and include some spacious and stylish rooms.

Rooms 32 (2 fmly) (5 smoking) **Facilities** STV ♫ Xmas New Year Wi-fi **Conf** Class 40 Board 30 Thtr 50 **Parking** 32 **Notes** ⊗ Civ Wed 140

Campanile Leicester

Campanile

BUDGET HOTEL

☎ 0116 261 6600 📠 0116 261 6601
St Matthew's Way, 1 Bedford Street North LE1 3JE
e-mail: leicester@campanile.com
dir: From A5460, right at end of road, left at rdbt on A594. Follow Vaughan Way, Burleys Way then St. Matthew's Way. Hotel on left

This modern building offers accommodation in smart, well-equipped bedrooms, all with en suite bathrooms. Refreshments may be taken at the informal bistro. See also the Hotel Groups pages.

Rooms 93 **Conf** Class 30 Board 30 Thtr 40

Holiday Inn Express - Walkers Stadium

BUDGET HOTEL

☎ 0116 249 4590 📠 0116 249 4591
Filbert Way, Raw Dykes Rd LE2 7FQ
e-mail: info@exhileicester.co.uk
web: www.hiexpress.com/leicesterwalke
dir: From A5460 follow signs to Walkers Stadium

A modern hotel ideal for families and business travellers. Fresh and uncomplicated, the spacious rooms include Sky TV, power shower and tea and coffee-making facilities. Continental buffet breakfast is included in the room rate; other meals may be taken at the nearby family pub or restaurant. See also the Hotel Groups pages.

Rooms 110 (12 smoking) **S** £59-£129; **D** £59-£129 (incl. bkfst)* **Conf** Class 100 Board 60 Thtr 160 Del from £119 to £189*

Ibis Leicester

BUDGET HOTEL

☎ 0116 248 7200 📠 0116 262 0880
St Georges Way, Constitution Hill LE1 1PL
e-mail: H3061@accor.com
web: www.ibishotel.com
dir: From M1/M69 junct 21, follow town centre signs, central ring road (A594)/railway station, hotel opposite Leicester Mercury

Modern, budget hotel offering comfortable accommodation in bright and practical bedrooms. Breakfast is self-service and dinner is available in the restaurant. See also the Hotel Groups pages.

Rooms 94 (15 fmly)

Premier Inn Leicester (Braunstone)

BUDGET HOTEL

☎ 0871 527 8590 📠 0871 527 8591
Meridian Business Park, Thorpe Astley, Braunstone LE19 1LU
dir: M1 junct 21, follow A563 (outer ring road) signs W to Thorpe Astley. At slip road after Texaco garage. Hotel on left

High quality, budget accommodation ideal for both families and business travellers. Spacious, en suite bedrooms feature tea and coffee making facilities, and Freeview TV in most hotels. Internet access and Wi-fi are available for a small fee. The adjacent family restaurant features a wide and varied menu. See also the Hotel Groups pages.

Rooms 51 **D** £45-£55*

Premier Inn Leicester (Braunstone South)

BUDGET HOTEL

☎ 0871 527 8588 📠 0871 527 8589
Braunstone Lane East LE3 2FW
dir: M1 junct 21, at M69 junct take A5460 towards city. After 1m right at lights to hotel

Rooms 170 **D** £45-£55*

Premier Inn Leicester Central (A50)

BUDGET HOTEL

☎ 0871 527 8594 📠 0871 527 8595
Heathley Park, Groby Rd LE3 9QE
dir: Off A50, city centre side of County Hall & Glenfield General Hospital

Rooms 76 **D** £45-£55*

Premier Inn Leicester City Centre

BUDGET HOTEL

☎ 0871 527 8596 📠 0871 527 8597
1 St Georges Way LE1 1AA
dir: Telephone for detailed directions

Rooms 135 **D** £49-£57*

Premier Inn Leicester (Forest East)

BUDGET HOTEL

☎ 0871 527 8592 📠 0871 527 8593
Hinckley Rd, Leicester Forest East LE3 3GD
dir: M1 junct 21, A5460. At major junct (Holiday Inn on right), left into Braunstone Lane. In 2m left onto A47 towards Hinkley. Hotel 400yds on left

Rooms 40 **D** £45-£55*

Premier Inn Leicester North West

BUDGET HOTEL

☎ 0871 527 8598 📠 0871 527 8599
Leicester Rd, Glenfield LE3 8HB
dir: M1 junct 21a N'bound, A46. Onto A50 for Glenfield & County Hall. Or M1 junct 22 S'bound onto A50 towards Glenfield. Into County Hall. Hotel on left adjacent to Gynsills

Rooms 43 **D** £45-£55*

Premier Inn Leicester South (Oadby)

BUDGET HOTEL

☎ 0871 527 8600 📠 0871 527 8601
Glen Rise, Oadby LE2 4RG
dir: M1 junct 21, A563 signed South. Right at Leicester racecourse. Follow Market Harborough signs. Dual carriageway, straight on at rdbt. Into single lane, hotel on right

Rooms 30 **D** £45-£55*

LEICESTER FOREST MOTORWAY SERVICE AREA (M1) Map 11 SK50
Leicestershire

Days Inn Leicester Forest East - M1

BUDGET HOTEL

☎ 0116 239 0534 📠 0116 239 0546
Leicester Forest East, M1 Junct 21 LE3 3GB
e-mail: leicester.hotel@welcomebreak.co.uk
web: www.welcomebreak.co.uk
dir: On M1 N'bound between junct 21 & 21A

This modern building offers accommodation in smart, spacious and well-equipped bedrooms, suitable for families and business travellers, and all with en suite bathrooms. Continental breakfast is available, and other refreshments may be taken at the nearby family restaurant. See also the Hotel Groups pages.

Rooms 92 (71 fmly) (10 smoking) **S** £39.95-£59.95; **D** £49.95-£69.95 **Conf** Board 10

LEIGH Map 15 SJ69
Greater Manchester

L

Park Inn Leigh

park inn by Radisson

★★★ 75% HOTEL

☎ 01942 366334 & 687111 📠 01942 366337
Altherleigh Way WN7 4JZ
e-mail: info.leigh@rezidorparkinn.com
dir: M6 junct 23, A580, 3.1m follow signs to Leigh Sports Village

A stylish modern hotel that is conveniently located close to the motorway network and a short drive from Manchester Airport and Warrington. The hotel is adjacent to Leigh Sports Village and the contemporary bedrooms are equipped with the latest in facilities including air conditioning, flat-screen TVs and Wi-fi. The hotel has a fitness suite, sauna and steam room along with modern meeting rooms and a business centre.

Rooms 135 (10 fmly) (10 smoking) **S** £59-£65; **D** £59-£65* **Facilities** FTV Gym Sauna Steam room Xmas New Year Wi-fi **Conf** Class 72 Board 40 Thtr 150 Del from £99 to £101* **Services** Lift Air con **Parking** 50 **Notes** LB Civ Wed 100

LENHAM
Kent Map 7 TQ85

INSPECTORS' CHOICE

Chilston Park
★★★★ ®® HOTEL

☎ 01622 859803 🖷 01622 858588
Sandway ME17 2BE
e-mail: chilstonpark@handpicked.co.uk
web: www.handpickedhotels.co.uk
dir: From A20 exit to Lenham, right into High St, pass station on right, 1st left, over x-roads, hotel 0.25m on left

This elegant Grade I listed country house is set in 23 acres of immaculately landscaped gardens and parkland. An impressive collection of original paintings and antiques creates a unique environment. The sunken Venetian-style restaurant serves modern British food with French influences. Bedrooms are individual in design, some have four-poster beds and many have garden views.

Rooms 53 (23 annexe) (2 fmly) (3 GF) **S** £87-£165; **D** £97-£165 (incl. bkfst)* **Facilities** STV FTV Fishing ⚘ Xmas New Year Wi-fi **Conf** Class 60 Board 50 Thtr 100 Del from £145 to £200* **Services** Lift **Parking** 100 **Notes** LB ⊗ Civ Wed 90

LEOMINSTER
Herefordshire Map 10 SO45

Best Western Talbot
★★★ 75% HOTEL

☎ 01568 616347 🖷 01568 614880
West St HR6 8EP
e-mail: talbot@bestwestern.co.uk
dir: From A49, A44 or A4112, hotel in town centre

This charming former coaching inn is located in the town centre and makes an ideal base for exploring this delightful area. Public areas feature original beams and antique furniture, and include an atmospheric bar and elegant restaurant. The bedrooms vary in size, but all are comfortably furnished and equipped. Facilities are available for private functions and conferences.

Rooms 28 (3 fmly) (2 GF) **S** £61.50-£78; **D** £73-£85.50* **Facilities** FTV Wi-fi **Conf** Class 60 Board 30 Thtr 130 Del from £95* **Parking** 26 **Notes** ⊗

LEWDOWN
Devon Map 3 SX48

INSPECTORS' CHOICE

Lewtrenchard Manor
★★★ ®®® HOTEL

☎ 01566 783256 & 783222 🖷 01566 783332
EX20 4PN
e-mail: info@lewtrenchard.co.uk
web: www.vonessenhotels.co.uk
dir: A30 from Exeter to Plymouth/Tavistock road. At T-junct turn right, then left onto old A30 (Lewdown road). Left in 6m signed Lewtrenchard

This Jacobean mansion was built in the 1600s, with many interesting architectural features, and is surrounded by its own idyllic grounds in a quiet valley close to the northern edge of Dartmoor. Public rooms include a fine gallery, as well as magnificent carvings and oak panelling. Meals can be taken in the dining room where imaginative and carefully prepared dishes are served using the best of Devon produce. Bedrooms are comfortably furnished and spacious.

Rooms 16 (2 fmly) (3 GF) **S** £125-£255; **D** £155-£395 (incl. bkfst)* **Facilities** FTV Fishing ⚘ Clay pigeon shooting Falconry Beauty therapies Xmas New Year Wi-fi **Conf** Class 40 Board 20 Thtr 50 **Parking** 50 **Notes** LB Civ Wed 100

LEWES
East Sussex Map 6 TQ41

Shelleys Hotel
★★★★ 76% ® HOTEL

☎ 01273 472361 & 483403 🖷 01273 483152
136 High St BN7 1XS
e-mail: reservations@theshelleys.co.uk
dir: A23 to Brighton onto A27 to Lewes. At 1st rdbt left for town centre, after x-rds hotel on left

Originally a coaching inn dating from the 16th century, this charming establishment is the perfect base for exploring the South Downs and when shopping in nearby Brighton. All bedrooms are comfortably furnished in a traditional style and equipped with modern amenities such as Wi-fi. As well as a cosy bar and lounge, a fine dining restaurant is available, and homemade cream teas in the stunning garden are a speciality.

Rooms 19 (1 fmly) **Facilities** STV ⚘ Xmas New Year Wi-fi **Conf** Class 20 Board 25 Thtr 60 **Parking** 20 **Notes** LB Civ Wed 60

LEYLAND
Lancashire Map 15 SD52

Best Western Premier Leyland

★★★★ 77% HOTEL

☎ 01772 422922 🖷 01772 622282
Leyland Way PR25 4JX
e-mail: leylandhotel@feathers.uk.com
web: www.feathers.uk.com
dir: M6 junct 28 turn left at end of slip road, hotel 100mtrs on left

This purpose-built hotel enjoys a convenient location, just off the M6, within easy reach of Preston and Blackpool. Spacious public areas include extensive conference and banqueting facilities as well as a smart leisure club.

Rooms 93 (4 fmly) (31 GF) **S** £59-£119; **D** £59-£119 (incl. bkfst)* **Facilities** STV FTV supervised Gym Xmas New Year Wi-fi **Conf** Class 250 Board 250 Thtr 500 Del from £105 to £185* **Parking** 150 **Notes** LB ⊗ Civ Wed 200

Farington Lodge

★★★★ 73% HOTEL

☎ 01772 421321 📠 01772 455388
Stanifield Ln, Farington PR25 4QR
e-mail: info.farington@classiclodges.co.uk
web: www.classiclodges.co.uk
dir: Left at rdbt at end of M65, left at next rdbt. Entrance 1m on right after lights

This Grade II listed Georgian house, ideally located close to the M6, M61 and M65, is set in three acres of quiet, mature gardens and offers a romantic getaway. The choice of bedroom styles range from classic and traditional rooms in the original house to the contemporary, purpose-built executive rooms; all are stylishly decorated to a very high standard. This hotel is a popular venue for weddings, private dining and other special occasions.

Rooms 27 (3 fmly) (6 GF) **S** £79-£115; **D** £89-£125 (incl. bkfst)* **Facilities** FTV Xmas New Year Wi-fi **Conf** Class 80 Board 60 Thtr 180 **Parking** 90 **Notes** LB ⊗ Civ Wed 150

LICHFIELD
Staffordshire — Map 10 SK10

INSPECTORS' CHOICE

Swinfen Hall

★★★★ ®® HOTEL

☎ 01543 481494 📠 01543 480341
Swinfen WS14 9RE
e-mail: info@swinfenhallhotel.co.uk
web: www.swinfenhallhotel.co.uk
dir: Set back from A38, 2.5m outside Lichfield, towards Birmingham

Dating from 1757, this lavishly decorated mansion has been painstakingly restored by the present owners. It is set in 100 acres of parkland which includes a deer park. Public rooms are particularly stylish, with intricately carved ceilings and impressive oil portraits. Bedrooms on the first floor boast period features and tall sash windows; those on the second floor (the former servants' quarters) are smaller and more contemporary by comparison. Service in the award-winning restaurant is both professional and attentive.

Rooms 17 (5 fmly) **S** £145-£300; **D** £170-£325 (incl. bkfst)* **Facilities** STV Fishing Jogging trail New Year Wi-fi **Conf** Class 50 Board 120 Thtr 96 Del from £180* **Parking** 80 **Notes** LB ⊗ Civ Wed 120

Best Western The George

★★★ 77% HOTEL

☎ 01543 414822 📠 01543 415817
12-14 Bird St WS13 6PR
e-mail: mail@thegeorgelichfield.co.uk
web: www.thegeorgelichfield.co.uk
dir: From Bowling Green Island on A461 take Lichfield exit. Left at next island into Swan Rd, as road bears left, turn right into Bird St for hotel car park

Situated in the city centre, this privately owned hotel provides good quality, well-equipped accommodation which includes a room with a four-poster bed. Facilities here include a large ballroom, plus several other rooms for meetings and functions.

Rooms 45 (5 fmly) **S** £45-£156; **D** £45-£156 (incl. bkfst) **Facilities** FTV Gym Wi-fi **Conf** Class 60 Board 40 Thtr 110 Del from £135 to £150* **Services** Lift **Parking** 45 **Notes** LB ⊗ Civ Wed 110

Cathedral Lodge Hotel

★★★ 67% HOTEL

☎ 01543 414500 📠 01543 415734
62 Beacon St WS13 7AR
e-mail: enquiries@cathedrallodgehotel.com
dir: From Birmingham, A38 to Lichfield. Hotel in city centre

Set within easy walking distance of the famous cathedral and just a short drive to the NEC, Belfry Golf course and many other attractions. The accommodation is modern, spacious and comfortable, and each room has a large, flat-screen TV with Sky Sports. There is a large function suite together with conference facilities.

Rooms 36 (2 fmly) (6 smoking) **S** £45-£79.50; **D** £45-£150 (incl. bkfst)* **Facilities** STV FTV Xmas New Year Wi-fi **Conf** Class 80 Board 70 Thtr 80 Del from £100 to £120* **Notes** LB ⊗

Holiday Inn Express Lichfield

BUDGET HOTEL

☎ 01543 482700 📠 01543 483106
Wall Island, Birmingham Rd, Shenstone WS14 0QP
e-mail: lichfield@morethanhotels.com
web: www.hiexpress.com/lichfielduk
dir: M6 junct 12/A5 towards Lichfield/Tamworth, to junct with A5127. Hotel on left on Wall Island

A modern hotel ideal for families and business travellers. Fresh and uncomplicated, the spacious rooms include Sky TV, power shower and tea and coffee-making facilities. Continental buffet breakfast is included in the room rate; other meals may be taken at the nearby family pub or restaurant. See also the Hotel Groups pages.

Rooms 102 (60 fmly) (25 GF) (7 smoking) **S** £43-£115; **D** £43-£115 (incl. bkfst)* **Conf** Class 16 Board 20 Thtr 30 Del from £105*

L

Premier Inn Lichfield

BUDGET HOTEL

☎ 0871 527 8602 📠 0871 527 8603
Fine Ln, Fradley WS13 8RD
dir: On A38, 3 NE of Lichfield

High quality, budget accommodation ideal for both families and business travellers. Spacious, en suite bedrooms feature tea and coffee making facilities, and Freeview TV in most hotels. Internet access and Wi-fi are available for a small fee. The adjacent family restaurant features a wide and varied menu. See also the Hotel Groups pages.

Rooms 30 **D** £52-£59*

LIFTON
Devon — Map 3 SX38

Arundell Arms

★★★ 80% ®® HOTEL

☎ 01566 784666 📠 01566 784494
PL16 0AA
e-mail: reservations@arundellarms.co.uk
dir: 1m off A30, 3m E of Launceston

This former coaching inn, boasting a long history, sits in the heart of a quiet Devon village. It is internationally famous for its country pursuits such as winter shooting and angling. The bedrooms offer individual style and comfort. Public areas are full of

continued

LIFTON *continued*

character with a relaxed atmosphere, particularly around the open log fire during colder evenings. Award-winning cuisine is a celebration of local produce.

Rooms 21 (3 fmly) (4 GF) **Facilities** STV Fishing Skittle alley Game shooting (in winter) Fly fishing school New Year Wi-fi **Conf** Class 30 Board 40 Thtr 100 **Parking** 70 **Notes** LB Civ Wed 80

Tinhay Mill Guest House and Restaurant

RESTAURANT WITH ROOMS

01566 784201 01566 784201
Tinhay PL16 0AJ
e-mail: tinhay.mill@talk21.com
web: www.tinhaymillrestaurant.co.uk
dir: A30/A388 approach Lifton, establishment at bottom of village on right

These former mill cottages are now a delightful restaurant with rooms of much charm. Beams and open fireplaces set the scene, with everything geared to ensure a relaxed and comfortable stay. Bedrooms are spacious and well equipped, with many thoughtful extras. Cuisine is taken seriously here, and uses the best local produce.

Rooms 6

LINCOLN Lincolnshire — Map 17 SK97

The Bentley Hotel & Spa

★★★ 85% HOTEL

01522 878000 01522 878001
Newark Rd, South Hykeham LN6 9NH
e-mail: info@bentleyhotellincoln.co.uk
web: www.bentleyhotellincoln.co.uk
dir: A1 onto A46 E towards Lincoln for 10m. Straight on at 1st rdbt on Lincoln Bypass. Hotel 50yds on left

This modern hotel is on a ring road, so it is conveniently located for all local attractions. Attractive bedrooms, most with air conditioning are well equipped and spacious. The hotel has a leisure suite with gym and large pool (with a hoist for the less able). Extensive conference facilities are available.

Rooms 80 (5 fmly) (26 GF) **S** £92-£102; **D** £107-£143 (incl. bkfst)* **Facilities** Spa STV Gym Steam room Sauna New Year Wi-fi **Conf** Class 150 Board 30 Thtr 300 Del from £118* **Services** Lift Air con **Parking** 170 **Notes** LB Civ Wed 120

Washingborough Hall

★★★ 79% COUNTRY HOUSE HOTEL

01522 790340 01522 792936
Church Hill, Washingborough LN4 1BE
e-mail: enquiries@washingboroughhall.com
dir: B1190 into Washingborough. Right at rdbt, hotel 500yds on left

This Georgian manor stands on the edge of the quiet village of Washingborough and is set in attractive gardens. Public rooms are pleasantly furnished and comfortable, while the restaurant offers interesting menus. Bedrooms are individually designed and most have views out over the grounds to the countryside beyond.

Rooms 12 (3 fmly) **S** £50-£85; **D** £80-£135 (incl. bkfst)* **Facilities** FTV Bicycles for hire New Year Wi-fi **Conf** Class 30 Board 26 Thtr 50 **Parking** 40 **Notes** LB Civ Wed 70

The Lincoln

★★★ 78% HOTEL

01522 520348 01522 510780
Eastgate LN2 1PN
e-mail: reservations@thelincolnhotel.com
web: www.thelincolnhotel.com
dir: Adjacent to cathedral

This privately owned modern hotel enjoys superb uninterrupted views of Lincoln Cathedral. There are ruins of the Roman wall and Eastgate in the grounds. Bedrooms are contemporary with up-to-the-minute facilities. An airy restaurant and bar, plus a comfortable lounge are provided. There are substantial conference and meeting facilities.

The Lincoln

Rooms 71 (4 fmly) (8 GF) **S** £75-£150; **D** £85-£160 (incl. bkfst) **Facilities** FTV Gym Wi-fi **Conf** Class 50 Board 40 Thtr 120 Del from £129 to £169 **Services** Lift **Parking** 120 **Notes** LB Civ Wed 150

Branston Hall

★★★ 75% COUNTRY HOUSE HOTEL

01522 793305 01522 790734
Branston Park, Branston LN4 1PD
e-mail: info@branstonhall.com
web: www.branstonhall.com
dir: On B1188

Dating back to 1885 this country house sits in 88 acres of beautiful grounds complete with a lake. There is an elegant restaurant, a spacious bar and a beautiful lounge in addition to impressive conference and leisure facilities. Individually styled bedrooms vary in size and include several with four-poster beds. The hotel is a popular wedding venue.

Rooms 50 (7 annexe) (3 fmly) (4 GF) **Facilities** Spa STV Gym Jogging circuit Xmas New Year Wi-fi **Conf** Class 54 Board 40 Thtr 200 **Services** Lift **Parking** 100 **Notes** Civ Wed 160

The White Hart

★★★ 73% HOTEL

01522 526222 & 563293 01522 531798
Bailgate LN1 3AR
e-mail: info@whitehart-lincoln.co.uk
web: www.whitehart-lincoln.co.uk
dir: A46 onto B1226, through Newport Arch. Hotel 0.5m on left as road bends left

Lying in the shadow of Lincoln's magnificent cathedral, this hotel is perfectly positioned for exploring the shops and sights of this medieval city. The attractive bedrooms are furnished and decorated in a traditional style and many have views of the cathedral. Hotel parking is a real benefit.

Rooms 50 (3 fmly) **S** £69-£95; **D** £89-£110 (incl. bkfst) **Facilities** FTV Xmas New Year Wi-fi **Conf** Class 80 Board 103 Thtr 160 **Services** Lift **Parking** 50 **Notes** LB Civ Wed 120

Tower Hotel

★★ 79% HOTEL

☎ 01522 529999 📠 01522 560596
38 Westgate LN1 3BD
e-mail: tower.hotel@btclick.com
dir: From A46 follow signs to Lincoln N then to Bailgate area. Through arch, 2nd right

This hotel faces the Norman castle wall and is in a very convenient location for the city. The relaxed and friendly atmosphere is very noticeable here. There's a modern conservatory bar and a stylish restaurant where contemporary dishes are available throughout the day.

Rooms 15 (1 fmly) **S** £65-£82; **D** £90-£100 (incl. bkfst)* **Facilities** STV FTV Wi-fi **Conf** Class 24 Board 16 Thtr 24 **Notes** Closed 24-27 Dec & 1 Jan

Holiday Inn Express Lincoln City Centre

BUDGET HOTEL

☎ 01522 504200 📠 01522 504210
Ruston Way, Brayford Park LN6 7DB
e-mail: gm@expresslincoln.co.uk
dir: M180 junct 4, A15 signed Lincoln, A46 (Lincoln bypass). Take exit signed A57/Lincoln Central. Over bridge. At rdbt 3rd exit. Hotel on left

A modern hotel ideal for families and business travellers. Fresh and uncomplicated, the spacious rooms include Sky TV, power shower and tea and coffee-making facilities. Continental buffet breakfast is included in the room rate; other meals may be taken at the nearby family pub or restaurant. See also the Hotel Groups pages.

Rooms 118 (96 fmly) **S** £65-£109; **D** £65-£109 (incl. bkfst)* **Conf** Class 20 Board 20 Thtr 40 Del from £95 to £145*

Ibis Lincoln

BUDGET HOTEL

☎ 01522 698333 📠 01522 698444
Runcorn Rd (A46), off Whisby Rd LN6 3QZ
e-mail: H3161@accor-hotels.com
web: www.ibishotel.com
dir: Off A46 (ring road) onto Whisby Rd. 1st left

Modern, budget hotel offering comfortable accommodation in bright and practical bedrooms. Breakfast is self-service and dinner is available in the restaurant See also the Hotel Groups pages.

Rooms 86 (19 fmly) (8 GF) **D** £29-£90* **Conf** Class 12 Board 20 Thtr 35

Premier Inn Lincoln

BUDGET HOTEL

☎ 0871 527 8604 📠 0871 527 8605
Lincoln Rd, Canwick Hill LN4 2RF
dir: Approx 1m S of city centre at junction of B1188 & B1131

High quality, budget accommodation ideal for both families and business travellers. Spacious, en suite bedrooms feature tea and coffee making facilities, and Freeview TV in most hotels. Internet access and Wi-fi are available for a small fee. The adjacent family restaurant features a wide and varied menu. See also the Hotel Groups pages.

Rooms 60 **D** £55-£60*

The Old Bakery

◎◎ RESTAURANT WITH ROOMS

☎ 01522 576057
26/28 Burton Rd LN1 3LB
e-mail: enquiries@theold-bakery.co.uk
dir: Exit A46 at Lincoln North follow signs for cathedral. 3rd exit at 1st rdbt, 1st exit at next rdbt

Situated close to the castle at the top of the town, this converted bakery offers well-equipped bedrooms and a delightful dining operation. The cooking is international and uses much local produce. Expect good friendly service from the dedicated staff.

Rooms 4 (1 fmly)

LIPHOOK Map 5 SU83
Hampshire

Old Thorns Hotel Golf & Country Estate

★★★★ 71% HOTEL

☎ 01428 724555 📠 01428 725036
Griggs Green GU30 7PE
e-mail: sales@oldthorns.com
dir: Take Griggs Green exit off A3. Hotel 0.5m

This hotel, with easy access to the A3, is peacefully located in 400 acres of rolling countryside that includes a championship golf course. The spacious bedrooms are stylish in design and offer high levels of comfort. The leisure facilities are extensive and include a health club and spa; in addition there is a sports bar, and the Kings Carvery Brasserie offers all-day dining.

Rooms 150 (2 fmly) (14 GF) **Facilities** Spa STV FTV supervised 18 Putt green Gym Xmas New Year Wi-fi **Conf** Class 100 Board 30 Thtr 250 **Parking** 100 **Notes** Civ Wed 250

LISKEARD
Cornwall
Map 2 SX26

Premier Inn Liskeard

BUDGET HOTEL

☎ 0871 527 8608 🖷 0871 527 8609
Liskeard Retail Park, Haviland Rd PL14 3FG
dir: Off A38, on A390 SW of Liskeard

High quality, budget accommodation ideal for both families and business travellers. Spacious, en suite bedrooms feature tea and coffee making facilities, and Freeview TV in most hotels. Internet access and Wi-fi are available for a small fee. The adjacent family restaurant features a wide and varied menu. See also the Hotel Groups pages.

Rooms 51 **D** £70*

LITTLEHAMPTON
West Sussex
Map 6 TQ00

Premier Inn Littlehampton

BUDGET HOTEL

☎ 0871 527 8610 🖷 0871 527 8611
Roundstone Ln, East Preston BN16 1EB
dir: A27 onto A280 signed Littlehampton/Rustington & Angmering. At next rdbt follow Littlehampton, Rustington/A259 signs. At next rdbt 1st exit signed East Preston. Hotel on left

High quality, budget accommodation ideal for both families and business travellers. Spacious, en suite bedrooms feature tea and coffee making facilities, and Freeview TV in most hotels. Internet access and Wi-fi are available for a small fee. The adjacent family restaurant features a wide and varied menu. See also the Hotel Groups pages.

Rooms 20 **D** £67*

LIVERPOOL
Merseyside
Map 15 SJ39

Thornton Hall Hotel and Spa

★★★★ 79% HOTEL

☎ 0151 336 3938 & 353 3717 🖷 0151 336 7864
Neston Rd CH63 1JF
e-mail: reservations@thorntonhallhotel.com
web: www.thorntonhallhotel.com

(For full entry see Thornton Hough)

Crowne Plaza Liverpool

★★★★ 79% HOTEL

☎ 0151 243 8000 🖷 0151 243 8111
St Nicholas Place, Princes Dock, Pier Head L3 1QW
e-mail: enquiries@cpliverpool.com
web: www.crowneplaza.co.uk

Situated right on the waterfront, yet still within striking distance of the city centre this hotel offers comprehensive leisure and meeting facilities, whether taking a snack in the spacious lounge or using the business centre. Contemporary in style with superb quality, this hotel offers a welcome to business or leisure guests alike.

Rooms 159 (11 fmly) **Facilities** Spa STV FTV Gym Sauna Steam room New Year Wi-fi **Conf** Class 340 Board 30 Thtr 500 **Services** Lift Air con **Parking** 150 **Notes** Civ Wed 500

Hope Street Hotel

★★★★ 78% HOTEL

☎ 0151 709 3000 🖷 0151 709 2454
40 Hope St L1 9DA
e-mail: sleep@hopestreethotel.co.uk
dir: Follow Cathedral & University signs on entering city. Telephone for detailed directions

This stylish property is located within easy walking distance of the city's cathedrals, theatres, major shops and attractions. Stylish bedrooms and suites are appointed with flat-screen TVs, DVD players, internet access and comfy beds with Egyptian cotton sheets; the bathrooms have rain showers and deep tubs. The London Carriage Works Restaurant specialises in local, seasonal produce and the adjacent lounge bar offers lighter all-day dining and wonderful cocktails.

Rooms 89 (16 fmly) (5 GF) **S** £89-£650; **D** £89-£650* **Facilities** STV FTV Gym Massage & beauty rooms New Year Wi-fi **Conf** Class 40 Board 30 Thtr 60 Del from £190* **Services** Lift Air con **Parking** 14 **Notes** Civ Wed 70

Crowne Plaza Liverpool - John Lennon Airport

★★★★ 75% HOTEL

☎ 0151 494 5000 🖷 0151 494 5050
Speke Aerodrome, Speke L24 8QD
e-mail: reservations.liverpool@kewgreen.co.uk
web: www.crowneplaza.com
dir: M62 junct 6, take Knowsley Expressway towards Speke. At end of Expressway right onto A561 towards Liverpool. Approx 4m, hotel on left just after Estuary Commerce Park

This stylish art decor hotel was originally part of the airport buildings and is just a few minutes' drive from the Liverpool John Lennon Airport. The bedrooms are comfortable and have air conditioning. The hotel day rooms are strikingly appointed with furnishings inspired by the 1930s. There is ample on-site parking.

Rooms 164 (50 fmly) (46 GF) **Facilities** STV supervised Gym Squash Xmas New Year Wi-fi **Conf** Class 120 Board 80 Thtr 280 **Services** Lift Air con **Notes** Civ Wed 280

Liverpool Marriott Hotel City Centre

Marriott HOTELS & RESORTS

★★★★ 75% HOTEL

☎ 0151 476 8000 🖷 0151 474 5000
1 Queen Square L1 1RH
e-mail: liverpool.city@marriotthotels.com
web: www.liverpoolmarriottcitycentre.co.uk
dir: End of M62 follow city centre signs, A5047, Edge Lane. From city centre follow signs for Queens Square parking

An impressive modern hotel located in the heart of the city. The elegant public rooms include a ground-floor café bar, a cocktail bar and stylish Oliver's Restaurant on the first floor. The hotel also boasts a well-equipped, indoor leisure health club with pool. Bedrooms are stylishly appointed and benefit from a host of extra facilities.

Rooms 146 (29 fmly) (12 smoking) **Facilities** Gym Xmas New Year Wi-fi **Conf** Class 90 Board 30 Thtr 300 **Services** Lift Air con **Parking** 137 **Notes** Civ Wed 300

Radisson Blu Hotel Liverpool

★★★★ 72% HOTEL

☎ 0151 966 1500 📠 0151 966 1415
107 Old Hall St L3 9LQ
e-mail: info.liverpool@radissonblu.com
dir: M62 W to end, follow signs to Albert Dock. Left onto Old Hall St from main Leeds St dual carriageway

This smart hotel is centrally located close to the city. Spacious public areas include the White Bar, an airy restaurant and an impressive lobby. Bedrooms are well equipped and include a number of business class rooms and suites. A good range of conference and meeting rooms is available, as well as a good range of leisure facilities.

Rooms 194 (4 smoking) **S** £79-£380; **D** £79-£380 **Facilities** STV FTV Gym Steam room Sauna Wi-fi **Conf** Class 120 Board 44 Thtr 180 Del from £126.95 to £250 **Services** Lift Air con **Parking** 25 **Notes** LB Civ Wed 180

Atlantic Tower, Liverpool

thistle

★★★★ 71% HOTEL

☎ 0871 376 9025 📠 0871 376 9125
Chapel St L3 9RE
e-mail: atlantictower@thistle.co.uk
web: www.thistle.com/atlantictower
dir: M6 onto M62, follow signs for Albert Dock, right at Liver Building. Stay in lane marked Chapel St, hotel on left

Designed to include the shape of a ship's prow, this notable hotel commands a prominent position overlooking Pier Head and the Liver Building. There's a choice of junior suites, executive and standard rooms, and although many are compact, all are of good quality and benefit from full air conditioning. Public areas include a choice of lounges and The Vu Bar which adjoins an attractive patio garden with superb river views. Thistle Hotels – AA Hotel Group of the Year 2011-12.

Rooms 225 (24 smoking) **Facilities** STV FTV Wi-fi **Conf** Class 40 Board 30 Thtr 120 Del from £135 to £150* **Services** Lift Air con **Parking** 50 **Notes** ⊗ Civ Wed 120

Novotel Liverpool

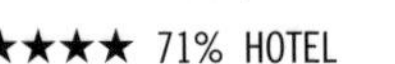

★★★★ 71% HOTEL

☎ 0151 702 5100 📠 0151 702 5110
40 Hanover St L1 4LY
e-mail: h6495@accor.com

This attractive and stylish city centre hotel is convenient for Liverpool Echo Arena, Liverpool One shopping centre and the Albert Dock; it is adjacent to a town centre car park. The hotel caters for conferences, and the leisure facilities include an indoor heated pool and fitness suite. The restaurant offers a contemporary style menu. Bedrooms are comfortable and stylishly designed.

Rooms 209 (127 fmly) **S** £75-£195; **D** £75-£195* **Facilities** STV FTV Gym Steam room Wi-fi **Conf** Class 60 Board 50 Thtr 90 Del from £125 to £265* **Services** Lift Air con

Malmaison Liverpool

★★★ 85% ⊛ HOTEL

☎ 0151 229 5000 📠 0151 229 5025
7 William Jessop Way, Princes Dock L3 1QZ
e-mail: liverpool@malmaison.com
dir: A5080 follow signs for Pier Head/Southport/ Bootle. Into Baln St to rdbt, 1st exit at rdbt, immediately left onto William Jessop Way

This is a purpose-built hotel with cutting edge and contemporary style. 'Mal' Liverpool, as its known, has a stunning location alongside the river and docks, which is in the heart of the city's regeneration area. Bedrooms are stylish and comfortable, and are provided with lots of extra facilities. The public areas are packed with fun and style, and there is a number of meeting rooms as well as private dining available, including a chef's table.

Rooms 130 **Facilities** STV Gym Wi-fi **Conf** Class 28 Board 22 Thtr 50 **Services** Lift Air con

Best Western Alicia Hotel

★★★ 78% HOTEL

☎ 0151 727 4411 📠 0151 727 6752
3 Aigburth Dr, Sefton Park L17 3AA
e-mail: aliciahotel@feathers.uk.com
web: www.feathers.uk.com
dir: From end of M62 take A5058 to Sefton Park, then left, follow park around

This stylish and friendly hotel overlooks Sefton Park and is just a few minutes' drive from both the city centre and John Lennon Airport. Bedrooms are well equipped and comfortable. Day rooms include a striking modern restaurant and bar. Extensive, stylish function facilities make this a popular wedding venue.

Rooms 41 (8 fmly) **S** £64-£124; **D** £69-£129 (incl. bkfst)* **Facilities** STV Xmas New Year Wi-fi **Conf** Class 80 Board 40 Thtr 120 Del from £129 to £169* **Services** Lift **Parking** 40 **Notes** ⊗ Civ Wed 120

Jurys Inn Liverpool

JURYS INNS

★★★ 75% HOTEL

☎ 0151 244 3777 📠 0151 244 3888
No 31 Keel Wharf L3 4FN
e-mail: jurysinnliverpool@jurysinns.com
dir: Follow City Centre & Albert Dock signs Hotel opposite BT Convention Centre

Located on the Kings Waterfront adjacent to the BT Convention Centre, Echo Arena, Albert Dock complex and a short walk from the very popular shopping district of Liverpool One, this hotel offers contemporary and spacious bedrooms. Guests have a choice of dining options - the Innfusion restaurant and the Inntro bar. There are ten dedicated meeting rooms and Wi-fi is available throughout. There is ample secure parking nearby.

Rooms 310 (58 fmly) **S** £62-£215; **D** £62-£215* **Facilities** Wi-fi **Conf** Class 50 Board 40 Thtr 100 Del from £128 to £145* **Services** Lift Air con **Notes** ⊗ Closed 24-25 Dec

L

Holiday Inn Liverpool City Centre

★★★ 74% HOTEL

☎ 0151 709 7090 📠 0151 709 0137
Lime St L1 1NQ
e-mail: enquiries@hiliverpool.com
web: www.hiliverpool.com
dir: M62 junct 4, follow edge lane A5047, left to Coppers Hill Lane (signed Post Lime St Station). Right onto Skelhorne St to hotel

Centrally located opposite Lime Street Train Station and within easy reach of all attractions. Bedrooms feature air conditioning, flat-screen TVs, high speed internet access and en suites with both bath and shower. The Lime Lounge on the second floor comprises a modern bar and restaurant with informal dining and fantastic views of the city. There is also a mini gym, and discounted rates at the adjacent car park are available.

Rooms 139 (20 smoking) **Facilities** STV Gym Xmas New Year Wi-fi **Conf** Class 250 Board 60 Thtr 400 Del from £110 to £360* **Services** Lift Air con **Notes** LB ⊗ Closed 25 Dec Civ Wed 270

LIVERPOOL *continued*

Campanile Liverpool

BUDGET HOTEL

☎ 0151 709 8104 🖷 0151 709 8725
Chaloner St, Queens Dock L3 4AJ
e-mail: liverpool@campanile.com
dir: Follow tourist signs marked Albert Dock. Hotel on waterfront

This modern building offers accommodation in smart, well-equipped bedrooms, all with en suite bathrooms. Refreshments may be taken at the informal bistro. See also the Hotel Groups pages.

Rooms 100 (4 fmly) (33 GF) **S** £62-£100; **D** £62-£100* **Conf** Class 18 Board 24 Thtr 35 Del from £85 to £100*

Holiday Inn Express Liverpool-Albert Dock

BUDGET HOTEL

☎ 0151 7026369 🖷 0151 709 1144
Britannia Building, Albert Dock L3 4AD
e-mail: reservations@exliverpool.com
web: www.exliverpool.com
dir: Follow signs for Liverpool City Centre and Albert Dock

A modern hotel ideal for families and business travellers. Fresh and uncomplicated, the spacious rooms include Sky TV, power shower and tea and coffee-making facilities. Continental buffet breakfast is included in the room rate; other meals may be taken at the nearby family pub or restaurant. See also the Hotel Groups pages.

Rooms 135

Holiday Inn Express Liverpool Knowsley

BUDGET HOTEL

☎ 0151 549 2700 🖷 0151 549 2800
Ribblers Ln, Knowsley L34 9HA
e-mail: liverpool@exhi.co.uk
web: www.hiexpress.com/lpool-knowsley
dir: M57 junct 4, last exit off rdbt, then 1st left. Hotel on left

Rooms 86 (62 fmly) (8 GF) (8 smoking) **S** £45-£85; **D** £45-£99 (incl. bkfst) **Conf** Class 24 Board 25 Thtr 40 Del from £75 to £125

Ibis Liverpool City Centre

BUDGET HOTEL

☎ 0151 706 9800 🖷 0151 706 9810
27 Wapping L1 8LY
e-mail: H3140@accor.com
web: www.ibishotel.com
dir: From M62 follow Albert Dock signs. Opposite Dock entrance

Modern, budget hotel offering comfortable accommodation in bright and practical bedrooms. Breakfast is self-service and dinner is available in the restaurant. See also the Hotel Groups pages.

Rooms 127 (15 fmly) (23 GF)

Premier Inn Liverpool (Aintree)

BUDGET HOTEL

☎ 0871 527 8612 🖷 0871 527 8613
Ormskirk Rd, Aintree L9 5AS
dir: M58, A57, A59 towards Liverpool. Pass Aintree Retail Park, left at lights into Aintree Racecourse. Hotel on left

High quality, budget accommodation ideal for both families and business travellers. Spacious, en suite bedrooms feature tea and coffee making facilities, and Freeview TV in most hotels. Internet access and Wi-fi are available for a small fee. The adjacent family restaurant features a wide and varied menu. See also the Hotel Groups pages.

Rooms 40 **D** £56-£59*

Premier Inn Liverpool Airport

BUDGET HOTEL

☎ 0871 527 8626 🖷 0871 527 8627
57 Speke Hall Av L24 1YQ
dir: A561 towards Liverpool follow 'Liverpool John Lennon Airport' signs into Seake Hall Ave, at 1st rdbt take 2nd left. Hotel 300mtrs on left

Rooms 10 **D** £58-£62*

Premier Inn Liverpool Albert Dock

BUDGET HOTEL

☎ 0871 527 8622 🖷 0871 527 8623
East Britannia Building, Albert Dock L3 4AD
dir: Follow signs for Liverpool City Centre & Albert Dock

Rooms 130 **D** £66-£69*

Premier Inn Liverpool City Centre

BUDGET HOTEL

☎ 0871 527 8624 🖷 0871 527 8625
Vernon St L2 2AY
dir: From M62 follow Liverpool City Centre & Birkenhead Tunnel signs. At rdbt 3rd exit into Dale St, right into Vernon St. Hotel on left

Rooms 165 **D** £65-£69*

Premier Inn Liverpool North

BUDGET HOTEL

☎ 0871 527 8628 🖷 0871 527 8629
Northern Perimeter Rd L30 7PT
dir: 0.25m from end of M58/M5, on A5207

Rooms 63 **D** £56-£59*

Premier Inn Liverpool (Roby)

BUDGET HOTEL

☎ 0871 527 8616 🖷 0871 527 8617
Roby Rd, Huyton L36 4HD
dir: Just off M62 junct 5 on A5080

Rooms 53 **D** £54-£57*

L

Premier Inn Liverpool (Tarbock)

BUDGET HOTEL

☎ 0871 527 8618 🖷 0871 527 8619
Wilson Rd, Tarbock L36 6AD
dir: At M62 & M57 junct. From M62 junct 6 take A5080 (Huyton). 1st right into Wilson Rd

Rooms 41 **D** £54-£57*

Premier Inn Liverpool (West Derby)

BUDGET HOTEL

☎ 0871 527 8620 🖷 0871 527 8621
Queens Dr, West Derby L13 0DL
dir: At end of M62 right under flyover onto A5058 (follow football stadium signs). Hotel 1.5m on left, just past Esso garage

Rooms 84 **D** £59*

LIVERSEDGE West Yorkshire Map 16 SE12

Healds Hall Hotel & Restaurant

THE INDEPENDENTS HOTEL ASSOCIATION

★★★ 77% ® HOTEL

☎ 01924 409112 🖷 01924 401895
Leeds Rd WF15 6JA
e-mail: enquire@healdshall.co.uk
web: www.healdshall.co.uk
dir: On A62 between Leeds & Huddersfield. 50yds on left after lights at Swan Pub

This 18th-century house, in the heart of West Yorkshire, provides comfortable and well-equipped accommodation and excellent hospitality. The hotel has earned a good local reputation for the quality of its food and offers a choice of casual or more formal dining styles, from a wide range of dishes on the various menus.

Rooms 24 (3 fmly) (3 GF) **S** £50-£95; **D** £60-£110 (incl. bkfst) **Facilities** FTV Wi-fi **Conf** Class 60 Board 45 Thtr 100 Del from £110 to £140 **Parking** 90 **Notes** LB Closed 1 Jan & BH Mon Civ Wed 100

LIZARD Cornwall Map 2 SW71

Housel Bay

★★★ 70% ® HOTEL

☎ 01326 290417 & 290917 🖷 01326 290359
Housel Cove TR12 7PG
e-mail: info@houselbay.com
dir: A39 or A394 to Helston, then A3083. At Lizard sign turn left, left at school, down lane to hotel

This long-established hotel has stunning views across the Western Approaches, equally enjoyable from the lounge and many of the bedrooms. Good cuisine is available in the stylish dining room, from where guests might enjoy a stroll to the end of the garden, which leads directly onto the Cornwall coastal path.

Rooms 20 (1 fmly) **Facilities** FTV Xmas New Year **Services** Lift **Parking** 35 **Notes** ⊗

London

Horse Guards Parade

Index of London Hotels

London Plan 1
0
2 miles
0
1
2
3 kilometres
Central London Congestion Charging Zone
A
B
C
D
1
2
3
4
5
Ruislip
RUISLIP
Ruislip Manor
West Ruislip
South Ruislip
Ickenham
Eastcote
Bayhurst Wood
Northwood Hills
Pinner
PINNER
North Harrow
HARROW
Harrow on the Hill
Roxeth
South Harrow
Headstone
Wealdstone
Belmont
Little Stanmore
Queensbury
KENTON
Greenhill
Kingsbury
The Hyde
HENDON
West Hendon
Staples Corner
BRENT
Dollis Hill
Cricklewood
Neasden
Dudden Hill
WILLESDEN
Willesden Green
Brondesbury
Brondesbury Park
Kensal Green
Harlesden
Wembley Park
North Wembley
Sudbury
WEMBLEY
Alperton
Stonebridge
Horsenden Hill
Perivale
Park Royal
North Acton
East Acton
ACTON
Acton Green
South Acton
Bedford Park
Shepherd's Bush
Notting Hill
HAMMERSMITH
Chiswick
Gunnersbury
Barnes
Mortlake
North Sheen
East Sheen
Roehampton
Putney Heath
PUTNEY
Putney Vale
Wimbledon Common
WIMBLEDON
Coombe
Kingston Vale
Kingston Hill
Cottenham Park
Raynes Park
New Malden
West Barnes
Old Malden
Motspur Park
Cannon Hill Common
Morden Cemetery
Lower Morden
Berrylands
SURBITON
KINGSTON UPON THAMES
Norbiton
Hampton Wick
Teddington
Petersham
Ham
Richmond Park
RICHMOND UPON THAMES
St Margarets
TWICKENHAM
Whitton
Isleworth
Old Deer Park
Syon Park
Kew Gardens
Brentford
Osterley
HOUNSLOW
Hounslow West
Hounslow Heath
Heston
North Hyde
Norwood Green
EALING
Hanwell
Brent Lodge Park
SOUTHALL
GREENFORD
NORTHOLT
HAYES
Yeading
Hayes Shrub
North Hillingdon
HILLINGDON
Colham Green
Hillingdon Heath
Yiewsley
West Drayton
Sipson
Harlington
Cranford
Hatton
HEATHROW AIRPORT
Heathrow Airport
North Feltham
FELTHAM
East Bedfont
Ashford
Chattern Hill
Lower Feltham
Feltham Hill
Ashford Common
Sunbury-on-Thames
Charlton
Lower Sunbury
Hanworth
Hampton
Hampton Hill
Strawberry Hill
Crane Park
Fulwell Park
Bushy Park
Hurst Park
East Molesey
West Molesey
Hampton Court
Hampton Court Park
Thames Ditton
Shepperton
Queen Mary Reservoir
Queen Elizabeth II Storage Reservoir
Island Barn Reservoir
Gunnersbury Park
Wormwood Scrubs Park
M4
M1
M3
A4
A40
A30
A312
A316
A406
A205
A3

HARINGEY
TOTTENHAM
WALTHAM FOREST
WALTHAMSTOW
REDBRIDGE
ILFORD
HAMPSTEAD
CAMDEN
HACKNEY
ISLINGTON
CITY
SEE LONDON PLANS 2 - 5
WESTMINSTER
LAMBETH
CHELSEA
TOWER HAMLETS
PLAN 6
PLAN 7
PLAN 8
PLAN 9
NEWHAM
BARKING
WOOLWICH
GREENWICH
SOUTHWARK
CLAPHAM
LEWISHAM
WANDSWORTH
STREATHAM
CATFORD
BECKENHAM
BROMLEY
MERTON
MITCHAM
LONDON CITY AIRPORT
River Thames
E
F
G
H

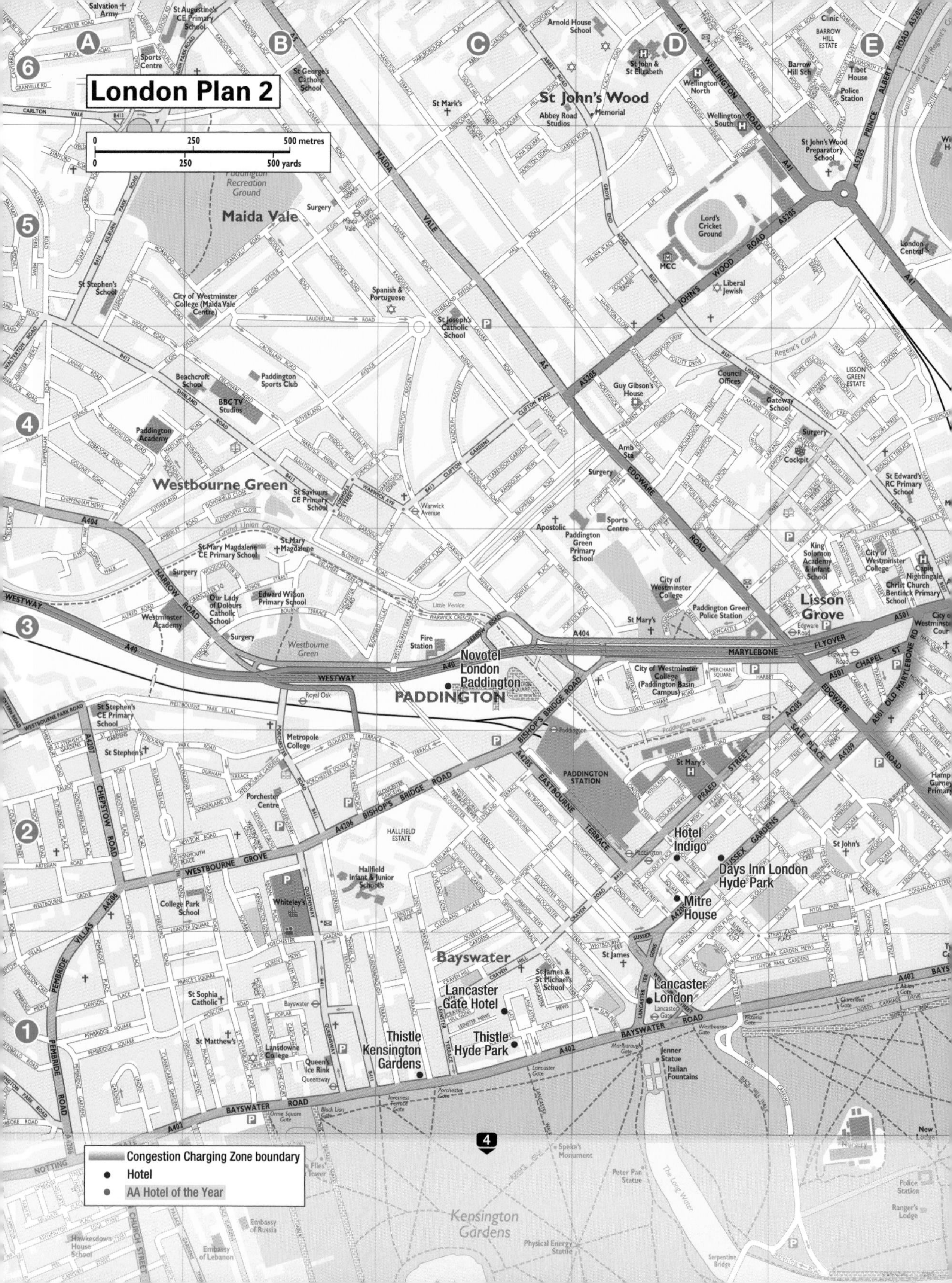

London Plan 2
0
250
500 metres
0
250
500 yards
A
B
C
D
E
6
5
4
3
2
1
St John's Wood
Maida Vale
Westbourne Green
PADDINGTON
Bayswater
Lisson Grove
Kensington Gardens
Novotel London Paddington
Hotel Indigo
Days Inn London Hyde Park
Mitre House
Lancaster London
Lancaster Gate Hotel
Thistle Hyde Park
Thistle Kensington Gardens
Paddington Recreation Ground
Lord's Cricket Ground
Abbey Road Studios
Paddington Station
St Mary's
Whiteley's
Little Venice
Westbourne Green
BBC TV Studios
Paddington Academy
Paddington Sports Club
Paddington Green Police Station
City of Westminster College
MCC
Liberal Jewish
Memorial
Arnold House School
St John & St Elizabeth
Wellington North
Wellington South
St John's Wood Preparatory School
London Central
Italian Fountains
Jenner Statue
Peter Pan Statue
Speke's Monument
Physical Energy Statue
Serpentine Bridge
Embassy of Russia
Embassy of Lebanon
MAIDA VALE
EDGWARE ROAD
BAYSWATER ROAD
WESTWAY
MARYLEBONE FLYOVER
BISHOP'S BRIDGE ROAD
WESTBOURNE GROVE
HARROW ROAD
ST JOHN'S WOOD ROAD
WELLINGTON ROAD
PRINCE ALBERT ROAD
PRAED STREET
SUSSEX GARDENS
CHEPSTOW ROAD
PEMBRIDGE VILLAS
QUEENSWAY
Grand Union Canal
Regent's Canal
4
Congestion Charging Zone boundary
Hotel
AA Hotel of the Year

F
G
H
J
K
London Zoo
Greater London House
Mayford Estate
Youth Centre
Somerstown Estate
St Aloysius School
SS Mary & Pancras School
Somers Town
Maria Fidelis Sch (Upper)
The Hub
Regent's Park
Christ Church School
St George's Cathedral
Cumberland Gate
St John's Lodge
Capel Manor College
Regent's Park Estate
Open-air
Queen Mary's Gardens
Inner Circle
Chester Road
The Holme
Boating Lake
London Business School
Regent's College
Tennis Centre
Netley Primary School
Schafer House
Police Station
Royal College of Physicians
Thistle Euston
Euston Station
Maria Fidelis
Ibis London Euston St Pancras
Friends Meeting House
Language College
Wellcome Collection
Euston Road
Meliá White House
HMRC
University College
UCL
Bloomsbury (UCL)
Inst of Archaeology
Gandhi Memorial
University College London (UCL)
Chinese Art Gallery
Park Square Gardens
Warren Street
Venezuela Embassy
Grafton Way
Gower Street
Tottenham Court Road
Hampstead Road
Albany Street
Francis Holland CE School
Sherlock Holmes
Lost Property Office
Royal Academy of Music
Marylebone Road
Regent's Park Crescent Gardens
Park Crescent
Portland
Royal National Orthopaedic
Holiday Inn London Regents Park
Fitzroy Square
YMCA
Petrie
Warburg Institute
Madame Tussauds
Baker Street
Princess Grace
St Marylebone CE School
The Clinic
Fitzrovia
BT Tower
The Landmark London
University of Westminster
Park Plaza Sherlock Holmes
University College London
York St
Paddington Street
Middlesex
Courtauld Institute of Bio-chemistry
Goodge Street
Cavendish College
College of Law
School of Hygiene & Tropical Medicine
St Mary's
Heart
Ten Manchester Street
All Souls Primary School
British Transport Police Station
College of Naturopathic Medicine
Fire Station
St Marylebone CE School
MARYLEBONE
Queen's College
Embassy of Switzerland
University of Westminster
Mortimer Street
Goodge Street
Wallace Collection
DLD College
The Langham London
Family Court
Holiday Inn London - Oxford Circus
University of Westminster
London Marriott Hotel Marble Arch
Radisson Blu Portman Hotel
School of Economic Science
The Mandeville Hotel
Royal College of Nursing
Animation Art Gal
The Plaza
100 Club
French Protestant
St Patrick's College
The Montcalm
Hyatt Regency London - The Churchill
London College of Fashion
Oxford Circus
London Palladium
Photographers' Gallery
Youth Hostel
Surgery
Best Western Premier Mostyn Hotel
Selfridges
Oxford Street
Thistle Marble Arch
Bond Street
Liberty
Soho
The Cumberland
Marble Arch
West London College
London Marriott Hotel Park Lane
Claridge's
Westminster Kingsway Coll
Queen's Soho Parish Sch
Madame Jo Jo's
Statue
Cumberland Gate
Speakers' Corner
London Marriott Hotel Grosvenor Square
Argentine Embassy
Italian Embassy
Canadian Embassy
Gielgud
Chinatown
Apollo
Lyric
Piccadilly
London Trocadero
US Embassy
The Westbury Hotel
Police Station
Thistle Piccadilly
Monument
Millennium Hotel London Mayfair
Ripley's Believe It or Not!
Piccadilly Circus
The Connaught
Mayfair
Haunch of Venison
Royal Academy of Arts
Le Meridien Piccadilly
Criterion
Grosvenor House, A JW Marriott Hotel
Holiday Inn London-Mayfair
Brown's Hotel
Jermyn Street
Grosvenor Chapel
St George's School
St James's
Regent Street
Haymarket
4
3
Cavendish London
White Cube Art Gallery
Chesterfield Mayfair
The Lookout
The Dorchester
The Washington Mayfair Hotel
The Ritz London
The London Library
Sofitel London St James
Crimean War
St James's Hotel and Club
Hyde Park
45 Park Lane
7th July Memorial
The Stafford London
Dukes
Pall Mall
Piccadilly
Park Lane

A
B
C
D
E
King's Cross
St Pancras International Station
King's Cross Station
Pentonville
Pentonville Road
White Lion Street
Premier Inn London King's Cross St Pancras
Somers Town
Renaissance St Pancras Hotel
Novotel London St Pancras
Premier Inn London Euston
St Pancras
FINSBURY
Holiday Inn London King's Cross / Bloomsbury
Clerkenwell
Holiday Inn London Bloomsbury
Hotel Russell
Bloomsbury
The Zetter Hotel
Malmaison Charterhouse Square
Bedford Hotel
The Montague on the Gardens
The Kingsley by Thistle
Holborn
Chancery Court Hotel London
St Giles
Crowne Plaza London - The City
Soho
Strand
The Savoy
Thistle Piccadilly
The Royal Trafalgar by Thistle
Charing Cross
CITY OF LONDON
River Thames
Victoria Embankment
Corinthia Hotel London
The Royal Horseguards
Mercure London City Bankside
Express by Holiday Inn London - Southwark
Sofitel London St James
Congestion Charging Zone boundary
Hotel
AA Hotel of the Year

London Plan 3
0
250
500 metres
0
250
500 yards
F
G
H
J
K
1
2
3
4
5
6
5
Hoxton
The RE London Shoreditch
Thistle City Barbican
Holiday Inn Express London City
SHOREDITCH
St Luke's
Spitalfields
ANdAZ Liverpool Street
Apex London Wall Hotel
Ibis London City
The Chamberlain
Whitechapel
Mint Hotel Tower of London
Novotel London Tower Bridge
Premier Inn London City (Tower Hill)
Apex City of London Hotel
Premier Inn London Southwark
Novotel London City South
All Seasons London Southwark Rose Hotel
London Bridge Hotel
The Tower
St Geor
Old Street Station
Liverpool Street Station
Moorgate Station
Cannon Street Station
The Barbican
Museum of London
Bank of England
The Gherkin
Tower of London
Old Spitalfields Market

London Plan 4
0
250
500 metres
0
250
500 yards
2
Thistle Kensington Gardens
Thistle Hyde Park
Jenner Statue
Italian Fountains
Kensington Gardens
Speke's Monument
Peter Pan Statue
The Long Water
Nursery
Police Station
Ranger's Lodge
Physical Energy Statue
Round Pond
Sunken Gardens
Kensington Palace
Kensington Palace Green
Serpentine Bridge
Isis Statue
The Serpentine
Serpentine Gallery
The Lido
Diana Princess of Wales Memorial Fountain
Bandstand
St Govor's Well
Mount Gate
Tennis Courts
Bowling Green
Albert Memorial
Embassy of Russia
Embassy of Lebanon
Romanian Embassy
Israel Em
Royal Garden Hotel
Fire Station
Hawkesdown House School
St Mary Abbots
St Mary Abbots CE Primary School
Kensington & Chelsea Town Hall
Milestone Hotel
KENSINGTON
High Street Kensington
Royal College of Art
Royal Albert Hall
Royal Geographical Society
Knightsbridge
Baglioni Hotel
Heythrop College
Thomas's Day School
Copthorne Tara Hotel London Kensington
Royal College of Music
Imperial College London
Prince's Gardens
Imperial College London
Imperial College London
Science
Royal College of Art
The Oratory
Brompton
Egerton House
Darwin Centre
Natural History
Victoria & Albert
Police Station
Health Centre
Baden Powell House
Superstore
Cromwell
Institute Français
Lycée Français
Millennium Bailey's Hotel London Kensington
Premier Inn London Kensington (Olympia)
London Marriott Kensington
Gloucester Road
Millennium Gloucester Hotel London Kensington
South Kensington
South Kensington
Premier Inn London Kensington
Harrington Hall
Our Lady of Victories RC Primary School
Marlborough Primary School
Police Station
K + K Hotel George
Best Western Burns Hotel
Earl's Court Station
Twenty Nevern Square
Earl's Court
St Cuthbert & St Matthais CE Primary School
Bousfield Primary School
Royal Marsden
Royal Marsden
Royal Cancer
Royal Brompton & Harefield
St Luke's
CHELSEA
Gems Hampshire School
Earls Court Exhibition Centre
West Brompton Station
St Luke's
Fire Station
Register Office
Sports Centre
Express by Holiday Inn London Earl's Court,
Ibis London Earl's Court
West Brompton
Brompton Cemetery
Servite RC Primary School
Chelsea & Westminster
Ambulance Station
Park Walk Primary School
Carlyle's House
Fulham Primary School
KENSINGTON ROAD
HYDE PARK GATE
KENSINGTON GORE
KENSINGTON HIGH STREET
KENSINGTON CHURCH STREET
NOTTING HILL GATE
CROMWELL ROAD
WEST CROMWELL ROAD
OLD BROMPTON ROAD
BROMPTON ROAD
THURLOE PLACE
FULHAM ROAD
KINGS ROAD
LILLIE ROAD
REDCLIFFE GARDENS
FINBOROUGH ROAD
EARL'S COURT ROAD
WARWICK ROAD
PEMBROKE ROAD
1
2
3
4
5
6
A
B
C
D
E

Millennium Hotel London Mayfair
The Connaught
Mayfair
Grosvenor House, A JW Marriott Hotel
Holiday Inn London-Mayfair
Brown's Hotel
Le Meridien Piccadilly
Thistle Piccadilly
The Royal by Thistle
2
Chesterfield Mayfair
Cavendish London
Sofitel London St James
The Dorchester
The Washington Mayfair Hotel
The Ritz London
St James's Hotel and Club
45 Park Lane
Hyde Park
Metropolitan London
The Stafford London by Kempinski
Dukes London
St James's
Athenaeum Hotel & Apartments
Four Seasons Hotel Park Lane
Green Park
5
St James's Park
The Lanesborough
Mandarin Oriental Hyde Park London
The Berkeley
Sheraton Park Tower
Buckingham Palace Gardens (private)
Buckingham Palace
The Halkin Hotel
The Capital
Millennium Hotel London Knightsbridge
The Levin
Harrods
Jumeirah Lowndes
Belgrave Square
Jumeirah Carlton Tower
51 Buckingham Gate
Taj Suites and Residences
St Ermins Hotel
The Rubens at the Palace
No 41
Crowne Plaza London St James
The Beaufort
The Goring
Thistle Westminster
WESTMINSTER
Cadogan
Victoria Station
The Grosvenor
Park Plaza Victoria London
Premier Inn London Victoria
Belgravia
The Draycott
Pimlico
Holiday Inn Express London - Victoria
Chelsea
Royal Hospital Chelsea
Ranelagh Gardens
River Thames
Grosvenor Bridge
Chelsea Bridge
Congestion Charging Zone boundary
Hotel
AA Hotel of the Year
F
G
H
J
K

LONDON
River Thames
Thistle Piccadilly
The Royal Trafalgar by Thistle
The Savoy
Charing Cross
Sofitel London St James
Corinthia Hotel London
The Royal Horseguards
Premier Inn London County Hall
London Marriott Hotel County Hall
Park Plaza County Hall
LAMBETH
H10 London Waterloo Hotel
Mercure London City Bankside
Express by Holiday Inn London - Southwark
Days Hotel London Waterloo
Novotel London Waterloo
Park Plaza Riverbank London
Mint Hotel Westminster
Plaza on the River - Club & Residence
Vauxhall
Kennington
Newington
WATERLOO STATION
WATERLOO EAST STATION
VAUXHALL STATION
The Oval (Surrey County Cricket Ground)
Imperial War
St Thomas'
Archbishop's Park
Tate Britain
Westminster Abbey
Houses of Parliament
Big Ben
London Eye
National
IBM
ITV
IMAX
Royal Festival Hall
Queen Elizabeth Hall
Hayward Gallery
BFI
Treasury
Home Office
Cenotaph
Horse Guards
Whitehall
Victoria Embankment
Albert Embankment
Millbank
Lambeth Bridge
Westminster Bridge
Vauxhall Bridge
Hungerford Bridge
Waterloo Bridge
Blackfriars Bridge
Lambeth Palace
New Covent Garden Market
Kennington Park
Vauxhall Park
Spring Gardens
Victoria Tower Gardens
Jubilee Gardens
St James's Park
St James's Lake
3
4
4
A
B
C
D
E

London Plan 5
Premier Inn London Southwark
Novotel London City South
All Seasons London Southwark Rose Hotel
London Bridge Hotel
Premier Inn London Tower Bridge
The Tower
The Borough
Walworth
River Thames
Tower of London
HMS Belfast
City Hall
London Bridge
Tower Bridge
Southwark Cathedral
Guy's
Borough Market
London Dungeon
The Shard
Burgess Park
0
250
500 metres
0
250
500 yards
Congestion Charging Zone boundary
Hotel
AA Hotel of the Year
F
G
H
J
K
1
2
3
4
5
6

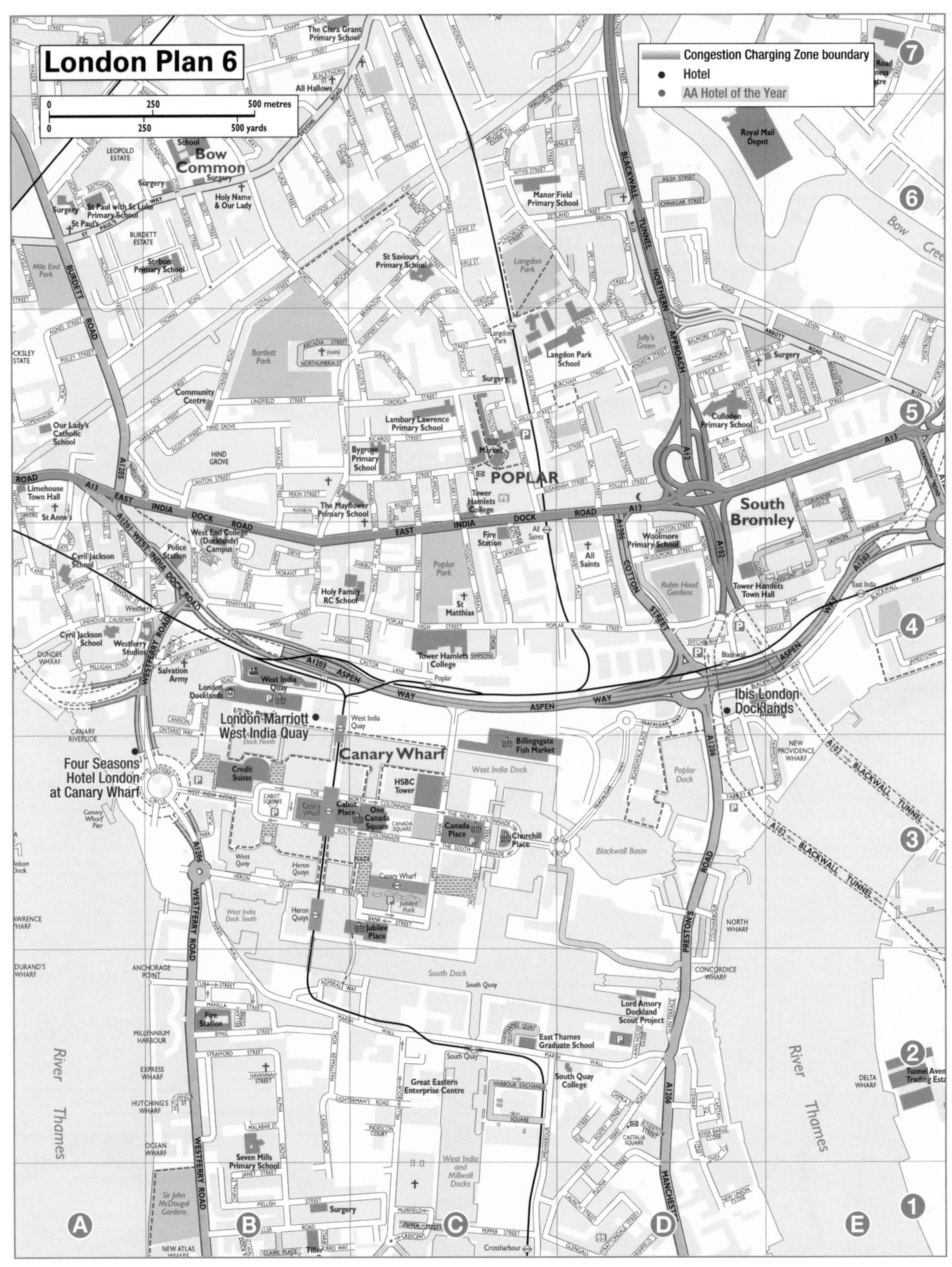

London Plan 6
0
250
500 metres
0
250
500 yards
Congestion Charging Zone boundary
Hotel
AA Hotel of the Year
The Clara Grant Primary School
All Hallows
Bow Common
School
Surgery
LEOPOLD ESTATE
Holy Name & Our Lady
St Paul with St Luke Primary School
St Paul's
BURDETT ESTATE
Stebon Primary School
Mile End Park
BURDETT ROAD
Manor Field Primary School
Langdon Park
St Saviours Primary School
Limehouse Cut
BLACKWALL TUNNEL NORTHERN APPROACH
Royal Mail Depot
Bow Creek
Bartlett Park
Jolly's Green
Langdon Park School
Community Centre
Our Lady's Catholic School
HIND GROVE
Lansbury Lawrence Primary School
Bygrove Primary School
Market
POPLAR
Culloden Primary School
South Bromley
Limehouse Town Hall
St Anne's
EAST INDIA DOCK ROAD
The Mayflower Primary School
Tower Hamlets College
Fire Station
All Saints
Woolmore Primary School
West End College (Docklands) Campus
Police Station
Cyril Jackson School
Holy Family RC School
Poplar Park
St Matthias
Robin Hood Gardens
Tower Hamlets Town Hall
East India
Westferry
Westferry Studios
Salvation Army
DUNDEE WHARF
London Docklands
West India Quay
Tower Hamlets College
ASPEN WAY
Poplar
Blackwall
Ibis London Docklands
London Marriott West India Quay
CANARY RIVERSIDE
Four Seasons Hotel London at Canary Wharf
Canary Wharf
Billingsgate Fish Market
West India Dock
Credit Suisse
HSBC Tower
Poplar Dock
NEW PROVIDENCE WHARF
Canary Wharf Pier
Cabot Place
One Canada Square
Canada Place
Churchill Place
Blackwall Basin
BLACKWALL TUNNEL
West Quay
Heron Quays
Jubilee Park
Jubilee Place
West India Dock South
WESTFERRY ROAD
PRESTON'S ROAD
NORTH WHARF
South Dock
South Quay
ANCHORAGE POINT
CONCORDICE WHARF
Lord Amory Dockland Scout Project
Fire Station
MILLENNIUM HARBOUR
East Thames Graduate School
River Thames
EXPRESS WHARF
Great Eastern Enterprise Centre
South Quay College
HUTCHING'S WHARF
DELTA WHARF
Tunnel Avenue Trading Estate
OCEAN WHARF
Seven Mills Primary School
West India and Millwall Docks
MANCHESTER
Sir John McDougal Gardens
Surgery
NEW ATLAS WHARF
Crossharbour
A
B
C
D
E
1
2
3
4
5
6
7

London Plan 7

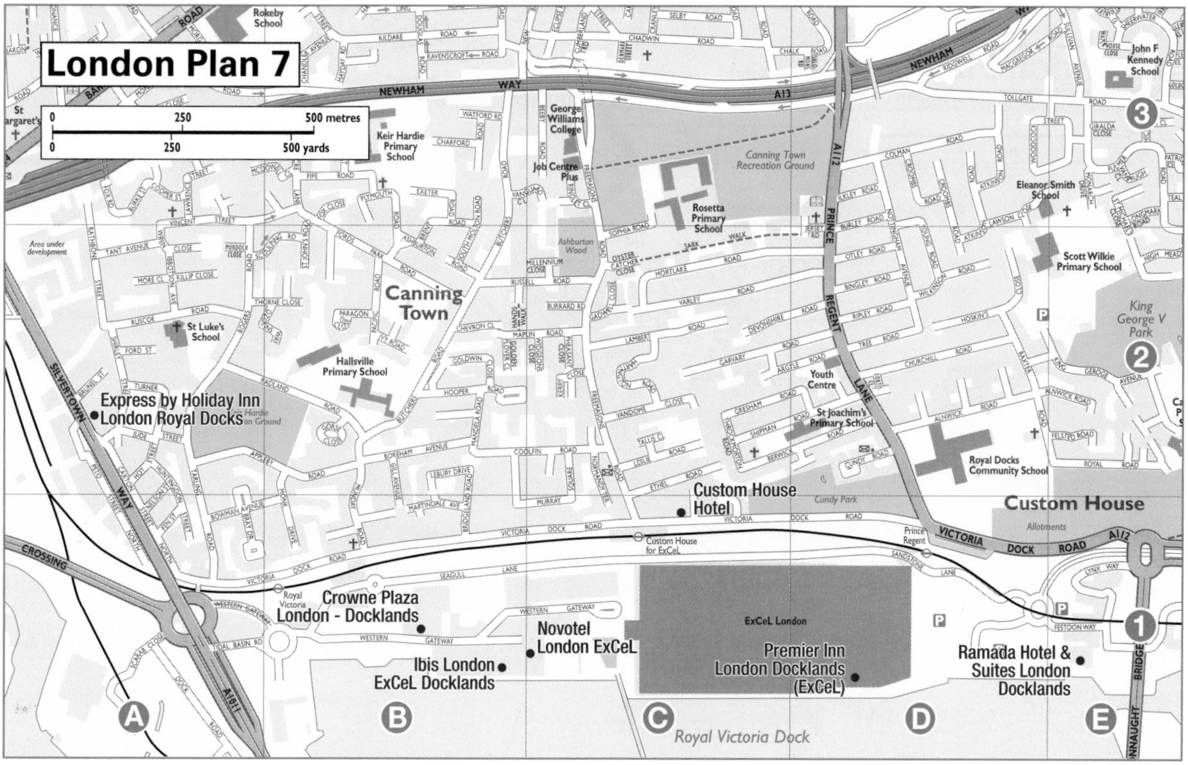

0 250 500 metres
0 250 500 yards

Canning Town

Custom House

Express by Holiday Inn London Royal Docks

Crowne Plaza London - Docklands

Novotel London ExCeL

Ibis London ExCeL Docklands

Premier Inn London Docklands (ExCeL)

Custom House Hotel

Ramada Hotel & Suites London Docklands

ExCeL London

Royal Victoria Dock

King George V Park

Rokeby School

Keir Hardie Primary School

George Williams College

Job Centre Plus

Canning Town Recreation Ground

Rosetta Primary School

Ashburton Wood

St Luke's School

Hallsville Primary School

Youth Centre

St Joachim's Primary School

Royal Docks Community School

Eleanor Smith School

Scott Wilkie Primary School

John F Kennedy School

Cundy Park

Allotments

Custom House for ExCeL

Royal Victoria

Prince Regent

A B C D E

1 2 3

London Plan 8

0 250 500 metres
0 250 500 yards

GREENWICH

Greenwich Park

Blackheath

Ibis London Greenwich

Novotel London Greenwich

Premier Inn London Greenwich

Cutty Sark

Trinity College of Music

University of Greenwich

Dreadnought

Greenwich Market

Maritime Greenwich

National Maritime

Devonport House Conference Centre

St Alfege

Picture House

Fan

James Wolfe Primary School

Alpha Meridian College

Greenwich College

Greenwich Playhouse

Police Station

Greenwich Dance Academy

Greenwich London College

Greenwich Community College

Greenwich West Community & Arts Centre

Our Lady Star of the Sea

St Ursula's Convent School

Greenwich Magistrates' Court

Fire Station

Brookmarsh Industrial Estate

Deptford Creek

GREENWICH STATION

MAZE HILL STATION

Arches Leisure Centre

Flamstead House

Statue

Royal Observatory

Peter Harrison Planetarium

Tea House

Bandstand

One Tree Hill

The Flower Gardens

The Wilderness (Deer Park)

Ranger's House (Wernher Collection)

The Point

John Roan School

War Memorial

A B C D E

1 2 3

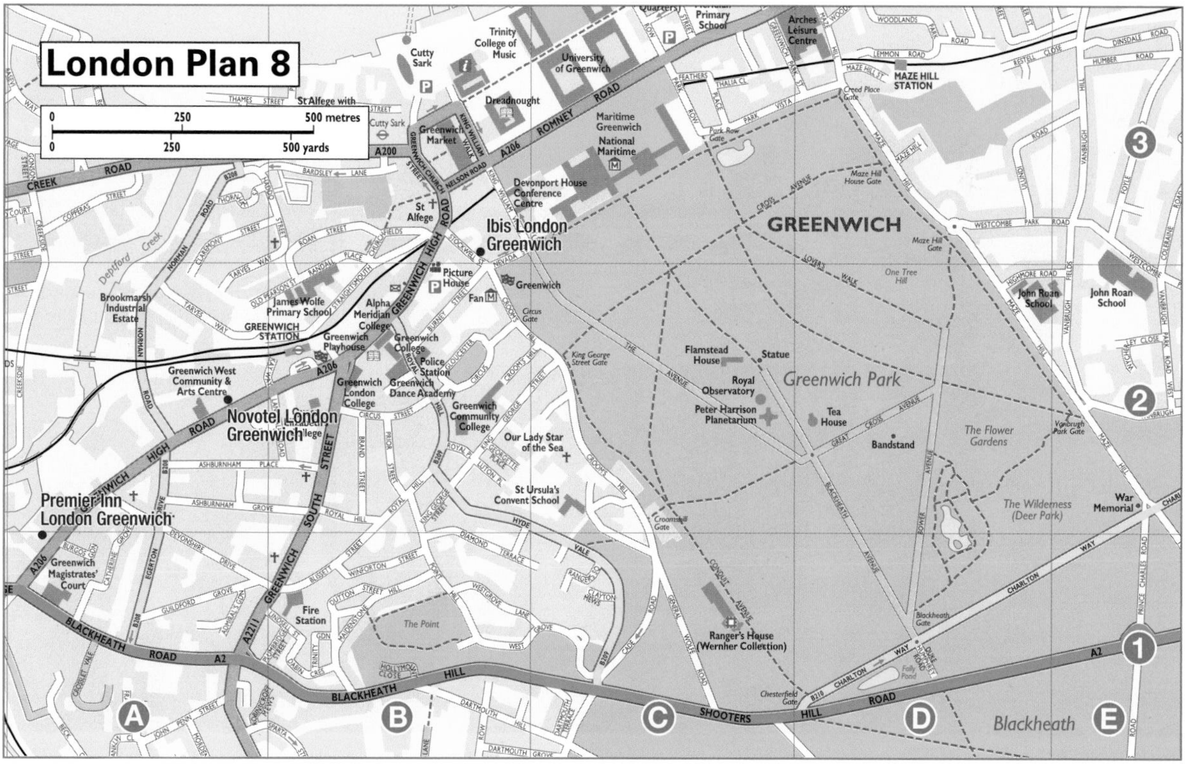

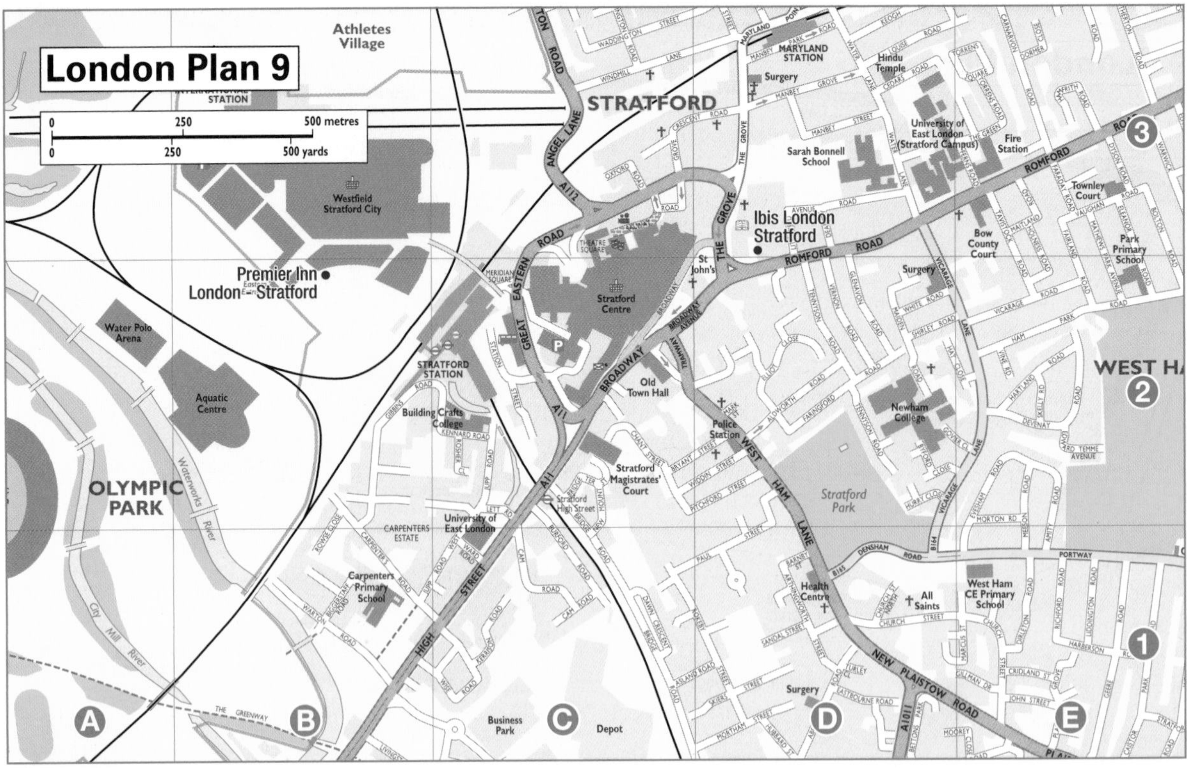
London Plan 9
0 250 500 metres
0 250 500 yards
Athletes Village
STRATFORD
Westfield Stratford City
Premier Inn London - Stratford
Ibis London Stratford
Water Polo Arena
Aquatic Centre
OLYMPIC PARK
Waterworks River
City Mill River
THE GREENWAY
STRATFORD STATION
Stratford Centre
Old Town Hall
Building Crafts College
CARPENTERS ESTATE
Carpenters Primary School
University of East London
Stratford Magistrates' Court
Police Station
Stratford Park
Health Centre
All Saints
West Ham CE Primary School
Newham College
University of East London (Stratford Campus)
Sarah Bonnell School
Hindu Temple
MARYLAND STATION
Fire Station
Townley Court
Bow County Court
Park Primary School
WEST HA
Business Park
Depot
Surgery
St John's
ROMFORD ROAD
BROADWAY
HIGH STREET
WEST HAM LANE
NEW PLAISTOW ROAD
GREAT EASTERN ROAD
ANGEL LANE
THE GROVE
PORTWAY
A
B
C
D
E
1
2
3

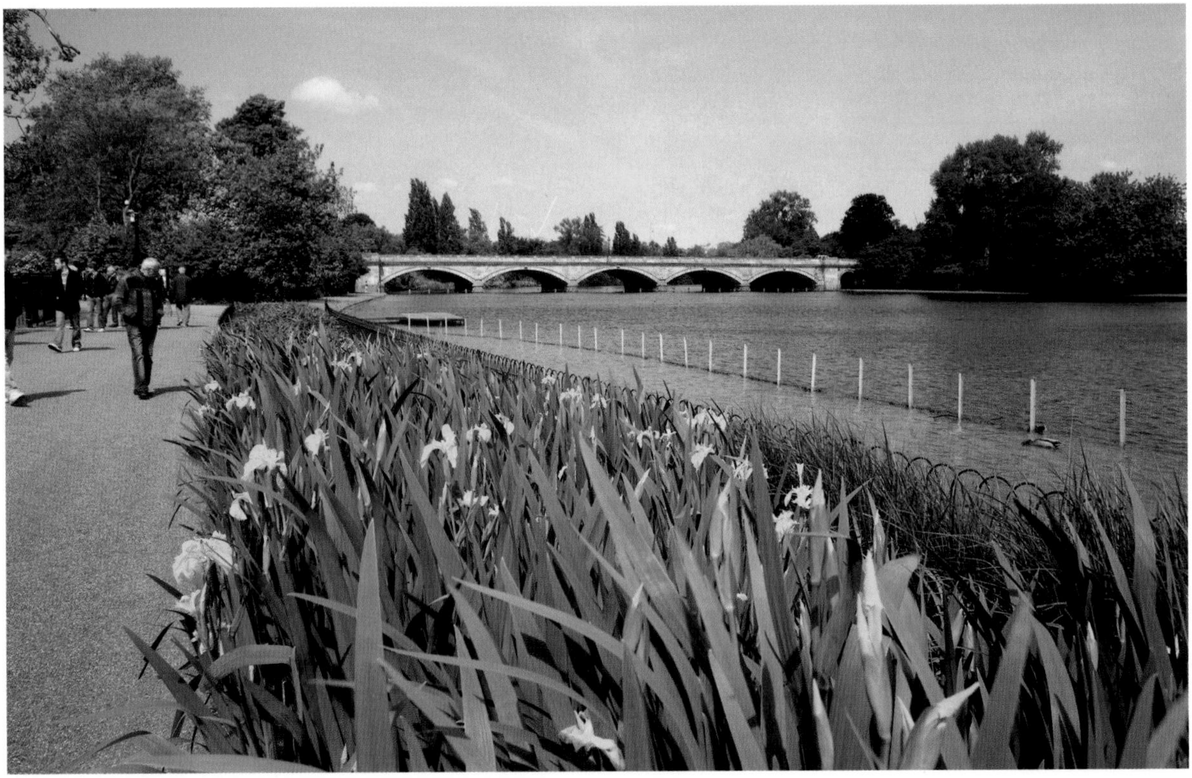

LONDON

LONDON

Greater London Plans 1-9, pages 274-286. (Small scale maps 6 & 7 at back of book.) Hotels are listed below in postal district order, commencing East, then North, South and West, with a brief indication of the area covered. Detailed plans 2-9 show the locations of AA-appointed hotels within the Central London postal districts. If you do not know the postal district of the hotel you want, refer to the index preceding the street plans for the entry and map pages. The plan reference for each AA-appointed hotel also appears within its directory entry.

E1 STEPNEY AND EAST OF THE TOWER OF LONDON

See also LONDON plan 1 G4

The Tower

★★★★ 72% HOTEL PLAN 5 J6

☎ 0870 333 9106 🖷 0870 333 9206
St Katherine's Way E1W 1LD
e-mail: tower@guoman.com
dir: Follow signs for Tower Bridge, left into St Katharine's Way. Car park under hotel (control barrier)

This extensive modern hotel enjoys superb views over the Thames, Tower Bridge and St Katherine's Docks. Public areas include several lounges, a modern, contemporary bar and a choice of restaurants. Bedrooms are traditionally furnished and include a selection of impressive suites.

Rooms 801 (34 fmly) (90 smoking) **Facilities** Gym Xmas New Year Wi-fi **Conf** Class 350 Board 65 Thtr 500 **Services** Lift Air con **Parking** 200 **Notes** ⊗ Civ Wed 500

Express by Holiday Inn London-Limehouse

BUDGET HOTEL

☎ 020 7791 3850 🖷 020 7791 3851
469-475 The Highway E1W 3HN
e-mail: jcniclas@exhi-limehouse.co.uk
web: www.hiexpress.com/limehouse

A modern hotel ideal for families and business travellers. Fresh and uncomplicated, the spacious rooms include Sky TV, power shower and tea and coffee-making facilities. Continental buffet breakfast is included in the room rate; other meals may be taken at the nearby family pub or restaurant. See also the Hotel Groups pages.

Rooms 150 **Conf** Class 26 Board 25 Thtr 60

Ibis London City

BUDGET HOTEL PLAN 3 J2

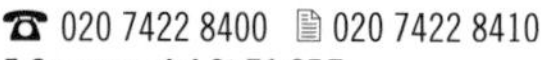

☎ 020 7422 8400 🖷 020 7422 8410
5 Commercial St E1 6BF
e-mail: H5011@accor.com
dir: M25 junct 30, A13, follow The City signs, then Aldgate signs

Modern, budget hotel offering comfortable accommodation in bright and practical bedrooms. Breakfast is self-service and dinner is available in the restaurant. See also the Hotel Groups pages.

Rooms 348

Premier Inn London City (Tower Hill)

BUDGET HOTEL PLAN 3 J1

☎ 0871 527 8646 🖷 0871 527 8641
22-24 Prescott St, Tower Hill E1 8BB
dir: Nearest tube: Tower Hill. 3 mins walk from Docklands Light Rail (DLR)

High quality, budget accommodation ideal for both families and business travellers. Spacious, en suite bedrooms feature tea and coffee making facilities, and Freeview TV in most hotels. Internet access and Wi-fi are available for a small fee. The adjacent family restaurant features a wide and varied menu. See also the Hotel Groups pages.

D £88-£119*

E2 BETHNAL GREEN

The RE London Shoreditch

★★★ 70% HOTEL PLAN 3 K6

☎ 020 7613 6501 🖷 020 7613 6501
419-437 Hackney Rd E2 8PP
e-mail: reservations@hotelshoreditch.com
web: www.hotelshoreditch.com
dir: Off A1208, 400mtrs from junct with Cambridge Heath Rd

A purpose-built hotel conveniently located for the financial district, the City Airport and the Olympic Village. The hotel offers comfortable and contemporary bedrooms with air-conditioning, Wi-fi and flat-screen TVs. The Executive Rooms have been designed to accommodate the needs of the business traveller. A secure car park is available.

Rooms 178 (53 fmly) (11 GF) **Facilities** STV FTV Xmas New Year Wi-fi **Conf** Class 30 Board 16 Thtr 50 **Services** Lift Air con **Parking** 23 **Notes** ⊗ Civ Wed 100

E4 CHINGFORD Map 6 TQ39

Express by Holiday Inn London Chingford

BUDGET HOTEL

☎ 0870 444 2789 🖷 0870 444 2790
5 Walthamstow Av, Chingford E4 8ST
e-mail: dgmchingford@expressholidayinn.co.uk
web: www.hiexpress.com/lonchingford
dir: On A406 (North Circular) at Crooked Billet rdbt, adjacent to A112 (Chingford-Walthamstow)

A modern hotel ideal for families and business travellers. Fresh and uncomplicated, the spacious rooms include Sky TV, power shower and tea and coffee-making facilities. Continental buffet breakfast is included in the room rate; other meals may be taken at the nearby family pub or restaurant. See also the Hotel Groups pages.

Rooms 102 (65 fmly) **Conf** Class 10 Board 16 Thtr 20

E6 EAST HAM

See LONDON SECTION plan 1 H4

Premier Inn London Beckton

BUDGET HOTEL

☎ 0871 527 8644 🖷 0871 527 8645
1 Woolwich Manor Way E6 5NT
dir: A13 onto A117 (Woolwich Manor Way) towards City Airport, hotel on left after 1st rdbt

High quality, budget accommodation ideal for both families and business travellers. Spacious, en suite bedrooms feature tea and coffee making facilities, and Freeview TV in most hotels. Internet access and Wi-fi are available for a small fee. The adjacent family restaurant features a wide and varied menu. See also the Hotel Groups pages.

Rooms 90 **D** £60-£76*

E14 CANARY WHARF & LIMEHOUSE

INSPECTORS' CHOICE

Four Seasons Hotel London at Canary Wharf

★★★★★ ® HOTEL PLAN 6 A3

☎ 020 7510 1999 📠 020 7510 1998
Westferry Circus, Canary Wharf E14 8RS
e-mail: reservations.caw@fourseasons.com
web: www.fourseasons.com/canarywharf
dir: From A13 follow Canary Wharf, Isle of Dogs & Westferry Circus signs. Hotel off 3rd exit of Westferry Circus rdbt

With superb views over the London skyline, this stylish modern hotel enjoys a delightful riverside location. Spacious contemporary bedrooms are particularly thoughtfully equipped. Public areas include the Italian Quadrato Bar and Restaurant, an impressive business centre and a gym. Guests also have complimentary use of the impressive Holmes Place health club and spa. Welcoming staff provide exemplary levels of service and hospitality.

Rooms 142 (20 smoking) **S** £160-£330; **D** £160-£330* **Facilities** Spa STV FTV supervised Gym Fitness centre Xmas New Year Wi-fi **Conf** Class 120 Board 56 Thtr 200 **Services** Lift Air con **Parking** 54 **Notes** Civ Wed 200

LONDON

London Marriott West India Quay

Marriott HOTELS & RESORTS

★★★★★ 80% HOTEL PLAN 6 B4

☎ 020 7093 1000 📠 020 7093 1001
22 Hertsmere Rd, Canary Wharf E14 4ED
web: www.londonmarriottwestindiaquay.co.uk
dir: Exit Aspen Way at Hertsmere Rd. Hotel opposite, adjacent to Canary Wharf

This spectacular skyscraper with curved glass façade is located at the heart of the docklands, adjacent to Canary Wharf and overlooking the water. The hotel is modern, but not pretentiously trendy; eye-catching floral displays add warmth to the public areas. Bedrooms, many of which overlook the quay, provide every modern convenience, including broadband and air conditioning. Curve Restaurant offers good quality cooking focusing on fresh fish.

Rooms 301 (22 fmly) **Facilities** STV Gym Xmas New Year Wi-fi **Conf** Class 132 Board 27 Thtr 290 **Services** Lift Air con **Notes** ⊗ Civ Wed 290

Ibis London Docklands

BUDGET HOTEL PLAN 6 D4

☎ 020 7517 1100 📠 020 7987 5916
1 Baffin Way E14 9PE
e-mail: H2177@accor.com
web: www.ibishotel.com
dir: From Tower Bridge follow City Airport and Royal Docks signs, exit for 'Isle of Dogs'. Hotel on 1st left opposite McDonalds

Modern, budget hotel offering comfortable accommodation in bright and practical bedrooms. Breakfast is self-service and dinner is available in the restaurant. See also the Hotel Groups pages.

Rooms 87 (15 GF) **S** £68-£153; **D** £68-£153*

E15 STRATFORD

Ibis London Stratford

BUDGET HOTEL

☎ 020 8536 3700 📠 020 8519 5161
1A Romford Rd, Stratford E15 4LJ
e-mail: h3099@accor.com
web: www.ibishotel.com

Modern, budget hotel offering comfortable accommodation in bright and practical bedrooms. Breakfast is self-service and dinner is available in the restaurant. See also the Hotel Groups pages.

Rooms 108 **S** £67-£140; **D** £67-£140*

Premier Inn London - Stratford

○ PLAN 9 B2

☎ 0871 527 8000
Westfield Stratfield City, Stratford E15 1AZ

This hotel is due to open in 2012.

Rooms 267

E16 SILVERTOWN

Crowne Plaza London - Docklands

★★★★ 77% ® HOTEL PLAN 7 B1

☎ 020 7055 2000 📠 020 7055 2001
Royal Victoria Dock, Western Gateway E16 1AL
e-mail: sales@crowneplazadocklands.co.uk
web: www.crowneplazadocklands.co.uk
dir: A1020 towards ExceL. Follow signs for ExceL West. Hotel on left 400mtrs before ExceL

Ideally located for the ExCeL exhibition centre, Canary Wharf and London City airport, this unique, contemporary hotel overlooking Royal Victoria Dock, offers accommodation suitable for both the leisure and business travellers. Rooms are spacious and equipped with all modern facilities. The hotel has a busy bar, a contemporary restaurant and health and fitness facilities with an indoor pool, jacuzzi and sauna.

Rooms 210 (12 fmly) **Facilities** STV supervised Gym Beauty treatments Sauna Steam room Xmas New Year Wi-fi **Conf** Class 140 Board 62 Thtr 275 **Services** Lift Air con **Parking** 75 **Notes** ⊗ Civ Wed 275

Novotel London ExCeL

★★★★ 75% HOTEL PLAN 7 C1

☎ 020 7540 9700 & 0870 850 4560
🖷 020 7540 9710
7 Western Gateway, Royal Victoria Docks E16 1AA
e-mail: H3656@accor.com
web: www.novotel.com/3656
dir: M25 junct 30, A13 towards 'City', exit at Canning Town. Follow ExCeL West signs. Hotel adjacent to ExCeL

This hotel is situated adjacent to the ExCeL exhibition centre and overlooks the Royal Victoria Dock. Design throughout the hotel is contemporary and stylish. Public rooms include a range of meeting rooms, a modern coffee station, indoor leisure facilities and a smart bar and restaurant, both with a terrace overlooking the dock. Bedrooms feature modern decor, a bathroom with separate bath and shower, and an extensive range of extras.

Rooms 257 (211 fmly) **S** £250; **D** £285* **Facilities** STV FTV Gym Sauna Steam room Relaxation room with massage bed Wi-fi **Conf** Class 55 Board 30 Thtr 70 **Services** Lift Air con **Parking** 160 **Notes** LB Civ Wed 50

Ramada Hotel & Suites London Docklands

RAMADA

★★★★ 71% HOTEL PLAN 7 E1

☎ 020 7540 4820 & 020 7540 4820
🖷 020 7540 4821
ExceL 2 Festoon Way, Royal Victoria Dock E16 1RH
e-mail: reservations@ramadadocklands.co.uk
dir: Follow signs to ExceL East & London City Airport. Over Connaught Bridge then immediate left at rdbt

This hotel benefits from a stunning waterfront location and is close to the events venue, ExCeL, the O2 Arena, Canary Wharf and London City Airport. The accommodation comprises a mix of spacious bedrooms and suites. The relaxed public areas consist of a modern restaurant and informal lounge area. Parking, a fitness room and meeting rooms are available on site.

Rooms 224 (71 fmly) (50 smoking) **Facilities** FTV Gym Xmas Wi-fi **Conf** Class 20 Board 25 Thtr 30 **Services** Lift Air con **Parking** 60 **Notes** Civ Wed 120

Custom House Hotel

★★★ 70% HOTEL PLAN 7 C1

☎ 020 7474 0011 & 7474 7472 🖷 020 7476 0005
272-283 Victoria Dock Rd E16 3BY
e-mail: reservations@customhouse-hotel.co.uk
dir: Nearest station: DLR. Custom House Station opposite hotel

Conveniently located for the ExceL Centre, the financial district and City Airport, the hotel offers comfortable accommodation to meet the requirements of the modern traveller. Superior bedrooms are air conditioned. There is a choice of dining options and a secure car park on a first-come-first-served basis.

Rooms 282 (12 smoking) **Facilities** STV FTV Xmas New Year Wi-fi **Conf** Class 50 Board 44 Thtr 110 **Services** Lift Air con **Parking** 70 **Notes** LB ⊗

Express by Holiday Inn London Royal Docks

BUDGET HOTEL PLAN 7 A2

☎ 020 7540 4040 🖷 020 7540 4050
1 Silvertown Way, Silvertown E16 1EA
e-mail: info@exhi-royaldocks.co.uk
web: www.hiexpress.com/londonroyal
dir: A13 onto A1011 towards Silvertown, City Airport & ExceL. Hotel on left

A modern hotel ideal for families and business travellers. Fresh and uncomplicated, the spacious rooms include Sky TV, power shower and tea and coffee-making facilities. Continental buffet breakfast is included in the room rate; other meals may be taken at the nearby family pub or restaurant. See also the Hotel Groups pages.

Rooms 136 (48 fmly) **Conf** Class 30 Board 30 Thtr 80

Ibis London ExCeL Docklands

BUDGET HOTEL PLAN 7 B1

☎ 020 7055 2300 🖷 020 7055 2310
9 Western Gateway, Royal Victoria Docks E16 1AB
e-mail: H3655@accor.com
web: www.ibishotel.com
dir: M25 then A13 to London, City Airport, ExCeL East

Modern, budget hotel offering comfortable accommodation in bright and practical bedrooms. Breakfast is self-service and dinner is available in the restaurant See also the Hotel Groups pages.

Rooms 278 (64 fmly)

Premier Inn London Docklands (ExCeL)

BUDGET HOTEL PLAN 7 D1

☎ 0871 527 8650 🖷 0871 527 8651
Excel East, Royal Victoria Dock E16 1SL
dir: A13 onto A1020. At Connaught rdbt take 2nd exit into Connaught Rd. Hotel on right

High quality, budget accommodation ideal for both families and business travellers. Spacious, en suite bedrooms feature tea and coffee making facilities, and Freeview TV in most hotels. Internet access and Wi-fi are available for a small fee. The adjacent family restaurant features a wide and varied menu. See also the Hotel Groups pages.

Rooms 202 **D** £67-£88*

EC1 CITY OF LONDON

The Zetter Hotel

★★★★ 80% ®® HOTEL PLAN 3 E4

☎ 020 7324 4444 🖷 020 7324 4445
St John's Square, 86-88 Clerkenwell Rd EC1M 5RJ
e-mail: info@thezetter.com
dir: From West A401, Clerkenwell Rd A5201. Hotel 200mtrs on left

This iconic hotel offers individually styled bedrooms with an impressive array of amenities, including the latest in-room entertainment. The Roof Top Studio rooms, some with a private patio, have amazing views over London's historic Clerkenwell and beyond. The Bistrot Bruno Loubet offers award-winning, imaginative and modern French cuisine, and the Atrium Bar and Lounge is the place to meet for coffee, have a light lunch or enjoy a drink. Two stylish rooms are available for private events.

Rooms 59 (13 smoking) **Facilities** STV Wi-fi **Conf** Class 28 Board 32 Thtr 50 **Services** Lift Air con **Parking** 1 **Notes** ⊗

Malmaison Charterhouse Square

★★★ 88% ®® HOTEL PLAN 3 E3

☎ 020 7012 3700 🖷 020 7012 3702
18-21 Charterhouse Square, Clerkenwell EC1M 6AH
e-mail: london@malmaison.com
web: www.malmaison.com
dir: Exit Barbican Station turn left, take 1st left. Hotel on far left corner of Charterhouse Square

Situated in a leafy and peaceful square, Malmaison Charterhouse maintains the same focus on quality service and food as the other hotels in the group. The bedrooms, stylishly decorated in calming tones, have

continued

EC1 CITY OF LONDON *continued*

all the expected facilities including power showers, CD players and free internet access. The brasserie and bar at the hotel's centre has a buzzing atmosphere and offers traditional French cuisine.

Rooms 97 (5 GF) **S** £255-£365; **D** £275-£385* **Facilities** STV Gym Wi-fi **Conf** Class 18 Board 16 Thtr 30 Del from £305 to £425* **Services** Lift Air con **Notes** LB

Thistle City Barbican

thistle

★★★ 75% HOTEL PLAN 3 F5

☎ 0871 376 9004 📠 0871 376 9104
Central St, Clerkenwell EC1V 8DS
e-mail: citybarbican@thistle.co.uk
web: www.thistlehotels.com/citybarbican
dir: From Kings Cross E, follow Pentonville Rd, right into Goswell Rd. At lights left into Lever St. Hotel at junct of Lever St & Central St

Situated on the edge of The City, this modern hotel offers a complimentary shuttle bus to Barbican, Liverpool Street and Moorgate tube stations at peak times. Bedrooms are well equipped and include some smart executive and superior rooms; public areas include a bar, a coffee shop and restaurant along with a smart Otium leisure club. Thistle Hotels – AA Hotel Group of the Year 2011-12.

Rooms 463 (166 annexe) (13 fmly) **Facilities** Spa STV FTV supervised Gym Sauna Steam room Xmas New Year Wi-fi **Conf** Class 75 Board 35 Thtr 175 **Services** Lift **Parking** 10 **Notes** LB

Holiday Inn Express London City

BUDGET HOTEL PLAN 3 H5

☎ 020 7300 4300 📠 020 7300 4400
275 Old St EC1V 9LN
e-mail: rescity@holidayinnlondon.com
web: www.hiexpress.com/londoncityex
dir: At City Rd rdbt turn left, hotel on left, next to fire station

A modern hotel ideal for families and business travellers. Fresh and uncomplicated, the spacious rooms include Sky TV, power shower and tea and coffee-making facilities. Continental buffet breakfast is included in the room rate; other meals may be taken at the nearby family pub or restaurant. See also the Hotel Groups pages.

Rooms 224 (132 fmly) (20 smoking) **Conf** Class 32 Board 32 Thtr 70

EC2

ANdAZ Liverpool Street

★★★★★ 82% HOTEL PLAN 3 H3

☎ 020 7961 1234 📠 020 7961 1235
40 Liverpool St EC2M 7QN
e-mail: info.londonliv@andaz.com
dir: On corner of Liverpool St & Bishopsgate, attached to Liverpool St station

This is an exciting and contemporary place to stay - no reception desk here so guests are checked-in by staff with laptops. Bedrooms are stylish, and designed very much with the executive in mind, with iPods and Wi-fi as well as a mini bar stocked with healthy choices. The dining options are varied and many - Miyako (1 AA Rosette) restaurant for Japanese cuisine, 1901 Restaurant and Wine Bar (3 AA Rosettes), St Georges pub, Catch and Champagne bar (1 AA Rosette), and the Eastway brasserie. There are also rooms for private dining and other events.

Rooms 267 (7 smoking) **S** £132-£378; **D** £162-£408* **Facilities** STV FTV Gym Steam room Treatment rooms New Year Wi-fi **Conf** Class 120 Board 24 Thtr 250 **Services** Lift Air con **Notes** Civ Wed 200

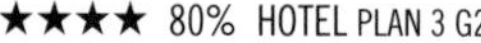

Apex London Wall Hotel

★★★★ 80% HOTEL PLAN 3 G2

☎ 0845 365 0000 & 020 7562 3030
📠 020 7256 2180
7-9 Copthall Av EC2R 7NJ
e-mail: london.reservations@apexhotels.co.uk
dir: Telephone for directions

A sister property to the nearby City of London Hotel. This hotel is situated in the heart of London's financial district and is close to many places of interest. This 'boutique' property offers contemporary accommodation for both the business and leisure travellers. Bedrooms and bathrooms have been fitted to a very high standard and feature some great guest comforts. Off the Wall restaurant features informal dining with a modern British menu.

Rooms 89 **Facilities** FTV Gym Xmas New Year Wi-fi **Services** Lift Air con **Notes** No children

EC3 CHEAPSIDE

Mint Hotel Tower of London

★★★★ 81% HOTEL PLAN 3 H1

☎ 020 7709 1000 & 0845 601 3009
📠 020 7709 1001
7 Pepys St EC3N 4AF
e-mail: toweroflondon.reservations@minthotel.com
dir: A100 From Tower Bridge, left into Tower Hill Terrace (A3211). Right into Trinity Sq, left into Savage Grdns, left into Pepys St

This property has been designed with comfort and style in mind. There's a truly uncompromising approach to both quality and innovation with genuine hospitality and good service. The hotel is energy efficient and includes a feature carbon-reducing living wall. Each stylish bedroom has a multimedia iMac, air conditioning and White Company toiletries. Award-winning cuisine is available in the City Café, together with a bar menu in the Frenchgate Lounge; there are impressive views over London from the penthouse SkyLounge. Free Wi-fi is available throughout.

Rooms 583 **S** £140-£365; **D** £140-£365* **Facilities** STV FTV Gym Wi-fi **Conf** Class 84 Board 80 Thtr 210 Del from £220 to £327* **Services** Lift Air con **Parking** 36 **Notes**

Apex City of London Hotel

★★★★ 80% HOTEL PLAN 3 H1

☎ 0845 365 0000 & 020 7702 2020
📠 020 7702 2217
No 1 Seething Ln EC3N 4AX
e-mail: london.reservations@apexhotels.co.uk
web: www.apexhotels.co.uk
dir: Opposite Tower of London

Situated close to Tower Bridge, this hotel is in the heart of the business district. Bedrooms are appointed to a high standard and have walk-in power showers in the en suites. The gym has the most up-to-date equipment, and there is a sauna room. The Addendum Restaurant offers a good dining option.

Rooms 179 (5 GF) (6 smoking) **Facilities** STV Gym Xmas Wi-fi **Conf** Class 36 Board 30 Thtr 80 **Services** Lift Air con **Notes**

LONDON

The Chamberlain

★★★★ 75% HOTEL PLAN 3 J2

☎ 020 7680 1500 📠 020 7702 2500
130-135 Minories EC3N 1NU
e-mail: thechamberlain@fullers.co.uk
web: www.thechamberlainhotel.com
dir: M25 junct 30, A13 W towards London. Follow into Aldgate, left after bus station. Hotel halfway down Minories

This smart hotel is ideally situated for the City, Tower Bridge, plus both Aldgate and Tower underground stations. The impressive bedrooms are stylish, well equipped and comfortable, and the modern bathrooms are fitted with TVs to watch from the bath. Informal day rooms include a popular pub, a lounge and an attractive restaurant.

Rooms 64 **S** £105-£325; **D** £115-£335 **Facilities** STV Wi-fi **Conf** Class 20 Board 22 Thtr 50 Del from £150 to £295 **Services** Lift Air con **Notes** LB ⊗ Closed 24-28 Dec

Novotel London Tower Bridge

★★★★ 73% HOTEL PLAN 3 J1

☎ 020 7265 6000 & 7265 6002 📠 020 7265 6060
10 Pepys St EC3N 2NR
e-mail: H3107@accor.com
web: www.novotel.com

Located near the Tower of London, this smart hotel is convenient for Docklands, the City, Heathrow and London City airports. Air-conditioned bedrooms are spacious, modern, and offer a great range of facilities. There is a smart bar and restaurant, a small gym, children's play area and extensive meeting and conference facilities.

Rooms 203 (130 fmly) **Facilities** STV FTV Gym Steam room Sauna Fitness room Xmas New Year Wi-fi **Conf** Class 56 Board 25 Thtr 100 **Services** Lift

EC4

Crowne Plaza London - The City

★★★★ 79% ® HOTEL PLAN 3 E1

☎ 0871 942 9190 📠 020 7438 8080
19 New Bridge St EC4V 6DB
e-mail: loncy.info@ihg.com
web: www.crowneplaza.co.uk/londonthecity
dir: Opposite Blackfriars station

This hotel has a 1919 façade, but is modern and bright inside; it is situated close to the north bank of the River Thames and also to Blackfriars station. Bedrooms are modern and well equipped. There is a small gym and valet parking is available. Booking for dinner are required.

Rooms 203 (60 fmly) (8 smoking) **S** £120-£440; **D** £140-£460* **Facilities** STV Gym Sauna ♫ Xmas New Year Wi-fi **Conf** Class 100 Board 50 Thtr 160 Del from £250 to £380* **Services** Lift Air con **Notes** LB ⊗ Civ Wed 150

N1 ISLINGTON

Premier Inn London King's Cross St Pancras

BUDGET HOTEL PLAN 3 B6

☎ 0871 527 8672 📠 0871 527 8673
26-30 York Way, Kings Cross N1 9AA
dir: M25 junct 16 onto M40 (becomes A40). Follow City signs, exit at Euston Rd, follow one-way system to York Way

High quality, budget accommodation ideal for both families and business travellers. Spacious, en suite bedrooms feature tea and coffee making facilities, and Freeview TV in most hotels. Internet access and Wi-fi are available for a small fee. The adjacent family restaurant features a wide and varied menu. See also the Hotel Groups pages.

Rooms 276 **D** £90-£114*

N3 FINCHLEY, GOLDERS GREEN

Express by Holiday Inn London Golders Green North

BUDGET HOTEL PLAN 1 E5

☎ 0870 770 4059 📠 020 7433 6667
58 Regents Park Rd N3 3JN
web: www.hiexpress.co.uk
dir: M1 junct 1, A404 (North Circular Rd) E to junct with A41. At lights left, then 1st right into Tillingbourne Grdns. Hotel entrance on right

A modern hotel ideal for families and business travellers. Fresh and uncomplicated, the spacious rooms include Sky TV, power shower and tea and coffee-making facilities. Continental buffet breakfast is included in the room rate; other meals may be taken at the nearby family pub or restaurant. See also the Hotel Groups pages.

Rooms 83

NW1 REGENT'S PARK, CAMDEN TOWN

See LONDON SECTION plan 1 E4

INSPECTORS' CHOICE

The Landmark London

★★★★★ ®® HOTEL PLAN 2 F3

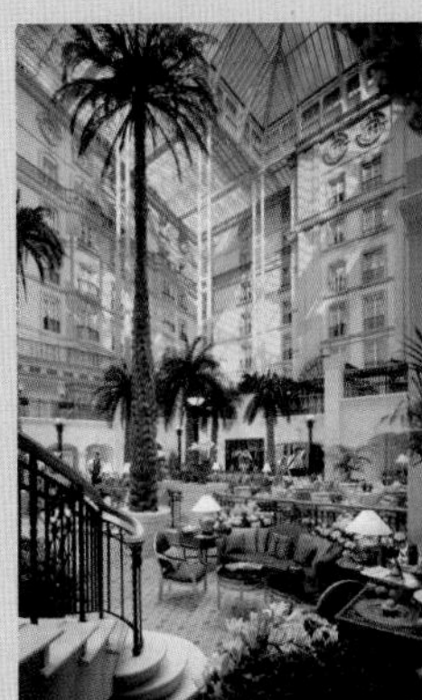

☎ 020 7631 8000 📠 020 7631 8080
222 Marylebone Rd NW1 6JQ
e-mail: reservations@thelandmark.co.uk
web: www.landmarklondon.co.uk
dir: Adjacent to Marylebone Station. Hotel on Marylebone Rd

Once one of the last truly grand railway hotels, The Landmark boasts a number of stunning features, the most spectacular being the naturally lit central atrium forming the hotel's focal point. When it comes to eating and drinking there are a number of choices, including the Cellars bar for cocktails and upmarket bar meals, the Mirror Bar, and The Gazebo - ideal for a business meeting or a quick snack. The Winter Garden Restaurant has the centre stage in the atrium and is a great place to watch the world go by; and the twotwentytwo restaurant and bar is a relaxing place to meet, eat and drink. The air-conditioned bedrooms are luxurious and have large, stylish bathrooms. The health club offers a complete wellbeing experience.

Rooms 300 (62 fmly) (50 smoking) **Facilities** Spa STV FTV Ⓢ Gym Beauty treatments & massages ♫ Xmas Wi-fi **Conf** Class 364 Board 50 Thtr 568 **Services** Lift Air con **Parking** 80 **Notes** ⊗ Civ Wed 300

NW1 REGENT'S PARK, CAMDEN TOWN *continued*

Meliá White House

★★★★ 80% ®® HOTEL PLAN 2 H4

☎ 020 7391 3000 📠 020 7388 0091
Albany St, Regents Park NW1 3UP
e-mail: melia.white.house@solmelia.com
dir: Opposite Gt Portland St underground station & next to Regents Park/Warren Street underground

Owned by the Spanish Solmelia company, this impressive art deco property is located opposite Great Portland Street tube station. Spacious public areas offer a high degree of comfort and include an elegant cocktail bar, a fine dining restaurant and a more informal brasserie. Stylish bedrooms come in a variety of sizes, but all offer high levels of comfort and are thoughtfully equipped.

Rooms 581 (7 fmly) (61 smoking) **Facilities** STV FTV Gym ♫ Xmas New Year Wi-fi **Conf** Class 80 Board 60 Thtr 140 **Services** Lift Air con **Notes** ® Civ Wed 140

Novotel London St Pancras

★★★★ 75% ® HOTEL PLAN 3 A5

☎ 020 7666 9000 & 7666 9010 📠 020 7766 9001
100-110 Euston Rd NW1 2AJ
e-mail: H5309@accor.com
web: www.novotel.com
dir: Between St Pancras & Euston stations

This hotel enjoys a central location adjacent to the British Library and close to some of London's main transport hubs. The style is modern and contemporary throughout. Bedrooms vary in size but are all very well equipped and many have views over the city. Open-plan public areas include a leisure suite and extensive conference facilities including the Shaw Theatre.

Rooms 312 (29 fmly) (25 smoking) **Facilities** Gym Steam room Sauna Xmas Wi-fi **Conf** Class 220 Board 80 Thtr 446 **Services** Lift Air con **Notes** ®

Thistle Euston

thistle

★★★★ 73% HOTEL PLAN 2 J5

☎ 0871 376 9017 📠 0871 376 9117
Cardington St NW1 2LP
e-mail: euston@thistle.co.uk
web: www.thistlehotels.com/euston
dir: From M40 continue to end of A40, follow Marylebone Rd, take Euston Rd to Melton St & into Cardington St

This smart, modern hotel is ideally located a short walk from Euston Station. Spacious public areas include a spacious bar/lounge, extensive meeting and function rooms and a bright basement restaurant. Bedrooms include a large number of deluxe and executive rooms that are spacious, comfortable and well equipped. The hotel also has limited on-site parking. Thistle Hotels – AA Hotel Group of the Year 2011-12.

Rooms 362 (18 fmly) (42 GF) **Facilities** STV FTV Wi-fi **Conf** Class 45 Board 35 Thtr 90 **Services** Lift Air con **Parking** 21 **Notes** ®

Renaissance St Pancras Hotel

U PLAN 3 B5

☎ 00800 1927 1927
Pancras Rd NW1 2QP

Currently the rating for this establishment is not confirmed. This may be due to a change of ownership or because it has only recently joined the AA rating scheme. For further details please see the AA website: theAA.com

Rooms 244

Ibis London Euston St Pancras

BUDGET HOTEL PLAN 2 J5

☎ 020 7388 7777 📠 020 7388 0001
3 Cardington St NW1 2LW
e-mail: H0921@accor-hotels.com
web: www.ibishotel.com
dir: From Euston Rd or station, right to Melton St & into Cardington St

Modern, budget hotel offering comfortable accommodation in bright and practical bedrooms. Breakfast is self-service and dinner is available in the restaurant. See also the Hotel Groups pages.

Rooms 380 **S** £80-£159; **D** £80-£159* **Conf** Class 40 Board 40 Thtr 100

York & Albany

®®® RESTAURANT WITH ROOMS PLAN 1 E4

☎ 020 7387 5700 📠 020 7255 9250
127-129 Parkway NW1 7PS
e-mail: yandareception@gordonramsay.com
dir: Telephone for detailed directions

Overlooking Regent's Park, the York & Albany had been stylishly appointed to retain many original features and with guest comfort in mind. The property showcases a restaurant, bar, Nonna's delicatessen and meeting space in addition to the very well appointed bedrooms and suites. Award-winning cuisine is served in the restaurant and showcases ingredients from some of the best suppliers. Picnics for the park can be ordered from Nonna's.

Rooms 10 en suite

NW2 BRENT CROSS & CRICKLEWOOD

See LONDON plan 1 D5

Crown Moran Hotel

★★★★ 77% HOTEL

☎ 020 8452 4175 📠 020 8452 0952
142-152 Cricklewood Broadway, Cricklewood NW2 3ED
e-mail: crownres@moranhotels.com
web: www.moranhotels.com
dir: M1 junct 1 follow signs onto North Circular (W) A406. Junct with A5 (Staples Corner). At rdbt take 1st exit onto A5 to Cricklewood

This striking hotel is connected by an impressive glass atrium to the popular Crown Pub. Features include excellent function and conference facilities, a leisure club, a choice of stylish lounges and bars and a contemporary restaurant. The air-conditioned bedrooms are appointed to a high standard and include a number of trendy suites.

Rooms 149 (35 GF) **S** £105-£170; **D** £115-£190 (incl. bkfst)* **Facilities** STV Gym ♫ Xmas New Year Wi-fi **Conf** Class 200 Board 80 Thtr 300 **Services** Lift Air con **Parking** 41 **Notes** LB ® Closed 24-26 Dec Civ Wed 300

Holiday Inn London - Brent Cross

★★★ 78% HOTEL

☎ 0871 942 9112 & 020 8967 6359
📠 020 8967 6372
Tilling Rd, Brent Cross NW2 1LP
web: www.holidayinn.co.uk
dir: At M1 junct 1. At rdbt after bridge turn left into Tilling Rd

Ideally located beside the M1 on the A406 North Circular, just a few minutes' walk from Brent Cross Shopping Centre and four miles from Wembley Stadium. The hotel offers well-appointed bedrooms with air conditioning and high-speed internet access; Wi-fi is available in the public areas. Conference rooms and a contemporary restaurant are available, plus there is ample parking.

Rooms 154 (87 fmly) (16 smoking) **Facilities** STV FTV New Year Wi-fi **Conf** Class 40 Board 32 Thtr 80 **Services** Lift Air con **Parking** 150 **Notes** ®

LONDON

NW3 HAMPSTEAD AND SWISS COTTAGE

See LONDON plan 1 E4

London Marriott Hotel Regents Park

★★★★ 75% HOTEL

☎ 020 7722 7711 & 0800 221222
📠 020 7586 5822
128 King Henry's Rd NW3 3ST
e-mail: london.regional.reservations@marriott.com
web: www.londonmarriottregentspark.co.uk
dir: 200yds off Finchley Rd on A41

Situated in a quieter part of town and close to the tube station, this hotel offers guests comfortably appointed, air-conditioned accommodation; all rooms boast balconies and are particularly well equipped to meet the needs of today's business traveller. The open-plan ground floor is spacious and airy and includes a well-equipped leisure centre with indoor pool. Secure parking is a bonus.

Rooms 304 (148 fmly) **Facilities** STV supervised Gym Hair & Beauty salon Steam room Sauna Wi-fi **Conf** Class 150 Board 120 Thtr 300 Del from £199 to £299* **Services** Lift Air con **Parking** 110 **Notes** Civ Wed 300

Premier Inn London Hampstead

BUDGET HOTEL

☎ 0871 527 8662 📠 0871 527 8663
215 Haverstock Hill, Hampstead NW3 4RB
dir: A41 to Swiss Cottage. Before junct take feeder road left into Buckland Cresent, into Belsize Ave. Left into Haverstock Hill

High quality, budget accommodation ideal for both families and business travellers. Spacious, en suite bedrooms feature tea and coffee making facilities, and Freeview TV in most hotels. Internet access and Wi-fi are available for a small fee. The adjacent family restaurant features a wide and varied menu. See also the Hotel Groups pages.

Rooms 143 **D** £83-£99*

NW4 HENDON

See LONDON plan 1 D5

Hendon Hall

★★★★ 75% HOTEL

☎ 020 8203 3341 📠 020 8457 2502
Ashley Ln, Hendon NW4 1HF
e-mail: reception.hendon@handpicked.co.uk
dir: M1 junct 2, A406. Right at lights into Parson St, right into Ashley Ln. Hotel on right

This impressive property was originally built in the 16th century when it was known as Hendon Manor, and is now a stylish hotel boasting smart, well-equipped, comfortable bedrooms with luxury toiletries, free Wi-fi and well-appointed en suites. Public areas include meeting and conference facilities, a contemporary cocktail bar and a richly decorated restaurant that opens onto a garden terrace. Staff are friendly and attentive.

Rooms 57 **S** £99-£129; **D** £109-£139 (incl. bkfst)* **Facilities** STV FTV Xmas New Year Wi-fi **Conf** Class 130 Board 76 Thtr 350 Del from £157 to £200* **Services** Lift Air con **Parking** 70 **Notes** LB Civ Wed 120

NW6 MAIDA VALE

London Marriott Maida Vale

★★★★ 75% HOTEL PLAN 1 D6

☎ 020 7543 6000 📠 020 7543 2100
Plaza Pde, Maida Vale NW6 5RP
e-mail: reservations.london.england.maidavale@marriotthotels.com
web: www.londonmarriottmaidavale.co.uk
dir: From M1 take A5 S'bound for 3m. Hotel on left. From Marble Arch take A5 N'bound. Hotel on right

This smart, modern hotel is conveniently located just north of central London. Air-conditioned bedrooms are tastefully decorated and provide a range of extras. The hotel also boasts extensive function facilities as well as an indoor leisure centre which has a swimming pool, gym and health and beauty salon.

Rooms 237 (40 fmly) **S** fr £119; **D** fr £119* **Facilities** STV Gym Hair & beauty salon Treatment rooms Exercise studio & classes Xmas Wi-fi **Conf** Class 70 Board 30 Thtr 200 Del from £215* **Services** Lift Air con **Parking** 28 **Notes** LB Civ Wed 100

SE1 SOUTHWARK AND WATERLOO

Plaza on the River - Club & Residence

★★★★★ 85% TOWN HOUSE HOTEL
PLAN 5 B2

☎ 020 7769 2525 📠 020 7769 2524
18 Albert Embankment SE1 7TJ
e-mail: guestrelations@plazaontheriver.co.uk
dir: From Houses of Parliament turn onto Millbank, at rdbt left onto Lambeth Bridge. At rdbt 3rd exit onto Albert Embankment

This is a superb modern townhouse overlooking London from the south bank of the Thames, with outstanding views of the capital's landmarks. The bedrooms are large and many are full suites with state-of-the-art technology and kitchen facilities; all are decorated in an elegant modern style. Service includes a full range of in-room dining options; additionally, the bar and restaurant in the adjacent Park Plaza are available to guests.

Rooms 65 **Facilities** STV FTV Gym Xmas New Year Wi-fi **Conf** Class 450 Board 40 Thtr 650 **Services** Lift Air con **Parking** 64 **Notes** Civ Wed 600

London Marriott Hotel County Hall

★★★★★ 82% HOTEL PLAN 5 C5

☎ 020 7928 5200 📠 020 7928 5300
Westminster Bridge Rd, County Hall SE1 7PB
e-mail: sales.countyhall@marriott.com
web: www.londonmarriottcountyhall.co.uk
dir: On Thames South Bank, between Westminster Bridge & London Eye

This impressive building, appointed to a very high standard, enjoys an enviable position on the south bank of the Thames, adjacent to the London Eye. Public areas have a traditional elegance and the crescent-shaped restaurant offers fine views of Westminster. All bedrooms are smartly laid out and thoughtfully equipped especially with the business traveller in mind.

Rooms 200 (58 fmly) **Facilities** Spa STV Gym Sauna Steam room Pilates classes Dance studio Xmas New Year Wi-fi **Conf** Class 40 Board 30 Thtr 80 **Services** Lift Air con **Parking** 70 **Notes** LB Civ Wed 80

SE1 SOUTHWARK AND WATERLOO *continued*

London Bridge Hotel

★★★★ 79% HOTEL PLAN 5 G6

☎ 020 7855 2200 📠 020 7855 2233
8-18 London Bridge St SE1 9SG
e-mail: sales@londonbridgehotel.com
web: www.londonbridgehotel.com
dir: Access through London Bridge Station (bus/taxi yard), into London Bridge St (one-way). Hotel on left, 50yds from station

This elegant, independently owned hotel enjoys a prime location on the edge of the city, adjacent to London Bridge station. Smartly appointed, well-equipped bedrooms include a number of spacious deluxe rooms and suites. Compact yet sophisticated public areas include a selection of meeting rooms and a well-equipped gym. The eating options are Londinium offering modern British food and the Borough Bar with an all-day menu. Free Wi-fi is available

Rooms 138 (12 fmly) (10 smoking) **S** £138-£343.20; **D** £138-£343.20* **Facilities** STV FTV Gym Wi-fi **Conf** Class 36 Board 36 Thtr 80 **Services** Lift Air con **Notes** LB ⊗

Park Plaza County Hall

★★★★ 78% ◎ HOTEL PLAN 5 C5

☎ 020 7021 1800 📠 020 7021 1801
1 Addington St SE1 7RY
e-mail: ppchsales@pphe.com
web: www.parkplazacountyhall.com
dir: From Houses of Parliament cross Westminster Bridge (A302). At rdbt turn left. 1st right into Addington St. Hotel on left

This hotel is located just south of Westminster Bridge near Waterloo international rail station. This contemporary design-led, air-conditioned establishment features studios and suites, most with kitchenettes and seating areas with a flat-screen TV. There are six meeting rooms, an executive lounge, a restaurant and bar plus a fully-equipped gym with sauna and steam room. Wi-fi is available.

Rooms 398 (303 fmly) **Facilities** STV FTV Gym Sauna Steam room Beauty therapy room Xmas New Year Wi-fi **Conf** Class 60 Board 40 Thtr 100 **Services** Lift Air con **Parking** 3 **Notes** LB ⊗

Park Plaza Riverbank London

★★★★ 77% HOTEL PLAN 5 C3

☎ 020 7958 8000 📠 020 7769 2400
18 Albert Embankment SE1 7SP
e-mail: rppres@pphe.com
web: www.parkplazariverbank.com
dir: From Houses of Parliament turn onto Millbank, at rdbt left onto Lambeth Bridge. At rdbt take 3rd exit onto Albert Embankment

Situated on the south side of the River Thames, this hotel offers guests the convenience of a central London location and high levels of comfort. Contemporary design coupled with a host of up-to-date facilities, the hotel is home to the Chino Latino brasserie. The air-conditioned bedrooms have flat-screen TVs and large work desks; some rooms and suites have stunning views of the Houses of Parliament. Other facilities include Wi-fi throughout, high-tech conference rooms, a business centre, and a fitness centre with cardiovascular equipment.

Rooms 394 **Facilities** Gym Wi-fi **Conf** Class 405 Board 40 Thtr 700 **Services** Lift Air con **Parking** 90 **Notes** ⊗ Civ Wed 150

H10 London Waterloo Hotel

★★★★ 75% HOTEL PLAN 5 E5

☎ 020 7928 4062 📠 020 7928 2264
284-302 Waterloo Rd SE1 8RQ
e-mail: h10.london.waterloo@h10hotels.com
dir: 450mtrs from Waterloo Station

This hotel, located close The National Theatre and Waterloo Station, has a host of features. Bedrooms are stylish and designed with the international traveller in mind. The bar provides a useful internet facility and the stylish restaurant offers fresh and interesting dishes. The staff are friendly and efficient.

Rooms 177 **S** £125-£245; **D** £145-£265* **Facilities** STV FTV Gym Treatment room Xmas New Year Wi-fi **Conf** Class 45 Board 24 Thtr 70 **Services** Lift Air con **Notes** ⊗

Novotel London City South

★★★★ 74% HOTEL PLAN 5 F6

☎ 020 7089 0400 📠 020 7089 0410
Southwark Bridge Rd SE1 9HH
e-mail: H3269@accor.com
web: www.novotel.com
dir: At junct at Thrale St, off Southwark St

Conveniently located for both business and leisure guests, with The City just across the Thames; other major attractions are also easily accessible. The hotel is contemporary in design with smart, modern bedrooms and spacious public rooms. There is a gym, sauna and steam room on the 6th floor, and limited parking is available at the rear of the hotel.

Rooms 182 (139 fmly) **Facilities** STV FTV Gym Steam room Sauna Wi-fi **Conf** Class 45 Board 40 Thtr 100 **Services** Lift Air con **Parking** 80

Mercure London City Bankside

★★★★ 71% HOTEL PLAN 5 E6

☎ 020 7902 0800 📠 020 7902 0810
71-79 Southwark St SE1 0JA
e-mail: H2814@accor.com
web: www.mercure.com
dir: A200 to London Bridge. Left into Southwark St.

This smart, contemporary hotel forms part of the rejuvenation of the South Bank. With the City of London just over the river and a number of tourist attractions within easy reach, the hotel is well located for business and leisure visitors alike. Facilities include spacious air-cooled bedrooms, a modern bar and the stylish Loft Restaurant.

Rooms 144 (15 fmly) (5 GF) **Facilities** STV Gym ♫ Wi-fi **Conf** Class 40 Board 30 Thtr 60 Del from £265 to £335* **Services** Lift Air con **Notes** LB

Novotel London Waterloo

★★★★ 71% HOTEL PLAN 5 C3

☎ 020 7793 1010 📠 020 7793 0202
113 Lambeth Rd SE1 7LS
e-mail: h1785@accor.com
web: www.novotel.com/1785
dir: Opposite Houses of Parliament on S bank of River Thames, off Lambeth Bridge, opposite Lambeth Palace

This hotel has an excellent location with Lambeth Palace, the Houses of Parliament and Waterloo Station all within a short walk. The bedrooms are spacious and benefit from comfort cooling; a number of rooms have been designed for less able guests. The open-plan public areas include the Garden Brasserie, Elements bar and restaurant, and also a children's play area.

Rooms 187 (80 fmly) **S** £109-£210; **D** £109-£210* **Facilities** STV Gym Steam room Sauna Wi-fi **Conf** Class 24 Board 24 Thtr 40 Del from £240 to £270* **Services** Lift Air con **Parking** 40

All Seasons London Southwark Rose Hotel

★★ 75% HOTEL PLAN 5 F6

☎ 020 7015 1480 & 7015 1491 📠 020 7015 1481
Southwark Rose, 47 Southwark Bridge Rd SE1 9HH
e-mail: h7465@accor.com
dir: From Westminster Bridge into Stamford Rd, into Southwark St, left into Southwark Bridge Rd

Conveniently located just south of the River Thames on Southwark Bridge, this modern hotel offers well equipped air-conditioned bedrooms, internet and ample work space. There is a pleasant restaurant, bar lounge and business area the 6th floor offering breakfast and dinner. The staff are friendly and welcoming. Limited parking is available at the rear of the hotel.

Rooms 84 (6 fmly) **S** £99-£250; **D** £101-£252 (incl. bkfst)* **Facilities** STV Gym Wi-fi **Conf** Class 35 Board 26 Thtr 60 Del from £199 to £340* **Services** Lift Air con **Parking** 44 **Notes** ⊗

Days Hotel London Waterloo

BUDGET HOTEL PLAN 5 D4

☎ 020 7922 1331 📠 020 7922 1441
54 Kennington Rd SE1 7BJ
e-mail: book@hotelwaterloo.com
web: www.daysinn.com
dir: On corner of Kennington Rd & Lambeth Rd. Opposite Imperial War Museum

This modern building offers accommodation in smart, spacious and well-equipped bedrooms, suitable for families and business travellers, and all with en suite bathrooms. Continental breakfast is available and other refreshments may be taken at the nearby family restaurant. See also the Hotel Groups pages.

Rooms 162 (15 fmly) (13 GF) **S** £99-£169; **D** £109-£169*

Express by Holiday Inn London - Southwark

BUDGET HOTEL PLAN 5 E6

☎ 020 7401 2525 📠 020 7401 3322
103-109 Southwark St SE1 0JQ
e-mail: stay@expresssouthwark.co.uk
web: www.hiexpress.com/lon-southwark
dir: A20 onto A2 to city centre towards Elephant & Castle. Right before Blackfriars Bridge at 1st large lights junct

A modern hotel ideal for families and business travellers. Fresh and uncomplicated, the spacious rooms include Sky TV, power shower and tea and coffee-making facilities. Continental buffet breakfast is included in the room rate; other meals may be taken at the nearby family pub or restaurant. See also the Hotel Groups pages.

Rooms 88 (10 fmly) **Conf** Board 12

Premier Inn London County Hall

BUDGET HOTEL PLAN 5 C5

☎ 0871 527 8648 📠 0871 527 8649
Belvedere Rd, Westminster SE1 7PB
dir: In County Hall building. Nearest tube: Waterloo

High quality, budget accommodation ideal for both families and business travellers. Spacious, en suite bedrooms feature tea and coffee making facilities, and Freeview TV in most hotels. Internet access and Wi-fi are available for a small fee. The adjacent family restaurant features a wide and varied menu. See also the Hotel Groups pages.

Rooms 313 **D** £109-£119*

Premier Inn London Southwark

BUDGET HOTEL PLAN 5 F6

☎ 0871 527 8676 📠 0871 527 8677
Bankside, 34 Park St SE1 9EF
dir: A3200 onto A300 (Southwark Bridge Rd), 1st left into Sumner St, right into Park St. From S: M3, A3 follow Central London signs

Rooms 59 **D** £99-£110*

Premier Inn London Tower Bridge

BUDGET HOTEL PLAN 5 H5

☎ 0871 527 8678 📠 0871 527 8679
159 Tower Bridge Rd SE1 3LP
dir: S of Tower Bridge on A100

Rooms 196 **D** £88-£110*

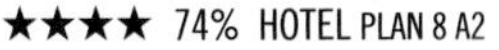

SE10 GREENWICH

Novotel London Greenwich

★★★★ 74% HOTEL PLAN 8 A2

☎ 020 8312 6800 📠 020 8312 6810
173-185 Greenwich High Rd SE10 8JA
e-mail: H3476@accor.com
web: www.novotel.com
dir: Adjacent to Greenwich Station

This purpose-built hotel is conveniently located for rail and DLR stations, as well as major attractions such as the Royal Maritime Museum and the Royal Observatory. Air-conditioned bedrooms are spacious and equipped with a host of extras, and public areas include a small gym, contemporary lounge bar and restaurant.

Rooms 151 (34 fmly) **Facilities** STV FTV Gym Steam room Wi-fi **Conf** Class 40 Board 32 Thtr 92 **Services** Lift Air con **Parking** 30

SE10 GREENWICH *continued*

Express by Holiday Inn London - Greenwich

BUDGET HOTEL PLAN 1 H3

☎ 020 8269 5000 🖷 020 8269 5069
162 Bugsby Park SE10 0DQ
e-mail: greenwich@expressholidayinn.co.uk
web: www.hiexpress.com/greenwicha102m

A modern hotel ideal for families and business travellers. Fresh and uncomplicated, the spacious rooms include Sky TV, power shower and tea and coffee-making facilities. Continental buffet breakfast is included in the room rate; other meals may be taken at the nearby family pub or restaurant. See also the Hotel Groups pages.

Rooms 162 **Conf** Class 55 Board 35 Thtr 80

Ibis London Greenwich

BUDGET HOTEL PLAN 8 B3

☎ 020 8305 1177 🖷 020 8858 7139
30 Stockwell St, Greenwich SE10 9JN
e-mail: H0975@accor.com
web: www.ibishotel.com
dir: From Waterloo Bridge, Elephant & Castle, A2 to Greenwich

Modern, budget hotel offering comfortable accommodation in bright and practical bedrooms. Breakfast is self-service and dinner is available in the restaurant. See also the Hotel Groups pages.

Rooms 82 (10 fmly) (12 GF)

Premier Inn London Greenwich

BUDGET HOTEL PLAN 8 A1

☎ 0871 527 9208
43-81 Greenwich High Rd, Greenwich SE10 8JL
dir: Telephone for detailed directions

High quality, budget accommodation ideal for both families and business travellers. Spacious, en suite bedrooms feature tea and coffee making facilities, and Freeview TV in most hotels. Internet access and Wi-fi are available for a small fee. The adjacent family restaurant features a wide and varied menu. See also the Hotel Groups pages.

Rooms 150 **D** £70-£85*

SW1 WESTMINSTER

INSPECTORS' CHOICE

The Berkeley

MAYBOURNE HOTEL GROUP

★★★★★ HOTEL PLAN 4 G5

☎ 020 7235 6000 🖷 020 7235 4330
Wilton Place, Knightsbridge SW1X 7RL
e-mail: info@the-berkeley.co.uk
dir: 300mtrs from Hyde Park Corner along Knightsbridge

This stylish hotel, just off Knightsbridge, boasts an excellent range of bedrooms; each furnished with care and a host of thoughtful extras. Newer rooms feature trendy, spacious glass and marble bathrooms and some of the private suites have their own roof terrace. The striking Blue Bar enhances the reception rooms, all adorned with magnificent flower arrangements. Various eating options include the Caramel Room for breakfast, an all-day menu from 11am and afternoon tea. Marcus Wareing at The Berkeley is awarded 5 AA Rosettes for stunning French cuisine, and here guests can also book the chef's table. The health spa offers a range of treatment rooms and includes a stunning open-air, roof-top pool.

Rooms 214 **Facilities** Spa STV FTV Gym Beauty/therapy treatments Xmas Wi-fi **Conf** Class 80 Board 52 Thtr 250 **Services** Lift Air con **Notes** Civ Wed 160

INSPECTORS' CHOICE

The Halkin Hotel

★★★★★ TOWN HOUSE HOTEL PLAN 4 G5

☎ 020 7333 1000 🖷 020 7333 1100
Halkin St, Belgravia SW1X 7DJ
e-mail: res@halkin.como.bz
dir: Between Belgrave Sq & Grosvenor Place. Via Chapel St into Headfort Place, left into Halkin St

This smart, contemporary hotel has an enviable and peaceful position just a short stroll from both Hyde Park and the designer shops of Knightsbridge. Service is attentive, friendly and very personalised. The stylish bedrooms and suites are equipped to the highest standard with white marble bathrooms and every conceivable extra. Each floor is discreetly designed following the themes of water, air, fire, earth and sky. There is the airy Halkin Bar that offers all day eating including an afternoon tea menu, and the famous, award-winning Thai restaurant, Nahm.

Rooms 41 **Facilities** STV FTV Complimentary use of gym & spa at sister hotel Wi-fi **Conf** Class 20 Board 26 Thtr 40 **Services** Lift Air con **Notes**

INSPECTORS' CHOICE

The Lanesborough

★★★★★ ®®® HOTEL PLAN 4 G5

☎ 020 7259 5599 📠 020 7259 5606
Hyde Park Corner SW1X 7TA
e-mail: pmccolgan@lanesborough.com
dir: At Hyde Park corner

Occupying an enviable position on Hyde Park Corner, this elegant hotel offers the highest international standards of comfort, quality and security, much appreciated by a loyal clientele. The stylish bedrooms and suites reflect the historic nature of the property, offering high levels of comfort and a superb range of complimentary facilities including laptops and high speed internet access. Services are equally impressive with personal butlers ensuring individual attention. Apsleys offers award-winning modern Italian cuisine, and afternoon tea is offered.

Rooms 93 (7 fmly) (6 GF) (38 smoking) **Facilities** STV FTV Gym ♫ Wi-fi **Conf** Class 48 Board 52 Thtr 100 **Services** Lift Air con **Parking** 40 **Notes** Civ Wed 100

INSPECTORS' CHOICE

Mandarin Oriental Hyde Park, London

★★★★★ ®®® HOTEL PLAN 4 F5

☎ 020 7235 2000 📠 020 7235 2001
66 Knightsbridge SW1X 7LA
e-mail: molon-reservations@mohg.com
web: www.mandarinoriental.com/london
dir: Harrods 400mtrs on right & Harvey Nichols directly opposite hotel

Situated in fashionable Knightsbridge and overlooking Hyde Park, this iconic venue is a popular destination for highfliers, celebrities and the young and fashionable. Bedrooms, many with park views, are appointed to the highest standards with luxurious features such as the finest Irish linen and goose down pillows. Guests have a choice of dining options - Bar Boulud (with 2 AA Rosettes) offering a contemporary bistro menu of seasonal, rustic French dishes; and Dinner by Heston Blumenthal (with 3 AA Rosettes) where the dishes are based on recipes dating as far back as the 14th century but have Heston's legendary modern twist. The Mandarin Bar serves light snacks and cocktails. The stylish spa is a destination in its own right and offers a range of innovative treatments.

Rooms 198 **S** £675-£12000; **D** £6755-£12000* **Facilities** Spa STV FTV Gym Sanarium Steam room Vitality pool Zen colour therapy Relaxation area ♫ Xmas New Year Wi-fi **Conf** Class 120 Board 60 Thtr 250 **Services** Lift Air con **Notes** ⊗ Civ Wed 250

INSPECTORS' CHOICE

St James's Hotel and Club

★★★★★ ®®® TOWN HOUSE HOTEL PLAN 4 J6

☎ 020 7316 1600 📠 020 7316 1602
7-8 Park Place SW1A 1LP
e-mail: info@stjameshotelandclub.com
web: www.stjameshotelandclub.com
dir: On A4 near Picadilly Circus & St James's St

Dating back to 1857 this elegant property with its distinctive neo-Gothic exterior is discreetly set in the heart of St James. Inside there is impressive decor created by interior designer Anne Maria Jagdfeld. Air-conditioned bedrooms are appointed to a very high standard and feature luxurious beds and a range of modern facilities. Stylish open-plan public areas include a smart bar/lounge, and the fine dining restaurant, Seven Park Place by William Drabble, that serves modern-French dishes created from mainly British ingredients.

Rooms 60 (8 fmly) (15 GF) **S** £285-£415; **D** £318-£3000* **Facilities** FTV Wi-fi **Conf** Class 30 Board 25 Thtr 40 **Services** Lift Air con **Notes** LB ⊗ Civ Wed

SW1 WESTMINSTER *continued*

INSPECTORS' CHOICE

The Goring

★★★★★ HOTEL PLAN 4 H4

☎ 020 7396 9000 020 7834 4393
Beeston Place SW1W 0JW
e-mail: reception@thegoring.com
web: www.thegoring.com
dir: Off Lower Grosvenor Place, just prior to Royal Mews

This icon of British hospitality for over 100 years is centrally located and within walking distance of the Royal Parks and principal shopping areas. Spacious bedrooms and suites, some contemporary in style with state-of-the-art technology and others more classically furnished, all boast high levels of comfort and quality. Catherine Middleton, now the Duchess of Cambridge, stayed in the newly created Royal Suite on the night before her marriage to HRH Prince William. Elegant day rooms include the Garden Bar and the drawing room, both popular for afternoon tea and cocktails. The stylish airy restaurant offers a popular menu of contemporary British cuisine and delightful private dining rooms are available. Guests will experience a personalised service from the attentive and friendly team.

Rooms 69 (9 fmly) **S** £275-£492; **D** £323-£3000* **Facilities** STV Free membership of nearby health club Xmas New Year Wi-fi **Conf** Class 30 Board 25 Thtr 50 **Services** Lift Air con **Parking** 16 **Notes** LB Civ Wed 50

INSPECTORS' CHOICE

Jumeirah Carlton Tower

★★★★★ HOTEL PLAN 4 F4

☎ 020 7235 1234 020 7235 9129
Cadogan Place SW1X 9PY
e-mail: jctinfo@jumeirah.com
web: www.jumeirahcarltontower.com
dir: A4 towards Knightsbridge, right onto Sloane St. Hotel on left before Cadogan Place

This impressive hotel, celebrating its 50th anniversary in 2011, enjoys an enviable position in the heart of Knightsbridge, overlooking Cadogan Gardens. The stunningly designed bedrooms, including a number of suites, vary in size and style; many have wonderful city views. Leisure facilities include a glass-roofed swimming pool, a well-equipped gym and a number of treatment rooms. The renowned Rib Room provides excellent dining, together with the other options of the Club Room, the Chinoiserie and the GILT Cocktail Lounge.

Rooms 220 (59 fmly) (70 smoking) **Facilities** Spa STV FTV supervised Gym Golf simulator (50 courses) Xmas New Year Wi-fi **Conf** Class 250 Board 30 Thtr 400 **Services** Lift Air con **Parking** 170 **Notes** Civ Wed 320

INSPECTORS' CHOICE

The Stafford London by Kempinski

★★★★★ HOTEL PLAN 4 J6

☎ 020 7493 0111 020 7493 7121
16-18 St James's Place SW1A 1NJ
e-mail: reservation.london@kempinski.com
web: www.kempinski.com/en/london
dir: Off Pall Mall into St James's St. 2nd left into St James's Place

Tucked away in a quiet corner of St James's, this classically styled boutique hotel retains an air of understated luxury. The American Bar is a fabulous venue in its own right, festooned with an eccentric array of celebrity photos, caps and ties. Afternoon tea is a long established tradition here. From the pristine, tastefully decorated and air-conditioned bedrooms, to the highly professional, yet friendly service, this exclusive hotel maintains the highest standards. 26 stunning mews suites are available.

Rooms 105 (38 annexe) (9 GF) (5 smoking) **Facilities** STV Gym Use of fitness club nearby Xmas Wi-fi **Conf** Class 20 Board 24 Thtr 60 **Services** Lift Air con **Notes** Civ Wed 44

INSPECTORS' CHOICE

51 Buckingham Gate, Taj Suites and Residences

★★★★★ TOWN HOUSE HOTEL PLAN 4 J4

☎ 020 7769 7766 020 7828 5909
SW1E 6AF
e-mail: info@51-buckinghamgate.co.uk
dir: From Buckingham Palace onto Buckingham Gate, 100mtrs, hotel on right

This all-suites hotel is a favourite with those who desire a quiet, sophisticated environment. Each of the suites has its own butler on hand plus a kitchen, and most have large lounge areas furnished in a contemporary style with modern accessories. There are one, two, three and four bedroom suites to choose from. The hotel has a spa and a well-equipped gym.

Rooms 86 (86 fmly) (4 GF) **D** £342-£702* **Facilities** Spa STV Gym Sauna Steam room Xmas New Year Wi-fi **Conf** Class 90 Board 60 Thtr 180 **Services** Lift Air con **Notes** LB ⊗ Civ Wed 150

INSPECTORS' CHOICE

No 41

THE RED CARNATION HOTEL COLLECTION

★★★★★
TOWN HOUSE HOTEL PLAN 4 H4

☎ 020 7300 0041 020 7300 0141
41 Buckingham Palace Rd SW1W 0PS
e-mail: book41@rchmail.com
web: www.41hotel.com
dir: Opposite Buckingham Palace Mews entrance

Small, intimate and very private, this stunning town house is located opposite the Royal Mews. Decorated in stylish black and white, bedrooms successfully combine comfort with state-of-the-art technology such as iPod docking stations, interactive TV and free high speed internet access. Thoughtful touches such as fresh fruit, flowers and scented candles add to the very welcoming atmosphere. The large lounge is the focal point; food and drinks are available as are magazines and newspapers from around the world plus internet access. Attentive personal service and a host of thoughtful extra touches make No 41 really special.

Rooms 30 (2 fmly) **D** £323-£467* **Facilities** STV Local health club Beauty treatments In-room spa Xmas New Year Wi-fi **Conf** Board 10 **Services** Lift Air con **Notes** LB

Sheraton Park Tower

★★★★★ 87% ®®® HOTEL
PLAN 4 F5

☎ 020 7235 8050 020 7235 8231
101 Knightsbridge SW1X 7RN
e-mail:
00412.central.london.reservations@sheraton.com
web: www.luxurycollection.com/parktowerlondon
dir: Adjacent to Harvey Nichols

Superbly located for some of London's most fashionable stores, the Park Tower offers stunning views over the city. Bedrooms combine a high degree of comfort with up-to-date decor and a super range of extras; the suites are particularly impressive. The hotel offers the intimate Knightsbridge lounge, the more formal Piano Bar and extensive conference and banqueting facilities. Restaurant One-O-One is renowned for its seafood.

Rooms 280 (280 fmly) (62 smoking) **Facilities** STV Gym Fitness room ♫ Wi-fi **Conf** Class 60 Board 26 Thtr 120 **Services** Lift Air con **Parking** 67 **Notes** Civ Wed 100

Sofitel London St James

SOFITEL

★★★★★ 86% ® HOTEL
PLAN 4 K6

☎ 020 7747 2200 020 7747 2210
6 Waterloo Place SW1Y 4AN
e-mail: H3144@sofitel.com
dir: 3 mins walk from Piccadilly Circus & Trafalgar Square

Located in the exclusive area of St James's, this Grade II listed, former bank is convenient for most of the city's attractions, theatres and the financial district. The modern bedrooms are equipped to a high standard and feature luxurious beds, whilst more traditional public areas, including the French restaurant, provide a taste of classical charm.

Rooms 185 (98 fmly) **S** £450-£2160; **D** £510-£2160 **Facilities** Spa STV Gym So spa So fit ♫ Xmas New Year Wi-fi **Conf** Class 125 Board 44 Thtr 170 Del from £600 to £2500 **Services** Lift Air con **Notes** Civ Wed 140

SW1 WESTMINSTER *continued*

Dukes London

★★★★★ 85% HOTEL PLAN 4 J6

☎ 020 7491 4840 🖷 020 7493 1264
35 St James's Place SW1A 1NY
e-mail: bookings@dukeshotel.com
dir: From Pall Mall turn into St James's St. 2nd left into St James's Place. Hotel in courtyard on left

Discreetly tucked away in St James's, Dukes is over 100 years old. Its style is understated with smart, well-equipped bedrooms and public areas. Facilities include a gym, marble steam room and body-care treatments. The intimate street-facing restaurant offers diners a good selection of British dishes. A smart lounge and a sophisticated and buzzing cocktail bar add to guests' enjoyment, and Martinis are a must!

Rooms 90 (4 GF) **Facilities** STV FTV Gym Steam room Health club Personal training Xmas New Year Wi-fi **Conf** Class 30 Board 30 Thtr 70 **Services** Lift Air con **Notes** LB ⊗ Civ Wed 60

See advert on opposite page

The Royal Horseguards

GUOMAN HOTELS

★★★★★ 81% ❁❁ HOTEL
PLAN 5 B6

☎ 0871 376 9033 🖷 0871 376 9133
2 Whitehall Court SW1A 2EJ
e-mail: royalhorseguards@guoman.co.uk
web: www.theroyalhorseguards.com
dir: Trafalgar Square to Whitehall, left to Whitehall Pl, turn right

This majestic looking hotel in the heart of Whitehall sits beside the Thames and enjoys unrivalled views of the London Eye and the city skyline. Bedrooms, appointed to a high standard, are well equipped and some of the luxurious bathrooms are finished in marble. Impressive public areas and outstanding meeting facilities are also available.

Rooms 280 (7 fmly) **Facilities** STV Gym ♫ Xmas New Year Wi-fi **Conf** Class 180 Board 84 Thtr 240 **Services** Lift Air con **Notes** ⊗ Civ Wed 228

The Rubens at the Palace

THE RED CARNATION HOTEL COLLECTION

★★★★ 83% ❁❁ HOTEL PLAN 4 H4

☎ 020 7834 6600 🖷 020 7233 6037
39 Buckingham Palace Rd SW1W 0PS
e-mail: bookrb@rchmail.com
web: www.rubenshotel.com
dir: Opposite Royal Mews, 100mtrs from Buckingham Palace

This hotel enjoys an enviable location close to Buckingham Palace. Stylish, air-conditioned bedrooms include the pinstripe-walled Savile Row rooms, which follow a tailoring theme, and the opulent Royal rooms, named after different monarchs. Public rooms include The Library fine dining restaurant and a comfortable stylish cocktail bar and lounge. The team here pride themselves on their warmth and friendliness.

Rooms 161 (13 fmly) (14 smoking) **S** £167-£299; **D** £179-£311* **Facilities** STV Health club & beauty treatment available nearby ♫ Xmas New Year Wi-fi **Conf** Class 40 Board 30 Thtr 90 Del from £264 to £396* **Services** Lift Air con **Notes** LB Civ Wed 80

Cavendish London

★★★★ 81% ❁ HOTEL PLAN 4 J6

☎ 020 7930 2111 🖷 020 7839 2125
81 Jermyn St SW1Y 6JF
e-mail: info@thecavendishlondon.com
web: www.thecavendishlondon.com
dir: From Piccadilly, (pass The Ritz), 1st right into Dukes St before Fortnum & Mason

This smart, stylish hotel enjoys an enviable location in the prestigious St James's area, just a short walk from Green Park and Piccadilly. Bedrooms have a fresh, contemporary feel, and there are a number of spacious executive rooms, studios and suites. Elegant public areas include a first-floor lounge and well-appointed conference and function facilities. The popular Petrichor restaurant is committed to sourcing sustainable ingredients, especially from British producers. A good value, pre-theatre menu is available.

Rooms 230 (12 fmly) **Facilities** STV Wi-fi **Conf** Class 50 Board 40 Thtr 80 **Services** Lift Air con **Parking** 50 **Notes** ⊗

Mint Hotel Westminster

minthotel

★★★★ 80% ❁❁ HOTEL
PLAN 5 B3

☎ 020 7630 1000 🖷 020 7233 7575
30 John Islip St SW1P 4DD
e-mail: westminster.reservations@minthotel.com
web: www.minthotel.com
dir: From Millbank into Horseferry Rd. 2nd left into John Islip St. Hotel approx 200mtrs on left

This hotel is set in the heart of Westminster close to the River Thames and the Houses of Parliament. Spacious, contemporary, air-conditioned bedrooms boast a wide range of facilities including iMacs and complimentary high speed Wi-fi. Striking public areas feature regularly changing modern art; and include a range of meeting rooms and the popular cocktail bar, the Millbank Lounge. The hotel's restaurant, City Café Art Street Terrace offers the option of alfresco dining in warmer months.

Rooms 460 (7 fmly) **Facilities** STV FTV Gym Xmas New Year Wi-fi **Conf** Class 70 Board 80 Thtr 180 **Services** Lift Air con **Parking** 35 **Notes** ⊗ Civ Wed 130

Park Plaza Victoria London

Park Plaza Hotels & Resorts

★★★★ 78% ❁ HOTEL PLAN 4 J3

☎ 020 7769 9999 & 7769 9800 🖷 020 7769 9998
239 Vauxhall Bridge Rd SW1V 1EQ
e-mail: info@victoriaparkplaza.com
web: www.parkplaza.com
dir: Turn right from Victoria Station

This smart modern hotel close to Victoria station is well located for all of central London's major attractions. Air-conditioned bedrooms are tastefully appointed and thoughtfully equipped for both business and leisure guests. Airy, stylish public areas include an elegant bar and restaurant, a popular coffee bar and extensive conference facilities complete with a business centre.

Rooms 299 **Facilities** Spa STV FTV Gym Sauna Steam room Xmas Wi-fi **Conf** Class 240 Board 45 Thtr 550 **Services** Lift Air con **Parking** 36 **Notes** ⊗ Civ Wed 500

LONDON

SW1 WESTMINSTER *continued*

Crowne Plaza London St James

★★★★ 76% HOTEL PLAN 4 J4

☎ 020 7834 6655 📠 020 7630 7587
Buckingham Gate SW1E 6AF
e-mail: reservations@cplonsj.co.uk
web: www.london.crowneplaza.com
dir: With Buckingham Palace facing, turn left to Buckingham Gate. After 100mtrs hotel on right

Enjoying a prestigious location, this elegant Victorian hotel is a few minutes' walk from Buckingham Palace. Air-conditioned bedrooms are smartly appointed and superbly equipped. Public areas include a choice of three restaurants - Bank, Bistro 51 and Quilon, two bars, conference and business facilities and a fitness club with Sodashi Spa. Service is attentive and friendly.

Rooms 342 (36 fmly) (26 smoking) **S** £355-£560; **D** £355-£560* **Facilities** Spa STV FTV Gym Steam room Sauna ♫ Xmas New Year Wi-fi **Conf** Class 90 Board 60 Thtr 180 **Services** Lift Air con **Notes** ® Civ Wed 180

Millennium Hotel London Knightsbridge

★★★★ 75% ® HOTEL PLAN 4 F4

☎ 020 7235 4377 📠 020 7235 3705
17 Sloane St, Knightsbridge SW1X 9NU
e-mail: reservations.knightsbridge@millenniumhotels.co.uk
web: www.millenniumhotels.co.uk
dir: From Knightsbridge tube station towards Sloane St. Hotel 70mtrs on right

This fashionable hotel boasts an enviable location in Knightsbridge's chic shopping district. Air-conditioned, thoughtfully equipped bedrooms are complemented by a popular lobby lounge and MU Restaurant and Lounge where the cuisine is French with Asian influences. Valet parking is available if pre-booked.

Rooms 222 (41 fmly) (38 smoking) **Facilities** STV FTV New Year Wi-fi **Conf** Class 80 Board 50 Thtr 120 **Services** Lift Air con **Parking** 11 **Notes** ®

Cadogan

★★★★ 74% HOTEL PLAN 4 F4

☎ 020 7235 7141 📠 020 7245 0994
75 Sloane St SW1X 9SG
e-mail: jsauri@cadogan.com
dir: A4 towards Knightsbridge, right at lights after Harrods into Sloane St

This smart hotel, once home to Lillie Langtry, enjoys a prime Knightsbridge location overlooking Cadogan Gardens; Sloane Square, Harrods and Harvey Nichols are just a stone's throw away. Bedrooms and suites vary in size and style but all are stylishly appointed and attractively furnished. Public rooms include the beautifully panelled drawing room, a stylish bar and restaurant.

Rooms 64 (1 fmly) **Facilities** STV FTV Gym Xmas Wi-fi **Conf** Class 30 Board 30 Thtr 50 **Services** Lift Air con **Notes** ® Civ Wed 70

Thistle Westminster

thistle

★★★★ 71% HOTEL PLAN 4 H4

☎ 0871 376 9039 📠 0871 376 9139
49 Buckingham Palace Rd SW1W 0QT
e-mail: westminster@thistle.co.uk
web: www.thistlehotels.com/westminster
dir: Opposite Buckingham Palace Mews

A purpose built hotel situated in the heart of London's political landmarks and close to Buckingham Palace. The spacious bedrooms come in a variety of styles; each one is smartly decorated and well equipped. Public rooms include a large lounge, a bar, a brasserie and a range of meeting rooms. Thistle Hotels – AA Hotel Group of the Year 2011-12.

Rooms 134 (66 fmly) **Facilities** FTV Wi-fi **Conf** Class 70 Board 45 Thtr 170 **Services** Lift **Parking** 7 **Notes** ®

Corinthia Hotel London

U PLAN 5 B6

☎ 020 7930 8181 📠 020 7321 3001
Whitehall Place SW1A 2BD
e-mail: london@corinthia.com
dir: M4 onto A4, follow Central London signs. Pass Green Park, right into Coventry St, 1st right into Haymarket, left into Pall Mall East, right into Trafalgar Sq, 3rd exit into Whitehall Place

Currently the rating for this establishment is not confirmed. This may be due to a change of ownership or because it has only recently joined the AA rating scheme. For further details please see the AA website: theAA.com

Rooms 294 (10 fmly) (46 smoking) **S** £330-£595; **D** £350-£900* **Facilities** Spa STV Gym Vitality pool Nail studio Daniel Galvin hair salon Relaxation sleep pod Xmas New Year Wi-fi **Conf** Class 120 Board 50 Thtr 250 **Services** Lift Air con **Notes** ® Civ Wed 250

The Grosvenor

U PLAN 4 H4

☎ 0871 376 9038 & 020 7834 9494
📠 0871 376 9138
101 Buckingham Palace Rd SW1W 0SJ
e-mail: grosvenor@guoman.co.uk
web: www.thistle.com
dir: Adjacent to Victoria Station

Currently the rating for this establishment is not confirmed. At the time of going to press The Grosvenor was undergoing a complete refurbishment, and unfortunately the AA was not able to make an inspection before guide deadlines. For further details please see the AA website: theAA.com

Rooms 357 (175 annexe) **Facilities** STV FTV ♫ Xmas New Year Wi-fi **Conf** Class 120 Board 70 Thtr 200 **Services** Lift **Notes** ® Civ Wed 80

Jumeirah Lowndes

U PLAN 4 F4

☎ 020 7823 1234 📠 020 7235 1154
21 Lowndes St SW1X 9ES
e-mail: jlhinfo@jumeirah.com
dir: M4 onto A4 into London. Left from Brompton Rd into Sloane St. Left into Pont St, Lowndes St next left. Hotel on right

This hotel is a smart modern townhouse set in the Belgravia area of Knightsbridge. Public areas are limited in scale but an all-day bar and restaurant with an outside terrace overlooking the leafy side street. The bedrooms vary in size, but all have a very modern style and have high spec facilities such as air-conditioning and iPod speakers. Guests can also enjoy the extensive facilities at the nearby Jumeirah Carlton Hotel.

Rooms 87 **Facilities** STV FTV Wi-fi **Conf** Class 12 Board 18 Thtr 25 **Services** Lift Air con **Notes** ®

St Ermins Hotel

PLAN 4 K4

☎ 020 7222 7888 & 0800 635 0438
020 7976 0710
2 Caxton St, St James Park, Westminster SW1H 0QW
e-mail: reservations@sterminshotel.co.uk
dir: Just off Victoria St, directly opposite New Scotland Yard

This hotel is located just a minute's walk from St James's Park, and has undergone a multi-million pound refurbishment. Accessed via a tree-lined courtyard, the hotel has retained many original features that create a uniquely stylish interior. There are 331 spacious bedrooms and suites that offer a sense of calm and luxury. The main restaurant is the Caxton Grill, but other options are the Caxton Bar, and the Caxton Terrace which overlooks the courtyard. Unfortunately the AA was unable to inspect the hotel before the guide went to press. See the AA website - the AA.com for up-to-date information.

Rooms 331 (18 fmly) (12 GF) **S** £149-£309; **D** £199-£359* **Facilities** STV FTV Gym Xmas New Year Wi-fi **Conf** Class 80 Board 60 Thtr 160 Del from £370 to £520* **Services** Lift Air con **Notes** LB Civ Wed 160

Holiday Inn Express London - Victoria

BUDGET HOTEL PLAN 4 J2

☎ 020 7630 8888 020 7828 0441
106-110 Belgrave Rd, Victoria SW1V 2BJ
e-mail: info@hiexpressvictoria.co.uk
web: www.hiexpress.com/londonvictoria
dir: 600mtrs from Pimlico Underground

A modern hotel ideal for families and business travellers. Fresh and uncomplicated, the spacious rooms include Sky TV, power shower and tea and coffee-making facilities. Continental buffet breakfast is included in the room rate; other meals may be taken at the nearby family pub or restaurant. See also the Hotel Groups pages.

Rooms 52 (9 fmly) (4 GF) (15 smoking)

Premier Inn London Victoria

BUDGET HOTEL PLAN 4 J3

☎ 0871 527 8680 0871 527 8681
82 - 83 Eccleston Square, Victoria SW1V 1PS
dir: From Victoria Station, right into Wilton Rd, 3rd right into Gillingham St, hotel 150mtrs

High quality, budget accommodation ideal for both families and business travellers. Spacious, en suite bedrooms feature tea and coffee making facilities, and Freeview TV in most hotels. Internet access and Wi-fi are available for a small fee. The adjacent family restaurant features a wide and varied menu. See also the Hotel Groups pages.

Rooms 110 **D** £90-£114*

SW3 CHELSEA, BROMPTON

INSPECTORS' CHOICE

The Capital

★★★★★ TOWN HOUSE HOTEL
PLAN 4 F5

☎ 020 7589 5171 020 7225 0011
Basil St, Knightsbridge SW3 1AT
e-mail: reservations@capitalhotel.co.uk
web: www.capitalhotel.co.uk
dir: 20yds from Harrods & Knightsbridge tube station

Personal service is assured at this small, family-owned hotel set in the heart of Knightsbridge. Beautifully designed bedrooms come in a number of styles, but all rooms feature antique furniture, a marble bathroom and a thoughtful range of extras. Cocktails are a speciality in the delightful, stylish bar, whilst afternoon tea in the elegant, bijou lounge is a must.

Rooms 49 **S** fr £220; **D** fr £295* **Facilities** STV FTV Xmas New Year Wi-fi **Conf** Class 24 Board 24 Thtr 30 **Services** Lift Air con **Parking** 12 **Notes** ⊗

Egerton House

★★★★★ 84%
TOWN HOUSE HOTEL PLAN 4 E4

☎ 020 7589 2412 020 7584 6540
17 Egerton Ter, Knightsbridge SW3 2BX
e-mail: bookeg@rchmail.com
web: www.egertonhousehotel.com
dir: Just off Brompton Rd, between Harrods & Victoria & Albert Museum, opposite Brompton Oratory

This delightful town house enjoys a prestigious Knightsbridge location, a short walk from Harrods and close to the Victoria & Albert Museum. Air-conditioned bedrooms and public rooms are appointed to the highest standards, with luxurious furnishings and quality antique pieces; an exceptional range of facilities include iPods, safes, mini bars and flat-screen TVs. Staff offer the highest levels of personalised, attentive service.

Rooms 28 (5 fmly) (2 GF) **D** £280-£895* **Facilities** STV Xmas New Year Wi-fi **Conf** Class 12 Board 10 Thtr 14 **Services** Lift Air con

The Draycott

★★★★★ 81% TOWN HOUSE HOTEL PLAN 4 F3

☎ 020 7730 6466 020 7730 0236
26 Cadogan Gardens SW3 2RP
e-mail: reservations@draycotthotel.com
web: www.draycotthotel.com
dir: From Sloane Sq station towards Peter Jones, keep to left. At Kings Rd take 1st right into Cadogan Gdns, 2nd right, hotel on left corner

Enjoying a prime location just yards from Sloane Square, this town house provides an ideal base in one

continued

LONDON

SW3 CHELSEA, BROMPTON ***continued***

of the most fashionable areas of London. Many regular guests regard this as their London residence and staff pride themselves on their hospitality. Beautifully appointed bedrooms include a number of very spacious suites and all are equipped to a high standard. Attractive day rooms, furnished with antique and period pieces, include a choice of lounges, one with access to a lovely sheltered garden.

Rooms 35 (9 fmly) (2 GF) **Facilities** STV Beauty treatments Massage Wi-fi **Conf** Class 12 Board 12 Thtr 20 **Services** Lift Air con

INSPECTORS' CHOICE

The Levin

★★★★ TOWN HOUSE HOTEL PLAN 4 F4

☎ 020 7589 6286 📠 020 7823 7826
28 Basil St, Knightsbridge SW3 1AS
e-mail: reservations@thelevin.co.uk
web: www.thelevinhotel.co.uk
dir: 20yds from Harrods & Knightsbridge tube station

This sophisticated town house is the sister property to the adjacent Capital Hotel and enjoys a prime location on the doorstep of Knightsbridge's stylish department and designer stores. Bedrooms and en suites offer stylish elegance alongside a host of up-to-date modern comforts; extra touches include champagne bars and state-of-the-art audio-visual systems. Guests can enjoy all-day dining in the stylish, popular, lower ground floor Metro Restaurant.

Rooms 12 (1 GF) **S** fr £270; **D** fr £270 (incl. bkfst)* **Facilities** STV FTV Xmas New Year Wi-fi **Services** Lift Air con **Parking** 8 **Notes** ®

The Beaufort

★★★★ 77% TOWN HOUSE HOTEL PLAN 4 F4

☎ 020 7584 5252 📠 020 7589 2834
33 Beaufort Gardens SW3 1PP
e-mail: reservations@thebeaufort.co.uk
web: www.thebeaufort.co.uk
dir: 100yds past Harrods on left of Brompton Rd

This friendly, attractive town house enjoys a peaceful location in a tree-lined cul-de-sac just a few minutes' walk from Knightsbridge. Air-conditioned bedrooms are thoughtfully furnished and equipped with CD players, movie channel access, safe and free Wi-fi. Guests are offered complimentary drinks and afternoon cream tea with homemade scones and clotted cream. A good continental breakfast is served in guests' own rooms.

Rooms 29 (3 GF) **Facilities** STV Wi-fi **Conf** Thtr 10 **Services** Lift Air con **Notes** ®

SW5 EARL'S COURT

London Marriott Kensington

Marriott HOTELS & RESORTS

★★★★ 82% HOTEL PLAN 4 B3

☎ 020 7973 1000 📠 020 7370 1685
Cromwell Rd SW5 0TH
e-mail: kensington.marriott@marriotthotels.com
web: www.londonmarriottkensington.co.uk
dir: On A4, opposite Cromwell Rd Hospital

This stylish contemporary hotel features a stunning glass exterior and a seven-storey atrium lobby. Fully air conditioned throughout, the hotel has elegant design combined with a great range of facilities, including indoor leisure, a range of conference rooms and parking. Smart bedrooms offer a host of extras including the very latest communications technology.

Rooms 216 (39 fmly) **Facilities** STV FTV ⓢ Gym Wi-fi **Conf** Class 80 Board 60 Thtr 150 **Services** Lift Air con **Parking** 20 **Notes** ®

Twenty Nevern Square

★★★★ 70% TOWN HOUSE HOTEL PLAN 4 A3

☎ 020 7565 9555 & 7370 4934 📠 020 7565 9444
20 Nevern Square, Earls Court SW5 9PD
e-mail: hotel@twentynevernsquare.co.uk
web: www.twentynevernsquare.co.uk
dir: From station take Warwick Rd exit, right, 2nd right into Nevern Sq. Hotel 30yds on right

This smart boutique-style town house hotel is discreetly located in Nevern Square and is ideally situated for both Earls Court and Olympia. The stylish, individually furnished bedrooms, which vary in shape and size, are appointed to a high standard and are well equipped. Public areas include a delightful lounge and Café Twenty where breakfast and light meals are served.

Rooms 20 (3 GF) **Facilities** FTV Wi-fi **Conf** Class 20 Board 20 Thtr 20 **Services** Lift **Parking** 4 **Notes** ®

See advert on opposite page

K + K Hotel George

★★★ 83% HOTEL PLAN 4 A3

☎ 020 7598 8700 & 7598 8707 📠 020 7370 2285
1-15 Templeton Place, Earl's Court SW5 9NB
e-mail: hotelgeorge@kkhotels.co.uk
web: www.kkhotels.com/george
dir: From Earls Court Rd (A3220) right into Trebovir Rd, right into Templeton Place

This smart hotel enjoys a central location, just a few minutes' walk from Earls Court and with easy access to London's central attractions. Stylish public areas include a bar/bistro, an executive lounge and meeting facilities and a restaurant that overlooks the attractive rear garden. Bedrooms are particularly well equipped with a host of useful extras including free, high-speed internet access.

Rooms 154 (38 fmly) (8 GF) (14 smoking) **Facilities** STV FTV Gym Wellness area with exercise machines Sauna Wi-fi **Conf** Class 14 Board 18 Thtr 35 **Services** Lift Air con **Parking** 20 **Notes** LB

LONDON

SW5 EARL'S COURT *continued*

Best Western Burns Hotel

★★★ 70% METRO HOTEL PLAN 4 B3

☎ 020 7373 3151 📠 020 7370 4090
18-26 Barkston Gardens, Kensington SW5 0EN
e-mail: burnshotel@vienna-group.co.uk
dir: Off A4, right to Earls Court Rd (A3220), 2nd left

This friendly Victorian hotel overlooks a leafy garden in a quiet residential area not far from the Earls Court exhibition centre and tube station. Bedrooms are attractively appointed, with modern facilities. Public areas, although not extensive, are stylish.

Rooms 105 (10 fmly) **Services** Lift **Notes** ⊗

Premier Inn London Kensington

BUDGET HOTEL PLAN 4 A3

☎ 0871 527 8666 📠 0871 527 8667
11 Knaresborough Place, Kensington SW5 0TJ
dir: Just off A4 (Cromwell Rd). Nearest tube: Earls Court

High quality, budget accommodation ideal for both families and business travellers. Spacious, en suite bedrooms feature tea and coffee making facilities, and Freeview TV in most hotels. Internet access and Wi-fi are available for a small fee. The adjacent family restaurant features a wide and varied menu. See also the Hotel Groups pages.

Rooms 184 **D** £87-£99*

Premier Inn London Kensington (Olympia)

BUDGET HOTEL PLAN 4 B3

☎ 0871 527 8668 📠 0871 527 8669
22-32 West Cromwell Rd, Kensington SW5 9QJ
dir: On N side of West Cromwell Rd, between juncts of Cromwell Rd, Earls Court Rd & Warwick Rd

Rooms 86 **D** £87-£99*

SW6 FULHAM

See also LONDON plan 1 D/E3

Millennium & Copthorne Hotels at Chelsea FC

★★★★ 76% HOTEL

☎ 020 7565 1400 📠 020 7565 1450
Stamford Bridge, Fulham Rd SW6 1HS
e-mail: reservations@chelseafc.com
web: www.millenniumhotels.co.uk
dir: 4 mins walk from Fulham Broadway tube station

A unique destination in a fashionable area of the city. Situated at Chelsea's famous Stamford Bridge football club the accommodation offered here is very up-to-the-minute. Bedroom facilities include flat-screen LCD TVs, video on demand, broadband, Wi-fi and good sized desk space; larger Club rooms have additional features. For eating there's a brasserie, the Bridge Bar and sports bar, and for corporate guests a flexible arrangement of meeting and event rooms is available.

Rooms 281 (64 fmly) **S** £80-£500; **D** £80-£500* **Facilities** Spa STV FTV Ⓢ Gym Health club Treatments Stadium tours Football packages Xmas New Year Wi-fi **Conf** Class 600 Board 30 Thtr 950 Del from £160 to £560* **Services** Lift Air con **Parking** 360 **Notes** LB ⊗ Civ Wed 50

Ibis London Earls Court

★★★ 70% HOTEL PLAN 4 A1

☎ 020 7610 0880 📠 020 7381 0215
47 Lillie Rd SW6 1UD
e-mail: h5623@accor.com
web: www.ibishotel.com
dir: From Hammersmith flyover towards London, keep in right lane, right at Kings pub on Talgarth Rd to join North End Rd. At mini-rdbt turn right. Hotel on left

Situated opposite the Earls Court Exhibition Centre, this large, modern hotel is popular with business and leisure guests. Bedrooms are comfortable and well equipped. There is a café bar open all day and a restaurant that serves evening meals. There are also extensive conference facilities and an underground car park.

Rooms 504 (20 fmly) **Facilities** FTV Health club & gym nearby Wi-fi **Conf** Class 750 Board 25 Thtr 1200 **Services** Lift **Parking** 130

Premier Inn London Putney Bridge

BUDGET HOTEL PLAN 1 D2

☎ 0871 527 8674 📠 0871 527 8675
3 Putney Bridge Approach SW6 3JD
dir: Nearest tube: Putney Bridge. Hotel on A219, N of River Thames

High quality, budget accommodation ideal for both families and business travellers. Spacious, en suite bedrooms feature tea and coffee making facilities, and Freeview TV in most hotels. Internet access and Wi-fi are available for a small fee. The adjacent family restaurant features a wide and varied menu. See also the Hotel Groups pages.

Rooms 154 **D** £79-£89*

SW7 SOUTH KENSINGTON

Baglioni Hotel

★★★★★ 88% ◎ HOTEL PLAN 4 C5

☎ 020 7368 5700 📠 020 7368 5701
60 Hyde Park Gate, Kensington Rd, Kensington SW7 5BB
e-mail: baglioni.london.@baglionihotels.com
dir: On corner of Hyde Park Gate & De Vere Gardens

Located in the heart of Kensington and overlooking Hyde Park, this small hotel buzzes with Italian style and chic. Bedrooms, mostly suites, are generously sized and designed in bold dark colours; they have espresso machines, interactive plasma-screen TVs and a host of other excellent touches. Service is both professional and friendly, with personal butlers for the bedrooms. Public areas include the main open-plan space with bar, lounge and Brunello restaurant, all merging together with great elan; there is a small health club and a fashionable private club bar downstairs.

Rooms 67 (7 fmly) (30 smoking) **S** £334-£474; **D** £334-£474 **Facilities** Spa STV FTV Gym Xmas New Year Wi-fi **Conf** Class 33 Board 34 Thtr 60 Del from £460 to £600 **Services** Lift Air con **Parking** 2 **Notes** LB Civ Wed 60

Millennium Bailey's Hotel London Kensington

★★★★ 75% HOTEL PLAN 4 C3

020 7373 6000 020 7370 3760
140 Gloucester Rd SW7 4QH
e-mail: reservations.baileys@millenniumhotels.co.uk
web: www.millenniumhotels.co.uk
dir: From A4 at Cromwell Hospital into Knaresborough Place, to Courtfield Rd to corner of Gloucester Rd, hotel opposite tube station

This elegant hotel has a town house feel and enjoys a prime location. Air-conditioned bedrooms are smartly appointed and thoughtfully equipped, particularly the club rooms which benefit from DVD players. Public areas include a stylish contemporary restaurant and bar. Guests may also use the facilities at the larger sister hotel which is adjacent.

Rooms 211 (3 smoking) **Facilities** STV Gym Wi-fi **Conf** Class 12 Board 12 Thtr 12 **Services** Lift Air con **Parking** 110 **Notes** ⊗

Millennium Gloucester Hotel London Kensington

★★★★ 74% HOTEL PLAN 4 C3

020 7373 6030 020 7373 0409
4-18 Harrington Gardens SW7 4LH
e-mail: reservations.gloucester@millenniumhotels.co.uk
web: www.millenniumhotels.co.uk
dir: Opposite Gloucester Rd tube station

This spacious, stylish hotel is centrally located, close to The Victoria & Albert Museum and Gloucester Road tube station. Air-conditioned bedrooms are furnished in a variety of contemporary styles and Clubrooms benefit from a dedicated club lounge with complimentary breakfast and snacks. A wide range of eating options includes Singaporean and Mediterranean cuisine.

Rooms 610 (8 fmly) (37 smoking) **Facilities** STV Gym Wi-fi **Conf** Class 300 Board 100 Thtr 500 **Services** Lift Air con **Parking** 110 **Notes** ⊗ Civ Wed 500

Harrington Hall

★★★★ 73% HOTEL PLAN 4 C3

020 7396 9696 020 7396 9090
5-25 Harrington Gardens SW7 4JW
e-mail: book.london@nh-hotels.com
web: www.nh-hotels.com
dir: 2 mins walk from Gloucester Road tube station

This splendid period property is centrally located just a stone's throw from Gloucester Road tube station and is convenient for visiting the museums and for shopping in Knightsbridge. Spacious bedrooms are smartly appointed and boast a host of extra touches. The public areas include extensive meeting facilities, a lounge bar and a restaurant.

Rooms 200 (4 fmly) **S** £115-£275; **D** £115-£275* **Facilities** STV FTV Gym Sauna Xmas New Year Wi-fi **Conf** Class 100 Board 50 Thtr 240 **Services** Lift Air con **Notes** LB ⊗ Civ Wed 200

SW10 WEST BROMPTON

Wyndham Grand London Chelsea Harbour

★★★★★ 84% HOTEL PLAN 1 E3

020 7823 3000 020 7351 6525
Chelsea Harbour SW10 0XG
e-mail: wyndhamlondon@wyndham.com
web: www.wyndham.com
dir: A4 to Earls Court Rd S towards river. Right into Kings Rd, left into Lots Rd to Chelsea Harbour

Against the picturesque backdrop of Chelsea Harbour's small marina, this modern hotel offers spacious, comfortable accommodation. All rooms are suites, which are superbly equipped; many enjoy splendid views of the marina. In addition, there are also several luxurious penthouse suites. Public areas include a modern bar and restaurant, excellent leisure facilities and extensive meeting and function rooms.

Rooms 158 (36 fmly) (46 smoking) **Facilities** Spa STV FTV Gym Sauna Steam room ♫ Xmas New Year Wi-fi **Conf** Class 115 Board 40 Thtr 600 **Services** Lift Air con **Parking** 2000 **Notes** LB Civ Wed 450

SW15 PUTNEY

See LONDON plan 1 D2

The Lodge Hotel

★★★ 75% METRO HOTEL

020 8874 1598 020 8874 0910
52-54 Upper Richmond Rd, Putney SW15 2RN
e-mail: res@thelodgehotellondon.com
dir: M25 junct 10/A3 towards central London. A219 to Putney, right to Upper Richmond, left at lights after 0.5m

This friendly hotel is conveniently located for East Putney tube station. Public areas include a bar/lounge with satellite TV and conference and banqueting facilities. A buffet breakfast is served in the garden conservatory. Thoughtfully equipped, comfortable bedrooms include a selection of executive rooms and suites. Parking for residents is an asset.

Rooms 60 (5 fmly) (15 GF) (4 smoking) **Facilities** STV FTV Wi-fi **Conf** Class 40 Board 30 Thtr 90 Del from £180 to £200* **Parking** 35 **Notes** Civ Wed 80

SW18 WANDSWORTH

Holiday Inn Express Wandsworth-Battersea

BUDGET HOTEL PLAN 1 D2

020 8877 5950 020 8877 0631
Smugglers Way, Wandsworth SW18 1EG
e-mail: wandsworth@morethanhotels.com
web: www.hiexpress.com/londonwandswth
dir: from S side of Wandsworth Bridge, take A3205 W. 0.5m to Smugglers Way on right

A modern hotel ideal for families and business travellers. Fresh and uncomplicated, the spacious rooms include Sky TV, power shower and tea and coffee-making facilities. Continental buffet breakfast is included in the room rate; other meals may be taken at the nearby family pub or restaurant. See also the Hotel Groups pages.

Rooms 148 (60 fmly) **Conf** Class 16 Board 15 Thtr 35

SW19 WIMBLEDON

See LONDON plan 1 D1

Cannizaro House

★★★★ 80% COUNTRY HOUSE HOTEL

020 8879 1464 020 8879 7338
West Side, Wimbledon Common SW19 4UE
e-mail: info@cannizarohouse.com
dir: From A3 follow A219 signed Wimbledon into Parkside, right into Cannizaro Rd, sharp right into West Side

This unique, elegant 18th-century house has a long tradition of hosting the rich and famous of London society. A few miles from the city centre, the landscaped grounds provide a peaceful escape and a country-house ambience; fine art, murals and stunning fireplaces feature throughout. Spacious bedrooms are individually furnished and equipped to a high standard. The award-winning restaurant menus proudly herald locally sourced, organic ingredients.

Rooms 46 (10 fmly) (5 GF) **D** £175-£485 (incl. bkfst)* **Facilities** STV Xmas New Year Wi-fi **Conf** Class 50 Board 40 Thtr 120 **Services** Lift **Parking** 95 **Notes** LB Civ Wed 100

LONDON

SW19 WIMBLEDON *continued*

Premier Inn London Wimbledon South

BUDGET HOTEL

☎ 0871 527 8684 📠 0871 527 8685
27 Chapter Way, Off Merantun Way, SW19 2RF
dir: A298 (Wimbledon) onto A238. Right onto A219, left onto A24 (Merantun Way). At rdbt 3rd exit signed Merton Abbey Mills

High quality, budget accommodation ideal for both families and business travellers. Spacious, en suite bedrooms feature tea and coffee making facilities, and Freeview TV in most hotels. Internet access and Wi-fi are available for a small fee. The adjacent family restaurant features a wide and varied menu. See also the Hotel Groups pages.

Rooms 132 **D** £68-£80*

W1 WEST END

INSPECTORS' CHOICE

The Connaught

MAYBOURNE HOTEL GROUP

★★★★★ ⓐⓐⓐⓐ HOTEL PLAN 2 G1

☎ 020 7499 7070 📠 020 7495 3262
Carlos Place W1K 2AL
e-mail: info@the-connaught.co.uk
dir: Between Grosvenor Sq & Berkeley Sq

This iconic hotel is truly spectacular with stunning interior design. There are sumptuous day rooms and stylish bedrooms with state-of-the-art facilities and marble en suites with deep tubs, TV screens and power showers. Butlers are available at the touch of a button and guests are pampered by friendly, attentive staff offering intuitive service. There is a choice of bars and restaurants including the Espelette bistro, and the award-winning cuisine of Hélène Darroze which is imaginative, inspired and truly memorable. The excellent Aman Spa at the hotel offers health and beauty treatments, a swimming pool and fitness centre.

Rooms 123 (17 smoking) **Facilities** Spa STV FTV Gym Wi-fi **Conf** Class 70 Board 60 Thtr 130 **Services** Lift Air con **Notes** ⊗ Civ Wed 20

INSPECTORS' CHOICE

Claridge's

MAYBOURNE HOTEL GROUP

★★★★★ ⓐⓐⓐ HOTEL PLAN 2 H1

☎ 020 7629 8860 📠 020 7499 2210
Brook St W1A 2JQ
e-mail: info@claridges.co.uk
dir: 1st turn after Green Park tube station to Berkeley Sq & 4th exit into Davies St. 3rd right into Brook St

Once renowned as the resort of kings and princes, Claridge's today continues to set the standards by which other hotels are judged. The sumptuous, air-conditioned bedrooms are elegantly themed to reflect the Victorian or art deco architecture of the building. Gordon Ramsay at Claridge's is now established as one of London's most popular dining venues, while the stylish cocktail bar is a hit with residents and non-residents alike. Service throughout is punctilious and thoroughly professional.

Rooms 203 (144 fmly) **Facilities** Spa STV Gym Beauty & health treatments Use of sister hotel's swimming pool ♫ Xmas New Year Wi-fi **Conf** Class 130 Board 60 Thtr 250 **Services** Lift Air con **Notes** ⊗ Civ Wed 200

INSPECTORS' CHOICE

The Ritz London

★★★★★ ⓐⓐⓐ HOTEL PLAN 4 J6

☎ 020 7493 8181 📠 020 7493 2687
150 Piccadilly W1J 9BR
e-mail: enquire@theritzlondon.com
web: www.theritzlondon.com
dir: From Hyde Park Corner E on Piccadilly. Hotel on right after Green Park

This renowned, stylish hotel offers guests the ultimate in sophistication whilst still managing to retain all its former historical glory. Bedrooms and suites are exquisitely furnished in Louis XVI style, with fine marble bathrooms and every imaginable comfort. Elegant reception rooms include the Palm Court with its legendary afternoon teas, the beautiful fashionable Rivoli Bar and the sumptuous Ritz Restaurant, complete with gold chandeliers and extraordinary trompe-l'oeil decoration.

Rooms 136 (44 fmly) (27 smoking) **S** £306-£696; **D** £360-£822* **Facilities** STV Gym Treatment room Hairdressing Fitness centre The Ritz Club Casino ♫ Xmas New Year **Conf** Class 40 Board 30 Thtr 60 **Services** Lift Air con **Parking** 10 **Notes** ⊗ Civ Wed 60

INSPECTORS' CHOICE

Athenaeum Hotel & Apartments

★★★★★ ◎◎ HOTEL PLAN 4 H6

☎ 020 7499 3464 📠 020 7493 1860
116 Piccadilly W1J 7BJ
e-mail: info@athenaeumhotel.com
web: www.athenaeumhotel.com
dir: On Piccadilly, overlooking Green Park

With a discreet address in Mayfair, this well-loved hotel offers bedrooms appointed to the highest standard; several boast views over Green Park. The delightful bar has an excellent stock of whiskies which complements the stunning Garden Lounge and stylish restaurant. A row of Edwardian townhouses adjacent to the hotel offers a range of spacious and well-appointed apartments. There is an extensive range of beauty treatments available along with conference and meeting facilities.

Rooms 156 (8 smoking) **Facilities** STV Gym Steam rooms Sauna Hairdressing salon Xmas New Year Wi-fi **Conf** Class 35 Board 36 Thtr 55 **Services** Lift Air con **Notes** ⊗ Civ Wed 80

INSPECTORS' CHOICE

Brown's Hotel

★★★★★ ◎◎ HOTEL PLAN 2 J1

☎ 020 7493 6020 📠 020 7493 9381
Albemarle St, Mayfair W1S 4BP
e-mail: reservations.browns@roccofortecollection.com
web: www.roccofortecollection.com
dir: A short walk from Green Park, Bond St & Piccadilly

Brown's is a London hospitality icon that retains much charm by the successful balance of the traditional and the contemporary. Bedrooms are luxurious, furnished to the highest standard and come with all the modern comforts expected of such a grand Mayfair hotel. The hotel has 29 suites including two Royal Suites and two Presidential Suites. The elegant, yet informal, HIX at the Albemarle serves a traditional selection of popular British dishes that are created with skill; it is home to a collection of works by leading British artists; the English Tea Room proves a great meeting place for afternoon tea.

Rooms 117 (12 smoking) **Facilities** Spa STV Gym ♫ Xmas New Year Wi-fi **Conf** Class 30 Board 30 Thtr 70 **Services** Lift Air con **Notes** ⊗ Civ Wed 70

INSPECTORS' CHOICE

The Dorchester

★★★★★ ◎◎ HOTEL PLAN 4 G6

☎ 020 7629 8888 📠 020 7629 8080
Park Ln W1K 1QA
e-mail: info@thedorchester.com
dir: Halfway along Park Ln between Hyde Park Corner & Marble Arch

One of London's finest. The Dorchester remains one of the best-loved hotels in the country and always delivers. The spacious bedrooms and suites are beautifully appointed and feature fabulous marble bathrooms. Leading off from the foyer, The Promenade is the perfect setting for afternoon tea or drinks. In the evening guests can relax to the sound of live jazz, whilst enjoying a cocktail in the stylish bar. Dining options include the sophisticated Chinese restaurant, China Tang (2 AA Rosettes); Alain Ducasse at The Dorchester from the world renowned French chef of the same name (3 AA Rosettes), and of course, The Grill (2 AA Rosettes).

Rooms 250 **Facilities** Spa STV FTV Gym Steam rooms Fitness suite ♫ Xmas New Year Wi-fi **Conf** Class 300 Board 42 Thtr 500 **Services** Lift Air con **Parking** 13 **Notes** ⊗ Civ Wed 500

W1 WEST END *continued*

INSPECTORS' CHOICE

Four Seasons Hotel Park Lane

★★★★★ ®® PLAN 4 G6

☎ 020 7499 0888 📠 020 7493 1895
Hamilton Place, Park Ln W1A 1AZ
e-mail: fsh.london@fourseasons.com
dir: From Piccadilly into Old Park Ln. Then Hamilton Place

This long-established popular hotel is discreetly located near Hyde Park Corner, in the heart of Mayfair. It successfully combines modern efficiencies with traditional luxury. Guest care is consistently of the highest order, even down to the smallest detail of the personalised wake-up call. The bedrooms are elegant and spacious, and the unique conservatory rooms are particularly special. Spacious public areas include extensive conference and banqueting facilities, Lane's bar and fine-dining restaurant and an elegant lounge where wonderful afternoon teas are served.

Rooms 219 **Facilities** Gym ♫ Xmas New Year Wi-fi **Conf** Class 180 Board 70 Thtr 400 **Services** Lift Air con **Parking** 72 **Notes** Civ Wed 180

LONDON

The Langham, London

★★★★★ 86% HOTEL PLAN 2 H3

☎ 020 7636 1000 📠 020 7323 2340
Portland Place W1B 1JA
e-mail: lon.info@langhamhotels.com
dir: N of Regent St, left opposite All Soul's Church

This hotel has a grand entrance which leads into restored interior elegance. Dating back to 1865 the building displays a contemporary, luxurious style. Situated on Regent Street it is ideally located for both theatreland and the principal shopping areas. Bedrooms are delightfully appointed and many have excellent views. The Landau restaurant and Artesian bar offer high standards of service, delivered by a friendly team. Palm Court is a great place for afternoon tea or a glass of champagne. There is also an extensive health club complete with a 16-metre pool.

Rooms 380 (5 fmly) (15 smoking) **S** £199-£7000; **D** £199-£7000* **Facilities** Spa STV supervised Gym Health club Sauna Steam room ♫ Xmas New Year Wi-fi **Conf** Class 148 Board 80 Thtr 300 **Services** Lift Air con **Notes** LB ⊗ Civ Wed 280

Metropolitan London

★★★★★ 84% ®® HOTEL PLAN 4 G6

☎ 020 7447 1000 📠 020 7447 1100
Old Park Ln W1K 1LB
e-mail: res.lon@metropolitan.como.bz
dir: On corner of Old Park Ln and Hertford St, within 200mtrs from Hyde Park corner

Overlooking Hyde Park this hotel is located within easy reach of the fashionable stores of Knightsbridge and Mayfair. The hotel's contemporary style allows freedom and space to relax. Understated luxury is the key here with bedrooms enjoying great natural light. There is also a Shambhala Spa, steam room and fully equipped gym. For those seeking a culinary experience, Nobu offers innovative Japanese cuisine with an upbeat atmosphere.

Rooms 150 (25 smoking) **S** £209-£390; **D** £209-£470* **Facilities** Spa STV FTV Gym Treatments Steam rooms Wi-fi **Conf** Class 25 Board 30 Thtr 40 **Services** Lift Air con **Parking** 8 **Notes** Civ Wed 30

London Marriott Hotel Park Lane

Marriott HOTELS & RESORTS

★★★★★ 83% ® HOTEL PLAN 2 F1

☎ 020 7493 7000 📠 020 7493 8333
140 Park Ln W1K 7AA
e-mail: mhrs.parklane@marriotthotels.com
web: www.londonmarriottparklane.co.uk
dir: From Hyde Park Corner left on Park Ln onto A4202, 0.8m. At Marble Arch into Park Ln. Take 1st left onto North Row. Hotel on left

This modern and stylish hotel is situated in a prominent position in the heart of central London. Bedrooms are superbly appointed and air conditioned. Public rooms include a popular lounge/bar, and there are excellent leisure facilities and an executive lounge.

Rooms 157 (31 smoking) **Facilities** STV Gym Steam room Xmas New Year Wi-fi **Conf** Class 33 Board 42 Thtr 72 **Services** Lift Air con **Notes** ⊗

Hyatt Regency London - The Churchill

★★★★★ 82% ®®® HOTEL PLAN 2 F2

☎ 020 7486 5800 📠 020 7486 1255
30 Portman Square W1H 7BH
e-mail: london.churchill@hyatt.com
dir: From Marble Arch rdbt, follow signs for Oxford Circus into Oxford St. Left after 2nd lights into Portman St. Hotel on left

This smart hotel enjoys a central location overlooking Portman Square. Excellent conference and in-room facilities, plus a fitness room make this the ideal choice for both corporate and leisure guests. To set the style guests are greeted by stunning floral displays in the sophisticated lobby. The Montagu restaurant offers contemporary dining, plus the option to sit at the Chef's Table for a front row seat to watch all the action in the kitchen. Bedroom refurbishment, plus the creation of six new suites, is due to be completed by 2012.

Rooms 434 (87 smoking) **S** £200-£460; **D** £200-£460* **Facilities** STV FTV Gym Jogging track ♫ Xmas New Year Wi-fi **Conf** Class 160 Board 68 Thtr 250 Del from £305 to £600* **Services** Lift Air con **Parking** 48 **Notes** ⊗ Civ Wed 250

Grosvenor House, A JW Marriott Hotel

GROSVENOR HOUSE A JW MARRIOTT HOTEL LONDON

★★★★★ 82% ® HOTEL PLAN 2 G1

☎ 020 7499 6363 & 7399 8400 📠 020 7493 3341
Park Ln W1K 7TN
e-mail: grosvenor.house@marriotthotels.com
web: www.londongrosvenorhouse.co.uk
dir: Centrally located on Park Ln, between Hyde Park Corner & Oxford St

This quintessentially British hotel overlooking Hyde Park, offers luxurious accommodation, warm hospitality and exemplary service that epitomises the fine hotel culture of London. The property boasts the largest ballroom in Europe, and there is a steakhouse and a cocktail bar. The Park Room and The Library make perfect settings for afternoon tea.

Rooms 494 (111 smoking) **Facilities** STV Gym Health & Fitness centre Xmas New Year Wi-fi **Conf** Class 800 Board 140 Thtr 1500 **Services** Lift Air con **Parking** 70 **Notes** ⊗ Civ Wed 1500

The Westbury Hotel

★★★★★ 81% ®® HOTEL PLAN 2 H1

☎ 020 7629 7755 📠 020 7495 1163
Bond St W1S 2YF
e-mail: reservations@westburymayfair.com
dir: From Oxford Circus S down Regent St, right onto Conduit St, hotel at junct of Conduit St & Bond St

A well-known favourite with an international clientele, The Westbury is located at the heart of London's finest shopping district and provides a calm atmosphere away from the hubbub. The standards of accommodation are high throughout. As we went to press we understood that there were to be changes concerning the eating options at the hotel. Please see the AA website theAA.com for up-to-date details.

Rooms 246 (80 fmly) **D** £190.80-£3000*
Facilities STV FTV Gym Fitness centre Steam room Sauna Xmas New Year Wi-fi **Conf** Class 100 Board 40 Thtr 200 **Services** Lift Air con **Notes** ⊗ Civ Wed 80

Le Meridien Piccadilly

★★★★★ 81% HOTEL PLAN 2 J1

☎ 0207 734 8000 📠 0207 437 7575
21 Piccadilly W1J 0BH
e-mail: reservations.picadilly@lemeridien.com
dir: 100mtrs from Piccadilly Circus

Situated in heart of Piccadilly this well established hotel is ideally located for both the west end and theatreland. Well equipped, air-conditioned bedrooms vary in shape and size, are modern and contemporary in style. Public areas include extensive leisure complete with pool, the trendy Longitude 0*8 cocktail bar and popoular Terrace restaurant which overlooks Piccadilly.

Rooms 266 **Conf** Class 160 Board 80 Thtr 250

INSPECTORS' CHOICE

Chesterfield Mayfair

★★★★ ®®
HOTEL PLAN 4 H6

☎ 020 7491 2622 📠 020 7491 4793
35 Charles St, Mayfair W1J 5EB
e-mail: bookch@rchmail.com
web: www.chesterfieldmayfair.com
dir: Hyde Park Corner along Piccadilly, left into Half Moon St. At end left & 1st right into Queens St, then right into Charles St

Quiet elegance and an atmosphere of exclusivity characterise this stylish Mayfair hotel where attentive, friendly service is paramount. The bedrooms, each with a marble-clad bathroom, have contemporary styles - perhaps with floral fabric walls, an African theme or with Savile Row stripes. In addition to these deluxe bedrooms there are 13 individually designed suites; some with four-poster beds and some with jacuzzis. The Butler's Restaurant is the fine dining option, and The Conservatory, with views over the garden, is just the place for cocktails, light lunches and afternoon teas. The hotel is air conditioned throughout.

Rooms 107 (7 fmly) **S** £168-£330; **D** £192-£450*
Facilities STV ♫ Xmas Wi-fi **Conf** Class 45 Board 45 Thtr 100 Del from £345 to £500*
Services Lift Air con **Notes** Civ Wed 120

London Marriott Hotel Grosvenor Square

Marriott HOTELS & RESORTS

★★★★ 84% ®® HOTEL PLAN 2 G1

☎ 020 7493 1232 📠 020 7514 1528
Grosvenor Square W1K 6JP
e-mail: philip.hyland@marriotthotels.com
web: www.londonmarriottgrosvenorsquare.co.uk
dir: M4 E to Cromwell Rd through Knightsbridge to Hyde Park Corner. Park Lane right at Brook Gate into Upper Brook St to Grosvenor Sq

Situated adjacent to Grosvenor Square in the heart of Mayfair, this hotel boasts convenient access to the city, West End and some of London's most exclusive shops. Bedrooms and public areas are furnished and decorated to a high standard and retain the traditional elegance for which the area is known. The hotel's eating options include the Maze Grill with 2 AA Rosettes.

Rooms 237 (26 fmly) **Facilities** Gym Exercise & fitness centre Xmas Wi-fi **Conf** Class 500 Board 120 Thtr 900 **Services** Lift Air con **Notes** ⊗ Civ Wed 600

London Marriott Hotel Marble Arch

Marriott HOTELS & RESORTS

★★★★ 84% HOTEL PLAN 2 F2

☎ 020 7723 1277 📠 020 7402 0666
134 George St W1H 5DN
e-mail: mhrs.lonma.sales.mkt.cood@marriotthotels.com
web: www.londonmarriottmarblearch.co.uk
dir: From Marble Arch turn into Edgware Rd, then 4th right into George St. Left into Dorset St for entrance

Situated just off the Edgware Road and close to the Oxford Street shops, this friendly hotel offers smart, well-equipped, air-conditioned bedrooms. Public areas are stylish, and include a smart indoor leisure club and an Italian themed restaurant. Secure underground parking is available.

Rooms 240 (100 fmly) (20 smoking) **Facilities** STV FTV ⓢ supervised Gym Xmas New Year Wi-fi **Conf** Class 75 Board 80 Thtr 150 **Services** Lift Air con **Parking** 83 **Notes** ⊗ Civ Wed 150

W1 WEST END *continued*

Millennium Hotel London Mayfair

★★★★ 81% ◎◎ HOTEL PLAN 2 G1

☎ 020 7629 9400 📠 020 7629 7736
Grosvenor Square W1K 2HP
e-mail: reservations@millenniumhotels.co.uk
web: www.millenniumhotels.co.uk
dir: S side of Grosvenor Square

This hotel benefits from a prestigious location in the heart of Mayfair, close to Bond Street. The smart bedrooms are generally spacious, and club-floor rooms have exclusive use of a lounge with complimentary refreshments. A choice of bars and dining options is available along with conference facilities and a fitness room.

Rooms 336 **S** £175-£425; **D** £185-£435* **Facilities** STV FTV Gym Fitness suite ♫ Xmas New Year Wi-fi **Conf** Class 250 Board 70 Thtr 500 Del from £354* **Services** Lift Air con **Notes** ⊗ Civ Wed 250

The Mandeville Hotel

★★★★ 80% ◎◎ HOTEL PLAN 2 G2

☎ 020 7935 5599 📠 020 7935 9588
Mandeville Place W1U 2BE
e-mail: sales@mandeville.co.uk
web: www.mandeville.co.uk
dir: 3 mins walk from Bond St tube station

This is a stylish and attractive boutique-style hotel with a very contemporary feel. Bedrooms have air conditioning, state-of-the-art TVs and large, very comfortable beds. One of the suites, The Penthouse, has a patio with views over London. The deVille Restaurant offers award-winning modern British cuisine, and the deVigne cocktail bar is always popular.

Rooms 142 **Facilities** STV FTV Xmas New Year Wi-fi **Conf** Class 20 Board 20 Thtr 40 **Services** Lift Air con **Notes** ⊗

Best Western Premier Mostyn Hotel

★★★★ 77% ◎◎◎ HOTEL PLAN 2 F2

☎ 020 7935 2361 📠 020 7487 2759
4 Bryanston St W1H 7BY
e-mail: info@mostynhotel.co.uk
web: www.bw-mostynhotel.co.uk
dir: Nearest tube stations: Marble Arch & Bond St

This well located, historic property has benefited from a fashionable, contemporary refurbishment. The bedrooms, including executive and deluxe club floor rooms, vary in size but all are smartly equipped, boast bright trendy soft furnishings and are air conditioned; the en suites are equally modern and stylish. The public areas include a cocktail bar/ lounge, Fire & Spice all-day dining concept, the acclaimed Texture Restaurant which delivers impressive, modern cooking, and the Trimiri Spa. The hotel offers free Wi-fi throughout.

Rooms 121 (15 fmly) (9 GF) **S** £200-£250; **D** £230-£270 **Facilities** Spa STV FTV Gym ♫ Xmas Wi-fi **Conf** Class 70 Board 50 Thtr 130 **Services** Lift Air con **Notes** ⊗

See advert on this page

Park Plaza Sherlock Holmes

★★★★ 76% ◎ HOTEL PLAN 2 F3

☎ 020 7486 6161 📠 020 7958 5211
108 Baker St W1U 6LJ
e-mail: info@sherlockholmeshotel.com
web: www.sherlockholmeshotel.com
dir: From Marylebone Flyover into Marylebone Rd. At Baker St turn right for hotel on left

Chic and modern, this boutique-style hotel is near a number of London underground lines and rail stations. Public rooms include a popular bar, sited just inside the main entrance, and Sherlock's Grill, where the mesquite-wood burning stove is a feature of the cooking. The hotel also features an indoor health suite and a relaxing lounge.

Rooms 119 (20 fmly) **Facilities** STV Gym ♫ Xmas Wi-fi **Conf** Class 50 Board 30 Thtr 80 **Services** Lift Air con **Notes** ⊗ Civ Wed 70

Thistle Marble Arch

thistle

★★★★ 74% HOTEL PLAN 2 G2

☎ 0871 971 1753 & 020 7629 8040
📠 0871 376 9127
Bryanston St W1A 4UR
e-mail: marblearch@thistle.co.uk
web: www.thistlehotels.com/marblearch
dir: From Marble Arch monument down Oxford St. 1st left onto Portman St, 1st left onto Bryanston St. Hotel entrance on left

This centrally located hotel, adjacent to a car park, is ideal for the attractions of Oxford Street and Knightsbridge. The spacious bedrooms come in a range of size and price options, but all are very well equipped and have air conditioning. The public areas include a fast food service, Co-Motion, and a more leisurely carvery restaurant, which also offers a carte menu. There is also a gym, a range of meeting rooms and an executive lounge. Thistle Hotels – AA Hotel Group of the Year 2011-12.

Rooms 692 (60 fmly) (97 smoking) **Facilities** STV FTV Gym ♫ Xmas New Year Wi-fi **Conf** Class 180 Board 94 Thtr 380 **Services** Lift Air con **Notes** ⊗

The Cumberland

★★★★ 73% ◉ HOTEL PLAN 2 F2

☎ 0871 376 9014 📠 0870 333 9281
Great Cumberland Place W1A 4RF
e-mail: enquiries@thecumberland.co.uk
dir: Behind Marble Arch monument, at top of Park Lane & Oxford St

This landmark hotel, occupying a prime position at Marble Arch, has a striking, airy lobby that is the focal point. A choice of bars, two Gary Rhodes restaurants (one with 3 AA Rosettes and the other with 1 Rosette) and extensive conference and meeting facilities are just some of what's on offer here. Bedrooms have a stylish contemporary feel and boast an excellent range of facilities.

Rooms 1019 (119 annexe) (8 fmly) (9 GF) **Facilities** Gym ♫ Xmas New Year Wi-fi **Conf** Class 170 Board 85 Thtr 350 **Services** Lift Air con **Notes** ⊗ Civ Wed 300

Radisson Blu Portman Hotel

★★★★ 73% HOTEL PLAN 2 F2

☎ 020 7208 6000 📠 020 7208 6001
22 Portman Square W1H 7BG
e-mail: reservations.london@radissonblu.com
web: www.radissonblu.co.uk
dir: 100mtrs N of Oxford St; 300mtrs E of Edgware Rd

This smart, popular hotel enjoys a prime location a short stroll from Oxford Street and close to all the city's major attractions. The spacious, well-equipped bedrooms are themed, ranging from Oriental through to classical and contemporary Italian decor. Public areas include extensive conference facilities, a bar and the modern European Portman Restaurant.

Rooms 272 (93 fmly) (14 smoking) **Facilities** FTV Gym Xmas Wi-fi **Conf** Class 280 Board 65 Thtr 600 **Services** Lift Air con **Parking** 400 **Notes** ⊗ Civ Wed 500

Ten Manchester Street

★★★★ 73%
TOWN HOUSE HOTEL PLAN 2 G3

☎ 0870 111 1627 & 7317 5900 📠 0870 111 1628
Ten Manchester St, Marylebone W1U 4DJ
e-mail: reservations@tenmanchesterstreethotel.com
dir: Nearest tube station: Baker Street

This smart, modern townhouse hotel is located in a quiet area just around the corner from the fashionable Marylebone High Street and a short walk from Oxford Street. All of the stylish bedrooms are comfortable but vary in shape and size due to the character of the building; some have their own garden terrace. Refreshments, snacks and evening meals are served in the relaxing lounge bar. The unique all-weather cigar terrace is popular.

Rooms 45 (4 fmly) (13 GF) **Facilities** STV Xmas New Year Wi-fi **Services** Lift Air con **Notes** LB ⊗

Holiday Inn London-Mayfair

★★★★ 72% HOTEL PLAN 2 H1

☎ 0870 400 9110 📠 020 7629 2827
3 Berkeley St W1J 8NE
e-mail: himayfair-reservations@ihg.com
web: www.holidayinn.co.uk
dir: At corner of Berkeley St & Piccadilly

Located in the heart of Mayfair and just minutes from Green Park tube station, this busy hotel has the benefit of well-proportioned, attractive bedrooms and elegant public areas. Options for dining include the graceful Nightingales Restaurant or choices from a substantial snack menu in the lounge bar.

Rooms 194 (63 fmly) (24 smoking) **Facilities** STV Xmas New Year Wi-fi **Conf** Class 32 Board 30 Thtr 65 **Services** Lift Air con **Parking** 18 **Notes** LB ⊗

The Washington Mayfair Hotel

★★★★ 72% HOTEL PLAN 4 H6

☎ 020 7499 7000 📠 020 7495 6172
5-7 Curzon St, Mayfair W1J 5HE
e-mail: sales@washington-mayfair.co.uk
web: www.washington-mayfair.co.uk
dir: From Green Park station take Piccadilly exit & turn right. 4th right into Curzon Street

Situated in the heart of Mayfair, this stylish independently owned hotel offers a very high standard of accommodation. Personalised, friendly service is noteworthy. Bedrooms are attractively furnished and provide high levels of comfort. The hotel is also a popular venue for afternoon tea and refreshments, served in the marbled and wood-panelled lounge.

Rooms 171 (32 smoking) **S** £150-£750; **D** fr £180* **Facilities** Gym Xmas New Year Wi-fi **Conf** Class 40 Board 36 Thtr 110 Del from £250 to £500* **Services** Lift Air con **Notes** LB ⊗

Holiday Inn London - Regents Park

★★★★ 71% HOTEL PLAN 2 H4

☎ 0871 942 9111 & 020 7388 2302
📠 020 7387 2806
Carburton St, Regents Park W1W 5EE
e-mail: reservations-londonregentspark@ihg.com
web: www.holidayinn.co.uk
dir: From E: from King's Cross, A50, left into Bolsover St. From W: A40, A501 (Regent's Pk Station on right). Left into Albany St, 1st right to cross Euston Rd. Pass Gt Portland St tube station to Bolsover St. Hotel on left

Well located and with the benefit of an adjacent public car park, this popular modern hotel provides a range of comfortable bedrooms equipped for both business and leisure guests. The attractive Junction Restaurant is the setting for brasserie-style eating and a comprehensive buffet breakfast provides a good start to the day. The hotel also provides excellent conference facilities within The Academy Centre.

Rooms 332 (28 smoking) **Facilities** STV FTV Wi-fi **Conf** Class 200 Board 50 Thtr 350 Del from £170 to £385* **Services** Lift Air con **Notes** LB ⊗

W1 WEST END *continued*

Holiday Inn London - Oxford Circus

★★★ 77% HOTEL PLAN 2 H2

☎ 020 7935 4442 📠 020 7487 3782
57 - 59 Welbeck St W1M 8HS
e-mail: dmelrose@holidayinnoxfordcircus.com
web: www.holidayinn.co.uk
dir: From M1, North Circular Rd, A41. Into Finchley Rd & Baker St to Portman Sq. Left on Wigmore St, left into Queen Anne St. Left into Wellbeck St

This Edwardian property enjoys a prime location only a few minutes' walk from Oxford Street and close to all of London's major theatres, shops and attractions. Bedrooms are particularly well equipped and include a number of spacious executive and junior suites. Public areas include a split-level bar, restaurant and mini-gym.

Rooms 164 (18 fmly) (18 smoking) **S** £110-£280; **D** £120-£300* **Facilities** STV Gym Wi-fi **Conf** Class 45 Board 32 Thtr 75 Del from £180 to £295* **Services** Lift Air con **Notes** LB ⊗

LONDON

Thistle Piccadilly

thistle

★★★ 77% METRO HOTEL PLAN 3 A1

☎ 0871 376 9031 📠 0871 376 9131
39 Coventry St W1D 6BZ
e-mail: piccadilly@thistle.co.uk
web: www.thistlehotels.com/piccadilly
dir: From Kings Cross follow signs for West End & Piccadilly

This popular hotel is centrally located between Leicester Square and Piccadilly Circus, ideal for all of the West End's attractions. Bedrooms vary in size and style but all are well equipped; deluxe and stylish executive rooms have air conditioning. Public areas include a cosy bar/lounge where snacks are available, and a smart breakfast room. Numerous restaurants are located within walking distance. Thistle Hotels – AA Hotel Group of the Year 2011-12.

Rooms 92 (2 fmly) **Facilities** STV FTV Wi-fi **Services** Lift Air con **Notes** ⊗

45 Park Lane

U PLAN 4 G6

☎ 0207 493 4545 📠 0207 4934544
45 Park Ln W1K 1BJ
e-mail: info45parklane@dorchestercollection.com

Opened in the summer of 2011, this new hotel offers luxurious and contemporary interiors. There are 45 bedrooms, including ten suites, all with a view of Hyde Park; the Penthouse Suite has its own roof terrace. A striking central staircase leads to a mezzanine featuring Bar 45, a library and a private media room. Other public areas include a lounge area and CUT at 45 Park Lane, a modern American steak restaurant. Unfortunately the AA was unable to inspect this hotel before guide deadlines. For further details please see the AA website: theAA.com

Rooms 45 **S** £395-£695; **D** £565-£865*

The Montcalm

U PLAN 2 F2

☎ 020 7402 4288 📠 020 7724 9180
Great Cumberland Place W1H 7TW
e-mail: reservations@montcalm.co.uk
dir: 2 mins' walk N from Marble Arch station

Currently the rating for this establishment is not confirmed. This may be due to a change of ownership or because it has only recently joined the AA rating scheme For further details please see the AA website: theAA.com

Rooms 143 (17 fmly) (7 GF) **Facilities** Spa STV supervised Gym Wi-fi **Services** Lift Air con **Notes** ⊗

W2 BAYSWATER, PADDINGTON

Lancaster London

★★★★ 83% ◎◎ HOTEL PLAN 2 D1

☎ 020 7262 6737 📠 020 7724 3191
Lancaster Ter W2 2TY
e-mail: book@lancasterlondon.com
web: www.lancasterlondon.com
dir: Adjacent to Lancaster Gate tube station

Located adjacent to Hyde Park, this large hotel offers a wide range of facilities. There are a broad variety of room types; higher floors have excellent panoramic views of the city and park whilst the suites are truly impressive. The hotel also offers two contrasting award-winning restaurants - the contemporary Island Restaurant & Bar, and Nipa restaurant with authentic Thai cuisine. Further enhancements include the spacious state-of-the-art flexible conference and banqueting facilities, a 24-hour business centre and secure parking. This is an environmentally conscious hotel which has instigated many initiatives including a honey farm on the roof.

Rooms 416 (11 fmly) **Facilities** STV Xmas New Year Wi-fi **Conf** Class 600 Board 40 Thtr 1400 **Services** Lift Air con **Parking** 65 **Notes** ⊗ Civ Wed 1000

Novotel London Paddington

★★★★ 78% HOTEL PLAN 2 C3

☎ 020 7266 6000 📠 020 7266 6010
3 Kingdom St, Paddington W2 6BD
e-mail: h6455@accor.com
dir: Easy access from Westway A40 & Bishops Bridge Rd A4206

Located in the Paddington Central area, this hotel is easily accessible by road, and is only a few minutes walk from Paddington Station. Ideal for business or leisure guests. The facilities include the Elements Restaurant, a bar, conference facilities, a swimming pool, sauna, plus steam and fitness rooms. An NCP car park is a 5-minute walk away.

Rooms 206 (24 fmly) **Facilities** STV Gym Steam room Sauna Wi-fi **Conf** Class 70 Board 40 Thtr 150 **Services** Lift

Thistle Hyde Park

thistle

★★★★ 74% HOTEL PLAN 2 C1

☎ 0871 376 9022 📠 0871 376 9122
90-92 Lancaster Gate W2 3NR
e-mail: hydepark@thistle.co.uk
web: www.thistlehotels.com/hydepark
dir: From Marble Arch rdbt take A404 (Bayswater Rd)

Delightful building ideally situated overlooking Hyde Park and just a short walk from Kensington Gardens. The stylish public areas include a piano bar, a lounge and a smart restaurant. Bedrooms are tastefully appointed and equipped with many thoughtful touches; some rooms have views of the park. Thistle Hotels – AA Hotel Group of the Year 2011-12.

Rooms 54 (12 fmly) **Facilities** STV FTV Wi-fi **Conf** Class 20 Board 20 Thtr 35 **Services** Lift Air con **Parking** 20 **Notes** LB ⊗

Hotel Indigo

★★★★ 72% HOTEL PLAN 2 D2

☎ 020 7706 4444 📠 020 7706 1100
16 London St, Paddington W2 1HL
e-mail: malcolm@lth-hotels.com

This smart hotel is located within a stone's throw of Paddington Station. Contemporary and stylish, bedrooms are equipped with all modern extras; they boast high quality comfy beds ensuring a great night's sleep and en suites with power showers and quality toiletries. Delightful public areas include a restaurant, bar and a coffee shop offering tempting cakes.

Rooms 64 **Facilities** STV FTV Gym Wi-fi **Services** Lift Air con **Notes** LB ⊗

Thistle Kensington Gardens

thistle

★★★★ 72% HOTEL PLAN 2 C1

☎ 0871 376 9024 📠 0871 376 9124
104 Bayswater Rd W2 3HL
e-mail: kensingtongardens@thistle.co.uk
web: www.thistle.com/kensingtongardens

Located beside Hyde Park, this modern hotel provides a contemporary, comfortable environment. Following substantial refurbishment both bedrooms and bathrooms are appointed to a high standard and are suitable for both the leisure and business traveller. The informal Brasserie provides a good range of dishes throughout the day. Secure parking is available on site, and the property is well located for the tube network. Thistle Hotels – AA Hotel Group of the Year 2011-12.

Rooms 175 (13 fmly) (11 smoking) **S** £118-£347; **D** £118-£347* **Facilities** FTV Wi-fi **Conf** Class 30 Board 30 Thtr 45 Del from £210 to £381* **Services** Lift Air con **Parking** 62 **Notes** ⊗

Lancaster Gate Hotel

★★★ 67% HOTEL PLAN 2 C1

☎ 020 7479 2500 & 7262 5090 📠 020 7723 1244
66 Lancaster Gate W2 3NA
e-mail: info@lghhydepark.co.uk
dir: Just off Bayswater Rd

This hotel is in a convenient location between Oxford Street and Knightsbridge and is also close to Hyde Park and Kensington Gardens. Bedrooms are well equipped, with broadband and safes, as well as a good range of TV channels. There is a comfortable bar and stylish restaurant; the hotel also has a range of meeting rooms.

Rooms 188 (3 fmly) (13 GF) **Facilities** STV FTV Off-site leisure facilities available Wi-fi **Conf** Class 18 Board 18 Thtr 35 **Services** Lift Air con **Notes** ⊗

Mitre House

★★ 67% METRO HOTEL PLAN 2 D2

☎ 020 7723 8040 📠 020 7402 0990
178-184 Sussex Gardens, Hyde Park W2 1TU
e-mail: reservations@mitrehousehotel.com
web: www.mitrehousehotel.com
dir: Parallel to Bayswater Rd & one block from Paddington Station

This family-run hotel continues to offers a warm welcome and attentive service. It is ideally located, close to Paddington station and near the West End and major attractions. Bedrooms include a number of family suites and there is a lounge bar.

Rooms 69 (7 fmly) (7 GF) (69 smoking) **Facilities** STV Wi-fi **Services** Lift **Parking** 20 **Notes** ⊗

Days Inn London Hyde Park

BUDGET HOTEL PLAN 2 D2

☎ 020 7723 2939 📠 020 7723 6225
148/152 Sussex Gardens W2 1UD
e-mail: reservations@daysinnhydepark.com
web: www.daysinn.com
dir: On N side of Hyde Park. 2 mins walk from Paddington Station

This modern building offers accommodation in smart, spacious and well-equipped bedrooms, suitable for families and business travellers, and all with en suite bathrooms. Continental breakfast is available and other refreshments may be taken at the nearby family restaurant. See also the Hotel Groups pages.

Rooms 57 (5 fmly) (11 GF)

W3 ACTON

See LONDON plan 1 D4

Ramada Encore London West

★★★ 74% HOTEL

☎ 020 8753 0800 📠 020 8753 0907
4 Portal Way, Gypsy Corner, A40 Western Av W3 6RT
e-mail: reservations@encorelondonwest.co.uk
web: www.encorelondonwest.co.uk

Conveniently situated on the A40 this modern, purpose-built, glass fronted hotel offers smartly appointed accommodation with en suite power shower rooms and air conditioning. Open-plan public areas include a popular Asian and European restaurant, Wok Around the World, and a 2go café and sandwich bar. Secure parking and a range of meeting rooms complete the picture.

Rooms 150 (35 fmly) (15 smoking) **Facilities** STV FTV Gym Wi-fi **Conf** Class 28 Board 26 Thtr 50 **Services** Lift Air con **Parking** 72 **Notes** ⊗

Holiday Inn Express London-Park Royal

BUDGET HOTEL

☎ 020 8896 4460 📠 020 8896 4461
Victoria Rd, Acton W3 6UB
e-mail: info@exhiparkroyal.co.uk
web: www.hiexpress.co.uk
dir: A40 towards North Acton. 1st right onto Portal Way. Left Wales Farm Rd, left Victoria Rd, hotel 100mtrs on right

A modern hotel ideal for families and business travellers. Fresh and uncomplicated, the spacious rooms include Sky TV, power shower and tea and coffee-making facilities. Continental buffet breakfast is included in the room rate; other meals may be taken at the nearby family pub or restaurant. See also the Hotel Groups pages.

Rooms 104 (35 fmly) **Conf** Class 30 Board 30 Thtr 50

W4 CHISWICK

See LONDON SECTION plan 1 D3

Chiswick Moran

★★★★ 75% HOTEL

☎ 020 8996 5200 📠 020 8996 5201
626 Chiswick High Rd W4 5RY
e-mail: chiswickres@moranhotels.com
web: www.moranhotels.com
dir: 200yds from M4 junct 2

This stylish, modern hotel is conveniently located for Heathrow and central London, with Gunnersby tube station just a few minutes' walk away. Airy, spacious public areas include a modern restaurant, a popular bar and excellent meeting facilities. Fully air-conditioned bedrooms are stylish and extremely well appointed with broadband, laptop safes and flat-screen TVs. All boast spacious, modern bathrooms, many with walk-in rain showers.

Rooms 123 (6 fmly) (7 smoking) **S** £79-£230; **D** £89-£335* **Facilities** STV Gym Xmas New Year Wi-fi **Conf** Class 45 Board 40 Thtr 90 **Services** Lift Air con **Parking** 40 **Notes** LB ⊗ Civ Wed 80

W5 EALING

Crowne Plaza London-Ealing

★★★★ 77% ® HOTEL PLAN 1 C4

☎ 0871 942 9114 & 020 8233 3200
📠 020 8233 3201
Western Av, Hanger Ln, Ealing W5 1HG
e-mail: info@cp-londonealing.co.uk
web: www.cp-londonealing.co.uk
dir: A40 from central London towards M40. Exit at Ealing & North Circular A406 sign. At rdbt take 2nd exit signed A40. Hotel on left

Appointed to a high standard, this hotel occupies a prime position on the A40 and North Circular at Hangar Lane; Wembley Stadium is easily accessible. Modern, well-equipped, air-conditioned and sound-proofed bedrooms offer good facilities. There is a smart gym, a steam room together with meeting facilities and the West 5 Brasserie. On-site parking is available.

Rooms 131 (17 GF) (15 smoking) **Facilities** FTV Gym Steam room Xmas New Year Wi-fi **Conf** Class 48 Board 35 Thtr 80 Del from £160 to £240* **Services** Lift Air con **Parking** 85 **Notes** ⊗

W5 EALING *continued*

Premier Inn London Hanger Lane

BUDGET HOTEL PLAN 1 C4

☎ 0871 527 8346 📠 0871 527 8347
1-6 Ritz Pde, Ealing W5 3RA
dir: M4 junct 2, A4 follow North Circular/A406 signs, for 0.5m. Take A406 for approx 2.5m. Right into Ashbourne Rd, immediately left into Ashbourne Parade, right into Ritz Parade. Hotel on right

High quality, budget accommodation ideal for both families and business travellers. Spacious, en suite bedrooms feature tea and coffee making facilities, and Freeview TV in most hotels. Internet access and Wi-fi are available for a small fee. The adjacent family restaurant features a wide and varied menu. See also the Hotel Groups pages.

Rooms 59 **D** £69-£85*

W6 HAMMERSMITH

See LONDON plan 1 D3

Novotel London West

★★★★ 70% HOTEL

☎ 020 8741 1555 📠 020 8741 2120
1 Shortlands W6 8DR
e-mail: H0737@accor.com
web: www.novotellondonwest.co.uk
dir: M4 (A4) & A316 junct at Hogarth rdbt. Along Great West Rd, left for Hammersmith before flyover. On Hammersmith Bridge Rd to rdbt, take 5th exit. 1st left into Shortlands, 1st left to hotel main entrance

A Hammersmith landmark, this substantial hotel is a popular base for both business and leisure travellers. Spacious, air-conditioned bedrooms have a good range of extras and many have additional beds, making them suitable for families. The hotel also has its own car park, business centre and shop, and boasts one of the largest convention centres in Europe.

Rooms 630 (148 fmly) **Facilities** STV Gym Wi-fi **Conf** Class 700 Board 200 Thtr 1700 **Services** Lift Air con **Parking** 240 **Notes** Civ Wed 1400

Holiday Inn Express London - Hammersmith

BUDGET HOTEL

☎ 020 8746 5100 📠 020 8746 5199
120 -124 King St W6 0QU
e-mail: info@expresshammersmith.co.uk
web: www.expresshammersmith.co.uk
dir: M4/A4 junct 1 to Hammersmith Broadway. 2nd left to A315 towards Chiswick (King St). Hotel on right

A modern hotel ideal for families and business travellers. Fresh and uncomplicated, the spacious rooms include Sky TV, power shower and tea and coffee-making facilities. Continental buffet breakfast is included in the room rate; other meals may be taken at the nearby family pub or restaurant. See also the Hotel Groups pages.

Rooms 135 (49 fmly) **Conf** Class 18 Board 20 Thtr 35

Premier Inn London Hammersmith

BUDGET HOTEL

☎ 0871 527 8660 📠 0871 527 8661
255 King St, Hammersmith W6 9LU
dir: From central London on A4 to Hammersmith, follow A315 towards Chiswick

High quality, budget accommodation ideal for both families and business travellers. Spacious, en suite bedrooms feature tea and coffee making facilities, and Freeview TV in most hotels. Internet access and Wi-fi are available for a small fee. The adjacent family restaurant features a wide and varied menu. See also the Hotel Groups pages.

Rooms 106 **D** £81-£97*

W8 KENSINGTON

INSPECTORS' CHOICE

Royal Garden Hotel

★★★★★ ◉◉◉ HOTEL PLAN 4 B5

☎ 020 7937 8000 📠 020 7361 1991
2-24 Kensington High St W8 4PT
e-mail: sales@royalgardenhotel.co.uk
web: www.royalgardenhotel.co.uk
dir: Adjacent to Kensington Palace

This landmark hotel, just a short walk from the Royal Albert Hall, has airy, stylish public rooms that include the Park Terrace Restaurant and Bar, Bertie's cocktail bar and the contemporary 10th-floor Min Jiang Restaurant, an exciting elegant restaurant offering authentic Chinese cuisine and enjoying breathtaking views of the city. The contemporary bedrooms are equipped with up-to-date facilities and include a number of spacious rooms and suites with super views over Kensington Gardens.

Rooms 394 **Facilities** Spa STV Gym Health & fitness centre Xmas New Year Wi-fi **Conf** Class 260 Board 80 Thtr 550 **Services** Lift Air con **Notes** ⊗ Civ Wed 400

INSPECTORS' CHOICE

Milestone Hotel

★★★★★ ®®
HOTEL PLAN 4 B5

☎ 020 7917 1000 📠 020 7917 1010
1 Kensington Court W8 5DL
e-mail: bookms@rchmail.com
web: www.milestonehotel.com
dir: From Warwick Rd right into Kensington High St. Hotel 400yds past Kensington tube station

This delightful town house enjoys a wonderful location opposite Kensington Palace and is near the elegant shops. The individually themed bedrooms include a selection of stunning suites that are equipped with every conceivable extra - fruit, cookies, chocolates, complimentary newspapers and even the next day's weather forecast. Up-to-the-minute technology includes high speed Wi-fi and interactive TV. Public areas include the luxurious Park Lounge where afternoon tea is served, the delightful split-level Stables Bar, a conservatory, the sumptuous Cheneston's restaurant and a fully equipped small gym, resistance pool and a spa treatment room.

Rooms 62 (3 fmly) (1 GF) (5 smoking) **S** £300-£432; **D** £336-£492* **Facilities** STV FTV Gym Health club ♫ Xmas New Year Wi-fi **Conf** Class 20 Board 20 Thtr 50 Del from £445 to £485* **Services** Lift Air con **Parking** 1 **Notes** LB Civ Wed 30

Copthorne Tara Hotel London Kensington

★★★★ 75% HOTEL PLAN 4 B4

☎ 020 7937 7211 & 7872 2000 📠 020 7937 7100
Scarsdale Place, Wrights Ln W8 5SR
e-mail: reservations.tara@millenniumhotels.co.uk
web: www.millenniumhotels.co.uk
dir: From Kensington High Street into Wrights Ln (NB for Sat Nav use postal code W8 5SY)

This expansive hotel that is ideally placed for the stylish shops and also the tube station. Smart public areas include a trendy coffee shop, a gym, a stylish brasserie and bar plus extensive conference facilities. Bedrooms include several well-equipped rooms for less mobile guests, in addition to a number of Connoisseur rooms that have the use of a club lounge with its many complimentary facilities.

Rooms 833 (3 fmly) **Facilities** STV Gym Xmas New Year Wi-fi **Conf** Class 160 Board 90 Thtr 280 **Services** Lift Air con **Parking** 101 **Notes** ® Civ Wed 280

W14 WEST KENSINGTON

K West Hotel & Spa

★★★★ 80% HOTEL PLAN 1 D3

☎ 020 8008 6600 📠 020 8008 6650
Richmond Way W14 0AX
e-mail: info@k-west.co.uk
web: www.k-west.co.uk
dir: From A40/M take Shepherd's Bush Exit. Holland Park rdbt 3rd exit. Take 1st left & left again. Hotel straight ahead

This stylish, contemporary hotel is conveniently located for Notting Hill, the exhibition halls and the BBC; Bond Street is only a 10-minute tube journey away. Funky, minimalist public areas include a trendy lobby bar and mezzanine-style restaurant. Spacious bedrooms and suites are extremely well appointed and offer luxurious bedding and a host of thoughtful extras such as CD and DVD players. Wi-fi is available throughout. The spa offers a comprehensive range of health, beauty and relaxation treatments.

Rooms 220 (31 GF) (44 smoking) **Facilities** Spa STV FTV Gym Hydrotherapy pool Sauna Snow room Solarium ♫ New Year Wi-fi **Conf** Class 20 Board 25 Thtr 55 Del from £150 to £200* **Services** Lift Air con **Parking** 100 **Notes** ®

Express by Holiday Inn London-Earl's Court

BUDGET HOTEL PLAN 4 A1

☎ 020 7384 5151 📠 020 7384 5152
295 North End Rd W14 9NS
e-mail: info@exhiearlscourt.co.uk
web: www.hiexpress.com/lonearlscourt

A modern hotel ideal for families and business travellers. Fresh and uncomplicated, the spacious rooms include Sky TV, power shower and tea and coffee-making facilities. Continental buffet breakfast is included in the room rate; other meals may be taken at the nearby family pub or restaurant. See also the Hotel Groups pages.

Rooms 100 (65 fmly) **Conf** Class 12 Board 12 Thtr 50

WC1 BLOOMSBURY, HOLBORN

Chancery Court Hotel, London

CHANCERY ·COURT· LONDON

★★★★★ 85% ®®® HOTEL PLAN 3 C3

☎ 020 7829 9888 📠 020 7829 9889
252 High Holborn WC1V 7EN
e-mail: rhi.loncc.sales.cord@renaissancehotels.com
web: www.renaissancechancerycourt.co.uk
dir: From Shaftesbury Ave into High Holborn, hotel on right

This is a grand place with splendid public areas, decorated from top to bottom in rare marble. Craftsmen meticulously restored the sweeping staircases, archways and stately rooms of this 1914 building. The result is a spacious, relaxed hotel offering everything from stylish, luxuriously appointed bedrooms to a health club and state-of-the-art meeting rooms. The sophisticated Pearl Restaurant & Bar offers an impressive standard of cooking.

Rooms 356 (68 fmly) (14 smoking) **Facilities** Spa Gym **Conf** Class 234 Board 40 Thtr 435 **Services** Lift Air con **Notes** ® Civ Wed 280

WC1 BLOOMSBURY, HOLBORN *continued*

The Montague on the Gardens

THE RED CARNATION HOTEL COLLECTION

★★★★ 85% HOTEL PLAN 3 B3

☎ 020 7637 1001 020 7637 2516
15 Montague St, Bloomsbury WC1B 5BJ
e-mail: bookmt@rchmail.com
web: www.montaguehotel.com
dir: Just off Russell Square, adjacent to British Museum

This stylish hotel is situated right next to the British Museum. A special feature is the alfresco terrace overlooking a delightful garden. Other public rooms include the Blue Door Bistro and Chef's Table, a bar, a lounge and a conservatory where traditional afternoon teas are served. The bedrooms are beautifully appointed and range from split-level suites to more compact rooms.

Rooms 100 (10 fmly) (19 GF) (5 smoking) **S** £174-£306; **D** £198-£330* **Facilities** STV Gym Xmas New Year Wi-fi **Conf** Class 50 Board 50 Thtr 120 Del from £255 to £385* **Services** Lift Air con **Notes** LB Civ Wed 90

Hotel Russell

principal hayley

★★★★ 73% HOTEL PLAN 3 B4

☎ 020 7837 6470 020 7837 2857
Russell Square WC1B 5BE
e-mail: russell.reservations@principal-hayley.com
web: www.principal-hayley.com
dir: From A501 into Woburn Place. Hotel 500mtrs on left

This landmark Grade II, Victorian hotel is located on Russell Square, within walking distance of the West End and theatre district. Many bedrooms are stylish and state-of-the-art in design, and others are more traditional. Spacious public areas include the impressive foyer with a restored mosaic floor, a choice of lounges and an elegant restaurant.

Rooms 373 (2 fmly) **Facilities** STV FTV Wi-fi **Conf** Class 200 Board 75 Thtr 450 **Services** Lift Air con **Notes** Civ Wed 300

The Kingsley by Thistle

thistle

★★★★ 71% HOTEL PLAN 3 B3

☎ 0871 376 9006 0871 376 9106
Bloomsbury Way WC1A 2SD
e-mail: thekingsley@thistle.co.uk
web: www.thistlehotels.com/thekingsley
dir: A40(M) to A501 (Marylebone Rd), take slip road before underpass to Holburn. Into Gower St, Bloomsbury St (A400). Left into Oxford St then into Bloomsbury Way

Well situated for theatregoers, this hotel enjoys a convenient central location. The well-equipped rooms are generally spacious with good quality fabrics and furnishings, with both family rooms and executive suites available. The ground-floor bar and lounge areas are well appointed. There is a public car park nearby. Thistle Hotels – AA Hotel Group of the Year 2011-12.

Rooms 129 **S** £109-£169; **D** £129-£299* **Facilities** STV FTV Wi-fi **Conf** Class 50 Board 30 Thtr 120 **Services** Lift Air con **Notes** LB

Holiday Inn London Kings Cross/Bloomsbury

★★★★ 70% HOTEL PLAN 3 C5

☎ 020 7833 3900 020 7917 6163
1 Kings Cross Rd WC1X 9HX
e-mail: sales@holidayinnlondon.com
web: www.holidayinn.co.uk
dir: On corner of King Cross Rd & Calthorpe St

Conveniently located for Kings Cross station and The City, this modern hotel offers smart, spacious air-conditioned accommodation with a wide range of facilities. There are versatile meeting rooms, a bar, a well-equipped fitness centre and a choice of restaurants including one serving Indian cuisine.

Rooms 405 (163 fmly) (126 smoking) **Facilities** STV FTV Gym **Conf** Class 120 Board 30 Thtr 220 **Services** Lift Air con **Parking** 15 **Notes**

Holiday Inn London Bloomsbury

★★★ 80% HOTEL PLAN 3 B4

☎ 0871 942 9222 020 7837 5374
Coram St WC1N 1HT
e-mail: bloomsbury@ihg.com
web: www.holidayinn.co.uk
dir: Off Upper Woburn Place

Centrally located, this modern and stylish hotel is within easy reach of many of London's tourist attractions and close to St Pancras International Rail Station. The bedrooms boast a pillow menu, air-conditioning and high-speed internet access. The Junction restaurant offers a modern menu whilst Callaghans is a traditional Irish pub featuring the best Irish beers. The meeting rooms can cater for many different events.

Rooms 311 (30 fmly) (14 smoking) **Facilities** STV Wi-fi **Conf** Class 180 Board 80 Thtr 300 **Services** Lift Air con **Notes**

Bedford Hotel

★★★ 71% HOTEL PLAN 3 B3

☎ 020 7636 7822 & 7692 3620 📠 020 7837 4653
83-93 Southampton Row WC1B 4HD
e-mail: info@imperialhotels.co.uk
web: www.imperialhotels.co.uk

Just off Russell Square, this intimate hotel is ideal for visits to the British Museum and Covent Garden. The bedrooms are well equipped with all the expected facilities including modem points if requested. The ground floor has a lounge, a bar and restaurant plus there's a delightful secret rear garden. The underground car park is a bonus.

Rooms 184 (1 fmly) **S** £82; **D** £110 (incl. bkfst)* **Facilities** FTV Xmas New Year Wi-fi **Conf** Board 12 **Services** Lift **Parking** 50 **Notes** LB ⊗

Premier Inn London Euston

BUDGET HOTEL PLAN 3 A5

☎ 0871 527 8656 📠 0871 527 8657
1 Duke's Rd, Euston WC1H 9PJ
dir: On corner of Euston Road & Duke's Road, between Kings Cross/St Pancras & Euston stations

High quality, budget accommodation ideal for both families and business travellers. Spacious, en suite bedrooms feature tea and coffee making facilities, and Freeview TV in most hotels. Internet access and Wi-fi are available for a small fee. The adjacent family restaurant features a wide and varied menu. See also the Hotel Groups pages.

Rooms 220 **D** £90-£114*

WC2 SOHO, STRAND

HOTEL OF THE YEAR

INSPECTORS' CHOICE

The Savoy

★★★★★ @@ HOTEL PLAN 3 C1

☎ 020 7836 4343 📠 020 7240 6040
Strand WC2R 0EU
e-mail: savoy@fairmont.com
dir: Halfway along The Strand between Trafalgar Sq and Aldwych

The Savoy Hotel has been at the fore of the London hotel scene since it opened in 1889. Now taken over by the Fairmont Group, the hotel has benefited from some loving restoration with much of its art deco and Edwardian heritage kept intact. The 268 bedrooms, including an extensive range of stunning suites, vary in style and size, and many overlook the Thames. The famous River Restaurant, Savoy Grill and American Bar remain as well loved favourites, the Thames Foyer is well known for its afternoon teas and the newly created Beaufort Bar offers a comprehensive range of champagnes. Immaculately presented staff offer excellent standards of hospitality and service. AA Hotel of the Year for London 2011-12.

Rooms 268 **Facilities** supervised Gym Health & beauty treatments Personal training ♫ Xmas New Year **Conf** Class 200 Board 32 Thtr 500 **Services** Lift Air con **Parking** 65

Charing Cross

★★★★ 80% HOTEL PLAN 3 B1

☎ 0871 376 9012 📠 0871 376 9112
The Strand WC2N 5HX
e-mail: charingcross@guoman.co.uk
web: www.guoman.com
dir: On The Strand towards Trafalgar Square, right into station forecourt

This centrally located and historic landmark hotel provides a friendly welcome. Spacious in design, the original grand architecture blends nicely with the modern interior, particularly in the bedrooms and bathrooms. There is a choice of dining options including The Brasserie at Charing Cross which has splendid views of London, especially at night. The hotel gym is exclusively for guests.

Rooms 239 (83 annexe) (12 fmly) (8 smoking) **Facilities** STV Gym ♫ Xmas New Year Wi-fi **Conf** Class 96 Board 46 Thtr 140 **Services** Lift Air con **Notes** LB Civ Wed 140

The Royal Trafalgar, London

thistle

★★★ 79% HOTEL PLAN 3 A1

☎ 0871 376 9037 📠 0871 376 9137
Whitcomb St WC2H 7HG
e-mail: theroyaltrafalgar@thistle.co.uk
web: www.thistle.com/theroyaltrafalgar
dir: 100mtrs from Trafalgar Sq adjacent to Sainsbury Wing of National Gallery

Quietly located, this handily placed hotel is just a short walk from Trafalgar Square and theatreland. Bedrooms offer good levels of comfort with a variety of standards available. Dining options include the Squares Restaurant offering a wide selection, or alternatively, light meals can be taken in the Gravity Lounge and Bar. Thistle Hotels – AA Hotel Group of the Year 2011-12.

Rooms 108 (12 fmly) **Facilities** STV FTV Wi-fi **Services** Lift Air con **Notes** ⊗

LONDON GATEWAY MOTORWAY SERVICE AREA (M1) Map 6 TQ19

Days Hotel London North - M1

★★★ 67% HOTEL

☎ 020 8906 7000 📠 020 8906 7011
Welcome Break Service Area NW7 3HU
e-mail: lgw.hotel@welcomebreak.co.uk
web: www.welcomebreak.co.uk
dir: On M1 between junct 2/4 N'bound & S'bound

This modern building offers accommodation in smart, spacious and well-equipped bedrooms, suitable for families and business travellers, and all with en suite bathrooms. Continental breakfast is available and other refreshments may be taken at the nearby family restaurant.

Rooms 200 (190 fmly) (80 GF) (20 smoking) **S** £59.95-£89.95; **D** £69.95-£99.95 **Facilities** FTV Wi-fi **Conf** Class 30 Board 50 Thtr 70 **Services** Lift Air con **Parking** 160 **Notes** LB Civ Wed 80

LONG EATON
Derbyshire
Map 11 SK43

Novotel Nottingham East Midlands

★★★ 67% HOTEL

☎ 0115 946 5111 📠 0115 946 5900
Bostock Ln NG10 4EP
e-mail: H0507@accor.com
web: www.novotel.com
dir: M1 junct 25 onto B6002 to Long Eaton. Hotel 400yds on left

In close proximity to the M1, this purpose-built hotel has much to offer. All bedrooms are spacious, have sofa beds and provide exceptional desk space. Public rooms include a bright brasserie, which is open all day and provides extended dining until midnight. There is a comprehensive range of meeting rooms.

Rooms 108 (40 fmly) (20 GF) **S** £45-£105; **D** £45-£105* **Facilities** Wi-fi **Conf** Class 100 Board 100 Thtr 250 Del from £99 to £135* **Services** Lift **Parking** 220 **Notes** LB

LONGHORSLEY
Northumberland
Map 21 NZ19

Macdonald Linden Hall, Golf & Country Club

★★★★ 82% HOTEL

☎ 01670 500000 & 0844 879 9084
📠 01670 500001
NE65 8XF
e-mail: lindenhall@macdonald.hotels.co.uk
web: www.macdonaldhotels.co.uk
dir: N'bound on A1 take A697 towards Coldstream. Hotel 1m N of Longhorsley

This impressive Georgian mansion lies in 400 acres of parkland and offers extensive indoor and outdoor leisure facilities including a golf course. The Dobson Restaurant provides a fine dining experience, or guests can eat in the more informal Linden Tree pub. The good-sized bedrooms have a restrained modern style. The team of staff are enthusiastic and professional.

Rooms 50 (3 fmly) (16 GF) **Facilities** Spa STV FTV supervised 18 Putt green Gym Steam room Sauna Xmas New Year Wi-fi **Conf** Class 120 Board 50 Thtr 300 Del from £130 to £180 **Services** Lift **Parking** 300 **Notes** Civ Wed 120

LONG MELFORD
Suffolk
Map 13 TL84

The Black Lion

★★★ 80% HOTEL

☎ 01787 312356 📠 01787 374557
Church Walk, The Green CO10 9DN
e-mail: enquiries@blacklionhotel.net
web: www.blacklionhotel.net
dir: At junct of A134 & A1092

This charming 15th-century hotel is situated on the edge of this bustling town overlooking the green. Bedrooms are generally spacious and each is attractively decorated, tastefully furnished and equipped with useful extras. An interesting range of dishes is served in the lounge bar or guests may choose to dine from the same innovative menu in the more formal restaurant.

Rooms 10 (1 fmly) **Facilities** Xmas New Year Wi-fi **Conf** Class 28 Board 28 Thtr 50 **Parking** 10 **Notes** Civ Wed 50

The Bull

★★★ 73% HOTEL

☎ 01787 378494 📠 01787 880307
Hall St CO10 9JG
e-mail: bull.longmelford@greeneking.co.uk
web: www.bull-hotel.com
dir: 3m N of Sudbury on A134

The public areas of this delightful 14th-century property feature a wealth of charm and character, including exposed beams, carvings, heraldic markings and huge open fireplaces. Bedrooms are smartly decorated, thoughtfully equipped and retain many original features. Snacks or light lunches are served in the bar, or guests can choose to dine in the more formal restaurant.

Rooms 25 (4 fmly) **S** £70-£80; **D** £110-£120 (incl. bkfst) **Facilities** FTV Xmas New Year Wi-fi **Conf** Class 40 Board 30 Thtr 100 Del from £120 to £135 **Parking** 35 **Notes** LB Civ Wed 100

LOOE
Cornwall
Map 2 SX25

See also **Portwrinkle**

Trelaske Hotel & Restaurant

★★★ 79% HOTEL

☎ 01503 262159 📠 01503 265360
Polperro Rd PL13 2JS
e-mail: info@trelaske.co.uk
dir: B252 signed Looe. Over Looe bridge signed Polperro. 1.9m, hotel signed on left, turn right

This small and welcoming hotel offers comfortable accommodation, professional yet friendly service and award-winning food. Set in its own very well-tended and pretty grounds, it is only two miles from Polperro and Looe.

Rooms 7 (4 annexe) (2 fmly) (2 GF) **S** £70-£105; **D** £95-£105 (incl. bkfst)* **Facilities** FTV Wi-fi **Conf** Class 30 Board 40 Thtr 100 Del from £130 to £145* **Parking** 50 **Notes** LB

Hannafore Point

THE INDEPENDENTS HOTEL ASSOCIATION

★★★ 71% HOTEL

☎ 01503 263273 📠 01503 263272
Marine Dr, West Looe PL13 2DG
e-mail: stay@hannaforepointhotel.com
dir: A38, left onto A385 to Looe. Over bridge turn left. Hotel 0.5m on left

With panoramic coastal views of St George's Island around to Rame Head, this popular hotel provides a warm welcome. The wonderful view is certainly a feature of the spacious restaurant and bar, creating a scenic backdrop for both dinners and breakfasts. Additional facilities include a heated indoor pool and gym.

Rooms 37 (5 fmly) **S** £55-£70; **D** £110-£150 (incl. bkfst)* **Facilities** STV Gym Spa pool Steam room Sauna Xmas New Year Wi-fi **Conf** Class 80 Board 40 Thtr 120 Del from £80 to £130* **Services** Lift **Parking** 32 **Notes** LB Civ Wed 150

Fieldhead Hotel & Horizons Restaurant

★★ 80% HOTEL

☎ 01503 262689
Portuan Rd, Hannafore PL13 2DR
e-mail: fieldheadhotel@gmail.com
web: www.fieldheadhotel.co.uk
dir: In Looe pass Texaco garage, cross bridge, left to Hannafore. At Tom Sawyer turn right & right again. Hotel on left

Overlooking the bay, this engaging hotel has a relaxing atmosphere. Bedrooms are furnished with care and many have sea views. Smartly presented public areas include a convivial bar and restaurant, and outside there is a palm-filled garden with a secluded patio and swimming pool. The fixed-price menu changes daily and features quality local produce.

Rooms 16 (2 fmly) (2 GF) **S** £46-£63; **D** £92-£160 (incl. bkfst)* **Facilities** FTV New Year Wi-fi Child facilities **Conf** Class 20 Board 16 Thtr 20 Del from £95 to £140 **Parking** 15 **Notes** LB Closed 1 day at Xmas

LOSTWITHIEL Map 2 SX15
Cornwall

Best Western Restormel Lodge

★★★ 75% HOTEL

☎ 01208 872223 01208 873568
Castle Hill PL22 0DD
e-mail: bookings@restormellodgehotel.co.uk
web: www.restormellodgehotel.co.uk
dir: On A390 in Lostwithiel

A short drive from the Eden Project, this popular hotel offers a friendly welcome to all visitors and is ideally situated for exploring the area. The older building houses the bar, restaurant and lounges, with original features adding to the character. Bedrooms are comfortably furnished, with a number overlooking the secluded outdoor pool.

Rooms 36 (12 annexe) (2 fmly) (9 GF) **S** £29-£69; **D** £39-£119 (incl. bkfst) **Facilities** FTV Xmas New Year Wi-fi **Conf** Class 12 Board 12 Thtr 12 **Parking** 40 **Notes** LB

Lostwithiel Hotel Golf & Country Club

★★★ 68% HOTEL

☎ 01208 873550 01208 873479
Lower Polscoe PL22 0HQ
e-mail: reception@golf-hotel.co.uk
web: www.golf-hotel.co.uk
dir: Off A38 at Dobwalls onto A390. In Lostwithiel turn right & hotel signed

This rural hotel is based around its own golf club and other leisure activities. The main building offers guests a choice of eating options, including all-day snacks in the popular Sports Bar. The bedroom accommodation, designed to incorporate beamed ceilings, has been developed from old Cornish barns that are set around a courtyard.

Rooms 27 (2 fmly) (16 GF) (2 smoking) **S** £45-£57; **D** £90-£114 (incl. bkfst)* **Facilities** FTV 18 Putt green Fishing Gym Undercover floodlit driving range Indoor golf simulator Xmas New Year Wi-fi **Conf** Class 40 Board 40 Thtr 120 Del from £75 to £95* **Parking** 120 **Notes** LB Civ Wed 120

LOUGHBOROUGH Map 11 SK51
Leicestershire

Quorn Country Hotel

★★★★ 76% HOTEL

☎ 01509 415050 & 415061 01509 415557
Charnwood House, 66 Leicester Rd LE12 8BB
e-mail: reservations@quorncountryhotel.co.uk
web: www.quorncountryhotel.co.uk

(For full entry see Quorn)

LOUTH Map 17 TF38
Lincolnshire

Brackenborough Hotel

★★★ 87% HOTEL

☎ 01507 609169 01507 609413
Cordeaux Corner, Brackenborough LN11 0SZ
e-mail: reception@brackenborough.co.uk
web: www.oakridgehotels.co.uk
dir: On A16 (Louth to Grimsby road), 1m from Louth

In an idyllic setting amid well-tended gardens, this hotel offers attractive bedrooms, each individually decorated with co-ordinated furnishings and many extras. The award-winning bistro offers informal dining and the menu is based on locally sourced produce. The hotel specialises in weddings, events and private functions and has excellent conference facilities. Free Wi-fi is available. Guests have free access to state-of-the-art leisure facilities (less than half a mile away).

Rooms 24 (2 fmly) (6 GF) **S** £84.50-£122.50; **D** £99.50-£157.50 (incl. bkfst)* **Facilities** FTV Xmas New Year Wi-fi **Conf** Class 40 Board 30 Thtr 70 **Services** Air con **Parking** 91 **Notes** LB Civ Wed 100

Best Western Kenwick Park

★★★ 77% HOTEL

☎ 01507 608806 01507 608027
Kenwick Park Estate LN11 8NR
e-mail: enquiries@kenwick-park.co.uk
web: www.kenwick-park.co.uk
dir: A16 from Grimsby, then A157 Mablethorpe/Manby Rd. Hotel 400mtrs down hill on right

This elegant Georgian house is situated on the 320-acre Kenwick Park estate, overlooking its own golf course. Bedrooms are spacious, comfortable and provide modern facilities. Public areas include a restaurant and a conservatory bar that overlook the grounds. There is also an extensive leisure centre and state-of-the-art conference and banqueting facilities.

Rooms 34 (5 annexe) (10 fmly) **Facilities** Spa supervised 18 Putt green Gym Squash Health & beauty centre Xmas New Year Wi-fi **Conf** Class 40 Board 90 Thtr 250 **Parking** 100 **Notes** Civ Wed 200

L

LOWER BARTLE
Lancashire
Map 18 SD43

Bartle Hall Hotel

★★★★ 71% HOTEL

☎ 01772 690506 📠 01772 690841
Lea Ln PR4 0HA
e-mail: recp@bartlehall.co.uk
dir: M6 junct 32 onto Tom Benson Way, follow signs for Woodplumpton

Ideally situated between Preston and Blackpool, Bartle Hall is within easy access of the M6 and the Lake District. Set in its own extensive grounds the hotel offers comfortable, well-equipped and renovated accommodation. The restaurant cuisine uses local produce and there is a large comfortable bar and lounge. There are also extensive conference facilities, and this hotel is a popular wedding venue.

Rooms 14 (1 annexe) (2 fmly) (1 GF) **Facilities** FTV New Year Wi-fi **Conf** Class 50 Board 40 Thtr 200 Del from £90 to £120* **Parking** 150 **Notes** ⊗ Closed 25-26 Dec Civ Wed 130

L

LOWER BEEDING
West Sussex
Map 6 TQ22

South Lodge Hotel

★★★★★ 87% ⊛⊛
COUNTRY HOUSE HOTEL

☎ 01403 891711 📠 01403 891766
Brighton Rd RH13 6PS
e-mail: enquiries@southlodgehotel.co.uk
web: www.exclusivehotels.co.uk
dir: On A23 left onto B2110. Turn right through Handcross to A281 junct. Turn left, hotel on right

This impeccably presented 19th-century lodge with stunning views of the rolling South Downs is an ideal retreat. There is the traditional and elegant Camellia Country Kitchen, with 2 AA rosettes, that offers memorable, seasonal dishes, and The Pass Restaurant, with 3 AA Rosettes, which is an innovative take on the chef's table concept - a mini-restaurant within the kitchen itself. The elegant lounge is popular for afternoon teas. Bedrooms are individually designed with character and quality throughout. The conference facilities are impressive.

Rooms 89 (11 fmly) (19 GF) **S** £275-£980; **D** £275-£980 **Facilities** STV ⛳ 36 ⛱ Putt green 🎾 Gym Mountain biking Archery Clay pigeon shooting Xmas New Year Wi-fi **Conf** Class 60 Board 50 Thtr 160 Del from £345 to £395 **Services** Lift **Parking** 200 **Notes** LB Civ Wed 130

LOWER SLAUGHTER
Gloucestershire
Map 10 SP12

INSPECTORS' CHOICE

Lower Slaughter Manor

★★★ COUNTRY HOUSE HOTEL

☎ 01451 820456 📠 01451 822150
GL54 2HP
e-mail: info@lowerslaughterter.co.uk
web: www.lowerslaughter.co.uk
dir: Off A429 signed 'The Slaughters'. Manor 0.5m on right on entering village

There is a timeless elegance about this wonderful manor, which dates back to the 17th century. Its imposing presence makes it very much the centrepiece of this famous Cotswold village. Inside, the levels of comfort and quality are immediately evident, with crackling log fires warming the many sumptuous lounges. Spacious and tastefully furnished bedrooms are either in the main building or in the adjacent coach house. The AA Rosette award is temporarily suspended due to a change of chef; a new award will be in place once our inspectors have completed their assessments of meals cooked by the new kitchen team.

Rooms 19 (8 annexe) (5 fmly) (4 GF) **S** £250-£780; **D** £390-£950 (incl. bkfst)* **Facilities** STV FTV ⛱ 🎾 Xmas New Year Wi-fi **Conf** Class 20 Board 22 Thtr 36 **Parking** 31 **Notes** LB ⊗ Civ Wed 70 No credit cards accepted (at th time of going to press)

Washbourne Court

★★★ 88% ⊛⊛
COUNTRY HOUSE HOTEL

☎ 01451 822143 📠 01451 821045
GL54 2HS
e-mail: info@washbournecourt.co.uk
web: www.vonessenhotels.co.uk
dir: Exit A429 at 'The Slaughters' sign, between Stow-on-the-Wold & Bourton-on-the-Water. Hotel in village centre

Beamed ceilings, log fires and flagstone floors are some of the attractive features of this part 17th-century hotel, set in four acres of immaculate grounds beside the River Eye. The hotel has an elegant, contemporary style and boasts stunning bedrooms with up-to-the-minute technology and marble bathrooms. Dining, whether in the restaurant or bar is memorable and utilises fine local produce.

Rooms 30 (9 GF) **Facilities** FTV Xmas New Year Wi-fi **Conf** Class 40 Board 30 Thtr 70 **Parking** 40 **Notes** Civ Wed 60

LOWESTOFT
Suffolk
Map 13 TM59

Ivy House Country Hotel

★★★ 83% ⊛⊛ HOTEL

☎ 01502 501353 & 588144 📠 01502 501539
Ivy Ln, Beccles Rd, Oulton Broad NR33 8HY
e-mail: aa@ivyhousecountryhotel.co.uk
web: www.ivyhousecountryhotel.co.uk
dir: On A146 SW of Oulton Broad turn into Ivy Ln beside Esso petrol station. Over railway bridge, follow private drive

A peacefully located, family-run hotel set in three acres of mature landscaped grounds and just a short walk from Oulton Broad. Public rooms include an 18th-century thatched barn restaurant where an interesting choice of dishes is served. The attractively decorated bedrooms are housed in garden wings, and many have lovely views of the grounds to the countryside beyond.

Rooms 20 (20 annexe) (1 fmly) (17 GF) **S** £99-£109; **D** £135-£175 (incl. bkfst)* **Facilities** FTV Wi-fi **Conf** Board 22 Thtr 55 Del from £135 to £175* **Parking** 50 **Notes** LB Closed 23 Dec-6 Jan Civ Wed 80

Hotel Victoria

★★★ 83% ⊛ HOTEL

☎ 01502 574433 📠 01502 501529
Kirkley Cliff NR33 0BZ
e-mail: info@thehotelvictoria.co.uk
dir: A12 to seafront on one-way system signed A12 Ipswich. Hotel on seafront

An attractive Victorian building situated on the esplanade overlooking the sea and with direct access to the beach. Bedrooms are pleasantly decorated and thoughtfully equipped; many rooms have sea views. Public rooms include modern conference and banqueting facilities, a choice of lounges, a comfortable bar and a restaurant, which overlooks the pretty garden.

Rooms 24 (4 fmly) **Facilities** FTV Xmas New Year Wi-fi **Conf** Class 150 Board 50 Thtr 200 **Services** Lift **Parking** 45 **Notes** ⊗ Civ Wed 200

Premier Inn Lowestoft

BUDGET HOTEL

☎ 0871 527 8688 📠 0871 527 8689
249 Yarmouth Rd NR32 4AA
dir: On A12, 2m N of Lowestoft

High quality, budget accommodation ideal for both families and business travellers. Spacious, en suite bedrooms feature tea and coffee making facilities, and Freeview TV in most hotels. Internet access and Wi-fi are available for a small fee. The adjacent family restaurant features a wide and varied menu. See also the Hotel Groups pages.

Rooms 60 **D** £65*

LOWESWATER Map 18 NY12
Cumbria

Grange Country House

★★ 74% SMALL HOTEL

☎ 01946 861211 & 861570
CA13 0SU
e-mail: info@thegrange-loweswater.co.uk
dir: Exit A5086 for Mockerkin, through village. After 2m left for Loweswater Lake. Hotel at bottom of hill on left

This delightful country hotel is set in extensive grounds in a quiet valley at the north-western end of Loweswater, and continues to prove popular with guests seeking peace and quiet. It has a friendly and relaxed atmosphere, and the cosy public areas include a small bar, a residents' lounge and an attractive dining room. The bedrooms are well equipped and comfortable, and include four-poster rooms.

Rooms 8 (2 fmly) (1 GF) **Facilities** FTV National Trust boats & fishing Xmas **Conf** Class 25 Board 25 Thtr 25 **Parking** 22 **Notes** RS Jan-Feb

LUDLOW Map 10 SO57
Shropshire

INSPECTORS' CHOICE

Fishmore Hall

★★★ ⓐⓐⓐ SMALL HOTEL

☎ 01584 875148 📠 01584 877907
Fishmore Rd SY8 3DP
e-mail: reception@fishmorehall.co.uk
web: www.fishmorehall.co.uk
dir: A49 into Henley Rd. 1st right, Weyman Rd, at bottom of hill right into Fishmore Rd

Located in a rural area within easy reach of town centre, this Palladian-style Georgian house has been sympathetically renovated and extended to provide high standards of comfort and facilities. The contemporary interior highlights many period features, and public areas include a comfortable lounge and restaurant, the setting for imaginative cooking.

Rooms 15 (1 GF) **Facilities** FTV Beauty treatments Massage Xmas New Year Wi-fi **Conf** Class 20 Board 30 Thtr 40 **Services** Lift **Parking** 48 **Notes** LB Civ Wed 80

Overton Grange Hotel and Restaurant

★★★ 86% ⓐⓐ HOTEL

☎ 01584 873500 & 0845 476 1000
📠 01584 873524
Old Hereford Rd SY8 4AD
e-mail: info@overtongrangehotel.com
dir: A49 onto B4361 to Ludlow, signed Ludlow & Richards Castle. Hotel 0.5m on left

This is a traditional country-house hotel with stylish, comfortable bedrooms, and high standards of guest care. Food is an important part of what the hotel has to offer and the restaurant serves classically based, French-style cuisine using locally sourced produce whenever possible.

Rooms 14 **S** £110-£240; **D** £145-£245 (incl. bkfst)* **Facilities** Spa FTV Xmas New Year Wi-fi **Conf** Class 50 Board 30 Thtr 100 **Parking** 45 **Notes** LB No children 7yrs Civ Wed 100

Dinham Hall

★★★ 80% ⓐⓐ HOTEL

☎ 01584 876464
By The Castle SY8 1EJ
e-mail: info@dinhamhall.com
dir: In town centre, opposite castle & market square

Built in 1792, this lovely house stands in attractive gardens immediately opposite Ludlow Castle; it has a well-deserved reputation for warm hospitality. The well-equipped bedrooms include two in a converted cottage, and some rooms have four-poster beds. The comfortable public rooms are elegantly appointed.

Rooms 13 (2 annexe) (2 fmly) (2 GF) **S** £110-£240; **D** £145-£245 (incl. bkfst)* **Facilities** FTV Xmas New Year Wi-fi **Conf** Class 20 Board 26 Thtr 40 **Parking** 16 **Notes** LB No children 7yrs

Feathers

★★★ 80% ⓐ HOTEL

☎ 01584 875261 📠 01584 876030
The Bull Ring SY8 1AA
e-mail: feathers.ludlow@btconnect.com
web: www.feathersatludlow.co.uk
dir: From A49 follow town centre signs to centre. Hotel on left

Famous for the carved woodwork outside and in, this picture-postcard 17th-century hotel is one of the town's best-known landmarks and is in an excellent location. Bedrooms are traditional both in style and decor. The public areas have retained much of the traditional charm, and the first-floor lounge is particularly stunning.

Rooms 40 (3 fmly) **S** £79-£89; **D** £99-£115 (incl. bkfst)* **Facilities** STV FTV Xmas New Year Wi-fi **Conf** Class 40 Board 40 Thtr 80 Del from £120 to £139* **Services** Lift **Parking** 33 **Notes** LB Civ Wed 80

LUDLOW *continued*

Cliffe

★★ 80% SMALL HOTEL

☎ 01584 872063 01584 873991
Dinham SY8 2JE
e-mail: thecliffehotel@hotmail.com
web: www.thecliffehotel.co.uk
dir: In town centre turn left at castle gates to Dinham, follow over bridge. Take right fork, hotel 200yds on left

Built in the 19th century and standing in extensive grounds and gardens, this privately owned and personally run hotel is quietly located close to the castle and the river. It provides well-equipped accommodation, and facilities include a lounge bar, a pleasant restaurant and a patio overlooking the garden.

Rooms 9 (2 fmly) **S** £50-£65; **D** £65-£90 (incl. bkfst)* **Facilities** FTV Wi-fi **Parking** 22 **Notes** LB

The Clive Bar & Restaurant with Rooms

RESTAURANT WITH ROOMS

☎ 01584 856565 & 856665 01584 856661
Bromfield SY8 2JR
e-mail: info@theclive.co.uk
web: www.theclive.co.uk
dir: 2m N of Ludlow on A49 in village of Bromfield

The Clive is just two miles from the busy town of Ludlow and is a convenient base for visiting the local attractions or for business. The bedrooms, located outside the main restaurant area, are spacious and very well equipped; some are suitable for families and many are on the ground-floor level. Meals are available in the well-known Clive Restaurant or in the bar areas. The property also has a small meeting room.

Rooms 15 (15 annexe) (9 fmly)

LUMBY North Yorkshire **Map 16 SE43**

Quality Hotel Leeds Selby

★★★ 66% HOTEL

☎ 01977 682761 01977 685462
A1/A63 Junction LS25 5LF
e-mail: enquiries@hotels-leeds-selby.com
dir: A1(M) junct 42/A63 signed Selby, hotel on A63 on left

A modern hotel situated in extensive grounds near the A1(M) and A63 junction. Attractive day rooms include the Woodlands Restaurant and the Leisure Club. The hotel offers an all-day lounge menu and 24-hour room service.

Rooms 97 (18 fmly) (40 GF) **Facilities** STV Putt green Gym Xmas New Year Wi-fi **Conf** Class 100 Board 80 Thtr 160 **Parking** 250 **Notes** Civ Wed 120

LUTON Bedfordshire **Map 6 TL02**

Luton Hoo Hotel, Golf and Spa

★★★★★ 89% HOTEL

☎ 01582 734437 & 698888 01582 485438
The Mansion House LU1 3TQ
e-mail: reservations@lutonhoo.com
dir: M1 junct 10A, 3rd exit to A1081 towards Harpenden/St Albans. Hotel approx 1m on left

A luxury hotel in more than 1,000 acres of 'Capability' Brown designed parkland and formal gardens, with an 18-hole, par 73 golf course and the River Lea meandering through. The centrepiece is the Grade I listed Mansion House that has architectural influences by many famous architects including Robert Adams. There are three sumptuous lounges where guests can enjoy afternoon tea and pre-dinner drinks, and two eating options - The Wernher Restaurant and the Adams Brasserie. The spacious bedrooms and impressive suites combine historic character with modern amenities. The Robert Adams Club House is the perfect place for relaxation, with the brasserie, a spa, golf, pool and gym together with two bars, and Warren Weir, at the foot of the estate, on the river bank is an exclusive retreat for weddings and meetings.

Rooms 228 (50 fmly) (65 GF) **D** £230-£895 (incl. bkfst)* **Facilities** Spa FTV 18 Putt green Fishing Gym Bird watching Cycling Snooker Jogging trails Xmas New Year Wi-fi **Conf** Class 220 Board 60 Thtr 388 Del from £250 to £340* **Services** Lift **Parking** 316 **Notes** LB Civ Wed 380

Best Western Menzies Strathmore

MenziesHotels

★★★★ 77% HOTEL

☎ 01582 734199 01582 402528
Arndale Centre LU1 2TR
e-mail: strathmore@menzieshotels.co.uk
web: www.menzieshotels.co.uk
dir: M1 junct 10a , follow town centre signs, hotel adjacent to Arndale Centre car park

Situated in the centre of town with adjacent parking, this hotel is convenient for the nearby shopping areas and many guests stay here prior to catching flights at the nearby airport. The bedrooms are comfortable and well equipped with good facilities. Public areas include a spacious lounge bar and a contemporary brasserie-style restaurant. Waves health and leisure club offers guests beauty and message therapies plus a pool, sauna and steam room.

Rooms 152 (6 fmly) (21 smoking) **Facilities** Spa Gym Beauty salon Xmas New Year Wi-fi **Conf** Class 120 Board 90 Thtr 250 **Services** Lift **Parking** 5 **Notes** Civ Wed 200

Icon Hotel

★★★ 81% HOTEL

☎ 01582 722123 01582 722424
15 Stuart St LU1 2SA
e-mail: reservations@iconhotelluton.com

This modern purpose-built hotel occupies a prominent position close to Luton town centre and is a short drive from the international airport. The contemporary open-plan bar is very comfortable and Capello's Restaurant offers a modern Mediterranean menu. Bedrooms are attractively presented and feature the latest in technology along with large LCD TVs and complimentary Wi-fi. There is a range of business suites and a well-equipped gym.

Rooms 60 **S** £85-£170; **D** £85-£170* **Conf** Class 40 Board 30 Thtr 50

LUTON AIRPORT
Bedfordshire Map 6 TL12

Express by Holiday Inn London - Luton Airport

BUDGET HOTEL

☎ 0870 444 8920 🖷 0870 444 8930
2 Percival Way LU2 9GP
e-mail: lutonairport@expressbyholidayinn.net
web: www.hiexpress.com/lutonairport
dir: M1 junct 10, follow signs for airport (hotel visable), right into Percival Way, hotel car park on right

A modern hotel ideal for families and business travellers. Fresh and uncomplicated, the spacious rooms include Sky TV, power shower and tea and coffee-making facilities. Continental buffet breakfast is included in the room rate; other meals may be taken at the nearby family pub or restaurant. See also the Hotel Groups pages.

Rooms 147 (87 fmly) **Conf** Class 30 Board 20 Thtr 60

Ibis London Luton Airport

BUDGET HOTEL

☎ 01582 424488 🖷 01582 455511
Spittlesea Rd LU2 9NH
e-mail: H1040@accor.com
web: www.ibishotel.com
dir: M1 junct 10, follow signs to Luton Airport. Hotel 600mtrs from airport

Modern, budget hotel offering comfortable accommodation in bright and practical bedrooms. Breakfast is self-service and dinner is available in the restaurant. See also the Hotel Groups pages.

Rooms 162 (8 fmly) (4 GF) **S** £53-£101; **D** £53-£101* **Conf** Class 64 Board 80 Thtr 114

Premier Inn Luton Airport

BUDGET HOTEL

☎ 0871 527 8690 🖷 0871 527 8691
Osborne Rd LU1 3HJ
dir: M1 junct 10, A1081 follow signs for Luton, at 3rd rdbt left into Gypsy Lane, left at next rdbt

High quality, budget accommodation ideal for both families and business travellers. Spacious, en suite bedrooms feature tea and coffee making facilities, and Freeview TV in most hotels. Internet access and Wi-fi are available for a small fee. The adjacent family restaurant features a wide and varied menu. See also the Hotel Groups pages.

Rooms 129 **D** £55-£69*

LYME REGIS
Dorset Map 4 SY39

Swallows Eaves

★★ 82% HOTEL

☎ 01297 553184 🖷 01297 553574
Swan Hill Rd EX24 6QJ
e-mail: info@swallowseaves.co.uk
web: www.swallowseaves.co.uk

(For full entry see Colyford, Devon)

Royal Lion

★★ 76% HOTEL

☎ 01297 445622 🖷 01297 445859
Broad St DT7 3QF
e-mail: enquiries@royallionhotel.com
web: www.royallionhotel.com
dir: From W on A35, take A3052 or from E take B3165 to Lyme Regis. Hotel in town centre, opposite The Fossil Shop

This 17th-century, former coaching inn is full of character and charm, and is situated a short walk from the seafront. Bedrooms vary in size; those in the newer wing are more spacious and some have balconies, sea views or a private terrace. In addition to the elegant dining room and guest lounges, a heated pool, jacuzzi, sauna and small gym are available. There is a car park at the rear.

Rooms 33 (14 fmly) (11 GF) **S** £70-£75; **D** £100-£148 (incl. bkfst)* **Facilities** FTV Gym Sauna Games room Snooker tables Table tennis Xmas New Year Wi-fi **Conf** Class 20 Board 20 Thtr 50 Del from £110 to £158* **Parking** 33 **Notes** LB

LYMINGTON
Hampshire Map 5 SZ39

Stanwell House

★★★ 86% HOTEL

☎ 01590 677123 🖷 01590 677756
14-15 High St SO41 9AA
e-mail: enquiries@stanwellhouse.com
dir: M27 junct 1, follow signs to Lyndhurst & Lymington

A privately owned Georgian house situated on the wide high street only a few minutes from the marina, and a short drive from the New Forest. Styling itself as a boutique hotel, the bedrooms are individually designed; there are Terrace rooms with garden access, four-poster rooms, and Georgian rooms in the older part of the building. The four suites include two with their own roof terrace. Dining options include the informal bistro and the intimate Seafood Restaurant. Service is friendly and attentive. A meeting room is available.

Rooms 30 (6 fmly) (5 GF) **S** £89-£99; **D** £99-£140 (incl. bkfst)* **Facilities** FTV Xmas New Year Wi-fi **Conf** Class 25 Board 20 Thtr 70 Del from £125 to £135 **Parking** 12 **Notes** LB Civ Wed 100

Passford House

★★★ 83% HOTEL

☎ 01590 682398 🖷 01590 683494
Mount Pleasant Ln SO41 8LS
e-mail: sales@passfordhousehotel.co.uk
web: www.passfordhousehotel.co.uk
dir: From A337 at Lymington over 2 mini rdbts. 1st right at Tollhouse pub, 1m right into Mount Pleasant Lane

A peaceful hotel set in attractive grounds on the edge of town. Bedrooms vary in size but all are comfortably furnished and well equipped. Extensive public areas include lounges, a smartly appointed restaurant and bar plus leisure facilities. The friendly and well motivated staff provide attentive service.

Rooms 51 (2 annexe) (10 GF) **S** £95-£115; **D** £135-£225 (incl. bkfst)* **Facilities** Putt green Gym Petanque Table tennis Pool table Xmas New Year **Conf** Class 30 Board 30 Thtr 80 Del from £140 to £155* **Parking** 100 **Notes** LB Civ Wed 80

LYMINGTON *continued*

Macdonald Elmers Court Hotel & Resort

★★★ 82% HOTEL

☎ 0844 879 9060 📠 01590 679780
South Baddesley Rd SO41 5ZB
e-mail: elmerscourt@macdonald-hotels.co.uk
web: www.macdonaldhotels.co.uk
dir: M27 junct 1, through Lyndhurst, Brockenhurst & Lymington, hotel 200yds right after Lymington ferry terminal

Originally known as The Elms, this Tudor manor house dates back to the 1820s. Ideally located at the edge of the New Forest and overlooking The Solent with views towards the Isle of Wight, the hotel offers suites and self-catering accommodation in the grounds, along with a host of leisure facilities.

Rooms 42 (42 annexe) (8 fmly) (22 GF) **Facilities** Spa supervised Putt green Gym Squash Steam room Aerobics classes Sauna Table tennis Xmas New Year Wi-fi **Conf** Class 40 Board 40 Thtr 100 **Parking** 100 **Notes** Civ Wed 100

Premier Inn Lymington (New Forest Hordle)

BUDGET HOTEL

☎ 0871 527 8692 📠 0871 527 8693
Silver St, Hordle SO41 0FN
dir: M27 junct 1, A337. 3.5m, left into High St (A35) right into Gosport Ln. Left into Clay Hill (A337). Right into Grigg Ln (B3055). Approx 8m, left into Barrows Ln, right into Silver St

High quality, budget accommodation ideal for both families and business travellers. Spacious, en suite bedrooms feature tea and coffee making facilities, and Freeview TV in most hotels. Internet access and Wi-fi are available for a small fee. The adjacent family restaurant features a wide and varied menu. See also the Hotel Groups pages.

Rooms 20 **D** £57*

LYMM — Cheshire — Map 15 SJ68

The Lymm Hotel

★★★ 73% HOTEL

☎ 01925 752233 📠 01925 756035
Whitbarrow Rd WA13 9AQ
e-mail: general.lymm@macdonald-hotels.co.uk
web: www.macdonaldhotels.co.uk/lymm
dir: M6 junct 20, B5158 to Lymm. Left at junct, 1st right, left at mini-rdbt, into Brookfield Rd, 3rd left into Whitbarrow Rd

In a peaceful residential area, this hotel benefits from both a quiet setting and convenient access to local motorway networks. It offers comfortable bedrooms equipped for both the business and leisure guest. Public areas include an attractive bar and an elegant restaurant. There is also extensive parking.

Rooms 62 (38 annexe) (5 fmly) (11 GF) **S** £60-£95; **D** £60-£95 **Facilities** STV Xmas New Year Wi-fi **Conf** Class 60 Board 40 Thtr 120 Del from £105 to £140 **Parking** 75 **Notes** Civ Wed 100

LYNDHURST — Hampshire — Map 5 SU30

INSPECTORS' CHOICE

Lime Wood

★★★★★ ◎◎◎
COUNTRY HOUSE HOTEL

☎ 023 8028 7177 📠 023 8028 7199
Beaulieu Rd SO43 7FZ
e-mail: info@limewood.co.uk
dir: A35 onto B3056 towards Beaulieu, hotel 1m on right

This meticulously restored country house situated deep in the New Forest, provides a wealth of facilities and much opulence. The hotel prides itself on its relaxed, friendly and attentive service, and has lots to interest and captivate. The luxurious bedrooms are notable; some are in the pavilion and some in the main house. There are choices for eating - the Scullery, styled on an 18th-century country kitchen which has a relaxed atmosphere, and the more formal Dining Room, overlooking the botanical gardens, that serves interesting cuisine. The Herb House spa offers a hydro therapy pool and many other excellent facilities along with a gym and steam room.

Rooms 29 (13 annexe) (8 fmly) (4 GF) **S** £245-£750; **D** £245-£750* **Facilities** Spa STV FTV Fishing Gym Xmas New Year Wi-fi **Conf** Board 16 Thtr 20 Del from £325 to £425* **Services** Lift **Parking** 60 **Notes** Civ Wed 80

Bell Inn

★★★ 83% ◎◎ HOTEL

☎ 023 8081 2214 📠 023 8081 3958
SO43 7HE
e-mail: bell@bramshaw.co.uk
web: www.bellinnbramshaw.co.uk

(For full entry see Brook (Near Cadnam))

Best Western Forest Lodge

NEW FOREST HOTELS

★★★ 83% ◎◎ HOTEL

☎ 023 8028 3677 📠 023 8028 2940
Pikes Hill, Romsey Rd SO43 7AS
e-mail: forest@newforesthotels.co.uk
web: www.newforesthotels.co.uk
dir: M27 junct 1, A337 towards Lyndhurst. In village, with police station & courts on right, take 1st right into Pikes Hill

Situated on the edge of Lyndhurst, this hotel is set well back from the main road. The smart, contemporary bedrooms include four-poster rooms and family rooms; children are very welcome here. The eating options are the Forest Restaurant and the fine-dining Glasshouse Restaurant. There is an indoor swimming pool and Nordic sauna.

Rooms 36 (11 fmly) (10 GF) **D** £120-£170 (incl. bkfst)* **Facilities** FTV Xmas New Year Wi-fi **Conf** Class 70 Board 60 Thtr 120 **Parking** 50 **Notes** LB Civ Wed 60

Best Western Crown

★★★ 75% HOTEL

☎ 023 8028 2922 📠 023 8028 2751
High St SO43 7NF
e-mail: reception@crownhotel-lyndhurst.co.uk
web: www.crownhotel-lyndhurst.co.uk
dir: In town centre, opposite church

The Crown, with its stone mullioned windows, panelled rooms and elegant period decor evokes the style of an Edwardian country house. Bedrooms are generally a good size and offer a useful range of facilities. Public areas have style and comfort and include a choice of function and meeting rooms. The pleasant garden and terrace are havens of peace and tranquillity.

Rooms 38 (8 fmly) **Facilities** FTV Xmas New Year Wi-fi **Conf** Class 30 Board 45 Thtr 70 **Services** Lift **Parking** 60 **Notes** LB Civ Wed 70

Lyndhurst Park

★★★ 74% HOTEL

☎ 023 8028 3923 📠 023 8028 3019
High St SO43 7NL
e-mail: lyndhurst.park@forestdale.com
web: www.lyndhurstparkhotel.co.uk
dir: M27 juncts 1-3 onto A35 to Lyndhurst. Hotel at bottom of High St

Although it is just by the High Street, this hotel is afforded seclusion and tranquillity from the town due to its five acres of mature grounds. The comfortable bedrooms include home-from-home touches. The bar offers a stylish setting for a snack whilst the oak-panelled Tudor restaurant provides a more formal dining venue.

Rooms 59 (3 fmly) **Facilities** FTV Sauna Xmas New Year Wi-fi **Conf** Class 120 Board 85 Thtr 300 **Services** Lift **Parking** 100 **Notes** LB Civ Wed 120

Penny Farthing Hotel

★★ 81% METRO HOTEL

☎ 023 8028 4422 📠 023 8028 4488
Romsey Rd SO43 7AA
e-mail: stay@pennyfarthinghotel.co.uk
dir: M27 junct 1, A337 to Lyndhurst. Hotel on left

This friendly, well-appointed establishment on the edge of town is suitable for business or for exploring the New Forest area. The attractive bedrooms are well-equipped, with some located in an adjacent cottage. There is a spacious breakfast room, a comfortable lounge bar and a bicycle store.

Rooms 20 (4 annexe) (1 fmly) (1 GF) **Facilities** FTV Wi-fi **Parking** 26 **Notes** ⊗ Closed Xmas week & New Year

LYNMOUTH
Devon — Map 3 SS74

See also **Lynton**

Tors Hotel

★★★ 71% HOTEL

☎ 01598 753236 📠 01598 752544
EX35 6NA
e-mail: info@torshotellynmouth.co.uk
web: www.torslynmouth.co.uk
dir: Adjacent to A39 on Countisbury Hill just before entering Lynmouth from Minehead

In an elevated position overlooking Lynmouth Bay, this friendly hotel is set in five acres of woodland. The majority of the bedrooms benefit from the superb views, as do the public areas which are generously proportioned and well presented. A fixed-price menu is offered with local, seasonal produce to the fore.

Rooms 31 (6 fmly) **S** £50-£200; **D** £80-£240 (incl. bkfst)* **Facilities** Table tennis Pool table Xmas New Year Wi-fi **Conf** Class 40 Board 25 Thtr 60 Del from £80 to £150* **Services** Lift **Parking** 40 **Notes** LB Closed 4-31 Jan RS Oct-Apr Civ Wed 125

Rising Sun

★★ 76% ® HOTEL

☎ 01598 753223 📠 01598 753480
Harbourside EX35 6EG
e-mail: reception@risingsunlynmouth.co.uk
web: www.risingsunlynmouth.co.uk
dir: M5 junct 23, A39 to Minehead. Hotel on harbour

This delightful thatched establishment, once a smugglers' inn, sits on the harbour front. Popular with locals and guests alike, there is the option of eating in either the convivial bar or the restaurant; a comfortable, quiet lounge is also available. Bedrooms, located in the inn and adjoining cottages, are individually designed and have modern facilities.

Rooms 14 (1 fmly) (1 GF) **Facilities** Xmas

Bath Hotel

★★ 71% HOTEL

☎ 01598 752238 📠 01598 753894
Sea Front EX35 6EL
e-mail: info@bathhotellynmouth.co.uk
dir: M5 junct 25, follow A39 to Lynmouth

This well established, friendly hotel, situated near the harbour offers lovely views from the attractive, sea-facing bedrooms and is an excellent starting point for scenic walks. There are two lounges and a sun lounge. The restaurant menu is extensive and features daily-changing specials that make good use of fresh produce and local fish.

Rooms 22 (9 fmly) **S** £45-£55; **D** £75-£115 (incl. bkfst)* **Facilities** Wi-fi **Parking** 12 **Notes** Closed Dec & Jan RS Nov & Feb

LYNTON
Devon — Map 3 SS74

See also **Lynmouth**

Lynton Cottage

★★★ 75% ®® HOTEL

☎ 01598 752342 📠 01598 754016
Northwalk EX35 6ED
e-mail: enquiries@lynton-cottage.co.uk
dir: M5 junct 23 to Bridgwater, A39 towards Minehead, follow signs to Lynton. 1st right after church, right again

Boasting breathtaking views, this wonderfully relaxing and friendly hotel stands some 500 feet above the sea and makes a peaceful hideaway. Bedrooms are individual in style and size, with the added bonus of the wonderful views; public areas have charm and character in equal measure. Accomplished cuisine is on offer with dishes created with care and skill.

Rooms 16 (1 fmly) (1 GF) **Facilities** FTV Wi-fi **Parking** 20 **Notes** Closed 2 Dec-12 Jan

L

LYTHAM ST ANNES
Lancashire — Map 18 SD32

Clifton Arms Hotel

★★★★ 75% ® HOTEL

☎ 01253 739898 🖷 01253 730657
West Beach, Lytham FY8 5QJ
e-mail: welcome@cliftonarms-lytham.com
web: www.cliftonarms-lytham.com
dir: On A584 along seafront

This well established hotel occupies a prime position overlooking Lytham Green and the Ribble estuary beyond. Bedrooms vary in size and are appointed to a high standard; front-facing rooms are particularly spacious and enjoy splendid views. There is an elegant restaurant, a stylish open-plan lounge and cocktail bar as well as function and conference facilities.

Rooms 48 (2 fmly) **S** £60-£140; **D** £80-£190 (incl. bkfst)* **Facilities** STV FTV Xmas New Year Wi-fi **Conf** Class 100 Board 60 Thtr 200 Del from £155 to £185* **Services** Lift **Parking** 50 **Notes** LB ® Civ Wed 100

Bedford Hotel

★★★ 80% HOTEL

☎ 01253 724636 🖷 01253 729244
307-313 Clifton Drive South FY8 1HN
e-mail: reservations@bedford-hotel.com
web: www.bedford-hotel.com
dir: From M55 follow signs for airport to last lights. Left through 2 sets of lights. Hotel 300yds on left

This popular family-run hotel is close to the town centre and the seafront. Bedrooms vary in size and style and include superior and club class rooms. The newer bedrooms are particularly elegant and tastefully appointed. Spacious public areas include a choice of lounges, a coffee shop, fitness facilities and an impressive function suite.

Rooms 45 (6 GF) **S** £60-£65; **D** £90-£160 (incl. bkfst)* **Facilities** FTV Gym Hydrotherapy spa bath Xmas New Year Wi-fi **Conf** Class 140 Board 60 Thtr 200 Del from £97.50* **Services** Lift **Parking** 25 **Notes** LB ® Civ Wed 200

Best Western Glendower Promenade Hotel

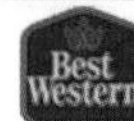

★★★ 77% HOTEL

☎ 01253 723241 🖷 01253 640069
North Promenade FY8 2NQ
e-mail: recp@theglendowerhotel.co.uk
web: www.theglendowerhotel.co.uk
dir: M55 follow airport signs. Left at Promenade to St Annes. Hotel 500yds from pier

Located on the seafront and with easy access to the town centre, this popular, friendly hotel offers comfortably furnished, well-equipped accommodation. Bedrooms vary in size and style, and include four-poster rooms and very popular family suites. Public areas feature a choice of smart, comfortable lounges, a bright, modern leisure club and function facilities.

Rooms 60 (17 fmly) **Facilities** FTV Gym Children's playroom Snooker ♫ Xmas New Year Wi-fi **Conf** Class 120 Board 50 Thtr 150 Del from £80 to £120* **Services** Lift **Parking** 45 **Notes** ® Civ Wed 150

Chadwick

THE INDEPENDENTS HOTEL ASSOCIATION

★★★ 77% HOTEL

☎ 01253 720061 🖷 01253 714455
South Promenade FY8 1NP
e-mail: info@thechadwickhotel.com
web: www.thechadwickhotel.com
dir: M6 junct 32 take M55 to Blackpool then A5230 to South Shore. Follow signs for St Annes, hotel on promenade south end

This popular, comfortable and traditional hotel enjoys a seafront location. Bedrooms vary in size and style, but all are very thoughtfully equipped; those at the front boast panoramic sea views. Public rooms are spacious and comfortably furnished and the smart bar is stocked with some 200 malt whiskies. The hotel has a well-equipped, air-conditioned gym and indoor pool.

Rooms 75 (28 fmly) (13 GF) **S** £67-£79; **D** £115-£139 (incl. bkfst & dinner) **Facilities** FTV ⓢ Gym Turkish bath Sauna Games room Wii room Soft play adventure area ♫ Xmas New Year Wi-fi **Conf** Class 24 Board 28 Thtr 72 Del from £89.50 to £94.50* **Services** Lift **Parking** 40 **Notes** LB ®

See advert on this page

MACCLESFIELD
Cheshire Map 16 SJ97

Barceló Shrigley Hall Hotel, Golf & Country Club

★★★★ 76% HOTEL

☎ 01625 575757 📠 01625 573323
Shrigley Park, Pott Shrigley SK10 5SB
e-mail: shrigleyhall@barcelo-hotels.co.uk
web: www.barcelo-hotels.co.uk
dir: Off A523 at Legh Arms towards Pott Shrigley. Hotel 2m on left before village

Originally built in 1825, Shrigley Hall is an impressive hotel set in 262 acres of mature parkland and commands stunning views of the countryside. Features include a championship golf course. There is a wide choice of bedroom sizes and styles. The public areas are spacious, combining traditional and contemporary decor, and include a well-equipped gym.

Rooms 148 (11 fmly) **Facilities** Spa STV supervised 18 Putt green Fishing Gym Beauty salon Hydro centre Xmas New Year Wi-fi **Conf** Class 110 Board 42 Thtr 180 **Services** Lift **Parking** 300 **Notes** Civ Wed 150

Legacy Hollin Hall Country House Hotel

★★★ 75% HOTEL

☎ 08444 119072 📠 08444 119073
Jackson Ln, Kerridge, Bollington SK10 5BG
e-mail: res-hollinhall@legacy-hotels.co.uk
dir: From Macclesfield A523 (The Silk Road) towards Bollington, at rdbt right onto B5090 signed Bollington. 1st right signed Kerridge. 2.5m, hotel entrance on left

Within easy reach of the Peak District and visitor attractions, this elegant Victorian hotel offers a combination of traditional and contemporary design. Beautifully maintained period features are complemented by stylish, smartly presented décor and furnishings. Bedrooms are well equipped and cater well for both leisure and business guests; complimentary Wi-fi is provided.

Rooms 58 (5 fmly) (16 GF) **S** £49.95-£104.95; **D** £49.95-£104.95* **Facilities** FTV Gym Xmas New Year Wi-fi **Conf** Class 50 Board 50 Thtr 120 Del from £120 to £145* **Services** Lift **Parking** 75 **Notes** LB Civ Wed 120

Premier Inn Macclesfield North

BUDGET HOTEL

☎ 0871 527 8694 📠 0871 527 8695
Tytherington Business Park, Springwood Way, Tytherington SK10 2XA
dir: On A523 in Tytherington Business Park

High quality, budget accommodation ideal for both families and business travellers. Spacious, en suite bedrooms feature tea and coffee making facilities, and Freeview TV in most hotels. Internet access and Wi-fi are available for a small fee. The adjacent family restaurant features a wide and varied menu. See also the Hotel Groups pages.

Rooms 41 **D** £52-£57*

Premier Inn Macclesfield South West

BUDGET HOTEL

☎ 0871 527 8696 📠 0871 527 8697
Congleton Rd, Gawsworth SK11 7XD
dir: M6 junct 17, A534 towards Congleton, A536 towards Macclesfield to Gawsworth. Hotel on left

Rooms 28 **D** £52-£57*

MAIDENCOMBE

See Torquay

MAIDENHEAD
Berkshire Map 6 SU88

INSPECTORS' CHOICE

Fredrick's Hotel Restaurant Spa

★★★★ @@ HOTEL

☎ 01628 581000 📠 01628 771054
Shoppenhangers Rd SL6 2PZ
e-mail: reservations@fredricks-hotel.co.uk
web: www.fredricks-hotel.co.uk
dir: M4 junct 8/9 onto A404(M) to Maidenhead West & Henley. 1st exit 9a to White Waltham. Left into Shoppenhangers Rd to Maidenhead, hotel on right

Just 30 minutes from London, this delightful hotel enjoys a peaceful location yet is within easy reach of the M4 and only 20 minutes' drive from Wentworth and Sunningdale golf courses. The spacious bedrooms are comfortably furnished and very well equipped. An enthusiastic team of staff ensure friendly and efficient service. The imaginative cuisine is a highlight, as is the luxurious spa that offers the ultimate in relaxation and wellbeing.

Rooms 34 (11 GF) **S** £135-£225; **D** £145-£275* **Facilities** Spa supervised supervised Gym Rasul suite Oriental steam Dead Sea floatation room Wi-fi **Conf** Class 80 Board 60 Thtr 120 Del from £200 to £320 **Services** Air con **Parking** 90 **Notes** LB Closed 24 Dec-3 Jan Civ Wed 120

Holiday Inn Maidenhead/ Windsor

★★★★ 71% HOTEL

☎ 0871 942 9053 & 01628 506000
📠 01628 506001
Manor Ln SL6 2RA
e-mail: reservations-maidenhead@ihg.com
web: www.holidayinn.co.uk
dir: A404 towards High Wycombe. Exit at junct 9A. Left at mini rdbt. Hotel on right

Located close to Maidenhead town centre with transport links to Windsor and the M4, this well sited

continued

M

MAIDENHEAD *continued*

hotel is suitable for both the business and leisure traveller. Public areas benefit from a spacious lounge bar, brasserie-style restaurant and extensive conference facilities. The popular leisure club includes swimming pool and full gym facilities.

Rooms 197 (23 fmly) (56 GF) (18 smoking) **Facilities** STV supervised Gym Steam room Sauna New Year Wi-fi **Conf** Class 200 Board 100 Thtr 400 **Services** Lift Air con **Parking** 250 **Notes** Civ Wed 400

Walton Cottage Hotel

★★★ 78% METRO HOTEL

☎ 01628 624394 01628 773851
Marlow Rd SL6 7LT
e-mail: res@waltoncottagehotel.co.uk
dir: A308 towards Marlow, hotel on right after passing town centre

Conveniently located close to the town centre, this hotel offers an extensive choice of very attractively presented bedrooms. Heathrow Airport is just a 20-minute drive away, with Windsor, Henley and Ascot also close by. The hotel has well-equipped conference and business suites, ample parking, and Wi-fi is available for guests.

Rooms 72 (8 fmly) (20 GF) **Facilities** FTV Discounted day membership at nearby David Lloyd Gym & Spa Wi-fi **Conf** Class 30 Board 25 Thtr 70 **Services** Lift **Parking** 65 **Notes** Closed 22 Dec-4 Jan

M

MAIDSTONE Map 7 TQ75
Kent

Tudor Park, a Marriott Hotel & Country Club

★★★★ 78% HOTEL

☎ 01622 734334 & 632004 01622 735360
Ashford Rd, Bearsted ME14 4NQ
e-mail: mhrs.tdmgs.salesadmin@marriotthotels.com
web: www.marriotttudorpark.co.uk
dir: M20 junct 8 to Lenham. At rdbt turn right, follow Bearsted & Maidstone signs on A20. Hotel 1m on left

Located on the outskirts of Maidstone in a wooded valley below Leeds Castle, this fine country hotel is set in 220 acres of parkland. Spacious bedrooms provide good levels of comfort and a comprehensive range of extras. Facilities include a championship golf course, a fully equipped gym and two dining options.

Rooms 120 (48 fmly) (60 GF) (8 smoking) **Facilities** Spa 18 Putt green Gym Driving range Beauty salon Steam room Xmas New Year Wi-fi **Conf** Class 100 Board 60 Thtr 250 **Services** Lift **Parking** 250 **Notes** Civ Wed 160

Grange Moor Hotel

★★★

☎ 01622 677623 01622 678246
4-8 St Michael's Rd ME16 8BS
e-mail: reservations@grangemoor.co.uk
dir: From town centre towards A26 (Tonbridge road). Hotel 0.25m on left, just after church

Rooms 50 (11 annexe) (5 fmly) (7 GF) **S** £48-£52; **D** £59-£69* **Facilities** FTV Wi-fi **Conf** Class 60 Board 40 Thtr 100 **Parking** 60 **Notes** Closed 23-30 Dec Civ Wed

Premier Inn Maidstone (A26/ Wateringbury)

BUDGET HOTEL

☎ 0871 527 8706 0871 527 8707
103 Tonbridge Rd, Wateringbury ME18 5NS
dir: M25 junct 3 onto M20. Exit at junct 4 onto A228 towards West Malling. A26 towards Maidstone, approx 3m

High quality, budget accommodation ideal for both families and business travellers. Spacious, en suite bedrooms feature tea and coffee making facilities, and Freeview TV in most hotels. Internet access and Wi-fi are available for a small fee. The adjacent family restaurant features a wide and varied menu. See also the Hotel Groups pages.

Rooms 40 **D** £56-£60*

Premier Inn Maidstone (Allington)

BUDGET HOTEL

☎ 0871 527 8698 0871 527 8699
London Rd ME16 0HG
dir: M20 junct 5, 0.5m on London Rd towards Maidstone

Rooms 40 **D** £59-£65*

Premier Inn Maidstone (Leybourne)

BUDGET HOTEL

☎ 0871 527 8702 0871 527 8703
Castle Way, Leybourne ME19 5TR
dir: M20 junct 4, A228, hotel on left

Rooms 40 **D** £59-£63*

Premier Inn Maidstone (Sandling)

BUDGET HOTEL

☎ 0871 527 8704 0871 527 8705
Allington Lock, Sandling ME14 3AS
dir: M20 junct 6, follow Museum of Kent Life signs

Rooms 40 **D** £59-£65*

MALMESBURY Map 4 ST98
Wiltshire

INSPECTORS' CHOICE

Whatley Manor

★★★★★ HOTEL

☎ 01666 822888 01666 826120
Easton Grey SN16 0RB
e-mail: reservations@whatleymanor.com
web: www.whatleymanor.com
dir: M4 junct 17, follow signs to Malmesbury, continue over 2 rdbts. Follow B4040 & signs for Sherston, hotel 2m on left

Sitting in 12 acres of beautiful countryside, this impressive country house provides the most luxurious surroundings. Spacious bedrooms, most with views over the attractive gardens, are individually decorated with splendid features such as Bang & Olufsen sound and vision systems, and unique works of art. Several eating options are available: Le Mazot, a Swiss-style brasserie, The Dining Room that serves classical French cuisine with a contemporary twist via carte and tasting menus, plus the Kitchen Garden Terrace for alfresco breakfasts, lunches and dinners. Guests might even like to take a hamper and a picnic rug and find a quiet spot in the grounds. The old Loggia Barn is ideal for wedding ceremonies, and the Aquarius Spa is magnificent.

Rooms 23 (4 GF) **D** £305-£865 (incl. bkfst)* **Facilities** Spa STV Fishing Gym Cinema Hydro pool (indoor & outdoor) Xmas New Year Wi-fi **Conf** Class 20 Board 25 Thtr 60 Del from £325 to £352* **Services** Lift **Parking** 100 **Notes** LB No children 12yrs Civ Wed 120

Old Bell

★★★ 81% @@ HOTEL

☎ 01666 822344 📠 01666 825145
Abbey Row SN16 0BW
e-mail: info@oldbellhotel.com
web: www.oldbellhotel.com
dir: M4 junct 17, follow A429 north. Left at 1st rdbt. Left at T-junct. Hotel next to Abbey

Dating back to 1220, the wisteria-clad Old Bell is reputed to be the oldest purpose-built hotel in England. Bedrooms vary in size and style; those in the main house tend to be more spacious and are traditionally furnished with antiques, while the newer bedrooms in the coach house have a contemporary feel. Guests have a choice of comfortable sitting areas and dining options, including the main restaurant where the award-winning cuisine is based on high quality ingredients.

Rooms 33 (15 annexe) (7 GF) **S** £89.55; **D** £115-£245 (incl. bkfst)* **Facilities** FTV Xmas New Year Wi-fi **Conf** Class 32 Board 32 Thtr 60 **Parking** 33 **Notes** LB Civ Wed 80

Best Western Mayfield House

★★★ 72% @ HOTEL

☎ 01666 577409 📠 01666 577977
Crudwell SN16 9EW
e-mail: reception@mayfieldhousehotel.co.uk
web: www.mayfieldhousehotel.co.uk
dir: M4 junct 17, A429 to Cirencester. 2m N of Malmesbury on left in Crudwell

This popular hotel is in an ideal location for exploring the many attractions that Wiltshire and The Cotswolds have to offer. Bedrooms come in a range of shapes and sizes, and include some on the ground-floor level in a cottage adjacent to the main building. In addition to outdoor seating, guests can relax with a drink in the comfortable lounge area where orders are taken for the carefully prepared dinner to follow.

Rooms 28 (8 annexe) (4 fmly) (8 GF) **S** £60-£75; **D** £83-£103 (incl. bkfst)* **Facilities** FTV Xmas New Year Wi-fi **Conf** Class 30 Board 25 Thtr 40 Del from £85 to £125* **Parking** 50 **Notes** LB

MALVERN
Worcestershire
Map 10 SO74

The Cottage in the Wood Hotel

★★★ 85% @@ HOTEL

☎ 01684 588860 📠 01684 560662
Holywell Rd, Malvern Wells WR14 4LG
e-mail: reception@cottageinthewood.co.uk
web: www.cottageinthewood.co.uk
dir: 3m S of Great Malvern off A449, 500yds N of B4209, on opposite side of road

Sitting high up on a wooded hillside, this delightful, family-run hotel boasts lovely views over the Severn Valley. The bedrooms are divided between the main house, Beech Cottage and the Pinnacles. The public areas are very stylishly decorated, and imaginative food is served in an elegant dining room, overlooking the immaculate grounds.

Rooms 30 (23 annexe) (9 GF) **S** £79-£121; **D** £99-£198 (incl. bkfst)* **Facilities** FTV Xmas New Year Wi-fi **Conf** Board 14 Thtr 20 **Parking** 40 **Notes** LB

Colwall Park Hotel, Bar & Restaurant

★★★ 81% @@ HOTEL

☎ 01684 540000 📠 01684 540847
Walwyn Rd, Colwall WR13 6QG
e-mail: hotel@colwall.com
web: www.colwall.co.uk
dir: Between Malvern & Ledbury in centre of Colwall on B4218

Standing in extensive gardens, this hotel was purpose built in the early 20th century to serve the local racetrack. Today the proprietors and loyal staff provide high levels of hospitality and service. The Seasons Restaurant has a well-deserved reputation for its cuisine. Bedrooms are tastefully appointed and public areas help to create a fine country-house atmosphere.

Rooms 22 (1 fmly) **S** £85-£100; **D** £110-£180 (incl. bkfst)* **Facilities** FTV Boules Xmas New Year Wi-fi **Conf** Class 80 Board 50 Thtr 150 **Parking** 40 **Notes** LB

Cotford Hotel & L'Amuse Bouche Restaurant

★★★ 79% @@ HOTEL

☎ 01684 572427 📠 01684 572952
51 Graham Rd WR14 2HU
e-mail: reservations@cotfordhotel.co.uk
web: www.cotfordhotel.co.uk
dir: From Worcester follow signs to Malvern on A449. Left into Graham Rd signed town centre, hotel on right

This delightful house, built in 1851, reputedly for the Bishop of Worcester, stands in attractive gardens with stunning views of The Malverns. Bedrooms have been authentically renovated, retaining many of the original features and with a good selection of welcome extras. Food, service and hospitality are all major strengths.

Rooms 15 (3 fmly) (1 GF) **Facilities** STV Wi-fi **Conf** Class 26 Board 12 Thtr 26 **Parking** 15 **Notes** LB

See advert on page 332

The Malvern Hills Hotel

★★★ 78% HOTEL

☎ 01684 540690 📠 01684 540327
Wynds Point WR13 6DW
e-mail: malhilhotl@aol.com
web: www.malvernhillshotel.co.uk
dir: 4m S, at junct of A449 & B4232

This 19th-century hostelry is situated to the west of Malvern, opposite the British Camp, which was fortified and occupied by the Ancient Britons. The bedrooms are well equipped and benefit from smart modern bathrooms. Public areas include a choice of

continued

MALVERN ***continued***

bars, retaining original features, modern conference facilities and an attractive restaurant.

Rooms 14 (1 fmly) (2 GF) **Facilities** STV FTV Xmas New Year Wi-fi **Conf** Class 24 Board 30 Thtr 40 **Parking** 45 **Notes** LB

Mount Pleasant

★★★ 68% HOTEL

☎ 01684 561837 01684 569968
Belle Vue Ter WR14 4PZ
e-mail: reception@mountpleasanthotel.co.uk
web: www.mountpleasanthotel.co.uk
dir: On A449, in town centre by x-rds opposite Priory Church

An attractive Georgian house in the town centre that occupies an elevated position and overlooks Priory Church and the picturesque Severn Valley. The bedrooms are spacious, and there is a smart bar and brasserie where guests can enjoy a full meal or just a drink or a snack. In warmer months the small terrace on the lawn makes a delightful place to relax.

Rooms 14 (1 fmly) **S** £50-£78; **D** £80-£115 (incl. bkfst) **Facilities** FTV Hair salon ♫ Xmas New Year Wi-fi **Conf** Class 40 Board 50 Thtr 90 Del from £80 to £95 **Parking** 20 **Notes** LB ⊗

Holdfast Cottage

★★ 82% ❁ HOTEL

☎ 01684 310288 01684 311117
Marlbank Rd, Welland WR13 6NA
e-mail: enquiries@holdfast-cottage.co.uk
web: www.holdfast-cottage.co.uk
dir: M50 junct 1, follow Upton Three Counties/A38 signs, onto A4104 to Welland

At the base of the Malvern Hills this delightful wisteria-covered hotel sits in attractive manicured grounds. Charming public areas include an intimate bar, a log fire enhanced lounge and an elegant dining room. Bedrooms vary in size but all are comfortable and well appointed. Fresh local and seasonal produce are the basis for the cuisine.

Rooms 8 (1 fmly) **Facilities** FTV Xmas New Year Wi-fi **Conf** Class 30 Board 30 **Parking** 15 **Notes** LB Civ Wed 35

The Great Malvern Hotel

★★ 71% HOTEL

☎ 01684 563411 01684 560514
Graham Rd WR14 2HN
e-mail: sutton@great-malvern-hotel.co.uk
dir: From Worcester on A449, left after fire station into Graham Rd. Hotel at end on right

Close to the town centre this privately owned and managed hotel is ideally situated for many of Malvern's attractions. The accommodation is spacious and well equipped. Public areas include a cosy bar area, popular with locals, and a quiet lounge area.

Rooms 13 (1 fmly) **S** £59.50-£65; **D** £79.50 (incl. bkfst)* **Facilities** STV FTV ♫ Wi-fi **Conf** Class 20 Board 20 Thtr 20 **Services** Lift **Parking** 9 **Notes** LB

MANCHESTER Map 16 SJ89
Greater Manchester

See also **Manchester Airport & Sale**

The Lowry Hotel

RF THE ROCCO FORTE COLLECTION

★★★★★ 83% ❁❁ HOTEL

☎ 0161 827 4000 0161 827 4001
50 Dearmans Place, Chapel Wharf, Salford M3 5LH
e-mail: enquiries.lowry@roccofortecollection.com
web: www.roccofortecollection.com
dir: M6 junct 19, A556/M56/A5103 for 4.5m. At rdbt take A57(M) to lights, right onto Water St. Left to New Quay St/Trinity Way. At 1st lights right into Chapel St for hotel

This modern, contemporary hotel, set beside the River Irwell in the centre of the city, offers spacious bedrooms equipped to meet the needs of business and leisure visitors alike. Many of the rooms look out over the river, as do the sumptuous suites. The River Room restaurant produces good brasserie cooking. Extensive business and function facilities are available, together with a spa to provide extra pampering.

Rooms 165 (7 fmly) **S** £387-£2500; **D** £423-£2500* **Facilities** Spa STV FTV Gym Swimming facilities available nearby ♫ Xmas New Year Wi-fi **Conf** Class 250 Board 60 Thtr 400 **Services** Lift Air con **Parking** 100 **Notes** LB Civ Wed 400

The Midland

★★★★ 85% ◎◎ HOTEL

☎ 0161 236 3333 📠 0161 932 4100
Peter St M60 2DS
e-mail: midlandsales@qhotels.co.uk
web: www.qhotels.co.uk
dir: M602 junct 3, follow Manchester Central Convention Complex signs, hotel opposite

This much loved, centrally located, well-established Edwardian-style hotel (Grade II listed) offers stylish, thoughtfully equipped bedrooms that have a contemporary feel. Elegant public areas are equally impressive and facilities include extensive function and meeting rooms. Eating options include the award-winning classical French Restaurant, the Colony Restaurant and the Octogan Lounge.

Rooms 312 (13 fmly) **S** £99-£250; **D** £99-£250* **Facilities** STV Gym Squash Hair & beauty salon Wi-fi **Conf** Class 300 Board 120 Thtr 600 Del from £169 to £229* **Services** Lift Air con **Notes** LB Civ Wed 600

Worsley Park, A Marriott Hotel & Country Club

★★★★ 80% ◎ HOTEL

☎ 0161 975 2000 📠 0161 799 6341
Worsley Park, Worsley M28 2QT
e-mail: uk.pennines.sales.office@marriotthotels.com
web: www.marriottworsleypark.co.uk
dir: M60 junct 13, over 1st rdbt take A575. Hotel 400yds on left

This smart, modern hotel is set in impressive grounds with a championship golf course. Bedrooms are comfortably appointed and well equipped for both leisure and business guests. Public areas include extensive leisure and conference facilities, and an elegant restaurant offering imaginative cuisine.

Rooms 158 (33 fmly) (49 GF) (6 smoking) **S** fr £99; **D** fr £109 (incl. bkfst)* **Facilities** Spa STV 18 Putt green Gym Fitness suite Aerobics studio Sauna Steam room Health & beauty salon Wi-fi **Conf** Class 150 Board 100 Thtr 250 Del from £139 to £175* **Services** Lift **Parking** 400 **Notes** Civ Wed 200

Macdonald Manchester

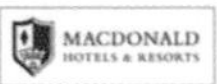

★★★★ 78% ◎ HOTEL

☎ 0844 879 9088 & 0161 272 3200
📠 0870 194 2237
London Rd M1 2PG
e-mail: general.manchester@macdonald-hotels.co.uk
web: www.macdonald-hotels.co.uk
dir: Opposite Piccadilly Station

Ideally situated just a short walk from Piccadilly Station, this hotel provides a handy location for both business and leisure travellers. Stylish, modern rooms have plasma TVs and iPod docking stations and the bathrooms offer walk-in power showers and luxury baths. The first-floor restaurant serves skilfully prepared dinners and hearty breakfasts. Staff throughout are cheerful and keen to please.

Rooms 338 (14 fmly) **S** £69-£185; **D** £69-£185* **Facilities** Spa FTV Gym Sauna New Year Wi-fi **Conf** Class 150 Board 80 Thtr 250 Del from £135 to £179 **Services** Lift Air con **Parking** 85 **Notes** LB Civ Wed 200

Mint Hotel Manchester

★★★★ 78% ◎ HOTEL

☎ 0161 242 1000 📠 0161 242 1001
One Piccadilly Place, 1 Auburn St M1 3DG
e-mail: manchester.reservations@minthotel.com
web: www.minthotel.com
dir: M56/A5103 signed city centre, at rdbt for A57(M) take 2nd exit into Medlock St (A5103). Right at lights into Whitworth St (B6469), bear left into Aytoun St, right into Auburn St

A large stylish, modern hotel set on the Piccadilly Place development which is ideally located for both the rail station and the city centre. Spacious, contemporary bedrooms offer city views and boast a wide range of facilities including iMacs and complimentary high speed Wi-fi. Striking public areas feature modern art and include a range of meeting rooms, a popular bar and city café which offers high quality modern, European cuisine.

Rooms 285 (22 fmly) **Facilities** STV FTV Gym Xmas New Year Wi-fi **Conf** Class 74 Board 70 Thtr 170 **Services** Lift Air con **Parking** 24 **Notes** Civ Wed 120

Marriott Manchester Victoria & Albert Hotel

Marriott HOTELS & RESORTS

★★★★ 78% HOTEL

☎ 0161 832 1188 📠 0161 834 2484
Water St M3 4JQ
e-mail: london.regional.reservations@marriott.com
web: www.manchestermarriottvictoriaandalbert.co.uk
dir: M602 to A57 through lights on Regent Rd. Pass Sainsbury's, left at lights onto ring road, right at lights into Water St

This uniquely converted warehouse, with an interior featuring exposed brickwork and iron pillars, is located on the banks of the River Irwell, just a short stroll from the city centre. There are stylish, comfortable and well-equipped bedrooms together with attractive public areas. A large bar lounge leads onto an intimate restaurant, and extensive conference facilities are available.

Rooms 148 (30 fmly) (7 smoking) **S** £129-£185; **D** £129-£185* **Facilities** FTV Complimentary use of Bannatynes Health Club (5 mins' walk) New Year Wi-fi **Conf** Class 120 Board 72 Thtr 250 Del from £145 to £159* **Services** Lift Air con **Parking** 100 **Notes** LB Civ Wed 200

M

Holiday Inn Manchester - MediaCityUK

★★★★ 77% HOTEL

☎ 0845 250 8458 📠 0845 250 8459
Media City UK, Salford M50 2HT
dir: M602 junct 2 onto A576 to Salford Quays

Located in the heart of the exciting media district on Salford Quays, this new hotel is adjacent to the main production studios and only minutes from Old Trafford and The Lowry Centre. The stylish Hub Bar features TV-themed murals and the attractive Green Room Restaurant is on the mezzanine floor. Bedrooms are well equipped with safes, mini-bars and many have views of the Manchester Shipping Canal. There's complimentary Wi-fi throughout, and a mini-gym is available to guests.

Rooms 218 (10 fmly) **Facilities** STV FTV Gym Xmas New Year Wi-fi **Conf** Class 25 Board 30 Thtr 44 Del from £145 to £199 **Services** Lift Air con **Notes**

MANCHESTER ***continued***

Copthorne Hotel Manchester

★★★★ 76% HOTEL

☎ 0161 873 7321 📠 0161 877 8112
Clippers Quay, Salford Quays M50 3SN
e-mail: reservations.manchester@millenniumhotels.co.uk
web: www.millenniumhotels.co.uk
dir: From M602 follow signs for Salford Quays & Trafford Park on A5063. Hotel 0.75m on right

This smart hotel enjoys a convenient location on the redeveloped Salford Quays close to Old Trafford, The Lowry Centre and The Imperial War Museum. Bedrooms are comfortably appointed and well equipped for both business and leisure guests. The informal Clippers Restaurant serves a wide range of modern dishes.

Rooms 166 (6 fmly) (23 GF) **Facilities** STV Wi-fi **Conf** Class 80 Board 70 Thtr 160 Del from £120 to £190* **Services** Lift **Parking** 120 **Notes** ⊗ Civ Wed 160

Crowne Plaza Manchester City Centre

★★★★ 76% HOTEL

☎ 0161 828 8660 📠 0161 828 8606
70 Shudehill M4 4AF
e-mail: reception@cpmanchester.com
web: www.cpmanchester.com
dir: In city centre

A stylish hotel located in the heart of Manchester in the trendy Northern Quarter, with Victoria and Piccadilly Stations, Shudehill Tram and Bus Interchange all within walking distance. The bedrooms, including Club Rooms and a Club Lounge, have either one or two queen-size, or king-sized beds. The contemporary bathrooms feature separate bath and shower. Complimentary internet access is provided and a mini gym is available 24 hours a day.

Rooms 228 **S** £69-£229; **D** £69-£229* **Facilities** STV FTV Gym Xmas New Year Wi-fi **Conf** Class 160 Board 60 Thtr 200 **Services** Lift Air con **Notes** LB ⊗ Civ Wed 200

Renaissance Manchester

★★★★ 76% HOTEL

☎ 0161 831 6000 📠 0161 835 3077
Blackfriars St M3 2EQ
e-mail: rhi.manbr.sales@renaissancehotels.com
web: www.renaissancemanchester.co.uk
dir: Follow signs to Deansgate, left into Blackfriars St at 2nd lights after Kendals, hotel on right

This smart hotel enjoys a central location just off Deansgate, within easy walking distance of The Arena and the city's many shops and attractions. Stylish, well-equipped bedrooms are extremely comfortable and those on higher floors offer wonderful views. Public areas include an elegant bar and restaurant plus an impressive conference and banqueting suite.

Rooms 203 **Facilities** Complimentary leisure facilities nearby Wi-fi **Conf** Class 300 Board 100 Thtr 400 **Services** Lift Air con **Parking** 80 **Notes** ⊗ Civ Wed 400

The Palace

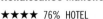

★★★★ 74% HOTEL

☎ 0161 288 1111 📠 0161 288 2222
Oxford St M60 7HA
e-mail: richard.grove@principal-hayley.com
web: www.principal-hayley.com
dir: Opposite Manchester Oxford Road rail station

Formerly the offices of the Refuge Life Assurance Company, this impressive neo-Gothic building occupies a central location. There is a vast lobby, spacious open-plan bar lounge and restaurant, and extensive conference and function facilities. Bedrooms vary in size and style but are all spacious and well equipped.

Rooms 275 (59 fmly) **Facilities** STV ♫ Wi-fi **Conf** Class 650 Board 200 Thtr 1000 **Services** Lift **Notes** ⊗ Civ Wed 600

Malmaison Manchester

★★★ 88% ◉ HOTEL

☎ 0161 278 1000 📠 0161 278 1002
Piccadilly M1 3AQ
e-mail: manchester@malmaison.com
web: www.malmaison.com
dir: Follow city centre signs, then signs to Piccadilly station. Hotel at bottom of station approach

Stylish and chic, Malmaison Manchester offers the very best incontemporary hotel keeping, in a relaxed and comfortable environment. Converted from a former warehouse it offers a range of bright meeting rooms, a gym and treatment rooms, as well as the ever popular bar and French-style brasserie. Air-conditioned suites combine comfort with stunning design. Expect the unusual in some of the rooms, for instance the Cinema Suites have a private screening room with 52" screen with surround-sound.

Rooms 167 **Facilities** STV Gym Xmas New Year Wi-fi **Conf** Class 48 Board 30 Thtr 100 **Services** Lift Air con

Best Western Willow Bank

★★★ 79% HOTEL

☎ 0161 224 0461 📠 0161 257 2561
340-342 Wilmslow Rd, Fallowfield M14 6AF
e-mail: gm-willowbank@feathers.uk.com
web: www.feathers.uk.com
dir: M60 junct 5, A5103, left onto B5093. Hotel 2.5m on left

This popular hotel is conveniently located three miles from the city centre, close to the universities. Bedrooms vary in size and style but all are appointed to impressively high standards; they are well equipped and many rooms benefit from CD players and PlayStations. Spacious, elegant public areas include a bar, a restaurant and meeting rooms.

Rooms 116 (4 fmly) **Facilities** STV Xmas New Year Wi-fi **Conf** Class 60 Board 70 Thtr 125 **Parking** 100 **Notes** ⊗ Civ Wed 125

Novotel Manchester Centre

★★★ 79% HOTEL

☎ 0161 235 2200 📠 0161 235 2210
21 Dickinson St M1 4LX
e-mail: H3145@accor.com
web: www.novotel.com
dir: From Oxford St into Portland St, left into Dickinson St. Hotel on right

This smart, modern property enjoys a central location convenient for theatres, shops, China Town and Manchester's business district. Spacious bedrooms are thoughtfully equipped and brightly decorated. Open-plan, contemporary public areas include an all-day restaurant and a stylish bar. Extensive conference and meeting facilities are available.

Rooms 164 (15 fmly) (10 smoking) **Facilities** STV FTV Gym Steam room Sauna Aromatherapy Wi-fi **Conf** Class 50 Board 36 Thtr 90 **Services** Lift Air con **Notes** LB

The Portland by Thistle, Manchester

thistle

★★★ 78% HOTEL

☎ 0871 376 9026 📠 0871 376 9126
3/5 Portland St, Piccadilly Gardens M1 6DP
e-mail: reservations.manchester@thistle.co.uk
web: www.thistlehotels.com/manchester
dir: M6 junct 19 onto M56, A5103 signed city centre, straight on at rdbt, right at 2nd lights, straight at next lights into Portland St, hotel on right

The hotel is located close to the Piccadilly Gardens and five minutes' walk from the central and financial districts. Rooms are compact and well equipped, and the Portland Bar and Restaurant offers a wide selection of meals, drinks and wines. There is also an Otium Leisure Centre, and conference facilities are available. Thistle Hotels – AA Hotel Group of the Year 2011-12.

Rooms 204 (1 fmly) **S** £49-£170; **D** £58-£180* **Facilities** STV supervised Gym Steam room Sauna Plunge pool Xmas New Year Wi-fi **Conf** Class 140 Board 40 Thtr 300 Del from £119 to £189* **Services** Lift Air con **Notes** LB ⊗ Civ Wed 220

Jurys Inn Manchester

JURYS INNS

★★★ 77% HOTEL

☎ 0161 953 8888 📠 0161 953 9090
56 Great Bridgewater St M1 5LE
e-mail: manchester_inn@jurysinns.com
web: www.jurysinns.com
dir: In city centre adjacent to Manchester Central & Bridgewater Hall

Enjoying a prime city centre location, this hotel offers good value, air-conditioned accommodation, ideal for both business travellers and families. Public areas include a smart, spacious lobby, the Inn Pub and the Infusion Restaurant. There are several conveniently located car parks with special rates available.

Rooms 265 (11 fmly) (16 GF) **S** £66-£250; **D** £66-£250* **Facilities** FTV Wi-fi **Conf** Class 25 Board 25 Thtr 50 **Services** Lift Air con **Notes** ⊗

Novotel Manchester West

NOVOTEL

★★★ 72% HOTEL

☎ 0161 799 3535 📠 0161 703 8207
Worsley Brow M28 2YA
e-mail: H0907@accor.com
web: www.novotel.com

(For full entry see Worsley)

Chancellors Hotel & Conference Centre

★★★ 70% HOTEL

☎ 0161 9077414
Moseley Rd, Fallowfield M14 6NN
dir: Telephone for detailed directions

A Grade II listed manor house set in five acres of landscaped gardens hidden in the heart of Fallowfield, well located for the city's shopping, business and commercial centres. Bedrooms offer modern facilities and the cuisine is enjoyable. Wi-fi and secure parking are available.

Rooms 69

Diamond Lodge

★★ 71% HOTEL

☎ 0161 231 0770 📠 0161 231 0660
Hyde Rd, Belle Vue M18 7BA
web: www.diamondlodge.co.uk
dir: On A57, 2.5m W of M60 junct 24

Offering very good value for money, this modern lodge provides comfortable accommodation near the city centre, motorway networks and football stadiums. Bright and airy, open-plan day rooms include a lounge and an informal dining room where complimentary breakfasts and a wide choice of evening meals are available.

Rooms 85 (13 fmly) (16 GF) (13 smoking) **S** £40.95; **D** £40.95 (incl. bkfst)* **Parking** 90 **Notes** ⊗ Closed 24-26 Dec RS 31 Dec

See advert on this page

M

MANCHESTER *continued*

Monton House

★★ 65% HOTEL

☎ 0161 789 7811 📠 0161 787 7609
116-118 Monton Rd, Eccles M30 9HG
e-mail: hotel@montonhousehotel.co.uk
web: www.montonhousehotel.co.uk
dir: M602 junct 2/A576, 2nd left onto B5229 (Half Edge Ln) right into Monton Rd, pass flats on left, hotel 100yds on right

A modern, purpose-built hotel conveniently situated for the motorway network, airport and city centre. The bedrooms are well equipped, and the brightly furnished restaurant offers an imaginative choice at dinner that is excellent value for money.

Rooms 60 (2 fmly) (1 GF) **Facilities** FTV New Year Wi-fi **Conf** Class 50 Board 50 Thtr 150 **Services** Lift **Parking** 100 **Notes** LB ⊗ Civ Wed 120

Macdonald Townhouse Manchester

U

☎ 0161 236 5122 📠 0161 236 4468
101 Portland St M1 6DF
e-mail: gm.townhouse@macdonald-hotels.co.uk
dir: From Piccadilly Station, along Piccadilly. Left into Portland St, hotel at junct with Princess St

Currently the rating for this establishment is not confirmed. This may be due to a change of ownership or because it has only recently joined the AA rating scheme. For further details please see the AA website: theAA.com

Rooms 85 (24 fmly) **S** £77-£165; **D** £77-£250* **Facilities** FTV ♫ Wi-fi **Conf** Class 26 Board 30 Thtr 48 Del from £135 to £165* **Services** Lift Air con

Campanile Manchester

BUDGET HOTEL

☎ 0161 833 1845 📠 0161 833 1847
55 Ordsall Ln, Regent Rd, Salford M5 4RS
e-mail: manchester@campanile.com
dir: M602 to Manchester, then A57. After large rdbt with Sainsbury's on left, left at next lights. Hotel on right

This modern building offers accommodation in smart, well-equipped bedrooms, all with en suite bathrooms. Refreshments may be taken at the informal bistro. See also the Hotel Groups pages.

Rooms 104 (25 GF) **Conf** Class 40 Board 30 Thtr 50

Express by Holiday Inn Manchester East

BUDGET HOTEL

☎ 0161 231 9900 📠 0161 220 8555
Hyde Rd M18 7LJ
e-mail: manchester@morethanhotels.com
web: www.hiexpress.co.uk
dir: 1m from M60 junct 24

A modern hotel ideal for families and business travellers. Fresh and uncomplicated, the spacious rooms include Sky TV, power shower and tea and coffee-making facilities. Continental buffet breakfast is included in the room rate; other meals may be taken at the nearby family pub or restaurant. See also the Hotel Groups pages.

Rooms 97 (58 fmly) (27 GF) (14 smoking) **S** £39-£199; **D** £39-£199 (incl. bkfst)* **Conf** Class 18 Board 18 Thtr 35 Del from £99 to £149*

Holiday Inn Express Manchester-Oxford Road

BUDGET HOTEL

☎ 0843 208 3005 📠 0843 208 3006
Oxford Road 2 M1 5QA
e-mail: info@hiemanchester.co.uk
dir: From A57(M) follow signs for Peters Fields & A5103, into Cambridge St. 1st right into Chester St. NCP car park on left at end (NB for Sat Nav use M1 5GE)

A modern hotel ideal for families and business travellers. Fresh and uncomplicated, the spacious rooms include Sky TV, power shower and tea and coffee-making facilities. Continental buffet breakfast is included in the room rate; other meals may be taken at the nearby family pub or restaurant. See also the Hotel Groups pages.

Rooms 147

Holiday Inn Express Manchester Salford Quays

BUDGET HOTEL

☎ 0161 868 1000 📠 0161 868 10 68
Waterfront Quay, Salford Quays M50 3XW
e-mail: info@expressmanchester.co.uk
web: www.hiexpress.com/salfordquays

Rooms 120 (72 fmly) (incl. bkfst) **Conf** Class 10 Board 12 Thtr 25

Ibis Manchester Charles Street

BUDGET HOTEL

☎ 0161 272 5000 📠 0161 272 5010
Charles St, Princess St M1 7DL
e-mail: H3143@accor.com
web: www.ibishotel.com
dir: M62, M602 towards Manchester Centre, follow signs for UMIST (A34)

Modern, budget hotel offering comfortable accommodation in bright and practical bedrooms. Breakfast is self-service and dinner is available in the restaurant. See also the Hotel Groups pages.

Rooms 126

Ibis Manchester City Centre

BUDGET HOTEL

☎ 0161 234 0600 📠 0161 234 0610
96 Portland St M1 4GY
e-mail: H3142@accor.com
web: www.ibishotel.com
dir: In city centre, between Princess St & Oxford St

Rooms 127 (16 fmly) (7 smoking)

Premier Inn Manchester Central

BUDGET HOTEL

☎ 0871 527 8742 📠 0871 527 8743
Bishopsgate, 7-11 Lower Mosley St M2 3DW
dir: M56 to end, A5103 towards city centre. Right at 2nd lights. At next lights left into Oxford Rd, left at junct of St Peters Sq. Hotel on left of Lower Mosley St

High quality, budget accommodation ideal for both families and business travellers. Spacious, en suite bedrooms feature tea and coffee making facilities, and Freeview TV in most hotels. Internet access and Wi-fi are available for a small fee. The adjacent family restaurant features a wide and varied menu. See also the Hotel Groups pages.

Rooms 147 **D** £62-£67*

Premier Inn Manchester City Centre (Deansgate)

BUDGET HOTEL

☎ 0871 527 8740 📠 0871 527 8741
Medlock St M15 5FJ
dir: M60 junct 24, A57(M) (Mancunian Way) towards city centre. Hotel adjacent on A5103 (Medlock St)

Rooms 200 **D** £59-£64*

Premier Inn Manchester City Centre (Portland Street)

BUDGET HOTEL

☎ 0871 527 8746 📠 0871 527 8747
The Circus, 112-114 Portland St M1 4WB
dir: M6 junct 19, A556. M56 junct 3 onto A5103 to Medlock St, right into Whitworth St, left into Oxford St, right into Portland St

Rooms 225 **D** £62-£67*

Premier Inn Manchester City MEN/ Printworks

BUDGET HOTEL

☎ 0871 527 8744 📠 0871 527 8745
North Tower, Victoria Bridge St, Salford M3 5AS
dir: M602 to city centre, A57(M) towards GMEX. 2nd exit follow A56 city centre signs. Left before MEN arena onto A6, 1st left

Rooms 170 **D** £62-£67*

Premier Inn Manchester (Denton)

BUDGET HOTEL

☎ 0871 527 8708 📠 0871 527 8709
Alphagate Dr, Manchester Rd South, Denton M34 3SH
dir: M60 junct 24, A57 signed Denton. 1st right at lights, right at next lights, hotel on left

Rooms 40 **D** £52-£58*

Premier Inn Manchester (Heaton Park)

BUDGET HOTEL

☎ 0871 527 8710 📠 0871 527 8711
Middleton Rd, Crumpsall M8 4NB
dir: M60 junct 19, A576 towards Manchester, through 2 sets of lights. Hotel on left

Rooms 45 **D** £53-£58*

Premier Inn Manchester North (Middleton)

BUDGET HOTEL

☎ 0871 527 8748 📠 0871 527 8749
818 Manchester Old Rd, Rhodes, Middleton M24 4RF
dir: M60/M62 junct 18 follow Manchester/Middleton signs. M60 junct 19 take A576 towards Middleton

Rooms 42 **D** £52-£58*

Premier Inn Manchester Old Trafford

BUDGET HOTEL

☎ 0871 527 8750 📠 0871 527 8751
Waters Reach, Trafford Park M17 1WS
dir: M6 junct 19, A556 towards Altrincham. Follow Stretford & Manchester City Centre signs (road becomes A56). Follow Manchester United Football Stadium signs. At stadium left at lights. Into Sir Matt Busby Way, after 1st lights hotel on right

Rooms 160 (8 GF) **D** £62-£65*

Premier Inn Manchester (Salford Quays)

BUDGET HOTEL

☎ 0871 527 8718 📠 0871 527 8719
11 The Quays, Salford Quays, Salford M50 3SQ
dir: M602 junct 3, A5063, on Salford Quays

Rooms 52 **D** £62-£65*

Premier Inn Manchester Trafford Centre North

BUDGET HOTEL

☎ 0871 527 8752 📠 0871 527 8753
18-20 Trafford Boulevard, Urmston M41 7JE
dir: M6, onto M62 at junct 21a, towards Manchester. M62 junct 1, M60 towards south. M60 junct 10, take B5214. Hotel on left just before Ellesmere Circle

Rooms 42 **D** £63*

Premier Inn Manchester Trafford Centre South

BUDGET HOTEL

☎ 0871 527 8754 📠 0871 527 8755
Wilderspool Wood, Trafford Centre M17 8WW
dir: M62 junct 21a towards Manchester. Or M62 junct 1 onto M60 S. Or M60 junct 10, B5124 towards Trafford Park. At 1st rdbt last exit for Trafford Centre parking. At 2nd rdbt straight on. Hotel on left

Rooms 59 **D** £63*

Premier Inn Manchester Trafford Centre West

BUDGET HOTEL

☎ 0871 527 8756 📠 0871 527 8757
Old Park Ln M17 8PG
dir: M60 junct 10 towards The Trafford Centre

Rooms 161 (20 GF) **D** £63*

Premier Inn Manchester (West Didsbury)

BUDGET HOTEL

☎ 0871 527 8722 📠 0871 527 8723
Christies Field Office Park, Derwent Ave, Didsbury M21 7QS
dir: M60 junct 5, A5103 (Princess Parkway) towards Manchester on A5103. Hotel approx 1m on left

Rooms 80 **D** £54-£59*

MANCHESTER AIRPORT Map 15 SJ88
Greater Manchester

See also **Altrincham**

Manchester Airport Marriott

Marriott HOTELS & RESORTS

★★★★ 80% HOTEL

☎ 0161 904 0301 🖷 0161 980 1787
Hale Rd, Hale Barns WA15 8XW
e-mail: london.regional.reservations@marriott.com
web: www.manchesterairportmarriott.co.uk
dir: M56 junct 6, in left lane (Hale, Altrincham). Left at lights, on approach to bridge into right lane. At rdbt 3rd exit into hotel car park

With good airport links and convenient access to the city, this sprawling modern hotel is a popular destination. The hotel offers extensive leisure and business facilities, a choice of eating and drinking options and ample parking. Bedrooms are situated around courtyards and have a comprehensive range of facilities.

Rooms 215 (22 fmly) (43 GF) (16 smoking) **Facilities** Spa STV supervised Gym Wi-fi **Conf** Class 70 Board 50 Thtr 160 **Services** Lift Air con **Parking** 400 **Notes** Civ Wed 110

M

Stanneylands

PRIMA HOTEL GROUP

★★★★ 79% HOTEL

☎ 01625 525225 🖷 01625 537282
Stanneylands Rd SK9 4EY
e-mail: reservations@stanneylandshotel.co.uk
web: www.stanneylandshotel.co.uk
dir: From M56 at airport exit follow Wilmslow signs. Left towards Handforth. Left at lights into Stanneylands Rd, hotel on left

This traditional hotel offers well-equipped bedrooms and delightful, comfortable day rooms. The cuisine in the restaurant is of a high standard and ranges from traditional favourites to more imaginative contemporary dishes. Staff throughout are friendly and obliging.

Rooms 56 (2 fmly) (10 GF) **Facilities** STV FTV Wi-fi **Conf** Class 50 Board 40 Thtr 120 **Services** Lift **Parking** 108 **Notes** LB Civ Wed 100

Radisson Blu Hotel Manchester Airport

★★★★ 78% HOTEL

☎ 0161 490 5000 🖷 0161 490 5100
Chicago Av M90 3RA
e-mail: sales.manchester@radissonblu.com
web: www.radissonblu.co.uk/hotel-manchesterairport
dir: M56 junct 5, follow signs for Terminal 2. At rdbt 2nd left, follow signs for railway station. Hotel adjacent to station

All the airport terminals are quickly accessed by covered, moving walkways from this modern hotel. There is an excellent and well-equipped leisure club complete with indoor pool, and extensive conference and banqueting facilities are available. Air-conditioned bedrooms are thoughtfully equipped and come in a variety of decorative themes. Super views of the runway can be enjoyed in the Phileas Fogg Restaurant that offers international cuisine; there's also an all-day brasserie.

Rooms 360 (2 fmly) (25 smoking) **Facilities** STV Gym Beauty treatments Sauna Steam room Xmas New Year Wi-fi **Conf** Class 150 Board 60 Thtr 350 Del from £135 to £165* **Services** Lift Air con **Parking** 222 **Notes** Civ Wed 300

Hallmark Hotel Manchester

★★★★ 76% HOTEL

☎ 0161 437 0511
Stanley Rd SK9 3LD
e-mail: linda.gregory@hallmarkhotels.co.uk
dir: M60 junct 3/A34 signed Cheadle/Wilmslow. Right at 3rd rdbt onto Stanley Rd (B5094). Hotel on left

Ideally located for Manchester Airport and just a few miles from both the Trafford Centre and the city's many shops, the hotel offers well appointed bedrooms. Guests can relax and unwind in the hotel's 20-metre pool, jacuzzi and steam rooms. The brasserie is open for both lunch and dinner and offers a range of international dishes.

Rooms 88 (12 fmly) (12 GF) **S** £50-£140; **D** £60-£150* **Facilities** Spa FTV Gym Steam room Sauna Hair salon New Year Wi-fi **Conf** Class 300 Board 150 Thtr 500 Del from £128 to £155* **Services** Lift **Notes** LB Civ Wed

Crowne Plaza Manchester Airport

★★★★ 72% HOTEL

☎ 0871 942 9055 🖷 0161 436 2340
Ringway Rd M90 3NS
e-mail: reservations-manchesterairport@ihg.com
web: www.crowneplaza.co.uk
dir: M56 junct 5 signed Manchester Airport. At airport, follow signs to Terminal 1 & 3. Hotel adjacent to Terminal 3. Long stay car park on left

Located by Terminal 3, this smart, modern hotel offers well equipped, comfortable bedrooms, all with fitted with air conditioning and effective double glazing. A choice of dining styles and bars is available, and the hotel has spacious leisure facilities and ample on-site parking. Hospitality is friendly with several long-serving staff members who greet regular customers as friends.

Rooms 294 (100 fmly) (51 GF) (25 smoking) **Facilities** STV Gym Saunas Wi-fi **Conf** Class 25 Board 20 Thtr 30 **Services** Lift Air con **Parking** 300

Etrop Grange Hotel

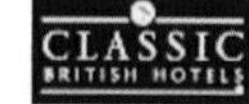

★★★★ 71% HOTEL

☎ 0844 855 9118 🖷 0161 499 0790
Thorley Ln M90 4EG
e-mail: gm@etrophotel.co.uk
dir: M56 junct 5 follow signs for Terminal 2, on slip road to rdbt take 1st exit. Immediately left, hotel 400yds

This Georgian country-house style hotel is close to Terminal 2 but one would never know once inside. Stylish, comfortable bedrooms provide modern comforts and good business facilities. Elegant day rooms include the Coach House Restaurant that serves creative dishes. Complimentary chauffeured transport to the airport is available for guests using the airport.

Rooms 64 (4 fmly) (9 GF) **Facilities** STV New Year Wi-fi **Conf** Class 35 Board 35 Thtr 80 **Parking** 80 **Notes** Civ Wed 90

Bewleys Hotel Manchester Airport

★★★ 78% HOTEL

☎ 0161 498 0333 & 498 1390 🖷 0161 498 0222
Outwood Ln M90 4HL
e-mail: man@bewleyshotels.com
web: www.bewleyshotels.com
dir: At Manchester Airport. Follow signs to Manchester Airport Terminal 3. Hotel on left on Terminal 3 rdbt

Located adjacent to the airport this modern, stylish hotel provides an ideal stop-off for air travellers and business guests alike. All bedrooms are spacious and well equipped and include a wing of superior rooms. Spacious, open-plan day rooms are stylishly appointed and include a large bar and restaurant along with a good range of meeting and conference facilities.

Rooms 365 (111 fmly) (30 GF) (19 smoking) **S** £59-£149; **D** £59-£149* **Facilities** Gym Wi-fi **Conf** Class 35 Board 18 Thtr 90 Del from £129 to £145* **Services** Lift **Parking** 300 **Notes** ®

Holiday Inn Manchester Airport

★★★ 75% HOTEL

☎ 0871 942 9096 📠 01625 531876
Altrincham Rd SK9 4LR
e-mail: himanchester@qmh-hotels.com
web: www.holidayinn.co.uk
dir: M56 junct 6, A538 towards Wilmslow. Approx 1m, over mini rdbt, hotel on left

Just a short distance from Manchester Airport and the M56, this pleasant hotel offers comfortable public areas, modern leisure and meeting facilities. The restaurant provides a wide choice of formal and informal dining options. Bedrooms are fully equipped and include air conditioning; 24-hour room service is available.

Rooms 126 (6 fmly) (19 GF) **S** £45-£169; **D** £45-£169 **Facilities** Gym Squash Sauna Steam room Xmas New Year Wi-fi **Conf** Class 150 Board 90 Thtr 300 Del from £99 to £169 **Services** Lift Air con **Parking** 529 **Notes** LB ® RS 23-31 Dec Civ Wed 300

Premier Inn Manchester Airport

BUDGET HOTEL

☎ 0871 527 8726 📠 0871 527 8727
Runger Ln, Wilmslow Rd M90 5DL
dir: M56 junct 6, follow Wilmslow & Hale signs. Merge onto M56 signed Warrington, Macclesfield & Hale. Left into Runger Ln (signed Freight Terminal)

High quality, budget accommodation ideal for both families and business travellers. Spacious, en suite bedrooms feature tea and coffee making facilities, and Freeview TV in most hotels. Internet access and Wi-fi are available for a small fee. The adjacent family restaurant features a wide and varied menu. See also the Hotel Groups pages.

Rooms 195 **D** £45*

Premier Inn Manchester Airport (FT)

BUDGET HOTEL

☎ 0871 527 8730 📠 0871 527 8731
Runger Ln, Wilmslow Rd M90 5DL
dir: M56 junct 6, follow Airport signs. 2nd exit at rdbt. Hotel on left. Through Travelodge car park. Hotel on right

Rooms 166 **D** £45*

Premier Inn Manchester (Handforth)

BUDGET HOTEL

☎ 0871 527 8732 📠 0871 527 8733
30 Wilmslow Rd SK9 3EW
dir: M56 junct 6, A538 towards Wilmslow. At main junct into town centre bear left. In 2m hotel at top of hill on right just after Wilmslow Garden Centre

Rooms 35 **D** £57-£59*

Premier Inn Manchester (Wilmslow)

BUDGET HOTEL

☎ 0871 527 8736 📠 0871 527 8737
Racecourse Rd SK9 5LR
dir: M6 junct 19 to Knutsford, follow Wilmslow signs. Left at 1st & 2nd lights towards Wilmslow. Through Mobberley, left just before Bird in Hand pub. At T-junct, right. Hotel 150yds on right

Rooms 37 **D** £57-£59*

MANSFIELD
Nottinghamshire — Map 16 SK56

Pine Lodge

★★ 70% SMALL HOTEL

☎ 01623 622308 📠 01623 656819
281-283 Nottingham Rd NG18 4SE
e-mail: enquiries@pinelodge-hotel.co.uk
web: www.pinelodge-hotel.co.uk
dir: On A60 (Nottingham to Mansfield road), hotel 1m S of Mansfield

Located on the edge of Mansfield, this hotel offers welcoming and personal service to its guests - many return time and again. The public rooms include a comfortable lounge bar, a cosy restaurant and a choice of meeting and function rooms. Bedrooms are thoughtfully equipped and are carefully maintained; a suite is available.

Rooms 20 (2 fmly) **S** £36-£62; **D** £67-£72 (incl. bkfst) **Facilities** STV FTV Wi-fi **Conf** Class 30 Board 35 Thtr 50 Del from £73 to £132 **Parking** 40 **Notes** ® Closed 25-26 Dec

MARAZION
Cornwall — Map 2 SW53

Mount Haven Hotel & St Michaels Restaurant

★★★ 84% @@ HOTEL

☎ 01736 710249 📠 01736 711658
Turnpike Rd TR17 0DQ
e-mail: reception@mounthaven.co.uk
web: www.mounthaven.co.uk
dir: A30 towards Penzance. At rdbt take onto A394. Next rdbt right into Marazion, hotel on left

This hotel enjoys spectacular views across the sea towards St Michaels Mount; all rooms have spacious balconies from where the views can be enjoyed - sunrises and sunsets can be spectacular. Bedrooms are contemporarily styled and have comfortable beds and exotic fabrics. Dining is a highlight with the freshest local seafood and fish used to create interesting menus. A range of holistic therapies is available. The attentive and friendly service helps make a relaxing and enchanting environment throughout.

Rooms 18 (1 fmly) (6 GF) **Facilities** FTV Aromatherapy Reflexology Massage Reiki Hot rocks Wi-fi **Parking** 30 **Notes** LB ® Closed 20 Dec-5 Feb

M

Marazion

★★ 74% SMALL HOTEL

☎ 01736 710334
The Square TR17 0AP
e-mail: enquiries@marazionhotel.co.uk
web: www.marazionhotel.co.uk
dir: A30 to Penzance, at rdbt follow St Michael's Mount signs. Hotel on left

Within 50 yards of one of Cornwall's safest beaches, this family run hotel, offers a relaxed atmosphere with friendly service. The individually furnished and decorated bedrooms are comfortable, many with the benefit of stunning views across to St Michael's Mount. The hotel incorporates the Cutty Sark public bar and restaurant, where a wide range of meals is offered to suit all palates and budgets.

Rooms 10 (3 fmly) **S** £72-£109; **D** £88-£134 (incl. bkfst)* **Facilities** FTV Xmas Wi-fi **Parking** 20 **Notes** ®

MARCH
Cambridgeshire
Map 12 TL49

Oliver Cromwell Hotel

★★★ 70% HOTEL

☎ 01354 602890 📠 01354 602891
High St PE15 9LH
e-mail: reception@olivercromwellhotel.co.uk
dir: In village centre

This purpose built hotel is ideally situated for touring the Cambridgeshire countryside, and within easy reach of Ely and Wisbech. The spacious bedrooms are pleasantly decorated and thoughtfully equipped. Public rooms include a smart lounge bar and a dining room as well as conference and banqueting facilities.

Rooms 42 (2 fmly) (8 GF) **Facilities** FTV Gym Sauna Steam room Wi-fi **Conf** Class 80 Board 40 Thtr 120 **Services** Lift Air con **Parking** 60 **Notes** Civ Wed 100

MARGATE
Kent
Map 7 TR37

Smiths Court

★★★ HOTEL

☎ 01843 222310 📠 01843 222312
Eastern Esplanade, Cliftonville CT9 2HL
e-mail: info@smithscourt.co.uk
dir: From clocktower on seafront, left onto A28 for approx 1m. Hotel on right Eastern Esplanade at junct with Godwin Rd

Rooms 43 (10 fmly) (4 GF) **Facilities** FTV Gym New Year Wi-fi **Conf** Class 50 Board 80 Thtr 80 **Services** Lift **Parking** 15 **Notes** Civ Wed 80

Premier Inn Margate

BUDGET HOTEL

☎ 0871 527 8762 📠 0871 527 8763
Station Green, Station Rd CT9 5AF
dir: M2, A299, A28 to Margate seafront. Hotel adjacent to Margate station

High quality, budget accommodation ideal for both families and business travellers. Spacious, en suite bedrooms feature tea and coffee making facilities, and Freeview TV in most hotels. Internet access and Wi-fi are available for a small fee. The adjacent family restaurant features a wide and varied menu. See also the Hotel Groups pages.

Rooms 44 **D** £69*

MARKET DRAYTON
Shropshire
Map 15 SJ63

Goldstone Hall

★★★ 83% HOTEL

☎ 01630 661202 📠 01630 661585
Goldstone TF9 2NA
e-mail: enquiries@goldstonehall.com
dir: 4m S of Market Drayton off A529 signed Goldstone Hall Hotel. 4m N of Newport signed from A41

Situated in extensive grounds, this period property is a family-run hotel. It provides traditionally furnished, well-equipped bedrooms with outstanding bathrooms and lots of thoughtful extras. Public rooms are extensive and include a choice of lounges, a snooker room and a conservatory. The hotel has a well deserved reputation for good food that utilises home-grown produce. A warm welcome is assured.

Rooms 12 (2 GF) **S** £140; **D** £210 (incl. bkfst & dinner)* **Facilities** STV FTV Snooker table New Year Wi-fi **Conf** Class 30 Board 30 Thtr 50 **Parking** 60 **Notes** LB Civ Wed 100

Ternhill Farm House & The Cottage Restaurant

RESTAURANT WITH ROOMS

☎ 01630 638984
Ternhill TF9 3PX
e-mail: info@ternhillfarm.co.uk
web: www.ternhillfarm.co.uk
dir: On junct A53 & A41, archway off A53

The elegant Grade II listed Georgian farmhouse stands in a large pleasant garden and has been modernised to provide quality accommodation. There is a choice of comfortable lounges, and the Cottage Restaurant features imaginative dishes using local produce. Secure parking is an additional benefit.

Rooms 5 (2 fmly)

MARKET HARBOROUGH
Leicestershire
Map 11 SP78

Best Western Three Swans

★★★ 77% HOTEL

☎ 01858 466644 📠 01858 433101
21 High St LE16 7NJ
e-mail: sales@threeswans.co.uk
web: www.bw-threeswanshotel.co.uk
dir: M1 junct 20, A304 to Market Harborough. Through town centre on A6 from Leicester, hotel on right

Public areas in this former coaching inn include an elegant fine dining restaurant and cocktail bar, a smart foyer lounge and popular public bar areas. Bedroom styles and sizes vary, but are very well appointed and equipped. Those in the wing are particularly impressive, offering high quality and spacious accommodation.

Rooms 61 (48 annexe) (8 fmly) (20 GF) **S** £50-£79; **D** £50-£90.50 (incl. bkfst) **Facilities** STV Xmas New Year Wi-fi **Conf** Class 90 Board 50 Thtr 250 Del from £120 to £145 **Services** Lift **Parking** 100 **Notes** LB Civ Wed 140

Premier Inn Market Harborough

BUDGET HOTEL

☎ 0871 527 8764 📠 0871 527 8765
Melton Rd, East Langton LE16 7TG
dir: On A6, N of Market Harborough. Hotel on rdbt junct of A6 & B6047

High quality, budget accommodation ideal for both families and business travellers. Spacious, en suite bedrooms feature tea and coffee making facilities, and Freeview TV in most hotels. Internet access and Wi-fi are available for a small fee. The adjacent family restaurant features a wide and varied menu. See also the Hotel Groups pages.

Rooms 40 **D** £49-£59*

MARKET RASEN Map 17 TF18
Lincolnshire

The Advocate Arms

RESTAURANT WITH ROOMS

☎ 01673 842364
2 Queen St LN8 3EH
e-mail: info@advocatearms.co.uk
dir: In town centre

Appointed to a high standard this 18th-century property is located in the heart of Market Rasen and combines historic character and contemporary design. The operation centres around the stylish restaurant where service is friendly yet professional and the food is a highlight. The attractive bedrooms are very well equipped and feature luxury bathrooms.

Rooms 10 (2 fmly)

MARKFIELD Map 11 SK40
Leicestershire

Field Head Hotel

OldEnglish

★★★ 70% HOTEL

☎ 01530 245454 📠 01530 243740
Markfield Ln LE6 9PS
e-mail: 9160@greeneking.co.uk
web: www.oldenglish.co.uk
dir: M1 junct 22, towards Leicester. At rdbt turn left, then right

This conveniently situated hotel dates back to the 17th century when it was a farmhouse; it has been considerably extended over the years. Within the public areas, the bar and lounge are the focal point for residents and non-residents alike, whilst meals can be taken either in the bar or the dining room. Bedrooms are modern and well furnished and offer good all-round comforts and facilities. Four large feature bedrooms are available.

Rooms 28 (1 fmly) (13 GF) **S** £90; **D** £100 (incl. bkfst) **Facilities** FTV ♫ Xmas New Year Wi-fi **Conf** Class 30 Board 36 Thtr 60 **Parking** 65 **Notes** LB Civ Wed 50

MARKINGTON Map 19 SE26
North Yorkshire

Hob Green Hotel

★★★ 82% COUNTRY HOUSE HOTEL

☎ 01423 770031 📠 01423 771589
HG3 3PJ
e-mail: info@hobgreen.com
web: www.hobgreen.com
dir: From A61, 4m N of Harrogate, left at Wormald Green, follow hotel signs

This hospitable country house is set in delightful gardens amidst rolling countryside midway between Harrogate and Ripon. The inviting lounges boast open fires in season and there is an elegant restaurant with a small private dining room. The individually designed bedrooms are very comfortable and come with a host of thoughtful extras.

Rooms 12 (1 fmly) **S** £95-£100; **D** £120-£135 (incl. bkfst) **Facilities** FTV Xmas New Year Wi-fi **Conf** Class 10 Board 10 Thtr 15 Del from £135 to £165 **Parking** 40 **Notes** LB Civ Wed 35

See advert on this page

MARLBOROUGH Map 5 SU16
Wiltshire

The Castle & Ball

OldEnglish

★★★ 70% HOTEL

☎ 01672 515201 📠 01672 515895
High St SN8 1LZ
e-mail: castleandballmarlboroughreservations@greeneking.co.uk
web: www.oldenglish.co.uk
dir: A338 and A4 to Marlborough

This traditional coaching inn in the town centre offers contemporary and very well equipped bedrooms. Open-plan public areas include a comfortable bar/lounge area and a smartly appointed restaurant, which serves food all day. Meeting rooms are also available.

Rooms 35 (1 annexe) (5 fmly) **Facilities** Xmas New Year Wi-fi **Conf** Class 30 Board 30 Thtr 45 **Parking** 48

M

MARLOW
Buckinghamshire
Map 5 SU88

INSPECTORS' CHOICE

Macdonald Compleat Angler

★★★★ ◉◉◉ HOTEL

☎ 0844 879 9128 🖷 01628 486388
Marlow Bridge SL7 1RG
e-mail: compleatangler@macdonald-hotels.co.uk
web: www.macdonald-hotels.co.uk/compleatangler
dir: M4 junct 8/9, A404(M) to rdbt, Bisham exit, 1m to Marlow Bridge, hotel on right

This well-established hotel enjoys an idyllic location overlooking the River Thames and the delightful Marlow weir. The bedrooms, which differ in size and style, are all individually decorated and are equipped with flat-screen satellite TVs, high speed internet and air conditioning; some rooms have balconies with views of the weir and some have four-posters. Aubergine (a sister restaurant to the restaurant of the same name in Chelsea) has three AA rosettes and offers modern French cuisine; Bowaters serves British dishes and has gained two AA rosettes. In summer guests can use two boats that the hotel has moored on the river and the fishing is, of course, a popular activity - a ghillie can accompany guests if prior arranged. Staff throughout are keen to please and nothing is too much trouble.

Rooms 64 (6 fmly) (6 GF) **D** £130-£270 (incl. bkfst) **Facilities** STV Fly & coarse fishing River trips (Apr-Sep) Xmas New Year Wi-fi **Conf** Class 65 Board 36 Thtr 150 Del from £220 to £280 **Services** Lift **Parking** 100 **Notes** LB Civ Wed 120

Crowne Plaza Marlow

★★★★ 82% ◉ HOTEL

☎ 01628 496800 🖷 01628 496959
Field House Ln SL7 1GJ
e-mail: enquiries@crowneplazamarlow.co.uk
web: www.crowneplazamarlow.co.uk
dir: A404 exit to Marlow, left at mini rdbt, left into Field House Lane

This hotel is in the Thames Valley not far from Windsor, Henley-on-Thames and the motorway. The public areas are air conditioned and include the Agua café and bar and the Glaze Restaurant. Leisure facilities include an up-to-the-minute gym and large pool. The bedrooms, including six contemporary suites, enjoy plenty of natural light and have excellent workstations; the Club Rooms have European and US power points

Rooms 168 (47 fmly) (56 GF) (11 smoking) **Facilities** Spa STV FTV Gym Sauna Steam room Dance studio Xmas New Year Wi-fi **Conf** Class 180 Board 30 Thtr 450 **Services** Lift Air con **Parking** 300 **Notes** LB ⊗ Civ Wed 400

Danesfield House Hotel & Spa

★★★★ 81% ◉◉◉◉ HOTEL

☎ 01628 891010 🖷 01628 890408
Henley Rd SL7 2EY
e-mail: reservations@danesfieldhouse.co.uk
web: www.danesfieldhouse.co.uk
dir: 2m from Marlow on A4155 towards Henley

Set in 65 acres of elevated grounds just 45 minutes from central London and 30 minutes from Heathrow, this hotel enjoys spectacular views across the River Thames. Impressive public rooms include the cathedral-like Great Hall, an impressive spa, and The Orangery for informal dining. The beautiful Oak Room Restaurant is an ideal setting to enjoy superb, imaginative fine dining. Some bedrooms have balconies and stunning views. Nothing is too much trouble for the team of committed staff.

Rooms 84 (3 fmly) (27 GF) **S** £135-£195; **D** £150-£345 (incl. bkfst)* **Facilities** Spa STV Putt green Gym Jogging trail Steam room Hydrotherapy room Treatment rooms Xmas New Year Wi-fi **Conf** Class 60 Board 50 Thtr 100 Del from £235 to £370* **Services** Lift **Parking** 100 **Notes** LB ⊗ Civ Wed 100

See advert on this page

Premier Inn Marlow

BUDGET HOTEL

☎ 0871 527 8767 📠 0871 5278767

The Causeway SL7 2AA

dir: M40 junct 4, A404 signed Marlow/Maidenhead. Left, follow A4155 signs to Marlow. At 3rd rdbt 1st exit into High St, signed Bisham. Straight on at mini rdbt. Hotel on left

High quality, budget accommodation ideal for both families and business travellers. Spacious, en suite bedrooms feature tea and coffee making facilities, and Freeview TV in most hotels. Internet access and Wi-fi are available for a small fee. The adjacent family restaurant features a wide and varied menu. See also the Hotel Groups pages.

D £60-£80*

MARSDEN — West Yorkshire — Map 16 SE01

The Olive Branch Restaurant with Rooms

RESTAURANT WITH ROOMS

☎ 01484 844487

Manchester Rd HD7 6LU

e-mail: eat@olivebranch.uk.com

web: www.olivebranch.uk.com

dir: 1m NE of Marsden on A62

The Olive Branch, once a roadside inn, was developed into a popular restaurant with three comfortable bedrooms. The menu features the best of seasonal produce cooked with flair and enthusiasm. The surrounding countryside has many historic attractions and offers pleasant walking opportunities.

Rooms 3

MARSTON — Lincolnshire — Map 11 SK84

The Olde Barn

★★★ 73% HOTEL

☎ 01400 250909 📠 01400 250130

Toll Bar Rd NG32 2HT

e-mail: reservations@theoldebarnhotel.co.uk

dir: From A1 N: left to Marston by petrol station. From A1 S: 1st right after Allington/Belton exit

Located in the countryside one mile from the A1, this sympathetically renovated and extended former period barn provides a range of thoughtfully furnished bedrooms, ideal for both business and leisure customers. Imaginative food is offered in the attractive beamed restaurant, and extensive leisure facilities include a swimming pool, sauna, steam room and a well-equipped gym.

Rooms 103 (11 fmly) (51 GF) (6 smoking) **S** £55-£65; **D** fr £65* **Facilities** Spa STV FTV Gym Xmas New Year Wi-fi **Conf** Class 180 Board 100 Thtr 300 Del from £135 to £145 **Services** Lift **Parking** 280 **Notes** LB Civ Wed 250

MASHAM — North Yorkshire — Map 19 SE28

INSPECTORS' CHOICE

Swinton Park

★★★★ HOTEL

☎ 01765 680900 📠 01765 680901

HG4 4JH

e-mail: reservations@swintonpark.com

web: www.swintonpark.com

dir: A1 onto B6267/8 to Masham. Follow signs through town centre & turn right into Swinton Terrace. 1m past golf course, over bridge, up hill. Hotel on right

Although extended during the Victorian and Edwardian eras, the original part of this welcoming castle dates from the 17th century. Bedrooms are luxuriously furnished and come with a host of thoughtful extras. Samuel's restaurant (built by the current owner's great-great-great grandfather) is very elegant and serves imaginative dishes using local produce. The majority of the food is sourced from the 20,000-acre Swinton Estate, as the hotel, winner of several green awards, is committed to keeping the 'food miles' to a minimum. The gardens, including a four-acre walled garden, have been gradually restored. The Deerhouse is the venue for the hotel's alfresco food festivals, summer BBQs and weddings.

Rooms 30 (5 fmly) **D** £180-£375 (incl. bkfst)* **Facilities** Spa FTV 9 Putt green Fishing Gym Shooting Falconry Pony trekking Cookery school Off-road driving Xmas New Year Wi-fi Child facilities **Conf** Class 60 Board 40 Thtr 120 **Services** Lift **Parking** 50 **Notes** LB Civ Wed 120

The Kings Head

★★ 72% HOTEL

☎ 01765 689295 📠 01765 689070

Market Place HG4 4EF

e-mail: kings.head.6395@thespiritgroup.com

dir: From A1 take B6267 or A6108 to Masham, follow Market Place signs

This historic hotel, with its uneven floors, beamed bars and attractive window boxes, looks out over the large market square. Guests have the option of choosing either the bedrooms in the main building or the spacious Coach House rooms at the rear of the property; all rooms are thoughtfully equipped. Public areas are traditional in style and include the restaurant serving interesting, freshly-prepared dishes.

Rooms 27 (15 annexe) (4 fmly) (10 GF) **Facilities** FTV Wi-fi **Conf** Class 24 Board 30 Thtr 54 **Parking** 3 **Notes**

MATFEN — Northumberland — Map 21 NZ07

Matfen Hall

PRIMA

★★★★ 81% HOTEL

☎ 01661 886500 & 855708 📠 01661 886055

NE20 0RH

e-mail: info@matfenhall.com

web: www.matfenhall.com

dir: Off A69 to B6318. Hotel just before village

This fine mansion lies in landscaped parkland overlooking its own golf course. Bedrooms are a blend of contemporary and traditional, but all are very comfortable and well equipped. Impressive public rooms include a splendid drawing room and the elegant Library and Print Room Restaurant, as well as a conservatory bar and very stylish spa, leisure and conference facilities.

Rooms 53 (11 fmly) **Facilities** Spa STV FTV supervised 27 Putt green Gym Sauna Steam room Salt grotto Ice fountain Aerobics Driving range Golf academy Xmas Wi-fi **Conf** Class 46 Board 40 Thtr 120 **Services** Lift **Parking** 150 **Notes** Civ Wed 120

M

MATLOCK
Derbyshire
Map 16 SK35

The Red House Country Hotel

★★ 85% SMALL HOTEL

☎ 01629 734854
Old Rd, Darley Dale DE4 2ER
e-mail: enquiries@theredhousecountryhotel.co.uk
web: www.theredhousecountryhotel.co.uk
dir: Off A6 onto Old Rd signed Carriage Museum, 2.5m N of Matlock

A peaceful country hotel set in delightful Victorian gardens. Rich colour schemes are used to excellent effect throughout. The well-equipped bedrooms include three ground floor rooms in the adjacent coach house. A comfortable lounge with delightful rural views is available for refreshments and pre-dinner drinks; service is friendly and attentive.

Rooms 9 (2 annexe) (2 GF) **S** £55-£70; **D** £105-£120 (incl. bkfst)* **Facilities** New Year Wi-fi **Conf** Class 10 Board 10 Thtr 10 Del from £135 to £155* **Parking** 12 **Notes** LB No children 12yrs Closed 1-14 Jan

MAWGAN PORTH
Cornwall
Map 2 SW86

M

The Scarlet Hotel

★★★★ 81% HOTEL

☎ 01637 861800 01637 861801
Tredragon Rd TR8 4DQ
e-mail: stay@scarlethotel.co.uk
dir: A39, A30 towards Truro. At Trekenning rdbt take A3059, follow Newquay Airport signs. Right after garage signed St Mawgan & Airport. Right after airport, right at T-junct signed Padstow (B3276). At Mawgan Porth left. Hotel 250yds on left

Built as an eco hotel, this strikingly modern property has a stunning cliff-top location with magnificent views and offers something a little different. The very stylish and well-equipped bedrooms are categorised in five types: Just Right, Generous, Unique, Spacious and Indulgent. The Ayurvedic spa is exceptional and encompasses the rejuvenation of the whole body and mind; relaxation is the key here. Cuisine is equally important, and in tune with the hotel's environment policies, daily changing menus feature fresh, seasonal and local produce. The team of 'hosts' offer a high level of hospitality and service.

Rooms 37 (5 GF) **S** £165-£415; **D** £180-£430 (incl. bkfst)* **Facilities** Spa FTV Yoga Xmas New Year **Conf** Board 16 **Services** Lift **Parking** 37 **Notes** LB No children 16yrs Closed 2 Jan-3 Feb Civ Wed 74

Bedruthan Steps Hotel

★★★★ 76% HOTEL

☎ 01637 860555 & 860860 01637 860714
TR8 4BU
e-mail: stay@bedruthan.com
dir: From A39/A30 follow signs to Newquay Airport. Past airport, right at T-junct to Mawgan Porth. Hotel at top of hill on left

With stunning views over Mawgan Porth Bay from the public rooms and the majority of the bedrooms, this is a child-friendly hotel. Children's clubs for various ages are provided in addition to children's dining areas and appropriate meals and times. A homage to architecture of the 1970s, with a modern, comfortable, contemporary feel, this hotel also has conference facilities. In the spacious restaurants, an imaginative fixed-price menu is offered; a short carte is available from Tuesdays to Saturdays.

Rooms 101 (60 fmly) (1 GF) **Facilities** Spa FTV Gym Jungle tumble ball pool Sauna Steam room Hydro pool Pool table Xmas New Year Wi-fi **Conf** Class 60 Board 40 Thtr 180 **Services** Lift **Parking** 100 **Notes** LB Closed 21-28 Dec Civ Wed 150

MAWNAN SMITH
Cornwall
Map 2 SW72

Budock Vean-The Hotel on the River

★★★★ 79% COUNTRY HOUSE HOTEL

☎ 01326 252100 & 0800 833927
01326 250892
TR11 5LG
e-mail: relax@budockvean.co.uk
web: www.budockvean.co.uk
dir: From A39 follow tourist signs to Trebah Gardens. 0.5m to hotel

Set in 65 acres of attractive, well-tended grounds, this peaceful hotel offers an impressive range of facilities. Convenient for visiting the Helford River Estuary and the many local gardens, or simply as a tranquil venue for a leisure break. Bedrooms are spacious and come in a choice of styles; some overlook the grounds and golf course.

Rooms 57 (2 fmly) **S** £69-£134; **D** £138-£268 (incl. bkfst & dinner)* **Facilities** Spa FTV 9 Putt green Private river boat & foreshore Xmas New Year Wi-fi **Conf** Class 40 Board 30 Thtr 60 **Services** Lift **Parking** 100 **Notes** Closed 3 wks Jan Civ Wed 65

Meudon

★★★ 85% COUNTRY HOUSE HOTEL

☎ 01326 250541 01326 250543
TR11 5HT
e-mail: wecare@meudon.co.uk
web: www.meudon.co.uk
dir: From Truro A39 towards Falmouth at Hillhead (Anchor & Cannons) rdbt, follow signs to Maenporth Beach. Hotel on left in 1m

This charming late Victorian mansion is a relaxing place to stay, with friendly hospitality and attentive service. It sits in impressive nine-acre, sub-tropical gardens that lead down to a private beach. The spacious and comfortable bedrooms are situated in a more modern building. The cuisine features the best local Cornish produce and is served in the conservatory restaurant.

Rooms 29 (2 fmly) (15 GF) **S** £94-£150; **D** £188-£300 (incl. bkfst & dinner)* **Facilities** FTV Fishing Private beach Hair salon Yacht for skippered charter Xmas Wi-fi **Conf** Class 20 Board 15 Thtr 30 Del from £ to £150* **Services** Lift **Parking** 50 **Notes** LB Closed 28 Dec-Jan

Trelawne

★★★ 77% HOTEL

☎ 01326 250226 01326 250909
TR11 5HS
e-mail: info@trelawnehotel.co.uk
web: www.trelawnehotel.co.uk
dir: A39 to Falmouth, right at Hillhead rdbt signed Maenporth. Past beach, up hill, hotel on left

This hotel is surrounded by attractive lawns and gardens, and enjoys superb coastal views. An informal atmosphere prevails, and many guests return year after year. Bedrooms, many with sea views, are of varying sizes, but all are well equipped. Dinner features quality local produce used in imaginative dishes.

Rooms 14 (2 fmly) (4 GF) **Parking** 20 **Notes** Closed end Nov-mid Feb

MELKSHAM
Wiltshire Map 4 ST96

Beechfield House Hotel, Restaurant & Gardens

★★★ 79% ® COUNTRY HOUSE HOTEL

☎ 01225 703700 📠 01225 790118
Beanacre SN12 7PU
e-mail: reception@beechfieldhouse.co.uk
web: www.beechfieldhouse.co.uk
dir: M4 junct 17, A350 S, bypass Chippenham, towards Melksham. Hotel on left after Beanacre

This is a charming, privately owned hotel set within eight acres of beautiful grounds that has its own arboretum. Bedrooms are individual styled and include four-poster rooms, and ground-floor rooms in the coach house. Relaxing public areas are comfortably furnished and there is a beauty salon with a range of pampering treatments available. At dinner there is a very good selection of carefully prepared dishes with an emphasis on seasonal and local produce.

Rooms 24 (6 fmly) (4 GF) **S** £; **D** £125-£175 (incl. bkfst)* **Facilities** FTV Beauty treatment room Xmas New Year Wi-fi **Conf** Class 60 Board 45 Thtr 100 **Parking** 70 **Notes** LB Civ Wed 70

Shaw Country

★★ 76% SMALL HOTEL

☎ 01225 702836 & 790321 📠 01225 790275
Bath Rd, Shaw SN12 8EF
e-mail: info@shawcountryhotel.com
web: www.shawcountryhotel.com
dir: 1m from Melksham, 9m from Bath on A365

Located within easy reach of both Bath and the M4, this relaxed and friendly hotel sits in its own gardens and includes a patio area ideal for enjoying a drink during the summer months. The house boasts very well-appointed bedrooms, a comfortable lounge and bar, and the Mulberry Restaurant, where a wide selection of innovative dishes make up both carte and set menus. A spacious function room is a useful addition.

Rooms 13 (2 fmly) **S** £65-£90; **D** £90-£110 (incl. bkfst)* **Facilities** FTV Wi-fi **Conf** Class 40 Board 20 Thtr 60 **Parking** 30 **Notes** RS 26-27 Dec & 1 Jan Civ Wed 90

MELTON MOWBRAY
Leicestershire Map 11 SK71

INSPECTORS' CHOICE

Stapleford Park

★★★★ ®® COUNTRY HOUSE HOTEL

☎ 01572 787000 📠 01572 787651
Stapleford LE14 2EF
e-mail: reservations@stapleford.co.uk
web: www.staplefordpark.com
dir: 1m SW of B676, 4m E of Melton Mowbray & 9m W of Colsterworth

This stunning mansion, dating back to the 14th century, sits in over 500 acres of beautiful grounds. Spacious, sumptuous public rooms include a choice of lounges and an elegant restaurant; an additional brasserie-style restaurant is located in the golf complex. The hotel also boasts a spa with health and beauty treatments and gym, plus horse-riding and many other country pursuits. Bedrooms are individually styled and furnished to a high standard. Attentive service is delivered with a relaxed yet professional style. Dinner, in the impressive dining room, is a highlight of any stay.

Rooms 55 (7 annexe) (10 fmly) **Facilities** Spa STV FTV 18 Putt green Fishing Gym Archery Croquet Falconry Horse riding Petanque Shooting Billiards Xmas New Year Wi-fi **Conf** Class 140 Board 80 Thtr 200 **Services** Lift **Parking** 120 **Notes** Civ Wed 150

Sysonby Knoll

★★★ 78% HOTEL

☎ 01664 563563 📠 01664 410364
Asfordby Rd LE13 0HP
e-mail: reception@sysonby.com
web: www.sysonby.com
dir: 0.5m from town centre on A6006

This well-established hotel is on the edge of town and set in attractive gardens. A friendly and relaxed atmosphere prevails and the many returning guests have become friends. Bedrooms, including superior rooms in the annexe, are generally spacious and thoughtfully equipped. There is a choice of lounges, a cosy bar, and a smart restaurant that offers carefully prepared meals.

Rooms 30 (7 annexe) (1 fmly) (7 GF) **S** £75-£103; **D** £95-£130 (incl. bkfst)* **Facilities** FTV Fishing Wi-fi **Conf** Class 25 Board 34 Thtr 50 **Parking** 48 **Notes** LB Closed 25 Dec-1 Jan

M

MELTON MOWBRAY *continued*

Scalford Hall

★★★ 74% HOTEL

☎ 0845 400 1403 🖹 01664 444487
Scalford Rd LE14 4UB
e-mail: sales@scalfordhall.co.uk
dir: A6006 towards Melton Mowbray. Left at 2nd lights into Scalford Rd, hotel 3m on left

Set in extensive grounds, Scalford Hall is just three miles north of Melton Mowbray. The bedrooms are tastefully furnished, and well equipped for both the business and leisure traveller; many have views over the gardens. Public rooms include a spacious lounge area and a small bar.

Rooms 88 (21 annexe) (6 fmly) (19 GF) **Facilities** FTV Putt green Gym New Year Wi-fi **Conf** Class 36 Board 40 Thtr 150 **Parking** 120 **Notes** LB Civ Wed 100

Quorn Lodge

★★★ 70% HOTEL

☎ 01664 566660 🖹 01664 480660
46 Asfordby Rd LE13 0HR
e-mail: quornlodge@aol.com
dir: From town centre take A6006. Hotel 300yds from junct of A606/A607 on right

Centrally located, this smart privately owned and managed hotel offers a comfortable and welcoming atmosphere. Bedrooms are individually decorated and thoughtfully designed. The public rooms consist of a bright restaurant overlooking the garden, a cosy lounge bar and a modern function suite. High standards are maintained throughout and parking is a bonus.

Rooms 19 (2 fmly) (3 GF) **S** £30-£66; **D** £55-£85 (incl. bkfst)* **Facilities** STV FTV Wi-fi **Conf** Class 70 Board 80 Thtr 100 **Parking** 38 **Notes** LB ⊗ Civ Wed 80

M

MEMBURY MOTORWAY SERVICE AREA (M4) — Map 5 SU37
Berkshire

Days Inn Membury - M4

BUDGET HOTEL

☎ 01488 72336 🖹 01488 72336
Membury Service Area RG17 7TZ
e-mail: membury.hotel@welcomebreak.co.uk
web: www.welcomebreak.co.uk
dir: M4 between junct 14 & 15

This modern building offers accommodation in smart, spacious and well-equipped bedrooms, suitable for families and business travellers, and all with en suite bathrooms. Continental breakfast is available and other refreshments may be taken at the nearby family restaurant. See also the Hotel Groups pages.

Rooms 38 (32 fmly) (17 GF) (5 smoking) **S** £39.93-£59.95; **D** £49.95-£59.95 **Conf** Board 10

MERIDEN — Map 10 SP28
West Midlands

Forest of Arden, A Marriott Hotel & Country Club

Marriott HOTELS & RESORTS

★★★★ 82% COUNTRY HOUSE HOTEL

☎ 01676 522335 🖹 01676 523711
Maxstoke Ln CV7 7HR
web: www.marriottforestofarden.co.uk
dir: M42 junct 6 onto A45 towards Coventry, over Stonebridge flyover. After 0.75m left into Shepherds Ln. Hotel 1.5m on left

The ancient oaks, rolling hills and natural lakes of the 10,000 acre Forest of Arden estate provide an idyllic backdrop for this modern hotel and country club. The hotel boasts an excellent range of leisure facilities and is regarded as one of the finest golfing destinations in the UK. Bedrooms provide every modern convenience and a full range of facilities.

Rooms 214 (65 GF) (5 smoking) **Facilities** Spa 18 Putt green Fishing Gym Floodlit golf academy New Year Wi-fi **Conf** Class 180 Board 40 Thtr 300 **Services** Lift **Parking** 300 **Notes** ⊗ Civ Wed 250

Manor Hotel

CLASSIC BRITISH HOTELS

★★★★ 73% HOTEL

☎ 01676 522735 🖹 01676 522186
Main Rd CV7 7NH
e-mail: reservations@manorhotelmeriden.co.uk
web: www.manorhotelmeriden.co.uk
dir: M42 junct 6, A45 towards Coventry then A452 signed Leamington. At rdbt take B4102 signed Meriden, hotel on left

A sympathetically extended Georgian manor in the heart of a sleepy village is just a few minutes away from the M6, M42 and National Exhibition Centre. The Regency Restaurant offers modern dishes, while Houston's serves lighter meals and snacks. The bedrooms are smart and well equipped.

Rooms 110 (20 GF) **S** £55-£150; **D** £55-£150* **Facilities** FTV Wi-fi **Conf** Class 150 Board 60 Thtr 250 Del from £110 to £180* **Services** Lift **Parking** 200 **Notes** LB RS 24 Dec-2 Jan Civ Wed 150

MEVAGISSEY — Map 2 SX04
Cornwall

Trevalsa Court Hotel

★★★ 78% HOTEL

☎ 01726 842468
School Hill, Polstreath PL26 6TH
e-mail: stay@trevalsa-hotel.co.uk
web: www.trevalsa-hotel.co.uk
dir: From St Austell take B3273 to Mevagissey. Pass sign to Pentewan. At top of hill left at x-rds. Hotel signed

Very well located above the town of Mevagissey with easy access to nearby attractions, this establishment is an Arts & Crafts style property appointed to a high standard throughout with lots of original features retained. Bedrooms, many with sea views, are comfortable and well presented; there is also a stylish guests' sitting room with views across the bay.

Rooms 13 (3 GF) **Facilities** FTV Wi-fi **Parking** 20 **Notes** Closed Dec & Jan

Tremarne

★★ 83% HOTEL

☎ 01726 842213 🖹 01726 843420
Polkirt PL26 6UY
e-mail: info@tremarne-hotel.co.uk
dir: From A390 at St Austell take B3273 to Mevagissey. Follow Portmellon signs through Mevagissey. At top of Polkirt Hill 1st right into Higherwell Park. Hotel drive facing

A very popular hotel, set in landscaped gardens with a swimming pool, that has superb views across to Mevagissey. The friendliness of Michael, Fitz and the team cannot be bettered. The hotel offers comfortable, individually styled bedrooms that either have views of the sea or the countryside, good service and freshly cooked food from a daily-changing menu.

Rooms 13 (2 fmly) **Facilities** FTV New Year Wi-fi **Parking** 14 **Notes** LB ⊗ No children 6yrs Closed Jan

MEXBOROUGH — Map 16 SE40
South Yorkshire

Best Western Pastures

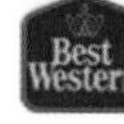

★★★ 80% HOTEL

☎ 01709 577707 🖹 01709 577795
Pastures Rd S64 0JJ
e-mail: info@pastureshotel.co.uk
web: www.pastureshotel.co.uk
dir: 0.5m from town centre on A6023, left by ATS Tyres, signed Denaby Ings & Cadeby. Hotel on right

This private hotel is in a rural setting beside a working canal with view of Conisbro Castle in the distance, and is convenient for Doncaster or the Dearne Valley with its nature reserves and leisure centre. Guests can dine in the Pastures Lodge pub and family restaurant situated opposite the hotel, or in Reeds fine dining restaurant in the hotel (open Tuesday-Saturday). Bedrooms, in a modern, purpose-built block, are quiet, comfortable and equipped with many modern facilities.

Rooms 60 (5 fmly) (28 GF) **S** fr £60; **D** fr £70 (incl. bkfst)* **Facilities** STV Xmas New Year Wi-fi **Conf** Class 170 Board 100 Thtr 250 Del from £100 to £118* **Services** Lift **Parking** 179 **Notes** LB ⊗ Civ Wed 200

MICHAELWOOD MOTORWAY SERVICE AREA (M5) — Map 4 ST79
Gloucestershire

Days Inn Michaelwood - M5

BUDGET HOTEL

☎ 01454 261513 📠 01454 269150
Michaelwood Service Area, Lower Wick GL11 6DD
e-mail: michaelwood.hotel@welcomebreak.co.uk
web: www.welcomebreak.co.uk
dir: M5 N'bound between junct 13 & 14

This modern building offers accommodation in smart, spacious and well-equipped bedrooms, suitable for families and business travellers, and all with en suite bathrooms. Continental breakfast is available and other refreshments may be taken at the nearby family restaurant. See also the Hotel Groups pages.

Rooms 38 (34 fmly) (5 smoking) **S** £39.95-£59.95; **D** £49.95-£69.95 **Conf** Board 10

MIDDLESBROUGH — Map 19 NZ41
North Yorkshire

Thistle Hotel Middlesbrough

thistle

★★★★ 73% HOTEL

☎ 0871 376 9028 & 01642 232000
📠 0871 376 9128
Fry St TS1 1JH
e-mail: middlesbrough@thistle.co.uk
web: www.thistlehotels.com/middlesbrough
dir: A19 onto A66 signed Middlesbrough. A66 after Zetland car park. 3rd exit at 1st rdbt, 2nd exit at 2nd rdbt

The staff here are committed to guest care and nothing is too much trouble. Located close to the town centre and football ground this establishment offers bedrooms of varying sizes, that are well furnished and comfortably equipped. The contemporary first-floor CoMotion café bar leads into the open-plan Gengis restaurant featuring an interesting range of globally inspired dishes. Guests have full use of the hotel's Otium health club. Thistle Hotels – AA Hotel Group of the Year 2011-12.

Rooms 132 (8 fmly) **S** £59-£179; **D** £59-£179* **Facilities** Spa STV FTV Gym Steam room Sauna Hair & beauty salon New Year Wi-fi **Conf** Class 144 Board 100 Thtr 400 Del from £125 to £145* **Services** Lift **Parking** 66 **Notes** LB Civ Wed 400

Best Western Middlesbrough

★★★ 72% HOTEL

☎ 01642 817638 📠 01642 821219
335 Marton Rd TS4 2PA
e-mail: middlesbrough@tavistockleisure.com
dir: From A66 onto A172 to Stokesley, right at rdbt, straight on at mini rdbt. Left at next mini rdbt, hotel 150yds on right

A modernised, small hotel in the residential suburbs offering comfortable and practical bedrooms. Informal dining is very popular in the Tavistock Italia restaurant where guests will find that is service is very friendly.

Rooms 32 (2 fmly) (9 GF) **S** £55-£78; **D** £65-£98 (incl. bkfst)* **Facilities** Wi-fi **Conf** Class 15 Board 15 Thtr 45 Del from £125 to £140* **Parking** 50 **Notes** LB ⊗

Premier Inn Middlesbrough Central South

BUDGET HOTEL

☎ 0871 527 8770 📠 0871 527 8771
Marton Way TS4 3BS
dir: Off A172 opposite South Cleveland Hospital complex

High quality, budget accommodation ideal for both families and business travellers. Spacious, en suite bedrooms feature tea and coffee making facilities, and Freeview TV in most hotels. Internet access and Wi-fi are available for a small fee. The adjacent family restaurant features a wide and varied menu. See also the Hotel Groups pages.

Rooms 74 **D** £54-£60*

MIDDLETON-IN-TEESDALE — Map 18 NY92
Co Durham

The Teesdale Hotel

★★ 65% HOTEL

☎ 01833 640264 📠 01833 640651
Market Place DL12 0QG
e-mail: enquiries@teesdalehotel.co.uk
web: www.teesdalehotel.co.uk
dir: From Barnard Castle take B6278, follow signs for Middleton-in-Teesdale & Highforce. Hotel in town centre

Located in the heart of the popular village, this family-run hotel offers a relaxed and friendly atmosphere. Bedrooms and bathrooms are well equipped and offer a good standard of quality and comfort. Public areas include a residents' lounge on the first floor, a spacious restaurant and a lounge bar which is popular with locals.

Rooms 14 (1 fmly) **S** £30-£45; **D** £55-£80 (incl. bkfst)* **Facilities** Wi-fi **Conf** Class 20 Board 20 Thtr 40 Del from £50 to £100* **Parking** 20 **Notes** LB

MIDDLETON STONEY — Map 11 SP52
Oxfordshire

Best Western Jersey Arms

★★ 76% HOTEL

☎ 01869 343234 & 343270 📠 01869 343565
OX25 4AD
e-mail: jerseyarms@bestwestern.co.uk
web: www.jerseyarms.co.uk
dir: 3m from A34, on B430, 10m N of Oxford, between junct 9 & 10 of M40

With a history dating back to the 13th century, the Jersey Arms combines old-fashioned charm with contemporary style and elegance. The individually designed bedrooms are well equipped and comfortable. The lounge has an open fire, and the smart and spacious restaurant provides a calm atmosphere in which to enjoy the popular cuisine.

Rooms 20 (14 annexe) (3 fmly) (9 GF) **S** £72-£79; **D** fr £79 (incl. bkfst)* **Facilities** FTV Xmas New Year Wi-fi **Conf** Class 20 Board 20 Thtr 20 Del from £95 to £150* **Parking** 55 **Notes** LB ⊗

M

MIDHURST
West Sussex Map 6 SU82

Spread Eagle Hotel and Spa

★★★ 81% ®® HOTEL

☎ 01730 816911 📠 01730 815668
South St GU29 9NH
e-mail: spreadeagle@hshotels.co.uk
web: www.hshotels.co.uk/spread/spreadeagle-main.htm
dir: M25 junct 10, A3 to Milford, take A286 to Midhurst. Hotel adjacent to market square

Offering accommodation since 1430, this historic property is full of character, evident in its sloping floors and inglenook fireplaces. Individually styled bedrooms provide modern comforts; those in the main house have oak panelling and include some spacious feature rooms. The hotel also boasts a well-equipped spa and offers noteworthy food in the oak beamed restaurant.

Rooms 38 (4 annexe) (8 GF) **S** £95-£340; **D** £125-£340 (incl. bkfst)* **Facilities** Spa STV FTV Gym Health & beauty treatment rooms Steam room Sauna Fitness trainer Xmas New Year Wi-fi **Conf** Class 40 Board 34 Thtr 80 Del from £135* **Parking** 75 **Notes** LB Civ Wed 120

MIDSOMER NORTON
Somerset Map 4 ST65

The Moody Goose at The Old Priory

®® RESTAURANT WITH ROOMS

☎ 01761 416784 📠 01761 417851
Church Square BA3 2HX
e-mail: info@theoldpriory.co.uk
dir: A362 for 1m left to High Street to lights, turn right to small rdbt by St John's church, turn right

Dating back to the 12th century, this relaxing establishment, with plenty of historic charm and character has been sensitively restored to maintain original features. The bedrooms, including one with a four-poster, are individually styled with plenty of welcome extras. The intimate, open-plan restaurant serves innovative, carefully prepared dishes utilising local produce whenever possible. There are two cosy lounges with log fires blazing in the colder months.

Rooms 6 (1 fmly)

MILDENHALL
Suffolk Map 12 TL77

The Olde Bull Inn

★★★ 83% ® HOTEL

☎ 01638 711001 📠 01638 712003
The Street, Barton Mills IP28 6AA
e-mail: bookings@bullinn-bartonmills.com
dir: Off A11 between Newmarket & Mildenhall, signed Barton Mills. Hotel by Five Ways rdbt

This delightful 16th-century coaching inn is lovingly care for by the owners. Public rooms offer a choice of bars, a brasserie-style restaurant and a further lounge area. The contemporary bedrooms are tastefully appointed with co-ordinated soft furnishings and many thoughtful touches.

Rooms 14 (2 annexe) (2 fmly) (2 GF) **S** £70-£99; **D** £85-£125 (incl. bkfst)* **Facilities** STV FTV Wi-fi **Conf** Class 20 Board 20 Thtr 30 **Parking** 60 **Notes** ® RS 25 Dec

See advert on page 363

MILFORD ON SEA
Hampshire Map 5 SZ29

Westover Hall Hotel

★★★ 88% ®® COUNTRY HOUSE HOTEL

☎ 01590 643044 📠 01590 644490
Park Ln SO41 0PT
e-mail: info@westoverhallhotel.com
dir: M3 & M27 W onto A337 to Lymington, follow signs to Milford on Sea onto B3058, hotel outside village centre towards cliff

Just a few moments' walk from the beach and boasting uninterrupted views across Christchurch Bay to the Isle of Wight in the distance, this late-Victorian mansion offers a relaxed, informal and friendly atmosphere together with efficient standards of hospitality and service. Bedrooms do vary in size and aspect, but all have been decorated with flair and style. Architectural delights include dramatic stained-glass windows, extensive oak panelling and a galleried entrance hall. The cuisine is prepared with much care and attention to detail.

Rooms 15 (3 annexe) (2 fmly) (2 GF) **S** £99-£210; **D** £120-£270 (incl. bkfst)* **Facilities** Xmas New Year Wi-fi **Conf** Class 14 Board 18 Thtr 35 Del from £200 **Parking** 50 **Notes** LB Civ Wed 90

See advert on opposite page

South Lawn

★★★ 67% HOTEL

☎ 01590 643911 📠 01590 645843
Lymington Rd SO41 0RF
e-mail: reservations.southlawn@ohiml.com
web: www.oxfordhotelsandinns.com
dir: M27 junct 1, A337 to Lymington, follow signs for Christchurch, in 3m left on B3058 signed Milford on Sea, hotel 1m on right

Close to the coast and enjoying a quiet location, this pleasant hotel is set in well tended and spacious grounds this hotel is a comfortable place to stay. Bedrooms are spacious and well appointed. Guests can relax or take afternoon tea in the lounge; the restaurant menu offers a good range of choice. Staff are friendly and attentive.

Rooms 24 (3 fmly) (3 GF) **Facilities** FTV Xmas New Year Wi-fi **Conf** Class 40 Board 30 Thtr 100 **Parking** 60 **Notes** Civ Wed 120

M

MILTON COMMON Map 5 SP60
Oxfordshire

The Oxfordshire

★★★★ 82% ® HOTEL

☎ 01844 278300 📠 01844 278003
Rycote Ln OX9 2PU
e-mail: gm@theoxfordshire.com
dir: M40 junct 7 N'bound (junct 8 S'bound), A329 towards Thame

Located within easy reach of the M40, this new hotel has been built at the championship golf course, The Oxfordshire, in the heart of the beautiful Chilterns. The accommodation offers impressive levels of comfort and quality and all rooms are air conditioned and have access onto a balcony. The Tempus Spa includes a 15-metre pool, modern gym and three treatment rooms. This resort makes an ideal location for a relaxing break.

Rooms 50 (18 GF) **Facilities** Spa FTV 18 Putt green Gym Sauna Steam room New Year Wi-fi **Conf** Class 66 Board 54 Thtr 180 Del from £165* **Services** Lift Air con **Parking** 150 **Notes** ⊗ Civ Wed

The Oxford Belfry

QHOTELS

★★★★ 79% HOTEL

☎ 01844 279381 📠 01844 279624
OX9 2JW
e-mail: oxfordbelfry@qhotels.co.uk
web: www.qhotels.co.uk
dir: M40 junct 7 onto A329 to Thame. Left onto A40, hotel 300yds on right

This modern hotel has a relatively rural location and enjoys lovely views of the countryside to the rear. The hotel is built around two very attractive courtyards and has a number of lounges and conference rooms, as well as indoor leisure facilities and outdoor tennis courts. Bedrooms are large and feature a range of extras.

Rooms 154 (20 fmly) (66 GF) **Facilities** Spa STV Gym Steam room Sauna Aerobics studio Xmas New Year Wi-fi **Conf** Class 180 Board 100 Thtr 450 Del from £135 to £190 **Services** Lift **Parking** 350 **Notes** LB Civ Wed 300

MILTON KEYNES Map 11 SP83
Buckinghamshire

See also **Aspley Guise**

Holiday Inn Milton Keynes

Holiday Inn

★★★★ 74% HOTEL

☎ 01908 698541 📠 01908 698685
500 Saxon Gate West MK9 2HQ
e-mail: reservations-miltonkeynes@ihg.com
web: www.holidayinn.co.uk/miltonkeynes
dir: M1 junct 14. Straight on at 7 rdbts. At 8th (Saxon South) turn right. Hotel after lights on left

Ideally located to explore central England, with both Oxford and Cambridge within an hour's drive, and central London just 40 minutes away by train. The hotel is a spacious, purpose-built, city-centre property offering a range of well-appointed bedrooms, conference rooms and a fully-equipped health club. The Junction restaurant offers a contemporary dining experience in a relaxing environment.

Rooms 166 (17 fmly) **S** £55-£252; **D** £55-£252 **Facilities** STV supervised Gym Sauna Beauty room Xmas New Year Wi-fi **Conf** Class 50 Board 50 Thtr 130 Del from £110 to £165 **Services** Lift Air con **Parking** 85 **Notes** LB ⊗ Civ Wed 70

Mercure Parkside

Mercure

★★★ 78% HOTEL

☎ 01908 661919 📠 01908 676186
Newport Rd, Woughton on the Green MK6 3LR
e-mail: H6627-gm@accor.com
web: www.mercure.com
dir: M1 junct 14/A509 towards Milton Keynes. 2nd exit on H6 follow signs to Woughton-on-the-Green

Situated in five acres of landscaped grounds in a peaceful village setting, this hotel is only five minutes' drive from the hustle and bustle of the town centre. Bedrooms are divided between executive rooms in the main house and standard rooms in the adjacent coach house. Public rooms include a range of meeting rooms, and Strollers bar. The Lanes Restaurant provides a comfortable venue where eclectic modern dishes are offered.

Rooms 49 (1 fmly) (19 GF) **Facilities** STV Free entry to health & fitness club (approx 2m) Xmas New Year Wi-fi **Conf** Class 60 Board 50 Thtr 150 **Parking** 75 **Notes** Civ Wed 120

Novotel Milton Keynes

★★★ 73% HOTEL

☎ 01908 322212 📠 01908 322235
Saxon St, Layburn Court, Heelands MK13 7RA
e-mail: H3272@accor.com
web: www.novotel.com
dir: M1 junct 14, follow Childsway signs towards city centre. Right into Saxon Way, straight across all rdbts, hotel on left

Contemporary in style, this purpose-built hotel is situated on the outskirts of the town, just a few minutes' drive from the centre and mainline railway station. Bedrooms provide ample workspace and a good range of facilities for the modern traveller, and

continued

M

MILTON KEYNES *continued*

public rooms include a children's play area and indoor leisure centre.

Rooms 124 (40 fmly) (40 GF) **Facilities** FTV Gym Steam bath Wi-fi **Conf** Class 75 Board 40 Thtr 120 Del from £120 to £165* **Services** Lift **Parking** 130 **Notes** Civ Wed 100

Ramada Encore Milton Keynes

★★★ 73% HOTEL

☎ 01908 545500 📄 01908 545530
312 Midsummer Boulevard MK9 2EA
e-mail: enquiries@encoremiltonkeynes.co.uk

This hotel is located in the heart of the town centre, close to the central railway station. The accommodation is stylish, contemporary and has all the modern comforts such as air conditioning and Wi-fi. There are two meeting rooms as well as an attractive bar and restaurant. Limited on-site parking is available, charged at a daily rate.

Rooms 159 (28 fmly) (16 smoking) **Facilities** STV Xmas New Year Wi-fi **Conf** Class 30 Board 30 Thtr 64 **Services** Lift Air con **Parking** 50 **Notes** LB

M

Broughton

OldEnglish

BUDGET HOTEL

☎ 01908 667726 📄 01908 604844
Broughton MK10 9AA
e-mail: broughtonhotel@greeneking.co.uk
web: www.oldenglish.co.uk
dir: M1 junct 14, at 1st rdbt A5130 signed Woburn, 600yds. Right for Broughton, hotel on left

This hotel is within easy reach of road networks and offers modern accommodation. Day rooms are dominated by an open-plan lounge bar and the Hungry Horse food concept, which proves particularly popular with young families.

Rooms 30 (2 fmly) (14 GF) **Conf** Class 30 Board 30 Thtr 80

Campanile Milton Keynes

Campanile

BUDGET HOTEL

☎ 01908 649819 📄 01908 649818
40 Penn Road (off Watling St), Fenny Stratford, Bletchley MK2 2AU
e-mail: miltonkeynes@campanile.com
dir: M1 junct 14, A4146 to A5. S'bound on A5. 4th exit at 1st rdbt to Fenny Stratford. Hotel 500yds on left

This modern building offers accommodation in smart, well-equipped bedrooms, all with en suite bathrooms. Refreshments may be taken at the informal bistro. See also the Hotel Groups pages.

Rooms 80 (26 GF) **Conf** Class 30 Board 30 Thtr 40

Holiday Inn Express Milton Keynes

BUDGET HOTEL

☎ 01908 681000 📄 01908 609429
Eastlake Park, Tongwell St MK15 0YA
e-mail: info@expressmiltonkeynes.co.uk
web: www.hiexpress.com/exmiltonkeynes
dir: M1 junct 14 follow sign for centre, at Northfields rdbt, straight across dual carriageway (H6) follow signs to Fox Milne 3rd exit V11

A modern hotel ideal for families and business travellers. Fresh and uncomplicated, the spacious rooms include Sky TV, power shower and tea and coffee-making facilities. Continental buffet breakfast is included in the room rate; other meals may be taken at the nearby family pub or restaurant. See also the Hotel Groups pages.

Rooms 178 (96 fmly) (47 GF) **S** £55-£120; **D** £55-£120 (incl. bkfst)* **Conf** Class 45 Board 45 Thtr 80 Del from £85 to £120*

Premier Inn Milton Keynes Central

BUDGET HOTEL

☎ 0871 527 8774 📄 0871 527 8775
Secklow Gate West MK9 3BZ
dir: M1 junct 14 follow H6 route over 6 rdbts, at 7th (South Secklow) turn right, hotel on left

High quality, budget accommodation ideal for both families and business travellers. Spacious, en suite bedrooms feature tea and coffee making facilities, and Freeview TV in most hotels. Internet access and Wi-fi are available for a small fee. The adjacent family restaurant features a wide and varied menu. See also the Hotel Groups pages.

Rooms 38 **D** £60-£72*

Premier Inn Milton Keynes East (Willen Lake)

BUDGET HOTEL

☎ 0871 527 8778 📄 0871 527 8779
Brickhill St, Willen Lake MK15 9HQ
dir: M1 junct 14 , H6 (Childsway). Right at 3rd rdbt into Brickhill St. Right at 1st mini rdbt, hotel 1st left

Rooms 41 **D** £52-£66*

Premier Inn Milton Keynes South

BUDGET HOTEL

☎ 0871 527 8780 📄 0871 527 8781
Lakeside Grove, Bletcham Way, Caldecotte MK7 8HP
dir: M1 junct 14, towards Milton Keynes on H6 (Childs Way). Straight on at 2 rdbts. Left at 3rd onto V10 (Brickhill St). Straight on at 5 rdbts, at 6th right onto H10 (Bletcham Way)

Rooms 41 **D** £52-£66*

Premier Inn Milton Keynes South West (Furzton Lake)

BUDGET HOTEL

☎ 0871 527 8776 📄 0871 527 8777
Shirwell Crescent, Furzton MK4 1GA
dir: M1 junct 14, A509 to Milton Keynes. Straight on at 8 rdbts, at 9th rdbt (North Grafton) left onto V6. Right at next onto H7. Over The Bowl rdbt, hotel on left

Rooms 120 **D** £52-£72*

MINEHEAD Somerset **Map 3 SS94**

Best Western Northfield

★★★ 74% HOTEL

☎ 01643 705155 & 0845 1302678
📄 01643 707715
Northfield Rd TA24 5PU
e-mail: reservations@northfield-hotel.co.uk
web: www.northfield-hotel.co.uk
dir: M5 junct 23, follow A38 to Bridgwater then A39 to Minehead

Located conveniently close to the town centre and the seafront, this hotel is set in delightfully maintained gardens and has a loyal following. A range of comfortable sitting rooms and leisure facilities, including an indoor, heated pool is provided. A fixed-price menu is served every evening in the oak-panelled dining room. The attractively co-ordinated bedrooms vary in size and are equipped to a good standard.

Rooms 30 (7 fmly) (4 GF) (6 smoking) **Facilities** STV FTV Putt green Gym Steam room Xmas New Year Wi-fi **Conf** Class 45 Board 30 Thtr 70 **Services** Lift **Parking** 34 **Notes** LB

Channel House

★★★ 74% SMALL HOTEL

☎ 01643 703229
Church Path TA24 5QG
e-mail: channelhouse@btconnect.com
dir: From A39 right at rdbt to seafront, left onto promenade. 1st right, 1st left to Blenheim Gdns,1st right into Northfield Rd

This family-run hotel offers relaxing surroundings, yet is only a short walk from the town centre. The South West coastal path starts from the hotel's two-acre gardens. Many of the exceptionally well-equipped bedrooms benefit from wonderful views. Imaginative menus are created from the best local produce. The hotel is totally non-smoking.

Rooms 8 **S** £98-£115; **D** £156-£190 (incl. bkfst & dinner)* **Facilities** FTV Wi-fi **Services** Air con **Parking** 10 **Notes** ⊗ No children 15yrs Closed Nov & 29 Dec-15 Mar

Alcombe House Hotel

★★ 85% HOTEL

☎ 01643 705130
Bircham Rd, Alcombe TA24 6BG
e-mail: alcombehouse@talktalkbusiness.net
web: www.alcombehouse.co.uk
dir: On A39 on outskirts of Minehead opposite West Somerset Community College

Located midway between Minehead and Dunster on the coastal fringe of Exmoor National Park, this Grade II listed, Georgian hotel offers a delightful combination of efficient service and genuine hospitality delivered by the very welcoming resident proprietors. Public areas include a comfortable lounge and a candlelit dining room where a range of carefully prepared dishes is offered from a daily-changing menu.

Rooms 7 **S** £45.50; **D** £71 (incl. bkfst)* **Facilities** FTV Xmas Wi-fi **Parking** 9 **Notes** No children 15yrs Closed 8 Nov-18 Mar

MONK FRYSTON — North Yorkshire — Map 16 SE52

Monk Fryston Hall

★★★ 81% COUNTRY HOUSE HOTEL

☎ 01977 682369 📠 01977 683544
LS25 5DU
e-mail: reception@monkfrystonhallhotel.co.uk
web: www.monkfrystonhallhotel.co.uk
dir: A1(M) junct 42/A63 towards Selby. Monk Fryston 2m, hotel on left

This delightful 16th-century mansion house enjoys a peaceful location in 30 acres of grounds, yet is only minutes' drive from the A1. Many original features have been retained and the public rooms are furnished with antique and period pieces. Bedrooms are individually styled and thoughtfully equipped for both business and leisure guests.

Rooms 29 (2 fmly) (5 GF) **S** £65-£79; **D** £115-£135 (incl. bkfst)* **Facilities** STV Xmas New Year Wi-fi **Conf** Class 30 Board 25 Thtr 70 Del from £125 to £140* **Parking** 80 **Notes** LB Civ Wed 72

MORECAMBE — Lancashire — Map 18 SD46

Clarendon

★★★ 71% HOTEL

☎ 01524 410180 📠 01524 421616
76 Marine Road West, West End Promenade LA4 4EP
e-mail: clarendon@mitchellshotels.co.uk
dir: M6 junct 34 follow Morecambe signs. At rdbt (with 'The Shrimp' on corner) 1st exit to Westgate, follow to seafront. Right at lights, hotel 3rd block

This traditional seafront hotel offers views over Morecambe Bay, modern facilities and convenient parking. An extensive fish and grill menu is offered in the contemporary Waterfront Restaurant and guests can relax in the comfortable lounge bar. Davy Jones Locker in the basement has a more traditional pub atmosphere and offers cask ales and regular live entertainment.

Rooms 29 (4 fmly) **S** £60; **D** £90 (incl. bkfst)* **Facilities** Xmas New Year Wi-fi **Conf** Class 40 Board 40 Thtr 90 **Services** Lift **Parking** 22 **Notes** Civ Wed 60

Hotel Prospect

★ 75% HOTEL

☎ 01524 417819 📠 01524 417819
363 Marine Road East LA4 5AQ
e-mail: peter@hotel-prospect.fsnet.co.uk

Situated on the promenade, this friendly, family-run establishment has panoramic views over the bay to the Lakeland mountains. Bedrooms are comfortably proportioned and thoughtfully furnished, and the bright dining room extends into a small lounge area which has a well-stocked bar and overlooks the sea.

Rooms 13 (4 fmly) (2 GF) **S** £25-£26; **D** £50-£52 (incl. bkfst)* **Facilities** Xmas **Parking** 14

MORETON — Merseyside — Map 15 SJ28

Leasowe Castle

★★★ 78% HOTEL

☎ 0151 606 9191 📠 0151 678 5551
Leasowe Rd CH46 3RF
e-mail: reservations@leasowecastle.com
web: www.leasowecastle.com
dir: M53 junct 1, 1st exit from rdbt onto A551. Hotel 0.75m on right

Located adjacent to Leasowe Golf Course and within easy reach of Liverpool, Chester and all of the Wirral's attractions, this historic hotel dates back to 1592. Bedrooms are smartly appointed and well equipped, many enjoying ocean views. Public areas retain many original features. Weddings and functions are well catered for.

Rooms 47 (3 fmly) **S** £60-£95; **D** £85-£120 (incl. bkfst)* **Facilities** FTV Gym Water sports Sea fishing Sailing Health club Xmas New Year Wi-fi **Conf** Class 200 Board 80 Thtr 400 Del from £99 to £125* **Services** Lift **Parking** 200 **Notes** Civ Wed 250

MORETONHAMPSTEAD — Devon — Map 3 SX78

Best Western The White Hart Hotel

★★★ 81% ◎ HOTEL

☎ 01647 441340 📠 01647 441341
The Square TQ13 8NQ
e-mail: enquiries@whitehartdartmoor.co.uk
dir: A30 towards Okehampton. At Whiddon Down take A382 for Moretonhampstead

Dating back to the 1700s, this former coaching inn is located on the edge of Dartmoor. A relaxed and friendly atmosphere prevails, with the staff providing attentive service. Comfortable bedrooms have a blend of traditional and contemporary styles with thoughtful extras provided. Dining is in either the brasserie restaurant or more informally in the bar where quality cuisine is served.

Rooms 28 (8 annexe) (6 fmly) (4 GF) (28 smoking) **Facilities** FTV Xmas New Year **Conf** Class 40 Board 40 Thtr 60 **Notes** Civ Wed 60

M

MORETON-IN-MARSH Map 10 SP23
Gloucestershire

Manor House

★★★★ 75% @@ HOTEL

☎ 01608 650501 📠 01608 651481
High St GL56 0LJ
e-mail: info@manorhousehotel.info
web: www.cotswold-inns-hotels.co.uk/manor
dir: Off A429 at south end of town. Take East St off High St, hotel car park 3rd right

Dating back to the 16th century, this charming Cotswold coaching inn retains much of its original character with stone walls, impressive fireplaces and a relaxed, country-house atmosphere. Bedrooms vary in size and reflect the individuality of the building; all are well equipped and some are particularly opulent. Comfortable public areas include a popular bar, a brasserie and the stylish Mulberry Restaurant where the chance to enjoy an evening meal should not be missed.

Rooms 35 (1 annexe) (3 fmly) (1 GF) **S** £120-£160; **D** £155-£195 (incl. bkfst)* **Facilities** Xmas New Year Wi-fi **Conf** Class 48 Board 54 Thtr 120 Del from £150* **Services** Lift **Parking** 24 **Notes** LB Civ Wed 120

White Hart Royal Hotel

★★★ 79% HOTEL

☎ 01608 650731 📠 01608 650880
High St GL56 0BA
e-mail: whr@bpcmail.co.uk
web: www.whitehartroyal.co.uk
dir: On High St at junct with Oxford Rd

This historic hotel has been providing accommodation for hundreds of years and has now completed a major refurbishment programme that has resulted in high standards of quality and comfort. Public areas are full of character, and the bedrooms, in a wide range of shapes and sizes, include several very spacious and luxurious rooms situated adjacent to the main building. A varied range of well prepared dishes is available throughout the day and evening in the main bar and the relaxing restaurant.

Rooms 28 (8 annexe) (2 fmly) (9 GF) **Facilities** STV FTV Xmas New Year Wi-fi **Conf** Class 40 Board 20 Thtr 55 **Notes** LB

Redesdale Arms

★★★ 78% @ HOTEL

☎ 01608 650308 📠 01608 651843
High St GL56 0AW
e-mail: info@redesdalearms.com
dir: On A429, 0.5m from rail station

This fine old inn has played a central role in the town for centuries. Traditional features combine successfully with contemporary comforts; bedrooms are located in the main building and in an annexe. Guests can choose from an imaginative menu in either in the stylish restaurant or the conservatory.

Rooms 24 (16 annexe) (2 fmly) (11 GF) **D** £65-£140 (incl. bkfst)* **Facilities** STV FTV Xmas New Year Wi-fi **Parking** 14 **Notes** LB ®

MORLEY Map 11 SK34
Derbyshire

The Morley Hayes Hotel

★★★★ 77% @ HOTEL

☎ 01332 780480 📠 01332 781094
Main Rd DE7 6DG
e-mail: hotel@morleyhayes.com
web: www.morleyhayes.com
dir: 4m N of Derby on A608

Located in rolling countryside this modern golfing destination provides extremely comfortable, stylish bedrooms with wide-ranging facilities, plasma TVs, and state-of-the-art bathrooms; the plush suites are particularly eye-catching. Creative cuisine is offered in the Dovecote Restaurant, and both Roosters and the Spikes sports bar provide informal eating options.

The Morley Hayes Hotel

Rooms 32 (4 fmly) (15 GF) **S** £80-£255; **D** £120-£276 (incl. bkfst)* **Facilities** STV ⛳ 27 Putt green Golf driving range Wi-fi **Conf** Class 50 Board 40 Thtr 120 Del from £147 to £169.95* **Services** Lift Air con **Parking** 245 **Notes** LB ® Civ Wed 90

MOTTRAM ST ANDREW Map 16 SJ87
Cheshire

De Vere Mottram Hall

DE VERE Hotels & Resorts

★★★★ 79% HOTEL

☎ 01625 828135 📠 01625 828950
Wilmslow Rd SK10 4QT
e-mail: dmh.sales@devere-hotels.com
web: www.devere.co.uk
dir: M6 junct 18 from S, M6 junct 20 from N, M56 junct 6, A538 Prestbury

Set in 272 acres of some of Cheshire's most beautiful parkland, this 18th-century Georgian country house is certainly an idyllic retreat. The hotel boasts extensive leisure facilities, including a championship golf course, swimming pool, gym and spa. Bedrooms are well equipped and elegantly furnished, and include a number of four-poster rooms and suites.

Rooms 131 (44 GF) **Facilities** Spa STV supervised ⛳ 18 Putt green Fishing Gym Squash Children's playground Rugby & football pitch Xmas New Year Wi-fi **Conf** Class 120 Board 60 Thtr 180 **Services** Lift **Parking** 300 **Notes** ® Civ Wed 160

MOUSEHOLE Map 2 SW42
Cornwall

Old Coastguard Hotel

★★ 82% HOTEL

☎ 01736 731222 📠 01736 731720
The Parade TR19 6PR
e-mail: bookings@oldcoastguardhotel.co.uk
dir: A30 to Penzance, coast road to Newlyn then Mousehole. 1st building on left on entering village

This hotel, with great views across Mounts Bay, has a good reputation and as popular as ever. The atmosphere is relaxed and informal, and staff are friendly and keen to help. Bedrooms are comfortable and well appointed, and many enjoy the fabulous views. Fresh local fish appears on the menus.

Rooms 14 (1 fmly) (6 GF) **S** £93.75-£161.25; **D** £125-£215 (incl. bkfst)* **Facilities** FTV Sub-tropical garden New Year Wi-fi **Parking** 14 **Notes** Closed 25 Dec & 9 Jan-2 Feb

The Cornish Range Restaurant with Rooms

RESTAURANT WITH ROOMS

01736 731488
6 Chapel St TR19 6BD
e-mail: info@cornishrange.co.uk
dir: From Penzance take B3315, through Newlyn to Mousehole. Along harbour, past Ship Inn, sharp right, left, establishment on right

This is a memorable place to eat and stay. Stylish rooms, with delightful Cornish home-made furnishings, and attentive, friendly service create a relaxing environment. Interesting and accurate cuisine relies heavily on freshly-landed, local fish and shellfish, as well as local meat and poultry, and the freshest fruit and vegetables.

Rooms 3

MUCH WENLOCK Map 10 SO69
Shropshire

Raven

★★★ 78% HOTEL

01952 727251 01952 728416
30 Barrow St TF13 6EN
e-mail: enquiry@ravenhotel.com
web: www.ravenhotel.com
dir: M54 junct 4 or 5, take A442 S, then A4169 to Much Wenlock

This town centre hotel is spread across several historic buildings with a 17th-century coaching inn at its centre. Accommodation is well furnished and equipped to offer modern comfort, with some ground floor rooms. Public areas feature an interesting collection of prints and memorabilia connected with the modern-day Olympic Games - an idea which was, interestingly, born in Much Wenlock.

Rooms 15 (7 annexe) **Facilities** Beauty salon **Conf** Board 16 Thtr 16 **Parking** 30 **Notes**

Gaskell Arms

★★★ 75% SMALL HOTEL

01952 727212 01952 728505
Bourton Rd TF13 6AQ
e-mail: maxine@gaskellarms.co.uk
web: www.gaskellarms.co.uk
dir: M6 junct 10A onto M54, exit at junct 4, follow signs for Ironbridge/Much Wenlock & A4169

This 17th-century former coaching inn has exposed beams and log fires in the public areas, and much original charm and character is retained throughout. In addition to the lounge bar and restaurant, offering a wide range of meals and snacks, there is a small bar which is popular with locals. Well-equipped bedrooms, some located in stylishly renovated stables, provide good standards of comfort.

Rooms 16 (3 fmly) (5 GF) **S** £70-£80; **D** £90-£115 (incl. bkfst)* **Facilities** FTV Wi-fi **Conf** Class 30 Board 20 Thtr 30 **Parking** 40 **Notes** LB

MUDEFORD

See Christchurch

MULLION Map 2 SW61
Cornwall

Mullion Cove Hotel

★★★ 79% HOTEL

01326 240328 01326 240998
TR12 7EP
e-mail: enquiries@mullion-cove.co.uk
dir: A3083 towards The Lizard. Through Mullion towards Mullion Cove. Hotel in approx 1m

Built at the turn of the last century and set high above the working harbour of Mullion, this hotel has spectacular views of the rugged coastline; seaward facing rooms are always popular. The stylish restaurant offers some carefully prepared dishes using local produce; an alternative option is to eat less formally in the bar. After dinner guests might like to relax in one of the elegant lounges.

Rooms 30 (3 fmly) (3 GF) **S** £60-£232.50; **D** £120-£310 (incl. bkfst)* **Facilities** FTV Xmas New Year Wi-fi **Conf** Class 20 Board 30 Thtr 50 Del from £100 to £150* **Services** Lift **Parking** 60 **Notes** LB

See advert on this page

M

MULLION *continued*

Polurrian

★★★ 77% HOTEL

☎ 01326 240421 🖹 01326 240083
TR12 7EN
e-mail: relax@polurrianhotel.com
web: www.polurrianhotel.com
dir: A394 to Helston, then follow The Lizard & Mullion signs, onto A3083. Approx 5m, right onto B3296 to Mullion. Follow one-way system to T-junct, turn left signed Mullion Cove. 0.5m turn right, follow hotel sign. Hotel at end of road

With spectacular views across St Mount's Bay, this is a well managed and relaxed hotel where guests are assured of a warm welcome from the friendly team of staff. In addition to the formal eating option, the High Point restaurant offers a more casual approach, open throughout the day and into the evening. The popular leisure club has a good range of equipment. Bedrooms vary in size, and the sea-view rooms are always in demand.

Rooms 39 (4 fmly) (8 GF) **S** £55-£104; **D** £110-£208 (incl. bkfst)* **Facilities** FTV Gym Children's games room & outdoor play area Xmas New Year Wi-fi Child facilities **Conf** Class 25 Board 26 Thtr 50 Del from £110 to £150* **Parking** 60 **Notes** Closed Jan-5 Feb Civ Wed 80

See advert on this page

M

NAILSWORTH Map 4 ST89
Gloucestershire

Wild Garlic Restaurant and Rooms

RESTAURANT WITH ROOMS

☎ 01453 832615
3 Cossack Square GL6 0DB
e-mail: info@wild-garlic.co.uk
dir: M4 junct 18. A46 towards Stroud. Enter Nailsworth, left at rdbt, immediate left. Establishment opposite Britannia Pub

Situated in a quiet corner of this charming Cotswold town, this restaurant with rooms offers a delightful combination of welcoming, relaxed hospitality and high quality cuisine. The spacious and well equipped bedrooms are situated above the restaurant. The small and friendly team of staff ensure guests are very well looked after throughout their stay.

Rooms 3 (2 fmly)

NANTWICH Map 15 SJ65
Cheshire

Rookery Hall Hotel and Spa

HandPICKED HOTELS

★★★★ 84% HOTEL

☎ 01270 610016 & 0845 072 7533
🖹 01270 615617
Main Rd, Worleston CW5 6DQ
e-mail: rookeryhall@handpicked.co.uk
web: www.handpickedhotels.co.uk/rookeryhall
dir: B5074 off 4th rdbt, on Nantwich by-pass. Hotel 1.5m on right

This fine 19th-century mansion is set in 38 acres of gardens, pasture and parkland. Bedrooms are spacious and appointed to a high standard with wide-screen plasma TVs and DVD players; many rooms have separate walk-in showers as well as deep tubs. Public areas are delightful and retain many original features. There is an extensive, state-of-the art spa and leisure complex.

Rooms 70 (39 annexe) (6 fmly) (23 GF) **S** £99-£162; **D** £109-£172 (incl. bkfst)* **Facilities** Spa STV Gym Sauna Crystal steam room Hydro therapy pool Xmas New Year Wi-fi **Conf** Class 90 Board 46 Thtr 200 Del from £139 to £159* **Services** Lift **Parking** 120 **Notes** Civ Wed 140

Alvaston Hall Hotel

Warner Leisure Hotels

★★★ 77% HOTEL

☎ 01270 624341 🖹 01270 623395
Middlewich Rd CW5 6PD

A Grade-II listed Victorian property located in the delightful Cheshire countryside and set in extensive grounds. Bedrooms vary in size and style; some have spacious seating areas and some have outdoor terraces. Outdoor and indoor leisure facilities include a 9-hole golf course, hair and beauty treatments, and a great range of entertainment and activities. Please note that this is an adults-only (over 21 years old) hotel. Warner Leisure Hotels – AA Small Hotel Group of the Year 2011-12.

Rooms 168 (52 annexe) (96 GF) **S** £56-£163; **D** £112-£326 (incl. bkfst & dinner)* **Facilities** Spa FTV supervised 9 Putt green Gym Archery Bowling green Floodlit driving range Xmas New Year Wi-fi **Conf** Class 24 Board 16 Thtr 30 Del from £70 to £110* **Services** Lift **Parking** 108 **Notes** LB No children

Crown Hotel & Casa Brasserie

★★ 73% HOTEL

☎ 01270 625283 📠 01270 628047
High St CW5 5AS
e-mail: info@crownhotelnantwich.com
web: www.crownhotelnantwich.com
dir: A52 to Nantwich, hotel in town centre

Ideally set in the heart of this historic and delightful market town, The Crown has been offering hospitality for centuries. It has an abundance of original features and the well-equipped bedrooms retain an old world charm. There is also a bar with live entertainment throughout the week and diners can enjoy Italian food in the atmospheric brasserie.

Rooms 18 (2 fmly) (1 smoking) **S** £55-£76; **D** £60-£88* **Facilities** FTV ♫ Wi-fi **Conf** Class 150 Board 70 Thtr 200 **Parking** 18 **Notes** Closed 25 Dec Civ Wed 140

Premier Inn Crewe/ Nantwich

BUDGET HOTEL

☎ 0871 527 8782 📠 0871 527 8783
221 Crewe Rd CW5 6NE
dir: M6 junct 16, A500 towards Chester, A534 towards Nantwich. Hotel approx 100yds on right

High quality, budget accommodation ideal for both families and business travellers. Spacious, en suite bedrooms feature tea and coffee making facilities, and Freeview TV in most hotels. Internet access and Wi-fi are available for a small fee. The adjacent family restaurant features a wide and varied menu. See also the Hotel Groups pages.

Rooms 37 **D** £58*

NETHER STOWEY Map 4 ST13
Somerset

Apple Tree Hotel

★★★ 68% HOTEL

☎ 01278 733238 📠 01278 732693
Keenthorne TA5 1HZ
e-mail: reservations@appletreehotel.com
web: www.appletreehotel.com
dir: A39 from Bridgwater towards Minehead. Hotel on left, 2m past Cannington

Parts of this cottage-style property, conveniently located for the coast and the M5, date back some 340 years. Bedrooms, which vary in character and style, are suited to both leisure and corporate guests; some are in a single storey annexe adjacent to the main building. Public areas include an attractive conservatory restaurant, a bar and a library lounge. The friendly owners and their staff make every effort to guarantee an enjoyable stay.

Rooms 16 (2 fmly) (6 GF) **S** £69.50; **D** £95-£105 (incl. bkfst)* **Facilities** FTV Wi-fi **Conf** Class 12 Board 12 Thtr 20 **Parking** 30 **Notes** ⊗

NEW ALRESFORD Map 5 SU53
Hampshire

Swan

THE INDEPENDENTS HOTEL ASSOCIATION

★★ 68% HOTEL

☎ 01962 732302 & 734427 📠 01962 735274
11 West St SO24 9AD
e-mail: swanhotel@btinternet.com
web: www.swanhotelalresford.com
dir: Off A31 onto B3047

This former coaching inn dates back to the 18th century and remains a busy and popular destination for travellers and locals alike. Bedrooms are situated in both the main building and the more modern wing. The lounge bar and adjacent restaurant are open all day; for more traditional dining there is another restaurant which overlooks the busy village street.

Rooms 23 (12 annexe) (3 fmly) (5 GF) **S** £45-£55; **D** £75-£85 (incl. bkfst)* **Facilities** FTV New Year Wi-fi **Conf** Class 60 Board 40 Thtr 90 Del from £70 to £80* **Parking** 25 **Notes** LB RS 25 Dec

See advert on this page

N

NEWARK-ON-TRENT Map 17 SK75
Nottinghamshire

The Grange Hotel

★★★ 82% ® HOTEL

☎ 01636 703399 📠 01636 702328
73 London Rd NG24 1RZ
e-mail: info@grangenewark.co.uk
web: www.grangenewark.co.uk
dir: From A1 follow signs to Balderton, hotel opposite Polish War Graves

Expect a warm welcome at this family-run hotel, situated just a short walk from the town. Bedrooms are attractively decorated with co-ordinated soft furnishings and equipped with many thoughtful extras. Public rooms include the Potters Bar, a residents' lounge and the Cutlers Restaurant, where enjoyable cuisine is presented. In the summer guests can enjoy the delightful terrace gardens.

Rooms 19 (9 annexe) (1 fmly) **S** £83-£120; **D** £97-£160 (incl. bkfst)* **Facilities** FTV Wi-fi **Parking** 17 **Notes** LB ® Closed 23 Dec-4 Jan

Premier Inn Newark

BUDGET HOTEL

☎ 0871 527 8784 📠 0871 527 8785
Lincoln Rd NG24 2DB
dir: At junct of A1 & A46 & A17, follow B6166 signs

High quality, budget accommodation ideal for both families and business travellers. Spacious, en suite bedrooms feature tea and coffee making facilities, and Freeview TV in most hotels. Internet access and Wi-fi are available for a small fee. The adjacent family restaurant features a wide and varied menu. See also the Hotel Groups pages.

Rooms 40 **D** £50-£60*

NEWBURY Map 5 SU46
Berkshire

See also **Andover**

INSPECTORS' CHOICE

The Vineyard at Stockcross

★★★★★ ®®® HOTEL

☎ 01635 528770 📠 01635 528398
Stockcross RG20 8JU
e-mail: general@the-vineyard.co.uk
web: www.the-vineyard.co.uk
dir: From M4 take A34 towards Newbury, exit at 3rd junct for Speen. Right at rdbt then right again at 2nd rdbt

A haven of style in the Berkshire countryside, this hotel prides itself on a superb art collection, which can be seen throughout the building. Bedrooms come in a variety of styles - many split-level suites that are exceptionally well equipped. Comfortable lounges lead into the stylish restaurant, which serves the award-winning, imaginative and precise cooking created by Daniel Galmiche, complemented by an equally impressive selection of wines from California and around the world. The welcome throughout the hotel is warm and sincere, the service professional yet relaxed.

Rooms 49 (15 GF) **S** £140-£195; **D** £140-£325* **Facilities** Spa STV Gym Treatment rooms Xmas New Year Wi-fi **Conf** Class 70 Board 30 Thtr 140 Del from £295 **Services** Lift Air con **Parking** 100 **Notes** LB ® Civ Wed 100

Donnington Valley Hotel & Spa

★★★★ 84% ®® HOTEL

☎ 01635 551199 📠 01635 551123
Old Oxford Rd, Donnington RG14 3AG
e-mail: general@donningtonvalley.co.uk
web: www.donningtonvalley.co.uk
dir: M4 junct 13, take A34 signed Newbury. Take exit signed Donnington/Services, at rdbt take 2nd exit signed Donnington. Left at next rdbt. Hotel 2m on right

In its own grounds complete with an 18-hole golf course, this stylish hotel boasts excellent facilities for both corporate and leisure guests; from the state-of-the-art spa offering excellent treatments, to an extensive range of meeting and function rooms. Air-conditioned bedrooms are stylish, spacious and particularly well equipped with fridges, lap-top safes and internet access. The Wine Press restaurant offers imaginative food complemented by a superb wine list.

Rooms 111 (3 fmly) (36 GF) **S** £99-£205; **D** £99-£205* **Facilities** Spa STV 18 Putt green Fishing Gym Aromatherapy Sauna Steam room Studio Xmas New Year Wi-fi **Conf** Class 60 Board 40 Thtr 140 Del from £295* **Services** Lift Air con **Parking** 150 **Notes** LB ® Civ Wed 85

Best Western West Grange

★★★★ 73% HOTEL

☎ 01635 273074 📠 01635 862351
Cox's Ln, Bath Rd, Midgham RG7 5UP
e-mail: reservations@westgrangehotel.co.uk
dir: M4 junct 12, A4 (Bath Rd), follow Newbury signs. Through Woolhampton, hotel on right in approx 2m

This former farmhouse has been turned into a smart and modern hotel that is set in well-managed grounds only a short drive away from Thatcham. Bedrooms offer a quiet and comfortable stay, and guests can relax in the large bar lounge and attractive restaurant. There is also a patio for warmer months.

Rooms 68 (2 fmly) (19 GF) **Facilities** STV New Year Wi-fi **Conf** Class 25 Board 30 Thtr 50 **Services** Lift **Parking** 70 **Notes** ®

Ramada Newbury Elcot Park

RAMADA JARVIS

★★★★ 71% HOTEL

☎ 01488 658100 & 0844 815 9060
📠 01488 658288
RG20 8NJ
e-mail: sales.elcotpark@ramadajarvis.co.uk
web: www.ramadajarvis.co.uk/newbury
dir: M4 junct 13, A338 to Hungerford, A4 to Newbury. Hotel 4m from Hungerford

Enjoying a peaceful location yet within easy access to both the A4 and M4, this country-house hotel is set in 16 acres of gardens and woodland. Bedrooms are comfortably appointed and include some located in an adjacent mews. Public areas include the Orangery Restaurant, which enjoys views over the Kennet Valley, a leisure club and a range of conference rooms.

Rooms 73 (17 annexe) (4 fmly) (25 GF) (5 smoking) **Facilities** FTV supervised Gym Sauna Steam room Xmas New Year Wi-fi **Conf** Class 45 Board 35 Thtr 110 **Services** Lift **Parking** 130 **Notes** Civ Wed 120

Newbury Manor Hotel

★★★ 81% HOTEL

☎ 01635 528838 📠 01635 523406
London Rd RG14 2BY
e-mail: enquiries@newbury-manor-hotel.co.uk
dir: On A4 between Newbury & Thatcham

This former Georgian watermill, which still features the original millrace, is situated beside the River Kennet in well tended grounds. The character bedrooms vary in style and size and offer many accessories. Guests can dine in the award-winning River Bar Restaurant.

Rooms 34 (4 fmly) (11 GF) **S** £60-£190; **D** £70-£200 (incl. bkfst) **Facilities** STV Fishing Xmas New Year Wi-fi **Conf** Class 140 Board 90 Thtr 190 Del from £125 to £145* **Parking** 100 **Notes** LB Civ Wed 180

Hare & Hounds Hotel

★★ 68% HOTEL

☎ 01635 521152 📠 01635 47708
Bath Rd, Speen RG14 1QY
e-mail: reservations@hareandhoundshotel.net
web: www.hareandhoundshotel.net
dir: A34 (Newbury bypass) onto A4 towards Newbury signed Speen. Hotel 300yds on right

A privately owned, historic hotel just a few minutes from the centre of Newbury. The hotel offers bedrooms in the coach house and in the mews, and all are modern and tastefully decorated. There is a relaxed, informal restaurant offering regularly changing menus, and the bar is popular with locals and guests alike.

Rooms 30 (23 annexe) (3 fmly) (11 GF) (6 smoking) **S** £49.50-£69.50; **D** £66.50-£89.50 (incl. bkfst)* **Facilities** STV FTV New Year Wi-fi **Parking** 64 **Notes** LB

The Chequers Hotel

U

☎ 01635 38000 📠 01635 37170
6-8 Oxford St RG14 1JB
e-mail: info@chequershotelnewbury.co.uk
web: www.chequershotelnewbury.co.uk
dir: M4 junct 13, A34 S onto A339 to Newbury. At 2nd rdbt right to town centre. At clock tower rdbt right, hotel on right

Currently the rating for this establishment is not confirmed. This may be due to a change of ownership or because it has only recently joined the AA rating scheme. For further details please see the AA website: theAA.com

Rooms 56

Premier Inn Newbury/ Thatcham

Premier Inn

BUDGET HOTEL

☎ 0871 527 8786 📠 0871 527 8787
Bath Rd, Midgham RG7 5UX
dir: M4 junct 12, A4 towards Newbury. Hotel 7m on right

High quality, budget accommodation ideal for both families and business travellers. Spacious, en suite bedrooms feature tea and coffee making facilities, and Freeview TV in most hotels. Internet access and Wi-fi are available for a small fee. The adjacent family restaurant features a wide and varied menu. See also the Hotel Groups pages.

Rooms 49 **D** £62-£72*

NEWBY BRIDGE Cumbria **Map 18 SD38**

Lakeside Hotel Lake Windermere

★★★★ 87% HOTEL

☎ 015395 30001 📠 015395 31699
Lakeside LA12 8AT
e-mail: sales@lakesidehotel.co.uk
web: www.lakesidehotel.co.uk
dir: M6 junct 36, A590 to Barrow, follow signs to Newby Bridge. Right over bridge, hotel 1m on right

This impressive hotel enjoys an enviable location on the southern edge of Lake Windermere and has easy access to the Lakeside & Haverthwaite Steam Railway and ferry terminal. Bedrooms are individually styled and many enjoy delightful lake views. Spacious lounges and a choice of restaurants are available. The state-of-the-art spa is exclusive to residents and provides a range of treatment suites. Staff throughout are friendly and nothing is too much trouble.

Rooms 75 (8 fmly) (8 GF) **S** £110-£430; **D** £160-£450 (incl. bkfst) **Facilities** Spa STV Fishing Gym Private jetty Rowing boats Xmas New Year Wi-fi **Conf** Class 50 Board 40 Thtr 100 Del from £140 to £230 **Services** Lift **Parking** 200 **Notes** LB Civ Wed 80

N

NEWBY BRIDGE *continued*

Whitewater Hotel

★★★★ 75% ® HOTEL

☎ 015395 31133 Fax 015395 31881
The Lakeland Village LA12 8PX
e-mail: enquiries@whitewater-hotel.co.uk
web: www.whitewater-hotel.co.uk
dir: M6 junct 36 follow signs for A590 Barrow, 1m through Newby Bridge. Right at sign for Lakeland Village, hotel on left

This tasteful conversion of an old mill on the River Leven is close to the southern end of Lake Windermere. Bedrooms, many with lovely river views, are spacious and comfortable. Public areas include a luxurious, well-equipped spa, squash courts, and a choice of comfortable lounges. The Dolly Blue bar overlooks the river and is a vibrant informal alternative to the fine dining restaurant.

Rooms 38 (10 fmly) (2 GF) **Facilities** Spa STV (indoor pool) supervised (outdoor pool) Putt green Gym Squash Beauty treatment Steam room Table tennis Xmas New Year Wi-fi **Conf** Class 32 Board 40 Thtr 80 **Services** Lift **Parking** 50 **Notes** (no smoking) Civ Wed 110

N

NEWCASTLE-UNDER-LYME Map 10 SJ84
Staffordshire

Holiday Inn Stoke-on-Trent

★★★ 75% HOTEL

☎ 01782 557000 & 557018 Fax 01782 717138
Clayton Rd, Clayton ST5 4DL
e-mail: reservations-stoke@ihg.com
web: www.holidayinn.co.uk
dir: Just off M6 junct 15. Follow Clayton Rd signs towards Newcastle-under-Lyme. Hotel 200yds on left

Stylish and contemporary, this modern hotel is well located just minutes from the motorway. Bedrooms are comfortable and boast an excellent range of facilities. Guests have the use of the leisure club.

Rooms 118 (38 fmly) **Facilities** STV (indoor pool) supervised Gym Xmas New Year Wi-fi **Conf** Class 30 Board 22 Thtr 70 **Services** Air con **Parking** 150 **Notes** (no smoking)

Premier Inn Newcastle-under-Lyme

BUDGET HOTEL

☎ 0871 527 8808 Fax 0871 527 8809
Talke Rd, Chesterton ST5 7AL
dir: M6 junct 12, A500, A34 to Newcastle-under-Lyme. Hotel 0.5m on right

High quality, budget accommodation ideal for both families and business travellers. Spacious, en suite bedrooms feature tea and coffee making facilities, and Freeview TV in most hotels. Internet access and Wi-fi are available for a small fee. The adjacent family restaurant features a wide and varied menu. See also the Hotel Groups pages.

Rooms 83 **D** £53-£60*

NEWCASTLE UPON TYNE Map 21 NZ26
Tyne & Wear

See also **Whickham**

INSPECTORS' CHOICE

Jesmond Dene House

★★★★ ®®® HOTEL

☎ 0191 212 3000 Fax 0191 212 3001
Jesmond Dene Rd NE2 2EY
e-mail: info@jesmonddenehouse.co.uk
web: www.jesmonddenehouse.co.uk
dir: A167 N to A184. Right, then right again into Jesmond Dene Rd, hotel on left

This grand house, overlooking the wooded valley of Jesmond Dene, yet just five minutes from the centre of town, has been sympathetically converted into a stylish, contemporary hotel destination. The bedrooms are beautifully designed and boast flat-screen TVs, sumptuous beds with Egyptian cotton linen, digital radios, well-stocked mini bars, free broadband, desk space and safes. Equally eye-catching bathrooms with under floor heating are equipped with high quality bespoke amenities. The stylish restaurant is the venue for innovative cooking which will prove a highlight of any stay.

Rooms 40 (8 annexe) (1 fmly) (4 GF) **S** £125-£165; **D** £145-£450* **Facilities** Wi-fi **Conf** Class 80 Board 44 Thtr 125 Del from £181 to £245* **Services** Lift **Parking** 64 **Notes** LB (no smoking) Civ Wed 100

Vermont

★★★★ 81% @ HOTEL

☎ 0191 233 1010 📠 0191 233 1234
Castle Garth NE1 1RQ
e-mail: info@vermont-hotel.co.uk
web: www.vermont-hotel.com
dir: City centre by high level bridge & castle keep

Adjacent to the castle and close to the buzzing quayside area, this imposing hotel enjoys fine views of the Tyne Bridge. Thoughtfully equipped bedrooms offer a variety of styles, including grand suites. The elegant reception lounge and adjoining bar invite relaxation, while the Bridge Restaurant is the focus for dining.

Rooms 101 (12 fmly) **S** £80-£190; **D** £80-£190* **Facilities** STV FTV Gym Xmas New Year Wi-fi **Conf** Class 60 Board 30 Thtr 200 **Services** Lift **Parking** 100 **Notes** LB Civ Wed 120

Hotel du Vin Newcastle

★★★★ 79% @@
TOWN HOUSE HOTEL

☎ 0191 229 2200 📠 0191 229 2201
Allan House, City Rd NE1 2BE
e-mail: lkelk@malmaison.com
dir: A1 junct 65 onto A184 Gateshead/Newcastle, Quayside to City Rd

The former maintenance depot of the Tyne Tees Shipping Company, this is a landmark building on the Tyne. It has been transformed into a modern and stylish hotel. Bedrooms are well equipped and deeply comfortable with all the Hotel du Vin trademark items such as Egyptian cotton sheets, plasma TVs, DVD players and monsoon showers. Guests can dine in the bistro or alfresco if the weather allows in the courtyard.

Rooms 42 (6 GF) **S** £110-£420; **D** £110-£420* **Facilities** STV Wi-fi **Conf** Board 20 Thtr 26 Del from £199 to £225* **Services** Lift Air con **Parking** 10 **Notes** LB Civ Wed 40

Newcastle Marriott Hotel Gosforth Park

Marriott HOTELS & RESORTS

★★★★ 78% HOTEL

☎ 0191 236 4111 📠 0191 236 8192
High Gosforth Park, Gosforth NE3 5HN
web: www.newcastlemarriottgosforthpark.co.uk
dir: Onto A1056 to Killingworth & Wideopen. 3rd exit to Gosforth Park, hotel ahead

Set within its own grounds, this modern hotel offers extensive conference and banqueting facilities, along with indoor and outdoor leisure. There is a choice of dining in the more formal Plate Restaurant or the relaxed Chat's lounge bar. Many of the air-conditioned bedrooms have views over the park. The hotel is conveniently located for the bypass, airport and racecourse.

Rooms 178 (17 smoking) **Facilities** Spa STV supervised Gym Squash Jogging trail New Year Wi-fi **Conf** Class 280 Board 60 Thtr 800 **Services** Lift Air con **Parking** 340 **Notes** Civ Wed 300

Newcastle Marriott Hotel MetroCentre

Marriott HOTELS & RESORTS

★★★★ 77% HOTEL

☎ 0191 493 2233 📠 0191 493 2030
MetroCentre NE11 9XF
e-mail: reservations.newcastle.england.metrocentre@marriotthotels.co.uk
web: www.newcastlemarriottmetrocentre.co.uk

(For full entry see Gateshead)

Copthorne Hotel Newcastle

★★★★ 71% HOTEL

☎ 0191 222 0333 📠 0191 230 1111
The Close, Quayside NE1 3RT
e-mail: sales.newcastle@millenniumhotels.co.uk
web: www.millenniumhotels.co.uk
dir: Follow signs to Newcastle city centre. Take B1600 Quayside exit, hotel on right

Set on the banks of the River Tyne close to the city centre, this stylish purpose-built hotel provides modern amenities including a leisure centre, conference facilities and a choice of restaurants for dinner. Bedrooms overlook the river, and there is a floor of 'Connoisseur' rooms that have their own dedicated exclusive lounge and business support services.

Rooms 156 (4 fmly) **S** £79-£220; **D** £89-£230 (incl. bkfst) **Facilities** STV supervised Gym Steam room Xmas New Year Wi-fi **Conf** Class 90 Board 60 Thtr 220 Del from £110 to £185 **Services** Lift **Parking** 180 **Notes** Civ Wed 150

Malmaison Newcastle

★★★ 88% @ HOTEL

☎ 0191 245 5000 📠 0191 245 4545
Quayside NE1 3DX
e-mail: newcastle@malmaison.com
dir: Follow signs for city centre, then for Quayside/Law Courts. Hotel 100yds past Law Courts

Overlooking the river and the Millennium Bridge, the hotel has a prime position in the very popular quayside district. Bedrooms have striking decor, CD/DVD players, mini-bars and a number of individual touches. Food and drink are an integral part of the operation here, with a stylish brasserie-style restaurant and café bar, plus the Café Mal, a deli-style café next door to the main entrance.

Rooms 122 (10 fmly) **Facilities** Spa STV Gym Wi-fi **Conf** Board 18 Thtr 30 **Services** Lift Air con **Parking** 50

Mercure Newcastle George Washington Hotel

Mercure

★★★ 81% HOTEL

☎ 0191 402 9988 📠 0191 415 1166
Stone Cellar Rd, High Usworth NE37 1PH
e-mail: reservations@georgewashington.co.uk
web: www.georgewashington.co.uk

(For full entry see Washington)

Eslington Villa Hotel

★★★ 79% @ HOTEL

☎ 0191 487 6017 & 420 0666 📠 0191 420 0667
8 Station Rd, Low Fell NE9 6DR
e-mail: home@eslingtonvilla.co.uk

(For full entry see Gateshead)

N

NEWCASTLE UPON TYNE *continued*

County Hotel, Newcastle

thistle

★★★ 79% HOTEL

☎ 0871 376 9029 📠 0871 376 9129
Neville St NE1 5DF
e-mail: newcastle@thistle.co.uk
web: www.thistlehotels.com/newcastle
dir: A1 onto A184. Cross Redheugh Bridge, right at 2nd lights, right after cathedral, left at pedestrian zone

A 19th-century listed building, the hotel enjoys a central location opposite the city's Central Station, which also has links to the Metro system. Bedrooms are comfortably appointed for both business and leisure guests. Limited free parking is available. Thistle Hotels – AA Hotel Group of the Year 2011-12.

Rooms 114 **Facilities** FTV Complimentary use of nearby gym New Year Wi-fi **Conf** Class 100 Board 100 Thtr 250 **Services** Lift **Parking** 19 **Notes** ⊗ Civ Wed 100

Horton Grange Country House Hotel

★★★ 79% HOTEL

☎ 01661 860686 📠 01661 860308
Berwick Hill, Ponteland NE13 6BU
e-mail: enquiries@horton-grange.co.uk
web: www.horton-grange.co.uk
dir: A1/A19 junct at Seaton Burn take 1st exit at 1st rdbt, after 1m turn left signed Ponteland/Dinnington. Hotel on right approx 2m along this road

A Grade II listed building set in its own grounds just a short distance from Newcastle Airport and Ponteland. The main house has traditionally styled executive bedrooms, and in addition there are four contemporary garden rooms that are elegant and spacious. All bedrooms have flat-screen TVs, digital radios and broadband access. Food is served in the light and airy restaurant and the lounge that both overlook the gardens.

Rooms 9 (1 fmly) (4 GF) **Facilities** FTV Xmas New Year Wi-fi **Conf** Class 40 Board 30 Thtr 120 **Parking** 50 **Notes** LB ⊗ Civ Wed 120

N

Holiday Inn Newcastle upon Tyne

★★★ 78% HOTEL

☎ 0871 423 4818 & 0191 201 9988
📠 0191 236 8091
Great North Rd, Seaton Burn NE13 6BP
e-mail: hinewcastle@qmh-hotels.com
web: www.holidayinn.com/newcastleuk
dir: A1/A19, 6m N of Newcastle. A190/Tyne Tunnel exit A1. Follow brown Holiday Inn signs

This modern hotel is set in 16 acres and is convenient for Newcastle International Airport, Tyne Tunnel and the North Sea Ferry Terminal. Each bedroom is fully equipped with all necessary facilities, and executive rooms are available. The Convivium Restaurant serves breakfast and dinner, and the Mercury Bar offers a snack menu from 11 to 11. A leisure club is available, and there are plenty of activities for children.

Rooms 154 (56 fmly) (72 GF) **S** £59-£180; **D** £59-£180 (incl. bkfst)* **Facilities** STV Gym Cardiovascular & weights room Sauna Steam room Beauty salon Xmas New Year Wi-fi **Conf** Class 150 Board 60 Thtr 400 Del from £99 to £142 **Services** Air con **Parking** 350 **Notes** LB ⊗ Civ Wed 300

Best Western New Kent Hotel

★★★ 74% HOTEL

☎ 0191 281 7711 📠 0191 281 3369
127 Osborne Rd NE2 2TB
e-mail: newkenthotel@hotmail.com
web: www.newkenthotel.com
dir: On B1600, opposite St Georges Church

This popular business hotel offers relaxed service and typical Geordie hospitality. The bright modern bedrooms are well equipped and the modern bar is an ideal meeting place. A range of generous, good value dishes is served in the restaurant, which doubles as a wedding venue.

Rooms 32 (4 fmly) **S** £71.50; **D** £91.50 (incl. bkfst)* **Facilities** STV FTV Xmas New Year Wi-fi **Conf** Class 30 Board 40 Thtr 60 **Parking** 22 **Notes** LB Civ Wed 90

The Caledonian Hotel, Newcastle

★★★ 71% HOTEL

☎ 0191 281 7881 📠 0191 281 6241
64 Osborne Rd, Jesmond NE2 2AT
e-mail: info@caledonian-hotel-newcastle.com
web: www.peelhotels.co.uk
dir: From A1 follow signs to Newcastle City, cross Tyne Bridge to Tynemouth. Left at lights at Osborne Rd, hotel on right

This hotel is located in the Jesmond area of the city, and offers comfortable bedrooms that are well equipped. The public areas include the trendy Billabong Bar and Bistro which serves food all day, and the terrace where a cosmopolitan atmosphere prevails. Alfresco dining is available.

Rooms 90 (6 fmly) (7 GF) (15 smoking) **Facilities** Xmas New Year Wi-fi **Conf** Class 50 Board 50 Thtr 100 Del from £95 to £110 **Services** Lift **Parking** 35 **Notes** LB ⊗ Civ Wed 70

Newgate Hotel

★★★ 63% METRO HOTEL

☎ 0191 232 6570 📠 0191 231 2053
Newgate St NE1 5SX
e-mail: enquiries@hotels-newcastle.com
dir: A184/A189 over bridge, 2nd lights turn right, left at 1st lights into Clayton St. 1st right to Fenkle St, 1st left to car park at end

Ideally located right in the heart of Newcastle, this hotel makes a good base for exploring the city. Bedrooms offer comfortable beds and free Wi-fi. Breakfast is served in the sixth-floor restaurant that has great views of the city.

Rooms 93 (8 fmly) **Facilities** STV Wi-fi **Conf** Board 12 Thtr 14 **Services** Lift **Parking** 120 **Notes** Closed 24-27 Dec

Kenilworth Hotel

★★ 76% SMALL HOTEL

☎ 0191 281 8111 & 281 9111 📠 0191 281 9476
44 Osborne Rd, Jesmond NE2 2AL
e-mail: info@thekenilworthhotel.co.uk
web: www.thekenilworthhotel.co.uk
dir: A1058 signed Tynemouth for 1m. Left at lights onto Osborne Rd, hotel 0.5m on right

This family-run hotel in the Jesmond area of the city features wooden floors and leather furniture. The smart bedrooms have satellite TVs, DVD players, beverage trays and hairdryers. There is relaxed and informal restaurant, and exterior seating in the summer allows guests to enjoy the café culture which popular in this area.

Rooms 11 (5 fmly) **S** £45-£58; **D** £65-£90 (incl. bkfst) **Facilities** FTV Access to leisure centre 1.5km away Xmas New Year Wi-fi **Conf** Class 60 Board 60 Thtr 80 **Parking** 11

Express by Holiday Inn Newcastle City Centre

BUDGET HOTEL

☎ 0870 4281488 📠 0870 4281477
Waterloo Square, St James Boulevard NE1 4DN
e-mail: gm.newcastle@expressholidayinn.co.uk
web: www.hiexpress.com/newcastlectyct

A modern hotel ideal for families and business travellers. Fresh and uncomplicated, the spacious rooms include Sky TV, power shower and tea and coffee-making facilities. Continental buffet breakfast is included in the room rate; other meals may be taken at the nearby family pub or restaurant. See also the Hotel Groups pages.

Rooms 130 (50 fmly) **Conf** Class 15 Board 16 Thtr 30

Premier Inn Newcastle Central

BUDGET HOTEL

☎ 0871 527 8802 📠 0871 527 8803
New Bridge Street West NE1 8BS
dir: Follow Gateshead & Newcastle signs on A167(M), over Tyne Bridge. A193 signed Wallsend & city centre, left to Carliol Square, hotel on corner

High quality, budget accommodation ideal for both families and business travellers. Spacious, en suite bedrooms feature tea and coffee making facilities, and Freeview TV in most hotels. Internet access and Wi-fi are available for a small fee. The adjacent family restaurant features a wide and varied menu. See also the Hotel Groups pages.

Rooms 172 **D** £59-£70*

Premier Inn Newcastle City Centre (Millennium Bridge)

BUDGET HOTEL

☎ 0871 527 8800 📠 0871 527 8801
City Rd, Quayside NE1 2AN
dir: At corner of City Rd (A186) & Crawhall Rd

Rooms 81 **D** £67-£70*

Premier Inn Newcastle (Holystone)

BUDGET HOTEL

☎ 0871 527 8790 📠 0871 5278791
The Stonebrook, Edmund Rd, Holystone NE27 0UN
dir: 3m N of Tyne Tunnel. From A19 take A191 signed Gosforth. Hotel on left

Rooms 40 **D** £53-£59*

Premier Inn Newcastle Quayside

BUDGET HOTEL

☎ 0871 527 8804 📠 0871 527 8805
The Quayside NE1 3AE
dir: S'bound: A1, A167(M), A186 signed Walker & Wallsend follow B1600 Quayside signs. N'bound: A1, A184, A189 (cross river). 1st exit, follow B1600 Quayside signs. Hotel at foot of Tyne Bridge in Exchange building

Rooms 152 **D** £67-£70*

NEWCASTLE UPON TYNE AIRPORT

Map 21 NZ17

Tyne & Wear

Novotel Newcastle Airport

★★★ 77% HOTEL

☎ 0191 214 0303 📠 0191 214 0633
Ponteland Rd, Kenton NE3 3HZ
e-mail: H1118@accor-hotels.com
web: www.novotel.com
dir: Off A1(M) airport junct onto A696, take Kingston Park exit

This modern, well-proportioned hotel lies just off the bypass and is just a five minute drive from the airport and has secure parking. The hotel has a scheduled shuttle service and flight information screens for air passengers. Bedrooms are spacious with a range of extras. The Elements Restaurant offers a flexible dining option and is open until late. There is a contemporary style lounge bar and also a small leisure centre for the more energetic guests.

Rooms 126 (36 fmly) **Facilities** Gym Wi-fi **Conf** Class 90 Board 40 Thtr 200 **Services** Lift **Parking** 260 **Notes** Civ Wed 200

Premier Inn Newcastle Airport

BUDGET HOTEL

☎ 0871 527 8796 📠 0871 527 8797
Newcastle Int Airport, Ponteland Rd, Prestwick NE20 9DB
dir: A1 onto A696, follow Airport signs. At rdbt take turn immediately after airport exit

High quality, budget accommodation ideal for both families and business travellers. Spacious, en suite bedrooms feature tea and coffee making facilities, and Freeview TV in most hotels. Internet access and Wi-fi are available for a small fee. The adjacent family restaurant features a wide and varied menu. See also the Hotel Groups pages.

Rooms 88 **D** £57-£58*

Premier Inn Newcastle Airport (South)

BUDGET HOTEL

☎ 0871 527 8798 📠 0871 527 8799
Callerton Lane Ends, Woolsington NE13 8DF
dir: Just off A696 on B6918, 0.3m from airport

Rooms 53 **D** £53-£56*

NEWENT Map 10 SO72
Gloucestershire

Three Choirs Vineyards

◎◎ RESTAURANT WITH ROOMS

☎ 01531 890223 📠 01531 890877
GL18 1LS
e-mail: info@threechoirs.com
web: www.threechoirs.com
dir: On B4215 N of Newent, follow brown tourist signs

This thriving vineyard continues to go from strength to strength and provides a wonderfully different place to stay. The restaurant, which overlooks the 100-acre estate, enjoys a popular following thanks to well-executed dishes that make good use of local produce. Spacious, high quality bedrooms are equipped with many extras, and each opens onto a private patio area which has wonderful views.

Rooms 11 (11 annexe) (1 fmly)

NEWHAVEN Map 6 TQ40
East Sussex

Premier Inn Newhaven

BUDGET HOTEL

☎ 0871 527 8810 📠 0871 527 8811
Avis Rd BN9 0AG
dir: From A26 (New Rd) through Drove Industrial Estate, left after underpass. Hotel in same complex as Sainsbury's

High quality, budget accommodation ideal for both families and business travellers. Spacious, en suite bedrooms feature tea and coffee making facilities, and Freeview TV in most hotels. Internet access and Wi-fi are available for a small fee. The adjacent family restaurant features a wide and varied menu. See also the Hotel Groups pages.

Rooms 70 **D** £58*

NEWICK Map 6 TQ42
East Sussex

INSPECTORS' CHOICE

Newick Park Hotel & Country Estate

★★★ ◎◎ HOTEL

☎ 01825 723633 📠 01825 723969
BN8 4SB
e-mail: bookings@newickpark.co.uk
web: www.newickpark.co.uk
dir: Exit A272 at Newick Green, 1m, pass church & pub. Turn left, hotel 0.25m on right

Delightful Grade II listed Georgian country house set amid 250 acres of Sussex parkland and landscaped gardens. The spacious, individually decorated bedrooms are tastefully furnished, thoughtfully equipped and have superb views of the grounds; many rooms have huge American king-size beds. The comfortable public rooms include a study, a sitting room, lounge bar and an elegant restaurant.

Rooms 16 (3 annexe) (5 fmly) (1 GF) **Facilities** FTV Fishing Badminton Clay pigeon shooting Helicopter rides Quad biking Tank driving Xmas Wi-fi **Conf** Class 40 Board 40 Thtr 80 **Parking** 52 **Notes** LB Civ Wed 100

NEWMARKET Map 12 TL66
Suffolk

Bedford Lodge Hotel

★★★★ 81% ◎◎ HOTEL

☎ 01638 663175 📠 01638 667391
Bury Rd CB8 7BX
e-mail: info@bedfordlodgehotel.co.uk
web: www.bedfordlodgehotel.co.uk
dir: From town centre take A1304 towards Bury St Edmunds, hotel 0.5m on left

Imposing 18th-century Georgian hunting lodge set in three acres of secluded landscaped gardens. Public rooms feature the elegant Orangery restaurant, a smart lounge bar and a small lounge. The hotel also features superb leisure facilities and self-contained conference and banqueting suites. Contemporary bedrooms have a light, airy feel, and each is tastefully furnished and well equipped.

Rooms 55 (3 fmly) (16 GF) (3 smoking) **Facilities** FTV Gym Steam room Sauna Spa bath Xmas New Year Wi-fi **Conf** Class 80 Board 60 Thtr 200 Del from £155 to £195 **Services** Lift **Parking** 120 **Notes** RS Sat lunch Civ Wed 150

Tuddenham Mill

★★★★ 81% ◎◎ HOTEL

☎ 01438 713552
High St, Tuddenham St Mary IP28 6SQ
e-mail: info@tuddenhammill.co.uk

A beautifully converted old watermill set amidst landscaped grounds between Newmarket and Bury St Edmunds. The contemporary style bedrooms are situated in separate buildings adjacent to the main building, each one is tastefully appointed with co-ordinated fabrics and soft furnishings. The public areas have a wealth of original features such as the water wheel and exposed beams; they include a lounge bar, a smart restaurant, a meeting room and choice of terraces.

Rooms 15 **S** £185-£395; (incl. bkfst)* **Conf** Class 36 Board 16 Thtr 50 **Notes** Civ Wed

Rutland Arms

★★★ 78% HOTEL

☎ 01638 664251 📠 01638 666298
High St CB8 8NB
e-mail: reservations.rutlandarms@ohiml.com
web: www.oxfordhotelsandinns.com
dir: A14 junct 37 onto A142, or M11 junct 9 onto A11 then A1304 - follow signs for town centre

Expect a warm welcome at this former coaching inn situated in the heart of town. The property is built around a 17th-century cobbled courtyard and still retains many original features. The public rooms include a large lounge bar and Carriages, a contemporary restaurant and wine bar. Bedrooms are smartly appointed and well equipped.

Rooms 46 (1 fmly) **Facilities** FTV Wi-fi **Conf** Class 40 Board 30 Thtr 70 **Parking** 40 **Notes** ⊗

Best Western Heath Court

★★★ 78% HOTEL

☎ 01638 667171 📠 01638 666533
Moulton Rd CB8 8DY
e-mail: quality@heathcourthotel.com
dir: Exit A14 for Newmarket & Ely onto A142. Follow town centre signs over mini rdbt. At clocktower left into Moulton Rd

A modern red-brick hotel situated close to Newmarket Heath and perfectly placed for the town centre. Public rooms include a choice of dining options - informal meals can be taken in the lounge bar or a modern carte menu is offered in the restaurant. The smartly presented bedrooms are mostly spacious and some have air conditioning.

Rooms 41 (2 fmly) **S** £35-£89.50; **D** £40-£182* **Facilities** STV FTV New Year Wi-fi **Conf** Class 50 Board 40 Thtr 130 Del from £100 to £115* **Services** Lift **Parking** 70 **Notes** LB Civ Wed 100

Cadogan

★★★ 73% SMALL HOTEL

☎ 01638 663814 & 07776 258688
📠 01638 561480
Fordham Rd CB8 7AA
e-mail: kgreed@btinternet.com
dir: A14, A142 to Newmarket. Straight on at 2 rdbts follow Town Centre signs. 1.5m. At 30mph limit, hotel 500mtrs on left

This small, friendly, family run hotel is situated just a short walk from the town centre within easy reach of Newmarket racecourse. Public rooms include an open-plan lounge bar with plush seating and a smart dining room. The bedrooms are pleasantly decorated with co-ordinated fabrics and have a good range of facilities.

Rooms 12 (2 fmly) (1 GF) **S** £65-£95; **D** £85-£145 (incl. bkfst) **Facilities** FTV Wi-fi **Parking** 18 **Notes** LB Closed 24 Dec-2 Jan

Premier Inn Newmarket

BUDGET HOTEL

☎ 0871 527 9296 📠 0871 527 9297
Fred Archer Way CB8 7XN
dir: A14 junct 37, A142 (Fordham Rd). 2.3m, straight on at 2 rdbts. At end of Fordham Rd, into right lane, turn right. Hotel on right

High quality, budget accommodation ideal for both families and business travellers. Spacious, en suite bedrooms feature tea and coffee making facilities, and Freeview TV in most hotels. Internet access and Wi-fi are available for a small fee. The adjacent family restaurant features a wide and varied menu. See also the Hotel Groups pages.

Rooms 75

N

NEW MILTON
Hampshire
Map 5 SZ29

INSPECTORS' CHOICE

Chewton Glen Hotel & Spa

★★★★★ ◎◎◎
COUNTRY HOUSE HOTEL

☎ 01425 275341 🖹 01425 272310
Christchurch Rd BH25 6QS
e-mail: reservations@chewtonglen.com
web: www.chewtonglen.com
dir: A35 from Lyndhurst for 10m, left at staggered junct. Follow tourist sign for hotel through Walkford, take 2nd left

This outstanding hotel has been at the forefront of British hotel-keeping for many years. Once past the wrought iron entrance gates, guests are transported into a world of luxury. Log fires and afternoon tea are part of the tradition here, and lounges enjoy fine views over sweeping croquet lawns. Most bedrooms are very spacious, with private patios or balconies. Dining is a treat, and the extensive wine lists are essential reading for the enthusiast. The spa and leisure facilities are among the best in the country.

Rooms 58 (11 GF) **D** £299-£677* **Facilities** Spa FTV Putt green Gym Hydrotherapy spa Dance studio Cycling & jogging trail Clay shooting Archery Xmas New Year Wi-fi Child facilities **Conf** Class 70 Board 40 Thtr 150 Del £395 **Services** Air con **Parking** 100 **Notes** Civ Wed 140

NEWPORT
Shropshire
Map 15 SJ71

Premier Inn Newport / Telford

BUDGET HOTEL

☎ 0871 527 8808 🖹 0871 527 8809
Stafford Rd TF10 9BY
dir: From A41 E of Newport take A518 towards Stafford. Hotel on right adjacent to Mere Park Garden Centre

High quality, budget accommodation ideal for both families and business travellers. Spacious, en suite bedrooms feature tea and coffee making facilities, and Freeview TV in most hotels. Internet access and Wi-fi are available for a small fee. The adjacent family restaurant features a wide and varied menu. See also the Hotel Groups pages.

Rooms 50 **D** £54-£61*

NEWPORT
Isle of Wight
Map 5 SZ58

Premier Inn Isle of Wight (Newport)

BUDGET HOTEL

☎ 0871 527 8556 🖹 0871 527 8557
Seaclose, Fairlee Rd PO30 2DN
dir: From Newport take A3054 signed Ryde. In 0.75m at Seaclose lights, turn left. Hotel adjacent to council offices

High quality, budget accommodation ideal for both families and business travellers. Spacious, en suite bedrooms feature tea and coffee making facilities, and Freeview TV in most hotels. Internet access and Wi-fi are available for a small fee. The adjacent family restaurant features a wide and varied menu. See also the Hotel Groups pages.

Rooms 68 **D** £68*

NEWPORT PAGNELL MOTORWAY SERVICE AREA (M1)
Buckinghamshire
Map 11 SP84

Days Inn Milton Keynes East M1

BUDGET HOTEL

☎ 01908 610878 🖹 01908 216539
Newport Pagnell MK16 8DS
e-mail: newport.hotel@welcomebreak.co.uk
web: www.daysinn.com
dir: M1 junct 14-15. In service area - follow signs to Barrier Lodge

This modern building offers accommodation in smart, spacious and well-equipped bedrooms, suitable for families and business travellers, and all with en suite bathrooms. Refreshments may be taken at the nearby family restaurant. See also the Hotel Groups pages.

Rooms 90 (54 fmly) **S** £49.95-£79.95; **D** £49.95-£79.95 **Conf** Class 12 Board 16 Thtr 40 Del from £79.95

NEWQUAY
Cornwall
Map 2 SW86

Headland

★★★★ 79% HOTEL

☎ 01637 872211 🖹 01637 872212
Fistral Beach TR7 1EW
e-mail: reservations@headlandhotel.co.uk
web: www.headlandhotel.co.uk
dir: A30 onto A392 at Indian Queens, approaching Newquay follow signs for Fistral Beach, hotel adjacent

This Victorian hotel enjoys a stunning location overlooking the sea on three sides - views can be enjoyed from most of the windows. Bedrooms are comfortable and spacious. The grand public areas, with impressive floral displays, include various lounges and in addition to the formal dining room, Sands Brasserie offers a relaxed alternative. Self-catering cottages are available, and guests staying in these can use the hotel facilities.

Rooms 96 (40 fmly) **S** £79-£359.10; **D** £89-£399 (incl. bkfst)* **Facilities** STV FTV Putt green Boules Surf school New Year Wi-fi **Conf** Class 120 Board 40 Thtr 250 Del from £152 to £208* **Services** Lift **Parking** 400 **Notes** LB Closed 24-27 Dec Civ Wed 250

N

Atlantic Hotel

★★★★ 74% HOTEL

☎ 01637 872244 📠 01637 874108

Dane Rd TR7 1EN

e-mail: info@atlantichotelnewquay.co.uk

Located on a cliff top with stunning views of Newquay and the Atlantic seascape, this imposing property dominates the skyline and offers traditional hotel keeping with modern comforts. All bedrooms are appointed to a high standard and offer ample modern comforts; balcony suites are available. Silks restaurant is popular with locals and residents alike.

Rooms 55 (10 fmly) **S** £45-£80; **D** £95-£240 (incl. bkfst)* **Facilities** FTV Xmas New Year Wi-fi **Conf** Class 300 Board 120 Thtr 300 Del from £95 to £180* **Services** Lift **Parking** 55 **Notes** Civ Wed 300

See advert on this page

Best Western Hotel Bristol

★★★ 77% HOTEL

☎ 01637 875181 📠 01637 879347

Narrowcliff TR7 2PQ

e-mail: info@hotelbristol.co.uk

web: www.hotelbristol.co.uk

dir: Off A30 onto A392, then onto A3058. Hotel 2.5m

This hotel is conveniently situated and many of the bedrooms enjoy fine sea views. Staff are friendly and provide a professional and attentive service. There is a range of comfortable lounges, ideal for relaxing prior to eating in the elegant dining room. There are also leisure and conference facilities.

Rooms 74 (23 fmly) **Facilities** FTV Table tennis New Year Wi-fi **Conf** Class 80 Board 30 Thtr 200 **Services** Lift **Parking** 105 **Notes** LB Closed 23-27 Dec & 4-18 Jan

See advert on page 366

Porth Veor Manor

★★★ 77% HOTEL

☎ 01637 873274 & 839542 📠 01637 879572

Porth Way, Porth TR7 3LW

e-mail: enquiries@porthveormanor.com

web: www.porthveormanor.com

dir: From A3058 at main rdbt onto B3276, hotel 0.5m on left

Overlooking Porth Beach and in a quiet location, this pleasant mid 19th-century manor house offers a relaxed and friendly atmosphere. The spacious bedrooms have satellite TVs, and many have views of the beach; superior rooms are available. The hotel has a fine dining restaurant, a lounge/bar, and an outdoor heated pool. There is direct access via a private path from the hotel grounds to the beach, and the coastal paths are just a short walk away.

continued

N

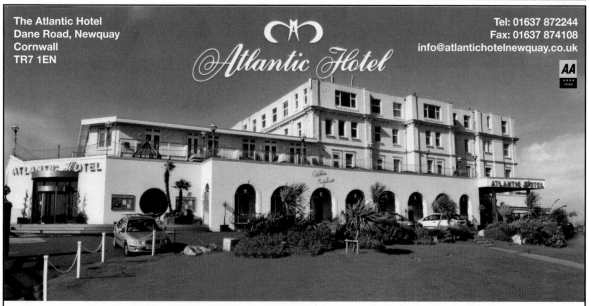

NEWQUAY ***continued***

Rooms 18 (6 fmly) **S** £60-£90; **D** £90-£138 (incl. bkfst) **Facilities** STV FTV Putt green Xmas New Year Wi-fi **Conf** Class 30 Board 40 Thtr 70 **Parking** 36 **Notes** No children 5yrs Civ Wed 60

Hotel Victoria

★★★ 75% HOTEL

01637 872255 01637 859295
East St TR7 1DB
e-mail: bookings@hotel-victoria.co.uk
dir: A30 towards Bodmin following signs to Newquay. Hotel next to Newquay's main post office

Standing on the cliffs, overlooking Newquay Bay, this hotel is situated at the centre of this vibrant town. The spacious lounges and bar areas all benefit from glorious views. Varied menus, using the best of local produce, are offered in the restaurant. Bedrooms vary from spacious superior rooms and suites to standard inland-facing rooms. Berties pub, a nightclub and indoor leisure facilities are also available.

Rooms 71 (23 fmly) (1 GF) (5 smoking) **S** fr £45; **D** fr £90 (incl. bkfst)* **Facilities** STV Gym Beauty room New Year Wi-fi **Conf** Class 130 Board 50 Thtr 200 Del from £103 **Services** Lift **Parking** 50 **Notes** LB Civ Wed 90

See advert on opposite page

Trebarwith

★★★ 75% HOTEL

01637 872288 & 0800 387520
01637 875431
Trebarwith Crescent TR7 1BZ
e-mail: trebahotel@aol.com
web: www.trebarwith-hotel.co.uk
dir: From A3058 into Mount Wise Rd. 3rd right into Marcus Hill, across East St into Trebarwith Cres. Hotel at end

With breathtaking views of the rugged coastline and a path leading to the beach, this friendly, family-run hotel is set in its own grounds close to the town centre. The public rooms include a lounge, ballroom, restaurant and cinema. The comfortable bedrooms include four-poster and family rooms, and many benefit from the sea views.

Rooms 41 (8 fmly) (1 GF) **S** £45-£75; **D** £69-£139 (incl. bkfst)* **Facilities** FTV Fishing Video theatre Games room Surf school Wi-fi **Conf** Class 30 Board 18 Thtr 45 Del from £100 to £200* **Parking** 41 **Notes** LB Closed Nov-5 Apr

Kilbirnie

★★★ 68% HOTEL

01637 875155 01637 850769
Narrowcliff TR7 2RS
e-mail: info@kilbirniehotel.co.uk
dir: On A392

With delightful views over the open space known as The Barrowfields and beyond to the sea, this privately-run hotel offers an impressive range of facilities. The reception rooms are spacious and comfortable, and during summer months host a programme of entertainment. Bedrooms vary in size and style, and some enjoy fine sea views.

Rooms 66 (6 fmly) (8 GF) **Facilities** Gym Fitness room Hair salon Xmas New Year Wi-fi **Conf** Class 50 Board 25 Thtr 100 **Services** Lift Air con **Parking** 58 **Notes**

Hotel California

★★★ 67% HOTEL

☎ 01637 879292 & 872798 📠 01637 875611
Pentire Crescent TR7 1PU
e-mail: info@hotel-california.co.uk
web: www.hotel-california.co.uk
dir: A392 to Newquay, follow signs for Pentire Hotels & Guest Houses

This hotel is tucked away in a delightful location, close to Fistral Beach and adjacent to the River Gannel. Many rooms have views across the river towards the sea, and some have balconies. There is an impressive range of leisure facilities, including indoor and outdoor pools, and ten-pin bowling. Cuisine is enjoyable and menus offer a range of interesting dishes.

Rooms 70 (27 fmly) (13 GF) **S** £40-£56; **D** £80-£107 (incl. bkfst) **Facilities** FTV Squash 4-lane American bowling alley Hairdresser Snooker & pool room Sauna Solarium Xmas New Year Wi-fi **Conf** Class 100 Board 30 Thtr 100 Del from £74 to £100 **Services** Lift **Parking** 66 **Notes** LB Closed 3 wks Jan Civ Wed 150

Glendorgal Resort

★★★ HOTEL

☎ 01637 874937 & 859981 📠 01637 851341
Lusty Glaze Rd, Porth TR7 3AD
e-mail: info@glendorgal.co.uk
dir: A30 onto A392, 2nd rdbt, right onto A3058, at mini rdbt straight on, right into Lusty Glaze Rd, follow signs for Glendorgal

Rooms 26 (8 fmly) **Facilities** FTV Gym Steam room Cardiovascular room Sauna Wi-fi **Conf** Class 36 Board 30 Thtr 60 Del from £70 to £95* **Parking** 100 **Notes** Civ Wed 110

Priory Lodge

★★ 75% HOTEL

☎ 01637 874111
30 Mount Wise TR7 2BN
e-mail: fionapocklington@tiscali.co.uk
dir: From lights in town centre onto Berry Rd, right onto B3282 Mount Wise, 0.5m on right

The hotel enjoys a central location close to the town centre, the harbour and the local beaches. Secure parking is available at the hotel along with a range of leisure facilities including a heated pool, sauna, games room and hot tub. Attractively decorated bedrooms vary in size and style with many offering sea views over Towan Beach.

Rooms 28 (6 annexe) (13 fmly) (1 GF) **S** £40-£50; **D** £80-£100 (incl. bkfst) **Facilities** Xmas New Year Wi-fi **Parking** 30 **Notes** Closed 18-22 Dec & 4 Jan-early Mar

Sandy Lodge

★★ 72% HOTEL

☎ 01637 872851 📠 01637 872851
6-12 Hilgrove Rd TR7 2QY
e-mail: info@sandylodgehotel.co.uk
dir: From Hever Rd into Hilgrove Rd (by Tesco).

This friendly, family-run hotel is ideally located for easy access to the seafront and surfing beaches, and is within walking distance of the town centre. Accommodation is comfortable with a choice of family, twin and double rooms. There is a spacious dining room and a choice of lounge areas; nightly entertainment is provided.

Rooms 80 (8 fmly) (12 GF) **S** £36-£49; **D** £72-£98 (incl. bkfst & dinner)* **Facilities** Gym Sauna Spa bath Xmas New Year Wi-fi **Conf** Class 40 Board 30 Thtr 100 **Services** Lift **Parking** 50 **Notes** Closed 5-23 Jan

Eliot Hotel

★★ 69% HOTEL

☎ 01637 878177 📠 01637 852053
Edgcumbe Av TR7 2NH
e-mail: eliot.newquay@alfatravel.co.uk
dir: A30 onto A392 towards Quintrell Downs. Right at rdbt onto A3058. 4m to Newquay, left at amusements onto Edgcumbe Av. Hotel on left

Located in a quiet residential area just a short walk from the beaches and the varied attractions of the town, this long-established hotel offers comfortable accommodation. Entertainment is provided most nights throughout the season and guests can relax in the spacious public areas.

Rooms 76 (10 fmly) **S** £36-£50; **D** £56-£84 (incl. bkfst)* **Facilities** FTV Pool table Table tennis Xmas New Year **Services** Lift **Parking** 20 **Notes** LB Closed Dec-Jan (ex Xmas) RS Nov & Feb-Mar

Premier Inn Quintrell Downs

BUDGET HOTEL

☎ 0871 527 8818 📠 0871 527 8819
Quintrell Downs TR8 4LE
dir: From A30 take A39. At rdbt 2nd exit signed Newquay A392. 4m, in Quintrell Downs take 1st exit at rdbt. Hotel on left

High quality, budget accommodation ideal for both families and business travellers. Spacious, en suite bedrooms feature tea and coffee making facilities, and Freeview TV in most hotels. Internet access and Wi-fi are available for a small fee. The adjacent family restaurant features a wide and varied menu. See also the Hotel Groups pages.

Rooms 75 **D** £70*

N

NEWTON ABBOT
Devon — Map 3 SX87

See also **Ilsington**

Passage House

★★★ 73% HOTEL

☎ 01626 355515 01626 363336
Hackney Ln, Kingsteignton TQ12 3QH
e-mail: hotel@passagehousegroup.co.uk
dir: A380 onto A381, follow racecourse signs

With memorable views of the Teign Estuary, this popular hotel provides spacious, well-equipped bedrooms. An impressive range of leisure and meeting facilities is offered and a conservatory provides a pleasant extension to the bar and lounge. A choice of eating options is available, either in the main restaurant, or the adjacent Passage House Inn for less formal dining.

Rooms 90 (52 annexe) (64 fmly) (26 GF) **Facilities** Spa STV supervised Gym Wi-fi **Conf** Class 50 Board 40 Thtr 120 **Services** Lift **Parking** 300 **Notes** RS 24-27 Dec Civ Wed 75

Best Western Queens Hotel

★★★ 70% METRO HOTEL

☎ 01626 363133 01626 354106
Queen St TQ12 2EZ
e-mail: reservations@queenshotel-southwest.co.uk
dir: A380. At Penn Inn turn right towards town, hotel opposite station

Pleasantly and conveniently located close to the railway station and racecourse, this hotel continues to be a popular venue for both business visitors and tourists. Bedrooms are comfortable and spacious. Light snacks and sandwiches are available in the café/bar and lounge.

Rooms 26 (3 fmly) **S** £60-£100; **D** £75-£120* **Facilities** FTV Chargeable gym Wi-fi **Conf** Class 20 Board 20 Thtr 40 Del from £105 to £150* **Parking** 6 **Notes** LB RS 24 Dec-2 Jan

NEWTON AYCLIFFE
Co Durham — Map 19 NZ22

Premier Inn Durham (Newton Aycliffe)

BUDGET HOTEL

☎ 0871 527 8336 0871 527 8337
Ricknall Ln, Great North Rd DL5 6JG
dir: On A167 E of Newton Aycliffe, 3m from A1(M)

High quality, budget accommodation ideal for both families and business travellers. Spacious, en suite bedrooms feature tea and coffee making facilities, and Freeview TV in most hotels. Internet access and Wi-fi are available for a small fee. The adjacent family restaurant features a wide and varied menu. See also the Hotel Groups pages.

Rooms 44 **D** £54-£58*

NEWTON-LE-WILLOWS
Merseyside — Map 15 SJ59

Holiday Inn Haydock M6 Jct 23

★★★ 78% HOTEL

☎ 0871 942 9039 01942 718419
Lodge Ln, Newton Le Willows WA12 0JG
e-mail: haydock@ihg.com
web: www.holidayinn.co.uk
dir: M6 junct 23, A49 to Ashton-in-Makerfield. Hotel 0.25m on right by racecourse

This hotel has an ideal location adjacent to Haydock Racecourse and within easy reach of most north-west cities and attractions. A variety of bedrooms is available and public areas include extensive meeting and conference facilities, a smart Spirit health and leisure club and a spacious bar and restaurant.

Rooms 136 (12 fmly) (23 GF) (38 smoking) **Facilities** STV Gym Xmas New Year Wi-fi **Conf** Class 70 Board 60 Thtr 180 **Services** Lift Air con **Parking** 204 **Notes** Civ Wed 120

NEWTON POPPLEFORD
Devon — Map 3 SY08

Moores' Restaurant & Rooms

RESTAURANT WITH ROOMS

☎ 01395 568100
6 Greenbank, High St EX10 0EB
e-mail: info.moores@btconnect.com
dir: On A3052 in village centre, 3m from Sidmouth

Centrally located in the village, this small restaurant offers very comfortable, practically furnished bedrooms. Guests are assured of a friendly welcome and relaxed, efficient service. Good quality, locally sourced ingredients are used to produce imaginative dishes full of natural flavours.

Rooms 3 (2 fmly)

NORMAN CROSS
Cambridgeshire — Map 12 TL19

Premier Inn Peterborough A1(M) Jct 16

BUDGET HOTEL

☎ 0871 527 8870 0871 527 8871
Norman Cross, A1(M) Junct 16 PE7 3TB
dir: A1(M) junct 16, A15 towards Yaxley, hotel in 100yds

High quality, budget accommodation ideal for both families and business travellers. Spacious, en suite bedrooms feature tea and coffee making facilities, and Freeview TV in most hotels. Internet access and Wi-fi are available for a small fee. The adjacent family restaurant features a wide and varied menu. See also the Hotel Groups pages.

Rooms 95 **D** £45-£55*

NORMANTON
Rutland — Map 11 SK90

Best Western Normanton Park

★★★ 70% HOTEL

☎ 01780 720315 01780 721086
Oakham LE15 8RP
e-mail: info@normantonpark.co.uk
web: www.normantonpark.com
dir: From A1 follow A606 towards Oakham, 5m. Turn left, 1.5m. Hotel on right

This hotel offers some of Rutland Water's best views over the south shore. The comfortable bedrooms are located in the main house and the courtyard. Public rooms include a conservatory dining room overlooking the water, and a cosy lounge is available for guests to relax in.

Rooms 30 (7 annexe) (6 fmly) (11 GF) **Facilities** FTV Xmas New Year Wi-fi **Conf** Class 60 Board 80 Thtr 200 **Parking** 100 **Notes** LB Civ Wed 100

NORTHAMPTON
Northamptonshire Map 11 SP76

Northampton Marriott Hotel

★★★★ 75% HOTEL

☎ 01604 768700 🗎 01604 769011
Eagle Dr NN4 7HW
e-mail: mhrs.ormnh.salesadmin@marriotthotels.com
web: www.northamptonmarriott.co.uk
dir: M1 junct 15, follow signs to Delapre Golf Course, hotel on right

Located on the outskirts of town, close to major road networks, this modern hotel caters to a cross section of guests. A self-contained management centre makes this a popular conference venue, and its spacious and well-designed bedrooms will suit business travellers particularly well. This makes a good base for exploring the attractions the area has to offer.

Rooms 120 (10 fmly) (52 GF) (5 smoking) **S** £90-£165; **D** £90-£175 (incl. bkfst)* **Facilities** STV supervised Gym Steam room Beauty treatment room Sauna Xmas New Year Wi-fi **Conf** Class 72 Board 30 Thtr 250 Del from £125 to £155* **Services** Air con **Parking** 200 **Notes** ⊗ Civ Wed 180

Best Western Lime Trees

★★★ 72% HOTEL

☎ 01604 632188 🗎 01604 233012
8 Langham Place, Barrack Rd NN2 6AA
e-mail: info@limetreeshotel.co.uk
web: www.limetreeshotel.co.uk
dir: From city centre 0.5m N on A508 towards Market Harborough, near racecourse & cathedral

This well presented hotel is popular with business travellers during the week and leisure guests at the weekend. Service is both efficient and friendly. Bedrooms are comfortable and in addition to all the usual facilities, many offer air conditioning. Notable features include an internal courtyard and a row of charming mews houses that have been converted into bedrooms.

Rooms 28 (8 annexe) (4 fmly) (5 GF) **Facilities** FTV Xmas New Year Wi-fi **Conf** Class 50 Board 45 Thtr 140 Del from £115 to £148 **Services** Air con **Parking** 25 **Notes** Civ Wed 140

Park Inn Northampton

★★★ 71% HOTEL

☎ 01604 739988 🗎 01604 739978
Silver St NN1 2TA
e-mail: reservations.northampton@rezidorparkinn.com
web: www.northampton.parkinn.co.uk
dir: In town centre

Ideally located within the city centre, the hotel is a spacious, purpose-built property offering a range of well-appointed bedrooms, conference rooms and a fully-equipped health club. The popular restaurant offers an open-plan contemporary dining experience in a relaxing environment.

Rooms 146 **S** £65-£190; **D** £65-£190* **Facilities** Spa FTV Gym New Year Wi-fi **Conf** Class 300 Board 100 Thtr 600 Del from £99 to £145* **Services** Lift Air con **Parking** 160 **Notes** ⊗ Civ Wed 600

Westone Manor Hotel

★★★ 70% HOTEL

☎ 01604 739955 🗎 01604 415023
Ashley Way, Weston Favell NN3 3EA
e-mail: enquiries@hotels-northampton.com

Ideally located with easy access to the motorway network and the city centre, this hotel, situated in peaceful gardens, offers a good range of accommodation to suit both business and leisure travellers. Built in 1924 for a shoe manufacturer, the house retains many original features. The bedrooms have free Wi-fi and TVs with Sky channels. There are banqueting facilities that cater for various functions from small business meetings to wedding receptions; the hotel holds a civil wedding licence.

Rooms 69 (30 annexe) (2 fmly) (15 GF) (6 smoking) **Facilities** FTV Xmas New Year Wi-fi **Conf** Class 50 Board 50 Thtr 140 **Services** Lift **Parking** 65 **Notes** Civ Wed 180

Campanile Northampton

★★★ 67% HOTEL

☎ 01604 662599 🗎 01604 622598
Cheaney Dr, Grange Park NN4 5FB
e-mail: northampton@campanile.com
dir: M1 junct 15, A508 towards Northampton. 2nd exit at 1st rdbt, 2nd exit at 2nd rdbt into Grange Park

This modern building offers accommodation in smart, well-equipped bedrooms, all with en suite bathrooms. Refreshments may be taken at the informal bistro.

Rooms 87 (18 fmly) **Facilities** STV FTV Xmas New Year Wi-fi **Conf** Class 60 Board 60 Thtr 150 **Services** Lift Air con **Parking** 100

Express by Holiday Inn Northampton M1 Jct 15

BUDGET HOTEL

☎ 01604 432800 🗎 01604 432832
Loake Close, Grange Park NN4 5EZ
e-mail: northampton@expressholidayinn.co.uk
web: www.hiexpress.com/exnorthampton
dir: Just off M1 junct 15, follow signs for Grange Park

A modern hotel ideal for families and business travellers. Fresh and uncomplicated, the spacious rooms include Sky TV, power shower and tea and coffee-making facilities. Continental buffet breakfast is included in the room rate; other meals may be taken at the nearby family pub or restaurant. See also the Hotel Groups pages.

Rooms 126 **S** £40-£95; **D** £40-£120 (incl. bkfst)* **Conf** Class 28 Board 28 Thtr 70

Ibis Northampton Centre

BUDGET HOTEL

☎ 01604 608900 🗎 01604 608910
Sol Central, Marefair NN1 1SR
e-mail: H3657@accor-hotels.com
web: www.ibishotel.com
dir: M1 junct 15/15a & city centre towards railway station

Modern, budget hotel offering comfortable accommodation in bright and practical bedrooms. Breakfast is self-service and dinner is available in the restaurant. See also the Hotel Groups pages.

Rooms 151 (14 fmly) **S** £39-£160; **D** £39-£169* **Conf** Board 10

Premier Inn Northampton Bedford Road/A428

BUDGET HOTEL

☎ 0871 527 8822 🗎 0871 527 8823
The Lakes, Bedford Rd NN4 7YD
dir: M1 junct 15, follow A508 (A45) signs to Northampton. A428 at rdbt take 4th exit (signed Bedford). Left at next rdbt. Hotel on right

High quality, budget accommodation ideal for both families and business travellers. Spacious, en suite bedrooms feature tea and coffee making facilities, and Freeview TV in most hotels. Internet access and Wi-fi are available for a small fee. The adjacent family restaurant features a wide and varied menu. See also the Hotel Groups pages.

Rooms 44 **D** £51-£64*

N

NORTHAMPTON *continued*

Premier Inn Northampton Great Billing/A45

BUDGET HOTEL

☎ 0871 527 8824 📠 0871 527 8825
Crow Ln, Great Billing NN3 9DA
dir: M1 junct 15, A508, A45 follow Billing Aquadrome signs

Rooms 60 **D** £51-£64*

Premier Inn Northampton South (Wootton)

BUDGET HOTEL

☎ 0871 527 8826 📠 0871 527 8827
Newport Pagnell Road West, Wootton NN4 7JJ
dir: M1 junct 15, A508 towards Northampton, exit at junct with A45. At rdbt take B526. Hotel on right

Rooms 45 **D** £51-£64*

Premier Inn Northampton West (Harpole)

BUDGET HOTEL

☎ 0871 527 8828 📠 0871 527 8829
Harpole Turn, Weedon Rd, Harpole NN7 4DD
dir: M1 junct 16, A45 towards Northampton. In 1m left into Harpole Turn. Hotel on left

Rooms 51 **D** £49-£64*

N

NORTH FERRIBY
East Riding of Yorkshire — Map 17 SE92

Hallmark Hotel Hull

★★★★ 71% HOTEL

☎ 01482 645212 📠 01482 643332
Ferriby High Rd HU14 3LG
dir: M62 onto A63 towards Hull. Follow North Ferriby signs, through village, hotel 0.5m on right

This fully refurbished property is situated just outside Hull city centre, with breathtaking views of the Humber Bridge. Service is attentive with a friendly atmosphere. The comfortable bedrooms are tastefully appointed and are suitable for both business and leisure guests. The restaurant and bar serve a good choice of dishes. Conference facilities available along with free Wi-fi and private parking.

Rooms 95 (3 fmly) (16 GF) **S** £59-£89; **D** £69-£99* **Facilities** STV FTV Xmas New Year Wi-fi **Conf** Class 85 Board 86 Thtr 200 Del from £105 to £120* **Parking** 150 **Notes** LB Civ Wed 200

NORTH KILWORTH
Leicestershire — Map 11 SP68

INSPECTORS' CHOICE

Kilworth House

★★★★ ⊛⊛ HOTEL

☎ 01858 880058 📠 01858 880349
Lutterworth Rd LE17 6JE
e-mail: info@kilworthhouse.co.uk
web: www.kilworthhouse.co.uk
dir: A4304 towards Market Harborough, after Walcote, hotel 1.5m on right

A restored Victorian country house located in 38 acres of private grounds offering state-of-the-art conference rooms. The gracious public areas feature many period pieces and original art works. The bedrooms are very comfortable and well equipped, and the large Orangery is now used for informal dining, while the opulent Wordsworth Restaurant has a more formal air.

Rooms 44 (2 fmly) (13 GF) **D** £140-£200* **Facilities** FTV Fishing Gym Beauty therapy rooms Xmas Wi-fi **Conf** Class 30 Board 30 Thtr 80 **Services** Lift **Parking** 140 **Notes** LB Civ Wed 130

NORTH SHIELDS
Tyne & Wear — Map 21 NZ36

Premier Inn North Shields

BUDGET HOTEL

☎ 0871 527 8818 📠 0871 527 8819
Coble Dene Rd NE29 6DL
dir: From all directions follow signs for Royal Quays (Outlet Centre) & International Ferry Terminal. From A187 take Coble Dene Rd. At 3rd rdbt right, 1st right at mini rdbt

High quality, budget accommodation ideal for both families and business travellers. Spacious, en suite bedrooms feature tea and coffee making facilities, and Freeview TV in most hotels. Internet access and Wi-fi are available for a small fee. The adjacent family restaurant features a wide and varied menu. See also the Hotel Groups pages.

Rooms 50 **D** £53-£59*

NORTH WALSHAM
Norfolk — Map 13 TG23

INSPECTORS' CHOICE

Beechwood Hotel

★★★ ⊛⊛ HOTEL

☎ 01692 403231 📠 01692 407284
Cromer Rd NR28 0HD
e-mail: info@beechwood-hotel.co.uk
web: www.beechwood-hotel.co.uk
dir: B1150 from Norwich. At North Walsham left at 1st lights, then right at next

Expect a warm welcome at this elegant 18th-century house, situated just a short walk from the town centre. The individually styled bedrooms are tastefully furnished with well chosen antique pieces, attractive co-ordinated soft fabrics and many thoughtful touches. The spacious public areas include a lounge bar with plush furnishings, a further lounge and a smartly appointed restaurant.

Rooms 17 (4 GF) **S** fr £82; **D** £90-£150 (incl. bkfst) **Facilities** FTV New Year Wi-fi **Conf** Class 20 Board 20 Thtr 20 Del from £136 **Parking** 20 **Notes** LB No children 10yrs

NORTH WALTHAM
Hampshire — Map 5 SU54

Premier Inn Basingstoke South

BUDGET HOTEL

☎ 0871 527 8064 📠 0871 527 8065
RG25 2BB
dir: M3 junct 7, A30 follow signs for Kingsworthy & crematorium. Hotel 2m on right, adjacent to Wheatsheaf

High quality, budget accommodation ideal for both families and business travellers. Spacious, en suite bedrooms feature tea and coffee making facilities, and Freeview TV in most hotels. Internet access and Wi-fi are available for a small fee. The adjacent family restaurant features a wide and varied menu. See also the Hotel Groups pages.

Rooms 28 **D** £55-£68*

NORTHWICH
Cheshire
Map 15 SJ67

Premier Inn Northwich (Sandiway)

BUDGET HOTEL

☎ 0871 527 8830 🖷 0871 527 8831
520 Chester Rd, Sandiway CW8 2DN
dir: M6 junct 19, A556 towards Chester. Hotel in 11m

High quality, budget accommodation ideal for both families and business travellers. Spacious, en suite bedrooms feature tea and coffee making facilities, and Freeview TV in most hotels. Internet access and Wi-fi are available for a small fee. The adjacent family restaurant features a wide and varied menu. See also the Hotel Groups pages.

Rooms 42 **D** £53-£58*

Premier Inn Northwich South

BUDGET HOTEL

☎ 0871 527 8832 🖷 0871 527 8833
London Rd, Leftwich CW9 8EG
dir: Just off M6 junct 19. Follow A556 towards Chester. Right at sign for Northwich & Davenham

Rooms 33 **D** £53-£58*

NORTON
Shropshire
Map 10 SJ70

Hundred House Hotel

★★ 84% ®® HOTEL

☎ 01952 580240 🖷 01952 580260
Bridgnorth Rd TF11 9EE
e-mail: reservations@hundredhouse.co.uk
web: www.hundredhouse.co.uk
dir: Between Telford & Bridgnorth on A442. In town centre

Primarily Georgian in origin, but with parts dating back to the 14th century, this friendly family owned and run hotel offers individually styled, well-equipped bedrooms which have period furniture and attractive soft furnishings. Public areas include cosy bars and intimate dining areas where memorable meals are served. There is an attractive conference centre in the old barn.

Rooms 10 (4 fmly) **Facilities** New Year Wi-fi **Conf** Class 30 Board 32 Thtr 80 **Parking** 45 **Notes** LB Closed 25 & 26 Dec nights Civ Wed 100

NORWICH
Norfolk
Map 13 TG20

See also **Hethersett**

Sprowston Manor, A Marriott Hotel & Country Club

★★★★ 82% ®® HOTEL

☎ 01603 410871 🖷 01603 423911
Sprowston Park, Wroxham Rd, Sprowston NR7 8RP
e-mail: mhrs.nwigs.frontdesk@marriotthotels.com
web: www.marriottsprowstonmanor.co.uk
dir: From A11/A47, 2m NE on A1151 (Wroxham road). Follow signs to Sprowston Park

Surrounded by open parkland, this imposing property is set in attractively landscaped grounds and is just a short drive from the city centre. Bedrooms are spacious and feature a variety of decorative styles. The hotel also has extensive conference, banqueting and leisure facilities. Other public rooms include an array of seating areas and the elegant Manor Restaurant.

Rooms 94 (3 fmly) (5 GF) (8 smoking) **S** £105-£135; **D** £140-£145 (incl. bkfst)* **Facilities** Spa FTV (indoor pool) supervised ⛳ 18 Putt green Gym Steam room Sauna Xmas New Year Wi-fi **Conf** Class 50 Board 50 Thtr 500 **Services** Lift **Parking** 150 **Notes** LB Civ Wed 300

St Giles House

★★★★ 81% ®® HOTEL

☎ 01603 275180 🖷 0845 299 1905
41-45 St Giles St NR2 1JR
e-mail: reception@stgileshousehotel.com
web: www.stgileshousehotel.com
dir: A11 into central Norwich. Left at rdbt (Chapelfield Shopping Centre). 3rd exit at next rdbt. Left onto St Giles St. Hotel on left

A stylish 19th-century, Grade II listed building situated in the heart of the city. The property has a wealth of magnificent original features such as wood-panelling, ornamental plasterwork and marble floors. Public areas include an open-plan lounge bar/restaurant, a smart lounge with plush sofas and a Parisian-style terrace. The spacious, contemporary bedrooms are individually designed and have many thoughtful touches.

Rooms 24 (incl. bkfst) **Facilities** Spa FTV Xmas New Year Wi-fi **Conf** Class 20 Board 24 Thtr 45 **Services** Lift **Parking** 30 **Notes** LB ⊗ Civ Wed 60

De Vere Dunston Hall

DE VERE Hotels & Resorts

★★★★ 79% ® HOTEL

☎ 01508 470444 🖷 01508 471499
Ipswich Rd NR14 8PQ
e-mail: dhreception@devere-hotels.com
web: www.devere.co.uk
dir: From A47 take A140 (Ipswich road). 0.25m, hotel on left

An imposing Grade II listed building set amidst 170 acres of landscaped grounds just a short drive from the city centre. The spacious bedrooms are smartly decorated, tastefully furnished and equipped to a high standard. The attractively appointed public rooms offer a wide choice of areas in which to relax, and the hotel also boasts a superb range of leisure facilities including an 18-hole PGA golf course, floodlit tennis courts and a football pitch.

Rooms 169 (16 fmly) (16 GF) (2 smoking) **S** £79-£159; **D** £99-£179 (incl. bkfst)* **Facilities** Spa (indoor pool) ⛳ 18 Putt green Gym Floodlit driving range Xmas New Year Wi-fi **Conf** Class 140 Board 80 Thtr 300 Del from £130 to £175 **Services** Lift **Parking** 500 **Notes** LB Civ Wed 90

The Maids Head Hotel

★★★★ 76% ® HOTEL

☎ 0844 855 9120 🖷 01603 613688
Tombland NR3 1LB
e-mail: gm@maidsheadhotel.co.uk
web: www.maidsheadhotel.co.uk
dir: Follow city centre signs past Norwich Castle. 3rd turn after castle into Upper King St. Hotel opposite cathedral

A 13th-century building situated close to the impressive Norman cathedral, the Anglian TV studios and within easy walking distance of the city centre. The bedrooms are pleasantly decorated and thoughtfully equipped; some rooms have original oak beams. The spacious public rooms include a Jacobean bar, a range of seating areas and the Courtyard Restaurant.

Rooms 84 (10 fmly) **S** £69-£149; **D** £79-£159 **Facilities** FTV Treatment room Use of nearby gym Xmas New Year Wi-fi **Conf** Class 30 Board 50 Thtr 100 Del from £110 to £175 **Services** Lift **Parking** 83 **Notes** LB ⊗ Civ Wed 100

NORWICH *continued*

Barnham Broom Hotel, Golf & Restaurant

★★★★ 74% HOTEL

☎ 01603 759393 01603 758224
NR9 4DD
e-mail: amortimer@barnham-broom.co.uk
web: www.barnham-broom.co.uk

(For full entry see Barnham Broom)

Holiday Inn Norwich-North

★★★★ 71% HOTEL

☎ 01603 410544 01603 487701
Cromer Rd NR6 6JA
e-mail: frontoffice@hinorwich.com
web: www.hinorwich.com
dir: A140 signed for Cromer, turn right at lights signed 'Airport Passengers'. Hotel on right

A modern, purpose-built hotel situated to the north of Norwich at the airport. Bedrooms are smartly decorated, equipped with modern facilities and have a good range of useful extras. Public areas include a large open-plan lounge bar and restaurant, as well as meeting rooms, a banqueting suite and leisure facilities.

Rooms 121 (8 fmly) (33 GF) (5 smoking) **Facilities** Gym Wi-fi **Conf** Class 200 Board 70 Thtr 600 Del from £120 to £180* **Services** Lift Air con **Parking** 200 **Notes** Civ Wed 500

Best Western Annesley House Hotel

★★★ 86% HOTEL

☎ 01603 624553 01603 621577
6 Newmarket Rd NR2 2LA
e-mail: annesleyhouse@bestwestern.co.uk
dir: On A11, 0.5m before city centre

Delightful Georgian property set in three acres of landscaped gardens close to the city centre. Bedrooms are split between three separate houses, two of which are linked by a glass walkway. Each is attractively decorated, tastefully furnished and thoughtfully equipped. Public rooms include a comfortable lounge/bar and a smart conservatory restaurant which overlooks the gardens.

Rooms 26 (8 annexe) (1 fmly) (7 GF) **S** £50-£80; **D** £75-£90* **Facilities** FTV Wi-fi **Parking** 25 **Notes** LB Closed 24 Dec-2 Jan

Holiday Inn Norwich

★★★ 79% HOTEL

☎ 0871 942 9060 & 0800 405060
01603 506400
Ipswich Rd NR4 6EP
e-mail: reservations-norwich@ihg.com
web: www.holidayinn.co.uk
dir: A47 (Great Yarmouth) then A140 (Norwich). 1m, hotel on right

A modern, purpose-built hotel situated just off the A140 which is a short drive from the city centre. Public areas include a popular bar, the Junction Restaurant and a large open-plan lounge. Bedrooms come in a variety of styles and are suited to the needs of both the business and leisure guest alike.

Rooms 119 (41 fmly) (39 GF) **S** £50-£145; **D** £50-£145* **Facilities** STV FTV supervised Gym Sauna Steam room Xmas New Year Wi-fi **Conf** Class 48 Board 40 Thtr 150 Del from £99 to £135 **Services** Air con **Parking** 250 **Notes** LB Civ Wed 120

Best Western George Hotel

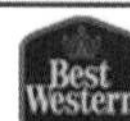

★★★ 75% HOTEL

☎ 01603 617841 01603 663708
10 Arlington Ln, Newmarket Rd NR2 2DA
e-mail: reservations@georgehotel.co.uk
web: www.arlingtonhotelgroup.co.uk
dir: From A11 follow city centre signs (becomes Newmarket Rd). Hotel on left

Within just 10 minutes' walk of the town centre, this friendly, family-run hotel is well placed for guests wishing to explore the many sights of this historic city. The hotel occupies three adjacent buildings; the restaurant, bar and most bedrooms are located in the main building, while the adjacent cottages have been converted into comfortable and modern guest bedrooms.

Rooms 43 (5 annexe) (4 fmly) (19 GF) **S** £65-£77; **D** £87-£97 (incl. bkfst)* **Facilities** Beauty therapist Holistic treatments Xmas New Year **Conf** Class 30 Board 30 Thtr 70 Del from £99 to £120* **Parking** 40 **Notes** LB

Stracey Hotel

★★★ 74% SMALL HOTEL

☎ 01603 628093 01603 753511
2 Stracey Rd NR1 1EZ
e-mail: info@straceyhotel.co.uk
dir: Telephone for detailed directions

Ideally situated close to the railway station, and within easy walking distance of the historic city centre, with its range of shops and amenities. The contemporary-style bedrooms are smartly decorated and well equipped. Public rooms include a smart open-plan lounge bar and an outside terrace.

Rooms 20 (2 fmly) (5 GF) **Facilities** FTV Xmas New Year Wi-fi **Notes**

INSPECTORS' CHOICE

The Old Rectory

★★ SMALL HOTEL

☎ 01603 700772 01603 300772
103 Yarmouth Rd, Thorpe St Andrew NR7 0HF
e-mail: enquiries@oldrectorynorwich.com
web: www.oldrectorynorwich.com
dir: From A47 southern bypass onto A1042 towards Norwich N & E. Left at mini rdbt onto A1242. After 0.3m through lights. Hotel 100mtrs on right

This delightful Grade II listed Georgian property is ideally located in a peaceful area overlooking the River Yare, just a few minutes' drive from the city centre. Spacious bedrooms are individually designed with carefully chosen soft fabrics, plush furniture and many thoughtful touches; many of the rooms overlook the swimming pool and landscaped gardens. Accomplished cooking is offered via an interesting daily-changing menu, which features skilfully prepared local produce.

Rooms 8 (3 annexe) **S** £95-£155; **D** £125-£155 (incl. bkfst)* **Facilities** FTV Wi-fi **Conf** Class 18 Board 16 Thtr 25 **Parking** 15 **Notes** LB Closed 23 Dec-3 Jan

Stower Grange

★★ 85% HOTEL

☎ 01603 860210 📠 01603 860464
School Rd, Drayton NR8 6EF
e-mail: enquiries@stowergrange.co.uk
web: www.stowergrange.co.uk
dir: Norwich ring road N to Asda supermarket. Take A1067 (Fakenham road) at Drayton, right at lights into School Rd. Hotel 150yds on right

Expect a warm welcome at this 17th-century, ivy-clad property situated in a peaceful residential area close to the city centre and airport. The individually decorated bedrooms are generally quite spacious; each is tastefully furnished and equipped with many thoughtful touches. Public rooms include a smart open-plan lounge bar and an elegant restaurant.

Rooms 11 (1 fmly) **S** fr £80; **D** £100-£150 (incl. bkfst) **Facilities** FTV New Year Wi-fi **Conf** Class 45 Board 30 Thtr 100 Del from £135 **Parking** 40 **Notes** LB Civ Wed 100

Express by Holiday Inn Norwich

BUDGET HOTEL

☎ 01603 780010 📠 01603 780011
Drayton High Rd, Hellesdon NR6 5DU
e-mail: gm@exhinorwich.co.uk
web: www.hiexpress.com/norwich
dir: At junct of A140 (ring road) & A1067 to Fakenham, follow brown tourist signs

A modern hotel ideal for families and business travellers. Fresh and uncomplicated, the spacious rooms include Sky TV, power shower and tea and coffee-making facilities. Continental buffet breakfast is included in the room rate; other meals may be taken at the nearby family pub or restaurant. See also the Hotel Groups pages.

Rooms 78 (45 fmly) (14 GF) (14 smoking) **Conf** Class 12 Board 12 Thtr 12

Premier Inn Norwich Airport

BUDGET HOTEL

☎ 0871 527 8836 📠 0871 527 8837
Delft Way NR6 6BB
dir: From Norwich take A140 signed Cromer & Airport. Right at lights into Amsterdam Way. At mini-rdbt turn right. Hotel on right

High quality, budget accommodation ideal for both families and business travellers. Spacious, en suite bedrooms feature tea and coffee making facilities, and Freeview TV in most hotels. Internet access and Wi-fi are available for a small fee. The adjacent family restaurant features a wide and varied menu. See also the Hotel Groups pages.

Rooms 40 **D** £62-£67*

Premier Inn Norwich Central South

BUDGET HOTEL

☎ 0871 527 8838 📠 0871 527 8839
Broadlands Business Park, Old Chapel Way NR7 0WG
dir: A47 onto A1042, 3m E of city centre

Rooms 92 **D** £58-£62*

Premier Inn Norwich City Centre (Duke Street)

BUDGET HOTEL

☎ 0871 527 8840 📠 0871 527 8841
Duke St NR3 3AP
dir: From A1074 straight on at lights at Toys'R'Us into St Benedict's St (or from A147 (A140/A11) right at lights. At next lights into Duke St (car park in St Andrews multi-storey on right - free to guests)

Rooms 117 **D** £65-£68*

Premier Inn Norwich Nelson City Centre

BUDGET HOTEL

☎ 0871 527 8842 📠 0871 527 8843
Prince of Wales Rd NR1 1DX
dir: Follow city centre, football ground & railway station signs. Hotel opposite station

Rooms 160 (27 GF) **D** £70-£74*

Premier Inn Norwich (Showground A47)

BUDGET HOTEL

☎ 0871 527 8834 📠 0871 527 8835
Longwater Interchange, Dereham Rd, New Costessey NR5 0TP
dir: A47 towards Dereham, take A1074 to City Centre. At rdbt 2nd exit, hotel on right. From N: A47 through Dereham. Straight on at 1st rdbt, at 2nd rdbt take 3rd exit. Hotel on left

Rooms 40 **D** £58-£62*

Brasteds

RESTAURANT WITH ROOMS

☎ 01508 491112 📠 01508 491113
Manor Farm Barns, Framingham Pigot NR14 7PZ
e-mail: enquiries@brasteds.co.uk
web: www.brasteds.co.uk
dir: A11 onto A47 towards Great Yarmouth, then A146. After 0.5m turn right onto Fox Rd, 0.5m on left

A lovely detached property set in 20 acres of mature, landscaped parkland on the outskirts of Norwich. The tastefully appointed bedrooms have beautiful soft furnishings and fabrics along with comfortable seating and many thoughtful touches. Public rooms include a cosy snug with plush sofas, and a smart dining room where breakfast is served. Dinner is available in Brasteds Restaurant, which can be found in an adjacent building.

Rooms 6 (1 fmly)

N

NOTTINGHAM
Nottinghamshire Map 11 SK53

See also **Langar**

Hart's Hotel
★★★★ 82% ◎◎ HOTEL

☎ 0115 988 1900 0115 947 7600
Standard Hill, Park Row NG1 6FN
e-mail: reception@hartsnottingham.co.uk
web: www.hartsnottingham.co.uk
dir: At junct of Park Row & Ropewalk

This outstanding modern building stands on the site of the ramparts of the medieval castle, overlooking the city. Many of the bedrooms enjoy splendid views. Rooms are well appointed and stylish, while the Park Bar is the focal point of the public areas; service is professional and caring. Fine dining is offered at nearby Hart's Restaurant. Secure parking and private gardens are an added bonus.

Rooms 32 (1 fmly) (7 GF) **D** £125-£260* **Facilities** STV FTV Small unsupervised exercise room Xmas New Year Wi-fi **Conf** Class 75 Board 30 Thtr 100 **Services** Lift **Parking** 16 **Notes** Civ Wed 100

Nottingham Belfry
★★★★ 79% HOTEL

☎ 0115 973 9393 0115 973 9494
Mellor's Way, Off Woodhouse Way NG8 6PY
e-mail: nottinghambelfry@qhotels.co.uk
web: www.qhotels.co.uk
dir: A610 towards Nottingham. A6002 to Stapleford/Strelley. 0.75m, last exit at rdbt, hotel on right

Set conveniently close to the motorway links, yet not far from the city centre attractions, this modern hotel has a stylish and impressive interior. Bedrooms and bathrooms are spaciously appointed and very comfortable. There are two restaurants and two bars that offer interesting and satisfying cuisine. Staff are friendly and helpful.

Rooms 120 (20 fmly) (36 GF) **S** £112-£132; **D** £145-£165 (incl. bkfst & dinner)* **Facilities** Spa STV FTV ⓢ Gym Sauna Steam room Treatment rooms Aerobic studio Xmas New Year Wi-fi **Conf** Class 360 Board 60 Thtr 700 Del from £ to £159* **Services** Lift **Parking** 250 **Notes** LB ⊗ Civ Wed 150

Crowne Plaza Nottingham

★★★★ 75% HOTEL

☎ 0115 936 9988 & 0870 787 5161
0115 947 5667
Wollaton St NG1 5RH
e-mail: cpnottingham@qmh-hotels.com
web: www.crowneplaza.co.uk
dir: Follow city centre signs on A6200 to Canning Circus. Down hill, straight on at lights

Located in the heart of the city centre this is a large, purpose-built hotel. Spacious public areas uniquely centre on a tree-lined avenue and include a popular bar and extensive meeting rooms. Air-conditioned bedrooms, which vary in size, include flat-screen TVs. The hotel also has a leisure club and extensive parking.

Rooms 210 (9 fmly) **Facilities** STV ⓢ Gym Beautician Hairdresser Dance studio Treatment rooms Xmas New Year Wi-fi **Conf** Class 300 Board 40 Thtr 400 **Services** Lift Air con **Parking** 600 **Notes** ⊗ Civ Wed 400

Park Plaza Nottingham

★★★★ 73% HOTEL

☎ 0115 947 7200 0115 947 7300
41 Maid Marian Way NG1 6GD
e-mail: ppnsales@pphe.com
web: www.parkplaza.com/nottinghamuk
dir: A6200 (Derby Rd) into Wollaton St. 2nd exit into Maid Marian Way. Hotel on left

This ultra modern hotel is located in the centre of the city within walking distance of retail, commercial and tourist attractions. Bedrooms are spacious and comfortable, with many extras, including laptop safes, high-speed phone lines and air conditioning. Service is discreetly attentive in the foyer lounge and the Chino Latino restaurant, where Pan Asian cooking is a feature.

Rooms 178 (10 fmly) (16 smoking) **Facilities** STV FTV Gym Complimentary fitness suite Wi-fi **Conf** Class 100 Board 54 Thtr 200 **Services** Lift Air con **Notes** ⊗

Colwick Hall Hotel
★★★★ 72% HOTEL

☎ 0115 950 0566 & 0870 755 7756
0115 924 3797
Colwick Park, Racecourse Rd NG2 4BH
e-mail: reservations@colwickhallhotel.com
web: www.colwickhallhotel.com
dir: From Nottingham Forest FC, left into Radciffe Rd (A6520), left at Lady Bay Bridge, at lights right into Meadow Ln, at rdbt 4th exit onto A612 (Daleside Rd) signed Southwell, at rdbt 2nd exit into Daleside Rd

This splendid palladian Georgian mansion sits in 60 acres of well established gardens and parkland, conveniently located for the adjacent racecourse and just two miles from the city centre. Character Grade II listed day rooms, which include the Georgetown Restaurant (specialising in colonial Malaysian cuisine) are complemented by some splendidly appointed accommodation. The superior bedrooms are luxurious and particularly spacious.

Rooms 16 (4 fmly) **Facilities** FTV Xmas New Year Wi-fi **Conf** Class 300 Board 200 Thtr 700 Del from £110 to £155* **Parking** 120 **Notes** ⊗ Civ Wed 350

Park Inn Nottingham
★★★ 72% HOTEL

☎ 0115 935 9988 0115 924 5227
Mansfield Rd NG5 2BT
e-mail: reservations.nottingham@rezidorparkinn.com
dir: Approx 1m from city centre on A60 (Mansfield Rd), at large rdbt, straight on at lights. Hotel on right

Ideally located to explore the city centre, the hotel is a spacious, purpose-built property offering a range of well-appointed bedrooms, conference rooms and a fully-equipped leisure club. The popular restaurant offers a contemporary dining experience in an airy environment.

Rooms 172 (11 fmly) **S** £55-£130; **D** £55-£130* **Facilities** STV FTV ⓢ supervised Gym Treatment room Sauna Steam room New Year Wi-fi **Conf** Class 45 Board 40 Thtr 180 Del from £99 to £177* **Services** Lift Air con **Parking** 410 **Notes** LB ⊗ Civ Wed 200

Best Western Bestwood Lodge

★★★ 71% HOTEL

☎ 0115 920 3011 Fax 0115 964 9678
Bestwood Country Park, Arnold NG5 8NE
e-mail: enquiries@bestwoodlodgehotel.co.uk
web: www.bw-bestwoodlodge.co.uk
dir: 3m N off A60. Left at lights into Oxclose Ln, right at next lights into Queens Bower Rd. 1st right. Keep right at fork in road

Set in 700 acres of parkland this Victorian building, once a hunting lodge, has stunning architecture that includes Gothic features and high vaulted ceilings. Bedrooms include all modern comforts, suitable for both business and leisure guests, and the popular restaurant serves an extensive menu.

Rooms 39 (5 fmly) **Facilities** FTV Guided walks Wi-fi **Conf** Class 65 Board 50 Thtr 200 **Parking** 120 **Notes** LB RS 25 Dec & 1 Jan Civ Wed 80

See advert on this page

Nottingham Gateway

★★★ 68% HOTEL

☎ 0115 979 4949 Fax 0115 979 4744
Nuthall Rd, Cinderhill NG8 6AZ
e-mail: sales@nottinghamgatewayhotel.co.uk
web: www.nottinghamgatewayhotel.co.uk
dir: M1 junct 26, A610, hotel on 3rd rdbt on left

Located approximately three miles from the city centre, and with easy access to the M1. This modern hotel provides spacious public areas, with the popular Bows Gallery Restaurant and lounge bar, and the contemporary accommodation is suitably well equipped. Ample parking is a bonus.

Rooms 108 (18 fmly) (6 smoking) **S** £49.95-£85; **D** £54.95-£100 (incl. bkfst)* **Facilities** STV FTV Xmas New Year **Conf** Class 150 Board 60 Thtr 250 Del from £90 to £135* **Services** Lift **Parking** 250 **Notes** LB Civ Wed 250

Rutland Square Hotel

★★★ 68% HOTEL

☎ 0115 941 1114 Fax 0115 941 0014
St James St NG1 6FJ
e-mail: rutland.square@forestdale.com
web: www.rutlandsquarehotel.co.uk
dir: Follow signs to castle. Hotel on right 50yds beyond castle

The enviable location in the heart of the city adjacent to the castle makes this hotel a popular choice with both leisure and business travellers. The hotel is modern and comfortable with excellent business facilities. Bedrooms offer a host of thoughtful extras to guests and the penthouse has its own jacuzzi. The contemporary Woods Restaurant offers a full range of dining options.

Rooms 87 (3 fmly) **Facilities** FTV Discounted day passes to nearby gym Xmas Wi-fi **Conf** Class 70 Board 45 Thtr 200 **Services** Lift **Parking** 30 **Notes** LB Civ Wed 110

Swans Hotel & Restaurant

★★★ 67% HOTEL

☎ 0115 981 4042 Fax 0115 945 5745
84-90 Radcliffe Rd, West Bridgford NG2 5HH
e-mail: enquiries@swanshotel.co.uk
web: www.swanshotel.co.uk
dir: On A6011. (For detailed directions telephone hotel or see website)

This privately owned hotel is located on the outskirts of the city, conveniently placed for the various

continued

N

NOTTINGHAM *continued*

sporting stadiums. Bedrooms vary in size, but are all equipped to meet the needs of both business and leisure visitors. An interesting range of dishes is served in either the cosy bar or, more formally, in the restaurant.

Rooms 30 (3 fmly) (1 GF) **S** £45-£55; **D** £60-£65 (incl. bkfst)* **Facilities** STV FTV Wi-fi **Conf** Class 10 Board 24 Thtr 30 **Services** Lift **Parking** 26 **Notes** ⊗ Closed 24-28 Dec

The Strathdon

★★ 69% HOTEL

☎ 0115 941 8501 📠 0115 948 3725
Derby Rd NG1 5FT
e-mail: info@strathdon-hotel-nottingham.com
web: www.strathdon-hotel-nottingham.com
dir: From M1 follow city centre signs. At Canning Circus into one-way system into Wollaton St, keep right, next right to hotel

N

This city-centre hotel has modern facilities and is very convenient for all city attractions. A popular themed bar has a large-screen TV and serves an extensive range of popular fresh food, while more formal dining is available in Bobbins Restaurant on certain evenings.

Rooms 68 (4 fmly) (16 smoking) **S** £39.50-£75; **D** £55-£105* **Facilities** FTV Xmas New Year Wi-fi **Conf** Class 60 Board 40 Thtr 150 Del from £85 to £110* **Services** Lift **Parking** 4 **Notes** LB Civ Wed 85

Ibis Nottingham Centre

BUDGET HOTEL

☎ 0115 985 3600 📠 0115 985 3610
16 Fletcher Gate NG1 2FS
e-mail: h6160@accor.com
dir: In Lace Market area of city centre

Modern, budget hotel offering comfortable accommodation in bright and practical bedrooms. Breakfast is self-service and dinner is available in the restaurant. See also the Hotel Groups pages.

Rooms 142 (33 fmly) **S** £54-£99; **D** £54-£99*

Premier Inn Nottingham Arena (London Rd)

BUDGET HOTEL

☎ 0871 527 8848 📠 0871 527 8849
Island Site, London Rd NG2 4UU
dir: M1 junct 25, A52 into city centre. Follow signs for A60 to Loughborough. Hotel adjacent to BBC building

High quality, budget accommodation ideal for both families and business travellers. Spacious, en suite bedrooms feature tea and coffee making facilities, and Freeview TV in most hotels. Internet access and Wi-fi are available for a small fee. The adjacent family restaurant features a wide and varied menu. See also the Hotel Groups pages.

Rooms 87 **D** £58-£63*

Premier Inn Nottingham Castle Marina

BUDGET HOTEL

☎ 0871 527 8844 📠 0871 527 8845
Castle Marina Park, Castle Bridge Rd NG7 1GX
dir: M1 junct 24, A453. Follow ring road & signs for Queen's Drive Industrial Estate. After Homebase left into Castle Bridge Rd, opposite Pizza Hut restaurant. Hotel adjacent to Boathouse Beefeater

Rooms 39 **D** £58-£66*

Premier Inn Nottingham City Centre (Goldsmith Street)

BUDGET HOTEL

☎ 0871 527 8846 📠 0871 527 8847
Goldsmith St NG1 5LT
dir: A610 to city centre. Follow signs for Nottingham Trent University into Talbot St. 1st left into Clarendon St. Right at lights. Hotel on right

Rooms 161 **D** £52*

Premier Inn Nottingham North (Daybrook)

BUDGET HOTEL

☎ 0871 527 8850 📠 0871 527 8851
101 Mansfield Rd, Daybrook NG5 6BH
dir: M1 junct 26, A610 towards Nottingham. Left onto A6514. Left onto A60 towards Mansfield. Hotel 0.25m on left

Rooms 64 **D** £54-£57*

Premier Inn Nottingham South

BUDGET HOTEL

☎ 0871 527 8854 📠 0871 527 8855
Loughborough Rd, Ruddington NG11 6LS
dir: M1 junct 24, follow A453 signs to Nottingham, A52 to Grantham. Hotel at 1st rdbt on left

Rooms 42 **D** £54-£57*

Premier Inn Nottingham West

BUDGET HOTEL

☎ 0871 527 8856 📠 0871 527 8857
The Phoenix Centre, Millennium Way West NG8 6AS
dir: M1 junct 26, 1m on A610 towards Nottingham

Rooms 86 **D** £52-£57*

INSPECTORS' CHOICE

Restaurant Sat Bains with Rooms

@@@@@ RESTAURANT WITH ROOMS

☎ 0115 986 6566 📠 0115 986 0343
Trentside, Lenton Ln NG7 2SA
e-mail: info@restaurantsatbains.net
dir: M1 junct 24 take A453 Nottingham S. Over River Trent in central lane to rdbt. Left then left again towards river. Establishment on left after bend

This charming restaurant with rooms, a stylish conversion of Victorian farm buildings, is situated on the river and close to the industrial area of Nottingham. The bedrooms create a warm atmosphere by using quality soft furnishings together with antique and period furniture; suites and four-poster rooms are available. Public areas are chic and cosy, and the delightful restaurant complements the truly outstanding cuisine.

Rooms 8 (4 annexe)

Cockliffe Country House

@ RESTAURANT WITH ROOMS

☎ 0115 968 0179 📠 0115 968 0623
Burntstump Country Park, Burntstump Hill, Arnold NG5 8PQ
e-mail: enquiries@cockliffehouse.co.uk

Expect a warm welcome at this delightful property situated in a peaceful rural location amidst neat landscaped grounds, close to Sherwood Forest. Public areas include a smart breakfast room, a tastefully appointed restaurant and a cosy lounge bar. The individually decorated bedrooms have co-ordinated soft furnishings and many thoughtful touches.

Rooms 11 (4 annexe)

NUNEATON Map 11 SP39
Warwickshire

Best Western Weston Hall

★★★ 73% HOTEL

☎ 024 7631 2989 024 7664 0846
Weston Ln, Bulkington CV12 9RU
e-mail: info@westonhallhotel.co.uk
dir: M6 junct 2, B4065 through Ansty. Left in Shilton, from Bulkington follow Nuneaton signs, into Weston Ln at 30mph sign

This Grade II listed hotel, with origins dating back to the reign of Elizabeth I, sits within seven acres of peaceful grounds. The original three-gabled building retains many original features, such as the carved wooden fireplace in the library. Friendly service is provided; and the bedrooms, that vary in size, are thoughtfully equipped.

Rooms 40 (1 fmly) (14 GF) **Facilities** FTV New Year Wi-fi **Conf** Class 100 Board 60 Thtr 200 **Parking** 300 **Notes** Civ Wed 200

Premier Inn Nuneaton/ Coventry

BUDGET HOTEL

☎ 0871 527 8858 0871 527 8859
Coventry Rd CV10 7PJ
dir: M6 junct 3, A444 towards Nuneaton. Hotel on B4113 on right, just off Griff Rdbt towards Bedworth

High quality, budget accommodation ideal for both families and business travellers. Spacious, en suite bedrooms feature tea and coffee making facilities, and Freeview TV in most hotels. Internet access and Wi-fi are available for a small fee. The adjacent family restaurant features a wide and varied menu. See also the Hotel Groups pages.

Rooms 48 **D** £47-£55*

OAKHAM Map 11 SK80
Rutland

INSPECTORS' CHOICE

Hambleton Hall

★★★★ @@@@
COUNTRY HOUSE HOTEL

☎ 01572 756991 01572 724721
Hambleton LE15 8TH
e-mail: hotel@hambletonhall.com
web: www.hambletonhall.com
dir: 3m E off A606

Established 30 years ago by Tim and Stefa Hart this delightful country house enjoys tranquil and spectacular views over Rutland Water. The beautifully manicured grounds are a delight to walk in. The bedrooms in the main house are stylish, individually decorated and equipped with a range of thoughtful extras. A two-bedroom folly, with its own sitting and breakfast room, is only a short walk away. Day rooms include a cosy bar and a sumptuous drawing room, both featuring open fires. The elegant restaurant serves very accomplished, award-winning cuisine with menus highlighting locally sourced, seasonal produce - some grown in the hotel's own grounds.

Rooms 17 (2 annexe) **S** £195-£215; **D** £235-£625 (incl. bkfst)* **Facilities** STV FTV Private access to lake Xmas New Year Wi-fi **Conf** Board 24 Thtr 40 Del from £300 to £400* **Services** Lift **Parking** 40 **Notes** LB Civ Wed 64

Barnsdale Lodge Hotel

★★★ 75% @ HOTEL

☎ 01572 724678 01572 724961
The Avenue, Rutland Water, North Shore LE15 8AH
e-mail: enquiries@barnsdalelodge.co.uk
web: www.barnsdalelodge.co.uk
dir: Off A1 onto A606. Hotel 5m on right, 2m E of Oakham

A popular and interesting hotel converted from a farmstead overlooking Rutland Water. The public areas are dominated by a successful food operation with a good range of appealing meals on offer for either formal or informal dining. Bedrooms are comfortably appointed with excellent beds enhanced by contemporary soft furnishings and thoughtful extras.

Rooms 44 (2 fmly) (15 GF) **S** £85-£90; **D** £100-£110 (incl. bkfst)* **Facilities** FTV Fishing Archery Beauty treatments Golf Sailing Shooting Xmas New Year Wi-fi **Conf** Class 120 Board 76 Thtr 330 Del from £112* **Parking** 200 **Notes** LB Civ Wed 160

O

OCKLEY Map 6 TQ14
Surrey

Gatton Manor Hotel & Golf Club

★★★ 80% HOTEL

☎ 01306 627555 01306 627713
Standon Ln RH5 5PQ
e-mail: info@gattonmanor.co.uk
web: www.gattonmanor.co.uk
dir: Exit A29 at Ockley into Cat Hill Ln, left into Standon Ln, follow signs for approx 1m

Gatton Manor enjoys a peaceful setting in private grounds. It is a popular golf and country club, with an 18-hole professional course, that offers a range of comfortable, modern bedrooms. The public areas include the main club bar and restaurant. Conference facilities are also available.

Rooms 18 (2 fmly) **Facilities** STV 18 Putt green Gym Treatments New Year Wi-fi **Conf** Class 22 Board 30 Thtr 80 **Parking** 250 **Notes** LB Closed 25 Dec Civ Wed 90

ODIHAM
Hampshire — Map 5 SU75

George

★★★ 73% HOTEL

☎ 01256 702081 📠 01256 704213
High St RG29 1LP
e-mail: reception@georgehotelodiham.com
web: www.georgehotelodiham.com
dir: M3 junct 5 follow Alton & Odiham signs. Through North Warnborough into Odiham left at top of hill, hotel on left

The George is over 450 years old and is a fine example of an old English inn. Bedrooms come in a number of styles; the older part of the property has beams and period features, whilst newer rooms have a contemporary feel. Guests can dine in the all-day bistro or the popular restaurant.

Rooms 28 (9 annexe) (1 fmly) (6 GF) (4 smoking) **S** £65-£95; **D** £85-£130 (incl. bkfst)* **Facilities** FTV Wi-fi **Conf** Class 10 Board 26 Thtr 30 **Parking** 20 **Notes** Closed 24-26 Dec

OKEHAMPTON
Devon — Map 3 SX59

Ashbury Hotel

★★ 74% HOTEL

☎ 01837 55453 📠 01837 55468
Higher Maddaford, Southcott EX20 4NL
dir: Off A30 at Sourton Cross onto A386. Left onto A3079 to Bude at Fowley Cross. After 1m right to Ashbury. Hotel 0.5m on right

With no less than five courses and a clubhouse with lounge, bar and dining facilities, The Ashbury is a golfers' paradise. The majority of the well-equipped bedrooms are located in the farmhouse and the courtyard-style development around the putting green. Guests can enjoy the many on-site leisure facilities or join the activities available at the nearby sister hotel.

Rooms 184 (79 fmly) (77 GF) **Facilities** FTV ⛳ 99 Putt green Fishing Gym Badminton Driving range Golf simulator Shooting range Ten-pin bowling New Year Wi-fi **Conf** Thtr 250 **Parking** 150 **Notes** LB

See advert on opposite page

Manor House Hotel

★★ 72% HOTEL

☎ 01837 53053 📠 01837 55027
Fowley Cross EX20 4NA
e-mail: reception@manorhousehotel.co.uk
web: www.manorhousehotel.co.uk
dir: Off A30 at Sourton Cross flyover, right onto A386. Hotel 1.5m on right

Enjoying views to Dartmoor in the distance, this hotel specialises in short breaks and is set in 17 acres of grounds, close to the A30. The superb range of sporting and craft facilities has been enhanced by an impressive swimming pool; golf is also offered at the adjacent sister hotel. Bedrooms, many located on the ground floor, are comfortable and well equipped.

Rooms 200 (91 fmly) (90 GF) **Facilities** Spa ⛳ 99 Putt green Fishing Gym Squash Craft centre Indoor bowls Shooting range Laser clay pigeon shooting Aerobics Xmas New Year Wi-fi **Parking** 200 **Notes** LB

See advert on opposite page

White Hart Hotel

★★ 72% HOTEL

☎ 01837 52730 & 54514 📠 01837 53979
Fore St EX20 1HD
e-mail: enquiry@thewhitehart-hotel.com
dir: In town centre, adjacent to lights, car park at rear of hotel

Dating back to the 17th century and situated on the edge of the Dartmoor National Park, the White Hart offers modern facilities. Bedrooms are well equipped and spacious. Locally sourced, home-cooked food is on offer in the bars and the Courtney Restaurant; or guests can choose to eat in Vines Pizzeria. Wi-fi is available in public areas.

Rooms 19 (2 fmly) **Facilities** FTV Xmas Wi-fi **Conf** Class 30 Board 40 Thtr 100 **Parking** 20

OLDBURY
West Midlands — Map 10 SO98

Express by Holiday Inn Birmingham Oldbury M5

BUDGET HOTEL

☎ 0121 511 0000 📠 0121 511 0051
Birchley Park B69 2BD
e-mail: oldbury@expressholidayinn.co.uk
web: www.hiexpress.com/bhx-oldbury
dir: Off M5 junct 2, behind Total Garage on Wolverhampton Rd

A modern hotel ideal for families and business travellers. Fresh and uncomplicated, the spacious rooms include Sky TV, power shower and tea and coffee-making facilities. Continental buffet breakfast is included in the room rate; other meals may be taken at the nearby family pub or restaurant. See also the Hotel Groups pages.

Rooms 109 (55 fmly) (16 GF) **Conf** Class 20 Board 25 Thtr 30

Premier Inn Birmingham Oldbury M5 Jct 2

BUDGET HOTEL

☎ 0871 527 8090 📠 0871 527 8091
Wolverhampton Rd B69 2BH
dir: M5 junct 2, A4123 (Wolverhampton Rd) N towards Dudley

High quality, budget accommodation ideal for both families and business travellers. Spacious, en suite bedrooms feature tea and coffee making facilities, and Freeview TV in most hotels. Internet access and Wi-fi are available for a small fee. The adjacent family restaurant features a wide and varied menu. See also the Hotel Groups pages.

Rooms 60 **D** £52-£62*

OLDHAM Map 16 SD90
Greater Manchester

Best Western Hotel Smokies Park

★★★ 80% HOTEL

☎ 0161 785 5000 🖹 0161 785 5010
Ashton Rd, Bardsley OL8 3HX
e-mail: sales@smokies.co.uk
web: www.smokies.co.uk
dir: On A627 between Oldham & Ashton-under-Lyne

This modern, stylish hotel offers smart, comfortable bedrooms and suites. A wide range of Italian and English dishes is offered in the Mediterranean-style restaurant and there is a welcoming lounge bar with live entertainment at weekends. There is a small yet well equipped, residents-only fitness centre and extensive function facilities are also available.

Rooms 73 (2 fmly) (22 GF) **S** £50-£99; **D** £70-£119* **Facilities** FTV Xmas New Year Wi-fi **Conf** Class 100 Board 40 Thtr 400 **Services** Lift **Parking** 120 **Notes** LB ㊗ RS 25 Dec-3 Jan Civ Wed 400

Premier Inn Oldham (Broadway)

BUDGET HOTEL

☎ 0871 527 8860 🖹 0871 527 8861
Broadway/Hollinwood Av, Chadderton OL9 8DW
dir: M60 (anti-clockwise) junct 21, signed Manchester city centre. Take A663, hotel 400yds on left

High quality, budget accommodation ideal for both families and business travellers. Spacious, en suite bedrooms feature tea and coffee making facilities, and Freeview TV in most hotels. Internet access and Wi-fi are available for a small fee. The adjacent family restaurant features a wide and varied menu. See also the Hotel Groups pages.

Rooms 40 **D** £52-£58*

Premier Inn Oldham Central

BUDGET HOTEL

☎ 0871 527 8862 🖹 0871 527 8863
Westwood Park, Chadderton Way, Chadderton OL1 2NA
dir: M62 junct 20, A627(M) to Oldham. Take A627 (Chadderton Way). Hotel on left opposite B&Q Depot

Rooms 40 **D** £53-£58*

OLD HARLOW Map 6 TL41
Essex

Premier Inn Harlow

BUDGET HOTEL

☎ 0871 527 8488 🖹 0871 527 8489
Cambridge Rd CM20 2EP
dir: M11 junct 7, A414, A1184 (Sawbridgeworth to Bishop's Stortford road)

High quality, budget accommodation ideal for both families and business travellers. Spacious, en suite bedrooms feature tea and coffee making facilities, and Freeview TV in most hotels. Internet access and Wi-fi are available for a small fee. The adjacent family restaurant features a wide and varied menu. See also the Hotel Groups pages.

Rooms 61 **D** £56-£67*

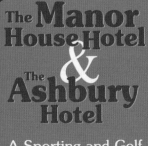

OLDSTEAD
North Yorkshire — Map 19 SE57

INSPECTORS' CHOICE

The Black Swan at Oldstead

@@@ RESTAURANT WITH ROOMS

☎ 01347 868387
YO61 4BL
e-mail: enquiries@blackswanoldstead.co.uk
dir: Exit A19, 3m S Thirsk for Coxwold, left in Coxwold, left at Byland Abbey for Oldstead

The Black Swan is set amidst the stunning scenery of the North Yorkshire National Park, with parts of the building dating back to the 16th century. Well appointed, very comfortable bedrooms and bathrooms provide the perfect get-away-from-it-all. Open fires, a traditional bar and a restaurant, serving award-winning food, is the icing on the cake for this little gem of a property.

Rooms 4

OLLERTON
Nottinghamshire — Map 16 SK66

Thoresby Hall Hotel

Warner Leisure Hotels

★★★★ 81% @@
COUNTRY HOUSE HOTEL

☎ 01623 821000 & 821033 Fax 01623 821069
Thoresby Park NG22 9WH
e-mail: reception.thoresbyhall@bourne-leisure.co.uk

This hotel is set in acres of rolling parklands on the edge of Sherwood Forest. Thoresby Hall is a magnificent Grade I Victorian country house. Guests can choose to relax in the spa, stroll around the beautiful gardens or just sit and relax in the Great Hall. Bedrooms vary in style and size. Please note that this is an adults-only (over 21 years old) hotel. Warner Leisure Hotels – AA Small Hotel Group of the Year 2011-12.

Rooms 221 (168 annexe) (72 GF) **Facilities** Spa (indoor pool) supervised (outdoor pool) Putt green Fishing Gym Rifle shooting Archery Outdoor bowls Fencing Laser clay Yoga Tai chi (entertainment) Xmas New Year **Conf** Class 200 Board 30 Thtr 400 **Services** Lift **Parking** 140 **Notes** (no smoking) No children Civ Wed 92

ORFORD
Suffolk — Map 13 TM45

The Crown & Castle

★★★ 86% @@ HOTEL

☎ 01394 450205
IP12 2LJ
e-mail: info@crownandcastle.co.uk
web: www.crownandcastle.co.uk
dir: Turn right from B1084 on entering village, towards castle

A delightful inn situated adjacent to the Norman castle keep. Contemporary style bedrooms are spilt between the main house and the garden wing; the latter are more spacious and have patios with access to the garden. The restaurant has an informal atmosphere with polished tables and local artwork; the menu features quality, locally sourced produce.

Rooms 19 (12 annexe) (1 fmly) (11 GF) **D** £130-£235 (incl. bkfst)* **Facilities** Xmas New Year Wi-fi **Conf** Board 10 Del from £200 to £300* **Parking** 20 **Notes** LB No children 8yrs

ORMSKIRK
Lancashire — Map 15 SD40

Premier Inn Southport (Ormskirk)

BUDGET HOTEL

☎ 0871 527 9010 Fax 0871 527 9011
544 Southport Rd, Scarisbrick L40 9RG
dir: From Southport follow Ormskirk/A570 signs. Hotel on right of A570 (Southport Rd) at 1st lights (entrance just after lights)

High quality, budget accommodation ideal for both families and business travellers. Spacious, en suite bedrooms feature tea and coffee making facilities, and Freeview TV in most hotels. Internet access and Wi-fi are available for a small fee. The adjacent family restaurant features a wide and varied menu. See also the Hotel Groups pages.

Rooms 20 **D** £60*

OSWESTRY
Shropshire — Map 15 SJ22

Lion Quays Waterside Resort

★★★★ 77% HOTEL

☎ 01691 684300 Fax 01691 684313
Moreton, Weston Rhyn SY11 3EN
e-mail: reservations@lionquays.com
dir: On A483, 3m N of Oswestry

This resort is situated beside the Llangollen Canal and is in a convenient location for visiting Chester to the north and the Snowdonia region to the west. The comfortable bedrooms have views over the countryside or the magnificent grounds and gardens. Guests can dine either in the Waterside Bar or the Country Club which offers the use of a stunning 25-metre swimming pool, a modern gym plus spa facilities. Extensive conference and meeting facilities are also available.

Rooms 82 (25 GF) **Facilities** Spa STV (indoor pool) supervised (outdoor pool) Gym Xmas New Year Wi-fi **Conf** Class 200 Board 150 Thtr 600 **Services** Lift Air con **Parking** 250 **Notes** LB (no smoking) Civ Wed 600

Wynnstay Hotel

★★★★ 74% @ HOTEL

☎ 01691 655261 Fax 01691 670606
Church St SY11 2SZ
e-mail: info@wynnstayhotel.com
web: www.wynnstayhotel.com
dir: B4083 to town, fork left at Honda Garage, right at lights. Hotel opposite church

This Georgian property was once a coaching inn and posting house and surrounds a unique 200-year-old Crown Bowling Green. Elegant public areas include a health, leisure and beauty centre, which is housed in a former coach house. Well-equipped bedrooms are individually styled and include several suites, four-poster rooms and a self-catering apartment. The Four Seasons Restaurant has a well deserved reputation for its food, and the adjacent Wilsons café/bar is a stylish, informal alternative.

Rooms 34 (5 fmly) **S** £65-£85; **D** £85-£110* **Facilities** Spa FTV (indoor pool) Gym Crown bowling green Beauty suite New Year Wi-fi **Conf** Class 150 Board 50 Thtr 290 Del from £104.57 to £120* **Parking** 80 **Notes** LB (no smoking) Civ Wed 90

See advert on opposite page

Pen-y-Dyffryn Country Hotel

★★★ 83% HOTEL

☎ 01691 653700 01978 211004
Rhydycroesau SY10 7JD
e-mail: stay@peny.co.uk
web: www.peny.co.uk
dir: A5 into town centre. Follow signs to Llansilin on B4580, hotel 3m W of Oswestry before Rhydycroesau

Peacefully situated in five acres of grounds, this charming old house dates back to around 1840, when it was built as a rectory. The tastefully appointed public rooms have real fires during cold weather, and the accommodation includes several mini-cottages, each with its own patio. This hotel attracts many guests for its food and attentive, friendly service.

Rooms 12 (4 annexe) (1 fmly) (1 GF) **S** £85-£92; **D** £120-£180 (incl. bkfst)* **Facilities** STV FTV Guided walks Wi-fi **Parking** 18 **Notes** LB No children 3yrs Closed 18 Dec-19 Jan

Premier Inn Oswestry

BUDGET HOTEL

☎ 0871 527 8864 0871 527 8865
SY10 8NN
dir: From rdbt junct of A483 & A5 (SE of Oswestry) take A5 signed Oswestry B4579. Hotel 500yds on left

High quality, budget accommodation ideal for both families and business travellers. Spacious, en suite bedrooms feature tea and coffee making facilities, and Freeview TV in most hotels. Internet access and Wi-fi are available for a small fee. The adjacent family restaurant features a wide and varied menu. See also the Hotel Groups pages.

Rooms 59 **D** £56-£60*

OTLEY
West Yorkshire — Map 19 SE24

Chevin Country Park Hotel & Spa

★★★ 74% HOTEL

☎ 01943 467818 01943 850335
Yorkgate LS21 3NU
e-mail: chevin@crerarhotels.com
dir: From Leeds/Bradford Airport rdbt take A658 N towards Harrogate, for 0.75m to 1st lights. Left, then 2nd left into Yorkgate. Hotel 0.5m on left

Peacefully located in its own woodland yet convenient for major road links and the airport. Bedrooms are split between the original main log building and chalet-style accommodation in the extensive grounds. Public areas include a bar and several lounges. The Lakeside Restaurant provides views over the small lake and good leisure facilities are available.

Rooms 49 (30 annexe) (7 fmly) (45 GF) **Facilities** Spa FTV Fishing Gym Steam room Xmas New Year Wi-fi **Conf** Class 90 Board 50 Thtr 120 **Parking** 100 **Notes** Civ Wed 100

OTTERBURN
Northumberland — Map 21 NY89

Otterburn Hall Hotel

★★★★ 72% COUNTRY HOUSE HOTEL

☎ 01830 520663 01830 520491
NE19 1HE
e-mail: info@otterburnhall.com
dir: A696 to Otterburn

Situated in the Northumberland National Park, this hotel sits in extensive grounds that are beautifully maintained. Both spacious, luxurious bedrooms and more practical rooms are offered. The impressive public rooms are a haven for relaxation and include a superb dining room and, for the more energetic, a small fitness room.

Rooms 65 (17 GF) **S** £85; **D** £144-£232 (incl. bkfst)* **Facilities** FTV Fishing Gym Xmas New Year Wi-fi **Conf** Class 150 Board 50 Thtr 250 Del from £110 to £180* **Parking** 70 **Notes** LB Civ Wed 130

The Otterburn Tower Hotel

★★★ 78% HOTEL

☎ 01830 520620 01830 521504
NE19 1NS
e-mail: info@otterburntower.com
web: www.otterburntower.com
dir: In village, on A696 (Newcastle to Edinburgh road)

Built by a cousin of William the Conqueror, this mansion is set in its own wooded grounds. The property is steeped in history, and Sir Walter Scott stayed here in 1812. Bedrooms come in a variety of sizes and some have huge ornamental fireplaces; though furnished in period style, they are equipped with all modern amenities. The restaurant features 16th-century oak panelling.

Rooms 18 (2 fmly) (2 GF) **Facilities** STV FTV Fishing Clay target shooting Xmas New Year Wi-fi Child facilities **Conf** Class 60 Board 60 Thtr 120 Del from £105 to £130* **Parking** 70 **Notes** Civ Wed 150

O

OTTERSHAW Surrey — Map 6 TQ06

Foxhills Club and Resort

★★★★ 80% HOTEL

01932 872050 & 704500 01932 874762
Stonehill Rd KT16 0EL
e-mail: reservations@foxhills.co.uk
web: www.foxhills.co.uk
dir: M25 junct 11, A320 to Woking. 2nd rdbt last exit into Chobham Rd. Right into Foxhills Rd, left into Stonehill Rd

This 19th-century mansion hotel enjoys a peaceful setting in extensive grounds, not far from the M25 and Heathrow. Spacious well-appointed bedrooms are provided in a choice of annexes situated a short walk from the main house. Golf, tennis, three pools and impressive indoor leisure facilities are available. There is a superb spa offering a range of treatments and therapies plus a health club with all the latest fitness equipment. The eating options are the Manor Restaurant, in the former music room, and the Summerhouse Brasserie.

Rooms 70 (8 fmly) (39 GF) **S** £100-£300; **D** £100-£300 (incl. bkfst)* **Facilities** Spa STV FTV 45 Putt green Gym Squash Children's adventure playground Country pursuits Off-road course Hairdresser Xmas New Year Wi-fi **Conf** Class 52 Board 56 Thtr 100 Del from £200 to £290* **Services** Lift **Parking** 500 **Notes** Civ Wed 75

O

OTTERY ST MARY Devon — Map 3 SY19

Tumbling Weir Hotel

★★ 78% SMALL HOTEL

01404 812752 01404 812752
Canaan Way EX11 1AQ
e-mail: reception@tumblingweirhotel.com
web: www.tumblingweir-hotel.co.uk
dir: A30 onto B3177 to Ottery St Mary, hotel signed from Mill St, access through old mill

Quietly located between the River Otter and its millstream and set in well-tended gardens, this family-run hotel offers friendly and attentive service. Bedrooms are attractively presented and equipped with modern comforts. In the dining room, where a selection of carefully prepared dishes makes up the carte menu, beams and subtle lighting help to create an intimate atmosphere.

Rooms 10 (1 fmly) **S** £55-£65; **D** £80-£100 (incl. bkfst) **Facilities** Wi-fi **Conf** Class 60 Board 50 Thtr 90 **Parking** 10 **Notes** LB Closed 19 Dec-5 Jan Civ Wed 80

OXFORD Oxfordshire — Map 5 SP50

INSPECTORS' CHOICE

Le Manoir Aux Quat' Saisons

★★★★★ HOTEL

01844 278881 01844 278847
Church Rd OX44 7PD
e-mail: lemanoir@blanc.co.uk
web: www.manoir.com

(For full entry see Great Milton)

Macdonald Randolph

★★★★★ 81% HOTEL

01865 256400 01865 792133
Beaumont St OX1 2LN
e-mail: randolph@macdonald-hotels.co.uk
web: www.macdonaldhotels.co.uk
dir: M40 junct 8, A40 signed Oxford/Cheltenham, 5m, at lights to ring road rdbt. Right signed Kidlington/ North Oxford. At next rdbt left towards city centre (A4165/ Banbury Rd). Through Summertown to lights at end of St Giles. Hotel on right

Superbly located near the city centre, The Randolph boasts impressive neo-Gothic architecture and tasteful decor. The spacious and traditional restaurant, complete with picture windows, is the ideal place to watch the world go by while enjoying freshly prepared, modern dishes. Bedrooms include a mix of classical and contemporary wing rooms, which have been appointed to a high standard. Parking is a real bonus.

Rooms 151 **Facilities** Spa STV Gym Treatment rooms Thermal suite Mini gym Xmas New Year Wi-fi **Conf** Class 130 Board 60 Thtr 300 **Services** Lift **Parking** 60 **Notes** LB Civ Wed 120

Barceló Oxford Hotel

★★★★ 77% HOTEL

01865 489988 01865 489952
Godstow Rd, Wolvercote Roundabout OX2 8AL
e-mail: oxford@barcelo-hotels.co.uk
web: www.barcelo-hotels.co.uk
dir: Adjacent to A34/A40, 2m from city centre

Conveniently located on the northern edge of the city centre, this purpose-built hotel offers bedrooms that are bright, modern and well equipped. Guests can eat in the Medio Restaurant or try the Cappuccino Lounge menu. There is the option to eat alfresco on the Patio Terrace when the weather is fine. The hotel offers impressive conference, business and leisure facilities.

Rooms 168 (11 fmly) (89 GF) **Facilities** Spa STV supervised Gym Squash Steam room Beauty treatments New Year Wi-fi **Conf** Class 130 Board 110 Thtr 320 **Parking** 250 **Notes** Civ Wed 250

The Old Bank Hotel

★★★★ 77% TOWN HOUSE HOTEL

01865 799599 01865 799598
92-94 High St OX1 4BN
e-mail: info@oldbank-hotel.co.uk
web: www.oldbank-hotel.co.uk
dir: From Magdalen Bridge into High St, hotel 50yds on left

Located close to the city centre and the colleges, this former bank benefits from an excellent location. An eclectic collection of modern pictures and photographs, many by well-known artists, are on display. Bedrooms are smart with excellent business facilities plus the benefit of air conditioning. Public areas include the vibrant all-day Quod Bar and Restaurant. The hotel has its own car park - a definite advantage in this busy city.

Rooms 42 (4 fmly) (1 GF) **S** £132-£250; **D** £132-£250* **Facilities** FTV Treatment room Free use of nearby gym Bicycles Xmas Wi-fi **Conf** Board 30 Thtr 50 **Services** Lift Air con **Notes** LB

Oxford Thames Four Pillars Hotel

★★★★ 76% HOTEL

0800 374 692 & 01865 334444
01865 334400
Henley Rd, Sandford-on-Thames OX4 4GX
e-mail: thames@four-pillars.co.uk
web: www.four-pillars.co.uk/thames
dir: M40 junct 8 towards Oxford, follow ring road. Left at rdbt towards Cowley. At rdbt with lights turn left to Littlemore, hotel approx 1m on right

Set in 30 acres of beautiful grounds beside the river, this mellow stone property provides a quiet retreat, yet is close to the city. The spacious and traditional River Room Restaurant has superb views of the hotel's own boat moored on the river. The gardens can be enjoyed from the patios or balconies in the newer bedroom wings. Public rooms include a beamed bar and lounge area with minstrels' gallery, and Jerome's Leisure Club. The hotel is popular as a wedding venue.

Rooms 62 (5 fmly) (30 GF) **S** £75-£195; **D** £90-£210 **Facilities** STV Gym Steam room Sauna Xmas New Year Wi-fi **Conf** Class 80 Board 40 Thtr 200 Del from £130 to £195 **Parking** 120 **Notes** LB Civ Wed 100

Old Parsonage

★★★★ 75% TOWN HOUSE HOTEL

☎ 01865 310210 01865 311262
1 Banbury Rd OX2 6NN
e-mail: info@oldparsonage-hotel.co.uk
web: www.oldparsonage-hotel.co.uk
dir: From Oxford ring road to city centre via Summertown. Hotel last building on right before entering St Giles

Dating back in parts to the 16th century, this stylish hotel offers great character and charm and is conveniently located at the northern edge of the city centre. Bedrooms are attractively styled and particularly well appointed. The focal point of the operation is the busy all-day bar and restaurant; the small garden areas and terraces prove popular in summer months.

Rooms 30 (4 fmly) (10 GF) **D** £132.50-£225* **Facilities** STV FTV In room beauty treatments Free use of nearby leisure facilities & house bikes Xmas New Year Wi-fi **Conf** Class 8 Board 12 Thtr 20 **Services** Air con **Parking** 14 **Notes** LB Civ Wed 60

Cotswold Lodge

★★★★ 75% HOTEL

☎ 01865 512121 01865 512490
66a Banbury Rd OX2 6JP
e-mail: info@cotswoldlodgehotel.co.uk
web: www.cotswoldlodgehotel.co.uk
dir: A40 (Oxford ring road) onto A4165 (Banbury road) signed city centre/Summertown. Hotel 2m on left

This Victorian property is located close to the centre of Oxford and offers smart, comfortable accommodation. Stylish bedrooms and suites are attractively presented and some have balconies. The public areas have an elegant country-house feel. The hotel is popular with business guests and caters for conferences and banquets.

Rooms 49 (14 GF) **S** £75-£160; **D** £85-£200 (incl. bkfst)* **Facilities** STV Xmas New Year Wi-fi **Conf** Class 45 Board 40 Thtr 100 Del from £130 to £195* **Parking** 40 **Notes** LB Civ Wed 100

Oxford Spires Four Pillars Hotel

★★★★ 74% HOTEL

☎ 0800 374 692 & 01865 324324
01865 324325
Abingdon Rd OX1 4PS
e-mail: spires@four-pillars.co.uk
web: www.four-pillars.co.uk/spires
dir: M40 junct 8 towards Oxford. Left towards Cowley. At 3rd rdbt follow city centre signs. Hotel in 1m

This purpose-built hotel is surrounded by extensive parkland, yet is only a short walk from the city centre. Bedrooms are attractively furnished, well equipped and include several apartments. Public areas include a spacious restaurant, open-plan bar/lounge, leisure club and extensive conference facilities.

Rooms 170 (10 annexe) (1 fmly) (54 GF) **S** £89-£195; **D** £89-£205 **Facilities** STV Gym Beauty Steam room Sauna Xmas New Year Wi-fi **Conf** Class 96 Board 76 Thtr 266 Del from £135 to £195 **Services** Lift **Parking** 95 **Notes** LB Civ Wed 200

Malmaison Oxford

★★★ 85% HOTEL

☎ 01865 268400 01865 268402
3 Oxford Castle, New Rd OX1 1AY
web: www.malmaison.com
dir: M40 junct 9, A34 N to Botley interchange. Follow city centre & rail station signs. At rail station straight ahead to 2nd lights. Turn right, at next lights left into Park End St. Straight on at next lights, hotel 2nd left

Once the city's prison, this is definitely a hotel with a difference. Many of the rooms are actually converted from the old cells. Not to worry though there have been many improvements since the previous occupants left! Exceedingly comfortable beds and luxury bathrooms are just two of the changes. The hotel has a popular brasserie with quality and value much in evidence. Limited parking space is available.

Rooms 95 (5 GF) **Facilities** STV Gym Xmas New Year Wi-fi **Conf** Class 40 Board 40 Thtr 80 Del from £200 to £300* **Services** Lift **Parking** 30 **Notes** Civ Wed 80

Mercure Eastgate

★★★ 81% HOTEL

☎ 01865 248332 & 248332 01865 794163
73 High St OX1 4BE
e-mail: h6668@accor.com
web: www.mercure.com
dir: A40 follow signs to Headington & Oxford city centre, over Magdalen Bridge, stay in left lane, through lights, left into Merton St, entrance to car park on left

Just a short stroll from the city centre, this hotel, as its name suggests, occupies the site of the city's medieval East Gate and boasts its own car park. Bedrooms are appointed and equipped to a high standard. Stylish public areas include the all-day Town House Brasserie and Bar.

Rooms 63 (3 fmly) (4 GF) **Facilities** Wi-fi **Conf** Board 16 **Services** Lift Air con **Parking** 40 **Notes**

Holiday Inn Oxford

★★★ 80% HOTEL

☎ 0870 942 9086 & 01865 888300
01865 888333
Peartree Roundabout, Woodstock Rd OX2 8JD
e-mail: oxford@ihg.com
web: www.hioxfordhotel.co.uk
dir: From A34 at Peartree Interchange follow Oxford & Services signs. Hotel on left

Located at The Peartree Roundabout, this purpose-built, modern hotel is ideal for business and leisure guests visiting Oxford. Bedrooms are spacious, well equipped and have air cooling. There is a smart bar and restaurant plus as a well-equipped gym and large swimming pool. There are meeting facilities and ample free parking.

Rooms 154 (33 fmly) (23 GF) (6 smoking) **Facilities** Spa STV FTV supervised Gym Sauna Steam room Wi-fi **Conf** Class 65 Board 40 Thtr 150 Del from £129 to £154* **Services** Lift Air con **Parking** 184 **Notes** Civ Wed 100

Westwood Country Hotel

★★★ 78% HOTEL

☎ 01865 735408 01865 736536
Hinksey Hill, Boars Hill OX1 5BG
e-mail: reservations@westwoodhotel.co.uk
web: www.westwoodhotel.co.uk
dir: Off Oxford ring road at Hinksey Hill junct towards Boars Hill & Wootton. At top of hill road bends to left. Hotel on right

This Edwardian country-house hotel is prominently set in terraced landscaped grounds and is within

continued

O

OXFORD *continued*

easy reach of the city centre by car. The hotel is modern in style with very comfortable, well-equipped and tastefully decorated bedrooms. Public areas include a contemporary bar, a cosy lounge and a restaurant overlooking the pretty garden.

Rooms 20 (5 fmly) (7 GF) **Facilities** FTV Arrangement with local health club, golf club & riding school Xmas New Year Wi-fi **Conf** Class 36 Board 35 Thtr 60 **Parking** 50 **Notes** LB Civ Wed 200

Hawkwell House

★★★ 77% HOTEL

☎ 01865 749988 🖷 01865 748525
Church Way, Iffley Village OX4 4DZ
e-mail: reservations@hawkwellhouse.co.uk
web: www.hawkwellhouse.co.uk
dir: A34 follow signs to Cowley. At Littlemore rdbt A4158 exit into Iffley Rd. After lights left to Iffley

Set in a peaceful residential location, Hawkwell House is just a few minutes' drive from the Oxford ring road. The spacious rooms are modern, attractively decorated and well equipped. Public areas are tastefully appointed and the conservatory-style restaurant offers an interesting choice of dishes. The hotel also has a range of conference and function facilities.

Rooms 66 (10 fmly) (4 GF) **Facilities** FTV Xmas New Year Wi-fi **Conf** Class 100 Board 80 Thtr 200 **Services** Lift **Parking** 120 **Notes** ⊗ Civ Wed 150

O

Best Western Linton Lodge

★★★ 75% HOTEL

☎ 01865 553461 🖷 01865 553691
11-13 Linton Rd OX2 6UJ
e-mail: sales@lintonlodge.com
web: www.lintonlodge.com
dir: Towards city centre on Banbury Rd. In 0.5m right into Linton Rd. Hotel opposite St Andrews Church

Located in a residential area, this hotel is within walking distance of the city centre. Bedrooms are modern, well equipped and comfortable. The oak-panelled Linton's Restaurant serves both set and carte menus, and the Dragon Bar, overlooking the extensive lawned gardens, is the ideal place to relax and have a drink.

Rooms 70 (2 fmly) (14 GF) **Facilities** FTV ⛳ Wi-fi **Conf** Class 50 Board 40 Thtr 120 **Services** Lift **Parking** 40 **Notes** LB ⊗ Civ Wed 120

Manor House

★★ 69% METRO HOTEL

☎ 01865 727627 🖷 01865 200478
250 Iffley Rd OX4 1SE
dir: On A4158, 1m from city centre

This family run establishment is easily accessible from the city centre and all major road links. The hotel provides informal but friendly and attentive service. The comfortably furnished bedrooms are well equipped. The hotel has a bar but there is a selection of restaurants and popular pubs within easy walking distance. Limited private parking is available.

Rooms 8 (2 fmly) **S** £69-£99; (incl. bkfst)* **Parking** 6 **Notes** ⊗ Closed 20 Dec-20 Jan

Bath Place Hotel

★★ 65% METRO HOTEL

☎ 01865 791812 🖷 01865 791834
4-5 Bath Place, Holywell St OX1 3SU
e-mail: info@bathplace.co.uk
dir: On S side of Holywell St (parallel to High St)

The hotel has been created from a group of 17th-century cottages originally built by Flemish weavers who were permitted to settle outside the city walls. This lovely hotel is very much at the heart of the city today and offers individually designed bedrooms, including some with four-posters.

Rooms 16 (3 fmly) (5 GF) **S** £89-£105; **D** £118-£148 (incl. bkfst)* **Facilities** FTV Wi-fi **Parking** 16

The Balkan Lodge Hotel

★★ 63% METRO HOTEL

☎ 01865 244524 🖷 01865 251090
315 Iffley Rd OX4 4AG
e-mail: balkanlodge@aol.co.uk
web: www.hometown.aol.com/balkanlodge
dir: From M40/A40 take eastern bypass, into city on A4158

Conveniently located for the city centre and the ring road, this family operated metro hotel offers a comfortable stay. Bedrooms are attractive and well equipped. Public areas include a lounge and bar. A secure private car park is located to the rear of the building.

Rooms 13 **S** £68-£72; **D** £85-£92* **Facilities** Wi-fi **Parking** 12 **Notes** ⊗

Holiday Inn Express Oxford - Kassam Stadium

BUDGET HOTEL

☎ 01865 780888 🖷 01865 780999
Grenoble Rd OX4 4XP
e-mail: reservations@expressoxford.com
web: www.hiexpress.com/oxfrdkassam
dir: M40 junct 8 onto A40 for 4m. Left at McDonald's onto A4142. After 3.5m left onto A4074, take 1st exit signed Science Park & Kassam Stadium

A modern hotel ideal for families and business travellers. Fresh and uncomplicated, the spacious rooms include Sky TVs, power showers and tea and coffee-making facilities. A continental buffet breakfast is included in the room rate; other meals may be taken at the nearby family pub or restaurant. See also the Hotel Groups pages.

Rooms 162 (131 fmly) (31 GF) **S** £49-£95; **D** £49-£95 (incl. bkfst) **Conf** Class 18 Board 28 Thtr 30 Del from £80 to £110*

Premier Inn Oxford

BUDGET HOTEL

☎ 0871 527 8866 🖷 0871 527 8867
Oxford Business Park, Garsington Rd OX4 2JZ
dir: On Oxford Business Park, just off A4142 & B480 junct

High quality, budget accommodation ideal for both families and business travellers. Spacious, en suite bedrooms feature tea and coffee making facilities, and Freeview TV in most hotels. Internet access and Wi-fi are available for a small fee. The adjacent family restaurant features a wide and varied menu. See also the Hotel Groups pages.

Rooms 121 **D** £64-£72*

OXFORD Map 5 SP60
MOTORWAY SERVICE AREA (M40)
Oxfordshire

Days Inn Oxford - M40

BUDGET HOTEL

☎ 01865 877000 🖷 01865 877016
M40 junction 8A, Waterstock OX33 1LJ
e-mail: oxford.hotel@welcomebreak.co.uk
web: www.welcomebreak.co.uk
dir: M40 junct 8a, at Welcome Break service area

This modern building offers accommodation in smart, spacious and well-equipped bedrooms, suitable for families and business travellers, and all with en suite bathrooms. Continental breakfast is available and other refreshments may be taken at the nearby family restaurant. See also the Hotel Groups pages.

Rooms 59 (56 fmly) (25 GF) (10 smoking) **S** £39.95-£59.95; **D** £49.95-£69.95* **Conf** Board 8

PADSTOW Map 2 SW97
Cornwall

The Metropole

★★★★ 73% HOTEL

☎ 01841 532486 01841 532867
Station Rd PL28 8DB
e-mail: info@the-metropole.co.uk
web: www.the-metropole.co.uk
dir: M5/A30 pass Launceston, follow Wadebridge & N Cornwall signs. Take A39, follow Padstow signs

This long-established hotel first opened its doors to guests back in 1904 and there is still an air of the sophistication and elegance of a bygone age. Bedrooms are soundly appointed and well equipped; dining options include the informal Met Café Bar and the main restaurant, with its enjoyable cuisine and wonderful views over the Camel estuary.

Rooms 58 (3 fmly) (2 GF) **S** £118; **D** £236 (incl. bkfst) **Facilities** FTV Swimming pool open Jul & Aug only Xmas New Year Wi-fi **Conf** Class 20 Board 20 Thtr 40 **Services** Lift **Parking** 36 **Notes** LB

St Petroc's Hotel and Bistro

★★ 85% SMALL HOTEL

☎ 01841 532700 01841 532942
4 New St PL28 8EA
e-mail: reservations@rickstein.com
dir: A39 onto A389, follow signs to town centre. Follow one-way system, hotel on right on leaving town

One of the oldest buildings in town, this charming establishment is just up the hill from the picturesque harbour. Style, comfort and individuality are all great strengths here, particularly so in the impressively equipped bedrooms. Breakfast, lunch and dinner all reflect a serious approach to cuisine, and the popular restaurant has a relaxed, bistro style. Comfortable lounges, a reading room and lovely gardens complete the picture.

Rooms 14 (4 annexe) (3 fmly) (3 GF) **D** £97-£280 (incl. bkfst)* **Facilities** FTV Cookery school New Year Wi-fi **Conf** Board 12 **Services** Lift **Parking** 12 **Notes** LB Closed 1 May & 25-26 Dec RS 24 Dec eve

The Old Ship Hotel

★★ 75% HOTEL

☎ 01841 532357 01841 533211
Mill Square PL28 8AE
e-mail: stay@oldshiphotel-padstow.co.uk
web: www.oldshiphotel-padstow.co.uk
dir: From M5 take A30 to Bodmin then A389 to Padstow, follow brown tourist signs to car park

This attractive inn is situated in the heart of the old town's quaint and winding streets, just a short walk from the harbour. A warm welcome is assured, accommodation is pleasant and comfortable, and public areas offer plenty of character. Freshly caught fish features on both the bar and restaurant menus. On site parking is a bonus.

Rooms 14 (4 fmly) **S** £39-£59; **D** £90-£130 (incl. bkfst)* **Facilities** STV Xmas New Year Wi-fi **Parking** 20

The Seafood Restaurant

RESTAURANT WITH ROOMS

☎ 01841 532700 01841 532942
Riverside PL28 8BY
e-mail: reservations@rickstein.com
dir: Into town centre down hill, follow round sharp bend, restaurant on left

Food lovers continue to beat a well-trodden path to this legendary establishment. Situated on the edge of the harbour, just a stone's throw from the shops, the Seafood Restaurant offers stylish and comfortable bedrooms that boast numerous thoughtful extras; some have views of the estuary and a couple have stunning private balconies. Service is relaxed and friendly; booking is essential for both accommodation and a table in the restaurant.

Rooms 20 (6 annexe) (6 fmly)

PAIGNTON Map 3 SX86
Devon

Redcliffe

★★★ 77% HOTEL

☎ 01803 526397 01803 528030
Marine Dr TQ3 2NL
e-mail: redclfe@aol.com
dir: On seafront at Torquay end of Paignton Green

Set at the water's edge in three acres of well-tended grounds, this popular hotel enjoys uninterrupted views across Tor Bay. Offering a diverse range of facilities including a leisure complex, beauty treatments and lots of outdoor family activities in the summer. Bedrooms are pleasantly appointed and comfortably furnished, while public areas offer ample space for rest and relaxation.

Rooms 68 (8 fmly) (3 GF) **S** £60-£70; **D** £120-£140 (incl. bkfst) **Facilities** Spa FTV supervised Putt green Fishing Gym Table tennis Carpet bowls Xmas New Year Wi-fi **Conf** Class 50 Board 50 Thtr 150 Del from £80 to £90 **Services** Lift **Parking** 80 **Notes** LB Civ Wed 150

Redcliffe Lodge Hotel

★★ 65% HOTEL

☎ 01803 551394 01803 551394
1 Marine Dr TQ3 2NJ
e-mail: davies.valleyview@tiscali.co.uk
dir: A3022 to Paignton seafront. Hotel at end of Marine Drive on right adjacent to Paignton Green

Handily placed across the road from the seafront, this is an ideal base for those visiting the Torbay area. Bedrooms are furnished in traditional style and some have sea views. The dining room has lovely views over the garden to the sea beyond, and guests also have a choice of lounges and bar.

Rooms 17 (2 fmly) (3 GF) **Facilities** FTV Xmas New Year Wi-fi **Conf** Class 38 Board 30 Thtr 50 **Parking** 17 **Notes** LB

See advert on page 386

P

PAIGNTON *continued*

Premier Inn (Goodrington Sands)

BUDGET HOTEL

☎ 0871 527 9206 📠 0871 527 9207
Tanners Rd, Goodrington TQ4 6LP
dir: From Newton Abbot take A380 S. Left onto A3022 (Totnes Rd), right at Hayes Rd into Penwill Way, right at B3199 into Dartmouth Rd, at lights left into Tanners Rd

High quality, budget accommodation ideal for both families and business travellers. Spacious, en suite bedrooms feature tea and coffee making facilities, and Freeview TV in most hotels. Internet access and Wi-fi are available for a small fee. The adjacent family restaurant features a wide and varied menu. See also the Hotel Groups pages.

Rooms 33 **D** £66*

PAINSWICK Gloucestershire **Map 4 SO80**

Cotswolds88 Hotel

★★★★ 81% ◎◎ SMALL HOTEL

☎ 01452 813688 📠 01452 814059
Kemps Ln GL6 6YB
e-mail: reservations@cotswolds88hotel.com
web: www.cotswolds88hotel.com
dir: From Stroud towards Cheltenham on A46, in Painswick centre right at St Marys Church into Victoria St. Left into St Marys St, right into Tibbiwell St, right into Kemps Lane

In the heart of a pretty village, this 18th-century house offers a range of beautifully presented and individually styled bedrooms. Most of the rooms have stunning countryside views and all are equipped to the highest standard. Residents have access to the private lounge with a balcony and the cosy library. The modern award-winning restaurant has a well deserved reputation, and the dishes feature the finest locally sourced and organic produce.

Rooms 17 (8 annexe) (2 fmly) **Facilities** FTV Treatment room Xmas New Year Wi-fi **Conf** Class 34 Board 30 Thtr 60 **Parking** 17 **Notes** Civ Wed 120

St Michaels

◎ RESTAURANT WITH ROOMS

☎ 01452 814555 📠 01452 814606
Victoria St GL6 6QA
e-mail: info@stmickshouse.co.uk

This 17th-century Grade II listed building has a wealth of character and overlooks the famous Church of St Michaels with its 99 Yew trees. Each stylish bedroom has its own theme and is equipped with a host of thoughtful extras. The award-winning restaurant has an imaginative menu based on the best local produce. A warm welcome is guaranteed and the delicious breakfasts should not be missed. Situated in the heart of the very pretty Cotswold village of Painswick this establishment makes an ideal base for exploring the beautiful Cotswolds.

Rooms 3

PANGBOURNE Berkshire **Map 5 SU67**

Elephant at Pangbourne

★★★ 78% ◎ HOTEL

☎ 0118 984 2244 📠 0118 976 7346
Church Rd RG8 7AR
e-mail: dominic@elephanthotel.co.uk
web: www.elephanthotel.co.uk
dir: A4 Theale/Newbury, right at 2nd rdbt signed Pangbourne. Hotel on left

Centrally located in this bustling village, just a short drive from Reading. Bedrooms are individual in style but identical in the attention to detail, with handcrafted Indian furniture and rich oriental rugs. Guests can enjoy award-winning cuisine in the restaurant or there is bistro-style dining in the bar area.

Rooms 22 (8 annexe) (2 fmly) (4 GF) **S** £100-£120; **D** £140-£160 (incl. bkfst)* **Facilities** FTV Xmas New Year Wi-fi **Conf** Class 40 Board 30 Thtr 60 Del from £140 to £155* **Parking** 10 **Notes** LB Civ Wed 70

PARKGATE Map 15 SJ27
Cheshire

The Ship Hotel

★★★ 62% HOTEL

☎ 0151 336 3931 📠 0151 203 1636
The Parade CH64 6SA
e-mail: info@the-shiphotel.co.uk
web: www.the-shiphotel.co.uk
dir: A540 (Chester towards Neston) left then immediately right onto B5136 (Liverpool Rd). In Neston town centre, left onto B5135. Follow to The Parade in Parkgate, hotel 50yds on right

This hotel is conveniently located in the village of Parkgate on the Wirral Peninsula, and benefits from magnificent views across the Dee Estuary to the North Wales coast. The bedrooms are warm and comfortable, and traditional food can either be enjoyed in the restaurant or popular bar.

Rooms 24 (1 fmly) **S** £35-£50; **D** £70-£150 (incl. bkfst)* **Facilities** STV FTV Wi-fi **Conf** Class 30 Board 20 Thtr 60 **Parking** 30 **Notes** ⊗

PATTERDALE Map 18 NY31
Cumbria

Patterdale

★★ 69% HOTEL

☎ 0845 458 4333 & 017684 82231
📠 01253 754222
CA11 0NN
e-mail: reservations@choice-hotels.co.uk
dir: M6 junct 40, A592 towards Ullswater. 10m to Patterdale

Patterdale is a real tourist destination and this hotel makes a good base for those taking part in the many activity pursuits available in this area. The hotel enjoys delightful views of the valley and fells, being located at the southern end of Ullswater. The modern bedrooms vary in style. In busier periods accommodation is let for a minimum period of two nights.

Rooms 57 (16 fmly) (6 GF) **Facilities** Free bike hire Xmas New Year Wi-fi **Services** Lift **Parking** 30 **Notes** ⊗

PATTINGHAM Map 10 SO89
Staffordshire

Patshull Park Hotel Golf & Country Club

★★★ 79% HOTEL

☎ 01902 700100 📠 01902 700874
Patshull Park WV6 7HR
e-mail: sales@patshull-park.co.uk
web: www.patshull-park.co.uk
dir: 1.5m W of Pattingham, at church take Patshull Rd, hotel 1.5m on right

Dating from the 1730s and sitting in 280 acres of parkland, with good golf and fishing, this comfortably appointed hotel has a range of modern leisure and conference facilities. Public rooms include a lounge bar, Earl's Brasserie and the Lakeside Restaurant with delightful views over the lake. Bedrooms are well appointed and thoughtfully equipped; most have good views of either the golf course or lake.

Rooms 49 (15 fmly) (16 GF) **S** £49-£99; **D** £59-£109 (incl. bkfst)* **Facilities** STV 18 Putt green Fishing Gym Beauty therapist Cardio suite Weights room Steam rooms Saunas Xmas New Year Wi-fi **Conf** Class 75 Board 44 Thtr 160 Del from £110 to £129* **Parking** 200 **Notes** LB Civ Wed 120

PEASMARSH Map 7 TQ82
East Sussex

Flackley Ash Hotel & Restaurant

★★★ 78% HOTEL

☎ 01797 230651 📠 01797 230510
TN31 6YH
e-mail: enquiries@flackleyashhotel.co.uk
web: www.flackleyashhotel.co.uk
dir: Exit A21 onto A268 to Newenden, next left A268 to Rye. Hotel on left on entering Peasmarsh

Five acres of beautifully kept grounds make a lovely setting for this elegant Georgian country house. The hotel is superbly situated for exploring the many local attractions, including the ancient Cinque Port of Rye. Stylishly decorated bedrooms are comfortable and boast many thoughtful touches. A sunny conservatory dining room, luxurious beauty spa and a swimming pool are available.

Rooms 45 (5 fmly) (19 GF) (10 smoking) **Facilities** Spa STV supervised Gym Beauty salon Steam room Saunas Xmas New Year Wi-fi **Conf** Class 60 Board 40 Thtr 100 **Parking** 80 **Notes** Civ Wed 100

PECKFORTON Map 15 SJ55
Cheshire

Peckforton Castle

★★★★ 76% HOTEL

☎ 01829 260930 📠 01829 261230
Stone House Ln CW6 9TN
e-mail: info@peckfortoncastle.co.uk
web: www.peckfortoncastle.co.uk
dir: A49. At Beeston Castle pub right signed Peckforton Castle. Approx 2m, entrance on right

Built in the mid 19th century by parliamentarian and landowner Lord John Tollemache and now lovingly cared for by The Naylor Family, this Grade I medieval-style castle has been sympathetically renovated to provide high standards of comfort without losing original charm and character. Bedrooms and public areas retain many period features, and dining in the 1851 Restaurant is a memorable experience. There is a falconry centre at the castle.

Rooms 48 (7 fmly) (2 GF) **S** £59-£105; **D** £65-£220 (incl. bkfst)* **Facilities** FTV Falconry Outdoor pursuits Land Rover experience Abseiling Beauty salon Xmas New Year Wi-fi **Conf** Class 80 Board 40 Thtr 180 Del from £120 to £200* **Services** Lift **Parking** 400 **Notes** LB ⊗ Civ Wed 165

PENDLEBURY Map 15 SD70
Greater Manchester

Premier Inn Manchester (Swinton)

BUDGET HOTEL

☎ 0871 527 8720 📠 0871 527 8721
219 Bolton Rd M27 8TG
dir: M60 junct 13 towards A572, at rdbt take 3rd exit towards Swinton. At next rdbt take A572. In 2m right onto A580. After 2nd lights A666 Kearsley, 1st left at rdbt. Pass fire station on right, 1st right

High quality, budget accommodation ideal for both families and business travellers. Spacious, en suite bedrooms feature tea and coffee making facilities, and Freeview TV in most hotels. Internet access and Wi-fi are available for a small fee. The adjacent family restaurant features a wide and varied menu. See also the Hotel Groups pages.

Rooms 31 **D** £53-£58*

P

PENKRIDGE
Staffordshire

Map 10 SJ91

Mercure Stafford South Hatherton House Hotel

★★★ 66% HOTEL

☎ 01785 712459 📠 01785 715532
Pinfold Ln ST19 5QP
e-mail: enquiries@hotels-stafford.com
dir: A449 to Wolverhampton. In Penkridge turn right into Pinfold Ln. Hotel on left in 300yds

The hotel offers comfortable accommodation suitable for both leisure and business guests. The leisure facilities consist of a pool, steam room and jacuzzi with a well-equipped gym and two squash courts. Conference facilities are also available. There is free parking and easy access to the city and countryside.

Rooms 51 (4 fmly) (18 GF) (4 smoking) **Facilities** FTV Gym Squash Sauna Steam room Xmas New Year Wi-fi **Conf** Class 160 Board 120 Thtr 260 **Parking** 200 **Notes** LB Civ Wed 200

PENRITH
Cumbria

Map 18 NY53

See also **Glenridding and Shap**

North Lakes Hotel & Spa

★★★★ 78% HOTEL

☎ 01768 868111 📠 01768 868291
Ullswater Rd CA11 8QT
e-mail: nlakes@shirehotels.com
web: www.northlakeshotel.com
dir: M6 junct 40 at junct with A66

With a great location, it's no wonder that this modern hotel is perpetually busy. Amenities include a good range of meeting and function rooms and excellent health and leisure facilities including a full spa. Themed public areas have a contemporary, Scandinavian country style and offer plenty of space and comfort. High standards of service are provided by a friendly team of staff.

Rooms 84 (6 fmly) (22 GF) **S** £100-£200; **D** £110-£210* **Facilities** Spa STV Gym Children's splash pool Steam room Activity & wellness studios Sauna Xmas New Year Wi-fi **Conf** Class 140 Board 30 Thtr 200 Del from £135 to £185* **Services** Lift **Parking** 150 **Notes** LB Civ Wed 200

Temple Sowerby House Hotel & Restaurant

★★★ 87% COUNTRY HOUSE HOTEL

☎ 017683 61578 📠 017683 61958
CA10 1RZ
e-mail: stay@templesowerby.com
web: www.templesowerby.com

(For full entry see Temple Sowerby)

Westmorland Hotel

★★★ 81% HOTEL

☎ 015396 24351 📠 015396 24354
Westmorland Place, Orton CA10 3SB
e-mail: reservations@westmorlandhotel.com
web: www.westmorlandhotel.com

(For full entry see Tebay)

George

LAKE DISTRICT HOTELS

★★★ 77% HOTEL

☎ 01768 862696 & 0800 840 1242
📠 01768 868223
Devonshire St CA11 7SU
e-mail: georgehotel@lakedistricthotels.net
dir: M6 junct 40, 1m to town centre. From A6/A66 to Penrith

This inviting and popular hotel dates back to a time when 'Bonnie' Prince Charlie made a visit. Extended over the years this town centre hotel offers well equipped bedrooms. The spacious public areas retain a timeless charm, and include a choice of lounge areas that make ideal places for morning coffees and afternoon teas.

Rooms 35 (4 fmly) **S** £80; **D** £80-£124 (incl. bkfst)* **Facilities** FTV Xmas New Year Wi-fi **Conf** Class 80 Board 50 Thtr 120 Del from £115 to £140 **Parking** 40 **Notes** LB Civ Wed 120

See advert on opposite page

PENZANCE
Cornwall
Map 2 SW43

Hotel Penzance

★★★ 85% @@ HOTEL

☎ 01736 363117 📠 01736 350970
Britons Hill TR18 3AE
e-mail: reception@hotelpenzance.com
web: www.hotelpenzance.com
dir: From A30 pass heliport on right, left at next rdbt for town centre. 3rd right onto Britons Hill. Hotel on right

This Edwardian house has been tastefully redesigned, particularly in the contemporary Bay Restaurant. The focus on style is not only limited to the decor, but is also apparent in the award-winning cuisine that is based on fresh Cornish produce. Bedrooms have been appointed to modern standards and are particularly well equipped; many have views across Mount's Bay.

Rooms 25 (2 GF) **S** £82-£89; **D** £120-£190 (incl. bkfst)* **Facilities** FTV Xmas New Year Wi-fi **Conf** Class 50 Board 25 Thtr 80 **Parking** 12 **Notes** LB Civ Wed 80

Queens

★★★ 73% HOTEL

☎ 01736 362371 📠 01736 350033
The Promenade TR18 4HG
e-mail: enquiries@queens-hotel.com
web: www.queens-hotel.com
dir: A30 to Penzance, follow signs for seafront pass harbour into promenade, hotel 0.5m on right

With views across Mount's Bay towards Newlyn, this impressive Victorian hotel has a long and distinguished history. Comfortable public areas are filled with interesting pictures and artefacts, and in the dining room guests can choose from the daily-changing menu. Bedrooms, many with sea views, vary in style and size.

Rooms 70 (10 fmly) **S** £60-£92; **D** £100-£180 (incl. bkfst)* **Facilities** FTV Xmas New Year Wi-fi **Conf** Class 200 Board 120 Thtr 200 Del from £85 to £110* **Services** Lift **Parking** 50 **Notes** LB Civ Wed 250

PETERBOROUGH
Cambridgeshire
Map 12 TL19

Peterborough Marriott

Marriott HOTELS & RESORTS

★★★★ 77% HOTEL

☎ 01733 371111 📠 01733 236725
Peterborough Business Park, Lynchwood PE2 6GB
e-mail: reservations.peterborough@marriotthotels.co.uk
web: www.peterboroughmarriott.co.uk
dir: From A1 exit at Alwalton Showground, Chesterton. Left at T-junct. Hotel on left at next rdbt

This modern hotel is opposite the East of England Showground, and a just few minutes' drive from the heart of the city. Alwalton is famous for being the birthplace of Sir Frederick Henry Royce, one of the founders of the Rolls-Royce company. Air-conditioned bedrooms are spacious and well designed for business use. Public rooms include the Garden Lounge, cocktail bar, Laurels Restaurant and a leisure club.

Rooms 163 (8 fmly) (74 GF) (6 smoking) **Facilities** Spa STV Gym Beauty therapist Hairdressing New Year Wi-fi **Conf** Class 160 Board 45 Thtr 300 Del from £145 to £157* **Services** Air con **Parking** 175 **Notes** Civ Wed 80

PETERBOROUGH *continued*

Bull

★★★★ 75% HOTEL

☎ 01733 561364 📠 01733 557304
Westgate PE1 1RB
e-mail: rooms@bull-hotel-peterborough.com
web: www.peelhotels.co.uk
dir: Off A1, follow city centre signs. Hotel opposite Queensgate shopping centre. Car park on Broadway adjacent to library

This pleasant city-centre hotel offers well-equipped, modern accommodation, which includes several wings of deluxe bedrooms. Public rooms include a popular bar and a brasserie-style restaurant serving a flexible range of dishes, with further informal dining available in the lounge. There is a good range of meeting rooms and conference facilities.

Rooms 118 (2 fmly) (5 GF) (4 smoking) **Facilities** STV Xmas New Year Wi-fi **Conf** Class 120 Board 40 Thtr 200 Del from £100 to £160* **Parking** 100 **Notes** LB ⊗ Civ Wed 200

P

Holiday Inn Peterborough West

★★★★ 74% HOTEL

☎ 0871 942 9186 & 01733 289988
📠 01733 262737
Thorpe Wood PE3 6SG
e-mail: hipeterborough@qmh-hotels.com
web: www.holidayinn.co.uk
dir: A1(M) junct 17, A1139 towards Peterborough into Fletton Parkway. Exit at junct 3 into Nene Parkway. Exit junct 33 at rdbt into Thorpe Wood. Hotel on right

Situated just over two miles from the town centre close to the River Nene, with ample parking and easy access to road networks. The hotel provides air-conditioned accommodation and extensive conference and banqueting facilities together with a modern leisure club.

Rooms 133 (10 fmly) (27 GF) **Facilities** Spa STV ⓢ supervised Gym Sauna Steam room Beauty salon Dance studio ♫ Xmas New Year Wi-fi **Conf** Class 150 Board 100 Thtr 400 **Services** Lift Air con **Parking** 250 **Notes** ⊗ Civ Wed 180

Bell Inn Hotel

★★★ 81% ◎ HOTEL

☎ 01733 241066 📠 01733 245173
Great North Rd PE7 3RA
e-mail: reception@thebellstilton.co.uk
web: www.thebellstilton.co.uk

(For full entry see Stilton)

Best Western Orton Hall

★★★ 81% ◎ HOTEL

☎ 01733 391111 📠 01733 231912
Orton Longueville PE2 7DN
e-mail: reception@ortonhall.co.uk
dir: Off A605 E, opposite Orton Mere

An impressive country-house hotel set in 20 acres of woodland on the outskirts of town and with easy access to the A1. The spacious and relaxing public areas include the baronial Great Room and the Orton Suite for banqueting and for meetings, and the oak-panelled, award-winning Huntly Restaurant. The on-site pub, Ramblewood Inn, is an alternative, informal dining option.

Rooms 73 (2 fmly) (15 GF) **S** £35-£130; **D** £35-£150* **Facilities** STV ⓢ Gym Sauna Steam room Xmas New Year Wi-fi **Conf** Class 70 Board 60 Thtr 160 Del from £105 to £150* **Parking** 200 **Notes** LB Civ Wed 150

Park Inn Peterborough

park inn by Radisson

★★★ 79% HOTEL

☎ 01733 353750 📠 01733 353755
Wentworth St PE1 1BA
e-mail: info.peterborough@rezidorparkinn.com
dir: Off A15, 4 mins walk from station

Situated adjacent to Queensgate Shopping Centre which has a range of stores and amenities, and within easy walking distance of the main train station. The spacious bedrooms are modern and equipped to a very good standard. Public rooms feature the open-plan Red Bar Grill, a cosy lounge and a range of meeting rooms.

Rooms 115 (9 fmly) **D** £60-£106* **Facilities** FTV Treatment room Use of gym facilities (1m) Wi-fi **Conf** Class 28 Board 28 Thtr 48 **Services** Lift Air con **Parking** 45 **Notes** LB ⊗ Civ Wed 30

Queensgate Hotel

★★★ 79% HOTEL

☎ 01733 562572
5-7 Fletton Av PE2 8AX
e-mail: reservations@thequeensgatehotel.co.uk
dir: In town centre

This hotel is ideally situated close to the centre of town with its range of shops and amenities. Bedrooms are contemporary in style, and ideally equipped for both business and leisure guests. The modern public rooms include a lounge bar, two dining areas and a beauty therapy suite.

Rooms 40 (2 fmly) (10 GF) **Facilities** FTV Beauty clinic Xmas New Year Wi-fi **Conf** Class 35 Board 26 Thtr 72 **Notes** ⊗

Ramada Peterborough

RAMADA JARVIS

U

☎ 01733 564240 📠 01733 565538
Thorpe Meadows, Off Longthorpe Parkway PE3 6GA
e-mail: reception@ramadapeterborough.co.uk
dir: A1139, junct 3 to A1260, 0.5m to rdbt, 3rd exit

Currently the rating for this establishment is not confirmed. This may be due to a change of ownership or because it has only recently joined the AA rating scheme. For further details please see the AA website: theAA.com

Rooms 70 **Conf** Class 45 Board 40 Thtr 80

Days Inn Peterborough - A1

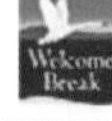

BUDGET HOTEL

☎ 01733 371540 📠 01733 391594
Peterborough Extra Services, A1 Junction 17, Great North Road, Haddon PE7 3UQ
e-mail: peterborough.hotel@welcomebreak.co.uk
dir: At A1(M) junct 17

This modern, purpose-built accommodation offers smartly appointed, particularly well-equipped bedrooms with good power showers. There is a choice of adjacent food outlets where guests can enjoy breakfast, snacks and meals. See also the Hotel Groups pages.

Rooms 82 (13 fmly) (40 GF) (13 smoking) **S** £39.95-£59.95; **D** £49.95-£69.95

Holiday Inn Express Peterborough

BUDGET HOTEL

☎ 01733 284450 📠 01733 284451
East of England Way, Orton Northgate PE2 6HE
e-mail: peterborough@morethanhotels.com
web: www.hiexpress.com/peterboroughex
dir: Follow signs on A1(M) for Peterborough Showground, hotel adjacent to showground

A modern hotel ideal for families and business travellers. Fresh and uncomplicated, the spacious rooms include Sky TV, power shower and tea and coffee-making facilities. Continental buffet breakfast is included in the room rate; other meals may be taken at the nearby family pub or restaurant. See also the Hotel Groups pages.

Rooms 80 (50 fmly) (37 GF) (4 smoking) **Conf** Class 20 Board 20 Thtr 30 Del from £ to £150

Premier Inn Peterborough (Ferry Meadows)

BUDGET HOTEL

☎ 0871 527 8872 📠 0871 527 8873
Ham Ln, Orton Meadows, Nene Park PE2 5UU
dir: A1(M) S junct 16, A15 through Yaxley, left at rdbt. A1(M) N junct 17, A1139 junct 3 right to Yaxley, right at 2nd rdbt

High quality, budget accommodation ideal for both families and business travellers. Spacious, en suite bedrooms feature tea and coffee making facilities, and Freeview TV in most hotels. Internet access and Wi-fi are available for a small fee. The adjacent family restaurant features a wide and varied menu. See also the Hotel Groups pages.

Rooms 40 **D** £51-£61*

Premier Inn Peterborough (Hampton)

BUDGET HOTEL

☎ 0871 527 8874 📠 0871 527 8875
Ashbourne Rd, off London Rd, Hampton PE7 8BT
dir: A1(M) S junct 16, A15 through Yaxley, hotel on left at 1st rdbt. Or A1(M) N junct 17, A1139, 2nd exit junct 3 follow Yaxley signs. Hotel on right at 2nd rdbt

Rooms 83 **D** £45-£55*

Premier Inn Peterborough North

BUDGET HOTEL

☎ 0871 527 8876 📠 0871 527 8877
1023 Lincoln Rd, Walton PE4 6AH
dir: A1, A47 towards Peterborough. In 7m exit at junct 17 signed city centre. At rdbt (bottom of slip road) straight on signed city centre. At next rdbt left onto dual carriageway. At next rdbt double back, follow signs for city centre. Hotel in 200mtrs

Rooms 40 **D** £49-£61*

PETERSFIELD Map 5 SU72
Hampshire

Langrish House

★★★ 75% ®® HOTEL

☎ 01730 266941 📠 01730 260543
Langrish GU32 1RN
e-mail: frontdesk@langrishhouse.co.uk
web: www.langrishhouse.co.uk
dir: A3 onto A272 towards Winchester. Hotel signed, 2.5m on left

Langrish House has been in the same family for seven generations. It is located in an extremely peaceful area just a few minutes' drive from Petersfield, halfway between Guildford and Portsmouth. Bedrooms are comfortable and well equipped with stunning views across the gardens to the hills. Guests can eat in the intimate Frederick's Restaurant with views over the lawn, or in the Old Vaults which have an interesting history dating back to 1644. The hotel is licensed for civil ceremonies and various themed events take place throughout the year.

Rooms 13 (1 fmly) (3 GF) **S** £45-£100; **D** £65-£170 (incl. bkfst)* **Facilities** Xmas New Year Wi-fi **Conf** Class 18 Board 25 Thtr 60 **Parking** 80 **Notes** LB Closed 2 weeks in Jan Civ Wed 80

Premier Inn Petersfield

BUDGET HOTEL

☎ 0871 527 8878 📠 0871 527 8879
Winchester Rd GU32 3BS
dir: At junct of A3 & A272 W'bound signed Services

High quality, budget accommodation ideal for both families and business travellers. Spacious, en suite bedrooms feature tea and coffee making facilities, and Freeview TV in most hotels. Internet access and Wi-fi are available for a small fee. The adjacent family restaurant features a wide and varied menu. See also the Hotel Groups pages.

Rooms 51 **D** £62-£64*

PICKERING Map 19 SE78
North Yorkshire

The White Swan Inn

★★★ 80% ® HOTEL

☎ 01751 472288 📠 01751 475554
Market Place YO18 7AA
e-mail: welcome@white-swan.co.uk
web: www.white-swan.co.uk
dir: In town, between church & steam railway station

This 16th-century coaching inn offers well-equipped, comfortable bedrooms, including suites, either of a more traditional style in the main building or modern in the annexe. Service is friendly and attentive. Good food is served in the attractive restaurant, in the cosy bar and the lounge, where a log fire burns in cooler months. A comprehensive wine list focuses on many fine vintages. A private dining room is also available.

Rooms 21 (9 annexe) (3 fmly) (8 GF) **D** £150-£260 (incl. bkfst)* **Facilities** FTV Xmas New Year Wi-fi **Conf** Class 18 Board 25 Thtr 35 **Parking** 45 **Notes** LB

Best Western Forest & Vale

★★★ 80% HOTEL

☎ 01751 472722 📠 01751 472972
Malton Rd YO18 7DL
e-mail: forestvale@bestwestern.co.uk
dir: On A169 towards York at rdbt on outskirts of Pickering

This lovely 18th-century hotel is an excellent base from which to explore the North Yorkshire Moors, one of England's most beautiful areas. A dedicated approach to upgrading means that the hotel is particularly well maintained, inside and out. Bedrooms vary in size and include some spacious 'superior' rooms; one has a four-poster bed.

Rooms 22 (5 annexe) (7 fmly) (5 GF) **S** £85-£115; **D** £85-£125* **Facilities** FTV Wi-fi **Conf** Class 50 Board 30 Thtr 120 Del from £160 to £190* **Parking** 40 **Notes** LB ⊗ Closed 24-26 Dec Civ Wed 90

P

PICKERING *continued*

Fox & Hounds Country Inn

★★ 82% ® HOTEL

☎ 01751 431577 🖹 01751 432791
Main St, Sinnington YO62 6SQ
e-mail: fox.houndsinn@btconnect.com
web: www.thefoxandhoundsinn.co.uk
dir: 3m W of Pickering, off A170, between Pickering & Helmsley

This attractive inn lies in the quiet village of Sinnington just off the main road. The smartly maintained, yet traditional public areas are cosy and inviting. The menu offers a good selection of freshly cooked, modern British dishes and is available in the restaurant or informally in the bar. Bedrooms and bathrooms are well equipped and offer a good standard of quality and comfort. Service throughout is friendly and attentive.

Rooms 10 (4 GF) **Facilities** New Year Wi-fi **Parking** 40 **Notes** Closed 25-26 Dec

Old Manse

★★ 76% HOTEL

☎ 01751 476484 🖹 01751 477124
19 Middleton Rd YO18 8AL
e-mail: info@oldmansepickering.com
web: www.oldmansepickering.co.uk
dir: A169, left at rdbt, through lights, 1st right into Potter Hill. Follow road to left. From A170 left at 'local traffic only' sign

A peacefully located house standing in mature grounds close to the town centre. It offers a combined dining room and lounge area, and comfortable bedrooms that are well equipped. Expect good hospitality from the resident owners.

Old Manse

Rooms 10 (2 fmly) (2 GF) **Facilities** New Year Wi-fi **Conf** Class 12 Board 10 Thtr 20 **Parking** 12 **Notes** Closed 24-27 Dec

PLYMOUTH Devon **Map 3 SX45**

Holiday Inn Plymouth

Holiday Inn

★★★★ 73% HOTEL

☎ 0871 942 9130 & 01752 63998
🖹 01752 673816
Armada Way PL1 2HJ
e-mail: hiplymouth@qmh-hotels.com
web: www.holidayinn.co.uk
dir: Exit A38 at Plymouth city centre & follow signs for Barbican/Hoe. Into Notte St, left into Hoe Approach, right into Citadel Rd. Hotel on right

Overlooking The Hoe with views towards Plymouth Sound, this modern, high-rise hotel offers extensive facilities, including a leisure club and impressive conference and function rooms. Most bedrooms are very spacious; sea-facing rooms are the most popular. Spectacular, panoramic views of the city can be enjoyed from the restaurant and bar on the top floor.

Rooms 211 (10 fmly) (12 GF) (21 smoking) **S** £53-£119; **D** £53-£119* **Facilities** STV Gym Beauty salon Dance studio Sauna Steam room Xmas New Year Wi-fi **Conf** Class 260 Board 60 Thtr 425 Del from £105 to £145* **Services** Lift Air con **Parking** 125 **Notes** LB Civ Wed 250

Invicta

★★★ 78% HOTEL

☎ 01752 664997 🖹 01752 664994
11-12 Osborne Place, Lockyer St, The Hoe PL1 2PU
e-mail: info@invictahotel.co.uk
web: www.invictahotel.co.uk
dir: A38 to Plymouth, follow city centre signs, then signs to The Hoe & Barbican. Hotel opposite Hoe Park on Lockyer St at junct with Citadel Rd

Just a short stroll from the city centre, this elegant Victorian establishment stands opposite the famous bowling green. The atmosphere is relaxed and friendly and bedrooms are neatly presented, well-equipped and attractively decorated. Eating options include meals in the bar or in the more formal setting of the dining room.

Rooms 23 (4 fmly) (1 GF) **Facilities** FTV Xmas Wi-fi **Conf** Class 30 Board 45 Thtr 45 **Parking** 14 **Notes** LB

Best Western Duke of Cornwall

★★★ 77% ® HOTEL

☎ 01752 275850 & 275855 🖹 01752 275854
Millbay Rd PL1 3LG
e-mail: enquiries@thedukeofcornwall.co.uk
web: www.thedukeofcornwall.co.uk
dir: Follow city centre, then Plymouth Pavilions Conference & Leisure Centre signs. Hotel opposite Plymouth Pavilions

A historic landmark, this city centre hotel is conveniently located. The spacious public areas include a popular bar, comfortable lounge and multi-functional ballroom. Bedrooms, many with far reaching views, are individually styled and comfortably appointed. The range of dining options includes meals in the bar, or the elegant dining room for a more formal atmosphere.

Rooms 71 (6 fmly) (20 smoking) **S** £65-£110; **D** £75-£130 (incl. bkfst) **Facilities** STV FTV Xmas New Year Wi-fi **Conf** Class 125 Board 84 Thtr 300 **Services** Lift **Parking** 50 **Notes** LB Civ Wed 300

Langdon Court Hotel & Restaurant

★★★ 77% ✿ HOTEL

☎ 01752 862358 🖷 01752 863428
Langdon, Wendbury PL9 0DY
e-mail: enquiries@langdoncourt.com
web: www.langdoncourt.com
dir: From Elburton follow hotel signs & tourist signs on A379

This magnificent Grade II listed Tudor manor, set in seven acres of lush countryside, has a direct path leading to the beach at Wembury and the coastal footpaths. Bedrooms enjoy countryside views while public areas include a stylish bar and brasserie restaurant where the contemporary menu incorporates local produce with excellent seafood.

Rooms 18 (3 fmly) **S** £69-£129; **D** £109-£199 (incl. bkfst) **Facilities** FTV ♫ Xmas New Year Wi-fi **Conf** Class 20 Board 20 Thtr 50 **Parking** 60 **Notes** LB ⊗ Civ Wed 100

New Continental

★★★ 75% HOTEL

☎ 01752 220782 & 276798 🖷 01752 227013
Millbay Rd PL1 3LD
e-mail: reservations@newcontinental.co.uk
web: www.newcontinental.co.uk
dir: A38, follow city centre signs for Continental Ferryport. Hotel before ferryport, adjacent to Plymouth Pavilions Conference Centre

Within easy reach of the city centre and The Hoe, this privately owned hotel continues to offer high standards of service and hospitality. A variety of bedroom sizes and styles is available, all with the same levels of equipment and comfort. The hotel is a popular choice for conferences and functions.

Rooms 99 (20 fmly) **S** £75-£110; **D** £85-£130 (incl. bkfst)* **Facilities** FTV ⓢ supervised Gym Sauna Steam room Wi-fi **Conf** Class 100 Board 70 Thtr 350 Del from £120 to £160 **Services** Lift **Parking** 100 **Notes** LB ⊗ Closed 24 Dec-2 Jan Civ Wed 140

Copthorne Hotel Plymouth

★★★ 74% HOTEL

☎ 01752 224161 🖷 01752 670688
Armada Way PL1 1AR
e-mail: sales.plymouth@millenniumhotels.co.uk
web: www.millenniumhotels.co.uk
dir: From M5 follow A38 to Plymouth city centre. Follow ferryport signs over 2 rdbts. Hotel on 1st exit left before 4th rdbt

This hotel is conveniently located adjacent to the city's main attractions and business area, and also well situated for the theatre and The Hoe. Bedrooms offer a good range of facilities and are available in a range of sizes. The restaurant provides enjoyable dining and there is an all day lounge and bar service. Secure parking is an asset.

Rooms 135 **Facilities** STV Gym New Year Wi-fi **Conf** Class 60 Board 60 Thtr 140 **Services** Lift **Parking** 50 **Notes** LB ⊗ Civ Wed 100

Elfordleigh Hotel, Golf & Country Club

★★★ 74% HOTEL

☎ 01752 336428 🖷 01752 344581
Colebrook, Plympton PL7 5EB
e-mail: reception@elfordleigh.co.uk
dir: Exit A38 for city centre, at Marsh Mills/ Sainsbury's rdbt into Plympton road. At 4th lights left into Larkham Ln, at end right then left into Crossway. At end left into The Moors, hotel 1m

Located in the beautiful Plym Valley, this well-established hotel is set in attractive wooded countryside. Bedrooms, many with lovely views, are spacious and comfortable. There is an excellent range of leisure facilities including an 18-hole golf course. A choice of dining options is available - a friendly brasserie and the more formal restaurant.

Rooms 34 (2 fmly) (7 GF) **Facilities** Spa STV FTV ⓢ ⛳ 18 ⓢ Putt green Fishing Gym Squash Hairdresser Beautician Dance & Aerobics studio Five-a-side football (hard) pitch Xmas New Year Wi-fi **Conf** Class 120 Board 50 Thtr 200 **Services** Lift **Parking** 200 **Notes** Civ Wed 200

The Legacy Plymouth International Hotel

★★★ 64% HOTEL

☎ 08444 119 097 🖷 08444 119 098
Marsh Mills PL6 8NH
e-mail: res-plymouthinternational@legacy-hotels.co.uk
web: www.legacy-hotels.co.uk
dir: Exit A38 at Marsh Mills, follow Plympton signs, hotel on left

Conveniently located on the outskirts of the city, close to Marsh Mills roundabout, this modern hotel offers good value accommodation. All bedrooms are spacious and designed with flexibility for family use. Public areas are open-plan with meals available throughout the day in either the Garden Brasserie, the bar, or from room service.

Rooms 100 (17 fmly) (18 GF) **Facilities** STV FTV Xmas New Year **Conf** Class 120 Board 100 Thtr 300 **Services** Lift **Parking** 140 **Notes** LB Civ Wed 200

Ibis Hotel Plymouth

BUDGET HOTEL

☎ 01752 601087 🖷 01752 223213
Marsh Mills, Longbridge Rd, Forder Valley PL6 8LD
e-mail: H2093@accor.com
web: www.ibishotel.com
dir: A38 to Plymouth, 1st exit after flyover towards Estover, Leigham and Parkway Industrial Est. At rdbt, hotel on 4th exit

Modern, budget hotel offering comfortable accommodation in bright and practical bedrooms. Breakfast is self-service and dinner is available in the restaurant. See also the Hotel Groups pages.

Rooms 52 (26 GF)

Premier Inn Plymouth Centre (Sutton Harbour)

BUDGET HOTEL

☎ 0871 527 8882 🖷 0871 527 8883
Sutton Rd, Shepherds Wharf PL4 0HX
dir: A38, A374 towards Plymouth. Follow Coxside & National Marine Aquarium signs. Right at lights after leisure park. Hotel adjacent to Lockyers Quay (NB there are 2 Premier Inns on this site, this hotel is the larger)

High quality, budget accommodation ideal for both families and business travellers. Spacious, en suite bedrooms feature tea and coffee making facilities, and Freeview TV in most hotels. Internet access and Wi-fi are available for a small fee. The adjacent family restaurant features a wide and varied menu. See also the Hotel Groups pages.

Rooms 107 **D** £68*

Premier Inn Plymouth City Centre (Lockyers Quay)

BUDGET HOTEL

☎ 0871 527 8880 🖷 0871 527 8881
1 Lockyers Quay, Coxside PL4 0DX
dir: From A38 (Marsh Mills rdbt) take A374 into Plymouth. Follow Coxside & National Marine Aquarium signs

Rooms 62 **D** £68*

P

PLYMOUTH *continued*

Premier Inn Plymouth East

BUDGET HOTEL

☎ 0871 527 8884 🖷 0871 527 8885
300 Plymouth Rd, Crabtree PL3 6RW
dir: From E: Exit A38 at Marsh Mill junct. Straight on at rdbt, exit slip road 100mtrs on left. From W: Exit A38 at Plympton junct, at rdbt exit slip road adjacent to A38

Rooms 41 **D** £63-£68*

POCKLINGTON Map 17 SE84
East Riding of Yorkshire

Feathers

★★ 68% HOTEL

☎ 01759 303155 🖷 01759 304382
56 Market Place YO42 2AH
e-mail: info@thefeathers-hotel.co.uk
dir: From York, B1246 signed Pocklington. Hotel just off A1079

This busy, traditional inn provides comfortable, well-equipped and spacious accommodation. Public areas are smartly presented. Enjoyable meals are served in the bar and the conservatory restaurant; the wide choice of dishes makes excellent use of local and seasonal produce.

Rooms 16 (10 annexe) (1 fmly) (10 GF) **S** £50; **D** £55 (incl. bkfst) **Facilities** FTV Wi-fi **Conf** Class 40 Board 30 Thtr 80 **Parking** 30 **Notes** ⊗

P

POLPERRO Map 2 SX25
Cornwall

Talland Bay Hotel

★★★ 87% ®® COUNTRY HOUSE HOTEL

☎ 01503 272667 🖷 01503 272940
Porthallow PL13 2JB
e-mail: info@tallandbayhotel.co.uk
web: www.tallandbayhotel.co.uk
dir: From Looe over bridge towards Polperro on A387, 2nd turn to hotel

This hotel has the benefit of a wonderful location, being situated in its own extensive gardens that run down almost to the cliff edge. A warm and friendly atmosphere prevails and many bedrooms have sea views. Public areas and bedrooms have under gone a major refurbishment with impressive and stylish results. Accomplished cooking, with an emphasis on carefully prepared local produce, remains a key feature here.

Rooms 20 (2 fmly) (5 GF) **S** £75-£110; **D** £100-£200 (incl. bkfst) **Facilities** FTV Xmas New Year Wi-fi **Conf** Class 20 Board 20 Thtr 20 Del from £140 to £200 **Parking** 22 **Notes** LB Civ Wed 180

PONTEFRACT Map 16 SE42
West Yorkshire

Wentbridge House

★★★★ 77% ®® HOTEL

☎ 01977 620444 🖷 01977 620148
Wentbridge WF8 3JJ
e-mail: info@wentbridgehouse.co.uk
web: www.wentbridgehouse.co.uk
dir: M62 junct 33 onto A1 S, hotel in 4m

This well-established hotel sits in 20 acres of landscaped gardens, offering spacious, well-equipped bedrooms and a choice of dining styles. Service in the Fleur de Lys restaurant is polished and friendly, and a varied menu offers a good choice of interesting dishes. The Brasserie has a more relaxed style of modern dining.

Rooms 41 (4 annexe) (4 GF) **S** £110-£190; **D** £140-£220 (incl. bkfst)* **Facilities** FTV Xmas New Year Wi-fi **Conf** Class 100 Board 60 Thtr 130 Del from £110 to £150* **Services** Lift **Parking** 100 **Notes** LB ⊗ Civ Wed 130

Premier Inn Pontefract North

BUDGET HOTEL

☎ 0871 527 8886 🖷 0871 527 8887
Pontefract Rd, Knottingley WF11 0BU
dir: M62 junct 33 onto A1 N. Exit at A645 Pontefract junct, to T-junct, right towards Pontefract. Hotel on right

High quality, budget accommodation ideal for both families and business travellers. Spacious, en suite bedrooms feature tea and coffee making facilities, and Freeview TV in most hotels. Internet access and Wi-fi are available for a small fee. The adjacent family restaurant features a wide and varied menu. See also the Hotel Groups pages.

Rooms 41 **D** £51-£57*

Premier Inn Pontefract South

BUDGET HOTEL

☎ 0871 527 8888 🖷 0871 527 8889
Great North Rd, Darrington WF8 3BL
dir: Just off A1, 2m S of M62 junct 33

Rooms 28 **D** £51-£57*

POOLE Map 4 SZ09
Dorset

Harbour Heights

★★★★ 80% ®® HOTEL

☎ 01202 707272 & 0845 337 1550
🖷 01202 708594
73 Haven Rd, Sandbanks BH13 7LW
e-mail: enquiries@fjbhotels.co.uk
web: www.harbourheights.net
dir: Follow signs for Sandbanks, hotel on left after Canford Cliffs

The unassuming appearance of this hotel belies a wealth of innovation, quality and style. The very stylish, contemporary bedrooms, many with sea views, combine state-of-the-art facilities with traditional comforts; all have spa baths. The smart public areas include the Harbar brasserie, popular bars and sitting areas where picture windows accentuate panoramic views of Poole Harbour. The sun deck is the perfect setting for watching the cross-channel ferries come and go.

Rooms 38 (2 fmly) **S** £75-£160; **D** £150-£320 (incl. bkfst)* **Facilities** STV Spa bath in all rooms Xmas New Year Wi-fi **Conf** Class 36 Board 22 Thtr 70 Del from £99 to £195* **Services** Lift Air con **Parking** 50 **Notes** LB ⊗ Civ Wed 120

Hotel du Vin Poole

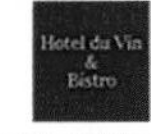

★★★★ 78% ◎ HOTEL

☎ 01202 785570 📠 01202 785571
Thames St BH15 1JN
e-mail: info.poole@hotelduvin.com
web: www.hotelduvin.com
dir: A31 to Poole, follow channel ferry signs. Left at Poole bridge onto Poole Quay, 1st left into Thames St. Hotel opposite St James Church

Offering a fresh approach to the well established company style, this property boasts some delightful rooms packed with comfort and all the expected Hotel du Vin features. Situated near the harbour the hotel offers nautically-themed bedrooms and suites that have plasma TVs, DVD players and bathrooms with power showers. The public rooms are light, open spaces, and as with the other hotels in this group the bar and restaurant form centre stage.

Rooms 38 (4 GF) **Facilities** STV Xmas New Year Wi-fi **Conf** Class 20 Board 20 Thtr 35 **Services** Air con **Notes** Civ Wed 40

Haven

★★★★ 76% ◎◎ HOTEL

☎ 01202 707333 & 0845 337 1550
📠 01202 708796
Banks Rd, Sandbanks BH13 7QL
e-mail: reservations@fjbhotels.co.uk
web: www.havenhotel.co.uk
dir: B3965 towards Poole Bay, left onto the Peninsula. Hotel 1.5m on left adjacent to Swanage Toll Ferry

Enjoying an enviable location at the water's edge with views of Poole Bay, this well established hotel was once the home of radio pioneer, Guglielmo Marconi. A friendly team of staff provide good levels of customer care. Bedrooms vary in size and style; many have balconies and wonderful sea views. The leisure facilities are noteworthy.

Rooms 77 (4 fmly) **S** £100-£195; **D** £200-£410 (incl. bkfst) **Facilities** Spa STV supervised Gym Dance studio Health & Beauty suite Sauna Steam room Xmas New Year Wi-fi **Conf** Class 70 Board 50 Thtr 160 Del from £115 to £195 **Services** Lift **Parking** 160 **Notes** LB Civ Wed 100

Sandbanks

★★★★ 75% ◎ HOTEL

☎ 01202 707377 & 0845 337 1550
📠 01202 708885
15 Banks Rd, Sandbanks BH13 7PS
e-mail: reservations@fjbhotels.co.uk
web: www.fjbhotels.co.uk
dir: A338 from Bournemouth onto Wessex Way, to Liverpool Victoria rdbt. Left, then 2nd exit onto B3965. Follow beach signs. Hotel on left

Set on the delightful Sandbanks Peninsula, this well loved hotel has direct access to the blue flag beach and stunning views across Poole Harbour. Most of the spacious bedrooms have sea views; some are air conditioned. There is an extensive range of leisure facilities, including an impressive crèche.

Rooms 110 (31 fmly) (4 GF) **S** £75-£140; **D** £150-£280 (incl. bkfst)* **Facilities** Spa STV FTV supervised Gym Sailing Mountain bikes Children's play area Massage room Watersports academy Xmas New Year Wi-fi Child facilities **Conf** Class 50 Board 80 Thtr 150 Del from £99 to £169* **Services** Lift **Parking** 120 **Notes** LB Civ Wed 70

Thistle Poole

thistle

★★★ 80% HOTEL

☎ 0871 376 9032 📠 0871 376 9132
The Quay BH15 1HD
e-mail: poole@thistle.co.uk
web: www.thistlehotels.com/poole
dir: On quay adjacent to Dolphin Marina

Situated on the quayside overlooking the harbour, this modern hotel is situated close to the ferry terminal and is also a good base for exploring the beautiful Dorset countryside. Many of the bedrooms have views of Poole harbour. There is a restaurant and two bars, plus two meeting rooms are available. Thistle Hotels – AA Hotel Group of the Year 2011-12.

Rooms 70 (22 GF) **Facilities** Xmas New Year Wi-fi **Conf** Class 80 Board 60 Thtr 120 **Services** Lift **Parking** 120 **Notes** Civ Wed 120

Arndale Court Hotel

★★★ 70% HOTEL

☎ 01202 683746 📠 01202 668838
62/66 Wimborne Rd BH15 2BY
e-mail: info@arndalecourthotel.com
web: www.arndalecourthotel.com
dir: On A349, opposite Poole Stadium

Ideally situated for the town centre and ferry terminal, this is a small, privately owned hotel. Bedrooms are well equipped, spacious and comfortable. Particularly well suited to business guests, this hotel has a pleasant range of stylish public areas and good parking.

Rooms 39 (7 fmly) (14 GF) (8 smoking) **S** £65-£83; **D** £80-£110 (incl. bkfst)* **Facilities** STV FTV Wi-fi **Conf** Class 20 Board 30 Thtr 50 **Parking** 40

Holiday Inn Express Poole

BUDGET HOTEL

☎ 01202 649222 📠 01202 649666
Walking Field Ln, Seldown Bridge Site BH15 1TJ
e-mail: reservations@exhipoole.co.uk
web: www.hiexpress.com/pooleuk
dir: A350 to town centre, pass bus station. Right at next rdbt, take slip road to left. Hotel adjacent to Dolphin Swimming Pool

A modern hotel ideal for families and business travellers. Fresh and uncomplicated, the spacious rooms include Sky TV, power shower and tea and coffee-making facilities. Continental buffet breakfast is included in the room rate; evening meals are available in the spacious café/bar. See also the Hotel Groups pages.

Rooms 85 (42 fmly) (10 GF) (7 smoking) **Conf** Class 16 Board 18 Thtr 30 Del from £100*

P

POOLE *continued*

Premier Inn Poole Centre (Holes Bay)

BUDGET HOTEL

☎ 0871 527 8892 🖷 0871 527 8893
Holes Bay Rd BH15 2BD
dir: S of A35 & A349 on A350 (dual carriageway). Follow Poole Channel Ferry signs

High quality, budget accommodation ideal for both families and business travellers. Spacious, en suite bedrooms feature tea and coffee making facilities, and Freeview TV in most hotels. Internet access and Wi-fi are available for a small fee. The adjacent family restaurant features a wide and varied menu. See also the Hotel Groups pages.

Rooms 83 **D** £75*

Premier Inn Poole North

BUDGET HOTEL

☎ 0871 527 8894 🖷 0871 527 8895
Cabot Ln BH17 7DA
dir: Follow Poole/Channel Ferries signs. At Darby's Corner rdbt take 2nd exit. At 2nd lights right into Cabot Ln. Hotel on right

Rooms 126 **D** £65-£68*

Milsoms Poole

RESTAURANT WITH ROOMS

☎ 01202 609000
47 Haven Rd, Canford Cliffs BH13 7LH
e-mail: poole@milsomshotel.co.uk

Milsoms Poole is located in the Canford Cliffs area, moments from some of the country's best beaches and the picturesque Purbeck Hills. This restaurant with rooms boasts comfortable and stylish en suite accommodation that is situated above the popular seafood Loch Fyne Restaurant. The friendly and helpful team provide a warm welcome. Limited on-site parking is available.

Rooms 8 (1 fmly)

PORLOCK
Somerset — Map 3 SS84

INSPECTORS' CHOICE

The Oaks

★★★ ® HOTEL

☎ 01643 862265 🖷 01643 863131
TA24 8ES
e-mail: info@oakshotel.co.uk
dir: From E of A39, enter village (road narrows to single track) then follow hotel sign. From W: down Porlock Hill, through village, hotel sign on right

A relaxing atmosphere is found at this charming Edwardian house, located near to the setting of R D Blackmore's novel *Lorna Doone*. Quietly located and set in attractive grounds, the hotel enjoys elevated views across the village towards the sea. Bedrooms are thoughtfully furnished and comfortable, and the public rooms include a charming bar and a peaceful drawing room. In the dining room, guests can choose from the daily-changing menu, which features fresh, quality local produce.

Rooms 8 **S** £150; **D** £220-£250 (incl. bkfst & dinner)* **Facilities** FTV Xmas New Year Wi-fi **Parking** 12 **Notes** LB ⊗ No children 8yrs Closed Nov-Mar (ex Xmas & New Year)

PORT GAVERNE
Cornwall — Map 2 SX08

Port Gaverne

★★ 75% HOTEL

☎ 01208 880244 🖷 01208 880151
PL29 3SQ
e-mail: graham@port-gaverne-hotel.co.uk
dir: Signed from B3314

In a quiet seaside port half a mile from the old fishing village of Port Isaac, this hotel has a romantic atmosphere, and retains flagstone floors, beamed ceilings and steep stairways. Bedrooms are available in a range of sizes. Local produce features on the restaurant menus, and bar meals always prove popular.

Rooms 14 (4 fmly) **S** £57.50-£67.50; **D** £95-£115 (incl. bkfst)* **Facilities** FTV Wi-fi **Parking** 30

PORTHLEVEN
Cornwall — Map 2 SW62

Kota Restaurant with Rooms

® RESTAURANT WITH ROOMS

☎ 01326 562407 🖷 01326 562407
Harbour Head TR13 9JA
e-mail: kota@btconnect.com
dir: B3304 from Helston into Porthleven. Kota on harbour opposite slipway

Overlooking the water, this 300-year-old building is the home of Kota Restaurant (Kota is the Maori word for shellfish). The bedrooms are approached via a granite stairway at the side of the building. The family room is spacious and has the benefit of harbour views, while the smaller, double room is at the rear of the property. The enthusiastic young owners ensure that guests will enjoy their stay, and a meal in the restaurant should not be missed. Breakfast features the best local produce.

Rooms 2 (2 annexe) (1 fmly)

PORT ISAAC
Cornwall — Map 2 SW98

The Longcross Hotel

★★ 76% HOTEL

☎ 01208 880243 🖷 01208 880560
Trelights PL29 3TF
e-mail: info@longcrosshotel.co.uk
dir: B3314 from Wadebridge towards Rock/Delabole, 5m, left signed Trelights, through village, follow hotel signs. Or B3266 from Camelford towards Delabole/Tintagel. 1.5m, left onto B3314. Through Delabole & Pendogget, right before church. Hotel in 1m

Located in a beautiful setting just minutes from Port Isaac, this hotel boasts a very friendly and relaxed atmosphere. The rooms are light and airy and there is a contemporary bar and separate lounge for guests. There are stunning views from the restaurant and many of the well-appointed bedrooms. Set in carefully tended gardens and grounds which are open to the public, it also offers a series of suites in a separate building. Food is locally sourced and menus offer a wide range of well cooked dishes.

Rooms 16 (5 annexe) (3 fmly) (7 GF) **Facilities** FTV Wi-fi **Conf** Class 100 Board 40 Thtr 150 Del from £50 to £80* **Parking** 30 **Notes** Closed Jan RS Nov-Dec & Feb-Mar Civ Wed 150

PORTISHEAD Map 4 ST47
Somerset

Premier Inn Portishead

BUDGET HOTEL

☎ 0871 527 8898 📠 0871 527 8899
Wyndham Way BS20 7GA
dir: M5 junct 19, A369 towards Portishead. Over 1st rdbt, hotel at next rdbt

High quality, budget accommodation ideal for both families and business travellers. Spacious, en suite bedrooms feature tea and coffee making facilities, and Freeview TV in most hotels. Internet access and Wi-fi are available for a small fee. The adjacent family restaurant features a wide and varied menu. See also the Hotel Groups pages.

Rooms 58 **D** £54-£65*

PORTLAND Map 4 SY67
Dorset

The Venue Hotel & Conference Centre

U

☎ 01305 826060
Southwell Park, DT5 2NA
e-mail: thevenuehotel12@yahoo.co.uk

Currently the rating for this establishment is not confirmed. This may be due to a change of ownership or because it has only recently joined the AA rating scheme. For further details please see the AA website: theAA.com

Rooms 77 **S** £60-£140; **D** £70-£160* **Conf** Class 100 Board 60 Thtr 200

PORTLOE Map 2 SW93
Cornwall

The Lugger Hotel

★★★ 82% ® HOTEL

☎ 01872 501322 📠 01872 501691
TR2 5RD
e-mail: reservations.lugger@ohiml.com
web: www.oxfordhotelsandinns.com
dir: A390 to Truro, B3287 to Tregony, A3078 (St Mawes Rd), left for Veryan, left for Portloe

This delightful hotel enjoys a unique setting adjacent to the slipway of the harbour where fishing boats still come and go. Bedrooms, some in adjacent buildings and cottages, are contemporary in style and well equipped. The sitting room, which reflects the original building's character, has beams and open fireplaces that create a cosy atmosphere. The modern restaurant enjoys superb views, and in warmer months a sun terrace overlooking the harbour proves a popular place.

The Lugger Hotel

Rooms 22 (17 annexe) (1 GF) **Facilities** FTV Xmas New Year Wi-fi **Parking** 26 **Notes** Civ Wed 50

PORTSCATHO Map 2 SW83
Cornwall

INSPECTORS' CHOICE

Driftwood

★★★ ®®® HOTEL

☎ 01872 580644 📠 01872 580801
Rosevine TR2 5EW
e-mail: info@driftwoodhotel.co.uk
dir: A390 towards St Mawes. On A3078 turn left to Rosevine at Trewithian

Poised on the cliff side with panoramic views, this contemporary hotel has a peaceful and secluded location. A warm welcome is guaranteed here, where professional standards of service are provided in an effortless and relaxed manner. Cuisine is at the heart of any stay, with quality local produce used in a sympathetic and highly skilled manner. The extremely comfortable and elegant bedrooms are decorated in soft shades reminiscent of the seashore. There is a sheltered terraced garden that has a large deck for sunbathing.

Rooms 15 (1 annexe) (3 fmly) (1 GF) **S** £157-£221; **D** £165-£260 (incl. bkfst)* **Facilities** FTV Private beach Treatments on request Wi-fi **Parking** 30 **Notes** LB ⊗ Closed 7 Dec-5 Feb RS Xmas & New Year

PORTSMOUTH & SOUTHSEA Map 5 SU60
Hampshire

Portsmouth Marriott Hotel

Marriott HOTELS & RESORTS

★★★★ 79% ® HOTEL

☎ 0870 400 7285 📠 0870 400 7385
Southampton Rd PO6 4SH
web: www.portsmouthmarriott.co.uk
dir: M27 junct 12, keep left off slip road & at lights. Hotel on left

Close to the motorway and ferry port, this hotel is well suited to the business trade. The comfortable and well laid-out bedrooms provide a comprehensive range of facilities including up-to-date workstations. The leisure club offers a pool, a gym, and a health and beauty salon.

Rooms 174 (77 fmly) (9 smoking) **D** £95-£170* **Facilities** STV FTV ⓢ supervised Gym Exercise studio Beauty salon Treatment room Xmas New Year Wi-fi **Conf** Class 180 Board 30 Thtr 350 Del from £135 to £170* **Services** Lift Air con **Parking** 196 **Notes** LB Civ Wed 350

Holiday Inn Portsmouth

★★★ 79% HOTEL

☎ 0870 400 9065 📠 023 9275 6715
Pembroke Rd PO1 2TA
e-mail: portsmouth@ihg.com
web: www.holidayinn.co.uk
dir: M275 into city centre, follow signs for seafront. Hotel on right after Kings Rd rdbt

This hotel occupies a great location close to Portsmouth seafront and near the Gunwharf Quays Shopping Centre. Restricted, complimentary parking is available on a first-come-first-served basis at the hotel. Accommodation is comfortable and very well maintained; some rooms have magnificent sea views. On-site facilities include a swimming pool, fitness room, a stylish restaurant and meeting rooms.

Rooms 165 (12 fmly) (6 GF) (13 smoking) **Facilities** FTV ⓢ supervised Gym Health club Steam room Sauna Xmas New Year Wi-fi **Conf** Class 70 Board 60 Thtr 160 **Services** Lift Air con **Parking** 66 **Notes** ⊗ Civ Wed 160

P

PORTSMOUTH & SOUTHSEA ***continued***

Best Western Royal Beach

★★★ 78% HOTEL

☎ 023 9273 1281 023 9281 7572
South Pde, Southsea PO4 0RN
e-mail: enquiries@royalbeachhotel.co.uk
web: www.royalbeachhotel.co.uk
dir: M27 to M275, follow signs to seafront. Hotel on seafront

This former Victorian seafront hotel is a smart and comfortable venue suitable for leisure and business guests alike. Bedrooms and public areas are well presented and generally spacious, and the smart Coast Bar is an ideal venue for a relaxing drink.

Rooms 124 (18 fmly) **Facilities** STV Xmas New Year Wi-fi **Conf** Class 180 Board 40 Thtr 280 **Services** Lift **Parking** 50 **Notes** LB Civ Wed

Westfield Hall Hotel

★★★ 74% HOTEL

☎ 023 9282 6971 023 9287 0200
65 Festing Rd, Southsea PO4 0NQ
e-mail: enquiries@whhotel.info
web: www.whhotel.info
dir: From M275 follow Southsea seafront signs. Left into Clarence Esplanade on South Parade, left into St Helens Parade, hotel 150yds

This hotel is situated in a quiet side road close to the seafront and town centre. The accommodation is split between two identical houses and all rooms are smartly appointed and well equipped. Public rooms are attractively decorated and include three lounges, a bar and a restaurant.

Rooms 25 (11 annexe) (12 fmly) (6 GF) **S** £48-£62; **D** £68-£120 (incl. bkfst)* **Facilities** STV FTV Wi-fi **Parking** 16 **Notes** ⊗

P

Seacrest

★★ 80% HOTEL

☎ 023 9273 3192 023 9283 2523
11/12 South Pde, Southsea PO5 2JB
e-mail: office@seacresthotel.co.uk
dir: From M27/M275 follow signs for seafront, Pyramids & Sea Life Centre. Hotel opposite Rock Gardens & Pyramids

In a premier seafront location, this smart hotel provides the ideal base for exploring the town. Bedrooms, many benefiting from sea views, are decorated to a high standard with good facilities. Guests can relax in either the south-facing lounge, furnished with large leather sofas, or the adjacent bar; there is also a cosy dining room popular with residents.

Rooms 28 (3 fmly) (3 GF) **S** £55-£79; **D** £65-£145 (incl. bkfst) **Facilities** STV FTV Wi-fi **Services** Lift **Parking** 12 **Notes** LB Closed 24 Dec-2 Jan

The Farmhouse & Innlodge Hotel

OldEnglish

BUDGET HOTEL

☎ 023 9265 0510 023 9269 3458
Burrfields Rd PO3 5HH
e-mail: farmhouse.portsmouth@greeneking.co.uk
web: www.farmhouseinnlodge.com
dir: A3(M)/M27 onto A27. Take Southsea exit, follow A2030. 3rd lights right into Burrfields Rd. Hotel 2nd car park on left

Located on the eastern fringe of the city, this purpose-built hotel is conveniently located for all major routes. The spacious, modern bedrooms are well equipped and include ground floor and family rooms. The Farmhouse Hungry Horse Pub offers a wide range of eating options, and there is an ActionZone adventure area.

Rooms 74 (6 fmly) (33 GF) **Conf** Class 64 Board 40 Thtr 150

Ibis Portsmouth Centre

ibis HOTEL

BUDGET HOTEL

☎ 023 9264 0000 023 9264 1000
Winston Churchill Av PO1 2LX
e-mail: h1461@accor.com
web: www.ibishotel.com
dir: M27 junct 12 onto M275. Follow signs for city centre, Sealife Centre & Guildhall. Right at rdbt into Winston Churchill Ave

Modern, budget hotel offering comfortable accommodation in bright and practical bedrooms. Breakfast is self-service and dinner is available in the restaurant. See also the Hotel Groups pages.

Rooms 144 **S** £60-£85; **D** £60-£85* **Conf** Class 20 Board 20 Thtr 30

Premier Inn Portsmouth (Horndean)

BUDGET HOTEL

☎ 0871 527 8902 0871 527 8903
2 Havant Rd PO8 0DT
dir: A3(M) junct 2, take B2149 signed Emsworth, Horndean. At rdbt left onto B2149, follow Horndean signs. At next rdbt left onto A3 towards Waterlooville. Hotel on left (behind Red Lion)

High quality, budget accommodation ideal for both families and business travellers. Spacious, en suite bedrooms feature tea and coffee making facilities, and Freeview TV in most hotels. Internet access and Wi-fi are available for a small fee. The adjacent family restaurant features a wide and varied menu. See also the Hotel Groups pages.

Rooms 25 **D** £67*

Premier Inn Portsmouth (Port Solent)

BUDGET HOTEL

☎ 0871 527 8906 0871 527 8907
Binnacle Way PO6 4FB
dir: M27 junct 12, left at lights onto Southampton Rd. Left after 200mtrs at lights onto Compass Rd. At mini-rdbt right onto Binnacle Way, hotel on right

Rooms 108 **D** £67-£70*

Premier Inn Portsmouth (Port Solent East)

BUDGET HOTEL

☎ 0871 527 8904 0871 527 8905
1 Southampton Rd, North Harbour PO6 4SA
dir: M27 junct 12, A3, left onto A27. Hotel on left

Rooms 64 **D** £67*

Premier Inn Southsea

BUDGET HOTEL

☎ 0871 527 9014 0871 527 9015
Long Curtain Rd, Southsea PO5 3AA
dir: M1 junct 24, A453. Follow ring road & Queen's Drive Industrial Estate signs. After Homebase left into Castle Bridge Rd, hotel opposite Pizza Hut restaurant

Rooms 40 **D** £69*

PORTWRINKLE
Cornwall **Map 3 SX35**

See also **Looe**

Whitsand Bay Hotel & Golf Club

★★★ 74% ® HOTEL

☎ 01503 230276 01503 230329
PL11 3BU
e-mail: whitsandbayhotel@btconnect.com
web: www.whitsandbayhotel.co.uk
dir: A38 from Exeter over River Tamar, left at Trerulefoot rdbt onto A374 to Crafthole/Portwrinkle. Follow hotel signs

An imposing Victorian stone building with oak panelling, stained-glass windows and a sweeping staircase. Bedrooms include family rooms and a suite with a balcony; many have superb sea views. Facilities include an 18-hole cliff-top golf course and an indoor swimming pool. The fixed-price menu offers an interesting selection of dishes.

Rooms 32 (7 fmly) **Facilities** 18 Putt green Gym Games room Lounge with wide screen TV Xmas **Parking** 60

POTTERS BAR Hertfordshire **Map 6 TL20**

Ponsbourne Park Hotel

★★★★ 71% HOTEL

01707 876191 & 879277 01707 875190
Newgate Street Village SG13 8QT
e-mail: reservations@ponsbournepark.co.uk
web: www.ponsbournepark.com
dir: M25 juncts 24 & 25. Hotel in Newgate Street Village

Set within 200 acres of quiet parkland, this 17th-century country house offers contemporary accommodation and public rooms, along with a flexible range of leisure and conference facilities. Smart modern bedrooms are located in the main house and adjacent annexe; each room is well equipped, but typically main house rooms are more spacious. The fine dining restaurant is supplemented by a bistro.

Rooms 50 (27 annexe) (8 fmly) (8 GF) **Facilities** STV 9 Gym New Year Wi-fi **Conf** Class 40 Board 40 Thtr 130 **Services** Air con **Parking** 80 **Notes** ⊗ Civ Wed 86

PRESTON Lancashire **Map 18 SD52**

See also **Garstang**

Barton Grange Hotel

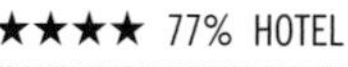

★★★★ 77% HOTEL

01772 862551 01772 861267
Garstang Rd PR3 5AA
e-mail: stay@bartongrangehotel.com
web: www.bartongrangehotel.co.uk

(For full entry see Barton)

Preston Marriott Hotel

★★★★ 75% HOTEL

01772 864087 01772 861728
Garstang Rd, Broughton PR3 5JB
e-mail: reservations.preston@marriotthotels.co.uk
web: www.prestonmarriott.co.uk
dir: M6 junct 32 to M55 junct 1, follow A6 towards Garstang. Hotel 0.5m on right

Exuding a country-club atmosphere this stylish hotel enjoys good links to both the city centre and motorway network. There are two dining options and the extensive leisure facilities ensure that there is plenty to do. The bedrooms are smartly decorated and equipped with a comprehensive range of extras.

Rooms 149 (41 fmly) (63 GF) **Facilities** Spa STV supervised Gym Steam room Beauty salon Hairdressing Xmas New Year Wi-fi **Conf** Class 100 Board 70 Thtr 220 **Services** Lift Air con **Parking** 250 **Notes** LB ⊗ Civ Wed 180

Pines

★★★ 82% HOTEL

01772 338551 01772 629002
570 Preston Rd, Clayton-Le-Woods PR6 7ED
e-mail: mail@thepineshotel.co.uk
dir: Exit M6 junct 28 N'bound towards Blackburn, 2.5m to hotel. M6 junct 2 S'bound towards Chorley, 1m. On A6

This unique and stylish hotel sits in four acres of mature grounds just a short drive from the motorway network. Elegant bedrooms are individually designed and offer high levels of comfort and facilities. Day rooms include a smart bar and the aptly named Rosette Restaurant, while extensive function rooms make this hotel a popular venue for weddings.

Rooms 35 (2 fmly) (14 GF) **S** £75-£175; **D** £85-£200 (incl. bkfst)* **Facilities** FTV Xmas New Year Wi-fi **Conf** Class 250 Board 100 Thtr 400 Del from £90 to £115* **Parking** 120 **Notes** ⊗ Civ Wed 250

Holiday Inn Preston

★★★ 79% HOTEL

01772 567000 & 567020
The Ringway PR1 3AU
e-mail: reservations@hipreston.com
web: www.hipreston.com
dir: M6 junct 31, A59 follow signs for town centre. Right at T-junct, hotel on left

Ideally situated in the city centre, yet accessible from the M6 which is just two miles away. The bedrooms are comfortable, well equipped and have useful accessories. The hotel offers Wi-fi, a conference centre and seminar venue, plus a small gym with excellent views across the city. Meals are served in the Ringway Bar and Grill Restaurant, and a bar offers light meals and live TV sport channels. Room service is available 24 hours a day.

Rooms 133 **Facilities** STV FTV Gym Wi-fi **Conf** Class 25 Board 30 Thtr 60 Del from £125 to £145* **Services** Lift Air con **Parking** 30 **Notes** ⊗

Macdonald Tickled Trout

★★★ 75% HOTEL

0844 8799053 01772 877463
Preston New Rd, Samlesbury PR5 0UJ
e-mail: general.tickledtrout@macdonald-hotels.co.uk
web: www.macdonald-hotels.co.uk
dir: M6 junct 31. Off A59 towards Preston

On the banks of the River Ribble, this hotel is conveniently located for the motorway, making it a popular venue for both business and leisure guests. Smartly appointed bedrooms are all tastefully decorated and equipped with a thoughtful range of extras. The hotel boasts a stylish wing of meeting rooms.

Rooms 98 (6 fmly) (10 GF) **Facilities** FTV Fishing Xmas New Year Wi-fi **Conf** Class 60 Board 50 Thtr 120 **Services** Lift **Parking** 180 **Notes** Civ Wed 90

The Legacy Preston International Hotel

★★★ 71% HOTEL

08444 119 028 08444 119 029
Marsh Ln PR1 2YF
e-mail: res-prestoninternational@legacy-hotels.co.uk
dir: M6 junct 31 or 32, A59 (ring road). Hotel in approx 3.5m (on one-way system)

This hotel is ideally located close to the town centre and the M6 making it a popular choice with both business and leisure guests. The contemporary bedrooms are very comfortable and well equipped, and free Wi-fi is available. The public areas include a light-filled lounge, and the menu in the restaurant offers a wide choice to suit most tastes. The hotel has secure parking.

Rooms 75 (12 fmly) **Facilities** FTV Wi-fi **Conf** Class 20 Board 20 Thtr 40 **Services** Lift **Parking** 40 **Notes** LB ⊗

P

PRESTON *continued*

Ibis Preston North

BUDGET HOTEL

☎ 01772 861800 📠 01772 861900
Garstang Rd, Broughton PR3 5JE
e-mail: H3162@accor.com
web: www.ibishotel.com
dir: M6 junct 32, then M55 junct 1. Left lane onto A6. Left at slip road, left again at mini-rdbt. 2nd turn, hotel on right past pub

Modern, budget hotel offering comfortable accommodation in bright and practical bedrooms. Breakfast is self-service and dinner is available in the restaurant. See also the Hotel Groups pages.

Rooms 82 (27 fmly) (16 GF) (12 smoking)
Conf Class 20 Board 20 Thtr 30

Premier Inn Preston Central

BUDGET HOTEL

☎ 0871 527 8908 📠 0871 527 8909
Fox St PR1 2AB
dir: Off Ridgway (A59). Telephone for detailed directions

High quality, budget accommodation ideal for both families and business travellers. Spacious, en suite bedrooms feature tea and coffee making facilities, and Freeview TV in most hotels. Internet access and Wi-fi are available for a small fee. The adjacent family restaurant features a wide and varied menu. See also the Hotel Groups pages.

Rooms 110 **D** £54-£63*

Premier Inn Preston East

BUDGET HOTEL

☎ 0871 527 8910 📠 0871 527 8911
Bluebell Way, Preston East Link Rd, Fulwood PR2 5PZ
dir: M6 junct 31a, follow ring road under motorway, hotel on left. (NB no exit for S'bound traffic so exit at M6 junct 31, onto M6 N'bound, exit at junct 31a)

Rooms 65 **D** £51-£55*

Premier Inn Preston South (Craven Drive)

BUDGET HOTEL

☎ 0871 527 8914 📠 0871 527 8915
Lostock Ln, Bamber Bridge PR5 6BZ
dir: M6 junct 29, A582 (Lostock Ln). Straight on at 1st lights, into left lane, hotel on left adjacent to B&Q

Rooms 74 **D** £57-£62*

Premier Inn Preston South (Cuerden Way)

BUDGET HOTEL

☎ 0871 527 8916 📠 0871 527 8917
Lostock Ln, Bamber Bridge PR5 6BA
dir: Off M65 junct 1 (0.5m from M6 junct 29) close to rdbt junct of A582 & A6

Rooms 42 **D** £57-£62*

Premier Inn Preston West

BUDGET HOTEL

☎ 0871 527 8918 📠 0871 527 8919
Blackpool Rd, Lea PR4 0XB
dir: Off A583, opposite Texaco garage

Rooms 38 **D** £51-£55*

PRESTWICH
Greater Manchester — Map 15 SD80

Premier Inn Manchester (Prestwich)

BUDGET HOTEL

☎ 0871 527 8714 📠 0871 527 8715
Bury New Rd M25 3AJ
dir: M60 junct 17, A56 signed Mancehseter City Centre, Prestwich & Whitefield. Hotel on left

High quality, budget accommodation ideal for both families and business travellers. Spacious, en suite bedrooms feature tea and coffee making facilities, and Freeview TV in most hotels. Internet access and Wi-fi are available for a small fee. The adjacent family restaurant features a wide and varied menu. See also the Hotel Groups pages.

Rooms 60 **D** £54-£58*

PUDDINGTON
Cheshire — Map 15 SJ37

Macdonald Craxton Wood

★★★★ 77% ® HOTEL

☎ 0844 879 9038 📠 0151 347 4040
Parkgate Rd, Ledsham CH66 9PB
e-mail: craxton@macdonald-hotels.co.uk
web: www.macdonald-hotels.co.uk
dir: From M6 take M56 towards N Wales, then A5117, A540 to Hoylake. Hotel on left 200yds past lights

Set in extensive grounds, this hotel offers a variety of bedroom styles; the modern rooms are particularly comfortable. The nicely furnished restaurant overlooks the grounds and offers a wide choice of dishes, whilst full leisure facilities and a choice of function suites complete the package.

Rooms 72 (8 fmly) (30 GF) **D** £62-£160*
Facilities Spa STV Gym Xmas New Year Wi-fi
Conf Class 200 Board 160 Thtr 300 **Services** Lift
Parking 220 **Notes** LB Civ Wed 350

Premier Inn Wirral (Two Mills)

BUDGET HOTEL

☎ 0871 527 9180 📠 0871 527 9181
Parkgate Rd, Two Mills CH66 9PD
dir: 5m from M56 junct 16 & M53 junct 5. On x-rds of A550 & A540

High quality, budget accommodation ideal for both families and business travellers. Spacious, en suite bedrooms feature tea and coffee making facilities, and Freeview TV in most hotels. Internet access and Wi-fi are available for a small fee. The adjacent family restaurant features a wide and varied menu. See also the Hotel Groups pages.

Rooms 31 **D** £53-£57*

PURTON
Wiltshire — Map 5 SU08

The Pear Tree at Purton

★★★ 81% ®® HOTEL

☎ 01793 772100 📠 01793 772369
Church End SN5 4ED
e-mail: stay@peartreepurton.co.uk
dir: M4 junct 16 follow signs to Purton, at Best One shop turn right. Hotel 0.25m on left

A charming 15th-century, former vicarage set amidst extensive landscaped gardens in a peaceful location in the Vale of the White Horse and near the Saxon village of Purton. The resident proprietors and staff provide efficient, dedicated service and friendly hospitality. The spacious bedrooms are individually decorated and have a good range of thoughtful extras such as fresh fruit, sherry and shortbread. Fresh ingredients feature on the award-winning menus.

Rooms 17 (2 fmly) (6 GF) **S** £120-£150; **D** £120-£180 (incl. bkfst) **Facilities** STV FTV Outdoor giant chess Vineyard Wi-fi **Conf** Class 30 Board 30 Thtr 70 Del from £185 to £220 **Parking** 60 **Notes** LB Civ Wed 50

QUORN Leicestershire **Map 11 SK51**

Quorn Country Hotel

PRIMA HOTEL GROUP

★★★★ 76% HOTEL

☎ 01509 415050 & 415061 01509 415557
Charnwood House, 66 Leicester Rd LE12 8BB
e-mail: reservations@quorncountryhotel.co.uk
web: www.quorncountryhotel.co.uk
dir: M1 junct 23 onto A512 into Loughborough. Follow A6 signs. At 1st rdbt towards Quorn, through lights, hotel 500yds from 2nd rdbt

Professional service is one of the key strengths of this pleasing hotel, which sits beside the river in four acres of landscaped gardens and grounds. The smart modern conference centre and function suites are popular for both corporate functions and weddings. Public rooms include a smart comfortable lounge and bar, and guests have the choice of two dining options: the formal Shires restaurant and the informal conservatory-style Orangery.

Rooms 36 (2 fmly) (11 GF) **Facilities** STV Fishing New Year Wi-fi **Conf** Class 162 Board 40 Thtr 300 Del from £150* **Services** Lift **Parking** 100 **Notes** ® Civ Wed 200

RADLETT Hertfordshire **Map 6 TL10**

Premier Inn St Albans/ Bricket Wood

BUDGET HOTEL

☎ 0871 527 9016 0871 527 9017
Smug Oak Ln, Bricketwood AL2 3PN
dir: M1 junct 6 (or M25 junct 21a) follow Watford signs, left at lights, turn left signed M1/Bricket Wood. 2nd left into Mount Pleasant Lane, straight on at 2 mini rdbts, right at The Gate pub. Hotel at end on left

High quality, budget accommodation ideal for both families and business travellers. Spacious, en suite bedrooms feature tea and coffee making facilities, and Freeview TV in most hotels. Internet access and Wi-fi are available for a small fee. The adjacent family restaurant features a wide and varied menu. See also the Hotel Groups pages.

Rooms 56 **D** £56-£69*

RAINHAM Greater London **Map 6 TQ58**

Manor Hotel & Restaurant

★★★ 79% HOTEL

☎ 01708 555586 01708 630055
Berwick Pond Rd RM13 9EL
e-mail: info@themanoressex.co.uk
web: www.themanoressex.co.uk
dir: M25 junct 30/31, A13, 1st exit signed Wennington, right, at main lights right onto Upminster Rd North, left into Berwick Pond Rd

Located in the countryside the former Berwick Manor has been lovingly restored, and today offers well-appointed, contemporary accommodation. The rooms are equipped with a good range of amenities including complimentary Wi-fi. Lunch and dinner are served in the attractive restaurant whilst alfresco dining is possible on the terrace. Two function suites provide the ideal events venue.

Rooms 15 (1 fmly) **S** £100-£115; **D** £130-£155 (incl. bkfst) **Facilities** STV Xmas New Year Wi-fi **Conf** Class 60 Board 40 Thtr 100 **Services** Lift **Parking** 60 **Notes** ® Civ Wed 60

Premier Inn Rainham

BUDGET HOTEL

☎ 0871 527 8920 0871 527 8921
New Rd, Wennington RM13 9ED
dir: M25 junct 30/31, A13 for Dagenham/Rainham, A1306 towards Wennington, Aveley, & Rainham. Hotel 0.5m on right

High quality, budget accommodation ideal for both families and business travellers. Spacious, en suite bedrooms feature tea and coffee making facilities, and Freeview TV in most hotels. Internet access and Wi-fi are available for a small fee. The adjacent family restaurant features a wide and varied menu. See also the Hotel Groups pages.

Rooms 61 **D** £59-£69*

RAINHILL Merseyside **Map 15 SJ49**

Premier Inn Liverpool (Rainhill)

BUDGET HOTEL

☎ 0871 527 8614 0871 527 8615
804 Warrington Rd L35 6PE
dir: Just off M62 junct 7, A57 towards Rainhill

High quality, budget accommodation ideal for both families and business travellers. Spacious, en suite bedrooms feature tea and coffee making facilities, and Freeview TV in most hotels. Internet access and Wi-fi are available for a small fee. The adjacent family restaurant features a wide and varied menu. See also the Hotel Groups pages.

Rooms 34 **D** £54-£59*

RAMSGATE Kent **Map 7 TR36**

Pegwell Bay

★★★ 77% HOTEL

☎ 01843 599590 01843 599591
81 Pegwell Rd, Pegwell CT11 0NJ
e-mail: reception@pegwellbayhotel.co.uk
dir: Telephone for detailed directions

Boasting stunning views over The Channel, this historic cliff-top hotel is suitable for guests either staying on business or for leisure. Spacious, comfortable bedrooms are well equipped and include Wi-fi. A modern lounge, majestic dining room and traditional pub offer a variety of options for eating and for relaxation.

Rooms 42 (1 fmly) (6 GF) **Facilities** FTV Xmas New Year Wi-fi **Conf** Class 65 Board 65 Thtr 100 **Services** Lift **Notes** ® Civ Wed 70

RAMSGATE *continued*

The Oak Hotel

★★ 84% HOTEL

☎ 01843 583686 & 581582 🖷 01843 581606
66 Harbour Pde CT11 8LN
e-mail: reception@oakhotel.co.uk
dir: Follow road around harbour, right into Harbour Parade

Located within easy reach of the railway station, ferry terminal and the town centre's shops, this stylish hotel enjoys spectacular views of the marina and harbour. The comfortable bedrooms are attractively presented and very well equipped. The Atlantis fish restaurant, Caffe Roma and the contemporary bar offer a variety of dining options.

Rooms 34 (9 fmly) (7 GF) **Facilities** STV FTV Wi-fi **Conf** Class 60 Board 50 Thtr 100 **Notes** ⊗

Royal Harbour

★★ 79% METRO HOTEL

☎ 01843 591514 🖷 01843 570443
10-11 Nelson Crescent CT11 9JF
e-mail: info@royalharbourhotel.co.uk
dir: A253 to Ramsgate. Follow signs to seafront. At Churchill Tavern, 1st left into Nelson Crescent

Dating back to 1799, this hotel is made up of adjoining Georgian Grade II listed townhouses, and occupies a prime position in the town's well known historic garden crescent. Many of the bedrooms boast magnificent views over the 'Royal Harbour', the yacht marina and the English Channel. The atmosphere is relaxed, the service is attentive and the breakfast is superb.

R

Rooms 19 (3 fmly) (1 GF) **S** £58-£98; **D** £78-£238 (incl. bkfst) **Facilities** FTV Wi-fi **Conf** Class 30 Board 25 Thtr 30 Del from £80 to £150 **Parking** 4 **Notes** LB

Express by Holiday Inn Kent International Airport-Minster

BUDGET HOTEL

☎ 01843 820250 🖷 01843 820263
Tothill St CT12 4AU
e-mail: reservations@express-kia.co.uk
web: www.hiexpress.co.uk
dir: On A299, off rdbt junct with B2048

A modern hotel ideal for families and business travellers. Fresh and uncomplicated, the spacious rooms include Sky TV, power shower and tea and coffee-making facilities. Continental buffet breakfast is included in the room rate; other meals may be taken at the nearby family pub or restaurant. See also the Hotel Groups pages.

Rooms 105 (62 fmly) (33 GF) (17 smoking) **Conf** Class 30 Board 20 Thtr 40

RANGEWORTHY — Map 4 ST68
Gloucestershire

Rangeworthy Court

★★ 72% HOTEL

☎ 01454 228347 🖷 01454 65089
Church Ln, Wotton Rd BS37 7ND
e-mail: reception@rangeworthycourt.com
dir: Signed from B4058. Hotel at end of Church Lane

This welcoming manor house hotel is peacefully located in its own grounds, and is within easy reach of the motorway network. The character bedrooms come in a variety of sizes and there is a choice of comfortable lounges in which to enjoy a drink before dinner. The relaxing restaurant offers a selection of carefully prepared, enjoyable dishes.

Rooms 13 (4 fmly) **S** £45-£82.25; **D** £60-£100* **Facilities** FTV ⥾ Wi-fi **Conf** Class 14 Board 16 Thtr 22 **Parking** 30 **Notes** Closed 24-30 Dec Civ Wed 50

RAVENGLASS — Map 18 SD09
Cumbria

Pennington

★★★ 82% HOTEL

☎ 01229 717222 & 0845 450 6445
🖷 01229 717598
CA18 1SD
e-mail: info@penningtonhotels.com
dir: In village centre

This hotel has a very relaxed atmosphere throughout and the public areas are open plan with high quality fabrics and artwork. The bedrooms are modern in design and have high spec fixtures and fittings in the bathrooms. Honest cooking, based on local and fine quality ingredients, is offered on the seasonal menus. Staff show exceptional customer awareness by providing very attentive and friendly service.

Rooms 21 (3 annexe) (6 fmly) (5 GF) **S** £90-£130; **D** £100-£145 (incl. bkfst) **Facilities** FTV Xmas New Year Wi-fi **Conf** Class 40 Board 40 Thtr 80 Del from £110 to £150* **Parking** 53 **Notes** LB Civ Wed 70

RAVENSCAR — Map 19 NZ90
North Yorkshire

Raven Hall Country House

★★★ 75% HOTEL

☎ 01723 870353 🖷 01723 870072
YO13 0ET
e-mail: enquiries@ravenhall.co.uk
web: www.ravenhall.co.uk
dir: A171 towards Whitby. At Cloughton turn right onto unclassified road to Ravenscar

This impressive cliff top mansion enjoys breathtaking views over Robin Hood's Bay. Extensive well-kept grounds include tennis courts, putting green, swimming pools and historic battlements. The bedrooms vary in size but all are comfortably equipped, many offer panoramic views. There are also eight environmentally-friendly Finnish lodges that have been furnished to a high standard.

Rooms 60 (8 annexe) (20 fmly) (5 GF) **S** £24-£51; **D** £48-£102 (incl. bkfst)* **Facilities** ⛾ ⛳ 9 ⛾ Putt green ⥾ Bowls Table tennis Xmas New Year Wi-fi **Conf** Class 80 Board 40 Thtr 100 Del from £115 to £135* **Services** Lift **Parking** 200 **Notes** LB Civ Wed 100

RAVENSTONEDALE — Map 18 NY70
Cumbria

The Fat Lamb

★★ 71% HOTEL

☎ 015396 23242 🖷 015396 23285
Crossbank CA17 4LL
e-mail: enquiries@fatlamb.co.uk
dir: On A683, between Kirkby Stephen & Sedbergh

Solid stone walls and open fires feature at this 17th-century inn, set on its own nature reserve. There is a choice of dining options with an extensive menu available in the traditional bar and a more formal dining experience in the restaurant. Bedrooms are bright and cheerful, and include family rooms and easily accessible rooms for guests with limited mobility.

Rooms 12 (4 fmly) (5 GF) **S** £58-£59; **D** £90-£98 (incl. bkfst)* **Facilities** Private 5-acre nature reserve Xmas Wi-fi Child facilities **Conf** Class 30 Board 30 Thtr 60 **Parking** 60 **Notes** LB

RAYLEIGH Essex Map 7 TQ89

Premier Inn Basildon (Rayleigh)

BUDGET HOTEL

☎ 0871 527 8058 📠 0871 527 8059
Rayleigh Weir, Arterial Road (A127) SS6 7XJ
dir: M25 junct 29, A127 towards Southend. Approx 13m exit at Rayleigh Weir junct onto A129 to Rayleigh. Straight on at 2 lights, 1st left (NB for Sat Nav use SS6 7XJ)

High quality, budget accommodation ideal for both families and business travellers. Spacious, en suite bedrooms feature tea and coffee making facilities, and Freeview TV in most hotels. Internet access and Wi-fi are available for a small fee. The adjacent family restaurant features a wide and varied menu. See also the Hotel Groups pages.

Rooms 49 **D** £53-£62*

READING Berkshire Map 5 SU77

See also **Sonning**

Forbury Hotel

von Essen hotels A PRIVATE COLLECTION www.vonessenhotels.com

★★★★★ 79% ® HOTEL

☎ 08000 789789 & 0118 958 1234
📠 0118 959 0806
26 The Forbury RG1 3EJ
e-mail: reservations@theforburyhotel.co.uk
dir: Telephone for detailed directions

The imposing exterior of this hotel belies the caring approach of the staff who provide helpful service with a smile. The up-to-the-minute bedrooms have very appealing designs and sensory appeal. For film buffs, a 30-seater cinema is also available, complete with refreshments! Cerise is the convivial and stylish venue for enjoying the award-winning cuisine.

Rooms 23 (1 fmly) (1 GF) **Facilities** ♫ Xmas New Year Wi-fi **Conf** Class 24 Board 24 Thtr 35 **Services** Lift **Parking** 20 **Notes** ⊗ Civ Wed 50

Crowne Plaza Reading

★★★★ 80% ®® HOTEL

☎ 0118 925 9988
Caversham Bridge, Richfield Av RG1 8BD
e-mail: info@cp-reading.co.uk
web: www.cp-reading.co.uk
dir: A33 to Reading. Follow signs for Caversham & Henley. Take 1st exit at rdbt onto Caversham Rd. Left at rdbt & entrance on right

Located on the banks of the River Thames, this hotel is well positioned for both business and leisure travellers. The air-conditioned bedrooms are smartly appointed and well equipped. Public areas include the stylish Acqua Restaurant, a lounge bar, extensive conference and business facilities and the Revive health club and spa. Secure parking is a real bonus.

Rooms 122 (9 fmly) **S** £85-£169; **D** £99-£189* **Facilities** Spa STV Ⓢ Gym Xmas New Year Wi-fi **Conf** Class 110 Board 60 Thtr 200 Del from £149 to £210* **Services** Lift Air con **Parking** 200 **Notes** ⊗ Civ Wed 180

Millennium Madejski Hotel Reading

★★★★ 79% ®® HOTEL

☎ 0118 925 3500 📠 0118 925 3501
Madejski Stadium RG2 0FL
e-mail: sales.reading@millenniumhotels.co.uk
web: www.millenniumhotels.co.uk
dir: M4 junct 11 onto A33, follow signs for Madejski Stadium Complex

A stylish hotel, that features an atrium lobby with specially commissioned water sculpture, is part of the Madejski stadium complex, home to both Reading Football and London Irish Rugby teams. Bedrooms are appointed with spacious workstations and plenty of amenities; there is also a choice of suites and a club floor with its own lounge. The hotel also has a fine dining restaurant.

Rooms 201 (39 fmly) (19 smoking) **D** £62-£240* **Facilities** Spa STV Ⓢ supervised Gym Wi-fi **Conf** Class 36 Board 30 Thtr 66 Del from £180 to £305* **Services** Lift Air con **Parking** 250 **Notes** LB RS Xmas & New Year

Novotel Reading Centre

★★★★ 78% HOTEL

☎ 0118 952 2600 📠 0118 952 2610
25b Friar St RG1 1DP
e-mail: h5432@accor.com
web: www.novotel.com
dir: M4 junct 11 or A33 towards Reading, left for Garrard St car park, at rdbt 3rd exit on Friar St

This attractive and stylish city centre hotel is convenient for Reading's business and shopping centre; it is adjacent to a town centre car park, and has a range of conference facilities and excellent leisure options. The restaurant offers a contemporary style menu and a good wine list too. Bedrooms are comfortable and stylishly designed.

Rooms 178 (15 fmly) **Facilities** STV FTV Ⓢ Gym Steam room Wi-fi **Conf** Class 50 Board 36 Thtr 90 **Services** Lift Air con **Parking** 15

Holiday Inn Reading M4 Jct 10

★★★★ 76% HOTEL

☎ 0118 944 0444 📠 0118 944 0033
Wharfedale Rd, Winnersh Triangle RG41 5TS
e-mail: reservations@hireadinghotel.com
web: www.meridianleisurehotels.com/reading
dir: M4 junct 10/A329 (N) towards Reading (E), 1st exit signed Winnersh/Woodley/A329, left at lights into Wharfesale Rd. Hotel on left

Situated in the Winnersh Triangle within close proximity of the M4, Reading, Bracknell and Wokingham, this hotel offers a range of contemporary and stylish bedrooms, eight state-of-the-art meeting rooms and extensive leisure facilities including a 19-metre indoor pool. The Caprice Restaurant offers relaxed dining throughout the day.

Rooms 174 (25 fmly) (16 smoking) **S** £42-£178; **D** £42-£178* **Facilities** FTV Ⓢ Gym Sauna Steam room Treatment room Xmas New Year Wi-fi **Conf** Class 160 Board 64 Thtr 260 Del from £140 to £160* **Services** Lift Air con **Parking** 120 **Notes** Civ Wed 260

Copthorne Hotel Reading

★★★★ 74% HOTEL

☎ 0118 950 0885 📠 0118 939 1996
Pingewood RG30 3UN
dir: A33 towards Basingstoke. At Three Mile Cross rdbt right signed Burghfield. After 300mtrs 2nd right, over M4, through lights, hotel on left

Enjoying a secluded and rural setting and yet just a few minutes south of Reading, this modern hotel was built around a man-made lake which is occasionally used for water sport. Bedrooms are generally spacious with good facilities, and most have balconies overlooking the lake and its wildlife.

Rooms 81 (23 fmly) **Facilities** STV Gym Watersports Wi-fi **Conf** Class 60 Board 60 Thtr 110 **Services** Lift **Parking** 250 **Notes** ⊗ Civ Wed 80

Malmaison Reading

★★★ 85% ® HOTEL

☎ 0118 956 2300 📠 0118 956 2301
Great Western House, 18-20 Station Rd RG1 1JX
e-mail: reading@malmaison.com
web: www.malmaison.com
dir: Opposite rail station

This historic hotel has been transformed to a funky, Malmaison style which reflects its proximity and long-standing relationship with the railway. Public areas feature rail memorabilia and excellent pictures, and

continued

R

READING ***continued***

include a Café Mal and a meeting room. Bedrooms here have all the amenities a modern executive would expect, plus comfort and quality in abundance. Dining is interesting too, with a menu that features home-grown and local produce accompanied by an impressive wine list.

Rooms 75 (6 fmly) **Facilities** Gym Xmas New Year Wi-fi **Conf** Board 16 **Services** Lift Air con

Holiday Inn Reading South M4 Jct 11

★★★ 73% HOTEL

☎ 0118 702 9067 📠 0118 931 1958
Basingstoke Rd RG2 0SL
e-mail: reading@ihg.com
web: www.holidayinn.co.uk
dir: A33 to Reading. 1st rdbt right onto Imperial Way. Hotel on left

This bright hotel provides modern accommodation and the addition of leisure facilities is a bonus at the end of a busy day. Meals are served in Traders restaurant, or snacks are available in the lounge. Callaghans, an Irish-style pub, offers live sports coverage. The business centre has a good range of conference and meeting rooms.

Rooms 202 (60 fmly) (99 GF) (10 smoking) **S** £79-£209; **D** £89-£219* **Facilities** FTV supervised Gym Health & fitness centre Treatment room New Year Wi-fi **Conf** Class 45 Board 50 Thtr 100 **Services** Air con **Parking** 300 **Notes** LB Civ Wed 100

Best Western Calcot Hotel

★★★ 72% HOTEL

☎ 0118 941 6423 📠 0118 945 1223
98 Bath Rd, Calcot RG31 7QN
e-mail: enquiries@calcothotel.net
web: www.calcothotel.co.uk
dir: M4 junct 12 onto A4 towards Reading, hotel in 0.5m

This hotel is conveniently located in a residential area just off the motorway. Bedrooms are well equipped with good business facilities, such as data ports and good workspace. There are attractive public rooms and function suites, and the informal restaurant offers enjoyable food in welcoming surroundings.

Rooms 78 (3 fmly) (6 GF) **Facilities** STV FTV New Year Wi-fi **Conf** Class 35 Board 35 Thtr 120 Del from £130 to £165 **Parking** 130 **Notes** Closed 25-27 Dec Civ Wed 200

Comfort Hotel Reading West

BUDGET HOTEL

☎ 0118 9713 282 📠 0118 971 4238
Bath Rd, Padworth RG7 5HT
e-mail: info@comfortreading.co.uk
web: www.comfortreading.co.uk
dir: M4 junct 12, A4 towards Newbury/Thatcham. Hotel approx 3m, after Fiesta Centre on left

This hotel is conveniently situated close to the A4 and M4 and offers easy access to Newbury and Reading. The good quality budget accommodation caters well for corporate guests, leisure guests and families. Enjoyable meals are served in the smart conservatory and comfortable, modern bar area. There is a beautiful small garden at the rear of the property; complimentary Wi-fi and parking are provided.

Rooms 33 (1 fmly) (20 GF) **S** £55-£85; **D** £60-£95* **Conf** Class 70 Board 50 Thtr 120 Del from £100 to £130*

Ibis Reading Centre

BUDGET HOTEL

☎ 0118 953 3500 📠 0118 953 3510
25A Friar St RG1 1DP
e-mail: H5431@accor.com
web: www.ibishotel.com
dir: A329 into Friar St. Hotel near central train station

Modern, budget hotel offering comfortable accommodation in bright and practical bedrooms. Breakfast is self-service and dinner is available in the restaurant. See also the Hotel Groups pages.

Rooms 182 (36 fmly)

Premier Inn Reading (Caversham Bridge)

BUDGET HOTEL

☎ 0871 527 8922 📠 0871 527 8923
Richfield Av RG1 8EQ
dir: M4 junct 11, A33 to Reading. A329 towards Caversham. Left at TGI Friday's. Left at Crowne Plaza. Hotel 200yds on right

High quality, budget accommodation ideal for both families and business travellers. Spacious, en suite bedrooms feature tea and coffee making facilities, and Freeview TV in most hotels. Internet access and Wi-fi are available for a small fee. The adjacent family restaurant features a wide and varied menu. See also the Hotel Groups pages.

Rooms 74 **D** £59-£79*

Premier Inn Reading Central

BUDGET HOTEL

☎ 0871 527 8924 📠 0871 527 8925
Letcombe St RG1 2HN
dir: M4 junct 11, A33 towards town centre, straight on at 3 rdbts (approx 3.5m). Right onto A329 signed The Oracle, Riverside Shopping Centre. Branch immediately left, hotel opposite The Oracle shopping centre

Rooms 151 **D** £59-£79*

Premier Inn Reading South

BUDGET HOTEL

☎ 0871 527 8926 📠 0871 527 8927
Goring Ln, Grazeley Green RG7 1LS
dir: M4 junct 11, A33 towards Basingstoke. At rdbt take exit towards Burghfield & Mortimer. 3rd right into Grazeley Green. Under rail bridge turn left. Hotel on left

Rooms 32 **D** £56-£73*

REDDITCH

Worcestershire

Map 10 SP06

Abbey Hotel Golf & Country Club

★★★★ 78% HOTEL

☎ 01527 406600 📠 01527 406514
Hither Green Ln, Dagnell End Rd, Bordesley B98 9BE
e-mail: info@theabbeyhotel.co.uk
web: www.theabbeyhotel.co.uk
dir: M42 junct 2, A441 to Redditch. End of carriageway turn left (A441), Dagnell End Rd on left. Hotel 600yds on right

With convenient access to the motorway and a proximity to many attractions, this modern hotel is popular with both business and leisure travellers. Bedrooms are well equipped and attractively decorated; the executive corner rooms are especially spacious. Facilities include an 18-hole golf course, pro shop, large indoor pool and extensive conference facilities.

Rooms 100 (20 fmly) (23 GF) **D** £45-£118* **Facilities** STV 18 Putt green Fishing Gym Beauty salon Golf driving range Xmas New Year Wi-fi **Conf** Class 60 Board 30 Thtr 170 Del from £125 to £170* **Services** Lift **Parking** 200 **Notes** LB Civ Wed 100

Campanile Redditch

Campanile

BUDGET HOTEL

☎ 01527 510710 📠 01527 517269
Far Moor Ln, Winyates Green B98 0SD
e-mail: redditch@campanile.com
dir: A435 towards Redditch, then A4023 to Redditch & Bromsgrove

This modern building offers accommodation in smart, well-equipped bedrooms, all with en suite bathrooms. Refreshments may be taken at the informal bistro. See also the Hotel Groups pages.

Rooms 46 (46 annexe) (20 GF) **Conf** Class 15 Board 15 Thtr 25

Holiday Inn Express Birmingham - Redditch

BUDGET HOTEL

☎ 01527 584658 📠 01527 597905
2 Hewell Rd, Enfield B97 6AE
e-mail: reservations@express.gb.com
web: www.meridianleisurehotels.com/redditch
dir: M42 junct 2/A441 follow signs to rail station. Before station turn right into Hewell Rd, 1st left into Gloucester Close

A modern hotel ideal for families and business travellers. Fresh and uncomplicated, the spacious rooms include Satellite channels, power shower and tea and coffee-making facilities. Complimentary hot breakfast is included in the room rate; with freshly prepared meals served in the GR Restaurant daily from 18:00-22:00.

Rooms 100 (75 fmly) (10 GF) (14 smoking) **S** £50-£99; **D** £50-£99 (incl. bkfst)* **Conf** Class 26 Board 20 Thtr 50 Del from £110 to £140.95*

Premier Inn Redditch

BUDGET HOTEL

☎ 0871 527 8928 📠 0871 527 8929
Birchfield Rd B97 6PX
dir: M5 junct 4, A38 towards Bromsgrove. At rdbt take A448 to Redditch. 1st exit for Webheath. At next rdbt 3rd exit, 1st right into Birchfield Rd

High quality, budget accommodation ideal for both families and business travellers. Spacious, en suite bedrooms feature tea and coffee making facilities, and Freeview TV in most hotels. Internet access and Wi-fi are available for a small fee. The adjacent family restaurant features a wide and varied menu. See also the Hotel Groups pages.

Rooms 33 **D** £49-£58*

REDHILL Map 6 TQ25
Surrey

Nutfield Priory

HandPICKED HOTELS

★★★★ 82% @@ HOTEL

☎ 01737 824400 & 0845 072 7485
📠 01737 824410
Nutfield RH1 4EL
e-mail: nutfieldpriory@handpicked.co.uk
web: www.handpicked.co.uk/nutfield
dir: M25 junct 6, follow Redhill signs via Godstone on A25. Hotel 1m on left after Nutfield Village. Or M25 junct 8, A25 through Reigate, Redhill & Godstone. Hotel on right 1.5m after rail bridge

This Victorian country house dates back to 1872 and is set in 40 acres of grounds with stunning views over the Surrey countryside. Bedrooms are individually decorated and equipped with an excellent range of facilities. Public areas include the impressive grand hall, Cloisters Restaurant, the library, and a cosy lounge bar area.

Rooms 60 (4 fmly) **Facilities** Spa STV Gym Squash Steam room Beauty therapy Aerobic & Step classes Saunas Wi-fi **Conf** Class 45 Board 40 Thtr 80 **Services** Lift Air con **Parking** 130 **Notes** Civ Wed 80

Premier Inn Redhill

BUDGET HOTEL

☎ 0871 527 8930 📠 0871 527 8931
Brighton Rd, Salfords RH1 5BT
dir: On A23, 2m S of Redhill; 3m N of Gatwick Airport

High quality, budget accommodation ideal for both families and business travellers. Spacious, en suite bedrooms feature tea and coffee making facilities, and Freeview TV in most hotels. Internet access and Wi-fi are available for a small fee. The adjacent family restaurant features a wide and varied menu. See also the Hotel Groups pages.

Rooms 48 **D** £54-£65*

REDRUTH Map 2 SW64
Cornwall

Penventon Park

★★★ 79% HOTEL

☎ 01209 203000 📠 01209 203001
TR15 1TE
e-mail: info@penventon.com
web: www.penventon.co.uk
dir: Off A30 at Redruth. Follow signs for Redruth West, hotel 1m S

Set in attractive parkland, this Georgian mansion is ideal for either the business or leisure guest. Bedrooms include twenty Garden Suites. Cuisine offers a wide choice and specialises in British, Cornish, Italian and French dishes. Leisure facilities include a fitness suite and health spa as well as function rooms and bars.

Rooms 64 (3 fmly) (25 GF) **Facilities** Spa FTV supervised Gym Masseuse Steam bath Beautician Solarium Pool table Xmas New Year Wi-fi **Conf** Class 100 Board 60 Thtr 200 Del from £110 to £115* **Parking** 100 **Notes** Civ Wed 150

Crossroads Lodge

THE INDEPENDENTS HOTEL ASSOCIATION

★★ 64% HOTEL

☎ 01209 820551 📠 01209 820392
Scorrier TR16 5BP
e-mail: crossroads@hotelstruro.com
web: www.crossroadstravelinn.co.uk
dir: A30 onto A3047 towards Scorrier

Situated on an historic stanary site and conveniently located just off the A30, this hotel has a smart appearance. Bedrooms are soundly furnished and include executive and family rooms. Public areas include an attractive dining room, a quiet lounge and a lively bar. Conference, banqueting and business facilities are also available.

Rooms 36 (2 fmly) (8 GF) **Facilities** Xmas New Year Wi-fi **Conf** Class 80 Board 60 Thtr 150 **Services** Lift **Parking** 140 **Notes** Civ Wed 70

R

REDWORTH
Co Durham
Map 19 NZ22

Barceló Redworth Hall Hotel

★★★★ 77%
COUNTRY HOUSE HOTEL

☎ 01388 770600 📠 01388 770654
DL5 6NL
e-mail: redworthhall@barcelo-hotels.co.uk
web: www.barcelo-hotels.co.uk
dir: From A1(M) junct 58/A68 signed Corbridge. Follow hotel signs

This imposing Georgian building includes a health club with state-of-the-art equipment and impressive conference facilities making this hotel a popular destination for business travellers. There are several spacious lounges to relax in along with the Conservatory Restaurant. Bedrooms are very comfortable and well equipped.

Rooms 143 (12 fmly) **Facilities** STV Gym Bodysense Health & Leisure Club Xmas New Year Wi-fi **Conf** Class 144 Board 90 Thtr 300 **Services** Lift **Parking** 300 **Notes** Civ Wed 240

REEPHAM
Norfolk
Map 13 TG12

Old Brewery House

★★★ 68% HOTEL

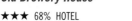

☎ 01603 870881 📠 01603 870969
Market Place NR10 4JJ
e-mail: reservations.oldbreweryhouse@ohiml.com
web: www.oxfordhotelsandinns.com
dir: A1067, right at Bawdeswell onto B1145 into Reepham, hotel on left in Market Place

This Grade II listed Georgian building is situated in the heart of this bustling town centre. Public areas include a cosy lounge, a bar, a conservatory and a smart restaurant. Bedrooms come in a variety of styles; each one is pleasantly decorated and equipped with a good range of facilities.

Rooms 23 (2 fmly) (7 GF) **Facilities** Gym Squash Xmas **Conf** Class 80 Board 30 Thtr 200 **Parking** 40 **Notes** Civ Wed 45

REIGATE
Surrey
Map 6 TQ25

Best Western Reigate Manor

★★★ 73% HOTEL

☎ 01737 240125 📠 01737 223883
Reigate Hill RH2 9PF
e-mail: hotel@reigatemanor.co.uk
web: www.reigatemanor.co.uk
dir: On A217, 1m S of M25 junct 8

On the slopes of Reigate Hill, the hotel is ideally located for access to the town and for motorway links. A range of public rooms is provided along with a variety of function rooms. Bedrooms are either traditional in style in the old house or of contemporary design in the wing.

Rooms 50 (1 fmly) **S** £55-£100; **D** £80-£120 **Facilities** STV Wi-fi **Conf** Class 80 Board 50 Thtr 200 Del from £125 to £165 **Parking** 130 **Notes** LB Civ Wed 200

RENISHAW
Derbyshire
Map 16 SK47

Sitwell Arms Hotel

★★★ 70% HOTEL

☎ 01246 641263 & 435226 📠 01246 433915
Station Rd S21 3WF
e-mail: info@sitwellarms.com
dir: On A6135 to Sheffield, W of M1 junct 30

This stone-built hotel, parts of which date back to the 18th century when it was a coaching inn, is conveniently situated close to the M1 and offers good value accommodation. Bedrooms are of a comfortable size and include modern facilities. There are extensive bars and a restaurant serving a wide range of meals and snacks. The hotel has a gym plus a hair and beauty salon.

Rooms 31 (8 fmly) (9 GF) **S** £39.50-£43; **D** £77.50-£110 (incl. bkfst)* **Facilities** STV Gym Fitness studio Hair & beauty salon Xmas New Year Wi-fi **Conf** Class 60 Board 60 Thtr 160 Del from £90 to £150* **Services** Lift **Parking** 150 **Notes** Civ Wed 150

RETFORD
Nottinghamshire
Map 17 SK78

Ye Olde Bell Hotel & Restaurant

★★★★ 74% HOTEL

☎ 01777 705121 📠 01777 860424
DN22 8QS
e-mail: enquiries@yeoldebell-hotel.co.uk
web: www.yeoldebell-hotel.co.uk

(For full entry see Barnby Moor)

Best Western West Retford

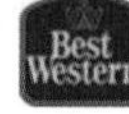

★★★ 77% HOTEL

☎ 01777 706333 📠 01777 709951
24 North Rd DN22 7XG
e-mail: reservations@westretfordhotel.co.uk
dir: From A1 take A620 to Ranby/Retford. Left at rdbt into North Rd (A638). Hotel on right

Stylishly appointed throughout, and set in very attractive gardens close to the town centre, this 18th-century manor house offers a good range of well-equipped meeting facilities. The spacious, well-laid out bedrooms and suites are located in separate buildings and all offer modern facilities and comforts.

Rooms 63 (15 fmly) (32 GF) **S** £105; **D** £125 (incl. bkfst) **Facilities** FTV Xmas New Year Wi-fi **Conf** Class 80 Board 40 Thtr 150 Del from £ to £140 **Parking** 150 **Notes** Civ Wed 150

RICHMOND
North Yorkshire
Map 19 NZ10

The Frenchgate Restaurant and Hotel

★★★★ 73% TOWN HOUSE HOTEL

☎ 01748 822087
59-61 Frenchgate DL10 7AE
e-mail: info@thefrenchgate.co.uk
dir: A1 into Richmond, on A6108 past war memorial on left at lights. 1st left into Lile Close for hotel car park

This sympathetic conversion of an 18th-century town house building offers an impressive level of contemporary, quality accommodation. Modern artworks by local artists adorn the walls of the house. The intimate dining room serves award-winning evening meals and memorable breakfasts. Personal, attentive and friendly staff are on hand to ensure a relaxing stay. Some off-road parking is available.

Rooms 9 (1 fmly) (1 GF) **S** £88-£190; **D** £118-£250 (incl. bkfst)* **Facilities** FTV Xmas New Year Wi-fi **Conf** Class 20 Board 20 Thtr 20 Del from £160 to £225* **Parking** 12 **Notes** LB Civ Wed 60

R

RICHMOND (UPON THAMES)
Greater London

See LONDON SECTION plan 1 C2

The Petersham Hotel

★★★★ 78% ◎◎ HOTEL

☎ 020 8940 7471 📠 020 8939 1098
Nightingale Ln TW10 6UZ
e-mail: enq@petershamhotel.co.uk
web: www.petershamhotel.co.uk
dir: From Richmond Bridge rdbt follow Ham & Petersham signs. Hotel in Nightingale Ln on left off Petersham Rd

Managed by the same family for over 25 years, this attractive hotel is located on a hill overlooking water meadows and a sweep of the River Thames. Bedrooms and suites are comfortably furnished, whilst public areas combine elegance and some fine architectural features. High quality produce features in dishes offered in the restaurant that looks out over the Thames below.

Rooms 60 (6 fmly) (3 GF) **S** fr £135; **D** fr £185 (incl. bkfst)* **Facilities** STV FTV Xmas New Year Wi-fi **Conf** Board 25 Thtr 35 Del from £235 to £299* **Services** Lift **Parking** 60 **Notes** ⊗ Civ Wed 40

The Richmond Hill Hotel

★★★★ 75% ◎ HOTEL

☎ 0208 940 2247 📠 0208 940 5424
Richmond Hill TW10 6RW
e-mail: info.richmond@kewgreen.co.uk
dir: A316 for Richmond, hotel at top of Richmond Hill

This attractive Georgian manor is situated on Richmond Hill, enjoying elevated views over the Thames, and the town and the park are within walking distance. Bedrooms vary in size and style but all are comfortable and contemporary in style. There is a well-designated heath club, and extensive conference and banqueting facilities.

Rooms 149 (1 fmly) (15 GF) **Facilities** Spa STV ⓢ Gym Steam room Health & beauty suite Sauna Xmas New Year Wi-fi **Conf** Class 80 Board 50 Thtr 180 **Services** Lift **Parking** 150 **Notes** ⊗ Civ Wed 182

The Richmond Gate Hotel

★★★★ 74% ◎◎ HOTEL

☎ 0845 906 9966 📠 020 8332 0354
152-158 Richmond Hill TW10 6RP
e-mail: reservations.richmondgate@akkeronhotels.com
web: www.akkeronhotels.com/richmondgate
dir: From Richmond to top of Richmond Hill. Hotel on left opposite Star & Garter home at Richmond Gate exit

This stylish Georgian hotel sits at the top of Richmond Hill, opposite the gates to Richmond Park and has a real country house feel to it. Bedrooms are equipped to a very high standard and include luxury doubles and spacious suites. Dinner in the Park Restaurant features bold, contemporary cooking and is the highlight of any visit. A smart leisure club and spa facilities complete the picture.

Rooms 68 **Facilities** Spa STV FTV ⓢ supervised Gym Health & beauty salon Steam room Sauna Wi-fi **Conf** Class 25 Board 28 Thtr 90 **Services** Air con **Parking** 50 **Notes** ⊗ Civ Wed 70

Bingham

★★★ 81% ◎◎◎ TOWN HOUSE HOTEL

☎ 020 8940 0902 📠 020 8948 8737
61-63 Petersham Rd TW10 6UT
e-mail: info@thebingham.co.uk
web: www.thebingham.co.uk
dir: On A307

This Georgian building, dating back to 1740, overlooks the River Thames and is within easy reach of the town centre, Kew Gardens and Hampton Court. The contemporary bedrooms feature bespoke art deco style furniture and up-to-the-minute facilities such as Wi-fi, a digital music library, flat-screen TVs and 'rain dance' showers. Public rooms have views of the pretty garden and river. Guests can choose from a selection of meals that range from light snacks to two or three-course dinners.

Rooms 15 (2 fmly) **S** £170; **D** £190-£285* **Facilities** FTV In room treatments Xmas New Year Wi-fi **Conf** Class 70 Board 40 Thtr 100 **Services** Air con **Parking** 8 **Notes** ⊗ Civ Wed 100

RICKMANSWORTH
Hertfordshire — Map 6 TQ09

See also **Chenies**

The Grove

★★★★★ 87% ◎◎◎ HOTEL

☎ 01923 807807 📠 01923 221008
Chandler's Cross WD3 4TG
e-mail: info@thegrove.co.uk
web: www.thegrove.co.uk
dir: M25 junct 19, A411 towards Watford. Hotel on right

Set amid 300 acres of rolling countryside, much of which is golf course, the hotel combines historic features with cutting-edge, modern design. The spacious bedrooms have the latest in temperature control and lighting technology; many have balconies. Suites in the original mansion are particularly stunning. Championship golf, a world-class spa and three dining options are just a few of the treasures to sample here. The hotel also has extensive crèche facilities. The hotel has three dining options - Collette's with 3 AA Rosettes that offers fine dining, and a more relaxed style in the Glasshouse and Stables restaurants. The walled garden is also well worth exploring.

Rooms 227 (69 fmly) (35 GF) **S** £285-£975; **D** £310-£1000 (incl. bkfst)* **Facilities** Spa STV FTV ⓢ ⛱ supervised ⛳ 18 Putt green Gym Walking & cycling trails Giant chess Orchid house Golf driving range Xmas New Year Wi-fi Child facilities **Conf** Class 300 Board 78 Thtr 450 Del from £395 to £650* **Services** Lift Air con **Parking** 400 **Notes** LB ⊗ Civ Wed 450

Long Island

OldEnglish

★★ 🅰 HOTEL

☎ 01923 779466 📠 01923 896248
2 Victoria Close WD3 4EQ
e-mail: office@longisland.fsbusiness.co.uk
web: www.oldenglish.co.uk
dir: M25 junct 18 onto A404, 1.5m. Turn left at rdbt onto Nightingale Rd, 1st left

Rooms 50 (3 fmly) (12 GF) **S** £45-£75; **D** £45-£75 (incl. bkfst)* **Facilities** ♫ **Conf** Class 15 Board 8 Thtr 12 Del from £99 to £129* **Parking** 120 **Notes** LB ⊗

R

RINGWOOD
Hampshire — Map 5 SU10

Tyrrells Ford Country House Hotel

★★★ 71% SMALL HOTEL

☎ 01425 672646 📠 01425 672262
Avon BH23 7BH
e-mail: info@tyrrellsford.co.uk
web: www.tyrrellsford.co.uk
dir: From A31 to Ringwood take B3347. Hotel 3m S on left

Set in the New Forest, this delightful family-run hotel has much to offer. Most bedrooms have views over the open country. Diners may eat in the formal restaurant, or sample the wide range of bar meals; all dishes are prepared using fresh local produce. The Gallery Lounge offers guests a peaceful area in which to relax.

Rooms 14 **Conf** Class 20 Board 20 Thtr 40 **Parking** 100 **Notes** ⊗ Civ Wed 60

RIPLEY
Derbyshire — Map 16 SK35

Premier Inn Ripley

BUDGET HOTEL

☎ 0871 527 8935 📠 0871 527 8935
Nottingham Rd DE5 3QP
dir: From S: M1 junct 26, A610 towards Ripley. Hotel off rdbt adjacent to Butterley Park. From N: M1 junct 28, A38, A610 towards Nottingham. Hotel on right at rdbt

High quality, budget accommodation ideal for both families and business travellers. Spacious, en suite bedrooms feature tea and coffee making facilities, and Freeview TV in most hotels. Internet access and Wi-fi are available for a small fee. The adjacent family restaurant features a wide and varied menu. See also the Hotel Groups pages.

Rooms 60 **D** £49-£56*

R

RIPON
North Yorkshire — Map 19 SE37

The Ripon Spa Hotel

★★★ 81% HOTEL

☎ 01765 602172 📠 01765 690770
Park St HG4 2BU
e-mail: sales@spahotelripon.co.uk
web: www.riponspa.com
dir: From A61 to Ripon, follow Fountains Abbey signs. Hotel on left after hospital. Or from A1(M) junct 48, B6265 to Ripon, straight on at 2 rdbts. Right at lights towards city centre. Left at hill top. Left at Give Way sign. Hotel on left

This privately owned hotel is set in extensive and attractive gardens just a short walk from the city centre. The bedrooms are well equipped to meet the needs of leisure and business travellers alike, while the comfortable lounges are complemented by the convivial atmosphere of the Turf Bar.

Rooms 40 (5 fmly) (4 GF) **S** £75-£134; **D** £84-£155 (incl. bkfst) **Facilities** FTV Xmas New Year Wi-fi **Conf** Class 35 Board 40 Thtr 150 **Services** Lift **Parking** 60 **Notes** LB Civ Wed 150

RISLEY
Derbyshire — Map 11 SK43

Risley Hall Hotel & Spa

★★★ 74% ® HOTEL

☎ 0115 939 9000 & 921 8523 📠 0115 939 7766
Derby Rd DE72 3SS
e-mail: reservations.risleyhall@ohiml.com
web: www.oxfordhotelsandinns.com
dir: M1 junct 25, Sandiacre exit into Bostock Ln. Left at lights, hotel on left in 0.25m

Set in 17 acres of private landscaped grounds and attractive mature gardens, this 11th-century manor house offers a good range of comfortable accommodation and relaxing day rooms. The friendly and attentive service complements the imaginative cuisine in the fine dining restaurant. The spa and beauty treatment rooms prove particularly popular with members and leisure guests alike.

Rooms 35 (8 GF) **Facilities** Spa STV FTV Xmas New Year **Conf** Class 22 Board 20 Thtr 100 **Services** Lift **Notes** ⊗ Civ Wed 100

ROCHDALE
Greater Manchester — Map 16 SD81

Mercure Norton Grange Hotel & Spa

★★★★ 77% HOTEL

☎ 0870 1942119 & 01706 630788
📠 01706 649313
Manchester Rd, Castleton OL11 2XZ
e-mail: h6631@accor.com
web: www.mercure.com
dir: M62 junct 20, follow A664/Castleton signs. Right at next 2 rdbts. Hotel 0.5m on left. (NB for Sat Nav use M24 2UB)

Standing in nine acres of grounds and mature gardens, this Victorian house provides comfort in elegant surroundings. The well-equipped bedrooms provide a host of extras for both the business and leisure guest. Public areas include the Pickwick bistro and smart Grange Restaurant, both offering a good choice of dishes. There is also an impressive leisure centre.

Rooms 81 (17 fmly) (10 GF) **Facilities** Spa Gym Leisure centre Indoor/Outdoor hydrotherapy pool Thermal suite Rock sauna Xmas New Year Wi-fi **Conf** Class 120 Board 70 Thtr 220 **Services** Lift **Parking** 150 **Notes** Civ Wed 150

Best Western Broadfield Park Hotel

★★★ 77% HOTEL

☎ 01706 639000 📠 01706 759398
Sparrow Hill OL16 1AF
e-mail: reservations@broadfieldparkhotel.co.uk
web: www.broadfieldparkhotel.co.uk
dir: M60 junct 20, follow signs for Rochdale & town centre. A640 onto Drake St, hotel signed 0.5m on left

Overlooking historic Broadfield Park and the town centre and only minutes away from the M60 and M62. Bedrooms are comfortably furnished and attractively decorated. The hotel offers a range of carefully prepared meals and snacks in either the formal restaurant, or the lounge bar. Service is friendly and attentive.

Rooms 29 (4 fmly) **S** £59-£89; **D** £59-£89 **Facilities** FTV Xmas New Year Wi-fi **Conf** Class 120 Board 80 Thtr 200 Del from £89 to £150 **Parking** 30 **Notes** RS 24-26 Dec Civ Wed 200

Premier Inn Rochdale

BUDGET HOTEL

☎ 0871 527 8936 🖷 0871 527 8937
Newhey Rd, Milnrow OL16 4JF
dir: M62 junct 21, at rdbt right towards Shaw, under motorway bridge, & 1st left

High quality, budget accommodation ideal for both families and business travellers. Spacious, en suite bedrooms feature tea and coffee making facilities, and Freeview TV in most hotels. Internet access and Wi-fi are available for a small fee. The adjacent family restaurant features a wide and varied menu. See also the Hotel Groups pages.

Rooms 40 **D** £53-£57*

ROCHESTER
Kent — Map 6 TQ76

Premier Inn Rochester

BUDGET HOTEL

☎ 0871 527 8938 🖷 0871 527 8939
Medway Valley Leisure Park, Chariot Way, Strood ME2 2SS
dir: M2 junct 2 follow Rochester, West Malling signs. At rdbt onto A228 signed Rochester, Strood. At next rdbt 2nd exit into Roman Way signed Medway Valley Park. At next rdbt 1st exit into Chariot Way, hotel in 100mtrs

High quality, budget accommodation ideal for both families and business travellers. Spacious, en suite bedrooms feature tea and coffee making facilities, and Freeview TV in most hotels. Internet access and Wi-fi are available for a small fee. The adjacent family restaurant features a wide and varied menu. See also the Hotel Groups pages.

Rooms 121 **D** £57-£65*

ROMALDKIRK
Co Durham — Map 19 NY92

Rose & Crown

★★★ 86% ❀❀ HOTEL

☎ 01833 650213 🖷 01833 650828
DL12 9EB
e-mail: hotel@rose-and-crown.co.uk
web: www.rose-and-crown.co.uk
dir: 6m NW from Barnard Castle on B6277

This charming 18th-century country inn is located in the heart of the village, overlooking fine dale scenery. The attractively furnished bedrooms, including suites, are split between the main house and the rear courtyard. Guests might like to have a drink in the cosy bar with its log fire, after returning from a long walk. Good local produce features extensively on the menus that can be enjoyed in the oak-panelled restaurant and in the brasserie and bar. Service is both friendly and attentive.

Rooms 12 (5 annexe) (1 fmly) (5 GF) **S** £95-£125; **D** £135-£210 (incl. bkfst)* **Facilities** STV New Year Wi-fi **Parking** 20 **Notes** LB Closed 24-26 Dec

ROMFORD
Greater London — Map 6 TQ58

Premier Inn Romford Central

BUDGET HOTEL

☎ 0871 527 8940 🖷 0871 527 8941
Mercury Gardens RM1 3EN
dir: M25 junct 28, A12 to Gallows Corner. Take A118 to next rdbt, turn left

High quality, budget accommodation ideal for both families and business travellers. Spacious, en suite bedrooms feature tea and coffee making facilities, and Freeview TV in most hotels. Internet access and Wi-fi are available for a small fee. The adjacent family restaurant features a wide and varied menu. See also the Hotel Groups pages.

Rooms 64 **D** £64-£72*

Premier Inn Romford West

BUDGET HOTEL

☎ 0871 527 8942 🖷 0871 527 8943
Whalebone Lane North, Chadwell Heath RM6 6QU
dir: 6m from M25 junct 28 on A12 at junct with A1112

Rooms 42 **D** £62-£70*

ROMSEY
Hampshire — Map 5 SU32

The White Horse Hotel & Brasserie

★★★ 85% ❀ HOTEL

☎ 01794 512431 🖷 01794 517485
19 Market Place SO51 8ZJ
e-mail: reservations@silkshotels.com
web: www.silkshotels.com
dir: In town centre close to Romsey Abbey

This hotel is located overlooking the market square of this historic town. Following an extensive refurbishment, this traditional former coaching inn provides comfortable and stylish bedrooms. Public areas boast relaxing day rooms and an elegant contemporary bar. Silks Brasserie features award-winning cuisine, with alfresco dining during the warmer summer months. Public car parks can be found close by, although the property does operate a valet parking service.

Rooms 31 (4 fmly) **S** £95-£115; **D** £115-£135* **Facilities** FTV Xmas New Year Wi-fi **Conf** Class 40 Board 30 Thtr 30 Del from £155 to £190* **Parking** 6 **Notes** Civ Wed 65

See advert on page 410

R

R

ROMSEY ***continued***

Potters Heron Hotel

★★★ 78% HOTEL

☎ 023 8027 7800 📠 023 8025 1359
Winchester Rd, Ampfield SO51 9ZF
e-mail: thepottersheron@pebblehotels.com
dir: M3 junct 12 follow Chandler's Ford signs. 2nd exit at 3rd rdbt follow Ampfield signs, over x-rds. Hotel on left in 1m

This distinctive thatched hotel retains many original features. In a convenient location with access to Winchester, Southampton and the M3, this establishment has modern accommodation and stylish, spacious public areas. Most of the bedrooms have their own balcony or terrace. The pub and restaurant both offer an interesting range of dishes that will suit a variety of tastes.

Rooms 54 (1 fmly) (29 GF) **S** £65-£95; **D** £75-£105 (incl. bkfst)* **Facilities** STV FTV Xmas New Year Wi-fi **Conf** Class 40 Board 30 Thtr 100 Del from £130 to £150* **Services** Lift **Parking** 120 **Notes** Civ Wed 100

Premier Inn Southampton West

BUDGET HOTEL

☎ 0871 527 9004 📠 0871 527 9005
Romsey Rd, Ower SO51 6ZJ
dir: Just off M27 junct 2. Take A36 towards Salisbury. Follow brown tourist signs 'Vine Inn'

High quality, budget accommodation ideal for both families and business travellers. Spacious, en suite bedrooms feature tea and coffee making facilities, and Freeview TV in most hotels. Internet access and Wi-fi are available for a small fee. The adjacent family restaurant features a wide and varied menu. See also the Hotel Groups pages.

Rooms 67 **D** £52-£62*

ROSSINGTON South Yorkshire **Map 16 SK69**

Best Western Premier Mount Pleasant Hotel

★★★★ 76% ® HOTEL

☎ 01302 868696 & 868219 📠 01302 865130
Great North Rd DN11 0HW
e-mail: reception@mountpleasant.co.uk
web: www.mountpleasant.co.uk
dir: On A638 between Bawtry & Doncaster

This charming 18th-century house stands in 100 acres of wooded parkland between Doncaster and Bawtry near Robin Hood Airport. The spacious public areas that include cosy lounges and an elegant restaurant have been designed for maximum comfort. The spacious bedrooms are beautifully furnished and individual in design; some rooms have four-poster beds, half-tester beds or sledge beds - one even has a five poster!

Rooms 56 (18 fmly) (27 GF) **S** £79-£99; **D** £99-£119 (incl. bkfst)* **Facilities** Spa STV Beauty salon Wi-fi **Conf** Class 70 Board 70 Thtr 200 Del from £135 to £170 **Services** Lift **Parking** 140 **Notes** LB Closed 25 Dec RS 24 Dec Civ Wed 180

ROSS-ON-WYE Herefordshire **Map 10 SO52**

Chase Hotel

★★★ 81% ® HOTEL

☎ 01989 763161 & 760644 📠 01989 768330
Gloucester Rd HR9 5LH
e-mail: res@chasehotel.co.uk
web: www.chasehotel.co.uk
dir: M50 junct 4, 1st left exit towards rdbt, left at rdbt towards A40. Right at 2nd rdbt towards town centre, hotel 0.5m on left

This attractive Georgian mansion sits in its own landscaped grounds and is only a short walk from the town centre. Bedrooms, including two four-poster rooms, vary in size and character; all rooms are appointed to impressive standards. There is a light and spacious bar, and also Harry's restaurant which offers an excellent selection of enjoyable dishes.

Rooms 36 (1 fmly) **S** £100-£205; **D** £120-£205 (incl. bkfst)* **Facilities** STV FTV New Year Wi-fi **Conf** Class 100 Board 80 Thtr 300 Del from £ to £145* **Parking** 75 **Notes** LB Closed 24-27 Dec Civ Wed 150

Pengethley Manor

★★★ 74% HOTEL

☎ 01989 730211 📠 01989 730238
Pengethley Park HR9 6LL
e-mail: reservations@pengethleymanor.co.uk
web: www.pengethleymanor.co.uk
dir: 4m N of Ross-on-Wye on A49

This fine Georgian mansion is set in extensive grounds with glorious views and two successful vineyards that produce over 1,000 bottles a year. The bedrooms are tastefully appointed and come in a wide variety of styles; all are well equipped. The elegant public rooms are furnished in a style that is in keeping with the character of the house. Dinner provides a range of enjoyable options and is served in the spacious restaurant.

Rooms 25 (14 annexe) (3 fmly) (4 GF) **Facilities** 9 Golf improvement course Xmas New Year Wi-fi **Conf** Class 25 Board 28 Thtr 70 Del from £109 to £130.80* **Parking** 70 **Notes** Civ Wed 75

Glewstone Court

★★★ 73% ® COUNTRY HOUSE HOTEL

☎ 01989 770367 📠 01989 770282
Glewstone HR9 6AW
e-mail: glewstone@aol.com
web: www.glewstonecourt.com
dir: From Ross-on-Wye market place follow A40/A49 Monmouth/Hereford signs, over Wilton Bridge to rdbt, left onto A40 towards Monmouth, in 1m turn right for hotel

This charming hotel enjoys an elevated position with views over Ross-on-Wye, and is set in well-tended gardens. Informal service is delivered with great enthusiasm by Bill Reeve-Tucker, whilst the kitchen is the domain of Christine Reeve-Tucker who offers an extensive menu of well executed dishes. Bedrooms come in a variety of sizes and are tastefully furnished and well equipped.

Rooms 8 (2 fmly) (1 GF) **S** £60-£85; **D** £100-£125 (incl. bkfst)* **Facilities** FTV New Year Wi-fi **Conf** Board 12 Thtr 18 Del from £150 to £165 **Parking** 25 **Notes** LB Closed 25-27 Dec Civ Wed 72

R

ROSS-ON-WYE *continued*

The Royal

★★★ 72% HOTEL

☎ 01989 565105 🖷 01989 768058
Palace Pound HR9 5HZ
e-mail: 6504@greeneking.co.uk
web: www.oldenglish.co.uk
dir: At end of M50 take A40 signed Monmouth. At 3rd rdbt, left to Ross-on-Wye, over bridge, follow The Royal Hotel sign

Close to the town centre, this imposing hotel enjoys panoramic views from its prominent hilltop position. Reputedly visited by Charles Dickens in 1867, the establishment has been sympathetically furnished to combine the ambience of a bygone era with the comforts of today. In addition to the bar and dining areas, there are function rooms, an elegant restaurant and an attractive garden.

Rooms 42 (1 fmly) **S** £30-£60; **D** £40-£130 (incl. bkfst) **Facilities** FTV Xmas New Year Wi-fi **Conf** Class 20 Board 28 Thtr 85 Del from £99 to £119* **Parking** 38 **Notes** LB Civ Wed 75

King's Head

★★★ 68% HOTEL

☎ 01989 763174 🖷 01989 769578
8 High St HR9 5HL
e-mail: enquiries@kingshead.co.uk
web: www.kingshead.co.uk
dir: In town centre, past market building on right

This establishment dates back to the 14th century and has a wealth of charm and character. Bedrooms are well equipped and comfortable with thoughtful guest extras provided; both four-poster and family rooms are available. The restaurant offers menus and a specials board that reflect a varied selection of local produce including fresh fish, free range beef and lamb. There is a well-stocked bar serving hand-pulled, real ales and along with the restaurant is popular with locals and visitors alike.

Rooms 15 (1 fmly) **S** £56; **D** £95 (incl. bkfst)* **Facilities** FTV Wi-fi **Parking** 13 **Notes** LB

Chasedale

★★ 74% SMALL HOTEL

☎ 01989 562423 & 565801 🖷 01989 567900
Walford Rd HR9 5PQ
e-mail: chasedale@supanet.com
web: www.chasedale.co.uk
dir: From town centre, S on B4234, hotel 0.5m on left

This large, mid-Victorian property is situated on the south-west outskirts of the town. Privately owned and personally run, it provides spacious, well-proportioned public areas and extensive grounds. The accommodation is well equipped and includes ground floor and family rooms, whilst the restaurant offers a wide selection of wholesome food.

Rooms 10 (2 fmly) (1 GF) **S** £45; **D** £90* **Facilities** FTV Xmas Wi-fi **Conf** Class 30 Board 25 Thtr 40 **Parking** 14 **Notes** LB

Premier Inn Ross-on-Wye

BUDGET HOTEL

☎ 0871 527 8944 🖷 0871 527 8945
Ledbury Rd HR9 7QJ
dir: M50 junct 4, towards town centre

High quality, budget accommodation ideal for both families and business travellers. Spacious, en suite bedrooms feature tea and coffee making facilities, and Freeview TV in most hotels. Internet access and Wi-fi are available for a small fee. The adjacent family restaurant features a wide and varied menu. See also the Hotel Groups pages.

Rooms 43 **D** £54-£59*

Orles Barn

◎◎ RESTAURANT WITH ROOMS

☎ 01989 562155 🖷 01989 768470
Wilton HR9 6AE
e-mail: reservations@orles-barn.co.uk
web: www.orles-barn.co.uk
dir: A49/A40 rdbt outside Ross-on-Wye, take slip road between petrol station & A40 to Monmouth. 100yds on left

The proprietors of this character property offer a warm welcome to all their guests. Older sections of the property date back to the 14th and 17th centuries when it was a farmhouse with a barn. The property offers comfortable bedrooms, a smart cosy lounge with a bar and a spacious restaurant. Dinner and Sunday lunch are offered on a balanced menu of fresh local and seasonal ingredients. Breakfast utilises quality local produce and makes a good start to the day.

Rooms 5 (1 fmly)

Wilton Court Restaurant with Rooms

◎◎ RESTAURANT WITH ROOMS

☎ 01989 562569 🖷 01989 768460
Wilton Ln HR9 6AQ
e-mail: info@wiltoncourthotel.com
dir: M50 junct 4, A40 towards Monmouth at 3rd rdbt left signed Ross-on-Wye, 1st right, hotel on right

Dating back to the 16th century, this establishment has great charm and a wealth of character. Standing on the banks of the River Wye and just a short walk from the town centre, there is a genuinely relaxed, friendly and unhurried atmosphere created by hosts Roger and Helen Wynn and their reliable team. Bedrooms are tastefully furnished and well equipped, while public areas include a comfortable lounge, traditional bar and pleasant restaurant with a conservatory extension overlooking the garden. High standards of food, using fresh, locally sourced ingredients, are offered.

Rooms 10 (1 fmly)

ROSTHWAITE Cumbria — Map 18 NY21

See also **Borrowdale**

Scafell Hotel

★★★ 78% HOTEL

☎ 017687 77208 🖷 017687 77280
CA12 5XB
e-mail: info@scafell.co.uk
web: www.scafell.co.uk
dir: M6 junct 40 to Keswick on A66. Take B5289 to Rosthwaite

A friendly hotel, popular with walkers and enjoying a peaceful location. Bedrooms have been tastefully appointed in a warm country house style with a contemporary twist; some have traditional antique furniture. Public areas include a residents' cocktail bar, lounge and spacious restaurant as well as the popular Riverside Inn pub, offering all-day menus in summer months.

Rooms 23 (2 fmly) (8 GF) **S** £39-£70; **D** £78-£140 (incl. bkfst)* **Facilities** FTV Guided walks Xmas New Year **Parking** 50 **Notes** LB Civ Wed 75

R

Royal Oak

★ 75% SMALL HOTEL

☎ 017687 77214 & 77695
CA12 5XB
e-mail: info@royaloakhotel.co.uk
web: www.royaloakhotel.co.uk
dir: 6m S of Keswick on B5289 in village centre

Set in a village in one of Lakeland's most picturesque valleys, this family-run hotel offers friendly and obliging service. There is a variety of accommodation styles, with particularly impressive rooms being located in a converted barn across the courtyard and backing onto a stream; family rooms are available. The cosy bar is for residents and diners only, and a set home-cooked dinner is served at 7pm.

Rooms 12 (4 annexe) (5 fmly) (4 GF) **S** £48-£62; **D** £96-£134 (incl. dinner)* **Parking** 15 **Notes** LB Closed 4-21 Jan & 5-28 Dec

ROTHERHAM
South Yorkshire — **Map 16 SK49**

Hellaby Hall

★★★★ 71% HOTEL

☎ 01709 702701 🖷 01709 700979
Old Hellaby Ln, Hellaby S66 8SN
e-mail: reservations@hellabyhallhotel.co.uk
web: www.hellabyhallhotel.co.uk
dir: 0.5m off M18 junct 1, onto A631 towards Maltby. Hotel in Hellaby. (NB do not use postcode for Sat Nav)

This 17th-century house was built to a Flemish design with high, beamed ceilings, staircases which lead off to private meeting rooms and a series of oak-panelled lounges. Bedrooms are elegant and well equipped, and guests can dine in the formal Attic Restaurant. There are extensive leisure facilities and conference areas, and the hotel holds a licence for civil weddings.

Rooms 90 (2 fmly) (17 GF) **S** £49-£106; **D** £49-£127* **Facilities** Spa STV FTV supervised Gym Beauty salon Exercise studio Spining studio Xmas New Year Wi-fi **Conf** Class 300 Board 150 Thtr 500 Del from £99 to £150* **Services** Lift **Parking** 250 **Notes** LB Civ Wed 200

Best Western Elton House Hotel

★★★ 80% HOTEL

☎ 01709 545681 🖷 01709 549100
Main St, Bramley S66 2SF
e-mail: reception@eltonhotel.co.uk
web: www.eltonhotel.co.uk
dir: M18 junct 1 follow A631 Rotherham signs, turn right to Ravenfield, hotel at end of Bramley, follow brown signs

A stone-built hotel set in well-tended gardens in a quiet village setting but less than a mile from the M18. Bedrooms are modern and well equipped with complimentary Wi-fi also provided. The stylish and contemporary bar and restaurant offer a good range of food. Function rooms are available for conferences, weddings or other special occasions.

Rooms 29 (16 annexe) (4 fmly) (11 GF) **S** fr £57; **D** fr £66 (incl. bkfst) **Facilities** STV FTV ♫ Wi-fi **Conf** Class 68 Board 48 Thtr 150 Del from £105 **Parking** 48 **Notes** LB Civ Wed 200

Carlton Park

★★★ 79% HOTEL

☎ 01709 849955 🖷 01709 368960
102/104 Moorgate Rd S60 2BG
e-mail: reservations@carltonparkhotel.com
web: www.carltonparkhotel.com
dir: M1 junct 33, onto A631, then A618. Hotel 800yds past District General Hospital

This modern hotel is situated in a pleasant residential area of the town, close to the hospital, yet within minutes of the M1. Bedrooms and bathrooms offer very modern facilities; three have separate sitting rooms. The restaurant and bar provide a lively atmosphere and there is a pool and leisure centre.

Rooms 80 (19 fmly) (16 GF) (7 smoking) **S** £49-£71; **D** £54-£77 (incl. bkfst)* **Facilities** STV FTV Gym ♫ Xmas New Year Wi-fi **Conf** Class 120 Board 60 Thtr 300 Del from £100 to £120* **Services** Lift **Parking** 120 **Notes** LB ⊗ Civ Wed 150

Best Western Consort Hotel

★★★ 78% HOTEL

☎ 01709 530022 🖷 01709 531529
Brampton Rd, Thurcroft S66 9JA
e-mail: info@consorthotel.com
web: www.consorthotel.com
dir: M18 junct 1, right towards Bawtry on A631. 250yds to rdbt, double back, in 200yds left. 1.5m to mini rdbt, hotel opposite

Bedrooms at this modern, friendly hotel are comfortable, attractive and air conditioned, and include ten superior rooms. A wide range of dishes is served in the open-plan bar and restaurant, and there is a comfortable foyer lounge. There are good conference and function facilities, and entertainment evenings are often hosted here.

Rooms 27 (2 fmly) (9 GF) **Facilities** FTV ♫ Wi-fi **Conf** Class 120 Board 50 Thtr 350 **Services** Air con **Parking** 90 **Notes** ⊗ Civ Wed 300

Park Inn Rotherham

★★★ 77% HOTEL

☎ 01709 760666 🖷 01709 760667
Express Park, Manvers Way, Wath-upon-Dearne S63 7EQ
e-mail: info.rotherham@rezidorparkinn.com
dir: M1 junct 36, follow signs for Doncaster then Manvers

Convenient for the Manvers Business Estate and M1, this purpose-built hotel provides versatile and well-equipped contemporary accommodation with Wi-fi throughout. Facilities include a spacious restaurant, comfortable lounge area, bar, fitness centre, sauna and steam room as well as meeting rooms.

Rooms 130 (30 fmly) **S** £39-£109; **D** £49-£119 (incl. bkfst)* **Facilities** STV FTV Gym Sauna Steam room Xmas New Year Wi-fi **Conf** Class 93 Board 60 Thtr 140 Del from £89 to £169 **Services** Lift Air con **Parking** 200 **Notes** LB Civ Wed 130

Restover Lodge

★★ 67% HOTEL

☎ 01709 700255 🖷 01709 545169
Hellaby Industrial Estate, Lowton Way, off Denby Way S66 8RY
e-mail: restovermarketing@btopenworld.com
dir: M18 junct 1. Follow signs for Maltby. Left at lights, 2nd on left

Located close to the M1 and M18, this hotel offers bedrooms in the main building and in an adjacent property, together with plenty of parking. Complimentary Wi-fi is provided in the open-plan bar and restaurant where there is a relaxed, friendly atmosphere. A conference room is available, and use of nearby leisure facilities is also offered.

Rooms 50 (12 fmly) **Facilities** Free use of nearby leisure facilities (by prior arrangement) Xmas Wi-fi **Conf** Class 35 Board 30 Thtr 40 **Parking** 40

R

ROTHERHAM *continued*

Ibis Rotherham East

BUDGET HOTEL

☎ 01709 730333 🖷 01709 730444
Moorhead Way, Bramley S66 1YY
e-mail: H3163@accor-hotels.com
web: www.ibishotel.com
dir: M18 junct 1, left at rdbt, left at 1st lights. Hotel adjacent to supermarket

Modern, budget hotel offering comfortable accommodation in bright and practical bedrooms. Breakfast is self-service and dinner is available in the restaurant. See also the Hotel Groups pages.

Rooms 86 (22 fmly) (8 GF) **S** £35-£56; **D** £35-£56* **Conf** Class 20 Board 20 Thtr 30

Premier Inn Rotherham

BUDGET HOTEL

☎ 0871 527 8946 🖷 0871 527 8947
Bawtry Rd S65 3JB
dir: On A631 towards Wickersley, between M18 junct 1 & M1 junct 33

High quality, budget accommodation ideal for both families and business travellers. Spacious, en suite bedrooms feature tea and coffee making facilities, and Freeview TV in most hotels. Internet access and Wi-fi are available for a small fee. The adjacent family restaurant features a wide and varied menu. See also the Hotel Groups pages.

Rooms 37 **D** £52-£58*

ROTHERWICK Map 5 SU75
Hampshire

INSPECTORS' CHOICE

Tylney Hall Hotel

★★★★ 🏵🏵 HOTEL

☎ 01256 764881 🖷 01256 768141
RG27 9AZ
e-mail: sales@tylneyhall.com
web: www.tylneyhall.com
dir: M3 junct 5, A287 to Basingstoke, over junct with A30, over rail bridge, towards Newnham. Right at Newnham Green. Hotel 1m on left

A grand Victorian country house set in 66 acres of beautiful parkland. The hotel offers high standards of comfort in relaxed yet elegant surroundings, featuring magnificently restored water gardens, originally laid out by the famous gardener, Gertrude Jekyll. Spacious public rooms include Italian and Wedgwood styled drawing rooms and the panelled Oak Room Restaurant, filled with stunning flower arrangements and warmed by log fires, that offers cuisine based on locally sourced ingredients. The spacious bedrooms are traditionally furnished and offer individual style and high degrees of comfort. The excellent leisure facilities include indoor and outdoor swimming pools, tennis courts, jogging trails, croquet lawns and a spa.

Rooms 112 (77 annexe) (1 fmly) (40 GF) **S** £190-£470; **D** £220-£500 (incl. bkfst)* **Facilities** Spa STV FTV Gym Clay pigeon shooting Archery Falconry Balloon rides Laser shooting Xmas New Year Wi-fi **Conf** Class 70 Board 40 Thtr 120 Del from £220 to £290* **Parking** 120 **Notes** LB Civ Wed 120

ROTHLEY Map 11 SK51
Leicestershire

Rothley Court

★★★ 73% HOTEL

☎ 0116 237 4141 🖷 0116 237 4483
Westfield Ln LE7 7LG
e-mail: 6501@greeneking.co.uk
web: www.oldenglish.co.uk
dir: On B5328

Mentioned in the Domesday Book, and complete with its own chapel, this historic property sits in seven acres of well-tended grounds. Public areas retain much of their original character and include an oak-panelled restaurant and a choice of function and meeting rooms. Bedrooms, some located in an adjacent stable block, are individually styled.

Rooms 30 (18 annexe) (3 fmly) (6 GF) **Facilities** Xmas **Conf** Class 35 Board 35 Thtr 100 **Parking** 100 **Notes** Civ Wed 85

ROWDE Map 4 ST96
Wiltshire

The George & Dragon

🏵🏵 RESTAURANT WITH ROOMS

☎ 01380 723053
High St SN10 2PN
e-mail: thegandd@tiscali.co.uk
dir: 1.5m from Devizes on A350 towards Chippenham

The George & Dragon dates back to the 14th century when it was a meeting house. Exposed beams, wooden floors, antique rugs and open fires create a warm atmosphere in the bar and restaurant. Bedrooms and bathrooms are very well decorated and equipped with some welcome extras. Dining in the bar or restaurant should not be missed, as local produce and fresh fish deliveries from Cornwall are offered on the daily-changing blackboard menu.

Rooms 3 (1 fmly)

R

ROWSLEY
Derbyshire Map 16 SK26

INSPECTORS' CHOICE

The Peacock at Rowsley

★★★ ◎◎◎ HOTEL

☎ 01629 733518 📠 01629 732671
Bakewell Rd DE4 2EB
e-mail: reception@thepeacockatrowsley.com
web: www.thepeacockatrowsley.com
dir: On A6 between Matlock & Bakewell

Owned by Lord Manners of Haddon Hall, this hotel combines stylish contemporary design by India Mahdavi with original period and antique features. Bedrooms are individually designed and boast DVD players, complimentary Wi-fi and smart marble bathrooms. Two rooms are particularly special - one with a four-poster and one with an antique bed originating from Belvoir Castle in Leicestershire. Imaginative cuisine, using local, seasonal produce, is a highlight. Guests are warmly welcomed and service is attentive. Fly fishing is popular in this area and the hotel has its own fishing rights on seven miles of the Rivers Wye and Derwent.

Rooms 16 (5 fmly) **S** £85-£140; **D** £150-£257.50* **Facilities** Fishing Free use of Woodlands Fitness Centre Free membership to Bakewell Golf Club New Year Wi-fi **Conf** Class 8 Board 16 Thtr 16 **Parking** 25 **Notes** No children 10yrs

See advert on this page

INSPECTORS' CHOICE

East Lodge Country House

★★★ ◎◎ HOTEL

☎ 01629 734474 📠 01629 733949
DE4 2EF
e-mail: info@eastlodge.com
web: www.eastlodge.com
dir: A6, 3m from Bakewell, 5m from Matlock

This hotel enjoys a romantic setting in ten acres of landscaped grounds and gardens. The stylish bedrooms are equipped with many extras such as TVs with DVD players, and most have lovely garden views. The popular restaurant serves much produce sourced from the area, and the conservatory lounge, overlooking the gardens, offers afternoon teas and light meals.

Rooms 12 (2 fmly) (1 GF) **Facilities** STV Xmas New Year Wi-fi **Conf** Class 20 Board 22 Thtr 75 **Parking** 40 **Notes** No children 7yrs Civ Wed 100

RUAN HIGH LANES
Cornwall Map 2 SW93

Hundred House

★★★ 74% ◎ COUNTRY HOUSE HOTEL

☎ 01872 501336 📠 01872 501151
TR2 5JR
e-mail: enquiries@hundredhousehotel.co.uk
web: www.hundredhousehotel.co.uk
dir: From B3287 at Tregony, left onto A3078 to St Mawes, hotel 4m on right

This Georgian house is set in attractive gardens and has good access to the Roseland Peninsula, which makes it an ideal base for a relaxing break and for touring the area. Bedrooms are well equipped, and the lounge and bar offer much comfort. Service is attentive as the staff are very much focused on their guests' needs. Both dinner and breakfast offer freshly cooked and appetising dishes.

Rooms 9 (1 GF) **Facilities** FTV Xmas New Year Wi-fi **Parking** 15 **Notes** LB No children 14yrs

R

RUBERY
West Midlands
Map 10 SO97

Premier Inn Birmingham South (Rubery)

BUDGET HOTEL

☎ 0871 527 8094 🖷 0871 527 8095
Birmingham Great Park, Ashbrook Dr, Parkway B45 9FP
dir: M5 junct 4, A38 towards Birmingham. Left at lights before Morrisons signed Great Park. Right at rdbt. Right at next rdbt, hotel on right

High quality, budget accommodation ideal for both families and business travellers. Spacious, en suite bedrooms feature tea and coffee making facilities, and Freeview TV in most hotels. Internet access and Wi-fi are available for a small fee. The adjacent family restaurant features a wide and varied menu. See also the Hotel Groups pages.

Rooms 62 **D** £49-£58*

RUGBY
Warwickshire
Map 11 SP57

Brownsover Hall Hotel

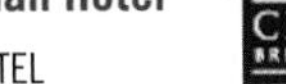

★★★ 78% HOTEL

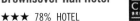

☎ 0844 855 9123 🖷 01788 535367
Brownsover Ln, Old Brownsover CV21 1HU
e-mail: reservations@brownsoverhall.co.uk
web: www.brownsoverhall.co.uk
dir: M6 junct 1, A426 to Rugby. After 0.5m at rdbt follow Brownsover signs, right into Brownover Rd, right again into Brownsover Ln. Hotel 250yds on left

A Grade II listed, Victorian Gothic hall designed by Sir Gilbert Scott, set in seven acres of wooded parkland. Bedrooms vary in size and style, including spacious and contemporary rooms in the converted stable block. The former chapel makes a stylish restaurant, and for a less formal meal or a relaxing drink, the Whittle Bar is popular.

Rooms 47 (20 annexe) (3 fmly) (11 GF) **S** £69-£130; **D** £69-£130* **Facilities** Xmas New Year Wi-fi **Conf** Class 36 Board 40 Thtr 70 Del from £99 to £165 **Parking** 100 **Notes** ⊗ Civ Wed 56

Golden Lion Hotel

★★★ 72% HOTEL

☎ 01788 833577 & 832265 🖷 01788 832878
Easenhall CV23 0JA
e-mail: reception@goldenlionhotel.org
web: www.goldenlionhotel.org
dir: A426 at Avon Mill rdbt follow Newbold-upon-Avon B4112 signs, approx 2m turn left at Harborough Parva sign, follow brown tourist signs, opposite agricultural showroom, 1m to Easenhall

This friendly, family-run, 16th-century inn is situated between Rugby and Coventry, and is convenient for access to the M6. Bedrooms, some in a smart extension, are equipped with both practical and homely items; one features a stunning Chinese bed. The beamed bar and restaurant retain many original features and a warm welcome is assured.

Rooms 20 (2 fmly) (6 GF) **Facilities** FTV Xmas New Year Wi-fi **Conf** Class 30 Board 24 Thtr 80 **Parking** 80 **Notes** ⊗ Civ Wed 100

Premier Inn Rugby North M6 Jct 1

BUDGET HOTEL

☎ 0871 527 8948 🖷 0871 527 8949
Central Park Dr, Central Park CV23 0WE
dir: M6 junct 1, S'bound onto A426. Hotel approx 1m on left at rdbt

High quality, budget accommodation ideal for both families and business travellers. Spacious, en suite bedrooms feature tea and coffee making facilities, and Freeview TV in most hotels. Internet access and Wi-fi are available for a small fee. The adjacent family restaurant features a wide and varied menu. See also the Hotel Groups pages.

Rooms 58 **D** £51-£64*

Premier Inn Rugby North (Newbold)

BUDGET HOTEL

☎ 0871 527 8950 🖷 0871 527 8951
Brownsover Rd CV21 1HL
dir: M6 junct 1, A426 follow Rugby signs. Straight on at 2 rdbts. At 3rd rdbt, hotel on right. (NB for Sat Nav use CV21 1NX)

Rooms 49 **D** £51-£64*

RUGELEY
Staffordshire
Map 10 SK01

Premier Inn Rugeley

BUDGET HOTEL

☎ 0871 527 9272 🖷 0871 527 9273
Tower Business Park WS15 2HJ
dir: M6 junct 14, A5013 towards Stafford. At rdbt 2nd exit onto A34. Take A513 signed Rugeley. At rdbt take 2nd exit onto A51. Left into Wolsley Rd, left into Powerstation Rd. Hotel off rdbt. (NB for Sat Nav use WS15 1PR)

High quality, budget accommodation ideal for both families and business travellers. Spacious, en suite bedrooms feature tea and coffee making facilities, and Freeview TV in most hotels. Internet access and Wi-fi are available for a small fee. The adjacent family restaurant features a wide and varied menu. See also the Hotel Groups pages.

Rooms 50 **D** £53-£60*

RUISLIP
Greater London

See LONDON SECTION plan 1 A5

Barn Hotel

★★★ 78% ◎◎ HOTEL

☎ 01895 636057 🖷 01895 638379
West End Rd HA4 6JB
e-mail: info@thebarnhotel.co.uk
web: www.thebarnhotel.co.uk
dir: From A40 take A4180 (Polish War Memorial) exit to Ruislip. 2m to hotel entrance at mini-rdbt before Ruislip tube station

Once a farm, with parts dating back to the 17th century, this impressive property sits in three acres of gardens. Bedrooms vary in style, from contemporary to traditional with oak-beams; all are comfortable and well appointed. The public areas provide a high level of quality and luxury.

Rooms 73 (3 fmly) (33 GF) (20 smoking) **S** £90-£160; **D** £115-£195 (incl. bkfst)* **Facilities** FTV Xmas New Year Wi-fi **Conf** Class 50 Board 30 Thtr 80 Del from £165 to £225* **Parking** 42 **Notes** ⊗ Civ Wed 74

See advert on opposite page

R

Premier Inn Ruislip

BUDGET HOTEL

☎ 0871 527 8952 📠 0871 527 8953
Ickenham Rd HA4 7DR
dir: From Ruislip High St into Ickenham Rd (B466). At mini rdbt 1st exit (The Orchard on left)

High quality, budget accommodation ideal for both families and business travellers. Spacious, en suite bedrooms feature tea and coffee making facilities, and Freeview TV in most hotels. Internet access and Wi-fi are available for a small fee. The adjacent family restaurant features a wide and varied menu. See also the Hotel Groups pages.

Rooms 20 **D** £53-£60*

RUNCORN Map 15 SJ58
Cheshire

Holiday Inn Runcorn

★★★ 72% HOTEL

☎ 0871 942 9070 📠 01928 714611
Wood Ln, Beechwood WA7 3HA
e-mail: adam.munday@ihg.com
web: www.holidayinn.co.uk
dir: M56 junct 12, left at rdbt, 100yds on left into Halton Station Rd under rail bridge, into Wood Ln

This modern hotel offers extensive conference, meeting and leisure facilities. The bedrooms are well equipped, and the spacious restaurant is open for lunch and dinner, and an all-day menu is provided in the lounge and bar. There is also a well-equipped leisure centre, and extensive conference facilities are available.

Rooms 153 (149 fmly) (31 GF) **Facilities** STV supervised Gym Xmas New Year Wi-fi **Conf** Class 250 Board 60 Thtr 500 **Services** Lift Air con **Parking** 250 **Notes** Civ Wed 500

Campanile Runcorn

Campanile HOTEL RESTAURANT

BUDGET HOTEL

☎ 01928 581771 📠 01928 581730
Lowlands Rd WA7 5TP
e-mail: runcorn@campanile.com
dir: M56 junct 12, A557, follow signs for Runcorn rail station/Runcorn College

This modern building offers accommodation in smart, well-equipped bedrooms, all with en suite bathrooms. Refreshments may be taken at the informal bistro. See also the Hotel Groups pages.

Rooms 53 (18 GF) **Conf** Class 24 Board 24 Thtr 35 Del from £65 to £75*

Premier Inn Runcorn

BUDGET HOTEL

☎ 0871 527 8954 📠 0871 527 8955
Chester Rd, Preston Brook WA7 3BB
dir: 1m from M56 junct 11, at Preston Brook

High quality, budget accommodation ideal for both families and business travellers. Spacious, en suite bedrooms feature tea and coffee making facilities, and Freeview TV in most hotels. Internet access and Wi-fi are available for a small fee. The adjacent family restaurant features a wide and varied menu. See also the Hotel Groups pages.

Rooms 43 **D** £50-£59*

RUSPER Map 6 TQ23
West Sussex

Ghyll Manor

★★★ 83% ® COUNTRY HOUSE HOTEL

☎ 0845 345 3426 📠 01293 871419
High St RH12 4PX
e-mail: enquiries@ghyllmanor.co.uk
web: www.ghyllmanor.co.uk
dir: A24 onto A264. Exit at Faygate, follow signs for Rusper, 2m to village

Located in the quiet village of Rusper, this traditional mansion house is set in 45 acres of idyllic, peaceful grounds. Accommodation is in either the main house or a range of courtyard-style cottages. A pre-dinner drink can be taken beside the fire, followed by an imaginative meal in the charming restaurant.

Rooms 29 (20 annexe) (7 fmly) (18 GF) **S** £148-£178; **D** £174-£234 (incl. bkfst)* **Facilities** STV FTV Gym Xmas New Year Wi-fi **Conf** Class 60 Board 40 Thtr 120 **Parking** 50 **Notes** LB Civ Wed 120

R

RYDE
Isle of Wight
Map 5 SZ59

Lakeside Park

★★★★ 79% ®® HOTEL

☎ 01983 882266 📠 01983 883380
High St PO33 4LJ
e-mail: reception@lakesideparkhotel.com
web: www.lakesideparkhotel.com
dir: A3054 towards Newport. Hotel on left after crossing Wotton Bridge

This hotel has picturesque views of the tidal lake and surrounding countryside. Bedrooms are well appointed with modern amenities, stylish design with guest comfort in mind. Public areas feature a comfortable open-plan bar and lounge, with dining options in two restaurants that showcase the best of island produce. Sizable conference and banqueting facilities are available whilst the leisure area includes an indoor pool and spa therapy.

Rooms 44 (2 fmly) (16 GF) **Facilities** Spa FTV Sauna Steam room Relaxation room Xmas New Year Wi-fi **Conf** Class 60 Board 40 Thtr 150 **Services** Lift Air con **Parking** 140 **Notes** Civ Wed 120

Yelf's Hotel

★★★ 73% HOTEL

☎ 01983 564062 📠 01983 563937
Union St PO33 2LG
e-mail: manager@yelfshotel.com
web: www.yelfshotel.com
dir: From Esplanade into Union St. Hotel on right

This former coaching inn has smart public areas including a busy bar, a separate lounge and an attractive dining room. Bedrooms are comfortably furnished and well equipped; some are located in an adjoining wing and some in an annexe. A conservatory lounge bar and stylish terrace are ideal for relaxing.

Rooms 40 (9 annexe) (5 fmly) (3 GF) (6 smoking) **Facilities** STV Spa & treatments at sister hotel nearby Wi-fi **Conf** Class 30 Board 50 Thtr 100 **Services** Lift **Parking** 23 **Notes** Civ Wed 100

R

Appley Manor Hotel

★★ 72% HOTEL

☎ 01983 564777 📠 01983 564704
Appley Rd PO33 1PH
e-mail: appleymanor@live.co.uk
web: www.appley-manor.co.uk
dir: A3055 onto B3330. Hotel 0.25m on left

A Victorian manor house located only five minutes from the town and set in peaceful surroundings. The spacious bedrooms are well furnished and decorated. Dinner can be taken in the popular adjoining Manor Inn.

Rooms 12 (2 fmly) **Conf** Class 40 Board 30 Thtr 40 **Parking** 60 **Notes**

RYE
East Sussex
Map 7 TQ92

George in Rye

★★★★ 76% ® HOTEL

☎ 01797 222114 📠 01797 224065
98 High St TN31 7JT
e-mail: stay@thegeorgeinrye.com
dir: M20 junct 10, A2070 to Brenzett, A259 to Rye

This attractive 16th-century property, situated in the heart of historic Rye, has been sympathetically styled to retain many original features including a stunning Georgian ballroom complete with a minstrels' gallery. The bedrooms are stylishly appointed and filled with an abundance of thoughtful touches. Contemporary public areas include a bar, lounge and dining room plus an excellent alfresco area for summer dining.

Rooms 34 (3 GF) **S** £95-£135; **D** £135-£295 (incl. bkfst)* **Facilities** FTV Xmas New Year Wi-fi **Conf** Class 65 Board 40 Thtr 100 Del from £165* **Notes** LB Civ Wed 100

Rye Lodge Hotel

★★★★ 75% METRO HOTEL

☎ 01797 223838 & 226688 📠 01797 223585
Hilders Cliff TN31 7LD
e-mail: info@ryelodge.co.uk
web: www.ryelodge.co.uk
dir: From one-way system follow signs for town centre, through Landgate arch, hotel 100yds on right

Standing in an elevated position, Rye Lodge has panoramic views across Romney Marshes and the Rother Estuary. Traditionally styled bedrooms come in a variety of sizes; they are attractively decorated and thoughtfully equipped. Public rooms feature indoor leisure facilities and the Terrace Room Restaurant where home-made dishes are offered. Lunch and afternoon tea are served on the flower-filled outdoor terrace in warmer months.

Rooms 19 (5 GF) **S** £75-£125; **D** £95-£195* **Facilities** STV FTV Aromatherapy Steam cabinet Sauna Exercise machines Wi-fi **Parking** 20 **Notes** LB

Mermaid Inn

★★★ 81% ® HOTEL

☎ 01797 223065 & 223788 📠 01797 225069
Mermaid St TN31 7EY
e-mail: info@mermaidinn.com
web: www.mermaidinn.com
dir: A259, follow signs to town centre, then into Mermaid St

Situated near the top of a cobbled side street, this famous smugglers' inn is steeped in history. The charming interior has many architectural features such as attractive stone work. The bedrooms vary in size and style but all are tastefully furnished. Delightful public rooms include a choice of lounges, cosy bar and smart restaurant.

Rooms 31 (5 fmly) **S** £90-£110; **D** £180-£260 (incl. bkfst)* **Facilities** Xmas New Year Wi-fi **Conf** Class 40 Board 30 Thtr 50 Del from £160* **Parking** 25 **Notes** LB

The Hope Anchor

★★★ 75% SMALL HOTEL

☎ 01797 222216 📠 01797 223796
Watchbell St TN31 7HA
e-mail: info@thehopeanchor.co.uk
web: www.thehopeanchor.co.uk
dir: From A268, Quayside, right into Wish Ward, into Mermaid St, right into West St, right into Watchbell St, hotel at end

This historic inn sits high above the town with enviable views out over the harbour and Romney Marsh, and is accessible via delightful cobbled streets. A relaxed and friendly atmosphere prevails within the cosy public rooms, while the attractively furnished bedrooms are well equipped and many enjoy good views over the marshes.

Rooms 16 (2 fmly) (1 GF) **S** £65-£140; **D** £95-£180 (incl. bkfst) **Facilities** FTV Xmas New Year Wi-fi **Conf** Class 30 Board 20 Thtr 40 Del from £120 to £200 **Parking** 12 **Notes** LB

White Vine House

RESTAURANT WITH ROOMS

☎ 01797 224748
24 High St TN31 7JF
e-mail: info@whitevinehouse.co.uk
dir: In town centre

Situated in the heart of the ancient Cinque Port town of Rye, this property's origins go back to the 13th century. The cellar is the oldest part, but the current building dates from 1560 and boasts an impressive Georgian frontage. The original timber framework is visible in many areas, and certainly adds to the house's sense of history. The bedrooms have period furniture along with luxury bath or shower rooms; one bedroom has an antique four-poster.

Rooms 7 (1 fmly)

ST AGNES Map 2 SW75
Cornwall

Rose-in-Vale Country House

★★★ 81% COUNTRY HOUSE HOTEL

☎ 01872 552202 📠 01872 552700
Mithian TR5 0QD
e-mail: reception@rose-in-vale-hotel.co.uk
web: www.rose-in-vale-hotel.co.uk
dir: A30 S towards Redruth. At Chiverton Cross at rdbt take B3277 signed St Agnes. In 500mtrs follow tourist sign for Rose-in-Vale. Into Mithian, right at Miners Arms, down hill. Hotel on left

Peacefully located in a wooded valley this Georgian manor house has a wonderfully relaxed atmosphere and abundant charm. Guests are assured of a warm welcome. Accommodation varies in size and style; several rooms are situated on the ground floor. An imaginative fixed-price menu featuring local produce is served in the spacious restaurant.

Rooms 23 (3 annexe) (1 fmly) (6 GF) **Facilities** FTV Xmas New Year Wi-fi **Conf** Class 50 Board 40 Thtr 75 Del from £135* **Services** Lift **Parking** 50 **Notes** No children 12yrs Civ Wed 80

Rosemundy House

★★★ 70% HOTEL

☎ 01872 552101 📠 01872 554000
Rosemundy Hill TR5 0UF
e-mail: info@rosemundy.co.uk
dir: A30 to St Agnes, approx 3m. On entering village 1st right signed Rosemundy, hotel at foot of hill

This elegant Queen Anne house has been carefully restored and extended to provide comfortable bedrooms and spacious, inviting public areas. The hotel is set in well-maintained gardens complete with an outdoor pool available in warmer months. There is a choice of relaxing lounges and a cosy bar.

Rooms 46 (3 fmly) (9 GF) **Facilities** FTV Putt green Xmas New Year **Conf** Board 80 **Parking** 50 **Notes** No children 5yrs

Beacon Country House Hotel

★★ 82% HOTEL

☎ 01872 552318
Goonvrea Rd TR5 0NW
e-mail: info@beaconhotel.co.uk
dir: From A30 take B3277 to St Agnes. At rdbt left into Goonvrea Rd. Hotel 0.75m on right

Set in a quiet and attractive area away from the busy village, this family-run, relaxed hotel has splendid views over the countryside and along the coast to St Ives. Hospitality and customer care are great strengths with guests assured of a very warm and friendly stay. Bedrooms are comfortable and well equipped, and many benefit from glorious views.

Rooms 11 (2 GF) **Facilities** FTV Xmas New Year Wi-fi **Conf** Class 20 Board 20 Del from £120 to £200* **Parking** 12 **Notes** LB No children 8yrs Closed 4-31 Jan

ST ALBANS Map 6 TL10
Hertfordshire

St Michael's Manor

★★★★ 77% HOTEL

☎ 01727 864444 📠 01727 848909
Fishpool St AL3 4RY
e-mail: reservations@stmichaelsmanor.com
dir: From St Albans Abbey follow Fishpool Street towards St Michael's village. Hotel 0.5m on left

Hidden from the street, adjacent to listed buildings, mills and ancient inns, this hotel, with a history dating back 500 years, is set in six acres of beautiful landscaped grounds. Inside there is a real sense of luxury, the high standard of decor and attentive service is complemented by award-winning food; the elegant restaurant overlooks the gardens and lake. The bedrooms are individually styled and have satellite TVs, DVDs and free internet access.

Rooms 30 (8 annexe) (3 fmly) (4 GF) (6 smoking) **S** £130-£350; **D** £160-£350 (incl. bkfst) **Facilities** STV FTV Licenced fishing in season Guided tours New Year Wi-fi **Conf** Class 20 Board 24 Thtr 30 Del from £240 to £460 **Parking** 60 **Notes** LB Civ Wed 140

Thistle St Albans

thistle

★★★★ 73% HOTEL

☎ 0871 376 9034 📠 0871 376 9134
Watford Rd AL2 3DS
e-mail: stalbans@thistle.co.uk
web: www.thistlehotels.com/stalbans
dir: M1 junct 6/M25 junct 21a, follow St. Albans signs, A405. Hotel 0.5m

Conveniently located for access to both the M1 and M25, this Victorian hotel lies within its own grounds and has secure parking. Bedrooms are neatly appointed in a traditional style. Public areas include a choice of restaurants, The Noke or the more informal Oak and Avocado, and there is also a small modern leisure club. Thistle Hotels – AA Hotel Group of the Year 2011-12.

Rooms 110 (2 fmly) (56 GF) (4 smoking) **S** £49-£109; **D** £49-£109* **Facilities** FTV supervised Gym Sauna Steam room Treatment room New Year Wi-fi **Conf** Class 30 Board 30 Thtr 300 Del from £109 to £159* **Parking** 150 **Notes** LB Civ Wed 100

Holiday Inn Luton South

Holiday Inn

★★★ 77% HOTEL

☎ 0871 942 9281 & 01582 449988
📠 01582 449041
London Rd, Markyate AL3 8HH
e-mail: hiluton@qmh-hotels.com
web: www.holidayinn.co.uk
dir: M1 junct 9 N towards Dunstable/Whipsnade, hotel 1m on right

Situated a short drive from the M1 and Luton Airport, this hotel has a pleasant setting with country views. There is a health and fitness club and a good range of air-conditioned conference and meeting facilities. The contemporary bedrooms are well appointed and have a good range of facilities.

Rooms 140 (12 fmly) (44 GF) **Facilities** STV Gym Sauna Beauty salon Steam room Wi-fi **Conf** Class 90 Board 50 Thtr 200 Del from £130 to £140* **Services** Lift Air con **Parking** 435 **Notes** Civ Wed 150

ST ALBANS *continued*

Quality Hotel St Albans

★★★ 71% HOTEL

☎ 01727 857858 📠 01727 855666
232-236 London Rd AL1 1JQ
e-mail: st.albans@quality-hotels.net
dir: M25 junct 22 follow A1081 to St Albans, after 2.5m hotel on left, before overhead bridge

This smartly presented property is conveniently situated close to the major road networks and the railway station. The contemporary style bedrooms have co-ordinated fabrics and a good range of useful facilities. Public rooms include an open-plan lounge bar and brasserie restaurant. The hotel has a leisure complex along with air-conditioned meeting rooms.

Rooms 81 (7 fmly) (14 GF) **S** £49-£95; **D** £60-£120 (incl. bkfst)* **Facilities** STV supervised Gym Saunarium Sunbed Beauty treatments Wi-fi **Conf** Class 40 Board 50 Thtr 220 Del from £80 to £140* **Services** Lift **Parking** 80 **Notes** LB

Ardmore House Hotel

THE INDEPENDENTS HOTEL ASSOCIATION

★★★ HOTEL

☎ 01727 859313 📠 01727 853642
54 Lemsford Rd AL1 3PR
e-mail: info@ardmorehousehotel.co.uk
web: www.ardmorehousehotel.co.uk
dir: A1081 signed St Albans, through 3 sets of lights & 2 mini rdbts. Right at 3rd mini rdbt, through 2 sets of lights. Hotel on right after 800yds

Rooms 40 (4 annexe) (5 fmly) (5 GF) **S** £64.50-£95; **D** £78-£145 (incl. bkfst) **Facilities** STV FTV Wi-fi **Conf** Class 50 Board 50 Thtr 130 Del from £125 to £155 **Parking** 40 **Notes** Civ Wed 150

Premier Inn Luton South M1 Jct 9

BUDGET HOTEL

☎ 0871 527 8334 📠 0871 527 8335
London Rd, Flamstead AL3 8HT
dir: M1 junct 9, A5 towards Dunstable

High quality, budget accommodation ideal for both families and business travellers. Spacious, en suite bedrooms feature tea and coffee making facilities, and Freeview TV in most hotels. Internet access and Wi-fi are available for a small fee. The adjacent family restaurant features a wide and varied menu. See also the Hotel Groups pages.

Rooms 75 **D** £50-£64*

ST ANNES

See Lytham St Annes

ST AUSTELL
Cornwall — Map 2 SX05

The Cornwall Hotel Spa & Estate

"bespoke" HOTELS

★★★★ 78% COUNTRY HOUSE HOTEL

☎ 01726 874050 📠 01726 66294
Pentewan Rd, Tregorrick PL26 7AB
e-mail: enquiries@thecornwall.com
dir: A391 to St Austell then B3273 towards Mevagissey. Hotel approx 0.5m on right

Set in 43 acres of wooded parkland, this manor house offers guests a real retreat. The restored White House has suites and traditionally styled bedrooms, and adjoining are the contemporary Woodland rooms ranging from standard, family, accessible, and also deluxe which have private balcony areas looking out to the Pentewan Valley. There are superb leisure facilities including the spa with luxury treatments, an infinity pool and state-of-the-art fitness centre. There is a choice of eating options - The Arboretum and the more informal Acorns plus the Drawing Room and Parkland Terrace for afternoon tea and cocktails. This is an ideal base for visiting The Eden Project, The Lost Gardens of Heligan and south Cornwall fishing villages.

Rooms 65 (4 fmly) **Facilities** Spa STV FTV Gym Xmas New Year Wi-fi Child facilities **Conf** Class 10 Board 14 Thtr 50 **Services** Lift **Parking** 200 **Notes** Civ Wed 120

The Carlyon Bay Hotel

★★★★ 77% HOTEL

☎ 01726 812304 & 811006 📠 01726 814938
Sea Rd, Carlyon Bay PL25 3RD
e-mail: reservations@carlyonbay.com
web: www.carlyonbay.com
dir: From St Austell, follow signs for Charlestown. Carlyon Bay signed on left, hotel at end of Sea Rd

Built in the 1920s, this long-established hotel sits on the cliff top in 250 acres of grounds which include indoor and outdoor pools, a golf course and a spa. Bedrooms are well maintained, and many have marvellous views across St Austell Bay. A good choice of comfortable lounges is available, whilst facilities for families include kids' clubs and entertainment.

Rooms 86 (14 fmly) **S** £90-£310; **D** £140-£310* **Facilities** Spa FTV 18 Putt green Gym 9-hole approach course Snooker room Sauna Steam room Xmas New Year Wi-fi Child facilities **Services** Lift **Parking** 100 **Notes** LB Civ Wed 100

See advert on opposite page

Porth Avallen

★★★ 77% HOTEL

☎ 01726 812802 📠 01726 817097
Sea Rd, Carlyon Bay PL25 3SG
e-mail: info@porthavallen.co.uk
web: www.porthavallen.co.uk
dir: A30 onto A391 to St Austell. Right onto A390. Left at lights, follow brown signs, left at rdbt, right into Sea Rd

This traditional hotel boasts panoramic views over the rugged Cornish coastline. It offers smartly appointed public areas and well-presented bedrooms, many with sea views. There is an oak-panelled lounge and conservatory; both are ideal for relaxation. Extensive dining options, including the stylish Reflections Restaurant, invite guests to choose from fixed-price, carte and all-day brasserie menus. The Olive Garden, inspired by the Mediterranean, is a lovely place to eat alfresco.

Rooms 28 (3 fmly) (3 GF) **Facilities** FTV Xmas New Year Wi-fi **Conf** Class 100 Board 80 Thtr 160 **Parking** 60 **Notes** Civ Wed 160

Cliff Head

★★★ 75% HOTEL

☎ 01726 812345 📠 01726 815511
Sea Rd, Carlyon Bay PL25 3RB
e-mail: info@cliffheadhotel.com
web: www.cliffheadhotel.com
dir: 2m E off A390

Set in extensive grounds and conveniently located for visiting the Eden Project, this hotel faces south and enjoys views over Carlyon Bay. A choice of lounges is provided, together with a swimming pool and solarium. Expressions restaurant offers a range of menus, which feature an interesting selection of dishes.

Rooms 57 (6 fmly) (11 GF) **Facilities** FTV ⛾ Xmas New Year Wi-fi **Conf** Class 130 Board 70 Thtr 150 Del from £50 to £70* **Parking** 60 **Notes** Civ Wed 120

Pier House

★★★ 73% HOTEL

☎ 01726 67955 📠 01726 69246
Harbour Front, Charlestown PL25 3NJ
e-mail: pierhouse@btconnect.com
dir: A390 to St Austell, at Mt Charles rdbt left into Charlestown Rd

This genuinely friendly hotel boasts a wonderful harbour location. The unspoilt working port has been the setting for many film and television productions. Most bedrooms have sea views, and the hotel's convivial Harbourside Inn is popular with locals and tourists alike. Locally caught fish features on the varied and interesting restaurant menu.

Rooms 28 (2 annexe) (3 fmly) (2 GF) **S** £67; **D** £108-£144* **Facilities** STV Wi-fi **Parking** 50 **Notes** LB ⊗ Closed 24-25 Dec

Boscundle Manor Country House Hotel

★★ 82% ◎ COUNTRY HOUSE HOTEL

☎ 01726 813557 📠 01726 814997
Tregrehan PL25 3RL
e-mail: reservations@boscundlemanor.co.uk
dir: 2m E on A390, 200yds on road signed Tregrehan

Set in beautifully maintained gardens and grounds, this handsome 18th-century stone manor house is a short distance from the Eden Project. Quality and comfort are apparent in the public areas and spacious, well-equipped bedrooms. A choice of eating options is available, with both fine dining and brasserie alternatives. Equally suitable for both leisure and business travellers, this hotel boasts both indoor and outdoor pools.

Rooms 14 (4 annexe) (4 fmly) (4 GF) **Facilities** FTV ⛾ ⛾ Treatment room Xmas New Year Wi-fi **Conf** Class 20 Board 20 Thtr 40 **Parking** 20 **Notes** LB ⊗ Civ Wed 60

Premier Inn St Austell

BUDGET HOTEL

☎ 0871 527 9018 📠 0871 527 9019
St Austell Enterprise Park, Treverbyn Rd PL25 4EL
dir: A30 onto A391 signed St Austell. Through Bugle. Continue on A391 at rdbt. Continue to follow St Austell signs. 1st exit at Carclaze rdbt. Hotel at St Austell Enterprise Park

High quality, budget accommodation ideal for both families and business travellers. Spacious, en suite bedrooms feature tea and coffee making facilities, and Freeview TV in most hotels. Internet access and Wi-fi are available for a small fee. The adjacent family restaurant features a wide and varied menu. See also the Hotel Groups pages.

Rooms 61 **D** £70*

ST HELENS Merseyside **Map 15 SJ59**

Premier Inn St Helens (A580/East Lancs)

BUDGET HOTEL

☎ 0871 527 9020 📠 0871 527 9021
Garswood Old Rd, East Lancs Rd WA11 7LX
dir: 3m from M6 junct 23, on A580 towards Liverpool

High quality, budget accommodation ideal for both families and business travellers. Spacious, en suite bedrooms feature tea and coffee making facilities, and Freeview TV in most hotels. Internet access and Wi-fi are available for a small fee. The adjacent family restaurant features a wide and varied menu. See also the Hotel Groups pages.

Rooms 44 **D** £52-£56*

Premier Inn St Helens South

BUDGET HOTEL

☎ 0871 527 9022 📠 0871 527 9023
Eurolink, Lea Green WA9 4TT
dir: M62 junct 7, A570 towards St Helens

Rooms 40 **D** £52-£59*

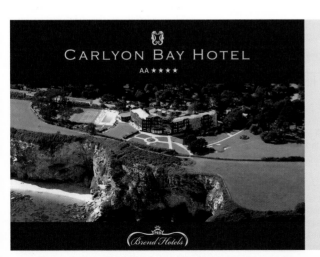

ST IVES
Cambridgeshire — Map 12 TL37

Slepe Hall Hotel

★★★ 79% HOTEL

☎ 01480 463122 📠 01480 300706
Ramsey Rd PE27 5RB
e-mail: reception@slepehallhotel.co.uk
dir: A14 junct 26 onto A1096, left at Toyota car showroom into Ramsey Rd

Ideally situated just a short walk from the town centre and only 20 minutes from Cambridge. The public areas have been appointed to a very high standard and are very smart; they include a brasserie, a lounge bar and a restaurant. The contemporary-style bedrooms are well equipped and have co-ordinated soft furnishings.

Rooms 16 (5 fmly) **S** £82-£92; **D** £92-£112 (incl. bkfst)* **Facilities** STV FTV ♫ Xmas New Year Wi-fi **Conf** Class 250 Board 250 Thtr 300 Del from £110 to £170* **Parking** 60 **Notes** LB ⊗ Civ Wed 250

Olivers Lodge

THE INDEPENDENTS HOTEL ASSOCIATION

★★★ 74% HOTEL

☎ 01480 463252 📠 01480 461150
Needingworth Rd PE27 5JP
e-mail: reception@oliverslodge.co.uk
web: www.oliverslodge.co.uk
dir: A14 towards Huntingdon/Cambridge, take B1040 to St Ives. Cross 1st rdbt, left at 2nd rdbt then 1st right. Hotel 500mtrs on right

A privately owned hotel situated in a peaceful residential area just a short walk from the town centre. Public rooms include a smart air-conditioned bar, a choice of lounges and a conservatory dining room. The pleasantly decorated bedrooms are equipped with modern facilities and have co-ordinated fabrics.

Rooms 17 (5 annexe) (3 fmly) (5 GF) **Facilities** Wi-fi **Conf** Class 30 Board 25 Thtr 65 **Notes** Civ Wed 65

The Dolphin Hotel

★★★ 70% HOTEL

☎ 01480 466966 📠 01480 495597
London Rd PE27 5EP
e-mail: enquiries@dolphinhotelcambs.co.uk
dir: A14 between Huntingdon & Cambridge onto A1096 towards St Ives. Left at 1st rdbt & immediately right. Hotel on left after 0.5m

This modern hotel sits by delightful water meadows on the banks of the River Ouse. Open-plan public rooms include a choice of bars and a pleasant restaurant offering fine river views. The bedrooms are modern and varied in style; some are in the hotel while others occupy an adjacent wing; all are comfortable and spacious. Conference and function suites are available.

Rooms 67 (37 annexe) (4 fmly) (22 GF) (2 smoking) **Facilities** FTV Fishing Gym **Conf** Class 50 Board 50 Thtr 150 Del from £130 to £150* **Parking** 400 **Notes** ⊗ RS 24 Dec-2 Jan Civ Wed 60

ST IVES
Cornwall — Map 2 SW54

Carbis Bay

★★★ 80% ◎ HOTEL

☎ 01736 795311 📠 01736 797677
Carbis Bay TR26 2NP
e-mail: carbisbayhotel@btconnect.com
web: www.carbisbayhotel.co.uk
dir: A3074, through Lelant. 1m, at Carbis Bay 30yds before lights, right into Porthrepta Rd to hotel

In a peaceful location with access to its own golden-sand beach, this hotel offers comfortable accommodation. Attractive public areas feature a smart bar and lounge, and a sun lounge overlooking the sea. Bedrooms, many with fine views, are well equipped. Interesting cuisine and particularly enjoyable breakfasts are offered. A small complex of luxury, self-catering apartments is available.

Rooms 40 (16 fmly) **Facilities** ⛱ Fishing Private beach ♫ Xmas New Year **Conf** Class 80 Board 60 Thtr 120 **Parking** 200 **Notes** ⊗ Civ Wed 120

See advert on opposite page

St Ives Harbour Hotel

★★★ 78% HOTEL

☎ 01736 795221 📠 01736 797043
The Terrrace TR26 2BN
e-mail: reception@porthminster-hotel.co.uk
web: www.porthminster-hotel.co.uk
dir: On A3074

This friendly hotel enjoys an enviable location with spectacular views of St Ives Bay. Extensive leisure facilities, a versatile function suite and a number of elegant and stylish lounges are available. The majority of bedrooms are appointed to a very high standard and many rooms have spectacular sea views, likewise the restaurant which looks out over the bay and golden sands below.

Rooms 42 (9 fmly) **Facilities** Spa FTV ⛆ Gym Steam room Xmas New Year Wi-fi Child facilities **Conf** Class 20 Board 35 Thtr 130 **Services** Lift **Parking** 43 **Notes** Civ Wed 160

Garrack Hotel & Restaurant

★★★ 77% ◎ HOTEL

☎ 01736 796199 📠 01736 798955
Burthallan Ln, Higher Ayr TR26 3AA
e-mail: aa@garrack.com
dir: Exit A30 for St Ives. From B3311 follow brown signs for Tate Gallery, then Garrack signs

Enjoying a peaceful, elevated position with splendid views across the harbour and Porthmeor Beach, the Garrack sits in its own delightful grounds and gardens. Bedrooms are comfortable and many have sea views. Public areas include a small leisure suite, a choice of lounges and an attractive restaurant, where locally sourced ingredients are used in the enjoyable dishes.

Rooms 18 (2 annexe) (2 fmly) (3 GF) **Facilities** FTV ⛆ Gym New Year Wi-fi **Conf** Class 10 Board 10 Thtr 20 **Parking** 30 **Notes** LB

Primrose Valley

★★★ 73% METRO HOTEL

☎ 01736 794939 📠 01736 794939
Porthminster Beach TR26 2ED
e-mail: info@primroseonline.co.uk
web: www.primroseonline.co.uk
dir: A3074 to St Ives, 25yds after town sign turn right onto Primrose Valley, left under bridge, along beach front, left back under bridge, property on left

St Ives is just a short walk from this stylish, friendly, family-run establishment close to Porthminster Beach. The property is light and airy, and modernisation has resulted in good levels of comfort; some bedrooms have balconies with stunning views. There is a lounge and bar area, and breakfast features local produce and home-made items.

Rooms 9 (1 fmly) **D** £105-£240 (incl. bkfst)* **Facilities** FTV Wi-fi **Parking** 11 **Notes** ⊗ No children 8 yrs Closed 19-27 Dec & 2-30 Jan

We invite you to experience a friendly, relaxed atmosphere in a unique, idyllic setting.
The CARBIS BAY Hotel
& Apartments
enjoyEngland.com
HOTEL
AA
HOTEL
AA Rosette for outstanding cuisine.
Carbis Bay · St. Ives · Cornwall · TR26 2NP
Tel: (01736) 795311 · email: info@carbisbayhotel.co.uk
www.carbisbayhotel.co.uk · Fax: (01736) 797677
enjoyEngland.com
Gold AWARD
enjoyEngland.com
SELF CATERING
"Carbis Bay Wins Gold Award"
The Hotel & Restaurant
"Award winning hotel on its own beach."
The Sands Hotel of Rosamund Pilcher's novels and films.
• Fully equipped en-suite rooms with child listening & room service
• Unsurpassed sea views
• Games & snooker room
• Ample parking
• Outdoor heated swimming pool & sun terrace
• Direct access to our own beach
• AA rosetted restaurant with superb choice of menu and wines
• Rail access
Bed & Breakfast from £65 per person per night.
Self Catering Holidays
• Choice of properties
• All year round availability
• Mid-week and weekend breaks
• Magnificent Seaviews
• Direct access to our own beach
• Use of all Hotel facilities
• Outdoor heated swimming pool & sun terrace
• AA Rosetted Restaurant
• Balcony or Terrace with many properties
• Games room and Entertainment
• New Luxury Granite Cottages now available
• Ample parking with every property
Suite Apartments
Beach House Interior
CARBIS BAY HOTEL
Blue Flag Beach

S

ST IVES *continued*

Tregenna Castle Hotel

★★★ 73% HOTEL

☎ 01736 795254 📠 01736 796066
TR26 2DE
e-mail: hotel@tregenna-castle.co.uk
web: www.tregenna-castle.co.uk
dir: A30 from Exeter to Penzance, at Lelant take A3074 to St Ives, through Carbis Bay, main entrance signed on left

Sitting at the top of town in beautiful landscaped sub-tropical gardens with woodland walks, this popular hotel boasts spectacular views of St Ives. Many leisure facilities are available, including indoor and outdoor pools, a gym and a sauna, and families are particularly welcome. The individually designed bedrooms are, in general, spacious. There are two restaurants, the Trelawny Room and the Godrevy Room, and the Brasserie provides lighter options in a less formal atmosphere.

Rooms 81 (12 fmly) (16 GF) **Facilities** Spa supervised 14 Putt green Gym Squash Steam room Badminton court Xmas New Year **Conf** Class 150 Board 30 Thtr 250 **Services** Lift **Parking** 200 **Notes** ⊗ Civ Wed 160

Chy-an-Albany

★★★ 71% HOTEL

☎ 01736 796759 📠 01736 795584
Albany Ter TR26 2BS
e-mail: info@chyanalbanyhotel.com
dir: A30 onto A3074 signed St Ives, hotel on left just before junct

Conveniently located, this pleasant hotel enjoys splendid sea views. The comfortable bedrooms come in a variety of sizes; some featuring balconies and sea views. Friendly staff and the relaxing environment mean that guests return on a regular basis. Freshly prepared and appetising cuisine is served in the dining room and a bar menu is also available.

Rooms 39 (11 fmly) **Facilities** FTV Wi-fi **Conf** Class 40 Board 30 Thtr 80 **Services** Lift **Parking** 33 **Notes** ⊗ Civ Wed 80

Hotel St Eia

★★ 69% HOTEL

☎ 01736 795531 📠 01736 793591
Trelyon Av TR26 2AA
e-mail: info@hotelsteia.co.uk
dir: A30 onto A3074, follow signs to St Ives, approaching town, hotel on right

This smart hotel is conveniently located and enjoys spectacular views over St Ives, the harbour and Porthminster Beach. The friendly proprietors provide a relaxing environment. Bedrooms are comfortable and well equipped, and some have sea views. The spacious lounge bar has a well-stocked bar and views can be enjoyed from the rooftop terrace.

Rooms 18 (3 fmly) (1 GF) **S** £40-£55; **D** £80-£110 (incl. bkfst)* **Facilities** FTV Wi-fi **Parking** 16 **Notes** ⊗ Closed Nov-Mar

Cottage Hotel

★★ 68% HOTEL

☎ 01736 795252 📠 01736 798636
Boskerris Rd, Carbis Bay TR26 2PE
e-mail: cottage.stives@alfatravel.co.uk
dir: From A30 take A3074 to Carbis Bay. Right into Porthreptor Rd. Just before rail bridge, left through railway car park into hotel car park

Set in quiet, lush gardens, this pleasant hotel offers friendly and attentive service. Smart bedrooms are pleasantly spacious and many rooms enjoy splendid views. Public areas are varied and include a snooker room, a comfortable lounge and a spacious dining room with views over the beach and Carbis Bay.

Rooms 80 (7 fmly) (2 GF) **S** £37-£52; **D** £58-£88 (incl. bkfst) **Facilities** FTV Snooker Xmas New Year **Services** Lift **Parking** 20 **Notes** LB ⊗ Closed Dec-Feb (ex Xmas) RS Nov & Mar

ST LEONARDS-ON-SEA

See Hastings & St Leonards

ST MARY CHURCH

See Torquay

ST MARY'S — Map 2 SV91
Cornwall (Isles of Scilly)

Tregarthen's Hotel

★★★ 77% HOTEL

☎ 01720 422540 📠 01720 422089
Hugh Town TR21 0PP
e-mail: reception@tregarthens-hotel.co.uk
dir: 100yds from town & quay

Opened in 1848 by Captain Tregarthen this is a well-established hotel. The impressive public areas provide wonderful views overlooking St Mary's harbour and some of the many islands, including Tresco and Bryher. Bedrooms are well equipped and neatly furnished. Traditional cuisine is served in the restaurant.

Rooms 33 (1 annexe) (5 fmly) **S** £120-£152; **D** £240-£326 (incl. bkfst & dinner)* **Notes** ⊗ Closed late Oct-mid Mar

ST MAWES — Map 2 SW83
Cornwall

Idle Rocks Hotel

RICHARDSON

★★★ 83% ®® HOTEL

☎ 01326 270771 📠 01326 270062
Harbour Side TR2 5AN
e-mail: reception@idlerocks.co.uk
web: www.idlerocks.co.uk
dir: A390 onto A3078, 14m to St Mawes. Hotel on left

This hotel has splendid sea views overlooking the attractive fishing port. The lounge and bar also benefit from the views and in warmer months service is available on the terrace. Bedrooms are individually styled and tastefully furnished to a high standard. The daily-changing menu served in the restaurant features fresh, local produce in imaginative cuisine.

Rooms 27 (4 annexe) (6 fmly) (2 GF) **D** £109-£209 (incl. bkfst)* **Facilities** FTV Xmas New Year Wi-fi **Parking** 4 **Notes** LB

ST MELLION — Map 3 SX36
Cornwall

St Mellion International

★★★★ 80% ®® HOTEL

☎ 01579 351351 📠 01579 352046
PL12 6SD
e-mail: stmellion@crown-golf.co.uk
dir: From M5/A38 towards Plymouth & Saltash. St Mellion off A38 on A388 towards Callington & Launceston

Set amidst 450 acres of Cornish countryside, this impressive golfing and leisure complex has much to offer. A vast range of leisure facilities are provided, including three pools, spa facilities and a health club. In addition, the hotel also boasts a choice of championship golf courses with the Jack Nicklaus signature course having hosted many PGA tour events. The bedrooms provide contemporary comforts and many have views across the course. Public areas are equally stylish with a choice of dining options including An Boesti, a fine-dining restaurant overlooking the 18th green.

Rooms 80 (20 fmly) (18 GF) **S** £70-£165; **D** £85-£165* **Facilities** Spa FTV supervised 36 Putt green Gym Studio classes Lawn bowls Xmas New Year Wi-fi Child facilities **Conf** Class 200 Board 80 Thtr 400 Del from £135 to £195* **Services** Lift Air con **Parking** 450 **Notes** LB ⊗ Civ Wed 300

ST NEOTS
Cambridgeshire Map 12 TL16

The George Hotel & Brasserie

★★★ 87% HOTEL

☎ 01480 812300 01480 813920
High St, Buckden PE19 5XA
e-mail: mail@thegeorgebuckden.com
web: www.thegeorgebuckden.com
dir: Just off A1 at Buckden, 2m S of A1 & A14 junct

Ideally situated in the heart of this historic town centre and just a short drive from the A1. Public rooms feature a bustling ground-floor brasserie, which offers casual dining throughout the day and evening; there is also an informal lounge bar with an open fire and comfy seating. Bedrooms are stylish, tastefully appointed and thoughtfully equipped.

Rooms 12 (1 fmly) **S** £95-£120; **D** £120-£150 (incl. bkfst)* **Facilities** STV Xmas Wi-fi **Conf** Class 30 Board 30 Thtr 50 Del from £150 to £200* **Services** Lift **Parking** 25 **Notes** LB Civ Wed 60

Abbotsley Golf Hotel

★★★ 68% HOTEL

☎ 01480 474000 01480 471018
Potton Rd, Eynesbury Hardwicke PE19 6XN
e-mail: manager@abbotsley.com

Situated in a rural location on the outskirts of St Neots, this property is set in 250-acre grounds with two golf courses, a golf school and leisure complex. The well-equipped bedrooms are situated in a courtyard and another adjacent block; some rooms have views over the golf course. Public rooms include two bars, a conservatory dining room and a choice of lounges.

Rooms 42 (42 annexe) (2 fmly) (29 GF) **Facilities** FTV 45 Putt green Gym Squash Xmas New Year Wi-fi **Conf** Thtr 80 Del from £85* **Parking** 200

Premier Inn St Neots (A1/Wyboston)

BUDGET HOTEL

☎ 0871 527 9024 0871 527 9025
Great North Rd, Eaton Socon PE19 8EN
dir: Just off A1 at rdbt junct of A428 & B1428 before St Neots, 1m from St Neots rail station

High quality, budget accommodation ideal for both families and business travellers. Spacious, en suite bedrooms feature tea and coffee making facilities, and Freeview TV in most hotels. Internet access and Wi-fi are available for a small fee. The adjacent family restaurant features a wide and varied menu. See also the Hotel Groups pages.

Rooms 65 **D** £52-£60*

Premier Inn St Neots (Colmworth Park)

BUDGET HOTEL

☎ 0871 527 9026 0871 527 9027
2 Marlborough Rd, Colmworth Business Park PE19 8YP
dir: From A1 N'bound: A428 towards Cambridge. 2nd exit at rdbt onto A4128 signed St Neots. Hotel on right. From A1 S'bound: follow A428 Cambridge signs. At rdbt 1st exit onto A4128 signed St Neots, hotel on right

Rooms 41 **D** £52-£60*

SALCOMBE
Devon Map 3 SX73

See also **Hope Cove**

Thurlestone Hotel

★★★★ 83% HOTEL

☎ 01548 560382 01548 561069
TQ7 3NN
e-mail: enquiries@thurlestone.co.uk
web: www.thurlestone.co.uk

(For full entry see Thurlestone)

Soar Mill Cove

★★★★ 79% HOTEL

☎ 01548 561566 01548 561223
Soar Mill Cove, Malborough TQ7 3DS
e-mail: info@soarmillcove.co.uk
web: www.soarmillcove.co.uk
dir: 3m W of town off A381 at Malborough. Follow Soar signs

Situated amid spectacular scenery with dramatic sea views, this hotel is ideal for a relaxing stay. Family-run, with a committed team, keen standards of hospitality and service are upheld. The bedrooms are well equipped and many have private terraces. There are different seating areas where, if guests wish, impressive cream teas can be enjoyed, and for the more active, there's a choice of swimming pools. Local produce and seafood are used to good effect in the restaurant.

Rooms 22 (5 fmly) (21 GF) **S** £115-£215; **D** £140-£240 (incl. bkfst)* **Facilities** FTV Putt green Table tennis Games room Wi-fi **Conf** Class 50 Board 50 Thtr 100 **Parking** 30 **Notes** Closed 2 Jan-8 Feb Civ Wed 150

Tides Reach

★★★ 82% HOTEL

☎ 01548 843466 01548 843954
South Sands TQ8 8LJ
e-mail: enquire@tidesreach.com
web: www.tidesreach.com
dir: Off A38 at Buckfastleigh to Totnes. Then A381 to Salcombe, follow signs to South Sands

Superbly situated at the water's edge, this personally run, friendly hotel has splendid views of the estuary and beach. Bedrooms, many with balconies, are spacious and comfortable. In the bar and lounge, attentive service can be enjoyed along with the view, and the Garden Room restaurant serves appetising and accomplished cuisine.

Rooms 32 (5 fmly) **S** £85-£144; **D** £140-£332 (incl. bkfst & dinner)* **Facilities** Spa STV FTV supervised Gym Squash Windsurfing Sailing Kayaking Scuba diving Hair & beauty treatment Wi-fi **Services** Lift **Parking** 100 **Notes** LB No children 8yrs Closed Dec-early Feb

SALCOMBE *continued*

Salcombe Harbour Hotel

U

☎ 01548 844444 01548 843109
Cliff Rd TQ8 8JH
e-mail: salcombe@harbourhotels.co.uk
web: www.salcombe-harbour-hotel.co.uk
dir: Into Salcombe along Main Rd (NB do not follow signs to town), becomes Bennet Rd, 0.25m, hotel on right

Currently the rating for this establishment is not confirmed. This may be due to a change of ownership or because it has only recently joined the AA rating scheme. For further details please see the AA website: theAA.com

Rooms 53 (8 fmly) **S** £45-£120; **D** £90-£300* **Facilities** FTV supervised Gym Sauna Steam room Table tennis Xmas New Year Wi-fi **Services** Lift **Parking** 40

SALE
Greater Manchester — Map 15 SJ79

Premier Inn Manchester (Sale)

BUDGET HOTEL

☎ 0871 527 8716 0871 527 8717
Carrington Ln, Ashton-upon-Mersey M33 5BL
dir: M60 junct 8, A6144(M) towards Carrington. Left at 1st lights, hotel on left

High quality, budget accommodation ideal for both families and business travellers. Spacious, en suite bedrooms feature tea and coffee making facilities, and Freeview TV in most hotels. Internet access and Wi-fi are available for a small fee. The adjacent family restaurant features a wide and varied menu. See also the Hotel Groups pages.

Rooms 43 **D** £52-£58*

SALISBURY
Wiltshire — Map 5 SU12

Mercure White Hart

★★★★ 72% HOTEL

☎ 0870 400 8125 & 01722 327476
01722 412761
St John St SP1 2SD
e-mail: H6616@accor.com
web: www.mercure.com
dir: M3 junct 7/8, A303 to A343 for Salisbury then A30. Follow city centre signs on ring road, into Exeter St, leading into St John St. Car park at rear

There has been a hotel on this site since the 16th century. Bedrooms vary - some are contemporary and some are decorated in more traditional style, but all boast a comprehensive range of facilities. The bar and lounge areas are popular with guests and locals alike for morning coffees and afternoon teas.

Rooms 68 (6 fmly) **Facilities** STV Xmas New Year Wi-fi **Conf** Class 40 Board 40 Thtr 100 **Parking** 60 **Notes** Civ Wed 100

Legacy Rose & Crown

LEGACY HOTELS

★★★★ 71% HOTEL

☎ 08444 119046 & 0330 333 2846
08444 119047
Harnham Rd, Harnham SP2 8JQ
e-mail: res-roseandcrown@legacy-hotels.co.uk
web: www.legacy-hotels.co.uk
dir: M3 junct 8, A303, follow Salisbury ring road & A338 towards Harnham. Hotel on right

This 13th-century coaching inn, situated beside the river, enjoys picturesque views of Salisbury Cathedral, especially from the Pavilion Restaurant which provides a good range of dishes. Many original features are still retained in the heavy oak-beamed bars. All bedrooms and bathrooms are beautifully appointed. Excellent conference and banqueting facilities are available.

Rooms 29 (5 fmly) (3 GF) **Facilities** STV FTV Xmas New Year Wi-fi **Conf** Class 30 Board 26 Thtr 90 **Parking** 60 **Notes** Civ Wed 120

Milford Hall

★★★ 80% HOTEL

☎ 01722 417411 & 424116 01722 419444
206 Castle St SP1 3TE
e-mail: reception@milfordhallhotel.com
web: www.milfordhallhotel.com
dir: Near junct of Castle St, A36 (ring road) & A345 (Amesbury road)

This hotel offers high standards of accommodation and is within easy walking distance of the city centre. There are two categories of bedroom - traditional rooms in the original Georgian house, and spacious, modern rooms in a purpose-built extension; all are extremely well equipped. Meals are served in the smart brasserie where a varied choice of dishes is provided.

Rooms 45 (2 fmly) (22 GF) **S** £65-£117.50; **D** £65-£197.50 (incl. bkfst) **Facilities** STV FTV New Year Wi-fi **Conf** Class 90 Board 60 Thtr 160 Del from £110 to £170 **Parking** 60 **Notes** LB Civ Wed 120

Best Western Red Lion

★★★ 77% HOTEL

☎ 01722 323334 01722 325756
Milford St SP1 2AN
e-mail: reception@the-redlion.co.uk
web: www.the-redlion.co.uk
dir: In city centre close to Guildhall Square

Dating from the 13th century, this hotel is full of character, with individually designed bedrooms that combine contemporary comforts with historic features; one room has a medieval fireplace dating back to 1220. The distinctive public areas include a bar, lounge and the elegant Vine Restaurant that serves an interesting mix of modern and traditional dishes.

Rooms 51 (1 fmly) **Facilities** Xmas New Year Wi-fi **Conf** Class 50 Board 40 Thtr 100 **Services** Lift **Notes** Civ Wed 80

Grasmere House Hotel

THE INDEPENDENTS HOTEL ASSOCIATION

★★★ 68% HOTEL

☎ 01722 338388 📠 01722 333710
Harnham Rd SP2 8JN
e-mail: info@grasmerehotel.com
web: www.grasmerehotel.com
dir: On A3094 on S side of Salisbury adjacent to Harnham church

This popular hotel, dating from 1896, has gardens that overlook the water meadows and the cathedral. The attractive bedrooms vary in size, some offer excellent quality and comfort, and some rooms are specially equipped for less mobile guests. In summer there is the option of dining on the pleasant outdoor terrace.

Rooms 38 (31 annexe) (16 fmly) (9 GF) **Facilities** STV FTV Fishing Xmas New Year Wi-fi **Conf** Class 45 Board 45 Thtr 110 **Parking** 64 **Notes** LB Civ Wed 120

Premier Inn Salisbury

BUDGET HOTEL

☎ 0871 527 8956 📠 0871 527 8957
Pearce Way, Bishopsdown SP1 3YU
dir: From Salisbury take A30 towards Marlborough. 1m. Hotel off Hampton Park at rdbt

High quality, budget accommodation ideal for both families and business travellers. Spacious, en suite bedrooms feature tea and coffee making facilities, and Freeview TV in most hotels. Internet access and Wi-fi are available for a small fee. The adjacent family restaurant features a wide and varied menu. See also the Hotel Groups pages.

Rooms 62 **D** £60-£62*

SALTASH
Cornwall — Map 3 SX45

China Fleet Country Club

★★★ 77% ® HOTEL

☎ 01752 854664 & 854661 📠 01752 848456
PL12 6LJ
e-mail: sales@china-fleet.co.uk
web: www.china-fleet.co.uk
dir: A38 towards Plymouth/Saltash. Cross Tamar Bridge, take slip road before tunnel. Right at lights, 1st right follow signs, 0.5m

Set in 180 acres of stunning Cornish countryside overlooking the beautiful Tamar estuary, ideal for access to Plymouth and the countryside, this hotel offers an extensive range of leisure facilities including an impressive golf course. The newly refurbished one and two-bedroom apartments are located in annexe buildings; each has a kitchen, lounge and flexible sleeping arrangements. The dining options include the brasserie, coffee shop and award-winning Farm House Restaurant.

Rooms 40 (24 fmly) (21 GF) **S** £80-£88; **D** £80-£88* **Facilities** Spa STV FTV supervised 18 Putt green Gym Squash 28-bay floodlit driving range Health & beauty suite Hairdresser Wi-fi Child facilities **Conf** Class 80 Board 60 Thtr 300 **Services** Lift **Parking** 400 **Notes** Civ Wed 300

SALTBURN-BY-THE-SEA
North Yorkshire — Map 19 NZ62

Hunley Hotel & Golf Club

★★★ 75% HOTEL

☎ 01287 676216 📠 01287 678250
Ings Ln, Brotton TS12 2QQ
e-mail: enquiries@hunleyhotel.co.uk
dir: From A174 bypass left at rdbt with monument, left at T-junct, pass church, turn right. 50yds right, through housing estate, hotel approx 0.5m

Spectacularly situated, this hotel overlooks the 27-hole golf course and beyond to the coastline. The members' bar is licensed and serves snacks all day, and the restaurant offers a wide choice of interesting dishes. The bedrooms are very comfortably equipped and some are particularly spacious.

Rooms 27 (2 fmly) (17 GF) **S** £66-£86; **D** £77-£102* **Facilities** STV FTV 27 Putt green Driving range Xmas New Year Wi-fi **Conf** Class 32 Board 28 Thtr 50 Del from £104 to £124* **Parking** 100 **Notes** LB Civ Wed 130

SANDBANKS

See Poole

SANDIACRE
Derbyshire — Map 11 SK43

Holiday Inn Derby/Nottingham

★★★ 73% HOTEL

☎ 0871 942 9062 📠 0115 949 0469
Bostocks Ln NG10 5NJ
e-mail: reservations-derby-nottingham@ihg.com
web: www.holidayinn.co.uk
dir: M1 junct 25 follow Sandiacre signs, hotel on right

This hotel is conveniently located by the M1, and ideal for exploring Derby and Nottingham. The bedrooms are modern and smart. The restaurant offers a wide range of dishes for breakfast, lunch and dinner. The lounge/bar area is a popular meeting place, with food served all day.

Rooms 92 (31 fmly) (53 GF) **Facilities** STV Xmas New Year Wi-fi **Conf** Class 32 Board 30 Thtr 75 Del from £89 to £139* **Services** Air con **Parking** 200 **Notes** LB Civ Wed 50

S

SANDIWAY Map 15 SJ67
Cheshire

INSPECTORS' CHOICE

Nunsmere Hall Hotel

PRIMA HOTEL GROUP

★★★★ ®®
COUNTRY HOUSE HOTEL

☎ 01606 889100 📠 01606 889055
Tarporley Rd CW8 2ES
e-mail: reception@nunsmere.co.uk
web: www.nunsmere.co.uk
dir: M6 junct 18, A54 to Chester, at x-rds with A49 turn left towards Tarporley, hotel 2m on left

In an idyllic and peaceful setting of well-kept grounds, including a 60-acre lake, this delightful house dates back to 1900. Spacious bedrooms are individually styled, tastefully appointed to a very high standard and thoughtfully equipped. Guests can relax in the elegant lounges, the library or the oak-panelled bar. Dining in the Crystal Restaurant is a highlight and both a traditional carte and a gourmet menu are offered.

Rooms 36 (2 GF) **Facilities** Xmas New Year Wi-fi **Conf** Class 24 Board 30 Thtr 50 **Services** Lift **Parking** 80 **Notes** Civ Wed 120

S

SANDOWN Map 5 SZ58
Isle of Wight

Melville Hall Hotel & Utopia Spa

★★★ 80% HOTEL

☎ 01983 400500 & 406526 📠 01983 407093
Melville St PO36 9DH
e-mail: enquiries@melvillehall.co.uk
dir: Exit A3055, hotel 30yds on left

Situated in the quiet semi-rural outskirts of Sandown, a few minutes walk from the seafront, railway station, cliffs and shops. There is a leisure suite, with both indoor and outdoor pool, and beauty treatment rooms are available. Bedrooms offer a good range of accessories and many have jacuzzi baths.

Rooms 30 (3 fmly) (4 GF) **Facilities** Spa STV Putt green Xmas New Year Wi-fi **Parking** 20 **Notes**

Sandringham

★★ 74% HOTEL

☎ 01983 406655 📠 01983 404395
Esplanade PO36 8AH
e-mail: info@sandringhamhotel.co.uk

With a prime seafront location and splendid views, this is one of the largest hotels on the island. Comfortable public areas include a spacious lounge and a heated indoor swimming pool and jacuzzi. Bedrooms vary in size and many sea-facing rooms have a balcony. Regular entertainment is provided in the ballroom.

Rooms 110 (39 fmly) (6 GF) **Facilities** Xmas **Services** Lift **Parking** 82 **Notes**

The Wight Montrene

★★ 74% HOTEL

☎ 01983 403722 📠 01983 405553
11 Avenue Rd PO36 8BN
e-mail: enquiries@wighthotel.co.uk
web: www.wighthotel.co.uk
dir: 100yds after mini-rdbt between High St & Avenue Rd

A family hotel, set in secluded grounds, that is only a short walk from Sandown's beach and high street shops. Bedrooms provide comfort and are either on the ground or first floor. Guests can relax in the heated swimming pool and enjoy the spa facility; there's also evening entertainment in the bar. The dinner menu changes nightly, and a plentiful breakfast is served in the colourful dining room.

Rooms 41 (18 fmly) (21 GF) **Facilities** Spa Gym Steam room Sauna Solarium Table tennis Full size snooker table Xmas New Year Wi-fi **Conf** Thtr 80 **Parking** 40

Bayshore Hotel

Leisureplex

★★ 72% HOTEL

☎ 01983 403154 📠 01983 406574
12-16 Pier St PO36 8JX
e-mail: bayshore.sandown@alfatravel.co.uk
dir: From Broadway into Melville St, follow Tourist Information Office signs. Across High St, right opposite pier. Hotel on right

This large hotel is located on the seafront opposite the pier and offers extensive public rooms where live entertainment is provided in season. The bedrooms are well equipped and staff very friendly and helpful.

Rooms 80 (18 fmly) (2 GF) **S** £37-£50; **D** £58-£84 (incl. bkfst) **Facilities** FTV Xmas New Year **Services** Lift **Notes** LB Closed Dec-Feb (ex Xmas) RS Mar & Nov

Riviera

★★ 71% HOTEL

☎ 01983 402518 📠 01983 406532
2 Royal St PO36 8LP
e-mail: enquiries@rivierahotel.org.uk
web: www.rivierahotel.org.uk
dir: At top of High St, beyond main Post Office

Guests return year after year to this friendly and welcoming family-run hotel. It is located near the High Street and just a short stroll from the beach, pier and shops. Bedrooms, including several at ground floor level, are very well furnished and comfortably equipped. Enjoyable home-cooked meals are served in the spacious dining room.

Rooms 43 (6 fmly) (11 GF) **S** £49-£56; **D** £98-£112 (incl. bkfst & dinner)* **Facilities** Xmas New Year **Parking** 30 **Notes** LB

Sandown Hotel

U

☎ 01983 402072
Culver Pde PO36 8AS
e-mail: info@sandown.co.uk
dir: In town centre

Currently the rating for this establishment is not confirmed. This may be due to a change of ownership or because it has only recently joined the AA rating scheme. For further details please see the AA website: theAA.com

Rooms 45

SANDWICH Kent — Map 7 TR35

The Bell

★★★ 83% HOTEL

☎ 01304 613388 📠 01304 615308
The Quay CT13 9EF
e-mail: reservations@bellhotelsandwich.co.uk
web: www.bellhotelsandwich.co.uk
dir: In town centre

The Bell has been welcoming travellers since the 14th century, when it looked out over a harbour, now the River Stour; the existing building dates mainly from the 19th century. The bedrooms to offer guests much style and comfort, and some have balconies with river views. The contemporary Old Dining Room Restaurant offers a seasonally changing menu that highlights locally caught fish and seafood, salt marsh lamb and produce from nearby farms. Dating from the Georgian era, the elegant Regency Room is ideal for conferences, wedding receptions and parties. Wi-fi is available throughout.

Rooms 37 (4 fmly) (3 GF) **S** £85-£120; **D** £110-£220 (incl. bkfst)* **Facilities** FTV Xmas New Year Wi-fi **Conf** Class 80 Board 50 Thtr 150 Del from £130 to £170* **Parking** 7 **Notes** LB Civ Wed 70

SAUNTON Devon — Map 3 SS43

Saunton Sands

★★★★ 79% HOTEL

☎ 01271 890212 & 892001 📠 01271 890145
EX33 1LQ
e-mail: reservations@sauntonsands.com
web: www.sauntonsands.com
dir: Off A361 at Braunton, signed Croyde B3231, hotel 2m on left

Stunning sea views and direct access to five miles of sandy beach are just two of the highlights at this popular hotel. The majority of sea-facing rooms have balconies, and splendid views can be enjoyed from all of the public areas, which include comfortable lounges. In addition to the dining room, in summer an outside grill has tables on the terrace overlooking the sea. Alternatively, The Sands café/bar, an informal eating option, is a successful innovation located on the beach.

Rooms 92 (39 fmly) **S** £170; **D** £478 (incl. bkfst & dinner)* **Facilities** Spa STV FTV Putt green Gym Squash Nursery Snooker room Games room Xmas New Year Wi-fi Child facilities **Conf** Class 180 Board 50 Thtr 200 Del from £125 to £160* **Services** Lift **Parking** 142 **Notes** LB Civ Wed 200

See advert on this page

SAWBRIDGEWORTH Hertfordshire — Map 6 TL41

Manor of Groves Hotel, Golf & Country Club

★★★ 74% HOTEL

☎ 01279 600777 & 0870 410 8833
📠 01279 600374
High Wych CM21 0JU
e-mail: info@manorofgroves.co.uk
web: www.manorofgroves.com
dir: A1184 to Sawbridgeworth, left to High Wych, right at village green & hotel 200yds left

Delightful Georgian manor house set in 150 acres of secluded grounds and gardens, with its own 18-hole championship golf course and superb leisure facilities. Public rooms include an imposing open-plan glass atrium that features a bar, lounge area and modern restaurant. The spacious bedrooms are smartly decorated and equipped with modern facilities.

Rooms 80 (2 fmly) (17 GF) **Facilities** Spa FTV supervised 18 Putt green Gym Dance studio Beauty salon Sauna Steam rooms Xmas New Year Wi-fi **Conf** Class 250 Board 50 Thtr 500 **Services** Lift **Parking** 350 **Notes** RS 24 Dec-2 Jan Civ Wed 300

SCARBOROUGH
North Yorkshire — Map 17 TA08

Crown Spa

★★★★ 77% HOTEL

☎ 01723 357400 📠 01723 357404
Esplanade YO11 2AG
e-mail: info@crownspahotel.com
web: www.crownspahotel.com
dir: On A64 follow town centre signs to lights opposite railway station, turn right over Valley Bridge, 1st left, right into Belmont Rd to cliff top

This well known hotel has an enviable position overlooking the harbour and South Bay and most of the front-facing bedrooms have excellent views. All the bedrooms, including suites, are contemporary and have the latest amenities including feature bathrooms. An extensive range of treatments is available in the outstanding spa.

Rooms 115 (20 fmly) **S** £50-£130; **D** £70-£210 **Facilities** Spa FTV Gym Fitness classes Massage Sauna Steam room Beauty treatments Xmas New Year Wi-fi **Conf** Class 100 Board 80 Thtr 260 Del from £99 to £199 **Services** Lift **Parking** 10 **Notes** LB Civ Wed 260

See advert on opposite page

S

Best Western Ox Pasture Hall Country Hotel

★★★★ 75% COUNTRY HOUSE HOTEL

☎ 01723 365295 📠 01723 355156
Lady Edith's Dr, Raincliffe Woods YO12 5TD
e-mail: oxpasture.hall@btconnect.com
web: www.oxpasturehall.com
dir: A171, left onto Lady Edith's Drive, 1.5m, hotel on right

This charming country hotel is set in the North Riding Forest Park and has a very friendly atmosphere. Bedrooms (split between the main house, townhouse and the delightful courtyard) are stylish, comfortable and well equipped. Public areas include a split-level bar, quiet lounge and an attractive restaurant. There is also an extensive banqueting area licensed for civil weddings.

Rooms 21 (1 fmly) (14 GF) **S** £79-£129; **D** £89-£199 (incl. bkfst) **Facilities** FTV Xmas New Year Wi-fi **Conf** Class 75 Board 50 Thtr 150 **Parking** 100 **Notes** LB Civ Wed 150

Palm Court

★★★ 79% HOTEL

☎ 01723 368161 📠 01723 371547
St Nicholas Cliff YO11 2ES
e-mail: info@palmcourt-scarborough.co.uk
dir: Follow signs for town centre & town hall, hotel before town hall on right

The public rooms are spacious and comfortable at this modern, town centre hotel. Traditional cooking is provided in the attractive restaurant and staff are friendly and helpful. Bedrooms are quite delightfully furnished and are also well equipped. Extra facilities include a swimming pool and free, covered parking.

Rooms 40 (11 fmly) **S** £60-£85; **D** £100-£140 (incl. bkfst)* **Facilities** FTV Xmas New Year Wi-fi **Conf** Class 70 Board 60 Thtr 80 Del from £119.50 to £145 **Services** Lift **Parking** 40 **Notes** LB Civ Wed

Wrea Head Country Hotel

★★★ 79% HOTEL

☎ 01723 378211 & 374374 📠 01723 371780
Barmoor Ln, Scalby YO13 0PB
e-mail: wreahead@englishrosehotels.co.uk
dir: A171 from Scarborough towards Whitby, hotel sign on left, turn into Barmoor Ln, through ford. Hotel entrance immediately left

This elegant country house is situated in 14 acres of grounds and gardens. Bedrooms are individually furnished and decorated; many have fine views. Public rooms include a conservatory, the oak-panelled lounge with inglenook fireplace and a beautiful library lounge that is full of books and games.

Rooms 20 (2 fmly) (1 GF) **S** £57.50-£77.50; **D** £115-£200 (incl. bkfst) **Facilities** Putt green Xmas New Year Wi-fi **Conf** Class 16 Board 20 Thtr 40 Del from £115 to £175 **Parking** 50 **Notes** LB Civ Wed 50

Royal Hotel

THE INDEPENDENTS HOTEL ASSOCIATION

★★★ 77% HOTEL

☎ 01723 364333 & 374374 📠 01723 371780
St Nicholas St YO11 2HE
e-mail: sales@englishrosehotels.co.uk
web: www.englishrosehotels.co.uk
dir: A64 into town. Follow town centre/South Bay signs. Hotel opposite town hall

This smart hotel enjoys a central location. Bedrooms are neatly appointed and offer a variety of styles from contemporary to traditional and include some suites. Public areas are elegant and include well-equipped conference and banqueting facilities, a leisure suite and the popular, modern Cafe Bliss where light snacks are served all day.

Rooms 118 (14 fmly) **S** £49.50-£69.50; **D** £80-£160 (incl. bkfst) **Facilities** supervised Gym Beauty treatments Steam room Sauna Xmas New Year Wi-fi **Conf** Class 125 Board 75 Thtr 300 Del from £105 to £175 **Services** Lift **Notes** LB Civ Wed 150

Beiderbecke's Hotel

★★★ 75% HOTEL

☎ 01723 365766 📠 01723 367433
1-3 The Crescent YO11 2PW
e-mail: info@beiderbeckes.com
dir: In town centre, 200mtrs from railway station

Situated in a Georgian crescent this hotel is close to all the main attractions. Bedrooms are very smart, well equipped and offer plenty of space and comfort. Some rooms have views over the town to the sea. Marmalade's, the restaurant, offers international cuisine with a modern twist and hosts live music acts at weekends, including the resident jazz band.

Rooms 27 (4 fmly) **S** £57.50-£130; **D** £95-£180 (incl. bkfst) **Facilities** STV FTV Xmas New Year Wi-fi **Conf** Class 40 Board 30 Thtr 80 Del from £99 to £149 **Services** Lift **Parking** 18 **Notes** LB

Ambassador Hotel

★★★ 75% HOTEL

☎ 01723 362841 📠 01723 366166
Centre of the Esplanade YO11 2AY
e-mail: ask@ambassadorhotelscarborough.co.uk
web: www.ambassadorhotelscarborough.co.uk
dir: A64, right at mini rdbt opposite B&Q, right at next mini rdbt, immediately left into Avenue Victoria to cliff top

Standing on the South Cliff with excellent views over the bay, this friendly hotel offers well-equipped bedrooms; some are executive rooms. An indoor swimming pool, sauna and solarium are also available. Entertainment is provided during the summer season.

Rooms 59 (10 fmly) (1 GF) **Facilities** FTV Sauna Spa bath Xmas New Year Wi-fi **Conf** Class 60 Board 40 Thtr 100 Del from £99 to £190* **Services** Lift Air con **Notes** Civ Wed 120

Esplanade

★★★ 68% HOTEL

☎ 01723 360382 📠 01723 376137
Belmont Rd YO11 2AA
e-mail: enquiries@theesplanade.co.uk
dir: From town centre over Valley Bridge, left then immediately right into Belmont Rd, hotel 100mtrs on right

This large hotel enjoys a superb position overlooking South Bay and the harbour. Both the terrace, leading from the lounge bar, and the restaurant, with its striking oriel window, benefit from magnificent views. Bedrooms are comfortably furnished and are well equipped. Touring groups are also well catered for.

Rooms 70 (7 fmly) **S** £45-£53; **D** £90-£116 (incl. bkfst)* **Facilities** Xmas New Year **Conf** Class 100 Board 30 Thtr 120 Del from £75 to £95* **Services** Lift **Parking** 15 **Notes** Closed 2 Jan-9 Feb

Brooklands

★★★ 66% HOTEL

☎ 01723 376576 📠 01723 341093
Esplanade Gardens, South Cliff YO11 2AW
e-mail: info@brooklands-scarborough.co.uk
dir: From A64 York, right at B&Q rdbt, right at lights, 1st left into Avenue Victoria, at end left, then 2nd left

Located on the South Cliff, overlooking the Esplanade Gardens and very close to the seafront, this is a contemporary hotel. There is a friendly team of staff and a range of stylish lounge areas, a games room and spacious restaurant. Entertainment is provided most evenings in the lower-ground floor bar.

Rooms 63 (13 fmly) (2 GF) **Facilities** FTV Xmas New Year Wi-fi **Conf** Class 90 Board 40 **Services** Lift **Notes** LB

See advert on page 432

S

SCARBOROUGH *continued*

The Mount

★★ 75% HOTEL

☎ 01723 360961 📠 01723 375850
Cliff Bridge Ter, Saint Nicholas Cliff YO11 2HA
e-mail: info@mounthotel.com
dir: On one-way system. From A165 (Valley Bridge Rd) left into Somerset Terrace, straight on at lights, straight on at rdbt (Palm Court Hotel on right). Next right into St Nicholas Cliff. Hotel at end on right

Standing in a superb, elevated position and enjoying magnificent views of the South Bay, this elegant Regency hotel is operated to high standards. The richly furnished and comfortable public rooms are inviting, and the well-equipped bedrooms have been attractively decorated. The spacious deluxe rooms are mini-suites.

Rooms 50 (5 fmly) **Facilities** Xmas **Services** Lift **Notes** Closed Jan-mid Mar

See advert on opposite page

Clifton Hotel

★★ 74% HOTEL

☎ 01723 375691 & 374374 📠 01723 364203
Queens Pde, North Cliff YO12 7HX
e-mail: clifton@englishrosehotels.co.uk
dir: On entering town centre, follow signs for North Bay

Standing in an impressive location with commanding fine views over the bay, this large holiday hotel is convenient for Peasholm Park and other local leisure attractions; tour groups are especially well catered for. Bedrooms are pleasant, and entertainment is provided in the spacious public rooms during the high season.

Rooms 71 (11 fmly) **Facilities** ♫ Xmas New Year **Conf** Class 50 Board 50 Thtr 120 **Services** Lift **Parking** 45 **Notes** ⊗

Park Manor

★★ 72% HOTEL

☎ 01723 372090 📠 01723 500480
Northstead Manor Dr YO12 6BB
e-mail: info@parkmanor.co.uk
web: www.parkmanor.co.uk
dir: Off A165, next to Peasholm Park

Enjoying a peaceful residential setting with sea views, this smartly presented, friendly hotel provides the seaside tourist with a wide range of facilities. Bedrooms vary in size and style but all are smartly furnished and well equipped. There is a spacious lounge, smart restaurant, games room and indoor pool plus a steam room for relaxation.

Rooms 42 (6 fmly) **S** £41.50-£50.50; **D** £83-£110 (incl. bkfst)* **Facilities** FTV Ⓢ Pool table Spa bath Steam room Table tennis New Year Wi-fi **Conf** Class 20 Board 20 Thtr 30 Del from £66 to £85* **Services** Lift **Parking** 20 **Notes** LB ⊗ No children 3yrs

Red Lea

★★ 72% HOTEL

☎ 01723 362431 📠 01723 371230
Prince of Wales Ter YO11 2AJ
e-mail: redlea@globalnet.co.uk
web: www.redleahotel.co.uk
dir: Follow South Cliff signs. Prince of Wales Terrace is off Esplanade opposite cliff lift

This friendly, family-run hotel is situated close to the cliff lift. Bedrooms are well equipped and comfortably furnished, and many at the front have picturesque views of the coast. There are two large lounges and a spacious dining room where good-value, traditional food is served.

Rooms 67 (7 fmly) (2 GF) **Facilities** FTV Ⓢ Gym Xmas New Year **Conf** Class 25 Board 25 Thtr 40 **Services** Lift **Notes** ⊗

S

The Cumberland

★★ 68% HOTEL

☎ 01723 361826 📠 01723 500081
Belmont Rd YO11 2AB
e-mail: cumberland.scarborough@alfatravel.co.uk
dir: A64 onto B1437, left at A165 towards town centre. Right into Ramshill Rd, right into Belmont Rd

On the South Cliff, convenient for the spa complex, beach and town centre shops, this hotel offers comfortably appointed bedrooms; each floor can be accessed by lift. Entertainment is provided most evenings and the meals are carefully cooked.

Rooms 81 (6 fmly) **S** £37-£47; **D** £58-£78 (incl. bkfst) **Facilities** FTV ♫ Xmas New Year **Services** Lift **Notes** LB ⊗ Closed Jan RS Nov-Dec & Feb

Delmont

★★ 65% HOTEL

☎ 01723 364500 📠 01723 363554
18/19 Blenheim Ter YO12 7HE
e-mail: enquiries@delmonthotel.co.uk
dir: Follow signs to North Bay. At seafront to top of cliff. Hotel near castle

Popular with groups, a friendly welcome is found at this hotel on the North Bay. Bedrooms are comfortable, and many have sea views. There are two lounges, a bar and a spacious dining room in which good-value, traditional food is served along with entertainment on most evenings.

Rooms 51 (18 fmly) (5 GF) **S** £20-£43; **D** £40-£86 (incl. bkfst)* **Facilities** FTV Games Room Pool table ♫ Xmas New Year **Services** Lift **Parking** 2 **Notes** LB

SCUNTHORPE
Lincolnshire **Map 17 SE81**

Forest Pines Hotel & Golf Resort

QHOTELS

★★★★ 79% ❀ HOTEL

☎ 01652 650770 📠 01652 650495
Ermine St, Broughton DN20 0AQ
e-mail: forestpines@qhotels.co.uk
web: www.qhotels.co.uk
dir: 200yds from M180 junct 4, on Brigg-Scunthorpe rdbt

This smart hotel provides a comprehensive range of leisure facilities. Extensive conference rooms, a modern health and beauty spa, and a championship golf course ensure that it is a popular choice with both corporate and leisure guests. The well-equipped bedrooms are modern, spacious, and appointed to a good standard. Extensive public areas include a choice of dining options, with fine dining available in The Eighteen57 fish restaurant, and more informal eating in the Grill Bar.

Rooms 188 (66 fmly) (67 GF) **Facilities** **Spa** STV FTV supervised ⛳ 27 Putt green Gym Mountain bikes Jogging track Xmas New Year Wi-fi **Conf** Class 170 Board 96 Thtr 370 **Services** Lift **Parking** 400 **Notes** Civ Wed 250

Premier Inn Scunthorpe

BUDGET HOTEL

☎ 0871 527 8960 📠 0871 527 8961
Lakeside Retail Park, Lakeside Parkway DN16 3UA
dir: M180 junct 4, A18 towards Scunthorpe. At Morrisons rdbt left onto Lakeside Retail Park, hotel behind Morrisons petrol station

High quality, budget accommodation ideal for both families and business travellers. Spacious, en suite bedrooms feature tea and coffee making facilities, and Freeview TV in most hotels. Internet access and Wi-fi are available for a small fee. The adjacent family restaurant features a wide and varied menu. See also the Hotel Groups pages.

Rooms 60 **D** £52-£60*

S

SEAHAM
Co Durham — Map 19 NZ44

INSPECTORS' CHOICE

Seaham Hall Hotel & Serenity Spa

★★★★★ ◎◎ HOTEL

☎ 0191 516 1400 🖷 0191 516 1410
Lord Byron's Walk SR7 7AG
e-mail: info@seaham-hall.co.uk
web: www.seaham-hall.co.uk
dir: From A19 take B1404 to Seaham. At lights straight over level crossing. Hotel approx 0.25m on right

This imposing house was the setting for Lord Byron's marriage to Annabella Milbanke in 1815. Now restored to their opulent glory, the bedrooms, including some stunning suites, offer cutting edge technology, contemporary artwork and a real sense of style. Bathrooms are particularly lavish, with two-person baths a feature. Public rooms are equally impressive. The White Room, with 2 AA Rosettes, offers a formal dining experience. The stunning Oriental Spa, accessed via an underground walkway, offers guests a wide range of treatments, plus the Ozone Restaurant which has been awarded 1 AA Rosette.

Rooms 20 (4 GF) **Facilities** Spa FTV Gym Xmas New Year Wi-fi **Conf** Class 48 Board 40 Thtr 100 Del from £175 to £195* **Services** Lift Air con **Parking** 122 **Notes** LB ⊗ Civ Wed 100

S

SEAHOUSES
Northumberland — Map 21 NU23

Beach House

★★ 78% HOTEL

☎ 01665 720337 🖷 01665 720921
Sea Front NE68 7SR
e-mail: enquiries@beachhousehotel.co.uk
web: www.beachhousehotel.co.uk
dir: Follow signs from A1 between Alnwick & Berwick

Enjoying a seafront location and views of the Farne Islands, this family-run hotel offers a relaxed and friendly atmosphere. Bedrooms come in a variety of sizes, but all are bright and airy. Dinner makes use of fresh produce and breakfast features local specialities. There is a well-stocked bar and comfortable lounge.

Rooms 27 (5 fmly) (4 GF) **Facilities** Xmas New Year **Conf** Thtr 50 **Parking** 20 **Notes** ⊗ No children 4yrs

SEASCALE
Cumbria — Map 18 NY00

Sella Park House Hotel

★★★ 85% COUNTRY HOUSE HOTEL

☎ 0845 450 6445 & 01946 841601
🖷 01946 841339
Calderbridge CA20 1DW
e-mail: info@penningtonhotels.com
dir: From A595 at Calderbridge, follow sign for North Gate. Hotel 0.5m on left

This property, which some believe dates back to the 13th century, is set in six acres of mature grounds which lead down to the River Calder. Inside the hotel, the massive refurbishment programme shows excellent results. The bedrooms are very well appointed and have many extras; public areas are comfortable and welcoming. Food is a highlight with local produce at the heart of each menu selection.

Rooms 16 (5 annexe) (2 GF) **S** £90-£120; **D** £110-£160 (incl. bkfst)* **Facilities** FTV Fishing Xmas New Year Wi-fi **Conf** Class 80 Board 80 Thtr 300 Del from £120 to £210* **Parking** 30 **Notes** LB Civ Wed 150

Cumbrian Lodge

◎ RESTAURANT WITH ROOMS

☎ 019467 27309 🖷 019467 27158
Gosforth Rd CA20 1JG
e-mail: cumbrianlodge@btconnect.com
web: www.cumbrianlodge.com
dir: Off A595 at Gosforth onto B5344 signed Seascale, 2m on left

A relaxed and friendly atmosphere prevails at this well-run restaurant with rooms, where tasty, well-prepared dinners prove popular locally. The decor and fixtures are modern throughout, and the bedrooms are well-equipped for both business and leisure guests. The thatched garden buildings provide a delightful opportunity for eating alfresco under canvas panels, for up to 12 diners.

Rooms 6 (1 fmly)

SEAVIEW
Isle of Wight — Map 5 SZ69

Priory Bay

★★★ 78% ◎ HOTEL

☎ 01983 613146 🖷 01983 616539
Priory Dr PO34 5BU
e-mail: enquiries@priorybay.co.uk
web: www.priorybay.co.uk
dir: B3330 towards Seaview, through Nettlestone. (NB do not follow Seaview turn, but continue 0.5m to hotel sign)

This peacefully located hotel has much to offer and comes complete with its own stretch of private beach and 6-hole golf course. Bedrooms are a wonderful mix of styles, all of which provide much comfort and character. Public areas are equally impressive with a choice of enticing lounges to relax and unwind. The kitchen creates interesting and imaginative dishes, using the excellent island produce as much as possible.

Rooms 22 (4 annexe) (6 fmly) (2 GF) **S** £90-£225; **D** £160-£300 (incl. bkfst)* **Facilities** FTV  6 Private beach Xmas New Year Wi-fi **Conf** Class 60 Board 40 Thtr 80 Del from £130 to £250* **Parking** 100 **Notes** LB ⊗ Civ Wed 100

SEDGEFIELD
Co Durham — Map 19 NZ32

Best Western Hardwick Hall

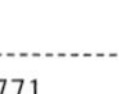

★★★★ 79% ◎ HOTEL

☎ 01740 620253 🖷 01740 622771
TS21 2EH
e-mail: info@hardwickhallhotel.co.uk
dir: Off A1(M) junct 60 towards Sedgefield, left at 1st rdbt, hotel 400mtrs on left

Set in extensive parkland, this 18th-century house suits both leisure and corporate guests. It is a top conference and function venue offering an impressive meeting and banqueting complex. Luxurious bedrooms include contemporary rooms and some with antique furnishings but all are appointed to the same high standard; many have feature bathrooms and some have stunning views over the lake. Both the modern lounge bar and cellar bistro have a relaxed atmosphere.

Rooms 51 (6 fmly) **S** £59-£205; **D** £59-£205* **Facilities** STV FTV **Conf** Board 80 Thtr 700 Del from £110 to £150* **Services** Lift **Parking** 200 **Notes** LB ⊗ Civ Wed 450

SEDGEMOOR MOTORWAY SERVICE AREA (M5) Map 4 ST35
Somerset

Days Inn Sedgemoor - M5

BUDGET HOTEL

☎ 01934 750831 📠 01934 750808
Sedgemoor BS24 0JL
e-mail: sedgemoor.hotel@welcomebreak.co.uk
web: www.welcomebreak.co.uk
dir: M5 northbound junct 21/22

This modern building offers accommodation in smart, spacious and well-equipped bedrooms, suitable for families and business travellers, and all with en suite bathrooms. Continental breakfast is available and other refreshments may be taken at the nearby family restaurant. See also the Hotel Groups pages.

Rooms 40 (39 fmly) (19 GF) (8 smoking) **S** £39.95-£59.95; **D** £49.95-£69.95

SHAFTESBURY Map 4 ST82
Dorset

Best Western Royal Chase

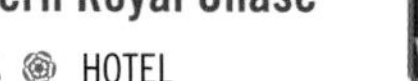

★★★ 72% ® HOTEL

☎ 01747 853355 📠 01747 851969
Royal Chase Roundabout SP7 8DB
e-mail: reception@theroyalchasehotel.co.uk
web: www.theroyalchasehotel.co.uk
dir: A303 to A350 signed Blandford Forum. Avoid town centre, follow road to 3rd rdbt

Equally suitable for both leisure and business guests, this well-known local landmark is situated close to the famous Gold Hill. Both Standard and Crown bedrooms offer good levels of comfort and quality. In addition to the fixed-price menu in the Byzant Restaurant, guests have the option of eating more informally in the convivial bar.

Rooms 33 (13 fmly) (6 GF) **S** £50-£95; **D** £50-£95 **Facilities** Ⓢ Turkish steam room New Year Wi-fi **Conf** Class 90 Board 50 Thtr 180 Del from £112.50 to £117.50 **Parking** 100 **Notes** LB Civ Wed 76

La Fleur de Lys Restaurant with Rooms

®® RESTAURANT WITH ROOMS

☎ 01747 853717 📠 01747 853130
Bleke St SP7 8AW
e-mail: info@lafleurdelys.co.uk
web: www.lafleurdelys.co.uk
dir: From junct of A30 & A350, 0.25m towards town centre

Located just a few minutes' walk from the famous Gold Hill, this light and airy restaurant with rooms combines efficient service in a relaxed and friendly atmosphere. Bedrooms, which are suitable for both business and leisure guests, vary in size but all are well equipped, comfortable and tastefully furnished. A relaxing guest lounge and courtyard are available for afternoon tea or pre-dinner drinks.

Rooms 7 (2 fmly)

SHANKLIN Map 5 SZ58
Isle of Wight

Channel View

★★★ 78% HOTEL

☎ 01983 862309 📠 01983 868400
Hope Rd PO37 6EH
e-mail: enquiries@channelviewhotel.co.uk
web: www.channelviewhotel.co.uk
dir: Exit A3055 at Esplanade & Beach sign. Hotel 250mtrs on left

With an elevated cliff-top location overlooking Shanklin Bay, several rooms at this hotel enjoy pleasant views and all are very well decorated and furnished. The hotel is family run, and guests can enjoy efficient service, regular evening entertainment, a heated indoor swimming pool and holistic therapy.

Rooms 56 (15 fmly) **S** £39-£58; **D** £78-£106 (incl. bkfst) **Facilities** Ⓢ Holistic therapies Aromatherapy ♫ **Services** Lift **Parking** 22 **Notes** LB Closed Jan-Feb

Luccombe Hall

★★★ 77% HOTEL

☎ 01983 869000 📠 01983 863082
8 Luccombe Rd PO37 6RL
e-mail: enquiries@luccombehall.co.uk
dir: Take A3055 to Shanklin, through old village then 1st left into Priory Rd, left into Popham Rd, 1st right into Luccombe Rd. Hotel on left

Appropriately described as 'the view with the hotel', this property was originally built in 1870 as a summer home for the Bishop of Portsmouth. Enjoying an impressive cliff-top location, the hotel benefits from wonderful sea views, delightful gardens and direct access to the beach. Well-equipped bedrooms are comfortably furnished and there is a range of leisure facilities.

Rooms 29 (15 fmly) (7 GF) **S** £49-£79; **D** £98-£208 (incl. bkfst)* **Facilities** STV Ⓢ ⊰ Putt green Gym Squash Games room Treatment room Sauna Xmas New Year Wi-fi Child facilities **Parking** 20 **Notes** LB ⊗

Melbourne Ardenlea Hotel

★★ 76% HOTEL

☎ 01983 862596 📠 01983 868927
4-6 Queens Rd PO37 6AP
e-mail: reservations@mahotel.co.uk
web: www.mahotel.co.uk
dir: A3055 to Shanklin. Then follow signs to Ventnor via A3055 (Queens Rd). Hotel just before end of road on right

This quietly located hotel is within easy walking distance of the town centre and the lift down to the promenade. Bedrooms are traditionally furnished and guests can enjoy the various spacious public areas including a welcoming bar and a large heated indoor swimming pool.

Rooms 54 (5 fmly) (6 GF) **S** £45-£80; **D** £70-£120 (incl. bkfst)* **Facilities** Ⓢ Sauna ♫ New Year Wi-fi **Conf** Class 24 Board 20 Thtr 80 Del from £59 to £89* **Services** Lift **Parking** 26 **Notes** LB Closed 21-28 Dec

Malton House

★★ 68% HOTEL

☎ 01983 865007 📠 01983 865576
8 Park Rd PO37 6AY
e-mail: couvoussis@maltonhouse.freeserve.co.uk
web: www.maltonhouse.co.uk
dir: Up hill from Hope Rd lights then 3rd left

A well-kept Victorian hotel set in its own gardens in a quiet area, conveniently located for cliff-top walks and the public lift down to the promenade. The bedrooms are comfortable and public rooms include a

continued

S

SHANKLIN *continued*

small lounge, a separate bar and a dining room where traditional homemade meals are served.

Rooms 12 (3 fmly) (2 GF) **S** £36-£40; **D** £62-£70 (incl. bkfst)* **Parking** 12 **Notes** LB ® No children 3 yrs Closed Oct-Apr

SHAP
Cumbria — **Map 18 NY51**

Best Western Shap Wells

★★★ 74% HOTEL

☎ 01931 716628 🖹 01931 716377
CA10 3QU
e-mail: manager@shapwells.com
dir: Between A6 & B6261, 4m S of Shap

This hotel occupies a wonderful secluded position amid trees and waterfalls. Extensive public areas include function and meeting rooms, a well-stocked bar, a choice of lounges and a spacious restaurant. Bedrooms vary in size and style but all are equipped with the expected facilities.

Rooms 98 (7 annexe) (10 fmly) (10 GF) **Facilities** FTV Games room Cardio vascular gym Xmas New Year Wi-fi **Conf** Class 80 Board 40 Thtr 170 **Services** Lift **Parking** 200 **Notes** Civ Wed 150

SHEDFIELD
Hampshire — **Map 5 SU51**

Meon Valley, a Marriott Hotel & Country Club

★★★★ 80% ® HOTEL

☎ 01329 833455 🖹 01329 834411
Sandy Ln SO32 2HQ
web: www.marriottmeonvalley.co.uk
dir: M27 junct 7 take A334 towards Wickham & Botley. Sandy Ln on left 2m from Botley

This modern, smartly appointed hotel and country club has extensive indoor and outdoor leisure facilities, including two golf courses. Bedrooms are spacious and well equipped, and guests have a choice of eating and drinking options. It is ideally suited for easy access to both Portsmouth and Southampton.

Rooms 113 (43 fmly) (29 GF) (10 smoking) **Facilities** Spa FTV ⓢ ⛳ 27 🎾 Putt green Gym Cardio-vascular aerobics Health & beauty salon Xmas New Year Wi-fi **Conf** Class 50 Board 32 Thtr 100 **Services** Lift **Parking** 360 **Notes** ® Civ Wed 90

SHEFFIELD
South Yorkshire — **Map 16 SK49**

Copthorne Hotel Sheffield

★★★★ 79% ® HOTEL

☎ 0114 252 5480 🖹 0114 252 5490
Sheffield United Football Club, Bramhall Ln S2 4SU
e-mail: orla.watt@millenniumhotels.co.uk
dir: M1 junct 33/A57. At Park Square rdbt follow A61 (Chesterfield Rd). Follow brown signs for Bramall Lane

This modern and stylish hotel is situated in the centre of Sheffield. Located next to the home of Sheffield United FC it offers contemporary public areas and its award-winning restaurant to the ground floor. A well-equipped gym is situated on the first floor. Bedrooms are spacious and comfortable. Ample parking is a plus in this central location.

Rooms 158 (23 fmly) **S** £69-£179; **D** £79-£199* **Facilities** STV FTV Wi-fi **Conf** Class 180 Board 40 Thtr 400 Del from £99 to £149 **Services** Lift Air con **Parking** 150 **Notes** LB ®

Whitley Hall Hotel

★★★★ 78% ®® HOTEL

☎ 0114 245 4444 & 246 0456 🖹 0114 245 5414
Elliott Ln, Grenoside S35 8NR
e-mail: reservations@whitleyhall.com
web: www.whitleyhall.com
dir: A61 past football ground, 2m, right just before Norfolk Arms, left at bottom of hill. Hotel on left

This 16th-century house stands in 20 acres of landscaped grounds and gardens. Public rooms are full of character and interesting architectural features, and command the best views of the gardens. The individually styled bedrooms are furnished in keeping with the country house setting, as are the oak-panelled restaurant and bar.

Rooms 32 (3 annexe) (2 fmly) (8 GF) **S** fr £80.25; **D** fr £90.50 (incl. bkfst)* **Facilities** STV FTV Wi-fi **Conf** Class 50 Board 34 Thtr 70 Del from £144* **Services** Lift **Parking** 100 **Notes** LB ® Civ Wed 100

Doubletree by Hilton

★★★★ 77% ® HOTEL

☎ 0114 282 9988 🖹 0114 237 8140
Chesterfield Road South S8 8BW
dir: From N: M1 junct 33, A630 Sheffield. A61 Chesterfield. After Graves Tennis Centre follow A6/Chesterfield/M1 South signs. Hotel 200yds on left. From S: M1 junct 29, A617 Chesterfield. Follow A61/Sheffield signs. After City of Sheffield boundary, double back at rdbt, hotel on left

A large modern hotel located on the ring road. The bedrooms are spacious and well equipped and include family rooms, suites and executive rooms. Other facilities include a leisure club, meeting rooms and ample secure parking.

Rooms 95 (20 GF) **S** £65-£135; **D** £65-£135 (incl. bkfst)* **Facilities** Spa STV FTV ⓢ Gym Steam room Sauna Xmas New Year Wi-fi **Conf** Class 200 Board 80 Thtr 500 Del from £95 to £145 **Services** Lift **Parking** 260 **Notes** LB ® Civ Wed 300

Mercure St Paul's Hotel & Spa

Mercure

★★★★ 77% HOTEL

☎ 0114 278 2000 🖹 0870 122 6586
119 Norfolk St S1 2JE
e-mail: h6628@accor.com
web: www.mercure.com
dir: M1 junct 33, 4th exit at rdbt, left at 1st lights, right at 2nd in front of Crucible Theatre

This modern, luxury hotel enjoys a central location close to key attractions in the city. Open-plan public areas are situated in a steel and glass atrium and include a popular Champagne bar, the Yard Restaurant and Zucca, an Italian Bistro. Bedrooms are superbly presented and richly furnished. The Vital health and beauty treatment centre provides a fabulous thermal suite.

Rooms 163 (40 fmly) **Facilities** Spa ⓢ Sauna Steam room Snail shower Ice fountain Fitness classes Xmas New Year Wi-fi **Conf** Class 400 Board 30 Thtr 600 **Services** Lift Air con **Notes** ® Civ Wed 350

S

Kenwood Hall

★★★★ 76% HOTEL

☎ 0114 258 3811 🖷 0114 255 4744
Kenwood Rd S7 1NQ
dir: A61 (Barnsley ring road) into St Mary's Rd. Straight over rdbt, left into London Rd, right at lights. 2nd exit at 2nd rdbt, hotel ahead

A smart, modern hotel peacefully located in a residential suburb a few miles from the city centre. The stylishly decorated bedrooms are spacious, quiet and well equipped. The hotel also has an extensive range of leisure and meeting facilities, and secure parking is located in extensive landscaped gardens.

Rooms 114 (8 fmly) **S** £61-£131; **D** £71-£141 (incl. bkfst)* **Facilities** STV Fishing Gym Steam room Sauna Solarium Treatment rooms New Year Wi-fi **Conf** Class 100 Board 60 Thtr 250 Del from £118 to £179* **Services** Lift **Parking** 150 **Notes** LB Civ Wed 260

Novotel Sheffield Centre

★★★★ 70% HOTEL

☎ 0114 278 1781 🖷 0114 278 7744
50 Arundel Gate S1 2PR
e-mail: h1348-re@accor.com
web: www.novotel.com
dir: Between Registry Office & Crucible/Lyceum Theatres, follow signs to Town Hall/Theatres & Hallam University

In the heart of the city centre, this hotel has stylish public areas including a very modern restaurant, indoor swimming pool and a range of meeting rooms. Spacious bedrooms are suitable for family occupation, and the Novation rooms are ideal for business users.

Rooms 144 (136 fmly) **Facilities** STV FTV Gym Steam room Xmas New Year Wi-fi **Conf** Class 180 Board 100 Thtr 220 **Services** Lift Air con **Parking** 60 **Notes** Civ Wed 180

Staindrop Lodge

★★★ 80% HOTEL

☎ 0114 284 3111 🖷 0114 284 3110
Lane End, Chapeltown S35 3UH
e-mail: info@staindroplodge.co.uk
dir: M1 junct 35, A629 for 1m, straight over 1st rdbt, right at 2nd rdbt, hotel approx 0.5m on right

This hotel, bar and brasserie offers smart modern public areas and accommodation. An art deco theme continues throughout the open-plan public rooms and the comfortably appointed, spacious bedrooms. Service is relaxed and friendly, and all-day menus are available.

Rooms 37 (5 annexe) (6 fmly) (3 GF) **Facilities** STV Wi-fi **Conf** Class 60 Board 40 Thtr 80 **Services** Air con **Parking** 80 **Notes** Civ Wed 80

Best Western Mosborough Hall

★★★ 80% HOTEL

☎ 0114 248 4353 🖷 0114 247 9759
High St, Mosborough S20 5EA
e-mail: hotel@mosboroughhall.co.uk
web: www.mosboroughhall.co.uk
dir: M1 junct 30, A6135 towards Sheffield. Follow Eckington/Mosborough signs 2m. Sharp bend at top of hill, hotel on right

This 16th-century, Grade II listed manor house is set in gardens not far from the M1 and is convenient for the city centre. The bedrooms offer very high quality and good amenities; some are very spacious. There is a galleried lounge and conservatory bar, and freshly prepared dishes are served in the traditional style dining room.

Rooms 43 (4 fmly) (16 GF) **S** £56-£95; **D** £56-£95* **Facilities** FTV Spa & beauty treatments Xmas New Year Wi-fi **Conf** Class 125 Board 70 Thtr 300 Del from £125 to £175* **Parking** 100 **Notes** LB Civ Wed 250

Best Western Cutlers Hotel

★★★ 71% HOTEL

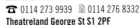

☎ 0114 273 9939 🖷 0114 276 8332
Theatreland George St S1 2PF
e-mail: enquiries@cutlershotel.co.uk
dir: M1 junct 33. At Park Sq follow signs to City Centre & Theatres. At top of Commercial St, left into Arundel Gate. Into right lane, at lights right into Norfolk St, 2nd right into George St. Hotel 50mtrs on left

Situated right in the heart of the city, near the theatres and only minutes away from the rail station. Public areas include a lower ground floor bistro, and room service is available if required. Discounted overnight parking is provided in the nearby public car park.

Rooms 45 (2 fmly) **Facilities** STV FTV Xmas New Year Wi-fi **Conf** Class 20 Board 25 Thtr 80 **Services** Lift **Notes** LB Civ Wed 60

Ibis Sheffield City Centre

BUDGET HOTEL

☎ 0114 241 9600 🖷 0114 241 9610
Shude Hill S1 2AR
e-mail: H2891@accor.com
web: www.ibishotel.com
dir: M1 junct 33, follow signs to Sheffield City Centre (A630/A57), at rdbt take 5th exit, signed Ponds Forge, for hotel

Modern, budget hotel offering comfortable accommodation in bright and practical bedrooms. Breakfast is self-service and dinner is available in the restaurant. See also the Hotel Groups pages.

Rooms 95 (15 fmly) (3 GF) (8 smoking) **S** £40-£89; **D** £40-£89*

Premier Inn Sheffield (Arena)

BUDGET HOTEL

☎ 0871 527 8964 🖷 0871 527 8965
Attercliffe Common Rd S9 2LU
dir: M1 junct 34, follow signs to city centre. Hotel opposite Arena

High quality, budget accommodation ideal for both families and business travellers. Spacious, en suite bedrooms feature tea and coffee making facilities, and Freeview TV in most hotels. Internet access and Wi-fi are available for a small fee. The adjacent family restaurant features a wide and varied menu. See also the Hotel Groups pages.

Rooms 61 **D** £60-£64*

Premier Inn Sheffield City Centre

BUDGET HOTEL

☎ 0871 527 8972 🖷 0871 527 8973
Young St, St Marys Gate S1 4LA
dir: M1 junct 33, A630, A57 follow Sheffield City Centre signs. At Park Square rdbt 3rd exit signed A61/ Chesterfield. At Granville Square right onto A61 signed Ring Rd. Keep in left lane. At rdbt 3rd exit signed A621. Left into Cumberland St. Left into South Lane. Right into Young St

Rooms 122 **D** £52*

S

SHEFFIELD *continued*

Premier Inn Sheffield City Centre Angel St

BUDGET HOTEL

☎ 0871 527 8970 📠 0871 527 8971
Angel St, (Corner of Bank Street) S3 8LN
dir: M1 junct 33, follow city centre, A630, A57 signs. At Park Square rdbt 4th exit (A61 Barnsley). Left at 4th lights into Snig Hill, right at lights into Bank St

Rooms 160 **D** £49*

Premier Inn Sheffield (Meadowhall)

BUDGET HOTEL

☎ 0871 527 8966 📠 0871 527 8967
Sheffield Rd, Meadowhall S9 2YL
dir: On A6178 approx 6m from city centre

Rooms 103 **D** £60-£64*

SHEPPERTON
Surrey

See LONDON SECTION plan 1 A1

Holiday Inn London - Shepperton

★★★★ 71% HOTEL

☎ 0871 942 9187 & 01932 899900
📠 01932 245231
Felix Ln TW17 8NP
e-mail: hishepperton@qmh-hotels.com
web: www.holidayinn.co.uk
dir: M3 junct 1, B375 to Lower Sunbury, 5th exit Green St, right at T-junct. Felix Ln 1.5m on left

This hotel has a range of modern, well-equipped leisure and conference facilities. Its hidden, tranquil location also makes it ideal for a family break. The spacious bedrooms are pleasantly appointed and have air conditioning. The restaurant offers a carte menu, and the bar provides an alternative dining venue.

Rooms 185 (11 fmly) (37 GF) **Facilities** STV Gym Beauty salon Sauna Wi-fi **Conf** Class 60 Board 40 Thtr 120 **Services** Lift Air con **Parking** 160 **Notes** Civ Wed 80

Harrisons Hotel

★★★ 66% HOTEL

☎ 01932 227320 📠 01932 226668
Rusell Rd TW17 9HX
e-mail: apreston@martynleisure.co.uk

Being located on the banks of the Thames, close to a number of visitor attractions and major transport networks makes this hotel suitable for both the leisure and business traveller. The tastefully appointed bedrooms and bathrooms are appointed to a high standard and have guest comfort very much in mind. The Bar and Bistro offers contemporary dining with popular favourites available for all tastes. Parking with CCTV is located nearby.

Rooms 32 **Conf** Class 45 Board 30 Thtr 100

SHERBORNE
Dorset **Map 4 ST61**

The Grange at Oborne

★★★ 80% HOTEL

☎ 01935 813463 📠 01935 817464
Oborne DT9 4LA
e-mail: reception@thegrange.co.uk
web: www.thegrangeatoborne.co.uk
dir: Exit A30, follow signs through village

Set in beautiful gardens in a quiet hamlet, this 200-year-old, family run, country-house hotel has a wealth of charm and character. It offers friendly hospitality together with attentive service. Bedrooms are comfortable and tastefully appointed. Public areas are elegantly furnished and the popular restaurant offers a good selection of dishes.

Rooms 18 (3 fmly) (2 GF) **S** £88-£135; **D** £105-£165 (incl. bkfst) **Facilities** STV Xmas New Year Wi-fi **Conf** Class 40 Board 30 Thtr 80 Del from £148.95 to £159.95* **Parking** 45 **Notes** LB Civ Wed 120

Eastbury

★★★ 78% HOTEL

☎ 01935 813131 📠 01935 817296
Long St DT9 3BY
e-mail: enquiries@theeastburyhotel.co.uk
web: www.theeastburyhotel.co.uk
dir: From A30 W'bound, left into North Rd, then St Swithin's, left at bottom, hotel 800yds on right

Much of the original Georgian charm and elegance is maintained at this smart, comfortable hotel. Just five minutes' stroll from the abbey and close to the town centre, the Eastbury's friendly and attentive staff ensure a relaxed and enjoyable stay. Award-winning cuisine is served in the attractive dining room, overlooking the walled garden, with an alfresco bistro option also available.

Rooms 23 (1 fmly) (3 GF) **Facilities** FTV New Year **Conf** Class 40 Board 28 Thtr 80 **Parking** 30 **Notes** Civ Wed 80

The Sherborne Hotel

★★ 69% HOTEL

☎ 01935 813191 📠 01935 816493
Horsecastles Ln DT9 6BB
e-mail: info@sherbornehotel.co.uk
dir: At junct of A30 & A352

This hotel is in a quiet location with attractive grounds yet only just off the main road. Bedrooms are spacious and well equipped. The open-plan lounge and bar area are comfortable and satellite TV is available. Cuisine offers a good range of choice and the dining room looks out to the garden.

Rooms 60 (24 GF) **S** £39-£69; **D** £39-£89 (incl. bkfst)* **Facilities** FTV Concessionary swimming rates at leisure centre opposite hotel Xmas New Year Wi-fi **Conf** Class 35 Board 30 Thtr 80 Del from £60 to £90* **Parking** 90 **Notes** LB

SHERINGHAM
Norfolk **Map 13 TG14**

Dales Country House Hotel

★★★★ 83% HOTEL

☎ 01263 824555 📠 01263 822647
Lodge Hill, Upper Sheringham NR26 8TJ
e-mail: dales@mackenziehotels.com
dir: On B1157 1m S of Sheringham, from A148 turn at entrance to Sheringham Park, 0.5m, hotel on left

Superb Grade II listed building situated in extensive landscaped grounds on the edge of Sheringham Park. The attractive public rooms are full of original character; they include a choice of lounges as well as an intimate restaurant and a cosy lounge bar. The spacious bedrooms are individually decorated with co-ordinated soft furnishings and many thoughtful touches.

Rooms 21 (5 GF) **Facilities** Giant garden games (chess & Jenga) Xmas New Year Wi-fi **Conf** Class 20 Board 27 Thtr 40 Del from £115* **Services** Lift **Parking** 50 **Notes** No children 14yrs

Roman Camp Inn

★★★ 79% SMALL HOTEL

☎ 01263 838291 📠 01263 837071
Holt Rd, Aylmerton NR11 8QD
e-mail: enquiries@romancampinn.co.uk
web: www.romancampinn.co.uk
dir: On A148 between Sheringham & Cromer, approx 1.5m from Cromer

A smartly presented hotel ideally placed for touring the north Norfolk coastline. The property provides spacious, pleasantly decorated bedrooms with a good range of useful facilities. Public rooms include a smart conservatory-style restaurant, a comfortable open-plan lounge/bar and a dining area.

Rooms 15 (1 fmly) (10 GF) **S** £60-£70; **D** £100-£120 (incl. bkfst)* **Facilities** Free use of nearby leisure complex & pool Wi-fi **Conf** Class 12 Board 16 Thtr 25 **Parking** 50 **Notes** LB ⊗ Closed 25-26 Dec

See advert on this page

Beaumaris Hotel

★★ 79% HOTEL

☎ 01263 822370 📠 01263 821421
South St NR26 8LL
e-mail: beauhotel@aol.com
web: www.thebeaumarishotel.co.uk
dir: Exit A148, left at rdbt, 1st right over rail bridge, 1st left by church, 1st left into South St

Situated in a peaceful side road just a short walk from the beach, town centre and golf course. This friendly hotel has been owned and run by the same family for over 60 years and continues to provide comfortable, thoughtfully equipped accommodation throughout. Public rooms feature a smart dining room, a cosy bar and two quiet lounges.

Rooms 21 (5 fmly) (2 GF) **S** £50-£60; **D** £100-£120 (incl. bkfst) **Facilities** FTV **Parking** 25 **Notes** LB ⊗ Closed mid Dec-1 Mar

S

SHIFNAL Map 10 SJ70
Shropshire

Park House

★★★★ 77% ◎ HOTEL

☎ 01952 460128 📠 01952 461658
Park St TF11 9BA
e-mail: reception@parkhousehotel.net
dir: M54 junct 4, A464 (Wolverhampton road) for approx 2m, under railway bridge, hotel 100yds on left

This hotel was created from what were originally two country houses of very different architectural styles. Located on the edge of the historic market town, it offers guests easy access to motorway networks, a choice of banqueting and meeting rooms, plus leisure facilities. Butlers Bar and Restaurant is the setting for imaginative food. Service is friendly and attentive.

Rooms 54 (16 annexe) (4 fmly) (8 GF) (4 smoking) **Facilities** STV FTV Gym Steam room Sauna Xmas New Year Wi-fi **Conf** Class 80 Board 40 Thtr 160 Del from £99 to £132.50* **Services** Lift **Parking** 90 **Notes** Civ Wed 200

Haughton Hall

★★★ 71% HOTEL

☎ 01952 468300 📠 01952 468313
Haughton Ln TF11 8HG
e-mail: reservations@haughtonhall.com
dir: M54 junct 4 take A464 into Shifnal. Turn left into Haughton Lane, hotel 600yds on left

This listed building dates back to 1718 and stands in open parkland close to the town. It is well geared for the conference trade and has a 9-hole par 4 golf course, a fishing lake and a leisure club with swimming pool, sauna, jacuzzi, steam room and gym. Oliver's Restaurant looks out over the grounds and offers extensive menus. The comfortable, well-equipped bedrooms include suites, one with a four-poster bed.

Rooms 36 (6 annexe) (5 fmly) (3 GF) **Facilities** FTV supervised 9 Fishing Gym Steam room Therapy room Solarium Treatment room Xmas New Year Wi-fi **Conf** Class 60 Board 25 Thtr 120 **Parking** 60 **Notes** Civ Wed 120

SHIPLEY Map 19 SE13
West Yorkshire

Hollins Hall, A Marriott Hotel & Country Club

★★★★ 76% ◎ HOTEL

☎ 01274 530053 📠 01274 534251
Hollins Hill, Baildon BD17 7QW
e-mail: mhrs.lbags.frontdesk@marriotthotels.com
web: www.marriotthollinshall.co.uk
dir: From A650 follow signs to Salt Mill. At lights in Shipley take A6038. Hotel 3m on left

The hotel is located close to Leeds and Bradford and is easily accessible from motorway networks. Built in the 19th-century, this Elizabethan-style building is set within 200 acres of grounds and offers extensive leisure facilities, including a golf course and gym. Bedrooms are attractively decorated and have a range of additional facilities.

Rooms 122 (50 fmly) (25 GF) **Facilities** Spa supervised 18 Putt green Gym Dance studio Swimming lessons **Conf** Class 90 Board 80 Thtr 200 Del from £135 to £155* **Services** Lift **Parking** 260 **Notes** Civ Wed 70

Ibis Bradford Shipley

ibis HOTEL

BUDGET HOTEL

☎ 01274 589333 📠 01274 589444
Quayside, Salts Mill Rd BD18 3ST
e-mail: H3158@accor.com
web: www.ibishotel.com
dir: Follow tourist signs for Salts Mill. Follow A650 signs through Bradford for approx 5m to Shipley

Modern, budget hotel offering comfortable accommodation in bright and practical bedrooms. Breakfast is self-service and dinner is available in the restaurant. See also the Hotel Groups pages.

Rooms 78 (20 fmly) (22 GF) **S** £29-£51; **D** £29-£51* **Conf** Class 16 Board 18 Thtr 20 Del from £70 to £140*

SHIPSTON ON STOUR Map 10 SO24
Warwickshire

The Old Mill

◎◎ RESTAURANT WITH ROOMS

☎ 01608 661421 📠 01608 610600
Mill St CV36 4AW
e-mail: jl@theoldmillshipston.co.uk
web: www.theoldmillshipston.com

This former mill sits of the banks of the fast flowing River Stour and is close to the centre of the pretty village of Shipston. The individually styled bedrooms are beautifully presented and very well equipped. The cosy bar has many original features and the potbelly stove creates a warm welcoming atmosphere. No stay here is complete with a visit to the award-winning restaurant and guests are assured of warm welcome and attentive service.

Rooms 5 (2 fmly)

SHREWSBURY Map 15 SJ41
Shropshire

See also **Church Stretton**

Albright Hussey Manor Hotel & Restaurant

★★★★ 75% ◎◎ HOTEL

☎ 01939 290571 & 290523 📠 01939 291143
Ellesmere Rd SY4 3AF
e-mail: info@albrighthussey.co.uk
web: www.albrighthussey.co.uk
dir: 2.5m N of Shrewsbury on A528, follow signs for Ellesmere

First mentioned in the Domesday Book, this enchanting medieval manor house is complete with a moat. Bedrooms are situated in either the sumptuously appointed main house or in the more modern wing. The intimate restaurant displays an abundance of original features and there is also a comfortable cocktail bar and lounge.

Rooms 26 (4 fmly) (8 GF) **Facilities** Xmas New Year Wi-fi **Conf** Class 180 Board 80 Thtr 250 **Parking** 100 **Notes** Civ Wed 180

Mercure Albrighton Hall Hotel & Spa

Mercure

★★★★ 74% COUNTRY HOUSE HOTEL

☎ 01939 291000 📠 01939 291123
Albrighton SY4 3AG
e-mail: H6629@accor.com
web: www.mercure.com
dir: From S: M6 junct 10a to M54 to end. From N: M6 junct 12 to M5 then M54. Follow signs Harlescott & Ellesmere to A528

Dating back to 1630, this former ancestral home is set in 15 acres of attractive gardens. Rooms are generally spacious and the stable rooms are particularly popular. Elegant public rooms have rich oak panelling and there is a modern, well-equipped health and fitness centre.

Rooms 87 (16 annexe) (6 fmly) (21 GF) **Facilities** Spa STV Gym Squash Beauty treatment rooms Thermal suite Relax room Spray tan Aerobics Xmas New Year Wi-fi **Conf** Class 150 Board 80 Thtr 300 Del from £129 to £159 **Services** Lift **Parking** 200 **Notes** Civ Wed 250

Rowton Castle Hotel

★★★ 88% ® HOTEL

☎ 01743 884044 📠 01743 884949
Halfway House SY5 9EP
e-mail: post@rowtoncastle.com
web: www.rowtoncastle.com
dir: From A5 near Shrewsbury take A458 to Welshpool. Hotel 4m on right

Standing in 17 acres of grounds where a castle has stood for nearly 800 years, this Grade II listed building dates in parts back to 1696. Many original features remain, including the oak panelling in the restaurant and a magnificent carved oak fireplace. Most bedrooms are spacious and all have modern facilities; some have four-poster beds. The hotel has a well deserved reputation for its food and is understandably a popular venue for weddings.

Rooms 19 (3 fmly) **Facilities** Wi-fi **Conf** Class 30 Board 30 Thtr 80 **Parking** 100 **Notes** ® Civ Wed 110

Prince Rupert

★★★ 83% HOTEL

☎ 01743 499955 📠 01743 357306
Butcher Row SY1 1UQ
e-mail: reservations@prince-rupert-hotel.co.uk
web: www.prince-rupert-hotel.co.uk
dir: Follow town centre signs, over English Bridge & Wyle Cop Hill. Right into Fish St, hotel 200yds

Parts of this popular town centre hotel date back to medieval times and many bedrooms have exposed beams and other original features. Luxury suites, family rooms and rooms with four-poster beds are all available. As an alternative to the main Royalist Restaurant, diners have a less formal option in Chambers, a popular brasserie. The Camellias Tea Rooms are adjacent providing snacks and afternoon teas. The hotel's valet parking service is also commendable.

Rooms 70 (4 fmly) **S** £79-£89; **D** £105-£175 (incl. bkfst) **Facilities** FTV Gym Weight training room Steam shower Sauna Snooker room Xmas New Year Wi-fi **Conf** Class 80 Board 40 Thtr 120 Del from £120 to £140 **Services** Lift **Parking** 70 **Notes** LB ®

The Lion

★★★ 78% ®® HOTEL

☎ 01743 353107 📠 01743 352744
Wyle Cop SY1 1UY
e-mail: info@thelionhotelshrewsbury.com
dir: From S cross English Bridge, fork right, hotel at hill top on left. From N follow Castle St into Dogpole

Sympathetically renovated in recent years, this Grade I listed, 16th-century former coach house boasts George IV, Charles Dickens (who wrote *Pickwick Papers* here) and Paganini as some of its illustrious visitors. Bedrooms are all different and many retain original features. There is a choice of comfortable lounges, the magnificent Adams Room, licensed for civil weddings, and Sam Hayward Room Restaurant, the setting for imaginative cooking.

Rooms 59 (3 fmly) **Facilities** Beauty & treatment service Xmas New Year Wi-fi **Conf** Class 80 Board 60 Thtr 180 **Services** Lift **Parking** 59 **Notes** ® Civ Wed 200

Lion & Pheasant Hotel

★★★ 77% ®® TOWN HOUSE HOTEL

☎ 01743 770345 📠 01743 770350
49-50 Wyle Cop SY1 1XJ
e-mail: info@lionandpheasant.co.uk

A city centre, 16th-century property stands on Wyle Cop which is part of the historic centre of Shrewsbury. A total refurbishment has now been completed; and the result is a minimalist style with natural materials such as limed oak, linens and silks. The high standard bedrooms include twin, double and family rooms. Award-winning food is offered in the first-floor restaurant and also in the ground-floor bar area.

Rooms 22 (1 fmly) **S** £75-£120; **D** £95-£175 (incl. bkfst)* **Facilities** FTV Wi-fi **Conf** Class 30 Board 30 Thtr 30 Del from £120 to £150* **Parking** 15 **Notes** ®

Mytton & Mermaid

★★★ 77% ®® HOTEL

☎ 01743 761220 📠 01743 761292
Atcham SY5 6QG
e-mail: reception@myttonandmermaid.co.uk
web: www.myttonandmermaid.co.uk
dir: From Shrewsbury over old bridge in Atcham. Hotel opposite main entrance to Attingham Park

Convenient for Shrewsbury, this former coaching inn enjoys a pleasant location beside the River Severn. Some bedrooms, including family suites, are in a converted stable block adjacent to the hotel. There is a large lounge bar, a comfortable lounge, and a brasserie that has gained a well-deserved local reputation for the quality of its food.

Rooms 18 (7 annexe) (1 fmly) (6 GF) **S** £85-£90; **D** £110-£175 (incl. bkfst)* **Facilities** Fishing ♫ New Year Wi-fi **Conf** Class 24 Board 28 Thtr 70 Del from £150 to £200* **Parking** 50 **Notes** LB ® Closed 25 Dec Civ Wed 80

Lord Hill

★★★ 74% HOTEL

☎ 01743 232601 📠 01743 369734
Abbey Foregate SY2 6AX
e-mail: reception@thelordhill.co.uk
web: www.thelordhill.co.uk
dir: From M54 take A5, at 1st rdbt left, 2nd rdbt take 4th exit into London Rd. At next rdbt (Lord Hill Column) take 3rd exit, hotel 300yds on left

This pleasant, attractively appointed hotel is located close to the town centre. Most of the modern bedrooms are set in a separate purpose-built property, but those in the main building include one with a four-poster, as well as full suites. Public areas include a conservatory restaurant and spacious function suites.

Rooms 35 (24 annexe) (2 fmly) (8 GF) **Facilities** FTV Wi-fi **Conf** Class 180 Board 180 Thtr 250 **Parking** 110 **Notes** Civ Wed 250

SHREWSBURY ***continued***

Abbots Mead Hotel

★★ 74% METRO HOTEL

☎ 01743 235281 📠 01743 369133
9 St Julian's Friars SY1 1XL
e-mail: res@abbotsmeadhotel.co.uk
dir: From S into town, 2nd left after English Bridge

This well maintained Georgian town house is located in a quiet cul-de-sac, near the English Bridge and close to both the River Severn and town centre with its many restaurants. Bedrooms are compact, neatly decorated and well equipped. Two lounges are available in addition to an attractive dining room, the setting for breakfasts, and dinner parties by prior arrangement.

Rooms 16 (2 fmly) **S** £59-£70; **D** £70-£80 (incl. bkfst)* **Facilities** Wi-fi **Parking** 10 **Notes** Closed certain days at Xmas

Premier Inn Shrewsbury (Harmers Hill)

BUDGET HOTEL

☎ 0871 527 8974 📠 0871 527 8975
Wem Rd, Harmer Hill SY4 3DS
dir: M54 junct 7, A5 signed Telford for approx 7m, at rdbt take A49, approx 3m. At next 2 rdbts 2nd exit, at next rdbt 4th exit signed Ellesmere & A528. In approx 3m hotel on left

High quality, budget accommodation ideal for both families and business travellers. Spacious, en suite bedrooms feature tea and coffee making facilities, and Freeview TV in most hotels. Internet access and Wi-fi are available for a small fee. The adjacent family restaurant features a wide and varied menu. See also the Hotel Groups pages.

Rooms 20 **D** £55*

Drapers Hall

@@ RESTAURANT WITH ROOMS

☎ 01743 344679
10 Saint Mary's Place SY1 1DZ
e-mail: goodfood@drapershallrestaurant.co.uk

This 16th-century timber-framed property is situated in the heart of the market town of Shrewsbury. It provides high quality accommodation, including two suites, with modern facilities. Careful renovation of the original beams and wood panels together with beautiful wooden furniture has created a harmony of the past and present. Accomplished dining, headed up by Nigel Huxley, can be enjoyed in the main restaurant, Huxleys at Drapers Hall.

Rooms 4 (2 fmly)

Mad Jack's Restaurant & Bar

@ RESTAURANT WITH ROOMS

☎ 01743 358870 & 761220 📠 01743 344422
15 Saint Mary's St SY1 1EQ
e-mail: info@madjacks.uk.com
dir: Follow one-way system around town, opposite St Mary's church

This fine property is located in the heart of the town. Its name comes from a eccentric squire in the 18th century who squandered a fortune and then landed in jail for his drunken and riotous behaviour. The four individually designed bedrooms, including a suite, are very comfortable and have spacious and contemporary bathrooms. Downstairs the award-winning, vibrant bar and restaurant specialises in British food with a classic twist. Breakfast offers a quality range of dishes. Secure parking is available in a nearby public car park.

Rooms 4 (1 fmly)

SIDLESHAM West Sussex — **Map 5 SZ89**

The Crab & Lobster

@ RESTAURANT WITH ROOMS

☎ 01243 641233
Mill Ln PO20 7NB
e-mail: enquiries@crab-lobster.co.uk
dir: A27 onto B2145 signed Selsey. 1st left after garage at Sidlesham into Rookery Ln to Crab & Lobster

Hidden away on the south coast near Pagham Harbour and only a short drive from Chichester is the stylish Crab & Lobster. Bedrooms are superbly appointed, and bathrooms are a feature with luxury toiletries and powerful 'raindrop' showers. Guests can enjoy lunch or dinner in the smart restaurant where the menu offers a range of locally caught fresh fish amongst other regionally-sourced, seasonal produce.

Rooms 4

SIDMOUTH Devon — **Map 3 SY18**

Victoria

Brend Hotels

★★★★ 83% @ HOTEL

☎ 01395 512651 📠 01395 579154
The Esplanade EX10 8RY
e-mail: reservations@victoriahotel.co.uk
web: www.victoriahotel.co.uk
dir: On seafront

This imposing building, with manicured gardens, is situated overlooking the town. Wonderful sea views can be enjoyed from many of the comfortable bedrooms and elegant lounges. With indoor and outdoor leisure facilities, the hotel caters to a year-round clientele. Carefully prepared meals are served in the refined atmosphere of the restaurant. The staff provide a professional and friendly service.

Rooms 65 (6 fmly) **S** £135-£155; **D** £175-£360* **Facilities** FTV Putt green Sauna Snooker room Games room Spa bath Treatment room Xmas New Year Wi-fi Child facilities **Conf** Thtr 60 **Services** Lift **Parking** 104 **Notes** LB

See advert on opposite page

S

SIDMOUTH *continued*

Riviera

★★★★ 82% HOTEL

☎ 01395 515201 📠 01395 577775
The Esplanade EX10 8AY
e-mail: enquiries@hotelriviera.co.uk
web: www.hotelriviera.co.uk
dir: M5 junct 30 & follow A3052

Overlooking the sea and close to the town centre, the Riviera is a fine example of Regency architecture. The large number of guests that become regular visitors here are testament to the high standards of service and hospitality offered. The front-facing bedrooms benefit from wonderful sea views, and the daily-changing menu places an emphasis on fresh, local produce.

Rooms 26 (6 fmly) **S** £132-£194; **D** £264-£368 (incl. bkfst & dinner)* **Facilities** FTV Xmas New Year Wi-fi **Conf** Class 60 Board 30 Thtr 85 **Services** Lift **Parking** 26 **Notes** LB

See advert on opposite page

Belmont Hotel

★★★★ 75% HOTEL

☎ 01395 512555 📠 01395 579101
The Esplanade EX10 8RX
e-mail: reservations@belmont-hotel.co.uk
web: www.belmont-hotel.co.uk
dir: On seafront

Prominently positioned on the seafront just a few minutes' walk from the town centre, this traditional hotel has many returning guests. A choice of comfortable lounges provides ample space for relaxation, and the air-conditioned restaurant has a pianist playing most evenings. Bedrooms are attractively furnished and many have fine views over the esplanade. Leisure facilities are available at the adjacent sister hotel, The Victoria.

Rooms 50 (4 fmly) (2 GF) **S** £120-£160; **D** £150-£235* **Facilities** STV Putt green Leisure facilities available at sister hotel Xmas New Year Wi-fi Child facilities **Conf** Thtr 50 **Services** Lift **Parking** 45 **Notes** LB Civ Wed 110

See advert on page 443

Westcliff

★★★ 79% HOTEL

☎ 01395 513252 📠 01395 578203
Manor Rd EX10 8RU
e-mail: stay@westcliffhotel.co.uk
web: www.westcliffhotel.co.uk
dir: Exit A3052 to Sidmouth then to seafront & esplanade, turn right, hotel directly ahead

This charming hotel is ideally located within walking distance of Sidmouth's elegant promenade and beaches. The spacious lounges and the cocktail bar open onto a terrace which leads to the pool and croquet lawn. Bedrooms, several with balconies and glorious sea views, are spacious and comfortable, whilst the restaurant offers a choice of well-prepared dishes.

Rooms 40 (1 fmly) (5 GF) **Facilities** FTV Putt green Pool table Table tennis Xmas New Year Wi-fi **Conf** Class 20 Board 15 Thtr 30 **Services** Lift **Parking** 40 **Notes** Civ Wed 80

Royal Glen

★★★ 74% HOTEL

☎ 01395 513221 & 513456 📠 01395 514922
Glen Rd EX10 8RW
e-mail: info@royalglenhotel.co.uk
dir: A303 to Honiton, A375 to Sidford, follow seafront signs, right onto esplanade, right at end into Glen Rd

This historic 17th-century, Grade I listed hotel has been owned by the same family for several generations. The comfortable bedrooms are furnished in period style. Guests may use the well-maintained gardens and a heated indoor pool, and can enjoy well-prepared food in the elegant dining room.

Rooms 32 (3 fmly) (3 GF) **S** £48-£72; **D** £96-£144 (incl. bkfst)* **Facilities** FTV Gym Wi-fi **Services** Lift **Parking** 22 **Notes** LB Closed Dec-1 Feb

Bedford Hotel

★★★ 73% HOTEL

☎ 01395 513047 & 0797 394 0671
📠 01395 578563
Esplanade EX10 8NR
e-mail: info@bedfordhotelsidmouth.co.uk
web: www.bedfordhotelsidmouth.co.uk
dir: M5 junct 30/A3052 & to Sidmouth. Hotel at centre of Esplanade

Situated on the seafront, this long established, family-run hotel provides a warm welcome and relaxing atmosphere. Bedrooms are well appointed and many have the added bonus of wonderful sea views. Public areas combine character and comfort with a choice of lounges in which to relax. In addition to the hotel dining room, Pyne's bar and restaurant offers an interesting range of dishes in a convivial environment.

Rooms 37 (1 GF) **Facilities** Xmas **Services** Lift **Parking** 6

Kingswood & Devoran Hotel

★★★ 73% HOTEL

☎ 01395 516367 & 08000 481731
📠 01395 513185
The Esplanade EX10 8AX
e-mail: kingswoodanddevoran@hotels-sidmouth.co.uk
web: www.hotels-sidmouth.co.uk
dir: M5 junct 30, A3052 signed Sidmouth on right, follow Station Rd down to Esplanade

This seafront hotel continues to offer friendly hospitality and service. Many bedrooms enjoy the sea views; all are well appointed and have smart bathrooms. Cuisine is pleasant and offers enjoyable dining featuring freshly prepared dishes.

Rooms 50 (8 fmly) (2 GF) **S** £85-£101; **D** £118-£168 (incl. bkfst & dinner)* **Facilities** FTV Xmas Wi-fi **Conf** Class 30 Board 20 Thtr 60 Del from £ to £120* **Services** Lift **Parking** 23 **Notes** LB Closed 27 Dec-10 Feb

Royal York & Faulkner

★★ 80% HOTEL

☎ 01395 513043 & 0800 220714
📠 01395 577472
The Esplanade EX10 8AZ
e-mail: stay@royalyorkhotel.co.uk
web: www.royalyorkhotel.co.uk
dir: M5 junct 30 take A3052, 10m to Sidmouth, hotel in centre of Esplanade

This seafront hotel, owned and run by the same family for over 60 years, maintains its Regency charm and grandeur. The attractive bedrooms vary in size, and many have balconies and sea views. Public rooms are spacious and traditional dining is offered, alongside Blinis Café-Bar, which is more contemporary in style and offers coffees, lunch and afternoon teas. The spa facilities include a hydrotherapy pool, steam room, sauna and a variety of treatments.

Rooms 70 (2 annexe) (8 fmly) (5 GF) **S** £57.50-£90.50; **D** £115-£181 (incl. bkfst & dinner)* **Facilities** **Spa** FTV Steam cabin Snooker table Sauna Xmas New Year Wi-fi **Services** Lift **Parking** 20 **Notes** LB Closed Jan

Hunters Moon

★★ 79% HOTEL

☎ 01395 513380 📠 01395 514270
Sid Rd EX10 9AA
e-mail: huntersmoon.hotel@virgin.net
dir: From Exeter on A3052 to Sidford, right at lights into Sidmouth, 1.5m, at cinema turn left. Hotel in 0.25m

Set amid three acres of attractive and well-tended grounds, this friendly, family-run hotel is peacefully located in a quiet area within walking distance of the town and esplanade. The light and airy bedrooms, some located at ground floor level, are comfortable and well equipped. There is a lounge and a cosy bar. The restaurant provides a choice of imaginative dishes, and, weather permitting tea may be taken on the lawn.

Rooms 33 (4 fmly) (11 GF) **S** £64-£67; **D** £120-£126 (incl. bkfst)* **Facilities** FTV Putt green Xmas Wi-fi **Parking** 33 **Notes** LB No children 3yrs Closed Jan-9 Feb RS Dec & Feb

Hotel Elizabeth

★★ 78% HOTEL

☎ 01395 513503 & 08000 481731
📠 01395 578000
The Esplanade EX10 8AT
e-mail: elizabeth@hotels-sidmouth.co.uk
web: www.hotels-sidmouth.co.uk
dir: M5 junct 30, then A3052 to Sidmouth. 1st exit on right to Sidmouth, then left onto esplanade

Occupying a prime location on the Esplanade, this elegant hotel attracts many loyal guests who return to enjoy the relaxed atmosphere and attentive service. Bedrooms are both comfortable and smartly appointed; all have sea views and some have balconies. The spacious lounge and sunny patio, with wonderful views across the bay, are perfect places to just sit and watch the world go by.

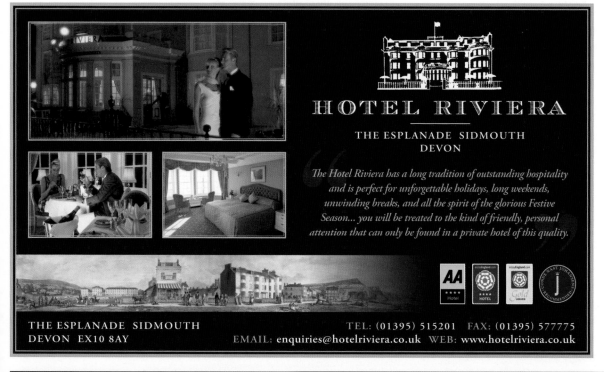

Rooms 28 (3 fmly) (1 GF) **Facilities** FTV Xmas Wi-fi **Services** Lift **Parking** 16 **Notes** Closed 28 Dec-10 Feb

SIDMOUTH *continued*

Mount Pleasant

★★ 78% HOTEL

☎ 01395 514694
Salcombe Rd EX10 8JA
dir: Exit A3052 at Sidford x-rds. In 1.25m left into Salcombe Rd, opposite Radway Cinema. Hotel on right after bridge

Quietly located within almost an acre of gardens, this modernised Georgian hotel is minutes from the town centre and seafront. Bedrooms and public areas provide good levels of comfort and high quality furnishings. Guests return on a regular basis, especially to experience the friendly, relaxed atmosphere. The light and airy restaurant overlooks the pleasant garden and offers a daily-changing menu of imaginative, yet traditional home-cooked dishes.

Rooms 17 (1 fmly) (3 GF) **S** £58-£73; **D** £116-£146 (incl. bkfst & dinner)* **Facilities** Putt green **Parking** 20 **Notes** ⊗ No children 8yrs Closed Dec-Feb

The Woodlands Hotel

★★ 74% HOTEL

☎ 01395 513120 🖷 01395 513348
Cotmaton Cross EX10 8HG
e-mail: info@woodlands-hotel.com
web: www.woodlands-hotel.com
dir: Follow signs for Sidmouth

Located in the heart of the town and ideally situated for exploring Devon and Dorset, this listed property has numerous character features. There is a spacious bar and a lounge where guests may relax. Freshly prepared dinners can be enjoyed in the smart dining room. Families with children are made very welcome and may dine early.

Rooms 20 (4 fmly) (8 GF) **S** £43-£73; **D** £74-£126 (incl. bkfst)* **Facilities** Wi-fi **Parking** 20 **Notes** LB Closed 20 Dec-15 Jan Civ Wed 70

The Salty Monk

◎◎ RESTAURANT WITH ROOMS

☎ 01395 513174
Church St, Sidford EX10 9QP
e-mail: saltymonk@btconnect.com
web: www.saltymonk.co.uk
dir: On A3052 opposite church

Set in the village of Sidford, this attractive property dates from the 16th century. There's oodles of style and appeal here and each bedroom has a unique identity. Bathrooms are equally special with multi-jet showers, spa baths and cosseting robes and towels. The output from the kitchen is impressive with excellent local produce very much in evidence, served in the elegant surroundings of the restaurant. A mini spa facility is available.

Rooms 6 (1 annexe)

SILLOTH — Map 18 NY15
Cumbria

Golf Hotel

★★ 71% HOTEL

☎ 016973 31438 🖷 016973 32582
Criffel St CA7 4AB
e-mail: info@golfhotelsilloth.co.uk

A friendly welcome waits at this hotel which occupies a prime position in the centre of the historic market town; it is a popular meeting place for the local community. Bedrooms are mostly well proportioned and are comfortably equipped. The lounge bar is a popular venue for dining, with a wide range of dishes on offer.

Rooms 22 (4 fmly) **S** £50-£87.50; **D** £97-£112 (incl. bkfst)* **Facilities** FTV Snooker & Games room **Conf** Class 50 Board 30 Thtr 100 Del from £99* **Notes** Closed 25 Dec RS 26 Dec, 1 Jan Civ Wed 100

SILVERSTONE — Map 11 SP64
Northamptonshire

Premier Inn Silverstone

Premier Inn

BUDGET HOTEL

☎ 0871 527 8976 🖷 0871 527 8977
Brackley Hatch, Syresham NN13 5TX
dir: On A43 near Silverstone

High quality, budget accommodation ideal for both families and business travellers. Spacious, en suite bedrooms feature tea and coffee making facilities, and Freeview TV in most hotels. Internet access and Wi-fi are available for a small fee. The adjacent family restaurant features a wide and varied menu. See also the Hotel Groups pages.

Rooms 41 **D** £55-£63*

SITTINGBOURNE — Map 7 TQ96
Kent

Hempstead House Country Hotel

★★★ 86% ◎ HOTEL

☎ 01795 428020 🖷 01795 436362
London Rd, Bapchild ME9 9PP
e-mail: info@hempsteadhouse.co.uk
web: www.hempsteadhouse.co.uk
dir: 1.5m from town centre on A2 towards Canterbury

Expect a warm welcome at this charming detached Victorian property, situated amidst four acres of mature landscaped gardens. Bedrooms are attractively decorated with lovely co-ordinated fabrics, tastefully furnished and equipped with many thoughtful touches. Public rooms feature a choice of elegant lounges as well as a superb conservatory dining room. In summer guests can eat on the terraces. There is a spa and fitness suite.

Rooms 34 (7 fmly) (1 GF) **Facilities** Spa STV FTV Gym Fitness studio Steam room Sauna Hydrotherapy pool Xmas New Year Wi-fi **Conf** Class 150 Board 100 Thtr 150 **Services** Lift **Parking** 100 **Notes** LB Civ Wed 150

Premier Inn Sittingbourne

BUDGET HOTEL

☎ 9871 527 8978 🖷 0871 527 8979
Bobbing Corner, Sheppy Way, Bobbing ME9 8RZ
dir: M2 junct 5, A249 towards Sheerness, approx 2m. Take 1st slip road after A2 underpass. At rdbt take 1st exit, hotel on left

High quality, budget accommodation ideal for both families and business travellers. Spacious, en suite bedrooms feature tea and coffee making facilities, and Freeview TV in most hotels. Internet access and Wi-fi are available for a small fee. The adjacent family restaurant features a wide and varied menu. See also the Hotel Groups pages.

Rooms 40 **D** £54-£64*

S

SIX MILE BOTTOM
Cambridgeshire
Map 12 TL55

Swynford Hotel

★★★ 79%  HOTEL

☎ 01638 570234 📠 01638 570283
CB8 0UE
e-mail: reception@swynfordhotel.com

This charming country house hotel is set in five acres of gardens and is short drive from both Newmarket and Cambridge. Each of the spacious bedrooms are individually styled, most with views over the grounds with its ancient trees. The award-winning conservatory restaurant serves an imaginative range of dishes and the cosy lounges make the ideal venue for afternoon tea.

Rooms 15 **Conf** Class 160 Board 45 Thtr 250

SKEGNESS
Lincolnshire
Map 17 TF56

Best Western Vine

★★★ 70% HOTEL

☎ 01754 763018 & 610611 📠 01754 769845
Vine Rd, Seacroft PE25 3DB
e-mail: info@thevinehotel.com
dir: A52 to Skegness, S towards Gibraltar Point, right into Drummond Rd, 0.5m, right into Vine Rd

Reputedly the second oldest building in Skegness, this traditional style hotel offers two character bars that serve excellent local beers. Freshly prepared dishes are served in both the bar and the restaurant; service is both friendly and helpful. The smartly decorated bedrooms are well equipped and comfortably appointed.

Rooms 25 (3 fmly) **Facilities** FTV Xmas New Year Wi-fi **Conf** Class 25 Board 30 Thtr 100 Del from £85 to £105* **Parking** 50 **Notes** Civ Wed 100

North Shore Hotel & Golf Course

★★★ 66% HOTEL

☎ 01754 763298 📠 01754 761902
North Shore Rd PE25 1DN
e-mail: info@northshorehotel.co.uk
dir: 1m N of town centre on A52, turn right into North Shore Rd (opposite Fenland laundry)

This hotel enjoys an enviable position on the beachfront, adjacent to its own championship golf course and only ten minutes from the town centre. Spacious public areas include a terrace bar serving informal meals and real ales, a formal restaurant and impressive function rooms. Bedrooms are smartly decorated and thoughtfully equipped.

Rooms 34 (3 annexe) (4 fmly) (3 GF) **S** £43-£70; **D** £65-£85 (incl. bkfst)* **Facilities** ⛳ 18 Putt green Xmas New Year Wi-fi **Conf** Class 60 Board 60 Thtr 220 Del from £90 to £110* **Parking** 200 **Notes** LB ⊗ Civ Wed 180

SKIPTON
North Yorkshire
Map 18 SD95

The Coniston

★★★★ 77% HOTEL

☎ 01756 748080 📠 01756 749487
Coniston Cold BD23 4EA
e-mail: info@theconistonhotel.com
dir: On A65, 6m NW of Skipton

This privately owned hotel set in 1,500 acres of prime country estate is a haven for guests staying or just visiting the hotel. All bedrooms and bathrooms are appointed to a very high standard; the bedroom wing offers large rooms with balconies. The reception, bar and restaurant have style and elegance, and the stunning spa adds to the impressive list of activities for guests.

Rooms 50 (13 fmly) (25 GF) **Facilities** STV Fishing Clay pigeon shooting Falconry Off-road Land Rover driving Archery Target golf Xmas New Year Wi-fi **Conf** Class 80 Board 50 Thtr 200 **Parking** 120 **Notes** LB Civ Wed 100

Herriots Hotel

★★★ 77% HOTEL

☎ 01756 792781 📠 01756 793967
Broughton Rd BD23 1RT
e-mail: info@herriotsforleisure.co.uk
web: www.herriotsforleisure.co.uk
dir: 2m off A59 at entrance to town & 50yds from railway station

Close to the centre of the market town, this friendly hotel offers tastefully decorated bedrooms that are well equipped. The open-plan brasserie is a relaxing place and offers a varied and interesting menu; meals and snacks are also available in the bar. The extension includes modern bedrooms and a stylish conservatory lounge.

Rooms 23 (3 fmly) **S** £55-£75; **D** £69-£99 (incl. bkfst)* **Facilities** FTV Private access onto Leeds Liverpool Canal Xmas New Year Wi-fi **Conf** Class 50 Board 52 Thtr 100 Del from £120 to £135* **Services** Lift **Parking** 26 **Notes** LB ⊗ Civ Wed 80

Rendezvous

★★★ 77% HOTEL

☎ 01756 700100 📠 01756 700107
Keighley Rd BD23 2TA
e-mail: reservations@rendezvous-skipton.com
dir: On A6131 (Keighley road) S from town centre

Located beside the canal just outside the town, the hotel has the advantage of plenty of parking and a leisure club with pool and gym. Bedrooms are well equipped and spacious, and have delightful views over the rolling countryside. There are extensive conference facilities. This hotel makes an ideal base for touring The Dales.

Rooms 80 (10 fmly) (13 GF) **Facilities** STV ⓢ supervised Gym Xmas New Year Wi-fi **Conf** Class 200 Board 120 Thtr 500 Del from £110 to £135* **Services** Lift **Parking** 120 **Notes** LB ⊗ Civ Wed 400

SKIPTON *continued*

Premier Inn Skipton North (Gargrave)

BUDGET HOTEL

☎ 0871 527 8980 📠 0871 527 8981
Hellifield Rd, Gargrave BD23 3NB
dir: NW of Skipton at rdbt junct of A59 & A65, take A65 signed Kendal, Settle & Gargrave. 3.5m. Through Gargrave. Hotel on left

High quality, budget accommodation ideal for both families and business travellers. Spacious, en suite bedrooms feature tea and coffee making facilities, and Freeview TV in most hotels. Internet access and Wi-fi are available for a small fee. The adjacent family restaurant features a wide and varied menu. See also the Hotel Groups pages.

Rooms 21 **D** £58*

SLEAFORD Lincolnshire **Map 12 TF04**

Carre Arms Hotel & Conference Centre

★★★ 68% SMALL HOTEL

☎ 01529 303156 📠 01529 303139
1 Mareham Ln NG34 7JP
e-mail: enquiries@carrearmshotel.co.uk
web: www.carrearmshotel.co.uk
dir: Take A153 to Sleaford, hotel on right at level crossing

This friendly, family run hotel is located close to the station and offers suitably appointed accommodation. Public areas include a smart brasserie and two spacious bars where a good selection of meals is offered. There is also a conservatory and a former stable that houses the spacious function room.

Rooms 13 (2 fmly) **Facilities** FTV Wi-fi **Conf** Class 70 Board 40 Thtr 120 **Parking** 80 **Notes** ® Civ Wed 80

SLOUGH Berkshire **Map 6 SU97**

Copthorne Hotel Slough-Windsor

★★★★ 75% HOTEL

☎ 01753 516222 📠 01753 516237
400 Cippenham Ln SL1 2YE
e-mail: sales.slough@millenniumhotels.co.uk
web: www.millenniumhotels.co.uk
dir: M4 junct 6, A355 towards Slough, at next rdbt left & left again for hotel entrance

Conveniently located for the motorway and for Heathrow Airport, this modern hotel offers visitors a wide range of indoor leisure facilities, and Turner's Grill, that serves a British menu. Bedrooms provide a useful range of extras including climate control, satellite TV and a trouser press. The hotel offers a discounted entrance fee to some of the attractions in the area.

Rooms 219 (47 fmly) (8 smoking) **S** fr £53; **D** fr £53* **Facilities** STV FTV Gym Steam room Sauna Wi-fi **Conf** Class 160 Board 60 Thtr 280 **Services** Lift **Parking** 303 **Notes** LB ® Civ Wed 280

The Pinewood Hotel

★★★★ 72% HOTEL

☎ 01753 896400 📠 01753 896500
Wexham Park Ln, George Green SL3 6AP
e-mail: info@pinewoodhotel.co.uk
web: www.pinewoodhotel.co.uk
dir: A4 N from Slough, A412 towards Uxbridge. Hotel 3m on left

This is a small luxury hotel on the outskirts of Slough. Excellent design is at the forefront throughout, together with good levels of comfort. The Eden brasserie specialises in quality produce, carefully prepared, including dishes cooked on the wood-burning stove. Service is friendly and attentive.

Rooms 49 (16 annexe) (4 fmly) (12 GF) **S** £65-£135; **D** £85-£155 (incl. bkfst) **Facilities** FTV Free use of nearby leisure facilities New Year Wi-fi **Conf** Class 46 Board 40 Thtr 120 Del from £150 to £210 **Services** Lift Air con **Parking** 40 **Notes** LB ® Civ Wed 110

Express by Holiday Inn Slough

BUDGET HOTEL

☎ 0844 499 2890 📠 0844 499 2910
Mill St SL2 5DD
e-mail: info@hiexslough.co.uk
web: www.hiexpress.co.uk
dir: Telephone for directions

A modern hotel ideal for families and business travellers. Fresh and uncomplicated, the spacious rooms include Sky TV, power shower and tea and coffee-making facilities. Continental buffet breakfast is included in the room rate; other meals may be taken at the nearby family pub or restaurant. See also the Hotel Groups pages.

Rooms 142 (110 fmly) **Conf** Class 25 Board 20 Thtr 30

Holiday Inn Express London Heathrow T5

BUDGET HOTEL

☎ 01753 684001 📠 01753 685767
London Rd SL3 8QB
e-mail: info@hiexheathrowt5.co.uk
web: www.hiexheathrowt5.co.uk
dir: M4 junct 5, follow signs for Colnbrook. Hotel 0.5m on right

A modern hotel ideal for families and business travellers. Fresh and uncomplicated, the spacious rooms include Sky TV, power shower and tea and coffee-making facilities. Continental buffet breakfast is included in the room rate; other meals may be taken at the nearby family pub or restaurant. See also the Hotel Groups pages.

Rooms 124 (124 fmly) **Conf** Class 50 Board 40 Thtr 100 Del from £120 to £160*

Premier Inn Slough

BUDGET HOTEL

☎ 0871 527 8982 📠 0871 527 8983
76 Uxbridge Rd SL1 1SU
dir: 2m from M4 junct 5, 3m from junct 6. Just off A4

High quality, budget accommodation ideal for both families and business travellers. Spacious, en suite bedrooms feature tea and coffee making facilities, and Freeview TV in most hotels. Internet access and Wi-fi are available for a small fee. The adjacent family restaurant features a wide and varied menu. See also the Hotel Groups pages.

Rooms 84 **D** £60-£85*

SNAINTON North Yorkshire **Map 17 SE98**

The Coachman Inn

RESTAURANT WITH ROOMS

☎ 01723 859231 📠 01723 850008
Pickering Road West YO13 9PL
e-mail: info@coachmaninn.co.uk
web: www.coachmaninn.co.uk
dir: From A170 in village onto B1258, establishment sign at side of road

This Grade II listed property was built in 1776 as a coaching inn and stands just on the outskirts of Snainton. It now offers comfortable, double, en suite rooms, fine dining in a wonderful large dining room, a locals' bar, a quiet lounge for residents and ample parking.

Rooms 6

S

SNETTISHAM
Norfolk
Map 12 TF63

Rose & Crown

★★ 80% HOTEL

☎ 01485 541382 📠 01485 543172
Old Church Rd PE31 7LX
e-mail: info@roseandcrownsnettisham.co.uk
dir: A149 towards Hunstanton. In Snettisham village centre turn into Old Church Rd, hotel 100yds on left

This lovely village inn provides comfortable, well-equipped bedrooms. A range of quality meals is served in the many dining areas, complemented by a good variety of real ales and wines. Service is friendly and a delightful atmosphere prevails. A walled garden is available on sunny days, as is a children's play area.

Rooms 16 (5 fmly) (2 GF) **S** £70-£95; **D** £85-£120 (incl. bkfst)* **Facilities** FTV Xmas New Year Wi-fi **Conf** Class 40 Board 40 Thtr 60 **Parking** 70 **Notes** LB

SOLIHULL
West Midlands
Map 10 SP17

See also **Dorridge**

St Johns Hotel

★★★★ 76% HOTEL

☎ 0121 711 3000 📠 0121 705 6629
651 Warwick Rd B91 1AT
dir: M42 junct 5, follow Solihull centre signs. 2nd left at rdbt (Warwick Rd). Straight on at 3rd lights (Barley Mow pub on left on approaching large rdbt). Straight ahead, hotel on right

With its town centre location, this modern hotel is conveniently situated for the NEC, Birmingham and many local attractions. Bedrooms are air conditioned, attractively decorated and equipped with a comprehensive range of extras. The hotel provides extensive conference facilities, an indoor leisure facility and extensive parking.

Rooms 180 (15 fmly) (9 GF) **Facilities** STV Gym Xmas New Year Wi-fi **Conf** Class 350 Board 60 Thtr 850 Del from £89 to £210 **Services** Lift Air con **Parking** 300 **Notes** Civ Wed 700

Holiday Inn Solihull

★★★★ 71% HOTEL

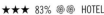

☎ 0871 942 9201 & 0121 623 9988
📠 0121 711 2696
61 Homer Rd B91 3QD
e-mail: hisolihull@qmh-hotels.com
web: www.holidayinn.co.uk
dir: M42 junct 5 follow signs to town centre, left at St Alphege Church into Church Hill Rd, continue to rdbt, hotel on right

Conveniently located for access to the NEC and motorway network, this modern hotel proves to be equally popular with both corporate and leisure guests. Bedrooms have been appointed to a smart contemporary standard, offering the benefits of air conditioning as standard. Public areas include the Club Moativation health and fitness club.

Rooms 120 (8 fmly) **Facilities** STV FTV supervised Gym Sauna Steam room Dance studio Xmas Wi-fi **Conf** Class 100 Board 100 Thtr 200 Del from £129 to £219* **Services** Lift Air con **Parking** 162 **Notes** Civ Wed 150

Premier Inn Solihull (Hockley Heath)

BUDGET HOTEL

☎ 0871 527 8984 📠 0871 527 8985
Stratford Rd, Hockley Heath B94 6NX
dir: On A3400, 2m S of M42 junct 4

High quality, budget accommodation ideal for both families and business travellers. Spacious, en suite bedrooms feature tea and coffee making facilities, and Freeview TV in most hotels. Internet access and Wi-fi are available for a small fee. The adjacent family restaurant features a wide and varied menu. See also the Hotel Groups pages.

Rooms 55 **D** £52-£60*

Premier Inn Solihull North

BUDGET HOTEL

☎ 0871 527 8988 📠 0871 527 8989
Stratford Rd, Shirley B90 3AG
dir: M42 junct 4 follow signs for Birmingham. Hotel in Shirley town centre on A34

Rooms 43 **D** £52-£60*

Premier Inn Solihull (Shirley)

BUDGET HOTEL

☎ 0871 527 8986 📠 0871 527 8987
Stratford Rd, Shirley B90 4EP
dir: M42 junct 4, A34N. Hotel in 1m

Rooms 51 **D** £52-£60*

SONNING
Berkshire
Map 5 SU77

The French Horn

★★★ 83% HOTEL

☎ 0118 969 2204 📠 0118 944 2210
RG4 6TN
e-mail: info@thefrenchhorn.co.uk
dir: From A4 into Sonning, follow B478 through village over bridge, hotel on right, car park on left

This long established Thames-side establishment has a lovely village setting and retains the traditions of classic hotel keeping. The restaurant is a particular attraction and provides attentive service. Bedrooms, including four cottage suites, are spacious and comfortable; many offer stunning views over the river. A private boardroom is available for corporate guests.

Rooms 22 (8 annexe) (4 GF) (4 smoking) **S** £125-£170; **D** £160-£215 (incl. bkfst)* **Facilities** FTV Fishing Affiliation with Nirvana Spa (15 mins by car) Wi-fi **Conf** Board 14 **Services** Air con **Parking** 40 **Notes** Closed 26-29 Dec

SOURTON
Devon
Map 3 SX59

Collaven Manor

★★ 79% COUNTRY HOUSE HOTEL

☎ 01837 861522 📠 01837 861614
EX20 4HH
e-mail: collavenmanor@supanet.com
dir: A30 onto A386 to Tavistock, hotel 2m on right

This delightful 15th-century manor house is quietly located in five acres of well-tended grounds. The friendly proprietors provide attentive service and ensure a relaxing environment. Charming public rooms have old oak beams and granite fireplaces, and provide a range of comfortable lounges and a well stocked bar. In the restaurant, a daily-changing menu offers interesting dishes.

Rooms 9 (1 fmly) **S** £59-£65; **D** £98-£146 (incl. bkfst)* **Facilities** FTV Bowls Wi-fi **Conf** Class 20 Board 16 Thtr 30 Del from £100 to £135* **Parking** 50 **Notes** LB Closed Dec-Jan Civ Wed 50

S

SOUTHAMPTON
Hampshire — Map 5 SU41

See also **Botley**

De Vere Grand Harbour

★★★★ 78% HOTEL

☎ 023 8063 3033 023 8063 3066
West Quay Rd SO15 1AG
e-mail: grandharbour@devere-hotels.com
web: www.devere.co.uk
dir: M27 junct 3 follow Waterfront signs. Keep in left lane of dual carrriageway, then follow Heritage & Waterfront signs onto West Quay Rd

Enjoying views of the harbour, this hotel stands alongside the medieval town walls and close to the West Quay centre. The modern design is impressive, with leisure facilities located in the dramatic glass pyramid. The spacious bedrooms are well appointed and thoughtfully equipped. For dining, guests can choose between two bars as well as fine dining in Allertons Restaurant and a more informal style in No 5 Brasserie.

Rooms 173 (22 fmly) (6 smoking) **Facilities** Spa STV Gym Beauty suite Sauna Steam room Xmas New Year Wi-fi **Conf** Class 200 Board 150 Thtr 500 **Services** Lift **Parking** 190 **Notes** Civ Wed 310

The Legacy Botleigh Grange Hotel

★★★★ 75% HOTEL

☎ 08444 119050 & 0330 333 2850
08444 119051
Grange Rd, Hedge End SO30 2GA
e-mail: res-botleighgrange@legacy-hotels.co.uk
web: www.legacy-hotels.co.uk
dir: M27 junct 7, A334 to Botley, hotel 0.5m on left

This impressive mansion, situated close to the M27, displays good quality throughout. The bedrooms are spacious with a good range of facilities. Public areas include a large conference room and a pleasant terrace with views overlooking the gardens and lake. The restaurant offers interesting menus using fresh, local produce.

Rooms 56 (8 fmly) (9 GF) **Facilities** Spa STV FTV Putt green Fishing Gym Sauna Steam room Relaxation room Xmas New Year Wi-fi **Conf** Class 175 Board 60 Thtr 500 **Services** Lift **Parking** 200 **Notes** Civ Wed 180

Mercure Southampton Centre Dolphin Hotel

★★★★ 71% HOTEL

☎ 023 8038 6460 023 8038 6470
34-35 High St SO14 2HN
e-mail: H7876@accor.com
dir: From A33 follow Docks & Old Town/I.O.W Ferry signs. At ferry terminal right into High St, hotel 400yds on left

Originally a coaching inn, this hotel enjoys a central location set almost in the heart of the town, yet close to the ferry terminals. Most bedrooms have now been refurbished to a high standard, and public areas include a traditional bar, popular restaurant and two meeting rooms. Parking at the rear of the hotel is an added bonus.

Rooms 90 (4 fmly) (22 GF) **Facilities** FTV Wi-fi **Conf** Del from £105 to £144* **Services** Lift **Parking** 80 **Notes** LB Civ Wed 120

Best Western Chilworth Manor

★★★ 79% HOTEL

☎ 023 8076 7333 023 8070 1743
SO16 7PT
e-mail: sales@chilworth-manor.co.uk
web: www.bw-chilworthmanor.co.uk
dir: 1m from M3/M27 junct on A27 (Romsey road) N from Southampton. Pass Chilworth Arms on left, in 200mtrs turn left at Southampton Science Park sign. Hotel immediately right

Set in 12 acres of delightful grounds, this attractive Edwardian manor house is conveniently located for Southampton and also the New Forest National Park. Bedrooms are located in both the main house and an adjoining wing. The hotel is particularly popular as both a conference and a wedding venue.

Rooms 95 (6 fmly) (23 GF) **Facilities** Spa STV FTV Gym Trail walking Giant chess Petanque New Year Wi-fi **Conf** Class 50 Board 50 Thtr 130 Del from £115 to £145* **Services** Lift **Parking** 200 **Notes** LB Civ Wed 105

Novotel Southampton

★★★ 74% HOTEL

☎ 023 8033 0550 023 8022 2158
1 West Quay Rd SO15 1RA
e-mail: H1073@accor.com
web: www.novotel.com
dir: M27 junct 3, follow city centre/A33 signs. In 1m take right lane for West Quay & Dock Gates 4-10. Hotel entrance on left. Turn at lights by McDonalds, left at rdbt, hotel straight ahead

A modern purpose-built hotel situated close to the city centre, railway station, ferry terminal and major road networks. The brightly decorated bedrooms are ideal for families and business guests; four rooms have facilities for the less mobile. The open-plan public areas include the Garden Brasserie, a bar and a leisure complex.

Rooms 121 (50 fmly) (9 smoking) **Facilities** STV FTV Gym Sauna New Year Wi-fi **Conf** Class 300 Board 150 Thtr 450 **Services** Lift **Parking** 300 **Notes** LB Civ Wed 300

Holiday Inn Southampton

★★★ 73% HOTEL

☎ 0871 942 9073 023 8063 4769
Herbert Walker Av SO15 1HJ
e-mail: southamptonhi@ihg.com
web: www.holidayinn.co.uk
dir: M27 junct 3 follow 'Dockgate 1-10 & Southampton Waterfront' signs. Hotel adjacent to Dock Gate 8

Convenient for both the port and town centre, this modern hotel is popular with both business and leisure guests. The well-equipped bedrooms are comfortably furnished. Public areas include an informal lounge bar and a contemporary restaurant offering an extensive range of popular dishes. Conference and leisure facilities are also available.

Rooms 130 (6 fmly) (15 smoking) **Facilities** STV supervised Gym New Year Wi-fi **Conf** Class 75 Board 60 Thtr 180 **Services** Lift Air con **Parking** 140 **Notes** LB Civ Wed

Southampton Park

★★★ 71% HOTEL

☎ 023 8034 3343 📠 023 8033 2538
Cumberland Place SO15 2WY
e-mail: southampton.park@forestdale.com
web: www.southamptonparkhotel.com
dir: At north end of Inner Ring Road, opposite Watts Park & Civic Centre

This modern hotel, in the heart of the city, provides well-equipped, smartly appointed and comfortable bedrooms. It boasts a well equipped spa with all modern facilities and a beauty salon for those who wish to pamper themselves. The public areas are spacious and include the popular MJ's Brasserie. Parking is available in a multi-storey behind the hotel.

Rooms 72 (10 fmly) **Facilities** Spa FTV supervised Gym New Year Wi-fi **Conf** Class 60 Board 50 Thtr 150 **Services** Lift **Notes** Closed 25 & 26 Dec nights

Elizabeth House

THE INDEPENDENTS HOTEL ASSOCIATION

★★ 78% HOTEL

☎ 023 8022 4327 📠 023 8033 9651
42-44 The Avenue SO17 1XP
e-mail: mail@elizabethhousehotel.com
web: www.elizabethhousehotel.com
dir: On A33, hotel on left after Southampton Common, before main lights

This hotel is conveniently situated close to the city centre, so provides an ideal base for both business and leisure guests. The bedrooms are well equipped and are attractively furnished with comfort in mind. There is also a cosy and atmospheric bistro in the cellar where evening meals are served.

Rooms 27 (7 annexe) (9 fmly) (8 GF) **S** £60-£67.50; **D** £70-£79.95 (incl. bkfst)* **Facilities** FTV Wi-fi **Conf** Class 24 Board 24 Thtr 40 **Parking** 31

Express by Holiday Inn Southampton - West

BUDGET HOTEL

☎ 023 8074 3100 📠 023 8073 1827
Adanac Park, Redbridge Ln SO16 0YP
e-mail: southampton@morethanhotels.com
web: www.hiexpress.com/southamptonuk
dir: M27 junct 3, onto M271. Exit at junct 1 (Lordshill Interchange), hotel on left via Redbridge Lane

A modern hotel ideal for families and business travellers. Fresh and uncomplicated, the spacious rooms include Sky TV, power shower and tea and coffee-making facilities. Continental buffet breakfast is included in the room rate; other meals may be taken at the nearby family pub or restaurant. See also the Hotel Groups pages.

Rooms 105 (63 fmly) **Conf** Class 20 Board 20 Thtr 35

Holiday Inn Express Southampton M27 Jct 7

BUDGET HOTEL

☎ 023 8060 6060 & 8060 6040 📠 023 8060 6050
Botley Rd, West End SO30 3XH
e-mail: reservations@expressbyholidayinn.uk.net
web: www.meridianleisurehotels.com/southampton
dir: M27 junct 7, follow brown Rose Bowl signs. Hotel 1m at The Rose Bowl entrance

This hotel, adjacent to the Rose Bowl, is conveniently located for Southampton Airport and Docks and has ample free parking. There is an air-conditioned restaurant serving conference lunches, evening meals and complimentary hot breakfasts, a fully licensed bar and lounge area with a 42" plasma TV with satellite channels. The hotel offers high speed Wi-fi throughout. Leisure facilities are available at the adjacent Esporta Leisure Centre for a nominal fee.

Rooms 176 (129 fmly) (38 GF) (18 smoking) **S** £49.46-£109; **D** £49.46-£109 (incl. bkfst)* **Conf** Class 26 Board 20 Thtr 52 Del from £104.50 to £212.50*

Ibis Southampton Centre

BUDGET HOTEL

☎ 023 8063 4463 📠 023 8022 3273
West Quay Rd, Western Esplanade SO15 1RA
e-mail: H1039@accor.com
web: www.ibishotel.com
dir: M27 junct 3, M271. Left to city centre (A35), follow Old Town Waterfront signs to 4th lights, left, left again, hotel opposite station

Modern, budget hotel offering comfortable accommodation in bright and practical bedrooms. Breakfast is self-service and dinner is available in the restaurant. See also the Hotel Groups pages.

Rooms 93 **S** £62-£140; **D** £62-£140* **Conf** Class 50 Board 40 Thtr 80 Del from £97 to £282*

Premier Inn Southampton Airport

BUDGET HOTEL

☎ 0871 527 8998 📠 0871 527 8999
Mitchell Way SO18 2XU
dir: M27 junct 5, A335 towards Eastleigh. Right at rdbt into Wide Ln. 1st exit at next rdbt into Mitchell Way

High quality, budget accommodation ideal for both families and business travellers. Spacious, en suite bedrooms feature tea and coffee making facilities, and Freeview TV in most hotels. Internet access and Wi-fi are available for a small fee. The adjacent family restaurant features a wide and varied menu. See also the Hotel Groups pages.

Rooms 121 **D** £60-£65*

Premier Inn Southampton City Centre

BUDGET HOTEL

☎ 0871 527 9266 📠 0871 527 9267
6 Dials, New Rd SO14 0YN
dir: M27 junct 5, A335 signed City Centre. At Charlotte Place rdbt take 3rd exit into East Park Terrace, 1st left into New Rd. Hotel on right

Rooms 172 **D** £60-£67*

Premier Inn Southampton North

BUDGET HOTEL

☎ 0871 527 9002 📠 0871 527 9003
Romsey Rd, Nursling SO16 0XJ
dir: M27 junct 3, M271 towards Romsey. At next rdbt take 3rd exit towards Southampton (A3057). Hotel 1.5m on right

Rooms 32 **D** £52-£62*

Premier Inn Southampton West Quay

BUDGET HOTEL

☎ 0871 527 9298 📠 0871 527 9299
Harbour Pde SO15 1ST
dir: M27 junct 3, follow M271(S)/Southampton/The Docks signs, onto M271, at Redbridge rdbt onto A35 follow Southampton/The Docks/A3024 signs. Merge onto A35 (Redbridge Rd), continue onto Millbrook Flyover/A3024, right at West Quay Rd/A3057, left after Ikea into Harbour Parade

Rooms 155

SOUTH BRENT
Devon
Map 3 SX66

Glazebrook House Hotel
★★ 78% HOTEL

☎ 01364 73322 📠 01364 72350
TQ10 9JE
e-mail: enquiries@glazebrookhouse.com
web: www.glazebrookhouse.com
dir: Exit A38 at South Brent, follow brown signs to hotel

Enjoying a tranquil and convenient location next to the Dartmoor National Park and set within four acres of gardens, this 18th-century former gentleman's residence offers a friendly welcome and comfortable accommodation. Elegant public areas provide ample space to relax and enjoy the atmosphere, whilst bedrooms are well appointed and include a number with four-poster beds. The dishes on the menus are created from interesting combinations of fresh, locally-sourced produce.

Rooms 10 **S** £50-£55; **D** £80-£137.50 (incl. bkfst)* **Facilities** FTV Reflexology Holistic therapies Xmas New Year Wi-fi **Conf** Class 60 Board 40 Thtr 80 Del from £83.50 to £91.50* **Parking** 40 **Notes** LB Closed 2-18 Jan RS 1 wk Aug Civ Wed 80

S

SOUTH CAVE
East Riding of Yorkshire
Map 17 SE93

Cave Castle Hotel & Country Club
★★★ 72% HOTEL

☎ 01430 422245 📠 01430 421118
Church Hill HU15 2EU
e-mail: info@cavecastlehotel.com
web: www.cavecastlehotel.com
dir: In village, opposite school

This beautiful Victorian manor retains original turrets, stone features and much charm together with modern comforts and style. It stands in 150 acres of meadow and parkland that provide a peaceful setting. Bedrooms are a careful mix of traditional and contemporary styles. Public areas include a well-equipped leisure complex and pool.

Rooms 70 (14 GF) **Facilities** Spa supervised 18 Putt green Gym New Year Wi-fi **Conf** Class 150 Board 100 Thtr 250 Del from £110* **Services** Lift **Parking** 100 **Notes** Civ Wed 150

SOUTH CERNEY
Gloucestershire
Map 5 SU09

Cotswold Water Park Four Pillars Hotel
★★★★ 77% HOTEL

☎ 0800 374692 & 01285 864000
📠 01285 864001
Lake 6 Spine Road East GL7 5FP
e-mail: waterpark@four-pillars.co.uk
web: www.cotswoldwaterparkhotel.co.uk
dir: Off A419, 3m from Cirencester (NB for Sav Nav use GL7 5TL)

This impressive hotel has well-appointed bedrooms and suites, conference facilities, a spa with an 11-metre pool, a gym, a hydro pool and treatment rooms. An excellent range of dining options is available. A large car park is provided.

Rooms 318 (57 fmly) (126 GF) **S** £79-£129; **D** £99-£149 (incl. bkfst)* **Facilities** Spa STV Fishing Gym Treatment rooms & therapies Steam room Sauna Xmas New Year Wi-fi **Conf** Class 204 Board 68 Thtr 370 Del from £135 to £185* **Services** Lift **Parking** 200 **Notes** LB Civ Wed 370

SOUTHEND-ON-SEA
Essex
Map 7 TQ88

Roslin Beach Hotel
★★★ 79% HOTEL

☎ 01702 586375 📠 01702 586663
Thorpe Esplanade SS1 3BG
e-mail: info@roslinhotel.com
web: www.roslinhotel.com
dir: A127, follow Southend-on-Sea signs. Hotel between Walton Rd & Clieveden Rd on seafront

This friendly hotel is situated at the quiet end of the esplanade, overlooking the beach and sea. The spacious bedrooms are pleasantly decorated and thoughtfully equipped; some rooms have superb sea views. Public rooms include a large lounge bar, the Mulberry Restaurant and a smart conservatory which overlooks the sea.

Rooms 57 (5 fmly) (7 GF) **Facilities** FTV Xmas New Year Wi-fi **Conf** Class 45 Board 39 Thtr 60 **Parking** 40 **Notes** Civ Wed 25

Park Inn by Radisson
park inn by Radisson

★★★ 78% HOTEL

☎ 01702 455100 📠 01702 455109
Church Rd SS1 2AL
e-mail: info.southend-on-sea@rezidorparkinn.com

This hotel, in the centre of the town's tourist area, has been completely refurbished and now offers comfortable and modern rooms to meet the needs of both leisure and business travellers; the front facing bedrooms have breathtaking sea views. The public areas include the all-day dining RBG Bar & Grill, both overlooking the mouth of the River Thames. There is a range of meeting rooms to cater for all occasions.

Rooms 137 (22 fmly) **S** £69-£149; **D** £79-£159* **Facilities** STV FTV Gym Squash Wi-fi **Conf** Class 90 Board 70 Thtr 300 Del from £99 to £160* **Services** Lift Air con **Notes** LB Civ Wed 300

Westcliff
★★★ 75% HOTEL

☎ 01702 345247 📠 01702 431814
Westcliff Pde, Westcliff-on-Sea SS0 7QW
e-mail: westcliff@zolahotels.com
dir: M25 junct 29, A127 towards Southend, follow signs for Cliffs Pavillion when approaching town centre

This impressive Grade II listed Victorian building is situated in an elevated position overlooking gardens and cliffs with views to the sea beyond. The spacious bedrooms are tastefully decorated and thoughtfully equipped; many have lovely sea views. Public rooms include a smart conservatory-style restaurant, a spacious lounge and a range of function rooms.

Rooms 55 (2 fmly) **Facilities** FTV ♫ Xmas New Year Wi-fi **Conf** Class 90 Board 64 Thtr 225 **Services** Lift **Notes** Civ Wed 120

Camelia

★★★ HOTEL

☎ 01702 587917 📠 01702 585704
176-178 Eastern Esplanade, Thorpe Bay SS1 3AA
e-mail: enquiries@cameliahotel.com
web: www.cameliahotel.com
dir: From A13 or A127 follow signs to Southend seafront; on seafront left, hotel 1m E of pier

Rooms 28 (8 annexe) (3 fmly) (8 GF) **S** £60-£100; **D** £76-£120 (incl. bkfst)* **Facilities** FTV New Year Wi-fi **Parking** 100 **Notes** LB

Premier Inn Southend Airport

BUDGET HOTEL

☎ 0871 527 9008 📠 0871 527 9009
Thanet Grange SS2 6GB
dir: At A127 & B1013 junct

High quality, budget accommodation ideal for both families and business travellers. Spacious, en suite bedrooms feature tea and coffee making facilities, and Freeview TV in most hotels. Internet access and Wi-fi are available for a small fee. The adjacent family restaurant features a wide and varied menu. See also the Hotel Groups pages.

Rooms 80 **D** £64*

Premier Inn Southend-on-Sea (Thorpe Bay)

BUDGET HOTEL

☎ 0871 527 9006 📠 0871 527 9007
213 Eastern Esplanade SS1 3AD
dir: Follow signs for A1159 (A13) Shoebury onto dual carriageway. At rdbt, follow signs for Thorpe Bay & seafront, at seafront turn right. Hotel on right

Rooms 43 **D** £64*

SOUTH MIMMS SERVICE AREA (M25) Map 6 TL20
Hertfordshire

Days Inn South Mimms - M25

BUDGET HOTEL

☎ 01707 665440 📠 01707 660189
Bignells Corner EN6 3QQ
e-mail: south.mimms@welcomebreak.co.uk
web: www.welcomebreak.co.uk
dir: M25 junct 23, at rdbt follow signs

This modern building offers accommodation in smart, spacious and well-equipped bedrooms, suitable for families and business travellers, and all with en suite bathrooms. Continental breakfast is available and other refreshments may be taken at the nearby family restaurant. See also the Hotel Groups pages.

Rooms 74 (55 fmly) (18 GF) (8 smoking) **S** £49.95-£69.95; **D** £59.95-£79.95 **Conf** Board 10

Premier Inn South Mimms/ Potters Bar

BUDGET HOTEL

☎ 0871 527 8990 📠 0871 527 8991
Swanland Rd EN6 3NH
dir: M25 junct 23 & A1 take services exit off main rdbt then 1st left & follow hotel signs

High quality, budget accommodation ideal for both families and business travellers. Spacious, en suite bedrooms feature tea and coffee making facilities, and Freeview TV in most hotels. Internet access and Wi-fi are available for a small fee. The adjacent family restaurant features a wide and varied menu. See also the Hotel Groups pages.

Rooms 142 **D** £45-£59*

SOUTH MOLTON Map 3 SS72
Devon

The George Hotel

★★ 76% HOTEL

☎ 01769 572514 📠 01769 579218
1 Broad St EX36 3AB
e-mail: info@georgehotelsouthmolton.co.uk
web: www.georgehotelsouthmolton.co.uk
dir: Off A361 at rdbt signed South Molton, 1.5m to centre

Retaining many of its original features, this charming 17th-century hotel is situated in the centre of town. Providing comfortable accommodation, complemented by informal and friendly service to all guests including children, this hotel is an ideal base for touring the area. Regularly changing menus, featuring local produce, are offered in the both the restaurant and the bar, which also serves real ales.

Rooms 9 (1 fmly) **S** £62.50; **D** £97.50-£112.50 (incl. bkfst)* **Facilities** FTV Wi-fi **Conf** Class 30 Board 30 Thtr 100 **Parking** 12 **Notes** LB RS 1st wk Jan

SOUTH NORMANTON Map 16 SK45
Derbyshire

The Derbyshire Hotel

★★★★ 72% HOTEL

☎ 01773 812000 📠 01773 813413
Carter Lane East DE55 2EH
e-mail: reservations.derbyshire@principal-hayley.com
dir: M1 junct 28, E on A38 to Mansfield

Conveniently located by the motorway, this hotel offers comfortable accommodation and a relaxed informal atmosphere through the lounge bar and restaurant. The conference and meeting rooms are appointed to a smart modern standard; delegates also have use of on-site sauna, jacuzzi and steam room in the spa.

Rooms 157 (10 fmly) (61 GF) **Facilities** Spa STV Gym Steam room Sauna New Year Wi-fi **Conf** Class 120 Board 25 Thtr 250 **Parking** 220 **Notes** Civ Wed 150

Premier Inn Mansfield

BUDGET HOTEL

☎ 0871 527 8758 📠 0871 527 8759
Carter Lane East DE55 2EH
dir: M1 junct 28, A38 signed Mansfield. Entrance 200yds on left

High quality, budget accommodation ideal for both families and business travellers. Spacious, en suite bedrooms feature tea and coffee making facilities, and Freeview TV in most hotels. Internet access and Wi-fi are available for a small fee. The adjacent family restaurant features a wide and varied menu. See also the Hotel Groups pages.

Rooms 82 **D** £49-£57*

S

SOUTHPORT
Merseyside Map 15 SD31

Vincent Hotel

★★★★ 81% TOWN HOUSE HOTEL

01704 883800 01704 883830
98 Lord St PR8 1JR
e-mail: manager@thevincenthotel.com
dir: M58 junct 3, follow signs to Ormskirk & Southport

This stylish, boutique property occupies a prime location on Southport's famous boulevard. Bedrooms, some with views of the beach, are appointed to a high standard with oversized beds, extremely well stocked mini-bars and stylish en suites with deep tubs. Public areas include a trendy cocktail bar, an all-day dining concept. Friendly staff offer personalised service.

Rooms 60 **S** £83-£199; **D** £83-£695* **Facilities** Spa STV FTV Gym Wi-fi **Conf** Class 96 Board 50 Thtr 196 Del from £130 to £160* **Services** Lift Air con **Parking** 50 **Notes** LB Civ Wed 150

Scarisbrick

★★★ 77% HOTEL

01704 543000 01704 533335
Lord St PR8 1NZ
e-mail: info@scarisbrickhotel.com
web: www.scarisbrickhotel.co.uk
dir: From S: M6 junct 26, M58 to Ormskirk then Southport. From N: A59 from Preston, well signed

Centrally located on Southport's famous Lord Street, this privately owned hotel offers a high standard of attractively furnished, thoughtfully equipped accommodation. A wide range of eating options is available, from the bistro style of Maloney's Kitchen to the more formal Knightsbridge Restaurant. Extensive leisure and conference facilities are also available.

Rooms 88 (5 fmly) (7 smoking) **Facilities** STV Gym Use of private leisure centre Beauty & aromatherapy studio Xmas New Year Wi-fi **Conf** Class 100 Board 80 Thtr 200 **Services** Lift **Parking** 68 **Notes** Civ Wed 170

Best Western Royal Clifton Hotel & Spa

★★★ 74% HOTEL

01704 533771 01704 500657
Promenade PR8 1RB
e-mail: sales@royalclifton.co.uk
dir: Adjacent to Marine Lake

This grand, traditional hotel benefits from a prime location on the promenade. Bedrooms range in size and style, but all are comfortable and thoughtfully equipped. Public areas include the lively Bar C, the elegant Pavilion Restaurant and a modern, well-equipped leisure club. Extensive conference and banqueting facilities make this hotel a popular function venue.

Rooms 120 (23 fmly) (6 GF) **S** £45-£90; **D** £70-£130 (incl. bkfst)* **Facilities** Spa STV supervised Gym Hair & beauty Steam room Aromatherapy Xmas New Year Wi-fi **Conf** Class 100 Board 65 Thtr 250 Del from £99 to £135* **Services** Lift **Parking** 60 **Notes** LB Civ Wed 150

Balmoral Lodge Hotel

★★ 74% HOTEL

01704 544298 01704 501224
41 Queens Rd PR9 9EX
e-mail: balmorallg@aol.com
dir: On edge of town on A565 (Preston road). E at rdbt at North Lord St, left at lights, hotel 200yds on left

Situated in a quiet residential area, this popular, friendly hotel is ideally situated just 50 yards from Lord Street. Bedrooms are comfortably appointed and family rooms are available. In addition to the restaurant which offers freshly prepared dishes, there is a choice of lounges including a comfortable lounge bar.

Rooms 15 (4 annexe) (3 fmly) (4 GF) **S** £30-£50; **D** £40-£90 (incl. bkfst) **Facilities** STV FTV Wi-fi **Conf** Class 30 Board 30 Thtr 30 Del from £60 to £100* **Parking** 12 **Notes** LB

Premier Inn Southport Central

BUDGET HOTEL

0871 527 9012 0871 527 9013
Marine Dr PR8 1RY
dir: From Southport follow Promenade & Marine Drive signs. Hotel at junct of Marine Parade & Marine Drive

High quality, budget accommodation ideal for both families and business travellers. Spacious, en suite bedrooms feature tea and coffee making facilities, and Freeview TV in most hotels. Internet access and Wi-fi are available for a small fee. The adjacent family restaurant features a wide and varied menu. See also the Hotel Groups pages.

Rooms 59 **D** £63-£65*

SOUTH RUISLIP
Greater London

See LONDON SECTION plan 1 B4

Days Hotel London South Ruislip

★★★ 73% HOTEL PLAN 1 A5

020 8845 8400 020 8845 5500
Long Dr, Station Approach HA4 0HG
e-mail: sales@daysinnheathrow.com
web: www.daysinnheathrow.com
dir: Exit A40 at Polish War Memorial, follow signs to Ruislip & South Ruislip

This modern building offers smart, spacious and well-equipped bedrooms, especially suitable for families and business travellers. Wings Restaurant offers a range of Indian and Italian dishes during the evening.

Rooms 78 (11 fmly) (7 GF) **Facilities** STV FTV Wi-fi **Conf** Class 40 Board 30 Thtr 60 Del from £110 to £140* **Services** Lift Air con **Parking** 100 **Notes** LB Civ Wed 70

SOUTHSEA

See Portsmouth & Southsea

SOUTH SHIELDS
Tyne & Wear Map 21 NZ36

Best Western Sea Hotel

★★★ 75% HOTEL

0191 427 0999 0191 454 0500
Sea Rd NE33 2LD
e-mail: info@seahotel.co.uk
dir: A1(M), past Washington Services onto A194. Then A183 through town centre along Ocean Rd. Hotel on seafront

Dating from the 1930s this long-established business hotel overlooks the boating lake and the Tyne estuary. Bedrooms are generally spacious and well equipped and include five annexe rooms with wheelchair access. A range of generously portioned meals is served in both the bar and restaurant.

Rooms 37 (5 annexe) (5 fmly) (5 GF) **S** £49-£69.50; **D** £59-£89.50 (incl. bkfst)* **Facilities** STV New Year Wi-fi **Conf** Class 100 Board 50 Thtr 200 Del from £89 to £109* **Parking** 70 **Notes** RS 26 Dec

S

Premier Inn South Shields (Port of Tyne)

BUDGET HOTEL

☎ 0871 527 8992 📠 0871 527 8993
Hobson Av, Newcastle Rd NE34 9PQ
dir: A1(M) onto A194(M). 2nd exit at rdbt into Leam Lane (A194). At next rdbt 2nd exit, next rdbt 3rd exit, next rdbt 2nd exit (A194), next rdbt 2nd exit. Hotel on left adjacent to Taybarns

High quality, budget accommodation ideal for both families and business travellers. Spacious, en suite bedrooms feature tea and coffee making facilities, and Freeview TV in most hotels. Internet access and Wi-fi are available for a small fee. The adjacent family restaurant features a wide and varied menu. See also the Hotel Groups pages.

Rooms 66 **D** £53-£59*

SOUTHWELL Nottinghamshire — Map 17 SK65

Saracens Head

★★★ 73% HOTEL

☎ 01636 812701 📠 01636 815408
Market Place NG25 0HE
e-mail: info@saracensheadhotel.net
web: www.saracensheadhotel.net
dir: From A1 to Newark exit. Follow B6386 for approx 7m

This half-timbered inn, rich in history, is set in the centre of town and close to the Minster. There is a relaxing atmosphere within the sumptuous public areas, which include a small bar, a comfortable lounge and a fine dining restaurant. Bedroom styles vary - all are appealing, comfortable and well equipped.

Rooms 27 (2 fmly) **S** £65-£75; **D** £85-£150 (incl. bkfst)* **Facilities** FTV ♫ Xmas New Year Wi-fi **Conf** Class 60 Board 40 Thtr 80 Del from £110 to £130* **Parking** 32 **Notes** LB ⊗ Civ Wed 70

The Old Vicarage

⊛ RESTAURANT WITH ROOMS

☎ 01636 815989 & 07787 534635
📠 0872 352 1940
Westhrope NG25 0NB
e-mail: reservations@vicarageboutiquehotel.co.uk

The Old Vicarage provides high standards of accommodation and service. The bedrooms and bathrooms are individually designed and retain many original features. The public areas have a real contemporary look and feel - wooden floors and highly polished tables etc. The dining room, overlooking the lovely gardens, is spacious with lots of natural light. Outside there is a hot tub and seating area. The establishment is owner managed ensuring first-class service and attention to detail.

Rooms 8 (2 fmly)

SOUTHWOLD Suffolk — Map 13 TM57

Swan Hotel

★★★★ 78% ⊛⊛ HOTEL

☎ 01502 722186 📠 01502 724800
Market Place IP18 6EG
e-mail: swan.hotel@adnams.co.uk
dir: A1095 to Southwold. Hotel in town centre. Parking via archway to left of building

A charming 17th-century coaching inn situated in the heart of this bustling town centre overlooking the market place. Public rooms feature an elegant restaurant, a comfortable drawing room, a cosy bar and a lounge where guests can enjoy afternoon tea. The spacious bedrooms are attractively decorated, tastefully furnished and thoughtfully equipped.

Rooms 42 (17 annexe) (11 fmly) (17 GF) **S** £95-£110.50; **D** £135-£252 (incl. bkfst)* **Facilities** STV FTV Treatment room Xmas New Year Wi-fi **Conf** Class 24 Board 12 Thtr 40 Del from £155 to £185* **Services** Lift **Parking** 42 **Notes** LB Civ Wed 60

The Blyth Hotel

★★ 85% ⊛ SMALL HOTEL

☎ 01502 722632 & 0845 348 6867
Station Rd IP18 6AY
e-mail: reception@blythhotel.com

Expect a warm welcome at this delightful family run hotel which is situated just a short walk from the town centre. The spacious public rooms include a smart residents' lounge, an open-plan bar and a large restaurant. Bedrooms are tastefully appointed with co-ordinated fabrics and have many thoughtful touches.

Rooms 13 **S** £65-£80; **D** £95-£150 (incl. bkfst)* **Facilities** FTV Xmas New Year Wi-fi **Conf** Class 20 Board 12 Thtr 20 Del from £100 to £150* **Parking** 8 **Notes** LB

The Crown

★★ 85% ⊛ HOTEL

☎ 01502 722275 📠 01502 727263
90 High St IP18 6DP
e-mail: crown.hotel@adnams.co.uk
dir: A12 onto A1095 to Southwold. Hotel on left in High Street

A delightful old posting inn situated in the heart of this bustling town. The property combines a pub, wine bar and restaurant with superb accommodation. The tastefully decorated bedrooms have attractive co-ordinated soft furnishings and many thoughtful touches. Public rooms feature an elegant lounge and a back room bar serving traditional Adnams ales.

Rooms 14 (2 fmly) **Facilities** FTV Xmas New Year Wi-fi **Conf** Board 8 **Parking** 23 **Notes** LB ⊗

S

SOUTHWOLD *continued*

Sutherland House

RESTAURANT WITH ROOMS

☎ 01502 724544
56 High St IP18 6DN
e-mail: enquiries@sutherlandhouse.co.uk
web: www.sutherlandhouse.co.uk
dir: A1095 into Southwold, on High St on left after Victoria St

A delightful 16th-century house situated in the heart of the bustling town centre with a wealth of character; there are oak beams, exposed brickwork, open fireplaces and two superb ornate plasterwork ceilings. The stylish bedrooms are tastefully decorated, have co-ordinated fabrics and many thoughtful touches. Public rooms feature a large open-plan contemporary restaurant with plush furniture.

Rooms 4 (1 fmly)

SPENNYMOOR
Co Durham — Map 19 NZ23

Best Western Whitworth Hall Hotel

★★★ 79% HOTEL

☎ 01388 811772 🖷 01388 818669
Whitworth Hall Country Park DL16 7QX
e-mail: enquiries@whitworthhall.co.uk
web: www.whitworthhall.co.uk
dir: A688 to Spennymoor, then Bishop Auckland. At rdbt right to Middlestone Moor. Left at lights, hotel on right

This hotel, peacefully situated in its own grounds in the centre of the deer park, offers comfortable accommodation. Spacious bedrooms, some with excellent views, offer stylish and elegant decor. Public areas include a choice of restaurants and bars, a bright conservatory and well-equipped function and conference rooms.

Rooms 29 (4 fmly) (17 GF) **Facilities** FTV Fishing Wi-fi **Conf** Class 40 Board 30 Thtr 100 **Parking** 100 **Notes** LB ⊗ Civ Wed 120

S

STAFFORD
Staffordshire — Map 10 SJ92

The Moat House

★★★★ 84% HOTEL

☎ 01785 712217 🖷 01785 715344
Lower Penkridge Rd, Acton Trussell ST17 0RJ
e-mail: info@moathouse.co.uk
web: www.moathouse.co.uk
dir: M6 junct 13 onto A449 through Acton Trussell. Hotel on right on exiting village

This 17th-century timbered building, with an idyllic canal-side setting, has been skilfully extended. Bedrooms are stylishly furnished, well equipped and comfortable. The bar offers a range of snacks and the restaurant boasts a popular fine dining option where the head chef displays his skills using top quality produce.

Rooms 41 (4 fmly) (15 GF) **Facilities** New Year Wi-fi **Conf** Class 60 Board 50 Thtr 200 **Services** Lift **Parking** 200 **Notes** ⊗ Closed 25 Dec Civ Wed 150

The Swan

★★★ 80% HOTEL

☎ 01785 258142 🖷 01785 223372
46 Greengate St ST16 2JA
e-mail: info@theswanstafford.co.uk
dir: From N on A34, access via Mill Street in town centre. From S take A449

This former coaching inn located in the town centre offers spacious, modern public areas that include a popular brasserie, a choice of elegant bars, a coffee shop and conference facilities. Individually styled bedrooms, many with original period features, are tastefully appointed and include two four-poster suites. Executive rooms are air conditioned.

Rooms 31 (3 fmly) **Facilities** FTV Wi-fi **Services** Lift **Parking** 40 **Notes** ⊗ Closed 25 Dec

Abbey Hotel

THE INDEPENDENTS HOTEL ASSOCIATION

★★ 74% HOTEL

☎ 01785 258531 🖷 01785 246875
65-68 Lichfield Rd ST17 4LW
web: www.abbeyhotelstafford.co.uk
dir: M6 junct 13 towards Stafford. Right at Esso garage, to mini-rdbt, follow Silkmore Lane to 2nd rdbt. Hotel 0.25m on right

This friendly privately owned and personally run hotel provides well-equipped accommodation and is particularly popular with commercial visitors. Family rooms are available. Facilities here include a choice of lounges and the spacious car park proves a real benefit to guests.

Rooms 17 (3 fmly) **Facilities** FTV Wi-fi **Parking** 21 **Notes** ⊗ Closed 22 Dec-7 Jan

Express by Holiday Inn Stafford M6 Jct 13

BUDGET HOTEL

☎ 01785 212244 🖷 01785 212377
Acton Gate, Acton Court ST18 9AP
e-mail: stafford@morethanhotels.com
web: www.hiexpress.com/stafford
dir: M6 junct 13. Hotel on A449 towards Stafford

A modern hotel ideal for families and business travellers. Fresh and uncomplicated, the spacious rooms include Sky TV, power shower and tea and coffee-making facilities. Continental buffet breakfast is included in the room rate; other meals may be taken at the nearby family pub or restaurant. See also the Hotel Groups pages.

Rooms 103 **Conf** Class 20 Board 20 Thtr 40

Premier Inn Stafford North (Hurricane)

BUDGET HOTEL

☎ 0871 527 9030 🖷 0871 527 9031
1 Hurrican Close ST16 1GZ
dir: M6 junct 14, A34 towards Stafford. Hotel approx 2m NW of town centre

High quality, budget accommodation ideal for both families and business travellers. Spacious, en suite bedrooms feature tea and coffee making facilities, and Freeview TV in most hotels. Internet access and Wi-fi are available for a small fee. The adjacent family restaurant features a wide and varied menu. See also the Hotel Groups pages.

Rooms 96 **D** £52-£57*

Premier Inn Stafford North (Spitfire)

BUDGET HOTEL

☎ 0871 527 9032 🖷 0871 527 9033
1 Spitfire Close ST16 1GX
dir: M6 junct 14, A34 N. Hotel approx 1m on left

Rooms 60 **D** £52-£57*

STAINES
Surrey Map 6 TQ07

Mercure Thames Lodge

★★★ 73% HOTEL

☎ 01784 464433 📠 01784 454858
Thames St TW18 4SJ
e-mail: h6620@accor.com
web: www.mercure.com
dir: M25 junct 13. Follow A30/town centre signs (bus station on right). Hotel straight ahead

Located on the banks of the River Thames in a bustling town, this hotel is well positioned for both business and leisure travellers. Meals are served in the Riverside Restaurant, and snacks are available in the spacious lounge/bar; weather permitting the terrace provides a good place for a drink on a summer evening. Onsite parking is an additional bonus.

Rooms 79 (17 fmly) (23 GF) **S** £79-£200; **D** £82-£210* **Facilities** STV Frontage moorings New Year Wi-fi **Conf** Class 40 Board 40 Thtr 50 **Parking** 40

STALLINGBOROUGH
Lincolnshire Map 17 TA11

Stallingborough Grange Hotel

THE INDEPENDENTS HOTEL ASSOCIATION

★★★ 73% HOTEL

☎ 01469 561302 📠 01469 561338
Riby Rd DN41 8BU
e-mail: grange.hot@virgin.net
web: www.stallingboroughgrange.com
dir: From A180 follow Stallingborough Interchange signs. Through village. From rdbt follow A1173/ Caistor signs. Hotel 1m on left just past windmill

This 18th-century country house has been tastefully extended to provide spacious and well-equipped bedrooms, including executive rooms. Run by the same family for over 20 years, the hotel is popular with locals and guests alike for the wide range of food offered in the restaurant, and for the real ales and wines in the bar.

Rooms 42 (6 fmly) (9 GF) **S** £65-£90; **D** £75-£115 (incl. bkfst)* **Facilities** STV FTV Gym Wi-fi **Conf** Class 40 Board 28 Thtr 60 **Parking** 100 **Notes** LB ⊗ Civ Wed 65

STAMFORD
Lincolnshire Map 11 TF00

The George of Stamford

★★★ 86% ◎ HOTEL

☎ 01780 750750 & 750700 (res)
📠 01780 750701
71 St Martins PE9 2LB
e-mail: reservations@georgehotelofstamford.com
web: www.georgehotelofstamford.com
dir: A1, 15m N of Peterborough onto B1081, hotel 1m on left

Steeped in hundreds of years of history, this delightful coaching inn provides spacious public areas that include a choice of dining options, inviting, lounges, a business centre and a range of quality shops. A highlight is afternoon tea, taken in the colourful courtyard when the weather permits. Bedrooms are stylishly appointed and range from traditional to contemporary in design.

Rooms 47 (24 fmly) **S** £95-£100; **D** £150-£230 (incl. bkfst)* **Facilities** STV ⛳ Complimentary membership to local gym Xmas New Year Wi-fi **Conf** Class 25 Board 25 Thtr 50 Del from £150 to £180* **Parking** 110 **Notes** LB Civ Wed 50

Crown

★★★ 79% HOTEL

☎ 01780 763136 📠 01780 756111
All Saints Place PE9 2AG
e-mail: reservations@thecrownhotelstamford.co.uk
web: www.thecrownhotelstamford.co.uk
dir: A1 onto A43, through town to Red Lion Sq, hotel behind All Saints Church

This small, privately owned hotel where hospitality is spontaneous and sincere, is ideally situated in the town centre. Unpretentious British food is served in the modern dining areas and the spacious bar is popular with locals. Bedrooms are appointed to a very high standard being quite contemporary in style and very well equipped; some have four-poster beds. Additional 'superior' rooms are located in a renovated Georgian town house just a short walk up the street.

Rooms 28 (9 annexe) (1 fmly) (1 GF) **S** £90-£120; **D** £120-£180 (incl. bkfst)* **Facilities** STV Use of local health/gym club Xmas New Year Wi-fi **Conf** Class 12 Board 12 Thtr 20 Del from £140 to £150* **Parking** 21 **Notes** LB ⊗

STAMFORD *continued*

Garden House Hotel

★★★ 75% HOTEL

☎ 01780 763359 📠 01780 763339
High St, St Martins PE9 2LP
e-mail: reservations@gardenhousehotel.com
web: www.gardenhousehotel.com
dir: A1 to South Stamford, B1081, signed Stamford & Burghley House. Hotel on left on entering town

Situated within a few minutes' walk of the town centre, this transformed 18th-century town house provides pleasant accommodation. Bedroom styles vary; all are well equipped and comfortably furnished. Public rooms include a charming lounge bar, conservatory restaurant and a smart breakfast room. Service is attentive and friendly throughout.

Rooms 20 (2 fmly) (4 GF) **S** £65-£85; **D** £95-£100 (incl. bkfst)* **Facilities** FTV New Year Wi-fi **Conf** Class 40 Board 30 Thtr 65 Del from £110 to £130* **Parking** 22 **Notes** LB RS 1-7 Jan Civ Wed 70

Candlesticks

RESTAURANT WITH ROOMS

☎ 01780 764033 📠 01780 756071
1 Church Ln PE9 2JU
e-mail: info@candlestickshotel.co.uk
dir: On B1081 High Street St Martins. Church Ln opposite St Martin Church

A 17th-century property situated in a quite lane in the oldest part of Stamford just a short walk from the centre of town. The bedrooms are pleasantly decorated and equipped with a good range of useful extras. Public rooms feature Candlesticks restaurant, a small lounge and a cosy bar.

Rooms 8

S

STANDISH — Map 15 SD51
Greater Manchester

Premier Inn Wigan North

BUDGET HOTEL

☎ 0871 527 9166 📠 0871 527 9167
Almond Brook Rd WN6 0SS
dir: M6 junct 27 follow signs for Standish. Left at T-junct, then 1st right

High quality, budget accommodation ideal for both families and business travellers. Spacious, en suite bedrooms feature tea and coffee making facilities, and Freeview TV in most hotels. Internet access and Wi-fi are available for a small fee. The adjacent family restaurant features a wide and varied menu. See also the Hotel Groups pages.

Rooms 36 **D** £50-£56*

STANLEY — Map 19 NZ15
Co Durham

Beamish Hall Country House Hotel

★★★★ 72% COUNTRY HOUSE HOTEL

☎ 01207 233733 📠 01207 299220
Beamish DH9 0YB
e-mail: info@beamish-hall.co.uk
dir: A693 to Stanley. Follow signs for hotel & Beamish Museum. Left at museum entrance. Hotel on left 0.2m after golf club

This hotel is set in 24 acres of impeccably maintained grounds and can trace its history back many centuries. The public areas are elegant and suitably appointed with leather suites and wooden floors. The beautifully decorated dining room gives that real feel of grandeur with high ceilings and wonderful views of the gardens. All the bedrooms are stylishly designed and well equipped, and include larger rooms that have jacuzzi baths and separate showers; some of the premier rooms are interconnecting, and there is also a two bedroom apartment with its own kitchen and family room.

Rooms 42 (18 fmly) (4 GF) **Facilities** STV FTV Xmas New Year Wi-fi **Conf** Class 160 Board 160 Thtr 300 **Services** Lift **Parking** 300 **Notes** ⊗ Civ Wed 200

STANSTED AIRPORT — Map 6 TL52
Essex

See also **Birchanger Green Motorway Service Area (M11)**

Radisson Blu Hotel London Stansted Airport

Radisson BLU HOTELS & RESORTS

★★★★ 78% HOTEL

☎ 01279 661012 📠 01279 661013
Waltham Close, Stansted Airport CM24 1PP
e-mail: info.stansted@radissonblu.com
web: www.radissonblu.co.uk/hotel-stanstedairport
dir: M11 junct 8 onto A120. Follow London Stansted Airport signs

This modern glass-fronted hotel, linked to the airport terminal by a covered walkway, is particularly well appointed. Facilities include a wide choice of restaurants, a smart leisure club and spa, extensive conference and meeting rooms, and the much talked about wine tower, complete with wine angels. Bedrooms follow a contemporary theme and include a host of thoughtful extras.

Rooms 500 (42 fmly) (51 smoking) **S** £89-£149; **D** £89-£159* **Facilities** Spa STV FTV ⓢ Gym Steam room Sauna Solarium ♫ Xmas New Year Wi-fi **Conf** Class 180 Board 36 Thtr 400 Del from £139 to £199* **Services** Lift Air con **Parking** 220 **Notes** LB ⊗

STANTON ST QUINTIN — Map 4 ST97
Wiltshire

Stanton Manor Hotel

★★★ 79% ❀ HOTEL

☎ 01666 837552 & 0870 890 02880
📠 01666 837022
SN14 6DQ
e-mail: reception@stantonmanor.co.uk
web: www.stantonmanor.co.uk
dir: M4 junct 17, A429 Malmesbury/Cirencester, 200yds, 1st left signed Stanton St Quintin, hotel entrance on left after church

Set in five acres of lovely gardens that includes a short golf course, this charming manor house, mentioned in the Domesday Book, has easy access to the M4. Public areas are a delight offering both character and comfort. The restaurant offers a short carte of imaginative dishes and an interesting wine selection.

Rooms 23 (4 fmly) (7 GF) **Facilities** FTV ⛳ 9 Putt green ⚘ Xmas New Year Wi-fi **Conf** Class 40 Board 32 Thtr 80 **Parking** 60 **Notes** LB Civ Wed 120

STANWICK — Map 11 SP97
Northamptonshire

The Courtyard Luxury Lodge

★★★ 74% SMALL HOTEL

☎ 01933 622233 📠 01933 622276
Rutland Lodge, West St NN9 6QY
e-mail: bookings@thecourtyard.me.uk
dir: A45 rdbt to Stanwick, entrance immediately on right

This charming family-run hotel is situated in the pretty village of Stanwick which is close to major road networks. Guests are guaranteed to receive a warm welcome along with attentive service. The bedrooms are all stylishly presented, very comfortable and benefit from complimentary Wi-fi. Good business and conference facilities are available, and there's ample secure parking.

Rooms 20 (13 annexe) (2 fmly) (17 GF) **S** £35-£75; **D** £45-£95 (incl. bkfst) **Facilities** FTV ♫ Xmas New Year Wi-fi **Conf** Class 180 Board 120 Thtr 250 Del from £110 to £150 **Parking** 60 **Notes** LB Civ Wed 250

STEEPLE ASTON
Oxfordshire — Map 11 SP42

The Holt Hotel

★★★ 72% HOTEL

☎ 01869 340259 📠 01869 340865
Oxford Rd OX25 5QQ
e-mail: info@holthotel.co.uk
web: www.holthotel.co.uk
dir: At junct of B4030 & A4260

This attractive former coaching inn has given hospitality to many over the centuries, not least to Claude Duval, a notorious 17th-century highwayman. Today guests are offered well-equipped, modern bedrooms and attractive public areas, which include a relaxing bar, restaurant and a well-appointed lounge. A selection of meeting rooms is available.

Rooms 86 (19 fmly) **S** £58.80-£82.80; **D** £70.80-£94.80 (incl. bkfst)* **Facilities** FTV Xmas New Year Wi-fi **Conf** Class 57 Board 32 Thtr 140 **Parking** 200 **Notes** LB Civ Wed 120

STEVENAGE
Hertfordshire — Map 12 TL22

Holiday Inn Stevenage

★★★★ 71% HOTEL

☎ 01438 722727 & 346060 📠 01438 727752
St George's Way SG1 1HS
e-mail: reservations@histevenage.com
dir: A1(M) junct 7, A602 to Stevenage, straight on at 1st rdbt, 1st exit at 2nd rdbt, 2nd exit at 3rd rdbt into St George's Way. Hotel 100yds on right

Situated in the heart of the town centre and just 25 minutes from central London by train. Bedrooms are air conditioned and well equipped; ideal for business and leisure travellers. Public areas are smart, capacious and stylish, and as well as a comfortable bar and restaurant there is a mini gym. Parking is limited, so it is advisable to call for details.

Rooms 140 (8 fmly) **Facilities** STV FTV Gym Xmas New Year Wi-fi **Conf** Class 180 Board 190 Thtr 400 Del from £85 to £160* **Services** Lift Air con **Parking** 23 **Notes** LB Civ Wed 400

Novotel Stevenage

★★★ 78% HOTEL

☎ 01438 346100 📠 01438 723872
Knebworth Park SG1 2AX
e-mail: H0992@accor.com
web: www.novotel.com
dir: A1(M) junct 7, at entrance to Knebworth Park

Ideally situated just off the A1(M) is this purpose built hotel, which is a popular business and conference venue. Bedrooms are pleasantly decorated and equipped with a good range of useful extras. Public rooms include a large open plan lounge bar serving a range of snacks, and a smartly appointed restaurant.

Rooms 101 (20 fmly) (30 GF) **Facilities** STV Use of local health club New Year Wi-fi **Conf** Class 80 Board 70 Thtr 150 **Services** Lift **Parking** 120 **Notes** Civ Wed 120

Best Western Roebuck Inn

★★★ 71% HOTEL

☎ 01438 365445 📠 01438 741308
London Rd, Broadwater SG2 8DS
e-mail: hotel@roebuckinn.com
dir: A1(M) junct 7, right towards Stevenage. At 2nd rdbt take 2nd exit signed Roebuck-London/Knebworth/B197. Hotel in 1.5m

Suitable for both the business and leisure traveller, this hotel provides spacious contemporary accommodation in well-equipped bedrooms. The older part of the building, where there is a restaurant and a cosy public bar with log fire and real ales, dates back to the 15th century.

Rooms 26 (8 fmly) (13 GF) **S** £59-£140; **D** £69-£180 **Facilities** STV FTV Xmas New Year Wi-fi **Conf** Class 20 Board 30 Thtr 50 Del from £125 to £155* **Parking** 50 **Notes** ⊗

Ramada Cromwell Stevenage

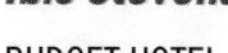

U

☎ 01438 779954 📠 01438 742169
High St, Old Town SG1 3AZ
e-mail: reception@cromwellhotelstevenage.co.uk
dir: A1(M) junct 8 signed Stevenage, over 2 rdbts. Join one-way system, 2nd exit, hotel 200yds on left

Currently the rating for this establishment is not confirmed. This may be due to a change of ownership or because it has only recently joined the AA rating scheme. For further details please see the AA website: theAA.com

Rooms 76 **Conf** Class 80 Board 56 Thtr 180

Holiday Inn Express Stevenage

BUDGET HOTEL

☎ 01438 344300 📠 01438 344301
Danestreet SG1 1XB
e-mail: reservations@morethanhotels.com
web: www.hiexpressstevenage.co.uk
dir: A1(M) junct 7, 1st exit at rdbt to A72, bear left then 3rd exit onto A1070, then 2nd exit to Danestrete

A modern hotel ideal for families and business travellers. Fresh and uncomplicated, the spacious rooms include Sky TV, power shower and tea and coffee-making facilities. Continental buffet breakfast is included in the room rate; other meals may be taken at the nearby family pub or restaurant. See also the Hotel Groups pages.

Rooms 129 (100 fmly) (5 GF) (23 smoking) **Conf** Class 30 Board 20 Thtr 40 Del from £110 to £150*

Ibis Stevenage Centre

BUDGET HOTEL

☎ 01438 779955 📠 01438 741880
Danestrete SG1 1EJ
e-mail: H2794@accor.com
web: www.ibishotel.com
dir: In town centre adjacent to Tesco & Westgate multi storey car park

Modern, budget hotel offering comfortable accommodation in bright and practical bedrooms. Breakfast is self-service and dinner is available in the restaurant. See also the Hotel Groups pages.

Rooms 98

Premier Inn Stevenage Central

BUDGET HOTEL

☎ 0871 527 9034 📠 0871 527 9035
Six Hills Way, Horizon Technology Park SG1 2DD
dir: A1(M) junct 7, follow Stevenage signs. Left into Gunnels Wood Rd. (NB do not use underpass). Left at next rdbt. Hotel in Horizon Technology Park on left

High quality, budget accommodation ideal for both families and business travellers. Spacious, en suite bedrooms feature tea and coffee making facilities, and Freeview TV in most hotels. Internet access and Wi-fi are available for a small fee. The adjacent family restaurant features a wide and varied menu. See also the Hotel Groups pages.

Rooms 115 **D** £45-£56*

STEVENAGE *continued*

Premier Inn Stevenage North

BUDGET HOTEL

☎ 0871 527 9036 🖷 0871 527 9037
Corey's Mill Ln SG1 4AA
dir: A1(M) junct 8, at intersection with A602 (Hitchin Rd & Corey's Mill Lane)

Rooms 41 **D** £54-£63*

STEYNING Map 6 TQ11
West Sussex

Best Western Old Tollgate Restaurant & Hotel

★★★ 78% HOTEL

☎ 01903 879494 🖷 01903 813399
The Street, Bramber BN44 3WE
e-mail: info@oldtollgatehotel.com
web: www.bw-oldtollgatehotel.com
dir: From A283 at Steyning rdbt to Bramber. Hotel 200yds on right

As its name suggests, this well-presented hotel is built on the site of the old toll house. The spacious bedrooms are smartly designed and are furnished to a high standard; eight rooms are air conditioned and have smart power showers. Open for both lunch and dinner, the popular carvery-style restaurant offers an extensive choice of dishes.

Rooms 38 (29 annexe) (5 fmly) (14 GF) **Facilities** STV New Year Wi-fi **Conf** Class 32 Board 26 Thtr 50 **Services** Lift **Parking** 60 **Notes** LB ⊗ Civ Wed 70

S

STILLINGTON Map 19 SE56
North Yorkshire

The Baytree

◎ RESTAURANT WITH ROOMS

☎ 01347 811394
High St YO61 1JU
e-mail: info@baytreestillington.com
web: www.baytreestillington.com
dir: A19 into Tollerton Rd (signed Huby, Public Weighbridge, Sutton Park). In Huby left into Main St, right into Stillington Rd. 1m, right into Roseberry Lane. 0.5m, left into Carr Lane (B1363), right into Main St

Just a 20-minute drive from York, the inn enjoys a quiet country village location. It is spacious with comfortable seating, a large conservatory restaurant, and a small, private dining area - perfect for small parties. The bar has open fires, stone-flagged floors and a great ambiance. The high-standard accommodation includes rooms suitable for families. The award-winning food is the highlight of any stay; the outside eating areas are delightful, and even if it's chilly, there are patio heaters.

Rooms 4 (2 fmly)

STILTON Map 12 TL18
Cambridgeshire

Bell Inn Hotel

★★★ 81% ◎ HOTEL

☎ 01733 241066 🖷 01733 245173
Great North Rd PE7 3RA
e-mail: reception@thebellstilton.co.uk
web: www.thebellstilton.co.uk
dir: A1(M) junct 16, follow Stilton signs. Hotel in village centre

This delightful inn is steeped in history and retains many original features, with imaginative food served in both the character village bar/brasserie and the elegant beamed first floor restaurant; refreshments can be enjoyed in the attractive courtyard and rear gardens when weather permits. Individually designed bedrooms are stylish and equipped to a high standard.

Rooms 22 (3 annexe) (1 fmly) (3 GF) **S** £76-£115; **D** £103-£135 (incl. bkfst)* **Facilities** STV FTV Wi-fi **Conf** Class 46 Board 50 Thtr 130 **Parking** 30 **Notes** ⊗ Closed 25 Dec pm RS 26 Dec pm Civ Wed 130

STOCK Map 6 TQ69
Essex

Greenwoods Hotel Spa & Retreat

★★★★ 75% HOTEL

☎ 01277 829990 & 829205 🖷 01277 829899
Stock Rd CM4 9BE
e-mail: info@greenwoodshotel.co.uk
dir: A12 junct 16 take B1007 signed Billericay. Hotel on right on entering village

Greenwoods is a beautiful 17th-century, Grade II listed manor house set in extensive landscaped gardens. All bedrooms are tastefully appointed, have a marbled bathroom and a wide range of extras; the premier rooms are equipped with spa baths and antique beds. The spa facilities are impressive offering the latest beauty treatments, together with saunas, a jacuzzi, steam rooms, a monsoon shower and a 20-metre pool.

Rooms 39 (6 GF) **Facilities** Spa STV 🏊 Gym Steam room Sauna Monsoon shower Xmas New Year Wi-fi **Conf** Class 70 Board 52 Thtr 110 **Services** Lift **Parking** 100 **Notes** ⊗ No children 16yrs Closed 24 & 26 Dec, 1 Jan Civ Wed 110

STOCKPORT Map 16 SJ89
Greater Manchester

See also **Manchester Airport**

Bredbury Hall Hotel & Country Club

★★★ 81% HOTEL

☎ 0161 430 7421 🖷 0161 430 5079
Goyt Valley SK6 2DH
e-mail: reservations@bredburyhallhotel.com
dir: M60 junct 25 signed Bredbury, right at lights, left onto Osbourne St, hotel 500mtrs on right

With views over open countryside, this large modern hotel is conveniently located for the M60. The well-equipped bedrooms offer space and comfort and the restaurant serves a very wide range of freshly prepared dishes.

Rooms 150 (2 fmly) (50 GF) **Facilities** STV FTV Fishing Gym Night club (Fri & Sat eve) ♫ Xmas New Year Wi-fi **Conf** Class 120 Board 60 Thtr 200 **Services** Lift **Parking** 450 **Notes** ⊗ Civ Wed 80

Alma Lodge Hotel

★★★ 74% HOTEL

☎ 0161 483 4431 📠 0161 483 1983
149 Buxton Rd SK2 6EL
e-mail: reception@almalodgehotel.com
web: www.almalodgehotel.com
dir: M60 junct 1 at rdbt take 2nd exit under rail viaduct at lights opposite. At Debenhams turn right onto A6. Hotel approx 1.5m on left

A large hotel located on the main road close to the town, offering modern and well-equipped bedrooms. It is family owned and run and serves a good range of quality Italian cooking in Luigi's restaurant. Good function rooms and free internet access are also available.

Rooms 52 (32 annexe) (2 fmly) **Facilities** FTV Wi-fi **Conf** Class 100 Board 60 Thtr 250 Del from £100 to £126* **Parking** 120 **Notes** ⊗ RS BHs Civ Wed 200

The Wycliffe Hotel

★★★ 73% HOTEL

☎ 0161 477 5395 📠 0161 476 3219
74 Edgeley Rd, Edgeley SK3 9NQ
e-mail: reception@wycliffe-hotel.com
web: www.wycliffe-hotel.com
dir: M60 junct 2 follow A560 towards Stockport, at 1st lights turn right, hotel 0.5m on left

This family-run, welcoming hotel provides immaculately maintained and well-equipped bedrooms in the main building, and more simply appointed rooms in the two houses opposite. There is a well stocked bar and a popular restaurant where the menu has an Italian bias. There is ample, convenient parking.

Rooms 20 (6 annexe) (3 fmly) (2 GF) **S** £55-£75.50; **D** £72-£87 (incl. bkfst)* **Facilities** FTV Wi-fi **Conf** Class 20 Board 20 Thtr 30 **Parking** 46 **Notes** ⊗ Closed 25-27 Dec RS BHs

Premier Inn Manchester Airport Heald Green

BUDGET HOTEL

☎ 0871 527 8734 📠 0871 527 8735
Finney Ln, Heald Green SK8 3QH
dir: M56 junct 5 follow signs to Terminal 1, at rdbt take 2nd exit, at next rdbt follow Cheadle signs. Left at lights, right at next lights

High quality, budget accommodation ideal for both families and business travellers. Spacious, en suite bedrooms feature tea and coffee making facilities, and Freeview TV in most hotels. Internet access and Wi-fi are available for a small fee. The adjacent family restaurant features a wide and varied menu. See also the Hotel Groups pages.

Rooms 66 **D** £57-£59*

Premier Inn Stockport Central

BUDGET HOTEL

☎ 0871 527 9040 📠 0871 527 9041
Churchgate SK1 1YG
dir: M60 junct 27, A626 towards Marple. Right at Spring Gardens

Rooms 46 **D** £55-£58*

Premier Inn Stockport South

BUDGET HOTEL

☎ 0871 527 9042 📠 0871 527 9043
Buxton Rd, Heaviley SK2 6NB
dir: On A6, 1.5m from town centre

Rooms 40 **D** £55-£58*

STOCKTON-ON-TEES
Co Durham — Map 19 NZ41

Best Western Parkmore Hotel & Leisure Club

★★★ 79% HOTEL

☎ 01642 786815 📠 01642 790485
636 Yarm Rd, Eaglescliffe TS16 0DH
e-mail: enquiries@parkmorehotel.co.uk
dir: Off A19 at Crathorne, follow A67 to Yarm. Through Yarm bear right onto A135 to Stockton. Hotel 1m on left

Set in its own gardens, this smart hotel has grown from its Victorian house origins to provide stylish public areas, as well as extensive leisure and beauty facilities including a hydrotherapy pool and conference facilities. The well-equipped bedrooms include junior suites. The restaurant known as J's@636 has a reputation for creativity meals. Service is friendly and obliging.

Rooms 55 (8 fmly) (9 GF) **Facilities** Spa STV 🏊 supervised Gym Beauty salon Badminton Aerobics studio Hydrotherapy Xmas New Year Wi-fi **Conf** Class 40 Board 40 Thtr 130 **Parking** 90 **Notes** LB Civ Wed 130

Premier Inn Stockton-on-Tees/Hartlepool

BUDGET HOTEL

☎ 0871 527 9044 📠 0871 527 9045
Coal Ln, Wolviston TS22 5PZ
dir: A1(M) junct 60, A689, follow Teeside then Hartlepool signs. Hotel on left at A89 & A19 junct

High quality, budget accommodation ideal for both families and business travellers. Spacious, en suite bedrooms feature tea and coffee making facilities, and Freeview TV in most hotels. Internet access and Wi-fi are available for a small fee. The adjacent family restaurant features a wide and varied menu. See also the Hotel Groups pages.

Rooms 49 **D** £54-£60*

Premier Inn Stockton-on-Tees/Middlesbrough

BUDGET HOTEL

☎ 0871 527 9048 📠 0871 527 9049
Whitewater Way, Thornaby TS17 6QB
dir: A19, A66 towards Stockton & Darlington. Take 1st exit signed Teeside Park/Teesdale. Right at lights over viaduct bridge rdbt & Tees Barrage

Rooms 62 **D** £54-£60*

Premier Inn Stockton-on-Tees West

BUDGET HOTEL

☎ 0871 527 9046 📠 0871 527 9047
Yarm Rd TS18 3RT
dir: A1(M) junct 60, A689 towards Teeside. Follow Hartlepool signs. Hotel on left at A689 & A19 interchange

Rooms 40 **D** £54-£60*

STOKE-BY-NAYLAND Map 13 TL93
Suffolk

The Crown

★★★ 86% ❀❀ SMALL HOTEL

☎ 01206 262001 & 262346 🖷 01206 264026
CO6 4SE
e-mail: reservations@crowninn.net
web: www.crowninn.net
dir: Follow Stoke-by-Nayland signs from A12 & A134. Hotel in village off B1068 towards Higham

Situated in a picturesque village this establishment, with an award-winning restaurant, has a reputation for making everyone feel welcome. It offers quiet, individually decorated rooms that look out over the countryside. Ground floor rooms, including three with a terrace, are of a contemporary design while upstairs rooms are in a country-house style; each room has Wi-fi, DVDs and luxury toiletries.

Rooms 11 (1 fmly) (8 GF) **S** £80-£140; **D** £80-£200 (incl. bkfst)* **Facilities** FTV New Year Wi-fi **Conf** Board 10 **Parking** 49 **Notes** LB ⊗

STOKE D'ABERNON Map 6 TQ15
Surrey

Woodlands Park Hotel

★★★★ 80% ❀❀ HOTEL

☎ 01372 843933 & 0845 072 7581
🖷 01372 842704
Woodlands Ln KT11 3QB
e-mail: woodlandspark@handpicked.co.uk
web: www.handpicked.co.uk
dir: A3 exit at Cobham. Through town centre & Stoke D'Abernon, left at garden centre into Woodlands Lane, hotel 0.5m on right

S

Originally built for the Bryant family, of the matchmaker firm Bryant & May, this lovely Victorian mansion enjoys an attractive parkland setting in ten and a half acres of Surrey countryside. Bedrooms in the wing are contemporary in style while those in the main house are more traditionally decorated. The hotel boasts two dining options, Benson's Brasserie and the Oak Room Restaurant.

Rooms 57 (4 fmly) **Facilities** STV Xmas New Year Wi-fi **Conf** Class 20 Board 50 Thtr 150 **Services** Lift Air con **Parking** 150 **Notes** ⊗ Civ Wed 200

STOKE-ON-TRENT Map 10 SJ84
Staffordshire

Best Western Stoke-on-Trent Moat House

★★★★ 73% HOTEL

☎ 0870 225 4601 & 01782 206101
🖷 01782 206101
Etruria Hall, Festival Way, Etruria ST1 5BQ
e-mail: reservations.stoke@qmh-hotels.com
web: www.bestwestern.co.uk
dir: M6 junct 15 (or junct 16), A500, A53 (Festival Park). Keep in left lane, take 1st slip road on left. Left at island, hotel opposite at next island

A large, modern hotel located in Stoke's Festival Park, that adjoins Etruria Hall, the former home of Josiah Wedgwood. The bedrooms are spacious and well equipped and include family rooms, suites and executive rooms. Public areas include a spacious lounge bar and restaurant as well as a business centre, extensive conference facilities and a leisure club.

Rooms 147 (63 fmly) (22 smoking) **Facilities** supervised Gym Beauty salon Sauna Steam room Solarium Dance studio Xmas New Year Wi-fi **Conf** Class 400 Board 40 Thtr 650 Del from £99 to £149 **Services** Lift Air con **Parking** 350 **Notes** ⊗ Civ Wed 80

Quality Hotel Stoke

★★★ 71% HOTEL

☎ 01782 202361 🖷 01782 286464
66 Trinity St, Hanley ST1 5NB
e-mail: enquiries@qualityhotelsstoke.co.uk
dir: M6 junct 15(S)/16(N) then A500 to city centre & Festival Park. A53 to Leek, keep in left lane, 3rd exit at rdbt for Hanley/City Centre/Cultural Quarter. Hotel on left at top of hill

This large city centre hotel provides a range of bedrooms and extensive public areas including a choice of popular bars. A well lit spacious car park and modern leisure facilities are additional benefits.

Rooms 136 (8 annexe) (54 fmly) (5 GF) **Facilities** supervised Gym Sports massage Hair salon Xmas New Year Wi-fi **Conf** Class 125 Board 60 Thtr 300 **Services** Lift **Parking** 150 **Notes** LB Civ Wed 250

Holiday Inn Express Stoke-on-Trent

BUDGET HOTEL

☎ 01782 377000 🖷 01782 377037
Sir Stanley Matthews Way, Trentham Lakes ST4 4EG
e-mail: info@expressstoke.co.uk
web: www.expressstoke.co.uk
dir: M6 junct 15, follow Uttoxeter/Derby signs to A50. Hotel adjacent to Britannia Stadium

A modern hotel ideal for families and business travellers. Fresh and uncomplicated, the spacious rooms include Sky TV, power shower and tea and coffee-making facilities. Continental buffet breakfast is included in the room rate; other meals may be taken at the nearby family pub or restaurant. See also the Hotel Groups pages.

Rooms 123 (73 fmly) **Conf** Class 16 Board 18 Thtr 35

Premier Inn Stoke (Trentham Gardens)

BUDGET HOTEL

☎ 9871 527 9050 🖷 0871 527 9051
Stone Rd, Trentham ST4 8JG
dir: M6 junct 15, A500, follow Trentham signs. At rdbt 3rd exit onto A34, 2m to hotel on right in Trentham Gardens

High quality, budget accommodation ideal for both families and business travellers. Spacious, en suite bedrooms feature tea and coffee making facilities, and Freeview TV in most hotels. Internet access and Wi-fi are available for a small fee. The adjacent family restaurant features a wide and varied menu. See also the Hotel Groups pages.

Rooms 119 **D** £55-£62*

Weathervane

OldEnglish

BUDGET HOTEL

☎ 01782 388799 🖷 01782 388804
Lysander Rd ST3 7WA
e-mail: 5305@greenking.co.uk
web: www.oldenglish.co.uk

A few minutes from A50 and convenient for both the city and industrial areas, this popular, modern pub and restaurant, under the 'Hungry Horse' brand, provides hearty, well-cooked food at reasonable prices. Adjacent bedrooms are furnished for both commercial and leisure customers.

Rooms 39 (8 fmly) (18 GF) **Conf** Class 20 Board 20 Thtr 20

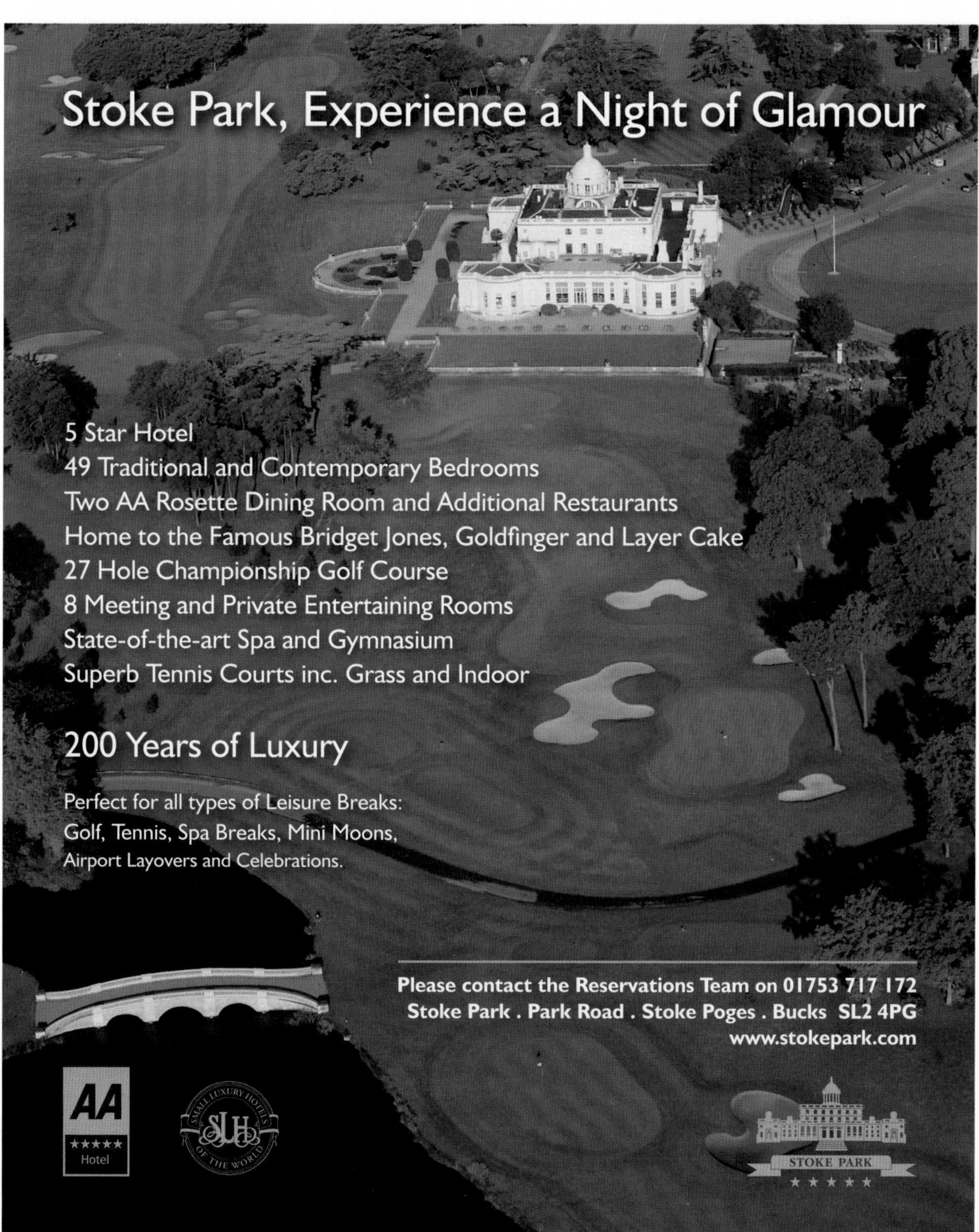
Stoke Park, Experience a Night of Glamour
5 Star Hotel
49 Traditional and Contemporary Bedrooms
Two AA Rosette Dining Room and Additional Restaurants
Home to the Famous Bridget Jones, Goldfinger and Layer Cake
27 Hole Championship Golf Course
8 Meeting and Private Entertaining Rooms
State-of-the-art Spa and Gymnasium
Superb Tennis Courts inc. Grass and Indoor
200 Years of Luxury
Perfect for all types of Leisure Breaks:
Golf, Tennis, Spa Breaks, Mini Moons,
Airport Layovers and Celebrations.
Please contact the Reservations Team on 01753 717 172
Stoke Park . Park Road . Stoke Poges . Bucks SL2 4PG
www.stokepark.com
AA
★★★★★
Hotel
SMALL LUXURY HOTELS OF THE WORLD
SLH
STOKE PARK
★ ★ ★ ★ ★

S

STOKE POGES Buckinghamshire **Map 6 SU98**

Stoke Park

★★★★★ 85% HOTEL

01753 717171 01753 717181
Park Rd SL2 4PG
e-mail: info@stokepark.com
dir: M4 junct 6, A355 towards Slough, B416 (Park Rd), hotel 1.25m on right

Located within 350 acres of beautiful parkland created by 'Capability' Brown and Humphry Repton, this hotel offers outstanding leisure and sporting facilities. Inside the stunning Mansion house, designed by George III's architect, the public areas display lavish opulence throughout and the bedrooms have a luxurious and classic feel. In contrast, the Pavilion features more contemporary bedrooms and public areas; here also are extensive state-of-the-art health and beauty facilities. The hotel has a championship golf course, tennis courts, and four restaurants, including the award-winning Dining Room and the more informal Italian brasserie, San Marco. There are bars, lounges and meeting rooms as well.

Rooms 49 (28 annexe) (14 fmly) **Facilities** Spa STV FTV 27 Putt green Fishing Gym New Year Wi-fi **Conf** Class 30 Board 38 Thtr 70 **Services** Lift **Parking** 460 **Notes** Closed 24-26 Dec Civ Wed 120

See advert on page 463

Stoke Place

★★★★ 79% HOTEL

01753 534790 01753 560209
Stoke Green SL2 4HT
e-mail: enquiries@stokeplace.co.uk
dir: A355, right at 1st lights to A4 Bath Rd. At 1st rdbt take 2nd exit onto Stoke Rd. B416 to Stoke Green. Hotel 200mtrs on right

Originally built in 1690 and set in 26 acres of 'Capability' Brown designed gardens, this William and Mary style manor house has undergone a major refurbishment. It now offers a range of stylish modern bedrooms that are equipped to a very high standard; rear-facing rooms have fantastic view of the garden. Guests can relax in the peaceful lounge and enjoy afternoon tea if they wish. The award-winning Garden Restaurant serves imaginative dishes and the tranquil bar area is ideal for post-dinner drinks.

Rooms 39 (15 annexe) (5 GF) **S** £130-£195; **D** £150-£225 (incl. bkfst) **Facilities** STV Fishing Outdoor jogging track Xmas New Year Wi-fi **Conf** Class 100 Board 60 Thtr 200 Del from £250 to £325 **Parking** 120 **Notes** LB Civ Wed 150

See advert on this page

STONE Staffordshire **Map 10 SJ93**

Stone House

★★★ 68% HOTEL

01785 815531 & 0844 414 6580
01785 814764
Stafford Rd ST15 0BQ
e-mail: reservations.stone@ohiml.com
web: www.oxfordhotelsandinns.com
dir: M6 junct 14 (N) or junct 15 (S). Hotel on A34

This former country house, set in attractive grounds, is located within easy reach of the M6. Attractive comfortable bedrooms and tastefully appointed public areas together with leisure and conference facilities make the hotel popular with both corporate and leisure guests. A light menu is offered in the bar and lounge areas, or guests can choose to dine in the stylish restaurant.

Rooms 50 (1 fmly) (15 GF) **Facilities** FTV supervised Gym New Year Wi-fi **Conf** Class 50 Board 40 Thtr 150 **Parking** 100 **Notes** Civ Wed 60

S

STON EASTON Map 4 ST65
Somerset

INSPECTORS' CHOICE

Ston Easton Park

★★★★ ®® COUNTRY HOUSE HOTEL

☎ 01761 241631 🖷 01761 241377
BA3 4DF
e-mail: info@stoneaston.co.uk
web: www.stoneaston.co.uk
dir: On A37

Surrounded by The Mendips this outstanding Palladian mansion lies in extensive parklands that were landscaped by Humphrey Repton. The architecture and decorative features are stunning; the state rooms include one of England's earliest surviving Print Rooms, and the Palladian Saloon considered one of Somerset's finest rooms. There is even an Edwardian kitchen that guests might like to take a look at. The helpful and attentive team provide a very efficient service, and the award-winning cuisine uses organic produce from the hotel's own kitchen garden. The bedrooms and bathrooms are all appointed to an excellent standard.

Rooms 22 (3 annexe) (2 fmly) **Facilities** STV Fishing Archery Clay pigeon shooting Quad bikes Hot air ballooning Xmas New Year Wi-fi **Conf** Class 60 Board 30 Thtr 100 **Parking** 120 **Notes** LB Civ Wed 100

STOURPORT-ON-SEVERN Map 10 SO87
Worcestershire

Menzies Stourport Manor
MenziesHotels

★★★★ 77% HOTEL

☎ 01299 289955 🖷 01299 878520
35 Hartlebury Rd DY13 9JA
e-mail: stourport@menzieshotels.co.uk
web: www.menzieshotels.co.uk
dir: M5 junct 6, A449 towards Kidderminster, B4193 towards Stourport. Hotel on right

Once the home of Prime Minister Sir Stanley Baldwin, this much extended country house is set in attractive grounds. A number of bedrooms and suites are located in the original building, although the majority are in a more modern, purpose-built section. Spacious public areas include a range of lounges, a popular restaurant, a leisure club and conference facilities.

Rooms 68 (17 fmly) (31 GF) (10 smoking) **Facilities** Putt green Gym Squash Xmas New Year Wi-fi **Conf** Class 110 Board 40 Thtr 350 **Parking** 300 **Notes** Civ Wed 300

STOWMARKET Map 13 TM05
Suffolk

Cedars
THE INDEPENDENTS HOTEL ASSOCIATION

★★★ 74% HOTEL

☎ 01449 612668 🖷 01449 674704
Needham Rd IP14 2AJ
e-mail: info@cedarshotel.co.uk
dir: A14 junct 15, A1120 towards Stowmarket. At junct with A1113 turn right. Hotel on right

Expect a friendly welcome at this privately owned hotel, which is situated just off the A14 within easy reach of the town centre. Public rooms are full of charm and character with features such as exposed beams and open fireplaces. Bedrooms are pleasantly decorated and thoughtfully equipped with modern facilities.

Rooms 25 (3 fmly) (9 GF) **S** £65-£68.50; **D** £70-£76 (incl. bkfst)* **Facilities** Wi-fi **Conf** Class 60 Board 40 Thtr 150 **Parking** 75 **Notes** LB Closed 25 Dec-1 Jan

STOW-ON-THE-WOLD Map 10 SP12
Gloucestershire

Number Four at Stow Hotel & Restaurant

★★★★ 80% ®® SMALL HOTEL

☎ 01451 830297 🖷 01451 831768
Fosseway GL54 1JX
e-mail: reservations@hotelnumberfour.co.uk

This hotel is situated in one of the most picturesque areas of the Cotswolds and has undergone a complete refurbishment. Service is relaxed and friendly, and the bedrooms are very stylish and beautifully presented. The award-winning Cutler's Restaurant serves imaginative dishes using the finest in local produce. Public areas include a contemporary lounge area and a well-equipped business suite.

Rooms 18 (5 fmly) (12 GF) **S** £90-£120; **D** £110-£150 (incl. bkfst)* **Facilities** FTV Wi-fi **Conf** Class 15 Board 28 Thtr 50 **Services** Air con **Parking** 50 **Notes** ®

The Wyck Hill House Hotel

★★★★ 74% ®® HOTEL

☎ 01451 831936 🖷 01451 832243
Burford Rd GL54 1HY
e-mail: info.wyckhillhouse@bespokehotels.com
dir: Exit A429. Hotel 1m on right

This charming 18th-century house enjoys superb views across the Windrush Valley and is ideally positioned for a relaxing weekend exploring the Cotswolds. The spacious and thoughtfully equipped bedrooms provide high standards of comfort and quality, located both in the main house and also the original coach house. Elegant public rooms include a cosy bar, library and the magnificent front hall with crackling log fire. The imaginative cuisine makes effective use of local produce.

Rooms 60 (4 GF) **S** £105-£190; **D** £145-£365 (incl. bkfst)* **Facilities** Spa FTV Sauna Steam room Xmas New Year Wi-fi **Conf** Class 50 Board 50 Thtr 150 Del from £145 to £165* **Services** Lift **Parking** 100 **Notes** LB ® Civ Wed 120

S

STOW-ON-THE-WOLD *continued*

Fosse Manor

★★★ 80% HOTEL

☎ 01451 830354 📠 01451 832486
GL54 1JX
e-mail: enquiries@fossemanor.co.uk
web: www.fossemanor.co.uk
dir: 1m S on A429, 300yds past junct with A424

Deriving its name from the historic Roman Fosse Way, this popular hotel is ideally situated for exploring the many delights of this picturesque area. Bedrooms, located both in the main building and the adjacent coach house, offer high standards of comfort and quality. Public areas include a small lounge, spacious bar and light and airy restaurant. Classy cuisine is on offer with quality produce used to create imaginative dishes.

Rooms 19 (8 annexe) (3 fmly) (5 GF) **Facilities** FTV Xmas New Year Wi-fi **Conf** Class 20 Board 26 Thtr 60 Del from £110 to £150* **Parking** 30 **Notes** LB

Stow Lodge

★★★ 77% SMALL HOTEL

☎ 01451 830485 📠 01451 831671
The Square GL54 1AB
e-mail: enquiries@stowlodge.com
web: www.stowlodge.com
dir: In town centre

Situated in smart grounds, this family-run hotel has direct access to the market square and provides high standards of customer care. Bedrooms are offered both within the main building and in the converted coach house, all of which provide similar standards of homely comfort. Extensive menus and an interesting wine list make for an enjoyable dining experience.

Rooms 21 (10 annexe) (1 fmly) **D** £85-£175 (incl. bkfst)* **Facilities** Wi-fi **Parking** 30 **Notes** LB No children 5yrs Closed Xmas-end Jan

Old Stocks

★★ 72% SMALL HOTEL

☎ 01451 830666 📠 01451 870014
The Square GL54 1AF
e-mail: aa@oldstockshotel.co.uk
web: www.oldstockshotel.co.uk
dir: Exit A429 to town centre. Hotel facing village green

Overlooking the old market square, this Grade II listed, mellow Cotswold-stone building is a comfortable and friendly base from which to explore this picturesque area. There's lots of character throughout, and the bedrooms offer individuality and charm. Facilities include a guest lounge, restaurant and bar, whilst outside, the patio is a popular summer venue for refreshing drinks and good food.

Rooms 18 (3 annexe) (5 fmly) (4 GF) **S** £36-£56; **D** £72-£112 (incl. bkfst)* **Facilities** FTV New Year Wi-fi **Parking** 12 **Notes** LB

STRATFORD-UPON-AVON
Warwickshire
Map 10 SP25

INSPECTORS' CHOICE

Ettington Park Hotel

HandPICKED HOTELS

★★★★ HOTEL

☎ 01789 450123 & 0845 072 7454
📠 01789 450472
CV37 8BU
e-mail: ettingtonpark@handpicked.co.uk
web: www.handpicked.co.uk
(For full entry see Alderminster)

Menzies Welcombe Hotel Spa & Golf Club

MenziesHotels

★★★★ 83% HOTEL

☎ 01789 295252 📠 01789 414666
Warwick Rd CV37 0NR
e-mail: welcombe@menzieshotels.co.uk
web: www.menzieshotels.co.uk
dir: M40 junct 15, A46 towards Stratford-upon-Avon, at rdbt follow signs for A439. Hotel 3m on right

This Jacobean manor house is set in 157 acres of landscaped parkland. Public rooms are impressive, especially the lounge with its wood panelling and ornate marble fireplace, and the gentleman's club-style bar. Bedrooms in the original building are stylish and gracefully proportioned; those in the garden wing are comfortable and thoughtfully equipped. The spa development incorporates advanced, luxurious facilities and treatments.

Rooms 78 (12 fmly) (11 GF) (6 smoking) **Facilities** Spa STV 18 Putt green Gym Xmas New Year Wi-fi **Conf** Class 75 Board 40 Thtr 200 **Parking** 200 **Notes** Civ Wed 120

The Arden Hotel

★★★★ 81% HOTEL

☎ 01789 298682 📠 0845 356 3047
Waterside CV37 6BA
e-mail: enquiries@theardenhotelstratford.com
web: www.theardenhotelstratford.com
dir: M40 junct 15 follow signs to town centre. At Barclays Bank rdbt left onto High St, 2nd left onto Chapel Lane (Nash's House on left). Hotel car park on right in 40yds

This property is on the same road as the world famous Royal Shakespeare and Swan theatres, and just a short walk from the town centre. The bedrooms and bathrooms have been tastefully designed and have quality fixtures and fittings. The dedicated team provide polite and professional service. Award-winning cuisine is served in the popular restaurant. Ample secure parking is available.

Rooms 45 (6 fmly) (17 GF) **Facilities** FTV Xmas New Year Wi-fi **Conf** Class 18 Board 28 Thtr 50 **Parking** 50 **Notes** LB Civ Wed 50

Macdonald Alveston Manor

★★★★ 79% HOTEL

☎ 0844 879 9138 📠 01789 414095
Clopton Bridge CV37 7HP
e-mail: sales.alvestonmanor@macdonald-hotels.co.uk
web: www.macdonald-hotels.co.uk
dir: On rdbt south of Clopton Bridge

A striking red-brick and timbered façade, well-tended grounds, and a giant cedar tree all contribute to the charm of this well-established hotel, just five minutes from Stratford. The bedrooms vary in size and character - the coach house conversion offers an impressive mix of full and junior suites. The superb leisure complex offers a 20-metre swimming pool, steam room, sauna, a high-tech gym and a host of beauty treatments.

Rooms 113 (8 fmly) (45 GF) **Facilities** Spa FTV supervised Gym Techno-gym Beauty treatments New Year Wi-fi **Conf** Class 80 Board 40 Thtr 140 Del from £140 to £185* **Services** Air con **Parking** 150 **Notes** Civ Wed 110

S

Barceló Billesley Manor Hotel

★★★★ 77% HOTEL

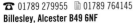

☎ 01789 279955 01789 764145
Billesley, Alcester B49 6NF
e-mail: billesleymanor@barcelo-hotels.co.uk
web: www.barcelo-hotels.co.uk
dir: A46 towards Evesham. Over 3 rdbts, right for Billesley after 2m

This 16th-century manor is set in peaceful grounds and parkland with a delightful yew topiary garden and fountain. The spacious bedrooms and suites, most in traditional country-house style, are thoughtfully designed and well equipped. Conference facilities and some of the bedrooms are found in the cedar barns. Public areas retain many original features, such as oak panelling, fireplaces and exposed stone.

Rooms 72 (29 annexe) (5 GF) **Facilities** Spa supervised Gym Steam room Beauty treatments Yoga studio Xmas New Year **Conf** Class 60 Board 50 Thtr 100 **Parking** 100 **Notes** Civ Wed 75

The Stratford

★★★★ 77% HOTEL

☎ 01789 271000 & 271007 01789 271001
Arden St CV37 6QQ
e-mail: thestratfordreservations@qhotels.co.uk
web: www.qhotels.co.uk
dir: A439 into Stratford. In town follow A3400/ Birmingham, at lights left into Arden St, hotel 150yds on right

Situated adjacent to the hospital, this eye-catching modern hotel with its red-brick façade is within walking distance of the town centre. The hotel offers modern, well-equipped and spacious bedrooms. The open-plan public areas include a comfortable lounge, a small, atmospheric bar and a spacious restaurant with exposed beams.

Rooms 102 (7 fmly) (14 GF) **S** £69-£159; **D** £99-£169 (incl. bkfst)* **Facilities** STV Gym Free use of Stratford Manor's leisure facilities Xmas New Year Wi-fi **Conf** Class 66 Board 54 Thtr 132 Del from £135 to £189* **Services** Lift Air con **Parking** 92 **Notes** LB Civ Wed 132

Stratford Manor

★★★★ 77% HOTEL

☎ 01789 731173 01789 731131
Warwick Rd CV37 0PY
e-mail: stratfordmanor@qhotels.co.uk
web: www.qhotels.co.uk
dir: M40 junct 15, A46 signed Stratford. At 2nd rdbt take A439 signed Stratford Town Centre. Hotel 1m on left. Or from Stratford centre take A439 signed Warwick & M40. Hotel 3m on right

Just outside Stratford, this hotel is set against a rural backdrop with lovely gardens and ample parking. Public areas include a stylish lounge bar and a contemporary restaurant. Service is both professional and helpful. Bedrooms are smartly appointed, spacious and have generously sized beds and a range of useful facilities. The leisure centre boasts a large indoor pool.

Rooms 104 (8 fmly) (24 GF) **Facilities** Gym Sauna Steam room Xmas New Year Wi-fi **Conf** Class 120 Board 100 Thtr 350 Del from £120 to £165* **Services** Lift **Parking** 220 **Notes** Civ Wed 150

Holiday Inn Stratford-upon-Avon

★★★★ 74% HOTEL

☎ 0871 942 9270 & 01789 279988
01789 298589
Bridgefoot CV37 6YR
e-mail: histratford@qmh-hotels.com
web: www.holidayinn.co.uk
dir: A439 to Stratford-upon-Avon. On entering town road bears left, hotel 200mtrs on left

This large modern hotel sits beside the River Avon in landscaped grounds and has ample parking. Bedrooms have a light contemporary feel and are equipped with a good range of facilities that include air conditioning and Wi-fi. Day rooms include a terrace lounge and bar, a carvery restaurant and the Club Moativation health and fitness facility that proves popular with both corporate and leisure guests.

Rooms 259 (8 fmly) **Facilities** STV supervised Gym Sauna Steam room Solarium Beauty Salon Xmas New Year Wi-fi **Conf** Class 340 Board 42 Thtr 550 **Services** Lift Air con **Parking** 350 **Notes** LB

Legacy Falcon

LEGACY HOTELS

★★★★ 71% HOTEL

☎ 08444 119005 & 0330 333 2805
08444 119006
Chapel St CV37 6HA
e-mail: res-falcon@legacy-hotels.co.uk
web: www.legacy-hotels.co.uk
dir: M40 junct 15, follow signs to town centre, towards Barclays Bank on rdbt. Turn into High St between Austin Reed & WH Smith. 2nd right into Scholars Ln, right into hotel car park

Situated in the heart of the town just a short walk from all the Shakespeare properties. The hotel dates back to 1500, and in the 17th century an extra storey was added. Bedrooms provide contemporary accommodation and the public areas are cosy. Service is provided by a friendly team. The restaurant provides good quality cuisine using fresh, local ingredients.

Rooms 83 (11 annexe) (6 fmly) (3 GF) **Facilities** STV Xmas New Year Wi-fi **Conf** Class 80 Board 50 Thtr 150 **Services** Lift **Parking** 120 **Notes** Civ Wed 150

Mercure Shakespeare

★★★★ 71% HOTEL

☎ 01789 294997 01789 415411
Chapel St CV37 6ER
e-mail: h6630@accor.com
web: www.mercure.com
dir: M40 junct 15. Follow signs for Stratford town centre on A439. Follow one-way system onto Bridge St. Left at rdbt, hotel 200yds on left opp HSBC bank

Dating back to the early 17th century, The Shakespeare is one of the oldest hotels in this historic town. The hotel name represents one of the earliest exploitations of Stratford as the birthplace of one of the world's leading playwrights. With exposed beams and open fires, the public rooms retain an ambience reminiscent of this era. Bedrooms are appointed to a good standard and remain in keeping with the style of the property.

Rooms 73 (11 annexe) (3 GF) **D** £79-£230 (incl. bkfst)* **Facilities** Xmas New Year Wi-fi **Conf** Class 60 Board 40 Thtr 80 **Services** Lift **Parking** 34 **Notes** Civ Wed 100

STRATFORD-UPON-AVON ***continued***

Macdonald Swan's Nest

★★★★ 71% HOTEL

☎ 0844 879 9140 📠 01789 414547
Bridgefoot CV37 7LT
e-mail: sales.swansnest@macdonald-hotels.co.uk
web: www.macdonald-hotels.co.uk/swansnest
dir: A439 towards Stratford, follow one-way system, turn left, over bridge (A3400), hotel on right

Dating back to the 17th century, this hotel is said to be one of the earliest brick-built houses in Stratford. It occupies a prime position on the banks of the River Avon and is ideally situated for exploring the town. Bedrooms and bathrooms are appointed to a high standard with some thoughtful guest extras provided.

Rooms 68 (2 fmly) (25 GF) **Facilities** FTV Use of facilities at Macdonald Alveston Manor New Year Wi-fi **Conf** Class 100 Board 60 Thtr 150 **Parking** 80 **Notes** Civ Wed 150

Best Western Grosvenor House

★★★ 78% HOTEL

☎ 01789 269213 📠 01789 266087
Warwick Rd CV37 6YT
e-mail: res@bwgh.co.uk
web: www.bwgh.co.uk
dir: M40 junct 15, follow Stratford signs to A439 (Warwick Rd). Hotel 7m, on one-way system

This hotel is a short distance from the town centre and many of the historic attractions. Bedroom styles and sizes vary, and the friendly staff offer an efficient service. Refreshments are served in the lounge all day, and room service is available. The Garden Room restaurant offers a choice of dishes from set priced and carte menus.

Rooms 73 (16 fmly) (25 GF) **S** £59-£140; **D** £59-£140 **Facilities** STV FTV Xmas New Year Wi-fi **Conf** Class 45 Board 50 Thtr 100 Del from £85 to £160 **Parking** 46 **Notes** LB ⊗ Civ Wed 100

Charlecote Pheasant Hotel

★★★ 78% HOTEL

☎ 0844 855 9126 📠 01789 470222
Charlecote CV35 9EW
dir: M40 junct 15, A429 towards Cirencester through Barford. In 2m right into Charlecote, hotel opposite Charlecote Park

Located just outside Stratford, this hotel is set in extensive grounds and is a popular conference venue. Various bedroom styles are available in the annexe wings, ranging from standard rooms to executive suites. The main building houses the restaurant and a lounge bar area.

Rooms 70 (39 fmly) **Facilities** FTV Children's play area Xmas New Year Wi-fi **Conf** Class 70 Board 40 Thtr 160 **Parking** 100 **Notes** Civ Wed 176

The New Inn Hotel & Restaurant

★★ HOTEL

☎ 01789 293402 📠 01789 292716
Clifford Chambers CV37 8HR
e-mail: thenewinn65@aol.com
web: www.thenewinnhotel.co.uk
dir: A3400 onto B4632, 500yds on left

Rooms 13 (2 fmly) (3 GF) **Facilities** New Year Wi-fi **Parking** 40 **Notes** ⊗ Closed 23-28 Dec

Premier Inn Stratford-upon-Avon Central

BUDGET HOTEL

☎ 0871 527 9282
Payton Rd CV37 6UQ
dir: A439, A4300 signed Stratford-upon-Avon. Hotel on left

High quality, budget accommodation ideal for both families and business travellers. Spacious, en suite bedrooms feature tea and coffee making facilities, and Freeview TV in most hotels. Internet access and Wi-fi are available for a small fee. The adjacent family restaurant features a wide and varied menu. See also the Hotel Groups pages.

Rooms 87 **D** £51-£63*

STREATLEY
Berkshire — **Map 5 SU58**

The Swan at Streatley

★★★★ 73% HOTEL

☎ 01491 878800 📠 01491 872554
High St RG8 9HR
e-mail: sales@swan-at-streatley.co.uk
web: www.swanatstreatley.co.uk
dir: From S right at lights in Streatley, hotel on left before bridge

A stunning location set beside the Thames, ideal for an English summer's day. The bedrooms are well appointed and many enjoy the lovely views. The hotel offers a range of facilities including meeting rooms, and the Magdalen Barge is moored beside the hotel making an unusual, yet perfect meeting venue. Motor launches are available for hire from April to October. The spa includes an indoor heated mineral pool and offers a range of treatments. Cuisine is accomplished and dining here should not be missed.

Rooms 45 (12 GF) **Facilities** Spa STV supervised Fishing Gym Electric motor launches for hire Apr-Oct Xmas New Year Wi-fi **Conf** Class 80 Board 60 Thtr 140 **Parking** 170 **Notes** Civ Wed 130

STREET
Somerset — **Map 4 ST43**

Wessex Hotel

★★★ 64% HOTEL

☎ 01458 443383 📠 01458 446589
High St BA16 0EF
e-mail: info@wessexhotel.com
dir: A303 into B3151. 7m, pass lights by Millfield School. Left at mini-rdbt

Centrally located in this popular town, with easy access to all the shops and attractions. The bedrooms and bathrooms vary slightly in size but most rooms provide good levels of quality and comfort. A wide range of snacks and refreshments is available throughout the day, including a regular carvery at dinner. Entertainment is often offered in the main season.

Rooms 51 (9 fmly) **S** £55-£65; **D** £75-£95 (incl. bkfst) **Facilities** FTV Xmas New Year Wi-fi **Conf** Class 120 Board 80 Thtr 400 **Services** Lift **Parking** 70 **Notes** LB ⊗

STROUD
Gloucestershire — **Map 4 SO80**

Burleigh Court

★★★ 79% HOTEL

☎ 01453 883804 📠 01453 886870
Burleigh, Minchinhampton GL5 2PF
e-mail: burleighcourt@aol.com
dir: From Stroud A419 towards Cirencester. Right after 2.5m signed Burleigh & Minchinhampton. Left after 500yds signed Burleigh Court. Hotel 300yds

Dating back to the 18th century, this former gentleman's manor house is in a secluded and elevated, though accessible, position with some wonderful countryside views. Public rooms are elegantly styled and include an oak-panelled bar for pre-dinner drinks beside a crackling fire. Combining comfort and quality, no two bedrooms are alike; some are in an adjoining coach house.

Rooms 18 (7 annexe) (2 fmly) (3 GF) **S** £90-£110; **D** £140-£200 (incl. bkfst)* **Facilities** New Year Wi-fi Child facilities **Conf** Class 30 Board 30 Thtr 50 **Parking** 40 **Notes** LB Closed 24-26 Dec Civ Wed 50

The Bear of Rodborough

★★★ 79% HOTEL

☎ 01453 878522 📠 01453 872523
Rodborough Common GL5 5DE
e-mail: info@bearofrodborough.info
web: www.cotswold-inns-hotels.co.uk/bear
dir: M5 junct 13, A419 to Stroud. Follow signs to Rodborough. Up hill, left at top at T-junct. Hotel on right

This popular 17th-century coaching inn is situated high above Stroud in acres of National Trust parkland. Character abounds in the lounges and cocktail bar, and in the Box Tree Restaurant where the cuisine utilises fresh local produce. Bedrooms offer equal measures of comfort and style with plenty of extra touches. There is also a traditional and well-patronised public bar.

Rooms 46 (2 fmly) **S** £80-£90; **D** £130-£140 (incl. bkfst)* **Facilities** STV Putt green Xmas New Year Wi-fi **Conf** Class 35 Board 30 Thtr 60 Del from £145* **Parking** 70 **Notes** LB Civ Wed 70

Premier Inn Stroud

BUDGET HOTEL

☎ 0871 527 9052 📠 0871 527 9053
Stratford Lodge, Stratford Rd GL5 4AF
dir: M5 junct 13, A419 to town centre, follow Leisure Centre signs. Hotel adjacent to Tesco superstore

High quality, budget accommodation ideal for both families and business travellers. Spacious, en suite bedrooms feature tea and coffee making facilities, and Freeview TV in most hotels. Internet access and Wi-fi are available for a small fee. The adjacent family restaurant features a wide and varied menu. See also the Hotel Groups pages.

Rooms 32 **D** £50-£59*

STUDLEY
Warwickshire — Map 10 SP06

Best Western Studley Castle

★★★ 73% HOTEL

☎ 01527 853111 & 855200 📠 01527 855000
Castle Rd B80 7AJ
e-mail: bookings@studleycastle.com
dir: A435 S into Studley, left at castle sign, hotel 1m on right

This hotel has a delightful parkland location close to Stratford. Specialising in providing meeting room venues, the hotel has an impressive range of public areas. The restaurant also offers a relaxing environment and lovely views across the countryside. Bedrooms are available in a range of sizes and all are well equipped.

Rooms 56 (2 fmly) **Facilities** STV Gym Xmas New Year Wi-fi **Conf** Class 66 Board 20 Thtr 150 **Services** Lift **Parking** 150 **Notes** LB Civ Wed 150

SUDBURY
Derbyshire — Map 10 SK13

The Boars Head

★★★ 75% HOTEL

☎ 01283 820344 📠 01283 820075
Lichfield Rd DE6 5GX
e-mail: enquiries@boars-head-hotel.co.uk
web: www.boars-head-hotel.co.uk
dir: A50 onto A515 towards Lichfield, hotel 1m on right

This popular hotel offers comfortable accommodation in well-equipped bedrooms. There is a relaxed atmosphere in the public rooms, which consists of a several bars and dining options. The beamed lounge bar provides informal dining thanks to a popular carvery, while the restaurant and cocktail bar offer a more formal environment.

Rooms 23 (1 annexe) (14 GF) **S** £59.95-£69.95; **D** £69.95-£79.95 (incl. bkfst)* **Facilities** STV Beauty salon Xmas New Year Wi-fi **Parking** 85 **Notes** LB

See advert on page 121

SUNBURY
Surrey

See LONDON SECTION plan A1

Premier Inn Sunbury (Kempton Park)

BUDGET HOTEL

☎ 0871 527 9054 📠 0871 527 9055
Staines Road West, Sunbury Cross TW16 7AT
dir: M25 junct 12, onto M3 signed London & Richmond. Exit at junct 1, take 1st exit at rdbt into Staines Road West (A308). 1st left into Crossways. Hotel on right

High quality, budget accommodation ideal for both families and business travellers. Spacious, en suite bedrooms feature tea and coffee making facilities, and Freeview TV in most hotels. Internet access and Wi-fi are available for a small fee. The adjacent family restaurant features a wide and varied menu. See also the Hotel Groups pages.

Rooms 109 **D** £51-£63*

SUNDERLAND
Tyne & Wear — Map 19 NZ35

Sunderland Marriott

★★★★ 73% HOTEL

☎ 0191 529 2041 📠 0191 529 4227
Queen's Pde, Seaburn SR6 8DB
e-mail: mhrs.nclsl.frontoffice@marriotthotels.com
web: www.sunderlandmarriott.co.uk
dir: A19, A184 (Boldon/Sunderland North), 3m. At rdbt left, then right. At rdbt left, follow to coast. Right, hotel on right

This seafront hotel provides comfortable and spacious bedrooms, some with fabulous views of the North Sea and vast expanses of sandy beach. Public rooms are bright and modern and a number of meeting rooms are available. The hotel is conveniently located for access to the local visitor attractions.

Rooms 82 (6 fmly) **Facilities** STV Gym Xmas New Year Wi-fi **Conf** Class 120 Board 70 Thtr 300 **Services** Lift **Parking** 110 **Notes** Civ Wed 80

S

SUNDERLAND *continued*

Best Western Roker

★★★ 77% HOTEL

☎ 0191 567 1786 & 567 8221 🖷 0191 510 0289
Roker Ter, Roker SR6 9ND
e-mail: info@rokerhotel.co.uk

This modern hotel offers stunning views of the coastline. Well-equipped bedrooms come in a variety of sizes, and several have feature bathrooms. Functions, conferences and weddings are all well catered for in the function suite. A choice of dining options is available including Restaurant Italia and Restaurant China, as well as an impressive range of bar meals in the R-bar.

Rooms 43 (8 fmly) (3 GF) **S** £50-£125; **D** £60-£175 (incl. bkfst) **Facilities** STV FTV ♫ Wi-fi **Conf** Class 150 Board 100 Thtr 300 Del from £90 to £150 **Services** Lift Air con **Parking** 150 **Notes** LB ⊗ Civ Wed 350

Premier Inn Sunderland A19/A1231

BUDGET HOTEL

☎ 0871 527 9058 🖷 0871 527 9059
Wessington Way, Castletown SR5 3HR
dir: From A19 take A1231 towards Sunderland. Hotel 100yds

High quality, budget accommodation ideal for both families and business travellers. Spacious, en suite bedrooms feature tea and coffee making facilities, and Freeview TV in most hotels. Internet access and Wi-fi are available for a small fee. The adjacent family restaurant features a wide and varied menu. See also the Hotel Groups pages.

Rooms 61 **D** £51-£58*

Premier Inn Sunderland North West

BUDGET HOTEL

☎ 0871 527 9056 🖷 0871 527 9057
Timber Beach Rd, off Wessington Way, Castletown SR5 3XG
dir: A1(M) junct 65, A1231 towards Sunderland, (cross over A19)

Rooms 63 **D** £51-£58*

SURBITON
Greater London

See **LONDON SECTION plan 1 C1**

Holiday Inn London - Kingston South

★★★★ 75% HOTEL

☎ 020 8786 6565 & 8786 6500 🖷 020 8786 6575
Kingston Tower, Portsmouth Rd KT6 5QQ
e-mail: enquiries@hikingston.co.uk
dir: M25 junct 10, A3, left onto A243, 3rd exit at rdbt. At lights left onto A307

This hotel occupies a convenient location overlooking the River Thames just outside Kingston-upon-Thames and close to Surbiton. Many front-facing bedrooms have beautiful river views; all are comfortable and stylish. The public areas include a small yet well-equipped fitness room. Complimentary parking and Wi-fi are also available.

Rooms 116 (2 fmly) **Facilities** STV FTV Gym Wi-fi **Conf** Class 125 Board 60 Thtr 250 Del from £129 to £169* **Services** Lift Air con **Parking** 120 **Notes** Civ Wed 300

SUTTON
Greater London — Map 6 TQ26

Holiday Inn London-Sutton

★★★ 79% HOTEL

☎ 020 8234 1100 & 8234 1104 🖷 020 8770 1539
Gibson Rd SM1 2RF
e-mail: sales-sutton@ihg.com
web: www.holidayinn.co.uk
dir: M25 junct 8, A217, B2230. Pass rail station, follow one-way system in right lane. At lights, right, immediately left, left into Gibson Rd

Well located for many famous attractions such as Chessington World of Adventure, All England Tennis Club at Wimbledon and Epsom Racecourse. This hotel offers air-conditioned bedrooms ranging from standard to executive, a variety of conference rooms, and leisure facilities with a swimming pool.

Rooms 119 (4 fmly) (6 smoking) **Facilities** Spa STV ③ Gym Xmas New Year Wi-fi **Conf** Class 100 Board 70 Thtr 180 Del from £99 to £135* **Services** Lift Air con **Parking** 105 **Notes** LB ⊗ Civ Wed 140

SUTTON COLDFIELD
West Midlands — Map 10 SP19

New Hall

★★★★ 80% ®® HOTEL

☎ 08450 727577 🖷 08450 727578
Walmley Rd B76 1QX
e-mail: newhall@handpicked.co.uk
dir: M42 junct 9, A4097, 2m to rdbt, take 2nd exit signed Walmley. Take 2nd exit from next 5 rdbts follow Sutton Coldfield signs. At 6th rdbt take 3rd exit follow Sutton Coldfield signs. Hotel on left

Situated in 26 acres of beautiful grounds this hotel is reputed to be the oldest inhabited, moated house in the country. The house's medieval charm and character combine well with 21st-century guest facilities. Executive and luxury suites are available. Public areas, with their fine panelling and mullioned stained-glass windows include the magnificent Great Chamber.

Rooms 60 (14 fmly) (25 GF) **Facilities** Spa STV FTV ③ supervised ⛳ 9 🎾 Fishing 🐎 Gym Steam room Pitch & putt Xmas New Year Wi-fi **Conf** Class 75 Board 35 Thtr 150 **Parking** 80 **Notes** ⊗ Civ Wed 70

Best Western Premier Moor Hall Hotel & Spa

★★★★ 75% HOTEL

☎ 0121 308 3751 🖷 0121 308 8974
Moor Hall Dr, Four Oaks B75 6LN
e-mail: mail@moorhallhotel.co.uk
web: www.moorhallhotel.co.uk
dir: A38 onto A453 towards Sutton Coldfield, right at lights into Weeford Rd. Hotel 150yds on left

Although only a short distance from the city centre this hotel enjoys a peaceful setting, overlooking extensive grounds and an adjacent golf course. Bedrooms are well equipped and executive rooms are particularly spacious. Public rooms include the formal Oak Room Restaurant, and the informal Country Kitchen which offers a carvery and blackboard specials. The hotel also has a well-equipped spa with pool, sauna, steam room, jacuzzi and treatment rooms.

Rooms 82 (5 fmly) (33 GF) **S** £58-£149; **D** £93-£169 (incl. bkfst)* **Facilities** Spa FTV Gym Aerobics studio Sauna Steam room Wi-fi **Conf** Class 120 Board 45 Thtr 250 Del from £139 to £190* **Services** Lift **Parking** 170 **Notes** LB Civ Wed 180

See advert on page 75

Premier Inn Birmingham North (Sutton Coldfield)

BUDGET HOTEL

☎ 0871 527 8088 🖷 0871 527 8089
Whitehouse Common Rd B75 6HD
dir: M42 junct 9, A446 towards Lichfield, then A453 to Sutton Coldfield. Left into Whitehouse Common Rd, hotel on left

High quality, budget accommodation ideal for both families and business travellers. Spacious, en suite bedrooms feature tea and coffee making facilities, and Freeview TV in most hotels. Internet access and Wi-fi are available for a small fee. The adjacent family restaurant features a wide and varied menu. See also the Hotel Groups pages.

Rooms 42 **D** £51-£58*

SUTTON ON SEA Map 17 TF58
Lincolnshire

The Grange & Links

★★★ 73% HOTEL

☎ 01507 441334 🖷 01507 443033
Sea Ln, Sandilands LN12 2RA
e-mail: grangeandlinkshotel@btconnect.com
web: www.grangeandlinkshotel.co.uk
dir: A1111 to Sutton-on-Sea, follow signs to Sandilands

This friendly, family-run hotel sits in five acres of grounds, close to both the beach and its own 18-hole links golf course. Bedrooms are pleasantly appointed and are well equipped for both business and leisure guests. Public rooms include ample lounge areas, a formal restaurant and a traditional bar, serving a wide range of meals and snacks.

Rooms 23 (10 fmly) (3 GF) **S** £69.50; **D** £94 (incl. bkfst)* **Facilities** 18 Putt green Gym Xmas New Year Wi-fi **Conf** Class 200 Board 100 Thtr 200 **Parking** 60 **Notes** LB Civ Wed 150

SUTTON SCOTNEY Map 5 SU43
Hampshire

Norton Park

QHOTELS

★★★★ 76% HOTEL

☎ 0845 074 0055 & 01962 763000
🖷 01962 760860
SO21 3NB
e-mail: nortonpark@qhotels.co.uk
web: www.qhotels.co.uk
dir: At junct of A303 & A34 follow Sutton Scotney signs. Hotel on Micheldever Station Rd (old A30), 1m from Sutton Scotney

Set in 54 acres of beautiful parkland in the heart of Hampshire, Norton Park offers both business and leisure guests a great range of amenities. Dating from the 16th century, the hotel is complemented by extensive buildings housing the bedrooms, and public areas which include a superb leisure club and numerous conference facilities. Ample parking is available.

Rooms 175 (11 fmly) (80 GF) **Facilities** Spa supervised Gym Steam room Sauna Experience shower Ice fountain Xmas New Year Wi-fi **Conf** Class 250 Board 80 Thtr 340 Del from £165 to £200 **Services** Lift **Parking** 220 **Notes** LB Civ Wed 340

SWAFFHAM Map 13 TF80
Norfolk

Best Western George Hotel

★★★ 77% HOTEL

☎ 01760 721238 🖷 01760 725333
Station Rd PE37 7LJ
e-mail: georgehotel@bestwestern.co.uk
web: www.arlingtonhotelgroup.co.uk
dir: Exit A47 signed Swaffham. Hotel opposite St Peter & St Paul church

A Georgian hotel situated in the heart of this bustling market town, which is ideally placed for touring north Norfolk. Bedrooms vary in size and style; each one is pleasantly decorated and well equipped. Public rooms include a cosy restaurant, a lounge and a busy bar where a range of drinks and snacks is available.

Rooms 29 (1 fmly) **Facilities** STV New Year Wi-fi **Conf** Class 70 Board 70 Thtr 150 **Parking** 100

SWANAGE Map 5 SZ07
Dorset

The Pines

★★★ 78% HOTEL

☎ 01929 425211 🖷 01929 422075
Burlington Rd BH19 1LT
e-mail: reservations@pineshotel.co.uk
web: www.pineshotel.co.uk
dir: A351 to seafront, left then 2nd right. Hotel at end of road

Enjoying a peaceful location with spectacular views over the cliffs and sea, The Pines is a pleasant place to stay. Many of the comfortable bedrooms have sea views. Guests can take tea in the lounge, enjoy appetising bar snacks in the attractive bar, and interesting cuisine in the restaurant.

Rooms 41 (26 fmly) (6 GF) **S** £66; **D** £132-£176 (incl. bkfst)* **Facilities** FTV Xmas New Year Wi-fi **Conf** Class 80 Board 80 Thtr 80 Del from £102.70* **Services** Lift **Parking** 60 **Notes** LB

See advert on page 472

Grand

★★★ 70% HOTEL

☎ 01929 423353 🖷 01929 427068
Burlington Rd BH19 1LU
e-mail: reservations@grandhotelswanage.co.uk
web: www.grandhotelswanage.co.uk

Dating back to 1898, this hotel is located on the Isle of Purbeck and has spectacular views across Swanage Bay and Peveril Point. Bedrooms are individually decorated and well equipped; public rooms offer a number of choices from relaxing lounges to extensive leisure facilities. The hotel also has its own private beach.

Rooms 30 (2 fmly) **S** £45-£85; **D** £90-£170 (incl. bkfst)* **Facilities** FTV supervised Fishing Gym Table tennis Treatment room Xmas New Year Wi-fi **Conf** Class 40 Board 40 Thtr 120 **Services** Lift **Parking** 15 **Notes** LB Closed 10 days in Jan (dates on application)

S

SWANLEY
Kent — Map 6 TQ56

Premier Inn Swanley

BUDGET HOTEL

☎ 0871 527 9288 📠 0871 527 9289
London Rd BR8 7QD
dir: M25 junct 3, B2173 towards Swanley. At rdbt 2nd exit onto B258 (High St). At next rdbt 4th exit into Swanley Ln, 1st exit into Bartholomew Way, at next rdbt 3rd exit into London Rd

High quality, budget accommodation ideal for both families and business travellers. Spacious, en suite bedrooms feature tea and coffee making facilities, and Freeview TV in most hotels. Internet access and Wi-fi are available for a small fee. The adjacent family restaurant features a wide and varied menu. See also the Hotel Groups pages.

Rooms 61

SWAY
Hampshire — Map 5 SZ29

Sway Manor Restaurant & Hotel

★★★ 75% HOTEL

☎ 01590 682754 📠 01590 682955
Station Rd SO41 6BA
e-mail: info@swaymanor.com
web: www.swaymanor.com
dir: Exit B3055 (Brockenhurst/New Milton road) into village centre

Built at the turn of the 20th century, this attractive mansion is set in its own grounds, and conveniently located in the village centre. Bedrooms are well appointed and generously equipped; most have views over the gardens and pool. The bar and conservatory restaurant, both with views over the gardens, are popular with locals.

Rooms 15 (3 fmly) **Facilities** Xmas New Year Wi-fi **Conf** Class 20 Board 15 **Services** Lift **Parking** 40 **Notes** Civ Wed 80

SWINDON
Wiltshire — Map 5 SU18

See also **Wootton Bassett**

Swindon Marriott Hotel

Marriott HOTELS & RESORTS

★★★★ 76% HOTEL

☎ 01793 512121 📠 01723 513114
Pipers Way SN3 1SH
e-mail: mhrs.swidt.frontdesk@marriotthotels.com
web: www.swindonmarriott.co.uk
dir: M4 junct 15, A419, A4259 to Coate rdbt & B4006 signed 'Old Town'

With convenient access to the motorway, this hotel is a good venue for meetings, and an ideal base from which to explore Wiltshire and the Cotswolds. The hotel offers a good range of public rooms, including a well-equipped leisure centre, Chats café bar and the informal Source Grill Restaurant, which serves a modern take on the region's finest flavours.

Rooms 156 (42 fmly) **Facilities** Spa Gym Aerobics studio Hairdresser Health & beauty salon Sauna Steam room Wi-fi **Conf** Class 100 Board 40 Thtr 280 **Services** Lift Air con **Parking** 300 **Notes** Civ Wed 280

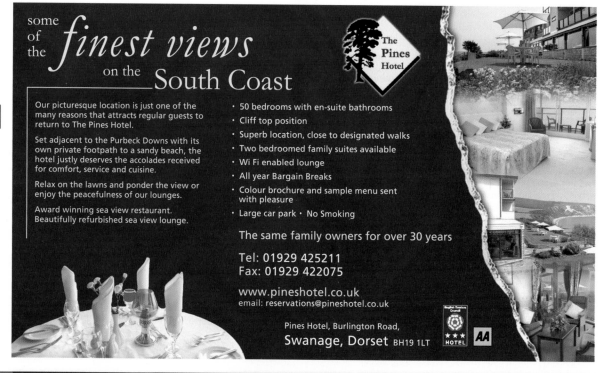

Best Western Premier Blunsdon House

★★★★ 74% HOTEL

☎ 01793 721701 🖷 01793 721056
Blunsdon SN26 7AS
e-mail: reservations@blunsdonhouse.co.uk
web: www.blunsdonhouse.co.uk
dir: 200yds off A419

Located just to the north of Swindon, Blunsdon House is set in 30 acres of well-kept grounds, and offers extensive leisure facilities and spacious day rooms. The hotel has a choice of eating and drinking options in three bars and two restaurants; the lively and informal Christopher's, and Nichols for fine dining. Bedrooms are comfortably furnished, and include family rooms with bunk beds and the contemporary spacious Pavilion rooms.

Rooms 108 (15 fmly) (27 GF) **S** £66.60-£149; **D** £66.60-£149* **Facilities** Spa STV FTV ⓢ ⛳ 9 ⛳ Putt green Gym Squash Beauty therapy Woodland walk Xmas New Year Wi-fi Child facilities **Conf** Class 200 Board 55 Thtr 300 Del from £99 to £152* **Services** Lift **Parking** 300 **Notes** LB ⊗ Civ Wed 200

Menzies Swindon

MenziesHotels

★★★★ 74% HOTEL

☎ 01793 528282 🖷 01793 541283
Fleming Way SN1 1TN
e-mail: swindon@menzieshotels.co.uk
web: www.menzieshotels.co.uk
dir: M4 junct 15/16, follow town centre signs

This modern hotel is conveniently located in the centre of the town with the added advantage of nearby parking. The hotel offers bedrooms and bathrooms that are well equipped with plenty of useful extras. The brasserie serves an exciting selection of dishes. There are also various conference and event facilities available.

Rooms 95 (2 fmly) **Facilities** FTV Xmas New Year Wi-fi **Conf** Class 80 Board 60 Thtr 200 **Services** Lift **Notes** ⊗ Civ Wed 200

The Pear Tree at Purton

★★★ 81% ⊛⊛ HOTEL

☎ 01793 772100 🖷 01793 772369
Church End SN5 4ED
e-mail: stay@peartreepurton.co.uk

(For full entry see Purton)

Stanton House

★★★ 77% HOTEL

☎ 0870 084 1388 🖷 01793 861857
The Avenue, Stanton Fitzwarren SN6 7SD
e-mail: reception@stantonhouse.co.uk
dir: A419 onto A361 towards Highworth, left towards Stanton Fitzwarren about 600yds past business park, hotel on left

Extensive grounds and superb gardens surround this Cotswold-stone manor house: the park and Stanton Lake are accessible to guests and provide great walks. Smart, well-maintained bedrooms have been equipped with modern comforts. Public areas include a conservatory, a bar and two eating options - The Rosemary Restaurant offering a wide choice of Japanese and European dishes, and the Mt Fuji Restaurant specialising in authentic Japanese food, in traditional surroundings. The friendly, multi-lingual staff create a relaxing atmosphere for their guests.

Rooms 82 (31 GF) **Facilities** STV Xmas New Year Wi-fi **Conf** Class 70 Board 40 Thtr 110 **Services** Lift **Parking** 110 **Notes** ⊗ Civ Wed 110

Chiseldon House

★★★ 75% ⊛⊛ HOTEL

☎ 01793 741010 & 07770 853883
🖷 01793 741059
New Rd, Chiseldon SN4 0NE
e-mail: info@chiseldonhousehotel.co.uk
web: www.chiseldonhousehotel.co.uk
dir: M4 junct 15, A346 signed Marlborough.In 0.5m right onto B4500, 0.25m, hotel on right

Conveniently located for the M4, Chiseldon House offers a quiet location and a relaxed ambience. Bedrooms, including a number of larger rooms, are comfortably furnished. Guests are welcome to enjoy the pleasant garden with outdoor seating. A selection of carefully prepared dishes utilising high quality produce is available in the restaurant.

Rooms 21 (8 fmly) **S** £95-£115; **D** £115-£135 (incl. bkfst)* **Facilities** STV Xmas New Year Wi-fi **Conf** Class 60 Board 25 Thtr 35 **Parking** 80 **Notes** LB ⊗ Civ Wed 120

Holiday Inn Swindon

★★★ 74% HOTEL

☎ 01793 817000 & 0871 942 9079
🖷 01793 512887
Marlborough Rd SN3 6AQ
e-mail: swindon@ihg.com
web: www.holidayinn.co.uk
dir: M4 junct 15, A419 towards Swindon. Take A4259 for 1m. Hotel on right opposite Sun Inn

With convenient access to both the M4 and Swindon's centre, this hotel provides an ideal base for business or leisure guests. Bedrooms are well decorated and have a good range of useful extras. Guests can enjoy the facilities of The Spirit Health and Fitness Club and then relax in the comfortable bar. A good selection of dishes is available whether by way of room service, lounge snacks or the welcoming, informal restaurant.

Rooms 99 (25 fmly) (48 GF) (9 smoking) **S** £49-£121; **D** £49-£121* **Facilities** STV FTV ⓢ supervised Gym Wi-fi **Conf** Class 30 Board 30 Thtr 60 Del from £85 to £140* **Services** Air con **Parking** 120 **Notes** LB ⊗ Civ Wed 40

Marsh Farm

★★★ 72% HOTEL

☎ 01793 842800 & 848044 🖷 01793 851528
Coped Hall SN4 8ER
e-mail: info@marshfarmhotel.co.uk
web: www.marshfarmhotel.co.uk
dir: M4 junct 16 onto A3102, straight on at 1st rdbt, right at 2nd rdbt. Hotel 200yds on left

The well decorated and comfortably furnished bedrooms at this hotel are situated in converted barns and extensions around the original farmhouse, which is set in its own grounds less than a mile from the M4. A relaxed and welcoming atmosphere prevails especially at dinner, when an extensive range of dishes to suit all tastes, is offered in the conservatory restaurant.

Rooms 50 (39 annexe) (1 fmly) (16 GF) **S** £65-£105; **D** £75-£135 (incl. bkfst) **Facilities** FTV Putt green Beauty salon Use of nearby leisure centre New Year Wi-fi **Conf** Class 60 Board 50 Thtr 120 **Parking** 100 **Notes** ⊗ Closed 26-30 Dec RS 25 Dec Civ Wed 100

S

SWINDON *continued*

Mercure Swindon South Marston Hotel & Spa

★★★ 72% HOTEL

☎ 01793 833700 🖷 01793 833775
Old Vicarage Ln, South Marston SN3 4SH
dir: M4 junct 15, take A419 N to Cirencester. Exit off 2nd junct signed A420 Oxford, turn left to South Marston. Hotel past pub on left

Located just outside Swindon, South Marston offers smart, modern, well-appointed bedrooms and spacious public areas. Free Wi-fi is available throughout. Leisure facilities include a spa with health and beauty treatments, a well-equipped gym and a 23-metre pool. The light and airy restaurant serves modern British cuisine.

Rooms 60 (7 fmly) (30 GF) **S** £59-£140; **D** £59-£140* **Facilities** Spa FTV Gym Squash Sauna Steam room Xmas New Year Wi-fi **Conf** Class 75 Board 60 Thtr 150 Del from £120 to £150* **Parking** 200 **Notes** LB Civ Wed 120

Campanile Swindon

BUDGET HOTEL

☎ 01793 514777 🖷 01793 514570
Delta Business Park, Great Western Way SN5 7XG
e-mail: swindon@campanile.com
web: www.campanile-swindon.co.uk
dir: M4 junct 16, A3102 towards Swindon. After 2nd rdbt, 2nd exit into Welton Rd; 1st left

This modern building offers accommodation in smart, well-equipped bedrooms, all with en suite bathrooms. Refreshments may be taken at the informal bistro. See also the Hotel Groups pages.

Rooms 120 (6 fmly) (22 GF) **Conf** Class 40 Board 40 Thtr 70

S

Express by Holiday Inn Swindon City Centre

BUDGET HOTEL

☎ 01793 602000 🖷 01793 602001
Bridge St SN1 5BT
e-mail: info@exhiswindon.co.uk
web: www.hiexpress.com/exhiswindon

A modern hotel ideal for families and business travellers. Fresh and uncomplicated, the spacious rooms include Sky TV, power shower and tea and coffee-making facilities. Continental buffet breakfast is included in the room rate; other meals may be taken at the nearby family pub or restaurant. See also the Hotel Groups pages.

Rooms 134 (71 fmly) **Conf** Class 30 Board 24 Thtr 50

Express by Holiday Inn Swindon West M4 Jct 16

BUDGET HOTEL

☎ 01793 818800 🖷 01793 818888
Frankland Rd, Blagrove SN5 8UD
e-mail: swindon@expressholidayinn.co.uk
web: www.hiexpress.com/swindonwest
dir: M4 junct 16, follow signs for town centre (A3102),1st left after rdbt

Rooms 121 (85 fmly) (10 GF) (10 smoking)
Conf Class 30 Board 27 Thtr 56

Premier Inn Swindon Central

BUDGET HOTEL

☎ 0871 527 9064 🖷 0871 527 9065
Kembrey Business Park, Kembrey St SN2 8YS
dir: M4 junct 15, A419 (Swindon bypass) towards Cirencester. In 6m at Turnpike Rdbt 1st left. Hotel on left in 2m

High quality, budget accommodation ideal for both families and business travellers. Spacious, en suite bedrooms feature tea and coffee making facilities, and Freeview TV in most hotels. Internet access and Wi-fi are available for a small fee. The adjacent family restaurant features a wide and varied menu. See also the Hotel Groups pages.

Rooms 50 **D** £52-£65*

Premier Inn Swindon North

BUDGET HOTEL

☎ 0871 527 9066 🖷 0871 527 9067
Broad Bush, Blunsdon SN26 8DJ
dir: N of Swindon. 5m from M4 junct 15. At junct of A419 & B4019

Rooms 62 **D** £50-£60*

Premier Inn Swindon West

BUDGET HOTEL

☎ 0871 527 9068 🖷 0871 527 9069
Great Western Way SN5 8UY
dir: M4 junct 16, A3102 to Lydiard Fields. Past Hilton, enterance on left. (NB for Sat Nav use SN5 8UB)

Rooms 63 **D** £52-£65*

SWINTON Greater Manchester — Map 15 SD70

Premier Inn Manchester (Worsley East/A580)

BUDGET HOTEL

☎ 0871 527 8724 🖷 0871 527 8725
East Lancs Rd M27 0AA
dir: M60 junct 13 (Swinton/Leigh), A580

High quality, budget accommodation ideal for both families and business travellers. Spacious, en suite bedrooms feature tea and coffee making facilities, and Freeview TV in most hotels. Internet access and Wi-fi are available for a small fee. The adjacent family restaurant features a wide and varied menu. See also the Hotel Groups pages.

Rooms 27 **D** £53-£58*

TADWORTH Surrey — Map 6 TQ25

Premier Inn Epsom South

BUDGET HOTEL

☎ 0871 527 8382 🖷 0871 527 8383
Brighton Rd, Burgh Heath KT20 6BW
dir: Just off M25 junct 8 on A217 towards Sutton

High quality, budget accommodation ideal for both families and business travellers. Spacious, en suite bedrooms feature tea and coffee making facilities, and Freeview TV in most hotels. Internet access and Wi-fi are available for a small fee. The adjacent family restaurant features a wide and varied menu. See also the Hotel Groups pages.

Rooms 76 **D** £65-£77*

TAMWORTH Staffordshire — Map 10 SK20

Drayton Court Hotel

★★ 82% HOTEL

☎ 01827 285805 🖷 01827 284842
65 Coleshill St, Fazeley B78 3RG
e-mail: draytoncthotel@yahoo.co.uk
web: www.draytoncourthotel.co.uk
dir: M42 junct 9, A446 to Lichfield, at next rdbt right onto A4091. 2m, Drayton Manor Theme Park on left. Hotel on right

Conveniently located close to the M42, this lovingly restored hotel offers bedrooms that are elegant and have been thoughtfully equipped to suit both business and leisure guests. Beds are particularly comfortable, and one room has a four-poster. Public areas include a panelled bar, a relaxing lounge and an attractive restaurant.

Rooms 19 (3 fmly) **S** £62.50-£82.50; **D** £62.50-£92.50* **Facilities** Wi-fi **Conf** Board 12 **Parking** 23 **Notes** ® Closed 22 Dec-1 Jan

Holiday Inn Express Tamworth

BUDGET HOTEL

☎ 01827 303220 🖹 01827 303221
Leisure Island, River Dr B79 7ND
e-mail: info@express-tamworth.com
dir: M42 junct 10, A5 to Tamworth. Hotel adjacent to Snowdome

A modern hotel ideal for families and business travellers. Fresh and uncomplicated, the spacious rooms include Sky TV, power shower and tea and coffee-making facilities. Continental buffet breakfast is included in the room rate; other meals may be taken at the nearby family pub or restaurant. See also the Hotel Groups pages.

Rooms 120 (83 fmly) (14 smoking) **S** £49-£159; **D** £49-£159 (incl. bkfst)* **Conf** Class 35 Board 36 Thtr 80 Del from £109 to £169*

Premier Inn Tamworth Central

BUDGET HOTEL

☎ 0871 527 9070 🖹 0871 527 9071
Bonehill Rd, Bitterscote B78 3HQ
dir: M42 junct 10, A5 towards Tamworth. Left in 3m onto A51 signed Tamworth. Straight on at 1st rdbt. At next rdbt 3rd exit. Hotel adjacent to Ladybridge Beefeater

High quality, budget accommodation ideal for both families and business travellers. Spacious, en suite bedrooms feature tea and coffee making facilities, and Freeview TV in most hotels. Internet access and Wi-fi are available for a small fee. The adjacent family restaurant features a wide and varied menu. See also the Hotel Groups pages.

Rooms 58 **D** £53-£60*

Premier Inn Tamworth South

BUDGET HOTEL

☎ 0871 527 9072 🖹 0871 527 9073
Watling St, Wilnecote B77 5PN
dir: M42 junct 10, A5 towards Tamworth. Left in 200yds signed Wilnecote/B5404. Left at next rdbt, hotel on left

Rooms 58 **D** £53-£60*

TANKERSLEY
South Yorkshire — Map 16 SK39

Tankersley Manor

★★★★ 77% HOTEL

☎ 01226 744700 🖹 01226 745405
Church Ln S75 3DQ
e-mail: tankersleymanor@qhotels.co.uk
web: www.qhotels.co.uk
dir: M1 junct 36 onto A61 (Sheffield road)

High on the moors with views over the countryside, this 17th-century residence is well located for major cities, tourist attractions and motorway links. Where appropriate, bedrooms retain original features such as exposed beams or Yorkshire-stone window sills. The hotel has its own traditional country pub, complete with old beams and open fires, alongside the more formal restaurant and bar. A well-equipped leisure centre is also available.

Rooms 99 (10 fmly) (16 GF) **S** £65-£149; **D** £65-£149* **Facilities** Spa STV FTV Gym Swimming lessons Beauty treatments Xmas New Year Wi-fi **Conf** Class 200 Board 100 Thtr 400 Del from £115 to £155* **Services** Lift **Parking** 350 **Notes** LB Civ Wed 250

Premier Inn Sheffield/ Barnsley M1 Jct 36

BUDGET HOTEL

☎ 0871 527 8968 🖹 0871 527 8969
Maple Rd S75 3DL
dir: M1 junct 35A (N'bound exit only), A616 for 2m. From M1 junct 36, A61 towards Sheffield

High quality, budget accommodation ideal for both families and business travellers. Spacious, en suite bedrooms feature tea and coffee making facilities, and Freeview TV in most hotels. Internet access and Wi-fi are available for a small fee. The adjacent family restaurant features a wide and varied menu. See also the Hotel Groups pages.

Rooms 62 **D** £50-£58*

TAPLOW
Buckinghamshire — Map 6 SU98

INSPECTORS' CHOICE

Cliveden Country House Hotel

★★★★★ ®® COUNTRY HOUSE HOTEL

☎ 01628 668561 🖹 01628 661837
SL6 0JF
e-mail: info@clivedenhouse.co.uk
web: www.clivedenhouse.co.uk
dir: M4 junct 7, A4 towards Maidenhead, in 1.5m take B476 towards Taplow, 2.5m, hotel on left

This wonderful stately home stands at the top of a gravelled boulevard. Visitors are treated as house-guests and staff recapture the tradition of fine hospitality. Bedrooms have individual quality and style, and reception rooms retain a timeless elegance. Exceptional leisure facilities include cruises along Cliveden Reach and massages in the Pavilion. The Terrace Restaurant with its delightful views has two AA Rosettes. The Rosette award for Waldo's, which offers innovative menus in discreet, luxurious surroundings, is temporarily suspended due to a change of chef; a new award will be in place once our inspectors have completed their assessments of meals cooked by the new kitchen team.

Rooms 39 (10 GF) **Facilities** Spa STV FTV Gym Squash Full range of beauty treatments 3 vintage boats Xmas New Year Wi-fi **Conf** Board 40 Thtr 80 **Services** Lift **Parking** 60 **Notes** Civ Wed 150

T

TAPLOW *continued*

Taplow House

★★★★ 76% ®® HOTEL

☎ 01628 670056 📠 01628 783985
Berry Hill SL6 0DA
e-mail: reception@taplowhouse.com
dir: Off A4 onto Berry Hill, hotel 0.5m on right

This elegant Georgian manor is set amid beautiful gardens and has been skilfully restored. Character public rooms are pleasing and include a number of air-conditioned conference rooms and an elegant restaurant. Comfortable bedrooms are individually decorated and furnished to a high standard.

Rooms 32 (8 fmly) (2 GF) **S** £65-£115; **D** £85-£195 (incl. bkfst)* **Facilities** STV FTV Complimentary use of private leisure facilities (1m) Xmas New Year Wi-fi **Conf** Class 50 Board 50 Thtr 120 Del from £160 to £200* **Services** Air con **Parking** 100 **Notes** LB Civ Wed 100

TARPORLEY Map 15 SJ56
Cheshire

Macdonald Portal

★★★★ 78% ®® HOTEL

☎ 0844 879 9082
Cobblers Cross Ln CW6 0DJ
dir: M6 junct 18, A54 towards Middlewich/Winsford. Left onto A49, through Cotebrook. In approx 1m follow signs for hotel

This hotel is located in beautiful rolling countryside and provides a luxury base for both the leisure and business guest. The spacious and well-equipped bedrooms have bathrooms with baths and power showers. Extensive leisure facilities include a superb spa, state-of-the-art fitness equipment, three golf courses and a golf academy. The Ranulf Restaurant delivers skilfully prepared, innovative cooking, as well as an excellent breakfast. Staff throughout are very friendly and nothing is too much trouble.

Rooms 83

T

TAUNTON Map 4 ST22
Somerset

The Mount Somerset

★★★ 83% ®® HOTEL

☎ 01823 442500 📠 01823 442900
Lower Henlade TA3 5NB
e-mail: info@mountsomersethotel.co.uk
web: www.vonessenhotels.co.uk
dir: M5 junct 25, A358 towards Chard/Ilminster, at Henlade right into Stoke Rd, left at T-junct at end, then right into drive

From its elevated and rural position, this impressive Regency house has wonderful views over Taunton Vale. Refurbishment has resulted in impressive quality and comfort levels throughout in the stylish bedrooms and bathrooms. The elegant public rooms combine elegance and flair with an engaging and intimate atmosphere. In addition to the daily-changing, fixed-price menu, a carefully selected seasonal carte is available in the restaurant.

Rooms 11 (1 fmly) **Facilities** Beauty treatments Xmas New Year Wi-fi **Conf** Class 30 Board 20 Thtr 60 **Services** Lift **Parking** 100 **Notes** Civ Wed 60

Farthings Country House Hotel and Restaurant

★★★ 74% ® SMALL HOTEL

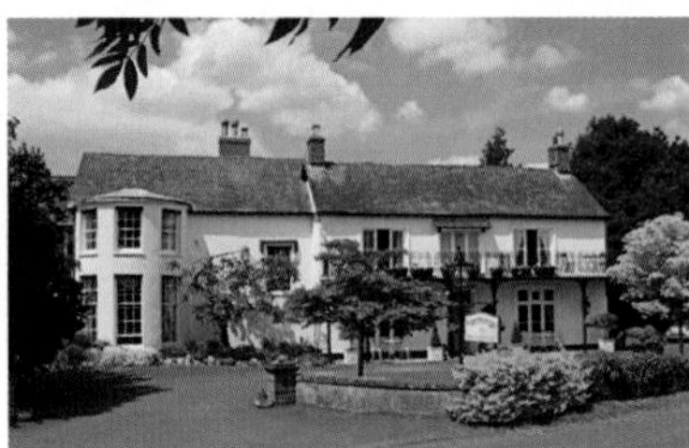

☎ 01823 480664 & 0785 668 8128
📠 01823 481118
Village Rd, Hatch Beauchamp TA3 6SG
e-mail: farthingshotel@yahoo.co.uk
web: www.farthingshotel.co.uk
dir: From A358, between Taunton & Ilminster, turn into Hatch Beauchamp. Hotel in village centre

This delightful hotel, set in its own extensive gardens in a peaceful village location, offers comfortable accommodation, combined with all the character and charm of a building dating back over 200 years. The calm atmosphere makes this a great place to relax and unwind. Dinner service is attentive, and menus feature best quality local ingredients prepared and presented with care.

Rooms 12 (2 annexe) (2 fmly) (3 GF) **S** £110-£155; **D** £130-£195 (incl. bkfst) **Facilities** FTV Xmas New Year Wi-fi **Conf** Class 25 Board 24 Thtr 50 Del from £140 to £225 **Parking** 25 **Notes** LB Civ Wed 175

Holiday Inn Taunton M5 Jct 25

★★★ 74% HOTEL

☎ 0871 942 9080 & 01823 281600
📠 01823 332266
Deane Gate Av TA1 2UA
web: www.hitauntonhotelm5.co.uk
dir: Adjacent to M5 junct 25, hotel before Harvester on right at entrance to business park

Handily located close to the M5, this is a popular choice for both business and leisure travellers. The open-plan public areas have a light and airy feel and include extensive leisure facilities. Bedrooms are well equipped and contemporary, with executive rooms also available. A choice of menus, with daily specials, is served in the relaxed restaurant.

Rooms 99 (68 fmly) (48 GF) (8 smoking) **D** £149* **Facilities** Gym Xmas New Year Wi-fi **Conf** Class 100 Board 30 Thtr 280 Del from £ to £169* **Services** Lift Air con **Parking** 300 **Notes** LB Civ Wed 200

Corner House Hotel

★★★ 71% HOTEL

☎ 01823 284683 📠 01823 323464
Park St TA1 4DQ
e-mail: res@corner-house.co.uk
web: www.corner-house.co.uk
dir: 0.3m from town centre. Hotel on junct of Park St & A38 Wellington Rd

The unusual Victorian façade of the Corner House, with its turrets and stained glass windows, belies a wealth of innovation, quality and style to be found inside. The contemporary bedrooms are equipped with state-of-the-art facilities but also offer traditional comforts. The smart public areas include the convivial bar and the 'Sausage and Wine' bistro, a relaxed and enjoyable dining venue.

Rooms 44 (9 annexe) (4 fmly) (5 GF) **Facilities** FTV Wi-fi **Conf** Class 30 Board 28 Thtr 50 **Parking** 30 **Notes**

Salisbury House

★★ 78% HOTEL

☎ 01823 272083 📠 01823 365978
14 Billetfield TA1 3NN
e-mail: res@salisburyhousehotel.co.uk
web: www.salisburyhousehotel.co.uk

Centrally and conveniently located, this elegant establishment dates back to the 1850s and retains many original features such as stained-glass windows and a wonderful oak staircase. Bedrooms provide impressive levels of comfort and quality with well-equipped, modern bathrooms. Public areas reflect the same high standards that are a hallmark throughout this hotel.

Rooms 17 (4 fmly) (6 GF) **S** £69-£88; **D** £75-£99 (incl. bkfst)* **Facilities** FTV Wi-fi **Parking** 17 **Notes** ⊗

Express by Holiday Inn Taunton M5 Jct 25

BUDGET HOTEL

☎ 01823 624000 📠 01823 624024
Blackbrook Business Park, Blackbrook Park Av TA1 2PX
e-mail: managertaunton@expressholidayinn.co.uk
web: www.hiexpress.com/taunton
dir: M5 junct 25. Follow signs for Blackbrook Business Park. Hotel 100yds on right

A modern hotel ideal for families and business travellers. Fresh and uncomplicated, the spacious rooms include Sky TV, power shower and tea and coffee-making facilities. Continental buffet breakfast is included in the room rate; other meals may be taken at the nearby family pub or restaurant. See also the Hotel Groups pages.

Rooms 92 (55 fmly) (22 GF) (8 smoking)
Conf Class 24 Board 16 Thtr 30

Premier Inn Taunton Central (North)

BUDGET HOTEL

☎ 0871 527 9076 📠 0871 527 9077
Massingham Park, Priorswood Rd TA2 7RX
dir: M5 junct 25, A358 into Taunton, at 2nd rdbt turn right onto Obridge Viaduct. Hotel at next rdbt

High quality, budget accommodation ideal for both families and business travellers. Spacious, en suite bedrooms feature tea and coffee making facilities, and Freeview TV in most hotels. Internet access and Wi-fi are available for a small fee. The adjacent family restaurant features a wide and varied menu. See also the Hotel Groups pages.

Rooms 40 **D** £58-£63*

Premier Inn Taunton East

BUDGET HOTEL

☎ 0871 527 9080 📠 0871 527 9081
81 Bridgwater Rd TA1 2DU
dir: M5 junct 25 follow signs to Taunton. Straight on at 1st rdbt, keep left at Creech Castle lights, hotel 200yds on right

Rooms 40 **D** £58-£63*

Premier Inn Taunton (Ruishton)

BUDGET HOTEL

☎ 0871 527 9074 📠 0871 527 9075
Ruishton Ln, Ruishton TA3 5LU
dir: Just off M5 junct 25 on A38

Rooms 38 **D** £56-£62*

TAVISTOCK
Devon — Map 3 SX47

Horn of Plenty

★★★ 85% ®® HOTEL

☎ 01822 832528 📠 01822 834390
Gulworthy PL19 8JD
e-mail: enquiries@thehornofplenty.co.uk
web: www.thehornofplenty.co.uk
dir: From Tavistock take A390 W for 3m. Right at Gulworthy Cross. In 400yds turn left, hotel in 400yds on right

With stunning views over the Tamar Valley, The Horn of Plenty maintains a good reputation as an excellent country-house hotel. Bedrooms are well equipped and have many thoughtful extras, with garden rooms offering impressive levels of both quality and comfort. Award-winning cuisine is prepared with skill and there is a passion to use the best ingredients the area has to offer.

Rooms 10 (6 annexe) (3 fmly) (4 GF) **S** £85-£215; **D** £95-£225 (incl. bkfst)* **Facilities** FTV Xmas New Year Wi-fi **Conf** Class 22 Board 14 Thtr 22 Del from £120 to £150* **Parking** 25 **Notes** LB Civ Wed 80

Bedford Hotel

★★★ 76% ® HOTEL

☎ 01822 613221 📠 01822 618034
1 Plymouth Rd PL19 8BB
e-mail: enquiries@bedford-hotel.co.uk
web: www.bedford-hotel.co.uk
dir: M5 junct 31, A30 (Launceston/Okehampton). Then A386 to Tavistock, follow town centre signs. Hotel opposite church

Built on the site of a Benedictine abbey, this impressive castellated building has been welcoming visitors for over 200 years. Very much a local landmark, the hotel offers comfortable and relaxing public areas, all reflecting charm and character throughout. Bedrooms are traditionally styled with contemporary comforts, whilst the Woburn Restaurant provides a refined setting for enjoyable cuisine.

Rooms 31 (2 fmly) (5 GF) **Facilities** FTV Xmas New Year **Conf** Class 100 Board 60 Thtr 160 **Parking** 45 **Notes** LB Civ Wed 120

TEBAY
Cumbria — Map 18 NY60

Westmorland Hotel

★★★ 81% ® HOTEL

☎ 015396 24351 📠 015396 24354
Westmorland Place, Orton CA10 3SB
e-mail: reservations@westmorlandhotel.com
web: www.westmorlandhotel.com
dir: Signed from Westmorland Services between M6 junct 38 & 39 (N'bound & S'bound)

With fine views over rugged moorland, this modern and friendly hotel is ideal for conferences and meetings. Bedrooms are spacious and comfortable, with the executive rooms being particularly well equipped. Open-plan public areas provide a Tyrolean touch and include a split-level restaurant.

Rooms 51 (5 fmly) (12 GF) **S** £87-£113; **D** £104-£124 (incl. bkfst)* **Facilities** FTV Xmas New Year Wi-fi **Conf** Class 24 Board 30 Thtr 120 Del from £135* **Services** Lift **Parking** 60 **Notes** LB RS 1 Jan Civ Wed 120

T

TEIGNMOUTH Map 3 SX97
Devon

Cliffden Hotel

★★★ 74% HOTEL

☎ 01626 770052 📠 01626 770594
Dawlish Rd TQ14 8TE
e-mail:
cliffden.hotel@actionforblindpeople.org.uk
dir: M5 junct 31, A380, B3192 to Teignmouth. Down hill on Exeter Rd to lights, left to rdbt (station on left). Left, follow Dawlish signs. Up hill. Hotel next right

Whilst this hotel mainly caters for visually impaired guests, their families, friends and guide dogs, it offers a warm welcome to all. This establishment is a listed Victorian building set in six acres of delightful gardens overlooking a small valley. Bedrooms are comfortable, very spacious and thoughtfully equipped. There's also leisure facilities and, of course, special provision for guide dogs.

Rooms 47 (5 fmly) (10 GF) **Facilities** FTV supervised Xmas New Year Wi-fi **Conf** Class 30 Board 30 Thtr 50 **Services** Lift **Parking** 25 **Notes** Civ Wed 60

TELFORD Map 10 SJ60
Shropshire

Telford Hotel & Golf Resort

QHOTELS

★★★★ 75% HOTEL

☎ 01952 429977 📠 01952 586602
Great Hay Dr, Sutton Heights TF7 4DT
e-mail: telford@qhotels.co.uk
web: www.qhotels.co.uk
dir: M54 junct 4, A442. Follow signs for Telford Golf Club

Set on the edge of Telford with panoramic views of the famous Ironbridge Gorge, this hotel offers excellent standards. Smart bedrooms are complemented by spacious public areas, large conference facilities, a spa with treatment rooms, a golf course and a driving range. Ample parking is available.

Rooms 114 (8 fmly) (50 GF) **S** £75-£165; **D** £95-£185 (incl. bkfst)* **Facilities** Spa STV 18 Putt green Gym Xmas New Year Wi-fi **Conf** Class 220 Board 100 Thtr 350 Del from £125 to £165* **Services** Lift **Parking** 200 **Notes** LB Civ Wed 250

Best Western Valley

★★★ 81% HOTEL

☎ 01952 432247 📠 01952 432308
TF8 7DW
e-mail: info@thevalleyhotel.co.uk
dir: M6, M54 junct 6 onto A5223 to Ironbridge

This privately owned hotel is situated in attractive gardens, close to the famous Iron Bridge. It was once the home of the Maws family who manufactured ceramic tiles, and fine examples of their craft are found throughout the house. Bedrooms vary in size and are split between the main house and a mews development; imaginative meals are served in the attractive Chez Maws restaurant.

Rooms 44 (3 fmly) (6 GF) **Facilities** FTV Wi-fi **Conf** Class 80 Board 60 Thtr 150 Del from £135 to £170* **Services** Lift **Parking** 80 **Notes** Closed 24 Dec-2 Jan RS 25 Dec Civ Wed 150

Hadley Park House

★★★ 81% HOTEL

☎ 01952 677269 📠 01952 676938
Hadley Park TF1 6QJ
e-mail: info@hadleypark.co.uk
dir: Off Hadley Park Island off A442 to Whitchurch

Located in Telford, but close to Ironbridge this elegant Georgian mansion is situated in three acres of its own grounds. Bedrooms are spacious and well equipped. There is a comfortable bar and lounge and meals are served in the attractive conservatory-style restaurant.

Rooms 22 (10 annexe) (6 fmly) (5 GF) **S** £105-£125; **D** £125-£150 (incl. bkfst)* **Facilities** STV FTV Xmas New Year Wi-fi **Conf** Class 80 Board 45 Thtr 200 Del from £135 to £165 **Parking** 60 **Notes** LB Civ Wed 200

Mercure Telford Madeley Court Hotel

★★★ 74% HOTEL

☎ 01952 680068 📠 01952 684275
Castlefields Way, Madeley TF7 5DW
e-mail: enquiries@hotels-telford.com
dir: A464 to Telford, A442, onto A4169 to Castlefields rdbt, 1st exit onto B4373. Hotel 200yds on left

This beautifully restored 16th-century manor house is set in extensive grounds and gardens. Bedrooms vary between character rooms and the newer annexe rooms. Public areas consist of two wood-panelled lounges, a lakeside bar and at the centre of the original manor house, The Priory restaurant. The 16th-century Grade I listed mill house makes a lovely location for wedding receptions.

Rooms 49 (49 annexe) (4 fmly) (21 GF) (6 smoking) **Facilities** FTV Xmas New Year Wi-fi **Conf** Class 150 Board 50 Thtr 175 Del from £127 to £155* **Parking** 100 **Notes** Civ Wed 175

Park Inn by Radisson, Telford

park inn by Radisson

★★★ 67% HOTEL

☎ 01952 429988 📠 01952 292012
Forgegate TF3 4NA
e-mail: info.telford@rezidorparkinn.com
dir: M54 junct 5

In a convenient location just off the motorway this is a comfortable place to stay. The facilities include an indoor swimming pool, conference rooms, and a car valet service as well as secure parking. The restaurant provides a relaxing setting with lots of natural daylight. Bedrooms are comfortably appointed.

Rooms 153 (1 fmly) (17 GF) (17 smoking) **S** £47-£124; **D** £47-£124* **Facilities** Gym Weights room Treatment rooms Xmas New Year Wi-fi **Conf** Class 200 Board 100 Thtr 400 Del from £65 to £150 **Services** Lift **Notes** Civ Wed 400

T

Premier Inn Telford Central

BUDGET HOTEL

☎ 0871 527 9082 📠 0871 527 9083
Euston Way TF3 4LY
dir: M54 junct 5 follow Central Railway Station signs. Hotel at 2nd exit off rdbt signed railway station

High quality, budget accommodation ideal for both families and business travellers. Spacious, en suite bedrooms feature tea and coffee making facilities, and Freeview TV in most hotels. Internet access and Wi-fi are available for a small fee. The adjacent family restaurant features a wide and varied menu. See also the Hotel Groups pages.

Rooms 62 **D** £53-£60*

Premier Inn Telford North (Donnington)

BUDGET HOTEL

☎ 0871 527 9084 📠 0871 527 9085
Donnington Wood Way, Donnington TF2 8LE
dir: From Telford M54 junct 4, B5060 (Redhill Way) signed Donnington. At rdbt straight on (becomes Donnington Wood Way then School Rd). At mini rdbt take 1st left into Wellington Rd (hotel adjacent to McDonalds & Shell garage)

Rooms 20 **D** £53-£60*

TELFORD SERVICE AREA (M54) Map 10 SJ70
Shropshire

Days Inn Telford - M54

BUDGET HOTEL

☎ 01952 238400 📠 01952 238410
Telford Services, Priorslee Rd TF11 8TG
e-mail: telford.hotel@welcomebreak.co.uk
web: www.welcomebreak.co.uk
dir: At M54 junct 4

This modern building offers accommodation in smart, spacious and well-equipped bedrooms, suitable for families and business travellers, and all with en suite bathrooms. Continental breakfast is available, and other refreshments may be taken at the nearby family restaurant. See also the Hotel Groups pages.

Rooms 48 (45 fmly) (21 GF) (8 smoking) **S** £39.95-£59.95; **D** £49.95-£69.95 **Conf** Board 8

TEMPLE CLOUD Map 4 ST65
Somerset

Cameley Lodge

★★★ 72% SMALL HOTEL

☎ 01761 452790 📠 01761 451112
Cameley, Temple Cloud BS39 5AH
e-mail: john@cameleylodge.co.uk
dir: A37 Bristol/Wells/Temple Cloud. Off A37 at Temple Cloud, 1m, hotel signed

A peacefully located property with views over a lake and surrounded by pleasant countryside. Being a small hotel, friendly and personal service is delivered by the resident proprietors and their staff. The bedrooms and bathrooms have been appointed to provide very good levels of quality and comfort. The modern and stylish restaurant offers a good selection of carefully prepared dishes, the conference and wedding facilities are popular.

Rooms 9 (2 fmly) **Facilities** Fishing Clay pigeon shooting Wi-fi **Conf** Class 64 Board 24 Thtr 80 **Services** Lift **Parking** 48 **Notes** ⊗ Civ Wed 100

TEMPLE SOWERBY Map 18 NY62
Cumbria

Temple Sowerby House Hotel & Restaurant

★★★ 87% ⊛⊛ COUNTRY HOUSE HOTEL

☎ 017683 61578 📠 017683 61958
CA10 1RZ
e-mail: stay@templesowerby.com
web: www.templesowerby.com
dir: 7m from M6 junct 40, midway between Penrith & Appleby, in village centre

The hotel is set in the heart of the Eden Valley, ideal for exploring the northern Lake District and Pennine Fells. Bedrooms are comfortable and stylish, most feature ultra-modern bathrooms, and there is a choice of pleasant lounges. The restaurant, with picture windows overlooking the beautiful walled garden, is a splendid place to enjoy the award-winning cuisine. Staff throughout are friendly and keen to please.

Rooms 12 (4 annexe) (2 GF) **S** £90-£110; **D** £135-£180 (incl. bkfst) **Facilities** FTV ⛳ New Year Wi-fi **Conf** Class 20 Board 20 Thtr 30 **Parking** 15 **Notes** LB ⊗ No children 12yrs Closed 20-29 Dec Civ Wed 40

The Kings Arms Hotel

★★ 83% HOTEL

☎ 017683 62944
CA10 1SB
e-mail: enquiries@kingsarmstemplesowerby.co.uk
dir: M6 junct 40, E on A66 to Temple Sowerby. Hotel in town centre

Located in the peaceful village of Temple Sowerby just a short drive from the A66 by-pass. This historic property dates back over 400 years and has now undergone a massive refurbishment programme. Highly enjoyable food, using quality local produce, and comfortable well-appointed bedrooms are on offer. This is an ideal location to touring the Lake District, Cumbria and Northumberland.

Rooms 9 (5 fmly) **S** £45-£50; **D** £70-£80 (incl. bkfst)* **Facilities** Fishing Xmas New Year Wi-fi **Parking** 20 **Notes** LB

TENBURY WELLS Map 10 SO56
Worcestershire

Cadmore Lodge Hotel & Country Club

★★ 74% ⊛ HOTEL

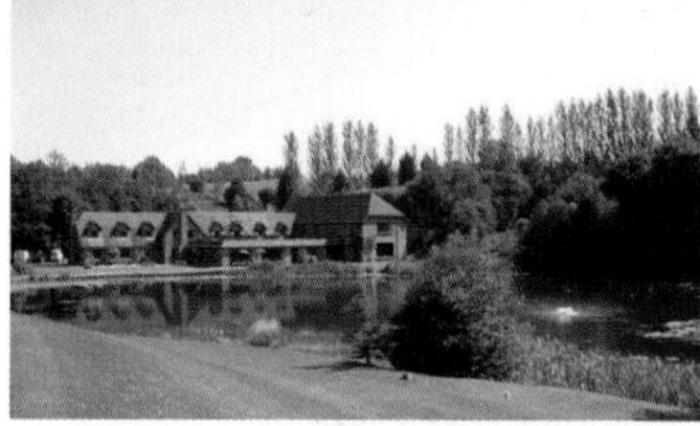

☎ 01584 810044 📠 01584 810044
Berrington Green, St Michaels WR15 8TQ
e-mail: reception.cadmore@cadmorelodge.com
web: www.cadmorelodge.com
dir: Off A4112 (Leominster-Tenbury Wells road), follow signs for Berrington

Cadmore Lodge is situated in an idyllic rural location overlooking a private lake. The 70-acre private estate features a 9-hole golf course and two fishing lakes. The traditionally styled bedrooms have modern amenities, and a large function room with lake views is popular for weddings and special occasions. The hotel has a well deserved reputation for its food.

Rooms 15 (1 fmly) **Facilities** ⛳ 9 Fishing Gym Bowling green Steam room Nature reserve Xmas New Year **Conf** Class 40 Board 20 Thtr 100 **Parking** 100 **Notes** ⊗ Civ Wed 160

T

TENTERDEN
Kent — Map 7 TQ83

Little Silver Country Hotel

★★★ 79% HOTEL

☎ 01233 850321 & 0845 166 2516
01233 850647
Ashford Rd, St Michael's TN30 6SP
e-mail: enquiries@little-silver.co.uk
web: www.little-silver.co.uk
dir: M20 junct 8, A274 signed Tenterden

Located just outside the charming town of Tenterden and within easy reach of many attractions in Kent, this charming hotel is ideal for leisure and business guests, as well as being a popular wedding venue. Bedrooms are spaciously appointed and well equipped; many boast spa baths. There is a spacious lounge, small bar and the modern restaurant overlooks beautifully tended gardens.

Rooms 16 (2 fmly) (6 GF) **S** £62-£125; **D** £97-£199 (incl. bkfst)* **Facilities** STV FTV Xmas Wi-fi **Conf** Class 50 Board 25 Thtr 75 **Parking** 70 **Notes** LB Civ Wed 120

London Beach Country Hotel, Spa & Golf Club

★★★ 73% HOTEL

☎ 01580 766279 01580 763884
Ashford Rd TN30 6HX
e-mail: enquiries@londonbeach.com
web: www.londonbeach.com
dir: M20 junct 9, A28 follow signs to Tenterden (10m). Hotel on right 1m before Tenterden

A modern purpose-built hotel situated in mature grounds on the outskirts of Tenterden. The spacious bedrooms are smartly decorated, have co-ordinated soft furnishings and most rooms have balconies with superb views over the golf course. The open-plan public rooms feature a brasserie-style restaurant, where a good choice of dishes is served.

Rooms 26 (2 fmly) (3 smoking) **Facilities** Spa 9 Putt green Fishing Driving range Health club Xmas New Year Wi-fi **Conf** Class 75 Board 40 Thtr 100 **Services** Lift **Parking** 100 **Notes** Civ Wed 100

TETBURY
Gloucestershire — Map 4 ST89

INSPECTORS' CHOICE

Calcot Manor

★★★★ HOTEL

☎ 01666 890391 01666 890394
Calcot GL8 8YJ
e-mail: reception@calcotmanor.co.uk
web: www.calcotmanor.co.uk
dir: 3m West of Tetbury at junct A4135/A46

Cistercian monks built the ancient barns and stables around which this lovely English farmhouse is set. No two rooms are identical, and each is beautifully decorated in a variety of styles and equipped with the contemporary comforts. Sumptuous sitting rooms, with crackling log fires in the winter, look out over immaculate gardens. There are two dining options: the elegant conservatory restaurant and the informal Gumstool Inn. There are also ample function rooms. The superb health and leisure spa includes an indoor pool, high-tech gym, massage tables, complementary therapies and much more. For children, a supervised crèche and 'playzone' are a great attraction.

Rooms 35 (23 annexe) (13 fmly) (17 GF) **D** £340-£540 (incl. bkfst & dinner)* **Facilities** Spa STV Gym Clay pigeon shooting Archery Cycling Running track Xmas New Year Wi-fi Child facilities **Conf** Class 40 Board 35 Thtr 120 Del from £290 to £330* **Parking** 150 **Notes** Civ Wed 100

Hare & Hounds

★★★★ 78% HOTEL

☎ 01666 880233 & 881000 01666 880241
Westonbirt GL8 8QL
e-mail: reception@hareandhoundshotel.com
web: www.hareandhoundshotel.com
dir: 2.5m SW of Tetbury on A433

This popular hotel, set in extensive grounds, is situated close to Westonbirt Arboretum and has remained under the same ownership for over 50 years. Bedrooms are individual in style; those in the main house are more traditional and the stylish cottage rooms are contemporary in design. Public rooms include the informal bar and light, airy lounges - one with a log fire in colder months. Guests can eat either in the bar or the attractive restaurant.

Rooms 42 (21 annexe) (8 fmly) (13 GF) **S** £95-£105; **D** £145-£179 (incl. bkfst)* **Facilities** FTV Xmas New Year Wi-fi **Conf** Class 80 Board 40 Thtr 120 Del from £165* **Parking** 85 **Notes** LB Civ Wed 200

The Priory Inn

★★★ 75% SMALL HOTEL

☎ 01666 502251 01666 503534
London Rd GL8 8JJ
e-mail: info@theprioryinn.co.uk
web: www.theprioryinn.co.uk
dir: On A433 (Cirencester to Tetbury road). Hotel 200yds from Market Square

A warm welcome is assured at this attractive inn where friendly service is a high priority to the team. Public areas and bedrooms have a contemporary style that mixes well with more traditional features, such as an open fireplace in the cosy bar dining room. Cuisine, using locally sourced produce, is offered on the menu that will suit all tastes.

Rooms 14 (1 fmly) (4 GF) **S** £59-£135; **D** £79-£135 (incl. bkfst)* **Facilities** FTV Beauty treatment rooms New Year Wi-fi **Conf** Class 28 Board 28 Thtr 30 **Parking** 35 **Notes** LB

Ormond at Tetbury

★★★ 68% HOTEL

☎ 01666 505690 📠 01666 505956
23 Long St GL8 8AA
e-mail: info@theormond.co.uk
dir: Exit A433 from Cirencester into Long St. Hotel approx 100yds on left

Located on the main street of this charming town, The Ormond provides a choice of individually styled and comfortably furnished bedrooms in a variety of shapes and sizes. The ambience is relaxed and friendly, and guests may chose to dine in either the popular bar area or in the adjoining restaurant. In warmer weather, outdoor seating is available in the courtyard.

Rooms 15 (3 fmly) **S** £55-£69; **D** £79-£160 (incl. bkfst)* **Facilities** FTV Xmas New Year Wi-fi Child facilities **Conf** Class 20 Board 20 Thtr 40 Del from £75 to £135* **Notes** LB Civ Wed 80

Snooty Fox

★★★ 68% SMALL HOTEL

☎ 01666 502436 📠 01666 503479
Market Place GL8 8DD
e-mail: res@snooty-fox.co.uk
web: www.snooty-fox.co.uk
dir: In town centre

Centrally situated this 16th-century coaching inn retains original features and is a popular venue for weekend breaks. The relaxed and friendly atmosphere, the high standard of accommodation, and the food offered in the bar and restaurant, are all very good reasons why many guests return here time and again.

Rooms 12 **S** £60-£130; **D** £70-£210 (incl. bkfst)* **Facilities** ♫ Xmas New Year **Conf** Class 12 Board 16 Thtr 24 Del from £90 to £112*

TEWKESBURY Map 10 SO83
Gloucestershire

Premier Inn Tewkesbury Central

BUDGET HOTEL

☎ 0871 527 9088 📠 0871 527 9089
Shannon Way, Ashchurch GL20 8ND
dir: M5 junct 9, A438 towards Tewkesbury, hotel 400yds on right

High quality, budget accommodation ideal for both families and business travellers. Spacious, en suite bedrooms feature tea and coffee making facilities, and Freeview TV in most hotels. Internet access and Wi-fi are available for a small fee. The adjacent family restaurant features a wide and varied menu. See also the Hotel Groups pages.

Rooms 40 **D** £50-£59*

THETFORD Map 13 TL88
Norfolk

Premier Inn Thetford

BUDGET HOTEL

☎ 0871 527 9090 📠 0871 527 9091
Lynn Wood, Maine St IP24 3PG
dir: From A11 N follow Thetford signs. At 3rd rdbt 1st exit for town centre into Brandon Rd. 1st exit into Maine St

High quality, budget accommodation ideal for both families and business travellers. Spacious, en suite bedrooms feature tea and coffee making facilities, and Freeview TV in most hotels. Internet access and Wi-fi are available for a small fee. The adjacent family restaurant features a wide and varied menu. See also the Hotel Groups pages.

Rooms 40 **D** £58-£65*

THORNBURY Map 4 ST69
Gloucestershire

INSPECTORS' CHOICE

Thornbury Castle

★★★ 

COUNTRY HOUSE HOTEL

☎ 01454 281182 📠 01454 416188
Castle St BS35 1HH
e-mail: info@thornburycastle.co.uk
web: www.thornburycastle.co.uk
dir: On A38 N'bound from Bristol take 1st turn to Thornbury. At end of High St left into Castle St, follow brown sign, entrance to Castle on left behind St Mary's Church

Henry VIII ordered the first owner of this castle to be beheaded! Guests today have the opportunity of sleeping in historical surroundings fitted out with all the modern amenities. Most rooms have four-poster or coronet beds and real fires. Tranquil lounges enjoy views over the gardens, while elegant, wood-panelled dining rooms make memorable settings for a leisurely award-winning meal.

Rooms 27 (3 fmly) (4 GF) **S** £120-£160; **D** £175-£535 (incl. bkfst)* **Facilities** STV FTV Archery Helicopter rides Clay pigeon shooting Massage treatment Xmas New Year Wi-fi **Conf** Class 40 Board 30 Thtr 70 Del from £160 to £260* **Parking** 50 **Notes** LB Civ Wed 70

T

THORNTON HOUGH
Merseyside
Map 15 SJ38

Thornton Hall Hotel and Spa

★★★★ 79% HOTEL

☎ 0151 336 3938 & 353 3717 📠 0151 336 7864
Neston Rd CH63 1JF
e-mail: reservations@thorntonhallhotel.com
web: www.thorntonhallhotel.com
dir: M53 junct 4, B5151/Neston onto B5136 to Thornton Hough (signed)

Dating back to the mid 1800s, this country-house hotel has been carefully extended and restored. Public areas include an impressive leisure spa boasting excellent facilities, a choice of restaurants and a spacious bar. Bedrooms vary in style and include feature rooms in the main house and more contemporary rooms in the garden wing. The highly accomplished cuisine is a repertoire of robustly-flavoured modern British dishes based on top-notch, locally supplied ingredients. The delightful grounds and gardens, and impressive function facilities make this a popular wedding venue.

Rooms 63 (6 fmly) (28 GF) **Facilities** Spa STV FTV Gym Beauty spa & clinic Hairdressing salon Wi-fi **Conf** Class 225 Board 80 Thtr 650 **Parking** 250 **Notes** Closed 1 Jan Civ Wed 500

THORPE (DOVEDALE)
Derbyshire
Map 16 SK15

Izaak Walton

★★★ 80% HOTEL

☎ 01335 350555 📠 01335 350539
Dovedale DE6 2AY
e-mail: reception@izaakwaltonhotel.com
web: www.izaakwaltonhotel.com
dir: A515 onto B5054 to Thorpe, straight over cattle grid & 2 small bridges, 1st right, sharp left

Peacefully situated, with magnificent views over the valley of Dovedale to Thorpe Cloud. Many of the bedrooms have lovely views; executive rooms are particularly spacious. Wi-fi access is available throughout. Food is a highlight, with an appealing choice in the bar area and more formal dining in the Haddon Restaurant. Fishing on the River Dove can be arranged.

Rooms 35 (6 fmly) (8 GF) **D** £70-£200 (incl. bkfst) **Facilities** FTV Fishing Xmas New Year Wi-fi **Conf** Class 40 Board 50 Thtr 50 Del from £140 to £160 **Parking** 80 **Notes** LB Civ Wed 120

THORPENESS
Suffolk
Map 13 TM45

Thorpeness Hotel

★★★ 80% HOTEL

☎ 01728 452176 📠 01728 453868
Lakeside Av IP16 4NH
e-mail: info@thorpeness.co.uk
web: www.thorpeness.co.uk
dir: A1094 towards Aldeburgh, take coast road N for 2m

Ideally situated in an unspoilt, tranquil setting close to Aldeburgh and Snape Maltings. The extensive public rooms include a choice of lounges, a restaurant, a smart bar, a snooker room and clubhouse. The spacious bedrooms are pleasantly decorated, tastefully furnished and equipped with modern facilities. An 18-hole golf course and tennis courts are also available.

Rooms 36 (36 annexe) (10 fmly) (10 GF) **S** £80-£124; **D** £98-£178 (incl. bkfst)* **Facilities** 18 Putt green Fishing Cycle hire Rowing boat hire Birdwatching Xmas New Year Wi-fi **Conf** Class 30 Board 24 Thtr 130 Del from £120 to £150* **Parking** 80 **Notes** LB Civ Wed 130

THURLASTON
Warwickshire
Map 11 SP47

Draycote

★★★ 64% HOTEL

☎ 01788 521800 📠 01788 521695
London Rd CV23 9LF
e-mail: mail@draycotehotel.co.uk
web: www.draycotehotel.co.uk
dir: M1 junct 17 onto M45, then A45. Hotel 500mtrs on left

Located in the picturesque Warwickshire countryside and within easy reach of motorway networks, this hotel offers modern, comfortable and well-equipped accommodation with a relaxed and friendly welcome. The hotel has a challenging golf course.

Rooms 49 (24 fmly) (24 GF) **Facilities** STV 18 Putt green Gym Golf driving range Chipping green New Year Wi-fi **Conf** Class 78 Board 72 Thtr 250 **Parking** 150 **Notes** Civ Wed 180

THURLESTONE
Devon
Map 3 SX64

Thurlestone Hotel

★★★★ 83% HOTEL

☎ 01548 560382 📠 01548 561069
TQ7 3NN
e-mail: enquiries@thurlestone.co.uk
web: www.thurlestone.co.uk
dir: A38, A384 into Totnes, A381 towards Kingsbridge, A379 towards Churchstow, onto B3197. Into lane signed to Thurlestone

This perennially popular hotel has been in the same family-ownership since 1896 and continues to go from strength to strength. A vast range of facilities is available for all the family including indoor and outdoor pools, a golf course and a beauty salon. Bedrooms are equipped to ensure a comfortable stay with many having wonderful views of the south Devon coast. The range of eating options includes the elegant and stylish restaurant with its stunning views.

Rooms 66 (23 fmly) **S** £75-£205; **D** £150-£410 (incl. bkfst)* **Facilities** STV supervised 9 Putt green Gym Squash Badminton courts Games room Toddler room Snooker room Xmas New Year Wi-fi Child facilities **Conf** Class 100 Board 40 Thtr 150 Del from £150 to £300 **Services** Lift **Parking** 121 **Notes** LB Closed 1-2 wks Jan Civ Wed 160

THURSFORD
Norfolk
Map 13 TF93

The Old Forge Seafood Restaurant

RESTAURANT WITH ROOMS

☎ 01328 878345
Seafood Restaurant, Fakenham Rd NR21 0BD
e-mail: sarah.goldspink@btconnect.com
dir: On A148 (Fakenham to Holt road)

Expect a warm welcome at this delightful relaxed restaurant with rooms. The open-plan public areas include a lounge bar area with comfy sofas, and an intimate restaurant with pine tables. Bedrooms are pleasantly decorated and equipped with a good range of useful facilities.

Rooms 3

TICEHURST
East Sussex — Map 6 TQ63

Dale Hill Hotel & Golf Club

★★★★ 81% HOTEL

☎ 01580 200112 01580 201249
TN5 7DQ
e-mail: info@dalehill.co.uk
web: www.dalehill.co.uk
dir: M25 junct 5, A21. 5m after Lamberhurst turn right at lights onto B2087 to Flimwell. Hotel 1m on left

This modern hotel is situated just a short drive from the village. Extensive public rooms include a lounge bar, a conservatory brasserie, a formal restaurant and the Spike Bar, which is mainly frequented by golf club members and has a lively atmosphere. The hotel also has two superb 18-hole golf courses, a swimming pool and gym.

Rooms 35 (8 fmly) (23 GF) **Facilities** STV 36 Putt green Gym Covered driving range Pool table Xmas New Year Wi-fi **Conf** Class 50 Board 50 Thtr 120 **Services** Lift **Parking** 220 **Notes** LB Civ Wed 150

TINTAGEL
Cornwall — Map 2 SX08

Atlantic View Hotel

★★ 76% SMALL HOTEL

☎ 01840 770221 01840 770995
Treknow PL34 0EJ
e-mail: atlantic-view@eclipse.co.uk
web: www.holidayscornwall.com
dir: B3263 to Tregatta, turn left into Treknow, hotel on road to Trebarwith Strand Beach

Conveniently located for all the attractions of Tintagel, this family-run hotel has a wonderfully relaxed and welcoming atmosphere. Public areas include a bar, comfortable lounge, TV/games room and heated swimming pool. Bedrooms are generally spacious and some have the added advantage of distant sea views.

Rooms 9 (1 fmly) **Facilities** FTV **Parking** 10 **Notes** LB Closed Nov-Feb RS Mar

TITCHWELL
Norfolk — Map 13 TF74

Titchwell Manor

★★★ 86% HOTEL

☎ 01485 210221 01485 210104
PE31 8BB
e-mail: margaret@titchwellmanor.com
web: www.titchwellmanor.com
dir: On A149 (coast road) between Brancaster & Thornham

Friendly family-run hotel ideally placed for touring the north Norfolk coastline. The tastefully appointed bedrooms are very comfortable; some in the adjacent annexe offer ground floor access. Smart public rooms include a lounge area, relaxed informal bar and a delightful conservatory restaurant, overlooking the walled garden. Imaginative menus feature quality local produce and fresh fish.

Rooms 26 (18 annexe) (4 fmly) (16 GF) **S** £45-£125; **D** £90-£250 (incl. bkfst)* **Facilities** FTV Xmas New Year Wi-fi **Conf** Class 50 Board 30 Thtr 30 Del from £170 to £270 **Parking** 50 **Notes** LB Civ Wed 80

TOLLESHUNT KNIGHTS
Essex — Map 7 TL91

Five Lakes Hotel, Golf, Country Club & Spa

★★★★ 77% HOTEL

☎ 01621 868888 01621 869696
Colchester Rd CM9 8HX
e-mail: enquiries@fivelakes.co.uk
web: www.fivelakes.co.uk
dir: Exit A12 at Kelvedon, follow brown signs through Tiptree to hotel

This hotel is set amidst 320 acres of open countryside, featuring two golf courses. The spacious bedrooms are furnished to a high standard and have excellent facilities. The public rooms offer a high degree of comfort and include five bars, two restaurants and a large lounge. The property also boasts extensive leisure facilities.

Rooms 194 (80 annexe) (4 fmly) (40 GF) **S** £75-£110; **D** £75-£110* **Facilities** Spa STV 36 Putt green Gym Squash Sauna Steam room Health & beauty spa Badminton Aerobics Studio Hairdresser Xmas New Year Wi-fi **Conf** Class 700 Board 60 Thtr 2000 Del from £131 to £195* **Services** Lift **Parking** 550 **Notes** LB Civ Wed 250

TONBRIDGE
Kent — Map 6 TQ54

Rose & Crown Hotel

★★★ 78% HOTEL

☎ 01732 357966 01732 357194
125 High St TN9 1DD
e-mail: rose.crown@bestwestern.co.uk

A 15th-century coaching inn situated in the heart of this bustling town centre. Following a refurbishment programme in 2011, the public areas have been transformed into a light and airy environment yet still retain much original character such as oak beams and Jacobean panelling. Food is served throughout the day in the Oak Room Bar & Grill. Bedrooms are stylishly decorated, spacious and well presented; amenities include free Wi-fi access.

Rooms 56 **Conf** Class 60 Board 60 Thtr 125

Premier Inn Tonbridge

BUDGET HOTEL

☎ 0871 527 9096 0871 527 9097
Pembury Rd TN11 0NA
dir: 11m from M25 junct 5. Follow A21 towards Hastings, pass A26 (Tunbridge Wells) junct. Exit at next junct, 1st exit at rdbt

High quality, budget accommodation ideal for both families and business travellers. Spacious, en suite bedrooms feature tea and coffee making facilities, and Freeview TV in most hotels. Internet access and Wi-fi are available for a small fee. The adjacent family restaurant features a wide and varied menu. See also the Hotel Groups pages.

Rooms 40 **D** £60-£65*

Premier Inn Tonbridge North

BUDGET HOTEL

☎ 0871 527 9098 0871 527 9099
Hilden Manor, London Rd TN10 3AN
dir: From A21 follow Seven Oaks & Hildenborough signs. At rdbt take 2nd exit onto B245 signed Hildenborough. In 2m hotel on right

Rooms 41 **D** £60-£65*

TORBAY

See Brixham, Paignton & Torquay

T

TORQUAY
Devon
Map 3 SX96

Barceló Torquay Imperial Hotel

★★★★ 80% HOTEL

☎ 01803 294301 📠 01803 298293
Park Hill Rd TQ1 2DG
e-mail: imperialtorquay@barcelo-hotels.co.uk
web: www.barcelo-hotels.co.uk
dir: A380 towards seafront. Turn left to harbour, right at clock tower. Hotel 300yds on right

This hotel has an enviable location with extensive views of the coastline. Traditional in style, the public areas are elegant and offer a choice of dining options including the Regatta Restaurant, with its stunning views over the bay. Bedrooms are spacious, most with private balconies, and the hotel has an extensive range of indoor and outdoor leisure facilities.

Rooms 152 (14 fmly) **Facilities** Spa STV supervised Gym Squash Beauty salon Hairdresser Steam room Xmas New Year Wi-fi **Conf** Class 200 Board 30 Thtr 350 **Services** Lift **Parking** 140 **Notes** Civ Wed 250

Grand

★★★★ 76% HOTEL

☎ 01803 296677 📠 01803 213462
Sea Front TQ2 6NT
e-mail: reservations@grandtorquay.co.uk
web: www.grandtorquay.co.uk
dir: A380 to Torquay. At seafront turn right, then 1st right. Hotel on corner, entrance 1st on left

Within level walking distance of the town, this large Edwardian hotel overlooks the bay and offers modern facilities. Many of the bedrooms, some with balconies, enjoy the best of the views; all are very well equipped. Boaters Bar also benefits from the hotel's stunning position and offers an informal alternative to the Gainsborough Restaurant.

Rooms 132 (32 fmly) (3 GF) **Facilities** FTV Gym Beauty clinic Car valeting Xmas New Year Wi-fi **Conf** Class 150 Board 60 Thtr 250 **Services** Lift **Parking** 57 **Notes** Civ Wed 250

Palace

★★★★ 72% HOTEL

☎ 01803 200200 📠 01803 299899
Babbacombe Rd TQ1 3TG
e-mail: info@palacetorquay.co.uk
web: www.palacetorquay.co.uk
dir: Towards harbour, left by clocktower into Babbacombe Rd, hotel on right after 1m

Set in 25 acres of stunning, beautifully tended wooded grounds, the Palace offers a tranquil environment. Suitable for business and leisure, the hotel boasts a huge range of well-presented indoor and outdoor facilities. Much of the original charm and grandeur is still in evidence, particularly in the dining room. Many of the bedrooms enjoy views of the magnificent gardens.

Rooms 141 (7 fmly) **Facilities** 9 Putt green Gym Squash Table tennis Xmas New Year Wi-fi **Conf** Class 800 Board 40 Thtr 1000 **Services** Lift **Parking** 140 **Notes** LB

Orestone Manor Hotel & Restaurant

★★★ 87% @@ HOTEL

☎ 01803 328098 📠 01803 328336
Rockhouse Ln, Maidencombe TQ1 4SX
e-mail: info@orestonemanor.com
web: www.orestonemanor.com
dir: A38 onto A380 then B3192

This country-house hotel is located on the fringe of Torbay and occupies a delightful rural location with distant sea views. There is a colonial theme throughout the public areas which creates a charming and comfortable environment. There are several lounges and a lovely terrace for drinks and alfresco eating. Bedrooms are individually styled and spacious; some have balconies. The cuisine offers an interesting range of dishes based on local ingredients.

Rooms 12 (3 fmly) (1 GF) **Facilities** FTV Xmas New Year Wi-fi **Conf** Class 20 Board 18 Thtr 40 **Parking** 40 **Notes** LB Closed 2-26 Jan Civ Wed 70

Best Western Hotel Gleneagles

★★★ 80% HOTEL

☎ 01803 293637 📠 01803 295106
Asheldon Rd, Wellswood TQ1 2QS
e-mail: enquiries@hotel-gleneagles.com
dir: A380 onto A3022 to A379, follow to St Mathias Church, turn right into Asheldon Rd

From its hillside location, looking out over Anstey's Cove towards Lyme Bay, this peacefully located hotel is appointed to an impressive standard. Stylish public areas combine comfort, flair and quality with ample space in which to find a quiet spot to unwind. Bedrooms also have a contemporary feel; many have balconies or patios. The pool area has a real Riviera feel with elegant Lloyd Loom sun loungers and palm trees.

Rooms 41 (2 fmly) (5 GF) **Facilities** Xmas New Year Wi-fi **Services** Lift **Parking** 21

Corbyn Head Hotel & Orchid Restaurant

★★★ 77% @@@ HOTEL

☎ 01803 213611 📠 01803 296152
Torbay Rd, Sea Front TQ2 6RH
e-mail: info@corbynhead.com
web: www.corbynhead.com
dir: Follow signs to Torquay seafront, turn right on seafront. Hotel on right with green canopies

This hotel occupies a prime position overlooking Torbay, and offers well-equipped bedrooms, many with sea views and some with balconies. The staff are friendly and attentive, and a well-stocked bar and comfortable lounge are available. Guests can enjoy fine dining in the award-winning Orchid Restaurant or more traditional dishes in the Harbour View Restaurant.

Rooms 45 (4 fmly) (9 GF) **Facilities** FTV Gym Squash ♫ Xmas New Year Wi-fi **Conf** Class 30 Board 30 Thtr 50 **Parking** 50 **Notes** Civ Wed 85

See advert on opposite page

Livermead House

★★★ 75% HOTEL

☎ 01803 294361 & 294363 📠 01803 200758
Torbay Rd TQ2 6QJ
e-mail: info@livermead.com
web: www.livermead.com
dir: From seafront turn right, follow A379 towards Paignton & Livermead, hotel opposite Institute Beach

Having a splendid waterfront location, this hotel dates back to the 1820s and is where Charles Kingsley is said to have written *The Water Babies*. Bedrooms vary in size and style, excellent public rooms are popular for private parties and meetings, and a range of leisure facilities is provided. Enjoyable cuisine is served in the impressive restaurant.

Rooms 67 (6 fmly) (2 GF) **Facilities** Gym Squash ♫ Xmas **Conf** Class 175 Board 80 Thtr 320 **Services** Lift **Parking** 131

See advert on page 486

Best Western Livermead Cliff

★★★ 72% HOTEL

☎ 01803 299666 📠 01803 294496
Torbay Rd TQ2 6RQ
e-mail: enquiries@livermeadcliff.co.uk
web: www.livermeadcliff.co.uk
dir: A379/A3022 to Torquay, towards seafront, turn right towards Paignton. Hotel 600yds on seaward side

Situated at the water's edge, this long-established hotel offers friendly service and traditional hospitality. The splendid views can be enjoyed from the lounge, bar and dining room. Alternatively, guests can take advantage of refreshment on the wonderful terrace and enjoy one of the best outlooks in the bay. Bedrooms, many with sea views and some with balconies, are comfortable and well equipped; a range of room sizes is available.

Rooms 65 (21 fmly) **S** £30-£97; **D** £60-£250 (incl. bkfst) **Facilities** FTV Fishing Use of facilities at sister hotel Xmas New Year Wi-fi **Conf** Class 60 Board 40 Thtr 120 Del from £65 to £185 **Services** Lift **Parking** 80 **Notes** LB Civ Wed 200

See advert on page 486

T

TORQUAY *continued*

Abbey Lawn Hotel

★★★ 66% HOTEL

☎ 01803 299199 & 203181 📠 01803 203181
Scarborough Rd TQ2 5UQ
e-mail: nicky@holdsworthhotels.freeserve.co.uk

Conveniently located for both the seafront and town centre, this is an ideal base for visiting the attractions of the 'English Riviera'. Many of the bedrooms, including the four-poster suite, benefit from lovely sea views. Facilities include a health club with extensive leisure activities and indoor and outdoor pools. Traditional cuisine is served in the elegant restaurant, and evening entertainment is a regular feature in the ballroom.

Rooms 57 (3 fmly) **Facilities** supervised supervised Gym Steam room Xmas New Year **Services** Lift **Parking** 20 **Notes** Closed Jan

Red House Hotel

★★ 72% HOTEL

☎ 01803 607811 📠 0871 5289455
Rousdown Rd, Chelston TQ2 6PB
e-mail: stay@redhouse-hotel.co.uk
web: www.redhouse-hotel.co.uk
dir: Follow signs for seafront & Chelston, turn into Avenue Rd, right at 1st lights. Pass shops & church, next left. Hotel on right

Set just a few minutes' drive from the town and seafront, this hotel is in an ideal location for exploring the Torbay area. The hotel offers comfortably appointed bedrooms, and facilities include indoor and outdoor swimming pools, plus a gym, sauna, steam room and a treatment room.

Rooms 9 (3 fmly) **Facilities** Gym Sun shower Beauty room Sauna Xmas New Year Wi-fi **Parking** 9 **Notes** LB

Anchorage Hotel

★★ 71% HOTEL

☎ 01803 326175 📠 01803 316439
Cary Park, Aveland Rd TQ1 3PT
e-mail: enquiries@anchoragehotel.co.uk

Quietly located in a residential area and providing a friendly welcome, this family-run establishment enjoys a great deal of repeat business. Bedrooms come in a range of sizes but all rooms are neatly presented. Evening entertainment is provided regularly in the large and comfortable lounge.

Rooms 56 (5 fmly) (17 GF) **S** £31.50-£52; **D** £63-£104 (incl. bkfst & dinner)* **Facilities** FTV Xmas New Year Wi-fi **Services** Lift **Parking** 26 **Notes** LB

Albaston House Hotel

★★ 69% HOTEL

☎ 01803 296758 📠 01803 209211
27 St Marychurch Rd TQ1 3JF
e-mail: albastonhousehotel@hotmail.com
dir: A380 left at lights then B3199, follow signs for Plainmoor to Westhill Rd. Right at lights. Hotel 0.5m on left

The Albaston is situated close to the town centre and is also convenient for the quieter attractions of Babbacombe. Public areas and bedrooms alike combine comfort and quality. Many guests return time after time to this welcoming, family-run hotel.

Rooms 13 (2 fmly) **S** £25-£36; **D** £50-£72 (incl. bkfst) **Facilities** FTV Wi-fi **Parking** 6 **Notes** LB

Coppice

★★ 69% HOTEL

☎ 01803 297786 & 211085 📠 01803 211085
Babbacombe Rd TQ1 2QJ
e-mail: reservations@coppicehotel.co.uk
web: www.coppicehotel.co.uk
dir: From harbour left at clock tower. Hotel in 0.75m on left

A friendly, comfortable and well-established hotel, The Coppice is a popular choice and provides a convenient location that is within walking distance of the beaches and shops. In addition to the indoor and outdoor swimming pools, evening entertainment is often provided in the spacious bar. Bedrooms are bright and airy with modern amenities.

Rooms 39 (16 fmly) (22 GF) **S** £40-£55; **D** £80-£110 (incl. bkfst & dinner)* **Facilities** FTV Putt green Gym Sauna Steam room Spa pool Boules Pool table Xmas New Year Wi-fi **Conf** Class 40 Board 40 Thtr 40 **Parking** 35 **Notes** LB

Frognel Hall

★★ 69% HOTEL

☎ 01803 298339 📠 01803 215115
Higher Woodfield Rd TQ1 2LD
e-mail: enquiries@frognel.co.uk
web: www.frognel.co.uk
dir: Follow signs to seafront, then follow esplanade to harbour, left to Babbacombe, right at lights towards Meadfoot Beach, 3rd left, hotel on left

Frognel Hall is a fine Victorian mansion set in its own quiet, landscaped gardens overlooking Torquay to the sea beyond. The hotel is a short walk from the marina and Meadfoot Beach. The comfortable bedrooms, including a four-poster room, are spacious and many have garden and sea views. Wi-fi is available throughout the hotel.

Rooms 26 (2 annexe) (6 fmly) (6 GF) **S** £27-£40; **D** £54-£100 (incl. bkfst)* **Facilities** FTV Hot stone therapy & massage Xmas New Year Wi-fi **Conf** Class 30 Board 15 Thtr 50 Del from £54 to £75 **Services** Lift **Parking** 28 **Notes** LB Closed Jan (ex New Year)

The Heritage Hotel

★★ 68% HOTEL

☎ 01803 299332 📠 01803 209191
Seafront, Shedden Hill TQ2 5TY
e-mail: enquiries@heritagehoteltorquay.co.uk
web: www.heritagehoteltorquay.co.uk
dir: A380 to Torquay follow signs to seafront. Hotel on left

In an elevated position overlooking Tor Abbey Sands, this hotel is a short walk from both the harbour and the shops. The bedrooms are traditionally furnished and come in various sizes; all have sea views except one. There is a variety of eating options based on American food themes, a large sun deck for relaxation in summer and also a ground-floor leisure complex.

Rooms 24 (24 fmly) (4 GF) **S** £35-£50; **D** £70-£90 (incl. bkfst)* **Facilities** STV FTV supervised Gym Wi-fi **Services** Lift **Parking** 40 **Notes**

T

TORQUAY *continued*

Regina

★★ 68% HOTEL

☎ 01803 292904 📠 01803 290270
Victoria Pde TQ1 2BE
e-mail: regina.torquay@alfatravel.co.uk
dir: Into Torquay, follow harbour signs, hotel on outer corner of harbour

This hotel enjoys a pleasant and convenient location right on the harbourside, a short stroll from the town's attractions. Bedrooms, some with harbour views, vary in size. Entertainment is provided on most nights and there is a choice of bars.

Rooms 68 (5 fmly) **S** £36-£50; **D** £56-£84 (incl. bkfst) **Facilities** FTV Xmas New Year **Services** Lift **Parking** 6 **Notes** LB Closed Jan & part Feb RS Nov-Dec (ex Xmas) & Feb-Mar

Shelley Court

★★ 68% HOTEL

☎ 01803 295642 📠 01803 215793
29 Croft Rd TQ2 5UD
e-mail: shelleycourthotel@hotmail.com
dir: From B3199 up Shedden Hill Rd, 1st left into Croft Rd

This hotel, popular with groups, is located in a pleasant, quiet area that overlooks the town towards Torbay. With a friendly team of staff, many guests return here time and again. Entertainment is provided most evenings in the season. Bedrooms come in a range of sizes and there is a large and comfortable lounge bar.

Rooms 27 (3 fmly) (6 GF) **Facilities** FTV Pool table Indoor skittle alley Xmas New Year **Parking** 20 **Notes** LB Closed 4 Jan-10 Feb

Ashley Court Hotel

★★ 67% HOTEL

☎ 01803 292417 📠 01803 215035
107 Abbey Rd TQ2 5NP
e-mail: reception@ashleycourt.co.uk
dir: A380 to seafront, left to Shedden Hill to lights, hotel opposite

Located close to the town centre and within easy strolling distance of the seafront, this hotel offers a warm welcome to guests. Bedrooms are pleasantly appointed and some have sea views. The outdoor pool and patio are popular with guests wishing to soak up some sunshine. Live entertainment is provided every night throughout the season.

Rooms 83 (12 fmly) (8 GF) (14 smoking) **Facilities** Games room Xmas New Year **Services** Lift **Parking** 51 **Notes** Closed 3 Jan-1 Feb

Maycliffe

★★ 67% HOTEL

☎ 01803 294964 📠 01803 201167
St Lukes Road North TQ2 5DP
e-mail: bob.west1@virgin.net
web: www.maycliffehotel.co.uk
dir: Left from Kings Dr, along seafront keep in left lane, at next lights (Belgrave Rd) up Shedden Hill, 2nd right into St Lukes Rd then 1st left

Set in a quiet and elevated position which is convenient for the town centre and attractions, the Maycliffe is a popular venue for leisure breaks. Bedrooms are individually decorated and equipped with modern facilities; there are two rooms on the ground floor suitable for less able guests. There is a quiet lounge for relaxation, whilst in the bar there is a cabaret on some nights during the season.

Rooms 28 (1 fmly) (2 GF) **Facilities** Xmas **Services** Lift **Parking** 10 **Notes** No children 4yrs Closed 2 Jan-12 Feb

Premier Inn Torquay

BUDGET HOTEL

☎ 0871 527 9102 📠 0871 527 9103
Seafront, Belgrave Rd TQ2 5HE
dir: On A380 into Torquay, continue to lights (Torre Station on right). Right into Avenue Road to Kings Drive. Left at seafront, hotel at lights

High quality, budget accommodation ideal for both families and business travellers. Spacious, en suite bedrooms feature tea and coffee making facilities, and Freeview TV in most hotels. Internet access and Wi-fi are available for a small fee. The adjacent family restaurant features a wide and varied menu. See also the Hotel Groups pages.

Rooms 83 **D** £65*

TRING Hertfordshire — Map 6 SP91

Pendley Manor

★★★★ 78% HOTEL

☎ 01442 891891 📠 01442 890687
Cow Ln HP23 5QY
e-mail: info@pendley-manor.co.uk
web: www.pendley-manor.co.uk
dir: M25 junct 20, A41 (Tring exit). At rdbt follow Berkhamsted/London signs. 1st left signed Tring Station & Pendley Manor

This impressive Victorian mansion is set in extensive and mature landscaped grounds where peacocks roam. The spacious bedrooms are situated in both the manor house and the wing, and offer a useful range of facilities. Public areas include a cosy bar, a conservatory lounge and an intimate restaurant as well as a leisure centre.

Rooms 73 (17 fmly) (17 GF) **S** £90-£140; **D** £110-£150 (incl. bkfst)* **Facilities** Spa Gym Steam room Dance Studio Sauna Snooker room Wi-fi **Conf** Class 80 Board 80 Thtr 250 Del from £160 to £230* **Services** Lift **Parking** 150 **Notes** LB Civ Wed 160

Premier Inn Tring

BUDGET HOTEL

☎ 0871 527 9104 📠 0871 527 9105
Tring Hill HP23 4LD
dir: M25 junct 20, A41 towards Aylesbury, at end of Hemel Hempstead/Tring bypass straight on at rdbt, hotel approx 100yds on right

High quality, budget accommodation ideal for both families and business travellers. Spacious, en suite bedrooms feature tea and coffee making facilities, and Freeview TV in most hotels. Internet access and Wi-fi are available for a small fee. The adjacent

T

family restaurant features a wide and varied menu. See also the Hotel Groups pages.

Rooms 30 **D** £52-£66*

TROWBRIDGE Wiltshire **Map 4 ST85**

Fieldways Hotel & Health Club

★★ 68% SMALL HOTEL

☎ 01225 768336 📠 01225 753649
Hilperton Rd BA14 7JP
e-mail: fieldwayshotel@yahoo.co.uk
dir: A361 from Trowbridge towards Melksham, Chippenham, Devizes. Hotel last property on left

Originally part of a Victorian mansion this hotel is quietly set in well-kept grounds and provides a pleasant combination of spacious, comfortably furnished bedrooms. There are two splendid wood-panelled dining rooms, one of which is impressively finished in oak, pine, rosewood and mahogany. The indoor leisure facilities include a gym, a pool and treatment rooms; 'Top to Toe' days are especially popular.

Rooms 13 (5 annexe) (2 fmly) (2 GF) **S** £60; **D** £80-£90 (incl. bkfst)* **Facilities** Spa Gym Range of beauty treatments/massage Specialists in pampering days Wi-fi **Conf** Class 40 Board 20 Thtr 40 **Parking** 70 **Notes** LB

TRURO Cornwall **Map 2 SW84**

Mannings

★★★ 85% HOTEL

☎ 01872 270345 📠 01872 242453
Lemon St TR1 2QB
e-mail: reception@manningshotels.co.uk
web: www.manningshotels.co.uk
dir: A30 to Carland Cross then Truro. Follow brown signs to hotel in city centre

This popular hotel is located in the heart of Truro and has an engaging blend of traditional and contemporary. Public areas offer a stylish atmosphere with the bar and restaurant proving popular with locals and residents alike. Bedrooms are pleasantly appointed. A wide choice of appetising dishes is available, including ethnic, classical and vegetarian as well as daily specials.

Rooms 43 (9 annexe) (4 fmly) (3 GF) **S** £79-£89; **D** £99-£109 **Facilities** STV Wi-fi **Parking** 43 **Notes** LB Closed 25-26 Dec

Alverton Manor

★★★ 78% HOTEL

☎ 01872 276633 📠 01872 222989
Tregolls Rd TR1 1ZQ
e-mail: reception@alvertonmanor.co.uk
web: www.alvertonmanor.co.uk
dir: From Carland Cross, take A39 to Truro

Formerly a convent, this impressive sandstone property stands in six acres of grounds, within walking distance of the city centre. It has a wide range of smart bedrooms, combining comfort with character. Stylish public areas include the library and the former chapel, now a striking function room. An interesting range of dishes, using the very best of local produce (organic whenever possible) is offered in the elegant restaurant.

Rooms 33 (3 GF) **S** £80-£95; **D** £120-£170 (incl. bkfst)* **Facilities** 18 Xmas Wi-fi **Conf** Class 60 Board 40 Thtr 80 **Services** Lift **Parking** 120 **Notes** Closed 28 Dec RS 4 Jan Civ Wed 80

Carlton Hotel

★★ 75% HOTEL

☎ 01872 272450 📠 01872 223938
Falmouth Rd TR1 2HL
e-mail: reception@carltonhotel.co.uk
dir: On A39 straight across 1st & 2nd rdbts onto bypass (Morlaix Ave). At top of sweeping bend/hill turn right at mini rdbt into Falmouth Rd. Hotel 100mtrs on right

This family-run hotel is pleasantly located a short stroll from the city centre. A friendly welcome is assured and both business and leisure guests choose the Carlton on a regular basis. A smart, comfortable lounge is available, along with leisure facilities. A wide selection of home-cooked dishes is offered in the dining room.

Rooms 29 (4 fmly) (4 GF) **Facilities** STV Wi-fi **Conf** Class 24 Board 36 Thtr 60 **Parking** 31 **Notes** Closed 21 Dec-3 Jan

Brookdale Hotel

THE INDEPENDENTS HOTEL ASSOCIATION

★★ 69% HOTEL

☎ 01872 273513 📠 01872 272400
Tregolls Rd TR1 1JZ
e-mail: brookdale@hotelstruro.com
web: www.hotelstruro.com
dir: From A30 onto A39, at A390 junct turn right into city centre. Hotel 600mtrs down hill

Pleasantly situated in an elevated position close to the city centre, the Brookdale provides a range of accommodation options; all rooms are pleasantly spacious and well equipped, and some are located in an adjacent annexe. Meals can be served in guests' rooms, or in the restaurant where an interesting selection of dishes is available.

Rooms 30 (2 fmly) (3 GF) **Facilities** STV FTV Xmas Wi-fi **Conf** Class 65 Board 30 Thtr 100 **Parking** 30

Premier Inn Truro

BUDGET HOTEL

☎ 0871 527 9106 📠 0871 527 9107
Old Carnon Hill, Carnon Downs TR3 6JT
dir: On A39 (Truro to Falmouth road), 3m SW of Truro

High quality, budget accommodation ideal for both families and business travellers. Spacious, en suite bedrooms feature tea and coffee making facilities, and Freeview TV in most hotels. Internet access and Wi-fi are available for a small fee. The adjacent family restaurant features a wide and varied menu. See also the Hotel Groups pages.

Rooms 62 **D** £70*

TUNBRIDGE WELLS (ROYAL) Kent **Map 6 TQ53**

The Spa

★★★★ 80% HOTEL

☎ 01892 520331 📠 01892 510575
Mount Ephraim TN4 8XJ
e-mail: reservations@spahotel.co.uk
web: www.spahotel.co.uk
dir: Off A21 to A26, follow signs to A264 East Grinstead, hotel on right

Set in 14 acres of beautifully tended grounds, this imposing 18th-century mansion offers spacious, modern bedrooms that are stylishly decorated and thoughtfully equipped. The public rooms include the Chandelier Restaurant, a champagne bar and the Orangery which complements the traditional lounge. There are extensive meeting and health club facilities, and the spa offers treatment rooms and is licensed for civil wedding ceremonies.

Rooms 70 (4 fmly) (1 GF) **S** £124.50-£134.50; **D** £189-£257 (incl. bkfst)* **Facilities** Spa STV FTV Gym Xmas New Year Wi-fi **Conf** Class 90 Board 90 Thtr 300 Del from £150 to £175* **Services** Lift **Parking** 150 **Notes** LB Civ Wed 150

T

TUNBRIDGE WELLS (ROYAL) *continued*

Brew House

★★★★ 77% HOTEL

01892 520587 01892 534979
1 Warwick Park TN2 5TA
e-mail: reception@brewhousehotel.com
web: www.brewhousehotel.com
dir: A267, 1st left onto Warwick Park, hotel immediately on left

Located adjacent to The Pantiles and a short walk from the historic town centre with its interesting boutiques, restaurants and bars. Built in the 18th-century and appointed in a contemporary style, this hotel offers accommodation of the highest quality including impressive bathrooms and hi-tech amenities. The popular, modern restaurant, brasserie and bar has mood lighting and chic furnishings creating an relaxed atmosphere.

Rooms 15 (5 annexe) (2 fmly) **D** £100-£199 (incl. bkfst)* **Facilities** STV FTV Gym Xmas New Year Wi-fi **Conf** Class 100 Board 50 Thtr 120 Del from £145 to £245 **Services** Lift Air con **Parking** 8 **Notes** LB

Ramada Tunbridge Wells

RAMADA JARVIS

★★★★ 72% HOTEL

01892 823567 01892 823931
8 Tonbridge Rd, Pembury TN2 4QL
e-mail: sales.tunwells@ramadajarvis.co.uk
web: www.ramadatunbridgewells.co.uk
dir: M25 junct 5, A21 S. Left at 1st rdbt signed Pembury Hospital. Hotel on left, 400yds past hospital

Built in the style of a traditional Kentish oast house, this well presented hotel is conveniently located just off the A21 with easy access to the M25. Bedrooms are comfortably appointed for both business and leisure guests. Public areas include a leisure club and a range of meeting rooms.

Rooms 84 (8 fmly) (40 GF) **Facilities** Steam room Sauna Xmas New Year Wi-fi **Conf** Class 150 Board 107 Thtr 390 **Parking** 200 **Notes** Civ Wed 70

Hotel du Vin Tunbridge Wells

Hotel du Vin & Bistro

★★★★ 71%
TOWN HOUSE HOTEL

01892 526455 01892 512044
Crescent Rd TN1 2LY
e-mail: reception.tunbridgewells@hotelduvin.com
web: www.hotelduvin.com
dir: Follow town centre signs to main junct of Mount Pleasant Rd & Crescent Rd/Church Rd. Hotel 150yds on right just past Phillips House

This impressive Grade II listed building dates from 1762, and as a princess, Queen Victoria often stayed here. The spacious bedrooms are available in a range of sizes, beautifully and individually appointed, and equipped with a host of thoughtful extras. Public rooms include a bistro-style restaurant, two elegant lounges and a small bar.

Rooms 34 **Facilities** STV Boules court in garden Wi-fi **Conf** Class 30 Board 25 Thtr 40 **Services** Lift **Parking** 30 **Notes** Civ Wed 84

Russell Hotel

★★ 63% METRO HOTEL

01892 544833 01892 515846
80 London Rd TN1 1DZ
e-mail: sales@russell-hotel.com
web: www.russell-hotel.com
dir: At junct A26 & A264, uphill onto A26, hotel on right

This detached Victorian property is situated just a short walk from the centre of town. The generously proportioned bedrooms in the main house are pleasantly decorated and well equipped. In addition, there are several smartly appointed self-contained suites in an adjacent building. The public rooms include a lounge and cosy bar.

Rooms 25 (5 annexe) (5 fmly) (1 GF) **S** £50-£85; **D** £65-£110 (incl. bkfst)* **Facilities** FTV Wi-fi **Conf** Class 10 Board 10 Thtr 10 **Parking** 14 **Notes** LB

TURNERS HILL
West Sussex

Map 6 TQ33

INSPECTORS' CHOICE

Alexander House Hotel & Utopia Spa

★★★★ HOTEL

01342 714914 01342 717328
East St RH10 4QD
e-mail: info@alexanderhouse.co.uk
web: www.alexanderhouse.co.uk
dir: 6m from M23 junct 10, on B2110 between Turners Hill & East Grinstead

Set in 175 acres of parkland and landscaped gardens, this delightful country house hotel dates back to the 17th century. Most of the bedrooms are very spacious and all have luxurious bathrooms; the rooms in the most recent wing are particularly stunning. There are two options for dining - AG's Grill which has been awarded AA Rosettes, or the lively Reflections which is set around an open courtyard, ideal for eating alfresco. The Utopia Spa has a state-of-the-art pool and gym, as well as specialised treatments.

Rooms 38 (12 fmly) (1 GF) **Facilities** Spa STV Gym Clay shooting Archery Mountain bikes Pony trekking Xmas New Year Wi-fi **Conf** Class 70 Board 40 Thtr 150 **Services** Lift **Parking** 100 **Notes** Civ Wed 100

T

TWICKENHAM
Greater London

See LONDON SECTION plan 1 C2

London Marriott Hotel Twickenham

Marriott HOTELS & RESORTS

★★★★ 79% HOTEL

☎ 020 8891 8200 📠 020 8891 8201
198 Whitton Rd TW2 7BA
e-mail: nathan.ridgwell@marriotthotels.com
dir: A316, exit Whitton Rd rdbt towards stadium. Hotel within South Stand of stadium

This purpose-built hotel occupies an area of the South Stand of the Twickenham Rugby Club Stadium. The bedrooms have the latest Marriott innovations including flat-screen LCD TVs and state-of-the-art technology; six suites even overlook the pitch. There is a popular Twenty Two South restaurant, the Side Step sports bar and a café lounge. Guests can use the health club and there's a wide range of meeting rooms and conference facilities. Hampton Court Palace, Kew Gardens and the River Thames are all close by.

Rooms 156 (76 fmly) **Facilities** STV FTV supervised Gym Sauna Steam room Soft climbing wall Xmas New Year Wi-fi **Conf** Class 100 Board 30 Thtr 240 **Services** Lift Air con **Parking** 150 **Notes**

Premier Inn Twickenham East

BUDGET HOTEL

☎ 0871 527 9108 📠 0871 527 9109
Corner Sixth Cross, Staines Rd TW2 5PE
dir: M25 junct 12 onto M3, follow Central London signs, at end of M3 becomes A316. Straight on at 1st rdbt. Hotel 500yds on left

High quality, budget accommodation ideal for both families and business travellers. Spacious, en suite bedrooms feature tea and coffee making facilities, and Freeview TV in most hotels. Internet access and Wi-fi are available for a small fee. The adjacent family restaurant features a wide and varied menu. See also the Hotel Groups pages.

Rooms 17 **D** £68-£83*

Premier Inn Twickenham Stadium

BUDGET HOTEL

☎ 0871 527 9110 📠 0871 527 9111
Chertsey Rd, Whitton TW2 6LS
dir: From M3 onto A316, then A305 signed Twickenham. At Hospital Bridge Rdbt 3rd exit into Hospital Bridge Rd. Take B358 signed Teddington. Becomes Sixth Cross Rd. Hotel on left

Rooms 31 **D** £68-£83*

TWO BRIDGES
Devon Map 3 SX67

Two Bridges Hotel

★★★ 78% HOTEL

☎ 01822 890581 📠 01822 892306
PL20 6SW
e-mail: enquiries@twobridges.co.uk
web: www.twobridges.co.uk
dir: At junct of B3212 & B3357

This wonderfully relaxing hotel is set in the heart of the Dartmoor National Park, in a beautiful riverside location. Three standards of comfortable rooms provide every modern convenience, and include four-poster rooms. There is a choice of lounges and fine dining is available in the restaurant, where menus feature local game and seasonal produce.

Rooms 33 (2 fmly) (6 GF) **Facilities** STV Fishing Xmas New Year **Conf** Class 60 Board 40 Thtr 130 **Parking** 100 **Notes** LB Civ Wed 130

TYNEMOUTH
Tyne & Wear Map 21 NZ36

Grand

★★★ 79% HOTEL

☎ 0191 293 6666 📠 0191 293 6665
Grand Pde NE30 4ER
e-mail: info20@grandhotel-uk.com
web: www.grandhotel-uk.com
dir: A1058 for Tynemouth. At coast rdbt turn right. Hotel on right approx 0.5m

This grand Victorian building offers stunning views of the coast. Bedrooms come in a variety of styles and are well equipped, tastefully decorated and have impressive bathrooms. In addition to the restaurant there are two bars; the elegant and imposing staircase is a focal point, and is a favourite spot for the bride and groom to have their photograph taken after their wedding here.

Rooms 45 (5 annexe) (11 fmly) (10 smoking) **Facilities** STV Xmas New Year Wi-fi **Conf** Class 40 Board 40 Thtr 130 **Services** Lift **Parking** 16 **Notes** RS Sun evening Civ Wed 120

UCKFIELD
East Sussex Map 6 TQ42

INSPECTORS' CHOICE

Buxted Park Hotel

HandPICKED HOTELS

★★★★ HOTEL

☎ 01825 733333 & 0845 458 0901
📠 01825 732 990
Buxted TN22 4AY
e-mail: buxtedpark@handpicked.co.uk
web: www.handpicked.co.uk
dir: From A26 (Uckfield bypass) take A272 signed Buxted. Through lights, hotel 1m on right

An attractive Grade II listed Georgian mansion dating back to the 17th century. The property is set amidst 300 acres of beautiful countryside and landscaped gardens. The stylish, thoughtfully equipped bedrooms are split between the main house and the modern Garden Wing. An interesting choice of dishes is served in the restaurant.

Rooms 44 (7 fmly) (16 GF) **Facilities** FTV Fishing Gym Orienteering Walking trail Snooker room Xmas New Year Wi-fi **Conf** Class 80 Board 42 Thtr 180 Del from £140 to £240* **Services** Lift **Parking** 100 **Notes** Civ Wed 120

East Sussex National Golf Resort & Spa

★★★★ 77% HOTEL

☎ 01825 880088 📠 01825 880066
Little Horsted TN22 5ES
e-mail: reception@eastsussexnational.co.uk
dir: M25 junct 6, A22 signed East Grinstead & Eastbourne. Straight on at rdbt junct of A22 & A26 (Little Horsted). At next rdbt right to hotel

This modern hotel is located in lovely country location and offers a super range of facilities with two golf courses and an impressive leisure suite. In addition there are also conference and meeting facilities. The bedrooms are spacious and have good facilities; all

continued

U

UCKFIELD *continued*

have delightful views across the golf course to the countryside beyond. The cuisine is enjoyable; particularly at breakfast, which is served in the restaurant that overlooks the course.

Rooms 104 (3 fmly) (36 GF) **S** £79-£170; **D** £85-£180 (incl. bkfst)* **Facilities** Spa STV FTV 36 Putt green Gym Academy of Golf Xmas New Year Wi-fi **Conf** Class 200 Board 50 Thtr 450 **Services** Lift Air con **Parking** 500 **Notes** LB Civ Wed 250

INSPECTORS' CHOICE

Horsted Place

★★★ HOTEL

01825 750581 01825 750459
Little Horsted TN22 5TS
e-mail: hotel@horstedplace.co.uk
dir: From Uckfield 2m S on A26 towards Lewes

This 17th-century property is one of Britain's finest examples of Gothic revivalist architecture. It is situated in extensive landscaped grounds, with a tennis court and croquet lawn, and is adjacent to the East Sussex National Golf Club. The spacious bedrooms are attractively decorated, tastefully furnished and equipped with many thoughtful touches such as flowers and books. Most bedrooms also have a separate sitting area.

Rooms 20 (3 annexe) (5 fmly) (2 GF) **S** £145-£360; **D** £145-£360 (incl. bkfst)* **Facilities** STV FTV 36 Free use of gym & indoor pool at nearby hotel Xmas New Year Wi-fi **Conf** Class 50 Board 40 Thtr 80 Del from £170* **Services** Lift **Parking** 32 **Notes** LB No children 7yrs Civ Wed 100

U

ULLESTHORPE
Leicestershire
Map 11 SP58

Best Western Ullesthorpe Court Hotel & Golf Club

Best Western

★★★★ 78% HOTEL

01455 209023 01455 202537
Frolesworth Rd LE17 5BZ
e-mail: bookings@ullesthorpecourt.co.uk
web: www.bw-ullesthorpecourt.co.uk
dir: M1 junct 20 towards Lutterworth. Follow brown tourist signs

Complete with its own golf club, this impressively equipped hotel is within easy reach of the motorway network, NEC and Birmingham airport. Public areas include both formal and informal eating options and extensive conference and leisure facilities. Spacious bedrooms are thoughtfully equipped for both the business and leisure guests, and a four-poster room is available.

Rooms 72 (3 fmly) (16 GF) **Facilities** Spa STV supervised 18 Putt green Gym Beauty room Steam room Sauna Snooker room New Year Wi-fi **Conf** Class 48 Board 30 Thtr 80 Del from £120 to £145* **Services** Lift **Parking** 280 **Notes** RS 25 & 26 Dec Civ Wed 120

ULLSWATER

See Glenridding & Patterdale

UPPER SLAUGHTER
Gloucestershire
Map 10 SP12

INSPECTORS' CHOICE

Lords of the Manor

★★★★ COUNTRY HOUSE HOTEL

01451 820243 01451 820696
GL54 2JD
e-mail: reservations@lordsofthemanor.com
web: www.lordsofthemanor.com
dir: 2m W of A429. Exit A40 onto A429, take 'The Slaughters' turn. Through Lower Slaughter for 1m to Upper Slaughter. Hotel on right

This wonderfully welcoming 17th-century manor house hotel sits in eight acres of gardens and parkland surrounded by Cotswold countryside. A relaxed atmosphere, underpinned by professional and attentive service is the hallmark here, so that guests are often reluctant to leave. The hotel has elegant public rooms that overlook the immaculate lawns, and the restaurant is the venue for consistently impressive cuisine. Bedrooms have much character and charm, combined with the extra touches expected of a hotel of this stature.

Rooms 26 (4 fmly) (9 GF) **Facilities** FTV Fishing Xmas New Year Wi-fi **Conf** Class 20 Board 20 Thtr 30 **Parking** 40 **Notes** Civ Wed 50

UPPINGHAM
Rutland
Map 11 SP89

The Lake Isle
RESTAURANT WITH ROOMS

☎ 01572 822951 📠 01572 824400
16 High Street East LE15 9PZ
e-mail: info@lakeisle.co.uk
web: www.lakeisle.co.uk
dir: From A47, turn left at 2nd lights, 100yds on right

This attractive townhouse centres round a delightful restaurant and small elegant bar. There is also an inviting first-floor guest lounge, and the bedrooms are extremely well appointed and thoughtfully equipped; spacious split-level cottage suites situated in a quiet courtyard are also available. The imaginative cooking and an extremely impressive wine list are highlights.

Rooms 12 (3 annexe) (1 fmly)

UPTON UPON SEVERN
Worcestershire
Map 10 SO84

White Lion Hotel
★★★ 71% HOTEL

☎ 01684 592551 📠 01684 593333
21 High St WR8 0HJ
e-mail: reservations@whitelionhotel.biz
dir: A422, A38 towards Tewkesbury. In 8m take B4104, after 1m cross bridge, turn left to hotel, past bend on left

Famed for being the inn depicted in Henry Fielding's novel *Tom Jones*, this 16th-century hotel is a reminder of 'Old England' with features such as exposed beams and wall timbers still remaining. The quality furnishing and the decor throughout enhance its character; the bedrooms are smart and include one four-poster room.

Rooms 13 (2 annexe) (2 fmly) (2 GF) **Facilities** FTV Wi-fi **Conf** Class 12 Board 12 Thtr 24 **Parking** 14 **Notes** Closed 1 Jan RS 25 Dec

UTTOXETER
Staffordshire
Map 10 SK03

Premier Inn Uttoxeter
BUDGET HOTEL

☎ 0871 527 9112 📠 0871 527 9113
Derby Rd ST14 5AA
dir: At junct of A50 & B5030 on outskirts of Uttoxeter, 7m S of Alton Towers Theme Park

High quality, budget accommodation ideal for both families and business travellers. Spacious, en suite bedrooms feature tea and coffee making facilities, and Freeview TV in most hotels. Internet access and Wi-fi are available for a small fee. The adjacent family restaurant features a wide and varied menu. See also the Hotel Groups pages.

Rooms 41 **D** £62*

UXBRIDGE
Greater London

See **Ruislip**

VENTNOR
Isle of Wight
Map 5 SZ57

The Royal Hotel
★★★★ 79% HOTEL

☎ 01983 852186 📠 01983 855395
Belgrave Rd PO38 1JJ
e-mail: enquiries@royalhoteliow.co.uk
web: www.royalhoteliow.co.uk
dir: A3055 into Ventnor follow one-way system, after lights left into Belgrave Rd. Hotel on right

This smart hotel enjoys a central yet peaceful location in its own gardens, complete with an outdoor pool. Spacious, elegant public areas include a bright conservatory, bar and lounge. Bedrooms, appointed to a high standard, vary in size and style. Staff are friendly and efficient, particularly in the smart restaurant, where modern British cuisine is offered.

Rooms 53 (9 fmly) **S** £115-£150; **D** £190-£290 (incl. bkfst)* **Facilities** Xmas New Year Wi-fi **Conf** Class 40 Board 24 Thtr 100 Del from £ to £250* **Services** Lift **Parking** 50 **Notes** LB Closed 1st 2 wks Jan Civ Wed 150

Eversley
★★★ 74% HOTEL

☎ 01983 852244 & 852462 📠 01983 856534
Park Av PO38 1LB
e-mail: eversleyhotel@yahoo.co.uk
web: www.eversleyhotel.com
dir: On A3055 W of Ventnor, next to Ventnor Park

Located west of Ventnor, this hotel enjoys a quiet location and has some rooms with garden and pool views. The spacious restaurant is sometimes used for local functions, and there is a bar, television room, lounge area, a card room as well as a jacuzzi and gym. Bedrooms are generally a good size.

Rooms 30 (8 fmly) (2 GF) **Facilities** Gym Pool table Xmas **Conf** Class 40 Board 20 **Parking** 23 **Notes** Closed 30 Nov-22 Dec & 2 Jan-8 Feb

Ventnor Towers Hotel
★★★ 72% HOTEL

☎ 01983 852277 📠 01983 855536
54 Madeira Rd PO38 1QT
e-mail: reservations@ventnortowers.com
web: www.ventnortowers.com
dir: From E, 1st left off A3055 just before pelican crossing

This mid-Victorian hotel, set in spacious grounds from where a path leads down to the shore, is high above the bay and enjoys splendid sea views. Many potted plants and fresh flowers grace the day rooms, which include two lounges and a spacious bar. Bedrooms include two four-poster rooms and some that have their own balconies.

Rooms 25 (4 fmly) (6 GF) **S** £55-£85; **D** £65-£110 (incl. bkfst)* **Facilities** 9 Putt green Xmas New Year Wi-fi **Conf** Class 60 Board 44 Thtr 100 Del from £85 to £135* **Parking** 20 **Notes** LB Civ Wed 150

V

VENTNOR *continued*

Wellington

★★★ HOTEL

☎ 01983 856600 📠 01983 856611
Belgrave Rd PO38 1JH
e-mail: enquiries@thewellingtonhotel.net
web: www.thewellingtonhotel.net

Rooms 28 (5 fmly) (7 GF) (14 smoking) **Facilities** STV Xmas New Year Wi-fi **Conf** Class 28 Board 28 Thtr 28 **Parking** 10 **Notes** Civ Wed 60

INSPECTORS' CHOICE

The Hambrough

RESTAURANT WITH ROOMS

☎ 01983 856333 📠 01983 857260
Hambrough Rd PO38 1SQ
e-mail: info@thehambrough.com
dir: Telephone for directions

A former Victorian villa set on the hillside above Ventnor and with memorable views out to sea, The Hambrough has a modern, stylish interior with well equipped and boutique style accommodation. The kitchen team's passion for food is clearly evident in the superb cuisine served in the minimalistic styled restaurant.

Rooms 7 (3 fmly)

VERYAN Map 2 SW93
Cornwall

INSPECTORS' CHOICE

The Nare Hotel

★★★★ COUNTRY HOUSE HOTEL

☎ 01872 501111 📠 01872 501856
Carne Beach TR2 5PF
e-mail: stay@narehotel.co.uk
web: www.narehotel.co.uk
dir: From Tregony follow A3078 for approx 1.5m. Left at Veryan sign, through village towards sea & hotel

This delightful hotel offers a relaxed, country-house atmosphere in a spectacular coastal setting. The elegantly designed bedrooms, many with balconies, have fresh flowers, carefully chosen artwork and antiques that contribute to their engaging individuality. A choice of dining options is available, from light snacks to superb local seafood.

Rooms 37 (7 fmly) (7 GF) **S** £136-£260; **D** £262-£746 (incl. bkfst)* **Facilities** Spa FTV Gym Health & beauty clinic Sauna Steam room Hotel sailing boat Shooting Xmas New Year Wi-fi **Services** Lift **Parking** 80 **Notes** LB

WADDESDON Map 11 SP71
Buckinghamshire

The Five Arrows

RESTAURANT WITH ROOMS

☎ 01296 651727 📠 01296 655716
High St HP18 0JE
e-mail: five.arrows@nationaltrust.org.uk

This Grade II listed building with elaborate Elizabethan chimney stacks, stands at the gates of Waddesdon Manor and was named after the Rothschild family emblem. Individually styled en suite bedrooms are comfortable and well appointed. Friendly staff are on hand to offer a warm welcome. Alfresco dining is possible in the warmer months.

Rooms 11

WAKEFIELD Map 16 SE32
West Yorkshire

See also **Liversedge**

Waterton Park

★★★★ 75% HOTEL

☎ 01924 257911 & 249800 📠 01924 259686
Walton Hall, The Balk, Walton WF2 6PW
e-mail: info@watertonparkhotel.co.uk
web: www.watertonparkhotel.co.uk
dir: M1 junct 39 towards Wakefield. At 3rd rdbt right for Crofton. At 2nd lights right & follow signs

This Georgian mansion, built on an island in the centre of a 26-acre lake is in an idyllic setting. The main house contains many feature bedrooms, and the annexe houses more spacious rooms, all equally well equipped with modern facilities; most of the bedrooms have views over the lake or the 18-hole golf course. The delightful beamed restaurant, two bars and leisure club are located in the old hall.

Rooms 65 (43 annexe) (5 fmly) (23 GF) **Facilities** STV FTV supervised Fishing Gym Steam room Sauna New Year Wi-fi **Conf** Class 80 Board 80 Thtr 150 **Services** Lift **Parking** 200 **Notes** Civ Wed 130

Cedar Court Hotel Wakefield

THE INDEPENDENTS HOTEL ASSOCIATION

★★★★ 73% HOTEL

☎ 01924 276310 📠 01924 280221
Denby Dale Rd WF4 3QZ
e-mail: sales@cedarcourthotels.co.uk
web: www.cedarcourthotels.co.uk
dir: Adjacent to M1 junct 39

This hotel enjoys a convenient location just off the M1. Traditionally styled bedrooms offer a good range of facilities while open-plan public areas include a busy bar and restaurant operation. Conferences and functions are extremely well catered for and a modern leisure club completes the picture.

Rooms 149 (2 fmly) (74 GF) (6 smoking) **Facilities** FTV supervised Gym Xmas New Year Wi-fi **Conf** Class 140 Board 80 Thtr 400 Del from £105 to £145* **Services** Lift **Parking** 350 **Notes** LB Civ Wed 250

V

Holiday Inn Leeds - Wakefield

★★★ 75% HOTEL

☎ 0871 942 9082 🖷 01924 230613
Queen's Dr, Ossett WF5 9BE
e-mail: reception-wakefield@ihg.com
web: www.holidayinn.co.uk/wakefield
dir: M1 junct 40 follow signs for Wakefield. Hotel on right in 200yds

Situated close to major motorway networks, this modern hotel offers well-equipped and comfortable bedrooms. Public areas include the popular Traders restaurant and a comfortable lounge where a menu is available throughout the day. Conference facilities are also available.

Rooms 104 (32 fmly) (35 GF) (9 smoking) **S** £39-£99; **D** £39-£99* **Facilities** STV Xmas New Year Wi-fi **Conf** Class 80 Board 80 Thtr 160 Del from £109 to £149 **Services** Lift Air con **Parking** 105 **Notes** LB Civ Wed 160

Campanile Wakefield

Campanile

BUDGET HOTEL

☎ 01924 201054 🖷 01924 290976
Monckton Rd WF2 7AL
e-mail: wakefield@campanile.com
dir: M1 junct 39, A636, 1m towards Wakefield, left into Monckton Rd, hotel on left

This modern building offers accommodation in smart, well-equipped bedrooms, all with en suite bathrooms. Refreshments may be taken at the informal bistro. See also the Hotel Groups pages.

Rooms 76 (76 annexe) (4 fmly) (25 GF) **Conf** Class 15 Board 15 Thtr 25

Premier Inn Wakefield Central

BUDGET HOTEL

☎ 0871 527 9114 🖷 0871 527 9115
Thornes Park, Denby Dale Rd WF2 8DY
dir: M1 junct 41, A650 towards Wakefield. Approx 1.5m. Hotel on right

High quality, budget accommodation ideal for both families and business travellers. Spacious, en suite bedrooms feature tea and coffee making facilities, and Freeview TV in most hotels. Internet access and Wi-fi are available for a small fee. The adjacent family restaurant features a wide and varied menu. See also the Hotel Groups pages.

Rooms 42 **D** £51-£59*

Premier Inn Wakefield South M1 Jct 39

BUDGET HOTEL

☎ 0871 527 9118 🖷 0871 527 9119
Calder Park, Denby Dale Rd WF4 3BB
dir: M1 junct 39, A636 towards Wakefield. At 1st rdbt 1st exit into Calder Park. Hotel on right

Rooms 74 **D** £51-£59*

WALLASEY Map 15 SJ29
Merseyside

Grove House

★★★ 80% HOTEL

☎ 0151 639 3947 & 630 4558 🖷 0151 639 0028
Grove Rd CH45 3HF
e-mail: reception@thegrovehouse.co.uk
dir: M53 junct 1, A554 (Wallasey New Brighton), right after church into Harrison Drive, left after Windsors Garage into Grove Rd

Pretty lawns and gardens provide the setting for this friendly hotel, conveniently situated about a mile from the M53. Attractively furnished, well-equipped bedrooms include family and four-poster rooms. Business meetings and weddings can be catered for. A wide choice of dishes is available in the restaurant that overlooks the garden.

Rooms 14 (7 fmly) **S** £69; **D** £90-£135 (incl. bkfst)* **Facilities** FTV Wi-fi **Conf** Class 30 Board 50 Thtr 50 Del from £104.90 to £117.90* **Parking** 28 **Notes** LB ⊗ RS BHs Civ Wed 50

WALLINGFORD Map 5 SU68
Oxfordshire

The Springs Hotel & Golf Club

★★★ 80% ◎ HOTEL

☎ 01491 836687 🖷 01491 836877
Wallingford Rd, North Stoke OX10 6BE
e-mail: info@thespringshotel.com
web: www.thespringshotel.com
dir: Off A4074 (Oxford-Reading road) onto B4009 (Goring). Hotel approx 1m on right

Set on its own 18-hole, par 72 golf course, this Victorian mansion has a timeless and peaceful atmosphere. The generously equipped, individually styled bedrooms vary in size but many are spacious. Some bedrooms overlook the pool and grounds while others have views of the spring-fed lake as does the elegant restaurant. There is also a comfortable lounge, with original features, to relax in.

Rooms 32 (3 fmly) (10 GF) **Facilities** FTV ⛳ 18 Putt green Fishing Boat trips on Thames Xmas New Year Wi-fi **Conf** Class 16 Board 26 Thtr 60 **Parking** 150 **Notes** Civ Wed 150

W

WALLINGFORD *continued*

The George

★★★ 77% HOTEL

☎ 01491 836665 📠 01491 825359
High St OX10 0BS
e-mail: info@george-hotel-wallingford.com
web: www.peelhotels.co.uk
dir: E side of A329, N end of Wallingford

Old world charm and modern facilities merge seamlessly in this former coaching inn. Bedrooms in the main house have character in abundance. Those in the wing have a more contemporary style, but all are well equipped and attractively decorated. Diners can choose between the restaurant and bistro, or relax in the cosy bar.

Rooms 39 (1 fmly) (9 GF) **S** £110-£148; **D** £138-£158* **Facilities** STV Xmas New Year Wi-fi **Conf** Class 60 Board 50 Thtr 150 Del from £128 to £148* **Parking** 60 **Notes** ⊗ Civ Wed 100

Shillingford Bridge

★★★ 73% HOTEL

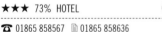

☎ 01865 858567 📠 01865 858636
Shillingford OX10 8LZ
e-mail: shillingford.bridge@forestdale.com
web: www.shillingfordbridgehotel.com
dir: M4 junct 12, A4 towards Newbury, A340 to Pangbourne, A329 to Winterbrook rbdt take unclassified road to Wallingford, straight on at lights towards Oxford. Hotel 1.5m. Or M40 junct 6, B4009 through Watlington & Benson, right onto A4074, left at Shillingford rbdt towards Wallingford. Hotel 0.5m

This hotel enjoys a superb position right on the banks of the River Thames, and benefits from private moorings and has a waterside open-air swimming pool. Public areas are stylish with a contemporary feel and have large picture windows making the best use of the view. Bedrooms are well equipped and furnished with guest comfort in mind.

Rooms 40 (8 annexe) (6 fmly) (9 GF) **Facilities** FTV supervised Fishing Table tennis Xmas New Year Wi-fi **Conf** Class 40 Board 36 Thtr 80 **Parking** 100 **Notes** LB Civ Wed 150

W

WALSALL
West Midlands
Map 10 SP09

Fairlawns Hotel & Spa

★★★ 85% ®® HOTEL

☎ 01922 455122 📠 01922 743148
178 Little Aston Rd WS9 0NU
e-mail: reception@fairlawns.co.uk
web: www.fairlawns.co.uk
dir: Off A452 towards Aldridge at x-roads with A454. Hotel 600yds on right

In a rural location with immaculate landscaped grounds, this constantly improving hotel offers a wide range of facilities and modern, comfortable bedrooms. Family rooms, one with a four-poster bed, and suites are also available. The Fairlawns Restaurant serves a wide range of award-winning seasonal dishes. The extensive comprehensively equipped leisure complex is mainly for adult use as there is restricted availability to young people.

Rooms 58 (8 fmly) (1 GF) (3 smoking) **S** £82.50-£167.50; **D** £110-£180 (incl. bkfst) **Facilities** Spa STV FTV supervised Gym Dance studio Beauty salon Bathing suite Floatation suite Sauna Aromatherapy room New Year Wi-fi **Conf** Class 40 Board 30 Thtr 80 Del from £109.50 to £165 **Services** Lift **Parking** 150 **Notes** LB RS 24 Dec-2 Jan Civ Wed 100

Beverley Hotel

★★★ 68% HOTEL

☎ 01922 622999 📠 01922 724187
58 Lichfield Rd WS4 2DJ
e-mail: info@beverley-hotel.com
dir: 1m N of town centre on A461 to Lichfield

This privately owned hotel dates back to 1880. Bedrooms are comfortably appointed, and the tastefully decorated public areas include a spacious bar combined with a conservatory. The restaurant offers guests a choice of carefully prepared, appetising dishes.

Rooms 31 (2 fmly) (4 GF) **S** £46.50-£75; **D** £57.50-£85 (incl. bkfst) **Facilities** FTV New Year Wi-fi **Conf** Class 30 Board 30 Thtr 80 Del from £95 to £125 **Parking** 68 **Notes** LB ⊗ Civ Wed 80

Holiday Inn Express Walsall M6 Jct 10

BUDGET HOTEL

☎ 01922 705250 📠 01922 705260
Tempus Ten, Tempus Dr WS2 8TJ
e-mail: admin@hiexwalsall.com
web: www.hiexpress.co.uk
dir: M6 junct 10/A454 to Walsall. Right at 1st lights, hotel 200mtrs on right

A modern hotel ideal for families and business travellers. Fresh and uncomplicated, the spacious rooms include Sky TV, power shower and tea and coffee-making facilities. Continental buffet breakfast is included in the room rate; other meals may be taken at the nearby family pub or restaurant. See also the Hotel Groups pages.

Rooms 120 (77 fmly) (30 GF) (19 smoking) **S** £49.95-£124.95; **D** £49.95-£124.95 (incl. bkfst) **Conf** Class 45 Board 36 Thtr 60 Del from £99.95 to £150

Premier Inn Walsall M6 Jct 10

BUDGET HOTEL

☎ 0871 527 9120 📠 0871 527 9121
Bentley Green, Bentley Road North WS2 0WB
dir: M6 junct 10, A454 signed Wolverhampton. 2nd exit (Ansons junct). Left at rdbt, 1st left at next rdbt, hotel on right

High quality, budget accommodation ideal for both families and business travellers. Spacious, en suite bedrooms feature tea and coffee making facilities, and Freeview TV in most hotels. Internet access and Wi-fi are available for a small fee. The adjacent family restaurant features a wide and varied menu. See also the Hotel Groups pages.

Rooms 40 **D** £50-£60*

WALTHAM ABBEY
Essex
Map 6 TL30

Waltham Abbey Marriott Hotel

Marriott HOTELS & RESORTS

★★★★ 73% HOTEL

☎ 01992 717170 📠 01992 711841
Old Shire Ln EN9 3LX
web: www.walthamabbeymarriott.co.uk
dir: M25 junct 26

This hotel benefits from convenient access to London and the major road networks. The air-conditioned bedrooms are spacious, tastefully decorated and offer a range of facilities for the modern business traveller. The hotel also provides a range of meeting rooms, a substantial parking area and a well-equipped indoor leisure centre.

Rooms 162 (16 fmly) (80 GF) **Facilities** STV Gym Xmas New Year Wi-fi **Conf** Class 120 Board 50 Thtr 280 **Services** Air con **Parking** 250 **Notes** Civ Wed 250

Premier Inn Waltham Abbey

BUDGET HOTEL

☎ 0871 527 9122 0871 527 9123
Sewardstone Rd EN9 3QF
dir: M25 junct 26, A121 towards Waltham Abbey. Left onto A112, hotel 0.5m on left

High quality, budget accommodation ideal for both families and business travellers. Spacious, en suite bedrooms feature tea and coffee making facilities, and Freeview TV in most hotels. Internet access and Wi-fi are available for a small fee. The adjacent family restaurant features a wide and varied menu. See also the Hotel Groups pages.

Rooms 93 **D** £59-£65*

WANSFORD Cambridgeshire **Map 12 TL09**

The Haycock Hotel

THE INDEPENDENTS HOTEL ASSOCIATION

★★★ 86% HOTEL

☎ 01780 782223 & 781124 01780 783508
PE8 6JA
e-mail: sales@thehaycock.co.uk
dir: A1 junct to A47 Leicester

A charming 17th-century coaching inn set amidst attractive landscaped grounds in a peaceful village location. The smartly decorated bedrooms are tastefully furnished and thoughtfully equipped. Public rooms include a choice of restaurants, a lounge bar, a cocktail bar and a stylish lounge. The hotel has a staffed business centre, and banqueting facilities are also available.

Rooms 48 (14 GF) **S** £69-£85; **D** £75-£135 (incl. bkfst)* **Facilities** FTV Wi-fi **Conf** Class 100 Board 45 Thtr 300 Del from £135 to £160* **Parking** 300 **Notes** LB Civ Wed

WANTAGE Oxfordshire **Map 5 SU38**

La Fontana Restaurant with Accommodation

RESTAURANT WITH ROOMS

☎ 01235 868287 01235 868019
Oxford Rd, East Hanney OX12 0HP
e-mail: anna@la-fontana.co.uk

Guests are guaranteed a warm welcome at this family-run Italian restaurant which is located on the outskirts of the busy town of Wantage. The stylish bedrooms are individually designed, well equipped and very comfortable. Dinner should not be missed - the menu features a wide range of regional Italian specialities.

Rooms 15 (7 annexe) (2 fmly)

WARE Hertfordshire **Map 6 TL31**

Hanbury Manor, A Marriott Hotel & Country Club

★★★★★ 81% COUNTRY HOUSE HOTEL

☎ 01920 487722 & 0870 400 7222
01920 487692
SG12 0SD
e-mail: mhrs.stngs.guestrelations@marriotthotels.com
web: www.marriotthanburymanor.co.uk
dir: M25 junct 25, A10 N, 12m, then A1170, right at rdbt, hotel on left

Set in 200 acres of landscaped grounds, this impressive Jacobean-style mansion boasts an enviable range of leisure facilities, including an excellent health club and championship golf course. Bedrooms are traditionally and comfortably furnished in the country-house style and have lovely marbled bathrooms. There are a number of food and drink options, including the renowned Zodiac and Oakes restaurants.

Hanbury Manor, A Marriott Hotel & Country Club

Rooms 161 (27 annexe) (60 fmly) **Facilities** Spa STV FTV supervised 18 Putt green Gym Health & beauty treatments Aerobics Yoga Dance class Xmas New Year Wi-fi **Conf** Class 86 Board 36 Thtr 150 **Services** Lift **Parking** 200 **Notes** Civ Wed 120

Roebuck

★★★ 72% HOTEL

☎ 01920 409955 01920 468016
Baldock St SG12 9DR
e-mail: roebuck@forestdale.com
web: www.theroebuckhotel.co.uk
dir: A10 onto B1001, left at rdbt, 1st left behind fire station

The Roebuck is a comfortable and friendly hotel situated close to the old market town of Ware, it is also within easy reach of Stansted Airport, Cambridge and Hertford. The hotel has spacious bedrooms, a comfortable lounge, bar and conservatory restaurant. There is also a range of air-conditioned meeting rooms.

Rooms 47 (1 fmly) (16 GF) **Facilities** FTV Wi-fi **Conf** Class 75 Board 60 Thtr 200 **Services** Lift **Parking** 64 **Notes** LB Civ Wed 80

WARMINSTER Wiltshire **Map 4 ST84**

Bishopstrow House Hotel

★★★★ 78% HOTEL

☎ 01985 212312 01985 216769
BA12 9HH
e-mail: info@bishopstrow.co.uk
web: www.vonessenhotels.co.uk
dir: A303, A36, B3414, hotel 2m on right

This is a fine example of a Georgian country home, situated in 27 acres of grounds. Public areas are traditional in style and feature antiques and open fires. Most bedrooms offer DVD players. A spa, a tennis court and several country walks ensure there is something for all guests. The restaurant serves top quality, contemporary cuisine.

Rooms 32 (2 annexe) (2 fmly) (7 GF) **Facilities** Spa Fishing Gym Clay pigeon shooting Archery Cycling Xmas New Year Wi-fi **Conf** Class 32 Board 36 Thtr 70 **Parking** 100 **Notes** Civ Wed 65

W

WARRINGTON
Cheshire
Map 15 SJ68

The Park Royal

★★★★ 78% HOTEL

☎ 01925 730706 📠 01925 730740
Stretton Rd, Stretton WA4 4NS
e-mail: parkroyalreservations@qhotels.co.uk
web: www.qhotels.co.uk
dir: M56 junct 10, A49 to Warrington, at lights turn right to Appleton Thorn, 1st right into Spark Hall Close, hotel on left

This modern hotel enjoys a peaceful setting, yet is conveniently located just minutes from the M56. The bedrooms are modern in style and thoughtfully equipped. Spacious, stylish public areas include extensive conference and function facilities, and a comprehensive leisure centre complete with outdoor tennis courts and an impressive beauty centre.

Rooms 146 (32 fmly) (34 GF) **Facilities** Spa FTV Gym Dance studio Xmas New Year Wi-fi **Conf** Class 180 Board 90 Thtr 400 **Services** Lift **Parking** 400 **Notes** Civ Wed 300

Best Western Fir Grove

★★★ 78% HOTEL

☎ 01925 267471 📠 01925 601092
Knutsford Old Rd WA4 2LD
e-mail: firgrove@bestwestern.co.uk
web: www.bw-firgrovehotel.co.uk
dir: M6 junct 20, follow signs for A50 to Warrington for 2.4m, before swing bridge over canal, turn right & right again

Situated in a quiet residential area, this hotel is convenient for both the town centre and the motorway network. Comfortable, smart bedrooms, including spacious executive rooms, offer some excellent extra facilities such as PlayStations and CD players. Public areas include a smart lounge/bar, a neatly appointed restaurant and excellent function and meeting facilities.

Rooms 52 (3 fmly) (20 GF) **Facilities** STV FTV Xmas New Year Wi-fi **Conf** Class 150 Board 50 Thtr 200 **Parking** 100 **Notes** LB Civ Wed 200

Holiday Inn Warrington

★★★ 73% HOTEL

☎ 0871 942 9087 📠 01925 838859
Woolston Grange Av, Woolston WA1 4PX
e-mail: nicola.crowley@ihg.com
web: www.holidayinn.co.uk
dir: M6 junct 21, follow signs for Birchwood

Ideally located within the M62 and M56 interchange, this hotel provides the ideal base for all areas of the north-west region for both corporate and leisure guests. Rooms are spacious and well equipped, and a wide choice of meals is available in the comfortable restaurant and cosy bar. Meeting and conference facilities are also available.

Rooms 96 (26 fmly) (9 GF) **Facilities** STV Xmas New Year Wi-fi **Conf** Class 10 Board 16 Thtr 30 Del from £88 to £124* **Services** Lift Air con **Parking** 101

Ramada Encore Warrington

★★★ 70% HOTEL

☎ 01925 847050 📠 01925 847060
Aston Avene, Birchwood Business Park WA3 6ZN
e-mail: gm@encorewarrington.co.uk
dir: M6 junct 21a, follow signs for Birchwood Park on A574

This purpose-built hotel makes a good base for both business and leisure guests. The bedrooms are spacious and bright with en suite power-shower rooms. Public areas include a restaurant, bar and lounge. Secure parking is available on site.

Rooms 103 (16 fmly) (7 GF) **S** £49-£99; **D** £49-£99* **Facilities** FTV Wi-fi **Conf** Class 40 Board 12 Thtr 35 Del from £89 to £129* **Services** Lift Air con **Parking** 94 **Notes** ⊗

Paddington House

★★ 74% HOTEL

☎ 01925 816767 📠 01925 816651
514 Old Manchester Rd WA1 3TZ
e-mail: hotel@paddingtonhouse.co.uk
web: www.paddingtonhouse.co.uk
dir: 1m from M6 junct 21, off A57, 2m from town centre

This busy, friendly hotel is conveniently situated just over a mile from the M6. Bedrooms are attractively furnished, and include four-poster and ground-floor rooms. Guests can dine in the wood-panelled Padgate Restaurant or in the cosy bar. Conference and function facilities are available.

Rooms 37 (9 fmly) (6 GF) (6 smoking) **Facilities** FTV New Year Wi-fi **Conf** Class 100 Board 40 Thtr 180 **Services** Lift **Parking** 50 **Notes** LB Civ Wed 150

Villaggio

★★ 63% HOTEL

☎ 01925 630106 📠 01925 631377
5-9 Folly Ln WA5 0LZ
e-mail: villaggiowarrington@hotmail.co.uk
dir: M62 junct 9, A49, through 2 rdbts to x-rds. Left at McDonalds, through lights, hotel on left

Conveniently located close to northwest motorway networks and only half a mile from the town centre. Bedrooms are simply furnished in a contemporary style with good quality accessories such as flat-screen TVs and complimentary Wi-fi. An extensive choice of meals is served in the spacious restaurant. Off-road parking is available.

Rooms 19 (2 fmly) **Facilities** FTV Xmas New Year Wi-fi **Conf** Class 180 Board 100 Thtr 230 **Parking** 30

Premier Inn Warrington A49/M62 Jct 9

BUDGET HOTEL

☎ 0871 527 9128 📠 0871 527 9129
Winwick Rd WA2 8RN
dir: M62 junct 9 towards Warrington, hotel 100yds

High quality, budget accommodation ideal for both families and business travellers. Spacious, en suite bedrooms feature tea and coffee making facilities, and Freeview TV in most hotels. Internet access and Wi-fi are available for a small fee. The adjacent family restaurant features a wide and varied menu. See also the Hotel Groups pages.

Rooms 74 **D** £49-£60*

Premier Inn Warrington Centre

BUDGET HOTEL

☎ 0871 527 9126 📠 0871 527 9127
1430 Centre Park, Park Boulevard WA1 1PR
dir: Take A49 to Brian Beven Island Rdbt, into Park Boulevard (Centre Park). Over bridge. Hotel on right

Rooms 42 **D** £54-£62*

Premier Inn Warrington (M6 Jct 21)

BUDGET HOTEL

☎ 0871 527 9124 📠 0871 527 9125
Manchester Rd, Woolston WA1 4GB
dir: Just off M6 junct 21 on A57 to Warrington

Rooms 105 **D** £52-£60*

W

Premier Inn Warrington North

BUDGET HOTEL

☎ 0871 527 9128 📠 0871 527 9129
Winwick Rd WA2 8RN
dir: M62 junct 9, A49 signed Warrington. At next rdbt follow Town Centre signs. Straight on at next rdbt, left into Warrington Collegiate Camp

Rooms 74 **D** £49-£60*

Premier Inn Warrington North East

BUDGET HOTEL

☎ 0871 527 9130 📠 0871 527 9131
Golborne Rd, Winwick WA2 8LF
dir: M6 junct 22, A573 towards Newton-le-Willows. Dual carriageway to end, take 3rd exit at rdbt. Hotel adjacent to church

Rooms 42 **D** £50-£60*

Premier Inn Warrington South

BUDGET HOTEL

☎ 0871 527 9134 📠 0871 527 9135
Tarporley Rd, Stretton WA4 4NB
dir: Just off M56 junct 10. Follow A49 to Warrington, left at 1st lights

Rooms 29 **D** £50-£60*

WARWICK
Warwickshire **Map 10 SP26**

See also **Leamington Spa (Royal) & Wroxall**

Chesford Grange

★★★★ 79% HOTEL

☎ 01926 859331 📠 01926 859272
Chesford Bridge CV8 2LD
e-mail: chesfordreservations@qhotels.co.uk
web: www.qhotels.co.uk

(For full entry see Kenilworth)

Ardencote Manor Hotel, Country Club & Spa

★★★★ 77% HOTEL

☎ 01926 843111 📠 01926 842646
The Cumsey, Lye Green Rd, Claverdon CV35 8LT
e-mail: hotel@ardencote.com
web: www.ardencote.com

(For full entry see Claverdon)

Holiday Inn Express Warwick

BUDGET HOTEL

☎ 01926 483000 📠 01926 483033
Stratford Rd CV34 6TW
e-mail: info@expresswarwick.co.uk
web: www.expresswarwick.co.uk
dir: M40 junct 15, follow signs A429 to Warwick. Take 1st right

A modern hotel ideal for families and business travellers. Fresh and uncomplicated, the spacious rooms include Sky TV, power shower and tea and coffee-making facilities. Continental buffet breakfast is included in the room rate; other meals may be taken at the nearby family pub or restaurant. See also the Hotel Groups pages.

Rooms 138 (35 fmly) (36 GF) **S** £49-£125; **D** £49-£125 (incl. bkfst)* **Conf** Class 16 Board 16 Thtr 35

WARWICK MOTORWAY SERVICE AREA (M40)
Warwickshire **Map 10 SP35**

Days Inn Warwick North - M40

BUDGET HOTEL

☎ 01926 651681 📠 01926 651634
Warwick Services, M40 N'bound Junction 12-13, Banbury Rd CV35 0AA
e-mail: warwick.north.hotel@welcomebreak.co.uk
web: www.welcomebreak.co.uk
dir: M40 N'bound between junct 12 & 13

This modern building offers accommodation in smart, spacious and well-equipped bedrooms, suitable for families and business travellers, and all with en suite bathrooms. Continental breakfast is available and other refreshments may be taken at the nearby family restaurant. See also the Hotel Groups pages.

Rooms 54 (45 fmly) (8 smoking) **S** £39.95-£59.95; **D** £49.95-£69.95 **Conf** Board 30

Days Inn Warwick South - M40

BUDGET HOTEL

☎ 01926 650168 📠 01926 651601
Warwick Services, M40 S'bound, Banbury Rd CV35 0AA
e-mail: warwick.south.hotel@welcomebreak.co.uk
web: www.welcomebreak.co.uk
dir: M40 S'bound between junct 14 & 12

Rooms 40 (38 fmly) (5 smoking) **S** £39.95-£59.95; **D** £49.95-£69.95

WASHINGTON
Tyne & Wear **Map 19 NZ35**

Mercure Newcastle George Washington Hotel

★★★ 81% HOTEL

☎ 0191 402 9988 📠 0191 415 1166
Stone Cellar Rd, High Usworth NE37 1PH
e-mail: reservations@georgewashington.co.uk
web: www.georgewashington.co.uk
dir: A1(M) junct 65 onto A194(M). Take A195 signed Washington North. Take last exit from rdbt for Washington then right at mini-rdbt. Hotel 0.5m on right

Popular with business and leisure guests, this purpose-built hotel boasts two golf courses and a driving range. Bedrooms are stylish and modern, generally spacious and comfortably equipped. Public areas include extensive conference facilities, a business centre and fitness club.

Rooms 103 (9 fmly) (41 GF) (6 smoking) **Facilities** **Spa** STV FTV supervised 18 Putt green Gym Squash Golf driving range Beauty salon Xmas Wi-fi **Conf** Class 80 Board 80 Thtr 200 **Parking** 180 **Notes** Civ Wed 180

Holiday Inn Washington

★★★ 75% HOTEL

☎ 0871 942 9084 📠 0191 415 3371
Emerson District 5 NE37 1LB
e-mail: washingtonhi@ihg.com
web: www.holidayinn.co.uk
dir: Just off A1(M) junct 64. Left at rdbt, hotel on left

This is an ideally located hotel, just off the A1(M), and located near historic Durham, Sunderland and Newcastle's city centre. It is a well established hotel noted for its friendly staff. Bedrooms are air conditioned and executive rooms are available. The eating options are Traders Restaurant and the lounge bar area.

Rooms 136 (6 GF) (6 smoking) **Facilities** STV Discounted leisure facilities at nearby club Xmas New Year Wi-fi **Conf** Class 60 Board 50 Thtr 100 **Services** Lift Air con **Parking** 200 **Notes** Civ Wed 150

WASHINGTON *continued*

Campanile Washington

BUDGET HOTEL

☎ 0191 416 5010 📠 0191 416 5023
Emerson Rd, District 5 NE37 1LE
e-mail: washington@campanile.com
dir: A1(M) junct 64, A195 to Washington, 1st left at rdbt into Emerson Rd. Hotel 800yds on left

This modern building offers accommodation in smart, well-equipped bedrooms, all with en suite bathrooms. Refreshments may be taken at the informal bistro. See also the Hotel Groups pages.

Rooms 79 (79 annexe) (1 fmly) (28 GF) **Conf** Class 15 Board 25 Thtr 40

Premier Inn Newcastle (Washington)

BUDGET HOTEL

☎ 0871 527 9136 📠 0871 527 9137
Emerson Rd NE37 1LB
dir: A1(M) junct 64, A195, follow Emerson signs. Left at rdbt, hotel 250yds left

High quality, budget accommodation ideal for both families and business travellers. Spacious, en suite bedrooms feature tea and coffee making facilities, and Freeview TV in most hotels. Internet access and Wi-fi are available for a small fee. The adjacent family restaurant features a wide and varied menu. See also the Hotel Groups pages.

Rooms 74 **D** £54-£59*

WATERMILLOCK Map 18 NY42
Cumbria

Macdonald Leeming House

★★★★ 75% ® HOTEL

☎ 0844 879 9142 📠 015394 43432
CA11 0JJ
e-mail: sales/oldengland@macdonald-hotels.co.uk
web: www.macdonald-hotels.co.uk
dir: M6 junct 40, A66 to Keswick. At rdbt A592 (Ullswater). 5m to T-junct, right (A592). Hotel on left in 3m

This hotel enjoys a superb location, being set in 20 acres of mature wooded gardens in the Lake District National Park, and overlooking Ullswater and the towering fells. Many rooms offer views of the lake and the rugged mountains beyond, with more than half having their own balcony. Public rooms include three sumptuous lounges, a cosy bar and library.

Rooms 41 (1 fmly) (10 GF) **Facilities** Fishing Xmas New Year Wi-fi **Conf** Class 40 Board 30 Thtr 80 **Parking** 50 **Notes** Civ Wed 80

INSPECTORS' CHOICE

Rampsbeck Country House

★★★ ®®® HOTEL

☎ 017684 86442 📠 017684 86688
CA11 0LP
e-mail: enquiries@rampsbeck.co.uk
web: www.rampsbeck.co.uk
dir: M6 junct 40, A592 to Ullswater, at T-junct (with lake in front) turn right, hotel 1.5m

This fine country house lies in 18 acres of parkland on the shores of Lake Ullswater, and is furnished with many period and antique pieces. There are three delightful lounges, an elegant restaurant and a traditional bar. Bedrooms come in three grades; the most spacious rooms are spectacular and overlook the lake. Service is attentive and the award-winning cuisine a real highlight.

Rooms 19 (1 fmly) (1 GF) **S** £97.50-£200; **D** £145-£300 (incl. bkfst)* **Facilities** STV FTV Putt green Private boat trips on Lake Ullswater Xmas New Year Wi-fi **Conf** Class 10 Board 15 Thtr 15 Del from £125 to £275* **Parking** 25 **Notes** LB Civ Wed 60

See advert on opposite page

WATFORD Map 6 TQ19
Hertfordshire

Best Western White House

★★★ 73% HOTEL

☎ 01923 237316 📠 01923 233109
Upton Rd WD18 0JF
e-mail: info@whitehousehotel.co.uk
web: www.whitehousehotel.co.uk
dir: From centre ring road into Exchange Rd, exit left into Upton Rd, hotel on left

This popular commercial hotel is situated within easy walking distance to the town centre. Bedrooms are pleasantly decorated and offer a good range of facilities that include interactive TV with internet. The public areas are open plan; they include a comfortable lounge/bar, cosy snug and an attractive conservatory restaurant with a sunny open terrace for summer dining. Functions suites are also available.

Rooms 57 (8 GF) **Facilities** STV FTV Wi-fi **Conf** Class 80 Board 50 Thtr 200 **Services** Lift **Parking** 50 **Notes** ® RS 25 Dec-2 Jan Civ Wed 120

Park Inn Watford

★★★ 66% HOTEL

☎ 01923 429988 & 429900 📠 01923 221175
30-40 St Albans Rd WD17 1RN
e-mail: info.watford@rezidorparkinn.com
web: www.watford.parkinn.co.uk
dir: On A412 between Town Hall & Watford Junction Station

Located within walking distance from Watford Junction main station with easy connections to London. This modern hotel has contemporary bedrooms and bathrooms which provide comfortable accommodation for both the leisure or business guest. A range of larger sized bedrooms is particularly suitable for the executive guest as well as families. The restaurant and lounge areas offer a substantial menu. A number of up-to-date conference rooms are available, and secure parking is an asset.

Rooms 100 (6 fmly) **S** £55-£145; **D** £55-£145* **Facilities** FTV Gym Xmas New Year Wi-fi **Conf** Class 90 Board 40 Thtr 180 Del from £125 to £155* **Services** Lift Air con **Parking** 92 **Notes** Civ Wed 180

Holiday Inn Express London-Watford Junction

BUDGET HOTEL

☎ 01923 288600 📠 01923 288605
19 Bridle Path WD17 1UE
e-mail: info@express-watford.com
dir: Telephone for directions

A modern hotel ideal for families and business travellers. Fresh and uncomplicated, the spacious rooms include Sky TV, power shower and tea and coffee-making facilities. Continental buffet breakfast is included in the room rate; other meals may be taken at the nearby family pub or restaurant. See also the Hotel Groups pages.

Rooms 98 **Conf** Class 14 Board 14 Thtr 24

Premier Inn Watford Centre

BUDGET HOTEL

☎ 0871 527 9140 🖷 0871 527 9141
Timms Meadow, Water Ln WD17 2NJ
dir: M1 junct 5, A41 into town centre. At rdbt take 3rd exit, stay in left lane through lights. Take 1st left into Water Ln. Hotel on left

High quality, budget accommodation ideal for both families and business travellers. Spacious, en suite bedrooms feature tea and coffee making facilities, and Freeview TV in most hotels. Internet access and Wi-fi are available for a small fee. The adjacent family restaurant features a wide and varied menu. See also the Hotel Groups pages.

Rooms 105 **D** £62-£73*

Premier Inn Watford (Croxley Green)

BUDGET HOTEL

☎ 0871 527 9138 🖷 0871 527 9139
2 Ascot Rd WD18 8AD
dir: M25 junct 18, A404 signed Watford/ Rickmansworth, left at 1st rdbt signed A412 Watford. Follow Croxley Green Business Park/Watford signs, at 4th rdbt, 3rd exit. M1 junct 5, A41 towards Watford, follow Watford West & Rickmansworth A412 signs. Then Croxley Green Business Park signs

Rooms 121 **D** £60-£71*

Premier Inn Watford North

BUDGET HOTEL

☎ 0871 527 9142 🖷 0871 527 9143
859 St Albans Rd, Garston WD25 0LH
dir: M1 junct 6, A405 towards Watford. At 2nd lights onto A412 (St Albans Rd). Into TGI Friday's car park. Hotel directly behind

Rooms 45 **D** £60-£69*

WATTON Norfolk — Map 13 TF90

Broom Hall Country Hotel

★★★ 77% COUNTRY HOUSE HOTEL

☎ 01953 882125 🖷 01953 885325
Richmond Rd, Saham Toney IP25 7EX
e-mail: enquiries@broomhallhotel.co.uk
web: www.broomhallhotel.co.uk
dir: From A11 at Thetford onto A1075 to Watton (12m), B1108 towards Swaffham, in 0.5m at rdbt turn right to Saham Toney, hotel 0.5m on left. From A47 take A1075, left onto B1108

A delightful Victorian country house situated down a private drive and set in mature landscaped gardens surrounded by parkland. The well-equipped bedrooms are split between the main house and an adjacent building. Public rooms include a relaxing lounge, a brasserie restaurant, a lounge bar, a conservatory and a smart restaurant. There is an indoor swimming pool.

Rooms 15 (5 annexe) (3 fmly) (5 GF) **S** £78-£150; **D** £95-£200 (incl. bkfst) **Facilities** FTV 🏊 Massage Reflexology Beauty treatments Wi-fi **Conf** Class 30 Board 22 Thtr 80 Del from £110 to £180 **Parking** 30 **Notes** LB Closed 24 Dec-4 Jan Civ Wed 70

WELLESBOURNE Warwickshire — Map 10 SP25

Barceló Walton Hall

★★★★ 81% 🏵🏵 HOTEL

☎ 01789 842424 🖷 01789 470418
Walton CV35 9HU
e-mail: waltonhall.mande@barcelo-hotels.co.uk
dir: A429 through Bradford towards Wellesbourne, right after watermill, follow signs to hotel

Sitting in 65 acres of beautiful countryside, this hotel is just 10 minutes from the M40. It has a fascinating history, with parts dating back to the 1500s. The property has been appointed in a style that combines both the traditional and modern. The individually designed bedrooms, many with stunning views over the lake and garden, have plasma screen TVs, DVD players and lap top-sized safes. Premium rooms and suites are available. The award-winning Moncreiffe Restaurant is situated in the hall and has views over the lovely gardens.

Rooms 56 (19 annexe) (11 GF) **Facilities** Spa STV FTV 🏊 supervised Gym Dance studio Beauty salon Xmas New Year Wi-fi **Conf** Class 60 Board 36 Thtr 240 **Services** Air con **Parking** 240 **Notes** ⊗ Civ Wed 240

W

WELLINGBOROUGH Map 11 SP86
Northamptonshire

Ibis Wellingborough

BUDGET HOTEL

☎ 01933 228333 🖷 01933 228444
Enstone Court NN8 2DR
e-mail: H3164@accor-hotels.com
web: www.ibishotel.com
dir: At junct of A45 & A509 towards Kettering, SW outskirts of Wellingborough

Modern, budget hotel offering comfortable accommodation in bright and practical bedrooms. Breakfast is self-service and dinner is available in the restaurant. See also the Hotel Groups pages.

Rooms 78 (20 fmly) (2 GF)

Premier Inn Wellingborough

BUDGET HOTEL

☎ 0871 527 9144 🖷 0871 527 9145
London Rd NN8 2DP
dir: 0.5m from town centre on A5193, near Dennington Industrial Estate

High quality, budget accommodation ideal for both families and business travellers. Spacious, en suite bedrooms feature tea and coffee making facilities, and Freeview TV in most hotels. Internet access and Wi-fi are available for a small fee. The adjacent family restaurant features a wide and varied menu. See also the Hotel Groups pages.

Rooms 40 **D** £49-£60*

WELLS Map 4 ST54
Somerset

Best Western Swan

★★★ 86% ⊛⊛ HOTEL

☎ 01749 836300 🖷 01749 836301
Sadler St BA5 2RX
e-mail: info@swanhotelwells.co.uk
dir: A39, A371, on entering Wells follow signs for Hotels & Deliveries. Hotel on right opposite cathedral

Situated in the shadow of Wells Cathedral, this privately owned hotel enjoys a truly stunning location and extends a genuinely friendly welcome. Full of character and with a rich history, the hotel has been restored and extended to provide high levels of quality and comfort. Guests can choose between the larger, period bedrooms in the main building or the more contemporary coach house rooms. Dinner in the oak-panelled restaurant should not be missed.

Rooms 49 (3 fmly) (4 GF) **S** £88-£98; **D** £140-£300 (incl. bkfst)* **Facilities** FTV Gym Health suite Xmas New Year Wi-fi **Conf** Class 45 Board 40 Thtr 120 **Parking** 25 **Notes** LB ⊗ Civ Wed 90

White Hart Hotel

THE INDEPENDENTS HOTEL ASSOCIATION

★★ 78% HOTEL

☎ 01749 672056 🖷 01749 671074
Sadler St BA5 2RR
e-mail: info@whitehart-wells.co.uk
web: www.whitehart-wells.co.uk
dir: Sadler St at start of one-way system. Hotel opposite cathedral

A former coaching inn dating back to the 15th century, this hotel offers comfortable, modern accommodation. Some bedrooms are in an adjoining former stable block and two are at ground floor level. Public areas include a guest lounge, a bar and the popular restaurant Brufani's where excellent steaks and gourmet burgers are in high demand.

Rooms 15 (3 fmly) (2 GF) **S** £90-£95; **D** £110-£125 (incl. bkfst)* **Facilities** Xmas New Year Wi-fi **Conf** Class 50 Board 35 Thtr 150 Del from £125 to £135* **Parking** 17 **Notes** LB Civ Wed 100

Coxley Vineyard

★★ 71% HOTEL

☎ 01749 670285 🖷 01749 679708
Coxley BA5 1RQ
e-mail: max@orofino.freeserve.co.uk
dir: A39 from Wells signed Coxley. Village halfway between Wells & Glastonbury

This privately owned and personally run hotel was built on the site of an old cider farm. It was later part of a commercial vineyard and some of the vines are still in evidence. It provides well equipped, modern bedrooms; most are situated on the ground floor. There is a comfortable bar and a spacious restaurant with an impressive lantern ceiling. The hotel is a popular venue for conferences and other functions.

Rooms 9 (5 fmly) (8 GF) **Facilities** FTV ⛱ Xmas Wi-fi **Conf** Class 50 Board 40 Thtr 90 **Parking** 50

Ancient Gate House Hotel

★★ 69% ⊛ HOTEL

☎ 01749 672029 🖷 01749 670319
20 Sadler St BA5 2SE
e-mail: info@ancientgatehouse.co.uk
dir: 1st hotel on left on cathedral green

Guests are treated to good old-fashioned hospitality in a friendly informal atmosphere at this charming hotel. Bedrooms, many with unrivalled cathedral views and four-poster beds, are well equipped and furnished in keeping with the age and character of the building. The Rugantino Restaurant remains popular, offering Italian specialities and traditional English dishes.

Rooms 9 **S** £90-£95; **D** £110-£125 (incl. bkfst)* **Facilities** FTV Xmas New Year Wi-fi **Notes** LB Closed 27-29 Dec

W

WELWYN GARDEN CITY Map 6 TL21
Hertfordshire

Tewin Bury Farm Hotel

★★★★ 75% HOTEL

01438 717793 01438 840440
Hertford Road (B1000) AL6 0JB
e-mail: reservations@tewinbury.co.uk
dir: From N: A1(M) junct 6, 1st exit signed A1000, at next rdbt 1st exit towards Digswell. 0.1m straight on at rdbt. 1m on B100. Hotel on left

Situated not far from the A1(M) and within easy reach of Stevenage and Knebworth House, this delightful country-house hotel is part of a thriving farm. Stylish, well-equipped bedrooms of varying sizes are perfectly suited for both leisure and business guests. An award-winning restaurant and meeting rooms are all part of this family-run establishment.

Rooms 39 (30 annexe) (6 fmly) (26 GF) **Facilities** STV FTV Fishing Cycling New Year Wi-fi **Conf** Class 180 Board 40 Thtr 500 **Services** Lift **Parking** 400 **Notes** ® Civ Wed 150

Best Western Homestead Court Hotel

★★★ 75% HOTEL

01707 324336 01707 326447
Homestead Ln AL7 4LX
e-mail: enquiries@homesteadcourt.co.uk
web: www.bwhomesteadcourt.co.uk
dir: Exit A1000, left at lights at Bushall Hotel. Right at rdbt into Howlands, 2nd left at Hollybush public house into Hollybush Lane. 2nd right at War Memorial into Homestead Lane

A friendly hotel ideally situated less than two miles from the city centre in a tranquil location adjacent to parkland. The property boasts stylish, brightly decorated public areas that include a smart lounge bar and a large restaurant. Bedrooms are pleasantly appointed and equipped with modern facilities. Conference rooms are also available.

Rooms 74 (8 annexe) (6 fmly) (2 GF) (2 smoking) **S** £49-£79; **D** £59-£85* **Facilities** STV Wi-fi **Conf** Class 60 Board 60 Thtr 200 **Services** Lift **Parking** 70 **Notes** LB ® Civ Wed 110

Premier Inn Welwyn Garden City

BUDGET HOTEL

0871 527 9146 0871 527 9147
Stanborough Rd AL8 6DQ
dir: A1(M) junct 4, A6129

High quality, budget accommodation ideal for both families and business travellers. Spacious, en suite bedrooms feature tea and coffee making facilities, and Freeview TV in most hotels. Internet access and Wi-fi are available for a small fee. The adjacent family restaurant features a wide and varied menu. See also the Hotel Groups pages.

Rooms 90 **D** £53-£65*

WEMBLEY
Greater London

See LONDON SECTION plan 1 C4

Quality Hotel Wembley

★★★ 71% HOTEL

020 8733 9000 020 8733 9001
Empire Way HA9 0NH
e-mail: sales@hotels-wembley.com
dir: M1 junct 6 onto A406, right onto A404. Right onto Empire Way, after rdbt at lights. Hotel on right

Conveniently situated within walking distance of both the Arena and conference centres this modern hotel offers smart, comfortable, spacious bedrooms; many are air conditioned. All rooms offer an excellent range of amenities. Air-conditioned public areas include a large restaurant serving a wide range of contemporary dishes.

Rooms 165 (70 fmly) (3 GF) (66 smoking) **S** £65-£325; **D** £70-£350 (incl. bkfst) **Facilities** STV FTV Wi-fi **Conf** Class 90 Board 90 Thtr 120 Del from £125 to £145* **Services** Lift Air con **Parking** 65 **Notes** ®

Ibis London Wembley

BUDGET HOTEL

020 8453 5100 020 8453 5110
Southway HA9 6BA
e-mail: H3141@accor.com
web: www.ibishotel.com
dir: From Hanger Lane on A40, take A406 N, exit at Wembley. A404 to lights junct with Wembley Hill Rd, right, 1st right into Southway. Hotel 75mtrs on left

Modern, budget hotel offering comfortable accommodation in bright and practical bedrooms. Breakfast is self-service and dinner is available in the restaurant. See also the Hotel Groups pages.

Rooms 210 (44 fmly)

Premier Inn London Wembley Stadium

BUDGET HOTEL

0871 527 8682 0871 527 8683
151 Wembley Park Dr HA9 8HQ
dir: A406 (North Circular) take A404 towards Wembley. 2m right into Wembley Hill Rd, keep right into Empire Way (B4565), pass Wembley Arena on right, keep right around petrol station. Hotel 200yds on left

High quality, budget accommodation ideal for both families and business travellers. Spacious, en suite bedrooms feature tea and coffee making facilities, and Freeview TV in most hotels. Internet access and Wi-fi are available for a small fee. The adjacent family restaurant features a wide and varied menu. See also the Hotel Groups pages.

Rooms 154 **D** £69-£80*

WEST AUCKLAND Map 19 NZ12
Co Durham

The Manor House Hotel

★★★ 80% HOTEL

01388 834834 01388 833566
The Green DL14 9HW
e-mail: enquiries@manorhousehotelcountydurham.co.uk
web: www.manorhousehotelcountydurham.co.uk
dir: A1(M) junct 58, A68 to West Auckland. At T-junct left, hotel 150yds on right

This historic manor house, dating back to the 14th century, is full of character. Welcoming log fires await guests on cooler evenings. Comfortable bedrooms are individual in style, tastefully furnished and well equipped. The brasserie and Juniper's restaurant both offer an interesting selection of freshly prepared dishes. Well-equipped leisure facilities are available.

Rooms 35 (11 annexe) (6 fmly) (3 GF) **S** £55-£75; **D** £70-£140 (incl. bkfst)* **Facilities** FTV Gym Steam room Sauna Xmas New Year Wi-fi **Conf** Class 80 Board 50 Thtr 100 Del from £115 to £135* **Parking** 150 **Notes** LB Civ Wed 120

W

WEST BAY

See Bridport

WEST BROMWICH
West Midlands — Map 10 SP09

Park Inn Birmingham West

★★★ 70% HOTEL

☎ 0121 609 9988 & 609 9931 📠 0121 525 7403
Birmingham Rd B70 6RS
e-mail: info.birminghamwest@rezidorparkinn.com
dir: From Birmingham Rd towards town centre, 1st right into Beechs Rd, 2nd right into Europa Ave. Hotel on right

Convenient for the M5, M42 and M6, this large, purpose-built hotel provides versatile and well-equipped contemporary accommodation. Facilities include a spacious restaurant, comfortable lounge areas, a bar and secure parking, as well as meeting rooms and function suites. There is also a modern leisure complex.

Rooms 168 (16 fmly) (33 GF) (9 smoking) **S** £40-£110; **D** £49-£120* **Facilities** STV FTV supervised Gym Treatment room Sauna Dance studio Wi-fi **Conf** Class 80 Board 60 Thtr 180 **Services** Lift Air con **Parking** 300

Premier Inn West Bromwich

BUDGET HOTEL

☎ 0871 527 9148 📠 0871 527 9149
New Gas St B70 0NP
dir: M5 junct 1, A41 (Expressway) towards Wolverhampton. At 3rd rdbt, hotel on right

High quality, budget accommodation ideal for both families and business travellers. Spacious, en suite bedrooms feature tea and coffee making facilities, and Freeview TV in most hotels. Internet access and Wi-fi are available for a small fee. The adjacent family restaurant features a wide and varied menu. See also the Hotel Groups pages.

Rooms 40 **D** £52-£62*

Premier Inn West Bromwich Central

BUDGET HOTEL

☎ 0871 527 9150 📠 0871 527 9151
144 High St B70 6JJ
dir: M5 junct 1 towards town centre, hotel 2m

Rooms 85 **D** £55-£62*

WEST CAMEL
Somerset — Map 4 ST52

Walnut Tree

★★ 81% HOTEL

☎ 01935 851292 📠 01935 852119
Fore St BA22 7QW
e-mail: info@thewalnuttreehotel.com
web: www.thewalnuttreehotel.com
dir: From Yeovil take A303 towards Exeter, pass Fleet Air Arm Museum turn right to West Camel. Hotel on right

This small hotel, where friendliness and personal service are high on the agenda, has the atmosphere of a village inn. The focus here is the imaginative cuisine offered in either the bar or the more formal dining room. The bar is traditional with oak beams and exposed brickwork. The modern bedrooms are well maintained.

Rooms 13 (6 GF) **S** £79-£85; **D** £110-£135 (incl. bkfst)* **Facilities** FTV New Year Wi-fi **Parking** 40 **Notes** LB Closed 25-26 Dec & 1 Jan

See advert on page 65

WEST DRAYTON

Hotels are listed under Heathrow Airport

WEST LULWORTH
Dorset — Map 4 SY88

Cromwell House

★★ 75% HOTEL

☎ 01929 400253 & 400332 📠 01929 400566
Lulworth Cove BH20 5RJ
e-mail: catriona@lulworthcove.co.uk
web: www.lulworthcove.co.uk
dir: 200yds beyond end of West Lulworth, left onto high slip road, hotel 100yds on left opposite beach car park

Built in 1881 by the Mayor of Weymouth, specifically as a guest house, this family-run hotel now provides visitors with an ideal base for touring the area and for exploring the beaches and coast. The house enjoys spectacular views across the sea and countryside. Bedrooms, many with sea views, are comfortable and some have been specifically designed for family use.

Rooms 18 (1 annexe) (3 fmly) (2 GF) **S** £45-£65; **D** £90-£120 (incl. bkfst) **Facilities** Access to Dorset coastal footpath & Jurassic Coast Wi-fi **Parking** 17 **Notes** LB Closed 22 Dec-3 Jan RS Xmas & New Year

W

WEST THURROCK Map 6 TQ57
Essex

Ibis London Thurrock

BUDGET HOTEL

☎ 01708 686000 📠 01708 680525
Weston Av RM20 3JQ
e-mail: H2176@accor.com
web: www.ibishotel.com
dir: M25 junct 31 to West Thurrock Services, right at 1st & 2nd rdbts, left at 3rd rdbt. Hotel on right in 500yds

Modern, budget hotel offering comfortable accommodation in bright and practical bedrooms. Breakfast is self-service and dinner is available in the restaurant. See also the Hotel Groups pages.

Rooms 102 (27 GF)

Premier Inn Thurrock East

BUDGET HOTEL

☎ 0871 527 9092 📠 0871 527 9093
Fleming Rd, Unicorn Estate, Chafford Hundred RM16 6YJ
dir: From A13 follow Lakeside Shopping Centre signs. Right at 1st rdbt, straight on at next rdbt, then 1st slip road. Left at next rdbt

High quality, budget accommodation ideal for both families and business travellers. Spacious, en suite bedrooms feature tea and coffee making facilities, and Freeview TV in most hotels. Internet access and Wi-fi are available for a small fee. The adjacent family restaurant features a wide and varied menu. See also the Hotel Groups pages.

Rooms 62 **D** £58-£68*

Premier Inn Thurrock West

BUDGET HOTEL

☎ 0871 527 9094 📠 0871 527 9095
Stonehouse Ln RM19 1NS
dir: From N: M25 junct 31, A1090 to Purfleet. (NB do not cross Dartford Bridge or follow signs for Lakeside). From S: M25 junct 31. On approach to Dartford Tunnel, bear far left signed Dagenham. After tunnel, hotel at top of slip road

Rooms 161 **D** £58-£68*

WEST WITTON Map 19 SE08
North Yorkshire

INSPECTORS' CHOICE

The Wensleydale Heifer

@@ RESTAURANT WITH ROOMS

☎ 01969 622322
Main St DL8 4LS
web: www.wensleydaleheifer.co.uk
dir: A1 to Leeming Bar junct, A684 towards Bedale for approx 10m to Leyburn, then towards Hawes 3.5m to West Wilton

Describing itself as 'boutique style', this 17th-century coaching inn is very much in the 21st-century. The bedrooms, with Egyptian cotton linen and Molton Brown toiletries as standard, are each designed with a unique and interesting theme - for example, Black Sheep, Night at the Movies, True Romantics and Shooters, and for chocolate lovers there the obvious choice of a bedroom where they can eat as much chocolate as they like! The food is very much the focus here in both the informal fish bar and the contemporary style restaurant. The kitchen prides itself on sourcing the freshest fish and locally reared meats. Winner of the AA Funkiest B&B of the Year Award 2011-12.

Rooms 13 (4 annexe)

WESTBURY Map 4 ST85
Wiltshire

The Cedar Hotel & Restaurant

★★★ 66% HOTEL

☎ 01373 822753 📠 01373 858423
114 Warminster Rd BA13 3PR
e-mail: info@cedarhotel-wiltshire.co.uk
dir: On A350, 0.5m S of town towards Warminster

Popular with both business and leisure guests, this hotel is located on the main Warminster Road with easy access to many local attractions. Bedrooms and bathrooms offer a variety of shapes and sizes and the hotel has a relaxed and traditional feel. A good range of options is available at dinner from the well chosen restaurant menu with a range of bar snacks also available. The hotel has a car park and pleasant garden to the rear.

Rooms 20 (12 annexe) **Notes** LB Closed 25 Dec-2 Jan

WESTLETON Map 13 TM46
Suffolk

Westleton Crown

★★★ 79% @@ HOTEL

☎ 01728 648777 📠 01728 648239
The Street IP17 3AD
e-mail: reception@westletoncrown.co.uk
web: www.westletoncrown.co.uk
dir: A12 N, turn right for Westleton just after Yoxford. Hotel opposite on entering Westleton

A charming coaching inn situated in a peaceful village location just a few minutes from the A12. Public rooms include a smart, award-winning restaurant, comfortable lounge, and busy bar with exposed beams and open fireplaces. The stylish bedrooms are tastefully decorated and equipped with many thoughtful little extras.

Rooms 34 (22 annexe) (5 fmly) (13 GF) **S** £80-£100; **D** £90-£215 (incl. bkfst)* **Facilities** FTV Xmas New Year Wi-fi **Conf** Class 40 Board 30 Thtr 60 **Parking** 34 **Notes** LB

WESTON-SUPER-MARE Map 4 ST36
Somerset

The Royal Hotel

★★★ 75% HOTEL

☎ 01934 423100 📠 01934 415135
1 South Pde BS23 1JP
e-mail: reservations@royalhotelweston.com
web: www.royalhotelweston.com
dir: M5 junct 21, follow signs to seafront. Hotel next to Winter Gardens Pavillion

The Royal, which opened in 1810, was the first hotel in Weston and occupies a prime seafront position. It is a grand building and many of the bedrooms, including some with sea views, are spacious and comfortable; family apartments are also available. Public areas include a choice of bars and a

continued

W

WESTON-SUPER-MARE ***continued***

restaurant which offers a range of dishes to meet all tastes. Entertainment is provided during the season.

Rooms 42 (3 annexe) (8 fmly) **S** £73-£83; **D** £105-£160 (incl. bkfst)* **Facilities** FTV Beauty room ♫ Wi-fi **Conf** Class 100 Board 60 Thtr 200 Del from £122* **Services** Lift **Parking** 152 **Notes** LB ⊗ Civ Wed 200

See advert on this page

Beachlands Hotel

★★★ 70% HOTEL

☎ 01934 621401 📠 01934 621966
17 Uphill Road North BS23 4NG
e-mail: info@beachlandshotel.com
web: www.beachlandshotel.com
dir: M5 junct 21, follow signs for hospital. At hospital rdbt follow signs for beach, hotel 300yds before beach

This popular hotel is very close to the 18-hole links course and a short walk from the seafront. Elegant public areas include a bar, a choice of lounges and a bright dining room. Bedrooms vary slightly in size, but all are well equipped for both the business and leisure guest. There is the added bonus of a 10-metre indoor pool and a sauna.

Rooms 21 (6 fmly) (11 GF) **S** £65-£97.50; **D** £92-£137.50 (incl. bkfst) **Facilities** FTV Sauna New Year Wi-fi **Conf** Class 20 Board 30 Thtr 60 Del from £92.25 to £115 **Parking** 28 **Notes** LB ⊗ Closed 23-29 Dec Civ Wed 110

Lauriston Hotel

★★★ 70% HOTEL

☎ 01934 620758 📠 01934 621154
6-12 Knightstone Rd BS23 2AN
e-mail: lauriston.hotel@actionforblindpeople.org.uk
dir: 1st right after Winter Gardens, hotel entrance opposite Cabot public house

A friendly welcome is assured at this pleasant hotel, located right on the seafront, just a few minutes' stroll from the pier. The hotel extends a warm welcome to everyone but caters especially for the visually impaired, their families, friends and guide dogs. There are comfortable and well-appointed bedrooms; special facilities for the guide dogs are, of course, available.

Rooms 37 (2 fmly) (8 GF) **Facilities** FTV ♫ Xmas New Year **Conf** Class 12 Board 10 Thtr 18 **Services** Lift **Parking** 16

New Birchfield

★★ 72% HOTEL

☎ 01934 621839 & 621829 📠 01934 626474
8-9 Manilla Crescent BS23 2BS
e-mail: info@newbirchfield.co.uk
dir: M5 junct 21/22. Hotel on seafront at N end of town

This establishment, popular with coach parties, is located just over the road from the beach. Bedrooms are individually sized and styled; some have sea views and some are located on the ground floor. There is a first-floor lounge and the dining room has large picture windows to make the most of the pleasant views. There is daily entertainment after dinner.

Rooms 30 (4 fmly) (4 GF) **S** £43-£55; **D** £86-£110 (incl. bkfst & dinner)* **Facilities** FTV ♫ Xmas New Year **Services** Lift **Parking** 10 **Notes** LB ⊗ Closed Jan

New Ocean

★★ 68% HOTEL

☎ 01934 621839 & 621829 📠 01934 626474
Madeira Cove BS23 2BS
e-mail: newoceanhotel@aol.com
web: www.newoceanhotel.co.uk
dir: M5 junct 21/22 follow signs for Seafront North

Ideally positioned on the seafront opposite the Marine Lake, this family-run hotel enjoys pleasant views over Weston Bay towards the Mendip and Quantock Hills; many of the bedrooms have a sea-facing aspect. In the downstairs restaurant, dinner offers traditional home cooking using fresh ingredients. The smart public areas include a well-furnished bar and lounge, where entertainment is regularly provided.

Rooms 53 (2 fmly) **S** £43-£55; **D** £86-£110 (incl. bkfst & dinner)* **Facilities** FTV ♫ Xmas New Year Wi-fi **Services** Lift **Parking** 6 **Notes** LB ⊗ RS Jan

W

Anchor Head Hotel

★★ 64% HOTEL

☎ 01934 620880 🖷 01934 621767
19 Claremont Crescent, Birnbeck Rd BS23 2EE
e-mail: anchor.weston@alfatravel.co.uk
dir: M5 junct 21, A370 to seafront, right towards N end of resort past Grand Pier towards Brimbeck Pier. Hotel at end of terrace on left

Enjoying a very pleasant location with views across the bay, the Anchor Head offers a varied choice of comfortable lounges and a relaxing outdoor patio area. Bedrooms and bathrooms are traditionally furnished and include several ground-floor rooms. Dinner and breakfast are served in the spacious dining room that also benefits from sea views.

Rooms 52 (1 fmly) (5 GF) **S** £36-£50; **D** £56-£84 (incl. bkfst) **Facilities** FTV ♫ Xmas New Year **Services** Lift **Notes** LB ⊗ Closed Dec-Feb (ex Xmas) RS Mar & Nov

Premier Inn Weston-Super-Mare East

BUDGET HOTEL

☎ 0871 527 9156 🖷 0871 527 9157
Hutton Moor Rd BS22 8LY
dir: M5 junct 21, A370 to Weston-Super-Mare. After 3rd rbt right at lights into Hutton Moor Leisure Centre. Left, into car park

High quality, budget accommodation ideal for both families and business travellers. Spacious, en suite bedrooms feature tea and coffee making facilities, and Freeview TV in most hotels. Internet access and Wi-fi are available for a small fee. The adjacent family restaurant features a wide and varied menu. See also the Hotel Groups pages.

Rooms 88 **D** £69*

WESTON-UNDER-REDCASTLE Map 15 SJ52
Shropshire

Hawkstone Park Hotel

★★★ 75% HOTEL

☎ 01948 841700 🖷 01939 200335
SY4 5UY
e-mail: enquiries@hawkstone.co.uk
dir: 1m E of A49 between Shrewsbury & Whitchurch

Built in the 1700 this splendid former coaching inn is set in 400 acres of lovely scenery which includes two championship golf course and the 18th-century follies. Bedrooms are comfortably appointed and equipped for both leisure and business guests. Public areas include conference facilities, and a pleasant dining room.

Rooms 67 (19 annexe) (2 fmly) (26 GF) **S** £42-£99; **D** £62-£129 (incl. bkfst)* **Facilities** STV ⛳ 42 Putt green Xmas New Year **Conf** Class 90 Board 50 Thtr 200 Del from £99 to £169* **Parking** 200 **Notes** LB Civ Wed 200

WETHERBY Map 16 SE44
West Yorkshire

INSPECTORS' CHOICE

Wood Hall Hotel

★★★★ ◎◎ HOTEL

☎ 01937 587271 🖷 01937 584353
Trip Ln, Linton LS22 4JA
e-mail: woodhall@handpicked.co.uk
web: www.handpicked.co.uk
dir: From Wetherby take Harrogate road N (A661) for 0.5m, left to Sicklinghall & Linton. Cross bridge, left to Linton & Wood Hall. Turn right opposite Windmill Inn, 1.25m to hotel

A long sweeping drive leads to this delightful Georgian house situated in 100 acres of parkland. Spacious bedrooms are appointed to an impressive standard and feature comprehensive facilities, including large plasma-screen TVs. Public rooms reflect the same elegance and include a smart drawing room and dining room, both with fantastic views. A state-of-the-art technogym is available.

Rooms 44 (30 annexe) (5 fmly) **D** £121-£274 (incl. bkfst)* **Facilities** Spa STV FTV Fishing Gym Beauty spa Xmas New Year Wi-fi **Conf** Class 70 Board 40 Thtr 100 Del from £140 to £265* **Services** Lift **Parking** 200 **Notes** LB ⊗ Civ Wed 100

The Bridge Hotel & Spa

★★★★ 75% HOTEL

☎ 01937 580115 🖷 01937 580556
Walshford LS22 5HS
e-mail: info@bridgewetherby.co.uk
web: www.bridgewetherby.co.uk
dir: From N exit A1(M) at junct 47 (York) or S junct 46 (Wetherby Race Centre), 1st left Walshford, follow brown tourist signs

A very conveniently located hotel close to the A1(M) with spacious public areas and a good range of services make this an ideal venue for business or leisure. The stylish bedrooms are comfortable and well equipped. The Bridge offers a choice of bars and a large open-plan restaurant. Conference and banqueting suites are also available.

Rooms 30 (2 fmly) (10 GF) **S** £60-£134; **D** £70-£140 (incl. bkfst) **Facilities** Spa FTV Gym Xmas New Year Wi-fi **Conf** Class 50 Board 50 Thtr 200 Del from £105 to £135 **Parking** 150 **Notes** LB Civ Wed 150

Days Inn Wetherby

BUDGET HOTEL

☎ 01937 547557 🖷 01937 547559
Junction 46 A1(M), Kirk Deighton LS22 5GT
e-mail: reservations@daysinnwetherby.co.uk
dir: A1(M) junct 46 at Moto Service Area

This modern building offers accommodation in smart, spacious and well-equipped bedrooms, suitable for families and business travellers, and all with en suite bathrooms. Continental breakfast is available and other refreshments may be taken at the nearby family restaurant. See also the Hotel Groups pages.

Rooms 129 (33 fmly) (35 GF) **Conf** Class 20 Board 20 Thtr 20

W

WEYBRIDGE
Surrey
Map 6 TQ06

Oatlands Park

★★★★ 73% HOTEL

☎ 01932 847242 📠 01932 842252
146 Oatlands Dr KT13 9HB
e-mail: info@oatlandsparkhotel.com
web: www.oatlandsparkhotel.com
dir: Through High Street to Monument Hill mini rdbt. Left into Oatlands Drive. Hotel 500yds on left

Once a palace for Henry VIII, this impressive building sits in extensive grounds encompassing tennis courts, a gym and a 9-hole golf course. The spacious lounge and bar create a wonderful first impression with tall marble pillars and plush comfortable seating. Most of the bedrooms are very spacious, and all are well equipped.

Rooms 144 (24 fmly) (39 GF) (8 smoking) **S** £190; **D** £220 **Facilities** STV ⛳ 9 🎾 Putt green Gym Jogging course Fitness suite Wi-fi **Conf** Class 150 Board 80 Thtr 300 Del from £ to £230 **Services** Lift Air con **Parking** 144 **Notes** LB Civ Wed 220

See advert on this page

Best Western Ship Hotel

★★★ 77% HOTEL

☎ 01932 848364 📠 01932 857153
Monument Green KT13 8BQ
e-mail: reservations@desboroughhotels.com
dir: M25 junct 11, at 3rd rdbt left into High St. Hotel 300yds on left

A former coaching inn retaining much period charm that is now a spacious and comfortable hotel. Bedrooms, some overlooking a delightful courtyard, are spacious and cheerfully decorated. Public areas include a lounge and cocktail bar, restaurant and a popular pub. The high street location and private parking are a bonus.

Rooms 76 (2 fmly) **Facilities** Wi-fi **Conf** Class 70 Board 60 Thtr 180 **Services** Lift **Parking** 65

Brooklands Hotel

U

☎ 01932 335700 📠 01932 335701
Brooklands Dr KT13 OSL
e-mail: info@brooklandshotelssurrey.com

Currently the rating for this establishment is not confirmed. This may be due to a change of ownership or because it has only recently joined the AA rating scheme. For further details please see the AA website: theAA.com

Rooms 120 **S** £130-£285; **D** £140-£295 (incl. bkfst)* **Conf** Class 86 Board 90 Thtr 174

W

WEYMOUTH Map 4 SY67
Dorset

Moonfleet Manor

★★★ 77% ®®
COUNTRY HOUSE HOTEL

☎ 01305 786948 📠 01305 774395
Fleet DT3 4ED
e-mail: info@moonfleetmanorhotel.co.uk
web: www.moonfleetmanor.com
dir: A354 to Weymouth, right on B3157 to Bridport. At Chickerell left at mini rdbt to Fleet

This enchanting hideaway, where children are especially welcome, is peacefully located at the end of the village of Fleet and enjoys a wonderful sea-facing position. The hotel is furnished with style and panache, particularly in the sumptuous lounges, and many of the well-equipped bedrooms overlook Chesil Beach. Accomplished cuisine is served in the beautiful restaurant.

Rooms 36 (6 annexe) (26 fmly) **Facilities** STV FTV supervised Squash Children's nursery Xmas Child facilities **Conf** Class 18 Board 26 Thtr 50 **Services** Lift **Parking** 50

Hotel Prince Regent

★★★ 74% HOTEL

☎ 01305 771313 📠 01305 778100
139 The Esplanade DT4 7NR
e-mail: info@princeregentweymouth.co.uk
web: www.princeregentweymouth.co.uk
dir: From A354 follow seafront signs. Left at Jubilee Clock, 25mtrs on seafront

Dating back to 1855, this welcoming resort hotel boasts splendid views over Weymouth Bay from the majority of public rooms and front-facing bedrooms. It is conveniently close to the town centre and harbour, and is opposite the beach. The restaurant offers a choice of menus, and entertainment is regularly provided in the ballroom during the season.

Rooms 70 (12 fmly) (5 GF) **S** £45-£89; **D** £65-£109 (incl. bkfst)* **Facilities** STV Xmas New Year Wi-fi **Conf** Class 150 Board 150 Thtr 180 Del from £89 to £99* **Services** Lift **Parking** 10 **Notes** LB ® Civ Wed 200

Hotel Rembrandt

THE INDEPENDENTS HOTEL ASSOCIATION

★★★ 74% HOTEL

☎ 01305 764000 📠 01305 764022
12-18 Dorchester Rd DT4 7JU
e-mail: reception@hotelrembrandt.co.uk
web: www.hotelrembrandt.co.uk
dir: On A354 from Dorchester, turn left at Manor rdbt & proceed for 0.75m

Only a short distance from the seafront and the town centre, this hotel is ideal for visiting the many local attractions. Facilities include indoor leisure, a bar and extensive meeting rooms. The restaurant offers an impressive carvery and carte menu which proves popular with locals and residents alike.

Rooms 78 (19 fmly) (7 GF) **S** £54-£112; **D** £108-£137 (incl. bkfst) **Facilities** STV FTV Gym Steam room Sauna Beautician Wi-fi **Conf** Class 100 Board 60 Thtr 200 Del from £100 to £118* **Services** Lift **Parking** 80 **Notes** LB ® Civ Wed 100

Hotel Rex

★★★ 71% HOTEL

☎ 01305 760400 📠 01305 760500
29 The Esplanade DT4 8DN
e-mail: rex@kingshotels.co.uk
web: www.kingshotels.co.uk
dir: On seafront opposite Alexandra Gardens

Originally built as the summer residence for the Duke of Clarence, this hotel benefits from a seafront location with stunning views across Weymouth Bay. Bedrooms, including several sea-facing rooms, are well equipped. A wide range of imaginative dishes is served in the popular and attractive restaurant.

Rooms 31 (2 fmly) **Facilities** FTV New Year Wi-fi **Conf** Class 30 Board 25 Thtr 40 **Services** Lift **Parking** 10 **Notes** ® Closed Xmas

Crown

★★ 72% HOTEL

☎ 01305 760800 📠 01305 760300
51-53 St Thomas St DT4 8EQ
e-mail: crown@kingshotels.co.uk
web: www.kingshotels.co.uk
dir: From Dorchester, A354 to Weymouth. Follow Back Water on left & cross 2nd bridge

This popular hotel is conveniently located adjacent to the old harbour and is ideal for shopping, local attractions and transportation links, including the ferry. Public areas include an extensive bar, ballroom and comfortable residents' lounge on the first floor. Themed events, such as mock cruises, are a speciality.

Rooms 86 (15 fmly) **S** £57-£63; **D** £108-£118 (incl. bkfst) **Facilities** ♫ New Year **Services** Lift **Parking** 14 **Notes** ® Closed Xmas

Hotel Central

★★ 71% HOTEL

☎ 01305 760700 📠 01305 760300
17-19 Maiden St DT4 8BB
e-mail: central@kingshotels.co.uk

Well located for the town, the beach and the ferries to the Channel Islands, and with off-road parking, this privately owned hotel has friendly staff. The bedrooms are comfortable, and three are designed for guests with limited mobility. The pleasant dining room offers a varied menu. Live entertainment is provided during the season.

Rooms 28 (5 fmly) (4 GF) (9 smoking) **S** £55-£57; **D** £96-£100 (incl. bkfst) **Facilities** ♫ **Services** Lift **Parking** 16 **Notes** ® Closed mid Dec-1 Mar

Fairhaven

★★ 69% HOTEL

☎ 01305 760200 📠 01305 760300
37 The Esplanade DT4 8DH
e-mail: fairhaven@kingshotels.co.uk
dir: On right just before Alexandra Gardens

A popular sea-facing, family-run hotel which has a friendly young team of staff. Bedrooms are comfortable and well maintained, and the hotel boasts two bars, one with panoramic views of the bay. Entertainment is provided most nights during the season.

Rooms 82 (23 fmly) (1 GF) (60 smoking) **S** £55-£57; **D** £96-£100 (incl. bkfst) **Facilities** ♫ **Services** Lift **Parking** 16 **Notes** ® Closed Nov-1 Mar

WEYMOUTH *continued*

Premier Inn Weymouth

BUDGET HOTEL

☎ 0871 527 9158 📠 0871 527 9159
Lodmoor Country Park, Preston Beach Rd, Green Hill DT4 7SX
dir: Follow signs to Weymouth then brown route signs to Lodmoor Country Park (height restriction of 9' 4" at barrier). Hotel adjacent to Lodmoor Brewers Fayre (NB for Sat Nav use DT4 7SL)

High quality, budget accommodation ideal for both families and business travellers. Spacious, en suite bedrooms feature tea and coffee making facilities, and Freeview TV in most hotels. Internet access and Wi-fi are available for a small fee. The adjacent family restaurant features a wide and varied menu. See also the Hotel Groups pages.

Rooms 64 **D** £73*

The Heritage Restaurant with Rooms

RESTAURANT WITH ROOMS

☎ 01305 783093 📠 01305 786668
8 East St, Chickerell DT3 4DS
e-mail: mail@the-heritage.co.uk
dir: In village centre

Located just three miles from Weymouth and less than a mile from the spectacular Chesil Beach, this building dates back to 1769. Attentive service and a friendly, caring approach are hallmarks here, with every effort made to ensure a relaxing stay. Excellent Dorset produce is featured on the menus that are offered in the elegant restaurant. After dinner, the comfortable bedrooms await, each individually styled and well appointed.

Rooms 6 (1 fmly)

WHICKHAM
Tyne & Wear — Map 21 NZ26

Gibside

★★★ 74% HOTEL

☎ 0191 488 9292 📠 0191 488 8000
Front St NE16 4JG
e-mail: reception@gibside-hotel.co.uk
web: www.gibside-hotel.co.uk
dir: Off A1(M) towards Whickham on B6317, into Front St, hotel 2m on right

Conveniently located in the village centre, this hotel is close to the Newcastle by-pass and its elevated position affords views over the Tyne Valley. Bedrooms come in two styles, classical and contemporary. Public rooms include the Egyptian-themed Sphinx bar and a more formal restaurant. Secure garage parking is available.

Rooms 44 (2 fmly) (13 GF) **S** £75-£110; **D** £85-£120* **Facilities** FTV Golf Academy at The Beamish Park ♫ New Year Wi-fi **Conf** Class 50 Board 50 Thtr 100 Del from £101.25 to £125* **Services** Lift **Parking** 18 **Notes** LB

WHITBY
North Yorkshire — Map 19 NZ81

Dunsley Hall

★★★ 82% ® COUNTRY HOUSE HOTEL

☎ 01947 893437 📠 01947 893505
Dunsley YO21 3TL
e-mail: reception@dunsleyhall.com
web: www.dunsleyhall.com
dir: 3m N of Whitby, signed off A171

Friendly service is found at this fine country mansion set in a quiet hamlet with coastal views north of Whitby. The house has Gothic overtones and boasts fine woodwork and panelling, particularly in the magnificent lounge. Two lovely dining rooms offer imaginative dishes and there is also a cosy bar.

Rooms 26 (2 fmly) (10 GF) **S** fr £105; **D** £159-£208 (incl. bkfst)* **Facilities** (indoor pool) Putt green Xmas New Year Wi-fi **Conf** Class 50 Board 40 Thtr 95 **Parking** 30 **Notes** LB ⊗ Civ Wed 100

Cliffemount

★★★ 80% ®® SMALL HOTEL

☎ 01947 840103 📠 01947 841025
Bank Top Ln, Runswick Bay TS13 5HU
e-mail: info@cliffemounthotel.co.uk
dir: Exit A174, 8m N of Whitby, 1m to end

Overlooking Runswick Bay this property offers a relaxed and romantic atmosphere with open fires and individual, carefully designed bedrooms; some have a private balcony overlooking the bay. Dining is recommended; the food is modern British in style and uses locally sourced fresh seafood, and game from nearby estates.

Rooms 20 (4 fmly) (5 GF) **S** £80-£180; **D** £115-£180 (incl. bkfst)* **Facilities** FTV Xmas New Year Wi-fi **Conf** Class 25 Board 16 Thtr 25 **Parking** 25 **Notes** LB

Saxonville

★★★ 77% HOTEL

☎ 01947 602631 📠 01947 820523
Ladysmith Av, Argyle Rd YO21 3HX
e-mail: newtons@saxonville.co.uk
web: www.saxonville.co.uk
dir: A174 to North Promenade. Turn inland at large four-towered building visible on West Cliff, into Argyle Rd, then 1st right

The friendly service is noteworthy at this long-established holiday hotel. Well maintained throughout it offers comfortable bedrooms and inviting public areas that include a well-proportioned restaurant where quality dinners are served.

Rooms 23 (2 fmly) (1 GF) **S** £40-£60; **D** £80-£140 (incl. bkfst)* **Facilities** Wi-fi **Conf** Class 40 Board 40 Thtr 100 Del from £65 to £80* **Parking** 20 **Notes** ⊗ Closed Dec-Jan RS Feb-Mar

Estbek House

®® RESTAURANT WITH ROOMS

☎ 01947 893424 📠 01947 893625
East Row, Sandsend YO21 3SU
e-mail: info@estbekhouse.co.uk
dir: From Whitby take A174. In Sandsend, left into East Row

A speciality seafood restaurant on the first floor is the focus of this listed building in a small coastal village north west of Whitby. There is also a small bar and breakfast room, and four individually appointed bedrooms offering luxury and comfort.

Rooms 4

WHITCHURCH
Shropshire — Map 15 SJ54

Macdonald Hill Valley Spa, Hotel & Golf

★★★★ 76% HOTEL

☎ 0844 879 9049 📠 01948 667373
Tarporley Rd SY13 4JH
e-mail: general.hillvalley@macdonald-hotels.co.uk
web: www.macdonald-hotels.co.uk/hillvalley
dir: 2nd exit off A41 towards Whitchurch

Located in rural surroundings on the town's outskirts, this modern hotel is surrounded by two golf courses and very well equipped leisure spa is also available. Spacious bedrooms, with country views, are furnished in minimalist style and public areas include a choice of bar lounges and extensive conference facilities.

Rooms 80 (27 GF) **S** £85-£180; **D** £95-£195 (incl. bkfst)* **Facilities** Spa STV (indoor pool) ⛳ 36 Putt green Gym

W

Crazy golf Xmas New Year Wi-fi **Conf** Class 150 Board 150 Thtr 300 Del from £135 to £170 **Services** Lift **Parking** 300 **Notes** LB Civ Wed 300

WHITEHAVEN Map 18 NX91
Cumbria

Premier Inn Whitehaven

BUDGET HOTEL

☎ 0871 527 9160 📠 0871 527 9161
Howgate CA28 6PL
dir: On A595 just outside Whitehaven

High quality, budget accommodation ideal for both families and business travellers. Spacious, en suite bedrooms feature tea and coffee making facilities, and Freeview TV in most hotels. Internet access and Wi-fi are available for a small fee. The adjacent family restaurant features a wide and varied menu. See also the Hotel Groups pages.

Rooms 47 **D** £60*

WHITSTABLE Map 7 TR16
Kent

Premier Inn Whitstable

BUDGET HOTEL

☎ 0871 527 9162 📠 0871 527 9163
Thanet Way CT5 3DB
dir: 2m W of town centre on B2205

High quality, budget accommodation ideal for both families and business travellers. Spacious, en suite bedrooms feature tea and coffee making facilities, and Freeview TV in most hotels. Internet access and Wi-fi are available for a small fee. The adjacent family restaurant features a wide and varied menu. See also the Hotel Groups pages.

Rooms 41 **D** £65-£67*

WHITTLEBURY Map 11 SP64
Northamptonshire

Whittlebury Hall

★★★★ 79% ❁❁ HOTEL

☎ 01327 857857 📠 01327 857987
NN12 8QH
e-mail: sales@whittleburyhall.co.uk
web: www.whittleburyhall.co.uk
dir: A43/A413 towards Buckingham, through Whittlebury, turn for hotel on right (signed)

A purpose-built, Georgian-style country house hotel with excellent spa and leisure facilities and pedestrian access to the Silverstone circuit. Grand public areas include F1 car racing memorabilia and the accommodation includes some lavishly appointed suites. Food is a strength, with a choice of various dining options. Particularly noteworthy are the afternoon teas in the spacious lounge and the fine dining in Murray's Restaurant.

Rooms 211 (3 fmly) (13 smoking) **Facilities** Spa FTV Gym Beauty treatments Relaxation room Hair studio Heat & Ice experience Leisure club ♫ Xmas New Year Wi-fi **Conf** Class 175 Board 40 Thtr 500 **Services** Lift **Parking** 450 **Notes** 🚭

WICKHAM Map 5 SU51
Hampshire

Old House Hotel & Restaurant

★★★ 80% ❁❁ HOTEL

☎ 01329 833049 📠 01329 833672
The Square PO17 5JG
e-mail: enquiries@oldhousehotel.co.uk
web: www.oldhousehotel.co.uk
dir: M27 junct 10, N on A32 for 2m towards Alton

This hotel, a Grade II listed building, occupies a convenient location in the heart of historic Wickham, which is not far from Portsmouth and Southampton. Bedrooms and bathrooms are smartly co-ordinated, and include stylish Garden Suites that look out on the delightful garden. The public areas have much character and charm, and the service is attentive and friendly. The award-winning cuisine utilises seasonal, local produce.

Rooms 12 (4 annexe) (1 fmly) (4 GF) **S** £70; **D** £95-£170 (incl. bkfst)* **Facilities** STV FTV Xmas New Year Wi-fi **Conf** Board 14 Thtr 24 Del from £220* **Parking** 8 **Notes** LB 🚭 Civ Wed 70

WIGAN Map 15 SD50
Greater Manchester

Wrightington Hotel & Country Club

★★★★ 75% ❁ HOTEL

☎ 01257 425803 📠 01257 425830
Moss Ln, Wrightington WN6 9PB
e-mail: info@wrightingtonhotel.co.uk
dir: M6 junct 27, 0.25m W, hotel on right after church

Situated in open countryside close to the M6, this privately owned hotel offers friendly hospitality. Accommodation is well equipped and spacious, and public areas include an extensive leisure complex complete with hair salon, boutique and sports injury lab. Blazers Restaurant, two bars and air-conditioned banqueting facilities appeal to a broad market.

Rooms 73 (6 fmly) (36 GF) **Facilities** Spa STV FTV Gym Squash Hairdressing salon Beauty spa Sports injury clinic New Year Wi-fi **Conf** Class 120 Board 40 Thtr 200 Del from £130 to £150* **Services** Lift **Parking** 240 **Notes** Civ Wed 100

Macdonald Kilhey Court

★★★★ 73% ❁ HOTEL

☎ 0870 1942122 📠 01257 422401
Chorley Rd, Standish WN1 2XN
e-mail: general.kilheycourt@macdonald-hotels.co.uk
web: www.macdonald-hotels.co.uk/kilheycourt
dir: M6 junct 27, A5209 Standish, over at lights, past church on right, left at T-junct, hotel on right 350yds. M61 junct 6, signed Wigan & Haigh Hall. 3m & right at T-junct. Hotel 0.5m on right

This hotel is peacefully situated in its own grounds yet conveniently located for the motorway network. The accommodation is comfortable and the rooms are split between the Victorian house and a modern extension. Public areas display many original features and the split-level restaurant has views over the Worthington Lakes. This hotel is a very popular venue for weddings.

Rooms 62 (18 fmly) (8 GF) **Facilities** STV FTV Gym Aerobics & yoga classes Private fishing arranged Beauty treatments Xmas New Year Wi-fi **Conf** Class 180 Board 60 Thtr 400 **Services** Lift **Parking** 200 **Notes** 🚭 Civ Wed 300

W

WIGAN *continued*

Mercure Wigan Oak Hotel

★★★ 73% HOTEL

☎ 01942 826888 🖷 01942 825800
Orchard St WN1 3SS
e-mail: enquiries@hotels-wigan.com
dir: From S: M6 junct 25, A49 (signed Wigan) then B5238, right after Grand Arcade Shopping. From N: M6 junct 27, A5209, onto A49, left at lights, hotel opposite Tesco

This modern and stylish hotel is situated in the centre of Wigan; easily accessed from the M6 and M61 and well positioned for public transport. The bedrooms are both comfortable and well equipped and public rooms include the restaurant, conservatory and popular bar. There is free Wi-fi throughout, and conference and events facilities are available. Ample parking is a plus in this central location.

Rooms 88 (7 fmly) (16 GF) **Facilities** FTV New Year Wi-fi **Conf** Class 80 Board 40 Thtr 160 Del from £80 to £120* **Services** Lift **Parking** 100 **Notes** Civ Wed 50

Premier Inn Haydock Park (Wigan South)

BUDGET HOTEL

☎ 0871 527 8502 🖷 0871 527 8503
53 Warrington Rd, Ashton-in-Makerfield WN4 9PJ
dir: Just off M6 junct 23, A49 towards Wigan

High quality, budget accommodation ideal for both families and business travellers. Spacious, en suite bedrooms feature tea and coffee making facilities, and Freeview TV in most hotels. Internet access and Wi-fi are available for a small fee. The adjacent family restaurant features a wide and varied menu. See also the Hotel Groups pages.

Rooms 30 **D** £55-£56*

Premier Inn Wigan M6 Jct 25

BUDGET HOTEL

☎ 0871 527 9164 🖷 0871 527 9165
Warrington Rd, Marus Bridge WN3 6XB
dir: M6 junct 25 (N'bound). At rdbt left, hotel on left

Rooms 40 **D** £50-£56*

Premier Inn Wigan West

BUDGET HOTEL

☎ 0871 527 9168 🖷 0871 527 9169
Orrell Rd, Orrell WN5 8HQ
dir: M6 junct 26 follow signs for Upholland & Orrell. At 1st lights turn left. Hotel on right behind Priory Wood Beefeater

Rooms 40 **D** £50-£56*

The Beeches

RESTAURANT WITH ROOMS

☎ 01257 426432 & 421316 🖷 01257 427503
School Ln, Standish WN6 0TD
e-mail: mail@beecheshotel.co.uk
dir: M6 junct 27, A5209 to Standish, into School Lane

Located a short drive from M6, this elegant Victorian house has been appointed to provide high standards of comfort. Bedrooms are equipped with practical and homely extras, and public areas include spacious lounges, a popular brasserie, and a self-contained function suite.

Rooms 10 (4 fmly)

WILLERBY — Map 17 TA03
East Riding of Yorkshire

Best Western Willerby Manor Hotel

★★★ 83% ❀ HOTEL

☎ 01482 652616 🖷 01482 653901
Well Ln HU10 6ER
e-mail: willerbymanor@bestwestern.co.uk
web: www.willerbymanor.co.uk
dir: Off A63, signed Humber Bridge. Right at rdbt by Waitrose. At next rdbt hotel signed

Set in a quiet residential area, amid well-tended gardens, this hotel was originally a private mansion; it has now been thoughtfully extended to provide very comfortable bedrooms, equipped with many useful extras. There are extensive leisure facilities and a wide choice of meals offered in the contemporary Figs Brasserie which has an impressive heated outdoor area.

Rooms 63 (6 fmly) (20 GF) (1 smoking) **S** £65-£98; **D** £106-£126 (incl. bkfst)* **Facilities** STV FTV supervised Gym Steam room Beauty therapist Aerobic classes New Year Wi-fi **Conf** Class 200 Board 100 Thtr 500 Del from £149.50 to £160* **Parking** 300 **Notes** LB Closed 24-26 Dec Civ Wed 150

WILMINGTON — Map 6 TQ50
East Sussex

Crossways

❀❀ RESTAURANT WITH ROOMS

☎ 01323 482455 🖷 01323 487811
Lewes Rd BN26 5SG
e-mail: stay@crosswayshotel.co.uk
web: www.crosswayshotel.co.uk
dir: On A27 between Lewes & Polegate, 2m E of Alfriston rdbt

Amidst stunning gardens and attractively tended grounds sits this well-established, popular restaurant. The well-presented bedrooms are tastefully decorated and provide an abundance of thoughtful amenities including free Wi-fi. Guest comfort is paramount and the naturally warm hospitality ensures guests often return.

Rooms 7

WILMSLOW

See **Manchester Airport**

WIMBORNE MINSTER — Map 5 SZ06
Dorset

Les Bouviers Restaurant with Rooms

❀❀ RESTAURANT WITH ROOMS

☎ 01202 889555 🖷 01202 639428
Arrowsmith Rd, Canford Magna BH21 3BD
e-mail: info@lesbouviers.co.uk
web: www.lesbouviers.co.uk
dir: A31 onto A349. In 0.6m turn left. In approx 1m right onto Arrowsmith Rd. Establishment approx 100yds on right

An excellent restaurant with rooms in a great location, set in six acres of grounds. Food is a highlight of any stay here as is the friendly, attentive service. Bedrooms are extremely well equipped and beds are supremely comfortable.

Rooms 6 (4 fmly)

W

WINCANTON Map 4 ST72
Somerset

Holbrook House

★★★ 82% COUNTRY HOUSE HOTEL

01963 824466 & 828844 01963 32681
Holbrook BA9 8BS
e-mail: enquiries@holbrookhouse.co.uk
web: www.holbrookhouse.co.uk
dir: From A303 at Wincanton left onto A371 towards Castle Cary & Shepton Mallet

This handsome country house offers a unique blend of quality and comfort combined with a friendly atmosphere. Set in 17 acres of peaceful gardens and wooded grounds, Holbrook House makes a perfect retreat. The restaurant provides a selection of innovative dishes prepared with enthusiasm and served by a team of caring staff.

Rooms 21 (5 annexe) (2 fmly) (5 GF) **S** £95-£150; **D** £95-£250 (incl. bkfst)* **Facilities** Spa FTV Gym Beauty treatment Exercise classes Sauna Steam room Fitness suite Xmas New Year Wi-fi **Conf** Class 50 Board 55 Thtr 200 **Parking** 100 **Notes** LB Civ Wed 150

WINCHCOMBE Map 10 SP02
Gloucestershire

Wesley House

RESTAURANT WITH ROOMS

01242 602366 01242 609046
High St GL54 5LJ
e-mail: enquiries@wesleyhouse.co.uk
web: www.wesleyhouse.co.uk
dir: In town centre

This 15th-century, half-timbered property is named after John Wesley, founder of the Methodist Church, who stayed here while preaching in the town. Bedrooms are small but full of character. In the rear dining room, a unique lighting system changes colour to suit the mood required, and also highlights the various floral creations by a world-renowned flower arranger. A glass atrium covers the outside terrace.

Rooms 5

WINCHESTER Map 5 SU42
Hampshire

INSPECTORS' CHOICE

Lainston House

★★★★ COUNTRY HOUSE HOTEL

01962 776088 01962 776672
Sparsholt SO21 2LT
e-mail: enquiries@lainstonhouse.com
web: www.exclusivehotels.co.uk
dir: 2m NW off B3049 towards Stockbridge

This graceful example of a William and Mary House enjoys a countryside location amidst mature grounds and gardens. Staff provide good levels of courtesy and care with a polished, professional service. Bedrooms are tastefully appointed and include some spectacular, spacious rooms with stylish handmade beds and stunning bathrooms. Public rooms include a cocktail bar built entirely from a single cedar and stocked with an impressive range of rare drinks and cigars.

Rooms 49 (6 fmly) (18 GF) **D** £245-£745* **Facilities** STV FTV Fishing Gym Archery Clay pigeon shooting Cycling Hot air ballooning Falconry Xmas New Year Wi-fi **Conf** Class 80 Board 40 Thtr 166 Del from £220 to £350* **Parking** 200 **Notes** LB Civ Wed 200

Holiday Inn Winchester

★★★★ 77% HOTEL

Holiday Inn

01962 670700 & 826280 01962 670701
Telegraph Way, Morn Hill SO21 1HZ
e-mail: info@hiwinchester.co.uk
dir: M3 junct 9, follow A31 Alton/A272 Petersfield signs. 1st exit at rdbt onto A31. After 1.6m 1st exit into Alresford Rd then left into Telegraph Way

Located a few miles from the historic city of Winchester and within easy reach of the south's transport links, this modern, purpose-built property is presented to a high standard. Bedrooms are spacious and well-equipped for both the business and leisure guest. Enjoyable cuisine is served in the restaurant and there is a very good range of freshly prepared dishes to choose from. Conference facilities and ample parking are available.

Rooms 141 (7 fmly) (60 GF) **Facilities** STV FTV Xmas New Year Wi-fi **Conf** Class 110 Board 120 Thtr 250 **Services** Lift Air con **Parking** 167 **Notes** Civ Wed 200

The Winchester Hotel

★★★★ 76% HOTEL

01962 709988 01962 859501
Worthy Ln SO23 7AB
e-mail: reservations@thewinchesterhotel.co.uk
web: www.pedersenhotels.com/winchester
dir: A33 then A3047, hotel 1m on right

This hotel is just a few minutes' walk from the city centre, is very smartly appointed throughout, and includes a great leisure centre. The staff are extremely friendly and helpful, and praiseworthy food is served in the contemporary Hutton's Brasserie.

Rooms 98 (2 fmly) (8 GF) **S** £79-£155; **D** £79-£155* **Facilities** FTV supervised Gym Sauna Steam room Spa bath Xmas New Year Wi-fi **Conf** Class 100 Board 40 Thtr 200 Del from £120 to £170* **Services** Lift Air con **Parking** 60 **Notes** LB Civ Wed 180

W

WINCHESTER *continued*

Hotel du Vin Winchester

★★★★ 74% ®® TOWN HOUSE HOTEL

☎ 01962 841414 📠 01962 842458
Southgate St SO23 9EF
e-mail: info@winchester.hotelduvin.com
web: www.hotelduvin.com
dir: M3 junct 11 towards Winchester, follow signs. Hotel in approx 2m on left just past cinema

Continuing to set high standards, this inviting hotel is best known for its high profile bistro. The individually designed bedrooms have all the Hotel du Vin signature touches including fine Egyptian cotton linen, power showers and Wi-fi. The bistro serves imaginative yet simply cooked dishes from a seasonal, daily-changing menu.

Rooms 24 (4 annexe) (4 GF) **Facilities** STV Xmas New Year Wi-fi **Conf** Class 30 Board 20 Thtr 40 **Parking** 35 **Notes** Civ Wed 60

Mercure Wessex

★★★★ 69% HOTEL

☎ 01962 861611 📠 01962 841503
Paternoster Row SO23 9LQ
e-mail: H6619@accor.com
web: www.mercure.com
dir: M3 junct 10, 2nd exit at rdbt signed Winchester/ B3330. Right at lights. Left at 2nd rdbt. Over small bridge, on at next rdbt into Broadway. Left at Guildhall Tavern into Colebrook St. Hotel 50yds on right

Occupying an enviable location in the centre of this historic city and adjacent to the spectacular cathedral, this hotel is quietly situated on a side street. Inside, the atmosphere is restful and welcoming, with public areas and some bedrooms enjoying unrivalled views of the hotel's centuries-old neighbour.

Rooms 94 (6 fmly) **S** £75-£147; **D** £85-£157* **Facilities** STV Gym Xmas New Year Wi-fi **Conf** Class 60 Board 60 Thtr 100 Del from £130 to £155* **Services** Lift **Parking** 42 **Notes** LB Civ Wed 120

The Winchester Royal Hotel

★★★ 78% ® HOTEL

☎ 01962 840840 📠 01962 841582
St Peter St SO23 8BS
e-mail: winchester.royal@forestdale.com
web: www.thewinchesterroyalhotel.co.uk
dir: M3 junct 9 to Winnall Trading Estate. Follow to city centre, cross river, left, 1st right. Onto one-way system, take 2nd right. Hotel immediately on right

Situated in the heart of the former capital of England, a warm welcome awaits at this friendly hotel, which in parts, dates back to the 16th century. The bedrooms may vary in style but all are comfortable and well equipped; the modern annexe rooms overlook the attractive well-tended gardens. The conservatory restaurant makes a very pleasant setting for enjoyable meals.

Rooms 75 (56 annexe) (1 fmly) (27 GF) **Facilities** FTV Xmas New Year Wi-fi **Conf** Class 50 Board 50 Thtr 120 **Parking** 50 **Notes** LB Civ Wed 100

Marwell

★★★ 73% HOTEL

☎ 01962 777681 📠 01962 777160
Thompsons Ln, Colden Common, Marwell SO21 1JY
e-mail: info@marwellhotel.co.uk
web: www.marwellhotel.co.uk
dir: B3354 through Twyford. 1st exit at rdbt (continue on B3354), left onto B2177 signed Bishop Waltham. Left into Thomsons Ln after 1m, hotel on left

Taking its theme from the adjacent zoo, this unusual hotel is based on the famous TreeTops safari lodge in Kenya. The well-equipped bedrooms, split between four lodges, convey a hint of safari style, while the smart public areas include an airy lobby bar and an 'Out of Africa' themed restaurant. There is also a selection of meeting and leisure facilities.

Rooms 66 (10 fmly) (36 GF) **Facilities** STV FTV supervised 18 Gym Sauna New Year Wi-fi **Conf** Class 60 Board 60 Thtr 175 **Parking** 120 **Notes** ® Civ Wed 150

WINDERMERE
Cumbria **Map 18 SD49**

INSPECTORS' CHOICE

Gilpin Hotel & Lake House

★★★★ ®®® HOTEL

☎ 015394 88818 📠 015394 88058
Crook Rd LA23 3NE
e-mail: hotel@gilpinlodge.co.uk
web: www.gilpinlodge.co.uk
dir: M6 junct 36, A590, A591 to rdbt N of Kendal, onto B5284, hotel 5m on right

This smart Victorian residence is set amidst delightful gardens leading to the fells, and is just a short drive from the lake. The individually designed bedrooms are stylish and a number benefit from private terraces; all are spacious and thoughtfully equipped, and each has a private sitting room. In addition there are luxury Garden Suites that lead out onto private gardens with cedar wood hot tubs. The welcoming atmosphere is notable and the attractive day rooms are perfect for relaxing, perhaps beside a real fire. Dining in any of the quartet of rooms is a must. AA Hotel of the Year for England 2011-12.

Rooms 26 (12 annexe) (12 GF) **S** £180-£510; **D** £290-£550 (incl. bkfst & dinner)* **Facilities** Free membership at local leisure club In-room spa treatment Xmas New Year **Parking** 40 **Notes** LB ® No children 7yrs

W

INSPECTORS' CHOICE

Holbeck Ghyll Country House Hotel

★★★★ ◎◎◎ COUNTRY HOUSE HOTEL

☎ 015394 32375 📄 015394 34743
Holbeck Ln LA23 1LU
e-mail: stay@holbeckghyll.com
dir: 3m N of Windermere on A591, right into Holbeck Lane (signed Troutbeck), hotel 0.5m on left

Holbeck Ghyll sits high up overlooking the majestic Lake Windermere surrounded by well maintained grounds. The original house was bought in 1888 by Lord Lonsdale, the first president of the AA, who used it as a hunting lodge. Guests today will find that this is a delightful place where the service is professional and attentive. There are beautifully designed, spacious bedrooms situated in the main house and also in lodges in the grounds; each has lake views and some have patios. There are also The Shieling and Miss Potter suites. Each bedroom has Egyptian cotton linens, fresh flowers, LCD satellite TV, CD & DVD players, bathrobes and a decanter of damson gin. The restaurant impresses with its award-winning cuisine. The hotel also has a health spa, gym and boutique store.

Rooms 26 (12 annexe) (5 fmly) (11 GF) **D** £250-£570 (incl. bkfst & dinner) **Facilities** Spa STV Gym Sauna Steam room Treatment rooms Beauty massage Xmas New Year Wi-fi **Conf** Class 40 Board 30 Thtr 60 **Parking** 34 **Notes** LB Civ Wed 60

INSPECTORS' CHOICE

Linthwaite House Hotel & Restaurant

★★★★ ◎◎ COUNTRY HOUSE HOTEL

☎ 015394 88600 📄 015394 88601
Crook Rd LA23 3JA
e-mail: stay@linthwaite.com
web: www.linthwaite.com
dir: A591 towards The Lakes for 8m to large rdbt, take 1st exit (B5284), 6m, hotel on left. 1m past Windermere golf club

Linthwaite House is set in 14 acres of hilltop grounds and enjoys stunning views over Lake Windermere. Inviting public rooms include an attractive conservatory and adjoining lounge, and an elegant restaurant which occupies three rooms and offers menus based on the finest local ingredients. Bedrooms, which are individually decorated, combine contemporary furnishings with classical styles; all are thoughtfully equipped and include CD players, radios and free Wi-fi. There is also a Garden Suite and the new luxurious Loft Suite which even has a retractable roof and telescope for star gazing. Service and hospitality are attentive and friendly.

Rooms 30 (1 fmly) (7 GF) **S** £129-£160; **D** £189-£531 (incl. bkfst)* **Facilities** STV FTV Putt green Fishing Beauty treatments Massage Access to nearby spa with pool & gym Xmas New Year Wi-fi **Conf** Class 22 Board 25 Thtr 54 **Parking** 40 **Notes** Civ Wed 64

Macdonald Old England Hotel & Spa

★★★★ 84% ◎◎ HOTEL

☎ 0844 879 9144 📄 015394 43432
Church St, Bowness LA23 3DF
e-mail: sales.oldengland@macdonald-hotels.co.uk
web: www.macdonaldhotels.co.uk
dir: Through Windermere to Bowness, straight across at mini-rdbt. Hotel behind church on right

This hotel stands right on the shore of England's largest lake and boasts superb views, especially through the floor-to-ceiling windows in the Vinand Restaurant. There are several bedroom types; standard, executive and suites; some rooms have been designed for wheelchairs users. The spa has a 20-metre pool, a gym, sauna and steam room.

Rooms 106 (6 fmly) (14 GF) **Facilities** Spa STV supervised Gym Private jetties Rock sauna Aromatherapy shower Steam room Ice room Xmas New Year Wi-fi **Conf** Class 60 Board 25 Thtr 150 **Services** Lift **Parking** 90 **Notes** LB Civ Wed 100

Lindeth Howe Country House Hotel & Restaurant

★★★★ 79% ◎◎ COUNTRY HOUSE HOTEL

☎ 015394 45759 📄 015394 46368
Lindeth Dr, Longtail Hill LA23 3JF
e-mail: hotel@lindeth-howe.co.uk
web: www.lindeth-howe.co.uk
dir: Exit A592, 1m S of Bowness onto B5284 (Longtail Hill) signed Kendal/Lancaster, hotel on right

Historic photographs commemorate the fact that this delightful house was once the family home of Beatrix Potter. Secluded in landscaped grounds, it enjoys views across the valley and Lake Windermere. Public rooms are plentiful and inviting, with the restaurant being the perfect setting for modern country-house cooking. Deluxe and superior bedrooms are spacious and smartly appointed.

Rooms 34 (3 fmly) (2 GF) **S** £95-£90; **D** £170-£360 (incl. bkfst)* **Facilities** STV Gym Sauna Fitness room Xmas New Year Wi-fi **Conf** Class 20 Board 18 Thtr 30 Del from £144 to £180* **Parking** 50 **Notes**

W

WINDERMERE *continued*

Storrs Hall

★★★★ 78% @@ HOTEL

☎ 015394 47111 📠 015394 47555
Storrs Park LA23 3LG
e-mail: storrshall@elhmail.co.uk
web: www.elh.co.uk/hotels/storrshall
dir: On A592, 2m S of Bowness, on Newby Bridge road

Set in 17 acres of landscaped grounds by the lake, this imposing Grade II Georgian mansion is delightful. The hotel has numerous lounges to relax in, each furnished with antiques and fine art, and a cosy bar ideal for pre-dinner drinks. The individually styled bedrooms are, in general, spacious and boast impressive bathrooms. Imaginative cuisine is served in the elegant Terrace Restaurant which offers fine views across the lawn to the lake and fells beyond. Guests can also request one of the chef's special picnics to enjoy while sitting by the lake. In the grounds there is a National Trust folly known as The Temple.

Rooms 30 **Facilities** FTV Fishing Use of nearby sports/beauty facilities Xmas New Year Wi-fi **Conf** Class 35 Board 24 Thtr 50 **Parking** 50 **Notes** LB No children 12yrs Civ Wed 94

Low Wood Bay

★★★★ 76% HOTEL

☎ 015394 33338 & 0845 850 3502
📠 015394 34275
LA23 1LP
e-mail: lowwood@elhmail.co.uk
dir: M6 junct 36, A590, A591 to Windermere, then 3m towards Ambleside, hotel on right

Benefiting from a lakeside location, this hotel offers an excellent range of leisure and conference facilities. Bedrooms, many with panoramic lake views, are attractively furnished, and include a number of larger executive rooms and suites. There is a choice of bars, a spacious restaurant and the more informal Café del Lago. The poolside bar offers internet access.

Rooms 111 (13 fmly) (21 GF) **S** £79-£160; **D** £98-£260 (incl. bkfst)* **Facilities** **Spa** supervised Fishing Gym Squash Water skiing Beauty salon Xmas New Year Wi-fi **Conf** Class 180 Board 150 Thtr 340 Del from £99 to £143* **Services** Lift **Parking** 204 **Notes** LB Civ Wed 280

See advert on opposite page

Beech Hill Hotel

★★★★ 74% @ HOTEL

☎ 015394 42137 📠 015394 43745
Newby Bridge Rd LA23 3LR
e-mail: reservations@beechhillhotel.co.uk
web: www.beechhillhotel.co.uk
dir: M6 junct 36, A591 to Windermere. Left onto A592 towards Newby Bridge

Located on the edge of Lake Windermere, the panoramic views are impressive. The bedrooms are well appointed and some have balconies overlooking the lake. The open areas, for enjoying coffee or drinks, prove very popular in the summer. There are cosy lounges with log fires, a fine restaurant, leisure facilities and landscaped gardens. High standards of service can be expected from the attentive, informative and very friendly staff.

Rooms 57 (4 fmly) (4 GF) **Facilities** FTV Fishing Solarium Xmas New Year Wi-fi **Parking** 70 **Notes** Civ Wed 130

INSPECTORS' CHOICE

The Samling

★★★ SMALL HOTEL

☎ 015394 31922 📠 015394 30400
Ambleside Rd LA23 1LR
e-mail: info@thesamlinghotel.co.uk
web: www.thesamlinghotel.co.uk
dir: M6 junct 36, A591 to Windermere. Hotel 300mtrs past Low Wood Water Sports Centre

This stylish house, built in the late 1700s, is situated in 67 acres of grounds and enjoys an elevated position overlooking Lake Windermere. The spacious, beautifully furnished bedrooms and suites, some in adjacent buildings, are thoughtfully equipped and all have superb bathrooms. Public rooms include a sumptuous drawing room, a small library and an elegant dining room. The Rosette award is temporarily suspended due to a change of chef; a new award will be in place once our inspectors have completed their assessments of meals cooked by the new kitchen team.

Rooms 11 (6 annexe) (2 GF) **S** fr £175; **D** £190-£560 (incl. bkfst)* **Facilities** STV FTV Xmas New Year **Conf** Board 12 Del from £280 to £340* **Parking** 15 **Notes** LB Civ Wed 30

Miller Howe Hotel

★★★ 86% @@ COUNTRY HOUSE HOTEL

☎ 015394 42536 📠 015394 45664
Rayrigg Rd LA23 1EY
e-mail: info@millerhowe.com
dir: M6 junct 36 , A591 past Windermere, left at rdbt towards Bowness

This long established hotel of much character enjoys a lakeside setting amidst delightful landscaped gardens. The bright and welcoming day rooms include sumptuous lounges, a conservatory and an opulently decorated restaurant. Imaginative dinners make use of fresh, local produce where possible and there is an extensive, well-balanced wine list. Stylish bedrooms, many with fabulous lake views, include well-equipped cottage rooms and a number with whirlpool baths.

Rooms 15 (3 annexe) (1 GF) **Facilities** Xmas New Year Wi-fi **Parking** 35 **Notes** Civ Wed 75

W

Lindeth Fell Country House Hotel

★★★ 85% COUNTRY HOUSE HOTEL

☎ 015394 43286 & 44287 🖷 015394 47455
Lyth Valley Rd, Bowness-on-Windermere LA23 3JP
e-mail: kennedy@lindethfell.co.uk
web: www.lindethfell.co.uk
dir: 1m S of Bowness on A5074

Enjoying delightful views, this smart Edwardian residence stands in seven acres of glorious, landscaped gardens. Bedrooms, which vary in size and style, are comfortably equipped. Skilfully prepared dinners are served in the spacious dining room that commands fine views. The resident owners and their attentive, friendly staff provide high levels of hospitality and service.

Rooms 14 (2 fmly) (1 GF) **S** £70-£120; **D** £140-£200 (incl. bkfst)* **Facilities** Putt green Fishing Bowling Xmas New Year Wi-fi **Conf** Class 12 Board 12 **Parking** 20 **Notes** LB Closed 3-29 Jan

Burn How Garden House Hotel

★★★ 80% HOTEL

☎ 015394 46226 🖷 015394 47000
Back Belsfield Rd, Bowness LA23 3HH
e-mail: info@burnhow.co.uk
web: www.burnhow.co.uk
dir: Exit A591 at Windermere, follow signs to Bowness. Pass Lake Piers on right, 1st left to hotel

Set in its own leafy grounds, this hotel is only a few minutes' walk from both the lake and the town centre. Attractive, spacious rooms, some with four-poster beds, are situated in modern chalets or in an adjacent Victorian house; many have private patios or terraces. Guests can enjoy creative meals in the stylish dining room, or just relax in the comfortable open-plan lounge areas.

Rooms 28 (28 annexe) (10 fmly) (6 GF) **S** £75-£125; **D** £80-£175 (incl. bkfst)* **Facilities** New Year Wi-fi **Parking** 30 **Notes** LB Closed 19-27 Dec, 4-11 Jan

Windermere Manor Hotel

★★★ 78% HOTEL

☎ 01539 445801 🖷 01539 448397
Rayrigg Rd LA23 1ES
e-mail: windermere@actionforblindpeople.org.uk
dir: A591 towards Ambleside. At mini-rdbt turn left, hotel 1st on left

Set above the shores of Lake Windermere in wooded landscaped gardens, this former manor house has been restored to its original splendour. The bedrooms and suites are smart and well appointed. The attractive dining room has an unusual barrel-vaulted wooden roof and serves delicious home cooking. The hotel extends a warm welcome to everyone but caters especially for the visually impaired, their families, friends and guide dogs. Special facilities for guide dogs are provided.

Rooms 28 (2 fmly) (5 GF) **S** £40-£68; **D** £80-£134 (incl. bkfst & dinner)* **Facilities** FTV supervised Gym Xmas New Year Wi-fi **Conf** Class 30 Board 15 Thtr 40 Del from £50 to £130* **Services** Lift **Parking** 28 **Notes** LB Civ Wed 40

Craig Manor

★★★ 77% HOTEL

☎ 015394 88877 🖷 015394 88878
Lake Rd LA23 2JF
e-mail: info@craigmanor.co.uk
dir: A590, then A591 into Windermere, left at Windermere Hotel, through village, pass Magistrates' Court, hotel on left

This establishment is situated in the heart of the Lake District in Bowness-on-Windermere. There is a relaxed and friendly atmosphere, with professional staff providing attentive service. Bedrooms are comfortable and well equipped, and some rooms have stunning views across the lake. The attractive and elegant lake-facing restaurant serves an excellent choice of quality dishes. The large car park is a further benefit at this popular tourist resort.

Rooms 16

Cedar Manor Hotel & Restaurant

★★ 84% HOTEL

☎ 015394 43192 & 45970 🖷 015394 45970
Ambleside Rd LA23 1AX
e-mail: info@cedarmanor.co.uk
dir: From A591 follow signs to Windermere. Hotel on left just beyond St Mary's Church

Built in 1854 as a country retreat this lovely old house enjoys a peaceful location that is within easy walking distance of the town centre. Bedrooms, some on the ground floor, are attractive and well equipped, with two bedrooms in the adjacent coach house. There is a comfortable lounge bar where guests can relax before enjoying dinner in the well-appointed dining room.

W

WINDERMERE *continued*

Rooms 10 (1 annexe) (1 fmly) (3 GF) **S** £80-£180; **D** £120-£350 (incl. bkfst)* **Facilities** FTV New Year Wi-fi **Conf** Board 12 Del from £200 to £300* **Parking** 11 **Notes** LB ⊗ Closed 3-21 Jan

The Hideaway at Windermere

⊛⊛ RESTAURANT WITH ROOMS

☎ 015394 43070
Phoenix Way LA23 1DB
e-mail: eatandstay@thehideawayatwindermere.co.uk
web: www.thehideawayatwindermere.co.uk
dir: Exit A591 at Ravensworth B&B, into Phoenix Way. The Hideaway 100mtrs on right

Tucked away quietly this beautiful Victorian Lakeland house is personally run by owners Richard and Lisa. Delicious food, individually designed bedrooms and warm hospitality ensure an enjoyable stay. There is a beautifully appointed lounge looking out to the garden, and the restaurant is split between two light and airy rooms; here guests will find the emphasis is on fresh, local ingredients and attentive, yet friendly service. Bedrooms vary in size and style - the larger rooms feature luxury bathrooms.

Rooms 11 (1 annexe)

Jerichos

⊛⊛ RESTAURANT WITH ROOMS

☎ 015394 42522 ⎙ 015394 88899
College Rd LA23 1BX
e-mail: info@jerichos.co.uk
dir: A591 to Windermere, 2nd left into Elleray Rd, 1st right into College Rd

Dating back to around 1870, this centrally located property has been lovingly restored by its current owners. All the elegantly furnished bedrooms are en suite and the top floor rooms have views of the fells. Breakfast is served in the Restaurant Room, and the comfortable lounge has a real fire to relax by on chillier days. The chef/proprietor has established a strong reputation for his creative menus that use the best local and seasonal produce. The restaurant is always busy so booking is essential. Wi-fi is available.

Rooms 10

WINDSOR
Berkshire — Map 6 SU97

Macdonald Windsor Hotel

★★★★ 81% HOTEL

☎ 0844 879 9101
High St SL4 1LH

Just across the street from Windsor Castle, this hotel is an ideal base for visiting not only the castle, but all the other famous attractions of the town. It has well-appointed bedrooms designed in soft shades to create a calm atmosphere. Caleys restaurant offers a relaxed and informal dining venue, and 24-hour room service is also available. Complimentary Wi-fi is available in the bedrooms and the conference rooms.

Rooms 120

Oakley Court

PH | principal hayley

★★★★ 78% HOTEL

☎ 01753 609988 & 609900 ⎙ 01628 637011
Windsor Rd, Water Oakley SL4 5UR
e-mail: oakley.reservations@principal-hayley.com
web: www.principal-hayley.com
dir: M4 junct 6, A355, then A332 towards Windsor, right onto A308 towards Maidenhead. Pass racecourse, hotel 2.5m on right

Built in 1859 this splendid Victorian Gothic mansion is enviably situated in extensive grounds that lead down to the Thames. All bedrooms are spacious, beautifully furnished and many enjoy river views. Extensive public areas include a range of comfortable lounges and the Oakleaf Restaurant. The comprehensive leisure facilities include a 9-hole golf course.

Rooms 118 (109 annexe) (5 fmly) (28 GF) **Facilities** Spa STV 🎾 ⛳ 9 ⛳ Putt green 🏋 Gym Boating Sauna Snooker Xmas New Year Wi-fi **Conf** Class 90 Board 50 Thtr 170 **Services** Air con **Parking** 120 **Notes** ⊗ Civ Wed 120

Mercure Castle

★★★★ 77% ⊛⊛ HOTEL

☎ 01753 851577 ⎙ 01753 856930
18 High St SL4 1LJ
e-mail: h6618@accor.com
web: www.mercure.com
dir: M4 junct 6/M25 junct 15, follow signs to Windsor town centre & castle. Hotel at top of hill opposite Guildhall

This is one of the oldest hotels in Windsor, beginning life as a coaching inn in the 16th century. Located opposite Windsor Castle, it is an ideal base from which to explore the town and its royal connections. Stylish bedrooms are thoughtfully equipped and include four-poster and executive rooms. Public areas are spacious and tastefully decorated.

Rooms 108 (70 annexe) (18 fmly) (3 GF) **Facilities** STV FTV Xmas New Year Wi-fi **Conf** Class 150 Board 50 Thtr 400 Del from £175 to £300* **Services** Lift Air con **Parking** 135 **Notes** LB ⊗ Civ Wed 300

The Harte & Garter Hotel & Spa

★★★★ 74% HOTEL

☎ 0845 609 9966 ⎙ 01753 830527
High St SL4 1PH
e-mail: reservations@akkeron-hotels.com
web: www.akkeron-hotels.com
dir: M4 junct 6, A332 follow town centre signs, hotel opposite front entrance to Windsor Castle

Enjoying an enviable location in the centre of Windsor, this hotel overlooks the magnificent castle. Bedrooms are comfortably appointed and interiors blend modern and classic styles well. Public areas include the Tower Brasserie and tea room which also enjoys views of the castle, a spa facility where guests can unwind, and a range of conference and meeting rooms.

Rooms 79 (40 annexe) (3 GF) **Facilities** Spa FTV Thermal suite & Hydro pool ♫ Xmas New Year Wi-fi **Conf** Class 80 Board 80 Thtr 260 **Services** Lift **Notes** ⊗ Civ Wed 180

W

Best Western Royal Adelaide Hotel

★★★★ 71% HOTEL

☎ 01753 863916 & 07710 473130
📠 01753 830682
46 Kings Rd SL4 2AG
e-mail: info@theroyaladelaide.com
web: www.theroyaladelaide.com
dir: M4 junct 6, A322 to Windsor. 1st left at rdbt into Clarence Rd. At 4th lights right into Sheet St, then Kings Rd. Hotel on right

This attractive Georgian-style hotel enjoys a quiet location yet is only a short walk from the town centre. Bedrooms vary in size. Public areas are tastefully appointed and include a range of meeting rooms, a bar and an elegant restaurant. Off-street parking is available.

Rooms 42 (4 annexe) (6 fmly) (8 GF) (5 smoking) **Facilities** STV Xmas New Year Wi-fi **Conf** Class 80 Board 50 Thtr 100 **Services** Air con **Parking** 16 **Notes** ⊗ Civ Wed 100

Christopher Hotel

★★★ 77% HOTEL

☎ 01753 852359 📠 01753 830914
110 High St, Eton SL4 6AN
e-mail: reservations@thechristopher.co.uk
web: www.thechristopher.co.uk
dir: M4 junct 5 (Slough E), Colnbrook Datchet Eton (B470). At rdbt 2nd exit for Datchet. Right at mini rdbt (Eton), left into Eton Rd (3rd rdbt). Left, hotel on right

This hotel benefits from an ideal location in Eton, being only a short stroll across the pedestrian bridge from historic Windsor Castle and the many other attractions the town has to offer. The hotel has comfortable and smartly decorated accommodation, and a wide range of dishes is available in the informal bar and grill. A stylish room is available for private dining or for meetings.

Rooms 34 (23 annexe) (10 fmly) (22 GF) **S** £112-£141; **D** £146-£186* **Facilities** FTV Xmas New Year Wi-fi **Conf** Board 10 Thtr 30 Del from £178* **Parking** 19 **Notes** LB

WINTERINGHAM
Lincolnshire — Map 17 SE92

INSPECTORS' CHOICE

Winteringham Fields

RESTAURANT WITH ROOMS

☎ 01724 733096 📠 01724 733898
DN15 9ND
e-mail: reception@winteringhamfields.co.uk
dir: In village centre at x-rds

This highly regarded restaurant with rooms, located deep in the countryside in Winteringham village, is six miles west of the Humber Bridge. Public rooms and bedrooms, some of which are housed in renovated barns and cottages, are delightfully cosseting. Award-winning food is served in the restaurant.

Rooms 11 (7 annexe) (2 fmly)

WISBECH
Cambridgeshire — Map 12 TF40

Crown Lodge

THE INDEPENDENTS HOTEL ASSOCIATION

★★★ 83% HOTEL

☎ 01945 773391 & 772206 📠 01945 772668
Downham Rd, Outwell PE14 8SE
e-mail: office@thecrownlodgehotel.co.uk
web: www.thecrownlodgehotel.co.uk
dir: On A1122 approx 5m from Wisbech

A friendly, privately owned hotel situated in a peaceful location on the banks of Well Creek a short drive from Wisbech. The bedrooms are pleasantly decorated, have co-ordinated fabrics and modern facilities. The public areas are very stylish; they include a lounge bar, brasserie restaurant and a large seating area with plush leather sofas.

Rooms 10 (1 fmly) (10 GF) **S** £79; **D** £99 (incl. bkfst)* **Facilities** FTV Squash Wi-fi **Conf** Class 60 Board 40 Thtr 80 **Services** Air con **Parking** 55 **Notes** LB Closed 25-26 Dec & 1 Jan

Elme Hall

★★★ 70% HOTEL

☎ 01945 475566 📠 01945 475666
Elm High Rd PE14 0DQ
e-mail: elmehallhotel@btconnect.com
web: www.elmehall.co.uk
dir: A47 onto A1101 towards Wisbech. Hotel on right

An imposing, Georgian-style property conveniently situated on the outskirts of the town centre just off the A47. Individually decorated bedrooms are tastefully furnished with quality reproduction pieces and equipped to a high standard. Public rooms include a choice of attractive lounges, as well as two bars, meeting rooms and a banqueting suite.

Rooms 8 (3 fmly) **Facilities** FTV ♫ Wi-fi **Conf** Class 200 Board 20 Thtr 350 **Parking** 200 **Notes** Civ Wed 350

WITHAM
Essex — Map 7 TL81

Rivenhall

★★★ 80% HOTEL

☎ 01376 516969 📠 01376 513674
Rivenhall End CM8 3HB
e-mail: info@rivenhallhotel.com
web: www.rivenhallhotel.com
dir: M25 junct 28 towards Chelmsford on A12, take exit for Silver End/Great Braxted. At T-junct turn right, then 1st right, hotel directly ahead

This modern hotel is ideally situated just off the A12 between Chelmsford and Colchester. Bedrooms are pleasantly decorated and equipped with modern facilities. Public rooms include a large restaurant and a comfortable lounge bar; conference and leisure facilities are also available.

Rooms 55 (37 annexe) (6 fmly) (42 GF) **Facilities** STV FTV Gym Sauna Steam room Xmas New Year Wi-fi **Conf** Class 70 Board 50 Thtr 150 **Parking** 150 **Notes** ⊗ Closed 26 Dec RS Xmas Civ Wed 150

WITNEY Oxfordshire **Map 5 SP31**

Oxford Witney Four Pillars Hotel

★★★★ 72% HOTEL

☎ 0800 374692 & 01993 779777
📠 01993 703467
Ducklington Ln OX28 4TJ
e-mail: witney@four-pillars.co.uk
web: www.four-pillars.co.uk/oxfordwitney
dir: M40 junct 9, A34 to A40, exit A415 Witney/Abingdon. Hotel on left, 2nd exit for Witney

This attractive modern hotel is close to Oxford and Burford and offers spacious, well-equipped bedrooms. The cosy Spinners Bar has comfortable seating areas and the popular Weavers Restaurant offers a good range of dishes. Other amenities include extensive function and leisure facilities, complete with indoor swimming pool.

Rooms 87 (14 fmly) (21 GF) **S** £80-£150; **D** £80-£150* **Facilities** FTV Gym Steam room Sauna Xmas New Year Wi-fi **Conf** Class 76 Board 44 Thtr 150 Del from £120 to £179* **Parking** 170 **Notes** LB Civ Wed 150

WOBURN Bedfordshire **Map 11 SP93**

The Inn at Woburn

★★★ 80% HOTEL

☎ 01525 290441 📠 01525 290432
George St MK17 9PX
e-mail: enquiries@theinnatwoburn.co.uk
dir: M1 junct 13, left towards Woburn. In Woburn left at T-junct, hotel in village

This inn provides a high standard of accommodation. Bedrooms are divided between the original house, a modern extension and some stunning cottage suites. Public areas include the beamed, club-style Tavistock Bar, a range of meeting rooms and an attractive restaurant with interesting dishes on offer.

Rooms 55 (7 annexe) (4 fmly) (21 GF) **S** £118; **D** £138* **Facilities** FTV 54 Concessionary rate to access Woburn Safari Park & Woburn Abbey Xmas Wi-fi **Conf** Class 40 Board 40 Thtr 60 **Parking** 80 **Notes** LB Civ Wed 60

WOKING Surrey **Map 6 TQ05**

Holiday Inn Woking

★★★ 79% HOTEL

☎ 01483 221000 📠 01483 221021
Victoria St GU21 8EW
e-mail: reservations@wokingholiday-inn.com
web: www.hiwoking.co.uk
dir: A320 to Woking. After last rdbt to town centre take slip road off dual carriageway. Hotel on left

Situated in a convenient town centre location with parking facilities and only ten minutes from Woking main line train station. Public areas are stylish and comfortable; dining options include bar snacks, a substantial restaurant meal or choices from room service. Bedrooms and bathrooms are generally spacious and offer good levels of comfort.

Rooms 161 (30 fmly) (17 smoking) **Facilities** FTV Gym Wi-fi **Conf** Class 180 Board 40 Thtr 300 Del from £159 to £199 **Services** Lift Air con **Parking** 50 **Notes** Civ Wed 60

Premier Inn Woking

BUDGET HOTEL

☎ 0871 527 9182 📠 0871 527 9183
Bridge Barn Ln, Horsell GU21 6NL
dir: From A324 at rdbt into Parley Drive. Left at next rdbt into Goldsworth Rd

High quality, budget accommodation ideal for both families and business travellers. Spacious, en suite bedrooms feature tea and coffee making facilities, and Freeview TV in most hotels. Internet access and Wi-fi are available for a small fee. The adjacent family restaurant features a wide and varied menu. See also the Hotel Groups pages.

Rooms 34 **D** £61-£77*

WOKINGHAM Berkshire **Map 5 SU86**

Best Western Reading Moat House

★★★★ 78% HOTEL

☎ 0870 225 0601 📠 0118 935 1646
Mill Ln, Sindlesham RG41 5DF
e-mail: ops.reading@qmh-hotels.com
web: www.bestwestern.co.uk/readingmoathouse
dir: Towards Reading on A329(M), take 1st exit to Winnersh. Follow Lower Earley Way North. Hotel on left

Located just off the M4 on the outskirts of Reading, this smart, modern hotel has been sympathetically built around a 19th-century mill house. Bedrooms are stylish and have a contemporary feel to them. Spacious public areas include good conference rooms, a spacious bar and restaurant, as well as a business centre and a small fitness area.

Rooms 129 (12 fmly) (22 GF) **S** £59-£124; **D** £59-£124* **Facilities** STV Fishing Gym Xmas New Year Wi-fi **Conf** Class 40 Board 40 Thtr 80 Del from £99 to £159* **Services** Lift Air con **Parking** 250 **Notes** LB Civ Wed 80

W

WOLVERHAMPTON
West Midlands
Map 10 SO99

See also **Pattingham**

Novotel Wolverhampton

★★★ 78% HOTEL

☎ 01902 871100 📠 01902 870054
Union St WV1 3JN
e-mail: H1188@accor.com
web: www.novotel.com
dir: 6m from M6 junct 10. A454 to Wolverhampton. Hotel on main ring road

This large, modern, purpose-built hotel stands close to the town centre. It provides spacious, smartly presented and well-equipped bedrooms, all of which contain convertible bed settees for family occupancy. In addition to the open-plan lounge and bar area, there is an attractive brasserie-style restaurant, which overlooks an attractive patio garden.

Rooms 132 (9 fmly) (6 smoking) **S** £59-£145; **D** £59-£145* **Facilities** STV Wi-fi **Conf** Class 100 Board 80 Thtr 200 Del from £99 to £145* **Services** Lift **Parking** 120 **Notes** LB RS 23 Dec-4 Jan Civ Wed 200

Holiday Inn Wolverhampton

★★★ 71% HOTEL

☎ 01902 390004 📠 01902 714364
Dunstall Park WV6 0PE
e-mail: holidayinn@wolverhampton-racecourse.com
web: www.holidayinn.co.uk
dir: Off A449, 1.5m from city centre. Follow brown sign for Dunstall Park

Located at Wolverhampton Racecourse, which is a floodlit racecourse with afternoon and evening meets, this modern hotel provides a range of well-equipped bedrooms and an open-plan public area with bar, lounge and brasserie-style restaurant.

Rooms 54 (18 fmly) **Facilities** STV Wi-fi **Services** Lift **Parking** 1500

The Connaught Hotel

★★★ 70% HOTEL

☎ 01902 424433 📠 01902 710353
Tettenhall Rd WV1 4SW
e-mail: info@theconnaughthotel.net
dir: A41 junct 3, 1st exit at rdbt. Follow signs for Tettenhall. In Tettenhall Rd, hotel on left

This hotel is located a short walk from the city centre and the railway station, with convenient access to the motorway networks. Bedrooms provide modern comfort with a contemporary decor. Wi-fi is available throughout the hotel. Swags Restaurant and Terrace Bar offer a traditional and European cuisine. There are seven air-conditioned conference and banqueting suites.

Rooms 87 (8 fmly) (3 GF) **Facilities** STV FTV Xmas New Year Wi-fi **Conf** Class 300 Board 60 Thtr 500 **Services** Lift **Parking** 120 **Notes** ⊗ Civ Wed 500

Mercure Wolverhampton Goldthorn Hotel

★★★ 68% HOTEL

☎ 01902 429216 📠 01902 710419
126 Penn Rd WV3 0ER
e-mail: enquiries@hotels-wolverhampton.com
dir: A454 then A449 signed Kidderminster. Hotel 1m on right

This hotel is situated just on the outskirts of the old town and offers easy access to major motorway networks. Bedrooms are comfortable and well equipped, with free Wi-fi available throughout. Leisure facilities include a swimming pool, steam and sauna. There is also free on-site parking.

Rooms 74 (16 annexe) (12 fmly) (4 GF) **Facilities** FTV Gym Sauna Steam room Xmas New Year Wi-fi **Conf** Class 70 Board 40 Thtr 140 **Parking** 100 **Notes** Civ Wed 100

Premier Inn Wolverhampton City Centre

BUDGET HOTEL

☎ 0871 527 9186 📠 0871 527 9187
Broad Gauge Way WV10 0BA
dir: M6 junct 10, A454 signed Wolverhampton for approx 2m. Right into Neachalls Ln (signed Wednesfield). 0.75m. At rdbt 1st exit onto A4124 (Wednesfield Way). 1st exit at next rdbt. 2nd exit at 3rd rdbt. At 2nd lights left into Sun St. 1st right, hotel at end of road

High quality, budget accommodation ideal for both families and business travellers. Spacious, en suite bedrooms feature tea and coffee making facilities, and Freeview TV in most hotels. Internet access and Wi-fi are available for a small fee. The adjacent family restaurant features a wide and varied menu. See also the Hotel Groups pages.

Rooms 88 **D** £52-£60*

Premier Inn Wolverhampton North

BUDGET HOTEL

☎ 0871 527 9184 📠 0871 527 9185
Greenfield Ln, Stafford Rd WV10 6TA
dir: M54 junct 2. Hotel at lights in approx 100yds

Rooms 77 **D** £52-£60*

WOMBWELL
South Yorkshire
Map 16 SE40

Premier Inn Barnsley (Dearne Valley)

BUDGET HOTEL

☎ 0871 527 8050 📠 0871 527 8051
Meadow Gate, Dearne Valley S73 0UN
dir: M1 junct 36 E'bound, A6195 towards Doncaster (5m). Hotel at rdbt adjacent to Meadows Brewers Fayre

High quality, budget accommodation ideal for both families and business travellers. Spacious, en suite bedrooms feature tea and coffee making facilities, and Freeview TV in most hotels. Internet access and Wi-fi are available for a small fee. The adjacent family restaurant features a wide and varied menu. See also the Hotel Groups pages.

Rooms 41 **D** £50-£58*

W

WOOBURN COMMON
Buckinghamshire — Map 6 SU98

Chequers Inn

★★★ 78% ❀ HOTEL

☎ 01628 529575 📠 01628 850124
Kiln Ln, Wooburn HP10 0JQ
e-mail: info@chequers-inn.com
web: www.chequers-inn.com
dir: M40 junct 2, A40 through Beaconsfield Old Town towards High Wycombe. 2m from town left into Broad Ln. Inn 2.5m

This 17th-century inn enjoys a peaceful, rural location beside the common. Bedrooms feature stripped-pine furniture, co-ordinated fabrics and an excellent range of extra facilities. The bar, with its massive oak post, beams and flagstone floor, and the restaurant, which overlooks a pretty patio, are very much focal points here.

Rooms 17 (8 GF) **Facilities** FTV Wi-fi **Conf** Class 30 Board 20 Thtr 50 Del from £155* **Parking** 60 **Notes** ⊗

WOODALL MOTORWAY SERVICE AREA (M1)
South Yorkshire — Map 16 SK48

Days Inn Sheffield - M1

BUDGET HOTEL

☎ 0114 248 7992 📠 0114 248 5634
Woodall Service Area S26 7XR
e-mail: woodall.hotel@welcomebreak.co.uk
web: www.welcomebreak.co.uk
dir: M1 S'bound between juncts 30 & 31, at Woodall Services,

This modern building offers accommodation in smart, spacious and well-equipped bedrooms, suitable for families and business travellers, and all with en suite bathrooms. Continental breakfast is available and other refreshments may be taken at the nearby family restaurant. See also the Hotel Groups pages.

Rooms 38 (32 fmly) (16 GF) (6 smoking) **S** £39.95-£59.95; **D** £49.95-£69.95 **Conf** Board 10

WOODBRIDGE
Suffolk — Map 13 TM24

Seckford Hall

★★★★ 76% ❀❀ HOTEL

☎ 01394 385678 📠 01394 380610
IP13 6NU
e-mail: reception@seckford.co.uk
web: www.seckford.co.uk
dir: Signed on A12. (NB do not follow signs for town centre)

An elegant Tudor manor house set amid landscaped grounds just off the A12. It is reputed that Queen Elizabeth I visited this property, and it retains much of its original character. Public rooms include a superb panelled lounge, a cosy bar and an intimate restaurant. The spacious bedrooms are attractively decorated, tastefully furnished and thoughtfully equipped.

Rooms 32 (10 annexe) (4 fmly) (7 GF) **S** £95; **D** £145-£220* **Facilities** Putt green Fishing Gym Beauty salon New Year Wi-fi **Conf** Class 46 Board 40 Thtr 100 Del from £170 to £190* **Parking** 100 **Notes** LB Closed 25 Dec Civ Wed 120

The Crown at Woodbridge

★★★ 86% ❀❀ HOTEL

☎ 01394 384242 📠 01394 387192
2 Thoro'fare IP12 1AD
e-mail: info@thecrownatwoodbridge.co.uk
dir: A12 follow signs for Woodbridge onto B1438. 1.25m from rdbt left into Quay St. Hotel on right approx 100yds

This 17th-century property offers contemporary-style accommodation throughout. The open-plan public areas are tastefully appointed and include a large lounge bar, a restaurant and a private dining room. The stylish bedrooms are tastefully appointed and equipped with modern facilities.

Rooms 10 (2 fmly) **Facilities** STV Wi-fi **Parking** 40 **Notes** ⊗

Best Western Ufford Park Hotel Golf & Spa

★★★ 82% HOTEL

☎ 01394 383555 📠 0844 4773727
Yarmouth Rd, Ufford IP12 1QW
e-mail: mail@uffordpark.co.uk
web: www.uffordpark.co.uk
dir: A12 N to A1152, in Melton left at lights, follow B1438, hotel 1m on right

A modern hotel set in open countryside boasting superb leisure facilities including a challenging golf course. The spacious public rooms provide a wide choice of areas in which to relax and include a busy lounge bar, a carvery restaurant and the Vista Restaurant. Bedrooms are smartly appointed and pleasantly decorated, and each is thoughtfully equipped; many overlook the golf course.

Rooms 87 (20 fmly) (32 GF) **Facilities** Spa FTV supervised 18 Putt green Fishing Gym Golf Academy with PGA tuition 2 storey floodlit driving range Dance Studio Xmas New Year Wi-fi **Conf** Class 120 Board 120 Thtr 300 Del from £99 to £119* **Services** Lift **Parking** 250 **Notes** Civ Wed 120

WOODBURY Devon Map 3 SY08

Woodbury Park Hotel and Golf Club

★★★★ 74% HOTEL

☎ 01395 233382 📠 01395 234701
Woodbury Castle EX5 1JJ
e-mail: enquiries@woodburypark.co.uk
web: www.woodburypark.co.uk
dir: M5 junct 30, A376 then A3052 towards Sidmouth, onto B3180, hotel signed

Situated in 500 acres of beautiful and unspoilt countryside, yet within easy reach of Exeter and the M5, this hotel offers smart, well-equipped and immaculately presented accommodation together with a host of sporting and banqueting facilities. There is a choice of golf courses, a Bodyzone beauty centre and enjoyable dining in the Atrium Restaurant.

Rooms 60 (4 annexe) (4 fmly) (28 GF) **S** £85-£110; **D** £95-£140 (incl. bkfst)* **Facilities** Spa STV FTV 27 Putt green Fishing Gym Squash Beauty salon Football pitch Driving range Fitness Studio Xmas New Year Wi-fi **Conf** Class 100 Board 40 Thtr 250 **Services** Lift **Parking** 400 **Notes** LB Civ Wed 150

WOODFORD BRIDGE Greater London Map 6 TQ49

Menzies Prince Regent

MenziesHotels

★★★★ 72% HOTEL

☎ 020 8505 9966 📠 020 8506 0807
Manor Rd IG8 8AE
e-mail: princeregent@menzieshotels.co.uk
web: www.menzieshotels.co.uk
dir: From A113 (Chigwell Rd) S of Chigwell into B173 (Manor Rd)

Situated on the edge of Woodford Bridge and Chigwell, this hotel with delightful rear gardens, offers easy access into London as well as the M11 and M25. There is a good range of spacious, well-equipped bedrooms. Extensive conference and banqueting facilities are particularly well appointed, and are very suitable for weddings and for business events.

Rooms 61 (4 fmly) (15 GF) (10 smoking) **Facilities** STV Xmas New Year Wi-fi **Conf** Class 150 Board 80 Thtr 350 **Services** Lift **Parking** 225 **Notes** Civ Wed 350

WOODHALL SPA Lincolnshire Map 17 TF16

Petwood

★★★ 74% HOTEL

☎ 01526 352411 📠 01526 353473
Stixwould Rd LN10 6QG
e-mail: reception@petwood.co.uk
web: www.petwood.co.uk
dir: From Sleaford take A153 (signed Skegness). At Tattershall turn left on B1192. Hotel is signed from village

This lovely Edwardian house, set in 30 acres of gardens and woodlands, is adjacent to Woodhall Golf Course. Built in 1905, the house was used by 617 Squadron, the famous Dambusters, as an officers' mess during World War II. Bedrooms and public areas are spacious and comfortable, and retain many original features. Weddings and conferences are well catered for in modern facilities.

Rooms 53 (3 GF) **S** fr £90; **D** fr £110 (incl. bkfst)* **Facilities** Putt green Xmas New Year Wi-fi **Conf** Class 100 Board 50 Thtr 250 **Services** Lift **Parking** 140 **Notes** LB Civ Wed 200

Golf Hotel

★★★ 66% HOTEL

☎ 01526 353535 📠 01526 353096
The Broadway LN10 6SG
e-mail: reception@thegolf-hotel.com
web: www.thegolf-hotel.com
dir: From Lincoln take B1189 to Metheringham onto B1191 towards Woodhall Spa. Hotel on left in approx 500yds from rdbt

Located near the centre of the village, this traditional hotel is ideally situated to explore the Lincolnshire countryside and coast. The adjacent golf course makes this a popular venue for golfers, and the hotel's hydrotherapy suite uses the original spa water supplies. Bedrooms vary in size.

Rooms 50 (2 fmly) (8 GF) (3 smoking) **Facilities** Spa FTV Xmas New Year Wi-fi **Conf** Class 50 Board 50 Thtr 150 Del from £129 to £175 **Services** Lift **Parking** 100 **Notes** Civ Wed 150

WOODSTOCK Oxfordshire Map 11 SP41

The Feathers Hotel

★★★★ 79% TOWN HOUSE HOTEL

☎ 01993 812291 📠 01993 813158
Market St OX20 1SX
e-mail: enquiries@feathers.co.uk
dir: From A44 (Oxford to Woodstock), 1st left after lights. Hotel on left

This intimate and unique hotel enjoys a town centre location with easy access to nearby Blenheim Palace. Public areas are elegant and full of traditional character from the cosy drawing room to the atmospheric restaurant. Individually styled bedrooms are appointed to a high standard and are furnished with attractive period and reproduction furniture.

Rooms 21 (5 annexe) (4 fmly) (2 GF) **S** £104-£189; **D** £104-£349 (incl. bkfst)* **Facilities** FTV Xmas New Year Wi-fi **Conf** Class 18 Board 20 Thtr 40 Del from £160 to £250* **Notes** LB

Macdonald Bear

★★★★ 76% HOTEL

☎ 0844 879 9143 📠 01993 813380
Park St OX20 1SZ
e-mail: gm.bear@macdonaldhotels.co.uk
web: www.macdonaldhotels.co.uk
dir: M40 junct 9 follow signs for Oxford & Blenheim Palace. A44 to town centre, hotel on left

With its ivy-clad façade, oak beams and open fireplaces, this 13th-century coaching inn exudes charm and cosiness. The bedrooms are decorated in a modern style that remains in keeping with the historic character of the building. Public rooms include a variety of function rooms, an intimate bar area and an attractive restaurant where attentive service and good food are offered.

Rooms 54 (18 annexe) (1 fmly) (8 GF) **Facilities** STV Xmas New Year Wi-fi **Conf** Class 12 Board 24 Thtr 40 **Parking** 40

WOODSTOCK *continued*

Kings Arms

★★★ 78% HOTEL

☎ 01993 813636 01993 813737
19 Market St OX20 1SU
e-mail: stay@kingshotelwoodstock.co.uk
web: www.kings-hotel-woodstock.co.uk
dir: In town centre, on corner of Market St & A44

This appealing and contemporary hotel is situated in the centre of town just a short walk from Blenheim Palace. Public areas include an attractive bistro-style restaurant and a smart bar. Bedrooms and bathrooms are comfortably furnished and well equipped, and appointed to a high standard.

Rooms 15 **S** £75-£100; **D** £140-£150 (incl. bkfst)* **Facilities** FTV Xmas New Year Wi-fi **Notes** LB No children 12yrs

WOODY BAY Map 3 SS64
Devon

Woody Bay Hotel

★★ 78% HOTEL

☎ 01598 763264 & 763563
EX31 4QX
e-mail: info@woodybayhotel.co.uk
dir: Signed off A39 between Blackmoor Gate & Lynton

Popular with walkers, this Victorian country style hotel is perfectly situated to enjoy sweeping views over Woody Bay. Bedrooms vary in style and size, but all boast truly magnificent views across dense woodland to the sea beyond. The same views can be enjoyed from the restaurant where local fish features prominently on the imaginative menus.

Rooms 7 (1 fmly) **Parking** 7 **Notes** No children 5yrs Closed Dec-Jan RS Nov & Feb

WOOKEY HOLE Map 4 ST54
Somerset

Wookey Hole Hotel

U

☎ 01749 672243
BA5 1BB
e-mail: witch@wookey.co.uk

Currently the rating for this establishment is not confirmed. This may be due to a change of ownership or because it has only recently joined the AA rating scheme. For further details please see the AA website: theAA.com

Rooms 58 (37 fmly) (27 GF) **D** £35-£85* **Facilities** FTV 9-hole adventure golf course Wi-fi **Services** Lift **Parking** 800 **Notes** LB

WOOLACOMBE Map 3 SS44
Devon

The Woolacombe Bay Hotel

★★★★ 74% HOTEL

☎ 01271 870388 01271 870613
South St EX34 7BN
e-mail: enquiries@woolacombebayhotel.co.uk
web: www.woolacombebayhotel.com
dir: A361 onto B3343 to Woolacombe. Hotel in centre

This family-friendly hotel is adjacent to the beach and the village centre, and has a welcoming environment. The public areas are spacious and comfortable, and many of the well-equipped bedrooms have balconies with splendid views over the bay. In addition to the elegant surroundings of Doyle's Restaurant, The Bay Brasserie is available for an informal alternative. Extensive leisure facilities also provided.

Rooms 68 (26 fmly) (2 GF) **S** £117-£166.50; **D** £234-£333 (incl. bkfst & dinner)* **Facilities** Spa FTV 9 Gym Squash Paddling pool Table tennis Snooker Steam room Outdoor short mat bowls Xmas New Year Wi-fi Child facilities **Conf** Class 150 Board 150 Thtr 200 **Services** Lift **Parking** 150 **Notes** Closed 2 Jan-5 Feb Civ Wed 150

Watersmeet Hotel

★★★ 87% HOTEL

☎ 01271 870333 01271 870890
Mortehoe EX34 7EB
e-mail: info@watersmeethotel.co.uk
web: www.watersmeethotel.co.uk
dir: Follow B3343 into Woolacombe, turn right onto esplanade, hotel 0.75m on left

With magnificent views, and steps leading directly to the beach, this popular hotel offers guests attentive service and a relaxing atmosphere. Bedrooms benefit from the wonderful sea views and some have private balconies. Diners in the attractive tiered restaurant can admire the beautiful sunsets while enjoying an innovative range of dishes offered on the fixed-price menu. Both indoor and outdoor pools are available.

Rooms 25 (4 fmly) (3 GF) **Facilities** FTV Steam room Xmas New Year Wi-fi **Conf** Board 20 Thtr 20 **Services** Lift **Parking** 38 **Notes** Civ Wed 60

WOOTTON BASSETT Map 5 SU08
Wiltshire

The Wiltshire

★★★ 78% HOTEL

☎ 01793 849999 01793 849988
SN4 7PB
e-mail: reception@the-wiltshire.co.uk
dir: M4 junct 16 follow Wootton Bassett signs. Hotel 1m S of Wootton Bassett on left of A3102 towards Lyneham

Surrounded by 220 acres of rolling countryside, this hotel, with easy access to the M4, offers golf enthusiasts two splendid courses - the 18-hole Lakes Course and the 9-hole Garden Course. The hotel has contemporary bedrooms with Freeview and free Wi-fi, and purpose-designed disabled access rooms are available. The air-conditioned Pavilion Restaurant & Lounge open onto a large patio overlooking the 18th green, and there are splendid leisure facilities including a techno-gym, 18-metre swimming pool, sauna and steam room.

Rooms 58 (29 GF) **Facilities** FTV 27 Putt green Gym Sauna Steam room New Year Wi-fi **Conf** Class 120 Board 30 Thtr 250 **Services** Lift **Parking** 250 **Notes** Closed 24-25 Dec Civ Wed 140

WORCESTER Map 10 SO85
Worcestershire

Pear Tree Inn & Country Hotel

★★★ 79% HOTEL

☎ 01905 756565 01905 756777
Smite WR3 8SY
e-mail: info@thepeartree.co.uk
dir: M5 junct 6 take A4538 towards Droitwich. In 200yds 3rd exit of Island (Brown Pear Tree sign), over canal bridge, up hill, hotel on left

Located close to M5 in pretty landscaped grounds, this traditional English inn and country hotel has spacious, air-conditioned bedrooms with attractive colour schemes and good facilities. Four suites are available. Guests can enjoy good food and a drink in relaxed surroundings; there is an excellent range of conference and function rooms.

Rooms 24 (2 fmly) (12 GF) **Facilities** Fishing Wi-fi **Conf** Class 150 Board 40 Thtr 250 **Services** Lift Air con **Parking** 200 **Notes** Closed 25-26 Dec RS 1 Jan Civ Wed 120

W

Premier Inn Worcester

BUDGET HOTEL

☎ 0871 527 9188 📠 0871 527 9189
Wainwright Way, Warndon WR4 9FA
dir: M5 junct 6. At entrance of Warndon commercial development area

High quality, budget accommodation ideal for both families and business travellers. Spacious, en suite bedrooms feature tea and coffee making facilities, and Freeview TV in most hotels. Internet access and Wi-fi are available for a small fee. The adjacent family restaurant features a wide and varied menu. See also the Hotel Groups pages.

Rooms 60 **D** £55-£62*

WORKINGTON Map 18 NY02
Cumbria

Washington Central Hotel

★★★★ 74% HOTEL

☎ 01900 65772 📠 01900 68770
Washington St CA14 3AY
e-mail: kawildwchotel@aol.com
web: www.washingtoncentralhotelworkington.com
dir: M6 junct 40, A66 to Workington. Left at lights, hotel on right

Enjoying a prominent town centre location, this modern hotel boasts memorably hospitable staff. The well-maintained and comfortable bedrooms are equipped with a range of thoughtful extras. Public areas include numerous lounges, a spacious bar, Caesars leisure club, a smart restaurant and a popular coffee shop. The comprehensive conference facilities are ideal for meetings and weddings.

Rooms 46 (4 fmly) **S** £95-£115; **D** £140-£220 (incl. bkfst)* **Facilities** FTV supervised Gym Mountain bikes Sauna Steam room Sunbed New Year Wi-fi **Conf** Class 200 Board 100 Thtr 300 **Services** Lift **Parking** 25 **Notes** LB Civ Wed 300

Hunday Manor Country House

★★★ 79% COUNTRY HOUSE HOTEL

☎ 01900 61798 📠 01900 601202
Hunday, Winscales CA14 4JF
e-mail: info@hunday-manor-hotel.co.uk
dir: A66 onto A595 towards Whitehaven, hotel 3m on right, signed

Delightfully situated and enjoying distant views of the Solway Firth, this charming hotel has well-furnished rooms with lots of extras. The open-plan bar and foyer lounge boast welcoming open fires, and the attractive restaurant overlooks the woodland gardens. The provision of a function suite makes the hotel an excellent wedding venue.

Rooms 24 (2 fmly) **S** £69-£99; **D** £99-£139 (incl. bkfst)* **Facilities** FTV Wi-fi **Conf** Class 180 Board 40 Thtr 200 **Parking** 50 **Notes** Civ Wed 250

WORKSOP Map 16 SK57
Nottinghamshire

Best Western Lion

★★★ 80% HOTEL

☎ 01909 477925 📠 01909 479038
112 Bridge St S80 1HT
e-mail: reception@thelionworksop.co.uk
web: www.thelionworksop.co.uk
dir: A57 to town centre, turn right at Sainsburys, follow to Norfolk Arms, turn left

This former coaching inn lies on the edge of the main shopping precinct, with a car park to the rear. It has been extended to offer modern accommodation that includes excellent executive rooms. A wide range of interesting dishes is offered in both the restaurant and bar.

Rooms 46 (3 fmly) (7 GF) **S** £50-£80; **D** £54-£89* **Facilities** STV FTV Xmas New Year Wi-fi **Conf** Class 80 Board 70 Thtr 160 Del from £90 to £145* **Services** Lift **Parking** 50 **Notes** LB Civ Wed 150

Clumber Park

★★★ 78% HOTEL

☎ 01623 835333 📠 01623 835525
Clumber Park S80 3PA
e-mail: reservations@clumberparkhotel.com
dir: M1 junct 30/31 follow signs to A57 & A1. From A1 take A614 towards Nottingham. Hotel 2m on left

Beside the A614, this hotel is situated in open countryside, edging on to Sherwood Forest and Clumber Park. Bedrooms are comfortably furnished and well equipped and public areas include a choice of formal and informal eating options. Dukes Tavern is lively and casual, while the restaurant offers a more traditional style of service.

Rooms 73 (5 fmly) (27 GF) **S** £69-£140; **D** £79-£150 (incl. bkfst)* **Facilities** Spa FTV Gym Sauna Steam room Free use of bikes Xmas New Year Wi-fi **Conf** Class 90 Board 40 Thtr 250 Del from £105 to £155* **Parking** 100 **Notes** LB Civ Wed 160

WORSLEY Map 15 SD70
Greater Manchester

Novotel Manchester West

★★★ 72% HOTEL

☎ 0161 799 3535 📠 0161 703 8207
Worsley Brow M28 2YA
e-mail: H0907@accor.com
web: www.novotel.com
dir: Adjacent to M60 junct 13

Well placed for access to the Peak District and the Lake District, as well as Manchester, this modern hotel successfully caters for both families and business guests. The spacious bedrooms have sofa beds and a large work area; the hotel has an outdoor swimming pool, children's play area and secure parking.

Rooms 119 (10 fmly) (41 GF) **S** £60-£130; **D** £60-£130* **Facilities** STV Gym Xmas New Year Wi-fi **Conf** Class 140 Board 25 Thtr 200 Del from £101 to £135* **Services** Lift **Parking** 95 **Notes** Civ Wed 140

WORTHING Map 6 TQ10
West Sussex

Ardington Hotel

★★★ 80% HOTEL

☎ 01903 230451 📠 01903 526526
Steyne Gardens BN11 3DZ
e-mail: reservations@ardingtonhotel.co.uk
web: www.ardingtonhotel.co.uk
dir: A27 to Lancing, then to seafront. Follow signs for Worthing. Left at church into Steyne Gardens

Overlooking Steyne Gardens adjacent to the seafront, this popular hotel offers well-appointed bedrooms with a good range of facilities. There's a stylishly modern lounge/bar with ample seating, where a light menu is available throughout the day. The popular restaurant offers local seafood and a choice of modern dishes. Wi-fi is available in lounge/bar.

Rooms 45 (4 fmly) (12 GF) **Facilities** STV FTV Wi-fi **Conf** Class 60 Board 35 Thtr 140 **Notes** LB Closed 25 Dec-4 Jan

WORTHING *continued*

Findon Manor Hotel

★★★ 70% HOTEL

☎ 01903 872733 🖷 01903 877473
High St, Findon BN14 0TA
e-mail: hotel@findonmanor.com
dir: 500yds off A24 between Worthing & Horsham. At sign for Findon follow signs to Findon Manor into village

Located in the centre of the village, Findon Manor was built as a rectory and has a beamed lounge which doubles as the reception area. Bedrooms, several with four-poster beds, are attractively decorated in a traditional style. The cosy bar offers a very good range of bar food, and is popular with locals, while the restaurant overlooks the garden and offers modern and traditional dishes.

Rooms 11 (2 GF) **S** £49.50-£130; **D** £49.50-£150 (incl. bkfst)* **Facilities** Boule Xmas New Year Wi-fi **Conf** Class 18 Board 25 Thtr 50 **Parking** 25 **Notes** LB RS 24-30 Dec Civ Wed 60

Kingsway

★★ 71% HOTEL

☎ 01903 237542 🖷 01903 204173
Marine Pde BN11 3QQ
e-mail: kingsway-hotel@btconnect.com
dir: A27 to Worthing seafront follow signs 'Hotel West'. Hotel 0.75m west of pier

Ideally located on the seafront and close to the town centre, this family-owned property extends a warm welcome to guests. Bedrooms vary in size, and some are very spacious with impressive sea views. Comfortable public areas include two modern lounges, a bright, stylish bar and well appointed restaurant.

Rooms 36 (7 annexe) (4 fmly) (3 GF) **Facilities** FTV Xmas Wi-fi **Conf** Class 25 Board 25 Thtr 50 **Services** Lift **Parking** 9

WOTTON-UNDER-EDGE Map 4 ST79
Gloucestershire

Tortworth Court Four Pillars

★★★★ 74% HOTEL

☎ 0800 374 692 & 01454 263000
🖷 01454 263001
Tortworth GL12 8HH
e-mail: tortworth@four-pillars.co.uk
web: www.four-pillars.co.uk/tortworth
dir: M5 junct 14, B4509 towards Wotton. 1st right into Tortworth Rd next right, hotel 0.5m on right

Set within 30 acres of parkland, this Gothic mansion displays original features cleverly combined with contemporary additions. Elegant public rooms include a choice of dining options, one housed within the library, another in the atrium and the third in the orangery. Bedrooms are well equipped, and additional facilities include a host of conference rooms and a leisure centre.

Rooms 190 (74 GF) **S** £95-£120; **D** £115-£140 (incl. bkfst)* **Facilities** Spa FTV Gym Beauty suite Steam room Sauna Xmas New Year Wi-fi **Conf** Class 200 Board 80 Thtr 400 Del from £145 to £189* **Services** Lift **Parking** 350 **Notes** Civ Wed 400

The Park Hotel

★★ 71% HOTEL

☎ 01454 260550 🖷 01454 269255
Whitfield GL12 8DR
e-mail: info@parkhotelfalfield.co.uk
web: www.parkhotelfalfield.co.uk
dir: M5 junct 14, A38, through Falfield. Hotel on left in 0.5m

Not far from the A38 and with easy access to the M5, this family-run hotel offers friendly service. Bedrooms, which vary in size, are located either in the main house or in the cottage annexe, just yards away. There is an informal bar where drinks and bar meals are served, and dinner, featuring homemade dishes, is available in the pleasant restaurant. The garden may be enjoyed during the warmer weather.

Rooms 18 (7 annexe) (2 fmly) (3 GF) **Facilities** Xmas New Year Wi-fi **Conf** Class 60 Board 40 Thtr 80 **Parking** 80 **Notes** Civ Wed 118

WROTHAM Map 6 TQ65
Kent

Holiday Inn Maidstone Sevenoaks

★★★ 74% HOTEL

☎ 0871 942 9054 & 01732 781510
🖷 01732 885850
London Rd, Wrotham Heath TN15 7RS
e-mail: reservations-maidstone@ihg.com
web: www.holidayinn.co.uk
dir: M26 junct 2A onto A20. Hotel on left

This purpose-built hotel is located within easy reach of the world famous Brands Hatch racing circuit as well as historic Leeds and Hever castles. Bedrooms are very spacious, comfortably furnished with many accessories. A fully equipped leisure centre, bar, restaurant and lounges are also available, as well as a range of modern meeting rooms.

Rooms 105 (16 fmly) (6 GF) (10 smoking) **Facilities** STV supervised Gym Steam room Sauna New Year Wi-fi **Conf** Class 35 Board 30 Thtr 70 **Services** Air con **Parking** 120 **Notes** Civ Wed 60

Premier Inn Sevenoaks/ Maidstone

BUDGET HOTEL

☎ 0871 527 8962 🖷 0871 527 8963
London Rd, Wrotham Heath TN15 7RX
dir: M26 junct 2a, A20 S. Left at lights onto A20 towards West Malling. Hotel on right

High quality, budget accommodation ideal for both families and business travellers. Spacious, en suite bedrooms feature tea and coffee making facilities, and Freeview TV in most hotels. Internet access and Wi-fi are available for a small fee. The adjacent family restaurant features a wide and varied menu. See also the Hotel Groups pages.

Rooms 40 **D** £56-£63*

WROXALL Warwickshire **Map 10 SP27**

Wroxall Abbey Estate

★★★ 76% HOTEL

☎ 01926 484470 & 486730 📠 01926 485206
Birmingham Rd CV35 7NB
e-mail: info@wroxall.com
dir: Between Solihull & Warwick on A4141

Situated in 27 acres of open parkland, yet only 10 miles from the NEC and Birmingham International Airport, this hotel is a magnificent Victorian mansion. Some of the individually designed bedrooms have traditional decor but there are some modern loft rooms as well; some rooms have four-posters. Sonnets Restaurant, with its impressive fireplace and oak panelling, makes the ideal setting for fine dining.

Rooms 70 (22 annexe) (10 GF) **S** £89-£99; **D** £99-£399* **Facilities** Spa STV Fishing Gym Ten-pin bowling Walking & jogging trail Xmas New Year Wi-fi **Conf** Class 80 Board 60 Thtr 160 Del from £149 to £169* **Services** Lift **Parking** 200 **Notes** No children 12yrs Civ Wed 200

WROXHAM Norfolk **Map 13 TG31**

Hotel Wroxham

★★ 71% HOTEL

☎ 01603 782061 📠 01603 784279
The Bridge NR12 8AJ
e-mail: reservations@hotelwroxham.co.uk
web: www.arlingtonhotelgroup.co.uk
dir: From Norwich take A1151 signed Wroxham & The Broads for approx 7m. Over bridge at Wroxham, 1st right, sharp right again. Hotel car park on right

Perfectly placed for touring the Norfolk Broads, this hotel is in the heart of the bustling town centre. The bedrooms are pleasantly decorated and well equipped; some rooms have balconies with lovely views of the busy waterways. The open-plan public rooms include the lively riverside bar, lounge, large sun terrace and restaurant.

Rooms 18 (2 fmly) **S** £55-£69.50; **D** £88.50-£98.50 (incl. bkfst)* **Facilities** STV FTV Fishing Boating facilities (by arrangement) Wi-fi **Conf** Class 50 Board 20 Thtr 200 **Parking** 45 **Notes** LB Civ Wed 40

WYBOSTON Bedfordshire **Map 12 TL15**

Wyboston Lakes Hotel

★★★ 73% HOTEL

☎ 01480 212625 & 479300 📠 01480 223000
Wyboston Lakes, Great North Rd MK44 3BA
e-mail: reservations@wybostonlakes.co.uk
dir: From A1, A428 follow brown Cambridge signs. Wyboston Lakes & hotel on right, marked by flags

Ideally located adjacent to the A1 on the Cambridgeshire/Bedfordshire border, Wyboston Lakes is easily accessible. The hotel is located within an extensive conference and leisure complex that includes a golf course. Bedrooms are tastefully decorated in a contemporary style, and offer a range of amenities to suit both the business and leisure traveller. The dining room overlooks the idyllic lake.

Rooms 103 (39 annexe) (18 fmly) (50 GF) **Facilities** FTV 18 Putt green Fishing Gym Golf driving range Wi-fi **Conf** Class 56 Board 40 Thtr 130 **Services** Lift **Parking** 200 **Notes** No children Closed 24 Dec-3 Jan Civ Wed 100

YARM North Yorkshire **Map 19 NZ41**

INSPECTORS' CHOICE

Judges Country House Hotel

★★★ HOTEL

☎ 01642 789000 📠 01642 782878
Kirklevington Hall TS15 9LW
e-mail: enquiries@judgeshotel.co.uk
web: www.judgeshotel.co.uk
dir: 1.5m from A19. At A67 junct, follow Yarm road, hotel on left

Formerly a lodging for local circuit judges, this gracious mansion lies in landscaped grounds through which a stream runs. Stylish bedrooms are individually decorated and come with 101 extras; four-poster bedrooms and suites are available. The Conservatory restaurant serves award-winning cuisine, and private dining for a small number of guests is available in the wine cellar. Judges is a popular wedding venue. The genuinely caring and attentive service from the staff is truly memorable.

Rooms 21 (3 fmly) (5 GF) **S** £95-£180; **D** £130-£220 (incl. bkfst)* **Facilities** STV FTV Gym Mountain bikes Nature trails Beauty treatment room Xmas New Year Wi-fi **Conf** Class 120 Board 80 Thtr 200 Del from £210 to £240* **Parking** 102 **Notes** LB Civ Wed 200

Y

YARMOUTH Map 5 SZ38
Isle of Wight

INSPECTORS' CHOICE

George Hotel
★★★ ◎◎ HOTEL

☎ 01983 760331 📠 01983 760425
Quay St PO41 0PE
e-mail: res@thegeorge.co.uk
dir: Between castle & pier

This delightful 17th-century hotel enjoys a wonderful location at the water's edge, adjacent to the castle and the quay. Public areas include a bright brasserie where organic and local produce are utilised, a cosy bar and an inviting lounge. Individually styled bedrooms, with many thoughtful extras, are beautifully appointed; some benefit from spacious balconies. The hotel's motor yacht is available for guests to hire.

Rooms 19 (1 GF) **S** £137.50; **D** £190-£287 (incl. bkfst)* **Facilities** STV Sailing from Yarmouth Mountain biking Xmas New Year Wi-fi **Conf** Class 20 Board 20 Thtr 40 Del from £185* **Notes** LB ⊗ No children 10yrs

YATELEY Map 5 SU86
Hampshire

Casa dei Cesari Restaurant & Hotel
★★★ 73% HOTEL

☎ 01252 873275 📠 01252 870614
Handford Ln GU46 6BT
e-mail: reservations@casadeicesari.co.uk
dir: M3 junct 4a, follow signs for town centre. Hotel signed

This delightful hotel where a warm welcome is guaranteed is ideally located for transport networks. It boasts rooms with quality and comfort, and the Italian-themed restaurant, which is very popular locally, serves an extensive traditional menu.

Rooms 63 (2 fmly) (15 GF) (33 smoking) **Facilities** Xmas New Year Wi-fi **Conf** Class 60 Board 60 Thtr 150 **Services** Lift **Parking** 80 **Notes** ⊗ Civ Wed 150

YATTON Map 4 ST46
Somerset

Bridge Inn
BUDGET HOTEL

OldEnglish

☎ 01934 839100 & 839101 📠 01934 839149
North End Rd BS49 4AU
e-mail: bridge.yatton@newbridgeinns.co.uk
web: www.oldenglish.co.uk
dir: M5 junct 20, take B3133 to Yatton. Take 1st left at rdbt, 1st left at 2nd rdbt. Hotel 2.5m on right

This establishment offers spacious, well-equipped bedrooms, and the bar/restaurant serves a variety of dishes throughout the day in a relaxed and informal environment. Breakfast is a self-service buffet plus a full English breakfast served at the table. There is also a play zone area for children.

Rooms 41 (4 fmly) (20 GF) **Conf** Class 30 Board 50 Thtr 100

YAXLEY Map 13 TM17
Suffolk

The Auberge
◎◎ RESTAURANT WITH ROOMS

☎ 01379 783604 📠 01379 788486
Ipswich Rd IP23 8BZ
e-mail: aubmail@the-auberge.co.uk
web: www.the-auberge.co.uk
dir: On A140 between Norwich & Ipswich at B1117 x-rds with Eye & Thornham Parva

A warm welcome awaits at this charming 15th-century property, which has been lovingly converted by the present owners into a smart restaurant with rooms. The public areas have a wealth of character, such as exposed brickwork and beams. The spacious bedrooms are tastefully appointed and have many thoughtful touches.

Rooms 11 (11 annexe) (2 fmly)

YELVERTON Map 3 SX56
Devon

Moorland Garden Hotel
★★★ 77% HOTEL

☎ 01822 852245 📠 01822 855004
PL20 6DA
e-mail: moorland.links@forestdale.com
web: www.moorlandlinkshotel.co.uk
dir: A38 from Exeter to Plymouth, then A386 towards Tavistock. 5m onto open moorland, hotel 1m on left

Set in nine acres in the Dartmoor National Park, this hotel offers spectacular views from many of the rooms across open moorland and the Tamar Valley. Bedrooms are well equipped and comfortably furnished, and some rooms have open balconies. The stylish restaurant looks out over the oak fringed lawns.

Rooms 44 (4 fmly) (17 GF) **Facilities** FTV Xmas New Year Wi-fi **Conf** Class 60 Board 50 Thtr 170 **Parking** 120 **Notes** LB Civ Wed 80

YEOVIL Map 4 ST51
Somerset

Lanes
★★★ 83% ◎◎ HOTEL

☎ 01935 862555 📠 01935 864260
West Coker BA22 9AJ
e-mail: stay@laneshotel.net
web: www.laneshotel.net
dir: 2m W of Yeovil on A30 in centre of West Coker

This splendid building, once a rectory, has a cleverly designed, contemporary extension. Guests are assured of a relaxed and friendly stay. The stylish, modern bedrooms, with their superb bathrooms, are equipped with many extras. The brasserie-style restaurant offers an imaginative range of dishes, using local produce whenever possible. There is also a luxury jacuzzi, sauna and small gym.

Rooms 27 (17 annexe) (3 fmly) (8 GF) **S** £90; **D** £130-£180 (incl. bkfst)* **Facilities** FTV Gym Sauna Spa pool Treatment room ♫ Xmas New Year Wi-fi **Conf** Class 40 Board 20 Thtr 60 **Services** Lift **Parking** 40 **Notes** LB

The Yeovil Court Hotel & Restaurant

★★★ 79% HOTEL

☎ 01935 863746 01935 863990
West Coker Rd BA20 2HE
e-mail: unwind@yeovilhotel.com
web: www.yeovilcourthotel.com
dir: 2.5m W of town centre on A30

This comfortable, family-run hotel offers a very relaxed and caring atmosphere. Bedrooms are well equipped and neatly presented; some are located in an adjacent building. Public areas consist of a smart lounge, a popular bar and an attractive restaurant. Menus combine an interesting selection that includes lighter options and dishes suited to special occasion dining.

Rooms 30 (12 annexe) (3 fmly) (11 GF) **S** £60-£120; **D** £85-£120 (incl. bkfst)* **Facilities** FTV Wi-fi **Conf** Class 18 Board 30 Thtr 50 Del from £90 to £150* **Parking** 65 **Notes** LB RS Sat lunch, 25 Dec eve & 26 Dec Civ Wed 70

Premier Inn Yeovil

BUDGET HOTEL

☎ 0871 527 9192 0871 527 9193
Alvington Ln, Brympton BA22 8UX
dir: M5 junct 25, A358, A303 follow Yeovil signs. At rdbt onto A3088. At next rdbt 1st left, at next rdbt turn left. Hotel on left

High quality, budget accommodation ideal for both families and business travellers. Spacious, en suite bedrooms feature tea and coffee making facilities, and Freeview TV in most hotels. Internet access and Wi-fi are available for a small fee. The adjacent family restaurant features a wide and varied menu. See also the Hotel Groups pages.

Rooms 20 **D** £60*

INSPECTORS' CHOICE

Little Barwick House

RESTAURANT WITH ROOMS

☎ 01935 423902 01935 420908
Barwick Village BA22 9TD
e-mail: littlebarwick@hotmail.com
dir: From Yeovil A37 towards Dorchester, left at 1st rdbt, 1st left, 0.25m on left

Situated in a quiet hamlet in three and half acres of gardens and grounds, this listed Georgian dower house is an ideal retreat for those seeking peaceful surroundings and good food. Just one of the highlights of a stay here is a meal in the restaurant, where good use is made of local ingredients. Each of the bedrooms has its own character, and a range of thoughtful extras such as fresh flowers, bottled water and magazines is provided.

Rooms 6

YORK
North Yorkshire
Map 16 SE65

See also **Aldwark & Escrick**

INSPECTORS' CHOICE

Middlethorpe Hall & Spa

★★★★ HOTEL

☎ 01904 641241 01904 620176
Bishopthorpe Rd, Middlethorpe YO23 2GB
e-mail: info@middlethorpe.com
dir: A1/A64 follow York West (A1036) signs, then Bishopthorpe, Middlethorpe racecourse signs

This fine house, dating from the reign of William and Mary, sits in acres of beautifully landscaped gardens. The bedrooms vary in size but all are comfortably furnished; some are located in the main house, and others are in a cottage and converted courtyard stables. Public areas include a small spa and a stately drawing room where afternoon tea is quite an event. The delightful panelled restaurant is a perfect setting for enjoying the imaginative cuisine.

Rooms 29 (19 annexe) (2 fmly) (10 GF) **S** £129-£159; **D** £199-£269 (incl. bkfst)* **Facilities** Spa FTV Gym Health & Beauty spa Xmas New Year Wi-fi **Conf** Class 30 Board 25 Thtr 56 Del from £170 to £190* **Services** Lift **Parking** 71 **Notes** LB No children 6yrs RS 25 & 31 Dec Civ Wed 56

YORK *continued*

Hotel du Vin York

★★★★ 81% ® HOTEL

☎ 01904 557350 📠 01904 557351
89 The Mount YO24 1AX
e-mail: info.york@hotelduvin.com
web: www.hotelduvin.com
dir: A1036 towards city centre, 6m. Hotel on right through lights.

This Hotel du Vin offers luxury and quality that will cosset even the most discerning guest. Bedrooms are decadent in design and the bathrooms have huge monsoon showers and feature baths. Dinner in the bistro provides a memorable highlight thanks to exciting menus and a superb wine list. Staff throughout are naturally friendly, nothing is too much trouble.

Rooms 44 (3 fmly) (14 GF) **Facilities** STV FTV Wi-fi **Conf** Class 8 Board 22 Thtr 22 **Services** Lift Air con **Parking** 18 **Notes** Civ Wed 50

The Grange

★★★★ 77% ®® HOTEL

☎ 01904 644744 📠 01904 612453
1 Clifton YO30 6AA
e-mail: info@grangehotel.co.uk
web: www.grangehotel.co.uk
dir: On A19 York/Thirsk road, approx 500yds from city centre

This bustling Regency town house is just a few minutes' walk from the centre of York. A professional service is efficiently delivered by caring staff in a very friendly and helpful manner. Public rooms are comfortable and have been stylishly furnished; these include two dining options, the popular and informal Cellar Bar, and main hotel restaurant The Ivy Brasserie, which offers fine dining in a lavishly decorated environment. The individually designed bedrooms are comfortably appointed and have been thoughtfully equipped.

Rooms 36 (6 GF) **S** £123-£198; **D** £137-£235 (incl. bkfst)* **Facilities** STV FTV Use of nearby health club Xmas New Year Wi-fi **Conf** Class 24 Board 24 Thtr 50 **Parking** 26 **Notes** Civ Wed 90

York Marriott Hotel

Marriott HOTELS & RESORTS

★★★★ 77% HOTEL

☎ 01904 701000 📠 01904 702308
Tadcaster Rd YO24 1QQ
e-mail: mhrs.qqyyk.pa@marriotthotels.com
web: www.yorkmarriott.co.uk
dir: From A64 at York 'West' onto A1036, follow signs to city centre. Approx 1.5m, hotel on right after church and lights

Overlooking the racecourse and Knavesmire Parkland, the hotel offers modern accommodation, including family rooms, all with comfort cooling. Within the hotel, guests enjoy the use of extensive leisure facilities including indoor pool, putting green and tennis court. For those wishing to explore the historic and cultural attractions, the city is less than a mile away.

Rooms 151 (14 fmly) (27 GF) (10 smoking) **Facilities** Spa STV Putt green Gym Beauty treatment New Year Wi-fi **Conf** Class 90 Board 40 Thtr 190 **Services** Lift Air con **Parking** 160 **Notes** Civ Wed 140

Best Western Dean Court

★★★★ 76% ® HOTEL

☎ 01904 625082 📠 01904 620305
Duncombe Place YO1 7EF
e-mail: sales@deancourt-york.co.uk
web: www.deancourt-york.co.uk
dir: In city centre opposite York Minster

This smart hotel enjoys a central location overlooking The Minster, and guests will find the service is particularly friendly and efficient. Bedrooms are stylishly appointed and vary in size. Public areas are elegant in a contemporary style and include the popular D.C.H. restaurant which enjoys wonderful views of the cathedral, and The Court café-bistro and bar where a more informal, all-day menu is offered. Valet parking is available.

Best Western Dean Court

Rooms 37 (4 fmly) **S** £85-£140; **D** £145-£240 (incl. bkfst)* **Facilities** FTV Xmas New Year Wi-fi **Conf** Class 12 Board 32 Thtr 50 Del from £136 to £155* **Services** Lift **Parking** 30 **Notes** LB ⊗ Civ Wed 50

Royal York Hotel & Events Centre

principal hayley

★★★★ 75% HOTEL

☎ 01904 653681 📠 01904 623503
Station Rd YO24 1AA
e-mail: royalyork.reservations@principal-hayley.com
web: www.principal-hayley.com
dir: Adjacent to railway station

Situated in three acres of landscaped grounds in the very heart of the city, this Victorian railway hotel has views over the city and York Minster. Contemporary bedrooms are divided between those in the main hotel and the air-conditioned garden mews. There is also a leisure complex and state-of-the-art conference centre.

Rooms 167 (8 fmly) **S** £79-£209; **D** £89-£209 (incl. bkfst)* **Facilities** supervised Gym Steam room Xmas New Year Wi-fi **Conf** Class 250 Board 80 Thtr 410 Del from £139 to £189* **Services** Lift **Parking** 80 **Notes** LB ⊗ Civ Wed 160

Marmadukes Hotel

★★★★ 74% TOWN HOUSE HOTEL

☎ 01904 623716
4 St Peters Grove, Bootham YO30 6AQ
e-mail: reservations@marmadukesyork.com
web: www.marmadukesyork.com
dir: A1036 signed York for approx 6m, past train station then signed Inner Ring Rd. Over Lendal bridge, at lights left onto A19 (Bootham Bar) for 0.4m, right into St Peters Grove

Quietly situated just a short walk from the Minster, Marmadukes is a classically furnished, period property with all the expected modern amenities. Steeped in history and with a Roman burial ground underneath the lawn, it also has a sauna and spa bath in the grounds. The bedrooms have antique

Y

furniture and many of the bathrooms have roll-top baths. The public areas, including the conservatory-style breakfast room, are equally impressive with an air of spaciousness.

Rooms 20 (1 fmly) (2 GF) **S** £50-£70; **D** £60-£150 (incl. bkfst)* **Facilities** FTV Sauna Wi-fi Child facilities **Conf** Class 20 Board 16 Thtr 20 Del from £85 to £120* **Parking** 14 **Notes** LB ® Civ Wed 50

Fairfield Manor

RAMADA JARVIS

★★★★ 72% COUNTRY HOUSE HOTEL

☎ 01904 670222 🖷 01904 670311
Shipton Rd, Skelton YO30 1XW
e-mail: sales.york@ramadajarvis.co.uk
web: www.ramadajarvis.co.uk
dir: Exit A1237 onto A19, hotel 0.5m on left

This stylish Georgian mansion stands in six acres of private grounds on the outskirts of the city. The contemporary bedrooms, styled in reds or blues, have broadband access and flat-screen TVs; some rooms have garden and courtyard views. The suites have either four-poster or king-size beds and a separate seating area. Kilby's Restaurant serves bistro food, and 24-hour room service is available. There are good conference facilities.

Rooms 89 (20 fmly) (24 GF) **Facilities** Xmas New Year Wi-fi **Conf** Class 72 Board 60 Thtr 180 **Services** Lift **Parking** 130 **Notes** LB ® Civ Wed 150

The Churchill Hotel

★★★ 81% ®® HOTEL

☎ 01904 644456 🖷 01904 663322
65 Bootham YO30 7DQ
e-mail: info@churchillhotel.com
dir: On A19 (Bootham), W from York Minster, hotel 250yds on right

A late Georgian manor house set in its own grounds, just a short walk from the Minster and other attractions. Period features and interesting artefacts relating to Winston Churchill are incorporated into smart contemporary design and up-to-date technology. Public areas include the Piano Bar & Restaurant, where innovative menus feature high quality, local produce.

The Churchill Hotel

Rooms 32 (4 fmly) (5 GF) **Facilities** ♫ Xmas New Year Wi-fi **Conf** Class 50 Board 30 Thtr 100 **Services** Lift **Parking** 40 **Notes** LB Civ Wed 70

Best Western Monkbar

★★★ 80% HOTEL

☎ 01904 638086 🖷 01904 629195
Monkbar YO31 7JA
e-mail: sales@monkbarhotel.co.uk
dir: A64 onto A1079 to city, turn right at city walls, take middle lane at lights. Hotel on right

This smart hotel enjoys a prominent position adjacent to the city walls, and just a few minutes' walk from the cathedral. Individually styled bedrooms are well equipped for both business and leisure guests. Spacious public areas include comfortable lounges, an American-style bar, an airy restaurant and impressive meeting and training facilities.

Rooms 99 (8 fmly) (2 GF) **S** £95-£120; **D** £110-£175 (incl. bkfst) **Facilities** STV FTV Xmas New Year Wi-fi **Conf** Class 80 Board 50 Thtr 140 Del from £140 to £175 **Services** Lift **Parking** 66 **Notes** LB Civ Wed 80

Holiday Inn York

★★★ 80% HOTEL

☎ 0871 942 9085 🖷 01904 702804
Tadcaster Rd YO24 1QF
e-mail: reservations-york@ihg.com
web: www.holidayinn.co.uk
dir: From A1(M) take A64 towards York. In 7m take A1036 to York. Straight over at rdbt to city centre. Hotel 0.5m on right

Located in a suburban area close to the city centre and overlooking York race course, this modern hotel caters equally well for business and leisure guests. Public areas include the spacious family friendly Junction Restaurant, lounge bar and the Cedar Tree Terrace. Seven function rooms are also available for meetings and social events.

Rooms 142 (50 fmly) (12 GF) **Facilities** STV Xmas New Year Wi-fi **Conf** Class 45 Board 55 Thtr 100 **Services** Lift Air con **Parking** 200

Novotel York Centre

★★★ 80% HOTEL

☎ 01904 611660 🖷 01904 610925
Fishergate YO10 4FD
e-mail: H0949@accor.com
web: www.novotel.com
dir: A19 north to city centre, hotel set back on left

Set just outside the ancient city walls, this modern, family-friendly hotel is conveniently located for visitors to the city. Bedrooms feature bathrooms with a separate toilet room, plus excellent desk space and sofa beds. Four rooms are equipped for less able guests. The hotel's facilities include indoor and outdoor children's play areas and an indoor pool.

Rooms 124 (124 fmly) **Facilities** STV Xmas New Year Wi-fi **Conf** Class 100 Board 120 Thtr 210 **Services** Lift **Parking** 140

Mount Royale

★★★ 79% ® HOTEL

☎ 01904 628856 🖷 01904 611171
The Mount YO24 1GU
e-mail: reservations@mountroyale.co.uk
web: www.mountroyale.co.uk
dir: W on A1036, 0.5m after racecourse. Hotel on right after lights

This friendly hotel, a William IV listed building, offers comfortable bedrooms in a variety of styles, several leading onto the delightful gardens. Public rooms include a lounge, a meeting room and a cosy bar; the hotel has an outdoor pool, a sauna and a hot tub plus a beauty therapist. There is a separate restaurant called One 19 The Mount and a cocktail lounge overlooking the gardens (all meals and drinks can be charged to room accounts).

Rooms 24 (3 fmly) (6 GF) **Facilities** Spa FTV supervised Beauty treatment centre Sauna Steam room ♫ Xmas New Year Wi-fi **Conf** Board 25 Thtr 35 **Parking** 27 **Notes** LB

YORK *continued*

Parsonage Country House Hotel

★★★ 78% COUNTRY HOUSE HOTEL

☎ 01904 728111 🖷 01904 728151
York Rd YO19 6LF
e-mail: reservations@parsonagehotel.co.uk
web: www.parsonagehotel.co.uk

(For full entry see Escrick)

Best Western Kilima Hotel

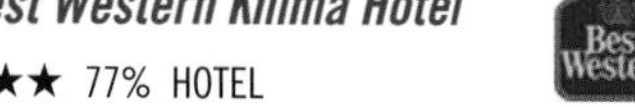

★★★ 77% HOTEL

☎ 01904 625787 🖷 01904 612083
129 Holgate Rd YO24 4AZ
e-mail: sales@kilima.co.uk
web: www.kilima.co.uk
dir: On A59, on W outskirts

This establishment, a former rectory, is conveniently situated within easy walking distance of the city centre. There is a relaxed and friendly atmosphere with professional, friendly staff providing attentive service. Bedrooms are comfortable and well equipped. There is an indoor pool, a fitness centre and a Turkish steam room.

Rooms 26 (2 fmly) (10 GF) **Facilities** FTV Gym Leisure complex Steam room Fitness suite Xmas New Year Wi-fi **Conf** Board 14 **Parking** 26 **Notes**

Best Western York Pavilion

★★★ 74% HOTEL

☎ 01904 622099 & 239900 🖷 01904 626939
45 Main St, Fulford YO10 4PJ
e-mail: reservations@yorkpavilionhotel.com
web: www.yorkpavilionhotel.com
dir: Exit A64 (York ring road) at A19 junct towards York. Hotel 0.5m on right opposite Pavilion Court

An attractive Georgian hotel situated in its own grounds. All the bedrooms are individually designed to a high specification; some are in the old house and some in the converted stables set around a garden terrace. There is a comfortable lounge, a conference centre and an inviting brasserie-style restaurant with a regularly changing menu.

Rooms 57 (4 fmly) (11 GF) **S** £79-£125; **D** £89-£135 (incl. bkfst) **Facilities** STV FTV Xmas New Year Wi-fi **Conf** Class 60 Board 45 Thtr 150 Del from £115 to £145 **Parking** 40 **Notes** Civ Wed 80

Park Inn York

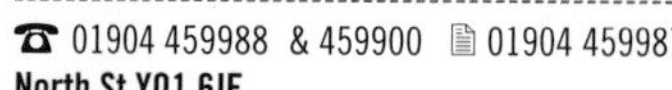

★★★ 73% HOTEL

☎ 01904 459988 & 459900 🖷 01904 459987
North St YO1 6JF
e-mail: info.york@rezidorparkinn.com
dir: A64/A1063 follow signs for city centre, into North St, hotel 250yds on right

Boasting spectacular views over the River Ouse in the heart of York this hotel is just minutes away from all the attractions of this historic, walled city. There are impressive conference rooms and leisure facilities, and the RBG Lounge Bar, overlooking the river, serves a wide-ranging menu throughout the day. Private parking is available.

Rooms 200 (8 fmly) **S** £59-£155; **D** £69-£165* **Facilities** FTV Gym Sauna Dance studio Exercise classes Beauty treatments Reflexology Sports therapy Xmas New Year Wi-fi **Conf** Class 150 Board 75 Thtr 400 Del from £99 to £165* **Services** Lift Air con **Parking** 92 **Notes** LB

Knavesmire Manor

★★ 74% SMALL HOTEL

☎ 01904 702941 🖷 01904 709274
302 Tadcaster Rd YO24 1HE
e-mail: enquire@knavesmire.co.uk
dir: A1036 into city centre. Hotel on right, overlooking racecourse

Commanding superb views across York's famous racecourse, this former manor house offers comfortable, well-equipped bedrooms, either in the main house or the garden rooms to the rear. Comfortable day rooms are stylishly furnished, whilst the heated indoor pool provides a popular addition.

Rooms 20 (9 annexe) (3 fmly) **S** £60-£89; **D** £79-£119 (incl. bkfst)* **Facilities** FTV New Year Wi-fi **Conf** Class 36 Board 30 Thtr 40 **Services** Lift **Parking** 28 **Notes** LB Closed 23-27 Dec

Lady Anne Middleton's Hotel

★★ 72% HOTEL

☎ 01904 611570 🖷 01904 613043
Skeldergate YO1 6DS
e-mail: bookings@ladyannes.co.uk
web: www.ladyannes.co.uk
dir: From A64 (Leeds) A1036 towards city centre. Right at City Walls lights, keep left, 1st left before bridge, then 1st left into Cromwell Rd. Hotel on right. (NB for Sat Nav use YO1 6DU)

This hotel has been created from several listed buildings and is very well located in the centre of York. Bedrooms are comfortably equipped. Among its amenities is a bar-lounge and a dining room where a satisfying range of food is served. An extensive fitness club is also available along with private parking.

Rooms 54 (17 annexe) (13 fmly) (12 GF) **S** £50-£100; **D** £80-£160 (incl. bkfst)* **Facilities** FTV Gym Fitness centre Beauty treatments Massage Wi-fi **Conf** Class 30 Board 30 Thtr 100 **Parking** 40 **Notes** LB Closed 24-29 Dec

Cedar Court Grand Hotel & Spa

U

☎ 01904 380038
Station Rise YO1 6HT
e-mail: info@cedarcourtgrand.co.uk
web: www.cedarcourtgrand.co.uk
dir: Near station

Currently the rating for this establishment is not confirmed. This may be due to a change of ownership or because it has only recently joined the AA rating scheme. For further details please see the AA website: theAA.com

Rooms 107 (14 GF) **S** £135-£1000; **D** £135-£1000 **Facilities** Spa FTV supervised Gym Sauna Steam room Xmas New Year Wi-fi **Conf** Class 60 Board 50 Thtr 120 **Services** Lift Air con **Notes** Civ Wed 120

Holiday Inn Express York

BUDGET HOTEL

☎ 01904 438660 🖷 01904 438560

Malton Rd YO32 9TE

web: www.hiexpressyorkeast.co.uk

dir: From A64 take A1036 towards York centre. Hotel on left behind The Hopgrove Toby Carvery

A modern hotel ideal for families and business travellers. Fresh and uncomplicated, the spacious rooms include Sky TV, power shower and tea and coffee-making facilities. Continental buffet breakfast is included in the room rate; other meals may be taken at the nearby family pub or restaurant. See also the Hotel Groups pages.

Rooms 49 (20 fmly) (21 GF) **S** £39-£150; **D** £39-£150 (incl. bkfst)*

Ibis York Centre

BUDGET HOTEL

☎ 01904 658301 🖷 01904 621224

77 The Mount YO24 1BN

e-mail: H6390@accor.com

dir: A64/A1036 follow signs to city centre, hotel on right

Modern, budget hotel offering comfortable accommodation in bright and practical bedrooms. Breakfast is self-service and dinner is available in the restaurant. See also the Hotel Groups pages.

Rooms 91 **Conf** Class 16 Board 16 Thtr 24

Premier Inn York City (Blossom St North)

BUDGET HOTEL

☎ 0871 527 9196 🖷 0871 527 9197

20 Blossom St YO24 1AJ

dir: 12m from A1 junct 47, off A59

High quality, budget accommodation ideal for both families and business travellers. Spacious, en suite bedrooms feature tea and coffee making facilities, and Freeview TV in most hotels. Internet access and Wi-fi are available for a small fee. The adjacent family restaurant features a wide and varied menu. See also the Hotel Groups pages.

Rooms 86 **D** £73-£78*

Premier Inn York City (Blossom St South)

BUDGET HOTEL

☎ 0871 527 9194 🖷 0871 527 9195

28-40 Blossom St YO24 1AJ

dir: From S, E & W: A64, A1036 (signed York West). From N: A1 (or A19), A59, follow city centre signs. At lights left onto A1036. Hotel on left just after cinema. (NB no drop-off point, parking at NCP, Queens St)

Rooms 91 **D** £75-£80*

Premier Inn York North

BUDGET HOTEL

☎ 0871 527 9198 🖷 0871 527 9199

Shipton Rd YO30 5PA

dir: From A1237 (ring road), A19 (Shipton Road South) signed York Centre. Hotel on right in Clifton Park

Rooms 49 **D** £65*

Premier Inn York North West

BUDGET HOTEL

☎ 0871 527 9200 🖷 0871 527 9201

White Rose Close, York Business Park, Nether Poppleton YO26 6RL

dir: On A1237 between A19 (Thirsk road) & A59 (Harrogate road)

Rooms 64 **D** £65*

Premier Inn York South West

BUDGET HOTEL

☎ 0871 527 9202 🖷 0871 527 9203

Bilbrough Top, Colton YO23 3PP

dir: On A64 between Tadcaster & York

Rooms 61 **D** £63*

YOXFORD
Suffolk **Map 13 TM36**

Satis House

★★★ 88% ◎◎ COUNTRY HOUSE HOTEL

☎ 01728 668418 🖷 01728 668640

IP17 3EX

e-mail: enquiries@satishouse.co.uk

web: www.satishouse.co.uk

dir: Off A12 between Ipswich & Lowestoft. 9m E Aldeburgh & Snape

Expect a warm welcome from the caring hosts at this delightful 18th-century, Grade II listed property set in three acres of parkland. The stylish public areas have a really relaxed atmosphere; they include a choice of dining rooms, a smart bar and a cosy lounge. The individually decorated bedrooms are tastefully appointed and thoughtfully equipped.

Rooms 10 (2 annexe) (1 fmly) (2 GF) **S** £65-£130; **D** £75-£210 (incl. bkfst)* **Facilities** STV FTV Xmas New Year Wi-fi **Conf** Class 40 Board 20 Thtr 40 Del from £80 to £120* **Parking** 30 **Notes** LB Civ Wed 50

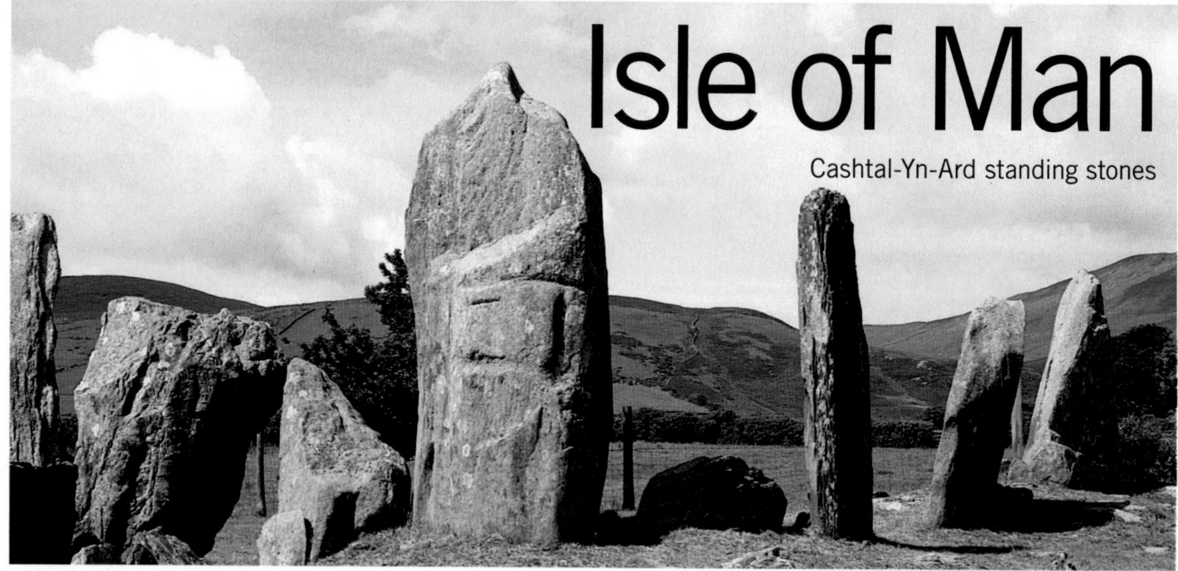

Isle of Man

Cashtal-Yn-Ard standing stones

DOUGLAS Map 24 SC37

Sefton

★★★★ 81% HOTEL

☎ 01624 645500 01624 676004
Harris Promenade IM1 2RW
e-mail: info@seftonhotel.co.im
web: www.seftonhotel.co.im
dir: 500yds from ferry dock on promenade

This Victorian hotel, extended over the years offers comfortably furnished bedrooms; many are spacious. Some have balconies overlooking the atrium water garden, while others enjoy sweeping views across the bay. A choice of comfortable lounges is available and freshly prepared dishes are served in the informal Gallery Restaurant.

Rooms 96 (3 fmly) **Facilities** Gym Cycle hire Steam room Library New Year Wi-fi **Conf** Class 30 Board 50 Thtr 150 **Services** Lift **Parking** 36 **Notes**

Mount Murray Hotel and Country Club

★★★★ 73% HOTEL

☎ 01624 661111 01624 611116
Santon IM4 2HT
e-mail: hotel@mountmurray.com
web: www.mountmurray.com
dir: 4m from Douglas towards airport. Hotel signed at Santon

This large, modern hotel and country club offers a wide range of sporting and leisure facilities, and a superb health and beauty salon. The attractively appointed public areas have a choice of bars and eating options. The spacious bedrooms are well equipped and many enjoy fine views over the 200-acre grounds and golf course. There is a very large conference suite.

Rooms 100 (4 fmly) (27 GF) **Facilities** STV 18 Putt green Gym Squash Driving range Wi-fi **Conf** Class 200 Board 100 Thtr 300 **Services** Lift **Parking** 400 **Notes**

PORT ERIN Map 24 SC16

Falcon's Nest

★★ 71% HOTEL

☎ 01624 834077 01624 835370
The Promenade IM9 6AF
e-mail: falconsnest@enterprise.net
web: www.falconsnesthotel.co.uk
dir: Follow coast road S from airport or ferry. Hotel on seafront, immediately after steam railway station

Situated overlooking the bay and harbour, this Victorian hotel offers generally spacious bedrooms. There is a choice of bars, one of which attracts many locals. Meals can be taken in the lounge bar, the conservatory or in the attractively decorated main restaurant.

Rooms 39 (9 fmly) (15 smoking) **Facilities** FTV Xmas New Year Wi-fi **Conf** Class 50 Board 50 Thtr 50 **Parking** 20

Channel Islands

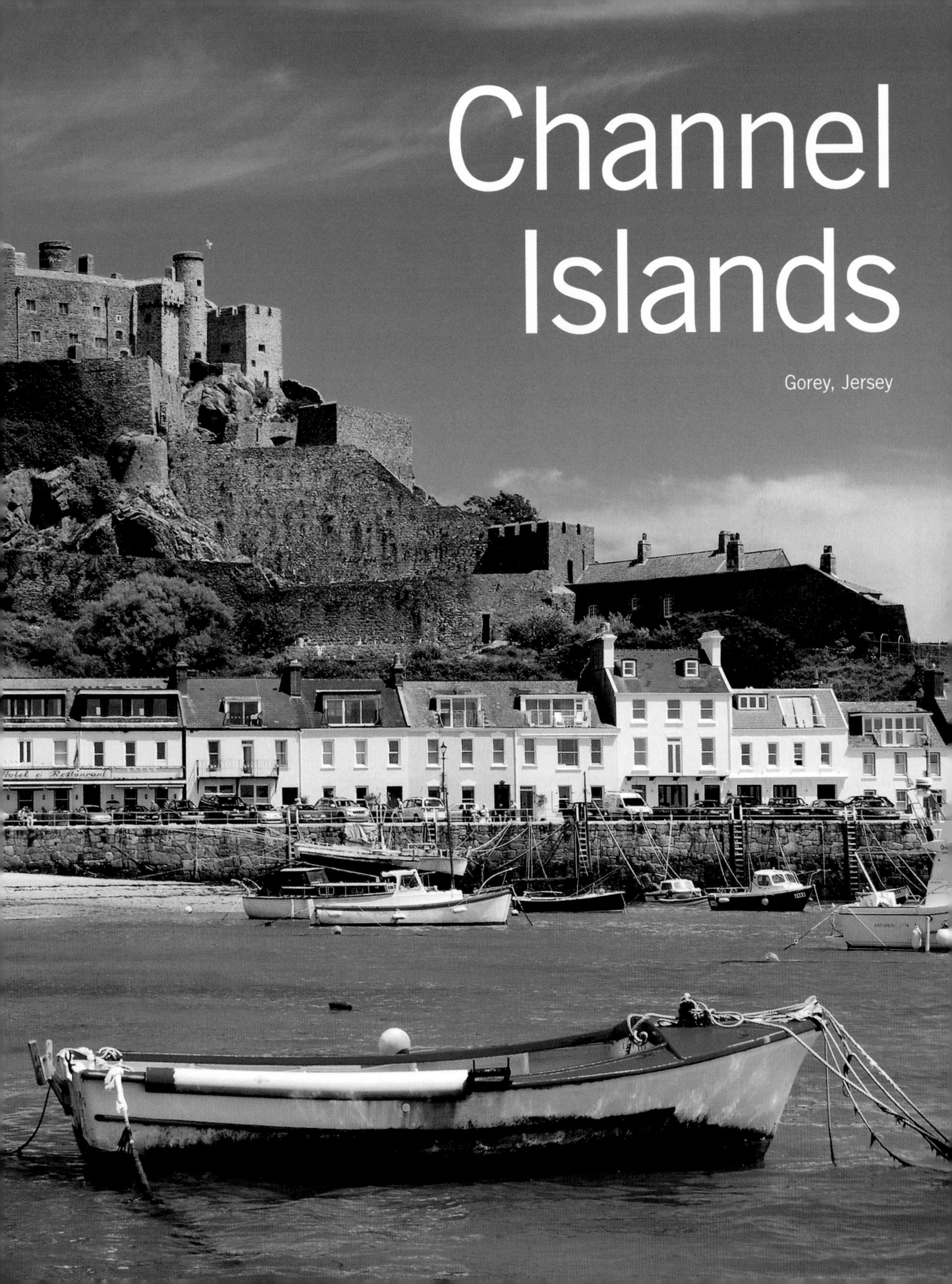

Gorey, Jersey

ALDERNEY

ALDERNEY Map 24

Braye Beach

★★★★ 71% ⊛ HOTEL

☎ 01481 824300 🖷 01481 824301
Braye St GY9 3XT
e-mail: reception@brayebeach.com
web: www.brayebeach.com
dir: Follow coast road from airport

Situated just a stone's throw from Braye's harbour and beach, this hotel provides comfortable yet stylish accommodation where many guest rooms have sea views; all bedrooms are well appointed and generously equipped. Public rooms include the popular bar and lounge, spacious terrace for the summer months and even a cinema. The well-appointed restaurant offers a varied seasonal menu often showcasing locally caught fish. Private dining can be catered for in the vaulted wine cellar.

Rooms 27 (2 fmly) **S** £80-£120; **D** £100-£200 (incl. bkfst) **Facilities** FTV Cinema Xmas New Year Wi-fi **Conf** Class 12 Board 16 Thtr 19 **Services** Lift **Notes** LB ⊗ Civ Wed 80

GUERNSEY

CASTEL Map 24

La Grande Mare Hotel Golf & Country Club

★★★★ 71% ⊛ HOTEL

☎ 01481 256576 🖷 01481 256532
The Coast Rd, Vazon Bay GY5 7LL
e-mail: reservations@lagrandemare.com
web: www.lgm.guernsey.net
dir: From airport turn right. At Coast Rd turn right

This hotel is located by a sandy bay and is set in 110 acres of private grounds that incorporates an 18-hole golf course and has a health suite. Bedrooms range from spacious studios to deluxe suites, and feature handcrafted furniture and impressive decor. The health suite features a 40ft-swimming pool that has dedicated children's swimming times.

Rooms 24 (13 fmly) (5 GF) **Facilities** supervised 18 Putt green Fishing Gym Xmas New Year Wi-fi **Conf** Class 21 Board 22 Thtr 48 **Services** Lift **Parking** 200 **Notes** ⊗

Cobo Bay

★★★ 82% ⊛⊛ HOTEL

☎ 01481 257102 🖷 01481 254542
Coast Rd, Cobo GY5 7HB
e-mail: reservations@cobobayhotel.com
web: www.cobobayhotel.com
dir: From airport turn right, follow road to W coast at L'Eree. Turn right onto coast road for 3m to Cobo Bay. Hotel on right

A popular hotel situated on the seafront overlooking Cobo Bay. The well-equipped bedrooms are pleasantly decorated; many of the front rooms have balconies and there is a secluded sun terrace to the rear. Public rooms include the Chesterfield Bar with its leather sofas and armchairs and a welcoming restaurant with stunning views of the bay.

Rooms 34 (4 fmly) **S** £49-£89; **D** £79-£190 (incl. bkfst) **Facilities** STV FTV Gym 2 Exercise bikes Sauna Wi-fi **Conf** Class 30 Board 30 Thtr 100 Del from £89 to £129 **Services** Lift **Parking** 60 **Notes** LB ⊗ Closed Jan-Feb

See advert on opposite page

FERMAIN BAY Map 24

Le Chalet Hotel

★★★ 74% HOTEL

☎ 01481 235716 🖷 01481 235718
St Martins GY4 6SD
e-mail: stay@lechaletguernsey.com
dir: Turn left from airport, follow Forest Rd, turn right onto Le Route de Sausmarez, right into Fermain Lane at Fermain Tavern. Hotel 150mtrs on right

A popular hotel that sits in a wooded valley within walking distance of Fermain Bay, ideal for those seeking a peaceful stay. Bedrooms vary in size and style; each one is pleasantly decorated and equipped with many thoughtful touches. Public areas include a panelled lounge, a bar area, a spacious restaurant and a stunning sun terrace adjoining a small indoor leisure facility.

Rooms 39 (4 fmly) **S** £49-£80; **D** £105-£140 (incl. bkfst)* **Facilities** Xmas New Year **Parking** 30 **Notes** LB RS Nov-Feb

FOREST Map 24

Le Chene

★★ 71% HOTEL

☎ 01481 235566 🖷 01481 239456
Forest Rd GY8 0AH
e-mail: info@lechene.co.uk
web: www.lechene.co.uk
dir: Between airport & St Peter Port. From airport left to St Peter Port. Hotel on right after 1st lights

This Victorian manor house is well located for guests wishing to explore Guernsey's spectacular south coast. The building has been skilfully extended to house a range of well-equipped, modern bedrooms. There is a swimming pool, a cosy cellar bar and a varied range of enjoyable freshly cooked dishes at dinner.

Rooms 26 (2 fmly) (1 GF) (1 smoking) **Facilities** Library Xmas New Year Wi-fi **Parking** 20 **Notes** ⊗

ST MARTIN Map 24

La Barbarie

★★★ 81% ⊛ HOTEL

☎ 01481 235217 🖷 01481 235208
Saints Rd, Saints Bay GY4 6ES
e-mail: reservations@labarbariehotel.com
web: www.labarbariehotel.com

This former priory dates back to the 17th century and retains much charm and style. Staff provide a very friendly and attentive atmosphere, and the modern facilities offer guests a relaxing stay. Excellent choices and fresh local ingredients form the basis of the interesting menus in the attractive restaurant and bar.

Rooms 26 (3 fmly) (8 GF) **S** £38.50-£75.50; **D** £77-£136 (incl. bkfst)* **Facilities** Wi-fi **Parking** 50 **Notes** ⊗ Closed Nov-11 Mar

Hotel Jerbourg

★★★ 78% HOTEL

☎ 01481 238826 📠 01481 238238
Jerbourg Point GY4 6BJ
e-mail: stay@hoteljerbourg.com
dir: From airport turn left to St Martin, right at filter, straight on at lights, hotel at end of road on right

This hotel boasts excellent sea views from its cliff-top location. Public areas are smartly appointed and include an extensive bar/lounge and bright conservatory-style restaurant. In addition to the fairly extensive carte, a daily-changing menu is available. Bedrooms are well presented and comfortable, and the luxury bay rooms are generally more spacious.

Rooms 32 (4 fmly) (5 GF) **S** £74-£159; **D** £89-£169 (incl. bkfst)* **Facilities** STV Petanque Xmas New Year Wi-fi **Parking** 50 **Notes** Closed 5 Jan-1 Mar

Saints Bay Hotel

★★★ 77% HOTEL

☎ 01481 238888 📠 01481 235558
Icart Rd GY4 6JG
e-mail: info@saintsbayhotel.com
dir: From St Martin take Saints Rd into Icart Rd

Ideally situated in an elevated position near Icart Point headland and above the fishing harbour at Saints Bay, this hotel has superb views. The spacious public rooms include a smart lounge bar, a first-floor lounge and a smart conservatory restaurant that overlooks the swimming pool. Bedrooms are pleasantly decorated and thoughtfully equipped.

Rooms 35 (2 fmly) (13 GF) **Facilities** Wi-fi **Parking** 15 **Notes** LB

La Villette Hotel & Leisure Suite

★★★ 77% HOTEL

☎ 01481 235292 📠 01481 237699
GY4 6QG
e-mail: reservations@lavillettehotel.co.uk
dir: Turn left from airport. Follow road past La Trelade Hotel. Take next right, hotel on left

Set in spacious grounds, this peacefully located, family-run hotel has a friendly atmosphere. The well-equipped bedrooms are spacious and comfortable. Live music is a regular feature in the large bar, while in the separate restaurant a fixed-price menu is provided. Residents have use of the excellent indoor leisure facilities, and there are also beauty treatments and a hairdressing salon.

Rooms 35 (3 fmly) (14 GF) **Facilities** STV supervised Gym Steam room Leisure suite Beauty salon Hairdresser Petanque Xmas New Year Wi-fi **Conf** Board 40 Thtr 80 **Services** Lift **Parking** 50 **Notes** LB

Hotel La Michele

★★ 81% HOTEL

☎ 01481 238065 📠 01481 239492
Les Hubits GY4 6NB
e-mail: info@lamichelehotel.com
web: www.lamichelehotel.com
dir: Approx 1.5m from St Peter Port

Expect a warm welcome from the caring hosts at this friendly family-run hotel, which is situated in a peaceful location. Bedrooms are particularly well equipped; each one is pleasantly decorated and has co-ordinated fabrics. Public areas include a conservatory and a cosy bar, and guests can relax in the well-tended gardens or around the pool.

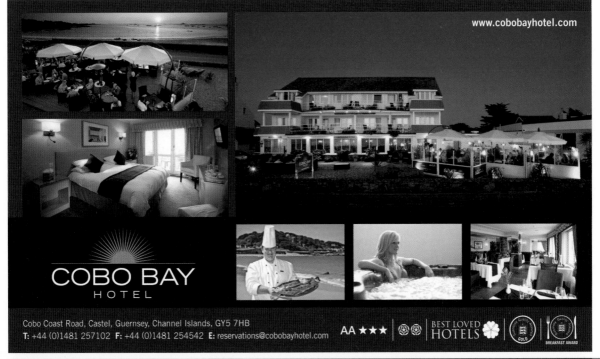

Rooms 16 (2 fmly) (6 GF) **S** £47-£67; **D** £94-£134 (incl. bkfst & dinner)* **Facilities** FTV Wi-fi **Parking** 16 **Notes** No children 10yrs Closed Nov-Mar

ST PETER PORT Map 24

INSPECTORS' CHOICE

Old Government House Hotel & Spa

THE RED CARNATION HOTEL COLLECTION

★★★★ HOTEL

☎ 01481 724921 📠 01481 724429
St Ann's Place GY1 2NU
e-mail: ogh@theoghhotel.com
web: www.theoghhotel.com
dir: At junct of St Julian's Ave & St Ann's Place

The affectionately known OGH is one of the island's leading hotels. Located in the heart of St Peter Port, it is the perfect base to explore Guernsey and the other islands of the Bailiwick. Bedrooms vary in size but are comfortable and offer high quality accommodation. There is an indulgent health club and spa, and the eating options are the OGH Brasserie, and award-winning Governor's that offers local produce with a French twist.

Rooms 62 (3 annexe) (6 fmly) **S** £113-£360; **D** £133-£380 (incl. bkfst)* **Facilities** Spa STV Gym Steam room Sauna Aerobics studio Xmas New Year Wi-fi **Conf** Class 100 Board 80 Thtr 200 Del from £203 to £450* **Services** Lift Air con **Parking** 20 **Notes** LB

Fermain Valley

★★★★ 77% HOTEL

☎ 01481 235666 & 0800 316 0314
📠 01481 235413
Fermain Ln GY1 1ZZ
e-mail: info@fermainvalley.com
dir: Turn left from airport, follow Forest Rd, turn right onto Le Route de Sausmarez, right into Fermain Lane at Fermain Tavern. Hotel 100mtrs on left

This hotel occupies an amazing location high above Fermain Bay with far reaching views out to sea; there are lovely walks along the cliff or down the lanes from the hotel. The delightfully furnished bedrooms, some with balconies, have either views of the sea, the valley or the well tended gardens. Informal eating is available in the stylish Rock Garden bar, and in summer on the terrace; the Valley Restaurant is the fine dining option. The leisure facilities include a pool, a sauna and a private cinema. The well-trained staff provide warm and friendly service.

Rooms 43 (11 annexe) (2 fmly) (6 GF) **S** £102-£184; **D** £135-£245 (incl. bkfst)* **Facilities** STV FTV Cinema Sauna Xmas New Year Wi-fi **Conf** Class 60 Board 40 Thtr 100 **Services** Lift **Parking** 40 **Notes** LB

St Pierre Park Hotel

★★★★ 73% HOTEL

☎ 01481 728282 📠 01481 712041
Rohais GY1 1FD
e-mail: reservations@stpierrepark.co.uk
dir: From harbour straight over rdbt, up hill through 3 sets of lights. Right at filter to lights. Straight ahead, hotel 100mtrs on left

Peacefully located on the outskirts of town amidst 45 acres of grounds, this well established hotel also features a 9-hole golf course. Most of the bedrooms overlook the pleasant gardens and have either a balcony or a terrace. Public areas include a choice of restaurants and a stylish bar which opens onto a spacious terrace, overlooking an elegant water feature.

Rooms 131 (5 fmly) (20 GF) **S** £74-£140; **D** £99-£165 (incl. bkfst)* **Facilities** Spa STV 9 Putt green Gym Birdwatching Children's playground Crazy golf Xmas New Year Wi-fi **Conf** Class 120 Board 70 Thtr 200 Del from £115 to £155* **Services** Lift **Parking** 150 **Notes** LB

Les Rocquettes

★★★ 79% HOTEL

☎ 01481 722146 📠 01481 714543
Les Gravees GY1 1RN
e-mail: rocquettes@sarniahotels.com
dir: From ferry terminal take 2nd exit at rdbt, through 5 sets of lights. After 5th lights straight on into Les Gravees. Hotel on right opposite church

This late 18th-century country mansion is in a good location close to St Peter Port and Beau Sejour. Bedrooms come in three grades - Deluxe, Superior and Standard, but all have plenty of useful facilities. Guests can eat in Oaks restaurant and bar. The hotel has attractive lounge areas on three levels; there is a health suite with a gym and swimming pool with an integrated children's pool.

Rooms 51 (5 fmly) **S** £74-£95; **D** £128-£170 (incl. bkfst & dinner)* **Facilities** supervised Gym Treatment rooms Sauna Steam room Xmas New Year Wi-fi **Conf** Class 60 Board 60 Thtr 100 **Services** Lift **Parking** 60 **Notes**

The Duke of Richmond

★★★ 79% HOTEL

☎ 01481 726221 📠 01481 728945
Cambridge Park GY1 1UY
e-mail: manager@dukeofrichmond.com
web: www.dukeofrichmond.com
dir: On corner of Cambridge Park & L'Hyvreuse Ave, opposite leisure centre

Peacefully located in a mainly residential area overlooking Cambridge Park, this hotel has comfortable, well-appointed bedrooms that vary in size. Public areas include a spacious lounge, a terrace and the unique Sausmarez Bar, with its nautical theme. The smartly uniformed team of staff provide professional standards of service.

Rooms 75 (7 fmly) **S** £69-£130; **D** £100-£170 (incl. bkfst)* **Facilities** STV Leisure centre nearby Xmas New Year Wi-fi **Conf** Class 50 Board 36 Thtr 150 Del from £128.50 to £189.50* **Services** Lift **Parking** 5 **Notes** LB

Best Western Hotel de Havelet

★★★ 78% HOTEL

☎ 01481 722199 📠 01481 714057
Havelet GY1 1BA
e-mail: havelet@sarniahotels.com
dir: From airport follow signs for St Peter Port through St. Martins. At bottom of 'Val de Terres' hill turn left at top of hill, hotel on right

This extended Georgian hotel looks over the harbour to Castle Cornet. Many of the well-equipped bedrooms are set around a pretty colonial-style courtyard. Day rooms in the original building have period elegance; the restaurant and bar are on the other side of the car park in converted stables.

Rooms 34 (4 fmly) (8 GF) (17 smoking) **S** £52-£125; **D** £88-£156 (incl. bkfst & dinner)* **Facilities** FTV Sauna Steam room Xmas New Year Wi-fi **Conf** Class 20 Board 18 Thtr 30 Del from £110 to £140* **Parking** 40 **Notes** LB

Duke of Normandie

★★★ 75% HOTEL

☎ 01481 721431 📠 01481 711763
Lefebvre St GY1 2JP
e-mail: dukeofnormandie@cwgsy.net
web: www.dukeofnormandie.com
dir: From harbour rdbt St Julians Ave, 3rd left into Anns Place, continue to right, up hill, then left into Lefebvre St, archway entrance on right

An 18th-century hotel situated close to the high street and just a short stroll from the harbour. Bedrooms vary in style and include some that have their own access from the courtyard. Public areas feature a smart brasserie, a contemporary lounge/lobby area and a busy bar with beams and an open fireplace.

Rooms 37 (17 annexe) (8 GF) **S** £50-£74; **D** £100-£148 (incl. bkfst)* **Facilities** STV Wi-fi **Conf** Class 30 Board 20 Thtr 40 **Parking** 15 **Notes**

CHANNEL ISLANDS

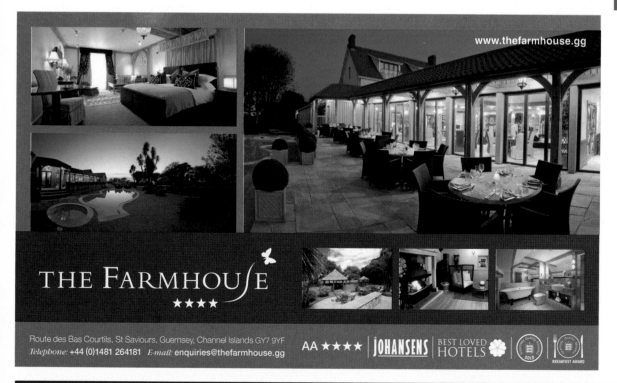

ST PETER PORT *continued*

Best Western Moores

★★★ 73% HOTEL

☎ 01481 724452 📠 01481 714037
Pollet GY1 1WH
e-mail: moores@sarniahotels.com
dir: Left at airport, follow signs to St Peter Port. Fort Road to seafront, straight on, turn left before rdbt, to hotel

An elegant granite town house situated in the heart of St Peter Port amidst the shops and amenities. Public rooms feature a smart conservatory restaurant which leads out onto a first-floor terrace for alfresco dining; there is also a choice of lounges and bars as well as a patisserie. Bedrooms are pleasantly decorated and thoughtfully equipped.

Rooms 49 (3 annexe) (8 fmly) (10 smoking) **S** £55-£122; **D** £96-£230 (incl. bkfst)* **Facilities** FTV Gym Sauna Solarium Xmas New Year Wi-fi **Conf** Class 20 Board 18 Thtr 40 Del from £110 to £140* **Services** Lift **Notes** LB ⊗

Sunnycroft Hotel

★★ 72% METRO HOTEL

☎ 01481 723008 & 0800 316 0314
📠 01481 712225
5 Constitution Steps GY1 2PN
e-mail: sunnycrofthotel@cwgsy.com
dir: In centre of town, past Salvation Army Building in Clifton

This property is located in one of St Peter Port's cobbled, stepped alleyways and has great views overlooking the marina. The bedrooms are cosy and provide a good level of comfort; many have sea views. An honesty bar is available and breakfast is served in the rooftop dining room. Access to the property is by foot only and might be unsuitable for those who are less steady on their feet.

Rooms 14 **S** £52-£72; **D** £81-£117 (incl. bkfst)*

ST SAVIOUR — Map 24

Farmhouse Hotel

★★★★ 82% ® SMALL HOTEL

☎ 01481 264181 📠 01481 266272
Route Des Bas Courtils GY7 9YF
e-mail: enquiries@thefarmhouse.gg
web: www.thefarmhouse.gg
dir: From airport, left to 1st lights. Left then left again around runway perimeter. After 1m left at x-rds. Hotel 100mtrs on right

This hotel provides spacious accommodation with amazingly comfortable beds and state-of-the-art bathrooms with under-floor heating. Guests can choose from various stylish dining options including alfresco eating in the warmer months. The outdoor swimming pool is available to guests in the summer and there are lots of countryside walks to enjoy.

Rooms 14 (7 fmly) **D** £69-£250 (incl. bkfst) **Facilities** STV Xmas New Year Wi-fi **Conf** Class 130 Board 30 Thtr 150 Del from £99 to £299 **Services** Air con **Parking** 80 **Notes** LB ⊗

VALE — Map 24

Peninsula

★★★ 75% HOTEL

☎ 01481 248400 📠 01481 248706
Les Dicqs GY6 8JP
e-mail: peninsula@guernsey.net
dir: On coast road at Grand Havre Bay

Adjacent to the sandy beach and set in five acres of grounds, this modern hotel provides comfortable accommodation. Bedrooms have an additional sofa bed to suit families and good workspace for the business traveller. Both fixed-price and carte menus are served in the restaurant, or guests can eat informally in the bar.

Rooms 99 (99 fmly) (25 GF) (5 smoking) **S** £72.50-£92.50; **D** £115-£155 (incl. bkfst)* **Facilities** STV Putt green Petanque Children's playground Xmas New Year Wi-fi **Conf** Class 140 Board 105 Thtr 250 Del from £100.45 to £120.45* **Services** Lift **Parking** 120 **Notes** LB ⊗ Closed Jan

See advert on page 539

HERM

HERM — Map 24

White House Hotel

★★★ 74% ® HOTEL

☎ 01481 750075 📠 01481 710066
GY1 3HR
e-mail: hotel@herm.com
web: www.herm.com
dir: Transport to island by catamaran ferry from St Peter Port, Guernsey

Enjoying a unique island setting, this attractive hotel is just 20 minutes from Guernsey by sea. Set in well-tended gardens, the hotel offers neatly decorated bedrooms, located in either the main house or adjacent cottages; the majority of rooms have sea views. Guests can relax in one of several lounges, enjoy a drink in one of two bars and choose from two dining options.

Rooms 40 (23 annexe) (23 fmly) (7 GF) **Facilities** Fishing trips Yacht & motor boat charters Wi-fi **Conf** Board 10 Thtr 50 **Notes** LB ⊗ Closed Nov-Mar

CHANNEL ISLANDS

JERSEY

GOREY Map 24

The Moorings Hotel & Restaurant

★★★ 73% HOTEL

☎ 01534 853633 📠 01534 857618
Gorey Pier JE3 6EW
e-mail: reservations@themooringshotel.com
web: www.themooringshotel.com
dir: At foot of Mont Orgueil Castle

Enjoying an enviable position by the harbour, the heart of this hotel is the restaurant where a selection of menus offers an extensive choice of dishes. Other public areas include a bar, coffee shop and a comfortable first-floor residents' lounge. Bedrooms at the front have a fine view of the harbour; three have access to a balcony. A small sun terrace at the back of the hotel is available to guests.

Rooms 15 **S** £57.50-£73.50; **D** £115-£147 (incl. bkfst)* **Facilities** FTV Xmas New Year Wi-fi **Conf** Class 20 Board 20 Thtr 20 Del from £140 to £170* **Notes** LB ⊗

Old Court House

★★★ 71% HOTEL

☎ 01534 854444 📠 01534 853587
JE3 9FS
e-mail: ochhotel@itl.net
web: www.ochhoteljersey.com

Situated on the east of the island, a short walk from the beach, this long established hotel continues to have a loyal following for its relaxed atmosphere and friendly staff. Bedrooms are of similar standard throughout and some have balconies overlooking the gardens. Spacious public areas include a comfortable, quiet lounge, a restaurant, and a large bar with a dance floor.

Rooms 58 (4 fmly) (9 GF) **S** £50-£69; **D** £100-£138 (incl. bkfst)* **Facilities** FTV ⛱ ♫ Wi-fi **Services** Lift **Parking** 40 **Notes** LB Closed Nov-Mar

Dolphin Hotel and Restaurant

★★ 74% HOTEL

☎ 01534 853370 📠 01534 855343
Gorey Pier JE3 6EW
e-mail: dolphinhotel@jerseymail.co.uk
dir: At foot of Mont Orgueil Castle

Located on the main harbour at Gorey, many bedrooms at this popular hotel enjoy views over the sea and beaches. The relaxed and friendly style is apparent from the moment of arrival, and the busy restaurant and bar are popular with locals and tourists alike. Outdoor seating is available in season, and fresh fish and seafood are included on the menu.

Rooms 16 **S** £36-£72; **D** £46.50-£93 (incl. bkfst)* **Facilities** STV ♫ Xmas New Year Wi-fi **Conf** Class 20 Board 20 Thtr 20 Del from £150 to £190* **Notes** LB ⊗

Maison Gorey

★★ 69% HOTEL

☎ 01534 857775 & 07797 715051
📠 01534 857779
Gorey Village Main Rd JE3 9EP
e-mail: maisongorey@jerseymail.co.uk
dir: Adjacent to Jersey Pottery

Located in the middle of Gorey this small, relaxing hotel provides well-equipped bedrooms and bathrooms. In addition to a spacious bar, a small TV lounge is available for guests. Some off-street parking is available in front of the hotel.

Rooms 26 (26 annexe) (2 fmly) **S** fr £35; **D** fr £80 (incl. bkfst) **Facilities** FTV ♫ Xmas New Year Wi-fi **Parking** 6 **Notes** ⊗ No children 5yrs Civ Wed 85

GROUVILLE Map 24

Beausite

★★★ 71% HOTEL

☎ 01534 857577 📠 01534 857211
Les Rue des Pres, Grouville Bay JE3 9DJ
e-mail: beausite@jerseymail.co.uk
web: www.southernhotels.com
dir: Opposite Royal Jersey Golf Course

This hotel is situated on the south-east side of the island; a short distance from the picturesque harbour at Gorey. With parts dating back to 1636, the public rooms retain original character and charm; bedrooms are generally spacious and modern in design. The indoor swimming pool, fitness room, saunas and spa bath are all added bonuses.

Rooms 75 (5 fmly) (18 GF) **Facilities** STV 🏊 Gym Wi-fi **Parking** 60 **Notes** LB Closed Oct-Mar

ROZEL Map 24

INSPECTORS' CHOICE

Château la Chaire

★★★ ®® HOTEL

☎ 01534 863354 📠 01534 865137
Rozel Bay JE3 6AJ
e-mail: res@chateau-la-chaire.co.uk
web: www.chateau-la-chaire.co.uk
dir: From St Helier on B38 turn left in village by Rozel Bay Inn, hotel 100yds on right

Built as a gentleman's residence in 1843, Château la Chaire is a haven of peace and tranquillity, set in a secluded wooded valley. Picturesque Rozel Harbour is within easy walking distance and the house is surrounded by terraced gardens and woods. There is a wonderful atmosphere here and the helpful staff deliver high standards of guest care. Imaginative menus, making the best use of local produce, are served in the oak-panelled dining room, in the conservatory or on the terrace when the weather permits. Bedroom and suite styles and sizes vary, but all are beautifully appointed and include many nice touches such as towelling robes, slippers, flowers and DVD players. Free Wi-fi is available throughout the hotel.

Rooms 14 (2 fmly) (1 GF) **Facilities** FTV Xmas New Year Wi-fi **Conf** Class 20 Board 20 Thtr 20 Del from £115 to £145* **Parking** 30 **Notes** ⊗ No children 7yrs Civ Wed 60

ST AUBIN Map 24

Somerville

★★★★ 78% HOTEL

☎ 01534 491906 01534 499574
Mont du Boulevard JE3 8AD
e-mail: somerville@dolanhotels.com
web: www.dolanhotels.com
dir: From village, follow harbour into Mont du Boulevard

Enjoying spectacular views of St Aubin's Bay, this friendly hotel is very popular. Bedrooms vary in style and a number of superior rooms offer higher levels of luxury. Public areas are smartly presented and include a spacious bar-lounge and elegant dining room; both take full advantage of the hotel's enviable views. An outdoor swimming pool is available in summer months.

Rooms 56 (4 GF) **S** £39.50-£94.50; **D** £79-£189 (incl. bkfst)* **Facilities** STV Xmas New Year Wi-fi **Conf** Class 33 Board 36 Thtr 55 **Services** Lift **Parking** 26 **Notes** No children 4yrs Civ Wed 40

ST BRELADE Map 24

INSPECTORS' CHOICE

The Atlantic

★★★★ HOTEL

☎ 01534 744101 01534 744102
Le Mont de la Pulente JE3 8HE
e-mail: info@theatlantichotel.com
web: www.theatlantichotel.com
dir: From Petit Port turn right into Rue de la Sergente, right again, hotel signed

Adjoining the manicured fairways of La Moye championship golf course, this hotel enjoys a peaceful setting with breathtaking views over St Ouen's Bay. Stylish bedrooms look out over the course or the sea, and offer a blend of high quality and reassuring comfort. An air of understated luxury is apparent throughout, and the attentive service achieves the perfect balance of friendliness and professionalism. The Ocean restaurant's very talented chef, Mark Jordan, uses the best island produce to create outstanding and impeccably modern cuisine.

Rooms 50 (8 GF) **S** £100-£200; **D** £150-£350 (incl. bkfst)* **Facilities** STV Gym Saunas Xmas New Year Wi-fi **Conf** Class 40 Board 20 Thtr 60 Del from £200 to £250* **Services** Lift **Parking** 60 **Notes** LB Closed 2 Jan-3 Feb Civ Wed 80

L'Horizon Hotel and Spa

HANDPICKED HOTELS

★★★★ 85% HOTEL

☎ 01534 743101 01534 746269
St Brelade's Bay JE3 8EF
e-mail: lhorizon@handpicked.co.uk
web: www.handpicked.co.uk/lhorizon
dir: From airport right towards St Brelades & Red Houses. Through Red Houses, hotel 300mtrs on right

The combination of a truly wonderful setting on the golden sands of St Brelade's Bay, a relaxed atmosphere and excellent facilities prove a winning formula here. Bedrooms are stylish and have a real contemporary feel, all with plasma TVs and a host of extras; many have balconies or terraces and superb sea views. Spacious public areas include a spa and leisure club, a choice of dining options and relaxing lounges.

Rooms 106 (1 fmly) (15 GF) **S** £58-£175; **D** £118-£290 (incl. bkfst)* **Facilities** Spa STV Gym Treatment rooms Windsurfing Water skiing Sauna Steam room Xmas New Year Wi-fi **Conf** Class 100 Board 50 Thtr 250 Del from £145 to £245* **Services** Lift **Parking** 125 **Notes** Civ Wed 240

St Brelade's Bay Hotel

★★★★ 80% HOTEL

☎ 01534 746141 01534 747278
JE3 8EF
web: www.stbreladesbayhotel.com
dir: SW corner of island

The hotel, in five-acre gardens, enjoys a fabulous location with unobstructed views overlooking St Brelade's Bay and with the sandy beach right on the doorstep. Having undergone a major refurbishment in 2011, the bedrooms are beautifully presented and equipped to a very high standard. The relaxing public areas include a stylish, comfortable lounge along with a spacious bar. The gardens feature a pool area and terraces for relaxing and eating. Attentive friendly service is guaranteed in the elegant restaurant.

Rooms 90 (8 fmly) **Facilities** STV Putt green Games room Table tennis Wi-fi **Conf** Board 12 **Services** Lift **Parking** 60 **Notes** LB Closed 12 Oct-2 Apr Civ Wed

Hotel La Place

★★★★ 71% HOTEL

01534 744261 01534 745164
Route du Coin, La Haule JE3 8BT
e-mail: reservations@hotellaplacejersey.com
dir: Off main St Helier/St Aubin coast road at La Haule Manor (B25). Up hill, 2nd left (to Red Houses), 1st right. Hotel 100mtrs on right

Developed around a 17th-century farmhouse and well placed for exploration of the island. Attentive, friendly service is the ethos here. A range of bedroom types is provided, some having private patios and direct access to the pool area. The cocktail bar is popular for pre-dinner drinks and a traditional lounge has a log fire in colder months. An interesting menu is offered.

Rooms 42 (1 fmly) (10 GF) **S** £50-£90; **D** £100-£150 (incl. bkfst)* **Facilities** STV Discount at Les Ormes Country Club, including golf, gym & indoor tennis Xmas Wi-fi **Conf** Class 40 Board 40 Thtr 100 Del from £90 to £140* **Parking** 100 **Notes** Civ Wed 100

Beau Rivage Hotel

★★★ 77% HOTEL

01534 745983 01534 747127
St Brelade's Bay JE3 8EF
e-mail: beau@jerseyweb.demon.co.uk
web: www.jersey.co.uk/hotels/beau
dir: Sea side of coast road in centre of St Brelade's Bay, 1.5m S of airport

With direct access to one of Jersey's most popular beaches, residents and non-residents alike are welcome to this hotel's bar and terrace. All of the well-equipped bedrooms are now suites, most have wonderful sea views, and some have the bonus of balconies. Residents have a choice of lounges, plus a sun deck exclusively for their use. A range of dishes, featuring English and Continental cuisine, is available from a selection of menus in either the bar or the main bistro restaurant.

Rooms 12 (12 fmly) (12 smoking) **S** £53-£165; **D** £86-£267* **Facilities** STV FTV Games room Wi-fi **Services** Lift **Parking** 16 **Notes** RS Nov-Mar Civ Wed 80

Hotel Miramar

★★ 72% HOTEL

01534 743831 01534 745009
Mont Gras d'Eau JE3 8ED
e-mail: reservations@miramarjersey.com
dir: From airport take B36 at lights, turn left onto A13, 1st right into Mont Gras d'Eau

A friendly welcome awaits at this family-run hotel set in delightful sheltered gardens, overlooking the beautiful bay. Accommodation is comfortable with well-appointed bedrooms; some are on the ground floor, and there are two on the lower ground with their own terrace overlooking the outdoor heated pool. The restaurant offers a varied set menu.

Rooms 38 (2 fmly) (12 GF) (4 smoking) **Facilities** Wi-fi **Parking** 30 **Notes** Closed Oct-mid Apr

ST CLEMENT Map 24

Pontac House

★★★ 77% HOTEL

01534 857771 01534 857031
St Clements Bay JE2 6SE
e-mail: info@pontachouse.com
web: www.pontachouse.com
dir: 10 mins from St Helier

Overlooking the sandy beach of St Clement's Bay, this hotel is located on the south eastern corner of Jersey. Many guests return on a regular basis to experience the friendly, relaxed style of service. The bedrooms, most with splendid views, are comfortable and well equipped. Varied menus, featuring local seafood, are on offer each evening.

Rooms 27 (1 fmly) (5 GF) **S** £35-£45; **D** £70-£108 (incl. bkfst)* **Facilities** FTV Wi-fi **Parking** 35 **Notes** Closed 18 Dec-1 Mar

The Samares Coast Hotel

★★★ 72% HOTEL

01534 723411 & 873006 01534 887906
St Clement's Coast Rd JE2 6SB
e-mail: admin@morvanhotels.com
dir: On main esplanade

This hotel is situated on the south coast in a prime seafront location with delightful views from the restaurant and many of the bedrooms. All the bedrooms are well appointed and the sea-facing, balcony rooms prove especially popular. Facilities include a leisure complex with swimming pool and gym, and there are pleasant gardens. Carefully prepared dishes are offered in the comfortable restaurant.

Rooms 52 (4 annexe) (5 fmly) (14 GF) **Facilities** STV FTV Gym Steam room Wi-fi **Services** Lift **Parking** 35 **Notes** LB Closed Nov-Mar

CHANNEL ISLANDS

ST HELIER Map 24

Grand Jersey

★★★★★ 82% ®®® HOTEL

☎ 01534 722301 🖷 01534 737815
The Esplanade JE2 3QA
e-mail: reservations@grandjersey.com

A local landmark, the Grand Hotel has pleasant views across St Aubin's Bay to the front and the bustling streets of St Helier to the rear. The hotel is elegant and contemporary in design with a real touch of grandeur throughout. The air-conditioned bedrooms, including six suites, come in a variety of designs, but all have luxurious beds, ottomans and LCD TVs. The spacious public areas, many looking out onto the bay, include the very popular Champagne Lounge, the Victorias brasserie, and the impressive and intimate Tassili fine-dining restaurant. There is a large terrace for alfresco eating in the summer months, and the spa offers an indoor pool, gym and treatment rooms.

Rooms 123 (18 fmly) (6 GF) **S** £99-£125; **D** £115-£450 (incl. bkfst)* **Facilities** Spa STV Gym Xmas New Year Wi-fi **Conf** Class 100 Board 50 Thtr 180 Del from £165 to £195* **Services** Lift Air con **Parking** 27 **Notes** LB Civ Wed 180

CHANNEL ISLANDS

INSPECTORS' CHOICE

The Club Hotel & Spa

★★★★ ®®®®
TOWN HOUSE HOTEL

☎ 01534 876500 🖷 01534 720371
Green St JE2 4UH
e-mail: reservations@theclubjersey.com
web: www.theclubjersey.com
dir: 5 mins walk from main shopping centre

This swish, town house hotel is conveniently located close to the centre of town and features stylish, contemporary decor throughout. All the guest rooms and suites have power showers and state-of-the-art technology including wide-screen LCD TV, DVD and CD systems. The choice of restaurants includes Bohemia, a sophisticated eating option that continues to offer outstanding cuisine. For relaxation there is an elegant spa with a luxurious range of treatments.

Rooms 46 (4 fmly) (4 GF) (5 smoking) **S** £99-£215; **D** £99-£215 (incl. bkfst)* **Facilities** Spa STV FTV Sauna Steam room Salt cabin Hydrothermal bench Rasul room New Year Wi-fi **Conf** Class 60 Board 34 Thtr 80 Del from £145 to £195* **Services** Lift Air con **Parking** 32 **Notes** LB Closed 24-30 Dec Civ Wed 84

The Royal Yacht

★★★★ 83% ®® HOTEL

☎ 01534 720511 🖷 01534 767729
The Weighbridge JE2 3NF
e-mail: reception@theroyalyacht.com
dir: In town centre, opposite marina & harbour

Overlooking the marina and steam clock, the Royal Yacht is thought to be the oldest established hotel on the island. Very much a 21st-century hotel, it has state-of-the-art technology in all the bedrooms and the two penthouse suites. There is a range of impressive dining options to suit all tastes with Sirocco's Restaurant offering high quality local produce. In addition to a choice of bars and conference facilities guests can enjoy the luxury spa with an indoor pool and gym.

Rooms 110 **S** £135; **D** £175-£750 (incl. bkfst)* **Facilities** Spa STV Gym Xmas New Year Wi-fi **Conf** Class 150 Board 40 Thtr 280 Del from £134 to £170* **Services** Lift Air con **Notes** LB Civ Wed 250

Radisson Blu Waterfront Hotel, Jersey

★★★★ 80% HOTEL

☎ 01534 671100 & 671173 🖷 01534 671101
The Waterfront, La Rue de L'Etau JE2 3WF
e-mail: info.jersey@radissonblu.com
web: www.radissonblu.com/hotel-jersey
dir: Follow signs to St Helier. From A2 follow signs to harbour. At rdbt just before harbour take 2nd exit, continue to hotel

Most of the bedrooms at this purpose-built hotel have fabulous views of the coastline. There is a popular brasserie, cocktail bar, lounges, indoor heated pool, gym, sauna and steam room. A wide range of meeting rooms provides conference facilities for delegates; parking is extensive.

Rooms 195 **S** £109-£185; **D** £109-£185 (incl. bkfst)* **Facilities** Spa STV Gym Sauna Steam room Xmas New Year Wi-fi **Conf** Class 184 Board 30 Thtr 400 Del from £138 to £189* **Services** Lift Air con **Parking** 95 **Notes** Civ Wed 400

Pomme d'Or

★★★★ 77% ⊛⊛ HOTEL

☎ 01534 880110 🖷 01534 737781
Liberation Square JE1 3UF
e-mail: enquiries@pommedorhotel.com
dir: Opposite harbour

This historic hotel overlooks Liberation Square and the marina and offers comfortably furnished, well-equipped bedrooms. Popular with the business fraternity, a range of conference facilities and meeting rooms are available. Dining options include the traditional fine dining in the Petite Pomme, the smart carvery restaurant and the coffee shop.

Rooms 143 (3 fmly) **D** £89-£200 (incl. bkfst)* **Facilities** STV Use of Aquadome at Merton Hotel. Xmas New Year Wi-fi **Conf** Class 100 Board 50 Thtr 220 Del from £165 to £195* **Services** Lift Air con **Notes** LB ⊗

Hotel Savoy

★★★★ 72% ⊛ HOTEL

☎ 01534 727521 🖷 01534 727521
37 Rouge Bouillon JE2 3ZA
e-mail: info@thesavoy.biz
web: www.thesavoy.biz
dir: From airport 1st exit at rdbt. At next rdbt take 2nd exit right, down Beaumont Hill. At bottom turn left, along coast onto dual carriageway. At 3rd lights turn 1st left. Right at end. Remain in right lane, into left lane before hospital. Hotel on left opposite police station

This family-run hotel, a manor house dating from the 19th century, sits peacefully in its own grounds, just a short walk from the main shopping area in St Helier. It offers spacious, comfortable accommodation and smart public rooms. The Montana Restaurant serves carefully prepared, imaginative cuisine. A car park and leisure facilities are also available.

Rooms 55 (2 fmly) (10 GF) **D** £80-£150 (incl. bkfst)* **Facilities** STV ⛳ Gym Treatment room ♫ Wi-fi **Conf** Class 70 Board 12 Thtr 120 Del from £137 to £149* **Services** Lift **Parking** 46 **Notes** LB

Best Western Royal

★★★ 79% ⊛ HOTEL

☎ 01534 726521 & 873006 🖷 01534 728873
David Place JE2 4TD
e-mail: enquiries@royalhoteljersey.com
web: www.royalhoteljersey.com
dir: From Airport: In St Helier on Victoria Ave, left by Grand Hotel into Peirson Rd. Follow one-way system into Cheapside. Left at filter, follow Ring Rd signs into Rouge Boullion (A14). At rdbt right, stay in right lane, right at lights into Midvale Rd. Through 2 lights, hotel on left

This long established hotel is located in the centre of town and is within walking distance of the business district and shops. Seasons Restaurant offers a modern approach to dining, and the adjoining bar provides a relaxed venue for residents and locals alike. The bedrooms are individually styled. Extensive conference facilities are available.

Rooms 89 (4 fmly) (9 smoking) **S** £60-£70; **D** £99-£139 (incl. bkfst)* **Facilities** Gym Xmas New Year Wi-fi **Conf** Class 120 Board 80 Thtr 300 **Services** Lift **Parking** 15 **Notes** LB ⊗ Civ Wed 30

Hotel Revere

★★★ 73% HOTEL

☎ 01534 611111 🖷 01534 611116
Kensington Place JE2 3PA
e-mail: reservations@revere.co.uk
web: www.revere.co.uk
dir: From Esplanade left after De Vere Grand Hotel

Situated on the west side of the town and convenient for the centre and harbour side, this hotel dates back to the 17th century and retains many period features. The style here is engagingly different, and bedrooms are individually decorated. There are three dining options and a small sun terrace.

Rooms 56 (2 fmly) (4 GF) **Facilities** STV ⛳ ♫ Xmas New Year Wi-fi **Conf** Class 100 Board 60 Thtr 100 **Notes** ⊗ Civ Wed 50

The Norfolk Lodge Hotel

★★★ 71% HOTEL

☎ 01534 722950 & 873006 🖷 01534 768804
Rouge Bouillon JE2 3ZB
e-mail: admin@morvanhotels.com

Centrally located and just a short walk to the main town, this popular hotel has a large number of regularly returning guests. Bedrooms are well decorated and equipped, and include some on the ground floor. In addition to an indoor swimming pool, the hotel offers regular evening entertainment during the main season. A range of well-prepared dishes is offered at dinner in the spacious restaurant.

Rooms 101 (11 annexe) (8 fmly) (22 GF) **Facilities** FTV 🏊 Children's pool Cycling machine ♫ Wi-fi **Services** Lift **Parking** 50 **Notes** LB ⊗ Closed Nov-Mar

The Monterey Hotel

★★★ 70% HOTEL

☎ 01534 724762 & 873006 🖷 01534 876424
St Saviour's Rd JE2 7LA
e-mail: admin@morvanhotels.com

Conveniently located for the town, this comfortable hotel has the added benefit of ample parking and a range of leisure facilities including an indoor pool. Bedrooms are well decorated and furnished, and include a number of superior rooms. The relaxing bar area is open all day, and a good range of freshly prepared dishes is offered each evening.

Rooms 73 (6 fmly) (9 GF) **Facilities** STV FTV 🏊 ⛳ Gym Xmas New Year Wi-fi **Conf** Class 12 Board 22 Thtr 40 **Services** Lift **Parking** 40 **Notes** LB ⊗

Uplands Hotel

★★★ 67% HOTEL

☎ 01534 730151 & 873006 🖷 01534 639899
St John's Rd JE2 3LE
e-mail: admin@morvanhotels.com
dir: Off A1 (main esplanade) into Pierson Rd by Grand Hotel, follow ring road for 200mtrs, 3rd on left into St John's Rd, hotel 0.5m

This hotel is situated on 12 acres of farmland just one mile from the centre of St Helier. Bedrooms are modern, spacious and comfortable; some overlook the swimming pool while others have country views. Plenty of parking and spacious public areas add to the attraction of this friendly and popular hotel.

Rooms 43 (3 fmly) (24 GF) **Facilities** STV FTV ⛳ Wi-fi **Parking** 35 **Notes** LB ⊗ Closed Nov-Mar

ST HELIER *continued*

Apollo Hotel

★★★ 64% HOTEL

☎ 01534 725441 📠 01534 722120
St Saviours Rd JE2 4GJ
e-mail: reservations@huggler.com
web: www.huggler.com
dir: On St Saviours Rd at junct with La Motte St

Centrally located, this popular hotel has a relaxed, informal atmosphere. Bedrooms are comfortably furnished and include useful extras. Many guests return regularly to enjoy the variety of leisure facilities including an outdoor pool with water slide and indoor pool with separate jacuzzi. The separate cocktail bar is an ideal place for a pre-dinner drink.

Rooms 85 (5 fmly) **S** £49-£119; **D** £79-£139 (incl. bkfst)* **Facilities** FTV supervised supervised Gym Xmas New Year Wi-fi **Conf** Class 100 Board 80 Thtr 150 **Services** Lift **Parking** 40 **Notes** LB

Millbrook House

★★ 76% HOTEL

☎ 01534 733036 📠 01534 724317
Rue De Trachy, Millbrook JE2 3JN
e-mail: millbrook.house@jerseymail.co.uk
web: www.millbrookhousehotel.com
dir: 1.5m W of town off A1

Peacefully located within its own grounds, this small, personally run hotel offers a friendly welcome and relaxing ambience. Bedrooms and bathrooms vary in size, but many of the rooms have pleasant, countryside views. In addition to outdoor seating in the warmer months, guests can relax in the library, maybe with a drink before dinner.

Rooms 24 (2 fmly) (6 GF) **S** £39-£49; **D** £78-£98 (incl. bkfst)* **Services** Lift **Parking** 20 **Notes** Closed Oct-13 May

Westhill Country Hotel

★★ 74% COUNTRY HOUSE HOTEL

☎ 01534 723260 📠 01534 766056
Mont-a-l'abbe JE2 3HB
e-mail: info@westhillhoteljersey.com
web: www.westhillhoteljersey.com
dir: Telephone for detailed directions

Set in its own beautifully landscaped gardens, this hotel enjoys a prominent position just on the outskirts of St Helier. Service is attentive and guests are guaranteed a warm welcome and genuine hospitality throughout. The bedrooms are spacious and well equipped; several rooms have commanding views over the gardens to the countryside beyond. Public areas include a stylish lounge bar and popular restaurant. Free Wi-fi is available in the public areas, and the swimming pool proves very popular with guests.

Rooms 90 (20 fmly) (16 GF) **S** £41.50-£55; **D** £83-£110 (incl. bkfst)* **Facilities** FTV Wi-fi **Parking** 75 **Notes** Closed early Oct-early Apr Civ Wed 75

Sarum

★★ 65% METRO HOTEL

☎ 01534 731340 📠 01534 758163
19/21 New St Johns Rd JE2 3LD
e-mail: sarum@jerseyweb.demon.co.uk
dir: On NW edge of St Helier, 0.5m from town centre

This hotel, just 600yds from the beach, offers self-catering bedrooms and a number of suites. The friendly staff provide a warm welcome, and there is a spacious recreational lounge with pool tables, plasma-screen TV and internet access. A garden and outdoor pool are also available. Local restaurants are just a short walk away, and bar snacks are available throughout the day.

Rooms 52 (5 annexe) (6 fmly) (2 GF) (52 smoking) **S** £37-£61; **D** £51-£93* **Facilities** STV FTV Games room Wi-fi **Services** Lift **Parking** 10 **Notes**

Hampshire Hotel

U

☎ 01534 724115
53 Val Plaisant JE2 4TB
e-mail: info@hampshirehotel.je

Currently the rating for this establishment is not confirmed. This may be due to a change of ownership or because it has only recently joined the AA rating scheme. For further details please see the AA website: theAA.com

Rooms 42 **S** £35-£50; **D** £60-£115 (incl. bkfst)* **Conf** Board 12 Del from £75 to £115* **Notes** Closed 1-3 Jan

ST MARY — Map 24

West View

★★ 69% HOTEL

☎ 01534 481643 📠 01534 483283
La Grande Rue JE3 3BD
e-mail: westview@jerseymail.co.uk
web: www.westviewhoteljersey.com
dir: At junct of B33 & C103

Located in the quiet parish of St Mary, this welcoming hotel is close to the delightful walks and cycle routes of the north coast. Bedrooms here are well equipped especially the larger, superior rooms. Entertainment is provided in the lounge bar during the summer months, when guests can also enjoy a swim in the heated outdoor pool.

Rooms 42 (3 fmly) (18 GF) **Facilities** Wi-fi **Parking** 38 **Notes** Closed Nov-Apr

ST PETER — Map 24

Greenhills Country Hotel

★★★★ 74% COUNTRY HOUSE HOTEL

☎ 01534 481042 📠 01534 485322
Mont de L'Ecole JE3 7EL
e-mail: reserve@greenhillshotel.co.uk
dir: From A1 signed St Peter's Valley (A11), in 4m right onto E112

Centrally located on the island and very close to The Living Legends display, this relaxing country house hotel has a lovely atmosphere and a delightful garden that surrounds it. Bedrooms extend from the main building around the courtyard; all are comfortable and well equipped. A varied menu, based on fresh local produce, is served in the spacious restaurant.

Rooms 31 (2 fmly) (9 GF) **Facilities** STV FTV Wi-fi **Conf** Class 12 Board 16 Thtr 20 Del from £100 to £150* **Parking** 40 **Notes** Closed mid Dec-early Feb Civ Wed 40

ST SAVIOUR Map 24

INSPECTORS' CHOICE

Longueville Manor

★★★★★ ®®® HOTEL

☎ 01534 725501 🖷 01534 731613
JE2 7WF
e-mail: info@longuevillemanor.com
web: www.longuevillemanor.com
dir: A3 E from St Helier towards Gorey. Hotel 1m on left

Dating back to the 13th century, there is something very special about Longueville Manor, which is why so many guests return time and again. It is set in 17 acres of grounds including woodland walks, a spectacular rose garden and a lake. Bedrooms have great style and individuality boasting fresh flowers, fine embroidered bed linen and a host of extras. The committed team of staff create a welcoming atmosphere and every effort is made to ensure a memorable stay. The very accomplished cuisine is also a highlight of any stay.

Rooms 30 (1 annexe) (7 GF) (6 smoking) **S** £195-£370; **D** £220-£630 (incl. bkfst)* **Facilities** STV Xmas New Year Wi-fi **Conf** Class 30 Board 30 Thtr 45 Del from £245 to £320* **Services** Lift **Parking** 40 **Notes** LB Civ Wed 40

TRINITY Map 24

Water's Edge Hotel

★★★ 74% HOTEL

☎ 01534 862777 🖷 01534 863645
Bouley Bay JE3 5AS
e-mail: mail@watersedgehotel.co.je
web: www.watersedgehotel.co.je
dir: On NE coast. 4m from St Helier & 7.4m from Jersey Airport

Set in the tranquil surroundings of Bouley Bay on the north coast, this hotel is situated exactly as its name conveys. The well-furnished bedrooms offer high standards of quality and comfort, and the vast majority enjoy the delightful views of either the garden or over the bay towards France. A range of modern British dishes, including fresh seafood, is offered in the comfortable dining room which also benefits from the splendid views. Free Wi-fi is available.

Rooms 50 (3 fmly) **S** £42.50-£62.50; **D** £85-£125 (incl. bkfst)* **Facilities** **Conf** Class 25 Board 20 Thtr 30 **Services** Lift **Parking** 20 **Notes** LB Closed mid Oct-mid Apr

SARK

SARK Map 24

Hotel Petit Champ

★★ 79% ®® SMALL HOTEL

☎ 01481 832046 🖷 01481 832469
GY10 1SF
e-mail: info@hotelpetitchamp.co.uk
web: www.hotelpetitchamp.co.uk
dir: Ferry from St Peter Port, Guernsey. From harbour through village, right at Gallery Stores. Pass church, left at x-rds. To Methodist Church, right, follow hotel signs

Guests can expect a warm welcome from the caring staff at this delightful small hotel, situated within a 20-minute walk of the main street. Wonderful views of the sea and neighbouring islands can be enjoyed from the lounges, the gardens and most of the bedrooms. A five-course dinner is included in the half-board terms, and a there's a well-stocked wine cellar and bar. An outdoor solar-heated swimming pool is available to residents.

Rooms 10 (2 fmly) **S** £57-£62; **D** £110-£124 (incl. bkfst)* **Facilities** Xmas New Year Wi-fi **Notes** ⊗ No children 10yrs

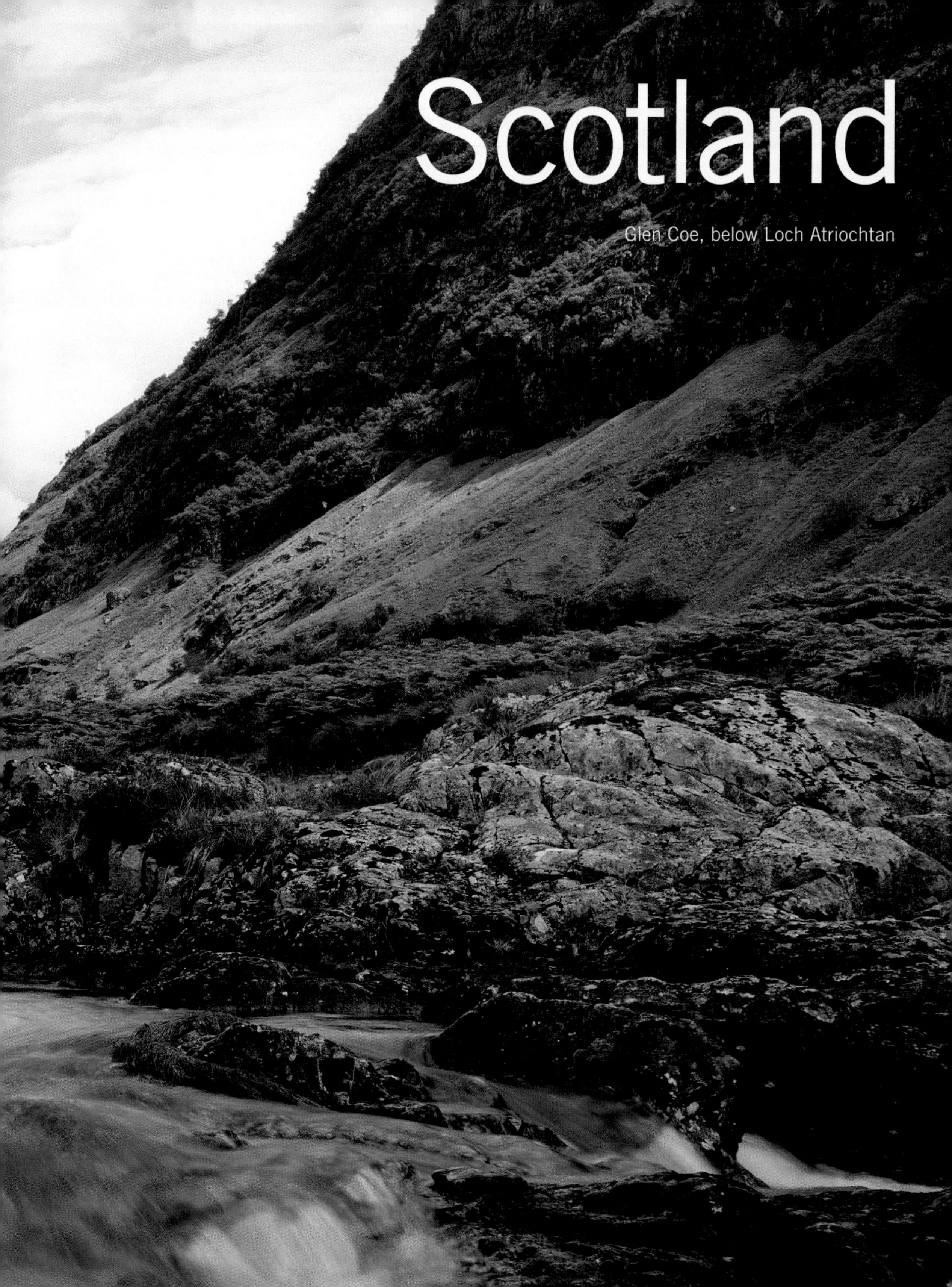

Scotland

Glen Coe, below Loch Atriochtan

A

ABERDEEN
City of Aberdeen — Map 23 NJ90

See also **Aberdeen Airport**

Norwood Hall

★★★★ 77% HOTEL

☎ 01224 868951 🖷 01224 869868
Garthdee Rd, Cults AB15 9FX
e-mail: info@norwood-hall.co.uk
web: www.norwood-hall.co.uk
dir: Off A90, at 1st rdbt cross Bridge of Dee, left at rdbt onto Garthdee Rd (B&Q & Sainsburys on left) continue to hotel sign

This imposing Victorian mansion has retained many of its original features, most notably the fine oak staircase, stained glass and ornately decorated walls and ceilings. Accommodation varies in style from individually designed bedrooms in the main house to the newest contemporary bedrooms. The extensive grounds ensure the hotel is popular as a wedding venue.

Rooms 73 (14 GF) **Facilities** STV FTV Xmas New Year Wi-fi **Conf** Class 100 Board 70 Thtr 200 **Services** Lift **Parking** 140 **Notes** ⊗ Civ Wed 150

Holiday Inn Aberdeen West

★★★★ 75% HOTEL

☎ 01224 270300 🖷 01224 270323
Westhill Dr, Westhill AB32 6TT
e-mail: info@hiaberdeenwest.co.uk
web: www.holidayinn.co.uk
dir: On A944 in Westhill

In a good location at the west side of the city, this modern hotel caters well for the needs of both business and leisure guests. The nicely appointed bedrooms and bathrooms have a contemporary feel. Luigi's restaurant serves modern Italian food, and the popular lounge offers more informal dining. There is a separate pub operation with wide-screen TVs showing a range of sporting events.

Rooms 86 (30 fmly) **Facilities** STV FTV Gym Wi-fi **Conf** Class 150 Board 80 Thtr 300 **Services** Lift Air con **Parking** 90 **Notes** Civ Wed 250

Mercure Ardoe House Hotel & Spa

Mercure

★★★★ 74% HOTEL

☎ 01224 860600 🖷 01224 861283
South Deeside Rd, Blairs AB12 5YP
e-mail: h6626@accor.com
web: www.mercure.com
dir: 4m W of city off B9077

From its elevated position on the banks of the River Dee, this 19th-century baronial-style mansion commands excellent countryside views. Beautifully decorated, thoughtfully equipped bedrooms are located in the main house, and in the more modern extension. Public rooms include a spa and leisure club, a cosy lounge and cocktail bar and impressive function facilities.

Rooms 109 **Facilities** Spa STV Gym Aerobics studio Xmas New Year Wi-fi **Conf** Class 200 Board 150 Thtr 600 **Services** Lift **Parking** 220 **Notes** ⊗ Civ Wed 250

Copthorne Hotel Aberdeen

MILLENNIUM HOTELS AND RESORTS MILLENNIUM • COPTHORNE

★★★★ 73% HOTEL

☎ 01224 630404 🖷 01224 640573
122 Huntly St AB10 1SU
e-mail: reservations.aberdeen@millenniumhotels.co.uk
web: www.millenniumhotels.co.uk/aberdeen
dir: West end of city centre, off Union St, up Rose St, hotel 0.25m on right on corner with Huntly St

Situated just outside of the city centre, this hotel offers friendly, attentive service. The smart bedrooms are well proportioned and guests will appreciate the added quality of the Connoisseur rooms. Mac's bar provides a relaxed atmosphere in which to enjoy a drink or to dine informally, whilst Poachers Restaurant offers a slightly more formal dining experience.

Rooms 89 (15 fmly) **S** £55-£300; **D** £55-£300* **Facilities** STV FTV New Year Wi-fi **Conf** Class 100 Board 70 Thtr 200 **Services** Lift **Parking** 15 **Notes** LB RS 24-26 Dec Civ Wed 180

Maryculter House Hotel

★★★★ 71% ⊛ HOTEL

☎ 01224 732124 🖷 01224 733510
South Deeside Rd, Maryculter AB12 5GB
e-mail: info@maryculterhousehotel.com
web: www.maryculterhousehotel.com
dir: Exit A90 S of Aberdeen onto B9077. Hotel 8m on right, 0.5m beyond Lower Deeside Caravan Park

Set in grounds on the banks of the River Dee, this charming Scottish mansion dates back to medieval times and is now a popular wedding and conference venue. Exposed stonework and open fires feature in the oldest parts, which house the cocktail bar and Priory Restaurant. Lunch and breakfast are taken overlooking the river; bedrooms are equipped especially with business travellers in mind.

Rooms 40 (1 fmly) (16 GF) **Facilities** STV FTV Fishing Clay pigeon shooting Archery Xmas New Year Wi-fi **Conf** Class 100 Board 50 Thtr 200 **Parking** 150 **Notes** ⊗ Civ Wed 132

The Calendonian, Aberdeen

thistle

★★★★ 71% HOTEL

☎ 0871 376 9003 🖷 0871 376 9103
10-14 Union Ter AB10 1WE
e-mail: aberdeencaledonian@thistle.co.uk
web: www.thistlehotels.com/thecaledonian
dir: Follow signs to city centre & Union St. Turn into Union Terrace. Hotel on left, parking behind hotel in Diamond St

Centrally located just off Union Street and overlooking Union Terrace Gardens this traditional hotel offers comfortable and well-appointed bedrooms, and public areas in keeping with the age of the building. The upbeat Café Bar Caley serves informal food, but for a more formal dining experience there's the Restaurant on the Terrace. A small car park is available to the rear. Thistle Hotels – AA Hotel Group of the Year 2011-12.

Rooms 83 (5 fmly) **Facilities** FTV Wi-fi **Conf** Class 40 Board 30 Thtr 80 **Services** Lift **Parking** 22 **Notes** ⊗ Civ Wed 40

Malmaison Aberdeen

★★★ 86% ⊛ HOTEL

☎ 01224 327370 🖷 01224 327371
49-53 Queens Rd AB15 4YP
e-mail: info.aberdeen@malmaison.com
dir: A90, 3rd exit into Queens Rd at 3rd rdbt, hotel on right

Popular with business travellers and as a function venue, this well-established hotel lies east of the city centre. Public areas include a reception lounge and an intimate restaurant, plus the extensive bar menu which remains a popular choice for many regulars. There are two styles of accommodation, with the superior rooms being particularly comfortable and well equipped.

Rooms 79 (8 fmly) (10 GF) **Facilities** Spa STV FTV Gym Steam room Xmas New Year Wi-fi **Conf** Class 30 Board 20 Thtr 40 **Services** Lift **Parking** 50 **Notes** LB

The Mariner Hotel

★★★ 79% HOTEL

☎ 01224 588901 🖷 01224 571621
349 Great Western Rd AB10 6NW
e-mail: info@themarinerhotel.co.uk
dir: E off Anderson Drive (A90) at Great Western Rd. Hotel on right on corner of Gray St

This well maintained, family operated hotel is located west of the city centre. The smart, spacious bedrooms are well equipped and particularly comfortable, with executive suites available. The public rooms are restricted to the lounge bar, which is food driven, and the Atlantis Restaurant that showcases the region's wide choice of excellent seafood and meats.

Rooms 25 (8 annexe) (4 GF) **S** £55-£100; **D** £85-£130 (incl. bkfst)* **Facilities** FTV New Year Wi-fi **Parking** 51 **Notes** ⊗

The Craighaar

★★★ 78% HOTEL

☎ 01224 712275 🖷 01224 716362
Waterton Rd, Bucksburn AB21 9HS
e-mail: info@craighaar.co.uk
dir: From A96 (Airport/Inverness) onto A947, hotel signed

Conveniently located for the airport, this welcoming hotel is a popular base for business people and tourists alike. Guests can make use of a quiet library lounge, and enjoy meals in the bar or restaurant. All bedrooms are well equipped, plus there is a wing of duplex suites that provide additional comfort.

Rooms 53 (6 fmly) (16 GF) (6 smoking) **S** £59-£109; **D** £65-£129 (incl. bkfst)* **Facilities** STV FTV Library Wi-fi **Conf** Class 33 Board 30 Thtr 90 Del from £129.50* **Parking** 80 **Notes** LB ⊗ Closed 25-26 Dec Civ Wed 40

Thistle Aberdeen Altens

thistle

★★★ 78% HOTEL

☎ 0871 376 9002 🖷 0871 376 9102
Souter Head Rd, Altens AB12 3LF
e-mail: aberdeenaltens@thistle.co.uk
web: www.thistle.com/aberdeenaltens
dir: A90 onto A956 signed Aberdeen Harbour. Hotel just off rdbt

Popular with oil industry personnel, this large purpose-built hotel lies in the Altens area, south east of the city. It's worth asking for one of the executive bedrooms that provide excellent space. Guests can eat in the restaurant, brasserie or the bar. Thistle Hotels – AA Hotel Group of the Year 2011-12.

Rooms 216 (96 fmly) (48 GF) **S** £85-£245; **D** £95-£255 (incl. bkfst)* **Facilities** FTV Gym Sauna Steam room Solarium Aerobic studio New Year Wi-fi **Conf** Class 144 Board 30 Thtr 400 Del from £165 to £205 **Services** Lift **Parking** 300 **Notes** LB ⊗ Civ Wed 150

A

ABERDEEN *continued*

Holiday Inn Express Aberdeen City Centre

BUDGET HOTEL

☎ 01224 623500 🖹 01224 623523
Chapel St AB10 1SQ
e-mail: info@hieaberdeen.co.uk
web: www.hiexpress.com/exaberdeencc
dir: In west end of city, just off Union Street

A modern hotel ideal for families and business travellers. Fresh and uncomplicated, the spacious rooms include Sky TV, power shower and tea and coffee-making facilities. Continental buffet breakfast is included in the room rate; other meals may be taken at the nearby family pub or restaurant. See also the Hotel Groups pages.

Rooms 155 (102 fmly) (30 smoking) **S** £48-£150; **D** £48-£150 (incl. bkfst)* **Conf** Class 18 Board 16 Thtr 35

Holiday Inn Express Aberdeen - Exhibition Centre

BUDGET HOTEL

☎ 01224 706878 🖹 01224 823923
Exhibition & Conference Centre, Parkway East, Bridge of Don AB23 8AJ
e-mail: info@hieaberdeenexhibitioncentre.co.uk

Rooms 135 (100 fmly) **Conf** Class 20 Board 24 Thtr 50

Premier Inn Aberdeen Central West

BUDGET HOTEL

☎ 0871 527 8006 🖹 0871 527 8007
North Anderson Dr AB15 6DW
dir: Into Aberdeen from S on A90 follow airport signs. Hotel 1st left after fire station. (NB for Sat Nav use AB15 6TP)

High quality, budget accommodation ideal for both families and business travellers. Spacious, en suite bedrooms feature tea and coffee making facilities, and Freeview TV in most hotels. Internet access and Wi-fi are available for a small fee. The adjacent family restaurant features a wide and varied menu. See also the Hotel Groups pages.

Rooms 62 **D** £54-£73*

Premier Inn Aberdeen City Centre

BUDGET HOTEL

☎ 0871 527 8008 🖹 0871 527 8009
Inverlair House, West North St AB24 5AS
dir: A90 onto A9013 into city centre. Take A956 towards King St, 1st left into Meal Market St

Rooms 162 **D** £55-£75*

Premier Inn Aberdeen North (Murcar)

BUDGET HOTEL

☎ 0871 527 8010 🖹 0871 527 8011
Ellon Rd, Murcar, Bridge of Don AB23 8BP
dir: From city centre take A90 N follow Peterhead signs. At rdbt 2m after Aberdeen Exhibition & Conference Centre, left onto B999. Hotel on right

Rooms 40 **D** £53-£70*

Premier Inn Aberdeen South

BUDGET HOTEL

☎ 0871 527 8012 🖹 0871 527 8013
Mains of Balquharn, Portlethen AB12 4QS
dir: From A90 follow Portlethen & Badentoy Park signs. Hotel on right

Rooms 40 **D** £53-£70*

Premier Inn Aberdeen (Westhill)

BUDGET HOTEL

☎ 0871 527 8004 🖹 0871 527 8005
Straik Rd, Westhill AB32 6HF
dir: On A944 towards Alford, hotel adjacent to Tesco

Rooms 61 **D** £53-£70*

ABERDEEN AIRPORT
City of Aberdeen
Map 23 NJ81

Thistle Aberdeen Airport

thistle

★★★★ 78% HOTEL

☎ 0871 376 9001 🖹 0871 376 9101
Aberdeen Airport, Argyll Rd AB21 0AF
e-mail: aberdeenairport@thistle.co.uk
web: www.thistle.com/aberdeenairport
dir: Adjacent to Aberdeen Airport

Ideally located at the entrance to the airport this hotel offers ample parking plus a courtesy bus service to the terminal. This is a well presented establishment that benefits from good-sized bedrooms and comfortable public areas. Just Gym offers a good variety of exercise equipment.

Rooms 147 (3 fmly) (74 GF) (18 smoking) **Facilities** FTV Gym Wi-fi **Conf** Class 350 Board 100 Thtr 600 **Parking** 300

Aberdeen Marriott Hotel

Marriott HOTELS & RESORTS

★★★★ 75% HOTEL

☎ 01224 770011 🖹 01224 722347
Overton Circle, Dyce AB21 7AZ
e-mail: reservations.scotland@marriotthotels.com
web: www.aberdeenmarriott.co.uk
dir: Follow A96 to Bucksburn, right at rdbt onto A947. Hotel in 2m at 2nd rdbt

Close to the airport and conveniently located for the business district, this purpose-built hotel is a popular conference venue. The well-proportioned bedrooms come with many thoughtful extras. Public areas include an informal bar and lounge, a split-level restaurant and a leisure centre that can be accessed directly from a number of bedrooms.

Rooms 155 (81 fmly) (61 GF) (10 smoking) **Facilities** STV (pool) supervised Gym Saunas (male & female) Solarium New Year Wi-fi **Conf** Class 200 Board 60 Thtr 400 **Services** Air con **Parking** 180 **Notes** (no smoking) Civ Wed 90

Menzies Dyce Aberdeen Airport

★★★ 78% HOTEL

☎ 01224 723101 📠 01224 773883
Farburn Ter, Dyce AB21 7DW
e-mail: dyce@menzieshotels.co.uk
dir: A96/A947 airport E after 1m turn left at lights. Hotel in 250yds

This hotel is very convenient for air travellers and for those wishing to explore this lovely Highland area. The spacious, well-equipped bedrooms have all the expected up-to-date amenities. The public areas are welcoming and include a contemporary brasserie. Secure parking and Wi-fi are also provided.

Rooms 198 (198 annexe) (3 fmly) (107 GF) (54 smoking) **Facilities** STV Xmas New Year Wi-fi **Conf** Class 160 Board 120 Thtr 400 **Parking** 150 **Notes** Civ Wed 220

ABERDOUR — Map 21 NT18
Fife

Woodside

★★★ HOTEL

☎ 01383 860328 📠 01383 860920
High St KY3 0SW
e-mail: reception@thewoodsidehotel.co.uk
web: www.thewoodsidehotel.co.uk
dir: M90 junct 1, E on A291 for 5m, hotel on left on entering village

Rooms 20 (3 fmly) **Facilities** FTV Wi-fi **Conf** Class 80 Thtr 60 Del from £110 to £120 **Parking** 22 **Notes** Closed 25 Dec & 1 Jan

ABERFOYLE — Map 20 NN50
Stirling

Macdonald Forest Hills Hotel & Resort

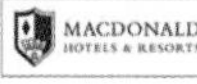

★★★★ 76% HOTEL

☎ 0844 879 9057 & 01877 389500
📠 01877 387307
Kinlochard FK8 3TL
e-mail: forest_hills@macdonald-hotels.co.uk
web: www.macdonald-hotels.co.uk/foresthills
dir: A84, A873, A81 to Aberfoyle onto B829

Situated in the heart of The Trossachs with wonderful views of Loch Ard, this popular hotel forms part of a resort complex offering a range of indoor and outdoor facilities. The main hotel has relaxing lounges and a restaurant that all overlook the landscaped gardens. A separate building houses the leisure centre, lounge bar and bistro.

Rooms 49 (16 fmly) (12 GF) **Facilities** Spa STV FTV Gym Children's club Snooker Watersports Quad biking Archery Clay pigeon shooting Xmas New Year Wi-fi **Conf** Class 60 Board 45 Thtr 150 **Services** Lift **Parking** 100 **Notes** Civ Wed 100

ABINGTON MOTORWAY SERVICE AREA (M74) — Map 21 NS92
South Lanarkshire

Days Inn Abington - M74

BUDGET HOTEL

☎ 01864 502782 📠 01864 502759
ML12 6RG
e-mail: abington.hotel@welcomebreak.co.uk
web: www.welcomebreak.co.uk
dir: M74 junct 13, accessible from N'bound and S'bound carriageways

This modern building offers accommodation in smart, spacious and well-equipped bedrooms, suitable for families and business travellers, and all with en suite bathrooms. Continental breakfast is available and other refreshments may be taken at the nearby family restaurant. See also the Hotel Groups pages.

Rooms 52 (50 fmly) (8 smoking) **S** £39.95-£59.95; **D** £49.95-£69.95 **Conf** Board 10

ANSTRUTHER — Map 21 NO50
Fife

The Waterfront

RESTAURANT WITH ROOMS

☎ 01333 312200 📠 01333 312288
18-20 Shore St KY10 3EA
e-mail: chris@anstruther-waterfront.co.uk
dir: Off A917 opposite marina

Situated overlooking the harbour, The Waterfront offers spacious, stylish, contemporary accommodation, with bedrooms located in lovingly restored buildings in a courtyard behind the restaurant. There is a comfortable lounge with a smartly fitted kitchen and dining room, and laundry facilities are available in the granary. Dinner and breakfast are served in the attractive restaurant that offers a comprehensive menu featuring the best of local produce.

Rooms 8 (8 annexe) (3 fmly)

ARCHIESTOWN — Map 23 NJ24
Moray

Archiestown Hotel

★★★ 77% SMALL HOTEL

☎ 01340 810218 📠 01340 810239
AB38 7QL
e-mail: jah@archiestownhotel.co.uk
web: www.archiestownhotel.co.uk
dir: A95 Craigellachie, follow B9102 4m to Archiestown

Set in the heart of this Speyside village this small hotel is popular with anglers and locals alike. It is rightly noted for its great hospitality, attentive service and good food. Cosy and comfortable public rooms include a choice of lounges (there is no bar as such) and a bistro offering an inviting choice of dishes at both lunch and dinner.

Rooms 11 (1 fmly) **S** £70-£80; **D** £70-£80 (incl. bkfst)* **Facilities** FTV New Year Wi-fi **Conf** Board 12 Thtr 20 Del from £126 to £136* **Parking** 20 **Notes** LB Closed 24-27 Dec & 3 Jan-9 Feb

ARDUAINE — Map 20 NM71
Argyll & Bute

Loch Melfort

★★★ 83% HOTEL

☎ 01852 200233 📠 01852 200214
PA34 4XG
e-mail: reception@lochmelfort.co.uk
web: www.lochmelfort.co.uk
dir: On A816, midway between Oban & Lochgilphead

Enjoying one of the finest locations on the West Coast, this popular, family-run hotel has outstanding views across Asknish Bay towards the Islands of Jura, Scarba and Shuna. The accommodation is provided in either the balcony rooms in the Cedar Wing or the more traditional rooms in the main hotel. The dining options are the main restaurant, which has stunning views, or the more informal bistro.

Rooms 25 (20 annexe) (2 fmly) (10 GF) **S** £102-£128; **D** £144-£196 (incl. bkfst)* **Facilities** 4 moorings Xmas New Year Wi-fi **Conf** Class 40 Board 20 Thtr 50 Del from £135* **Parking** 50 **Notes** Closed 4-20 Jan RS Winter Civ Wed 100

A

AUCHENCAIRN Map 21 NX75
Dumfries & Galloway

Balcary Bay Hotel

★★★ 86% ◎◎ HOTEL

☎ 01556 640217 & 640311 🖷 01556 640272
DG7 1QZ
e-mail: reservations@balcary-bay-hotel.co.uk
web: www.balcary-bay-hotel.co.uk
dir: On A711 between Dalbeattie & Kirkcudbright, hotel 2m from village

Taking its name from the bay on which it lies, this hotel has lawns running down to the shore. The larger bedrooms enjoy stunning views over the bay, whilst others overlook the gardens. The comfortable public areas invite relaxation. Imaginative dishes feature at dinner, accompanied by a good wine list.

Rooms 20 (1 fmly) (3 GF) **S** £65-£75; **D** £134-£164 (incl. bkfst)* **Facilities** FTV **Parking** 50 **Notes** LB Closed 1st Sun Dec-last Fri Jan

AUCHTERARDER Map 21 NN91
Perth & Kinross

INSPECTORS' CHOICE

The Gleneagles Hotel

★★★★★ ◎◎◎◎ HOTEL

☎ 01764 662231 🖷 01764 662134
PH3 1NF
e-mail: resort.sales@gleneagles.com
web: www.gleneagles.com
dir: Off A9 at exit for A823 follow signs for Gleneagles Hotel

With its international reputation for high standards, this grand hotel provides something for everyone. Set in 850 acres of glorious countryside, Gleneagles offers a peaceful retreat, as well as many sporting activities, including the famous championship golf courses. All bedrooms are appointed to a high standard and offer both traditional and contemporary styles. Stylish public areas include various dining options - the Deseo 'Mediterranean Food Market' eaterie, The Strathearn, with two AA Rosettes, as well as inspired cooking at Andrew Fairlie at Gleneagles, a restaurant with four AA Rosettes. There's also the Clubhouse and many bars. The award-winning EPSA spa offers the very latest treatments to restore both body and soul. Service is always professional - the staff are friendly and nothing is too much trouble. Chairman, Peter Lederer CBE has been awarded the AA Lifetime Achievement Award for 2011-12.

Rooms 232 (115 fmly) (11 GF) **S** fr £315; **D** fr £315 (incl. bkfst)* **Facilities** Spa STV FTV supervised 54 Putt green Fishing Gym Falconry Off-road driving Golf Archery Clay target shooting Gundog School Xmas New Year Wi-fi Child facilities **Conf** Class 240 Board 60 Thtr 360 Del from £ to £525* **Services** Lift **Parking** 277 **Notes** Civ Wed 360

AVIEMORE Map 23 NH81
Highland

Macdonald Highlands

MACDONALD HOTELS & RESORTS

★★★★ 75% HOTEL

☎ 01479 815100 🖷 01479 815101
Aviemore Highland Resort PH22 1PN
e-mail: general@aviemorehighlandresort.com
web: www.aviemorehighlandresort.com
dir: From N: Exit A9 to Aviemore (B970). Right at T-junct, through village. Right (2nd exit) at 1st rdbt into Macdonald Aviemore Highland Resort, follow reception signs. From S: Exit A9 to Aviemore, left at T-junct. Immediately after Esso garage, turn left into Resort

This hotel is part of the Aviemore Highland Resort which boasts a wide range of activities including a championship golf course. The modern, well-equipped bedrooms suit business, leisure guests and families, and Aspects Restaurant is the fine dining option. In addition there is a state-of-the-art gym, spa treatments and a 25-metre pool with a wave machine and flume.

Rooms 151 (10 fmly) (44 GF) **S** £84-£225; **D** £89-£230 (incl. bkfst) **Facilities** Spa STV FTV supervised 18 Putt green Fishing Gym Steam room Sauna Children's indoor & outdoor playgrounds Xmas New Year Wi-fi **Conf** Class 610 Board 38 Thtr 1000 Del from £110 to £260 **Services** Lift **Parking** 500 **Notes** Civ Wed 300

AYR Map 20 NS32
South Ayrshire

The Western House Hotel

★★★★ 84% ◎◎ HOTEL

☎ 0870 055 5510 🖷 01292 294990
2 Whitletts Rd KA8 0HA
e-mail: info@westernhousehotel.co.uk
dir: From Glasgow M77 then A77 towards Ayr. At Whitletts rdbt take A719 towards town centre

This impressive hotel is located in its own attractive gardens on the edge of Ayr racecourse. Bedrooms in the main house are superbly appointed, and the courtyard rooms offer much comfort too. Nicely appointed day rooms include the light and airy restaurant with views across the course. The staff are attentive and welcoming.

Rooms 49 (39 annexe) (39 fmly) (16 GF) **Facilities** STV Xmas New Year Wi-fi **Conf** Class 300 Board 50 Thtr 1200 Del from £110 to £180* **Services** Lift **Parking** 250 **Notes** Civ Wed 200

Fairfield House

★★★★ 79% ®® HOTEL

☎ 01292 267461 📠 01292 261456
12 Fairfield Rd KA7 2AR
e-mail: reservations@fairfieldhotel.co.uk
dir: From A77 towards Ayr South (A30). Follow town centre signs, down Miller Rd, left, then right into Fairfield Rd

Situated in a leafy cul-de-sac close to the esplanade, this hotel enjoys stunning seascapes towards to the Isle of Arran. Bedrooms are in either modern or classical styles, the latter featuring impressive bathrooms. Public areas provide stylish, modern rooms in which to relax. Skilfully prepared meals are served in the casual brasserie or elegant restaurant.

Rooms 44 (4 annexe) (3 fmly) (9 GF) **S** £79-£150; **D** £89-£160 (incl. bkfst)* **Facilities** FTV supervised Gym Fitness room Sauna Steam room Xmas New Year Wi-fi **Conf** Class 80 Board 40 Thtr 120 Del from £130* **Services** Lift **Parking** 50 **Notes** LB Civ Wed 150

Enterkine Country House

★★★★ 76% ®® COUNTRY HOUSE HOTEL

☎ 01292 520580 📠 01292 521582
Annbank KA6 5AL
e-mail: mail@enterkine.com
dir: 5m E of Ayr on B743

This luxurious art deco country mansion dates from the 1930s and retains many original features, notably some splendid bathroom suites. The focus is very much on dining, and in country house tradition there is no bar, drinks being served in the elegant lounge and library. The well-proportioned bedrooms are furnished and equipped to high standards, many with lovely countryside views.

Rooms 14 (8 annexe) (6 fmly) (5 GF) **S** £60-£100; **D** £80-£120 (incl. bkfst)* **Facilities** FTV Xmas New Year Wi-fi **Conf** Class 140 Board 140 Thtr 200 **Parking** 40 **Notes** LB Civ Wed 70

Express by Holiday Inn Ayr

BUDGET HOTEL

☎ 01292 272300 📠 01292 272315
Wheatpark Place KA8 9RT
e-mail: info@hiexpressayr.com
web: www.hiexpress.co.uk

A modern hotel ideal for families and business travellers. Fresh and uncomplicated, the spacious rooms include Sky TV, power shower and tea and coffee-making facilities. Continental buffet breakfast is included in the room rate; other meals may be taken at the nearby family pub or restaurant. See also the Hotel Groups pages.

Rooms 84 (44 fmly) (3 GF) **S** £49-£120; **D** £49-£120 (incl. bkfst)* **Conf** Class 12 Board 12 Thtr 23

Premier Inn Ayr/Prestwick Airport

BUDGET HOTEL

☎ 0871 527 8038 📠 0871 527 8039
Kilmarnock Rd, Monkton KA9 2RJ
dir: At Dutch House Rdbt (at junct of A77 & A78) at Monkton

High quality, budget accommodation ideal for both families and business travellers. Spacious, en suite bedrooms feature tea and coffee making facilities, and Freeview TV in most hotels. Internet access and Wi-fi are available for a small fee. The adjacent family restaurant features a wide and varied menu. See also the Hotel Groups pages.

Rooms 64 **D** £55-£60*

BALLACHULISH Highland — Map 22 NN05

The Isles of Glencoe Hotel & Leisure Centre

★★★ 72% HOTEL

☎ 0845 906 9966 & 0844 855 9134
📠 01855 811 770
PH49 4HL
e-mail: reservations@akkeronhotels.com
web: www.akkeronhotels.com
dir: A82 N, slip road on left into village, 1st right, hotel in 600yds

This hotel enjoys a spectacular setting beside Loch Leven. This friendly modern establishment has spacious bedrooms and guests have a choice of Loch or Mountain View rooms. Public areas include a popular restaurant and a family friendly leisure centre.

Rooms 59 (21 fmly) (21 GF) **S** £59-£155; **D** £59-£165 (incl. bkfst)* **Facilities** STV Gym Hydroseat Bio-sauna Xmas New Year Wi-fi **Conf** Class 40 Board 20 Thtr 40 Del from £70 to £140* **Parking** 100 **Notes** LB Civ Wed 100

BALLANTRAE South Ayrshire — Map 20 NX08

INSPECTORS' CHOICE

Glenapp Castle

★★★★★ ®®®® COUNTRY HOUSE HOTEL

☎ 01465 831212 📠 01465 831000
KA26 0NZ
e-mail: enquiries@glenappcastle.com
web: www.glenappcastle.com
dir: S through Ballantrae, cross bridge over River Stinchar, 1st right, hotel in 1m

Friendly hospitality and attentive service prevail at this stunning Victorian castle, set in extensive private grounds to the south of the village. Impeccably furnished bedrooms are graced with antiques and period pieces, and include two master rooms and a ground-floor family suite. Breathtaking views of Arran and Ailsa Craig can be enjoyed from the delightful, sumptuous day rooms and from many of the bedrooms. The outstanding cuisine is a great draw here; dinner is offered on a well crafted and imaginative fixed six-course menu. Much of the fruit, vegetables and herbs come from the hotel's own garden. Guests should make a point of walking round the wonderful 36-acre grounds, and take a look at the azalea pond, walled vegetable gardens and restored Victorian greenhouses.

Rooms 17 (2 fmly) (7 GF) **S** £265-£450; **D** £415-£620 (incl. bkfst & dinner)* **Facilities** STV FTV New Year Wi-fi **Conf** Class 12 Board 17 Thtr 17 Del from £295 to £500* **Services** Lift **Parking** 20 **Notes** LB Closed Jan-mid Mar & Xmas wk Civ Wed 40

B

BALLATER Aberdeenshire **Map 23 NO39**

INSPECTORS' CHOICE

Darroch Learg

★★★ ®®® SMALL HOTEL

☎ 013397 55443 📠 013397 55252
Braemar Rd AB35 5UX
e-mail: enquiries@darrochlearg.co.uk
web: www.darrochlearg.co.uk
dir: On A93, W of Ballater

Set high above the road in extensive wooded grounds, this long-established hotel offers superb views over the hills and countryside of Royal Deeside. Nigel and Fiona Franks are caring and attentive hosts who improve their hotel every year. Bedrooms, some with four-poster beds, are individually styled, bright and spacious. Food is a highlight of any visit, whether it is a freshly prepared breakfast or the fine cuisine served in the delightful conservatory restaurant.

Rooms 12 (1 GF) **S** £120-£195; **D** £190-£320 (incl. bkfst & dinner)* **Facilities** New Year **Conf** Board 12 Thtr 25 Del from £150 to £220* **Parking** 15 **Notes** LB Closed Xmas & Jan (ex New Year)

Loch Kinord

★★★ 80% ® HOTEL

☎ 013398 85229 📠 013398 87007
Ballater Rd, Dinnet AB34 5JY
e-mail: stay@kinord.com
dir: Between Aboyne & Ballater, on A93, in Dinnet

Family-run, this roadside hotel is well located for leisure and sporting pursuits. It has lots of character and a friendly atmosphere. There are two bars, one outside and a cosy one inside, plus a dining room with a bold colour scheme. Bedrooms are stylish and have smart bathrooms.

Rooms 20 (3 fmly) (4 GF) **Facilities** Pool table Xmas **Conf** Class 30 Board 30 Thtr 40 **Parking** 20 **Notes** Civ Wed 50

The Green Inn

®®® RESTAURANT WITH ROOMS

☎ 013397 55701
9 Victoria Rd AB35 5QQ
e-mail: info@green-inn.com
web: www.green-inn.com
dir: In village centre

A former temperance hotel, the Green Inn enjoys a central location in the pretty village of Ballater. Bedrooms are of a high standard and attractively presented. The kitchen has a strong reputation for its fine cuisine, which can be enjoyed in the stylish conservatory restaurant. Breakfast is equally enjoyable and should not be missed. Genuine hospitality from the enthusiastic proprietors is a real feature of any stay.

Rooms 2

The Auld Kirk

®® RESTAURANT WITH ROOMS

☎ 01339 755762 & 07918 698000
📠 0700 6037 559
Braemar Rd AB35 5RQ
e-mail: info@theauldkirk.com
dir: From A93 Braemar, on right just before town centre

A Victorian Scottish Free Church building that is now a contemporary restaurant with rooms boasting well-appointed bedrooms and bathrooms. Many original features of this kirk have been restored and incorporated in the design. The Spirit Restaurant with its high ceilings and tall windows provides a wonderful setting to enjoy the award-winning, seasonal food. There is a stylish bar with a good selection of malts and a terrace for alfresco eating when the weather permits.

Rooms 7 (1 fmly)

BALLOCH West Dumbartonshire **Map 20 NS38**

Cameron House on Loch Lomond

DE VERE Hotels & Resorts

★★★★★ 85% ® HOTEL

☎ 01389 755565 📠 01389 759522
G83 8QZ
e-mail: reservations@cameronhouse.co.uk
web: www.devere.co.uk
dir: M8 (W) junct 30 for Erskine Bridge. A82 for Crianlarich. 14m, at rdbt signed Luss, hotel on right

Enjoying an idyllic location on the banks of Loch Lomond in over 100 acres of wooded parkland, this stylish hotel offers an excellent range of leisure facilities. These include two golf courses, a world-class spa and a host of indoor and outdoor sporting activities. A choice of restaurants and bars cater for all tastes and include the Scottish-themed Cameron Grill and a fine dining operation, Martin Wishart at Loch Lomond (3 AA Rosettes). Bedrooms are stylish, well equipped and many boast wonderful loch views.

Rooms 96 (9 fmly) **Facilities** Ⓢ ⛳ 9 🎾 Fishing 🐎 Gym Squash Outdoor sports Motor boat on Loch Lomond Hairdresser Xmas **Conf** Class 80 Board 80 Thtr 300 **Services** Lift **Parking** 200 **Notes** ⊗ Civ Wed 200

BANCHORY Map 23 NO69
Aberdeenshire

Best Western Burnett Arms Hotel

★★★ 70% SMALL HOTEL

☎ 01330 824944 📠 01330 825553
25 High St AB31 5TD
e-mail: theburnett@btconnect.com
dir: Town centre on N side of A93

This popular hotel is located in the heart of the town centre and gives easy access to the many attractions of Royal Deeside. Public areas include a choice of eating and drinking options, with food served in the restaurant, bar and foyer lounge. Bedrooms are thoughtfully equipped and comfortably modern.

Rooms 18 (1 fmly) **Facilities** STV FTV Xmas New Year Wi-fi **Conf** Class 50 Board 50 Thtr 100 **Parking** 23 **Notes** LB Civ Wed 100

See advert on this page

Raemoir House Hotel

U

☎ 01330 824884
Raemoir AB31 4ED
e-mail: hotel@raemoir.com

Currently the rating for this establishment is not confirmed. This may be due to a change of ownership or because it has only recently joined the AA rating scheme. For further details please see the AA website: theAA.com

Rooms 20 (6 annexe) (2 fmly) **S** fr £125; **D** fr £140 (incl. bkfst) **Facilities** FTV Putt green ⛳ Xmas New Year Wi-fi **Conf** Class 50 Board 40 Thtr 80 **Parking** 20 **Notes** LB Civ Wed 50

BATHGATE Map 21 NS96
West Lothian

Premier Inn Livingston (Bathgate)

BUDGET HOTEL

☎ 0871 527 8630 📠 0871 527 8631
Starlaw Rd EH48 1LQ
dir: M8 junct 3A. At 1st rdbt 1st exit (Bathgate). Over bridge, at 2nd rdbt take 1st exit. Hotel 200yds on left

High quality, budget accommodation ideal for both families and business travellers. Spacious, en suite bedrooms feature tea and coffee making facilities, and Freeview TV in most hotels. Internet access and Wi-fi are available for a small fee. The adjacent family restaurant features a wide and varied menu. See also the Hotel Groups pages.

Rooms 74 **D** £55-£63*

BEAULY Map 23 NH54
Highland

Priory

★★★ 74% HOTEL

☎ 01463 782 309 📠 01463 782531
The Square IV4 7BX
e-mail: reservations@priory-hotel.com
web: www.priory-hotel.com
dir: Signed from A832, into Beauly, hotel in square on left

This popular hotel occupies a central location in the town square. Standard and executive rooms are on offer, both providing a good level of comfort and range of facilities. Food is served throughout the day in the open-plan public areas, with menus offering a first rate choice.

Rooms 37 (3 fmly) (1 GF) **S** £55-£62.50; **D** £70-£95 (incl. bkfst)* **Facilities** STV FTV Xmas New Year Wi-fi **Conf** Class 40 Board 30 Thtr 40 Del from £75 to £85* **Services** Lift **Parking** 20 **Notes** LB ⊗

Lovat Arms

★★★ 73% HOTEL

☎ 01463 782313 📠 01463 782862
IV4 7BS
e-mail: info@lovatarms.com
web: www.lovatarms.com
dir: From The Square past Royal Bank of Scotland, hotel on right

This fine family run hotel enjoys a prominent position in this charming town which is a short drive from Inverness. The bedrooms are comfortable and well

continued

B

BEAULY ***continued***

appointed. The spacious foyer has a real fire and comfortable seating, while the Strubag lounge is ideal for informal dining.

Rooms 33 (12 annexe) (4 fmly) (6 GF) **Facilities** STV FTV Xmas New Year Wi-fi **Conf** Class 26 Board 40 Thtr 80 Del from £120 to £150* **Parking** 25 **Notes** Civ Wed 60

BLAIR ATHOLL Map 23 NN86
Perth & Kinross

Atholl Arms Hotel

★★★ 72% HOTEL

☎ 01796 481205 📠 01796 481550
Old North Rd PH18 5SG
e-mail: hotel@athollarms.co.uk
web: www.athollarmshotel.co.uk
dir: Off A9 to B8079, 1m into Blair Atholl, hotel near entrance to Blair Castle

Situated close to Blair Castle and conveniently adjacent to the railway station, this stylish hotel has historically appointed public rooms that include a choice of bars, and a splendid baronial-style dining room. Bedrooms vary in size and style. Staff throughout are friendly and very caring.

Rooms 30 (3 fmly) **S** £51.50-£67; **D** £82-£97 (incl. bkfst)* **Facilities** Fishing Rough shooting ♫ New Year Wi-fi **Conf** Class 80 Board 60 Thtr 120 **Parking** 103 **Notes** LB Civ Wed 120

BOAT OF GARTEN Map 23 NH91
Highland

Boat Hotel

★★★ 80% ◎◎ HOTEL

☎ 01479 831258 & 831696 📠 01479 831414
PH24 3BH
e-mail: info@boathotel.co.uk
dir: Off A9 N of Aviemore onto A95, follow signs to Boat of Garten

A well established hotel situated in the heart of this pretty village. Public areas include a choice of comfortable lounges and The Osprey Bistro & Bar is inviting and relaxed, with appealing menus and a well deserved reputation for food. Individually styled bedrooms reflect the unique character of the hotel; all are comfortable and well equipped.

Rooms 34 (2 fmly) **Facilities** FTV Xmas New Year Wi-fi **Conf** Class 30 Board 25 Thtr 40 **Parking** 36 **Notes** Civ Wed 40

BOTHWELL Map 20 NS75
South Lanarkshire

Bothwell Bridge Hotel

★★★ 80% HOTEL

☎ 01698 852246 📠 01698 854686
89 Main St G71 8EU
e-mail: reception@bothwellbridge-hotel.com
web: www.bothwellbridge-hotel.com
dir: M74 junct 5 & follow signs to Uddingston, right at mini-rdbt. Hotel just past shops on left

This red-sandstone mansion house is a popular business, function and conference hotel conveniently placed for the motorway. Most bedrooms are spacious and all are well equipped. The conservatory is a bright and comfortable restaurant serving an interesting variety of Italian influenced dishes. The lounge bar offers a comfortable seating area that proves popular as a stop for coffee.

Rooms 90 (14 fmly) (26 GF) **Facilities** STV ♫ Xmas New Year Wi-fi **Conf** Class 80 Board 50 Thtr 200 Del from £90 to £103* **Services** Lift **Parking** 125 **Notes** ⊗ Civ Wed 250

BRACHLA Map 23 NH53
Highland

Loch Ness Lodge

◎◎ RESTAURANT WITH ROOMS

☎ 01456 459469 📠 01456 459439
Loch Ness-Side IV3 8LA
e-mail: escape@loch-ness-lodge
dir: From A9 Inverness onto A82 signed Fort William, after 9m & 30mph speed sign, Lodge on right immediately after Clansman Hotel

This house enjoys a prominent position overlooking Loch Ness, and each of the individually designed bedrooms enjoys views of the loch. The bedrooms are of the highest standard, and are beautifully presented with a mix of traditional luxury and up-to-date technology, including Wi-fi. There is a spa with a hot tub, sauna and a therapy room offering a variety of treatments. Award-winning evening meals are served restaurant, and guests have a choice of attractive lounges which feature real fires in the colder months.

Rooms 7

BRORA Map 23 NC90
Highland

Royal Marine Hotel, Restaurant & Spa

★★★★ 75% ◎ HOTEL

☎ 01408 621252 📠 01408 621181
Golf Rd KW9 6QS
e-mail: info@royalmarinebrora.com
web: www.royalmarinebrora.com
dir: Off A9 in village towards beach & golf course

A distinctive Edwardian residence sympathetically extended, the Royal Marine attracts a mixed market. Its leisure centre is popular, and the restaurant, Hunters Lounge and café bar offer three contrasting eating options. A modern bedroom wing complements the original bedrooms, which retain period style. There are also luxury apartments just a short walk away.

Rooms 21 (1 fmly) (2 GF) **Facilities** FTV Putt green Fishing Gym Steam room Sauna Xmas New Year Wi-fi **Conf** Class 40 Board 40 Thtr 70 **Parking** 40 **Notes** Civ Wed 60

BURNTISLAND Map 21 NT28
Fife

Kingswood

★★★ 75% HOTEL

☎ 01592 872329 📠 01592 873123
Kinghorn Rd KY3 9LL
e-mail: enquiries@kingswoodhotel.co.uk
web: www.kingswoodhotel.co.uk
dir: A921 (coast road) at Burntisland, right at rdbt, left at T-junct, at bottom of hill to Kinghorn Rd, hotel 0.5m on left

Lying east of the town, this hotel has views across the Firth of Forth to Edinburgh. Public rooms feature a range of cosy sitting areas, and a spacious, attractive restaurant serving good value meals. There is also a good-size function room and multi-purpose conservatory. Bedrooms include two family suites and front-facing rooms with balconies.

Rooms 13 (3 fmly) (1 GF) **S** £59-£69; **D** £60-£115 (incl. bkfst)* **Facilities** FTV New Year Wi-fi **Conf** Class 20 Board 40 Thtr 150 **Parking** 50 **Notes** LB ⊗ Closed 26 Dec & 1 Jan Civ Wed 120

CALLANDER Map 20 NN60
Stirling

INSPECTORS' CHOICE

Roman Camp Country House

★★★ ◎◎◎ COUNTRY HOUSE HOTEL

☎ 01877 330003 🖷 01877 331533
FK17 8BG
e-mail: mail@romancamphotel.co.uk
web: www.romancamphotel.co.uk
dir: N on A84, left at east end of High Street. 300yds to hotel

Built in the 17th century, and originally used as a shooting lodge, this charming country house has a rich history; it has now been in the same ownership for over two decades. The twenty acres of gardens and grounds lead down to the River Teith, and the town centre and its attractions are only a short walk away. Each bedroom is individually and elegantly designed, and offers much pampering comfort. Food is a highlight of any stay, and menus are dominated by high-quality Scottish produce that is sensitively treated by the talented kitchen team. Real fires warm the atmospheric public areas and service is friendly yet professional.

Rooms 15 (4 fmly) (7 GF) **S** £95-£100; **D** £150-£200 (incl. bkfst) **Facilities** STV FTV Fishing Xmas New Year Wi-fi **Conf** Class 60 Board 30 Thtr 120 Del from £200 to £250 **Parking** 80 **Notes** LB Civ Wed 150

Callander Meadows

◎ RESTAURANT WITH ROOMS

☎ 01877 330181
24 Main St FK17 8BB
e-mail: mail@callandermeadows.co.uk
web: www.callandermeadows.co.uk
dir: M9 junct 10 onto A84 to Callander, on main street just past A81 junct

Located on the high street in Callander, this family-run business offers comfortable accommodation and a restaurant that has quickly become very popular with the locals. The bedrooms have been appointed to a high standard. Private parking is available to the rear.

Rooms 3

CARNOUSTIE Map 21 NO53
Angus

Carnoustie Golf Hotel & Spa

OXFORD HOTELS & INNS

★★★★ 73% ◎ HOTEL

☎ 0844 414 6520 🖷 0844 414 6519
The Links DD7 7JE
e-mail: reservations.carnoustie@ohiml.com
web: www.oxfordhotelsandinns.com
dir: Adjacent to Carnoustie Golf Links

This fine hotel enjoys an enviable location and is adjacent to the 1st and 18th green of the famous Championship Course of Carnoustie. All bedrooms are spacious and attractively presented; most overlook the magnificent course and enjoy breathtaking coastal views. Fine dining can be enjoyed in the restaurant with more informal meals served in the comfortable bar.

Rooms 85 (11 fmly) **Facilities** Spa STV FTV ⓢ Putt green Gym Xmas New Year Wi-fi **Conf** Class 200 Board 100 Thtr 350 **Services** Lift Air con **Parking** 100 **Notes** ⊗ Civ Wed 325

CLYDEBANK Map 20 NS47
West Dumbartonshire

Beardmore Hotel

★★★★ 77% ◎ HOTEL

☎ 0141 951 6000 🖷 0141 951 6018
Beardmore St G81 4SA
e-mail: info@beardmore.scot.nhs.uk
dir: M8 junct 19, follow signs for Clydeside Expressway to Glasgow road, then A814 (Dumbarton road), then follow Clydebank Business Park signs. Hotel on left

Attracting much business and conference custom, this stylish modern hotel lies beside the River Clyde and shares an impressive site with a hospital (although the latter does not intrude). Spacious and imposing public areas include the stylish Arcoona Restaurant providing innovative contemporary Scottish cooking. The lounge bar offers a more extensive choice of lighter dishes. The leisure facilities include a 15-metre swimming pool, sauna and steam room.

Rooms 166 **Facilities** STV ⓢ supervised Gym Sauna Steam room Whirlpool Xmas New Year Wi-fi **Conf** Class 84 Board 27 Thtr 240 **Services** Lift Air con **Parking** 300 **Notes** ⊗ Civ Wed 170

C

COMRIE Map 21 NN72
Perth & Kinross

Royal

★★★ 83% HOTEL

☎ 01764 679200 📠 01764 679219
Melville Square PH6 2DN
e-mail: reception@royalhotel.co.uk
web: www.royalhotel.co.uk
dir: Off A9 on A822 to Crieff, then B827 to Comrie. Hotel in main square on A85

A traditional façade gives little indication of the style and elegance inside this long-established hotel located in the village centre. Public areas include a bar and library, a bright modern restaurant and a conservatory-style brasserie. Bedrooms are tastefully appointed and furnished with smart reproduction antiques.

Rooms 13 (2 annexe) **Facilities** STV Fishing Shooting arranged New Year Wi-fi **Conf** Class 10 Board 20 Thtr 20 **Parking** 22 **Notes** LB Closed 25-26 Dec

CONNEL Map 20 NM93
Argyll & Bute

Falls of Lora Hotel

THE INDEPENDENTS HOTEL ASSOCIATION

★★★ 77% HOTEL

☎ 01631 710483 📠 01631 710694
PA37 1PB
e-mail: enquiries@fallsoflora.com
web: www.fallsoflora.com
dir: From Glasgow take A82, A85. Hotel 0.5m past Connel sign (5m before Oban)

Personally run and welcoming, this long-established and thriving holiday hotel enjoys inspiring views over Loch Etive. The spacious ground floor takes in a comfortable, traditional lounge and a cocktail bar with over a hundred whiskies and an open log fire. Guests can eat in the popular, informal bistro, which is open all day. Bedrooms come in a variety of styles, ranging from the cosy standard rooms to high quality luxury rooms.

Rooms 30 (4 fmly) (4 GF) (30 smoking) **S** £29.50-£69.50; **D** £55-£151 (incl. bkfst)* **Facilities** FTV Wi-fi Child facilities **Conf** Class 20 Board 15 Thtr 45 **Parking** 40 **Notes** LB Closed mid Dec & Jan

See advert on this page

CRAIGELLACHIE Map 23 NJ24
Moray

Craigellachie

★★★★ 72% HOTEL

☎ 01340 881204 📠 01340 881253
AB38 9SR
e-mail: reservations.craigellachie@ohiml.com
web: www.oxfordhotelsandinns.com
dir: On A95 between Aberdeen & Inverness

This impressive and popular hotel is located in the heart of Speyside, so it is no surprise that malt whisky takes centre stage in the Quaich Bar with over 700 varieties featured. Bedrooms come in various sizes but all are tastefully decorated and bathrooms are of a high specification. Creative dinners showcase local ingredients in the traditionally styled dining room.

Rooms 26 (1 fmly) (6 GF) **Facilities** Xmas New Year Wi-fi **Conf** Class 35 Board 30 Thtr 60 **Parking** 30 **Notes** Civ Wed 60

CRAIL Fife Map 21 NO60

Balcomie Links Hotel

★★ 74% SMALL HOTEL

☎ 01333 450237 📠 01333 450540
Balcomie Rd KY10 3TN
e-mail: mikekadir@balcomie.co.uk
web: www.balcomie.co.uk
dir: A917 into Crail to village shops, right into Market Gate, becomes Balcomie Rd, hotel on left

Especially popular with visiting golfers, this family-run hotel on the east side of the village represents good value for money and has a relaxing atmosphere. Bedrooms come in a variety of sizes and styles and offer all the expected amenities. Food is served from midday in the attractive lounge bar, and also in the bright cheerful dining room in the evening.

Rooms 14 (3 fmly) **S** £59-£69; **D** £79-£89 (incl. bkfst) **Facilities** FTV Games room Xmas New Year Wi-fi **Parking** 20 **Notes** LB ® Closed Jan-Feb Civ Wed 45

CRIANLARICH Stirling Map 20 NN32

The Crianlarich Hotel

★★★ 77% ® HOTEL

☎ 01838 300272 📠 01838 300329
FK20 8RW
e-mail: info@crianlarich-hotel.co.uk
web: www.crianlarich-hotel.co.uk
dir: At junct of A85 & A82

Standing at what has been an important transport junction for many years, this hotel continues to cater to travellers' needs. The ground-floor areas are impressive, and the pleasant bedrooms are smartly appointed and offer all the usual amenities. Friendly relaxed service and high quality food makes this an enjoyable place to stay especially as it is close to Loch Lomond and the Trossachs National Park.

Rooms 36 (1 fmly) **Facilities** FTV ♫ Xmas New Year Wi-fi **Conf** Class 60 Board 40 Thtr 100 **Services** Lift **Parking** 30 **Notes** LB

CULLEN Moray Map 23 NJ56

Cullen Bay Hotel

★★★ 75% ® SMALL HOTEL

☎ 01542 840432 📠 01542 840900
A98 AB56 4XA
e-mail: stay@cullenbayhotel.com
web: www.cullenbayhotel.com
dir: On A98, 1m west of Cullen

This family-run hotel sits on the hillside west of the town and has lovely views of the golf course, beach and Moray Firth. The spacious restaurant, which offers a selection of fine dishes, makes the most of the view, as do many of the bedrooms. There is a comfortable modern bar, a quiet lounge and a second dining room where breakfasts are served.

Rooms 14 (3 fmly) **Facilities** New Year Wi-fi **Conf** Class 80 Board 80 Thtr 200 **Parking** 100 **Notes** ® Civ Wed 200

CUMBERNAULD North Lanarkshire Map 21 NS77

The Westerwood Hotel & Golf Resort

QHOTELS

★★★★ 81% ® HOTEL

☎ 01236 457171 📠 01236 738478
1 St Andrews Dr, Westerwood G68 0EW
e-mail: westerwood@qhotels.co.uk
web: www.qhotels.co.uk

This stylish, contemporary hotel enjoys an elevated position within 400 acres at the foot of the Camspie Hills. Accommodation is provided in spacious, bright bedrooms, many with super bathrooms, and day rooms include sumptuous lounges and an airy restaurant; extensive golf, fitness and conference facilities are available.

Rooms 148 (15 fmly) (49 GF) **Facilities** Spa STV 18 Putt green Gym Beauty salon Relaxation room Sauna Steam room Xmas New Year Wi-fi **Conf** Class 120 Board 60 Thtr 400 Del from £115 to £190 **Services** Lift **Parking** 250 **Notes** Civ Wed 350

Premier Inn Glasgow (Cumbernauld)

BUDGET HOTEL

☎ 0871 527 8424 📠 0871 527 8425
4 South Muirhead Rd G67 1AX
dir: From A80, A8011 follow Cumbernauld & town centre signs. Hotel opposite Asda & McDonalds

High quality, budget accommodation ideal for both families and business travellers. Spacious, en suite bedrooms feature tea and coffee making facilities, and Freeview TV in most hotels. Internet access and Wi-fi are available for a small fee. The adjacent family restaurant features a wide and varied menu. See also the Hotel Groups pages.

Rooms 37 **D** £54-£60*

DINGWALL Highland Map 23 NH55

Tulloch Castle

★★★★ 74% HOTEL

☎ 01349 861325 📠 01349 863993
Tulloch Castle Dr IV15 9ND
e-mail: reservations.tulloch@ohiml.com
web: www.oxfordhotelsandinns.com
dir: A9 N, Tore rdbt 2nd left signed Dingwall, at Dingwall turn left at 4th lights, hotel signed

Overlooking the town of Dingwall this 12th-century castle is still the gathering place of the Clan Davidson and boasts its own ghost in the shape of the Green Lady. The friendly team are very helpful and love to tell you about the history of the castle; the ghost tour after dinner is a must. The hotel has a self contained suite and a number of bedrooms with four-posters.

Rooms 20 (2 fmly) **Facilities** FTV Xmas New Year Wi-fi **Conf** Class 70 Board 70 Thtr 120 Del from £160 to £180* **Parking** 50 **Notes** Civ Wed 110

D

DORNOCH
Highland
Map 23 NH78

Dornoch Castle Hotel

★★★ 75% HOTEL

☎ 01862 810216 01862 810981
Castle St IV25 3SD
e-mail: enquiries@dornochcastlehotel.com
web: www.dornochcastlehotel.com
dir: 2m N of Dornoch Bridge on A9, turn right to Dornoch. Hotel in village centre

Situated opposite the cathedral, this fully restored ancient castle has become a popular wedding venue. Within the original castle are some splendid themed bedrooms, and elsewhere the more modern bedrooms have all of the expected facilities. There is a character bar and a delightful conservatory restaurant overlooking the garden.

Rooms 22 (3 fmly) (4 GF) **Facilities** FTV New Year Wi-fi Child facilities **Conf** Class 40 Board 30 Thtr 60 **Parking** 16 **Notes** LB Closed 24-26 Dec & 2nd wk Jan

DRYMEN
Stirling
Map 20 NS48

Best Western Buchanan Arms Hotel & Spa

★★★ 79% HOTEL

☎ 01360 660588 01360 660943
23 Main St G63 0BQ
e-mail: info@buchananarms.co.uk

This former coaching inn has benefited from on-going investment and refurbishment. Located in the quiet conservation village of Drymen, the hotel provides a perfect base for touring this area, with Loch Lomond just a few miles away. There are well-appointed bedrooms and welcoming public areas. Good leisure facilities are an added benefit.

Rooms 52 (9 fmly) (3 GF) **S** £40-£120; **D** £60-£160 (incl. bkfst)* **Facilities** Spa FTV supervised Gym Squash Xmas New Year Wi-fi **Conf** Class 140 Board 60 Thtr 250 Del from £109 to £159* **Parking** 120 **Notes** LB Civ Wed 100

Winnock Hotel

★★★ 75% HOTEL

☎ 01360 660245 01360 660267
The Square G63 0BL
e-mail: info@winnockhotel.com
web: www.winnockhotel.com
dir: From S: M74 onto M8 junct 16b through Glasgow. Follow A809 to Aberfoyle

Occupying a prominent position overlooking the village green, this popular hotel offers well-equipped bedrooms of various sizes and styles. The public rooms include a bar, a lounge and an attractive formal dining room that serves dishes of good, locally sourced food.

Rooms 73 (18 fmly) (19 GF) **Facilities** FTV Xmas New Year Wi-fi **Conf** Class 60 Board 70 Thtr 140 **Parking** 60 **Notes** Civ Wed 100

DUMBARTON
East Dunbartonshire
Map 20 NS37

Premier Inn Dumbarton

Premier Inn

BUDGET HOTEL

☎ 0871 527 9274 0871 527 9275
Lomondgate Dr G82 2QU
dir: From Glasgow follow A82 towards Crianlarich, right at Lomondgate rdbt onto A813, hotel on right. From N: A82 towards Glasgow, left at Lomondgate rdbt onto A813, hotel on right

High quality, budget accommodation ideal for both families and business travellers. Spacious, en suite bedrooms feature tea and coffee making facilities, and Freeview TV in most hotels. Internet access and Wi-fi are available for a small fee. The adjacent family restaurant features a wide and varied menu. See also the Hotel Groups pages.

Rooms 60 **D** £55-£59*

DUMFRIES
Dumfries & Galloway
Map 21 NX97

See also **Kirkbean**

Cairndale Hotel & Leisure Club

★★★ 80% HOTEL

☎ 01387 254111 01387 240288
English St DG1 2DF
e-mail: sales@cairndalehotel.co.uk
web: www.cairndalehotel.co.uk
dir: From S on M6 take A75 to Dumfries, left at 1st rdbt, cross rail bridge to lights, hotel 1st building on left

Within walking distance of the town centre, this hotel provides a wide range of amenities, including leisure facilities and an impressive conference and entertainment centre. Bedrooms range from stylish suites to cosy singles. There's a choice of eating options in the evening. The Reivers Restaurant is smartly modern with food to match.

Rooms 91 (22 fmly) (5 GF) **S** £59-£89; **D** £79-£159 (incl. bkfst) **Facilities** supervised Gym Steam room Sauna Xmas New Year Wi-fi **Conf** Class 150 Board 50 Thtr 300 Del from £79 to £119* **Services** Lift **Parking** 100 **Notes** LB Civ Wed 200

Best Western Station Hotel

★★★ 79% HOTEL

☎ 01387 254316 🖷 01387 250388
49 Lovers Walk DG1 1LT
e-mail: info@stationhotel.co.uk
web: www.stationhoteldumfries.co.uk
dir: A75, follow signs to town centre, hotel opposite railway station

This friendly hotel built in the Victorian era offers stylish, well-equipped bedrooms that feature flat-screen satellite TVs and free Wi-fi; three rooms have four-poster beds and spa baths. The Courtyard restaurant creates an informal atmosphere where, each evening, guests can enjoy a popular range of dishes; in addition good-value meals are served at lunchtime in either the lounge bar or on the patio in warmer weather. There is a delightful small garden to relax in.

Rooms 32 **Facilities** Use of local gym Xmas New Year Wi-fi **Conf** Class 35 Board 30 Thtr 60 **Services** Lift **Parking** 34 **Notes** Civ Wed 50

Premier Inn Dumfries

BUDGET HOTEL

☎ 0871 527 8316 🖷 0871 527 8317
Annan Rd, Collin DG1 3JX
dir: At rdbt junct of Euroroute bypass (A75) & A780

High quality, budget accommodation ideal for both families and business travellers. Spacious, en suite bedrooms feature tea and coffee making facilities, and Freeview TV in most hotels. Internet access and Wi-fi are available for a small fee. The adjacent family restaurant features a wide and varied menu. See also the Hotel Groups pages.

Rooms 40 **D** £62*

DUNDEE
City of Dundee **Map 21 NO43**

Apex City Quay Hotel & Spa

★★★★ 77% HOTEL

☎ 0845 365 0000 & 01382 202404
🖷 01382 201401
1 West Victoria Dock Rd DD1 3JP
e-mail: dundee.reservations@apexhotels.co.uk
web: www.apexhotels.co.uk
dir: A85/Riverside Drive to Discovery Quay. Exit rdbt for City Quay

This stylish, purpose-built hotel occupies an enviable position at the heart of Dundee's regenerated quayside area. Bedrooms, including a number of smart suites, feature the very latest in design. Warm hospitality and professional service are an integral part of the hotel's appeal. Open-plan public areas with panoramic windows and contemporary food options complete the package.

Rooms 151 (17 fmly) **Facilities** Spa FTV Gym Steam room, Sauna Xmas New Year Wi-fi **Conf** Class 180 Board 120 Thtr 375 **Services** Lift Air con **Parking** 150 **Notes** Civ Wed 300

The Landmark Hotel

★★★★ 74% HOTEL

☎ 01382 641122 🖷 01382 631201
Kingsway West DD2 5JT
e-mail: sales@thelandmarkdundee.co.uk
web: www.thelandmarkdundee.co.uk
dir: From A90 (Kingsway) at rdbt junct with A85, follow hotel signs

Well located off Kingsway West with ample parking, this hotel offers contemporary bedrooms that are equipped with many thoughtful extras. The restaurant overlooks the gardens which are a feature at this hotel. A good leisure club includes a gym, jacuzzi, steam room and sauna. The hotel is a popular wedding venue.

Rooms 95 (11 fmly) (45 GF) **Facilities** STV FTV supervised Gym Sauna Steam room Xmas New Year Wi-fi **Conf** Class 50 Board 45 Thtr 100 **Parking** 140 **Notes** Civ Wed 100

Holiday Inn Express Dundee

BUDGET HOTEL

☎ 01382 314330 🖷 01382 314343
Dock St DD1 3DR
e-mail: dm1@hiexpressdundee.com
dir: Telephone for directions

A modern hotel ideal for families and business travellers. Fresh and uncomplicated, the spacious rooms include Sky TV, power shower and tea and coffee-making facilities. Continental buffet breakfast is included in the room rate; other meals may be taken at the nearby family pub or restaurant. See also the Hotel Groups pages.

Rooms 95 (49 fmly) **Conf** Class 25 Board 25 Thtr 30

Premier Inn Dundee Centre

BUDGET HOTEL

☎ 0871 527 8320 🖷 0871 527 8321
Discovery Quay, Riverside Dr DD1 4XA
dir: Follow signs for Discovery Quay, hotel on waterfront

High quality, budget accommodation ideal for both families and business travellers. Spacious, en suite bedrooms feature tea and coffee making facilities, and Freeview TV in most hotels. Internet access and Wi-fi are available for a small fee. The adjacent family restaurant features a wide and varied menu. See also the Hotel Groups pages.

Rooms 40 **D** £65-£70*

Premier Inn Dundee East

BUDGET HOTEL

☎ 0871 527 8322 🖷 0871 527 8323
115-117 Lawers Dr, Panmurefield Village, Broughty Ferry DD5 3UP
dir: From N: A92 (Dundee & Arbroath). Hotel 1.5m after Sainsbury's. From S: A90. At end of dual carriageway follow Dundee to Arbroath signs

Rooms 60 **D** £49-£55*

Premier Inn Dundee (Monifieth)

BUDGET HOTEL

☎ 0871 527 8318 🖷 0871 527 8319
Ethiebeaton Park, Arbroath Rd, Monifieth DD5 4HB
dir: From A90 (Kingsway Rd) follow Carnoustie/Arbroath (A92) signs

Rooms 40 **D** £49-£55*

Premier Inn Dundee North

BUDGET HOTEL

☎ 0871 527 8324 🖷 0871 527 8325
Camperdown Leisure Park, Dayton Dr, Kingsway DD2 3SQ
dir: 2m N of city centre on A90 at junct with A923, adjacent to cinema. At entrance to Camperdown Country Park

Rooms 78 **D** £49-£55*

DUNDEE *continued*

Premier Inn Dundee West

BUDGET HOTEL

☎ 0871 527 8326 🖷 0871 527 8327
Kingsway West DD2 5JU
dir: On A90 towards Aberdeen adjacent to Technology Park rdbt

Rooms 64 **D** £49-£58*

D

DUNFERMLINE Map 21 NT08
Fife

Pitbauchlie House

★★★ 79% HOTEL

☎ 01383 722282 🖷 01383 620738
Aberdour Rd KY11 4PB
e-mail: info@pitbauchlie.com
web: www.pitbauchlie.com
dir: M90 junct 2, A823, then B916. Hotel 0.5m on right

Situated in three acres of wooded grounds this hotel is just a mile south of the town and has a striking modern interior. The bedrooms are well equipped, and the deluxe rooms have 32-inch LCD satellite TVs and CD micro systems; there is one bedroom designed for less able guests. The eating options include Harvey's Conservatory bistro and Restaurant 47 where Scottish and French influenced cuisine is offered.

Rooms 50 (3 fmly) (19 GF) **Facilities** STV FTV Gym Wi-fi **Conf** Class 80 Board 60 Thtr 150 **Parking** 80 **Notes** Civ Wed 150

King Malcolm

★★★ 73% HOTEL

☎ 01383 722611 🖷 01383 730865
Queensferry Rd KY11 8DS
e-mail: info@kingmalcolm-hotel-dunfermline.com
web: www.peelhotels.co.uk
dir: On A823, S of town

Located to the south of the city, this purpose-built hotel remains popular with business clientele and is convenient for access to both Edinburgh and Fife. Public rooms include a smart foyer lounge and a conservatory bar, as well as a restaurant. Bedrooms, although not large, are well laid out and well equipped.

Rooms 48 (2 fmly) (24 GF) **Facilities** ♫ Xmas New Year Wi-fi **Conf** Class 60 Board 50 Thtr 150 **Parking** 60 **Notes** Civ Wed 120

Holiday Inn Express Dunfermline

BUDGET HOTEL

☎ 01383 748220 🖷 01383 748221
Lauder College, Halbeath KY11 8DY
e-mail: info@hiexpressdunfermline.co.uk
web: www.hiexpress.com/dunfermline
dir: M9 junct 7 signed A994/A907, 3rd exit Lynebank rdbt or M90 junct 3, 2nd exit for A907, next rdbt 3rd exit, next rdbt 1st exit

A modern hotel ideal for families and business travellers. Fresh and uncomplicated, the spacious rooms include Sky TV, power shower and tea and coffee-making facilities. Continental buffet breakfast is included in the room rate; other meals may be taken at the nearby family pub or restaurant. See also the Hotel Groups pages.

Rooms 82 **Conf** Class 8 Board 16 Thtr 25

Premier Inn Dunfermline

BUDGET HOTEL

☎ 0871 527 8328 🖷 0871 527 8329
4-12 Whimbrel Place, Fife Leisure Park KY11 8EX
dir: M90 junct 3 (Forth Road Bridge exit) 1st left at lights signed Duloch Park. 1st left into Fife Leisure Park

High quality, budget accommodation ideal for both families and business travellers. Spacious, en suite bedrooms feature tea and coffee making facilities, and Freeview TV in most hotels. Internet access and Wi-fi are available for a small fee. The adjacent family restaurant features a wide and varied menu. See also the Hotel Groups pages.

Rooms 40 **D** £52-£58*

DUNOON Map 20 NS17
Argyll & Bute

Selborne

★★ 74% HOTEL

☎ 01369 702761 🖷 01369 704032
Clyde St, West Bay PA23 7HU
e-mail: selborne.dunoon@alfatravel.co.uk
dir: From Caledonian MacBrayne pier. Past castle, left into Jane St, right into Clyde St

This holiday hotel is situated overlooking the West Bay and provides unrestricted views of the Clyde Estuary towards the Isles of Cumbrae. Tour groups are especially well catered for in this good-value establishment, which offers entertainment most nights. Bedrooms are comfortable and many have sea views.

Rooms 98 (6 fmly) (14 GF) **S** £36-£49; **D** £56-£82 (incl. bkfst) **Facilities** FTV Pool table Table tennis ♫ Xmas New Year **Services** Lift **Parking** 30 **Notes** LB ⊗ Closed Dec-Feb (ex Xmas) RS Nov & Mar

EAST KILBRIDE Map 20 NS65
South Lanarkshire

Holiday Inn Glasgow-East Kilbride

★★★★ 75% HOTEL

☎ 01355 236300 🖷 01355 233552
Stewartfield Way G74 5LA
e-mail: salesmgr@hieastkilbride.com
web: www.hieastkilbride.com
dir: M74 junct 5, A725 then A726

A modern hotel located in East Kilbride but within easy striking distance of Glasgow. Bedrooms are nicely appointed and cater well for the needs of the modern traveller. Food is served in La Bonne Auberge with a definite French and Mediterranean bias. Good leisure facilities are an added bonus.

Rooms 101 (4 fmly) (26 GF) (8 smoking) **S** £39-£149; **D** £39-£149* **Facilities** Spa STV Gym Aerobics studio Spin-cycle studio Sauna Steam room Xmas New Year Wi-fi **Conf** Class 120 Board 60 Thtr 400 Del from £99 to £145* **Services** Lift Air con **Parking** 200 **Notes** Civ Wed 200

Macdonald Crutherland House

★★★★ 74% HOTEL

☎ 0844 879 9039 📠 01355 577047
Strathaven Rd G75 0QZ
e-mail: crutherland@macdonald-hotels.co.uk
web: www.macdonaldhotels.co.uk
dir: Follow A726 signed Strathaven, straight over Torrance rdbt, hotel on left after 250yds

This mansion is set in 37 acres of landscaped grounds two miles from the town centre. Behind its Georgian façade is a very relaxing hotel with elegant public areas plus extensive banqueting and leisure facilities. The bedrooms are spacious and comfortable. Staff provide good levels of attention and enjoyable meals are served in the restaurant.

Rooms 75 (16 fmly) (16 GF) **S** £60-£175; **D** £70-£185 **Facilities** Spa STV Gym Sauna Steam room Xmas New Year Wi-fi **Conf** Class 100 Board 50 Thtr 500 Del from £135 to £235 **Services** Lift **Parking** 200 **Notes** LB Civ Wed 300

Premier Inn Glasgow East Kilbride

BUDGET HOTEL

☎ 0871 527 8446 📠 0871 527 8447
5 Lee's Burn Court, Nerston G74 3XB
dir: M74 junct 5, follow East Kilbride/A725 signs. Into right lane, follow Glasgow/A749 signs. At lights left onto A749 signed East Kilbride Town Centre (A725). Take slip road to Lee's Burn Court

High quality, budget accommodation ideal for both families and business travellers. Spacious, en suite bedrooms feature tea and coffee making facilities, and Freeview TV in most hotels. Internet access and Wi-fi are available for a small fee. The adjacent family restaurant features a wide and varied menu. See also the Hotel Groups pages.

Rooms 44 **D** £52-£60*

Premier Inn Glasgow East Kilbride Central

BUDGET HOTEL

☎ 0871 527 8450 📠 0871 527 8451
Brunel Way, The Murray G75 0LD
dir: M74 junct 5, follow East Kilbride A725 signs, then Paisley A726 signs, left at Murray Rdbt, left into Brunel Way

Rooms 40 **D** £52-£60*

Premier Inn Glasgow East Kilbride (Peel Park)

BUDGET HOTEL

☎ 0871 527 8448 📠 0871 527 8449
Eaglesham Rd G75 8LW
dir: 8m from M74 junct 5 on A726 at rdbt of B764

Rooms 42 **D** £52-£60*

EDDLESTON
Scottish Borders **Map 21 NT24**

The Horseshoe Inn

RESTAURANT WITH ROOMS

☎ 01721 730225 📠 01721 730268
EH45 8QP
e-mail: reservations@horseshoeinn.co.uk
web: www.horseshoeinn.co.uk
dir: A703, 5m N of Peebles

This inn is five miles north of Peebles and only 18 miles south of Edinburgh. Originally a blacksmith's shop, it is run by Vivienne Steele and her partner, chef-director Patrick Bardoulet. It is a restaurant with rooms with a very good reputation for its delightful atmosphere and excellent classical, French inspired cuisine. There are eight luxuriously appointed and individually designed bedrooms.

Rooms 8 (1 fmly)

EDINBURGH
City of Edinburgh **Map 21 NT27**

INSPECTORS' CHOICE

Balmoral

THE ROCCO FORTE COLLECTION

★★★★★ HOTEL

☎ 0131 556 2414 📠 0131 557 3747
1 Princes St EH2 2EQ
e-mail: reservations.balmoral@roccofortecollection.com
web: www.roccofortecollection.com
dir: Follow city centre signs. Hotel at E end of Princes St, adjacent to Waverley Station

This elegant hotel enjoys a prestigious address at the top of Princes Street, with fine views over the city and the castle. Bedrooms and suites are stylishly furnished and decorated, all boasting a thoughtful range of extras and impressive marble bathrooms. Hotel amenities include a Roman-style health spa, extensive function facilities, a choice of bars and two very different dining options - Number One (3 AA Rosettes) offers inspired fine dining whilst Hadrian's (1 AA Rosette) is a bustling, informal brasserie.

Rooms 188 (22 fmly) (15 smoking) **S** £325-£2100; **D** £395-£2100 **Facilities** Spa STV Gym Xmas New Year Wi-fi **Conf** Class 180 Board 60 Thtr 350 **Services** Lift Air con **Parking** 100 **Notes** Civ Wed 120

E

EDINBURGH ***continued***

INSPECTORS' CHOICE

Prestonfield

★★★★★ ◎◎ TOWN HOUSE HOTEL

☎ 0131 225 7800 📠 0131 220 4392
Priestfield Rd EH16 5UT
e-mail: reservations@prestonfield.com
web: www.prestonfield.com
dir: A7 towards Cameron Toll. 200mtrs beyond Royal Commonwealth Pool, into Priestfield Rd

This centuries-old landmark has been lovingly restored and enhanced to provide deeply comfortable and dramatically furnished bedrooms. The building demands to be explored: from the tapestry lounge and the whisky room to the restaurant, where the walls are adorned with pictures of former owners. Facilities and services are up-to-the-minute, and the award-winning Rhubarb restaurant serves carefully prepared meals. Rhubarb is the Winner of the AA Wine Award for Scotland 2011-12.

Rooms 23 (6 GF) **D** £295-£365 (incl. bkfst)* **Facilities** STV FTV ⛳ 18 Putt green Free bike hire Xmas New Year Wi-fi **Conf** Class 500 Board 40 Thtr 700 **Services** Lift **Parking** 250 **Notes** Civ Wed 350

Hotel Missoni Edinburgh

★★★★★ 84% HOTEL

☎ 0131 220 6666 📠 0131 226 6660
1 George IV Bridge EH1 1AD
e-mail: info.edinburgh@hotelmissoni.com
dir: At corner of Royal Mile & George IV Bridge

Located in the heart of the old town, this hotel's design is strikingly different. Bold use of black and white and vivid colours together with strong patterns creates a stunning impression. Stylish bedrooms, some with great city views, have iPod/AV hook-up, Wi-fi, coffee machines, and bathrooms with walk-in showers as standard. The buzzing cocktail bar and Cucina Missoni, for modern Italian cuisine, attract locals and residents alike.

Rooms 136 **D** £140-£300 (incl. bkfst)* **Facilities** Spa STV FTV Gym Xmas New Year Wi-fi **Conf** Class 24 Board 24 Thtr 63 **Services** Lift Air con **Parking** 13

The Howard

★★★★★ 83% TOWN HOUSE HOTEL

☎ 0131 537 3500 📠 0131 557 6515
34 Great King St EH3 6QH
e-mail: reserve@thehoward.com
web: www.thehoward.com
dir: E on Queen St, 2nd left, Dundas St. Through 3 lights, right, hotel on left

Quietly elegant and splendidly luxurious, The Howard provides an intimate and high quality experience for the discerning traveller. It comprises three linked Georgian houses and is situated just a short walk from Princes Street. The sumptuous bedrooms, in a variety of styles, include spacious suites, well-equipped bathrooms and a host of thoughtful touches. Ornate chandeliers and lavish drapes adorn the drawing room, while the Atholl Dining Room contains unique hand-painted murals dating from the 19th century.

Rooms 18

The Scotsman

★★★★★ 82% ◎ TOWN HOUSE HOTEL

☎ 0131 556 5565 📠 0131 652 3652
20 North Bridge EH1 1YT
e-mail: reservations@thescotsmanhotelgroup.co.uk
web: www.thescotsmanhotel.co.uk
dir: A8 to city centre, left onto Charlotte St. Right into Queen St, right at rdbt onto Leith St. Straight on, left onto North Bridge, hotel on right

Formerly the headquarters of The Scotsman newspaper this is a stunning hotel conversion. The classical elegance of the public areas, complete with a marble staircase, blends seamlessly with the contemporary bedrooms and their state-of-the-art technology. The superbly equipped leisure club includes a stainless steel swimming pool and large gym. Dining arrangements can be made in the popular North Bridge Brasserie where afternoon tea is also served.

Rooms 69 (4 GF) **Facilities** Spa STV supervised Gym Beauty treatments Xmas New Year Wi-fi **Conf** Class 50 Board 40 Thtr 100 **Services** Lift **Notes** Civ Wed 70

Sheraton Grand Hotel & Spa

Sheraton HOTELS & RESORTS

★★★★★ 78% HOTEL

☎ 0131 229 9131 📠 0131 228 4510
1 Festival Square EH3 9SR
e-mail: grandedinburgh.sheraton@sheraton.com
dir: Follow City Centre signs (A8). Through Shandwick Place, right at lights into Lothian Rd. Right at next lights. Hotel on left at next lights

This modern hotel boasts one of the best spas in Scotland - the external top floor hydro pool is definitely worth a look whilst the thermal suite provides a unique venue for serious relaxation. The spacious bedrooms are available in a variety of styles, and the suites prove very popular. There is a wide range of eating options including Santini's which has a loyal following, and One Spa Café for light meals and snacks.

Rooms 269 **S** £120-£265; **D** £120-£285* **Facilities** Spa STV FTV Gym Indoor/Outdoor hydropool Kinesis studio Thermal suite Fitness studio Xmas New Year Wi-fi **Conf** Class 350 Board 120 Thtr 485 Del from £255 to £340* **Services** Lift Air con **Parking** 122 **Notes** LB Civ Wed 485

INSPECTORS' CHOICE

Norton House

★★★★ ◎◎◎ HOTEL

☎ 0131 333 1275 📠 0131 333 5305
Ingliston EH28 8LX
e-mail: nortonhouse@handpicked.co.uk
web: www.handpicked.co.uk
dir: Off A8, 5m W of city centre

This extended Victorian mansion, set in 55 acres of parkland, is peacefully situated just outside the city and is convenient for the airport. The original building dates from 1840, and it was bought nearly 40 years later by John Usher of the Scottish brewing family. Today both the contemporary bedrooms and the very spacious, traditional ones have an impressive range of accessories including large flat-screen satellite TVs, DVD/CD players and free high speed internet access; executive rooms have more facilities, of course, including MP3 connection and 'tilevision' TVs at the end of the baths. Public areas take in a choice of lounges as well as dining options, with a popular brasserie and Ushers Restaurant, the intimate award-winning restaurant. There is a health club, and a spa which offers a long list of treatments.

Rooms 83 (10 fmly) (20 GF) **Facilities** Spa STV Gym Archery Laser Clay shooting Quad biking Xmas New Year Wi-fi **Conf** Class 100 Board 60 Thtr 300 Del from £149 to £239* **Services** Lift **Parking** 200 **Notes** Civ Wed 140

INSPECTORS' CHOICE

Channings

★★★★ ◎ TOWN HOUSE HOTEL

☎ 0131 315 2226 📠 0131 332 9631
15 South Learmonth Gardens EH4 1EZ
e-mail: reserve@channings.co.uk
web: www.channings.co.uk
dir: From A90 & Forth Road Bridge, follow signs for city centre

Just minutes from the city centre, this elegant town house occupies five Edwardian terraced houses. Interestingly, one of the properties was the home of Sir Ernest Shackleton at the time he was Secretary of the Royal Scottish Geographical Society; top floor bedrooms are named after him and his fellow explorers. The public areas include sumptuous, inviting lounges, a wine bar for a pre-dinner drink or cocktail, and Channings Restaurant that offers various menus throughout the day. The attractive and individually designed bedrooms have a hi-tech spec for business guests.

Rooms 41 (4 GF) **S** £85-£145; **D** £120-£240 (incl. bkfst)* **Facilities** STV FTV Xmas New Year Wi-fi **Conf** Class 40 Board 30 Thtr 60 Del from £125 to £185* **Services** Lift **Notes**

Marriott Dalmahoy Hotel & Country Club

Marriott HOTELS & RESORTS

★★★★ 80% ◎◎ HOTEL

☎ 0131 333 1845 📠 0131 333 1433
Kirknewton EH27 8EB
e-mail: mhrs.edigs.frontdesk@marriotthotels.com
web: www.marriottdalmahoy.co.uk
dir: A720 (Edinburgh City Bypass) onto A71 towards Livingston, hotel on left in 2m

The rolling Pentland Hills and beautifully kept parkland provide a stunning setting for this imposing Georgian mansion. With two championship golf courses and a health and beauty club, there is plenty here to occupy guests. Bedrooms are spacious and most have fine views, while public rooms offer a choice of formal and informal drinking and dining options.

Rooms 215 (172 annexe) (59 fmly) (6 smoking) **Facilities** Spa STV 36 Putt green Gym Health & beauty treatments Steam room Dance studio Driving range Golf lessons Xmas New Year Wi-fi **Conf** Class 200 Board 120 Thtr 300 **Services** Lift Air con **Parking** 350 **Notes** Civ Wed 250

Hotel du Vin Edinburgh

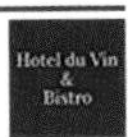

★★★★ 80% ◎
TOWN HOUSE HOTEL

☎ 0131 247 4900 📠 0131 247 4901
11 Bristo Place EH1 1EZ
dir: M8 junct 1, A720 (signed Kilmarnock/W Calder/ Edinburgh W). Right at fork, follow A720 signs, merge onto A720. Take exit signed A703. At rdbt take A702/ Biggar Rd. 3.5m. Right into Lauriston Pl which becomes Forrest Rd. Right at Bedlam Theatre. Hotel on right

Situated on the site of a former lunatic asylum, this hotel offers very stylish and comfortable accommodation; all bedrooms display the Hotel du Vin trademark facilities - air conditioning, free Wi-fi, plasma TVs, monsoon showers and Egyptian cotton linen to name but a few. Public areas include a whisky snug, a mezzanine bar that overlooks the brasserie where modern Scottish cuisine is served. For the wine connoisseur there's La Roche tasting room where wines from around the world can be appreciated.

Rooms 47 **S** £125-£495; **D** £125-£495* **Facilities** STV Wi-fi **Services** Lift Air con

E

E

EDINBURGH *continued*

Edinburgh Marriott Hotel

Marriott HOTELS & RESORTS

★★★★ 80% HOTEL

☎ 0131 334 9191 📠 0131 316 4507
111 Glasgow Rd EH12 8NF
e-mail: edinburgh@marriotthotels.com
web: www.edinburghmarriott.co.uk
dir: M8 junct 1 for Gogar, at rdbt turn right for city centre, hotel on right

This smart, modern hotel is located on the city's western edge which is convenient for the bypass, airport, showground and business park. Public areas include an attractive marbled foyer, extensive conference facilities and a restaurant serving a range of international dishes. The air-conditioned bedrooms are spacious and equipped with a range of extras.

Rooms 245 (76 fmly) (64 GF) (6 smoking) **Facilities** Spa STV FTV Ⓢ Gym Steam room Sauna Massage & beauty treatment room Hairdresser Xmas New Year Wi-fi **Conf** Class 120 Board 50 Thtr 250 Del from £130 to £200* **Services** Lift Air con **Parking** 300 **Notes** ⊗ Civ Wed 80

Apex International Hotel

★★★★ 79% ®® HOTEL

☎ 0845 365 0000 & 0131 300 3456
📠 0131 220 5345
31/35 Grassmarket EH1 2HS
e-mail: edinburgh.reservations@apexhotels.co.uk
web: www.apexhotels.co.uk
dir: Into Lothian Rd at west end of Princes St, 1st left into King Stables Rd, leads into Grassmarket

A sister to the Apex City Hotel close by, the International lies in a historic yet trendy square in the shadow of Edinburgh Castle. It has a versatile business and conference centre, and also Yu Time leisure and fitness facility with a stainless steel ozone pool. Bedrooms are contemporary in style and very well equipped. The fifth-floor restaurant boasts stunning views of the castle.

Rooms 169 (99 fmly) **Facilities** FTV Ⓢ Gym Tropicarium Xmas New Year Wi-fi **Conf** Class 80 Board 40 Thtr 200 **Services** Lift **Parking** 60 **Notes** ⊗ Civ Wed 200

George Hotel Edinburgh

PH principal hayley

★★★★ 79% HOTEL

☎ 0131 225 1251 📠 0131 226 5644
19-21 George St EH2 2PB
e-mail: enquiries.thegeorge@principal-hayley.com
web: www.principal-hayley.com/thegeorge
dir: In city centre

A long-established hotel, the George enjoys a city centre location. The splendid public areas have many original features such as intricate plasterwork, a marble-floored foyer and chandeliers. The Tempus Bar offers menus that feature a wide range of dishes to suit most tastes. The elegant, modern bedrooms come in a mix of sizes and styles; the upper ones having fine city views.

Rooms 249 (20 fmly) (4 GF) **Facilities** STV Xmas New Year Wi-fi **Conf** Class 120 Board 50 Thtr 300 **Services** Lift **Notes** ⊗ Civ Wed 300

Apex Waterloo Place Hotel

★★★★ 78% HOTEL

☎ 0845 365 0000 & 0131 523 1819
📠 0871 221 1432
23 - 27 Waterloo Place EH1 3BH
e-mail: edinburgh.reservations@apexhotels.co.uk
dir: At E end of Princes St. Telephone for detailed directions

This stunning hotel provides a state-of-the-art experience with slick interior design. Bedrooms, many with city views, are well appointed for both the business and leisure guest; stunning duplex suites provide extra space, surround-sound TV systems and luxurious feature bathrooms. The restaurant provides an appealing menu both at dinner and breakfast. There is also a well-equipped fitness centre and indoor pool. The hotel has direct, pedestrian access to Edinburgh's Waverley Station.

Rooms 187 (5 fmly) (15 GF) **Facilities** FTV Ⓢ Gym Sauna Steam rooms Xmas New Year Wi-fi **Conf** Class 70 Board 40 Thtr 150 **Services** Lift Air con **Notes** ⊗ Civ Wed 80

Apex City Hotel

★★★★ 77% ® HOTEL

☎ 0845 365 0000 & 0131 243 3456
📠 0131 225 6346
61 Grassmarket EH1 2JF
e-mail: edinburgh.reservations@apexhotels.co.uk
web: www.apexhotels.co.uk
dir: Into Lothian Rd at west end of Princes St, 1st left into King Stables Rd. Leads into Grassmarket

This modern, stylish hotel lies in a historic yet trendy square dominated by Edinburgh Castle above. The design-led bedrooms are fresh and contemporary and each has artwork by Richard Demarco. Agua Bar and Restaurant is a smart open-plan area in dark wood and chrome that serves a range of meals and cocktails. Residents can use the spa at a sister hotel, the International, which is nearby.

Rooms 119 (10 smoking) **Facilities** FTV Complimentary use of leisure facilities at Apex International Hotel Xmas New Year Wi-fi **Conf** Class 30 Board 34 Thtr 70 **Services** Lift **Notes** ⊗ Civ Wed 60

Novotel Edinburgh Park

★★★★ 77% HOTEL

☎ 0131 446 5600 📠 0131 446 5610
15 Lochside Av EH12 9DJ
e-mail: h6515@accor.com
dir: Near Hermiston Gate shopping area

Located just off the city by-pass and within minutes of the airport, this modern hotel offers bedrooms that are spacious and comfortable. The public areas include the open-plan lobby, bar and a restaurant where some tables have their own TVs.

Rooms 170 (130 fmly) **Facilities** Ⓢ Gym Wi-fi **Conf** Class 60 Board 40 Thtr 150 Del from £135 to £165* **Services** Lift **Parking** 96 **Notes** Civ Wed 90

Radisson Blu Hotel Edinburgh

★★★★ 77% HOTEL

☎ 0131 557 9797 & 557 6523 📠 0131 557 8789
80 High St, The Royal Mile EH1 1TH
e-mail: sales.edinburgh@radissonblu.com
web: www.radissonblu.com/hotel-edinburgh
dir: On Royal Mile

Centrally located in the heart of the old town on the Royal Mile, the spacious and comfortable bedrooms cater well for both leisure and corporate guests. The staff provide very attentive service. Leisure facilities, parking and complimentary Wi-fi are all assets at this hotel.

Rooms 238 (5 fmly) **Facilities** STV FTV Ⓢ supervised Gym Saunas Wi-fi **Conf** Class 105 Board 52 Thtr 240 **Services** Lift Air con **Parking** 131 **Notes** ⊗ Civ Wed 180

The Royal Terrace

★★★★ 76% HOTEL

☎ 0131 557 3222 📠 0131 557 5334
18 Royal Ter EH7 5AQ
e-mail: sales@royalterracehotel.co.uk
web: www.royalterracehotel.co.uk
dir: A8 to city centre, follow one-way system, left into Charlotte Sq. At end right into Queens St. Left at rdbt. At next island right into London Rd, right into Blenheim Place leading to Royal Terrace

Forming part of a quiet Georgian terrace in the heart of the city, this hotel offers bedrooms that successfully blend the historic architecture of the building with state-of-the-art facilities. Although most rooms afford lovely views, the top floor rooms provide excellent panoramas over the city to the Firth of Forth; for something unusual book an Ambassador Suite with a glass bathroom. The hotel's leisure club has a swimming pool, sauna and steam room, and award-winning dinners are served in the Terrace Brasserie.

Rooms 107 (13 fmly) (7 GF) **Facilities** Gym Steam room Sauna Aromatherapy shower Xmas New Year Wi-fi **Conf** Class 40 Board 40 Thtr 100 **Services** Lift **Notes** Civ Wed 80

Novotel Edinburgh Centre

★★★★ 76% HOTEL

☎ 0131 656 3500 📠 0131 656 3510
Lauriston Place, Lady Lawson St EH3 9DE
e-mail: H3271@accor.com
web: www.novotel.com
dir: From Edinburgh Castle right onto George IV Bridge from Royal Mile. Follow to junct, then right into Lauriston Place. Hotel 700mtrs on right

This modern hotel is located in the centre of the city, close to Edinburgh Castle. Smart and stylish public areas include a cosmopolitan bar, brasserie-style restaurant and indoor leisure facilities. The air-conditioned bedrooms feature a comprehensive range of extras and bathrooms with baths and separate shower cabinets.

Rooms 180 (146 fmly) **Facilities** STV Gym Sauna Steam room Xmas Wi-fi **Conf** Class 50 Board 32 Thtr 80 **Services** Lift Air con **Parking** 15

Holiday Inn Edinburgh

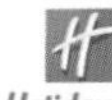

★★★★ 75% HOTEL

☎ 0871 942 9026 📠 0131 334 9237
Corstorphine Rd EH12 6UA
e-mail: edinburghhi@ihg.com
web: www.holidayinn.co.uk
dir: On A8, adjacent to Edinburgh Zoo

A modern hotel situated three miles west of Edinburgh and near Edinburgh Business Park. The hotel enjoys panoramic views of the Pentland Hills and makes a good base for visiting the attractions of the city. Bedrooms include family and executive rooms. The eating options are Traders Restaurant or Sampans Oriental Restaurant, as well as a café and bar. The Spirit Health and Fitness Club has a gym, swimming pool, sauna, spa and beauty treatments. There is also a conference centre.

Rooms 303 (76 fmly) (41 smoking) **Facilities** Spa STV FTV supervised Gym New Year Wi-fi **Conf** Class 60 Board 45 Thtr 120 Del from £99 to £185* **Services** Lift Air con **Parking** 105 **Notes** Civ Wed 80

Macdonald Holyrood

★★★★ 75% HOTEL

☎ 0870 1942106 📠 0131 550 4545
Holyrood Rd EH8 8AU
e-mail: general.holyrood@macdonald-hotels.co.uk
web: www.macdonaldhotels.co.uk/holyrood
dir: Parallel to Royal Mile, near Holyrood Palace & Dynamic Earth

Situated just a short walk from Holyrood Palace, this impressive hotel lies next to the Scottish Parliament building. Air-conditioned bedrooms are comfortably furnished, whilst the Club floor boasts a private lounge. Full business services complement the extensive conference suites.

Rooms 156 (16 fmly) (13 GF) **Facilities** Spa STV Gym Beauty treatment rooms Sauna Steam room Library Xmas New Year Wi-fi **Conf** Class 100 Board 80 Thtr 200 **Services** Lift Air con **Parking** 38 **Notes** LB Civ Wed 100

Barceló Carlton Hotel

★★★★ 74% HOTEL

☎ 0131 472 3000 📠 0131 556 2691
North Bridge EH1 1SD
e-mail: carlton@barcelo-hotels.co.uk
web: www.barcelo-hotels.co.uk
dir: On North Bridge which links Princes St to The Royal Mile

The Carlton occupies a city centre location just off the Royal Mile. Inside, it is modern and stylish in design, with an impressive open-plan reception/lobby, spacious first-floor lounge, bar and restaurant, plus a basement leisure club. Bedrooms, many air-conditioned, are generally spacious, with an excellent range of accessories.

Rooms 189 (20 fmly) **Facilities** STV supervised Gym Squash Table tennis Dance studio Exercise classes Treatment rooms Crèche Xmas New Year Wi-fi **Conf** Class 110 Board 60 Thtr 220 **Services** Lift **Notes** Civ Wed 160

E

The King James, Edinburgh

thistle

★★★★ 74% HOTEL

☎ 0871 376 9016 📠 0871 376 9116
107 Leith St EH1 3SW
e-mail: edinburgh@thistle.co.uk
web: www.thistlehotels.com/edinburgh
dir: M8/M9 onto A8 signed city centre. Hotel at end of Princes St adjacent to St James shopping centre

This purpose-built hotel adjoins one of Edinburgh's premier shopping malls at the east end of Princes Street. The friendly team of staff are keen to please whilst stylish, well-equipped bedrooms provide excellent levels of comfort and good facilities. Public areas include a spacious restaurant, popular bar and an elegant lobby lounge. Thistle Hotels – AA Hotel Group of the Year 2011-12.

Rooms 143 (12 fmly) **Facilities** STV FTV Xmas New Year Wi-fi **Conf** Class 160 Board 50 Thtr 250 **Services** Lift **Parking** 18 **Notes** LB

The Roxburghe Hotel

★★★★ 74% HOTEL

☎ 0844 879 9063 & 0131 240 5500
📠 0131 240 5555
38 Charlotte Square EH2 4HQ
e-mail: general.roxburghe@macdonald-hotels.co.uk
web: www.macdonaldhotels.co.uk/roxburghe
dir: On corner of Charlotte Sq & George St

This long-established hotel lies in the heart of the city overlooking Charlotte Square Gardens. Public areas are inviting and include relaxing lounges, a choice of bars (in the evening) and an inner concourse that looks onto a small lawned area. Smart bedrooms come in both classic and contemporary styles. There is a secure underground car park.

Rooms 199 (3 fmly) **S** £90-£240; **D** £95-£320* **Facilities** Spa STV FTV Gym Dance studio Sauna Steam room Xmas New Year Wi-fi **Conf** Class 160 Board 50 Thtr 300 **Services** Lift Air con **Parking** 20 **Notes** LB Civ Wed 280

EDINBURGH ***continued***

Malmaison Edinburgh

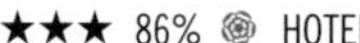
★★★ 86% HOTEL

☎ 0131 468 5000 🖷 0131 468 5002
One Tower Place EH6 7DB
e-mail: edinburgh@malmaison.com
web: www.malmaison.com
dir: A900 from city centre towards Leith, at end of Leith Walk, through 3 sets of lights, left into Tower St. Hotel on right at end of road

The trendy Port of Leith is home to this stylish Malmaison. Inside, bold contemporary designs create a striking effect. Bedrooms are comprehensively equipped with CD players, mini-bars and loads of individual touches. Ask for one of the stunning superior rooms for a really memorable stay. The smart brasserie and a café bar are popular with the local clientele.

Rooms 100 (18 fmly) **Facilities** STV Gym Xmas New Year Wi-fi **Conf** Class 30 Board 40 Thtr 55 **Services** Lift **Parking** 50

Apex European Hotel

★★★ 83% HOTEL

☎ 0845 365 0000 & 0131 474 3456
🖷 0131 474 3400
90 Haymarket Ter EH12 5LQ
e-mail: edinburgh.reservations@apexhotels.co.uk
web: www.apexhotels.co.uk
dir: A8 to city centre, 100m from Haymarket Railway Station

Lying just west of the city centre, close to Haymarket Station and handy for the Conference Centre, this modern hotel is popular with business travellers. Smart, stylish bedrooms offer an excellent range of facilities and have been designed with work requirements in mind. Public areas include Metro, an informal bistro. Service is friendly and pro-active.

Rooms 66 (3 GF) (8 smoking) **Facilities** FTV New Year Wi-fi **Conf** Class 30 Board 36 Thtr 80 **Services** Lift **Parking** 10 **Notes** ® Closed 24-27 Dec

Dalhousie Castle and Aqueous Spa

★★★ 82% HOTEL

☎ 01875 820153 🖷 01875 821936
Bonnyrigg EH19 3JB
e-mail: info@dalhousiecastle.co.uk
web: www.dalhousiecastle.co.uk
dir: A7 S from Edinburgh through Lasswade/ Newtongrange, right at Shell Garage (B704), hotel 0.5m from junct

A popular wedding venue, this imposing medieval castle sits amid lawns and parkland and even has a falconry. Bedrooms offer a mix of styles and sizes, including richly decorated themed rooms named after various historical figures. The Dungeon restaurant provides an atmospheric setting for dinner, and the less formal Orangery serves food all day. The spa offers many relaxing and therapeutic treatments and hydro facilities.

Rooms 36 (7 annexe) (3 fmly) **Facilities** Spa FTV Fishing Falconry Clay pigeon shooting Archery Laserday Xmas New Year Wi-fi **Conf** Class 60 Board 45 Thtr 120 **Parking** 110 **Notes** Civ Wed 100

Best Western Braid Hills Hotel

★★★ 82% HOTEL

☎ 0131 447 8888 🖷 0131 452 8477
134 Braid Rd EH10 6JD
e-mail: bookings@braidhillshotel.co.uk
web: www.braidhillshotel.co.uk
dir: 2.5m S A702, opposite Braid Burn Park

From its elevated position on the south side, this long-established hotel enjoys splendid panoramic views of the city and castle. Bedrooms are smart, stylish and well equipped. The public areas are comfortable and inviting, and guests can dine in either the restaurant or popular bistro/bar.

Rooms 67 (14 fmly) (14 GF) **Facilities** STV Xmas New Year Wi-fi **Conf** Class 50 Board 30 Thtr 100 **Parking** 38 **Notes** ® Civ Wed 100

Old Waverley

★★★ 81% HOTEL

☎ 0131 556 4648 🖷 0131 557 6316
43 Princes St EH2 2BY
e-mail: reservations@oldwaverley.co.uk
web: www.oldwaverley.co.uk
dir: In city centre, opposite Scott Monument, Waverley Station & Jenners

Occupying a commanding position opposite Sir Walter Scott's famous monument on Princes Street, this hotel lies right in the heart of the city close to the station. The comfortable public rooms are all on first-floor level and along with front-facing bedrooms enjoy the fine views.

Rooms 85 (5 fmly) **Facilities** Leisure facilities at sister hotel Wi-fi **Services** Lift **Notes** ®

Best Western Kings Manor

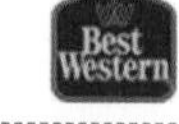

★★★ 79% HOTEL

☎ 0131 669 0444 & 468 8003 🖷 0131 669 6650
100 Milton Road East EH15 2NP
e-mail: reservations@kingsmanor.com
web: www.kingsmanor.com
dir: A720 E to Old Craighall junct, left into city, right at A1/A199 junct, hotel 400mtrs on right

Lying on the eastern side of the city and convenient for the by-pass, this hotel is popular with business guests, tour groups and for conferences. It boasts a fine leisure complex and a bright modern bistro, which complements the quality, creative cooking in the main restaurant.

Rooms 95 (8 fmly) (13 GF) **S** £60-£125; **D** £70-£180 **Facilities** Spa STV FTV Gym Health & beauty salon Steam room Sauna Wi-fi **Conf** Class 80 Board 60 Thtr 160 Del from £98 to £168* **Services** Lift **Parking** 130 **Notes** LB Civ Wed 100

The Point Hotel, Edinburgh

★★★ 78% HOTEL

☎ 0131 221 5555 📠 0131 221 9929
34 Bread St EH3 9AF
e-mail: enquiries@pointhoteledinburgh.co.uk
dir: A71 to Haymarket Station. Straight on at junct & right on Torphichen St, left onto Morrison St, straight on to Bread St, hotel on right

Built in 1892 as a Co-op which once employed Sean Connery as a milkman, the hotel has won many awards for its design and presentation. Bedrooms are spacious and cater well for the needs of the modern guest. Open-plan public areas are enhanced with coloured lighting and an array of artwork. The Point Restaurant offers imaginative dishes. The Glass Box Penthouse conference room affords fantastic views of the city.

Rooms 139 **Facilities** FTV Wi-fi **Conf** Class 60 Board 40 Thtr 120 Del from £130 to £160* **Services** Lift **Notes** ⊗ Civ Wed 90

Holiday Inn Edinburgh West

★★★ 75% HOTEL

☎ 0871 942 9025 📠 0131 332 3408
107 Queensferry Rd EH4 3HL
e-mail: reservations-edinburghcitywest@ihg.com
web: www.holidayinn.co.uk
dir: On A90 approx 1m from city centre

Situated on the north-west side of the city, close to Murrayfield Stadium and just five miles from the airport, this purpose-built hotel has a bright contemporary look. The colourful, modern bedrooms are well equipped and three specifications are available - with two double beds; with a double bed and sofa; or with a double bed and separate lounge. Some have great views of the city too. There is limited free parking.

Rooms 101 **Facilities** STV New Year Wi-fi **Conf** Class 60 Board 50 Thtr 140 Del from £79 to £265* **Services** Lift Air con **Parking** 80 **Notes** ⊗ Civ Wed 120

Express by Holiday Inn Edinburgh Waterfront

BUDGET HOTEL

☎ 0131 555 4422 📠 0131 555 4646
Britannia Way, Ocean Dr, Leith EH6 6JJ
e-mail: info@hiex-edinburgh.com
web: www.hiexpress.com/exedinburghwat
dir: Follow signs for Royal Yacht Britannia. Hotel just before Britannia on right

A modern hotel ideal for families and business travellers. Fresh and uncomplicated, the spacious rooms include Sky TV, power shower and tea and coffee-making facilities. Continental buffet breakfast is included in the room rate; other meals may be taken at the nearby family pub or restaurant. See also the Hotel Groups pages.

Rooms 145 (36 fmly) **Conf** Class 15 Board 18 Thtr 35

Holiday Inn Express Edinburgh City Centre

BUDGET HOTEL

☎ 0131 558 2300 📠 0131 558 2323
Picardy Place EH1 3JT
e-mail: info@hieedinburgh.co.uk
web: www.hiexpress.com/edinburghctyct
dir: Follow signs to city centre & Greenside NCP. Hotel off Picardy Place rdbt (E end of Princes St)

A modern hotel ideal for families and business travellers. Fresh and uncomplicated, the spacious rooms include Sky TV, power shower and tea and coffee-making facilities. Continental buffet breakfast is included in the room rate; other meals may be taken at the nearby family pub or restaurant. See also the Hotel Groups pages.

Rooms 161 (53 fmly) (27 GF) (13 smoking) **D** £69-£299 (incl. bkfst)* **Conf** Class 8 Board 18 Thtr 20

Holiday Inn Express Edinburgh Royal Mile

BUDGET HOTEL

☎ 0131 524 8400 📠 0131 524 8401
South Grays Close, Cowgate EH1 1NA
e-mail: info@hiexpressedinburgh.co.uk
web: www.hiexpressedinburgh.co.uk

Rooms 78 (50 fmly) (10 GF) **S** £39.99-£299.99; **D** £39.99-£299.99 (incl. bkfst)* **Conf** Class 20 Board 20 Thtr 40

Ibis Edinburgh Centre

BUDGET HOTEL

☎ 0131 240 7000 📠 0131 240 7007
6 Hunter Square, (off The Royal Mile) EH1 1QW
e-mail: H2039@accor.com
web: www.ibishotel.com
dir: M8/M9/A1 over North Bridge (A7) & High St, take 1st right off South Bridge, into Hunter Sq

Modern, budget hotel offering comfortable accommodation in bright and practical bedrooms. Breakfast is self-service and dinner is available in the restaurant. See also the Hotel Groups pages.

Rooms 99 (2 GF)

Premier Inn Edinburgh Airport (Newbridge)

BUDGET HOTEL

☎ 0871 527 9284 📠 0871 527 9285
2A Kirkliston Rd, Newbridge EH28 8SL
dir: M9 junct 1, A89 signed Broxburn. At lights turn right, then 2nd right

High quality, budget accommodation ideal for both families and business travellers. Spacious, en suite bedrooms feature tea and coffee making facilities, and Freeview TV in most hotels. Internet access and Wi-fi are available for a small fee. The adjacent family restaurant features a wide and varied menu. See also the Hotel Groups pages.

Rooms 119 **D** £54*

Premier Inn Edinburgh City Centre (Haymarket)

BUDGET HOTEL

☎ 0871 527 8368 📠 0871 527 8369
1 Morrison Link EH3 8DN
dir: Adjcent to Edinburgh International Conference Centre

Rooms 281 **D** £74*

Premier Inn Edinburgh City Lauriston Place

BUDGET HOTEL

☎ 0871 527 8366 📠 0871 527 8367
82 Lauriston Place, Lady Lawson St EH3 9DG
dir: A8 onto A702 (Lothian Rd). Left into Lauriston Place. Hotel on left

Rooms 112 **D** £74*

E

EDINBURGH *continued*

Premier Inn Edinburgh East

BUDGET HOTEL

☎ 0871 527 8370 🖷 0871 527 8371
228 Willowbrae Rd EH8 7NG
dir: M8 junct 1, A720 S for 12m, then A1. At Asda rdbt turn left. In 2m, hotel on left before Esso garage

Rooms 39 **D** £62-£65*

Premier Inn Edinburgh (Inveresk)

BUDGET HOTEL

☎ 0871 527 8358 🖷 0871 527 8359
Carberry Rd, Inveresk, Musselburgh EH21 8PT
dir: From A1 follow Dalkeith (A6094) signs. At rdbt turn right, hotel 300yds on right

Rooms 40 **D** £62-£65*

Premier Inn Edinburgh (Leith)

BUDGET HOTEL

☎ 0871 527 8360 🖷 0871 527 8361
51-53 Newhaven Place, Leith EH6 4TX
dir: From A1 follow coast road through Leith. Pass Ocean Terminal, straight ahead at mini-rdbt, 2nd exit signed Harry Ramsden's car park

Rooms 60 **D** £65*

21212

◎◎◎ RESTAURANT WITH ROOMS

☎ 0131 523 1030 & 0845 222 1212
🖷 0131 553 1038
3 Royal Ter EH7 5AB
e-mail: reservations@21212restaurant.co.uk

A real gem in Edinburgh's crown, this establishment takes its name from the numbers of choices at each course on the five-course dinner menu. Located on the prestigious Royal Terrace this is a light and airy, renovated Georgian townhouse stretching over four floors. The four individually designed bedrooms epitomise luxury living and the bathrooms have the wow factor. At the heart of this restaurant with rooms is the creative, award-winning cooking of Paul Kitching. Service throughout is friendly and very attentive.

Rooms 4

INSPECTORS' CHOICE

The Witchery by the Castle

◎ RESTAURANT WITH ROOMS

☎ 0131 225 5613 🖷 0131 220 4392
352 Castlehill, The Royal Mile EH1 2NF
e-mail: mail@thewitchery.com
web: www.thewitchery.com
dir: Top of Royal Mile at gates of Edinburgh Castle

Originally built in 1595, The Witchery by the Castle is situated in a historic building at the gates of Edinburgh Castle. The two luxurious and theatrically decorated suites, known as the Inner Sanctum and the Old Rectory are located above the restaurant and are reached via a winding stone staircase. Filled with antiques, opulently draped beds, large roll-top baths and a plethora of memorabilia, this ancient and exciting establishment is often described as one of the country's most romantic destinations.

Rooms 8 (5 annexe)

ELGIN Moray **Map 23 NJ26**

Mansion House

★★★ 79% HOTEL

☎ 01343 548811 🖷 01343 547916
The Haugh IV30 1AW
e-mail: reception@mhelgin.co.uk
web: www.mansionhousehotel.co.uk
dir: Exit A96 into Haugh Rd, then 1st left

Set in grounds by the River Lossie, this baronial mansion is popular with leisure and business guests as well as being a popular wedding venue. Bedrooms are spacious and many have views of the river. Extensive public areas include a choice of restaurants, with the bistro contrasting with the classical main restaurant. There is an indoor pool and a beauty and hair salon.

Rooms 23 (2 fmly) (5 GF) **Facilities** STV FTV supervised Fishing Gym Hair studio New Year Wi-fi **Conf** Thtr 180 **Parking** 50 **Notes** Civ Wed 160

Premier Inn Elgin

BUDGET HOTEL

☎ 0871 527 8372 🖷 0871 527 8373
15 Linkwood Way IV30 1HY
dir: On A96, 1.5m E of city centre

High quality, budget accommodation ideal for both families and business travellers. Spacious, en suite bedrooms feature tea and coffee making facilities, and Freeview TV in most hotels. Internet access and Wi-fi are available for a small fee. The adjacent family restaurant features a wide and varied menu. See also the Hotel Groups pages.

Rooms 40 **D** £54-£60*

ERISKA Argyll & Bute **Map 20 NM94**

INSPECTORS' CHOICE

Isle of Eriska Hotel, Spa & Golf

★★★★★ ◎◎◎
COUNTRY HOUSE HOTEL

☎ 01631 720371 🖷 01631 720531
Eriska PA37 1SD
e-mail: office@eriska-hotel.co.uk
dir: Exit A85 at Connel onto A828, 4m, follow hotel signs from N of Benderloch

Situated on its own private island with delightful beaches and walking trails, this hotel is in a tranquil setting, perfect for total relaxation. The spacious bedrooms are very comfortable and boast some fine antique pieces. Local seafood, meats and game feature prominently on the award-winning menu, as do vegetables and herbs grown in the hotel's kitchen garden. Leisure facilities include an indoor pool, gym and spa treatment rooms.

Rooms 23 (6 fmly) (2 GF) **S** £250-£460; **D** £330-£460 (incl. bkfst)* **Facilities** Spa FTV supervised 9 Putt green Fishing Gym Squash Sauna Steam room Skeet shooting Nature trails Xmas New Year Wi-fi **Conf** Class 30 Board 30 Thtr 30 **Parking** 40 **Notes** Closed Jan Civ Wed 50

FALKIRK Falkirk Map 21 NS88

Premier Inn Falkirk Central

BUDGET HOTEL

☎ 0871 527 8388 🖷 0871 527 8389
Main St, Camelon FK1 4DS
dir: From Falkirk take A803 signed Glasgow. At mini-rdbt right, continue on A803. At Rosebank rdbt 2nd exit signed Glasgow & Stirling

High quality, budget accommodation ideal for both families and business travellers. Spacious, en suite bedrooms feature tea and coffee making facilities, and Freeview TV in most hotels. Internet access and Wi-fi are available for a small fee. The adjacent family restaurant features a wide and varied menu. See also the Hotel Groups pages.

Rooms 31 **D** £59*

Premier Inn Falkirk (Larbert)

BUDGET HOTEL

☎ 0871 527 8390 🖷 0871 527 8391
Glenbervie Business Park, Bellsdyke Rd, Larbert FK5 4EG
dir: Just off A88. Approx 1m from M876 junct 2

Rooms 60 **D** £52-£58*

FINTRY Stirling Map 20 NS68

Culcreuch Castle Hotel & Estate

★★★ 79% HOTEL

☎ 01360 860555 & 860228 🖷 01360 860556
Kippen Rd G63 0LW
e-mail: info@culcreuch.com
web: www.culcreuch.com
dir: On B822, 17m W of Stirling

Peacefully located in 1,600 acres of parkland, this ancient castle dates back to 1296. Tastefully restored accommodation is in a mixture of individually themed castle rooms, some with four-poster beds, and more modern courtyard rooms which are suitable for families. Period-style public rooms include an elegant lounge, a bar serving light meals, and a wood-panelled dining room.

Rooms 14 (4 annexe) (4 fmly) (4 GF) **D** £102-£190 (incl. bkfst) **Facilities** STV FTV Fishing New Year Wi-fi **Conf** Class 70 Board 30 Thtr 140 Del from £119 to £129 **Parking** 100 **Notes** LB ⊗ Closed 4-18 Jan & 25-26 Dec Civ Wed 110

FORT AUGUSTUS Highland Map 23 NH30

Inchnacardoch Lodge Hotel

★★★ 73% ⊛ SMALL HOTEL

☎ 01456 450900 🖷 01320 366294
Inchnacardoch Bay PH32 4BL
e-mail: info@inchhotel.com

This 150-year-old former hunting lodge is set on the hillside looking over the south end of Loch Ness, making it a perfect base for exploring the Highlands. Guests can expect the finest of highland hospitality here from staff that are always eager to please. The bedrooms are very individual in style; the Bridal Suite is a very well appointed room with stunning views. The award-winning Yard Restaurant serves dishes based on the plentiful supply of local game and seafood.

Rooms 14 (2 fmly) **S** £69.99-£89.99; **D** £69.99-£140 (incl. bkfst)* **Facilities** FTV Fishing Xmas New Year Wi-fi **Conf** Class 26 Board 18 Thtr 20 Del from £179 to £239* **Parking** 30 **Notes** LB Civ Wed 40

FORTINGALL Perth & Kinross Map 20 NN74

Fortingall

★★★★ 78% ⊛⊛ SMALL HOTEL

☎ 01887 830367 & 830368 🖷 01887 830367
PH15 2NQ
e-mail: hotel@fortingallhotel.com
dir: B846 from Aberfeldy for 6m, left signed Fortingall for 3m. Hotel in village centre

Appointed to a very high standard, this hotel has plenty of charm. It lies at the foot of wooded hills in the heart of Glen Lyon. All the bedrooms are very well equipped and have an extensive range of thoughtful extras. The comfortable lounge, with its log fire, is ideal for pre-dinner drinks, and the small bar is full of character.

Rooms 10 (1 fmly) **Facilities** STV Fishing Stalking ♫ Xmas New Year Wi-fi **Conf** Board 16 Thtr 30 **Parking** 20 **Notes** Civ Wed 30

FORT WILLIAM Highland Map 22 NN17

INSPECTORS' CHOICE

Inverlochy Castle

★★★★★ ⊛⊛⊛
COUNTRY HOUSE HOTEL

☎ 01397 702177 🖷 01397 702953
Torlundy PH33 6SN
e-mail: info@inverlochy.co.uk
web: www.inverlochycastlehotel.com
dir: Accessible from either A82 (Glasgow-Fort William) or A9 (Edinburgh-Dalwhinnie). Hotel 3m N of Fort William on A82, in Torlundy

With a backdrop of Ben Nevis, this imposing and gracious castle sits amidst extensive gardens and grounds overlooking the hotel's own loch. Lavishly appointed in classic country-house style, spacious bedrooms are extremely comfortable and boast flat-screen TVs and laptops with internet access. The sumptuous main hall and lounge provide the perfect setting for afternoon tea or a pre-dinner cocktail, while imaginative modern British cuisine is served in one of three dining rooms. A snooker room and DVD library are also available.

Rooms 17 (6 fmly) **S** £375-£695; **D** £440-£695 (incl. bkfst)* **Facilities** STV Fishing on loch Massage Riding Hunting Stalking Clay pigeon shooting Archery ♫ Xmas New Year Wi-fi **Conf** Class 20 Board 20 Thtr 50 **Parking** 17 **Notes** LB Civ Wed 80

F

F

FORT WILLIAM *continued*

Moorings

★★★ 82% HOTEL

☎ 01397 772797 📠 01397 772441
Banavie PH33 7LY
e-mail: reservations@moorings-fortwilliam.co.uk
web: www.moorings-fortwilliam.co.uk
dir: Take A830 (N from Fort William), cross Caledonian Canal, 1st right

Located on the Caledonian Canal next to a series of locks known as Neptune's Staircase and close to Thomas Telford's house, this hotel with its dedicated team offers friendly service. Accommodation comes in two distinct styles and the newer rooms are particularly appealing. Meals can be taken in the bars or the spacious dining room.

Rooms 27 (2 fmly) (1 GF) **S** £49-£138; **D** £70-£148 (incl. bkfst)* **Facilities** STV Gym New Year Wi-fi **Conf** Class 60 Board 40 Thtr 140 Del from £90 to £120* **Parking** 60 **Notes** LB Closed 24-26 Dec Civ Wed 120

Lime Tree Hotel & Restaurant

★★★ 78% SMALL HOTEL

☎ 01397 701806 📠 01397 701806
Lime Tree Studio, Achintore Rd PH33 6RQ
e-mail: info@limetreefortwilliam.co.uk
dir: On A82 at entrance to Fort William

A charming small hotel with an inspirational art gallery on the ground floor, with lots of original artwork displayed throughout. Evening meals can be enjoyed in the restaurant which has a loyal following. The hotel's comfortable lounges with their real fires are ideal for pre or post dinner drinks or maybe just to relax in. Individually designed bedrooms are spacious with some nice little personal touches courtesy of the artist owner.

Rooms 9 (4 fmly) (4 GF) **S** £110; **D** £110 (incl. bkfst)* **Facilities** New Year Wi-fi **Conf** Class 40 Board 30 Thtr 60 Del from £200* **Parking** 9 **Notes** Closed 24-26 Dec

Alexandra Hotel

★★★ 75% HOTEL

☎ 01397 702241 📠 01397 705554
The Parade PH33 6AZ
e-mail: salesalexandra@strathmorehotels.com
dir: Off A82. Hotel opposite railway station

This charming old hotel enjoys a prominent position in the town centre and is just a short walk from all the major attractions. Front-facing bedrooms have views over the town and the spectacular Nevis mountain range. There is a choice of restaurants, including a bistro serving meals until late, along with several stylish and very comfortable lounges.

Rooms 93 (2 fmly) **S** £69-£89; **D** £99-£120 (incl. bkfst)* **Facilities** Free use of nearby leisure club ♫ Xmas New Year Wi-fi **Conf** Class 100 Board 40 Thtr 120 **Services** Lift **Parking** 50 **Notes** LB

See advert on page 550

Ben Nevis Hotel & Leisure Club

★★ 75% HOTEL

☎ 01397 702331 📠 01397 700132
North Rd PH33 6TG
e-mail: bennevismanager@strathmorehotels.com
dir: Off A82

This popular hotel is ideally situated on the outskirts of Fort William. It provides comfortable, well equipped bedrooms; many with views of the impressive Nevis mountains. The hotel's leisure centre is a firm favourite with guests at the hotel.

Rooms 119 (3 fmly) (30 GF) **Facilities** supervised Gym Beauty salon ♫ Xmas New Year Wi-fi **Conf** Class 60 Board 40 Thtr 150 **Parking** 100 **Notes** Civ Wed 60

See advert on page 550

Croit Anna

★★ 71% HOTEL

☎ 01397 702268 📠 01397 704099
Achintore Rd, Drimarben PH33 6RR
e-mail: croitanna.fortwilliam@alfatravel.co.uk
dir: From Glencoe on A82 into Fort William, hotel 1st on right

Located on the edge of Loch Linnhe, just two miles out of town, this hotel offers some spacious bedrooms, many with fine views over the loch. There is a choice of two comfortable lounges and a large airy restaurant. The hotel appeals to coach parties and independent travellers alike.

Rooms 92 (5 fmly) (13 GF) **S** £37-£52; **D** £58-£88 (incl. bkfst) **Facilities** FTV Pool table ♫ Xmas New Year **Parking** 25 **Notes** LB Closed Dec-Jan (ex Xmas) RS Nov, Feb, Mar

Premier Inn Fort William

BUDGET HOTEL

☎ 0871 527 8402 📠 0871 527 8403
Loch Iall, An Aird PH33 6AN
dir: N end of Fort William Shopping Centre, just off A82 (ring road)

High quality, budget accommodation ideal for both families and business travellers. Spacious, en suite bedrooms feature tea and coffee making facilities, and Freeview TV in most hotels. Internet access and Wi-fi are available for a small fee. The adjacent family restaurant features a wide and varied menu. See also the Hotel Groups pages.

Rooms 40 **D** £69*

FOYERS Highland — **Map 23 NH52**

Craigdarroch House

RESTAURANT WITH ROOMS

☎ 01456 486400 📠 01456 486444
IV2 6XU
e-mail: info@hotel-loch-ness.co.uk
dir: Take B862 from either end of loch, then B852 signed Foyers

Craigdarroch is located in an elevated position high above Loch Ness on the south side. Bedrooms vary in style and size but all are comfortable and well equipped; those that are front-facing have wonderful views. Dinner is well worth staying in for, and breakfast is also memorable.

Rooms 8 (1 fmly)

GALASHIELS
Scottish Borders **Map 21 NT43**

Kingsknowes

★★★ 77% HOTEL

☎ 01896 758375 🖷 01896 750377
Selkirk Rd TD1 3HY
e-mail: enq@kingsknowes.co.uk
web: www.kingsknowes.co.uk
dir: Off A7 at Galashiels/Selkirk rdbt

An imposing turreted mansion, this hotel lies in attractive gardens on the outskirts of town close to the River Tweed. It boasts elegant public areas and many spacious bedrooms, some with excellent views. There is a choice of bars, one with a popular menu to supplement the restaurant.

Rooms 12 (2 fmly) **Facilities** Wi-fi **Conf** Class 40 Board 30 Thtr 60 **Parking** 65 **Notes** Civ Wed 75

GATEHOUSE OF FLEET
Dumfries & Galloway **Map 20 NX55**

Cally Palace

★★★★ 76% ◎ COUNTRY HOUSE HOTEL

☎ 01557 814341 🖷 01557 814522
DG7 2DL
e-mail: info@callypalace.co.uk
web: www.callypalace.co.uk
dir: From M6 & A74, signed A75 Dumfries then Stranraer. At Gatehouse-of-Fleet right onto B727, left at Cally

A resort hotel with extensive leisure facilities, this grand 18th-century building is set in 500 acres of forest and parkland that incorporates its own golf course. Bedrooms are spacious and well equipped, whilst public rooms retain a quiet elegance. The short dinner menu focuses on freshly prepared dishes; a pianist plays most nights and the wearing of jacket and tie is obligatory.

Rooms 55 (7 fmly) **Facilities** STV FTV 18 Putt green Fishing Gym Table tennis Practice fairway Xmas New Year Wi-fi **Conf** Class 40 Board 25 Thtr 40 **Services** Lift **Parking** 100 **Notes** Closed Jan-early Feb

GLASGOW
City of Glasgow **Map 20 NS56**

See also **Clydebank & Uplawmoor**

HOTEL OF THE YEAR

Blythswood Square

★★★★★ 88% ◎◎ HOTEL

☎ 0141 248 8888
11 Blythswood Square G2 4AD
e-mail: reserve@blythswoodsquare.com
dir: Telephone for detailed directions

Built in 1821, and restored to its former glory, this was the headquarters of the Royal Scottish Automobile Club and was one of the official starting points for the 1955 Monte Carlo Rally. The bedrooms and bathrooms are sumptuous, and include suites and a stunning penthouse suite. Afternoon tea and cocktails are served in the 35-metre, first-floor Salon Lounge, and the award-winning restaurant occupies the old RSAC's ballroom. The spa includes a fantastic thermal suite. AA Hotel of the Year for Scotland 2011-12.

Rooms 100 **Facilities** Wi-Fi Spa **Conf** Board 52 Thtr 100 **Notes** Civ Wed 40

INSPECTORS' CHOICE

Hotel du Vin at One Devonshire Gardens

★★★★ TOWN HOUSE HOTEL

☎ 0141 339 2001 🖷 0141 337 1663
1 Devonshire Gardens G12 0UX
e-mail: reservations.odg@hotelduvin.com
web: www.hotelduvin.com
dir: M8 junct 17, follow signs for A82, 1.5m turn left into Hyndland Rd, 1st right, right at mini rdbt, right at end

Situated in a tree lined Victorian terrace this luxury 'boutique' hotel has stunning, individually designed bedrooms and suites that have the trademark Egyptian linens and seriously good showers. Naturally, wine is an important part of the equation here, and knowledgeable staff can guide guests around the impressive wine list. The Rosette award is temporarily suspended due to a change of chef; a new award will be in place once our inspectors have completed their assessments of meals cooked by the new kitchen team. Please see the AA website theAA.com for up-to-date information.

Rooms 49 (7 GF) **Facilities** Gym Tennis & Squash facilities at nearby club Xmas New Year Wi-fi **Conf** Class 30 Board 30 Thtr 50 **Notes** Civ Wed 70

GLASGOW *continued*

Glasgow Marriott Hotel

Marriott HOTELS & RESORTS

★★★★ 78% HOTEL

☎ 0141 226 5577 ▯ 0141 221 9202
500 Argyle St, Anderston G3 8RR
e-mail: cork.regional.reservations@marriott.com
web: www.glasgowmarriott.co.uk
dir: M8 junct 19, turn left at lights, then left into hotel

Conveniently located for all major transport links and the city centre, this hotel benefits from extensive conference and banqueting facilities and a spacious car park. Public areas include an open-plan lounge/bar and a Mediterranean style restaurant. High quality, well-equipped bedrooms benefit from air conditioning and generously sized beds; the suites are particularly comfortable.

Rooms 300 (89 fmly) **Facilities** Gym Beautician Poolside steam room Sauna New Year Wi-fi **Conf** Class 300 Board 50 Thtr 800 **Services** Lift Air con **Parking** 180 **Notes**

G

Beardmore Hotel

★★★★ 77% HOTEL

☎ 0141 951 6000 ▯ 0141 951 6018
Beardmore St G81 4SA
e-mail: info@beardmore.scot.nhs.uk

(For full entry see Clydebank)

Mint Hotel Glasgow

minthotel

★★★★ 77% HOTEL

☎ 0141 240 1002 & 227 1026 ▯ 0141 248 2754
Finnieston Quay G3 8HN
e-mail: glasgow.reservations@minthotel.com
web: www.minthotel.com
dir: M8 junct 19 follow signs for SECC. Hotel on left 200yds before entrance to SECC

A contemporary hotel sitting alongside the River Clyde and the 'Squinty Bridge'. Modern, well-equipped bedrooms and bathrooms have many thoughtful extras for guests. Alfresco dining and drinking are a possibility; the restaurant has panoramic views of the Clyde. The hotel is ideally located for the SECC & Science Centre.

Rooms 164 **S** £69-£209; **D** £69-£209 **Facilities** STV FTV Gym Free use of nearby health club Xmas New Year Wi-fi **Conf** Class 36 Board 40 Thtr 60 Del from £120 to £250 **Services** Lift Air con **Parking** 120 **Notes** LB Civ Wed 60

Menzies Glasgow

MenziesHotels

★★★★ 76% HOTEL

☎ 0141 222 2929 & 270 2323 ▯ 0141 270 2301
27 Washington St G3 8AZ
e-mail: glasgow@menzieshotels.co.uk
web: www.menzieshotels.co.uk
dir: M8 junct 19 follow signs for SECC & Broomielaw. Left at lights

Centrally located, this modern hotel is a short drive from the airport and a short walk from the centre of the city. Bedrooms are generally spacious and boast a range of facilities, including high-speed internet access. Facilities include a brasserie restaurant and an impressive indoor leisure facility.

Rooms 141 (16 fmly) (15 smoking) **Facilities** STV supervised Gym Sauna Steam room Hair & beauty salon Xmas New Year Wi-fi **Conf** Class 60 Board 70 Thtr 160 **Services** Lift Air con **Parking** 50 **Notes** Civ Wed 150

Thistle Glasgow

thistle

★★★★ 75% HOTEL

☎ 0871 376 9043 ▯ 0871 376 9143
36 Cambridge St G2 3HN
e-mail: glasgow@thistle.co.uk
web: www.thistle.com/glasgow
dir: In city centre, just off Sauchiehall St

Ideally located within the centre of Glasgow and with ample parking, this hotel is well presented with the lobby area that gives a great impression on arrival. It also benefits from having a well-presented leisure club along with the largest ballroom in Glasgow. Service is friendly and attentive. Thistle Hotels – AA Hotel Group of the Year 2011-12.

Rooms 300 (38 fmly) (1 smoking) **Facilities** STV FTV Gym Sauna Steam room New Year Wi-fi **Conf** Class 800 Board 15 Thtr 1000 **Services** Lift Air con **Parking** 216 **Notes** LB Civ Wed 720

Millennium Hotel Glasgow

MILLENNIUM HOTELS AND RESORTS MILLENNIUM • COPTHORNE

★★★★ 74% HOTEL

☎ 0141 332 6711 ▯ 0141 332 4264
George Square G2 1DS
e-mail: glasgow.reservations@millenniumhotels.co.uk
web: www.millenniumhotels.co.uk
dir: M8 junct 15 through 4 sets of lights, at 5th left into Hanover St. George Sq directly ahead, hotel on right

Right in the heart of the city, this hotel has pride of place overlooking George Square. Inside, the property has a contemporary air, with a spacious reception concourse and a glass veranda overlooking the square. There is a stylish brasserie and separate lounge bar, and bedrooms come in a variety of sizes.

Rooms 116 (17 fmly) **Facilities** STV New Year Wi-fi **Conf** Class 24 Board 32 Thtr 40 **Services** Lift **Notes** Closed 25 Dec Civ Wed 120

Grand Central Hotel

PH | principal hayley

★★★★ 72% HOTEL

☎ 0141 240 3720 ▯ 0141 240 3701
99 Gordon St G1 3SF
e-mail: grandcentralhotel@principal-hayley.com
dir: M8 junct 19 towards city centre turn left at Hope St. Hotel 200 mtrs on right

This is the place where John Logie Baird transmitted the world's first long-distance television pictures in 1927, and this 'grand old lady' of the Glasgow hotel scene has been completely updated and refurbished throughout to a very good standard. The result is a blend of contemporary, art deco and original Victorian styles. Bedrooms are well equipped and suit business travellers especially. There is Champagne Central, a glamorous bar, the Tempus Bar and Restaurant, and Deli Central (with direct access to the Central Station) which is an eat-in deli and a take-away. Ample meeting facilities are available, and NCP car parks are nearby.

Rooms 186 (13 fmly) **Facilities** Wi-fi **Conf** Class 350 Board 60 Thtr 500 **Services** Lift **Notes** Civ Wed 500

Crowne Plaza Glasgow

CROWNE PLAZA HOTELS & RESORTS

★★★★ HOTEL

☎ 0871 942 9091 ▯ 0141 221 2022
Congress Rd G3 8QT
e-mail: cpglasgow@qmh-hotels.com
web: www.crowneplaza.co.uk
dir: M8 junct 19, follow signs for SECC, hotel adjacent to centre

Rooms 283 (15 fmly) **Facilities** Spa STV supervised Gym Beauty salon Xmas New Year Wi-fi **Conf** Class 482 Board 68 Thtr 800 **Services** Lift Air con **Parking** 300 **Notes** Civ Wed 120

Holiday Inn Glasgow City Centre-Theatreland

★★★ 83% HOTEL

☎ 0141 352 8300 📠 0141 332 7447
161 West Nile St G1 2RL
e-mail: reservations@higlasgow.com
web: www.holidayinn.co.uk
dir: M8 junct 16, follow signs for Royal Concert Hall, hotel opposite

Built on a corner site close to the Theatre Royal Concert Hall and the main shopping areas, this contemporary hotel features the popular La Bonne Auberge French restaurant, a bar area and conservatory. Bedrooms are well equipped and comfortable; suites are available. Staff are friendly and attentive.

Rooms 113 (20 fmly) (10 smoking) **S** £65-£180; **D** £70-£190* **Facilities** STV FTV Wi-fi **Conf** Class 60 Board 60 Thtr 100 Del from £125 to £195* **Services** Lift Air con **Notes** ⊗

Malmaison Glasgow

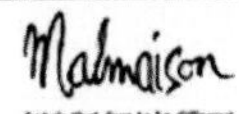

★★★ 82% HOTEL

☎ 0141 572 1000 📠 0141 572 1002
278 West George St G2 4LL
e-mail: glasgow@malmaison.com
web: www.malmaison.com
dir: From S & E: M8 junct 18 (Charing Cross). From W & N: M8 city centre

Built around a former church in the historic Charing Cross area, this hotel is a smart, contemporary establishment offering impressive levels of service and hospitality. Bedrooms are spacious and feature a host of modern facilities, such as CD players and mini bars. Dining is a treat here, with French brasserie-style cuisine, backed up by an excellent wine list, served in the original crypt.

Rooms 72 (4 fmly) (19 GF) **Facilities** STV Gym Cardiovascular equipment New Year Wi-fi **Conf** Board 22 Thtr 30 **Services** Lift **Notes** LB Civ Wed 80

Uplawmoor Hotel

★★★ 80% HOTEL

☎ 01505 850565 📠 01505 850689
Neilston Rd G78 4AF
e-mail: info@uplawmoor.co.uk
web: www.uplawmoor.co.uk

(For full entry see Uplawmoor)

Novotel Glasgow Centre

★★★ 79% HOTEL

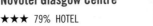

☎ 0141 222 2775 📠 0141 204 5438
181 Pitt St G2 4DT
e-mail: H3136@accor.com
web: www.novotel.com
dir: M8 junct 18 for Charing Cross. Follow to Sauchiehall St. 3rd right

Enjoying a convenient city centre location and with limited parking spaces, this hotel is ideal for both business and leisure travellers. Well-equipped bedrooms are brightly decorated and offer functional design. Modern public areas include a small fitness club and a brasserie serving a range of meals all day.

Rooms 139 (139 fmly) **Facilities** Gym Sauna Steam room Xmas Wi-fi **Conf** Class 20 Board 20 Thtr 40 **Services** Lift Air con **Parking** 19

Best Western Glasgow City Hotel

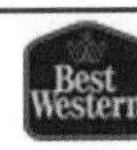

★★★ 75% TOWN HOUSE HOTEL

☎ 0141 227 2772 📠 0141 227 2774
27 Elmbank St G2 4PB
e-mail: glasgowcity@mckeverhotels.co.uk
dir: M8 junct 18, Charing Cross into Sauciehall St, 1st right into Elmbank St, pass petrol station, hotel on right

Situated in the heart of the city, this hotel offers spacious and well-equipped accommodation suitable for both families and business guests. Staff are friendly and helpful, and are mindful of the needs of the modern traveller. There is a secure pay car park close to the hotel.

Rooms 52 (4 fmly) (12 GF) **Facilities** FTV Xmas Wi-fi **Notes** ⊗

Argyll Hotel

★★★ 70% HOTEL

☎ 0141 337 3313 📠 0141 337 3283
973 Sauchiehall St G3 7TQ
e-mail: info@argyllhotelglasgow.co.uk
web: www.argyllhotelglasgow.co.uk
dir: M8 junct 18, stay in right lane, straight ahead to 2nd lights. Right into Berkley St, right into Elderslie St, 1st left into Sauchiehall St

Enjoying a prime city-centre location this popular hotel is within easy reach of the main shopping district, the university and the Scottish Exhibition & Conference Centre. The bedrooms are attractively presented with a good range of facilities including flat-screen TVs and free Wi-fi. The public areas include Sutherlands Restaurant and a cosy bar.

Rooms 38 (8 fmly) (5 GF) **S** £45-£65; **D** £60-£95 (incl. bkfst)* **Facilities** FTV Wi-fi **Conf** Class 16 Board 20 Thtr 25 Del from £110 to £150* **Services** Lift **Parking** 5 **Notes** ⊗

Campanile Glasgow

BUDGET HOTEL

☎ 0141 287 7700 📠 0141 287 7701
10 Tunnel St G3 8HL
e-mail: glasgow@campanile.com
dir: M8 junct 19, follow signs to SECC. Hotel adjacent to SECC

This modern building offers accommodation in smart, well-equipped bedrooms, all with en suite bathrooms. Refreshments may be taken at the informal bistro. See also the Hotel Groups pages.

Rooms 106 (2 fmly) (21 GF) **Conf** Class 60 Board 90 Thtr 150

Holiday Inn Express, Glasgow Theatreland

BUDGET HOTEL

☎ 0141 331 6800 📠 0141 331 6828
165 West Nile St G1 2RL
e-mail: frontoffice.exp@higlasgow.com
web: www.hiexpressglasgow.co.uk
dir: Follow signs to Royal Concert Hall

A modern hotel ideal for families and business travellers. Fresh and uncomplicated, the spacious rooms include Sky TV, power shower and tea and coffee-making facilities. Continental buffet breakfast is included in the room rate; other meals may be taken at the nearby family pub or restaurant. See also the Hotel Groups pages.

Rooms 118 (34 fmly) (17 smoking) **S** £49-£139.95; **D** £49-£139.95 (incl. bkfst)* **Conf** Board 12 Thtr 20

Holiday Inn Express Glasgow City Centre - Riverside

BUDGET HOTEL

☎ 0141 548 5000 📠 0141 548 5048
122 Stockwell St G1 4LT
e-mail: info@expressglasgow.co.uk
web: www.expressglasgow.co.uk
dir: M8 junct 19 (E & S), left at end of exit, follow river under Central Station bridge to Stockwell St

Rooms 128 (79 fmly) (13 smoking) **Conf** Class 16 Board 16 Thtr 30 Del from £85 to £125

GLASGOW *continued*

Ibis Glasgow

BUDGET HOTEL

☎ 0141 225 6000 🖷 0141 225 6010
220 West Regent St G2 4DQ
e-mail: H3139@accor-hotels.com
web: www.ibishotel.com

Modern, budget hotel offering comfortable accommodation in bright and practical bedrooms. Breakfast is self-service and meals are also available in the café-bar 24 hours. See also the Hotel Groups pages.

Rooms 141 **S** £55-£85; **D** £55-£85*

Premier Inn Glasgow (Bearsden)

BUDGET HOTEL

☎ 0871 527 8418 🖷 0871527 8419
279 Milngavie Rd G61 3DQ
dir: M8 junct 16, A81. Pass Asda on right. Hotel on left, behind The Burnbrae

High quality, budget accommodation ideal for both families and business travellers. Spacious, en suite bedrooms feature tea and coffee making facilities, and Freeview TV in most hotels. Internet access and Wi-fi are available for a small fee. The adjacent family restaurant features a wide and varied menu. See also the Hotel Groups pages.

Rooms 61 **D** £52-£60*

Premier Inn Glasgow (Bellshill)

BUDGET HOTEL

☎ 0871 527 8421 🖷 0871 527 8421
New Edinburgh Rd, Bellshill ML4 3PD
dir: M74 junct 5, A725. Follow Bellshill A721 signs, bear left. At rdbt left, follow Tannochside signs. At next rdbt left into Bellziehill Rd. Hotel on right

Rooms 40 **D** £54-£60*

Premier Inn Glasgow (Cambuslang/M74 Jct 1)

BUDGET HOTEL

☎ 0871 527 8422 🖷 0871 527 8423
Cambuslang Investment Park, Off London Rd G32 8YX
dir: At end of M74, turn right at rdbt. At 1st lights turn right, at 2nd lights straight ahead. Hotel on right

Rooms 40 **D** £54-£60*

Premier Inn Glasgow City Centre Argyle St

BUDGET HOTEL

☎ 0871 527 8436 🖷 0871 527 8437
377 Argyle St G2 8LL
dir: From S: M8 junct 19, at pedestrian lights left into Argyle St. Hotel 200yds on right

Rooms 121 **D** £59*

Premier Inn Glasgow City Centre (Charing Cross)

BUDGET HOTEL

☎ 0871 527 8438 🖷 0871 527 8439
10 Elmbank Gardens G2 4PP
e-mail: glasgow@premierlodge.co.uk
dir: Telephone for directions

Rooms 278 **D** £55*

Premier Inn Glasgow City Centre (George Square)

BUDGET HOTEL

☎ 0871 527 8440 🖷 0871 527 8441
187 George St G1 1YU
dir: M8 junct 15, into Stirling Rd. Right into Cathedral St. At 1st lights left into Montrose St. Hotel after 1st lights

Rooms 239 **D** £65*

Premier Inn Glasgow City Centre South

BUDGET HOTEL

☎ 0871 527 8442 🖷 0871 527 8443
80 Ballater St G5 0TW
dir: M8 junct 21 follow East Kilbride signs, right onto A8 into Kingston St. Right into South Portland St, left into Norfolk St, through Gorbals St into Ballater St

Rooms 114 **D** £60*

Premier Inn Glasgow East

BUDGET HOTEL

☎ 0871 527 8444 🖷 0871 527 8445
601 Hamilton Rd, Uddington G71 7SA
dir: At entrance to Glasgow Zoo, adjacent to junct 4 of M73 & M74

Rooms 66 **D** £54-£60*

GLASGOW AIRPORT
Renfrewshire **Map 20 NS46**

Holiday Inn Glasgow Airport

Holiday Inn

★★★ 79% HOTEL

☎ 0871 942 9031 & 0141 887 1266
🖷 0141 887 3738
Abbotsinch PA3 2TR
e-mail: operations-glasgow@ihg.com
web: www.holidayinn.co.uk
dir: From E: M8 junct 28, follow hotel signs. From W: M8 junct 29, airport slip road to hotel

Located within the airport grounds and within walking distance of the terminal. Bedrooms are well appointed and cater for the needs of the modern traveller. The open-plan public areas are relaxing as is the restaurant which offers a carvary and a carte menu. Wi-fi is available in the public areas with LAN in all bedrooms.

Rooms 300 (6 fmly) (54 smoking) **D** £51-£149* **Facilities** STV FTV Wi-fi **Conf** Class 150 Board 75 Thtr 300 Del from £89 to £199* **Services** Lift Air con **Parking** 56 **Notes** LB Civ Wed 250

Holiday Inn Express Glasgow Airport

BUDGET HOTEL

☎ 0141 842 1100 🖷 0141 842 1122
St Andrews Dr PA3 2TJ
e-mail: info@expressglasgowairport.co.uk
web: www.expressglasgowairport.co.uk
dir: M8 junct 28, at 1st rdbt turn right, hotel on right

A modern hotel ideal for families and business travellers. Fresh and uncomplicated, the spacious rooms include Sky TV, power shower and tea and coffee-making facilities. Continental buffet breakfast is included in the room rate; other meals may be taken at the nearby family pub or restaurant. See also the Hotel Groups pages.

Rooms 143 (65 fmly) (11 GF) **S** £39-£89; **D** £39-£89 (incl. bkfst)* **Conf** Class 20 Board 30 Thtr 70

Premier Inn Glasgow Airport

BUDGET HOTEL

☎ 0871 527 8434 🖷 0871 527 8435
Whitecart Rd, Glasgow Airport PA3 2TH
dir: M8 junct 28, follow airport signs for Long Stay & Car Park 3 (Premier Inn signed). At 1st rdbt right into St Andrews Drive. At next rdbt right into Whitecart Rd. Under motorway. Left at garage. Hotel on right

High quality, budget accommodation ideal for both families and business travellers. Spacious, en suite bedrooms feature tea and coffee making facilities, and Freeview TV in most hotels. Internet access and Wi-fi are available for a small fee. The adjacent family restaurant features a wide and varied menu. See also the Hotel Groups pages.

Rooms 104 **D** £54-£58*

Premier Inn Glasgow (Paisley)

BUDGET HOTEL

☎ 0871 527 8432 🖷 0871 527 8433
Phoenix Retail Park PA1 2BH
dir: M8 junct 28a, A737 signed Irvine, take 1st exit signed Linwood, left at 1st rdbt to Phoenix Park

Rooms 40 **D** £54-£58*

GLENEAGLES

See Auchterarder

GLENFINNAN Map 22 NM98
Highland

The Prince's House

★★★ 75% ®® SMALL HOTEL

☎ 01397 722246 🖷 01397 722323
PH37 4LT
e-mail: princeshouse@glenfinnan.co.uk
web: www.glenfinnan.co.uk
dir: On A830, 0.5m on right past Glenfinnan Monument. 200mtrs from railway station

This delightful hotel enjoys a well deserved reputation for fine food and excellent hospitality. The hotel has inspiring views and sits close to where 'Bonnie' Prince Charlie raised the Jacobite standard. Comfortably appointed bedrooms offer pleasing decor. Excellent local game and seafood can be enjoyed in the restaurant and the bar.

Rooms 9 **S** £65-£75; **D** £95-£140 (incl. bkfst)* **Facilities** STV FTV Fishing New Year Wi-fi **Conf** Class 20 Thtr 40 **Parking** 18 **Notes** LB Closed Xmas & Jan-Feb (ex New Year) RS Nov-Dec & Mar

GLENROTHES Map 21 NO20
Fife

Express by Holiday Inn Glenrothes

BUDGET HOTEL

☎ 01592 745509 🖷 01592 743377
Leslie Roundabout, Leslie Rd KY6 3EP
e-mail: ebhi-glenrothes@btconnect.com
web: www.hiexpress.com/glenrothes
dir: M90 junct 2A, onto A911 for Leslie. Through 4 rdbts, hotel on left

A modern hotel ideal for families and business travellers. Fresh and uncomplicated, the spacious rooms include Sky TV, power shower and tea and coffee-making facilities. Continental buffet breakfast is included in the room rate; other meals may be taken at the nearby family pub or restaurant. See also the Hotel Groups pages.

Rooms 49 (40 fmly) (21 GF) **Conf** Class 16 Board 16 Thtr 30

Premier Inn Glenrothes

BUDGET HOTEL

☎ 0871 527 8454 🖷 0871 527 8455
Beaufort Dr, Bankhead Roundabout KY7 4UJ
dir: M90 junct 2a N'bound, A92 to Glenrothes. At 2nd rbt (Bankhead) take 3rd exit. Hotel on left

High quality, budget accommodation ideal for both families and business travellers. Spacious, en suite bedrooms feature tea and coffee making facilities, and Freeview TV in most hotels. Internet access and Wi-fi are available for a small fee. The adjacent family restaurant features a wide and varied menu. See also the Hotel Groups pages.

Rooms 41 **D** £50-£57*

GLENSHEE (SPITTAL OF) Map 21 NO17
Perth & Kinross

Dalmunzie Castle

★★★ 80% ®® COUNTRY HOUSE HOTEL

☎ 01250 885224 🖷 01250 885225
PH10 7QG
e-mail: reservations@dalmunzie.com
web: www.dalmunzie.com
dir: On A93 at Spittal of Glenshee, follow signs to hotel

This turreted mansion house sits in a secluded glen in the heart of a glorious 6,500-acre estate, yet is within easy reach of the Glenshee ski slopes. The Edwardian style bedrooms, including spacious tower rooms and impressive four-poster rooms, are furnished with antique pieces. The drawing room enjoys panoramic views over the lawns, and the restaurant serves the finest Scottish produce.

Rooms 17 (2 fmly) **D** £190-£290 (incl. bkfst & dinner)* **Facilities** FTV ⛳ 9 Fishing Clay pigeon shooting Estate tours Grouse shooting Hiking Mountain bikes Stalking New Year Wi-fi **Conf** Class 20 Board 20 Thtr 20 **Services** Lift **Parking** 43 **Notes** ⊗ Closed 20-28 Dec RS Nov-Jan Civ Wed 70

GRANGEMOUTH Map 21 NS98
Falkirk

The Grange Manor

★★★★ 76% HOTEL

☎ 01324 474836 🖷 01324 665861
Glensburgh FK3 8XJ
e-mail: info@grangemanor.co.uk
web: www.grangemanor.co.uk
dir: E: M9 junct 6, hotel 200mtrs to right. W: M9 junct 5, A905 for 2m

Located south of town and close to the M9, this stylish hotel, popular with business and corporate clientele, benefits from hands-on family ownership. It offers spacious, high quality accommodation with superb bathrooms. Public areas include a comfortable foyer area, a lounge bar and a smart restaurant. Wallace's bar and restaurant is adjacent to the main house in the converted stables. Staff throughout are very friendly.

Rooms 36 (30 annexe) (6 fmly) (15 GF) **S** £68-£148; **D** £68-£148 **Facilities** STV FTV New Year Wi-fi **Conf** Class 68 Board 40 Thtr 120 Del from £115 to £145 **Services** Lift **Parking** 154 **Notes** ⊗ Civ Wed 120

G

G

GRANTOWN-ON-SPEY Map 23 NJ02
Highland

Grant Arms Hotel

★★★ 79% HOTEL

☎ 01479 872526 📠 01479 873589
25-27 The Square PH26 3HF
e-mail: info@grantarmshotel.com
web: www.grantarmshotel.com
dir: Exit A9 N of Aviemore onto A95

Conveniently located in the centre of the town, this fine hotel has now been refurbished and upgraded to a high standard yet still retains the building's traditional character. The spacious bedrooms are stylishly presented and very well equipped. The Garden Restaurant is a popular venue for dinner, and lighter snacks can be enjoyed in the comfortable bar. Modern conference facilities are available and the hotel is very popular with birdwatchers and wildlife enthusiasts.

Rooms 50 (4 fmly) **S** £45-£80; **D** £90-£160 (incl. bkfst) **Facilities** STV FTV Home to Birdwatching & Wildlife Club ♫ Xmas New Year Wi-fi **Conf** Class 30 Board 16 Thtr 70 Del from £95 to £125 **Services** Lift **Notes** LB

GREENOCK Map 20 NS27
Inverclyde

Holiday Inn Express Greenock

BUDGET HOTEL

☎ 01475 786666 📠 01475 786777
Cartsburn PA15 1AE
e-mail: greenock@holidayinnexpress.org.uk
web: www.hiexpressgreenock.co.uk
dir: M8 junct 31, A8 to Greenock, right at 5th rdbt, hotel on right

A modern hotel ideal for families and business travellers. Fresh and uncomplicated, the spacious rooms include Sky TV, power shower and tea and coffee-making facilities. Continental buffet breakfast is included in the room rate; other meals may be taken at the nearby family pub or restaurant. See also the Hotel Groups pages.

Rooms 71 (15 fmly) (6 GF) (20 smoking) **Conf** Class 48 Board 32 Thtr 70

Premier Inn Greenock

BUDGET HOTEL

☎ 0871 527 8476 📠 0871 527 8477
The Point, 1-3 James Watt Way PA15 2AD
dir: A8 to Greenock. At rdbt junct of East Hamilton St & Main St (McDonalds visable on right) take 3rd exit. Hotel on left

High quality, budget accommodation ideal for both families and business travellers. Spacious, en suite bedrooms feature tea and coffee making facilities, and Freeview TV in most hotels. Internet access and Wi-fi are available for a small fee. The adjacent family restaurant features a wide and varied menu. See also the Hotel Groups pages.

Rooms 17 **D** £57-£78*

GRETNA SERVICE AREA (A74(M)) Map 21 NY36
Dumfries & Galloway

Days Inn Gretna Green - M74

BUDGET HOTEL

☎ 01461 337566 📠 01461 337823
Welcome Break Service Area DG16 5HQ
e-mail: gretna.hotel@welcomebreak.co.uk
web: www.welcomebreak.co.uk
dir: Between junct 21/22 on M74 - accessible from both N'bound & S'bound carriageway

This modern building offers accommodation in smart, spacious and well-equipped bedrooms suitable for families and business travellers, and all with en suite bathrooms. Continental breakfast is available and other refreshments may be taken at the nearby family restaurant. See also the Hotel Groups pages.

Rooms 64 (54 fmly) (64 GF) **S** £39.95-£59.95; **D** £49.95-£69.95

GRETNA (WITH GRETNA GREEN) Map 21 NY36
Dumfries & Galloway

Smiths at Gretna Green

★★★★ 74% ® HOTEL

☎ 01461 337007 📠 01461 336000
Gretna Green DG16 5EA
e-mail: info@smithsgretnagreen.com
web: www.smithsgretnagreen.com
dir: From M74 junct 22 follow signs to Old Blacksmith's Shop. Hotel opposite

Located next to the World Famous Old Blacksmith's Shop Centre just off the motorway linking Scotland and England. The bedrooms offer a spacious environment, complete with flat-screen TVs, DVD players and broadband. Family rooms feature a separate children's area with bunk beds, each with its own TV. Three suites and a penthouse apartment are also available. Open-plan contemporary day rooms lead to the brasserie restaurant; impressive conference and banqueting facilities are provided.

Rooms 50 (8 fmly) **Facilities** STV FTV New Year Wi-fi **Conf** Class 100 Board 40 Thtr 250 **Services** Lift Air con **Parking** 115 **Notes** Civ Wed 150

The Gables Hotel

★★★ 75% HOTEL

☎ 01461 338300 📠 01461 338626
1 Annan Rd DG16 5DQ
e-mail: reservations@gables-hotel-gretna.co.uk
dir: M74 S or M6/M74 N follow signs for Gretna. At rdbt at Gretna Gateway take exit onto Annan Rd, hotel 200yds on right

This Grade II listed hotel is located close to the Gretna Gateway and is ideally located to explore both Galloway and the Border City of Carlisle. Bedrooms offer comfortable and well-appointed accommodation. The main restaurant offers a carte menu with a range of freshly prepared dishes, whilst Saddlers bar provides light snacks and meals.

Rooms 31 (5 fmly) (10 GF) **S** £79-£84; **D** £110-£115 (incl. bkfst)* **Facilities** FTV Xmas New Year Wi-fi **Conf** Class 60 Board 48 Thtr 100 Del from £99 to £119* **Parking** 60 **Notes** LB ⊗ Civ Wed 100

Garden House

★★★ 75% HOTEL

☎ 01461 337621 📠 01461 337692
Sarkfoot Rd DG16 5EP
e-mail: info@gardenhouse.co.uk
web: www.gardenhouse.co.uk
dir: Just off M6 junct 45

This purpose-built modern hotel lies on the edge of the village. With a focus on weddings its landscaped gardens provide an ideal setting, while inside corridor walls are adorned with photographs portraying that 'special day'. Accommodation is well presented including bedrooms that overlook the Japanese water gardens.

Rooms 38 (11 fmly) (14 GF) **Facilities** 🏊 supervised ♫ Xmas New Year **Conf** Class 80 Board 40 Thtr 150 **Services** Lift **Parking** 105 **Notes** ⊗ Civ Wed 150

HAMILTON
South Lanarkshire Map 20 NS75

Express by Holiday Inn Hamilton

BUDGET HOTEL

☎ 0141 419 3500 📠 0141 419 3500
Keith St ML3 7BL
web: www.hiexpress.com/hamilton

A modern hotel ideal for families and business travellers. Fresh and uncomplicated, the spacious rooms include Sky TV, power shower and tea and coffee-making facilities. Continental buffet breakfast is included in the room rate; other meals may be taken at the nearby family pub or restaurant. See also the Hotel Groups pages.

Rooms 104

HAWICK
Scottish Borders Map 21 NT51

Mansfield House Hotel

★★★ 81% HOTEL

☎ 01450 360400 📠 01450 372007
Weensland Rd TD9 8LB
e-mail: reception@themansfieldhousehotel.co.uk
dir: A7 to Hawick onto A698 (Weensland road). Hotel 1.2km on right

Set in its own mature grounds at the top of a hill with spectacular views over Hawick, this hotel has undergone a complete refurbishment. The bedrooms, located on the basement level and on the first floor, differ in size and include the fantastic Tower Room accessed via a steep, narrow staircase - but well worth the effort! Public areas are welcoming and the style is in keeping with the age of the building. The restaurant proudly uses local, quality ingredients for the menus.

Rooms 16 (2 fmly) **S** £70-£75; **D** £100-£110 (incl. bkfst)* **Facilities** FTV Xmas New Year Wi-fi **Conf** Class 160 Board 60 Thtr 160 Del from £95 to £105* **Parking** 25 **Notes** LB ⊗ Civ Wed 120

HOWWOOD
Renfrewshire Map 20 NS36

Bowfield Hotel & Country Club

★★★ 80% ◎ HOTEL

☎ 01505 705225 📠 01505 705230
PA9 1DZ
e-mail: enquiries@bowfieldhotel.co.uk
web: www.bowfieldhotel.co.uk
dir: M8 junct 28a/29, A737 for 6m, left onto B787, right in 2m, 1m to hotel

This former textile mill is now a popular hotel which has become a convenient stopover for travellers using Glasgow Airport. The leisure club offers very good facilities. Public areas have beamed ceilings, brick and white painted walls, and welcoming open fires. Bedrooms are housed in a separate wing and offer good modern comforts and facilities.

Rooms 23 (3 fmly) (7 GF) **Facilities** Spa FTV supervised 18 Gym Squash Children's soft play area Aerobics studio Health & beauty Xmas New Year Wi-fi **Conf** Class 60 Board 40 Thtr 100 **Parking** 120 **Notes** ⊗ Civ Wed 80

HUNTLY
Aberdeenshire Map 23 NJ53

Gordon Arms Hotel

★★ 64% SMALL HOTEL

☎ 01466 792288 📠 01466 794556
The Square AB54 8AF
e-mail: reception@gordonarms.demon.co.uk
dir: Off A96 (Aberdeen to Inverness road) at Huntly. Hotel immediately on left after entering town square

This friendly, family-run hotel is located in the town square and offers a good selection of tasty, well-portioned dishes served in the bar, and also in the restaurant at weekends or midweek by appointment. Bedrooms come in a variety of sizes, but all have a good range of accessories.

Rooms 13 (3 fmly) **Facilities** FTV Wi-fi **Conf** Class 80 Board 60 Thtr 160

INVERGARRY
Highland Map 22 NH30

Glengarry Castle

★★★ 82% ◎ COUNTRY HOUSE HOTEL

☎ 01809 501254 📠 01809 501207
PH35 4HW
e-mail: castle@glengarry.net
web: www.glengarry.net
dir: On A82, 0.5m from A82/A87 junct

This charming country-house hotel is set in 50 acres of grounds on the shores of Loch Oich. The spacious day rooms include comfortable sitting rooms with lots to read and board games to play. The classical dining room boasts an innovative menu that showcases local Scottish produce. The smart bedrooms vary in size and style but all boast magnificent loch or woodland views.

Rooms 26 (2 fmly) **S** £67-£77; **D** £118-£180 (incl. bkfst) **Facilities** FTV Fishing Wi-fi **Parking** 30 **Notes** Closed mid Nov-mid Mar

I

INVERGORDON
Highland Map 23 NH76

Kincraig Castle Hotel

★★★★ 78% ◎◎ COUNTRY HOUSE HOTEL

☎ 01349 852587 📠 01349 852193
IV18 0LF
e-mail: info@kincraig-house-hotel.co.uk
web: www.kincraig-house-hotel.co.uk
dir: Off A9 past Alness towards Tain. Hotel on left 0.25m past Rosskeen Church

This mansion house is set in well-tended grounds in an elevated position with views over the Cromarty Firth. It offers smart well-equipped bedrooms and inviting public areas that retain the original features of the house. However it is the friendly service and commitment to guest care that will leave a lasting impression.

Rooms 15 (1 fmly) (1 GF) **Facilities** STV Xmas Wi-fi **Conf** Class 30 Board 24 Thtr 50 **Parking** 30 **Notes** Civ Wed 70

INVERKEILOR Angus Map 23 NO64

Gordon's

RESTAURANT WITH ROOMS

01241 830364 01241 830364
Main St DD11 5RN
e-mail: gordonsrest@aol.com
dir: Off A92, follow signs for Inverkeilor

It's worth a detour off the main road to this family-run restaurant with rooms set in the centre of the village. It has earned AA Rosettes for dinner, and the excellent breakfasts are equally memorable. A huge fire dominates the restaurant on cooler evenings, and there is a small lounge with limited seating. The attractive bedrooms are tastefully decorated and thoughtfully equipped; the larger two are furnished in pine. AA Restaurant of the Year for Scotland 2011-12.

Rooms 5 (1 annexe)

INVERNESS Highland Map 23 NH64

Culloden House

★★★★ 80% HOTEL

01463 790461 01463 792181
Culloden IV2 7BZ
e-mail: info@cullodenhouse.co.uk
web: www.cullodenhouse.co.uk
dir: A96 from Inverness, right for Culloden. 1m after 2nd lights, left at church

Dating from the late 1700s this impressive mansion is set in extensive grounds close to the famous Culloden Battlefield. High ceilings and intricate cornices are particular features of the public rooms, including the elegant Adam dining room. Bedrooms come in a range of sizes and styles, with a number situated in a separate house.

Rooms 28 (5 annexe) (1 fmly) (3 GF) **S** £95-£175; **D** £125-£270 (incl. bkfst)* **Facilities** FTV Putt green Boules Badminton Golf driving net Putting green New Year Wi-fi **Conf** Class 40 Board 30 Thtr 60 Del from £120 to £170* **Parking** 50 **Notes** LB No children 10yrs Closed 24-28 Dec Civ Wed 65

Loch Ness Country House Hotel

★★★★ 79% SMALL HOTEL

01463 230512 01463 224532
Loch Ness Rd IV3 8JN
e-mail: info@lochnesscountryhousehotel.co.uk
web: www.lochnesscountryhousehotel.co.uk
dir: On A82, 1m from Inverness town boundary

Built in the Georgian era, this fine house is perfectly situated in its own six acre private Highland estate. The hotel has luxurious bedrooms, four of which are in the garden suite cottages. The stylish restaurant serves the best of local produce and guests have a choice of cosy well-appointed lounges for after dinner drinks. The garden terrace is ideal for relaxing and has splendid views over the landscaped gardens towards Inverness.

Rooms 13 (2 annexe) (8 fmly) (3 GF) **S** £85-£165; **D** £125-£215 (incl. bkfst)* **Facilities** FTV Xmas New Year Wi-fi **Conf** Class 30 Board 20 Thtr 50 Del from £135 to £175* **Parking** 50 **Notes** Civ Wed 120

The New Drumossie

★★★★ 78% HOTEL

01463 236451 & 0870 194 2110
01463 712858
Old Perth Rd IV2 5BE
e-mail: stay@drumossiehotel.co.uk
dir: From A9 follow signs for Culloden Battlefield, hotel on left after 1m

Set in nine acres of landscaped hillside grounds south of Inverness, this hotel has fine views of the Moray Firth towards Ben Wyvis. Art deco style decoration together with a country-house atmosphere are found throughout. Service is friendly and attentive, the food imaginative and enjoyable and the bedrooms spacious and well presented. The main function room is probably the largest in this area.

Rooms 44 (10 fmly) (6 GF) **Facilities** STV Fishing New Year Wi-fi **Conf** Class 200 Board 40 Thtr 500 Del from £145* **Services** Lift **Parking** 200 **Notes** Civ Wed 400

Glenmoriston Town House Hotel

★★★★ 76% HOTEL

01463 223777 01463 712378
20 Ness Bank IV2 4SF
e-mail: reception@glenmoristontownhouse.com
web: www.glenmoristontownhouse.com
dir: On riverside opposite theatre

Bold contemporary designs blend seamlessly with the classical architecture of this stylish hotel, situated on the banks of the River Ness. Delightful day rooms include a piano bar and two eating options. Abstract Restaurant features accomplished modern French cuisine based on the finest Scottish produce, and Contrast Brasserie is ideal for relaxed meals from breakfast through to dinner, and when the weather warms up guests can eat alfresco here. The sleek, modern, individually designed bedrooms have many facilities including free Wi-fi, DVD players and flat-screen TVs.

Rooms 30 (15 annexe) (1 fmly) (6 GF) **Facilities** STV Xmas New Year Wi-fi **Conf** Class 10 Board 10 Thtr 15 **Parking** 40 **Notes** Closed 26-28 Dec & 4-6 Jan Civ Wed 70

See advert on opposite page

Bunchrew House

★★★★ 74% ◎◎ COUNTRY HOUSE HOTEL

☎ 01463 234917 📠 01463 710620
Bunchrew IV3 8TA
e-mail: welcome@bunchrewhousehotel.com
web: www.bunchrewhousehotel.com
dir: W on A862. Hotel 2m after canal on right

Overlooking the Beauly Firth this impressive mansion house dates from the 17th century and retains much original character. Individually styled bedrooms are spacious and tastefully furnished. A wood-panelled restaurant is the setting for artfully constructed cooking and there is a choice of comfortable lounges complete with real fires.

Rooms 16 (4 fmly) (1 GF) **S** £115-£139; **D** £170-£178 (incl. bkfst)* **Facilities** FTV Fishing New Year Wi-fi **Conf** Class 30 Board 30 Thtr 80 Del from £128.50 to £144.50* **Parking** 40 **Notes** LB ⊗ Closed 24-27 Dec Civ Wed 92

Columba

★★★★ 74% HOTEL

☎ 08444 146 522 📠 08444 146 521
Ness Walk IV3 5NF
e-mail: reservations.columba@ohiml.com
web: www.oxfordhotelsandinns.com
dir: From A9, A96 follow signs to town centre, pass Eastgate shopping centre into Academy St. At bottom left into Bank St, right over bridge, hotel 1st left

Originally built in 1881 and with many original features retained, the Columba Hotel lies in the heart of Inverness overlooking the fast flowing River Ness. The bedrooms are very stylish, and public areas include a first-floor restaurant and lounge. A second dining option is the ever popular McNabs bar bistro, which is ideal for less formal meals.

Rooms 76 (4 fmly) **Facilities** FTV ♫ Xmas New Year Wi-fi **Conf** Class 100 Board 60 Thtr 200 **Services** Lift **Notes** Civ Wed 120

Royal Highland

★★★ 77% HOTEL

☎ 01463 231926 & 251451 📠 01463 710705
Station Square, Academy St IV1 1LG
e-mail: info@royalhighlandhotel.co.uk
web: www.royalhighlandhotel.co.uk
dir: From A9 into town centre. Hotel next to rail station & Eastgate Retail Centre

Built in 1858 adjacent to the railway station, this hotel has the typically grand foyer of the Victorian era with comfortable seating. The contemporary ASH Brasserie and bar offers a refreshing venue for both eating and drinking throughout the day. The generally spacious bedrooms are comfortably equipped especially for the business traveller.

Rooms 85 (12 fmly) (2 GF) (25 smoking) **Facilities** FTV Xmas New Year Wi-fi **Conf** Class 80 Board 80 Thtr 200 **Services** Lift **Parking** 8 **Notes** Civ Wed 200

I

INVERNESS *continued*

Thistle Inverness

thistle

★★★ 77% HOTEL

☎ 0871 376 9023 📠 0871 376 9123
Millburn Rd IV2 3TR
e-mail: inverness@thistle.co.uk
web: www.thistlehotels.com/inverness
dir: From A9 take Raigmore Interchange exit (towards Aberdeen), 3rd left towards centre. Hotel opposite

Well located within easy distance of the town centre. This well presented hotel offers modern bedrooms including three suites. There is a well equipped leisure centre along with an informal brasserie and open-plan bar and lounge. Ample parking is an added benefit. Thistle Hotels – AA Hotel Group of the Year 2011-12.

Rooms 118 **Facilities** supervised Gym Sauna Steam room Xmas New Year Wi-fi **Conf** Class 70 Board 50 Thtr 120 **Services** Lift **Parking** 80 **Notes** Civ Wed 120

Best Western Palace Hotel & Spa

★★★ 75% HOTEL

☎ 01463 223243 📠 01463 236865
8 Ness Walk IV3 5NG
e-mail: palace@miltonhotels.com
web: www.invernesspalacehotel.co.uk
dir: A82 Glenurquhart Rd onto Ness Walk. Hotel 300yds on right opposite Inverness Castle

Set on the north side of the River Ness close to the Eden Court theatre and a short walk from the town, this hotel has a contemporary look. Bedrooms offer good levels of comfort and equipment, and a smart leisure centre attracts a mixed market.

Rooms 88 (48 annexe) (3 fmly) (5 smoking) **S** £69.90-£189.90; **D** £99.90-£249.90 **Facilities** Spa FTV supervised Gym Beautician Sauna Steam room Xmas New Year Wi-fi **Conf** Class 40 Board 30 Thtr 80 Del from £129.90 to £159.90 **Services** Lift **Parking** 38 **Notes** LB

Ramada Encore Inverness City Centre

★★★ 75% HOTEL

☎ 01463 228850 📠 01463 228879
63 Academy St IV1 1LU
e-mail: reservations@encoreinverness.co.uk
dir: A9, A82, B865, hotel on right

This hotel is ideally located, as its name suggests, close to the main shopping district, railway station and the tourist attractions of Inverness. The contemporary bedrooms have a bright stylish design and all rooms are equipped with Wi-fi along with an extensive choice of TV channels and movies. Public areas include a modern restaurant and a light-filled lounge area with comfortable seating. There is a choice of ground-floor business suites which makes the hotel popular with corporate guests.

Rooms 90 (20 fmly) **Facilities** STV FTV Wi-fi **Conf** Class 20 Board 20 Thtr 34 **Services** Lift **Notes**

Glen Mhor

★★★ 72% HOTEL

☎ 01463 234308 📠 01463 218018
8-15 Ness Bank IV2 4SG
e-mail: enquires@glen-mhor.com
web: www.glen-mhor.com
dir: On east bank of River Ness, below Inverness Castle

This hotel is a short walk from the city centre and overlooks the beautiful River Ness. This fine old property offers bedrooms and several suites that are up-to-the-minute in design. The public areas include a cosy bar and a comfortable lounge with a log fire.

Rooms 52 (34 annexe) (3 fmly) (12 GF) **S** £39-£89; **D** £59-£149 (incl. bkfst)* **Facilities** FTV ♫ Xmas New Year Wi-fi **Conf** Class 30 Board 35 Thtr 60 **Parking** 26 **Notes** LB Civ Wed 60

Express by Holiday Inn Inverness

BUDGET HOTEL

☎ 01463 732700 📠 01463 732732
Stoneyfield IV2 7PA
e-mail: inverness@expressholidayinn.co.uk
web: www.hiexpress.com/inverness
dir: From A9 follow A96 & Inverness Airport signs, hotel on right

A modern hotel ideal for families and business travellers. Fresh and uncomplicated, the spacious rooms include Sky TV, power shower and tea and coffee-making facilities. Continental buffet breakfast is included in the room rate; other meals may be taken at the nearby family pub or restaurant. See also the Hotel Groups pages.

Rooms 94 (43 fmly) (24 GF) (10 smoking) **Conf** Class 20 Board 15 Thtr 35

Premier Inn Inverness Centre (Milburn Rd)

BUDGET HOTEL

☎ 0871 527 8544 📠 0871 527 8545
Millburn Rd IV2 3QX
dir: From A9 & A96 junct (Raigmore Interchange, signed Airport/Aberdeen), take B865 towards town centre, hotel 100yds after next rdbt

High quality, budget accommodation ideal for both families and business travellers. Spacious, en suite bedrooms feature tea and coffee making facilities, and Freeview TV in most hotels. Internet access and Wi-fi are available for a small fee. The adjacent family restaurant features a wide and varied menu. See also the Hotel Groups pages.

Rooms 55 **D** £65-£70*

Premier Inn Inverness East

BUDGET HOTEL

☎ 0871 527 8546 📠 0871 527 8547
Beechwood Business Park IV2 3BW
dir: From A9 follow Raigmore Hospital, Police HQ & Inshes Retail Park signs

Rooms 60 **D** £65-£70*

INVERURIE Aberdeenshire **Map 23 NJ72**

Macdonald Pittodrie House

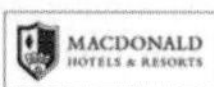

★★★★ 74% HOTEL

☎ 0870 1942111 & 01467 681744
📠 01467 681648
Chapel of Garioch, Pitcaple AB51 5HS
e-mail: pittodrie@macdonald-hotels.co.uk
web: www.macdonald-hotels.com/pittodrie
dir: From A96 towards Inverness, pass Inverurie under bridge with lights. Turn left & follow signs

Set in extensive grounds this house dates from the 15th century and retains many historic features. Public rooms include a gracious drawing room, restaurant, and a cosy bar boasting an impressive selection of whiskies. The well-proportioned bedrooms are found in both the original house and in the extension that was designed to match the existing building.

Rooms 27 (3 fmly) **Facilities** STV Clay pigeon shooting Quad biking Outdoor activities Xmas New Year Wi-fi **Conf** Class 75 Board 50 Thtr 150 **Parking** 200 **Notes** Civ Wed 120

IRVINE
North Ayrshire Map 20 NS33

Menzies Irvine
MenziesHotels

★★★★ 76% HOTEL

☎ 01294 274272 📠 01294 277287
46 Annick Rd KA11 4LD
e-mail: irvine@menzieshotels.co.uk
web: www.menzieshotels.co.uk
dir: From A78 at Warrix Interchange follow Irvine Central signs. At rdbt 2nd exit (town centre). At next rdbt right onto A71/Kilmarnock. Hotel 100mtrs on left

Situated on the edge of Irvine with good transportation links (including Prestwick Airport just seven miles away), this is a well-presented hotel that has an extremely friendly team with good customer care awareness. After major refurbishment the decor is contemporary throughout, and there is a brasserie-style restaurant, cocktail bar and spacious lounge.

Rooms 128 (14 fmly) (64 GF) **Facilities** STV Fishing Xmas New Year Wi-fi **Conf** Class 140 Board 100 Thtr 280 **Parking** 220 **Notes** Civ Wed 200

KELSO
Scottish Borders Map 21 NT73

The Roxburghe Hotel & Golf Course

★★★★ 77% ® COUNTRY HOUSE HOTEL

☎ 01573 450331 📠 01573 450611
Heiton TD5 8JZ
e-mail: hotel@roxburghe.net
web: www.roxburghe.net
dir: From A68 Jedburgh take A698 to Heiton, 3m SW of Kelso

Outdoor sporting pursuits are popular at this impressive Jacobean mansion owned by the Duke of Roxburghe, and set in 500 acres of woods and parkland bordering the River Teviot. Gracious public areas are the perfect settings for afternoon teas and carefully prepared meals. The elegant bedrooms are individually designed, some by the Duchess herself, and include superior rooms, some with four posters and log fires.

Rooms 22 (6 annexe) (3 fmly) (3 GF) **Facilities** Spa STV ⛳ 18 Putt green Fishing 🐟 Clay shooting Health & beauty salon Mountain bike hire Falconry Archery Xmas New Year Wi-fi **Conf** Class 20 Board 20 Thtr 50 **Parking** 150 **Notes** Civ Wed 60

Ednam House

★★★ 80% HOTEL

☎ 01573 224168 📠 01573 226319
Bridge St TD5 7HT
e-mail: contact@ednamhouse.com
web: www.ednamhouse.com
dir: From S: A1 to Berwick, A698 or A7 to Hawick, A698 to Kelso. From N: A68 to Carfraefmill, A6089 to Kelso

Overlooking a wide expanse of the River Tweed, this fine Georgian mansion has been under the Brooks family ownership for over 75 years. Accommodation styles range from standard to grand, plus The Orangerie, situated in the grounds, that has been converted into a gracious two-bedroom apartment. Public areas include a choice of lounges and an elegant dining room that has views over the gardens.

Rooms 32 (2 annexe) (4 fmly) (3 GF) **Facilities** FTV 🐟 Free access to Abbey Fitness Centre Wi-fi **Conf** Board 200 Thtr 250 **Parking** 60 **Notes** Closed 22 Dec-6 Jan Civ Wed 100

KENMORE
Perth & Kinross Map 21 NN74

Kenmore Hotel

★★★ 78% ® HOTEL

☎ 01887 830205 📠 01887 830262
The Square PH15 2NU
e-mail: reception@kenmorehotel.co.uk
web: www.kenmorehotel.com
dir: Off A9 at Ballinluig onto A827, through Aberfeldy to Kenmore, hotel in village centre

Dating back to 1572, this riverside hotel is Scotland's oldest inn and has a rich and interesting history. Bedrooms have tasteful decor, and meals can be enjoyed in the restaurant which has panoramic views of the River Tay. The choice of bars includes one with real fires.

Rooms 40 (13 annexe) (4 fmly) (7 GF) **S** £69.50-£79.50; **D** £109-£129 (incl. bkfst)* **Facilities** STV Salmon fishing on River Tay Xmas New Year Wi-fi **Conf** Class 60 Board 50 Thtr 80 **Services** Lift **Parking** 40 **Notes** LB Civ Wed 150

KILCHRENAN
Argyll & Bute Map 20 NN02

Taychreggan

★★★★ 76% ®® COUNTRY HOUSE HOTEL

☎ 01866 833211 & 833366 📠 01866 833244
PA35 1HQ
e-mail: info@taychregganhotel.co.uk
dir: W from Crianlarich on A85 to Taynuilt, S for 7m on B845 (single track) to Kilchrenan

Surrounded by stunning Highland scenery this stylish and superbly presented hotel, once a drover's cottage, enjoys an idyllic setting in 40 acres of wooded grounds on the shores of Loch Awe. The hotel has a smart bar with adjacent courtyard Orangerie and a choice of quiet lounges with deep, luxurious sofas. A well earned reputation has been achieved by the kitchen for the skilfully prepared dinners that showcase the local and seasonal Scottish larder. Families, and also dogs and their owners, are welcome.

Rooms 18 (1 fmly) **S** £91-£176; **D** £122-£292 (incl. bkfst) **Facilities** FTV Fishing 🐟 Air rifle range Archery Clay pigeon shooting Falconry Mock deer stalk Xmas New Year Wi-fi Child facilities **Conf** Class 15 Board 20 **Parking** 40 **Notes** Closed 3 Jan-9 Feb Civ Wed 70

KILCHRENAN *continued*

INSPECTORS' CHOICE

The Ardanaiseig

★★★ ◎◎◎ COUNTRY HOUSE HOTEL

☎ 01866 833333 📠 01866 833222
by Loch Awe PA35 1HE
e-mail: ardanaiseig@clara.net
dir: A85 at Taynuilt onto B845 to Kilchrenan. Left in front of pub (road very narrow) signed 'Ardanaiseig Hotel' & 'No Through Road'. Continue for 3m

Set amid lovely gardens and breathtaking scenery beside the shore of Loch Awe, this peaceful country-house hotel was built in a Scottish baronial style in 1834. Many fine pieces of furniture are evident in the bedrooms and charming day rooms, which include a drawing room, a library bar and an elegant dining room. The bedrooms are individually designed including some with four posters, some with loch views and some with access to the garden; standing on its own by the water is the Boat Shed, a delightful one bedroom suite. Guests can certainly look forward to the award-winning, skilfully cooked dishes that make excellent use of local, seasonal produce.

Rooms 18 (4 fmly) (5 GF) **S** £73-£113; **D** £146-£226 (incl. bkfst)* **Facilities** FTV Fishing Boating Clay pigeon shooting Bikes for hire Xmas New Year Wi-fi **Parking** 20 **Notes** LB Closed 2 Jan-1 Feb Civ Wed 50

KILDRUMMY Map 23 NJ41
Aberdeenshire

Kildrummy Castle Hotel

★★★★ 75% COUNTRY HOUSE HOTEL

☎ 019755 71288 📠 019755 71345
AB33 8RA
e-mail: kildrummy@btconnect.com
web: www.kildrummycastlehotel.co.uk
dir: Off A97 (Huntly to Ballater road)

Set in landscaped gardens and accessed via a tree lined drive, Kildrummy Castle enjoys a peaceful rural location in the heart of the beautiful Grampian Highlands, yet is only a 35-minute drive from Aberdeen. The comfortable bedrooms have fabulous views, often with the ruin of the original castle as a backdrop. The current owners have sympathetically restored much of the original features, and the cosy lounges provide a perfect setting for afternoon tea or a post dinner drink. Dinner features the best of local produce, along with an extensive wine list. The relaxed atmosphere, supported by friendly service, is an obvious attraction here.

Rooms 16 (2 fmly) **S** £97.50; **D** £134-£217 (incl. bkfst) **Facilities** FTV Fishing Xmas New Year Wi-fi **Conf** Board 18 Del from £150 to £185 **Parking** 25 **Notes** LB Closed 3-24 Jan RS 5-15 Nov

KILLIECRANKIE Map 23 NN96
Perth & Kinross

INSPECTORS' CHOICE

Killiecrankie House Hotel

★★★ ◎◎ SMALL HOTEL

☎ 01796 473220 📠 01796 472451
PH16 5LG
e-mail: enquiries@killiecrankiehotel.co.uk
dir: Exit A9 at Killiecrankie, onto B8079, hotel 3m on right

Originally built in the 1840, Killiecrankie sits in fours acres of wooded grounds with beautifully landscaped gardens; it enjoys a tranquil location by the Pass of Killiecrankie and the River Garry. Public areas include a wood-panelled bar and a cosy sitting room with original artwork and a blazing fire in colder months. Each of the bedrooms is individually decorated, well equipped and have wonderful countryside views.

Rooms 10 (2 GF) **Facilities** FTV Xmas New Year Wi-fi **Parking** 20 **Notes** Closed 3 Jan-12 Mar

KILMARNOCK Map 20 NS43
East Ayrshire

The Fenwick Hotel

★★★ 78% HOTEL

☎ 01560 600478 📠 01560 600334
Fenwick KA3 6AU
e-mail: info@thefenwickhotel.co.uk
web: www.thefenwickhotel.co.uk
dir: M77 junct 8, B7061 towards Fenwick, follow hotel signs

Benefiting from a great location alongside the M77 and offering easy links to Ayr, Kilmarnock and Glasgow. The spacious bedrooms are thoughtfully equipped; complimentary Wi-fi is available throughout the hotel. The bright restaurant offers both formal and informal dining and there are two bars to choose from.

Rooms 30 (1 fmly) (9 GF) **Facilities** STV Xmas New Year Wi-fi **Conf** Class 280 Board 150 Thtr 280 **Parking** 64 **Notes** Civ Wed 110

Premier Inn Kilmarnock

BUDGET HOTEL

☎ 0871 527 8566 📠 0871 527 8567
Moorfield Roundabout, Annadale KA1 2RS
dir: M74 junct 8 signed Kilmarnock (A71). From M77 onto A71 to Irvine. At next rdbt right onto B7064 signed Crosshouse Hospital. Hotel on right

High quality, budget accommodation ideal for both families and business travellers. Spacious, en suite bedrooms feature tea and coffee making facilities, and Freeview TV in most hotels. Internet access and Wi-fi are available for a small fee. The adjacent family restaurant features a wide and varied menu. See also the Hotel Groups pages.

Rooms 40 **D** £52-£59*

KINCARDINE Map 21 NS98
Fife

Premier Inn Falkirk North

BUDGET HOTEL

☎ 0871 527 8394 📠 0871 527 8395
Bowtrees Roundabout, Houghs of Airth FK2 8PJ
dir: From N: M9 junct 7 (or from S: M876) towards Kincardine Bridge. On rdbt at end of slip road

High quality, budget accommodation ideal for both families and business travellers. Spacious, en suite bedrooms feature tea and coffee making facilities, and Freeview TV in most hotels. Internet access and Wi-fi are available for a small fee. The adjacent family restaurant features a wide and varied menu. See also the Hotel Groups pages.

Rooms 40 **D** £52-£58*

KINCLAVEN Map 21 NO13
Perth & Kinross

Ballathie House Hotel

★★★★ 78% ®® COUNTRY HOUSE HOTEL

☎ 01250 883268 📠 01250 883396
PH1 4QN
e-mail: email@ballathiehousehotel.com
web: www.ballathiehousehotel.com
dir: From A9, 2m N of Perth, onto B9099 through Stanley, follow signs. Or from A93 at Beech Hedge follow signs for hotel, 2.5m

Set in delightful grounds, this splendid Scottish mansion house combines classical grandeur with modern comfort. Bedrooms range from well-proportioned master rooms to modern standard rooms, and many boast antique furniture and art deco bathrooms. It might be worth requesting one of the Riverside Rooms, a purpose-built development right on the banks of the river, complete with balconies and terraces. The elegant restaurant has views over the River Tay.

Rooms 41 (16 annexe) (2 fmly) (10 GF) **S** £65-£130; **D** £130-£290 (incl. bkfst)* **Facilities** FTV Putt green Fishing Xmas New Year Wi-fi **Conf** Class 20 Board 30 Thtr 50 **Services** Lift **Parking** 50 **Notes** Civ Wed 90

KINGUSSIE Map 23 NH70
Highland

INSPECTORS' CHOICE

The Cross at Kingussie

®®® RESTAURANT WITH ROOMS

☎ 01540 661166 📠 01540 661080
Tweed Mill Brae, Ardbroilach Rd PH21 1LB
e-mail: relax@thecross.co.uk
dir: From lights in Kingussie centre along Ardbroilach Rd, 300yds left onto Tweed Mill Brae

Situated in the valley near Kingussie, this former tweed mill sits next to a river, with wild flower gardens and a sunny terrace. Hospitality and food are clearly highlights of any stay at this special restaurant with rooms. Locally sourced produce is carefully prepared with passion and skill. Bedrooms are spacious and airy, and little touches such as fluffy towels and hand-made toiletries providing extra luxury.

Rooms 8 (1 fmly)

KINLOCH RANNOCH Map 23 NN65
Perth & Kinross

Dunalastair Hotel

★★★ 78% ® HOTEL

☎ 01882 632323 & 632218 📠 01882 632371
PH16 5PW
e-mail: info@dunalastair.co.uk
dir: A9 to Pitlochry, on N side take B8019 to Tummel Bridge then A846 to Kinloch Rannoch

Surrounded by unspoilt and beautiful countryside, this family-owned hotel, offers a warm and friendly welcome and great hospitality. The public areas are inviting, with fires lit on colder days. The restaurant offers a fine dining experience whilst the lounge and conservatory have a more informal and relaxed atmosphere. The bedrooms are well appointed.

Rooms 28 (4 fmly) (9 GF) **Facilities** Fishing 4x4 safaris Rafting Clay pigeon shooting Bike hire Archery Xmas New Year **Conf** Class 35 Board 30 Thtr 60 **Parking** 33 **Notes** Civ Wed 70

Macdonald Loch Rannoch Hotel

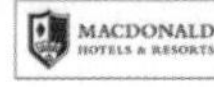

★★★ 75% HOTEL

☎ 0844 879 9059 & 01882 632201
📠 01882 632203
PH16 5PS
e-mail: loch_rannoch@macdonald-hotels.co.uk
web: www.macdonald-hotels.co.uk
dir: Off A9 onto B847 Calvine. Follow signs to Kinloch Rannoch, hotel 1m from village

Set deep in the countryside with elevated views across Loch Rannoch, this hotel is built around a 19th-century hunting lodge and provides a great base for exploring this beautiful area. The superior bedrooms have views over the loch. There is a choice of eating options - The Ptarmigan Restaurant and the Schiehallan Bar for informal eating. The hotel provides both indoor and outdoor activities.

Rooms 48 (25 fmly) **Facilities** FTV Fishing Gym Xmas New Year Wi-fi **Conf** Class 80 Board 50 Thtr 160 Del from £95 to £130 **Services** Lift **Parking** 52 **Notes** Civ Wed 130

K

KINROSS Map 21 NO10
Perth & Kinross

The Green Hotel

★★★★ 73% ® HOTEL

☎ 01577 863467 📠 01577 863180
2 The Muirs KY13 8AS
e-mail: reservations@green-hotel.com
web: www.green-hotel.com
dir: M90 junct 6, A922 follow Kinross signs to hotel

A long-established hotel offering a wide range of indoor and outdoor activities. Public areas include a classical restaurant, a choice of bars and a well-stocked gift shop. The comfortable, well-equipped bedrooms, most of which are generously proportioned, boast attractive colour schemes and smart modern furnishings.

Rooms 46 (3 fmly) (14 GF) **S** £62-£92; **D** £72-£132 (incl. bkfst)* **Facilities** STV supervised 36 Putt green Fishing Gym Petanque Curling (Sep-Apr) Cycling Shooting Xmas New Year Wi-fi **Conf** Class 75 Board 60 Thtr 130 **Parking** 60 **Notes** LB Civ Wed 100

KINROSS *continued*

The Windlestrae Hotel & Leisure Centre

★★★ HOTEL

☎ 01577 863217 📠 01577 864733
The Muirs KY13 8AS
e-mail: reservations@windlestraehotel.com
web: www.windlestraehotel.com
dir: M90 junct 6 into Kinross, left at 2nd mini rdbt. Hotel 400yds on right

Rooms 45 (13 GF) **S** £50-£110; **D** £60-£130 (incl. bkfst) **Facilities** STV supervised 36 Gym Beautician Steam room Toning tables Xmas New Year Wi-fi **Conf** Class 100 Board 80 Thtr 250 Del from £105 to £160 **Parking** 80 **Notes** LB Civ Wed 100

KIRKBEAN Dumfries & Galloway **Map 21 NX95**

INSPECTORS' CHOICE

Cavens

★★★ COUNTRY HOUSE HOTEL

☎ 01387 880234 📠 01387 880467
DG2 8AA
e-mail: enquiries@cavens.com
web: www.cavens.com
dir: Enter Kirkbean on A710, hotel signed

Set in six acres of parkland gardens, Cavens encapsulates all the virtues of an intimate country-house hotel. Quality is the keynote, and the proprietors spared no effort when they renovated the house. Bedrooms are delightfully individual and very comfortably equipped; choose between the Country rooms or the more spacious Estate rooms. The charming lounges invite peaceful relaxation. The menu at dinner offers dishes using the best local and home-made produce.

Rooms 6 (2 fmly) (1 GF) **S** £80-£130; **D** £80-£180 (incl. bkfst)* **Facilities** FTV Shooting Fishing Horse riding New Year Wi-fi **Conf** Class 20 Board 20 Thtr 20 **Parking** 20 **Notes** LB Closed Jan Civ Wed 100

KIRKCALDY Fife **Map 21 NT29**

Dean Park

★★★ 78% HOTEL

☎ 01592 261635 📠 01592 261371
Chapel Level KY2 6QW
e-mail: reception@deanparkhotel.co.uk
dir: Signed from A92 (Kirkcaldy West junct)

Popular with both business and leisure guests, this hotel has extensive conference and meeting facilities. Executive bedrooms are spacious and comfortable, and all are well equipped with modern decor and amenities. Twelve direct access, chalet-style rooms are set in the grounds and equipped to the same specification as main bedrooms. Public areas include a choice of bars and a restaurant.

Rooms 34 (2 fmly) (5 GF) (12 smoking) **Facilities** STV FTV Wi-fi **Conf** Class 125 Board 54 Thtr 250 **Services** Lift **Parking** 250 **Notes** Civ Wed 200

KIRKCUDBRIGHT Dumfries & Galloway **Map 20 NX65**

Arden House Hotel

★★ 75% HOTEL

☎ 01557 330544 📠 01557 330742
Tongland Rd DG6 4UU
dir: Exit A57, 4m W of Castle Douglas onto A711. Follow Kirkcudbright signs, over Telford Bridge. Hotel 400mtrs on left

Set well back from the main road in extensive grounds on the northeast side of town, this spotlessly maintained hotel offers attractive bedrooms, a lounge bar and adjoining conservatory serving a range of popular dishes, which are also available in the dining room. It boasts an impressive function suite in its grounds.

Rooms 9 (7 fmly) (5 smoking) **S** £60; **D** £80 (incl. bkfst)* **Conf** Class 175 Thtr 175 **Parking** 70 **Notes** No credit cards

LANARK South Lanarkshire **Map 21 NS84**

Best Western Cartland Bridge Hotel

★★★ 75% COUNTRY HOUSE HOTEL

☎ 01555 664426 📠 01555 663773
Glasgow Rd ML11 9UF
e-mail: sales@cartlandbridge.co.uk
dir: A73 through Lanark towards Carluke. Hotel 1.25m

Situated in wooded grounds on the edge of the town, this Grade I listed mansion continues to be popular with both business and leisure guests. Public areas feature wood panelling, a gallery staircase and a magnificent dining room. The well-equipped bedrooms vary in size.

Rooms 20 (2 fmly) **S** £40-£80; **D** £70-£120* **Facilities** FTV Xmas New Year Wi-fi **Conf** Class 180 Board 50 Thtr 250 Del from £65 to £140* **Parking** 120 **Notes** LB Civ Wed 200

LANGBANK Renfrewshire **Map 20 NS37**

Best Western Gleddoch House

★★★★ 73% HOTEL

☎ 01475 540711 📠 01475 540201
PA14 6YE
e-mail: reservations.gleddochhouse@ohiml.com
web: www.oxfordhotelsandinns.com
dir: M8 to Greenock, onto A8, left at rdbt onto A789, follow for 0.5m, turn right, 2nd on left

This hotel is set in spacious, landscaped grounds high above the River Clyde with fine views. The period house is appointed to a very high standard. The modern extension is impressive and offers spacious and very comfortable bedrooms. Warm hospitality and attentive service are noteworthy along with the hotel's parkland golf course and leisure club.

Rooms 70 (22 fmly) (17 GF) **Facilities** Spa FTV 18 Putt green Gym Steam room Sauna Xmas New Year Wi-fi **Conf** Class 70 Board 40 Thtr 150 **Parking** 150 **Notes** Civ Wed 120

LARGS North Ayrshire **Map 20 NS25**

Willowbank Hotel

★★★ 75% HOTEL

☎ 01475 672311 & 675435 📠 01475 689027
96 Greenock Rd KA30 8PG
e-mail: iaincsmith@btconnect.com
dir: On A78

A relaxed, friendly atmosphere prevails at this well maintained hotel where hanging baskets are a feature in summer months. The nicely decorated bedrooms are, in general, spacious and offer comfortable modern appointments. The public areas include a large, well-stocked bar, a lounge and a dining room.

Rooms 30 (4 fmly) **S** £70-£100; **D** £80-£140 (incl. bkfst) **Facilities** STV ♫ Xmas New Year **Conf** Class 100 Board 40 Thtr 200 Del from £100 to £140 **Parking** 40 **Notes** LB

LAUDER
Scottish Borders — Map 21 NT54

Lauderdale

★★★ 70% HOTEL

☎ 01578 722231 📠 01578 718642
1 Edinburgh Rd TD2 6TW
e-mail: enquiries@lauderdalehotel.co.uk
web: www.lauderdalehotel.co.uk
dir: On A68 from S, through Lauder centre, hotel on right. From Edinburgh, hotel on left at 1st bend after passing Lauder sign

Lying on the north side of the village with spacious gardens to the side and rear, this friendly hotel is ideally placed for those who don't want to stay in Edinburgh itself. The refurbished bedrooms and bathrooms are well equipped and well appointed. A good range of meals is served in both the bar and the restaurant.

Rooms 10 (1 fmly) **S** £55-£60; **D** £85-£90 (incl. bkfst)* **Facilities** STV FTV ♫ Xmas New Year Wi-fi **Conf** Class 200 Board 100 Thtr 200 Del from £150 to £160 **Parking** 200 **Notes** Civ Wed 180

LIVINGSTON
West Lothian — Map 21 NT06

Premier Inn Livingston M8 Jct 3

BUDGET HOTEL

☎ 0871 527 8632 📠 0871 527 8633
Deer Park Av, Deer Park, Knightsbridge EH54 8AD
dir: At M8 junct 3. Hotel opposite rdbt

High quality, budget accommodation ideal for both families and business travellers. Spacious, en suite bedrooms feature tea and coffee making facilities, and Freeview TV in most hotels. Internet access and Wi-fi are available for a small fee. The adjacent family restaurant features a wide and varied menu. See also the Hotel Groups pages.

Rooms 83 **D** £55-£63*

LOCHGILPHEAD
Argyll & Bute — Map 20 NR88

Cairnbaan

★★★ 78% ® HOTEL

☎ 01546 603668 📠 01546 606045
Crinan Canal, Cairnbaan PA31 8SJ
e-mail: info@cairnbaan.com
web: www.cairnbaan.com
dir: 2m N, A816 from Lochgilphead, hotel off B841

Located on the Crinan Canal, this small hotel offers relaxed hospitality in a delightful setting. Bedrooms are thoughtfully equipped, generally spacious and benefit from stylish decor. Fresh seafood is a real feature in both the formal restaurant and the comfortable bar area. Alfresco dining is popular in the warmer months.

Rooms 12 **Facilities** Xmas **Conf** Class 100 Board 80 Thtr 160 **Parking** 53 **Notes** Civ Wed 120

LOCHINVER
Highland — Map 22 NC02

INSPECTORS' CHOICE

Inver Lodge

★★★★ ®® HOTEL

☎ 01571 844496 📠 01571 844395
IV27 4LU
e-mail: stay@inverlodge.com
web: www.inverlodge.com
dir: A835 to Lochinver, through village, left after village hall, follow private road for 0.5m

Genuine hospitality is a noteworthy at this delightful, purpose-built hotel, set high on the hillside above the village. All bedrooms and public rooms enjoy stunning views. There is a choice of lounges and a restaurant where the chefs make use of the abundant local produce. Bedrooms are spacious, stylish and come with an impressive range of accessories. There is no night service between 11pm and 7am.

Rooms 21 (11 GF) **S** £115-£150; **D** £215-£480 (incl. bkfst)* **Facilities** FTV Sauna Wi-fi **Parking** 30 **Notes** LB Closed Nov-Mar Civ Wed 50

LOCKERBIE
Dumfries & Galloway — Map 21 NY18

Dryfesdale Country House

★★★★ 73% HOTEL

☎ 01576 202427 📠 01576 204187
Dryfebridge DG11 2SF
e-mail: reception@dryfesdalehotel.co.uk
web: www.dryfesdalehotel.co.uk
dir: From M74 junct 17 follow Lockerbie North signs, 3rd left at 1st rdbt, 1st exit left at 2nd rdbt, hotel 200yds on left

Conveniently situated for the M74, yet discreetly screened from it, this friendly hotel provides attentive service. Bedrooms, some with access to patio areas, vary in size and style; all offer good levels of comfort and are well equipped. Creative, good value dinners make use of local produce and are served in the airy restaurant that overlooks the manicured gardens and rolling countryside.

Rooms 29 (5 fmly) (20 GF) **S** £65-£89; **D** £99-£129* **Facilities** STV FTV Putt green Clay pigeon shooting Fishing ♫ Xmas New Year Wi-fi **Conf** Class 100 Board 100 Thtr 150 Del from £99 to £129* **Parking** 60 **Notes** Civ Wed 150

Kings Arms Hotel

★★ 78% HOTEL

☎ 01576 202410 📠 01576 202410
High St DG11 2JL
e-mail: reception@kingsarmshotel.co.uk
web: www.kingsarmshotel.co.uk
dir: A74(M), 0.5m into town centre, hotel opposite town hall

Dating from the 17th century this former inn lies in the town centre. Now a family-run hotel, it provides attractive well-equipped bedrooms with Wi-fi access. At lunch a menu ranging from snacks to full meals is served in both the cosy bars and the restaurant at dinner.

Rooms 13 (2 fmly) **S** £50; **D** £83 (incl. bkfst) **Facilities** FTV Xmas New Year Wi-fi **Conf** Class 40 Board 30 Thtr 80 **Parking** 8

L

LOCKERBIE *continued*

Ravenshill House

★★ 74% HOTEL

☎ 01576 202882
12 Dumfries Rd DG11 2EF
e-mail: aaenquiries@ravenshillhotellockerbie.co.uk
web: www.ravenshillhotellockerbie.co.uk
dir: From A74(M) Lockerbie junct onto A709. Hotel 0.5m on right

Set in spacious gardens on the fringe of the town, this friendly, family-run hotel offers cheerful service and good value, home-cooked meals. Bedrooms are generally spacious and comfortably equipped, including a two-room unit ideal for families.

Rooms 8 (2 fmly) **S** £40-£65; **D** £78-£85 (incl. bkfst)* **Facilities** FTV Wi-fi **Conf** Class 20 Board 12 Thtr 30 **Parking** 35 **Notes** LB Closed 1-3 Jan

LUSS Map 20 NS39
Argyll & Bute

The Lodge on Loch Lomond

★★★★ 76% 🏵🏵 HOTEL

☎ 01436 860201 📠 01436 860203
G83 8PA
e-mail: res@loch-lomond.co.uk
web: www.loch-lomond.co.uk
dir: Off A82, follow sign for hotel

This hotel is idyllically set on the shores of Loch Lomond. Public areas consist of an open-plan, split-level bar and fine dining restaurant overlooking the loch. The pine-finished bedrooms also enjoy the views and are comfortable, spacious and well equipped; all have saunas and some have DVDs and internet access. There is a stunning state-of-the-art leisure suite.

Rooms 47 (17 annexe) (20 fmly) (13 GF) **Facilities** Spa STV FTV Fishing Boating Xmas New Year Wi-fi **Conf** Class 80 Board 60 Thtr 150 **Parking** 120 **Notes** Civ Wed 100

MARKINCH Map 21 NO20
Fife

INSPECTORS' CHOICE

Balbirnie House

★★★★ 🏵🏵 COUNTRY HOUSE HOTEL

☎ 01592 610066 📠 01592 610529
Balbirnie Park KY7 6NE
e-mail: info@balbirnie.co.uk
web: www.balbirnie.co.uk
dir: Off A92 onto B9130, entrance 0.5m on left

The perfect venue for a business trip, wedding or romantic break, this imposing Georgian mansion lies in formal gardens and grounds amidst scenic Balbirnie Park. Delightful public rooms include a choice of inviting lounges. Accommodation features some splendid well-proportioned bedrooms with the best overlooking the gardens. But even the smaller standard rooms include little touches such as sherry, shortbread, fudge and mineral water. There is a choice of eating options, the Orangery with a chef's table for watching the action in the kitchen, or the more informal Bistro.

Rooms 30 (9 fmly) (7 GF) **Facilities** STV Woodland walks Jogging trails Treatment room Xmas New Year Wi-fi **Conf** Class 100 Board 60 Thtr 220 **Parking** 120 **Notes** LB Civ Wed 200

Town House

RESTAURANT WITH ROOMS

☎ 01592 758459 📠 01592 755039
1 High St KY7 6DQ
e-mail: townhousehotel@aol.com
web: www.townhousehotel-fife.co.uk
dir: In town centre opposite railway station

Well situated on the edge of town and close to the railway station, this friendly establishment offers well presented bedrooms with pleasant colour schemes, modern furnishings, and a good range of facilities and extras. The attractive bar-restaurant is popular with locals and serves a choice of good-value dishes.

Rooms 3 (1 fmly)

MELROSE Map 21 NT53
Scottish Borders

Burt's

★★★ 78% 🏵🏵 HOTEL

☎ 01896 822285 📠 01896 822870
Market Square TD6 9PL
e-mail: enquiries@burtshotel.co.uk
web: www.burtshotel.co.uk
dir: A6091, 2m from A68 3m S of Earlston

Recognised by its distinctive black and white façade and colourful window boxes, in the heart of a small market town, this hotel has been under the same family ownership for almost 40 years. The genuine warmth of hospitality is notable. The smart bedrooms have been individually styled and include Wi-fi. Food is important at Burt's and the elegant restaurant is well complemented by the range of tasty meals in the bar.

Rooms 20 **S** £72-£90; **D** £133-£140 (incl. bkfst)* **Facilities** STV FTV Salmon fishing Shooting New Year Wi-fi **Conf** Class 20 Board 20 Thtr 38 Del from £100 to £120* **Parking** 40 **Notes** LB Closed 24-26 Dec & 2-3 Jan

MILNGAVIE Map 20 NS57
East Dunbartonshire

Premier Inn Glasgow (Milngavie)

BUDGET HOTEL

☎ 0871 527 8428 📠 0871 527 8429
103 Main St G62 6JQ
dir: M8 junct 16, follow Milngavie (A879) signs. Approx. 5m. Pass Murray Park Training Ground. Left at lights. Hotel on A81 adjacent to West Highland Gate Beefeater

High quality, budget accommodation ideal for both families and business travellers. Spacious, en suite bedrooms feature tea and coffee making facilities, and Freeview TV in most hotels. Internet access and Wi-fi are available for a small fee. The adjacent family restaurant features a wide and varied menu. See also the Hotel Groups pages.

Rooms 60 **D** £52-£60*

MOFFAT Dumfries & Galloway Map 21 NT00

Annandale Arms Hotel

★★★ 78% HOTEL

☎ 01683 220013 📠 01683 221395
High St DG10 9HF
e-mail: reception@annandalearmshotel.co.uk
web: www.annandalearmshotel.co.uk
dir: M74 junct 15/A701. Hotel on west side of central square that forms High St

With a history dating back 250 years old, this family run hotel in the heart of Moffat provides well-appointed, modern bedrooms and bathrooms, located away from the hustle and bustle of the high street. There is a welcoming bar and restaurant serving real ales and quality food. Wi-fi and off-road parking are added benefits.

Rooms 16 (2 fmly) (5 GF) (5 smoking) **S** £70; **D** £110 (incl. bkfst) **Facilities** FTV New Year Wi-fi **Conf** Class 40 Board 40 Thtr 60 Del from £120 **Parking** 20 **Notes** LB Closed 25-26 Dec

MOTHERWELL North Lanarkshire Map 21 NS75

Alona Hotel

★★★★ 78% HOTEL

☎ 01698 333888 📠 01698 338720
Strathclyde Country Park ML1 3RT
e-mail: gm@alonahotel.co.uk
web: www.alonahotel.co.uk
dir: M74 junct 5, hotel approx 250yds on left

Alona is a Celtic word meaning 'exquisitely beautiful'. This hotel is situated within the idyllic beauty of Strathclyde Country Park, with tranquil views over the picturesque loch and surrounding forests. There is a very contemporary feel, from the open-plan public areas to the spacious and well-appointed bedrooms. Wi-fi is available throughout. M&D's, Scotland's Family Theme Park, is just next door.

Rooms 51 (24 fmly) (17 GF) **Facilities** FTV ♫ Xmas New Year Wi-fi **Conf** Class 100 Board 76 Thtr 140 **Services** Lift Air con **Parking** 100 **Notes** ⊗ Civ Wed 250

Express by Holiday Inn Strathclyde Park

BUDGET HOTEL

☎ 01698 858585 📠 01698 852375
Hamilton Rd, Hamilton ML1 3RB
e-mail: isabella.little@ichotelsgroup.com
web: www.hiexpress.com/strathclyde
dir: M74 junct 5 follow signs for Strathclyde Country Park

A modern hotel ideal for families and business travellers. Fresh and uncomplicated, the spacious rooms include Sky TV, power shower and tea and coffee-making facilities. Continental buffet breakfast is included in the room rate; other meals may be taken at the nearby family pub or restaurant. See also the Hotel Groups pages.

Rooms 120 (58 fmly) **Conf** Class 10 Board 18 Thtr 30

Premier Inn Glasgow (Motherwell)

BUDGET HOTEL

☎ 0871 527 8430 📠 0871 527 8431
Edinburgh Rd, Newhouse ML1 5SY
dir: From S: M74 junct 5, A725 towards Coatbridge. Take A8 towards Edinburgh, exit at junct 6, follow Lanark signs. Hotel 400yds on right

High quality, budget accommodation ideal for both families and business travellers. Spacious, en suite bedrooms feature tea and coffee making facilities, and Freeview TV in most hotels. Internet access and Wi-fi are available for a small fee. The adjacent family restaurant features a wide and varied menu. See also the Hotel Groups pages.

Rooms 40 **D** £54-£60*

MUIR OF ORD Highland Map 23 NH55

Ord House

★★ 72% SMALL HOTEL

THE CIRCLE

☎ 01463 870492 📠 01463 870297
IV6 7UH
e-mail: admin@ord-house.co.uk
dir: Off A9 at Tore rdbt onto A832. 5m, through Muir of Ord. Left towards Ullapool (A832). Hotel 0.5m on left

Dating back to 1637, this country-house hotel is situated peacefully in wooded grounds and offers brightly furnished and well-proportioned accommodation. Comfortable day rooms reflect the character and charm of the house, with inviting lounges, a cosy snug bar and an elegant dining room where wide-ranging, creative menus are offered.

Rooms 12 (3 GF) **S** £60-£85; **D** £100-£150 (incl. bkfst)* **Facilities** Putt green Clay pigeon shooting Wi-fi **Parking** 30 **Notes** LB Closed Nov-Apr

MUTHILL Perth & Kinross Map 21 NN81

Barley Bree Restaurant with Rooms

RESTAURANT WITH ROOMS

☎ 01764 681451 📠 01764 910055
6 Willoughby St PH5 2AB
e-mail: info@barleybree.com
dir: A9 onto A822 in centre of Muthill

Situated in the heart of the small village of Muthill, and is just a short drive from Crieff, genuine hospitality and quality food are obvious attractions at this charming restaurant with rooms. The property has been transformed by the current owners, and the stylish bedrooms are appointed to a very high standard. The restaurant has a rustic feel and boasts a log burning fire.

Rooms 6 (1 fmly)

NAIRN Highland **Map 23 NH85**

Newton

★★★★ 74% ® HOTEL

OXFORD HOTELS & INNS

☎ 01667 453144 🖷 01667 454026
Inverness Rd IV12 4RX
e-mail: newton.frontdesk@ohiml.com
web: www.oxfordhotelsandinns.com
dir: A96 from Inverness to Nairn, through 3 sets of lights, at 4th right to Newton Gate

This former mansion house, set in 21 acres of mature parkland and bordering Nairn's championship golf course, was a favourite with the actor Charlie Chaplin who often visited with his family. Originally built as a family home in 1872 the hotel has been extensively refurbished over the years, including the addition of the Highland Conference Centre. Bedrooms are of a high standard, and many of the front-facing rooms having splendid sea views.

Rooms 56 (4 fmly) **Facilities** STV Xmas New Year Wi-fi **Conf** Class 220 Board 90 Thtr 450 Del from £130 to £180* **Services** Lift **Parking** 150 **Notes** Civ Wed 250

Golf View Hotel & Leisure Club

★★★★ 72% ® HOTEL

☎ 01667 452301 🖷 01667 455267
The Seafront IV12 4HD
e-mail: golfview@crerarhotels.com
dir: Off A96 into Seabank Rd, hotel at end on right

This fine hotel has wonderful sea views and overlooks the Morey Firth and the Black Isle beyond. The championship golf course at Nairn is adjacent to the hotel and guests have direct access to the long sandy beaches. Bedrooms are of a very high standard and the public areas are charming. A well-equipped leisure complex and swimming pool are also available.

Rooms 42 (6 fmly) **S** £95-£130; **D** £130-£200 (incl. bkfst)* **Facilities** **Spa** FTV ⓢ supervised ⛳ Gym Sauna Steam room Xmas New Year Wi-fi **Conf** Class 40 Board 40 Thtr 100 Del from £125 to £195* **Services** Lift **Parking** 40 **Notes** LB Civ Wed 100

INSPECTORS' CHOICE

Boath House

★★★ ®®®® HOTEL

☎ 01667 454896 🖷 01667 455469
Auldearn IV12 5TE
e-mail: info@boath-house.com
web: www.boath-house.com
dir: 2m past Nairn on A96, E towards Forres, signed on main road

Standing in its own grounds, this splendid Georgian mansion has been lovingly restored. Hospitality is first class. The owners are passionate about what they do, and have an ability to establish a special relationship with their guests that will be particularly remembered. The food is also memorable here - the five-course dinners are a culinary adventure, matched only by the excellence of breakfasts. The house itself is delightful, with inviting lounges and a dining room overlooking a trout loch. Bedrooms are striking, comfortable, and include many fine antique pieces.

Rooms 8 (1 fmly) (1 GF) **S** £260-£330; **D** £345-£450 (incl. bkfst & dinner) **Facilities** FTV Fishing 🎣 Beauty salon Xmas New Year Wi-fi **Conf** Class 10 Board 10 Thtr 15 **Parking** 20 **Notes** LB Civ Wed 28

NETHY BRIDGE Highland **Map 23 NJ02**

Nethybridge

★★★ 68% HOTEL

☎ 01479 821203 🖷 01479 821686
PH25 3DP
e-mail: salesnethybridge@strathmorehotels.com
dir: A9 onto A95, onto B970 to Nethy Bridge

This popular tourist and coaching hotel enjoys a central location amidst the majestic Cairngorm Mountains. Bedrooms are stylishly furnished in bold tartans whilst traditionally styled day rooms include two bars and a popular snooker room. Staff are friendly and keen to please.

Rooms 69 (3 fmly) (7 GF) **Facilities** Putt green Bowling green ♫ Xmas New Year **Conf** Thtr 100 **Services** Lift **Parking** 80

See advert on page 550

The Mountview Hotel

★★ 78% ®® HOTEL

☎ 01479 821248 🖷 01479 821515
Grantown Rd PH25 3EB
e-mail: info@mountviewhotel.co.uk
dir: From Aviemore follow signs through Boat of Garten to Nethy Bridge. On main road through village, hotel on right

Aptly named, this country-house hotel enjoys stunning panoramic views from its elevated position on the edge of the village. It specialises in guided holidays and is a favoured base for birdwatching and for walking groups. Public rooms include inviting lounges, while imaginative, well-prepared dinners are served in a bright and modern restaurant extension.

Rooms 12 (1 GF) **Facilities** FTV **Parking** 20 **Notes** ⊗

N

NEWBURGH Map 23 NJ92
Aberdeenshire

The Udny Arms Hotel

U

☎ 01358 789444 📠 01358 789012
Main St AB41 6BL
e-mail: enquiries@udnyarmshotel.com
web: www.udnyarmshotel.com
dir: A90 N, 8m N of Aberdeen turn right to Newburgh (A975), hotel in village centre

Currently the rating for this establishment is not confirmed. This may be due to a change of ownership or because it has only recently joined the AA rating scheme. For further details please see the AA website: theAA.com

Rooms 30 (1 fmly) (4 GF) **S** £57-£70; **D** £67-£89 (incl. bkfst)* **Facilities** STV FTV Fishing Xmas New Year Wi-fi **Conf** Class 50 Board 20 Thtr 80 Del from £90 to £150* **Parking** 40 **Notes** LB Civ Wed 80

NEW LANARK Map 21 NS84
South Lanarkshire

New Lanark Mill Hotel

★★★ 83% HOTEL

☎ 01555 667200 📠 01555 667222
Mill One, New Lanark Mills ML11 9DB
e-mail: hotel@newlanark.org
web: www.newlanark.org
dir: Signed from all major roads, M74 junct 7 & M8

Originally built as a cotton mill in the 18th century, this hotel forms part of a fully restored village, now a UNESCO World Heritage Site. There's a bright modern style throughout which contrasts nicely with features from the original mill. There is a comfortable foyer-lounge with a galleried restaurant above. The hotel enjoys stunning views over the River Clyde.

Rooms 38 (5 fmly) (6 smoking) **S** £59-£99; **D** £69-£119 (incl. bkfst) **Facilities** STV Gym Beauty room Steam room Sauna Aerobics studios Xmas New Year Wi-fi **Conf** Class 60 Board 40 Thtr 200 Del from £99 to £139 **Services** Lift **Parking** 75 **Notes** LB Civ Wed 120

NEWTON STEWART Map 20 NX46
Dumfries & Galloway

INSPECTORS' CHOICE

Kirroughtree House

★★★ @@ COUNTRY HOUSE HOTEL

☎ 01671 402141 📠 01671 402425
Minnigaff DG8 6AN
e-mail: info@kirroughtreehouse.co.uk
web: www.kirroughtreehouse.co.uk
dir: A75 onto A712, hotel entrance 300yds on left

This imposing mansion enjoys a peaceful location in eight acres of landscaped gardens near Galloway Forest Park. It is said that Robert Burns sat on the staircase at Kirroughtree and recited his poems. The inviting day rooms comprise a choice of lounges, and two elegant dining rooms where guests can enjoy the delightful cuisine which is firmly based on top quality, locally sourced ingredients. Well-proportioned, individually styled bedrooms include some suites and mini-suites and many rooms enjoy fine views. Service is very friendly and attentive.

Rooms 17 **S** £80-£120; **D** £120-£260 (incl. bkfst)* **Facilities** FTV 9-hole pitch & putt Xmas New Year Wi-fi **Conf** Class 20 Board 20 Thtr 30 **Services** Lift **Parking** 50 **Notes** LB No children 10yrs Closed 2 Jan-mid Feb

The Bruce Hotel

★★★ 73% HOTEL

☎ 01671 402294 📠 01671 402294
88 Queen St DG8 6JL
e-mail: mail@the-bruce-hotel.com
web: www.the-bruce-hotel.com
dir: Exit A75 at Newton Stewart rdbt towards town. Hotel 800mtrs on right

Named after the Scottish patriot Robert the Bruce, this welcoming hotel is just a short distance from the A75. One of the well-appointed bedrooms features a four-poster bed, and popular family suites contain separate bedrooms for children. Public areas include a traditional lounge, a formal restaurant and a lounge bar, both offering a good choice of dishes.

Rooms 20 (3 fmly) **S** £50-£70; **D** £60-£90 (incl. bkfst) **Facilities** FTV New Year Wi-fi **Conf** Class 50 Board 14 Thtr 100 Del from £75 to £105 **Parking** 14 **Notes** LB

NORTH BERWICK Map 21 NT58
East Lothian

Macdonald Marine Hotel & Spa

★★★★ 82% @@ HOTEL

☎ 0844 879 9130 📠 01620 894480
Cromwell Rd EH39 4LZ
e-mail: sales.marine@macdonald-hotels.co.uk
web: www.macdonaldhotels.co.uk
dir: From A198 turn into Hamilton Rd at lights then 2nd right

This imposing hotel commands stunning views across the local golf course to the Firth of Forth. Stylish public areas provide a relaxing atmosphere; creative dishes are served in the restaurant and lighter bites in the lounge/bar. Bedrooms come in a variety of sizes and styles, all are well equipped and some are impressively large. The hotel boasts extensive leisure and conference facilities.

Rooms 83 (4 fmly) (4 GF) **Facilities** Spa STV supervised Putt green Gym Indoor & outdoor salt water hydro pool Xmas New Year Wi-fi **Conf** Class 120 Board 60 Thtr 300 Del from £135 to £155* **Services** Lift **Parking** 50 **Notes** Civ Wed 150

N

OBAN
Argyll & Bute — Map 20 NM82

Manor House

★★★ 83% HOTEL

☎ 01631 562087 🖹 01631 563053
Gallanach Rd PA34 4LS
e-mail: info@manorhouseoban.com
web: www.manorhouseoban.com
dir: Follow MacBrayne Ferries signs, pass ferry entrance for hotel on right

Handy for the ferry terminal and with views of the bay and harbour, this elegant Georgian residence was built in 1780 as the dower house for the family of the Duke of Argyll. Comfortable and attractive public rooms invite relaxation, whilst most of the well-equipped bedrooms are furnished with period pieces.

Rooms 11 (1 GF) **Facilities** New Year Wi-fi **Parking** 20 **Notes** No children 12yrs Closed 25-26 Dec Civ Wed 30

O

Falls of Lora Hotel

THE INDEPENDENTS HOTEL ASSOCIATION

★★★ 77% HOTEL

☎ 01631 710483 🖹 01631 710694
PA37 1PB
e-mail: enquiries@fallsoflora.com
web: www.fallsoflora.com

(For full entry see Connel)

Royal

★★★ 75% HOTEL

☎ 01631 563021 🖹 01631 562811
Argyll Sqaure PA34 4BE
e-mail: salesroyaloban@strathmorehotels.com
dir: A82 from Glasgow towards Loch Lomond & Crianlarich then A85 (pass Loch Awe) to Oban

Well situated in the heart of Oban, just minutes from the ferry terminal and with all the shops on its doorstep, this hotel really is central. The comfortable and well-presented bedrooms differ in size, and all public areas are smart. There is a first-floor restaurant overlooking the town square.

Rooms 91 (5 fmly) **S** £35-£70; **D** £70-£140 (incl. bkfst)* **Facilities** ♫ Xmas New Year Wi-fi **Conf** Class 60 Board 30 Thtr 140 **Services** Lift **Parking** 25 **Notes** Civ Wed 70

See advert on page 550

The Oban Caledonian Hotel

★★★ 74% HOTEL

☎ 0845 855 9135 🖹 01631 562998
Station Square PA34 5RT
e-mail: reservations.caledonian@akkeronhotels.com
web: www.akkeronhotels.com
dir: Opposite rail & ferry terminals

This Victorian hotel, overlooking the bay, has an enviable location close to the ferry terminal and parking facilities, as well as Oban's many attractions. Public areas are modern and stylish and include a smart restaurant, spacious lounges and an informal dining option in Café Caledonian. Attractive bedrooms come in a number of different styles and grades, some with comfortable seating areas, feature bathrooms and fine sea views.

Rooms 59 (6 fmly) **D** £59-£185* **Facilities** Xmas New Year Wi-fi **Conf** Class 90 Board 50 Thtr 100 **Services** Lift **Notes** Civ Wed 100

The Columba Hotel

★★★ 72% HOTEL

☎ 01631 562183 🖹 01631 564683
The Esplanade PA34 5QD
e-mail: columba@mckeverhotels.co.uk
dir: A85 to Oban, at 1st lights in town turn right

One of Oban's landmarks, this Victorian hotel is located on the seafront with stunning views out over the Firth of Lorne to the Isle of Mull. The well-appointed, contemporary bedrooms offer guests comfortable accommodation. Alba Restaurant provides a menu of modern Scottish dishes.

Rooms 49 (5 fmly) **Facilities** FTV ♫ Xmas New Year Wi-fi **Services** Lift **Parking** 6 **Notes** LB ⊗

OLDMELDRUM
Aberdeenshire — Map 23 NJ82

Meldrum House Hotel Golf & Country Estate

★★★★ 78% COUNTRY HOUSE HOTEL

☎ 01651 872294 🖹 01651 872464
AB51 0AE
e-mail: enquiries@meldrumhouse.co.uk
dir: 11m from Aberdeen on A947 (Aberdeen to Banff road)

Set in 350 acres of wooded parkland this imposing baronial country mansion has a golf course as its centrepiece. Tastefully restored to highlight its original character it provides a peaceful retreat. Bedrooms are massive, and like the public rooms, transport guests back to a bygone era, but at the same time provide stylish modern amenities including smart bathrooms.

Meldrum House Hotel Golf & Country Estate

Rooms 22 (13 annexe) (1 fmly) (6 GF) **D** £120-£180 (incl. bkfst)* **Facilities** FTV 18 Putt green Xmas New Year Wi-fi **Conf** Class 20 Board 30 Thtr 80 **Parking** 70 **Notes** LB Civ Wed 100

ONICH
Highland — Map 22 NN06

Onich

★★★ 78% HOTEL

01855 821214 01855 821484
PH33 6RY
e-mail: enquiries@onich-fortwilliam.co.uk
web: www.onich-fortwilliam.co.uk
dir: Beside A82, 2m N of Ballachulish Bridge

Genuine hospitality is part of the appeal of this hotel, which lies right beside Loch Linnhe with gardens extending to its shores. Nicely presented public areas include a choice of inviting lounges and contrasting bars, and views of the loch can be enjoyed from the attractive restaurant. Bedrooms, with pleasing colour schemes, are comfortably modern.

Rooms 26 (6 fmly) **Facilities** STV Games room Xmas New Year Wi-fi **Conf** Board 40 Thtr 150 **Parking** 50 **Notes** LB Civ Wed 120

PEAT INN
Fife — Map 21 NO40

INSPECTORS' CHOICE

The Peat Inn

RESTAURANT WITH ROOMS

01334 840206 01334 840530
KY15 5LH
e-mail: stay@thepeatinn.co.uk
dir: At junct of B940 & B941, 5m SW of St Andrews

This 300-year-old former coaching inn enjoys a rural location, yet is close to St Andrews. The spacious accommodation is very well appointed and all rooms have lounge areas. The inn is steeped in history and is a real haven for food lovers. The three dining areas create a romantic setting. Expect open fires and a relaxed ambiance.

Rooms 8 (8 annexe) (3 fmly)

PEEBLES
Scottish Borders — Map 21 NT24

INSPECTORS' CHOICE

Cringletie House

★★★★ COUNTRY HOUSE HOTEL

01721 725750 01721 725751
Edinburgh Rd EH45 8PL
e-mail: enquiries@cringletie.com
web: www.cringletie.com
dir: 2m N on A703

This romantic baronial mansion, built in 1861, is set in 28 acres of beautiful gardens and woodland; there is a walled garden with a 400-year-old yew hedge (perhaps the oldest in Scotland), a waterfall, sculptures and croquet lawn. In 1971 Scottish Heritage granted the property a Grade B listing, and in the same year the house became a hotel. The delightful public rooms, with welcoming fires, include a cocktail lounge with adjoining conservatory, and there are service bells in each room which still work. The award-winning, first-floor restaurant is graced by a magnificent hand-painted ceiling. The individually designed bedrooms have grace and charm, and for the ultimate luxury there's the Selkirk Suite.

Rooms 13 (2 GF) **S** £130-£230; **D** £160-£260 (incl. bkfst)* **Facilities** FTV Putt green Petanque Giant chess & draughts In-room therapy treatments Xmas New Year Wi-fi **Conf** Class 20 Board 24 Thtr 45 Del from £169 to £209* **Services** Lift **Parking** 30 **Notes** LB Civ Wed 60

P

PEEBLES *continued*

Macdonald Cardrona Hotel & Golf Course

★★★★ 77% ® HOTEL

☎ 01896 833600 📠 01896 831166
Cardrona EH45 8NE
e-mail: general.cardrona@macdonald-hotels.co.uk
web: www.macdonald-hotels.co.uk/cardrona
dir: On A72 between Peebles & Innerleithen, 3m S of Peebles

The rolling hills of the Scottish Borders are a stunning backdrop for this modern, purpose-built hotel. Spacious bedrooms are traditional in style, equipped with a range of extras, and most enjoy fantastic countryside. The hotel features some impressive leisure facilities, including an 18-hole golf course, 18-metre indoor pool and state-of-the-art gym.

Rooms 99 (24 fmly) (16 GF) **S** £95-£175; **D** £105-£185 (incl. bkfst)* **Facilities** Spa STV 18 Putt green Fishing Gym Sauna Steam room Xmas New Year Wi-fi **Conf** Class 120 Board 90 Thtr 250 Del from £110 to £150* **Services** Lift **Parking** 200 **Notes** LB Civ Wed 200

Tontine

★★★ 82% HOTEL

☎ 01721 720892 📠 01721 729732
High St EH45 8AJ
e-mail: info@tontinehotel.com
web: www.tontinehotel.com
dir: In town centre

Conveniently situated in the main street, this long-established hotel offers comfortable public rooms including the elegant Adam Restaurant and an inviting lounge and 'clubby' bar. Bedrooms, contained in the original house and the river-facing wing, offer a smart, classical style of accommodation. The lasting impression is of the excellent level of hospitality and guest care.

Rooms 36 (3 fmly) (10 smoking) **S** fr £55; **D** £85-£110 (incl. bkfst) **Facilities** STV FTV Xmas New Year Wi-fi **Conf** Class 24 Board 24 Thtr 40 **Parking** 24 **Notes** LB

P

PERTH
Perth & Kinross — Map 21 NO12

Murrayshall House Hotel & Golf Course

★★★★ 76% ®® HOTEL

☎ 01738 551171 📠 01738 552595
New Scone PH2 7PH
e-mail: info@murrayshall.co.uk
dir: From Perth take A94 (Coupar Angus), 1m from Perth, right to Murrayshall just before New Scone

This imposing country house is set in 350 acres of grounds, including two golf courses, one of which is of championship standard. Bedrooms come in two distinct styles: modern suites in a purpose-built building contrast with more classic rooms in the main building. The Clubhouse bar serves a range of meals all day, whilst more accomplished cooking can be enjoyed in the Old Masters Restaurant.

Rooms 41 (14 annexe) (17 fmly) (5 GF) **S** £77-£100; **D** £120-£150 (incl. bkfst)* **Facilities** STV 36 Putt green Driving range New Year Wi-fi **Conf** Class 60 Board 30 Thtr 150 Del from £150 to £160* **Parking** 120 **Notes** LB Civ Wed 130

Parklands Hotel

★★★★ 73% ®® SMALL HOTEL

☎ 01738 622451 📠 01738 622046
2 St Leonards Bank PH2 8EB
e-mail: info@theparklandshotel.com
web: www.theparklandshotel.com
dir: M90 junct 10, in 1m left at lights at end of park area, hotel on left

Ideally located close to the centre of town with open views over the South Inch. The enthusiastic proprietors continue to invest heavily in the business and the bedrooms have a smart contemporary feel. Public areas include a choice of restaurants with a fine dining experience offered in Acanthus.

Rooms 15 (3 fmly) (4 GF) **S** £92.50-£132.50; **D** £112.50-£162.50 (incl. bkfst)* **Facilities** STV Wi-fi **Conf** Class 18 Board 20 Thtr 24 Del from £124.50 to £154.50* **Parking** 30 **Notes** LB Closed 26 Dec-7 Jan Civ Wed 40

The New County Hotel

★★★ 77% ®® HOTEL

☎ 01738 623355 📠 01738 628969
22-30 County Place PH2 8EE
e-mail: enquiries@newcountyhotel.com
web: www.newcountyhotel.com
dir: A9 junct 11 Perth. Follow signs for town centre. Hotel on right after library

This is a smart hotel in the heart of the beautiful garden city of Perth. The bedrooms have a modern and stylish appearance and public areas include a popular bar and contemporary lounge area. No stay here is complete without a visit to the award-winning Opus One Restaurant, which has a well deserved reputation for fine dining.

Rooms 23 (4 fmly) **S** £60-£75; **D** £70-£140 (incl. bkfst)* **Facilities** New Year Wi-fi **Conf** Class 80 Board 24 Thtr 120 Del from £130 to £150* **Parking** 10 **Notes**

Best Western Queens Hotel

★★★ 75% HOTEL

☎ 01738 442222 📠 01738 638496
Leonard St PH2 8HB
e-mail: enquiry@queensperth.co.uk
dir: From M90 follow to 2nd lights, turn left. Hotel on right, opposite railway station

This popular hotel benefits from a central location close to both the bus and rail stations. Bedrooms vary in size and style with top floor rooms offering extra space and excellent views of the town. Public rooms include a smart leisure centre and versatile conference space. A range of meals is served in both the bar and restaurant.

Rooms 50 (4 fmly) **Facilities** STV FTV Gym Steam room Xmas New Year Wi-fi **Conf** Class 70 Board 50 Thtr 200 **Services** Lift **Parking** 50 **Notes** Civ Wed 220

Salutation

★★★ 70% HOTEL

☎ 01738 630066 📠 01738 633598
South St PH2 8PH
e-mail: salessalutation@strathmorehotels.com
dir: At end of South St on right before River Tay

Situated in heart of Perth, the Salutation is reputed to be one of the oldest hotels in Scotland and has been welcoming guests through its doors since 1699. It offers traditional hospitality with all the modern comforts. Bedrooms vary in size and are thoughtfully equipped. An extensive menu is available in the Adam Restaurant with its impressive barrel vaulted ceiling and original features.

Rooms 84 (5 fmly) **Facilities** ♫ Xmas New Year Wi-fi **Conf** Class 180 Board 60 Thtr 300 **Services** Lift **Notes** Civ Wed 100

See advert on page 550

Holiday Inn Express Perth

BUDGET HOTEL

Holiday Inn Express

☎ 01738 636666 📠 01738 633363
200 Dunkeld Rd, Inveralmond PH1 3AQ
e-mail: info@hiexpressperth.co.uk
web: www.hiexpressperth.co.uk
dir: Off A9 (Inverness to Stirling road) at Inveralmond rdbt onto A912 signed Perth. Right at 1st rdbt, follow signs for hotel

A modern hotel ideal for families and business travellers. Fresh and uncomplicated, the spacious rooms include Sky TV, power shower and tea and coffee-making facilities. Continental buffet breakfast is included in the room rate; other meals may be taken at the nearby family pub or restaurant. See also the Hotel Groups pages.

Rooms 81 (43 fmly) (19 GF) (8 smoking) **Conf** Class 15 Board 16 Thtr 30

PETERHEAD
Aberdeenshire — Map 23 NK14

Buchan Braes Hotel

★★★★ 75% ® HOTEL

☎ 01779 871471 📠 01779 871472
Boddam AB42 3AR
e-mail: info@buchanbraes.co.uk
dir: From Aberdeen take A90, follow Peterhead signs. 1st right in Stirling signed Boddam. 50mtrs, 1st right

A contemporary hotel located in Boddam that is an excellent base for exploring the attractions of this wonderful part of Scotland. There is an open-plan lounge for drinks and snacks and the Grill Room with an open kitchen that offers a weekly changing, seasonal menu of locally sourced produce. All the bedrooms, including three suites, have 32" flat-screen TVs with satellite channels, king-sized beds and free Wi-fi.

Rooms 47 (1 fmly) (26 GF) **S** £90-£130; **D** £100-£130 (incl. bkfst)* **Facilities** Xmas New Year Wi-fi **Conf** Class 100 Board 130 Thtr 250 Del from £150 to £170* **Services** Lift **Parking** 40 **Notes** ⊗ Civ Wed

Palace

★★★ 80% HOTEL

☎ 01779 474821 📠 01779 476119
Prince St AB42 1PL
e-mail: info@palacehotel.co.uk
web: www.palacehotel.co.uk
dir: A90 from Aberdeen, follow signs to Peterhead, on entering town turn into Prince St, then right into main car park

This town centre hotel is popular with business travellers and for social events. Bedrooms come in two styles, with the executive rooms being particularly smart and spacious. Public areas include a themed bar, an informal diner reached via a spiral staircase, and a brasserie restaurant and cocktail bar.

Rooms 64 (1 fmly) (14 GF) **S** £70-£85; **D** £80-£95 (incl. bkfst)* **Facilities** Snooker & Pool table ♫ New Year Wi-fi **Conf** Class 100 Board 60 Thtr 250 Del from £120 to £135* **Services** Lift **Parking** 50 **Notes** Civ Wed

PITLOCHRY
Perth & Kinross — Map 23 NN95

See also **Kinloch Rannoch**

Knockendarroch House Hotel

★★★★ 74% ® SMALL HOTEL

☎ 01796 473473 📠 01796 474056
Higher Oakfield PH16 5HT
e-mail: bookings@knockendarroch.co.uk
dir: Just off the A9

This secluded hotel has outstanding views over the town and surrounding hills. The individually styled bedrooms are spacious and very well appointed - all have plasma TVs. The traditional, country-style public rooms have large sofas, welcoming open fires and an excellent whisky cabinet. Dinner is served every evening in the award-winning restaurant with only the best of Scottish produce being used. The staff are friendly and attentive.

Rooms 12 (1 GF) **D** £138-£198 (incl. bkfst & dinner)* **Facilities** FTV Wi-fi **Parking** 12 **Notes** LB No children 10yrs Closed Dec-Jan

Green Park

★★★ 87% ® COUNTRY HOUSE HOTEL

☎ 01796 473248 📠 01796 473520
Clunie Bridge Rd PH16 5JY
e-mail: bookings@thegreenpark.co.uk
web: www.thegreenpark.co.uk
dir: Exit A9 at Pitlochry, follow signs 0.25m through town

Guests return year after year to this lovely hotel that is situated in a stunning setting on the shores of Loch Faskally. Most of the thoughtfully designed bedrooms, including a splendid wing, the restaurant and the comfortable lounges enjoy these views. Dinner utilises fresh produce, much of it grown in the kitchen garden.

Rooms 51 (3 fmly) (16 GF) **S** £66-£103; **D** £132-£206 (incl. bkfst & dinner)* **Facilities** FTV Putt green New Year Wi-fi **Services** Lift **Parking** 51 **Notes** LB

PITLOCHRY *continued*

Dundarach

★★★ 77% HOTEL

☎ 01796 472862 🖷 01796 473024
Perth Rd PH16 5DJ
e-mail: inbox@dundarach.co.uk
web: www.dundarach.co.uk
dir: S of town centre on main road

This welcoming, family-run hotel stands in mature grounds at the south end of town. Bedrooms come in a variety of styles, including a block of large purpose-built rooms that will appeal to business guests. Well-proportioned public areas feature inviting lounges and a conservatory restaurant giving fine views of the Tummel Valley.

Rooms 39 (19 annexe) (7 fmly) (12 GF) **Facilities** Wi-fi **Conf** Class 40 Board 40 Thtr 60 **Parking** 39 **Notes** ⊗ Closed Jan RS Dec-early Feb

Moulin Hotel

★★★ 75% HOTEL

☎ 01796 472196 🖷 01796 474098
11-13 Kirkmichael Rd, Moulin PH16 5EW
e-mail: enquiries@moulinhotel.co.uk
web: www.moulinhotel.co.uk
dir: Off A9 take A924 signed Braemar into town centre. Hotel 0.75m from Pitlochry

Steeped in history, original parts of this friendly hotel date back to 1695. The Moulin bar serves an excellent choice of meals as well as real ales from the hotel's own microbrewery. Alternatively, the comfortable restaurant overlooks the Moulin Burn. Bedrooms are well equipped.

Rooms 15 (3 fmly) **S** £45-£77; **D** £60-£92 (incl. bkfst) **Facilities** FTV New Year Wi-fi **Conf** Class 12 Board 10 Thtr 15 Del from £95 to £110 **Parking** 30 **Notes** LB ⊗

PLOCKTON
Highland — Map 22 NG83

The Plockton

★★★ 75% SMALL HOTEL

☎ 01599 544274 🖷 01599 544475
41 Harbour St IV52 8TN
e-mail: info@plocktonhotel.co.uk
dir: 6m from Kyle of Lochalsh. 6m from Balmacara

This very popular hotel occupies an idyllic position on the waterfront of Loch Carron. Stylish bedrooms offer individual, pleasing decor and many have spacious balconies or panoramic views. There is a choice of three dining areas and seafood is very much a speciality. The staff and owners provide a relaxed and informal style of attentive service. A self-contained cottage is available for group bookings.

Rooms 15 (4 annexe) (1 fmly) (1 GF) **S** £55-£90; **D** £80-£130 (incl. bkfst)* **Facilities** STV Pool table ♫ New Year Wi-fi **Notes** ⊗ Closed 25 Dec & 1 Jan

POLMONT
Falkirk — Map 21 NS97

Macdonald Inchyra Grange

★★★★ 72% HOTEL

☎ 01324 711911 🖷 01324 716134
Grange Rd FK2 0YB
e-mail: inchyra@macdonald-hotels.co.uk
web: www.macdonaldhotels.co.uk
dir: Just beyond BP Social Club on Grange Rd

Ideally placed for the M9 and Grangemouth terminal, this former manor house has been tastefully extended. It provides extensive conference facilities and a choice of eating options: the relaxed atmosphere of the Café Crema or the Opus 504 Restaurant, which provides a more formal dining experience. Bedrooms are comfortable and mostly spacious.

Rooms 98 (6 annexe) (35 fmly) (33 GF) **Facilities** Spa STV Gym Steam room Sauna New Year **Conf** Class 300 Board 80 Thtr 750 **Services** Lift **Parking** 500 **Notes** Civ Wed 450

Premier Inn Falkirk East

BUDGET HOTEL

☎ 0871 527 8392 🖷 0871 527 8393
Beancross Rd FK2 0YS
dir: M9 junct 5, Polmont A9 signs. Hotel on left

High quality, budget accommodation ideal for both families and business travellers. Spacious, en suite bedrooms feature tea and coffee making facilities, and Freeview TV in most hotels. Internet access and Wi-fi are available for a small fee. The adjacent family restaurant features a wide and varied menu. See also the Hotel Groups pages.

Rooms 40 **D** £52-£58*

P

PORT APPIN Map 20 NM94
Argyll & Bute

INSPECTORS' CHOICE

Airds Hotel

★★★★ ◎◎◎ SMALL HOTEL

☎ 01631 730236 🖷 01631 730535
PA38 4DF
e-mail: airds@airds-hotel.com
web: www.airds-hotel.com
dir: From A828 (Oban to Fort William road), turn at Appin signed Port Appin. Hotel 2.5m on left

The views are stunning from this small, luxury hotel on the shores of Loch Linnhe and where the staff are delightful and nothing is too much trouble. The well-equipped bedrooms provide style and luxury whilst many bathrooms are furnished in marble and have power showers. Expertly prepared dishes, utilising the finest of ingredients, are served in the elegant dining room. Comfortable lounges with deep sofas and roaring fires provide the ideal retreat for relaxation. A real get-away-from-it-all experience.

Rooms 11 (3 fmly) (2 GF) **D** £260-£460 (incl. bkfst & dinner)* **Facilities** FTV Putt green Xmas New Year Wi-fi **Conf** Class 16 Board 16 Thtr 16 **Parking** 20 **Notes** LB RS Nov-Jan Civ Wed 40

Pierhouse

★★★ 80% ◎ SMALL HOTEL

☎ 01631 730302 & 730622 🖷 01631 730509
PA38 4DE
e-mail: reservations@pierhousehotel.co.uk
web: www.pierhousehotel.co.uk
dir: A828 from Ballachulish to Oban. In Appin right at Port Appin & Lismore ferry sign. After 2.5m left after post office, hotel at end of road

Originally the residence of the Pier Master, with parts of the building dating back to the 19th century, this hotel is located on the shores of Loch Linnhe with picture-postcard views to the islands of Lismore and Mull. The beautifully appointed, individually designed bedrooms have Wi-fi access and include Arran Aromatics toiletries. The hotel has a Finnish sauna, and also offers a range of treatments. Babysitting can be arranged.

Rooms 12 (3 fmly) (6 GF) **Facilities** FTV Aromatherapy Massage Sauna New Year Wi-fi **Conf** Class 20 Board 20 Thtr 20 **Parking** 20 **Notes** LB Closed 25-26 Dec Civ Wed 80

PORT OF MENTEITH Map 20 NN50
Stirling

The Lake of Menteith Hotel

★★★ 74% ◎◎ SMALL HOTEL

☎ 01877 385258 🖷 01877 385671
FK8 3RA
e-mail: enquiries@lake-hotel.com
dir: M9 junct 10, A84. At Blairdrummond take A873. Left onto A81 to Port of Mentieth. Left onto B8034, hotel 200yds on right

This hotel is situated on the shores of the Lake of Menteith in the Trossachs National Park, within an hour's drive of either Glasgow or Edinburgh. The converted 19th-century manse house has stylish bedrooms with great views over the lake or the countryside. All rooms offer a very good range of accessories. Dining is a highlight with two dining options on offer. There's the fine dining restaurant with its spectacular views, and also the Port Bar that has outdoor seating for the summer months; both menus are based on well-sourced produce.

Rooms 17 (5 GF) **S** £60-£155; **D** £80-£195 (incl. bkfst)* **Facilities** FTV Xmas New Year Wi-fi **Conf** Board 18 Thtr 30 Del from £120 to £150* **Parking** 50 **Notes** LB Civ Wed 50

PORTPATRICK Map 20 NW95
Dumfries & Galloway

INSPECTORS' CHOICE

Knockinaam Lodge

★★★ ◎◎◎ HOTEL

☎ 01776 810471 🖷 01776 810435
DG9 9AD
e-mail: reservations@knockinaamlodge.com
web: www.knockinaamlodge.com
dir: From A77 or A75 follow signs to Portpatrick. Through Lochans. After 2m left at signs for hotel

Any tour of Dumfries & Galloway would not be complete without a stay at this haven of tranquillity and relaxation. Knockinaam Lodge is an extended Victorian house set in an idyllic cove with its own pebble beach, ideal for a private swim in the summer, and sheltered by majestic cliffs and woodlands. Surrounded by 30 acres of delightful grounds, the lodge was the location for a meeting between Churchill and General Eisenhower in World War II. Today, a warm welcome is assured from the proprietors and their committed team, and much emphasis is placed on providing a sophisticated but intimate home-from-home experience. There are just ten suites - each individually designed and all with flat-screen TVs with DVD players, luxury toiletries and complimentary bottled water. The cooking is a real treat and showcases prime Scottish produce treated with respect on the daily-changing, four-course set menus; guests can always discuss the choices in advance if they wish.

Rooms 10 (1 fmly) **Facilities** FTV Fishing Shooting Walking Sea fishing Clay pigeon shooting Xmas New Year Wi-fi **Conf** Class 10 Board 16 Thtr 30 **Parking** 20 **Notes** Civ Wed 40

P

POWFOOT Map 21 NY16
Dumfries & Galloway

Powfoot Golf Hotel

★★★ 78% HOTEL

☎ 01461 700254 & 207580 📠 01461 700288
Links Av DG12 5PN
e-mail: reception@thepowfootgolfhotel.co.uk
dir: A75 onto B721, through Annan. B724, approx 3m, left onto unclassified road

This hotel has well presented and comfortable modern bedrooms, many of which overlook the championship golf course. Public areas have panoramic views onto the Solway Firth and the Lakeland hills beyond. The service is friendly and relaxed, and quality food is served in a choice of locations.

Rooms 24 (9 fmly) (5 GF) **Facilities** STV FTV Putt green Xmas New Year Wi-fi **Conf** Class 80 Board 80 Thtr 80 **Parking** 30 **Notes** ⊗ Civ Wed 100

PRESTWICK Map 20 NS32
South Ayrshire

Parkstone

★★★ 77% HOTEL

☎ 01292 477286 📠 01292 477671
Esplanade KA9 1QN
e-mail: info@parkstonehotel.co.uk
web: www.parkstonehotel.co.uk
dir: From Main St (A79) W to seafront, hotel in 600yds

Situated on the seafront in a quiet residential area only one mile from Prestwick Airport, this family-run hotel caters for business visitors as well as golfers. Bedrooms come in a variety of sizes; all are furnished in a smart, contemporary style. The attractive, modern look of the bar and restaurant is matched by an equally up-to-date menu.

Rooms 30 (2 fmly) (7 GF) **S** £59-£79; **D** £84-£92 (incl. bkfst)* **Facilities** FTV Xmas New Year Wi-fi **Conf** Thtr 100 **Parking** 34 **Notes** LB ⊗ Civ Wed 100

RENFREW

For hotels see Glasgow Airport

RHU Map 20 NS28
Argyll & Bute

Rosslea Hall Hotel

★★★ 78% HOTEL

☎ 01436 439955 📠 01436 820897
Ferry Rd G84 8NF
dir: On A814, opposite church

Overlooking the Firth of the Clyde and close to Helensburgh, this imposing mansion is set in its own well tended gardens. Bedrooms and bathrooms are of a good size, well appointed and cater well for the modern traveller. The eating options include The Conservatory Restaurant, overlooking the grounds, and the Clyde which offers dishes prepared with imagination and flair. The hotel is a popular wedding venue.

Rooms 30 (3 fmly) (2 GF) **Facilities** FTV Xmas New Year Wi-fi **Conf** Class 60 Board 80 Thtr 150 **Parking** 30 **Notes** ⊗ Civ Wed 110

ROY BRIDGE Map 22 NN28
Highland

Best Western Glenspean Lodge Hotel

★★★ 83% HOTEL

☎ 01397 712223 📠 01397 712660
PH31 4AW
e-mail: reservations@glenspeanlodge.co.uk
web: www.glenspeanlodge.com
dir: 2m E of Roy Bridge, exit A82 at Spean Bridge onto A86

With origins as a hunting lodge dating back to the Victorian era, this hotel sits in gardens in an elevated position in the Spean Valley. Accommodation is provided in well laid out bedrooms, some suitable for families. Inviting public areas include a comfortable lounge bar and a restaurant that enjoys stunning views of the valley.

Rooms 17 (4 fmly) **Facilities** Gym Sauna Xmas New Year Wi-fi **Conf** Class 16 **Parking** 60 **Notes** Civ Wed 60

The Stronlossit Inn

★★★ 77% SMALL HOTEL

☎ 01397 712253 📠 01397 712641
PH31 4AG
e-mail: stay@stronlossit.co.uk
web: www.stronlossit.co.uk
dir: Exit A82 at Spean Bridge onto A86, signed Roy Bridge. Hotel on left

Appointed to modern standards with the character and hospitality of a traditional hostelry, The Stronlossit Inn is proving quite a draw for the discerning Highland tourist. The spacious bar is the focal point, with a peat burning fire providing a warm welcome in cooler months; guests can eat in the attractive restaurant. Bedrooms come in a mix of sizes and styles, most being smartly modern and well equipped.

Rooms 10 (5 GF) **Facilities** Wi-fi **Parking** 30 **Notes** ⊗ No children 17yrs Closed 1-15 Dec

ST ANDREWS Map 21 NO51
Fife

INSPECTORS' CHOICE

The Old Course Hotel, Golf Resort & Spa

★★★★★ ◎◎◎ HOTEL

☎ 01334 474371 📠 01334 477668
KY16 9SP
e-mail: reservations@oldcoursehotel.co.uk
dir: M90 junct 8, A91 to St Andrews

A haven for golfers, this internationally renowned hotel sits adjacent to the 17th hole of the championship course. Bedrooms vary in size and style but all provide decadent levels of luxury. Day rooms include intimate lounges, a bright conservatory, a spa and a range of pro golf shops. The fine dining Road Hole Restaurant, the Sands Grill specialising in seafood and steaks, and the informal Jigger Inn are all popular eating venues. Staff throughout are friendly and services are impeccably delivered.

Rooms 144 (5 fmly) (3 GF) **S** £170-£1535; **D** £200-£1535 (incl. bkfst) **Facilities** Spa STV FTV 18 Putt green Gym Thermal suite Xmas New Year Wi-fi **Conf** Class 473 Board 259 Thtr 950 Del from £250 to £1395 **Services** Lift **Parking** 125 **Notes** LB ⊗ Civ Wed 180

Fairmont St Andrews, Scotland

★★★★★ 85% @@ HOTEL

☎ 01334 837000 📠 01334 471115
KY16 8PN
e-mail: standrews.scotland@fairmont.com
dir: Approx 2m from St Andrews on A917 towards Crail

Sitting just a few miles from St Andrews, overlooking the rugged Fife coastline and the championship golf courses, The Fairmont is situated on a 520-acre estate. There are spacious bedrooms and bathrooms. The eating options are The Squire for brasserie-style food, Esperante for Mediterranean dishes, and The Clubhouse and The Atrium with all-day menus. The hotel has an impressive spa and health club. Good standards of service are found throughout.

Rooms 209 **Facilities** Spa STV FTV 36 Putt green Gym Xmas New Year Wi-fi **Conf** Class 450 Board 168 Thtr 500 **Services** Lift Air con **Parking** 150 **Notes** Civ Wed 350

INSPECTORS' CHOICE

Rufflets Country House

★★★★ @@ HOTEL

☎ 01334 472594 📠 01334 478703
Strathkinness Low Rd KY16 9TX
e-mail: reservations@rufflets.co.uk
web: www.rufflets.co.uk
dir: 1.5m W on B939

This charming property is set in extensive gardens a few minutes' drive from the town centre. Stylish, spacious bedrooms are individually decorated. Public rooms include a well-stocked bar, a choice of inviting lounges and the delightful Terrace Restaurant that serves imaginative, carefully prepared cuisine. Impressive conference and banqueting facilities are available in the adjacent Garden Suite.

Rooms 24 (5 annexe) (2 fmly) (5 GF) **S** £125-£255; **D** £130-£265 (incl. bkfst)* **Facilities** STV FTV Putt green Golf driving net Children's outdoor games Xmas New Year Wi-fi **Conf** Class 60 Board 60 Thtr 200 Del from £175 to £280* **Parking** 50 **Notes** Civ Wed 130

Macdonald Rusacks

MACDONALD HOTELS & RESORTS

★★★★ 75% @@ HOTEL

☎ 0844 879 9136 & 01334 474321
📠 01334 477896
Pilmour Links KY16 9JQ
e-mail: general.rusacks@macdonald-hotels.co.uk
web: www.macdonald-hotels.co.uk
dir: From A91 W, straight on at rdbt into St Andrews. Hotel 220yds on left

This long-established hotel enjoys an almost unrivalled location with superb views across the famous golf course. Bedrooms, though varying in size, are comfortably appointed and well equipped. Classically styled public rooms include an elegant reception lounge are contrasted with a modern restaurant and brasserie bar.

Rooms 70 (1 annexe) **Facilities** STV FTV New Year Wi-fi **Conf** Class 35 Board 20 Thtr 80 Del from £185 to £485* **Services** Lift **Parking** 21 **Notes** Civ Wed 60

Best Western Scores

★★★ 79% HOTEL

☎ 01334 472451 📠 01334 473947
76 The Scores KY16 9BB
e-mail: reception@scoreshotel.co.uk
web: www.bw-scoreshotel.co.uk
dir: M90 junct 2a onto A92 E'bound. Follow Glenrothes signs then St Andrews signs. Straight on at 2 rdbts, then left into Golf Place, right into The Scores

Enjoying views over St Andrews Bay, this well presented hotel is situated only a short pitch from the first tee of the famous Old Course. Bedrooms are impressively furnished and come in various sizes; many are quite spacious. Smart public areas include Champions Grill offering food all day from breakfast to dinner; Scottish High Teas are served here from 4.30-6.30pm. Alexander's Restaurant opens Thursday, Friday and Saturdays evenings.

Rooms 30 (1 fmly) **S** £87-£206; **D** £128-£295 (incl. bkfst)* **Facilities** FTV Xmas New Year Wi-fi **Conf** Class 60 Board 40 Thtr 180 Del from £142 to £199* **Services** Lift **Parking** 12 **Notes** LB Civ Wed 100

Russell Hotel

★★ 81% @ HOTEL

☎ 01334 473447 📠 01334 478279
26 The Scores KY16 9AS
e-mail: russellhotel@talk21.com
dir: From A91 left at 2nd rdbt into Golf Place, right in 200yds into The Scores, hotel in 300yds on left

Lying on the east bay, this friendly, family-run Victorian terrace hotel provides well appointed bedrooms in varying sizes; some enjoy fine sea views. Cosy public areas include a popular bar and an intimate restaurant, both offering a good range of freshly prepared dishes. Situated in St Andrews, said to be 'The Home of Golf', this hotel offers a comprehensive range of golfing breaks, and is convenient for visits to the castle, cathedral and university.

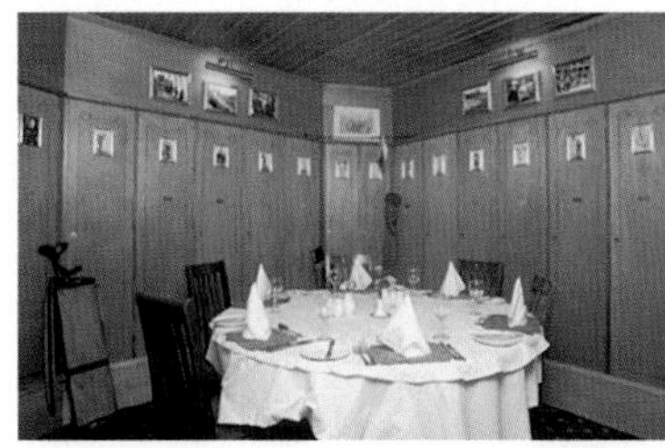

Rooms 10 (3 fmly) **Facilities** New Year **Notes**

S

ST BOSWELLS
Scottish Borders
Map 21 NT53

Dryburgh Abbey Hotel

★★★★ 73% COUNTRY HOUSE HOTEL

01835 822261 01835 823945
TD6 0RQ
e-mail: enquiries@dryburgh.co.uk
web: www.dryburgh.co.uk
dir: B6356 signed Scott's View & Earlston. Through Clintmains, 1.8m to hotel

Found in the heart of the Scottish Borders, and sitting beside to the ancient ruins of Dryburgh Abbey and the majestic River Tweed. This country house hotel, dating from the mid-19th century, offers comfortable public areas and an array of bedrooms and suites, each still displaying original features. The award-winning Tweed Restaurant, overlooking the river, showcases the chef's dedication to producing modern Scottish cuisine, and The Abbey Bistro offers food from noon until 9pm.

Rooms 38 (31 fmly) (8 GF) **Facilities** FTV Putt green Fishing Sauna Xmas New Year Wi-fi **Conf** Class 80 Board 60 Thtr 150 **Services** Lift **Parking** 70 **Notes** Civ Wed 120

ST FILLANS
Perth & Kinross
Map 20 NN62

The Four Seasons Hotel

★★★ 83% HOTEL

01764 685333 01764 685444
Loch Earn PH6 2NF
e-mail: info@thefourseasonshotel.co.uk
web: www.thefourseasonshotel.co.uk
dir: On A85, towards W of village

Set on the edge of Loch Earn, this welcoming hotel and many of its bedrooms benefit from fine views. There is a choice of lounges, including a library, warmed by log fires during winter. Local produce is used to good effect in both the Meall Reamhar restaurant and the more informal Tarken Room.

Rooms 18 (6 annexe) (7 fmly) **S** £54-£108; **D** £108-£166 (incl. bkfst) **Facilities** FTV Xmas New Year Wi-fi **Conf** Class 45 Board 38 Thtr 95 **Parking** 40 **Notes** LB Closed 2 Jan-mid Feb RS Nov, Dec, Mar Civ Wed 80

Achray House Hotel

★★★ 77% HOTEL

0845 557 0774
PH6 2NF
e-mail: info@achrayhouse.com
dir: End of M9 onto A9. At Greenloaning take B822. Through Braco, left onto B827 to Comrie. Left onto A85 to St Fillans

Overlooking the tranquil Loch Earn and surrounded by lush green hills, Achray House offers wonderful panoramic views and a chance to 'get away from it all'. It is in an ideal location to explore the Trossachs National Park and southern Highlands. The well equipped bedrooms come in various sizes and include a suite with a lounge area; most rooms have loch views. The restaurant serves imaginative dishes on a monthly-changing menu. The service is friendly and helpful.

Rooms 8 (3 GF) **S** £60-£80; **D** £80-£150 (incl. bkfst) **Facilities** Xmas New Year Wi-fi **Conf** Class 20 Board 20 Thtr 20 **Parking** 30 **Notes** LB Closed Jan-2 Feb Civ Wed 50

S

SANQUHAR Dumfries & Galloway **Map 21 NS70**

Blackaddie House Hotel

★★★ 79% @@ COUNTRY HOUSE HOTEL

☎ 01659 502700
Blackaddie Rd DG4 6JJ
e-mail: ian@blackaddiehotel.co.uk
dir: Exit A76 just N of Sanquhar at Burnside Service Station. Take private road to hotel 300mtrs on right

Overlooking the River Nith and in two acres of secluded gardens, this family run country house hotel offers friendly and attentive hands-on service. The bedrooms and suites, including family accommodation, are all well presented and comfortable with many useful extras provided as standard. The award-winning food, served in the restaurant, with its lovely garden views, is based on prime Scottish ingredients.

Rooms 9 (3 annexe) (2 fmly) (3 GF) **Facilities** Xmas New Year Wi-fi **Conf** Class 12 Board 16 Thtr 20 **Parking** 20 **Notes** Civ Wed 24

See advert on opposite page

SCOURIE Highland **Map 22 NC14**

Scourie

★★★ 73% SMALL HOTEL

☎ 01971 502396 🖷 01971 502423
IV27 4SX
e-mail: patrick@scourie-hotel.co.uk
dir: N'bound on A894. Hotel in village on left

This well-established hotel is an angler's paradise with extensive fishing rights available on a 25,000-acre estate. Public areas include a choice of comfortable lounges, a cosy bar and a smart dining room offering wholesome fare. The bedrooms are comfortable and generally spacious. The resident proprietors and their staff create a relaxed and friendly atmosphere.

Rooms 20 (2 annexe) (2 fmly) (5 GF) **S** £43-£54; **D** £82-£102 (incl. bkfst)* **Facilities** Fishing Wi-fi **Parking** 30 **Notes** LB Closed mid Oct-end Mar RS winter evenings

SELKIRK Scottish Borders **Map 21 NT42**

Best Western Philipburn Country House

★★★★ COUNTRY HOUSE HOTEL

☎ 01750 20747 🖷 01750 21690
Linglie Rd TD7 5LS
e-mail: info@philipburnhousehotel.co.uk
dir: From A7 follow signs for A72/A707 Peebles/Moffat. Hotel 1m from town centre

Rooms 12 (2 fmly) **S** £90-£140; **D** £100-£185 (incl. bkfst)* **Facilities** FTV Xmas New Year Wi-fi **Conf** Class 12 Board 24 Thtr 40 **Parking** 52 **Notes** LB Closed 6-15 Jan Civ Wed 85

SHIEL BRIDGE Highland **Map 22 NG91**

Grants at Craigellachie

@ RESTAURANT WITH ROOMS

☎ 01599 511331
Craigellachie, Ratagan IV40 8HP
e-mail: info@housebytheloch.co.uk
dir: From A87 exit for Glenelg, 1st right to Ratagan, opposite Youth Hostel sign

Sitting on the tranquil shores of Loch Duin and overlooked by the Five Sisters Mountains, Grants really does occupy a stunning location. The restaurant has a well deserved reputation for its cuisine, and the bedrooms are stylish and have all the creature comforts. Guests are guaranteed a warm welcome at this charming house.

Rooms 4 (2 annexe)

SHIELDAIG Highland **Map 22 NG85**

INSPECTORS' CHOICE

Tigh an Eilean

★ @@ SMALL HOTEL

☎ 01520 755251 🖷 01520 755321
IV54 8XN
e-mail: tighaneilean@keme.co.uk
dir: Exit A896 & follow Shieldaig signs, hotel in village centre

A splendid location by the sea, with views over the bay, is the icing on the cake for this delightful small hotel. It can be a long drive to reach Sheildaig but guests remark that the journey is more than worth the effort. The brightly decorated bedrooms are comfortable though don't expect television, except in one of the lounges. For many, it's the food that attracts, with fish and seafood featuring strongly.

Rooms 11 (1 fmly) **S** fr £70; **D** fr £140 (incl. bkfst)* **Facilities** Birdwatching Kayaks Astronomical telescope Xmas New Year Wi-fi **Parking** 15 **Notes** LB RS late Oct-mid Mar

S

SORN East Ayrshire **Map 20 NS52**

The Sorn Inn

@@ RESTAURANT WITH ROOMS

☎ 01290 551305 🖷 01290 553470
35 Main St KA5 6HU
e-mail: craig@sorninn.com
dir: A70 from S or A76 from N onto B743 to Sorn

Centrally situated in this rural village, which is convenient for many of Ayrshire's attractions, this inn has a fine dining restaurant with a cosy lounge area. There is also a popular chop house with a pub-like environment. The freshly decorated bedrooms have comfortable beds and good facilities.

Rooms 4 (1 fmly)

SOUTH BALLACHULISH
Highland — Map 22 NN05

The Ballachulish Hotel

★★★ 77% HOTEL

☎ 0845 609 9966 📠 01855 811629
PH49 4JY
e-mail: reservations@akkeron-hotels.com
web: www.akkeron-hotels.com
dir: On A828 (Fort William-Oban road), 3m N of Glencoe

On the shores of Loch Linnhe and at the foot of dramatic Glencoe, guests are assured of a warm welcome here. A selection of bar meals is available at lunchtime, and evening meals are served in the Bulas Bistro which overlooks the stunning mountain scenery. The tastefully decorated bedrooms include the six Chieftain Rooms which are particularly comfortable.

Rooms 53 (2 fmly) (7 GF) **Facilities** Xmas New Year Wi-fi **Conf** Board 20 **Parking** 60 **Notes** Civ Wed 65

SOUTH QUEENSFERRY
City of Edinburgh — Map 21 NT17

Premier Inn Edinburgh (Newcraighall)

BUDGET HOTEL

☎ 0871 527 8362 📠 0871 527 8363
91 Newcraighall Rd, Newcraighall EH21 8RX
dir: At junct of A1 & A6095 follow Musselburgh signs

High quality, budget accommodation ideal for both families and business travellers. Spacious, en suite bedrooms feature tea and coffee making facilities, and Freeview TV in most hotels. Internet access and Wi-fi are available for a small fee. The adjacent family restaurant features a wide and varied menu. See also the Hotel Groups pages.

Rooms 42 **D** £62-£65*

Premier Inn Edinburgh (South Queensferry)

BUDGET HOTEL

☎ 0871 527 8364 📠 0871 527 8365
Builyeon Rd EH30 9YJ
dir: M8 junct 2 follow M9 Stirling signs, exit at junct 1A take A8000 towards Forth Road Bridge, at 3rd rdbt 2nd exit into Builyeon Rd (NB do not go onto Forth Road Bridge)

Rooms 70 **D** £60-£63*

SPEAN BRIDGE
Highland — Map 22 NN28

Smiddy House

🏵🏵 RESTAURANT WITH ROOMS

☎ 01397 712335 📠 01397 712043
Roy Bridge Rd PH34 4EU
e-mail: enquiry@smiddyhouse.co.uk
web: www.smiddyhouse.co.uk
dir: In village centre, A82 onto A86

Set in the Great Glen which stretches from Fort William to Inverness, this was once the village smithy, and is now a very friendly establishment. The attractive bedrooms, named after places in Scotland, are comfortably furnished and well equipped. A relaxing garden room is available for guest use. Delicious evening meals are served in Russell's restaurant.

Rooms 4 (1 fmly)

STEPPS
North Lanarkshire — Map 20 NS66

Premier Inn Glasgow North East (Stepps)

BUDGET HOTEL

☎ 0871 527 8452 📠 0871 527 8453
Crowood Roundabout, Cumbernauld Rd G33 6HN
dir: M8 junct 12, A80 (becomes dual carriageway) to Crowwood rdbt, 4th exit back onto A80, hotel 1st left. Or exit M80 at Crowwood rdbt, 3rd exit signed A80 West. Hotel 1st left

High quality, budget accommodation ideal for both families and business travellers. Spacious, en suite bedrooms feature tea and coffee making facilities, and Freeview TV in most hotels. Internet access and Wi-fi are available for a small fee. The adjacent family restaurant features a wide and varied menu. See also the Hotel Groups pages.

Rooms 80 **D** £54-£60*

STIRLING
Stirling — Map 21 NS79

Barceló Stirling Highland Hotel

★★★★ 75% HOTEL

☎ 01786 272727 📠 01786 272829
Spittal St FK8 1DU
e-mail: stirling@barcelo-hotels.co.uk
web: www.barcelo-hotels.co.uk
dir: A84 into Stirling. Follow Stirling Castle signs to Albert Hall. Left, left again, follow Castle signs

Enjoying a location close to the castle and historic town, this atmospheric hotel was previously a high school. Public rooms have been converted from the original classrooms and retain many interesting features. Bedrooms are more modern in style and comfortably equipped. Scholars Restaurant serves traditional and international dishes, and the Headmaster's Study is the ideal venue for enjoying a drink.

Rooms 96 (4 fmly) **Facilities** Spa STV supervised Gym Squash Steam room Dance studio Beauty therapist Xmas New Year Wi-fi **Conf** Class 80 Board 60 Thtr 100 **Services** Lift **Parking** 96 **Notes** Civ Wed 100

Holiday Inn Express - Stirling

BUDGET HOTEL

☎ 01786 449922 📠 01786 449932
Springkerse Business Park FK7 7XH
e-mail: info@expressstirling.co.uk
web: www.hiexpress.com/stirling
dir: M9, M80 junct 9, A91 (Stirling/St Andrews exit). 2.8m, at 4th rdbt, take 2nd exit to sports stadium, 3rd exit to hotel

A modern hotel ideal for families and business travellers. Fresh and uncomplicated, the spacious rooms include Sky TV, power shower and tea and coffee-making facilities. Continental buffet breakfast is included in the room rate; other meals may be taken at the nearby family pub or restaurant. See also the Hotel Groups pages.

Rooms 80 (36 fmly) **S** £59-£119; **D** £59-£129 (incl. bkfst)* **Conf** Class 14 Board 18 Thtr 30

S

Premier Inn Stirling

BUDGET HOTEL

☎ 0871 527 9038 📠 0871 527 9039
Glasgow Rd, Whins of Milton FK7 8EX
dir: On A872, 0.25m from M9/M80 junct 9

High quality, budget accommodation ideal for both families and business travellers. Spacious, en suite bedrooms feature tea and coffee making facilities, and Freeview TV in most hotels. Internet access and Wi-fi are available for a small fee. The adjacent family restaurant features a wide and varied menu. See also the Hotel Groups pages.

Rooms 60 **D** £59-£65*

STRACHUR Map 20 NN00
Argyll & Bute

Creggans Inn

★★★ 82% ◎◎ HOTEL

☎ 01369 860279 📠 01369 860637
PA27 8BX
e-mail: info@creggans-inn.co.uk
web: www.creggans-inn.co.uk
dir: A82 from Glasgow, at Tarbet take A83 towards Cairndow, left onto A815 to Strachur

Benefiting from a superb location on the shores of Loch Fyne, this well established family-run hotel caters well for both the leisure and corporate market. Many of the bedrooms are generous in size and enjoy picture postcard views of the loch. During the cooler months open log fires are lit in the bar lounge and restaurant. Wi-fi is available throughout.

Rooms 14 (2 fmly) **Facilities** New Year Wi-fi **Parking** 16 **Notes** Civ Wed 80

STRANRAER Map 20 NX06
Dumfries & Galloway

Corsewall Lighthouse Hotel

★★★ 80% ◎ HOTEL

☎ 01776 853220 📠 01776 854231
Corsewall Point, Kirkcolm DG9 0QG
e-mail: lighthousehotel@btinternet.com
web: www.lighthousehotel.co.uk
dir: A718 from Stranraer to Kirkcolm (approx 8m). Follow hotel signs for 4m

Looking for something completely different? This is a unique hotel converted from buildings that adjoin a Grade A listed, 19th-century lighthouse set on a rocky coastline. Situated on the headland to the west of Loch Ryan, the lighthouse beam still functions to warn approaching ships. Bedrooms come in a variety of sizes, some reached by a spiral staircase, and like the public areas, are cosy and atmospheric. The cottage suites in the grounds offer greater space. The restaurant menus are based on Scottish produce such as venison and salmon.

Rooms 11 (5 annexe) (4 fmly) (2 GF) (3 smoking) **Facilities** FTV Xmas New Year Wi-fi **Conf** Thtr 20 **Parking** 20 **Notes** ⊗ Civ Wed 28

STRATHAVEN Map 20 NS74
South Lanarkshire

Rissons at Springvale

◎ RESTAURANT WITH ROOMS

☎ 01357 521131 & 520234 📠 01357 521131
18 Lethame Rd ML10 6AD
e-mail: rissons@msn.com
dir: A71 into Strathaven, W of town centre off Townhead St

Guests are assured of a warm welcome at this charming establishment close to the town centre. The bedrooms and bathrooms are stylish and well equipped. The main attraction here is the food - a range of interesting, well-prepared dishes served in Rissons Restaurant.

Rooms 9 (1 fmly)

STRATHBLANE Map 20 NS57
Stirling

Strathblane Country House

★★★ 78% COUNTRY HOUSE HOTEL

☎ 01360 770491 📠 01360 770345
Milngavie Rd G63 9EH
e-mail: info@strathblanecountryhouse.co.uk
dir: On A81 (Milngavie Rd) S of Strathblane. Hotel 0.75m past Mugdock Country Park on right

Set in 10-acre grounds looking out on the beautiful Campsie Fells, this majestic property, built in 1874, offers a get-away-from-it-all experience, yet is just a 20-minute drive from Glasgow. Lunch and dinner are served in the relaxed Brasserie Restaurant, and guests can visit the falconry or just kick back and relax in front of the fire with a book and a dram of whisky. Weddings are especially well catered for.

Rooms 10 (3 fmly) **S** £65-£99; **D** £84-£180 (incl. bkfst)* **Facilities** FTV Falconry ♫ Xmas New Year Wi-fi **Conf** Class 60 Board 60 Thtr 180 Del from £115 to £135 **Parking** 120 **Notes** LB ⊗ Civ Wed 180

STRATHYRE Map 20 NN51
Stirling

INSPECTORS' CHOICE

Creagan House

◎◎ RESTAURANT WITH ROOMS

☎ 01877 384638 📠 01877 384319
FK18 8ND
e-mail: eatandstay@creaganhouse.co.uk
web: www.creaganhouse.co.uk
dir: 0.25m N of Strathyre on A84

Originally a farmhouse dating from the 17th century, Creagan House has operated as a restaurant with rooms for many years. The baronial-style dining room provides a wonderful setting for the cuisine which is classic French with some Scottish influences. Warm hospitality and attentive service are the highlights of any stay.

Rooms 5 (1 fmly)

STRONTIAN
Highland — Map 22 NM86

INSPECTORS' CHOICE

Kilcamb Lodge

★★★ @@ COUNTRY HOUSE HOTEL

☎ 01967 402257 📠 01967 402041
PH36 4HY
e-mail: enquiries@kilcamblodge.co.uk
web: www.kilcamblodge.co.uk
dir: Off A861, via Corran Ferry

This historic house on the shores of Loch Sunart was one of the first stone buildings in the area, and was used as military barracks around the time of the Jacobite uprising. It is situated on the beautiful and peaceful Ardamurchan Peninsula where otters, red squirrels and eagles can be spotted. The suites and bedrooms, with either loch or garden views, are stylishly decorated using designer fabrics and have flat-screen TVs, DVD/CD players, plus bath robes, iced water and even guest umbrellas. Accomplished cooking, utilising much local produce, can be enjoyed in the stylish dining room. Warm hospitality is assured.

Rooms 10 (2 fmly) **S** £145-£208; **D** £229-£369 (incl. bkfst & dinner)* **Facilities** FTV Fishing Boating Hiking Bird, whale & otter-watching Stalking Clay pigeon shooting Xmas New Year Wi-fi **Conf** Class 18 Board 18 Thtr 18 Del from £ to £195* **Parking** 20 **Notes** LB No children 10yrs Closed 2 Jan-1 Feb Civ Wed 120

TAIN
Highland — Map 23 NH78

INSPECTORS' CHOICE

Glenmorangie Highland Home at Cadboll

★★★ @@ COUNTRY HOUSE HOTEL

☎ 01862 871671 📠 01862 871625
Cadboll, Fearn IV20 1XP
e-mail: relax@glenmorangie.co.uk
web: www.theglenmorangiehouse.com
dir: Exit A9 onto B9175 towards Nigg. Follow tourist signs

This historic highland home superbly balances top class service with intimate customer care. Evenings are dominated by the highly successful 'house party' where guests are introduced in the drawing room, sample whiskies then take dinner (a set six-course meal) together around one long table. Conversation can extend well into the evening. Stylish bedrooms are divided between the traditional main house and some cosy cottages in the grounds. This is an ideal base from which to enjoy the world famous whisky tours.

Rooms 9 (3 annexe) (4 fmly) (3 GF) **S** £225; **D** £350-£400 (incl. bkfst & dinner)* **Facilities** FTV Archery Beauty treatments Clay pigeon shooting Falconry Xmas New Year Wi-fi **Conf** Board 12 **Parking** 60 **Notes** LB ⊗ No children 15yrs Civ Wed 60

TARBERT LOCH FYNE
Argyll & Bute — Map 20 NR86

Stonefield Castle

★★★★ 73% @ HOTEL

☎ 01880 820836 📠 01880 820929
PA29 6YJ
e-mail: reservations.stonefieldcastle@ohiml.com
web: www.oxfordhotelsandinns.com
dir: From Glasgow take M8 towards Erskine Bridge, onto A82, follow Loch Lomond signs. From Arrochar follow signs for A83 through Inveraray & Lochgilphead, hotel on left, 2m before Tarbert

This fine baronial castle commands a superb lochside setting amidst beautiful woodland gardens renowned for their rhododendrons - visit in late spring to see them at their best. Elegant public rooms are a feature, and the picture-window restaurant offers unrivalled views across Loch Fyne. Bedrooms are split between the main house and a purpose-built wing.

Rooms 32 (2 fmly) (10 GF) **Facilities** Xmas New Year Wi-fi **Conf** Class 40 Board 50 Thtr 120 **Services** Lift **Parking** 50 **Notes** Civ Wed 100

S

THURSO
Highland Map 23 ND16

Forss House

★★★★ 76% ◎◎ SMALL HOTEL

☎ 01847 861201 📠 01847 861301
Forss KW14 7XY
e-mail: anne@forsshousehotel.co.uk
web: www.forsshousehotel.co.uk
dir: On A836 between Thurso & Reay

This delightful country house is set in its own 20 acres of woodland and was originally built in 1810. The hotel offers a choice of bedrooms from the traditional styled rooms in the main house to the more contemporary annexe rooms in the grounds. All rooms are very well equipped and well appointed. The beautiful River Forss runs through the grounds and is a firm favourite with fishermen.

Rooms 14 (6 annexe) (1 fmly) (7 GF) **S** £97-£115; **D** £130-£165 (incl. bkfst)* **Facilities** FTV Fishing Wi-fi **Conf** Class 12 Board 14 Thtr 20 Del from £155 to £170 **Parking** 14 **Notes** LB Closed 23 Dec-3 Jan Civ Wed 26

See advert on this page

T

TORRIDON
Highland
Map 22 NG95

INSPECTORS' CHOICE

The Torridon

★★★★ ®®®
COUNTRY HOUSE HOTEL

☎ 01445 791242 📠 01445 712253
By Achnasheen, Wester Ross IV22 2EY
e-mail: info@thetorridon.com
web: www.thetorridon.com
dir: From A832 at Kinlochewe, take A896 towards Torridon. (NB do not turn into village) 1m, hotel on right

Delightfully set amidst inspiring loch and mountain scenery, this elegant Victorian shooting lodge has been beautifully restored to make the most of its many original features. The attractive bedrooms are all individually furnished and most enjoy stunning Highland views. Comfortable day rooms feature fine wood panelling and roaring fires in cooler months. The first class, modern Scottish cuisine of 'Bruno' Birkbeck can be enjoyed in the restaurant which has magnificent oak-panelling and views to match. The whisky bar is aptly named, boasting over 300 malts and in-depth tasting notes. Outdoor activities include shooting, cycling and walking.

Rooms 19 (2 GF) **S** £140; **D** £215-£425 (incl. bkfst)* **Facilities** STV Fishing Abseiling Archery Climbing Falconry Kayaking Mountain biking Xmas New Year Wi-fi **Conf** Board 16 Thtr 42 Del from £325 to £425* **Services** Lift **Parking** 20 **Notes** Closed 2 Jan-9 Feb RS Nov-14 Mar Civ Wed 42

T

TROON
South Ayrshire
Map 20 NS33

INSPECTORS' CHOICE

Lochgreen House Hotel

★★★★ ®®® COUNTRY HOUSE HOTEL

☎ 01292 313343 📠 01292 318661
Monktonhill Rd, Southwood KA10 7EN
e-mail: lochgreen@costley-hotels.co.uk
web: www.costley-hotels.co.uk
dir: From A77 follow Prestwick Airport signs. 0.5m before airport take B749 to Troon. Hotel 1m on left

Set in immaculately maintained grounds, Lochgreen House is graced by tasteful extensions which have created stunning public rooms and spacious, comfortable and elegantly furnished bedrooms. Extra facilities include a coffee shop, gift shop and beauty treatments in The Retreat. The magnificent Tapestry Restaurant provides the ideal setting for dinners that are immaculately presented.

Rooms 38 (7 annexe) (17 GF) **Facilities** STV Beauty treatments Xmas New Year Wi-fi **Conf** Class 50 Board 50 Thtr 70 **Services** Lift **Parking** 50 **Notes** Civ Wed 140

Barceló Troon Marine Hotel

★★★★ 78% ®® HOTEL

☎ 01292 314444 📠 01292 316922
Crosbie Rd KA10 6HE
e-mail: marine@barcelo-hotels.co.uk
web: www.barcelo-hotels.co.uk
dir: A77, A78, A79 onto B749. Hotel on left after golf course

A favourite with conference and leisure guests, this hotel overlooks Royal Troon's 18th fairway. The cocktail lounge and split-level restaurant enjoy panoramic views of the Firth of Clyde across to the Isle of Arran. Bedrooms and public areas are attractively appointed.

Rooms 89 **Facilities** Spa STV supervised Gym Squash Steam room Beauty room Xmas New Year Wi-fi **Conf** Class 100 Board 40 Thtr 200 **Services** Lift **Parking** 200 **Notes** Civ Wed 100

TURNBERRY
South Ayrshire
Map 20 NS20

INSPECTORS' CHOICE

Turnberry Resort, Scotland

★★★★★ ®® HOTEL

☎ 01655 331000 📠 01655 331706
KA26 9LT
e-mail: turnberry@luxurycollection.com
web: www.luxurycollection.com/turnberry
dir: From Glasgow take A77/M77 S towards Stranraer, 2m past Kirkoswald follow signs for A719/Turnberry. Hotel 500mtrs on right

This famous hotel enjoys magnificent views over to Arran, Ailsa Craig, and the Mull of Kintyre. Facilities include a world-renowned golf course, the excellent Colin Montgomerie Golf Academy, a luxurious spa, and a host of outdoor pursuits. Some superbly modern rooms together with more traditional elegant bedrooms and suites are located in the main hotel, while adjacent lodges provide spacious, well-equipped accommodation. The public areas are stunning. The Ailsa Lounge is very welcoming, and in addition to the elegant 1906 restaurant for dining, there is the fine-dining James Miller room and chef's table.

Rooms 207 (89 annexe) (2 fmly) (12 GF) **Facilities** Spa STV supervised 36 Putt green Fishing Gym Leisure club Outdoor activity centre Colin Montgomerie Golf Academy New Year Wi-fi **Conf** Class 145 Board 80 Thtr 300 **Services** Lift **Parking** 200 **Notes** Closed 25 Dec Civ Wed 220

Malin Court

★★★ 83% HOTEL

☎ 01655 331457 📠 01655 331072
KA26 9PB
e-mail: info@malincourt.co.uk
web: www.malincourt.co.uk
dir: On A74 to Ayr then A719 to Turnberry & Maidens

Forming part of the Malin Court Residential and Nursing Home Complex, this friendly and comfortable hotel enjoys delightful views over the Firth of Clyde and Turnberry golf courses. Standard and executive rooms are available; all are well equipped. Public areas are plentiful, with the restaurant serving high teas, dinners and light lunches.

Rooms 18 (9 fmly) **Facilities** STV Putt green Wi-fi **Conf** Class 60 Board 30 Thtr 200 **Services** Lift **Parking** 110 **Notes** RS Oct-Mar Civ Wed 80

UPHALL
West Lothian
Map 21 NT07

Macdonald Houstoun House

★★★★ 78% ® HOTEL

☎ 0844 879 9043 📠 01506 854220
EH52 6JS
e-mail: houstoun@macdonald-hotels.co.uk
web: www.macdonaldhotels.co.uk
dir: M8 junct 3 follow Broxburn signs, straight over rdbt, at mini-rdbt turn right towards Uphall, hotel 1m on right

This historic 17th-century tower house lies in beautifully landscaped grounds and gardens, and features a modern leisure club and spa, a choice of dining options, a vaulted cocktail bar and extensive conference and meeting facilities. Stylish bedrooms, some located around a courtyard, are comfortably furnished and well equipped.

Rooms 73 (47 annexe) (12 fmly) (12 GF) **Facilities** Spa STV FTV Gym Health & beauty salon Xmas New Year Wi-fi **Conf** Class 80 Board 80 Thtr 400 **Parking** 250 **Notes** Civ Wed 200

UPLAWMOOR
East Renfrewshire
Map 20 NS45

Uplawmoor Hotel

★★★ 80% ® HOTEL

☎ 01505 850565 📠 01505 850689
Neilston Rd G78 4AF
e-mail: info@uplawmoor.co.uk
web: www.uplawmoor.co.uk
dir: M77 junct 2, A736 signed Barrhead & Irvine. Hotel 4m beyond Barrhead

Originally a coaching inn, this friendly hotel is set in a village off the Glasgow to Irvine road. The relaxed restaurant (with cocktail lounge adjacent) features imaginative dishes, whilst the separate lounge bar is popular for freshly prepared bar meals. The modern bedrooms are both comfortable and well equipped.

Rooms 14 (1 fmly) (2 smoking) **S** £60-£70; **D** £85-£95 (incl. bkfst)* **Facilities** STV Wi-fi **Conf** Class 12 Board 20 Thtr 40 Del from £85 to £105* **Parking** 40 **Notes** LB Closed 26 Dec & 1 Jan

WHITEBRIDGE
Highland
Map 23 NH41

Whitebridge Hotel

★★ 69% HOTEL

☎ 01456 486226 📠 01456 486413
IV2 6UN
e-mail: info@whitebridgehotel.co.uk
dir: A9 onto B851, follow signs to Fort Augustus. Or A82 onto B862 at Fort Augustus

Close to Loch Ness and set amid rugged mountain and moorland scenery, this hotel is popular with tourists, fishermen and deerstalkers. Guests have a choice of more formal dining in the restaurant or lighter meals in the popular cosy bar. Bedrooms are thoughtfully equipped and brightly furnished.

Rooms 12 (3 fmly) **S** £50-£60; **D** £75-£85 (incl. bkfst)* **Facilities** Fishing Wi-fi **Parking** 32 **Notes** Closed 11 Dec-9 Jan

WICK
Highland
Map 23 ND35

Mackay's

★★★ 75% HOTEL

☎ 01955 602323 📠 01955 605930
Union St KW1 5ED
e-mail: info@mackayshotel.co.uk
dir: Opposite Caithness General Hospital

This well-established hotel is situated just outside the town centre overlooking the River Wick. MacKay's provides well-equipped, attractive accommodation, suited to both the business and leisure guest. There is a stylish bistro offering food throughout the day and a choice of bars that also offer food.

Rooms 30 (2 fmly) **S** £75-£85; **D** £99-£150 (incl. bkfst)* **Facilities** FTV Wi-fi **Conf** Class 100 Board 60 Thtr 100 Del from £115 to £150* **Services** Lift **Notes** LB Closed 24-26 Dec & 1-3 Jan

Scottish Islands

Quiraing Stones, Trotternish, Isle of Skye

ISLE OF ARRAN

BLACKWATERFOOT Map 20 NR92

Best Western Kinloch

★★★ 80% HOTEL

☎ 01770 860444 📠 01770 860447
KA27 8ET
e-mail: reservations@kinlochhotel.eclipse.co.uk
web: www.bw-kinlochhotel.co.uk
dir: Ferry from Ardrossan to Brodick, follow signs for Blackwaterfoot, hotel in village centre

Well known for providing an authentic island experience, this long established stylish hotel is in an idyllic location. Smart public areas include a choice of lounges, popular bars and well-presented leisure facilities. Bedrooms vary in size and style but most enjoy panoramic sea views and several family suites offer excellent value. The spacious restaurant provides a wide ranging menu, and in winter when the restaurant is closed, the bar serves a choice of creative dishes.

Rooms 37 (7 fmly) (7 GF) **Facilities** STV Gym Squash Beauty therapy New Year Wi-fi **Conf** Class 20 Board 40 Thtr 120 **Services** Lift **Parking** 2 **Notes** Civ Wed 60

SCOTTISH ISLANDS

BRODICK Map 20 NS03

INSPECTORS' CHOICE

Kilmichael Country House

★★★ COUNTRY HOUSE HOTEL

☎ 01770 302219 📠 01770 302068
Glen Cloy KA27 8BY
e-mail: enquiries@kilmichael.com
web: www.kilmichael.com
dir: From Brodick ferry terminal towards Lochranza for 1m. Left at golf course, follow signs

Reputed to be the oldest on the island, this lovely house lies in attractive gardens in a quiet glen less than five minutes' drive from the ferry terminal. It has been lovingly restored to create a stylish, elegant country house, adorned with ornaments from around the world. There are two inviting drawing rooms and a bright dining room, serving award-winning contemporary cuisine. The delightful bedrooms are furnished in classical style; some are contained in a pretty courtyard conversion.

Rooms 8 (3 annexe) (7 GF) **S** £78-£98; **D** £130-£163 (incl. bkfst)* **Facilities** Wi-fi **Parking** 14 **Notes** LB No children 12yrs Closed Nov-Feb (ex for prior bookings)

ISLE OF HARRIS

SCARISTA (SGARASTA BHEAG) Map 22 NG09

Scarista House

RESTAURANT WITH ROOMS

☎ 01859 550238 📠 01859 550277
HS3 3HX
e-mail: timandpatricia@scaristahouse.com
dir: On A859, 15m S of Tarbert

A former manse, Scarista House is a haven for food lovers who seek to explore this magnificent island. It enjoys breathtaking views of the Atlantic and is just a short stroll from miles of golden sandy beaches. The house is run in a relaxed country-house manner by the friendly hosts. Expect wellies in the hall and masses of books and CDs in one of two lounges. Bedrooms are cosy, and delicious set dinners and memorable breakfasts are provided.

Rooms 5 (2 annexe)

TARBERT Map 22 NB10

Hotel Hebrides

★★★★ 78% HOTEL

☎ 01859 502364 📠 01839 502578
Pier Rd HS3 3DG
e-mail: stay@hotel-hebrides.com
dir: To Tarbert via ferry from Uig (Isle of Skye); or ferry from Ullapool to Stornaway, A859 to Tarbert; or by plane to Stornaway from Glasgow, Edinburgh or Inverness

Benefiting from an elevated position overlooking the town this hotel is just a few minutes' walk from the centre. The small, hands-on team extend wonderful hospitality and customer care. The bedrooms are stylishly designed and include Wi-fi, high speed internet access and flat-screen TVs; the deluxe rooms have iPod docking stations and some rooms have loch and harbour views. Award-winning food is served in the Pierhouse Restaurant. A complimentary bus service is provided to the theatre in the summer months.

Rooms 21

ISLE OF ISLAY

PORT ASKAIG Map 20 NR46

Port Askaig

★★ 62% SMALL HOTEL

☎ 01496 840245 📠 01496 840295
PA46 7RD
e-mail: hotel@portaskaig.co.uk
web: www.portaskaig.co.uk
dir: At ferry terminal

The building of this endearing family-run hotel dates back to the 18th-century. The lounge provides fine views over the Sound of Islay to Jura, and there is a choice of bars that are popular with locals. Traditional dinners are served in the bright restaurant and a full range of bar snacks and meals is also available. The bedrooms are smart and comfortable.

Rooms 8 (1 fmly) (8 GF) **Parking** 21

ISLE OF MULL

TOBERMORY Map 22 NM55

INSPECTORS' CHOICE

Highland Cottage

★★★ ®® SMALL HOTEL

☎ 01688 302030
Breadalbane St PA75 6PD
e-mail: davidandjo@highlandcottage.co.uk
web: www.highlandcottage.co.uk
dir: A848 Craignure/Fishnish ferry terminal, pass Tobermory signs, straight on at mini rdbt across narrow bridge, turn right. Hotel on right opposite fire station

Providing the highest level of natural and unassuming hospitality, this delightful little gem lies high above the island's capital. Don't be fooled by its side street location, a stunning view over the bay is just a few metres away. 'A country house hotel in town' it is an Aladdin's Cave of collectables and treasures, as well as masses of books and magazines. There are two inviting lounges, one with an honesty bar. The cosy dining room offers memorable dinners and splendid breakfasts. Bedrooms are individual; some have four-posters and all are comprehensively equipped to include TVs and music centres.

Rooms 6 (1 GF) **S** £110-£150; **D** £150-£185 (incl. bkfst)* **Facilities** FTV Wi-fi **Parking** 6 **Notes** LB No children 10yrs Closed Nov-Mar

Tobermory

★★ 80% ® HOTEL

☎ 01688 302091 📠 01688 302254
53 Main St PA75 6NT
e-mail: tobhotel@tinyworld.co.uk
web: www.thetobermoryhotel.com
dir: On waterfront

This friendly hotel, with its pretty pink frontage, sits on the seafront amid other brightly coloured, picture-postcard buildings. There is a comfortable and relaxing lounge where drinks are served prior to dining in the stylish restaurant (there is no bar). Bedrooms come in a variety of sizes; all are bright and vibrant.

Rooms 16 (2 fmly) (2 GF) **S** £38-£65; **D** £76-£128 (incl. bkfst)* **Facilities** FTV New Year Wi-fi **Conf** Class 26 Board 15 Thtr 26 **Notes** Closed Xmas

ORKNEY

ST MARGARET'S HOPE Map 24 ND49

The Creel Restaurant with Rooms

®® RESTAURANT WITH ROOMS

☎ 01856 831311
Front Rd KW17 2SL
e-mail: alan@thecreel.freeserve.co.uk
web: www.thecreel.co.uk
dir: A961 into village, establishment on seafront

With wonderful sea views, The Creel enjoys a prominent position in the pretty fishing village of St Margaret's Hope. The award-winning restaurant has a well deserved reputation for the quality of its seafood and a window seat is a must in the charming restaurant. The stylish bedrooms are appointed to a high standard and most enjoy views over the bay. Breakfasts should not be missed, with local Orkney produce and freshly baked breads on the menu.

Rooms 3

SHETLAND

LERWICK Map 24 HU44

Shetland

★★★ 73% HOTEL

☎ 01595 695515 📠 01595 695828
Holmsgarth Rd ZE1 0PW
e-mail: reception@shetlandhotel.co.uk
dir: Opposite ferry terminal, on main road N from town centre

This purpose-built hotel, situated opposite the main ferry terminal, offers spacious and comfortable bedrooms on three floors. Two dining options are available - the informal Oasis bistro and Ninians Restaurant. Service is prompt and friendly.

Rooms 64 (4 fmly) **S** £89; **D** £120 (incl. bkfst)* **Facilities** FTV Wi-fi **Conf** Class 75 Board 50 Thtr 300 **Services** Lift **Parking** 150 **Notes** ®

ISLE OF SKYE

ARDVASAR Map 22 NG60

Ardvasar Hotel

★★★ 74% SMALL HOTEL

☎ 01471 844223 📠 01471 844495
Sleat IV45 8RS
e-mail: richard@ardvasar-hotel.demon.co.uk
web: www.ardvasarhotel.com
dir: From ferry, 500mtrs, turn left signed Ardvasar

The Isle of Skye is dotted with cosy, welcoming hotels that make touring the island easy and convenient. This hotel ranks highly amongst its peers thanks to great hospitality and a preservation of community spirit. The hotel sits less than five minutes' drive from the Mallaig ferry and provides comfortable bedrooms and a cosy bar lounge for residents. Seafood is prominent on menus, and meals can be enjoyed in either the popular bar or the attractive dining room.

Rooms 10 (4 fmly) **Facilities** FTV ♫ Xmas New Year Wi-fi **Conf** Board 24 Thtr 50 **Parking** 30 **Notes** LB

See advert on oppostie page

BROADFORD Map 22 NG62

Broadford Hotel

★★★★ 74% SMALL HOTEL

☎ 01471 822204 📠 01471 822414
IV49 9AB
e-mail: broadford@macleodhotels.co.uk
dir: From Skye Bridge take A87 towards Portree. Hotel at end of village on left

A stylish modern hotel, in the centre of this charming town, that has been appointed to a high standard and offers all the creature comforts. Many of the spacious bedrooms have wonderful sea views and all are attractively presented and very well equipped. Meals can be enjoyed in the fine-dining restaurant or more informal options are served in traditional bar.

Rooms 11 (1 fmly) **Facilities** STV Fishing ♫ Xmas New Year Wi-fi **Conf** Class 80 Board 50 Thtr 150 **Parking** 20 **Notes** LB Civ Wed 100

COLBOST Map 22 NG24

INSPECTORS' CHOICE

The Three Chimneys and House Over-By

◎◎◎ RESTAURANT WITH ROOMS

☎ 01470 511258
IV55 8ZT
e-mail: eatandstay@threechimneys.co.uk
dir: 4m W of Dunvegan village on B884 signed Glendale

A visit to this delightful property will make a trip to Skye even more memorable. The stunning food is the result of a deft approach using quality local ingredients. Breakfast is an impressive array of local fish, meats and cheeses, served with fresh home baking and home-made preserves. The new stylish lounge-breakfast area has the real wow factor. Bedrooms, in the House Over-By, are creative and thoughtfully equipped - all have spacious en suites and wonderful views across Loch Dunvegan.

Rooms 6 (1 fmly) (6 GF)

ISLEORNSAY Map 22 NG71

Duisdale House

★★★★ 80% ◎◎ SMALL HOTEL

☎ 01471 833202 📠 01471 833404
IV43 8QW
e-mail: info@duisdale.com
web: www.duisdale.com
dir: 7m S of Bradford on A851 towards Armadale. 7m N of Armadale ferry

This grand Victorian house stands in its own landscaped gardens overlooking the Sound of Sleat. The hotel has a contemporary chic style which complements the original features of the house. Each bedroom is individually designed and the superior rooms have four-poster beds. The elegant lounge has sumptuous sofas, original artwork and blazing log fires in the colder months.

Rooms 18 (1 fmly) (1 GF) **S** £90-£180; **D** £170-£260 (incl. bkfst) **Facilities** STV Private yacht Outdoor hydropool Xmas New Year Wi-fi **Conf** Board 28 Thtr 50 Del from £167 to £230 **Parking** 30 **Notes** LB ® Civ Wed 58

See advert on opposite page

SCOTTISH ISLANDS

ISLEORNSAY *continued*

INSPECTORS' CHOICE

Kinloch Lodge

★★★ ®®® COUNTRY HOUSE HOTEL

☎ 01471 833214 & 833333 🖹 01471 833277
IV43 8QY
e-mail: reservations@kinloch-lodge.co.uk
web: www.kinloch-lodge.co.uk
dir: 6m S of Broadford on A851, 10m N of Armadale on A851

Owned and ran in a hands-on fashion by Lord and Lady MacDonald and their family, this hotel enjoys a picture postcard location surrounded by hills and a sea loch. Bedrooms and bathrooms are well appointed and comfortable, and public areas boast numerous open fires and relaxing areas to sit. There is a cookery school run by Claire MacDonald and a shop that sells her famous cookery books and produce.

Rooms 15 (8 annexe) (1 GF) **S** £240-£290; **D** £300-£420 (incl. bkfst & dinner)* **Facilities** STV FTV Fishing New Year Wi-fi **Conf** Class 20 Board 20 Thtr 20 **Parking** 40

Toravaig House Hotel

★★★ 81% ®® SMALL HOTEL

☎ 01471 820200 & 833231 🖹 01471 833231
Knock Bay IV44 8RE
e-mail: info@skyehotel.co.uk
web: www.skyehotel.co.uk
dir: From Skye Bridge, left at Broadford onto A851, hotel 11m on left. Or from ferry at Armadale take A851, hotel 6m on right

Set in two acres and enjoying panoramic views to the Knoydart Hills, this hotel is a haven of peace, with stylish, well-equipped and beautifully decorated bedrooms. There is an inviting lounge complete with deep sofas and an elegant dining room where delicious meals are the order of the day. The hotel provides a sea-going yacht for guests' exclusive use from April to September.

Rooms 9 **S** £75-£190; **D** £130-£230 (incl. bkfst) **Facilities** STV Daily excursions Apr-Sep on hotel yacht (residents only) Xmas New Year Wi-fi **Conf** Board 10 Thtr 15 Del from £100 to £200 **Parking** 15 **Notes** LB ⊗ Civ Wed 25

See advert on page 615

Hotel Eilean Iarmain

★★★ 78% ®® SMALL HOTEL

☎ 01471 833332 🖹 01471 833275
IV43 8QR
e-mail: hotel@eileaniarmain.co.uk
web: www.eileaniarmain.co.uk
dir: A851, A852, right to Isleornsay harbour

A hotel of charm and character, this 19th-century former inn sits by the pier and enjoys fine views across the sea loch. Bedrooms are individual and retain a traditional style, and a stable block has been converted into four delightful suites. Public rooms are cosy and inviting, and the restaurant offers award-winning menus showcasing the island's best produce, especially seafood and game.

Rooms 16 (10 annexe) (4 fmly) (3 GF) **S** £75-£145; **D** £110-£250 (incl. bkfst) **Facilities** FTV Fishing Shooting Exhibitions Whisky tasting ♫ Xmas New Year Wi-fi **Conf** Class 10 Board 14 Thtr 25 Del from £150 to £195 **Parking** 20 **Notes** LB Civ Wed 30

See advert on opposite page

PORTREE Map 22 NG44

Cuillin Hills

★★★★ 77% HOTEL

☎ 01478 612003 01478 613092
IV51 9QU
e-mail: info@cuillinhills-hotel-skye.co.uk
web: www.cuillinhills-hotel-skye.co.uk
dir: Right 0.25m N of Portree off A855. Follow hotel signs

This imposing building enjoys a superb location overlooking Portree Bay and the Cuillin Hills. Accommodation is provided in smart, well-equipped rooms that are generally spacious; some bedrooms are found in an adjacent building. Public areas include a split-level restaurant that takes advantage of the views. Service is particularly attentive.

Rooms 26 (7 annexe) (3 fmly) (8 GF) **Facilities** STV Xmas New Year Wi-fi **Conf** Class 60 Board 40 Thtr 100 **Parking** 56 **Notes** Civ Wed 45

Rosedale

★★★ 73% HOTEL

☎ 01478 613131 01478 612531
Beaumont Crescent IV51 9DF
e-mail: rosedalehotelsky@aol.com
web: www.rosedalehotelskye.co.uk
dir: Follow directions to village centre & harbour

The atmosphere is wonderfully warm at this delightful family-run waterfront hotel. A labyrinth of stairs and corridors connects the comfortable lounges, bar and charming restaurant, which are set on different levels. The restaurant offers fine views of the bay. Modern bedrooms offer a good range of amenities.

Rosedale

Rooms 18 (1 fmly) (3 GF) **S** £40-£65; **D** £70-£150 (incl. bkfst)* **Facilities** Wi-fi **Parking** 2 **Notes** LB Closed Nov-mid Mar

SCOTTISH ISLANDS

SKEABOST BRIDGE Map 22 NG44

Skeabost Country House

★★★ 75% ® COUNTRY HOUSE HOTEL

☎ 01470 532202 & 08444 146572
📠 01470 532761
IV51 9NP
e-mail: manager.skeabost@ohiml.com
web: www.oxfordhotelsandinns.com
dir: From Skye Bridge on A87, through Portree towards Uig. Left onto A850, hotel on right

This delightful property stands in mature, landscaped grounds at the edge of Loch Snizort. Originally built as a hunting lodge by the MacDonalds and steeped in history, Skeabost offers a welcoming environment from the caring and helpful staff. The hotel provides award-winning food, charming day rooms and well appointed accommodation. The pretty grounds include a challenging 9-hole golf course, and there is salmon and trout fishing nearby. Wi-fi is available.

Rooms 14 (5 GF) **Facilities** STV FTV ⛳ 9 Xmas New Year Wi-fi **Conf** Class 20 Board 20 Thtr 40 Del from £100 to £180* **Parking** 40 **Notes** LB Civ Wed 100

STAFFIN Map 22 NG46

Flodigarry Country House

★★★ 78% ® COUNTRY HOUSE HOTEL

☎ 01470 552203 📠 01470 552301
IV51 9HZ
e-mail: info@flodigarry.co.uk
web: www.flodigarry.co.uk
dir: A855 from Portree, through Staffin to Flodigarry, hotel signed on right

This hotel is located in woodlands on The Quiraing in north-east Skye overlooking the sea towards the Torridon Mountains. The dramatic scenery is a real inspiration here, and this charming house was once the home of the Scotland's heroine, Flora MacDonald. Guests are assured of real Highland hospitality and there is an easy going atmosphere throughout. A full range of activities is offered, with mountain walks, fishing and boat trips proving to be the most popular.

Rooms 18 (7 annexe) (3 fmly) (4 GF) **S** £80-£135; **D** £100-£210 (incl. bkfst)* **Facilities** FTV Xmas New Year Wi-fi **Parking** 40 **Notes** LB Closed Nov-15 Dec & Jan Civ Wed 80

The Glenview

® RESTAURANT WITH ROOMS

☎ 01470 562248
Culnacnoc IV51 9JH
e-mail: enquiries@glenviewskye.co.uk
dir: 12m N of Portree on A855

The Glenview is located in one of the most beautiful parts of Skye with stunning sea views; it is close to the famous rock formation, the Old Man of Storr. The individually styled bedrooms are very comfortable and front-facing rooms enjoy the dramatic views. Evening meals should not to be missed as the restaurant has a well deserved reputation for its locally sourced produce.

Rooms 5

STRUAN Map 22 NG33

INSPECTORS' CHOICE

Ullinish Country Lodge

®®® RESTAURANT WITH ROOMS

☎ 01470 572214 📠 01470 572341
IV56 8FD
e-mail: ullinish@theisleofskye.co.uk
dir: N on A863

Set in some of Scotland's most dramatic landscape, with views of the Black Cuillin and MacLeod's Tables, this lodge has lochs on three sides. Samuel Johnson and James Boswell stayed here in 1773 and were impressed with the hospitality even then! Hosts Brian and Pam hope to extend the same welcome to their guests today. As you would expect, all bedrooms have amazing views, and come with half-tester beds. The cuisine in the restaurant is impressive and uses the best of Skye's produce including locally sourced seafood and game.

Rooms 6

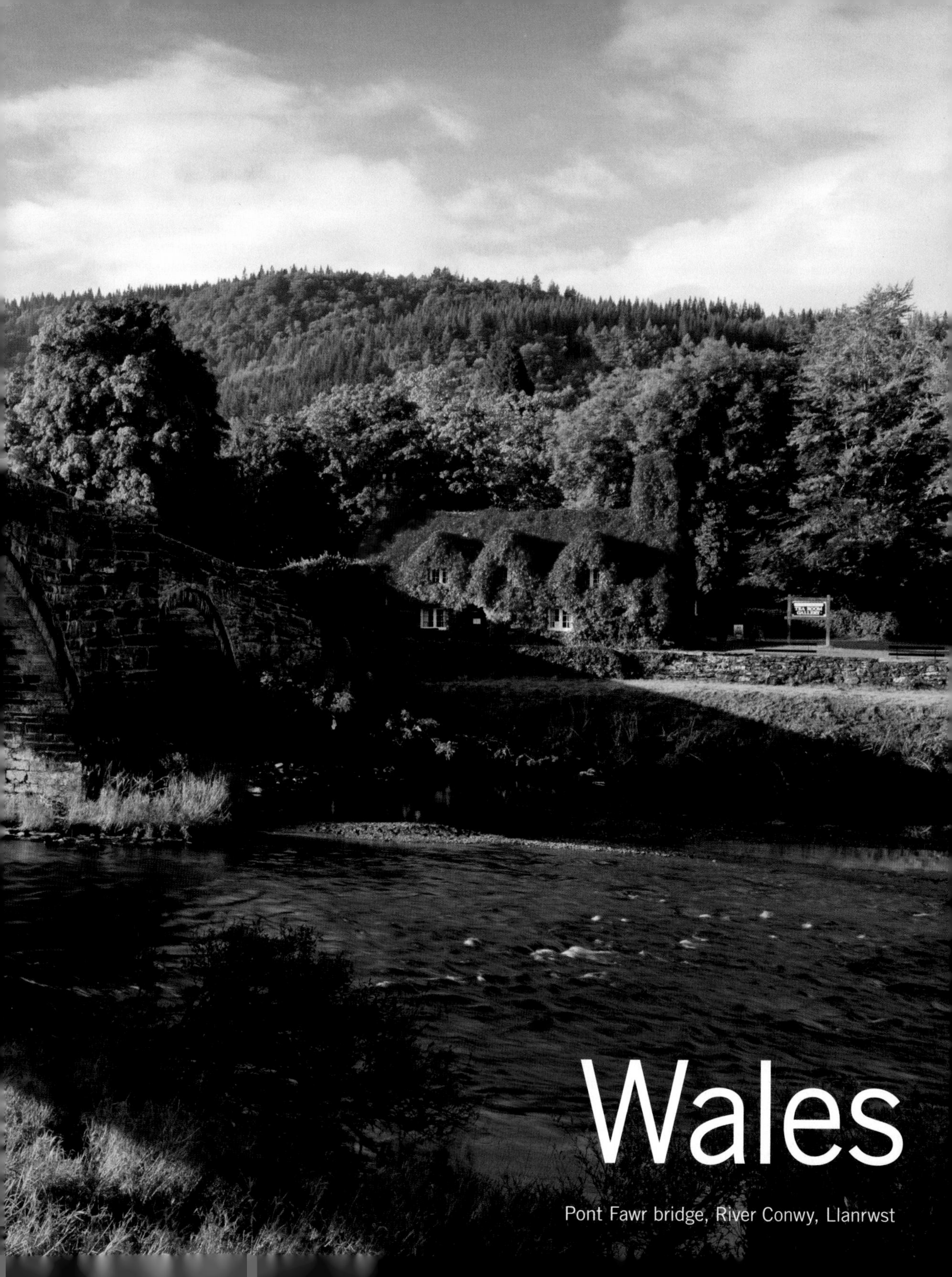

Wales

Pont Fawr bridge, River Conwy, Llanrwst

A

ABERAERON Map 8 SN46
Ceredigion

Ty Mawr Mansion

RESTAURANT WITH ROOMS

☎ 01570 470033
Cilcennin SA48 8DB
e-mail: info@tymawrmansion.co.uk
web: www.tymawrmansion.co.uk
dir: On A482 (Lampeter to Aberaeron road), 4m from Aberaeron

Surrounded by rolling countryside in its own naturally beautiful gardens, this fine country mansion house is a haven of perfect peace and tranquillity. Careful renovation has restored it to its former glory and, combined with lush fabrics, top quality beds and sumptuous furnishings, the accommodation is spacious, superbly equipped and very comfortable. Award-winning chefs create mouth-watering dishes from local and seasonal produce. There is also a 27-seat cinema with all the authenticity of the real thing. Martin and Cath McAlpine offer the sort of welcome which makes every visit to Ty Mawr a memorable one.

Rooms 9 (1 annexe) (1 fmly)

ABERDARE Map 9 SO00
Rhondda Cynon Taff

Premier Inn Aberdare

BUDGET HOTEL

☎ 0871 527 8002 0871 527 8003
Riverside Retail Park, Tirfounders Field CF44 0AH
dir: M4 junct 32, A470 signed Merthyr Tydfil. In approx 10m take A4059 signed Aberdare. Straight on at 1st rdbt, 3rd exit at next rdbt into Ffordd Tirwaun signed Riverside Retail Park, hotel in park

High quality, budget accommodation ideal for both families and business travellers. Spacious, en suite bedrooms feature tea and coffee making facilities, and Freeview TV in most hotels. Internet access and Wi-fi are available for a small fee. The adjacent family restaurant features a wide and varied menu. See also the Hotel Groups pages.

Rooms 28 **D** £49-£59*

ABERGAVENNY Map 9 SO21
Monmouthshire

Llansantffraed Court

WELSH RAREBITS Hotels of Distinction

★★★★ 78% COUNTRY HOUSE HOTEL

☎ 01873 840678 01873 840674
Llanvihangel Gobion, Clytha NP7 9BA
e-mail: reception@llch.co.uk
web: www.llch.co.uk
dir: At A465/A40 Abergavenny junct take B4598 signed Usk (NB do not join A40) towards Raglan, hotel on left in 4.5m

In a commanding position and in its own extensive grounds, this very impressive property, a privately owned country-house hotel, has enviable views of the Brecon Beacons. Extensive public areas include a relaxing lounge and a spacious restaurant offering imaginative and enjoyable award-winning dishes. Bedrooms vary in size and reflect the individuality of the building; all are comfortably furnished and provide some thoughtful extras. Extensive parking is available.

Rooms 21 (1 fmly) **S** £97-£105; **D** £125-£175 (incl. bkfst)* **Facilities** STV FTV Putt green Fishing Clay pigeon shooting school Wi-fi Child facilities **Conf** Class 120 Board 100 Thtr 220 Del from £140 to £180 **Services** Lift **Parking** 250 **Notes** LB Civ Wed 150

Angel Hotel

★★★ 78% HOTEL

☎ 01873 857121 01873 858059
15 Cross St NP7 5EN
e-mail: mail@angelhotelabergavenny.com
web: www.angelhotelabergavenny.com
dir: From A40 & A465 junct follow town centre signs, pass rail & bus stations

Once a coaching inn this has long been a popular venue for both local people and visitors; the two traditional function rooms and a ballroom are in regular use. In addition there is a comfortable lounge, a relaxed bar and a smart restaurant. In warmer weather the central courtyard is ideal for alfresco eating. The bedrooms include a four-poster room and some that are suitable for families.

Rooms 35 (4 annexe) (2 fmly) **S** £74-£140; **D** £96-£190 (incl. bkfst)* **Facilities** FTV New Year Wi-fi **Conf** Class 60 Board 60 Thtr 180 Del from £140* **Services** Lift **Parking** 30 **Notes** LB Closed 25 Dec RS 24 & 26-30 Dec Civ Wed 180

ABERGELE Map 14 SH97
Conwy

Kinmel Manor

THE INDEPENDENTS HOTEL ASSOCIATION

★★★ 73% HOTEL

☎ 01745 832014 01745 832014
St George's Rd LL22 9AS
e-mail: reception@kinmelmanorhotel.co.uk
dir: A55 junct 24, hotel entrance on rdbt

Rurally located at the end of a long drive leading from the A55, parts of this notable, family-run hotel date from the 16th century. The smart bedrooms vary from standard to superior and executive rooms. The public areas include a popular lounge bar, the stylish Seasons Brasserie, open from 11 until late, the restaurant and leisure facilities which include a gym, indoor pool, jacuzzi, steam room and sauna.

Rooms 51 (3 fmly) (22 GF) **S** £70-£85; **D** £90-£120 (incl. bkfst)* **Facilities** FTV Gym Steam room Sauna Spa bath Xmas New Year Wi-fi **Conf** Class 100 Board 100 Thtr 250 Del from £113 to £125* **Services** Lift **Parking** 120 **Notes** Civ Wed 250

The Kinmel Arms

RESTAURANT WITH ROOMS

☎ 01745 832207 01745 822044
The Village, St George LL22 9BP
e-mail: info@thekinmelarms.co.uk
dir: From A55 junct 24a to St George. E on A55, junct 25. 1st left to Rhuddlan, then 1st right into St George. Take 2nd right

This converted 17th-century coaching inn stands close to the church in the village of St George in the beautiful Elwy Valley. The popular restaurant specialises in produce from Wales and north-west England, and the friendly and helpful staff ensure an enjoyable stay. The four attractive suites are luxuriously furnished and feature stunning bathrooms. Substantial continental breakfasts are served in the rooms.

Rooms 4

ABERSOCH Map 14 SH32
Gwynedd

Porth Tocyn

★★★ 80% @@ COUNTRY HOUSE HOTEL

☎ 01758 713303 & 07789 994942
📠 01758 713538
Bwlch Tocyn LL53 7BU
e-mail: bookings@porthtocyn.fsnet.co.uk
web: www.porthtocynhotel.co.uk
dir: 2.5m S of Abersoch, after Sarnbach, follow Porth Tocyn signs

Located above Cardigan Bay with fine views over the area, Porth Tocyn is set in attractive gardens. Several elegantly furnished sitting rooms are provided and bedrooms are comfortably furnished. Children are especially welcome and a playroom is provided. Award-winning food is served in the restaurant.

Rooms 17 (1 fmly) (3 GF) **S** £72-£88; **D** £99-£176 (incl. bkfst)* **Facilities** FTV Table tennis Wi-fi **Conf** Class 15 **Parking** 50 **Notes** LB Closed mid Nov-wk before Etr

Neigwl

★★ 81% @ HOTEL

☎ 01758 712363 📠 01758 712544
Lon Sarn Bach LL53 7DY
e-mail: relax@neigwl.com
web: www.neigwl.com
dir: On A499, through Abersoch, hotel on left

This delightful, small hotel is privately owned and personally run. It is conveniently located for access to the town, harbour and beach. It has a deservedly high reputation for its food and warm hospitality. Both the attractive restaurant and the pleasant lounge bar overlook the sea, as do several of the tastefully appointed bedrooms.

Rooms 9 (2 fmly) (2 GF) **S** £45-£75; **D** £80-£115 (incl. bkfst)* **Parking** 20 **Notes** ® Closed Jan

ABERYSTWYTH Map 8 SN58
Ceredigion

Richmond

★★★ 77% SMALL HOTEL

☎ 01970 612201 📠 01970 626706
44-45 Marine Ter SY23 2BX
e-mail: reservations@richmondhotel.uk.com
web: www.richmondhotel.uk.com
dir: On entering town follow signs for Promenade

This privately owned and personally run, friendly hotel offers good sea views from its day rooms and many of the bedrooms. Good standards of comfort and facilities are found throughout; bedrooms have smart, modern bathrooms. An attractive dining room is the setting for imaginative dinners and comprehensive breakfasts.

Rooms 15 (2 fmly) **S** £50-£65; **D** £80-£95 (incl. bkfst)* **Facilities** FTV Wi-fi **Conf** Class 22 Board 28 Thtr 60 **Parking** 22 **Notes** LB ® Closed 20 Dec-3 Jan

BANGOR Map 14 SH57
Gwynedd

Premier Inn Bangor

BUDGET HOTEL

☎ 0871 527 8046 📠 0871 527 8047
Parc Menai, Ffordd Y Parc LL57 4FA
dir: A55 junct 9 (Holyhead, Ysbyty Gwynedd Hospital). Take 3rd exit off rdbt. Hotel next left

High quality, budget accommodation ideal for both families and business travellers. Spacious, en suite bedrooms feature tea and coffee making facilities, and Freeview TV in most hotels. Internet access and Wi-fi are available for a small fee. The adjacent family restaurant features a wide and varied menu. See also the Hotel Groups pages.

Rooms 40 **D** £60*

BARMOUTH Map 14 SH61
Gwynedd

Bae Abermaw

★★★ 82% @ HOTEL

☎ 01341 280550 📠 01341 280346
Panorama Hill LL42 1DQ
e-mail: enquiries@baeabermaw.com
web: www.baeabermaw.com
dir: Off A496 above Barmouth Bridge

Situated on attractive landscaped grounds in an elevated position overlooking the sea, this impressive Victorian house provides high standards of comfort and facilities. The interior is furnished and decorated in minimalist style and many bedrooms have stunning views.

Rooms 14 (4 fmly) **Facilities** FTV Xmas New Year Wi-fi **Conf** Class 75 Board 20 Thtr 100 **Parking** 35 **Notes** ® Civ Wed 100

BARRY Map 9 ST16
Vale of Glamorgan

Best Western Mount Sorrel

★★★ 73% HOTEL

☎ 01446 740069 📠 01446 746600
Porthkerry Rd CF62 7XY
e-mail: reservations@mountsorrel.co.uk
dir: M4 junct 33, A4232. Follow signs for A4050 through Barry. At mini-rdbt (with church opposite) turn left, hotel 300mtrs on left

Situated in an elevated position above the town centre, this extended Victorian property is ideally placed for exploring Cardiff and the nearby coast. The public areas include a choice of conference rooms, a restaurant with a bar called Strings, and smart leisure facilities with an indoor swimming pool and multi-gym. There is a separate, cosy lounge.

Rooms 42 (3 fmly) (5 GF) **S** £39.50-£99; **D** £54.50-£137* **Facilities** STV Gym Xmas Wi-fi **Conf** Class 100 Board 50 Thtr 150 **Services** Lift **Parking** 17 **Notes** ® Civ Wed 150

BEAUMARIS Map 14 SH67
Isle of Anglesey

B

Best Western Bulkeley Hotel

★★★ 77% HOTEL

☎ 01248 810415 🖷 01248 810146
Castle St LL58 8AW
e-mail: reception@bulkeleyhotel.co.uk
web: www.bulkeleyhotel.co.uk
dir: A55 junct 8a to Beaumaris. Hotel in town centre

A Grade I listed hotel built in 1832, the Bulkeley is just 100 yards from the 13th-century Beaumaris Castle in the centre of town; the friendly staff create a relaxed atmosphere. Many rooms, including 18 of the bedrooms, have fine panoramic views across the Menai Straits to the Snowdonian Mountains. The well-equipped bedrooms and suites, some with four-posters, are generally spacious, and have pretty furnishings. There is a choice of bars, a coffee shop, a restaurant and bistro.

Rooms 43 (5 fmly) **Facilities** FTV Xmas New Year Wi-fi **Conf** Class 40 Board 25 Thtr 180 Del from £95 to £105* **Services** Lift **Parking** 25 **Notes** Civ Wed 140

Bishopsgate House Hotel

★★ 85% ⊛ SMALL HOTEL

☎ 01248 810302 🖷 01248 810166
54 Castle St LL58 8BB
e-mail: hazel@bishopsgatehotel.co.uk
dir: From Menai Bridge onto A545 to Beaumaris. Hotel on left in main street

This immaculately maintained, privately owned and personally run small hotel dates back to 1760. It features fine examples of wood panelling and a Chinese Chippendale staircase. Thoughtfully furnished bedrooms are attractively decorated and two have four-poster beds. Quality cooking is served in the elegant restaurant and guests have a comfortable lounge and cosy bar to relax in.

Rooms 9 **S** £58-£68; **D** £95-£107 (incl. bkfst)* **Facilities** FTV Xmas New Year Wi-fi **Parking** 8 **Notes** LB

BEDDGELERT Map 14 SH54
Gwynedd

The Royal Goat

★★★ 77% HOTEL

☎ 01766 890224 🖷 01766 890422
LL55 4YE
e-mail: info@royalgoathotel.co.uk
web: www.royalgoathotel.co.uk
dir: On A498 at Beddgelert

An impressive building steeped in history, the Royal Goat provides well-equipped accommodation, and carries out an annual programme of refurbishment that includes the smart, modern bathrooms. Attractively appointed, comfortable public areas include a choice of bars and restaurants, a residents' lounge and function rooms.

Rooms 32 (4 fmly) **S** £53-£60; **D** £70-£110 (incl. bkfst)* **Facilities** FTV Fishing Xmas New Year Wi-fi **Conf** Class 40 Board 30 Thtr 70 Del from £120* **Services** Lift **Parking** 100 **Notes** LB Closed Jan-1 Mar RS Nov-1 Jan

BETWS-Y-COED Map 14 SH75
Conwy

See also **Llanrwst**

Craig-y-Dderwen Riverside Hotel

★★★★ 75% ⊛ COUNTRY HOUSE HOTEL

☎ 01690 710293 🖷 01690 710362
LL24 0AS
e-mail: info@snowdoniahotel.com
web: www.snowdoniahotel.com
dir: A5 to Betws-y-Coed, cross Waterloo Bridge, 1st left

This Victorian country-house hotel is set in well-maintained grounds alongside the River Conwy, at the end of a tree-lined drive. Very pleasant views can be enjoyed from many rooms, and two of the bedrooms have four-poster beds. There are comfortable lounges and the atmosphere throughout is tranquil and relaxing.

Rooms 18 (2 fmly) (1 GF) (2 smoking) **S** £105-£115; **D** £120-£200 (incl. bkfst)* **Facilities** STV FTV Fishing Badminton Volleyball New Year Wi-fi **Conf** Class 50 Board 50 Thtr 100 **Parking** 50 **Notes** LB Closed 23-26 Dec & 2 Jan-1 Feb Civ Wed 100

Royal Oak

★★★ 86% ⊛ HOTEL

☎ 01690 710219 🖷 01690 710603
Holyhead Rd LL24 0AY
e-mail: royaloakmail@btopenworld.com
web: www.royaloakhotel.net
dir: On A5 in town centre, adjacent to St Mary's church

Centrally situated in the village, this elegant, privately owned hotel started life as a coaching inn and now provides very comfortable bedrooms with smart, modern en suite bathrooms. The extensive public areas retain original charm and character. The choice of eating options includes the Grill Bistro, the Stables Bar which is much frequented by locals, and the more formal Llugwy Restaurant.

Rooms 27 (1 fmly) **S** £77.50-£80; **D** £95-£180 (incl. bkfst)* **Facilities** STV ♫ New Year Wi-fi **Conf** Class 40 Board 20 Thtr 80 Del from £100 to £150* **Parking** 90 **Notes** ⊗ Closed 25-26 Dec Civ Wed 60

See advert on opposite page

Best Western Waterloo

★★★ 78% HOTEL

☎ 01690 710411 🖷 01690 710986
LL24 0AR
e-mail: reservations@waterloo-hotel.info
web: www.waterloo-hotel.info
dir: On A5, S of village centre

This long-established hotel, named after the nearby Waterloo Bridge, is ideally located for visiting Snowdonia. Stylish accommodation is split between rooms in the main hotel and modern, cottage-style rooms located in buildings to the rear. The attractive

Garden Room Restaurant serves traditional Welsh specialities, and the vibrant Bridge Inn provides a wide range of food and drink throughout the day and evening.

Best Western Waterloo

Rooms 45 (34 annexe) (12 fmly) (31 GF) **Facilities** Gym Steam room Sauna Hair & beauty salon New Year Wi-fi **Conf** Class 18 Board 12 Thtr 40 **Parking** 100 **Notes** LB Closed 25-26 Dec

Fairy Glen

★★ 74% SMALL HOTEL

☎ 01690 710269
LL24 0SH
e-mail: fairyglenho@sky.com
web: www.fairyglenhotel.co.uk
dir: A5 onto A470 S'bound (Dolwyddelan road). Hotel 0.5m on left by Beaver Bridge

This privately owned and personally run former coaching inn is over 300 years old. It is located near the Fairy Glen beauty spot, south of Betws-y-Coed. The modern accommodation is well equipped and service is willing, friendly and attentive. Facilities include a cosy bar and a separate comfortable lounge.

Rooms 8 (1 fmly) **Parking** 10 **Notes** Closed Nov-Jan RS Feb

BODELWYDDAN Map 14 SJ07
Denbighshire

Bodelwyddan Castle Hotel

Warner Leisure Hotels

★★★ 70% HOTEL

☎ 01745 585088 01745 585089
LL18 5YA
dir: At A55 junct 25

This Grade II listed Victorian castle is located on the north Wales coast less than an hour from the Snowdonian mountains. The famous Bodelwyddan marble church, set in the valley below, can be seen from the grounds and The National Portrait Gallery is also situated on site. The hotel offers a great range of leisure facilities and numerous daily in-house and external activities. Packages range from a minimum two-night, half board stay. Please note that this is an adults-only (over 21 years old) hotel. Warner Leisure Hotels – AA Small Hotel Group of the Year 2011-12.

Rooms 186 **Facilities** Putt green 4-rink bowls complex All weather Crown Bowling green Archery Cycling Fitness studio Xmas New Year **Notes** No children

BRECON Map 9 SO02
Powys

The Castle of Brecon Hotel

★★★ 72% HOTEL

☎ 01874 624611 01874 623737
Castle Square LD3 9DB
e-mail: hotel@breconcastle.co.uk
dir: In town centre

This former coaching inn occupies an elevated position overlooking the town and the River Usk, with the ruins of the 11th-century castle in the grounds. Lovely views can be enjoyed from the restaurant and some of the bedrooms. The remaining public areas are roomy and relaxed in a contemporary style. Function and meeting rooms are available and even incorporate one of the castle walls. There is ample parking to the front of the property.

Rooms 38 (8 annexe) (9 fmly) (2 GF) **Facilities** STV FTV New Year Wi-fi **Conf** Class 100 Board 40 Thtr 140 **Parking** 35 **Notes** LB RS 24/26 Dec Civ Wed 120

Peterstone Court

RESTAURANT WITH ROOMS

☎ 01874 665387
Llanhamlach LD3 7YB
e-mail: info@peterstone-court.com
dir: 3m from Brecon on A40 towards Abergavenny

Situated on the edge of the Brecons Beacons this establishment affords stunning views and overlooks the River Usk. The style is friendly and informal. No two bedrooms are alike, but all share comparable levels of comfort, quality and elegance. Public areas reflect similar standards, eclectically styled with a blend of the contemporary and the traditional. Quality produce is cooked with care in a range of enjoyable dishes.

Rooms 12 (4 annexe) (2 fmly)

B

BRIDGEND
Bridgend
Map 9 SS97

Coed-Y-Mwstwr
THE INDEPENDENTS HOTEL ASSOCIATION

★★★★ 79% COUNTRY HOUSE HOTEL

☎ 01656 860621 📠 01656 863122
Coychurch CF35 6AF
e-mail: hotel@coed-y-mwstwr.com
web: www.coed-y-mwstwr.com
dir: Exit A473 at Coychurch, right at petrol station. Follow signs at top of hill

This Victorian mansion, set in 17 acres of grounds, is an inviting retreat. The public areas are full of character and feature an impressive, contemporary restaurant. The bedrooms have individual styles and offer a good range of extras; two full suites and the Coach House bedrooms in a separate building are also available. Other facilities include a large and attractive function suite with syndicate rooms, a gym, an outdoor pool and a tennis court.

Rooms 35 (2 fmly) **Facilities** STV Gym Xmas New Year Wi-fi **Conf** Class 120 Board 50 Thtr 180 **Services** Lift **Parking** 100 **Notes** Civ Wed 200

Best Western Heronston

★★★ 75% HOTEL

☎ 01656 668811 & 666085 📠 01656 767391
Ewenny Rd CF35 5AW
e-mail: reservations@bestwesternheronstonhotel.co.uk
web: www.bw-heronstonhotel.co.uk
dir: M4 junct 35, follow signs for Porthcawl, at 5th rdbt left towards Ogmore-by-Sea (B4265), hotel 200yds on left

Situated within easy reach of the town centre and the M4, this large modern hotel offers spacious well-equipped accommodation, including ground floor rooms. Public areas include an open-plan lounge/bar, attractive restaurant and a smart leisure and fitness club. The hotel also has a choice of function and conference rooms, and ample parking is available.

Best Western Heronston

Rooms 75 (4 fmly) (37 GF) (4 smoking) **S** £55-£110; **D** £65-£135 (incl. bkfst)* **Facilities** STV Gym Steam room Sauna Spa pool New Year Wi-fi **Conf** Class 80 Board 60 Thtr 250 Del from £99.50 to £125* **Services** Lift **Parking** 160 **Notes** LB Civ Wed 200

Court Colman Manor

★★★ 71% COUNTRY HOUSE HOTEL

☎ 01656 720212 📠 01656 724544
Pen-y-Fai CF31 4NG
e-mail: experience@court-colman-manor.com
dir: M4 junct 36, A4063 towards Maesteg, after lights 1st exit to Bridgend, under motorway, next right, follow hotel signs

Dating back to the Tudor times this fine mansion is set in its own peaceful grounds outside Bridgend, and is just a short distance from the M4. The spacious, comfortable bedrooms include ten that are themed on an exotic location - India, Japan, Morocco etc. The award-winning food served in Bokhara Brasserie is imaginative, and Indian and Mediterranean cuisine form are part of the choices. Diners can view their meals being prepared in the open-plan kitchen.

Rooms 30 (2 fmly) **Facilities** FTV Xmas New Year Wi-fi **Conf** Class 60 Thtr 100 **Parking** 180 **Notes** Civ Wed 150

Premier Inn Bridgend Central

BUDGET HOTEL

☎ 0871 527 8146 📠 0871 527 8147
The Derwen CF32 9ST
dir: M4 junct 36, A4061 (signed Bridgend & Pen-y-Bont). Hotel at next rdbt

High quality, budget accommodation ideal for both families and business travellers. Spacious, en suite bedrooms feature tea and coffee making facilities, and Freeview TV in most hotels. Internet access and Wi-fi are available for a small fee. The adjacent family restaurant features a wide and varied menu. See also the Hotel Groups pages.

Rooms 68 **D** £49-£60*

Premier Inn Bridgend M4 Jct 35

BUDGET HOTEL

☎ 0871 527 8144 📠 0871 527 8145
Pantruthyn Farm, Pencoed CF35 5HY
dir: At M4 junct 35, behind petrol station & McDonalds

Rooms 40 **D** £49-£60*

BUILTH WELLS
Powys
Map 9 SO05

Caer Beris Manor
THE INDEPENDENTS HOTEL ASSOCIATION

★★★ 77% COUNTRY HOUSE HOTEL

☎ 01982 552601 📠 01982 552586
LD2 3NP
e-mail: caerberis@btconnect.com
web: www.caerberis.com
dir: From town centre follow A483/Llandovery signs. Hotel on left

Guests can expect a relaxing stay at this friendly and privately owned hotel that has extensive landscaped grounds. Bedrooms are individually decorated and furnished to retain an atmosphere of a bygone era. The spacious and comfortable lounge and a lounge bar continue this theme, and there's an elegant restaurant, complete with 16th-century panelling.

Rooms 23 (2 fmly) (3 GF) **S** £73.95-£83.95; **D** £127.90-£147.90 (incl. bkfst)* **Facilities** FTV Fishing Clay pigeon shooting Birdwatching Xmas New Year Wi-fi Child facilities **Conf** Class 75 Board 50 Thtr 100 Del from £ to £97.95 **Parking** 100 **Notes** LB Civ Wed 200

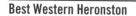

BURTON Pembrokeshire **Map 8 SM90**

Beggars Reach

★★★ 79% HOTEL

☎ 01646 600700 📠 01646 600560
SA73 1PD
e-mail: stay@beggars-reach.com
web: www.beggars-reach.com
dir: 8m S of Haverfordwest, 6m N of Pembroke, off A477

This privately owned and personally run hotel was a rectory in Georgian times; it stands in eight acres of grounds peacefully located close to the village of Burton. It provides modern, well-equipped bedrooms; two located in former stables which date back to the 14th century. Milford Haven and the ferry terminal at Pembroke Dock are both within easy reach.

Rooms 30 (16 annexe) (4 fmly) (8 GF) (1 smoking) **S** £81.50-£102; **D** £120-£175 (incl. bkfst)* **Facilities** STV FTV Wi-fi **Conf** Class 60 Board 60 Thtr 100 Del from £120* **Parking** 80 **Notes** LB ⊗ Civ Wed 160

CAERNARFON Gwynedd **Map 14 SH46**

INSPECTORS' CHOICE

Seiont Manor

HandPICKED HOTELS

★★★ ◎◎ COUNTRY HOUSE HOTEL

☎ 01286 673366 📠 01286 672840
Llanrug LL55 2AQ
e-mail: seiontmanor@handpicked.co.uk
web: www.handpickedhotels.co.uk
dir: E on A4086, 2.5m from Caernarfon

A splendid hotel created from authentic farm buildings, set in the tranquil countryside near Snowdonia; the River Seiont flows through the 150-acre grounds. The bedrooms, including junior suites, are individually decorated and have luxurious extra touches; each has either a balcony or patio. The comfortable public rooms are cosy and furnished in country-house style. The kitchen team use the best of local produce to provide exciting takes on traditional dishes, and guests can choose to eat in either the award-winning Llwyn y Brain Restaurant or the conservatory brasserie. The hotel is a popular wedding venue.

Rooms 28 (2 fmly) (14 GF) **S** £75-£158; **D** £87-£168 (incl. bkfst)* **Facilities** STV FTV ⓢ Fishing Gym Xmas New Year Wi-fi **Conf** Class 40 Board 40 Thtr 100 Del from £125 to £165* **Parking** 60 **Notes** LB ⊗ Civ Wed 100

Celtic Royal Hotel

★★★ 80% HOTEL

☎ 01286 674477 📠 01286 674139
Bangor St LL55 1AY
e-mail: reservations@celtic-royal.co.uk
web: www.celtic-royal.co.uk
dir: Exit A55 at Bangor onto A487 towards Caernarfon

This large, impressive, privately owned hotel is situated in the town centre. It provides attractively appointed accommodation, which includes family rooms and bedrooms for less able guests. The spacious public areas include a bar, a choice of lounges and a pleasant split-level restaurant. Guests also have the use of the impressive health club.

Rooms 110 (12 fmly) **S** £80-£120; **D** £120-£160 (incl. bkfst)* **Facilities** ⓢ Gym Steam room Sauna ♫ Xmas New Year Wi-fi **Conf** Class 120 Board 120 Thtr 300 Del from £125 to £135* **Services** Lift **Parking** 180 **Notes** LB ⊗ Civ Wed 200

Premier Inn Caernarfon

Premier Inn

BUDGET HOTEL

☎ 0871 527 8180 📠 0871 527 8181
Victoria Dock, Balaclava Rd LL55 1SQ
dir: A55 junct 9, at rdbt 1st exit follow Caernarfon signs. In Caernarfon at rdbt (Morrisons on right) 1st exit, keep in right lane, at next rdbt 4th exit to mini rdbt, hotel opposite

High quality, budget accommodation ideal for both families and business travellers. Spacious, en suite bedrooms feature tea and coffee making facilities, and Freeview TV in most hotels. Internet access and Wi-fi are available for a small fee. The adjacent family restaurant features a wide and varied menu. See also the Hotel Groups pages.

Rooms 49 **D** £60*

C

CAERNARFON *continued*

Rhiwafallen Restaurant with Rooms

RESTAURANT WITH ROOMS

01286 830172
Rhiwafallen, LLandwrog LL54 5SW
e-mail: ktandrobjohn@aol.com
dir: Off A499

Located south of Caernarfon on the Llyn Peninsula link, this former farmhouse has been tastefully renovated to provide high levels of comfort and facilities. Quality bedrooms are furnished in minimalist style with a wealth of thoughtful extras. The original modern art in public areas adds vibrancy to the interior. Warm hospitality and imaginative cooking ensure a memorable stay at this owner-managed establishment.

Rooms 5

CAERPHILLY — Caerphilly — Map 9 ST18

Premier Inn Caerphilly (Corbetts Lane)

BUDGET HOTEL

0871 527 8182 0871 527 8183
Corbetts Ln CF83 3HX
dir: M4 junct 32, A470, 2nd left signed Caerphilly. At rdbt 4th exit, at next rdbt 2nd exit. Straight on at next rdbt & at Pwllypant Rdbt, hotel on left

High quality, budget accommodation ideal for both families and business travellers. Spacious, en suite bedrooms feature tea and coffee making facilities, and Freeview TV in most hotels. Internet access and Wi-fi are available for a small fee. The adjacent family restaurant features a wide and varied menu. See also the Hotel Groups pages.

Rooms 42 **D** £52-£60*

Premier Inn Caerphilly (Crossways)

BUDGET HOTEL

0871 527 8184 0871 527 8185
Crossways Business Park, Pontypandy CF83 3NL
dir: M4 junct 32, A470 towards Merthyr Tydfil (junct 4 take A458 towards Caerphilly). At Crossways Business Park (5th rdbt). Hotel on right at McDonald's rdbt

Rooms 40 **D** £52-£60*

CAERSWS — Powys — Map 15 SO09

The Talkhouse

RESTAURANT WITH ROOMS

01686 688919 & 07876 086183
Pontdolgoch SY17 5JE
e-mail: info@talkhouse.co.uk
dir: 1.5m NW of Caersws on A470

A highlight of this delightful 19th-century inn is the food - home-made dishes make good use of local produce. The bedrooms offer luxury in every area and the cosy lounge, filled with sofas, is the place to while away some time with a glass of wine or a pot of tea. The bar features a large fireplace.

Rooms 3

CAPEL CURIG — Conwy — Map 14 SH75

Cobdens

★★ 60% SMALL HOTEL

01690 720243 01690 720354
LL24 0EE
e-mail: info@cobdens.co.uk
dir: On A5, 4m N of Betws-y-Coed

Situated in the heart of Snowdonia, this hotel has been a centre for mountaineering and other outdoor pursuits for many years. A wide range of meals, using local produce, is served in the restaurant. There are two bars including the aptly names Mountain Bar, built in the side of the mountain. A sauna room is also available.

Rooms 17 (4 fmly) **S** £30.50-£37.50; **D** £61-£75 (incl. bkfst)* **Facilities** STV FTV Fishing Sauna Pool table New Year Wi-fi **Conf** Class 25 Board 30 Thtr 50 Del from £75 to £100* **Parking** 40 **Notes** LB Closed Jan RS 24-25 & 31 Dec

CARDIFF — Cardiff — Map 9 ST17

See also **Barry**

St David's Hotel & Spa

PH | principal hayley

★★★★★ 81% HOTEL

029 2045 4045 029 2031 3075
Havannah St CF10 5SD
e-mail: stdavids.reservations@principal-hayley.com
web: www.thestdavidshotel.com
dir: M4 junct 33, A4232 for 9m, follow Cardiff Bay signs, then Techniquest signs, at top exit slip road, 1st left at rdbt, 1st right

This imposing contemporary building sits in a prime position on Cardiff Bay and has a seven-storey atrium creating a dramatic impression. Leading from the atrium are the practically designed and comfortable bedrooms. Tides Restaurant, adjacent to the stylish cocktail bar, has views across the water to Penarth, and there is a quiet first-floor lounge for guests seeking peace and quiet. A well-equipped spa and extensive business areas complete the package.

Rooms 132 (24 smoking) **S** £79-£330; **D** £89-£350* **Facilities** Spa FTV Gym Fitness studio Hydrotherapy pool Aerobics studio Xmas New Year Wi-fi **Conf** Class 110 Board 76 Thtr 270 Del from £140 to £250* **Services** Lift Air con **Parking** 80 **Notes** LB Civ Wed 270

The Parc Hotel, Cardiff

thistle

★★★★ 85% HOTEL

0871 376 9011 0871 376 9111
Park Place CF10 3UD
e-mail: cardiff@thistle.co.uk
web: www.thistle.com/theparchotel
dir: M4 junct 29, A48, 4th exit signed City Centre/A470. At rdbt 2nd exit signed City Centre/A470

Ideally located in the very centre of Cardiff, this bustling hotel retains an exterior of Victorian splendour while the interior is contemporary. The bedrooms are spacious, modern and well equipped, and a range of dining options is available including the Harlech Lounge & Bar and the modern Crown Social Restaurant which offers quality food with efficient service. Thistle Hotels – AA Hotel Group of the Year 2011-12.

Rooms 140 (5 fmly) **Facilities** STV Xmas New Year Wi-fi **Conf** Class 100 Board 50 Thtr 225 **Services** Lift Air con **Parking** 60 **Notes** Civ Wed 225

Cardiff Marriott Hotel

★★★★ 80% ❁ HOTEL

☎ 029 2039 9944 📠 029 2039 5578
Mill Ln CF10 1EZ
web: www.cardiffmarriott.co.uk
dir: M4 junct 29, A48M E follow signs city centre & Cardiff Bay. 3m, right into Mill Lane

Centrally located in the Café Quarter of the city, this modern hotel has spacious public areas and a good range of services to suit both business and leisure guests. The eating options include the informal Chats Café Bar, and the Brasserie Centrale for contemporary French cuisine that uses locally sourced ingredients. The well-equipped bedrooms are comfortable and air conditioned. The leisure suite includes a multi-gym and a good size swimming pool.

Rooms 184 (68 fmly) **Facilities** STV Gym Steam room Sauna Spa bath Xmas New Year Wi-fi **Conf** Class 200 Board 100 Thtr 400 Del from £140 to £180* **Services** Lift Air con **Parking** 146 **Notes** Civ Wed 200

Park Plaza Cardiff

★★★★ 80% HOTEL

☎ 029 2011 1111 & 2011 1101 📠 029 2011 1112
Greyfriars Rd CF10 3AL
e-mail: ppcres@parkplazahotels.co.uk
web: www.parkplazacardiff.com
dir: From M4 follow city centre (A470) signs. Left into Boulevard de Nantes, immediately left into Greyfriars Rd. Hotel on left by New Theatre

A smart hotel located in the city centre that features eye-catching, contemporary decor, a state-of-the-art indoor leisure facility, extensive conference and banqueting facilities and the spacious Laguna Kitchen and Bar. Bedrooms are also up-to-the-minute in style and feature a host of extras including a private bar, a safe and modem points.

Rooms 129 (20 fmly) **S** £89-£320; **D** £99-£330* **Facilities** Spa FTV Gym Dance studio Steam room New Year Wi-fi **Conf** Class 80 Board 60 Thtr 150 Del from £160 to £195* **Services** Lift Air con **Notes** LB Closed 24-25 Dec Civ Wed 120

Novotel Cardiff Central

★★★★ 77% HOTEL

☎ 029 2047 5000 📠 029 2048 1491
Schooner Way, Atlantic Wharf CF10 4RT
e-mail: h5982@accor.com
web: www.novotel.com
dir: M4 junct 33, A4232 follow Cardiff Bay signs to Atlantic Wharf

Situated in the heart of the city's development area, this hotel is equally convenient for the centre and Cardiff Bay. Bedrooms vary between standard rooms in the modern extension and executive rooms in the original wing. The hotel offers good seating space in public rooms, a popular leisure club and the innovative 'Elements' dining concept.

Rooms 138 (100 fmly) **Facilities** supervised Gym Wi-fi **Conf** Class 90 Board 65 Thtr 250 **Services** Lift Air con **Parking** 120 **Notes** Civ Wed 250

Mercure Holland House Hotel & Spa

★★★★ 76% HOTEL

☎ 029 2043 5000 📠 029 2048 8894
24/26 Newport Rd CF24 0DD
e-mail: h6622@accor.com
web: www.mercure.com
dir: M4 junct 33, A4232 to city centre, right at lights facing prison, straight through next lights, hotel car park at end of lane facing Magistrates Court

Conveniently located just a few minutes' walk from the city centre, this exciting hotel combines contemporary styling with a genuinely friendly welcome. Bedrooms, including five luxurious suites, are spacious and include many welcome extras. A state-of-the-art leisure club and spa is available in addition to a large function room. An eclectic menu provides a varied range of freshly prepared, quality dishes.

Rooms 165 (80 fmly) (8 smoking) **Facilities** Spa STV supervised Gym Wi-fi **Conf** Class 140 Board 42 Thtr 700 **Services** Lift Air con **Parking** 90 **Notes** Civ Wed 500

Copthorne Hotel Cardiff-Caerdydd

★★★★ 75% ❁ HOTEL

☎ 029 2059 9100 📠 029 2059 9080
Copthorne Way, Culverhouse Cross CF5 6DA
e-mail: reservations.cardiff@millenniumhotels.co.uk
web: www.millenniumhotels.co.uk
dir: M4 junct 33, A4232 for 2.5m towards Cardiff West. Take A48 W to Cowbridge

A comfortable, popular and modern hotel, conveniently located for the airport and city. Bedrooms are a good size and some have a private lounge. Public areas are smartly presented and include a gym, pool, meeting rooms and a comfortable restaurant with views of a lake.

Rooms 135 (7 fmly) (27 GF) **S** £42-£210; **D** £42-£210* **Facilities** STV Gym Sauna Steam room Treatment room Xmas New Year Wi-fi **Conf** Class 140 Board 80 Thtr 300 Del from £99 to £160 **Services** Lift **Parking** 225 **Notes** Civ Wed 200

Barceló Cardiff Angel Hotel

★★★★ 68% HOTEL

☎ 029 2064 9200 📠 029 2039 6212
Castle St CF10 1SZ
e-mail: angel@barcelo-hotels-co.uk
web: www.barcelo-hotels.co.uk/hotels/wales/barcelo-cardiff-angel-hotel
dir: Opposite Cardiff Castle

This well-established hotel is in the heart of the city overlooking the famous castle and almost opposite the Millennium Stadium. All bedrooms offer air conditioning and are appointed to a good standard. Public areas include an impressive lobby, a modern restaurant and a selection of conference rooms. There is limited parking at the rear of the hotel.

Rooms 102 (3 fmly) **Facilities** STV Xmas New Year Wi-fi **Conf** Class 120 Board 50 Thtr 300 **Services** Lift Air con **Parking** 60 **Notes** Civ Wed 200

Holiday Inn Cardiff City

★★★ 79% HOTEL

☎ 0800 40 50 60 & 0871 942 9240
📠 029 2038 9255
Castle St CF10 1XD
e-mail: cardiffcity@ihg.com
web: www.hicardiffcitycentre.co.uk
dir: M4 junct 29 E, A48(M), follow city centre signs, onto A470. Turn left to hotel

This hotel has a fantastic location in the heart of the city and is just a short walk from the Millennium Stadium, Cardiff Castle and Cardiff Bay. There are banqueting rooms, and state-of-the-art conference and meeting facilities. The air-conditioned accommodation is modern with many guest extras provided. The restaurant offers a good menu choice, or guests can take a snack in the lounge/bar area.

Rooms 157 (20 fmly) (10 smoking) **Facilities** Xmas New Year Wi-fi **Conf** Class 60 Board 50 Thtr 180 **Services** Lift Air con **Parking** 85 **Notes** Civ Wed 50

C

CARDIFF *continued*

Park Inn Cardiff City Centre

★★★ 77% HOTEL

☎ 029 2034 1441 & 2072 7026 📠 029 2072 7025
Mary Ann St CF10 2JH
e-mail: info.cardiff-city@rezidorparkinn.com
dir: In city centre adjacent to John Lewis building & Motorpoint Arena Cardiff. Follow signs to St Davids car park adjacent to hotel

This hotel is ideal for both business and leisure guests, being situated in the centre of the city, close to the shops and the Millennium Stadium. The accommodation has been appointed in a contemporary style, with guest comfort as the key consideration. The friendly restaurant provides a good range of contemporary dishes, including grill specialities. Secure, limited parking is available.

Rooms 146 (9 fmly) **S** fr £65; **D** fr £65 **Facilities** STV Arrangement with local gym nearby ♫ Xmas New Year Wi-fi **Conf** Class 120 Board 50 Thtr 300 Del from £125 **Services** Lift **Parking** 40 **Notes** LB ⊗ Civ Wed 300

Best Western St Mellons Hotel & Country Club

★★★ 70% HOTEL

☎ 01633 680355 📠 01633 680399
Castleton CF3 2XR
e-mail: reservations.stmellons@ohiml.com
web: www.oxfordhotelsandinns.com
dir: M4 junct 28 follow A48 Castleton/St Mellons signs. Hotel on left past garage

This Regency mansion has been tastefully converted into an elegant hotel with an adjoining leisure complex that attracts a strong local following. Bedrooms, some in purpose-built wings, are spacious and smart. The public areas retain pleasing architectural proportions and include relaxing lounges and a restaurant serving a varied choice of carefully prepared, enjoyable dishes.

Rooms 41 (20 annexe) (9 fmly) (5 GF) **S** £60-£150; **D** £70-£180* **Facilities** Spa Ⓢ Gym Squash Beauty salon Xmas Wi-fi **Conf** Class 185 Board 179 Thtr 480 Del from £120 to £150* **Parking** 100 **Notes** LB Civ Wed 160

The Legacy Cardiff International Hotel

★★★ 70% HOTEL

☎ 0844 411 9074 & 0330 333 2874
📠 0844 411 9075
Merthyr Rd, Tongwynlais CF15 7LD
e-mail: res-cardiffinternational@legacy-hotels.co.uk
dir: M4 junct 32, follow Tongwynlais/A4054 signs at large rdbt, hotel on right

This modern hotel is conveniently located off the M4 and with easy access to Cardiff and the Millennium Stadium. Guests can enjoy the spacious open-plan public areas and relax in the well proportioned and well equipped bedrooms, which include some suites. A good range of meeting rooms makes this hotel a popular conference venue. There is ample parking in the area around the hotel.

Rooms 95 (38 fmly) (20 GF) **Facilities** FTV Xmas New Year Wi-fi **Conf** Class 120 Board 60 Thtr 180 **Services** Lift **Notes** ⊗ Civ Wed

Park Inn Cardiff North

★★★ 70% HOTEL

☎ 029 2058 9988 📠 029 2054 9092
Circle Way East, Llanedeyrn CF23 9XF
e-mail: info.cardiff@rezidorparkinn.com
web: www.cardiff.parkinn.co.uk

This hotel is ideal for both business and leisure guests, being situated just a short distance from the M4 and convenient for city-centre shopping and the Millennium Stadium. The accommodation has been appointed in a contemporary style, with comfort as the key consideration. The friendly restaurant provides a good range of dishes, including charcoal-grill specialities. There is a complimentary gym and parking is extensive and secure.

Rooms 132 (16 fmly) (20 GF) **Facilities** STV FTV Ⓢ supervised Gym Treatment room Xmas New Year Wi-fi **Conf** Class 160 Board 160 Thtr 200 **Services** Lift Air con **Parking** 200 **Notes** ⊗ Civ Wed

Sandringham

★★ 71% HOTEL

☎ 029 2023 2161 📠 029 2038 3998
21 St Mary St CF10 1PL
e-mail: mm@sandringham-hotel.com
dir: M4 junct 29, follow 'city centre' signs. Opposite castle left into High St; leads to St Mary St (pedestrianised). Hotel on left

This friendly, privately owned and personally run hotel is near the Millennium Stadium and offers a convenient base for access to the city centre. Bedrooms are well equipped, and diners can relax in Café Jazz, the hotel's adjoining restaurant, where live music is provided most week nights. There is also a separate lounge/bar for residents, and an airy breakfast room.

Rooms 28 (1 fmly) **S** £35-£100; **D** £40-£145 (incl. bkfst)* **Facilities** FTV ♫ Wi-fi **Conf** Class 70 Board 60 Thtr 100 Del from £55 to £85* **Notes** ⊗ Closed 24-26 Dec (pm) & 1 Jan (pm)

Mercure Cardiff Centre

U

☎ 029 2089 4000 📠 029 2049 3695
Wharf Road East, Tyndall St CF10 4BB
e-mail: h6623@accor.com
web: www.mercure.com
dir: M4 juncts 29 & 33 follow city centre signs

Currently the rating for this establishment is not confirmed. This may be due to a change of ownership or because it has only recently joined the AA rating scheme. For further details please see the AA website: theAA.com

Rooms 100 (48 fmly) (27 GF) (5 smoking) **S** £45-£160; **D** £45-£160* **Facilities** STV Leisure facilities at sister hotel (Mercure Holland House) Wi-fi **Services** Lift Air con **Parking** 90 **Notes** LB

Campanile Cardiff

BUDGET HOTEL

☎ 029 2054 9044 📠 029 2054 9900
Caxton Place, Pentwyn CF23 8HA
e-mail: cardiff@campanile.com
dir: Take Pentwyn exit from A48(M), follow signs for hotel

This modern building offers accommodation in smart, well-equipped bedrooms, all with en suite bathrooms. Refreshments may be taken at the informal bistro. See also the Hotel Groups pages.

Rooms 47 (47 annexe) **Conf** Class 18 Board 16 Thtr 35

Holiday Inn Express Cardiff Airport

BUDGET HOTEL

☎ 01446 711117 🖷 01446 713290
Port Rd, Rhoose CF62 3BT
e-mail: sales@exhicardiffairport.co.uk
web: www.hiexpress.com/cardiffairport
dir: M4 junct 33, follow signs for Barry & Cardiff Airport. Hotel adjacent to airport terminal

A modern hotel ideal for families and business travellers. Fresh and uncomplicated, the spacious rooms include Sky TV, power shower and tea and coffee-making facilities. Continental buffet breakfast is included in the room rate; other meals may be taken at the nearby family pub or restaurant. See also the Hotel Groups pages.

Rooms 111 (60 fmly) (22 GF) (7 smoking)
Conf Class 20 Board 20 Thtr 40

Ibis Cardiff City Centre

BUDGET HOTEL

☎ 029 2064 9250 🖷 029 2920 9260
Churchill Way CF10 2HA
e-mail: H2936@accor.com
web: www.ibishotel.com
dir: M4 junct 29, to junct 29A, A48(M), A48, 2nd exit A4232. Follow signs to City Centre on Newport Rd, left after rail bridge, left after Queen St station

Modern, budget hotel offering comfortable accommodation in bright and practical bedrooms. Breakfast is self-service and dinner is available in the restaurant. See also the Hotel Groups pages.

Rooms 102 (19 GF) **S** £39-£230; **D** £39-£230*

Ibis Cardiff Gate

BUDGET HOTEL

☎ 029 2073 3222 🖷 029 2073 4222
Malthouse Av, Cardiff Gate Business Park, Pontprennau CF23 8RA
e-mail: H3159@accor.com
web: www.ibishotel.com
dir: M4 junct 30, follow Cardiff Service Station signs. Hotel on left

Rooms 78 (19 fmly) (22 GF) (7 smoking)
Conf Class 24 Thtr 25

Premier Inn Cardiff City Centre

BUDGET HOTEL

☎ 0871 527 8196 🖷 0871 527 8197
Helmont House, 10 Churchill Way CF10 2NB
dir: M4 junct 29 onto A48(M) towards Cardiff (East & South), 4.5m. Follow Cardiff (East), Docks & A4232 signs. Left at A4161 (Eastern Avenue North). At rdbt 2nd exit onto A4161 (Newport Rd). 2m, left into Station Terrace. Right into Churchill Way

High quality, budget accommodation ideal for both families and business travellers. Spacious, en suite bedrooms feature tea and coffee making facilities, and Freeview TV in most hotels. Internet access and Wi-fi are available for a small fee. The adjacent family restaurant features a wide and varied menu. See also the Hotel Groups pages.

Rooms 200 **D** £65*

Premier Inn Cardiff City South

BUDGET HOTEL

☎ 0871 527 8198 🖷 0871 527 8199
Keen Rd CF24 5JT
dir: Follow Cardiff Docks & Bay signs from A48(M), over flyover. At 5th rdbt 3rd exit. Hotel 1st right, 1st right again

Rooms 77 **D** £65*

Premier Inn Cardiff East

BUDGET HOTEL

☎ 0871 527 8200 🖷 0871 527 8201
Newport Rd, Castleton CF3 2UQ
dir: M4 junct 8, A48 signed Castleton. 3m, hotel on right

Rooms 49 **D** £49-£59*

Premier Inn Cardiff North

BUDGET HOTEL

☎ 0871 527 8202 🖷 0871 527 8203
Pentwyn Rd, Pentwyn CF23 7XH
dir: W'bound: M4 junct 29, A48(M). (E'bound: M4 junct 30, A4232 signs, A48(M) towards Cardiff). Follow Pentwyn signs, 3rd exit at rdbt. Hotel 200yds on right

Rooms 142 **D** £56-£63*

Premier Inn Cardiff (Roath)

BUDGET HOTEL

☎ 0871 527 8194 🖷 0871 527 8195
Ipswich Rd, Roath CF23 9AQ
dir: W'bound: M4 junct 29, A48(M) (or E'bound: M4 junct 30 A48(M)). Follow Cardiff (E) Docks & Cardiff Bay signs. Then follow brown signs for David Lloyd Tennis Centre. Into David Lloyd Leisure Club car park, follow hotel signs

Rooms 75 **D** £53-£60*

Premier Inn Cardiff West

BUDGET HOTEL

☎ 0871 527 8204 🖷 0871 527 8205
Port Rd, Nantisaf, Wenvoe CF5 6DD
dir: M4 junct 33, S on A4232. Take 2nd exit (signed Airport), 3rd exit at Culverhouse Cross rdbt. Hotel 0.5m on Barry Rd (A4050)

Rooms 39 **D** £53-£61*

CARMARTHEN
Carmarthenshire — Map 8 SN42

Ivy Bush Royal

★★★ 75% HOTEL

☎ 01267 235111 🖷 01267 234914
Spilman St SA31 1LG
e-mail: reception@ivybushroyal.co.uk
web: www.ivybushroyal.co.uk
dir: A48 to Carmarthen, over 1st rdbt, at 2nd rdbt right. Straight on at next 2 rdbts. Left at lights. Hotel on right at top of hill

This hotel offers spacious, well-equipped bedrooms and bathrooms, a relaxing lounge with outdoor patio seating and a comfortable restaurant serving a varied selection of carefully prepared meals. Weddings, meetings and conferences are all well catered for at this friendly, family-run establishment.

Rooms 70 (4 fmly) **S** £60-£115; **D** £80-£150 (incl. bkfst)* **Facilities** FTV Gym Xmas New Year Wi-fi **Conf** Class 50 Board 40 Thtr 200 Del from £99 to £145* **Services** Lift **Parking** 83 **Notes** LB ® Civ Wed 150

C

CARMARTHEN *continued*

Falcon

★★ 80% HOTEL

☎ 01267 234959 & 237152 🖹 01267 221277
Lammas St SA31 3AP
e-mail: reception@falconcarmarthen.co.uk
web: www.falconcarmarthen.co.uk
dir: In town centre pass bus station, turn left, hotel 200yds on left

This friendly hotel has been owned and run by the Exton family for over 45 years, and it is well placed in the centre of the town. Bedrooms, some with four-poster beds, are tastefully decorated with good facilities. There is a comfortable lounge with adjacent bar, and the restaurant offers a varied selection of enjoyable dishes at both lunch and dinner.

Rooms 16 (1 fmly) **Conf** Class 50 Board 40 Thtr 80 **Parking** 36 **Notes** Closed 26 Dec RS Sun

CHEPSTOW Monmouthshire — Map 4 ST59

St Pierre, A Marriott Hotel & Country Club

★★★★ 79% COUNTRY HOUSE HOTEL

☎ 01291 625261 🖹 01291 629975
St Pierre Park NP16 6YA
e-mail: mhrs.cwlgs.frontdesk@marriotthotels.com
web: www.marriottstpierre.co.uk
dir: M48 junct 2, A466 for Chepstow. At next rdbt take 1st exit signed Caerwent/A48. Hotel approx 2m on left

This 14th-century property offers an extensive range of leisure and conference facilities. The comfortable bedrooms are well equipped and located in adjacent wings or in a lakeside cottage complex. The main bar, popular with golfers, overlooks the 18th green; diners can choose between an elegant, traditional restaurant or a modern brasserie.

Rooms 148 (16 fmly) (75 GF) **D** fr £105* **Facilities** Spa STV 36 Putt green Fishing Gym Chipping green Floodlit driving range Sauna Steam room Xmas New Year Wi-fi **Conf** Class 120 Board 90 Thtr 240 Del from £135 to £185* **Parking** 440 **Notes** Civ Wed 220

Castle View

★★★ 68% HOTEL

☎ 01291 620349 🖹 01291 627397
16 Bridge St NP16 5EZ
e-mail: castleviewhotel@btconnect.com
dir: M48 junct 2, A466 for Wye Valley, at 1st rdbt right onto A48 towards Gloucester. Follow 2nd sign to town centre, then to Chepstow Castle, hotel directly opposite

This hotel was built around 300 years ago and offers unrivalled views of Chepstow Castle. Accommodation is comfortable - there are family rooms, double-bedded rooms, and some bedrooms that are situated in a separate building; a good range of guest extras is provided. There is a cosy bar area and a small restaurant where home-cooked food using fresh, local ingredients is offered.

Rooms 13 (4 annexe) (7 fmly) **S** £30-£60; **D** £68-£90 (incl. bkfst) **Facilities** Xmas New Year Wi-fi

CHIRK Wrexham — Map 15 SJ23

Moreton Park Lodge

★★★ 75% HOTEL

☎ 01691 776666 🖹 01691 776655
Moreton Park, Gledrid LL14 5DG
e-mail: reservations@moretonpark.com
web: www.moretonpark.com
dir: 200yds from rdbt junct of A5 & B5070

Located on the town's outskirts and convenient for the A5, this very well maintained property provides a range of spacious, well-equipped bedrooms ideal for both business and leisure guests. Breakfast, lunch and dinner are available in the adjacent Lord Moreton Bar & Restaurant. Service is friendly and attentive.

Rooms 45 (20 fmly) **S** £29-£45; **D** £29-£45* **Facilities** STV Free use of facilities at sister hotel (0.5m) Wi-fi **Conf** Class 50 Board 20 Thtr 60 **Parking** 200 **Notes**

CONWY Conwy — Map 14 SH77

Castle Hotel Conwy

WELSH RAREBITS Hotels of Distinction

★★★★ 79% TOWN HOUSE HOTEL

☎ 01492 582800 🖹 01492 582300
High St LL32 8DB
e-mail: mail@castlewales.co.uk
web: www.castlewales.co.uk
dir: A55 junct 18, follow town centre signs, cross estuary (castle on left). Right then left at mini-rdbts onto one-way system. Right at Town Wall Gate, right into Berry St then High St

This family-run, 16th-century hotel is one of Conwy's most distinguished buildings and offers a relaxed and friendly atmosphere. Bedrooms are appointed to an impressive standard and include a stunning suite. Public areas include a popular modern bar and the award-winning Shakespeare's restaurant.

Rooms 28 (2 fmly) **S** £82-£92; **D** £130-£250 (incl. bkfst) **Facilities** FTV Xmas New Year Wi-fi **Conf** Class 20 Board 20 Thtr 30 Del from £125 to £175 **Parking** 34 **Notes** LB

CRICCIETH Map 14 SH43
Gwynedd

Bron Eifion Country House

★★★ 87% COUNTRY HOUSE HOTEL

☎ 01766 522385 01766 523796
LL52 0SA
e-mail: enquiries@broneifion.co.uk
dir: A497 between Porthmadog & Pwllheli, 0.5m from Criccieth, on right towards Pwhelli

This delightful country house built in 1883, is set in extensive grounds to the west of Criccieth. Now a privately owned and personally run hotel, it provides warm and very friendly hospitality as well as attentive service. The interior style highlights the many retained period features; there is a choice of lounges and the very impressive central hall features a minstrels' gallery.

Rooms 18 (1 fmly) (1 GF) **S** £95-£135; **D** £135-£185 (incl. bkfst) **Facilities** FTV Xmas New Year Wi-fi **Conf** Class 150 Board 60 Thtr 150 **Parking** 50 **Notes** LB ⊗ Civ Wed 150

George IV

★★ 64% HOTEL

☎ 01766 522168 01766 523340
23-25 High St LL52 0BS
e-mail: georgeiv.criccieth@alfatravel.co.uk
dir: On A497 in town centre

This hotel which stands back from the A497 in the town centre. Generally spacious bedrooms are attractively furnished and equipped to meet the needs of both business guests and holidaymakers. George's Brasserie serves a menu based on locally sourced ingredients.

Rooms 47 (11 fmly) **S** £38-£52; **D** £60-£88 (incl. bkfst) **Facilities** FTV ♫ Xmas New Year **Services** Lift **Parking** 16 **Notes** LB ⊗ Closed Jan RS Nov & Feb-Mar

CRICKHOWELL Map 9 SO21
Powys

Bear Hotel

★★★ 75% HOTEL

☎ 01873 810408 01873 811696
NP8 1BW
e-mail: bearhotel@aol.com
dir: On A40 between Abergavenny & Brecon

A favourite with locals as well as visitors, the character and friendliness of this 15th-century coaching inn are renowned. The bedrooms come in a variety of sizes and standards including some with four-posters. The bar and restaurant are furnished in keeping with the style of the building and provide comfortable areas in which to enjoy some of the very popular dishes that use the finest locally-sourced ingredients.

Rooms 34 (13 annexe) (6 fmly) (6 GF) **Facilities** STV FTV Wi-fi **Conf** Class 20 Board 20 Thtr 40 Del from £130 to £150* **Parking** 45 **Notes** RS 25 Dec

Manor

★★★ 75% HOTEL

☎ 01873 810212 01873 811938
Brecon Rd NP8 1SE
e-mail: info@manorhotel.co.uk
web: www.manorhotel.co.uk
dir: On A40, 0.5m from Crickhowell

This impressive manor house, set in a stunning location, was the birthplace of Sir George Everest. The bedrooms and public areas are elegant, and there are extensive leisure facilities. The restaurant, with panoramic views, is the setting for exciting modern cooking, and the family farm supplies meat and poultry to the hotel. This is a popular wedding venue.

Rooms 23 (2 fmly) **S** £60-£90; **D** £80-£160 (incl. bkfst)* **Facilities** STV FTV Gym Fitness assessment Sunbed Xmas New Year Wi-fi **Conf** Class 250 Board 150 Thtr 300 Del from £120 to £140* **Parking** 200 **Notes** LB Civ Wed 150

CWMBRAN Map 9 ST29
Torfaen

Best Western Parkway

★★★★ 78% HOTEL

☎ 01633 871199 01633 869160
Cwmbran Dr NP44 3UW
e-mail: enquiries@parkwayhotel.co.uk
web: www.bw-parkwayhotel.co.uk
dir: M4 junct 25A/26, A4051 follow Cwmbran-Llantarnam Park signs. Right at rdbt then right for hotel

This purpose-built hotel, in over seven acres of grounds, offers comfortable bedrooms and public areas that will suit a wide range of guests. The coffee shop is an informal eating option, open throughout the day, and there is fine dining in Ravello's Restaurant. The bedrooms, including suites, interconnecting family rooms and wheelchair access rooms, are stylishly appointed. Additional facilities include a sports centre and conference and meeting facilities.

Rooms 70 (4 fmly) (34 GF) **S** £58-£120; **D** £68-£160* **Facilities** STV Gym Steam room Sauna Solaria Spa bath ♫ Xmas New Year Wi-fi **Conf** Class 240 Board 100 Thtr 500 Del from £140 to £163* **Parking** 350 **Notes** LB ⊗ Closed 27-30 Dec Civ Wed 250

Premier Inn Cwmbran

BUDGET HOTEL

☎ 0870 111 2851
Avondale Rd, Pontrhydyrun NP44 1DE
dir: M4 junct 26, A4501 signed Cwmbran, straight on at next 5 rdbts. At 6th take Pontrhydyrun Rd exit, left into Avondale Rd

High quality, budget accommodation ideal for both families and business travellers. Spacious, en suite bedrooms feature tea and coffee making facilities, and Freeview TV in most hotels. Internet access and Wi-fi are available for a small fee. The adjacent family restaurant features a wide and varied menu. See also the Hotel Groups pages.

Rooms 40 **D** £63*

D

DEGANWY Conwy — Map 14 SH77

Quay Hotel & Spa

★★★★ 82% ® HOTEL

☎ 01492 564100 🖷 01492 464115
Deganwy Quay LL31 9DJ
e-mail: info@quayhotel.com
dir: M56, A494, A55 junct 18, straight across 2 rdbts. At lights bear left into The Quay. Hotel on right

This boutique hotel occupies a stunning position beside the estuary on Deganwy's Quay. What was once an area for railway storage is now a property of modern architectural design offering hotel-keeping of the highest standard. Spacious bedrooms, many with balconies and wonderful views, are decorated in neutral colours and boast a host of thoughtful extras, including up-to-the-minute communication systems. The friendly staff provide a fluent service in a charmingly informal manner.

Rooms 74 (15 fmly) (30 GF) **Facilities** Spa supervised Gym Steam & sauna room Xmas New Year Wi-fi **Conf** Class 240 Board 90 Thtr 240 **Services** Lift **Parking** 96 **Notes** LB ⊗ Civ Wed 100

DEVIL'S BRIDGE Ceredigion — Map 9 SN77

The Hafod Hotel

★★★ 68% HOTEL

☎ 01970 890232 🖷 01970 890394
SY23 3JL
e-mail: hafodhotel@btconnect.com
dir: Exit A44 in Ponterwyd signed Devil's Bridge/ Pontarfynach onto A4120, 3m, over bridge. Hotel opposite

This former hunting lodge dates back to the 17th century and is situated in six acres of grounds. Now a family-owned and run hotel, it provides accommodation suitable for both business and leisure guests. Family rooms and a four-poster room are available. In addition to the dining area and lounge, there are tea rooms.

Rooms 17 (2 fmly) **S** £55; **D** £85-£100 (incl. bkfst)* **Facilities** Xmas New Year Wi-fi **Conf** Class 70 Board 40 Thtr 100 **Parking** 200 **Notes** Civ Wed 40

DOLGELLAU Gwynedd — Map 14 SH71

INSPECTORS' CHOICE

Penmaenuchaf Hall

WELSH RAREBITS Hotels of Distinction

★★★ ® COUNTRY HOUSE HOTEL

☎ 01341 422129 🖷 01341 422787
Penmaenpool LL40 1YB
e-mail: relax@penhall.co.uk
web: www.penhall.co.uk
dir: Off A470 onto A493 to Tywyn. Hotel approx 1m on left

Built in 1860, this impressive hall stands in 20 acres of formal gardens, grounds and woodland, and enjoys magnificent views across the River Mawddach. Sympathetic restoration has created a comfortable and welcoming hotel with spacious day rooms and thoughtfully furnished bedrooms, some with private balconies. Fresh produce cooked in modern British style is served in an elegant conservatory restaurant, overlooking the countryside.

Rooms 14 (2 fmly) **S** £100-£150; **D** £160-£250 (incl. bkfst)* **Facilities** STV FTV Complimentary salmon & trout fishing Coracling Xmas New Year Wi-fi **Conf** Class 30 Board 22 Thtr 50 Del from £125 to £215* **Parking** 30 **Notes** LB No children 6yrs Civ Wed 65

EBBW VALE Blaenau Gwent — Map 9 SO10

Premier Inn Ebbw Vale

BUDGET HOTEL

☎ 0871 527 8356 🖷 0871 527 8357
Victoria Business Park, Waunllwyd NP23 8AN
dir: M4 junct 28, A467 signed Risca, then Brynmawr. At rdbt at Brynithel 1st exit onto A4046, signed Ebbw Vale. At rdbt 3rd exit towards Waunllwyd. At rdbt 1st exit, next left. Hotel adjacent

High quality, budget accommodation ideal for both families and business travellers. Spacious, en suite bedrooms feature tea and coffee making facilities, and Freeview TV in most hotels. Internet access and Wi-fi are available for a small fee. The adjacent family restaurant features a wide and varied menu. See also the Hotel Groups pages.

Rooms 44 **D** £49-£57*

EGLWYS FACH Ceredigion — Map 14 SN69

INSPECTORS' CHOICE

Ynyshir Hall

★★★ ®®®
COUNTRY HOUSE HOTEL

☎ 01654 781209 & 781268 🖷 01654 781366
SY20 8TA
e-mail: ynyshir@relaischateaux.com
web: www.ynyshir-hall.co.uk
dir: Off A487, 5.5m S of Machynlleth, signed from main road

Set in beautifully landscaped grounds and surrounded by the RSPB Ynys-hir Nature Reserve, Ynyshir Hall is a haven of calm. The house was once owned by Queen Victoria and it is surrounded by mountain scenery. Lavishly styled bedrooms, each individually themed around a great painter, provide high standards of luxury and comfort. The lounge and bar, adorned with an abundance of fresh flowers, have different moods. The dining room offers highly accomplished cooking using the best, locally sourced ingredients including herbs, soft fruit and vegetables from the hotel's own kitchen garden and wild foods gathered nearby. Ynyshir Hall is an idyllic location for weddings.

Rooms 9 (2 annexe) **S** £245-£335; **D** £315-£405 (incl. bkfst)* **Facilities** Xmas New Year **Conf** Class 20 Board 18 Thtr 25 **Parking** 20 **Notes** LB No children 9yrs Civ Wed 40

FISHGUARD Map 8 SM93
Pembrokeshire

The Cartref Hotel

★★ 65% HOTEL

☎ 01348 872430 & 0781 330 5235
01348 873664
15-19 High St SA65 9AW
e-mail: cartrefhotel@btconnect.com
web: www.cartrefhotel.co.uk
dir: On A40 in town centre

Personally run by the proprietor, this friendly hotel offers convenient access to the town centre and ferry terminal. Bedrooms are well maintained and include some family rooms. There is also a cosy lounge bar and a welcoming restaurant that looks out onto the high street.

Rooms 10 (2 fmly) **Facilities** FTV **Parking** 4

GWBERT-ON-SEA Map 14 SN69
Ceredigion

The Cliff Hotel

★★★ 75% HOTEL

☎ 01239 613241 01239 615391
SA43 1PP
e-mail: reservations@cliffhotel.com
dir: Exit A487 into Cardigan, take B4548 towards Gwbert, 2m to hotel

Set in 30 acres of grounds with a 9-hole golf course, this hotel commands superb sea views from its cliff-top location overlooking Cardigan Bay. Bedrooms in the main building have excellent views and there is also a wing of modern rooms. Public areas are spacious and comprise a choice of bars, lounges and a fine dining restaurant. The spa offers a wide range of up-to-the-minute leisure facilities.

Rooms 70 (6 fmly) (5 GF) **S** £59-£85; **D** £75-£135 (incl. bkfst) **Facilities** Spa FTV 9 Putt green Fishing Gym Xmas New Year **Conf** Class 150 Board 140 Thtr 250 Del from £89.50 to £125 **Services** Lift **Parking** 100 **Notes** LB Civ Wed 200

HAY-ON-WYE Map 9 SO24
Powys

The Swan-at-Hay Hotel

★★★ 73% HOTEL

☎ 01497 821188 01497 821424
Church St HR3 5DQ
e-mail: stay@swanathay.co.uk
dir: In town centre

This former coaching inn, now a privately owned hotel, has plenty of character and overlooks well-tended gardens. The bedrooms are comfortable and a good range of guest extras is provided. The food, based on fresh local ingredients, is offered on a well-balanced menu. The Swan's location between The Black Mountains and the Brecon Beacons is ideal for walkers of course, but it is also convenient for leisure and business guests visiting the area. Wi-fi is available.

Rooms 17 **S** £75-£89; **D** £99-£145 (incl. bkfst)* **Notes** LB

HENSOL
Vale of Glamorgan — Map 9 ST07

Vale Resort

★★★★ 85% HOTEL

01443 667800 | 01443 667801
Hensol Park CF72 8JY
e-mail: reservations@vale-hotel.com
web: www.vale-hotel.com
dir: M4 junct 34 towards Pendoylan, hotel signed from junct

A wealth of leisure facilities is offered at this large and modern, purpose-built complex, including two golf courses and a driving range plus an extensive health spa with a gym, swimming pool, squash courts, orthopaedic clinic and a range of treatments. Public areas are spacious and attractive, whilst bedrooms, many with balconies, are well appointed. Meeting and conference facilities are available. Guests can dine in the traditional Vale Grill, a brasserie-style restaurant serving quality fresh ingredients.

Rooms 143 (114 annexe) (15 fmly) (36 GF) **Facilities** Spa STV 36 Putt green Fishing Gym Squash Children's club (Sat mornings & school holidays) Xmas New Year Wi-fi **Conf** Class 280 Board 60 Thtr 700 Del from £130 to £160* **Services** Lift Air con **Parking** 450 **Notes** Civ Wed 700

See advert on page 635

KNIGHTON
Powys — Map 9 SO27

Milebrook House

★★★ 79% COUNTRY HOUSE HOTEL

01547 528632 | 01547 520509
Milebrook LD7 1LT
e-mail: hotel@milebrook.kc3ltd.co.uk
web: www.milebrookhouse.co.uk
dir: 2m E of Knighton, on A4113

Set in three acres of grounds and gardens in the Teme Valley, this charming house dates back to 1760. Over the years since its conversion into a hotel, it has acquired a well-deserved reputation for its warm hospitality, comfortable accommodation and the quality of its cuisine, that uses local produce and home-grown vegetables.

Rooms 10 (2 fmly) (2 GF) **Facilities** Table tennis Trout fly fishing Xmas New Year Wi-fi **Conf** Class 30 **Parking** 21 **Notes** LB No children 8yrs RS Mon lunch

LAMPETER
Ceredigion — Map 8 SN54

The Falcondale Hotel & Restaurant

★★★★ 75% COUNTRY HOUSE HOTEL

01570 422910 | 01570 423559
SA48 7RX
e-mail: info@fthefalcondale.co.uk
web: www.thefalcondale.co.uk
dir: 800yds W of High St (A475) or 1.5m NW of Lampeter (A482)

Built in the Italianate style, this charming Victorian property is set in extensive grounds and beautiful parkland. The individually-styled bedrooms are generally spacious, well equipped and tastefully decorated. Bars and lounges are similarly well appointed with additional facilities including a conservatory and function room. Guests have a choice of either the Valley Restaurant for fine dining or the less formal Peterwells Brasserie.

Rooms 19 (2 fmly) **S** £99-£149; **D** £139-£189 (incl. bkfst)* **Facilities** FTV Xmas New Year Wi-fi **Conf** Class 26 Board 26 Thtr 60 **Services** Lift **Parking** 60 **Notes** LB Civ Wed 200

LLANBEDR Map 14 SH52
Gwynedd

Ty Mawr

★★ 74% SMALL HOTEL

☎ 01341 241440 📠 01341 241440
LL45 2NH
e-mail: info@tymawrhotel.com
web: www.tymawrhotel.com
dir: From Barmouth A496 (Harlech road). In Llanbedr turn right after bridge, follow brown signs, hotel 50yds on left

Ty Mawr means 'Big House' in Welsh. Located in a picturesque village within Snowdonia National Park, this family-run hotel has a relaxed, friendly atmosphere. The attractive grounds opposite the River Artro provide a popular beer garden during fine weather. The attractive, rustically furnished bar offers a blackboard selection of food and a good choice of real ales; a more formal menu is available in the restaurant. Bedrooms are smart and brightly decorated.

Rooms 10 (2 fmly) **S** £50; **D** £80 (incl. bkfst)* **Facilities** STV **Conf** Class 25 Del from £150 to £200* **Parking** 30 **Notes** LB Closed 24-26 Dec

LLANBERIS Map 14 SH56
Gwynedd

Legacy Royal Victoria

LEGACY HOTELS

★★★ 70% HOTEL

☎ 08444 119 003 & 0330 333 2803
📠 08444 119 004
LL55 4TY
e-mail: res-royalvictoria@legacy-hotels.co.uk
web: www.legacy-hotels.co.uk
dir: On A4086 (Caernarfon to Llanberis road), directly opposite Snowdon Mountain Railway

This well-established hotel sits near the foot of Snowdon, between the Peris and Padarn Lakes. The pretty gardens and grounds make an attractive setting for the many weddings held here. Bedrooms are well equipped and there are spacious lounges and bars, and a large dining room with a conservatory looking out over the lakes.

Rooms 106 (14 annexe) (7 fmly) **Facilities** FTV ♫ Xmas New Year **Conf** Class 60 Board 50 Thtr 100 **Services** Lift **Parking** 100 **Notes** Civ Wed 100

LLANDEGLA Map 15 SJ15
Denbighshire

Bodidris Hall Hotel

★★★ 73% ◎ COUNTRY HOUSE HOTEL

☎ 01978 790434 📠 01978 790335
LL11 3AL
e-mail: reception@bodidrishall.com
dir: In village take A5104 towards Chester. Hotel 2m on left, signed

This impressive manor house is in a quiet location surrounded by ornamental gardens and mature woodlands. It has an interesting history and a wealth of original features including gallery ceilinged bedrooms and inglenook fireplaces. Quality decor and furnishing schemes include some fine antique pieces which add to the intrinsic character of this notable property. Service is friendly and attentive.

Rooms 9 (1 fmly) **Facilities** Fishing Xmas New Year Wi-fi **Conf** Class 30 Board 30 Thtr 60 **Parking** 50 **Notes** No children 10yrs Civ Wed 90

LLANDEILO Map 8 SN62
Carmarthenshire

The Plough Inn

★★★★ 77% ◎ HOTEL

☎ 01558 823431 📠 01558 823969
Rhosmaen SA19 6NP
e-mail: info@ploughrhosmaen.com
web: www.ploughrhosmaen.com
dir: 0.5m N of Llandeilo on A40

This privately owned hotel has memorable views over the Towy Valley and the Black Mountains. Bedrooms, situated in a separate wing, are tastefully furnished, spacious and comfortable. The public lounge bar is popular with locals, as is the spacious restaurant where freshly prepared food can be enjoyed. There are also conference facilities, a gym and a sauna.

Rooms 14 (8 fmly) (5 GF) **Facilities** FTV Gym Sauna Xmas New Year Wi-fi **Conf** Class 60 Board 30 Thtr 100 **Services** Air con **Parking** 70 **Notes** Civ Wed 120

White Hart Inn

★★ 71% HOTEL

☎ 01558 823419 📠 01558 823089
36 Carmarthen Rd SA19 6RS
e-mail: info@thewhitehartinnwales.co.uk
web: www.whitehartinnwales.co.uk
dir: Off A40 onto A483, hotel 200yds on left

This privately owned, 19th-century roadside hostelry is on the outskirts of town. The modern bedrooms are well equipped and tastefully furnished, and family rooms are available. Public areas include a choice of bars where a wide range of grilled dishes is available. There are several function rooms, including a large self-contained suite.

Rooms 11 (6 fmly) **S** £40-£45; **D** £60-£70 (incl. bkfst) **Facilities** STV FTV New Year Wi-fi **Conf** Class 80 Board 40 Thtr 100 Del from £65 to £80 **Parking** 50 **Notes** ⊗ Civ Wed 70

LLANDRILLO Map 15 SJ03
Denbighshire

Tyddyn Llan Restaurant

◎◎ RESTAURANT WITH ROOMS

☎ 01490 440264 📠 01490 440414
LL21 0ST
e-mail: info@tyddynllan.co.uk
web: www.tyddynllan.co.uk

Tyddyn Llan is a very well appointed property set in the Edeyrnion Valley at the gateway to Snowdonia. Whilst not all the individually styled bedrooms are spacious, they do offer many home comforts. The public areas are beautiful furnished and have open fires in the colder months. Susan runs the front of the house with friendly informed staff; service is formal and in keeping to the style of the establishment. Husband and chef Bryan sources ingredients as locally as possible and his cooking is sympathetic to the produce. An extensive breakfast menu is available.

Rooms 13

LLANDRINDOD WELLS Map 9 SO06
Powys

The Metropole

★★★★ 77% HOTEL

01597 823700 01597 824828
Temple St LD1 5DY
e-mail: info@metropole.co.uk
web: www.metropole.co.uk
dir: On A483 in town centre

The centre of this famous spa town is dominated by this large Victorian hotel, which has been personally run by the same family for well over 100 years. The lobby leads to Spencers Bar and Brasserie and to the comfortable and elegantly styled lounge. Bedrooms vary in style, but all are spacious and well equipped. Facilities include an extensive range of modern conference and function rooms, as well as the impressive leisure centre. Extensive parking is provided to the rear of the hotel.

Rooms 120 (11 fmly) **S** £82-£98; **D** £105-£125 (incl. bkfst) **Facilities** Spa FTV Gym Beauty & holistic treatments Sauna Steam room Xmas New Year Wi-fi **Conf** Class 200 Board 80 Thtr 300 Del from £95 to £105 **Services** Lift **Parking** 150 **Notes** LB Civ Wed 300

LLANDUDNO Map 14 SH78
Conwy

INSPECTORS' CHOICE

Bodysgallen Hall and Spa

★★★★ COUNTRY HOUSE HOTEL

01492 584466 01492 582519
LL30 1RS
e-mail: info@bodysgallen.com
web: www.bodysgallen.com
dir: A55 junct 19, A470 towards Llandudno. Hotel 2m on right

Situated in idyllic surroundings of its own parkland and formal gardens, this 17th-century house is in an elevated position, with views towards Snowdonia and across to Conwy Castle. The lounges and dining room have fine antiques and great character. Accommodation is provided in the house, but also in delightfully converted cottages, together with a superb spa. Friendly and attentive service is discreetly offered, whilst the restaurant features fine local produce prepared with great skill.

Rooms 31 (16 annexe) (4 fmly) (4 GF) **S** £155-£349; **D** £169-£425 (incl. bkfst)* **Facilities** Spa STV Gym Beauty treatments Steam room Relaxation room Sauna Xmas New Year Wi-fi **Conf** Class 30 Board 22 Thtr 50 **Parking** 50 **Notes** LB No children 6yrs Civ Wed 50

St George's Hotel

★★★★ 80% HOTEL

01492 877544 & 862184 01492 877788
The Promenade LL30 2LG
e-mail: sales@stgeorgeswales.co.uk
dir: A55, A470, follow to promenade, 0.25m, hotel on corner

This large and impressive seafront property was the first hotel to be built in the town. Restored it to its former glory, the accommodation is of very high quality. Its many Victorian features include the splendid, ornate Wedgwood Room restaurant. The terrace restaurant and main lounges overlook the bay; hot and cold snacks are available all day. Many of the thoughtfully equipped bedrooms enjoy sea views.

Rooms 75 **S** £90-£180; **D** £115-£225 (incl. bkfst) **Facilities** STV FTV In-room beauty treatments Xmas New Year Wi-fi **Conf** Class 200 Board 45 Thtr 250 Del from £130 to £145 **Services** Lift Air con **Parking** 36 **Notes** LB Civ Wed 200

See advert on this page

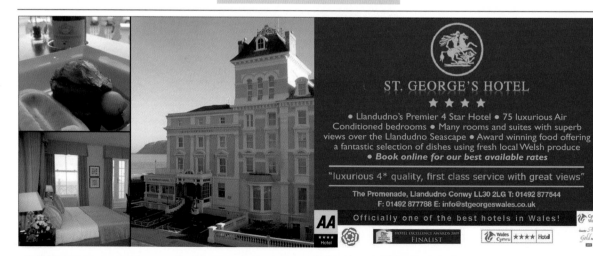

Imperial Hotel

★★★★ 79% HOTEL

☎ 01492 877466 📠 01492 878043
The Promenade LL30 1AP
e-mail: reception@theimperial.co.uk
web: www.theimperial.co.uk
dir: A470 to Llandudno

The Imperial is a large and impressive hotel, situated on the promenade with lovely views out over the blue flag beaches to the bay, and within easy reach of the town centre and other amenities. Many of the bedrooms have the sea views and there are also several suites available. The elegant Chantrey's Restaurant offers a fixed-price, monthly-changing menu that utilises local produce, and The Terrace is the place to relax and enjoy a leisurely lunch or a snack during the day.

Rooms 98 (10 fmly) **Facilities** FTV Gym Beauty therapist Hairdressing Xmas New Year Wi-fi **Conf** Class 50 Board 50 Thtr 150 Del from £145 to £165* **Services** Lift **Parking** 25 **Notes** Civ Wed 150

See advert on this page

Empire Hotel & Spa

★★★★ 75% HOTEL

☎ 01492 860555 📠 01492 860791
Church Walks LL30 2HE
e-mail: reservations@empirehotel.co.uk
web: www.empirehotel.co.uk
dir: From Chester, A55 junct 19 for Llandudno. Follow signs to Promenade, turn right at war memorial & left at rdbt. Hotel 100yds on right

Run by the same family for over almost 60 years, the Empire offers luxuriously appointed bedrooms with every modern facility. The 'Number 72' rooms in an adjacent house are particularly sumptuous. The indoor pool is overlooked by a lounge area where snacks are served all day, and in summer an outdoor pool and roof garden are available. The Watkins restaurant offers an interesting fixed-price menu.

Rooms 60 (8 annexe) (1 fmly) (2 GF) **S** £74.30-£89.60; **D** £99.95-£128.15 (incl. bkfst)* **Facilities** Spa STV FTV Gym Sauna Steam room Fitness suite New Year Wi-fi **Conf** Class 20 Board 20 Thtr 24 Del from £100 to £121* **Services** Lift Air con **Parking** 44 **Notes** LB Closed 16-30 Dec

INSPECTORS' CHOICE

St Tudno Hotel and Restaurant

★★★ HOTEL

☎ 01492 874411 📠 01492 860407
The Promenade LL30 2LP
e-mail: sttudnohotel@btinternet.com
web: www.st-tudno.co.uk
dir: On Promenade towards pier, hotel opposite pier entrance

An excellent family-owned hotel with friendly and attentive staff, that enjoys fine sea views. The stylish bedrooms are well equipped with mini-bars, robes, satellite TVs and many other thoughtful extras. Public rooms include a lounge, a welcoming bar and a small indoor pool. The Terrace Restaurant, where seasonal and daily-changing menus are offered, has a delightful Mediterranean atmosphere. Afternoon tea is a real highlight.

Rooms 18 (4 fmly) **S** £67.50-£100; **D** £95-£215 (incl. bkfst) **Facilities** FTV Xmas New Year Wi-fi **Conf** Class 25 Board 20 Thtr 40 **Services** Lift **Parking** 12 **Notes** LB Civ Wed 70

LLANDUDNO *continued*

INSPECTORS' CHOICE

Osborne House

★★★ TOWN HOUSE HOTEL

☎ 01492 860330 📠 01492 860791
17 North Pde LL30 2LP
e-mail: sales@osbornehouse.com
web: www.osbornehouse.com
dir: Exit A55 junct 19. Follow signs for Llandudno then Promenade. Continue to junct, turn right. Hotel on left opposite pier entrance

Built in 1832, this Victorian house was restored and converted into a luxurious townhouse by the Maddocks family. Spacious suites offer unrivalled comfort and luxury, combining antique furnishings with state-of-the-art technology and facilities. Each suite provides super views over the pier and bay. Osborne's café grill is open throughout the day and offers high quality food, whilst the bar blends elegance with plasma screens, dazzling chandeliers and gilt framed mirrors.

Rooms 7 **S** £143.50-£170; **D** £143.50-£170 (incl. bkfst)* **Facilities** STV FTV Use of swimming pool & sauna at Empire Hotel (100yds) New Year Wi-fi **Services** Air con **Parking** 6 **Notes** ⊗ No children 11yrs Closed 16-30 Dec

Dunoon

★★★ 81% HOTEL

☎ 01492 860787 📠 01492 860031
Gloddaeth St LL30 2DW
e-mail: reservations@dunoonhotel.co.uk
web: www.dunoonhotel.co.uk
dir: Exit Promenade at war memorial by pier into Gloddaeth St. Hotel 200yds on right

This impressive, privately owned hotel is centrally located and offers a variety of well-equipped bedrooms. Elegant public areas include a tastefully appointed restaurant where competently prepared dishes are served together with a good choice of notable, reasonably priced wines. The caring and attentive service is noteworthy.

Rooms 49 (4 fmly) **S** £64-£98; **D** £108-£130 (incl. bkfst) **Facilities** FTV Pool table Wi-fi **Services** Lift **Parking** 24 **Notes** LB Closed 17 Dec-early Mar

Tynedale Hotel

★★★ 79% HOTEL

☎ 01492 877426 📠 01492 871213
Central Promenade LL30 2XS
e-mail: enquiries@tynedalehotel.co.uk
web: www.tynedalehotel.co.uk
dir: On Promenade opposite bandstand

Tour groups are well catered for at this privately owned and personally run hotel, and regular live entertainment is a feature. Vibrant modern public areas create a unique and comfortable setting, and an attractive seafront patio garden is an additional asset. The bedrooms provide good comfort levels, and the staff are friendly and efficient.

Rooms 54 (1 fmly) **S** £40-£43; **D** £80-£122 (incl. bkfst)* **Facilities** FTV ♫ Xmas New Year Wi-fi **Services** Lift **Parking** 20 **Notes** LB ⊗

Cae Mor Hotel

★★★ 75% HOTEL

☎ 01442 878101 📠 01492 876545
5-6 Penrhyn Crescent LL30 1BA
e-mail: info@caemorhotel.co.uk
dir: Exit A55 junct 19, follow A470/Llandudno/Town Centre signs. Straight on at 3 rdbts, right at 4th. Into right lane, right at next rdbt, follow Promenade signs. Straight on at next rdbt, left at next rdbt onto Promenade. 200yds, pass Venue Cwmru

Located in a stunning seafront position adjacent to Venue Cwmru, this tastefully renovated Victorian hotel provides a range of thoughtfully furnished bedrooms in minimalist style with smart modern bathrooms. Public areas include a choice of lounges and a stylish restaurant, the setting for imaginative dinners featuring the best of local seasonal produce.

Rooms 23 (2 fmly) (2 GF) **Facilities** FTV Xmas New Year Wi-fi **Conf** Board 28 Thtr 60 Del from £125.75* **Services** Lift **Parking** 26 **Notes** Civ Wed 50

Merrion

★★★ 75% HOTEL

☎ 01492 860022 📠 01492 860379
Promenade, South Pde LL30 2LN
e-mail: enquiries@merrion-hotel.co.uk
dir: A55 follow Llandudno signs onto Llandudno Promenade then towards pier

Located on the seafront opposite the Victorian Pier and close to the town centre, this constantly improving owner-managed hotel offers comfortable, well-equipped accommodation; many rooms have sea views. Stylish air-conditioned public areas provide high standards of comfort and regular evening entertainment is a feature.

Rooms 65 (6 fmly) (3 GF) **Facilities** STV FTV ♫ Xmas Wi-fi **Conf** Class 40 Board 20 Thtr 30 **Services** Lift **Parking** 24 **Notes** ⊗ Closed Jan

Hydro Hotel

Leisureplex

★★ 71% HOTEL

☎ 01492 870101 📠 01492 870992
Neville Crescent LL30 1AT
e-mail: hydro.llandudno@alfatravel.co.uk
dir: Follow signs for theatre to seafront, towards pier

This large hotel is situated on the promenade overlooking the sea, and offers good, value-for-money, modern accommodation. Public areas are quite extensive and include a choice of lounges, a games/snooker room and a ballroom where entertainment is provided every night. The hotel is a popular venue for coach tour parties.

Rooms 120 (4 fmly) (9 GF) **S** £37-£52; **D** £74-£88 (incl. bkfst) **Facilities** Table tennis Snooker ♫ Xmas New Year **Services** Lift **Parking** 10 **Notes** LB ⊗ Closed Jan-mid Feb RS Nov-Dec (ex Xmas) & mid Feb-Mar

The Broadway Hotel

★★ 🅰 HOTEL

☎ 01492 876398 📠 01492 860460
Mostyn Broadway LL30 1YL
e-mail: sales@thebroadwayhotel.com
web: www.thebroadwayhotel.com
dir: A55 junct 19 towards Llandudno, follow signs to town centre. Approaching town centre right, hotel on opposite corner

Rooms 28 (4 fmly) **S** £30-£39; **D** £60-£78 (incl. bkfst)* **Facilities** FTV Xmas New Year **Conf** Class 12 Board 16 Thtr 30 Del from £75 to £95* **Services** Lift **Parking** 5 **Notes** LB Closed 2 & 31 Jan

Premier Inn Llandudno North (Little Orme)

BUDGET HOTEL

☎ 0871 527 8636 📠 0871 527 8637
Colwyn Rd LL30 3AL
dir: A55 junct 20 follow Rhos-on-Sea/Llandrillo-Yn-Rhos/B5115 signs. Onto B5115 (Brompton Ave). Straight on at next 2 rdbts. Hotel on left

High quality, budget accommodation ideal for both families and business travellers. Spacious, en suite bedrooms feature tea and coffee making facilities, and Freeview TV in most hotels. Internet access and Wi-fi are available for a small fee. The adjacent family restaurant features a wide and varied menu. See also the Hotel Groups pages.

Rooms 19 **D** £59*

The Lilly Restaurant with Rooms

◎ RESTAURANT WITH ROOMS

☎ 01492 876513
West Pde, West Shore LL30 2BD
e-mail: thelilly@live.co.uk

Located on the seafront on the West Shore with views over the Great Orme, this establishment has bedrooms that offer high standards of comfort and good facilities. Children are very welcome here, and a relaxed atmosphere can be found in Madhatters Brasserie, which takes its name from Lewis Caroll's *Alice in Wonderland* which was written on the West Shore. A fine dining restaurant is also available.

Rooms 12 (2 fmly)

LLANDUDNO JUNCTION Conwy — Map 14 SH77

Premier Inn Llandudno (Glan-Conwy)

BUDGET HOTEL

☎ 0871 527 8634 📠 0871 527 8635
Afon Conwy LL28 5LB
dir: A55 junct 19. Exit rdbt at A470 (Betws-y-Coed). Hotel immediately on left, opposite petrol station

High quality, budget accommodation ideal for both families and business travellers. Spacious, en suite bedrooms feature tea and coffee making facilities, and Freeview TV in most hotels. Internet access and Wi-fi are available for a small fee. The adjacent family restaurant features a wide and varied menu. See also the Hotel Groups pages.

Rooms 41 **D** £60*

LLANELLI Carmarthenshire — Map 8 SN50

Best Western Diplomat Hotel

★★★ 78% HOTEL

☎ 01554 756156 📠 01554 751649
Felinfoel SA15 3PJ
e-mail: reservations@diplomat-hotel-wales.com
web: www.diplomat-hotel-wales.com
dir: M4 junct 48, A4138 then B4303, hotel 0.75m on right

This Victorian mansion, set in mature grounds, has been extended over the years to provide a comfortable and relaxing hotel. The well-appointed bedrooms are located in the main house and there is also a wing of comfortable modern bedrooms. Public areas include Trubshaw's Restaurant, a large function suite and a modern leisure centre.

Rooms 50 (8 annexe) (2 fmly) (4 GF) **S** £85-£110; **D** £85-£110 (incl. bkfst) **Facilities** FTV 🏊 supervised Gym Sauna Steam room Sun beds Hairdresser ♫ Xmas New Year Wi-fi **Conf** Class 150 Board 100 Thtr 450 **Services** Lift **Parking** 250 **Notes** LB Civ Wed 300

LLANELLI *continued*

Ashburnham Hotel

★★ 75% HOTEL

☎ 01554 834343 & 834455 01554 834483
Ashburnham Rd, Pembrey SA16 0TH
e-mail: info@ashburnham-hotel.co.uk
web: www.ashburnham-hotel.co.uk
dir: M4 junct 48, A4138 to Llanelli, A484 W to Pembrey. Follow brown information signs

Amelia Earhart stayed at this friendly hotel after finishing her historic trans-Atlantic flight in 1928. Public areas include the brasserie restaurant and the conservatory lounge bar that serve an extensive range of bar meals. Bedrooms, varying from standard to superior, have modern furnishings and facilities. The hotel is licensed for civil ceremonies, and function and conference facilities are also available.

Rooms 13 (2 fmly) **S** £55-£90; **D** £65-£100 (incl. bkfst)* **Facilities** STV FTV Wi-fi **Conf** Class 150 Board 80 Thtr 150 **Parking** 100 **Notes** RS 24-26 Dec Civ Wed 130

L

Premier Inn Llanelli Central East

BUDGET HOTEL

☎ 0871 527 8638 0871 527 8639
Llandafen Rd SA14 9BD
dir: M4 junct 48, A4138, approx 3m. Hotel on left

High quality, budget accommodation ideal for both families and business travellers. Spacious, en suite bedrooms feature tea and coffee making facilities, and Freeview TV in most hotels. Internet access and Wi-fi are available for a small fee. The adjacent family restaurant features a wide and varied menu. See also the Hotel Groups pages.

Rooms 50 **D** £53-£59*

LLANFYLLIN Map 15 SJ11
Powys

Cain Valley

★★ 78% HOTEL

☎ 01691 648366 01691 648307
High St SY22 5AQ
e-mail: info@cainvalleyhotel.co.uk
dir: At end of A490. Hotel in town centre, car park at rear

This Grade II listed coaching inn has a lot of charm and character including features such as exposed beams and a Jacobean staircase. The comfortable accommodation includes family rooms, and a wide range of food is available in the bars, or in the restaurant, which has a well-deserved reputation for its locally sourced steaks.

Rooms 13 (2 fmly) (13 smoking) **Facilities** FTV Wi-fi **Parking** 10 **Notes** LB

LLANGAMMARCH WELLS Map 9 SN94
Powys

INSPECTORS' CHOICE

The Lake Country House & Spa

★★★ COUNTRY HOUSE HOTEL

☎ 01591 620202 & 620474 01591 620457
LD4 4BS
e-mail: info@lakecountryhouse.co.uk
web: www.lakecountryhouse.co.uk
dir: W from Builth Wells on A483 to Garth (approx 6m). Left for Llangammarch Wells, follow hotel signs

Expect good old-fashioned values and hospitality at this Victorian country house hotel. In fact, the service is so traditionally English, guests may believe they have a butler! The establishment offers a 9-hole, par 3 golf course, 50 acres of wooded grounds and a spa where the hot tub overlooks the lake. Bedrooms, some located in an annexe, and some at ground-floor level, are individually styled and have many extra comforts. Traditional afternoon teas are served in the lounge and award-winning cuisine is provided in the spacious and elegant restaurant.

Rooms 30 (7 GF) **Facilities** Spa FTV 9 Putt green Fishing Gym Archery Horse riding Mountain biking Quad biking Xmas New Year Wi-fi **Conf** Class 30 Board 25 Thtr 80 **Parking** 70 **Notes** No children 8 Civ Wed 100

LLANGATTOCK Map 9 SO21
Powys

The Old Rectory Country Hotel & Golf Club

★★★ 75% HOTEL

☎ 01873 810373
NP8 1PH
e-mail: oldrectoryhotel@live.com
dir: In Llangattock turn right 60mtrs after Horseshoe Inn, follow narrow lane, approx 0.25m. Hotel on right

Dating back to the 16th century this house was once the home of poet Henry Vaughan. It retains all the character of an elegant country house whilst offering contemporary bedrooms and bathroom facilities; there are ground-floor bedrooms, family rooms and suites. Guests receive complimentary use of the par three, 9-hole golf course which forms part of the extensive grounds. This hotel is a popular choice for weddings, and the large function room also caters for corporate events.

Rooms 23 **S** fr £55; **D** £85-£159 (incl. bkfst)* **Facilities** STV 9 Wi-fi **Conf** Class 80 Board 30 Thtr 100 **Parking** 50 **Notes** LB Civ Wed

LLANRWST Map 14 SH86
Conwy

See also **Betws-y-Coed**

Maenan Abbey

★★★ 75% HOTEL

☎ 01492 660247 01492 660734
Maenan LL26 0UL
e-mail: reservations@manab.co.uk
dir: 3m N on A470

Set in its own spacious grounds, this privately owned hotel was built as an abbey in 1850 on the site of a 13th-century monastery. It is now a popular venue for weddings as the grounds and magnificent galleried staircase make an ideal setting for photographs. Bedrooms include a large suite and are equipped with modern facilities. Meals are served in the bar and restaurant.

Rooms 14 (3 fmly) (4 smoking) **Facilities** Fishing Guided mountain walks Xmas New Year Wi-fi **Conf** Class 30 Board 30 Thtr 50 **Parking** 60 **Notes** Civ Wed 55

LLANTRISANT Map 9 ST39
Monmouthshire

Premier Inn Llantrisant

BUDGET HOTEL

☎ 0871 527 8640 📠 0871 527 8641
Gwaun Elai, Magden Park CF72 8LL
dir: M4 junct 34, A4119 towards Llantrisant & Rhondda. At 1st rdbt take 2nd exit. At 2nd rdbt take 1st exit

High quality, budget accommodation ideal for both families and business travellers. Spacious, en suite bedrooms feature tea and coffee making facilities, and Freeview TV in most hotels. Internet access and Wi-fi are available for a small fee. The adjacent family restaurant features a wide and varied menu. See also the Hotel Groups pages.

Rooms 51 **D** £51-£61*

LLANWDDYN Map 15 SJ01
Powys

Lake Vyrnwy Hotel & Spa

★★★★ 76% ®
COUNTRY HOUSE HOTEL

☎ 01691 870692 📠 01691 870259
Lake Vyrnwy SY10 0LY
e-mail: info@lakevyrnwyhotel.co.uk
web: www.lakevyrnwy.com
dir: On A4393, 200yds past dam turn sharp right into hotel drive

This elegant Victorian country-house hotel lies in 26,000 acres of woodland above Lake Vyrnwy, and provides a wide range of bedrooms, most with superb views and many with four-poster beds and balconies. Extensive public rooms retain many period features and more informal dining is available in the popular Tower Tavern. Relaxing and rejuvenating treatments are a feature of the stylish health spa.

Rooms 52 (12 fmly) **S** £100-£181; **D** £125-£206 (incl. bkfst)* **Facilities** Spa STV FTV Gym Archery Birdwatching Canoeing Kayaking Clay shooting Sailing Fly fishing Cycling Xmas New Year Wi-fi **Conf** Class 80 Board 60 Thtr 200 Del from £148 to £168* **Services** Lift **Parking** 70 **Notes** LB Civ Wed 200

LLANWRTYD WELLS Map 9 SN84
Powys

Carlton Riverside

®® RESTAURANT WITH ROOMS

☎ 01591 610248
Irfon Crescent LD5 4SP
e-mail: info@carltonriverside.com
dir: In town centre beside bridge

Guests become part of the family at this character property, set beside the river in Wales's smallest town. Carlton Riverside offers award-winning cuisine for which Mary Ann Gilchrist relies on the very best of local ingredients. The set menu is complemented by a well-chosen wine list and dinner is served in the delightfully stylish restaurant which offers a memorable blend of traditional comfort, modern design and river views. Four comfortable bedrooms have tasteful combinations of antique and contemporary furniture, along with welcome personal touches.

Rooms 4

Lasswade Country House

®® RESTAURANT WITH ROOMS

☎ 01591 610515 📠 01591 610611
Station Rd LD5 4RW
e-mail: info@lasswadehotel.co.uk
dir: Exit A483 into Irfon Terrace, right into Station Rd, 350yds on right

This friendly establishment on the edge of the town has impressive views over the countryside. Bedrooms are comfortably furnished and well equipped, while the public areas consist of a tastefully decorated lounge, an elegant restaurant with a bar, and an airy conservatory which looks towards the neighbouring hills. The kitchen utilises fresh, local produce to provide an enjoyable dining experience.

Rooms 8

LLYSWEN Map 9 SO13
Powys

Llangoed Hall Hotel

von Essen hotels

★★★★ 85% ®®
COUNTRY HOUSE HOTEL

☎ 01874 754525 📠 01874 754545
LD3 0YP
e-mail: drayson.kohli@llangoedhall.co.uk

Set against the stunning backdrop of the Black Mountains and the Wye Valley, this imposing country house is a haven of peace and quiet. The interior no less impressive, with a noteworthy art collection complementing the many antiques featured in day rooms and bedrooms. Comfortable, spacious bedrooms and suites are matched by equally inviting lounges.

Rooms 23 **D** £195-£400 (incl. bkfst) **Facilities** FTV Snooker table Xmas New Year Wi-fi **Conf** Class 30 Board 30 Thtr 80 **Parking** 50 **Notes** Civ Wed 80

MAESYCWMMER Map 9 ST19
Caerphilly

Bryn Meadows Golf, Hotel & Spa

★★★★ 80% HOTEL

☎ 01495 225590 📠 01495 228272
Maesycwmmer, Ystrad Mynach CF82 7SN
e-mail: reception@brynmeadows.co.uk
web: www.brynmeadows.com
dir: M4 junct 28, A467 signed Brynmawr, 10m to Newbridge. Take A472 signed Ystrad Mynach. Hotel off Crown rdbt signed 'golf course'. (NB for Sat Nav use NP12 2BR)

Surrounded by its own mature parkland and 18-hole golf course, this impressive hotel complex provides a range of high quality, well-equipped bedrooms; several have their own balconies or patio areas. The attractive public areas include a pleasant restaurant which, like many of the bedrooms, enjoys striking views of the golf course and beyond. There are impressive function facilities and the hotel is a popular venue for weddings.

Rooms 43 (1 annexe) (4 fmly) (21 GF) **Facilities** Spa FTV supervised 18 Putt green Gym Sauna Steam room Aromotherapy suite New Year Wi-fi **Conf** Class 70 Board 60 Thtr 120 Del from £100 to £150 **Services** Air con **Parking** 120 **Notes** Civ Wed 250

MANORBIER Pembrokeshire **Map 8 SS09**

Castlemead

RESTAURANT WITH ROOMS

☎ 01834 871358 📠 01834 871358
SA70 7TA
e-mail: castlemeadhotel@aol.com
web: www.castlemeadhotel.com
dir: A4139 towards Pembroke, B4585 into village, follow signs to beach & castle, establishment on left

Benefiting from a superb location with spectacular views of the bay, the Norman church and Manorbier Castle, this family-run property is friendly and welcoming. Bedrooms, which include some in a converted former coach house at ground floor level, are generally quite spacious and have modern facilities. The public areas include a cosy bar, a sea-view residents' lounge and a restaurant which is also open to non-residents. There are extensive gardens to the rear.

Rooms 8 (3 annexe) (2 fmly)

MERTHYR TYDFIL Merthyr Tydfil **Map 9 SO00**

Premier Inn Merthyr Tydfil

BUDGET HOTEL

☎ 0871 527 8768 📠 0871 527 8769
Pentrebach CF48 4BB
dir: M4 junct 32, A470 to Merthyr Tydfil. At rdbt right to Pentrebach (A4060). At next rdbt 3rd exit signed Abergavenny, (dual carriageway). Double back at next rdbt by Pentrebach Co-op onto A4060 towards Pentrebach. Left after layby, hotel adjacent to Pentrebach House

High quality, budget accommodation ideal for both families and business travellers. Spacious, en suite bedrooms feature tea and coffee making facilities, and Freeview TV in most hotels. Internet access and Wi-fi are available for a small fee. The adjacent family restaurant features a wide and varied menu. See also the Hotel Groups pages.

Rooms 40 **D** £50-£59*

MISKIN Rhondda Cynon Taff **Map 9 ST08**

Miskin Manor Country Hotel

★★★★ 75% ®® COUNTRY HOUSE HOTEL

☎ 01443 224204 📠 01443 237606
Pendoylan Rd CF72 8ND
e-mail: reservations@miskin-manor.co.uk
web: www.miskin-manor.co.uk
dir: M4 junct 34, A4119, signed Llantrisant, hotel 300yds on left

This historic manor house is peacefully located in 22-acre grounds, yet is only minutes away from the M4. Bedrooms are furnished to a high standard and include some located in converted stables and cottages. Public areas are spacious and comfortable and include a variety of function rooms. The relaxed atmosphere and the surroundings ensure this hotel remains popular for wedding functions as well as with business guests. There is a separate modern health and fitness centre which includes a gym, sauna, steam room and swimming pool.

Rooms 43 (9 annexe) (2 fmly) (7 GF) **Facilities** FTV Gym Wi-fi **Conf** Class 80 Board 65 Thtr 160 **Parking** 200 **Notes** Civ Wed 120

MOLD Flintshire **Map 15 SJ26**

Beaufort Park Hotel

★★★ 74% HOTEL

☎ 01352 758646 📠 01352 757132
Alltami Rd, New Brighton CH7 6RQ
e-mail: info@beaufortparkhotel.co.uk
web: www.beaufortparkhotel.co.uk
dir: A55, A494, through Alltami lights, over mini rdbt by petrol station towards Mold, A5119. Hotel 100yds on right

This large, modern hotel is conveniently located a short drive from the North Wales Expressway and offers various styles of spacious accommodation. There are extensive public areas, and several meeting and function rooms are available. There is a wide choice of meals in the formal restaurant and in the popular Arches bar.

Rooms 106 (8 fmly) (32 GF) **S** £50-£80; **D** £60-£110 (incl. bkfst)* **Facilities** FTV Squash ♫ Xmas New Year Wi-fi **Conf** Class 120 Board 120 Thtr 250 Del from £100 to £120* **Parking** 200 **Notes** Civ Wed 250

MONTGOMERY Powys **Map 15 SO29**

Dragon Hotel

★★ 79% ® HOTEL

☎ 01686 668359 📠 0870 011 8227
SY15 6PA
e-mail: reception@dragonhotel.com
web: www.dragonhotel.com
dir: In town centre behind town hall

This fine 17th-century coaching inn stands in the centre of Montgomery. Beams and timbers from the nearby castle, which was destroyed by Cromwell, are visible in the lounge and bar. A wide choice of soundly prepared, wholesome food is available in both the restaurant and bar. Bedrooms are well equipped and family rooms are available.

Rooms 20 (6 fmly) (2 smoking) **S** £57.20-£67.40; **D** £96.50-£106.80 (incl. bkfst)* **Facilities** FTV Sauna ♫ Xmas New Year Wi-fi **Conf** Class 30 Board 25 Thtr 40 Del from £88 to £130* **Parking** 21 **Notes** LB

NARBERTH Pembrokeshire **Map 8 SN11**

The Grove

®® RESTAURANT WITH ROOMS

☎ 01834 860915
Molleston SA67 8BX
e-mail: info@thegrove-narberth.co.uk
web: www.thegrove-narberth.co.uk
dir: A48 to Carmarthen, then A40 to Haverfordwest. At A478 rdbt 1st exit to Narberth, through town towards Tenby. At bottom of hill right, 1m, The Grove on right

An elegant 18th-century country house set on a hillside in 24 acres of rolling countryside. The enthusiastic owners have lovingly restored this building with care, combining period features with excellent modern decor. There are six bedrooms in the main house and six additional rooms in separate buildings; all are appointed with quality and comfort. Some bedrooms are on the ground floor, and most have fantastic views out over the Preseli Hills. There are two sumptuous lounge areas, one with an open fire and a small bar, and two separate dining rooms that offer award-winning cuisine. Self catering cottages are available.

Rooms 12 (6 annexe) (4 fmly)

NEATH
Neath Port Talbot
Map 9 SS79

Castle Hotel

★★★ 71% HOTEL

☎ 01639 641119 📠 01639 641624
The Parade SA11 1RB
e-mail: info@castlehotelneath.co.uk
web: www.castlehotelneath.co.uk
dir: M4 junct 43, follow signs for Neath, 500yds past rail station, hotel on right. Car park on left in 50yds

Situated in the town centre, this Georgian property, once a coaching inn, has a wealth of history and much character. Lord Nelson and Lady Hamilton are reputed to have stayed here, and it is where the Welsh Rugby Union was founded in 1881. The hotel provides well-equipped accommodation and pleasant public areas. Bedrooms include family bedded rooms and one with a four-poster. Green's restaurant provides a good range of dishes at both lunch and dinner. Function and meeting rooms are available.

Rooms 29 (3 fmly) (14 smoking) **Facilities** STV FTV ♫ Xmas New Year Wi-fi **Conf** Class 75 Board 50 Thtr 160 Del from £80 to £120* **Parking** 26 **Notes** ⊗ Civ Wed 120

NEWCASTLE EMLYN
Carmarthenshire
Map 8 SN34

Gwesty'r Emlyn Hotel

★★★ 78% HOTEL

☎ 01239 710317 📠 01239 710792
Bridge St SA38 9DU
e-mail: reception@gwestyremlynhotel.co.uk
web: www.gwestyremlynhotel.co.uk
dir: In town centre

This hotel, in the heart of a busy market town, dates back some 300 years. Now refurbished to a high standard, the stylish, comfortable bedrooms have luxury bathrooms. The public areas comprise a choice of bars, a cosy seating area and a modern restaurant offering dishes created from good, locally sourced ingredients. There is a gym, sauna and spa pool plus a large function suite for weddings and parties.

Rooms 21 (3 fmly) (1 GF) **S** £65; **D** £90-£155 (incl. bkfst)* **Facilities** FTV Gym Sauna Xmas New Year Wi-fi **Conf** Class 100 Board 50 Thtr 150 Del from £102.50 to £140* **Parking** 25 **Notes** LB ⊗ Civ Wed

NEWPORT
Newport
Map 9 ST38

See also **Cwmbran**

The Celtic Manor Resort

★★★★★ 85% @@@ HOTEL

☎ 01633 413000 📠 01633 412910
Coldra Woods NP18 1HQ
e-mail: postbox@celtic-manor.com
web: www.celtic-manor.com
dir: M4 junct 24, take B4237 towards Newport. Hotel 1st on right

This hotel is in the outstanding Celtic Manor Resort. Here there are three challenging golf courses including the Twenty Ten Course specifically designed for the 2010 Ryder Cup, a huge convention centre, superb leisure clubs and two hotels. This hotel has excellent bedrooms, including suites and two Presidential suites, offering good space and comfort; stylish extensive public areas are set around a spectacular atrium lobby that includes several eating options; The Crown at Celtic Manor is the award-winning, fine dining restaurant. There is a choice of shops and boutiques as well.

Rooms 400 (34 fmly) **S** £268-£1500; **D** £268-£1500 **Facilities** Spa STV FTV 🏊 ⛳ 54 🏌 Putt green Gym Golf Academy Clay pigeon shooting Mountain bike trails Table tennis ♫ Xmas New Year Wi-fi Child facilities **Conf** Class 150 Board 60 Thtr 1200 **Services** Lift Air con **Parking** 1300 **Notes** LB ⊗ Civ Wed 100

Manor House

★★★★ 74% @ HOTEL

☎ 01633 413000 📠 01633 410236
The Celtic Manor Resort, Coldra Woods NP18 1HQ
e-mail: bookings@celtic-manor.com
dir: M4 junct 24, B4237 towards Newport. Hotel 1st on right

Part of the complex of the Celtic Manor Resort (see previous entry), this hotel, built in the 19th century, offers country house charm combined with modern comforts. Sitting in beautiful landscaped gardens it has traditionally styled bedrooms, three with four-posters. Several eating options are available both at Manor House and at the Resort, where guests have access to all the hotel and leisure facilities; three challenging golf courses and superb leisure clubs among them.

Rooms 69 **Facilities** Spa 🏊 supervised ⛳ 54 (at Celtic Manor Resort) 🏌 Putt green Gym ♫ Xmas New Year **Conf** Class 80 Thtr 200 **Services** Lift Air con **Notes** LB Civ Wed

Holiday Inn Newport

★★★ 70% HOTEL

☎ 01633 412777 📠 01633 413087
The Coldra NP6 2YG
web: www.holidayinn.co.uk
dir: M4 junct 24, follow signs for B4237 towards Newport. Hotel 200yds on left

A purpose-built and modern hotel, in a very convenient location near to the M4, that caters equally well for both leisure and business guests. There is Harpers, the informal restaurant, a small leisure complex and a business centre.

Rooms 119

N

NEWPORT *continued*

Holiday Inn Express Newport

BUDGET HOTEL

☎ 01633 819850 🖷 01633 819998
Lakeside Dr, Coedkernew NP10 8BB
e-mail: gm@expressnewport.co.uk
web: www.hiexpress.com/exnewport
dir: M4 junct 28 at junct take St Mellons/Castleton exit. Remain in right lane, at lights turn right. Hotel on left

A modern hotel ideal for families and business travellers. Fresh and uncomplicated, the spacious rooms include Sky TV, power shower and tea and coffee-making facilities. Continental buffet breakfast is included in the room rate; other meals may be taken at the nearby family pub or restaurant. See also the Hotel Groups pages.

Rooms 125 (70 fmly) (34 GF) **S** £49-£89; **D** £49-£89 (incl. bkfst)* **Conf** Class 15 Board 15 Thtr 50

Premier Inn Newport South Wales

BUDGET HOTEL

☎ 0871 527 8814 🖷 0871 527 8815
Coldra Junction, Chepstow Rd, Langstone NP18 2NX
dir: M4 junct 24, A48 to Langstone, at next rdbt return towards junct 24. Hotel 50mtrs on left

High quality, budget accommodation ideal for both families and business travellers. Spacious, en suite bedrooms feature tea and coffee making facilities, and Freeview TV in most hotels. Internet access and Wi-fi are available for a small fee. The adjacent family restaurant features a wide and varied menu. See also the Hotel Groups pages.

Rooms 63 **D** £52-£62*

NEWPORT Map 8 SN03
Pembrokeshire

Llysmeddyg

RESTAURANT WITH ROOMS

☎ 01239 820008
East St SA42 0SY
e-mail: contact@llysmeddyg.com
dir: On A487 in centre of town on Main St

Llysmeddyg is a Georgian townhouse offering a blend of old and new, with elegant furnishings, deep sofas and a welcoming fire. The owners of this property employed local craftsmen to create a lovely interior that has an eclectic style. The focus of the quality restaurant menu is the use of fresh, seasonal, locally sourced ingredients. The spacious bedrooms are comfortable and contemporary in design; bathrooms vary in style.

Rooms 8 (3 annexe) (3 fmly)

PARKMILL (NEAR SWANSEA) Map 8 SS58
Swansea

Maes-Yr-Haf Restaurant with Rooms

RESTAURANT WITH ROOMS

☎ 01792 371000 🖷 01792 234922
SA3 2EH
e-mail: enquiries@maes-yr-haf.com
dir: Take A4118 W from Swansea

Set in the peaceful location on The Gower in the small village of Parkmill, this property is well situated for easy access to Swansea and the coast. It offers contemporary, individually styled bedrooms with a very good range of guest extras, where comfort is the key. Each bathroom has a bath and shower. The food is created from high quality, locally sourced ingredients; dinner is a highlight, served in the modern restaurant, and breakfast provides a very good start to the day.

Rooms 5

PEMBROKE Map 8 SM90
Pembrokeshire

Best Western Lamphey Court Hotel & Spa

★★★ 80% HOTEL

☎ 01646 672273 🖷 01646 672480
Lamphey SA71 5NT
e-mail: info@lampheycourt.co.uk
web: www.lampheycourt.co.uk
dir: A477 to Pembroke. Left at Milton for Lamphey, hotel on right

This Georgian mansion, on an elevated site, is set in attractive countryside and is perfectly situated for exploring the stunning Pembrokeshire coast, the beaches and the Preseli Hills. Well-appointed bedrooms and family suites are situated in a converted coach house within the grounds. The elegant public areas include both formal and informal dining rooms that feature dishes inspired by the local produce. Leisure facilities include a state-of-the-art spa with a swimming pool, gym, sauna, treatment rooms and much more.

Rooms 38 (12 annexe) (7 fmly) (6 GF) **Facilities** Spa FTV Gym Yacht charter Xmas New Year Wi-fi **Conf** Class 40 Board 30 Thtr 60 Del from £125 to £165* **Parking** 50 **Notes** LB Civ Wed 80

Lamphey Hall

★★★ 77% HOTEL

☎ 01646 672394 📠 01646 672369
Lamphey SA71 5NR
e-mail: andrewjones1990@aol.com
dir: From Carmarthen A40 to St Clears. Follow signs for A477, left at Milton

Set in a delightful village, this very friendly, privately owned and efficiently run hotel offers an ideal base from which to explore the surrounding countryside. Bedrooms are well equipped, comfortably furnished and include family rooms and ground floor rooms. Diners have a choice of three restaurant areas offering an extensive range of dishes. There is also a small lounge, a bar and attractive gardens.

Rooms 10 (1 fmly) (2 GF) **Facilities** FTV Wi-fi **Parking** 32 **Notes** ®

PENCOED Map 9 SS98
Bridgend

St Mary's Hotel & Country Club

★★★ 72% HOTEL

☎ 01656 861100 📠 01656 863400
St Marys Golf Club CF35 5EA
e-mail: stmarysgolfhotel@btinternet.com
dir: M4 junct 35, on A473

This charming 16th-century farmhouse has been converted and extended into a modern and restful hotel, surrounded by its own golf courses. The well-equipped bedrooms are generously appointed and most feature whirlpool baths. Guests have a choice of bars which prove popular with club members too, plus there's a good range of dining options.

Rooms 24 (19 fmly) (10 GF) **Facilities** STV ⛳ 30 Putt green Floodlit driving range New Year Wi-fi **Conf** Class 60 Board 40 Thtr 120 **Parking** 140 **Notes** ® Civ Wed 120

PONTYPOOL Map 9 SO20
Torfaen

Premier Inn Pontypool

Premier Inn

BUDGET HOTEL

☎ 0871 527 8890 📠 0871 527 8891
Tyr'felin, Lower Mill Field NP4 0RH
dir: At junct of A4042 & A472

High quality, budget accommodation ideal for both families and business travellers. Spacious, en suite bedrooms feature tea and coffee making facilities, and Freeview TV in most hotels. Internet access and Wi-fi are available for a small fee. The adjacent family restaurant features a wide and varied menu. See also the Hotel Groups pages.

Rooms 49 **D** £52-£60*

PONTYPRIDD Map 9 ST08
Rhondda Cynon Taff

Llechwen Hall

★★★ 74% ® COUNTRY HOUSE HOTEL

☎ 01443 742050 & 743020 📠 01443 742189
Llanfabon CF37 4HP
e-mail: enquiries@llechwenhall.co.uk
dir: A470 N towards Merthyr Tydfil. At large rdbt take 3rd exit. At mini rdbt take 3rd exit, hotel signed 0.5m on left

Set on top of a hill with a stunning approach, this country house hotel has served many purposes in its 200-year-old history including a private school and a magistrates' court. The spacious, individually decorated bedrooms are well equipped; some are situated in the separate coach house nearby. There are ground-floor, twin, double and family bedrooms on offer. The Victorian-style public areas are attractively appointed and the hotel is a popular venue for weddings.

Rooms 20 (8 annexe) (6 fmly) (4 GF) **Facilities** FTV Xmas New Year Wi-fi **Conf** Class 80 Board 40 Thtr 200 **Parking** 150 **Notes** Civ Wed 80

PORTHCAWL Map 9 SS87
Bridgend

Seabank Hotel

Leisureplex

★★ 64% HOTEL

☎ 01656 782261 📠 01656 785363
Esplanade CF36 3LU
e-mail: seabank@alfatravel.co.uk
dir: M4 junct 37, A4229 to Porthcawl seafront

This large hotel stands in a prime location on the promenade of this seaside town, with panoramic sea views from the majority of bedrooms, all of which are spacious. There is a restaurant, lounge bar and a choice of lounges with sea views. The hotel is a popular venue for coach tour parties, as well as weddings and conferences. There is ample parking in the area around the hotel.

Rooms 87 (2 fmly) (5 smoking) **S** £39-£55; **D** £62-£94 (incl. bkfst) **Facilities** STV ♫ Xmas New Year **Services** Lift **Parking** 60 **Notes** LB ® Closed 2 Jan-10 Feb

PORTHMADOG Map 14 SH53
Gwynedd

Royal Sportsman

★★★ 80% ®® HOTEL

☎ 01766 512015 📠 01766 512490
131 High St LL49 9HB
e-mail: enquiries@royalsportsman.co.uk
dir: At rdbt junct of A497 & A487

Ideally located in the centre of Porthmadog, this former coaching inn dates from the Victorian era and is a friendly, privately owned and personally run hotel. Rooms are tastefully decorated and well equipped, and some are in an annexe close to the hotel. There is a large comfortable lounge and a wide range of meals is served in the bar and in the restaurant.

Rooms 28 (9 annexe) (7 fmly) (9 GF) **S** £59-£83; **D** £85-£99 (incl. bkfst)* **Facilities** STV FTV Xmas New Year Wi-fi **Conf** Class 50 Board 30 Thtr 50 **Parking** 17 **Notes** LB

PORTMEIRION Map 14 SH53
Gwynedd

The Hotel Portmeirion

WELSH RAREBITS Hotels of Distinction

★★★★ 78% ®® HOTEL

☎ 01766 770000 📠 01766 770300
LL48 6ET
e-mail: hotel@portmeirion-village.com
web: www.portmeirion-village.com
dir: 2m W, Portmeirion village is S off A487

Saved from dereliction in the 1920s by Clough Williams-Ellis, the elegant Hotel Portmeirion enjoys one of the finest settings in Wales, located beneath the wooded slopes of the village, overlooking the sandy estuary towards Snowdonia. Many rooms have private sitting rooms and balconies with spectacular views. The mostly Welsh-speaking staff provide a good mix of warm hospitality and efficient service.

Rooms 42 (28 annexe) (4 fmly) **Facilities** Spa STV ⥼ Xmas New Year Wi-fi **Conf** Class 40 Board 30 Thtr 100 **Services** Lift **Parking** 40 **Notes** ® Civ Wed 130

P

PORTMEIRION ***continued***

Castell Deudraeth

WELSH RAREBITS *Hotels of Distinction*

★★★★ 77% ® HOTEL

☎ 01766 770000 🖷 01766 771771
LL48 6EN
e-mail: castell@portmeirion-village.com
web: www.portmeirion-village.com
dir: A4212 for Trawsfynydd/Porthmadog. 1.5m beyond Penrhyndeudraeth, hotel on right

A castellated mansion that overlooks Snowdonia and the famous Italianate village featured in the 1960's cult series *The Prisoner*. An original concept, Castell Deudraeth combines traditional materials, such as oak and slate, with state-of-the-art technology and design. Dynamically styled bedrooms boast underfloor heating, real-flame gas fires, wide-screen TVs with DVDs and cinema surround-sound. The brasserie-themed dining room provides an informal option at dinner.

Rooms 11 (5 fmly) **Facilities** Spa STV Xmas New Year Wi-fi **Conf** Class 18 Board 25 Thtr 30 **Services** Lift **Parking** 30 **Notes** ® Civ Wed 30

PORT TALBOT — Map 9 SS78
Neath Port Talbot

Best Western Aberavon Beach Hotel

★★★ 79% HOTEL

☎ 01639 884949 🖷 01639 897885
Neath SA12 6QP
e-mail: sales@aberavonbeach.com
web: www.aberavonbeachhotel.com
dir: M4 junct 41, A48 & follow signs for Aberavon Beach & Hollywood Park

This friendly, purpose-built hotel enjoys a prominent position on the seafront overlooking Swansea Bay. Bedrooms, many with sea views, are comfortably appointed and thoughtfully equipped. Public areas include a leisure suite with swimming pool, open-plan bar and restaurant plus a choice of function rooms.

Rooms 52 (6 fmly) **Facilities** FTV All weather leisure centre Sauna Xmas New Year Wi-fi **Conf** Class 200 Board 100 Thtr 300 Del from £95 to £130* **Services** Lift **Parking** 150 **Notes** LB Civ Wed 300

Premier Inn Port Talbot

BUDGET HOTEL

☎ 0871 527 8896 🖷 0871 527 8897
Baglan Rd, Baglan SA12 8ES
dir: M4 junct 41 W'bound. Hotel just off 4th exit at rdbt. M4 junct 42 E'bound, left towards Port Talbot. Take 2nd exit off 2nd rdbt

High quality, budget accommodation ideal for both families and business travellers. Spacious, en suite bedrooms feature tea and coffee making facilities, and Freeview TV in most hotels. Internet access and Wi-fi are available for a small fee. The adjacent family restaurant features a wide and varied menu. See also the Hotel Groups pages.

Rooms 42 **D** £49-£59*

RAGLAN — Map 9 SO40
Monmouthshire

The Beaufort Arms Coaching Inn & Brasserie

WELSH RAREBITS *Hotels of Distinction*

★★★ 75% ® HOTEL

☎ 01291 690412 🖷 01291 690935
High St NP15 2DY
e-mail: enquiries@beaufortraglan.co.uk
web: www.beaufortraglan.co.uk
dir: M4 junct 24, A449/A40 junct Monmouth/Abergavenny, 0.5m into village opposite church

This friendly, family-run village inn dating back to the 15th century has historic links with nearby Raglan Castle. The bright, stylish and beautifully appointed bedrooms in the main house are suitably equipped for both tourists and business guests. Food is served in either the Brasserie restaurant or traditional lounge, and both offer a relaxed service with an enjoyable selection of carefully prepared dishes.

Rooms 15 (5 annexe) (1 fmly) (5 GF) **Facilities** Use of facilities at golf club in village Wi-fi **Conf** Class 60 Board 30 Thtr 120 **Parking** 30 **Notes** ® RS 25-26 Dec

REYNOLDSTON — Map 8 SS48
Swansea

INSPECTORS' CHOICE

Fairyhill

®® RESTAURANT WITH ROOMS

☎ 01792 390139 🖷 01792 391358
SA3 1BS
e-mail: postbox@fairyhill.net
web: www.fairyhill.net
dir: M4 junct 47, A483, at next rdbt right onto A484. At Gowerton take B4295, 10m

Peace and tranquillity are never far away at this charming Georgian mansion set in the heart of the beautiful Gower peninsula. Bedrooms are furnished with care and are filled with many thoughtful extras. There is also a range of comfortable seating areas with crackling log fires, and the smart restaurant offers menus based on local produce and complemented by an excellent wine list.

Rooms 8

RHUDDLAN — Map 15 SJ07
Denbighshire

Premier Inn Rhuddlan

BUDGET HOTEL

☎ 0871 527 8932 🖷 0871 527 8933
Castle View Retail Park, Marsh Rd LL18 5UA
dir: A55 junct 27, A525 signed Rhyl. At next rdbt 3rd exit into Station Rd. Next left into Marsh Rd. Hotel on left

High quality, budget accommodation ideal for both families and business travellers. Spacious, en suite bedrooms feature tea and coffee making facilities, and Freeview TV in most hotels. Internet access and Wi-fi are available for a small fee. The adjacent family restaurant features a wide and varied menu. See also the Hotel Groups pages.

Rooms 44 **D** £60*

RHYL Map 14 SJ08
Denbighshire

Barratt's at Ty'n Rhyl

RESTAURANT WITH ROOMS

01745 344138 & 0773 095 4994
01745 344138
Ty'n Rhyl, 167 Vale Rd LL18 2PH
e-mail: ebarratt5@aol.com
dir: A55 onto A525 to Rhyl, pass Sainsburys & B&Q, pass Roger Jones on left, 50yds on right

This delightful 16th-century house lies in a secluded location surrounded by attractive gardens. The quality of the food reflects the skill of the owner-chef. Public areas are smartly furnished and include a panelled lounge, cosy library and an attractive conservatory. Bedrooms are comfortable and equipped with lots of thoughtful extras.

Rooms 3

ROCKFIELD Map 9 SO41
Monmouthshire

The Stonemill & Steppes Farm Cottages

RESTAURANT WITH ROOMS

01600 775424
NP25 5SW
e-mail: michelle@thestonemill.co.uk
dir: A48 to Monmouth, B4233 to Rockfield. 2.6m from Monmouth

Located in a small hamlet just west of Monmouth, close to the Forest of Dean and the Wye Valley, this operation offers accommodation comprising six very well-appointed cottages. The comfortable rooms (for self-catering or on a B&B basis) are architect designed and lovingly restored to retain many original features. In a separate, converted 16th-century barn is Stonemill Restaurant with oak beams, vaulted ceilings and an old cider press. Breakfast is served in the cottages on request. This establishment's location proves handy for golfers with a choice of many courses in the area.

Rooms 6 (6 fmly)

ROSSETT Map 15 SJ35
Wrexham

Best Western Llyndir Hall

Best Western

★★★ 81% HOTEL

01244 571648 01244 571258
Llyndir Ln LL12 0AY
e-mail: llyndirhallhotel@feathers.uk.com
dir: 5m S of Chester on B5445 follow Pulford signs

Located on the English/Welsh border within easy reach of Chester and Wrexham, this elegant manor house lies in several acres of mature grounds. The hotel is popular with both business and leisure guests, and facilities include conference rooms, an impressive leisure centre, a choice of comfortable lounges and a brasserie-style restaurant.

Rooms 48 (3 fmly) (20 GF) **Facilities** Spa FTV supervised Gym Beauty salon Sauna Xmas New Year Wi-fi **Conf** Class 60 Board 40 Thtr 120 Del from £125 to £150 **Parking** 80 **Notes** Civ Wed 120

ST ASAPH Map 15 SJ07
Denbighshire

The Oriel

★★★★ 74% HOTEL

01745 582716 01745 585208
Upper Denbigh Rd LL17 0LW
e-mail: mail@theorielhotel.com
web: www.theorielhotel.com
dir: A55 onto A525, right at cathedral, 1m on right

Set in several acres of mature grounds south of St Asaph, Oriel House offers generally spacious, well-equipped bedrooms and has a friendly and hospitable staff. The Terrace restaurant serves imaginative food with an emphasis on local produce. Extensive function facilities cater for business meetings and weddings, and the leisure club is available to guests.

Rooms 33 (3 fmly) (13 GF) **S** £79-£89; **D** £89-£160 (incl. bkfst) **Facilities** Spa STV FTV Gym Steam room Sauna Xmas New Year Wi-fi **Conf** Class 100 Board 50 Thtr 220 Del from £115 to £145 **Parking** 200 **Notes** LB Civ Wed 200

ST DAVID'S Map 8 SM72
Pembrokeshire

Warpool Court

WELSH RAREBITS Hotels of Distinction

★★★ 81% COUNTRY HOUSE HOTEL

01437 720300 01437 720676
SA62 6BN
e-mail: info@warpoolcourthotel.com
web: www.warpoolcourthotel.com
dir: At Cross Square left by The Bishops Restaurant (Goat St). Pass Farmers Arms pub, left in 400mtrs, follow hotel signs, entrance on right

Originally the cathedral choir school, this hotel is set in landscaped gardens looking out to sea and is within easy walking distance of the Pembrokeshire Coastal Path. The lounges are spacious and comfortable, and the bedrooms are well furnished and equipped with modern facilities. The restaurant offers delightful cuisine.

Rooms 22 (3 fmly) **S** £165-£210; **D** £240-£480 (incl. bkfst & dinner)* **Facilities** Table tennis Pool table Xmas New Year Wi-fi **Conf** Class 25 Board 25 Thtr 40 **Parking** 100 **Notes** LB Closed Nov & 1st half Dec Civ Wed 120

SARN PARK MOTORWAY SERVICE AREA (M4) Map 9 SS98
Bridgend

Days Inn Bridgend Cardiff - M4

BUDGET HOTEL

01656 659218 01656 768665
Sarn Park Services, M4 Junct 36 CF32 9RW
e-mail: sarn.hotel@welcomebreak.co.uk
web: www.welcomebreak.co.uk
dir: M4 junct 36

This modern building offers accommodation in smart, spacious and well-equipped bedrooms, suitable for families and business travellers, and all with en suite bathrooms. Continental breakfast is available and other refreshments may be taken at the nearby family restaurant. See also the Hotel Groups pages.

Rooms 40 (39 fmly) (20 GF) (5 smoking)
S £39.95-£59.95; **D** £49.95-£69.95

S

SAUNDERSFOOT Map 8 SN10
Pembrokeshire

HOTEL OF THE YEAR

St Brides Spa Hotel

★★★★ 82% HOTEL

☎ 01834 812304 📠 01834 811766
St Brides Hill SA69 9NH
e-mail: reservations@stbridesspahotel.com
web: www.stbridesspahotel.com
dir: A478 onto B4310 to Saundersfoot. Hotel above harbour

Set overlooking Carmarthen Bay this contemporary hotel and spa takes prime position. Many of the stylish, modern bedrooms enjoy sea views and have balconies; there are also luxury apartments in the grounds. The hotel is open plan and has excellent views of the bay from the split-level lounge areas. Fresh local seafood is a speciality in the modern airy restaurant which has a terrace for eating alfresco when the weather allows. The destination spa enjoys some of the very best views from the double treatment room and spa pool. AA Hotel of the Year for Wales 2011-12.

Rooms 46 (12 annexe) (6 fmly) (9 GF) **S** £125-£190; **D** £150-£280 (incl. bkfst) **Facilities** Spa FTV Gym Thermal suite Xmas New Year Wi-fi **Conf** Class 40 Board 26 Thtr 80 Del from £170 to £200 **Services** Lift **Parking** 65 **Notes** LB ⊗ Civ Wed 80

See advert on opposite page

S

Gower Hotel

★★★ 67% HOTEL

☎ 01834 813452 📠 01834 813452
Milford Ter SA69 9EL
e-mail: enquiries@gower-hotel.com
dir: A478 onto B4316 to Saundersfoot. Hotel on one-way system in village

This hotel, set back from the town, is just a stroll of the harbour, sandy beaches and beautiful countryside; there are many tourist attractions and amenities within the vicinity. On offer are comfortable twin, double or family rooms, and there is a lift to all floors. The popular bar provides entertainment on a regular basis, and the Orangery Restaurant serves an imaginative menu.

Rooms 20 (2 fmly) **S** £65; **D** £85-£94 (incl. bkfst)* **Facilities** FTV Xmas New Year Wi-fi **Conf** Class 30 Board 30 Thtr 40 **Services** Lift **Parking** 16 **Notes** LB ⊗

SKENFRITH Map 9 SO42
Monmouthshire

INSPECTORS' CHOICE

The Bell at Skenfrith

◎◎ RESTAURANT WITH ROOMS

☎ 01600 750235 📠 01600 750525
NP7 8UH
e-mail: enquiries@skenfrith.co.uk
web: www.skenfrith.co.uk
dir: On B4521 in Skenfrith, opposite castle

The Bell is a beautifully restored, 17th-century former coaching inn which still retains much original charm and character. It is peacefully situated on the banks of the Monnow, a tributary of the River Wye, and is ideally placed for exploring the numerous delights of the area. Natural materials have been used to create a relaxing atmosphere, while the bedrooms, which include full suites and rooms with four-poster beds, are stylish, luxurious and equipped with DVD players. The garden produces much of the fresh ingredients used in the kitchen where award-winning quality food is produced for relaxed dining in the welcoming restaurant. Overall Winner and Winner for Wales of the AA Wine Award 2012.

Rooms 11 (2 fmly)

SWANSEA Map 9 SS69
Swansea

See also **Port Talbot**

Swansea Marriott Hotel

Marriott HOTELS & RESORTS

★★★★ 80% HOTEL

☎ 0870 400 7282 📠 0870 400 7382
The Maritime Quarter SA1 3SS
web: www.swanseamarriott.co.uk
dir: M4 junct 42, A483 to city centre past Leisure Centre, then follow signs to Maritime Quarter

Just opposite City Hall in the bustling Maritime Quarter, this busy hotel enjoys fantastic views over the bay and marina. The air-conditioned bedrooms are spacious and equipped with a range of extras. Public rooms include a popular leisure club with a gym, whirlpool, sauna and swimming pool, and Abernethy's restaurant which overlooks the marina. It is worth noting, however, that lounge seating is limited.

Rooms 119 (49 fmly) (11 GF) **Facilities** STV ⛆ Gym New Year Wi-fi **Conf** Class 120 Board 30 Thtr 300 **Services** Lift Air con **Parking** 122 **Notes** LB ⊗ Civ Wed 200

Dragon

CLASSIC BRITISH HOTELS

★★★★ 76% ◎ HOTEL

☎ 01792 657100 & 0870 4299 848
📠 01792 456044
The Kingsway Circle SA1 5LS
e-mail: info@dragon-hotel.co.uk
web: www.dragon-hotel.co.uk
dir: A483 follow signs for city centre. After lights at Sainsbury's right into The Strand then left. Hotel straight ahead

This privately owned hotel is located in the city centre and offers spacious modern accommodation with well-equipped, comfortable bedrooms. There is a bar and lounge facility on the first floor along with the dining room for breakfast. On the ground floor, the Dragons Brasserie provides good food from a vibrant continental menu for both residents and non-residents. The health and fitness club offers an excellent choice of facilities and there is a good range of conference rooms.

Rooms 106 (5 fmly) **S** £58.65-£149; **D** £58.65-£149* **Facilities** STV supervised Gym Beauty therapist Xmas New Year Wi-fi **Conf** Class 120 Board 60 Thtr 230 Del from £129 to £149* **Services** Lift Air con **Parking** 52 **Notes** Civ Wed 200

Express by Holiday Inn Swansea - West

BUDGET HOTEL

☎ 01792 818700 01792 818718
Neath Rd, Llandarcy SA10 6JQ
e-mail: gm.swansea@expressholidayinn.co.uk
web: www.expressswansea.co.uk
dir: Off M4 junct 43

A modern hotel ideal for families and business travellers. Fresh and uncomplicated, the spacious rooms include Sky TV, power shower and tea and coffee-making facilities. Continental buffet breakfast is included in the room rate; other meals may be taken at the nearby family pub or restaurant. See also the Hotel Groups pages.

Rooms 91 (60 fmly) (18 GF) **Conf** Class 20 Board 16 Thtr 25

Premier Inn Swansea City Centre

BUDGET HOTEL

☎ 0871 527 9060 0871 527 9061
Salubrious Place, Wind St SA1 1EE
dir: M4 junct 42, A483 towards the city centre. Pass Sainsburys on left, right into Salubrious Place, 2nd right, then 3rd exit at mini rdbt

High quality, budget accommodation ideal for both families and business travellers. Spacious, en suite bedrooms feature tea and coffee making facilities, and Freeview TV in most hotels. Internet access and Wi-fi are available for a small fee. The adjacent family restaurant features a wide and varied menu. See also the Hotel Groups pages.

Rooms 116 **D** £60*

Premier Inn Swansea North

BUDGET HOTEL

☎ 0871 527 9062 0871 527 9063
Upper Forest Way, Morriston SA6 8WB
dir: M4 junct 45, A4067 towards Swansea. 0.5m, at 2nd exit left into Clase Rd. Hotel 400yds on left

Rooms 40 **D** £54-£60*

Premier Inn Swansea Waterfront

BUDGET HOTEL

☎ 0871 577 9212 0871 527 9213
The Waterfront Development, Langdon Rd SA1 8PL
dir: M4 junct 42, A483 towards Swansea/Abertawe (signed Fabian Way). Approx 4.5m. At 2nd lights, left into SA1 Waterfront development. At rdbt take 2nd exit into Langdon Rd. Hotel on left

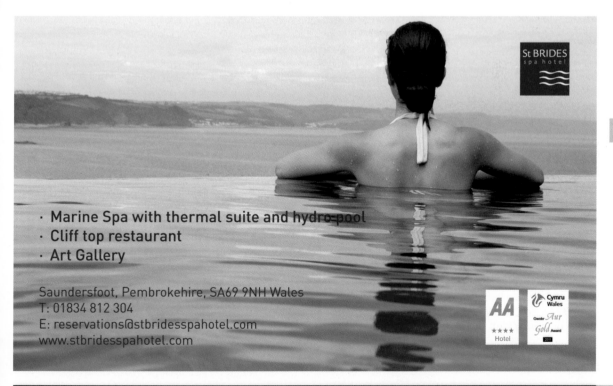

Rooms 132 **D** £56*

S

TENBY Map 8 SN10
Pembrokeshire

Atlantic Hotel

★★★ 80% HOTEL

☎ 01834 842881 📠 01834 840911
The Esplanade SA70 7DU
e-mail: enquiries@atlantic-hotel.uk.com
web: www.atlantic-hotel.uk.com
dir: A478 into Tenby & follow town centre signs (keep town walls on left). Right at Esplanade, hotel on right

This privately owned and personally run, friendly hotel has an enviable position looking out over South Beach towards Caldy Island. Bedrooms vary in size and style, but all are well equipped and tastefully appointed. The comfortable public areas include a choice of restaurants and, in fine weather guests can also enjoy the cliff-top gardens.

Rooms 42 (11 fmly) (4 GF) **S** £82-£93; **D** £114-£195 (incl. bkfst) **Facilities** FTV Steam room Spa bath Wi-fi **Conf** Board 8 **Services** Lift **Parking** 25 **Notes** LB Closed mid Dec-late Jan

Clarence House

★★ 63% HOTEL

☎ 01834 844371 📠 01834 844372
Esplanade SA70 7DU
e-mail: clarencehotel@freeuk.com
dir: From South Parade by town walls into St Florence Parade & Esplanade

Owned by the same family for over 50 years, this hotel has superb views from its elevated position. Many of the bedrooms have sea views and all are comfortably furnished. The bar leads to a sheltered rose garden or a number of lounges. Entertainment is provided in high season, and this establishment is particularly popular with coach tour parties.

Rooms 76 (6 fmly) **Facilities** ♫ **Services** Lift **Notes** Closed 18-28 Dec

See advert on this page

TINTERN PARVA Map 4 SO50
Monmouthshire

Best Western Royal George

★★★ 78% HOTEL

☎ 01291 689205 📠 01291 689448
Wye Valley Rd NP16 6SF
e-mail: royalgeorgetintern@hotmail.com
web: www.bw-royalgeorgehotel.co.uk
dir: Off M48 junct 2, A466, 4m to Tintern, 2nd left

This privately owned and personally run hotel provides comfortable, spacious accommodation, including bedrooms with balconies overlooking the well-tended garden; there are a number of ground-floor bedrooms. The public areas include a lounge bar and a large function room, and a varied and popular menu is available in either the bar or restaurant. This hotel is an ideal base for exploring the counties of Monmouthshire and Herefordshire.

Rooms 15 (14 annexe) (6 fmly) (10 GF) **S** £65-£95; **D** £75-£120 (incl. bkfst)* **Facilities** FTV Xmas New Year Wi-fi **Conf** Class 40 Board 30 Thtr 100 Del from £95 to £135* **Parking** 50 **Notes** LB Civ Wed 70

Tintern Abbey Hotel

★★★ 66% HOTEL

☎ 01291 680020
Monmouth Rd NP16 6SF
e-mail: abbeyhotel@live.com
dir: Opposite Tintern Abbey, off A466

Situated in the heart of the Wye Valley, this hotel offers many bedrooms that have views of Tintern Abbey. In addition to the main restaurant, a comfortable bar area is available for lighter dining options. Two function rooms are available and the hotel is a popular venue for weddings.

Rooms 22 (2 fmly) **Facilities** FTV Xmas New Year Wi-fi **Conf** Class 80 Board 40 Thtr 100 **Parking** 60 **Notes** LB Civ Wed 120

TREARDDUR BAY Map 14 SH27
Isle of Anglesey

Trearddur Bay Hotel

★★★ 82% HOTEL

☎ 01407 860301 📠 01407 861181
LL65 2UN
e-mail: enquiries@trearddurbayhotel.co.uk
web: www.trearddurbayhotel.co.uk
dir: A55 junct 2, turn left, over 1st rdbt, left at 2nd rdbt, left after approx 2m

This seaside hotel stands 100 yards from the Blue Flag beach, offering stunning views of the bay. The very comfortable bedrooms are well appointed and have flat-screen TVs. Guests have a choice of dining options, the more formal Bay Restaurant, or the Inn at The Bay, which also has an outdoor area for summer dining. Facilities include an indoor swimming pool and a children's play area.

Rooms 42 (6 annexe) (3 GF) **S** £60-£150; **D** £155-£220 (incl. bkfst)* **Facilities** FTV Wi-fi **Conf** Class 80 Board 60 Thtr 140 Del from £95 to £140* **Parking** 200 **Notes** LB Civ Wed 140

USK Map 9 SO30
Monmouthshire

Glen-yr-Afon House

★★★ 79% HOTEL

☎ 01291 672302 & 673202 📠 01291 672597
Pontypool Rd NP15 1SY
e-mail: enquiries@glen-yr-afon.co.uk
web: www.glen-yr-afon.co.uk
dir: A472 through High St, over river bridge, follow to right. Hotel 200yds on left

On the edge of this delightful old market town, Glen-yr-Afon, a unique Victorian villa, offers all the facilities expected of a modern hotel combined with the warm atmosphere of a family home. Bedrooms are furnished to a high standard and several overlook the well-tended gardens. There is a choice of comfortable sitting areas and a stylish and spacious banqueting suite.

Rooms 28 (1 annexe) (2 fmly) **S** £99-£123; **D** £136-£159 (incl. bkfst)* **Facilities** STV FTV Complimentary access to Usk Tennis Club New Year Wi-fi **Conf** Class 200 Board 30 Thtr 100 Del from £140 to £160* **Services** Lift **Parking** 151 **Notes** LB Civ Wed 150

The Three Salmons Hotel

★★★ 78% ◎◎ HOTEL

☎ 01291 672133 📠 01291 673979
Bridge St NP15 1RY
e-mail: general@threesalmons.co.uk
dir: M4 junct 24, A449, 1st exit signed Usk. On entering town hotel on main road

A 17th-century coaching inn located in the centre of a small market town with friendly, efficient staff who help create a welcoming atmosphere. Many changes have taken place these past years with quality and comfort the key to any guest stay. The food in the contemporary restaurant proves popular. Bedrooms are comfortable and a good range of extras are provided. There is a large function suite ideal for weddings and parties. Parking is secure.

Rooms 24 (14 annexe) (3 fmly) (4 GF) **S** £75-£105; **D** £85-£115 (incl. bkfst)* **Facilities** FTV Wi-fi **Conf** Class 80 Board 40 Thtr 110 Del from £115 to £125* **Parking** 25 **Notes** Civ Wed 100

Newbridge on Usk

◎ RESTAURANT WITH ROOMS

☎ 01633 451000 & 410262
Tredunnock NP15 1LY
e-mail: newbridgeonusk@celtic-manor.com
dir: M4 junct 24 signed Newport, onto B4236. At Ship Inn turn right, over mini-rdbt onto Llangybi/Usk road. Turn right opposite Cwrt Bleddyn Hotel, signed Tredunnock, through village & down hill

This cosy, gastro-pub is tucked away in a beautiful village setting with the River Usk nearby. The well-equipped bedrooms, in a separate building, provide comfort and a good range of extras. Guests can eat at rustic tables around the bar or in the upstairs dining room where award-winning, seasonal food is served; there is also a small private dining room. Breakfast is one of the highlights of a stay with quality local ingredients offered in abundance.

Rooms 6 (2 fmly)

WELSHPOOL Map 15 SJ20
Powys

Royal Oak

WELSH RAREBITS Hotels of Distinction

★★★ 77% ◎ HOTEL

☎ 01938 552217 📠 01938 556652
The Cross SY21 7DG
e-mail: relax@royaloakhotel.info
web: www.royaloakhotel.info
dir: By lights at junct of A483 & A458

This traditional market town hotel dates back over 350 years. The public areas are furnished in a minimalist style that highlight the many retained period features, including exposed beams and open fires. Three different bedroom styles provide good comfort levels and imaginative food is served in the elegant Red Room or adjacent all day café/bar.

Rooms 25 (3 fmly) **S** £68-£94; **D** £89-£132 (incl. bkfst)* **Facilities** FTV Xmas New Year Wi-fi **Conf** Class 60 Board 60 Thtr 150 **Parking** 19 **Notes** Ⓝ Civ Wed

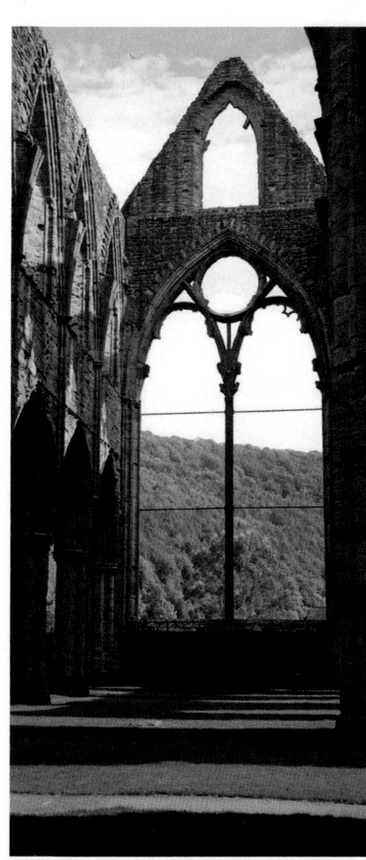

W

WHITEBROOK
Monmouthshire — Map 4 SO50

INSPECTORS' CHOICE

The Crown at Whitebrook

RESTAURANT WITH ROOMS

☎ 01600 860254 📠 01600 860607
NP25 4TX
e-mail: info@crownatwhitebrook.co.uk
dir: 4m from Monmouth on B4293, left at sign to Whitebrook, 2m on unclassified road, Crown on right

In a secluded spot in the wooded valley of the River Wye, this former drover's cottage dates back to the 17th century. Individually decorated bedrooms boast a contemporary feel with smart modern facilities. The restaurant and lounge combine many original features with a bright fresh look. The memorable cuisine features locally sourced ingredients, skilfully prepared. AA Restaurant of the Year for Wales 2011-2012.

Rooms 8

WOLF'S CASTLE
Pembrokeshire — Map 8 SM92

Wolfscastle Country Hotel

WELSH RAREBITS Hotels of Distinction

★★★ 78%
COUNTRY HOUSE HOTEL

☎ 01437 741688 & 741225 📠 01437 741383
SA62 5LZ
e-mail: enquiries@wolfscastle.com
web: www.wolfscastle.com
dir: On A40 in village at top of hill. 6m N of Haverfordwest

This large stone house, a former vicarage, dates back to the mid-19th century and is a friendly, privately owned and personally run hotel. It provides stylish, modern, well-maintained and well-equipped bedrooms. There is a pleasant bar and an attractive restaurant, which has a well deserved reputation for its food.

Rooms 20 (2 fmly) **Facilities** FTV New Year Wi-fi **Conf** Class 100 Board 30 Thtr 100 **Parking** 60 **Notes** LB Closed 24-26 Dec Civ Wed 70

WREXHAM
Wrexham — Map 15 SJ35

Best Western Cross Lanes Hotel & Restaurant

Best Western

★★★ 75% HOTEL

☎ 01978 780555 📠 01978 780568
Cross Lanes, Bangor Rd, Marchwiel LL13 0TF
e-mail: guestservices@crosslanes.co.uk
dir: 3m SE of Wrexham, on A525, between Marchwiel & Bangor-on-Dee

This hotel was built as a private house in 1890 and stands in over six acres of beautiful grounds. Bedrooms are well equipped and meet the needs of today's traveller; two rooms have four-poster beds. A fine selection of well prepared food is available in Lanes Bar and Restaurant.

Rooms 16 (1 fmly) **Facilities** FTV Putt green New Year Wi-fi **Conf** Class 60 Board 40 Thtr 120 **Parking** 80 **Notes** Closed 25 & 26 Dec (nights) Civ Wed 120

Premier Inn Wrexham

BUDGET HOTEL

☎ 0871 527 9190 📠 0871 527 9191
Chester Rd, Gresford LL12 8PW
dir: On B5445, just off A483 (dual carriageway) near Gresford

High quality, budget accommodation ideal for both families and business travellers. Spacious, en suite bedrooms feature tea and coffee making facilities, and Freeview TV in most hotels. Internet access and Wi-fi are available for a small fee. The adjacent family restaurant features a wide and varied menu. See also the Hotel Groups pages.

Rooms 38 **D** £53-£59*

W

Ireland

Rock of Cashel, Co. Tipperary

Additional Information for Northern Ireland & the Republic of Ireland

Licensing Regulations

Northern Ireland: Public houses open Mon-Sat 11.30-23.00. Sun 12.30-22.00. Hotels can serve residents without restriction. Non-residents can be served 12.30-22.00 on Christmas Day. Children under 18 are not allowed in the bar area and may neither buy nor consume liquor in hotels.

Republic of Ireland: General licensing hours are Mon-Thu 10.30-23.30, Fri & Sat 10.30-00.30. Sun 12.30-23.00 (or 00.30 if the following day is a Bank Holiday). There is no service (except for hotel residents) on Christmas Day or Good Friday.

The Fire Services (NI) Order 1984

This covers establishments accommodating more than six people, which must have a certificate from the Northern Ireland Fire Authority. Places accommodating fewer than six people need adequate exits. AA inspectors check emergency notices, fire fighting equipment and fire exits here.

The Republic of Ireland safety regulations are a matter for local authority regulations. For your own and others' safety, read the emergency notices and be sure you understand them.

Telephone numbers

Area codes for numbers in the Republic of Ireland apply only within the Republic. If dialling from outside check the telephone directory (from the UK the international dialling code is 00 353). Area codes for numbers in Britain and Northern Ireland cannot be used directly from the Republic.

For the latest information on the Republic of Ireland visit the AA Ireland's website: www.AAireland.ie

NORTHERN IRELAND

AGHADOWEY Map 1 C6
Co Londonderry

Brown Trout Golf & Country Inn

IRISH COUNTRY HOTELS

★★★ 71% HOTEL

☎ 028 7086 8209 📠 028 7086 8878
209 Agivey Rd BT51 4AD
e-mail: jane@browntroutinn.com
dir: At junct of A54 & B66 junct on road to Coleraine

Set alongside the Agivey River and featuring its own 9-hole golf course, this welcoming inn offers a choice of spacious accommodation. Comfortably furnished bedrooms are situated around a courtyard area whilst the cottage suites also have lounge areas. Home-cooked meals are served in the restaurant and lighter fare is available in the charming lounge bar which has entertainment at weekends.

Rooms 15 (11 fmly) (4 smoking) **S** £60-£70; **D** £70-£110 (incl. bkfst)* **Facilities** STV FTV ⛳ 9 Putt green Fishing Gym Game fishing ♫ Xmas New Year Wi-fi **Conf** Class 24 Board 28 Thtr 40 **Parking** 80 **Notes** LB

ANTRIM Map 1 D5
Co Antrim

Express by Holiday Inn Antrim M2 Jct 1

BUDGET HOTEL

☎ 028 9442 5500 📠 028 9442 5509
Ballymena Rd BT4 1LL
e-mail: reception.antrim@holidayinnexpress.org.uk
web: www.hiexpress.com/antrim
dir: At Junction One Shopping Outlet

A modern hotel ideal for families and business travellers. Fresh and uncomplicated, the spacious rooms include Sky TV, power shower and tea and coffee-making facilities. Continental buffet breakfast is included in the room rate; other meals may be taken at the nearby family pub or restaurant. See also the Hotel Groups pages.

Rooms 90 (52 fmly) (10 GF) **Conf** Class 20 Board 20 Thtr 40

BALLYMENA Map 1 D5
Co Antrim

Galgorm Resort & Spa

★★★★ 82% ®® HOTEL

☎ 028 2588 1001 📠 028 2588 0080
BT42 1EA
e-mail: mail@galgorm.com
dir: 1m from Ballymena on A42, between Galgorm & Cullybackey

Standing in 85 acres of private woodland and sweeping lawns beside the River Maine, this 19th-century mansion offers spacious, comfortable bedrooms. Public areas include a welcoming cocktail bar and elegant restaurant, as well as Gillies, a lively and atmospheric locals' bar. Also on the estate is an equestrian centre and a conference hall.

Rooms 75 (14 fmly) (8 GF) **Facilities** **Spa** STV FTV Fishing Gym Clay pigeon shooting Archery Horseriding ♫ Xmas New Year Wi-fi **Conf** Class 170 Board 30 Thtr 500 **Services** Lift **Parking** 300 **Notes** LB Civ Wed 500

BANGOR
Co Down Map 1 D5

The Old Inn

★★★★ 82% ®® HOTEL

☎ 028 9185 3255 ▤ 028 9185 2775
15 Main St BT19 1JH
e-mail: info@theoldinn.com
dir: A2 from Belfast (pass Belfast City Airport & Transport Museum). 2m, left at lights onto B20. 1.2m to hotel

This delightful hotel enjoys a peaceful rural setting just a short drive from Belfast. This property dates from 1614, and many of the day rooms exude charm and character. The individually styled, comfortable bedrooms, some with feature beds, offer modern facilities. The popular bar and intimate restaurant both offer creative menus, and staff throughout are keen to please.

Rooms 31 (1 annexe) (7 fmly) (6 GF) **S** £60-£150; **D** £60-£200 (incl. bkfst)* **Facilities** STV FTV In-room spa/massage treatments ♫ Xmas New Year Wi-fi **Conf** Class 120 Board 40 Thtr 150 Del from £77* **Services** Lift **Parking** 84 **Notes** LB ® Civ Wed 100

Clandeboye Lodge

★★★★ 80% ® HOTEL

☎ 028 9185 2500 ▤ 028 9185 2772
10 Estate Rd, Clandeboye BT19 1UR
e-mail: info@clandeboyelodge.co.uk
web: www.clandeboyelodge.com
dir: A2 from Belfast right at Blackwood Golf Centre & Hotel sign. 500yds into Ballysallagh Rd, left into Crawfordsburn Rd. Hotel 200yds on left

This hotel is located three miles west of Bangor, and sits in delightful landscaped grounds adjacent to the Clandeboye Estate. The bedrooms have a contemporary design and all have flat-screen, satellite TVs and Wi-fi. There are extensive conference, banqueting and wedding facilities which are separate from the main hotel. Public areas include a bright open-plan foyer bar and attractive lounge area.

Rooms 43 (2 fmly) (13 GF) **S** £75-£115; **D** £85-£145 (incl. bkfst)* **Facilities** FTV Wi-fi **Conf** Class 150 Board 50 Thtr 450 Del from £115 to £140* **Services** Lift **Parking** 250 **Notes** LB ® Closed 24-26 Dec Civ Wed 500

BELFAST
Belfast Map 1 D5

Merchant

★★★★★ 84% ® HOTEL

☎ 028 9023 4888 ▤ 028 9024 7775
16 Skipper St BT1 2DZ
e-mail: info@themerchanthotel.com
dir: In city centre, 2nd left at Albert Clock into Waring St. Hotel on left

A magnificent hotel situated in the historic Cathedral Quarter of the city centre. This Grade I listed building has been lovingly and sensitively restored to reveal its original architectural grandeur and interior opulence. All the bedrooms, including five suites, have air-conditioning, hi-speed internet access, flat-screen TVs and luxury bathrooms. There are several eating options including the grand and beautifully decorated Great Room Restaurant.

Rooms 63 (17 fmly) **S** £115-£240; **D** £125-£240 (incl. bkfst)* **Facilities** Spa FTV Gym ♫ Xmas New Year Wi-fi **Conf** Class 80 Board 20 Thtr 200 Del from £220 to £270* **Services** Lift Air con **Parking** 35 **Notes** LB ® Civ Wed 130

Radisson Blu Hotel Belfast

★★★★ 75% HOTEL

☎ 028 9043 4065 & 9082 0107 ▤ 028 9043 4066
3 Cromac Place BT7 2JB
e-mail: reservations.belfast@radissonblu.com
dir: On corner of Ormeau Rd & Cromac St

This modern hotel is in the centre of the regenerated urban area close to the city centre. The bedrooms are stylishly presented, well equipped and all have are air conditioning; there is a choice of business suites. Public areas include a spacious lounge bar and the Filini Restaurant, which serves good Italian and Sardinian cuisine. Ample secure parking, and free Wi-Fi (throughout the hotel) are available.

Rooms 120 (11 fmly) (4 smoking) **S** £83-£150; **D** £83-£150* **Facilities** FTV Access to LA Fitness (passes available at reception) Xmas New Year Wi-fi **Conf** Class 70 Board 50 Thtr 150 Del from £135 to £195* **Services** Lift Air con **Parking** 120 **Notes** LB Civ Wed 90

Malone Lodge

★★★★ 74% ® HOTEL

☎ 028 9038 8000 ▤ 028 9038 8088
60 Eglantine Av BT9 6DY
e-mail: info@malonelodgehotel.com
web: www.malonelodgehotelbelfast.com
dir: At hospital rdbt exit towards Bouchar Rd, left at 1st rdbt, right at lights at top, then 1st left

Situated in the leafy suburbs of the university area of south Belfast, this stylish hotel forms the centrepiece of an attractive row of Victorian terraced properties. The unassuming exterior belies an attractive and spacious interior with a smart lounge, popular bar and stylish Green Door restaurant. The hotel also has a small, well-equipped fitness room.

Rooms 46 (5 fmly) (1 GF) **S** £70-£160; **D** £70-£200 (incl. bkfst)* **Facilities** FTV Gym Wi-fi **Conf** Class 90 Board 40 Thtr 150 **Services** Lift **Parking** 35 **Notes** LB ® Civ Wed 120

Malmaison Belfast

★★★ 83% ® HOTEL

☎ 028 9022 0200 ▤ 028 9022 0220
34 - 38 Victoria St BT1 3GH
e-mail: lsteele@malmaison.com
web: www.malmaison.com
dir: M1 along Westlink to Grosvenor Rd. Follow city centre signs. Pass City Hall on right, left into Victoria St. Hotel on right

Situated in a former seed warehouse, this luxurious, contemporary hotel is ideally located for the city centre. Comfortable bedrooms, boast a host of modern facilities, whilst the deeply comfortable, stylish public areas include a popular bar lounge. The 'Home Grown and Local' menu in the brasserie showcases local seasonal ingredients. The warm hospitality is notable.

Rooms 64 (8 fmly) **S** £85-£160; **D** £95-£200* **Facilities** STV Gym Wi-fi **Conf** Board 22 Del from £145 to £175* **Services** Lift **Notes** LB

BELFAST *continued*

Ramada Encore Belfast City Centre

★★★ 79% HOTEL

☎ 0844 801 0331 & 028 9026800
Fax 0844 801 0332
20 Talbot St BT1 2LD
e-mail: reception@encorebelfast.co.uk
dir: On Dunbar Link behind St Annes Cathedral

This stylish modern hotel is ideally located in the city's Cathedral Quarter and is a short walk from the main shopping and business district. The open-plan public areas feature the SQ Bar & Grill, which is ideal for a relaxed lunch or an intimate dinner. The popular Hub Bar serves an extensive choice of cocktails and there's free Wi-fi in the bar area. The spacious bedrooms are very well appointed and have bathrooms with power showers.

Rooms 169 (20 fmly) **Facilities** FTV ♫ Xmas New Year Wi-fi **Conf** Class 75 Board 30 Thtr 110 **Services** Lift **Parking** 860 **Notes** LB ⊗

Holiday Inn Belfast

Holiday Inn

★★★ 78% HOTEL

☎ 0871 942 9005 Fax 028 9062 6546
22 Ormeau Av BT2 8HS
e-mail: belfast@ihg.com
web: www.holidayinn.co.uk
dir: M1/M2 onto West Link at Grosvenor Rd rdbt, follow city centre signs. 1st right, 2nd left into Hope St, at 2nd lights left into Bedford St, at next lights right into Ormeau Ave, hotel on right

This contemporary hotel is located in the heart of the city centre's 'golden mile' which makes it ideal for business visitors, for shopping and for exploring the tourist attractions. The air-conditioned bedrooms are modern in style and offer a comprehensive range of facilities. Public rooms include a staffed business centre and state-of-the-art health club.

Rooms 170 **Facilities** Spa Gym ♫ Wi-fi **Services** Lift Air con

Park Inn Belfast

park inn by Radisson

★★★ 77% HOTEL

☎ 028 9067 7700 Fax 028 9067 7701
4 Clarence Street West BT2 7GP
e-mail: info.belfast@rezidorparkinn.com
dir: M1 into Belfast, which becomes A12 (Westlink). Right into Grosvenor Rd (B38), follow City Centre signs. Right into Durnham St (B503), left into Hope St, which becomes Bruce St. Left into Bedford St (A1). Left into Clarence St, hotel on left

This hotel is well located in the city centre and a short walk from the main shopping, entertainment and business districts. The contemporary bedrooms are stylishly presented and the ten spacious business rooms have complimentary Wi-fi. The hotel also provides the RBG Bar and Grill, a sauna, steam room and conference facilities.

Rooms 145 (5 fmly) **Facilities** FTV Gym Sauna Steam room ♫ Xmas New Year Wi-fi **Conf** Class 60 Board 44 Thtr 120 **Services** Lift Air con **Parking** 15 **Notes** ⊗

Fitzwilliam Hotel

U

☎ 028 9044 2080 Fax 028 9044 2090
Great Victoria St BT2 7BQ
e-mail: enq@fitzwilliamhotelbelfast.com
dir: From Belfast Airport: A57, M2 S'bound towards Belfast. Onto Westlink towards Dublin. Exit at Divis St slip road. 1st right into Durham St, 2nd left into Atol St, at end left into Grosvenor Rd, hotel on right

Currently the rating for this establishment is not confirmed. This may be due to a change of ownership or because it has only recently joined the AA rating scheme. For further details please see the AA website: theAA.com

Rooms 130 **S** £100-£190; **D** £100-£190 **Facilities** STV FTV Gym ♫ Xmas New Year Wi-fi **Conf** Class 20 Board 25 Thtr 55 Del from £180 to £220 **Services** Lift Air con **Parking** 39

Premier Inn Belfast City Cathedral Quarter

BUDGET HOTEL

☎ 0871 527 8070 Fax 0871 527 8071
2-6 Waring St BT1 1XY
dir: M1 or M2 to Westlink to Grosvenor Rd rdbt, signed city centre. Into Grosvenor Rd. At 2nd lights left, take right lane, right (pass City Hall on right). At end of Chichester St left into Victoria St. Through next 2 lights, left into Waring St. Hotel 300yds on right

High quality, budget accommodation ideal for both families and business travellers. Spacious, en suite bedrooms feature tea and coffee making facilities, and Freeview TV in most hotels. Internet access and Wi-fi are available for a small fee. The adjacent family restaurant features a wide and varied menu. See also the Hotel Groups pages.

Rooms 171 **D** £59*

Premier Inn Belfast City Centre Alfred St

BUDGET HOTEL

☎ 0871 527 8068 Fax 0871 527 8069
Alfred St BT2 8ED
dir: M1 or M2 to Westlink. Follow city centre signs. 1st right, 2nd left into Hope St. At 2nd lights left into Bedford St. At next lights right into Ormeau Ave. Left into Alfred St. Underground car park (chargeable) on left

Rooms 148 **D** £59*

Premier Inn Belfast Titanic Quarter

BUDGET HOTEL

☎ 0871 527 9210 Fax 0871 527 9211
2A Queens Rd BT3 9FB
dir: From all major routes follow Odyssey Arena signs. From M3 junct 1 exit onto Queens Island, to lights. Hotel on left

Rooms 102 **D** £60*

BUSHMILLS Co Antrim — **Map 1 C6**

Bushmills Inn Hotel

★★★★ 77% ⊛ HOTEL

☎ 028 2073 3000 & 2073 2339 Fax 028 2073 2048
9 Dunluce Rd BT57 8QG
e-mail: mail@bushmillsinn.com
web: www.bushmillsinn.com
dir: On A2 in village centre

Enjoying a prominent position in the heart of the village, this hotel offers a range of bedroom styles including spacious, creatively designed rooms that have the latest technology and a small dressing room. The charming public areas feature inglenook turf-burning fires, cosy snugs along with a very popular traditional bar. The restaurant has a well deserved reputation for its food. The hotel is very popular with golfers; it is close to the Giants Causeway, Bushmills Distillery and the stunning scenery of the Antrim Coast.

Rooms 41 (2 fmly) (20 GF) **Facilities** STV ♫ New Year Wi-fi **Conf** Class 30 Board 18 Thtr 40 Del from £123.33 to £181.66 **Services** Lift **Parking** 70 **Notes** ⊗ Closed 25 Dec

CARNLOUGH
Co Antrim Map 1 D6

Londonderry Arms

★★★ 74% HOTEL

☎ 028 2888 5255 028 2888 5263
20 Harbour Rd BT44 0EU
e-mail: lda@glensofantrim.com
dir: 14m N from Larne on A2 (coast road)

This delightful hotel was built in the mid-19th century by Lady Londonderry, whose grandson, Winston Churchill, also owned it at one time. Today the hotel's Georgian architecture and rooms are still evident, and spacious bedrooms can be found in the modern extension. The hotel enjoys a prime location in this pretty fishing village overlooking the Antrim coast.

Rooms 35 (15 fmly) **Facilities** Fishing New Year Wi-fi **Conf** Class 60 Board 40 Thtr 120 Del from £99 to £120* **Services** Lift **Parking** 50 **Notes** Closed 24-25 Dec Civ Wed 60

CARRICKFERGUS
Co Antrim Map 1 D5

Premier Inn Carrickfergus

BUDGET HOTEL

☎ 0871 527 8214 0871 527 8215
The Harbour, Alexandra Pier BT38 8BE
dir: Exit at M2 junct 2, take M5 N onto A2 towards Carrickfergus. Follow Castle/Maritime Area signs. Right at rdbt adjacent to castle. Hotel straight ahead, adjacent to harbour

High quality, budget accommodation ideal for both families and business travellers. Spacious, en suite bedrooms feature tea and coffee making facilities, and Freeview TV in most hotels. Internet access and Wi-fi are available for a small fee. The adjacent family restaurant features a wide and varied menu. See also the Hotel Groups pages.

Rooms 49 **D** £54-£60*

CLOGHER
Co Tyrone Map 1 C5

Corick House Hotel

★★★ 80% COUNTRY HOUSE HOTEL

☎ 028 8554 8216 028 8554 9531
20 Corick Rd BT76 0BZ
e-mail: reservations@corickcountryhouse.com
dir: Off A4 (Augher & Clogher road)

A warm welcome is guaranteed at Corick House, a charming 17th-century William and Mary house set amid meandering streams and winding country roads in the heart of the beautiful Clogher Valley. The bedrooms are very spacious and many have breathtaking views of the valley and mountains. Public areas reflect much period charm and include a large dining room, a sun lounge and a cosy bar.

Rooms 19 (9 fmly) (3 GF) **S** £80; **D** £110-£130 (incl. bkfst)* **Facilities** STV FTV Xmas New Year Wi-fi **Conf** Class 150 Board 60 Thtr 400 **Parking** 200 **Notes** LB Civ Wed 350

COLERAINE
Co Londonderry Map 1 C6

Premier Inn Coleraine

BUDGET HOTEL

☎ 0871 527 8262 0871 527 8263
3 Riverside Park North, Castleroe Rd BT51 3GE
dir: A26 towards Colraine. At rdbt left on A29 (ring road) signed Cookstown/Garragh. At rdbt A54 (Castleroe Rd). Hotel on right

High quality, budget accommodation ideal for both families and business travellers. Spacious, en suite bedrooms feature tea and coffee making facilities, and Freeview TV in most hotels. Internet access and Wi-fi are available for a small fee. The adjacent family restaurant features a wide and varied menu. See also the Hotel Groups pages.

Rooms 49 **D** £55-£60*

DUNGANNON
Co Tyrone Map 1 C5

Cohannon Inn & Auto Lodge

★★ 72% HOTEL

☎ 028 8772 4488 028 8775 2217
212 Ballynakilly Rd BT71 6HJ
e-mail: info@cohannon.com
dir: 400yds from M1 junct 14

Handy for the M1 and the nearby towns of Dungannon and Portadown, this hotel offers well-maintained bedrooms, located behind the inn complex in a smart purpose-built wing. Public areas are smartly furnished and wide-ranging menus are served throughout the day.

Rooms 42 (20 fmly) (21 GF) (5 smoking) **S** fr £39.95; **D** fr £49.95* **Facilities** New Year **Conf** Class 100 Board 40 Thtr 160 **Parking** 160 **Notes** RS 25 Dec

ENNISKILLEN
Co Fermanagh Map 1 C5

Lough Erne Resort

★★★★★ 86% HOTEL

☎ 028 6632 3230 028 6634 5758
Belleek Rd BT93 7ED
e-mail: info@lougherneresort.com
web: www.lougherneresort.com
dir: A46 from Enniskillen towards Donegal, hotel in 3m

This delightful resort enjoys a peaceful and idyllic setting and boasts championship golf courses, a wonderful Thai spa and a host of outdoor and leisure pursuits. Bedrooms and en suites are spacious, particularly well appointed and include a number of luxury suites. Day rooms are spacious, luxurious and include lounges, bars and restaurants with splendid views. Service is friendly and extremely attentive.

Rooms 120 (61 annexe) **S** £112-£478; **D** £132-£498 (incl. bkfst)* **Facilities** Spa STV 18 Fishing Gym Xmas New Year Wi-fi **Conf** Class 200 Board 80 Thtr 400 **Services** Lift **Parking** 240 **Notes** LB Civ Wed 300

Manor House Country Hotel

★★★★ 80% COUNTRY HOUSE HOTEL

☎ 028 6862 2200 028 6862 1545
Killadeas BT94 1NY
e-mail: info@manorhouseresorthotel.com

This charming country house hotel enjoys a stunning location on the banks of Lower Lough Erne and is a short drive from the busy town of Enniskillen. Bedrooms are equipped to a very high standard with front-facing rooms having the fabulous lough views. There is a choice of restaurants, and afternoon tea is served in the comfortable lounge with its open fire. The hotel has first-class business, conference and leisure facilities including its own air-conditioned cruiser for tours and corporate events.

Rooms 81 (12 fmly) (12 GF) **S** £73-£125; **D** £81-£325 (incl. bkfst)* **Facilities** FTV Gym Sauna Xmas New Year Wi-fi **Conf** Class 120 Board 100 Thtr 400 **Services** Lift **Parking** 300 **Notes** Civ Wed

NORTHERN IRELAND

ENNISKILLEN *continued*

Killyhevlin Hotel & Health Club

★★★★ 79% HOTEL

☎ 028 6632 3481 🖷 028 6632 4726
BT74 6RW
e-mail: info@killyhevlin.com
web: www.killyhevlin.com
dir: 2m S of Enniskillen, off A4

This modern, stylish hotel is situated on the shores of Lough Erne, south of the town. The well-equipped bedrooms are particularly spacious and enjoy fine views of the gardens and lake. The restaurant, informal bar and comfortable lounges all share the views. Staff are friendly and helpful. There are extensive leisure facilities and a spa.

Rooms 70 (42 fmly) (22 GF) **S** fr £65; **D** fr £75 (incl. bkfst) **Facilities** **Spa** STV supervised Fishing Gym Aerobic studio Steam room Sauna Hydrotherapy area New Year Wi-fi **Conf** Class 160 Board 100 Thtr 500 Del from £90 to £125 **Services** Lift **Parking** 500 **Notes** LB Closed 25 Dec RS 24 & 26 Dec Civ Wed 250

FIVEMILETOWN — Map 1 C5
Co Tyrone

Valley Hotel

★★★ 73% HOTEL

☎ 028 8952 1505 🖷 028 8952 1688
60 Main St BT75 0PW
e-mail: info@thevalleyhotel.com
web: www.thevalleyhotel.com

This family-run hotel offers smartly presented bedrooms that are appointed to a very high standard. Comfortable public areas include a cosy residents' lounge and the popular bar where an excellent range of bar meals is served. More formal dining can be enjoyed in the Bordeaux Restaurant. The hotel has extensive conference facilities.

Rooms 22 (1 fmly) **Facilities** Fishing New Year Wi-fi **Conf** Class 30 Board 30 Thtr 50 **Services** Lift **Parking** 150 **Notes** Closed 25 Dec RS 26 Dec Civ Wed 200

LIMAVADY — Map 1 C6
Co Londonderry

Radisson Blu Roe Park Resort

★★★★ 75% HOTEL

☎ 028 7772 2222 🖷 028 7772 2313
BT49 9LB
e-mail: reservations@radissonroepark.com
web: www.radissonblu.co.uk/resort-limavady
dir: On A2 (Londonderry-Limavady road), 1m from Limavady

This impressive, popular hotel is part of a modern golf resort. The spacious, contemporary bedrooms are well equipped and many have excellent views of the fairways and surrounding estate. The Greens Restaurant provides a refreshing dining experience and the Coach House brasserie offers a lighter menu. The leisure options are extensive.

Rooms 118 (15 fmly) (37 GF) (5 smoking) **Facilities** **Spa** FTV supervised 18 Putt green Fishing Gym Driving range Indoor golf academy Xmas New Year Wi-fi **Conf** Class 190 Board 140 Thtr 450 **Services** Lift **Parking** 350 **Notes** Civ Wed 300

LISBURN — Map 1 D5
Co Antrim

Premier Inn Lisburn

BUDGET HOTEL

☎ 0871 527 8606 🖷 0871 527 8607
136-144 Hillsborough Rd BT27 5QY
dir: M1 onto A1 (Sprucefield Rd). Left into Hillsborough Rd. Approx 1.5m. Hotel on left

High quality, budget accommodation ideal for both families and business travellers. Spacious, en suite bedrooms feature tea and coffee making facilities, and Freeview TV in most hotels. Internet access and Wi-fi are available for a small fee. The adjacent family restaurant features a wide and varied menu. See also the Hotel Groups pages.

Rooms 60 **D** £55-£62*

LONDONDERRY — Map 1 C5
Co Londonderry

City Hotel

★★★★ 73% HOTEL

☎ 028 7136 5800 🖷 028 7136 5801
Queens Quay BT48 7AS
e-mail: reservations@cityhotelderry.com
dir: Follow city centre signs. Hotel on waterfront

In a central position overlooking the River Foyle, this stylish, contemporary hotel will appeal to business and leisure guests alike. All bedrooms have excellent facilities including internet access; the executive rooms make particularly good working environments. Meeting and function facilities are extensive and there are good leisure options.

Rooms 146 (16 fmly) (11 smoking) **S** £59-£152; **D** £66-£159 (incl. bkfst) **Facilities** supervised Gym Steam room New Year Wi-fi **Conf** Class 150 Board 80 Thtr 350 Del from £99 to £114 **Services** Lift Air con **Parking** 48 **Notes** LB Closed 25 Dec Civ Wed 350

Beech Hill Country House Hotel

★★★ 79% COUNTRY HOUSE HOTEL

☎ 028 7134 9279 🖷 028 7134 5366
32 Ardmore Rd BT47 3QP
e-mail: info@beech-hill.com
web: www.beech-hill.com
dir: From A6 (Londonderry to Belfast road) exit at Faughan Bridge. Hotel signed. 1m to Ardmore Chapel. Hotel entrance opposite

Dating back to 1729, Beech Hill is an impressive mansion, standing in 32 acres of glorious woodlands and gardens. Traditionally styled day rooms provide much comfort, and meals are served in the attractively extended dining room. The splendid bedroom wing provides spacious, well-equipped rooms in addition to the more classically designed bedrooms in the main house.

Rooms 27 (10 annexe) (4 fmly) (12 GF) **Facilities** FTV New Year Wi-fi **Conf** Class 50 Board 30 Thtr 100 **Services** Lift **Parking** 75 **Notes** Closed 24-25 Dec Civ Wed 80

REPUBLIC OF IRELAND

ADARE Map 1 B3
Co Limerick

Dunraven Arms

★★★★ 82% ◎◎ HOTEL

☎ 061 605900 ▤ 061 396541
e-mail: reservations@dunravenhotel.com
dir: On N21, follow signs Cork/Tralee. 1st hotel on right

This charming hotel, established in 1792, is a traditional country inn situated in the heart of one of Ireland's prettiest villages. The comfortable lounges have log fires and most of the spacious bedrooms and suites have four-poster beds. The lovely gardens, leisure and beauty facilities, a conference centre and good cuisine all add up to creating an enjoyable visit. Golf, horse racing and equestrian sports are available nearby.

Rooms 86 (6 fmly) (40 GF) **S** €80-€120; **D** €138-€170 (incl. bkfst)* **Facilities** STV FTV supervised Fishing Gym Beauty salon Xmas New Year Wi-fi **Conf** Class 60 Board 12 Thtr 180 Del from €108 to €180* **Services** Lift **Parking** 90 **Notes** LB Civ Wed 250

ARDMORE Map 1 C2
Co Waterford

Cliff House

★★★★ 82% ◎◎◎ HOTEL

☎ 024 87800 & 87801 ▤ 024 87820
e-mail: info@thecliffhousehotel.com
dir: From Dungarvan: N25, signed Cork. Left onto R673. From Youghal: N25 signed Waterford. Right onto R673 signed Ardmore. In Ardmore take Middle Rd to hotel

This is a unique property that is virtually sculpted into the cliff face overlooking Ardmore Bay, just a few minutes' walk from the village. Most of the individually designed bedroom suites and the public rooms enjoy the same great views, as do the relaxing leisure and spa facilities. Dinner in the award-winning House Restaurant is a particular highlight of any visit here; the menu features seasonal and local produce that are cooked with flair.

Rooms 39 (8 fmly) (7 GF) **Facilities** Spa STV FTV Fishing Gym Sauna Steam room Relaxation room Outdoor pursuits New Year Wi-fi **Conf** Class 30 Board 20 Thtr 50 **Services** Lift Air con **Parking** 52 **Notes** LB Closed 2 wks in Jan

ATHY Map 1 C3
Co Kildare

Clanard Court

★★★★ 76% HOTEL

☎ 059 8640666 ▤ 059 8640888
Dublin Rd
e-mail: sales@clanardcourt.ie
web: www.clanardcourt.ie
dir: N7 from Naas to M9 junct 11 signed Athy. Right onto N78. Hotel on right

Located just one kilometre from Athy on the Dublin road, this family owned hotel enjoys a well earned reputation for hosting weddings and family celebrations. Concerts and events are also a regular feature here. Bedrooms are spacious and attractively decorated. Bailey's is a popular bar serving food throughout the day.

Rooms 38 (2 fmly) (17 GF) (5 smoking) **S** €69-€119; **D** €89-€178 (incl. bkfst)* **Facilities** STV FTV Putt green Use of leisure facilities at affiliated club New Year Wi-fi Child facilities **Conf** Class 300 Board 20 Thtr 450 Del from €130 to €143 **Services** Lift **Parking** 250 **Notes** LB Closed 25-26 Dec Civ Wed 250

BALLINA Map 1 B4
Co Mayo

Mount Falcon Estate

★★★★ 83% ◎◎ HOTEL

☎ 096 74472 ▤ 096 74473
Mount Falcon Estate
e-mail: info@mountfalcon.com
dir: On N26, 6m from Foxford & 3m from Ballina. Hotel on left

Dating from 1876, this house has been lovingly restored to its former glory, and has a bedroom extension that is totally in keeping with the original design. Relaxing lounges look out on the 100-acre estate, which has excellent salmon fishing on The Moy plus well-stocked trout lakes. Dinner is served in the original kitchen with choices from a varied and interesting menu; for lunch there is also the Boathole Bar. An air-conditioned gym is available.

Rooms 32 (3 fmly) **S** €120-€480; **D** €120-€480 (incl. bkfst)* **Facilities** Spa STV supervised Fishing Gym Sauna Steam room New Year Wi-fi **Conf** Class 120 Board 80 Thtr 200 Del from €165 to €225* **Services** Lift **Parking** 260 **Notes** LB Closed 24-27 Dec Civ Wed 200

The Ice House

★★★★ 79% ◎◎ HOTEL

☎ 096 23500 ▤ 096 23598
The Quay
e-mail: chill@theicehouse.ie
dir: On Sligo road turn right at Judge's Garage into Riverside Estate. Right at T-junct into Quay Rd. Hotel on left

With a fascinating history, this property, a mile or so from the town centre, is a stunning mix of old and new. The contemporary decor features lots of wood, steel and glass creating a very light and airy interior, contrasted with a Victorian features and furnishing in the original house. The stylish bedrooms include suites that have river views from their balconies. An interesting menu is offered at dinner in the vaulted Pier Restaurant, once the ice store for the Moy fishery, with lighter fare offered during the day in the bright riverside bar.

Rooms 32 (7 fmly) (10 GF) **Facilities** Spa STV Laconium Steam room New Year Wi-fi **Conf** Class 35 Board 30 Thtr 70 **Services** Lift **Parking** 32 **Notes** Closed 25-26 Dec Civ Wed 150

Hotel Ballina

★★★★ 75% HOTEL

☎ 096 23600 ▤ 096 23623
N26 Dublin Rd
e-mail: info@hotelballina.ie
dir: S of town centre

Located just south of the town, this modern spacious hotel is ideally suited to those who enjoy fishing and golf. Bedrooms are spacious and appointed to a high standard. McShanes is a vibrant and welcoming bar and bistro that serves food all day. The hotel regularly hosts concerts and other live entertainment events. Guests have complimentary use of the Tranquillity leisure facilities.

Rooms 87 (2 fmly) (29 GF) **Facilities** Spa FTV supervised Gym New Year Wi-fi **Conf** Class 500 Board 100 Thtr 700 **Services** Lift **Parking** 400 **Notes** Closed 24-26 Dec Civ Wed

B

REPUBLIC OF IRELAND

BALLINA *continued*

Ballina Manor Hotel

U

☎ 096 80900
At the Moy Ridgepool
e-mail: info@ballinamanorhotel.ie

Currently the rating for this establishment is not confirmed. This may be due to a change of ownership or because it has only recently joined the AA rating scheme. For further details please see the AA website: theAA.com

Rooms 66 (4 fmly) (10 smoking) **S** €60-€200; **D** €90-€240 (incl. bkfst)* **Facilities** STV Gym Treatment rooms New Year Wi-fi **Conf** Class 110 Board 150 Thtr 220 Del from €109 to €210 **Services** Lift **Parking** 70 **Notes** LB Closed 25-26 Dec RS 24 & 27 Dec Civ Wed 160

BALLINASLOE Map 1 B4
Co Galway

Carlton Shearwater Hotel

CARLTON HOTEL GROUP

★★★★ 76% HOTEL

☎ 090 9630400 📠 090 9630401
Marina Point
e-mail: info.shearwater@carlton.ie
dir: N6 junct 14 or 15 to Ballinasloe, hotel at marina

Striking in its design, this hotel is situated at Marine Point in Ballinasloe. The spacious public areas are contemporary in style with a range of lounges to relax in, a bar, and an outdoor patio where bistro-style food is served throughout the day. The Carvery is popular at lunch time, and dinner is served in Marengo's Restaurant. Bedrooms are comfortably furnished, and the deluxe and Presidential Suites are particularly stylish. There are extensive conference, meeting and banqueting facilities, plus a spa and leisure centre. Ample underground parking is available.

Rooms 104 (44 fmly) (8 smoking) **S** €69-€144; **D** €98-€204 (incl. bkfst)* **Facilities** Spa STV FTV Gym Aerobics studio New Year Wi-fi Child facilities **Conf** Class 440 Board 96 Thtr 900 **Services** Lift Air con **Parking** 303 **Notes** LB Closed 23-26 Dec Civ Wed 160

BALLINGEARY Map 1 B2
Co Cork

Gougane Barra

★★★ 75% HOTEL

☎ 026 47069 📠 026 47226
Gougane Barra
e-mail: gouganebarrahotel@eircom.net
dir: On L4643. Exit R584 between N22 at Macroom & N71 at Bantry

Picturesquely situated on the shore of Gougane Barra Lake and at the entrance to the National Park, the Lucey family have run this hotel for five generations. The bedrooms are very comfortable. Dinner is a treat, and there is a cosy, traditional bar and lounges. Guests can experience the unique theatre during high season, and bikes and boats are available together with action-packed activity weekends.

Rooms 26 (12 GF) **Facilities** STV FTV Fishing Boating Cycling Wi-fi **Parking** 26 **Notes** Closed 10 Oct-18 Apr

BALLYBOFEY Map 1 C5
Co Donegal

Jackson's Hotel

U

☎ 074 9131021 📠 074 9131096
e-mail: enquiry@jacksons-hotel.ie

Currently the rating for this establishment is not confirmed. This may be due to a change of ownership or because it has only recently joined the AA rating scheme. For further details please see the AA website: theAA.com

Rooms 138 (55 fmly) (68 smoking) **Facilities** Spa STV FTV supervised Gym Xmas New Year Wi-fi **Conf** Class 800 Board 60 Thtr 1500 **Services** Lift **Parking** 550 **Notes** LB Civ Wed 800

BALLYCOTTON Map 1 C2
Co Cork

INSPECTORS' CHOICE

Bayview Hotel

★★★ HOTEL

☎ 021 4646746 📠 021 4646075
e-mail: res@thebayviewhotel.com
dir: Exit N25 at Castlemartyr, through Ladysbridge & Garryvoe to Ballycotton

The gardens of this hotel seem to hang onto the cliffs overlooking the fishing port and Ballycotton Bay. The comfortable public rooms and bedrooms with balconies take in the breathtaking coastline views. Dinner in the Capricho Room is a special delight and guests will find locally landed fish on the menus. The warm and friendly team certainly impress with their standards of customer care.

Rooms 35 (5 GF) (10 smoking) **D** €72-€149* **Facilities** STV Pitch and putt Sea angling Use of swimming pool at sister hotel Wi-fi **Conf** Class 30 Board 24 Thtr 60 **Services** Lift Air con **Parking** 40 **Notes** Closed Nov-Apr Civ Wed 100

BALLYLICKEY
Co Cork Map 1 B2

INSPECTORS' CHOICE

Sea View House Hotel

★★★ 🏵🏵 HOTEL

☎ 027 50073 & 50462 📠 027 51555
e-mail: info@seaviewhousehotel.com
web: www.seaviewhousehotel.com
dir: 5km from Bantry, 11km from Glengarriff on N71

Colourful gardens and glimpses of Bantry Bay through the mature trees frame this delightful country house. Owner Kathleen O'Sullivan's team of staff are exceptionally pleasant and there is a relaxed atmosphere in the cosy lounges. Guest comfort and good cuisine are the top priorities. Bedrooms are spacious and individually styled; some on the ground floor are appointed to suit less able guests.

Rooms 25 (3 fmly) (5 GF) **S** €75-€95; **D** €150-€170 (incl. bkfst)* **Conf** Class 30 Board 25 Thtr 25 Del from €95 to €110* **Parking** 32 **Notes** LB Closed mid Nov-mid Mar Civ Wed 75

BALLYLIFFIN
Co Donegal Map 1 C6

Ballyliffin Lodge & Spa

★★★★ 75% HOTEL

☎ 074 9378200 📠 074 9378985
Shore Rd
e-mail: info@ballyliffinlodge.com
dir: From Derry take A2 towards Moville, exit for Carndonagh at Quigleys Point. Ballyliffin 10km

Located in the heart of the village, this property offers a range of very comfortable bedrooms, many of which enjoy panoramic views of Malin Head and the famed Ballyliffin Golf Club. The Holly Tree offers a menu of the best local produce presented with international flair. The popular bar serves less formal meals throughout the day. Guests are welcome to use the leisure facilities in the adjoining Crystal Rock Spa.

Rooms 40 (28 fmly) **Facilities** **Spa** STV ⓢ supervised Gym ♫ New Year Wi-fi **Conf** Class 200 Board 100 Thtr 300 **Services** Lift **Parking** 80 **Notes** ⊗ Civ Wed 150

BALLYSHANNON
Co Donegal Map 1 B5

Creevy Pier Hotel

★★ 68% HOTEL

☎ 071 9858355 📠 071 9858356
Kildoney Glebe, Creevy
e-mail: info@creevy.ie

This charming family run hotel overlooks the pier at Creevy, and is just four kilometres north of Ballyshannon. It offers breathtaking views of Donegal Bay from the atmospheric Captains Bar and airy Pier Restaurant. The bedrooms are cosy and well appointed, brightly decorated with colourful fabrics. The food is good, and served with efficiency and friendliness. This warm and inviting house is an ideal base for activity holidays such as walking, watersports and golf.

Rooms 10 (5 fmly) (10 GF) **S** €50-€75; **D** €60-€120 (incl. bkfst) **Facilities** FTV ♫ Xmas New Year **Conf** Class 80 Board 60 Thtr 120 Del from €80 to €120* **Services** Air con **Parking** 60 **Notes** LB ⊗ Civ Wed 80

BALLYVAUGHAN
Co Clare Map 1 B3

HOTEL OF THE YEAR

INSPECTORS' CHOICE

Gregans Castle

★★★ 🏵🏵🏵 COUNTRY HOUSE HOTEL

☎ 065 7077005 📠 065 7077111
e-mail: stay@gregans.ie
dir: 3.5m S of Ballyvaughan on N67

This hotel is a hidden gem in The Burren area, and the delightful restaurant and bedrooms enjoy splendid views towards Galway Bay. The Haden family, together with their welcoming staff, offer a high level of personal service. Bedrooms are individually decorated; superior rooms and suites are particularly comfortable; some are on the ground floor and have patio gardens. There are welcoming fires in the comfortable drawing room and the cosy cocktail bar where afternoon tea is served. Dinner is a highlight of any visit; the chef shows a real passion for food which is evident in his cooking of top quality local and organic produce. The area is rich in archaeological, geological and botanical interest, and cycling and walking tours can be organised. There is a beautiful garden to relax in. AA Hotel of the Year for the Republic of Ireland 2011-12.

Rooms 20 (3 fmly) (7 GF) **Facilities** ♫ Wi-fi **Conf** Class 25 Board 14 Thtr 25 **Parking** 25 **Notes** LB Closed Jan-12 Feb & 30 Nov-Dec Civ Wed 65

B

REPUBLIC OF IRELAND

BANTRY
Co Cork — Map 1 B2

Westlodge Hotel

★★★ 74% HOTEL

☎ 027 50360 📠 027 50438
e-mail: reservations@westlodgehotel.ie
web: www.westlodgehotel.ie
dir: N71 to Bantry

A superb leisure centre and good children's facilities make this hotel very popular with families, and the friendly team of staff ensure a memorable visit. Dinner is a special treat and the menu includes organic and local seafood. The hotel's location on the outskirts of Bantry makes it an ideal base for touring west Cork and south Kerry, and there are lovely walks in the grounds.

Rooms 90 (20 fmly) (20 GF) **S** €65-€80; **D** €120-€140 (incl. bkfst) **Facilities** STV supervised Putt green Gym Squash 2 treatment rooms Pitch & putt New Year Wi-fi Child facilities **Conf** Class 200 Board 24 Thtr 400 **Services** Lift Air con **Parking** 400 **Notes** LB Closed 23-27 Dec Civ Wed 300

BARNA
Co Galway — Map 1 B3

The Twelve

★★★★ 79% HOTEL

☎ 091 597000 📠 091 597003
Barna Village
e-mail: enquire@thetwelvehotel.ie
dir: On outskirts of Barna

Located just ten minutes west of Galway city, this hotel looks as if it has been on the site for decades. However, once inside the decor is striking and contemporary. The bedrooms come in a number of different sizes, but all are furnished with taste and with guest comfort in mind. The Pins is a vibrant and popular bar and bistro where food is served throughout the day. West Restaurant opens during the evening, and features fine dining from a well-compiled menu of local and seasonal produce. Le Petit Spa offers treatments based on seaweed products.

Rooms 47 (12 fmly) **S** €90-€145; **D** €100-€155 (incl. bkfst)* **Facilities Spa** STV FTV Children's cookery programme Xmas New Year Wi-fi Child facilities **Conf** Class 70 Board 60 Thtr 80 Del from €150 to €180* **Services** Lift Air con **Parking** 140 **Notes** LB RS 22-27 Dec Civ Wed 100

BLARNEY
Co Cork — Map 1 B2

Blarney Golf Resort

★★★★ 76% HOTEL

☎ 021 4384477 📠 021 4516453
Tower
e-mail: reservations@blarneygolfresort.com
dir: Exit N20 for Blarney, 4km to Tower, right into Old Kerry Rd. Hotel 2km on right

This resort includes a John Daly designed golf course. The hotel is situated close to Tower village and the famous Blarney Castle. Bedrooms are well equipped and comfortable; some have balconies and spacious lounges. Early Bird and carte dinner menus are served nightly in the Inniscarra Restaurant, with more casual dining available in the golf club bar. There are excellent leisure facilities in the Sentosa Spa.

Rooms 117 (56 annexe) (56 fmly) (30 GF) **Facilities Spa** FTV supervised 18 Putt green Gym Steam room Sauna Xmas New Year Wi-fi **Conf** Class 150 Board 40 Thtr 300 **Services** Lift Air con **Parking** 250 **Notes** LB

BRAY
Co Wicklow — Map 1 D4

Royal Hotel & Leisure Centre

★★★ 73% HOTEL

☎ 01 2862935 & 2724900 📠 01 2867373
Main St
e-mail: royal@regencyhotels.com
dir: From N11, 1st exit for Bray, 2nd exit from rdbt, through 2 sets of lights, across bridge, hotel on left

Located in the town centre and walking distance from the seafront at Bray and close to Dun Laoighaire ferry port. Public areas offer comfortable lounges, a traditional bar and The Heritage Restaurant. Bedrooms vary in size but all are well appointed. There is a well-equipped leisure centre and a supervised car park.

Rooms 130 (10 fmly) **Facilities** supervised Gym Massage & beauty clinic Therapy room Whirlpool spa Creche Xmas Wi-fi **Conf** Class 300 Board 200 Thtr 500 **Services** Lift **Parking** 60 **Notes** Civ Wed 300

BUNCLODY
Co Wexford — Map 1 D3

Carlton Millrace Hotel

CARLTON HOTEL GROUP

★★★★ 79% HOTEL

☎ 053 9375100 & 1890 288288 📠 053 9375124
Riversedge
e-mail: reservations.millrace@carlton.ie
dir: On N80 (Carlow to Wexford road) in town

Located on the edge of the picturesque town of Bunclody, this modern hotel offers spacious well-appointed bedrooms that have comfort in mind. The public rooms are smartly presented, not least of which is the rooftop Lady Lucy restaurant where dinner and breakfast are served. Less formal dining takes place throughout the day in the Mill Bistro and bar. The hotel is popular for leisure breaks and has a good reputation for wedding celebrations.

Rooms 72 (12 annexe) (15 fmly) **S** €69-€99; **D** €129-€169 (incl. bkfst)* **Facilities Spa** STV FTV supervised Gym Sauna Steam room Xmas New Year Wi-fi Child facilities **Conf** Class 125 Board 60 Thtr 350 Del from €105 to €165* **Services** Lift Air con **Parking** 120 **Notes** LB Closed 24-25 Dec Civ Wed 120

CAHERDANIEL (CATHAIR DÓNALL)
Co Kerry — Map 1 A2

Derrynane

★★★ 75% HOTEL

☎ 066 9475136 📠 066 9475160
e-mail: info@derrynane.com
dir: Just off N70

This family run hotel has a super cliff top location overlooking Derrynane Bay on the Ring of Kerry. Many of the comfortable bedrooms have spectacular views as do the relaxing lounge and open-plan restaurant. The outdoor leisure facilities include cliff top walks, a heated 15-metre pool (in season), tennis court and gardens overlooking the ocean. Indoors there is a gym, natural seaweed bath, plus a steam and sauna room. Guests can also use the laundry and drying facility.

Rooms 50 (30 fmly) (32 GF) **Facilities** supervised Gym Seaweed therapy room Wi-fi **Parking** 60 **Notes** Closed 4 Oct-15 Apr

CARLOW
Co Carlow Map 1 C3

Seven Oaks

★★★ 78% HOTEL

☎ 059 9131308 📠 059 9132155
Athy Rd
e-mail: info@sevenoakshotel.com

This hotel is conveniently situated within walking distance of the town centre. Public areas include comfortable lounges, library, bar and a restaurant where food is available all day. There is a traditional Irish music session on Monday nights in the Oak Bar. Bedrooms are spacious and very well appointed. There are extensive leisure and banqueting facilities and a secure car park.

Rooms 89 (5 fmly) (7 GF) **S** €50-€90; **D** €80-€140 (incl. bkfst) **Facilities** STV supervised Gym Aerobic studio Steam room Wi-fi **Conf** Class 150 Board 80 Thtr 400 Del from €100 to €135 **Services** Lift Air con **Parking** 200 **Notes** LB Closed 25-26 Dec RS Good Fri Civ Wed 200

CARRICKMACROSS
Co Monaghan Map 1 C4

Nuremore

★★★★ 80% HOTEL

☎ 042 9661438 📠 042 9661853
e-mail: info@nuremore.com
web: www.nuremore.com
dir: M1 junct 14, N2. Hotel 3km S of Carrickmacross

Overlooking its own golf course and lakes, the Nuremore is a quiet retreat with excellent facilities. Bedrooms are spacious and many overlook the well-tended gardens. Public areas are spacious and include an indoor pool and gym. Chef Ray McArdle's food in the restaurant continues to impress, with an imaginative range of dishes on offer.

Rooms 72 (6 fmly) (42 smoking) **S** €100-€180; **D** €160-€350 (incl. bkfst)* **Facilities** Spa STV FTV supervised 18 Putt green Fishing Gym Beauty treatments Aromatherapy Massage Xmas New Year Wi-fi **Conf** Class 300 Board 50 Thtr 600 Del from €150 to €275 **Services** Lift **Parking** 200 **Notes** LB Civ Wed 200

Shirley Arms Hotel

★★★★ 75% HOTEL

☎ 042 9673100 📠 042 9664645
Main St
e-mail: reception@shirleyarmshotel.ie
dir: N2 to Derry, take Ardee Rd to Carrickmacross

Set at the top of the town, this long established hotel is an imposing stone building with a contemporary interior. Bedrooms, in a purpose-built block, are spacious and have clean, modern lines; there is also a comfortable suite in the original house overlooking the square. Food is an important element of the business here, with options available throughout the day.

Rooms 25 (2 fmly) **S** €85-€125; **D** €100-€200 (incl. bkfst) **Facilities** STV New Year Wi-fi **Conf** Class 150 Board 200 Thtr 200 Del from €105 to €165 **Services** Lift **Parking** 80 **Notes** LB Closed 24-26 Dec RS 6 Apr Civ Wed 150

CARRICK-ON-SHANNON
Co Leitrim Map 1 C4

The Landmark

★★★★ 74% HOTEL

☎ 071 9622222 📠 071 9622233
e-mail: reservations@thelandmarkhotel.com
dir: From Dublin on N4. Entering Carrick-on-Shannon, 1st exit at rdbt, hotel on right

Boasting breathtaking views, this wonderfully relaxing and friendly hotel stands some 500 feet above the sea and makes a peaceful hideaway. Bedrooms are individual in style and size, with the added bonus of the wonderful views; public areas have charm and character in equal measure. Eating options are the Broadwalk Café overlooking the River Shannon and serving accomplished cuisine, and the conservatory Aroma's café for tea, coffee, sweet and savoury snacks. The staff are happy to arrange river cruises, golf, angling and other activities.

Rooms 60 (4 fmly) (4 smoking) **S** €79-€128; **D** €135-€198 (incl. bkfst) **Facilities** STV Wi-fi **Conf** Class 210 Board 100 Thtr 550 **Services** Lift **Parking** 125 **Notes** LB Closed 24-25 Dec RS 26-Dec Civ Wed 300

CASHEL
Co Galway Map 1 A4

INSPECTORS' CHOICE

Cashel House

★★★ COUNTRY HOUSE HOTEL

☎ 095 31001 📠 095 31077
e-mail: res@cashel-house-hotel.com
web: www.cashel-house-hotel.com
dir: S off N59, 1.5km W of Recess, well signed

Cashel House is a mid-19th century property, standing at the head of Cashel Bay in the heart of Connemara, and set amidst secluded, award-winning gardens with woodland walks. Attentive service comes with the perfect balance of friendliness and professionalism from McEvilly family and their staff. The comfortable lounges have turf fires and antique furnishings. The restaurant offers local produce such as the famous Connemara lamb, and fish from the nearby coast.

Rooms 29 (4 fmly) (6 GF) (4 smoking) **Facilities** STV FTV Garden school Xmas New Year Wi-fi **Parking** 40 **Notes** Civ Wed 80

C

REPUBLIC OF IRELAND

C

REPUBLIC OF IRELAND

CASHEL *continued*

Zetland Country House

★★★ 78% HOTEL

☎ 095 31111 📠 095 31117
Cashel Bay
e-mail: info@zetland.com
dir: N59 from Galway towards Clifden, right after Recess onto R340, left after 4m onto R341, hotel 1m on right

Standing on the edge of Cashel Bay in Connemara, this former sporting lodge dating from the early 1800s, is a cosy and relaxing hotel that exudes charm. Many of the comfortable bedrooms have sea views, as has the restaurant where country-house and seafood cooking is a particular feature. Johnny O'Loughlins is atmospheric bistro and bar which stocks a very large range of Irish whiskey. This property is a popular base for fishing and shooting parties, with access to over 17,000 acres of diverse countryside.

Rooms 19 (10 fmly) (3 GF) **Facilities** STV FTV Fishing Shooting Cycling Xmas New Year Wi-fi **Conf** Class 40 Board 20 Thtr 80 **Parking** 32

CASTLEMARTYR Map 1 C2
Co Cork

Castlemartyr Resort

★★★★★ 88% HOTEL

☎ 021 4219000 📠 021 4623359
e-mail: reception@castlemartyrresort.ie
dir: N25, 3rd exit signed Rosslare. Continue past Carrigtwohill & Midleton exits. Right at lights in village

Castlemartyr Resort is an impressively restored 18th-century property, where old world grandeur and contemporary styles marry well. The individually decorated bedrooms in the Manor House make luxurious retreats, while the modern wing rooms are furnished in a more contemporary style. The hotel offers fine dining in the Bell Tower Restaurant and more casual eating in Knights Bar and the Clubhouse. The estate grounds offer a myriad of outdoor pursuits including golf on the Ron Kirby designed inland links style course, cycling, boating on the lake, and walking or jogging along the nature trails. There is also a stunning spa facility.

Rooms 109 (98 annexe) (6 fmly) (30 GF)
S €205-€285; **D** €220-€295 (incl. bkfst)*
Facilities Spa STV FTV supervised 18 Gym Bicycles Horse & carriage rides Target archery Clay pigeon shooting New Year Wi-fi **Conf** Class 150 Board 75 Thtr 250 Del from €260 to €315*
Services Lift Air con **Parking** 200 **Notes** LB Closed 16-27 Dec Civ Wed 190

CAVAN Map 1 C4
Co Cavan

Cavan Crystal

★★★★ 80% HOTEL

☎ 049 4360600 📠 049 4360699
Dublin Rd
e-mail: info@cavancrystalhotel.com
web: www.cavancrystalhotel.com
dir: N3 towards Cavan, at 1st rdbt take N55 signed Athlone

Contemporary design using native timber and handcrafted brickwork together with crystal chandeliers make this a particularly distinctive hotel. Expect excellent hospitality from all the highly trained staff. Located on the southern edge of the town, the hotel also features a well-equipped health plus beauty clinic and extensive banquet and conference facilities.

Rooms 85 (2 fmly) (9 GF) **Facilities** supervised Gym Beauty & massage treatment Salon Gym New Year Wi-fi **Conf** Class 300 Board 100 Thtr 500 **Services** Lift **Parking** 216 **Notes** Closed 24 & 25 Dec

Kilmore

★★★ 79% HOTEL

☎ 049 4332288 📠 049 4332458
Dublin Rd
e-mail: sales@hotelkilmore.ie
dir: Approx 3km from Cavan on N3

Located on the southern outskirts of Cavan, easily accessible from the N3, this comfortable hotel has spacious and welcoming public areas. Quality food is available throughout the day in the bar, including a carvery at lunchtime in the Annalee Restaurant.

Rooms 38 (16 fmly) (19 GF) **Facilities** Free use of facilities at Slieve Russell Golf & Country Club New Year Wi-fi **Conf** Class 200 Board 60 Thtr 500 **Services** Air con **Parking** 450 **Notes** Closed 25 Dec Civ Wed 200

CLANE Map 1 C4
Co Kildare

Westgrove Hotel

★★★★ 77% HOTEL

☎ 045 989900 📠 045 989911
Abbeylands
e-mail: info@westgrovehotel.com
dir: From M4 (W of Dublin) follow Naas/Maynooth signs. At rdbt 2nd exit signed Naas/Straffan. At rdbt 3rd exit signed Clane (R403). At next rdbt (before Clane) 1st exit. At next rdbt 2nd exit, hotel on right

Located on the outskirts of the village, this hotel is ideally suited to those with an interest in horseracing and golf as so many good sporting facilities are within easy reach. A range of bedroom styles is on offer; all are well appointed and comfortable. The spacious public rooms include a choice of dining options, bars, a popular leisure club and an Elemis Spa.

Rooms 99 (14 fmly) (30 smoking) **Facilities** Spa STV FTV supervised Gym New Year Wi-fi **Conf** Class 220 Board 100 Thtr 500 **Services** Lift **Parking** 550 **Notes** LB Closed 24-25 Dec Civ Wed 300

CLAREMORRIS Map 1 B4
Co Mayo

McWilliam Park Hotel

★★★★ 77% HOTEL

☎ 094 9378000 📠 094 9378001
e-mail: info@mcwilliamparkhotel.ie
dir: Take Castlebar/Claremorris exit off N17, straight over rdbt. Hotel on right

This fine hotel is situated on the outskirts of Claremorris which is close to the Knock Shrine and the airport. Public areas offer comfortable lounges, together with extensive conference, leisure and health facilities. The bedrooms are spacious and well appointed. Food is served all day in Kavanagh's bar, and dinner nightly in J.G's restaurant. Traditional music and social dancing evenings are held regularly in the McWilliam Suite.

Rooms 103 (19 fmly) (15 GF) (44 smoking)
S €60-€140; **D** €80-€240 (incl. bkfst) **Facilities** Spa STV FTV Gym Xmas New Year Wi-fi **Conf** Class 250 Board 80 Thtr 600 Del from €100 to €150 **Services** Lift **Parking** 320 **Notes** Civ Wed 200

CLIFDEN Co Galway **Map 1 A4**

Abbeyglen Castle Hotel

★★★★ 80% ® HOTEL

☎ 095 21201 📠 095 21797
Sky Rd
e-mail: info@abbeyglen.ie
dir: N59 from Galway towards Clifden. Hotel 1km from Clifden on Sky Road

The tranquil setting overlooking Clifden, matched with the dedication of the Hughes's father and son team and their attentive staff, combine to create a magical atmosphere here. Now into its 5th decade, Abbeyglen Castle has a well earned reputation, with many guests returning year after year. Well-appointed rooms and very comfortable suites are available, together with a range of relaxing lounge areas. The restaurant features a daily-changing menu of traditional and more modern dishes; many guests enjoy impromptu sessions around the piano in the bar following dinner. Treatment rooms are available.

Rooms 45 (9 GF) **S** €130-€156; **D** €198-€250 (incl. bkfst)* **Facilities** STV Putt green Beauty treatment & relaxation centre Xmas New Year Wi-fi **Conf** Class 50 Board 40 Thtr 100 Del from €215 to €235* **Services** Lift **Parking** 50 **Notes** LB No children 10yrs Closed 8 Jan-2 Feb

CLONAKILTY Co Cork **Map 1 B2**

Inchydoney Island Lodge & Spa

★★★★ 83% ®® HOTEL

☎ 023 8833143 📠 023 8835229
e-mail: reservations@inchydoneyisland.com
dir: Follow N71 (West Cork road) to Clonakilty. At rdbt in Clonakilty take 2nd exit, follow signs to hotel

Benefiting from a stunning location on Inchydoney Island, this welcoming hotel has much to offer guests that are looking for a truly relaxing experience. All of the comfortably appointed bedrooms and suites have sea views with balconies or terraces. The public rooms are spacious and decorated with an interesting range of specially commissioned furniture and artwork. Guests can choose between the informal atmosphere of the popular Dunes pub and bistro, or The Gulfstream Restaurant where the emphasis is on locally landed seafood cooked with care. The Island Spa offers a range of thalassotherapy treatments, using sea water pumped daily from the shore.

Rooms 67 (24 fmly) (18 GF) **S** €110-€175; **D** €150-€250 (incl. bkfst)* **Facilities** Spa supervised Fishing Gym Sauna Steam room Snooker room Surfing Ocean safari Wi-fi **Conf** Board 50 Thtr 300 **Services** Lift **Parking** 200 **Notes** Closed 24-25 Dec Civ Wed 300

Quality Hotel & Leisure Club, Clonakilty

★★★ 73% HOTEL

☎ 023 883 6400 📠 023 883 5404
Skibbereen Rd
e-mail: info.clonakilty@qualityhotels.ie
web: www.qualityhotelclonakilty.com
dir: In Clonakilty 2nd exit at mini rdbt into Skibbereen Bypass Rd. Hotel on left in approx 1m

A short distance from the town, in the heart of west Cork, this is good base for exploring the rich history and landscapes of the area. Families are particularly well catered for with a choice of bedroom styles and sizes. Oscars is a lively bar with entertainment at weekends. Use of the facilities of Club Vitae is complimentary to guests.

Rooms 96 (63 fmly) (41 GF) (10 smoking) **S** €65-€134; **D** €78-€218 (incl. bkfst) **Facilities** Spa STV supervised Gym 3-screen cinema Sauna Steam room New Year Wi-fi Child facilities **Conf** Class 75 Board 40 Thtr 140 Del from €99 to €130 **Services** Lift **Parking** 200 **Notes** LB Closed 24-26 Dec

CLONMEL Co Tipperary **Map 1 C2**

Hotel Minella

IRISH COUNTRY HOTELS

★★★★ 77% HOTEL

☎ 052 22388 📠 052 24381
e-mail: frontdesk@hotelminella.ie
web: www.hotelminella.ie
dir: S of river in town

This family-run hotel is set in nine acres of well-tended gardens on the banks of the Suir River. The hotel originates from the 1860s, and the public areas include a cocktail bar and a range of lounges; some of the bedrooms are particularly spacious. The leisure centre in the grounds is noteworthy. Two-bedroom holiday homes are also available.

Rooms 70 (8 fmly) (14 GF) **Facilities** Fishing Gym Aerobics room **Conf** Class 300 Board 20 Thtr 500 **Services** Lift **Parking** 100 **Notes** Closed 24-28 Dec

CONG Co Mayo **Map 1 B4**

Ashford Castle

★★★★★ 86% ®® HOTEL

☎ 094 9546003 📠 094 9546260
e-mail: ashford@ashford.ie
web: www.ashford.ie
dir: In Cross left at church onto R345 signed Cong. Left at hotel sign, through castle gates

Set in over 300 acres of beautifully grounds, this magnificent castle, dating from 1228, occupies a stunning position on the edge of Lough Corrib. Bedrooms vary in style but all benefit from a pleasing combination of character, charm and modern comforts. The hotel offers an extensive range of both indoor and outdoor leisure pursuits including falconry, golf, shooting, fishing and an equestrian centre.

Rooms 83 (6 fmly) (22 GF) **D** €275-€950 (incl. bkfst) **Facilities** Spa STV 9 Putt green Fishing Gym Archery Clay pigeon shooting Falconry Horse riding Bike hire Lake cruises Xmas New Year Wi-fi **Conf** Class 65 Thtr 110 **Services** Lift **Parking** 200 **Notes** Civ Wed 150

C

REPUBLIC OF IRELAND

CONG *continued*

The Lodge at Ashford

★★★★ 78% HOTEL

☎ 094 9545400 094 9545424
The Quay
e-mail: lodge@lisloughrey.ie
dir: N84 from Galway to Cross. Left at Cong sign. Left at hotel sign

Situated in an elevated position overlooking the quay and Lough Corrib, this delightful property combines contemporary luxury with a traditional country house setting. The individually-styled bedrooms and suites are in a quiet courtyard linked to the main house; each is named after a wine region of the world. The rooms have flat-screen TVs, goose down duvets and bathrooms with under floor heating. Cuisine is taken seriously here, with dinner in the award-winning Salt Restaurant being the highlight of a visit.

Rooms 50 (44 annexe) (5 fmly) (21 GF) **S** €95-€185; **D** €135-€225 (incl. bkfst)* **Facilities** Spa STV FTV Fishing Gym Outdoor sauna Beauty salon Screening room New Year Wi-fi **Conf** Class 70 Board 40 Thtr 180 **Services** Lift **Parking** 100 **Notes** LB Closed 24-26 Dec, 1 Jan Civ Wed 150

COOTEHILL Co Cavan Map 1 C4

Errigal Country House

★★★★ 77% HOTEL

☎ 049 5556901 049 5556902
Cavan Rd
e-mail: info@errigalhotel.com
web: www.errigalhotel.com
dir: 1km from town centre on R188 (Cavan Rd)

This modern hotel is located in landscaped gardens and within walking distance of Cootehill. Bedrooms are appointed to a high standard and public areas are very comfortable and attractively decorated. Reynards Restaurant serves dinner each evening, and a more informal fare is available in The Brewery Bar. The Eden Health & Wellness suite offers a range of treatments.

Rooms 29 (2 fmly) **S** €70-€90; **D** €100-€150 (incl. bkfst)* **Facilities** Spa STV New Year Wi-fi **Conf** Class 215 Board 130 Thtr 420 **Services** Lift Air con **Parking** 350 **Notes** LB Civ Wed 350

CORK Co Cork Map 1 B2

Maryborough Hotel & Spa

★★★★ 80% HOTEL

☎ 021 4365555 021 4365662
Maryborough Hill
e-mail: info@maryborough.com
dir: From Jack Lynch Tunnel take 2nd exit signed Douglas. Right at 1st rdbt, follow Rochestown signs to fingerpost rdbt. Left, hotel on left in 0.5m

Dating from 1715, this house was renovated and extended to become a fine hotel with beautifully landscaped grounds featuring rare plant species. There are stylish suites in the main house and the bedrooms in the wing are comfortably furnished. The bar and lounge are very popular for the range of food which is served throughout the day; Zings restaurant offers a mix of classic and contemporary dishes. There are impressive spa, leisure and conference facilities plus activities for children.

Rooms 93 (6 fmly) **S** €115-€145; **D** €130-€190 (incl. bkfst)* **Facilities** Spa STV supervised Gym Sauna Steam room New Year Wi-fi **Conf** Class 250 Board 60 Thtr 500 Del from €170 to €210 **Services** Lift **Parking** 300 **Notes** LB Closed 24-26 Dec Civ Wed 100

Silver Springs Moran

MORAN HOTELS

★★★★ 78% HOTEL

☎ 021 4507533 021 4507641
Tivoli
e-mail: silverspringsres@moranhotels.com
web: www.silverspringshotel.ie
dir: N8 S, take Silver Springs exit. Right, then right again, hotel on left

Located on the main approach to the city this hotel has spacious, contemporary public areas. The lobby lounge is very popular for all-day dining, with more formal meals served in the Watermarq Restaurant. Bedrooms and suites are comfortable, many offering good views over the River Lee. Excellent conference and leisure facilities are available in separate buildings in the grounds.

Rooms 109 (29 fmly) (12 smoking) **S** €79-€109; **D** €79-€109 **Facilities** supervised Gym Squash Aerobics classes New Year Wi-fi **Conf** Class 400 Board 30 Thtr 800 **Services** Lift **Parking** 325 **Notes** LB Closed 24-27 Dec Civ Wed 800

CURRY Co Sligo Map 1 B4

Yeats County Inn Hotel

★★ 72% HOTEL

☎ 094 9255050 094 9255053
e-mail: mail@yeatscountyinn.com
dir: On N17, S of Sligo

This family-run hotel offers a relaxing and friendly atmosphere. The traditional bar, with its open and welcoming fire, is comfortably furnished and serves food throughout the day. The bedrooms are attractively decorated and well appointed. Knock Shrine, the international airport, Strokestown Park and Foxford Woollen Mills are all close by.

Rooms 11 (2 fmly) (2 smoking) **Facilities** STV FTV Xmas New Year Wi-fi **Services** Lift **Parking** 120 **Notes** LB

DELGANY Co Wicklow Map 1 D3

Glenview

★★★★ 77% HOTEL

☎ 01 2873399 01 2877511
Glen O' the Downs
e-mail: sales@glenviewhotel.com
dir: From Dublin city centre follow signs for N11, past Bray on N11 S'bound

This hotel is set in lovely terraced gardens overlooking the Glen o' the Downs. The comfortable bedrooms are spacious, and many enjoy the great views over the valley. The impressive public areas include a conservatory bar, lounge and choice of dining options including the first-floor Woodlands Restaurant where dinner is served. The hotel has an excellent range of leisure and conference facilities. A championship golf course and horse riding can be found nearby.

Rooms 70 (11 fmly) (16 GF) **Facilities** Spa STV supervised Gym Aerobics studio Massage Beauty treatment room Xmas New Year Wi-fi **Conf** Class 100 Board 80 Thtr 270 **Services** Lift **Parking** 200 **Notes** LB Civ Wed 120

DINGLE (AN DAINGEAN) Map 1 A2
Co Kerry

Dingle Skellig Hotel & Peninsula Spa

★★★★ 78% HOTEL

☎ 066 9150200 📠 066 9151501
e-mail: reservations@dingleskellig.com
dir: N86 to Dingle, hotel on harbour

This modern hotel, close to the town, overlooks Dingle Bay and has spectacular views from many of the comfortably furnished bedrooms and suites. Public areas offer a spacious bar and lounge and a bright, airy restaurant. There are extensive health and leisure facilities, and many family activities are organised in the Fungi Kids Club.

Rooms 113 (10 fmly) (31 GF) **S** €84-€135; **D** €118-€210 (incl. bkfst)* **Facilities** Spa STV FTV supervised Gym New Year Wi-fi Child facilities **Conf** Class 120 Board 100 Thtr 250 **Services** Lift **Parking** 110 **Notes** Closed Jan RS Nov-Dec Civ Wed 230

Dingle Benners

★★★ 70% HOTEL

☎ 066 9151638 📠 066 9151412
Main St
e-mail: info@dinglebenners.com
dir: In town centre

Located in the centre of the town with parking to the rear, this long-established property has an old world charm. There are a selection of relaxing lounges, open turf fires and comfortable bedrooms that are furnished with antique pine; some have four-poster beds. Food is available in Mrs Benner's traditional bar.

Rooms 52 (2 fmly) (9 GF) **S** €85-€170; **D** €120-€250 (incl. bkfst) **Facilities** STV FTV Wi-fi **Services** Lift **Parking** 32 **Notes** LB Closed 19-27 Dec Civ Wed 90

DONABATE Map 1 D4
Co Dublin

Waterside House

★★★ 71% HOTEL

☎ 01 8436153 📠 01 8436111
e-mail: info@watersidehousehotel.ie
web: www.watersidehousehotel.ie
dir: Exit M1 junct 4 (Donabate/Portrane), 3rd exit at rdbt (pass Newbridge House Demesne on left) over rail bridge, right at sign for golf courses & hotel. Hotel on left

This family owned hotel is situated in an enviable position overlooking Lambay Island and the beach at Donabate. The public areas and bedrooms are appointed in a contemporary style, with the comfortable lounge bar and restaurant taking advantage of the breathtaking views. Close to Dublin Airport and a variety of golf courses.

Rooms 35 (8 fmly) (8 GF) **S** €40-€280; **D** €60-€280 (incl. bkfst)* **Facilities** STV FTV Xmas New Year Wi-fi **Conf** Class 150 Board 100 Thtr 350 Del from €75 to €150 **Services** Lift Air con **Parking** 100 **Notes** LB Civ Wed 250

DONEGAL Map 1 B5
Co Donegal

Harvey's Point Country Hotel

★★★★ 87% @@ HOTEL

☎ 074 9722208 📠 074 9722352
Lough Eske
e-mail: sales@harveyspoint.com
web: www.harveyspoint.com
dir: N56 from Donegal, then 1st right (Loch Eske/ Harvey's Point)

Situated by the lake shore, this hotel is an oasis of relaxation; comfort and attentive guest care are the norm here. A range of particularly spacious suites and bedrooms is available, together with smaller rooms in the courtyard annexe. The kitchen brigade maintains consistently high standards in The Restaurant, with less formal dining in The Steakhouse at peak periods. A very popular Sunday buffet lunch is served weekly, with dinner entertainment on selected dates.

Rooms 70 (34 GF) **Facilities** Treatment rooms Pitch 'n' putt Bicycle hire Walking tours Xmas New Year Wi-fi **Conf** Class 200 Board 50 Thtr 200 **Services** Lift **Parking** 300 **Notes** LB Closed Mon & Tue Nov-Mar Civ Wed 250

The Central Hotel Conference & Leisure Centre

★★★ 77% HOTEL

☎ 074 9721027 📠 074 9722295
The Diamond
e-mail: info@centralhoteldonegal.com

Located right in the centre of the town, this long established hotel is a gem. The public rooms are decorated to a high standard; a popular carvery lunch is served in The Just William, and an all-day menu of European dishes and authentic Thai specialities is available in the atmospheric Upper Deck Bar. Afternoon tea is served on the first-floor mezzanine from where guests can look down on the bustling town below. Bedrooms vary in style and many have views over Donegal Bay. There is also a contemporary banqueting suite where occasional concerts are held.

Rooms 112 (26 fmly) **S** €60-€70; **D** €98-€120 **Facilities** STV FTV supervised Gym Xmas New Year Wi-fi **Conf** Class 160 Board 70 Thtr 380 Del from €99 **Services** Lift **Notes** LB Civ Wed

Mill Park Hotel

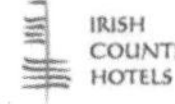

★★★ 75% HOTEL

☎ 074 9722880 📠 074 9722640
The Mullins
e-mail: info@millparkhotel.com
dir: Take N15 signed Lifford. 2nd exit at rdbt to N56 signed Killybegs. Hotel on right

The gentle flow of the millstream and the open fires create a welcoming atmosphere at this hotel which is within walking distance of the town centre. Wood and stone are incorporated with flair in the design of the public areas, as in the first-floor Granary Restaurant and the less formal café bar where food is served all day. Bedrooms are spacious and well appointed. There are extensive leisure and banqueting facilities.

Rooms 100 (10 fmly) (44 GF) (12 smoking) **S** €65-€250; **D** €80-€200 (incl. bkfst) **Facilities** Spa supervised Gym Wi-fi **Conf** Class 100 Board 30 Thtr 450 **Services** Lift **Parking** 250 **Notes** LB Civ Wed 300

D

REPUBLIC OF IRELAND

D

REPUBLIC OF IRELAND

DUBLIN Dublin **Map 1 D4**

INSPECTORS' CHOICE

The Merrion Hotel

★★★★★ @@@@ HOTEL

☎ 01 6030600 📠 01 6030700
Upper Merrion St
e-mail: info@merrionhotel.com
dir: At top of Upper Merrion St on left, beyond Government buildings on right

This terrace of gracious Georgian buildings, reputed to have been the birthplace of the Duke of Wellington, embraces the character of many changes of use over 200 years. Bedrooms and suites are spacious, offering comfort and a wide range of extra facilities. The lounges retain the charm and opulence of days gone by, while the Cellar bar area is a popular meeting point. Dining options include The Cellar Restaurant specialising in prime local ingredients and, for that very special occasion, award-winning Restaurant Patrick Guilbaud is Dublin's finest.

Rooms 142 (21 GF) (20 smoking) **S** €460-€3000; **D** €480-€3000* **Facilities** Spa STV FTV ⓢ Gym Steam room Xmas New Year Wi-fi **Conf** Class 25 Board 25 Thtr 60 **Services** Lift Air con **Parking** 60 **Notes** ⊛ Civ Wed 50

The Shelbourne Dublin, a Renaissance Hotel

★★★★★ 86% @ HOTEL

☎ 01 6634500 📠 01 6616006
27 St Stephen's Green
e-mail: rhi.dubbr.reservations@renaissancehotels.com
web: www.theshelbourne.ie
dir: M1 to city centre, along Parnell St to O'Connell St towards Trinity College, 3rd right into Kildare St, hotel on left

This Dublin landmark exudes elegance and a real sense of history. The public areas are spacious and offer a range of dining and bar options. There is a selection of bedroom styles and suites available, many with commanding views over St. Stephen's Green. The Saddle Room is the main restaurant featuring a steak and seafood menu with a contemporary twist, while afternoon tea is served in the elegant Lord Mayor's Lounge.

Rooms 265 (20 smoking) **S** €198-€650; **D** €198-€650* **Facilities** STV FTV Xmas Wi-fi **Conf** Class 180 Board 60 Thtr 500 Del from €299 to €600* **Services** Lift Air con **Notes** Civ Wed 350

Westbury

★★★★★ 86% HOTEL

☎ 01 6791122 📠 01 6797078
Grafton St
e-mail: westbury@doylecollection.com
dir: In city centre

Located just off Grafton Street, Dublin's premier shopping district, this is an oasis of calm; guests are well cared for amid the hotel's smart, contemporary surroundings. Spacious public areas include the relaxing Gallery Lounge where afternoon tea is popular with shoppers taking a break. Café Novo is the hotel's buzzing street-level brasserie bar, while Wilde-The Restaurant is an elegant grill with an emphasis on seasonal and artisan fare. A range of stylish suites and bedrooms is on offer; many overlook the roofs of the city. Valet parking is available.

Rooms 205 (9 fmly) (17 smoking) **S** €179-€499; **D** €179-€499* **Facilities** STV Gym Wi-fi **Conf** Class 100 Board 46 Thtr 220 Del from €300 to €434* **Services** Lift Air con **Parking** 100 **Notes** LB ⊛

INSPECTORS' CHOICE

The Clarence

★★★★ @@ HOTEL

☎ 01 4070800 📠 01 4070818
6-8 Wellington Quay
e-mail: reservations@theclarence.ie
web: www.theclarence.ie
dir: From O'Connell Bridge, W along Quays, through 1st lights (at Ha'penny Bridge) hotel 500mtrs

Located on the banks of the River Liffey in the Temple Bar area, The Clarence is within walking distance of the shops and visitor attractions. This is a very distinctive property - the character of the 1850 building has been successfully combined with contemporary design in the bedrooms and suites. The friendly service team provides unobtrusive yet professional and personable service. The eating options include The Tea Room, a spectacularly bright and airy room with a 20-foot high ceiling that serves innovative dishes cooked with flair and based on excellent ingredients. More casual dining can be found in the Octagon Bar, or in the cosy Study Café with its log fire.

Rooms 49 (3 fmly) (7 smoking) **Facilities** STV Gym Treatment & massage room New Year Wi-fi **Conf** Class 24 Board 35 Thtr 50 **Services** Lift **Parking** 15 **Notes** LB ⊛ Closed 24-26 Dec Civ Wed 50

Castleknock Hotel & Country Club

★★★★ 81% HOTEL

☎ 01 6406300 01 6406303
Porterstown Rd, Castleknock
e-mail: info@chcc.ie
web: www.castleknockhotel.com
dir: From airport/Blanch exit, left, right, right again into Castleknock. At Myos pub left, right at x-rds, follow signs

This modern hotel is set on a golf course yet it is only 15 minutes from Dublin. The bedrooms are very comfortable, with all the expected modern guest facilities. The spacious public rooms have an airy feel, and some rooms open onto a terrace that overlooks the golf course. The range of food and beverage outlets includes The Park Room, a steak house, a busy all-day brasserie, and The Lime Tree which is open in the evening. Excellent conference and banqueting facilities are available, together with a popular leisure centre.

Rooms 143 (6 fmly) (25 smoking) **Facilities** **Spa** FTV supervised 18 Gym Sauna Steam room Xmas New Year Wi-fi **Conf** Class 200 Board 80 Thtr 500 **Services** Lift **Parking** 200 **Notes** LB Closed 24-25 Dec Civ Wed 200

Clontarf Castle

★★★★ 79% HOTEL

☎ 01 8332321 & 8534336 01 8330418
Castle Av, Clontarf
e-mail: mlong@clontarfcastle.ie
dir: M1 towards centre, left at Whitehall Church, left at T-junct, straight on at lights, right at next lights into Castle Ave, hotel on right at rdbt

Dating back to the 12th century, this castle retains many historic architectural features which have been combined with contemporary styling in the well-equipped bedrooms. Public areas offer relaxing lounges, and modern cuisine is served in Fahrenheit Grill, Indigo Lounge and Knights Bar. The Great Hall is a versatile venue for banqueting and conferences.

Rooms 111 (7 fmly) (11 GF) (23 smoking) **Facilities** STV Gym Xmas New Year Wi-fi **Conf** Class 250 Board 90 Thtr 600 **Services** Lift Air con **Parking** 134 **Notes** Civ Wed 400

Crowne Plaza Hotel

★★★★ 78% HOTEL

☎ 01 8977777 01 8977750
The Blanchardstown Centre
e-mail: info@cpireland.crowneplaza.com
dir: Exit at M50 junct 6 (Blanchardstown)

This landmark building is on the doorstep of a wide range of shops in Blanchardstown. Bedrooms are stylishly decorated with generously sized beds and well appointed en suites. The Sanctuary Bar serves an international range of informal dishes from lunchtime through to the evening, with Italian specialities at dinner in Forchetta Restaurant. Secure underground parking is provided.

Rooms 188 (60 fmly) (15 smoking) **Facilities** STV Day gym Sauna New Year Wi-fi **Conf** Class 300 Board 300 Thtr 500 **Services** Lift Air con **Parking** 200 **Notes** LB Civ Wed 200

Gresham

GRESHAM HOTELS

★★★★ 78% HOTEL

☎ 01 8746881 01 8787175
O'Connell St
e-mail: info@thegresham.com
dir: Telephone for detailed directions

This elegant hotel enjoys a prime location right in the centre of the city, close to theatres, restaurants and plenty of shops. The wide range of bedrooms and suites are all comfortably appointed. Public areas are spacious, and include excellent conference facilities. Afternoon tea is a feature of the Writers Bar amid contemporary artwork and sculpture. The hotel has multi-storey car park at the rear, with special rates for resident guests.

Rooms 288 (1 fmly) (50 smoking) **Facilities** STV FTV Gym Fitness room Wi-fi **Conf** Class 150 Board 80 Thtr 350 **Services** Lift Air con **Parking** 150 **Notes**

Stillorgan Park

★★★★ 77% HOTEL

☎ 01 2001800 01 2831610
Stillorgan Rd, Stillorgan
e-mail: sales@stillorganpark.com
web: www.stillorganpark.com
dir: From N11 follow signs for Wexford (pass RTE studios on left) through 5 sets of lights. Hotel on left

This modern hotel is situated on the southern outskirts of the city, close to UCD, Dundrum and Stillorgan shopping centres. Comfortable public areas include a spacious lobby, The Purple Sage Restaurant and a traditional style bar. There are extensive air-conditioned banqueting and conference facilities plus a gym and spa with treatment rooms.

Rooms 150 (8 fmly) **S** €69-€149; **D** €69-€149* **Facilities** **Spa** STV Gym Beauty treatment room New Year Wi-fi **Conf** Class 220 Board 130 Thtr 500 Del from €138 to €170* **Services** Lift Air con **Parking** 300 **Notes** LB Closed 25 Dec RS 24 Dec Civ Wed 300

D

Red Cow Moran

★★★★ 76% HOTEL

☎ 01 4593650 01 4591588
Red Cow Complex, Naas Rd
e-mail: redcowres@moranhotels.com
web: www.moranhotels.com
dir: At junct of M50 & N7 on city side of motorway

Located just off the M50, this hotel is 20 minutes from the airport and only minutes away from the city centre via the Luas light rail system. The dedicated team of staff show a genuine willingness to create a memorable stay. Bedrooms are well equipped and comfortable, and the public areas and conference rooms are spacious. Ample free parking is available.

Rooms 123 (21 fmly) (48 smoking) **S** €89-€380; **D** €89-€380 (incl. bkfst) **Facilities** FTV New Year Wi-fi **Conf** Class 350 Board 150 Thtr 750 Del from €99.50 to €140 **Services** Lift Air con **Parking** 700 **Notes** Closed 24-26 Dec Civ Wed 200

REPUBLIC OF IRELAND

Ashling Hotel, Dublin

★★★★ 75% HOTEL

☎ 01 6772324 01 6793783
Parkgate St
e-mail: info@ashlinghotel.ie
dir: Close to River Liffey, opposite Heuston Station

Situated on the banks of the River Liffey close to the city centre, railway station and law courts; it is also just a five-minute walk from Phoenix Park. The hotel has been completely refurbished to a high standard in a contemporary style. Bedrooms are comfortably furnished; the newer ones are more spacious. Food is available in the Ivy Bar throughout the day and at lunch there is a popular carvery; Chesterfields Brasserie offers a carte menu in the evening. Staff are very friendly and service is attentive and professional. Secure indoor parking is available.

Rooms 225 (23 fmly) (10 smoking) **Facilities** STV Wi-fi **Conf** Class 110 Board 50 Thtr 220 Del from €115 to €200* **Services** Lift **Parking** 100 **Notes** Closed 25-26 Dec

DUBLIN *continued*

Bewleys Hotel Ballsbridge

★★★ 75% HOTEL

☎ 01 6681111 🖷 01 6681999
Merrion Rd, Ballsbridge
e-mail: ballsbridge@bewleyshotels.com
dir: On corner of Merrion Rd & Simmonscourt Rd

This stylish hotel is a restored 19th-century Masonic school situated near the RDS, Aviva Stadium and the city centre. It offers comfortable, good-value, well-appointed accommodation. The Brasserie serves an interesting menu with a very popular carvery lunch and breakfast; snacks are available in Tom's Bar throughout the day. There is secure underground parking, and Thomas Prior Hall is a unique venue for banquets and conferences.

Rooms 304 (64 fmly) (45 GF) (45 smoking) **S** €69-€199; **D** €69-€199 **Facilities** Xmas New Year Wi-fi **Conf** Class 150 Board 80 Thtr 250 Del from €135 **Services** Lift **Parking** 220 **Notes** LB ⊗ Civ Wed

Cassidys

★★★ 75% HOTEL

☎ 01 8780555 🖷 01 8780687
6-8 Cavendish Row, Upper O'Connell St
e-mail: stay@cassidyshotel.com
dir: In city centre at north end of O'Connell St

This family-run hotel is located at the top of O'Connell Street, in a terrace of red-brick Georgian townhouses, directly opposite the famed Gate Theatre. The warm and welcoming atmosphere created by the hospitable team in Groomes Bar and Bistro adds to the traditional atmosphere. Bedrooms are individually styled and well appointed; many have air conditioning. A residents' gym, conference facilities and limited parking are all available.

Rooms 113 (26 annexe) (3 fmly) (12 GF) (30 smoking) **Facilities** STV Gym Fitness suite Wi-fi **Conf** Class 45 Board 45 Thtr 80 **Services** Lift **Parking** 8 **Notes** ⊗ Closed 24-26 Dec

Bewleys Hotel Leopardstown

★★★ 74% HOTEL

☎ 01 2935000 & 2935001 🖷 01 2935099
Central Park, Leopardstown
e-mail: leop@bewleyshotels.com
dir: M50 junct 13/14, follow signs for Leopardstown. Hotel on right.

This hotel is conveniently situated close to the Central Business Park and Leopardstown racecourse, and serviced by the Luas light rail system and Aircoach. Contemporary in style, the open-plan public areas include a spacious lounge bar, brasserie and a selection of conference rooms. Bedrooms are well appointed. Underground parking is available.

Rooms 352 (70 fmly) (50 smoking) **S** €69-€149; **D** €69-€149 **Facilities** STV FTV Affiliation with local gym Wi-fi **Conf** Class 50 Board 50 Thtr 160 Del from €89 to €99 **Services** Lift **Parking** 228 **Notes** ⊗ Closed 23-25 Dec

Mespil Hotel

★★★ 74% HOTEL

☎ 01 4884600 🖷 01 6671244
Mespil Rd
e-mail: mespil@leehotels.com
dir: N81, right at Grove Rd (R111), hotel on right

This comfortable hotel is situated within walking distance of the city centre and overlooks the banks of the Grand Canal with the RDS and Ballsbridge close by. Public areas include an open-plan lobby and restaurant with a very cosy Terrace Bar where food is available throughout the day. Bedrooms are comfortably furnished and spacious. Secure parking is available at the rear.

Rooms 255 (100 annexe) (7 fmly) (10 GF) (26 smoking) **Facilities** STV Wi-fi **Conf** Class 12 Board 20 Thtr 25 **Services** Lift **Parking** 50 **Notes** ⊗ Closed 24-29 Dec RS 23 & 30 Dec

Sandymount Hotel

★★★ 74% HOTEL

☎ 01 6142000 🖷 01 6607077
Herbert Rd, Sandymount
e-mail: info@sandymounthotel.ie
dir: Adjacent to Aviva Stadium, 200mtrs from Dart Rail Station

This hotel (previously known as the Mount Herbert Hotel) has been run by the Loughran family for three generations, and is located close to the Aviva Stadium, the RDS and Sandymount village. The comfortable bedrooms are well appointed, as are the lounge areas. The bistro restaurant and bar overlook the lovely garden. There are conference facilities and ample free parking is available.

Rooms 168 (3 fmly) (56 GF) **S** €59-€240; **D** €59-€240 **Facilities** STV Wi-fi **Conf** Class 60 Board 40 Thtr 100 **Services** Lift **Parking** 90 **Notes** LB ⊗ Closed 21-27 Dec

Bewleys Hotel Newlands Cross

★★★ 72% HOTEL

☎ 01 4640140 & 4123301 🖷 01 4640900
Newlands Cross, Naas Rd
e-mail: newlands@bewleyshotels.com
web: www.bewleyshotels.com
dir: M50 junct 9, N7 (Naas road). Hotel near junct of N7 & Belgard Rd

This modern hotel is situated on the outskirts of Dublin and offers a pricing structure that is particularly popular with families. Bedrooms are well furnished and the brasserie restaurant is open for casual dining all day, with more formal meals in the evening. There is a comfortable lounge bar and conference facilities plus ample parking.

Rooms 299 (176 fmly) (63 GF) **S** €50-€199; **D** €50-€199 **Facilities** ♫ Wi-fi **Conf** Class 18 Board 14 Thtr 50 Del from €100* **Services** Lift **Parking** 200 **Notes** LB ⊗ Closed 24-26 Dec

Temple Bar

FBD Hotels

★★★ 72% HOTEL

☎ 01 6773333 🖷 01 6773088
Fleet St, Temple Bar
e-mail: reservations@tbh.ie
web: www.templebarhotel.com
dir: From Trinity College towards O'Connell Bridge. 1st left into Fleet St. Hotel on right

This hotel is situated right in the heart of Dublin's Temple Bar area, and is close to the main shopping districts, restaurants and the nightlife of the city. Bedrooms are comfortable and well equipped, with more spacious executive rooms available at a small surcharge. Food is served throughout the day in Buskers themed bar, with the Rendezvous a more peaceful option. Alchemy is the smart night club which becomes a music venue at weekends and at other peak periods. Parking is available in a multi-storey opposite at a reduced rate for hotel guests.

Rooms 129 (6 fmly) (34 smoking) **S** €76-€165; **D** €82-€240 (incl. bkfst)* **Facilities** Wi-fi **Conf** Class 40 Board 40 Thtr 70 **Services** Lift **Notes** LB ⊗ Closed 23-25 Dec RS Good Fri

West County Hotel

★★ 72% HOTEL

☎ 01 6264011 & 6264647 📠 01 6231378
Chapelizod
e-mail: info@westcountyhotel.ie
dir: From city centre follow signs for N4(W), 4m from city centre between Palmerstown & Ballyfermot on N4

This family run hotel is situated just off the N4 and is within walking distance of Chapelizod. The bedrooms are well appointed, and public areas include a comfortable lobby lounge and bar where carvery lunches are served daily; dinner is available in the Pine Restaurant.

Rooms 48 (10 fmly) (18 smoking) **Facilities** ♫ New Year Wi-fi **Conf** Class 100 Board 60 Thtr 200 **Services** Lift **Parking** 200 **Notes** LB ⊗ Closed 24-26 Dec Civ Wed 80

Carlton Hotel Blanchardstown

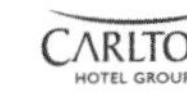

U

☎ 01 8275600 📠 01 8275601
Tyrrelstown
e-mail: reservationsblanchardstown@carlton.ie
dir: Take Blanchardstown exit on M50 onto N3, 2nd exit & follow signs for Tyrelstown

Currently the rating for this establishment is not confirmed. This may be due to a change of ownership or because it has only recently joined the AA rating scheme. For further details please see the AA website: theAA.com

Rooms 155 (22 fmly) (20 smoking) **S** €69-€129; **D** €79-€139* **Facilities** STV Gym New Year Wi-fi **Conf** Class 400 Board 100 Thtr 500 Del from €129 to €159 **Services** Lift Air con **Parking** 200 **Notes** LB ⊗ Closed 25-26 Dec Civ Wed 300

Ibis Hotel Dublin Red Cow

BUDGET HOTEL

☎ 01 464 1480 📠 01 464 1484
Naas Rd, Monastery Rd, Clondalkin
e-mail: H0595@accor.com

Close to Dublin airport and the M50, this hotel is modern in style. Bedrooms have contemporary furnishings including large desks. Public rooms include a restaurant and a lounge. Breakfast is self-service and a 24-hour snack service is also available.

Rooms 150 (39 fmly) (35 GF) **S** €41-€85; **D** €41-€85 **Conf** Class 25 Board 18 Thtr 35 Del from €70 to €110

DUBLIN AIRPORT

Dublin — Map 1 D4

Carlton Hotel Dublin Airport

★★★★ 76% HOTEL

☎ 01 8667500 & 8667501 📠 01 8623314
Old Airport Rd
e-mail: info.dublin@carlton.ie
dir: From city centre take M1 to airport rdbt then 1st exit S towards Santry. Hotel 800mtrs on right

Conveniently located next to Dublin Airport this modern hotel offers every facility for business and leisure guests. The spacious air-conditioned bedrooms are well appointed; some have balconies. Public areas include a comfortable lobby lounge, Kittyhawks Bar and Bistro where food is served throughout the day. There is extensive banqueting and conference facilities and a fitness centre. Ample parking is available, and a complimentary, 24-hour shuttle coach service operates to and from the airport.

Rooms 100 (10 fmly) (13 GF) (13 smoking) **S** €89-€159; **D** €89-€299 **Facilities** STV Gym Xmas New Year Wi-fi **Conf** Class 150 Board 80 Thtr 400 Del from €150 to €200 **Services** Lift Air con **Parking** 270 **Notes** LB Civ Wed 200

Bewleys Hotel Dublin Airport

★★★ 75% HOTEL

☎ 01 8711000 & 8711200 📠 01 8711001
Baskin Ln
e-mail: dublinairport@bewleyshotels.com
dir: At end of M50 N'bound, 2nd exit at rdbt (N32), left at next rdbt

Conveniently situated for Dublin Airport, this hotel has the added advantage of secure underground parking and a complimentary shuttle bus to the airport. Bedrooms are spacious and suitable for families; there is a comfortable lounge bar and brasserie with a wide selection of dishes on offer. Good quality meeting and banqueting rooms are available.

Rooms 466 (232 fmly) (36 smoking) **S** €69-€129; **D** €69-€139* **Facilities** FTV Fitness room Xmas Wi-fi **Conf** Class 150 Board 12 Thtr 300 Del from €114 to €159* **Services** Lift **Parking** 1150 **Notes** LB Civ Wed 250

Crowne Plaza Dublin Northwood

U

☎ 01 8628888 📠 01 8628800
Northwood Park, Santry Demesne, Santry
e-mail: info@crowneplazadublin.ie
web: www.cpdublin.crowneplaza.com
dir: M50 junct 4, left into Northwood Park, 1km, hotel on left

Currently the rating for this establishment is not confirmed. This may be due to a change of ownership or because it has only recently joined the AA rating scheme. For further details please see the AA website: theAA.com

Rooms 204 (17 fmly) (9 smoking) **S** €70-€220; **D** €70-€250* **Facilities** STV FTV Gym Xmas New Year Wi-fi **Conf** Class 450 Board 100 Thtr 850 Del from €140 to €220* **Services** Lift Air con **Parking** 400 **Notes** ⊗ Civ Wed 300

Premier Inn Dublin Airport

BUDGET HOTEL

☎ 0871 527 8312 📠 0871 527 8313
Airside Retail Park
dir: M1 junct 2 for Dublin Airport. At main airport rdbt 3rd exit, follow Drogheda & Belfast signs. 2nd exit at Cloghran rdbt. Right at lights signed Airside Industrial Estate/Retail Park. Hotel on right

High quality, budget accommodation ideal for both families and business travellers. Spacious, en suite bedrooms feature tea and coffee making facilities, and Freeview TV in most hotels. Internet access and Wi-fi are available for a small fee. The adjacent family restaurant features a wide and varied menu. See also the Hotel Groups pages.

Rooms 155 **D** €69*

D

REPUBLIC OF IRELAND

DUNDALK Map 1 D4
Co Louth

Ballymascanlon House Hotel

★★★★ 79% HOTEL

☎ 042 9358200 042 9371598
e-mail: info@ballymascanlon.com
dir: M1 junct 18 onto N52 signed Dundalk North/R173 at Carlingford. Exit at Faughart rdbt. 1st left at next rdbt. Hotel in approx 1km on left

This Victorian mansion is set in 130 acres of woodland and landscaped gardens at the foot of the Cooley Mountains. The elegant house and the modern extension make this a very comfortable hotel that has really stylish bedrooms. Public areas include a spacious restaurant, lounge and bar, together with relaxing reading rooms that retain many original architectural features. There is a well-equipped leisure centre, and The Oak Room banqueting facility proves to be very popular for weddings and family occasions.

Rooms 90 (11 fmly) (5 GF) (34 smoking) **Facilities** STV FTV supervised 18 Putt green Gym Steam room Sauna Plunge pool Xmas New Year Wi-fi **Conf** Class 220 Board 100 Thtr 400 **Services** Lift **Parking** 250 **Notes** Civ Wed 200

DUNFANAGHY Map 1 C6
Co Donegal

Arnold's Hotel

★★★ 74% HOTEL

☎ 074 9136208 074 9136352
e-mail: enquiries@arnoldshotel.com
dir: N56 from Letterkenny, hotel on left on entering village

This hotel is noted for its warm welcome and good food and is situated in a coastal village with sandy beaches and beautiful scenery. Public areas and bedrooms are very comfortable; there is a traditional cosy bar with turf fires and the Seascapes Restaurant serves good food especially local seafood and lamb. Links golf, horse riding, photographic and painting breaks are all available.

Rooms 30 (10 fmly) **S** €49.50-€85; **D** €99-€130 (incl. bkfst)* **Facilities** FTV Fishing New Year Wi-fi **Parking** 60 **Notes** LB Closed Nov-mid Apr RS Apr/Oct Civ Wed 80

DUNGARVAN Map 1 C2
Co Waterford

Lawlors

★★★ 68% HOTEL

☎ 058 41122 058 41000
e-mail: info@lawlorshotel.com
dir: Off N25

This town centre hotel has very attractive and comfortable public areas with a busy bar where food is served throughout the day. A good value dinner menu is available in Davit's Restaurant. The bedrooms vary in size but all are well appointed. Conference and meeting rooms plus secure parking are available.

Rooms 89 (8 fmly) **Facilities** New Year Wi-fi **Conf** Class 215 Board 420 Thtr 420 **Services** Lift **Notes** Closed 25 Dec

DUNKINEELY Map 1 B5
Co Donegal

Castle Murray House and Restaurant

RESTAURANT WITH ROOMS

☎ 074 9737022 074 9737330
St Johns Point
e-mail: info@castlemurray.com
dir: From Donegal take N56 towards Killybegs. Left to Dunkineely

Situated on the coast road of St Johns Point, this charming family-run house and restaurant overlooks McSwynes Bay and the castle. The bedrooms are individually decorated and appointed with guest comfort very much in mind, as is the cosy bar and sun lounge. There is a strong French influence in the cooking; locally landed fish, and prime lamb and beef are featured on the menus.

Rooms 10 (2 fmly)

DURRUS Map 1 B2
Co Cork

Blairscove House & Restaurant

RESTAURANT WITH ROOMS

☎ 027 61127 027 61487
e-mail: mail@blairscove.ie
dir: From Durrus on R591 towards Crookhaven, 2.4km, house (blue gate) on right

Blairscove comprises four elegant suites located in the courtyard of a Georgian country house outside the pretty village of Durrus near Bantry; they are individually decorated in a contemporary style and have stunning views over Dunmanus Bay and the mountains. The restaurant is renowned for its wide range of hors d'oeuvres and its open wood-fire grill. The piano playing and candle light add to a unique dining experience.

Rooms 4 (4 annexe) (1 fmly)

ENNIS Map 1 B3
Co Clare

Temple Gate

★★★ 80% HOTEL

☎ 065 6823300 065 6823322
The Square
e-mail: info@templegatehotel.com
dir: Exit N18 onto Tulla Rd for 0.25m, hotel on left

This smart hotel is owned and run by the Madden family and is located in the centre of the town. It incorporates a 19th-century, Gothic-style Great Hall banqueting room. The public areas are well planned and include a comfortable library lounge, popular traditional pub and Legends Restaurant. Bedrooms are attractive and well equipped with some executive rooms and suites available.

Rooms 70 (3 fmly) (11 GF) (20 smoking) **Facilities** STV FTV New Year Wi-fi **Conf** Class 100 Board 80 Thtr 250 **Services** Lift **Parking** 52 **Notes** Closed 25-26 Dec RS 24 Dec Civ Wed 200

ENNISKERRY Map 1 D3
Co Wicklow

The Ritz Carlton Powerscourt

★★★★★ 86% HOTEL

☎ 01 2748888 01 2749999
Powerscourt Estate
e-mail: powerscourtreservations@ritzcarlton.com
dir: From Dublin take M50, M11, then N11, follow Enniskerry signs. In Enniskerry left up hill, hotel on right

This very stylish hotel, built in the Palladian style, has a tranquil setting with stunning views over the gardens and woodlands to the Sugar Loaf. The bedrooms and suites are particularly spacious and well appointed with very impressive bathrooms that have TVs, deep tubs and walk-in showers. The luxuriously appointed public areas are airy and spacious with a variety of food options that includes the Gordon Ramsay at Powerscourt restaurant. The hotel also has a stunning spa, two golf courses, and includes fly fishing and equestrian pursuits among its many leisure facilities.

Rooms 200 (39 GF) **D** €255-€5000* **Facilities** Spa STV 36 Putt green Fishing Gym Cycling Mega chess Xmas New Year Wi-fi **Conf** Class 240 Board 72 Thtr 500 Del from €169* **Services** Lift Air con **Parking** 384 **Notes** LB Civ Wed 400

GALWAY
Co Galway Map 1 B3

Ardilaun Hotel & Leisure Club

★★★★ 81% HOTEL

☎ 091 521433 📠 091 521546
Taylor's Hill
e-mail: info@theardilaunhotel.ie
web: www.theardilaunhotel.ie
dir: M6 to Galway City West, then follow signs for N59 Clifden, then N6 towards Salthill

This very smart country-house style hotel, appointed to a high standard, is located on the outskirts of the city near Salthill and has lovely landscaped gardens. The bedrooms have been thoughtfully appointed and the deluxe rooms and suites are particularly spacious. Public areas include a selection of comfortable lounges, the Camilaun Restaurant that overlooks the garden, Blazers bistro and bar, and extensive banqueting and leisure facilities. This hotel is the winner of AA Ireland's Courtesy & Care Award 2011-12.

Rooms 125 (17 fmly) (8 GF) (16 smoking) **Facilities** Spa STV supervised Gym Treatment & analysis rooms Beauty salon Spin-cycle room New Year Wi-fi **Conf** Class 300 Board 100 Thtr 650 **Services** Lift **Parking** 380 **Notes** LB Closed 24-26 Dec RS Closed pm 23 Dec Civ Wed 650

Park House Hotel & Park Room Restaurant

★★★★ 78% HOTEL

☎ 091 564924 📠 091 569219
Forster St, Eyre Square
e-mail: parkhousehotel@eircom.net
web: www.parkhousehotel.ie
dir: In city centre

Situated just off Eyre Square, this well established hotel offers comfortable facilities to suite business or leisure guests. Public areas and bedrooms are well appointed and attractively decorated. The Park Restaurant has been a popular spot for the people of Galway for many years; less formal food is available throughout the day in Boss Doyle's bar. Parking for hotel guests is available at the rear.

Rooms 84 (4 smoking) **Facilities** STV FTV Wi-fi **Services** Lift Air con **Parking** 48 **Notes** Closed 24-26 Dec

Claregalway

★★★ 79% HOTEL

☎ 091 738300 & 738302 📠 091 738311
Claregalway Village
e-mail: stay@claregalwayhotel.ie
dir: At junct of N17 (Galway/Sligo) & N18 (Dublin/Limerick)

Just 12 kilometres from Galway, this modern hotel offers comfortable bedrooms and spacious public areas. Run by the Gill family and their dedicated team, guests are sure to feel welcome and at home here. Food is served throughout the day in the popular Ti Cusack's Bar and Grill. Leisure facilities are complimentary to residents.

Rooms 48 (8 fmly) (3 smoking) **S** €50-€300; **D** €50-€300 (incl. bkfst)* **Facilities** Spa supervised Gym Sauna Steam room Sunbeds New Year Wi-fi **Conf** Class 250 Board 100 Thtr 400 **Services** Lift Air con **Parking** 160 **Notes** LB Closed 23-26 Dec Civ Wed 300

Carlton Hotel Galway City

★★★ 77% HOTEL

☎ 091 381200 📠 091 753187
Dublin Rd
e-mail: reservations.galwaycity@carlton.ie
dir: M6 left onto R446, last exit off Martin rdbt onto R338. Continue on R388 & through Steritt rdbt, hotel on left

This hotel is located a short drive from the city centre. It features a wide range of bedroom styles, many interconnected and suitable for family groups. The food options include all-day dining in Bar Solo, with dinner in Reubens Restaurant. There are a number of conference and meeting rooms for up to 120 delegates, and Active Fitness is available to resident guests.

Rooms 363 (150 fmly) (80 GF) (80 smoking) **S** €69-€250; **D** €78-€260 (incl. bkfst)* **Facilities** STV FTV supervised Gym Sauna Steam room Aerobics studio New Year Wi-fi Child facilities **Services** Lift **Notes** Closed 20-26 Dec

The G Hotel

U

☎ 091 865200 📠 091 865203
Wellpark, Dublin Rd
e-mail: info@theg.ie
dir: Telephone for detailed directions

Currently the rating for this establishment is not confirmed. This may be due to a change of ownership or because it has only recently joined the AA rating scheme. For further details please see the AA website: theAA.com

Rooms 101 (2 fmly) **S** €140-€2500; **D** €140-€2500 (incl. bkfst) **Facilities** Spa STV FTV Gym New Year Wi-fi **Conf** Class 42 Board 40 Thtr 120 **Services** Lift Air con **Parking** 349 **Notes** Closed 23-26 Dec Civ Wed 90

GARRYVOE
Co Cork Map 1 C2

Garryvoe

★★★★ 75% HOTEL

☎ 021 4646718 📠 021 4646824
Ballycotton Bay, Castlemartyr
e-mail: res@garryvoehotel.com
dir: N25 onto L72 at Castlemartyr (between Midleton & Youghal). 6km to hotel

In a delightful location facing the beach and overlooking Ballycotton Island and Bay, this is a comfortable, family-run hotel with caring staff. The bedrooms are appointed to a very high standard; some have balconies. The popular bar serves light meals throughout the day, while a more formal menu at dinner is available in the dining room. There are extensive banqueting and excellent health club facilities.

Rooms 82 (17 fmly) (5 smoking) **D** €74-€149* **Facilities** STV supervised Putt green Gym Sauna Steam room Wi-fi **Conf** Class 150 Board 12 Thtr 300 **Services** Lift **Parking** 100 **Notes** LB Closed 24-25 Dec Civ Wed 150

G

REPUBLIC OF IRELAND

GLASLOUGH Map 1 C5
Co Monaghan

The Lodge at Castle Leslie Estate

★★★★ 78% HOTEL

047 88100 047 88256
e-mail: info@castleleslie.com
dir: M1 junct 14 onto N2 to Monaghan, then N12 to N185 to Glaslough

Set in 1,000 acres of rolling countryside, the lodge is part of the Castle Leslie Estate which has been in the Leslie family since the 1660s. Bedrooms are in both the original hunting lodge and the converted stable block. Resident guests have two dining options including the fine dining restaurant in the castle. With a successful equestrian centre and a private fishing lake, this is an ideal location for those who enjoy country pursuits.

Rooms 29 (5 fmly) (10 GF) **S** €125-€150; **D** €180-€240 (incl. bkfst) **Facilities** Spa STV FTV Fishing Equestrian centre Wi-fi **Conf** Class 25 Board 24 Thtr 40 Del from €150 to €200 **Services** Lift **Parking** 100 **Notes** LB Closed 22-28 Dec RS Oct-1 Apr Civ Wed 40

GLENDALOUGH Map 1 D3
Co Wicklow

The Glendalough

★★★ 71% HOTEL

0404 45135 0404 45142
e-mail: info@glendaloughhotel.ie
dir: N11 to Kilmacongue, right onto R755, straight on at Laragh, right onto R756

Mountains and forest provide the setting for this long-established hotel at the edge of the famed monastic site, and many of the comfortably appointed bedrooms have superb forest views. Food is served daily in the very popular bar and on the terrace when weather permits; the renovated Glendasan River Restaurant is a stylish bistro where dinner is served. The atmospheric Glendalough Tavern is a popular meeting place for visitors and locals alike.

Rooms 44 (3 fmly) **Facilities** STV Fishing Wi-fi **Conf** Class 150 Board 50 Thtr 200 **Services** Lift **Parking** 100 **Notes** RS Dec-Jan, Mon-Fri

GOREY Map 1 D3
Co Wexford

Amber Springs Hotel

★★★★ 78% HOTEL

053 9484000 053 9484494
Wexford Rd
e-mail: info@ambersprings.ie
dir: 500mtrs from Gorey by-pass at junct 23

This hotel, on the Wexford road, is within walking distance of the town. Bedrooms are spacious and very comfortable, and guests have full use of the leisure facilities. Dining in Kelby's Bistro is a highlight of a visit, with a combination of interesting food and really friendly service.

Rooms 80 (18 fmly) **S** €65-€140; **D** €110-€230 (incl. bkfst)* **Facilities** Spa STV supervised Gym New Year Wi-fi Child facilities **Conf** Class 450 Board 30 Thtr 700 Del from €160 to €300 **Services** Lift Air con **Parking** 178 **Notes** LB Closed 25-26 Dec Civ Wed 700

Ashdown Park Hotel

★★★★ 76% HOTEL

053 9480500 053 9480777
The Coach Rd
e-mail: info@ashdownparkhotel.com
web: www.ashdownparkhotel.com
dir: N11 junct 22, on approaching Gorey, 1st left (before railway bridge), hotel on left

Situated on an elevated position overlooking the town, this modern hotel has excellent health, leisure and banqueting facilities. There are comfortable lounge areas and two dining options – Ivy, a popular carvery bar, and The Rowan Tree, the first-floor fine dining restaurant open in the evenings. Bedrooms are available in a number of styles; all are spacious and well equipped. Close to a number of golf courses, this property is popular with golfers, and also with families as it is near the beaches.

Ashdown Park Hotel

Rooms 79 (12 fmly) (20 GF) **Facilities** FTV supervised Gym Leisure centre Massage rooms New Year Wi-fi **Conf** Class 315 Board 100 Thtr 800 **Services** Lift **Parking** 150 **Notes** Closed 25 Dec Civ Wed 300

INSPECTORS' CHOICE

Marlfield House Hotel

★★★ COUNTRY HOUSE HOTEL

RELAIS & CHATEAUX

053 9421124 053 9421572
e-mail: info@marlfieldhouse.ie
web: www.marlfieldhouse.com
dir: N11 junct 23, follow signs for Courtown. At Courtown Rd rdbt left for Gorey. Hotel 1m on left

This Regency-style building has been gracefully extended and developed into an excellent hotel. An atmosphere of elegance and luxury permeates every corner of the house, underpinned by truly friendly and professional service led by the Bowe family who are always in evidence. The bedrooms are decorated in keeping with the style of the house, with some really spacious rooms and suites on the ground floor. Dinner in the restaurant is always a highlight of a stay at Marlfield.

Rooms 19 (3 fmly) (6 GF) **Facilities** FTV In-room treatments Xmas New Year Wi-fi **Conf** Board 24 Thtr 60 **Parking** 100 **Notes** LB Closed 2 Jan-28 Feb Civ Wed 100

KENMARE
Co Kerry Map 1 B2

INSPECTORS' CHOICE

Sheen Falls Lodge

★★★★★ @@ COUNTRY HOUSE HOTEL

☎ 06466 41600 📠 06466 41386
e-mail: info@sheenfallslodge.ie
dir: From Kenmare take N71 to Glengarriff over suspension bridge, take 1st left

This former fishing lodge has been developed into a beautiful hotel with a friendly team of professional staff. The cascading Sheen Falls are floodlit at night, forming a romantic backdrop to the enjoyment of award-winning cuisine in La Cascade Restaurant. Less formal dining is available in Oscar's Bistro, and the Sun Lounge serves refreshments and light snacks throughout the day. The bedrooms are very comfortably appointed; many of the suites are particularly spacious. The leisure centre and beauty therapy facilities offer a number of exclusive treatments, and outdoor pursuits include walking, fishing, tennis, horse riding and clay pigeon shooting.

Rooms 66 (14 fmly) (14 GF) **S** €310-€455; **D** €310-€455* **Facilities** Spa STV supervised Fishing Gym Table tennis Steam room Clay pigeon shooting Cycling Vintage car rides Library Xmas New Year Wi-fi **Conf** Class 65 Board 50 Thtr 120 **Services** Lift **Parking** 76 **Notes** LB Closed 2 Jan-1 Feb RS Midwk in Feb, Mar, Nov & Dec Civ Wed 100

KILKENNY
Co Kilkenny Map 1 C3

Kilkenny River Court Hotel

★★★★ 78% @ HOTEL

☎ 056 7723388 📠 056 7723389
The Bridge, John St
e-mail: reservations@rivercourthotel.com
dir: In town centre, opposite castle

Hidden behind archways on John Street, this is a very comfortable and welcoming establishment. The restaurant, bar and many of the well-equipped bedrooms command great views of Kilkenny Castle and the River Nore. Attentive, friendly staff ensure good service throughout the hotel. Excellent corporate and leisure facilities are provided.

Rooms 90 (4 fmly) **Facilities** Spa supervised Gym Beauty salon Treatment rooms Wi-fi **Conf** Class 110 Board 45 Thtr 260 Del from €155 to €250 **Services** Lift **Parking** 84 **Notes** Closed 23-26 Dec Civ Wed 250

Pembroke Hotel

★★★★ 72% HOTEL

☎ 056 7783500 📠 056 7783535
Patrick St
e-mail: info@pembrokekilkenny.com

This hotel enjoys an ideal location right at the heart of the city. Bedrooms are spacious and furnished to a high standard, some with views of the famed Kilkenny Castle. Stathams bar and grill is open throughout the day; the menu features firm favourites, together with a range of home-made desserts and bakery items. Bright, airy meeting and training rooms are located in the courtyard and secure, complimentary parking is available to residents.

Rooms 74 (16 fmly) (5 GF) **Facilities** STV FTV Gym New Year Wi-fi **Services** Lift Air con **Parking** 80 **Notes** LB Civ Wed 100

Langton House Hotel

★★★ 75% HOTEL

☎ 056 7765133 & 5521728 📠 056 7763693
69 John St
e-mail: reservations@langtons.ie
dir: N9 & N10 from Dublin, follow city centre signs on outskirts of Kilkenny, left to Langtons. Hotel 500mtrs on left after lights

This hotel has a long and well-founded reputation for its genuine hospitality as an entertainment venue, nightclub and bar. The most recent addition to the facilities is Set, an intimate theatre space. There is a range of bedroom options, many in the garden annexe; all are very comfortable, tastefully decorated and well appointed. The Langton is a busy restaurant serving dinner, with more casual all-day dining in 67, the lively bar that is popular with visitors and locals alike.

Rooms 34 (16 annexe) (4 fmly) (8 GF) (22 smoking) **Facilities** STV New Year Wi-fi **Conf** Class 250 Board 30 Thtr 400 **Services** Air con **Parking** 60 **Notes** LB Closed 24-25 Dec Civ Wed 100

KILLARNEY
Co Kerry Map 1 B2

Muckross Park Hotel & Cloisters Spa

★★★★ 84% HOTEL

☎ 064 6623400 📠 064 6631965
Lakes of Killarney
e-mail: sales@muckrosspark.com
dir: From Killarney take N71 towards Kenmare

Dating originally from 1795, this fine property offers spacious accommodation and excellent public areas. The bedrooms and suites are beautifully appointed. Casual dining is available throughout the day in the old world atmosphere of Molly Darcy's pub, while The Cloisters Spa is an oasis of calm and tranquillity.

Rooms 68 (3 fmly) **S** €130-€299; **D** €160-€299 (incl. bkfst)* **Facilities** Spa STV supervised Fishing Gym Archery Cycling Yoga Wi-fi **Conf** Class 280 Board 30 Thtr 350 Del from €285 to €400* **Services** Lift Air con **Parking** 80 **Notes** LB Civ Wed 80

Cahernane House

MANOR HOUSE

★★★★ 80% @@ HOTEL

☎ 064 6631895 📠 064 6634340
Muckross Rd
e-mail: info@cahernane.com
web: www.cahernane.com
dir: On N22 to Killarney, take 1st exit off rdbt then left at church, 1st exit at next rdbt to Muckross Rd

This fine country mansion, former home of the Earls of Pembroke, has a magnificent mountain backdrop and panoramic views from its lakeside setting. Elegant period furniture is complemented by more modern pieces to create a comfortable hotel offering a warm atmosphere with a particularly friendly team dedicated to guest care.

Rooms 38 (26 annexe) **Facilities** Fishing Wi-fi **Conf** Class 10 Board 10 Thtr 15 **Services** Lift Air con **Parking** 50 **Notes** Closed 21 Dec-Jan Civ Wed 60

KILLARNEY ***continued***

Randles Court

★★★★ 80% HOTEL

☎ 064 6635333 🖷 064 6639301
Muckross Rd
e-mail: info@randlescourt.com
dir: N22 towards Muckross, right at T-junct. From N72 3rd exit on 1st rdbt into town, follow signs for Muckross, hotel on left

Owned and run by the Randles family, this charming hotel is situated close to the town, the lakes and Killarney National Park. The Drawing room and Wiggs bar are elegantly furnished and very relaxing. Bedrooms are spacious, and great care has been taken in the choice furnishings and decor. Dinner is served nightly in Checkers restaurant. There is a swimming pool, spa treatment rooms and secure underground parking.

Rooms 78 (4 fmly) (6 GF) **S** €60-€190; **D** €100-€300 (incl. bkfst) **Facilities Spa** STV supervised Sauna Steam room Hydrotherapy suite New Year Wi-fi **Conf** Class 50 Board 40 Thtr 90 Del from €120 to €150 **Services** Lift **Parking** 110 **Notes** LB Closed 22-27 Dec Civ Wed 140

Lake

★★★★ 78% HOTEL

☎ 064 6631035 🖷 064 6631902
Lake Shore, Muckross Rd
e-mail: info@lakehotel.com
dir: N22 to Killarney. Hotel 2km from town on Muckross Rd

Enjoying a delightful location on the shores of Killarney's lake shore, this hotel is run by the second generation of the Huggard family together with a dedicated and friendly team. There is a relaxed atmosphere with log fires and stunning views from the lounges and restaurant, and guests could be lucky enough to see a herd of red deer wander by. The smartly furnished bedrooms have either lake or woodland views; some have balconies and four-poster beds. The spa offers good facilities, and there are cycle paths and lovely walks to enjoy.

Rooms 130 (6 fmly) (23 GF) **S** €72-€240; **D** €104-€320 (incl. bkfst) **Facilities Spa** STV FTV Fishing Gym Sauna Steam room Wi-fi **Conf** Class 60 Board 40 Thtr 80 **Services** Lift **Parking** 140 **Notes** LB Closed 6 Dec-Jan Civ Wed 60

Castlerosse Hotel & Golf Resort

★★★ 79% HOTEL

☎ 064 6631144 🖷 064 6631031
e-mail: res@castlerosse.ie
web: www.castlerosse.ie
dir: From Killarney take R562 signed Killorglin & The Ring of Kerry. Hotel 1.5km from town on left

This hotel is situated on 6,000 acres overlooking the Lakes of Killarney with the Magillycuddy Mountains as a backdrop. At times guests will be able to spot deer in Killarney National Park. Bedrooms and junior suites are well appointed and comfortable. There is live entertainment most nights in Mulligan's pub. Leisure facilities include a 9-hole parkland golf course, tennis courts, a leisure centre and treatment rooms.

Rooms 120 (27 fmly) **S** €60-€90; **D** €85-€180 (incl. bkfst)* **Facilities Spa** STV FTV supervised 9 Putt green Gym Golfing & riding arranged Wi-fi Child facilities **Conf** Class 100 Board 40 Thtr 200 **Services** Lift **Parking** 100 **Notes** LB Closed Dec-Feb Civ Wed 80

Killeen House

★★★ 78% HOTEL

☎ 064 6631711 & 6631773 🖷 064 6631811
Lakes of Killarney, Aghadoe
e-mail: charming@indigo.ie
dir: In Aghadoe, just off Dingle road

Dating back to 1838 this charming Victorian country house is situated close to Killarney National Park and the lakes. Stylishly decorated public areas include a cosy sitting room and bar where 'golf' is spoken! Good cuisine is served in the restaurant which overlooks the beautifully manicured garden. Bedrooms are well appointed and comfortable. The Rosney family and their staff take particular pride in extending a warm welcome to their guests.

Rooms 23 (8 fmly) (10 GF) (10 smoking) **S** €60-€100; **D** €110-€200 (incl. bkfst) **Facilities** STV FTV Wi-fi **Parking** 30 **Notes** LB Closed 21 Oct-19 Apr Civ Wed 50

KILLENARD Co Laois **Map 1 C3**

The Heritage Golf & Spa Resort

U

☎ 057 8645500 🖷 057 8695037
e-mail: info@theheritage.com
dir: From Dublin M7 to Cork. Exit at Monesterevin, through village, 3km, right at Bollands Pub. Killenard in 3km

Currently the rating for this establishment is not confirmed. This may be due to a change of ownership or because it has only recently joined the AA rating scheme. For further details please see the AA website: theAA.com

Rooms 98 (10 fmly) (20 GF) (23 smoking) **S** €120-€350; **D** €120-€350 (incl. bkfst)* **Facilities Spa** Putt green Fishing Gym Wi-fi Child facilities **Conf** Class 250 Board 50 Thtr 400 Del from €160 to €185* **Services** Lift Air con **Parking** 600 **Notes** LB Closed 19-26 Dec Civ Wed 170

KILLINEY Co Dublin **Map 1 D4**

Fitzpatrick Castle

★★★★ 81% HOTEL

☎ 01 2305400 🖷 01 2305430
e-mail: reservations@fitzpatricks.com
web: www.fitzpatrickcastle.com
dir: From Dun Laoghaire port turn left, on coast road right at lights, left at next lights. Follow to Dalkey, right at Ivory Pub, immediate left, up hill, hotel at top

This family-owned, 18th-century castle is situated in lovely gardens with mature trees and spectacular views over Dublin Bay. The original castle rooms are appointed to a high standard and have four-poster beds, while the rooms in the modern wing are spacious and some have balconies. Lounges are comfortably furnished and PJ's restaurant serves dinner on certain days of the week; more casual fare is available each night in the trendy Dungeon bar and grill. There are extensive leisure and conference facilities.

Rooms 113 (36 fmly) (12 smoking) **Facilities** STV supervised Gym Beauty/hairdressing salon Sauna Steam room Fitness centre New Year Wi-fi **Conf** Class 250 Board 80 Thtr 500 **Services** Lift **Parking** 300 **Notes** RS 25-Dec Civ Wed 400

K REPUBLIC OF IRELAND

KILMESSAN Map 1 C/D4
Co Meath

The Station House Hotel

★★★ 75% HOTEL

☎ 046 9025239 & 9025586 046 9025588
e-mail: info@thestationhousehotel.com
web: www.thestationhousehotel.com
dir: M50, N3 towards Navan. At Dunshaughlin left at end of village, follow signs

While the Station House saw its last train in the early sixties, it still retains much of its railway history and atmosphere. Some of the accommodation is located in the old carriage house, and the signal box is the bridal suite; the station itself hosts diners in the station master's office. The bedrooms are comfortably appointed, and the lounge areas are very relaxing. Set in attractively landscaped gardens and woodlands, this is a popular wedding venue. Dinner is always a highlight, featuring well-sourced ingredients cooked with both flair and care.

Rooms 20 (14 annexe) (3 fmly) (5 GF) **Facilities** Xmas New Year Wi-fi **Conf** Class 300 Board 100 Thtr 400 Del from €99 to €250 **Parking** 200 **Notes** Civ Wed 100

KILTIMAGH Map 1 B4
Co Mayo

Kiltimagh Park Hotel

★★★ 75% HOTEL

☎ 094 9374922 094 9374924
e-mail: info@parkhotelmayo.com
dir: N17 onto R322 or R323 (or N60 onto R320) to Kiltimagh

This smart hotel overlooks the Wetlands Wildlife Park and is within walking distance of Kiltimagh, and just 15 minutes from Ireland West Knock Airport and Knock Marian Shrine. The spacious bedrooms are well appointed. Public areas are attractively decorated and include comfortable lounges, Café Bar, Park Restaurant and banqueting facilities. The Aroma Beauty Spa offers a range of treatments and there is also a fitness centre and steam room. A shuttle coach service operates to the airport, and for guests using the airport, parking can be arranged at the hotel.

Rooms 46 (40 fmly) **S** €60-€200; **D** €70-€200 (incl. bkfst) **Facilities** Spa Gym New Year Wi-fi **Conf** Class 120 Board 60 Thtr 450 **Services** Lift **Parking** 300 **Notes** LB Civ Wed 350

Cill Aodain Court Hotel

★★★ 70% HOTEL

☎ 094 9381761 094 9381838
Main St
e-mail: info@cillaodain.ie
dir: In town centre opposite Market Square

Situated in the heart of historic Kiltimagh and close to Marian Shrine at Knock and also the airport, this smart, contemporary hotel offers comfortable well-appointed bedrooms. Public areas include The Gallery Restaurant, Court Bar & Bistro. Off-street parking is available opposite the hotel.

Rooms 17 (4 fmly) (7 smoking) **S** €40-€70; **D** €70-€140 (incl. bkfst) **Facilities** STV New Year Wi-fi **Conf** Class 30 Board 25 Thtr 50 Del from €79 to €99 **Notes** LB Closed 24-25 Dec

KINSALE Map 1 B2
Co Cork

Carlton Hotel Kinsale

★★★★ 79% HOTEL

☎ 021 4706000 021 4706001
Rathmore Rd
e-mail: reservations.kinsale@carlton.ie
dir: R600 to Kinsale, turn left signed Charles Fort. 3kms, (pass rugby club), hotel on left

This newly built hotel is set on an elevated position overlooking Oysterhaven Bay in 90 acres of mature parkland. All the bedrooms are spacious and well appointed, and many have spectacular views over the bay. Two-bedroom holiday apartment options are available in the grounds. The contemporary first-floor public rooms include the Rockpool Restaurant where guests can cook Aberdeen Angus steaks on lava stones at their own table. The staff are very guest focused and make families particularly welcome.

Rooms 130 (20 fmly) (24 GF) **Facilities** Spa STV FTV supervised Gym New Year Wi-fi **Conf** Class 120 Board 40 Thtr 300 Del from €180 to €220 **Services** Lift Air con **Parking** 140 **Notes** Closed 23-27 Dec Civ Wed 200

Blue Haven

★★★ 74% HOTEL

☎ 021 4772209 021 4774268
3 Pearse St
e-mail: info@bluehavenkinsale.com
dir: In town centre

At the heart of this historic town, this vibrant hotel offers a comfortable lounge and café, a very popular and stylish bar with an airy bistro plus an elegant restaurant. Live music is a feature seven days a week in high season, and there is a pizza and disco bar at the rear. Bedrooms vary in size and are furnished to a high standard.

Rooms 17 **Facilities** New Year Wi-fi **Conf** Class 35 Board 25 Thtr 100 **Notes** Closed 25 Dec Civ Wed 70

The White House

RESTAURANT WITH ROOMS

☎ 021 4772125 021 4772045
Pearse St, The Glen
e-mail: whitehse@indigo.ie
dir: In town centre

Centrally located among the narrow, twisting streets of the charming town of Kinsale, this restaurant with rooms dates from 1850, and is a welcoming hostelry with modern, smart, comfortable bedrooms. The bar and bistro are open for lunch and dinner, and the varied menu features local fish and beef. The courtyard makes a perfect setting in summer and there is traditional music in the bar most nights.

Rooms 10 (2 fmly)

KNOCK Co Mayo — Map 1 B4

Knock House Hotel

★★★ 70% HOTEL

☎ 094 9388088 📠 094 9388044
Ballyhaunis Rd
e-mail: info@knockhousehotel.ie
dir: 0.5km from Knock

Adjacent to the Marian Shrine and Basilica at Knock, this creatively designed limestone-clad building is surrounded by landscaped gardens. There is a relaxing lounge bar, and lunch and dinner are served in the Four Seasons Restaurant daily. Bedrooms are spacious and well appointed, and some rooms are adapted to facilitate wheelchair users. Conference facilities are available.

Rooms 68 (12 fmly) (40 GF) **Facilities** FTV Xmas New Year Wi-fi **Conf** Class 90 Board 45 Thtr 150 **Services** Lift **Parking** 150 **Notes** ⊛

LEENANE Co Galway — Map 1 A4

Delphi Mountain Resort

U

☎ 095 42208 📠 095 42223
e-mail: info@delphiescape.com

Currently the rating for this establishment is not confirmed. This may be due to a change of ownership or because it has only recently joined the AA rating scheme. For further details please see the AA website: theAA.com

Rooms 39 (4 fmly) (12 GF) **Facilities** Spa Thermal suite Xmas **Conf** Class 40 Board 60 Thtr 80 **Services** Lift **Parking** 40 **Notes** LB ⊛ Closed Jan Civ Wed 150

LETTERKENNY Co Donegal — Map 1 C5

Radisson Blu Hotel Letterkenny

★★★★ 79% ❁ HOTEL

☎ 074 9194444 📠 074 9194455
Paddy Harte Rd
e-mail: info.letterkenny@radissonblu.com
dir: N14 into Letterkenny. At Polestar Rdbt take 1st exit, to hotel

Letterkenny is an ideal base for visiting the many peninsulas of County Donegal. Within walking distance of the town and the retail parks, this hotel offers a range very comfortable rooms, with all the facilities that today's traveller expects. Guests can dine throughout the day in the popular Oakk Bar & Grill, or, in the evening, enjoy seafood delights and other good dishes in Brasserie TriBeCa, where there is a live TV link to the kitchen to see the action! Well-equipped meeting rooms are available, together with a large conference and banqueting hall. The leisure facilities are complimentary to resident guests.

Rooms 114 (5 fmly) (6 smoking) **Facilities** STV Gym Sauna Steam room Sunbed Olympic weights room Xmas New Year Wi-fi **Conf** Class 270 Thtr 600 **Services** Lift **Parking** 150 **Notes** LB ⊛ Civ Wed 600

Downings Bay

★★★ 74% HOTEL

☎ 074 9155586 & 9155770 📠 074 9154716
Downings
e-mail: info@downingsbayhotel.com
dir: 23m N of Letterkenny on R245. Hotel in village centre

This hotel is situated on Sheephaven Bay in the picturesque village of Downings. There is a cosy lounge, traditional style bar and a restaurant where food is available all day. The bedrooms are comfortable and well appointed. Guests have complimentary use of the local leisure centre, and the night club is open at weekends.

Rooms 40 (8 fmly) (4 smoking) **S** €35-€80; **D** €60-€140 (incl. bkfst) **Facilities** supervised Gym Sauna Steam room Indoor adventure play area New Year Wi-fi **Conf** Class 175 Board 50 Thtr 350 Del from €80 to €110 **Services** Lift Air con **Parking** 40 **Notes** LB ⊛ Closed 25-26 Dec

LIMERICK Co Limerick — Map 1 B3

Carlton Castletroy Park Hotel

★★★★ 79% ❁ HOTEL

☎ 061 335566 & 508700 📠 061 331117
Dublin Rd
e-mail: reservations.castletroy@carlton.ie
dir: On Dublin road, 3km from city, opposite University of Limerick

This modern hotel is close to the University of Limerick. The attractively decorated public areas include the atmospheric Merry Pedler Bar & Bistro that serves food throughout the day, and the fine-dining McLaughlin's Restaurant overlooking the gardens and which opens in the evening. Bedrooms are very well equipped to suit both leisure and business guests. The banqueting and conference facilities are extensive. Complimentary underground parking is available opposite the hotel.

Rooms 107 (80 fmly) (5 smoking) **S** €79-€229; **D** €89-€249 (incl. bkfst) **Facilities** Spa STV FTV supervised Gym Sauna Steam room Xmas New Year Wi-fi Child facilities **Conf** Class 270 Board 80 Thtr 400 Del from €135 to €300 **Services** Lift **Parking** 150 **Notes** ⊛ Civ Wed 300

LISDOONVARNA Co Clare — Map 1 B3

Sheedys Country House

★★★ 78% ❁❁ HOTEL

☎ 065 7074026 📠 065 7074555
e-mail: info@sheedys.com
dir: 200mtrs from The Square in town centre

Dating in part from the 17th century and set in an unrivalled town centre location on the edge of The Burren, this house is full of character and has an intimate atmosphere. Fine cuisine can be enjoyed in the contemporary restaurant, and bedrooms are spacious and well appointed. This makes an ideal base for touring as it is close to Doolin, Lahinch Golf Course, and the Cliffs of Moher.

Rooms 11 (1 fmly) (5 GF) **S** €80-€120; **D** €99-€170 (incl. bkfst)* **Facilities** STV Wi-fi **Parking** 40 **Notes** ⊛ Closed mid Oct-Apr

LISMORE Co Waterford Map 1 C2

Lismore House Hotel

★★★ 72% HOTEL

☎ 058 72966 & 54304 📠 058 53068
Main St
e-mail: info@lismorehousehotel.com
dir: On main road between Dungarvan & Fermay directly opposite Lismore Castle

Located in the heart of the heritage town of Lismore and built in 1797 by the Duke of Devonshire, this property is Ireland's oldest purpose-built hotel; it was carefully restored to reveal its former Georgian style. The bedrooms are well appointed and many enjoy views of the castle and Millennium Park. Food is available throughout the day in the comfortable Malt Bar and lounge, and dinner served in the Riverbank Restaurant at weekends.

Rooms 29 (3 fmly) (12 GF) (4 smoking) **S** €50-€59; **D** €89-€99 (incl. bkfst)* **Facilities** FTV Fishing ♫ Xmas Wi-fi **Conf** Class 120 Board 60 Thtr 160 Del from €90 to €110* **Services** Lift Air con **Parking** 40 **Notes** LB ⊗ Civ Wed 170

LUCAN Co Dublin Map 1 D4

Finnstown Country House Hotel

★★★ 79% ® HOTEL

☎ 01 6010700 & 6010708 📠 01 6281088
Newcastle Rd
e-mail: edwina@finnstown-hotel.ie
dir: From M1 onto M50 S'bound. 1st exit for N4. Take slip road signed Newcastle/Adamstown. Straight on at rdbt, through lights, hotel on right

Set in 45 acres of wooded grounds, Finnstown is a calm and peaceful country house in an urban setting. The elegant bar and drawing room is where informal meals are served throughout the day, with more formal dining at lunch and dinner in the restaurant. There is a wide choice of bedroom styles, situated both in the main house and in the annexes. Staff members are all very guest focussed.

Rooms 81 (54 annexe) (6 fmly) (9 GF) (17 smoking) **S** €60-€190; **D** €60-€250 (incl. bkfst) **Facilities** STV Gym Turkish bath ♫ New Year Wi-fi **Conf** Class 150 Board 50 Thtr 300 Del from €140 to €180 **Services** Lift Air con **Parking** 300 **Notes** LB Closed 24-26 Dec Civ Wed 160

Lucan Spa

★★★ 63% HOTEL

☎ 01 6280494 📠 01 6280841
e-mail: info@lucanspahotel.ie
dir: N4 junct 4a, approx 11km from city centre

Set in its own grounds, 20 minutes from Dublin Airport and close to the M50, the Lucan Spa is a lovely Georgian house with a modern extension. Bedrooms vary in size but all are well equipped. There are two dining options; there's casual dining in the Earl Bistro, and dinner is served in Honora D Restaurant. A conference centre is also available.

Rooms 71 (15 fmly) (9 GF) (12 smoking) **S** €50-€80; **D** €65-€120 (incl. bkfst) **Facilities** STV FTV ♫ New Year Wi-fi Child facilities **Conf** Class 250 Board 80 Thtr 600 Del from €100 to €500 **Services** Lift Air con **Parking** 200 **Notes** LB ⊗ Closed 24-25 Dec Civ Wed 100

MACREDDIN Co Wicklow Map 1 D3

BrookLodge Hotel & Wells Spa

★★★★ 86% ®® HOTEL

☎ 0402 36444 📠 0402 36580
e-mail: info@brooklodge.com
web: www.brooklodge.com
dir: N11 to Rathnew, R752 to Rathdrum, R753 to Aughrim, follow signs to Macreddin Village

A luxury country-house hotel in a village-style setting which includes an 18-hole golf course, a pub, café and food shop. There is a choice of dining options - the award-winning Strawberry Tree Restaurant specialising in organic and wild foods and a more casual Italian restaurant. Bedrooms and lounges in the original house are very comfortable; there are also bedrooms in Brookhall, tailored for guests attending weddings and conferences. The Wells Spa offers extensive treatments and leisure facilities, and there are many outdoor activities including horse riding and off-road driving.

Rooms 90 (32 annexe) (27 fmly) (4 GF) **Facilities** Spa STV FTV 18 Putt green Gym Archery Clay pigeon shooting Falconry Off road driving Xmas New Year Wi-fi **Conf** Class 120 Board 40 Thtr 300 **Services** Lift **Parking** 200 **Notes** Civ Wed 180

MALLOW Co Cork Map 1 B2

Springfort Hall Country House Hotel

★★★ 75% HOTEL

☎ 022 21278 📠 022 21557
e-mail: stay@springfort-hall.com
web: www.springfort-hall.com
dir: N20 onto R581 at Two Pot House, hotel 500mtrs on right

This 18th-century country manor is tucked away amid tranquil woodlands just six kilometres from Mallow. There is an attractive oval dining room, a cosy drawing room and lounge bar where bistro-style food is served. The spacious bedrooms are comfortably furnished. There are extensive banqueting and conference facilities. Local amenities include championship golf courses, fishing on Blackwater and Ballyhass Lakes, and horse racing at Cork racecourse.

Rooms 49 (5 fmly) (17 GF) **S** €55-€90; **D** €80-€150 (incl. bkfst)* **Facilities** STV FTV ♫ **Conf** Class 200 Board 50 Thtr 300 Del from €129 to €225 **Parking** 200 **Notes** LB ⊗ Closed 23-26 Dec Civ Wed 250

MOHILL Co Leitrim Map 1 C4

Lough Rynn Castle

★★★★ 78% ® HOTEL

☎ 071 9632700 & 9632714 📠 071 9632710
e-mail: enquiries@loughrynn.ie

Once the ancestral home of Lord Leitrim, set in 300 acres of parkland, the castle offers a range of luxurious rooms and suites. The award-winning Sandstone Restaurant is an elegant dining option, and the many lounges are individually decorated; some feature antique furniture.

Rooms 43 (16 annexe) (5 fmly) (6 GF) **S** €99-€175; **D** €119-€190 (incl. bkfst) **Facilities** STV FTV ♫ Xmas New Year Wi-fi **Conf** Class 200 Board 30 Thtr 450 Del from €125 to €175 **Notes** LB ⊗ Civ Wed 320

REPUBLIC OF IRELAND M

MOLVILLE
Co Donegal

Redcastle Hotel, Golf & Spa Resort

U

074 9385555 9385444
e-mail: info@redcastlehotel.com
dir: On R238 between Derby & Greencastle

Currently the rating for this establishment is not confirmed. This may be due to a change of ownership or because it has only recently joined the AA rating scheme. For further details please see the AA website: theAA.com

Rooms 93 (17 fmly) (16 GF) (8 smoking) **Facilities** Spa STV FTV 9 Putt green Fishing Gym Thalasso therapy pool New Year Wi-fi **Conf** Class 150 Board 50 Thtr 300 Del from €90 to €169* **Services** Lift **Parking** 200 **Notes** Civ Wed 250

MULLINGAR
Co Westmeath
Map 1 C4

Mullingar Park

★★★★ 80% HOTEL

044 9344446 & 9337500 044 9335937
Dublin Rd
e-mail: info@mullingarparkhotel.com
web: www.mullingarparkhotel.com
dir: N4 junct 15, take exit for Mullingar

Situated off the N4 close to Mullingar this imposing modern hotel is contemporary in design and has much to offer including spacious public areas, flexible banqueting suites, extensive meeting rooms and a business area, complemented by a well-equipped leisure centre. Bedrooms are well appointed. The Terrace Restaurant is particularly popular for its lunch buffet and fine dining at night.

Rooms 95 (12 fmly) (39 smoking) **Facilities** Spa STV supervised Gym Aerobic studio Children's pool Hydrotherapy pool Sauna Steam room New Year Wi-fi **Conf** Class 750 Board 60 Thtr 1200 Del from €160* **Services** Lift **Parking** 500 **Notes** Closed 24-26 Dec Civ Wed 500

Bloomfield House Hotel, Leisure Club & Spa

★★★ 75% HOTEL

044 93440894 044 9343767
Belvedere
e-mail: info@bloomfieldhouse.com
dir: N4 junct 15, N52 signed Tullamore/Belvedere. Take exit for Belvedere House, 0.5km. Hotel on left

Located in lovely parkland overlooking Lough Ennell, Bloomfield House is next to the Belvedere Estate on the outskirts of Mullingar. Bedrooms vary in style with the wing and suites enjoying the spectacular views. Public areas include comfortable and relaxing lounges with open fires. Informal food is available from the bar and carvery, while the smart restaurant serves dinner nightly. There are extensive leisure and banqueting facilities.

Rooms 111 (21 fmly) (26 smoking) **Facilities** Spa STV supervised Gym Sauna Steam room Free kids club New Year Wi-fi **Conf** Class 200 Board 60 Thtr 450 **Services** Lift **Parking** 400 **Notes** LB Closed 25 Dec Civ Wed 400

MULRANY
Co Mayo
Map 1 B4

Mulranny Park Hotel

★★★★ 79% HOTEL

098 36000 098 36899
e-mail: info@mulrannyparkhotel.ie
dir: R311 from Castlebar to Newport onto N59. Hotel on right

Set on an elevated site, this property has commanding views over Clew Bay. Originally a railway hotel dating from the late 1800s, it has a range of smart public rooms that retain many of the period features. Bedrooms vary in size but are comfortable and decorated in a contemporary style. Dinner in the Nephin Restaurant is a highlight of any stay, with casual dining available throughout the day in the Waterfront Bar. A programme of activities is offered weekly for resident guests, in addition to a well appointed leisure club.

Rooms 61 (25 fmly) (10 GF) (4 smoking) **Facilities** supervised Gym Steam room Health & Beauty suites Hairdressing Kayaking Fishing Cycling New Year Wi-fi **Conf** Class 140 Board 50 Thtr 400 **Services** Lift **Parking** 200 **Notes** Closed 4-21 Jan Civ Wed 150

NAAS
Co Kildare
Map 1 D3

Maudlins House Hotel

★★★ 79% HOTEL

045 896999 045 906411
Dublin Rd
e-mail: info@maudlinshousehotel.ie
dir: M7 junct 9, R445 towards town centre. Hotel on right 200mtrs from Globe rdbt

Situated on the outskirts of Naas, this is a modern property that incorporates the original country house. Bedrooms are well appointed with a choice of classic and deluxe rooms; the annexed coach rooms are popular with long stay guests. The Virginia Restaurant, a series of comfortable rooms to the front of the house, offers fine dining from a creative menu; less formal options are served in the bar throughout the day. This hotel is located near two racecourses and many of the bloodstock agencies of County Kildare.

Rooms 25 (5 annexe) (5 GF) **S** €79-€129; **D** €99-€250 (incl. bkfst) **Facilities** STV FTV Hair salon New Year Wi-fi **Conf** Class 50 Board 50 Thtr 100 Del from €99 to €159 **Services** Lift Air con **Parking** 70 **Notes** LB Closed 24-25 Dec

NEWMARKET-ON-FERGUS Map 1 B3
Co Clare

INSPECTORS' CHOICE

Dromoland Castle

★★★★★ ®® HOTEL

☎ 061 368144 📠 061 363355
e-mail: sales@dromoland.ie
dir: N18 to Ennis/Galway from Shannon for 8km to 'Dromoland Interchange' signed Quin. Take slip road left, 4th exit at 1st rdbt, 2nd exit at 2nd rdbt. Hotel 500mtrs on left

Dromoland Castle, dating from the early 18th century, stands on a 375-acre estate and offers extensive indoor leisure activities and outdoor pursuits. The team are wholly committed to caring for guests. The thoughtfully equipped bedrooms and suites vary in style but all provide excellent levels of comfort, and the magnificent public rooms, warmed by log fires, are no less impressive. The hotel has several dining options - the elegant fine-dining Earl of Thomond, the less formal Fig Tree in the golf clubhouse, and The Gallery which offers a menu all day.

Rooms 99 (20 fmly) **S** €238-€607; **D** €238-€607* **Facilities** Spa STV supervised 18 Putt green Fishing Gym Hair salon Archery Clay shooting Mountain bikes Driven shoots Falconry New Year Wi-fi **Conf** Class 220 Board 80 Thtr 450 Del from €345 to €445* **Services** Lift **Parking** 120 **Notes** LB Closed 25-26 Dec Civ Wed 70

PORTLAOISE Map 1 C3
Co Laois

Killeshin

★★★★ 73% HOTEL

☎ 057 8681870 📠 057 8681871
Dublin Rd
e-mail: info@thekilleshin.com
web: www.thekilleshin.com

This long established hotel, located within walking distance of the town, is a smart contemporary property. It has well-appointed, spacious bedrooms and comfortable public areas. Cedarooms is the hotel's bar and restaurant facility where a range of dining options is on offer throughout the day. There are impressive banqueting and business facilities. Within walking distance are the Zest Health Club (complimentary to residents) and secure underground parking.

Rooms 91 **Facilities** Gym Steam room New Year Wi-fi **Conf** Class 100 Board 50 Thtr 200 **Services** Lift **Parking** 174 **Notes** Closed 23-27 Dec

RATHMULLAN Map 1 C6
Co Donegal

Rathmullan House

★★★★ 79% ®® COUNTRY HOUSE HOTEL

☎ 074 9158188 📠 074 9158200
e-mail: info@rathmullanhouse.com
dir: From Letterkenny, through Ramelton to Rathmullan, R243. Left at Mace shop, through village, hotel gates on right

Dating from the 18th-century, this fine property has been operating as a country-house hotel for the last 40 years or so under the stewardship of the Wheeler family. Guests are welcome to wander around the well-planted grounds and the walled garden, from where much of the ingredients for the Weeping Elm Restaurant's menus are grown. The many lounges are relaxing and comfortable, while many of the bedrooms benefit from balconies and patio areas.

Rooms 34 (4 fmly) (9 GF) **S** €93.50-€148.50; **D** €187-€297 (incl. bkfst) **Facilities** Spa New Year Wi-fi Child facilities **Conf** Class 90 Board 40 Thtr 135 Del from €125 to €170 **Parking** 80 **Notes** LB Closed 11 Jan-5 Feb RS 15 Nov-12 Mar Civ Wed 135

RATHNEW Map 1 D3
Co Wicklow

Hunter's Hotel

★★★ 75% ® HOTEL

☎ 0404 40106 📠 0404 40338
e-mail: reception@hunters.ie
dir: 1.5km from village off N11

One of Ireland's oldest coaching inns, this charming country house was built in 1720 and is full of character and atmosphere. The comfortable bedrooms have wonderful views over prize-winning gardens that border the River Vartry. The restaurant has a good reputation for carefully prepared dishes which make the best use of high quality local produce, including fruit and vegetables from the hotel's own garden.

Rooms 16 (2 fmly) (2 GF) **Conf** Class 40 Board 16 Thtr 40 **Parking** 50 **Notes** Closed 24-26 Dec

RECESS (SRAITH SALACH) Map 1 A4
Co Galway

Ballynahinch Castle

★★★★ 85% ®® COUNTRY HOUSE HOTEL

☎ 095 31006 📠 095 31085
Recess, Connemara
e-mail: info@ballynahinch-castle.com
dir: W from Galway on N59 towards Clifden. After Recess turn left for Roundstone

Open log fires and friendly professional service are just some of the delights of staying at this 16th-century castle. Set in 450 acres of woodland, rivers and lakes, this hotel has many suites and bedrooms with stunning views. There is a selection of comfortable lounges, a cosy Fisherman's Pub and dinner is served in the Owenmore Restaurant overlooking the winding Ballynahinch River (which boasts some of the finest fly fishing in Ireland). There is an on-site walking guide to give an insight into the rich history, archaeology and ecology of the estate.

Rooms 40 (8 fmly) (3 GF) **S** €140-€350; **D** €160-€400 (incl. bkfst) **Facilities** STV FTV Fishing Bicycles for hire River & lakeside walks New Year Wi-fi **Conf** Class 20 Board 20 Thtr 30 Del from €240 to €400 **Parking** 55 **Notes** LB Closed 1-23 Feb & 18-27 Dec RS Good Fri Civ Wed 40

RECESS (SRAITH SALACH) *continued*

INSPECTORS' CHOICE

Lough Inagh Lodge

★★★ ® COUNTRY HOUSE HOTEL

MANOR HOUSE HOTELS

☎ 095 34706 & 34694 📠 095 34708
Inagh Valley
e-mail: inagh@iol.ie
dir: From Recess take R344 towards Kylemore

Dating from 1880, this former fishing lodge is akin to a family home, where guests are encouraged to relax and enjoy the peace. Overlooking Lough Inagh, and situated amid the mountains of Connemara, it is in an ideal location for those who enjoy walking and fishing. Bedrooms are individually decorated, some with spacious seating areas, and each is dedicated to an Irish literary figure. There are two cosy lounges where welcoming turf fires are often lit. Informal dining from a bar menu is available during the day. Dinner is a highlight of a visit to the lodge; the menus feature locally sourced produce cooked with care - seafood is a speciality.

Rooms 13 (1 fmly) (4 GF) **Facilities** Hill walking Fly fishing Cycling **Conf** Class 20 Board 20 Thtr 20 **Services** Air con **Parking** 16 **Notes** Closed mid Dec-mid Mar

ROSCOMMON
Co Roscommon — Map 1 B4

Abbey Hotel

★★★★ 76% HOTEL

☎ 090 6626240 📠 090 6626021
Galway Rd
e-mail: info@abbeyhotel.ie
dir: From Roscommon take Galway Rd, 1st left after rdbt, to hotel

The Grealy family have tastefully restored this fine manor house. The spacious bedrooms are tastefully furnished and overlook the magnificent gardens. The smart lounge, bar and Terrace Restaurant have views of the 12th-century Dominican Abbey, and the carvery is very popular at lunchtime. There are extensive leisure and conference facilities.

Rooms 50 (8 fmly) (10 GF) **S** €69-€180; **D** €89-€300 (incl. bkfst)* **Facilities** supervised Gym Sauna Steam room Treatment room Plunge pool Children's pool Wi-fi **Conf** Class 160 Board 60 Thtr 350 Del from €129 to €199* **Services** Lift Air con **Parking** 100 **Notes** LB Closed 24-26 Dec Civ Wed 200

ROSSCARBERY
Co Cork — Map 1 B2

Celtic Ross

★★★ 75% HOTEL

☎ 023 884 8722 📠 023 884 8723
e-mail: info@celticrosshotel.com
dir: N71 from Cork, through Bandon towards Clonakilty. Follow signs for Skibbereen

This hotel is situated on the edge of the village overlooking Rosscarbery Bay. Public areas are relaxing places with a variety of lounges, a library, and the Warren Suite which enjoys panoramic views to Gally Head. Bistro-style food is available in the bar throughout the day, and dinner is served in Druids Restaurant. The spacious bedrooms are comfortable and well appointed. There are extensive leisure and banqueting facilities plus music and dancing events at weekends.

Rooms 66 (30 fmly) **Facilities** supervised Gym Steam room **Conf** Class 150 Board 60 Thtr 300 **Services** Lift Air con **Parking** 200 **Notes** Closed 24-26 Dec & mid Jan-mid Feb

ROSSLARE
Co Wexford — Map 1 D2

INSPECTORS' CHOICE

Kelly's Resort Hotel & Spa

★★★★ ® HOTEL

☎ 053 9132114 📠 053 9132222
e-mail: info@kellys.ie
dir: N25 onto Rosslare/Wexford road, signed Rosslare Strand

The Kelly family have been offering hospitality here since 1895, where together with a dedicated team, they provide very professional and friendly service. The resort overlooks the sandy beach and is within minutes of the ferry port at Rosslare. Bedrooms are thoughtfully equipped and comfortably furnished. The extensive leisure facilities include a smart spa, swimming pools, a crèche, young adults' programme and spacious well-tended gardens. Both the eating options, La Marine Bistro and Beaches restaurant, have been awarded an AA Rosette for the quality of their cuisine.

Rooms 118 (15 fmly) (20 GF) **Facilities** Spa STV FTV supervised Putt green Gym Bowls Plunge pool Badminton Crazy golf Table tennis Snooker Wi-fi **Conf** Class 30 Board 20 Thtr 30 **Services** Lift **Parking** 120 **Notes** Closed mid Dec-late Feb

SALTHILL

See Galway

REPUBLIC OF IRELAND

R

SLIGO
Co Sligo Map 1 B5

Radisson Blu Hotel & Spa Sligo

★★★★ 79% ® HOTEL

☎ 071 9140008 📠 071 9140005
Rosses Point Rd, Ballincar
e-mail: info.sligo@radissonblu.com
dir: From N4 into Sligo to main bridge. Take R291 on left. Hotel 1.5m on right

Located three kilometres north of the town overlooking Sligo Bay, this contemporary hotel offers standard and business class bedrooms which are all appointed with up-to-date facilities. The Benwiskin bar offers tasty casual dining throughout the day, and for formal dining in the evening there's Classiebawn Restaurant. Residents are welcome to use Healthstyles leisure club during their stay, and spa treatment facilities are also available. A range of eleven rooms are provided for meetings and events.

Rooms 132 (13 fmly) (32 GF) (19 smoking) **Facilities** Spa STV Gym Steam room Treatment rooms Thermal suite Xmas New Year Wi-fi **Conf** Class 420 Board 40 Thtr 750 **Services** Lift Air con **Parking** 395 **Notes** LB Civ Wed 750

Glasshouse

★★★★ 76% ® HOTEL

☎ 071 9194300 📠 071 9194301
Swan Point
e-mail: info@theglasshouse.ie
dir: From N4 right at 2nd junct. Left at Post Office in Wine St. Hotel on right

This landmark building in the centre of town makes a bold statement with its cutting edge design and contemporary decor. Cheerful colours are used throughout the hotel; the bedrooms have excellent facilities including LCD TVs, workspace and internet access. There is a first-floor café bar, a ground-floor bar and a Mediterranean-style restaurant with great river views. Secure underground parking is complimentary to residents.

Rooms 116 **Facilities** STV FTV New Year Wi-fi **Conf** Class 100 Board 60 Thtr 120 **Services** Lift **Parking** 250 **Notes** Closed 24-25 Dec Civ Wed 120

Sligo Park

★★★★ 74% HOTEL

☎ 071 9190400 📠 071 9169556
Pearse Rd
e-mail: sligo@leehotels.com
dir: N4 to Sligo take Carrowroe/R287 exit. Follow signs for Sligo/R287. Hotel 1m on right

Set in seven acres on the southern side of town, this hotel is well positioned for visiting the many attractions of the north west and Yeats' Country. Bedrooms are spacious and appointed to a high standard. There are two dining options, plus good leisure and banqueting facilities.

Rooms 137 (10 fmly) (52 GF) (23 smoking) **S** €190; **D** €310 (incl. bkfst) **Facilities** supervised Gym Holistic treatment suite Plunge pool Steam room Xmas New Year Wi-fi **Conf** Class 290 Board 80 Thtr 520 **Services** Lift **Parking** 200 **Notes** LB RS 24-26 Dec Civ Wed 520

STRAFFAN
Co Kildare Map 1 D4

INSPECTORS' CHOICE

The K Club

★★★★★ ®®® COUNTRY HOUSE HOTEL

☎ 01 6017200 📠 01 6017298
e-mail: resortsales@kclub.ie
dir: From Dublin take N4, exit for R406, hotel on right in Straffan

The K Club is set in 700 acres of rolling woodland. There are two magnificent championship golf courses and a spa facility that complements the truly luxurious hotel that is the centrepiece of the resort. Public areas and bedrooms are opulently furnished, and have views of the formal gardens. Award-winning food is served in the elegant Byerly Turk Restaurant, with more informal dining options offered in the River Room and in Legends in the Golf Pavilion.

Rooms 79 (10 annexe) (10 fmly) **Facilities** Spa supervised 36 Putt green Fishing Gym Beauty salon Fishing tuition Clay pigeon shooting Xmas New Year Wi-fi **Conf** Class 300 Board 160 Thtr 300 **Services** Lift **Parking** 205 **Notes**

Barberstown Castle

★★★★ 80% ®® HOTEL

☎ 01 6288157 📠 01 6277027
e-mail: info@barberstowncastle.ie
web: www.barberstowncastle.ie
dir: R406, follow signs for Barberstown

With parts dating from the 13th century, this castle hotel provides the very best in standards of comfort. The inviting public areas range from the original keep, which houses one of the restaurant areas, to the warmth of the drawing room and its cocktail bar. Bedrooms, some in a purpose-built wing, are elegantly appointed with relaxing seating areas. The airy Tea Room serves light meals throughout the day.

continued

STRAFFAN *continued*

The Castle is a popular venue for weddings and other family occasions.

Rooms 58 (21 GF) **S** €150-€200; **D** €230-€280 (incl. bkfst)* **Facilities** STV New Year Wi-fi **Conf** Class 100 Board 70 Thtr 200 Del from €185 to €285* **Services** Lift **Parking** 200 **Notes** LB Closed 24-26 Dec & Jan Civ Wed 300

THOMASTOWN
Co Kilkenny — Map 1 C3

INSPECTORS' CHOICE

Mount Juliet Hotel

★★★★ COUNTRY HOUSE HOTEL

☎ 056 7773000 📠 056 7773019
e-mail: info@mountjuliet.ie
dir: M7 from Dublin, N9 towards Waterford, exit at junct 9/Danesfort for hotel

Mount Juliet is set in 1,500 acres of parkland with a Jack Nicklaus designed golf course and an equestrian centre. The elegant and spacious public areas retain much of the original architectural features including ornate plasterwork and Adam fireplaces. Bedrooms, in both the main house and the Hunters Yard annexe, are comfortable and well appointed. Fine dining is on offer in the Lady Helen restaurant (2 AA Rosettes), overlooking the river, and French brasserie cuisine is available in Kendals (1 AA Rosette), and there is also all day dining in the President's Bar. The hotel has an excellent spa and health club. Self-catering is also available.

Rooms 57 (26 annexe) (14 GF) **Facilities** Spa STV supervised 18 Putt green Fishing Gym Archery Cycling Clay pigeon shooting Equestrian Xmas Wi-fi **Conf** Class 40 Board 20 Thtr 75 **Parking** 200 **Notes** LB Civ Wed 60

THURLES
Co Tipperary — Map 1 C3

Horse & Jockey Hotel

★★★★ 79% HOTEL

☎ 0504 44192 📠 0504 44747
Horse & Jockey
e-mail: info@horseandjockeyhotel.com
dir: 800mtrs from M8 junct 6

Located just off the motorway, this hotel offers smart and well-appointed bedrooms which are very comfortable. Dining options are the Enclosure Bar with a varied menu, and for more formal dining in the evening there is Silks Restaurant. There is also a well-equipped leisure centre with spa treatments and an equestrian themed gift shop. The conference facilities include ten self-contained meeting rooms and a tiered auditorium seating 200 delegates.

Rooms 67 (4 fmly) (15 GF) (7 smoking) **Facilities** Spa STV FTV supervised Gym Sauna Steam room Hydro therapy area Wi-fi **Conf** Class 24 Board 25 Thtr 200 **Services** Lift **Parking** 450 **Notes** Closed 25 Dec RS 24 & 26 Dec

TRALEE
Co Kerry — Map 1 A2

Ballygarry House Hotel and Spa

★★★★ 80% HOTEL

☎ 066 7123322 📠 066 7127630
Killarney Rd
e-mail: info@ballygarryhouse.com
web: www.ballygarryhouse.com
dir: 1.5km from Tralee, on N21

This charming hotel offers the complete country house experience, where courtesy and care is paramount from the friendly team. There are comfortably furnished lounges with open log fires, food is served throughout the day in the Leebrook bar and fine dining is available in Brooks Restaurant which overlooks the lovely six-acre gardens. Bedrooms and suites are spacious and elegantly decorated. Spa treatments and relaxation areas are available in the Nadur Spa.

Rooms 64 (10 fmly) (16 GF) **S** €80-€140; **D** €140-€195 (incl. bkfst) **Facilities** Spa STV Steam room Sauna New Year Wi-fi **Conf** Class 100 Board 50 Thtr 200 Del from €130 to €175 **Services** Lift **Parking** 200 **Notes** LB Closed 20-26 Dec Civ Wed 350

Carlton Hotel Tralee

CARLTON HOTEL GROUP

★★★★ 78% HOTEL

☎ 066 7119986 & 7199100 📠 066 7119987
Fels Point, Dan Spring Rd
e-mail: kmurphy@carlton.ie

This contemporary hotel is situated on the ring road and is within walking distance of the town centre. Public areas include a stylish lobby lounge where a grand piano is played at weekends. Bistro food is served in Clarets Bar all day, with fine dining available in Morels Restaurant at night. The smart bedrooms are air conditioned and have LCD TVs and high-speed internet connections. There are extensive conference, banqueting and leisure facilities.

Rooms 165 (5 fmly) (29 smoking) **Facilities** STV FTV Gym New Year Wi-fi **Conf** Class 250 Board 50 Thtr 350 **Services** Lift Air con **Parking** 227 **Notes** Closed 24-26 Dec Civ Wed 200

Manor West

★★★★ 77% HOTEL

☎ 066 7194500 📠 066 7194545
Killarney Rd
e-mail: info@manorwesthotel.ie
web: www.manorwesthotel.ie

Just five minutes from the centre of town, this hotel is part of a large retail park with many shopping opportunities. Spacious well-equipped bedrooms are matched by smart public areas, including a high spec leisure facility. There is a spa with pools, steam room and sauna, and a variety of treatments is offered in the Harmony Wellness suites. The popular Mercantile Bar serves food throughout the day, with fine dining available in The Walnut Room in the evening.

Rooms 75 **Facilities** Spa STV FTV supervised Gym Sauna Steam room Theray pools New Year Wi-fi **Conf** Class 150 Board 60 Thtr 200 **Services** Lift Air con **Parking** 200 **Notes** LB Closed 24-26 Dec

TRAMORE Co Waterford Map 1 C2

Majestic

★★★ 77% HOTEL

☎ 051 381761 051 381766
e-mail: info@majestic-hotel.ie
dir: Exit N25 through Waterford onto R675 to Tramore. Hotel on right, opposite lake

A warm welcome awaits visitors to this long established, family friendly hotel in the holiday resort of Tramore. Many of the comfortable and well-equipped bedrooms have sea views; some have balconies. Public areas offer relaxing comfortable lounges, a smartly decorated bar, a garden patio and a spacious restaurant where guests can enjoy the spectacular sea views. A discounted rate at Splashworld across from the hotel is available to residents.

Rooms 60 (4 fmly) **Facilities** STV FTV ♫ New Year Wi-fi **Conf** Class 100 Board 50 Thtr 100 **Services** Lift **Parking** 10 **Notes** LB ® Civ Wed 250

TULLOW Co Carlow Map 1 D3

Mount Wolseley Hotel, Spa & Country Club

★★★★ 80% ® HOTEL

☎ 059 9180100 059 9152123
e-mail: info@mountwolseley.ie
dir: N7 from Dublin. In Naas, N9 towards Carlow. In Castledermot left for Tullow

Located on a vast, well landscaped estate long associated with the Wolseley family of motoring fame, this hotel has much to offer. Public areas are very spacious with a large range of suites and bedrooms. Leisure pursuits include a championship golf course together with a popular health centre and Sanctuary Spa facilities. The hotel offers a number of dining options including Aaron's lounge, Fredrick's with 1 AA Rosette, and The Wolseley Lounge in the Golf Pavillion.

Rooms 143 (10 fmly) (5 smoking) **Facilities** Spa STV supervised 18 Putt green Gym Childrens play area ♫ New Year Wi-fi **Conf** Class 288 Board 70 Thtr 750 Del from €129 to €149 **Services** Lift Air con **Parking** 160 **Notes** LB ® Closed 25-26 Dec Civ Wed 400

VIRGINIA Co Cavan Map 1 C4

The Park Hotel

★★★ 73% ® HOTEL

☎ 049 8546100 049 8547203
Virginia Park
e-mail: info@parkhotelvirginia.com
web: www.parkhotelvirginia.com
dir: Exit N3 onto R194 in Virginia. Hotel 500yds on left

A charming hotel, built in 1750 as the summer retreat of the Marquis of Headford. Situated overlooking Lake Ramor on a 100-acre estate, it has a 9-hole golf course, lovely mature gardens and woodland. This hotel brings together generous hospitality and a relaxed leisurely way of life. The Marquis Dining room is renowned for good food, and fruit, herbs and vegetables are grown in the estate's organic gardens.

Rooms 26 (1 fmly) (8 GF) **Facilities** 9 Fishing ♫ Xmas New Year Wi-fi **Conf** Class 40 Board 40 Thtr 100 **Parking** 150 **Notes** ® Closed 25 Dec Civ Wed 100

WATERFORD Co Waterford Map 1 C2

INSPECTORS' CHOICE

Waterford Castle

★★★★ ®® HOTEL

☎ 051 878203 051 879316
The Island
e-mail: info@waterfordcastle.com
dir: From city centre into Dunmore East Rd, 1.5m, pass hospital, 0.5m left after lights. Ferry at bottom of road

This enchanting and picturesque castle dates back to Norman times and is located on a 320-acre island just a five-minute journey from the mainland by chain-link ferry. Bedrooms vary in style and size, but all are individually decorated and offer high standards of comfort. Dinner is served in the oak-panelled Munster Room, with breakfast taken in the conservatory. The 18-hole golf course is set in beautiful parkland where deer can be seen.

Rooms 19 (2 fmly) (4 GF) **Facilities** 18 Putt green Boules Archery Clay pigeon shooting ♫ New Year Wi-fi **Conf** Board 15 Thtr 30 **Services** Lift **Parking** 50 **Notes** LB ® Closed 24-26 Dec Civ Wed 110

Faithlegg House

FBD Hotels

★★★★ 76% ® HOTEL

☎ 051 382000 051 382010
Faithlegg
e-mail: reservations@fhh.ie
web: www.faithlegg.com
dir: From Waterford follow Dunmore East Rd then Cheerpoint Rd

This hotel is surrounded by a championship golf course and overlooks the estuary of the River Suir. The house has 14 original bedrooms, and the others are in an adjacent modern block. There is a range of comfortable lounges together with comprehensive meeting facilities. The leisure and treatment rooms are the perfect way to work off the excesses of the food offered in the Roseville Restaurant.

Rooms 82 (6 fmly) (30 GF) (16 smoking) **Facilities** FTV supervised 18 Putt green Gym Sauna Steam room New Year Wi-fi **Conf** Class 90 Board 44 Thtr 180 **Services** Lift **Parking** 100 **Notes** LB ® Closed 20-27 Dec Civ Wed

Granville

★★★ 80% HOTEL

☎ 051 305555 051 305566
The Quay
e-mail: stay@granville-hotel.ie
web: www.granville-hotel.ie
dir: N25 to waterfront, hotel opposite clock tower

Centrally located on the quayside, this long established hotel was originally a coaching house. It is appointed to a very high standard, and retains

continued

REPUBLIC OF IRELAND W

WATERFORD *continued*

much of its original character. The bedrooms come in a choice of standard or executive grades; all are well equipped and very comfortable. The Meagher Bar offers food throughout the day, and is a popular lunch venue with shoppers and the business community of Waterford. The Bianconi is an elegant restaurant where evening dinner is served. Friendliness and hospitality are hallmarks of a stay here.

Rooms 100 (5 fmly) (10 smoking) **Facilities** STV ♫ New Year **Conf** Class 150 Board 30 Thtr 200 Del from €100 to €150 **Services** Lift **Parking** 300 **Notes** ⊗ Closed 25-26 Dec

See advert on this page

Tower

FBD Hotels

★★★ 79% HOTEL

☎ 051 875801 & 862300 📠 051 870129
The Mall
e-mail: info@thw.ie
web: www.fbdhotels.com
dir: Opposite Reginald's Tower in town centre. Hotel at end of quay

With a commanding position on The Mall opposite Reginald's Tower, this well established hotel has much to offer. The spacious public areas include conference suites, a choice of dining options and a popular leisure club. Health and beauty treatments are available. A range of bedrooms is on offer, all are comfortably appointed and stylishly decorated. Secure parking is provided to the rear of the building.

Rooms 136 (6 fmly) **Facilities** supervised Gym Treatment rooms ♫ New Year Wi-fi **Conf** Class 250 Board 80 Thtr 500 **Services** Lift **Parking** 100 **Notes** LB ⊗ Closed 24-28 Dec Civ Wed 400

Dooley's

★★★ 78% HOTEL

☎ 051 873531 📠 051 870262
30 The Quay
e-mail: hotel@dooleys-hotel.ie
dir: On N25, adjacent to Discover Ireland Centre

This hotel has been family run for three generations. It is situated on the quay overlooking the River Suir at the harbour's mouth. Dinner is served in New Ship Restaurant and casual dining is available in the Dry Dock Bar. Bedrooms are attractively decorated and offer a good standard of comfort. There is a convenient public car park opposite the hotel.

Rooms 113 (3 fmly) (29 smoking) **S** €70-€130; **D** €80-€198 (incl. bkfst) **Facilities** STV ♫ New Year Wi-fi **Conf** Class 150 Board 100 Thtr 240 Del from €110 **Services** Lift **Notes** ⊗ Closed 25-27 Dec

Waterford Manor

★★★ 74% HOTEL

☎ 051 377814 📠 051 354545
Killotteran, Butlerstown
e-mail: sales@waterfordmanorhotel.ie
dir: N25 from Waterford to Cork, turn right 2m after Waterford Crystal, left at end of road, hotel on right

Dating back to 1730 this manor house is set in delightful landscaped and wooded grounds. It provides high quality accommodation as well as extensive conference and banqueting facilities. Public areas include a charming drawing room and restaurant for intimate dining, plus a brasserie with its own bar that serves a carvery lunch daily.

Rooms 21 (3 fmly) **Facilities** **Conf** Class 300 Board 40 Thtr 600 **Parking** 400 **Notes** LB ⊗ RS 25 Dec

WESTPORT Co Mayo **Map 1 B3**

Knockranny House Hotel

MANOR HOUSE HOTELS

★★★★ 83% HOTEL

☎ 098 28600 📠 098 28611
e-mail: info@khh.ie
web: www.khh.ie
dir: On N5 (Westport-Castlebar road)

Overlooking the town, with Clew Bay and Croagh Patrick in the distance, the reception rooms of this family-run hotel take full advantage of the stunning views. The comfortable furnishings create an inviting and relaxing atmosphere throughout the lounges, bar and restaurant. Two styles of bedrooms are available, with the newer ones being particularly spacious. Dinner in the award-winning La Fougere Restaurant is a highlight of a visit. Spa Salveo features a thermal suite with hydrotherapy stations in a vitality pool.

Rooms 97 (4 fmly) **S** €90-€195; **D** €110-€320 (incl. bkfst) **Facilities** Spa STV Gym ♫ New Year Wi-fi **Conf** Class 350 Board 40 Thtr 600 **Services** Lift **Parking** 150 **Notes** ⊗ Closed 24-26 Dec Civ Wed 250

Hotel Westport Leisure, Spa & Conference

★★★★ 78% HOTEL

☎ 098 25122 & 0870 876 5432 📠 098 25122
Newport Rd
e-mail: reservations@hotelwestport.ie
web: www.hotelwestport.ie
dir: N5 to Westport. Right at end of Castlebar St, 1st right before bridge, right at lights, left before church. Follow to end of street

Located in seven acres of woodlands and just a short riverside walk to the town, this hotel offers spacious public areas, including The Islands restaurant and the all-day Maple Bar. Bedrooms come in a range of styles, and are all comfortable and well appointed. Both leisure and business guests are well catered for by the enthusiastic and friendly team who go to great lengths to ensure residents enjoy their stay. This hotel is a popular choice with special interest groups and also families, who enjoy the leisure facilities, and in summer time, the children's club.

Rooms 129 (67 fmly) (42 GF) (12 smoking) **S** €59-€159; **D** €70-€270 (incl. bkfst) **Facilities** Spa STV supervised Gym Children's pool Lounger pool Steam room Sauna Fitness suite ♫ Xmas New Year Wi-fi Child facilities **Conf** Class 150 Board 60 Thtr 500 Del from €99 to €199 **Services** Lift **Parking** 220 **Notes** LB Civ Wed 300

Carlton Atlantic Coast

CARLTON HOTEL GROUP

★★★★ 76% HOTEL

☎ 098 29000 📠 098 29111
The Quay
e-mail: info@carltonatlanticcoasthotel.com
dir: From N5 follow signs into Westport then Louisburgh on R335. 1m from Westport

This distinctive hotel is in a renovated mill that has been appointed to a good contemporary standard. It is located on the quay, a short drive from the town of Westport. Many of the rooms have sea views, as has the award-winning Blue Wave restaurant on the fourth floor. The ground floor has comfortable lounge areas and a lively bar, Fishworks, where food is served throughout the day. The leisure centre is complimentary to resident guests, and spa treatments are offered in the C Spa.

Rooms 85 (6 fmly) **S** €69-€109; **D** €98-€178 (incl. bkfst)* **Facilities** Spa supervised Gym Treatment rooms Sauna Steam room Fitness suite ♫ New Year Wi-fi **Conf** Class 100 Board 70 Thtr 180 Del from €89 to €149* **Services** Lift **Parking** 140 **Notes** LB Closed 23-27 Dec Civ Wed 140

The Wyatt

★★★ 72% HOTEL

☎ 098 25027 📠 098 26316
The Octagon
e-mail: info@wyatthotel.com
dir: Follow one-way system in town. Hotel by tall monument

This stylish, welcoming hotel is situated in the famous town-centre Octagon. Bedrooms are attractively decorated and well equipped. Public areas are very comfortable with open fires and include a lively, contemporary bar and the traditional Cobblers Bar is very cosy. JW Bistro serves food all day and in high season The Wyatt Restaurant offers more formal dining.

Rooms 51 (2 GF) (5 smoking) **Facilities** Complimentary use of nearby leisure park ♫ New Year Wi-fi **Conf** Class 200 Board 80 Thtr 300 **Services** Lift **Parking** 20 **Notes** LB Closed 25-26 Dec Civ Wed 200

Mill Times Hotel Westport

★★★ 71% HOTEL

☎ 098 29200 & 29130 📠 098 29250
Mill St
e-mail: info@milltimeshotel.ie
dir: N59 signed town centre, in Bridge St keep in left lane, left at top into Mill St, hotel on left

This family run hotel is situated in the centre of Westport, close to the shops and many pubs of this bustling town. It is ideal for visiting north Mayo with its many beaches and golf courses, or as a base for climbing the pilgrimage mountain of Croagh Patrick. Bedrooms are traditional in style and public areas are comfortable. Uncle Sam's café bar is a lively venue with entertainment at weekends. Temptations Restaurant offers good value meals during the evening, and is where a hearty breakfast is served. Underground parking is provided.

Rooms 34 (6 fmly) **S** €49-€150; **D** €59-€240 **Facilities** ♫ New Year Wi-fi **Conf** Class 60 Board 60 Thtr 200 Del from €100 to €200* **Services** Lift Air con **Parking** 25 **Notes** LB Closed 24-25 Dec Civ Wed 100

WEXFORD Co Wexford **Map 1 D3**

Whitford House Hotel Health & Leisure Club

★★★★ 75% HOTEL

☎ 053 9143444 📠 053 9146399
New Line Rd
e-mail: info@whitford.ie
web: www.whitford.ie
dir: Just off N25 (Duncannon rdbt) take exit for R733 (Wexford), hotel immediately left

This is a friendly family-run hotel located just three kilometres from the town centre and within easy reach of the Rosslare Ferry. Comfortable bedrooms range from standard to the spacious deluxe rooms. Public areas include a choice of lounges and the popular Forthside Bar Bistro where a carvery is served at lunch. More formal meals are on offer during the evening in the award-winning Seasons Restaurant. Leisure and fitness facilities are complimentary to resident guests.

Rooms 36 (28 fmly) (18 GF) **S** €59-€99; **D** €90-€218 (incl. bkfst)* **Facilities** Spa FTV supervised Gym Children's playground Football area Hairdresser ♫ Xmas New Year Wi-fi **Conf** Class 12 Board 25 Thtr 50 Del from €95 to €147* **Parking** 200 **Notes** LB RS 24-27 Dec Civ Wed 100

Gibraltar

Rock of Gibraltar, view towards Spain

GIBRALTAR

Caleta

★★★★ 79% ®® HOTEL

☎ 00 350 200 76501 📠 00 350 200 42143
Sir Herbert Miles Rd, PO Box 73
e-mail: sales@caletahotel.gi
web: www.caletahotel.com
dir: Enter Gibraltar via Spanish border & cross runway. At 1st rdbt turn left, hotel in 2kms

For travellers arriving to Gibraltar by air the Caleta is an eye catching coastal landmark that can be spotted by planes arriving from the east. This imposing and stylish hotel sits on a cliff top and all sea-facing rooms enjoy panoramic views across the straights to Morocco. Bedrooms vary in size and style with some boasting spacious balconies, flat-screen TVs and mini bars. Several dining venues are available but Nunos provides an award-winning fine-dining Italian experience. Staff are friendly, service is professional.

Rooms 161 (89 annexe) (13 fmly) (80 smoking) **S** 120-189; **D** 120-189* **Facilities** **Spa** STV FTV supervised Gym Health & beauty club Xmas New Year Wi-fi **Conf** Class 172 Board 85 Thtr 200 Del from 140 to 170 **Services** Lift Air con **Parking** 32 **Notes** Civ Wed 300

The Rock Hotel

★★★★ 78% ®® HOTEL

☎ 00 350 200 73000 📠 00 350 200 73513
Europa Rd
e-mail: rockhotel@gibtelecom.net
web: www.rockhotelgibraltar.com
dir: From airport follow tourist board signs. Hotel on left half way up Europa Rd

Enjoying a prime elevated location directly below the Rock, this long established art deco styled hotel has been the destination of celebrities and royalty since it was built in 1932. Bedrooms are spacious and well equipped and many boast stunning coastal views that stretch across the Mediterranean to Morocco. Staff are friendly and service is delivered with flair and enthusiasm. Creative dinners and hearty breakfasts can be enjoyed in the stylish restaurant.

Rooms 104 (25 smoking) **D** 165* **Facilities** STV supervised Xmas New Year Wi-fi **Conf** Class 24 Board 30 Thtr 70 **Services** Lift Air con **Parking** 40 **Notes** LB RS 5 Oct-1 Apr Civ Wed 40

O'Callaghan Eliott

★★★★ 76% HOTEL

☎ 00 350 200 70500 & 200 75905
📠 00 350 200 70243
2 Governor's Pde
e-mail: eliott@ocallaghanhotels.com
web: www.ocallaghanhotels.com

Located in the heart of the old town, this hotel provides a convenient central base for exploring the duty free shopping district and other key attractions on foot. The bedrooms are stylish, spacious and well equipped. The roof-top restaurant provides stunning bay views whilst guests can also take a swim in the roof-top pool.

Rooms 120 **S** 240-340; **D** 240-340 **Facilities** STV Gym Xmas New Year Wi-fi **Conf** Class 80 Board 70 Thtr 180 Del from 210 to 410 **Services** Lift Air con **Parking** 17 **Notes** LB Civ Wed 120

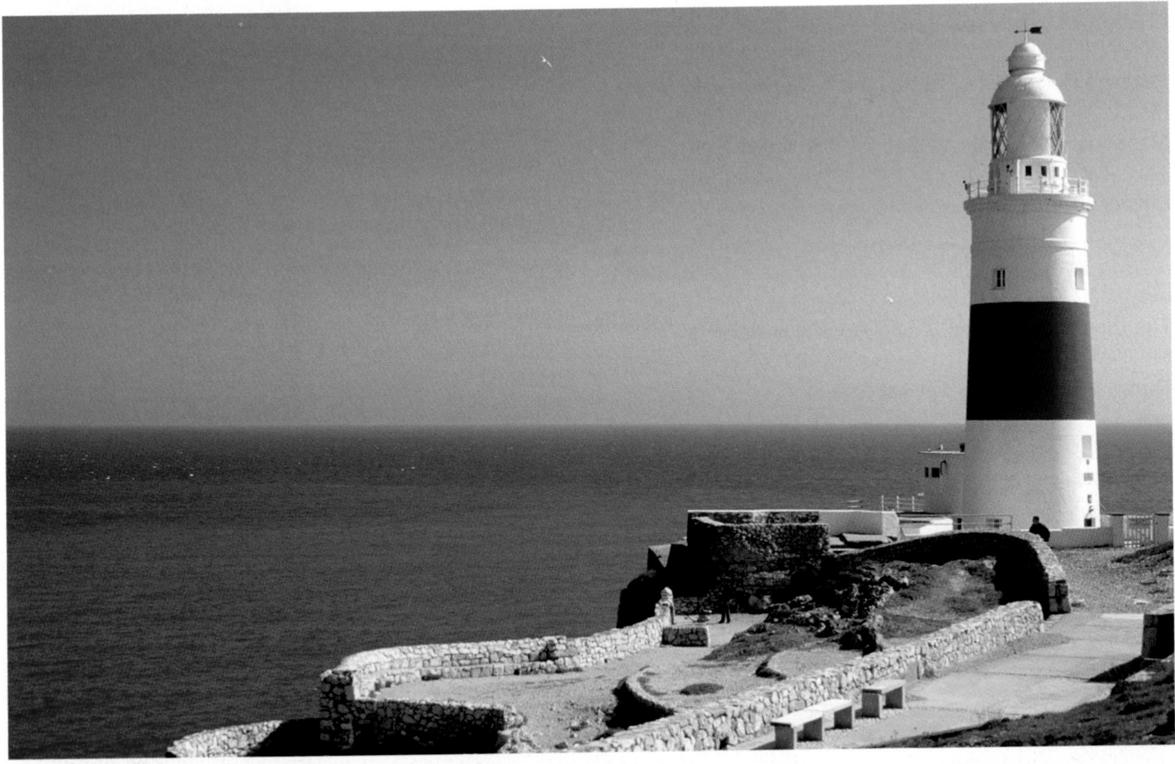

Inspectors' Choice

Assessed and announced annually, the AA's Inspectors' Choice awards recognise the very best hotels in Britain and Ireland. These hotels offer consistently outstanding levels of quality, comfort, cleanliness and customer care.

The full entries for these hotels are listed in their country section under their location name.

ENGLAND

BERKSHIRE

MAIDENHEAD

Fredrick's Hotel Restaurant Spa ★★★★ @@

NEWBURY

The Vineyard at Stockcross ★★★★★ @@@

BUCKINGHAMSHIRE

AYLESBURY

Hartwell House Hotel, Restaurant & Spa ★★★★ @@@

MARLOW

Macdonald Compleat Angler ★★★★ @@@

TAPLOW

Cliveden Country House Hotel ★★★★★ @@

CHESHIRE

CHESTER

The Chester Grosvenor & Spa ★★★★★ @@@@

SANDIWAY

Nunsmere Hall Hotel ★★★★ @@

CORNWALL

BRYHER (Isles of Scilly)

Hell Bay Hotel ★★★ @@@

PORTSCATHO

Driftwood ★★★ @@@

FOWEY

The Old Quay House Hotel ★★ @@

VERYAN

The Nare Hotel ★★★★ @

COUNTY DURHAM

SEAHAM

Seaham Hall Hotel & Serenity Spa ★★★★★ @@

CUMBRIA

BASSENTHWAITE

Armathwaite Hall ★★★★ @

BRAMPTON

Farlam Hall Hotel ★★★ @@

GRANGE-OVER-SANDS

Clare House ★ @

HOWTOWN

Sharrow Bay Country House Hotel ★★★ @@

WATERMILLOCK

Rampsbeck Country House Hotel ★★★ @@@

WINDERMERE

Gilpin Hotel & Lake House ★★★★ @@@

Holbeck Ghyll Country House Hotel ★★★★ @@@

Linthwaite House Hotel & Restaurant ★★★★ @@

The Samling ★★★

DERBYSHIRE

BASLOW

Fischer's Baslow Hall ★★★ @@@

ROWSLEY

East Lodge Country House Hotel ★★★ @@

The Peacock at Rowsley ★★★ @@@

DEVON

BURRINGTON

Northcote Manor ★★★ @@

CHAGFORD

Gidleigh Park ★★★★★ @@@@

HONITON

Combe House - Devon ★★★ @@

LEWDOWN

Lewtrenchard Manor ★★★ @@@

DORSET

EVERSHOT

Summer Lodge Country House Hotel & Spa ★★★★ @@@

ESSEX

DEDHAM
Maison Talbooth ★★★ ◎◎

GLOUCESTERSHIRE

BUCKLAND
Buckland Manor ★★★ ◎◎
CIRENCESTER
Barnsley House ★★★★ ◎◎
COLN ST-ALDWYNS
The New Inn at Coln ★★ ◎◎
CORSE LAWN
Corse Lawn House Hotel ★★★ ◎◎
LOWER SLAUGHTER
Lower Slaughter Manor ★★★
TETBURY
Calcot Manor ★★★★ ◎◎
THORNBURY
Thornbury Castle Hotel ★★★ ◎◎
UPPER SLAUGHTER
Lords of the Manor ★★★★ ◎◎◎

HAMPSHIRE

BROCKENHURST
Cloud Hotel ★★
The Pig ★★★ ◎◎
Rhinefield House ★★★★ ◎◎
DOGMERSFIELD
Four Seasons Hotel Hampshire ★★★★★ ◎
LYNDHURST
Lime Wood ★★★★★ ◎◎◎
NEW MILTON
Chewton Glen Hotel & Spa ★★★★★ ◎◎◎
ROTHERWICK
Tylney Hall Hotel ★★★★ ◎◎
WINCHESTER
Lainston House Hotel ★★★★ ◎◎◎

KENT

ASHFORD
Eastwell Manor ★★★★ ◎
LENHAM
Chilston Park Hotel ★★★★ ◎◎

LANCASHIRE

LANGHO
Northcote ★★★★ ◎◎◎◎

LEICESTERSHIRE

MELTON MOWBRAY
Stapleford Park ★★★★ ◎◎
NORTH KILWORTH
Kilworth House Hotel ★★★★ ◎◎

LONDON

LONDON E14
Four Seasons Hotel Canary Wharf ★★★★★ ◎
LONDON NW1
The Landmark London ★★★★★ ◎◎
LONDON SW1
51 Buckingham Gate, Taj Suites and Residences ★★★★★
The Berkeley ★★★★★ ◎◎◎◎◎
The Goring ★★★★★ ◎◎
The Halkin Hotel ★★★★★ ◎◎◎
Jumeirah Carlton Tower ★★★★★ ◎◎
The Lanesborough ★★★★★ ◎◎◎
Mandarin Oriental Hyde Park, London ★★★★★ ◎◎◎
No 41 ★★★★★
St James's Hotel and Club ★★★★★ ◎◎◎
The Stafford London by Kempinski ★★★★★ ◎
LONDON SW3
The Capital ★★★★★
The Levin ★★★★
LONDON W1
Athenaeum Hotel & Apartments ★★★★★ ◎◎
Brown's Hotel ★★★★★ ◎◎
The Chesterfield Mayfair ★★★★ ◎◎
Claridge's ★★★★★ ◎◎◎
The Connaught ★★★★★ ◎◎◎◎
The Dorchester ★★★★★ ◎◎
Four Seasons Hotel Park Lane ★★★★★ ◎◎
The Ritz London ★★★★★ ◎◎◎
LONDON W8
Milestone Hotel ★★★★★ ◎◎
Royal Garden Hotel ★★★★★ ◎◎◎
LONDON WC2
The Savoy ★★★★★ ◎◎

Inspectors' Choice *continued*

NORFOLK

BLAKENEY
Morston Hall ★★★ @@@
GRIMSTON
Congham Hall Country House Hotel ★★★ @@
NORTH WALSHAM
Beechwood Hotel ★★★ @@
NORWICH
The Old Rectory ★★ @@

NORTHAMPTONSHIRE

DAVENTRY
Fawsley Hall ★★★★

OXFORDSHIRE

GREAT MILTON
Le Manoir Aux Quat' Saisons ★★★★★ @@@@@

RUTLAND

OAKHAM
Hambleton Hall ★★★★ @@@@

SHROPSHIRE

LUDLOW
Fishmore Hall ★★★ @@@

SOMERSET

BATH
The Queensberry Hotel ★★★ @@@
HINTON CHARTERHOUSE
Homewood Park Hotel ★★★
PORLOCK
The Oaks Hotel ★★★ @
STON EASTON
Ston Easton Park ★★★★ @@

STAFFORDSHIRE

LICHFIELD
Swinfen Hall Hotel ★★★★ @@

SUFFOLK

BILDESTON
The Bildeston Crown ★★★ @@@
HINTLESHAM
Hintlesham Hall Hotel ★★★★ @@
IPSWICH
Salthouse Harbour Hotel ★★★★ @@

SURREY

BAGSHOT
Pennyhill Park Hotel & The Spa ★★★★★ @@@@@

SUSSEX, EAST

FOREST ROW
Ashdown Park Hotel & Country Club ★★★★ @@
NEWICK
Newick Park Hotel & Country Estate ★★★ @@
UCKFIELD
Buxted Park Hotel ★★★★ @@
Horsted Place ★★★ @

SUSSEX, WEST

AMBERLEY
Amberley Castle Hotel ★★★★ @@@
CLIMPING
Bailiffscourt Hotel & Spa ★★★ @@
CUCKFIELD
Ockenden Manor ★★★ @@@
GATWICK AIRPORT (LONDON)
Langshott Manor ★★★★ @@
TURNERS HILL
Alexander House Hotel & Utopia Spa ★★★★ @@

TYNE & WEAR

NEWCASTLE UPON TYNE
Jesmond Dene House ★★★★ @@@

WARWICKSHIRE

ALDERMINSTER
Ettington Park Hotel ★★★★ @@
LEAMINGTON SPA (ROYAL)
Mallory Court Hotel ★★★ @@@

WIGHT, ISLE OF

YARMOUTH
George Hotel ★★★ ◎◎

WILTSHIRE

CASTLE COMBE
Manor House Hotel and Golf Club ★★★★ ◎◎◎
COLERNE
Lucknam Park Hotel & Spa ★★★★★ ◎◎◎
MALMESBURY
Whatley Manor ★★★★★ ◎◎◎◎

WORCESTERSHIRE

CHADDESLEY CORBETT
Brockencote Hall Country House Hotel ★★★ ◎◎

YORKSHIRE, NORTH

BOLTON ABBEY
The Devonshire Arms Country House Hotel & Spa ★★★★ ◎◎◎◎
CRATHORNE
Crathorne Hall Hotel ★★★★ ◎◎
HARROGATE
Rudding Park Hotel, Spa & Golf ★★★★ ◎◎
HELMSLEY
Feversham Arms Hotel & Verbena Spa ★★★★ ◎◎◎
MASHAM
Swinton Park ★★★★ ◎◎◎
YARM
Judges Country House Hotel ★★★ ◎◎◎
YORK
Middlethorpe Hall & Spa ★★★★ ◎◎

YORKSHIRE, WEST

WETHERBY
Wood Hall Hotel ★★★★ ◎◎

CHANNEL ISLANDS

GUERNSEY

ST PETER PORT
Old Government House Hotel & Spa ★★★★ ◎◎

JERSEY

ROZEL
Chateau la Chaire ★★★ ◎◎
ST BRELADE
The Atlantic Hotel ★★★★ ◎◎◎◎
ST HELIER
The Club Hotel & Spa ★★★★ ◎◎◎◎
ST SAVIOUR
Longueville Manor Hotel ★★★★★ ◎◎◎

SCOTLAND

ABERDEENSHIRE

BALLATER
Darroch Learg Hotel ★★★ ◎◎◎

ARGYLL & BUTE

ERISKA
Isle of Eriska Hotel, Spa & Golf ★★★★★ ◎◎◎
KILCHRENAN
The Ardanaiseig Hotel ★★★ ◎◎◎
PORT APPIN
Airds Hotel ★★★★ ◎◎◎

CITY OF EDINBURGH

EDINBURGH
The Balmoral ★★★★★ ◎◎◎
Channings ★★★★ ◎
Norton House Hotel ★★★★ ◎◎◎
Prestonfield ★★★★★ ◎◎

CITY OF GLASGOW

GLASGOW
Hotel du Vin at One Devonshire Gardens ★★★★

Inspectors' Choice *continued*

DUMFRIES & GALLOWAY

KIRKBEAN
Cavens ★★★ ❀
NEWTON STEWART
Kirroughtree House ★★★ ❀❀
PORTPATRICK
Knockinaam Lodge ★★★ ❀❀❀

FIFE

MARKINCH
Balbirnie House ★★★★ ❀❀
ST ANDREWS
The Old Course Hotel, Golf Resort & Spa ★★★★★ ❀❀❀
ST ANDREWS
Rufflets Country House ★★★★ ❀❀

HIGHLAND

FORT WILLIAM
Inverlochy Castle Hotel ★★★★★ ❀❀❀
LOCHINVER
Inver Lodge Hotel ★★★★ ❀❀
NAIRN
Boath House ★★★ ❀❀❀❀
SHIELDAIG
Tigh an Eilean ★ ❀❀
STRONTIAN
Kilcamb Lodge Hotel ★★★ ❀❀
TAIN
The Glenmorangie Highland Home at Cadboll ★★★ ❀❀
TORRIDON
The Torridon ★★★★ ❀❀❀

PERTH & KINROSS

AUCHTERARDER
The Gleneagles Hotel ★★★★★ ❀❀❀❀
KILLIECRANKIE
Killiecrankie House Hotel ★★★ ❀❀

SCOTTISH BORDERS

PEEBLES
Cringletie House ★★★★ ❀❀

SOUTH AYRSHIRE

BALLANTRAE
Glenapp Castle ★★★★★ ❀❀❀❀
TROON
Lochgreen House Hotel ★★★★ ❀❀❀
TURNBERRY
Turnberry Resort, Scotland ★★★★★ ❀❀

STIRLING

CALLANDER
Roman Camp Country House Hotel ★★★ ❀❀❀

SCOTTISH ISLANDS

ISLE OF ARRAN

BRODICK
Kilmichael Country House Hotel ★★★ ❀❀

ISLE OF MULL

TOBERMORY
Highland Cottage ★★★ ❀❀

ISLE OF SKYE

ISLEORNSAY
Kinloch Lodge ★★★ ❀❀❀

WALES

CEREDIGION

EGLWYS FACH
Ynyshir Hall ★★★ ❀❀❀

CONWY

LLANDUDNO
Bodysgallen Hall and Spa ★★★★ ❀❀❀
Osborne House ★★★ ❀
St Tudno Hotel and Restaurant ★★★ ❀❀

GWYNEDD

CAERNARFON

Seiont Manor Hotel ★★★ ⊛⊛

DOLGELLAU

Penmaenuchaf Hall Hotel ★★★ ⊛

POWYS

LLANGAMMARCH WELLS

The Lake Country House & Spa ★★★ ⊛⊛

REPUBLIC OF IRELAND

CO CLARE

BALLYCOTTON

Bay View Hotel ★★★ ⊛⊛

BALLYLICKEY

Sea View House Hotel ★★★ ⊛⊛

BALLYVAUGHAN

Gregans Castle ★★★ ⊛⊛

NEWMARKET-ON-FERGUS

Dromoland Castle Hotel ★★★★★ ⊛⊛

DUBLIN

The Clarence ★★★★ ⊛⊛

The Merrion Hotel ★★★★★ ⊛⊛⊛⊛

CO GALWAY

CASHEL

Cashel House Hotel ★★★ ⊛⊛

RECESS

Lough Inagh Lodge Hotel ★★★ ⊛

CO KERRY

KENMARE

Sheen Falls ★★★★★ ⊛⊛

CO KILDARE

STRAFFAN

The K Club ★★★★★ ⊛⊛⊛

CO KILKENNY

THOMASTOWN

Mount Juliet Conrad Hotel ★★★★ ⊛⊛

CO WATERFORD

WATERFORD

Waterford Castle Hotel ★★★★ ⊛⊛

CO WEXFORD

GOREY

Marlfield House Hotel ★★★ ⊛⊛

ROSSLARE

Kelly's Resort Hotel & Spa ★★★★ ⊛

RESTAURANTS WITH ROOMS

These establishments are inspected under the AA's B&B scheme. They have been awarded the highest accommodation rating under this scheme.

ENGLAND

CUMBRIA CARTMELL

L'Enclume ⊛⊛⊛⊛⊛

DEVON ASHWATER

Blagdon Manor Hotel & Restaurant ⊛⊛

LINCOLNSHIRE WINTERINGHAM

Winteringham Fields ⊛⊛

NOTTINGHAMSHIRE NOTTINGHAM

Restaurant Sat Bains with Rooms ⊛⊛⊛⊛⊛

SOMERSET YEOVIL

Little Barwick House ⊛⊛⊛

WIGHT, ISLE OF VENTNOR

The Hambrough ⊛⊛⊛

YORKSHIRE, NORTH OLDSTEAD

The Black Swan at Oldstead ⊛⊛⊛

SCOTLAND

CITY OF EDINBURGH EDINBURGH

The Witchery by The Castle ⊛

FIFE PEAT INN

The Peat Inn ⊛⊛⊛

HIGHLAND KINGUSSIE

The Cross at Kingussie ⊛⊛⊛

STIRLING STRATHYRE

Creagan House ⊛⊛

SCOTTISH ISLANDS

ISLE OF SKYE COLBOST

The Three Chimneys & The House Over-By ⊛⊛⊛

ISLE OF SKYE STRUAN

Ullinish Country Lodge ⊛⊛⊛

WALES

MONMOUTHSHIRE SKENFRITH

The Bell at Skenfrith ⊛⊛

MONMOUTHSHIRE WHITEBROOK

The Crown at Whitebrook ⊛⊛⊛

SWANSEA REYNOLDSTON

Fairyhill ⊛⊛

Maps

Borrowdale, Lake District National Park

COUNTY MAPS

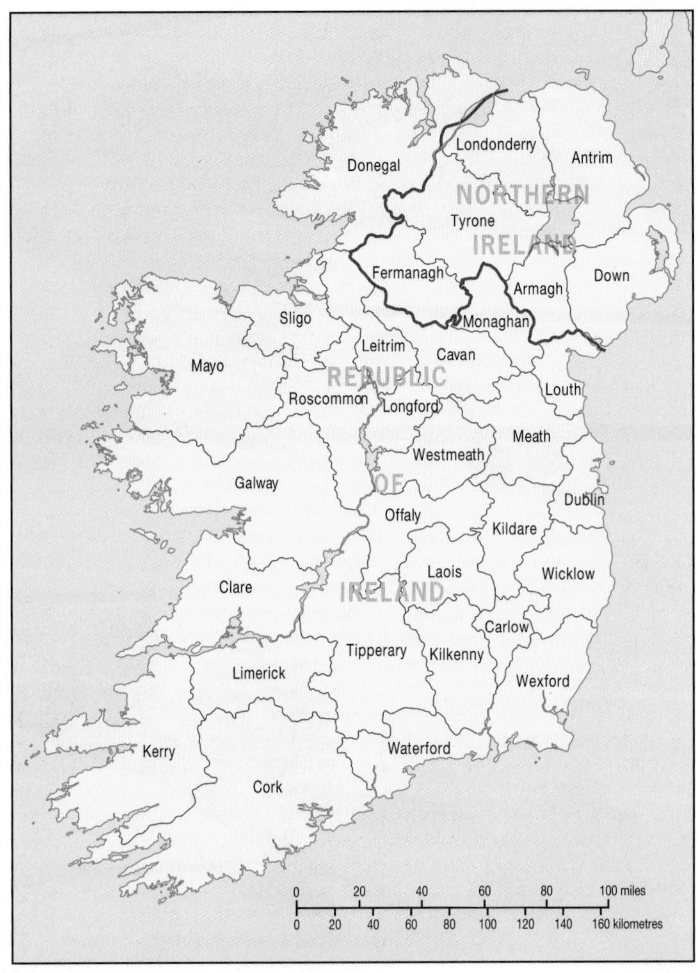

England

1 Bedfordshire
2 Berkshire
3 Bristol
4 Buckinghamshire
5 Cambridgeshire
6 Greater Manchester
7 Herefordshire
8 Hertfordshire
9 Leicestershire
10 Northamptonshire
11 Nottinghamshire
12 Rutland
13 Staffordshire
14 Warwickshire
15 West Midlands
16 Worcestershire

Scotland

17 City of Glasgow
18 Clackmannanshire
19 East Ayrshire
20 East Dunbartonshire
21 East Renfrewshire
22 Perth & Kinross
23 Renfrewshire
24 South Lanarkshire
25 West Dunbartonshire

Wales

26 Blaenau Gwent
27 Bridgend
28 Caerphilly
29 Denbighshire
30 Flintshire
31 Merthyr Tydfil
32 Monmouthshire
33 Neath Port Talbot
34 Newport
35 Rhondda Cynon Taff
36 Torfaen
37 Vale of Glamorgan
38 Wrexham

Na h-Eileanan an Iar
Orkney Islands
Shetland Islands
Moray
Highland
City of Aberdeen
Aberdeenshire
SCOTLAND
Angus
Perth & Kinross
Argyll & Bute
Stirling
City of Dundee
Fife
East Lothian
North Ayrshire
19
24
Scottish Borders
South Ayrshire
Dumfries & Galloway
Northumberland
Tyne & Wear
Cumbria
Durham
Isle of Man
North Yorkshire
East Riding of Yorkshire
Lancashire
West Yorkshire
Isle of Anglesey
6
South Yorkshire
Merseyside
Conwy
30
Cheshire
Derbyshire
Lincolnshire
29
38
11
Gwynedd
ENGLAND
13
Norfolk
Shropshire
9
12
WALES
15
5
Ceredigion
Powys
14
10
16
Suffolk
7
1
Pembrokeshire
Carmarthenshire
8
Essex
Gloucestershire
4
Swansea
Oxfordshire
Greater London
3
2
Wiltshire
Kent
Surrey
Somerset
Hampshire
West Sussex
East Sussex
Devon
Dorset
Isle of Wight
Cornwall
Isles of Scilly
Guernsey
Jersey
Argyll & Bute
Stirling
18
22
Fife
25
20
Falkirk
Inverclyde
City of Edinburgh
23
17
North Lanarkshire
West Lothian
Midlothian
North Ayrshire
21
Scottish Borders
19
South Lanarkshire
33
31
26
32
36
35
28
34
27
Cardiff
37
0 20 40 60 80 100 miles
0 20 40 60 80 100 120 140 160 kilometres

KEY TO ATLAS

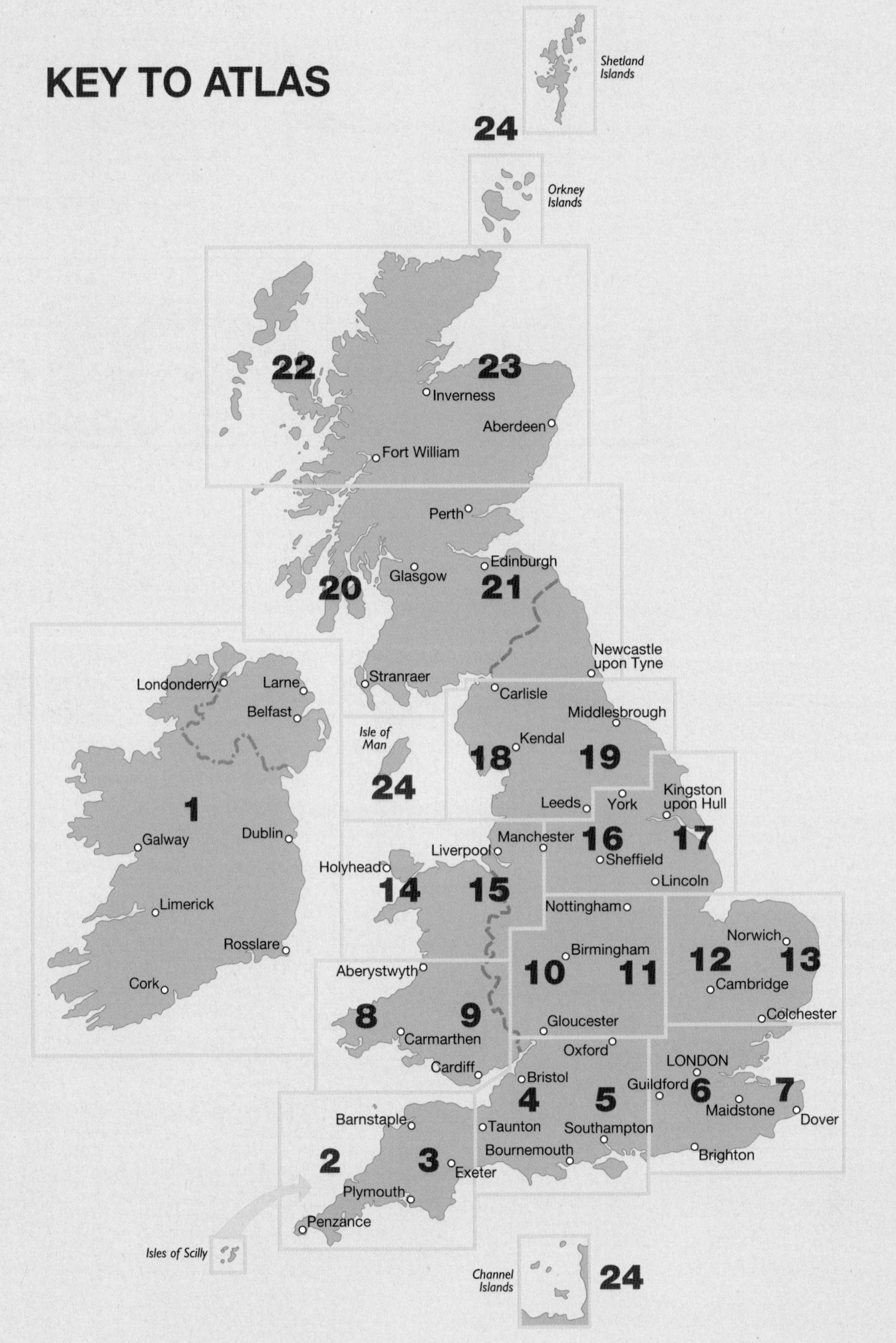

24
Shetland Islands
Orkney Islands
22
23
Inverness
Aberdeen
Fort William
Perth
Edinburgh
Glasgow
20
21
Newcastle upon Tyne
Stranraer
Carlisle
Londonderry
Larne
Belfast
Isle of Man
24
Middlesbrough
Kendal
18
19
1
Leeds
York
Kingston upon Hull
Galway
Dublin
Manchester
Liverpool
16
17
Sheffield
Holyhead
14
15
Lincoln
Limerick
Nottingham
Rosslare
Norwich
Birmingham
12
13
10
11
Cork
Aberystwyth
Cambridge
8
9
Colchester
Gloucester
Carmarthen
Oxford
Cardiff
LONDON
Bristol
Guildford
6
7
4
5
Maidstone
Barnstaple
Dover
Taunton
Southampton
Bournemouth
Brighton
2
3
Exeter
Plymouth
Penzance
Isles of Scilly
Channel Islands
24

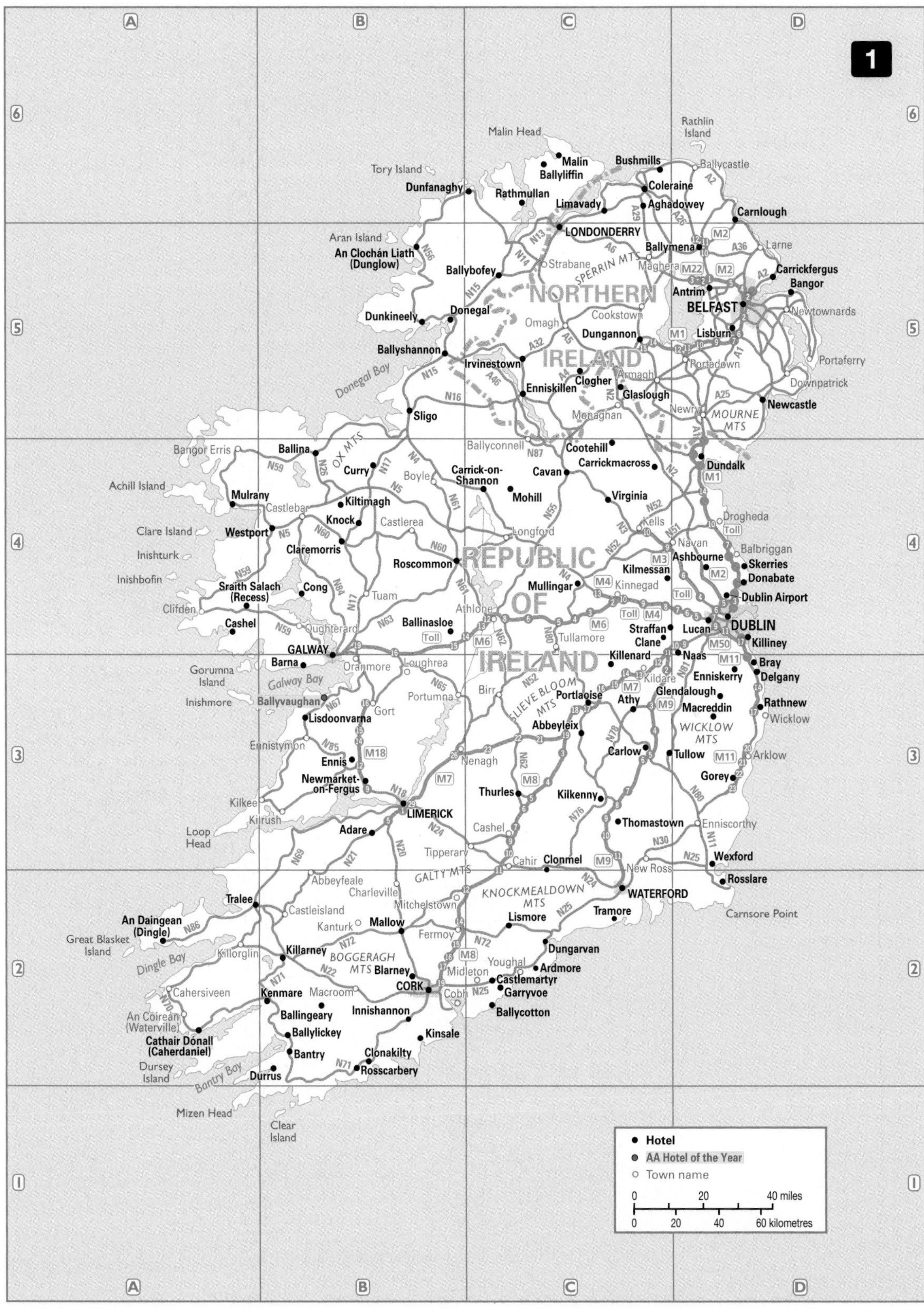
1
A
B
C
D
6
5
4
3
2
1
Malin Head
Rathlin Island
Malin
Ballyliffin
Bushmills
Ballycastle
Tory Island
Dunfanaghy
Rathmullan
Coleraine
Limavady
Aghadowey
Carnlough
LONDONDERRY
Aran Island
An Clochán Liath (Dunglow)
Ballymena
Larne
Strabane
SPERRIN MTS
Maghera
Carrickfergus
Ballybofey
Bangor
NORTHERN
Antrim
BELFAST
Dunkineely
Donegal
Omagh
Cookstown
Newtownards
Dungannon
Lisburn
Ballyshannon
IRELAND
Portaferry
Donegal Bay
Irvinestown
Armagh
Portadown
Clogher
Downpatrick
Enniskillen
Glaslough
Newry
Newcastle
Sligo
Monaghan
MOURNE MTS
Bangor Erris
Ballina
OX MTS
Ballyconnell
Cootehill
Carrickmacross
Dundalk
Achill Island
Curry
Boyle
Carrick-on-Shannon
Cavan
Mohill
Virginia
Mulrany
Castlebar
Kiltimagh
Drogheda
Knock
Castlerea
Kells
Clare Island
Westport
Longford
Navan
Balbriggan
Claremorris
Inishturk
REPUBLIC
Ashbourne
Skerries
Roscommon
Kilmessan
Donabate
Inishbofin
Mullingar
Kinnegad
Sraith Salach (Recess)
Cong
Dublin Airport
Tuam
Clifden
OF
Athlone
DUBLIN
Cashel
Ballinasloe
Tullamore
Straffan
Lucan
Oughterard
Clane
Killiney
GALWAY
IRELAND
Naas
Bray
Barna
Killenard
Oranmore
Loughrea
Gorumna Island
Enniskerry
Delgany
Kildare
Galway Bay
Birr
Glendalough
SLIEVE BLOOM MTS
Portumna
Ballyvaughan
Portlaoise
Inishmore
Athy
Rathnew
Gort
Macreddin
Lisdoonvarna
Wicklow
Abbeyleix
WICKLOW MTS
Ennistymon
Carlow
Ennis
Tullow
Arklow
Nenagh
Newmarket-on-Fergus
Gorey
Thurles
Kilkenny
Kilkee
Kilrush
LIMERICK
Thomastown
Enniscorthy
Loop Head
Cashel
Adare
Tipperary
Wexford
Cahir
Clonmel
New Ross
GALTY MTS
Abbeyfeale
Rosslare
KNOCKMEALDOWN MTS
WATERFORD
Charleville
Tralee
Mitchelstown
Castleisland
Carnsore Point
Tramore
An Daingean (Dingle)
Lismore
Kanturk
Mallow
Great Blasket Island
Fermoy
Dungarvan
Dingle Bay
Killorglin
Killarney
BOGGERAGH MTS
Youghal
Ardmore
Blarney
Midleton
Castlemartyr
CORK
Cahersiveen
Kenmare
Macroom
Cobh
Garryvoe
Ballingeary
Innishannon
Ballycotton
An Coireán (Waterville)
Ballylickey
Kinsale
Cathair Dónall (Caherdaniel)
Bantry
Clonakilty
Dursey Island
Bantry Bay
Rosscarbery
Durrus
Mizen Head
Clear Island
Hotel
AA Hotel of the Year
Town name
0
20
40 miles
0
20
40
60 kilometres

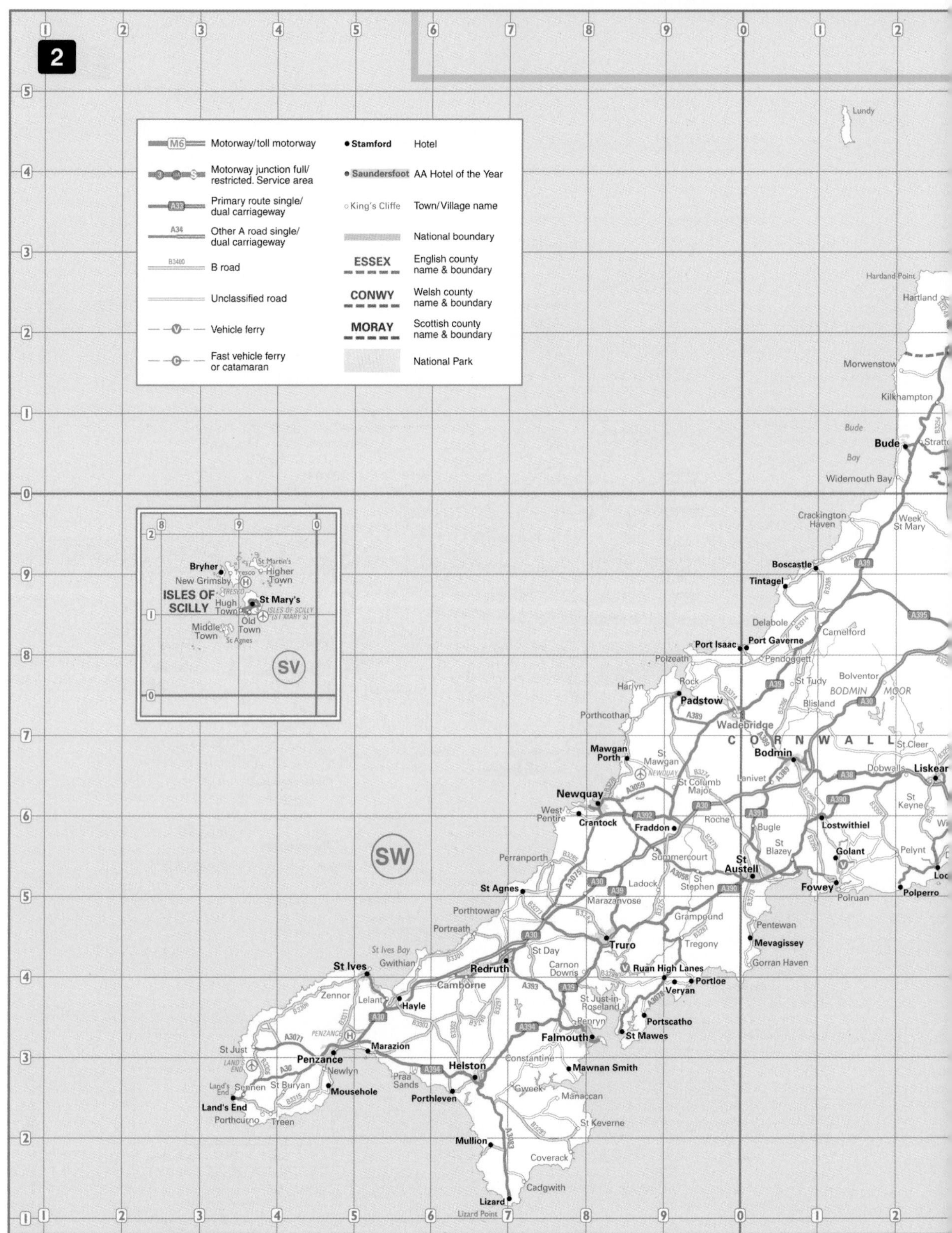

For continuation pages refer to numbered arrows

3
SUPER-MARE
Bleadon
Winscombe
Sedgemoor Services
Brent Knoll
Berrow
Burnham-on-Sea
Highbridge
Mark
Wedmore
Bridgwater Bay
BRISTOL CHANNEL
9
Woody Bay
Lynton
Lynmouth
Ilfracombe
Combe Martin
Mortehoe
Lee
Woolacombe
Georgeham
Croyde
Saunton
Braunton
Barnstaple or Bideford Bay
Parracombe
Brendon
EXMOOR
NATIONAL
PARK
Porlock Weir
Porlock
Minehead
Dunster
Blue Anchor
Watchet
Wootton Courtenay
Carhampton
Challacombe
Simonsbath
Exford
Withypool
Wheddon Cross
Kilve
Stogursey
West Huntspill
Holford
Nether Stowey
Cannington
QUANTOCK HILLS
Bridgwater
Glastonbury
Ashcott
Walton
Middlezoy
Othery
North Petherton
Goathurst
SOMERSET
Bratton Fleming
Muddiford
Barnstaple
Brayford
Winsford
Brompton Regis
Elworthy
Crowcombe
Sampford Brett
Appledore
Instow
Northam
Westward Ho!
Bideford
Clovelly
Horns Cross
SS
South Molton
North Molton
Dulverton
Exbridge
Wiveliscombe
Fitzhead
Bishops Lydeard
Milverton
Petton
Bampton
Taunton
ST
Lyng
Curry Rivel
North Curry
Langport
Long Sutton
Monkleigh
Great Torrington
Umberleigh
Chittlehamholt
Rackenford
Wellington
Sampford Arundel
Corfe
Staple Fitzpaine
Hatch Beauchamp
South Petherton
Ilminster
Little Torrington
Burrington
Beaford
Stibb Cross
Chulmleigh
Chawleigh
Witheridge
Bradworthy
Merton
Dolton
Tiverton
Halberton
Culmstock
Hemyock
Uffculme
Willand
Milton Damerel
Shebbear
Black Torrington
Sheepwash
Meeth
Winkleigh
Eggesford
Lapford
Cheriton Fitzpaine
Morchard Bishop
Cullompton
Bickleigh
Upottery
Chard
Crewkerne
Yarcombe
Winsham
Mosterton
Chilsworthy
Holsworthy
Highampton
Hatherleigh
Copplestone
Silverton
Tytherleigh
Broadwindsor
Beaminster
Halwill Junction
Beaworthy
Clawton
Crediton
Stoke Canon
Fenny Bridges
Honiton
Wilmington
Shute
Axminster
DEVON
Newton St Cyres
Tedburn St Mary
Broadclyst
Whimple
Ottery St Mary
Colyton
Uplyme
North Chideock
Ashwater
Okehampton
South Zeal
Whiddon Down
Crockernwell
EXETER
Newton Poppleford
Colyford
Seaton
Axmouth
Lyme Regis
Charmouth
Bridport
Bratton Clovelly
Sourton
Bridestowe
Dunsford
Clyst St Mary
Topsham
Woodbury
Branscombe
Beer
West Bay
Burton Bradstock
Launceston
Lewdown
Lifton
Lydford
Chagford
DARTMOOR
Moretonhampstead
Kennford
Exminster
Otterton
Sidmouth
Budleigh Salterton
Lyme Bay
Milton Abbot
Kenton
Exmouth
Bovey Tracey
Chudleigh
Lamerton
Mary Tavy
Postbridge
Widecombe in the Moor
Haytor Vale
Ideford
Dawlish
Tavistock
Two Bridges
Ilsington
Chudleigh Knighton
Bishopsteignton
Teignmouth
Princetown
Kingsteignton
Gunnislake
Pensilva
Callington
Horrabridge
Hexworthy
Ashburton
Newton Abbot
Dousland
Kingskerswell
Maidencombe
Bere Alston
Yelverton
Holne
PARK
Buckfastleigh
St Mellion
Bere Ferrers
Ipplepen
SY
Pillaton
Shaugh Prior
Dartington
TORQUAY
Landrake
Cornwood
South Brent
Totnes
Paignton
Saltash
Plympton
Wrangaton
Stoke Gabriel
Tor Bay
Polbathic
Ivybridge
Harbertonford
Churston Ferrers
Torpoint
Dittisham
Brixham
Portwrinkle
Crafthole
PLYMOUTH
Ugborough
Millbrook
Heybrook Bay
Brixton
Yealmpton
Modbury
Halwell
Kingswear
Cawsand
Dartmouth
Wembury
Holbeton
Aveton Gifford
Newton Ferrers
Stoke Fleming
SX
Bigbury-on-Sea
Bigbury Bay
Kingsbridge
Slapton
Strete
Thurlestone
Chillington
Start Bay
Torcross
Hope
Malborough
Hope Cove
Salcombe
Beesands
Start Point
East Prawle
10 miles
10
20 kilometres

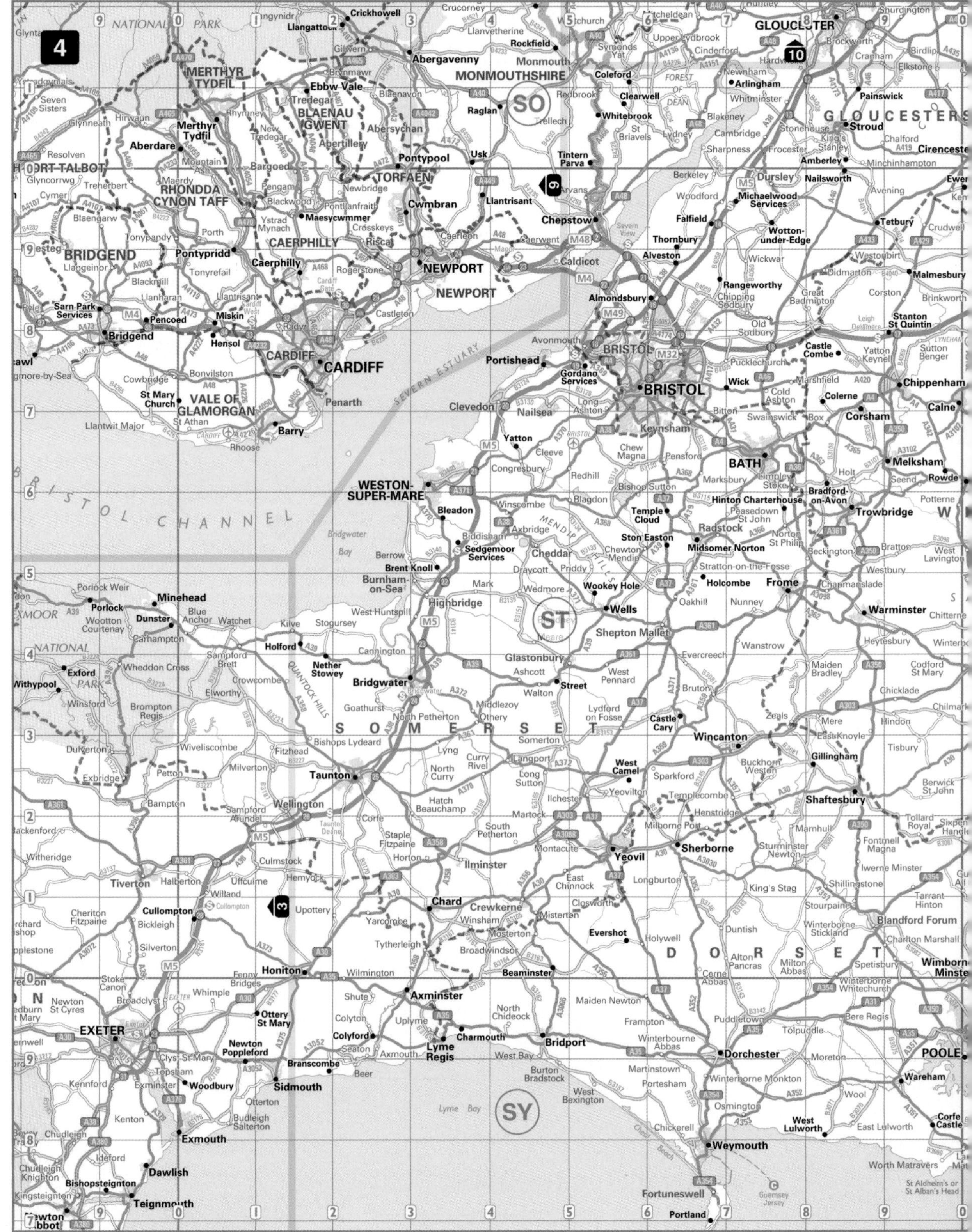

For continuation pages refer to numbered arrows

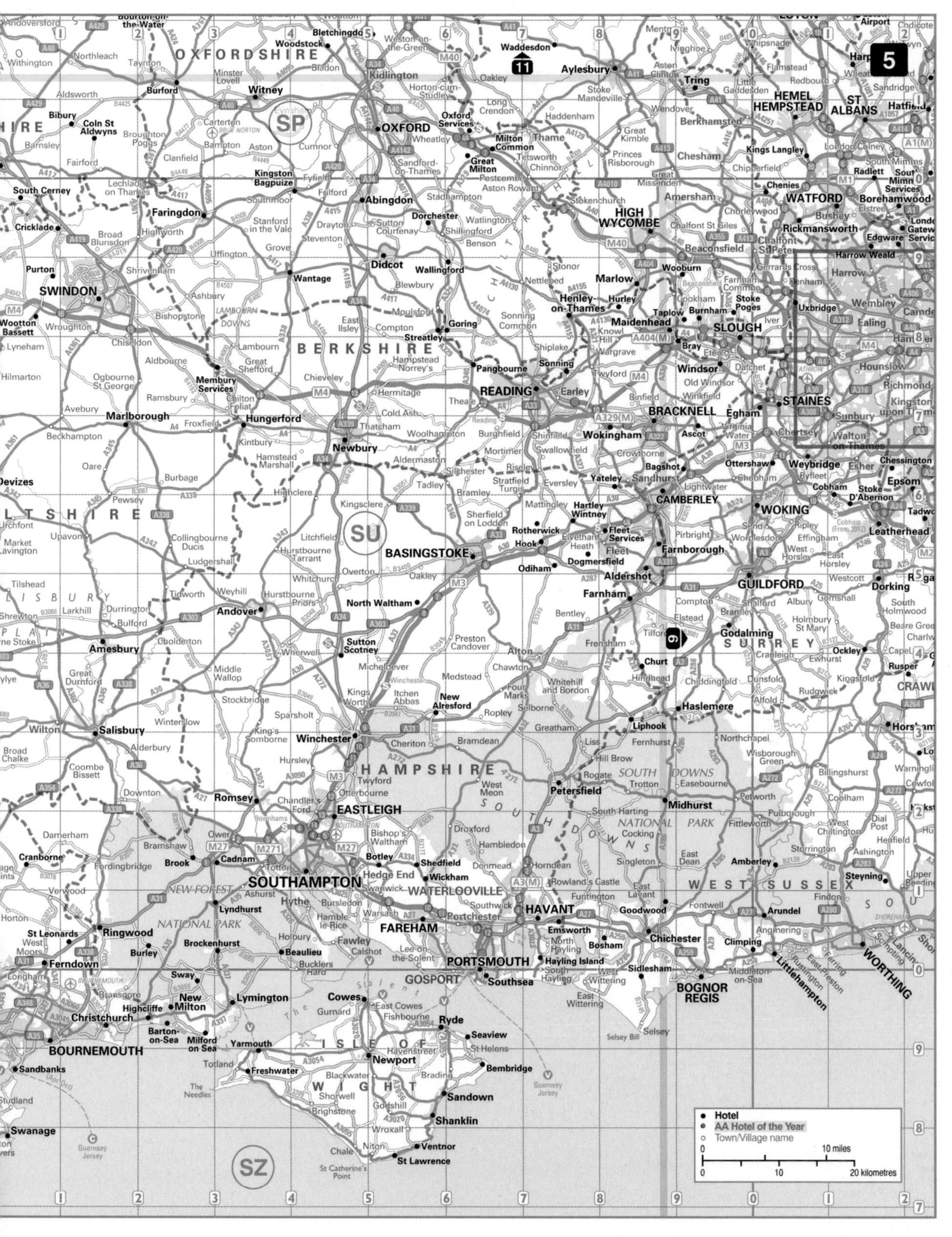
5
OXFORDSHIRE
BERKSHIRE
HAMPSHIRE
SURREY
WEST SUSSEX
ISLE OF WIGHT
SP
SU
SZ
11
6
Waddesdon
Aylesbury
Bletchingdon
Woodstock
Kidlington
Witney
Burford
Bibury
Coln St Aldwyns
Carterton
OXFORD
Oxford Services
Thame
Milton Common
Great Milton
Abingdon
Kingston Bagpuize
Faringdon
South Cerney
Cricklade
Dorchester
Didcot
Wallingford
Wantage
SWINDON
Purton
Wootton Bassett
Membury Services
Marlborough
Hungerford
Newbury
Goring
Streatley
Pangbourne
READING
Sonning
Henley-on-Thames
Marlow
HIGH WYCOMBE
Beaconsfield
Wooburn
Taplow
Burnham
Stoke Poges
Maidenhead
SLOUGH
Bray
Windsor
Egham
STAINES
BRACKNELL
Ascot
Wokingham
Bagshot
Sandhurst
CAMBERLEY
Yateley
Hartley Wintney
Rotherwick
Fleet Services
Hook
Odiham
BASINGSTOKE
Dogmersfield
Farnborough
Aldershot
Farnham
GUILDFORD
WOKING
Ottershaw
Weybridge
Cobham
Stoke D'Abernon
Chessington
Epsom
Leatherhead
Dorking
Ockley
Rusper
Godalming
Churt
Haslemere
Liphook
Midhurst
Petersfield
North Waltham
Andover
Amesbury
Sutton Scotney
New Alresford
Winchester
Salisbury
Romsey
EASTLEIGH
Cadnam
Brook
SOUTHAMPTON
Shedfield
Wickham
Botley
Lyndhurst
Cranborne
Ringwood
St Leonards
Ferndown
Burley
Brockenhurst
Beaulieu
Sway
New Milton
Lymington
Highcliffe
Christchurch
BOURNEMOUTH
Sandbanks
Swanage
FAREHAM
PORTSMOUTH
Southsea
HAVANT
Emsworth
Bosham
Hayling Island
Chichester
Sidlesham
Goodwood
BOGNOR REGIS
Arundel
Amberley
Climping
Littlehampton
WORTHING
Steyning
Cowes
Ryde
Seaview
Bembridge
Newport
Yarmouth
Freshwater
Sandown
Shanklin
Ventnor
St Lawrence
Berkhamsted
Tring
Kings Langley
Chenies
WATFORD
Rickmansworth
Borehamwood
Radlett
HEMEL HEMPSTEAD
ST ALBANS
Harrow Weald
Uxbridge
Denham
Hounslow
Richmond
SOUTH DOWNS NATIONAL PARK
NEW FOREST NATIONAL PARK
Hotel
AA Hotel of the Year
Town/Village name
10 miles
20 kilometres

For continuation pages refer to numbered arrows

7
TM
TR
Halstead
Braintree
COLCHESTER
Coggeshall
Witham
Maldon
Tolleshunt Knights
Great Totham
Tollesbury
West Mersea
Brightlingsea
Wivenhoe
Harwi
Walton on the Naze
Frinton-on-Sea
CLACTON-ON-SEA
St Osyth
Thorrington
Bradwell-on-Sea
Southminster
Burnham-on-Crouch
South Woodham Ferrers
Hockley
Rayleigh
Rochford
Great Wakering
SOUTHEND-ON-SEA
Canvey Island
Sheerness
Minster
Eastchurch
Leysdown-on-Sea
Isle of Sheppey
ROCHESTER
GILLINGHAM
CHATHAM
Sittingbourne
Faversham
Whitstable
Herne Bay
Reculver
MARGATE
Kingsgate
Broadstairs
Ramsgate
Sandwich
Canterbury
Deal
Kingsdown
St Margaret's at Cliffe
DOVER
Hawkinge
CHANNEL TUNNEL TERMINAL
FOLKESTONE
Hythe
Lympne
Ashford
K E N T
Wye
Lenham
Charing
Tenterden
Hamstreet
Dymchurch
St Mary's Bay
New Romney
Lydd
Camber
Dungeness
Rye
Winchelsea
Peasmarsh
HASTINGS
St Leonards
STRAIT OF DOVER
Channel Tunnel (Rail)
Hotel
AA Hotel of the Year
Town/Village name
0
10 miles
10
20 kilometres

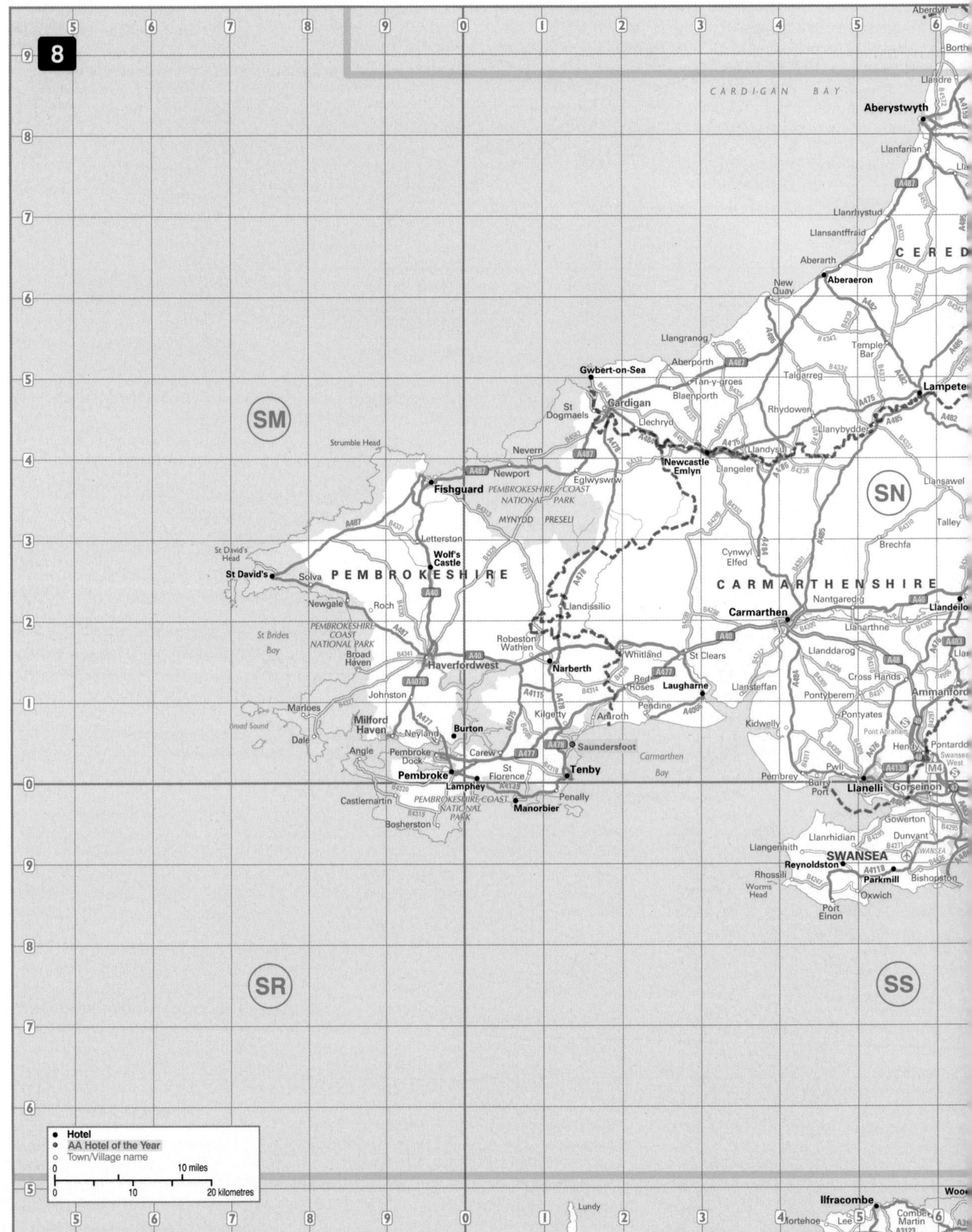

For continuation pages refer to numbered arrows

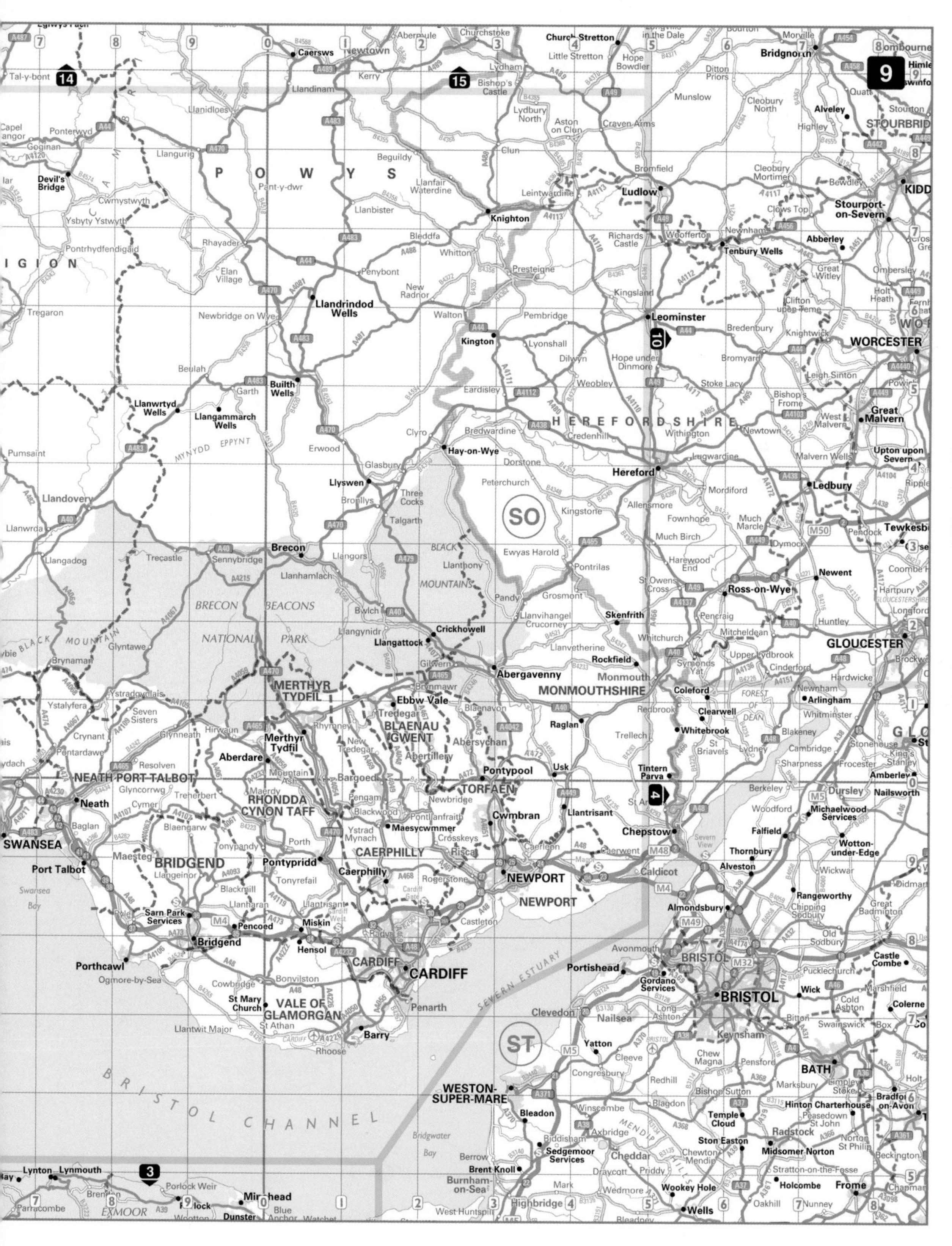

9
14
15
10
4
3
POWYS
HEREFORDSHIRE
MONMOUTHSHIRE
MERTHYR TYDFIL
BLAENAU GWENT
TORFAEN
NEATH PORT TALBOT
RHONDDA CYNON TAFF
BRIDGEND
CAERPHILLY
NEWPORT
VALE OF GLAMORGAN
CARDIFF
BRISTOL
SO
ST
BRECON BEACONS NATIONAL PARK
BLACK MOUNTAINS
BLACK MOUNTAIN
MYNYDD EPPYNT
SEVERN ESTUARY
BRISTOL CHANNEL
Swansea Bay
Bridgwater Bay
FOREST OF DEAN
EXMOOR
MENDIP HILLS
Caersws
Newtown
Abermule
Churchstoke
Church Stretton
Little Stretton
Hope Bowdler
Bridgnorth
Morville
Ditton Priors
Munslow
Cleobury North
Alveley
Highley
Stourton
STOURBRIDGE
Kerry
Lydham
Bishop's Castle
Llandinam
Llanidloes
Tal-y-bont
Capel Bangor
Ponterwyd
Goginan
Llangurig
Devil's Bridge
Cwmystwyth
Ysbyty Ystwyth
Pontrhydfendigaid
Tregaron
Beguildy
Llanfair Waterdine
Pant-y-dwr
Llanbister
Lydbury North
Aston on Clun
Clun
Craven Arms
Bromfield
Leintwardine
Ludlow
Cleobury Mortimer
Bewdley
Stourport-on-Severn
Clows Top
Knighton
Richards Castle
Woofferton
Newnham
Tenbury Wells
Abberley
Great Witley
Ombersley
Holt Heath
Rhayader
Elan Village
Bleddfa
Whitton
Penybont
New Radnor
Presteigne
Kingsland
Clifton upon Teme
Llandrindod Wells
Newbridge on Wye
Walton
Pembridge
Leominster
Bredenbury
Knightwick
WORCESTER
Kington
Lyonshall
Dilwyn
Hope under Dinmore
Bromyard
Leigh Sinton
Beulah
Garth
Builth Wells
Llanwrtyd Wells
Llangammarch Wells
Eardisley
Weobley
Stoke Lacy
Bishop's Frome
Great Malvern
West Malvern
Clyro
Bredwardine
Credenhill
Withington
Newtown
Upton upon Severn
Malvern Wells
Pumsaint
Erwood
Hay-on-Wye
Dorstone
Lugwardine
Glasbury
Hereford
Ledbury
Llyswen
Peterchurch
Mordiford
Llandovery
Three Cocks
Bronllys
Allensmore
Kingstone
Fownhope
Much Marcle
Tewkesbury
Pendock
Llanwrda
Talgarth
Much Birch
Dymock
Llangadog
Trecastle
Sennybridge
Brecon
Llangors
Llanthony
Ewyas Harold
Harewood End
Newent
Coombe Hill
Llanhamlach
Pontrilas
St Owens Cross
Ross-on-Wye
Hartpury
Longford
Pandy
Grosmont
Bwlch
Llanvihangel Crucorney
Skenfrith
Pencraig
Huntley
Llangynidr
Crickhowell
Llangattock
Whitchurch
Mitcheldean
GLOUCESTER
Glyntawe
Brynamman
Llanvetherine
Rockfield
Symonds Yat
Upper Lydbrook
Cinderford
Gilwern
Abergavenny
Monmouth
Hardwicke
Brynmawr
Ystradgynlais
Ebbw Vale
Tredegar
Blaenavon
Coleford
Newnham
Arlingham
Ystalyfera
Seven Sisters
Redbrook
Clearwell
Whitminster
Rhymney
Raglan
Whitebrook
Trellech
St Briavels
Blakeney
Crynant
Glynneath
Hirwaun
Merthyr Tydfil
New Tredegar
Abersychan
Lydney
Cambridge
Stonehouse
Pontardawe
Resolven
Aberdare
Abertillery
King's Stanley
Mountain Ash
Bargoed
Pontypool
Usk
Tintern Parva
Sharpness
Frocester
Amberley
Glyncorrwg
Treherbert
Maerdy
Pengam
Berkeley
Dursley
Nailsworth
Neath
Cymer
Blackwood
Newbridge
Cwmbran
Llantrisant
St Arvans
Woodford
Michaelwood Services
Baglan
Blaengarw
Ystrad Mynach
Maesycwmmer
Pontllanfraith
Crosskeys
Caerleon
Chepstow
Falfield
SWANSEA
Maesteg
Tonypandy
Porth
Risca
Magor
Caerwent
Thornbury
Wotton-under-Edge
Port Talbot
Llangeinor
Pontypridd
Caerphilly
Rogerstone
Caldicot
Alveston
Wickwar
Tonyrefail
Blackmill
Llanharan
Llantrisant
Rangeworthy
Sarn Park Services
Pencoed
Miskin
Castleton
Almondsbury
Chipping Sodbury
Great Badminton
Bridgend
Hensol
Radyr
Old Sodbury
Porthcawl
Ogmore-by-Sea
Bonvilston
Avonmouth
Portishead
Gordano Services
Pucklechurch
Castle Combe
Cowbridge
St Mary Church
Penarth
Clevedon
Nailsea
Long Ashton
Wick
Marshfield
Cold Ashton
Colerne
Llantwit Major
St Athan
Barry
Rhoose
Cardiff
Bitton
Swainswick
Box
Yatton
Cleeve
Keynsham
Chew Magna
Pensford
BATH
Congresbury
Redhill
Marksbury
Limpley Stoke
Holt
Bradford-on-Avon
WESTON-SUPER-MARE
Bishop Sutton
Blagdon
Hinton Charterhouse
Bleadon
Winscombe
Temple Cloud
Peasedown St John
Axbridge
Radstock
Norton St Philip
Biddisham
Sedgemoor Services
Cheddar
Ston Easton
Chewton Mendip
Midsomer Norton
Beckington
Berrow
Brent Knoll
Draycott
Priddy
Stratton-on-the-Fosse
Burnham-on-Sea
Mark
Wedmore
Wookey Hole
Holcombe
Frome
Chapmanslade
Highbridge
Oakhill
Nunney
Wells
West Huntspill
Lynton
Lynmouth
Porlock Weir
Porlock
Minehead
Brendon
Parracombe
Dunster
Blue Anchor

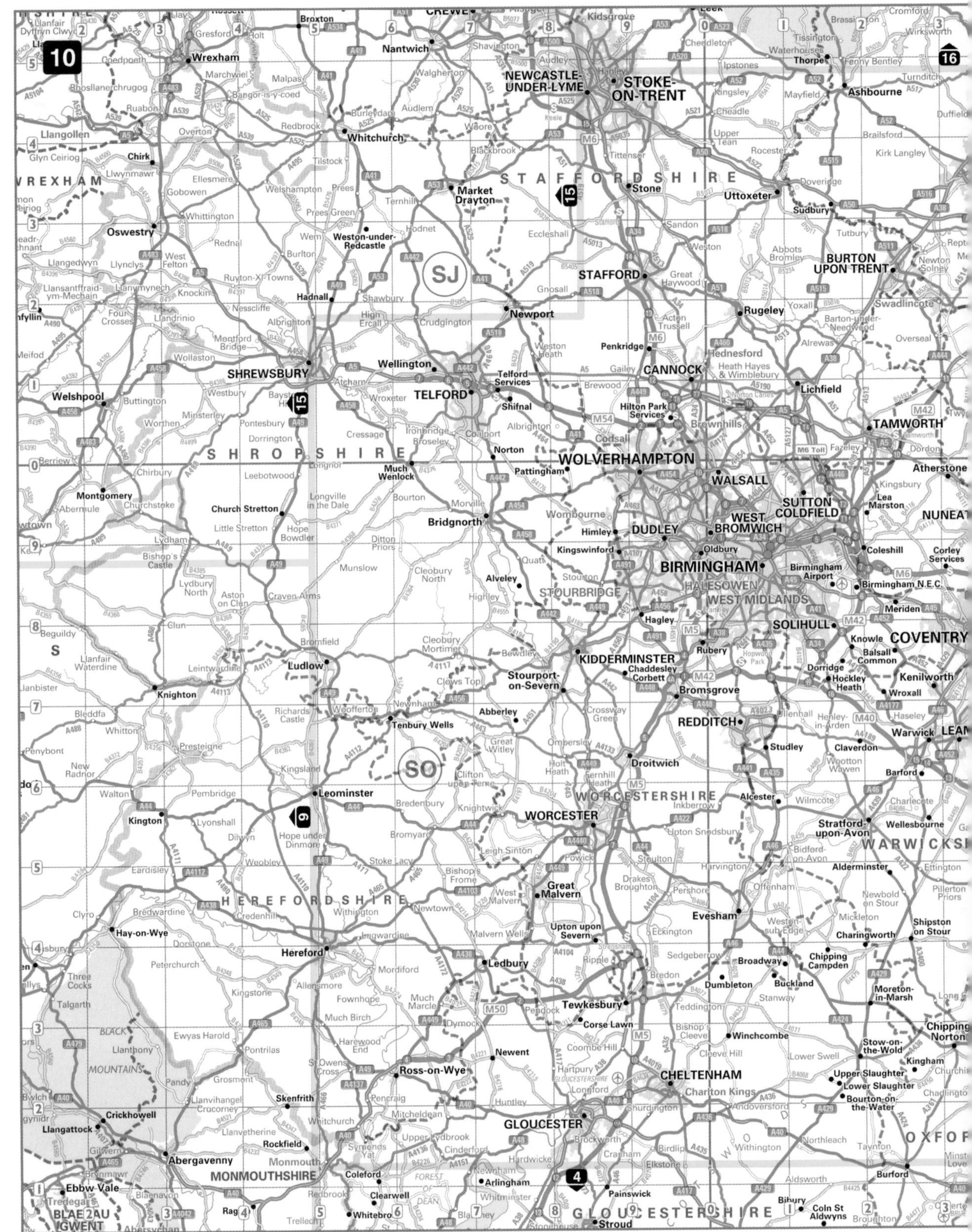

For continuation pages refer to numbered arrows

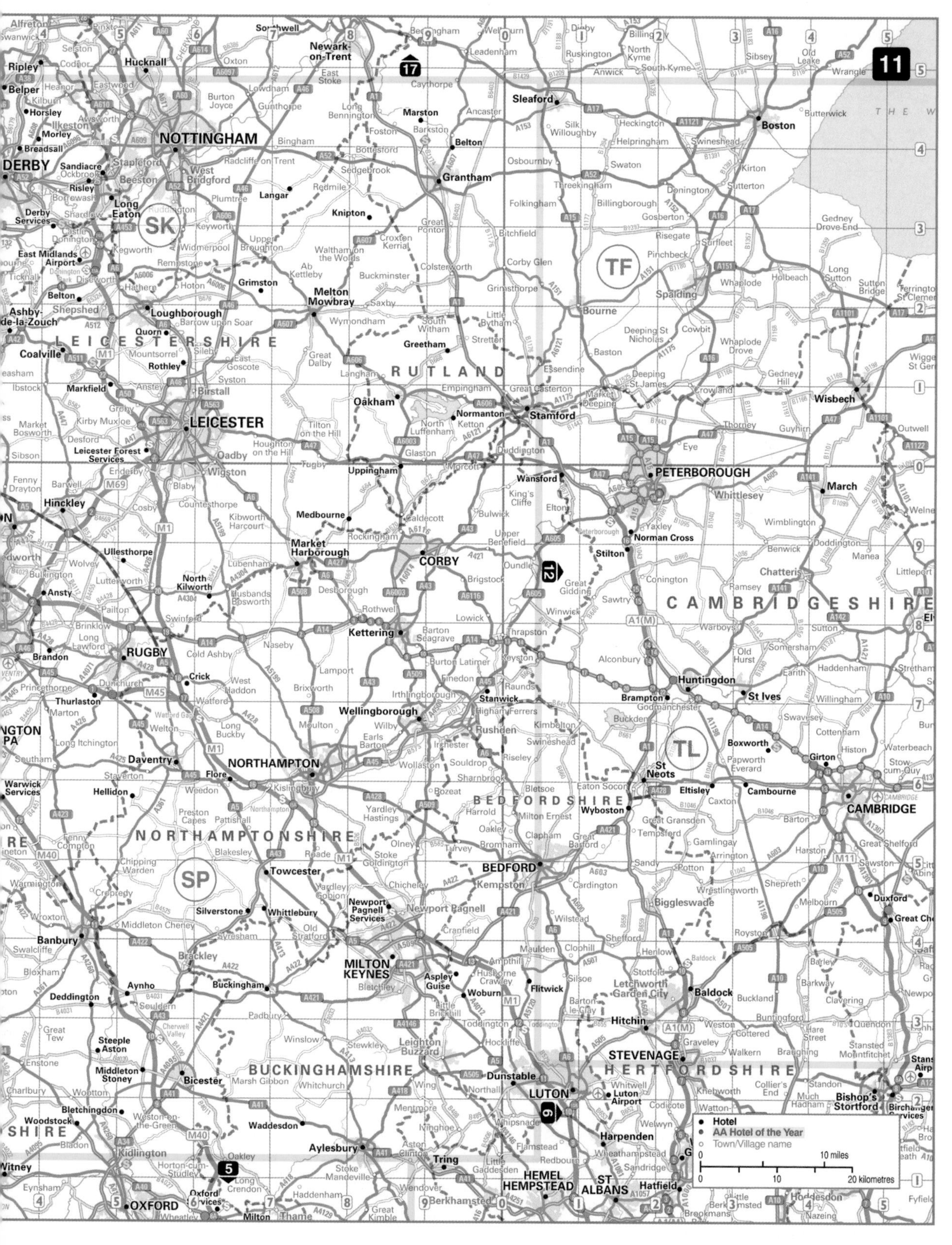

11
NOTTINGHAM
DERBY
LEICESTER
PETERBOROUGH
NORTHAMPTON
CAMBRIDGE
MILTON KEYNES
BEDFORD
LUTON
STEVENAGE
OXFORD
HEMEL HEMPSTEAD
ST ALBANS
CORBY
Grantham
Boston
Sleaford
Newark-on-Trent
Melton Mowbray
Loughborough
Stamford
Oakham
Kettering
Wellingborough
Huntingdon
St Ives
St Neots
Wisbech
March
Spalding
Rugby
Daventry
Banbury
Bicester
Aylesbury
Towcester
Market Harborough
Hinckley
Coalville
Hucknall
Ripley
Belper
Long Eaton
Stapleford
West Bridgford
Oadby
Wigston
Uppingham
Rushden
Kempston
Biggleswade
Baldock
Letchworth Garden City
Hitchin
Harpenden
Dunstable
Leighton Buzzard
Tring
Bishop's Stortford
Royston
Newport Pagnell
Buckingham
Brackley
Kidlington
Witney
Woodstock
Hatfield
Whittlesey
Bourne
LEICESTERSHIRE
RUTLAND
CAMBRIDGESHIRE
NORTHAMPTONSHIRE
BEDFORDSHIRE
BUCKINGHAMSHIRE
HERTFORDSHIRE
SK
TF
SP
TL
THE W
East Midlands Airport
Luton Airport
Leicester Forest Services
Newport Pagnell Services
Oxford Services
M1
M40
M11
M45
M69
A1(M)
A1
A14
A43
A45
A47
5
6
9
12
17
Hotel
AA Hotel of the Year
Town/Village name
0
10 miles
0
10
20 kilometres

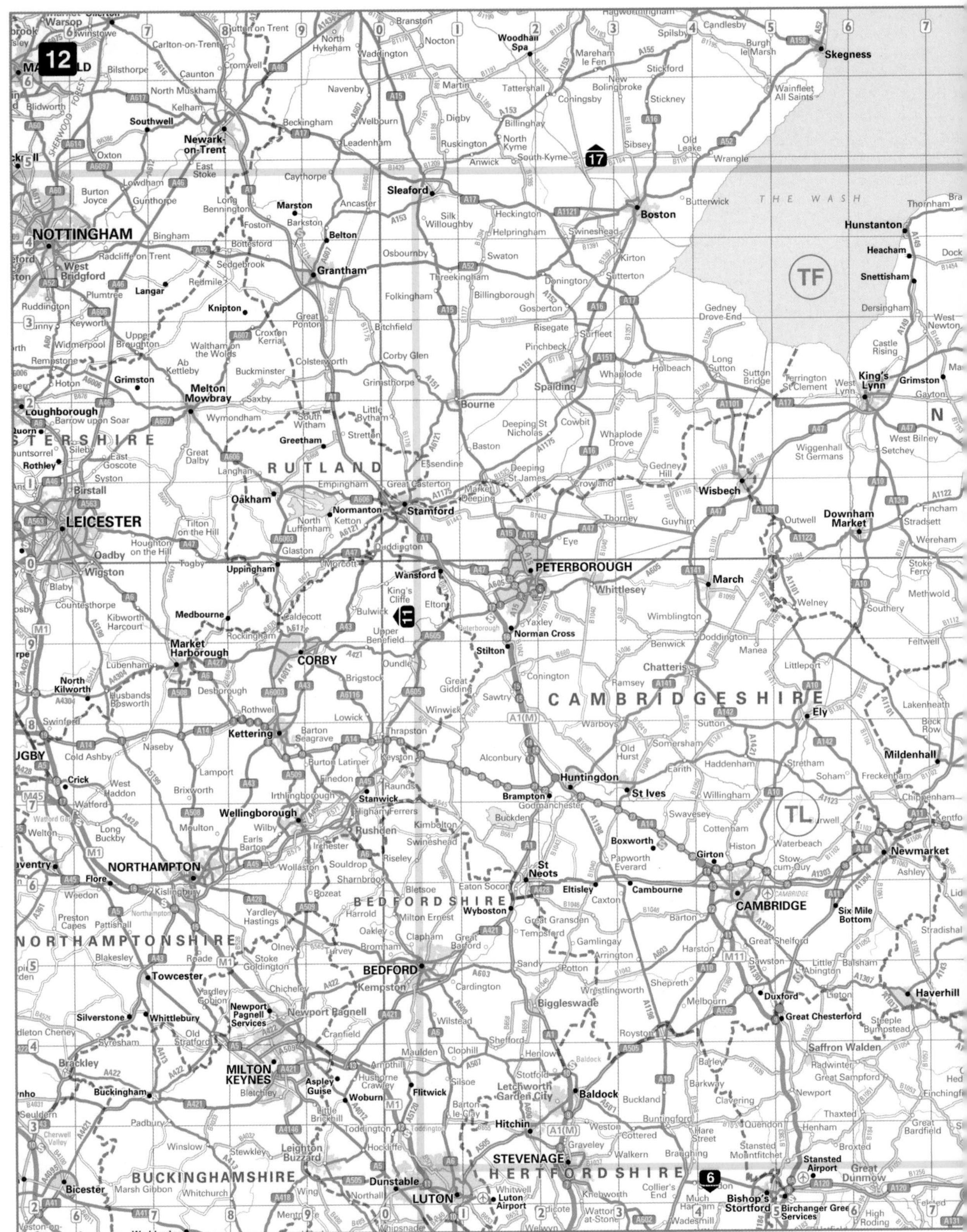

For continuation pages refer to numbered arrows

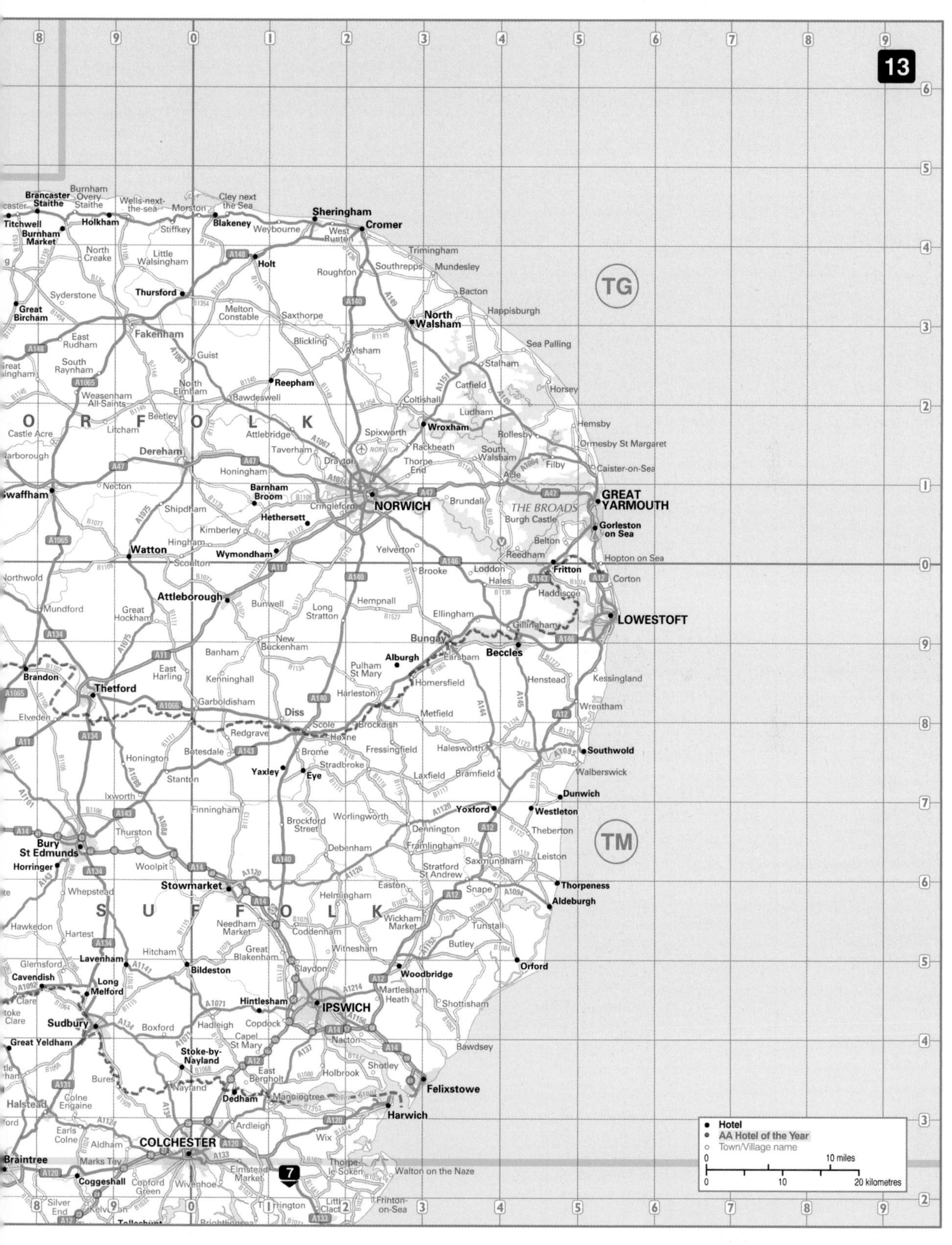
13
TG
TM
N O R F O L K
S U F F O L K
Brancaster Staithe
Burnham Overy Staithe
Wells-next-the-sea
Cley next the Sea
Morston
Titchwell
Holkham
Stiffkey
Blakeney
Weybourne
Sheringham
Cromer
West Runton
Burnham Market
North Creake
Little Walsingham
Holt
Trimingham
Southrepps
Mundesley
Roughton
Bacton
Thursford
Syderstone
Great Bircham
Melton Constable
Saxthorpe
North Walsham
Happisburgh
Fakenham
East Rudham
South Raynham
Blickling
Aylsham
Sea Palling
Guist
Stalham
Weasenham All Saints
North Elmham
Reepham
Bawdeswell
Catfield
Horsey
Coltishall
Ludham
Hemsby
Beetley
Litcham
Castle Acre
Attlebridge
Spixworth
Wroxham
Rollesby
Ormesby St Margaret
Dereham
Taverham
Drayton
Rackheath
South Walsham
Filby
Honingham
Thorpe End
Acle
Caister-on-Sea
Swaffham
Necton
Barnham Broom
NORWICH
Brundall
THE BROADS
GREAT YARMOUTH
Shipdham
Cringleford
Burgh Castle
Gorleston on Sea
Hethersett
Kimberley
Belton
Hingham
Yelverton
Reedham
Watton
Wymondham
Scoulton
Hopton on Sea
Fritton
Brooke
Loddon
Hales
Corton
Northwold
Haddiscoe
Attleborough
Hempnall
Mundford
Great Hockham
Bunwell
Long Stratton
Ellingham
LOWESTOFT
Gillingham
New Buckenham
Bungay
Banham
Alburgh
Earsham
Beccles
East Harling
Pulham St Mary
Brandon
Kenninghall
Henstead
Kessingland
Thetford
Homersfield
Harleston
Garboldisham
Wrentham
Elveden
Diss
Metfield
Scole
Brockdish
Redgrave
Hoxne
Botesdale
Brome
Fressingfield
Halesworth
Southwold
Honington
Stradbroke
Walberswick
Stanton
Yaxley
Eye
Laxfield
Bramfield
Ixworth
Dunwich
Finningham
Yoxford
Westleton
Brockford Street
Worlingworth
Dennington
Theberton
Bury St Edmunds
Thurston
Framlingham
Debenham
Leiston
Horringer
Woolpit
Saxmundham
Stratford St Andrew
Stowmarket
Thorpeness
Whepstead
Easton
Snape
Helmingham
Aldeburgh
Wickham Market
Hawkedon
Needham Market
Hartest
Tunstall
Coddenham
Witnesham
Butley
Great Blakenham
Glemsford
Hitcham
Lavenham
Orford
Bildeston
Claydon
Cavendish
Woodbridge
Long Melford
Martlesham Heath
Clare
Hintlesham
IPSWICH
Shottisham
Stoke Clare
Sudbury
Boxford
Hadleigh
Copdock
Nacton
Capel St Mary
Great Yeldham
Bawdsey
Stoke-by-Nayland
East Bergholt
Shotley
Bures
Holbrook
Felixstowe
Nayland
Colne Engaine
Dedham
Manningtree
River Stour
Halstead
Harwich
Ardleigh
Earls Colne
Aldham
COLCHESTER
Wix
Braintree
Marks Tey
Thorpe-le-Soken
Walton on the Naze
Coggeshall
Copford Green
Wivenhoe
Elmstead Market
7
Silver End
Kelvedon
Thorrington
Little Clacton
Frinton-on-Sea
Tollesbury
Brightlingsea
A148
A140
A149
A1151
A1067
A47
A146
A143
A12
A11
A1075
A1065
A134
A1066
A140
A144
A145
A1095
A1088
A1101
A14
A1120
A1141
A1092
A1071
A1214
A1156
A137
A131
A120
A133
A1124
A1152
A1094
A1062
B1105
B1110
B1149
B1354
B1145
B1150
B1159
B1108
B1077
B1113
B1134
B1527
B1332
B1136
B1074
B1127
B1123
B1126
B1125
B1122
B1119
B1116
B1117
B1118
B1078
B1079
B1069
B1084
B1083
B1106
B1115
B1064
B1068
B1070
B1080
B1352
B1035
B1414
B1024
B1022
0 1 2 3 4 5 6 7 8 9
6 5 4 3 2 1 0 9 8 7 6 5 4 3 2
Hotel
AA Hotel of the Year
Town/Village name
0
10 miles
10
20 kilometres

For continuation pages refer to numbered arrows

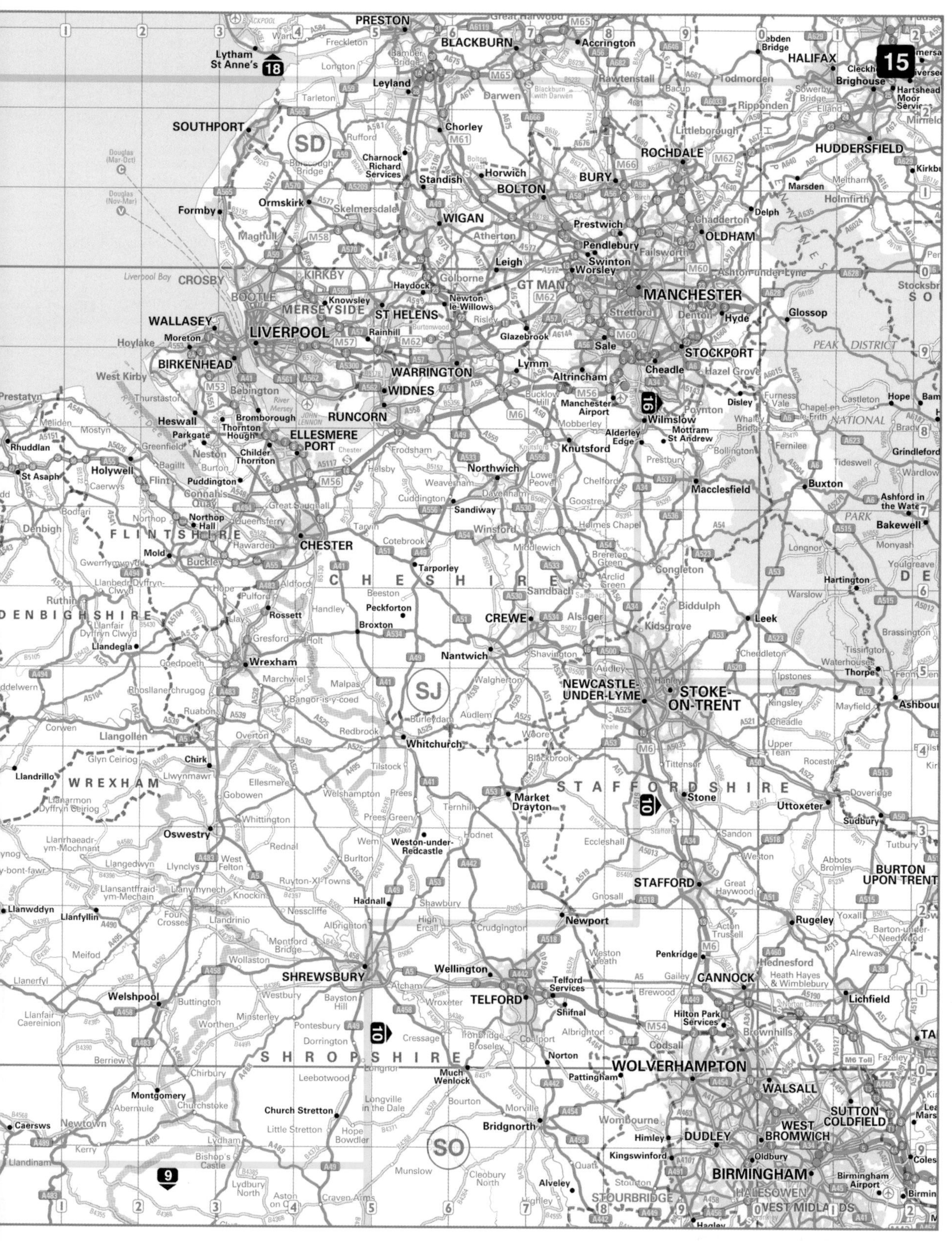

15
PRESTON
BLACKBURN
Accrington
Hebden Bridge
HALIFAX
Brighouse
Lytham St Anne's
18
Freckleton
Longton
Leyland
Bamber Bridge
Darwen
Rawtenstall
Bacup
Todmorden
Ripponden
Tarleton
SOUTHPORT
Rufford
Chorley
Littleborough
SD
Charnock Richard Services
Horwich
ROCHDALE
HUDDERSFIELD
Burscough Bridge
Standish
BOLTON
BURY
Marsden
Formby
Ormskirk
Skelmersdale
WIGAN
Prestwich
Chadderton
Delph
Holmfirth
Maghull
Atherton
Pendlebury
OLDHAM
Leigh
Swinton
Worsley
Failsworth
Liverpool Bay
CROSBY
KIRKBY
Golborne
GT MAN
Ashton-under-Lyne
BOOTLE
Haydock
MANCHESTER
Knowsley
MERSEYSIDE
ST HELENS
Newton-le-Willows
Stretford
Denton
Hyde
Glossop
WALLASEY
Moreton
LIVERPOOL
Rainhill
Risley
Glazebrook
Sale
Hoylake
BIRKENHEAD
WARRINGTON
Lymm
STOCKPORT
PEAK DISTRICT
West Kirby
Bebington
WIDNES
Altrincham
Cheadle
Hazel Grove
Prestatyn
Thurstaston
Manchester Airport
16
Disley
Chapel-en-le-Frith
Castleton
Hope
Heswall
Bromborough
RUNCORN
Wilmslow
Whaley Bridge
NATIONAL
Rhuddlan
Parkgate
Thornton Hough
ELLESMERE PORT
Mobberley
Alderley Edge
Mottram St Andrew
Neston
Childer Thornton
Frodsham
Knutsford
Prestbury
Bollington
Fernilee
St Asaph
Holywell
Flint
Helsby
Northwich
Tideswell
Puddington
Connah's Quay
Macclesfield
Buxton
Weaverham
Chelford
Cuddington
Sandiway
Goostrey
Ashford in the Water
Northop Hall
Queensferry
Great Saughall
Winsford
Holmes Chapel
Bakewell
Denbigh
FLINTSHIRE
Hawarden
CHESTER
Tarvin
Cotebrook
Middlewich
PARK
Mold
Buckley
Tarporley
Brereton Green
Congleton
Longnor
Monyash
Youlgreave
CHESHIRE
Arclid Green
Hartington
Ruthin
Hope
Pulford
Aldford
Beeston
Sandbach
Warslow
DENBIGHSHIRE
Rossett
Peckforton
Handley
Biddulph
Llanfair Dyffryn Clwyd
Broxton
CREWE
Alsager
Leek
Kidsgrove
Llandegla
Gresford
Holt
Nantwich
Shavington
Cheddleton
Waterhouses
Thorpe
Wrexham
Audley
Coedpoeth
Marchwiel
Malpas
NEWCASTLE-UNDER-LYME
STOKE-ON-TRENT
Hanley
Ipstones
Ashbourne
Rhosllanerchrugog
SJ
Walgherton
Bangor-is-y-coed
Kingsley
Mayfield
Corwen
Ruabon
Audlem
Burleydam
Cheadle
Llangollen
Overton
Redbrook
Whitchurch
Woore
Keele
Upper Tean
Chirk
Glyn Ceiriog
Blakenhall
Tittensor
Rocester
Llandrillo
WREXHAM
Llwynmawr
Ellesmere
Tilstock
STAFFORDSHIRE
Stone
Doveridge
Llanarmon Dyffryn Ceiriog
Gobowen
Welshampton
Prees
Market Drayton
Uttoxeter
Whittington
Prees Green
Ternhill
Sudbury
Oswestry
Weston-under-Redcastle
Hodnet
Sandon
Llanrhaeadr-ym-Mochnant
Rednal
Wem
Eccleshall
Tutbury
West Felton
Burlton
Weston
Abbots Bromley
BURTON UPON TRENT
Llangedwyn
Llynclys
Ruyton-XI-Towns
Great Haywood
STAFFORD
Llansantffraid-ym-Mechain
Llanymynech
Knockin
Hadnall
Shawbury
Gnosall
Llanwddyn
Llanfyllin
Four Crosses
Nesscliffe
Llandrinio
Albrighton
High Ercall
Crudgington
Newport
Acton Trussell
Rugeley
Yoxall
Barton-under-Needwood
Meifod
Montford Bridge
Weston Heath
Penkridge
Hednesford
Alrewas
Wollaston
Wellington
SHREWSBURY
Llanerfyl
Telford Services
Gailey
CANNOCK
Heath Hayes & Wimblebury
Welshpool
Westbury
Atcham
Brewood
Buttington
Bayston Hill
TELFORD
Shifnal
Hilton Park Services
Lichfield
Llanfair Caereinion
Wroxeter
Worthen
Minsterley
Pontesbury
10
Cressage
Albrighton
Brownhills
Dorrington
Ironbridge
Broseley
Coalport
Codsall
Berriew
SHROPSHIRE
Norton
WOLVERHAMPTON
Chirbury
Much Wenlock
Leebotwood
Pattingham
WALSALL
Montgomery
Abermule
Churchstoke
Longville in the Dale
Bourton
Morville
Church Stretton
SUTTON COLDFIELD
Caersws
Newtown
Wombourne
WEST BROMWICH
Little Stretton
Hope Bowdler
Bridgnorth
Himley
DUDLEY
Kerry
Lydham
SO
Oldbury
Llandinam
Bishop's Castle
Kingswinford
9
Munslow
Cleobury North
Quatt
BIRMINGHAM
Birmingham Airport
Lydbury North
Alveley
Aston on Clun
Craven Arms
Stourton
STOURBRIDGE
Highley
HALESOWEN
WEST MIDLANDS
Hagley

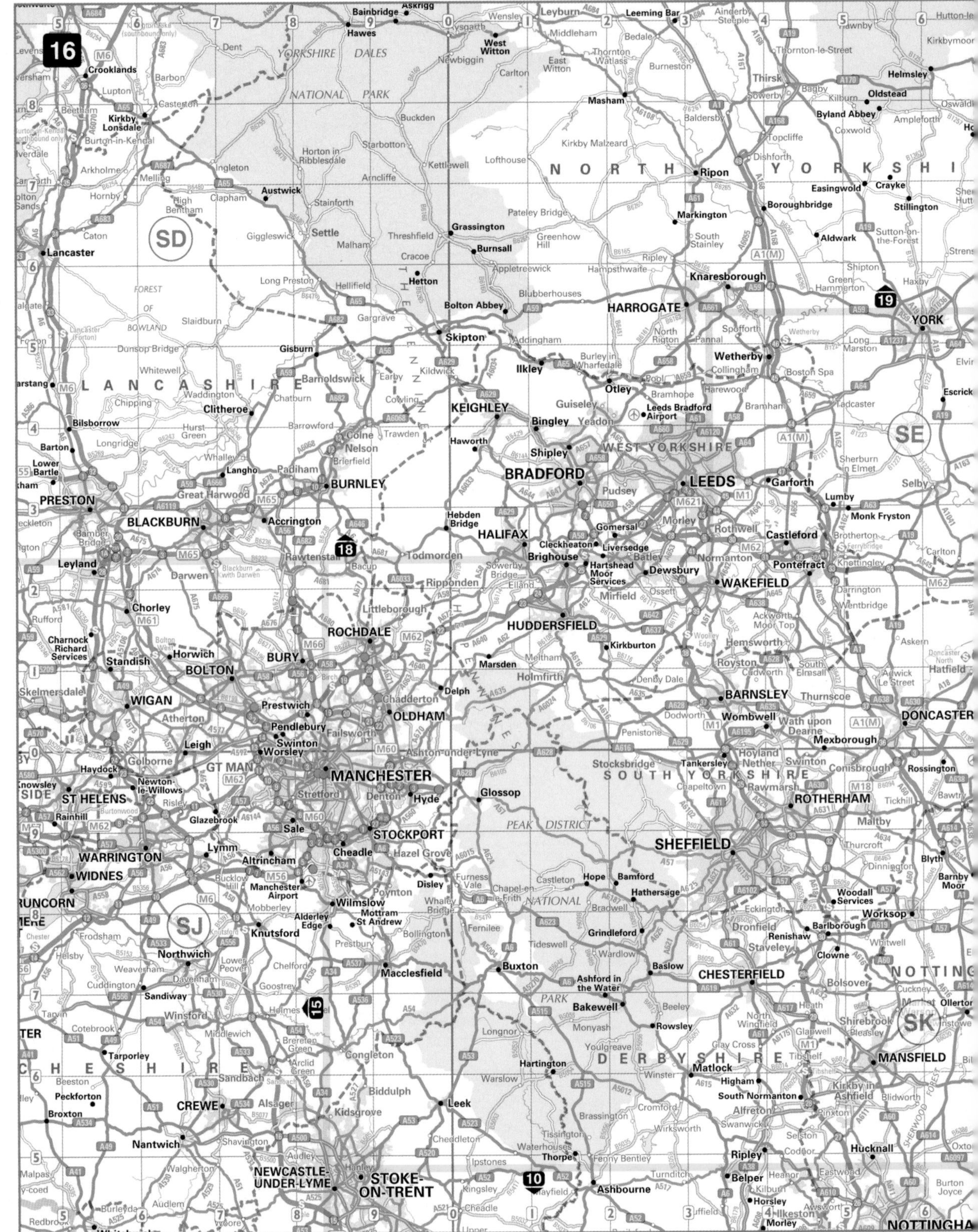

For continuation pages refer to numbered arrows

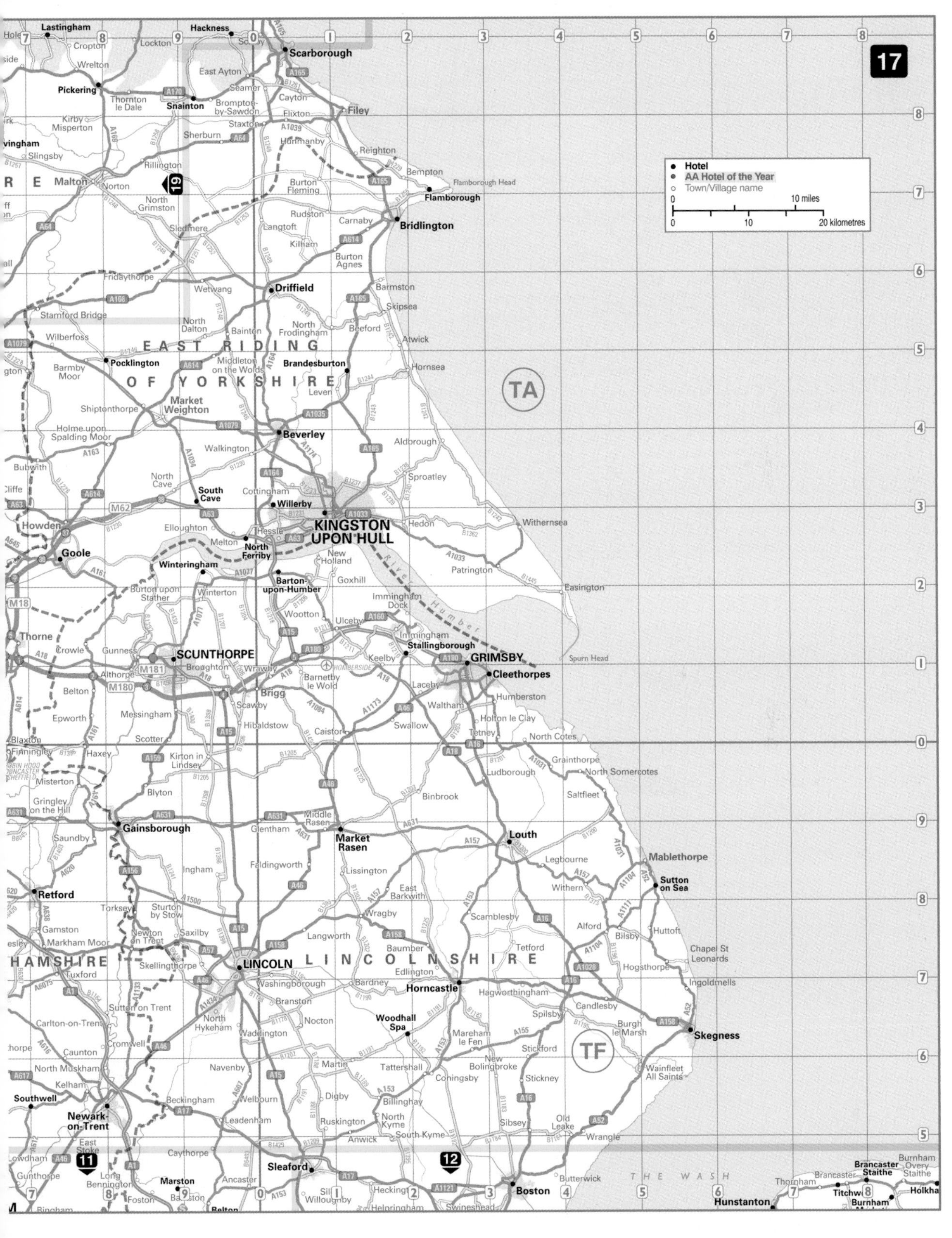

17
Hotel
AA Hotel of the Year
Town/Village name
10 miles
20 kilometres
TA
TF
Lastingham
Cropton
Wrelton
Pickering
Thornton le Dale
Lockton
Hackness
Scalby
Scarborough
East Ayton
Seamer
Snainton
Brompton-by-Sawdon
Cayton
Filey
Flixton
Staxton
Sherburn
Kirby Misperton
Slingsby
Rillington
Malton
Norton
North Grimston
Hunmanby
Reighton
Bempton
Flamborough Head
Flamborough
Burton Fleming
Rudston
Carnaby
Bridlington
Langtoft
Kilham
Sledmere
Burton Agnes
Fridaythorpe
Wetwang
Driffield
Barmston
Skipsea
Stamford Bridge
North Dalton
Bainton
North Frodingham
Beeford
Atwick
Wilberfoss
EAST RIDING OF YORKSHIRE
Pocklington
Middleton on the Wolds
Brandesburton
Hornsea
Barmby Moor
Leven
Market Weighton
Shiptonthorpe
Holme upon Spalding Moor
Beverley
Aldbrough
Walkington
Bubwith
North Cave
Sproatley
South Cave
Cottingham
Willerby
Howden
Ellough ton
Hessle
KINGSTON UPON HULL
Hedon
Withernsea
Melton
North Ferriby
Goole
Winteringham
New Holland
Barton-upon-Humber
Patrington
Goxhill
Easington
Burton upon Stather
Winterton
Immingham Dock
River Humber
Wootton
Ulceby
Thorne
Crowle
Gunness
SCUNTHORPE
Immingham
Stallingborough
Keelby
GRIMSBY
Spurn Head
Cleethorpes
Althorpe
Broughton
Wrawby
Barnetby le Wold
Belton
Brigg
Scawby
Laceby
Humberston
Waltham
Epworth
Messingham
Hibaldstow
Caistor
Swallow
Holton le Clay
Tetney
North Cotes
Blaxton
Finningley
Haxey
Scotter
Kirton in Lindsey
Grainthorpe
North Somercotes
Ludborough
Misterton
Blyton
Binbrook
Saltfleet
Gringley on the Hill
Gainsborough
Glentham
Middle Rasen
Market Rasen
Louth
Saundby
Mablethorpe
Legbourne
Ingham
Faldingworth
Lissington
Sutton on Sea
Withern
East Barkwith
Retford
Torksey
Sturton by Stow
Wragby
Scamblesby
Alford
Huttoft
Gamston
Newton on Trent
Saxilby
Langworth
Bilsby
Markham Moor
Baumber
Tetford
Chapel St Leonards
LINCOLNSHIRE
LINCOLN
Edlington
Hogsthorpe
Skellingthorpe
Tuxford
Washingborough
Bardney
Horncastle
Ingoldmells
Hagworthingham
Branston
Candlesby
Sutton on Trent
Spilsby
North Hykeham
Nocton
Woodhall Spa
Burgh le Marsh
Skegness
Carlton-on-Trent
Waddington
Mareham le Fen
Cromwell
Caunton
Stickford
New Bolingbroke
North Muskham
Navenby
Martin
Tattershall
Coningsby
Wainfleet All Saints
Kelham
Stickney
Southwell
Beckingham
Welbourn
Digby
Billinghay
Newark-on-Trent
Leadenham
Ruskington
North Kyme
Sibsey
Old Leake
East Stoke
South Kyme
Wrangle
Anwick
Lowdham
Caythorpe
Gunthorpe
Long Bennington
Marston
Sleaford
Ancaster
Barkston
Foston
Silk Willoughby
Heckington
Helpringham
Swineshead
Boston
Butterwick
THE WASH
Thornham
Brancaster
Brancaster Staithe
Burnham Overy Staithe
Titchwell
Holkham
Burnham Market
Hunstanton
Bingham
Belton
HAMSHIRE
Humberside

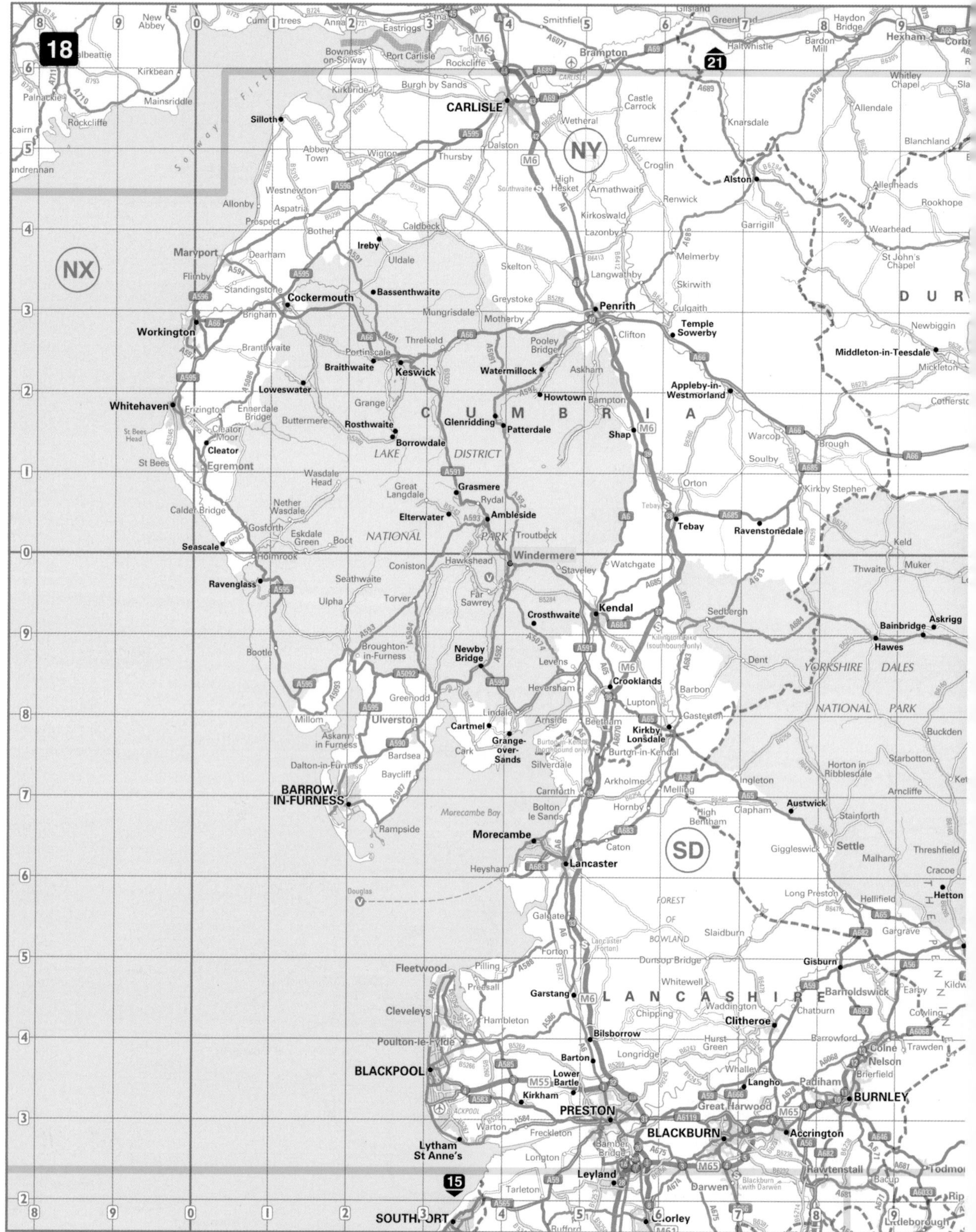

For continuation pages refer to numbered arrows

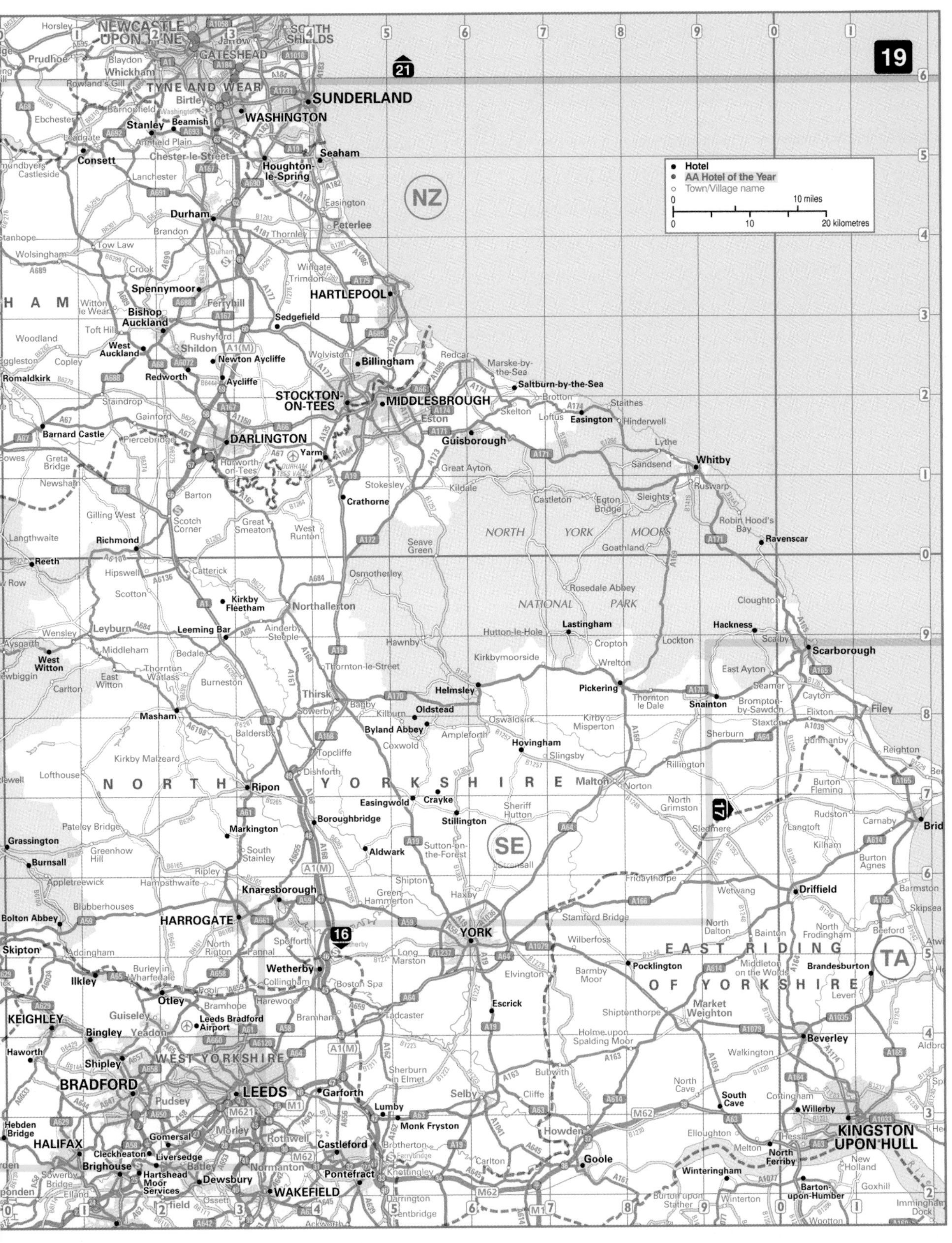

19
Hotel
AA Hotel of the Year
Town/Village name
10 miles
20 kilometres
NZ
SE
TA
NEWCASTLE UPON TYNE
GATESHEAD
SOUTH SHIELDS
TYNE AND WEAR
SUNDERLAND
WASHINGTON
Prudhoe
Blaydon
Whickham
Birtley
Stanley
Beamish
Consett
Chester-le-Street
Seaham
Houghton-le-Spring
Lanchester
Durham
Easington
Peterlee
Brandon
Thornley
Stanhope
Tow Law
Wolsingham
Crook
Wingate
Trimdon
Spennymoor
HARTLEPOOL
Ferryhill
Bishop Auckland
Sedgefield
Woodland
West Auckland
Shildon
Rushyford
Newton Aycliffe
Wolviston
Billingham
Redcar
Marske-by-the-Sea
Saltburn-by-the-Sea
Romaldkirk
Redworth
Aycliffe
STOCKTON-ON-TEES
MIDDLESBROUGH
Staindrop
Gainford
Eston
Skelton
Brotton
Loftus
Easington
Staithes
Hinderwell
Barnard Castle
Piercebridge
DARLINGTON
Yarm
Guisborough
Lythe
Sandsend
Whitby
Bowes
Greta Bridge
Hurworth-on-Tees
Great Ayton
Stokesley
Kildale
Castleton
Egton Bridge
Sleights
Ruswarp
Newsham
Barton
Crathorne
Robin Hood's Bay
Gilling West
Scotch Corner
Great Smeaton
West Rounton
NORTH YORK MOORS
Seave Green
Goathland
Ravenscar
Langthwaite
Richmond
Reeth
Hipswell
Catterick
Osmotherley
Rosedale Abbey
Scotton
Kirkby Fleetham
Northallerton
NATIONAL PARK
Cloughton
Leyburn
Wensley
Leeming Bar
Ainderby Steeple
Hutton-le-Hole
Lastingham
Hackness
Aysgarth
West Witton
Middleham
Bedale
Hawnby
Cropton
Lockton
Scalby
Scarborough
Thornton Watlass
Thornton-le-Street
Kirkbymoorside
Wrelton
East Ayton
Newbiggin
Carlton
East Witton
Burneston
Thirsk
Helmsley
Pickering
Thornton le Dale
Snainton
Seamer
Brompton-by-Sawdon
Cayton
Filey
Masham
Sowerby
Bagby
Kilburn
Oldstead
Byland Abbey
Ampleforth
Oswaldkirk
Kirby Misperton
Sherburn
Staxton
Flixton
Hunmanby
Baldersby
Coxwold
Hovingham
Slingsby
Rillington
Reighton
Kirkby Malzeard
Topcliffe
Lofthouse
Dishforth
NORTH YORKSHIRE
Ripon
Malton
Norton
Burton Fleming
Easingwold
Crayke
North Grimston
Sheriff Hutton
Pateley Bridge
Boroughbridge
Stillington
Sledmere
Rudston
Langtoft
Carnaby
Grassington
Markington
Kilham
Greenhow Hill
South Stainley
Aldwark
Sutton-on-the-Forest
Burton Agnes
Burnsall
Appletreewick
Ripley
Strensall
Hampsthwaite
Shipton
Fridaythorpe
Wetwang
Driffield
Barmston
Knaresborough
Green Hammerton
Haxby
Skipsea
Blubberhouses
Bolton Abbey
HARROGATE
Stamford Bridge
North Dalton
Bainton
North Frodingham
Beeford
YORK
Skipton
Addingham
Spofforth
North Rigton
Pannal
Long Marston
Wilberfoss
EAST RIDING OF YORKSHIRE
Wetherby
Elvington
Pocklington
Barmby Moor
Middleton on the Wolds
Brandesburton
Ilkley
Burley in Wharfedale
Collingham
Boston Spa
Otley
Pool
Harewood
Escrick
Leven
KEIGHLEY
Guiseley
Bramhope
Leeds Bradford Airport
Bramham
Tadcaster
Shiptonthorpe
Market Weighton
Bingley
Yeadon
Holme upon Spalding Moor
Beverley
Haworth
Shipley
WEST YORKSHIRE
Walkington
BRADFORD
Sherburn in Elmet
Bubwith
North Cave
LEEDS
Garforth
Pudsey
Selby
Cliffe
South Cave
Cottingham
Willerby
Lumby
Monk Fryston
Hebden Bridge
Gomersal
Morley
Howden
Ellougton
KINGSTON UPON HULL
HALIFAX
Cleckheaton
Liversedge
Rothwell
Castleford
Brotherton
Melton
North Ferriby
Hessle
Brighouse
Batley
Normanton
Carlton
Goole
New Holland
Hartshead Moor Services
Dewsbury
Pontefract
Knottingley
Winteringham
Barton-upon-Humber
Goxhill
Elland
WAKEFIELD
Darrington
Burton upon Stather
Winterton
Immingham Dock
Ossett
Wentbridge
Ackworth
Wootton

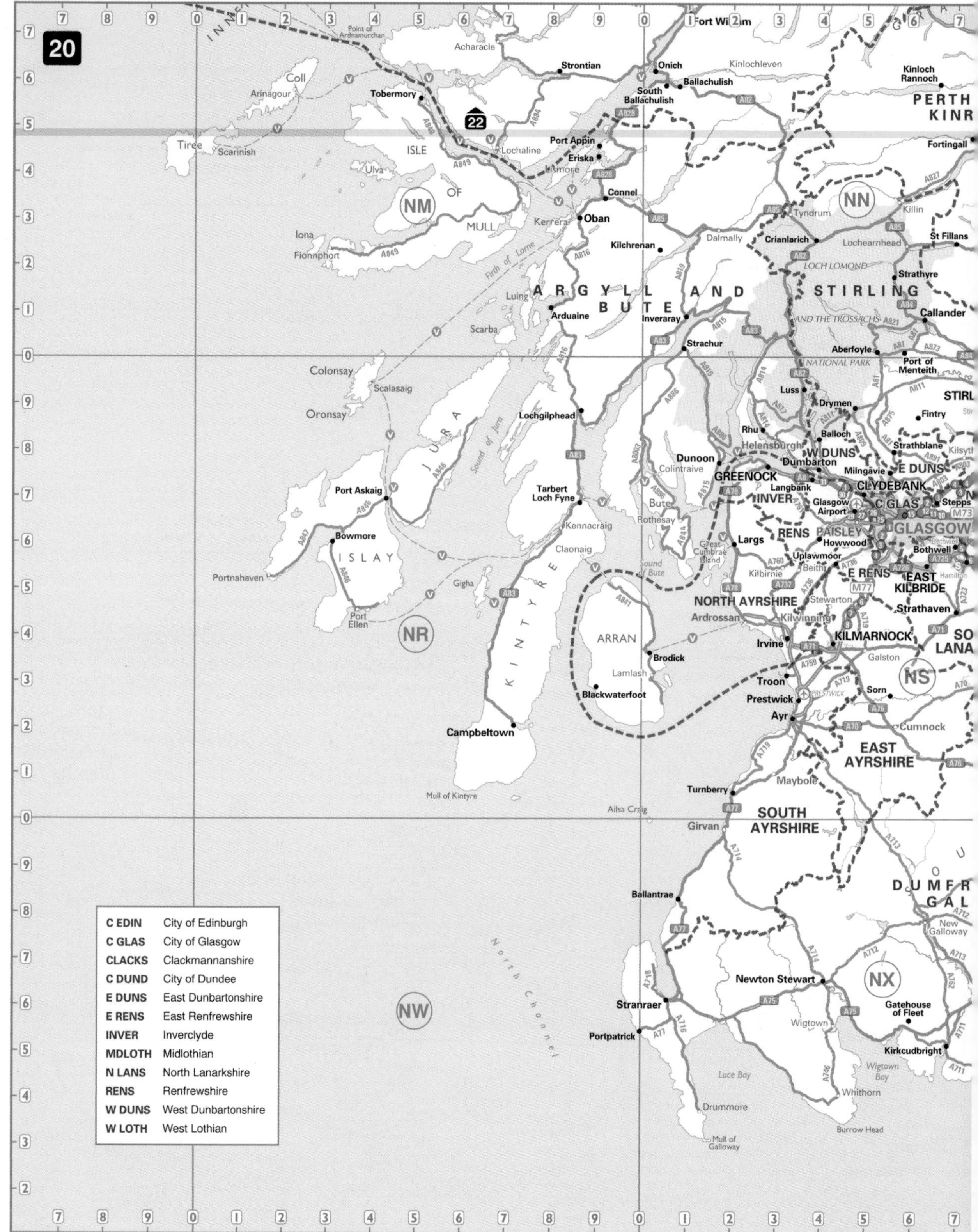

For continuation pages refer to numbered arrows

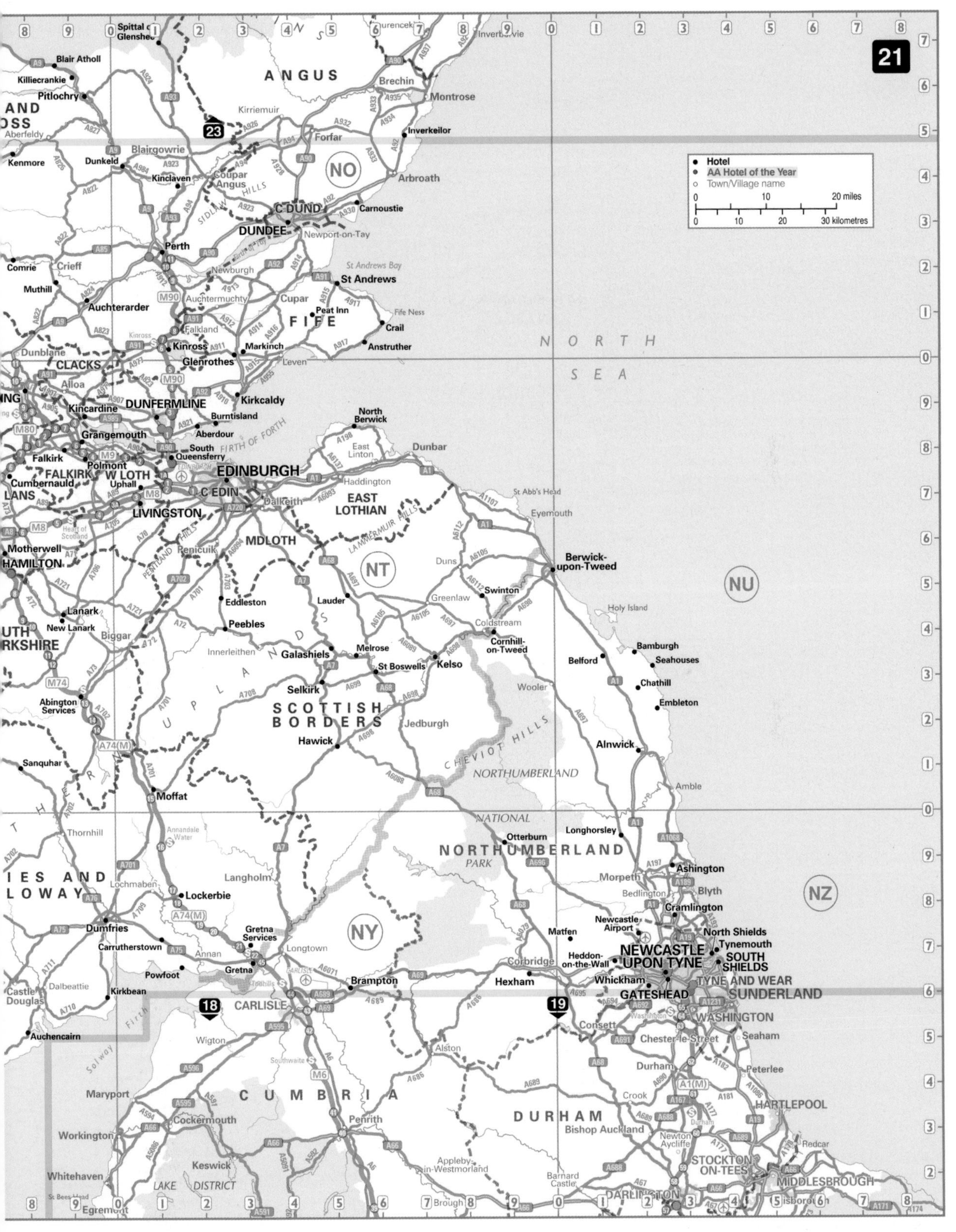
Hotel
AA Hotel of the Year
Town/Village name
0
10
20 miles
0
10
20
30 kilometres
NO
NT
NU
NY
NZ
NORTH
SEA
ANGUS
FIFE
CLACKS
DUNFERMLINE
FALKIRK
W LOTH
C EDIN
EDINBURGH
LIVINGSTON
MDLOTH
EAST LOTHIAN
SCOTTISH BORDERS
UPLANDS
LAMMERMUIR HILLS
PENTLAND HILLS
SIDLAW HILLS
CHEVIOT HILLS
NORTHUMBERLAND
NORTHUMBERLAND NATIONAL PARK
CUMBRIA
DURHAM
LAKE DISTRICT
TYNE AND WEAR
C DUND
DUNDEE
Blair Atholl
Killiecrankie
Pitlochry
Aberfeldy
Kenmore
Dunkeld
Blairgowrie
Kinclaven
Coupar Angus
Kirriemuir
Forfar
Brechin
Montrose
Inverkeilor
Arbroath
Carnoustie
Newport-on-Tay
Perth
Comrie
Crieff
Muthill
Auchterarder
Newburgh
Auchtermuchty
Cupar
St Andrews
St Andrews Bay
Peat Inn
Fife Ness
Crail
Anstruther
Kinross
Falkland
Markinch
Glenrothes
Leven
Dunblane
Alloa
Kincardine
Kirkcaldy
Burntisland
Aberdour
Grangemouth
Falkirk
Polmont
South Queensferry
FIRTH OF FORTH
Cumbernauld
Uphall
Dalkeith
Haddington
North Berwick
East Linton
Dunbar
St Abb's Head
Eyemouth
Motherwell
HAMILTON
Penicuik
Eddleston
Peebles
Lanark
New Lanark
Biggar
Innerleithen
Galashiels
Lauder
Duns
Swinton
Greenlaw
Coldstream
Cornhill-on-Tweed
Berwick-upon-Tweed
Holy Island
Bamburgh
Seahouses
Belford
Chathill
Embleton
Melrose
St Boswells
Kelso
Wooler
Selkirk
Jedburgh
Hawick
Alnwick
Amble
Abington Services
Sanquhar
Moffat
Thornhill
Annandale Water
Langholm
Lochmaben
Lockerbie
Dumfries
Carrutherstown
Gretna Services
Gretna
Annan
Powfoot
Longtown
Brampton
Dalbeattie
Castle Douglas
Kirkbean
Auchencairn
CARLISLE
Wigton
Southwaite
Otterburn
Longhorsley
Morpeth
Ashington
Bedlington
Blyth
Cramlington
Newcastle Airport
Matfen
Heddon-on-the-Wall
Corbridge
Hexham
NEWCASTLE UPON TYNE
Whickham
GATESHEAD
North Shields
Tynemouth
SOUTH SHIELDS
SUNDERLAND
WASHINGTON
Consett
Chester-le-Street
Seaham
Durham
Peterlee
Alston
Crook
HARTLEPOOL
Bishop Auckland
Newton Aycliffe
Redcar
STOCKTON-ON-TEES
MIDDLESBROUGH
DARLINGTON
Barnard Castle
Appleby-in-Westmorland
Brough
Maryport
Cockermouth
Workington
Keswick
Whitehaven
St Bees Head
Egremont
Penrith
Solway Firth
18
19
23

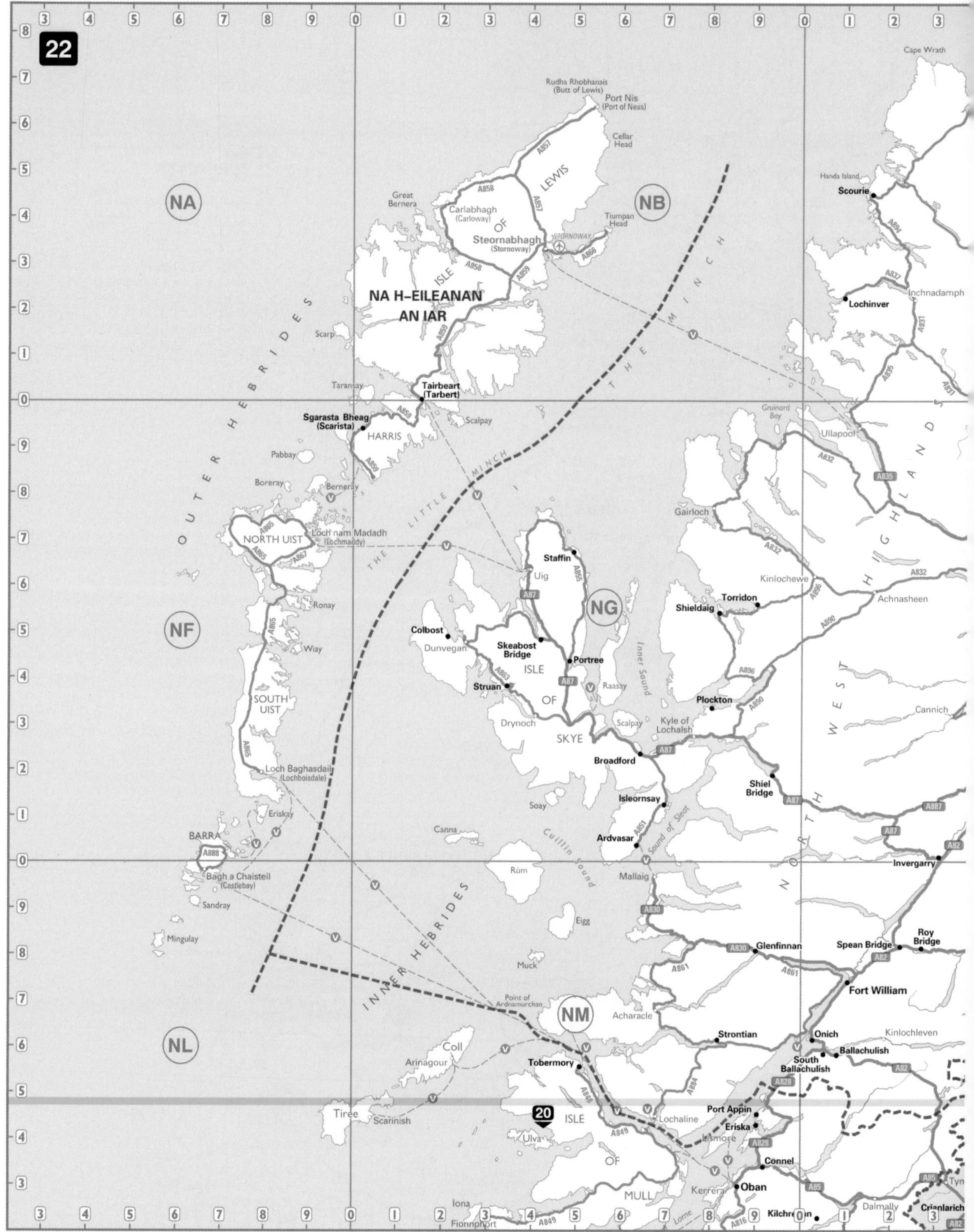

Cape Wrath
Rudha Rhobhanais
(Butt of Lewis)
Port Nis
(Port of Ness)
Cellar Head
LEWIS
Great Bernera
Carlabhagh
(Carloway)
Steornabhagh
(Stornoway)
STORNOWAY
Tiumpan Head
NA
NB
ISLE OF
NA H-EILEANAN
AN IAR
Scarp
Taransay
Tairbeart
(Tarbert)
Sgarasta Bheag
(Scarista)
HARRIS
Scalpay
Pabbay
Boreray
Berneray
OUTER HEBRIDES
THE MINCH
THE LITTLE MINCH
NORTH UIST
Loch nam Madadh
(Lochmaddy)
Ronay
NF
Wiay
SOUTH UIST
Loch Baghasdail
(Lochboisdale)
Eriskay
BARRA
Bagh a Chaisteil
(Castlebay)
Sandray
Mingulay
Handa Island
Scourie
Inchnadamph
Lochinver
Gruinard Bay
Ullapool
Gairloch
Kinlochewe
Torridon
Shieldaig
Achnasheen
Staffin
Uig
NG
Colbost
Dunvegan
Skeabost Bridge
Portree
ISLE OF SKYE
Struan
Drynoch
Raasay
Inner Sound
Scalpay
Kyle of Lochalsh
Plockton
Broadford
Soay
Isleornsay
Shiel Bridge
Canna
Ardvasar
Sound of Sleat
Cuillin Sound
Rùm
Mallaig
Eigg
Invergarry
Cannich
NORTH WEST HIGHLANDS
Glenfinnan
Spean Bridge
Roy Bridge
Fort William
Muck
INNER HEBRIDES
Point of Ardnamurchan
NM
Acharacle
Strontian
Onich
Kinlochleven
Ballachulish
South Ballachulish
NL
Coll
Arinagour
Tobermory
Tiree
Scarinish
20
ISLE OF MULL
Lochaline
Port Appin
Eriska
Lismore
Ulva
Connel
Kerrera
Oban
Iona
Fionnphort
Lorne
Kilchrenan
Dalmally
Tyndrum
Crianlarich

23
Hotel
AA Hotel of the Year
Town/Village name
20 miles
30 kilometres
Stromness
Dunnet Head
PENTLAND FIRTH
Island of Stroma
St Margaret's Hope
Duncansby Head
John o' Groats
Scrabster
Thurso
Gills
Strathy Point
Durness
Melvich
Bettyhill
Tongue
Wick
Lybster
Dunbeath
Altnaharra
Helmsdale
Lairg
Golspie
Brora
Bonar Bridge
Dornoch
Tain
HIGHLAND
Alness
Invergordon
Cromarty
MORAY FIRTH
Dingwall
Fortrose
Nairn
Muir of Ord
Beauly
INVERNESS
INVERNESS (DALCROSS)
Abriachan
Brachla
Drumnadrochit
Foyers
Invermoriston
Whitebridge
Fort Augustus
Monadhliath Mountains
Lossiemouth
Elgin
Forres
Buckie
Cullen
Portsoy
Banff
Fraserburgh
MORAY
Rothes
Archiestown
Craigellachie
Aberlour
Dufftown
Keith
Aberchirder
Turriff
Huntly
Peterhead
Grantown-on-Spey
Carrbridge
Nethy Bridge
Boat of Garten
Tomintoul
Aviemore
Kildrummy
Alford
Oldmeldrum
Ellon
Newburgh
Inverurie
Kintore
Aberdeen Airport
Dyce
CITY OF ABERDEEN
ABERDEEN
Kirkwall
Lerwick
CAIRNGORMS
CAIRNGORM MOUNTAINS
NATIONAL PARK
Kingussie
Newtonmore
ABERDEENSHIRE
Peterculter
Aboyne
Ballater
Banchory
Braemar
Stonehaven
GRAMPIAN MOUNTAINS
Spittal of Glenshee
Laurencekirk
Inverbervie
ANGUS
Brechin
Montrose
Blair Atholl
Killiecrankie
Kinloch Rannoch
Pitlochry
PERTH AND KINROSS
Aberfeldy
Kirriemuir
Forfar
Inverkeilor
Fortingall
Kenmore
Dunkeld
Blairgowrie
Coupar Angus
Kinclaven
SIDLAW HILLS
Arbroath
Carnoustie
C DUND
DUNDEE
Newport-on-Tay
Killin
St Fillans
Lochearnhead
Perth
Comrie
Crieff
St Andrews Bay
NC
ND
NH
NJ
NK
NN
NO
21

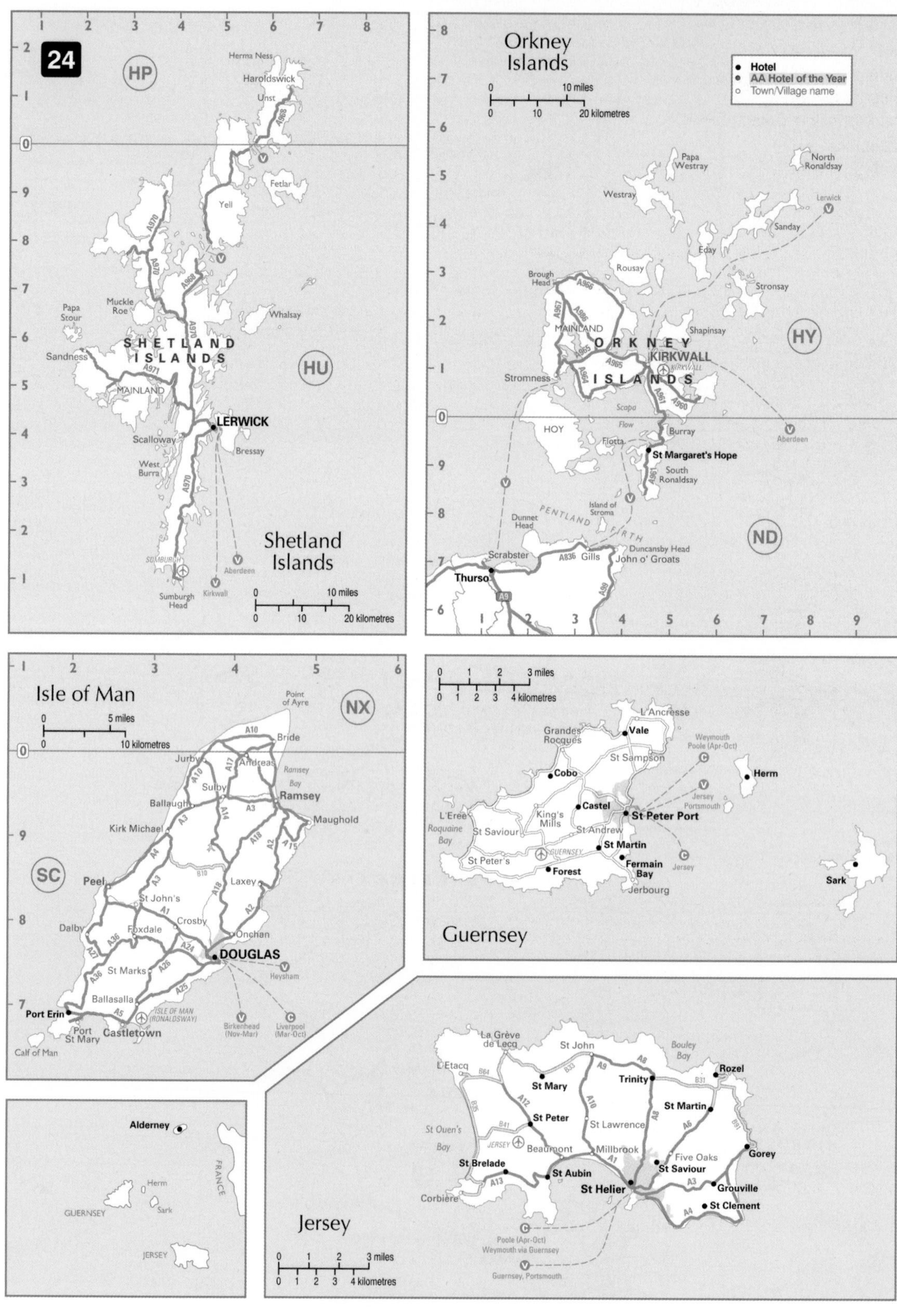
Shetland Islands
0 10 miles
0 10 20 kilometres
Herma Ness
Haroldswick
Unst
Fetlar
Yell
Whalsay
Papa Stour
Muckle Roe
SHETLAND ISLANDS
Sandness
MAINLAND
LERWICK
Scalloway
Bressay
West Burra
Sumburgh Head
Kirkwall
Aberdeen
Orkney Islands
Hotel
AA Hotel of the Year
Town/Village name
Papa Westray
North Ronaldsay
Westray
Lerwick
Sanday
Eday
Rousay
Stronsay
Brough Head
MAINLAND
Shapinsay
ORKNEY ISLANDS
KIRKWALL
Stromness
Scapa Flow
HOY
Burray
Flotta
St Margaret's Hope
South Ronaldsay
Aberdeen
Island of Stroma
Dunnet Head
PENTLAND FIRTH
Duncansby Head
John o' Groats
Scrabster
Gills
Thurso
Isle of Man
0 5 miles
0 10 kilometres
Point of Ayre
Bride
Jurby
Andreas
Ramsey Bay
Sulby
Ballaugh
Ramsey
Maughold
Kirk Michael
Peel
Laxey
St John's
Crosby
Dalby
Foxdale
Onchan
DOUGLAS
Heysham
St Marks
Ballasalla
Port Erin
Port St Mary
Castletown
Calf of Man
Birkenhead (Nov-Mar)
Liverpool (Mar-Oct)
Guernsey
0 1 2 3 miles
0 1 2 3 4 kilometres
L'Ancresse
Grandes Rocques
Vale
St Sampson
Weymouth Poole (Apr-Oct)
Cobo
Herm
Jersey Portsmouth
Castel
St Peter Port
L'Eree
Rocquaine Bay
King's Mills
St Saviour
St Andrew
St Martin
St Peter's
Fermain Bay
Forest
Jersey
Jerbourg
Sark
Alderney
Herm
Sark
GUERNSEY
JERSEY
FRANCE
Jersey
La Grève de Lecq
St John
Bouley Bay
L'Etacq
Rozel
St Mary
Trinity
St Martin
St Peter
St Lawrence
St Ouen's Bay
Beaumont
Millbrook
Five Oaks
Gorey
St Brelade
St Aubin
St Saviour
St Helier
Grouville
Corbière
St Clement
Poole (Apr-Oct) Weymouth via Guernsey
Guernsey, Portsmouth
0 1 2 3 miles
0 1 2 3 4 kilometres

Readers' Report Form

Please send this form to:
Editor, The Hotel Guide,
Lifestyle Guides,
The Automobile Association,
Fanum House,
Basingstoke RG21 4EA

or fax: 01256 491647
or e-mail: lifestyleguides@theAA.com

Please use this form to recommend any hotel where you have stayed, whether it is included in the guide or not currently listed. You can also help us to improve the guide by completing the short questionnaire on the reverse.

The AA does not undertake to arbitrate between guide readers and hotels, or to obtain compensation or engage in protracted correspondence.

Date:

Your name (block capitals)

Your address (block capitals)

....

....

....

....

....

....

e-mail address:

Name of hotel:

Comments ....

....

....

....

....

....

....

....

(please attach a separate sheet if necessary)

Please tick here if you DO NOT wish to receive details of AA offers or products

PTO

Have you bought this guide before? Yes No

Have you bought any other accommodation, restaurant, pub or food guides recently?
If yes, which ones?

....

....

....

Why did you buy this guide? (circle all that apply)

holiday short break business travel special occasion
overnight stop find a venue for an event e.g. conference
other ....

How often do you stay in hotels? (circle one choice)

more than once a month once a month once in 2-3 months
once in six months once a year less than once a year

Please answer these questions to help us make improvements to the guide:
Which of these factors are most important when choosing a hotel?

price location awards/ratings service
decor/surroundings previous experience recommendation
other (please state) ....

Do you read the editorial features in the guide? Yes No

Do you use the location atlas? Yes No

What elements of the guide do you find the most useful when choosing somewhere to stay?

description photo advertisement star rating

Can you suggest any improvements to the guide?

....

....

....

....

Please send this form to:
Editor, The Hotel Guide,
Lifestyle Guides,
The Automobile Association,
Fanum House,
Basingstoke RG21 4EA

Readers' Report Form

or fax: 01256 491647
or e-mail: lifestyleguides@theAA.com

Please use this form to recommend any hotel where you have stayed, whether it is included in the guide or not currently listed. You can also help us to improve the guide by completing the short questionnaire on the reverse.

The AA does not undertake to arbitrate between guide readers and hotels, or to obtain compensation or engage in protracted correspondence.

Date:

Your name (block capitals)

Your address (block capitals)

....

....

....

....

....

....

e-mail address:

Name of hotel:

Comments ....

....

....

....

....

....

....

....

(please attach a separate sheet if necessary)

Please tick here if you DO NOT wish to receive details of AA offers or products

PTO

Have you bought this guide before? Yes No

Have you bought any other accommodation, restaurant, pub or food guides recently?
If yes, which ones?

....

....

....

Why did you buy this guide? (circle all that apply)

holiday	short break	business travel	special occasion
overnight stop	find a venue for an event e.g. conference		

other ....

How often do you stay in hotels? (circle one choice)

more than once a month	once a month	once in 2-3 months
once in six months	once a year	less than once a year

Please answer these questions to help us make improvements to the guide:

Which of these factors are most important when choosing a hotel?

price	location	awards/ratings	service
decor/surroundings	previous experience	recommendation	

other (please state) ....

Do you read the editorial features in the guide? Yes No

Do you use the location atlas? Yes No

What elements of the guide do you find the most useful when choosing somewhere to stay?

description	photo	advertisement	star rating

Can you suggest any improvements to the guide?

....

....

....

....

HG12

Please send this form to:
Editor, The Hotel Guide,
Lifestyle Guides,
The Automobile Association,
Fanum House,
Basingstoke RG21 4EA

Readers' Report Form

or e-mail: lifestyleguides@theAA.com

Please use this form to recommend any hotel where you have stayed, whether it is included in the guide or not currently listed. You can also help us to improve the guide by completing the short questionnaire on the reverse.

The AA does not undertake to arbitrate between guide readers and hotels, or to obtain compensation or engage in protracted correspondence.

Date:

Your name (block capitals)

Your address (block capitals)

....

....

....

....

....

....

e-mail address:

Name of hotel:

Comments ....

....

....

....

....

....

....

....

(please attach a separate sheet if necessary)

Please tick here if you DO NOT wish to receive details of AA offers or products

PTO

Have you bought this guide before? Yes No

Have you bought any other accommodation, restaurant, pub or food guides recently?
If yes, which ones?

....

....

....

Why did you buy this guide? (circle all that apply)

holiday	short break	business travel	special occasion
overnight stop	find a venue for an event e.g. conference		

other ....

How often do you stay in hotels? (circle one choice)

more than once a month	once a month	once in 2-3 months
once in six months	once a year	less than once a year

Please answer these questions to help us make improvements to the guide:

Which of these factors are most important when choosing a hotel?

price	location	awards/ratings	service
decor/surroundings	previous experience	recommendation	

other (please state) ....

Do you read the editorial features in the guide? Yes No

Do you use the location atlas? Yes No

What elements of the guide do you find the most useful when choosing somewhere to stay?

description	photo	advertisement	star rating

Can you suggest any improvements to the guide?

....

....

....

....

AA Media Limited wishes to thank the following photographers and organisations for their assistance in the preparation of this book.

Abbreviations for the picture credits are as follows – (t) top; (b) bottom; (l) left; (r) right; (c) centre; (AA) AA World Travel Library

1 Gilpin Hotel & Lake House, Windermere; 2 Le Manoir Aux Quat' Saisons, Great Milton; 3 The Strathdon Hotel, Nottingham; 7 Brown's Hotel, London; 8 AA/T Mackie; 9l Gilpin Hotel & Lake House, Windermere; 9r The Savoy, London; 10l Blythswood Square, Glasgow; 10r Blythswood Square, Glasgow; 11l Gregans Castle, Ballyvaughn; 11r AA/K Blackwell; 12 The Grand, Bristol; 13t Cricket St Thomas Hotel, Chard; 13c Thoresby Hall Hotel & Spa, Ollerton; 13b Littlecote House Hotel, Hungerford; 14 AA/M Kipling; 15l The Red Carnation Hotel Collection; 15tr AA; 15cr David Chalmers; 15br The Lancaster, London; 16/17 The Goring, London; 18 The Goring, London; 19l The Goring, London; 19r R Trussell; 20/21 R Trussell; 22 The Goring, London; 23t R Trussell; 23c The Goring, London; 24l Ivy House Country Hotel, Lowestoft; 24c Marmadukes Hotel, York; 24r Driftwood, Portscatho; 25t Eastwell Manor, Ashford; 25bc Brook Lodge Hotel & Wells Spa, Wicklow; 25br Pennyhill Park Hotel & Spa, Bagshot; 26 AA/J Hunt; 27 AA/S Montgomery; 36 AA/S Day; 38 AA/M Jourdan; 40/41 AA/M Kipling; 267 AA/J Wood; 268/269 AA/J Tims; 286 AA/S Montgomery; 534 AA/V Bates; 535 Peter Brogden/Alamy; 542 JLImages/Alamy; 547 BL Images Ltd/Alamy; 548/549 AA/S Anderson; 586 AA/S Anderson; 607 AA/J Henderson; 608 AA/K Paterson; 610/611 AA/S Whitehorne; 619 AA/S Whitehorne; 620/621 AA/M Bauer; 653 AA/R Duke; 655 AA/S Lewis; 656/657 AA/S McBride; Design Pics Inc./Alamy; 692 Design Pics Inc./Alamy; 693 David R. Frazier Photolibrary, Inc./Alamy; 700/701 AA/A Mockford & N Bonetti; 735 AA/A Burton

Every effort has been made to trace the copyright holders, and we apologise in advance for any unintentional omissions or errors. We would be pleased to apply any corrections in a following edition of this publication.

Notes